HAWAIIAN
DICTIONARY

HAWAIIAN DICTIONARY

Hawaiian-English
English-Hawaiian

Revised and Enlarged Edition

Mary Kawena Pukui

Samuel H. Elbert

UNIVERSITY OF HAWAII PRESS
Honolulu

© 1986 UNIVERSITY OF HAWAII PRESS

PREVIOUS EDITIONS © 1957, 1961, 1964, 1965, 1971
BY UNIVERSITY OF HAWAII PRESS

98   99   00   01   11   10   9

Library of Congress Cataloging-in-Publication Data

Pukui, Mary Kawena, 1895–
Hawaiian dictionary.

Bibliography: p.
1. Hawaiian language—Dictionaries—English.
2. English language—Dictionaries—Hawaiian.
I. Elbert, Samuel H., 1907– . II. Title.
PL6446.P795   1986   499'.4   85–24583
ISBN 0–8248–0703–0

University of Hawai'i Press books are printed on acid-free paper
and meet the guidelines for permanence and durability
of the Council on Library Resources

Contents

Preface

Authors rarely have the privilege, after twenty-five years, of revising a work of considerable size. We are grateful to have had this privilege, because the need for a complete revision of the *Hawaiian Dictionary* has long been evident, judging from the response of scholars and of many other readers, not only in Hawai'i, but from all parts of the world. Work of revision, begun in 1972, has taken so long that the compilers often wondered if they would live to see the final form of this labor of love. In this preface we review the additions and changes that have been incorporated in this latest edition.

About 3,000 new entries have been added to the Hawaiian-English section, bringing the total number of entries in that section to about 29,000. Almost certainly it is the largest and most complete of any Polynesian dictionary. Partly because of the increased interest in Hawaiiana, many books have appeared since the first edition was compiled in the early 1950s. Those sources most productive of new entries and additional meanings of old entries include the following (see the References for bibliographic details): Handy and Pukui 1958, Ii 1959, Gosline and Brock 1960, Kamakau 1961, 1964, 1976, Neal 1965, Johnson and Mahelona 1970, Pukui, Haertig, and Lee 1972, Elbert and Pukui 1979, St. John 1982.

In addition to entirely new entries and meanings, many changes have been effected that, we hope, will increase the usefulness of the book. These include a means of showing stress groups to facilitate pronunciation of words with more than three syllables; indication of Hawaiian parts of speech; scientific names of plants changed since the early 1950s; additional ancestral reconstructions; classical origins of Hawaiian borrowings;

corrections of previous entries that were made as knowledge of the language progressed; and many more cross references that, when consulted, should enhance understanding of words and their many nuances.

Hawaiian-language newspapers—excellent sources for names of rains, stars, winds, *lua* fighting holds, and much else—were reexamined, as well as the important old books in Hawaiian by Kelekona and by Nakuina, and volumes 5 and 6 of the Fornander series. Many legal and land terms from about the middle of the last century were uncovered by William H. Wilson and Ray Kalā Enos, as they translated Hawaiian-language documents at the Hawai'i State Archives.

Effort has been extended, through careful cross-referencing, to make the English-Hawaiian section a more detailed "index" of the riches, many of them hidden, on the Hawaiian-English side. Here are some comparisons of the number of epithets and cross references to sayings in the Hawaiian-English section (the number of examples in the present edition precedes the number in the previous editions): insults (45, 20), laziness (48, 0), love (18, 8), rain names (138, 17), warriors (20, 5), wind names (160, 138). These topics are also entered: 94 *lua* fighting holds (most of them are poetic and have no obvious connection with combat), 67 hula terms, and 22 epithets for vagabonds.

Hula masters and students have called the dictionary their bible, perhaps because of the many citations from chants, songs, and ancient prayers, the poetic sayings and epithets, and the abundance of pithy proverbs that comment on many aspects of ancient Hawaiian life. Perhaps no other Polynesian dictionary contains as much poetry, folklore, and ethnology.

In the revised dictionary we have attempted to credit Greek, Hebrew, and Latin as sources of many loan words in Hawaiian, drawing on Elbert and Knowlton's unpublished paper (1985) that lists words probably from Greek (mostly in the New Testament), Hebrew (mostly in the Old Testament), and Latin (mostly of non-Hawaiian animals and terms for Christian services).

We found that the meanings of Hawaiian words in the King James Version (KJV) differed considerably from those in the Revised Standard Version (RSV) of 1946–1952 (Old Testament) and 1971 (New Testament). In such cases both definitions are given, the RSV meanings appearing first, as presumably based on later research. There is no assurance that *all* such differences in the two versions are noted.

In the table below are listed a few of the many words from Greek, Hebrew, and Latin with RSV glosses that differ from KJV glosses. Notice that in every case the alternate spelling (with non-Hawaiian letters) clearly reflects the source language. Notice also that the Hawaiian loan words of Greek origin in this short list end in *o;* this is probably because of the frequency of Greek words ending in *os,* the singular nominative suffix.

For other words from Hebrew with contrasting RSV and KJV glosses, see *keakula, kikala, kikima, kileka, kinola, kipoka, kome, leʻema, lekema, lokema,* and others.

A few names of non-Hawaiian animals were taken from the Latin names of the family (in roman) or, more commonly, the genus (in italics), for example:

> *ʻalekea, aredea* 'heron', Ardeidae
> *kikonia* 'stork', *Ciconia*
> *lana, rana* 'frog', *Rana*
> *lepu* 'hare', *Lepus*
> *mukuela, mutuela* 'weasel', *Mustela*

Many words used in Christian services (but not necessarily found in the Bible) are of Latin origin. See *ʻepikekole, ʻepikopo, ʻEpipania, ʻEukalikia, komunio, kopilimakio, likānia,* and probably *lōkālio.*

For a more extensive discussion of loan words, see Schütz 1976 and Elbert and Pukui's *Hawaiian Grammar,* pp. 27–34.

Names of plants and animals. The scientific names of plants and animals have been updated. References to Neal's *In Gardens of Hawaii* have been changed to conform with the 1965 edition of this classic work. Many Niʻihau plant names (St. John 1982) have been included for the first time.

The metric system. As of 1991 Americans were accepting meters if they were athletes, and kilometers whenever they traveled outside the borders of the United States. This dictionary, too, now uses the metric system. The most commonly used metric measurements occur in the descriptions of plants: centimeters for width and length of leaves and fronds and heights of shrubs, and meters for heights of trees and for elevations where

Loan words from classical languages.

HAWAIIAN ENTRY	RSV	KJV	SOURCE
ʻaeko, aeto	vulture	eagle	Greek *aetos*
ʻanaka	gekko	polecat, ferret	Hebrew *ʻanaqa*
ʻaneko, aneto	dill	anise	Greek *anethon*
kikona, disona	ibex	pygarg	Hebrew *dison*
lalu, laru	gull (?)	cuckoo	Latin *larus*
pelakano, pelatano	plane tree	chestnut	Greek *platanos*

certain plants grow. Here are some of the most common measurements:

1 inch = 2.54 centimeters
1 foot = 30.48 centimeters
1 mile = 1.6 kilometers

1 centimeter = 0.39 inches
1 meter = 39.37 inches
1 kilometer = 0.6 mile

Reconstructions. In the 1957 edition of the dictionary, the origins of numerous Hawaiian words were traced back three thousand years or so to ancestral Proto Malayo-Polynesian (now called Proto Austronesian). For this new volume, in view of the tremendous advancements during the last three decades in Indonesian studies, we have traced words back only to Proto Polynesian, a hypothetical language spoken at about the time of Christ, probably near Fiji or Tonga, and before the 50 or 60 Polynesian languages known today had developed from it. In the 1957 edition only words known in Proto Austronesian were reconstructed; in this volume we have tried to reconstruct Hawaiian words with cognates anywhere in Polynesia, without consideration of Proto Austronesian.

For the dictionaries consulted, see in the References: Churchward (Tongan), Carroll and Soulik (Nukuoro), Dordillon (Marquesan), Elbert (Rennell and Bellona), Englert (Easter Island), Fuentes (Easter Island), Lemaître (Tahitian), Lieber and Dikepa (Kapingamarangi), McEwen (Niuean), Milner (Samoan), Pukui and Elbert (Hawaiian), Savage (Rarotongan), Stimson and Marshall (Tuamotuan), Williams (Maori). Also see Biggs 1972, 1978.

The spelling system. The orthography in this revision differs in one way from that used in the 1957 edition of the dictionary. The *-w-* following *o* or *u* is treated as a predictable glide; there is no difference in the pronunciation of the pairs listed below—the *-w-* is superfluous. In general, entries in the new dictionary show both forms, and the definition follows the form without the glide. Thus

auē, auwē, exclamation . . .
auwē. See *auē.*

kauā, kauwā 'outcast . . .'
kauwā. See *kauā.*

koali, kowali 'morning glory . . .'
kowali. See *koali.*

'uala, 'uwala 'sweet potato . . .'
'uwala. See *'uala.*

Unfortunately, it was not possible to be entirely consistent in doing this, partly because of the writing habits of older Hawaiian speakers.

An exception: if the *-w-*, even after *o* or *u,* is the initial letter of a semantically related base, the *-w-* is retained, thus: *kūwili* 'to move restlessly' and *wili* 'to twist', *mōwaho* 'afar' and *waho* 'outside', *'uwī'uwī* 'to squeak' and *wī* 'to squeal'.

The following section on provisional spelling recommendations was prepared by Emily Hawkins, president of the 'Ahahui 'Ōlelo Hawai'i ('A'ŌH), a committee of Hawaiian language teachers, formed to address the entire scope of spelling rules, including capitalization, use of non-native letters, use of hyphens, and compound words. In a few instances these rules result in different spellings than those preferred in the dictionary. Most of the differences can be attributed to the separate purposes of the dictionary and the 'A'ŌH spelling recommendations. The dictionary serves as a reference within which meanings are sought for spellings that have been found in reading, while the primary goal of the 'A'ŌH rules is to set a standard orthography to be used in teaching the language. To that end, the 'A'ŌH advocates spelling using the following guidelines:

(a) Spell each word in one way only.
(b) Spell without using hyphens.
(c) Spell with non-native letters when

so pronounced consistently by native speakers.

(d) Write prepositions separate from the word that follows.

(e) Write contractions as one word (e.g., *ia'u, maila, akula, a'ela, ihola, kai*).

(f) Use /w/ only to represent the consonant, not the glide.

(g) Capitalize all words in their use as names.

(h) Write a compound term as one word if the meaning is not evident from its parts.

Following these guidelines, a few discrepancies with the dictionary arise. The greatest differences are found in compound words and vowel length in grammatical particles. More detail can be found in "Recommendations and Comments on the 'Ahahui 'Ōlelo Hawai'i 1978 Hawaiian Spelling Project" by Hawkins and Wilson. The 'A'ŌH committee believes that considerable work remains to be done in these and other areas before the spelling of Hawaiian can be thought to be as firmly established as the spelling of English.

The concept "rare." It is not surprising that half or perhaps more of the words in the revised dictionary are not known today to fluent speakers of Hawaiian. Because language reflects culture, when a culture goes, so too goes much of the language. In the 1957 dictionary many words were labeled "obsolete," but subsequent research found examples of some of them in old texts. The term "obsolete" has therefore been rejected, and "rare" substituted, but only for words not pertaining to the old culture; there is no need to label such words (concerning religion, sorcery, canoe and house making, tapa, tattooing, weapons, diseases and their remedies), as most of them are rare. The term "rare" is reserved for non-cultural words for which no examples have been found in texts, and that have been found only in the dictionaries by Andrews and by Andrews and Parker, and for which no recognizable base

has been noted. Then why keep them? Hawaiian research is just beginning, and unequivocal examples of the words marked "rare" may be discovered some day. They are too precious to discard.

Have any Hawaiian words been "invented"? Over the years hundreds of words have been taken from English and have been rewritten with Hawaiian sounds (Elbert and Pukui, pp. 27–30). Some are not obvious, as *penikila* 'painkiller', *kikane* 'jitney', and *kini,* which in Hawaiian does for 'gin, guinea, Jane, Jean, Jennie, kin, king, tin, zinc'. In some instances, new ideas and inventions fit easily into Hawaiian:

'airport'	*kahua ho'olulu* place anchor *mokulele* flying ship
'air raid'	*pākaha mai ka lewa* raid from the atmosphere
'cleptomania'	*kuko 'aihue* lust to steal
'computer'	*lolo uila* brain electric
'escalator'	*alapi'i lawe 'ōhua* stairs carry passenger
'outer space'	*lewa luna loa* atmosphere high very
'radio broadcast'	*ho'olele leo* cause to fly voice

It is not difficult, either, to invent names of sciences, as:

'anthropology'	*huli kanaka* study man
'archaeology'	*noi'i 'ike hana* research know work *lima* manual

'botany'   *'ike   na'auao i*
                   know wisdom in
                   nā   ā'au like
                   the (pl.) plant same
                   'ole
                   not

'geology'   *'ike   no'eau i*
                   know wise   in
                   nā   pōhaku
                   the (pl.) stone

'linguistics'   *kālai   'ōlelo*
                   carve up language

Some of the early missionary inventions
for terms that the old culture did not need are
picturesque, as *'ike hana no'eau* 'knowing
wise work' for "art," *kahuna pule* 'prayer
expert', for "preacher," *luna 'ike hala* 'officer knowing mistakes' for "conscience," or
moekalohe 'mischievous sleep' for "fornica-
tion."

It is hoped that this edition, like its prede-
cessors, will benefit Hawaiian studies for
many years.

It may be appropriate to conclude these
remarks, written while the book is in press,
with a saying (number 1498) from Mary
Kawena Pukui's classic collection, *'Ōlelo
No'eau:*

> *Kani ke 'ō, he ihona pali.*
> 'One may shout with joy, as this is a going
> down hill.'

Minor corrections have been made for the
third printing of this dictionary. Typographical and alphabetical errors have been cor-
rected, and glosses that have come to my
attention since the original publication have
been added.

S.H.E.
January 1991

On Translating into Hawaiian

He ala ehu aku kēnā.
'A misty pathway, that!'

Partly because of its few phonemes, Hawaiian has more words with multiple meanings than almost any other language. One wishing to name a child, a house, a T-shirt, or a painting, should be careful that the chosen name does not have a naughty or vulgar meaning. The name of a justly respectable children's school, Hana Hauʻoli, means happy activity and suggests a missionary author, but among older Hawaiians it has another, less "innocent" meaning that should not concern little children. A Honolulu street (and formerly the name of a hotel) is Hale Leʻa 'joyous house', but *leʻa* also means orgasm. The Hawaiian name for Frank is Palani, but the *palani* is a strong-smelling surgeonfish and the word has come to mean rancid. Even the common toast in Hawaii that is a translation of "bottoms up" is *ʻōkole maluna* 'buttocks up', not a pretty picture.

But perhaps more common are names with bad grammar. For example, glottal stops are sometimes inserted where none belong, as Hale ʻO Pua and Hui ʻO Kamalei, the names of a flower shop and a hula studio. With the glottal stop, these names mean nothing. Hale O Pua (without the glottal stop) means 'a house belonging to [someone named] Pua'. If the meaning 'house of flowers' is intended, the Hawaiian would be *hale o nā pua,* just as a women's club would be *hui o nā wāhine.*

An artist may spend weeks, months, or years on a painting, and then give it a meaningless title, as " *ʻŌlapa a "* meaning 'Dance of'. ' *ʻŌlapa*-style hula' would be just *"Hula ʻŌlapa."*

The Hawaiian praise of Maui *(Maui nō ka ʻoi)* is well known and is believed to have great sales appeal. The pronunciation is sometimes mangled as *Maui nou ka owe.* A favorite of enterprising businessmen, we have No Ka Oi Appliance, No-Ka-Oi Floral, No Ka Oi Ice, No-Ka-Oi Liquor, No Ka Oi R & R, No Ka Oi Realty, No Ka Oi Termite and Pest Control. All, bad grammar. *Nō ka ʻoi,* which may be translated 'indeed the best', *follows* the noun. Are these as good salesmanship as they are good grammar: Appliance Nō Ka ʻOi, Floral Nō Ka ʻOi, and Ice Nō Ka ʻOi?

A 1984 hula ballet was "He Makana No ʻOe." Understandable, yes, but what bad grammar! The old timer would say *He Makana Nāu* 'a gift for you'.

A few simple rules as to Hawaiian structure, however, may help those who are seeking translations of easy utterances.

1. Adjectives follow nouns. 'Royal child' is *kama lani* or *lei lani*. The place name Lani Kai 'sea heaven' is probably a mistake for Kai Lani 'heavenly sea'. A hula studio is named Halau O Na Maoli Pua 'studio of flower natives'. Could the owner have wished the studio to be called Hālau O Nā Pua Maoli 'studio of native flowers [or children]?

2. The definite or specific articles (*ka* or *ke* in the singular, *nā* in the plural) and the indefinite or non-specific article *he* precede nouns, even nouns that in English do not take articles, as *ka hanohano* 'glory', *ke aloha* 'love', *ka hilahila* 'embarrassment', *he pilikia* 'trouble'.

3. A verb *commonly* precedes its subject. 'The girl is pretty' is *nani ka wahine* (pretty the woman).

Hint: Some Hawaiian words have very many English meanings. The student should study carefully such long entries as *aloha, ʻano, hou, kuleana, lāʻau, lilo, loaʻa, paʻa, pilikia*. All of these are common words and may be used in many contexts—learning to use them wisely will quickly increase one's vocabulary and speaking proficiency.

Acknowledgments

In 1972 Robert Sparks, director of the University of Hawaii Press, suggested that a revision and expansion of the 1971 edition of the dictionary would benefit future generations of the people of Hawai'i. We accepted this challenge, little realizing how many years of research, preparation, and finally proofreading would be necessary, and how many people we would need to consult.

Five persons who spent countless hours on the book will be mentioned first. John Charlot, folklorist and tireless reader of Hawaiian, found a seemingly endless number of new entries and nuances during his perusal of hundreds of Hawaiian pages, including volumes 5 and 6 of the Fornander series, and the books by Green and Pukui, and by Nakuina. (Finally, to cheer a weary Elbert, Charlot said he was leaving Hawaiian and switching to Baudelaire. But of course he didn't.)

David L. Dressel prepared the first versions of the English-Hawaiian section of the dictionary and proofread large portions of both the Hawaiian-English and English-Hawaiian sections—a task even more demanding than the one he performed in the early 1960s for the first *English-Hawaiian Dictionary*.

Derral Herbst carefully examined and proofread the approximately 2,000 plant names and updated the scientific names that had been changed since Marie Neal's 1948 volume.

Esther T. Mookini, who is co-author with the present compilers of earlier books, and who has written important contributions of her own, again devoted her great energies to the new book.

Harlan Murphy, whose work, in range and exactitude, rivals that of a computer, looked up every Hawaiian word listed in the English-Hawaiian section of the dictionary and checked to see that every English gloss was included in the Hawaiian entries.

Then, too, there was Dolores Springer who bravely faced the immense task of typing the enormous coded manuscript for the computer typesetter, a task which, in spite of many untidy pages, she accomplished with great accuracy.

Albert J. Schütz devised a way to indicate stress units of Hawaiian words (to facilitate pronunciation) and described this novel method (see "Pronunciation of Hawaiian," pp. xvii–xviii). Emily A. Hawkins wrote of the spelling system advocated provisionally by the 'Ahahui 'Ōlelo Hawai'i, a committee of teachers of Hawaiian chaired by William H. Wilson (see "The Spelling System," pp. ix–x).

Dorothy B. Barrère generously shared her voluminous gleanings, collected during many years of translating and editing, particularly from Ii 1959, and Kamakau 1961, 1964, and 1976. She and William H. Davenport greatly increased the reliability of the ancient Hawaiian terms for rank, such as *naha, nī'aupi'o,* and *wohi.*

Others who made important contributions include Alison Kay, who verified nomenclature of marine invertebrates; Edgar C. Knowlton, who checked words of Hebrew, Greek, and Latin origin; and Harold St. John, who supplied many not previously recorded Ni'ihau plant names.

Others who suggested entries and helped when needed include Patience Bacon, Andrew Berger, Elizabeth K. Bushnell, Malcolm Chun, Kenneth Emory, Michel Kaiser, Larry Kimura, Michael La Gory, Paki Neves, John Randall, Lee Rogers, Kalena Silva, Cecelia Rapu of Easter Island, and Eleanor Williamson.

To all of you, *mahalo* for helping to make the book possible.

Pronunciation of Hawaiian

Consonants

p, k   about as in English but with less aspiration.

h, l, m, n   about as in English; *l* may be dental-alveolar and *n* dental.

w   after *i* and *e* usually a lax *v;* after *u* and *o* usually like *w;* after *a* or initially, like *w* or *v*.

'   a glottal stop, similar to the sound between the *oh*'s in English *oh-oh*.

Vowels

Unstressed

a like *a* in above
e like *e* in bet
i like *y* in city
o like *o* in sole }
u like *oo* in moon }   but without off-glides.

Stressed

a, ā   like *a* in far   ⎫
e   like *e* in bet   ⎪   but without off-glides; vowels marked
ē   like *ay* in pay   ⎬   with macrons are somewhat longer than
i, ī   like *ee* in see   ⎪   other vowels and are always stressed.
o, ō   like *o* in sole   ⎪
u, ū   like *oo* in moon   ⎭

Rising Diphthongs

ei, eu, oi, ou, ai, ae, ao, au   always stressed on the first element, but the second element has more vowel quality than the off-glide in an English diphthong.

Even Diphthong

iu

Stress (or accent)

As an additional guide to pronunciation, on-line periods are used in many entry words to separate longer words into smaller units, making it possible (for the first time in a dictionary of a Polynesian language) for the reader to stress unfamiliar words properly. The following explanation of this system was prepared by Albert J. Schütz, who devised it.

Stress is a system that marks one syllable as more prominent than those around it.

Contrary to many statements about Polynesian languages, there are no rules to predict which syllable will be stressed in words of more than four syllables. For example, one need only look at a pair of words like

> *'èlemakúle* 'old man'
> *makùahíne* 'mother'

to see that the placement of stress cannot be predicted by counting syllables. For shorter words, however, stress *is* predictable. In the following words, the stress is on the second syllable from the end:

máka, púle, wahíne, kanáka

Stress is placed also on syllables with:

a long vowel, as: *lā̆, kā̆ne*

a diphthong (long or short), as: *kéiki, 'ā̆ina* 'meal'

Thus, there are these kinds of stress units: (1) a dissyllable (such as *maka* 'eye'); (2) a syllable with a long vowel or a diphthong (such as *lā* 'sun' or *kai* 'sea'); and (3) either of these two types preceded by an unstressed syllable (such as *mahalo* 'thank you' or *makai* 'toward the sea'). For such short words, the stress is always predictable: on the last vowel or diphthong, or (if the syllables are short) on the second-to-last syllable.

To show the stress pattern of longer words, we follow this simple premise: long words are composed of a series of two or more such units, each of which has one stress. Thus, the entries for the first examples given are marked as follows: *'ele.makule, makua.hine*

Other examples are:

hei.au 'place of worship'
hō.'ala 'to perfume' (cf. *'ala* 'fragrance'; *ho'āla* 'to awaken someone', and *ala* 'awake'; *ho'āla* is a single stress group, *hō.'ala* is two)
ho'o.ulu 'to inspire' (cf. *uluulu* 'growing')
kana.iwa 'ninety'
Kau.a'i   island name
kū.kae.nalo 'beeswax'

pā.hoe.hoe 'smooth lava'
pule.lehua 'butterfly'

Proper names are not entered in the Dictionary, but when they occur in the quotations, hyphens may separate the words embodied in the name. *These hyphens have nothing to do with pronunciation,* but are useful to those wishing to know the meaning of the names. The pronunciation is shown by stress groups, as in these familiar names:

ETYMOLOGICAL GUIDE	PRONUNCIATION GUIDE
Hana-uma	Hanauma
Ka-imu-kī	Kai.mukī
Ka-mehameha	Kameha.meha
Ka-'ahu-manu	Ka'ahu.manu
Ka-lā-kaua	Kalā.kaua
Ka-pi'o-lani	Kapi'o.lani

Long words that have been borrowed from English show that one cannot rely on meaning or syllable count to determine the correct stress placement:

'Aukeku.lehia 'Australia'
'ekale-sia 'church organization'
kalena.kalio 'calendar'
Kaliki.ano 'Christian'
Kaliki.maka 'Christmas'
Kā.pala.kiko 'San Francisco'
Pā.kī.pika 'Pacific'
pele-kikena 'president'

This marking system is not a change in the spelling system; it is only a guide to placement of stress in pronunciation. It is used in this Dictionary *only* for Hawaiian-English entries.

Glossary of Grammatical and Other Technical Terms Used in the Dictionary

ACCENT. See STRESS.

ACCENT UNIT. See STRESS UNIT.

a-CLASS POSSESSIVE. A possessive containing or consisting of *a, ka,* or *kā* indicating that the possessor controlled or acquired the relationship of the possessed object, as child *(keiki)*/his child *(kāna keiki).*

ARTICLE. A particle preceding nouns *(ka/ ke, he, wahi, nā, nāhi).*

CAUSATIVE/SIMULATIVE (caus./sim.). A derivative formed by a base preceded by *hoʻo, hoʻ, hōʻ, ho,* or *hō;* a common function is to transitivize the meaning of the base *(makaʻu* 'fear, to fear' and *hoʻomakaʻu* 'to frighten'). Less commonly the meaning indicates similarity *(haole* 'white person' and *hoʻohaole* 'to act like a white person').

CONJUNCTION (conj.). A particle connecting sentences, phrases, and words.

DEMONSTRATIVE (demon.). A word denoting relative proximity in space of speaker and hearer; many may replace nouns: *Ua maikaʻi ka hale* 'the house is good'. *Ua maikaʻi kēia* 'this is good'.

DIRECTIONAL. A particle *(mai, iho, aʻe, aku)* following a head word that indicates relative proximity in space or time of speaker and hearer.

EXCLUSIVE. A pronoun or possessive containing *mā,* indicating that the person addressed is excluded, as *kā **mā**ua keiki,* the child belonging to me and someone else but not to you. Cf. INCLUSIVE.

IDIOM. Any short expression with meaning not deducible from the meanings of the parts.

INCLUSIVE. A pronoun or possessive containing *kā,* indicating that the person addressed is included; a husband and wife could say *kā **kā**ua keiki,* the child belonging to the two of us. Cf. EXCLUSIVE.

INTERJECTION (interj.). A short expression that does not fit into the normal patterns of the language, often expressing emotion, but also including salutations, taunts, song refrains, calls to animals, and onomatopoeic sounds.

INTERROGATIVE (interr.). A question word, such as *hea* 'which'.

INTRANSITIVE VERB (vi.). A type of verb that does not take a direct object but that may take a marker of the imperative or passive/imperative, and commonly takes *o*-class possessives. *(Hele!* 'Go!' *Hele ʻia ke ala* 'the road is gone upon'.)

LOCATIVE NOUN (loc. n.). A noun indicating location in space or time. One class of locative nouns includes those not preceded by articles *(ʻō* 'there'); nouns of the other class (preceded by articles) have meanings that differ from those of the same word without preceding articles *(i kai* 'at the sea', *ke kai* 'the sea').

NOMINALIZER (nom.). The particle *ʻana* and the suffixes *na, hana, kana, lana* that change verbs into nouns, as *hele* 'to go', and *hele ʻana* and *helena,* 'going, departure'.

NOUN (n.). A base that may be preceded by an article (especially *ka* or *ke*) or a preposition (especially *ma*); they are often names of persons, places, or things.

NOUN-VERB (nv.). A base commonly used as both noun (without the nominalizer *ʻana*) and verb, as *ka pilikia* 'the trouble', *ua pilikia* 'to be troubled'.

o-CLASS POSSESSIVE. A possessive containing or consisting of *o, ko,* or *kō* indicating that the possessor did not control or acquire the relationship of the possessed object, as parent *(makua)*/his parent *(kona makua).*

OFF-GLIDE. An audible tongue-shifting following a vowel, as in English pronunciation of *e* as *ei,* and *o* as *ou;* Hawaiian *e* and *o* have no off-glides (that is, they are not diphthongized).

PARTICLE. A small item that is not intelligible if used alone and that occurs before and after nouns, pronouns, demonstratives, and verbs, usually with grammatical rather than lexical meaning.

PASSIVE/IMPERATIVE (pas/imp.). The common particle *'ia* and the suffixes *a, na, hia, kia, lia, mia,* and *nia* that passivize a preceding base, or, rarely, change it to a command *(maka'u* 'fear', and *makaū* '**ia** *ke ali'i* 'the chief is feared'; *ha'ina mai ka puana* 'tell the song refrain'; *hukia ka waha o ka 'upena* 'pull the opening of the net'.

POSSESSIVE (poss.). A form denoting ownership. Most Hawaiian possessives contain *a* or *o* (see *a*-CLASS and *o*-CLASS POSSESSIVES).

PREPOSITION (prep.). A particle, often followed by an article, introducing a noun.

PROTO CENTRAL POLYNESIAN (PCP). A reconstruction of a word or sound found in more than one Central Polynesian language, such as Hawaiian, Marquesan, Rarotongan, Maori, and Tahitian, but not occurring in the language of Easter Island.

PROTO EAST POLYNESIAN (PEP). A reconstruction of a word or sound occurring in the Easter Island language and one or more Central Polynesian languages.

PROTO NUCLEAR POLYNESIAN (PNP). A reconstruction of a word or sound occurring in Samoan, Rennellese, East Futunan, or other closely related language.

PROTO POLYNESIAN (PPN). A reconstruction of a word or sound occurring in Tongan or Niue and one or more other Polynesian language.

RARE. A term applied to any entry for which no references have been discovered other than the Andrews and the Andrews and Parker dictionaries. Terms referring to prehistoric culture no longer in existence are not so labeled because their rarity in 1984 is obvious.

RECONSTRUCTION. An ancestral form of a sound or word posited by comparison with similar forms in related languages.

REDUPLICATION (redup.). The repetition of all or part of a base, commonly but not always indicating repeated or continuing action or state. Some reduplications are diminutives.

STATIVE VERB (vs.). A type of verb that is rarely passivized and that generally marks condition or state, as *maika'i* 'to be good, good' and *maopopo* 'to understand'.

STRESS. A system that marks one syllable as more prominent than those around it (also called ACCENT).

STRESS UNIT. A stretch of speech with one accent: in prosodic terms, a *foot.* Hawaiian has the following types: a dissyllable (such as *maka* 'eye'), a syllable with a long vowel or a diphthong (such as *lā* 'sun' or *kai* 'sea'), either of these two types preceded by an unstressed syllable (such as *mahalo* 'thank you' or *makai* 'toward the sea'). For such short words, the stress is predictable: on the long vowel or diphthong, or (if the syllables are short) on the second-to-last syllable.

TRANSITIVE VERB (vt.). A type of verb that may take direct objects and passive/imperative markers.

TRANSITIVIZERS. The suffixes *ka'i, la'i, na'i, a'i, hi, ki, 'i,* and *i* that seem to emphasize the transitive nature of the preceding base.

VERB. A base that may follow certain markers, especially *ua,* usually marking an action or state. See INTRANSITIVE VERB, STATIVE VERB, and TRANSITIVE VERB.

Arrangement of the Hawaiian-English Dictionary

Alphabetization: A hyphen after an entry indicates that the entry occurs only with a following element. A hyphen before an entry indicates that the entry does not occur initially. In determining alphabetical order, entries with following hyphens precede entries with preceding hyphens. Short vowels precede long vowels. The glottal stop is ignored in determination of alphabetical order except that, for example, *a* precedes *'a,* and *kau* precedes *kāu* and *-ka'u.* (Examples: *kau, kāu, ka'u, -ka'u; n-, na, na-, nā-, -na, nā; nana, nanā, nānā; pau, pa'u, pa'ū, pā'ū.*) Single-word entries precede entries consisting of more than one word *('ahamele* before *'aha mele,* but *'ai kū* before *'ā'īkū,* because the latter begins with a long vowel).

Type style: Entries and causative/simulative forms *(ho'o-* and its alternants) are in bold-face type. Hawaiian words in English definitions or translations are italicized, except heiau, hula, lei, poi, and 'ukulele, which are in roman type and are defined only when occurring as entry words.

Stress units: Periods, used in entry words only, set off stress units. See "Pronunciation of Hawaiian," pp. xvii–xviii.

Capitalization: Initial letters are capitalized in names of people, places, institutions, winds, stars, rains, months, *lua* fighting holds, days of the week, and months of the year. If an entry is not capitalized, later numbered homonyms within the entry that require initial capital letters are preceded by the note *(Cap.):* see *'a'ā 3.* Conversely, if an entry is capitalized, later numbered homonyms within the entry that do not require an

initial capital letter are preceded by the note *(Not cap.):* see *Ka'ula.*

Hyphenization: To designate genus and species of flora and fauna, the scientific system (without hyphens) is used: thus *'ohi'a, 'ohi'a 'ai,* and *'ohi'a lehua* for types of *'ohi'a* trees. The same for sociological terms, as for types of gatherings: *anaina, anaina ho'olewa,* and *anaina ho'omana.* Components of long personal names are separated by hyphens, as are parts of names of winds, rains, stars, *lua* fighting holds, and tapa and mat designs. Many long names are poetic and are unwieldy in colloquial conversation. The hyphens make them more intelligible.

Variant spellings. The following types of variant spellings may follow the entry: spellings of loan words *(pailaka, pailata);* spellings with and without the *w*-glide described in "The Spelling System," pp. ix–x *(koali, kowali);* words sometimes spelled with single long vowels and sometimes with double vowels *(oloolo, olōlo).*

Parts of speech. Abbreviations of parts of speech follow entries but are not given for *ho'o-* forms, for reduplications, for entries followed by "Var. of—" or "Same as—," or for entries credited to And. or AP.

Definitions. A definition is generally entered only once. Thus for the following types of entries there will often be only cross references to the entry where the definition is to be found: reduplicated forms in less common use than the base, bases in less common use than the reduplications, passive/imperative forms, variant forms, *ho-* or *ho'o-* forms.

Cross references are also given to examples of the headword elsewhere in the Dictionary. Homonyms are numbered according to frequency of use, except that semantically close words are adjoining, and loan words follow native words.

The elements following the definition of each homonym are listed in the following order (not every entry has all these parts, of course):

1. Hawaiian phrases and sentences illustrating the glosses (using dictionary spelling), followed by the source references if available (see "Abbreviations Used in the Dictionary," pp. xxv–xxvi).

2. Source of loans, as English, Greek, Hebrew, Latin, or other, with English translation if not readily apparent.

3. Variants of the entry, usually preceded by *"Also."*

4. Cross references. *"See"* references are more numerous and more pertinent than *"Cf."* references.

5. References to *Hawaiian Grammar.*

6. *"Rare."* See "The Concept 'Rare'," p. x.

7. Names of Hawaiian islands to which the homonym is confined.

8. Reconstructions: PPN, PNP, PEP, and PCP (see "Abbreviations Used in the Dictionary," pp. xxv–xxvi).

Arrangement of the English-Hawaiian Dictionary

The glosses are arranged in order of approximate frequency of use. Some entries are quite detailed. Extremely rare glosses are given last, often preceded by *"Also":* or *"Rare":*

Caution is urged in use of Hawaiian words that one may find in the English-Hawaiian section. Many have two or more meanings, some of which may have unfavorable connotations (for example, *hala, 'ole, paoa)* or prove embarrassing (see *kali, lua).* For this reason one must look up any Hawaiian word listed on the English side and note all its possible meanings before using it. The English-Hawaiian section is in some ways an "index" to Hawaiian words, but remember:

Mālama o pā 'oe. 'Be careful lest the result be disastrous to you.' (Saying 2122 in Pukui 1983).

Abbreviations Used in the Dictionary

Abbreviations other than Biblical

(See "Glossary of Gramatical Terms" and the References)

And.	Andrews dictionary, 1865; reference is given only if no evidence is available other than that in Andrews and Andrews-Parker (AP)
AP	Andrews-Parker dictionary, 1922; reference is given only if no evidence is available other than that in Andrews (And.) and Andrews-Parker
Cap.	beginning with a capital letter
caus/sim.	causative/simulative
conj.	conjuction
demon.	demonstrative
Eng.	word borrowed from English
ex.	example, examples
f.	form (in names of plants)
fig.	figuratively
For.	Fornander, *Hawaiian Antiquities* (For. 4:297 = Fornander Vol. 4, p. 297)
FS	Elbert, *Selections from Fornander*
GP	Green and Pukui, *Legend of Kawelo*
Gr.	word probably borrowed from Greek
Gram.	Elbert and Pukui, *Hawaiian Grammar*
Heb.	word probably borrowed from Hebrew
HM	Beckwith, *Hawaiian Mythology*
HP	Handy, *Hawaiian Planter*
Ii	Ii, *Fragments of Hawaiian History*
interr.	interrogative
interj.	interjection
Kam. 1964	Kamakau, *Ka Poʻe Kahiko*

Kam. 1976	Kamakau, *The Works of the People of Old*
Kel.	Kelekona, *Kaluaikoolau*
Kep.	Beckwith, *Kepelino*
KJV	King James Version of the Bible
KL.	Beckwith, *Kumulipo*
Laie	Beckwith, *Laieikawai*
lit.	literally
loc. n.	locative noun
Malo	Malo, *Hawaiian Antiquities,* 1951
MK	*Ke Alanui o ka Lani, Oia ka Manuale Kakolika*
n.	noun
n.v.	noun-verb
Nak.	Nakuina, *Moolelo Hawaii . . .*
Nānā	Pukui, Haertig, Lee, *Nānā i ke Kumu*
Neal	Neal, *In Gardens of Hawaii,* 1965
num.	numeral
par.	particle
pas/imp.	passive/imperative
PH	Emerson, *Pele and Hiiaka*
pl.	plural
PCP	Proto Central Polynesian
PEP	Proto East Polynesian
PNP	Proto Nuclear Polynesian
poss.	possessive
PPN	Proto Polynesian
prep.	preposition
RC	Kamakau, *Ruling Chiefs*
redup.	reduplication (for meanings of reduplications, see Gram. 6.2.2)
RSV	*Holy Bible, Revised Standard Version*
sg.	singular

sp., spp.	species	var.	variant, variety
TC	*Taro Collection*	vi.	intransitive verb
UL	Emerson, *Unwritten Literature*	vs.	stative verb
v.	verb	vt.	transitive verb

Biblical Abbreviations and References

(See *Ka Baibala,* 1941, in the References)

Am.	Amosa (Amos)	Lunk.	Lunakanawai (Judges)
Dan.	Daniela (Daniel)	Mal.	Malaki (Malachi)
Epeso	(Ephesians)	Mar.	Mareko (Mark)
Eset.	Esetera (Esther)	Mat.	Mataio (Matthew)
Ezek.	Ezekiela (Ezekiel)	Mele	Mele a Solomona (Songs of Solomon)
Ezera	(Ezra)		
Gal.	Galatia (Galatians)	Mika	(Micah)
Hagai	(Haggai)	Nah.	Nahelu (Numbers)
Hal.	Halelu (Psalms)	Nal.	Nalii (Kings)
Heb.	Hebera (Hebrews)	Neh.	Nehemia (Nehemiah)
Hoik.	Hoikeana (Revelation)	Oih.	Oihana (Acts)
Hos.	Hosea (Hosea)	Oihk.	Oihanakahuna (Leviticus)
Iak.	Iakobo (James)	Oihn.	Oihanaalii (Chronicles)
Ier.	Ieremia (Jeremiah)	Pet.	Petero (Peter)
Ioane	(John)	Pilipi	(Philippians)
Ioba	(Job)	Puk.	Pukaana (Exodus)
Ioela	(Joel)	Roma	(Romans)
Ios.	Iosua (Joshua)	Ruta	(Ruth)
Isa.	Isaia (Isaiah)	Sam.	Samuela (Samuel)
Iuda	(Jude)	Sol.	Solomona (Proverbs)
Kanl.	Kanawailua (Deuteronomy)	Tes.	Tesalonike (Thessalonians)
Kekah.	Kekahuna (Ecclesiastes)	Tim.	Timoteo (Timothy)
Kin.	Kinohi (Genesis)	Tito	(Titus)
Kol.	Kolosa (Colosians)	Zek.	Zekaria (Zechariah)
Kor.	Korineto (Corinthians)	Zep.	Zepania (Zephaniah)
Luka	(Luke)		

HAWAIIAN-ENGLISH

Periods indicate stress units and are only in entry words. See ʻā.ʻā. Hyphens divide long entries into meaningful units. See ʻaʻai-ʻanuhe-a-Kāne, and pp. xvii–xviii.

A

All nouns beginning with a- *or* ā- *may be preceded by the article* ke. *Nouns beginning with* ʻa- *or* ʻā- *may be preceded by the article* ka, *unless otherwise stated.*

a. 1. prep. Of, acquired by. This *a* forms part of the possessives, as in *kaʻu,* mine, and *kāna,* his. (Gram. 9.6.1.) *ʻUmi-a-Līloa,* ʻUmi, [son] of Līloa. *Hale-a-ka-lā,* house acquired [or used] by the sun [mountain name]. (PPN *ʻa.*) **2.** *(Cap.)* nvs. Abbreviation of *ʻākau,* north, as in surveying reports.

-a. Pas/imp. suffix. (Gram. 6.6.3.) (PPN *-a.*)

ā. 1. nvi. Jaw, cheekbone. *Fig.,* to talk a lot, jabber, jibber jabber. *Ke ā nui, ke ā iki,* big jaw, little jaw [bragging and wheedling, as of a man seeking the favor of a woman]. **hoʻā.** To talk a lot, jabber. (PCP *aa.*) **2.** n. An instrument made of smooth bone, formerly used for abortion, lancing, or bleeding. Also *ā ʻōʻō,* piercing *ā.* **3.** nvs. Mold found in souring foods, especially poi, generally known as *Oidium lactis* or *Oospora lactis,* but now called *Geotrichum candidum.* **4.** conj. and prep. When, at the time when, until, to, as far as, and, or *(rare),* and then, but (usually preceding verbs, whereas *a me* usually precedes nouns; *ā* may also connect words translated by English adjectives, as *he poʻe kuli ā ʻāʻā,* a people deaf and dumb; *nani ā pumehana kēia kakahiaka,* this morning is beautiful and warm). (Gram. 9.5, 11.1.) *Ā* also connects verb + noun compounds: see *ʻai ā manō, holoāiʻa,* Gram. 8.7.2. *Ā hiki mai ia,* when he arrives. *Hola ʻelua ā ʻoi,* a little after two oʻclock. *Noho ʻoia malaila ā make,* he lived there until death. Prolonged *ā* may designate a protracted period of time or distance, a long continued action, or emphasis. *Aloha ā nui,* much, much aloha. *Mahalo ā nui,* thanks very, very much. *Holo aʻela ia ā hiki i ka ʻāina kahiki,* he sailed and sailed and sailed until he reached a foreign country. *Hele ā uka,* go clear to the uplands. (PCP *a.*)

-ā. 1. Pejorative suffix, often written *wā* after *o* or *u.* See *ʻaiā, haiā, hainā, huā (huwā), kauā (kauwā), lonoā (lonowā), makoeā, naʻauʻauā (naʻauʻauwā), poluā (poluwā),* Gram. 6.5. (PPN *-haʻa;* cf. Tonga *kaihaʻa* ʻsteal.*.) **2.** Personal article occurring only after the preposition *i,* written *ia.* (Gram. 9.3.1.) (PPN *(ʻ)a.*)

-ā-. Simulative ligature in the sequence ʻverb + nounʼ compounds. See *ʻai ā manō, holoāiʻa,* Gram. 8.7.2. (PPN *aa.*)

ʻa-. 1. Prefix to numbers from one through nine, especially for counting in series. See *ʻalua, ʻakolu, Pōʻahā.* (Gram. 10.3.) (PNP *kaa-.*) **2.** Same as *ʻā-.*

ʻā. 1. nvi. Fiery, burning; fire; to burn, blaze. *Fig.,* to glitter or sparkle, as a gem; to burn, as with jealousy or anger. *ʻĀ akaaka,* to shine brightly, as stars. *ʻĀ ke kaimana,* the diamond sparkles. **hoʻā.** To set on fire, burn, ignite; to light, as a lamp. *Fig.,* to incite, arouse. *Ua hoʻā ʻia kona inaina,* his anger was aroused. *Hoʻā imu,* to light an oven; one who lights an oven. (PPN *kakaha,* PNP *kaa.*) **2.** nvi. *Aa* lava, or lava rock, as distinguished from smooth unbroken *pāhoehoe* lava (formerly preceded by *ke*); to flow, as *aa* lava. **3.** Same as *ʻaʻa 1,* to dare. *ʻAʻole ʻoia i ʻā e noho,* he did not dare to stay. **4.** n. Red-footed booby bird *(Sula sula rubripes),* brown booby *(Sula leucogaster plotus),* masked or blue-faced booby *(Sula dactylatra personata);* all indigenous and also breeding elsewhere. Also *ʻaʻa.* Legendary birds believed to have taken the shape of this bird are *ʻā ʻaia, ʻā-ʻai-ʻanuhe-a-Kāne* and *ʻā-ʻaia-nui-nū-keu; ʻā* by some were considered *ʻaumākua.* See also Kep. 33. **5.** n. Young stage of damselfish *(ʻāloʻiloʻi).* Also *ʻaʻā. ʻĀ ʻaki maunu,* baittaking *ʻā* [said of petty thieves; a var. phrase is *ʻā ʻaki makau,* hook-taking *ʻā*]. **6.** interj. Oh! Well! Ah! Er . . . (Gram. 12.) (PNP *kaa.*) **7.** vt. To drive, as fish or cattle. **hoʻā.** Caus/sim. **8.** n. The letter "a." *Eng.*

ʻā-. In the nature of (as *hina,* white, *ʻāhina,* somewhat white, gray; *pali,* cliff, *ʻāpali,* like a cliff). There are many examples, as *ʻālewalewa, ʻālualua, ʻāmokumoku, ʻāoʻo, ʻāpono, ʻāwela.* (Gram. 6.3.1.) (PNP *kaa-.*)

aʻa. 1. n. Small root, rootlet, vein, artery, nerve, tendon, muscle. *Fig.,* womb, offspring. See ex., *cerebral hemorrhage. Aʻa koni,* throbbing vein or artery, pulse; throbbing, as with excitement or passion. *Aʻa lewalewa,* aerial roots, as put forth by *ʻōhiʻa* trees at high altitudes or in damp climates. *ʻŌ kuʻu aʻa kēia,* this is my offspring. *Kuʻu kaikaina i ke aʻa hoʻokahi,* my younger sibling of the same womb. *Ke koko maloko o nā aʻa,* blood in the veins. **hoʻo.aʻa.** To cause a plant or slip to take root; to take root. (PPN *aka, waka.*) **2.** nvt. To send greetings or love; joyous hospitality; joy at greeting a loved one. Cf. *haaʻa. Makamaka aʻa,* friend who is warmly hospitable. *Ā e aʻa ana ʻo mea mā iāʻoe,* then they send their regards to you.

ʻaʻa. 1. vt. To brave, dare, challenge, defy (1 Sam. 17.10), check, venture; to accept a challenge; to volunteer, involving a difficulty; to act wickedly or presumptuously (Kanl. 1.43); bold, venturesome, valiant, intrepid. See ex., *mea 1. He poʻe ʻaʻa hewa,* a people acting wickedly. *He ʻaʻa ka manaʻo, he wiwo ʻole,* thoughts are full of courage, fearless. **2.** nvt. Belt, girdle, waist; to gird, tie on. *Kākiʻi maila ʻo Ka-haka-loa i kāna laʻau pālau, a loaʻa ihola ka ʻaʻa o Ka-welo* (FS 89), Ka-haka-loa brandished his war club so as to reach Ka-welo's waist. **3.** n. Bag, pocket, caul, envelope for a foetus, scrip (1 Sam. 17.40); fiber from coconut husk; clothlike sheath at base of coconut frond; cloth; chaff, hull (Ier. 23.28); skin covering eyeballs. See *ʻaʻa moni. ʻAʻa haole,* foreign cloth. *ʻAʻa maluna o ke ake,* caul above the liver. *Ka ʻaʻa o ke au ma ke akepaʻa* (Oihk. 3.4), the caul of the bile and the liver. *ʻA ʻole kanaka ʻaʻa ʻole,* no man without his scrip. (PPN *kaka.*) **4.** *(Cap.)* Same as *Maʻaʻa,* a wind. **5.** Same as *ʻā 4,* booby bird.

ʻaʻā. 1. nvi. To burn, blaze, glow; fire; staring, as eyes (see *ʻaʻā maka*). *Fig.,* angry; fury. *ʻAʻā koke,* combustible, inflammable. *Ua ʻaʻā ka puʻu,* the throat is on fire [with great thirst]. *Ke ʻaʻā maila ka wahine,* the woman burns hither [Pele and her volcanic fires approach]. *Ua ʻaʻā ʻia au i ke aloha* (FS 21), I burn with love. **hoʻa.ʻā.** To kindle, light. *Mea hoʻaʻā,* fire kindling. (PNP *kakaa*.) **2.** nvs. ʻA *ʻā* lava; stony, abounding with *aʻā* lava. **3.** *(Cap.)* n. Sirius, a zenith star that passes over Tahiti and Raʻi-ātea, formerly believed used by navigators; one of the brightest stars in the heavens. See *Sirius* for var. names. **4.** n. Young stage of damselfish *(ʻaloʻiloʻi)*. Also *ʻā*.

ʻā.ʻā. 1. nvs. Dumbness, inability to speak intelligibly, a dumb person (Puk. 4.11); dumb, silent, still; to stutter and stammer, as a dumb person. *Poʻe kuli a ʻāʻā,* deaf mutes. *Ua ʻāʻā ka leo,* the voice is unintelligible. *He ʻāʻā kō ka hale,* the people of the house are silent. *I lohe ʻia e nā ʻāʻā lololohe; i mau ʻāʻā lōlōkuli,* it was heard from the dumb one who could hear, about those who were deaf and dumb. **2.** nvs. Dwarf, small person; dwarfish, small. *Kanaka poupou ʻāʻā,* a short stout person. *He ʻīlio ʻāʻā* (KL line 577), a short-legged dog. **3.** vs. Demented, panic-stricken. See *ʻaʻā maka, ʻaʻaia. Holo ʻāʻā,* to run about in a panic. *hō.ʻā.ʻā.* To look about or search in confusion, stray, wander; disconcerted. *E hōʻāʻā ana i nā makaaniani,* looking in confusion for the spectacles. **4.** Probable var. of *ʻā 4,* booby bird. **5.** n. Male *ʻōʻō* bird. (PPN *ka(a)kaa*.)

aʻaʻa. n. Network of veins.

ʻaʻaʻa. nvs. Clothlike sheath at base of coconut frond; vascular bundles in taro corm, chaff, tissue; fibrous, stringy. Also *hāʻaʻa*.

ʻaʻa.ʻā. 1. Redup. of *ʻaʻā 1;* lava cave. **2.** Redup. of *ʻāʻā 1*.

ʻaʻa.ʻaʻa. Redup. of *ʻaʻaʻa. ʻAʻaʻaʻa hoʻi kēia ʻuala,* this sweet potato is full of fibers.

aʻaahi. n. Scion or shoot of sandalwood.

ʻaʻa.ahi. n. Bag for carrying fire-making equipment *(ʻaʻa,* bag, and *ahi,* fire).

ʻaʻa.ʻaki. Redup. of *ʻaʻaki*.

ʻaʻae. n. Second or third crop, as of taro; taro patch where the taro has been pulled up. Also *ʻae*.

ʻaʻa.ea. interj. The sound *ay* that infants make in calling for attention; to make this sound.

ʻaʻaha. n. Netted carrier for a calabash, made of sennit or *olonā* cord. More commonly called *kōkō.* Cf. *ʻaha,* sennit.

ʻaʻahi. Same as *ʻiliahi,* sandalwood. (And.)

ʻā ahi. n. Burning fire. *hoʻā ahi.* To set on fire.

aʻa.hia. Pas/imp. of *aʻa 2*.

ʻaʻaho. 1. n. Thatch purlin; rails, as in a fence. See *ʻahohui, ʻahopiʻo, ʻahopueo. Pā ʻaʻaho,* corral, rail fence. **2.** nvt. Container, as for *pia,* arrowroot starch; to put *pia* in small packages so that it may keep sweet. *Rare.*

ʻaʻahu.kau. Same as *haupia,* coconut and arrowroot pudding.

ʻaʻahu. nvt. Clothing in general, garment, array, attire, costume, mantle, gown; to put on or wear clothing, especially shirt, suit, or coat; to cover or wrap, as the body with a blanket. *E ʻaʻahu aku ʻoe i kēia,* wear this. *ʻAʻahu hoʻohiwahiwa,* festive attire, evening gown. *ʻAʻahu i kau lula ʻia,* formal attire. *ʻAʻahu au i ka pono,* I have clothed myself in righteousness. *hō.ʻaʻahu.* To put clothing on someone else; to dress, supply with clothing, clothe.

ʻaʻa.hua. Pas/imp. of *ʻaʻahu*.

ʻaʻa.huā, ʻaʻahuwā. nvi. To speak reproachfully, contemptuously, deride, jeer; jealous challenge. (Gram. 6.5.) *ʻAʻahuā nohoʻi kāna mau ʻōlelo,* his words are contemptuous.

ʻaʻahu aliʻi. n. Regal attire, a royal robe, a type of colored tapa worn by people of rank.

ʻĀ.ʻā.hua.liʻi. n. A fabulous being said to have had extraordinary strength, to have come from the center of the earth, and to have been the creator of all dwarfs. Cf. *haʻakualiki.*

ʻaʻahu a poʻo. n. Head shield; protection for the head in war, as helmet, shield. (Epeso 6.16.)

aʻa.huʻi. n. Aching veins, varicose veins.

ʻaʻahu kaua. n. Armor, war garment.

ʻaʻa.huki. n. Tendon. *Lit.,* pulled vein. See ex., *wikani*.

ʻaʻahu maka.loa. nv. A long *malo* or ornamented band made of the soft *makaloa* rush; to put on or wear this garment.

ʻaʻahu ʻoi.hana piha. n. Full regalia, dress uniform. *Lit.,* full professional garment.

ʻaʻahu pā.wehe. n. Garment made of *pāwehe,* patterned mat; mat made of soft material and woven in the *pāwehe* pattern; to put on and wear this garment. *No laila i ʻōlelo ʻia ai he ʻaʻahu pāwehe hiwa na ka makani,* so it was called the choice patterned mat made by the spirits.

ʻaʻahu ʻula. Var. of *ʻahu ʻula*.

ʻa.huwā. Var. spelling of *ʻahuā*.

ʻaʻai. 1. Redup. of *ʻai 1;* eating, spreading, festering, increasing, as a sore; ulcerous, cancerous, malignant; to eat away, corrode; to take bait readily, as fish; erosion. See *ʻaʻaiole. He maʻi ʻaʻai,* a spreading sore, infection, or cancer. *ʻAʻai ka hīnālea i ka ʻōpae,* the hīnālea fish takes the shrimp [bait] readily. *Nā manaʻo ʻaʻai ʻawa kaniʻuhū,* heartbreaking, sad thoughts. **2.** vs. Bright, vivid, as of contrasting colors. *ʻAʻai ka lei hulu melemele i ka holokū ʻeleʻele,* a yellow feather lei appears brighter on a black Mother Hubbard. **3.** Same as *ʻaʻei,* a net.

ʻaʻaia. vs. Demented. *ʻO Moikeha, mai Kahiki ka hele ʻana mai, i ʻaʻaia i ke aloha o Luʻukia* (For. 4:161), Moikeha was from Kahiki, where he was mad with love for Luʻukia.

ʻā ʻaia. n. Legendary bird believed to have taken the shape of the *ʻā,* booby bird. See *ʻā 4*.

ʻaʻai-ʻanuhe-a-Kāne. n. Legendary bird. *Lit.,* caterpillar eater of Kāne. See *ʻā 4*.

ʻaʻa.ʻina. Redup. of *ʻaʻina*.

ʻaʻai.ole. nvs. Inferior, weak, said of breadfruit or fruit with a weak stem that may fall before maturity; weak object. (Kep. 93.) *Fig.,* of persons dying before their time. *Mai lou i ka ʻulu i luna loa, o lou hewa i ka ʻaʻaiole, eia nō ka ʻulu i ke alo,* don't pluck the breadfruit on top or you will pluck one not securely fastened, there is the breadfruit in front.

ʻaʻaka. 1. vs. Surly, cranky, roiled, complaining, irritable, peevish, bad tempered, cantankerous, cross; severe, as labor. See ex., *papaioa. Kai ʻaʻaka* (Kep. 103), roiled sea. *hō.ʻaʻaka.* To act surly, to pretend to be cross. **2.** vs. Dry, as coral of the reef at low tide; parched, wrinkled, dry and thirsty; peeling off, as the tough skin of such fish as the *humuhumu* after it has been in the fire; to crackle, burst, as a ripe melon. **3.** n. Rocky undersea cavern, (PH 219, Malo 26.) **4.** n. Wood of the *naio,* bastard sandalwood.

ʻaʻaki. Redup. of *ʻaki 1;* to nip repeatedly; to take a nip and hold on (cf. *nahu,* to bite with the whole mouth, and *nau,* to chew); a bite, nibble. *Fig.,* thick, obscure, dark, penetrating; to feel pangs, as of love or childbirth. *Ka naho manini nui, ke ʻaʻaki nei i ka limu,* the cleft with the large *manini* fish, nibbling now at the seaweed. *ʻAʻaki ke kuʻi,* to close the mouth so tightly that the molars cling, as in lockjaw. *Ua ʻaʻaki paʻa ʻia ke aloha wela i luna o Ka-ʻōnohi-o-ka-lā* (Laie 595), hot love was firmly clutched upon Ka-ʻōnohi-o-ka-lā. *Ke ʻaʻaki nei ka pō ʻeleʻele,* all-engulfing utter blackness of night. (PNP *kakati*.)

ʻaʻaki makau. n. A hook nibbler, said of small fish that nibble away the bait; to nibble at a hook.

ʻaʻako. Redup. of *ʻako 1, 2;* repeated plucking; insatiable lust; to get into action *(rare). ʻAʻako aku i ka hana,* get going with the work.

ʻaʻa koko. n. Vein, blood vessel.

ʻaʻa kolo. n. A root running horizontally that produces roots below and above; a rhizome, creeping root.

ʻaʻa.kū. n. Name of a combination of diseases: liver complication resulting in hardening of the veins, bloody dysentery accompanied by fever.

aʻa kū.kū.kū. n. Varicose veins. *Lit.,* raised veins.

ʻaʻala. 1. nvs. Fragrant, sweet-smelling; fragrance, perfume, aroma, sweet scent. *Fig.*, of high rank, royal. *He 'a'ala nō 'o Ka-'ahu-manu*, Ka-'ahu-manu is of sweet high rank. *Pupuka ho'i paha, he 'a'ala ka inoa*, ugly perhaps, but a noble name. (PPN *kakala*.) **2.** *(Cap.)* n. Winds.

'A'ala Honua. n. Name of a wind accompanied by rain associated with Hilo. *Lit.*, earth fragrance. *Ke honi maila kō Hilo pali kū, kū ka makani he 'A'ala Honua ki'i ua*, those of Hilo with its sheer precipices inhale as the rain-bringing Earth-Fragrance wind blows.

'a'a.lai.hau. n. A fish (no data; perhaps a local name for one of the chaetodons).

'a'ala.'ihi. n. Young of the *ala'ihi* fishes.

'a'alai.oa. nvs. Wild, demented person; uncivilized.

'a'ala.kai. vs. **1.** Insipid, unsavory, tasteless. **2.** Large, plump. Cf. *'u'ulukai.*

'A'ala Loloa. n. Wind name.

'a'olo.'ula. Velvety-green, succulent-appearing seaweeds, one of several species of *Codium*. It yields a red liquid when placed in a container overnight with brine, after chopping or pounding. Both the liquid and the seaweed are well liked, being eaten plain or with other food. (KL line 47.) *'A'ala'ula* is the common name on Kaua'i and Maui, *wāwae'iole* elsewhere.

a'a.lele. n. Pulse, leaping vein.

'a'ali. Redup. of *'ali 1*; scarred, marked, grooved; depression, groove; wattles of a fowl; slight depression under the gills of a fish.

'a'a.li'i. n. Native hardwood shrubs or trees (*Dodonaea*, all species), 30 cm to 10 m high, more or less sticky at branch tips; leaves narrow, 2 to 10 cm long; flowers small; fruit a yellow, red, or brown papery capsule about 1 cm long and with two to four wings. Fruit clusters are made into leis with their own leaves or ferns and worn in the hair. A boast of the people of Ka'ū, is: *He 'a'ali'i au, 'a'ohe makani e hina ai*, I am an *'a'ali'i* shrub, no wind can push me over. See similar ex., *'ula'a*. (Neal 536-7, FS 57.) Also *'a'ali'i kū makani* (*'a'ali'i* standing [in] wind), *'a'ali'i kū ma kua* (*'a'ali'i* standing in back).

'a'a.li'i mahu. Same as *pūkiawe*, shrubs.

'a'a.lina. vs. **1.** Scarred. (PH 218.) **2.** Large, fat, weak, as a fat person.

'a'alo. Redup. of *'alo 1, 2*.

'a'a lole. n. Clothlike sheath at base of coconut frond; European cloth.

a'a.lolo. n. Nerve. *Lit.*, brain vein. *A'alolo ho'ā'o*, taste bud. *A'alolo kuli*, deafness, deaf mute. *A'alolo lohe*, auditory nerve.

'a'alu. n. Ravine, small stream, valley, depression. Cf. *'alu*, depression.

'a'ama. **1.** n. A large, black, edible crab (*Grapsus grapsus tenuicrustatus*) that runs over shore rocks. *'A'ama kua lenalena*, rock crab with yellow back; *fig.*, swift, strong warrior. (PPN *kamakama*.) **2.** vi. To spread and relax, as the fingers. [The *'a'ama* crab was offered in sacrifices so that the gods would loosen (*'a'ama*) and grant the request.] **3.** Redup. of *ama 1*; to talk.

'a'ā maka. nv. To stare or glare with wide-open eyes, as in desire, fear, or intent to frighten; one who does so. **hō.'a'ā maka.** To stare.

'a'a manu. n. Coconut-leaf or pandanus-leaf bag used for carrying birds.

'a'amo. Same as *'amo 2*; contraction of anal muscles.

a'a moku. n. Broken blood vessel.

'a'a moni. n. Purse. *Biblical*.

'a'a.mo'o. n. **1.** Young clothlike sheath at base of coconut frond; gauze, as of a veil; diaphanous cloth. *Lit.*, *'a'a* portion. **2.** Snakeskin; slime, as on fresh water. *Lit.*, lizard *'a'a*.

'a'ana. vi. To use abusive language, revile, malign. Cf. *'a'a*, daring. *Mai 'a'ana mai 'oe*, don't use defiant language. **hō.'a'ana.** Caus/sim.

'a'a.nai. Redup. of *'anai*.

'a'ana.li'i. Var. of *kakanali'i*, stunted.

'a'ana.pu'u. Redup. of *'anapu'u*, bumpy.

'a'a.nema. vt. To criticize maliciously; malign.

'a'a niu. Clothlike sheath at base of coconut frond.

'a'ano. vs. Overbearing, arrogant, bold, defiant, daring; bully. Cf. *'a'a. hō.'a'ano*. To act the bully, bluff, defy, boast of courage that may be lacking; to challenge, take risks, act bold or defiant, dare.

'a'ao. **1.** vs. Greedy, voracious. **2.** n. Uncultivated bananas. *Rare*.

'a'ao ho'o.kahi. Same as *'ao kahi. E hele ke kalo ā 'a'ao ho'okahi*, the taro grew until there was only one leaf left.

'a'apa. Redup. of *'apa*. *Rare*. Cf. *'apa'apa*.

a'a.pau. n. Valve of a vein.

'a'ā pele. nvs. *'A'ā* lava or flow, volcanic.

'a'api. vs. Warped, curved.

'a'apo. vt. To learn quickly, to catch the meaning quickly, apt. Cf. *'apo, 'apo'apo*.

a'a.pū. Same as *a'apau*.

'a'apu. **1.** nvs. Coconut-shell cup; cuplike. Also *'apu.* **hō.'a'apu.** To form a cup of the hollow of the hand; to fold a leaf into a cup. **2.** vi. To warp, bend, ruffle.

'a'a pua. n. Arrow case, quiver.

a'a pū.haka. n. Girdle, belt. *Lit.*, loin belt.

a'a pu'u.pu'u. n. **1.** Capsular ligament. **2.** Knots in a fish net.

'a'ā pu'u.pu'u. n. Sharp or waterworn, coarse gravel or rock.

'a'apu.wai. Same as *'apuwai*, a variety of taro.

'a'au. **1.** vi. To move here and there, wander, rove; to ripple, as the sea. *Ka lele 'a'au o ka manu*, the flight here and there [as in fright] of the bird. **2.** Redup. of *'au*, stalk. *'A'au loa* (Malo 59, 63), long stalks; *fig.*, long-suffering and patient, as of a chief who cared for his people. (PPN *kakau*.)

'ā.'aua. vs. Coarse, as wrinkled or blotched skin; lean, as fish. Also *'aua, mā'aua. Pua'a 'a'aua*, old tough pig.

'a'awa. **1.** n. Wrasse fishes, Hawaiian hogfish (*Bodianus bilunulatus*), considered *'aumākua* by some. The name *'a'awa* may be qualified by the terms *'e'a, hai'e'u, lelo, ule holu* (pliable penis). Also *po'ou*. (PPN *kawakawa*.) **2.** Same as *'a'awa hua kukui*. **3.** Name given for an insect that destroys potatoes. (And.)

'a'awa hua kukui. n. A native tree (*Pittosporum hosmeri* and its varieties), about 6 m high, with leaves 10 to 25 cm by 1.5 to 6 cm, shiny and wrinkled above, brown-wooly beneath; small, clustered, cream-colored flowers; ovoid fruits about 5 cm long, each with two to four thick valves containing orange pulp and black oily seeds. Also *hō'awa, hā'awa*. (Neal 382-4.)

'a'awe. Same as *'awe*, to carry.

a'e. **1.** n. Several native trees, the soapberry (*Sapindus saponaria* f. *inaequalis*), and all species of *Zanthoxylum* (also known as *Fagara, Zanthoxylum* having yellowish wood formerly used for digging sticks and spears); seeds of all (largest in the soapberry) are black, round, and used for leis. Also *mānele*. (PPN *ake*.) **2.** *(Cap.)* n. Northeast tradewind. Cf. *A'e Loa, Moa'e, na'e*. **3.** n. Blight. (Malo 199.) **4.** directional. Upward, sideways, nearby, contiguous, adjoining, next, approaching (often expresses space and time near the addressee, table 2, Gram. 7.2). *Hele a'e*, to go up, sideways. *Kanaka 'ē a'e*, different person. *Kēia pule a'e*, next week. *Ko'u mua a'e*, the one born just before me [older sibling, the one before me]. *'O wai hou a'e?* Who will be next? *Ā he aha a'e?* And what next? *'O āu keiki a'e kēia*, here come your children. *Ia lā a'e, ia lā a'e*, from day to day. *A'e* also commonly expresses the comparative degree: *maika'i a'e*, better. Followed by *nei, a'e* indicates recent past: *Ua hele a'e nei no Maui*, [he] has just gone to Maui. *A'e* + demon. *lā* is pronounced and written as a single word, *a'ela*. *'Ī a'ela 'oia*, he said to someone nearby (cf. *aku 2*). (PPN *hake*.) **5.** Replacement of *e* in songs (commonly written *a e*, but a glottal stop is pronounced before '*e*). *'A'ole* *mākou a'e minamina i ka pu'u kālā a ke aupuni* (song), we do not care about the government's sum of money. **6.** n. Maui name for *maua 2*, trees.

'ae. 1. vt., interj. Yes; to say yes, consent, conform, grant, agree, approve, let, confirm, admit, permit, allow, accept, yield; approval, admission, permission. Cf. *a'e nei. 'Ae waha,* oral agreement. *'Ae wale,* to agree easily; pliable. *Ua 'ae mai 'oia i ko'u hele,* he consented to my going. (PCP *(')a(a)e.*) **2.** n. Sap wrung from seaweed or leaves of plants such as taro; liquid remaining after dregs have settled, as of *pia,* arrowroot starch; saliva, drooling of the mouth. *'Ae limu,* juice remaining on the pounding board after seaweed *(limu)* is pounded; mixed with salt it is used to flavor sauce for *'ō'io* or other fish. *Kahe ka 'ae o ka waha,* mouth saliva flows [mouth waters; *fig.,* to desire avidly]. **3.** vs. Fine, mashed, comminuted, as dust or powder; silky soft, as down; smooth, as well-mixed poi or bread dough. *'Ae moa,* downy chicken feathers. **hō.'ae.** To make fine, pulverize, refine, soften. *He ahi 'ā nopu hō'ae,* a hot glowing fire that pulverizes. **4.** vi. To rise, of the tide. **hō.'ae.** Caus/sim. **5.** n. A native fern *(Polypodium pellucidum)* commonly seen at Kī-lau-ea Volcano. It has oblong fronds 15 to 40 cm long, once divided into about fifteen or more pairs of oblong segments, each of which bears many round fruit dots. (Neal 25.) Cf. *'ae lau nui.* **6.** Same as *'a'ae.* **7.** n. Shoots from main root portion of the *wauke* plant. See *ohi 3.* **8.** See *'ae kai,* water's edge.

'a'e. nvt. To step over, get on top of, tread upon, trespass; to raise; to massage the back with the feet; to break a taboo or violate a law; counter sorcery; to inflict sorcery on a sorcerer; to get into by stepping up, as into a car; step. *Fig.,* oppressed. *'A'e kū, 'a'e kapu,* to trespass, break a law or taboo deliberately; disrespectful of taboo. *'A'e loa,* long step, long journey. *Ua 'a'e lākou i luna o kahi la'a,* they trespassed on a taboo place; they broke an agreement, law, taboo. *'A'ohe i 'a'e i ka wela a ka lā,* not oppressed by the heat of the sun. **hō.'a'e.** Caus/sim. (PPN *kake.*)

aea. vi. To rise up; to raise the head; to come up from under water. *Lu'u aku a aea mai* (song), dive down and come up.

'aea. n. Cord, as used in joining two or more nets into a larger one. *Rare.*

'ae'a. nvi. Wandering, shiftless, unstable; to wander, stray; tramp. Cf. *hōkū 'ae'a. 'Ae'a hauka'e,* vagrant person, tramp, beachcomber, trespasser; to trespass *(lit.,* defiled wanderer). *Kanaka 'ae'a,* wanderer, drifter, tramp (less pejorative than *'ae'a hauka'e*). One *'ae'a,* shifting sands. **hō.'ae'a.** To cause to wander; to wander. *Na ke kaumaha i hō'ae'a iāia mai ke one hānau mai,* it was grief that caused him to wander from his homeland.

'a'ea. Pas/imp. of *'a'e 1.*

ae.ae. 1. nvi. A prolonged sound, wail; to prolong, stretch. **ho'āe.ae.** A style of chanting with prolonged vowels and fairly short phrases, much used in love chants; to chant in this fashion; to read or recite Bible passages or multiplication tables. **2.** n. Andante.

a'e.a'e. 1. vt. Mixing of a dark or brilliant color with a lighter one, as feathers in a lei; of dark hair of a young person with streaks of gray; to mix, as drinks. *A'ea'e mōhala i luna o ke kukui,* streaks of silvery gray showing on the candlenut tree [said of a graying person]. **2.** n. A kind of banana with green and white striped leaves and fruits. (Neal 249.) Also *koa'e* and *manini.* **3.** n. A fish (no data).

'ae.'ae. 1. Redup. of *'ae 3.* See *lole, mehelu.* *Hulu 'ae'ae,* downy feathers. *Ka 'ai 'ae'ae,* soft food or poi. **hō.- 'ae.** To make soft, fine, etc. **2.** n. A small native shrub *(Lycium sandwicense)* growing near salt marshes and among rocks near the sea. It has light-colored

bark; succulent, narrow pale-green leaves about 2.6 cm long; small white to blue-tinted flowers; and small red berries. (Neal 740.) Also *'ākulikuli 'ae'ae, 'ākulikuli 'ōhelo,* and *'ōhelo kai.* **3.** n. Water hyssop, a succulent herb *(Bacopa monnieria).* Ni'ihau. Cf. Neal 759. **4.** Redup. of *'ae 4. 'Ae'ae kai,* rise of the tide; froth of the sea.

'a'e.'a'e. Redup. of *'a'e.*

ae.ā.ea. n. A small green fish resembling the *hīnālea,* used as *pani* (food or drink taken to finish a medical treatment) for certain diseases of children of the *'ea* type.

'Ae.'ae-a-hiwa. n. Name of a star (no data).

'ae'a hau.ka'e. 1. See *'ae'a.* **2.** n. A variety of wild sweet potato, good only as pig food.

'a'ei. n. Fine net, as used for *'ōpelu* and *maomao* fish; it was held open at the mouth by *kuku,* stretching poles.

ā.ē.ī.ē. interj. Chant refrain.

ā.ē.ī eia. interj. Chant ending.

'a'e ka'a. n. A step, as on a carriage; running board of an automobile.

'ae kai. n. Place where sea and land meet; water's edge.

'ae.kai mokiha. n. Ancient type of tapa (no data).

'aeke.lona, aeselona. n. Falcon, vulture.

'aeko, aeto. n. **1.** Eagle. *Lio hulu 'aeko,* dark-gray horse; *lit.,* eagle-feather horse. (Gr. *aetos.*) **2.** Alto. *Eng.* See *'aleko.*

'aeko kula. n. Golden eagle.

a'ela. Directional part. *a'e* + demon. *lā.* See ex., *a'e 4.*

'ae lau niu. Same as *'ae 5,* with large leaves.

'ae.like. nvi. Agreement, contract, truce, accord, deal; to come to an agreement; contracted. *Palapala 'aelike,* contract. *Nā mea 'aelike,* terms or conditions of agreement. *'Aelike ho'oku'u ma kahi,* compromise, one side gives up.

ā.elo. vs. Rotten, of eggs that do not hatch due to infertility. *Fig.,* spoiled, worthless. *Hua āelo,* rotten egg; *fig.,* in vain, worthless. *E mālama ho'i o hua āelo ka luhi o ka ho'oikaika 'ana,* be careful, lest the wearisomeness of the effort be in vain. (PPN *'elo.*)

A'e Loa. n. Name for the trade wind. See ex., *ki'eki'e.* Cf. *A'e 2, Moa'e, welo 1.*

a'e nei. Just now, lately; nearby, not far; ordinary, insignificant. *E like me ka'u i 'ōlelo a'e nei,* just what I just said. *Ua hele a'e nei,* just now gone. *Ma'ō a'e nei nō,* just over there, not far. *Kahi 'eha a'e nei nō,* just a minor pain. *Kahi 'ike a'e nei nō,* nothing outstanding about the knowledge.

ae'o. n. **1.** Stilts. **2.** Hawaiian stilt bird *(Himantopus mexicanus knudseni),* an endemic subspecies of stilt, formerly common on the main Hawaiian Islands, endangered. Also *kukuluae'o.* **3.** Same as *kīholo 1,* wood fishhook. *Kaua'i.*

'ae o hope. n. Train of a dress (origin uncertain). (Kam. 76:99.)

'ae.'oia. vi. To be well supplied with comforts and necessities. *He nohona 'ae'oia,* a well-supplied way of life. *Ua 'ae'oia a'ela ka 'ohana,* the family has all it needs.

'ae-o-kaha-loa. n. A kind of fine tapa, used in *kuni* and other ceremonies, as for divining with pebbles. Also *kaha-loa, pālau-anahu.*

'ae one. n. Sandy beach.

ā.ewa. vi. **1.** Thin, tall, spindly; to weave to and fro, as seaweed; to sway, as a branch or sea eddy. Cf. *ewa, māewa. Ulu maika'i a āewa hua 'ole* (Kep. 159), growing well but spindly and fruitless [of bananas]. **2.** Possessing a family or lineage. Cf. *ēwe 1. Hānau ka huelo māewa, he āewa kona* (KL line 525), born [those of] tail-end [junior] rank, they have their lineage.

aha. inter. Why? What? For what reason? To do what? To ask what? *(Aha* frequently follows *he* and is often written *heaha;* cf. Gram. 4.6, 8.5.) *He aha?* What is it? What? *He aha kēlā?* What is that? *He aha kāna?* What has he got there? What does he have to say about it?

What business is it of his [sarcastic]? *I ke aha?* Why? What for? *He aha ia mea?* What of it [frequently spoken with an outward gesture of the right hand with palm upwards]? *He . . . aha?* What kind of? For what purpose? *He hale aha kēlā?* What kind of a house is that? What is it used for? *He mea aha?* What's it used for [annoyance]? Why? *He aha ihola lā,* no one knows why, for no apparent reason. *He aha ihola lā 'o ka ua nō ia,* for no reason it's raining. To what? Why? *E hele ana 'oe i ke aha?* Why are you going? *No ke aha?* Why? *E aha ana 'oe?* What are you doing? *E aha 'ia ana?* What is being done? *E aha ana lā lāua nei?* (FS 231) What are the two doing here? *I aha 'ia ke ka'a?* What happened to the car? *I aha ai ka hele 'ana?* (pronounced *iahai*), Why go? *E kama'ilio ā e aha?* What's the use of talking? *Aha maila ke kahuna, "He mea aha?"* (Kep. 21) The priest asked, "What's that?" *O aha?* Lest what? What will happen then? *O aha'ina* (contraction of *o aha 'ia ana*)? Lest what happen? (PPN *haa* and probably *hafa,* PEP *afa.*)

ā.hā. interj. Aha (exclamation of surprise). *Āhā, loa'a pono ke kolohe!* Ah, the culprit is caught redhanded!

'aha. 1. n. Meeting, assembly, gathering, convention, court, party. Many types of *'aha* are listed below. **2.** nvi. Sennit; cord braided of coconut husk, human hair, intestines of animals; string for a musical instrument; to stretch the *'aha* cord for the outline of a house so that the posts may be properly placed; measurement of an edge or border. *Ua like nā 'aha,* the sides are of equal length [as of a rectangle]. *E ki'i i ke kaula e 'aha ai,* get a cord to stake out the house with. *hō.'aha.* To make or braid *'aha;* to tie up a calabash. (PPN *kafa.*) **3.** n. A prayer or service whose efficacy depended on recitation under taboo and without interruption. The priest was said to carry a cord *('aha).* (Malo 180–1.) *Ua ka'i ka 'aha,* the prayer is rendered. *Loa'a kā kākou 'aha,* our prayer is rendered successfully. *Ua lilo ka 'aha, ā laila pule hou,* the prayer has not been successfully given, so pray again. **4.** n. Millepede, so called because it coils itself up like a string. **5.** n. Any of the needlefishes of the family Belonidae. The young are called *'aha'aha.* Varieties are qualified by the terms *holowī, mele,* and *uliuli.* **6.** n. Design supposed to resemble the continuing track of a duck, carved on tapa beaters. Also *'ahaana* and *kapua'i-koloa.*

'ahā. num. Four (usually in counting in series): four times. *Pō'ahā,* Thursday.

ahaaha. vi. To pant, to breathe hard with heat, as a dog. Cf. *hā,* breath.

'aha.'aha. 1. n. Cordage. **2.** vi. To sit with back stiff and upright, arms akimbo, head up, as with haughty air of superiority; to sit cross-legged; to stand with hands on hips (considered rude and overbearing). *He aha lā ho'i kā ia nei e kū 'aha'aha mai nei?* What's he standing here haughtily with hands on hips for? *hō.'aha.'aha.* To sit or stand thus. (Perhaps PPN *kafa.*) **3.** n. Young of the *'aha,* a fish.

'aha.'aina. nvi. Feast, dinner party, banquet; to feast. *Lit.,* meal gathering. Many types of *'aha'aina* are listed below. *hō.'aha.'aina.* To feast, give a feast.

'Aha.'aina a ka Haku. n. Holy Communion, Lord's Supper; feast of the Lord.

'aha.'aina hepe.koma (hebedoma). n. Feast of weeks. (Puk. 34.22.)

'aha.'aina ho'o.la'a. n. Feast of consecration or dedication, as of a house, church, canoe, or fish net.

'aha.'aina ho'o.lilo. n. Feast of dedication. (Ioane 10.22.)

'aha.'aina ho'o.mana'o. n. Commemorative or anniversary feast.

'aha.'aina kahe. n. Feast given at the time of a boy's subincision. Called in Christian times *'aha'aina 'oki poepoe.*

'aha.'aina kahu.kahu. n. Feast given at the completion of a student's first work (as mat, quilt, tapa, net), or of

a child's first fish catch; one purpose w; gods to grant greater knowledge and skill man. *Lit.,* feast to care for. Cf. *kahukahu.*

'aha.'aina kala hala. n. Feast given to ask p; gods. *Lit.,* feast to forgive sins.

'Aha.'aina Kau.hale.lewa. n. Feast of T *Biblical.*

'aha.'aina komo. n. Initiation feast.

'aha.'aina lau.lima. n. Feast held after comp joint project or cooperative undertaking, harvest.

'aha.'aina lima luhi. Similar to *'aha'aina maka*

'aha.'aina maka luhi. n. Feast given to honor t prepared the feast and served, the workers bei by those who had celebrated before; also a celebrate completion of a particularly labori(ject. *Lit.,* feast for tired persons.

'aha.'aina make. n. Funeral feast, intended to (the mourners.

'aha.'aina male (mare). n. Wedding feast or rece;

'aha.'aina mā.wae.wae. n. Feast given shortly a; birth of the first child, intended to clear th *(māwaewae)* of misfortune for that child and i others to follow.

'Aha.'aina Mō.lia.ola. n. Feast of the Passover. *lical.*

'Aha.'aina Pelena (Berena). n. Holy Communion. feast of bread.

'aha.'aina piha maka.hiki. n. Feast on the first b day of a child, or to celebrate any anniversary. i feast for completion of the year.

'aha.'aina pī wai. n. Feast given principally to break monotony of country life; those instigating the fe would sprinkle *(pī wai)* their friends with a little wat those sprinkled brought food to the feast or, later, gi of coins.

'aha.'aina puka. n. Graduation feast.

'aha.'aina 'ū.niki. n. Graduation feast, as for hula dan(ing or *lua* fighting.

'aha.'aina wai.maka. n. Feast of tears, held on the firs anniversary of a death, a happy occasion, as the deatl by this time has been accepted by the family (Nānā 138).

'ahaana. n. Design said to resemble duck tracks, carved on tapa beaters. Also *'aha* and *kapua'i-koloa.*

'aha 'ā.pana. n. District court.

'aha 'elele. n. Convention of delegates; name for American presidential conventions.

ahā.hā. Var. of *ahahana.* (FS 13.)

aha.hana. interj. Syllables repeated in chants, usually at ends of verses, similar to *ēhē;* a taunting singsong teasing phrase, used especially by children, meaning "Oh! Oh! Aha! Shame on you! You are going to catch it!" As a verb, to tease. See ex., *lei 1, 'uhene.* Also *ahana* and *ahana kōkō lele,* both meaningless. *Mai ahahana 'oe i kou pōki'i,* don't tease your young brother.

'aha hā.wele. n. Cord support for gourd water bottles.

'aha hele honua. n. Ceremonial measuring of the dimensions of a *mana* house within a place of worship; a priest carried a line to the four corner posts of the *mana,* and the chief sacrificed a pig; name of the line. (Malo 166–7.)

'aha hī.meni. n. Song festival, concert.

'aha hō.'ike maka.hiki. n. Annual meeting of Sunday Schools, as of Congregationalists.

'aha ho'o.kō kau.oha. n. Probate court.

'aha ho'o.kolo.kolo. n. General name for court assembly. Names of several types of courts are listed below.

'aha ho'o.kolo.kolo 'ā.pana. n. District court.

'aha ho'o.kolo.kolo ho'o.malu. n. Police court.

'aha ho'o.kolo.kolo ka'a.puni. n. Circuit court.

'aha ho'o.kolo.kolo kā.kau. n. Old name for *'aha kākau,* court of records.

'aha ho'o.kō. n. Executive council.

'Aha Ho'o.kolo.kolo Ki'e.ki'e. n. Supreme Court.

ha ho'o.kolo.kolo koa. n. Military court, court martial.

ha ho'o.kolo.kolo ko'i.ko'i. n. Superior court.

aha ho'o.kolo.kolo malalo iho. n. Lower court.

aha ho'o.malu. n. Administrative body, assembly.

aha ho'o.pono.pono i ka nohona. n. Court of domestic relations.

aha ho'o.pono.pono wai.wai ho'o.ilina. n. Probate court. *Lit.,* court settling inheritance property.

'aha.hui. n. Society, club, association, organization, company, convention. Various types are listed below.

'Aha.hui 'Euane.lio Pae 'Āina. n. A term used in 1911 for evangelical conference of all the islands.

'Aha.hui Hō.'ikaika Kaliki.ano. n. Christian Endeavor Society.

'aha.hui ho.'ole wai 'ona. n. Temperance union. *Lit.,* society forbidding intoxicating liquor.

'aha.hui 'imi na'au.ao. n. Academy, learned society.

'Aha.hui Kanu Kō Hawai'i. n. Hawaiian Sugar Planters' Association.

'aha.hui kula Kā.paki (Sabati). n. Sunday School association.

'aha.hui malū. n. Secret society.

'Aha.hui Māmaka.kaua. n. Sons and Daughters of Hawaiian Warriors. *Lit.,* warriors' society.

'Aha.hui Mo'o.lelo Hawai'i. n. Hawaiian Historical Society.

'aha.huina. 1. n. Corporation, association. 2. *(Cap.)* vs. Congregational. *Rare.*

'Aha.hui Wāhine Kaliki.ano Hō.'ole Wai 'Ona. n. Women's Christian Temperance Union.

'aha hula.hula. n. 1. Assembly for ballroom dancing; a ball. 2. Ancient assembly for the *hulahula* religious ceremony.

'aha.hulu.hulu. n. Bristle worm, a hairy sea creature *(Eurythoe complanata).*

'ā.hai. n. Commemorative wooden or stone pillar (probably short for 'ā *hailona,* symbolic stone).

'ā.ha'i. vt. To carry off, chase, rout; to flee, run away. *Ka 'āha'i 'ana i nā po'e ha'iha'i kānāwai,* the pursuit of lawbreakers.

'ā.ha'i.ha'i. Redup. of *'āha'i. Na ka manu 'āha'iha'i, kanu lau 'awa o uka* (song), it was the birds who carried, planting kava leaf in the upland.

'ā.ha'i.kapu.puhi. vi. To go with the wind, to disappear completely. *Ua 'āha'ikapupuhi mua akula ku 'eu'eu Ko'olau* (Kel. 55), clever Ko'olau had completely vanished.

'aha iki. n. Small gathering for private conversation; small or secret council, as called in an emergency.

'ā.ha'i.lono. nv. Reporter, messenger, bringer of news; in legends, the sole survivor of a disastrous defeat who reports the news; to tell news.

aha.'ina. Short for *aha 'ia ana.* See *aha.*

'ā.ha'ina. Same as *'āha'i.*

'aha inu. n. Drinking party, as *'aha inu waina,* wine-drinking party, *'aha inu lama,* rum party.

'ā.ha'i 'ō.lelo. nv. Messenger; to carry word.

'aha ka'a.puni. n. Circuit court.

'aha kā.kau. n. Court of records.

'aha kapu. n. 1. A sacred assembly. 2. Sacred sennit cord belonging to a high chief and kept on a high place before his house; trespassers entering the house were killed if the cord remained in place, but if it fell down and the stranger stepped over it, this was a token of the stranger's high rank or kinship with the owner of the cord. Some chiefs had several such cords, each given a name, and some were used after the owner's death in making the *kā'ai,* container for his bones.

'aha kau kā.nā.wai. n. Session of the legislature.

'aha kau.like. n. An 1854 name for the highest court.

'aha kau.oha. n. Probate court.

'aha.kea. n. 1. Native trees (species of *Bobea*) with small to medium-sized, oblong leaves; small greenish or white flowers; and small, purple-to-black juicy fruits.

The wood is yellow and formerly was used for poi boards and canoe rims. *I ke aha ho'i? I ka 'ahakea.* Why then? The *'ahakea* [a saucy retort containing a pun on the word *aha,* what]. 2. Same as *haokea,* a taro.

'aha.kea lau li'i. n. A small-leafed *'ahakea (Bobea elatior* var. *brevipes).*

'aha.kea lau nui. n. A large-leafed *'ahakea (Bobea elatior).*

'aha kene.koa. n. Senate.

'Aha Ki'e.ki'e. n. Supreme Court.

'aha kiule ki'e.ki'e. n. Grand jury.

'Aha Ko'i.ko'i. Same as *'Aha Ho'okolokolo Ki'eki'e. Lit.,* powerful court.

'aha.kū. n. Cord used for measuring, as in laying out a garden or house. *Ho'omoe 'ia mai ka 'ahakū,* now lay down the measuring line.

'aha kuhina. n. Cabinet, assembly of ministers.

'aha kū.kā. n. Council meeting, discussion meeting, advisory council, conference.

'aha kū.kā malū. n. Privy council, secret deliberative meeting.

'aha lima.lima. See *limalima.*

'aha.lua.like. n. Rectangle. *Lit.,* two equal sides.

'aha luna.kahiko. n. Presbytery, meeting of elders.

'aha luna.kā.nā.wai. n. Judiciary session, meeting of judges.

'aha maha. n. Place or assembly for practice of athletic games, as sham fights. *Lit.,* assembly for relaxation.

'aha.maka. n. 1. Hammock, as of tapa, fastened to the *manuea,* center support of a house; hammock in general. *Lit.,* sennit meshes. 2. Cord with which edges of cracks in gourd bowls were sewn together in crisscross patterns suggestive of net mesh; the technique for such repair. 3. Strangling in *lua* fighting, as with green vines. 4. Secret meeting of priests to pray for a chief.

'aha.mele. n. A yellow-spotted needlefish.

'aha mele. n. Concert, song concert, song festival.

'aha.moa. n. 1. An assembly watching a *lua* contest of the kind called *hakakā-a-moa.* 2. A cord made from the entrails of an enemy killed in a *lua* fight of the *hakakā-a-moa* type.

'aha moku.puni. n. Island conference, with representatives from a single island, especially of Congregationalists.

ahana. Same as *ahahana.*

'aha ni.ele. n. Inquisition, inquest. *'Aha nīele kumu make,* coroner's inquest.

'aha nina.ninau. n. Court of inquiry.

'aha.niu. n. A native sedge *(Machaerina mariscoides* subsp. *meyenii)* with pointed, leathery leaves about 90 by 1.6 cm, mostly basal around a more or less zigzag spike, which bears light-brown scattered flower clusters. See also *'uki,* all species of *Cladium* and *Machaerina.* (Neal 89.)

'a.hao. Probably similar to *hao 3, 4.* (For. 6:472.)

'aha.'ō.lelo. nv. Legislature, assembly, council meeting, congress; to hold such meetings; to serve in the legislature.

'aha.'ō.lelo kau kā.nā.wai. n. Legislature, lawmaking body.

'aha.'ō.lelo lā.hui. n. Congress of the United States; national assembly.

'aha.'ō.lelo luna.kahiko. n. Conference of elders.

'aha.'ō.lelo nui. n. Congress.

'aha o nā luna.kā.nā.wai 'ā.pana. n. District court.

'aha pae.'āina. n. Convention of delegates from all the islands, especially as held by the Hawaiian Evangelical Association of Congregational Christian Churches.

'aha.pi'i. n. A kind of tapa dyed with *kukui* bark and decorated with fine lines, for chiefs.

'aha pule. n. Congregation, prayer assembly.

'aha 'uao ('uwao). n. Board of arbitration.

'aha 'ula. n. Council of chiefs. *Lit.,* regal meeting.

'ahawa. Waterhead, beginning of a water-course; to overflow. (AP.)

ahe. nvi. Breeze; to blow or breathe gently, waft; softly blowing. *Ke ahe makani Pu'u-lena,* the gently wafting Pu'u-lena breeze.

ā.hē. vi., interj. To exclaim, to oh and ah; yes, so that's it, so, oh. *Āhē, pēlā kou mana'o, 'eā?* So that's your opinion, is it [in indignation]? *'Oia ka malama a ka po'e mahi 'ai e āhē ai i ka ulu maika'i a nā mea kanu* (Kep. 91), this is the month the farmers exclaim about the fine growth of the crops.

'ahē. nvi. A hacking cough; to cough. Also *'ehē.* Cf. *'ahē'ahē, 'ehē'ehē.*

'ā.hē. 1. vs. Timid, shy, wary. 2. n. Wild taro. *Kaua'i.* Varieties are qualified by the colors *ke'oke'o* and *'ula'ula.* Called *'āweu* on Hawai'i.

ā.hea. 1. Pas/imp. of *ahe. Lohe lau āhea,* hearing of the many breezes [rumor]. 2. inter. When (future). (Gram. 11.2.) (PPN *'afea,* PNP *aafea.*)

'ahea. Same as *'āheahea 2.*

ahe.ahe. Redup. of *ahe;* soft, gentle in sound; weak. *Pā mai ka makani aheahe,* the gentle wind blows. *He kamumu o ke aheahe mālie,* rustle of the gentle breeze, sound of quiet whispers. *Aheahe kahi 'ōpū i ka pōloli,* the stomach feels weak with hunger.

'ahē.'ahē. Redup. of *'ahē. I ka manawa 'ahē'ahē, kau maila ka 'ahē'ahē make maluna o lāua,* at the time of coughing, a deadly coughing seized upon the two of them.

'ā.hea.hea. 1. vi. To wilt, as a plant; warm, insipid. 2. n. A native shrub *(Chenopodium oahuense)* and an introduced weedy herb *(C. album),* both with narrow to triangular or rhomboidal, thickish leaves; flowers small, in panicles. Young plants, leaves, and plant tips are used for greens, wrapped in ti leaves and cooked on hot coals. Also *'ahea, 'āhewahewa, alaweo; alaweo huna (Ni'ihau), 'āweoweo.* (Neal 331.) 3. Var. name for *pakai 2.* 4. Same as *heahea,* to call.

'ahele. nvt. Snare; to snare. Also *pahele. 'Ahele pulu niu,* snare of coconut fibers, as for *'a'ama,* a crab.

'ā.hewa. 1. nvi. To condemn, blame, censure, reproach, convict; condemnation, blame, conviction. *Mamuli o kona 'āhewa 'ia 'ana ua hopu hou 'ia,* after his conviction [he] was rearrested. **ho.'ā.hewa.** To find guilty, blame, condemn, pronounce guilty, convict, curse (Gal. 3.13). *Ho'āhewa kumu 'ole,* to bring false accusation. 2. vs. Walleyed, cross-eyed (with *maka*). 3. n. O'ahu name for the *mānā* fern. 4. A mimosa tree. (AP.)

'ā.hewa.hewa. Same as *'āheahea 2,* a shrub.

ahi. nvs. Fire, match, lightning; to burn in a fire, destroy by fire. See *ahikao, ahikoe, ahi koli, ahimakani, ipo, limu ahi, pau ahi. Leho ahi,* a cowry shell used for octopus fishing, colored red by toasting over fire. *Ahi wela,* hot fire, love hot as fire. *Hō'ā ahi,* to light a fire. *Ipo ahi,* fiery, ardent lover. *Ke ahi o Ka-maile,* the famous firebrands thrown over cliffs at Ka-maile, Kaua'i. *Ho'opau ahi, kinai ahi,* to put out a fire. *Ahi 'auhau,* firebrand. (PPN *afi.*)

'ahi. n. Hawaiian tuna fishes, especially the yellow-fin tuna *(Thunnus albacares),* an important fish in the Honolulu market. The name *'ahi* may be qualified by the terms *hi'u wīwī* (thin tail) or *kala'alā'au, kaha uli* (dark stripe), *kananā* (young stage, *lit.,* the defiant one; cf. *he aha sananā), kihikihi* or *'ōpū hemo* (loose belly), *lepalepa, maha 'ō'ō* (piercing brow), *mālailena, maoli, pālaha,* and *po'o nui* (large head). (PNP *kasi.*)

ahia. vs. Faded.

'ahia. 1. Same as *'āhiahia.* 2. inter. How many.

'ā.hia. n. Tinder resulting from plowing with the fire plow; the powdery rubbings that ignite.

ahi.ahi. nvi. Evening, late afternoon; to become evening. *Ua mana'o māua e hiki 'ē i 'ane'i, 'o ke ahiahi 'ia 'ana ihola ia,* we thought of arriving here earlier but were overtaken by evening. **ho.'āhi.ahi, ho'o.ahi.ahi.** To become evening; to spend an evening; to detain until evening; to darken, obscure. *Aia a hele aku au e*

ho'āhiahi me 'olua, when I get there I'll spend the evening with you two. *E kali kāua a ho'āhiahi iho,* let's wait until evening begins to fall. (PPN *afiafi.*)

'ahi.'ahi. nvt. To defame, slander, tattle against; false report, defamation, slander. *He po'e . . . e hele ana me ka 'ahi'ahi* (Ier. 6.28), people . . . walking with slanders.

'ā.hia.hia. vs. Faint, obscure, faded; dim, as colors in tapa or cloth. *'Ula'ula 'āhiahia,* faded red.

ahi.ahi.hia. Pas/imp. of *ahiahi;* overtaken by evening. (Gram. 6.6.3.)

Ahi.ahi Kaliki.maka. n. Christmas Eve, Christmas night.

Ahi.ahi Maka.hiki Hou. n. New Year's Eve.

ahi 'ai honua. n. Volcano, volcanic fire. *Lit.,* fire destroying land.

'ā.hie.hie. vs. Silvery gray, faded. *Ni'ihau.*

'ā.hihi. n. 1. A low spreading bush *(Metrosideros* sp.), formerly numerous in Nu'u-anu. Also *'āhihi lehua, lehua 'āhihi, 'āhihi kū ma kua.* 2. Any plant with long runners or creepers, as cup of gold; any creeping vine. Cf. *hihi,* entangled.

'ahi kananā. Same as *kananā;* a shark or a fierce and courageous fighter. See *nanā. Ka pūkaua 'ahi kananā,* the warrior, fierce as an *'ahi* fish.

ahi.kao. n. Fireworks (perhaps from Eng. scow *[kao],* as fireworks were first displayed from ships of explorers). Also *kao lele.*

ahi.kao lele. n. Skyrocket, rocket.

ahi.koe. n. Match. Also *ahipele, kūkaepele. Lit.,* scratching fire.

ahi koli. v. To pass fire from one candlenut to the next on a chain *(koli)* or candlenut torch. *Lit.,* to fire the torch.

'ahiku. num. Seven (especially in counting in a series); seven times.

ahi lele. n. Fire fountain, firebrands thrown over cliffs at Ka-maile, Kaua'i. See *ahi* and chant, *Ka-ua-hae.*

'ā.hilu. n. Bits of crustacea and bones found at the opening of an octopus burrow.

ahi.makani. n. Gasoline. *Lit.,* wind fire.

'ā.hina. 1. vs. Gray, gray- or white-haired. 2. n. Blue denim cloth, dungarees, blue jeans.

'ā.hina.hina. 1. Same as *'āhina 1, 2.* 2. n. The silversword *(Argyroxiphium sandwicense),* a native plant found only at altitudes of 1,870 m or more on Maui and Hawai'i; the many long silvery leaves forming a rounded rosette to 60 cm in diameter; about a hundred purplish, daisy-like flowers borne on an erect, leafy stem, which is about 1.8 m high. (Neal 845–7.) Also *hinahina.* 3. n. A native spreading shrub to 1 m high, *(Artemisia australis);* leaves divided into narrow segments, hoary on under side; flowers in panicles, small, daisy-like. Pounded leaves are used for asthma. (Neal 852.) Also *hinahina.* 4. Same as *hinahina 2,* Florida moss.

'ā.hina kua.hiwi. n. A native fern *(Cyrtomium caryotideum),* with fronds 25 to 35 cm long, once divided into 6 to 18 broadly sickle-shaped pinnae, lobed at the base. Also *kā'ape'ape.*

ahio. vi. Lazy, indolent; to shirk work, loiter.

'ahi pā.laha. n. Albacore, *Thunnus alalunga* (family Scombridae). *Lit.,* flat *'ahi.*

ahi.pele. n. Match.

ahi pō.ka'u.wili. n. Pinwheel (fireworks).

'ā.hiu. 1. vs. Wild, untamed, as animals or plants. 2. *(Cap.)* n. Name of a wind common in the mountains of Kahana, O'ahu and by the sea. *I aloha a'e au i ka 'Āhiu o Kahana,* I greet the Wild Wind of Kahana.

'ā.hiu.hiu. Redup. of *'āhiu 1.*

'ā.hiwa. vs. Dark, dusky, somber.

aho. 1. n. Line, cord, lashing, fishing line, thong, kite string. *Aho kākele, aho kālewa,* trolling line. *Aho loa,* long line, as with several hooks for deep-sea fishing or for sounding. (PPN *afo.*) 2. nvi. Breath; to breathe.

See *ahonui, pauaho, paupauaho. Aho loa,* to hold the breath for a long time, as divers and chanters, or as children playing in the water (cf. *nā'ū*); a long breath (cf. *aholoa*). **ho.'āho.** A narrow escape; to escape by a slim margin; to have courage; to put forth great effort. (PCP *af(f,s)o.*) **3.** idiom. It is better or preferable (used after *e,* sometimes in comparisons). See *ahona,* Gram. 4.6. *E aho ia,* that's better. *E aho nō ia, hala no ka lā,* it's good enough, the day passes [it is good enough for the needs of the day]. *E aho ka hele 'ana mamua o ka noho 'ana,* it is better to go than to stay. *E aho nāu,* it's better for you.

'aho. n. Thatch purlin. Also *'a'aho.* See *'ahohui, 'ahokele, 'ahopi'o kuahui, 'ahopueo. 'Aho 'ai 'ole,* a thatch purlin that is too short. **hō.'aho.** To tie *'aho* to the frame of the roof. (PPN *kaso.*)

'aho.hui. n. Thatch purlin support.

'aho kā. n. Small lashing on the *pueo* main purlin.

'aho.kele. n. Horizontal thatch purlin. (Kep. 183.)

'aho kope.kope. n. Name given for roof thatching on top of the ridgepole. Also *we'o.* (For. 5:645.)

ā.hole. n. An endemic fish *(Kuhlia sandvicensis)* found in both fresh and salt water. The mature stage is *āhole,* the young stage *āholehole.* Because of the meaning of *hole,* to strip away, this fish was used for magic, as to chase away evil spirits and for love magic. It was also called a "sea pig" *(pua'a kai)* and used ceremonially as a substitute for pig. Foreigners were sometimes called *āhole* because of the light skin of the fish. *He āhole ka i'a, hole ke aloha, āhole* is the fish, love is restless [of *āhole* fish used in love magic].

Aho-lehia. n. Stroke in *lua* fighting. See *Ke-aho-lehi.*

ā.hole.hole. n. Young stage of the *āhole,* Hawaiian flagtail.

'aholo. n. Sliding rock, landslide, avalanche. (For. 6:472.)

aho.loa. Same as more common *ahonui. Lit.,* longbreath. For *aho* loa see *aho 1.*

aho lolo. See *lolo 4.*

ahona. vs. Better, well, well-being, fortunate, improved; to need *(aho 3 + -na). Pehea 'oe? Ua ahona iki.* How do you feel? A little better. *Ke ahona ihola nō ia,* she's a little better just now. *Ahona mākou i ka 'ike 'ia e ka uka,* we were fortunate to be seen by those on shore. *Hahana ka 'āina, i ahona i ka makani,* the heat of the land was relieved by the breeze. *I ahona iki nō au lā ia mau kānaka* (Nak. 118), I do have some need for these men.

aho.nui. nvs. Patience; patient, enduring, long suffering; to tolerate. *Lit.,* great breath. Cf. *aholoa, pauaho, paupauaho;* see ex., *lawe 2, makua. Ahonui 'ole,* impatient. *Ua ahonui nō 'oe i nā pōpilikia,* you have been patient in the times of trouble. **ho.'āho.nui.** Caus/sim. *E ho'āhonui a'e ā pau kēia pilikia,* be patient until this trouble is over.

aho 'ō.wili. n. Lashing fastening *kaupaku* roof to *kua 'iole,* upper ridgepole.

'aho pi'o kua.hui. n. Thatch purlin support.

aho pueo. n. Lashing on the *pueo* main purlin.

'aho pueo. n. Main purlin in a house. Also *pueo.*

ahu. nvs. Heap, pile, collection, mound, mass; altar, shrine, cairn; a traplike stone enclosure made by fishermen for fish to enter; laid, as the earth oven. Cf. *ahu waiwai, ahuwale, O'ahu. Ahu kele,* mud heap; muddy. *Ahu ka pala!* A heap of excreta [hence worthless; sometimes shortened to *ahu* only or to *e ahu ana*]! *Ahu ka 'ala'ala!* A heap of squid ink! Not worth much! *Ahu wawā,* a great din. *Ahu ili,* a large inheritance or transfer [said of reward, vengeance]. *Ahu 'ena'ena,* a red-hot heap [an oven]. *Ahu kupanaha iā Hawai'i 'imi loa* (Kep. 143), a mass of wondrous things in deepdelving Hawai'i. **ho.'āhu.** To pile, gather, accumulate, heap up; to lay away, as goods for the future; collect; collection, mound. *Fig.,* to resent, dislike. *Hale ho'āhu,* storehouse, warehouse. *Lumi ho'āhu,* storeroom. *E ho'āhu ana i ka huhū maluna o kēlā po'e,* heaping up anger against those people. (PPN *afu.*)

'ahu. nvt. Garment or covering for the upper part of the body and shoulders, as a cape, shirt, coat; to put on or wear such; fine soft mat, formerly often used as a cloak; mat used as a canoe cover; short for *'ahu 'ula.* Cf. *'a'ahu, 'ahu 'ao, 'ahu hīnano, 'ahu moena, 'ahunāli'i 1, 'ahu 'o'eno, 'ahu ua, 'ahu uhi wa'a, 'ahu 'ula. 'Ahu 'ili kanaka,* commoner's skin cloak [commoner]. (PPN *kafu.*)

'ā.hua. 1. nvi. To swell, as a wave; heap, mound, hillock, knoll, pile; heaped, heaped, humped; tremendous. *'Āhua one,* sand dune, sandbank. *Kau 'āhua maha'oi* (Kel. 43), fantastically brazen. **ho'āhua.** To pile or heap up; embankment. 2. n. Young, as of the *aku, kawakawa,* and *moano* fishes. Cf. *'ōhua.*

ahu.ahu. nvi. Healthy, vigorous; strength and vigor, as of animal or plant; to grow rapidly, thrive. Also *ehuehu. Ulu ahuahu,* to grow fast, to be big for one's age. *Ke ahuahu kō* (For. 5:646), a healthy sugar-cane plant.

ahu 'ai. vi. To overeat, waste food, squander. *Mai ahu 'ai,* don't overeat. *Ka ahu 'ai wale 'ana i ka nui o kona waiwai,* the senseless waste of most of his property.

ahu.ake. Rare var. of *ahuwale.* (For. 5:533.)

'ā.hua lā.lā kukui. *Kukui* branches strewn about, as after a storm.

'ahu 'ao. n. Choice mat of fine strands of soft white young pandanus leaves, about 3 cm mesh.

'ahu.'awa. n. 1. A sedge *(Cyperus javanicus)* about .3 to 1.3 m high, with a basal tuft of long narrow leaves and a radiating inflorescence borne at the tip of a long slender stem. (Neal 86-7.) Also *'ehu'awa, pu'uka'a haole. Ōpū 'ahu'awa hānau,* born in a clump of *'ahu'awa* [of a humble birthplace]. 2. Another coarse sedge *(Cyperus hypochlorus)* similar to the preceding one, but with green instead of brown flowers.

ahu 'awa. n. Kava dregs. See ex., *hoka 2.*

'ahu.'awa haole. n. The umbrella plant, a leafless ornamental sedge *(Cyperus alternifolius),* 30 to 180 cm high, the umbrella-shaped flowering head with about 20 grasslike rays at the top of a slender stalk. (Neal 84-5.) Also *pu'uka'a haole.*

ahue. vt. To make two thicknesses by folding; to double up, fold, as paper or tapa.

'ahu hī.nano. n. Soft, fine mat garment plaited from fine strands of dried bracts of male pandanus flowers.

'ā.hui. n. Bunch or cluster, as of bananas, grapes; whole pandanus fruit consisting of keys. *'Āhui waina,* cluster of grapes. (PEP *kaafui;* cf. Penrhyn.)

'ā.hui hala. n. 1. Pandanus fruit. 2. Protuberance of the vagina resulting from syphilis; the roughness of the skin was thought to suggest the pandanus fruit.

ahu.kū. nvt. To stone to death; slaughter by burying the victim under a pile of stones. Hākau, half brother of 'Umi, was killed in this fashion (FS 141), and this method was used unsuccessfully against the hero Kawelo (FS 107). *Ho'okahi wale nō kumu e make ai 'o Ka-welo, 'o ke kaua i ke ahukū,* there was only one way to kill Ka-welo, burial beneath stones.

ahu lā.'ī. n. Ti-leaf raincoat or cape.

ahu.lau. nvs. Pestilence, epidemic; heaped up, as dead bodies. *Ahulau ihola nā kānaka i ka make,* slaughtered bodies were heaped up.

ahu.li'u. vs. Overheated, as oven stones; white-hot. *Ahuli'u ka imu,* the oven is white-hot.

ahulu. vs. Overdone, overcooked; overcultivated, as soil. *'Ai ahulu,* overcooked food; *fig.,* to pray to death, poison. (PPN *afulu.*)

'ahulu. vi. Discolored, foamy, feathery, choppy, uneven, mussed.

'ā.hulu.hulu. 1. n. Young of the *kūmū* fish. (PNP *'afulu.*) 2. Same as *huluhulu 2. Ko'i 'āhuluhulu,* planing adze, as for rough *('āhuluhulu)* lumber.

'ahu moena. n. Fine patterned mat, plaited with materials of different colors.

ahuna. n. Pile, heap. *Ahuna iwi* (Kep. 47), heap of bones.

'ahuna. n. Coat, garment, ti-leaf raincoat.

ahu.nā.li'i. n. A land division.

'ahu.nā.li'i. n. **1.** A tapa for chiefs, colored with candlenut and *noni* and striped red. **2.** Issue of a union of a male chief and a commoner. Also *waikī* and *kūkae pōpolo.*

ā.huni.huni. n. Name given for a fish of the *'ōpakapaka* type.

'ahu 'o'eno. n. Matting with twilled pattern, associated with Kaua'i. (Laie 479.)

ahup. Abbreviation for *ahupua'a.*

'ahu po'o nui. n. Cloth bound about the head of warriors. (Ellis 102.)

ahu.pua'a. n. **1.** Land division usually extending from the uplands to the sea, so called because the boundary was marked by a heap *(ahu)* of stones surmounted by an image of a pig *(pua'a),* or because a pig or other tribute was laid on the altar as tax to the chief. The landlord or owner of an *ahupua'a* might be a *konohiki.* **2.** The altar on which the pig was laid as payment to the chief for use of the *ahupua'a* land.

'ahu ua. nvi. Old type of raincoat made of dried ti leaves fastened to an *olonā* net, or consisting of a small mat about 1.2 by 1.8 m, made of *makaloa* sedge, and so supple that it could be rolled up; to wear this garment. Today, raincoat is *kukaweke* and *kuka ua.*

'ahu uhi wa'a. n. Mat canoe covering that protected paddlers in storms.

'ahu 'ula. n. **1.** Feather cloak or cape made of the feathers of the *'ō'ō, 'i'iwi* and other birds, usually red or yellow trimmed with black or green, formerly worn by high chiefs and kings. Today about 160 have been located in museums and collections of the world, the largest being in the Bishop Museum, Honolulu. Imitation cloaks of plush, felt, paper, or dyed feathers (rare) are worn today in pageants and by members of Hawaiian societies. *Lit.,* royal cloak. **2.** *(Cap.)* Same as *Ka-'ahu-'ula.* **3.** See *limu 'ahu 'ula.*

ahuulu. See *'upena ahuulu.*

ahu wai.wai. n. Storehouse, heap of goods. *Hale ahu waiwai,* storehouse.

ahu.wale. vs. Exposed, conspicuous, prominent, obvious, in plain view; heaped up. *Ahuwale ka mana'o,* real thoughts or nature are exposed, as of something revealed in its true colors.

ai. **1.** nvt. Coition; to have sexual relations, cohabit (frequently pronounced *ei*). **hō.'ai.** To breed, as a horse. (Probably PPN *ha'i.*) **2.** Same as *wai,* inter. pronoun. (PPN *hai.*) **3.** Linking or anaphoric part. frequently pronounced *ei.* (Gram. 7.3.) (PPN *ai.*) **4.** Short for *aia,* there. Cf. *ai loa, ai luna. Ai i loko o ka hale,* there in the house.

aī. interj. of surprise.

a'i. **1.** Same as *a'ia'i 1.* **2.** Part. replacing *i* often in songs; usually written *a i.* Cf. *a'e, a'o. Malihini ka 'ikena a'i nā Kona,* seeing the Kona districts for the first time.

-a'i. nonproductive transitive suffix. See *hua'i, lua'i, luma'i,* Gram. 6.6.4. Cf. *Kaua'i, kaula'i.* (PPN *-'aki.*)

'ai. **1.** nvt. Food or food plant, especially vegetable food as distinguished from *i'a,* meat or fleshy food; often *'ai* refers specifically to poi; harvest (Oihk. 19.9); to eat, destroy or consume as by fire; to erode; to taste, bite, take a hook, grasp, hold on to; edible. *Fig.,* to rule, reign, or enjoy the privileges and exercise the responsibilities of rule, and one who does so, as *'ai ahupua'a:* to rule an *ahupua'a,* the ruler of one; *'ai 'āina:* to own, control, and enjoy land; the owner of land; *'ai ali'i, 'ai lani,* and *'ai li'i,* to enjoy the comforts and honors and exercise the responsibilities of being a chief; *'ai 'ili:* to control an *'ili* land division, one who does control the *'ili; 'ai moku:* to rule a district or island *[moku],* one

who rules one. Cf. *'aialo, 'ai kanaka, 'ai nui, 'ai 'oko'a, 'ai pa'a, 'ai pala maunu, 'ai pilau, 'ai 'uha-'uha, 'ai waiū.* Various ways of eating may qualify *'ai,* as *'ai hele, 'ai lau,* and *'ai noa,* to eat freely and without observance of taboos (see also *'ai kū); 'ai kapu,* to eat under taboo; *'ai kau,* to feed by dropping poi directly from the fingers into the mouth, especially to feed a favorite child this way; *'ai maka,* to eat raw; *'ai pau,* to eat all. *Hiki ke 'ai 'ia,* edible. *'Ai 'aha,* to tie with sennit. *Mōhai 'ai* (Oihk. 2.14), cereal offering. *Pā'ū 'ai kaua* (For. 4:53), sarong worn in battle. *'A 'ohe kapu o ka'u pā hula, he 'ai kū, he 'ai hele,* there are no taboos in my hula troupe, eat standing, eat on the run. *'A 'ohe 'ai 'o ka ma'i,* the disease makes no advance. *Kāna 'ai,* his food. *Kona 'ai,* his eating. **hō.'ai.** To feed, give food to, board. (PPN *kai.*) **2.** n. Score, points in a game, stake, wager. *'Ehia 'ai e eo ai?* How many points to win? (PPN *kai.*) **3.** n. Dancing style or type. Cf. *'ai 'ami, 'ai ha'a.* **4.** n. Stroke or hold in *lua* fighting; spear thrust. *Ka 'ai a ke kumu i koe iā 'oukou* (For. 5:409), the teacher's stroke that you do not have [have not been taught]. *Ka 'ai a ka u'i,* the stroke of the youth. **5.** n. Stone used in the *kimo* game other than the stone that is tossed and caught, which is the *pōhaku kimo.*

'ā.'ī. n. Neck, neck of a shirt or dress, neck of the *iheihe* fish net. Cf. *'ā'īkū, 'ā'īlepe, 'ā'ī oeoe, 'ā'ī 'olo'olo, 'ā'ī pahāha, 'ā'ī pala'e, 'ā'īpau, 'ā'ī pu'u, 'ā'ī uaua. Lei 'ā'ī,* necktie. (PNP *ka(a)kii.*)

aia. idiom. **1.** There, there it is, there are (sometimes shortened to *ai,* with loss of the following part. *i;* see *ai lalo, ai luna*). Cf. also *aia ho'i, aia kā, aia lā, aia na'e, ai lā, ai loa,* Gram. 4.6. *Aia kēia,* furthermore, besides. *Aia malaila ka hale,* the house is there, there's the house. *Aia i hea ka hale?* Where is the house? **2.** Depending on, only if, only when, whatever, whenever. *Aia nō ia ia'oe,* depending on you; as you want; it's up to you; suit yourself. *Aia nō ia i kāu ho'oholo 'ana,* whatever you decide. *Aia nō i kahi e hana ana,* it doesn't matter where the work is done; depending on where the work is done. *Aia nō i kāu hele 'ana mai,* whenever you want to come; depending on your coming. *Alia wau e 'ae aku, aia 'ae mai 'o 'A-i-wohi-kupua* (Laie 485), before I consent, 'A-i-wohi-kupua must agree. *Aia ā pau ka uhi 'ana o ka noe . . . ia manawa e 'ike aku ai i nā mea apau* (Laie 499), when the mist covering is gone, then everything may be seen. *Aia ā pau kēia hana,* when [or whenever] this work is done. *Aia ā hele aku au,* when I go. *'A 'ole 'oe e ola i ka mele ho'okahi, aia 'elua mele* (FS 239), you won't be saved by one song, only with two songs. *Aia aku ā aia mai, 'ai kākou i ka na'aukake,* every now and then we eat weiners. *Aia i hea ka puke?* Where's the book?

'ai.ā. nvs. Ungodly, godless, irreligious, wicked, unbelieving, careless of observance of taboos; wickedness. **hō.'aiā.** To act wickedly or lead others astray. (PPN *kaiha'a.*)

ai'a. interj. Here! Here it is!

aia ho'i. interj. Behold! See there! Lo! Suddenly. *'Ī maila ke Akua, Aia ho'i* (Kin. 1.29), and God said, Behold.

ai.ā.hua, ai.ā.hulu. Same as *'aiā.*

a'i.a'i. **1.** nvs. Bright as moonlight; fair, white, clear, pure, brilliant, shining; brightness, clearness. *Pōhaku a'ia'i,* crystal. *Wahine 'ili a'ia'i,* woman with skin that is fair and clear. **ho'ā'i.a'i.** to whiten, clear, shine, whitewash, remove rust or dirt; white, clear, shining. *Fig.,* to clarify, brighten, as a tarnished reputation. See ex., *kāhela 1.* (Probably PNP *akiaki.*) **2.** n. A native tree or shrub (*Streblus sandwicensis* [*Pseudomorus sandwicensis* and *P. brunoniana* are synonyms]), with narrow-ovate leaves, and milky sap; a member of the fig family. (Neal 299.)

'ai.'ai. **1.** See *'ōpū 'ai'ai.* **2.** n. Dependent, one living on the resources of another.

-'ai'ai. hō.'ai.'ai. To release, as war captives.

'ai.'ai.ā. Redup. of 'aiā. *He ali'i 'ino a me ka 'ai'aiā* (Kep. 63), a chief wicked and impious. hō.'ai.'ai.ā. Caus/sim.

'ai.'aiele. nvs. Swinging, unsteady motion.

'ai 'āina. v. To rule or own land. hō.'āi.'āina. To award land, as by a chief. (Nak. 27.)

'ai.'aio.hua. Name given for persons sacrificed for not observing taboos during the offering of prayers by the priest (pronunciation not certain). (Kep. 139.)

aia kā. interj. There now! So it's there after all!

'ai-a-ka-honu. Same as *hulu manu*, a seaweed. *Lit.*, food of the turtle.

'ai-a-ka-nē.nē. n. A native trailing, woody plant *(Coprosma ernodeoides)*, with narrow, tiny leaves and black, berry-like fruits. (Neal 803.) *Lit.*, food of the *nēnē* goose. Also *kūkaenēnē, leponēnē, pūnēnē.*

aia lā. interj. There! I told you so! There it is!

'ā.'ī 'ala.'ala. Same as *'ā'ī pala'e.*

'ai ali'i. v. To rule (or eat) as a chief.

'ai.alo. n. Attendant of the chief's household, intimate of a chief. *Lit.*, eating [in the] presence.

'ai ā manō. vi. To eat like a shark. *Fig.*, to have a ravenous appetite. (Gram. 8.7.2.)

'ai.'ami. nvi. Type of hula with little foot movement, but with hip revolving throughout the dance; to dance thus.

'ai.ana. nvt. Clothes iron; to iron, press, as clothes. *Eng.*

aia na'e. conj. But, furthermore.

'ai ā pua'a. vi. To eat like a pig; to eat greedily; to wolf food.

'ai.au. 1. vi. To look about with covetous or jealous eyes; to practice sorcery or poisoning. 2. vs. Weary, discouraged by long continued work. See ex., *kupali'i 2.*

'ai.'ē. nvt. Debt; to owe. See *'ao'ao 'ai'ē, lawe 'ai'ē. 'Ai'ē pohō, 'ai'ē ka'a 'ole, 'ai'ē pono 'ole,* bad debt. *Hā'awi 'ai'ē,* to lend on usury. hō.'ai.'ē. To lend, loan, charge on account, borrow, ask for credit; charge account, loan, credit. *Hale hō'ai'ē,* pawnshop. *Ua hō'ai'ē nō anei 'oe i ka hale kū'ai?* Did you charge to the store?

'ai.ea. n. 1. All species of the endemic Hawaiian genus *Nothocestrum,* soft-wooded shrubs and trees with ovate or oblong leaves, yellowish flowers, and whitish to reddish berries. One slender species was used for thatching sticks *('aho)* and fire-making. 2. Same as *kāwa'u,* a native *Ilex;* holly. *Kaua'i.* 3. Exhaustion. *Rare.*

'ai.eana. Same as *'aiea 3.*

'ai ha'a. 1. nvi. Hula step danced with bended knees; the chanting for this dance is usually bombastic and emphatic (UL 266); to dance thus. *Lit.*, low style. 2. vs. Allegro.

'ai hamu. See *hamu 2.*

'aihē. Center of a taro corm. (Kep. 16.5.)

ai hea, aia i hea. inter. Where? See *hea 5.*

'ai hele. Similar to *'ai kū.* (Kam. 64:87.) *Lit.*, to eat walking.

'ai ho'o.kano. vt. To eat proudly of high-priced food, as a rich person; *fig.*, to have many women. *Na nei selamoku e 'ai ho'okano* (song), this sailor who has so much to eat.

ai.hua.wa'a. Vagabond; to wander, roam. (And.)

'ai.hue. nvt. To steal, rob, pilfer, filch, cheat; thief, robber, theft, larceny. (PPN *kaiha'a.*) Cf. Marquesan *kaihue.*

'ai.hue.ea, 'ai.hue.hia, 'ai.hue.lia, 'ai.hue.nia. Pas/imp. forms of *'aihue.*

'aihue kanaka. nv. To kidnap; kidnapper.

'ai.humu.humu. vt. To eat in order to destroy; to destroy wantonly or by violence or sorcery.

'ai 'ili loko. v. To have the use of fish ponds *(loko);* to control the interior *(loko)* land division known as *'ili.*

'aika. vs. Hard and poor tasting, as thin or inferior fish.

ai.kaha.'ula. See *kaha'ula* and cf. FS 251.

'ā.'ī.kala. n. Collar. *Lit.*, neck collar *(Eng.).*

'ā.'ī.kala kū. n. Stiff collar.

'ai.kalima. n. Ice cream. *Eng.*

'ai kalo pa'a. n. Unpounded taro. *Fig.*, difficult problem that must be chewed, as whole taro.

'Ai-kanaka. n. Name of a star.

'ai kanaka. nv. Cannibal, man-eater; to eat human flesh.

ai.kāne. nvs. Friend; friendly; to become a friend. See *hale aikāne. Kāna aikāne,* his friend. *Moe aikāne,* to commit sodomy *(rare).* ho.'ai.kāne. To be a friend, make friends, befriend.

'ai.kapa. nvs. A privileged friend who shares the profits of a friend's land, sometimes sharing in the work; one who shares a friend's spouse; to share land or spouse; to pay part of a debt but withhold the remainder. *Lit.*, eat [on the] border.

'ai kapu. v. To eat under taboo; to observe eating taboos.

'ai kā.wele. See *kāwele 2.*

'ai.kena. vs. Sick and tired of a person or situation, surfeited, exhausted, discouraged, fatigued.

'ai kepa. vt. To cut or tear obliquely, as with teeth or edged instrument; to seize or tear with the teeth; to fit by rabbeting, rabbet.

'ai.kepa.kepa. Redup. of *'ai kepa;* to snap the jaws; to speak rapidly, as with overlapping words; to talk too much or too fast; to jabber.

'ā.iki. vi. To light up dimly; to look furtively, peek, peer. ho.'ā.iki. To make shine a little; to open the eyes a little to see; to peek.

'A-iki-kau-e-lono. n. Name of a star, possibly Sirius. Also called *Hiki-kau-e-lono.*

'Ai.kiopa, Aitiopa. Ethiopia; Ethiopian. (Gr. *Aethiops.*)

'ai.kola. nvs. Interj. of scorn or derision, especially rejoicing over others' misfortunes, with meaning "serves you right" or "I told you so"; as a verb, to use this term. hō.'ai.kola. To treat contemptuously; to rejoice over the misfortunes of others; sarcastic, contemptible. *Hō'aikola noho'i nā lā'au ka'a maluna ou* (Isa. 14.8), the fir trees rejoice at thee. *Hō'aikola noho'i kāu hana,* you do such contemptible things. (PCP *kaitoa.*)

'Ai.ko'o. n. Name of a wind at Nu'alolo, Kaua'i. (For. 5:95.)

'ai kū. vt. To eat freely; to do as one wishes; to break taboos or transgress. (Kam. 64:87.) See ex., *'ai 1. 'O ka hula 'ai kū 'ai hele,* a dance completely free of taboos [a saying often said by hula teachers].

'ā.'ī.kū. n. 1. High collar, stiff collar. 2. Spasmodic affection of the neck muscles which draws the head toward the affected side, a torticollis; stiff neck. 3. Croup.

'ai kū.pele. n. Medicinal juices mixed with poi or mashed sweet potato, used to build up strength. *Lit.*, kneaded poi.

'Ai.kupika, Aigupita. nvs. Egypt; Egyptian. Perhaps Gr. *Aigyptios.*

ai lā. Short for *aia lā.*

'aila. nvt. Any oil, grease, lard; to oil, grease, lubricate. *Eng.* Many kinds of oil and grease are listed below. *'Aila hamo,* rubbing oil, grease, ointment; to oil, lubricate.

'ai lā. v. Scorched or sunburned.

'aila.ea. Same as *'ailea.*

'aila.honua. Kerosene. *Lit.*, earth oil.

'aila ho'o.malo'o pena. n. Turpentine. *Lit.*, oil for drying paint.

'aila ho'o.nahā. Castor oil. *Lit.*, purge oil.

ai laila, aia i laila. There, to be there. *Ai laila lākou e noho nei,* they are living in that place.

'aila kē.pama (sepama). n. Sperm oil. *Eng.*

'aila koka (koda). n. Cod-liver oil.

'aila kolī. n. Castor oil. *Lit.*, castor-bean oil.

ai lalo, aia i lalo. Down there.

'aila māhu. n. Kerosene. *Lit.*, steam oil.

'ai.lana. 1. vs. In love. *'Ailana ka mana'o,* loving thoughts. 2. n. Island. *Eng.*

'aila pa'a. n. Thick grease.

'aila palai. n. Frying oil. *Eng.*

'aila pua'a. n. Lard, pork grease.

'ai lau. 1. vt. To eat a great deal. **2.** n. A bundle of cooked taro wrapped in ti leaves.

'ai.lea. n. Gasoline (contraction of *'aila,* oil, and *ea,* air).

'ā.'ī.lepe. Ruffles, folds, gathers about the neck; to make ruffles; to ruffle feathers, as a grouse. (AP.)

'ai lepo. v. To eat filth (insulting).

'ā.'ili. 1. vi. To struggle for breath; to breathe with convulsions, gasp, pant, twitch, jerk. **2.** vt. To pull, as weeds. (Kep. 157.)

'a.'īlia. Pas/imp. of *'ā'ili.*

'ai.lihi. Same as *'aikapa.*

'ā.'ili.'ili. Redup. of *'ā'ili;* spasm.

'Ai.liki, Airisi. nvs. Irish. *Eng.*

'Ai-lima-iki. nv. A method of *lua* fighting; to grab the little finger of an adversary and twist it.

ai loa, aia i loa. vi. Away off in the distance.

'Ai-loli. n. Name of a wind at Kau-pō, Maui. (For. 5:101.) *Lit.,* sea cucumber food.

'ai.lolo. 1. nvt. Ceremony usually marking the end of training, so called because the student ate *('ai)* a portion of the head, and especially the brains *(lolo),* of a fish, dog, or hog offered to the gods; to partake of the ceremony. *Ua 'ailolo i ka pua'a hiwa,* taking part in the ceremony marking the completion of training by eating a portion of the head of an entirely black pig. **hō.ai.lolo.** Caus/sim. **2.** vt. Skilled, adept, expert, trained, proficient. *Ua 'ailolo 'oia i ka hula,* he is trained in the hula.

-'ailona. hō.'ai.lona. Sign, symbol, representation, insignia, emblem, mark, badge, signal, omen, portent, target, credential, token of recognition, a lot that is cast; title (legal); depth sounding; to mark; to take a depth sounding; to draw lots. Cf. *hailona, kila 2. Hō'ailona helu,* plural sign or marker, algebra. *Hō'ailona mahele,* measure signature in music. *Hō'ailona kū'auhau, hō'ailona no ke kūlana,* family crest or coat of arms. *Hō'ailona mō'ī,* badge or emblem of royalty, sceptre. *Hō'ailona pa'i,* printed stamp. *Hō'ailona manawa,* time signature in music. *Hō'uilonu lunukilu,* emblem or trophy of victory, trophy. *Ka pana 'ana aku i ka hō'ailona* (1 Sam. 20.20), shooting at the mark. (PPN *faka'ilonga.*)

ai luna, aia i luna. vi. Up there.

'ai mā.mā. nv. Light meal, snack; to eat such.

'Ai-maunu. n. Name of a wind at Hāna, Maui. (For. 5:101.) *Lit.,* bait eating.

'ai.mī.kana. n. Linnet, California house finch, papaya bird *(Carpodacus mexicanus frontalis),* an early introduction to Hawai'i, now well established throughout the Hawaiian Islands. *Lit.,* papaya eater.

'ai moku. nv. Ruler of a *moku,* district or island; to rule a *moku.*

aina. n. Sexual intercourse. (PCP *kainga.*)

'aina. 1. n. Meal. Cf. *'aina ahiahi, 'aina awakea, 'aina kakahiaka,* and *'ai,* to eat. *Hale 'aina,* restaurant. (PNP *kainga.*) **2.** Pas/imp. of *'ai 1;* eaten, consumed devoured. See ex., *nūpolupolu.* **3.** vs. Rejected, as refuse, especially of sugar cane. *Kō 'aina,* sugar-cane refuse or bagasse after juice is extracted. *Ipu 'aina,* slop basin. **4.** See *'aina kea, 'aina kea melemele.*

'ai.nā. nvi. Sore aching; stiffness, as from overexercise.

'āina. 1. n. Land, earth. Cf. *'ai,* to eat; *'aina, kama'āina. Kō nā 'āina like 'ole,* belonging to foreign lands, foreign, international. *'Āina ho'oilina,* inherited property or estate. *Ua mau ke ea o ka 'āina i ka pono* (motto of Hawai'i), the life of the land is preserved in righteousness. (PEP *kaainga.*)

'a'ina. n. Crackling, snapping; an explosive sound, sharp report, bang *(rare),* loud prolonged sound, peal (less common than *'u'ina*). Cf. *'a'a'ina. Kani 'a'ina,* to crackle, peal.

'aina ahi.ahi. n. Evening meal, supper, dinner.

'aina awa.kea. n. Noon meal, lunch.

'āina 'ē. n. Foreign land, *Kō nā 'āina 'ē* (Mat. 10.5), of the Gentiles; international. *Ma ka 'āina 'ē,* in a foreign land, abroad.

'āina hā.nau. n. Land of one's birth, native land, homeland, birthplace. See *one hānau.*

'āina haole. n. Foreign land, mainland United States.

'Āina-Hemo.lele. n. Holy Land.

'a'ina.hia. Pas/imp. of *'a'ina.*

'Āina-hō.'ano. n. Holy Land.

'āina ho'o.kū.'ono.'ono. n. Homestead, homesteading land. *Lit.,* land for security.

'āina ho'o.pula.pula. See *pulapula.*

'a'ina.'ina. Redup. of *'a'ina.*

'aina kaka.hiaka. n. Morning meal, breakfast.

'aina kea. n. A good-looking variety of sugar cane, of medium height, striped red and green or yellow, pith white and brown, leaves and leaf sheaths with white markings; used in medicine. Also *pū kea.*

'aina kea mele.mele. n. A variety of sugar cane, the yellow mutant of *'aina kea.*

'aina.kini. n. Navy blue cotton cloth.

'āina kō. n. Cane trash, bagasse. Cf. *'aina 3.*

'āina kū.'ai. n. Land purchased or for sale; land in fee simple.

'āina kū.pono. n. Land free from all rent and taxes.

'āina lei ali'i. n. Crown lands.

'āina makua. n. Fatherland, mainland.

'āinana. Short for *maka'āinana.* (For. 6:39.)

'āina noho kahu 'ia. n. Trust territory.

'āina nui. n. Great power, great land, mainland.

'aina 'ole. vs. Not eaten or consumed; without vegetable foods. *He makau 'aina 'ole,* a hook that a fish will not bite.

'Āina-'ō.ma'o.ma'o. n. Greenland.

'āina pua. n. Poetic name for China. *Lit.,* flower land.

'āina.puni.'ole. n. Continent. *Lit.,* land not surrounded.

'Āina-wohi. n. Said to be a name for the New Hebrides. (RC 293.) See *Nānā-pua.*

'ai.nea. vs. Exhausted by strain and trouble, tired, weary.

'ai.nema.nema. vt. To criticize severely, hunt for flaws, split hairs.

'ai.niha. nvs. Bad temper; bad tempered, cross. See *niha* and ex., *kūpalaiki.*

'ai noa. vt. To eat freely, without observance of taboos.

'ā.inu, hō.'ā.inu. Same as *hāinu, ho'ohāinu,* to give to drink. *Ka'ū.*

'ai nui. nvi. Principle or staple food; to eat a lot.

ā.io. Same as *ioio,* grooves.

'aiō. 1. n. A wave that rises and falls without breaking; a swell. **2.** interj. Heigh-ho. *Eng.*

'ā.'ī oe.oe. nvs. Slim-necked; a slim or slender neck. Nickname for wives of early missionaries because their bonnets made their necks appear slim.

'ai 'oko'a. n. Cooked unpounded taro. *Lit.,* whole taro. *Kaua'i.* Also *kalo pa'a.*

a i 'ole. conj. Or. *Ua makemake anei 'oe i kēlā pāpale a i 'ole i kēia?* Do you want this hat or that [one]?

'ā.'ī 'olo.'olo. n. Sagging of the chin and throat, as in old age; double chin; goiter.

'ā.'ī 'o.o.le'a. nvs. Stiff neck. *Fig.,* disobedience, obstinacy; obstinate.

'ai pa'a. n. Cooked taro pounded into a hard mass not mixed with water, sometimes preserved in ti-leaf bundles. *Fig.,* a difficult problem. *Lit.,* hard poi.

'ā.'ī.pahā.ha. n. Mumps. *Lit.,* swollen neck.

'ā.'ī pala'e. n. Scrofula, a scrofulous neck, abscess on neck. Also *'ā'ī 'ala'ala.*

'ai pala maunu. nv. To eat a dab of bait. *Fig.,* to take the leavings of others, to steal another's mate, one who does so; a beggar. *He 'ai pala maunu na ka po'e loa'a* (Kep. 103), an eater of bait dabs belonging to people with possessions [a scavenger, beggar].

'ai pala niho. Same as *'ai pala maunu. Lit.,* to eat tooth tartar.

'ā.'ī.pau. n. Glandular swelling in the neck, thyroid.

'ai pilau. nv. Eater of filth, scavenger; to eat rotten food;

rotten food; an insulting epithet for a sorcerer who prays others to death. See *manu 'ai pilau.*

'ai pō.'ala. vt. To gulp, choke, suffocate. *Rare.*

'ai.po'o.lā. n. Feast to celebrate the completion of a hard task or project. *Lit.,* food [for] workers [in the] sun.

'ai pū. vt. To eat together (both sexes), formerly tabu.

'ai.puni. vt. To encircle, go around, encompass, environ. Cf. *pō'ai puni.*

'ā.'ī pu'u. n. Lumped, calloused, or swollen neck; swelling of the neck or shoulder, said to be caused by carrying heavy burdens; one with a calloused neck.

'ai pu'u.pu'u. n. Lumpy poi.

'ā.'ī.pu'u.pu'u. n. Steward, butler, said to be so called because the chief's steward got calluses *(pu'upu'u)* on his shoulders from carrying food. *Wa'a 'ā'īpu'upu'u* (Laie 461), canoe with provisions. **ho'ā.'ī.pu'u.pu'u.** To appoint or make one a steward; to act as one, as by waiting on the table; to issue provisions.

'ā.'ī ua.ua. n. Stiff neck. *Fig.,* stubborn.

'ai 'uha.'uha. nvt. To eat wastefully; a wasteful or riotous eater.

ā.iwa. Same as *āiwaiwa. Kapu-āiwa* (name of Kamehameha V), mysterious taboo.

'a.iwa. num. Nine (usually in counting in a series); nine times.

'ai wai.ū. nv. Nursing, suckling, as an infant; to nurse, suckle; a nursing child, unweaned animal. *Lit.,* to eat milk.

ā.iwaiwa. vs. Inexplicable, mysterious, marvelous, strange, amazing, fantastic, fathomless, incomprehensible, wonderful because of divinity; wonderfully proficient or skilled; weirdly bad, notorious. See ex., *kapolakā.* **ho'ā.iwa.iwa.** Mystifying, causing wonder; to mystify.

Ak. Abbreviation of *'ākau,* north.

aka. 1. n. Shadow. Cf. *hoaka 4. Aka lehulehu,* shadow of the multitude; *fig.,* a well-worn path. *Ili i ke aka,* to cast a shadow. *'Ōlelo i ke aka ka hele ho'okahi,* one going alone talks to the shadow. **ho'o.aka.** To cast a shadow. (PPN *ata*.) **2.** nvi. Reflection, image, likeness (Nah. 12.8); faint glimmer preceding the rising of the moon; essence of an offering rather than the flesh; to appear, of moonlight. Many words compounded with *aka* express clarity, brightness, related to this meaning. Cf. *hoaka 3. 'O ke aka kā 'oukou, ē ke akua, 'o ka 'i'o kā mākou,* yours is the essence, O god, ours the material part. (PPN *ata*.) **3.** n. Embryo at the moment of conception. **4.** n. Newly hatched fish in the stage in which its body is still transparent. Cf. *hāuli, mana, kākau.* **5.** n. Knuckles, as of hands or ankles; joints of the backbone; node and stalk of kava; kava slip for planting.

aka-. Carefully, slowly. Cf. *aka'ai, akahai, akahana, akahao, akahele, akahoe, akaholo, akaku'u, akalewa, akaluli, akanahe, akanoho, aka'ōlelo,* Gram. 6.3.3. (PCP *ata-*.)

akā. conj. But, however, nevertheless, on the other hand, notwithstanding.

'aka. nvi. To laugh; laughter. See *'aka hene. Kū i ka 'aka,* funny. *'Aka iki,* sly laughter: to laugh a little, giggle, chuckle. **hō.'aka.** To provoke laughter; laughter. Cf. *ho'omāke'aka.* (PPN *kata*.)

'ā.ka'a. vt. To tear off, peel; to break open, as a seal (Hoik. 5.2); to fall off or down, as old thatching of a house; to break up, as the sides of a house; to uproot, ruffled, as feathers. *Niu 'āka'a,* coconut with flesh that shakes; such coconut flesh. **ho'ā.ka'a.** Caus/sim.

aka-'a'amo. n. A type of fine white tapa. (GP 8.) Cf. *akaaka 2.*

aka.'ai. vt. To eat slowly, carefully. Cf. Easter *'aka kai,* eat more.

akaaka, akaka. 1. vs. Clear, luminous, transparent, visible, manifest, plain, intelligible; thin, as cloth; shining, bright, distinct. Cf. *mōakaaka.* **ho'ā.kaaka.** To clarify, explain, render or make intelligible, provide clearly for, prescribe, describe; explanation, clarification.

'Ōlelo ho'ākaaka mua, preface. *Nā mea apau i ho'ākaaka 'ole 'ia ma ke kānāwai,* all things not expressly provided for by law. **2.** n. A white and very thin tapa. Cf. *aka-'a'amo.* **3.** n. A downy, thorny branching plant *(Solanum aculeatissimum),* 30 to 90 cm high, from tropical America. It bears round scarlet fruits 2.6 cm in diameter, which are strung for leis. (Neal 742–3.) Also *kīkānia lei.* **4.** Same as *aka 5.*

'aka.'aka. nvi. To laugh, ridicule; laughter, merriment. **hō.'aka.'aka.** To cause laughter, create mirth, jeer, ridicule, pretend to laugh; comic. *'Ōlelo hō'aka'aka,* witticism, amusing speech. *Ki'i hō'aka'aka,* cartoon. (PPN *katakata*.)

'ā.ka'a.ka.a. Redup. of *'āka'a;* peeled, as the skin by sunburn or by drinking kava; peeling; ruffled. *Fig.,* exhausted, thin. *Kūkae 'āka'aka'a,* pellet-like excreta, as of rabbits. *Ua māhuna i ka 'awa, ua 'āka'aka'a,* scaly with kava, peeling.

aka.'aka.'awa. n. An endemic begonia *(Hillebrandia sandwicensis),* a succulent herb with oblique, rounded, lobed leaves 10 to 20 cm in diameter and with sprays of small pink or white flowers, found only in shaded, damp ravines. (Neal 602.) *Kaua'i.* Also *pua maka nui.*

akaaka.hi'u. Same as *akahi'u.*

'aka.'a.kai. n. **1.** The great bulrush *(Scirpus validus,* formerly called *S. lacustris)* that grows on the edge of fresh or brackish water marshes in Hawai'i. The plants have unbranched, slender, green stems, 1 to 3 m high, looking like giant onion plants. Formerly Hawaiians used them for house thatch or plaited them into mats for the lower layers of beds or for some temporary purpose, as the material is not durable. (Neal 88.) *S. californicus* on Ni'ihau. *'Ai 'aka'akai,* to eat bulrushes [fresh poi, which was not liked]. **2.** The common onion *(Allium cepa);* the tops look like those of the great bulrush. (Neal 198.)

'aka'a.kai (or **akaakai?**). An ambiguous passage in For. 4:157: *maluna o ka wa'a naku akaakai . . . kona wa'a akaakai,* in the bulrush canoe . . . his bulrush canoe. (Reference is to a canoe bound for Kahiki to search for 'Olopana. Thrum's note [For. 4:156] says that canoes were not made of bulrushes and thinks *naku* here is 'to search' [see *naku 2*]. An alternative interpretation of *akaakai* is *akaaka,* clear, + *-i,* transitivizer, which might also mean 'search' in the sense of clarification.)

'aka'a.kai kī.kā.nia. n. A common variety of onion.

'aka'a.kai kula.pe.peiao. n. Big, yellowish onion. *Lit.,* earring onion.

'aka'a.kai kū.maka.hiki. n. A purplish annual onion.

'aka'a.kai lau. n. Green onion *(Allium fistulosum);* its leaves are eaten with salt salmon. (Neal 198.) *Lit.,* leaf onion.

'aka'a.kai mahina. n. A wild onion, used for sore throat. *Lit.,* moon onion, so called because the curve of the section of the bulb suggests a crescent moon.

'aka'a.kai naku. n. Bulrush.

'aka'a.kai pilau. n. Garlic *(Allium sativum).* (Neal 198–9.)

'aka'a.kai pū.pū. n. Garlic. *Lit.,* bunched onion.

akaaka.lani. n. Afterglow.

akaaka 'ole. vs. Not clear, vague, indistinct.

'ā.ka'a.loa. n. A variety of seaweed.

aka.'awa. n. A tall endemic climber *(Smilax sandwicensis)* with tendrils and shiny, leathery, heart-shaped leaves; used for tying rafters. (Neal 211.) Also *hoi kuahiwi.*

'ā.kaha. Same as *'ēkaha,* bird's-nest fern.

aka.hai. nvs. Modest, gentle, unassuming, unpretentious, unobtrusive, docile, decorous, meek, suave; meekness, modesty. *Pōmaika'i ka po'e akahai, no ka mea, e lilo ka honua iā lākou* (Mat. 5.5), blessed are the meek for they shall inherit the earth. (PCP *ata-* + PPN *fai*.)

aka-ka-na'i. n. Name of a kind of white tapa.

aka.hana. vt. To work carefully or slowly.

aka.hao. vt. To pick up carefully, as food.

aka.hele. vi. Slow or moderate, cautious, careful, prudent (see ex., *pukapai*). *Me ke akahele,* circumspectly, prudently. *Ka noʻonoʻo akahele,* careful consideration. *E hikiwawe mai i ka lohe, e akahele hoʻi i ka ʻōlelo,* be quick to hear but slow to speak. **ho.ʻā.kahele.** Caus/sim.; precautionary; to take precautions.

ʻaka hene, ʻaka hene.hene. vt. To laugh at teasingly, jeer. *ʻAka hene iki,* to titter.

ʻakahi. 1. num. One (especially in counting in a series). *Pōʻakahi,* Monday. *ʻAkahi kahi ana, ʻo ka ʻEwa iki, ʻo ka ʻEwa nui,* a single unit, then lesser ʻEwa and greater ʻEwa. **2.** idiom. For the first time, never before (usually followed by *nō*). (Gram. 4.6.) *ʻAkahi nō ʻoe ā hiki maʻaneʻi?* Is this the first time you have come here? Have you ever been here before? *ʻAkahi nō au ā ʻike iā Hilo,* this is the first time I've seen Hilo. *ʻAkahi nō au ā lohe i ka hekili,* I've never heard such thunder. **3.** idiom. To have just. *ʻAkahi nō ā pau kaʻu haʻawina,* my lesson is just finished.

ʻakahi akahi. idiom. Inexperienced, trying out for the first time; novice, beginner. *E akahele ka mea ʻakahi akahi i ka luʻu,* let the inexperienced be careful in diving. *ʻA ʻole nō i ʻike loa no ka mea ʻakahi akahi,* [I] did not know much because of inexperience.

aka.hiʻu. n. Base of caudal fin. Also *akaakahiʻu.*

aka.hoe. vt. To paddle carefully, silently.

aka.holo. vi. To sail or run cautiously.

a kai. By the sea. *Kō a kai,* those by the sea.

ʻā.kaʻi.kaʻi. vs. Large, potbellied, plump.

aka iki. nvi. To laugh a little, snicker.

akaka. Var. spelling of *akaaka 1.*

ʻakaka. 1. nvi. A rent, split, chink, separation; to crack, split, scale. **2.** Also **agata.** n. Agate. *Eng.*

ʻaka.kane. n. Hawaiʻi *ʻākepa* (honey creeper), *Loxops coccinea coccinea,* endangered. See *ʻākepa.*

ʻakake, agate. n. Agate. *Eng.*

ʻaka.ke. vs. Spry, quick, nimble, especially about getting into people's way or into trouble.

ʻakaki, agati. n. Agate. *Eng.*

ʻaka.kihi. Same as *ʻakakē. Rare.*

aka kiʻi. n. Negative of a photograph.

aka.kole. nvs. Destitution, poverty; poor.

aka.kū. vs. Vision, trance; reflection, as in a mirror; hallucination; to see a vision. **ho.ʻāka.kū.** Caus/sim. **2.** See *kino aka.*

aka.kū ā.nue.nue. n. The phenomenon known as the Specter of the Brocken, seen at Hale-a-ka-lā Crater. *Lit.,* rainbow apparition. **ho.ʻāka.kū ā.nue.nue.** Caus/sim.

aka.kuʻu. vi. Lessened, diminished, mitigated; to cease, abate, grow calm, stop, as wind, surf, rain, anger, grief, pain; settled, calmed, quieted, appeased. *Ua akakuʻu mai ke aliʻi, ʻaʻole inu lama hou,* the chief has calmed down, he doesn't drink any more.

ʻā.kala. 1. vs. Pink. **2.** n. Two endemic raspberries *(Rubus hawaiensis* and *R. macraei);* and the thimbleberry *(R. rosaefolius),* from southeastern Asia. (Neal 390–1.) Also *ʻākalakala, ʻōlaʻa.* **3.** n. Dye made from *ʻākala* juice. **4.** n. A pink tapa. **5.** Same as *kala,* a seaweed.

ʻā.kala.kala. 1. Same as *ʻākala 2, 3.* **2.** vs. Pinkish. *Rare.*

aka.lani. Same as *akaakalani.*

aka.lau. n. The ghost or spirit of a living person seen by others, a sign of calamity. *Lit.,* many shadows.

aka.lei. n. String of multicolored glass beads. *Lit.,* bead reflections.

aka.lewa. vi. To sway the hips daintily, deliberately, and gracefully. See *aka-, lewa 2.*

ʻaka.lio, asario. n. Farthing. (Latin *assarius.)*

aka.luli. vi. To move slowly, carefully. See *aka-, luli.*

ʻakama, adama. vs. Adamant. *Eng.*

aka.mai. nvs. Smart, clever, expert; smartness, skill, wit. Cf. *akeakamai. Nā ʻōlelo akamai a Kolomona,* the proverbs of Solomon. **ho.ʻāka.mai.** To make wise or smart; to make a pretense of wisdom; to show off, display erudition; theorist. (PPN *ʻatamai.)*

ʻAkamu, Adamu. n. Adam. *Eng.*

aka.nahe. vs. Careful, gentle in behavior and speech. See *aka-, nahe.*

aka.noho. vi. To sit quietly, live cautiously. See *aka-, noho 2.*

aka.ʻōlelo. vt. To speak cautiously, deliberately, in moderation. See *aka-, ʻōlelo.*

aka.oʻo. vs. Stingy, miserly, hard.

ʻaka.pane. Same as *ʻapapane,* a bird.

ʻā.kau. 1. nvs. Right (not *left).* Cf. *mākaukau, hema. Ma ka ʻākau, huli,* right, face; *nānā ma ka ʻākau,* dress right [military commands]. *Lālau ka ʻākau, lū ka hema* (saying), the right [hand] grabs, the left throws away [of a spendthrift]. (PPN *mataʻu,* PCP *katau.)* **2.** n. North (when one faces west, the direction of the sun's course, the right hand is to the north).

akaua.helo. nvi. To go here and there, vagabond; vagabond.

aka.ʻula. n. Red sunset, looked upon as a sign that rain will clear. *Lit.,* red shadow.

ake. 1. n. Liver. Cf. *akeloa, akemāmā. Maʻi ʻai ake,* tuberculosis. (PPN *ʻate.)* **2.** vt. To desire, wish, be eager, yearn [the emotions and intelligence were thought to be centered within the body]. *ʻAke hoʻoipoipo,* amorous, "horny". *Ake nui nō lākou e hāʻule ka ua,* they want very much for rain to fall.

ʻā.kē. vt. To find fault, criticize, slander. See *kē.*

ā.kea. 1. nvs. Broad, wide, spacious, open, unobstructed, public, at large; full, as a skirt; breadth, width. *Fig.,* liberal. *Piliwaiwai ākea,* open gambling. *Ākea ka noʻonoʻo,* broad-minded. *Hōʻike ākea,* a public report; to lay before the public. *Ke hoʻolaha ʻia aku nei ma ke ākea,* there is being widely advertised hereby. **ho.ʻā.kea.** To widen, broaden, extend, enlarge, make public; broadening, expansion; extension; to escape *(rare). E hoʻākea i ke kolone,* extend the column [a military command]. **2.** *(Cap.)* n. Var. of *Wākea.*

ʻā.kea. n. Starboard or outer hull of a double canoe. (PPN *katea.)*

ake.aka.mai. nvs. A lover of wisdom, seeker after knowledge, philosopher, scientist, scholar; philosophy, science; scientific. *Lit.,* to desire wisdom.

ake.ake. vs. Quick, ready, as to do a kindly deed, helpful.

ʻakē.ʻakē. n. Hawaiian storm petrel *(Oceanodroma castro cryptoleucura).*

ā.kea.kea. **1.** Same as *hākeakea,* faded; to fade. **2.** n. A kind of gray tapa.

ʻā.keʻa.keʻa. nvt. To block, hinder, obstruct, interfere; obstruction, block.

ā.kē.kē. 1. Var. of *kēkē,* potbellied. **2.** n. Name given for the *ʻoʻopu hue,* puffer fish, and listed by Malo. (Malo 46.)

ʻā.keke. n. Cindery or pebbly soil; cinder.

ʻake.keʻe. n. A honey creeper *(Loxops coccinea caeruleirostris).* Usually called *ʻākepa* in Eng. Also *ʻōʻūholowai.*

ʻake.keke. 1. n. Ruddy turnstone *(Arenaria interpres),* a winter migrant to Hawaiʻi, occurring in small flocks which rise and wheel together. Also *keke.* **2.** vi. To talk loquaciously in a friendly, hospitable manner, bidding a guest to feel at home, make himself comfortable, eat plenty. Cf. *heahea.* **3.** Redup. of *ʻakeke,* cinder.

ʻAke.lanika, Atelanika. nvs. Atlantic. *Eng.*

ʻakele, akere. n. Acre. *Eng.*

ʻā.kele.kele. nvi. To escape from danger or sickness; to have a narrow escape.

ʻake.lika, akerida. See *ʻūhini ʻakelika.*

ake.loa. n. Spleen. *Lit.,* long liver.

ake maka. n. Edible raw liver.

ake.makani. n. Lung. Also *akemāmā, akepāhola. Lit.,* wind liver.

ake.mā.mā. n. Lung. *Lit.,* light liver.

akena. vt. To boast, brag, admire, praise. *Kūʻē akena,* to taunt, defy. *Keiki akena ā haʻanui,* child boaster and exaggerator.

'ā.kena, agena. n. Agent, factor. *Eng.*
'ā.kena hō.'oia'i'o pala.pala. n. Notary public.
'ā'kena kā.lepa ka'a.hele. n. Traveling salesman, commercial traveler.
ā.kena.kena. Redup. of *akena.*
ake.nī'au. Spleen. *Lit.,* coconut-midrib liver.
Ake-o-Milu. n. See *Ke-ake-o-Milu.*
'ā.kepa. 1. n. Group of small scarlet or yellow-green Hawaiian honey creepers *(Loxops coccinea).* See *'akakane, 'akeke'e, 'akepeu'ie.* 2. vs. Quick, nimble, sprightly, active.
ake.pa'a. n. Liver (more specific than *ake).* (Oihk. 3.4.) *Lit.,* firm liver.
ake.paha.ola. n. Lung.
ake.pā.hola. n. Lung.
ā.kepa.kepa. 1. vs. Unkempt, as hair; oblique. *'Oki ākepakepa,* to cut obliquely, as fish. 2. Rare var. of *kepakepa 1.*
ake.pau. n. Tuberculosis, consumption. *Lit.,* finished liver.
'ake.peu.'ie. n. O'ahu *'ākepa* (honey eater), *Loxops coccinea rufa,* presumed extinct; Maui *'ākepa, L. c. ochracea,* endangered.
'akeu. vs. Active, lively, quick; pleasant, sociable.
'ā.keu.keu. Redup. of *'akeu.*
'ā.ke'u.ke'u. vt. To find fault, contradict, criticize, hinder.
'aki. 1. nvt. To take a nip and let go, snap; to nibble, as fish; to bite off the bark of sugar cane; to heal, as a wound; to scar over; sharp recurring pain, as in head or stomach. *Fig.,* to attack, taunt, malign, snap at; slander (Hal. 50.20); backbiter (Roma 1.30). *'Ōpū 'aki,* severe stomach-ache. *'Aki ka nuku,* to press the lips tightly together. *Pēlā e lilo ai ia i mea i hō'ino 'ia ai, i mea e 'aki ai* (Ezek. 5.15), so it shall be a reproach and a taunt. hō.'aki. Caus/sim. (PNP *kati.)* 2. n. Height, tip, top (preceded by *ke). Kū i ke 'aki,* to stand at the top [to have success]. 3. n. Pillow. 4. n. Block on which a canoe is placed on the shore. Also *Iona.* 5. vs. Filled, as a canoe with waves. 6. Same as *'aki'aki 2,* a rush. (KL line 66.)
'ā.kī. 1. nvi. Hair switch; knot fastening plaits or braids of hair; to add long strands of hair. *Ua 'ākī 'ia ka lauoho, ua like ka lō'ihi o ka 'ākī me ka pūpū olonā,* the hair is lengthened with long switches; the switches are as long as *olonā* bunches. 2. vt. To furl, as sails. 3. Same as *kikī,* fast. *Rare.*
'ā.kia. 1. n. Endemic shrubs and trees *(Wikstroemia* spp.) with small leaves, tiny yellowish flowers, and yellow to red, small, ovoid one-seeded fruits. The bark yields a fiber; the bark, roots, and leaves (as *W. oahuensis)* a narcotic used for fish poisoning (Neal 616), and according to Kep., used in *'anā'anā* sorcery. Varieties are qualified by the terms *lau nui, mānalo,* and *pehu.* Also *kauhi.* 2. n. *Solanum nelsoni.* Ni'ihau. 3. vi. To ferment; very sour, as poi. *'Ai 'ākia,* sour poi. 4. Pas/imp. of *'aki 1.* 5. Also *Asia.* nvs. Asia; Asian, Asiatic. *Eng.*
akia.hala. Same as *kanawao 1,* small endemic trees.
'aki.'aki. 1. Redup. of *'aki 1;* to nibble, as a fish; constant snapping at, attacking. (PPN *katikati.)* 2. n. Seashore rush grass *(Sporobolus virginicus),* a coarse grass growing on sandy beaches; used to exorcise spirits. (Neal 66-7.) Also *mānienie 'aki'aki, mānienie māhikihiki,* and *mānienie maoli.* 3. n. A kind of coarse red seaweed *(Ahnfeltia concinna)* which because of its toughness must be eaten in little bites; a good source of carrageenin, a colloid. (KL line 41.) Called *'eleau* on Maui.
'aki.'aki haole. n. Buffalo grass *(Stenotaphrum secundatum),* an American grass used for lawns. Some people believed that buffalo grass could be used to exorcise spirits because it had been given the same name *('aki-'aki)* as the seashore rush grass, which was used for this purpose. (Neal 72-3.) Also *mānienie 'aki'aki.*
'akia.loa. n. A group of Hawaiian honey creepers with

long, curved bill, olive or yellow-green above, lighter below *(Hemignathus obscurus),* with subspecies on Hawai'i *(H. o. o.),* Lā-na'i *(H. o. lanaiensis),* O'ahu *(H. o. ellisianus),* and Kaua'i *(H. procerus).* The latter is endangered; it has the longest curved beak, for sipping honey at the base of *'ie'ie* and *hala pepe* leaves. Cf. *'iwi, 'i'iwi.* Also *'akihi loa, kipi.*
'akia pō.lā.'au. Same as *'akihi po'o lā'au.*
'akihi, 'aki.hia. n. Birds. See below.
'akihi a loa. Same as *'akialoa* and *'akihi loa.* (Malo 39.)
'akihi ke'ehi 'ale. n. A small black sea bird, probably a stormy petrel *(Oceanodroma),* of which two dark, sooty species are known about the Hawaiian Islands, especially those to the northwest. *Lit.,* billow-treading *'akihi.*
'akihi loa. Same as *'akialoa.*
'akihi pō.lena. n. A bird listed by Malo. (Malo 39.)
'akihi po'o lā.'au. n. The *nuku pu'u* honey creeper of Hawai'i *(Hemignathus wilsoni).* See *nuku pu'u.*
'aki.ho'o.lana. n. Drydock. *Lit.,* floating canoe-rest.
'ā.ki'i.ki'i. n. Dip net, as used in fishing *uhu.* Also *'upena pāki'iki'i.*
'akika, acida. nvs. Acid. *Eng. E mālama pono iho 'oe i ke kī'aha wai 'akika* (song), watch carefully for the glassful of acid.
'akika kapo.lika, asida cabolika. n. Carbolic acid. *Eng.*
'akiki. 1. nvs. Dwarfed; dwarf. Cf. *'ukiki.* 2. Same as *'ūkīkiki,* young of *'ōpakapaka* fish.
'aki.kiki. n. The endemic Kaua'i creeper *(Loxops maculata bairdi,* formerly *Paroreomyza bairdi).*
'aki.lolo. n. 1. A wrasse fish of the *hīnālea* type *(Gomphosus varius).* Also *hīnālea 'akilolo.* This fish was used by priests as the *pani* or closing medicine for head diseases. The taro or sugar cane of the same name might substitute. *Lit.,* brain biting. 2. A variety of sugar cane, striped with green and deep purplish-red when young, with yellow and red when older; named for the fish. 3. A variety of taro.
'aki.lolo 'ula.'ula. n. A variety of sugar cane, with purplish leaves. See *nānahu.*
'aki lou. v. To take with a *lou* or fruit-plucking stick.
'akima, azima. n. Feast of unleavened bread.
'aki.malala, adimarala. n. Admiral. *Eng.*
'aki.mona. Same as *'inamona, kukui* nut relish.
'akina. nvi. Biting; bite.
'akio.hala, 'akia.hala. n. An endemic, small, hairy, pink-flowered shrub *(Hibiscus youngianus),* usually found in marshy places. (Neal 560.) Also *hau hele.*
'aki.oma. n. Axiom. *Eng.*
'aki.pī.hopa. n. Archbishop. *Eng.*
'aki.pohe. 1. vt. To nip. *'Akipohe nā manu i ka lehua,* the birds nip at the fringes of the *lehua* flowers. 2. vs. Round, as a leaf; compact, concise. *'Akipohe ke 'ike aku i ka nani o Wai-pi'o,* compact the view of the beauty of Wai-pi'o. 3. *(Cap.)* n. Name of a wind of Wai-he'e, Maui. 4. vi. To center or concentrate in one place, as wind, rain. *Rare.*
'akiu. vt. To search, seek, probe, penetrate, spy.
'ā.kiu.kiu. Redup. of *'akiu. A me ka makani 'ākiukiu kīpē pua hala o Puakei,* and the penetrating wind pelting the pandanus blossoms of Puakei.
ako. nvt. Thatching; to thatch. *Mea ako hale,* thatcher. *Ako 'ia ka hale,* the house is thatched [if during an emergency it was impossible to erect a temple, the priest merely gestured that the house was completed and thatched]. (PPN *'ato.)*
'ako. 1. vt. To cut, shear, clip, trim, as hair; to break or pluck, as flowers. *Kanaka 'ako lauoho,* barber. *Nā mea 'ako hulu hipa* (I Sam. 25.7), wool shearers. (PEP *kato.)* 2. nvs. Itch, throat irritation, venereal disease. *Fig.,* lust.
'akoa. n. A small tree resembling *koa;* dye was made from its bark, and used to color tapa. (And.) But cf. *kū'oulena.*
'ako.'ako. 1. Redup. of *'ako 1, 2.* 2. nvi. Crest of a

wave; to break or swell, as waves. *Pipipi'i i ka 'ako'ako nā li'i nui i ka 'ako'ako, i ka 'iu lani* (chant for Kua-kini), the great chiefs ascend to the crest of the waves, to the crest, to the heavenly height.

'ā.koa.koa. vi. To assemble; assembled, collected, heaped. *Pau 'ākoakoa,* all gathered together. **ho'ā.koa.koa.** To assemble, congregate, muster, throng; to collect, gather. *'Imi ā ho'ākoakoa,* to search for and gather, as data. (PPN *ka(a)toa.*)

'ā.ko'a.ko'a. n. Coral in general, coral head.

'ā.ko'a.ko'a kohe. n. Mushroom coral *(Fungia scutaria). Lit.,* vagina coral.

'ā.kohe.kohe. n. The crested honey creeper *(Palmeria dolei),* formerly endemic on Maui, endangered.

'akohi. n. A variety of taro. (Heb. *egowz.*)

'akoka, agoza. n. A nut.

'akoki. n. A variety of sugar cane, deep-red and green when young, changing to purple and brown-yellow; pith dark-brown; larger and stronger than *'akilolo,* especially in wet districts.

'akoko. n. Endemic shrubs and trees *(Euphorbia* spp.) with jointed stems, opposite leaves, and milky sap (Neal 515–6). Buds and leaves of one species *(E. multiformis)* were chewed for debility. Also *ēkoko, koko, kōkōmālei.*

'ā.kokoko. vs. Bloody. Also *kokoko.*

'akola. Same as *'aikola,* gesture and expression of contempt.

'akole. 1. vs. Poor, destitute, shiftless. **2.** n. A large endemic fern *(Dryopteris unidentata),* 1 m or more high, with triangular-oblong fronds much subdivided.

'ā.kō.lea. n. **1.** A native fern *(Athyrium microphyllum* syn. *A. poiretianum)* with beautiful, large, lacy fronds. See *hākonakona 1.* (Neal 25.) **2.** A small mollusk *(Epitonium perplexum).* Often called *pipipi 'ākōlea* or *kōlea.*

'akole.ana. n. Accordion. *Eng.*

'ako.lika. n. Ostrich. *Eng.*

'akolo. vi. To creep, attempt to creep; to put out small roots, as potatoes.

'akolu. num. Three (as in counting in a series); three times. *Pō'akolu,* Wednesday *(lit.,* third day).

'ako.mika. vs. Atomic. *Eng.*

'ako.pie, adobie. vs. Adobe. *Eng.*

aku. 1. nvi. Bonito, skipjack *(Katsuwonus pelamis),* an important food; to run, of *aku.* Young of this fish are called *kīna'u* and *'āhua. Ua aku 'o Mahai-'ula* (FS 287), bonitos are running at Mahai-'ula [place at Keāhole quadrangle, Kona, Hawai'i]. (PPN *'atu.*) **2.** Part. expressing direction away from the speaker, and time either past (with *nei)* or future (without *nei,* sometimes translated *soon).* (Table 12 in Gram. 7.2.) *Aku* contrasts with *mai* and sometimes may be translated *away. Hele aku,* go away. *Kū'ai aku,* to sell. *Kēlā makahiki aku nei,* last year. *Kēlā pule aku nei,* last week. *'Apōpō ā ia lā aku,* day after tomorrow. *Nehinei ā ia lā aku,* day before yesterday. *Kēia lā aku,* later today, sometime today. *I aha 'ia aku nei?* What happened a while ago? *Na Ioane aku i nā 'ekalekia* (Hoik. 1.4), John said to the churches. *Aku* + demon. *lā* is pronounced and written as a single word, *akula. 'Ī akula 'oia,* he said to someone far away (cf. *a'e 4). Aku* sometimes expresses the comparative degree: *Nā mea nui aku i kēia,* things larger than this. In an idiom, *aku* is sometimes used as a noun after the plural definite article *nā: I nā aku,* right away, soon. *He mea 'ai i nā aku* (Kep. 121), food will be here soon. (PPN *atu.*)

'akū. n. An endemic lobelia *(Cyanea tritomantha),* a small tree 2 to 3 m high, with clustered leaves (up to 78 by 20 cm), somewhat downy beneath. The leaves were cooked and eaten like cabbage. Cf. *'akū'akū.*

akua. 1. vs. God, goddess, spirit, ghost, devil, image, idol, corpse; divine, supernatural, godly. *Akua* might mate with humans and give birth to normal humans, *mo'o,* or *kupua* (Nānā 23). Children of Ka-mehameha by Ke-ōpu-o-lani were sometimes referred to as *akua* because of their high rank. *Kauā,* or outcasts, were sometimes called *akua* because they were despised as ghosts. *Kona akua,* his god. *Akua nō kona 'ike,* his knowledge is indeed divine. *'Ai akua,* to have a prodigious appetite, as though possessed of gods [as youthful heroes in legends]. *Nāna nō i hā'awi i ke akua,* through her given to the god [death by sorcery, cursed]. **ho'ā.kua.** To deify, make a god of; godlike, supernatural, extraordinary, divine. Cf. *hoa kua. Ho'ākua noho'i kāna hana,* his deeds are marvelous. *Ho'ākua ke kai,* a dangerous sea. (PPN *'atua.*) **2.** *(Cap.)* n. God (Christian). **3.** n. "It" in a game of tag or hide-and-seek. **4.** *(Cap.)* Name of the 14th night of the full moon. (PEP *'Atua.*) **5.** Same as *mai'a Polapola,* a banana.

akua 'ai hamu. n. Spirit eater of scraps, designation of a god sent on errands of destruction by sorcerers.

akua 'ai kahu. n. A spirit that destroys its keeper; a god sent on an evil errand who returns to destroy his keeper rather than the victim; any evil practice, as excessive drinking, gossiping. *He akua 'ai kahu ka holoholo-'ōlelo,* bearing gossip is a spirit who destroys its keeper.

akua 'ai pilau. n. Spirit eater of filth. Same as *akua 'ai hamu.*

akua 'au.makua. n. Supernatural with dual roles as *akua* to unrelated persons and *'aumakua* to relatives, as formerly the four major gods to high ranking chiefs, and later only as Pele, Hi'iaka, and Laka to mortals. (Nānā 36.)

akua hana. n. A god to whom one appealed with offerings for help, as in fishing, farming, or killing an enemy. *Lit.,* work god.

akua hā.nai, n. **1.** Spirits, as of a recently dead kinsman, who were fed *(hānai)* offerings (such as food) and sent out to destroy an enemy. **2.** The *kauila, nioi,* and *'ohe* "poison" woods of Moloka'i, which were kept by sorcerers in their houses, wrapped in tapa, and to which food offerings were made daily; scraps of these woods were used as poison, and poison itself was sometimes called *akua hānai.*

akua ho'o.una.una. n. God sent on errands of destruction.

akua hulu. n. Feather image. (Ii 39.)

akua kā.'ai. n. Stick image (general name); image wrapped in tapa; image consisting of a carved staff, with a tuft of feathers at the top, bound to its bearer by a sash *(kā'ai)* (Malo 80) and carried into battle; staff with a carved figure at the head, used in ceremonies to procure offspring (Malo 135, 139).

Akua kahi.kolu. n. Holy Trinity. (Kep. 175.)

akua kahu.kahu. n. A god to whom offerings and sacrifices were made.

akua kī.hei pua. n. Same as *'uhane kīhei pua.*

akua ki'i. n. Image representing a god.

'akū.'akū. 1. vi. Swaying, as a canoe in rough sea; not steady; bumpy, as a road. *'Akū'akū ka ihu o ka wa'a,* the prow of the canoe rises and falls. **2.** vi. Hasty, poorly done, rash. **3.** n. An endemic lobelia *(Cyanea rollandioides)* 1 to 1.4 m high, with rough leaves to 50 by 15 cm. The leaves were cooked like cabbage or taro tops or sweet potato leaves, with pork or salt beef. Cf. *'akū.*

akua kumu haka. n. Similar to *akua hānai 1, 2;* sent out in the shape of fireballs to kill, or inserted in a victim's food, water, or tobacco. (Kam. 64:134–5.)

akua lapu. n. Ghost, specter, apparition, evil spirit.

akua lele. n. Flying god, usually a poison god sent to destroy, sometimes in the form of fireballs *(pōpō ahi).* See *akua hānai.*

akua loa. n. A tall image, especially an image of Lono carried on a circuit of the island during the *makahiki,* harvest festival; it was called *loa,* long, because of its "long" travels. The image consisted of a staff about two fathoms long. Pieces of *pala* fern, feather leis, and skins of the *ka'upu* bird were fastened to a crosspiece tied near the top of the staff, in the center of which was a tiny carved head. A long white tapa banner was attached to the crosspiece. (Malo 143–5, but see Malo text, chapter 36, sections 22–4.) Tribute was collected. Also *Lono Makua.*

akua mali.hini. n. Foreign god, epithet often applied to Pele because she had come from a foreign land.

akua noho. n. A spirit that takes possession of people and speaks through them as a medium. (Malo 115–7.)

akua pā.'ani. n. Image representing the god of sports that accompanied the *akua loa* on its circuit, to preside at the sport festivals. (Malo 145, 154.)

akua pahulu. n. The god of nightmares; a god who carried persons to distant places in their sleep, especially if they had eaten certain fish, as the *weke.*

akua panau.ea. n. Last and slow-moving image in a procession during *kauila nui* ceremonies. (Ii 41.)

akua pepei.ao. Same as *pepeiao akua.*

akua poko. Similar to *akua loa,* except that it was taken to a *poko.* See *poko 3.*

akua ulu. n. A god that inspires or possesses people.

akua wahine. n. Goddess.

aku'e. nvs. Club-footed; deformity of the feet. Cf. *kuku'e.*

'ā.kuhe.kuhe. Same as *'ōkuhekuhe,* a fish; fish form of the god Kāne-milo-hai (HM 452).

'ā.ku'i 1. vt. To pound. **2.** Probably similar to *'āku'iku'i 2. He lā'au 'āku'i . . . no ka wā 'upena ku'u,* (For. 5:621), sticks used with gill nets.

'ā.ku'i.ku'i. 1. vt. To pound. See *ku'i 1.* **2.** nvt. A long fish net; to drive fish into the net by striking the water with sticks. Also *pāku'iku'i.*

aku.ila. Same as *kihe,* a red seaweed.

'aku.kana. nvs. Adjutant. *Eng.*

'aku.kana kene.lala (generala). n. Adjutant general. *Eng.*

'akuku. vt. To beat, as tapa. (Kep. 99.)

'a.kū.kū. nvi. Tossing about, agitated; jolting, as a vehicle on a rough road. *He 'akūkū nalu lā i po'i,* an agitation of waves that broke.

akula. Directional part. *aku* + demon. *lā.* See ex., *aku 2.*

akule. n. Big-eyed or goggle-eyed scad fish *(Trachurops crumenophthalmus).* Stages of growth are *pā'ā'ā, halalū* or *hahalalū,* and *akule. Ua wehe ke akule i ka hohonu,* the *akule* has fled to the depths [of escape]. (PPN *atule.*)

'ā.kule.ana. vt. To give property or a right to it; to delegate responsibility. **ho'ā.kule.ana,** Caus/sim. *He hō'ailona ia o ka luhi a me ka ho'ākuleana* (Kep. 117), this is a sign of toil and of obtaining property.

'akule.kele, aduletere. n. Adultery. *Eng.*

'ā.kuli. nvi. To collect, as leaves in a stream; to dam a stream thus; forest pool where leaves and rubbish have accumulated. *Fig.,* to cast a reflection. *Ākuli ke aka o ka lā'au i ka wai,* the reflection of trees is cast on the water.

'ā.kuli.kuli. n. **1.** General name for succulent plants. (PCP *ka(a)tuli.*) **2.** A coastal herb *(Sesuvium portulacastrum),* known in many warm regions, somewhat like wild portulaca *(ākulikuli kula),* but with longer, narrower leaves, and with small white to magenta flowers at leaf axils. (Neal 340.) **3.** *Portulaca cyanosperma.* Ni'ihau.

'ā.kuli.kuli 'ae.'ae. Same as *'ae'ae 2.*

'ā.kuli.kuli kai, 1. n. A tropical American, low succulent *(Batis maritima),* commonly forming a continuous green cover by salt marshes. Locally called pickleweed. (Neal 339.) **2.** Same as *'ae'ae 2.*

'ā.kuli.kuli kula. n. Purslane *(Portulaca oleracea),* a cosmopolitan weed, a small succulent, prostrate herb, with spatula-shaped leaves and yellow flowers. It is eaten by people, poultry, and stock. (Neal 342.) *Lit.,* plain succulent.

'ā.kuli.kuli lau li'i. Same as *'ākulikuli kula.*

'ā.kuli.kuli lei. n. Ice plant *(Lampranthus glomeratus)* from Africa, a low succulent, with thick, narrow leaves, and pink, rose, or orange flowers (used for leis). (Neal 341.)

'ā.kuli.kuli-'ō.helo. Same as *'ae'ae 2.*

'akumu. vs. Broken or cut off, as a pencil point; blunt, stumpy.

'ā.kumu.kumu Redup. of *'akumu.*

aku nei. A while ago, last. See *aku 2.*

'akupa. 1. Same as *'ōkuhe,* an *'o'opu* fish. **2.** n. A small endemic tree *(Bobea mannii).* Cf. *'ahakea.*

ala. 1. n. Path, road, trail. Cf. *alaloa, alanui, alawai. Ala iki,* narrow or small path. *Ala i hiki ai,* access, approach. *Ala ho'i 'ole mai,* a pathway on which there is no returning [death]. *Ala a ka manu,* a bird's trail [a life difficult to emulate]. *Ala iki a kāhuna,* the small path of priests [a difficult way of life]. (PPN *hala.*) **2.** vi. To waken, stay awake; awake. **ho'āla, ho'o.ala.** To awaken someone. *Mele ho'āla,* a chant intended to awaken a sleeper. (PPN *ara.*) **3.** vi. To rise up, arise, get up, come forward. *Ala kū'ē,* to rise in revolt. Cf. *ala hou.* **ho'āla.** To arouse, stir up, incite, renew, restore, revive, raise; to restore, as a building; summons. *Ho'āla i ke kumuhana,* to bring up a subject. *Ho'āla i ke kiko,* cock a gun. *Ā na lākou noho'i kēia ho'āla ia'u* (GP 10), this summons to me was from them. *Ke ho'āla mai nei 'oia i ko'u 'uhane* (Hal. 23.3), he restoreth my soul. *Ho'āla kuahu,* a chant said at the construction of a hula altar *(kuahu hula),* calling on the gods, especially Laka, to possess the altar. **4.** Rare var. of *ale 1.* Cf. *alaō, alapoho. Ua ala ka i'a i ka makau,* the fish takes the hook whole. **5.** demon. There (same as the more frequent *lā* and *-la*). Cf. *e lākou ala, e lauala, e* (verb) *ala,* Gram. 7.4, 8.2. *Ua kanaka ala,* the person there. (PEP *ala.*)

ala-. Fast, quickly. Cf. *alaheo, alamimo, alapine, alawiki,* Gram. 6.3.3.

'ala. 1. vs. Fragrant, sweet-smelling, perfumed; fragrance, perfume (preceded by *ke*). *Fig.,* esteemed, chiefly. *Mea 'ala,* ointment, perfume. *Ke 'ala kūpaoa,* a strong heady fragrance. *Ke 'ala punia,* a fragrance so strong that it causes dizziness. Cf. *'a'ala.* **hō.'ala.** To perfume. (PNP *kala.*) **2.** n. A variety of taro, said to be pungent-smelling when cooked. Varieties are qualified by the terms *'ele'ele, ke'oke'o, 'ōpelu;* cf. also *'ala-o-Puna.*

'alā. n. Dense waterworn volcanic stone, as used for poi pounders, adzes, hula stones; hard lava, basalt. Kinds of *'alā* rock, as used for adzes, are qualified by the phrases *pia maka hinu,* shiny-faced arrowroot; *māhinu,* shiny; and *maka hinu,* shiny face. (Kam. 76: 122) *'alā haumeku 'olokele, 'alā lelekepue. 'Alā o ka ma'a,* slingstone. *Ka-'alā-wai* (place name, Honolulu), the watery basalt. (PPN *fatukalaa,* PNP *kalaa.*)

'ā.la'a. 1. n. A large endemic tree *(Planchonella* spp.) with smooth, oblong leaves, shiny-green above, bronze beneath, the fruit yellow or black, to 5 cm long. The sticky, milky sap was used to trap birds, the wood for spears and *'ō'ō* handles. (Neal 668.) Also *āulu, 'ēla'a.* (PPN *kalaka.*) **2.** nvt. *'Ō'ō* digging stick made of *'āla'a* or any wood; to prod or dig with a stick, as in taro cultivation. *Fig.,* to dig into the mind; to be dislodged, as by the wind. **3.** n. Small corm, as of taro.

'Ā.la'a-honua. n. A strong Hilo wind. *Lit.,* landprodding.

-alaala. ho'ā.laala. Redup. of *ho'āla;* to keep awake; to awaken or reawaken; to incite to action. Cf. *'oālaala. He mea ho'ālaala ke kope,* coffee is something that keeps [one] awake. (PPN *araara.*)

ā la'a lā. See *la'a 2.*

'ala'ala. 1. n. Ink sac in octopus or squid; after salting, drying, and broiling on the fire, it is mixed with *'inamona* or chili peppers and eaten; mixed with *'auhuhu* juice it is used as bait. *Fig.,* useless. *Ahu ka 'ala'ala!* Just a pile of squid ink sac [no use]! *He aha ka 'ala'ala o kēnā mea āu i ho'iho'i mai nei?* What's the good of that octopus ink sac you've brought home? *He aha kāna 'ala'ala?* What's he good for? *He aha kō 'ala'ala* (For. 5:569)? What's your reason? **2.** nvs. Scar of a scrofulous sore; to be so scarred; perhaps tuberculosis adenitis (Kam. 64:115). *Mai ʻalaʻala paha auaneʻi i ka ua o Kawaʻahia,* perhaps his neck will be scarred in the rain of Kawaʻahia [in trouble]. (PNP *kakala;* cf. Rennellese *kakaga.*) **3.** n. Aerial tubers of bitter yam, *hoi (Dioscorea bulbifera).*

ʻalā.ʻalā. n. Small *ʻalā* stones.

ā.laʻa.laʻa. n. Small tubers, as of taro.

ā.laʻa.lae. vs. Lukewarm; half-cooked.

-alaala.hia. hoʻā.laala.hia. Pas/imp. of *hoʻālaala.*

ʻala.ʻala.hua. Same as *māhoe 2,* kinds of trees.

alaʻa.lai. 1. Redup. of *ālai 1,* to hinder. **2.** n. Type of taro patch built on artificial mounds, known near Hilo as *kipi* (HP 125); mucky claylike soil, as in this type of patch. **3.** Same as *waimakanui,* a kind of large coarse endemic fern *(Thelypteria keraudreniana).*

ʻala.ʻala pū loa. Same as *ʻuhaloa,* a weed. *Aia i kula, i ka ʻalaʻala pū loa,* there in the fields, for *ʻalaʻala pū loa* [a wild-goose chase].

ʻala.ʻalawa. Redup. of *ʻalawa. ʻAlaʻalawa ka maka o ka ʻaihue,* the eyes of the thief glance this way and that.

ʻala.ʻala wai nui. n. **1.** All species of *Peperomia,* small native succulent forest herbs, related to *ʻawa.* (Neal 293.) The name is qualified by the terms *kāne* (on Oʻahu) or *kupa liʻi* (on Hawaiʻi), *pehu, pōhina.* Also *ʻawa-lau-a-Kāne.* **2.** A small weedy herb *(Plectranthus parviflorus),* in the mint family. (Neal 736.) This name may be qualified by the terms *pua kī, wahine.*

ā.laʻa.papa. 1. v. To tell publicly, as of the past. **2.** n. Type of ancient dramatic hula. (UL, chapter IX.) **3.** n. Long cloud formation.

ala.ʻau. n. River ford; place on a trail where one swims or wades across a stream.

ʻala.au.moe. n. A West Indian shrub, night cestrum *(Cestrum nocturnum),* Chinese inkberry, with narrow leaves and narrow, tubular, green-to-creamy white flowers, which are most fragrant at night. (Neal 751.) Also *kūpaoa, onaona lapana.*

ʻalae. 1. n. Mudhen or Hawaiian gallinule *(Gallinula chloropus sandvicensis),* a black wading bird with red frontal plate; cry of this bird is believed a bad omen; some considered the *ʻalae* an *ʻaumakua;* endangered. For the coot, see *ʻalae kea.* Also *koki.* See saying, *keʻu.* (PPN *kalae.*) **2.** Same as *ʻiwa,* a fern.

ʻalaea. n. **1.** Water-soluble colloidal ocherous earth, used for coloring salt, for medicine, for dye, and formerly in the purification ceremony called *hiʻuwai;* any red coloring matter; according to Dr. Frank Tabrah (Kam. 76:149), brick-red soil containing hematite. See *ʻiʻo ʻalaea, kuhi ʻalaea. Ua ʻalaea* (For. 4:399), red rain [red of the rainbow]. (PCP *kalaea.*) **2.** Fleshlike redness, especially the dark red meat close to the spine of some fish, as of the *aku.* **3.** Annatto dye plant *(Bixa orellana),* a tropical American shrub or small tree, bearing fruit with scarlet seeds, used for dyeing. Sometimes called *ʻalaea lāʻau* to distinguish from the earth; locally also called lipstick plant. (Neal 589.) Also *kūmauna.* **4.** Tribe or clan; people in a district who have intermarried. **5.** Bad breath, halitosis. **6.** Fore part of thigh; long narrow thigh muscle. (And.)

ʻalaea kāne. n. Dark-red *ʻalaea. Lit.,* male *ʻalaea 3.*

ʻalaea wahine. n. Light-red *ʻalaea. Lit.,* female *ʻalaea 3.*

ʻalae awī. n. The introduced Australian gallinule *Porphyrio poliocephalus, P. p. melanotus.* Also applied to a form of *ʻalae kea,* with brownish frontal knob.

ʻalae hua.pī. Same as *ʻalae ʻula.*

ʻala.ʻeke. n. An edible crab of the *Portunus* sp., sand-colored, and found in shallow water.

ʻalae kea. n. Hawaiian coot *(Fulica americana alai),* a marsh and pond bird, distinguished from *ʻalae ʻula* by its ivory-white frontal knob; endangered.

ʻalae keʻo.keʻo. Same as *ʻalae kea.*

ā.lae.lae. Same as *ʻōlaelae 1;* having a number of capes and land points.

ā.laʻe.laʻe. Var. of *mālaʻelaʻe.*

Ala-ʻeli. n. A wind of Mānoa Valley, Honolulu. *Kuʻu kāne mai nā makani anu o ka ʻāina, he Mālualua me ke*

Ala-ʻeli, my husband from the cool winds of the land, the Mālualua and the Ala-ʻeli.

ʻalae nū kea. Same as *ʻalae kea. Lit.,* white-beaked *ʻalae.*

ʻalae ʻula. n. Hawaiian gallinule or mudhen *(Gallinula chloropus sandvicensis),* distinguished from *ʻalae kea* by its reddish bill and frontal plate; endangered.

ala.haka. n. Plank bridge, rough road over ravines or chasms, trestle, ladder (Kin. 28:12).

ala.haka-o-Nuʻa-lolo. n. Type of braid used in the *pāpale ʻie.*

ala.haki. n. Mountain ladder or steps cut into a cliff.

ala.hao. n. Railway, railroad track. *Lit.,* iron road.

ala.heʻe, wala.heʻe. n. A large native shrub or small tree *(Canthium odoratum;* synonym *Plectronia odorata)* with shiny leaves and small, fragrant, white flowers. The wood is hard and was formerly used in making the *ʻōʻō* digging stick; also used medicinally. (Neal 797.) Also *ʻōheʻe.*

ala.heʻe haole. n. Mock orange *(Murraya paniculata),* an ornamental hedge plant (Neal 480) with shiny, dark-green leaves, small fragrant white flowers, and red berries. Also *walaheʻe haole.*

ala hele. n. Pathway, route, road, way to go, itinerary, trail, highway, means of transportation. *Hoʻokahi ala hele,* one way [of a plane trip]. *Pono ala hele,* right of way. *Kuleana ala hele e hiki aku ai,* right of way of access. *ʻO ka pono koʻu ala hele,* my course is righteousness.

ala hele wā.wae. n. Pedestrian's road, sidewalk.

ala.heo. vi. Gone, departed. *Ua alaheo ka iʻa,* the fish is gone.

ala.hia. Pas/imp. of *ala 2, 3. Rare.* **hoʻāla.hia.** Caus/ sim.; to awaken; wakefulness, insomnia. *I ka hiki hoʻālahia nei lā, ē ala, ē ala mai ʻoe* (prayer), the time to be awakened comes, awake, awake. (PPN *ʻarafia.*)

ala.hiʻi. n. Hem or finished border of a plaited mat or hat.

ala holo papa. n. Wooden bridge.

ala honua. vi. To wake up early for no reason.

ʻAla-honua. n. Name of a light Hilo breeze. *Lit.,* land fragrance. Also *ʻA ʻala-honua.*

Ala-hou. n. Name of a Molokaʻi wind. (For. 5:103.)

ala hou. nvi. Resurrection; to rise again, resurrect. *Ka lā i ala hou ai ka Haku,* Easter [Protestant; *lit.,* the day the Lord rose again]. **hoʻāla hou,** to restore, revive. (PPN *ʻara* + PPN *foʻou.*)

ala.huki.moku. n. Marine railway. *Lit.,* road to pull ships.

ala.hula. nvi. A frequented and well-known path; to frequent such; to tread or trample, as on a taboo being broken (And.). *Alahula Puʻu-loa he ala hele na Kaʻahupāhau,* everywhere in Pearl Harbor lies the path of Kaʻahu-pāhau. *Ua alahula kēia wahi iaʻu,* I am very familiar with this place.

ā.lai. 1. nvt. Obstruction, hindrance, block, blockade, bar, screen; to obstruct, hinder, block, defend, stand in the way, oppose, hamper. Cf. *alaʻalai, ānai. Ālai maka,* to fascinate the eyes, as beauty. *Ua ālai ʻia ʻoia e ka hilahila ā hiki ʻole ke pane aku,* he was hindered by embarrassment and could not answer. (PPN *aarai.*) **2.** n. Two sticks carried with the *akua loa* in the *makahiki* festival; they were used to mark the boundary of the taboo area.

ā.laʻi. vs. Gentle, as a breeze. Cf. *laʻi.*

alaia. n. Small thin surfboard, as of breadfruit or *koa* wood, and heavier than the *olo* board. Also *omo.*

ʻalai.aha. n. An upland bird, gray, about the size of the *ʻelepaio,* reported in 1863. See *ʻeʻea.* (KL line 308.)

ʻala.ʻihi. n. **1.** Various species of squirrelfishes of the family Holocentridae, including *Flammeo sammara* (spotfin squirrelfish, 185 mm), *Adioryx lacteoguttatus* (whitespotted, 117 mm), *A. diadema,* (crown, 109 mm), *A. xanterythrus* (Hawaiian, 132 mm), *A. tiere* (Tahitian, 259 mm). The young are called *ʻaʻalaʻihi.* Unidentified kinds are qualified by the terms *ʻakoʻakoʻa, kala loa* or *kanaloa, lā kea, māhū, maoli,* and *pilikoʻa.* **2.**

Pale pink tapa; any faded color. **3.** A variety of sugar cane named for the fish, either a deep-red mutant of *'āwela* or related to it; internodes barrel-shaped, leaves purple. (HP 221, 224.)

alā.iki. nvt. Appropriation of property by force, as practiced by some chiefs on their travels; to do so.

a laila. See *laila.*

ā.laina n. Obstacle, obstruction.

Ā.laka. n. Alaska. *Eng.*

ala kai. Sea course, path where one must swim past a projecting cliff.

ala.ka'i. nvt. To lead, guide, direct; leader, guide, conductor, head, director (a putative PCP *ala,* to lead [cf. Maori *arahi*] + *-ka'i,* transitivizer: Gram. 6.6.4). *Alaka'i hīmeni, alaka'i mele,* song leader. *Alaka'i hula,* hula leader. *Alaka'i ho'opaipai,* cheerleader. *Alaka'i pāna,* band leader. *Kī alaka'i,* tonic, keynote. *Kumu alaka'i,* leading teacher; exemplary teacher, pattern, or example. (PPN *alataki.*)

'ala.kai. vs. Potbellied, bloated.

ala.ka'ina. n. Leadership, guidance.

ala kā.pae. n. Detour.

'ala.kapaika. n. Allspice. (Neal 634–5.) *Eng.*

'ala.kē. vi. To jump, hurry from place to place.

Ala-kea. n. **1.** Name of a star, probably used in navigation. **2.** Name of a downtown Honolulu street. *Lit.,* white road.

'ala.kenika, arasenika. n. Arsenic. *Eng.*

ala.kō. **1.** vt. To drag, pull along. **2.** n. Bird-catching pole. Also *'auku'u.*

'ala.kuma. n. A large crab *(Carpilius maculatus),* with 11 dark red spots on its back, usually found concealed in rocks or under stones.

ala.ku'u.ku'u. n. Place for climbing a cliff, usually with ropes.

-alala. Var. spelling of *-alaala.*

ā.lā.lā. n. Sweet potatoes that bear from branch *(lālā)* vines.

'ala.lā. **1.** nvi. To bawl, bleat, squeal, cry, caw, yelp, wail, scream; such noises. *Hele ka makuahine, 'alalā keiki i kauhale,* when the mother goes, children bawl at home [a neglectful mother]. **hō.ala.lā.** Caus/sim. *He aha lā kāu i hō'alalā mai nei i kēlā keiki?* Why did you make that child cry? **2.** n. Hawaiian crow *(Corvus tropicus),* named for its caw; endangered. *He 'alalā, he manu leo nui,* a crow, a bird with much talk [a talkative person]. **3.** nvt. A style of chanting with open mouth, vibration and tremor of the voice, and prolonged vowels; to chant thus. **4.** vt. To gargle. *Rare.*

ala.lai. Redup. of *ālai. Ua alalai mai 'oia i ko'u hele 'ana,* he obstructed my going.

'ala.lāna. n. Bleating, wailing. See *'alalā 1.*

'ala.lau.ā, 'alalauwā. n. Young of the red *'āweoweo* fish. Appearance of schools of this fish near shore was an omen that royalty would die. Also *'alauwā.*

'ala.lehe. nvs. Sickly, weak, fretful, as a child; fretfulness. *He ukuhi 'ōhemo nā keiki, 'ōmino 'alalehe, ka 'alalehe, ka uwē wale,* weaning children are sickly, crying and fretful, weak, just crying.

'ala.lī. nvi. Sharp shrill yelp, sudden screech; to yelp, screech.

ala.loa. n. Highway, main road, belt road around an island, a long road.

'alama, arama. n. Protection, defense. (*Eng.* arms.)

ala maika. n. Bowling alley.

'ala.mea. **1.** vs. Ripe. **2.** vs. Precious, as a child. **3.** n. A bird (no data). **4.** See *iki 'alamea.*

'alā mea. n. Hard volcanic stone, used for adzes.

'ala.mihi. n. A common black crab *(Metopograpsus thukuhar).* Also *'elemihi, 'elepī. 'Alamihi 'ai kupapa'u,* corpse-eating black crab [a scavenger]. (PPN *kalamisi.*)

ala.mimo. vs. Quick, fast. *Nā kapua'i alamimo o nā kini maka lehua o nā 'ōpio,* nimble soles [dancing feet] of the many *lehua* blossoms of youth.

'ala.mo'o. n. An endemic fresh-water *'o'opu* fish *(Lentipes concolor). Hilo.* Also *hi'u 'ula* and *hi'u kole.*

ala muku. n. Cut off or unfinished road, dead-end road. *Fig.,* an incomplete rainbow, rainbow fragment.

alana. nvi. Awakening, rising. See *ala 2, 3. 'Ike 'ia ke alana o ka pua,* the upward flight of the arrow was seen. *Alana 'ia* (Kel. 29)! Rise up!

'alā.na. See *kīkē 'alāna.*

'ā.lana. **1.** nvt. Offering, especially a free-will offering, contrasting with a *mōhai* that was prescribed by a priest; to offer. *He 'ālana ka mea e hā'awi aku ai e kala 'ia mai ai ka hala o ka mea lawehala,* an *'āana* is the thing given so that the sin of a transgressor will be pardoned. *Ē ke kahuna 'i'o a me ka 'ālana 'i'o,* O true priest and true victim [of Christ]. *Mo'oka'ao . . . 'ālana ā ho'ola'a 'ia i mua o ka lāhui Hawai'i,* a story . . . offered and dedicated to the Hawaiian people. **2.** vs. Light, buoyant, easily floating. See *lana.*

'ā.lana aloha. n. Peace offering, offering of love.

'ā.lana kuni. n. Burnt offering, offering to procure death by sorcery.

'ala.neo. **1.** nvs. Clear, calm, serene, unclouded, free from impediment; clearness, calm, stillness; emptiness, nothing; desolate (Ier. 50.3). *'Alaneo ka 'ole ao, 'a'ole ao,* clear were the uplands, without clouds. *Ē Lono i ka pō la'ila'i, ku'ua mai ka 'alaneo* (Malo 183). O Lono of the clear night, let down clear skies. *Hāhā nā lima i kahi e loa'a ai, a ho'oku'i me ka 'alaneo* (Kel. 136), the hands grope at places to find things and collide with nothing at all. **2.** vs. Of a single color or texture, especially of a feather cloak without design and made of feathers of a single kind and color. **3.** N. Swelling disease, dropsy, generalized edema, kidney disease. **4.** n. Name of a class of 12 male supernatural beings called *papa pae māhū,* said to be hermaphrodite healers from Kahiki. One at least was according to legend turned to stone and has been moved to Kuhiō Park, Wai-kīkī, O'ahu. See *Pae-māhū* in Pukui, Elbert, and Mookini, 1974.

alani. n. **1.** Brown seaweeds *(Dictyota* spp.), regularly divided into narrow segments. They are so bitter that they will taint other seaweeds put with them and can be eaten but little and by some are considered poisonous. Medical *kahunas* used them in small quantities to treat asthma. This name is sometimes qualified by the terms *kai* and *'ula.* Also *maka* and false *līpoa.* Cf. *kūālani.* **2.** An O'ahu tree *(Pelea sandwicensis* or *P. oahuensis),* with oblong, fragrant leaves (like the *mokihana* of Kaua'i), which were used for scenting tapa. The bark was used for medicine. Also other species of *Pelea.* (PPN *alani.*) **3.** An upland moss.

'alani. n. Any kind of orange, both fruit and tree, as *Citrus sinensis.* (Neal 483.) *Eng. Melemele 'ili 'alani,* orange-yellow color.

ala.nia. vs. Smooth, even, not rough.

'alani 'awa.'awa. n. Calamondin *(Citris mitis),* a small tree with flattened-globose fruits to 2.6 cm in diameter, orange-colored, few-seeded, sour. (Neal 484.)

ala-niho. n. Long tattoo stripe. *Lit.,* tooth path.

'alani kua'.hiwi. n. All species of *Pelea.* Also *kūkaemoa.*

'alani wai. n. Tangerine, mandarin *(Citrus reticulata* cv. 'deliciosa'), a small tree with small leaves and small, loose-skinned, orange, flattened-globose, sweet fruits. (Neal 482.) *Lit.,* Chinese orange. On Ni'ihau, identified as *C. grandis;* cf. Neal 481.

alani wai. n. A low native shrub *(Pelea waialealae),* found only on high, wet parts of Kaua'i. Also *'anonia.*

ala.nui. n. Street, road, highway, thoroughfare, waterway, course. *Lit.,* large path. *Alanui hele,* any traversed road. *Alanui o ke ke'a,* station of the cross. Poetic names for the equator are *alanui a ke ku'uku'u,* road of the spider, and *alanui i ka piko o Wākea,* road at Wākea's navel. *Alanui polohiwa a Kanaloa,* the dark path of Kanaloa [southern limit of the sun in its yearly cycle, about the 15th and 16th days of the month Hilina Mā]. *Alanui polohiwa a Kāne,* the dark path of

Kāne [northern limit of the sun, about the middle of the month Kaulua]. *Alanui ma'awe 'ula a Kanaloa,* road of the scarlet footprint of Kanaloa [the western sky]. (PCP *alanui.*)

ala.nui ā.kea. n. Avenue, boulevard, wide street.

ala.nui hele 'ao.'ao, ala.nui hele wā.wae. n. Sidewalk.

ala.nui-o-nā-hō.kū-ho'o.kele. n. Pathway of the navigator stars; star course followed by navigators. Probably also *hōkū 'ai 'āina.*

ala.ō. 1. vt. To swallow whole, as a fish or shrimp. Also *ala'oma. Ke alaō mai nō i nā wahi 'o'opu a me nā wahi 'ōpae,* swallowing whole small *'o'opu* fish and shrimps. 2. n. Heiau or temple that had no *lele* altar.

ala 'oki. n. Road cut, short cut.

Ala-'oli. n. Name of a Kaua'i wind, said to bring good weather. (For. 5:97.) *Lit.,* happy path.

ala 'olo.lī. n. Narrow path, lane, alley.

ala.'oma. Var. of *alaō 1,* and *ala'ume.*

'ala-o-Puna. n. A variety of taro, growing wild, also cultivated dry in Puna, Hawai'i; fragrant when cooked, like *welowelo-lā.* Also *welowelo-lā.*

'ā.lapa. nvs. Athletic, active; athlete; an epithet for Ka-mehameha I; name of a company of Ka-lani-'opu'u's warriors. *Nā 'ālapa e mākaukau ana no ka moko-moko,* the athletes skilled in boxing.

'ala.pahi. nvt. Slander, falsehood, deceit; slanderer; to slander, defame, deceive, lie. *He 'alapahi moe ipo kā nāna,* so it is a lie of his about sleeping with the sweetheart.

'ala.paka. n 1. Alpaca. *Eng.* 2. Also *alabata,* Alabaster, ointment vase of alabaster. (Luka 7:37.) *Eng.*

'ala.pakelo, alabatero. Same as *'alapaka 2.* (Probably Gr. *alabastros.*)

ala.pao. n. Tunnel.

'ala.papa. n. Alfalfa. *Eng.*

'ā.lapa pi'i mo'o Kū. n. Athletic person aspiring to the lineage of Kū (said of Ka-mehameha).

'Ala.pia. 1. nvs. Arabia, Arabian. *Eng.* 2. *(Not cap.)* n. A heavy cloth resembling serge.

ala.pi'i. n. Stairs, steps, ladder, stile, doorstep, ascent, scale (musical). See ex., *'o'opu 1.*

Ala-pi'i-a-ka-'ōpae. n. *Lua* fighting stroke. *Lit.,* stairway of the shrimp.

ala.pi'i kū. n. Steep road or path.

ala.pi'i lawe 'ōhua. n. Escalator, moving stairs.

ala.pi'i mele. n. Musical scale.

ala.piko. n. Belly of a fish, considered choice.

ala.pine. vs. 1. Quick, fast. *He 'uleu nā po'e o ke kai, alapine nā lima i ke kaula,* the boys of the sea are spry, quick hands on the lines. 2. Frequent, often. Cf. *ala-, pinepine.*

ala.pine.pine. Redup. of *alapine 1, 2.*

ala pō. n. Night awakening. **ho'āla pō.** A summons sent at night. (GP 10.)

ala pō.'ai. n. Orbit of the stars, circular road.

ala.poho. vt. To gulp, swallow whole.

ala.poki. vs. Shipwrecked. *Rare.* Same as *'ōlulo.*

'alā po'o malu. n. Name of a dark basalt. Also *kai 'anu'u.*

ala.puka. nvs. Body sores; to have such sores; affected with dry rot, as taro. *Rare.*

'ala.pu'u. n. Small, young, of creatures. *'Alapu'u mo'o,* scalawag of a baby grandchild. *'Alapu'u he'e,* baby squid.

alau. vs. Dividing, branching, as of winds and lineages. *He makani alau kō kēia wahi,* the wind here in this spot divides.

'alaua. Var. spelling of *'alawa,* to glance.

'alau.ā, 'alauwā. Same as *'alalauā,* young *'āweoweo* fish. *Pupū ke kai i ka 'alauā,* the sea is congested with *'alauā* fish [of difficulties; omen of death of royalty].

'alaua.hio. n. Endemic Hawaiian honey creepers *(Lox-ops maculata),* O'ahu creeper *(L. m. maculata),* endangered; Lā-na'i creeper *(L. m. montana),* presumed

extinct; Maui creeper *(L. m. newtoni);* Hawai'i creeper *(L. m. mana),* endangered.

'ala.'uka. nvs. Homely, vile, slovenly, worthless; homeliness, vileness, dregs of society. *He hana 'ino'ino, pu-puka, 'ala'uka,* it is wicked, nasty, vile conduct.

alaula. n. Light of early dawn, sunset glow. *Lit.,* flaming road. *Ke alaula a Kāne,* the flaming path of Kāne [the eastern sky]. *Ka wehe 'ana o ke alaula, 'oia ka paoa,* the opening of the flaming pathway is the dawn.

'ala.'ula. n. Red dust in a road, red dust.

'ala.'ula. Same as *'a'ala'ula,* a seaweed *(Codium* spp.).

ā.lau.lau. nvt. Clothes, tapa, mats; to envelop, clothe. *Rare.* Cf. *laulau,* wrapper.

ala 'ū.lili. n. Sheer trail as for climbing a cliff. Also *hūlili.*

ala.'ume. vt. To draw, pull, attract, as a magnet. *Malalo ka huila e niniu ai, ala'ume nā 'ili i ka nui hao* (hula song), the wheels revolve below, the fan belts pull the immensity of the metal.

'alau.wā. Var. spelling of *'alauā.*

'alau.wahio. Var. spelling of *'alauahio,* a bird.

'alau.wī. Same as *'alauahio.*

'alawa. 1. nvt. To glance, look quickly; glance. *'Alawa maka* (Kam. 64:98), to see at a glance; to diagnose by insight. *He 'alawa nā maka i hope e 'ike i ka po'e e hele mai ana,* the eyes glance back to see the people coming along. **hō.'alawa.** Caus/sim. 2. n. A bird (no data).

ala wa'a. n. Canoe course.

ala waele. n. Road, highway. *Lit.,* cleared road.

ala.wai. n. Channel, canal.

ala.wela. n. Dark lines on stomach of a pregnant woman, converging near the navel. *Lit.,* burned path.

ala.weo. Same as *'āheahea 2,* a shrub.

ala.weo huna. Same as *'āheahea 2,* a shrub, Ni'ihau.

ala.wī. 1. vi. To shriek; shrill. Cf. *wī,* to squeal. *Alawī ka niho no ka pa'akikī i ka hele,* [he'll] shriek through the teeth for being so insistent on going. 2. n. Upland bird, reported to be the young of the *'anianiau,* and on Kaua'i, the *'amakihi.*

ala.wiki. vi. To hurry; quick, fast. Cf. *wiki. Mai lohi mai 'oe, e alawiki mai,* don't be slow, be fast.

ale. 1. vt. To swallow, engulf, gulp, absorb. *Huaale,* pill. 2. n. Hollow or cavern on the sea floor. (PCP *ale.*) 3. n. An endemic mountain plant *(Plantago princeps),* 60 cm to 2 m high, rarely branching, stem woody, with long narrow leaves at top; related to the *laukahi.*

'ale. 1. nvt. Wave, crest of a wave, billow; to ripple, form waves, stir; to well, as tears in the eyes; rippling, stirring. See *poale.* Many types of billows are listed below. *'Ale lau loa,* wave long and large. *'Ale po'i,* breaking wave. *'Ale pā pua'a,* pig-pen wave, of a wave striking the side of a canoe. *Ka 'ale wai hau a ke kua,* the snow water wave of the gods [it was believed that the gods made snow]. **hō.'ale.** Caus/sim.; to surge (PH 51). (PCP *kale.*) 2. n. Gust. *Rare.* 3. Also **are.** n. Are, a unit of measure. *Eng.*

'alē. nvs. Marshy; marsh, swamp.

alea. 1. Pas/imp. of *ale 1.* 2. n. A fish, said to be short for *hīnalea* or a kind of *hīnalea.* Also *ālealea.*

'alea, area. n. Area. *Eng.*

'ale'a. vs. Sweet-voiced.

'ale 'aki. n. A swamping wave, as one striking a canoe broadside from prow to stern. See *'aki 5.*

ale.ale. vs. Wounded, pierced; wound, sore. Less common than *pōaleale.*

'ale.'ale. Redup. of *'ale 1;* stirring, moving, undulating, tossing, rippling, full to the brim. *Ā ka wai, ua piha ā 'ale'ale ke ka'eka'e,* the water is full, the edge is brimful. **hō.'ale.'ale.** To stir up waves, agitate, confuse; to cause tumult. (PCP *kalekale.*)

ā.lea.lea. n. 1. A shellfish *(Turbo sandwicensis);* its shell. 2. Same as *alea 2.*

'alehe. n. Snare, noose; to snare. Also *'ahele.*

alehu. Same as *pūlehu,* to broil.

ā.lehu. n. Ashes. (For. 6:482.)

'ale.'ihi. Var. of *'ala'ihi,* a fish.

'aleka, areza. n. Large tree of the pine family, cedar, fir. *Biblical.* (Hebrew *'erez.*)
'ale.kanika, aresanika. n. Arsenic. *Eng.*
'ale.kea, aredea. n. Heron. (Oihk. 11.19.) (Latin Ardeidae, a family.)
'aleko, aleto. nvs. Alto. *Eng.*
'ale.kohola. n. Alcohol. *Eng.*
'ale kua.kea. n. Whitecaps, white spray.
'ale kua loloa. n. Long-backed billow.
'ale.kuma, aleguma. n. Algum tree. *Biblical. Eng.*
'ale kū.pī.pī. n. Dashing billow.
'ā.lela. See *uhi 'ālela,* a yam.
'alele. Var. of *'elele,* messenger. (PCP *kalele.*)
'ale.lele. vi. To skip, jump, fly.
alelo. n. 1. Tongue, language. Also *elelo.* Cf. *pelu.* (PPN *'alelo.*) 2. Meat of the sea egg or sea urchin *(wana),* so called because of resemblance to a tongue. 3. Concave curve of the lower portion of the *lei palaoa,* whaletooth pendant, suggestive of a tongue. 4. Point at the tip of a paddle.
alelo.ahi. n. A kind of introduced flower (no data).
alelo pala. n. Coated tongue.
alelo pelu. vs. Tongue-tied, paralyzed tongue.
alelo pu'u. n. Paralysis of the tongue, believed sometimes caused by a *kahuna.* Also *alelo pehu, alelo pelu, lelo pu'u.*
Ale.mamaka. n. Alma Mater. *Eng.*
'ale.manaka. n. Almanac, calendar. *Eng.*
'Ale.menia, Aremenia. nvs. Armenia; Armenian. *Eng.*
'ale.mone, alemona. nvs. Almond *(Prunus dulcis)* (Neal 396), hazel tree [KJV], almond [RSV] (Kin. 30.37.) *Eng.*
'ale.muka, alemuga. Same as *'alekuma.*
alena. n. A lowland perennial weed *(Boerhaavia repens),* with long, thin, prostrate branches, bearing small leaves and flowers. The swollen roots were used medicinally, acting as a diuretic. (Neal 336–7.) *Anena* on Ni'ihau.
ale.nale. Same as *kōnane,* clear.
'ale'o. nvs. Tower, high lookout, gazebo; towering. *'Ale'o puhi 'ohe,* bandstand. *Nā pali 'ale'o,* towering cliffs.
'ale olo.walu. n. Billows that follow one after the other.
'alepa. n. Alpha. *Eng.*
'ale.papeka, alepabeta. n. Alphabet. *Eng.*
'ā.leu.leu. nvs. Old, worn-out, as tapa, mats, clothing; worn-out tapa, clothing; objects of inferior quality. Also *pāleuleu. He moku 'āleuleu,* districts of ragamuffins [said of Ka'ū and Puna by Kamehameha's followers because the farmers worked hard and wore old clothes].
'ā.lewa. Same as *'ālewalewa.*
'ā.lewa.lewa. vs. Buoyant, floating.
ali. Same as *aliali.* (PPN *'ali.*)
-ali. (Perhaps a var. of *ani.*) ho'āli. (a) To signal, wave; to stir, as coffee or a fire; signal, stirring; wavy, undulating. (PPN *angi.*) (b) To make an offering to the gods with signals and signs or prayers with gestures. Cf. *mōhai ho'āli.*
'ali. 1. n. Scar, depression, groove, imbedded mark. Also *'eli.* Cf. *'a'ali, 'ālina.* 2. Var. of *'eli,* to dig. (PPN *kali.*)
alia. idiom. To wait, stop; before; usually as a command: stop! wait a minute! *Alia kāu puke,* away with your book. *Alia wau e 'ae aku* (Laie 485), before I agree. ho'ā.lia. To stop, check, restrain, wait.
ā.lia. 1. nvs. Salt bed, salt-encrusted area; salty, brackish. *He ālia ho'oha'aha'a pa'akai; lo'i 'ale nō i ke ālia o loko,* it is a low salt bed; water comes in to flood the salt bed inside. (PCP *aalia.*) 2. n. Name of two *kauila* or *māmane* sticks carried by priests before the *makahiki* god; also the two crossed spears with upright spear in the center, used as insignia for the present-day Māmakakaua society; small flag or streamer. See *'Ahahui Māmakakaua.*
ali.ali. nvs. Crystal clear, white; clarity, whiteness. Also *aniani.* hoāli.ali. To whiten, cause to shine. (PNP *'ali'ali.*)

-ali.ali. hoāli.āli. Redup. of *ho'āli.*
'ali.'ali. Redup. of *'ali 1;* scarred, grooved; profound. Cf. *'eli'eli. E 'ali'ali kapu, e 'ali'ali noa* (Kep. 184), profound the taboo, profound the release to freedom. hō.'ali.'ali. To scar, deface.
ā.lia.lia. Same as *ālia. He ālialia pa'akai, he ālialia manu, nā ālialia o nā waipuna hu'ihu'i,* it is a salt bed, a salt bed for birds, salt-encrusted places with cool springs.
ali.ana. Same as *'oliana,* let me see.
'alihi. 1. n. Cords or fine ropes threaded through marginal meshes of upper and lower edges of nets, to which were attached floats and sinkers; loops at the top of a *kōkō* net holding a calabash. See below and *'upena 'alihi.* (PCP *kalifi.*) 2. n. Horizon (sometimes qualified by *lani* or *moana*). Cf. *lihi,* edge. 3. Deceit, trickery; to deceive, cheat. (AP.)
'alihi.kaua. n. General, commander in battle, strategist.
'alihi.kaua nui. n. Commander in chief.
'alihi kē.pau. n. Lower cord in a net to which lead sinkers were attached.
'alihi.lele. n. Dragnet, mullet net.
'alihi pā.'ū. n. Line for lashing down the *pā'ū* mat covering of a canoe.
'alihi pī.koi. n. Upper cord in a net to which floats were attached.
'alihi pō.haku. n. Lower cord in a net to which stone sinkers were attached.
ali'i. nvs. Chief, chiefess, officer, ruler, monarch, peer, headman, noble, aristocrat, king, queen, commander; royal, regal, aristocratic, kingly; to rule or act as a chief, govern, reign; to become a chief. *Fig.,* kind (see *na'au ali'i, 'ōpū ali'i*). *Ali'i nui,* high chief. *Kāna ali'i,* his chief (controlled directly or raised by him). *Kona ali'i,* his hereditary chief; his chieftainship. *Ali'i kū'oko'a,* independent chief, autocrat. *Ua lilo ia i ali'i no Kaua'i ia wā, ā malalo mai ona nā kānaka o Kaua'i, pēlā i ali'i ai 'o Makali'i* (FS 233), he then became chief of Kaua'i, with the people of Kaua'i beneath him, thus Makali'i became chief. ho'ā.li'i. To make a chief, establish royalty in office; to imitate royalty; to treat as royalty; regal, royal, kingly; to be made an officer, be commissioned. *Ua ho'āli'i aku 'oia i kāna kāne,* she treats her husband like a king. (PPN *'ariki.*)
ali'i 'ai moku. n. Chief who rules a *moku* (district).
ali'i ā.nela. n. Archangel.
ali'i ho'o.malu. n. Presiding officer, ruling officer; chairman, viceroy.
ali'i kāne. n. Male chief, king; husband (polite, not said of one's own husband or to him). *Pehea kāu ali'i kāne?* How is your noble husband?
ali'i koa. n. Military officer, officer of army or navy.
ali'i koa i komikina 'ia, n. Commissioned officer.
ali'i koa uku. n. Warrant officer.
ali'i kū.'oko'a. n. Independent chief, aristocrat.
ali'i maoli. n. True chief, commissioned officer (old term).
ali'i ku'i. n. Power behind the throne. *Lit.,* supplementary king.
Ali'i-o-Kona-i-ka-lewa. Same as *Ke-ali'i-o-Kona-i-ka-lewa.*
ali'i pala.pala ho'o.kohu 'ole. n. Non-commissioned officer, petty officer (old term).
ali'i papa. n. Offspring of a high chiefess and commoner (or lesser chief) father. Cf. *papa ali'i.*
ali'i.poe. n. The ornamental cannas *(Canna indica,* forms and hybrids), large tropical American herbs, with large oval or narrow leaves and large red or red and yellow flowers. The round black seeds are worn in leis and are also placed in fruit shells of the *la'amia* for hula rattles. Cannas are both cultivated and wild in Hawai'i. Also *li'ipoe.* (Neal 263–4.)
ali'i po'e kau.ā. n. Lesser chiefs who served other chiefs. Cf. *kauā.*
ali'i pū.'ō lani. n. An exalted chief (probably from *pū'ō'ā,* tower). (For. 6:303.)
ali'i wa'a.pā. n. Boatswain.

ali'i wahine. n. Chiefess, queen; wife (polite, not said of one's own wife or to her).

'Ā.lika, Arika. nvs. Arctic. *Eng. Aia i 'Ālika ka ihu o ka moku* (song), the prow of the ship turns to the Arctic.

'ā.lika.lika. vs. Clammy, sticky, tenacious, tough. *Fig.,* stingy. Cf. *lina, linalina, nina, ninanina, 'ūlika, 'ūlika-lika.*

'ā.like. vs. Alike (often repeated: *'ālike 'ālike, like 'ālike,* alike, just alike, identical, equally, midway. *E hiamoe ana ke keiki ā hiki 'ālike 'ālike o ka pō,* the child slept until the middle of the night).

'ali.kekoa, aligetoa. n. Alligator. *Eng.*

'ā.liki.liki. vt. To tighten, tie tightly. ho.'**ā.liki.liki.** Caus/sim. Cf. *liki 2.*

'alī.lea. n. The common turbo shell *(Turbo sandwicensis).*

'alili. Same as *ho'olili,* sparkling.

'alima. num. Five (especially in counting in a series); five times. *Pō'alima,* Friday.

'ali.makika, arimatika. n. Arithmetic. *Eng.*

'ā.lina. nvs. Scar, blemish; scarred, disfigured, injured, maimed (FS 93) (preceded by *ke*). *Fig.,* low, disgraced, degraded, dishonored. *Kau ke 'ālina* (FS 93), blemished. *Ua 'ālina ka inoa,* the name is dishonored.

'ā.lina.lina. n. Limpet *(Cellana sandwicensis).*

alo. n. Front, face, presence; upper surface, as of a bowl; leeward. Cf. *'aialo, aloali'i, pali. (Alo* refers to a wife: cf. *pilialo.) Ka mo'opuna i ke alo,* the favorite grandchild, a grandchild reared by grandparents. *He alo ā he alo,* face to face. *Eia 'oe i ke alo o ka 'aha,* here you are in the presence of the assembly. *Ua laupa'i ko'u alo i nā mo'opuna,* I have many grandchildren with me here. **ho'o.alo, ho'alo.** Caus/sim. *I ka ho'alo 'ana,* presentation, as to a monarch. (PPN *'aro.*)

'alo. 1. vt. To dodge, evade, elude, avoid. *'Alo 'ana,* dodging, avoidance, oversight, omission. *'A'ole e hiki ke alo a'e,* it can't be helped. **hō.'alo.** To shun, dodge, avoid, escape, omit, skip; omission; to alternate or place irregularly, as strips of thatch (For. 5:651). (PPN *kalo.)* **2.** vt. To be with, come near, go with, attend, escort, accompany, share an experience, endure, resist. *Ku'u hoa 'alo i ke anu,* my companion who shared the cold. *Kū ana 'o Mauna Loa, kuahiwi 'alo ehuehu* (song), stands Mauna Loa, mountain that resists storms. *E 'alo a'e 'oe iā mākou ā hiki aku i Moloka'i* (FS 267), escort us to Moloka'i.

'ā.loa. 1. Same as *maka'āloa,* a crab. **2.** n. Name recorded for *olonā* fiber. **3.** vt. To lengthen, enlarge.

alo.ali'i. nvi. In the presence of chiefs; royal court.

alo.alo. 1. n. All kinds of hibiscus, including the native white hibiscus *(Hibiscus arnottianus);* often called *pua aloalo, pualoalo.* A law was passed in 1923 making the *aloalo* the flower of the Territory of Hawai'i. Qualifying terms: *hua moa* (egg) or *pele* (bell) *(Abutilon pictum,* Neal 550), *ko'ako'a (Hibiscus schizopetalus* or coral hibiscus, Neal 558; see also *kulapepeiao); lahilahi* (all single-flowered forms), *pahūpahū (Malvaviscus arboreus* var. *penduliflorus; lit.,* firecracker, Neal 554), *ponimō'ī (Hibiscus,* an introduced variety with red double flowers 8 cm. wide or less, *lit.,* coronation, carnation, Neal 556), *pupupu (Hibiscus,* all double-flowered forms), *waikāhuli (Hibiscus mutabilis,* Neal 558-9, during the day flowers changed from white to pink or red). Formerly the blossoms were used as laxatives. **2.** n. Squilla *(Pseudosquilla ciliata, Lysiosquilla maculata),* highly desired as food. Also *Squilla* sp. **3.** Loved and served by many persons, as a chief or favorite child; esteemed. Cf. *alo. Haku o Hawai'i he inoa, hānau aloalo a'u a Ke'elikōlani* (chant for Prince of Hawai'i), his title is Prince of Hawai'i, child of Ke-'elikōlani, mine, born with many to serve and love [him]. **4.** n. Tapa made from *māmaki* mixed with *wauke.* (Kam. 76:115.) (Perhaps PNP *aloalo.)*

'alo.'alo. 1. Redup. of *'alo 1;* to dodge rapidly or continuously; to look about slyly; evasive. **hō.'alo.'alo.** Caus/sim. *'Ōlelo hō'alo'alo.* Excuse, pretext. (PPN *kalokalo.)* **2.** Redup. of *'alo 2;* one who follows, escorts, accompanies. *He 'alo'alo ua au no ke Ko'olau* (chant), I am one who follows rainfall in the Ko'olau [mountains]. **3.** vs. Lumpy, as poi. *Rare.* **4.** n. A kind of small inshore fish (no data).

'ā.loa.loa. vs. Far, at a distance. **ho.'ā.loa. loa.** To keep at a distance.

'ā.lo'a.lo'a. 1. Same as *hālo'alo'a,* turbulent, rough. **2.** vs. Pitted, as rocks. Also *lo'alo'a.*

alodio. Var. spelling of *'alolio.*

'aloe. n. Aloe, any plant of the genus *Aloe;* also the *pānini 'awa'awa. Eng.*

aloha. nvt, nvs. Aloha, love, affection, compassion, mercy, sympathy, pity, kindness, sentiment, grace, charity; greeting, salutation, regards; sweetheart, lover, loved one; beloved, loving, kind, compassionate, charitable, lovable; to love, be fond of; to show kindness, mercy, pity, charity, affection; to venerate; to remember with affection; to greet, hail. Greetings! Hello! Good-by! Farewell! Alas! The common greetings follow: *Aloha 'oe,* may you be loved or greeted, greetings (to one person). *Aloha kāua,* may there be friendship or love between us, greetings (to one person); dear Sir. *Aloha kākou,* same as above, but to more than one person. *Ke aloha nō! Aloha!* Greetings! (The *nō* may be prolonged for emphasis.) (Gram. 4.6.) The following greetings were introduced after European times; *Aloha ahiahi,* good evening. *Aloha kakahiaka,* good morning. Cf. *aloha 'āina, hana aloha. Aloha ali'i,* royalist, royal love. *Aloha 'ino!* What a pity! Alas! [Expression of regret, either great or small.] *Aloha akua,* love of god; divine love, pity, charity. *Mea aloha,* loved one, beloved. *Aloha makua,* considerate and thoughtful of parents and elders, filial. *Aloha 'ia,* beloved, pitied. *Aloha pumehana,* warm aloha, affection. *Me ke aloha o Ka-wena,* with the love (or greeting) of Ka-wena. *'O wau iho nō me ke aloha,* I remain, with very best regards. *Aloha 'oe, ē Maria, ua piha 'oe i ka maika'i,* hail, Mary, full of grace. *Ē Maria hemolele, e aloha mai 'oe iā mākou,* Holy Mary, have mercy on us. *Aloha a'e ana mākou i ke ehu wāwae o ka lani* (chant for Ka-lā-kaua), we remember fondly the footprints of the king. *E aloha aku au i ka mea a'u e mana'o ai e aloha aku* (Puk. 33.19), I show mercy to those I want to show mercy to. *Aloha nō ia mau lā o nā makahiki he kanalima i kūnewa akula!* Affectionate [memories] of these days of fifty years past! **hō.aloha.** Rare var. of *ho'ālohaloha.* Cf. *hoaloha.* (PPN *alofa.)*

aloha hoa.hā.nau. n. Brotherhood.

aloha 'āina. nv. Love of the land or of one's country, patriotism; the name of a Hawaiian-language newspaper published 1893-1920; *aloha 'āina* is a very old concept, to judge from the many sayings (perhaps thousands) illustrating deep love of the land. (Pukui, Elbert, and Mookini 268-9.) Cf. the song *Kaulana nā Pua* (Elbert and Mahoe 62-4).

aloha'i. vi. Bible spelling of *aloha ai.* (Mele 5.6.)

aloha kaka.hiaka. See *aloha.*

ā.loha.loha. Redup. of *aloha* (less used than *hō-'ālohaloha).* **ho.'ā.loha.loha.** To make love, express affection, gratitude or compassion; expression of love or affection (FS 93); to give thanks (I Kor. 11.24); friendly, loving, lovable. *Lā Ho'ālohaloha,* Thanksgiving Day. *Palapala ho'ālohaloha,* written condolence.

aloha.lua. n. Name given to the *kāmole* plant used in *hana aloha* sorcery. *Lit.,* mutual love.

aloha 'oe. See *aloha.*

aloha 'ole. vs. Pitiless, merciless, ungrateful, without love or affection.

'alohi. nvi. To shine, glitter, sparkle; bright, brilliant; splendor, brilliancy. *'Alohi e like me ka lā i ke awakea,* bright as the sun at noon. *Ke 'alohi kea o ke ano kakahiaka,* the white light of morning, (PCP *kalo(f,s)i.)*

'alo.hia. Pas/imp. of *'alo.*

alo.hiki. n. Families united by marriage, in-laws.

'alohi lani. n. Brightness of heaven, a term applied to the heavenly courts of the goddesses Uli and Kapo.

'ā.lohi.lohi. Redup. of *'alohi;* radiant. *Maka 'ālohilohi,* eyes bright and sparkling, blue or light brown eyes. *Ka haole nui maka 'ālohilohi, ē Kama lepo pua'a* (FS 201), big stranger with bright eyes, O Kama with excreta of a pig [said to the pig-god, Kama-pua'a].

ā.lo'i. n. Mud puddle, pool. Cf. *lo'i.*

'ā.lo'i. Same as *'ālo'ilo'i.*

'ā.lo'i.lo'i. 1. n. A damselfish *(Dascyllus albisella).* Also *lo'ilo'i.* The young stage is *'ā* or *'a'ā. He 'ālo'ilo'i ka i'a waha iki o ke kai,* a damsel, small-mouthed fish of the sea [one with little to say]. 2. vs. Humble. *Kū 'ālo'ilo'i i ka hale o ke akua* (prayer to Pele), standing humbly in the house of the god. 3. Same as *lo'ilo'i 1.*

alo.kahi. n. Single weft in plaiting; mat of a single thickness, with only one shiny side. Cf. *alolua. Lit.,* single side.

alo.kele. 1. vs. Attractive, of fine appearance. *Alokele ke 'ike aku i ke alo o ia kuahiwi* (hula song), a pleasure to see the face of that mountain. 2. n. A red bird reported by Kepelino (no data).

'alo.kio, alodio, 'alo.lio, arosio. nvs. Alodial title, alodium, fee simple. *Eng. Kuleana malalo o ke 'ano 'alokio,* freehold less than alodial. *'Alolio i ke 'ano 'ae like,* conditioned alodial. *Ho'olimalima ma ke 'ano alolio,* conditional lease.

alo.lio. See *limu alolio.*

ā.lolo. Same as *'aikola.*

alo.lua. 1. vs. Two-sided, two-faced; facing one another, as cliffs on opposite sides of a valley. 2. n. Double weft in plaiting; plaiting with a reversible side, with two thicknesses. Cf. *alokahi.*

'aloma, aroma. n. Aroma. *Eng.*

'alopa.lopā. vs. Shiftless, dependent on others for a livelihood. Cf. *lōpā.*

'alo.peke, alopeka. n. Fox. (Luka 13.32.) (Gr. *alopeks.*)

alo.pihe. n. Persons shouting, as in mourning. *Ua hiki aku i ke alopihe,* went to the lamenting people.

alo.piko. n. Belly of a fish, choice to Hawaiians.

alu. vs. Combined, acting together; to cooperate, act together. *Alu like mai!* Work in unity! Work together! *E alu, e alu, e kui lima!* Cooperate! Cooperate! Join hands! *E alu ka pule iā Hakalau,* combine prayers to overcome Hakalau. *He mau 'īlio alu i ka hākākā,* dogs that combine in fighting. (PPN *'alu.*)

'alu. vi. Depression, gutter, ravine; lines of the hand, loose skin over the eyeball; tuck in a garment, shirring, ruffling; descent, as of trail or road; of low rank (Kep. 125); to bend, duck, hang, sag, slacken, stoop; to relax; to ruff, as a mat. Cf. *pū'alu. Ho'ailona 'alu,* tuck creaser, of a sewing machine. *Ho'onoho 'alu,* to make tucks, shirring; tucker on a sewing machine. *Mea hana 'alu,* tucker. *Wela ka hao, 'alu ka uwea,* the iron is hot, bend the wire [now is the time for fun, a saying originating at the Honolulu Iron Works]. *Ua 'alu ihola ka paniolo e lālau i ka pū'olo,* the cowboy leaned down to pick up the package. **hō.'alu.** To slacken, loosen, hang down, bend down, stoop; depression, slack. *Kī hō'alu,* slack key. (PPN *kalu.*)

'alua. num. Two, twice. *Pō'alua,* Tuesday; *lit.,* second day. *'Alua a'u hele 'ana i kēlā wahi,* I've been to that place twice.

'ā.lu'a. vs. Old, worn-out, faded, dilapidated; old and wrinkled, as a person.

alu.alu. vi. To follow, pursue, chase; to run, as for political office. *Alualu loloa,* to run after persistently. **ho'ālu.alu.** Caus/sim. (PPN *'alu'alu.*)

'alu.'alu. nvs. Loose, flabby; misshapen, as a premature baby; slack, as a rope; to sag; wrinkled, uneven, rough, lined; foetus; skin, rind, peel. *Hua 'alu'alu,* egg with very soft shell. *Keiki 'alu'alu,* premature baby. *Pala 'alu'alu ka 'ai a kamali'i,* mostly peel when matured are the food crops of children [infants are not strong enough to make good farmers]. **hō.'alu.'alu.** To slacken, loosen; to make gathers, as in a skirt; a gatherer, as on sewing machines; yielding, loose, flexible, soft. (PPN *kalukalu.*)

'ā.lua.lua. 1. vs. Rough, bumpy, as a road; full of knotholes, as a board; pitted with holes, as a reef. Cf. *lua,* hole. *He 'ālualua 'ino'ino ke alanui,* the road is badly pitted. 2. n. Multiplication tables. *Hua 'ālualua,* code writing (with numbers).

'alu.he'e. vs. Loose, as a bundle not securely tied; flabby, ill-fitting, loose-jointed.

'ā.luka. nvs. Crowd, heap; mixed, crowded, heaped. *'Āluka moku,* group of irregular-lying islands. *'Āluka ka pala a ka 'ōhi'a,* mountain apples ripen everywhere. *Kaua 'āluka* (For. 5:151), widespread war. **hoā.luka.** Caus/sim.; to bring together, collect.

'ā.luku. vt. To destroy; destructive.

ā.lula. n. An endemic member of the lobelia family *(Brighamia* spp.), presently known only on Moloka'i and Kaua'i, believed extinct on Maui and Ni'ihau, an unbranched, succulent, thick-stemmed perennial about 1.5 m high, topped with a rosette of large oval leaves and racemes of long, white, fragrant flowers. (Neal 815–7.) Also *hāhā.* See *pua 'ala, 'ōlulu.*

'ā.luli. vi. To incline the head, sway.

alu like. See *alu.*

ā.lulu. vi. Quickly, hastily (used after *hele, hana, holo, holoholo, hopuhopu*). *Holo hopuhopu ālulu mākou,* we grabbed and fled in great haste.

'ā.luna. n. Descent, loosening, slackening, stooping. See *'alu 1.*

'ā.luna ahi.ahi. n. Late afternoon or early evening.

'ā.luna awa.kea. n. Early afternoon (For. 6:379.)

'ā.lunu. nvs. Greedy, covetous, rapacious; greed, greedy person. Also *'ānunu.*

ama. n. Outrigger float; port hull of a double canoe, so called because it replaces the float. Also *iama.* (PPN *hama.*)

'ama. 1. nvs. Talkative, prattling, tattling. Cf. *'a'ama. He waha 'ama iā ha'i,* a mouth prattling about others. (PCP *kama.*) 2. vs. Light, bright. (Kep. 25.) Cf. *mā'ama'ama.* (PCP *kama.*), 3. n. Young *'ama'ama* fish, usually called *pua 'ama.*

-'ama. hō.'ama. To begin to ripen. *Fig.,* adolescents beginning to mature. Usually called *hā'ama.*

'ama.'ama. 1. n. Mullet *(Mugil cephalus),* a very choice indigenous fish. Stages are (finger length) *pua 'ama, pua 'ama'ama, pua po'olā, 'o'olā;* (hand length) *kahaha* (or *pahaha*); (20 cm) *'ama'ama;* (30 cm or more) *'anae. Fig.,* an easy mark (modern slang). See *'ōpele 2. Mai pi'ikoi i ka 'ama'ama!* Don't strive for the *'ama'ama* fish! [be satisfied with what you have, why look for a rich person?] (PCP *kamakama.*) 2. Redup. of *'ama 1, 2.*

'ā.ma'a.mau. vi. In rapid succession. Cf. *ma'amau. 'Āma'amau ka holo o nā ka'a,* the cars followed one behind the other very quickly.

'ā.make. vt. To cause death, defeat.

'ama.kihi. n. A group of small endemic Hawaiian honey creepers, *Loxops virens;* abundant on Hawai'i *(L. v. v.),* Maui *(L. v. wilsoni),* and Kaua'i, uncommon on O'ahu *(L. v. chloris)* and Moloka'i, rare on Lā-na'i. The feathers are yellow and greenish, and were formerly used in feather capes. The Kaua'i form was also called *alawī kihi. 'Amakihi 'awa'awa,* sour *'amakihi* [person with a sour disposition].

'ā.mala, amara. n. Armorer, blacksmith. *Eng.*

'ā.mama. vt. Finished, of a pre-Christian prayer (said almost at the end of a prayer); to finish a prayer, to pray and sacrifice. *'Āmama, ua noa,* the prayer is said, the taboo is over. *Ua 'āmama aku 'o 'Umi i ke kino o Hākau i mua o Kā'ili, kona akua,* 'Umi offered the body of Hākau in sacrifice to Kā'ili, his god.

'ā.mana. n. Y-shaped crosspiece at the end of a pole (as of a *lā'au kia*); horizontal line on an upright; branches of a tree in the form of a Y; gallows; T-shaped; shaft of an octopus lure (Kam. 76:68). Cf. *ke'a, ko'oko'o 'āmana, noho 'āmana, pe'a,* and *mana,* branch.

-āmana. ho'ā.mana. To give authority, authorization; to empower, authorize, commission. *Na wai 'oe i ho'ā-mana mai?* Who gave you permission?

'ama'u. n **1.** All species of an endemic genus of ferns *(Sadleria)*, with trunk more or less evident. The fronds are narrower, smaller, and less divided than those of the *hāpu'u*. At least one species has at the top of the trunk a mass of soft scales *(pulu)* used as pillow stuffing. Formerly, in times of famine, the tasteless pith of the trunk was cooked and eaten. The fronds were used to mulch dry-land taro, the stems for plaiting and as sizing for tapa. The *'ama'u* was one of the forms that Kama-pua'a, the pig god, could take at will. Also *ma'uma'u, ma'u.* See *ma'uma'u.* (Neal 22-3.) **2.** Place where *ama'u* ferns are found.

'ā.maui. n. O'ahu thrush *(Phaeornis obscurus oahuensis)*, dusky, olive-brown above, ashy-gray beneath, endemic, presumed extinct, with subspecies on Hawai'i *(ōma'o)*, Lā-na'i *(oloma'o)*, Moloka'i *(oloma'o)*, and Kaua'i.

amau.mau. Similar to *maumau 1. Ke amaumau a'ela i nā kīkīao,* (chant) gusts blow steadily.

'ama'u.ma'u. n. Young *'ama'u* ferns; many *'ama'u* ferns, ferny, abounding in *'ama'u* ferns; a covering of *'ama'u* ferns (preceded by *ke*). (FS 215.)

ā me. conj. And (sometimes written *ame*). (Gram. 11.1.)

'ameki, ameti. n. Amethyst. *Eng.*

'ame.ku.keke, ametusete, ametuseto. n. Amethyst. (Puk. 28.19.) (Probably Gr. *amethystos*.)

'Ame.lika, America. nvs. America; American. *Eng.*

'Ame.lika 'Ā.kau. nvs. North America, North American.

'Ame.lika Hema. nvs. South America, South American.

'Ame.lika Hui.pū. nvs. United States of America, American.

'Ame.lika Waena. nvs. Central America, Central American.

'amene. interj. and vi. Amen; to say amen. *Eng.*

'ame.pela, amebera. n. Amber. *Eng.*

'ami. 1. nvi. Hinge, joint; to turn on hinges. *Ihu 'ami,* nose with irregularly shaped bridge. **2.** nvi. A hula step with hip revolutions; to do this step. Three types are *'ami kāhela, 'ami kūkū,* and *'ami 'ōniu.* See also *'ami honua, 'ami ku'upau, 'ami 'ōpū,* and *'ami poepoe.* **3.** n. Measuring worm.

'ami.'ami. Redup. of *'ami 1, 2;* elastic, pendulous, springy; jerking of the hips back and forth in a crude or vulgar *'ami* hula; motion of sexual intercourse; to move on hinges.

'ā.miha.miha. Same as *āwihiwihi.*

'ami honua. nvi. Exaggerated and rapid revolving of the hips in the hula; to do so. Also *'ami ku'upau.*

'ami ho'o.ku'i. n. Joint. *Lit.,* connecting joint.

'ami ho'o.ku'ina lewa. n. Ball-and-socket joint. *Lit.,* swinging connecting joint.

'ami hue. Similar to *'ami ku'upau.* See *hue 3.*

'ā.mika. Same as *āmikamika.*

'ami kā.hela. nvi. Hula step; hip rotations with weight on the right hip as the left heel lifts very slightly, then reversing; to do this *'ami.* See *'ami kūkū.*

'ami kai. n. An amphipod *(Caprellid amphipods)* that clings to seaweeds or hydroids; it has a long slender body and is the color of the seaweed or hydroid on which it feeds.

'ā.mika.mika. n. A relish, morsel, or bit of food, scraps of food. *E ho'ohui a'e i nā 'āmikamika e kupa me ka pipi kū,* mix the scraps to make soup with the beef stew.

'ami kū.kū. nvi. A hula step with *'ami;* like the *'ami kāhela* except that the revolutions are smaller and faster and in groups of three; sometimes two slower *kāhela* revolutions are followed by three faster *kūkū* revolutions; to perform this step.

'ami ku'u.pau. nvi. Very rapid revolution of the hips in the hula; an uninhibited *(ku'upau) 'ami;* to do so. Also *'ami honua, 'ami hue.*

'ā.mimi. n. Name recorded for a type of lava rock on Lehua Island. *Ni'ihau.*

ā.mio. 1. nvi. Narrow channel, as to a sea pool; to move through such a channel; to blow in a current; to pass in and out; gusty. *Fig.,* to die. Cf. *mio. Kō ke akua ha'i āmio,* god reveals through narrow channels. *Hē āmio ka makani, e pio auane'i,* the wind blows a draft, [the light] may go out. (PPN *'a(a)mio*.) **2.** See *Ke-āmio.*

ā.mio.mio. Redup. of *āmio.*

'ami 'ō.niu. nvi. The figure-eight hula step; the revolving hips *('ami)* form an eight, with weight shifting; to perform this step. *Lit.,* spinning *'ami.*

'ami 'ō.pū. nvi. An *'ami* hula step with abdomen thrust forward, considered in poor taste; to do this step. *Lit.* stomach *'ami.*

'ami poe.poe. Same as *'ami kāhela* but a new term. Lit., round *'ami.*

'ami puka. n. Hinge of door or gate.

amo. nvt. To carry a burden on the shoulders, to lift weights; a burden. *Fig.,* responsibility. Cf. *'auamo. E amo pū!* Shoulder arms! (PPN *'amo*.)

'amo. 1. nvi. Wink, sparkle; to wink, sparkle, glimmer, twinkle. (PPN *kamo*.) **2.** n. Contraction of the anal muscles, anal opening, vagina. Cf. *pī ka 'amo* under *pī 2. 'Amo hulu,* rectum, vagina.

amoa. Pas/imp. of *amo.*

amo.amo. vi. To raise or mount high, as waves; high, raised.

'amo.'amo. Redup. of *'amo 1, 2. Hōkū 'amo'amo,* twinkling star or eyes.

amo kau. n. A stick for carrying burdens on the shoulder.

'ā.moke.moke. vs. Irregular, uneven.

'amo.ki'i. n. **1.** Stem of fruits or tubers; small end of sweet potato tuber. **2.** Genitals of male. Also *'anaki'i, 'anaki'u, 'anami'u.*

'ā.moku.moku. vs. Abounding in islets or rocks, as a reef; full of stumps; cutting, severing.

'amomo. n. Amomum, a genus of plants in the ginger family. (Gr. *amomon*.)

'amo.nia. n. Ammonia. *Eng.*

'ā.mo'o.mo'o. n. **1.** Small strip of tapa or matting such as can serve as a sample. **2.** Young stage of the *'ō'io* fish.

'amo.pu'u. vs. Thin, emaciated, lean. *Lit.,* protruding anal opening.

amu. 1. vt. To curse, revile. Cf. *kūamuamu.* (PPN *(amu)amu*.) **2.** vt. To eat. Cf. *hamu.* (PCP *amu*.) **3.** *(Cap.)* n. Name of a Kaua'i wind. (For. 5:97.)

ā.mū. vt. To trim, shear, shave; shaving, shearing. *Pahi āmū,* razor. *Lauoho āmū,* trimmed hair.

amu.amu. Redup. of *amu 1. Ke amuamu 'ana i ke ali'i me ka ho'ohiki 'ino,* reviling the chief with profane oaths. (PPN *amuamu*.)

ā.mū.ā.mū. Redup. of *āmū.*

'ā.mu'e.mu'e. nvs. Suffering from penetrating cold, bitter cold, bitter to taste.

ā.muka. Reported as a var. name for the *kāhala* fish.

'ā.muku. vs. Cut off. Same as *'āpahu.*

'ā.muku.muku. Same as *āmokumoku.*

amu.mū. nvs. Dull, blunt; dullness, bluntness.

ana. 1. nvt. To measure, survey, evaluate, rate, fathom; survey, measurement, standard, pattern, design, plan, model, meter, gauge, die. Cf. *anana, ana 'ole,* and numerous types of measurements listed below. See *lani 2. Kaula ana* (Ier. 31.39), measuring line. *Ana i ka hohonu,* to sound the depths. **ho'o.ana, ho'āna.** To make measurements, rearrange, put in order. (PPN *hanga*.) **2.** vi. To have enough or too much, satisfied, satiated, surfeited. *Ā ana nā kūpuna o Ka-welo i ke kāhumu 'ai na Ka-welo* (FS 33), the grandparents of Ka-welo had had enough of tending the food ovens for Ka-welo. *Ua hele au ā ana,* I've had all I can take; I'm disgusted. *'A'ole e 'ōlelo mai ana ke ahi ua ana ia,* fire will never say that it has enough [of love]. **3.** n. Cave, grotto, cavern. *Kokoke aku i kahi ana o ka pō* (GP 34), near the cavern of the night /depths of the night/. (PPN *'ana*.) **4.** n. Larynx. **5.** Part. after *e* (verb). See *e* (verb) *ana,* Gram. 5.3. (PEP *ana*.) **6.** Demon. following verbs indicating a single event, whether a command or a statement, whether completed or incompleted.

(Gram. 7.4.) *Iāia nō ā hala, kū ana ke kaʻa,* as soon as he had gone, the car came. *Nou ana kēia hale,* this house will be yours. *ʻOia ana nō,* it's the same; regardless. *He ʻaukai ana ʻoia nei,* he will be a seafarer. See also *e l.* (Probably PNP *ana(a).*)

āna. poss. His, her, hers (singular, *a*-form, zero-class; Gram. 9.6.3). (PPN *haʻana.*)

ʻana. 1. n. Pumice, used as a rubber. (PPN *kana.*) **2.** n. Siliceous sponge *(Leiodermatium),* used as medicine and as sandpaper. **3.** Nominalizing part. (Gram. 6.6.2.) *Kona hele ʻana mai,* his coming here.

ana ʻāina. nv. Land surveying; to survey.

ʻana ʻalaea. n. Red pumice.

ʻana.ʻana. vs. **1.** Pellet-shaped, as goat dung. **2.** To shiver, tremble. (And.)

ʻanā.ʻanā. nvt. Black magic, evil sorcery by means of prayer and incantation; to practice this. See *kahu ʻanāʻanā, kahuna ʻanāʻanā. ʻO ke kahu ʻanāʻanā akamai ma ke kala ʻana i ka ʻanāʻanā ʻia mai e kekahi,* the master of black magic skillful in countering the sorcery being directed at him by another.

ʻā.na'a.nai. Redup. of *ʻānai.*

ʻana.ʻanapa. Redup. of *ʻanapa.*

anaana.pau. Redup. of *anapau;* to move briskly. *Ua ʻike au i ka mokuahi Kī-lau-ea anaanapau ka holo,* I saw the ship Kī-lau-ea briskly sailing along.

ʻana.ʻana.puʻu. Redup. of *ʻanapuʻu. ʻAnaʻanapuʻu ka uila,* the jagged lightening flashes.

ʻā.naʻa.nau. Redup. of *ʻanau.*

ʻā.na'a.nea. Idiotic, foolish, as one under the spell of sorcery.

ana.ʻē. vt. To save for future use. **hoʻā.na.ʻē.** To withhold for the future. *Ka hoʻoilina . . . ua hoʻānaʻē ʻia ma ka lani* (1 Pet. 1.4), inheritance . . . reserved in heaven.

ʻanae. n. Full-sized *ʻamaʻama* mullet fish. (PPN *kanahe.*)

ana.hā. Reflection of light. (And.)

ā.nahe.nahe. Same as *nahenahe,* soft, gentle.

ana hola. n. Hourglass.

ana.honua. n. Geometry.

ana honua. nv. Surveying, to measure the surface of the earth.

ana hoʻo.hā.like. n. Model, pattern.

ʻana.hua. vs. Deformed, disfigured, stoop-shouldered, lopsided; such a person. **hō.ʻana.hua.** Caus/sim.

ana.huina.kolu. n. Trigonometry. *Lit.,* triangular measurement.

ana.hulu. 1. nvi. Period of ten days; for ten days; to pass ten days. *Kū anahulu ka moku,* the ship arrives once in ten days; the ship stays for ten days. (PPN *hangafulu.*) **2.** n. Large *moana,* a fish, from 30 to 80 cm long.

ā.nai. Same as *ālai l;* screen; attraction. *Ke ānai maila ka ʻiwa ānai maka* (UL 197), the frigate bird that fascinates the eyes is attracting attention.

ʻā.nai. nvt. **1.** To rub, scrub, scour, polish, grind, grate, blot out, lay waste, destroy; rubbing, scrubbing, etc.; friction. Cf. *ʻaʻanai, ʻanaʻanai, ānainai.* **2.** To curse.

anaina. nvs. Congregation, audience, assembly, gathering, crowd; to assemble.

anaina hoʻo.lewa. n. Funeral wake or gathering.

anaina hoʻo.mana. n. Congregation for worship.

ʻā.nai.nai. Redup. of *ʻānai.*

anaina ʻike aliʻi. n. Royal reception or audience.

ʻanaka. n. Gekko (RSV); polecat, ferret (KJV). (Oihk. 11.30.) (Heb. *ʻanaqa.*)

ʻana.kā. n. Anchor. *Eng. Leikō ka ʻanakā,* let go the anchor.

ana.kahi. n. Unit of measurement.

ʻana.kala. n. Uncle. *Eng.*

ana kau.maha. nv. To weigh; weight.

ʻana.kē, anate. n. Aunt, auntie. *Eng.*

ʻana.keʻe. vs. Bent, crooked, misshapen.

ʻana.kia. nvs. Anarchy, anarchist. *Eng.* Also *ʻanekomio.*

ʻana.kiʻi, ʻanakiʻu. Same as *ʻamokiʻi.* (For. 5:533.)

ʻana.koe. vi. Nothing remains to be done. *A pau a ʻana-*

koe, kū ana kēlā mea kēia mea i luna o ka waʻa, when all was done, each one stood up in the canoe.

ʻana.koʻi. n. Inflammatory swelling of a lymph gland, venereal tumor, bubo.

ʻana.komia, anatomia. n. Anatomy. *Eng.*

ana.kuʻu. Var. of *akakuʻu.*

ʻana.liʻi. 1. vs. Wee, stunted. Also *ʻaʻanaliʻi, kakanaliʻi.* **2.** n. A native fern *(Asplenium lobulatum)* with narrow fronds to 45 cm long, having many narrow lobes along two opposite sides of the axis. Also *piʻipiʻilaumanamana.*

ana.lio. n. **1.** Tail feathers. **2.** Same as *analipo.*

ana.lipo. n. Distance, faraway space, beyond the horizon. Cf. *kumulipo.*

ana loa. n. Measurement of length.

ana manawa. n. Tempo marker in music; Maelzel's metronome marker.

ana mekela (metera). n. Metric weight and measure.

ʻana.mi'u. Same as *ʻamokiʻi.*

anana. n. Fathom: formerly the distance between tips of longest fingers of a man, measured with arms extended on each side; Catholic writers equated *anana* with one meter (Kam. 76:50-1); to count by this measurement or by fathoms. Cf. *ana l.*

ʻā.nana. nvt. To strain, as juice or poi. Same as *kānana.*

ʻana.nalu. n. A variety of *hīnālea* fish.

ʻana.nau. Redup. of *ʻanau.*

ana.nea. vs. Leafless, bare.

ʻana.niʻo. Same as *ʻamokiʻi.*

ananū. n. Turnip.

ananū pilau. n. Daikon. *Lit.,* bad-smelling turnip.

ʻana.nuʻu. vi. To collapse or deflate, as a balloon.

ana ʻō.la'i, mī.kini ana ʻō.la'i. n. Seismograph. *Lit.,* machine to measure earthquakes.

ʻana ʻō.laʻi. n. White pumice with fine pores.

ana ʻole. vs. Without equal, unsurpassed, immeasurable, incomparable (in this sense, similar to *launa ʻole* and *lua ʻole*), limitless, unlimited, never satisfied. See ex., *lani 2.*

ʻanapa. nvi. To shine, gleam, glitter, flash, sparkle; brightness, gleam. **hoʻanapa.** Caus/sim. (PCP *kanapa.*)

ana.paʻa. n. Cubic measure. See ex., *paʻa l.*

ʻā.napa.napa. 1. Redup. of *ʻanapa.* **2.** n. Hawaiian soap plant *(Colubrina asiatica),* a twining shrub, distributed from Africa, India, and Australia to Polynesia, with ovate- to heart-shaped leaves and small round fruits. The leaves form a lather in water and have long been used as soap on Pacific islands. The plant is mistakenly reported to be poisonous. (Neal 541.) Also *kauila ʻanapanapa, kukuku; kolokolo* on Niʻihau. **3.** n. Red seaweeds *(Gelidium* spp.); small, stiff, branching, edible plants. Also *limu loloa.*

ana paona. vt. Scales, balance; to weigh. *Lit.,* pound *(Eng.)* measure.

ʻana.pau. vi. To leap, frisk, frolic; frisky. [Now heard only in the song: *He aha ka hana a ʻAnapau (mele maʻi* for Queen Liliʻu-o-ka-lani)? What does Frisky do?] **hō.ʻana.pau.** To caper, cavort; to twist and turn the body, especially in the finale of a hula with rapid hip movements.

ana piha. n. Measurement of capacity.

ana piwa. nv. Thermometer, for taking temperatures; to take temperature. *Lit.,* fever *(Eng.)* measure.

ʻanapu. Same as *ʻanapa. ʻAnapu ma ka honua mea,* flashing hot on the reddened earth.

ana puka. nvi. Underground passage, tunnel.

ʻā.napu.napu. Redup. of *ʻanapu.*

ana.puni. nv. Boundary, circumference, perimeter; to encircle, go around. *Komo akula i ke anapuni a Limaloa,* entered the circle of Long-arm [where others have the upper hand].

ʻana.puʻu. vs. Bumpy, lumpy, jagged, uneven; bump, hump; to hump along, buck; to project, as the bones of a thin animal. Cf. *ʻaʻanapuʻu, anaʻanapuʻu.* **hō.ʻana.puʻu.** Caus/sim.

'anau. vi. To move with a jerky motion; to go gadding from place to place. Cf. *'ananau, 'āna'anau. 'Anau noho'i 'oe i kauhale,* how you go gadding from house to house.

ana ua. nv. Rain gauge; to measure rainfall.

anaua.ni'i. Same as *'anianiau,* a honey creeper.

'anau hele. vs. To go here and there, gad.

ana.'uku. n. Mealybug (Coccidae) and scale insects.

anauna. Same as *hanauna,* generation.

'ā.nau.nau. 1. Same as *naunau 3,* shellfish. **2.** n. A small shrubby mustard, called peppergrass (probably a native species, *Lepidium bidentatum* var. *o-waihiense);* the root was used medicinally. (Neal 370.) Also *kūnānā, naunau.* **3.** n. According to Rock (1913) a large native peppergrass *(Lepidium serra),* with narrower leaves, found only on Kaua'i.

ana.waena. n. Diameter. *Lit.,* middle measure. *Anawaena loa,* traverse diameter of an ellipse. *Anawaena poko,* conjugate diameter of an ellipse.

ana wai. n. Water meter.

ana waina. n. Liquid measure.

ana wela. nv. Thermometer, measurement of heat; to measure heat.

ane. n. **1.** A dermestid beetle that destroys feathers in feather-work; mites, as in chickens; ringworm; insect-eaten, gnawed. *Lehu ane,* fine ashes. (PPN *ane.)* **2.** The breath of life, passing of a breeze. Cf. *aneane.* **3.** Pimple, scabies.

'ane. 1. Same as *'ane'ane,* to draw near. *Ua 'ane hiki mai,* almost here. *Ua 'ane aku i ka manawa,* it is almost time. **2.** Var. of *'ana 1,* pumice.

ā.nea. 1. vs. Insipid, tasteless. **2.** n. Vibration caused by heat. **3.** Pas/imp. of *ane 1;* moth-eaten. *Fig.,* a battered tramp. (PPN *anea.)* **4.** vs. Bare, leafless. **5.** Pas/imp. of *ane 2;* gentle, as a breeze.

'ane.alika, anearika. n. Antarctic. *Eng.*

ane.ane. nvs. Faint, feeble, exhausted; nauseous dizziness. Cf. *aneaneane.*

'ane.'ane. vs. Nearly, almost, scarcely, hardly, not quite, fairly; near. *Ua 'ane'ane ho'i e pa'a,* it is almost finished. *'Ane'ane i ka make,* near death.

ā.nea.nea. Redup. of *ānea.*

'ā.ne'e. vi. **1.** To move along by jerks, hitch along, sidle. **2.** To go where one is not welcome, to wear out a welcome.

'ā.ne'e ali'i. n. Parasite or sponger on a chief; royalist (disparaging).

'ā.ne'e.ne'e. 1. Redup. of *'āne'e 1, 2.* **2.** n. Old clothing; small mat that is carried about to sit on.

ā.nehe. vi. To come upon quietly, move stealthily, poise. *Ānehe akula ia e ku'i,* he stole up quietly to strike a blow. *Ānehe mai nā kānaka e kaua* (FS 71), the people were poised for fighting.

ā.nehe.nehe. Redup. of *ānehe.*

ā.neho. Transgression of the law, wrong, fault; to transgress. (And.)

anei. Part. indicating that a question may be answered by yes or no, always following a word or phrase. (Gram. 7.5.) *'O ia anei?* Isn't it so? Isn't it? *Pēlā anei?* Is it that way? Is that so? *E hele ana anei 'oe i ke kaona?* Are you going to town? (PCP *a(a)nei.)*

'ane'i. loc. n. Here (usually after *ma-, i,* or *kō:* Gram. 8.6.). See ex., *nei 3, 'oi. Ē ku'u aloha, ma'ane'i mai, ne'ene'e mai nō ā pili* (song), my loved one, come here, sidle up close. *'A 'ohe o 'one'i wahine e like me 'oe, ā inā noho'i no 'ane'i aku nei, 'a'ole nō e hele mai i 'ane'i; he kapu o 'ane'i, he make* (FS 259), none of the local women are like you, and had [you] been of this place, [you] would not have come here; it is taboo here, death. **2.** Part. Doubtful (used idiomatically). Same as *auane'i 2.* (Gram. 7.5.) *He pa'akai 'ane'i e hehe'e ai,* so, like salt that melts [said by one who doesn't mind going into the rain].

Āne.kali.kana, Anegalikana. vs. Anglican. *Eng.*

'ane.kaliko. Var. of *'anikelikeko.*

'Aneke, Anede. n. Andes. *Eng.*

'ane.kelo. n. Angle. *Eng.*

'ane.kelopa, anetelopa, anekelope. n. Antelope; gazelle (RSV), roebuck (KJV) (1 Nal. 4.23). *Eng.*

'aneko, aneto. n. Dill (RSV), anise (KJV). (Mat. 23.23.) (Gr. *anethon.)*

'ane.komio, anetomio. Var. of *'anakomia,* anatomy. (For. 5:543.)

'ā.nela. n. Angel; designation for Hawaiian gods and spirits by those converts to Christianity who had kept some of the old gods. *Eng. 'Ānela kia'i,* guardian angel.

'ane.moku. n. Peninsula. *Lit.,* near island (perhaps a translation of French *presqu'île)*

anena. Same as *alena,* an herb. *Ni'ihau.*

ā.neo. n. A game; the stone called *hiu* was said to have been used in this game.

ā.ne'o.ne'o. vi. To itch. Cf. *mane'o.*

ā.newa. vi. Dizzy, unsteady, as one ill or intoxicated. Cf. *newa,* dizzy.

ā.newa.newa. Redup. of *ānewa.*

ani. vt. To beckon, wave; to blow softly, as a breeze; to draw a net over the surface of water; to pass over the surface, as a hand; beckoning. *'Upena ani,* draw net. **ho'āni.** To beckon, wave, signal; to let wind. *Ho'āni pākī,* to threaten to throw at, as a dog. (PPN *angi.)*

ania. 1. Pas/imp. of *ani;* breezy. See ex., *nāhāhā.* **2.** vs. Smooth.

'ā.nia. vs. Scorched, singed, parched; hot, as an oven.

ani.ani. 1. nvs. Mirror, glass; clear, transparent, obvious. Cf. *makaaniani, pukaaniani.* Several types of *aniani* are listed below. *Aniani nā hana i ka Naukilo* (song), techniques are clear to the Nautilus. (PPN *ali.)* **2.** vs. Cool, refreshing; to blow softly, gently. *Fig.,* to travel swiftly. (PPN *angiangi.)*

ā.nia.nia. vs. Smooth, calm.

'ā.nia.nia. Redup. of *'ānia.*

'ania.niau. n. A small, bright olive or yellowish-green Hawaiian honey creeper *(Loxops* [formerly *Chlorodrepanis] parva),* endemic to Kaua'i, and related to the *'amakihi.* The young birds which are confused with young *'amakihi,* were reported to have been called *alawī.* The greater *'amakihi (L. satittirostris)* is presumed extinct.

ani.ani ho'o.nui 'ike. n. Magnifying glass, microscope, telescope. *Lit.,* glass to enlarge vision.

Ani.ani-i-ka-lani. n. Name of a star said to be in the Milky Way.

ani.ani ipu kukui. n. Lamp chimney.

ani.ani kilohi. n. Mirror looking glass.

ani.ani kū. n. Standing mirror.

ani.ani kukui uila. n. Electric-light bulb. *Lit.,* electric-light glass.

ani.ani nā.nā. n. Mirror, looking glass.

ani.ani pa'a lima. n. Hand mirror.

'ā.niha. vs. Unfriendly, angry, hardhearted, hostile. Cf. *kamaniha.*

'ā.niha.niha. 1. Redup. of *'āniha.* **2.** vi. Nearly, almost. *'Anihaniha mākou ā pae, loa'a i ka makani,* we were almost landing when [we were] caught by the wind.

'ā.nihi.nihi. 1. vs. Precarious. Cf. *nihi. 'Anihinihi i ke ola,* life hanging [as by a thread]. **2.** n. Small taro tubers. Less used than *'ōnihinihi.*

'ā niho loa. n. A small fish (no data).

'ani.keli.keko, anikristo, anikeriseto. nvs. Antichrist. Also shortened to *'anekaliko.* (Gr. *antichristos.)*

ā.nini. n. *Eurya sandwicensis,* a native tree or shrub in the tea family. Also *wānini.* (Neal 582.)

'anini. 1. vs. Dwarfish, stunted, tiny. *Rare.* **2.** vi. To vary, as great and small waves. *Rare.* **3.** n. Awning. *Eng.*

ani pe.'ahi. vi. To wave or beckon, as with the hand, fan.

'ā.ni'u.ni'u. n. Root connecting sweet potato to vine.

ano. 1. nvi. Awe, reverence, peacefulness, sacredness, holiness; feeling of awe, fear, or oppression; weird solitude, oppressive quiet; awestruck, lost in thought.

Ke ano mai nei ka nahele, 'a'ohe manu o ke kula (song), the forest is silent, there are no birds in the plains. *Ano wale mai nō kō aloha,* your love overpowers me. **hō.ano.** Holy, devoted to sacred use, hallowed, solemn; to reverence, sanctify, attribute divine honor, hallow. *Po'e Hōano o nā Lā Hope Nei,* Latter-Day Saints. *Hōano, Hōano, Hōano* (Hoik. 4.8), Holy, Holy, Holy. *Ē kō mākou Makua i loko o ka lani, e hōano 'ia kou inoa* (Mat. 6.9), our Father which art in Heaven, hallowed be Thy name. **2.** n. Time (in songs, and usually before *ahiahi,* rarely before *kakahiaka*).

'ano. 1. n. Kind, variety, nature, character, disposition, bearing, type, brand, likeness, sort, way, manner, shape, tendency, fashion, style, mode, circumstance, condition, resemblance, image, color, moral quality, denomination, meaning (preceded by *ke*). *Ke 'ano o ka nohona,* way of life, standard of living. *He aha ke 'ano?* What is [it] like [sometimes said scornfully]? What kind of nonsense is that? *He aha nō lā kou 'ano?* What's the matter with you? **hō.'ano.** To cause to take a definite shape, produce a resemblance. (PPN *kano.*) **2.** vs. Somewhat, rather; to show signs of. *'Ano maika'i,* somewhat good, pretty good, fair. *'Ano maika'i 'ole,* not very good. *'Ano 'ino,* wicked, disorderly (of conduct). *'Ano poepoe,* somewhat round. *Ke 'ano mālie mai nei,* beginning to clear up now. *E 'ano ua aku ana,* it looks like rain.

'ā.nō. loc. n. Now, present. (Gram. 8.6.)

anoa. 1. nvi. Dry, parched, barren. Same as *panoa.* **2.** Pas/imp. of *ano 1.* Rare.

'ā.noa. vi. To end, give up.

'ano.'ai. 1. nvt. Greeting, salutation, news; to greet. *'Ano'ai kākou,* greetings (to more than two persons). *Nā 'ano'ai o Kona 'Ākau,* news of North Kona. **2.** vi. Unexpected. *'Ano'ai kō māua hui 'ana,* our meeting was unexpected. **3.** part. Perhaps. *'Ano'ai aia paha i laila ka hale noho a ka 'i'ini* (chant for Ka-lā-kaua), perhaps there the dwelling house of desire.

'ano akua. nvs. Godlike, divine; godly form.

ano.ano. Redup. of *ano 1.* *Kula anoano kanaka 'ole,* solitary uninhabited plain. **ho'āno.ano.** Redup. of *ho'āno.* *Ho'ānoano wale mai nō mehe haili lā e kau iho maluna,* awe-struck as though a spirit has descended from above. *I Wai-lua ā ho'ānoano ka ihu o ka wa'a* (GP 62), [turn] the prow of the canoe to Wai-lua and place under taboo.

'ano.'ano. n. Seed, kernel, germ; dried and salted Chinese watermelon seed. *Fig.,* progeny, offspring.

'ano 'ē. vs. Strange, odd, unusual, uncommon, grotesque, peculiar, eccentric, freakish, queer, quaint, different, uncomfortable. **hō.'ano 'ē.** Caus/sim. *Hō'ano 'ē iki a'e kona helehelena,* and altered his features.

ano.hale. n. Individual presiding over the *'ume* game. (Malo 215.)

'ano hana. n. Method, case, technique, as in solving problems.

'ā.noho. n. Sitting taboo. (Kep. 137.)

'ano hou. nvs. New variety, fashion, or kind; new, unusual. **hō.'ano hou.** To renew, change the nature or character.

'ano hui. n. Compound, as of fractions.

'ano hui.kau. vs. Complex, as of fractions.

'ano'i. nvt. Desire, longing, love, desired one, lover (see ex., *pouli 1*); to desire, yearn; loved, beloved. *'Ano'i pua,* cherished flower, sweetheart. *'Ano'i ka mana'o,* hope. *Ka mele i 'ano'i nui 'ia,* the greatly beloved song. *'Ano'i aku e 'ike iāia,* great desire to see her.

'ano lani. vs. Of heavenly or royal character, celestial, noble, royal, pure.

'ano like. nvs. Resembling, of similar nature or type; resemblance, similarity. *Nā mea 'ano like 'ole,* assortment, miscellany.

'ā.nona.nona. Same as *naonao* and *nonanona,* ant. *E hele 'oe i ka 'ānonanona, e nānā i kona 'ao'ao e ho'ona'auao iho* (Sol. 6.6), go to the ant, study her

ways and learn. The newspaper Ka Nonanona (1841–5) was named for this saying.

'ā.noni. vt. To mix, interweave, intertwine, mixed. *Fig.,* confused, doubtful. *Koko 'ānoni,* mixed blood. *'Ānoni 'ia me ke koko Pākē,* mixed with Chinese blood. *'Ānoni ka mana'o,* a confused, doubting mind. (PCP *kaanoni.*)

'ano.nia. 1. Pas/imp. of *'anoni.* **2.** Same as *alani wai,* a plant.

'ā.noni.noni. Redup. of *'ānoni,* perplexity.

'ano.noni. Same as *ānoninoni.*

'ano nui. nvs. Important, vital, main; importance. *Mea 'ano nui,* important person, loved one, V.I.P., celebrity.

'ano 'ole. nvs. Insignificant, trivial, of no consequence, unattractive; nonsense. *He wahi kumu 'ano 'ole, 'o ka huhū nō ia,* it was such a trifling reason for anger.

'ano pili. n. Property, as of a number; fraction.

anu. nvs. **1.** Cool, cold; coolness, temperature. *Nu'uanu* (place name), cool elevation. **ho'ānu.** To cool. (PCP *anu.*) **2.** nvi. Cold, influenza; to have a cold. *Ua loa'a i ke anu,* to get a cold.

'anu'a. n. Heap, mass, pile.

anu.anu. Redup. of *anu,* cold; chilly. **ho'ānu.anu.** Caus/sim.

ā.nue.nue. 1. nvi. Rainbow. *E wai ānuenue ana nā wāwae o nā koa,* the feet of the soldiers form a rainbow pattern [of marching soldiers in colored uniforms]. (PNP *nuanua.*) **2.** n. Scallop-like design on tapa and tapa beater.

'anuhe. n. Caterpillar. Also called *'enuhe, nuhe.* (PPN *'anufe.*)

anu.hea. nvs. Cool, soft fragrance, as of upland forests; sweetness; to be cool, fragrant, and sweet. Also *waianuhea.* *Kō 'ala anuhea ka'u i honi aku* (song), your cool soft fragrance I inhaled.

'ā.nuhe.nuhe. 1. vs. Infested with caterpillars. **2.** vi. Wrinkled, furrowed; to pucker, wrinkle, shrivel. **3.** Var. name for *nenue* fish. (AP.)

'anu.iki, 'anuiti. n. Annuity. Eng.

'ā.nulu, 'ānunu. Variants of *'ālunu,* greed. *Palapala 'ānunu me ka pākaha* (song Elbert and Mahoe 63), greedy document of extortion.

'ā.nunu. n. A native genus of cucurbit vines *(Sicyos).* (Neal 808.) Cf. *kūpala.*

'anu'u. 1. n. Stairs, jogs, steps, terrace, dais, ledge (1 Nal. 6.6). **2.** n. Tower in ancient heiau, about 7 m high and 5.5 m square, as enclosed with white *'ōloa* tapa. Cf. *nu'u 1.* **3.** nvi. Sprain, strain, disjointed vertebra; to stumble, trip, sprain; to land heavily or jar, as when one steps down but there is no step; jarred. *Fig.,* error, slip; to err. Cf. *māui.* **4.** n. A step between two notes on a musical staff. *Pili 'anu'u,* to go up an interval (in music). **5.** Noun indicating comparison of adjectives. *'Anu'u kumu,* basic stage. *'Anu'u waena,* comparative degree. *'Anu'u loa,* superlative degree.

'anu'u hapa. n. Half-step in music.

'anu'u maoli. n. Full step in music.

'anu'u hapa a me nā 'anu'u maoli. n. An augmented second in music.

'ā.nu'u.nu'u. vi. Having steps; wavy, curly, vibrating, undulating; to beat with regular rhythm; to jerk the body, as by osteopaths or masseurs. *Alapi'i 'ānu-'unu'u,* stairs. **ho'ā.nu'u.nu'u.** To vibrate, undulate, wave, jerk, make steps; wavy, as hair. *Leo ho'ānu-'unu'u,* quavering, trilling voice.

ao. 1. nvi. Light, day, daylight, dawn; to dawn, grow light; enlightened; to regain consciousness. Cf. *aokanaka.* *Piliwaiwai lākou ā ao ka pō,* they gambled until night became day [all night long, until dawn]. *Kēlā pō ā ao a'e i nehinei,* night before last; *lit.,* that night that dawned yesterday. *Ā ao ka pō ā pō ke ao,* when night becomes day until the day becomes night [for a night and a day]. *Ua ao mai ka no'ono'o,* the mind is functioning. **ho'āo.** To marry; marriage (old term, probably *lit.,* to stay until daylight). **(b)** *(Cap.)* Night of the day called Huna, eleventh night of the month, when the *ho'āo* nuptials took place. (PPN *'aho*.) **2.** n. Any kind of a cloud, including *'ōpua*, but specifically, high clouds that when wind-blown scud along *(ka'a)*. See ex., *pūnohu 1*, and cf. *aokū, ao loa, ao 'ōnohi, aouli, 'ōpua, pālāmoa, pāpalamoa, puapua'a. Ao kai lilo a Kāne*, a cloud over the distant sea of Kāne [away out, where only cloud and sea are seen]. (PPN *'ao*.) **3.** n. World, earth, realm. *Ke ao o Milu*, the realm of the underworld. **4.** vt. To be careful, beware, watch out. *E ao na'e 'oe iā Kalahumoku* (For. 5:413), beware then of Kalahumoku. *E ao 'oe o 'eha*, be careful or you'll be hurt. **5.** Rare var. of *wao*, upland area. **6.** idiom. The exact image of (preceded by *a 'e*). *'O ka makuahine nō a 'e ao*, the image of the mother. **7.** n. A kind of fine mat. **8.** n. A kind of fish (no data). (KL line 149.)

a'o. 1. nvt. Instruction, teaching, doctrine, learning, instruction book, manual, advice, counsel; to learn, teach, advise, instruct, train, tutor, coach, prescribe, admonish. Many kinds of instruction are listed below as *a'o heluhelu, a'o hōkū, a'o kiko, a'o loko, a'o palapala, a'o pili'ōlelo*. See *lohe* for idioms. *A 'o ikaika, a'o 'o'ole'a*, teach harshly, discipline. *'Ōlelo a'o*, advice, precept, instruction. *A'o poko*, briefly taught; to learn a little [said of lowly individuals]. *E a'o kākou iā 'oe i ke kino lele o kō wahine* (For. 4:73), we will teach you the flying power [*lit.*, body] of your wife. *Na wai 'oe i a'o?* Who taught you? **ho'ā'o.** To test, try, attempt, taste, undertake, experiment, endeavor, tempt (Kin. 22.1); to do a little (equivalent of the pidgin English "try" before verbs; see ex., *kuhi hewa*). *E ho'ā'o ana*, contestants. *E ho'ā'o mai ana 'oe e hīmeni?* Won't you sing a little? [Pidgin, "try sing"] *Lohe mai ke a'o*, idiomatic intensifier, as in *Kalohe ā lohe mai ke a'o*, mischievous beyond boundary. *Nani ā lohe mai ke a'o*, extremely beautiful. (PPN *ako*.) **2.** Part. replacing *o*, of, and *'o*,. subject marker, in songs. (Gram. 2.8, 9.13.) *'O nā pali a'o Ko'olau Loa*, the cliffs of Ko'olau Loa. *Lapakū ka wahine a'o Pele*, the woman, Pele, is very active.

'ao. n. 1. A new shoot, leaf, or bud, especially of taro. (UL 17.) Cf. *'ahu 'ao, 'ao kahi, 'ao lū'au.* (PCP *kao*.) **2.** Dried baked taro or sweet potato; in Ka'ū this food was hung in baskets in the wind so that it dehydrated; it was used on sea journeys and is perhaps related to *ō*, sea rations. (PCP *kao*.) **3.** Ship biscuit, pilot bread, hardtack.

'a'o. n. Newell's puffin or shearwater *(Puffinus puffinis newelli)*, said to be the only sea bird endemic to Hawai'i, and to breed only in Hawai'i; glossy black above, white beneath; endangered. Also *li'o. Ho'okahi nō hua a ka 'a'o*, the *'a'o* lays but a single egg [said of an only child].

'aoa. 1. nvi. To bark, as a dog; to howl (Ioela 1.5), bowwow; lamentation, cry of distress; doleful creature (Isa. 13.21), sad (perhaps *aoa*). **hō.aoa.** To make a dog bark or howl. (PCP *(k)aoa*.) **2.** n. A small shellfish *(Melampus castaneus)*, strung in leis. Also *maka'aoa.* (PCP *ka(',l)oa*.) **3.** Same as *'iliahi*, sandalwood. (AP.) **4.** n. Name for sacrificial places near fishponds where semiannual offerings were made, as of taro, bananas, mullet, *kohekohe* sedge, and black pigs. (Ii 26.) **5.** *(Cap.)* n. Name of a sea breeze associated with Honolulu and elsewhere. Also *'Ao'aoa* or *Ulu-mano.* **6.** n. Hour. *Eng.* (Ka Nonanona, 1844.)

ao akua. n. Godly cloud. *Fig.*, rainbow.

'Aoa Lae.nihi. n. A rainy wind at Ni'ihau, said to be so-called because it creeps *(nihi)*.

'ao.'ao. n. 1. Side, boundary, hemisphere. See ex., *'ānonanona. Ma kahi 'ao'ao*, on the side, sideways. *Ma kekahi 'ao'ao*, on the other side, on the other hand. *Ma kēlā 'ao'ao*, on that side, across. (PPN *kaokao*.) **2.** Group, team, denomination; party (political). *Ke koho 'ana o nā 'ao'ao*, option of the parties [to an agreement]. **3.** Page. **4.** Way (Sol. 6.6), habit, mode of living, education. *'O kona mau 'ao'ao āpau he maika'i wale*

nō, all his ways are very good. **5.** Family gods, *'aumākua. He 'ao'ao pueo kō mākou*, we have the owl as our family god.

a'o.a'o. n. Stratagem, plot, advice, counsel.

ao.aoa. n. A small seaside shrub *(Wikstroemia* sp.). The root bark is used externally for sores, and stems and bark of branches for coughs. Branches and leaves are mixed with rasped seeds of *Barringtonia asiatica* (syn. *B. speciosa)* to stupefy fish. See *'ākia 1*. (PNP *'aoa*.)

'ao.'aoa. 1. Redup of *'aoa 1*. **2.** *(Cap.)* Same as *'aoa 5*, a sea breeze.

'ao.'ai.'ē. n. Debit side (in bookkeeping).

'ao.'ao 'ā.kau. n. Right or leeward side of an island. See *Kona*.

'ao.'ao ho'o.ma'e.ma'e. n. Reform party.

'ao.'ao kā.lai.'āina. n. Political party.

'ao.'ao kū.'ē. n. Opposition, opponent, as in a trial; minority party.

'ao.'ao kū.pale. n. Defense, as in a trial.

'ao.'ao kū.pono. vs. Perpendicular, of a triangle.

'ao.'ao leo nui. n. A variety of taro (no data).

'ao.'ao loa. n. Hypotenuse.

'ao.'ao makani. n. Windward side.

'ao.'ao mau o ka honua. n. Death, afterlife. *Lit.*, everlasting side of the earth.

'ao.'ao moe. n. Base, as of a triangle.

'ao.'ao nui. n. Young of the *kūpīpī* fish, or alternate name.

'ao.'ao pale. Same as *'ao'ao kūpale.*

'ao.'ao.wela. n. A green fish. (And.)

'a'oe. Same as *'a'ole*, not. See chant, *wāhia. 'A 'oe e 'ole!* Certainly not! *'A 'oe ho'i e 'ole!* Absolutely not! *'A 'oe au e hele*, I will not go.

'a'ohe. interj. None; no, not; to have or be none; there is no one who (in subordinate phrases). *'A 'ohe* is a contraction of the negative *'a'ole* and *he*, the indefinite article (Gram. 10.2). It is often followed by zero possessives, as *'a'ohe āna hana*, he has no work; *'a'ohe o'u makemake i poi*, I don't want any poi. Today a gesture is commonly used by all races to replace *'a'ohe koena*, there isn't any more, or *'a'ole*, no. The gesture, taken from Hawaiians, is a quick flick of the hand with the palm turned downward and away from the body, originally significant of an empty hand. *'Oia kama'ilio aku ā 'ea ka waha, 'a'ohe lohe 'ia mai*, while talking until the tongue is coated, [yet] no one is listened to.

a'o hele. vt. To teach while traveling; to act as itinerant teacher, preacher, missionary.

a'o helu.helu. nvt. Reader, primer; to learn or teach to read.

Ao-hō.kū. n. Name of a star, possibly Jupiter. *Lit.*, star light. Cf. *Hōkū-ao.*

a'o hō.kū. nvt. Astronomy, astronomer; to teach or learn astronomy.

'ā.oka. n. Same as *oka*, dregs.

'ao kahi. n. One remaining leaf *('ao)* on an old taro stalk, said of an old taro about to die.

ao.kanaka. nvi. To think or behave reasonably; human enlightment, civilization; rational.

'ā.oka.oka. Redup. of *'āoka.*

a'o kepela (sepela). nv. Spelling book; to learn or teach spelling.

a'o kiko. nv. Manual of punctuation; to learn or teach punctuation.

ao.kū. n. Rain cloud, mist.

ao kuewa. n. Realm of homeless spirits.

'a'ole. interj. No, not, never; to be none, to have none, -un. Commonly pronounced *'a'ale* (Gram. 2.7). Cf. *'a'ohe. 'A'ole loa!* Certainly not! Not at all! I should say not! Never! *'A'ole loa anei 'oe i hele i Hilo?* Have you ever been to Hilo? *'A'ole paha*, probably not, perhaps not (polite). *'A'ole i ma'ama'ahia*, unfamiliar. (PCP *kakole*.)

'ā.olo. Same as *ālai. I 'apa kāua i ka 'āolo o ka 'ōka'i me ka pulelehua i kō kāua ala hele*, we were delayed by the obstruction of the moths and butterflies in our way.

ao loa. n. Long cloud; high or distant cloud; stratus cloud along the horizon. *Fig.,* a distinguished person.

aʻo loko. n. Innermost teaching, inspiration. *I ka haʻalele ʻana aku i Kou aʻo loko ʻana mai,* from the neglect of Thy inspirations.

ʻao lū.ʻau. nv. Unexpanded leaf blade of taro; to offer as a sacrifice. *E ʻao lūʻau a kaulima,* offer young taro leaves five times as sacrifice.

ʻā.one. nvs. Sandy; sandy soil.

ʻa.ono. num. Six, especially in counting in a series; six times. *Pōʻaono,* Saturday; *lit.,* sixth day.

ā ʻō.ʻō. See *ā 2.*

ʻā.o.ʻo. vs. Elderly, middle-aged. Cf. *oʻo.*

ao ʻō.nohi. n. Cloud with rainbow *(ʻōnohi)* colors.

aʻo pala.pala. nvt. Instruction, education; to teach or learn writing.

aʻo pili.ʻō.lelo. nvt. Grammar, instruction in grammar; to teach or learn grammar.

aouli. n. **1.** Firmament, sky, blue vault of heaven. **2.** Var. of *ʻouli.*

Ap. Abbreviation for *ʻāpana,* land parcel, used in surveying.

ʻapa. 1. vt. To delay, waste time, tarry, linger, keep others waiting. *Kahuli ihola lāua, a lilo ihola lāua i ke kā, i ka hoe, pēlā lāua i ʻapa ai* (FS 49), the two upset, and were occupied with the bailer and paddles, in this way they were delayed. *Mai ʻapa mai ʻoe, e hele kākou,* don't dillydally, let's go. *Kū ka ʻapa iā Hawaiʻi, he moku nui,* it is fitting for Hawaiʻi to tarry [do as it wants], a big island. **hō.ʻapa.** Caus/sim. **2.** Ephah. *Biblical.* **3.** *(Cap.)* Also **Aba.** Abba. (Mar. 14.36.) *Eng.*

ʻā.pā. n. **1.** Roll or ream, as of paper; bolt, as of cloth. **2.** See *lima ʻāpā.*

ʻā.paʻa. 1. nvs. Arid, dry; dry area, clod of dirt. *Pili hoʻōla ka ua i ka ʻāpaʻa,* akin to a healer is the rain to the arid plains. (PPN *pakaka.*) **2.** n. Land one has lived on for a long time (a term of affection related to *paʻa,* firmly bound). **3.** Same as *wao ʻilima.*

ʻā.paʻa.kuma. n. Native of a place and descendant from its earliest line of chiefs. (Malo 24.)

ʻapa.ʻapa. 1. Redup. of *ʻapa 1;* to procrastinate, deliberate, slow. **hō.ʻapa.ʻapa.** To slow down others; to lag, dillydally, bother. *He ʻaumakua hoʻoluhi, hōʻapaʻapa i ke kahuna,* a family god who bothers and interferes with the priest. (1 Pet. 2.22, Roma 1.25.) See *ʻapakeʻe.* **2.** nvt. Guile, deceit; to practice such. (1 Pet. 2.22, Roma 1.25.) See *ʻapakeʻe.*

ʻĀ.paʻa.paʻa. 1. n. Name of a strong wind associated with Kohala, Hawaiʻi. **2.** *(Not cap.)* vs. Dry, parched. **3.** *(Not cap.)* Same as *ʻāpaʻa 2.* **4.** *(Not cap.)* n. A kind of lobster (no data). **5.** *(Not cap.)* vs. Firm, hard, compact. See ex., *mahani.*

ʻā.paʻa.pana. n. Small pieces, fragments. Cf. *ʻāpana.*

ʻā.paʻa.pāna. n. Delay, procrastination.

ʻā.paʻa.pani. nvi. Quick, effective repartee; to retort thus. *Rare.*

ā . . . paha. See *paha 6.*

ʻā.paha. vi. To doubt; perhaps, maybe. *Rare.*

ʻapa.hū. Rare var. of *pahū,* explosion.

ʻā.pahu. 1. nvt. To cut squarely off, chop; a piece cut off at right angles. *Poʻo ʻāpahu,* head with receding forehead. **2.** Same as *kūnehi,* a sunfish. **3.** Conspicuous, as one dressed oddly. (And.) **4.** To cram, pack full, stuff (And.)

ʻapai. Same as *pai 5,* a fish trap.

ʻapa.kau. vt. To seize, lay hold of, disarrange, displace; to spread, as sunlight. *Ka ʻapakau ʻana iho o nā kukuna o ka lā maluna o ka ʻili o ke kai,* the spreading of the rays of the sun on the surface of the sea.

ʻapa.keʻe. nvs. Deceit, dishonesty; deceitful, corrupt, inaccurate.

ʻā.pala. n. Apple *(Pyrus malus* syn. *M. sylvestris).* (Neal 388.) *Eng.* Also *poma.*

ʻā.pali. vs. Hilly, craggy. *Fig.,* impertinent, rude.

ʻā.pali.pali. 1. Redup. of *ʻāpali.* **2.** To hurry, hasten. (And.)

ʻā.pana. 1. Piece, slice, portion, fragment, section, segment, installment, part, land parcel, lot, district, sector, ward, precinct; chop, as of lamb. A *kuleana,* land division, may consist of several *ʻāpana.* Cf. *kapa ʻāpana. Kōmike komo ʻāpana,* visiting committee, as of a church. (PCP *(k)a(a)pana:* cf. Marquesan *apana.*) **2.** Same as *mile 1.* (Kam. 76:45.)

ʻā.pana ipu lepo. n. Potsherd. (Ioba 2.8.) *Lit.,* portion of earthen container.

ʻā.pana kā.nā.wai. n. Phylactery.

ʻā.pana.pana. Redup. of *ʻāpana;* fragments, pieces; to cut into pieces (For. 5:591). *Nā pōkā ʻāpanapana,* shrapnel.

ʻā.pana pō.ʻai. n. Segment of a circle.

ʻā.pane. 1. n. A kind of *lehua* tree with dark-red flower. **2.** Short for *ʻapapane,* a bird. See *ʻōhiʻa ʻāpane.* **3.** vs. Red, flushed, blushing.

ʻā.pani. nvt. To block, shut. *Fig.,* an unwelcome visitor who monopolizes conversation.

ʻā.pani ani.ani. n. Window pane.

ʻā.pani.pani. Redup. of *ʻāpani,* to block.

ʻā.papa. n. Stratum, flat, especially a coral flat.

ʻā.papa lani. n. **1.** Legendary upper stratum and abode of the gods (preceded by *ke*). **2.** Chiefs of the highest rank, as *nīʻaupiʻo;* gods. *E ala, ē ʻāpapa nuʻu, e ala, ē ke ʻāpapa lani!* (UL 196). Awake, gods of high station, awake, gods of highest station!

ʻapa.pane. n. A Hawaiian honey creeper *(Himatione sanguinea),* with crimson body and black wings and tail, found on all the main Hawaiian Islands. Its feathers occasionally were used for featherwork. Also *ʻakakane.*

ʻapa.papa. Same as *laupapa 1,* reef.

āpau. idiom. All, entirely. *Nā kānaka āpau,* all the people, everyone, everybody.

ʻape. n. Large taro-like plants *(Alocasia macrorrhiza, Xanthosoma robustum).* (Neal 156, 162.) A number of beliefs concerning *ʻape* have been recorded. *ʻApe* was planted by a gate or fence because the irritating sap of the leaves was thought to ward off evil spirits; leaves were placed under tapas or mats on which the sick lay for the same reason. *ʻApe* was not planted near the house for fear the residents might become sick. Varieties are qualified by the colors *kea* or *keʻokeʻo* (white), or *hiwa* or *ʻeleʻele* (dark). (PPN *kape.*)

ʻape.ʻape. 1. n. All endemic species of *Gunnera,* huge-leafed forest perennial herbs, with thick, prostrate stems rising at the tip to about 120 cm. (Neal 651.) Called *hāhā* on Kauaʻi. **2.** vs. Elastic, flexible, limber. *Rare.*

ʻā.peʻa.peʻa. 1. Same as *peʻapeʻa,* bat. **2.** n. An unidentified cephalopod. **3.** Same as *ʻōpeʻapeʻa 3,* half leaf.

ʻā.peʻe.peʻe. Rare var. of *līpeʻepeʻe,* a seaweed.

ʻā.peke.peke. n. The Kauaʻi *ʻelepaio (Chasiempis sandwichensis sclateri).*

ʻā.pela. vs. Old, aged. *Rare.*

ʻā pele. n. Volcanic lava or ejecta of any kind, rough lava, lava flow.

apele.koka, aperekoka. n. Apricot *(Prunus armeniaca).* (Neal 396.) *Eng.*

ʻApe.lika, Aferika. Africa; African. *Eng.*

ʻApe.lila, Aperila. April. *Eng.*

ʻā.peu. Same as *ʻāleuleu;* long coarse mats used to hold food.

ʻape.ʻula. n. Kind of tapa, wrapped about images. (Kam. 64:12.)

ʻā.peu.peu. Same as *ʻāleuleu. He wahi ʻāpeupeu moena kaʻu i lawe mai nei,* I've just brought some ordinary coarse mats [a polite way to disparage a gift that may actually be fine].

ʻapi. 1. n. Soft spot in the temples; soft part of the human body between the pelvic cone and the lowest rib; under part of an animal's body (sometimes preceded by *ke*). **2.** nvi. A surgeonfish *(Acanthurus guttatus),* 20 cm long. (PPN *hapi.*) **3.** nvi. Fish gills; to breathe through gills. **4.** vi. To palpitate, throb, tremble, shake, quiver;

to beat, as the pulse; to stir, as waves; palpitation, quivering. **5.** n. A decoy stick basket with a wide opening; it was baited, and after the fish were accustomed to coming for food, a trap was substituted. *Ke ao 'ō'ō, ke 'api wai* (FS 201), the sharp-pointed cloud, the water basket [a cloud full of rain]. **6.** To gather together, as people or things. (And.)

-āpī. hō.'ā.pī. Stingy; to withhold.

'api.'api. 1. Redup of *'api 4;* elastic, springy; short of breath. **2.** Redup. of *'api 3.* **3.** vs. Filled, as a basket; abundant, as a feast. *'Aha'aina ka lani i ka lolo o Kūka-huila-lani, 'api'api kanalani* (For. 6:398), the chief feasts at the *lolo* ceremony of Kū-the-heavenly-lightning, abundant repletion.

'ā.pi'i. 1. vs. Curly. **2.** n. Tapa-beater design. **3.** n. A variety of taro in the *piko* group, having light-colored corms which are good for poi or table taro; red *('ula)* and white *(kea)* forms exist; it is called "curly" *('āpi'i)* because of crinkles under the leaf. **4.** n. A ti plant with green, crinkly leaves.

'ā.pi'i.pi'i. 1. vs. Wavy, crimpy, kinky, very curly; tempestuous, as waves. **2.** n. A kind of seaweed that is tough and not eaten much, perhaps *Amansia glomerata.*

'ā.pika.pika. nvs. Having suction cups, as the tentacles of the octopus; suction cups; spotted.

'ā.piki. nvs. Crafty, cunning, mischievous, deceitful, dishonest, naughty, treacherous, peculiar, strange; trickery, treachery, rogue, rascal, mischief-maker, humbug. *Ka mea 'āpiki,* however, but, yet. *Lei 'āpiki,* a name given to the *'ilima* lei because it was believed to attract mischievous spirits; some did not wear this lei but others considered it lucky.

'ā.piki.piki. 1. vs. Troubled, agitated, as the sea. Cf. *kūpikipiki'ō.* **2.** nvt. Fold, pleat; to fold, pleat. (PPN *kapitipiti.*) **3.** vt. To clean taro greens by peeling the stems. *Rare.* **4.** n. A kind of variegated or spotted tapa.

'apipa, abiba. n. Abib, a Hebrew month. (Puk. 13.4.) (Heb. *abhibh.*)

'ā.pipi. vs. United, joined, coupled; double. *He wa'a 'āpipi,* a double canoe. **ho'ā.pipi.** To join, couple.

apo. 1. nvt. Circle, circuit, hoop, loop, band, bracelet, hoop-shaped earring, girdle, belt, ring, embrace; to span, reach around, embrace, put an arm around, clasp. Many compounds with *apo* are listed below. Cf. *kahaapo.* (PPN *apo.*) **2.** n. Union of the molar or cheekbone with the temporal bone.

'apo. 1. nvt. To catch, grasp, grab, hug, seize and retain, catch, acceptance, admission. *Fig.,* to perceive, understand. Cf. *'a'apo, 'apoa, 'apo'apo. E 'apo 'ia e nā kila,* covered by patents. (PNP *kapo.*) **2.** n. A variety of sweet potato (no data). (For. 5:664–5.) **3.** n. A variety of taro (no data).

'apoa. Pas/imp. of *'apo. Ua 'apoa e ka ua nahua o nā pali,* caught by the pelting rain of the cliffs.

apo.'ā.'ī 'ī.lio. n. Dog collar.

apo.ā.lewa. n. Highest heavens or space. *Rare.*

apo.apo. nvt. Hill, as of sweet potatoes; bunch, as of taro; to hill up plants.

'apo.'apo. 1. Redup. of *'apo;* catching, grasping; attack, fit, heart palpitation, agitation; to have an attack, fit. *Ā lohe a'ela 'o Heloke ke ali'i, 'apo'apo a'ela kona 'ō'ili* (Mat. 2.3), when Herod the king heard, his heart was troubled. (PNP *kapokapo.*) **2.** n. Half-grown stage of the *āhole,* a fish.

'ā.po'e.po'e. vi. To assemble.

'apo.hā. Same as *'ōkuhe,* an *'o'opu,* a fish.

apo hao. n. Iron hoop or band, named for the king's guard under the monarchy.

apo hele. n. Orbit, as of stars and planets.

'ā.poho. nvs. Depression, hollow, hollowed, pitted.

'ā.poho.poho. 1. Redup. of *'āpoho.* **2.** vi. Pounding, slapping, as the sea. Cf. *poho, 'ūpoho.*

'ā.po'i.po'i. vt. To pounce; to crouch in order to conceal (UL 203); to attempt to conceal an article rather than share it.

'apo.kaka. n. Apostate. (Latin *apostata.*)

'apo.kau. Var. of *'apakau.*

'ā.poke. vt. A short piece; cut, broken off; to cut into short pieces.

'apoke.kolo, aposetole. n. Apostle. (Gr. *apostolos.*)

'Apoke.lupo, Apokerupa. n. Apocrypha. (Gr. *apocryphos.*)

'apo.kolo, apotolo. n. Apostle. *Eng.*

apo kula (gula). n. Gold bracelet; formerly a gold ring.

'ā.pole. vs. Smooth. Also *molemole.*

'apo leo. 1. v. To record a voice. *Mīkini 'apo leo,* recorder. **2.** nv. Magical voice snatching (a sorcerer was believed able to snatch a victim's voice so that he could not chant or sing); to snatch a voice thus.

'ā.pole.pole. Redup. of *'āpole.*

apo lima. n. Bracelet, signet. (Kin. 38.18.)

'ā.pona. vs. Embracing, grasping, catching. Cf. *'apo 1.*

'ā.pono. vi. To approve, confirm, justify, ratify, recommend, commend, consent, accept, endorse, adopt; to pass, as a bill. Cf. *pono,* proper, right. *'Āpono 'ole 'ia,* disqualified, not approved or confirmed. **ho'ā.pono.** To approve, accept, justify, find not guilty in a trial; approved, worthy; approbation, sanction, approval. *Palapala ho'āpono,* credentials, letter of recommendation.

'āpono 'ana. n. Approval (sometimes preceded by *ke*). See ex., *ka'a malalo 2.*

'ā.pono ola. n. Guarantee, assurance. *Nani ka mahalo i nā ku'ikahi, mehe 'āpono ola e pa'a ai ke aupuni,* much impressed by the treaties that seem to assure the security of the nation.

'ā.po'o. nvi. To hide, seek shelter; to gad about, a gadder.

'ā.po'o.po'o. nvs. Hollow, cavity; depressed.

apo pā.pale. n. Hatband.

apo pepei.ao. n. Hoop earring.

'apō.pō. loc. n. Tomorrow (often preceded by *kēlā,* that; perhaps related to *pō,* night, since the Hawaiian "day" began at nightfall). Sometimes shortened to *pōpō.* (Gram. 8.6.) *'Apōpō ia lā aku,* day after tomorrow. (PEP *aapoopoo.*)

apo.waena. n. Parentheses. Cf. *kahaapo.*

'apo.wai. 1. n. Type of Hawaiian dog with solid grayish-brown body and nose tip and eyes of the same color, believed to love water and consequently offered as a sacrifice to *mo'o* water spirits. **2.** vs. To be a grayish-brown color, as a horse, perhaps bay.

'apo.wale. n. A native variety of wet-land taro grown chiefly for poi. *Ē! loa'a akula ke kalo, 'o ka 'apowale,* O, you get taro, the *'apowale* [a waste of time, pun on *'apo wale,* to grasp needlessly].

apu. nvt. **1.** To snap or snatch with the teeth; snatching. *Fig.,* to destroy, ravage, ruin. (PNP *apu.*) **2.** Same as *apuapu 2.*

'apu. nv. **1.** Coconut shell cup; to drink (For. 6:471). (PPN *kapu.*) **2.** General name for medical potions, as made of taro, yam, or herbs. *Kalo 'apu,* taro used as medicine. **3.** A taro cultivar, perhaps related to the *'apuwai.* (TC3.)

'ā.pua. 1. Same as *pai 5,* a fish trap. *Puka ma ka 'āpua,* got out of the trap [of one going scot free]. **2.** n. Handle, as of a *laulau* food package; shank knob of a fishhook (also *puapua);* twisted top of a paper sack that may serve as a handle. *Hemo ma ka 'āpua,* to get away through the handle [to escape]. **3.** nvs. Disloyal, disobedient, rebellious; such a person. *'Āpua pale leo,* to disregard orders; one who does so, as a chief or priest.

'ā.pua kā.'e'e. Same as *pai 5,* a fish trap.

'Ā.pua-kea. n. Rain name associated with Ko'olau Poko, O'ahu, said to be named for a beautiful woman, 'Āpua-kea, changed to rain by the goddess Hi'iaka. See song, Elbert and Mahoe 61.

apu.apu. 1. Redup. of *apu 1.* **2.** nvt. File, rasp; to smooth or sharpen with a file. **3.** Beard of a fishhook. (And.)

'apu.'apu. 1. vs. Cup-shaped. (PPN *kapukapu*.) 2. n. Type of agricultural land, as for sweet potatoes, mentioned in 1848 land claims, perhaps a pocket-like area.

apu.apu 'ā.nai makau. n. File or polisher for fishhook.

'apu 'au.huhu. n. Cup containing 'auhuhu plant concoction used for stupefying fish; poison cup.

'ā.pu'e. Same as *'āpu'epu'e*.

'ā.pu'e.pu'e. nvt. Difficult; difficulty; to struggle, strive (preceded by *ke*). *Komo 'āpu'epu'e*, barely able to get in; to enter with difficulty. *'Āpu'epu'e nā kānaka i ka 'ai i ka wā wī*, the people struggled to get food in time of famine. *Ke 'āpu'epu'e o ka loa'a 'ana mai o ka 'ike kūpono i ka 'ōlelo haole*, the difficulties of getting proper knowledge of English.

'apuhi. vt. To deceive, lie, cheat.

apu.hihi. n. A shellfish resembling the *hīhīwai*, found in brackish water.

'ā.puka. 1. nvt. To swindle, cheat, defraud; forgery, embezzlement; fraudulent. *Kālā 'āpuka*, money gained through fraud or embezzlement. *Palapala 'āpuka*, false or forged document. ho.'ā.puka. Caus/sim. 2. vi. To emerge, come into light. *Wai-'āpuka* (place name), water coming through a tunnel. ho.'ā.puka. Caus/sim.

'ā.puka.puka. vs. Pitted. *Rare*.

'apuki. vs. Short. *Rare*.

'apu kō.heo.heo. n. Deadly poison, as given to prisoners.

'ā.puku. Same as *hāpuku*, to collect.

'ā.pulu. vs. Worn out, as a garment; to show wear and tear; rough, dingy. *Hale 'āpulu*, shack.

'ā.pulu.pulu. Redup. of *'āpulu*.

'ā.puni. 1. nvi. Angry or noisy dispute, quarrel, wrangle, brawl; to brawl. 2. vs. Ill-omened, inauspicious.

'apu'u. n. 1. An endemic fern (*Sadleria squarrosa*), 30 to 60 cm high, with short trunk, narrow oblong leaves; related to *'ama'u*. 2. Hill, mound. Cf. *'āpu'upu'u*.

'ā.pu'u.pu'u. 1. vs. Lumpy, bumpy, pimply, rough, hilly, rugged. 2. n. Young stage of *hāpu'u* fish. Also *hāpu'upu'u*.

'apu.wai. n. A variety of taro: its corm is used for poi and table taro, its leaves for *lū'au*. Varieties are white *(kea)* and red *('ula)*.

au. 1. nvi. Period of time, age, epoch, cycle, the passing of time. See *aumoe, au nele. I ke au o Ka-lani*, in the time of Ka-lani. *Ke au hou*, the new era. *O kēia au*, of this time, contemporary, current. *Au pau 'ole*, eternity, endless time. *Ua au wale ka pō*, the night has passed on. *E kala kahiko i au wale*, gone a long time ago, long past. *Na ke au o ka manawa e hō'ike mai*, the passing of time will tell. 2. nvi. Current; to flow, as a current. *Au kanai'i*, strong current; *fig.*, a strong warrior. *Au kō malalo*, undertow. (PPN *'au*.) 3. nvi. Movement, eddy, tide, motion; to move, drift, float, walk, hurry, stir; succession or rates, as of thought, trend. *Ke au nei ka mana'o, pehea 'o Niakala* (song), the thought comes to mind, how fares Niagara. *E au, ā e wiki mai*, hasten, hurry here. ho.'āu. Caus/sim.; to cause to float, as timber. 4. n. Gall, bile (Oihk. 3.4); gall bladder. *'Awa ke au*, bitter bile [rank ingratitude]. *Mālama o kpū ke au*, take care not to break the gall bladder [do not cause bitterness]. (PPN *'ahu*.) 5. n. Weather. See ex., *Ko'olau 1. Wānana i ke au o ka manawa*, forecast of weather. 6. n. Small sweet potatoes of poor quality that grow from the vine. 7. n. Pumice. 8. n. Grain of wood. 9. vt. To weed. 10. vt. To rub, massage, polish. 11. vt. To set, as a net or fish trap. ho.'āu. Same as above; fishermen who set nets in *ku'u* fishing. 12. Same as *heau* (*Exocarpus* spp.) 13. n. *Hedyotis acuminata*, a native shrub (coffee family), with small green flowers, and unpleasant-smelling, ovate or narrower leaves. Cf. *pilo 2*. 14. Also *wau*. pronoun. I. (Gram. 2.1.) *'O au pū*, so do I; me too. (PPN *au*.)

-au. ho.'āu. To dedicate, set apart, as in a housewarming. *Rare*.

āu. poss. Your, yours (singular, *a*-form, zero-class; Gram. 9.6.3). (PPN *ha'au*.)

a'u. 1. n. Swordfish, sailfish, marlin, spearfish (Istiophoridae). See sayings, *la'a 2, 'olo'olo 3*. (PPN *haku*.) 2. pronoun. Me (used after *e* and *me* and fusing with *ia* to form *ia'u*; Gram. 9.6.3). *Hana 'ia e a'u*, done by me. *Noho 'oia me a'u*, he stayed with me. *Nānā mai 'oia ia'u*, he looked at me. (PNP *aku*.) 3. poss. My, mine (*a*-form, zero-class; Gram. 9.6.3). (PPN *ha'aku*.)

'au. 1. vi. To swim, travel by sea. *'Au-i-ke-kai-loa* (personal name), travel in the distant seas. *Ua 'au 'ia nā kai loa*, the distant seas were traveled. hō.'au. To teach to swim, learn to swim; to swim with a drowning person; to douse, as clothes being washed; the man who sets a *ku'u*, drop net. (PPN *kau*.) 2. vi. To jut out into the sea, as a land point; to project. *Aloha Maka-pu'u, 'au i ke kai*, greetings to Maka-pu'u [Point], reaching out into the sea. 3. n. Handle, staff, stem, stalk, shaft; bone of lower arm or leg. See *'au ki, 'au lima, 'au wāwae. 'Au loa*, long bones in arm or leg; long-limbed, long-shanked. *'Au kīpāpali* (For. 6:61), shaft-like cliff slope. (PPN *kau*.) 4. n. Group (followed by a qualifier, as *moku, wa'a*.) Cf. *'aumakua*. (PPN *kau*.)

aua. vi. To look, observe. *Rare*.

'aua. 1. Same as *'ā'aua*; lean, as fish. *Lau 'aua*, wrinkled leaf; *fig.*, experienced, as warrior or strategist. 2. n. Cawing, as of the *'alalā*, crow. 3 (*Cap*.) n. Name recorded for the star Betelgeuse.

'au'a. 1. nvi. Stingy, selfish, to withhold, detain, grudge, refuse to part with; stinginess; sparingly. *Home ho'opa'a 'au'a 'ia*, detention home. *Mai ho'i mai māua i nehinehi, 'o ka 'au'a ho'i o ka makamaka*, we would have returned yesterday, but were detained by friends. *Ua 'au'a ke kahuna*, the sorcerer refuses to part with his knowledge. 2. n. A kind of *'ōpelu* fish said to be larger than others in a school and hence more visible. When net fishermen see an *'au'a* they know a school is present; the *'au'a* then can not be caught [he refuses].

auahi, auwahi. This word is related to *uahi*, smoke. One source says it refers to lowly or humble persons. Malo 109 says it may refer to a distant relationship. (PPN *'ahu + afi*.)

aua.'ina. n. An unknown herb, the bark and leaves of which were used as medicine.

aua.ke'e. vs. Dishonest. See *ke'e 1*.

au.akua. nvs. Ghost-ridden; haunted or unfriendly land. *Lit.*, ghost bile. (Cf. Isa. 13.9.) *'A 'ohe maika'i kānaka o kēia wahi, he auakua*, the people of this place are not good, they are most unkind.

auala.liha. n. A variety of *'o'opu* goby fish found in both brackish and fresh water. Also *kāni'o*.

auala.lo'i. n. Terraced taro patches.

aua.li'i. vs. Royal, chiefly. *Ua noho aloha lāua me ka lani auali'i*, they lived in friendliness with the high chief.

auā.lipo. vs. Overcome by intense emotion, as love, grief.

'au.amo. nvt. Pole or stick used for carrying burdens across the shoulders; yoke, palanquin, burden; to carry on the *'auamo*. *Lit.*, carrying handle. Also *'aumaka* and *māmaka*. See *amo, pipi 'auamo. 'Auamo ki'i*, carrying pole with carved heads near the ends. hō.'au.amo. Caus/sim. (PCP *kauamo*.)

'au.ana, 'auwana. vi. To wander, drift, ramble, go from place to place; to stray morally or mentally. Cf. *hula 'auana. 'Auana ka no'ono'o*, delirium. hō.'auana. To cause to wander, disperse, as a conqueror disperses an enemy.

aua.ne'i. 1. postposed temporal part. Soon, by-and-by, presently, shortly, just. (Gram. 7.5.) 2. postposed dubitative part. Probably, merely, probably not, possibly, doubtful. (Gram. 7.5.) *He lohe mai auane'i i ka makua!* Actually paying attention to [his] parent [implication that he is not]. *'O ka 'ike auane'i iāia, ua lawa ia i ka makemake*, just seeing him, the desire was satisfied. *Pehea auane'i ka pono?* What then is right?

a'ua.ne'i. Var. of *auane'i.*

au 'ā.pa'a.pa'a. n. Passing of much time on a piece of land, as an old family.

au.au. 1. Same as *au 1;* to walk lightly and swiftly. *'O kāne hānau i ke auau pō 'ele'ele,* man born in the age of darkness. **2.** Redup. of *au 3.* **ho'āu.au.** To hasten, hurry, rush, excite to action. **3.** Redup of *au 10.* **4.** Same as *au 11.* **ho'āu.au.** Same as *ho'āu.*

a'u.a'u. n. Small *a'u* fish.

'au.'au. 1. vi. To bathe. Cf. *'au 1, wai 'au'au. 'Au'au kai,* to bathe in the sea. *'Au'au wai,* to bathe in fresh water. *Hale 'au'au,* bathhouse. **hō.'au.'au.** To give a bath. (PPN *kaukau.*) **2.** n. Stick, stem (as of ti plant); spear made of *loulu* palm, with shark teeth on its end; extra ridgepole. **3.** Trap, snare, as for catching birds. (And.)

'au.'aua. Same as *'ā'aua,* coarse. *'Ili 'au'aua lena,* yellow wrinkled skin.

'au.'au.kī. 1. n. Young eel. **2.** A fish said to resemble *weke* (no data).

'au.'au.ko'i. Same as *'auko'i,* a weed.

a'u.a'u papa-'ohe. Same as *a'u-papa-'ohe.* (And.)

'au.'au.waha. Redup. of *'auwaha;* furrowed.

au 'awa. n. Bitter gall. *Fig.,* ingratitude.

aue. Same as *ue 3.*

auē, auwē. interj. and vi. Oh! Oh dear! Oh boy! Alas! Too bad! Goodness! (Much used to express wonder, fear, scorn, pity, affection; see ex., *hu'ahu'a 1,* Gram. 12.) To groan, moan, grieve, bewail. *Auē noho'i ē!* Goodness! Alas! Oh! *Auē kākou!* Alas for us! Woe betide us! *Auē ho'i au!* Woe is me! *Auē! Nānā aku 'oe iā Lei mā!* Say! You should see Lei and the others! *E auē ana i ke aloha keiki,* grieving for love of the child. (PPN *aue(e).*)

auele. Same as *au wale. Rare.*

auē.uē. n. A calling, crying, humming, buzzing.

au.hā. n. **1.** Molting, of a chicken. (For. 5:495.) *Rare.* **2.** Outhouse, as for storing canoes; shed, shelter. *Rare.*

Au-haele. n. Name of a star, companion to Hōkū-'ula and Pai-kauhale. Perhaps the three are Sigma, Antares, and Tau Scorpii.

'au.haka. nvs. Spindle-legged; spindleshanks; an animal with slender legs.

Au-haku. n. Name of a star (no data).

'au.hau. 1. nvt. Tax, assessment, levy, charge, tariff, toll, tribute, price; to levy a tax, pay tribute, tax. *'Auhau kino, 'auhau po'o,* poll tax. *Kū i ka 'auhau,* taxable. *'Auhau helu waiwai,* excise tax. *Hale 'auhau,* building where taxes are collected. *Kou 'auhau,* your tax (that you pay). *Kāu 'auhau,* your tax (that you impose). *Luna 'auhau,* tax collector. *Nā po'e ho'oka'a 'auhau,* taxpayers. *He aha kāu 'auhau no ka pāpale loulu?* What is your price for the *loulu* hat? **2.** n. Femur and humerus bones of the human skeleton. **3.** n. Stems of plants whose bark can be stripped, such as *wauke* and *olonā,* but not *maile. Inā e kua 'ia ka wauke, ā hohole 'ia ka 'auhau, . . .* if the *wauke* is cut and the stems stripped, . . .

'au hau. n. Stalk of a *hau* tree, spear made of *hau* wood. *Ahi 'au hau,* firebrand (of light wood, as *hau*).

'au.hau.hui. Var. of *uhau hui,* a prayer.

'au.hau ma'ule. Misplaced or concealed *no'a* stone in the game of *pūhenehene.* (And.)

'au.hau Pō.'alua. n. Tuesday tax, a term used in 1852, probably an educational tax.

'au.hau.puka. nvi. Beggar; to go from door to door asking for charity.

'au.hea. 1. inter. Where (in questions). (Gram. 8.5.) **2.** idiom. Listen (in commands, common in songs). See ex., *'aumakua 2. 'Auhea 'oukou* (Laie 473)! Hear ye! *'Auhea wale ana 'oe, ē ka pua o ka lokelani,* now pay attention, O blossom of the rose. (PNP *fea.*) **3.** idiom. Sir [formal beginning of a letter].

'au.hea ho'i. idiom. Where indeed (with implication of

neglect or indifference)? Where's the interest? Where's the care? *'Auhea ho'i ka hele mai o lākou e kōkua,* they'll never come and help, they don't care.

'au.he'e. vt. To flee from danger; routed, dispersed, defeated. *'Auhe'e pū'iwa,* to flee in fright, stampede. *E 'auhe'e i ka 'ino,* refrain from evil. **hō.'au.he'e.** To rout, put to flight, flee.

'au.he'e.he'e. Redup. of *'auhe'e.*

au.hele. vi. To go looking from place to place without any definite course, to drift or sail aimlessly, drifting. *Ma ke auhele o ka hewahewa* (Kel. 99), on the drifting path of error.

au.hili. vi. To turn off the course, wander, deviate. *Ua lili ke Akua ia wā no ke auhili 'ia o nā kānaka i ka 'ino* (Kep. 35), God was jealous then because of the turning away of men to wickedness.

'au.hola. Same as *'auhuhu,* a shrub.

au.honua. n. Ancient age, era, epoch. See *mauliauhonua. I ke auhonua hānau o Papa i kēia mau moku,* in the ancient time Papa gave birth to these islands. *I ke auhonua o nā Kaikala,* in the age of the Caesars.

'au.huhu. n. A slender, shrubby legume *(Tephrosia purpurea* syn. *T. piscatoria),* 30 to 60 cm high, with small, compound leaves, small white or purplish flowers, and narrow pods, used for poisoning fish. The plant is known from tropical Asia eastward into Polynesia. (Neal 448–9.) Also *'auhola, hola.* Cf. *pōpō 'auhuhu.*

'Au.huhu-pa'ina. n. Var. name for the month of Makali'i, a time so dry that the *'auhuhu* plant became brittle *(pa'ina).* See *month.*

'au hula.'ana. nvt. To swim around a *hula'ana,* or precipice facing the sea; course or route for swimming here.

au.huli. vt. To overturn, overthrow, upset; to till. **ho'āu.huli.** Caus/sim. *Ka ho'āuhuli 'ana,* revolution, upset.

au.huli.hia. Pas/imp. of *auhuli. Kaua auhulihia,* revolutionary war.

'aui. 1. vi. To turn aside, digress, deviate, pass by, decline, bend down. Cf. *auinalā. Nā 'aui 'ana,* variations, deviations. **hō.'aui.** Caus/sim. *Ke hō'aui maila ka lā,* the sun is beginning to descend to the west. **2.** nvi. To swell and roll, as the sea; to pitch; billow, roller. *'Aui 'ale,* large swell, billow. **3.** nvi. Declension, case; to name declensions or conjugations (term devised by Andrews based on Latin *declinare,* to turn aside); never used extensively and not entered in Hitchcock's 1887 English-Hawaiian Dictionary. **hō.'aui.** To conjugate, decline. *Ka hō'aui 'ana,* declension, conjugation. **4.** nvi. A hula step: the dancer turns to the side and points out one foot once or several times, drawing the foot well back between each pointing; at the same time the body is tipped, with a lowered hand pointing to the outpointing toes, and the other hand raised in the opposite direction; to dance thus. Cf. *ue.*

auī, auwī. interj. Ouch!

'auia. Pas/imp. of *'aui.*

'aui.alo. n. Accusative case. *Lit.,* front case.

'aui.'aui. Redup. of *'aui 1.*

'aui.hea. n. Vocative case. *Lit.,* calling case.

'aui.hele. n. Case denoting separation, as shown by *mai,* from, ablative.

'aui.hui. n. Case denoting association. *Lit.,* joined case.

'aui.ia. n. Agentive case.

'aui.iki. n. Genetive or possessive case.

'aui.kō.ha'i. n. Possessive case. *Lit.,* case belonging to someone else.

'aui.kumu. n. Nominative case.

'aui.moe. n. Locative case.

'auina, auwina. n. Bending, sloping; descent, slope.

'auina.lā. n. Afternoon. *Lit.,* declining sun.

'auina.pō. n. Midnight, late night.

'aui.pa'ewa. n. Dative case.

'aui.pili. n. Possessive case. *'Auipili laulā, o*-form of the possessive. *'Auipili pa'a, a*-form of the possessive.

'aui.pō. Similar to *'auina pō.* (For. 6:420).

auka. vs. Weary, exhausted. *Ua auka au i ka 'u'umi* (Ier. 6.11), I am weary with holding in.

'auka. vs. Out (in games). *Eng. Rare.*

'au.kā. n **1.** Bar, as of soap or gold, nugget; ridge or strip between the flutes of a column, facet, fillet, capstan bar, bar across a roadway; stump. **2.** Long stems, as of some species of mangoes. **3.** Wood woven through sticks in *'ie kala* fish trap. **4.** Stools, feces.

au.kaha. vs. Desolate, dreary, nonproductive.

au.kahi. vs. **1.** Even, smooth, clear. *Fig.*, suave and pleasant in speech and manner. *Aukahi ka pua'a,* a smooth pig [a sacrificial hog with uncracked skin, believed perfect for sacrifice; *fig.*, of perfection]. **2.** United, flowing together. *Ua aukahi mai nā 'ale, ua malino ka Pākīpika* (chant for Ka-lā-kaua), the waves move with one accord, the Pacific is calm.

'au.kai. nvi. To travel or swim by sea; seafaring; sailor, seafarer.

au.kaka. n. Deep coral bed with overlapping ledges where fishes hide. *Rare.*

'Au.kake. n. August. *Eng.*

'au.kā kopa. n. Bar of soap. *Lit.*, bar soap. *Eng.*

au.kana. Short for *au kanai'i* (see *au* 2). *Ke ali'i i makana ai, he koa a he aukana ia,* the chief who gave the gift, a warrior and a strong soldier he.

au.kanaka. nvs. Inhabited place, settlement; inhabited. *Nā wahi aukanaka apau* (Mat. 24.14), all inhabited places.

āu.kauka. n. Inland; fishing grounds, identified by lining up with landmarks ashore.

'Aukeku.lalia, Auseturalia. nvs. Australia; Australian. *Eng.*

'Aukeku.lia, Auseturia. nvs. Austria; Austrian. *Eng.*

Au-kele. Short for *'Au-kele-nui-a-Iku,* a hero.

a'u.kī. n. A fish, perhaps a marlin.

'au kī. n. Stem of a ti plant.

Au.koa'e-ua-mā.lie. n. Name of a stroke in *lua* fighting. *Lit.*, tropic bird hastens, it is calm.

'au.ko'i. 1. n. Coffee senna *(Cassia occidentalis),* a tropical American shrubby legume, each leaf with eight to ten leaflets, and with yellow flowers and narrow, many-seeded pods. Used medicinally for ringworm. (Neal 422.) Also *'au'auko'i, mikipalaoa, pī hohono.* **2.** Same as *'awaiāhiki.*

'au ko'i. n. Axe handle. *Pili 'au ko'i,* a trusted friend or relationship.

'au kolo. nvi. Crawl (swimming); to swim thus.

au kō malalo. n. Undertow.

au.kū. 1. vi. To pitch and toss; to raise, lift. **2.** n. Uphill path. **3.** Shallow. (AP.)

a'u kū. n. Broadbill swordfish *(Xiphias gladius).*

'au kū. vi. To tread water.

'au.kuku. n. Tapa beater.

au.kukū. vs. Crowded, close.

au.kū.kū. nvi. Agitated; agitation.

au.kukui. n. Apprentice canoe maker. *Rare.*

'au.ku'u. 1. n. Black-crowned night heron *(Nycticorax nycticorax hoactli),* a non-migratory land bird, which feeds on small fish and the larvae of insects in water. See sayings, *heron.* (PCP *kautuku.*) **2.** n. Kind of fishhook with a long slender shaft, perhaps named for its resemblance to the heron's neck. **3.** n. A long bamboo pole with two *maile* stalks across the top that were gummed with lime to catch birds. Also *alakō.* **4.** vi. To vomit, retch. **5.** n. Cords held by the fishermen *(ho'āu)* who managed the net in *ku'u* fishing. Also *kāwelewele.*

'au.ku'u kā.hili, 'au.ku'u kō.hili. n. A variety of *'auku'u* heron.

'au.ku'u pili 'āina. n. Name given by Kepelino for a bird resembling the *kioea,* and not an *'auku'u.*

au.lā. vs. Stunted, sun-baked.

'ā.'ula. 1. vs. Reddish, brownish. Cf. *hā'ula.* **2.** n. An edible seaweed, perhaps the same as *limu hā'ula.*

'au.lama. v. To light with a torch.

'au.lani. n. Messenger of a chief. *Rare.*

au.lau. vt. To gather leaves to wrap fish in for cooking, as leaves of *pōhuehue, mānewanewa, laua'e,* ti; to frighten fish into a net with leaves.

'au.lau. n. Leaves strung on lines at ends of seines, as ti leaves.

au.lele. vi. To fly, as a frightened flock of birds.

'au.lena. n. A variety of native banana. (HP 177.)

a'u lepe. n. Sailfish *(Istiophorus orientalis).*

'ā.uli. vs. Dark. *Hānau ke po'o āuli, he uliuli kona* (KL line 509), the dark heads are born, they are dark.

au.lia. Pas/imp. of *au* 2, 3. *Aulia manu,* flight of birds. *Wai aulia,* flowing water.

'au.lia. Pas/imp. of *'au,* to swim.

'au.li'i. 1. vs. Dainty, neat, trim, cute, exquisite, nice, perfect. **hō.'au.li'i.** To make attractive, neat. **2.** n. A small staff. *Hila 'auli'i,* high heels.

au.like. 1. vs. Even, smooth, as timber. **2.** vt. To treat kindly. *He po'e aulike i nā malihini* (Kep. 75), a people who treat visitors kindly. *He ho'okipa a me ke aulike kekahi i kekahi,* hospitable and helpful one to another.

'au like. vi. To swim evenly or abreast.

'au lima. n. 1. Bone of arm below elbow. (PPN *kaulima.*) **2.** Stick held in the hand and rubbed in the fire-plow to produce fire by friction. Cf. *'aunaki.*

au.loli. n. Mildew. Also *kūkaeloli.*

ā.ulu. 1. vi. Rough, raging, as sea or wind; to injure, harm, rage. **2.** vi. To grow. **3.** n. A tall endemic tree *(Pisonia sandwicensis),* with large, oblong, dark-green leaves; small, rounded flower heads, narrow, sticky fruits, and very soft wood. Cf. *kaulu, pāpala kēpau.* **4.** Same as *'ala'a 1, Planchonella* spp. **5.** Same as *lonomoea, Sapindus oahuensis.*

au.mai.ewa. n. Large-mouthed net placed at the wings of the *papa hului* net to receive fish; used in deep water. (Malo 212.)

'au.maka. Same as *'auamo,* carrying pole.

'au.makiki. n. A variety of sweet potato.

'au.makua. 1. nvt. Family or personal gods, deified ancestors who might assume the shape of sharks (all islands except Kaua'i), owls (as at Mānoa, O'ahu and Ka'ū and Puna, Hawai'i), hawks (Hawai'i), *'elepaio, 'iwi,* mudhens, octopuses, eels, mice, rats, dogs, caterpillars, rocks, cowries, clouds, or plants. A symbiotic relationship existed; mortals did not harm or eat *'aumākua* (they fed sharks), and *'aumākua* warned and reprimanded mortals in dreams, visions, and calls. (Beckwith, 1970, pp. 124–43, 559; Nānā 38.) *Fig.*, a trustworthy person. (Probably *lit.*, *'au 4,* group, + *makua,* parent.) See *pulapula 2.* **hō.'au.makua.** To acquire or contact *'aumākua.* **2.** vt. To offer grace to *'aumākua* before eating; to bless in the name of *'aumākua. 'Auhea 'oe, ē ke kanaka o ke akua, eia kā kāua wahi 'ai, ua loa'a maila mai ka pō mai; no laila nāu e 'aumakua mai i ka 'ai a kāua* (prayer), hearken, O man who serves the god, here is food for you [*lit.*, our food], received from the night, so bless our food in the name of the *'aumakua.* **3.** vt. To ask someone to hula; the request was not refused without giving the caller a lei or flower. *'Aumakua iā Kamuela,* Samuel must dance!

'au.mākua. Plural of *'aumakua.*

'ā.'ume.'ume. nvt. Opposition, struggle, contention, strife; to struggle, oppose. Also *'ā'u'ume. Ola 'ā'ume'ume,* struggle between life and death.

au.miha. nvi. To float off in the air, as miasma; evil spirits thought to attend graves.

au.mihi. vt. To grieve, regret, be sorry. Cf. *mihi.*

au.miki. 1. n. Outgoing current. **2.** n. Fresh water mixed with *noni* juice, drunk after kava. **3.** Same as *miki 2;* to sip. *Aumiki aku i ka 'apu 'awa,* sipping in the kava bowl.

au.moa. vi. To care for; protected. Cf. *moamoa 1. 'O ka 'ape aumoa ka hiwa uli* (KL line 379), the protected *'ape,* the black sacredness.

'au.moana. 1. nvi. To travel on the open sea; sailor. **2.** n. Name of laws enacted by Queen Ka-'ahu-manu, so called in commemoration of her attempt to commit suicide by swimming out to sea. She was saved by a child who swam after her and refused to leave her. She returned to shore rather than cause his death. **3.** n. Nautilus. Usually called *'au-wa'a-lā-lua, moamoa, moamoa wa'a.*

au.moe. n. Late at night, as about midnight. *Lit.,* time to sleep. **hō.'au.moe.** To pass the night.

'au moku. n. Fleet of ships.

'ā.una. n. Large group, flock. *He kohu 'āuna manu o ke kula,* like flocks of birds of the plains. *'Āuna kumu kula,* school faculty. **ho'ā.una.** To flock, collect (intransitive).

'au.naki. n. **1.** Stick rubbed in obtaining fire by friction. Cf. *'au lima.* (PPN *kaunatu,* PCP *kaunati.*) **2.** Also *'aunake, 'auneki.* Ounce. *Eng.*

'ā.una.una. n. A common gastropod *(Nassa serta),* a shellfish.

au nele. n. Hard times, depression, recession.

au.olo. n. Shelter or shed, as for canoes; outhouse, temporary house; tabernacle. *Ke ke'ena auolo mua o ka hale ali'i,* the front reception hall of the palace.

au.paka. n. **1.** Some representatives of an endemic genus *(Isodendrion),* members of the violet family. They are small shrubs bearing greenish-white or reddish flowers, which have equal petals and none spurred. Cf. *wahine noho kula.* **2.** Ni'ihau name for *naupaka kahakai.*

'au.papa. nvs. Everything, as of things taken or lost; destitute. *He mea lawe 'aupapa ke kaua,* the war deprives one of everything. *He 'ohina 'aupapa maoli nō kāna,* he gathered up absolutely everything.

a'u papa.'ohe. n. A variety of *a'u* fish.

au.po'i.pū. n. According to Kepelino and Kamakau, a relationship extending back 24 generations. (For. 6:268.)

au.pula. n. Fishing with a *pula* stick or *pūlale* to drive fish into a net.

au.puni. nvs. Government, kingdom, dominion, nation, people under a ruler; national. *Aupuni 'emepela,* empire. *Aupuni koloniala,* colonial government. *Aupuni hui,* union of nations, confederation. *Nā 'Aupuni Hui 'Ia,* United Nations, League of Nations. *Aupuni kāko'o,* ally. *'Aupuni maka'āinana,* commonwealth. *Aupuni a ka lehulehu,* democracy. *Aupuni kūikawā,* provisional government. *Aupuni mō'ī,* monarchy. *Aupuni pelekikena,* republic. *Aupuni pekelala,* federal government. *Luna aupuni,* government official. *Hana o ke aupuni,* official or government business *Nā lā o kona noho aupuni 'ana,* the days of his reign.

au.pū.pū. n. **1.** Same as *makaloa 2,* a shellfish. **2.** Same as *mo'opuna-a-ka-līpoa,* a common seaweed.

'au uma.uma. nvi. Breast stroke (swimming); to swim thus.

'a.'u'ume. Same as *'ā'ume'ume* (For. 5:553).

'au wa'a. n. Canoe fleet.

au-wa'a-lā-lua. n. Paper nautilus *(Argonauta argo).* *Lit.,* fleet of canoes with two sails. See *'aumoana 3.*

'au.wae. **1.** nvs. Chin. *Fig.,* indifferent, scornful. Cf. *papa 'auwae.* *'Auwae o'o,* matured chin [unsocial, unfriendly]. *'Elemakule 'auwae lenalena,* old man with yellowed chin [of the very old]. **hō.'au.wae.** To show no interest; scornful, disrespectful of taboo (Kep. 139). (PPN *kauwa'e* 'leg', PNP *kauwa'e* 'jaw'.) **2.** n. Curved notch cut on the outer side of a post below the base of a tenon, also called *ma'i wahine* (For. 5:643). **3.** n. Portion of the point of a pearl-shell lure which overhangs the shank.

au.waea. vs. Distant, remote, deep. *Pō nui auwaea* (Kep. 9), the remote great darkness [age of the mythical beginning of the earth].

'au.wae.'āina. nv. Tribute of the best selected *(wae)* hogs or fruits of the land to the landlord; to inspect land. *E hele ana i ka 'auwae'āina o lākou nei,* going to look over their land.

'Au.wae-lewa. See *Ka-'auwae-lewa.*

'au.wae.pa'a. vi. Firmly opposed, set against. *Lit.,* firm chin. *He mea 'auwaepa'a 'ia ihola ia e 'oukou, 'o ke*

ki'i ho'i i ke kāne, you all were dead set against my sending for the man.

'au.wae.pahā.ha. n. Mumps. *Lit.,* puffed chin.

'au.wae.pili. n. Close relative. (Malo 199, Emerson note.)

'au.wae.pu'u. **1.** nvs. Indifference to work, discouraged. *Lit.,* chin lump. **hō.'au.wae.pu'u.** To thrust out the chin and twist the lips to the side, or stick the tongue under the lower lip to form a lump (a gesture of refusal or contempt); to sulk, act indifferent or hostile. **2.** vi. To squat.

'au.waha. **1.** nvi. Ditch, furrow, trench, gutter, canal, channel; groove, as in a tapa beater; to notch, as tops of house posts (For. 5:643). *Hā'ule nō i kāna 'auwaha i 'eli ai,* fallen in the ditch he himself dug [caught in his own trap]. **hō.'au.waha.** To make a ditch, plow a furrow; to cut a wedge or fork. **2.** Outhouse, as for storing canoes.

-'au.waha.waha. hō.'au.waha.waha. Redup. of *hō-'auwaha.*

auwahi. Var. spelling of *auahi.*

'au.wai. n. Ditch, canal. *'Auwai lawe mea 'ino,* sewer; *lit.,* ditch carrying rotten things. (PPN *kau + wai.*)

'au.wai.hiki. Same as *'awaiāhiki.*

'au.wai pa'a. n. Conduit, solid ditch.

'au.wai papa. n. Flume.

au.wala.kī. vs. **1.** Entangled, snarled, as fishline. **2.** Destitute, especially of the rich who lose everything.

au wale. See *au 1.*

'au.wana. Var. spelling of *'auana,* to wander.

'au wā.wae. n. Leg bone.

auwe. interj., vi. Same as *ue 3.*

auwē. Var. spelling of *auē.*

'auwē.'āina. Var. of *'auwae'āina.*

au.wehe.wehe.kika. n. Name recorded for *kauā,* outcasts.

auwē.uwē. n. Var. spelling of *auēuē.*

auwī. interj. Var. spelling of *auī.*

'au.wina. Var. spelling of *'auina.*

'au.wini.wini. n. Sharp end of a leaf; term of raillery applied to men, referring to the male member. Cf. *wini 1,* sharp.

awa. n. **1.** Port, harbor, cove; channel or passage, as through a reef. *Awa lua,* double channel [dual natured]. *Awa pae,* landing place. *Ke awa lau o Pu'uloa,* the many channels [or lochs] of Pearl Harbor. (PPN *awa*). **2.** Milkfish *(Chanos chanos).* Stages of growth are *pua awa (puawa),* young; *awa 'aua,* medium size; *awa,* commercial size; *awa kalamoho,* very large. (PPN *'awa*).

ā.wā. vi. Noisy, loud; to talk loudly.

'awa. **1.** n. The kava *(Piper methysticum),* a shrub 1.2 to 3.5 m tall with green jointed stems and heart-shaped leaves, native to Pacific islands, the root being the source of a narcotic drink of the same name used in ceremonies (Neal 291), prepared formerly by chewing, later by pounding. The comminuted particles were mixed with water and strained. When drunk to excess it caused drowsiness and, rarely, scaliness of the skin and bloodshot eyes. Kava was also used medicinally. *Kapu 'awa* (FS 57), to perform ceremony of offering kava to the gods [an unusual reference, as kava was not taken ceremonially, as in Samoa]. *'Awa kau lā'au,* the tree-resting kava, growing in tree crotches and famous in poetry concerning Puna, Hawai'i. Many varieties of kava are listed below. (PPN *kawa*). **2.** vs. Sour, bitter, poisonous. *'Awa ka 'upena,* the net is sour [of a net into which fish will not enter]. *'Awa ke au,* how bitter the gall [a sour disposition]. **hō.'awa.** To make bitter, to make a concoction of leaves or bark to extract dye colors. (PPN *kakawa,* PCP *kawa*.) **3.** n. Cold mountain rain, fog, mist; to rain or mist. *Fig.,* tragic misfortune or ordeal; in PH this word is preceded by *ke* and may refer to volcanic eruption: *Uwē au, puni 'ā i ke 'awa* (PH 193), I weep, surrounded by lava in the downpour. *'O ka uahi noe lehua, 'o ke 'awa nui i ka mauna* (PH 205), the *lehua* mist smoke, the great outburst on the mountain. **4.** n. A premature infant, believed caused by a "sour" condition of the mother. **5.** n. A kind of bitter seaweed.

'ā.wa'a. nvt. Long, narrow excavation, trench, ditch, gully; to dig a ditch or furrow.

'ā.wa'a.hia. Pas/imp. of *'āwa'a. Papaioa 'āwa'ahia ka lani* (chant), the high chief is a furrowed reef.

'awa-a-Kāne. Same as *'awa li'i,* a variety of kava. It is said that the god Kāne brought the first *'awa* to Hawai'i.

'awa ā.kea. n. A variety of kava with long, light-green internodes and reddish nodes. Also *'awa maha kea, 'awa mākea.*

'awa 'apu. n. A variety of kava.

awa 'aua. n. A herring-like fish, sometimes called tenpounder or tarpon *(Elops hawaiensis);* according to some, a medium-sized *awa* fish.

awaawa. Var. spelling of *awāwa.*

'awa.'awa. 1. Redup. of *'awa 2;* bitter, sour, tart, acid, fermented, brackish; bitterness, sourness. *Fig.,* unpleasant, disagreeable, harsh, bad-tempered; unpleasant or tragic experience, anguish. (Ioba 7.11.) *Iā Makali'i lau 'awa'awa o Puna* (FS 217), during the Makali'i season, innumerable disasters in Puna. **hō.'awa.awa.** To embitter, make bitter or sour; bitter tasting. (PPN *kawakawa.*) **2.** Redup. of *'awa 3. Pō Puna i ka ua a ka 'awa'awa* (FS 225), Puna is darkened in the bitterly cold rain.

'ā.wa'a.wa'a. vs. **1.** Uneven, furrowed, craggy. **2.** Muscular.

'awa.'awa.hia. Pas/imp. of *'awa'awa 1, 2.* (PNP *kawakawasia.*)

'awa.'awa.hua. vs. Bitter, sour. *Fig.,* crabbed in nature, bitter, ungrateful.

'awa.'awa.ina. n. Bitterness.

'ā.waha. nvi. To speak in a rude, harsh manner; rudeness. *Pule 'āwaha,* a prayer to bring misfortune.

'awa.hia. Pas/imp. of *'awa 2, 3. 'Awahia noho'i ka 'ōlelo!* What bitter words! (PPN *kawasia.*)

'awa hiwa. n. A variety of kava with long internodes.

'awa.hua. Similar to *'awa'awahua;* ingratitude, meanness; to be mean, ungrateful, embittered, resentful. See *make 'awahua iho. Mana'o 'awahua o lākou* (Nak. 110), their bitter thoughts.

'ā.wai. 1. n. Rostrum, pulpit, speaker's platform, dais, scaffold. *Ka 'āwai lā'au* (Neh. 8.4), a pulpit of wood. **2.** n. Bundle, bunch, cluster, as of tied objects. **3.** See *'awaiāhiki.*

'awai.ā.hiki. nvi. Swelling in the groin, bubo; to have such a swelling. Also *'auko'i, 'auwaihiki, 'āwai, 'ēwai, haha'i.*

awai.ā.ulu. vt. To bind securely, fasten, as of the marriage tie. *Ua awaiāulu 'ia nā 'ōpio,* the young people were united in one. *Awaiāulu 'ia ke aloha me ku'u lei pikake,* bound securely is my love for my *pikake* lei [my child].

awai.kū. n. Good spirits, as the messengers of Kāne, who guarded people from evil ghosts and managed the rain, winds, and weather. (Malo 104.)

'awa-i-kū. n. Kava root dug ceremonially by a priest and held up *(kū)* towards heaven while chanting a prayer of consecration and eulogy, after which the root was termed *'awa-i-lani.*

awa kala.moho. n. A large *awa,* milkfish.

'awa Kana.loa. n. Same as *makou 1,* all kinds of buttercups.

awa.kea. nvi. Noon, midday; to be at noon, to become noon. *E awīwī ke awakea maila kākou,* hurry, we are almost at noon. (PCP *awatea.*)

'awa ke'o.ke'o. Probably same as *'awa papa kea.* (HP 202.)

'awa kua 'ea. Same as *'awa nēnē,* a spotted variety of kava.

'awa-kū-ma-kua. n. A variety of kava with green internodes of medium length.

awa kū moku. n. Ship harbor or anchorage, port.

'awa.kupoi. n. Avoirdupois. *Eng.*

'ā.wala. vt. **1.** To throw a knife or stock with a back flip; to throw back the head so as to grab dangling food with an open mouth. Cf. *wala,* to tilt. *'O ka 'āwala 'ana me nā miki poi,* throwing back the head to grab dabs of poi. **2.** To pull back steadily, as a line. *Fig.,* to throw oneself into work.

awa lau. See *awa 1.*

'awa lau. n. A young kava plant (root, stem, and leaves) used as an offering to the gods.

'awa-lau-a-Kāne. Same as *'ala'ala wai nui 1,* a succulent related to kava.

'ā wale. vi. To burn for no particular reason; susceptible to combustion; spontaneous combustion; overcooked. *E 'ā wale loa auane'i ho'i ka i'a ā 'ono 'ole ka 'ai 'ana,* the fish may be cooked too much and not delicious to eat.

'awa.li'i. n. Type of hard stone from which adzes were made.

'awa li'i. Same as *'awa-a-Kāne,* a variety of kava.

awa.loa. n. Place where bones of chiefs were hidden, as in a cave. *Lit.,* eternal harbor.

'awalu. num. Eight (usually in counting in a series).

'awa maha kea. n. Name for *'awa ākea, 'awa mākea* at Ka'ū, Hawai'i.

'awa mā.kea. n. A variety of kava.

'awa mamaka. n. A variety of kava with short internodes and light-green stalk, reported at Wai-niha, Kaua'i. (HP 202.)

'awa mā.nie.nie. n. A variety of kava with smooth, white stalk.

'awa mō.'ī. n. A variety of kava with short, dark-green internodes and whitish nodes, called *'awa papa mō'ī* at Ka'ū, Hawai'i.

'awa moki.hana. n. A variety of kava with short yellowish-green internodes and hairlike roots, named for the *mokihana* plant because of its fragrance, and yielding a strong brew; famous on Kaua'i. (HP 202.)

'awa nē.nē. n. A variety of kava with long, spotted internodes. Also *'awa kua 'ea.*

'awa papa. n. A variety of kava with short internodes and spotted stalk. This name may be qualified by the terms *'ele'ele, mō'ī,* and *kea* (or *ke'oke'o*), the last being the commonest variety, and whitish in general appearance.

'awa.puhi. n. **1.** Wild ginger *(Zingiber zerumbet),* a forest herb with narrow leaves arranged along a stalk 30 to 60 cm high, bearing on a separate stalk small yellowish flowers in an oblong head, and having aromatic underground stems; a native of India. (Neal 257.) The root was used to scent and dye tapa. Also *'awapuhi kuahiwi, 'ōpuhi.* Several varieties are listed below. *'Awapuhi lau pala wale,* ginger leaves yellow quickly [of things that pass too soon]. (PNP *kawapu(s)i.*) **2.** A variety of sweet potato. **3.** A type of taro (no data). (For. 5.683.)

'awa.puhi 'ai. Same as *'awapuhi Pākē. Lit.,* edible ginger.

'awa.puhi-a-Kana.loa. n. *Liparis hawaiensis,* a small, endemic orchid with two large ovate leaves and small flowers. (Neal 273, 274.)

'awa.puhi kā.hili. Same as *kāhili 4.*

'awa.puhi ke'o.ke'o. n. The white ginger *(Hedychium coronarium),* a large herb from India, both wild and cultivated in Hawai'i. White fragrant flowers, popular for leis and perfume, are borne in heads at tips of leafy stems. (Neal 252–3.)

'awa.puhi ko'o.ko'o. n. Torch ginger *(Phaeomeria speciosa),* a large herb, from the East Indies, grown in Hawai'i for its ornamental pink or red cone-shaped flower heads. These are borne on long stems separate from the longer leafy stems. (Neal 258–9.) *Lit.,* walking-stick ginger.

'awa.puhi kua.hiwi. See *'awapuhi.*

'awa.puhi luhe.luhe. n. The shell ginger *(Catimbium speciosum),* a large ornamental herb from East Indies.

won't hurt the Kaua'i lad. *E 'eha ana 'oia ia'u,* I will hurt him. *'Eha o ke kua,* backache. *Nāna wale nō ka 'eha, ā koe ke kaikua'ana huhū* (For. 4:37), only he inflicted pain, until [only] the angry older brother was left. **hō.'eha.** To inflict pain or punishment, to hurt, oppress.

hā. num. Four; four times. See ex., *hā 1.*

ha.'eha. Redup. of *'eha;* great pain, agony, tribulation, many small pains; painful. *'Eha'eha ka na'au,* feelings are hurt. **hō.'eha'eha.** Redup. of *hō'eha;* to torment, distress. *Hō'eha'eha na'au,* heart-breaking, tragic.

haha. vi. To breathe hard, pant. Cf. *hā,* breath.

eha.kō. n. The Chinese lace-necked, or ring-necked dove *(Streptopelia chinensis),* an early introduction to Hawai'i, said to be named for its call *'eha kō,* prolonged pain.

'eha wale. vs. Easily hurt, sensitive, having feelings easily hurt; to hurt for no reason.

ē.hē. interj. Syllables repeated in chants at ends of verses, affording pleasure by repetition or sameness of sound harmonizing with repetition of sameness of drum beat; similar in function to English tra-la-la but different in mood, tending to be more serious. Cf. *ēhā. Eia nō 'o Kāwika, ēhē, ka heke a'o nā pua, ēhē* (chant for Ka-lā-kaua), here is David, ah, ah, the greatest of descendants, ah, ah.

'ehē. nvi. A hard, dry cough; to cough. *He kunu 'ehē,* a racking cough.

'ehē.'ehē. Redup. of *'ehē.*

ehehe. interj. Song refrain. (Elbert and Mahoe 67.)

ehe.hene. 1. nvi. To laugh merrily, giggle in glee; laughter. *Ehehene kō 'aka i ka le'ale'a,* your laughter is merry because of joy. 2. interj. Syllables repeated for musical effect at end of verses, similar to *ēhē.*

'ehe.hene. Var. of *ehehene 2.*

'ehe.heu. n. Wings. Cf. *'ēheu.*

ehe.ho'o.pi'i. n. Carved parallel or undulating lines on a tapa beater and on tapa. (AP.)

'ē.heu. 1. nvi. Wing, as of bird, kite, or airplane; winged, soaring on wings; to fly, take wings (Kel. 140). Also *'ēkeu, pēkeu.* Cf. *'eheheu, 'ekekeu, pekekeu. Ka uhi 'ana mai o nā 'eheu o ka pō,* the covering of the wings of night [nightfall]. **ho'ē.heu.** To flap the wings; to lift up or stretch the wings; to undulate the arms in a hula imitating a bird in flight; to flap the arms, shrug the shoulders; to pull up shoulders proudly, hence to be proud. (PCP *ke(e)(f,s)eu.*) 2. n. Rim of a hat. 3. n. Pectoral fin, as of a shark. *Rare.* 4. n. Flipper, as of turtle. *Rare.* 5. *(Cap.)* See *Ka-'ēheu.*

ehe.'ula. n. Name recorded for adult stage of *hāpu'u* fish.

'ehia. num. inter. How many, how much, what price; also used with the meaning of no matter how many or much, so very much or many, just a few. *'Ehia ou pāpale?* How many hats have you? *'Ehia o kou pāpale?* How much [money did you pay] for your [own] hat? *'Ehia o kāu pāpale?* How much [money] for your hat? *Hola 'ehia?* What time is it? *'Ehia ka luhi, he mea 'ole ia iāia,* however tired, it doesn't matter to him. *'Ehia nō lā, pau kēlā hana nui,* in just a few days that big project was finished. *'Ehia nō lū 'ana, pau ke kālā,* just a few reckless spendings, the money was gone. *'Ehia ua mea aloha, 'o wau!* Woe is me! *'Ehia mea aloha i ke keiki* (Nak. 104), so much pity for the child. (Gram. 10.4; PNP *efia.*)

'ehiku. num. Seven; seven times.

'ehipa. vs. Somewhat crooked, warped; not in sound mind. *Rare.* (Similar to but perhaps less strong than *hipa* and *hepa.*)

'eho. 1. n. Stone pile (FS 107), especially as used to mark land boundaries; stone image; heap of stones under water (at times fishermen block one end with a net and drive the fish in from the other end), also *umu, imu;* pillar (Kin. 35.20); red-hot stones put inside dressed animals in cooking (also *pōhaku 'eho*). *Lono-ka-'eho* (FS 209), Lono-the-stone [name of the god with eight stone foreheads, vanquished by Kama-pua'a]. (PEP *ke(f,s)o.*) 2. n. Swelling or ulcerous sore, as caused by friction under the arm, tumor. See *kua'eho.*

'eho.'eho. Redup. of *'eho,* stone pile. (And.)

E-ho'i-ka-u'i-o-Mānoa-ua-ahiahi. n. Name of a *lua* stroke. *Lit.,* let the hero of Mānoa return, [it's] evening. (*E-* is sometimes omitted.)

ehu. 1. Same as *'ehu 1-4.* See *kēhu.* (PPN *efu,* dust.) 2. Same as *ehuehu 2,* thriving. (PPN *efu.*) **ho'o.ehu.** Caus/sim. 3. n. Water or water mixed with fragrant herbs used in sprinkling or gently rubbing a patient to revive him from fainting. 4. Var. name for *'olapa 2, Cheirodendron* trees.

-ēhu. ho'ē.hu. To drive or shoo away; to stir, as a fire. Cf. *ehuehu 1.*

'ehu. 1. n. Spray, foam, mist. (Many older people say *ehu* for *'ehu 1-4,* which is probably the older form; note lack of glottal stops in such forms as *ehuehu, 'ehuehu, kaiehu, kēhu, kuehu, luehu, puehu.*) See ex., *moi 1. Ka 'ehu kēhau* (Kel. 48), the dew spray. *'Ehu moi,* foam of sea where *moi* fish are found. *I ka 'ehu nō o ka lā'au,* in the spray of the war club [of a swift or terrible blow]. *Kū ka 'ehu,* to send spray flying [to lose one's temper]. *Na ke kea ka 'ai, kū ka 'ehu o nā wa'a li'ili'i i ke keiki o Kuai-he-lani* (For. 4:57), the white [pebble] wins, the child of Kuai-he-lani stirs the spray of small canoes [an old *kōnane* game chant]. 2. nvs. Dust; dusty. *Kū ka 'ehu,* the dust rises. *He ala 'ehu,* a dusty path [this might also be interpreted as a faint path: see *'ehu 4*]. (PPN *efu.*) 3. n. Pollen. 4. nvs. Faint, difficult to see; wisp. *Wāwae 'ehu,* faint footprint. *He 'ehu wāwae no ka lani,* a trace of the high chief's steps [rain, rainbow]. 5. nvs. Reddish tinge in hair, of Polynesians and not of Caucasians; one with *'ehu* hair; reddish-brown complexion said to be characteristic of some *'ehu* people; ruddy. (This *'ehu* is invariably pronounced with an initial glottal stop.) Cf. *'e'ehu, 'ehu-'ehu. He 'ehu, he nani kona mau maka* (I Sam. 16.12), ruddy and of a beautiful countenance. (PPN *kefu.*)

'ehu ahi.ahi. n. The dust of evening. *Fig.,* twilight, old age.

'ehu.'awa. Same as *'ahu'awa (Cyperus javanicus).*

ehu.ehu. 1. nvs. Animation varying from fury and storm to power and majesty; violent, furious, powerful, animated; violence, fury, anger, majesty, animation. *Waiho kāhela i ka la'i ā ahiahi ehuehu mai,* lying stretched out in the calm until at evening full of animation. *Ā ka la'i a 'Ehu lā, ehuehu 'oe ē ka lani lā* (song for Ka-lā-kaua), and the calm of 'Ehu, you, o chief, appeared with majesty. *Kū ana 'o Mauna Loa, kuahiwi 'alo ehuehu* (song), stands Mauna Loa, hill resisting storms. 2. vs. Healthy, vigorous. Less used than *ahuahu.* 3. n. A kind of rock, used for adzes. (Malo 19.)

'ehu.ehu. Redup. of *'ehu 1-4* (this form was perhaps once *ehuehu* and is sometimes pronounced thus still). *Ku'u hoa i ka 'ehuehu a ka noe,* my companion in the spray of mist. *Ke 'ehuehu nei nā 'ale,* the billows rise in waves [of flaring temper]. *'Ehuehu kai, noho ka moi,* where the sea foams, the *moi* fish lives. (PPN *kefukefu.*)

'ehu.'ehu. Redup. of *'ehu 5. 'Ehu'ehu nā lihilihi,* reddened eyelash.

'ehu hī.nano. n. *Hīnano*-blossom pollen.

'Ehu-kai. n. Name of a wind of Hālawa, Moloka'i. (For. 5:103.)

'ehu kai. n. Sea spray, foam.

'ehu kaka.hiaka. n. The dust of morning. *Fig.,* dawn, youth, a shower that clears quickly.

'ehu kumu uli. n. Hair black at the roots that shades out to reddish at the tips, said to be characteristic of some *'ehu* people.

'ehu lepo. nvs. Dust; dusty.

'ehu pua. n. Flower pollen.

'ehu wai. n. Spray from water.

ei. 1. Var. of *eia,* especially before words beginning with

Clusters of irregularly bell-shaped flowers that are white and marked with red and yellow bend downward from the top of leafy, arching stems, which are 1.5 to 3.5 m high. *Lit.,* drooping ginger. (Neal 259–60.)

'awa.puhi mele.mele. n. The yellow ginger *(Hedychium flavescens),* similar to *'awapuhi ke'oke'o* and similarly used, but the flowers are yellow. (Neal 252.)

'awa.puhi Pā.kē. n. Ginger *(Zingiber officinale),* yielding a valuable commercial root spice. The plant looks much like *'awapuhi kuahiwi* and probably comes from southeast Asia. (Neal 257–8.) *Lit.,* Chinese ginger. Also *'awapuhi 'ai.*

'awa.puhi 'ula.'ula. n. The red ginger *(Alpinia purpurata),* an ornamental plant having a long flower spike with many red bracts. It is a native of some islands of the western Pacific. (Neal 260.)

awāwa. n. Valley, gulch, ravine. Cf. *kuawa.* **ho.'ā.wāwa.** To make a groove, furrow.

'awa-wai-a-ka-manu. n. A variety of kava, an offshoot of *'awa hiwa,* with joints green on one side and dark on the other. (HP 202.) *Lit.,* watery kava of the bird.

awe. 1. nvs. Strand, thread; thin, soft. (Probably PPN, PCP *awe.*) 2. n. Wake of a ship. (Note both *awe* and *'awe* in Hawaiian, *awe* and *kawe* in PCP.)

'awe 1. nvt. Pack, knapsack carried on the back; to carry on the back. Cf. *'auamo, hā'awe.* **hō.'āwe.** To carry on the back; a burden so carried. (PPN *kawe.*) 2. n. Tentacle. Cf. *'awe puhi, 'awe ule.* (PPN *kawe.*)

'awea. Pas/imp. of *'awe 1.*

awe.awe. 1. vs. Tenacious, sticky, threadlike, adhesive; glueyness, threads. Cf. *aweawe poi. Ke aweawe 'ōnohi i ke kula* (chant), the sun's rays on the plain. **hō.'awe.awe.** Caus/sim. 2. Wake, as of a ship.

'awe.'awe. Redup. of *'awe 1;* pack knapsack; straps for a bundle; strips, as of *wauke;* runners, as on a vine; tentacles. (PPN *kawekawe.*)

'ā.we'a.we'a. 1. nvs. Faint trace, spot, glimpse; faint, dim; streaked, faded. *'Āwe'awe'a koko ali'i* (Kep. 127), trace of royal blood. *'Āwe'awe'a lono,* dim recollection. *'Ike 'āwe'awe'a,* to see fleetingly, to know but have slight knowledge; faint glimpsing, slight knowledge. *Ua 'ike 'āwe'awe'a a'e nei au i ua manu nei,* I caught but a fleeting glimpse of this bird. **ho.'ā.we'a.we'a.** Caus/sim. 2. n. A kind of seaweed.

'ā.we'a.we'a koko. n. Traces of blood, as in vomit.

awe.awe poi. n. Drip of poi; an insult to the chiefs of Hawai'i, playing on the name of their chiefs, Keawe, with implication that poi is excreted in a sticky chain.

'aweka. vt. To hide rather than share wealth (perhaps related to *weka,* squid ink).

'ā.wela. 1. n. Young stage of the *hou* fish, Christmas wrasse *(Thalassoma fuscum).* 2. vs. Heated, hot. 3. n. A flowerless variety of sugar cane, named for the fish; it is green and yellow striped, becoming flushed with rose in the sun; the internodes are barrel-shaped and the leaves variegated. (HP 221, 224.) Also *pua'ole.*

'ā.wela mele.mele. n. A variety of sugar cane, a bronze-yellow mutant of *'āwela.* Also *ule'ohi'u, uluhui.* (HP 221.)

'ā.wela.wela. Redup. of *'āwela 2.*

'ā.wele. 1. Same as *hāwele,* to tie. 2. Goal, mark, line, goal post. (AP.)

'awe.lika, averiga. nvs. Average, pro rata. *Eng.*

'ā.welu. nvs. Ragged, worn-out, torn; worn-out garment. *'Āwelu moena,* ragged mat.

'ā.welu.welu. Redup. of *'āwelu.*

'ā.weo.weo. n. 1. Various Hawaiian species of *Priacanthus,* red fishes, sometimes called bigeye. Young are called *'alalauā* and *'alauwā.* 2. A variety of sugar cane named for the fish. 3. Same as *'āheahea (Chenopodium oahuense).* 4. A seaweed.

'awe puhi. n. Eel tentacle, but referring to the octopus, a euphemism for *'aweule.*

'ā.weu, 'ā.weu.weu. n. A native variety of taro, often growing wild; good for poi, but too acrid for table taro; the corms are shaggy and fibrous outside, the flesh white with yellow fibers. Also *mā'auea.*

'awe.ule. n. Lone octopus tentacle, said to wave in order to entice and ensnare a victim. *Lit.,* penis tentacle.

'ā.weu.weu. Same as *'āweu.*

'awī.'awī. Same as *'uwī'uwī,* an herb.

'ā.wiha. Same as *'āwe'awe'a.*

'ā.wiha.wiha. Redup. of *'āwiha.*

'ā.wihi. vi. To wink, ogle. See saying, *lihilihi 2. Kō 'oukou po'e 'āwihi ho'owalewale* (Ier. 27.9), your deceiving enchanters.

'ā.wihi.wihi. Redup. of *'āwihi.*

'ā.wiki. vi. To hurry, be quick, swift. *E 'āwiki mai 'oe!* Hurry up!

'ā.wiki.wiki. 1. Redup. of *'āwiki.* 2. n. A vine *(Canavalia* spp.), native to Hawai'i, related to the *maunaloa (C. cathartica),* but with narrower pods; used for small, temporary fish traps. Also *puakauhi.* 3. Same as *kō'ele'ele,* a seaweed.

'ā.wili. 1. vt. To mix, interweave, entwine; mixed, agitated. Cf. *ko'i 'āwili. Koko 'āwili,* mixed blood. (PCP *kaawili.*) 2. n. Alligation (an old arithmetic term). *'Āwili kaulua,* alligation alternate.

'ā.wili.wili. Redup. of *'āwili 1.*

'ā.wini. vs. Sharp, bold, forward. Cf. *kīwini, wini.*

'ā.wiwi. n. A small native herb *(Centaurium sebaeoides,* syn. *Erythraea sebaeoides),* with white or pale pink flowers, in the gentian family. (Neal 684.)

'ā.wī.wī. vi. To hurry; speedy, swift, quick, fast.

B

All loan words from English sometimes spelled with initial *b-* are entered under *p-*. For example: *Baibala,* see *Paipala,* Bible; *balota,* see *pālota,* ballot; *bele,* see *pele,* bell; *bila,* see *pila,* bill; *bipi,* see *pipi,* beef; *buke,* see *puke,* book.

D

All loan words from English sometimes spelled with initial *d-* are entered under *k-*. For example: *dala,* see *kālā,* dollar; *dia,* see *kia,* deer; *diabolo,* see *kiapolo,* devil.

E

Nouns beginning with e- *are preceded by the article* ke, *and are often pronounced with fusion of the two* e's *into a single long vowel. Nouns beginning with* ‘e- *are preceded by the article* ka. *In some words there is today variation of* ke e- *and* ka ‘e-; *see* ea, ‘ehu.

e. 1. Part. marking imperative/intentive mood. See *e* (verb) *ai, e* (verb) *ana,* Gram. 5.4. (PCP *e.*) **2.** Agentive part. By, by means of (follows a pas/imp.). (Gram. 9.9.) *Ua ‘āhewa ‘ia ‘oia e ke ali‘i,* he was blamed by the chief. (PPN *e.*) **3.** Infinitive part. used before certain subordinate verbs. (Gram. 5.4.) *Makemake au e hele,* I want to go (PCP *e.*) 4. See *ē 1.*

ē. 1. Vocative part.; a second *ē* often follows the head word for emphasis. *Ē Pua; ē Pua ē,* O Pua. *Ē ke ali‘i o Maui,* O chief of Maui. *Ē* is shortened to *e* before third-person pronouns: see *e ia nei, e lākou ala.* (PPN *(‘e)e.*) **2.** Intensifying part., as in the common exclamation *Auē noho‘i ē!* (Gram. 7.5.) **3.** interj. Alas!

‘e-. Prefix to numerals, inanimate, as *‘ekahi, ‘elua, ‘ekolu.* (PPN *e.*)

‘ē. 1. nvs. Different, strange, peculiar, unusual, heathen (Biblical), other; away off, elsewhere; beforehand, already, before, premature, in advance (sometimes translated ‘had’ and called by Andrews [Gram. 1.4] a sign of the pluperfect tense, although it is used after the imperative mood). Cf. *‘ē a‘e, ‘ano ‘ē, mea ‘ē. ‘Āina ‘ē,* foreign land. *He ‘ē!* How strange! [It] is gone, past! *Holo ‘ē lākou,* they fled beforehand (away, elsewhere). *Keiki hānau ‘ē,* prematurely born child. *Hele ma kahi ‘ē!* Go away! Get out! *‘Ike ‘ē lākou,* they already knew. *I kahi ‘ē ka ua, waele ‘ē ke pulu* (saying), when the rain is elsewhere, open up beforehand the mulch [prepare for rain before it comes]. (PPN *kese,* PEP *kee.*) **2.** interj. Yes (unemphatic, as in mild agreement and indicating that one has heard; cf. *‘ae*). **3.** n. The letter "e". *Eng.* **4.** n. Key of A (music). *Eng.*

ea. 1. n. Sovereignty, rule, independence. *Lā Ho‘iho‘i Ea,* Restoration Day. *Ho‘iho‘i i ke ea o Hawai‘i,* restore the sovereignty of Hawai‘i. **2.** n. Life, air, breath, respiration, vapor, gas; fumes, as of tobacco; breeze, spirit (Isa. 42.5). This *ea,* as well as *ea 1, 3, 4,* is sometimes pronounced or sung *‘ea.* Cf. *eamāmā, eaolamāmā. Kaha ea,* to deprive of rights of livelihood. *Wai ea,* aerated waters. *Ho‘opuka ea,* exhaust fumes. *Ua mau ke ea o ka ‘āina i ka pono* (motto of Hawai‘i), the life of the land is preserved in righteousness. *He palupalu lākou, he ea hele wale aku* (Hal. 78.39), they were flesh, a wind that passes away. *Kā‘ili ‘ia aku ke ea o ‘Aberahama* (Kin. 25.8), Abraham gave up the ghost; *lit.,* the breath of life was snatched away. **3.** vi. To rise, go up, raise, become erect. Cf. *aea, e‘ea, hō‘ea. Kai ea* (Kep. 183), rising sea. *Ua ea kona po‘o,* his head was raised. *Ke ea ‘ana o ka ‘ai, ka i‘a* (Kep. 97), the obtaining of poi, fish. *‘A ‘ole ho‘i au e ea maluna o ko‘u wahi moe* (Hal. 132.3), I will not go up into my bed. (PPN *e‘a.*) **4.** vi. To smell. Also *‘ea.* Cf. *maea, māeaea. Ea ‘ino‘ino, ea pilau,* evil-smelling, rotten-smelling. (Perhaps PEP *ea.*)

-ea. Pejorative suffix. See *hanaea, luea, nanaiea, poluea,* Gram. 6.5. (PNP *-ea:* cf. Rennellese *-ea.*)

‘ea. 1. n. Hawksbill turtle *(Chelone imbricata),* both land and sea species; the shell of this turtle. (PNP *kea.*) **2.** vs. Reddish-brown, as the color of the *‘ea* shell. Cf. *‘ea mālani, ‘ea ‘ula.* **3.** n. A general term for infections and infectious diseases; coated tongue, sometimes accompanied by sore throat, the thrush disease of children. Many diseases of miscellaneous nature begin with *‘ea* and are listed below. *‘Ea ka waha,* the tongue is coated. *‘Oia kama‘ilio aku a ‘ea ka waha, ‘a‘ohe lohe ‘ia mai,* while talking on until the tongue is coated, yet no one pays any attention [a metaphor to show exasperation]. (PPN *keakea,* PCP *kea.*) **4.** n. Spray. Cf. *‘e‘a,* dust. These words are sometimes interchanged. *Kū ka ‘ea i ka moana,* the spray rises in the sea. **5.** Vocative interj. usually at the beginning or end of utterances. (Gram. 12, 1 Sam. 9.5; Lunk. 7.3.) *‘Ea, hele mai!* Say, come here! *Ho‘olohe mai ‘oukou, ‘ea,* all of you there, listen. **6.** Var. of *ea 4,* to smell. **7.** nvi. Noisy; to yell, whoop; whoop. *E kani ana ka ‘ea,* a whoop sounded. **8.** Var. of *ea 2, 3. A waiho i ka ‘ea nā iwi o kama hele* (RC 367), the traveler's bones are left in the air [said of one dying in a foreign land].

‘eā. interj. **1.** Isn't that so? That's it! *‘Oia, ‘eā?* Is that so? *Ua hele aku ‘oia i Honolulu, ‘eā,* she went to Honolulu, you know. *‘Eā, e aha ana ‘oukou?* Say, what are you up to? *Pēlā, ‘eā?* It's that way, is it? **2.** Song refrain. See ex., *wawalo* and Gram. 12. Also *‘eā‘eā.*

‘e‘a. 1. nvs. Dust, dirt, dust cloud, spray (*‘e‘a* and *‘ea 4* are probably interchanged at times). *Kōwelo ‘e‘a,* dust streamer. *Kū ka ‘e‘a i ke kula,* the dust cloud rose over the plain. *‘Ōka‘i ka ‘e‘a, ‘ōka‘i huaka‘i ‘ula,* a marching cloud of dust, a red procession on the march [warriors with feather cloaks]. **2.** n. Mountain banana patch. *Līlā ka mai‘a o ka ‘e‘a, wili ka ‘ōka‘i,* spindly is the growth of the mountain banana patch, the blossom container twists [even a spindly plant may bear fruit]. **3.** n. A fish similar to *‘a‘awa,* but with dark flesh.

ea.‘a‘ā. n. Gas. *Lit.,* burning air.

‘ē a‘e. vs. Different, other, another, else.

ea.ea. 1. n. Air, breath, air current. Some confusion exists in the uses of *eaea, ‘ea‘ea,* and *‘e‘a‘e‘a.* **2.** Redup. of *ea 3;* to rise; high waves. *He i‘a no ka papa‘u, he loa‘a wale i ka hopu lima; he i‘a no ka hohonu, noho i ke eaea,* fish of the shallows, gotten merely by catching in the hands; fish of the depths stay in the high waves [some tasks are easier than others]. (PPN *e‘ae‘a.*) **3.** Redup. of *ea 4;* a smell, as of seaweed; to smell.

‘ea.‘ea. 1. Redup. of *‘ea 4,* spray; encrusted with spray (sometimes confused with *eaea* and *‘e‘a‘e‘a*). *Ka lawai‘a nui i ‘ea‘ea nā ku‘emaka, i ‘ehu‘ehu nā lihilihi,* the great fisherman whose brows are sprayed with sea and whose lashes are reddened [admiration of a fisherman]. **2.** Dignified, honorable. (And.) **3.** n. A bird (no data).

-‘ea.ea. ho‘ea.ea. To approach.

‘eā.‘eā. Interj. at end of verses in some chants that maintains rhythm and affords pleasure in repetition, something like English tra-la-la. *Nani wale nā hala, ‘eā‘eā, o Naue i ke kai, ‘eā‘eā* (song), beautiful indeed the pandanus, tra-la, of Naue by the sea, tra-la.

‘e‘a.‘e‘a. Redup. of *‘e‘a 1,* dust; dusty; obscure, dark-

ened, cloudy, shady; to cloud, overshadow (sometimes confused with *eaea* and *‘ea‘ea*).

‘ea hanu pa‘a. n. Condition of frequent colds. *Lit., ‘ea* with hardened breath.

‘ea houpo lewa.lewa. n. Great hunger, perhaps due to diabetes. *Lit.,* loose-hanging diaphragm *‘ea.*

‘ea huna. n. Dizzy spells, dizziness; latent *‘ea* disease (Kam. 64:103).

e (verb) **ai.** Particles indicating imperative/intentive mood and accompanying subordinate verbs (*ai* in this case is the anaphoric *ai*). (Gram. 5.4, 7.3.)

‘ea kai wawaka. n. Impaired vision, perhaps labyrinthitis.

‘ea kā.kua. n. A disease, perhaps secondary lues (Kam. 64:115).

‘ea kā.molo.wā. n. Condition of listlessness.

‘ea kua neneke. n. A variety of *‘ea,* a land tortoise. *Lit.,* tortoise with back fitted into sections.

‘ea kū.ka‘a. n. Disease with swelling symptoms.

‘ea kū manawa. n. Severe headaches, perhaps due to high blood pressure. *Lit., ‘ea* at fontanel.

e (verb) **ala.** Same as *e* (verb) *lā. ‘Oia ia lepo ‘ula āu e ‘ike ala,* it's that red dirt you see over there.

‘ea mā.hani. n. A type of *‘ea* described as evanescent. (Kam. 64:103.)

‘ea mā.lani. nvs. Light-brown in color. See *‘ea 2.*

ea.mā.mā. n. Gas. *Lit.,* light air.

e (verb) **ana.** Particles indicating incompleted action and future. Gram. 5.2. (PCP *‘e* verb *‘ana.*)

ea.ola.mā.mā. n. Oxygen. *Lit.,* light life breath.

‘ea ‘ō.lena. n. Jaundice, hepatitis.

‘ea pō.niu. n. Dizziness, vertigo.

‘ea ‘ula. nvs. Wine-colored, such a color.

‘ea wāhi pa‘a. n. Osteomalacia, gradual softening of the bones.

‘ea wawaka. n. Acute childhood *‘ea* disease. (Kam. 64:105.)

e‘e. 1. nvi. To climb on, mount, get on, go aboard, board, embark; one who climbs, mounts, boards; step. Cf. *e‘e kuahiwi, e‘e moku, hikie‘e. Kai e‘e,* tidal wave. **ho.‘ē‘e.** To rise or swell, as surf; to mount, as a surfer mounts a wave. (2 Oihn. 35.24.) *Kai ho‘ē‘e,* tidal wave, deep sea. *Ho‘ē‘e akula ia i ka noho maluna o kona hoki* (Kin. 22.3), he saddled his ass. (PPN *heke.*) **2.** Same as *a‘a 2,* to extend greetings.

‘e‘e. vs. Hard, stiff, dry. Cf. *ka‘e‘e.*

‘ē.‘ē. 1. Redup. of *‘ē 1;* contrary, peculiar, opposite; adversely. *He ‘ē‘ē wale nō kona mana‘o,* his opinion is in opposition. *E pale ana i ka wawā lapuwale, a me ke kū ‘ē‘ē ‘ana i ka mea i kapa hewa ‘ia he na‘auao* (I Tim. 6.20), avoiding profane babblings and oppositions of the thing falsely called science. **ho.‘ē.‘ē.** To keep away from, avoid. (PPN *kesekese,* PEP *keekee.*) **2.** n. Yellow underwing feathers of the *‘ō‘ō,* a bird, as used in featherwork. **3.** n. Armpit. Also *pō‘ae‘ae, po‘ē‘ē;* see *kui‘ē‘ē.* (PCP *keekee.*).

e‘ea. Redup. of *ea 3;* to rise up frequently, as in water; to bob up and down. *E‘ea a‘e ke po‘o o ka honu i ka ‘ilikai,* the head of the turtle appeared again and again on the surface of the sea.

‘e‘ea. 1. vs. Quick ready, expert. *He ‘e‘ea nō kona kūlana,* he is quick in his ways. **2.** n. A bird, said to be an adult *‘alaiaha.* (KL line 307.)

‘e‘e‘e. Redup. of *e‘e 1;* to keep climbing over everything, as an active child; mischievous.

‘e‘ehi. Same as *hehi,* to step on. *‘E‘ehi ihola ia a pa‘a,* he placed his feet down and stood firm.

‘e‘e.hia. nvs. Overcome with fearful reverence, terror-stricken, awe-stricken; awe-inspiring, solemn; fear, reverence, awe, terror; wierd. *Ka ‘e‘ehia iā Iēhowa* (2 Oihn. 17.10), fear of Jehovah. *Piha au i ka ‘e‘ehia,* I am filled with awe.

e‘ehu. Same as *ehuehu,* healthy.

‘e‘ehu. Redup. of *‘ehu 5;* reddish; a number of *‘ehu* persons. *Pala ‘e‘ehu,* to turn red or yellow, as leaves or fruit (riper than *pala hā‘ama*).

‘e‘ei. Offensive, filthy, fly-ridden. (And.)

‘e‘ei.ao. Rare var. of *pepeiao,* ear. *Mō pua‘a,* cut off is the ear of the pig.

‘e‘ei.ehi.ehi. Same as *‘e‘ei.* (AP.)

‘e‘e.‘ina. vi. To creak, crackle. Cf. *‘a‘ina,*

‘E‘eka. Same as *‘Eka 2,* a wind.

‘e‘eke. 1. Redup. of *‘eke 2.* Cf. *mū‘e‘eke. ka wela o ke ahi,* shrinking back from tl fire. **2.** n. Name given for a hard-shelled c

‘e‘eke.loi. vt. To tap a drum slowly, as to chant.

‘e‘eku. Same as *‘eku‘eku. Ē Kāne-pua‘a, e ‘ pa, e ho‘owali,* o Kāne-pua‘a, root, and and furrows.

e‘e kua.hiwi. v. To climb mountains; mounta

‘e‘ele. Same as *‘ele‘ele 1,* but used chiefly in *Ka manu ‘e‘ele koi* (For. 5:99), the black bird

‘e‘ele.koa. vs. Stormy. *Kū ‘ia ka malama* weathered the stormy month [to have endu ships].

‘e‘ele.kū. Redup. of *‘elekū;* blackened or dark leaves or fruit due to maturity or to pelting by dark, gloomy, as clouds. *Ma ia malama ua ‘e‘ lani i nā ao ua . . . a ua ‘e‘elekū ho‘i nā lau o nā me nā mea ulu i ke o‘o* (Kep. 93), in this month is dark with rain clouds . . . and the leaves of tr growing things are dark with maturity. *Ma ia ma Nana, ua pau ka ‘e‘elekū o ka lau o nā lā‘au i ka ka ua ma nā lā o ka ho‘oilo* (Kep. 89), in this mo Nana, the dark bruising of the leaves of trees b pelting of the rains of the days of winter has cease

‘e‘elo. 1. Redup. of *‘elo;* drenched, soaked. **hō.‘e** To wet, drench, soak; tearfully sulky, as a crying c *Ua hō‘e‘elo,* drenching rain. **2.** vs. Loitering; to d dally. *Rare.*

‘E‘elo-koa. Name of a storm from the northeast of W mea, Hawai‘i. (And.)

e‘e moku. nvi. To board a ship; ship passenger; imi grant.

‘e‘ena. vs. **1.** Shy, timid, wary, wild, afraid, fearsom untamed; to shy away. Cf. *‘ena 2, hā‘e‘ena. ‘E‘en Hā‘ena i ke ehu kai,* Hā‘ena is fearsome because of se spray. **2.** Extraordinary. Cf. *‘ē 1. He ‘e‘ena a mīkolo hua ka ‘ōlelo,* impressive and eloquent in speech. *Kan ‘e‘ena ka pahu i ka moana,* the drum sounds weirdly over the ocean.

‘e‘epa. nvs. Extraordinary, incomprehensible, abnormal, deceitful, peculiar, as persons with miraculous powers; such persons. Many *‘e‘epa* characters in mythology were born in strange forms, as a plant, an animal, or a piece of rope. Cf. *‘epa 1, ‘epa‘epa, kino ‘e‘epa.* The *menehune, Nāwā,* and *Nāmū* of Wao-lani in Nu‘u-anu Valley were *‘e‘epa.* Trickery or deceit that passes comprehension is also *‘e‘epa.* **hō.‘e‘epa.** Mysterious, mystifying, incomprehensible. *Hō‘e‘epa wale ho‘i nā hana a kēlā keiki,* that boy's behavior is certainly mysterious.

‘e‘eu. 1. vi. To crawl, creep, as an insect. Cf. *‘eu 2.* (PCP *kekeu.*) **2.** nvi. Shuddering sensation of revulsion (less strong than *mania*); to rise in horror, flinch (sometimes interpreted as a portent). *‘E‘eu ka ‘ili o ke po‘o,* the scalp of the head flinches. *‘E‘eu a‘ela ka hulu o ka ‘īlio,* the dog's hair bristles [in anger].

‘e‘ewa. vi. To make a wry face, pout, as in derision; to protrude the lips mockingly.

ē.hā. Same as *ēhē. He wahi ma‘i ēhē, ēhā, no ‘Io-lani, ēhē, ēhā* (chant), a genital chant, oh, oh, for ‘Io-lani, oh, oh.

‘eha. nvs. Hurt, in pain, painful, aching, sore, pained; pain, injury, ailment, suffering, soreness, aching; to hurt, pain, cause suffering or pang. See *mea ‘eha.* Gram. 4.4. *‘Eha koni,* throbbing ache; *fig.,* throbbing love. *He ‘eha konikoni i ka pu‘uwai,* the heart throbs with agony [of love]. *‘Eha i ka ‘eha lima ‘ole,* aching with an ache not inflicted by [human] hands [love]. *‘A‘ole e ‘eha ke keiki o Kaua‘i iā‘oe* (For. 5:411), you

a-. *Ei au, ē Laka,* here I am, O Laka. **2.** Var. of *ai 1,* coition. **3.** Rather frequent variation of the anaphoric *ai (ai 3)* in fast speech, but seldom if ever found so in printed form.

eia. 1. idiom. Here, here is, here are, present (as response to roll call). Cf. *'ei'a,* Gram. 4.6. Numerous idioms are listed below. *Eia 'oe,* so you have come; well, here you are. (In a kindly voice *eia 'oe* may be an affectionate welcome, but in an angry voice it indicates displeasure.) *Eia 'oe ke hō'ike 'ia aku ŋei,* you are hereby notified. (PCP *eia:* cf. Marquesan *eia.*) **2.** n. This place. *Ke eia me ke eia aku,* the here and the hereafter [phrase introduced by missionaries; sometimes pronounced *ka 'eia*].

'ei'a. Emphatic variation of *eia:* here! here it is!

eia a'e. idiom. Here close by, here approaching. *'O Kama-pua'a eia a'e, ua hiki mai nei* (FS 247), here comes Kama-pua'a, he's coming now.

eia aku. idiom. Approaching, nearby, soon. *Eia aku 'o Nā-maka,* here is Nā-maka coming. *Kō mākou noho 'ana me Winona mā, eia aku nō a eia mai,* our dwelling and that of Winona and her family, they are close. *Eia aku nō a eia mai, pa'a kēia mea hana,* in no time this work will be finished. *He hele mai nō a 'ike, eia aku, eia mai,* does come to visit every once in a while (every so often).

eia ala. idiom. Here, here it is; you over there, you. Cf. *e ia nei.*

eia ho'i. idiom. And, finally, behold. *Eia ho'i, ua hewa wau* (2 Sam. 24.17), lo, I have sinned.

eia hou ho'i. idiom. And again, furthermore. (Heb. 1.6.)

eia iho. idiom. Wait a moment. *Eia iho a hō'ea mai,* wait a moment, [it] will be arriving.

eia kā. idiom. So at last, then. *Ko'u moe akula nō ia i ka 'ona a ka 'awa, eia kā, ua hapai 'ia mai au a loko nei o kou hale,* I was just sleeping then with the drunkenness of the kava, and then I was carried here to the inside of your house.

eia kekahi. idiom. But withal, moreover, furthermore.

eia lā. Same as *eiu ulu.*

e ia nei. pronoun. You (sg.), you there (as between husband and wife, often affectionate and replacing such Eng. terms as darling; shortened vocative *e* + pronoun *ia* + zero-demon., Gram. 8.2).

eia (nō) na'e. idiom. But, furthermore, however.

elna. vs. Scorched.

ei nei. Short for *e ia nei.*

ei ne'i, eiā i 'ane'i. idiom. Here, here it is. *Ei ne'i ka wai,* here's the water.

'e.iwa. 1. num. Nine, nine times. **2.** See *wao'eiwa.*

'eka. 1. nvs. Dirty, foul, fecal (Kam. 64:109); filth, dirt, soil. See ex., *kūlepe 1. Kaha 'eka,* foul spot [poor soil]. *Ua ho'oleilei nā wai ona i ka wai 'eka* (Isa. 57.20), whose waters cast up mire. **hō.'eka.** To soil, make dirty. **2.** *(Cap.)* n. Name of a wind at Kona, Hawai'i. *Ka makani kūkulu pe'a nui, he 'Eka,* the 'Eka wind, that sets up big sails [good for fishing]. *He 'Eka, ka makani ho'olale wa'a o nā Kona,* the 'Eka breeze calls forth the canoes of the Kona districts [good fishing]. **3.** n. A variety of bananas. (PH 173.) **4.** n. Acre. *Eng.*

'ē.kā. n. Hand of bananas. Compare *mai'a* for pejorative connotations. *E painu'u 'oe me nā mahalo a pala hinu nā 'ēkā mai'a* (Kel. 138), you brag with praise of bright and ripe banana hands [worthless bragging].

'eka.'eka. 1. Redup. of *'eka 1.* Cf. *hā'eka'eka. 'Eka'eka ka lole,* the dress is dirty. *'Eka'eka nā hana,* filthy deeds. **2.** n. Hawaiian name for a Japanese variety of taro *(adado)* grown in Hawai'i. (HP 32.)

'ē.kaha. n. **1.** The bird's-nest fern *(Asplenium nidus),* widespread in the tropics, forming large rosettes and in some forests perching on branches of trees. The fronds are large, entire, sword-shaped. The black midrib is used like the *'ama'u* fern for decorating pandanus hats. (Neal 21.) Also *'ākaha.* This fern is sometimes called *'ēkaha kuahiwi,* mountain *'ēkaha,* to distinguish it from the mosses or from *'ēkaha kū moana.* (PCP

ke(e)ta(f,s)a.) **2.** A moss growing on rotted trees. Also *limu 'ēkaha.* **3.** Same as *'ēkaha kū moana.*

'ē.kaha 'ā.kō.lea. Same as *pākahakaha,* a small fern. (Neal 25.)

'ē.kaha.kaha. n. **1.** Juvenile or small form of bird's-nest fern. Cf. *'ēkaha.* **2.** Var. name for *limu loloa* and *limu uaua loli.*

'ē.kaha kua.hiwi. See *'ēkaha 1.*

'ē.kaha kū moana. n. "Black coral" *(Antipathes grandis),* used medicinally.

'ē.kaha-loa. n. Type of tapa.

'ē.kaha 'ula. n. A native fern *(Elaphoglossum alatum),* with entire, narrow fronds 24 to 64 cm long and with close, parallel veins. The spore-bearing fronds are similar but smaller. Cf. *hoe-a-Māui.*

'ekahi. num. One, once. Cf. *kahi, 'akahi.*

'ē.kake. Var. of *kēkake,* donkey. *Eng.* See *iākake.*

'ekale.kia, ekalesia. n. Church (the organization, not the building; usually pronounced *'ekalesia*). *(Gr. ekklesia.)*

'eke. n. **1.** Sack, pocket, bag, basket; bag-shaped fish net; scrotum. (Often preceded by *ke;* many types are listed below.) (PPN *kete.*) **2.** vi. To cringe, shrink from, draw away from, flinch, wince; to become smaller, shrink.

-eke. ho'o.eke. Var. of *ho'oweke (weke 1).*

'ē.kea. Var. of *'ākea,* canoe hull; boom on the right side of a double canoe (Ii 129).

'eke.'eke. 1. n. Small bag or sack, pocket, purse, scrotum. **2.** Redup. of *'eke 2;* fussy, overexacting, cranky, particular. **3.** n. A herringbone design, as in mat plaiting or in the *pāpale 'ie.* **4.** *(Cap.)* n. Name of a wind of the island of Ka-'ula. (For. 5:99.)

'eke.'eke kā.lā. n. Billfold, wallet, small purse.

'eke.'eke ma'a. n. Holder for stone in the sling *(ma'a),* sometimes a kind of woven basket, but in smaller slings merely a kind of noose.

'eke.'ekemu. Redup. of *'ekemu. 'A'ohe 'eke'ekemu wale 'o kēlā kanaka,* that person hardly answers at all.

'eke hau. n. Icecap.

'eke ho'o.pa'a laho. n. Male supporter, jockstrap. *Lit.,* basket supporting scrotum.

'eke hulu.hulu. n. Gunny sack. *Lit.,* hairy sack.

'eke.ke'i. vs. Short, as a dress or fishline (probably a redup. of *'eke 2* + -*'i,* transitivizer: Gram. 6.6.4). Cf. *mū'ekeke'i. Lima 'ekeke'i,* short sleeve. *Lole wāwae 'ekeke'i,* shorts. *Ihu 'ekeke'i,* short wrinkled nose. **hō.'eke.ke'i.** To shorten; to pucker up, wrinkle, as the nose.

'Eke.kemō, Esekemo. nvs. Eskimo. *Eng.*

'eke.kēmu. Short for *'eke'ekemu.* Rare.

'eke.keu. n. Wings. See *'ēheu 1. Nā hulu 'ekekeu,* wing feathers.

'eke kū.kae.nalo. n. Flour sack or sack of unbleached muslin *(kūkaenalo),* as formerly used for poi.

ekele. n. Plant listed (no data). (KL line 78.)

'eke leka (leta). n. Mail pouch, mailbag.

'ekeli.uma, eteriuma. n. Ethereum. *Eng.*

'ekelo. See *piha'ekelo,* mynah bird.

'Eke.loa. n. Wind name. See *'Olu-'Ekeloa-ho'oka'a-moena.*

'eke.mau'u. n. Gunny sack, burlap. *lit.,* grass sack.

'ekemo. vs. Akimbo. *Eng.*

'ekemu. vi. To answer briefly, speak but little; taciturn. (Kin. 24.21.) *'A'ole i hiki ke 'ekemu iki mai kona po'e hoahānau* (Kin. 45.3), and his brethren could not answer. *'Ekemu 'ole,* tacit.

'ē.kena, egena. n. **1.** Agent. *Eng. Uku 'ēkena,* commission, agent's fee. **2.** *(Cap.)* Also **Edena.** Eden. *Eng. Kīhāpai o 'Ekena,* garden of Eden.

'eke pa'a lima, 'eke.'eke pa'a lima. n. Handbag, hand basket, briefcase.

'eke.pue. vi. To bend over, crouch, as to hide oneself or an object. *Fig.,* secretive, as in love affairs; to keep a secret. **hō.'eke.pue.** Caus/sim. *E hō'ekepue ana 'oe i ke aha?* Why are you so secretive?

'**eke.pu'u.** n. A bird (no data). (KL line 355.)

'**ē.keu.** Same as '*ēheu 1, 2.* (Cf. Easter *keke'u,* shoulder.)

'**eke.'ula.** n. A type of banana. (Kam. 76:38.)

'**eke wai wela.** n. Hot-water bag.

'**eki.** n. Ace. *Eng. 'Eki pihulu,* ace of spades.

'**ekī.** n. **1.** Bayonet. Cf. *kī,* to shoot, and *'ēlau waikī.* **2.** Place where ti plants grow.

'**eki.'eki.** n. Hawaiian tern *(Anous* sp.*).*Cf. *noio.*

ekiki.lau. nvs. A stench that draws flies; bad-smelling.

eko. Var. of *weko,* bad-smelling.

'**ē.koa.** Same as *koa haole,* false koa *(Leucaena leucocephala),* a plant.

eko.eko. Redup. of *eko;* extremely bad-smelling.

'**ekoko.** Same as '*akoko* and *koko,* shrubs and trees.

'**ekolu.** num. Three; three times. Cf. *kolu, 'akolu.*

'**eku.** nvt. To root, as a pig. *Fig.,* prow of a canoe. (PEP *ketu.)*

'**ekua.** Pas/imp. of '*eku. Ē Kāne-pua'a, 'ekua i uka, 'ekua i kai* (Kep. 59), O Pig-Kāne, root inland, root seaward. (PCP *ketua.)*

'**Ekua.kola, Ekuadora.** nvs. Ecuador; Ecuadorian. *Eng.*

'**eku.'eku.** Redup. of '*eku;* to soften the earth, as for planting (Kep. 155).

'**eku.lē.kū.** n. Digging place. *Aia i 'ō ka 'ekulēkū a lākou,* over there is their digging place.

e (verb) **lā.** Similar to *e* (verb) *nei,* except that *lā* indicates action away. See Gram. 5.2.

'**ela.** n. Ale. *Eng.*

'**ē.la'a.** Var. of '*āla'a,* a tree.

'**ela kinika.** n. Ginger ale. *Eng.*

e lā.kou ala. Similar to *e lākou nei,* but persons addressed are farther away.

e lā.kou nei. pronoun. You (pl.), you there (usually affectionate). (Shortened vocative *e* + pronoun *lākou* + zero demon.: Gram. 8.2.) *E lākou nei e pe'e ho'opue nei, 'a'ole 'o 'oukou lohe i ke kani o nā pū* (Kel. 81)? O you who are hiding crouched over here, don't you hear the sound of the guns?

'**ē.lama.** Same as *lama 1,* ebony. *Rare.*

'**ē.lau.** n. **1.** Tip, point, end, top, extremity, extreme, snapper (of whip). Also *wēlau.* **2.** Wisp of breeze. **3.** Bayonet, spear point, short spear.

'**ē.lau alelo.** n. Tongue tip.

'**ē.lau wai.kī.** n. Gun bayonet.

-ele. See '*iele, lauele, luaiele, nīele, nīnauele.*

'**ele.** nvs. Black (less used than '*ele'ele),* also '*e'ele, pā'ele.* (PPN *kele.)* **2.** n. Embryo. '*Ele Kū,* embryo of Kū [said of a child born on the night or day of Kū]. **3.** Short for *'ea'ele 1.* **4.** n. Water hole, dark spring covered with growth. Cf. *kele.*

'**ele-.** **1.** Old. See '*elehine, 'elekule, 'elemakule, lā'ele.* **2.** Prefix to names of directions used by priests; see below.

'**ele.ao.** n. **1.** Plant louse, aphid; germ; blight; blighted, as by *'eleao. Fig.,* troublemaker. *Ua 'eleao 'ia ke kalo,* the taro is blighted by insects. **2.** A native fungus *(Gnomonia iliau),* parasitic on leaf sheaths of sugar cane. **3.** Time of light, daylight, a term used in *kuwā* prayers, as to indicate that a new house is free from taboo and may be occupied. Cf. *'eleua, kuwā 2.* **4.** n. Door at the leeward end of a house. Cf. *'eleua.*

'**ele.au.** n. **1.** Period of darkness. **2.** Perhaps same as *'aki'aki,* a seaweed. *Maui.*

'**ele.'ele.** **1.** nvs. Black, dark, the black color of Hawaiian eyes. Also *'ene'ene.* **hō.'ele.'ele.** To blacken, darken, become dark. (PPN *kelekele.)* **2.** n. Variety of tapa said to have originated at Kau-makani, Maui; it was dyed with candlenut, *pā'ihi,* and black mud. **3.** n. Long, filamentous, green, edible seaweeds *(Enteromorpha prolifera).* Some kinds are among the most popular in Hawai'i, being eaten raw as condiments at feasts. Called *pīpīlani* on Maui. **4.** n. A cooking banana (a form of *Musa xparadisiaca),* valued for shiny black skin of trunk, used for designs worked into pandanus mats and hats. (Neal 249.) Also *hinupua'a.* **5.** Same as *hinupua'a* and *naioea,* varieties of taro. **6.** Same as

māikoiko, a variety of sugar cane. **7.** n. A variety of sweet potato.

'**ele.'ele kani.kau.** n. Black crepe worn for mourning.

'**ele.'ele.kū.** Redup. of '*elekū;* unattractively dark and ugly, coal-black.

'**ele.'ele mā.koko.** n. A taro cultivar. (TC 3.)

'**ele.'ele pa'a.** n. Coal-black.

'**ele.'ele.pī.** nvs. Agitated, turbulent, tumultuous. '*Ele-'elepī ka waha,* blabber-mouth. **2.** Same as '*elepī.*

'**ele'e.leu.** Redup. of '*eleu;* vivacious, energetic, lively. **hō.'ele'e.leu.** Caus/sim.; vivacious, energetic, full of life.

'**ele.he'i.** Var. of '*ekeke'i,* short.

'**ele.he'u.** **1.** nvs. Mutilated, deprived of some essential part; mayhem. *Rare.* Cf. *manuhe'u.* **2.** Angry. (AP.)

'**ele.hine.** n. Old woman. *Rare.* See *luahine.*

'**ele hiwa.** nvs. Coal-black, jet-black, all black. See chant, '*elemoe.*

'**ele.honua.** nvs. Priests' name for west.

elehu. n. Slate or ash-colored pumice. *Rare.* Cf. *lehu.*

'**ele.ī.** nvs. Blue-black, shiny black. *Fig.,* select, choice. *He mea 'ele'ī kēia i ko'u mana'o,* this is choice, in my opinion.

'**elei.ā.honua.** Same as '*elehonua.*

'**elei.ā.lani.** Same as '*elelani.*

'**ele.iki.** vt. To bear a grudge. *Ua 'eleiki wale aku nō ia i nā hoahānau,* he nursed a little grudge against the cousins.

'**ele.'io.** nvi. To go after secretly and speedily; agile, spry; the name of a famous runner on Maui (For. 4:483-7).

'**ēleka.** n. Elk. *Eng.*

'**ele.ke'i.** Var. of '*ekeke'i,* short.

'**ele.kū.** **1.** n. Coarse vesicular basalt. (PEP *keletuu;* cf. Marquesan *ke'etu.)* **2.** n. Stone polisher or rubber made of this rock. **3.** nvs. Entirely black, coal-black, said jokingly of dark people, including Negroes. See chant, '*elemoe.* **4.** n. Priests' name for north.

'**ele.kule.** n. Old fellow, old chap. Cf. the common '*elemakule. 'Eleu nō kahi 'elekule,* the old fellow is spry.

'**ele.kuma.** n. Small crabs *(Xanthidae* spp.).

'**ele.lani.** nvs. Priests' name for east.

'**ele.lau.** Var. of *welelau,* tip.

'**elele.** n. Messenger, delegate, ambassador, envoy, any diplomatic representative. Also '*alele.* (PCP *kelele.)*

'**elele waha 'ole.** n. Letter, written message. *Lit.,* messenger without mouth.

elelo. Same as *alelo,* tongue.

elelo lua. nvs. Double-tongued, deceitful; trickster. *Mai puni 'oe, he elelo lua,* don't believe, [he] is deceitful.

'**ele.lū.** n. Cockroaches (Blattidae).

'**ele.lū kea.** n. A cockroach that has shed its skin and is light *(kea)* in color; a term of ridicule for an unclean white person.

'**ele.lū kī.kē.kē.** n. A large American cockroach *(Periplaneta americana). Lit.,* knocking cockroach.

'**ele.lū la'a loa.** n. A cockroach, kitchen roach.

'**ele.lū lepo.** n. Burrowing cockroach *(Pycnoscelus indicus). Lit.,* earth cockroach.

elelū papa. n. A cockroach. (Malo 41.)

'**ele.lū 'ula.'ula.** n. Large, brown cockroaches, such as the American cockroach *(Periplaneta americana),* and the somewhat smaller Australasian cockroach *(P. australasiae).*

'**ele.makai.ā.uli.** n. An expert taro farmer (no data). (For. 5:681.)

'**ele.makule.** nvs. Old man; to become an old man; old (of males). See saying, *hopena.* **hō.'ele.makule.** To behave like an old man; to pretend to be an old man.

'**ele.mā.kule.** Plural of '*elemakule.*

'**ele.mihi.** Same as '*alamihi* and '*elepī,* a small black crab.

'**ele.mika, eremita.** Hermit. (MK 7.) Probably French.

'**ele.mimo.** Var. of *alamimo,* quick.

'**ele.mio.** **1.** vs. Tapering. **2.** vt. To snatch without being seen, as by a thief. *Ma'ane'i iho nei nō ku'u 'eke'eke,* *eia kā ua 'elemio 'ia aku nei,* my purse was right here, and then it is snatched away.

'ele.moe. 1. vs. Dark, still, as sea or forest. *Kai 'ōma'o, 'elekū, 'ele hiwa, 'elemoe, 'elewawā* (chant for Ka-lā-kaua), sea green, jet-black, sacred black, silent black, tumultuous black. **2.** n. Priests' name for south.

'ē.lemu. n. Buttocks.

'ele.paio. 1. nvi. A species of flycatcher with subspecies on Hawai'i *(Chasiempis sandwichensis sandwichensis),* Kaua'i *(C. sandwichensis sclateri),* and O'ahu *(C. sandwichensis gayi).* The Kaua'i subspecies is also called *'apekepeke.* This bird was believed to be the goddess of canoe makers, hence the saying *ua 'elepaio 'ia ka wa'a,* the canoe is [marked] by the *'elepaio* [an *'elepaio* bird pecking slowly on a tree trunk for insects signified that the trunk was insect-ridden and not suitable for a canoe (see *kani 1*); the saying may be applied to any failure]. The name also refers to one who craves fish but does not go fishing, as the cry of the bird was thought to suggest *'ono ka i'a, 'ono ka i'a,* fish is delicious, fish is delicious. **2.** n. A native variety of taro; the leaves are mottled with white. (HP 17).

'ele.pani, elepani. nvs. Elephant. *Eng. Ka niho 'elepani* (1 Nal. 10.22), ivory.

'ele.pani kai. n. Sea elephant.

'ele.pī. Same as *'alamihi, ele'elepī,* and *'elemihi,* a small black crab. See *kono 'elepī.*

'eleu. vs. Active, alert, energetic, lively, nimble, quick, dexterous, agile, spry, sprightly, prompt. Also *'uleu.* **hō.'eleu.** Caus/sim.; to animate, stir into action, animated.

'Ele.'ū. 1. n. A dark-skinned people said to be descended from a chief of this name. **2.** *(Not cap.)* A hard stone, sometimes used as a fish god.

'eleua. n. **1.** Darkness of rain or rain clouds. **2.** A new house before it has beem made *noa,* or free from taboo. Cf. *'eleao 3.* **3.** Door on the weather end of a house. Cf. *'eleao 4.* **4.** Ancestor or aged male of a family. **5.** A major illness (no data).

'ele.uli. 1. nvs. Grayish black. **2.** A rare type of dark-gray or perfumed tapa. (FS 18-9).

'ele.wawā. nvs. Dark and tumultuous, as sea or forest. See chant, *'elemoe.*

'ele.weka. n. Elevator. *Eng.*

ele.wiki. Same as *alawiki,* to hurry.

'eli. vt. To dig, excavate. Also *'ali, pā'eli.* (PPN *keli).*

'elia. Pas/imp. of *'eli.*

'eli.'eli. Redup. of *'eli;* to dig often. *Fig.,* firmly rooted, profound, deep, as a taboo, or its removal; reverence. *'Amama, 'eli'eli kapu, 'eli'eli noa* (Kep. 55), the taboo is over, profound has been the taboo, profound is the freeing. *'Eli'eli kau mai,* may a profound reverence alight [solemn supplication at the end of prayers]. *Ā 'eli'eli kūlana i Hawai'i,* and are firmly rooted in Hawai'i.

'elima. num. Five; five times. Cf. *lima, 'alima.*

'eli ua. v. To dig a trench so that rain water will run off. (FS 211.)

'elo. vs. Wet, soggy. *Pulu 'elo,* soaked, drenched. **hō.'elo.** Caus/sim.

'elo.'elo. Redup. of *'elo,* very wet, drenched. See ex., *Kū-lani-hāko'i.* **hō.'elo.'elo.** Caus/sim. *Ka ua hō'elo-'elo,* a drenching rain.

'elua. num. Two; twice Cf. *lua, 'alua. 'Elua a'u hele 'ana i laila,* I went there twice.

elu.ehe. n. A Moloka'i name for *'ūlei,* a shrub.

'eme.lala, emerala. n. Emerald. *Eng.*

'eme.paea. n. Empire. *Eng.*

'eme.pake, emebase. n Embassy. *Eng.*

'eme.pake.koa, emebasedoa. n. Ambassador. *Eng.*

'eme.pela, emepera. nvs. Emperor. *Eng. Aupuni 'eme-pela,* empire.

emi. 1. nvs. To diminish, reduce, depreciate, grow smaller, subside, wane, decrease, recede, ebb; to lose vigor, droop, lower; low, reduced, thin; reduction, decrease, loss; mitigated. See ex., *manoninia. Emi iho,* to go

down, settle (as earth). *Emi ke kino,* to lose weight. *Emi mau nō ke olakono,* the health keeps failing. *Emi hope,* to back up. **ho'ēmi, ho'o.emi.** To reduce, diminish (Puk. 21.10), lessen, draw back, curtail, discount. *Ho'ēmi kino, ho'ēmi momona,* reduce in weight. (PCP *emi.)* **2.** vs. Cheap. **ho'ēmi.** To lower the price, cheapen; cheap. *Kū'ai ho'ēmi,* reduction sale. *Ho'ēmi panakō,* bank discount. **3.** n. Flat (in music).

emi.emi. Redup. of *emi 1, 2;* lowering, decreasing, diminishing, dwindling, lagging slowly; backward. **ho-'ēmi.emi.** Caus/sim.; to retreat, lag, hesitate; to lower a price, to bargain.

emi hope. vi. To return, go backward, withdraw, back up. **ho'ēmi hope.** Caus/sim. *Ho'ēmi hope i ka wa'a,* to back water.

emi kua. vi. To go backward with stooped back, as from the presence of a chief.

'emila, emira. n. Emir. *Eng.*

emi pū. vs. To lose weight rapidly, as due to sickness.

'emo. nvi. A waiting, delay; to wait, delay (often used with a negative). *'A'ohe i 'emo, hiki ana ke ka'a,* in hardly any time at all, the car arrived. (PCP *kemo.)*

'emo.loa. n. A native grass *(Eragrostis variabilis)* 30 to 90 cm high, with long narrow flowering panicles, growing on open slopes and ridges. Also *kalamālō, kāwelu.*

'emo 'ole. conj. Without delay, immediately, suddenly, in no time at all, quickly. (FS 11, Oih. 2.2.) (Gram. 11.1.)

emo.wai. n. An addition of water, as for mixing poi. *Kaua'i.*

emu. vt. **1.** To shoo away. **2.** To rid plants of weeds. **ho'ēmu.** Caus/sim. (Malo 199.)

'ena. 1. nvi. Red-hot, glowing. *Fig.,* raging, angry; anger. *'Ena aloha,* intense affection or longing. *Pi'i ka 'ena,* to feel anger. **hō.'ena.** Caus/sim. (PCP *kena;* cf. Marquesan *kena.)* **2.** vt. Shy; to shy. *Mai 'ena i ke kanaka i laka aku,* do not shy away from a person who is attracted [treat kindness with kindness]. **3.** n. Abundance, plenty. Cf. *One-lau-'ena.* **4.** n. Opening in the clouds said to be like the jaw of the *a'u* swordfish and a sign of rain. (Malo text, chapter 6, section 6.)

'ena.'ena. 1. Redup. of *'ena 1, 2;* glowing, red-hot, raging. *'Ena'ena pilau,* unbearable stench. *'Ena'ena ulu o Malama i ka 'ilima* (chant), growth at Malama glowing with *'ilima* [leis]. **hō.'ena.'ena.** To cause heat; heat; to rouse to anger. *Ua hō'a'ā 'ia ke ahi e ku'u inaina, a 'e 'ena'ena 'ia* (Kanl. 32.22), a fire is kindled by my anger and shall burn. (PCP *kenakena.)* **2.** n. All species of cudweeds *(Gnaphalium),* members of the daisy family, small herbs having small inconspicuous flowers and more or less white woolly stems and leaves. Formerly Hawaiians stored feather standards, *kāhili,* with native species *(G. sandwicensium* and *G. hawaiiense)* to repel insects. (Neal 836.) Called *pūheu* on Ni'ihau.

'ena.kō.ī. nvi. To break wind foully; such action. Probably *lit.,* flowing abundance. *E hele 'oe i ka 'enakōī,* go and break wind [a vulgar insult].

'ena makani. n. **1.** Stormy wind. *Mahina 'ino kēia, ke kau nei ka 'ena makani,* this is a stormy month that wind furies come. **2.** Windmill. *Rare.*

'ena.mela, enamela. n. Enamel. *Eng.*

ene. nvi. First attempts of an infant to move; to draw up knees and push elbows, to crawl, creep.

'ene. Rare var. of *'ele'ele,* black.

'ene.'enemi. Redup. of *'enemi. Ā 'ene'enemi ho'i i kona noho hanohano* (Nak. 30), opposing his position of honor.

e (verb) **nei.** Particles indicating imperfect aspect and future tense and accompanying subordinate verbs. The *nei* indicates action here or now. See Gram. 5.2.

'Ene.kelea, Enekerea. n. Incarnation. *Ma ka miterio o Kou 'Enekerea Hemolele,* through the mystery of Thy Holy Incarnation.

'ene.kini. n. Engine. *Eng.*

'ene.kinia kī.wila. n. Civil engineer. *Eng.*

'enemi. nvi. Enemy; to feel enmity; to be an enemy.

Eng.: note that the Hawaiian stress is on the second syllable, contrasting with Eng. stress on the first syllable. *He wahine 'enemi wale 'ia* (Kep. 105), a woman who has enemies without cause. *Kona po'e 'enemi* (For. 5:385), his enemies. *E lilo wau i 'enemi no kou po'e 'enemi* (Puk. 23.22), I will be an enemy of your enemies. **hō.'enemi.** To feel animosity or enmity; to make an enemy.

enene. 1. Redup. of *ene. Enene akula ke kama iki,* the little child makes creeping movements. **2.** vi. To dilate, as nostrils. *Rare.*

ene.nue. Var. of *nenue,* a fish.

'eni.kini. Var. of *'enekini,* engine. *Eng.*

'eno. vs. Wild, untamed, fearful of people, shy. **hō.-'eno.** Easily frightened, shy, wary, coy; to cause to be wild.

'eno.'eno. Redup. of *'eno;* very wild, etc. Cf. *mā'eno'eno. No ke aha 'oia i 'eno'eno ai?* Why was he so wildly excited?

'enuhe. n. Caterpillar, as of hawk or sphinx moths (Sphingidae). *Fig.,* a rapacious person. Also *'anuhe, nuhe. He 'enuhe au* (Hal. 22.6), I am a worm.

'enuhe kilika (silika). n. The introduced silkworm *(Bombyx mori).*

eo. vs. To lose, be defeated, beaten (if followed immediately by an animate subject and then by *i-iā* marking agent); to win, beat; winning, victory (in other environments). *Mea eo,* winner, victor. *Inā kāua i kilu a i eo 'oe ia'u, alaila, 'o kou kino ka uku, a i eo wau iā 'oe, 'o ko'u kino ka uku* (FS 275), and if we play quoits, and I defeat you (*lit.,* you are defeated by me), your body is the pay, and if you defeat me (*lit.,* I am defeated by you), my body is the pay. *Eo ia'u ka hākōkō,* I won the wrestling match. *Nā 'ai eo* (FS 283), the winning points. *Ua eo au,* I won. (PCP *eo.*)

eō. 1. interj. Yes, I am here (in answer to a call by name, or to a name chant in one's honor). **2.** nvt. Call; to call, answer (Ioba 13.22). *Ua eō aku au i ku'u makua,* I called to my parent. *Eō e Lili'u i kou inoa,* Lili'u, answer to your name song.

'eo. vs. **1.** Full of food, as a calabash (but not as full as *piha'ū*). *'Umeke ka 'eo,* a full calabash [a well-filled mind]. **2.** vt. To agree. *Ua 'eo like lāua e hele,* they agreed to go.

'e'oe. Rare var. of *'a'oe,* no, not. *'E'oe au e hele,* I'm not going.

'eo.'eo. Same as *'eho 1.*

'e'ole. conj. If not for . . . would not have. *'E'ole ko'u holo, pakele au,* if it were not for my running, I would not have escaped. *'E'ole nō ia,* if it weren't for him [in derision, meaning that he thinks nothing can be done without him].

'e'ole . . . inā. conj. If not . . . would have. (Gram. 11.1.) *'E'ole au e 'ike aku nei iā'oe, inā ua make 'oe* (FS 101), if I hadn't seen you here, you would have been killed.

'eono. num. Six; six times. Cf. *ono.*

'epa. 1. nvt. Tricky, mischievous, dishonest; deceit; to deceive. Cf. *'e'epa, haku 'epa. Lā 'Epa o 'Apelila,* April Fools' Day. *'O ka po'e ho'oki'eki'e ua 'epa wahahe'e mai lākou ia'u* (Hal. 119.69), the proud have forged a lie against me. **hō.'epa.** To deceive, cheat. **2.** n. Also **epa.** Ephah. See ex., *hua pale,* Puk. 16.36. *Eng.*

epa.epa. n. Part of a fish's tail above and below the cleft. Cf. *epaepa huila.*

'epa.'epa. Redup. of *'epa 1;* frequentative and intensive. (GP 46.)

epa.epa huila. n. Propeller blade.

'epaka, epata, epeta. v. Ephphatha; let it be opened (Mar. 7.34.) (Probably Aramaic *ephathah.*)

'epane, epani. n. Apron. *Eng.*

'epe. n. Stanza. *Rare.*

'Epeko.pala. nvs. Episcopal; Episcopalian. *Eng.* Less common than *Ho'omana Pīhopa.*

'epi.kekole, epistetole; 'epi.kekolo, episetolo. n. Epistle. (Probably Latin *epistola.*)

'epi.kopo. Same as *pīhopa,* bishop. (Latin *episcopus.*)

'Epipa.nia. n. Epiphany. (Probably late Latin *epiphania.*)

'ē.poka, epoda. n. Ephod. *Pūliki 'ia i ka 'ēpoka olonā* (1 Sam. 22.18), did wear a linen ephod. *Eng.*

'ē.poni, eboni. nvs. Ebony. *Eng.* (Ezek. 27.15.)

'epu.kane. n. Spouse. *Ka 'epukane o ka Virigine Hemolele,* the spouse of the Holy Virgin. (Possibly French *époux,* husband, *kāne,* male.)

eu. Spelling occasionally found for *e,* part. + *u,* plural prefix (see For. 5:507). *No ke kāne a me ka wahine eu ka'awale ai* (Kep. 65), for the man and wife to be separated.

'eu. 1. nvi. Mischievous, naughty, playful, as a child; rogue, rascal, scamp; mischief; hoot of an owl *'aumakua* warning of imminent danger (also same as *hō'eu (a)).* Cf. *hū'eu. E 'eu,* get going; get a move on. *Piha 'eu,* roguish scamp; full of fun or humor. *Nui ka 'eu o nā maka,* eyes full of mischief. **hō.'eu. (a).** To stir up, incite, animate, encourage, bestir. *Kōmike hō'eu,* revival committee. *Hō'eu, kukupu, 'īnana, kū i luna o ka moku* (ancient prayer, For. 6:267), bestir, grow, animate, rule the island. (PCP *keu;* cf. Marquesan *keu.*) **(b)** *(Cap.)* Name of a star. **2.** vi. To crawl along; to rise, rising. *Ka 'eu o ka noe,* the rising of the mist. (PPN *keu.*)

'eu.ane.lika, euanelita, ewanelika. nvs. Evangelist; evangelistic.

'eu.ane.lio. nvs. Evangelical; gospel (Mat. 11.5). *Ha'i 'euanelio,* to preach the gospel.

e ue. See *ue,* hula step. (This is sometimes said today as a chant ending, but is probably an innovation.)

'eu.'eu. vs. Exciting, rousing, alert, lively, animated, aroused. *'Eu'eu ka puapua o ka moa,* animated tall feathers of the chicken [full of exuberance]. **hō.'eu.'eu.** To encourage, stir, rouse, excite; vivacious, spirited. See chant, *pu'uwai. Hālāwai hō'eu'eu,* rally. *Kō ma'i hō'eu'eu* (chant), your animated genital. (PPN *keukeu.*)

'Eukali.kia, eukaritia. n. **1.** Eucharist. (Latin *eucharistia.*) **2.** *(Not cap.)* Also **eukalitia.** Eucalyptus tree. Also *nuhōlani, palepiwa.*

'Eu.lopa, Europa. nvs. Europe; European. *Eng.*

ē.ulu. 1. nvt. Top of tree or plant; trimmed hedge top; cutting; to top, cut or crop off, as top branches. **2.** n. A kind of taro, qualified by the terms *ke'oke'o* and *kohu uauahi.*

'eu.nuha. n. Eunuch. *Biblical.*

ewa. Unstable, swaying, wandering; strayed. Cf. *māewa.* (PPN *'ewa.*)

'ewa. 1. vs. Crooked, out of shape, imperfect, ill-fitting. *Fig.,* incorrect, unjust. Cf. *pa'ewa. Ua 'ewa ka pilina a ka nihoniho* (song), the fitting of the scallops is imperfect. **hō.'ewa.** One-sided, crooked; to cause not to fit. **2.** *(Cap.)* n. Place name west of Honolulu, used as a direction term. See ex., *kuhi 1, 'ū 1. Hele ma 'Ewa,* to go in the direction of 'Ewa. **3.** *(Cap.)* n. Eve. *Fig.,* woman.

'ewa.'ewa. 1. Redup. of *'ewa 1;* irregular, biased, unequal, unjust. *Maka 'ewa'ewa 'ia,* looked at with disfavor, eyed askance. *O'ahu maka 'ewa'ewa,* O'ahu with indifferent eyes [a term of reproach to O'ahu people, said to have been said by Hi'iaka when her O'ahu relatives refused to help her mend a canoe for a journey to Kaua'i]. *'A'ole anei 'ewa'ewa 'ole ko'u mau 'ao'ao? 'A'ole anei 'o kō 'oukou mau 'ao'ao ka i 'ewa'ewa?* (Ezek. 18.25) Is not my way just? Are not your ways unjust? *Ho'okō au ia kauoha me ka 'ewa'ewa 'ole* (Kel. 125), I carried out this instruction without a flaw. **2.** n. Sooty tern *(Sterna fuscata oahuensis);* forehead and sides of head white, rest of head black; upper parts black, white beneath. Also *'ewa'ewa iki.*

'ewai. Perhaps a var. of *'auwai,* ditch (noted in 1848 land claim, Hāmākua, Hawai'i).

'ē.wai. Same as *'awaiāhiki,* swelling in the groin.

'ewalu. num. Eight; eight times. Cf. *walu, 'awalu.* (PPN *walu.*)

won't hurt the Kaua'i lad. *E 'eha ana 'oia ia'u,* I will hurt him. *'Eha o ke kua,* backache. *Nāna wale nō ka 'eha, ā koe ke kaikua'ana huhū* (For. 4:37), only he inflicted pain, until [only] the angry older brother was left. **hō.'eha.** To inflict pain or punishment, to hurt, oppress.

'ehā. num. Four; four times. See ex., *hā 1.*

'eha.'eha. Redup. of *'eha;* great pain, agony, tribulation, many small pains; painful. *'Eha'eha ka na'au,* feelings are hurt. **hō.'eha'eha.** Redup. of *hō'eha;* to torment, distress. *Hō'eha'eha na'au,* heart-breaking, tragic.

ehaha. vi. To breathe hard, pant. Cf. *hā,* breath.

'eha.kō. n. The Chinese lace-necked, or ring-necked dove *(Streptopelia chinensis),* an early introduction to Hawai'i, said to be named for its call *'eha kō,* prolonged pain.

'eha wale. vs. Easily hurt, sensitive, having feelings easily hurt; to hurt for no reason.

ē.hē. interj. Syllables repeated in chants at ends of verses, affording pleasure by repetition or sameness of sound harmonizing with repetition of sameness of drum beat; similar in function to English tra-la-la but different in mood, tending to be more serious. Cf. *ēhā. Eia nō 'o Kāwika, ēhē, ka heke a'o nā pua, ēhē* (chant for Ka-lā-kaua), here is David, ah, ah, the greatest of descendants, ah, ah.

'ehē. nvi. A hard, dry cough; to cough. *He kunu 'ehē,* a racking cough.

'ehē.'ehē. Redup. of *'ehē.*

ehehe. interj. Song refrain. (Elbert and Mahoe 67.)

ehe.hene. 1. nvi. To laugh merrily, giggle in glee; laughter. *Ehehene kō 'aka i ka le'ale'a,* your laughter is merry because of joy. 2. interj. Syllables repeated for musical effect at end of verses, similar to *ēhē.*

'ehe.hene. Var. of *ehehene 2.*

'ehe.heu. n. Wings. Cf. *'ēheu.*

ehe.ho'o.pi'i. n. Carved parallel or undulating lines on a tapa beater and on tapa. (AP.)

'ē.heu. 1. nvi. Wing, as of bird, kite, or airplane; winged, soaring on wings; to fly, take wings (Kel. 140). Also *'ēkeu, pēkeu.* Cf. *'eheheu, 'ekekeu, pekekeu. Ka uhi 'ana mai o nā 'eheu o ka pō,* the covering of the wings of night [nightfall]. **ho'ē.heu.** To flap the wings; to lift up or stretch the wings; to undulate the arms in a hula imitating a bird in flight; to flap the arms, shrug the shoulders; to pull up shoulders proudly, hence to be proud. (PCP *ke(e)(f,s)eu.*) 2. n. Rim of a hat. 3. n. Pectoral fin, as of a shark. *Rare.* 4. n. Flipper, as of turtle. *Rare.* 5. *(Cap.)* See Ka-'ēheu.

ehe.'ula. n. Name recorded for adult stage of *hāpu'u* fish.

'ehia. num. inter. How many, how much, what price; also used with the meaning of no matter how many or much, so very much or many, just a few. *'Ehia ou pāpale?* How many hats have you? *'Ehia o kou pāpale?* How much [money did you pay] for your [own] hat? *'Ehia o kāu pāpale?* How much [money] for your hat? *Hola 'ehia?* What time is it? *'Ehia ka luhi, he mea 'ole ia iāia,* however tired, it doesn't matter to him. *'Ehia nō lā, pau kēlā hana nui,* in just a few days that big project was finished. *'Ehia nō lū 'ana, pau ke kālā,* just a few reckless spendings, the money was gone. *'Ehia ua mea aloha, 'o wau!* Woe is me! *'Ehia mea aloha i ke keiki* (Nak. 104), so much pity for the child. (Gram. 10.4; PNP *efia.*)

'ehiku. num. Seven; seven times.

ehipa. vs. Somewhat crooked, warped; not in sound mind. *Rare.* (Similar to but perhaps less strong than *hipa* and *hepa.*)

'eho. 1. n. Stone pile (FS 107), especially as used to mark land boundaries; stone image; heap of stones under water (at times fishermen block one end with a net and drive the fish in from the other end), also *umu, imu;* pillar (Kin. 35.20); red-hot stones put inside dressed animals in cooking (also *pōhaku 'eho*). *Lono-ka-'eho*

(FS 209), Lono-the-stone [name of the god with eight stone foreheads, vanquished by Kama-pua'a]. (PEP *ke(f,s)o.*) 2. n. Swelling or ulcerous sore, as caused by friction under the arm, tumor. See *kua'eho.*

'eho.'eho. Redup. of *'eho,* stone pile. (And.)

E-ho'i-ka-u'i-o-Mānoa-ua-ahiahi. n. Name of a *lua* stroke. *Lit.,* let the hero of Mānoa return, [it's] evening. (*E-* is sometimes omitted.)

ehu. 1. Same as *'ehu 1-4.* See *kēhu.* (PPN *efu,* dust.) 2. Same as *ehuehu 2,* thriving. (PPN *efu.*) **ho'o.ehu.** Caus./vt. 3. n. Water or water mixed with fragrant herbs used in sprinkling or gently rubbing a patient to revive him from fainting. 4. Var. name for *'olapa 2, Cheirodendron* trees.

-ēhu. ho'ē.hu. To drive or shoo away; to stir, as a fire. Cf. *ehuehu 1.*

'ehu. 1. n. Spray, foam, mist. (Many older people say *ehu* for *'ehu 1-4,* which is probably the older form; note lack of glottal stops in such forms as *ehuehu, 'ehuehu, kaiehu, kēhu, kuehu, luehu, puehu.*) See ex., *moi 1. Ka 'ehu kēhau* (Kel. 48), the dew spray. *'Ehu moi,* foam of sea where *moi* fish are found. *I ka 'ehu nō o ka lā'au,* in the spray of the war club [of a swift or terrible blow]. *Kū ka 'ehu,* to send spray flying [to lose one's temper]. *Na ke kea ka 'ai, kū ka 'ehu o nā wa'a li'ili'i i ke keiki o Kuai-he-lani* (For. 4:57), the white [pebble] wins, the child of Kuai-he-lani stirs the spray of small canoes [an old *kōnane* game chant]. 2. nvs. Dust; dusty. *Kū ka 'ehu,* the dust rises. *He ala 'ehu,* a dusty path [this might also be interpreted as a faint path: see *'ehu 4*]. (PPN *efu.*) 3. n. Pollen. 4. nvs. Faint, difficult to see; wisp. *Wāwae 'ehu,* faint footprint. *He 'ehu wāwae no ka lani,* a trace of the high chief's steps [rain, rainbow]. 5. nvs. Reddish tinge in hair, of Polynesians and not of Caucasians; one with *'ehu* hair; reddish-brown complexion said to be characteristic of some *'ehu* people; ruddy. (This *'ehu* is invariably pronounced with an initial glottal stop.) Cf. *'e'ehu, 'ehu-'ehu. He 'ehu, he nani kona mau maka* (I Sam. 16.12), ruddy and of a beautiful countenance. (PPN *kefu.*)

'ehu ahi.ahi. n. The dust of evening. *Fig.,* twilight, old age.

'ehu.'awa. Same as *'ahu'awa (Cyperus javanicus).*

ehu.ehu. 1. nvs. Animation varying from fury and storm to power and majesty; violent, furious, powerful, animated; violence, fury, anger, majesty, animation. *Waiho kāhela i ka la'i ā ahiahi ehuehu mai,* lying stretched out in the calm until at evening full of animation. *Ā ka la'i na 'Ehu lā, ehuehu 'oe ē ka lani lā* (song for Ka-lā-kaua), and the calm of 'Ehu, you, o chief, appeared with majesty. *Kū ana 'o Mauna Loa, kuahiwi 'alo ehuehu* (song), stands Mauna Loa, hill resisting storms. 2. vs. Healthy, vigorous. Less used than *ahu-ahu.* 3. n. A kind of rock, used for adzes. (Malo 19.)

'ehu.ehu. Redup. of *'ehu 1-4* (this form was perhaps once *ehuehu* and is sometimes pronounced thus still). *Ku'u hoa i ka 'ehuehu a ka noe,* my companion in the spray of mist. *Ke 'ehuehu nei nā 'ale,* the billows rise in waves [of flaring temper]. *'Ehuehu kai, noho ka moi,* where the sea foams, the *moi* fish lives. (PPN *kefukefu.*)

'ehu.'ehu. Redup. of *'ehu 5. 'Ehu'ehu nā lihilihi,* reddened eyelash.

'ehu hī.nano. n. *Hīnano*-blossom pollen.

'Ehu-kai. n. Name of a wind of Hālawa, Moloka'i. (For. 5:103.)

'ehu kai. n. Sea spray, foam.

'ehu kaka.hiaka. n. The dust of morning. *Fig.,* dawn, youth, a shower that clears quickly.

'ehu kumu uli. n. Hair black at the roots that shades out to reddish at the tips, said to be characteristic of some *'ehu* people.

'ehu lepo. nvs. Dust; dusty.

'ehu pua. n. Flower pollen.

'ehu wai. n. Spray from water.

ei. 1. Var. of *eia,* especially before words beginning with

ened, cloudy, shady; to cloud, overshadow (sometimes confused with *eaea* and *'ea'ea*).

'ea hanu pa'a. n. Condition of frequent colds. *Lit., 'ea* with hardened breath.

'ea houpo lewa.lewa. n. Great hunger, perhaps due to diabetes. *Lit.,* loose-hanging diaphragm *'ea*.

'ea huna. n. Dizzy spells, dizziness; latent *'ea* disease (Kam. 64:103).

e (verb) **ai**. Particles indicating imperative/intentive mood and accompanying subordinate verbs (*ai* in this case is the anaphoric *ai*). (Gram. 5.4, 7.3.)

'ea kai wawaka. n. Impaired vision, perhaps labyrinthitis.

'ea kā.kua. n. A disease, perhaps secondary lues (Kam. 64:115).

'ea kā.molo.wā. n. Condition of listlessness.

'ea kua neneke. n. A variety of *'ea,* a land tortoise. *Lit.,* tortoise with back fitted into sections.

'ea kū.ka'a. n. Disease with swelling symptoms.

'ea kū manawa. n. Severe headaches, perhaps due to high blood pressure. *Lit., 'ea* at fontanel.

e (verb) **ala**. Same as *e* (verb) *lā. 'Oia ia lepo 'ula āu e 'ike ala,* it's that red dirt you see over there.

'ea mā.hani. n. A type of *'ea* described as evanescent. (Kam. 64:103.)

'ea mā.lani. nvs. Light-brown in color. See *'ea 2*.

ea.mā.mā. n. Gas. *Lit.,* light air.

e (verb) **ana**. Particles indicating incompleted action and future. Gram. 5.2. (PCP *'e* verb *'ana*.)

ea.ola.mā.mā. n. Oxygen. *Lit.,* light life breath.

'ea 'ō.lena. n. Jaundice, hepatitis.

'ea pō.niu. n. Dizziness, vertigo.

'ea 'ula. nvs. Wine-colored, such a color.

'ea wāhi pa'a. n. Osteomalacia, gradual softening of the bones.

'ea wawaka. n. Acute childhood *'ea* disease. (Kam. 64:105.)

e'e. 1. nvi. To climb on, mount, get on, go aboard, board, embark; one who climbs, mounts, boards; step. Cf. *e'e kuahiwi, e'e moku, hikie'e. Kai e'e,* tidal wave. **ho.'ē'e.** To rise or swell, as surf; to mount, as a surfer mounts a wave. (2 Oihn. 35.24.) *Kai ho'ē'e,* tidal wave, deep sea. *Ho'ē'e akula ia i ka noho maluna o kona hoki* (Kin. 22.3), he saddled his ass. (PPN *heke*.) **2.** Same as *a'a 2,* to extend greetings.

'e'e. vs. Hard, stiff, dry. Cf. *ka'e'e*.

'ē.'ē. 1. Redup. of *'ē 1;* contrary, peculiar, opposite; adversely. *He 'ē'ē wale nō kona mana'o,* his opinion is in opposition. *E pale ana i ka wawā lapuwale, a me ke kū 'ē'ē 'ana i ka mea i kapa hewa 'ia he na'auao* (I Tim. 6.20), avoiding profane babblings and oppositions of the thing falsely called science. **ho.'ē.'ē.** To keep away from, avoid. (PPN *kesekese,* PEP *keekee*.) **2.** n. Yellow underwing feathers of the *'ō'ō,* a bird, as used in featherwork. **3.** n. Armpit. Also *pō'ae'ae, po'ē'ē;* see *kui'ē'ē*. (PCP *keekee*.).

e'ea. Redup. of *ea 3;* to rise up frequently, as in water; to bob up and down. *E'ea a'e ke po'o o ka honu i ka 'ilikai,* the head of the turtle appeared again and again on the surface of the sea.

'e'ea. 1. vs. Quick ready, expert. *He 'e'ea nō kona kūlana,* he is quick in his ways. **2.** n. A bird, said to be an adult *'alaiaha*. (KL line 307.)

'e'e. Redup. of *e'e 1;* to keep climbing over everything, as an active child; mischievous.

'e'ehi. Same as *hehi,* to step on. *'E'ehi ihola ia a pa'a,* he placed his feet down and stood firm.

'e'e.hia. nvs. Overcome with fearful reverence, terrorstricken, awe-stricken; awe-inspiring, solemn; fear, reverence, awe, terror; wierd. *Ka 'e'ehia iā Iēhowa* (2 Oihn. 17.10), fear of Jehovah. *Piha au i ka 'e'ehia,* I am filled with awe.

e'ehu. Same as *ehuehu,* healthy.

'e'ehu. Redup. of *'ehu 5;* reddish; a number of *'ehu* persons. *Pala 'e'ehu,* to turn red or yellow, as leaves or fruit (riper than *pala hā'ama*).

'e'ei. Offensive, filthy, fly-ridden. (And.)

'e'ei.ao. Rare var. of *pepeiao,* ear. *Mō ka 'e'eiao o ka pua'a,* cut off is the ear of the pig.

'e'ei.ehi.ehi. Same as *'e'ei*. (AP.)

'e'e.'ina. vi. To creak, crackle. Cf. *'a'ina, 'u'ina*.

'E'eka. Same as *'Eka 2,* a wind.

'e'eke. 1. Redup. of *'eke 2*. Cf. *mū'e'eke. 'E'eke maila i ka wela o ke ahi,* shrinking back from the heat of the fire. **2.** n. Name given for a hard-shelled crab (no data).

'e'eke.loi. vt. To tap a drum slowly, as to accompany a chant.

'e'eku. Same as *'eku'eku. Ē Kāne-pua'a, e 'e'eku e kūlapa, e ho'owali,* o Kāne-pua'a, a root, and make ridges and furrows.

'e'e kua.hiwi. v. To climb mountains; mountain climber.

'e'ele. Same as *'ele'ele 1,* but used chiefly in old chants. *Ka manu 'e'ele koi* (For. 5:99), the black bird begged.

'e'ele.koa. vs. Stormy. *Kū 'ia ka malama 'e'elekoa,* weathered the stormy month [to have endured hardships].

'e'ele.kū. Redup. of *'elekū;* blackened or darkened, as leaves or fruit due to maturity or to pelting by storms; dark, gloomy, as clouds. *Ma ia malama ua 'e'elekū ka lani i nā ao ua . . . a ua 'e'elekū ho'i nā lau o nā lā'au a me nā mea ulu i ke o'o* (Kep. 89), in this month the sky is dark with rain clouds . . . and the leaves of trees and growing things are dark with maturity. *Ma ia malama o Nana, ua pau ka 'e'elekū o ka lau o nā lā'au i ka noke a ka ua ma nā lā o ka ho'oilo* (Kep. 89), in this month of Nana, the dark bruising of the leaves of trees by the pelting of the rains of the days of winter has ceased.

'e'elo. 1. Redup. of *'elo;* drenched, soaked. **hō.'e'elo.** To wet, drench, soak; tearfully sulky, as a crying child. *Ua hō'e'elo,* drenching rain. **2.** vs. Loitering; to dillydally. *Rare*.

'E'elo-koa. Name of a storm from the northeast of Waimea, Hawai'i. (And.)

e'e moku. nvi. To board a ship; ship passenger; immigrant.

'e'ena. vs. **1.** Shy, timid, wary, wild, afraid, fearsome, untamed; to shy away. Cf. *'ena 2, hā'e'ena. 'E'ena Hā'ena i ke ehu kai,* Hā'ena is fearsome because of sea spray. **2.** Extraordinary. Cf. *'ē 1. He 'e'ena a mīkolohua ka 'ōlelo,* impressive and eloquent in speech. *Kani 'e'ena ka pahu i ka moana,* the drum sounds weirdly over the ocean.

'e'epa. nvs. Extraordinary, incomprehensible, abnormal, deceitful, peculiar, as persons with miraculous powers; such persons. Many *'e'epa* characters in mythology were born in strange forms, as a plant, an animal, or a piece of rope. Cf. *'epa 1, 'epa'epa, kino 'e'epa.* The *menehune, Nāwā,* and *Nāmū* of Wao-lani in Nu'u-anu Valley were *'e'epa*. Trickery or deceit that passes comprehension is also *'e'epa.* **hō.'e'epa.** Mysterious, mystifying, incomprehensible. *Hō'e'epa wale ho'i nā hana a kēlā keiki,* that boy's behavior is certainly mysterious.

'e'eu. 1. vi. To crawl, creep, as an insect. Cf. *'eu 2*. (PCP *kekeu*.) **2.** nvi. Shuddering sensation of revulsion (less strong than *mania*); to rise in horror, flinch (sometimes interpreted as a portent). *'E'eu ka 'ili o ke po'o,* the scalp of the head flinches. *'E'eu a'ela ka hulu o ka 'īlio,* the dog's hair bristles [in anger].

'e'ewa. vi. To make a wry face, pout, as in derision; to protrude the lips mockingly.

ē.hā. Same as *ēhē. He wahi ma'i ēhē, ēhā, no 'Io-lani, ēhē, ēhā* (chant), a genital chant, oh, oh, for 'Io-lani, oh, oh.

'eha. nvs. Hurt, in pain, painful, aching, sore, pained; pain, injury, ailment, suffering, soreness, aching; to hurt, pain, cause suffering or pang. See *mea 'eha.* Gram. 4.4. *'Eha koni,* throbbing ache; *fig.,* throbbing love. *He 'eha konikoni i ka pu'uwai,* the heart throbs with agony [of love]. *'Eha i ka 'eha lima 'ole,* aching with an ache not inflicted by [human] hands [love]. *'A'ole e 'eha ke keiki o Kaua'i iā 'oe* (For. 5:411), you

E

Nouns beginning with e- *are preceded by the article* ke, *and are often pronounced with fusion of the two* e's *into a single long vowel. Nouns beginning with* 'e- *are preceded by the article* ka. *In some words there is today variation of* ke e- *and* ka 'e-; *see* ea, 'ehu.

e. **1.** Part. marking imperative/intentive mood. See *e* (verb) *ai, e* (verb) *ana,* Gram. 5.4. (PCP *e.*) **2.** Agentive part. By, by means of (follows a pas/imp.). (Gram. 9.9.) *Ua 'ahewa 'ia 'oia e ke ali'i,* he was blamed by the chief. (PPN *e.*) **3.** Infinitive part. used before certain subordinate verbs. (Gram. 5.4.) *Makemake au e hele,* I want to go (PCP *e.*) **4.** See *ē 1.*
ē. **1.** Vocative part.; a second *ē* often follows the head word for emphasis. *Ē Pua; ē Pua ē,* O Pua. *Ē ke ali'i o Maui,* O chief of Maui. *Ē* is shortened to *e* before third-person pronouns: see *e ia nei, e lākou ala.* (PPN *('e)e.*) **2.** Intensifying part., as in the common exclamation *Auē noho'i ē!* (Gram. 7.5.) **3.** interj. Alas!
'e-. Prefix to numerals, inanimate, as *'ekahi, 'elua, 'ekolu.* (PPN *e.*)
'ē. **1.** nvs. Different, strange, peculiar, unusual, heathen (Biblical), other; away off, elsewhere; beforehand, already, before, premature, in advance (sometimes translated 'had' and called by Andrews [Gram. 1.4] a sign of the pluperfect tense, although it is used after the imperative mood). Cf. *'ē a'e, 'ano 'ē, mea 'ē. 'Āina 'ē,* foreign land. *He 'ē!* How strange! [It] is gone, past! *Holo 'ē lākou,* they fled beforehand (away, elsewhere). *Keiki hānau 'ē,* prematurely born child. *Hele ma kahi 'ē!* Go away! Get out! *'Ike 'ē lākou,* they already knew. *I kahi 'ē ka ua, waele 'ē ke pulu* (saying), when the rain is elsewhere, open up beforehand the mulch [prepare for rain before it comes]. (PPN *kese,* PEP *kee.*) **2.** interj. Yes (unemphatic, as in mild agreement and indicating that one has heard; cf. *'ae*). **3.** n. The letter "e". *Eng.* **4.** n. Key of E *A* (music). *Eng.*
ea. **1.** n. Sovereignty, rule, independence. *Lā Ho'iho'i Ea,* Restoration Day. *Ho'iho'i i ke ea o Hawai'i,* restore the sovereignty of Hawai'i. **2.** n. Life, air, breath, respiration, vapor, gas; fumes, as of tobacco; breeze, spirit (Isa. 42.5). This *ea,* as well as *ea 1, 3, 4,* is sometimes pronounced or sung *'ea.* Cf. *eamāmā, eaolamāmā. Kaha ea,* to deprive of rights of livelihood. *Wai ea,* aerated waters. *Ho'opuka ea,* exhaust fumes. *Ua mau ke ea o ka 'āina i ka pono* (motto of Hawai'i), the life of the land is preserved in righteousness. *He palupalu lākou, he ea hele wale aku* (Hal. 78.39), they were flesh, a wind that passes away. *Kā'ili 'ia aku ke ea o 'Aberahama* (Kin. 25.8), Abraham gave up the ghost; *lit.,* the breath of life was snatched away. **3.** vi. To rise, go up, raise, become erect. Cf. *aea, e'ea, hō'ea. Kai ea* (Kep. 183), rising sea. *Ua ea kona po'o,* his head was raised. *Ke ea 'ana o ka 'ai, ka i'a* (Kep. 97), the obtaining of poi, fish. *'A 'ole ho'i au e ea maluna o ko'u wahi moe* (Hal. 132.3), I will not go up into my bed. (PPN *e'a.*) **4.** vi. To smell. Also *'ea.* Cf. *maea, māeaea. Ea 'ino'ino, ea pilau,* evil-smelling, rotten-smelling. (Perhaps PEP *ea.*)
-ea. Pejorative suffix. See *hanaea, luea, nanaiea, poluea,* Gram. 6.5. (PNP *-ea:* cf. Rennellese *-ea.*)
'ea. **1.** n. Hawksbill turtle (*Chelone imbricata*), both land and sea species; the shell of this turtle. (PNP *kea.*) **2.** vs. Reddish-brown, as the color of the *'ea* shell. Cf. *'ea*

mālani, 'ea 'ula. **3.** n. A general term for infections and infectious diseases; coated tongue, sometimes accompanied by sore throat, the thrush disease of children. Many diseases of miscellaneous nature begin with *'ea* and are listed below. *'Ea ka waha,* the tongue is coated. *'Oia kama'ilio aku a 'ea ka waha, 'a'ohe lohe 'ia mai,* while talking on until the tongue is coated, yet no one pays any attention [a metaphor to show exasperation]. (PPN *keakea,* PCP *kea.*) **4.** n. Spray. Cf. *'e'a,* dust. These words are sometimes interchanged. *Kū ka 'ea i ka moana,* the spray rises in the sea. **5.** Vocative interj. usually at the beginning or end of utterances. (Gram. 12, 1 Sam. 9.5; Lunk. 7.3.) *'Ea, hele mai!* Say, come here! *Ho'olohe mai 'oukou, 'ea,* all of you there, listen. **6.** Var. of *ea 4,* to smell. **7.** nvi. Noisy; to yell, whoop; whoop. *E kani ana ka 'ea,* a whoop sounded. **8.** Var. of *ea 2, 3. A waiho i ka 'ea nā iwi o kama hele* (RC 367), the traveler's bones are left in the air [said of one dying in a foreign land].
'eā. interj. **1.** Isn't that so? That's it! *Oia, 'eā?* Is that so? *Ua hele aku 'oia i Honolulu, 'eā,* she went to Honolulu, you know. *'Eā, e aha ana 'oukou?* Say, what are you up to? *Pēlā, 'eā?* It's that way, is it? **2.** Song refrain. See ex., *wawalo* and Gram. 12. Also *'eā'eā.*
'e'a. **1.** nvs. Dust, dirt, dust cloud, spray (*'e'a* and *'ea 4* are probably interchanged at times). *Kōwelo 'e'a,* dust streamer. *Kū ka 'e'a i ke kula,* the dust cloud rose over the plain. *'Ōka'i ka 'e'a, 'oka'i huaka'i 'ula,* a marching cloud of dust, a red procession on the march [warriors with feather cloaks]. **2.** n. Mountain banana patch. *Līlā ka mai'a o ka 'e'a, wili ka 'ōka'i,* spindly is the growth of the mountain banana patch, the blossom container twists [even a spindly plant may bear fruit]. **3.** n. A fish similar to *a'awa,* but with dark flesh.
ea.'a'ā. n. Gas. *Lit.,* burning air.
'ē a'e. vs. Different, other, another, else.
ea.ea. **1.** n. Air, breath, air current. Some confusion exists in the uses of *eaea, 'ea'ea,* and *'e'a'e'a.* **2.** Redup. of *ea 3;* to rise; high waves. *He i'a no ka papa'u, he loa'a wale i ka hopu lima; he i'a no ka hohonu, noho i ke eaea,* fish of the shallows, gotten merely by catching in the hands; fish of the depths stay in the high waves [some tasks are easier than others]. (PPN *e'ae'a.*) **3.** Redup. of *ea 4;* a smell, as of seaweed; to smell.
'ea.'ea. **1.** Redup. of *'ea 4,* spray; encrusted with spray (sometimes confused with *eaea* and *'e'a'e'a*). *Ka lawai'a nui i 'ea'ea nā ku'emaka, i 'ehu'ehu nā lihilihi,* the great fisherman whose brows are sprayed with sea and whose lashes are reddened [admiration of a fisherman]. **2.** Dignified, honorable. (And.) **3.** n. A bird (no data).
-'ea.ea. ho'ea.ea. To approach.
'eā.'eā. Interj. at end of verses in some chants that maintains rhythm and affords pleasure in repetition, something like English tra-la-la. *Nani wale nā hala, 'eā'eā, o Naue i ke kai, 'eā'eā* (song), beautiful indeed the pandanus, tra-la, of Naue by the sea, tra-la.
'e'a.'e'a. Redup. of *'e'a 1,* dust; dusty; obscure, dark-

Clusters of irregularly bell-shaped flowers that are white and marked with red and yellow bend downward from the top of leafy, arching stems, which are 1.5 to 3.5 m high. *Lit.,* drooping ginger. (Neal 259-60.)

'awa.puhi mele.mele. n. The yellow ginger *(Hedychium flavescens),* similar to *'awapuhi ke'oke'o* and similarly used, but the flowers are yellow. (Neal 252.)

'awa.puhi Pā.kē. n. Ginger *(Zingiber officinale),* yielding a valuable commercial root spice. The plant looks much like *'awapuhi kuahiwi* and probably comes from southeast Asia. (Neal 257-8.) *Lit.,* Chinese ginger. Also *'awapuhi 'ai.*

'awa.puhi 'ula.'ula. n. The red ginger *(Alpinia purpurata),* an ornamental plant having a long flower spike with many red bracts. It is a native of some islands of the western Pacific. (Neal 260.)

awāwa. n. Valley, gulch, ravine. Cf. *kuawa.* **ho.- 'ā.wāwa.** To make a groove, furrow.

'awa-wai-a-ka-manu. n. A variety of kava, an offshoot of *'awa hiwa,* with joints green on one side and dark on the other. (HP 202.) *Lit.,* watery kava of the bird.

awe. 1. nvs. Strand, thread; thin, soft. (Probably PPN, PCP *awe.)* **2.** n. Wake of a ship. (Note both *awe* and *'awe* in Hawaiian, *awe* and *kawe* in PCP.)

'awe 1. nvt. Pack, knapsack carried on the back; to carry on the back. Cf. *'auamo, hā'awe.* **hō.'āwe.** To carry on the back; a burden so carried. (PPN *kawe.)* **2.** n. Tentacle. Cf. *'awe puhi, 'awe ule.* (PPN *kawe.)*

'awea. Pas/imp. of *'awe 1.*

awe.awe. 1. vs. Tenacious, sticky, threadlike, adhesive; glueyness, threads. Cf. *aweawe poi. Ke aweawe 'ōnohi i ke kula* (chant), the sun's rays on the plain. **hō.'awe.awe.** Caus/sim. **2.** n. Wake, as of a ship.

'awe.'awe. Redup. of *'awe 1;* pack knapsack; straps for a bundle; strips, as of *wauke;* runners, as on a vine; tentacles. (PPN *kawekawe.)*

'ā.we'a.we'a. 1. nvs. Faint trace, spot, glimpse; faint, dim; streaked, faded. *'Āwe'awe'a koko ali'i* (Kep. 127), trace of royal blood. *'Āwe'awe'a lono,* dim recollection. *'Ike 'āwe'awe'a,* to see fleetingly, to know but have slight knowledge; faint glimpsing, slight knowledge. *Ua 'ike 'āwe'awe'a a'e nei au i ua manu nei,* I caught but a fleeting glimpse of this bird. **ho.'ā.we'a.we'a.** Caus/sim. **2.** n. A kind of seaweed.

'ā.we'a.we'a koko. n. Traces of blood, as in vomit.

awe.awe poi. n. Drip of poi; an insult to the chiefs of Hawai'i, playing on the name of their chiefs, Keawe, with implication that poi is excreted in a sticky chain.

'aweka. vt. To hide rather than share wealth (perhaps related to *weka,* squid ink).

'ā.wela. 1. n. Young stage of the *hou* fish, Christmas wrasse *(Thalassoma fuscum).* **2.** vs. Heated, hot. **3.** n.

A flowerless variety of sugar cane, named for the fish; it is green and yellow striped, becoming flushed with rose in the sun; the internodes are barrel-shaped and the leaves variegated. (HP 221, 224.) Also *pua'ole.*

'ā.wela mele.mele. n. A variety of sugar cane, a bronze-yellow mutant of *'āwela.* Also *ule'ohi'u, uluhui.* (HP 221.)

'ā.wela.wela. Redup. of *'āwela 2.*

'ā.wele. 1. Same as *hāwele,* to tie. **2.** Goal, mark, line, goal post. (AP.)

'awe.lika, averiga. nvs. Average, pro rata. *Eng.*

'ā.welu. nvs. Ragged, worn-out, torn; worn-out garment. *'Āwelu moena,* ragged mat.

'ā.welu.welu. Redup. of *'āwelu.*

'ā.weo.weo. n. **1.** Various Hawaiian species of *Priacanthus,* red fishes, sometimes called bigeye. Young are called *'alalauā* and *'alauwā.* **2.** A variety of sugar cane named for the fish. **3.** Same as *'āheahea (Chenopodium oahuense).* **4.** A seaweed.

'awe puhi. n. Eel tentacle, but referring to the octopus, a euphemism for *'aweule.*

'ā.weu, 'ā.weu.weu. n. A native variety of taro, often growing wild; good for poi, but too acrid for table taro; the corms are shaggy and fibrous outside, the flesh white with yellow fibers. Also *mā'auea.*

'awe.ule. n. Lone octopus tentacle, said to wave in order to entice and ensnare a victim. *Lit.,* penis tentacle.

'ā.weu.weu. Same as *'āweu.*

awī.'awī. Same as *'uwī'uwī,* an herb.

'ā.wiha. Same as *'āwe'awe'a.*

'ā.wiha.wiha. Redup. of *'āwiha.*

'ā.wihi. vi. To wink, ogle. See saying, *lihilihi 2. Kō 'oukou po'e 'āwihi ho'owalewale* (Ier. 27.9), your deceiving enchanters.

'ā.wihi.wihi. Redup. of *'āwihi.*

'ā.wiki. vi. To hurry, be quick, swift. *E 'āwiki mai 'oe!* Hurry up!

'ā.wiki.wiki. 1. Redup. of *'āwiki.* **2.** n. A vine *(Canavalia* spp.), native to Hawai'i, related to the *maunaloa (C. cathartica),* but with narrower pods; used for small, temporary fish traps. Also *puakauhi.* **3.** Same as *kō'ele'ele,* a seaweed.

'ā.wili. 1. vt. To mix, interweave, entwine; mixed, agitated. Cf. *ko'i 'āwili. Koko 'āwili,* mixed blood. (PCP *kaawili.)* **2.** n. Alligation (an old arithmetic term). *'Āwili kaulua,* alligation alternate.

'ā.wili.wili. Redup. of *'āwili 1.*

'ā.wini. vs. Sharp, bold, forward. Cf. *kīwini, wini.*

'ā.wiwi. n. A small native herb *(Centaurium sebaeoides,* syn. *Erythraea sebaeoids),* with white or pale pink flowers, in the gentian family. (Neal 684.)

'ā.wī.wī. vi. To hurry; speedy, swift, quick, fast.

B

All loan words from English sometimes spelled with initial *b-* are entered under *p-.* For example: *Baibala,* see *Paipala,* Bible; *balota,* see *pālota,* ballot; *bele,* see *pele,* bell; *bila,* see *pila,* bill; *bipi,* see *pipi,* beef; *buke,* see *puke,* book.

D

All loan words from English sometimes spelled with initial *d-* are entered under *k-.* For example: *dala,* see *kālā,* dollar; *dia,* see *kia,* deer; *diabolo,* see *kiapolo,* devil.

'ewane.lika. Var. spelling of 'euanelika.
ewane.lio. Var. spelling of 'euanelio.
ewe. n. Eve. *Eng.*
ēwe. **1.** nvi. Sprout, rootlet; lineage, kin; birthplace; family trait; to sprout. Cf. *ēweewe, ēwe kapu, ēwe lani.* *Hookahi nō o māua ēwe,* we are of the same lineage. *Ēwe hānau o ka 'āina,* natives of the land. *Kū nō ke ēwe,* true to the family traits. *E kolo ana nō i ēwe i ke ēwe,* rootlet creeps to rootlet [kinfolk seek and love each other]. *I ke ēwe 'āina o ke kupuna,* in the ancestors' family homeland. ho'ēwe. Caus/sim. *Ua ho'ēwe pa'a 'ia i loko o kona papa houpo ali'i,* firmly fixed in the heart of the chiefly class. **2.** n. Navel string; abdominal aorta, mature birth. **3.** Same as *'iewe 1,* afterbirth.

Hānau ēwe, premature birth. (PCP *eewe.*) **4.** n. White of an egg. *Ke ēwe o ka hua moa* (Ioba 6.6), the white of an egg.
ē.weewe. nvs. Kinsmen, lineage; pertaining to the family, having a family. *Hānau ke ēweewe, he ēweewe kona* (KL line 524), born were those of the lineage, of the lineage they. (PCP *e(e)weewe.*)
'ewe.'ewe. interj. Cry of 'Ewe'ewe-iki, a legendary woman who died in childbirth and who is said to return at night as a ghost and make this cry, which is followed by a *nā* cry like that of an infant, an omen that a birth is imminent.
ēwe kapu. n. Sacred or taboo lineage.
ēwe lani. n. Chiefs of divine descent.

F

All loan words from English sometimes spelled with initial *f-* are entered under *p-*. For example: *falu,* see *palū,* flu; *fea,* see *pea,* fair; *fiku,* see *piku,* fig; *fila,* see *pila,* fiddle; *fiwa,* see *piwa,* fever.

G

All loan words from English sometimes spelled with initial *g-* are entered under *k-*. For example: *gita,* see *kīkā,* guitar; *gula,* see *kula,* gold.

ha-. Same as *ha'a-*.

hā. 1. num. Four, fourth (commonly preceded by the numeral-marking prefixes, as '*ehā keiki*, four children; *Pō'ahā*, Thursday; *lit.*, fourth day). *Hā* and multiples of four are sacred or formulistic numbers. Rarely used as an intensifier, as *Wai-a-lua, la'i 'ehā*, Wai-a-lua, of fourfold calm. Cf. *kāuna*. *'O nā manu kolo e hele ana ma nā hā* (Oihk. 11.20), the fowls that creep, going upon all four. (PPN *faa*.) **2.** nvi. To breathe, exhale; to breathe upon, as kava after praying and before prognosticating; breath, life. *Hā ke akua i ka lewa*, god breathed into the open space. *Ka hā o kona waha* (2 Tes. 2.8), the spirit of his mouth; (Ioba 15.30), the breath of his mouth. **3.** nvs. Hoarse; hoarseness. (PPN *faa*.) **4.** nvs. Stalk that supports the leaf and enfolds the stem of certain plants, as taro, sugar cane; layers in a banana stump. Cf. *'ohana*. (PPN *fa'a*.) **5.** nvi. Trough, ditch, sluice; to form a ditch or trough. *Hā wai*, water ditch or trough. *Hā ka iwi*, the bones are a trough [of a thin person or of one straining in work]. **6.** n. Stick or furrowed stone used as a sinker, with hooks attached. Also *hā lawai'a*. **7.** n. A native tree *(Eugenia [Syzygium] sandwicensis)*, with red, edible fruit about 8.5 mm. in diameter, related to the mountain apple, *'ōhi'a 'ai*. The bark was used to color tapa black. Also *'ōhi'a hā*, and *pā'ihi* (on Maui). (Neal 635.) **8.** n. Fourth note in the musical scale, fa. Eng. **9.** interj. See *'oia ho'i hā*.

hā-. Same as *ha'a-*. (PPN *faa*.; cf. Fijian *vā*.)

ha'a. 1. nvs. Low; dwarf; man or animal of short stature. **ho'o.ha'a.** To lower; humble. See the more common *ho'oha'aha'a*. (PNP *saka*.) **2.** n. A dance with bent knees; dancing (1 Sam. 18.6); called hula after mid 1800s. (PPN *saka*.) **3.** n. A short variety of banana.

ha'a-. A prefix similar in meaning to the causative/simulative *ho'o-*. Before short vowels and glottal stop the form is usually *hā-*, as *hāinu*, to give to drink, and *hā'awe*, to carry. Before consonants, both *ha'a-* and *hā-* occur, as *ha'alele* and *hāku'i*. Before glottal stop plus a long vowel, *ha-* occurs, as *ha'āpuka*. For a few bases, derivatives with both *ha'a-* and *ho'o* occur, as *ha'ako'o* and *ho'oko'o*, which have the same meanings; with a few bases, meanings differ, as *ha'alele* (described with the *h*'s) and *ho'olele* (under *lele*). A few bases with *ha'a-* may form another derivative with *ho'o-*, as *inu, hāinu*, and *ho'ohāinu; heo, ha'aheo, ho'oha'aheo*. Before colors the meaning is "-ish, somewhat," as *hākea, ha'akea, hā'ele'ele, hāuliuli*. For clear understanding, delete *ha'a-* and look up the base. (Gram. 6.3.1.) (PPN *faka-*.)

ha'ā. Same as *hame 1*, native trees.

haa'a. Same as *a'a 2*.

hā.'a'a. Same as *a'a'a*, fibrous.

hā.'ae. 1. nvi. Saliva, spittle; to slobber, drool. *Kahe ka hā'ae, moni i ka hā'ae*, to drool or water at the mouth. **2.** n. A variety of sweet potato used to make beer.

ha'a.ha'a. Redup. of *ha'a 1*; low, lowly, minimum, humble, degraded, meek, unpretentious, modest, unassuming, unobtrusive; lowness, humility. Cf. *lani ha'aha'a. Ha'aha'a loa*, minimum, servile, abject. *'O wau nō me ka ha'aha'a*, I am, humbly yours [formerly a common closing to a letter]. *He ho'olimalima makahiki ha'aha'a*, minimum annual rental. *Ka pū'ulu ha'aha'a iho o nā koi*, lower group requirements. **ho'o.ha'a.ha'a.** To lower, debase, humiliate, humble (Kanl. 8.2), disgrace, underrate, belittle; humble, lowly, modest. *Ho'oha'aha'a aku*, to condescend. *E ho'oha'aha'a 'ia ho'i ka mana'o ki'eki'e o ke kanaka* (Isa. 2.17), the

haughtiness of men shall be made low. (PNP *sakasaka*.)

ha'a.heo. nvi. Proud, haughty; to strut; to cherish with pride; pride, vanity, haughtiness. Cf. *heo. Hele ha'aheo*, walk proudly, strut. *Ha'aheo aka me ka hanohano*, maestoso (musical term used by Henry Berger). *Ha'aheo Kaimana-hila*, pride in Diamond Head. *Ā e wāhi aku au i ka ha'aheo o kō 'oukou mana* (Oihk. 26.19), and I will break the pride of your power. **ho'o.ha'a.heo.** Caus/sim.; to act haughty.

ha'a.hui. vs. United. (For. 6:403.) Cf. *hui 2*.

ha'a.ikaika. Same as *haikaika*.

ha'a.iwi. n. Bachelor. *Rare*.

ha'a.kē. Same as *ho'okē*.

ha'a.kea. 1. nvs. Whitish, pale; pallor. **2.** Same as *haokea*, a native taro. *Mō'ī puni ha'akea* (song), king fond of white taro.

ha'a.kei. vs. Proud, haughty, rude, snobbish, snooty, vain; to scorn, scoff. *Ka noho o ka po'e ha'akei* (Hal. 1.1), the seat of the scornful.

ha'a.kei.kei. Redup. of *ha'akei*.

ha'a.kekē. Same as *ho'okekē*.

ha'a.ko'a. vs. Short, as a bantam. *Rare*.

ha'a.koa'e. vs. Like the tropic bird. See *koa'e. Pali ha'akoa'e*, an inaccessible cliff where *koa'e* birds fly.

ha'a.kōhi. Same as *kōhi. Ha'akōhi ihola e Rāhela, a pu'ua iho i ka hānau keiki 'ana* (Kin. 35.16). Rachel travailed and had hard labor in childbirth.

ha'a.koi. nvi. **1.** Egotistic; egotism; proud; to brag, boast, show off. Cf. *pi'ikoi*. **2.** vi. To force, urge, insist. **3.** vi. To practice onanism.

ha'a.koi.koi. Redup. of *ha'akoi 1–3*.

ha'a.kokoe. Same as *ho'okokoe*.

ha'a.kokōhi. 1. Redup. of *ha'akōhi;* to travail. See *kōhi 4. Ka 'eha e like me kō ka wahine ha'akokōhi* (Hal. 48.6), pain, as of a woman in travail. *Kani ha'akokōhi o nā leo*, emphatic sound of the voices. **2.** vt. To bring out the natural grain of wood, as by careful use of oil.

ha'a.koni. n. Female *kāhili*-bearer for a chief.

ha'a.ko'o. Same as *ho'oko'o*.

ha'a.ko'o.ko'o. Same as *ho'oko'oko'o*.

ha'a.kua. 1. vs. To struggle to right oneself, as a turtle turned over. **2.** n. Male *kāhili*-bearer for a chiefess.

ha'a.kua.li'i. n. A class of dwarfish people of great strength and valor. (Malo 201.) Cf. *'Ā'ahuali'i*.

ha'a.kua.liki. An officer who preceded a chief and his train and announced his rank and the object of his approach. (AP.)

ha'a.ku'e. 1. vs. To shift or ripple; to and fro, back and forth. **2.** A *kāhili*-bearer for a chief or chiefess of the same sex. (AP.)

ha'a.ku'ia. Same as *ho'oku'ia*. See ex., *ku'iku'ia. Ha'aku'ia ka mana'o*, disturbed thoughts.

ha'a.kula manu. Same as *ho'okula manu*.

ha'a.kū.lipo. Same as *ho'okūlipo*, dark.

ha'a.kū.lou. Same as *ho'okūlou*, to bow.

ha'a.lau. vs. To produce leaves.

hā.'ale. vs. Completely full and ready to overflow; rippling. Cf. *'ale*. *Ua hā'ale ka wai i ka lau o ke pili*, the stream rose up to the very *pili* grass. *Hā'ale i ka wai a ka manu*, rippling in the water of birds [an attractive person likened to rippling waters that attracts birds].

hā.'ale.'ale. Redup. of *hā'ale. Hā'ale'ale i ka pu'uwai*, a heart full to the brim [as with love].

ha'a.lei. Same as *ho'olei*.

ha'a.lele. vt. To leave, desert, abandon, forsake, quit, resign, abdicate, discard, give up, reject, leave unfinished. Cf. *ho'olele*. *Ha'alele i ke ola*, to leave life, pass away. *Ha'alele noho ali'i*, to resign or abdicate as monarch. *Keiki ha'alele kula*, truant. *Palapala ha'alele 'oihana*, letter of resignation. *Ua ha'alele ka 'aha kuhina*, the cabinet has resigned. **ho'o.ha'a.lele**. To pretend to quit or leave; to cause to quit. (PPN *fakalele*.)

ha'a.lelea. 1. Pas/imp. of *ha'alele*. 2. n. Man sacrificed when cutting an *'ōhi'a* tree for an image.

ha'a.lelele. Redup. of *ha'alele;* to desert repeatedly.

ha'a.lele loa. 1. vt. To abandon permanently or completely. 2. vs. Extremely, exceedingly. *Pupuka ha'alele loa*, extremely ugly. *Kauwā ha'alele loa* (Kep. 11), a *kauwā*, outcast, of the worst and most abandoned sort. *Hūpō ha'alele loa maoli nō 'oe*, you are extremely ignorant.

ha'a.lele noho ali'i. v. To abdicate a throne.

ha'a.lele wale. 1. vt. To abandon for no reason. 2. Same as *ha'alele loa 2*. *Uwā ka pihe a ha'alele wale* (FS 35-7), to shout oneself hoarse.

ha'a.lewa. Same as *lewa 2*, and *ho'olewa*. See ex., *ninipo*. *Kai ha'alewa*, swaying sea.

hā.'ali. n. Fish gills. *Rare*.

hā.'ali'ali. n. 1. Fish gills. *Rare*. 2. End of penis. *Rare*.

ha'a.li'i. Same as *hāli'i*. *Loa'a iā Hezekia ia mau palapala . . . ā ha'ali'i akula i mua o Iēhowa* (Isa. 37.14), Hezekiah received the letters . . . and spread [them] before Jehovah.

ha'a.liki. nvt. To brag, boast; braggart.

ha'a.lili. Same as *ho'olili*. See *-lili*.

ha'a.lilio. vs. Tight, taut. Cf. *lio 2*. *Ha'alilio ka 'ōpū i ka 'ai nui loa*, the stomach is tight from overeating.

ha'a.lilo. vs. Far off, distant. *Kani ha'alilo*, sound in the distance.

ha'a.lipo. Same as *ho'onipo;* to be darkened; to bow the head, as in grief. *Eia 'o Ka-pili ē, ke ha'alipo nei ana lipo walohia* (lament for Lele-iō-Hoku), here is Ka-pili, her grief and anguish darkened.

ha'a.lohi. Same as *'alohi*, sparkling.

ha'a.loku. Same as *ho'oloku*, downpour; emotion.

ha'a.loku.loku. Same as *ho'olokuloku*.

ha'a.lo'u. vi. To bend over, as a heavy branch; to droop, as in sorrow.

ha'a.lo'u.lo'u. Redup. of *ha'alo'u*. *Uwē ha'alo'ulo'u*, to bow the head and sob with grief. *Noke ihola i ka 'aka'aka ha'alo'ulo'u*, to keep bending over and rocking with laughter.

hā.'alu. Same as *hō'alu*.

ha'a.lulu. vi. To shake, quake, totter, tremble, quiver. Cf. *lulu*. *E lo'ohia noho'i ka po'e . . . i ka ha'alulu* (Puk. 15.15), trembling shall take hold of the people. **ho'o.ha'a.lulu**. Caus/sim.

ha'a.lululu. Same as *ha'alulu*. (Nak. 78.)

hā.'ama. vs. To begin to turn yellow, as ripening mango or papaya. Cf. *-'ama*.

ha'ā.maile. Same as *hame 1*, trees.

Ha'a.moa. Same as *Kāmoa*, Samoa.

ha'a.momoe. Similar to *momoe*. (For. 6:445.)

hā.'ana.'ana. n. Short strips of *wauke* bark, as used for tapa.

ha'a.napu. vi. To sway, as in a dance. *Rare*.

ha'a.nepu. Same as *ho'onepu*, plump.

ha'a.nipo. Var. of *ho'onipo*. *Na ka ua Kuahine o Wa'ahila e noho ha'anipo lā i ka wao* (chant), by the Kuahine rain of Wa'ahila [Mānoa, O'ahu] that dwells in love with the uplands.

hā.'ano. Same as *'a'ano*.

ha'a.noa.noa. Var. of *ho'onoanoa*, to free from taboo.

ha'a.nopu. vi. To swell, surge, as the sea.

ha'a.nou. Same as *ho'onou*. *E ha'anou ana 'o Mea e ho'owā lua'i*, Mea is straining to retch [and] vomit.

ha'a.no'u. nvt. To exaggerate, gush, boast, speak forcefully; to chant with emphasis and force on stressed syllables.

ha'a.nu'a. Same as *ho'onu'a*.

ha'a.nui. vt. To boast, brag, exaggerate, gloat. (See *nui* and 2 Sam. 1.20.) *I kō lākou ha'anui 'ana ma ka mea*

lapuwale (2 Pet. 2.18), their speaking great swelling words of vanity. **ho'o.ha'a.nui**. Caus/sim.

hā.'ao. n. 1. Sections or divisions following in the procession after a high chief. 2. *(Cap.)* Name of a rain at 'Au'au-lele, Ka'ū and at Nu'u-anu, O'ahu, so called because its showers follow one another like members of a chief's retinue. 3. Name of a tapa pattern. Also *uahā'ao*, *nao-ua-hā'ao*.

ha'a.papa'a. vs. Firm, tight. Cf. *pa'a*.

ha'a.pā.pa'a. Same as *ho'opāpa'a*.

hā.'apu.'apu. Same as *hā'upu'upu*, sweet potato sprouts.

ha'ā.puka. Same as *ho'āpuka*. *E hele li'ili'i ka waiwai i ha'āpuka wale 'ia* (Sol. 13.11), wealth gotten by vanity shall be diminished.

ha'a.pupū. Same as *ho'opupū*. *Aloha wale ka maka o a'u pao'o, e ha'apupū, e ha'apapa'a mai nei e 'ai paha*, alas, the face of my *pao'o* fish, holding back, grasping tight, taking the bait maybe.

ha'a.pu'u. 1. Rare var. of *ho'opu'u*. 2. Same as *hāpu'upu'u 4*, mound.

ha'a.uē. Same as *auē*.

hā.'awa. Same as *hō'awa*, trees.

ha'a.wale. See *pāki'i ha'awale*, a flatfish.

hā.'awe. 1. nvt. To carry a burden on the back, pack; a bundle or burden so carried, backpack. See *'awe 1*. *Nā hā'awe kaumaha* (Isa. 58.6), heavy burdens. **ho'o.hā.-'awe**. To have something carried on the back; to load on the back. 2. nvi. A tumbling game: a player lies face down, reaches back and grasps his ankles, pulling them back and up to form a loop; the second player, lying at right angles to the first, slips his arm in that loop and tumbles the player over his head; to play this game.

hā.'awe.awe. Same as *hō'aweawe*.

hā.'awe.'awe. 1. n. Runners on plants. 2. Redup. of *hā'awe 1*. 3. vs. Sharp abdominal pains.

hā.'awi. nvt. To give, grant, allot, hand, present; to bid, as at auction; to offer; to deal, as cards; a deal. Cf. *ha'awina*. *Hā'awi lokomaika'i*, to give freely, open-handed. *Hā'awi wale*, to give freely, gratis.

hā.'awi 'āina. n. Land grant.

hā.'awi.kea. Same as *haokea*, a taro.

ha'a.wina. n. Lesson, assignment, task, gift (Rom. 11.29), appropriation, allowance, grant, or contribution, honorarium, allotment, award, as of money; donation, portion, deal or hand in cards, dream, article (section in a law). *Ha'awina* is used broadly by Kel. as blessings, results, symptoms, burdens, pangs, feelings, happenings, revelations. *Nā ha'awina o ua ma'i . . . nei* (Kel. 18), the symptoms of this disease. *He ha'awina ka'u i ka pō nei*, I had a dream last night. *Hā'awi ha'awina*, to assign a lesson.

ha'a.wina ho'i hope. n. Review lesson. *Lit.*, lesson going backward.

ha'a.wina hō.'ike. n. Examination, test. *Lit.*, showing lesson.

ha'a.wina ho'o.hano.hano. n. Honorarium.

ha'a.wina ho'o.mau. n. Life pension.

ha'a.wina 'ike. The gift of second sight, a gift of knowledge.

hā.'awi.pio. To give up, surrender. *Hā'awipio 'oko'a*, unconditional surrender.

hae. 1. nvs. Wild, fierce, vicious, furious, savage, ferocious; fury, rage; to rage. *Hae ka inaina*, enraged. *Hae i ka pōloli*, famished. *Hae ka pu'u i ka 'ai*, ravenous with hunger. *Hae i ka wai* (Kel. 48), very thirsty. **ho'o.hae**. To make wild or savage; to provoke, tease, exasperate, stir up wrath. (PCP *(f,s)ae*.) 2. vi. To bark (Isa. 56.10), growl, snap, as a dog; to chirp noisily or scold, as a mynah bird. **ho'o.hae**. To cause to bark, growl, scold. 3. vt. To tear. (PPN *sae*.) 4. n. Flag, banner (perhaps so called because a piece of torn *[hae]* tapa was used as a banner). *E kau ai kākou i ka hae* (Hal. 20.5), we will set up the banners. 5. n. Flowers. See below.

ha'e. nvt. Yearning, longing; to yearn. *Rare.*

haea. 1. Pas/imp. of *hae 3.* (PPN *saea*). **2.** See *limu haea.*

hā.'ea. Rare var. *kaha'ea,* clouds.

hā.'e'ena. vs. Shy. Cf. *'ena.*

hae.hae. 1. Redup. of *hae 2, 3;* to tear to bits, tease. *Ua pau 'o Iosepa i ka 'īlio hihiu, 'oia'i'o nō, ua haehae 'ia 'o Iosepa* (Kin. 37.33), Joseph is devoured by a wild beast; Joseph is without doubt rent in pieces. **2.** Redup. of *hae 1.* **ho'o.hae.hae.** Caus/sim.; to drive into a fury; to decoy *uhu* fish by tying an *uhu* to a line; to tease. *Ka 'iwa ho'ohaehae nāulu,* an *'iwa,* frigate bird, teases the showers [an attractive person provokes envy]. **3.** n. A variety of taro in the *piko* group, characterized by having the two basal lobes of the leaf blade separated up to the *piko* (point of joining with the leaf stem); a hardy taro often grown commercially for poi, formerly common at Kā'ana-pali, Maui, where strong winds tore the leaves (hence *haehae*). (HP 29, 32.) Also *piko uliuli.*

ha'e.ha'e. Redup. of *ha'e;* strong affection and desire. *Ā e hā'awi 'ia aku kāu mau keiki . . . i nā kānaka 'ē, a e ha'eha'e wale nā maka ou i ka nānā aku* (Kanl. 28.32), thy sons . . . shall be given unto other people, and thy eyes shall look and fail with longing for them.

Hae.hae-ka-manu-o-Kāne-aloha. n. A *lua* fighting stroke. *Lit.,* the birds of Kāne-aloha tear to bits.

hae Hawai'i. n. **1.** Hibiscus. *Lit.,* Hawaiian flag, from having red petals striped with white. (Neal 556.) **2.** Carnation *(Dianthus caryophyllus),* petals red with white stripes, formerly a great favorite with Hawaiians (Neal 345). **3.** A variety of plumeria.

hae.hia. Pas/imp. of *hae 1–3.*

hā.ehu. Same as *ehuehu, ahuahu,* to grow well.

hā.'ehu.'ehu. vs. Reddish-brown, as hair.

hā.'ei. vi. To peep. *Rare.*

hā.'eka.'eka. vs. Dirty, drab; smudged, as by smoke.

hae.koko. vs. Bloodthirsty. (Kel. 42.)

haele. vi. To go, come (dual or plural) *Haele mai,* come. *Pali haele a māua,* the cliffs traveled by the two of us. *Kohala makani 'Āpa'apa'a, 'āina o nā pu'u haele lua o Pili me Ka-lā-hiki-ola,* Kohala with its 'Āpa'apa'a wind, land where the hills Pili and Ka-lā-hiki-ola go by twos. (PPN *sa'ele.*)

hā.'ele. Same as *hā'ele'ele.*

hae.leele. Redup. of *haele;* to go or come to and fro together.

hā.'ele.'ele. nvs. Blackish.

hā.'ele.lepo. n. A variety of sweet potato. (HP 141.)

haena. n. *Na-* form with *hae 1–3;* wildness; barking; tearing.

hā.'ena. 1. nvs. Red-hot, burning, red. *Hā'ena nā ihu,* a red nose (with blood). **2.** *(Cap.)* Place names on Hawai'i, Kaua'i, and O'ahu. **3.** Same as *hā'e'ena. Ua lū 'ia e ka manu, hā'ena wale i ka nahele* (song), scattered by the birds, shy in the forest. **4.** n. Kind of tapa wrapped about images. (Kam. 64:12.)

hae.ola. vs. Murderous. (Kel. 45.)

-haha. 1. Redup. of *hā 2;* to breathe hard, pant. **2.** vs. Proud, haughty. *Rare.* **ho'o.haha.** To parade, strut. **3.** Same as *haha kā 'upena, una.* (PNP *'afa.*)

-haha. ho'o.haha. Overcast, calm.

hā.hā. 1. vt. To grope, feel, as with the hands. (For. 6:111.) *Kahuna hāhā,* an expert who diagnoses, as sickness or pain, by feeling the body. (PPN *faafaa.*) **2.** Same as *hā,* stalk; striped taro leaves boiled or baked and eaten. **3.** n. Trap made of twigs and small branches, for fresh-water fish. **4.** n. Lobelias. See below and *ālula, 'ohā, 'ōhā kēpau, 'ohā wai nui.* **5.** n. Kaua'i name for *'ape'ape.*

hāhā-. ho'o.hā.hā. To beat, pound, as tapa; to harden. (PPN *sasa.*)

hā.hā-'ai-a-ka-manu. n. A native lobelia *(Clermontia clermontioides),* found only in high mountains of Kaua'i, a shrub or small tree with many branches; oblong and narrow leaves; greenish-purple, curved flowers; and sweet, edible yellow berries. *Lit., hāhā,* food

of the birds, so called because the thick sap was used for catching birds.

hahae. 1. Same as *haehae,* to tear; to strip, as pandanus leaves for plaiting. Cf. *kīhae.* (PPN *sasae.*) **2.** n. Small sweet potatoes removed in thinning a hill. *Ka'ū.*

haha.hana. Redup. of *hana 1;* to work, of many persons.

hā.hā hele. vt. To grope here and there, feel.

hahahi. Redup. of *hahi.*

hahai. nvt. Persons following, pursuit (FS 31); to follow, pursue, chase, hunt; to accompany, go with (For. 4:47). *Kuahaua o ke 'ano e hahai 'ia ai,* declaration of policy. **ho'o.hahai.** To cause to follow, entice; to pretend to follow.

haha'i. 1. Redup. of *ha'i 1, 2;* to break into pieces; to break off, as to thin sweet potato vines. (PPN *fafaki.*) **2.** n. Painful swelling, as in the groin. Also *'awaiāhiki.*

haha'i.anana. Same as *'awaiāhiki,* also a name for syphilis. *Rare.*

haha'i lua. vt. To break in two. *Fig.,* bad luck. *A 'o ke kuapa'a i loa'a mai ia hele 'ana, ua kapa 'ia he kuapu'u haha'i lua,* a hunchback encountered on the trip is considered an unlucky hunchback.

haha'i malū. vt. To follow secretly, "tail", stalk.

hahai manu. nv. Bird hunter, fowler; to hunt birds.

hahaka. Redup. of *haka 4.*

haha kā 'upena. n. Net spacer or mesh stick, gauge used in making meshes in nets, made of wood, turtle shell, bone, bamboo, whale rib, coconut shell, or metal.

hahaki. Redup. of *haki,* to break. *Hahaki kū,* to break without permission or recklessly. See ex., *'oi'oi 1.*

hahaku. Redup. of *haku,* to compose.

hahala.lū. Same as *halalū,* young *akule* fish. See ex., *pākī 2.*

hahale. Same as *halehale;* high, as waves.

hahalu. vs. Empty, void; somewhat deflated, as a balloon; half rotten, as wood, taro. *Fig.,* hungry.

hā.hā.lua. n. Manta ray, sea devil, family Mobulidae *(Manta alfredi). Lit.,* two mouths (two flap-like appendages extend forward on each side of the mouth). (PNP *faafaalua;* cf. Tahitian *faafaapiti.*)

hā.hā lua. n. A native tree lobelia *(Cyanea leptostegia),* found only on Kaua'i. The trunk is slender, unbranched, to 12 m high, and bears a crown of narrow leaves that are up to 60 cm long. The many flowers are purplish-red, the fruits yellow berries.

hā.hā.mau. vt. To catch fish with the hands, as in crevices.

hahana. nvs. Heat, warmth; warm, sultry, hot. *Hahana ke kaua,* the battle waxes hot. See *hana 4. Hahana ka wela,* the heat is hot [anger]. *Holo ka hahana i ku'u piko* (FS 41), heat rushes to my navel [moved with emotion, as sorrow, love, fear]. **ho'o.hahana.** To create heat; to rouse to fury.

hahani. Redup. of *hani 1;* to touch.

hahano. Redup. of *hano 1, 4, 6;* enema.

hā.hā nui. n. A native shrubby lobelia *(Cyanea horrida),* from Maui, with thorny branches and rough, lobed leaves.

hahao. vt. To insert, put in. (Oihk. 10.1.) *Hahao iho i nā mea maika'i i loko o nā ipu* (Mat. 13.48), gathered the good into vessels. (PPN *fafa'o.*)

hā.hā.pa'a.kai. nv. Salt bed or pool; to gather salt. **ho'o.hā.hā.pa'a.kai.** To gather salt. *Po'e ho'ohāhāpa'akai,* salt-gatherers [fig., those who do easy work not requiring stamina or courage].

hahape. Same as *awa 1. Kaua'i.*

hahau. 1. nvt. To strike, hit, whip, beat, switch, smite, wield, thrash; to throw down, as a playing card with force; to trump; to play, as a card or *kōnane* pebble; to insert; whip, lash, stroke; to bat, as a ball; a blow. *Hahau ikaika,* to lambaste, wallop. *Pepa hahau,* playing cards. (PPN *sasau.*) **2.** vt. To offer a prayer or sacrifice; to lay before. (FS 205.) **3.** vt. To build, as by laying bricks.

hahaua. Pas/imp. of *hahau.*

-hahau.hia. ho'o.hahau.hia. To be struck: see *hahau.*

Ua hoʻohahauhia ka lāʻau e ke kanaka, the stick was struck by the man.
hahau.hui. Same as *uhauhui,* a prayer.
hahau kā.kua. vt. To hurl a blow by swinging from the shoulders. (FS 169.)
hahei. 1. Same as *kīkepa,* a type of pig. *Rare.* **2.** vs. Plump, fleshy. *Rare.* **3.** vi. To be bound fast.
hahi. Same as *hehi. Kahua hahi* (Ruta 3.2), threshing floor.
hahi.hahi. Redup. of *hahi.*
hahili. A kind of fish. (And.)
hahina. Same as *hehina.*
haho. vs. Lacking in flesh, thin; to fail, of an invalid. *Rare.*
hahoma. Same as *homa 1, 2. Rare.*
hā.hoʻo.ili. n. Hereditary stalk; established people with inherited land. *Rare.*
hahu. 1. Var. of *hehu,* seedling or plant (see ex., *mānewanewa 2*). **2.** vt. To clear, smooth; to purge, as the bowels. **hoʻo.hahu.** To smooth, level off; to give a purge; cathartic purge. (PPN *safu.*)
hahu.alo. Same as *halo 1.* (AP.)
hahu.hahu. Redup. of *hahu 2.*
hai. 1. nvt. Offering, sacrifice; to offer, sacrifice. Cf. *hai ʻai, haialo, haiau, haipule, heiau. Hai nō ʻo ʻAi-kanaka iāʻoe i luna o ka lele* (FS 87), ʻAi-kanaka will sacrifice you on the altar. *Hai kanaka,* to offer human sacrifice; to kill for a human sacrifice. (PNP *fai.*) **2.** Same as *hahai,* to follow. (PCP *(f,s)ai.*) **3.** vt. To hire, employ. *Eng. Ka hai ʻana,* the employment, hiring.
hai-. 1. Simulative prefix similar to *haʻa-.* See *haikea, hailawe, hailepo, hailuku, haipule, haiʻula, haiwa,* Gram. 6.3.3. **2.** See *akahai.* (PPN *fai.*)
haʻi. 1. nvt. To break or snap, as a stick; broken; fracture, joint, break. (Cf. *haki, moku, nahā, wāhi.*) **hoʻo.haʻi.** To cause a break. (PPN *faki.*) **2.** vt. To say, tell, mention, state, declare, confess. Cf. *haʻina, haʻi pōkole. Ka haʻi ʻana,* the telling, annunciation. *Kona haʻi maoli ʻana i kona hewa,* the true confession of his offense. (PNP *fa(a)ki.*) **3.** loc. n. Edge, border (not used with the articles). *Lepo ma haʻi o ke kalo* (Kep. 155), dirt on the edge of the taro. **4.** vi. Coquettish, flirtatious; to flirt. *Ke holo mai nei ʻo Halaki haʻi ʻē nā pua i ke kula,* as Charlotte rides along, the youngsters of the plains had become coy. **hoʻo.haʻi.** Caus/sim. **5.** vi. To sway, bend. *Kāna hele hoʻohaʻi lua ʻana ma ka ʻaluheʻe nohoʻi maʻō a maʻaneʻi,* her swaying walk, sagging this way and that. **6.** n. House. *Kauaʻi. Rare.* **7.** pronoun. Someone else, another person; another place, elsewhere *(rare).* (Not used with articles: Gram. 8.2.) *No haʻi,* for someone else. *Aia nō ia haʻi nā ʻāina o mākou* (Neh. 5.5), other men have our lands. *Hoʻolei ke ʻaʻā apau ma haʻi ā maikaʻi,* throw all the stones somewhere else so [the garden] will be fine.
haia. Pas/imp. of *hai 2,* to pursue.
hai.ā. 1. n. Retainer or follower of a chief. Cf. *haiā kāne, haiā wahine.* **2.** Same as *haihaiā.*
haiʻai. nv. Food offering; to offer vegetable food.
hai.ā kāne. n. Male retainer of a chief.
haiʻale. v. To break, of billows. *Fig.,* to surge, of emotion.
haiʻi.aliʻi. n. Name of a hard rock used for making adzes.
hai.alo. Same as *haiā 1. Lit.,* follow the presence.
haia.mū. vi. To gather, crowd, flock; in great numbers, as ripening fruit. Cf. *mū 3. Ua haiamū ʻia aʻe nā huina alanui,* the street intersections are crowded.
haia.mua. Pas/imp. of *haiamū.*
haiʻi.ʻano. n. Adjective.
haiʻi.ʻano. v. To describe, tell the nature of.
hai ao. nv. Day sacrifice; to sacrifice by daylight.
haiʻi aʻo. nv. Sermon, lecture, instructive discourse; to give advice.
haiau. Var. of *heiau.* Cf. *hai,* to sacrifice.
hai.ā wahine. n. **1.** Female retainer of a chief. *Papai-ʻawa aʻela ʻo ʻAi-wohi-kupua me kona mau kaukaualiʻi a me nā haiā wāhine ona e hoʻopau i kāna ʻōlelo hoʻohiki* (Laie 475), ʻAi-wohi-kupua and his lesser

chiefs and the women of the household made ceremonial kava offerings to put an end to his oath. **2.** Wicked woman, concubine (Lunk. 19.1).
haiʻeʻa. n. A variety of *ʻaʻawa lelo,* a fish.
hai.ehu. Var. of *kaiehu 1.*
haʻi ʻeuane.lio. nv. To preach the gospel; evangelist.
hai.hai. Same as *hahai,* to follow.
haʻi.haʻi. 1. Redup. of *haʻi 1;* brittle; limbering exercises, as for the hula; massage in chiropractic; quavering; breaking, rising and falling of the voice; a style of singing with a breaking voice; to break, as a law. *Kauka haʻihaʻi iwi,* chiropractor. *E haʻihaʻi i ke kanaka* (For. 4:35), to break the bones of people [in fighting]. *E haʻihaʻi iho ʻoe i kāna ʻauamo* (Kin. 27.40), you break his yoke. **hoʻo.haʻi.haʻi.** Caus/sim.; to break, as waves. *Ma ka leo kauō, hoʻānuʻunuʻu, ā hoʻohaʻihaʻi,* with loud voice, vibrating, rising and falling. **2.** Redup. of *haʻi 2;* to speak quietly back and forth; to murmur (Kel. 70). *Kuʻu hoa haʻihaʻi leo,* my friend [with whom I] talk flirtatiously.
hai.hai.ā. nvs. Wicked person; wicked, unholy. *Ka poʻe haihaiā* (1 Tim. 1.9), the unholy. *E māhuahua ai ka haihaiā* (2 Tim. 2.16), to increase unto more ungodliness. **2.** vi. To prevent the gods from hearing a rival's curses by acting insane (eating poison, going naked), thus diverting the god's curses to himself and freeing the victim; with his superior mana he turns the curses away from himself and on to the rival sorcerer (Kam. 64:140-1); to prevent gods from hearing by offering herbs and medicine (And.).
haʻi.haʻi iwi. nv. By holding the shoulders, to make a person's bones crack audibly; a form of chiropractic; to do so; to break bones.
haʻi.hana. n. Verb (old name).
haʻi.inoa. n. Noun. *Lit.,* name telling.
haʻi.inoa lau.lā. n. Common noun.
haʻi.inoa pili kahi. n. Proper noun. *Lit.,* noun referring to someone or place.
haika. 1. Same as *haikaika.* **2.** vi. To gasp. *Rare.*
hai.kaika. nvi. To make faces; a grimace of defiance and contempt; the corners of the mouth were drawn back tightly, the teeth separated, chin and lower teeth twisting from side to side; perhaps the figure-eight mouthed images were inspired by this violent fighting expression. Cf. *ikaika,* strong. **hoʻo.hai.kaika.** A less violent grimace than *haikaika;* to make faces, cause to make faces.
hai.kala. n. **1.** Severe cramps, said to have often proved fatal. **2.** Asthma. (For. 6:451.)
hai.kala muku. n. Cramps, less severe than *haikala.*
hā.ʻike. Same as *hōʻike,* to show.
hai.kea. 1. Same as *hākea,* pale, and *hākea,* a type of banana. **2.** n. A type of tapa (no data).
hā.ʻike.ʻike. Same as *hōʻikeʻike.*
hā.iki. nvs. Narrow, pinched; limitation, restriction (in fast speech, *haiki*). *Hāiki ka noʻonoʻo, hāiki ka ʻike,* narrow-minded. *Aia nō i kahi hāiki,* just there in a narrow place [said of an unborn child]. *Ka hāiki o ka manawa,* limitations of time. *Kona wā i hāiki ai i ka pōloli* (Mar. 2.25), the time he was pinched with hunger. *Haʻihaʻi pua o kuʻu manawa ē, eia wau lā ua hāiki* (Laie 521), broken flowers of my heart, here I am in straits. **hoʻo.hā.iki.** To contract, shrink, restrict, curtail, narrow. *Kekahi mau hoʻohāiki o ka lawaiʻa ʻana,* certain restrictions on fishing.
hā.iki.iki. Redup. of *hāiki.*
hai.kina. n. Hyacinth. *Eng.*
haʻi.kū. 1. n. The *kāhili* flower *(Grevillea banksii),* so named because first planted near the town of Haʻi-kū, Maui. (Neal 321.) Also *kāhili,* and *ʻoka pua ʻulaʻula* on Niʻihau. **2.** vs. Haughty, conceited. *Rare.*
haʻi.kū keʻokeʻo. Same as *ʻoka kilika,* silk oak.
haʻi kūpuna. nv. To tell of ancestors; a chant concerning ancestors, genealogy.
haʻi.kū.uma.uma. n., interj. A call to lift a canoe or to rally together in any work.
hai.lapu. Same as *hōlapu. Hailapu ke aloha,* love flares.

hai.lawe. vt. To exchange, barter. *Rare.*

ha'i.le'a. vt. To tell clearly.

hai.lepo. 1. nvs. Ash-gray pallor; to have this pallor. *He limu ka i'a, hailepo ka lani,* if seaweed is the marine food, the chief pales [sometimes *limu* is a bad omen]. **2.** n. An ancient pestilence. (Malo 246.) **3.** n. One of the sting rays, perhaps *hīhīmanu.* (PPN *fai.*)

haili. 1. Same as *hali'a. Ke kau mai nei ka haili aloha* (FS 41), the loving memory returns. *Haili moe,* premonition, as in a dream. *Haili 'ōpua,* a cloud bank that recalls to mind. *ho'o.haili.* To cause, produce a recollection or premonition; to challenge (Nak. 12). **2.** nvs. Spirit, ghost; dim, indistinct. *ho'o.haili.* To assume a ghostly form; dim. **3.** n. Yellow band, as on the tail of *ono,* the fish.

hā.'ili. Same as *hā'ili'ili. Ka pali hā'ili kauā* (KL line 2094), the cliff that curses the outcast.

hai.lia. Pas/imp. of *haili 1.*

haili aka. n. Shadowy form of a ghost.

hā.'ili.'ili. vt. To revile, curse (Puk. 21.17), blaspheme, speak evilly.

ha'i liki. vt. To boast.

hai.lili. Same as *lili,* jealous.

ha'i.lima. n. Distance from the elbow to the end of the fingers.

haili.moa. n. A shellfish resembling the *wana,* but with short spines, possibly *Tripneustes* or *Echinometra.*

haili moe. n. Recollected dream, vision.

haili-o-Pua. n. A small native fern *(Schizaea robusta)* found in high mountain wet areas believed to be the plant form of the sorcery goddess Pua; sometimes used as a psychological remedy to ward off the evil influence of Pua. (Neal 8.) *Lit.,* Pua's memory. *Hawai'i.* Also *'oāli'i makali'i.*

hai.lipo. Var. of *hailepo 3,* a sting ray.

ha'i.loa'a. n. Answer to a problem, solution, key. *'O ka ha'iloa'a o ka hope o ka helo na'au,* key to the supplement of the mental arithmetic.

hai-lō-keaka. n. The card game high-low-jack-and-the-game. *Eng.*

hai.lona. nvi. Divination, casting lots, throwing dice; to test (also used interchangeably with *hō'ailona*). *Hailona 'o Moikeha i nā keiki āna, i akaaka kō lākou mea ikaika a koa* (For. 4:161), Moikeha tested his children to discover their strength and valor.

ha'i.lono. 1. v. To tell the news, to spread a report. **2.** *(Cap.)* n. Name of a star.

-ha'i.lua. ho'o.ha'i.lua. vt. To flirt; loose-jointed.

hai.luku. vt. To stone. *Fig.,* to hurt the feelings. *Ua kokoke lākou e hailuku mai ia'u* (Puk. 17.4), they be almost ready to stone me.

ha'i.malule. Same as *malule,* weak, limp.

ha'i mana'o. v. To state an opinion, testify.

ha'i.manawa. n. A thin, delicate white tapa.

ha'i manawa. 1. v. To tell of the times. **2.** *(Cap.)* n. *The Times* (name of a publication).

ha'i.moe.ipo. n. Fascination, interest. *Ka ha'imoeipo o kona mau ho'oka'au,* the fascination of his wit.

haina. n. Offering, sacrifice. Cf. *hai,* to sacrifice. *Ka haina 'awa,* offering of kava. *Ka haina kanaka* (KL line 2098), human sacrifice.

hai.nā. vt. Cruel, unmerciful, heartless; to abuse, treat cruelly. *Mai hainā wale i ka holoholona,* do not abuse the animal. *Mea haina,* cruel person, tyrant.

ha'ina. 1. nvi. A saying, declaration, statement, explanation; answer, as to a riddle; confession; solution; the two (or sometimes more) last verses of a song that usually begin with the word *ha'ina* and that repeat the theme of the song, or the name of the person to whom the song is dedicated; to sing the *ha'ina* of a song; to tell, confess. Cf. *ha'i,* to speak. *Ha'ina hou,* to sing the *ha'ina* again. *Ha'ina 'ia mai ana ka puana:* see *puana 1.* **2.** n. A breaking, as of a stick or law; a break. **3.** n. Verb. Cf. *ha'ina keke'e, ha'ina kōkua, ha'ina 'oko'a, ha'ina pili.*

hai.nakā. n. Handkerchief, napkin *(rare). Eng.*

hai.nakā 'ā.'ī. n. Neckerchief.

hai.nakā lei. n. Neckerchief.

hai.nakā pa'eke. n. Pocket handkerchief. *Eng.*

hai.nakā pakeke. n. Pocket handkerchief. *Eng.*

hai.nakā pepa. n. Paper handkerchief, cleaning tissue.

ha'ina keke'e. n. Irregular verb.

hai.naki. 1. n. Prayer removing the taboo on land after the taxes had been collected (an example of a *pule hainaki* is in Malo 146-7). **2.** nvt. Quarter of a roasted pig reserved for priests at the *laukini* service (Malo 174); to offer such.

ha'ina kō.kua. n. Helping or auxiliary verb.

ha'ina.le'a. n. Adverb. *Lit.,* clarifying verb.

ha'ina kuhi.kuhi. n. Directional adverbs, as *mai, iho, aku, a'e. Lit.,* pointing adverbs.

ha.ī.nana. vi. To talk with animation. *Rare.*

ha'ina nalu. n. Breaking wave.

ha'ina 'oko'a. n. Neuter or intransitive verb.

ha'ina pili, ha'ina pili aku. n. Transitive verb, active verb.

ha'ina pili ha'i.inoa. n. Verbal adjective.

ha'ina pili iā ha'i. n. Transitive active verb. *Lit.,* verb referring to another person.

ha'ina pili 'ia mai. n. Transitive passive verb.

ha'ina pili 'ole aku. n. Intransitive verb.

ha'ina pule. n. Recitation of prayers.

ha'i.nau. vt. To bend the head forward.

hai.nikā. Var. of *hainakā. Pāpale hainikā* (Puk. 28.4), turban (RSV), mitre (KJV).

ha'i.noa. Same as *ha'iinoa.*

hai.nole. Same as *nīnole,* pliant.

ha'i.nole. vt. To incite, encourage, stimulate. *Rare.*

hā.inu, ho'o.hā.inu. vt. To give drink. *Pali hāinu kai,* the cliff that drinks of the sea [rising from the sea]. *Ā ho'ohāinu ihola i nā hipa* (Kin. 29.3), and watered the sheep.

ha'i ola. nv. To preach salvation or eternal life; one who so preaches.

ha'i 'ole. vs. Unbreakable, inflexible, stubborn.

ha'i.'ō.lelo. nv. Speech, address, lecture, sermon; to orate, preach, make a speech; speaker. See ex., *lūlā.*

ha'i.'ō.lelo ho'o.le'a. n. Eulogistic speech.

ha'i 'ō.uli. nv. To tell omens, prognosticate, as by observing clouds; soothsayer. *Nā mea ha'i 'ōuli ma ka malama* (Isa. 47.13), the monthly prognosticators.

hai pō. n. Night religious service, sacrifice. (For. 6:377.)

ha'i pō.kole. vt. To speak or report briefly, *Ha'i pōkole mai ma ka waha,* orally summarize.

hā ipu. n. Stem of a gourd leaf, as used in medicine.

hai.pule. nvi. Religious, devout, pious, reverent; piety, a pious person; to worship; to hold prayers or service, as to consecrate a heiau; church service. *Ka pule a kāu kauā nei e haipule ai i mua o kou alo* (1 Nal. 8.28), the prayer which thy servant prays before thee.

hā.'iu.'iu. nvs. High, height. Cf. *'iu'iu.* (FS 201.)

hai.'ula. Same as *hā'ula.*

hai.wā. vt. To plant far apart, as taro, coconuts. *Rare.*

ha'i waha. vt. Word-of-mouth, verbal, oral; to tell verbally.

ha'i.wale. n. All native species of *Cyrtandra,* slender soft-wooded forest shrubs with white tubular flowers. (Neal 773.) Sometimes called *kanawao ke'oke'o.* See *'ilihia.*

ha'i wale. 1. vs. Easily broken, brittle. **2.** vt. To tell without reason. **3.** vt. To flirt readily, with little reason.

haka. 1. n. Shelf, perch, platform; roost, as for chickens; fish spear rack; rack for suspending water gourds and other household objects; rack attached to booms of double canoe to hold spears and other objects; ladder (see *alahaka, haka 'ūlili*). *Haka kau a ka manu,* a perch for birds to light upon [a promiscuous woman]. (PPN *fata.*) **2.** n. Recipient; medium, oracle, one possessed. *Haka waiwai* (Kep. 117), recipient of wealth. **3.** n. Crested feather helmet, so called because the crest perches on the helmet. **4.** nvs. Hole, breach, open space, vacancy; empty, vacant, full of holes or spaces. Cf. *hakahaka, 'olohaka. ho'o.haka.* To make openings, holes, spaces; to create space; full of holes. *Fig.,* hungry. **5.** nvt. To stare, gaze. (Hal. 22.17.) *Haka hele,* to stare or examine carefully as one walks. *Ua haka malū aku kona mau maka i ka mea 'ilihune* (Hal. 10.8), his eyes are privily set against the poor. **6.** vt. To place wood in a ground oven, to lay an oven fire. **7.** n. Heart, hearts, in a deck of cards. *Eng.*

hā.kā. Same as *hakakā.*

haka.'ano. n. **1.** Breach, as in mist. *Rare.* **2.** Wind associated with Hālawa, Moloka'i.

hā.ka'e. Same as *hakaka'e.*

hā.kaha. To delay, detain. (And.)

haka.haka. 1. Redup. of *haka 4;* vacant space, vacancy, room; blanks, as in a questionnaire; gap; thin, emaciated, especially of one with hollow chest or sunken features. *He lawa ke kino, 'a'ohe hakahaka,* a strong body, not emaciated. Cf. *pani hakahaka. Hakahaka nā maka,* hollow-eyed. *Niho hakahaka,* teeth with gaps. *Uea hakahaka,* wire screen, window screen. *Kohala ihu hakahaka,* Kohala of the extended nostrils [climbing the Kohala mountains makes one breathe hard]. ho'o.- **haka.haka.** Full of openings and spaces; to make open spaces, holes. *'A 'ole i ho'ohakahaka 'ia kou pepeiao* (Isa. 48.8), thine ear was not opened. (PEP *(f,s)ata-(f,s)ata.)* **2.** Same as *haka 1. Rare.* Cf. *ke'ahakahaka.* (PEP *(f,s)ata(f,s)ata).*

haka.haka.ea. n. Rainbow with much green color. *Rare.*

haka.haka leo. n. Ghostly voice, spirit voice. *Rare.*

hakai, hagai. n. Container, bag, named for Haggai (Hagai 1.6), who carried a bag with holes [spoken humorously]. *Eng.*

hā.kai. 1. n. Stem, stalk. **2.** Rare var. of *hākui 1, 2.*

hā.ka'i. Probably similar to *ka'i 1;* to move along, as rain. *Hāka'i lua nei i ke anu o Wai-'ale'ale* (For. 5:705), venturing again into the cold of Wai-'ale'ale.

haka ipu. n. Shelf for calabashes; frame from which calabashes were hung.

hakaka, hadasa. n. Myrtle. (Isa. 41.19.)

haka.kā. vt. To fight, quarrel; fight, duel, strife. *Hakakā 'ōlelo,* dispute, argument. (Kin. 26.20.) ho'o.- **haka.kā.** To provoke a fight.

haka.kā-a-moa. n. **1.** Cockfight. Also *hākā moa.* **2.** *(Cap.)* n. Type of *lua* fighting in which the contestants did not use their hands, but fought with feet, legs, shoulders, head.

haka.ka'e. vs. Frail, weak; thin, as tapa or a dress.

haka.kai. vs. Bloated, swollen. *Rare.*

haka.kā pahi kaua. n. Duel with swords.

haka.kā pū.pana.pana. n. Pistol duel.

haka.kau. nvt. To straddle. *Fig.,* a tall thin person.

haka kau. n. Perch, shelf.

haka kau.la'i. n. Drying frame or rack.

haka.kau.luna. Same as *lona,* canoe rest.

haka.kau.pili. vi. To stand intently watching, as a thief [said to be the name of a legendary rat thief]; to stand precariously, as at the edge of a cliff.

haka.kē. 1. vs. Crowded, overlapping, entangled. **2.** vi. To stand on stilts, as a spider.

haka.kī. vs. Plump. *Rare.*

haka.kū. n. Frame, platform, as for drying fish.

hā.kala. n. Ends of a house, gable. Also *kala.*

haka lā.'au. n. Wooden trough, flume. (For. 6:546.)

hā.kala.lū. vs. Debilitated, weak, as from age or sickness.

Haka-lau-'ai. n. Name of a star associated with Hanakau-luna, considered a sign of pestilence or calamity; also the name of a legendary place.

haka lele. n. Altar platform, especially where human sacrifices were laid.

haka.lī. vs. High. *Mai pi'i a'e 'oe i ka lālā kau hakalī o 'ike 'ia kou wahi hilahila,* don't climb to the topmost branch lest your private parts be seen [do not act superior].

hā.kā.lia. vs. Slow, dilatory [used idiomatically]. *Hākālia nō ā,* as soon as. *Hākālia nō ā ao, 'o kō mākou hele nō ia,* as soon as it became day, we went. *'A 'ole hākālia pau kēia,* not long, this will be finished. *E hākālia anei*

kekahi mea iā Iēhowa? (Kin. 18.14.) Does Jehovah have to wait for anything? **ho'o.hā.kā.lia.** To delay, slow down; slow, dilatory; hesitation. *Mai ho'ohākālia aku 'oe,* don't delay.

haka.lina. vs. Showy, pompous, vain, as of one's attire.

haka.lū. Var. of *hakanū.*

haka.lunu. Same as *hākalalū.*

Haka.moa. n. Name of a constellation. *Lit.,* chicken roost.

hā.kā moa. Same as *hakakā-a-moa 1,2.* **ho'o.hā.kā moa.** Caus/sim.

haka.kane. Same as *ho'okanea.*

haka.nea. Same as *ho'okanea.*

haka.nele. nvs. To be worthless, useless; uselessness. See *nele. He hakanele kēlā,* that's worthless.

hā.kanelo. Same as *hākaneno.*

haka.neno. vs. Weak, sick.

haka.nū. vs. Silent, sullen; struck dumb, as in amazement. **ho'o.haka.nū.** To cause silence; silent.

hā.ka'o. vs. Naked, nude.

hā.kao.kao. 1. vs. Decaying, as taro in the field or a few days after cooking. Cf. *kaokao.* **2.** n. Hole for inserting mast in a canoe. *Rare.*

hā.ka'o.ka'o. n. Net that enclosed a calabash. (Malo 91.)

haka 'ō.lelo. n. Medium or one possessed, who speaks; one who reports to a chief, especially the misdeeds of others.

hā.kā 'ō.lelo. v. To quarrel, argue violently.

haka.pō. n. Darkness. (For. 6:371.)

haka pono. vt. To observe carefully, stare. (2 Nal. 8.11.)

hā.kau. 1. vs. To protrude, as bones or cliff ridges. See ex., *kōlīlā.* **2.** Same as *haka kau,* perch, shelf.

haka 'ula a Kāne. n. Poetic name for the rainbow. *Lit.,* red perch of Kāne.

haka 'ū.lili. n. Ladder, trestle.

hakē. vs. Packed full, protruding, bulging, cramfull, swollen. *Hakē ka pa'i 'ai o ka Malu-lani,* the Malu-lani [ship] is overloaded with bundles of hard poi [uncomplimentary reference to a pregnant woman]. **ho'o.- hakē.** To pack full, cram, push; to break, as a boil.

hā.kea. 1. Same as *ha'akea 1.* **2.** n. A variety of banana.

hā.kea.kea. Same as *hākea 1;* faded, wan, fair, blond.

hā.kei. Same as *ha'akei. Hākei nā moku kaiāmū* (For. 6:398), the hushed islands are in glory.

hā.kelo. nvs. Slimy, snotty; mucus, slime. Cf. *kelo.*

hā.ke'o.ke'o. nvs. Whitish.

haki. Same as *ha'i 1. Haki wale,* easily broken, fragile. *He ko'oko'o haki wale,* an easily broken staff [a weak leader]. (PPN *fati.*)

hā.kī. Same as *ho'okī. 'O kō lāua 'i'o, hākī koko nei 'o Kalua* (chant), their own flesh was Kalua, [their] blood issue.

hakia. Pas/imp. of *haki.*

hā.kia. nvt. Pin, nail, spike; to fasten, nail. Cf. *kākia.*

hakia koko. n. Bloody stools. (Kam. 64:111.)

haki.haki. Same as *ha'iha'i 1. Malaila ia i hakihaki ai i nā pua* (Hal. 76.3), there he broke the arrows.

haki.hana. Same as *hakina.*

hā.ki'i. vt. To tie, bind. Cf. *-ki'i.*

hā.ki'i.ki'i. Redup. of *hāki'i.* See *nīki'i.*

hā.kikila. Same as *kikila,* thunder. (PNP *fatutili.*)

hā.kilo. vt. To observe closely, spy on, reconnoiter, snoop, eavesdrop. Cf. *kilo. Hākilo ihola lākou iāia* (Luka 14.1), they watched him.

hakina. n. Broken piece, remnant, portion, balance, section, scrap, fragment; fraction, as in arithmetic. See ex., *palena. Hakina 'āina aupuni,* portion of government land.

hakina 'ai. n. Food fragment, scrap, morsel.

hakina kū.pa'ewa. n. Improper fraction.

hakina kū.pono. n. Proper fraction.

hakina maoli. n. Common fraction.

hakina 'ō.lelo. n. Portion of a word, syllable.

hakina pā.na'i. n. Reciprocal number.

hakina pā.'umi. n. Decimal fraction.

hakina pili. n. Mixed number.

haki.nau. Var. of *ha'inau.*

haki.'opa. vi. To limp, hobble, amble. *Rare.*

hā.kiu. vt. To spy, examine, look.

hako. vs. Dignified, noble, honorable. *Rare.*

hā.kō. vt. To carve out a pathway, as a passage through coral or as a water course. *Rare.*

hā.ko'a.ko'a. Same as *'āko'ako'a,* coral.

hako.hako. Redup. of *hako.*

hā.ko'i. Same as *hakuko'i;* agitated; paraphimosis. See *Kū-lani-hāko'i. Hāko'i ka wai a ka neki,* water agitated among the rushes [one in love]. **ho'o.hā.ko'i.** Caus/ sim.

hā.ko'i.ko'i. Redup. of *hāko'i. 'O ka 'ale hāko'iko'i,* agitated billows.

hā.kō.kō. nvt. Wrestling; to wrestle. *Mea hākōkō,* wrestler, fighter. (Kin. 32.24, For. 6:369.)

hā.kō.kō noho. nv. Ancient type of sitting wrestling, the object being to topple over the opponent; to wrestle thus.

hā.kona. Same as *hākonakona.* (Perhaps PPN *tona.*)

hā.kona.kona. 1. vs. Parched, as a blemished breadfruit; unhealthy condition of a banana when the skin adheres to the pulp, supposedly after the plant has been touched by the *'ākōlea* fern. 2. Same as *kākonakona 1. Ni'ihau.*

hā.ko.ko'o. Same as *ho'oko'oko'o.*

haku. 1. n. Lord, master, overseer, employer, owner, possessor, proprietor. A chief was often addressed as *ē ku'u haku,* my master. See *Haku-o-Hawai'i. Kona haku,* his lord. *'O Iēhowa ka Haku* (Isa. 50.5), the Lord Jehovah. **ho'o.haku.** To act as *haku,* dominate; to treat as a *haku;* to rule others, sometimes without authority; bossy. *'A 'ole 'oe e ho'ohaku maluna ona me ka 'o'olea* (Oihk. 25.43), you shall not rule over him with rigor. (PCP *fatu.*) 2. vt. To compose, invent, put in order, arrange; to braid, as a lei, or plait, as feathers. Cf. *haku mele. Ka mahiole 'ie i haku 'ia i ka hulu o nā 'i'iwi* (Laie 479), plaited helmet made with *'i'iwi* feathers. (PPN *fatu.*) 3. n. Core, lump, as of poi; stone, coconut sponge. Cf. *pōhaku, haku maka, haku 'ōnohi. Haku ipu,* pulp and seeds of melon. *Haku kā ko'i* (Malo 51), stone for chipping. (PPN *fatu.*)

hakū. Same as *ho'okū;* rising, bulging; bulge; to rise, as the moon. **ho'o.hakū.** Caus/sim.

hakua. Pas/imp. of *haku 2, 3.*

haku 'āina. n. Landowner; landlord.

haku.alo. n. Belly, lower abdomen; belly fin and flesh of fish. *He 'i'o momona ia, he 'i'o hakualo* (For. 6:395), fat flesh, the belly flesh.

haku.'apa. Same as *haku 'epa.*

hā.ku'e. Same as *hā'uke,* sea urchin. (Malo 45.) (PEP *(f,s)atuke.*)

hā.ku'e.ku'e. Same as *hā'uke'uke.*

haku.'epa. nvt. To deceive, fabricate; liar; malicious gossip; deceitful. *Ka po'e haku 'epa i kō 'oukou noho pono 'ana i loko o Kristo* (1 Pet. 3.16), the people that falsely accuse your good life within Christ. *'A 'ole pēlā ka 'oia'i'o, haku 'epa loko 'ino* (song), that is not the truth, malicious fabrications.

haku.haku. 1. vs. Lumpy, as poi. (Kep. 165.) Cf. *haku 3.* 2. vt. To fold, as tapa; to arrange, put in order. *Rare.* (PPN *fatu.*)

haku hale. n. Landlord, house owner, host, hostess.

haku.hana. Same as *hākuma.*

haku hana. n. Overseer, superintendent, employer, boss.

Haku.hiwa. n. Fatu Hiva.

haku hulu. nv. To plait, as feathers; featherworker.

hā.kui. 1. vt. To steam, as by placing fish, meat, or vegetables in a sealed calabash with hot stones and a little hot water. (Kep. 161.) 2. n. Spike, as of the *hā'uke'uke.*

hā.ku'i. vt. To beat, pound, pummel; to echo, reverberate; to flutter, palpitate, thump; to puff, as smoke. **ho'o.hā.ku'i.** Caus/sim. *Ho'ohāku'i i ko'u na'au,* shocking to my heart. *Ho'ohāku'i nākolo,* blow echoing and reechoing.

hā.ku'i.ku'i. Redup of *hāku'i.* **ho'o.hā.ku'i.ku'i.** Caus/ sim.

haku.kele. vs. Wet, lumpy, as poi. (Kep. 163.)

haku.ko'i. vt. Disturbed, agitated, excited; to surge, excite, rush. *Hakuko'i ka wai i ka pali* (chant), the water rushes over the cliff. *E hakuko'i nei i ka pu'uwai,* pulling at the heart.

haku.kole. nvt. To defame, ridicule, as in figurative language and chant; defamer.

hā.kuma. vs. 1. Pock-marked, as by smallpox; ravaged, as by leprosy; coarse, rough, lumpy, pitted; moss-grown. 2. Dark, thick, as clouds. *Fig.,* intense, as love. Cf. *mākuma.*

haku maka. Same as *haku 'ōnohi.*

hā.kuma.kuma. Redup. of *hākuma 1, 2. Ua 'ula'ula mai ke ao, ua hākumakuma* (Mat. 16.3), the sky is red and lowering.

haku mele. nvi. Poet, composer; to compose song or chant; those that speak in proverbs (Nah. 21.27). Cf. *haku o ke mele,* owner of the chant, the one for whom a chant was composed rather than the composer.

haku mo'o.lelo. n. Author, story writer.

haku nui. n. Manager, as of a plantation or firm.

Haku-o-Hawai'i. n. Prince Albert, only son of Kamehameha IV and Queen Emma who died at the age of four in 1862, "leaving his father and mother heartbroken and the native community in desolation" (Daws 1968:158). *Lit.,* lord of Hawai'i. See chant, *kiakahi.*

haku 'ōhi'a. n. *'Ōhi'a* log to be carved into a canoe (also *malu 'ōhi'a,* Kam. 76:136); main *'ōhi'a* image in a heiau.

haku 'ō.lelo. nv. Author, writer, reporter; to compose, as narrative or story; to slander, fabricate.

haku.one. n. 1. Small land division, as cultivated for a chief. Also *kō'ele.* 2. Inland pond. *Rare.*

haku 'ō.nohi. n. Eyeball.

haku.pa'a. n. New taro patch. *Lit.,* hard core. *Rare.*

haku.papa. vt. To sew feathers to a band, as for a hat.

hā.kupe. vs. Slow, feeble, hesitating.

haku.pehe. vt. Hesitating, slow; to walk or speak with hesitation; to stalk. (For. 6:296.)

hakupe.'o'i. vi. To limp.

Haku-pō-kano. n. Name of a star. *Lit.,* lord of dark night.

haku puke. n. Author.

haku wahine. n. Wife of a chief, lady, woman of high rank; female employer or supervisor.

haku wai.ū. n. Hard core in a breast.

haku wale. nvt. To make up, invent, fabricate, improvise; fabricator. Cf. *mo'olelo hakuwale.*

hala. 1. nvi. Sin, vice, offense, fault, error; to sin (Kan. 9.21), err. See *-hala manawa. Ke kala mai i ka 'ino a me ka hala* (Puk. 34.7), forgiving iniquity and transgression and sin. **ho'o.hala.** To cause to sin, lead astray; to fail to do. (PPN *sala.*) 2. vi. To pass, elapse, as time; to pass by; to miss; to pass away, die. *Ua hala ka manawa,* time has passed; it is late. *Hala nō ka lā,* the day indeed passes [enough for the day]. *A hala i ka lani* (Kanl. 9.1), up to heaven. *He 'elua mano a me kona hala,* eight thousand and more. *Kainoa a hala,* it did happen; I thought it would happen. *Nome hala 'ole* (Kel. 42), going on without stopping. **ho'o.hala.** To cause to miss; to dodge, turn aside; to pass, as time. *Ho'ohala lā,* to spend the day. *Mai ho'ohala 'oe iāia,* do not miss him. (PPN *sala.*) 3. n. The pandanus or screw pine *(Pandanus odoratissimus),* native from southern Asia east to Hawai'i, growing at low altitudes, both cultivated and wild. It is a tree with many branches, which are tipped with spiral tufts of long narrow, spine-edged leaves; its base is supported by a clump of slanting aerial roots. The pineapple-shaped fruits are borne on female trees whereas the spikes of fragrant, pollen-bearing flowers are borne separately on male trees. Many uses: leaves *(lau hala)* for mats, baskets, hats; the yellow to red fruit sections for leis, brushes; male flowers to scent tapa, their leaflike bracts to plait mats (see *hīnano*). (Neal 51.) The aerial root *(uleule)* tip is a good source of vitamin B and cooked in ti leaves was used medicinally, although unpleasant tasting. The tree is called *pū hala*. The *hala* lei is much liked today but formerly was not worn on important ventures because *hala* also means failure. For the same reason some persons will not compose songs about *hala*. Types of *hala* are listed below. Pineapples are *hala* plus qualifier. See ex., *pō 2. Puna paia ʻala i ka hala,* Puna, its walls fragrant with pandanus [fragrant flowers were placed indoors in house thatching and under mats]. (PPN *fara.*)

hala ʻai. 1. n. Older name for *hala kahiki*, pineapple. *Lit.,* edible *hala*. **2.** nv. Sin of eating forbidden vegetable or fruit; failure to offer essence of such food to the gods before consuming it; to commit such offense. Cf. *hala iʻa.*

Hala.aliʻi. Var. spelling of *Halāliʻi.*

hala.hala. 1. Redup. of *hala 1, 2;* correction, criticism, complaint, reproach. **hoʻo.hala.hala.** To criticize, complain, find fault, correct, negotiate *(rare)*, suggest; correction, complaint; critical. *Hoʻohalahala ʻole,* uncomplaining. **2.** n. Young stage of *kāhala* fish. (KL line 147.) (PCP *falafala.*) **3.** vs. Bitter, sour, brackish. *Rare.*

hala.hala.kau. Redup. of *halakau. Ua halahalakau nā manu pūnua mai kō lākou pūnana aku* (Kep. 89), the young birds perch far away from their nests.

hala.hala.wai. vs. Watery, wet, tearful, weeping.

hala.hī. vi. To buzz, whiz by, as in missing a mark.

hala.hiʻa. vt. To fail to hit, miss.

hala hī.nano. n. A male pandanus bearing the *hīnano* blossom.

hala.hū. Similar to *halahī;* to fail, err, miss.

hala hua. n. **1.** A female pandanus bearing fruit, contrasting with *hala hīnano*. **2.** Nut in a pandanus key.

hala.hula. n. Consideration of grievances, disputes; councils for such consideration. *Rare.*

hā.la.ʻi. Same as *laʻi*, calm. *Ke kai hālaʻi lana mālie* (chant), the calm sea floating peacefully.

hala iʻa. nv. Sin of eating a forbidden fish or meat; failure to offer essence of fish or flesh to the gods before consuming it; to commit such offenses. Cf. *hala ʻai.*

hala ʻī.koi. n. A variety of *hala* with keys 7 cm long, lemon-colored at base, changing abruptly to bright-orange in upper half; when cut for leis, a rim of orange is left at top of each key used.

hala ʻiʻo. n. Pandanus key that is ripe and soft, suitable for leis. Cf. *ʻiʻo hala.*

hala iwi nui. nvs. Hard pandanus key, not suitable for leis. *Fig.,* hard-appearing, dissatisfied.

hala.kā. See *pāʻū halakā.*

hala kahiki. n. The pineapple *(Ananas comosus),* probably originating in Brazil, of great commercial importance. *Lit.,* foreign *hala*. See *hala kea* and *hala ʻula* for what some Hawaiians call native varieties, still said to be growing wild in the forests at Puna, Hawaiʻi. Called *hala* on Niʻihau.

hala kapa. nv. Sin of breaking clothing taboos; to sin thus.

hala.kau. 1. vi. To perch high, as a bird. *Halakau ka manu i ka lāʻau,* the bird perches high in the tree [a person not easily gotten]. **2.** vs. Large, as a pregnant woman. *Rare.*

hala.kea. 1. vs. Fair, light. **2.** n. A yellowish tapa dyed with coconut oil. *I hoʻoluʻu halakea ʻia e Ka-pua* (chant), tapa dyed by Ka-pua.

hala kea. n. Said by some Hawaiians to be a native variety of pineapple; plant spreading vinelike; leaves with thorny edges; fruit plain green when unripe, yellow when ripe, small, fragrant, good-tasting; pieces of the skin were used for hat leis (HP 214.) *Lit.,* white *hala*.

hala.keʻa. n. Temporary support or prop in the middle of the house ridgepole.

hala.kī. vi. To go off course, miss the way.

hala.kū. Same as *holokū;* plump.

hā.lala. 1. vs. Big, large, overgrown, oversized. *E hānai i nui, i hālala ka ʻahui,* raise until large, and big the banana bunch. **2.** *(Cap.)* n. Name of Ka-lā-kaua's genital. See Elbert and Mahoe 67. **3.** vi. To bend low (For. 4:283); to travel far. (PPN *falala.*)

hā.lā.la.ʻi. Redup. of *hālaʻi. He au hālālaʻi kēia,* this is a time of tranquillity.

hala.lani. n. High heavens, atmosphere. *Nā manu i halalani,* the birds in the high heavens.

hala.lē. vs. To slurp, as soup; to eat noisily; to swish, as the sea; to spill or slop over; fat; not clear, as speech. *ʻAi halalē,* to gobble. *Lomaloma ʻai halalē,* lazy glutton. *Kani halalē,* to squawk. *ʻO ka ʻōʻio halalē ke kai lā* (song), as for the *ʻōʻio* fish, smacking good the sauce.

hala.lī. vs. Far away and small. *Ka lālā kau halalī,* topmost branches.

hala lihi.lihi ʻula. n. Variety of *hala* with keys bright yellow at base, grading to bright orange-red at top, and smaller than *hala ʻīkoi. Lit.,* red-edged *hala*.

Halā.liʻi. n. **1.** Name of a pleasure-loving chief of Niʻihau in ancient times. His name became synonymous with fun-making. *E hele mai i ka pō leʻa o Halāliʻi,* come to the joyous night of Halāliʻi [an invitation to a party]. **2.** *(Not cap.)* A variety of sugar cane, vigorous, large, of the Lahaina type, perhaps named for Halāliʻi, Niʻihau, where a famous sugar cane once grew in the sand dunes. This cane was used in ceremonies for remission of sins *(uku hala, wehe hala).* Also *pakaiea*. See saying, *kō 1.*

hā.lalo. 1. vt. To place under, lift up from beneath; to give an enema, douche. *Kau lī lua i ke anu Wai-ʻaleʻale, he maka hālalo ka lehua maka noe* (UL 105), the keen chill of the cold of Wai-ʻaleʻale settles, centers of *lehua* blossoms are overturned, misty centers. **2.** n. Medicine. Cf. *hālalo poʻi.* **3.** vt. To gaze upon, reflect. *Hālalo ihola kona maka e ʻimi iā Iēhowa* (2 Oihn. 20.3), set himself to seek Jehovah. *Hālalo kuʻu naʻau i nā hana* (Kekah. 8.9), applied my heart to the tasks.

hala.loa. n. A fish (no data).

hala loa. vs. Gone a long distance or time; far.

hā.lalo poʻi. n. Steaming decoction of herbs, as prescribed for sickness.

hala.lū. 1. n. Young of the *akule,* a fish, about 14 or 15 cm long. **2.** vs. Weak, in poor health. **3.** vt. To rumble; to strum, as an *ʻukulele* (Kel. 137).

-hala manawa. hoʻo.hala manawa. To pass the time, agreeably or otherwise; to loaf; pastime. See *hala 2.*

hala maoli. Same as *hala melemele.*

hala mele.mele. n. A common form of pandanus with bright yellow keys.

hala mō.ʻī wahine. n. A variety of pineapple. *Lit.,* queen pineapple.

hā.lana. vi. **1.** To overflow, flood. Cf. *lana 1. Hālana ka manaʻo,* to be hopeful. **hoʻo.hā.lana.** Caus/sim. *Me aʻu i hoʻohiki ai, ʻaʻole e hoʻohālana hou nā wai o Noa i ka honua* (Isa. 54.9), I have sworn that the waters of Noah shall go no more over the land. **2.** vs. Quiet. *Hālana mālie,* calm tranquillity.

hā.lana.lana. Redup. of *hālana 1, 2. Hālo ʻiloʻi me ka hālanalana o kō lākou waimaka,* their tears welled and flooded.

hā.la.ʻo. Same as *laʻo*, mote.

hala.ʻō. Var. of *halaʻoʻa.*

hala.ʻoʻa. vt. To project, extend; to appear dimly, as in a vision; to see dimly. *Fig.,* presumptuous. *"Halaʻoʻa ʻoe, ē ke kāne." Ke ʻano o ia, mahaʻoi.* (For. 4:99.) "You are protruding, husband." The meaning of this, impertinent.

hā.la.ʻo.la.ʻo. 1. Redup. of *hālaʻo*. **2.** vs. Stunted, poor, thin.

hā.lapa. Same as *hoʻolapa;* ridge; active; flashing brightly. See *lapa 1, 2. Hālapa ka ʻōpū,* uneasy stomach.

hala pepe. n. Native trees *(Dracaena [Pleomele]* spp.) in the lily family, with narrow leaves in tufts at branch ends and with clustered round yellow fruits. (Neal 205–6.) This was one of the five standard plants used in the hula altar to Laka. See more under *palai* (Neal 12). Also *leʻie*.

hala pia. n. An indigenous variety of pandanus, with keys 4 cm long, canary-yellow and small; head small, about 15 by 12 cm., used in medical prescription and for exorcising evil spirits. It was much prized for leis. *He ʻili hala pia* (Kep. 67), light-colored skin.

hala Pola.pola. n. A kind of pandanus. *Lit.,* Borabora [Tahitian] *hala.*

hā.lau. 1. n. Long house, as for canoes or hula instruction; meeting house. *Malu hālau loa,* shade of the long house; *fig.,* shade of trees. *Ā ua nui Hilo, hālau lani i ke ao* (chant), and Hilo rains so much, a heavenly shed in the clouds. (PNP *folau.*) **2.** vs. Large, numerous; much. *Ka wai hālau o Wai-lua* (For. 4:163), expansive waters of Wai-lua. **hoʻo.hā.lau.** To make numerous. *Hoʻohālau i ka hale a piha i nā makamaka,* fill the house full with friends.

hala ʻuha.loa. n. Probably the same as the weed *ʻuhaloa,* a plant form of the pig god Kama-puaʻa, mentioned repeatedly in an 1851 version of the legend of Kama-puaʻa.

hala ʻula. n. **1.** Pandanus with fruit sections entirely orange-red; same size as *hala ʻĪkoi.* **2.** A variety of pineapple similar to *hala kea,* but leaves and unripe fruit red-tinged. (HP 214.)

Hālau-lani. n. A star, said to be observed in the month of Hilinehu.

hala ʻula.ʻula. Same as *hala ʻula 1, 2.*

hā.lawa. Same as *kālawa 1–3.*

hā.lā.wai. 1. nvi. Meeting; to meet. **hoʻo.hā.lā.wai.** To arrange a meeting. (Kin. 27.20; Hal. 59.4.) **2.** n. Horizon. *Mai ka hoʻokuʻi a ka hālāwai,* from zenith to horizon.

hā lawaiʻa. See *hā 6,* sinker.

hā.lā.wai hō.ʻeu.ʻeu. n. Rally; inspirational meeting.

hā.lawa.lawa. Redup. of *hālawa.*

halawi. To scrutinize. (And.)

hale. 1. nvi. House, building, institution, lodge, station, hall; to have a house. Many types of *hale* are listed below. *Ua hale mākou,* we have a house. *Hale i luna a i lalo,* a two-story house. **hoʻo.hale.** To lodge in a house; to receive in a house. *E hoʻohale ʻia aku, he makamaka ola,* extend the hospitality of the house, [he is] a friend who extends appreciation. (PPN *fale.*) **2.** n. Host, hospitable person. Cf. *hale aikāne, hale kipa. He hale leo ʻole aku ia,* he is a kindly hospitable friend. **3.** n. Name listed by Brigham for a *pāwehe* mat pattern; there is a central large lozenge with an enclosed rectangular figure internally enhanced with red on alternate weft crossings. **4.** Also *hare.* Hare. (Oihk. 11.6.)

hale ʻaha.ʻaina. n. Restaurant.

Hale ʻAha.ʻō.lelo Aliʻi. n. House of Nobles.

hale ahu.wai.wai. n. Warehouse.

hale ai.kāne. n. A close family friend, house with friends.

hale ʻaina. n. Restaurant, cafe, eating house, boardinghouse; in ancient times, the eating house for women.

hale-a-ka-iʻa. Same as *pōniu* and *ʻinalua,* the balloon vine. *Lit.,* house of the fish, so called because the vine was used in making small fish basket traps. *Niʻihau.*

hale aliʻi. n. Chief's house, royal residence, palace.

hale ʻā.mala. n. Blacksmith shop.

hale ʻā.pulu. n. Shack.

hale ʻau.amo. n. Palanquin.

hale ʻau.ʻau. n. Bathhouse.

hale ʻauhau. n. House where taxes are paid; tax building.

hale aupuni. n. Capitol building, government building.

hale.haka. n. Hollyhock *(Althaea rosea),* introduced. (Neal 552.) *Eng.* Halehaka pupupu, double form of the hollyhock.

hale hā.lā.wai. n. Meetinghouse, synagogue.

hale.hale. nvs. High, towering, as a housetop, cliff, or waves; cavernous. *Fig.,* emptiness, hunger. *Poʻi halehale ka nalu,* the waves break high as a house. *Pali e halehale mai ana* (FS 21), cliffs towering up. *Halehale*

---

ke aloha (song), deep, deep love. **hoʻo.hale.hale.** Caus/sim.

hale hana. n. Workshop, factory.

hale hana hao. n. Ironworks.

hale hana ʻili. n. Tannery.

hale hana pia (bia). n. Brewery.

hale hana uila. n. Powerhouse. *Lit.,* electricity-making house.

hale hau. n. **1.** House built with posts and thatch sticks of *hau* wood and thatch tied with *hau* cord; said to be used for healing the sick. **2.** Icehouse.

hale hei.au. n. House for keeping images and for worship; house in a heiau.

hale ho.āhu. n. Warehouse, storehouse, shed.

hale ho.āhu puke. n. Library.

hale hoʻo.ʻai.ʻē. n. Pawnshop.

hale hō.ʻai.ʻē kā.lā. n. Credit union. *Lit.,* house for loaning money.

hale hō.ʻike.ʻike. n. Exhibition hall, museum, art academy. *Hale Hōʻikeʻike o Ka-mehameha,* Bishop Museum.

hale hō.ʻike.ʻike iʻa. n. Aquarium. Cf. *pahu iʻa.*

hale holo.holona. n. Barn.

hale hoʻo.kama.kama. n. House of prostitution, brothel.

hale hoʻo.kipa. n. Guest house, lodging house, inn.

hale hoʻo.kolo.kolo. n. Court house.

hale hoʻo.komo kini. n. Cannery.

hale hoʻo.lako kaua. n. Armory.

hale hoʻo.lewa. n. Funeral parlor, undertaker's establishment.

hale hoʻo.luhi. n. House of bondage. (Puk. 13.3.)

hale hoʻo.lulu. n. Railway depot or terminal, waiting station.

hale hoʻo.lulu kaʻa. n. Bus station or terminal.

hale hoʻo.lulu kaʻa.ahi. n. Train station or terminal.

hale hoʻo.lulu moku.lele. n. Airport.

hale hoʻo.luʻu. n. Dyehouse.

hale hoʻo.luʻu ʻili. n. Tannery.

hale hoʻo.maha. n. Resthouse.

hale hoʻo.malu. n. Quarantine house or station.

hale hoʻo.nā. n. Building where land claims were adjudicated by the Board of Commissioners to Quiet Land Titles.

hale hoʻo.pono.pono. n. Administrative building.

hale hoʻo.ulu mea kanu. n. Greenhouse, conservatory.

halei. Rare var. of *helei 1, 2.*

hale imu. n. Shelter for the ground oven; cookhouse.

hale inu kī. n. Teahouse, teashop. *Lit.,* tea- *(Eng.)* drinking house.

hale inu kope. n. Coffeehouse.

hale inu lama. n. Saloon, tavern, bar. *Lit.,* rum-drinking house.

hale inu pia. n. Beer parlor.

hale ipu.kukui. n. Lighthouse.

hale kaʻa. n. **1.** Garage, house for a vehicle. **2.** Carriage, chariot (Hoik. 18.13; Puk. 14.7).

hale kā.hiko kaua. n. Armory.

hale kahu. n. **1.** House of a pastor. **2.** Same as *hale kāhumu.*

hale kā.humu. n. Cookhouse.

hale kā.mala. n. Temporary shed, booth, shelter.

hale kā.piʻo. n. Lean-to shelter; house without walls. This name may be qualified by the terms *ʻalaneo, auolo, hālau, kāmala, kele, kōlea, Oʻahu a Lua.* (Kam. 76: 123.)

hale kā.piʻo ʻili lā.ʻau. n. Rude hut made of bent branches or uprights covered with bark. Cf. *kāpiʻo.*

hale kaua. n. Fort, fortification; tower (Lunk. 9.51, 52).

hale kā.wili lā.ʻau. n. Pharmacy, drug store.

hale keaka. n. Theater.

hale kia. n. Portico; veranda with pillars; porch of pillars (1 Nal. 7.6).

hale kiaʻi. n. Watchtower, tower (Lunk. 8.9).

hale kilo. n. Observatory.

hale kilo hō.kū. n. Star observatory.

hale kinai ahi. n. Fire station.

hale kipa. n. **1.** Guesthouse, lodginghouse, inn (Puk. 4.24), house of hospitality. **2.** Hospitable friend. *E hale kipa kāua e pono ai* (song), it's best for us to be hospitable to one another. **hoʻo.hale kipa.** To entertain, as a guest or friend; hospitable.

hale koa. n. Armory, barracks.

hale.koko. n. House where the *hoa aliʻi,* chief's companions, slept; house where prisoners were held until sacrificed. *Lit.,* blood house.

hale kua. n. **1.** Log cabin. **2.** House where tapa was made.

hale kū.ʻai. n. Store, shop.

hale kū.ʻai lā.ʻau. n. Drugstore, pharmacy.

hale kū.ʻai lole. n. Clothing store, dry goods store.

hale kū.ʻai mea ʻai. n. Grocery store.

hale kū.ʻai palaoa. n. Bakery.

hale kū.ʻai puke. n. Bookstore.

hale.kuʻi. n. Building with many stories, tower. *Lit.,* added house. *Ka Halekuʻi o Papela,* the Tower of Babel.

hale kuʻi hao. n. Blacksmith shop.

hale kuke. n. Customhouse, cookhouse.

hale kuku. n. House for beating tapa.

hale kula. n. Schoolhouse.

hale kupa.paʻu. n. Tomb, sepulcher (1 Nal. 13.22), grave; undertaking parlor. *Lit.,* corpse house.

hale laʻa. n. Temple, house dedicated to God.

hale lā.ʻau. n. Wooden or frame building.

hale lā.lā lā.ʻau. n. House made of branches, booth (Oihk. 23.42), shanty. *Lit.,* tree-branch house.

hale lama. n. House built of *lama* wood, completed during daylight *(lama)* hours and used for treating sick chiefs and for convalescence.

hale lana. n. Floating house, ark, houseboat. *Ka hale lana i ke kai,* the house floating on the sea [a ship].

hale lana.lana. n. House built on a double canoe, as for chiefs.

hale lapa.ʻau. n. Hospital.

hale lau. n. **1.** House thatched with leaves rather than with *pili* grass. **2.** Same as *hale lama;* taboo house for training *kahuna hāhā.* (Kam 64:106.)

hale lau hau. n. Taboo sleeping house for chief and chiefess.

hale lau lama. Same as *hale lama.*

hale leka. n. Post office. *Lit.,* letter *(Eng.)* house.

hā.lelelo. Redup. of *hālelo 1–3.*

hale lepo. n. Mud house, adobe house; dirty house.

hale.lewa. n. Tent, portable house, tabernacle (Mar. 9.5).

hale liʻi.liʻi. n. Outhouse. *Lit.,* small house.

hale lio. n. Stable, barn. *Lit.,* horse house.

hā.lelo. **1.** Jagged, rocky; rocks. See ex., *papaioa. Kū ka hālelo, ke ʻā o kahawai,* rocks and lava in the streams appear [as after a storm; *fig.,* angry words]. **2.** n. Coral sea cavern. **3.** nvs. Yellowish.

hale.loke. n. A kind of lavender or purplish-red chrysanthemum. Probably *lit.,* rose house, and named for someone called Rose, or whose house was called *Haleloke.* Also *wailuku.*

hale lole. n. Cloth house, tent. *He poʻe humuhumu hale lole* (Oih. 18.3), tentmakers.

hale lole holo.holona. n. Slaughterhouse. *Lit.,* house for skinning animals.

hā.lelo.lelo. Redup. of *hālelo 1–3.*

hale.lū. nvt. Psalm, in the Bible; to sing psalms (Hal. 148.1). (Probably Heb. *hallelu-yah.*)

hale lua. n. Cave house; house or vault over a grave; grave (1 Sam. 2.6); outhouse. *Lit.,* pit house.

hale lua liʻi.liʻi. n. Outhouse. *Lit.,* house with little pit.

hale.luia. Hallelujah. (Heb. *hallelu-yah.*)

hā.lema, harema. n. Harem. *Eng.*

hale maʻi. n. Hospital.

hale mā.kaʻi. n. Police station.

hale malu, hale malu.malu. n. Shaded house, shed.

hale mana. n. Largest house in a *luakini* temple. (Summers, 1971, ix.)

hale mana hoʻo.kō. n. Administrative building.

hale manawa. n. House belonging to the high chief where he held secret conferences with the *kālaimoku. Lit.,* temporary house. (Malo 196.)

hale manu. n. Birdhouse, aviary.

Hale-mau.ʻu. n. Name of a Hāna wind. *Lit.,* grass house.

hale moa. n. Chicken house.

hale moe. n. Sleeping house, dormitory.

hale mō.neka. n. Monastery. *Lit.,* monk *(Eng.)* house.

hā.lena. **1.** nvt. Yellowish, pale yellow; to bleach, as tapa. See *lena 1.* **2.** Same as *ʻaiea 1,* native shrubs and trees. **3.** Same as *lena 3;* to draw tight. See *kalena 1. Hālena pono ʻoi i ke kaula ʻili,* draw the lasso tight.

hale nau.ā (nauwa). See *nauā.*

hale noa. n. House without taboo, where the family mingled and slept.

hale noho. n. Dwelling house, residence.

hale ʻoi.hana. n. Shop, workshop.

hale o Lono. n. House where prayers to Lono were offered, as for rain and good crops; on all the islands heiau were so named. See Pukui, Elbert, and Mookini, 1974, 38.

hale olo papa. n. Sawmill.

hale o Papa. n. House of the goddess Papa, i.e., house where religious services were held for women, said to be outside the heiau walls.

hale ʻope.ʻope. n. House for keeping chief's clothes and possessions; house for keeping bones of chiefs. *Lit.,* bundle house.

hale.pā. n. Cupboard, safe. *Lit.,* dish house.

hale paʻa.hana. n. Workshop, tool house.

hale paʻa.hao. n. Jail, prison.

hale pahu. n. Drum house, especially in a heiau where prayers were uttered (Malo 162); a place of refuge in time of war (AP).

hale paʻi. n. Publishing house, print shop, printing establishment.

hale pā.kuʻi. n. Tower (Kin. 11.4), fortified house; addition to a house, annex.

hale pale hau. n. Snowshed.

hale papaʻa. n. Storehouse (Kin. 41.56). *Lit.,* secure house. **hoʻo.hale papaʻa.** To convert into a storehouse; to store in a house; to serve as a storehouse.

hale papaʻi. n. Apartment building. *He poʻe hale kēia i hoʻolimalima ʻia i nā ʻohana he 60 ka nui, a ua kapa ʻia he hale papaʻi,* these are houses rented to families, 60 in number, and are called apartment houses. *Lit.,* uplifted house.

hale peʻa. n. **1.** Tent. **2.** Menstrual house.

hale pele. n. Belfry. *Lit.,* bell *(Eng.)* house.

hale pepehi holo.holona. n. Slaughterhouse. *Lit.,* house for killing animals.

hale pili. n. House thatched with *pili* grass.

hale piʻo. n. Type of ancient house, probably same as *hale kāpiʻo.*

hale pipipi. n. House for convalescence; small, low house.

hale poki. n. Shrine where bones of dead chiefs were kept, as the Hale-o-Keawe at Kona, Hawaiʻi. (Malo 106.)

hale poʻo ʻoi.hana au.puni. n. Capitol. *Lit.,* head house for government business.

hale pua niu. n. House where offerings of bananas, coconuts, and kava were kept, said to be offered in ceremonies deifying a deceased person or making him into a lizard god. *Lit.,* coconut-blossom house.

hale puhi kō. n. Sugar mill; boiling house of a sugar mill. *Lit.,* cane cooking house.

hale puhi palaoa. n. Bakery.

hale pū.kaua. n. Fort, tower, castle.

hale pule. n. Church, chapel. *Lit.,* prayer house.

hale puna. n. House built of limestone or coral.

hale pupupu. n. Makeshift or temporary house, shed, shelter, lodge (Isa. 1.8).

hale puʻu.one. n. Temporary booth, as in a *luakini* temple enclosure (Malo 163), probably used for divinations.

hā.leu. nvt. Toilet paper or anything so used; to wipe, as with toilet paper. *Ua hāleu 'ole,* a rain without toilet paper [so sudden that there is not time to use toilet paper]. (PPN *fa'elu.)*

hale ukana. n. Warehouse, storehouse.

hale umu. n. Oven house, cookhouse.

hale 'u'uku. n. Small house, cottage, cabin.

hale 'uwī wai.ū. n. Dairy.

hale wai. n. Prison, jail. *Lit.,* house [for]retention.

hale wai ea. See *wai ea 2.*

hale weu.weu. n. Grass house.

hale wili. n. Mill. *Lit.,* turning house.

hale wili kō. n. Sugar mill.

hale wili palaoa. n. Flour mill.

hale wili papa. n. Planing mill.

hali. vt. To carry, fetch, bear (Nah. 10.17). Cf. *hali ukana. I ka mea nāna i hali kāna mea kaua* (1 Sam. 31.4), to his armor-bearer. **ho'o.hali.** To cause to carry. *He 'ōlelo ho'ohali,* a roundabout suggestion or hint. *Ho'ohali 'ōlelo,* to hint, suggest indirectly.

hali'a. nvt. Sudden remembrance, memory, especially of a loved one; fond recollection; premonition; to recall, recollect fondly. *Hali'a aloha,* cherished or loving memory; to remember fondly. **ho'o.hali'a.** To evoke reminiscence or recollection; remembrance; to remind.

halia. 1. Pas/imp. of *hali.* 2. Same as *hākālia.*

hā.li'a.li'a. Redup. of *hāli'a.* See ex., *manawa 2.* **ho'o.hā.li'a.li'a.** Caus/sim.

hali.hali. Redup. of *hali;* to transport, transmit. *Moku halihali,* ferry. *Moku halihali koa,* troop transport. *Moku halihali mokulele,* aircraft carrier. *'O wau wale nō ke halihali i kēia po'e kānaka apau* (Nah. 11.14), I alone bear all these people.

hali hele. vt. To carry from place to place.

hā.li'i. nvt. A covering, spread; to spread, as a sheet. *E hāli'i ana ka hau mai ka piko o Mauna Kea* (Laie 479), the snow from the summit of Mauna Kea was spread. *Hāli'i ihola i ka palaoa* (2 Sam. 17.19), to spread wheat. *Kā hāli'i,* asphalt surface. (PPN *faaliki.)*

ha.li'i kuli. v. 1. To spread the knees. 2. Stingy.

hā.li'i.li'i. Redup. of *hāli'i.*

hā.li'i moe. n. Bedspread or sheet.

hā.li'i pela. n. Mattress cover.

hā.li'i pili. nv. To spread over *pili* grass, said poetically of a rain shower.

hā.like. vs. Alike, similar. **ho'o.hā.like.** To compare, contrast, make alike, resemble, copy; artificial. *Ho'o-hālike kolohe,* counterfeit resemblance. *Ho'ohālike me ka haole,* to ape a white person. *Ho'ohālike mai 'oe e like me kēia ki'i,* make a copy of this picture. *'A 'ole ho'i 'oe i ho'ohālike a'e nei me Dāvida ka'u kauā* (1 Nal. 14.8), you are not like David, my servant.

hā.like.like. Redup. of *hālike;* to exemplify. **ho'o.hā.like.like.** Redup. of *ho'ohālike;* comparison, resemblance, similarity, impersonation; to equalize, match, impersonate. *Mea ho'ohālikelike,* example.

hā.liko. vi. To bud, spring forth; to shed a shell, as a crab.

hā.lili. n. Sundial shell, members of the Architectonicidae family.

hā.lina. 1. n. Appearance, bearing, resemblance. 2. vs. Weak, as plants. (Kep. 95.)

hā.lina.lina. Redup. of *hālina 1, 2.*

hā.liu. vi. To turn, look, hearken, incline, have regard. **ho'o.hā.liu.** Caus/sim. *E ho'ohāliu a'e 'oia i kō kākou na'au iāia e hele ma kona mau 'ao'ao apau* (1 Nal. 8.58), that he may incline our hearts towards him, to walk in all his ways. (PPN *fa(a)liu.)*

hā.liua. Pas/imp. of *hāliu. Ē Lono ē, hāliua mai kō alo i o'u nei* (prayer to Lono), O Lono, turn your face to me here.

hali ukana. nv. To carry baggage; porter.

hā.liu.liu. Redup. of *hāliu.*

halo. 1. n. Fins between gill plate and ventral fin. 2. nvt. Motion of the fins or hands in swimming; motion of rubbing; to rub, polish. *E like me ka mea 'au'au, i halo aku i nā lima e 'au* (Isa. 25.11), as the swimmer spreads

forth his hands to swim. (PPN *sa'alo.)* 3. n. Harrow. *Eng.*

hā.lō. vt. To peer, as with the hands shading the eyes; to peep. *He ao hālō* (Malo 146), a peering cloud.

hā.loa. 1. vs. Far-reaching, long. *Hāloa ka hale o ke aloha,* the house with love reaches far. 2. n. Poetic name for *lauloa* taro. 3. n. A variety of sweet potato. 4. n. A type of prayer. (For. 6:37.) *Lit.,* long breath.

Hā-loa. n. 1. A son of Wākea. 2. Star name.

hā.loa kea. Same as *hāloa 2.*

hā.lo'a.lo'a. vi. Turbulent, rough, crowded, jammed.

hā.lo'i. vi. To well with tears, form pools.

hā.lo'i.lo'i. Redup. of *hālo'i;* tearful.

haloke. vi. Loose-fitting, not tight.

hā.loke.loke. Redup. of *haloke.*

hā.loko. nvi. Puddle, pool, pond; to form a pool. *Kai hāloko,* sea almost surrounded by land.

hā.loko i'a. n. Small fishpond.

hā.loko.loko. Redup. of *hāloko. Ka hālokoloko mai o nā waimaka* (FS 279), the welling forth of tears.

hā.loko.loko li'u. Same as *loko li'u.*

hā.loku. vi. To ripple.

halo.lani. vi. To move quietly, as a soaring bird.

hā.loli.'ili. vs. Indolent, idle, useless.

hā.lona. vi. Peering; place from which to peer, place to peer at, lookout. (For. 5:91, For. 6:389.)

hā.lona.ipu. n. A variety of sweet potato.

halu. Same as *puhalu, uhalu.* **ho'o.halu.** Caus/sim. (PPN *salu.)*

hā.lua. 1. nvs. Hollow, dip, furrow, groove, pit; pitted, full of holes. 2. nvt. To ambush, lie in wait, waylay, spy, provoke trouble. **ho'o.hā.lua.** Same as above; ambush. *'Ōlelo 'olu'olu aku kekahi i kona hoalauna me ka waha, akā ma ka na'au, ua ho'ohālua iāia* (Ier. 9.8), one speaks peaceably to his neighbor with the mouth, but in [his] heart, [he] lies in wait.

hā.lu'a. 1. nvs. Stripe, ripple; striped, ridged, seamed, streaked, wrinkled. Cf. *'alu'a.* 2. n. Pattern on the surface of a tapa beater or tapa. This term may follow types of beaters, as *ko'eau hālu'a, mole hālu'a, pū'ili hālu'a.* It also precedes types of beaters, as listed below. 3. Var. of *hānu'a;* see *nu'a 1.* 4. vs. Empty, as the stomach. *O'ahu.*

hā.lu'a-ko'e.au. n. Tapa-beater design.

hā.lu'a-lei-hala. n. Tapa-beater design, said to resemble a pandanus lei and consisting of interlocked triangles.

hā.lu'a.lu'a. Same as *lu'alu'a.*

hā.lu'a-maka-'upena. Same as *hālu'a-manamana.*

hā.lu'a-mana.mana. n. Tapa-beater design.

hā.lu'a-niho-manō. n. Tapa-beater design. The panels between the *hālu'a* lines are enhanced by regularly spaced small triangles. *Lit.,* sharktooth *hālu'a.*

hā.lu'a-pā.wehe-niho-manō. n. A tapa-beater design. The triangles of the *niho manō* pattern are bordered by oblique lines *(pāwehe).*

hā.lua.pou. vi. To make sturdy, as a banana plant (a word used in ancient prayers). *E hāluapou ka pa'a o ka 'āhui,* sturdy the holding of the banana bunch.

hā.lu'a-pū.'ili. n. Tapa-beater design.

hā.lu'a-pū.'ili. n. A tapa-beater pattern with circular motifs *(pūpū).* Also *kōnane pūpū.*

halu.halu. 1. Redup. of *halu.* (PPN *salusalu.)* 2. vi. To breathe heavily.

haluku. vi. 1. To clatter, bang, thud, rattle, plop; to strike the side of the canoe with the paddle. 2. To wallow, as a hog *... i kona haluku 'ana i loko o ke ki'o lepo* (2 Pet. 2.22), the pig . . . to her wallowing in the mire. 3. To crowd, rush; crowded. *Haluku ka 'ai a ke aku,* the bonito rush to eat.

hā.luku.luku. Redup. of *haluku 1-3. Kekahi wahi hālukuluku o ke alanui,* a crowded part of the street.

hā.lula. n. A sea urchin with longer spines than those of the *wana.* (KL line 21.)

hā.lū.lā. Same as *lūlā,* calm, slack, at ease.

hā.lule.lule. Same as *lulelule.*

hā.luli. Same as *luli.*

halulu. **1.** nvi. To roar, thunder; roar, explosion, loud noise, racket. (Isa. 5.30.) *Leo halulu,* deep voice. **hoʻo.halulu.** Same as above; to produce a roaring noise. (PCP *(f,s)alulu.*) **2.** *(Cap.)* n. A legendary man-eating bird. (For. 4:65.)

hā.luna. **1.** Same as *haluhalu 2.* **2.** vt. To summon men to work. *Rare.*

hā.lupa. Same as *lupalupa,* flourishing.

hama.hamau. Redup. of *hāmau.*

Hā.mā.kua-i-ka-paia-ʻala-i-ka-hala. n. Name of a *lua* fighting stroke. *Lit.,* Hāmākua of the bowers fragrant with pandanus.

hama.kuʻu. vt. To tie the hair in a topknot.

hā.male, hamare. nvt. Hammer (Lunk. 4.21), mallet; to hammer. *Eng.*

hā.male kuʻi hao. n. Sledge hammer. *Lit.,* iron-driving hammer.

hā.male lā.ʻau. n. Wooden mallet or hammer.

hā.mama. vi. Open, as a door or obstruction; to open, gape, yawn. *Uē hāmama,* to cry loudly. *Hāmama ka puka,* the door is open. *Uwoki ʻoe e hāmama ana ka waha i ka makani,* be careful lest your mouth be open to the wind [and you will have cause for weeping]. **hoʻo.hā.mama.** To open, expose; to pretend to open, yawn. *Ua hoʻohāmama loa lākou i kō lākou waha iaʻu* (Hal. 35.21), they opened wide their mouth against me. (PCP *faamama.*)

hā.mana. nvs. Fork; branching, forked.

hā.mani. Same as *mani 1.* *Hapawalu liʻiliʻi, hāmani wale nō,* tiny eighth of a dollar, so smooth [a mere nothing].

hama.paka. nvt. Humbug; to humbug. *Eng. Hamapaka ʻia kahi kāpena, pau ka ʻike i ka ʻāina* (song), the captain was humbugged, no more was land to be seen.

hā.mau. vi. Silent; silence; hush. Cf. *iʻa hāmau leo, lehua hāmau.* *Hāmau ē nā kānaka, mele mai nā ʻānela* (hymn), hark, people, the angels sing. **hoʻo.hā.mau.** To silence, hush.

hā.mau.ā.ua. vi. To concentrate, as silently.

hame. n. **1.** The two native species of *Antidesma,* medium-sized trees with hard wood, in the euphorbia family; leaves more or less ovate, fruits in grapelike clusters, purple, one-seeded. Formerly the wood was used for anvils for preparing *olonā* fiber, the fruit to color tapa red. (Neal 500.) Also *haʻā, haʻāmaile, hamehame, mehame.* **2.** Ham. *Eng.* Also *ʻūhā hame, puaʻa hame.*

hame.hame. Same as *hame 1.*

hā.miha. vs. Calm, quiet. *Rare.*

hamo. **1.** vt. Anointed, smeared; to anoint, stain, rub, as with oil; to besmear, plaster, stroke gently, pet, fondle, caress; to struggle, as a drowning man; to put on, as gloves (Kel. 134); to spread, as butter; to plane smooth. *Fig.,* to flatter; compassion. *Mea hamo, lāʻau hamo,* ointment, salve, balm. *Nā papa hū ʻole i hamo ʻia i ka ʻaila* (Puk. 29.2), unleavened wafers anointed with oil. *Nā hale ulaʻau i hamo ʻia ā hinuhinu* (Kel. 135), wooden houses planed beautifully smooth. **hoʻo.hamo.** Caus/sim. **2.** vt. To thrust through or split asunder, as with a spear. *E hamo ʻia iho ana ua koa nei* (For. 5:703), this fighter was split asunder. *E hamo iho ana ʻo Ka-welo i ka ihe* (For. 5:707), Ka-welo thrust his spear through. **3.** n. A variety of sweet potato. (HP 141.) (PCP *(f,s)amo.*)

hamo.hamo. Redup. of *hamo 1;* to pat. See saying, Pukui, Elbert, and Mookini, 1974: *Hamohamo. Ua huli pū aʻela ka waʻa, ā hamohamo ana ʻoia me ka hokua,* the canoe upset, and he struggled at the crest of the waves. *Me kona leo kū i ke aloha e ʻī aku ana ma ka hamohamo ʻana,* in his voice filled with compassion [he] spoke soothingly. **hoʻo.hamo.hamo.** Caus/sim.

hā.mole. Same as *mole 2;* smooth, plain features.

hamo puna. nv. Whitewash, plaster; to plaster; one who plasters, bricklayer.

hamo.ʻula. nvt. Ribbed tapa; to stain or dye with red, as tapa.

hamu. vt. **1.** To eat voraciously, devour, eat scraps; fragments, scraps. Cf. *amu 2.* (PPN *samu.*) **2.** To destroy; to consume, as by fire. *ʻAi hamu,* to destroy, as by sorcery. *Ua pau aku ka hapa nui o kō lāua lako hale i ka hamu ʻia e ke ahi,* most of their household goods were destroyed by fire.

hamu.hamu. Redup. of *hamu 1, 2. Maʻaneʻi nō kahi puaʻa a mākou kahi i hamuhamu ai,* here is where our pig was eating all sorts of things.

hamu.ʻili. n. Personal attendant of a chief, as a taster. *Lit.,* rind consumer.

hamumu. nvi. To whisper, murmur, hum; whispering.

hamu.mumu. Redup. of *hamumu. Ka hamumumu a nā kauwā āna* (2 Sam. 12.19), the whispering of his servants.

hana. **1.** nvt. Work, labor, job, employment, occupation, duty, office, activity, function, practice, procedure, process, deal, incident, reason, action, act, deed, task, service, behavior; to work, labor, do, behave, commit, make, manufacture, create, transact, perform, prepare, happen; to develop, as a picture; to have a love affair (FS 115); to induce by sorcery; to handle (as a court case); to conduct (as a class). (Translated by many English words, but seldom by 'work'.) Cf. *hana wale,* Puk. 12.47, and many examples below. *Hana ʻia,* made, completed, wrought. *Ka haʻi ʻana i ka hana aku,* active voice. *Poʻe hana,* workers, employees. *Maikaʻi ka hana,* well done. *Hana ā maikaʻi,* fix. *Ka haʻi ʻana i ka hana ʻia mai,* passive verb. *I . . . hana,* when; as; while; at the time that. *I hele aku kona hana, ua lilo ka pāpale,* when he went, the hat was gone. *Mea hana,* tool; task; offering to ʻaumākua gods. *Ke hana mai ʻo Pele i kāna hana,* when Pele does her work. *Ka hana ia a ka loea, ʻo ke akamai paheʻe ʻulu* (chant), that is the way an expert does, smart in bowling. *ʻO ka hana, ua hana ʻia,* the work has been done [a completed task]. *Hana maikaʻi i ka ʻāina,* clear the soil well. *ʻA ʻohe kona he maʻi maoli, he maʻi hana ʻia,* his is not a natural sickness, it is induced by sorcery. *Hana ʻia maila ka wai ā ʻono* (Puk. 15.25), the waters were made sweet. **hoʻo.hana.** To use, employ, cause to work, carry out, administer, manage, encourage; use, employment, management, administration. *Luna hoʻohana,* manager, administrative head. *Noho hoʻohana,* to act or serve as manager. *Nā mea hoʻohana,* tools, implements, or anything to work with. (PNP *sanga;* cf. Fijian.) **2.** vs. Worthless; provoked. Cf. *hana wale. ʻAi mai nei nā hana kanaka a waiho mai nei i nā pā naʻu e holoi,* this worthless person ate and left the dishes for me to wash. **hoʻo.hana.** To tease, provoke, nag, plague; one who teases or provokes. **3.** Same as *kilohana,* a tapa. **4.** Same as *hahana,* warm. *Rare.* Cf. *hanahana, kōhanahana, mahana, pumehana.* (PPN *fana.*) **5.** n. Notch, as in a tree. (PPN *kausanga.*)

Hana-. Bay, valley (only in place names, as Hanalei, Hanapēpē. Also *Hono-,* as in Honolulu). (Gram. 8.1; Pukui, Elbert, and Mookini, 1974, 245–7.) (PPN *fanga.*)

-hana. Nominalizing suffix. Cf. *ʻana 3,* Gram. 6.6.2. (PPN *-fanga* [see *kilohana 2*] and PNP *-sanga* [see *hauhana*].)

hāna. vs. **1.** Alert. *I hāna ka pō, i hāna ke ao,* so the night may be alert, the day alert. **2.** *(Cap.)* n. Name of a district and town, East Maui.

hā.nā. n. **1.** Ridgepost supporting each end of the ridgepole. **2.** Wood shavings (Kamakau). *Rare.*

hana aloha. nvt. Love magic; to practice love magic. There follows a *pule hana aloha,* prayer to evoke love. *E hiaala, e hele iāia e ulukū ai, e moe ʻole ai kona pō,* keep awake, go to him and disturb, so his night is sleepless.

hanaea. vs. Willful, disobedient. (Gram. 6.5.) *Rare.*

hana.hana. vs. **1.** Hot, warm, vehement. *Ua hanahana loa ka wī* (Kin. 47.13), the famine was violent. See *hana 4, hahana, mahana 1, pumehana.* (PPN *fanafana.*) **2.** Sour, stinking.

hana.hanai. n. Edge of a precipice or slope, brow of a hill. *Rare.*

hana.hanauna. Same as *hanauna;* contemporary.

hana hemo. vt. To loosen, let go.

hana hewa. v. To do wrong, err. Cf. *hana i ka hewa,* to commit adultery.

hana.hihi. vs. Rank-growing, wild, branchy. *Fig.,* untamed, uncivil, crude.

hana hoʻo.hano.hano. n. Ceremony, ritual.

hana hoʻo.hiwa.hiwa. n. Celebration to honor someone or something.

hana hoʻo.hala manawa. n. Hobby, pastime.

hana hoʻo.nanea. n. Pleasant pastime, hobby, avocation.

hana hou. vt. To do again, repeat, renew, repair, mend; encore.

hā.nai. 1. nvs. Foster child, adopted child; foster, adopted. *Keiki hānai,* foster child. *Lawe hānai,* to adopt a child. *Makua hānai,* foster parent. *Kāna hānai,* his adopted child. **2.** nvt. To raise, rear, feed, nourish, sustain; provider, caretaker (said affectionately of chiefs by members of the court). Cf. *akua hānai, hanai-āhuhu, hanaina. Hānai holoholona,* to feed and care for domestic animals. *Makamaka hānai,* generous and hospitable friend. *Hānai ā momona,* to fatten. *Hānai maila ʻoia iāia i ka meli* (Kanl. 32.13), he fed him the honey. (PPN *faangai.*) **3.** n. Body of a *kōkō* net carrier, and cords attached to it; fish net or trap, as for *ʻoʻopu* fish; kite. **4.** Same as *hanahanai.* **5.** n. Hawaiʻi name for *mānai,* needle. **6.** vi. To skim along.

hā.nai.ā.huhu. nvt. To make a pet of an animal; to care for well, as a pet; cherished plans, pet projects. *Eia kekahi mau hānaiāhuhu a ke aupuni,* here are some favorite plans of the government.

hā.nai ʻai. nv. To feed, give food to; food provider.

Hā.nai-a-ka-malama. n. **1.** The Southern Cross. **2.** Name of a benevolent goddess. **3.** Name of Queen Emma's residence in Nuʻu-anu Valley.

hā.nai kahu. n. Offering for a pastor, of Congregationalists. *Lit.,* feeding pastor.

hana ikaika. nv. Hard or strenuous labor or activity; to do such.

hā.nai kuahu. nv. To renew offerings on a *kuahu* altar; one who does so.

hana ʻili. nv. Tanner; to tan.

hanaina. n. Feeding. *Eia mai ka moa i hanaina lā* (GP 42), here is the rooster fed in the sun [Ka-welo likens himself to a fighting cock; the cock fed in the sun was believed strong because of turning his head to avoid heat; in FS 63 and 65 the verb is *hānai ʻia i ka lā,* fed in the sun].

hana ʻino. nvt. To mistreat, abuse, mutilate, injure, mar, treat cruelly or carelessly; cruelty; cruel, wicked; evil deed, torment. *Hana ʻino ʻoe i ka lole,* you are treating the dress carelessly.

hana.ʻi'o. vs. Serious about what one does; to consummate, as a love affair. *Lit.,* to do truly. *Mai kolohe aku ʻoe i kā ke aliʻi, o hanaʻiʻo mai auaneʻi,* don't tamper with the chief's [things], or [he] will do something drastic. *Hanaʻiʻo ka ua iā Kohala* (song), rain really poured at Kohala.

hā.nai.pū. n. Title of the bearer of an image, who ate the food offered to the god.

Hana.kahi. n. An ancient chief of Hilo whose name was used in poetry to designate the Hilo district. See ex., *hananeʻe, Kani-lehua.*

Hana-kaʻi-luna. n. Name of a *lua* stroke.

hana kala.kalai. n. Trifling, inconsequential action, as a casual love affair. *Lit.,* carving act.

Hana-ka.lau-ʻai. n. Name of a star associated with Hana-kau-luna, and the name of a legendary place. *Lit.,* Hana, the abundant food.

hana kama.liʻi. vs. Childishness; childish; so easy that a child can do it.

hana.kapahu. n. Smallpox (perhaps short for *hana i ka pahu,* build the coffin).

Hana-kau-luna. n. **1.** Name of a star associated with *Hana-kalau-ʻai,* and *Haka-lau-ʻai;* all were omens of pestilence or calamity. **2.** Name of a death stroke in *lua* fighting.

hana keaka. See *keaka 1.*

hana kī.wila. Civil service.

hana kolohe. nv. Mischief, trick; to do mischief, misbehave.

hana kuli. See *kuli 2.*

Hanale. 1. n. Henry. *Eng.* See saying, *pulu 5.* **2.** *(Not cap.)* nvi. Hungry, hunger. *Eng.*

Hana.lei. n. Name of a large valley on Kauaʻi. *Lit.,* lei valley. See saying *kaupoku 1.* **2.** *(Not cap.)* vi. Hurled forth. *Kēia huhū hanalei ʻana,* this vented anger.

hana lepo. nv. Dirty work; to do dirty work; excrement; to excrete.

hana lima. nv. Handmade, manual; manual labor; to work with the hands. *Nā mea hana lima,* handicraft. *Hana lima ʻike,* skilled labor.

hana luhi. nvs. Tiresome activity or work, bother, toil.

hana maʻa. n. Customary or usual activity. *Mea hana maʻa,* habit.

hana maʻi. nvi. Sexual intercourse; to perform such. *Lit.,* genital activity.

hana make. nvt. Thing of destruction, as a weapon of sorcery; to kill, destroy; deathly.

hana mana. n. Miracle, supernatural deed, witchcraft.

hana mau. nvi. Customary activity; to work constantly, diligent. *Hana mau ʻia,* commonly done, usual activity. *ʻŌlelo hana mau ʻia,* common word.

hana mua ʻia. vs. Second hand, done before.

hanana. n. Occasion, event, occurrence, incident, time. *I hele mai nā malihini i kēlā hanana i ka male ʻana o nā keiki,* the visitors come on that occasion of the marriage of the children.

hā.nana. Var. of *hālana 1;* to overflow.

hana.nai. Same as *nanai 1;* to strut.

hana.neʻe. Same as *hāneʻeneʻe 1. Hananeʻe ke kīkala o kō Hilo kini; hoʻi luʻuluʻu i ke one o Hanakahi,* sagging hips of Hilo's multitudes; return burdened to the sands of Hanakahi [of grief or heavy burdens].

hana noʻeau. n. Art. *ʻIke hana noʻeau,* art; artistic.

hana nui. vs. Difficult, hard, laborious.

hana.nuʻu. vs. Short, plump. *Wahine poupou pou hananuʻu* (song), woman stout, very short and plump.

hana ʻoi. nvt. To sharpen; cutlery. See ex., *puʻu lele.*

hana paʻa. 1. vt. To make secure, fasten, shut up. *Hana paʻa ʻoia iā Ioane i loko o ka hale paʻahao* (Luka 3.20), he shut up John in prison. **2.** n. Steady employment.

hana.pē.pē. vt. To bruise, crush. (Hal. 44.19.)

hana.pilo. Var. of *hanopilo.*

hana pipi. nv. To work with cattle, especially as a cowboy; such work.

hana puna.hele. n. Favorite pastime, hobby.

hā.nau. 1. nvt. To give birth; to lay (an egg); born; offspring, child, childbirth; productive, fertile. *Hānau ʻo Hina,* Hina gave birth. *Hānau ʻia ʻo Hina,* Hina was born. *ʻIliʻili hānau,* reproducing pebbles. *He keiki hānau ʻē,* premature baby. *Lā hānau,* birthday. *Hānau ka moa i ka hua,* the chicken lays an egg. *Hānau ʻia. To act as midwife, deliver a baby; to reproduce. (PPN *faanau.*) **2.** interj. Happy birthday (used in toasts). **3.** Short for *hoahānau,* cousin. *Rare.*

hanaua. Rare pas/imp. of *hānau 1.* (For. 6:502.)

hā.nau ʻe.epa. nvi. Peculiar or unusual birth; born with a strange sign or mark.

hā.nau ēwe. n. Premature birth.

hā.nau hope. n. Younger brother or sister; the lastborn.

hā.nau hou. nvs. Reborn, born again, rebirth; baptism. *hoʻo.hā.nau hou.* To cause a rebirth, baptize.

hā.nau kahi. n. Only child. (Sol. 4.3.)

hā.nau kama. nvs. Childbearing, prolific, fertile, having many children; mother of one's children, wife. *Kāna hānau kama,* his wife.

hā.nau keiki ʻana. n. Childbirth.

hā.nau mua. n. First-born child, especially the eldest living member of the senior branch of a family; senior, older brother or sister.

hanauna. n. Generation; relative whose relationship was established several generations previously; ancestry, birth. *Hanauna like,* relative of the same generation; of the same generation, contemporary. *Makuahine hanauna,* aunt, female cousin of one's father or mother. *Keiki hanauna,* nephew, niece. *Kaikuahine hanauna,* female cousin of a male. *Pili ma ka hanauna,* related through having a common ancestor. *Nā makua kāne hanauna* (For. 4:161), uncles, fathers, brothers and male cousins. *ʻŌpio ʻAmelika o ka hanauna Kepanī,* American youth of Japanese ancestry. (PPN *fanaunga.*)

hā.nau pā.hā. n. Quadruplets.

hā.nau pā.kolu. n. Triplets.

hā.nau pā.lima. n. Quintuplets.

hana.wai. 1. nvt. Irrigation; to irrigate, water. 2. nvi. Menstruation; to menstruate. 3. nvi. Urine; to urinate. See *ʻōpū hanawai.*

hana wale. vt. 1. To work aimlessly, gratuitously, to no avail, uselessly. 2. To tease, annoy needlessly.

hana walea. vt. To do with ease, as of long custom.

hā.nawa.nawa. Rare var. of *hāwanawana.*

hā.nau wawā. nvs. Reincarnation; to be born repeatedly, as Haumea, an earth mother. (Kam. 64:44, note 1.) *Lit.,* repeated birth.

hane. 1. vs. Ghostly, soft, and indistinct sounding. Cf. *ʻuhane.* See ex., *hinihini 2.* 2. vi. To give life and spirit. *ʻO ka hua a Kama i hane, nā lani ka hua* (For. 6:412), the fruit of Kama was given life, the high chiefs were the fruits.

hā.neʻe. vi. To fall, as a building; to collapse, slide, cave in, slip. See chant, *hanuʻu. Hāneʻe ka mauna,* landslides on the mountain. **hoʻo.hā.neʻe.** To cause an avalanche, slide; to flatten.

hā.neʻe.neʻe. 1. Redup. of *hāneʻe.* 2. Same as *neʻeneʻe,* moving along. 3. Same as *kīkala hāneʻeneʻe.*

hane.hane. 1. Redup. of *hane 1, 2;* ghostly. *Na leo wawalo o ka hanehane,* calling voices of the spirit.

hā.nei. Rare var. of *hānai.*

hanele, haneri. num. Hundred. *Eng.*

hā.nene. Same as *nene 1,* to stir.

hā.nē.nē. Same as *nēnē,* to chirp; rumor.

hane.o.o. n. Strong blow, as of the fist. *Rare.*

hā.newa.newa. vs. 1. Weak, giddy. 2. Same as *hāwanawana. Rare.*

hani. 1. vi. To step or move lightly or softly; to graze, touch; soft, light. *Fig.,* to hint, suggest, act coy or flirtatious. Cf. *māhani, makahani. Hani ka helena a ka ʻaihue,* soft the step of the thief. **hoʻo.hani.** To touch, graze, hint. 2. Same as *hanahanai. I kukupu i ka hani pali,* sprouting on the cliff side. 3. vi. To know well. *Ua aʻo i nā mele a hani wale,* the songs were learned perfectly.

hani.hani. Redup. of *hani 1.*

hanile. vt. To prepare for or receive company.

hanina. 1. Same as *hani 1. Nā manu hanina i ka laʻi.* the birds moving lightly in the calm. 2. Yellow sarong, as dyed with turmeric. (And.)

hanini. vi. To overflow, spill, pour out, slop over; to pour down, as rain; to disappear. (Isa. 45.8.) **hoʻo.hanini.** To overflow, etc.; to cause an overflow. *Hoʻohanini i Mānā ka wai ʻōpua,* the water of the cloud banks pours down at Mānā. *Ua hanini anei kō lākou akamai?* (Ier. 49.7.) Is their wisdom vanished?

hā.nini.nini. Redup. of *hanini.*

hā niu. n. Heavy end of a coconut frond.

hano. 1. Same as *hanohano.* Cf. *pūhano. Kau i ka hano,* placed in a position of honor. *Leo hano,* voice of authority and respect. **hoʻo.hano.** Same as *hoʻohanohano.* 2. nvs. Hoarse; humming sound of chanting. Cf. *hanopilo.* (PCP *(f,s)ango.*) 3. n. Nose flute. (Probably PPN *fangu.*) 4. nvt. Enema, syringe; to inject, use as a

syringe. 5. n. Fish net, as for *mālolo* fish or *ʻiao;* bag net. 6. n. Container, as for water or tobacco.

hā.nō. nvi. Asthma; to wheeze.

hanoa, hanowa. vs. Fermented. *ʻO nā ʻumeke piʻialiʻi, nohu, . . . ua hanowa i loko o ke kūmau,* the bowls with *piʻialiʻi* and *nohu* taros . . . had fermented in the poi bowls.

hanoalewa. n. Temporary altar where offerings were made to the gods.

hano.hano. nvs. Glorious, magnificent, noble, honored, stately, dignified, grand, distinguished, honorable, honorary; honor, pomp, glory, prestige. *I ka mea hanohano, ka luna hoʻomalu,* to the honorable speaker. *Ka Mea Hanohano, ke Kiaʻaina,* his Excellency, the Governor. **hoʻo.hano.hano.** To honor, exalt, glorify; to conduct oneself with distinction. *Mea hoʻohanohano, hōʻailona hoʻohanohano,* insignia of distinction, regalia, decoration. *Kekele hoʻohanohano,* honorary degree. *Medala hoʻohanohano,* medal, as a military medal for merit.

hano hā.weo. See *hāweo.*

hanona. 1. Same as *hano 5.* 2. To determine by lot the virtue or value of a thing. (AP.)

hā.nono, hā.nonono. Same as *nono 1, 2.*

hano paka. n. Tobacco box or container.

hano.pilo. vi. Hoarse, wheezy, weak-voiced. *Hanopilo ka leo o ka ʻalae,* hoarse is the voice of the mudhen [a person who talks himself hoarse].

hanowa. Var. spelling of *hanoa.*

hano wai. Same as *hue wai.*

hanu. nvt. To breathe, smell, sniff, inhale; breath, respiration, transpiration, last breath of life; vanity (Biblical). Cf. *hanuāpuaʻa, pūhanu. ʻĪlio hanu kanaka,* bloodhound. *Omo i ka hanu,* suck in the breath, gasp. *Eia ua lani a Hā-loa i pili ai ka hanu i ke kapu,* here is a chief descended from Hā-loa, whose taboo makes one hold his breath [as in terror]. *He hanu wale nō kuʻu mau lā* (Ioba 7.16), my days are vanity. *Nāna nō i hāʻawi mai nei ke ola . . . a me ka hanu* (Oih. 17.25), he has given life . . . and breath. *Hanu lipo o ka palai* (song), breathing deep of the *palai* fern. *Nui nei ka hanu* (Kel. 52), breathing hard; to puff, sigh. *Paʻa ka hanu,* breathing is stifled; smothering; to gasp. *Hanu i loko,* inhalc. *Hanu i wuho,* exhale. **hoʻo.hanu.** To cause to breathe, resuscitate, administer an inhalant. *I ka hoʻohanu ʻana o kou mau pukaihu* (Puk. 15.8), with the blast of your nostrils. (PPN *fangu.*)

hanua. Pas/imp. of *hanu.*

hā.nuʻa. Same as *nuʻa 1.*

hanu.ā.puaʻa. vi. To breathe like a pig; to gasp for breath, as a strangled pig.

hanu.hanu. Redup. of *hanu.* **hoʻo.hanu.hanu.** Redup. of *hoʻohanu. Lāʻau hoʻohanuhanu,* inhalant. *Paʻakai hoʻohanuhanu,* smelling salts.

hā.nui. Same as *mokumoku hā nui,* a damselfish.

Hanu-i-piʻi. n. A stroke in *lua* fighting. *Lit.,* rising breath.

hā.nuna. vi. To snore, to talk with nasalized sounds; blurred, as sound.

hā.nuna.nuna. 1. Redup. of *hānuna.* 2. First fermentation of fresh poi (AP.)

hā.nū.nē. Similar to *nūnē,* speculation.

hanunu. vs. Steep, bent-over, stooped, round-shouldered; stooping. *Rare.*

hanu nui. n. Deep breath.

hā.nupa. vi. Surging, swollen; choppy, as the sea; slippery, muddy.

hanu paʻa. nvi. A head cold; stifled breathing; to have such.

hā.nupa.nupa. Redup. of *hānupa. Ke awa hānupanupa,* the surging channel.

hanu.paoa. Same as *naʻenaʻe 1,* plants. *Lit.,* fragrant breath.

hanu.pau. n. A disease, perhaps pneumonia.

hanu pau. nvi. Last breath or gasp; to give the last breath, as of one dying.

hanu pī. vi. To sniffle. Cf. *pī 2.*

hanu pilo. nvi. Bad breath, halitosis; to have such.

hanu'u. nvi. To flow in spurts, ebb, fluctuate; fluctuation, ebb. *Ka pali mākō i hāne'e, i hanu'u* (chant), the rock cliff that slid, that moved in spurts. *Kaha i ka hanu'u,* to mark fluctuation, as the high-water mark of the tide. **2.** vs. Short, stunted, thick. Cf. *hananu'u.*

hā.nu'u.nu'u. Redup. of *hanu'u 1, 2.*

hao. **1.** n. Iron, general name for metal tools, a bit; brand, as on a horse. Cf. *hao kuni.* See sayings, *'alu, wela 1. Mea hao,* hardware. (PPN *fa'o.*) **2.** n. All native species of a genus of small trees *(Rauvolfia)* related to the *maile* and the *hōlei,* four or five narrow branches are borne together at joints of branches; many small, yellowish flowers develop, and then small, black, flattened, twinned, inverted, heart-shaped fruits. (Neal 691.) (PPN *fao.*) **3.** nvt. To scoop, dish, or pick up; to grasp, gouge, pillage, plunder, loot; robber. (Perhaps PPN *sa'o.*) **4.** vt. To come with force, as wind or rain; to do with force and energy. See ex., *pa'ihi. Hao wale,* to strike at random; violent. *Hao mai i ka pu'upu'u,* deliver a blow of the fist. *Hao maila ka mana* (FS 265), power was in full force. *Hao mai nā koa 'Amelika!* On come the American soldiers! *Hao mai ka makani, kuakea ka moana; hao mai ke kai, kū ke ko'a i uka,* the wind blows, the sea is white with foam; the sea rises and coral is washed ashore [anger]. **ho'o.hao.** Caus/sim. *Ke ho'ohao nei ke ahe makani,* the wafted breeze comes with force. **5.** Same as *mai'a 'oa,* a variety of banana. **6.** n. Horn, as of a goat. **7.** Rare var. of *haohao 2.*

ha'o. **1.** Same as *ha'oha'o. He ha'o wale ho'i,* how unusual; surprising. **2.** vt. To long for, desire; to miss, whether desirable or not. *'Ōpū ha'o,* hunger pains. **3.** *(Cap.)* n. Name of a star.

haoa. **1.** Pas/imp. of *hao 3, 4.* **2.** nvs. Scorching, bitter; heartburn, sour stomach. **3.** Same as *haoa puhi.* Also *ha'oa, laoa, la'oa.* See ex., *kilokilohia.* **ho'o.haoa.** Caus/sim. Also *ho'oha'oa, ho'olaoa, ho'ola'oa.*

hao'a. vs. Rocky, as of broken lava or coral rubble; scraggly, uneven; choppy, as the sea. *Rare.*

hao.'ao'a. Redup. of *hao'a. Rare.*

haoa puhi. n. Gorge used for catching eels: when the eel took the baited stick it was pulled by a string, and lodged in the throat of the eel.

hao'e. Var. of *hao'a. Hao'e nā 'ale o Hōpoe i ka 'ino,* the billows of Hōpoe rise in the storm [anger mounting; the seas at Hōpoe, Puna, were notoriously rough].

hā.o'e.o'e. Redup. of *hao'e. 'O Pana-'ewa nui, moku lehua, 'ōhi'a kupu hāo'eo'e i ka ua* (PH 32), great Pana-'ewa, district with *lehua* flowers, *'ōhi'a* trees growing scraggly in the rain.

hao haka.haka. n. Grate, grill.

hao.hana. Scooping; handful. *Rare.* (Probably *hao 3 + -hana,* nominalizer.)

hao.hao. **1.** Redup. of *hao 3, 4.* (PPN *sa'osa'o.*) **2.** nvs. Soft meat that can be scooped from young coconuts. *He 'ono ka wai o ka niu haohao* (song), delicious is the water of the young coconut with soft meat.

ha'o.ha'o. vs. Strange, puzzling, astonishing; astonished, puzzled, surprised; to wonder, marvel. Cf. *maha'oha'o, pāha'oha'o.* **ho'o.ha'o.ha'o.** To arouse wonder, surprise, puzzlement.

hao.haoa. Redup. of *haoa 1, 2. Haohaoa lani,* royal heat [taboo of a chief]. *He ahi kāoko o nā ali'i, loa'a i ka pili haohaoa* (chant), hot fire of the chiefs obtained by the [one who] approaches the heat [dangerous to approach a taboo chief].

hao.haoa. Same as *haohao 1.*

ha'o.ha'ona. n. Astonishment, wonder.

hao.hia. Pas/imp. of *hao 3,4.*

hao ho'o.pa'a lima. n. Manacle. *Lit.,* hand-binding iron.

hao ho'o.pa'a wahie. n. Andiron. *Lit.,* iron for holding fuel.

hao hou puka. n. Metal punch.

hā.'o'i. vi. To limp.

hao.kanu. nvt. Seedbed; to prepare a seedbed. *Rare.*

hao kaula waha. n. Bit of a bridle.

hao.kea. n. A rather common native variety of taro; the leaves are narrow, the *piko,* leaf attachment, light, and petioles light green. This taro supplies some gray commercial poi and *lū'au* greens. It was formerly used both medicinally and in religious ceremonies, as for dedicating new fish nets. According to HP 17, it is a domesticated form of wild *'āweu.* The name may be qualified by the colors *hā'ula'ula* and *ke'oke'o.* Var. names reported include *'ahakea, ha'akea,* and *hā'awikea.*

hao ke'ehi. n. Stirrups.

hao.kila. vs. To be sturdy as steel. *Lit.,* iron steel *(Eng.). Umauma haokila* (Kel. 24), steel-hard chest.

hao ku'e. n. Piston.

hao kuni. n. Branding iron.

haole. nvs. White person, American, Englishman, Caucasian; American, English; formerly, any foreigner; foreign, introduced, of foreign origin, as plants, pigs, chickens; entirely white, of pigs (Malo 37; perhaps Malo actually means of foreign introduction). See *kolea 1.* References in traditional literature are few, but these have been noted: *He haole nui maka 'ālohilohi* (FS 201), a big foreigner with bright eyes [referring to Kama-pua'a, the pig demigod]. *Hānau ke po'o haole, he haole kēlā* (KL line 505), born was the stranger's head, that was strange. *Ho'okahi o Tahiti kānaka, he haole* (Kua-li'i chant, For. 4:375), only one people in Tahiti, foreigners. *'Āina haole,* foreign land. *'Ōlelo haole,* European language, especially English. **ho'o.-haole.** To act like a white person, to ape the white people, or assume airs of superiority [often said disparagingly, especially of half-whites]. *Ho'ohaole 'ia,* Americanized, Europeanized; to have become like a white person or have adopted the ways of a white man. (Marquesan *hao'e* is probably a loan from Hawaiian.)

hā.'olo.'olo. Probably similar to *'olo'olo 1–3. Ke hā-'olo'olo 'ē lā ke ao* (UL 85, 86, 88), light floods forth.

haoma. n. Name of a fish (no data).

hao mā.kē.neki (mageneti). n. Magnet.

hao mana.mana. n. Grate, grill, gridiron. *Lit.,* branched iron.

haona. Same as *hao 3, 4;* handful, scoopful; receptacle, as a dipper for kava.

hā 'o'opu. n. Trap for *'o'opu* fish.

hao waha. n. Bit of a bridle. *Lit.,* mouth iron.

hao wili. n. Wrench.

hapa. **1.** nvs. Portion, fragment, part, fraction, installment; to be partial, less. (Eng. *half.*) Cf. *hapahā, hapalua,* etc. *Ka 'ike hapa,* limited knowledge. *Ua hapa nā hae,* the flags are at half-mast. **ho'o.hapa.** To lessen, diminish. **2.** nvs. Of mixed blood, person of mixed blood, as *hapa Hawai'i,* part Hawaiian. See *hapa haole.* **3.** n. A-minor in music. See *lele 7.*

hāpa. n. Harp. *Eng.* See *pila hāpa.*

hapa.hā. num. One fourth, one quarter, quarter, twenty-five cents; quarterly; tribute (Kin. 30:14). *Lit.,* fourth part. *Hapahā i hala ka hola 'eiwa,* a quarter after nine o'clock. *Hō'ike hapahā,* quarterly report.

hapa.hā kini. n. Five-dollar gold piece. *Lit.,* guinea *(Eng.)* quarter. *Rare.*

hapa.haneli. nvs. **1.** Hundredth part, percentage. *Iwakālua hapahaneli no ke kālā,* twenty per cent on the dollar. **2.** n. A copper penny issued by Ka-mehameha III in 1847.

hapa haole. nvs. Part-white person; of part-white blood; part white and part Hawaiian, as an individual or phenomenon. *Hula hapa haole,* a hula danced to a *mele hapa haole* (a Hawaiian type of song with English words and perhaps a few Hawaiian words).

hapa.hapai. Redup. of *hāpai 1;* to toss up, as a child; to heave or breathe heavily; to glorify, praise. *Nou paha ka inoa e ka'ika'ikū ana, pā i ka nuku ā hapahapai a'e,* yours perhaps the name chant carried to and fro, and that is on everyone's lips in praise.

hapa.hiku. num. One seventh.

hā.pai. 1. vt. To carry, bear, lift, elevate, raise, hoist, hold up; to support, as another's testimony. (Nah. 23.7.) *Hāpai pū,* to carry together; carry arms [a military command]. *Hāpai i ka leo,* to lift up the voice, as in song. *No ka hoʻohanohano ʻana iaʻu, i koʻu hāpai ʻia ʻana i kiaʻāina,* honoring me in my elevation to the governorship. Caus/sim. (PPN *sapai,* PCP *saapai.*) **2.** vi. Pregnant; to conceive. *Kou hāpai ʻana* (Kin. 3.16), your conception. **hoʻo.hā.pai.** To cause conception; to perform ceremonies or take treatment to induce conception. **3.** n. A native variety of banana with trunk of medium height, the fruit maturing within it, about two-thirds of the way up. The fruits are small, finger length, and ten or less; their skin is yellow, and the flesh yellow, sweet, and edible raw. (HP 175, Neal 250.) Also *hua waena.* **4.** vt. To encourage, support. *Ua hāpai ʻoia e inu ka ʻāina apau i ka lama,* he encouraged everyone in the land to drink rum.

hā.pai kanaka. vt. To carry or lift, as an invalid unable to raise himself in bed or walk.

hapa iki. Same as *hapa ʻuʻuku.*

hā.pai kō. v. To carry sugar cane bundles on the back, as formerly done by plantation workers.

hā.pai malule. Same as *mākoi kanaka,* a sport.

hā.pai.memeue. vt. To praise, laud.

hapaina. n. Carrying, lifting, carrier; pregnancy. *He hoa manu nēnē, he hapaina ʻino* (chant), a goose bird companion, carrier of filth.

hapai.pū. nvi. Heavy breathing, as of one with asthma; to breathe heavily.

hapa Kepa.nī. n. One of part Japanese ancestry.

hapa.kolu. num. Third; one third. *ʻElua hapakolu,* two thirds.

hapa.kuʻe. nvs. Crooked, deformed, crippled, defective; speech impediment; to speak with an impediment, as one who has had a stroke; crippling, defection. *Lele mai he mokulele i ʻano hapakuʻe kona mau ʻenekina . . . me ʻelua wale nō mau ʻenekina e kakaʻa ana,* an airplane came, the motors of which were somewhat crippled . . . only two motors were turning over.

hā.pala. 1. vt. To daub, blot, besmear; to spread, as butter. *Fig.,* to defile, defame. *Lā Hāpala Lehu,* Ash Wednesday. *Hāpala ka ʻele, na ke kea ka ʻai* (For. 4.273), the black is smeared, the white gets the score [in a *kōnane* game]. *Ka makani hāpala lepo o Pāʻia,* dust-smearing wind of Pāʻia. *Ua hāpala ʻia i ke kaikea* (Isa. 34.6), smeared with fat. **hoʻo.hā.pala.** To besmear, etc. **2.** Same as *pala 1,* ripe. *Rare.*

hā.pala.pala. Redup. of *hāpala.*

hā.pale. n. Shovel, trowel. *Rare.*

hapa.lima. num. Fifth; one fifth.

hapa loa. n. A small portion, very few. Cf. *hapa nui. He nui ka waiwai i lilo no ka ʻīlio, ā he hapa loa ka waiwai loaʻa hou mai ā ia,* a lot of wealth is spent on dogs, very little value is obtained in return.

hapa.lua. num. Half, half dollar; in two portions. *Hapalua like,* even half, exactly half. *Hapalua hola ʻelua,* half-past two o'clock.

hapa.lua kini. n. Ten-dollar gold piece. *Lit.,* guinea *(Eng.)* half.

hapa maka.hiki. n. Semiannual. *Ma ka hapa makahiki e uku ai,* to be paid semiannually.

hapa nui. n. Majority, most; quorum; greatest or largest portion. Cf. *hapa loa. Ka hapa nui o ka manawa,* most of the time.

hapa.ono. num. One sixth.

hā.papa. 1. n. Rock stratum covered with thin earth; shoal; shoal water, coral flat; shallow. *Fig.,* superficial. **2.** vt. To grope, feel the way, reach for, extend out; to experience, feel. *Hāpapa hewa ka malihini makamaka ʻole,* a stranger without friends gropes vainly. *ʻO ka makapō wale nō ka mea hāpapa i ka pō uli,* only the blind grope in the dark night. *ʻA ʻole hoʻi i hāpapa ikaika loa mai nā ʻeheu ʻiniʻini a ke kēhau* (Kel. 17), did not feel very strongly the pinching wings of

dew. **3.** n. Stick for catching ʻio hawks; the crosspieces were gummed and a live bird was tied as a decoy.

hā.papapa. Same as *hāpapa 1, 3.*

hapa.pū. vs. Partly finished, incomplete, as work.

hapa.pū.lima. n. Signature, handwriting, autograph.

hā.pau.ea. nvi. Feeble with age; aged person.

hapa ʻuku. Same as *hapa ʻuʻuku.*

hapa.ʻumi. num. Tenth part, tithe; five cents, nickel. *Hapaʻumi o kō ʻoukou waiwai* (Kanl. 12.6), tithe.

hā.paʻu.paʻu. vs. Shabby, dingy, sooty, dilapidated.

hapa ʻuʻuku. nvs. Minority, small portion; less.

hapa.wai. n. A shellfish, *Theodoxus vespertinus.*

hapa.walu. num. One eighth; eighth part; a coin worth twelve and a half cents; a piece of silver money (Luka 15.8).

hape. 1. vs. Incorrect, faulty, inaccurate; to break, transgress (Kep. 49). **hoʻo.hape.** Caus/sim. *ʻŌlelo hoʻo-hape mai,* to speak incorrectly. (PPN *sape.*) **2.** See *hapenuia.*

hā.peʻe.peʻe. vi. To limp. *ʻO ka hāpeʻepeʻe o ka hele, e ʻōnaha ai nā wāwae* (For. 5:111), going with a limp and bowlegged. See also Nak. 79.

hā.pele. Same as *napele,* soft. Cf. *pele 2.*

hape.nu.ia. interj. Happy New Year. *Eng. Lā-naʻi, Molokaʻi nui a Hina, hape hapenuia* (song). Lā-naʻi, great Molokaʻi [child] of Hina, happy, happy New Year.

hā.poko.poko. vs. Short, as a piece of wood or clouds (see ex., *wehiwa 2*).

hā.pō.pō. vs. Partially blind.

hā.pua. n. Flowering season. *Rare.*

hā.pue. 1. vi. To huddle. *Rare.* Cf. *pupue 1.* **2.** n. A medicinal plant (no data); a kind of fiber used for nets. *Rare.*

hapuee. A kind of fish. (And.)

hā.puku. 1. vt. To collect, gather together in haste or indiscriminately and usually for oneself. *Makapehu ke ao, ke hāpuku wale lā nō i ke koʻekoʻe,* swollen clouds collecting aimlessly in the chill. **2.** vs. Indiscriminately, foolishly. *Hāpuku ʻohiʻohi,* to talk foolishly. *ʻOhi hāpuku ka makapehu o Ka-unu,* the hungry ones of Ka-unu grab at anything [of gossip]. **3.** n. Crane (for moving objects); bucket attached to a crane.

hā.pou. 1. Same as *pou,* short. **2.** Same as *ōlaʻi,* pumice.

hā.pou.pou. Redup. of *hāpou 1.*

hā.puna. n. **1.** Spring, pool, puddle. *Fig.,* as representing continuation of life. **2.** Harpoon. *Eng.*

hā.puna.puna. Redup. of *hapuna 1.* (Nak. 82.)

hā.puʻu. n. 1. An endemic tree fern *(Cibotium splendens,* formerly called *C. chamissoi),* common in many forests of Hawaiʻi, as at Kī-lau-ea Volcano, and now frequently cultivated. These ferns grow about 5 m high, and the trunks are crowned with large, triangular, lacy-looking fronds up to 2.7 m long, their light brown stems rising from a mass of silky, golden *pulu* (wool). Young stems were formerly used to make hats; the *pulu* was used as a dressing and to embalm the dead and later as stuffing for pillows and mattresses. The starchy trunk core has been used for cooking and laundry, the outer fibrous part to line or form baskets for plants. Young shoots are called *pepeʻe.* (Neal 10.) Also *hāpuʻu pulu.* **2.** Grouper, a fish *(Epinephelus quernus).* The young stage is *hāpuʻupuʻu* or *ʻāpuʻupuʻu.* See *ʻeheʻula.* (PPN *faapuku (rare).* **3.** Budding. *Fig.,* child, baby; young, as of squid *(rare).* **4.** A variety of taro, also *hāpuʻu-puʻu,* that may be qualified by the colors *ʻeleʻele, hāuli-uli* (favored by planters), *kea* or *keʻokeʻo, lena,* and *ʻulaʻula.* (HP 17, 18, 32.)

hā.puʻu ʻiʻi. n. 1. An endemic tree fern *(Cibotium chamissoi,* formerly called *C. menziesii)* much like the *hāpuʻu* and also known as *hāpuʻu,* but bearing stiff blackish hairs on the frond stems. (Neal 10-1.) Also *ʻiʻi.* **2.** *Dryopteris paleacea* var. *fusco-atra,* a much smaller endemic fern (not a tree) with dark hairs at stems' base. Also *ʻiʻi.*

hā.puʻu pulu. Same as *hāpuʻu 1.*

hā.puʻu.puʻu. 1. n. Young *hāpuʻu* ferns that have not yet developed trunks. **2.** n. Young stage of *hāpuʻu* fish. **3.** Same as *ʻapuʻupuʻu;* rough, bumpy, pimpled; impediment, as of speech; to speak with an impediment; obscured, as by mist. **4.** n. A mound, as for playing marbles. Also *haʻapuʻu, hoʻopuʻupuʻu.* **5.** Same as *hāʻupuʻupu,* sweet potato sprouts. **6.** Same as *hāpuʻu,* taro: the plant is said to be distinguished by its leaf stems: yellow-green above, and dark brownish on lower half. The corms yield good light-colored poi, the leaves good greens. This name is qualified by the terms *ʻeleʻele, keʻokeʻo,* and *maoli.* (HP 17, 32.)

hau. 1. n. A lowland tree *(Hibiscus tiliaceus),* found in many warm countries, some spreading horizontally over the ground forming impenetrable thickets, and some trained on trellises. The leaves are rounded and heart-shaped, the flowers cup-shaped, with five large petals that change through the day from yellow to dull-red. Formerly the light, tough wood served for outriggers of canoes, the bast for rope, the sap and flowers for medicine. (Neal 559–60.) Of the two varieties of *hau,* a rare erect one *(hau oheohe)* was grown for its bast and a creeping one *(hau)* was planted for windbreaks. (HP 196.) See *ʻau hau.* (PPN *fau.*) **2.** nvs. Cool, iced; ice, frost, dew, snow (see ex., *ʻale l*); a cool breeze; to blow, of a cool breeze. Cf. *kēhau. Wai hua ʻai hau,* iced fruit punch. (PPN *sau.*) **3.** Same as *hahau l;* to hit, smite, beat, tap. (PPN *faʻu, sau.*) **4.** Same as *hahau 2;* to lay before; to offer, as a sacrifice or prayer. **5.** n. A soft porous stone, as used for polishing calabashes. *Rare.* **6.** n. Mother-of-pearl shell. *Rare.*

hau-. 1. Dirty, unpleasant. Cf. *hauʻeka, haukaʻe, haumia, hauna,* Gram. 6.3.3. (PCP *fau.*) **2.** Ruler (nonproductive, mostly in proper names, such as in the common names *Haulani* and *Haunani).* (Gram. 6.3.3.) (PPN *sau.*)

haʻu. vi. To snort (Ier. 8.16), bray, puff; to chatter, as the teeth; to choke with sobs. Cf. *puhaʻu. Haʻu ka waha,* to puff for breath. *Haʻu ka waha i ka makani,* to puff to the wind [of one who scolds]. *ʻO Kona i ka paka ʻona, ke haʻu iho ʻoe, kūnewanewa,* Kona with the intoxicating tobacco, a draw and you stagger [a Kona lover is not forgotten]. *He hoki hihiu . . . e haʻu ana i ka makani* (Ier. 2.24), a wild ass . . . that snuffeth up the wind.

haua. 1. Pas/imp. of *hau 3;* a blow, stripe; to whip. *ʻO ka haua hoʻi no ke kua o ka poʻe lapuwale* (Sol. 19.29), stripes indeed for the backs of fools. *Haua iho nei au e kō aloha* (chant), I've been smitten by your love. **2.** Pas/imp. of *hau 4. Aloha ʻoe, ē Hiʻiaka . . . i haua ʻia i ka ihu o ka puaʻa* (prayer), greetings to you, O Hiʻiaka . . . to whom is sacrificed a pig nose [a whole pig].

haʻua. Pas/imp. of *haʻu.*

haua.ʻiliki. 1. vs. Bitter, cold. *Ke anu hauaʻiliki,* the bitter cold. **2.** *(Cap.)* n. Name of a handsome surfer of Kauaʻi who vainly wooed Lāʻie-i-ka-wai (Elbert, 1970, 214–5); also a place name on Kauaʻi.

haua.laoʻa. Var. spelling of *hauwalaoʻa.*

hau.ʻeka. vs. Defiled, filthy, smutty.

hau.ʻeli. n. Glauber salts, sulphate of soda.

hau.ene. n. Calcareous earth resembling chalk or plaster.

hā.ʻue.ʻue. 1. n. Slate pencil sea urchin *(Heterocentrotus mammillatus).* Also *hāʻueʻue peni, pūnohu.* **2.** Name in some localities for *hāʻukeʻuke,* sea urchin. **3.** Ringworm.

hau.hala.kī. vs. Tangled, snarled; untidy, confused.

hau.hana. nvt. Lashing, as of adze to handle; to lash. *(hau 3 + -hana,* nominalizer: Gram. 6.6.2.) Cf. *imu hau hana. Pale hauhana,* cloth protecting *(pale)* lashing of *ʻiako,* outrigger boom, to the canoe float. (PNP *faʻusanga.*)

hau.hau. 1. Redup. of *hau 3,* to hit. **hoʻo.hau.hau.** Same as above. *E hoʻohauhau mai ʻoe i ka lau hala a kāua i palupalu,* beat our pandanus leaf so as to soften

it. (PPN *faʻufaʻu.*) **2.** vs. Cool, as food. Cf. *hau 2.* **3.** Same as *hauna,* bad odor. (PCP *sausau.*)

haʻu.haʻu. 1. Redup. of *haʻu.* **2.** interj. A refrain in dance songs, usually fast, and perhaps related to *haʻu. Hoʻolewa aʻe ʻoe, haʻuhaʻu ē* (song), dance, puff, puff.

hau.haua. Pas/imp. of *hauhau l. Koʻi hauhaua,* tapping adze.

hau.hau.hali. vt. To carry to and from, as gossip. *Rare.*

hau.hau.hili. Redup. of *hauhili.*

hau.hau.koʻi. n. Swelling of the groin.

hau.hauna. Same as *hauna.*

hau.hā.una. Same as *hāuna.*

haʻu.haʻu.uwē. v. To sob.

hau heheʻe. n. Slush.

hau hele. 1. Same as *ʻakiohala,* a shrub. **2.** n. A shrub or herb *(Abutilon grandifolium).* Niʻihau. *Lit.,* traveling *hau.*

hau hele ʻula. n. An endemic genus of small trees *(Kokia,* four species), in the hibiscus family. The leaves are leathery, round, with three to seven shallow lobes. The flowers are large and red, and have three broad bracts at the base. (Neal 567–8.) See *kokiʻo 2.*

hau hele wai. n. A kind of *hau hele* shrub.

hau.hia. Pas/imp. of *hau 3.*

hau.hili. 1. Same as *hilikau.* Cf. *huikau. Hauhili ka hana,* disorderly work. *Hauhili kāna ʻōlelo,* mixed, contradictory in his speech. *Hauhili ka ʻai a ke kāweleʻā,* the *kāweleʻā* fish takes the hook and tangles [the lines; of a tangled situation]. **hoʻo.hau.hili.** Caus/sim.; to cause confusion, as in speech. **2.** Probably similar to *hauhilikī.*

hau.hili.kī. vt. To snarl, entangle.

hau.hō. Var. of *hauhoa.*

hau.hoa. vt. To tie, lash, bind; to saddle, as a horse.

hau.hole. nvs. Slang term for *haole,* perhaps related to *hole,* to fidget, squirm; it might also be said of a drunk, over-persistent lover, or mischievous child.

haui. A word known only in the chant called *Haui ka lani* (For. 6:368–410); according to Andrews (For. 6:368), an ancient, poetical name for *hāʻule* which he translates "fallen" but more probably *hau,* to strike + *-i,* transitivizer. A more accurate translation of the chant's title is "the chief is struck down." (Gram. 6.6.4.) A less plausible interpretation is *hau i ka lani,* offer to the royal chief.

hau.ʻina. n. Tapa sarong dyed with *ʻōlena.*

hauka. nvs. Out (said in gambling). *Eng.*

hau.kaʻe. nvt. Stained, smeared, smudged, defaced, sordid; to besmirch, stain, smear; defiled, as taboo food cooked with common food; babbler (Oih. 17.18). Cf. *ʻaeʻa.* **hoʻo.hau.kaʻe.** Caus/sim.; to spoil, as a ballot. *Fig.,* to defile a reputation.

hau kaʻe.kaʻe. n. A kind of *hau* tree.

hau.kala.lī. vi. To strut. Cf. *kalalī l.*

hau.kalī. vs. Dressed in one's best.

hau.kamumu. Same as *kamumu.*

hau.kapila. n. Hospital. *Eng.*

hau.kau. Choppy, as the sea. (And.)

hā.ʻuka.ʻuka. Var. of *hāʻukeʻuke 1–3.*

hau.kawewe. Same as *kawewe. Haukawewe ke kolopā, nāueue nā hao pine,* the crowbars clitter-clatter; the iron pegs shake. *Haukawewe hoʻi nā ʻōmaka wai o Kū-lani-hākoʻi,* the stream sources of Kū-lani-hākoʻi pour down.

hā.ʻuke. 1. Same as *hāʻukeʻuke 1–3.* **2.** Same as *nāʻuke,* to search for lice. Cf. *hāʻule 4.*

hau kea. n. White snow, snow.

haʻu.keke, haʻu.kekeke. vi. To quiver, shiver. (Nak. 78.)

hā.ʻuke.ʻuke. n. **1.** An edible variety of sea urchin *(Colobocentrotus atratus).* The teeth were used for medicine. (KL line 23.) Varieties are qualified by the terms *kau pali* (cliff-perching), *kai ʻina,* and *ʻulaʻula.* **2.** Ringworm. **3.** Motif on tapa stamp.

hā.ʻukē.ʻukē. vi. To swing back and forth with a bang

or clatter; to click as the teeth; to bounce back and forth, as breasts.

hā.'uke.'uke iwi loloa. Same as *hā'ue'ue 1. Lit.,* long-boned *hā'uke'uke.*

hau.kī. n. Pudding made of arrowroot starch and juice extracted from baked ti root. Cf. *haukō, haupia.*

hau.kō. n. A pudding made of arrowroot starch, coconut cream, and sugar-cane juice. Cf. *haupia.*

hau.kōhi. n. Icecap, as at the Arctic. (Kep. 183.) *Lit.,* checked ice.

hau.koi. n. Floater, as on a fish net.

hau ko'i'i. n. A kind of hard *hau* tree.

Hau-komo. n. See *Ka-hau-komo.*

hau kua.hiwi. n. Five species of a native genus *(Hibiscadelphus)* of medium-sized trees, related to the *hau;* rare plants, with heart-shaped leaves and curved, red, yellow, and green flowers. (Neal 566–7.)

hā.'ula. 1. nvs. Reddish. **2.** See *limu hā'ula.*

hau.lalapa. vi. To blaze, scorch, sear. *Nā 'ōlelo haulalapa a ka waha,* scorching, sizzling words of the mouth.

hau.lana. n. Iceberg, floating ice.

hau.lani. vi. To surge, as the sea; to plunge, as a canoe; to ply back and forth; restless, constantly on the move. *Fig.,* to dissipate. *Haulani i ke alahao,* speeding on the train.

Hau-lani. n. A personal name. *Lit.,* ruling royal chief (this meaning is based solely on historical evidence: see *hau- 2).*

hā.'ula.'ula. nvs. Reddish, pink.

hā.'ule. 1. vi. To fall, drop, tumble down; dropped. Cf. *hina,* to fall from an upright position, and *hā'ule,* to drop down. *Hā'ule hua,* to lay an egg. *Hā'ule lio,* to fall off a horse. *Hā'ule wale,* to fall prematurely, as fruit. *He keiki hā'ule wale,* a miscarriage. *Hā'ule ka ua,* the rain falls. **ho'o.hā.'ule.** To drop, cause to fall. (1 Sam. 31.4.) *E ho'ohā'ule au i ka ua maluna o ka 'ili o ka honua* (1 Nal. 18.1), I will send rain upon the earth. **2.** nvi. To lose, fail, forget, die, neglect; loss, failure, defeat. *Ka hā'ule 'ole o ka manawa,* without loss of time. *Hā'ule ka heihei,* to lose a race. *No ka hā'ule o ka uku,* because of failure to pay. *Kekahi mea hā'ule* (Oihk. 6.3), that which was lost. **3.** vi. To begin to do. *Hā'ule i ka hewa,* to fall into sin, as by adultery. *Pau kā mo'olelo hō'inā'inau, hā'ule ihola lākou kōnane* (For. 4:57), after the interesting story, they began to play *kōnane* checkers. **4.** vt. To delouse, look for louse. See *hā'uke,* For. 5:541. (PPN *sakule,* PNP *saakule.)*

hā.'ule.hia. Pas/imp. of *hā'ule.*

hā.'ule hope. vt. To miss, fall or lag behind. *Ua hā'ule hope mākou i ke ka'a,* we missed the car.

hā.'ule.lani. n. **1.** A variety of sweet potato. *Lit.,* fallen from the sky. **2.** A fresh-water alga found in taro patches.

hā.'ule lau. n. Fall, autumn. *Lit.,* leaf falling.

ha'u.lena. n. A falling, dropping. *Hō'ili'ili i nā ha'ulena o kāu 'ai* (Oihk. 19.9), to gather the gleanings of your harvest.

hā.'ule.pio. vi. To fall, surrender.

hā.'ule.'ule. Redup. of *hā'ule 1–3.*

hauli. n. This word is used idiomatically with *lele* and *ho'olele,* and may be related to *mauli. Lele ka hauli,* greatly shocked, astonished, moved, startled, frightened. *Auwē! lele kā ho'u ko'u hauli,* oh, how startled I am. *He kaua ho'olele hauli,* alarm; shocking events.

hā.uli. 1. nvs. Blackish, swarthy, dark. **2.** n. Bruise. *Ka hāuli o ka mea hewa 'ole, he nalowale koke,* a bruise inflicted on an innocent person vanishes quickly. **3.** n. Small fish with formerly transparent body beginning to darken; embryo of human or animal.

ha'u.lili. vs. To shiver. Cf. *lili.*

hā.uli.uli. 1. Redup. of *hāuli 1.* **ho'o.hā.uli.uli.** To darken. **2.** n. A fish *(Gempylus serpens),* sometimes called the snake mackerel.

hā.uli.uli puhi. n. A variety of *hāuliuli,* a fish. *Lit.,* eel *hāuliuli.*

hau.loli'i. n. Descendant, offspring. *Rare.*

hau.maka.'iole. nvs. Blurred eyes of a rat, said of very old persons; an aged person.

hau.malu. nvs. Quiet.

hau.mana, hau.māna. n. Student, pupil, apprentice, recruit, disciple (Mat. 10.1). Perhaps *lit.,* to lay before one a ball of masticated food *(māna);* also see *hau- 2. Haumana a'o 'oihana,* technological student, trainee, apprentice. *Haumana komo hou,* new student, freshman. **ho'o.hau.māna.** To act as a pupil, become a pupil; to make pupils of.

hau.manu. Probably similar to *haumanumanu.*

hau.manu.manu. Same as *manumanu,* irregular, dull; ugly. *Haumanumanu ka ipu 'ino'ino,* misshapen is the imperfect gourd [an ugly person; a warning to a mother to mold the body of her baby].

hau.mekū. n. A kind of stone used for adzes. *Rare.*

hau.mia. nvs. Uncleanliness, filth, defilement, abomination; defiled, indecent, obscene, vile, lewd, unclean (Oihk. 15.2), contaminated, sordid. *(hau- 1 + -mia,* pas/imp.) **ho'o.hau.mia.** To pollute, defile, befoul, besmirch, contaminate. *Moe ihola me ia, a ho'ohaumia iāia* (Kin. 34.2), sleeping with her and defiling her.

hauna. nv. Unpleasant odor, as of spoiling fish or meat, or volcanic sulphur; stench; tainted. *(Hau- 1 + -na,* nominalizer.) **ho'o.hauna.** To cause an offensive odor; to use strong-smelling bait to attract fish; to smell such an odor. *I'a ho'ohauna,* same as *i'a ho'omelu;* see *melu.* (PNP *saunga.)*

hā.una. Same as *hau 3, 4;* stroke; blow; offering; to mend a net; to toss, as a *kilu* quoit (Laie 483). See *hāuna lā'au.*

hau.naele. n. Panic, riot, roughhouse, brawl, tumult, commotion, confusion, hubbub. *Ka leo o kēia haunaele* (1 Sam. 4.14), the noise of this tumult. **ho'o.-hau.naele.** To provoke panic, riot; agitator. *Ho'ohaunaele i nā ahu ho'okolokolo,* contempt of court.

Hauna-'Ī.loli. n. Wind name.

Hau.na.kele.kele. n. Name of a star in the Milky Way.

hau.naku. Same as *naku 1,* to root, wallow.

hā.una lā.'au. n. Stroke or thrust of the war club.

hau.nama. n. A slightly offensive odor. *Rare.*

Hau.none. n. Name of a cold wind.

hā.unu. nvi. A line, as used in lashing a mat canoe cover; to add a new weft in plaiting. *Moena hāunu 'ole o ka nahele,* mats of the forest without added wefts [a bed of forest ferns and greenery].

hā.unu kupu.kupu. Same as *unu kupukupu;* see *unu 2,* altar.

-haunu'u. ho'o.hau.nu'u. Proud.

hau ohe.ohe. n. A rare variety of *hau,* a tree, with a straight trunk.

ha'u.oi. Var. spelling of *ha'uōwī.*

hau 'ō 'iao. n. *Hau* wood handle attached to net used for *'iao* fishing.

hau.'oki. 1. nvs. Chilled to the bone, stiff with cold; frost, ice, cold; icy wind. **2.** n. A medicine made of *hau* bark for women in labor.

hau.'oli. nvs. Happy, glad, gay, joyful; happiness, enjoyment, joy. The common expressions *Hau'oli Makahiki Hou,* Happy New Year, and *hau'oli lā hānau,* happy birthday, are translations from English. *Hau'oli mau,* always happy, cheerful. **ho'o.hau.'oli.** To cause happiness, gaiety, joy. *Mea ho'ohau'oli,* entertainment, pleasure, treat.

hau.'oli.'oli. Redup. of *hau'oli. 'O kou kānāwai ka'u e hau'oli'oli nei* (Hal. 119.77), thy law is my delight.

Hau-o-Mā.'ihi. n. Name of a wind associated with Kailua quadrangle, Hawai'i. *Lit.,* cool [wind] of Mā'ihi (a wind goddess whose full name was Mā'ihi-'ala-kapu-a-Lono, fragrant sacred Mā'ihi [child] of Lono).

hau 'ō mā.lolo. n. *Hau*-stick handle of *mālolo* (flying fish) net.

hau.one. n. Soft limestone.

hau.'opo. Same as *'opo. Rare.*

ha'u.ō.wī, ha'uoi. Same as *ōwī 1,* a verbena. *Ni'ihau.*

haupa. vt. To eat heartily or voraciously. *Rare. Ka haupa 'ana,* feasting.

ha'u.pā. vi. To open and shut, as scissors, jaws.

Hau-palemo. See *Ka-hau-palemo.*

hau.pe'e.pe'e. nvi. To play hide-and-seek; hide-and-seek.

hau.pia. n. Pudding formerly made of arrowroot *(pia)* and coconut cream, now usually made with cornstarch. Cf. *haukō.*

hau.poa. vt. To soften the earth, as for planting. *Rare.*

hā.'upu. vt. To recollect, recall, remember. *'O 'oe ka'u i hā'upu a'e nei* (song), you are what I have remembered. *ho'o.hā.'upu.* To cause to recollect, recall.

hau pū.ehu.ehu. n. Snowflake.

hau.pu'u. Same as *pu'uhau. Rare.*

hā.'upu.'upu. 1. Redup. of *hā'upu;* to recall again and again. 2. n. Sprouts from sweet potatoes. Also *hāpu'upu'u, hā'apu'apu.*

hau.pu'u.pu'u. Redup. of *haupu'u.*

hau.wala.'au. vt. To gabble, gossip, chatter, babble, hubbub, fuss.

hau.wala.o'a, haualao'a. nvi. A confused, excited din; to sound thus. (The following words are confused at times: *uluao'a, wala'au, wanao'a.*)

hau.wala.wala.'au. Redup. of *hauwala'au.*

hau.wana.o'a. Same as *wanao'a.*

hau.wawā. Same as *wawā;* medley of simultaneous talking. **ho'o.hau.wawā.** Caus/sim.; provocative of loud noise.

hau.wene. vt. To cry, tease, nag, fret. **ho'o.hau.wene.** Caus/sim.; to tease others.

hawa. vs. Defiled, unclean, filthy, daubed with excrement. (PPN *sawa.*)

hā.wa'a.wa'a. vi. To wallow in troughs, as a rough sea.

hā.wa'e. n. 1. A sea urchin *(Tripneustes gratilla). Fig.,* of no character or substance, perhaps so used because of the sayings *hāwa'e kai nui,* sea urchin with much juice [and little meat, hence useless], and *he hāwe'a 'i'o 'ole,* sea urchin without meat [or brains]. Varieties of sea urchin are qualified by the terms *maoli* (natural) and *po'o hina* (gray-head). (PNP *saawak(e,i).*) 2. A kind of stone, used as sinkers for octopus lures. 3. Sprouts from sweet potatoes. 4. *(Cap.)* Name of a famous evil sorcerer. See *lauhue 1,* for figurative meaning.

hā.wa'e.wa'e. n. 1. General name for small lobsters. 2. Sprouts from sweet potatoes.

hawa.hawa. Redup. of *hawa;* a taunt in a children's game. (PPN *sawasawa.*)

hā.wai. 1. vt. To generate steam in an earth oven by pouring on water (Kep. 163); to purify with water. 2. n. Temporary long, gabled house in which priestesses assembled for purification ceremonies. (Malo 178.) 3. n. Sewer. 4. n. A variety of sweet potato.

hā wai. n. Water trough or pipe, aqueduct, flume.

Hawai'i. nvs. Hawai'i (both the island and the group of islands); Hawaiian person; Hawaiian. Elsewhere in Polynesia, Hawai'i or a cognate is the name of the underworld or of the ancestral home, but in Hawai'i the name has no meaning; see Pukui, Elbert, and Mookini, 1974. See saying, *kuauli.* **ho'o.hawai'i.** To act as a Hawaiian; to ape or imitate Hawaiians. (PPN *Sawaiki.*)

Hawai'i-loa. n. 1. Name of a legendary figure believed by some to have discovered Hawai'i, but see Barrère, 1969; place name. 2. *(Not cap.)* Name of a line for *ulua* fishing in 17 or more fathoms of water.

Hawai'i piha. n. Full-blooded Hawaiian.

hā wai lawe 'ino. n. Sewerage pipes, sewage system.

hā.wale. vt. To lie, bluff. *Rare.*

hā.wali. vs. Weak, soft, boggy. Cf. *nāwali.*

hā.wali.wali. Redup. of *hāwali.*

hā.wana. Same as *hāwanawana.*

hā.wana.wana. nvi. To whisper; whispering. (Hal. 41.7.) See *kānāwai.* (PPN *fanafana.*)

hā.wane. n. 1. Nut of the *loulu,* native palm, considered delicious to eat; also the tree itself. Also *wāhane. Lau hāwane* (Nak. 77), *loulou* leaves. 2. A small, fine, red seaweed *(Polysiphonia* spp.), consisting of branching filaments forming dense tufts.

hā.wā.wā. nvs. Unskilled, awkward, clumsy, incompetent, blundering; blunder, incompetence. Cf. *wa-'awa'a.* See saying, *'ō 2. Na'au hāwāwā* (Rom. 1.21), foolish heart. *I make nō he hāwāwā, 'auhea noho'i nā lima e 'au mai?* The unskilled die, where are arms to swim with? [Skill saves life.] *A ke ho'omake nei ka huhū i ka mea hāwāwā* (Ioba 5.2), anger kills the foolish man.

hā.wele. 1. nvt. To tie, bind, lash, make fast; to snub, as cattle; net lashing, as for a *hue wai,* gourd; thong. *Fig.,* umbilical cord; to eat. *E hāwele 'oukou 'o kēlā kanaka kēia kanaka i kāna pahi kaua* (1 Sam. 25.13), gird ye on every man his sword. 2. n. A type of tapa (no data).

hā.wena. n. White lime, as used for dressing hair and turning the hair brown. *Hāpala 'ia i ka hāwena,* bedaubed with white lime [one whose gray hairs have not brought wisdom].

hā.weo. vs. Glowing. *Fig.,* distinguished, honored (used after *hano). Kau i ka hano hāweo,* placed in a position of glittering honor.

hā.weo.weo. Redup. of *hāweo.*

hawewe. nvi. 1. To rumble, clatter, patter, as rain; rumbling. (GP 78.) Cf. *kawewe.* 2. To pour down, as the sun; to vibrate, as heat.

he. indefinite article. A, an; to be a, have (with a possessive). (Gram. 10.2.) *He kanaka maika'i ia,* he is a good person. *He ka'a ko'u,* I have a car. (PPN *sa.*)

hē. 1. n. Grave. *Ka 'eho no ka hē o Rāhela* (Kin. 35.20), the pillar for Rachel's grave. 2. n. General name for caterpillar. Cf. *'anuhe, kāhē.* (PCP *fee.*) 3. vt. To scrape, rub, polish. 4. nvi. Swish, as of a whip; murmuring sound of wind or running water; to swish, sough. *Ka hē o ka makani,* the swish of the wind. 5. n. Upper part of a crab's leg. *Rare.* 6. n. Poi from the center or core of taro, formerly reserved for chiefs, as it had not come into contact with dirt (Kep. 165). 7. n. Edges of the mouth of the square *uhu* (parrot fish) net. *Rare.* 8. n. Dividing line between lands. *Rare.* 9. n. Hollow container in which canoe paint was mixed. 10. n. The letter "h." *Eng.* 11. n. Hay. *Eng.*

-hē. ho'ohē. Same as *hōhē,* cowardly.

hea. 1. vt. To call, name; to sing or recite a name chant; to give a name to. Cf. *'auihea, kāhea. Ua hea aku au i kona inoa 'o La'a-kea,* I named him La'a-kea. *Ke hea mai 'oukou ia'u, he kumu* (Ioane 13.13), ye call me, teacher. (PPN *sea.*) 2. vs. Misty, clouded, smoky, obscure. Cf. *Kona Hea.* 3. n. Bank, as of a river. (Kep. 91.) 4. interr. Which (in questions and after other words). Cf. *'āhea, ināhea. Ka mea hea?* Which thing? *Ka manawa hea?* Which time? When? *Ka hale hea?* Which house? (Gram. 8.5.) (PPN *fea.*) 5. inter. Where? (Usually following prepositions *i, ma, mai, no, 'o; mahea* is often written as one word.) *I hea ka puke?* Just where is the book? *Mahea ka puke?* Whereabouts is the book? *Mai hea mai?* Where from? *No hea 'oe?* Where are you from? *Ā e hele ana 'oe 'o hea* (For. 5:219)? Where are you going? *Aia i hea ka puke?* Where's the book (sometimes shortened to *aihea*)? *'O kēia lio ā 'o kēlā lio, mahea 'oe?* This horse or that horse, which for you? (See also *'auhea.*) (PPN *fea.*)

he'a. nvs. Stained red, inflamed, reddened; flattened and destroyed, as by lava; blood red; a blood sacrifice, as hog or man. Cf. *heka, kilihe'a, kīpalahe'a. Kā ia he'a hala o Ka-li'u* (song), this destroyed pandanus of Ka-li'u is struck [Pele's destruction of Hi'iaka's pandanus trees].

hea'e. Kaua'i name for *kāwa'u,* a kind of *Zanthoxylum.* Cf. *a'e.*

he aha, heaha. See *aha.*

he aha sana.nā. interj. of scorn. What does it amount to? It's of no value. (Perhaps *nanā* is from *he 'ahi kananā,* a phrase describing a fierce fighter; cf. *nanā.*)

Also *wesenanā. He aha sananā, he mauʻu Hilo* (Kel. 138)? What does it amount to? It's just Hilo grass.

hea.hea. 1. vt. To call frequently and hospitably; to welcome; friendly, hospitable, genial. *He leo heahea,* a hospitable calling voice. *Kēlā pali heahea, walowalo i ke kanaka,* that calling cliff summoning men. (PPN *seasea.*) **1.** vs. Warm, tepid, insipid. Cf. *ʻāheahea, mūhea, ʻōheahea.*

heʻa.heʻa. vt. To imprint with spots, stains; smeared, as with red earth. *Pulu au i ka huna kai, kai heʻaheʻa i ka ʻili* (song), wet by spray of sea, sea that reddens the skin. (PNP *fekafeka.*)

hea inoa. nvi. To give a name; to chant a name chant; to call a name in hospitable welcome; to call the roll; roll call; name chant.

heana. n. **1.** Corpse, especially of one slain in battle; victim, human sacrifice; carcass (Mat. 24.28), remains. *Kou heana* (Kanl. 28.26), your corpse. *Kāu heana,* your victim. (PEP *(f,s)eana;* cf. Marquesan *heana.*) **2.** Calling, as in greeting. *He heana kanaka, he pihana kamaliʻi,* a calling of people, a gathering of children.

heana kanaka. n. Human carcass, human sacrifice, an insulting name for *kauwā,* outcasts.

heau. n. **1.** Place where fishermen set a basket fish trap, as for *hīnālea.* **2.** *Exocarpus* spp., native shrubs and small trees (sandalwood family), with more or less leafless, jointed branches. (Neal 325.) Also *au 12.*

heʻe. 1. n. Octopus (*Polypus* sp.), commonly known as squid. *Heʻe mahola,* octopus given for sickness caused by sorcery, as octopus *(heʻe)* would cause the sickness to flee *(heʻe)* or spread out *(mahola).* (PPN *feke.*) **2.** vi. To slide, surf, slip, flee (Kin. 14.10). Cf. *heʻe nalu, pūheʻe.* See ex., *puʻe one. ʻO ka mea i hilinaʻi aku iāia, aʻole ia e heʻe* (Isa. 28.16), he that believed did not make haste. **hoʻo.heʻe.** To cause to slip, slide, flee; to put to flight, rout. *Hoʻoheʻe kī,* ti leaf sliding. (PPN *seke.*) **3.** vi. To melt, flow, drip, soften; to skim, as milk. Cf. *heʻeheʻe, heheʻe.* **4.** vi. To hang down, as fruit; to sag; to bear breadfruit. See ex., *ule 1. Laho heʻe,* hernia rupture. (Probably PNP *seke.*) **5.** n. Line that supports the mast, stay.

heehe. vi. To bleat.

heʻe.heʻe. 1. Redup. of *heʻe 2-4;* avalanche *(rare).* **hoʻo.heʻe.heʻe.** Redup. of *hoʻoheʻe;* to slide, slip. **2.** n. Breast disease, with caking and great pain during nursing. (PPN *fekefeke.*)

heʻe hō.lua. See *hōlua.*

heʻe koko. n. Flow of blood, hemorrhage, menstrual flow (Oihk. 15.25).

heʻe mā.koko. n. A variety of large red octopus *(Octopus ornatus);* it was rarely eaten because of its bitter taste, but was sometimes used as medicine.

heʻe mā.kole. n. Squid beginning to decompose, with a pinkish color and a bad odor, liked by some.

heʻe nalu. nv. To ride a surfboard; surfing; surf rider. *Lit.,* wave sliding.

Heʻe-nehu. n. Name of a misty rain observed off the coast of Hilo when *nehu* fish are running.

heʻe nehu. nv. Season when *nehu* fish run; to run in schools, of *nehu. Ke kai heʻe nehu o ʻEwa,* the sea of ʻEwa with its *nehu* schools.

hee.pā.laha. n. Each of two posts at the back wall of the ancient house, visible at the door. *Rare.*

Heʻe-pā.laha. n. A stroke in *lua* fighting.

heʻe pā.laha. n. An octopus settled on the ocean floor with tentacles spread out.

heʻe pali. n. Tiny, young octopus that clings to rocks along sea pools, especially in certain seasons.

heʻe puʻe.wai. v. To surf toward the mouth of a stream or up the stream.

heʻe pū loa. n. A long-headed, long-tentacled octopus *(Octopus ornatus),* very tough, tenderized only by much pounding; now called the night octopus. *Lit.,* long-headed octopus.

heʻe pulu. n. Octopus slightly decomposed. Also *heʻe mākole.*

heʻe uma.uma. nvi. Body surfing; to body surf.

heʻe.wale. nvi. Miscarriage; to have a miscarriage.

heha. nvs. Lazy, indolent, drowsy; weariness following sexual gratification. *ʻŌpū heha,* indolent character. *Heha Wai-piʻo i ka noe,* Wai-piʻo is drowsy in the mist. *He hoʻopunipuni mau kō Kerete . . . ʻōpū heha* (Tito 1.12), the Cretans always lie and are . . . slow bellies.

hehe. n. A kind of bird (no data). (KL line 348.)

hehē. nvi. Burst of laughter, guffaw; to guffaw. *Ka ʻaka hehē a ka manu o Kaiona* (song), the loud laughter of the birds [people] of Kaiona.

hē.hē. nvs. A boil, running sore; ulcerous; botch [KJV], boils [RSV] (Kanl. 28.27).

heheʻe. 1. Redup. of *heʻe 2-4;* to slide, sag, fade; landslide, avalanche; soft, watery, melting. *E heheʻe auaneʻi ka poʻe āpau e noho ana ma Kanaʻana* (Puk. 15.15), all the people of Canaan shall melt away. **hoʻo.heheʻe.** To melt, liquefy, cast, dissolve, soften; to slide, especially to slide by jerks, as on a *hōlua,* sled, or ti-leaf slide. *Wahi hoʻoheheʻe hao,* foundry. *Wai hoʻoheheʻe,* digestive juice. *E hoʻoheheʻe ʻoe i ʻehā ʻapo gula* (Puk. 25.12), thou shalt cast four rings of gold. **2.** nvs. Discharge, as of pus; fluid. *He maʻi heheʻe* (Oihk. 13.18), a boil.

hehe.heʻe. Redup. of *heheʻe 1, 2.*

hehe.hewa. Redup. of *hewa;* a mistake by many. *I hehehewa kākou iāia lā, i ke koi huhuki a ka manaʻo* (chant), we were in the wrong because of him, and the insistent urging of the thought.

hehei. 1. Redup. of *hei 1,* to entangle. **2.** n. Type of *pāʻū (no data).*

heheia. Pas/imp. of *hehei.*

hehele.leʻi. Redup. and intensifier of *heleleʻi. Ua wāwahia, ua nāhāhā, ua heheleleʻi ka papa i Pua-lei ē* (chant by Hiʻiaka), shattered, broken, the foundation at Pua-lei crumbles.

hehelo. Redup. of *helo;* reddish, bright, showy. **hoʻo.hehelo.** Caus/sim. *Nā pāpale hulu manu like ʻole o nā aliʻi e hoʻohehelo ana i ka ʻōnohi o ka lā,* the hats of the varying bird feathers of the chiefs shining brightly within the eyeball [sight] of the sun.

-hehelo. hoʻo.hehelo. Proud, especially of one's appearance or dress.

hehena. nvs. Insane, raving mad, crazy, possessed; insanity, madness; lunatic, maniac. (1 Sam. 21.13, 14). *Kai hehena,* raging sea. *E hahau mai ʻo Iēhowa iāʻoe i ka hehena* (Kanl. 28.28), and Jehovah shall smite you with madness. **hoʻo.hehena.** Caus/sim. *ʻO kāna mau hana lapuwale, he mea hoʻohehena i ka noʻonoʻo maikaʻi,* his wretched actions drive a sane mind mad.

heheo. nvi. A swaggering or swishing walk; swishing, as of a skirt; to whirl, swish, strut. **hoʻo.heheo.** Caus/sim.; to swish, swirl; to swish up and down on the foot, as a child.

hehi. nvt. To stamp, tread, trample, pedal, step on; trampling. *Fig.,* to repudiate, deny, desecrate, loathe, break (as taboo). Also *hahi. Hehi ʻia,* downtrodden. *Hehi berita,* to trample on a covenant. *Kaʻa hehi wāwae,* bicycle. *Kahi hehi palaoa* (Nah. 15.20), threshing floor. *Ka hehi ʻana i ka lā Kāpaki,* desecration of the Sabbath day. *Hehi nō ka mea māʻona i ka waihona meli* (Sol. 27.7), the person full of food loathes the honeycomb. *Hehi i ka pili,* to repudiate a relationship, as to in-laws after a spouse's death.

hehia. Pas/imp. of *hehi.*

hehi.hehi. Redup. of *hehi.*

hehi hewa. nvi. Misstep; to make a misstep.

hehi ʻino. vt. To step firmly, stamp; to make a misstep and come down hard. *Ua hehi ʻino ʻoia no ka huhū,* he stamped his foot in anger.

hehi.kū. nvt. To break rules or taboos, disregard the rights of others, trample on their rights, trespass; willful; trespassing, violation. *Ka hehikū wale ʻia o kekahi ʻōlelo hoʻoholo,* the breach of any regulation.

hehina. n. Footrest; any place on which to step or tread; a stepping, treading.

hehi palaoa. nv. To thresh wheat; threshing. *Lit.*, tread flour *(Eng.).*

Hehi-pua-hala. n. Rain name associated with Poʻo-kū, Kauaʻi. *Lit.*, stepping upon pandanus flowers.

hehu. 1. vt. To uproot, dig up, put to flight, drive away, evict, shoo. *E hehu aʻe ʻoia i ka ʻIseraʻela mai loko aʻe o kēlā ʻāina maikaʻi* (1 Nal. 14.15), and he shall root up Israel out of this good land. **2.** n. Young seedlings or plants, as for transplanting; sucker. Cf. *ilo 2.* **3.** nvt. A purge, as of water and juice of gourd stems used as an enema; to purge. **4.** n. Ceremony to drive away evil influence. **5.** n. Pile, as of rocks. (GP 100.)

hei. 1. nvt. Net, snare, stratagem, ruse; to ensnare, entangle, catch in a net; to festoon with leis. See *kāhei 1, 2;* Luka 5.4. **hoʻo.hei.** To snare, tangle, rope, lasso; to beset with difficulties; to infatuate, be enraptured. *Hoʻohei manaʻo,* to infatuate, beguile; spellbound. *Hoʻohei pipi,* to rope cattle. *Ka hoʻohei ʻana i nā pua,* catching fish fry. *E hoʻohei aʻe ʻoe i kānaka* (Luka 5.10), you shall catch [by fishing] men. *Hoʻohei manaʻo,* to cast a spell, enchant, beguile. **2.** nvi. String figure, cat's cradle; to make such. Many kinds are listed by Dickey. **3.** n. Motion of hands and fingers, especially of the dying. (Some persons did not make string figures, *hei,* at night because of the association of the figures with the motions of death.) **4.** vs. Adept, deft; to absorb, as knowledge or skill. *Ka ʻike a ka makua, he hei na ke keiki,* the knowledge of the parent is absorbed by the child. **5.** Var. of *hai,* to sacrifice. Cf. *haiau, heiau. Hei kapu,* sacred place. (Probably PPN *fai.*) **6.** n. Water oozing from a cliff and trickling down. Cf. *hī 2.*

he- . . . **-i.** See *heleleʻi.*

hē.ʻī. 1. Same as *mīkana,* papaya. (Neal 600–1.) **2.** n. A variety of sweet potato usually called *ʻuala hēʻī.* **3.** Same as *maiʻa Polapola,* a wild banana. (PCP *feekii.*)

heia. 1. Pas/imp. of *hei 1.* **2.** n. Piece of hair, tooth, fingernail, small bone, or the like of a deceased beloved, kept and offered as food in order to please the spirit of the deceased.

hei.au. n. Pre-Christian place of worship, shrine; some heiau were elaborately constructed stone platforms, others simple earth terraces. Many are preserved today. Several types are listed below. In Isa. 15.2, heiau is a high place of worship. See *hei 5. Hale heiau,* house of worship. (PPN *fai.*)

hei.au hoʻōla. n. Heiau for treating sick.

hei.au hoʻo.ulu ʻai. Heiau where first fruits were offered to insure further growth. *Lit.*, heiau for the increase of food crops.

hei.au hoʻo.ulu iʻa. n. Heiau where fish were offered to insure good fishing.

hei.au hoʻo.ulu ua. Heiau where offerings were made to insure rain.

hei.au kā.lua ua. n. Heiau for stopping rain, or (less frequently) for bringing rain. One such heiau named Imu-kālua-ua (rain-baking oven) was in the Kaunakakai quadrangle, Molokaʻi; a land section in Puna, Hawaiʻi, also has this name. Rain in leaf packages is said to have been baked in an oven.

hei.au maʻo. n. Small temporary heiau covered with tapa stained green *(maʻo),* used for the *hoʻoulu ʻai* ceremony to bring food. (Malo 158.)

hei.au poʻo kanaka. Heiau where human sacrifices were offered. (FS 159.)

hei.au wai.kaua. n. A heiau used for services to bring success in war.

hei.ē. n. Helper or apprentice to a priest.

hei.hei. 1. nvi. Race, as foot race, canoe race, horse race; to race. *He kanaka ikaika e heihei ana* (Hal. 19.5), a strong man running a race. **hoʻo.hei.hei.** To run swiftly, take part in a race, pretend to race, cause to race. **2.** Redup. of *hei 1–3;* to festoon, drape. Cf. *pāʻū heihei.* **hoʻo.hei.hei.** To ensnare, entrap; to mend, as a net or wire fence. **3.** vt. To enthrall, enchant. *Noho ʻoia mehe*

mea lā ua heihei ʻia, he sat like one entranced; enchanted; in a daze. **hoʻo.hei.hei.** Caus/sim.; to fascinate, flirt; to ward off possible sorcery by imitating the gestures of the *kahuna.*

-hei.hei. hoʻo.hei.hei. To beat, as a heiau drum; sound of heiau drum.

hei.hei kū.kini. n. Footrace.

hei kapu. n. A sacred place, as one where a priest stayed in seclusion to await a message from the gods, usually a small house on the heiau. (UL 74.)

heka. vs. Red, sore, inflamed, bleary. Cf. *heʻa, pīheka.*

heka.heka. Redup. of *heka.*

hekau. 1. nvt. Anchor, stone anchor, towline, line for fastening boats; warp; to anchor, make fast, tow; taut, stretched, anchored. *Hekau o ka pōloli,* the taut intensity of hunger. **2.** vi. To come upon, happen, befall, strike. *Hekau auaneʻi i ka lae ʻaʻā,* you will strike a rocky point [trouble]. *He nui nā pōʻino i hekau aku maluna o kekahi poʻe,* lots of trouble happens to some people. *ʻO ka lanakila kiʻekiʻe i hekau iho,* complete victory resulted.

heke. 1. n. Best, greatest, foremost. See ex., *manomano. Eia nō ʻo Kāwika, ēhē, ka heke o nā pua, ēhē* (chant for Ka-lā-kaua), here comes David, oh, oh, the greatest of descendants, oh, oh. **2.** n. Top gourd in a hula gourd drum. Cf. *ʻolo 1.* **3.** n. Feathered top of an *ʻulīʻulī,* hula rattle. **4.** n. Nail, pin, rack, as for hanging objects in a house. **5.** n. Triangular sail, topsail. Also *peʻa heke.* **6.** vs. Shy, sensitive. Cf. *ʻōheke.* **7.** Same as *hekeheke.* Cf. *ʻuheke.*

heke.heke. vs. Plump.

heke.kē. vs. Plump.

heki.kili. Redup. of *hekili. Ke kau nei ka malu, hekikili i luna,* a shade spreads, thundering above.

hekili. 1. nvi. Thunder; to thunder. *Fig.,* passion, rage. See *hakikila. Kuʻi ka hekili,* thunder roars. *Ua hekili,* rain consisting of big drops, so called because of the noise of their falling. *Nā hekili o ke kuko ʻino,* passions of lust. *Ke hekili mai nei ke Akua nani* (Hal. 29.3), the God of glory thunders. **hoʻo.hekili.** To cause thunder; threatening thunder storm. *Hoʻohekili maila ʻo Iēhova,* Jehovah thunders. (PNP *fatitili.*) **2.** n. A variety of taro. **3.** n. A variety of sweet potato.

hekili pā.malō, hekili pā.maloʻo. n. Thunder without rain.

hē.kuawa, heku.awawa. Same as *kuawa 1,* valley. *Malu hekuawa,* valley shade.

hē kupa.paʻu. n. Grave. (Nah. 19.16.)

hela. 1. nvi. Redness of the eyelids; rawness, as of scraped skin; to be red or raw. (PPN *fela.*) **2.** vi. To spread, as the arms. Cf. *helahela, kāhela.* (PPN *fela.*) **3.** nvi. Hula step: one foot is placed at about a 45-degree angle to the front and side, with the weight on the opposite hip and with that knee bent; the foot is then returned to the original position and the step is repeated with the other foot; to dance thus.

hela.hela. Redup. of *hela 1, 2;* widespread.

hele. 1. nvi. To go, come, walk; to move, as in a game; going, moving; a gadabout. *Fig.,* to die. Cf. *hele wale, hele wāwae. Hele mai,* come. *Hele aku,* go; go away. *Hele pololei,* to go straight ahead. *Hele nō ā ka poʻe ʻōpiopio,* extending even to the young people. *Kāu hele kēia,* this is your move [as in the kōnane game]. *Hele a ka lā,* the path of the sun; circuit of the sun. *Hele i lalo,* go down, descend. **hoʻo.hele.** To cause to move, set in motion; to start, as a clock; to manage; to walk someone else or force oneself to walk. *Kō kākou mau hoʻohele ʻana,* our management. *E hoʻohele aku ʻoe i ka uaki,* start the watch. (PPN *saʻele,* PCP *sele.*) **2.** vi. To become, get; like, in a state of, similar (frequently followed by *ā*). *Hele loa i ka ʻono,* really delicious. *Ua hele ʻoia ā huhū, momona, ʻona,* he has become angry, fat, drunk. *I uhi pākaukau nui, i hele loa aku kēia lumi i ka maikaʻi,* [bring] a fresh tablecloth, so that this room will be greatly improved. **hoʻo.hele.** To imitate, pretend; imitative, pretending. *ʻAi hoʻohele,* to eat in an imitative fashion. *Nīnau hoʻohele,* indirect questioning. **3.** vi. When, by the time that (usually followed by *ā*). *Hele ā pau kēia, ua hala nā makahiki ʻelua,* by the time this is finished, two years will be gone. **4.** vs. following other bases, imparting idea of everywhere, here and there, continuously. *Holo hele,* to run here and there or continuously. *Huli hele,* to search everywhere. *Nui nō kona hoʻounauna hele i kāna keiki,* he continuously sends his child on errands. **5.** n. A relationship term. See *hele hope, hele mua.* **6.** nvt. To tie, bind, lash, make fast; noose, snare. *Ua kama ʻia i nā kaula a i hele ʻia,* tied with ropes and bound. (PPN *sele.*) **7.** vt. To divide, cut apart. *Rare.* Cf. *mahele.* (PPN *sele.*)

helē. n. Priest's helper.

helea. Pas/imp. of *hele 1, 6. Helea kāua* (Nak. 117), let's go.

hele.ā.wai. vi. To flow like water. *Ke heleāwai nei ke koko,* blood flows like water.

hele au. vi. To go drifting along. (For. 5:509.)

Helee.kela, Hereekela. n. The planet Uranus, formerly called Hershel for its discoverer, Sir William Hershel, in 1781.

hele.hele. Redup. of *hele 7;* to cut up, divide; divided; filled with ruts, as a road. (PPN *selesele.*)

-hele.hele. hoʻo.hele.hele. To help someone walk; to take walking, as a dog. Cf. *hele 1.*

hele.helei. Redup. and intensifier of *helei 1, 2.*

hele.helena. n. Features, face. *Kona helehelena maka* (Dan. 10.6), his face.

-hele.hele ʻō.lelo. hoʻo.hele.hele ʻō.lelo. To lead up to a subject in a roundabout way, hint, suggest.

hele hewa. vi. To go wrong, take the wrong path, go astray, err.

hele honua. 1. vi. To go suddenly, early, or for no apparent reason. **2.** vt. To tie or bind beforehand, as in preparation for a journey.

hele hope. nvi. Younger brother or sister; descendant of a younger brother or sister; to go behind.

helei. 1. vi. To straddle. **hoʻo.helei.** Caus/sim. *Noho hoʻohelei i ka ʻūhā,* to sit with legs stretched far apart [considered indecent]. **2.** nvi. Stretched sideways, as the mouth; pulled down, as an eyelid with a finger (these were signs of contempt); inflammatory disease of the eye with a drawing down of the lower lid. See saying, *maka helei.* **hoʻo.helei.** To pull down, as the eyelid; to stretch, as the mouth. (PCP *felei.*)

hele kau.hale. vi. To go from house to house, gad.

hele.kika, heretika. n. Heretic. *Eng.*

hele kikī. vi. To go quickly, fast.

hele.kū. vi. To walk upright, wade.

hele kū.kū. vi. To go by fits and starts, jerk.

helela, herela. n. Herald. *Eng.*

hele.lei. n. Quick-bearing kind of sweet potato. (Kam. 76:27.)

hele.leʻi, hele.lei. nvs. Falling; scattered, as rain, tears, grain; crumbling, as the earth; dilapidated; to shed, as a dog's hair. Cf. *heheleleʻi. Mea heleleʻi,* small change [money]. *I kāna lūlū ʻana, heleleʻi ihola kekahi ma kapa alanui* (Mat. 13.4), in his sowing, some fell by the wayside. **hoʻo.hele.leʻi.** To scatter, sow; to fall, as rain. *Ke hoʻohelelēʻi mai nei,* it's beginning to rain. (Probably PPN *felelei,* a reciprocal derivative of *lele.*)

hele loa. vi. To go or come far; to go with no hope of returning. *Haʻina ka puana, no ka lani hele loa,* tell the refrain, for the king gone forever [song for Ka-lā-kaua, who died at San Francisco]. *Kū ā hele loa,* to get up and go without thought of returning [spoken in anger this can mean: get out and stay out].

hele lua. vi. To travel together, of two.

hele mali.hini. vi. To go to a place for the first time or as a stranger. *Ka hele malihini ʻana mai kēia ao aku a hiki i kēlā ao,* going for the first time from this world to that world [the Hawaiian title of *The Pilgrim's Progress*].

hele.mauna. n. A rare native variety of dry-land taro, with dark purplish petioles and white corms; grown on Hawaiʻi. (HP 18, 32.) Also *piko ʻeleʻele.*

hele mauna. nvi. To travel in the mountains; mountain climber.

hele mua. nvi. **1.** To go ahead; older sibling, descendant of an older sibling, senior. **2.** Da capo (musical term).

helena. 1. n. Going. (See idiom, *oneʻā* and below.) *Hoʻokahi helena, pau ka hana,* in no time at all the work was finished. *Niau kololani ka helena,* going quickly and silently. **2.** Same as *helemauna. Ka helena o ia pua,* the appearance of this flower.

Helene. nvs. Greek, Grecian, Greece. (Gr. *Hellenes.*)

-hele ʻō.lelo. See *-helehele ʻōlelo.*

hele pē.lā. interj. Get out! Go away!

hele pū. vi. To go with, accompany.

hē.leu. Var. of *hāleu.*

hele.uma. n. Stone anchor, anchor. (Heb. 6.19.) *Huki i ka heleuma,* to weigh anchor.

hele wale. vi. To go naked; to go without fixed purpose or far and wide; to go empty-handed; to go without recompense. *Hele wale ka wāwae,* to go barefoot. *ʻA ʻohe uʻi hele wale o Kohala,* no youth of Kohala goes empty-handed [a saying complimenting Kohala on the industry of its youth, who are well supplied with goods as a result]. *Ua hele wale ʻia nō kēia kai e aʻu,* this sea has been sailed far and wide by me.

hele wā.wae. nvi. To walk, go on foot, hike; pedestrian. (Hawaiian pidgin 'walk feet' is probably a loan translation.)

hele wiki. nvi. Quick step, quick time; to go fast.

helio.kalope, hilio.kalupa. n. Introduced, sweet-scented heliotrope *(Heliotropium arborescens* syn. *H. corymbosum).* (Neal 718.) *Eng.* Cf. *hinahina 3.*

helo. 1. vi. To move back and forth rapidly; jerky pushing or sawing motion. Cf. *helohelo, hula helo, ʻilihelo, ʻōhelo 2, 3.* **2.** n. Ramrod. **3.** nvs. Red, as *ʻōhelo* berries; rosy. Cf. *hehelo, helohelo, ʻōhelo. Kai helo,* a red sauce made of fermented shrimps, salt, and coconut cream. (Probably PPN *felo.*)

helo.helo. Redup. of *helo 1, 3;* rosy, as cheeks. (Probably PPN *felofelo.*)

helu. 1. nvt. To count, number, compute, take a census, figure, enumerate, list, include, impute (Oihk. 7.18); to assess, as taxes; to chant a list of names, as of genealogy; including, counting, enumeration, census, list, rate, number, figure, total, inventory; statistics. Cf. *heluhelu, huahelu, uē helu. Helu ʻekahi,* number one, best. *Helu ʻole ʻia,* not counted, excluded. *Poʻe helu ukana,* shipping clerks. *He mau mea helu bālota,* election tellers. *Mīkina helu,* adding machine; comptometer. *He lehulehu loa kēia poʻe, ke helu ʻia nā kāne, a me nā wāhine,* these people are very many, counting men and women. **hoʻo.helu.** Caus/sim.; numerator, in fractions; a telling, explanation. **2.** nvs. Arithmetic, score, reckoning, account; serial; volume (in a series); numbered. *Pona helu,* serial bond. *Aʻo i ka helu,* to learn arithmetic. *Helu a nā kamaliʻi,* children's counting [a game]. **3.** *He mau lā helu wale nō i koe,* only a few days left. **4.** vt. To scratch the earth, as a hen; to dig with the fingers; to paw the earth, as an angry bull. See *māhelu. Neʻepapa ka helu a ka lā i Puna-hoa,* the sun scratched everywhere at Puna-hoa [a long fight]. (PPN *selu.*) **5.** vt. To grumble, list offenses or complaints, especially about lack of gratitude or appreciation.

helua. Pas/imp. of *helu 1, 4, 5. Ua helua e ka manawa a weluwelu* (chant), scratched and torn by time.

helu ʻai. nv. Scorekeeper; to keep score.

helu ʻano hui. n. Uneven totals, as ten bushels and three pecks.

helu ʻano like. n. Even numbers and totals, without fractions.

helu 'ekahi. n. Best, "number one."

helu 'ekale.kia. n. Church census.

helu.hana. n. Factor, as in arithmetic.

helu hana 'ia. n. Composite number.

helu.hana kumu. n. Prime factor.

helu.helu. 1. v. To read, count. (2 Nal. 23.2.) *Mea helu-helu,* reader (either a book, or a person who reads). *Po'e heluhelu,* reader (person). *A 'o heluhelu,* reader (book); to learn to read. **2.** Redup. of *helu 4;* to scratch.

helu.helu ho'o.pono.pono. vt. To proofread.

helu.helu ka'a.hele. vt. To take turns reading, read in turn.

helu hō.'ike. n. Abacus.

helu ho'o.lawe. n. Subtrahend.

helu ho'o.nui. n. Multiplier.

helu ho'o.nui 'ia. n. Multiplicand.

helu hou. vt. To recount; recount.

helu kama.li'i. n. Children's arithmetic.

helu kanaka. nv. Census; to take a census.

helu kau.like. n. Even number.

helu komo. n. Divisor.

helu komo 'ia. n. Multiple.

helu kuala. n. Rate of interest.

helu kumu. n. Prime number.

helu lua. n. Double number; dual number, as in grammar.

heluna. n. Number, count, total sum, amount; grade or mark (evaluation). *He aha ka heluna o kāna po'e moa?* What is the total number of his chickens?

helu na'au. n. Mental arithmetic.

heluna papa. n. Grade or mark, as in school; number of a grade (class), enumeration.

helu nui. n. Large number; plural number.

helu nui ka'a.wale. n. Exclusive plural, as in Hawaiian grammar.

helu nui pili. n. Inclusive plural, as in Hawaiian grammar.

helu 'oko'a. n. Whole number.

helu pā-. vt. To count by, as *helu pālua,* to count by twos; *helu pākolu,* to count by threes; *helu pā'umi,* to count by tens.

helu pā.'ani. nv. Counting game with chants; to play this game.

helu pa'ewa. n. Odd number.

helu pā.loka (balota). nv. To count ballots; election teller.

helu papa. vt. To count or recite in order or consecutively.

helu pō. nv. List of the nights of the moon in the old Hawaiian calendar; to count the nights.

helu po'o.kela. n. Perfect number.

helu puka. n. Quotient, in division.

helu wai.wai. n. Inventory.

Hem. Abbreviation used in surveying for *hema,* south.

hema. nvs. **1.** Left, left side. *Nānā i ka hema,* left, dress. *Ma ka hema, huli,* left, face. [Military commands.] (PPN *sema.*) **2.** South, southern.

hema.hema. nvs. **1.** Awkward, clumsy, unskilled, inexpert, incompetent, unprepared, inefficient, inexperienced; lack of skill; to not know well. *'Ike hemahema,* to know imperfectly. **ho'o.hema.hema.** To neglect, not care for; careless, negligent, defective, deficient, ignorant (Roma 1.31). *Nui kona ho'ohemahema i ke a'o a nā kūpuna,* he was most neglectful of the teachings of the grandparents. *Ke kā waiho ho'ohemahema,* a bailer left unnoticed [a skilled person whose services are not used]. (PPN *semasema.*) **2.** Want, need, necessity; lacking, destitute (Oihk. 22.23), needy. *Ua hemo nā hemahema,* the needs are met.

hemo. vs. **1.** Loose, separated, untied, unfastened, open, satisfied (see ex., *hemahema 2*), discharged, divorced, opened, weaned; taken off, as clothes. (Cf. *puhemo 1,* Puk. 19.21.) *Kuli hemo,* dislocated knee. *Hemo ka hale kū'ai i ka pō,* the store is open in the evening. *Ua hemo akula ke kāma'a,* the shoes are off. *Ua hemo nā kāma'a a Pua iā Kū,* Kū took off Pua's shoes.

ho'o.hemo. To loosen, undo, unfasten, disconnect, take off, set at liberty, liberate, free, abort. *Ho'ohemo i ka 'ono o ka lama,* freed of taste for liquor. (PCP *(f,s)emo.*) **2.** Var. of *'ōhemo 1,* weak, feeble. Cf. *puhemo 2. Nā kuli e hemo ana* (Ioba 4.4), feeble knees. (PCP *(f,s)emo.*)

hemo.'ē. vs. Faint, scanty, feeble, hungry, gasping, as of one near death.

hemo.hemo. Redup. of *hemo 1;* separation, loosening. **ho'o.hemo.hemo.** Caus/sim.; to take off. (Puk. 14.25.) (PCP *(f,s)emo(f,s)emo.*)

hemo.lele. 1. nvs. Perfect, faultless, flawless, holy, immaculate, saintly, pure in heart; complete; perfection, virtue, goodness, holiness; angel, person without fault. *Ma'ema'e wale nō 'o Kaua'i, hemolele wale i ka mālie* (song), perfectly beautiful is Kaua'i, flawless in the calm. *Kō māua hemolele iho* (Oih. 3.12), our holiness. **ho'o.hemo.lele.** To make holy; to feign holiness. *Ua ho'ohemolele lākou i kou nani* (Ezek. 27.4), they have perfected your beauty. **2.** vs. Without restraint. *Hā'awi hemolele,* to give freely and without stint or reward; gratis.

hemū. interj. Shoo, be off, scat (perhaps from Eng. *move*). **ho'o.hemū.** To drive off, scare away, as hens.

hemu.wā. vi. To sound indistinctly, as a voice. *Ka leo o ka lawai'a e hemuwā mai ana,* the indistinct voice of the fisherman.

hena. n. Buttocks; mons pubis; hollow of the thigh; nakedness. *E wehe 'ia auane'i kou hena* (Isa. 47.3), your nakedness shall be uncovered. **ho'o.hena.** To see, feel, or handle the *hena;* to take off one's clothing and expose the *hena.*

hena.hena. **1.** Var. of *henehene 1.* **2.** Redup. of *hena.*

hene. 1. n. Mons pubis. (PCP *(f,s)ene.*) **2.** n. Slope, as of a hill. *'Ike 'oe i ka nani a 'o Himela, ka hene wai'olu lawe mālie* (song), you see the beauty of the Himalayas, gentle slopes that become so calm [note *hene 1* for alternate translation]. **3.** Same as *henehene;* to snicker. Cf. *pūhene 1. Hene iki,* to laugh a little, giggle, snicker. *Hene ka 'aka,* to giggle. **ho'o.hene.** Same as *ho'ohenehene,* to tease. **4.** Rare var. of *kīhene,* basket.

hene.hene. 1. nvt. To laugh at, ridicule, mock, tease, snicker, giggle; mockery, laughter. *Henehene kou 'aka, kou le'ale'a paha* (song), your laughter is merry, perhaps your gaiety. *Ua henehene aku iā'oe* (Isa. 37.22), has despised you. *Ua henehene mai iā'oe ka mea lohe* (Sol. 25.10), lest he that hears put you to shame. **ho'o.hene.hene.** To tease, laugh at, jeer, banter, ridicule. **2.** Redup. of *hene,* slope. (KL line 545.)

hene 'ū.hā. n. Inner side of the thighs where they join the body on either side of the genitals; groins.

heno. Same as *henoheno.* **ho'o.heno.** To cherish, love, caress; affectionate, demonstrative of affection; expression of affection, as a song. *Ho'oheno ho'i kēia wahi keiki,* this little child is so affectionate. *Nona nei ho'oheno,* this song is for him.

-heno. **ho'o.heno.** Decorative plaiting on mat, fan; to decorate thus.

heno.heno. vs. Lovable, sweet. **ho'o.heno.heno.** Caus/sim.

heo. 1. n. Knob of any kind, as of a door; end of the penis, prepuce. Cf. *pūheheo; pūheoheo 2.* **2.** vi. To depart in haste. *I 'ane'i iho nei 'o Kū ā ua heo aku lā,* Kū was here and departed quickly. **3.** vs. Proud, haughty (less common than *ha'aheo*). Cf. *heheo.* **ho'o.heo.** Proud, vaunting, vain; to show off, boast.

heo.heo. Same as *heo 1,* and *pōheoheo,* knob. *Eia kāu 'o ka heoheo,* so much for you, a knob [a curse, usually accompanied by a vulgar gesture imitative of the genitalia].

hepa. nvs. Idiot, moron, imbecile; partial paralysis of the vocal organs causing indistinct articulation; feeble-minded, moronic. *Hepa ka 'ōlelo,* indistinct speech; to make a slip of the tongue. **ho'o.hepa.** Caus/sim. *'Ōlelo ho'ohepa,* idiotic talk; to mispronounce or misconstrue language.

hepa.hepa. Redup. of *hepa.* **ho'o.hepa.hepa.** Caus/sim. *Rare.*

hepe.koma, hebedoma. n. Week; seven years. Cf. *pule.* (Gr. *hebdomas.*)

Hepela, Hebera. nvs. Hebrew. *Ma'i Hepela,* smallpox. *Eng.*

hē.pia. nvs. Pale yellow, of the domesticated *'ilima* flower. Also *pia.*

heu. nvs. Down or fine hair, fuzz, loose fibers on certain fruits or leaves, quicksilver or mercury on back of a mirror, hairlike growths or spines on sugar cane stalks or cactus; fuzzy, downy; to begin to grow, as a youth's beard or pubic hair; to sprout, of seedlings. *Kū ka heu, pi'i ka heu,* the fuzz bristles [anger]. *Ku'u keiki o ka lā heu 'ole,* child of my beardless youth [Ka-mehameha's term for his first child, Ka-ōlei-o-Kū]. *'Ōkalakala heu pānini,* bristling with fine cactus spines. **ho'o.heu.** Caus/sim.; to grow, sprout, germinate; pubescence. (PEP *feu.*)

-heu. ho'o.heu. (a) To bleach. **(b)** *(Cap.)* Name of a strong wind threatening to be a gale.

he'u. nvi. 1. Hoot, as of an owl; to croak, hoot. 2. Deep-throated sounds made in Hawaiian chants and prayers; to chant thus.

heu ani.ani. n. Fine bits of broken or ground glass; mercury on glass made into a mirror.

heu.heu. Redup. of *heu.* (PEP *feufeu.*)

he'u.he'u. Redup. of *he'u 1, 2.*

heu.miki. Beautiful, comely, attractive. (AP.)

he'u.pueo. n. 1. A reedlike grass, a bent grass *(Agrostis avenacea,* synonyms *A. retrofracta* and *Calamagrostis forsteri),* originally found in Australia, and now found through Polynesia; *Panicum heupueo* on Ni'ihau. *Lit.,* owl hoot. 2. Probable Hawaiian name for *pili uka,* a grass.

hewa. 1. nvs. Mistake, fault, error, sin, blunder, defect, offense, guilt, crime, vice; wrong, incorrect, wicked, sinful, guilty; to err, miss, mismanage, fail, miss. *Ko'u hewa,* my mistake. *Hewa haumia,* filthy sin, immorality. *Hana i ka hewa,* to do wrong, commit adultery. *Hele hewa,* to go wrong. *Ua 'ai hewa au i ka mea 'ono,* I ate the cake by mistake. *Nā hewa i kūpono i ka make,* offenses punishable by death. *Kū ka hewa iāia,* he is guilty. *Ua hewa 'o Pua iā Kū,* Kū treated Pua wrongly. *E hele ana 'oe i hea? E au i ke hewa.* Where are you going? Just drifting aimlessly [said if one doesn't choose to answer the question]. **ho'o.hewa.** To cause one to do wrong, cause or feign a mistake; to blame, condemn. (Cf. the more common *ho'āhewa,* to condemn.) *Ho'ohewa 'ia,* convicted. *'Ōlelo ho'ohewa,* to make errors in speech on purpose. *Mai 'ai 'oe ia mea, ua ho'ohewa ka 'āina nou* (Kin. 3.17), eat not this thing, cursed is the ground for your sake. (PCP *(f,s)ewa.*) 2. n. Is it wrong to? Then why not? *He hewa kā 'oe ke kū'ai i 'āina, loa'a ke kahua pa'a?* Why not then buy land and get security? 3. vs. Offended, annoyed. *E hūnā 'oe i ke aloha, mai ha'i, o lohea 'ia auane'i, hewa kahi po'e* (song), conceal the love, don't tell, lest it be heard, and some people be offended. 4. vs. To the point of satiety; to be in great quantities; to do excessively. See ex., *wai 1. Hewa ka maka,* to look until one can see no more; to flirt with the eyes. *Hewa ka waha,* to speak too much or hastily. *E hea i ke kanaka e komo maloko e hānai ai a hewa ka waha,* call the person to come in and feed until his mouth can take no more [hospitality].

hewa.hewa. 1. nvs. A great many, very, vast, in great quantities. *He nui hewahewa nā mea nani o kēia home,* there are many, many beautiful things in this home. *'A'ole o kana mai i ka hewahewa o nā mea 'ai,* there were boundless quantities of food. 2. vs. Crazy, demented, wild, aimless; to fail to recognize (Ier. 29.26). Cf. *kala hewahewa. Kā hewahewa, he ua* (FS 37), hit wildly, it's raining [let the fight begin]. **ho'o.-hewa.hewa.** To fail to recognize. (PEP *(f,s)ewa;* cf. Blixen 1977; PCP *(f,s)ewa(f,s)ewa.*)

-hewahewa. ho'o.hewa.hewa. Twill plaiting.

hī. 1. vt. To cast or troll, as for bonito, *'ahi,* and *kala.* (PPN *sii.*) 2. nvt. Dysentery, diarrhea; to flow, hiss; to purge. *Ka hī koko* (Oih. 28.8), a bloody flux. **ho'o.hī.** Caus/sim.; to purge. (PPN *sii.*)

-hi. A rare transitivizer. See *kilohi, ukuhi,* Gram. 6.6.4. (PPN *-fi.*)

hia. n. Desire, delight. Cf. *hiamoe. 'A'ole i pau ko'u hia i ka nani o Hilo,* my delight in the beauties of Hilo is endless. *Ua mau ka hia o ka po'e o ka hale e noho,* it was still the desire of the people of the house to stay. (PPN *fia.*) **ho'o.hia.** Caus/sim. (For. 6:419.)

-hia. 1. inter. How many? How much? (Follows *'a-, 'e-,* or *pā-.*) (Gram. 10.3.) (PPN *fiha.*) 2. Pas/imp. (Gram. 6.6.3.) (PPN *-fia* [see *ilihia, kilohia*] and PPN *-sia* [see *'awa'awahia, hulihia*].)

hi'a. nvt. 1. To make fire with the fire-plow; the act of making fire thus. (PPN *sika.*) 2. Shuttle or needle for making nets; to knot or fasten the meshes of a net; to form a network; to bind, as house rafters (For. 5:651). (PPN *sika.*)

hia.'ā. nvs. Indisposed to sleep, wakeful, sleepless; insomnia. *E hia'ā ana no kona aloha,* sleepless because of his being in love. **ho'o.hia.'ā.** To cause sleeplessness. *He mea ho'ohia'ā ke kope,* coffee causes sleeplessness.

hia.'ai. vs. Pleased with, delighted with; delightful, pleasing. *Hia'ai ka mana'o ke honi aku i kou ala* (song), thought is delighted when inhaling your fragrance. **ho'o.hia.'ai.** To delight, enchant, entrance.

hia.'ai.'ono. nvs. Greatly pleased or delighted, most delightful; appetite for delicious food. (PPN *fia kai.*)

hia.ala. Same as the more common *hia'ā.* See ex., *hana aloha.*

hia.hia. 1. vs. Faded, gray, hazy. Cf. *ahia,* faded. 2. Var. of *hiehie.* **ho'o.hia.hia.** Caus/sim.

hi'a.hi'a. Redup. of *hi'a 1, 2.*

hi'a kā 'upena. n. Shuttle or needle for making a fish net, sometimes of bone.

hī aku. nv. To cast for bonito; bonito casting. *Pā hī aku,* mother-of-pearl lure for bonito. *'O ka hī aku ka lawai'a nui a 'Umi a-Līloa* (FS 173), casting for bonito was the principal means of fishing of 'Umi [son] of-Līloa. (PPN *sii 'atu.*)

hiala.'ai. 1. Same as *hia'ai.* **ho'o.hiala.'ai.** Caus/sim. *Ko'u nanea ho'ohiala'ai,* my delightful relaxation. 2. vt. To eat heartily.

hia.lele. vi. Restless, furtive. *Maka 'ā hialele* (Kep. 184), staring, furtive eyes.

hi'ai. 1. n. Food offering to the gods. 2. vt. To stir, as a fire; to signal with the hands. *Rare.*

hia.loa. vs. Well trained, skilled. *'O mākou nā 'ōlohe āiwaiwa hialoa ma ka lā,* we are the most wondrously skilled experts of the day.

hi'a.loa. n. 1. Bald temple. 2. Same as *'uhaloa,* a weed.

hia.moe. nvi. Sleep; to sleep, fall asleep, asleep. *Kona hiamoe 'ana,* his sleeping. *Holoholona hiamoe,* sloth. *Hiamoe i ka make,* to sleep in death, die. **ho'o.-hia.moe.** To put to sleep, lull to sleep, to pretend to sleep; soporific. *Lā'au ho'ohiamoe,* sleeping tablet or drug. (PPN *fiamohe.*)

hia.moe iki. nvi. A little sleep, nap; to take a nap.

hia.moe loa. nvi. To oversleep, sleep deeply; death, eternal sleep. Cf. *moe loa.*

hia.moe pa'a loa. nvi. Fast asleep; deep sleep. (Lunk. 4.21.)

hiana. n. Depression or hole, as under water. *Hiana ulua,* hole frequented by *ulua.*

hi'ana.ki'u. n. Stems by which tubers are attached to vines. (Kep. 99.) Cf. *'anaki'u.*

hia.pa'i.'ole. n. Foremost, expert. *He āiwaiwa, a he hiapa'i'ole aku kēlā ma nā mea apau, he palena 'ole ka 'ike me ka ikaika,* a wonder, a foremost expert in all things, unlimited knowledge and strength.

hiapo. n. First-born child; first born, oldest. *E pepehi nō wau i nā hiapo apau* (Puk. 12.12), I will smite all the first-born. **ho'o.hiapo.** To have the privileges of a first-born; to act as a first-born; to treat as a first-born.

hie. nvs. Attractive, distinguished, dignified, noble, becoming. Cf. *māhie.* *'A'ohe hie o kēnā pāpale iā'oe,* that hat is not becoming to you. *Pau ka hie,* no longer attractive. **ho'o.hie.** To make or cause to appear distinguished; distinguished, stately, regal; delightful.

hie.hie. Redup. of *hie;* superb. **ho'o.hie.hie.** To beautify, make distinctive, beautiful, elegant; distinguished in manner or appearance. *'O ke aloha . . . 'a'ole ho'i e ho'ohiehie* (1 Kor. 13.4, 5), charity . . . does not act elegantly. *Ho'ohiehie launa 'ole,* showy, superlatively decorated, gaudy, gorgeous.

hiena. n. **1.** Kind of soft porous stone used to smooth and polish utensils; it is harder than the *'ana* stone, which is used on wood. **2.** Hyena. *Eng.* **3.** Speckled bird of prey. (Ier. 12.9.)

hī.he'e. vi. Obliquely, indirectly, sideways. (For. 6:495.)

hihi. 1. nvi. To entangle, creep, spread, intertwine, intermingle; entanglement, web, snare. Cf. *pohihihi. Hihi ka lani,* intermarried, of chiefly families. *Lā'au hihi,* vine. **ho'o.hihi.** To cause entanglement; to entwine, entangle. (PPN *fihifihi.)* **2.** n. A large-meshed fish net.

-hihi. ho'o.hihi. To take a fancy to, admire greatly, be enraptured with. *Ho'ohihi ka mana'o i ka nani o Kahana,* the mind is entranced with the beauty of Kahana.

hī.hī. Redup. of *hī 2;* to hiss. (PPN *sisi.)*

hihia. 1. nvs. Entangled, interwoven, involved, perplexed, hampered, rank, snarled, obscure and difficult to understand (Kep. 167); snarl, entanglement, kink, thicket, difficulty, problem, trouble. *Ka hihia pa'a o ka nahele,* the dense thicket of the forest. *Nui nā kumu hihia ma nā maka, lima, wāwae, kino (ma ka hula),* there are many sources of difficulties [immoralities] from the eyes, hands, feet, body (in the hula). **ho'o.hihia.** To get into difficulties, entangle, perplex, beset with trouble (Mat. 26.31), complicate. *Ka ho'ohihia 'ana o kēia kanaka iā kākou* (Puk. 10.7), this man is a snare to us. **2.** n. Lawsuit or case before the court, trial. Cf. *hihia kalaima, hihia waiwai.* (PCP *fifia.)*

hihia kalaima. n. Criminal case.

hihia.lou. A plant with small yellow flowers. (And.)

hihia.wai. n. The swamp fern *(Ceratopteris thalictroides),* an edible, somewhat succulent fern, distributed through the tropics. It grows in mud or water, as around taro patches, in tufts about 30 cm high. The fronds are triangular and are finely divided into long, narrow parts. Young fronds are eaten with fresh-water shrimps. (Neal 12.) Also *palai kahawai.*

hihia wai.wai. n. Civil case.

hihihi. Redup. of *hihi 1.*

hihi.hiki. vi. To come or go, of many people. Cf. *hiki 3, hihiki.*

hihi.hina. Redup. and intensifier of *hina,* to fall.

hihiki. Redup. of *hiki,* to come, go. *'Akahi a hihiki ka makemake* (chant), at last has come desire.

hihi.kolo. 1. Same as *kākalaioa 2, 3,* kinds of brambles. **2.** n. Name of a legendary *koa* tree on Kaua'i that was said to have no trunk. **3.** See *Ka-hili-kolo.*

hihi manō. Net made of strong cord used for shark fishing. (Malo 213.) Also *kāhala.*

hī.hī.manu. 1. n. Various sting rays (Dasyatidae) and eagle rays *(Actobatus narinari).* Also *lupe.* **2.** nvs. Lavish, magnificent, elegant; elegance. *He nui ka hīhīmanu o kā lāua mau anaina ho'okipa i hā'awi ai,* they gave very lavish receptions. *Hīhīmanu noho'i nā hale kū'ai i nā mea kū'ai o nā mea like 'ole,* the stores are magnificent with all sorts of things for sale. **3.** *(Cap.)* n. A Kaua'i peak. (FS 75.) See saying, *keha.*

hihina. 1. Redup. and plural of *hina,* to fall. **ho'o.hihina.** To cause to fall; to sway to and fro. *E ho'ohihina noho'i ke kino i maua a i hope, i ka 'ākau a i ka hema,* the body sways forward and back, to the right and to the left. **2.** n. Entanglement, spreading. Cf. *hihi.*

hihio. nvi. Soft whistling sound, gust or draft of wind; to whistle.

hihi'o. nvi. A dream or vision (Kin. 15.1), as while dozing; to dream while dozing; to whistle or sough, as wind.

hihi.pe'a. nvs. Jungle, tangled thicket; entangled. *Fig.,* bewilderment, grief.

hihi pū.nā.wele, hihi pūnā.wele.wele. n. Spider web, cobweb. *Maka hihi pūnāwelewele,* dim, lifeless eyes.

hihiu. vs. **1.** Wild, untamed. **ho'o.hihiu.** To cause fear, frighten. **2.** Rare, uncommon. *Hana hihiu,* unusual or rare work. *Maka hihiu,* a person of exceptional merit or lineage.

hī.hī.wai. n. **1.** Endemic grainy snail *(Neritina granosa),* in both fresh and brackish water, eaten both cooked and raw. Also *wī,* if in fresh water. See *hūai 1.* **3.** A night for *hīhīwai* [a lucky time]. (PPN *sisi,* PNP *sisiwai:* cf. Samoan *sisivai* in Pratt.) **2.** A shellfish *(Nerita vespertina).* Also *hapawai.* See *hūai 1.* **3.** A pelagic grapsid crab, probably *Grapsus tenuicrustatus.* **4.** A tide in the high-tide zone.

hi'i. 1. vt. To hold or carry in the arms, as a child; to bear; to nurse or tend a child (Hawaiians did not carry children unrelated to them, and commoners did not touch a chief's child; carrying a child symbolized love, kinship, and affection). Cf. *Hi'iaka, hi'ialo, hi'ikua, hi'ilani, hi'ilei, hi'imo'opuna, hi'ipaka, hi'ipoi.* **ho'o.hi'i.** Caus/sim. (PPN *siki.)* **2.** Same as *kūpoki,* a plaiting process. **3.** vs. Tall, as cliff or mountain. *Ku'u kaikua'ana o ka pali hi'i,* my older brother of the tall cliff.

hi'ia. Pas/imp. of *hi'i 1. Ē nā keiki o . . . Hawai'i, hi'ia i ka hana mau 'ia e ka makani anu Ka-la'i-ākea* (chant), o children of Hawai'i, sustained by the constant action of the cool Ka-la'i-ākea wind.

Hi'i.aka. n. **1.** First part of the names of the twelve younger sisters of the goddess Pele; the youngest and most famous was *Hi'iaka-i-ka-poli-o-Pele.* See PH. **2.** *(Not cap.)* A rare variety of taro with bronze-red leaf and stem, used in medicine. **3.** *(Not cap.)* A variety of sweet potato.

hi'i.alo. 1. vi. Carried in the arms, as a beloved child. *Ku'u lei i hi'ialo 'ia,* my beloved child carried in my arms. **2.** loc. n. Nearby, in front. See ex., *hi'ikua.*

hi'i.kala. n. Hook used for *kala,* a fish, and baited with *kala,* a seaweed.

hi'i.kua. 1. vi. Carried on the shoulders, as a beloved child. **2.** loc. n. In back, far. *Hele 'ia i hi'ikua i hi'ialo,* gone far and near. **3.** *(Cap.)* n. Name of a star said to rise on the night of Hoaka and to vanish on the night of Muku in the month of Welehu.

hi'i.lani. nvt. To nurse or care for, as an infant; to admire, exalt, praise, extol in poetry; praise. *E halelū aku 'oukou iā Iēhova, ē kō nā 'āina apau, e hi'ilani aku iāia* (Hal. 117.1), oh sing psalms of praise to Jehovah, those of all nations, praise him.

hi'i.lawe. 1. vt. To lift, carry. **2.** *(Cap.)* n. Name of the highest waterfall in Hawai'i, and one of the highest in the world, with a vertical drop of about 300 m, at Waipi'o Valley, Hawai'i. See Elbert and Mahoe, p. 49, for a famous song.

hi'i.lei. v. To carry, tend, and cherish a beloved child *(lei).*

Hi'i-Lei. n. Name of a star that rises and vanishes at the same times as *Hi'ikua.*

hi'i.mo'o.puna. nv. To bear a grandchild in the arms; to be a grandparent (a term of pride and affection). *Ua hi'imo'opuna 'oia,* he has the joy of being a grandparent.

hi'i.paka. vt. To care for a child; to instruct a child.

hi'i.poi. vt. To tend, feed, cherish, as a child. *E hi'ipoi 'oe iā lākou ma kou umauma* (Nah. 11.12), carry them in your bosom.

hi'i.poi.poi. Redup. of *hi'ipoi. Mālama pono 'oe i ku'u aloha, hi'ipoipoi 'ia ma kō alo* (love song), take good care of my love, cherishing always in your presence.

Hik. Abbreviation for *hikina,* east.

hī.kā. Same as *hīkākā. E hele hīkā ana maluna o nā kukuluae'o,* going unsteadily on the stilts. *He au e hīkā ana i ka 'āina,* a current spreading about the land.

hika'a. vt. To tilt back, as the head. *Hika'a lani,* to look heavenward.

hī.kā.kā. nvi. To stagger, totter, reel; spreading, as vines (Kep. 157); unsteady gait. *Ka mea i 'ona, e hīkākā ana maloko o kona lua'i* (Isa. 19.14), a drunken man staggering in his vomit. **ho'o.hī.kā.kā.** Caus/sim. *Ā e ho'ohīkākā aku 'oia iā lākou mehe mea 'ona lā* (Ioba 12.25), and he makes them stagger like a drunken man.

hī.kapala.lē. nvi. Gibberish; to talk gibberish; to speak a foreign language, especially English.

hī.kau. vt. To pelt, throw. *Lā'au hīkau pe'a* (FS 93), blows hurled crosswise.

Hikaua. n. Name of an unknown person, used something like so-and-so, usually followed by *mā. Ua lalau aku i kauhale o Hikaua mā* (Kel. 134), [he] has wandered off to So-and-so's house.

Hikauhi. n. Name of the wife of the famous legendary navigator, Pāka'a and of the coastal area, Moloka'i, where she lived. She was lost during labor pains and her husband searched vainly for her, hence the saying applied to fruitless endeavors, *Hikauhi i Kau-manamana,* Hikauhi is at Kau-manamana [another place on Moloka'i].

hī.ke'a. Similar to *ke'a 1, 2. Na Pele ia hīke'a maila i Kīlau-ea,* Pele blocked [the way] at Kī-lau-ea.

hiki. 1. nvs. Can, may; to be able; ability; possible. Cf. *hiki nō, hikiwale, hikiwawe,* Gram. 4.4. *Hiki 'ole,* impossible, can't do. *Pau ka hiki,* no longer able to do; impotent. *Hiki iāia ke hele mai,* he can come; he may [has permission to] come. *E hiki ana,* when possible. *Ka lā e hiki ana,* any possible day. *Ka manawa e hiki ana,* any possible time. 2. interj. All right, O.K. (in sense of "able to do"), certainly, surely (used alone or preceding *mā*). 3. vi. To get to or reach a place, come, arrive, approach, appear, arise. Cf. *hikina. Ā + hiki* followed by a word expressing time or place, is often translated: to, until. *Ho'i maila ia ā hiki i Wai-kīkī* (FS 41), he came back to [until arrived at] Wai-kīkī. *Ua pa'a ia 'ōlelo ā hiki i keia wā,* this story has been preserved until this time. *Ā hiki lāua malaila* (FS 45), when they got there. *'A 'ole i hiki mai,* did not come, absent. *Hiki honua,* to happen suddenly, unexpectedly, by chance. *Ua hiki ka lā, aia i luna* (FS 39), the sun has risen, there [it] is above. **ho'o.hiki.** To cause to come, arrive, appear. *Ho'ohiki wawe,* to rush, come fast, speed up, expedite. (PPN *fiti.*) 4. vi. Next. *Nā makahiki kanalima e hiki mai ana,* the next fifty years. 5. vt. To fetch, carry back and forth (less used than *lawe*). *E hiki mai 'oe i ka pakeke,* fetch the bucket.

hiki-. Names of cardinal directions, stars, and portions of the sky, perhaps because of movement *(hiki 3)* of the sun. See below.

-hiki.ho'o.hiki. (a). To vow, swear, take an oath, promise; to administer an oath; vow, oath, promise, pledge. See *'ōlelo ho'ohiki. Ho'ohiki kūpa'a,* pledge of allegiance. *Ho'ohiki pa'a,* firm oath; to bind under oath. *Keiki hānai ho'ohiki,* legally adopted child. *Ho'ohiki 'ino,* a violent oath [such as *pau Pele,* translated under *manō*]. *Nāna au i ho'ohiki,* he administered the oath to me. *Nā haole ho'ohiki a me nā haole ho'ohiki 'ole,* foreigners naturalized and not naturalized [or alien]. *Make i ka ho'ohiki i kānāwai* (Kep. 45), death for breaking a law. *Ho'ohiki ihola ia i ka ho'ohiki* (1 Sam. 1.11), she vowed a vow. **(b)** vt. To peel, pry off. See *mahiki 5* and *'ōhiki 1.*

hikia. vt. To aim carefully, as with stone, spear, or gun.

hiki.alo.alo. n. Zenith. *Rare.*

hiki.'ala.mea. Probably the same as *iki'alamea,* a disease.

hiki.anako.pili. n. Spittle passed from a dying master, according to the belief that his knowledge was thereby handed on. *Na'u kekahi wahi hikianakopili,* give me a little knowledge [before you die].

Hiki.ana.lia. n. Name of a star, described as medium-bright and near the equator; visible from April to September; used as a guide to mariner and fisherman.

Hiki-'au-moana. n. Kaua'i name for the star Hikianalia.

hiki.e'e. n. Large Hawaiian couch. *Lit.,* possible to mount. *Maluna o kou hikie'e* (Puk. 8.3), upon your bed.

hiki.hiki. 1. Redup. of *hiki 3;* to come repeatedly, as voices. **ho'o.hiki.hiki.** Caus/sim. 2. Redup. of *hiki 5,* to fetch and carry; to fetch repeatedly or a little at a time. **ho'o.hiki.hiki.** Caus/sim.

hī.ki'i. nvt. Binding, tying; to tie, bind, make fast. Cf. *hīki'iki'i, nāki'i, mūki'i. Hīki'i ihola ia i kāna keiki iā 'Ika'aka* (Kin. 22.9), he bound his son Isaac. (PEP *fitiki.*)

hī.ki'i.ki'i. Redup. of *hīki'i.* (Mat. 27.2.)

hī.ki'i.lia. Pas/imp. of *hīki'i.*

Hiki.kau.elia, Hikikaulia. n. Name of a star; according to some, Sirius.

Hiki-kau-e-lono. n. Name of a star. Also *'Ā-iki-kau-e-lono.*

Hiki-kau-lono-meha. n. The star Sirius.

hiki.ki'i. vi. 1. To lean back, relax. *Ua 'ia kāua e ka ua, hikiki'i kāua i Kananā,* we are rained on, let's lean back and relax at Kananā [pun on *kāua,* we two, and *ka ua,* the rain]. 2. To spread, as mist; to rain, especially a slanting rain. *Hikiki'i ka noe i nā pali,* the fog slants by the cliffs.

hiki kū. n. Portion of the sky immediately above the horizon.

hiki.lele. nvi. To jump or start from shock, to gasp; shock, perturbation. *Hikilele'ela 'o La'ie-i-ka-wai, he moe'uhane kā* (Laie 523), La'ie-i-ka-wai awoke startled, but it was a dream. **ho'o.hiki.lele.** To startle, shock. *He mea hou ho'ohikilele,* shocking news.

Hikili-i-maka-o-Unu.lau. n. Star name, perhaps morning star. (For. 5:119.)

hiki.moe. West. *Lit.,* come to rest. *Rare.*

hiki.mua. nvi. Progress, advance; to progress.

hiki mua. vi. To come ahead or beforehand.

hikina. n. 1. East. 2. *(Cap.)* Orient. 3. Coming, advent.

hikina 'ā.kau. n. Northeast.

hikina hema. n. Southeast.

hiki nō. interj. All right, O.K., certainly, surely, it can be done. Cf. *hiki 2.*

hiki 'ole. nvs. Impossible, unable, can't or unable to do; inability, regrets.

hIki.pua. 1. vi. To force one's way, as through a crowd or undergrowth. *Rare.* 2. *(Cap.)* n. Wind name associated with Hālawa, Moloka'i.

hiki.wale. vs. Easy. *He mea hikiwale nō kēia,* this is easy to do.

hiki wale. vi. To come accidentally, alone, or without any particular purpose or reason.

hiki.wawe. vs. Quickly, speedily, suddenly, prompt, quickly done; possible to do quickly; doubletime (military command). *He huhū hikiwawe,* quick anger. *Hikiwawe ka 'ike,* learning very fast. *Hikiwawe ka hele 'ana,* to travel fast. **ho'o.hiki.wawe.** To accelerate, hurry, hasten.

hī koko. n. Bloody dysentery, hemorrhoids; ulcers (RSV), emerods (KJV) (Kanl. 28.27.)

hikoni. n. Tattoo brand on the forehead of a *kauā* outcast, or on the forehead of the caught seducer of a high chief's wife. (See figure 1, Malo 70.)

hiku. num. Seven, seventh (usually preceded by the numerical prefix *'e*). Cf. *Nā-hiku,* the Big Dipper. (PPN *fitu.*)

hikua. vt. To throw aimlessly, carelessly.

hiku.hiku. 1. n. Many. *He hikuhiku nā kini akua,* the hosts of gods are many, many. 2. Confusion of sounds. (And.)

hila. 1. Same as *hilahila 1.* **ho'o.hila.** Caus/sim. (PCP *sila.*) 2. n. Heel. *Eng. Hila 'auli'i,* high heels. *Hila ha'aha'a,* low heels. 3. n. Hill. *Eng.* Cf. *kuahiwi, mauna. Kaimana Hila,* Diamond Head.

hila.hila. 1. nvs. Bashful, shy, ashamed (2 Nal. 2.17), abashed, embarrassed; shame, bashfulness. Cf. *puahilahila. Kou wahi hilahila,* your private parts. *Hilahila 'ole,* shameless, brazen. *He ma'i nui ka hilahila,* shyness is a great disease. **ho'o.hila.hila.** To make ashamed or embarrassed; to disgrace, humiliate; shameful, bashful, timid. *Hana ho'ohilahila,* disgraceful behavior or acts. *Ho'ohilahila noho'i 'oe ia'u,* you've made me ashamed; I'm ashamed of you. **2.** Same as *iholena,* a banana.

hila'i. vt. To exalt, praise. *Rare.*

hilala. vi. To reel, lean or tilt sideways. *Ua hele ā hilala nā kia, kiki'i ka pe'a i ka makani,* the masts lean over, the sails tilt in the breeze. **ho'o.hilala.** Caus/sim.; to cause to swing back and forth; to lean over, tilt.

hī lau.lele. n. Dysentery caused by eating *laulele* greens; name of a famine during the sandalwood-cutting days when farms were neglected and the people lived on *laulele* greens.

hī.lea. vs. Careless, shiftless (named for the people of Hīlea village, Ka'ū, Hawai'i, reported to have brought poorly prepared poi to a chief). *Hīlea i kalo 'eka'eka,* Hīlea of the dirty taro [a saying applied to anyone careless or inefficient in work].

hili. 1. nvt. To braid or plait, as a lei or candlenuts; a braid, plaiting, string. See *lei hili. Ka hili 'ana i ka lauoho* (1 Pet. 3.3), the plaiting of the hair. (PPN *firi.*) **2.** vi. To turn aside, deviate, miss the way, wander, stray. Cf. *hilikau, pūhili. Mea hili i hope,* straggler. *Ua pā hili,* rain blown by wind in various directions. *Mai hili 'i'o paha au inā 'a'ole kēia kama'āina,* I might have gone quite astray had it not been for this native of the place. **ho'o.hili.** Caus/sim.; to lead astray. (PPN *fili.*) **3.** nvt. To whip, smite, thrash, switch, bat; batter, as in baseball; stroke, as in fighting. *Mea hili kinipōpo,* batter. **ho'o.hili.** Caus/sim.; to pretend to whip, to whip gently. **4.** n. Bark used in dyeing, as *hili kukui, hili kōlea, hili noni;* the dark-brown dye made from this bark; a tapa dyed with *hili;* to dye with *hili.*

hī.lia. 1. nvt. *He kī'oki o ke kīkākapu, 'o ka i'a kapu hīlia au 'awahia,* stripes of the *kīkākapu,* the sacred fish, smitten with bitter bile. **2.** n. A native bird (no data).

hili.au. vi. In devious ways; to ramble; be indirect. See ex., *ne'ikū.*

hili.e'e. Var. of *'ilie'e,* plumbago.

hili hā. nvt. Four-strand braid; to braid thus.

hili hewa. nvi. Tangled, confused; entanglement, confusion; to become entangled; to trip or fall. *Hili hewa ka no'ono'o,* mental confusion. *Hili hewa ka wāwae,* to stumble, trip.

hili.hili. 1. Redup. of *hili 1–3.* **ho'o.hili.hili.** Redup. of *ho'ohili.* **2.** Redup. of *hili 4;* dark red or brown (less dark than *hili 4*). *Hilihili honu,* turtle coloring; *fig.,* wealthy. **ho'o.hili.hili.** To dye.

hili.hua. vi. To grope here and there. *Rare.*

hili.kau. vs. Mixed, snarled, entangled; to mix, snarl. See saying *makau. Hilikau nā wāwae,* to stumble. *Hilikau ka no'ono'o,* to have confused or bewildered thoughts. **ho'o.hili.kau.** Caus/sim. *Ho'ohilikau i nā wāwae,* to trip someone.

hili.kī. vt. To hit carelessly, at random. (Gram. 6.5.)

hili.kolo. Var. of *hihikolo 2,* a legendary tree.

Hili-kolo. Same as *Ka-hili-kolo* and *Ka-hihi-kolu.*

hili kolu. nvt. A three-strand braid; to braid such.

hili.kua. nvt. To lash against, whip. *Makani hilikua 'e'ena nā pali* (song), wind lashing furiously against the cliffs.

Hilina Ehu. n. Name of a star and of a Hawaiian month (same as *Māhoe Mua;* see *month*). (PPN *silinga.*)

hili.na'i. nvt. To believe, trust; to lean on, rely on; trust, confidence. *'Ōlelo ho'oholo hilina'i,* vote of confidence. *He aha kēia hilina'i āu e hilina'i nei?* (2 Nal. 18.19) What confidence is this wherein you trust? *Hilina'i Ka'ū, kālele iā Puna; Hilina'i Puna, kālele iā Ka'ū* (saying), Ka'ū is dependent, supported by Puna; Puna

is dependent, supported by Ka'ū [Ka'ū and Puna depend on one another, said also of persons who do so].

Hilina Mā. n. Name of the eleventh month (Moloka'i), eighth (Kaua'i), or tenth (Alexander); same as *Māhoe Hope.* Cf. *alanui*

Hili.nehu. Same as *Hilina Ehu.*

hilio.kalupe. Same as *heliokalope,* heliotrope. *Eng.*

hili.'ō.'ū. 1. Square braid of eight or sixteen strands. (And.) **2.** Ailment of the bowels or stomach, accompanied by gas pains. (And.)

hili pā.hā. nvt. Four-strand braid; to braid such.

hili pā.kolu. nvt. Three-strand braid; to braid such.

hili pō. vi. To wander or grope aimlessly in the dark.

hiliu. n. Sound or call of a wind instrument, as the conch shell. *Rare.* **ho'o.hiliu.** To blow a conch or wind instrument. *Rare.*

hilo. 1. nvt. To twist, braid, spin; twisted, braided; threadlike; faint streak of light. See *lei hilo. Ua hilo 'ia i ke aho a ke aloha,* braided with the cords of love. *He olonā i hilo 'ia* (Puk. 26.1), fine twined linen. **ho'o.hilo.** Caus/sim. *Rare.* (PPN *filo.*) **2.** *(Cap.)* n. First night of the new moon. See Malo 35. (PCP *filo.*) **3.** *(Cap.)* n. Name of a famous Polynesian navigator for whom the city and district may have been named. See sayings, *Hilo* (Eng.-Hawaiian) (PCP *filo.*) **4.** Same as *mau'u Hilo,* Hilo grass. **5.** n. Gonorrhea; a running sore (Oihk. 15.3). **6.** n. A variety of sweet potato. **7.** See *iwi hilo.*

hilo.hilo. 1. vt. To lengthen a speech or story by inserting new matter; to embroider or spin out a tale. **2.** Sweet juice of ti root. (And.)

hilu. 1. n. Various species of reef fishes of the genus *Coris.* The name *hilu* may be qualified by the terms *'ele'ele, lauwili, melemele, moelola, pano* (probably same as *uli), pāni'o, piliko'a (Paracirrhites forsteri,* hawkfish*), 'ula, uli.* See saying, *no'eno'e 2.* **2.** nvs. Quiet, reserved, well-behaved, decorous, unobtrusive, easygoing; such a person (a child born to a woman who craved *hilu* fish during her pregnancy was thought to be of this desirable type). **3.** vs. Strange. *Eia ka mea hilu loa,* here is something unusual.

-hilu. ho'o.hilu. (a) To decorate, beautify. **(b)** To praise, exalt, dignify.

hilu.hilu. vs. Elegant, beautiful. **ho'o.hilu.hilu.** To beautify, bedeck, decorate. *Ho'ohiluhilu kula,* golden finery, jewelry.

Himela. n. Himalayas. *Eng.* See song, *hene 2.*

hī.meni. nvt. Hymn, any song not used for hulas; to sing a *hīmeni. Eng. Hīmeni wae,* selected hymn or anthem. *Ā hīmeni aku ka po'e hīmeni* (2 Oihn. 29.28), the singers sang.

hī.meni kū pā.kahi. n. Vocal solo.

hī.meni kū pā.kolu. n. Trio (musical).

hina. 1. nvs. To fall, tumble, or topple over from an upright position (cf. *hā'ule,* to drop); to be "controlled," as a disease (Kam. 64:102); to fall morally; to throw down; a falling (a *loa'a*-type word; see Gram. 4.4). *'A'ole na'e he hina o ke kanaka o Kā-kuhihewa i nā kaikua'ana o Ka-welo* (FS 35), but the older brothers of Ka-welo did not throw Kā-kuhihewa's man. **ho'o.-hina.** To throw, cause to fall, knock down; to lean over. *Ho'ohina ihola ka daimonio iāia* (Luka 4.35), the devil threw him. (PPN *singa.*) **2.** n. Italics, probably so called because italics slant. **3.** vi. To blow in a straight course, of wind. *Ke hina maila ka makani mai uka mai,* the wind is now blowing steadily from the uplands. **4.** vs. Gray- or white-haired; gray. Cf. *'āhina. Ko'u oho hina* (Kin. 44.29), my gray hairs. (PPN *sina.*) **5.** n. Hin (a Hebrew measure). (Puk. 29.40.) *Eng.* **6.** A goddess. (PPN *Sina.*)

hina-'ai-ka-malama. 1. Same as *na'ena'e,* shrubs or trees. **2.** *(Cap.)* n. Name of a legendary goddess. (PPN *Sina.*)

hina.hina. 1. n. The silversword *(Argyroxiphium sandwicense).* See *'āhinahina 2.* **2.** n. Florida moss *(Tillandsia usneoides),* an air plant, growing on tree branches and hanging baskets, forming masses of gray, thread-like stems and leaves. It is often substituted for the heliotrope (below) as the flower of Ka-hoʻolawe, and so called. (Neal 169–71.) Also *ʻāhinahina* and *ʻumiʻumi-o-Dole*, Dole's whiskers. **3.** n. Native heliotrope *(Heliotropium anomalum* var. *argenteum),* a low, spreading beach plant, with narrow, clustered, silvery leaves and small, white, fragrant flowers. As designated by the Territorial legislature in 1923, it represents Ka-hoʻolawe in the leis of the islands; it is used for tea and medicine. (Neal 717.) Called *nohonoho puʻuone* on Niʻihau. **4.** n. Native geraniums *(Geranium cuneatum* var. *tridens* and other native silvery geraniums), shrubs or small trees of the high mountains, with ovate, toothed leaves and red or white flowers. (Neal 469.) Cf. *nohoanu.* **5.** n. Native artemisia *(Artemisia australis).* See *ʻāhinahina 3.* **6.** vs. Gray, grayish. **7.** n. A variety of sugar cane, gray-green with a rosy flush, the whole covered with a wax bloom; pith dark brown; looks like *lahi 2.* (HP 224, 225.) **8.** Redup. of *hina 1. Rare.*

hina.hina ʻa·ala. n. Dusty miller *(Artemisia stelleriana),* a perennial herb in the daisy family, from northeastern Asia and eastern North America. The leaves and stems have a white, velvety covering and are aromatic. (Neal 852.)

hina.hina kaha.kai. n. A native Hawaiian plant of the water-leaf family *(Nama sandwicensis).* Niʻihau. Cf. Neal 712.

hina.hina kolo. Same as *pōhinahina 2,* the beach vitex.

hina.hina kua.hiwi. Same as *hinahina 5,* artemisia.

hina.hina kū kaha.kai. Same as *hinahina 3,* a beach *(kahakai)* heliotrope.

hina.hina kula. An unidentified plant.

hina.hina kū loa. An unidentified plant.

hī.naʻi. n. Basket or container made of braided *ʻie* vine, pandanus, or other material; a kind of basket fish trap, as used for shrimps, eels, *hīnāleu* and *ʻoʻopu.* Also *hīnaʻi hoʻoluʻuluʻu* or *hīnaʻi hoʻomoe a ʻia.* (PPN *fiinaki.)*

Hinaia.ʻele.ʻele. n. A Hawaiian star and month name. See *ʻumeke, month.*

hī.naʻi poe.poe. n. A round basket or container, as braided around a calabash.

hī.naʻi uea. n. Wire fish trap.

hina.kā. n. Handkerchief. *Eng.*

hina.kā ʻā.ʻī. n. Neckerchief. *Niʻihau.*

hina.kā paʻeke. n. Pocket handkerchief. *Niʻihau.*

hina.kea. n. Type of stone laid near the coral pile *(umu)* to attract fish; it was flat on one side and rounded on the other, and was believed to attract *manini* and young of other fish which resembled it in color. *Lit.,* white gray.

Hina-lani. n. Name of a star.

hī.nale. vs. Thin, sickly.

hina leʻa. vi. To blow favorably, as wind. See ex., *pēlā 1.*

hī.nā.lea. n. **1.** Small- to moderate-sized, brightly colored wrasses, family Labridae. In addition to those listed below, *hīnālea* may be qualified by the terms *ʻeleʻele, līpoa, lolo, nīʻau, nuku ʻiʻiwi, nuku ʻiʻiwi ʻula, nuku ʻiʻiwi uli, nuku loa, nuku loa ʻeleʻele.* Cf. *ʻōpule. Hīnālea* was eaten raw as an aftertaste for kava. It was prepared in the *iʻa hoʻomelu* fashion with *kukui* nuts and chili pepper; as this had a somewhat offensive smell, the phrase *ipu kai hīnālea,* dish of *hīnālea* sauce, was applied rudely to one with unpleasant breath, especially if he had the *iʻa kui,* nasal discharge. **2.** A variety of taro.

hī.nā.lea ʻaki.lolo. n. Yellowtail coris, *Coris gaimard,* up to 46 cm. See *ʻakilolo.*

hī.nā.lea ʻiʻiwi. n. Bird wrasse, *Gomphosus varius,* 23 cm.

hī.nā.lea lauwili. n. A saddle wrasse up to 20 cm. long *(Thalassoma duperreyi).*

hī.nā.lea lua.hine. n. A blacktail wrasse up to about 18 cm. long *(Thalassoma ballieui). Lit.,* old-lady wrasse.

Hina.liʻi. n. **1.** Name of a chief in whose time occurred a

famous deluge called *kai a ka Hinaliʻi;* the Biblical flood (Kin. 6.17). See saying *ʻiliki 1.* **2.** Name of a star that appears in the month of Hilinehu and follows in its course the star Polo-wehi-lani.

hī.nalo. Var. of *hīnano.*

Hina-mā.lai.lena. n. Name of a star, said to be the tutelary star of Hāna, Maui.

hina moe. vi. To lie down to sleep; to lie low, as of smoke; to drop dead.

hinana. n. Young of *ʻoʻopu,* a fish, formerly caught in nets and greatly relished. *ʻAi wale i ka hinana, ka iʻa kaulana o ka ʻāina,* eat readily of the *hinana,* the famous fish of the land. See saying, *pā ʻili.*

hina.nau.ō. Same as *hīnau. Rare.*

hī.nano. n. Male pandanus blossom. *Moena hīnano,* very fine mat made of the bracts of the *hīnano.* Cf. *ʻahu hīnano.* (PPN *singano,* PCP *hi(i)nano.)*

hinao. n. Type of *pāʻū* (no data).

Hina.ona-lai.lena. Var. of *Hina-mālailena,* a star.

hina.pā. Var. of *hinapē.*

hina.pē. vs. Too weak to stand alone.

hina.pū. n. **1.** A rare native variety of upland taro, with green leaves, reddish leaf juncture *(piko),* dark-green petioles, and white corm. (HP 18, 32.) Perhaps same as *lauloa uliuli.* **2.** A variety of sweet potato.

hina pū. vi. To fall together, of several; to topple.

hī.nau. vs. Thin, fine, as hair. Probably obsolete except in names.

hina.ʻula. n. A kind of seaweed.

hina ulu. vs. To begin to gray, of hair.

hī.nawa.nawa.ū. Same as *hīnawe, nānawaū, hīnewane-waū.*

hī.nawe. Same as *hīnawenawe.*

hī.nawe.nawe. vs. Thin, feeble, weak, spindling, slender, puny, debilitated.

hine. vs. Gaudy, showy, splendid.

-hine. Female, feminine. Cf. *wahine, kaikamahine, kaikuahine, luahine.* (PPN *fine.)*

hine.hine.ʻula. n. A moss listed by Rock.

Hine.kū, Hinedu. nvs. Hindu. *Eng.*

hī.newa.newa, hī.newa.newa.ū. Var. of *hīnawenawe.*

hini. vs. Weak, feeble, delicate. (PCP *(f,s)ini.)*

hini.hini. 1. Redup. of *hini;* indistinct, faint, as a voice. (PCP *(f,s)ini(f,s)ini.)* **2.** n. A variety of land shell. See *hinihini konouli, hinihini kua mauna.* See ex., *māpu. Mehe leo no ka hinihini, ka pā hane i ke ahe mālie* (chant), like the voice of a *hinihini,* blown softly by the gentle breeze. **3.** n. Cooked greens, as of *ʻāheahea, pōpolo, pakai.*

hini.hini kono.uli. n. A land shell *(Succinea casta orophila).*

hini.hini kua mauna. n. A land shell *(Succinea casta).*

hini.hini ʻula. n. An upland moss (no data).

hinu. nvs. Oil, grease, ointment; oily, greasy; smooth and polished, lustrous, slick. Cf. *maka hinu. Puaʻa hinu,* a greasy pig [human sacrifice]. (PPN *sinu;* cf. Fijian.)

hinua. Pas/imp. of *hinu. I hinua i ke kukui o Lilikoʻi a paheʻe,* polished smooth with the *kukui* of Lilikoʻi.

hinu.hinu. 1. Intensification of *hinu;* bright, glossy, shining, lustrous, glittering, as of polished stones or shells; splendid; splendor. *A me ka ʻaila hoʻi, i mea e hinuhinu ai kona maka* (Hal. 104.15), and oil to make his face to shine. **hoʻo.hinu.hinu.** To shine, polish; to show off (Kel. 130). *Keiki hoʻohinuhinu kāmaʻa,* shoe shiner, bootblack. *Hoʻohinuhinu mikiʻao,* fingernail polish. *E hoʻohinuhinu ana ʻo Ke-ola i kona kāmaʻa,* Ke-ola is polishing his shoes. (PPN *sinusinu.)* **2.** Var. of *hiluhilu.* **hoʻo.hinu.hinu.** Var. of *hoʻohiluhilu. Ua hoʻohinuhinu loa ʻo Makaliʻi i kāna wahine, ā ua nani loa* (For. 4:81), Makaliʻi bedecks his wife and [she is] very beautiful.

hinu.puaʻa. 1. Same as *maiʻa ʻeleʻele* or *ʻeleʻele,* a mountain banana with shiny black trunk. See also *hinu.* **2.** n. A native variety of upland taro. Also *ʻeleʻele.*

hio. 1. nvi. A sweep or gust of wind; to blow in gusts.

(PPN *fio.*) **2.** n. Inside corners of a house, said to be so named because ghosts came whistling in at the corners. *Hio kala* (FS 29), inside angle of gables. **3.** vi. To break wind silently. Cf. *pūhiʻu.*

hiō. vi. To fall sideways, lean, slant, slope, incline, leaning, oblique, diagonal. See *pahiō, wele 1. Kaha hiō,* an x signifying "times" in multiplication. hoʻo.hiō. Caus/sim.

hī.ʻō. vi. Restless, active, flighty. See ex., *palawili.*

hio.hio. 1. vi. To whistle softly; to blow softly, draw in the breath, as of one eating hot food. **2.** nvi. Gibberish; to jabber. See *hiohio haole. Namu hiohio,* English talk. **3.** n. Lure for trolling, said to be named for its whistling sound tripping over the water.

hiō.hiō. vi. To lean every which way. hoʻo.hiō.hiō. Redup. of *hoʻohiō.*

hiʻo.hiʻo. vs. Ruddy, bright red. *Rare.*

hio.hio haole. vi. To jibber jabber in the white man's language, so called because English seemed full of whistling *(hiohio),* sibilant sounds. *Palalē ka leo o ka ua i luna o ka nahele, e hiohio haole ana* (chant for Ka Haku o Hawaiʻi), indistinct voice of rain on the plants, shishing English.

hiʻo.hiʻo.lani. vt. To level off, as a flower bed. (Kep. 157.)

hio.hiolo. Redup. of *hiolo.* hoʻo.hio.hiolo. Caus/sim.; to hang or drape festively.

hio.hiona. Redup. of *hiona.*

hiʻo.hiʻona. n. Features, as of a face or landscape; sight, aspect.

hiʻo.lani. vi. To sleep, lie at ease, lounge, relax (this word sometimes replaces *moe* in poetry because *moe* suggests the sleep of death). *Ua kau ke keha i ka uluna, ua hiʻolani i ka moena* (UL 130), the head rests on the pillow, stretching out on the mat [relax after work is done].

hiolo. nvi. To tumble down, collapse; overthrown, defeated; collapse, landslide, falling. *E hiolo ana nā kapu kahiko,* the ancient taboos collapse. hoʻo.hiolo. To overthrow, demolish, raze.

hiolo.hia. Pas/imp. of *hiolo.* hoʻo.hiolo.hia. Caus/sim.

hiona. n. Leaning, slanting. *ʻAno ʻē hoʻi ka hiona o kēlā kumu niu,* what a peculiar angle that coconut tree has.

hiʻona. n. General appearance, as of a person; impression. Cf. *hiʻohiʻona. Pehea kāu hiʻona ʻana i kēia mea?* How does this appear to you?

hī.ʻō.ʻō. Redup. of *hīʻō.*

hipa. 1. vs. Var. of *hepa,* imbecilic. **2.** n. Sheep. *Eng.* (Ioane 10.2.) *Hulu hipa,* wool. *ʻIli hipa,* sheepskin. *ʻĪlio kiaʻi hipa,* sheep dog. *ʻIʻo hipa,* mutton. *Kahu hipa,* shepherd.

hipa.hipa. 1. Same as *puka wai,* a coconut eye that is or may be pierced for drinking. **2.** interj. Hip, hip, hurrah! Cheers! *(Eng.,* hip.) *ʻEkolu hipahipa no ka mōʻī,* three cheers for the king!

Hipa-kāne. n. The star Aries.

hipa kāne. n. Ram. *Lit.,* male sheep. *Hipa kāne ʻakolu ona makahiki* (Kin. 15.9), three-year-old ram. *Hipa kāne wāwahi* (Ezek. 4.2), battering ram.

hipa keiki. n. Lamb.

hipopo.kamu, hipopotamu. n. Hippopotamus. *Eng.*

hipū. n. Resting place, as in the shelter of a tree or cave. *Rare.*

hī.puka. n. A concealed snare for plovers. *Rare.*

hī.puʻu. nvt. **1.** Knot, bond, fastening; to tie a knot. *Hīpuʻu o ka male,* bonds of matrimony. hoʻo.hī.puʻu. To tie, bind. **2.** Tied bundle, purse (Sol. 1.14, Isa. 3.22); to bundle up.

hī.puʻu.puʻu. Redup. of *hīpuʻu 1, 2.*

hiu. 1. vi. To throw or fling violently; to haul energetically with ropes; to get into action, as play or sport; to pursue with energy, as love-making. *Hiu ā wela,* ardent and persistent love-making; to take by storm. *Hiu aku nei ʻoia i ka puʻupuʻu,* he swung into action with his fists. *E kū i ka malo ā hiu* (Malo 146), stand up with [your] *malo* and go to it. *Hiu nō au ā naʻu ʻoe,* I'll sweep you off your feet. hoʻo.hiu. Caus/sim. (PCP

fiu.) **2.** vt. To elevate, hoist, as by block and tackle. hoʻo.hiu. Caus/sim. *Ua hoʻohiu ʻia ka moku i luna o ke alahukimoku,* the ship was lifted onto the marine railway. **3.** n. Stones used in games of *kōnane, kinipeki,* and *āneo,* usually polished and flat.

hiʻu. 1. n. Hind part or tail section of a fish, considered less delicious than the head or front section. See saying, *pau 1. Hiʻu kahi,* a single fishtail; limited knowledge *(fig.).* (PPN *siku.*) **2.** n. Caudal fin. **3.** vi. To break wind. Same as *pūhiʻu.* **4.** vi. To motion with the hands in a way destructive to the addressee. (Kam. 64:141.)

hiua. 1. n. A game something like checkers, played on a board with five squares. **2.** vs. Menstrual. *He koko hiua,* menstrual blood.

hiu.hiu. Redup. of *hiu 1, 2;* to pelt repeatedly; to tug, lift again and again.

hiʻu.hiʻu. n. Last bits of odds and ends; remnants of matting strips that must be cut off after plaiting is finished; ends of knots in plaiting; wispy end of a braid. Cf. *hiʻu,* tail. (PPN *sikusiku.*)

hiʻu.iʻa. n. Fishtail fern *(Nephrolepis biserrata* cv. *furcans),* a kind of sword fern, with forked divisions (pinnae). In Kaʻū, leis are made by combining pinnae of this fern (or whole frond) with flower sprays of *wāpine* (lemon verbena). (Neal 14, 15.)

hiʻu.kā. n. Whole fish used as bait for trolling. *Rare.*

hiʻu kahi. n. A single fishtail. *Fig.,* limited knowledge.

hiʻu.kole. n. A fresh-water *ʻoʻopu* fish with a pinkish tail *(hiʻu kole).* It is taboo to some because it is believed related to the *moʻo* lizard gods. Also *ʻalamoʻo, hiʻuʻula,* and *nuʻukole.*

hiʻu waʻa. n. Canoe stern. *Fig.,* a straight tree suitable for a canoe.

hiʻu.wai. 1. n. Water purification festivities on the second night of the month of Welehu (near the end of the year). The people bathed and frolicked in the sea or stream after midnight, then put on their finest tapa and ornaments for feasting and games. (Kep. 97, 193–4.) **2.** vs. "Water-tailed," said of one allegedly descended from a shark. (GP 10-1.)

hiʻu.wī.wī. n. A kind of *ʻahi,* a tuna fish. *Lit.,* thin tail.

hiwa. 1. nvs. Entirely black, as of pigs offered to the gods, a desirable blackness contrasting with *uli* and *ʻeleʻele,* which have pejorative connotations. See *polohiwa* and its associations with the god Kāne. (PCP *(f,s)iwa.*) **2.** vs. Choice. See *hiwahiwa.* **3.** A term qualifying coconuts and kava; see *niu, ʻawa.* **4.** See *ʻAeʻae-a-hiwa.*

hī.waʻa.waʻa. vs. Corpulent, fat. Cf. *ʻawaʻawaʻa 2.*

hiwa.hiwa. nvs. Precious, beloved, esteemed, petted, darling, indulged; favorite. See ex., *luxury. Ka Mesia, ka hiwahiwa a ke Akua* (Luka 23.35), the Messiah, the chosen of God. hoʻo.hiwa.hiwa. To honor, adorn, decorate; to display, as the flag; to treat as a favorite; festive. *He mea hoʻohiwahiwa i ke akua,* a thing to honor the gods. *ʻO ka mea hoʻohiwahiwa i kāna kauā mai kona wā ʻuʻuku mai* (Sol. 29.21), he who delicately brings up his servant from his childhood.

hiwa.kea. n. An all-black pig with white hoofs and white tips of tail, ears, and nose.

hiwa lani. n. Esteemed chief; beloved child or favorite; royal favorite.

hiwa paʻa. nvs. Coal-black, entirely black, solid-black. (A *puaʻa hiwa* might have a few white hairs, but none at all were on a *puaʻa hiwa paʻa.*)

hiwi. 1. vi. Skinny, bony, thin, angular. Cf. *iwi.* hoʻo.hiwi. To be downright skin and bones. **2.** n. Sharp ridge of a mountain. Cf. more common *kuahiwi.* (PNP *siwi.*)

hiwi.hiwi. Redup. and intensifier of *hiwi 1.*

hō. 1. vt. To give, transfer, go (followed by directionals). (Hal. 15.5.) No caus/sim. derivation with *hō* has been noted. For the word often written *hooho,* see *oho. E hō mai i ka ʻai* (Kin. 43.31), set on food. *Hō mai i wai noʻu,* give me some water. *Ē ke aloha, hō mai he leo* (FS 275), O my love, give your voice. *E hō aʻe kāua,* let us go. *Hō aʻe kāua i ka ihu o ka lio i ka ulu kukui*

In causative/simulative forms beginning with ho-, hō-, ho'-, *or* hō', *delete the prefix and look for the stem.*

(song), let's turn the nose of the horse toward the candlenut grove. (PPN *foaki,* PCP *soo:* cf. Penrhyn *soo,* Yasuda 15.) **2.** vi. To wheeze, breathe hard. **3.** n. Hoe, colter of a plow. *Eng. Me kāna hō, a me kāna ko'ilipi* (1 Sam. 13.20, with his colter and his axe.

ho-. Marker of the caus/sim.; same as *ho'o-,* but commonly found before words beginning with a glottal stop followed by a long vowel, as *'āpuka, ho'āpuka.*

hō-. Caus/sim. marker before glottal stop and short vowel or before long vowel or vowels, as *'ike, hō'ike, 'ā, hō'ā, hō'ā'ā.* Gram. 6.4.

ho'-. Marker of the caus/sim.; same as *ho'o-,* but commonly found before words beginning with a- or e- (or sometimes i-), with lengthening of the first vowel of the word, as *ano, ho'āno; emi, ho'ēmi; inu, ho'īnu,* or before words beginning with a long vowel, as *ō, ho'ō.*

hō'-. Marker of the caus/sim.; same as *ho'o-;* occasionally found before words beginning with i-, as *ikaika, hō'ikaika.*

hoa. 1. n. Companion, friend, associate, colleague, comrade, partner, mate, peer, fellow, antagonist (if followed by a word such as *kaua* or *paio*). Cf. *hoahānau, hoa hele, hoaloha, hoa paio,* and saying, *cold 1. Kona hoa,* his friend. *Hoa o ka Hale o nā Lunamaka'āinana,* member of the House of Representatives. *ho'o.hoa.* To make friends. (PPN *soa.*) **2.** nvt. To tie, bind, secure, rig; rigging, lashing. See *hoa wa'a.* **3.** nvt. To strike with a stick or club; to club; a club. (PPN *foa.*) **4.** Same as *mamo 1,* the honey-creeper.

-hoa. ho'o.hoa. To challenge, dare, provoke; daring, defiant. Cf. *uahoa. Ho'ohoa nā manu hanina,* the quiet birds are daring. *Hana ka iwi a kanaka makua, ho'ohoa mai,* get maturity into the bones before issuing a challenge.

hō.'ā. 1. vt. To set on fire, burn, ignite, etc. See *'ā 1.* **2.** vt. To drive, as cattle or fish; to herd. See -*'ā.* **3.** vi. To talk much. See *ā 1.* **4.** See *hō'ā īpuka hale.*

hō.'a'a. See *a'a 1,* root, vein, etc.

hō.'a'ā. vt. To kindle, light. See *'a'ā 1.*

hō.'ā.'ā. vi. To blunder, stray. See *'ā'ā,* demented.

hō.'ā ahi. v. To kindle fire.

hō.'a'ahu. vt. To clothe. See *'a'ahu.*

hoa 'ai. Eating or dinner companion.

hoa.'āina. n. Tenant, caretaker, as on a *kuleana. Ou po'e hoa'āina* (FS 141), your tenants.

hō.'a'aka. vs. Surly. See *'a'aka 1.*

hoa ali'i. n. Companion of a chief, fellow chief, chief descended from the god Kāne (For. 6:266). *Fig.,* the gods.

hoa aloha. Var. spelling of *hoaloha.*

hō.'a'ā maka. v. To stare, etc. See *'a'ā maka.*

hō.'a'ano. vt. To boast, defy. See *'a'ano.*

hō.'a'apu. See *'a'apu.*

hō.'ae. 1. vt. To make fine, soft. See *'ae 3.* **2.** vi. To rise. See *'ae 4.*

hō.'a'e. vt. To break taboo. See *'a'e.*

hō.'ae'a. vt. To cause to wander. See *'ae'a.*

ho'āe.ae. n. A chant with lengthened vowels. See *aeae.*

hō.'aha. vt. To braid. See *'aha 2.*

hō.'aha.'aha. Same as *'aha'aha 2.*

hoa hana. n. Fellow worker, colleague, partner, accomplice.

hoahā.nau. n. Cousin; brother or sister, as a church member. *Kona hoahānau,* his cousin. *Hoahānau Kamika,* Smith Brothers [as the name of a firm].

hoa hanauna. n. Relative of one's own generation.

hoa hau.mana. n. Schoolmate.

hoa hele. n. Traveling companion, fellow traveler. (In Iosua 14.8 *"ko'u hoa hele"* seems to be the Hawaiian translation of "my brethren.")

ho'ā.hewa. vt. To blame, condemn. See *'āhewa.*

ho'āhi.ahi. See *ahiahi,* evening.

ho'āho. See *aho,* breath.

hō.'aho. See *'aho,* thatch.

hoa.hoa. Redup. of *hoa 3;* a rounded tapa beater (also called *hohoa, pepehi*); rapid beating, striking, as of tapa or pandanus leaves; a stick beater for washing clothes. *Fig.,* bad-tempered. *Keu ho'i kēia a ke kanaka hoahoa,* this person certainly beats the beater [in rage]. *ho'o.hoa.hoa.* Caus/sim.

hoa.hoaka. 1. Redup. of *hoaka 3–5.* **2.** n. Comb of a rooster.

hoa holo.moku. n. Shipmate.

ho'āho.nui. See *ahonui.*

ho'āhu. vt. To collect, pile. See *ahu.*

hoa.hui. n. Associate.

hoai. n. Joining, suture, joint. *Rare.* Cf. *hoa 2,* and below.

hō.'ai. vt. To feed. See *'ai,* food.

hō.'ai.'ē. See *'ai'ē.*

hoai kala. n. Lambdoidal suture.

hoai kau.paku. n. Sagital suture.

hoa ikū. Similar to *hoa ali'i.* (PH 53, 65.)

hō.'ai.lona. See -*'ailona.*

hō.'ai.lona lana.kila. n. Sign or emblem of victory. See -*'ailona.*

hoai maha. n. Temporal suture.

hoai manawa. n. Coronal suture.

hoa 'inau. n. Sweetheart, mate, spouse.

hō.'ā 'ī.puka hale. Same as *hoaka 'īpuka hale.*

hoaka. 1. n. Crescent; arch, as over door of ancient house (Kep. 101); crescent-shaped design at base of temple drum; crest, as on a helmet. **2.** *(Cap.)* n. Second day of the month. (Kep. 101.) (PCP *(F,S)oata,* cf. Easter *o'ata.*) **3.** nvi. Brightness; shining, glittering, splendid; to glitter, shine, flash as lightning, become daylight; to flame. *Fig.,* glory. Also *'oaka. Lele hoaka,* to fly glittering, as fire sparks. (PCP *(f,s)oata.*) **4.** v. To cast a shadow; to brandish, as a spear (2 Sam. 23.18), to drive away, ward off, frighten. Cf. *aka 1. Mai hele ma'ō e hoaka ai i ke kai o holo ka i'a,* don't go over there and cast your shadow in the sea lest the fish run away. **5.** vt. To open, as the mouth. (Hoik. 13.6.) **6.** n. Spirit, apparition, ghost (For. 6:370). *Lele ka hoaka,* the spirit has flown [of death; the glory of the land has departed]. **7.** n. Disease of the abdomen, perhaps appendicitis, rupture (followed by a qualifier). See *hoaka 'īpuka hale, hoaka kākala.* Other qualifiers reported are *hāwele, kū, kū kahi, kū lua.*

hō.'aka. See *'aka,* to laugh.

ho'ā.kaaka, hoakaaka. vt. To clarify. See *akaaka,* clear.

hō.'aka.'aka. See *'aka'aka,* to laugh.

ho'ā.kahele. See *akahele.*

hoaka 'ī.puka hale. n. Ruptured appendix, appendicitis (not certain).

hoaka kā.kala. n. A disease (ruptured appendix?).

hoaka.kala. 1. Bracelet of tusks of hog or dog. **2.** Same as *hoaka kākala.*

hoa kā.kau. Coauthor, writing associate.

hoaka.ke'a. n. Arch over a door, lintel.

hoa kā.ko'o. n. Ally, supporter.

hoa kama.li'i. n. Childhood playmate.

hoa kanaka. n. Fellow man. *E 'ike iā kāua hoa kanaka, o kipa hewa ke aloha i ka 'īlio* (chant), recognize us [who are] fellow men, lest love be wasted on a dog.

hoa kaua. n. Fellow soldier, enemy.

hoa kā.unu. n. Lover, delightful companion.

ho'ā.kea. See *ākea.*

hō.'aki. See *'aki,* to nip.

ho'ā.koa.koa. See *'ākoakoa.*

hoa kua. n. Companion of a god, godly companion.

hoa kū.kā, hoa kū.kā.kū.kā. n. Consultant, counselor, adviser, one with whom one confers and deliberates. *Kona hoa kūkākūkā* (Rom. 11.34), his counselor.

hoa kula. n. Schoolmate.

In causative/simulative forms beginning with ho-, hō-, ho'-, *or* hō', *delete the prefix and look for the stem.*

ho'āla. See *ala,* to waken, rise up.
hō.'ala. See *'ala,* fragrant.
hoa.launa. n. Neighbor, close associate or friend (2 Sam. 15.37).
hoa lawe.hana. n. Fellow laborer or worker, helper.
hoa lawe pū. n. Sharer, partner. *Mau hoa lawe pū i kona hewa* (Hoik. 18.4), partakers of her sins.
hō.'ale.'ale. See *'ale'ale.*
ho'āli. See *-ali.*
ho'ā.lia. See *alia,* to wait.
ho'āli.ali. See *aliali,* clear.
hō.'ali.'ali. See *'ali'ali,* scarred.
hoa li'i. Same as *hoa ali'i.*
ho'ā.li'i. See *ali'i,* chief.
hoa like. n. Companion or contemporary of equal status.
hō.'alo. See *'alo,* to dodge.
hoa loa'a. n. Fellow sharer, receiver, partaker.
hoa.loha, hoa aloha. n. Friend. *Lit.,* beloved companion. Cf. *aloha. Kona hoaloha,* his friend. **ho'o.-hoa.loha.** To make friends, be friendly, befriend.
ho'ā.loha.loha. See *ālohaloha.*
hō.'alu. See *'alu,* depression.
hō.'alu.'alu. See *'alu'alu,* loose.
hoa luhi. n. Fellow worker, especially one helping to rear a child. Cf. *luhi.*
hoa lumi. n. Roommate.
hō.'ama. See *-'ama.*
hoa maka.'āi.nana. n. Fellow citizen.
ho'ā.mana. See *-'āmana.*
hoa moe. n. Sleeping companion, bedfellow.
hoana. 1. nvt. Hone, whetstone, grindstone; to rub, grind. (PCP *(f,s)oana.*) **2.** vt. To brandish, as a whip; to threaten. *Hoana e hō'eha,* assault and battery. **3.** n. Joining, joint, binding. See *hoa 2.* **4.** See *puhi hoana.* **5.** Same as *kōkala,* porcupine fish.
ho'āna. See *ana,* to measure.
ho'ana.'ē. See *ana'ē.*
hoana ka'a. n. Grindstone, rolling grindstone.
ho'āni. See *ani,* to beckon.
ho'āno. See *ano,* awe.
hō.'ano. See *'ano,* somewhat.
hoa noho. n. Neighbor, one who lives with or near another.
ho'ānu. See *anu,* cool.
ho'ā.nu'u.nu'u. See *'ānu'unu'u.*
ho'āo. n. Marriage. See *ao 1,* light.
ho'ā'o. vt. To try, taste. See *a'o,* instruction.
hoa 'ō.lelo. vt. Companion with whom one converses or consults.
hoa pa'a.hana. n. Fellow worker.
hoa pā.'ani. n. Playmate.
hoa paio. Opponent, antagonist, adversary, enemy, rival.
hoa pā.oni.oni. n. Enemy, contestant, rival.
hō.'ā.pī. See *-āpī.*
hoa pili. n. Close, intimate, or personal friend.
ho'ā.pipi. See *'āpipi.*
ho'ā.pono. vt. To approve. See *'āpono.* Cf. *hoa pono,* true friend.
ho'āu. See *au 11,* to set; and *-au.*
hō.'au. See *'au,* to swim.
hō.'auana, ho'o.'auwana. See *'auana,* to wander.
hō.'au.'au. See *'au'au,* to bathe.
hō.'au.he'e. See *'auhe'e.*
hō.'āu.huli. See *auhuli.*
hō.'au.li'i. See *'auli'i,* dainty.
hoa una. n. One accompanying a messenger.
ho'ā.una. vi. To flock, collect. See *'āuna.*
hō.'au.waha. See *'auwaha,* ditch.
hō.'awa. 1. n. All Hawaiian species of the genus *Pittosporum,* trees and shrubs with narrow leaves clustered at branch ends, and thick-valved fruits containing many seeds surrounded by a sticky substance (Neal 382–4); considered poisonous (Kam. 64:124, 140). Cf. *'a'awa hua kukui.* Also *hā'awa.* **2.** See *'awa,* bitter.
hoa wa'a. n. **1.** Canoe companion, mate. **2.** Canoe rigging, tackle.
hō.'awa lau nui. n. A kind of *hō'awa (Pittosporum kauaiense),* a tree to 12 m high, found only on Kaua'i, with large leaves to 25 by 8 cm, more or less downy beneath, and with quadrangular fruits 1.3 cm in diameter.
ho'ā.wāwa. See *awāwa,* valley.
hō.'awe. vt. To carry. See *'awe,* pack, burden.
hoe. 1. nvt. Paddle, oar; to paddle, row. *Fig.,* to travel, get to work, continue working. *Kāna hoe* (FS 21), his paddle. *Hoe aku i ka wa'a,* paddle ahead the canoe [do your share; continue; keep going]. **ho'o.hoe.** Caus/sim.; to have a canoe paddled. (PPN *fohe.*) **2.** vi. To draw in the breath and expel it with a whistling sound, as when tired. **3.** n. A bird reported by Kepelino as being the size of the *'ō'ō* and black and gray.
hoea. Pas/imp. of *hoe 1;* let's get started, go ahead.
hō.'ea. vi. To arrive. *Pōmaika'i e hō'ea mai ana,* blessings to come.
hoe-a-Mā.ui. n. Probably same as *'ēkaha 'ula* fern, but according to some it is *Elaphoglossum pellucidum,* a smaller *Elaphoglossum* than the *'ēkaha 'ula. Lit.,* Māui's paddle.
hō.'eha. vt. To hurt. See *'eha.*
hoe.ha'a. Same as *'oeha'a. Fig.,* unreliable, unstable. *Hoeha'a noho'i ua O'ahu maka 'ewa'ewa,* unreliable are the O'ahu people who avert the eyes.
hō.'eha.pu'u.wai. n. A West African vine, the bleeding heart *(Clerodendrum thomsonae),* with red and white flowers, grown for ornament. (Neal 730–1.) *Lit.,* heart aching.
ho'ē.heu. See *'ēheu,* wing.
hoe.hoe. 1. Redup. of *hoe 1;* paddling back and forth. (PNP *foefoe.*) **2.** Redup. of *hoe 2;* a plaintive prolonged sound, as of the nose flute. Cf. *hoene 1.* **3.** n. Shoulder blade (used after *iwi*). **4.** See *lipi hoehoe.*
hoe.hoena. Same as *hoe 2.*
hoe.hoene. 1. Redup. of *hoene 1. Kai hoehoene i nā pali* (chant), sea singing softly to the cliffs. **2.** To pierce the ear lobes with acid. (And.) **3.** Poor, destitute, sick. (And.)
hoe.hoe-pā.kea. n. A name for a Ni'ihau *pāwehe* design in plaiting.
ho'ēhu. vt. To drive, stir. See *-ehu.*
hō.'eka. vt. To soil. See *'eka.*
hoe kala. n. A paddle with a blade narrower than the *hoe nanue. Lit.,* pointed paddle.
hō.'eke.ke'i. vt. To shorten. See *'ekeke'i.*
hō.'ele.'ele. vt. To blacken. See *'ele'ele.*
hō.'eleu. vt. To animate. See *'eleu.*
hoelo. vt. To stir, poke, as a fire. (PH 42.)
ho'ēmi. vt. To reduce, diminish, cheapen. See *emi 1, 2.*
hoena. n. Paddling. *Aia nō i kāu hoena,* it's up to you to paddle [to decide, start].
hoe nanue. Same as *hoe nenue.*
hoene. 1. nvi. A soft sweet sound, as of song; to sound softly, rustle, sough, as the wind. **2.** Var. of *'owā 5. Mākahi hoene,* a net mesh somewhat larger than the width of a finger. **3.** nvt. To use a douche or enema; enema, medicine, injection, abortion. *Nā hoene wai 'akika ho'omake 'ano'ano puponika,* acid solution for killing bubonic germs.
hoe nenue. n. A type of paddle named for *nenue* fish, with broad and round blade.
hō.'epa. vt. To deceive. See *'epa.*
hō.'eu. 1. vt. To stir up. See *'eu.* **2.** n. A bird name (no data).

In causative/simulative forms beginning with **ho-, hō, ho'-,** *or* **hō',** *delete the prefix and look for the stem.*

hoe uli. n. Steering paddle or oar, rudder, helm. *He hoe uli,* just a steering paddle [a wagging tongue].
hō.'ewa. See *'ewa,* crooked.
hoe wa'a. nv. Oarsman, paddler; to paddle a canoe. *'Elua nō āna mau hoe wa'a,* he has only two paddlers.
hohani. Same as *hani 1. Hohani me ka 'ō'ō i ka pu'e,* soften the hill with the digging stick.
hō.hē, ho'o.hē. nvs. Cowardly; coward, cowardice. (FS 81.) *He kaua kamali'i, he hōhē wale,* a battle of children, just cowards [quarrels of children are not worth worrying about].
hohiu. n. A native fern *(Dryopteris glabra)* with rather finely divided fronds.
hohō. vi. To snore, snort, bray, heehaw, splash, gurgle, breathe hard, draw in mucus. **ho'o.hohō.** Caus/sim.; to cause a snort.
hohoa. Same as *hoahoa,* tapa beater, washing stick.
hoho.ho'i. Redup. and plural of *ho'i 1,* to leave.
hoho'i. Redup. of *ho'i 1,* to leave; to return often.
hohoi.ea. vs. Wheezy. Cf. For. 4:169.
hohoka. Redup. of *hoka 1, 2.* **ho'o.hohoka.** Caus/sim.
hohola. vi. To spread out, unfold, unfurl, as tapa, mats, clouds, wings; to extend, stretch, diffuse. Cf. *hola, ma'ihohola, pāhola.* (PPN *fofola.)*
hohole. Redup. of *hole 1, 2.* (PCP *sosole.)*
hoholo. Redup. of *holo,* to run, sail. **ho'o.hoholo.** Caus/sim. *Ho'ohoholo 'ia akula ka hūpē i loko,* snuffle up mucus.
hoholu. Redup. of *holu 1. Hoholu ka 'āhihi i ka makani* (chant), the *'āhihi* shrub sways in the wind.
hohoma. Redup. of *homa.*
hohono. nvi. Acrid odor, unpleasant body odor of perspiration; to smell thus. Cf. *honohono 5; pepeiao hohono.* **ho'o.hohono.** To cause or produce such an odor. (PPN *sosongo.)*
hohonu. nvs. Deep, profound; depth, soundings. *He kanaka hohonu o ka 'ike,* a man with profound knowledge. **ho'o.hohonu.** To deepen. (Probably PPN *fonu,* full, as of liquid; PCP *fofonu,* deep.)
hohopa. vs. Tall, thin. *Rare.*
hoi. 1. n. Bitter yam *(Dioscorea bulbifera,* synonym *D. sativa),* a vine with cylindrical stem, heart-shaped leaves, small tuberous root, round aerial tubers. The tubers, used only in times of famine, need long washing to make them fit to eat. (HP 167, Neal 230.) Called *pi'oi* on Kaua'i. *Ua ua paha, ke ulu nei ka hoi,* perhaps it's been raining, the *hoi* is growing [said when someone looks happy, a play on *hoi 1* and *hoi 2*]. See *Kaulu-hoi.* (PPN *soi.)* 2. Same as *hoihoi. Kū 'ole i ka hoi,* not suiting; displeasing.
ho'i. 1. vi. To leave, go or come back; to cause to come back. Cf. *ho'i hou. Ho'i loa,* to go or come permanently. *E ho'i ana au,* I'm leaving. *O ho'i,* go then. *E ho'i mai,* come back. *'A'ole e ho'i kō wahine ia mau hana* (FS 273), these things won't cause your wife to return. (PPN *foki.)* 2. vi. To enter, as an institution or last resting place. *Ua ho'i i ke kula,* has entered school. 3. n. A parting chant to which hula dancers dance as they leave the audience. 4. nvt. Marriage of a chief with the daughter of a brother or sister; to do so (a means of increasing the rank of the offspring). (Malo 55.) 5. Part. intensifying preceding base. See *kāho'i, noho'i,* Gram. 7.5. *'Elua ho'i,* just two; two indeed. *'A'ohe ho'i au i lohe,* I certainly did not hear. (PPN *foki.)* 6. part. Also, too, besides. (Gram. 7.5.) *'A'ole ho'i,* neither. (PPN *foki.)* 7. Part. expressing doubt, uncertainty. (Gram. 7.5.) *Pehea ho'i,* how indeed, I don't know. *He mea aha ho'i!* What indeed for!
hoi'a. n. Ni'ihau name of a sea tern.
ho'ia. Pas/imp. of *ho'i,* to leave.
ho'i.hā. Intensive of *ho'i 5* (often written as two words). (Gram. 7.5.) *E hele ho'ihā kāua,* well, let's go then.

Maika'i ho'ihā, very good indeed. *I Hawai'i ho'ihā me Pele e noho ai* (FS 239), then stay at Hawai'i with Pele.
hō.'ihi. See *'ihi,* sacred.
ho'iho. See *iho,* to go down, and *-iho.*
hoi.hoi. nvi. Pleased, interesting, entertaining, happy, joyful, amused; pleasure, happiness, joy, delight, enjoyment, interest, cheerfulness (Rom. 12.8). *Hoihoi 'ole,* unpleasant, unenthusiastic, unhappy, uninterested, dispirited, dull, boring, to dislike. *Mea e hoihoi ai,* treat, pleasure. **ho'o.hoi.hoi.** To entertain, amuse, charm, delight, encourage, please.
ho'i.ho'i. vt. To return, send back, restore. Cf. *ho'i 1. E ho'iho'i aku 'oe i ka lio iā Kale,* take the horse back to Charles. *Pēlā anei 'oukou e ho'iho'i aku ai iā Iēhowa?* (Kanl. 32.6) Do you thus requite Jehovah? (PNP *fokifoki.)*
ho'i.ho'i ea. nv. Restoration, as of sovereignty; to restore sovereignty. *Lā Ho'iho'i Ea,* Restoration Day.
ho'i hope. vi. To go back, return, retreat, revert, backslide, deteriorate morally. (In Ier. 3.22 *ho'i hope* seems to be the translation of "faithless" and "faithlessness" and in Ier. 6.28 the translation of "revolter.") *Po'e lālā ho'i hope,* backsliding members [of a church].
ho'i hou. 1. vi. To go or come back, return. 2. n. Repeat sign in music.
hō.'ī.'ī. See *'ī'ī,* tight.
hō.'ī.'ī. See *'ī'ī,* sour.
hō.'ikaika. See *ikaika,* strong.
ho'i.kau. part. Pert. Very, great (often written as two words). *He u'i ho'i kau,* very beautiful indeed. (Gram. 7.5.)
Ho'i-ka-u'i-o-Mā-noa-ua-ahi.ahi. See *E-ho'i-ka-u'i-o-Mānoa-ua-ahiahi.*
hō.'ike. v. To show, exhibit. For the many important meanings see *'ike.*
Hō.'ike 'Ana. n. Revelation (Biblical). See *'ike.*
hō.'ike honua. n. Geography.
hō.'ike.'ike. n. Display. See *'ike'ike* for the many meanings.
hoi kua.hiwi. n. A native vine *(Smilax sandwicensis),* growing wild in the mountains; the leaves are heart-shaped, shiny, with longitudinal veins, much like the *hoi* but bearing tendrils; the roots are tuberous and not palatable. (Neal 211.) Also *aka'awa.*
hō.'ike manawa. n. Chronology.
hō.'ī.lewa. n. Pain of hunger. *Rare.* Cf. *houpo lewalewa.*
hō.'ili. See *ili 1, 2.*
hō.'ili. See *-'ili.*
hō.'ili.hune. See *'ilihune,* poor.
hō.'ili.'ili. vt. To collect. See *'ili'ili 2.*
ho'i.lina. n. Heir. See *ilina.*
ho'i.lo. 1. v. Var. spelling of *ho'oilo.* See *ilo 2* and *-ilo. Ka hale ho'ilo* (Ier. 36.22), the winter house. 2. n. Land term of unknown meaning used in the 1840s, perhaps a winter-time plot.
ho'i loa. vi. To go or come with no thought of returning; to go permanently.
ho'i.loli. See *'īloli 1.*
hō.'imi. See *'imi,* to look for.
hō.'imo. See *'imo,* to wink.
ho'ina. n. 1. Returning, coming back; return. 2. Farewell gift, as to a parting guest after a feast.
hō.'inaina. See *inaina 1,* wrath, and *inaina 2.*
hō.'inā.'inau. See *'inā'inau.*
hoī.nana. See *'īnana.*
hō.'ino. See *'ino 1-4.*
ho'inu. See *inu,* to drink.
hō.'io. Same as *'ua'u kani. Rare.*
hō.'i'o. 1. n. A large native fern *(Diplazium* [*Athyrium*] *arnottii)* with subdivided fronds. The young fronds are eaten raw, much liked with raw fresh-water shrimps or with salted salmon. Only Orientals cook this fern. It was formerly sold in the market. It will not grow at low

altitudes (HP 214, Neal 25.) Cf. *pohole,* the Maui name. **2.** See *'i'o l.*

hō.'i'o kula. n. A native fern *(Dryopteris stegnogrammoides* syn. *Stegnogramma sandwicensis),* resembling the *kikawaiō,* having large pinnate fronds, but the tip tapering to a point instead of forming a separate lobe. Young fronds are eaten raw, like those of the *hō'i'o.*

hoka. 1. nvi. Disappointed, thwarted, baffled; disappointment, frustration (Hal. 9.18). *Ā hoka!* Serves you right! Good for you [insulting]! **ho'o.hoka.** To cause disappointment, chagrin; to frustrate, thwart, put to shame (Hal. 44.7). **2.** vt. To squeeze, strain, as kava or liquids through fibers. *Hoka ana lākou i ke ahu 'awa* (Ii 150–1), they were straining kava dregs [they were disappointed, a pun on *hoka l*]. (PPN *fota.*)

hō.kā. Same as *ho'okā.* See *kā 1. Ua 'ane hōkā ke anu i ka malama o Kā'elo* (Kep. 89), the cold really strikes during the month of Kā'elo.

hō.ka'a. nvs. Dizzy; a dull ache, as in head or stomach.

hoka 'awa. nv. To strain kava; a kava strainer.

hō.ka'e. vt. To smudge, smear, blot.

hō.ka'e.ka'e. Redup. of *hōka'e.*

hoka.hoka. Redup. of *hoka 1, 2.* **ho'o.hoka.hoka.** Caus/sim.

hoka.hokai. 1. Redup. of *hōkai.* **2.** vt. To mix, as ingredients. *Kuha ihola ia ma ka lepo, ā hokahokai ihola i ke kuha ma ka lepo* (Ioane 9.6), he spat on the ground and made clay of the spittle.

hō.kai. nvt. To confuse, disturb, meddle, mix up, spoil, interfere; to blunder along; nuisance, bother, confusion, disorder. *Hōkai ua lawai'a o ke kai pāpa'u, he po'opa'a ka i'a e ho'i ai,* a fisherman who blunders about in shallow water, takes home *po'opa'a* fish [easy to catch but not desirable]. **ho'o.hō.kai.** To cause confusion, mix up, bother; to blot out the memory.

hō.kake. vt. To interfere, disturb, as would a child; to annoy. See *kake 1.*

hō.kake.kake. Redup. of *hōkake;* to roil, as mud.

hō.kale. 1. Same as *kakale,* watery. **2.** n. Mastoid infection.

hō.kana, hosana. interj. Hosanna. (Gr. *hōsanna.*)

hō.kelo. Same as *hōkeo 1. Hōkelo ua,* container for catching rain.

Hokene.koka, Hotenetota. nvs. Hottentot. *Eng.*

hō.keo. 1. n. Long gourd calabash, as used to hold food, clothing, fishing gear; any cooking pot. *Fig.,* an empty container, a trifle. Cf. *hōkeo kani. He wahi hōkeo wale nō,* just an empty container [to have or know nothing]. (PCP *(f,s)ooteo:* cf. Maori *hooteo.*) **2.** vt. To cherish secretly, as love. *E hōkeo iho i ke aloha* (song), cherish the love. **3.** n. A variety of sweet potato.

hō.keo kani. n. Wind instrument, as in a band.

hoki. 1. n. Mule, ass (Nah. 16.15). *(Eng.* horse.) **2.** vs. Barren, of a woman. *Modern.*

hō.kī. Same as *ho'okī.* See *kī 3.*

hō.ki'i. nvs. Thin, wasted; tuberculosis, wasting sickness; consumption (Oihk. 26.16). Cf. Isa. 10.18.

hō.kī.kī. Probable redup. of *hōkī.* (PH 121.)

hō.kilo. Same as *hōki'i.*

hō.kio. n. Small gourd whistle; flute [RSV], pipe [KJV] (1 Sam. 10.5); to whistle.

hō.kio.kio. n. Gourd whistle; flute [RSV], pipe [KJV] (Isa. 5.12); to whistle.

hō.kio pū.eo.eo. nvi. To whistle with hands cupped over the mouth; such a whistle. *(Pūeoeo* is said to be the sound of the whistle.)

hoko. 1. vs. Fat, fleshy, as thighs, buttocks, or calf. *Rare.* **2.** vt. To strike, threaten. *Rare.* (PCP *(f,s)oto:* cf. Maori *hoto.*)

hoko.hoko. Redup. of *hoko 1, 2.*

Hoku. n. Night of the full moon. When this moon set before daylight it was called *Hoku Palemo,* Hoku that slips away. When it set after daylight it was called *Hoku Ili,* grounded Hoku. (Malo 32.) Cf. *hōkū,* star. *Ka mahina o Hoku,* the full moon of the night Hoku. (PEP *(F,S)otu.*)

-hoku. Ho'o.hoku-i-ka-lani. n. Name of the daughter of Wākea and Papa. *Hoku* may be compared to Tahitian *hotu,* to produce fruit and Tongan *fotu,* to appear. (PPN *fotu.*)

hō.kū. n. Star. (PPN *fetu'u.*)

hokua. 1. n. Nape of the neck, shoulder (Puk. 12.34); main stem of a vine (Kep. 157). *He kanaka hokua kano,* a person with hard, strong shoulders. *He nalu ha'aheo i ka hokua o ke kanaka,* the proud surf at the nape of a man's neck [a wind from the back, and a pun on *hokua 2*]. **2.** n. Tip of high waves, crest. See ex., *hamohamo.* **3.** vt. To lift up. (Kel. 152.)

hō.kū 'ae'a. n. Planet. *Lit.,* wandering star.

hō.kū 'ai 'āina. n. Probably same as *alanui-o-nā-hōkū-ho'okele. Lit.,* stars ruling land.

hō.kū ala. Same as *hōkū 'ae'a. Lit.,* rising star.

hō.kū-ali'i. Same as *Hōkū-loa.* Called *Hōkū-ali'iwahine* in Kep. 83.

Hō.kū-ao. n. Morning Star, Venus when seen in the morning. Also *Hōkū-loa, Hōkū-ali'i.*

hō.kū hele. Same as *hōkū 'ae'a. Lit.,* traveling star.

hō.kū-hele.le'i. n. A design on Ni'ihau mats. *Lit.,* falling star.

hō.kū-ho'o.kele-wa'a. n. The star Sirius. *Lit.,* canoe-guiding star.

Hoku Ili. See *Hoku.*

hō.kū-'iwa. n. A Hawaiian constellation, perhaps Boötes. *Lit.,* frigate-bird star.

hō.kū kai. n. Starfish. Cf. more common *pe'a.*

Hō.kū-kau-ahiahi. n. Evening Star.

Hō.kū-kau-'ō.pae. n. Evening Star or Sirius. Also *Hōkū-'ōpae.*

Hō.kū-ke'a. n. Southern Cross. *Lit.,* cross star.

Hō.kū-komo.hana. n. Morning Star. (Kep. 83.) *Lit.,* western star.

hō.kū.kū. nvi. Discomfort preceding bowel discharge; to suffer this. *Fig.,* angry, agitated.

Hō.kū-le'a. n. A navigational star, probably Arcturus; a zenith star above Hawai'i. (Kep. 83.) *Lit.,* clear (or happy) star. Also *Le'a.*

hō.kū-lei. n. An unidentified star.

hō.kū lele. n. Shooting star, meteor, any moving star.

hō.kū lewa. n. Moving star, planet.

hō.kū lī'ili'i. n. Small star, asteroid.

Hō.kū-loa. Same as *Hōkū-ao.* (Kep. 83.)

Hō.kū-noho-aupuni. n. A name for the Milky Way. (Kep. 83.) *Lit.,* ruling star.

Hō.kū-ō.pae. Same as *Hōkū-kau-'ōpae.* (GP 34.)

Hō.kū-pā. n. Name of a constellation, perhaps Leo or the head of Cetus. *Lit.,* fence star.

Hō.kū-pa'a. n. North Star. *Lit.,* immovable star.

Hoku Palemo. See *Hoku.*

Hō.kū-pō.kano. n. Name of a star. *Lit.,* very dark star.

hō.kū puhi.paka. n. Comet. *Lit.,* tobacco-smoking star. *Modern.*

hō.kū ukali. Satellite star. *Lit.,* accompanying star.

Hō.kū-'ula. n. A star, perhaps Mars, but see *Auhaele. Lit.,* red star.

hō.kū welo.welo. n. Shooting star, comet. *Lit.,* streaming star.

hola. 1. Same as *hohola,* to spread. Cf. *kauhola, mahola, pāhola.* (PPN *fola.*) **2.** Same as *'auhuhu;* to drug fish with this poison. *'Upena hola,* net used with this poison. *Hele nō i ka hola i'a i ka lā,* go to poison fish in the daytime [more efficient to work by day]. *Ni'ihau.* **3.** n. Groin (rare, in chants, Kam. 64:124). **4.** n. Hour, time, o'clock. *Eng. Hola 'ehia kēia?* What time is it?

hola.hia. Pas/imp. of *hola. He kapa kea i holahia lā i ke kai* (chant), a white tapa spread over the sea. (PPN *folasia.*)

hola.hola. Redup. of *hola 1, 2.* See *papa holahola kānāwai la'a.* (PPN *folafola.*)

holā.holā. vi. To blossom, as a flower or adolescent growing into maturity. *Ka'ū. Holāholā wale 'ia a'e nō ā pau ka pupuka,* just having blossomed with an end to ugliness.

holana. Same as *hola 1.*

Hō.lani. 1. n. Name of a mythical place. Stars observed by priests were *Hōlani-aliʻi* and *Hōlani-kū*. **2.** Holland; Dutch. *Eng.*

hō.laʻo. vi. To pass by, refuse to recognize. *Rare.*

hō.lapa. Same as *hoʻolapa*. See *lapa 1, 2.*

hō.lapu. vi. To disturb, roil; to spread, as fire. *Fig.,* to flare, as anger. See saying, *makaʻā*. *Ua hōlapu aʻe ke ahi ma Alanui Fremont,* the fire spread on Fremont Street.

hole. 1. nvt. To skin, peel, file, rasp, make a groove; to strip, as sugar-cane leaves from the stalk; furrow. Cf. *papa hole, pohole, puhole, penis. Hole Wai-mea i ka ihe a ka makani* (name song for Ka-mehameha I, Elbert and Mahoe 52), Wai-mea strips the spear of the wind [the wind refers to warriors, and the song describes their making of spears]. (PNP *sole;* cf. Penrhyn *sosore,* Yasuda 66.) **2.** vi. To squirm, twist, turn, fidget; to caress passionately. Cf. *pīhole.*

holea. Pas/imp. of *hole 1, 2.* (PEP *solea.*)

hō.leha. vt. To nibble at food. *Rare.*

hole.hole. 1. Redup. of *hole 1, 2. ʻŌlelo ka waha, holehole ka lima,* the mouth talks, the hand strips [of one who speaks as a friend but does unfriendly deeds]. (PNP *solesole.*) **2.** vt. To mix different feathers in a lei; mingling, as feathers. *Rare.*

hole.hole.hia. Pas/imp. of *hole 1.* (For. 5:509.)

hole.hole iwi. v. To strip flesh from the bones, as formerly done with the dead. *Fig.,* to tell evil of one's relatives or reveal confidences.

hō.lei. 1. n. A small native tree *(Ochrosia compta)* related to the *hao (Rauvolfia)* and closely resembling it, but the leaves thicker, the yellow flowers fragrant, and the twinned fruits yellow and much larger. Formerly, bark and roots yielded a yellow dye for tapa. (Neal 691.) **2.** nvt. Tapa dyed with *hōlei;* to dye thus. **3.** n. An introduced yellow dotted cloth. **4.** n. A variety of sweet potato.

hole iʻe. v. To groove or carve figures in the *iʻe* tapa beater.

hole ʻie. v. To strip aerial roots of the *ʻieʻie* vine for baskets or plaiting.

hole.lola. n. Holy Roller. *Eng.*

hō.leʻo.leʻo. Same as *hoʻoleʻoleʻo.*

holi. vi. **1.** To sprout, as plants or a youth's beard. **2.** To ask indirectly, seek to open conversation, search. *ʻOi holi mai nei ʻo Lei, a noi maoli,* Lei started with indirect hints, then asked directly. (Perhaps PCP *(f,s)oli:* Maori *hori,* speak falsely.)

holili. 1. vs. Weak, spindly, puny. (KL line 371.) **2.** See *-lili.*

holina. vs. Immature and inferior, as breadfruit falling prematurely.

hō.lina. interj. Haul in! Help! *Eng.*

hō.lio. 1. n. Two species of small, rare, endemic trees *(Cryptocarya)* in the laurel family, found only on Kauaʻi and Oʻahu. (Neal 361.) **2.** vs. Constantly in mind and thought. *Rare.*

hō.liʻo. 1. Same as *hōliʻoliʻo.* **2.** *(Cap.)* n. Rain name associated with Hawaiʻi and Oʻahu.

hō.liʻo.liʻo. Same as *liʻoliʻo 1;* dazzled, as the eyes by sunlight.

holo. 1. vi. To run, sail, ride, go; to flow, as water; to run, as for political office; to slide, as an avalanche; fleet, fast; double time; landslide; to fare, progress. Cf. *holoholo, holo i mua, holo lio, holomoku. Holo nui,* to run fast, gallop. *Holo ka hana,* fast work. *Ua holo ka ulu ʻana o ka pēpē,* the baby is growing fast. *Ka mea e holo ana,* whatever goes; however it goes or happens. *Pehea ka holo ʻana?* How is it going? What fortune? **hoʻo.holo.** To sail, run; to cause to run, sail, run free, as a horse; to ride, as a horse; to add water, as to poi; to flush, as a toilet; to drive, as a carriage. *Hoʻoholo ʻāwīwī,* to speed up, accelerate. *Hoʻoholo moa,* to slide the *moa* dart. *Hoʻoholo kāmelo* (1 Sam. 30.17), to ride camels. *Hoʻoholo i ka wai o ka lua,* to flush the toilet. (PPN *solo.*) **2.** vs. Decided, determined, agreed upon, settled, approved, passed, enacted. *Ua holo kō kāua*

manaʻo, we have agreed. *Ua holo ke kumu kūʻai,* the price is agreed upon. **hoʻo.holo.** To decide, determine, enact, pass, resolve, enforce, appraise, settle, conclude; to manage, as a business; decision, judgment. Cf. *ʻōlelo hoʻoholo. E hoʻoholo ʻia,* be it resolved. *Ka hoʻoholo kūʻokoʻa,* independent judgment. *Kōkua ʻia a hoʻoholo ʻia,* seconded and carried. *E hoʻoholo ʻia e ka Mōʻī,* be it enacted by the King. *Hoʻoholo i ke kānāwai,* enforce the law. *Hoʻoholo hou ʻana i ka waiwai,* reappraisal of property. *Hoʻoholo ʻia ka ʻōlelo hoʻopaʻi no ka hewa,* convicted of an offense. **3.** n. Noose. **4.** n. Running hula step to the side; similar to *kāholo* except that the feet are not necessarily brought together. **5.** n. A long bundle, as of hard poi. **6.** vt. To sew, as a break in a gourd calabash. See *holoholo 2,* and *kāholo 2.* (PPN *solosolo.*) **7.** n. Holes in edge of a canoe, through which lashings were passed to hold a canoe cover in place. (Malo 135.) **8.** n. Diagonal pole or strut attached to the inner side of the roof framework and extending obliquely from the upper end of a rafter at one corner to the lower end of the rafter at the other corner. **9.** n. Loss of a pebble in the *kōnane* game. (For. 4:57.) **10.** n. Hall. *Eng.*

-holo. hoʻo.holo. Grooved piece above the door frame, in which the door slides.

holoa. Pas/imp. of *holo 1, 2.*

holo.aʻa. Var. spelling of *holowaʻa.*

holo ʻā.ʻā. See *ʻāʻā 3.*

holo ahi. vs. Steam-driven.

holo ʻai. n. Food bundle, especially ti-leaf bundle of hard poi. Cf. *paʻi ʻai, pūkeleʻai.*

holo.ā.iʻa. nvi. To swim like a fish; to get the bends; to drown, sink; the bends, caisson disease. (Gram. 8.7.2.) *Inu ʻoe ā holoāiʻa* (Kel. 138), drink until [you] swim like [a] fish. **hoʻo.holo.ā.iʻa.** Caus/sim. *ʻO ke ʻano e hoʻoholoāiʻa ʻia ai ka moku kaua, mamuli ia o kona hoʻopahū ʻia ana aʻe,* the way the warship was sunk, because of being bombed.

holo.ʻanai. v. To gallop.

holo.ā.wai. vi. To flow like water. See *limu holoāwai,* Gram. 8.7.2.

holo.hau. vi. To ice skate, ski. *Lit.,* ice run. *Kinipōpō holohau,* ice hockey.

holo hele. vi. To run to and fro; bustle.

holo.hiʻa. vi. To dart this way and that, as children at play; to veer at an angle, miss. *Hoʻokūkū, hoʻonānā, nānā kō maka i ka mahina, holohiʻa aku, holohiʻa mai, nui nō ʻoe, nui kō kino* (child's game chant), stand about, look about, let your eyes see the moon, run this way, run that way, you are big, big your body.

holo.holo. 1. vi. To go for a walk, ride, or sail; to go out for pleasure, stroll, promenade. *Holoholo wale,* ride anywhere or aimlessly, stray. *He pule holoholo ʻana,* a continuous prayer. *E holoholo ana ma ka mahina ʻai* (Kin. 3.8), walking in the garden. **hoʻo.holo.holo.** To take someone out for a drive or excursion; to escort; to help walk, as a child or invalid. *Hoʻoholoholo waʻa* (For. 4:161), to sail canoes. (PPN *solosolo.*) **2.** nvt. Basting; to baste, sew. **hoʻo.holo.holo.** Caus/sim.; to make large running stitches. *Lopi hoʻoholoholo,* basting thread. **3.** nvi. A net into which fish run *(holoholo)* after being frightened; to fish with this net. **4.** nvi. An old Hawaiian game of kicking a ball to which feathers were attached; to play this game.

Holo.holo.ʻā. n. Star name (no data). (Kuhelani.)

holo.holoi. Redup. of *holoi.* (PPN *solosoloʻi.*)

holo.holo kaʻa. v. To go for a drive or ride. See song in Elbert and Mahoe 53–4. **hoʻo.holo.holo kaʻa.** To take someone for a drive or ride.

holo.holo.kake. Redup. of *holokake;* blown, as by wind.

holo.holo.kē. Redup. of *holokē.*

holo.holo lio. Redup. of *holo lio;* to go horseback riding.

holo.holo.moku. Redup. of *holomoku 1, 2;* ocean trip, cruise.

holo.holona. n. **1.** Animal, beast, insect. **2.** A trip, excursion, ride. *Rare.* Cf. *ipu holoholona.*

holo.holona 'ai 'i'o. n. Carnivorous animal.

holo.holona 'ai weu.weu. n. Herbivorous animal.

holo.holona hia.moe. n. Sloth, sleeping animal.

holo.holona lele. n. Insect, flying creature.

holo.holo.'ō.lelo. nv. To gossip, slander, bear tales, tattle; tattler, talebearer, spreader of gossip. (Oihk. 19.16.) **ho'o.holo.holo.'ō.lelo.** Caus/sim.

Holo.holo-pī.na'au. n. Name of a star, perhaps Mars.

holo hō.lua. n. Course for *hōlua,* sledding.

holo.hu'a. vi. To glance off, fly off obliquely, miss, fail to hit the mark. *Lit.,* run edge.

holoi. nvt. To wash, clean, scour, scrub, rub, erase, wipe (Biblical); washing, erasure. (2 Nal. 21.13.) *Mea holoi,* washing, laundry, eraser. *Holoi ā nalo,* erase completely, blot out. **ho'o.holoi.** To have washed, cleaned; to pretend to wash. (PPN *solo'i.*)

Holo-i-Kahiki. n. Name of a legendary star (Kep. 77) that guided Hawai'i-nui on his return to Kahiki-honua-kele after discovering Hawai'i.

holoi lau.oho. n. Shampoo.

holo i mua, holoi.mua. nvi. To progress, advance, surpass, go ahead; progress, advancement; successful. Also *holomua.* **ho'o.holo i mua.** To promote, cause progress; advancement, success.

holo 'ino. vi. To speed recklessly.

holo ka'a. v. To ride in a car or carriage. (Hal. 45.4.) **ho'o.holo ka'a.** To drive a car or carriage. *Rare.*

holo.kahiki. nv. Sailor; to sail to foreign lands. *Kauwō ulupau ka holokahiki,* the sailor drags anchor everywhere.

holo.kai. nvt. Seaman, seafarer; to sail on the sea; sea voyage or cruise. *Nā holokai* (Ezek. 26.17), seafaring men.

holo.kake. vs. Not secure, loose, not tight.

holo.kē. vi. To run here and there; helter-skelter.

hō.loke.loke. Same as *hālokeloke,* loose.

holo.kia. vi. To dart, as a bird.

holo.kikī. vi. To run or sail swiftly; headlong. Cf. *kikī holo.*

holo.kū. **1.** n. A loose, seamed dress with a yoke and usually with a train, patterned after the Mother Hubbards of the missionaries. Cf. the *mu'umu'u,* which formerly was not yoked and has no train or seam. Both garments are frequently made of gaily patterned material. **2.** n. Cloak (Isa. 59.17), mantle (Hal. 109.29). **3.** vs. Evenly plump, stout and symmetrical. Cf. *kolopū, pahupū.*

holo.kū kua poe.poe. n. A round-yoked *holokū.*

holo.kuku. n. Upper edge of an *'ōpelu* fish net.

holo kū.kū. vi. To trot, as a horse; to jounce.

holo.lani. n. Mission. *Ho'opau akula 'oia i kona hololani 'ana,* he finished his mission.

holo le'a. vi. To succeed, fare well; successful. *Holo le'a 'ole,* unsuccessful.

holo.leka. v. To correspond.

holo lio. nv. To ride horseback; horseman, rider (Isa. 36.8). *Ka wahine holo lio,* the woman rider. **ho'o.holo lio.** Same as above; horseman (Puk. 14.9); to make a horse run.

holo lua. vi. To run, sail, move in two ways. *Fig.,* hypocrite; deceitful.

holo.makani. vs. Breezy, airy. *Lit.,* wind running.

holo mana'o. v. To decide, determine. See *holo 2.* **ho'o.holo mana'o.** Caus/sim. *Ka po'e i ho'oholo mana'o* (Isa. 30.1), those who took counsel.

holo.moana. Same as *holokai.*

holo.moku. **1.** n. Sailor, passenger, anyone who sails; to sail, take a sail or ocean trip. **ho'o.holo.moku.** To sail. **2.** n. Rush or torrent, as of water; to rush, break forth, overflow. *Fig.,* overwhelming. *Holomoku ke koho 'ia 'ana o ka mō'ī,* the king was elected by an overwhelming majority. *Ua holomoku a'ela ka heluna nui a kō Honolulu mau kini no kekahi hale kū'ai,* most of the Honolulu populace rushed to a certain store.

holo.mokuna. Same as *holomoku 2.*

holo.mū. n. A long fitted dress, a combination of *holokū* and *mu'umu'u,* a name probably coined after World War II.

holo.mua. Same as *holo i mua;* improvement, progress.

holona. n. **1.** A running, sailing, traveling; performance. *Ka holona a ku'u lio,* the running of my horse. **2.** A double bar to show the end of a piece of music.

hō.lona. nvs. Unskilled, far from expert; novice, amateur, beginner. (For. 4:293.)

hō.lono. Rare var. of *ho'olono,* to hear.

holo.'oko'a. nvs. Whole, entire, complete, total, all, absolute, altogether; entirely; paramount, supreme; entity. *He ali'i holo'oko'a,* a chief over all. **holo.'ō.lelo.** Same as *holoholo'ōlelo.* **ho'o.holo.-'ō.lelo.** Caus/sim.

holo pahe'e. vi. To skate, skid.

holo.pani. n. A pain that nearly shuts off *(pani)* the breath.

holo.papa. **1.** n. Shelf, ledge, rack, frame on which tapa and other articles were laid; flooring. *Kau holopapa,* to place on the rack; one of chiefly blood (even though he did not know his genealogy), so called because he was entitled to place his belongings on a separate rack so that they might not be defiled by the possessions of others (Malo 56). **2.** vi. To spread, overrun, prevail, overcome, control, defeat; everywhere, completely. *Holopapa ka hana,* work done successfully. *He niuhi 'ai holopapa o ka moku,* the niuhi shark that devours all the island [a powerful warrior].

-holopau. **ho'o.holo.pau.** To finish, complete. *'A 'ole i ho'oholopau 'ia,* not finished; incomplete.

holo pā.'ū. nv. To ride horseback while wearing the sarong known as *pā'ū;* a *pā'ū* rider.

holo.peki. vi. To trot. *Lit.,* pace *(Eng.)* run.

holo pono. nvi. To pass off successfully, succeed, accomplish; successful; success. *Ua holo pono ka'u huaka'i,* my mission was successful.

Holo.po'o.po'o. n. Wind famous at Wai-pi'o, Hawai'i. *Lit.,* running in the hollows.

holo puni. nvi. To sail or travel around, circumnavigate; everywhere. *Alanui holo puni,* belt road. *He pilikia holo puni kēia,* this is a trouble that goes everywhere.

holo pupule. nvi. Reckless, mad running; to tear madly, as a frightened horse; to speed recklessly, as an auto.

holo.uka. n. Draft, air current, as in the mountains. *Rare.*

holo.wā. **1.** Same as *holokē. Rare.* **2.** n. Thrust through a cleft. *Rare.* **3.** n. War engine. *Rare.*

holo.wa'a, holo.a'a. n. **1.** Trough, especially vessel in which kava was mixed; oblong box, coffin, chest, cradle; furrow, as for planting sugar cane. *Holowa'a waiho aniani,* handmade mirror fitted into a wooden frame, as of *wiliwili* wood. *Kau i ka lani ka holowa'a ua o Hilo,* placed in the heavens is the rain trough of Hilo [admiration for one of regal bearing]. **2.** Sheath covering coconut flowers. Also *lolo.* **3.** Shuttle into which the bobbin of a sewing machine is slipped after it is filled with thread. **4.** A kind of fish net.

holo.wa'a lepo. n. Form or mold, as for making adobe bricks.

holo.wai. nvi. Water ditch or course; to run in such courses; watery. *Ua holowai nā kahawai,* the streams run swiftly.

holo.wī. vs. Long, thin. *Rare.* Cf. *'aha 5.*

holu. **1.** vi. Springy, pliable, resilient, as a mattress; to sway, as palm fronds; to ripple, as waves; to play back and forth; bumpy, as an airplane ride. Cf. *hoholu, holu nape, nolu. Ke one holu,* the sand carried back and forth [by the sea]. *Ua holu mai ke kai i kō lāua mau kino,* the sea lapped upon their bodies. **ho'o.-holu.** Caus/sim.; to bend, move up and down, sway. (PPN *soru.*) **2.** *(Cap.)* n. Name of a star. **3.** *(Cap.)* n. Name of a fish god. **4.** See *ko'i holu.*

hō.lū. vs. Soft; to soften. *Pāpa'i hōlū,* soft-shelled crab.

holua. 1. Pas/imp. of *holu 1*. **2.** n. Prayer for *luakini* dedication. (For. 6:27.)
hō.lua. n. Sled, especially the ancient sled used on grassy slopes; the sled course. *Papa hōlua*, sled. *He'e hōlua*, to ride a *hōlua* sled; the *hōlua* course; *fig.*, an expression of pride in descent from certain chiefly families at Wai-pi'o, Hawai'i, who were famous for their skill with the *hōlua* sled.
hō.lua kī. nv. Sliding downhill on ti leaves; to do so (a children's sport).
holu.holu. Redup. of *holu 1*; flexible. *Kai holuholu*, sea rising and falling. **ho'o.holu.holu.** Caus/sim. *Rare.*
hō.lule. 1. vs. Soft, flexible, limp; soft-shelled, as an egg or crab; hanging loose, as fat. **2.** n. A variety of sweet potato.
hō.lulo. Var. of *hōlule 1*.
holulu. To oppress. (And.)
hō.lū.lū. 1. n. Mid-tide. **2.** Redup. of *hōlū;* corpulent.
holu.lule. Redup. of *hōlule 1*.
holu nape. nvi. To sway, wave; swaying. *Ka holu nape a ka lau o ka niu* (song), the swaying of the fronds of the coconut.
homa. 1. vs. Disappointed. *Kū mawaho o ka pā o Homa*, standing outside Holmes's yard [said of one who is disappointed, a play on the name Holmes]. **2.** vs. Thin, flabby; hollow, as cheeks. *Rare.* **3.** vt. To hold a canoe to its course in a rough sea. *Rare.* **4.** n. Beat of paddle on canoe side, as in rhythmic paddling while fish are driven into a net. *Rare.*
homa.homa. Redup. of *homa 1-4*.
hō.male, hō.mali. vs. Emaciated, thin.
home. n. Home. *Eng. Ka home kaupoku 'ole*, the home without a ridgepole [a prison, ship, or place occupied by man that is not actually a home; an unhappy home].
home ho'o.kū.'ono'ono. n. Homestead.
home ho'o.pa'a. n. Detention home.
homeka, hometa. n. Sand lizard (RSV), snail (KJV). (Oihk. 11.30.)
home lula. Home rule; the name of the political party composed of native Hawaiians formed in the early years of Hawai'i as a territory. This party ended in 1912 after Kuhiō was elected delegate to Congress. (Daws 294-5.) *Eng.* See ex., *wela 1*.
homeo.pakika, homepakika, homepatita. Homeopathic. *Eng.*
Home Rula Republa.Ilka. n. Semi-weekly newspaper in Hawaiian and Eng. published 1901-02.
hō.mī. vi. Withered, stunted, puny, feeble; to wither, dry or shrivel up.
hō.mī.mī. Redup. of *hōmī*.
hona. 1. Same as *hōpue*, a tree. **2.** n. A variety of taro. (HP 24.)
hone. 1. vi. Sweet and soft, as music; sweetly appealing, as perfume or a memory of love; to sound softly; to tease, play pranks; mischievous. *Ke kani hone a ka waiolina*, the sweet sound of a violin. *Na ka moani lā i hali mai, hone ana i ke kai* (song), brought by the *moani* breeze, spreading sweetly to the sea. *Kani hone kēia keiki*, this child keeps up a teasing cry. **ho'o.hone.** Caus/sim. **2.** n. Honey. *Eng. Wili i ka hone*, to extract honey. **3.** n. Tenon of a wall post (Kam. 76:97.)
hone.hone. Redup. of *hone 1*; melodious.
hone.kakala. n. Honeysuckle, a low, twining shrub *(Lonicera japonica)*, from East Asia, with short-stemmed, oval leaves and fragrant tubular flowers that open white and turn yellow. (Neal 805-6.) *Eng.*
hone.koa. vs. Saucy, impudent.
hō.nē.nē. vt. To attract. *He lāhui kanaka hōnēnē i nā mea 'ino* (Kep. 75), a race of people attracted persistently by sinful things.
honi. 1. nvt. To kiss; a kiss; formerly, to touch noses on the side in greeting. *Hele akula 'o Iakoba, a honi a'ela iāia* (Kin. 27.27), Jacob came near and kissed him. **ho'o.honi.** To cause or pretend to kiss. (PPN *songi*.) **2.** nvt. To smell, sniff; scent; a scent. **ho'o.honi.**

Caus/sim. (PPN *songi*.) **3.** vt. To touch, as a match to a combustible. (Lunk. 16.9.)
honia. Pas/imp. of *honi 1-3*. *Ua honia wale i ke 'ala o ka maile*, to have inhaled indeed the fragrance of *maile*.
honi.honi. Redup. of *honi 1-3*; to kiss or smell repeatedly, sniff. (PPN *songisongi*.)
honi.kā. nvt. A loud kiss; to kiss loudly. *Rare.*
honi lima. nvt. To throw a kiss; such a kiss.
honina. 1. Same as *honi 1-3*. **2.** n. Name of a tapa dyed with turmeric and worn as a sarong.
hō.nina.nina. vi. Soft, yielding. Cf. *lina*.
honi pā.ha'o.ha'o. n. A "puzzling" smell: said if the smell is out of place, as that of gardenias in a canoe at sea, interpreted as a warning of danger (Nānā 58.)
hono. 1. nvi. To stitch, sew, mend, patch; a joining, as of mountains. Cf. *pāhonohono. E hono ana i kā lākou mau 'upena* (Mat. 4.21), mending their nets. (PPN *fono*.) **2.** n. Back of the neck, brow of a cliff. **3.** vs. Bad smelling (less common than *hohono*). Cf. *mimi hono*. **4.** n. Rite at the end of *kapu loulu* rituals during which chiefs sat without shifting positions while a kahuna prayed for as long as an hour. (Ii 44.) (PPN *fono*.)
Hono-. Bay, gulch, valley (as a part of place names such as Honolulu, Honokōhau, Honoli'i, Honomanu; also in the poetic phrase *nā Hono- a Pi'i-lani*, the bays beginning with Hono- of *Pi'i-lani* [a chief who ruled the bays on Maui, Moloka'i, and Lā-na'i that were visible from Lahaina]. *Hana-* occurs similarly as in Hanalei and Hanauma. See Gram. 8.1. (PPN *fanga-*.)
hono.ā, hono.wā. Same as *kūkae*, excrement, and an insulting epithet for commoners.
-hōnō.ai, -hōnō.wai. Rare var. for *-hūnōai*.
hono.hina. n. Wild spiderflower *(Gynandropsis gynandra)*, a cosmopolitan tropical hairy annual weed, native to Africa, in the caper family, 30 to 90 cm high, leaves five-parted; flowers spider-like, white with a purple tinge; fruit narrow, cylindrical capsule with many seeds. (Neal 369.) Also *'ili'ohu*.
hono.hono. 1. n. Short for *honohono kukui*. (PPN *hongohongo*.) **2.** n. The wandering Jew or dayflower *(Commelina diffusa)*, known in many temperate and tropical countries, a creeping weed, rooting at the joints, and bearing grasslike, ovate leaves and small bright-blue flowers. (Neal 185.) Also *honohono wai*, and *mākolokolo*. Cf. *honohono 'ula*. **3.** n. A very rare native mint *(Haplostachys haplostachya)*, a downy erect herb with oblong or narrower leaves and white flowers. (Neal 732.) **4.** See *'okika honohono*. **5.** Same as *hohono*, bad-smelling. **6.** n. A children's game; the child locked fingers of two hands and thrust them into the sand, letting the sand out through a small opening.
hono.hono kukui. n. The basket grass *(Oplismenus hirtellus)*, a creeping grass that originated in America, called *kukui* because it is often found under *kukui* trees. (Neal 73-4.) Also *honohono maoli*. (Neal 73-4.)
hono.hono kū mau. n. A variety of *honohono*.
hono.hono maoli. Same as *honohono kukui*.
hono.hono 'ula. n. Wandering Jew or zebrina, an ornamental, now naturalized, native to Mexico *(Zebrina pendula)*. (Neal 183-4.)
hono.hono wai. Same as *honohono 2*.
hono.ka'a. 1. Cavern, sea cave. (AP.) **2.** *(Cap.)* n. Town name, Hāmākua, Hawai'i.
Hono.kaona. n. Hong Kong. *Eng.*
hono.koī. n. A hard lump beside the mons pubis. (And., Kam. 64:115.)
honole. vs. Mischievous, teasing; to tease. *Rare.*
Hono.lulu. n. Name of the capital city in the Hawaiian Islands. *Lit.*, sheltered bay. (For PPN see *Hono-* and *lulu*.)
hono makani. n. Windbreak. *Rare.*
hono.pū. Mob, angry crowd. (AP.)
hono.wā. Var. spelling of *honoā*.
-hōnōwai. Rare var. for *-hunōai*.
honu. 1. n. General name for turtle and tortoise, as *Chelonia mydas*. *Hula honu*, an ancient dance imitating the

In causative/simulative forms beginning with hoʻo-, *delete the prefix* hoʻo- *and look for the stem.*

movements of a turtle. *Honu neʻe pū ka ʻāina,* the land moves like the turtle [land passes slowly but inexorably from owner to heir]. (PPN *fonu.*) **2.** n. Name of a design for Niʻihau mats. **3.** Rare var. of *hohonu,* deep. **hoʻo.honu.** To deepen. (PPN *fonu,* full, as of liquid; PCP *fofonu,* deep.)

honua. 1. nvs. Land, earth, world; background, as of quilt designs; basic, at the foundation, fundamental. See *lani. Kaua honua,* world war. *Ka wahine ʻai honua,* the earth-eating woman [Pele]. **hoʻo.honua.** To establish land, act as land; to scoop out earth, as for a fireplace; firmly established. *Fig.,* rich *(rare).* (PPN *fanua.*) **2.** part. Suddenly, abruptly and without reason. Cf. *kūhonua. Huhū honua ihola nō,* suddenly angry and for no reason. *Makaʻu honua ihola nō ia,* sudden fear. **3.** n. Middle section of a canoe; central section of a canoe fleet, as fishing *iheihe* fish; main section, as of an army.

honua nalu. n. Base of a breaker.

honua.ʻula. n. A variety of sugar cane, a dark brown-red mutant of *manulele,* with purple leaf sheaths and leaves. (HP 221, 225.) It was formerly used in medicine, and is one of the best canes for eating raw.

honu ʻea. n. Hawksbill turtle *(Chelonia);* the shell of this turtle was used as medicine for the disease called *ʻea* and was used for combs and fans.

honu.honu. 1. nvi. A game in which player and opponent sat with legs crossed and tried to unseat each other; to play this game. (For. 4:35.) **2.** nvi. A game in which one boy sat astride the back of another who was down on all fours; to play this game. (Malo 233.) **3.** A tapa pattern said to have its surface raised in ridges like corduroy. (AP.)

honu kahiki. n. A tortoise, perhaps the introduced land tortoise of the genus *Gopherus. Lit.,* foreign turtle.

honu mā.ea.ea. n. A variety of turtle.

honu peʻe.kue. 1. n. A variety of thick-shelled turtle. *Lit.,* coarse turtle. *Ka honu peʻekue wakawaka, pipiʻi ka unahi ma ke kua, hiolo ka unahi ma ke alo* (turtle dance chant), turtle with rough, coarse shell, scales climb up the back, scales slide down the front. **2.** vs. Crowded, thick. *Honu peʻekue ka paʻa pono o ke kai i ua ulu waʻa nei,* this canoe fleet covers the sea like the coarse shell of a turtle.

honu poʻo kea. n. A variety of turtle. *Lit.,* white-headed turtle.

hoʻo-. A very active former of caus/sim. derivatives; see Gram. 6.4. *Hoʻo-* is treated as a prefix because it occurs only before bases; unlike prefixes, however, it takes the stress of a word, as does the following base; thus *hoʻo.una,* to send, bears stress on the *u* and on the first *o. Hoʻo-* usually precedes bases beginning with the vowels *i-* and *u-* and all the consonants except the glottal stop. Important meanings follow: **(1)** Causation and transitivization, as *pono,* correct; *hoʻoponopono,* to correct. **(2)** Pretense, as *kuli,* deaf; *hoʻokuli,* to feign deafness. **(3)** Similarity, as *kamaliʻi,* children; *hoʻokamaliʻi,* childish. **(4)** No meaning, as *kāholoholo,* to hurry; *hoʻokāholoholo,* to hurry. The meanings of some *hoʻo-* derivatives are quite different from the meanings of the stems, as *maikaʻi,* good; *hoʻomaikaʻi,* to congratulate. *Hoʻo-* derivatives are defined under the bases. Delete *hoʻo-* and see the bases. (PPN *faka-.*)

hoʻō. See *ō,* food, and *ʻō* 2.

hoʻo.ā. Same as *hōʻoā.* See *ʻoā* and *ʻowā.*

hoʻō.ʻā. vt. To mix. See *ʻōʻā.*

ho.ʻōe.oe. See *oeoe* 1.

hoʻo.haʻa.haʻa. See *haʻahaʻa,* low, humble.

hoʻo.haʻa.heo. See *haʻaheo,* proud.

hoʻo.haʻa.lulu. See *haʻalulu,* to shake.

hoʻo.haʻa.nui. See *haʻanui,* to boast.

hoʻo.hae. See *hae,* wild, and *hae,* to bark.

hoʻo.hā.hā. vt. To beat. See *hāhā.*

hoʻo.hahana. See *hahana,* warm.

hoʻo.hahu. See *hahu,* to clear, purge.

hoʻo.haʻi. See *haʻi,* to break, and *haʻi,* coquettish.

hoʻo.hā.iki. See *hāiki,* narrow.

hoʻo.hā.inu. See *hāinu,* to give a drink.

hoʻo.haka. See *haka,* hole.

hoʻo.haka.kā.lia. See *hākālia,* slow.

hoʻo.haka.nū. See *hakanū,* silent.

hoʻo.hakē. See *hakē,* packed.

hoʻo.haku. See *haku,* lord.

hoʻo.hala. See *hala,* to sin, and *hala,* to pass.

hoʻo.hala.hala. vt. To criticize. See *halahala.*

hoʻo.hala manawa. v. To pass the time. See *-hala manawa.*

hoʻo.hale. See *hale,* house.

hoʻo.haliʻa. See *haliʻa,* recollection.

hoʻo.hā.like. See *hālike,* alike.

hoʻo.hā.lua. See *hālua,* to ambush.

hoʻo.hā.mama. See *hāmama,* open.

hoʻo.hamo. See *hamo,* anointed.

hoʻo.hana. See *hana,* work, and *hana,* worthless.

hoʻo.hani. vt. To touch. See *hani.*

hoʻo.hano.hano. See *hanohano,* glorious.

hoʻo.haʻo.haʻo. See *haʻohaʻo,* puzzling.

hoʻo.hape. See *hape,* incorrect.

hoʻo.hau.kaʻe. See *haukaʻe,* stained.

hoʻo.hā.ʻule. See *hāʻule,* to fall.

hoʻo.hau.mia. See *haumia,* defilement.

hoʻo.hau.naele. See *haunaele,* panic.

hoʻo.hē. Same as *hōhē,* coward.

hoʻo.heʻe. See *heʻe,* to slide.

hoʻo.hehe. See *heheʻe* 1.

hoʻo.hei. See *hei,* snare.

hoʻo.hei.hei. See *heihei,* race, and *heihei* 2, 3.

hoʻō.heke. See *ʻōheke.*

hoʻo.hele. See *hele* 1, 2.

hoʻo.hele.leʻi. See *heleleʻi,* falling.

hoʻo.hemo. See *hemo,* loose.

hoʻo.hene.hene. vt. To tease. See *henehene.*

hoʻo.heno. vt. To cherish. See *heno.*

hoʻo.heu. See *heu,* down.

hoʻo.hewa. See *hewa,* mistake.

hoʻō.hewa. See *ʻōhewa,* delicious.

hoʻō.hia.moe. See *hiamoe,* sleep.

hoʻo.hie. See *hie,* attractive.

hoʻo.hihia. See *hihia,* entangled.

hoʻo.hiki. vi. To vow, swear. See *-hiki.*

hoʻo.hila.hila. See *hilahila,* bashful.

hoʻo.hili. See *hili,* to turn, and *hili,* to whip.

hoʻo.hina. See *hina,* to fall.

hoʻo.hinu.hinu. See *hinuhinu* 1, 2.

hoʻo.hiwa.hiwa. See *hiwahiwa,* precious.

hoʻōho. See *oho,* to call.

hoʻo.hoa. See *hoa,* companion, and *-hoa.*

hoʻo.hohono. See *hohono,* acrid odor.

hoʻo.hohonu. See *hohonu,* deep.

hoʻo.hoi.hoi. See *hoihoi,* pleased.

hoʻo.hoka. See *hoka,* disappointed.

Ho.ʻo.hoku. See *-hoku.*

hoʻo.holo. See *holo,* to run; *holo,* decided; and *-holo.*

hoʻo.hopo.hopo. See *hopohopo,* anxiety.

hoʻo.hū. See *hū,* to swell.

hoʻo.hua. See *hua,* fruit.

hoʻo.huʻa. See *-huʻa.*

hoʻo.huhū. See *huhū,* angry.

hoʻo.huhuki. See *huhuki,* to pull.

hoʻo.hui. See *hui,* club, and *hui,* to join.

hoʻo.huʻi.huʻi. See *huʻihuʻi,* cold.

hoʻo.hui.kau. See *huikau,* mixed.

In causative/simulative forms beginning with ho'o-, *delete the prefix* ho'o- *and look for the stem.*

ho'o.huki. See *huki*, to pull, and *-huki*.
ho'o.huli. See *huli*, to turn, and *huli*, to look for.
ho'o.hulu. See *hulu*, esteemed.
ho'o.hū.nā. See *hūnā*, to hide.
ho'o.huoi. See *huoi*, suspicion.
hō.'oia. See *oia*, truth.
hō.'oia.'i'o. See *oia'i'o*, true.
ho'o.ī.kā. See *īkā*, to drift.
ho'o.iki. See *iki*, small.
ho'o.ili. See *ili*, stranded, and *ili*, inheritance.
ho'o.ilina. See *ilina*, recipient.
ho'o.ilo. n. 1. Winter, rainy season. See *-ilo*. *Ua hala ka ho'oilo, ua mālie*, winter is gone, it is calm [trouble is over]. 2. A strong, bitter purgative. (Kam. 64:109.) 3. See *ilo 2*.
ho'o.inu. See *inu*, to drink.
hō.'oio. See *-'oio*.
hō.'oi.'oi. See *'oi'oi*.
ho'o.kā. vt. To shatter. See *kā 1*.
ho'o.ka'a. See *ka'a 1, 4*.
ho'o.ka'a.wale. See *ka'awale*.
ho'o.kae. vt. To despise. See *kae*.
ho'o.kahe. See *kahe*, to flow.
ho'o.kahi. See *kahi 1*.
ho'o.kahua. See *kahua*.
ho'o.kahuli. See *kahuli*, overthrow.
ho'o.kala. See *kala 1, 4*.
ho'o.kala.kupua. See *kalakupua*.
ho'o.kali. See *kali*, to wait.
ho'o.kama.kama. See *-kamakama*.
ho'o.kamani. See *kamani 2*.
ho'o.kani. vt. To play. See *kani*, sound.
ho'o.kano. See *kano 1*, and *-kano*.
ho'o.kau.like. See *kaulike*, equality.
ho'o.kē. vi. To crowd. See *kē 1*.
ho'o.kē.kē. See *-kēkē*.
ho'o.kele. See *kele*, watery, and *kele*, to sail.
ho'o.kepa. See *kepa*.
ho'o.ōki. See *oki*, to stop.
hō.'oki. See *'oki*, to cut.
ho'o.ki'e.ki'e. See *ki'eki'e*, height.
ho'o.kī.kī. See *kīkī*.
ho'o.kina. See *-kina*.
ho'o.kī.nā. See *kīnā*, blemish.
ho'o.kino. See *kino*, body.
ho'o.kipa. To entertain. See *kipa*.
ho'o.kipi. See *kipi*, rebellion.
ho'o.kō. See *kō*, to fulfill.
ho'o.koe. vt. To save. See *koe*, to remain.
ho'o.kohu. See *kohu*, resemblance, and *-kohu*.
ho'o.ko'i.ko'i. See *ko'iko'i*, weight.
ho'o.kokoke. See *kokoke*, near.
ho'o.kolo.kolo. See *kolokolo*.
ho'o.komo. See *komo*, to enter, and *komo*, to dress.
ho'o.kū. See *kū*, to stand, and *kū*, in a state of.
ho'o.kū.'ē. See *kū'ē*, to oppose.
ho'o.ku'i. See *ku'i*, to pound.
ho'o.kū.kū. See *kūkū*, to shake, and *-kūkū*.
ho'o.kuli. See *kuli*, deaf.
ho'o.kumu. See *kumu*, beginning.
ho'o.kū.'ono.'ono. See *kū'ono'ono*, well-off.
ho'o.kupa. See *kupa*, citizen.
ho'o.kupu. See *kupu*, sprout, and *-kupu*.
ho'o.ku'u. See *ku'u*, to release.
ho'o.lā. See *lā*, sun.
ho'ōla. 1. See *ola*, life. 2. n. Small piece of tapa; tapa in general (Kaua'i).
ho'o.la'a. vt. To consecrate. See *la'a 1*.
ho'o.lā.'au. See *lā'au*, tree, and *-lā'au*.
ho'o.laha. See *laha*, extended.
ho'o.laka. vt. To tame. See *laka*.

ho'o.lako. vt. To supply. See *lako*.
ho'o.lalau. See *lalau*, mistake.
ho'o.lā.lau. See *lālau*, to seize.
ho'o.lana. See *lana*, floating, and *-lana*.
hō.'olā.'olā. See *'olā'olā*.
ho'o.lapa. See *lapa*, ridge, and *lapa*, energetic.
ho'ōla pā.na'i. See *ola pāna'i*.
ho'o.lapu. See *lapu*, ghost.
ho'o.lau. See *lau*, leaf; *lau*, dragnet; and *lau*, much.
ho'o.lau.lā. See *laulā*, broad.
ho'o.lau.le'a. n. Celebration. See *laule'a*.
ho'o.launa. See *launa*, friendly.
ho'o.lawa. vt. To supply. See *lawa 1*.
ho'o.lawe. vt. To subtract. See *lawe 1*.
ho'o.lawe.hala. See *lawehala*, sin.
hō.'ole. vt. To deny, repudiate. See *'ole*.
hō.'olei. vt. To throw. See *lei 2*.
ho'o.lele. vt. To fly. See *lele 1*. Cf. *ha'alele*.
ho'o.lepe. vt. To cut, stir. See *lepe*.
hō.'olepe. See *'ōlepe*, to turn.
Hō.'ole.Pope. nvs. Protestant. *Lit.*, Denier of the Pope.
ho'o.lewa. See *lewa*, to float, and *-lewa*.
ho'o.lilo. See *lilo 1, 3*.
ho'o.lima.lima. vt. To rent. See *limalima*.
ho'o.lohe. See *lohe*, to hear, obey.
ho'o.loli. See *loli*, to change.
ho'o.lono. vt. To listen. See *lono 1*.
hō.'olo.pū. See *'olopū*.
hō.'olu. See *'olu*, cool.
ho'o.lua. See *lua 1, 3*, and *-lua*.
ho'o.lu'a. See *-lu'a*.
ho'o.luhi. vt. To bother. See *luhi 1*.
ho'o.luli. See *luli*, to shake.
hō.'olu.'olu. See *'olu'olu*.
ho'o.lu'u. See *lu'u*, to dive.
ho'o.ma'a.ma'a. See *ma'ama'a*.
ho'o.ma'awe. See *ma'awe*, fibre.
ho'o.ma'e.ma'e. vt. To clean. See *ma'ema'e*.
ho'o.maha. See *maha*, rest.
ho'o.mahana. vt. To warm. See *mahana 1*.
ho'o.mahua. vt. To mock. See *mahua*.
ho'o.mā.hua. vt. To increase. See *māhua*.
ho'o.mai.ka'i. See *maika'i*, good.
ho'o.maka. vt. To begin. See *maka 3*.
ho'o.mā.ka'i.ka'i. See *māka'ika'i*, to visit.
ho'o.maka'u. vt. To frighten. See *maka'u*.
ho'o.mā.kau.kau. vt. To prepare. See *mākaukau*.
ho'o.make. vt. To kill. See *make*, to die.
ho'o.mā.ke'aka. vs. Funny. See *-māke'aka*.
ho'o.mā.lama.lama. See *mālamalama 1*.
ho'o.mali.mali. vt. To flatter. See *malimali*.
ho'o.malolo. See *malolo*, to rest.
ho'o.malu. See *malu*, shade.
ho'o.mā.luhi.luhi. vt. To tire. See *māluhiluhi*.
ho'o.mamao. See *mamao*, far.
ho'o.mana. See *mana*, power, and *-mana*.
ho'o.mā.nalo. See *mānalo*, sweet, and *mānalo*, appeased.
ho'o.mana.mana. vs. Superstitious. See *manamana*.
ho'o.mana'o. vt. To remember. See *mana'o*.
ho'o.manawa.nui. See *-manawanui*, patience.
ho'o.mao.popo. vt. To understand. See *maopopo*.
ho'o.mau. See *mau 1-3*.
ho'o.meheu. See *meheu*, track.
ho'o.melu. See *melu*, soft.
ho'o.mo'a. See *mo'a*, cooked.
ho'o.moana. See *moana*, campground, and *moana*, broad.
ho'o.moe. See *moe*, to sleep, and *moe*, to marry.
hō.'omo.'omo. vt. To mold. See *'omo'omo*.
ho'o.mū. See *mū 2, 3*.

In causative/simulative forms beginning with ho'o-, *delete the prefix* ho'o- *and look for the stem.*

ho'o.nā. See *nā,* calmed.
ho'o.na'au.ao. vt. To educate. See *na'auao.*
ho'o.nanea. See *nanea 1.*
ho'o.nane.nane. vs. Puzzling. See *nanenane.*
ho'o.nani. vt. To beautify. See *nani 1.*
ho'o.nē. See *nē,* teasing.
ho'ōne. See *one,* sand.
ho'o.ne'e. See *ne'e,* to move along.
hō.'oni. See *'oni,* to move.
ho'o.nipo. See *nipo 1, 2.*
hō.'ono. See *'ono,* delicious.
ho'o.noho. See *noho.*
ho'o.nui. vt. To enlarge. See *nui 1.*
hō.'oma. See *'o'oma,* concave.
hō.'o'opa. See *'o'opa,* lame.
ho'o.pā. See *pā,* to touch, and *pā,* barren.
ho'o.pa'a. vt. To make fast. See *pa'a 1.*
ho'o.pa'a.pa'a. vt. To argue. See *pa'apa'a 1, 4.*
ho'o.pae. See *pae,* cluster, and *pae,* to land.
ho'o.pahe'e. See *pahe'e,* slippery.
ho'o.pai. vt. To encourage. See *pai.*
ho'o.pa'i. See *pa'i,* to slap.
ho'o.pai.lua. See *pailua,* nausea.
ho'o.pakele. See *pakele,* to escape.
ho'o.pala. See *pala,* ripe, and *pala,* dab.
ho'o.pale. vt. To ward off. See *pale 1.*
ho'o.pā.na'i. See *pāna'i,* revenge.
ho'o.pā.pā. See *pāpā,* to touch.
ho'o.pau. See *pau,* finished.
ho'o.pau.manawa. v. To waste time. See *-paumanawa.*
ho'o.pē. See *pē,* crushed; *pē,* perfumed; and *pē,* drenched.
hō.'ope. See *'ope,* bundle.
ho'o.piha. See *piha,* full.
ho'o.pi'i. See *pi'i 1, 2, 5,* and *-pi'i.*
ho'o.pili. See *pili,* to cling, and *pili,* to refer.
ho'o.pono.pono. vt. To correct. See *ponopono 1.*
ho'o.pū.'iwa. See *pū'iwa,* startled.
ho'o.puka. See *puka 1-3.*
ho'o.pula.pula. See *pulapula,* seedling.
ho'o.pulu. See *pulu,* wet, and *pulu,* mulch.
ho'o.puna.hele. See *punahele.*
ho'o.puni. See *puni 1-3.*
ho'o.u'i. vt. To beautify. See *u'i.*
ho'o.uka. See *-uka.*
ho'o.uku. See *uku,* pay.
ho'o.uli. See *uli 1,* dark.
ho'o.ulu. See *ulu 1, 2.*
ho'o.una. vt. To send. See *-una.*
ho'o.wā. See *wā,* roar.
hō.'owā. Var. spelling of *ho'oā.*
ho'o.wae. See *wae,* to choose.
ho'o.wahā.wahā. See *wahāwahā.*
ho'o.wale.wale. vt. To tempt. See *walewale.*
ho'o.weli.weli. vt. To frighten. See *weli.*
ho'o.wili. See *wili,* to turn.
hopai. Same as *pai 5,* a fishing basket.
hō.pa'i. Same as *ho'opa'i,* to slap, punish, chastise.
hope. 1. loc. n. After, behind, last, late, younger, subsequent, residue, next, back, rear, aft, posterior, stern of a vessel, fate (see ex., *nalu 2*); afterwards; those behind. (This common word usually occurs without a preceding *k*-word; it frequently follows *ma-,* usually then pronounced *mahape* but not so written. Gram. 8.6. *Mahope, mahope aku,* afterwards, by-and-by, late, later, hereafter, behind [referring to both time and place]. *I hope,* in back, behind, astern [does not refer to time]. *Hope loa,* youngest, very last, final, ultimate. *Kāhāhā 'o hope* (FS 255), those behind were astonished. *Ke keiki hope loa,* the very last child, the youngest. *Mahope mākou a Lili'u-lani* (song), we are supporters of Lili'u-lani. *No'ono'o 'o hope nei . . .* (FS

255), the people in the rear thought . . . *Mahope aku au,* I'll come later. *Ma keia hope iho,* from now on. (PPN *sope.*) 2. n. Result, conclusion, end, purpose, sequel, consequence, supplement. *Nā hana hope 'ole,* inconsequential deeds, deeds without result. *Ka hope o ka helu na'au,* the supplement of the mental arithmetic. 3. n. Deputy, substitute, assistant, adjutant, representative, surety, successor, proxy, acting officer, supporter, vice-, agent, factor. *Hope kenelale,* adjutant general. 4. n. Posterior, buttocks. *Malo ma kō 'Umi hope* (FS 123), loincloth on 'Umi's buttocks. 5. n. Second brew of kava.
hope.'a'ei. n. Part of an *'ōpelu* net.
hope.'eha. Same as *hope'ō. Lit.,* pain-inflicting rear.
hope ha'ina. n. Object of a sentence.
hope kia.'āina. n. Lieutenant governor.
hope kumu. n. Substitute or assistant teacher.
hopena. n. Result, conclusion, sequel, ending, destiny, fate, consequence, effect, last. *He hopena 'elemakule,* the result of being an old man. *He hopena luahine,* the result of being an old woman. (Both of these sayings are said jokingly of oneself as he advances in years.) *Hopena pō'ino,* doom, evil fate.
hopena ala.hao. n. Railroad terminus.
hope.'ō. n. Wasp, yellow jacket, hornet.
hō.pē.pē. Same as *ho'opēpē.*
hope pele.kikena (peresidena). n. Vice-president.
hope po'o. n. Acting or deputy head, director, leader.
hope pu'u.kū. n. Assistant or deputy treasurer.
hope wai.wai. n. Assignee (term in will 303, 1875, State Archives).
hō.pilo. 1. vs. Barely able to speak; to whisper. *Rare.* 2. To relapse after recovery from illness, often sick. (And.)
hopi.lole. To eat slowly, as an invalid. (And.)
hopo. Same as *hopohopo.* (Probably PPN *sopo.*)
hō.poe. 1. vs. Fully developed, as a *lehua* flower. See *poepoe, popohe. Hōpoe lehua ki'eki'e i luna,* well-rounded mighty *lehua* bloom above. 2. *(Cap.)* n. A dancer who was turned into a balancing rock by Pele at Puna, Hawai'i.
hopo.hopo. nvs. Anxiety, uncertainty, doubt, fright; uncertain, anxious, in doubt, fearful, perturbed, alarmed, uneasy. *Me ka hopohopo ho'okamani 'ole,* with unfeigned diffidence. ho'o.hopo.hopo. To evoke or produce doubt, fear, anxiety. (PPN *soposopo.*)
hopo'i. Transitive form of *hopo.*
hopu. nvt. To seize, grasp, take, catch, capture, arrest; seizure, taking, arrest. *Palapala hopu,* warrant of arrest. *Pakele mai ka hopu 'ia,* freedom from arrest. (PCP *(f,s)opu.*)
hopua. Pas/imp. of *hopu. Hopua mai ka 'īlio,* catch the dog.
hō.pue. n. 1. Orange finch *(Psittirostra palmeri),* the largest of the Hawaiian finchlike forms, found only in the Kona and Ka'ū districts, Hawai'i. 2. A native tree, endemic to Kaua'i *(Urera sandvicensis* var. *kauaiensis),* in the nettle family, with broad-ovate, long-stemmed leaves, and red, clustered, male flowers. Also *hona, ōpuhe.*
hopu.hia. Pass/imp. of *hopu. 'O kou maka kūnou, ā, ua hopuhia* (PH 66), your bowed head is caught.
hopu.hopu. Redup. of *hopu.* See ex., *ālulu.* (PCP *(f,s)opu(f,s)opu.*)
hopu.hopu.ā.lulu. Same as *pupuāhulu.*
hopuna. n. 1. Grasping, seizing, taking; arrest. 2. Pronunciation, accent.
hopuna 'ō.lelo. n. 1. Pronunciation, enunciation. 2. Paragraph. 3. Syllable.
hō.pū.pū. vs. Emotionally excited, as with hate, love, lust.
hou. 1. vs. New, fresh, recent. *Ka-puna-hou* (place

name), the new spring. (PPN *fo'ou.*) **2.** vs. Again, more, re- (as in *ho'oponopono hou,* re-edit). *Hana hou,* do again, repeat; encore. **3.** vt. To push, thrust, poke, stab, shove, prick, plunge, ram, jab, drill, bore, pierce, inject. See also *houhou. Hou kui,* injection needle. *Ka hou 'ana o ka ihe* (FS 55), the hurling of the spear. (PPN *fohu.*) **4.** nvi. Perspiration, sweat; to perspire, sweat. (PCP *(f,s)ou.*) **5.** n. Varieties of wrasse *(Thalassoma)* shallow-water fish, as *T. purpureum.* The following names have been recorded for the young stages of the *hou:* *'āwela, kanaloa, 'ōlali, 'ōlani, pāhouhou, pākaiele, pākaueloa, palae'a, pā'ou'ou.* **6.** Same as *pakaweli,* a variety of sugar cane.

hō.'ū. vi. To grunt. See *'ū 1.*

hou.hewa. vi. To turn this way and that, as in panic.

hou.hou. Redup. of *hou 3. Fig.,* to make cutting or cruel remarks. *Ka makani houhou 'ili* (song), the wind that makes the skin tingle. (PEP *foufou.*)

hou kui. See *hou 3.*

hō.'ulu.'ulu. See *'ulu'ulu,* collection.

hō.una. n. Scooping. See *'upena hōuna.*

hou pahi. v. To stab with a knife.

houpo. n. Diaphragm, chest, solar plexus. *Lelele ka houpo i ka 'oli'oli,* the heart leaps for joy. *Pa'a ka houpo,* the stomach is full. *Houpo lewalewa,* sagging chest [hunger]. (PCP *(f,s)oupo:* cf. Tuamotu *houpo.*)

houpo 'ume pau. n. Strong pulsation in solar plexis, heart attack.

hou puka. v. To drill a hole, bore or pierce through.

hō.wai. vs. Watery, as thin poi; soggy. *Pā hōwai,* a dish containing liquids.

hō.wai-a-ulu. n. A perennial herb *(Lagenophora maviensis),* found only in marshy high parts of West Maui. The leaves form a basal rosette, from which rises a stalk bearing a round daisy-like flower head with yellow center and white rays.

hū. 1. nvi. To rise or swell, as yeast or souring poi; to ferment, leaven, overflow (Isa. 8.7), percolate, effervesce, boil over; to surge or rise to the surface, as emotion; to gush forth; rising, swelling, outburst. Cf. *hua'i. Perena hū 'ole,* unleavened bread. *Hū ka 'aka,* to burst into laughter, guffaw. *Hū ka pele,* to pour forth lava, erupt. *Inā hū aku kou 'uhane i ka po'e pōloli* (Isa. 58.10), if your soul has compassion for the hungry people. *Hū mai ke aloha no ka 'āina,* love for the homeland swells forth. *He hū wale mehe wai lā* (Kin. 49.4), unstable as water. *ho'o.hū.* To leaven, cause to rise, inflate, swell, overflow; yeast, baking powder. **2.** vi. and interj. To roar, grunt, hum, whistle; huh [interj.)! *Hū ka makani,* the wind whistles or roars [of things going at great speed]. *Hū wawā ka nahele,* din roaring in the forest [gossip]. (PPN *fuu.*) **3.** n. A spinning top. *Hū oeoe,* humming top. *Kaula hū,* cord used to spin a top. *Ho'oniniu i ka hū,* to spin a top. **4.** vi. To depart from the proper course, miss the way. *Hū ā pua'a,* off the course like a pig [of one who does not follow a straight and narrow path, as of a drunkard]. *ho'o.hū.* To cause someone to deviate from the path; to shoo, drive away, rout. **5.** n. Gum, as of the *'ōlapa* tree. **6.** n. Commoners as a mass. *Ē ka hū, ē ka maka'āinana, aloha 'oukou* (chant by Ka-māmalu bidding farewell to Hawai'i), O commoners, O citizenry, farewell to you. **7.** Var. of *hui 2,* to unite, join. *Ē Lono, e hū 'ia mai ka lani me ka honua* (prayer), O Lono, join heaven and earth.

hua. 1. nvi. Fruit, tuber, egg, produce, yield, ovum, seed, grain, offspring; meat as in *'opihi* shell or *'alamihi* crab; to bear fruit, tuber or seed; to bear a child; fruitful. For kinds of eggs, see *hua 'alu'alu, huamakani, hua moa. Hua mo'a loa,* hard-boiled egg. *Hua mo'a hapa,* soft-boiled egg. *Hua 'ai,* fruit. *Hua kanu,* seed. *Ā e hana aku 'oe iā 'oukou e hua a'e* (Oihk. 26.9), and will make you fruitful. *ho'o.hua.* To bear fruit, reproduce, produce, yield; to sire or give birth; to swell high, as a wave (UL 36). *Nalu ho'ohua,* a swelling wave. *Ho'ohua kawowo,* a medicine for women to induce conception. (PPN *fua.*) **2.** n. Round object, as pill or bead. Cf. *huaale.* **3.** n. Result, effect; credit, as for a

university course. *Ka hua o kā 'oukou hana,* the result of your work. *ho'o.hua.* To have as a result, because of, ever since (followed by *nō). Ho'ohua nō ka make 'ana o ka makua kāne, pau kō mākou 'ike 'ana iāia,* ever since his father's death, we've never seen him again. *Ho'ohua nō i ka huhū 'ana o ke kupuna, 'o ka hele nō ia,* because of his grandparent's anger, he departed. **4.** n. Testicles. *Ka hele ā pala nā hua i ka moana,* testicles rot at sea [a sailor lacks a sex partner]. *He hua pēpē 'ia* (Oihk. 21.20), broken testicles. (PNP *fua.*) **5.** Same as *huahua 3,* a vulgar gesture. *Ho'opu'u ka hua,* to make this gesture. **6.** nvi. Word, letter, figure, watchword, rallying cry, note in music; winning word in the Chinese gambling game of *chee-fah;* type; to speak. Cf. *hua helu, hua 'ōlelo. Ho'onoho hua,* to set type. *Kāne kū i ke kala, kala i ka hua o ka waha* (prayer), Kāne stand to forgive, forgive the words of the mouth. *Ā hua* (For. 5:43), then speak [cf. *pane 1*]. (PPN *fua.*) **7.** *(Cap.)* n. Name of the thirteenth night of the lunar month. (Malo 35.) (PEP *(f,s)ua.) Kapu Hua,* monthly taboo nights of Mōhalu and Hua. **8.** *(Cap.)* Name of a star. **9.** n. The bulging of the broadest part of a paddle blade. **10.** See *pai hua.* **11.** See *pa'i hua.*

huā, huwā. nvi. Envy, jealousy; envious, jealous; to stir up trouble due to envy. Cf. *māhuā. ho'o.huā.* To provoke anger or jealousy. (PPN *hua'a.*)

hu'a. n. **1.** Foam, froth, bubble, suds, scum. *Hu'a o ka wai,* water bubble. (PCP *(f,s)uka.*) **2.** Rim, border, edge, side, hem; ruffles and tucks at the bottom of a dress; tucks in a mat; train of a gown. See *mānele hu'a ho'ohiwahiwa. Ākea ka hu'a o ka lole,* the bottom of the dress is wide [a full skirt]. *Ka hu'a o ka lā'au* (FS 99), the reach of the club. **3.** Suburb, boundary. **4.** Pile, as of mats or tapa. (For. 4:63.) Also *nu'a.* **5.** Same as *ma'a 4.*

-hu'a. ho'o.hu'a. To insist, persist. *Ho'ohu'a noho'i i ka inu lama,* persisting in drinking intoxicants.

hua.'ā. vs. Very sour, of poi.

hū.'a'ā. vi. To burn intensely.

hua 'ai. n. Edible fruit or seed. *Hua 'ai mālili* (Kanl. 28.22), blasted fruit.

hua.ala. n. Nutmeg, spice. *Lit.,* fragrant fruit.

hua ala.ka'i. n. A leading note in music, the major seventh of any scale, a semitone below the tonic.

hua.ale. n. Pill, tablet. *Lit.,* seed to swallow.

hua.ale ho'o.moe. n. Sleeping tablet.

hua 'alo. n. Missing letter.

hua 'alu.'alu. n. Egg with a very soft shell.

hua 'ā.lua.lua. See *'ālualua 2.*

hua ani.ani. n. Glass bead.

hua 'ē. n. Child born out of wedlock, that is accepted by the husband or wife of the parent and treated as his own. *Lit.,* strange fruit. *Ka'ū.*

huā.elo. Var. spelling of *hua āelo.* See *āelo.*

hua hapa. n. Half note, as in music.

hua hapa.hā. n. Quarter note, as in music.

hua hā.'ule. nvs. Fallen fruit or seed. *Fig.,* friendless, uncared for by parents or chief; bastard, illegitimate child (modern); foetus lost through miscarriage.

hua hā.ule wale. Same as *hua hā'ule.* Also said of a sweet potato produced from the extended vine as distinguished from the product in the hill.

hua.hekili. n. **1.** Hail. *Lit.,* thunder fruit. (Puk. 9.18.) **2.** Rare name for the beach *naupaka (Scaevola)* plant.

hua.hekili uka. n. A small native *naupaka (Scaevola kilaueae)* found only on dry lava near Kī-lau-ea Volcano. It does not exceed a height of 80 cm, has narrow, thick leaves, dull-yellow flowers, and small black fruits that were used to dye tapa. Also *papa'ahekili.* (Neal 819-20.)

hua helu. n. **1.** Figure, number (the character). **2.** A few, little. *'Ehia āu lei? He mau hua helu nō.* How many leis for sale have you? Just a few. *He wahi hua helu ia,* it's of some help [financial].

hua hō.'ai.lona. n. Abbreviation.

hua ho'o.ne'e. n. Combination, as of a safe. *Lit.,* number to make move.

hua ho'o.noho. n. Type.

hua.hua. 1. vi. Fruitful, productive, prolific; to bear many fruits; to lay many eggs. (PPN *fuafua*.) **2.** Testicles. See insult, *loa'a . . . kāu.* **3.** n. A vulgar gesture of contempt made by thrusting the thumb between index and middle fingers with the fist clenched, or the fist held up to the face and the eyelid drawn down. With the gesture one sometimes said, *"Eia kāu 'o ka huahua,"* "Here's your *huahua* gesture." **ho'o.hua.hua.** To make the *huahua* gesture.

huā.huā, huāhuwā. Redup. of *huā.* See ex., *pe'a 1,* For. 4:129, 131. *Ā huāhuā maila kō Pilisetia iāia* (Kin. 26.14), and the Philistines envied him.

hu'a.hu'a. 1. Redup. of *hu'a 1;* foam, froth, lather, bubbling, frothing. *Ua lo'ohia 'oia e kekahi 'uhane, auē koke nō ia . . . ā hu'ahu'a a'e* (Luka 9.39), a spirit seizes him, and he suddenly cried out . . . until [he] foams. **ho'o.hu'ahu'a.** Caus/sim. *Rare.* (PCP *(f,s)uka(f,s)uka;* perhaps PEP.) **2.** n. Jelly. *Rare.* **3.** See *hu'ahu'a kai.*

hua.hua'i. Redup. of *hua'i;* to boil up, as water in a spring; to gush forth, effervesce; culmination of sexual passion. *Kāua i ka huahua'i, e 'uhene lā i pili ko'olua* (song, UL 166), we two in passionate outpour, giggling, clinging two and two.

hu'a.hu'a kai. n. **1.** Sponge *A ho'oma'ū i ka hu'ahu'a kai i ka vinega* (Mar. 15.36), and soaked a sponge with vinegar. **2.** Sea foam; crest of a wave breaking into foam. **3.** A variety of seaweed.

hu'a.hu'a.kō. n. A coarse, weedy native dock *(Rumex albescens)* in the buckwheat family. See also *pāwale.*

hu'a.hu'a kopa (sopa). n. Soapsuds.

hu'a.hu'a lana. n. Floating froth. *Fig.,* an ignoramus.

hua.hua.lau. nvt. Interrogation to incriminate, ensnare, or obtain information by roundabout methods, to question or quiz indirectly. **ho'o.hua.hua.lau.** Caus/sim.; to cross-examine. (Kin. 42.7.) *Na'u na'e i ho'o-huahualau aku, ā no laila, hū mai ko'u aloha* (Laie 607), I used devious methods and then my love poured forth. *Ua ho'ohuahualau mai ia iā mākou me kāna 'ōlelo 'ino'ino* (3 Ioane 10), he prattles against us with his evil words.

hua.huwā. Var. spelling of *huāhuā.*

hū.ai, hū.wai. n. **1.** A shellfish of the *hīhīwai* family. **2.** A kind of seaweed *(Codium).*

hua'i. vt. To disclose, reveal, uncover, as an oven; to disinter, dig up, pour forth, break forth; to churn water, as a ship propeller (*hū 1 + -a'i,* transitivizer: Gram. 6.6.4). Cf. *po'o hua'i. Ke lepo ke kumu wai, e hua'i ana ka lepo i kai,* when the source of water is dirty, dirt is seen in the lowlands [one with dirty thoughts hears dirty words].

hua iki. n. Small letter, small fruit.

hua.'ina. nvi. Boiling up, opening, uncovering; to gush forth, as lava.

huaka. 1. vs. Clear as crystal, bright, dazzling, white, shining, flashing. **ho'o.huaka.** To cause a gleam of light, flash, glimmer. **2.** n. Shadow, reflection. **ho'o.-huaka.** To cast a shadow or reflection.

hua kahi. n. An only child or offspring. (PPN *fuatasi.*)

hua kai. n. Scrambled eggs.

hu'a kai. n. Sponge, foam.

hua.ka'i. nvi. Trip, voyage, journey, mission, procession, parade; to travel, parade. Cf. *ka'i,* to lead. *Ua huli a'e nā huaka'i* (Ioba 6.18), the caravans turn aside.

hua.ka'i hele. nvi. Travels, a long trip; to keep traveling.

hua.ka'i ho'o.hano.hano. n. Honor escort.

hua.ka'i ka'a.hele. nvi. Tour; to make a tour.

hua.ka'i pō. n. Night procession or parade, especially the night procession of ghosts that is sometimes called *'oi'o.*

hua kala.kala. n. Bur.

-hua kama. ho'o.hua kama. To sire a child.

hua kani. n. Tone in music.

hua kanu. n. Seed, as of mango; bulb.

hu'a kapa. n. Pile of tapas. See *hu'a 4.*

hu'a kapu. n. Taboo borders, as of a taboo place, or of the taboo enclosure where hula was taught.

-hua.kawowo. ho'o.hua.kawowo. To induce pregnancy.

hua.kē. vs. Full and plump, as a healthy person; well-proportioned, as a properly built canoe.

-huake'eo, -huake'o, ho'o.hua.ke'eo. Hurt, angry, displeased, resentful. Also *ho'okuake'eo, ka'eo, ho'o-ke'eo, ho'oke'eke'e.*

hua kē.pau. n. Printer's type. See ex., *'ōniu 3.*

hū ā keu. vs. Excessive. *Hū ā keu i ka 'ino,* extremely wicked.

hua kineko, huakineto. n. Jacinth. (Hoik. 21.20.)

hua kō.kua. n. Grace note in music.

hu'a kopa. n. Soap bubble.

hū ā kū. Same as *hū ā keu. He 'ōlelo hū ā kū i ka pono,* a word completely just.

hua kukaima, hua kudaima. n. Mandrake. (Kin. 30.14.) (Hebrew *dudoim.*)

hua kukui. n. *Kukui* (candlenut) nuts. *Hua kukui ka i'a,* the fish resemble *kukui* nuts [describing schools of fish with noses protruding from the water].

hua kumu. n. Alphabet. *Lit.,* basic letters.

hū.ala.kē. vs. Loose; to tie loosely; round, full, swelling; to sag, as cheeks.

hua.lala. vs. Curved, warped, oval, twisted.

hua.lani. n. A variety of sweet potato.

hua.lani. n. Offspring of a chief.

hua.lau. n. A variety of banana. *Lit.,* many fruits.

huāle. Var. spelling of *huaale.*

hua.lele. n. **1.** Seeds of the *laulele* plant. **2.** Hernia. *Lit.,* flying testicles.

hua leo hui. See *hua palapala leo hui.*

hua leo kahi. See *hua palapala leo kahi.*

hu'a.lepo. vi. To scatter dust, especially a method of fighting with a club or spear in which the opponent was blinded by stirring up dust; to hit an underhanded blow. Also *hu'elepo. Wili a'ela 'o Pūpū-ākea i kāna lā'au, a hu'alepo akula ma nā wāwae o Maka-kū-i-ka-lani* (For. 4:349), Pūpū-ākea twirled his club and scattered dust at the feet of Maka-kū-i-ka-lani.

hua lewa. n. *'Ōhi'a* or *'ōhi'a 'ai* fruit used as medicine (Kam. 64:103, 141); perhaps also a kind of wood.

huali. vs. Bright, polished, clean, pure, white, glittering, gleaming; morally pure. *Ua huali kona kapa e like me ka hau* (Mat. 28.3), his raiment was white as snow. **ho'o.huali.** Caus/sim.; to polish (Ezek. 21.10). *Mehe 'ōlinolino lā ke nānā aku, a me ke keleawe ho'ohuali 'ia* (Ezek. 8..2), like the brightness of the sun to look upon, and gleaming bronze.

hua li'i. 1. nvs. Small or inferior fruit; runt; small, puny. **2.** n. Small letter.

hua li'i.li'i. 1. n. Berry. **2.** nvs. Grace note in music.

hua lili. n. Blasted fruit.

hua loa'a. n. Product, answer, as in arithmetic.

hu'a lole. n. Trimmings or borders of a garment; hem of a dress.

hū.'alu. n. Loose skin over the eyeball; slight viscous membrane covering the eye.

hua.lua. n. *mai'a hua lua.*

hua.lū.kini. n. Musk, as used in making perfume. See *wai Lūkini.*

hua mā.hoe. n. A two-note chord.

hua-mai-lani. Same as *kūkaeakua. Lit.,* fruit from heaven.

hua.makani. n. Tiny, yolkless egg. *Lit.,* wind egg.

hua mele. n. Notes in music; words of a song.

hua.moa. n. **1.** Round-ended bone entering the hip socket. **2.** Type of house with thatch purlins separated by a width of three fingers. (For. 5:645.) **3.** Same as *moa,* a native variety of banana. **4.** A variety of sweet potato.

hua moa. n. Chicken egg. (PPN *fua moa.*)

hu'a moena. n. Pile of mats. (For. 4:63.)

hua mua. n. **1.** Offering to a Congregational church of the first earnings in a new job or undertaking; offerings in gratitude for a particular success, as a big fish catch. *Lit.,* first fruit. **2.** Initial letter, first word.

huana. n. Gushing forth, overflow. *Hala ka huana wai,* gone is the rush of water.

hua nanai. n. Name of the *hinahina* root when used in *hana aloha,* love sorcery.

hua nui. 1. nvi. Large fruit; to be fruitful, productive. **2.** n. Capital letter.

hua 'oko'a. n. Whole note in music.

hua 'ole. vs. Fruitless, unproductive, worthless, sterile, unrewarding.

hua 'ō.lelo. n. **1.** Word, term. **2.** An affront to a family *'aumakua* god. *E no'ono'o noho'i i ka hua 'ōlelo,* then think of the affront [that caused the god's displeasure].

hua 'ō.lelo ho'o.hui 'ia. n. Compound word.

hua.'ono. n. A variety of sweet potato.

hua pā.kā. n. Scrambled eggs, omelet.

hua.pala. 1. n. Orange trumpet or sweetheart vine *(Pyrostegia venusta* syn. *Bignonia venusta, B. ignea),* an ornamental climber from Brazil, bearing early in the year many deep-orange flowers, hence chestnut-colored or light brown. (Neal 764.) *Lit.,* ripe fruit. **2.** nvs. Sweetheart, lover; pretty, handsome. *Ē Kohala i ka huapala kau i ka nuku,* O Kohala with the handsome folk to delight the eyes [*lit.,* to appear at the mouth]. **3.** nvs. Chestnut brown.

huapalaoa. n. Wheat. *Lit.,* flour *(Eng.)* grain. *'Ai 'ia nā pu'u huapalaoa* (Puk. 22.6), the stacked grain is consumed.

hua palaoa 'ele.'ele. n. Rye *(Secale cereale).*

hua pala.pala. n. Letter of the alphabet. *Lit.,* writing letter.

hua pala.pala hiō. n. Italics.

hua pala.pala leo hui, hua leo hui. n. Consonant. *Lit.,* letter joined in pronunciation.

hua pala.pala leo kahi, hua leo kahi. n. Vowel. *Lit.,* letter pronounced separately.

hua pala.pala nui. n. Capital letter.

hua pale (bale). n. Barley *(Hordeum vulgare). Ho'okahi paha 'epa hua bale* (Ruta 2.17), about an ephah of barley.

hua pāma. n. Date. *Lit.,* fruit of *pāma,* date palm.

hua.pī. Same as *'alae huapī.*

hua.po'o. n. Bones of the side of the head; side of the head.

hua pō.polo. n. *Pōpolo* berry. Also *'olohua.*

hua.'ula.'ula. n. The red sandalwood tree *(Adenanthera pavonina),* from parts of tropical Asia and Malaysia, of moderate height and with rather widespreading branches. The tree is planted in parks, and its round, lens-shaped, red seeds are used for leis, and their long, yellow-lined pods for decorative arrangements. (Neal 414.)

hua.waena. Same as *hāpai,* a variety of banana.

hua.wai. Var. of *hue wai,* water gourd container.

hua.wai.maka. n. Collection of dew or rain water, pool.

hua waina. n. Grape, grapes *(Vitis* spp.). (Neal 540–3.) *Lit.,* wine *(Eng.)* fruit. *'O ka manawa ia o ka hua waina pala mua* (Nah. 13.20), it was the time of the first ripe grapes.

hua waina malo'o. n. Raisins. *Lit.,* dry grapes.

hue. 1. n. Gourd, water calabash, any narrow-necked vessel for holding water, flask. Cf. *ipu, pōhue.* (PPN *fue,* a creeper; PEP *fue,* gourd.) **2.** nvi. Quick, as in stealing or deception; light-fingered; to steal, filch, move fast; to work the rope fast in skipping rope; theft *(rare).* Cf. *'aihue.* (Probably PPN *fue.*) **3.** nvi. A type of hula dancing, usually at the end of a program, a kind of *'ai 'ami* with a revolving of the hips as fast as the drummer can beat time, to see who can dance longest; to dance thus. **4.** n. A way of connecting net sections by interlocking meshes.

hu'e. vt. To remove, lift off, uncover, expose; to unload, as a ship; to open, as an oven; to exhume, push, force,

prod; to wash out, as flood waters; to reveal. *Hu'e i ke kaona,* reveal the hidden meaning. *Ua hu'e ka wai i ke pili,* the water flowed out over the *pili* grass. *E hu'e mai 'oe i ke koai'e o Maka-wao,* uproot the *koai'e* tree of Maka-wao [a boast and challenge of the native of Maka-wao, Maui]. (PPN *fuke.*)

huea. Rare var. of *'aihue.* (For. 6:424.)

hu'ea. Pas/imp. of *hu'e. Hu'ea maila nā piha'ā moe wai o uka,* the flotsam in the upland stream comes pouring down [of gossip]. *Hu'ea pau 'ia e ka wai,* all washed away by water.

hue 'awa.'awa. n. Type of bitter gourd, as used for utensils.

Huehu. 1 n. Name of a strong northwesterly wind of the winter months. Also *Kiu Inu Wai* and *Mālua Ki'i Wai.* **2.** *(Not cap.)* vs. Chilled, benumbed, as of one shivering in this wind.

hue.hue. 1. nvi. Pimples, acne; to have pimples. (PPN *fuafua.*) **2.** n. A native climber *(Cocculus ferrandianus),* with oval leaves and bluish one-seeded fruits. The stems were used for twine and for funnel-mouthed fish traps. (Neal 354.) Also *hue 'ie.*

hu'e.hu'e. 1. Redup. of *hu'e;* to keep removing; to take out and put in again, as furniture; to overflow repeatedly. (PPN *fukefuke.*) **2.** See *hu'ehu'e kai.*

hue.hue haole. n. A wild passionflower *(Passiflora suberosa)* with small greenish-yellow flowers, small three-lobed or undivided leaves, and blackish fruits 1.3 cm in diameter. (Neal 597.) *Lit.,* introduced *huehue.*

hu'e.hu'e kai. Same as *hu'ahu'a kai 1, 2.*

hue.huelo. n. Tail end, as of a strip of pandanus plaiting. Cf. *huelo. He wahi huehuelo mana'o kēia,* this is a trivial bit of idea.

hue 'ie. 1. Same as *huehue 2.* **2.** n. Demijohn.

hue 'ili. n. Container or bag for liquids made of animal skin. *Nā hue 'ili waina kahiko* (Iosua 9.4), old wineskins.

hu'e.lepo. 1. Var. of *hu'alepo.* (FS 89.) **2.** n. Small hula graduating exercises held at noon outside in the dust *(lepo).*

huelo. 1. nvs. Tail, as of dog, cat, or pig; train of a dress; tail-end, last. *Fig.,* inferior. Cf. *huehuelo, pewa, hi'u, puapua. He po'e kanaka huelo ia* (Kel. 119), these are the tail ends of Hawaiians. **ho'o.huelo.** To lengthen, continue, make a tail; to stream down, as water over a cliff. **2.** A hop vine. (AP.)

huelo.'awa. n. Sting of a scorpion. *Lit.,* bitter tail.

huelo.elo. vs. Tail-like, having tails.

huelo.'ī.lio. n. A small shrub *(Buddleja asiatica),* native of southeastern Asia to Java, growing wild in Hawai'i, related to the summer lilac. It has narrow leaves and small white flowers growing in long narrow clusters. (Neal 683.) *Lit.,* dog tail.

huelo mā.ewa. n. Tail end, especially of a junior line of a lineage. (KL line 525.)

huelo.poki (boti). n. Whaleboat. *Eng.*

huelo.pō.poki. n. Australian bluegrass, *Andropogon sericeus. Lit.,* cat tail. *Ni'ihau.*

hue mā.nalo. n. An edible sweet gourd.

hu'ena. n. Opening, unloading, flowing, pushing. Cf. *hu'e. Ho'okahi nō hu'ena a nā kānaka i kā lākou māpuna hoe,* just one push by the men of their paddle stroke.

hū.'ena. vs. Very angry.

huene. n. A wheezing sound, as of asthmatic persons; a prolonged shrill cry.

hue nuku pueo. n. A variety of gourd with a short beak.

hū.'eu. nvs. Witty, comical, amusing, funny, mischievous; rascal, rogue.

hue wai. n. Gourd water container, water bottle.

hue wai 'ihi, hue wai 'ihi loa. n. Long-necked water container.

hue wai pū.'ali. n. Gourd water container with constriction about the middle.

hue wai pu.eo. n. Water gourd shaped like an hourglass. *Lit.,* owl water gourd.

hū.hā. **1.** nvi. Chat, talk, rumor; to chat, talk. **2.** nvs. Fat, unwieldy; such a person.

hū.hewa. vi. To miss the course, digress, fail to penetrate or grasp. *Hūhewa ka pōkā,* the shot missed the mark. *Hūhewa kō lākou lohe, a me kō lākou 'ike a'o 'ia* (Kep. 15), what they heard and were taught was not maintained. *Ua hūhewa paha ke Kīna'u* (song), the Kīna'u [ship] has perhaps gone off her course.

hū honua. vi. To come out of the earth as a spring or an outcrop of *'alaea* dirt. *Fig.,* to rise in revolt.

huhu. **1.** n. A wood-boring insect, termite; worm-eaten, rotten. *E 'ai noho'i ka huhu iā lākou e like me ka hulu hipa* (Isa. 51.8), and the worm shall eat them like wool. (PCP *(f,s)u(f,s)u.*) **2.** vt. To pet, cherish, as animal pets. *Hānai ā huhu,* to raise a pet. *Moe kō a ka huhu,* dream fulfilled and cherished.

huhū. nvi. Angry, offended, indignant, mad, scolding; anger, wrath; to scold, become angry. See ex., *pau pū. Huhū wela loa,* very great anger, fury. *Pi'i ka huhū,* to become angry. **ho'o.huhū.** To provoke anger, pretend anger. *Mai ho'ohuhū aku iāia* (Puk. 23.21), do not rebel against him.

hū.hū. Redup. of *hū 1;* to bulge; to effervesce. (PPN suusuu.)

huhu-'ai-lā'au. n. Wood-eating borer. (For. 5:169.)

huhue. Possibly a redup. of *hue 2,* fast. *Huhue nā keiki paniolo* (chant), the cowboys were fast.

huhu'e. Probably a redup. of *hu'e;* to cease, quit. *Huhu'e aku kāua, moe i ke awakea* (FS 94-5), let's stop [fighting], sleep at noon.

huhuhu. vi. Insect-eaten, rotten, worm-eaten, wormy.

huhu.hue. Redup. of *hue 2;* to filch repeatedly, to steal in company.

huhu.hui. Redup. of *hui 1;* to meet as equals, as two beautiful persons.

huhu.hula. nvi. Hawaiian hula by many persons; to hula, of many.

huhu.hulei. Redup. of *hulei;* lifting, tossing about, trotting, sporting, leaping, twisting.

huhu.huli. Redup. of *huhuli;* to turn, seek frequently. See *huli 1, 2.*

huhu.hume. Redup. of *huhume.*

huhu.huna. Redup. of *huhuna.*

huhu.hune. Redup. of *hunehune* and *hune 1, 2;* fine, dainty; stripped of all property.

huhui. n. **1.** Cluster, collection, swarm, bunch. Also *huihui. E noho malalo o ka lā'au maka, iho mai ka huhui, mā'ona ka 'ōpū,* sit under a green tree, the cluster falls, stomach is filled [serve a worthy person and you will be rewarded]. **2.** *(Cap.)* Pleiades. Also *Huihui. Ho'opa'a i nā mea pa'a o nā Huhui* (Ioba 38.31), bind the chains of the Pleiades.

huhui helu. n. Logarithm. *Lit.,* number collection.

huhui palaoa. n. Ears of grain. (Mat. 12.1.)

huhui waina. n. Cluster of grapes. *A 'o kā lākou hua waina, he hua waina make, a 'o nā huhui waina a lākou, he 'awa'awa ia* (Kanl. 32.32), their grapes are grapes of poison, their grape clusters are bitter.

huhuki. Redup. of *huki;* to pull hard or frequently. *Pau ke kalo i ka huhuki 'ia,* all the taro was pulled up. *Koi huhuki,* compelling, insistent urge. **ho'o.huhuki.** To pull, cause to pull. *Fig.,* headstrong. (PPN *fufuti.*)

huhuku. Redup. of *huku.*

huhula. nvt. Hula dance by many; to dance the hula, of many.

huhuli. Redup. of *huli 1, 2;* to seek, turn, of many and repeatedly.

huhulu. vs. Bristling, tousled, as feathers, fur, body hair.

huhulu i'i. Intensifier of *huhulu. Huhulu i'i ka hulu o ka manu i ka ua kakahiaka* (chant), tousled were the feathers of the bird in the morning rain.

huhulu kū. vi. To rise, as fur of an angry dog.

huhulu weo. Same as *huluhulu weo.*

huhume. Redup. of *hume.*

huhuna. Redup. of *huna;* particles, fragments.

huhune. **1.** Redup. of *hune 1, 2.* **2.** nvi. Skin eruption on animals, as hog, dog; to have such.

huhu-pao-lā'au. n. A wood borer. *Fig.,* slanderer, defamer. *Lit.,* borer that digs wood.

huhū wale. vi. Short-tempered, peevish, cantankerous, angry without cause.

hui. **1.** nvi. Club, association, society, corporation, company, institution, organization, band, league, firm, joint ownership, partnership, union, alliance, troupe, team; to form a society or organization; to meet, intermingle, associate, congregate. (Probably *hū 7 + -i,* transitivizer; cf. Gram. 6.6.4.) *Ā hui hou aku,* goodby; till [we] meet again. **ho'o.hui.** To form a society. *Palapala ho'ohui,* charter, as of an association. (PPN *fuhi.*) **2.** nvi. To join, unite, combine, mix; combination. See *hui pū* and saying, *nāwao 1. Hui 'ia,* united, joined, joint. *Nā mahele i hui 'ia,* combined divisions, precincts. *Hui ka 'aha,* to press together, of a crowd; to mingle, as two sides at the conclusion of an athletic competition (For. 5:407). *Ka hui 'ia o ka loa a me ka laulā, pēlā e loa'a mai ai ka 'alea,* the multiplication of the length and the width, thus is obtained the area. **ho'o.hui.** To join, as two words; to add a prefix or suffix; to add on, annex, append, unite; to introduce one person to another; meeting of persons; binder. *Ho'ohui 'ia,* united, allied. *Ho'ohui ā ho'opa'a,* to bring together, consolidate. *Ho'ohui 'ana,* union, joining. *Ho'ohui 'āina,* joining of lands, annexation. *Ho'ohui helu,* to connect, as telephone numbers by a telephone operator. *Ka ho'ohui o ka mīkini humuhumu,* sewing machine binder. (PPN *fuhi.*) **3.** n. A plus sign. **4.** n. Cluster, as of grapes or coconuts; bunch, as of bananas. Also *huhui, huihui.* **5.** n. Chorus of a song. **6.** n. Flippers of a turtle. *Ua loha nā hui o Hā'upu,* the flippers of Hā'upu droop [an aged person, a reference to the story of *Kana* and *Niheu,* in which a turtle lifted up Hā'upu hill on Moloka'i]. **7.** Var. of *huli,* to turn, seek. *Hui iho nei ka wa'a a Ka-moho-ali'i* (chant), Ka-moho-ali'i's canoe turned. **8.** n. Small uniting stick in a thatched roof, supporting rod for purlins. **9.** vi. To disperse, as a meeting. **10.** A prayer on the morning after *'anā'anā* sorcery. (For. 6:17.) (Pronunciation uncertain: perhaps *hu'i.*)

hūi. interj. Halloo.

hu'i. **1.** nvs. Ache, pain; aching. *Niho hu'i,* toothache. (PPN *suki.*) **2.** n. A prayer.

huia. **1.** Pas/imp. of *hui 2. 'O 'oe ka i huia ihola, ē ke aloha* (song), you are the one who was met, O love. (PPN *fuhia.*) **2.** *(Cap.)* n. Name of a surfing wave. (Laie 505.)

hui.'apa. n. A kind of stone, as used for making *maika* stones.

Hui Hei.hei Moku Pā.kī.pika. n. Pacific Yacht Club. *Lit.,* Pacific ship racing club.

hui hali ukana. n. Express company.

hui hō.'ai.'ē kā.lā (dala). n. Credit union. *Lit.,* society [for] loaning money.

hui ho'o.pa'a. n. Insurance company.

hui.hui. **1.** vi. Mixed, mingled, united, joined; to pool together, as to buy cooperatively. **ho'o.hui.hui.** Caus/sim. *Ho'ohuihui lā'au,* chemistry, pharmacist. *Mea ho'ohuihui,* alloy, anything mixed. *Mea inu ho'ohuihui,* mixed drink, punch. **2.** n. Cluster, collection, bunch. (PPN *fuhifuhi.*) **3.** n. Constellation. *Nā hōkū o ka lani a me nā huihui ona* (Isa. 13.10), the stars of the heavens and their constellations. **4.** *(Cap.)* n. Pleiades. Also *Huihui.*

hu'i.hu'i. nvi. Cold, cool, chilly; numbing, tingling, as love. *He aloha hu'ihu'i konikoni ana i loko o u'u,* ardent, tingling love within me. *Ke kī'aha wai hu'ihu'i* (Mat. 10.42), the cup of cold water. **ho'o.hu'i.hu'i.** To make cold, chill, as by refrigeration. *Mea inu ho'ohu'ihu'i,* iced or chilled drink.

hui.hui ā kō.lea. vi. To gather together like a flock of *kōlea* birds. *Fig.,* to gather together to help one another in time of trouble.

Hui.hui-kō.kō-a-Maka.li'i-kau-i-luna. n. A name for Pleiades. *Lit.,* Makali'i's net hanging above. (HM 368.)
hui.hui maka li'i. n. A kind of seaweed.
hui.huini. Redup. of *huini 1, 2.*
hui 'ia. vs. Incorporated, united, joined.
huika, huita. n. Wheat. *Eng. Palaoa o ka huita* (Puk. 29.2), wheat flour.
hui kahi. vs. 1. United in one; in accord and agreement. 2. Girded in *malo* or *pā'ū* tightly fastened with a single hitch.
hui.ka'i. vt. To mix or jumble, make disagreeing statements, put several stories into one. (*hui 2 + -ka'i,* transitivizer; cf. Gram. 6.6.4.)
hui.kala. nvt. To absolve entirely, forgive all faults, excuse, cleanse and purify morally; pardon, atonement, absolution; ceremonial cleansing. Cf. Malo 199. *E huikala 'oukou iā 'oukou iho* (Oihk. 20.7), sanctify yourselves.
hui kā.lepa. n. Trading company, mercantile firm.
hui.kau. nvs. Mixed, confused, haphazard, blurred; mix-up, confusion, jumble; to mix. *Huikau ka makau a ka lawai'a,* the fisherman's hook is tangled [of confusion]. **ho'o.hui.kau.** Caus/sim., to mix, confuse, complicate, perplex, scramble.
Hui Ke'a 'Ula.'ula. n. Red Cross.
hui kinai ahi. n. Fire department.
huila. 1. Rare var. of *uila. Huila nā pū,* the guns flashed. See ex., *'api'api 3.* **2.** n. Wheel. *Eng. Ke 'ano o nā huila* (Ezek. 1.16), the appearance of the wheels.
huila kau.like. n. Disc wheel of a sewing machine.
huila makani. n. Pinwheel. *Lit.,* wind wheel.
huila niho.niho. n. Stitch regulator of a sewing machine.
huila nui. n. Large wheel; flywheel, as of a sewing machine.
huila.palala, huilapalela. n. Wheelbarrow. *Eng.*
huila pō.niu.niu. Same as *ka'a pōniuniu,* Ferris wheel.
huila wai. n. Water wheel, windmill.
hu'i lele. n. Darting pain. (Kam 64:108.)
hui malū. nvi. Any secret society or fraternity, as the Masons; Masonic; to meet secretly.
Hui Moku Holo Pili.'āina. n. Inter-Island Steam Navigation Company.
Hui Moku.lele Pili.'āina. n. Inter-Island Airways Company.
huina. n. **1.** Sum, total, amount. (2 Sam. 24.9.) *E ho'oku'i i ka huina,* add up the total. *Ho'oku'i i ka huina o lākou me nā mamo a Isera'ela* (Nah. 1.49), add up a census of them among the descendants of Israel. **2.** Unit, cluster; military detail or detachment. *Ka huina lawe hae,* color detachment, color-bearing unit. **3.** Angle; corner, as of a house or street; crossroads, intersection, junction, juncture. **4.** Tie or slur (music).
huina-. Geometric figure. See *huinahā, huinakolu,* and others.
huina ala.nui. n. Crossroads, street corner.
huina.hā. n. Quadrangle, quadrilateral.
huina.hā hiō. n. Figure with four equal sides but oblique angles, rhombus.
huina.hā hiō lō.'ihi. n. Oblique parallelogram.
huina.hā kau.like. n. Square.
huina.hā like. n. Square. *Lit.,* equal square.
huina.hā like 'ole. n. Quadrangle with unequal sides.
huina.hā loa. n. Rectangle.
huina.hā lua like. n. Quadrangle with only two sides parallel, trapezoid.
huina.hā pā.'ani. n. Children's blocks.
huina helu. n. **1.** Sum of several numbers, total. *Huina helu 'oko'a* (Nah. 14.29), the whole number, sum total. **2.** General arithmetic.
huina.hiku. n. Heptagon.
huina koho. n. Purchase price, as at an auction.
huina.kolu. n. Triangle.
huina.kolu 'ao.'ao like 'ole. n. Irregular triangle.
huina.kolu 'elua 'ao.'ao like. n. Isosceles triangle.

huina.kolu kū.pono. n. Right-angle triangle.
huina.kolu like. n. Equilateral triangle.
huina.kolu 'oi. n. Acute triangle.
huina.kolu pele.leu. n. Obtuse triangle.
huina kū.pono. n. Right angle.
huina.lā.'au.lana. n. Raft. (1 Nal. 5.9). *Lit.,* collection of floating logs.
huina.lima. n. **1.** Pentagon. **2.** Joining of two hands, especially in hand wrestling *(uma).*
huina loa'a. n. Gross profit.
huina 'oi. n. Acute angle.
huina.ono. n. Hexagon.
huina.papa.lana. n. Raft. *Lit.,* collection of floating boards.
huina pele.leu. n. Obtuse angle.
huina pū kuni ahi. n. Battery (artillery).
huina.wai. n. Pool, meeting place of two or more streams. *Ma nā loko, a ma nā huinawai apau* (Puk. 7.19), over the ponds and all the pools of water.
huina waina. n. Cluster of grapes.
huina.walu. n. Octagon.
huini. 1. vs. Needle-pointed, sharp-pointed. **ho'o.huini.** To carve or sharpen into a point. **2.** nvi. Sharp, shrill sounds; to make such shrill cries. **3.** n. Wooden peg used in mending bowls. Also *kui lā'au.*
hui o Papa. n. Chorus of Papa, a prayer for the purification of women uttered in the early morning at the *Hale o Papa,* house of Papa, a temple reserved for women.
huipa. 1. n. Kind of hard, black stone used for *maika* stones. **2.** nvi. Whip; to whip. *Eng.*
hui.pa'a. n. Syntax. *Loina huipa'a,* rules of syntax.
hui.pū. n. Conjunction (the part of speech).
hui pū. vt. To mix, unite, blend, assemble, combine, mingle. See *'Amelika Huipū 'Ia. Hui pū 'ia,* united, joined.
hui puhi 'ohe. n. Band.
hui.pu'u. n. Type of *pā'ū* (no data).
hui 'uwī wai.ū. n. Dairy.
huka. 1. nvt. Hook, as on a door, shoes, clothes; to hook. *Eng.* **2.** Advice, information. (And.) **3.** A balm. (And.)
hū.kā. vt. To guzzle and gobble, as a hog; a call to hogs to come. *Hūkā noho'i ka 'ai 'ana,* such hoglike gobbling.
hū.ka'a. n. Pitch, resin, gum from a tree; resinous timber drifting to Hawai'i from the northwest coast of America.
huka.hukā. Redup. of *hūkā.*
huka.hū.kai. vs. Somewhat insipid, brackish. See *hūkākai.*
hū.kai. Same as *hūkākai.*
hū.kai.kai. Rare var. of *hūkākai.*
hukai.loloa. One who has long served a chief. (And.)
hū.kā.kai. 1. vs. Insipid, tasteless, bland, as food or poi made of immature taro; brackish. Also *'ōkākai.* **2.** Same as *'u'ulukai,* bloated.
huka pihi. nv. Buttonhook; to hook a button.
hū.kē. vt. To blow the nose. Also *ho'okē.*
Huke.kona, Hudesona. n. Hudson, as the river or bay. *Eng.*
hū.keu. n. Bulge, cheek of the buttocks.
huki. 1. vt. To pull or tug, as on a rope; to draw, stretch, reach; to support, as a political party. See ex., below. *Huki i luna,* to pull up, hoist. *O huki mamuli o kona 'ao'ao,* lest preference be shown to his side. *Huki i ka lani, ka lae o Ka-lā'au* (chant by Hi'iaka), reaching to the sky is point Ka-lā'au. **ho'o.huki.** Caus/sim.; to pull gently. (PPN *futi.*) **2.** nvi. A fit of any kind, convulsion, stroke, spasm, epileptic fit; twitching, cramp, as in the leg; to have a fit or cramp. Cf. *huki leo pa'a.* **3.** nvi. A hula step: one foot steps to the side, the other foot is pulled toward it so that the heels almost touch, and then is taken to the opposite side. **4.** vs. Soft, tender, as cooked meat that pulls apart when picked up. **5.** vs. Twisted, drawn at the mouth, as a result of illness.

-huki. hoʻo.huki. Willful, headstrong.
hukia. Pas/imp. of *huki 1, 2. Hukia ka waha o ka ʻupena,* pull the opening of the net. (PNP *futia.)*
huki.heʻe. 1. nvs. Smooth. **2.** n. Fine-meshed net used for fish fry. (FS 167.)
huki.huki. 1. nvt. To pull or draw frequently, or by many persons; to pull by jerks or continuously, as in the tug-of-war game; to gather, as taro; friction, dissension. *Hele maila lākou ā hukihuki i ka wai* (Puk. 2.16), they came to draw water. (PPN *futifuti.)* **2.** nvi. To disagree, quarrel; disagreement; not cooperative, headstrong, obstinate. *Pili hukihuki,* a relationship with constant quarrels, as in a family. **hoʻo.-huki.huki.** Caus/sim. **3.** nvi. Tug-of-war game; to play the game.
huki ʻino. vt. To jerk, pull hard or suddenly.
hukiki. Same as *ʻukiki,* small.
huki.kū. vi. **1.** Snobbish, haughty. **2.** Uncooperative.
huki.lau. nvi. A seine; to fish with the seine. *Lit.,* pull ropes *(lau).*
huki leo paʻa. n. Stroke that impedes speech.
huki like. vt. To pull or work together, cooperate.
hukina. n. A pulling. (Kep. 153.)
huki wai. nv. To draw water; one who draws water. *Hele aʻela kekahi wahine no Samaria e huki wai* (Ioane 4.7), there came a woman of Samaria to draw water.
hukopa, husopa. n. Hyssop. (Oihk. 14.4.) *Eng.*
huku. nvi. Protuberance, lump, projection, elevation, jutting out, heap; to protrude, jut. *Hehihehi ana i ka huku ʻale* (song for Ka-lā-kaua), treading on the swelling billows. **hoʻo.huku.** To project, protrude.
Hukue.noka, Huguenota. nvs. Huguenot. *Eng.*
huku liʻi. nvs. Small protuberance; small, little.
hula. 1. nvt. The hula, a hula dancer; to dance the hula. For types of hula see below and *ʻai haʻa, ʻala ʻapapa, ʻami, hapa haole, hue, kiʻelei, kōlani, kuhi, kuʻi, muʻumuʻu, ʻōhelo, ʻōlapa, ʻōniu, pahua, paʻi umauma, ʻūlili,* UL 275–6. For hulas named for instruments see *ʻiliʻili, kāʻekeʻeke, kā lāʻau, pahu, pā ipu, papa hehi, pūʻili, ʻulīʻulī.* For hulas named for creatures see below or *honu, ʻīlio, kōlea, manō, peʻepeʻemakawalu, puaʻa. He hula* (For. 5:479), a hula dancer. *Kumu hula,* hula master or teacher. *Hula mai ʻoe* (song), come to me dancing the hula. *Haihai akula nā wāhine apau mamuli ona, me nā mea kuolokani, a me ka hula* (Puk. 15.20), all the women followed after her with timbrels and dancing. **hoʻo.hula.** To cause someone to dance; to pretend to hula. (PCP *(f,s)ula.)* **2.** nvt. Song or chant used for the hula; to sing or chant for a hula. **3.** vi. To twitch, as a muscle or eyelid; to palpitate, throb. (PCP *(f,s)ula.)*
hulā. vi. To prod, pry, uproot, pierce and penetrate, expel, reject. Also *hulaʻa, kulaʻa, ʻulaʻa. ʻO mai maʻanei a hulā maʻō,* to pierce in on this side and come out on that. *E poholalo aʻe ana ʻo ʻAi-ohi-kupua i kāna puʻupuʻu . . . a hulā ma ke kua,* ʻAi-ohi-kupua gave an undercut blow with his fist . . . and it came out at the back. **hoʻo.hulā.** Caus/sim. *Rare.*
hulaʻa. Same as *hulā.*
hula.ʻana. n. Place where it is necessary to swim past a cliff that blocks passage along a beach or coast; sheer cliff where the sea beats.
hū lā.ʻau. n. Pitch, resin.
hula ʻau.ana. n. Informal hula without ceremony or offering, contrasted with the *hula kuahu;* modern hula.
hula.hē. vi. To jump for joy, cavort with happiness.
hula helo. Same as *hula ʻōhelo; see ʻōhelo.*
hula honu. n. Hula in which the dancer imitates the motions of a turtle.
hula hoʻo.nā.nā. n. Any hula for amusement. (UL 244.)
hula.hula. 1. nvt. Ballrom dancing with partners, American dancing, ball; massed hula dancing; to dance. (PEP *(f,s)ula(f,s)ula.)* **2.** Rare redup. of *hula 1–3;* twitching, fluttering. *Hulahula ka maka,* throbbing of an eyelid [considered by some a sign of rain or of coming grief]. **3.** nvt. Ceremonial killing of a pig and offer-

ing it to the gods during the long ceremonies dedicating a *luakini* temple. (Malo 170, 183.)
hulā.hulā. Same as *hulehulei.*
hula ʻili.ʻili. n. Hula in which smooth water-worn stones are used as clappers or castanets; the pebble hula.
hula ʻī.lio. n. A hula imitative of the movements of a dog. (UL 223.)
hula kiʻi. 1. nvi. Dance of the images in which the dancers postured stiffly like images; to dance thus. *Kauaʻi.* **2.** n. A dance with marionettes. (UL 91–102.)
hula kō.lea. n. A kneeling hula imitative of the *kōlea,* plover. (UL 219.)
hula kolili. n. A dance with love forfeits, similar to those in the *kilu* and *ʻume* games. (UL 247.)
hula kuahu. n. Altar hula, any hula taught with ceremonies and an altar, contrasting with *hula ʻauana.*
hula kuhi lima. See *kuhi 1.*
hula kuʻi. See *kuʻi,* joined.
hula kuʻi Molo.kaʻi. n. The punch *(kuʻi)* hula of Molokaʻi, an ancient, fast dance with stamping, heel twisting, thigh slapping, dipping of knees, doubling of fists as in boxing, vigorous gestures imitative of such pursuits as dragging fish nets, and unaccompanied by instruments. This dance originated on Molokaʻi, an island famous for sports. Many of the songs contain taunts, as *a laʻa kō kū i ke aʻu,* now you are jabbed by the swordfish. Cf. *hula kuʻi* under *kuʻi,* joined.
hula kuolo. n. Sitting chant dance; the performer beats the gourd drum *(ipu)* and chants. Also *pā ipu.*
hula lā.ʻau pili. n. Name of hulas performed for the coronation of Ka-lā-kaua, probably stick hulas.
hulali. 1. nvs. Shining, glittering, glossy, slippery; to shine, glitter, sparkle, reflect light. Cf. *ali, lali. Ka ʻōpuʻu kaimana e hulali nei lā* (song), diamond pendant sparkling here. **hoʻo.hulali.** Caus/sim. **2.** n. A kind of *loli,* sea cucumber. Also *kūnounou.*
hū.lali.lali. 1. Redup. and intensification of *hulali 1.* **2.** Same as *hulali 1.*
hula mā.nai. n. Dance with a thin flexible stick with which the squatting dancer beats time as by striking the floor.
hula manō. n. Sitting dance imitative of sharks. (UL 221.)
hula muʻu.muʻu. See *muʻumuʻu 1.*
hula nema.nema. n. Name of hulas performed for Ka-lā-kauaʻs coronation.
hū.lani. vt. To praise extravagantly, gush.
hula noho. nvi. Any sitting hula; to perform such.
hula ʻō.helo. See *ʻōhelo 3.*
hula ʻō.lepe.lepe. n. Name of hulas performed for Ka-lā-kauaʻs coronation.
hula pahu. See *pahu 1.*
hula Pahua. nvi. A kind of fast hula that increases to a frenzy, said to have been named originally for a *mele maʻi* named *Pahua* (shoved). Emerson (UL 183–5) calls it a stick dance and gives an example. To perform this dance.
hula Palani paʻi uma.uma. n. Name of chest-slapping hulas performed for Ka-lā-kauaʻs coronation.
hula papa hehi. n. Dance in which the dancers use the *papa hehi,* treadle boards; this dance is said to have originated on Niʻihau.
hula peʻe.peʻe.maka.walu. n. A spider dance with stiff legs, dancers hopped, right foot forward and left in reverse; then opposite, keeping time with a boisterous chant and with hands fluttering vigorously.
hula Pele. n. Sacred dance in honor of the goddess Pele.
hula puaʻa. n. A hula dance in which the hips sway from side to side in imitation of a fat hogʻs waddling. Also *ʻami puaʻa.*
hula ʻulī.ʻulī. n. Hula with *ʻulīʻulī,* gourds.
hule.hulei. Redup. of *hulei;* repeated motions or lifting; to seesaw.
hulei. vt. To lift, raise, draw up, as a skirt; to pull, pry; to pitch and toss, as a ship on the waves; to move along, as a ship; to flap wings; to trot, as a horse. Cf.

papa hulei. **ho'o.hulei.** Caus/sim. to trot, cause to trot, move back and forth. (PPN *fule*.)

hule.'ia. n. A kind of soft pumice stone. Also *'ana, 'ōla'i*.

hū.lei.lei. Redup. of *hulei*. **ho'o.hū.lei.lei.** Caus/sim.; to toss, as a child on one's foot.

hulei.lua. Intensifier of *hulei;* to toss and pitch, trot, swing. *Walawala ka pumi mahope, huleilua i ka 'ilikai*, the boom teetered at the stern, pitching on the surface of the sea. *Huleilua i nā nalu o Lau-niu-poko* [of one not sure of himself].

huli. 1. vi. To turn, reverse; to curl over, as a breaker; to change, as an opinion or manner of living. *E huli loa*, about face [military command]. *Ma ka 'ākau, huli*, right, face. *Kai huli*, a sea that dashes and recedes. *Huli i luna ke alo*, turning the front up [an early stage of infancy when the infant lies on its back]. *Pau ka 'ai 'ana, huli ke alo i luna*, after eating, turn over [relax]. **ho'o.huli.** To turn, change, affect, overturn, convert, reform. *Ho'ohuli kū'ē*, to alienate. (PPN *fuli*.) 2. nvt. To look for, search, explore, seek, study; search, investigation; scholarship (see *huli honua, huli kanaka*). **ho'o.huli.** Caus/sim. *Ho'ohuli pipi*, to drive cattle; cattle roundup. Also *huli pipi*. (Possibly PCP *(f,s)juli:* cf. Marquesan *hu'iahia*.) 3. n. Section, as of a town, place, or house. 4. n. Taro top, as used for planting; shoot, as of *wauke* (see *'ae 7*). See ex., *'ōmaka 1*. (PPN *suli*.) 5. n. Trump or winning card. *'A'ohe huli*, no trumps. 6. Same as *hului*, bag net.

hulia. Pas/imp. of *huli 1, 2*.

hulia.lana. v. To remove the bitterness, especially to pour off the bitter liquid and add fresh water to the preparation of arrowroot *(pia)*. *I pau ka hulialana* (a prayer; Malo 199), to remove the bitterness. *Ka pō luluka me ka hulialani, ma'ema'e ka 'āina, kōnalenale ka noho* (For. 6:403), the night of peace and returned tranquillity, clean the land, calm the dwelling.

huli alo. v. To turn toward; to face one another. *Iā 'Olopana me ke kahuna e huli alo ana* (FS 207), while 'Olopana and the priest faced each other.

Huli-alo-pali. n. Name of a wind at Lahaina, Maui. *Lit.*, turn to the face of the cliff.

huli.ā.mahi. 1. vi. To join together in great numbers to cooperate; to act with unanimity, as a political party. 2. vs. Strong, as the sea. See Gram. 8.7.2.

huli 'ao.'ao. v. To lean over to one side, tilt, turn to the side.

huli.au. 1. n. Turning point, time of change. *'O ka ho'ohui 'āina, he huliau ia no Hawai'i*, annexation was a turning point for Hawai'i. 2. vi. To think of the past, recall the past. *Ua 'ākoakoa mākou no ka huliau 'ana*, we gathered together to recall the past.

huli hana. v. Diligent in work; to seek work.

huli hele. vt. To search here and there. *Ua huli hele au i ku'u puke, 'a'ole i loa'a*, I looked everywhere for my book, [but] didn't find [it].

huli.hia. Pas/imp. of *huli 1, 2;* overturned; a complete change, overthrow; turned upside down. Chants about Pele with verses beginning with the word *"hulihia"* are referred to as *hulihia*. See prayer, *kualakai 2*. *Hulihia ka mauna, wela i ke ahi* (PH 204, 225), mountain overturned, hot with fire. *Hulihia Kī-lau-ea, pō i ka uahi* (PH 197), Kī-lau-ea [Volcano] is overturned, darkened by smoke. *Kaua hulihia*, revolutionary war. (PNP *fulisia*.)

huli honua. nv. Profound study of the earth, geology; to do such. Cf. RC 433.

huli hope. vi. To turn back; inverse, as in math.

huli.huli. Redup. of *huli 1, 2;* to search repeatedly or long; searching by many people; to turn repeatedly. *Kōmike hulihuli*, reference committee, as in the legislature. *E hulihuli mai 'oia iā 'oukou* (Ioba 13.9), he searches you out. **ho'o.huli.huli.** Caus/sim.; to convert. (PPN *fulifuli*.)

huli kanaka. nv. Profound studies of any kind, moral philosophy, social science, anthropology; to do such.

huli.ko'a. nvt. To seek into the depths of a matter, to describe fully; description. *"He Wahi Huliko'a Manu Hawai'i"* (title of an article about birds), "A Short Study of Hawaiian Birds."

huli.kua. n. Ornamental comb decorated with feathers, with ornaments turned towards the back. (Malo 77.)

huli kua. 1. nv. To turn one's back, refuse to help, ignore; one who does so, as one who is offended. 2. n. Back section, as back house wall.

huli.lau. n. 1. A variety of large gourd or calabash, used as receptacle for tapa or garments, or for food offerings. *Fig.*, a woman, mother, wife. *'O ka po'e hulilau 'ole o hope*, those with no large gourd calabashes in the back [without wives]. 2. Border, boundary. *Ke 'ike maila nō 'o Lā'ie-ka-wai i ka 'aha kanaka mai kēlā hulilau a kēia hulilau o ke kaha o Kea'au*, Lā'ie-ka-wai looked at the assembly of people from that border to this border of the arena at Kea'au.

huli.lawa. vt. To find enough material goods, as food. *Hiki ke hulilawa i ka i'a*, possible to get enough meat.

hulili. nvs. Dazzling light, vibration, undulation; to blaze, sparkle, dazzle, glare, vibrate, swell. **ho'o.-hulili.** Caus/sim.

hū.lili. 1. nvt. Ladder, bridge, as to scale a cliff or cross a gully; trestle; log or plank serving as a bridge; steep trail; to lay sticks, as for a bridge or trestle. See ex., *wāhia*. 2. n. Garrison, fort, tower, altar, strong high place. 3. n. Bracelet of hog's or dog's teeth. (For. 5.419.) 4. n. A type of tapa.

huli.lī. vi. To shiver. Cf. *lī*.

huli lua. vi. To turn in two directions or twice; to shift, as the wind; unstable, shifting. *Nā pali huli lua*, cliffs facing each other. *Mehe makani huli lua lā, huli ka mana'o*, like a shifting wind, the mind changes.

huli.mai'a. n. Name of a reddish-brown honey-sucking bird (no data). *Lit.*, banana seeker.

huli mana'o. v. To seek an opinion; to change an opinion. **ho'o.huli mana'o.** To induce change of opinion, influence, convert.

huli mio. n. Taro stalk with spent strength.

huli.moku. vi. To turn and rush; to pour forth, as a cloudburst; to stampede.

hulina. 1. n. Turning, overturning, turning place, reversing, frontage. *Ka hulina i ke Ko'olau*, the side facing the Ko'olau. 2. n. A searching, seeking; search. 3. vs. Soft and sticky, glutinous, gluey. Also *'ūlina*.

hulina alo. n. Facing, face to face, opposite. *Ka Mauna 'Oliweka ma ka hulina alo o ka luakini* (Mar. 13.3), Mount of Olives opposite the temple.

huli.nu'u. n. Highest rank or grade.

huli.pahu. n. Second mate of a vessel. *Lit.*, binnacle turner.

huli pau. vt. To overturn completely; to search everywhere; said sometimes as equivalent to modern "bottoms up" toast, instead of the vulgar " '*ōkole maluna.'*"

huli.peua. nvs. Greedy; a greedy person.

huli pewa. n. Twists of the tail; *fig.*, passing of time. See *pawa 1* and *pewa 1*.

huli.poe.poe. n. Globe. *Lit.*, revolving sphere.

huli.pū. Same as *ulua kihikihi*, a fish.

huli pū. vt. To overturn, turn upside down, overthrow.

huli.pū.loa. n. A variety of taro. (HP 32.)

hulō, huro. interj. Hurrah, cheers. *Eng.* See ex., *kiliwehi, pa'apa'ina*. **ho'o.hulō.** Caus/sim. *Rare*.

hulu. 1. n. Feather, quill, plumage. (PPN *fulu*.) 2. nvs. Esteemed, choice, precious; esteemed older relative, as of parents or grandparents' generations. (This meaning may be connected with the high value attached to featherwork.) *He hulu ali'i*, an elderly chief who is loved and esteemed. *Nā hulu maka'āinana o nā ali'i*, the most precious of the chiefs' citizenry. **ho'o.hulu.** To esteem, prize. *Inā ho'i 'oe he manu lele i luna, ho'ohulu aku ua hoa nei* (chant for Ka-mehameha III), if you then were a bird flying above, this companion would nurse great esteem. **3.** n. Fur, wool, fleece, human body hair (contrasting with *lauoho*, head hair). *Ka hulu 'ako mua o kāu po'e hipa* (Kanl. 18.4), the fleece first shorn of your sheep. (PPN *fulu*.) **4.** n. Kind, nature, color, *Ho'okahi nō hulu like o kēlā po'e,* those people are of the same sort. (PEP *fulu*.) **5.** n. Hackle; fishhook with barb on the outside (Malo 79). *Rare.* **6.** n. Brush. *Rare.* **7.** n. Muscle attaching a bivalve to rocks. *Rare.* **8.** n. Seal, named for its valuable fur. *Rare.* **9.** n. Cloth. See *hulu hipa, hulumanu.* **10.** Same as *hulu 'īlio 1, nahawele 2, pūhuluhulu 2,* a seaweed.

hulu 'ā.'īlio. n. Horse's mane.

hulu 'aina 'ole. n. An esteemed, beloved person well cared for. *Lit.,* choice one not rejected.

hulu ali'i. n. Royal favorite and loved one; royal feather.

hulu.'ā.nai. n. **1.** Scrubbing or painting brush, formerly made of a coconut husk. **2.** A variety of sea urchin.

hulu hipa. n. Sheep wool, fleece; woolen cloth. *Nā mea 'ako hulu hipa* (1 Sam. 25.7), wool shearers.

hulu.hulu. nvs. Body hair, hair of eyelashes, fleece (Lunk. 6.37), wool, fur; hairy. (PPN *fulufulu*.) **2.** vs. Frayed, splintered, rough, not smooth, shaggy, bristling, feathery. Also *'āhuluhulu. 'Eke huluhulu,* gunny sack. *Lopi huluhulu,* worsted thread. *Papa huluhulu,* rough lumber. **3.** n. Blanket. *Kūwili me kahi huluhulu moe kēhau o Milo-li'i,* moving restlessly on a blanket lying on the dew of Milo-li'i [poetic]. **4.** n. Feathers. Cf. *kauila huluhulu. Kū ā huluhulu Pana'ewa* (chant), Pana'ewa has trees like plumes. (PPN *fulufulu*.) **5.** n. Down or fuzz on plant stems, rootlet. **6.** Short for *'aha huluhulu,* a bristle worm. **7.** Same as *ma'o,* cotton. **8.** n. Kinds of seaweeds and mosses. **9.** n. Flannel.

hulu.hulu-a-'ī.lio. n. A green, velvety, carpet-like mountain moss. The spore cases rise above the plants. *Lit.,* fur like a dog's.

hulu.hulu-a-'iole. Same as *hulu 'iole.*

hulu.hulu 'i'i. Same as *hulu 'i'i.*

hulu.hulu waena. n. An irregularly branching, dark-red seaweed *(Grateloupia filicina)* with many narrow segments. It is commonly eaten and is sold in some markets. Also *pakele-a-wa'a.*

hulu.hulu weo. vs. Bristling, glowing. *'Ele'ele ka lani huluhulu weo* (birth chant for Ka-mehameha III), the sky is dark and bristles and glows.

hului. 1. nvi. A kind of bag fish net; to drag such a net. Also *huli, papa hului. He kai hului kō Kālia,* a sea for dragnet fishing at Kālia. **2.** vt. To take or grab, as winnings. *Ua hului 'ia aku nei ka 'ulu a kākou,* our breadfruit has been taken away.

hulu 'i'i. n. A kind of seaweed.

hulu 'ī.lio. n. **1.** A fine, red seaweed *(Centroceras clavulatum),* forming short, dense, regularly branching tufts, with tiny forked tips; not edible. Also *hulu, pūhuluhulu, wāwae'iole. Lit.,* dog fur. **2.** Fine, branching, edible brown seaweeds *(Ectocarpus* spp.), forming short, olive-brown clumps. **3.** A fine, branching, green seaweed *(Cladophora nitida),* forming flexible, long, bright-green tufts; said to be edible. **4.** A fine, feathery, green, fresh-water alga *(Stigeoclonium amoenum),* found in streams and ditches; said to be edible. **5.** A fine, unbranched, green seaweed *(Chaetomorpha antennina),* looking much like 3 above. Also *'īlio, nahawele.* **6.** A fine, nonedible, brown seaweed *(Sphacelaria tribuloides),* densely tufted, shorter and darker brown than *Ectocarpus.* **7.** Some kinds of *Polysiphonia* seaweeds.

hulu 'iole. Same as *wāwae'iole,* a plant.

hulu.'iwi. n. A pig that is reddish-colored about the hams. (Malo 37.) *Lit., 'iwi* bird feather.

hulu kā.kau. n. A pen, quill for writing.

hulu.koa. n. Bird crest.

hulu.koa'e. n. A kind of grass.

hulu ko'o. n. Long tail feathers, as of a rooster.

hulu ku'e.maka. n. Eyebrow. *E koli 'oia i kona lauoho apau . . . a me kona 'umi'umi, a me kona hulu ku'e-*

maka (Oihk. 14.9), he shall shave off all his hair . . . and his beard, and his eyebrows.

hulu kupu. n. Pinfeathers, new-grown fur.

hulu kupuna. n. The precious few living blood relatives of the grandparent's generation (a term of affection and pride).

hulu.lua. n. Hook with two barbs.

hulu makua. n. Precious parent or relative of the parent's generation. Cf. *hulu kupuna.*

hulu.manu. n. Tick used for mattresses and pillow covers, so called because they were stuffed with bird feathers.

hulu manu. n. **1.** Bird feathers. **2.** Green seaweeds *(Caulerpa* spp.), growing like land plants, with roots, prostrate stems, and leaflike divided fronds; not edible. Also *'ai-a-ka-honu, hulu moa, līmoa.* **3.** Court favorites of Ka-mehameha III.

hulu.moa. n. The Hawaiian mistletoes *(Korthalsella* spp., formerly called *Viscum),* small plants perching on trees and extracting part of their food from them. They have flat or cylindrical jointed green stems. (Neal 324–5.) *Lit.,* chicken feathers. Also *kaumahana.*

hulu moa. Same as *hulu manu 2.*

hulu-o-Ka'au.hele.moa. n. A moss said to grow only in Pālolo Valley, Honolulu, named for Ka'au-hele-moa, a legendary cock defeated in battle by a hen. She pulled out his feathers, which fell and became this moss. It is used in leis.

hulu.pala. vs. Light brown, bay, as a horse. *Inā 'o ku'u lio hulupala,* if it had been my bay horse.

hulu pena. n. Paintbrush.

hulu.peu. Rare var. of *hulu weuweu.*

hulu pi'i. n. Body hair, animal hair, or feathers standing on end.

hulu.pua'a. n. Beard hanging from the breast of mature turkey males. *Lit.,* hog hair.

hulu pua'a. n. A small, matted, red seaweed *(Spyridia spinella),* its many branches covered with short bristles. It is rather common in shallow water near shore. It is eaten in South Hawai'i, but not generally elsewhere.

hulu waena. Same as *huluhulu waena.*

hulu weu.weu. n. Downy feathers or beard, fuzz.

hume. vt. To bind about the loins, as a *malo;* to put on a *malo;* to wear a sanitary napkin. *Mea hume,* sanitary napkin. **ho'o.hume.** To put a loincloth on another. (PCP *(f,s)ume.*)

humea. Pas/imp. of *hume. O humea ka malo lani o Līloa* (chant), gird on the divine loincloth of Līloa.

hume.hume. Redup. of *hume.*

humena. n. A girding on of a loincloth; part of the loins covered by the *malo.*

humu. 1. nvt. To sew, stitch; seam, stitch; to bind together parts of a fishhook; to bind, as a book. *Nā puke i humu 'ia,* the books that were bound. **ho'o.-humu.** To make someone sew. (PNP *sumu.*) **2.** n. Hole by which parts of a hook were bound together. **3.** *(Cap.)* n. The star Altair, in Aquila, said to have been used for navigation from Hawai'i to Tahiti. Also *Ho'ohumu.* (PNP *Sumu.*) **4.** Short for *paehumu,* taboo enclosure.

humu ho'i. nvt. Back stitching; to sew with back stitching.

humu (humu.humu) ho'o.holo.holo. n. Running stitch, basting. Also *humu kāholo.*

humu.humu. 1. Redup. of *humu;* to sew, of many or continuously. *E ho'ouna ana mākou i nā puke a pa'i 'ia a e humuhumu 'ia,* we are sending the books to be printed and bound. **2.** n. Trigger fish. The name *humuhumu* is qualified by the following terms (in addition to those listed separately as identified): *kapa* or *kapu, lei, māne'one'o* (said to be irritating to the mouth), *'uwī'uwī* (thought by some to be the young of the *māne'one'o*). (PPN *sumusumu.*) **3.** n. A variety of taro with coloring like that of the *humuhumu* (fish); the leaf stem is pink at base, dark-purple midway and green above. (HP 18, 32.) **4.** n. A dark-colored birthmark, believed to be the result of the pregnant mother's eating *humuhumu* (fish). **5.** vt. To destroy, ravage. *ʻAi humuhumu ka maʻi i nā kānaka,* the disease ravaged the people. **6.** n. Seam. See *komo humuhumu.*

humu.humu ʻele.ʻele. n. Black triggerfish *(Melichthys niger),* used as fuel when fuel was scarce.

humu.humu hiʻu kole. n. Pinktail durgon *(Melichthys vidua). Lit.,* red-tailed triggerfish.

humu.humu lei. n. Lei triggerfish *(Sufflamen bursa).*

humu.humu meʻe.meʻe. Same as *humuhumu-nuku-nuku-ā-puaʻa.* (And.)

humu.humu mimi. n. Bridled triggerfish *(Sufflamen fraenatus). Lit.,* urine triggerfish, so called because of its odor.

humu.humu-nuku.nuku-ā-puaʻa. n. Varieties of *humuhumu (Rhinecanthus aculeatus, R. rectangulus). Lit., humuhumu* with a snout like a pig.

humu.humu puke. n. Bookbinding.

humu.humu puke ʻili lole. n. Cloth bookbinding.

humu.humu puke ʻili pepa. n. Paper bookbinding.

humu.humu ulana. vt. To darn, as socks.

humu.humu uli. Same as *humuhumu hiʻu kole.*

humu.humu uma.uma lei. n. A variety of *humuhumu* fish *(Balistes bursa). Lit., humuhumu* with leis on its chest.

humu.kā. nvt. Cross-stitching; to do cross-stitching.

humu kā.holo (kā.holo.holo). Same as *humu hoʻo-holoholo.*

humu kaula.hao. nvt. Chain stitch; to make chain stitches.

humu lala. vt. To sew in a diagonal line.

humu.lau. vt. To embroider. *He holokū kilika i humulau ʻia me ka pua Pākē,* it is a silk gown *(holokū)* embroidered with Chinese flowers.

Humu-mā. n. Name for the cluster of three stars in a row in the constellation Aquila. *Lit.,* Humu and companions.

humuna. n. Sewing, seam.

humu.niki. n. Pattern in *pāwehe* plaiting, said to consist of a continuous row of red lozenges with their lateral angles touching.

humu.ʻō.mou. n. Stitch used in tacking.

humu.paʻa. nvt. Lock stitch, a stitch that does not loosen easily; to sew thus.

humu.papa. vt. To sew to a backing, as feather leis.

humu peʻa. nv. Sail-making; to sew sails.

humu puka pihi. n. Buttonhole stitch.

humu.ʻula. n. **1.** Red jasper stone, as used for adzes. **2.** *(Cap.)* Name of a place on the slopes of Mauna Kea.

humu.wili. n. Overcasting stitch; to hem.

huna. 1. nvs. Minute particle, grain, crumb, gram, speck, tiny bit, scrap, minutia; small, little, powdery. (This word is similar to *hune 2.*) Cf. *hunaahi, huna kai, huna kaua, huna lepo, hunalewa, huna olonā. Ka hāʻule ʻana o kekahi huna o ke kānāwai* (Luka 16.17), the voiding of one dot of the law. **2.** nvs. Hidden secret; hidden. Cf. *huna,* a stative usually following .nouns, and the transitive verb *hūnā. Wahi huna,* hidden place, sexual part. *Lua huna,* secret cave. *Mea huna,* secret. *Kahi huna* (Oihk. 18.7), nakedness. (PNP *funa.*) **3.** *(Cap.)* n. Eleventh night of the month. (Malo 35.) **4.** n. Common, fine, red seaweeds *(Hypnea* spp.), irregularly and more or less densely branching, thorny looking; eaten cooked, furnishes a good colloid when boiled.

hū.nā. vt. To hide, conceal, disguise, secrete; confidential; covert. Cf. *huna 2, peʻe 1. He mea ia i hūnā ʻia,* this was a hidden thing. *He manaʻo e hūnā,* a thought to be hidden. *Hoʻo.hū.nā.* To hide deliberately. *Ua hoʻohūnā ʻoe i ka naʻauao mai kō lākou naʻau aku* (Ioba 17.4), you have closed their minds to understanding. (PPN *fuu,* PNP *fuuna-* (Rennell *huunaki*), PEP *naʻa.*)

hunaahi. n. Fire spark, live cinder. (Isa. 1.31.)

huna.huna. n. Fragments, particles, crumbs, scraps. *Hunahuna mea hou,* bits of news.

hunā.hunā. Redup. of *hūnā;* to hide frequently or be hidden by many persons; secretly. *Hunāhunā ʻole,* frank, open. **hoʻo.hunā.hunā.** Caus/sim. *Nīnau hoʻohunāhunā,* to ask in a roundabout way.

huna.huna ʻō.lelo. n. A particle, as *ua, e, i* in Hawaiian.

huna.kai. n. **1.** White-flowered beach morning-glory *(Ipomea stolonifera);* synonym, *I. acetosaefolia),* distributed in tropical regions, with oblong to lyre-shaped leaves, and white flowers with yellow centers. (Neal 705.) **2.** Sanderling *(Calidris alba),* a small winter migrant to Hawaiʻi, cinnamon brown with dark markings. *Lit.,* sea foam, so called from the bird's habit of following close behind receding waves.

huna kai. n. Sea spray, sea foam. Also *hune kai.*

Huna.kalia, Hunagaria. nvs. Hungary; Hungarian. Eng.

huna.kā.naʻi. n. A kind of tapa with white and yellow dots.

huna kaua. n. A battle unit, either a single individual or a group of men; host of an army (Iosua 10.5).

hū.nā.kele. vt. To hide in secret, as the body of a loved one in a secret cave; to keep a secret, conceal. *Ua hūnākele ʻoia i ka moʻolelo kupuna,* she has hidden the family records.

huna lepo. n. Dust particle. *Helu i nā huna lepo o Iakoba* (Nah. 23.10), count the dust of Jacob.

huna.lewa. n. Van of an army, front ranks. Cf. *hunapaʻa.*

huna olonā. n. Waste and refuse of *olonā* after the fiber is cleaned. *E lilo nō ka mea ikaika i huna olonā* (Isa. 1.31), the strong shall become tow.

huna.paʻa. n. Rear guard of an army.

huna pakē.pakē. n. A species of *Hypnea,* a seaweed. *Lit.,* brittle *huna.*

huna palai. Same as *pai,* a native fern.

huna wai. n. Drop of water, spray, mist.

huna wai.lele. n. Spray from a waterfall.

hune. 1. nvs. Poor, destitute; a poor person. Cf. *ʻilihune, māhune. He hune kō lākou nohona,* their way of life is poverty-stricken. **hoʻo.hune.** To cause poverty, impoverish. *E hoʻohune iā mākou* (Lunk. 14.15), to impoverish us. **2.** vs. Fine, tiny. Cf. *huna, kilihune, Menehune.*

-hune. hoʻo.hune. To persist, nag, tease; to do with avidity and persistence. See ex., *nē 1. Koi hoʻohune* (Nak. 101), keep asking. *He mea hoʻohune loa ka iʻa i ka makani hou,* the fish are constantly going into the fresh wind.

hune.hune. 1. Redup. and intensification of *hune 2,* very fine, delicate. *Palai lau hunehune,* fine-leafed fern. *Kilika hunehune,* fine quality silk. *Hunehune ka lau o kēia lole,* the design of the cloth of this dress is delicate. **2.** n. Bits, as of news, gossip; minutia. *Nā hunehune mea hou,* bits of news. **3.** Same as *huna,* a seaweed.

hune kai. n. Sea spray, sea foam. Also *huna kai.*

hune one. n. Fine-grained sand, sand particles.

hū.nō-. Relationship between parent- and child-in-law. See *hūnōna, -hūnōai.* (PNP *funo.*)

-hū.nō.ai. Father- or mother-in-law, usually after *makua* and followed by *kāne* or *wahine* for specific designation of sex. These terms apply also to uncle and aunt by marriage. (PCP *fungawai.*)

hū.nō.na. Son- or daughter-in-law, followed by *kāne* or *wahine* for specific designation of sex. These terms also apply to nephew or niece by marriage. (PPN *funoo-nga.*)

hū.nunu. vs. Lumpy, coarse, as of certain skin diseases; humped; lumps.

Huo. n. Name of an unidentified star.

huoi. n. Suspicion. *Rare.* **hoʻo.huoi.** To suspect, surmise, distrust; suspicion. *Ka huwā, ka paio, ka nuku, ka hoʻohuoi ʻino* (1 Tim. 6:4), envy, strife, railings, evil surmisings.

hū ʻō.lapa. n. Gum of the *ʻōlapa* tree, formerly used for embalming.

hū 'ole. vs. Unfermented, unleavened. *Ka 'aha'aina o ka pelena hū 'ole* (Puk. 34.18), the feast of unleavened bread.

hū 'ono 'ole. n. Unpalatable ferment.

hupa. n. Hoop. *Eng. Ka hupa pahu,* the barrel hoop.

hū pā ipu. n. Small bulging upper part of a gourd. *He hū pā ipu anei, e pa'a ai i ka humu?* Is this a gourd top that is to be fixed by being sewed [of family rifts hard to mend]?

hupau. vt. To draw together. *He nahā ipu auane'i o pa'a i ka hupau humu* (RC 404)? Is it a broken gourd that can be mended by drawing together and sewing? [It is hard to repair a family rift.]

hū.pē. n. Mucus from the nose. Also *'ūpē.* (PPN *isupe'e,* PEP *suupe'e.*)

hū.pē.koho.lā. n. 1. Ambergris. 2. A variety of seaweed.

hū.pē.kole. nvi. Running nose; to sniffle; snotty.

hū.pī. vt. To squeeze, as to remove water; to wring. *Rare.* Also *'uwī.*

hupilo. n. A kind of *pilo 3 (Coprosma).*

hū.pō. nvs. Ignorant, foolish, unintelligent, stupid; fool, foolishness. *Lit.,* swelling darkness. *Hūpō nui,* grossly ignorant. *Ka po'e hūpō* (Hal. 119.130), the simple folk.

hū.poe.nui. n. Name for one with one *kauwā* (outcast) parent.

hū.pō kaliko (karito). n. Hypocrite (early used by translators of the New Testament, but replaced in later editions by *ho'okamani*).

hupu. n. Collection; catch, as of fish. (This rare word is not clear. *'O nā mea hupu apau loa, ua kapu ia mau mea, 'a'ole e hiki ke ki'i ā lawe wale,* as for everything caught [?], these things are taboo and cannot be sought and carried off without permission.

huwā. Var. spelling of *huā.*

hū.wai. Var. spelling of *hūai 1, 2.*

-huwā.ke'o. ho'o.huwā.ke'o. Same as *ho'ohuake'eo.*

I

i. **1.** Part. marking direct and indirect object, agent, source (indefinite), instrument, causation. To, towards, at, in, on, by, because of, for, due to, by means of. (After *loa'a*-type words *i* marks the agent. Before pronouns, the interrogative *wai*, who, names of people, and sometimes before names of places and titles of songs or stories, *i* is replaced by *iā*.) (Gram. 9.3.) (PPN *'i, ki*.) **2.** Part. preceding subordinate verbs and marking completed or past action and state or condition; sometimes the anaphoric *ai* follows the verb or verb phrase. (Gram. 5.2.) (PCP *i*.) **3.** Part. preceding subordinate verbs and marking imperative/exhortative mood and purpose. (Gram. 5.4.) **4.** conj. If. (Gram. 11.1.) *Ā i 'ino mai ke koko, pau pū ka hale i ka 'ino*, if the blood is bad, the house is at the same time bad. **5.** conj. While, at the time that, when, no sooner than, as soon as (replaced by *iā* in the same contexts as *i* 1). (Gram. 11.1.) *I ka makua kāne nō a make, pau ke kālā i ka lū 'ia*, no sooner had the father died than the money was squandered.

-i. Transitivizer suffix. Cf. *haui, kālai, minoi*, Gram. 6.6.4. (PPN *-i, -hi*: cf. *hui 2*.)

-'i. Transitivizer suffix. Cf. *pana'i, puku'i*, Gram. 6.6.4. (PPN *-ki*.)

'Ī. **1.** nvi. To say, speak, suppose; saying. *'Ī ihola ke Akua* (Kin. 1.3), God said. *He 'Ī mai kāu e ō hele mai ho'i nā keiki*, you would think the children would come. (PPN *kii*.) **2.** n. Supreme, great, best (frequently a part of names, as *Ka'Ī-i-mamao* (KL title), the supreme one at a distance; *'Ī-lālā-'ole*, supreme without branches). *'O kela nō ka 'Ī*, that is the best. **3.** vs. Hard, close, stingy. Cf. *'Ī'Ī 1*. **4.** Interj. of scorn, used idiomatically. *No hea ke a'o 'ana i ka hula? I ka 'Ī!* Where learn the hula? Much [she] knows about it! Stuff and nonsense! **5.** n. The letter "i".

ia. **1.** pronoun. He, she, it. Cf. *'oia, 'o . . . ia*, Gram. 8.2. *He inoa ia*, it's a name. *No ia ho'i*, therefore; for this reason. (See *e ia nei* for use of *ia* as a second person vocative.) (PPN *ia*.) **2.** demon. This, that, aforementioned. (Gram. 7.4.) (PPN *ia*.)

-ia. Pas/imp. Cf. *malaia*, Gram. 6.6.3. (PPN *-ia*.)

iā. **1.** Yard (unit of measure). *Eng. Iā pa'a'ili ono*, cubic yard. **2.** Yard (spar on a sailing vessel). *Eng.* **3.** Part. replacing *i 1, 5*, and sometimes used before *kai, uka, 'ō, ne'i*, and after *mai*; coalescing with *a'u (ia'u)* and joined to *ia (iāia)*, and usually joined to *'oe (iā'oe)*. *Hele iā Maui*, go to Maui. *'Ike wau iā'oe*, I see you. *He kua ke 'ano, 'a'ole e make iā'oe* (FS 205), a god in nature, not to be killed by you. *Mai iā Kanaloa*, from Kanaloa. *Ke nānā ihola iā kai* (Kep. 95), looking down to the sea. *Iā'oe ia wahi?* Is that your business? Is it any business of yours? *Iāia nō ā hala, kū ana ke ka'a*, as soon as he had gone, the car came. (PEP *iaa*.)

'ia. Part. marking pas/imp. (sometimes written as a part of modified word). (Gram. 6.6.3.) *'Ai 'ia ka mai'a*, the banana was eaten; eat the banana *E hele 'ia e kāua*, we should go; let's go. *Nānā 'ia ke kanaka*, the person was looked at; look at the person. (PNP *kia*.)

i'a. n. **1.** Fish or any marine animal, as eel, oyster, crab, whale. *Ka i'a kīnohinohi pōhaku*, the sea creature that adorns rocks [periwinkles and *Nerita*]. (PPN *ika*.) **2.** Meat or any flesh food. **3.** Any food eaten as a relish with the staple (poi, taro, sweet potato, breadfruit), including meat, fish, vegetable, or even salt. Also *'Ina'i. Ka i'a lauoho loloa o ke kuahiwi*, the long-haired relish of the mountain [greens]. **4.** *(Cap.)* Milky Way. *Ka I'a ui o ka lani*, the turning Milky Way of the heavens. *Ua huli ka I'a*, the Milky Way has turned [changed position; it is past midnight].

ia ala. pronoun. The one there, you (Gram. 8.2). Also *iala. E ia ala, hele mai kāua . . .* (For. 5:715), say, you, let's come . . .

i aha. See *aha*.

ia.hai. Fast pronunciation of *i aha ai*, sometimes written *i aha'i*. See *aha*.

i'a hā.mau leo. n. Pearl oyster, once numerous at Pearl Harbor. *Lit.*, sea creature that silences the voice, so called for a taboo of silence maintained by fishermen there.

I'a-ho'o.pā.pā-'ili-kanaka. n. Name of a stroke in *lua* fighting. *Lit.*, fish touching skin of man.

i (verb) ai. Particles indicating completed aspect or state or condition and accompanying subordinate verbs; *this* is the anaphoric *ai*. Gram. 7.3.

iā.ia. **1.** Him, her; to him, to her; because of or due to him or her (the particle *iā* and *ia*, he, her; see *i 1*). **2.** While he or she, as soon as he or she, at the time that he or she (the particle *iā* and *ia*, he, she; see *i 5*).

I'a-iki. n. Name of a wind at Wai-luku, Maui, at Ho'olehua, Moloka'i (For. 5:101), and at Hāna, Maui. *Lit.*, little fish.

i'a inu. n. Fish or relish eaten after kava. (For. 6:503.) Usually called *pūpū*.

iaka. n. Yak. *Eng.*

iā.kake. n. Jackass. *Eng.* See *donkey*.

iā.kala. n. Jackal. *Eng.*

iā.kepi, iasepi. n. Jasper. (Puk. 28.20.) *Eng.*

'iako. **1.** n. Outrigger boom. (PPN *kiato*.) **2.** num. Forty, as in counting tapas, canoes, or feathers. (Gram. 10.3.)

i'a kū. n. Run or school of fish. *I'a kū o ka 'āina*, fish running in the area; fish common in the area (cf. *kū 5*).

iā.kua, iagua. n. Jaguar. *Eng.*

i'a.kui. n. Ozena, a discharge of fetid matter from the nostril accompanied by vile smell; if a pregnant woman strung out fish (*i'a kui*) to dry, it was believed that if some of the fish spoiled, her future offspring would acquire the affliction. Also *ihu kīlu, ihu pilau*.

iala. Same as *ala*. See ex., *kīko'o*.

I'a-lele-i-aka. n. Milky Way. *Lit.*, fish jumping in shadows.

i'a.loa. **1.** nvt. Embalmed body, mummy; to embalm, stuff. *Nā holoholona i i'aloa 'ia*, stuffed animals [as at a museum]. **2.** n. Human sacrifice.

i'a loko. n. Fish raised in ponds *(loko)*.

iama. Same as *ama*, outrigger float.

i'a maka. n. Raw fish.

i'a makika. n. Mosquito fish *(Gambusia affinis)*, introduced from Texas after 1905.

lā.meka. n. Jamaica. *Eng.*

'iamo. vi. To jump into water from a height, feet first, without causing a splash. Also *'iomo*.

iana. n. Ostrich (RSV), owl (KJV). (Isa. 13.21.)

ia nei. pronoun. This person, he, she (after *'o*, subject marker; Gram. 8.2). Cf. *eia nei. 'Ī mai 'oia nei, "mai hana pēlā."* He said, "don't act like that."

i 'ane'i. See *ane'i*.

'Ianu.ali, Ianuari. n. January. *Eng.*

'iao. n. **1.** Silversides *(Pranesus insularum)*, a fish 5 to 8 cm long, in shallow pools, used as bait for such fish as *aku*. Also *'i'iao, 'iomo*. **2.** *(Cap.)* Name of Jupiter appearing as the morning star; *fig.*, dawn. *Wehe a'ela ka 'Iao* (FS 59), dawn breaks. **3.** *(Cap.)* Valley and peak, West Maui. **4.** A bird said to resemble the *moho* (no data).

i'a Pā.kē. n. An introduced fish *(Ophiocephalus striatus)* found in rice or taro patches and streams. *Lit., Chinese fish.*

lā.pana. n. Japan. *Eng.* Cf. *Kepanī.*

ia'u. pronoun. **1.** Me, to me; because of or due to me (the particle *iā* and *a'u,* me; see *i 1*). *'Ike mai 'oia ia'u,* he saw me. (Gram. 8.2.) **2.** conj. While I, at the time that I, when I, as soon as I, no sooner than I (the particle *iā* and *a'u,* me; see *i 5*). *Ia'u i puka aku ai mai ka hale aku nei* (Laie 433), when I emerged from this house.

i'a 'ula.'ula. n. Goldfish *(Carassius auratus),* introduced from China or Japan in the time of Ka-'ahu-manu. *Lit., red fish.*

i'a 'ula.'ula kea. n. Pale-red goldfish or carp.

i'a 'ula.'ula lā kea. n. White-marked goldfish. *Lit.,* white-finned red fish.

i'a 'ula.'ula uli. n. Probably the introduced carp *(Cyprinus carpio). Lit.,* dark-red fish.

lawa, lava. n. Java. *Eng.*

'iawe. Same as *'iewe.*

i'e. n. Tapa beater. For types of beaters, see Buck 169–79 and *pepehi 2* and *ho'opa'i (b).* A beater with a smooth surface was used finally *(ho'ōki)* to smooth out the cloth. (PPN *ike.*)

'ie. **1.** n. Aerial root of the *'ie'ie* vine; the vine itself. *Pua ka 'ie,* the *'ie* vine blossoms [royalty is born]. (PPN *kie.*) **2.** n. A woven basket. **3.** nvs. A flat, plaited braid as used in hats; braided. *Kāma'a 'ie,* braided shoes. *Mahiole 'ie* (Laie 479), plaited feather helmet. **4.** nvs. Wicker. *He noho 'ie,* a wicker chair. **5.** n. Name for fish traps, combined with the particle *lā,* as *'ie kala, 'ie palani.* **6.** Same as *'ie'ie 3.* **7.** nvs. Canvas, cotton, linen. *Rare.* **8.** nvs. Corduroy. *Rare.*

lē.howa, lehova. n. Jehovah. (Heb. *Yehowah.*)

'ie.'ie. **1.** n. An endemic woody, branching climber *(Freycinetia arborea)* growing luxuriantly in forests at altitudes of about 300 to 600 m. The ringed stems end in tufts of long, narrow, spiny leaves, in the center of which flowers are borne on cylindrical spikes surrounded by leafy bracts, which are orange or green with orange bases. (Neal 54.) *'Ie'ie* was one of five plants used on the hula altar (see *palai*). Also *'ie.* (PNP *kiekie.*) **2.** n. A native variety of taro with leaf blades and flowers suggesting *'ie'ie 1;* the leaves are dark and glossy, the petioles reddish with yellow-green stripes. (HP 18, 32.) **3.** vs. High, conceited. **hō.'ie.'ie, ho'o.'ie.'ie.** Caus/ sim.

'ie.'iea. nvs. Barbed, as a hook; barb.

'ie.'iewe. Rare var. of *'iewe.*

i'e-io.io-kaha-loa. n. Kind of brown tapa made at Waipi'o, Hawai'i. *Lit.,* tapa beater with ridges of long stripes.

lē.kuiko, lesuito, lesuita. n. Jesuit. *Eng.*

i'e kuku. n. Tapa beater.

i'e kuku ho.'ōki. n. Tapa beater, as used to finish the tapa. *Lit.,* finishing-beating mallet.

'ie lawe. n. Fish-trap basket made of *'ie* vine. *Lit.,* portable *'ie.*

-iele. pejorative suffix. *Rare.* See *lōiele, luaiele, luluaiele, maiele, noiele.*

'iele. n. Person of distinction, chief. (And.) Cf. *'ī,* supreme.

lelu.kalema, lerusalema. n. Jerusalem. *Eng.*

'ie 'ō.pala. n. Wastebasket.

'ie palaoa. n. Breadbasket.

lesū. n. Jesus. (Probably Heb. *Yeshua.*)

'iewe. n. **1.** Afterbirth, placenta. Also *ēwe.* **2.** Infant. (Kanl. 28.57.) **3.** Relatives of a common ancestry. *E kolo ana nō ka ēwe i ka 'iewe,* descendants of the same ancestors crawl together [seek out one another].

'iha. Same as *'iha'iha.*

'iha.'iha. nvs. Feeling of discomfort of one needing to relieve himself; tight, taut, tense. *'Iha'iha ke kaula,* the rope is taut. *No'ono'o 'iha'iha,* mental anxiety, trouble, discomfort. **ho'o.'iha.'iha** Bloated, uncomfortable. (PCP *ki(f,s)a.*)

ihe. n. **1.** Spear, javelin, dart. Various types of *ihe* are listed below. (PCP *i(f,s)e.*) **2.** Same as *iheihe,* a fish. (PPN *ise.*)

'ihe. Var. of *'iha'iha.*

i hea. inter. Where (indefinite), why, why not. *I hea 'oia?* Where is he? *I hea lā 'olua kama'ilio mai?* Why didn't you two speak of it?

ī.he'e. vi. To spread out, prevail, as of calm, peace. *Rare.*

ī.he'e.he'e. vi. To flow. *Rare.*

ī.he'e.kai. n. Turmeric or ocher with salt water, used as a daub by guardians of shark gods and other priests. (Malo 116.)

ihe.ihe. n. **1.** One of several halfbeaks *(Hemirampus depauperatus).* (PPN *iseise.*) **2.** A variety of taro. (HP 32.)

'ihe.'ihe. Same as *'iha'iha.*

ihe.ihe lei. n. A variety of *iheihe* taro.

ihe lau.meki, ihe lau.maki. n. Barbed spear.

ihe 'ō. n. Dart; piercing spear.

'ī.hepa. Same as *hepa,* imbecilic.

ihe pahe'e. n. Short spear, lance; stick used in the game *pahe'e.*

ihe pakelo. n. Lance.

ihi. vt. To strip, peel, as bark or fruit; to tear off, remove. (PPN *hisi.*)

'ihi. **1.** vs. Sacred, holy, majestic, dignified; treated with reverence or respect. **hō.'ihi. (a)** To treat thus; to hallow. **(b)** Tapa or pandanus fitted into a hoop and placed on the head of an attendant *(kahu),* serving as a holder for a food container from which the chief or favorite child was served, a means of bestowing high honor. **2.** n. Wood sorrels *(Oxalis,* all species), perennial weedy herbs, creeping or not, and bearing cloverlike leaves and yellow, white, red, or pink bell-shaped flowers. The plants have a pleasant sour taste due to oxalic acid. (Neal 473–4.) Known to some as *Portulaca* spp. (PPN *kisi.*) **3.** See *hue wai 'ihi.*

'ihi 'ai. n. A kind of *'ihi (Oxalis corniculata).* (Neal 473.) *Lit.,* edible *'ihi.*

ihi.akala. Same as *holomoku 2.* (Kam. 76:10.)

'ihi 'awa. Same as *'ihi 'ai.*

'ihi.'awa.'awa. n. Storm accompanied by much thunder and lightning, and an epithet for the gods of thunder and lightning. *Lit.,* stormy sacred ones.

ihi.hī. vi. To neigh, whinny. **hō.ihi.hī.** To imitate neighing; to make a horse neigh.

'ihi.'ihi. **1.** Redup. of *'ihi 1;* revered. **2.** An unknown plant formerly growing at 'Ihi'ihi-lau-ākea, the western side of Hanauma Bay, O'ahu.

'ihī.'ihī. Same as *ihihī. 'A 'ike i ke kumulau, 'ihī'ihī launa 'ole* (song), seeing the mare, such a neighing.

'ihi.'ihi-i-one. n. A mustard plant, *Coronopus didymus. Ni'ihau.*

'ihi kū.kae hipa. Same as *kūkaehipa,* spiny bur *(Acanthospermum australe).* (Neal 837.) Also *pipili 3.*

'ihi kū kē.pau. n. Same as *pā'ihi,* a weed related to watercress.

'ihi kū ma kua. n. A weedy sorrel. *(Oxalis* sp.).

'ihi lā'au. *Marsilea villosa. Lit.,* medicinal sorrel. *Ni'ihau.*

'ihi lani. n. Heavenly splendor; sacredness of a chief; reverence due a chief.

ihiloa. n. Small, long-necked gourd as used for holding water.

'ihi maka 'ula. Same as *'ihi mākole.*

'ihi mā.kole. n. A creeping variety of *'ihi* with red stems (differing in this from *'ihi 'awa*), yellow flowers, and no bulbs; used medicinally. *Lit.,* red-eyed *'ihi.* Also *'ihi maka 'ula.*

'ihi pehu. n. A kind of sorrel *(Oxalis martiana)* with large leaves, pink flowers, bulbous scaly root, used medicinally. (Neal 473.)

'ihi pua kea. n. Shamrock. *Lit.,* white-flowering *Oxalis.*

iho. **1.** nvi. To go down, descend; downhill; towards the sea; to subside; go south or before the wind; descent.

ho'o.iho. Caus/sim. (PPN *hifo*.) **2.** n. Core, as of an apple, breadfruit, or pandanus; cob, as of corn; heart, as of celery; spongy white growth in the center of a sprouted coconut, sometimes called coconut sponge (cf. *lolo niu*); pith, spadix; flesh of the octopus after the skin is removed; axis, as of the earth; axle, as of a wheel. *Iho 'ole*, without core, said of *koa* trees easily shaped into canoes. Also *haku*. (PPN *uso*, PCP *iso*.) **3.** n. Collective terms for inner layers of white sleeping tapas below the *kilohana*. **4.** n. Block used in plaiting a hat to give shape to the crown. Also *pahu pāpale*. **5.** n. Battery, electric plug. **6.** directional. Down, below. (Table 12, Gram. 7.2.) *Maluna iho*, just barely on top. *Hele iho*, go down, descend. *Iho* + demon. lā is pronounced and written as a single word, *ihola*. (PPN *hifo*.) **7.** Same part. and reference as above but with reflexive meaning, often following words describing activities of the body, as eating, drinking, thinking. *'Ai iho*, to eat. *No'ono'o iho*, to think. *Make wai ihola 'o Kāwika* (Oihn. 11.17), David was thirsty. (PPN *hifo*.) **8.** Same part. and reference as above, with meaning "self"; personally. *E hana ana 'oia nona iho*, he will work for himself. *Pa'akiki ma kāna iho* (Kep. 103), stubborn with his own self. *'O au iho nō me ka mahalo*, I am, yours respectfully. **9.** Same part. and reference as *iho 6–8*, but used with words of time, usually present or future, but past if followed by *nei*. *Mahope iho*, afterwards. *Kēia Lāpule iho*, this coming Sunday. *'O ka manawa ihola nō ia*, it's just the time. *'Ānō iho nei*, just now, just a short time ago, recently. *I kēia mau lā iho nei*, a few days ago.

-iho. ho'o.iho, ho.'īho. Besides that, also, furthermore. *He kanaka waiwai 'oia, a ho'īho nō, he wahine waiwai kāna*, he is a rich man and, besides that, has a rich wife.

'ī.hoe. n. Canoe paddler. *Me nā 'īhoe ali'i o kō ke ali'i mō'ī mau wa'a*, with the chiefly paddlers of the ruler's canoes.

iho huila. n. Wheel axis.

iho.iho. 1. Redup. of *iho 1*. **2.** n. Candle, torch. **3.** n. Heart or heavy core of a tree.

-iho.iho. ho'o.iho.iho. In quilting, to make running stitches towards the sewer. Cf. *ho'opi'ipi'i*.

iho.iho kukui. n. *Kukui*-nut candle; candle.

iho kū.lina. n. Corn cob.

ihola. Directional and reflexive part. *iho* + demon. *-la*. (Gram. 7.2.)

iho.lena. n. A favorite and common native variety of banana, eaten raw or cooked. The fruit bunches are small, the skin thin, ripening yellow, the flesh salmon-pink. (HP 175.) This was one of the few bananas permitted women. Also *hilahila*. *Lit.*, yellow core.

ihona. n. Descent, incline. **ho'o.ihona.** Descent, slope; to descend, go south. (PPN *hifonga*.)

i hope. See *hope*.

iho wai. n. Descent of water, as a stream.

ihu. n. **1.** Nose, snout, beak, bill, trunk of an elephant, toe of a shoe; a kiss. Often qualified, as with the following: *'ami*, irregular-shaped bridge; *kikiwi*, hooked; *kū*, *pi'i*, tilted (*fig.*, haughty); *lapalapa*, high-bridged; *manana*, *mene*, *papa*, *pepe*, *'ū*, broad and flat; *manana*, distended, of nostrils; *meumeu*, snub; *nanā*, snarling (*fig.*, quarrelsome); *winiwini*, sharp. See ex., *kaninonino* and sayings, *mau 1*, *ma'u 1*. *Moe ka ihu o ka pua'a*, the nose of the pig is laid down [a pig offered as a sacrifice]. *Kū ka ihu*, elevated nose; *fig.*, superior, proud. *'Elepani ihu peleleu* (song), long-trunked elephant. *'Ume i ka ihu*, to draw on the nose [with the hand, i.e., to weep]. *La'a ka ihu iā Kekalukalu-o-kēwā* (Laie 505), reserve the kiss for Kekalukalu-o-kēwā. *Aia i ka ihu o ka lio ka 'ai*, the food is at the horse's nose [in the direction the horse is going]. (PPN *isu*.) **2.** Prow or bow of a canoe or ship. **3.** Thick end of pearl-shell shank.

ihu.anu. n. Name of an odoriferous tree or shrub.

ihu-anu. n. Name of a wind blowing down from the uplands of Ka-wela, O'ahu. *Lit.*, cold nose.

ihu 'e'eke. vi. To wrinkle up the nose, as to show scorn.

ihu 'eka. n. Dirty nose, a disparaging epithet.

ihu hā.nuna. vi. To snore or speak with nasalized sounds.

ihu.ihu. vi. Rising upward, as the prow of a canoe. *Fig.*, scornful.

ihu kā.ma'a. n. Toe of shoes.

ihu kilu. Same as *kilu 3* and *i'akui*.

Ihu-kū. n. Name reported for a Hawaiian star, although it may be a general term for any guiding star standing (*kū*) above the bow (*ihu*) of a canoe.

ihu kū. nvs. Tilted nose, pug nose. *Fig.*, haughty, snobbish, snooty, contemptuous.

ihu.ma'a. vs. Disobedient, impudent.

Ihu-moe. n. Name of a star.

ihu nā. nvi. To snore with prolonged sounds; such snoring. *Lit.*, moaning nose.

ihu nui. n. **1.** Large nose. **2.** Canoe with a large bow, hollowed from the large end of a log instead of from the butt end, as was customary. (Malo 131, 135.)

Ihu-o-ka-pua'a. n. **1.** Deadly stroke in *lua* fighting. *Lit.*, nose of the pig. **2.** (*Not cap.*) Type of coarse-grained stone. **3.** (*Not cap.*) See *ihu 1*.

ihu 'ole. n. Possibly a syphilitic saddlenose or damage from leprosy. (Kam. 64:115.) *Lit.*, no nose.

ihu 'olā.'olā. nvi. To snore with short puffs; such snoring. *Lit.*, gurgling nose.

ihu.pani. n. Expert, wise person, wisdom. *Lit.*, closed nose, perhaps referring to deep diving and hence profound knowledge. Cf. *ihu pōhue*.

ihu papa'a. n. Scab nose, an insulting term for a lunkhead.

ihu pī. vi. To breathe with difficulty due to partial obstruction of the nostrils, as of one with a cold. See *pī 2*.

ihu pi'i. nvs. Elevated nose. *Fig.*, scornful, haughty, aloof, contemptuous, disdainful, snobbish, snooty.

ihu pilau. Same as *i'akui*.

ihu pō.hue. n. Gourd nose, said of one with superficial knowledge or lack of skill, perhaps so called because one floats like a gourd rather than descends to the depths of knowledge (*ihupani*).

ihu.'ū. n. A variety of rarely cultivated banana, wild in forests of Kaua'i and Hawai'i, with short, slender, green trunk, and yellow fruit with yellow flesh, edible only when cooked. (HP 175.)

ihu 'ū. Snub-nosed.

ihu wa'a. n. Bow of a canoe, bowsprit.

i'i. vs. Bristling, dishevelled (follows *hulu*, *huhulu*, *huluhulu*).

'i'i. 1. vs. Small, stunted, undersized, dwarf. *Pua 'i'i*, tiny fry of fish. *Kioea 'ai pua 'i'i o Hilia*, the *kioea* bird that eats the tiny spawn of Hilia [of big persons gobbling up little ones]. **2.** n. Admired deep, rasping sound in chanting; tremor; guttural quality of some sounds, as when vowels are strongly aspirated "h." *Inā e ho'oko'iko'i i ka leo, e loa'a nō ka 'i'i*, if the voice is stressed, the guttural quality is obtained. **3.** Same as *'i'ini*. *Nānā aku au iā 'oe, noho pono ka 'i'i iā loko* (song), I looked at you, desire settles deep within. **4.** vt. To gather, collect. *Ua 'i'i kānaka i ka hunahuna mea 'ai*, the people collected the scraps of food. **5.** Short for *hāpu'u 'i'i 1, 2*, ferns; *'ama'u 'i'i*, a fern; *pala 'i'i*, a taro. **6.** vs. Reddish-brown, as a dog's hair. **7.** Same as *'apapane*, a bird.

'i'ī. 1. vs. Tight, difficult to extract, as a plug; stiff. *E 'i'ī ana, ēhē, āhā, e mamau ana, ēhē, āhā* (chant for Kamehameha IV), fitted tightly, tra-la, remaining firm, tra-la. **hō.'i'ī.** To strain and grunt as during real or false pain or exertion; labor pains. *Fig.*, stingy. *No ka nui o ka i'a, hō'i'ī nā lawai'a i ka huki 'ana i ka 'upena*, because of the great number of fish, the fishermen groaned as they pulled on the net. **2.** vi. To frown, scowl. **hō.'i.'ī.** Caus/sim. (often used with *maka*). **3.** vi. To move swiftly. *Kaua'i*. **4.** vs. Lost, as old knowledge. *Rare*.

'Ī.'Ī. **1.** vs. Sour, rancid, moldy, musty. **hō.'Ī.'Ī.** Caus/sim.; to cause to sour. **2.** *(Cap.)* n. Family name of John Papa 'Ī'Ī.

'i.'i.aao. n. Cooked and partly dried taro or sweet potato that becomes sour or ferments.

'i.'iao. Same as *'iao*, a fish.

'i'i. **1.** Intensification of *'i'i 1*, small, tiny. *Pua'a 'i'i'i,* tiny pig. **2.** Same as *'i'i 5, 6;* small *hāpu'u 'i'i* and *'ama'u 'i'i* ferns.

'i.'i.'Ī. vi. To restrain, choke back; to groan, as with exertion.

'i'ika. vi. Contracted, drawn, as facial features; wincing, as in pain; to contract, wince, shrivel, as octopus that writhes or turns while being broiled. **ho'o.'i'ika.** To contort the features; to pucker, shrink, contract, wrinkle, scowl.

'i'ike. vt. To see well; observant; to recognize and accost in a friendly way.

'i'imi. nvt. To seek again and again; one seeking everywhere, as for knowledge. Cf. *'imi, 'imi'imi. Kanaka 'i'imi 'ike,* one constantly seeking knowledge.

'i'imo. vi. To blink. Cf. *'imo, 'imo'imo.* **ho.'i'imo.** To blink rapidly; to twinkle, to cause a twinkling.

i (verb phrase) **inā.** Same as *inā* (phrase) *inā. I 'ai 'ia iho nei e 'oe, inā 'a'ole e 'eha kō po'o,* if you had eaten, then your head would not be aching.

'i'ini. nvt. To desire, crave, yearn for, wish; desire, liking.

'i'iwi. n. **1.** Scarlet Hawaiian honey creeper *(Vestiaria coccinea),* found on all the main islands; its feathers were used extensively in feather work. Also *'iwi, 'i'iwi pōlena, olokele.* Cf. also *'i'iwi pōpolo* and *kikiwi. Ka mahiole 'ie i haku 'ia i ka hulu o nā 'i'iwi* (Laie 479), plaited helmet made of *'i'iwi* feathers. **2.** Same as the honey creeper called *'akialoa* on O'ahu *(Hemignathus obscurus ellisianus).*

'i'iwi haole. n. Cape honeysuckle *(Tecomaria capensis),* a climbing shrub bearing narrow, curved, tubular, scarlet flowers and fernlike leaves (Neal 765), introduced to Ka'ū by George Jones.

'i'iwi pō.lena. Same as *'i'iwi 1.*

'i'iwi pō.polo. n. Immature, greenish-yellow, black-spotted stage of the *'i'iwi* bird. *Lit.,* pōpolo berry honey creeper.

ika. vs. Strong. Cf. *ikaika, lima ika.*

'Ī.kā. **1.** nvi. To drift upon, strike against; to turn aside from a straight course; flotsam and jetsam. *Pa'a 'ia iho i ka hoe uli i 'ole e īkā i ke ko'a,* grasp the steering paddle lest [we] strike the coral head. *Īkā ihola lākou i lalo i kahi wiliau, ili ihola ka moku* (Oih. 27.41), and falling into a place where two seas met [currents mixed] they ran the ship aground. **ho'o.Ī.kā.** To put or throw ashore; to float, strike, drift. **2.** n. Sides of taro patch or garden. *Rare.*

i kai. See *kai*, sea.

i ka 'Ī. See '*Ī 4.*

ikaika. **1.** nvs. Strong, powerful, sturdy, stalwart, potent; strength, force, energy, might, vigor, determination *(rare)* (usually pronounced *ikeika;* Gram. 2.7). **ho'o.ikaika, hō.'ikaika.** To make a great effort, work hard, encourage, animate, strengthen, fortify, try, strive, strain; calisthenics. *Ho'oikaika Kalikiano,* Christian Endeavor Society. *Ho'oikaika kino,* bodybuilding exercise. *Pili ho'oikaika kino,* relating to body building, athletic. *Pōhaku ho'oikaika,* stones lifted as a test of strength. *E ho'oikaika ana au e hana i kēia,* I'm going to make a great effort to do this. *Ua ho'omaka 'ia nā ho'oikaika pāloka 'ana mawaena o nā kālai'āina 'ekolu,* political campaigns were begun by three political cal parties; *lit.,* ballot strengthening. **2.** n. A name reported for Jupiter.

ikaika lio. n. Horsepower.

Ikalia, Italia. nvs. Italy; Italian. *Italian.*

ikamu, itamu. n. Item. *Eng. Ikamu mea hou,* news item.

ikā.mū. n. Gathering together, as of fish about a hook. Cf. *mū 3.*

i kana mai. See *kana 2.*

ikāna wai. n. Bank of a stream. *Rare.*

I-ka-wao-lani. n. Name of a star. *Lit.,* in the mountain area occupied by gods or high chiefs.

'ike. **1.** nvt. To see, know, feel, greet, recognize, perceive, experience, be aware, understand; to know sexually (For. 4:275); to receive revelations from the gods; knowledge, awareness, understanding, recognition, comprehension and hence learning; sense, as of hearing or sight; sensory, perceptive, vision. Cf. *anaina 'ike ali'i, 'ike loa. 'Ike nui 'ia,* well known, famous. *'Ike 'ē,* foresee. *'Ike mamao,* far-sighted. *'Ike pōkole,* nearsighted. *'Ike wale 'ia,* easily seen, conspicuous. *Aniani ho'onui 'ike,* magnifying glass, telescope, microscope. *Hāiki ka 'ike,* narrow-minded. *'Ike aku, 'ike mai,* to recognize one another. *Ē Leo, e hele mai e 'ike i kō hoahānau,* Leo, come and greet your cousin. *Pau ka 'ike,* to lose consciousness. *'Ike ho'omaopopo,* conscious, consciousness. *Ua hele au e 'ike i ku'u hoaloha; ua pau ka 'ike, pau ka lohe,* I went to see my friend, he was in a coma, neither seeing or hearing. *He 'ike kumu, he 'ike lau, he 'ike lono, he 'ike pū 'awa hiwa; ka 'ike ia āu ē ke akua* (hula prayer), a knowledge basic, a knowledge flowering, a knowledge heard, a knowledge from kava offerings; this is the knowledge from you, O god. **hō.'ike. (a)** To show, make known, display, tell, exhibit, reveal, indicate, inform, report, notify, explain, testify, cause to know or see, discover, announce, allege; acquaint; testimony, notice, information; identifying characteristics, as of land claims; proof, token, guide, exhibition. *Hō'ike maopopo aku,* to demonstrate clearly. *Hō'ike 'ōlelo,* grammar. *Ha'awina hō ike,* examination, test. *Hō'ike ā maka, hō'ike ākea,* to reveal openly and clearly. *Hō'ike 'ana,* show, exhibition, *(cap.)* Revelation (Biblical). *Hō'ike 'ano,* description, example, illustration; to tell the nature of, describe. *Hō'ike honua,* geography. *Hō'ike ho'opōkole,* shortened review, synopsis, sketch, summary, outline, resumé. *Hō'ike manawa,* chronology. *Hō'ike panakō,* bank statement or report. *Palapala hō'ike,* affidavit, report. **(b)** Witness, as in court. *Hō'ike ho'opunipuni, hō'ike wahahe'e,* false witness; to lie, commit perjury. *Hō'ike pa'a,* witness, one who confirms. *Hō'ike pāku'i,* rebuttal. **(c)** School commencement; to hold commencement. **(d)** Congregational convention of various Sunday Schools with singing and recitation. *Nā hō'ike makahiki,* the annual conventions. (PPN *kite.)* **2.** interj. of scorn in the phrase: *I ka 'ike!* What does [he, she] know!

'ikea. Pas/imp. of *'ike 1.* **hō.'ikea.** Pas/imp. of *hō'ike. Ē Kāne-i-ka-wai-ola hō'ikea mai i ke ola* (prayer), O Kāne-of-the-living-water, bring forth life. (PPN *kitea.)*

'ike hana lima. nvs. Skilled craftsman, craftsmanship; deft.

'ike hā.nau. n. Instinct. (Kep. 11.) *Lit.,* birth knowledge.

'ike.'ike. Rare redup. of *'ike 1.* **hō.'ike.'ike.** To display, exhibit, as in a museum or show; entertainment, play, fair, exposition, circus, carnival, show of almost any kind; demonstration. *Hale hō'ike'ike,* museum, art academy, exhibition hall. *Hō'ike'ike honua nui,* world's fair. *He nūpepa hō'ike'ike ki'i,* illustrated newspaper. (PPN *kitekite.)*

'ike ka'a kaua. nv. Strategy, knowledge pertaining to war; to know the strategy of war.

'ike kū.hohonu. n. Deep knowledge or insight.

'ike kumu. n. Basic or fundamental knowledge.

'Ike.la'ela, Iseraela. nvs. Israel. (Heb. *Yisraayl.)* (For the Hawaiian glottal stop, cf. Gram. 2.9.3.)

'ike lihi. vt. To glimpse.

'ike loa. vi. To know very well indeed, knowledgeable, versed, wise.

'ike mahu'i. nvt. To glimpse; inkling.

'ike maka. nvt. Eyewitness, witness as to a will, eyesight, visual knowledge; visible; to see or witness personally.

'ikena. n. View, seeing, knowing, association, scenery, knowledge. *E ho'oma'amau i ka 'ikena* (song), continue forever seeing [one another]. *Nalo ka 'ikena a ka maka,* lost from view. (PCP *kitenga.*)

'ike.oma. nvs. Idiom; idiomatic. *Eng.*

'ike pā.pā.lua. nvt. To see double; to have the gift of second sight and commune with the spirits; supernatural knowledge, extrasensory perception.

'ike pono. nvt. To see clearly; to know definitely; certain knowledge.

iki. nvs. Small, little, slightly; a little, trifle; not at all (with a negative). Cf. *'auiiki. Ua 'eha iki,* slightly hurt. *He mea iki,* it's a trifle; you are welcome; don't mention it. *'A 'ole kohu iki,* not the least fitting; most inappropriate. *'A 'ole au i hele iki i laila,* I've never been there. *He iki pua mau'u,* a small blade of grass. **ho'o.iki.** To lessen, diminish, make small. (PPN *'iti.*)

iki.'ala.mea. n. Name given for a disease, probably stomach ulcers. Cf. *hiki'alamea.*

ikiiki. 1. nvi. Stifling heat and humidity; acute discomfort, pain, grief, suffering; to be weary, stifling, sultry, stuffy. *Ikiiki o ke kaua,* fury and heat of war. *Ikiiki au i ka ho'omanawanui 'ana* (Ier. 20.9), I am weary with forbearing. **2.** *(Cap.)* n. Name of a month in the summer season. (FS 281.) See *month.* **3.** *(Cap.)* n. Name for the planet Jupiter.

iki.makua. n. A kind of stone, as used for making *maika* stones.

iki.pua.hola. n. A pestilence said to have come in the reign of Waia, believed the same as the *'ōku'u* disease of 1804. (Malo 245.)

ikō. To imitate, copy. (And.)

'i.koi. 1. Same as *pīkoi 1, 2;* breadfruit or pandanus core; tripper. **2.** n. Float, as on a fish net; buoy.

'i.koi pua. n. Spadix.

'i.koko. nvs. Bloodless, wan, pale; anemia. *Rare.*

ikū. n. Officer, as in a society. Several types are listed below. *Rare.*

I kū. interj. Stand! Take your places! Get ready! Let's go!

'iku.ā, 'ikuwā. 1. nvs. Noisy, clamorous, loud-voiced; to make a din; din, clamor; voices of the gods in the elements. *'Ikuwā nā manu i ka nahele,* the birds make a din in the forest. **2.** *(Cap.)* n. Month of the Hawaiian year, named, according to Kepelino, for the roar of surf, thunder, and cloudbursts of this month. (Kep. 95.) *'O 'Ikuwā i pohā kō'ele'ele, 'ikuwā ke kai, 'ikuwā ka hekili, 'ikuwā ka manu,* 'Ikuwā is the month when dark storms arise, sea roars, thunder roars, birds roar. *Pohā-kō'ele'ele* is a var. name: see *month.*

ikū ha'i. n. Chairman. *Lit.,* speaking officer.

'iku.'iku. nvs. Stench; foul-smelling.

ikū kau. n. Secretary.

ikū lani. n. Highest officer, head, president.

ikū.mau.maua. *nvt.* To offer a prayer of thanksgiving; such a prayer.

ikū nu'u. n. Chief of rank below the *hoa ali'i* descendants of Kāne; chiefs of this rank could rule as *mō'ī* but were not considered divine. (For. 6:266.) But cf. *mō'ī.*

ikū.one. n. Treasurer.

ikū pau. n. Genealogy of chiefs of the *hoa ali'i* class (descendants of Kāne), the highest of all. (For. 6:266.)

'iku.wā. Var. spelling of *'ikuā.*

iku.wai. Var. of *ukuwai;* visiting place in a grass house.

ila. 1. n. A dark birthmark. *Ke hele nei ā kūka'i na ila o Pūpū-kea* (FS 195), the birthmark of Pūpū-kea appears [believed to indicate strength]. (PPN *'ila.*) **2.** vs. Dark. *Pau ka wao mai'a a pala ila* (chant), all the bananas of the uplands are ripened black. **3.** n. Changing colors of an octopus skin. *'O ka ila o ka he'e e holo ana i'ō ā i 'ane'i o ka he'e,* the changing colors of the octopus

move here and there on the octopus. **4.** Same as *kawowo,* seedling.

i laila. See *laila.*

'I lā.lā 'ole. n. Mighty one without branches [i.e. descendants, a reference to Ka-mehameha, who had no children by Ka-'ahu-manu].

i lalo. See *lalo.*

ilā.muku. n. Executive officer, marshal, sheriff. (PPN *'ilaamuku.*)

'ilau. vi. To do together. *'Ilau hoe,* to paddle together. *E 'ilau mai kākou,* let's work together.

'Ile.lani, Irelani. nvs. Ireland; Irish. *Eng.* Cf. *'Ailiki.*

ili. 1. nvi. Stranded, aground or wrecked, as a ship; to run aground; to run over, as with a car; to set, as the sun. Cf. *Hoku Ili,* Oih. 27.41, *īkā 1. Ili ke aka,* to cast a shadow. **ho.'īli, ho'o.ili.** To land upon, load, as freight on a ship; to transfer, consign, transmit; to set on shore. *Ho'īli kaua,* to attack in war. *Ho'oili kolohe,* fraudulent exporting. *Ho'īli iā ha'i,* delegate to someone else. (PPN *hili.*) **2.** nvi. Inheritance; to inherit. Cf. *ilina. Ili aku mai ka makua a ke keiki,* passing in inheritance from father to son. **ho.'īli, ho'o.ili.** To bequeath or leave in a will; to lay aside, save. *He mā'ona ho'oili,* filled to satiety. **3.** nvi. To fall upon, as sorrow, responsibility, blessings (Kanl. 28.2), curses (Kanl. 28.15). *E ili ai ka hewa o ke ke'ena kapu* (Nah. 18.1), shall bear the iniquity of the sanctuary. *Ua ili maluna o mea ke kanikau 'ana no ka make 'ana o kō lāua pōki'i,* there befell so-and-so a sorrow for the death of their younger brother.

'ili. n. 1. Skin, complexion, hide, pelt, scalp, bark, rind, peel. See ex., *kūakā. Ho'okae 'ili,* race prejudice; to have race prejudice. *Ka 'ili o ke po'o,* scalp. *Kāne i ka 'ili,* husband. *'A 'ohe mea 'ē a'e, 'o ka lole wale nō i ka 'ili,* there was nothing else except the clothing on the back. (PPN *kili.*) **2.** Leather. *'Ili lahilahi,* thin leather. *'Ili mānoanoa,* thick leather. **3.** Surface, area. Cf. *'ili 'āina, 'ilikai.* **4.** Binding, cover. *'Ili pa'a,* hard cover (of a book). **5.** Land section, next in importance to *ahupua'a* and usually a subdivision of an *ahupua'a.* **6.** Strap of any kind, as reins, harness, fan belt, machine belt; hose. Cf. *ala'ume.* **7.** Pebble (less used than *'ili'ili); kōnane* pebble. **8.** vs. Square, as in measurements. *Ana 'ili,* square measurements.

-'ili. hō.'ili. To collect; to bunch together, as fish in a net.

'ili.'ā. n. A variety of taro.

'ili 'a'ai. n. A skin or complexion prone to infection. *Lit.,* corrosive skin. Cf. *'ili 'awa.*

'ili.ahi. n. 1. All Hawaiian kinds of sandalwood *(Santalum* spp.), shrubs and trees, with fragrant heart wood, small pale-green or gray-green leaves, small, dull-red or greenish flowers, and small purple fruits. From about 1790 to 1830 sandalwood trees were cut and exported to China. (Neal 325-6.) Also *'aoa.* (PPN *asi.*) **2.** One whose clothes wear out fast, as due to carelessness.

'ili ahi. n. A fiery surface. *Wai 'ula 'ili ahi,* red water with surface of fire [a poetic description of the waters of Wai-mea Stream, Kaua'i, the waters of which after a storm are said to be red along one bank].

'ili.ahi-a-lo'e. n. A small shrubby form of Hawaiian sandalwood *(Santalum ellipticum),* found rarely and near the beach. (Neal 325.)

ili 'āina. n. Land inheritance.

'ili 'āina. n. **1.** Land area. *Ka 'ili 'āina o 0.75 'eka,* an area of 0.75 acre. **2.** An *'ili* land division whose chief pays tribute to the chief of the *ahupua'a* of which it is a part, rather than directly to the king. Cf. *'ili kūpono.*

ili.au. n. An endemic woody plant *(Wilkesia gymnoxiphium),* related to the *'āhinahina* or silversword, found only in western mountains of Kaua'i. It is 1 to 4 m high, unbranched, the stems ending in clumps of long narrow leaves. (Neal 845.) See ex., *pū'olo. 'O ka iliau loha i ka lā* (For. 4:283), the *iliau* drooping in the sun.

'ili 'awa. n. Skin not easily bruised or infected; one with such a skin is said to emit an acrid *('awa)* odor; a strong-smelling fish caught by him (as *pualu* or *palani*) is said to become more offensive in odor.

'ili.e'e. n. Wild plumbago *(Plumbago zeylanica),* a native of tropics of the Eastern Hemisphere to Hawai'i, a shrub with white tubular flowers and thin, oval leaves that were used medicinally; the sap was used to blacken tattoo marks. (Neal 667.) Also *'ilihe'e, hilie'e; lauhihi* on Ni'ihau.

'ili e'e. n. Contagious skin disease.

'ili 'ele.'ele. n. Black *kōnane* stone.

'ili hau. n. Bark of the *hau* tree, as used for rope and for modern grass skirts.

'ili.he'e. Same as *'ilie'e.*

'ili.helo. Unsystematic or unskilled in farming, working spasmodically. (And.)

ili.hia. 1. Pas/imp. of *ili;* to have gone aground. 2. vi. Stricken with awe, reverence, dread (PH 33); overcome, thrilled, as by beauty. *Ā 'e ho'oneoneo aku au i ka 'āina, ā no laila e ilihia ai kō 'oukou po'e 'enemi* (Oihk. 26.32), and I will bring the land into desolation; and your enemies shall be astonished. (PPN *ilifia.*)

'ili.hia. n. A kind of *ha'iwale (Cyrtandra begoniaefolia),* on East Maui, having unequal heart-shaped leaves.

'ili hinu.hinu. n. Patent leather. *Lit.,* shiny leather.

'ili.holo. Same as *'ilihelo.*

'ili holo.holona. n. Leather; fur, as about the neck.

'ili honua. n. Surface of the earth.

'ili.hune. nvs. Poor, destitute; poverty, poor person. *Lit.,* tiny skin. **hō.'ili.hune.** To cause poverty; to behave as if poor. *He hō'ilihune kona noho 'ana,* he lives as if in poverty.

'ili.'ili. 1. n. Pebble, small stone, as used in dances or *kōnane. Hula 'ili'ili,* pebble dance. *Ho'onoho i ka 'ili'ili,* to arrange pebbles on a mat in the shape of a man and his vital organs, to teach anatomy. (PPN *kilikili.*) 2. vi. To pile, overlap. **hō.'ili.'ili.** To gather, collect, pile up, save, store away, glean, assemble; collection. *Aia hō'ili'ili 'oe i nā huawaina* (Kanl. 24.21), when you gather the grapes. *He hō'ili'ili po'oleka,* a stamp collection.

'ili.'ili 'ele.'ele. n. Black *kōnane* pebble.

'ili.'ili kea. n. White *kōnane* pebble.

'ili.'ili hā.nau. n. The birth pebbles of Kō-loa (a small section of the beach at Puna-lu'u, Ka'ū), which were believed to reproduce themselves, the smooth non-porous ones being male, the porous ones female. These stones were best liked for the pebble hula. *Ka 'ili'ili hānau o Kō-loa, ka nalu ha'i o Kāwā* (song), the birth pebbles of Kō-loa, the breaking waves of Kāwā.

ili.ili.hia. Redup. of *ilihia.*

'ili.'ili maka.li'i. n. Gravel, small stones.

'ili.ka'a. n. Harness.

'ili.kai. 1. n. Surface of the sea. 2. vs. Horizontal. *He kaha 'ilikai,* a horizontal line.

'ili kala. n. Skin of *kala,* a fish, sometimes stretched over a coconut shell to form the top of the small *pūniu,* knee drum.

'ili.kala.kala. n. A bird (no data).

'ili.kana. n. Corm immediately under the skin, as of taro.

'ili kani. n. 1. A skin that sounds, as used in drums. 2. Tough skin.

'ili kapu. n. Taboo against contact with clothing or bedding of others; one with such a taboo.

'ili kau.ō. Reins. *Lit.,* pulling strap.

'ili kea. n. 1. Fair skin, of Hawaiians less dark than *'ili kou.* Cf. *'ilipuakea.* 2. White *kōnane* pebble.

'ili ke'ehi. n. Stirrup.

'iliki. 1. nvt. To strike suddenly, pour down, as rain; onset, striking, downpour. *'Iliki ke kai i ka 'ope'ope lā, lilo,* sea strikes the bundles, gone. *Ka 'iliki a ka ua a hana mao 'ole i ke kai a ka Hinali'i,* sudden downpour of rain, constant without cessation in the flood of

Hinali'i. 2. n. A varnish, as made of candlenut bark, ti root, banana stump, and other plants.

'Ili.kini. nvs. 1. Indian (of America). *Eng.* Also *'Inikini.* 2. *(Not cap.)* Naked, nude.

'iliki.uma, iridiuma. n. Iridium. *Eng.*

'ili.kole. 1. nvs. Poverty-stricken, very poor, destitute; pauper (stronger than *'ilihune*). *Lit.,* bare skin. **hō.'ili.kole.** To cause poverty. *He keiki hō'ilikole,* a child that makes paupers [of the parents, as with expenses]. 2. n. Flesh of half-ripe coconut.

'ili.kona. n. Wart. *Lit.,* hard skin.

'ili.kone. Rare var. of *'ilikole.*

'ili kou. vs. Dark-skinned, as dark Hawaiians. *Lit., kou*-wood skin.

'ili.kū. Short for *'ili kūpono.*

'ili kuapo. n. Belt.

'ili kū.pono. n. A nearly independent *'ili* land division within an *ahupua'a,* paying tribute to the ruling chief and not to the chief of the *ahupua'a.* Transfer of the *ahupua'a* from one chief to another did not include the *'ili kūpono* located within its boundaries. Also *'ilikū.*

'ili lā.'au. n. Tree bark.

ili.lani. nvi. Unexpected rain, as from a sunny sky; to rain thus.

'ili lele. n. Portion of an *'ili* land division separated from the main part of the *'ili* but considered a part of it. Also *lele.*

'ili lua. n. New skin, as over a sore; new bark.

'ili luna. n. Epidermis; outer bark.

'ilima. n. 1. Small to large native shrubs (all species of *Sida,* especially *S. fallax*), bearing yellow, orange, greenish, or dull-red flowers; some kinds strung for leis. The flowers last only a day and are so delicate that about 500 are needed for one lei. Fruits of the *ma'o (Abutilon grandifolium),* when green and soft, are used with *'ilima* leis, one fruit at each end of the lei; or the pale-green, cap-like calyx of the *'ilima* flower is used. A mild laxative for babies is made by squeezing out the juice of flowers; this is called *kanakamaika'i.* The *'ilima* was designated in 1923 by the Territorial Legislature as the flower of O'ahu. It is related to the hibiscus. (Neal 552–3.) See songs, *nōweo, pue 1;* cf. *'āpiki. Ola nō i ka pua o ka 'ilima,* healing in the *'ilima* flower [reference to its medicinal use]. 2. Area where *'ilima* plants may grow.

'ili mā.'ila. Same as *'ili kea.*

'ilima koli kukui. A rare *'ilima* with bronze-red flowers, domesticated on O'ahu. (Neal 553.) *Lit., kukui* candle *'ilima.* Also *kolikukui.*

'ilima kua.hiwi. n. A kind of *'ilima.*

'ili mā.ku'a.ku'a. n. Dark-red bark, especially of *koa* trees.

'ili mā.ku'e. vs. Dark-skinned. *Kanaka 'ili māku'e o ka moana Pākīpika,* dark-skinned native of the Pacific Ocean.

'ilima kū kaha.kai. n. A kind of *'ilima* creeping on sand on which beach dodder *(kauna'oa)* grows. (Neal 553.) *Lit., 'ilima* standing on beach.

'ilima kū kula. n. A wild form of *'ilima,* not so often used for leis as *'ilima lei,* the cultivated form. *Lit., 'ilima* standing on plains. Also *'ilima papa.* (Neal 553.)

'ilima lei. n. Domesticated form of *'ilima.*

'ilima makana.'ā. n. A wild *'ilima* growing on old lava beds in Ka'ū, with small flowers; of medium height. (HP 213.)

'ilima mamo. n. A kind of *'ilima,* probably same as *'ilima lei.*

'ili mā.noa.noa. nvs. Callus, calloused skin, thick leather; calloused.

'ilima ō.kea. n. A domesticated *'ilima,* light yellow in color.

'ilima papa. Same as *'ilima kū kula.*

-ili.mo'o. ho'o.ili.mo'o. n. A service for *luakini* dedications. (For. 6:23.)

ilina. n. 1. Grave, tomb, sepulcher, cemetery, mausoleum, plot in a cemetery. Cf. *ili 1. Pā ilina,* cemetery. *Ka ilina o nā ali'i,* royal mausoleum. **2.** Recipient. **ho.ʻo.ilina, ho.ʻī.lina.** Heir, inheritance, legacy, estate, heritage, bequest; successor (so used in the official English version of the Constitution of 1852, Article 25). *Hoʻoilina mōʻī,* heir to the throne, crown prince or princess. *Palapala hoʻoilina,* will. *Hoʻoilina ʻōlelo,* a will made verbally; one entrusted to speak for another. *Kona mau hoʻoilina,* his heirs.

ilina wai. n. Place where a stream goes underground.

ʻili.nia. Same as *ʻinia 2,* the pride of India flower and plant.

ʻī.lio. n. **1.** Dog (brought to Hawaiʻi by early Polynesians, considered an *ʻaumakua* by some). Cf. *ʻapowai, hula ʻīlio, nūkea,* Gram. 2.9, Titcomb 1969, Hal. 22.16, Hoik. 22.15. Many types of dogs are listed below. *ʻĪlio moʻo, ʻīlio peʻelua,* brindled dog. (PPN *kulii;* the Hawaiian term may have come from Tuamotu *kurio,* with replacement of *-u-* by *-i-.*) **2.** A generic term for foreign quadruped. See below and Gram. 2.9.2. **3.** Cloud (poetic, or cloud with an omen). *ʻĪlio ʻehu,* cloud with a ruddy tint. *ʻO ʻīlio uli, ʻo ʻīlio mea, ʻo Kū ke ao iki, ʻo Kū ke ao loa, ʻo Kū ke ao poko* (PH 144), dark dog-cloud, reddish dog-cloud, Kū the small cloud, Kū the long cloud, Kū the short cloud. See *kū 11,* the god. **4.** Tie beam in a house, brace that holds rafter to crossbeam. **5.** A seaweed, same as some of the *hulu ʻīlio 5.*

ʻī.lio ʻau.kai. n. **1.** Sea dog, experienced sailor. **2.** Warship.

ili.oha. n. Horseweeds (*Conyza* spp.), tall, slender coarse weeds of the daisy family, established in Hawaiʻi; used medicinally. One species is *laniwela.* (Neal 834.) Also *ʻawīʻawī, puamana, ʻuwīʻuwī.*

ʻī.lio.ha'a. Same as *līpahapaha, pahapaha,* sea lettuce (*Ulva* and related genera).

ʻī.lio hae. n. Fierce or vicious dog; wolf, jackal.

ʻī.lio hahai. n. Greyhound. (Sol. 30.31.) *Lit.,* chasing dog.

ʻī.lio hahai holo.holona. n. Hunting dog.

ʻī.lio hahai manu. n. Bird dog.

ʻī.lio hanu kanaka. n. Bloodhound. *Lit.,* dog that smells man.

ili.ohe. n. Name reported for a green fresh-water moss.

ʻī.lio hihiu hae. n. Wild, fierce dog; wolf.

ʻī.lio hipa. n. Sheep dog, shepherd dog.

ʻī.lio hohono. n. Bad-smelling dog; skunk.

ʻī.lio-holo-I-ka-ua.ua. n. Seal. *Lit.,* quadruped running in the rough [seas].

ʻili.ʻohu. Same as *honohina,* wild spiderflower. *Lit.,* mist skin.

ʻī.lio hulu pā.pale. n. Beaver. *Lit.,* hat-fur dog.

ʻī.lio ʻiʻi. n. Small curly-haired native dog, said to be in four colors; reddish-brown (as the fibers of the *hāpuʻu ʻiʻi* tree fern), cream-colored, ashy-gray, and wine-colored.

ʻī.lio iole. n. Rat terrier.

ʻī.lio kawa.ū. n. A damp dog. *Fig.,* one shivering with cold (said in fun).

ʻī.lio kekeko. n. Pug-nosed dog.

ʻī.lio kiaʻi hipa. n. Sheep dog, shepherd dog.

ʻī.lio kula ʻō.lohe.lohe. n. Prairie dog. *Lit.,* hairless dog of the plains.

ili ʻō.lelo. nv. A tattletale, talebearer, gossip; to tattle, gossip.

ʻili ʻō.maka. n. Foreskin.

ʻī.lio mā.kuʻe. n. Native dog, brown dog.

ʻī.lio moʻo. n. Brindled dog. (HM 139.)

ʻili omo wai. n. Suction tube.

ʻī.lio ʻō.lohe. n. Hairless dog; *fig.,* skilled in fighting and robbery. *ʻĪlio ʻōlohe kona ʻāina* (GP 6–7), his land is fierce as a hairless dog.

ʻili.ʻō.pua. n. A variety of sugar cane like the *kea* but dwarfed. (HP 224, 225.)

ʻī.lio pulu. n. Bulldog. *Lit.,* bull *(Eng.)* dog.

ʻī.lio wahine. n. Bitch.

ʻili paʻa. n. An *ʻili* land division complete in one section, as distinguished from an *ʻili lele.*

ʻili paka.lua. n. Thick, coarse, or wrinkled skin or bark.

ʻili pala.pala. n. Parchment. (2 Tim. 4.13.)

ʻili pala uli. vs. Dark-complexioned.

ʻili pale o kā.maʻa. n. Sole of shoes.

ʻili pā.paʻa, ʻili pā.paʻa lā. Sunburned or tanned skin.

ʻili pilo. Smelly skin, said approvingly of industrious farmers.

ʻili pipi. n. Leather, cowhide.

ʻili poʻo. n. Scalp.

ʻili poʻo.poʻo. nvs. Concave surface; hollow. *Pono ʻiʻo nō i ka makaaniani ʻili poʻopoʻo,* good enough for the one with concave glasses [sarcastic].

ʻili.pua.kea. n. White person. *Lit.,* white flower skin. Poetic.

ʻili.ua.ua. n. A variety of taro with large, thick, firm leaf blades. The corms are very large, with white flesh tinged with pink; good as table taro but not for poi; leaves good for *lūʻau. Lit.,* tough hide. Also *kalo Pākē.*

ʻIli-ʻula. n. Name of a star.

ʻili wahī. n. Scabbard, sheath.

ʻili.wai. **1.** nvs. Surface, as of water; level, horizontal, flat. *ʻĪliwai,* completely level. **hō.ʻili.wai.** To grade or level, as a road. **2.** n. Carpenter's or surveyor's level. **3.** n. Water hose.

ilo. nvi. Maggot, grub, worm; to creep, as worms, to be beset by maggots. Cf. *kuailo. Ua paʻapū koʻu kino i ka ilo* (Ioba 7.5), my body is covered with worms. (PNP *ʻilo;* cf. Fijian.) **2.** Young shoot; to germinate, sprout. Cf. *hehu, ʻōilo.* **hoʻo.ilo.** To cause germination or sprouting.

-ilo. hoʻo.ilo, hoʻīlo. Rainy, winter-like months, winter.

ilo.ilo. Redup. of *ilo 1, 2;* wormy, maggoty; sprouting, germinating. Sorcerers cursed by saying that maggots would eat a victim's body (Kam. 64:123–4).

-iloilo. hoʻo.ilo.ilo, hoīlo.ilo. To predict disaster or misfortune.

i loko. See *loko.*

ʻī.loli. **1.** nvi. Unpleasant sensations of pregnancy; emotional disturbances; intense yearning, longing, desire; to suffer such. *He loli ka iʻa, ʻīloli ke aloha,* sea cucumber, the sea creature, passionate the love [in *hana aloha* prayers with *loli* as an offering, a play on words]. **ho.ʻī.loli.** To feel the discomforts of pregnancy; to suffer emotional disturbance; to yearn for an absent lover; to be imbued with (often used favorably). *Ka leo ʻolu hoʻīloli o ka waipahē* (Kel. 10), sweet voice alive with tenderness. *Hoʻīloli ke kai,* the sea rages. **2.** vs. Spotted, daubed with color, as tapa; speckled, as overripe pandanus keys. **3.** n. Unpleasant odor, as of shark.

i luna. See *luna.*

ʻī.maka. n. Watchtower; lookout, observation point.

ʻime.peli.ala, imeperiala. vs. Imperial. *Eng.*

ʻimi. v. To look, hunt, search, seek. Cf. *ʻiʻimi, ʻimiʻimi,* and other phrases with *ʻimi* listed below. **hō.ʻimi.** Caus/sim. (PPN *kumi,* PEP *kimi.*)

ʻimia. Pas/imp. of *ʻimi. ʻImia aku ā loaʻa,* search until found.

ʻimi ā loaʻa. nvs. Discoverer; to discover; to seek until found. Cf. *ʻimi loaʻa. ʻImi ā loaʻa ka waiwai,* seek until [you] obtain wealth. *Lilo ʻoe me Kāpena Kuke ka ʻimi ā loaʻa o Hawaiʻi* (song), you and Captain Cook have become the discoverers of Hawaiʻi.

ʻimi ʻepa. n. Deceit, troublemaker.

ʻimi haka.kā. nvi. To look for a fight; one doing so, antagonistic.

ʻimi haku. nv. To seek a chief, as of a lesser chief or priest wishing a new master; one who seeks a chief; a chief who marries one of higher rank than himself, or a sister or half sister so that their child will be of still higher rank.

'imi hala. vt. To find fault with, blame, seek condemnation. *Ua 'imi hala 'oia i kona kaikua'ana,* he looked for faults in his older brother.

'imi hale. nv. **1.** To establish, as a dynasty; to acquire authority, power, property; one who does so; to look for a house. *'O Ka-mehameha ka 'imi hale, 'o Liholiho ka noho hale,* Ka-mehameha established the rule; Liholiho was the legatee. **2.** To form a friendship so close that one feels welcome in the house of the other. *Rare today.*

'imi hana. v. **1.** To seek work. *Kōmike 'imi hana,* employment committee. **2.** To stir up trouble.

'imi-hau. n. Name of a stormy wind at Lahaina, Maui. *Lit.,* dew seeker.

'imi.hia. Pas/imp. of *'imi. Ua 'imihia ka hohonu,* the depths have been searched [of search for knowledge].

'imi 'ike. nv. To seek knowledge; a seeker of knowledge.

'imi.'imi. Redup. of *'imi.* (PPN *kumikumi,* PCP *kimikimi.*)

'imi.'imi.hia. Pas/imp. of *'imi'imi.* See ex., *lanalanahia.*

'imi kā.lā. nv. To seek money, to earn a livelihood; commercial.

'imi loa. vi. To seek far, explore; distant traveler, explorer. *Fig.,* one with great knowledge or avaricious for knowledge. *Ahu kupanaha iā Hawai'i 'imi loa* (Kep. 143), a heap of marvellous things in Hawai'i [and its] profound knowledge.

'imi loa'a. nv. Money-earner, as for a family; breadwinner. Cf. *'imi ā loa'a. Kā mākou 'imi loa'a kēlā,* he's our breadwinner.

'imina. n. Looking, seeking; search. *Ho'onui ka 'imina o ka pono* (song), increase the search for righteousness. (PCP *kuminga.*)

'imi na'au.ao. nv. To seek knowledge or education; ambitious to learn; one seeking education or learning, research, learning. *Po'e 'imi na'auao,* scientist, scholar, philosopher, learned man. *Hana 'imi na'auao,* science, scholarship, work of learning.

'imi 'ō.lelo. v. To lie, slander, stir up trouble by gossip.

'imi pono. v. To seek or strive for righteousness; endeavor. *'Ahahui 'Ōpiopio 'Imi Pono o Karisto,* Young People's Christian Endeavor Society [old name].

'imo. nvi. To wink, twinkle; winking, twinkling. Cf. *'i'imo,* Hal. 35.19. **hō.'imo.** To cause to wink; to wink to get one to wink back. (PPN *kimo.*)

'imo.'imo. Redup. of *'imo.* (Ioba 15.12.) *Hōkū 'imo-'imo,* twinkling star. (PPN *kimokimo.*)

'imona. n. Twinkling.

imu. n. **1.** Underground oven; food cooked in an *imu.* Also *umu.* (PPN *'umu.*) **2.** Rock and coral fish trap; the fisherman might insert a branch into an opening at one side to frighten the fish into a surrounding net. Also *ahu, umu.*

i mua. See *mua.*

imu hau hana. n. Oven in which *hau* wood was heated *(hana)* to be bent for a canoe outrigger.

imu ho'o.ma'a.lili. n. Oven with food intended as an offering to appease *(ho'oma'alili)* a god.

imu kā.lua loa. n. Oven for baking a long time; oven for baking human sacrifice. *Ku'u imu kālua loa: make* (riddle), my oven for baking forever: death.

i muli. See *muli.*

imu loa. n. Oven used as a sweat bath: the hot rocks of the oven were covered with a thick layer of greenery (as ginger, maile, ti); the patient lay here and was covered with more leaves and tapa; the treatment was said to last ten days and included prayers; its purpose was to remove the influence of sorcery. *Lit.,* long oven [with idea that a long life would follow].

imu ō nui. n. Well-filled *imu,* a breadbasket.

imu pao. n. Hawaiian oven built above the ground, with an opening through which wood could be stoked *(pao).*

ina. 1. vt. To pry, as with a lever. **2.** To vary or modulate the tone of voice; to sound, as from a distance. (And.)

3. interj. In! (Cry of children in a marble game when the marble is "in" a hole.) *Eng.*

inā. 1. interj. Let's go! *Inā kākou, e hana kākou i nā pōhaku 'ula* (Kin. 11.3), let's get going and make bricks. **2.** conj. If, would that; unless, whether (with a negative). (Gram. 11.1.) *Inā 'a'ole 'oe e ho'oikaika, 'a'ole e holomua,* unless you make great efforts, [you] will not progress. *Inā 'oe e hele, e hele nō au me 'oe,* if you go, I'll go with you. *Inā 'oe e hana, ā e hana 'ole,* whether you work or not. *Inā nō au i make nou!* Would that I had died in your stead! *Inā e like au me nā malama mamua* (Ioba 29.2), Oh, that I were as in months past.

'ina. 1. n. Small sea urchin *(wana),* as *Echinometra* spp. Qualifying terms are *'ele'ele* or *uli, kea* or *ke'oke'o,* and *'ula* or *'ula'ula.* Some of these are listed below. (PPN *kina.*) **2.** n. Kind of stone, used to make octopus sinkers. **3.** Contraction of *'ia ana* in the idiom *e aha 'ia ana?* What is being done? See *aha.*

inā.hea. inter. When (in questions in the past). Cf. Gram. 8.5. *Ināhea 'oe i hele mai ai?* When did you come? (Probably PPN *na + fea:* see Pawley, 1966, 58.)

'ī.na'i. nvi. Accompaniment to poi, usually meat, fish, or vegetable; to serve as *'īna'i. Fig.,* to flavor, garnish, spice. *Ku'u lā pōloli, ā ola i kou aloha, 'īna'i pū me ka waimaka* (PH 86), on my day of hunger, your love saves me, seasoned with tears. (PNP *kinaki.*)

inaina. 1. nvt. Anger, wrath, rage, hatred, enmity (Kin. 3.15), malice; to hate (Kin. 37.4), abhor; moved with hatred, angry. See ex., *'ena'ena 1;* cf. *mainaina. Kēia mau mea inaina 'ia* (Oihk. 18.29), these abominations. **ho'o.inaina.** To stir up anger, rouse hate. **2.** Redup. of *ina 1, 2.* **ho'o.inaina.** To sooth as by soft music. *Rare.*

inā (phrase) **inā.** conj. If . . . would.(Gram. 11.1.) *Inā he nui ke kālā, inā ua holomua ka hana,* if there were much money, the work would progress. *Inā i a'o maika'i 'ia kāua, inā ua holomua ka hana,* if we had been taught properly, the work would have succeeded.

'ina.'ina. 1. n. Reddish discharge preceding labor in childbirth, amniotic fluid. *Ua hemo ka 'ina'ina o ke keiki, ua kokoke paha i ka manawa e hānau ai,* the prebirth matter has been discharged, perhaps the time of birth is near. **2.** vs. Tiny *'ina.* See *'ina 1.*

'inā.'inau. To make love; pleasant, agreeable, sprightly. **hō.'inā.'inau.** Caus/sim. See ex., *hā'ule'a, ho'okokoe. He mau hō'inā'inau no nā keiki ho'opāpā,* interesting bits concerning the boys who played at contests of wit.

'ina.leo. n. Prep. (part of speech). *Rare.* Also *'inawaena.*

'ina.lua. 1. Same as *pōniu,* a vine. See *naomakalua. He 'inalua, he lā'au hihi, he mea hopu i'a,* an *'inalua,* vines for catching fish. **2.** Another name for *huehue 2.*

'ina.mona. n. Relish made of the cooked kernel of candlenut *(kukui)* mashed with salt (perhaps a contraction of *'īna'i momona,* sweet garnish). (Neal 506.) Also *'akimona.*

'ī.nana. nvi. To come to life or activity, as of a sick person; to show liveliness, as of young birds about to fly; animated; stirring of life. Cf. *kīnana, pūnana. Hō'eu, kukupu, 'īnana, kū i luna o ka moku* (ancient prayer, For. 6.527), bestir, grow, come to life, rule the island. *Ke 'īnana lā mehe 'ōpae 'oeha'a,* active there like freshwater shrimps [of scattered foes]. *Wahi piopio moa i ka hua e 'īnana nei i loko ou,* little chicken in the egg coming to life within you. **hō.'ī.nana.** To animate, give life to. *'O ka honua nui a Kāne i ho'īnana a 'ahu kīnohinohi* (Kep. 123), the great earth that Kāne gave life to and clothed decoratively. *Ō ho'ūlu 'oe, ō 'īnana 'oe, ho'īnana i ke ola* (prayer, PH 150), inspire, animate, give life.

inane! interj. Let me see! Show it to me! (Cf. *'oia ana, 'oliana.*)

'ī.nane. Var. of *'īnana.*

'inau. Same as *'inā'inau. Hoa 'inau,* sweetheart, mate, spouse. **hō.'inau.** Caus/sim. *Hōkū 'imo'imo hō'inau* (Kel. 10), stars twinkling merrily.

'ina 'ula. n. A red 'ina, perhaps young of *Heterocentrotus mammillatus.*

'ina uli. n. Black 'ina, perhaps young of *Echinometra oblonga,* or one of several other sea urchins.

'ina.waena. n. Preposition (part of speech). Also *'inaleo. Rare.*

'ī.nawe.nawe. Same as *hīnawenawe.*

ine. Var. of *ina,* to pry. *Rare.*

'ī.nea. nvi. Hardship, suffering, distress; to suffer discomfort. See ex., *pūlua. Hoa 'īnea,* a companion who shares hardships. *He hana 'īnea ka hewa,* sin is a work that brings suffering. ho.'ī.nea. To cause hardship, distress.

i nehi.nei. See *nehinei,* yesterday.

i ne'i. See *ne'i,* here.

'ine.kui.kikio, inekuisitio. n. Inquisition. (Latin *inquisitio.*)

'ini-. See *'ini'ini, 'iniki.* (PPN *kini.*)

'ī.nia. 1. nvs. India; East Indian. *Eng.* 2. *(Not cap.)* n. The pride of India *(Melia azedarach),* a tree from the Old World, naturalized in Hawai'i. It has much-divided fernlike leaves, and bears large clusters of purplish flowers and fruits like golden balls. (Neal 491–2.) Also *'ilinia.*

'Ini.ana. nvs. Indian, as Indian Ocean. *Eng.*

'ī.niha. n. Inch. *Eng.*

'ini.'ini. vt. To pinch. See ex., *hāpapa 2.* (PPN *kinikini,* strike; PNP *kinikini,* pinch.)

'ini.'iniki. 1. vt. To pinch or nip repeatedly; tingling, as with cold. *Ka 'ini'iniki mālie a ke kēhau,* gentle chill [or pang] of misty rain. 2. n. A way of catching small eels by holding bait on the palm of the hand and clenching the fist when the eels come.

'ī.niki. n. 1. Ink. *Eng.* 2. Malabar nightshade or Ceylon spinach *(Basella alba),* a succulent vine with thick, heart-shaped leaves, and spikes bearing black, berry-like fruits. It is eaten as greens. It is a native of tropical Asia or of Africa. (Neal 343–4.)

'iniki. vi. To pinch, nip; sharp and piercing, as wind or pangs of love. (Probably *'ini-* + *-ki,* transitivizer.) Cf. *'ini'iniki, 'īnikiniki. 'Iniki welawela,* a sharp pinch. (PPN *kiniti.*)

'Ini.kini. Same as *'Ilikini,* Indian. *Eng.*

'ī.niki.niki (sometimes pronounced *'īnisinini* in songs). Same as *'ini'iniki. Makani houhou 'ili, 'īnikiniki mālie* (song), wind that pierces the skin, a gentle pang.

'ini.kō. n. Indigo *(Indigofera suffruticosa),* a West Indian legume with compound leaves, small reddish flowers, and small, clumped, curved seed pods, introduced to Hawai'i about 1850 for commercial purposes. It was not a financial success. (Neal 447–8.) *Eng.* Also *'inikoa, kolū 4.*

'ini.koa. Same as *'inikō.*

'ini.kua. nvs. Insurance. *Eng. Palapala 'inikua,* insurance policy.

'ini.kua home. n. Home insurance. *Eng.*

'ini.kua ka'a. n. Automobile insurance.

'ini.kua ola. n. Life insurance.

'ini.kua pau ahi. n. Fire insurance.

'ini.kua ulia. n. Accident insurance.

'ini.pā.keke. n. In the pocket (used in the phrase: *komo ma ka 'inipākeke,* put in the pocket [pocketed]). *Eng.*

-ino. See *māino.*

'ino. 1. nvs. Wicked, immoral, sinful, unwholesome, unclean, bad, vicious, evil, unprincipled; hate, sin, decomposition (For. 5:713). See *kahi 'ino* and ex., *'oi 2. 'Ino loa,* very bad or wicked, horrible, abominable. *Kā i ka 'ino,* curse. hō.'ino, ho'o.'ino. To insult, malign, persecute, abuse, dishonor, defame, speak evil. *Hō'ino wale,* needlessly defame, damn. *Ho'opau ho'o'ino 'ia,* dishonorably discharged [as from the armed services]. (PNP *kino.*) 2. nvi. Spoiled, contaminated, bad-smelling, of poor quality, ugly; spoiled object, pollution. *Pau ka 'ino,* the foul period is over [of a child after toilet training]. 3. vt. To injure, hurt,

harm, break. *'O ka inu wai 'ona, he mea ia e 'ino ai ke kino,* the drinking of intoxicants injures the body. ho'o.'ino. To harm, injure, damage. 4. nvs. Storm; stormy. *'O ka uhiwai nō ka i 'ike i ka 'ino o ka wai,* the mists are those that know of storm on the water [those close by know what is going to happen]. 5. n. A commoner. (Kep. 141.) 6 part. Very, very much, intensely. (Sometimes pejorative; Gram. 7.5.) *Aloha 'ino,* too bad, what a shame. *Nui 'ino,* very, very many or much. *Holo 'ino ke ka'a,* the car races terrifically. *Makemake 'ino au i kēlā mea,* I want that thing very much.

inoa (in fast speech often preceded by *ke*). n. 1. Name, term, title. *Inoa laula, inoa nui,* general name. *Ola ka inoa,* the name lives [a family name is given to a child]. (PPN *hingoa.*) 2. Namesake. *E hele aku māua me Inoa,* we'll go with Namesake [said only by one of his *own* namesake; the possessive may be omitted; also used in the vocative]. 3. An affectionate term for affinal relatives, or in-laws or in-laws, or relatives usually not related by blood; *inoa* may be followed by a kinship term indicative of generation (as *mo'opuna, kaikamahine, keiki, makua, kupuna*), or of the common relative (as *puluna, hūnōna.*) A grandchild's spouse's relatives united by affection to the speaker might thus be called *inoa mo'opuna.* Similarly the cousins of a *puluna* (parents-in-law of an offspring) might be *inoa puluna,* and the cousins or in-laws of a parent might be *inoa makua.* The relationship might also extend to close family friends. 4. Name chant or song. *He inoa no ka lani* (chant), a name chant in honor of the chief.

inoa 'ala. n. Esteemed name, especially of a chief. *Lit.,* fragrant name.

inoa kapa.kapa. See *kapakapa 2.*

inoa makua. See *inoa 3.*

inoa 'ohana. n. Family name, surname.

inoa papa. n. Denomination, as in arithmetic.

inoa pō. n. Dream name, as a name for an infant believed received in a dream; it was thought that if such a name were not given, the child would be sickly or die.

inoa puluna. See *inoa 3.*

inoa 'ū.lā.leo. n. A name given to a child by a supernatural voice, usually heard just before the child's birth; a voice name.

'ino.'ino. 1. vi. Spoiled, contaminated, rotten, foul, broken, damaged; wretched. *'Ino'ino keia 'i'o pipi,* this beef is spoiled. *Paloka 'ino'ino,* spoiled ballot. hō.'ino.'ino. To mar, deface, disfigure, break, damage, ruin, speak evil of. (PNP *kinokino.*) 2. nvi. Stormy; storm. 3. nvi. Wicked, sinful; sin. 4. vi. Angry. *No ke aha lā i 'ino'ino ai kou maka* (Neh. 2.2)? Why is thy countenance angry? (The Neh. translation "sad" seems an error.) *Ka 'ino'ino o nā maka* (For. 5:555), the wrath of your eyes.

inu. nvt. To drink; a drink, drinking. Also *unu, rare. Kāna mea inu,* his beverage. *Kona inu,* his drinking. *Mea inu ho'ohuihui,* mixed drink. *Mea inu ho'ohu'ihu'i,* cold or iced beverage. *Pākela inu,* to drink to excess. *Pū'ali inu wai,* army of water drinkers (name of a temperance society). ho.'īnu, ho'o.inu. To give to drink. (PPN *(i,u)nu.*)

inu 'awa. nv. Kava drinker; to drink kava.

inu.hia. Pas/imp. of *inu.*

inu ho'o.mai.ka'i. vi. To toast (as before drinking).

inu lama. nv. To drink rum or other alcoholic drink; one who drinks.

inu li'i.li'i. vt. To drink but a little, sip.

inu.mia. Pas/imp. of *inu.* (PPN *inumia.*)

inu 'ona. v. To drink until intoxicated.

Inu-wai. n. Name of a sea breeze. *Lit.,* water drinking. See sayings, *lomia, milika'a. Hao ka Inu-wai, malo'o ka lau lā'au,* the Inu-wai blows, the tree leaves wither [of pillage].

io. n. Short rib extending upward from the tip of a paddle, on the forward surface. Also *'upe.* (PPN *io.*)

iō. Same as the particle *iā* and replacing *i 5* before proper nouns. (Gram. 9.3.2.) *Ā hiki i lalo iō Milu* (FS 91), going down to Milu. (PCP *ioo:* cf. Marquesan *io.*)

i 'ō. See *'ō,* yonder.

'io. 1. n. Hawaiian hawk *(Buteo solitarius),* an endemic and endangered hawk with dark and light color phases, confined to forests on the island of Hawai'i, where it is regarded by some as an *'aumakua.* The *'io* signified royalty because of its lofty flight, and hence occurs in such names as *'Io-lani,* royal hawk. Cf. *'io mea, 'io uli, māpumāpu, mio 1. Kaha ka 'io i ka mālie,* the *'io* hawk poises in the calm [admiration of a handsome person]. (PPN *kio.*) **2.** nvi. To twitter, chirp, peep; peeping. (PPN *kio.*) **3.** vi. To flee. (PEP *kio;* cf. Marquesan *'i'o.*) **4.** nvi. A round, light-colored bitter gourd *(Lagenaria siceraria),* about 30 cm in diameter. Cf. *ipu.* **5.** nvi. Tag; a Hawaiian game similar to tag; to play these games. **6.** nvi. Bundle or food package; loaded with such bundles. Cf. *'io pa'akai.* **7.** n. One who announces the presence of a chief; herald. **8.** *(Cap.)* n. Probably the name of a stroke in *lua* fighting; also a low stroke in club fighting (RC 59).

'i'o. 1. n. Flesh, meat, flesh and blood, muscle, sinew, essence, substance. *Fig.,* a relative; heart or gist of a matter. Many compounds and phrases with *'i'o* are listed below. For the fern *hō'i'o* see *hō'i'o. 'Ai 'i'o,* carniverous. *Make nō 'o Pā-mano i ka 'i'o pono'ī,* Pā-mano died of his own flesh and blood [said of harm done by relatives]. **hō.'i'o.** To become fleshy; to form a corm, fruit, tuber; to grow thick, as a stem. *Mai ka pō mai ka 'oia'i'o, i hō'i'o i luna, i hua i luna* (hula prayer), truth from out of the night, formed flesh above, formed fruit above. (PPN *kiko.*) **2.** vs. True, genuine, significant, real; really, truly, surely, actually; true worth. Cf. *'oia'i'o, hana'i'o. 'A'ohe 'i'o ho'i?* Not really? *No laila, 'i'o akula!* Fine! *Ka mea 'i'o makamae,* the truly precious thing. *He akua 'i'o nō Lono,* Lono is a true god. *E uhaele 'i'o aku kākou,* let's do go. *Ke ali'i ke pi'i i ka 'i'o,* the chief is the one ascending to true significance. **hō.'i'o.** To take things in earnest or seriously. **3.** n. Grain of wood. Cf. *'i'o lau mai'a. 'I'o lau li'i,* grain with slight curliness. *'I'o nalu,* wavy grain. *'I'o pū mai'a,* grain straight as a banana stalk.

'i'o 'alaea. n. Blood kin (but not children or siblings).

'i'o.awe.awe. n. A variety of taro. (HP 33.)

iō.ē. vi. To respond to a chant. *Iōē maila 'o Ka-welo* (FS 39), Ka-welo answered.

iō.'ena. vs. Wild, savage, untamed. Cf. *'ena,* to burn. *Maka iō'ena,* furious eyes.

'i'o hala. n. Small white seeds in a *hala* key, eaten by children and used as medicine. Cf. *hala 'i'o.*

'i'o hipa. n. Mutton, flesh of sheep.

'i'o holo.holona. n. Meat.

'i'o huki. n. Muscle.

io.io. nvs. Rounded grooves in carving, as in *kukui* nuts used in necklaces; depression made by stitches in quilting; grooved. **ho'o.io.io.** To cut grooves; to sew a quilt so that stitches settle in grooves. (PPN *ioio.*)

io.'io. 1. Redup. of *'io 2;* cheeping, peeping. Cf. *mā'io-'io. Manu 'io'io* (Isa. 38.14), swallow. *'A'ohe mea i hā-mama ka waha ā 'io'io* (Isa. 10.14), none opened the mouth or peeped. (PPN *kiokio.*) **2.** vi. To project, taper.

'i'o.'i'o. n. Clitoris. (PPN *kiko.*)

'io.'iole. vs. Mousy, like a rat. **ho.'io.'iole.** Caus/sim.

io.io.le'a. vs. Brisk, spirited, lively, quick-tempered, angry.

'io'io.lepo. nvi. Tattletale; to gossip or tattle maliciously.

'io.ko'o. n. Young pandanus leaves, white at the base and light green at the apex, as used in fine mats.

'i'o kupu. n. Disease of the nose, gumboil; growth on the roof of a horse's mouth.

'i'o lā.'au. n. Grain of wood; heart of wood.

'io.lana. nvi. To soar, poise, as a hawk; soaring hawk.

'Io-lani. n. Name of the Palace and of a school in Honolulu; also the names of Ka-mehameha II and IV: see Pukui, Elbert, and Mookini, 1974. *Lit.,* royal hawk (the high flight of the hawk symbolized royalty).

'i'o lau mai'a. n. Yellowish grain in wood, especially *koa,* named for its resemblance to the yellow color of a banana leaf *(lau mai'a).*

i'ole. conj. So that not, in order not. (Gram. 11.1.) *Ua kapa aku kō Hawai'i nei i ke akua ma nā inoa lehulehu, i'ole ai paha e nalowale ke akua 'i'o* (Kep. 15), those of Hawai'i called god with many names, in order not to forget by chance the true god.

'iole. 1. n. Hawaiian rat *(Rattus exulans);* introduced rat, mouse (Oihk. 11.29); rodent (see *'iole lāpaki, 'iole manakuke, 'iole pua'a);* mole (Isa. 2.20); considered by some an *'aumakua.* Cf. *piko pau 'iole, haumaka'iole, pa'ipa'i'iole, papa'iole, 'uwī'uwī 3.* **hō.'iole.** To behave like a rat; ratlike. *Fig.,* to steal, cheat, lie in wait in order to assail. (PNP *kiole.*) **2.** Classifier for rodents. See below. **3.** Name for a sinker of an octopus lure and the lure.

'iolea. vs. Unsocial.

'iole.holo.kula. n. Extinct variety of small, sweet gourd with long stem, formerly used as medicine. (HP 208.) *Lit.,* rat running on plains.

'iole lā.paki (rabati). n. Rabbit.

'iole li'i.li'i. n. Small rat, mouse.

'iole mana.kuke. n. Mongoose.

iō.lena. Var. of *iō'ena.* (UL 100.)

'iole.niho. n. Octopus lure. *Lit.,* rat tooth.

'iole nui. n. Introduced large rat.

'iole po'o wai. n. Introduced large rat, probably Norway rat. *Lit.,* water-source rat.

'iole pua'a. n. Guinea pig.

'i'o.liu. n. Tenderloin.

'iolo. vi. To vibrate, whiffle, sough. (For. 6:476.)

'i'o lū.'au. n. Greenish meat of turtles, considered the best, so named because its color resembled cooked taro tops *(lū'au).*

'i'o maha. n. Temple muscle.

'io mea. n. A variety of *'io* hawk without dark markings.

'iomo. 1. Same as *'iamo.* **2.** Same as *'iao,* a fish.

i ona. To him, her; him, her. (Gram. 9.6.3; Luka 23.15.) *Lit.,* to his, hers. *Ua holo akula au i ona lā,* I ran to him.

'i'o nī.oi. n. Condiment of boiled pulp of chili peppers *(nīoi),* often mixed with relish such as *'inamona.*

'i'o niu. n. Flesh of coconut.

'i'o nui. 1. nvs. Meaty, fleshy, as of some fish, or as the soft part of pandanus keys that are strung for leis. **2.** n. A fern known in many countries *(Dryopteris parallelogramma* syn. *D. paleacea),* up to 80 cm high, with feather-shaped fronds clustered on a short trunk, the frond stems clothed with long brown to black scales.

'i'o 'ō.hi'a. n. *'Ōhi'a* wood grain; reddish grain of *koa* wood.

'io pa'a.kai. n. Container for salt, as made of pandanus leaves.

'i'o pale niho. n. Gums. *Lit.,* tooth-protecting flesh.

'i'o pipi. n. Beef.

'i'o pipi i wili 'ia. n. Hamburger, ground round steak. *Lit.,* ground beef flesh.

'i'o pipi keiki. n. Veal.

'io po'i moa. n. Chicken-stealing hawk. *Fig.,* a clever thief, especially of another's sweetheart.

'i'o pono. n. Blood relative.

'i'o pono.ī. n. One's own relative.

'i'o pua'a uahi. n. Bacon. *Lit.,* smoked pork flesh.

i ou. Toward you, to you; you. (Gram. 9.6.3.) *Lit.,* to your.

i o'u. To me, me. *Lit.,* to my. (Gram. 9.6.3.)

'io uli. n. A dark *'io,* hawk.

'i'o ulu. n. Growth, tumor.

'ipeka, ibeka. n. Ibex. *Eng. Ka 'ipeka 'olu'olu* (Sol. 5.19), pleasant doe (RSV), roe (KJV).

ipo. n. Sweetheart, lover. *Kāna ipo,* his or her sweet-

heart. *Ipo ahi,* ardent lover. *Ipo laua'e,* sweet-natured lover. *Ipo manuahi,* extramarital lover, mistress.
ho'o.ipo. To make love, court, woo. (PCP *ipo.*)
ipo.ipo. vt. To make love (less used than *ho'oipoipo*).
ho'o.ipo.ipo. To make love, court, woo; love; romantic. *Ho'okela o ka ho'oipoipo,* fantastic love making. *Ho'oipoipo 'ana,* courtship. *Mele ho'oipoipo,* love song. *Ka 'aha'aina ho'oipoipo* (1 Pet. 4.3), revelings. *Ka po'e ho'oipoipo* (Heb. 13.4), whoremongers. (PEP *ipoipo.*)
ipu. n. **1.** The bottle gourd *(Lagenaria siceraria,* also *L. vulgaris),* a wide-spreading vine, with large-angled or lobed leaves, white, night-blooming flowers, and smooth green and mottled or white fruits varying widely in shape and size. The plant is a native of tropical Asia or Africa. Hawaiians have long used gourds as receptacles, small gourds with thin walls to hold water or food, or for rattles for dances (the *ipu* has a fine tone, halfway between that of *niu* and *la'amia*), larger ones with thin to thick walls to hold tapa and other articles or to serve as drums. Orientals cook and eat the white pulp of green fruits. Hawaiians have distinguished between a kind with bitter pulp, used medicinally, and a kind with nonbitter pulp. (Neal 812-3.) For gourds classified according to shape and color see *hōkeo, hue, hulilau, kūkae'iwa, 'olo, po'okanaka.* Cf. *pule ipu.* (PPN *ipu.*) **2.** The watermelon *(Citrullus lanatus),* a wide-spreading vine from tropical Africa, with large, lobed leaves and yellow flowers. It is grown for its edible fruits, which are round or oblong, green or green with light stripes, and full of sweet, juicy, rose-colored pulp surrounding flat, black seeds. The watermelon was introduced to Hawai'i about 1792 and thrived until the melon fly arrived about 1910. Among many varieties that were developed were three outstanding ones: *ipu huluhulu, ipu po'o kanaka,* and *ipu oloolo.* Today watermelons are again cultivated successfully because the fruits are commonly wrapped in paper or cloth during early stages. (Neal 810-1.) Also *ipu 'ai maka, ipu 'ai waha, ipu haole.* **3.** General name for vessel or container, as dish, mug, calabash, pot, cup, utensil, urn, bowl, basin, pipe. *Ka ipu o ka 'ike,* a container of knowledge [a learned person]. **4.** Drum consisting of a single gourd or made of two large gourds of unequal size joined together. See *ipu hula, ipu pa'i, ipu wai.* **5.** Crown of a hat.
ipu ahi. n. Censer, vessel for burning incense. (Nah. 4.14.)
ipu 'ai. n. **1.** An edible melon. **2.** Calabash or vessel for food or food offering.
ipu 'ai maka. n. Watermelon, melon (Nah. 11.5). *Lit.,* melon to eat raw. See *ipu 2.*
ipu 'aina. n. Scrap bowl, slop basin, refuse container.
ipu 'ai waha. Same as *ipu 'ai maka. Lit.,* melon to eat in mouth.
ipu akua. Same as *ipu huluhulu. Lit.,* ghost melon.
ipu 'ala. n. **1.** Cantaloupe melon *(Cucumis melo* var. *cantalupensis).* (Neal 811.) **2.** Container for perfume or other fragrant matter. *Lit.,* fragrant gourd.
ipu 'au.'au. n. Washbasin; container of water for a bath. *Ipu 'au'au keleawe* (Puk. 30.18), a laver of brass.
ipu 'au.makua. n. Large gourd calabash in which food was offered to the *'aumakua* family gods.
ipu 'awa, ipu 'awa.'awa. n. A variety of gourd *(Lagenaria siceraria)* with bitter-tasting pulp, used medicinally. (Neal 812.) Its strong odor is eradicated by soaking in sea water.
ipu 'ā.wa'a.wa'a. n. A kind of introduced muskmelon *(Cucumis melo).*
ipu hana lepo, iho hanawai. n. Chamber pot.
ipu hao. n. Iron pot; kettle or saucepan of any sort, skillet, whether glass, aluminum, or enamel. *Lit.,* iron container. *Ka ipu hao nui* (2 Nal. 4.38), the great pot.
ipu haole. n. Watermelon. *Lit.,* foreign gourd. See *ipu 2.*

ipu hao puhi. n. Still, for distilling.
ipu heke. n. Gourd drum with a top section *(heke).*
ipu heke 'ole. n. Gourd drum consisting of a single gourd without a top section.
ipu hoe.hoe. Same as *hoehoe,* gourd whistle.
ipu hō.kio.kio. Same as *hōkiokio,* gourd whistle. Also *pu'a.*
ipu holo.holona. n. Gourd containing fisherman's gear and bait, or a traveler's possessions. *Lit.,* traveling container.
ipu holoi. n. Washbasin.
ipu holoi lima. n. Finger bowl. *Lit.,* container wash hand.
ipu ho'o.lapa.lapa. n. Boiler.
ipu ho'o.mo'a kō. n. Sugar boiler.
ipu hula. n. Dance drum made of two gourds sewed together. Cf. *'olo.*
ipu hulu.hulu. n. A variety of watermelon with a slightly fuzzy *(huluhulu)* skin, and with whitish or pale-pink pulp; it is edible but not greatly liked; it formerly grew wild at Ka'ū. Also *ipu akua.* (Neal 810.)
ipu i'a. n. Meat dish; fleshpot (Puk. 16.3).
ipu 'ī.nika. n. Inkwell, inkstand.
'ī.puka. n. Door, entrance, exit, gate, gateway, opening in the wall for the admission of light or air. Cf. *puka,* hole. *Ka 'Īpuka Gula,* Golden Gate [San Francisco]. *Kū i ka 'īpuka o kou hale,* stand at the door of your house [attend to your own affairs, not other people's]. *A ho'i mai, ma kēlā 'īpuka ā kēia 'īpuka o kahi ho'omoana* (Puk. 32.27), and go out from gate to gate throughout the camp.
ipu kai. n. A dish for meat or any dish deep enough to hold gravy *(kai);* gravy boat. *Fig.,* lowland areas, often an affectionate term and with a connotation of bountiful sea food. Cf. also *hīnālea.*
ipu kā.lua. n. Baked pumpkin or squash.
ipu kā.ni'o. See *kāni'o 3.*
ipu kapu ahi. n. Same as *ipu ahi.*
ipu kī. n. Teapot.
ipu kī.'o'e. n. Dipper.
ipu kua.'aha. n. Container for sacred objects; gourd calabash covered with a sennit net and suspended by a handle composed of four cords; food offerings were placed inside for the god Lono. (Neal 748.) Also *ipu-o-Lono.*
ipu kū.'aha. Short for *ipu kua'aha.*
ipu kuha. n. Spittoon.
ipu ku'i wai.ū.paka. n. Churn. *Lit.,* container for pounding butter.
ipu.kukui. n. Lamp, candlestick. *Hale ipukukui,* lighthouse. *Ipukukui manamana he gula maika'i* (Puk. 25.31), a branched candlestick of pure gold.
ipu.kukui hele pō. n. Lantern. *Lit.,* light for going at night.
ipu kula. n. The cup of gold *(Solandra hartwegi,* often called *S. guttata),* a large climbing shrub from Mexico, with long-stemmed, oblong leaves. The large, showy, fragrant flowers bloom in winter, are about 23 cm long, goblet-shaped with five shallow lobes, and are yellow with five narrow purple longitudinal streaks. *Lit.,* golden *(Eng.)* container. (Neal 748.)
ipu kū.li'u. n. Salt container. *Lit.,* seasoning container.
ipu kuni 'ala. n. Incense burner, censer (Nah. 16.6). *Lit.,* container burning fragrance.
ipu lei. n. Container for leis.
ipu lē.'ī. n. Fishhook container. *Rare.*
ipu lepo. n. Earthenware pot, clay pot, vessel of earth (Oihk. 15.12), potter's vessel (Hal. 2.9); chamber pot. *Lit.,* dirt container.
ipu māhu. n. Boiler.
ipu mā.nalo. n. A variety of gourd with nonbitter pulp. (Neal 812.) *Lit.,* sweet gourd.
ipu mimi. n. Chamber pot, container for urine.
ipu nui. n. A large container; the great bronze laver in Solomon's temple. (2 Nal. 25.16.)
ipu oe.oe. n. Same as *ipu hōkiokio.*

ipu-o-Kāne. n. Shell container of the *hiwa* green coconut used in ceremonies honoring the god Kāne.

ipu ʻō.lelo. n. Speaking gourd, a gourd containing pebbles and other objects used in divination; oracle.

ipu-o-Lono. n. **1.** A variety of taro used as offering to the gods; it may be qualified by the terms *kea* and *ʻulaʻula*. **2.** An agricultural heiau; a heiau where ceremonies seeking to obtain rain were held. **3.** Shell of the yellow-husked or *lelo* coconut. **4.** Same as *ipu kuaʻaha*.

ipu oloolo. n. A variety of watermelon with fruit like that of *ipu poʻo kanaka*, but ovoid and larger. (Neal 810.)

ipu paʻi. n. Gourd drum. *Lit.*, gourd to beat.

ipu pā.ʻina. n. A variety of cantaloupe. *Lit.*, feast melon.

ipu paka (baka). n. Tobacco pipe.

ipu pā.wehe. n. Gourd calabash decorated with designs.

ipu poʻo kanaka. n. A variety of watermelon with round, small fruit, smooth skin, and red pulp. (Neal 810.) *Lit.*, human head melon.

ipu pū. Same as *pū 3*, a general name for pumpkin and squash.

ipu pueo. n. Gourd with hourglass shape.

ipu.wai. n. Wood rollers laid under a canoe being hauled to prevent it from being scratched or damaged.

ipu wai. n. **1.** Water container or bottle. **2.** Gourd drum. (This word is actually *ipu uai [uwai]*, movable gourd.)

ipu wai ʻau.ʻau. n. Washbasin. *Fig.*, chiefs' genealogists who were supposed to keep the characters of their masters clean.

iū. pronoun. You. *Eng. Inā ʻo iū maʻaneʻi* (song), if you were here.

ʻiu. nvs. Lofty, sacred, revered, consecrated; such a place. *Ka-ʻiu-lani* (personal name), the royal sacred one. *Noho ihola ke kahuna nui i ka ʻiu* (For. 6:41), the high priest occupied the high consecrated spot [while others marched in the *makahiki* circuit]. **hō.ʻiu.** To make lofty, sacred; to elevate; shy, reserved. **2.** n. Taboo isolating menstruating women in a special hut.

ʻiui. n. Ceremonial feeding by the high chief of the messenger carrying the image Lono about the island during the *makahiki* festivals. (Malo 148.)

ʻiu.ʻiu. Intensification of *ʻiu 1*; majestic, lofty, very high; distant, far away; long absent and out of sight; a distant realm of the gods. Cf. *hoʻomāʻiuʻiu*. *ʻIuʻiu wale*, so long away, so far.

i uka. See *uka*.

Iu.kaio, Iudaio. nvs. Jew; Jewish. (Gr. *Iudaios*.)

Iulai. n. July. *Eng.*

Iune. n. June. *Eng.*

iuni.pela, iunipera. n. Broom tree (RSV), juniper (KJV). (Neal 49, 1 Nal. 19.4.) *Eng.*

Iupika, Iupita. n. The planet Jupiter, originally known as *Ka-ʻā-wela*. *Eng.*

iupi.lē, iubile. n. Jubilee. *Eng. Ka pū iubile* (Oihk. 25.9), trumpet of the jubilee.

iwa. num. Ninth, ninth. Cf. *ʻaiwa*, *ʻeiwa*. *Hapa iwa*, one ninth. *Kanaiwa*, ninety. (PPN *hiwa*.)

ʻiwa. n. **1.** Frigate or man-of-war bird *(Fregata minor palmerstoni);* it has a wing span of 12 m. *Fig.*, thief, so called because it steals food by forcing other birds to disgorge; also used figuratively for a handsome person, as follows: *Kīkaha ka ʻiwa, he lā makani*, poises the frigate bird, a windy day [of a handsome person who draws attention, as does the ʻiwa bird poised aloft]. *Ka ʻiwa ālai maka*, the frigate bird that fascinates the eye [an attractive person]. *He iwa ka hoa e like ai* (Kel. 134), just like one's friend the ʻiwa bird (of one dressed up in finery). See ex., *maʻoha*; see sayings, *ʻānai*, *haehae 2*. (PCP *kiwa*.) **2.** A native fern *(Asplenium horridum)* with narrow, feather-shaped fronds 45 to 95 cm long, their dark stems bearing dark-brown hairs and scales. The stems were formerly used for making hats. Also *ʻalae*. (PCP *kiwa*.)

i waena. See *waena*.

i waho. See *waho*.

ʻiwa.ʻiwa. n. **1.** All maidenhair ferns *(Adiantum* spp.), from warm regions of the world, many grown ornamentally. The stems are dark, commonly shiny, slender, wiry; the fronds' subdivisions are four-sided, oblong, or wedge-shaped. (Neal 17–9.) *ʻA ʻohe i ana iho koʻu makemake i nā ʻiwaʻiwa o ka ua o Hāʻao* (hula), my desire is not satisfied for the maidenhair ferns in the Hāʻao rain. (PCP *kiwakiwa*.) **2.** A small, high-mountain fern *(Asplenium adiantum-nigrum)*, with shiny, brown stems and triangular or ovate, subdivided, stiff fronds, the spores numerous, often found covering the under side of the fronds. Known in many countries. **3.** Var. name for *manawahua 2*, ferns *(Doryopteris* spp.), listed by Rock and Hillebrand.

ʻiwa.ʻiwa-a-Kāne. n. An endemic fern *(Asplenium rhipidoneuron)* with narrow, feather-shaped fronds, which are stiff, 10 to 30 cm long, dark-green, the divisions pointed and obliquely cut, their stems bearing many dark scales.

ʻiwa.ʻiwa ʻā.piʻi.piʻi. n. The curly-leaved maidenhair *(Adiantum tenerum* f. *farleyense)*, an ornamental fern much like the ʻiwaʻiwa hāuli, but the leaf subdivisions much larger, more deeply cut, fringed and overlapping. (Neal 18.) *Lit.*, curly maidenhair. Also *ʻiwaʻiwa ʻAukekulalia*.

ʻiwa.ʻiwa ʻAukeku.lalia. Same as *ʻiwaʻiwa ʻāpiʻipiʻi*. *Lit.*, Australian maidenhair.

ʻiwa.ʻiwa hā.uli. n. The fan maidenhair fern *(Adiantum tenerum)*, with each of the last fan-shaped subdivisions split into five to ten segments.

ʻiwa.ʻiwa hā.wai. n. The Venus-hair, a kind of maidenhair fern *(Adiantum capillus-veneris)*, known in many warm countries, both wild and cultivated in Hawaiʻi. The fronds are subdivided into many small, bright-green, fan-shaped divisions, borne on slender, black stems. (Neal 18.) Also *ʻiwaʻiwa kahakaha*.

ʻiwa.ʻiwa kaha.kaha. Same as *ʻiwaʻiwa hāwai*. *Lit.*, striped *ʻiwaʻiwa*.

ʻiwa.ʻiwa lau liʻi. n. A native fern *(Asplenium macraei)* with narrow, feather-shaped fronds 30 to 60 cm long, with subdivisions of each frond lobed or scalloped. *Lit.*, small-leafed *ʻiwaʻiwa*. Also *iwa lau liʻi*.

ʻiwa.ʻiwa lau nui. n. An endemic fern *(Tectaria gaudichaudii)* with thin, triangular fronds 30 cm to 1.2 m long, much divided into rather broad lobes. *Lit.*, large-leafed *ʻiwaʻiwa*.

iwa.kā.lua. num. Twenty, twentieth.

iwa.kā.lua kū.mā.hā. num. Twenty-four.

iwa.kā.lua kū.mā.hiku. num. Twenty-seven.

iwa.kā.lua kū.mā.iwa. num. Twenty-nine.

iwa.kā.lua kū.mā.kahi. num. Twenty-one.

iwa.kā.lua kū.mā.kolu. num. Twenty-three.

iwa.kā.lua kū.mā.lima. num. Twenty-five.

iwa.kā.lua kū.mā.lua. num. Twenty-two.

iwa.kā.lua kū.mā.ono. num. Twenty-six.

iwa.kā.lua kū.mā.walu. num. Twenty-eight.

ʻiwa lau liʻi. Same as *ʻiwaʻiwa lau liʻi*.

ʻiwa pua.kea. Same as *mānā 2*, a fern. Maui.

iwi. n. **1.** Bone; carcass (as of a chicken); core (as of a speech). The bones of the dead, considered the most cherished possession, were hidden, and hence there are many figurative expressions with *iwi* meaning life, old age: *Na wai e hoʻōla i nā iwi?* Who will save the bones? [Who will care for one in old age and in death?] *Maʻaneʻi au me ʻoe a waiho nā iwi*, here I am with you until leaving the bones [death]. *ʻO ʻoe nō kuʻu iwi, a me kuʻu ʻiʻo* (Kin. 29.14), thou art my bone and my flesh. *Holehole iwi*, to strip bones of flesh [to speak ill of one's kin]. *Pili i nā iwi*, to wager one's bones [one's life]. Many phrases and compounds with *iwi* are listed below. Cf. *kaulaʻi iwi*. *Kona iwi*, his [own] bone. *Kāna iwi*, his bone [as a chicken bone he is chewing on]. *Iwi koko*, bloody bones [a living person]. *Iwi koko ʻole*, bones without blood [a dead person]. *Kō iwi*, your own interests, your own. *Hana nō i kā kō iwi*, do for your own bones [take care of your own interests]. *Kō kō iwi ʻāina hānau,* your own land of birth (PPN *iwi.*) **2.** Shell, as of coconut, candlenut, gourd, egg, shellfish. Cf. *iwi hala.* **3.** Remnants, pieces, as of coral in a lime pit after lime is extracted by burning, or as pieces of broken glass. **4.** Corncob. **5.** Stones or earth ridge marking land boundary. **6.** Long line, as of surf. **7.** Midrib, as of *pili* grass or ti leaf.

'iwi. **1.** Var. of *ʻiʻiwi,* a bird; considered by some an *ʻaumakua.* (PCP *kiwi.*) **2.** nvs. Reddish. **3.** n. Twitching of the eye, sometimes accompanied by contraction of the mouth. **hō.ʻiwi.** Caus/sim. (PPN *kiwi.*)

iwi **ā.** n. Jawbone. *Ka iwi ā o ka hoki* (Lunk. 15.15), jawbone of an ass.

iwi **akua.** n. A deified bone of an ancestor, an *unihipili.* **hoʻo.iwi akua.** To impart mana to a human bone.

iwi **ʻao.ʻao.** n. **1.** Rib, rib bone, spareribs. (2 Sam. 2.23.) **2.** Wife (so-called because Eve is said to have been taken from Adam's rib); assistant leader in a hula troupe. Also *paepae.*

iwi ʻaui. n. Sprain.

iwi **elelo.** n. Hyoid bone at the base of the tongue. *Lit.,* tongue bone.

iwi **hala.** n. Hard, upper part of pandanus key.

iwi **hilo.** n. Thighbone, femur, the last rib bone; poetically the very core of one's being. *Konikoni ana i ka iwi hilo,* throbbing to the very depths of the chest.

iwi hoe.hoe. n. Shoulder blade.

iwi **honua.** n. Rock or shoal projecting on a coral reef. (UL 61.) *Lit.,* earth shell.

iwi **hope.** n. Bone forming the posterior segment of the skull.

iwi **hua.** n. Hipbone; round bone fitting into a socket.

iwiiwi. nvs. Bony, skinny, emaciated. (PPN *iwiiwi.*)

iwi kā. n. Ischium, seat bone; spines on a fish fin.

iwi kaʻele. n. Keel, as of a ship.

iwi kala. Same as *iwi kaʻele;* spines on fish fins.

iwi kala kua. n. Spines on dorsal fins of fish.

iwi kā lalo. n. Spines on ventral fins of fish.

iwi kamumu. n. Cartilage. Also *iwi kumumumu.*

iwi kanaka. n. Human bone or skeleton.

iwi kā.nana. n. Bone of the anterior part of the skull, forming the skeleton of the forehead.

iwi **kani.** nvs. Strong bones; possessing strong bones, strength. *E hana paha ʻoe a iwi kani, i kohu ai kāu*

kaena iho (song), you should, perhaps, have strong bones to match your boasting.

iwi kano. n. Preaxial bone of the forearm.

Iwi-kau-i-ka-ua. n. Name of a star and of an ancient chief of Hawaiʻi.

iwi kele. Same as *iwi kaʻele.*

iwi koko. See *iwi l.*

Iwi-koʻo. n. Name of a *lua* stroke.

iwi.kū. n. Bone of the lower leg.

iwi.kua.mo'o. n. **1.** Spine, backbone. **2.** Near and trusted relative of a chief who attended to his personal needs and possessions, and executed private orders; family. *Hoʻi hou i ka iwikuamoʻo,* return to the family [as after long absence or estrangement].

iwi kumu.mumu. See *kumumumu.*

iwi lā.ʻī. n. Stem and midrib of a ti leaf.

iwi.lei. n. **1.** Collarbone. (PNP *iwilei.*) **2.** Measure of length from the collarbone to the tip of the middle finger with the arm extended; yard. (PNP *iwilei.*)

iwi loa. n. A tall bone. *Fig.,* a tall person.

iwi ʻō. n. Wishbone.

iwi.ole. n. Kind of adze. *Lit.,* fang bone.

iwi ʻō.peʻa.peʻa. n. Two bones between the occipital and frontal bones forming a part of the top and sides of the cranium; parietal bone.

iwi pā.uma. n. Breastbone, as of a fowl.

iwi pili. n. **1.** Midrib of a blade of *pili* grass. **2.** Double or united bone of arm of leg.

iwi poʻi. n. Kneecap.

ʻiwi pō.lena. Same as *ʻiʻiwi pōlena,* a honey creeper.

iwi pona. n. Hollow bone, as the eye socket; socket at a joint into which a round end of a bone fits.

iwi poʻo. n. Skull, head bone; leader *(rare). Ka-iwi-poʻo,* Calvary (partial loan translation of Latin *calvaria,* bare skull).

iwi pū.haka. n. Pelvic bone.

iwi-puhi. n. Design on a tapa beater and on tapa consisting of a herringbone figure with a long ridge in the center; design in plaited hat braids, as forming the *pāpale ʻie. Lit.,* eel bone.

iwi pū.niu. n. Coconut shell. *Fig.,* skull.

iwi uluna. n. Humerus or bone of the upper arm. *Lit.,* pillow bone.

iwi umauma. n. Breastbone, sternum.

J

For loan words from English beginning with j-, *substitute* i- *or* k-. *For example: for June, July, see* Iune, Iulai; *for Japanese, jury, see* Kepanī, kiule.

K

k-. Marker of *k*-words (definite articles, possessives, demonstratives), with meaning singular/definite. (Gram. 10.1.) (PPN *t*-.)

ka. **1.** Definite singular article replaced by *ke* before words beginning with *a, e, o,* and *k,* and before some words beginning with the glottal stop and *p* (ka ʻaka, the laugh, *ke ʻala,* the fragrance; *ka pā,* the yard, *ke pā,* the dish). In documents in the State Archives dating from the 1850s, *ke* was used also before words beginning with other letters. *Ka* is sometimes used before nouns that are obviously plural and instead of possessives (see ex., *mae*). *Ka* is usually translated 'the' except that it is not translated before English mass nouns and status titles, as *ka hanohano,* glory, and *ke Akua,* God. (Gram. 10.2.) (PNP *te*.) **2.** The one who, the person in question (usually followed by *i,* completed aspect, and a verb, a shortening of *ka mea:* Gram. 10.2; see *ke 2*).

kā. **1.** nvt. To hit, strike, throw, smite, hack, thrust, toss, fling, hurl, dash, especially with a quick hard stroke; to bail water, as from a canoe; to clean, as weeds or mud from a pond; to fling the arms or swing them while walking; to make net meshes; to tie, as thatch battens; to knit; to fish with a pole; to turn the soil; to turn a rope for children to jump; to remove, as a cataract from the eye with the edge of a blade of *kūkae puaʻa* grass; to snare, as birds; to curse (especially if used with *ʻino;* cf. *kāmalū*); to murder; murderous; murderer, dead shot. *Kā i ka hoe,* to pull on a paddle with all one's strength. *Kā make loa,* to dash to death, hurl down, as a foe in *lua* fighting; to doom to death. *Kā i ka ʻino,* to curse, do evil to. *Kā i ka nele loa,* to take away everything, utterly deprive, to be without. *Limu kā kanaka o Manuʻa-kepa,* the man-striking moss of Manuʻa-kepa [name of a famous slippery alga growing on the beach at Hanalei, Kauaʻi]. *Kā makau,* to make a fishhook of bone or other material. *Kā kēhau,* to rub tapa on grass or shrubbery to absorb the dew as a means of gathering moisture in arid places such as Kaʻū. *Kā koʻi,* to make adzes. *Kā liliko,* to burn, sear. For *kā i ka waha,* see *waha. I ke kā ʻana* (For. 5:650), in tying [thatch]. **hoʻo.kā.** To dash down, shatter, break, strike. (PPN *taa*.) **2.** nvt. Canoe bailer; to bail. (PPN *taa*.) **3.** n. Beater, knee-drum beater made of dried ti leaves or braided fiber. **4.** n. Cross-stitching. **5.** nv. Vine, as of sweet potato; to send out a vine, to vine, to grow into a vine. Cf. *hīkākā, kāhihi. Ua kā nā ʻuala a kākou,* our sweet potatoes have grown into vines. **6.** nvi. Root cutting, as of breadfruit; to send forth shoots. **7.** n. Pelvic bone. *He kā manu* (For. 4:287), thigh of a bird [perhaps a mistranslation; *ʻūhā manu* in the preceding line is mistranslated *leg of a bird*]. **8.** n. Incoming, of a current *(au).* **9.** n. Container, hanger. Cf. *kā ipu, kā paka, kā ʻumeke.* **10.** interj. of mild disapproval, annoyance, or surprise. Oh! So! Goodness! So that's it! Is that so! (If spoken alone it is frequently pronounced *Chā!* or *Sah!*) (Gram. 12.) *ʻO ʻoe kā!* So it's you! *ʻOia kā!* Is that it! *Eia aʻe nō kā!* Still here! *ʻO kā mākou kā kāu mea i manaʻo ai* (For. 4.297), so ours is what you wanted. **11.** poss. Of, belonging to (*a*-class, Gram. 9.6), as in the possessives *kā kākou,* our (inclusive), *kā mākou,* our (exclusive); *kā ka haumana puke,* the student's book. (PNP *taʻa*.) **12.** n. Czar. *Eng.* **13.** Also *tā.* n. Tar, asphalt. *Eng.*

kā-. **1.** Inclusiveness, in the first person dual and plural pronouns *kāua, kākou.* (PPN *ta,* PNP *taa*.) **2.** Non-productive caus/sim. prefix similar to *hoʻo-*. Cf.

kāhea, kāhili, kāhinu, kākoʻo, kāmaʻa, kāwili, and many others, and Gram. 6.3.1. (PPN *ta(a)-*.)

kaʻa. **1.** vi. To roll, turn, twist, wallow, wind, braid, revolve; to scud or move along, as clouds; to wield, as a club; rolling, twisting, turning, sloping. See ex., *pōhaku 1. Puʻu kaʻa,* sloping, rolling hill. *Kaʻa i ka lepo,* to wallow in the mud or dirt. *Kaʻa ka lolo,* the brain spins; dizziness; perturbation; *fig.,* destitution, poverty. **hoʻo.kaʻa.** To cause a rolling, turning. (PPN *taka*.) **2.** n. Vehicle, carriage, wagon, automobile, car, cart, coach, buggy. *Uku kaʻa,* carfare, transportation charge. *Nui nā kaʻa,* many cars, heavy traffic. **3.** vi. To go past, pass by, reach; to be in a state of; to be located at; to take effect, as medicine; gone, absent, past, turned over, transferred, delivered. *Kaʻa loa lākou i waena o ka waha o ua moʻo nei* (For. 5:413), they went straight into the middle of the mouth of this lizard. *Ua kaʻa ʻoia i ka maʻi,* he is confined with illness. *Kaʻa iho nō ā kaʻa iho nō i ka maʻi,* sick again and again. *Kaʻa i ka lawa,* it's enough, sufficient. *He mau lā e kaʻa aʻe,* several days gone by. *Kaʻa ka pilikia mahope,* the trouble is gone. **4.** vi. To pay; paid. *Ua kaʻa kuʻu ʻaiʻē,* my debt is paid. **hoʻo.kaʻa.** To pay a debt, disburse, avenge (FS 85). *Hoʻokaʻa hapa,* partial payment. **5.** vi. To manage, run, be in charge of; given, as work to a person; well versed, skilled (used very broadly to indicate custom, nature, character, habit: see *kaʻa hele, kaʻa kaua, kaʻa lolohi, kaʻa maʻi, kaʻa moena, kaʻa nema, kaʻa nemo*). *Ka poʻe i kaʻa aku ka mālama ʻana i nā mea ana ua,* the people charged with taking care of the rain instruments. *Ua kaʻa ka hana iāʻoe,* the work has passed on to you. (Probably PPN *taka*.) **6.** n. Resin. Cf. *hūkaʻa, lāʻau-kaʻa, kēpau kaʻa.* **7.** vt. To wipe dry with a cloth, as dishes. *Kaʻū.* **8.** n. Pulley. **9.** See *hoana kaʻa.* **10.** n. Tale, legend (now replaced by *kaʻao*).

kaʻā. nvt. Thread, line, as of *olonā* fiber; snell of a fishline, snood; ply, twist, strand; to make thread, as of *olonā* (Nak. 62). Cf. *kaʻā kolu, kaʻā lua.*

kaʻaahi. n. Train, railroad, locomotive engine. *Lit.,* fire wagon. *Kaʻaahi kau i ka lewa,* elevated train.

kaʻa.ʻei. n. Star name.

Kaʻa-ʻē-nā-aliʻi. n. A *lua* fighting stroke.

kā.ʻaha. n. Stick, rod, or wand with leaves and tapa at one end, held by the priest while sacrificing in the temple.

kā.ʻaha.ʻaha. vi. To grow thriftily, of plants.

kaʻa hale. n. Trailer, house on wheels.

kaʻa hali ʻō.hua. n. Passenger conveyance. *Lit.,* vehicle carrying passengers.

kaʻa hali ukana. n. Freight *(ukana)* conveyance.

kaʻa hapa.ʻumi. n. Horse-drawn trolley car. *Lit.,* five-cent vehicle.

kaʻa.hē. vs. Feeble, near death; to labor for breath. Cf. *-nākū.*

kaʻa.hea. vi. To languish, pine. (For. 4:27.) **hoʻo.kaʻa.-hea.** To soothe.

kaʻa hehi wā.wae. n. Bicycle, tricycle. *Lit.,* vehicle press feet.

kaʻa.hele. vi. To make a tour, travel about; a tour; in turns. *Kahuna pule kaʻahele,* traveling preacher. *Heluhelu kaʻahele,* to read in turn. *Ua kaʻahele au a puni ke kaona,* I have gone all around the town.

kā.ʻahi. Short for *kaʻaahi.*

kaʻa.hili. vi. To struggle; to pant, as for breath. *Ua kaʻahili mauliʻawa,* struggling, gasping.

ka'a.hina. vi. To fall down and roll.

ka'a.hō.kai. vt. To mix up, disturb. Cf. *hōkai.*

ka'a.holo. vi. To speed ahead, run.

ka'a holo hau. *n.* Sled. *Lit.,* car riding snow.

ka'a hope. Arrears in a payment; to pass by. *Ma ka Sabati iho nei i ka'a hope a'e,* on the past Sabbath.

ka'a huila kahi. n. Wheelbarrow.

ka'a huila lua. n. Any two-wheeled vehicle, as cart or buggy.

ka'a huki. n. Handcart. *Lit.,* pull vehicle.

Ka-'ahu-'ula. n. A *lua* fighting stroke. *Lit.,* the feather cloak. (Also without *Ka-*.)

kā.'ai. **1.** nvt. Sash, belt, girdle of any kind; sennit casket alleged to contain the bones of Līloa and Lono-i-ka-makahiki, in Bishop Museum in 1976; protective cloth wrapped around an object; to bind, tie around, encircle, gird on; to put on, as armor or a mourning garment. Also *kā'ei, kāhei.* See *akua kā'ai. Ho'i 'o Keawe, kū i ke kā'ai* (saying), Keawe returns, [his remains] bound in the sennit container [formerly said of newly dead]. (PPN *takai.*) **2.** vt. To dig food crops, as taro, sweet potatoes.

ka'aka. n. Fellow, chap, wretch, person. *Slang.* (Possibly Tahitian, but see *mahumahu, 'ōkole ka'aka.*)

ka'a.ka'a. **1.** vt. To open, as the eyes; open, watching. *E noho 'oe e ka'aka'a i ka hale,* stay and watch the house. *Ē ka Haku ē, i ka'aka'a ko'u mau maka* (Mar. 10.51), Lord, that I might receive sight. **ho'o.ka'a.ka'a.** Caus/sim. *Rare.* (PCP *takataka.*) **2.** *(Cap.)* n. Name of a star or constellation, said to be on the border of the Milky Way. (KL line 1865.) **3.** Rare variant of *ko'a,* coral head, fishing grounds.

-ka'a.ka'a. ho'o.ka'a.ka'a. To cause to roll repeatedly. Also *ho'okaka'a.* (PPN *takataka.*)

ka'a.ka'a.hiki. vs. Actively and gainfully employed, successful; to make progress. *Rare.*

ka'a.ka'a.lā.'au. Same as *hi'u wīwī,* an *'ahi,* a fish.

ka'a.ka'a.lalo. Redup. of *ka'alalo.* (Kep. 101.)

ka'a.ka'a.lawa. vs. To have enough, especially of material goods; ample. *Ka'aka'alawa ka papa e pa'a ai ka hale,* there is ample lumber to complete the house.

ka'a.ka'a.lina. vs. Tough, stringy, as of banana trees; viscid, gluey.

ka'a.ka'a.ana. Redup. of *ka'ana.*

ka'a.ka'a.wili. Redup. of *ka'awili.* **ho'o.ka'a.ka'a.wili.** Redup. of *ho'oka'awili. Ho'oka'aka'awili ihola 'oia no kona 'eha'eha,* he writhed much in his pain.

ka'a ka lolo. See *ka'a 1.*

ka'a kaua. **1.** nvi. Skilled in warfare; strategist, war maneuvers, strategy. **2.** n. War tank; war chariot. (Puk. 14.25.)

ka'a kau.ō (kauwō). n. Trailer, tractor.

ka'a.kepa. nvt. Diagonal, cut at an angle; to avoid, shy away from, take a short cut. See ex., *keha. No laila e ka'akepa nei, 'e'ena i ka pili kēpau* (hula song), that's the reason for being so shy, fearful of the sticky gum.

ka'a kewe. n. Cable car.

ka'a kinai ahi. Fire engine. *Lit.,* vehicle extinguish fire.

ka'ā kolu. vs. Three-stranded; threefold.

ka'a.ko'o. vt. To belt. *E pono e ka'ako'o i ka lole ma ke kino me ke kā'ei,* the garment should be belted on the body with a belt.

ka'a.kua. nvi. Violent dizziness; to lie down or lean back in pain, to roll over backwards. *Ka'akua ka lani, ho'īloli ka honua* (chant for Ka-māmalu), heaven leans back in pain, earth is in travail.

ka'a.kukua. Redup. of *ka'akua.*

ka'a.kū.mā.kena. nvi. Period of mourning, especially wailing in grief; to mourn and wail.

ka'a.kumu. vs. Dull, of tools.

ka'a.kupa.pa'u. n. Hearse.

kaala. n. Widow, widower. (And.)

ka'a.lā. **1.** Same as *mo'o 'alā,* a lizard. **2.** vs. Blind (used with *maka*). *Rare.*

kā.'ala. n. An *'opihi,* a limpet.

kā.'alā. nv. Sling; to hurl stones with a sling. *He nui ka po'e i a'o i ke kā'alā,* many persons learned to use a sling.

ka'a.la'a. Rare var. of *kā'ala'ala.*

kā.'ala.'ala. vs. Vigorous, sturdy, healthy, as of an infant or young animal. *I ke kā'ala'ala 'ana a'e o ke keiki . . .* (Nak. 6), upon the vigorous growth of the child . . .

ka'a lā.'au. v. To wield a war club; to send a curse by playing with seeming innocence with four or five sticks held in the hand (Kam. 64:141).

ka'a.lalo. vi. To sail to leeward. *Fig.,* full of lies, underhanded, deceitful. Cf. *ka'aka'alalo.*

ka'a.lani. n. Those about a chief; members of the royal court. *Honi nā kini i ka makani Pa'ala'a, he hanu no ke ka'alani ē* (chant for Ka-mehameha I), the multitude smell the *Pa'ala'a* breeze, a breath of air for those about the chief.

ka'a.lau. Same as *hukilau.*

ka'a lau niu. n. Coconut-leaf thatching. *'O ka hana ho'i a nā ali'i wāhine 'o ka ulana i ka'a lau niu hale no ke ali'i,* the work the chiefesses did was to plait coconut thatching for the house of the chief.

ka'a lawe ma'i. n. Ambulance.

ka'a.lele. vi. To sway, reel; to fly or soar, as birds.

ka'a.lelewa. Redup. and intensifier of *ka'alewa. Nā ao ka'alelewa* (1 Tes. 4.17), floating clouds.

ka'a.leo. vi. To speak loudly.

ka'a.lewa. vi. **1.** To revolve. **2.** To drift, sail off and on. Cf. *kālewa.*

ka'a.lia. Pas/imp. of *ka'a 1, 3–5. Rare.* **ho'o.ka'a.lia.** Pas/imp. of *ho'oka'a. Ho'oka'alia mai ke alo o ka moku ia'u nei* (Kep. 184), let the front of the island be turned toward me.

kā ali'i. nv. Ceremonial throwing of spears at a high chief returning from a voyage; he dodges or catches the spears to show his courage and skill; to hurl thus.

ka'a.lina. vt. To bruise; to pelt, as rain. Cf. *'ālina.*

ka'a lio. n. Horse-drawn vehicle, wagon, carriage.

kā.'alo. vt. To pass by, go by. Cf. *mā'alo.* **ho'o.kā.'alo.** To pass to and fro, to cause to pass. (PPN *ta(a)kalo.*)

kā.'alo.'alo. Redup. of *kā'alo.*

ka'a.lohi. Same as *ka'alolohi.*

ka'a.loku.loku. nvs. Intrepid, fearless, as of one unafraid to brave the elements; bravery. (FS 239.) Cf. *loku.*

Ka'a-lolo. n. Name of a star, said to be the tutelary star of Ni'ihau.

ka'a.lolohi. vs. Slow-moving, slow to anger. *Kū i ka 'ena o ka lani nei ali'i, 'o ka lani ka'a lolohi, ka'a ka lani* (chant for Ka-mehameha I), this chief is filled with regal fury, the chief usually slow to anger, the way of a chief.

ka'ā lua. vs. Two-ply, two-stranded.

ka'a.luna. vi. To sail or turn against the wind. *Fig.,* to dominate; overbearing. Cf. *ka'alalo.*

ka'a māhu. n. Steam-propelled vehicle.

ka'a ma'i. nv. Siege of sickness, a long or chronic illness; to suffer such. *Lō'ihi ke ka'a ma'i 'ana,* the siege of sickness was long.

ka'a malalo. vi. **1.** To fall in (military command), to serve others, to roll beneath. **2.** To be subject to. *Kōmike e ka'a aku malalo o ke 'āpono 'ana . . . ,* committee subject to approval . . .

ka'a malo'o. vt. To wipe dry, as dishes with a cloth.

ka'a maluna. vi. To rise in station, to come up from under; to rule others.

ka'a mea. vi. To change, as the wind or an idea. *Rare.*

ka'a.meha'i. Var. of *kāmeha'i.*

ka'a moena. nv. Bedridden. *Rare.*

ka'a mola. vi. To turn around loosely, as a screw or peg that does not fit; loose, unsteady.

ka'ana. **1.** vi. To divide, share, apportion. **ho'o.ka'ana.** To divide equally among, share. **2.** vi. To decoy, especially to attract *uhu* fish with a live *uhu* decoy; to proselyte. *Ke pō'ai haele nei 'oukou i ke kai a me ka 'āina, i ka'ana mai ai na 'oukou kekahi haumana* (Mat. 23:15), you encompass the seas and lands to make one proselyte; *lit.,* so one pupil is decoyed by you. **3.** n. A rolling, as of stones.

kā.'ana.'ana. n. Constipation. *Rare.* Cf. *'ana'ana.*

ka'ā.nani.'au. Same as *ahupua'a,* the altar marking the land division. *O'ahu. Rare.*

ka'ane. n. Strangling cord.

ka'a.ne'i. Interj. of surprise or scorn. *'Oia ka'ane'i!* Is that so! So that's it! *He lio ka'ane'i, he pipi!* So a horse, a cow [scornful]!

kā 'ane'i. poss. The local, as *kā 'ane'i paia,* the walls here 'a-class; cf. *kō 'ane'i*).

ka'a nema. Same as *nemanema.*

ka'a nemo. vs. Smooth, rounded, as seeds. (Kep. 159.)

ka'a niau. vi. To move or walk quietly.

ka'a.nī.'au. vs. Freed, as of a taboo.

ka'a.nini. vi. To writhe, squirm, as a fidgety child or one in a tantrum; to run after in agitation; to go round and round, as a dog greeting a friend. Cf. *niniu,* spin.

ka'a.nini.au. Var. of *ka'anini.* See saying, *wiliwai. Ua ka'aniniau i ka wai,* whirling in the water.

ka'a.nu'a. n. An elevated place; sleeping place in a grass house.

ka'ao. nvt. Legend, tale, novel, romance, usually fanciful; fiction; tell a fanciful tale. **ho'o.ka'ao.** To tell tales; story telling. (PCP *t(a,e)kao.*)

kā.'ao. **1.** nvi. Ripe, of pandanus fruit; ripe pandanus. Cf. *puhalu 1.* **2.** *(Cap.)* n. A favorable Hālawa, Moloka'i, wind mentioned in For. 5:123; also associated with Hanamā'ulu, Kaua'i (For. 5:97).

kā.'ao.'ao. n. Name for a garden patch.

ka'a 'ō.hua. n. Vehicle carrying passengers for hire, as bus, taxi, stagecoach.

ka'a.oki. vt. To finish or complete, as a canoe; to put on the last touches. Cf. *kā'oko'a, oki. Ka'aoki iho 'oe i kahi pū niu a hā'awi mai,* finish the work on the coconut shell and give it to me.

ka'a.'oko'a. **1.** Var. of *kā'oko'a. Ka'a'oko'a nō kona mana'o,* his thinking is independent. **ho'o.ka'a.'oko-'a.** To separate, set apart, refrain, abstain from. *'O ka mea ho'oka'a'oko'a i ka lā'au hahau, 'oia ke aloha 'ole i kāna keiki* (Sol. 13.24), he who spares the rod has no love for his son. **2.** vi. Entirely paid, as a debt.

ka'a 'oko.mopila (otomobila). n. Automobile. *Lit.,* automobile *(Eng.)* vehicle.

Ka'a.ona. **1.** n. Name of a month. See *month.* **2.** *(Not cap.)* nvs. Red or reddish-brown, due to being smoked, especially of fish, or of the stem of sugar-cane tassel to be used in a dart. **3.** *(Not cap.)* vs. Attractive, of a child (children born in the month of *Ka'aona* were thought to be attractive and lovable). Cf. *pua ka'aona.* **4.** n. Name of a star. (KL line 1881.)

ka'a.'owē. nvi. To roll along with a rustling sound *('owē).* *Fig.,* a person with no property or means of support.

ka'a.pā. vi. To toss from side to side, as a restless child in bed; in spasms. *Eia ku'u hanu lā ke ka'apā wale nei nō i ka houpo,* here is my breath, panting within the chest.

ka'a pahu. n. Pushcart.

ka'ā.pahu. vt. To cut off squarely or crosswise *(kā,* strike, and *'āpahu,* cut off short).

ka'a paiki.kala. n. Bicycle. *Lit.,* bicycle *(Eng.)* vehicle.

ka'a palaoa. Same as *kāwili palaoa.*

ka'a pau ahi. n. Fire engine. Also *ka'a wai.*

ka'a.pē. vs. Servile, humble, fawning, cringing.

kā.'ape. vs. Headstrong, willful, obstinate (perhaps related to the *'ape* plant which holds its leaves upright).

kā.'ape.'ape. **1.** Same as *'āhina kuahiwi,* a fern. **2.** n. A seaweed. **3.** n. Same as *ka'ape'apehā.*

ka'a.pe'a.pehā. n. A deep-sea fish said to resemble the *moano.*

ka'a.peha. **1.** nvs. Large mass of clouds; impressively

big, large, even corpulent in a distinguished manner; influential and important. **2.** vi. To spread wings or tail feathers. (For. 6:381.) **3.** vt. To fold over, as a bundle. (For. 6:381.)

ka'a.pehā. n. Castor bean, more commonly known as *koli* or *pā'aila.*

ka'a.pi'o. n. Hack (carriage). *Lit.,* bent vehicle, so called because of the top.

ka'a.pola. n. Taboo night in the ruling chief's heiau during October.

ka'a pō.niu.niu. n. Ferris wheel. Also *huila pōniuniu.*

ka'a.puni. **1.** nvt. To make a tour, go around, surround, encircle, rotate, revolve, travel; circuit. *Kekimala ka'apuni,* circulating decimal. *'Aha ka'apuni,* circuit court. *Ua hele māua i ke ka'apuni honua,* we went on a tour around the world. **2.** nvt. The hula step now called "around the island": the dancer pivots on the ball of one foot in a complete circle; the other foot takes four or more steps to complete the circuit; to do this step. **3.** n. Revolution, revolving.

ka'au. **1.** num. Forty. See *pāka'au.* (PPN *tekau.*) **2.** *(Cap.)* n. A fine rain in Kohala, Hawai'i.

-kā'au. ho'o.kā.'au. Witty, clever, funny, entertaining, humorous; to pass the time pleasantly; entertaining time. *Ho'okā'au 'ana,* time spent pleasantly.

kā.'au.'au.pu'u. n. Hard, mottled stone, as used for *'ulu maika* stones. *Rare.*

ka'a uila. n. Streetcar, electric bus, electric vehicle.

ka'a ukana. n. Truck.

Ka-'au.wae-lewa. n. A *lua* fighting stroke. *Lit.,* the floating chin. (Also without *Ka-.*)

kā.'awa. n. Large bowl in which kava was mixed and strained (short for *kānoa 'awa*).

ka'a wai. n. Vehicle carrying water, fire engine.

ka'a.wale. nvt. Separate, free, different, apart, spare, alone, unoccupied, empty; to separate, isolate or reserve, withdraw; free time, opportunity; to take interval (military command); distance separating places or objects. *Kahi ka'awale, wahi ka'awale,* empty space or place, secluded or isolated place, aside. *Manawa ka'awale,* spare or free time. *'Eono mile ke ka'awale,* six miles away. *Kū ka'awale,* to stand apart, entirely different; independent. *'A'ohe wahi ka'awale o kēia pahu,* there's no room left in this box. *'A'ohe wahi ka'awale o kēia keiki i ka makua kāne,* this boy is the exact image of his father [nothing independent or different]. *Mawaena o lāua, 'ewalu anana ke ka'awale* (FS 145), eight fathoms distance between the two. **ho'o.ka'a.wale.** To separate, distinguish (1 Nal. 3.9); to cause a division; to keep a distance or distinction; to establish as a separate entity; to set aside, appropriate, sort, segregate, reserve, discriminate, differentiate. *Ma'i ho'oka'awale,* leprosy. *Ho'oka'awale i ka pu'u kālā,* to appropriate a sum of money.

ka'a wale. vi. To turn or roll freely, independently, or without control. (PPN *taka wale.*)

kā.'awe. nvt. To tie anything tightly around the neck, to choke, strangle, hang; necktie. *Ua kā'awe 'oia a make,* he hanged himself until dead. *Kā'awe 'ā'ī,* name of the *manulele* sugar cane when prayed over in *hana aloha,* love-making sorcery, to induce an absent person to fall in love; cf. *manu lele.*

kā.'awe.'awe. Redup. of *kā'awe;* choking, strangling sensation.

Ka-'ā-wela. n. Name of a planet, probably Venus or Jupiter. (KL line 1851.) (Probably the same as *Hōkū-loa* (Kep. 82), *Hōkū-ao* and *Ka-lani-'ōpu'u.*)

ka'a.wele.kā. vi. To repeat, do over and over. *Ke ka'awelekā nei nō ia mea kahiko i loko o mākou,* this old thing is still being mulled over within us.

ka'a.wili. vt. To turn, twist, writhe as in pain; to knead, as bread (Ier. 7.18). (*'Ōpelu* fish that form a vertical wall as they swim, flapping to maintain this unusual position, are said to *ka'awili.*) Cf. *pāka'awili.* **ho'o.ka'a.wili.** To cause pain (Ier. 4.19); to torture; to cause to twist or writhe; to fondle or pet in ardent love-making.

ka'a.wili lā.'au. n. **1.** Lathe. **2.** Perfumer (RSV), apothecary (KJV). (Puk. 37.29.) More commonly *kāwili lā'au.*

kae. 1. n. Refuse or rubbish, waste, excrement (cf. *kūkae*); refuse from fibers, as of *olonā;* raw bast and refuse of the *wauke* plant after soaking. (PPN *ta'e.*) **2.** vi. Treated with contempt, scorn. *Ke kae 'ia o ka inoa,* contempt shown the name. **ho'o.kae.** To despise, detest, treat with contempt or scorn; destroy, devastate (Oihk. 26.31); to refrain from doing, as due to horror. *Ho'okae 'ili,* race prejudice. *Ho'okae 'ino,* to abhor.

ka'e. 1. n. Brink, border, margin, rim, brim, fringe, curb, bank, edge; toothless gums;.projecting brow of a hill. Cf. *ka'eka'e, hakaka'e.* *He ka'e wale nō,* only gums and no teeth. (PNP *take.*) **2.** Idiom following *'a'ole* and possessive *o. 'A'ole o ka'e mai,* without limit. For a similar idiom, see *kana 2.* **3.** vi. To sulk, fuss; sullen, cross. **4.** vi. To smudge, dab, besmear. **hō.ka'e, ho'o.ka'e.** To daub, smudge, soil, smear. Cf. *hauka'e. Hōka'e a'ela ku'u pepa i ka 'īnika,* my paper is smeared by ink.

kaea. 1. n. Cessation or lack of appetite or desire. *'A'ole kahe mai 'o ka waimaka, 'o ke kaea pū wale a'ela nō ia* (Laie 523), the tears do not flow, the desire was just gone. **2.** vi. Tired. *Eng.*

ka'e'a. Same as *kā'e'a'e'a.*

kā.'e'a.'e'a. n. Expert, hero, fighter. *He kā'e'a'e'a pulu 'ole nō ka he'e nalu,* an expert on the surfboard does not get wet.

ka'e'e. vi. Hard, stiff, not soft or pliable; dried up, withered as by heat; evaporated. *He wahi wai 'a'ohe i ka'e'e i ka lā,* a little water not evaporated by the sun.

kā.'e'e. n. **1.** A sea bean *(Mucuna gigantea),* native from southeast Asia, east into Polynesia, a high-growing vine, bearing greenish flowers and large pods, each pod containing two to four round and flattened seeds, black-spotted or brown. In Hawai'i, the seeds, known as *pēka'a,* are found on the beaches, and are used medicinally for their strong purgative effect and are also strung for leis (Neal 462). **2.** Hand net hanging on an ellipsoidal wooden frame with one end pointed, used for *'ōhua* and other inshore fish; to use this net or a skirt of a dress in this type of fishing; to strain, as through a strainer. (PCP *taakeke.*)

kā.'ō.'ō. vs. Joyful, glad, hospitable, friendly. Same as *a'a 2.*

kā.'e'e'e. Var. of *kā'e'ē 1.*

kā.'ō.'ē'e. Redup. of *kā'ē'ē;* very joyful, glad, etc.

Ka'e.'ele. Rare var. of *Ka'ele 2,* a wind.

Ka-'ō.heu. n. A *lua* fighting stroke. *Lit.,* the wing. (Also *'Ēheu.*)

kā.ehu. Rare var. of *kaiehu.*

kā.'ei. Var. of *kā'ai;* belt, sash; zone; ring for bobbin winder of sewing machine. *Kā'ei kapu o Līloa,* a sacred cordon, baldric, or sash, the highest symbol of authority, on display in 1976 at the Bishop Museum. It is made of a net of *olonā* fibre with red *'i'iwi* feathers on the sides and a lei of *'ō'ō* feathers on the borders. The end, hanging in front of the body, is ornamented with human and fish teeth. The other end was brought over the shoulders and passed twice around the waist. According to tradition it was made by Līloa for his son 'Umi in the late 15th century. A copy, without the teeth, is on the statue of Ka-mehameha in front of Ali'i-o-lani Palace, Honolulu.

Kā.'ei-anu. n. Arctic Circle.

kā.'ei pā.pale. n. Hatband.

kā.'ei po'o. n. Diadem, turban.

kā.'ekā. vi. Entangled, confused, twisted; to interweave. *Wili kā'ekā ke aho,* the line is tangled. *Hihi kā'ekā,* obscure confusion, tangle.

kae.kae. 1. vs. Smooth, polished, perfect, as a new canoe without knots or knobs; young, attractive,

plump, desirable, as of a woman; tasty, mellow, soft, as of sweet potatoes; to rub smooth, polish, finish. Cf. *mōkaekae. Kaekae ke olonā,* the *olonā* fibers are perfectly cleaned. *Kaekae ka 'umeke,* the wooden bowl is smoothly polished. **2.** *(Cap.)* n. Name of a star.

ka'e.ka'e. 1. Same as *ka'e 1.* **2.** Redup. of *ka'e 4.* **hō.ka'e.ka'e, ho'o.ka'e.ka'e.** Redup. of *ho'oka'e. Mai ho'oka'eka'e wale 'oe i ka paia,* don't stain the wall.

kae.kaea. Pas/imp. of *kaekae 1.* Rare.

kā.'eke. Same as *kā'eke'eke.*

kā.'eke.'eke. nvt. Bamboo pipes, varying in length from .3 to about 1 m; usually with one end open. A player held one vertically in each hand tapping down on a mat or on the ground. The tone varied according to the size of the tube. Several musicians might play at once. (UL 143-4, Roberts 53.) Barrèrre suggests (Barrèrre, Pukui, and Kelly 11) that *kā'eke'eke* as the name for bamboo pipes seems to have originated with Emerson. She quotes Andrews (who refers to Laie) as saying the name applied to coconut-tree drums. It is also used as a verb. Also *'ohe kā'eke'eke* or *pahūpahū.*

Kā.'eke.loi, Kā.'eke.'eke.loi. Same as *Kā'eleloli.*

kā.'eko. vs. Peeved, offended.

kaela. Rare var. of *kaola.*

ka'ele. 1. nvs. Empty and hollow, as of a bowl, poi board, drum, canoe hull; hull; inside bottom as of a calabash or poi board. Also *'ele. Ka'ele papa,* dug-in poi board. *Iwi ka'ele,* keel. *Mehe ka'ele papa lā Hilo, i lalo ka noho, kā'ele wale Hilo i ke ālai 'ia e ka ua* (UL 60), like a poi board Hilo, dwelling below, darkened Hilo by the blocking rain. (PPN *takele.*) **2.** *(Cap.)* n. Name of a wind of Ka-lele-wa'a, Moloka'i. (For. 5:101.)

kā.'ele. 1. vs. Darkened; cf. *'ele,* black. See ex., *ka'ele 1.* **2.** vs. Numerous. *Kā'ele ho'i kānaka o kēlā wahi!* So many people in that place! **3.** vs. Slow, delaying. *Kā'ele noho'i kō 'oukou hele 'ana mai,* how slowly you came. **4.** n. A seaweed.

Ka-'elele-o-ka-wana.'ao. n. Star name, probably the same as *Hōkū-loa,* Venus. (Kep. 82.) *Lit.,* the messenger of the dawn.

kā.'ele.loi. n. Roll, ruffle, as of a drum.

Kā.'ele-loli. n. Name of a rain at Makiki, O'ahu.

kā.'elo. 1. vs. Name of a wet month. Cf. *'elo,* saturated. *'O Kā'elo ka malama, kāpule ke kōlea* (saying), Kā'elo is the month, the plovers are fat. **2.** Name of a star, possibly Betelgeuse.

kaena. vt. To boast, brag, glorify, praise; boastful, conceited, proud. *No ko'u 'ike i ka maika'i, ko'u mea nō ia i 'ōlelo kaena ai* (saying), as for my knowledge of beauty, that's something I brag about.

ka'eo. vs. Resentful, peeved, indignant, angry.

kā.'eo. 1. vs. Full, as a food calabash. *Fig.,* full of knowledge. See ex., *'umeke.* **2.** vs. Strong, zealous. **3.** n. Hair gathered in a topknot on the head, as by priests in ceremonies. (For. 6:401.)

kā.'eo.'eo. Redup. of *ka'eo,* and *kā'eo.*

ka'eo lau. n. A variety of taro.

ka'eo nui. n. A variety of taro.

ka'e pa'a. n. Selvage of cloth. *Lit.,* solid edge.

kā.'eu.'eu. vs. Helpful, cooperative; joyous, active; larger, bigger. Cf. *'eu.* **ho'o.kā.'eu.'eu, hō.kā.'eu.- 'eu.** To encourage and bestir to action.

ka'e.umu. n. A variety of sweet potato.

kaha. 1. nvt. To scratch, mark, check, draw, sketch, cut, cut open or slice lengthwise, as fish or animals; to operate, as on the sick; to give a grade or mark to; to engrave; a line in mathematics; punctuation or other mark, as an accent mark; stripe, as in the flag or of enlisted men in the Armed Forces; a grade, as in school; checkmark, long striped cloth. See *kaha ki'i, kaha palapala'āina. He hana kaha ea,* deprivation of livelihood; *lit.,* life-cutting activity. *He aha ko'u kaha?* What was my grade? **ho'o.kaha.** Caus/sim. (PPN *tafa.*) **2.** loc. n. Place (often followed by a qualifier, as *kahakai, kahaone, kahawai,* and used without *ke,* as *hele i kahakai,* go to the beach); in legends, a hot dry shore (PH 74, 84; FS 173). (Gram. 8.6.) *'O kēia ka mea ulu o ko'u kaha,* this is what grows on my place. (PPN *tafa.*) **3.** vi. To swoop, as a kite; to be poised, soar, as a bird (less used than *kīkaha*); to go by, pass by, to turn and go on; to surf, body surf (FS 153). *Kaha ka lā ma ke kua o Lehua* (UL 238), the sun passes to the back of Lehua [Island]. **ho'o.kaha.** Caus/sim. (PEP *ta(f,s)a.*) **4.** vt. To desolate, plunder, cheat. Cf. *pākaha. Ua kaha akula ka nalu o ku'u 'āina,* the waves of my land have swept everything away [said of famine]. **ho'o.kaha.** Caus/sim.; to extort. **5.** n. Stage of a foetus in which limbs begin to develop. Also *mana.* **6.** vs. Proud, haughty. *Rare.* See *ho'okahakaha.* **7.** n. A kind of tapa. (Kam. 76:111.)

kā.hā. vs. Large, fat, plump, as of a well-fed dog. *Rare.*

kaha akua. n. **1.** A track of a god. **2.** Abode of gods or spirits.

kaha.apo. n. Circumference, parentheses, brackets. *Lit.,* mark embrace.

kaha ea. See *kaha 1.*

kaha.'ea. n. Cumulus clouds, often colored, thought to be a sign of rain. Cf. *ao, 'ōpua. Kau kaha'ea i ka hana waele; palepale nā 'auwai o lalo,* the cumulus clouds appear during the task of weeding; clean the watercourses down below.

kaha.'ea.'ea. Redup. of *kaha'ea. I ke kau kaha'ea'ea a ke aloha,* the cumulus clouds of love are set.

kaha emi. n. Minus sign.

kahaha. **1.** n. Young growth stage of the fish *'ama'ama,* about a hand's length. Also *pahaha.* **2.** Same as *aukaha,* desolate.

kā.hā.hā. interj., n., and vi. Interj. of surprise, wonder, displeasure; to wonder, be surprised, astonished, amazed, puzzled; surprise, astonishment. *Kāhāhā i ka 'ino,* shocked, aghast, horrified. *Kū i ke kāhāhā nui* (Kel. 104), most astonishing. **ho'o.kā.hā.hā.** Surprising, astonishing; to cause astonishment.

kaha.hā.nai. n. **1.** Radius of a circle. **2.** Strings securing upper part of the net surrounding a calabash *(kōkō).*

kaha.hiō. n. Multiplication sign, crisscross mark; slanting lines.

kaha ho'o.lawe. n. Minus sign.

kaha ho'o.nui. n. Multiplication sign.

kaha.hui. n. Bracket combining two items, as male and female voices in music; tenor clef; plus sign in arithmetic. *Lit.,* joining mark.

kā.hai. Var. of *kā'ai.*

Kaha'i. n. A culture hero. (PNP *Tafaki.*)

kā.ha'i. Same as *kanaha'i.*

kā.ha'i.ha'i. **1.** Redup. of *kāha'i.* **2.** Same as *'āweoweo,* a native shrub.

Kaha-i-Kaha'i. n. Star name, said to be the twentieth in the Milky way. *Lit.,* going to Kaha'i [hero's name].

kā ha'i make mai ho'i. n. Death by sorcery. *Lit.,* death indeed from someone else. (Kam. 64:43.)

kaha.'ino. nvs. Evil, evil place. *Haele ana nō kānaka i ke kaha, alualu ana i ke ka'i o kaha'ino ē* (For. 6:469), people go to the place, following the marks of evil.

kahaka. n. Plant said to have been used for medicine (no data).

kaha.kā. vs. Disagreeable, unpleasant. *Ka'ū.*

kaha.kaha. **1.** Redup. of *kaha 1;* to mark frequently, to draw lines, scratch; to cut lengthwise or into strips; to scarify, engrave; striped, lined. *Pepa kahakaha,* scratchpaper, lined paper. **ho'o.kaha.kaha.** Caus/sim. *Me ka ho'okahakaha 'ana i ka lau i ka lima* (For. 5:663), with the separation of the leaves in the hands. (PPN *tafatafa.*) **2.** Redup. of *kaha 3.* **ho'o.kaha.kaha.** Caus/sim.; to parade back and forth, make a display or exhibition; to show off, act the dandy; to drill, as a fire drill; parade, celebration, exhibition, display, vanity, pomp; superb, showy. *Lā ho'okahakaha,*

holiday. (PEP *ta(f,s)ata(f,s)a.*) **3.** n. Small stone larger than a pebble. *Rare.*

kaha.kahana. n. Markings, scratchings, lines, stripes; narrow strip of cloth, usually white. *Kahakahana lole* (Ioane 11.44), napkin. *Kahakahana kaumaha,* marks of worry, as on the face.

kaha.kai. loc. n. Beach, seashore, seacoast, seaside, strand. (Gram. 8.6.) (PEP *tafatai.*)

kaha kau.pale. n. Boundary.

kaha.kea. vs. High, inaccessible, as a cliff. (For. 6:412.)

kaha kele.awe. nv. To cut or engrave in copper or brass; a worker in copper or brass; engraver.

kaha ki'i. nv. To draw or paint a picture or draw plans; artist.

kaha ki'i hale. nv. Architect; to draw building plans.

kaha.kikī. nvs. Roaring sound, as of wind, rain, or rushing waters; to roar. *Ua lohe akula lākou i ke kahakikī a ka wai,* they heard the roar of rushing water.

kaha.kō. **1.** vs. Steep, sheer. *Ka pali kahakō lele a koa'e,* sheer cliff reached by tropic bird. **2.** n. Macron.

kaha.kū. **1.** vi. To turn off one's course; to go where one pleases, trespass. *He kahakū wau no kēia 'āina, ia'u o uka, ia'u o kai* (FS 235), I may go where I please on this land, inland is mine, seaward is mine. **2.** n. A unit of measure, usually said to be about 2.5 m, but in FS 97 called fifteen feet (4.5 m).

kaha kuhi. n. Reference mark in writing or printing to direct attention, as asterisk, dagger, arrow, blaze.

kā.hala. **1.** n. Amberjack or yellowtail *(Seriola dumerilii). Kāhala 'ōpio* is *S. aureovittata.* The name may be qualified also by *maoli* and *moku lei. Āmuka* is a variant name or a name for the adult stage. Another name is *mokule'ia.* See also *halahala 2.* **2.** vs. Ripe, said of a gourd with stem beginning to wither. *Ua kāhala ka ipu,* the gourd is ripe. **3.** n. Net made of strong cord, used for sharks. (Malo 213.) Also *hihi manō.*

kā.hala.hala. vs. Tasteless, insipid, flavorless, unpleasant tasting. Cf. *hala,* fault.

kaha lalo. nvi. Underscore, underline.

kaha lelele.pō. n. Famine during wartime, with persons seeking food at night for fear of being seen. *Lit.,* cut leap about night.

kaha.lili. **1.** n. Sanctified stone used by a priest in *'anā'anā* sorcery. **2.** vi. To exhibit wrath or displeasure due to jealousy.

kaha.loa. **1.** Short for *'ae-o-kaha-loa,* a tapa. **2.** A stone brought before a priest in sorcery prayers. (And.)

kaha loa. nvi. To turn and then go straight for a long distance; long detour or digression.

kaha.maha. vt. To interrupt, break into a conversation.

kaha maha. n. Dash (punctuation mark). *Lit.,* mark to rest.

kaha mekala. nv. To engrave; engraver.

kaha moe. n. Hyphen. *Lit.,* horizontal mark.

kahana. n. Cutting, drawing of a line; turning point. Cf. *kaha 1, 3. Eia ma'ane'i ke kahana alanui e iho ai i kahakai,* here's the turn of the road to go down to the beach.

kā.hana.hana. n. Clearing, as in a forest; redup. of *kahana* (For. 6:61). *Ka'ū.*

kā.hana.hana pali. n. Cliff ledge. (For. 6:61.)

kaha nalu. nvs. Body surfing. Cf. *kaha 3.*

kaha.nia. vs. **1.** Smooth-shaven, smooth, unclouded. *Kahania ke po'o o ka 'ōhule,* the head of the bald man is smooth. **2.** Sour, as of poi.

kaha.one. loc. n. Sandy beach.

kaha pala.pala.'āina. v. To draw a map. *Mea kaha palapala'āina,* cartographer, topographer.

kaha pe'a. nv. To make a cross or *X,* especially in black magic (the victim becomes gravely or mortally ill by stepping on or over the mark); to crisscross; a cross or *X.*

kaha.pili. n. Tangent of a circle. *Lit.,* line that touches.

kaha.pō.'ai. n. Circumference of a circle. *Lit.*, mark surround.

kaha po'o.hiwi. n. Fat or muscle on the shoulder blade. *Lit.*, shoulder fat.

kaha.pouli. n. Taboo on menstruating women, restricting them to the menstruating house. *Lit.*, place of dark night.

kaha pu'u.naue. n. Division sign.

kahau. 1. nv. The sport of hurling lightweight *hau* wood spears; to hurl such spears. *Lit.*, hurl *hau* wood. 2. v. To catch edible locusts by striking *(kā)* the dew *(hau)* on bushes.

kā.ha'u. vi. To diminish, abate, lessen, as a storm or sickness. *Ua kāha'u mai ka 'eha*, the pain has grown less. *Ua kāha'u ka wai o ke kahawai*, the water in the stream has subsided.

Ka-hau-komo. n. A *lua* fighting stroke. *Lit.*, the blow enters. (Also without *Ka-*.)

kaha.'ula. 1. nvi. Sensual dream (sickness or bad luck, as in fishing, was believed to follow shortly); to have sexual relations in a dream (Laie 459). *Aikaha'ula*, a dream of coition. *Moe kaha'ula*, lascivious dream. 2. *(Cap.)* n. Name of a sexual goddess.

kaha ule. vt. To subincise or circumcise (less used than *kahe ule* or Biblical *'oki poepoe*). *Lit.*, slit penis.

kaha.uli. n. A kind of *'ahi*, a tuna. It is small, has a long pectoral fin, and reaches about 35 kilos in weight. *Lit.*, dark-striped.

Ka-hau-palemo. n. A *lua* fighting stroke. *Lit.*, the drowned blow. (Also without *Ka-*.)

kaha.wai. n. Stream, creek, river; valley, ravine, gulch, whether wet or dry.

kahe. 1. nvi. To flow, trickle, drop, melt, menstruate; in heat, of a bitch; a run or school of fish. See ex., *kaea. Kahe ka hā'ae*, to drool at the mouth. *Kahe ka hu'a o ka waha*, to froth at the mouth. **ho'o.kahe.** To water or irrigate; to cause to flow, discharge, drain. (PPN *tafe*.) 2. vt. To cut or slit longitudinally; to subincise or circumcise. See *kahe ule*. (PPN *tafa*.)

kā.hē. nvi. First appearance of young caterpillars on vines, especially of sweet potatoes; to be eaten by caterpillars. *Ka'ū*. Cf. *hē*, caterpillar. *Ua kāhē ka 'uala*, the caterpillars are beginning to eat the sweet-potato leaves.

kā.hea. nvt. To call, cry out, invoke, greet, name; recital of the first lines of a stanza by the dancer as a cue to the chanter; to recite the *kāhea;* to give a military command; to summon; a call, alarm *(kā-*, caus. + *hea*, call).

kā.he'a. nvs. Red stains or streaks, as at dawn; bloody. (Malo 13.)

kā.hea 'ai. nv. A call to come and eat; a prayer calling on the gods to come and share the food.

kā.hea kua. vt. To call to someone who is leaving (this was believed to bring bad luck, because the departing person had to change his plans).

kā.hea pau ahi. n. Fire alarm.

kahe.ā.wai. vi. To flow like water. *Fig.*, to move in great crowds. (Gram. 8.7.2.)

kā.he'e. vi. 1. To pour. 2. To catch fish with a scoop or hand net. See *'upena kāhe'e*. 3. To slip flowers from the stringing needle to the string. 4. To train or practice, as for foot races. (Malo 219.)

Ka-he'e-pā.laha. n. A *lua* fighting stroke.

kā.hehi. vi. To make a misstep, stumble. Cf. *hehi*.

kā.hei. 1. nvt. Hurling, as firebrands at Ka-maile, Kaua'i; to hurl; to put on a lei. (PCP *taasei*.) 2. Var. of *kā'ai*.

kā.heka. n. Pool, especially a rock basin where the sea washes in through an opening and salt forms; salt pan.

kahe.kahe. 1. Redup. of *kahe 1.* **ho'o.kahe.kahe.** Redup. of *ho'okahe.* (PPN *tafetafe*.) 2. nvt. Method of fishing with a large net placed in deep water where fish fed or where bait had been strewn; to fish thus. (Malo 212.) 3. nvi. A method of birdcatching: all save a few

lehua blossoms were plucked and the remaining flowers were gummed so that birds would be stuck; to catch birds thus.

kā.heka.heka. Plural and diminutive of *kāheka;* small sea pool or pools; artificial salt pan.

kahe.kahe wai. Same as *na'ina'i mimi.* **ho'o.kahe.-kahe wai.** Irrigation, to irrigate; also same as *na'ina'i mimi* (FS 35).

kahe.kawai. Similar to *kaheāwai;* abundance.

kahe koko. nv. Flow of blood, hemorrhage; to have such. **ho'o.kahe koko.** To shed blood; bloodshed.

kā.hela. 1. vi. To lie spread out, as an individual or a wide expanse of land or sea; to sweep backward and forward, as great billows that do not break; prone, spread out, flat; summation of productive forces of land and sea (Kam. 76:30, 51). Cf. *lipi kāhela. Kāhela ai ka uha* (saying), eating, intestines inflate [said of one who has eaten a good meal]. *Kāhela ka nalu o ka pae lau hala, hō'a'i'a'i ke kai ko'o o Maliu ē*, waves sweep up to the leaves of pandanus rows; white-capped is the rough sea of Maliu. 2. See *'ami kāhela*, a hula step. 3. n. Gourd drumbeat: the gourd is thumped down on a pad; it is then raised with the left hand and is struck with two quick slaps of the fingers of the right hand. *Pā kāhela*, to perform this beat. 4. *(Cap.)* n. Name of a star, seen in the month *'Ikuwā.*

kā.hela.hela. Redup. and intensifier of *kāhela 1–3;* to sprawl.

kahele. Adze. (And.)

kā.hele. 1. nvi. Decorated for a journey, as with a lei. *He lei kāhele no ke ala*, a lei decoration for traveling the road. 2. vi. To flow.

kā.hele.hele. vi. To be entangled.

kahele.lani. n. 1. Species of small colored shells, found particularly on Ni'ihau; perhaps so called because the shells were used by chiefs. 2. *(Cap.)* Name of an ancient chief associated with Ni'ihau. *Lit.*, the royal going.

kahena. n. Flowing. Cf. *kahe 1. Kahena wai*, stream bed, stream. (PPN *tafenga*.)

kā.heu. vt. To weed and stir up the soil.

kahe ule. v. To subincise or circumcise. *Lit.*, cut penis. Cf. *'oki poepoe.*

kā.hewa. vi. To miss, fail, not succeed; to hit by mistake; foiled or thwarted in an attempt.

kahi. 1. nvt. To cut longitudinally, shave, plane, comb, press, rub or stroke, as in a massage, with gentle pressure of the open palm of the hand; to scrape; to run the fingers along the sides of a poi bowl so as to remove the poi clinging to the sides; comb; scraper, as for *olonā* fiber. *Hale kahi olonā* (Laie 607), fiber-combing house. **ho'o.kahi.** Caus/sim. (PPN *tafi*, but cf. Fijian *tasi*, to scrape.) 2. num. One, only one, alone, lone, some (sometimes following the numeral classifiers *'a-* and *'e-*, or *ho'o-*); also, besides, too, single; fellow worker, wife, companion; someone, someone else, a certain (less common than *kekahi*); unit. See ex., *kāmau 1. 'O au kahi e hele*, I'm going too. *Na'u kahi*, give me some. *Pehea kahi o 'olua?* How is your companion (wife, spouse, colleague)? *Ka 'āina o kahi* (Kep. 159), someone else's land. **ho'o.kahi.** One, one only, alone; oneness, separately, single, singular, solitude, sole; together as a unit, at the same time; to make one, unite; to be similar; same; a, an. *Noho ho'okahi*, to live alone. *Hele ho'okahi*, to go alone. *E 'imi kākou ma ka mea e ho'okahi ai ka mana'o 'ana*, let us seek to unite our thoughts into one. *Ho'okahi kō kāua noho pū 'ana*, let us live together. *Ho'okahi nō makua kāne*, the same father. *Ho'okahi nō 'ano*, of similar nature; synonym, synonymous. *O ia lā ho'okahi nō*, that very day. (PPN *taha* [cf. Pawley 1966:54], *tasi*.) 3. loc. n. Place, location (contraction of *ka wahi*, not preceded by *ke* with this meaning); duty; where; in case of, approximately, about. (For use of possessives *o* and *a* with *kahi*, see Gram. 8.6.) *Kahi 'ē*, elsewhere. *Ma kahi 'ē, ma kahi 'oko'a*, absent. *Hele ma kahi 'ē!* Go away!

Get out! *Aia ka ʻai i kahi ʻē kahi i waiho ai* (Kep. 157), the food is left elsewhere. *Mai kahi ʻē ā noho mai,* from far away but yet sitting here [said rudely of intruders or uninvited guests]. *ʻAuhea kahi e hele ai?* Where's the place to go? *ʻAuhea kahi o Kupa mā?* Where's the residence of Kupa and his family? *Ma kahi hoʻokahi,* at the same place, at one place. *A koe ʻo kahi wale nō e paʻa ana i ka lima* (For. 5:711), only the handle [of the spear] was left. *Ma kahi o ʻumi kapuaʻi,* approximately ten feet. *Ka mea iāia kahi i paʻa ai kona komo ʻana,* the one whose duty it was to register his entrance. *Ā ma kahi o ke komohewa,* in case of trespassing.

kahi.aka. Old var. of *kakahiaka,* morning.

kahi.au. vt. **1.** To give generously or lavishly with the heart and not with expectation of return. *Rare.* **2.** To polish, as a bowl. *Rare.*

kahi ʻē. See *kahi 3.*

kā.hihi. nvi. Entanglement, perplexity, involvement, blocking; entangled, choked, as by weeds; blocked, involved, as with the law (Mat. 5.40), trapped, framed (slang). Cf. *hihi.* **hoʻo.kā.hihi.** To entrap, ensnare, entangle, etc.

kā.hī.hī. Interj. of disapproval or disbelief; the vowels are sometimes nasalized and the last two greatly lengthened, spoken with rising inflection. Horrors! Cf. *kāhāhā, kāhūhū. Nui koʻu kāhīhī ʻana!* I couldn't believe it [*lit.,* much my disbelief]!

kahi.hihi. Redup. of *kāhihi.*

ka hihi kolu. Same as *ka hili kolo.*

Ka-hihi-kolu. Same as *Ka-hili-kolo.*

kahi hō.ʻike.ʻike holo.holona. n. Zoo.

kahi holoi pā. n. Sink (basin).

kahi hoʻo.maʻe.maʻe. n. Place for cleansing; purgatory.

kahi ʻino. n. Buttocks. (For. 5:703.)

kahi.kahi. Redup. of *kahi 1.* (PPN *tafitafi.*)

kahi kā.lena. vt. To stretch out smooth by rubbing, as in making tapa. *Lit.,* rub stretch out.

Kahiki. 1. n. Tahiti. Cf. *holokahiki. Holo i Kahiki,* sail to Tahiti. The sky was divided (Malo 10) into five areas beginning with the term Kahiki: *Kahiki-moe,* horizon; *lit.,* prostrate Kahiki. *Kahiki-kū,* sky just above the horizon; *lit.,* upright Kahiki. *Kahiki-ka-papa-nuʻu,* the next layer; *lit.,* Kahiki the elevated stratum. *Kahiki-kapapa-lani,* high in the sky, almost directly overhead; *lit.,* Kahiki the sky (or god) stratum. *Kahiki-kapu-i-Hōlani-ke-kuʻina,* the sky directly overhead; *lit.,* sacred Kahiki at Hōlani the meeting place. (See Malo 10.) (PEP *Tafiti.*) **2.** *(Not cap.)* nvs. Any foreign country, abroad, foreign. (PCP *tafiti.*) **3.** n. A variety of banana, common wild on Maui. Kinds are *kahiki hae, kahiki mauki,* and *kahiki puhi.*

Ka-hiki-kolo. n. Name of a legendary tree and place in the uplands of Kauaʻi (FS 233), probably a var. of *Kahili-kolo.* Kama-puaʻa used the tree as a club with which he knocked away *(kuehu)* his foes' clubs from their hands, enabling him to kill them.

Kahiki-nui. n. Name of a navigation star, said to be named for one of the eight steersmen of Hawaiʻi-loa.

Kahiki Nui. n. Name of a district or *ahupuaʻa* on Maui. (Malo 6.) *Lit.,* great Tahiti. (PEP *Tafiti Nui.*)

kahiko. 1. nvs. Old, ancient, antique, primitive, long ago, beforehand; to age; old person. (Usually in the singular; cf. *kāhiko 2, puka kahiko.*) *Wā kahiko,* old times. *Wahi a kahiko* (Kel. 50), said the old people. *Kahiko ʻē,* prematurely old. *E kala kahiko,* gone a long time. *E paupauaho a manakā kahiko ʻoe iaʻu* (Kel. 60), you would be disheartened, weary, and old before me. *He wahine hoʻokahiko,* an old-fashioned woman. (PPN *tafito,* base; PCP *tafito,* ancient.) **2.** *(Cap.)* n. Name of the first Hawaiian. (Malo 4.)

kā.hiko. 1. nvi. Finery, ornaments; to wear finery, dress up; to harness (Ier. 46.4). *Kāhiko o ke akua,* adornment of the gods [rain]. *Kāhiko o ka hale,* house adornments

and furniture. **hoʻo.kā.hiko.** To dress someone in finery; to adorn, decorate, deck, trim, array; to wear fine clothes. **2.** Plural of *kahiko 1.*

kā.hiko.hiko. 1. vs. Somewhat old. **2.** Redup. of *kāhiko,* finery. **hoʻo.kā.hiko.hiko.** Caus/sim.

kā.hiko kaua. n. War finery, formerly shield, helmet, feather cape.

kahi.kole. vi. To have lost the red glow of dawn. Cf. *kahikū. Ua kahikole ka lā,* the sun is up and has lost the glow of dawn.

Kahi.kolu. n. Trinity, three in one. See *Kū-kaua-kahi.*

Ka-hiku. n. Star name (no data). (Kuhelani.)

kahi.kū. vi. To rise higher, of the sun, to a stage between *kahikole* and *kau i ka lolo* (noon).

kā.hili. 1. nvt. Feather standard, symbolic of royalty; segment of a rainbow standing like a shaft (also a sign of royalty); to brush, sweep, switch *(kā- 2 + hili).* See *uhao* and *kāhili* chants, *ʻouʻou 1* and *uluaoʻa 2. Paʻa kāhili, kāhili* bearer. *Kū kāhili,* one standing by a *kāhili* or carrying it. *Kāhili pulu,* to clear away mulch. *Haku ʻia naʻe hoʻi ka hulu o ka moa i kāhili i mua o nā aliʻi; kāhili ʻia naʻe hoʻi kō kua* (FS 101), chicken feathers indeed are woven into a standard for the presence of the chiefs; your back is brushed by the *kāhili.* **hoʻo.kā.hili.** Caus/sim., to brush or fan gently. **2.** n. The crape myrtle *(Lagerstroemia indica),* an ornamental shrub from China, with small oval leaves and panicles of pink, white, or purple crapy flowers. (Neal 618.) **3.** n. A small tree *(Grevillea banksii)* from Australia, related to the silky oak, *ʻoka kilika,* but the leaves with fewer subdivisions and the flowers red or cream-white. This is a later application of *kāhili* to a plant. Flowers not used for leis on head or around neck because of irritating hairs, but made into leis for hats by sewing alternate rows of flower clusters and own leaves on pandanus band. (Neal 321.) See *haʻikū.* **4.** n. *Kāhili* ginger *(Hedychium gardnerianum),* from the Himalaya region; much like the white ginger but with a more open flower head, the flowers with narrow yellow segments and one bright-red stamen apiece. (Neal 253–4.) Also *ʻawapuhi kāhili.* **5.** n. A seaweed, probably *Turbinaria ornata.*

kā.hili.hili. Redup. of *kāhili 1;* to spray. *Kāhilihili ke kai a ka heʻe nalu* (UL 36), spraying sea of surfrider.

kā.hili kā.popo. n. Medical combination of juices of the gourd and the *puʻukaʻa* sedge.

ka hili kolo. n. Name of a legendary *koa* tree on Kauaʻi said to consist of branches without a trunk. *Lit.,* the creeping tangle.

Ka-hili-kolo. n. *Lua* fighting stroke. (Also without *Ka-;* also *Kāhili-kolo.*)

kahi lio. n. Currycomb. *Lit.,* horse comb.

kā.hili paʻa lima. n. Small *kāhili* carried in the hand.

kahi moe. n. Place to sleep, bed, cot.

kahina. n. Wood shavings; rubbing, cutting, etc. Cf. *kahi 1.* (PNP *tafinga.*)

kā.hina. vt. To knock down, take advantage of, deceive.

Kahina.liʻi. n. Name of a legendary chief in whose time was a great sea flood (HM 315), perhaps a *tsunami.* See *kānāwai. Kai a Kahinaliʻi,* flood.

kahi noho. n. Residence, address.

kā.hinu. vt. To rub with oil, grease, petroleum jelly; to anoint *(kā- 2 + hinu).* Cf. *hinuhinu.* **hoʻo.kā.hinu.** Caus/sim.

kā.hiō. vi. To lean to one side *(kā- 2 + hiō).* Cf. the more common *hiō.* **hoʻo.kā.hiō.** Caus/sim.

kā.hiʻo. vi. Tipsy.

kahi ʻō. n. High-backed comb with long prongs *(ʻō)* such as worn by the Spanish.

kā.hiō.hiō. Redup. of *kāhiō.*

kā.hiʻo.hiʻo. Redup. of *kāhiʻo;* drunk.

kahi ʻō.mou. n. Back or side comb used to hold the hair in place. *Lit.,* comb to pin down.

kā.hiu. See *pule kāhiu.*

kahi ʻuku. n. Fine-toothed comb, as used for removing dandruff or head lice *(ʻuku).*

kahi ʻumiʻumi. nv. To shave the whiskers; barber.

kā.hiwa (uli). n. Dark pupil, as of the eye *(kā- + hiwa).* *'O ka 'ōnohi o ka lani nui, 'o ke kāhiwa uli o ka 'ōnohi lani* (chant for Lili'u-o-ka-lani), the eyeball of the high chiefess, the dark pupil of the royal eyeball.

kā hiwa. n. Sacred vine. (KL line 379.)

kā.hoa. 1. vt. To strike, break; to strike of a fish at a hook *(kā- 2 + hoa).* *E kāhoa aku 'oe i ke po'o,* strike the head. **2.** Same as *kāhoahoa.* **3.** nvt. Beginning of a chant, with others then joining in; to begin a chant. **4.** Same as *kāhoahoa,* to appeal.

kā.hoa.hoa. vi. **1.** To appeal, intercede. *E kāhoahoa aku kāu pule i mua o Kāne i loa'a mai ke ola iki, ke ola nui, a me ke ola ā kau i ka pūaneane,* may your prayer to Kāne appeal for the obtaining of, small life, big life, and life extending to vast old age. **2.** Redup. of *kāhoa 1.*

kā.hoaka. n. **1.** Phantom, specter, spirit of a living person; sign in the heavens. **2.** Kind of sorcery prayer spoken in a moderate or natural voice.

Ka-hoana-kū. n. Unidentified star. (Johnson and Mahelona 43.)

Kaho.'ea. n. Name of a star.

kā.hō.hō. Interj. of surprise or anger. Cf. *kāhāhā, kāhīhī, kāhūhū.*

kāho'i. Interj. indicating surprise, following bases. *'O 'oukou kāho'i* (For. 5:129)? What of all of you? *He aha kāho'i kāna i hana ai?* What on earth did he do?

kā.holo. 1. vi. Hasty, nimble, swift, quick; to move fast, progress rapidly. Cf. *holo,* to run; *pule kāholo.* *Ko'i kāholo,* planing adze. *Kāholo ka 'ōlelo,* to speak generally and vaguely without committing oneself. *Kāholo ka 'ike o kēlā wahi keiki 'u'uku,* that little boy is quick in learning. **ho'o.kā.holo.** To cause to hurry; to speed, hurry. **2.** vt. To sew with long stitches; basting; sennit lashings on royal canoes (Malo 131). *Lopi kāholo,* basting thread. **3.** nvi. The "vamp" hula step, more common in modern than in ancient dance, consisting of four counts: (1) one foot is extended to the side, (2) the other is brought alongside, (3, 4) this is repeated on the same side; then the four steps are repeated on the opposite side; to execute this step. **4.** *(Cap.)* n. Name of a star.

kā.holo.holo. Redup. of *kāholo 1, 2.* **ho'o.kā.holo.holo.** Redup. of *ho'okāholo,* to exercise, as a horse; to practice racing; skittering in fishing. *E ho'okāholoholo ana ua wahi pua'a nei,* this little pig hurried.

kāhonua. n. **1.** Globe of the earth. **2.** Level landing place, as after fording a stream or coming down from a cliff. **3.** Dirt embankment.

Ka-ho'o.lawe. n. The only uninhabited major Hawaiian Island. In prehistoric times 80 men, sent from Hawai'i, dug a well ten fathoms deep at Ke-ana-pou (For. 5:200–3). *Lit.,* the taking away [as by currents]. See *Kanaloa 4* and saying, *kūpala 4.*

kahu. 1. n. Honored attendant, guardian, nurse, keeper of *'unihipili* bones, regent, keeper, administrator, warden, caretaker, master, mistress; pastor, minister, reverend, or preacher of a church; one who has a dog, cat, pig, or other pet. According to J. S. Emerson 92:2, *kahu* "implies the most intimate and confidential relations between the god and its guardian or keeper, while the word *kahuna* suggests more of the professional relation of the priest to the community." Cf. *kahu hipa, kahu ho'oponopono, kahu mālama, kahu waiwai,* and ex., *'anā'anā. Kona kahu,* his attendant. *'O ka 'īlio kahu,* the dog's master. *Ho'i nō 'ai i kou kahu,* return and destroy your keeper [sending a curse or evil back to the original sender]. **ho'o.kahu.** To act as a *kahu;* to appoint a *kahu. Mea kaho'okahu 'ia,* ward, beneficiary of an estate. (Probably PEP *ta(f,s)u.)* **2.** vn. To tend or cook at an oven; to build an oven fire; to burn, as lime in a pit; one who tends an oven, a cook. *Fig.,* to seethe with hot rage. *E hana ana kō ia nei inaina,* the rage of this [man] here is seething. *Kahu ka 'ena,* to attend the heat [to be angry]. **ho'o.kahu.** To make a fire for cooking in the oven; to act as *kahu.* (PPN *tafu.)* **3.** Similar to *kahukahu. Kahu ma ka paha 'ana* (GP 52), pray in chant.

kahua. n. **1.** Foundation, base, site, location, grounds, background, platform, as of a house; an open place, as for camping or for sports, as for *'ulu maika* or *hōlua* sliding; playground, arena, stand, stage, courtyard; course, camp; bed, as of a stream. *Fig.,* declaration of principles or policy, doctrine, platform. *Ka Monroe kahua kālai 'āina,* Monroe doctrine about land division. *E hana mua ā pa'a ke kahua, mamua o ke a'o 'ana iā ha'i* (saying), work first to make firm the foundation before teaching others. **ho'o.kahua.** To lay a foundation, establish, found; to camp or be stationed, as soldiers; to settle down and develop a place, as homesteaders. *Ho'okahua ka no'ono'o,* settle down to a task with determination to see it through. *Ko'u noho ali'i i ho'okahua 'ia maluna o kahi pu'u pele,* my kingdom established on a lava hill. (PEP *ta(f,s)u'a.)* **2.** Base of a quilt on which the pattern *(lau)* is appliquéd; this base is above the layer of cotton or wool. The *pili* is below it.

kāhua. See *moekāhua.*

Kahu'a. n. Name of a star.

kahua hale. n. House foundation or site.

kahua hana. n. Subject, as of a discussion, basis for work; foundation principles, as a political platform; work site.

kahua hehi. n. Threshing floor.

kahu ahi. nv. Fire builder; to build and tend a fire.

kahua hō.'ike.'ike holo.holona. n. Zoo.

kahua hō.lua. n. Sledding course.

kahua ho'o.lele leo. n. Radio broadcasting station. *Lit.,* site for making voice fly.

kahua ho'o.lulu. n. Meeting place. Cf. *hale ho'olulu.* *Lit.,* site for shelter.

kahua ho'o.lulu moku.lele. n. Airport.

kahua ho'o.moana. n. Staging area, as in warfare.

kahua ho'o.uka. n. Battleground; place used for competitive sports or contests. *Lit.,* site for attack.

kahu 'ai. vt. To cook taro or vegetable food; to keep the store of such food; to make poi; a keeper or cook. Cf. *kahu 2.* Same as *kahu umu* or *kahūmu.*

kahu 'āina. n. Headman of a land division.

kahua kaua. n. Battlefield.

kahua kaua lewa. n. Air base.

kahua kenika. n. Tennis court.

kahua kinai ahi. n. Fire station. *Lit.,* place quench fire.

kahua kini.pō.pō. n. Any ball-playing area, as a baseball diamond, football field, tennis court.

kahua kolepa. n. Golf course.

kahu akua. n. One who takes care of an image or a god; priest.

kahua le'a, kahua le'a.le'a. n. Playground.

kahu ali'i. n. Royal guardian in the family of a high chief.

kahua moku.lu'u. n. Submarine base.

kahu 'anā.'anā. n. Master or practitioner of sorcery and counter sorcery. See ex., *'anā'anā.* Cf. *kahuna 'anā-'anā.*

kahua 'ole. nvs. Ignoramus, one without background, trade, profession, knowledge; to be such.

kahua 'olo.hū. n. Bowling alley.

kahua o Mali'o. n. Place of happiness, comfort, pleasure (named for Mali'o, a mythical woman renowned for entertaining with music and for her ability in love magic).

kahua o nā hōkū. n. Solar system.

kahua pa'a. n. Terra firma, the solid earth. *Fig.,* security.

kahua pā.'ani. n. Stadium; playground or athletic field of any kind. *Lit.,* site for play.

kahu au.puni. n. Deputy or regent in the days of the monarchy. *Lit.,* government caretaker.

kahu 'ekale.kia (ekalesia). n. Pastor of a church.

Ka-huelo-iki. n. Unidentified star name. (Johnson and Mahelona 43.)

Ka-huelo-kū. n. Unidentified star name. (Johnson and Mahelona 43.)

kahu hā.nai. n. Foster parent (of adopted children).

kahu hipa. n. Shepherd.

kahu hoʻo.pono.pono. n. Administrator.

kā.hū.hū. Interj. of surprise or anger. Cf. *kāhāhā, kāhīhī.*

Ka-hui.hui-o-Maka.liʻi. n. Pleiades. (Kuhelani.)

kahu kaʻa. n. Coachman.

kahu.kahu. vt. To offer food and prayers to a god or to the spirit of a deified person. Cf. *ʻahaʻaina kahukahu.*

kahu keiki. n. One who tends a child, as a nurse.

kahuki. Same as *palahuki.*

kahu kula. n. Schoolmaster, school supervisor. Cf. *papa o nā kahu kula.*

kahu kula nui. n. School superintendent.

kahuli. vt. To overturn, overthrow, capsize, upset. **hoʻo.kahuli.** Caus/sim. (PPN *tafuli.*)

kā.huli. 1. vi. To change, alter. *Ua kāhuli ke ʻano,* the appearance is changed. **hoʻo.kā.huli.** Caus/sim. *ʻO Pāʻao ka mea nāna i hoʻokāhuli i ka lāhui Hawaiʻi nei ma ka hoʻomana kiʻi* (Kep. 21), Pāʻao was the one who converted the Hawaiian people to idol worship. (PPN *tafuli.*) 2. n. Land shells (*Philonesia* spp.). 3. n. Sport or mutant, as of sweet potato.

Kahuli-aliʻi. n. Name of a star. Cf. *Ke-kau-hiwa-kā.*

kahuli au.puni. nv. Revolution, revolutionist; to overthrow the government. Also *hoʻokahuli aupuni.*

kā.huli.huli. vi. Unsteady, shaky, rickety, variable, unsettled; to sway, reel, tip, rock, totter; tossed about, as a ship. (PPN *tafulifuli.*)

kahu lio. n. Coachman, groom.

kahuli pū. vi. Turned completely over, upside down.

kahu.lui. n. 1. Athletic contest, especially championship match. 2. Crescent-shaped disposition of soldiers on a battlefield. (Malo 203, Emerson note.) 3. Variety of sweet potato. 4. *(Cap.)* A *lua* fighting stroke.

kahu maʻi. n. Nurse.

kahu mā.lama. n. Custodian, caretaker.

kahu mā.lama ʻā.pana. n. Warden of a district.

kahu mā.lama hale. n. Housekeeper.

kahu mā.lama kino. n. Legal guardian of minors.

kahu mā.lama maʻi. n. Nurse.

kahu mā.lama paʻa.hao. n. Warden of a prison.

kahu moka. n. Person who cared for the chief's excrement so that it would not fall into the possession of a sorcerer. Also *kahu poka.*

kahu moku. n. Mate of a ship.

kahūmu. Var. spelling of *kahu umu. E kahūmu ʻai ana kākou,* we are going to bake vegetable foods in the oven.

kahuna. nvi. 1. Priest, sorcerer, magician, wizard, minister, expert in any profession (whether male or female); in the 1845 laws doctors, surgeons, and dentists were called *kahuna.* See *kahu* and many examples below; for plural see **kāhuna. hoʻo.kahuna.** To cause to be a *kahuna* or pretend to be one; to ordain or train as a *kahuna.* (PPN *tufunga,* PCP *t(a,o)funga.*) 2. Oven cooking; to cook. Cf. *kahu 2.*

kā.huna. 1. Plural of *kahuna 1.* See ex., *ʻololī.* 2. Same as *kāhunahuna.*

kahuna ʻai pilau. n. Filth-eating sorcerer [insulting term].

kahuna ʻanā.ʻanā. n. Sorcerer who practices black magic and counter sorcery, as one who prays a person to death. Cf. *kahu ʻanāʻanā.*

kahuna aʻo. n. Teaching preacher, minister, sorcerer.

kahuna hā.hā. See *hāhā.*

kahuna haʻi.ʻō.lelo. n. Preacher, especially an itinerant preacher.

kahuna hoʻo.hā.pai keiki. n. Medical expert who induced pregnancy. (Kam. 64:98.)

kahuna hoʻo.piʻo.piʻo. n. Malevolent sorcerer, as one who inflicts illness by gesture, as rubbing his own head to give the victim a severe headache or head injury.

Sometimes the victim might imitate the gesture and send the affliction back to the sorcerer. Cf. *hoʻoheihei.*

kahuna hoʻo.ulu ʻai. n. Agricultural expert.

kahuna hoʻo.ulu lā.hui. n. Priest who increased population by praying for pregnancy.

kahuna hui. n. A priest who functioned in ceremonies for the deification of a king (Malo 105) or who detected symptoms of sorcery in one sick or dead (Handy 72: 322).

kā.huna.huna. vi. To sprinkle lightly, especially with salt. Cf. *huna,* fine.

kāhuna imu. n. Place where food is cooked in an underground oven, as in a cookhouse; tending of the oven.

kahuna kā.lai. n. Carving expert, sculptor.

kahuna kā.lai waʻa. n. Canoe builder.

kahuna kiʻi. n. Caretaker of images, who wrapped, oiled, and stored them, and carried them into battle ahead of the chief.

kahuna kilo.kilo. n. Priest or expert who observed the skies for omens.

kahuna lapa.ʻau. n. Medical doctor, medical practitioner, healer. *Lit.,* curing expert.

kahuna makani. n. A priest who induced spirits to possess a patient so that he might then drive the spirits out, thus curing the patient. *Lit.,* spirit priest. (Kam. 64:138.)

kahuna nui. n. High priest and councilor to a high chief; office of councilor.

kahuna poʻo. n. High priest.

kahuna pule. n. Preacher, pastor, minister, parson, priest. *Lit.,* prayer expert.

kahu paka. n. High chief's trusted attendant of royal blood who had charge of his tobacco and pipes; he lighted them and drew a few puffs before presenting them to the chief. *Lit.,* guardian of tobacco *(Eng.)*

kahu pipi. nv. Herdsman, keeper of cattle, cattle owner, rancher; to care for cattle.

kahu poka. Same as *kahu moka.*

kahu puke (buke). n. Librarian, custodian of books. Also *mea mālama puke.*

kahu ʻū.hā. n. The high chief who attended an infant chief, carried him, and sat him on his lap *(ʻūhā).* Also *ʻūhā.* (Kep. 127.)

kahu umu. nv. Oven tender; to tend an oven.

kahu wai. n. One in charge of water rights and division, water master.

kahu wai.ū. n. Wet nurse (also *kahu wale*). (Kep. 127.)

kahu wai.wai. n. Trustee, executor. *Lit.,* custodian of wealth or property.

kahu wale. n. Same as *kahu waiū.* (Kep. 123.)

kai. 1. nvs. Sea, sea water; area near the sea, seaside, lowlands; tide, current in the sea; insipid, brackish, tasteless. *I kai,* towards the sea. *Makai,* on the seaside, toward the sea, in the direction of the sea. *O kai,* of the lowland, of the sea, seaward. *Nā kānaka o kai,* shore dwellers. *Nā kai ʻewalu,* the eight seas [a poetic expression for the channels dividing the eight inhabited islands]. *Kai lalo,* lower sea, i.e., western sea, where the sun sets. *Ka mokupuni kai lalo, ʻo Kauaʻi,* Kauaʻi, the island of the western sea. *Kō a kai,* people from the shore district. (PPN *tahi,* PNP *tai.*) 2. n. Gravy, sauce, dressing, soup, broth. 3. Interj. similar to *keu.* My, how much! How very! How terrific! *Kai ka nani!* How beautiful! *Kai ke kolohe!* Oh, how mischievous. Cf. *kainō.*

ka i, kai. Contraction *ka mea i,* the one who did. Cf. *ka i. ʻO ʻoe ka i hele i ka hale,* you're the one who went to the house. Cf. *ke,* the one who will or should. (Gram. 10.2, 11.3.)

kai-. Prefix to six kinship terms used as terms of reference: *kaikaina, kaikoʻeke, kaikuaʻana, kaikunāne, kaikuahine, kaikamahine.* (Gram. 8.1.)

-kai. Swollen, bloated. *Hakakai,* swollen, excessive fat. Cf. *kuakaikai, kūhākakai, ʻuʻulukai.* (Gram. 6.5.)

kaī, kaīī. Interj. of displeasure, vexation, annoyance, prolonged to indicate greater force. *Kaīī! Chā! ʻIno-*

'ino maoli kāna hana! Oh, oh, his work is downright wicked!

kā.ī. n. A variety of taro, the corms of which are fragrant when cooked and, though tough, yield excellent poi. Kinds are qualified by the terms *'ele'ele, kea, ke'oke'o* (said to be reserved for chiefs), *koi, nenene, pala, 'ula'ula, uliuli, welo 'eka. Ua 'ai i ke kāī koi o 'Ewa,* having eaten of the very choice *kāī koi* taro of 'Ewa [said of a sweetheart one can't forget].

ka'i. 1. nvt. To lead, direct, lift up and carry; to walk or step in a row or procession, or as a child learning to walk; to come dancing out before an audience; the chant during which dancers appear and leave; to train, as for racing (Malo 219). Cf. *'aha 3, alaka'i, hāka'i, huaka'i. Ka'i 'āuna,* to move in a flock, herd, company. *Ka'i . . . i ke ka'a* (2 Sam. 6.3), to drive . . . a cart. *Hou mai ua ihe āu, a ka'i a'e i ka pola o ka malo* (FS 87), thrust your spear, directing towards the flap of the loincloth. (PPN *taki*.) 2. vt. To pull, as weeds. 3. Fish net or seine; snare or noose for birds. (And.) 4. n. Snood of a fishhook. 5. n. A decayed tooth that requires extraction.

-ka'i. Perhaps a transitivizer. Cf. *alaka'i,* Gram. 6.6.4. (PPN *-taki*.)

kāia. vi. 1. Fast asleep (used with *hiamoe.*) Kāia loa 'ia ihola 'o Wākea mā i ka hiamoe (Kep. 65), Wākea and his companion were fast asleep. 2. To swing, as arms.

kā ia. Same as *kāna,* possessive. (Gram. 8.4.1.) *He wahine kā ia ala* (Laie 485), he has a wife. *'Ae mai 'o Māhinahina i kā ia nei 'ōlelo* (For. 5:507), Māhinahina agreed to his word.

ka'i.ahea. vi. To resound from a distance.

Ka-i'a-ho'o.pā.pā-'ili-kanaka. n. A *lua* fighting stroke. *Lit.,* fish touching human skin. (Also without *Ka-*.)

ka'i ā hui.hui. vi. To come in flocks, as followers to a generous chief. (Nak. 28.)

kai.aka. nvi. Weakened and watery fluid, as coffee, thinned-down milk; to be watery. *Kaiaka ke koko,* anemic blood.

kai a Kahina.li'i. See *Kahinali'i.*

kai a Kahulu.manu. Same as *kai a Kahinali'i* (Kin. 6.17.)

kai akua. n. Raging sea so dangerous that man cannot survive. *Lit.,* supernatural sea.

ka'i.ā.lana. n. Large traveling company. (For. 6:490.)

kai.ali'i. n. Hard type of rock, used for adzes.

kaia.lile. nvs. Indolent, lazy, unskilled; such a person. *He kaialile, he mea mana'o hana 'ole,* a lazy person without a thought of working.

ka'i.ā.lupe. vt. To support a sick or intoxicated person between two other persons. *Lit.,* lead like a kite. Same as *kauālupe.*

kai a malō, kai a malo'o. n. An extreme low tide with reef exposed. *Lit.,* dry sea.

kai.ā.mū. vi. To sit in silence, as at a meeting. Cf. *mū,* silence. See ex., *hākei.*

kai.ā.noa. n. Bonito lure made of shell; bone fishhook; barbless deep-sea hook composed of two small hooks. (Malo 219.)

kai.'anu'u. Same as *'alā po'o malu,* a basalt.

kai.ao. nvi. Dawn; to dawn; to enlighten (used without the article). Cf. *ao,* daylight. See ex., *kainu'u. Ke wehewehe maila kaiao,* the dawn is opening. *Ua kaiao kākou,* it is dawn for us; we are enlightened. (PNP *taiao*.)

kai.apa. n. Diaper. *Eng.*

kai a Pele. n. Tidal wave. *Lit.,* sea of Pele. Also *kai ho'ē'e.*

kai apo. n. Rising or high tide. *Lit.,* encircling sea.

kai-a-pō-kea. n. Name of a long prayer used after the *kauila* celebration at a temple dedication, probably short for *po'o kea,* white head or bleached skull, since the sea water *(kai)* used was held in a skull (Malo 167, 168, 181.)

kai au. n. Sea where a moving current is visible. *Lit.,* current sea.

kai 'au. n. Sea too deep to walk in. *Lit.,* swimming sea.

kai.ā.ulu. n. 1. Community, neighborhood, village. *'Oia nō kekahi o nā kānaka waiwai nui a kū'ono'ono ma iā mau kaiāulu,* he was one of the wealthiest and most prosperous persons of these communities. 2. *(Cap.)* Name of a pleasant, gentle trade-wind breeze, famous in song, at Wai-'anae, O'ahu. *'Olu'olu i ka pā a ke Kaiāulu* (song), cool with the touch of the *Kaiāulu.* Also *Pua-kaiāulu.*

ka'i.awe. vi. To move slowly along. *Ka'iawe ka huila wai* (song), the water wheel keeps turning.

kai ea. n. Rising tide; sea washing higher on land than usual. *Lit.,* rising sea.

kai e'e. n. Tidal wave. *Lit.,* mounting sea. Also *kai ho'ē'e, kai a Pele.*

kai.ehu. 1. vt. To scatter or stir up, as dust or dirt; tossed, as spray; to moisten or sprinkle with fine drops of water, as of poi being pounded. Cf. *ehu. 'A 'ole pono ke kaiehu ka 'ō'ō ma ia apoapo 'ana* (Kep. 157), it is not right to stir up dust while digging and hilling [sweet potatoes]. 2. vt. To prod or poke sideways, as in digging, to prod loose; to discharge, as a servant. 3. *(Cap.)* n. Star name. (Johnson and Mahelona 44.)

kai.ele. vt. To disturb, bother. *'A 'ole mea nāna i kaiele i kō lāua mana'o 'i'ini,* there was nothing to disturb their desire for each other.

kai.elo. Same as *kai helo.*

kai emi. n. Ebbing sea. *Lit.,* decreasing sea.

kai.ena. vi. To walk with feet far apart, as an infant; to straddle, as on a horse.

kai.ewa. vi. To take life philosophically as it comes, sometimes in poverty, sometimes in wealth.

kai 'ewalu. n. A poetic expression referring to the channels between the islands; always follows *nā.* Eight is a formulistic number. (FS 273.)

kā.'iewe. n. Group of relatives who faithfully serve and care for a chief during illness; perhaps related to *'iewe,* placenta.

kai ha'a.nalu. n. *Makahiki* festivals prayer. (For. 6:45.)

kai he'e. n. Receding sea or wave.

kai hehe'e. n. Taboo place along the shore where outcasts *(kauwā)* or breakers of certain taboos were drowned that they might be offered as sacrifices; one such place was at Kewalo in Honolulu. *Lit.,* slippery sea.

ka'i hele. vi. To walk, move, proceed, walk in line or in succession, as of a parade; to walk holding on to something or with uncertainty, as a child learning to walk; to move, as in checkers. *Ka'i hele ho'i paha kāu pōhaku i hiki i ka'u pōhaku ke hele aku,* be so good as to move your stone so that my stone can go forward [as in the *kōnane* game].

kai hele kū. n. Any place in the sea or on the reef where a footing may be obtained. *Lit.,* sea walk upright.

kai helo. n. Sauce, as made of crushed shrimp and coconut cream. *Lit.,* red sauce.

ka'i hemo. Same as *ka'i ho'i.*

kai hī. n. Flowing sea, especially one that goes through a sluice gate into fish ponds.

kā.'ihi. 1. nvi. Dizzy, dizziness. 2. vi. To refuse to pay losses or forfeit, as in a game; to use another's property without permission; to usurp. 3. n. A fine-meshed fish net, similar to *kā'ili.* (Malo 213.)

kai ho.'ē'e. Var. of *kai e'e.*

kai hohonu. n. Deep sea; high tide.

kai ho'i. n. Ebbing sea. *Lit.,* returning sea.

ka'i ho'i. vi. To exit dancing, as in a hula.

kai holo. n. Running sea or current.

kai ho'o.lulu. n. Calm sea water, especially as left to evaporate in a pool so as to form a crust of salt.

ka'i hua.ka'i. nvi. Parade, procession; to march in a parade.

kai huki. n. Sea with strong current, undertow.

ka-ihu-o-ka-pua'a. n. 1. A type of stone (no data). *Lit.,* the snout of the pig. 2. *(Cap.)* A *lua* fighting stroke. (Also without *Ka-*.)

ka'i.hulu.hulu. vt. To drag along; to force to go against one's will.

ka'i'i. 1. vs. Smooth, unwrinkled. *Rare.* 2. n. Small-meshed net. Cf. *'i'i*, small.

kā.'i'ī. vi. Hard, rigid; stingy, close-fisted, hard-hearted, harsh; to refuse help; to deny a request; to strut pompously; persistent. Cf. *'i'ī*, hard. *'Olu'olu 'ole au e noho nei ke kani kā'i'ī a ke oeoe* (chant for Ka-pi'olani), I sit here in discomfort, with the persistent, hard blowing of the whistle.

kai 'ina. 1. n. Sea-urchin sauce (the crushed shells were placed in salted water; afterwards the liquid was usually strained and added to the flesh of the *'ina*). 2. nvs. Lavender, reddish-purple, so called because of the color of the sauce.

kā 'i'iwi. n. A climber *(Strongylodon ruber,* misidentified locally as *S. lucidus),* in the bean family, endemic in Hawai'i, with three-parted leaves and large seeds. The flowers are clustered, red, and shaped like narrow beaks. (Neal 440, 461.) Also *nuku 'i'iwi.*

kaika, saida. n. Cider. *Eng.*

kai.kā. n. Cultivated patch; bank of taro patch.

ka'i.kahi. Rare var. of *kaka'ikahi.*

ka'i.ka'i. vt. To lead, support, lift up; raise. Cf. *ka'i 1. Ka'ika'i i ka leo,* to raise the voice. *Ka'ika'i hope* (Kel. 118), recede backwards, as in time. *Ka hele ka'ika'i mālie o nā wāwae* (Kel. 48), walking along slowly. (PPN *takitaki.)*

ka'i.ka'i.kū. vt. To lead against the will, as a young child; to lead here and there without permission; to waddle, move with difficulty; to carry about everywhere. *Ka inoa e ka'ika'ikū ana,* a name carried everywhere.

kai.kaina. n. Younger sibling or cousin of the same sex, as younger brother or male cousin of a male, or younger sister or female cousin of a female; sibling or cousin of the same sex of the junior line, whether older or younger. Cf. *kaina,* Gram. 2.7. *Ko'u kaikaina,* my younger sibling. **ho'o.kai.kaina.** To claim a *kaikaina* relationship; to act as a *kaikaina,* to address and treat as *kaikaina,* as from affection. (PPN *t(e,a)hina.)*

ka'i.ka'ina. n. Carrying, leading, etc.

kai.kaina hoa.hā.nau. n. Relative of a junior sibling line.

Kai.kala. Caesar. *Biblical.* Gr. *Kaisar.*

kai kala. n. Salt water and *'ōlena* root used to remove evil influences. *Lit.,* freeing salt water.

kaika.mahine. n. Girl, daughter, niece, lass. *Hana kaikamahine,* woman's work [said of an easy task, somewhat like English "There's nothing to it!"] *Kaikamahine hoa wahine,* bridesmaid. (PNP *tama'afafine.)*

kaika.mā.hine. Plural of *kaikamahine.*

kai kāne. n. Strong sea. *Lit.,* male sea.

kai.kapū. vs. Creeping with age; aged (a proper name in some legends for an old hag). (HM 263–4.)

kai.kea. n. 1. Sap, sapwood. (And.) 2. Fat, as of pork. (Isa. 34.6.) 3. White sea foam, especially as washed up on a beach. 4. Enema composed of sea water and raw crushed *kukui* nuts. Also *kaikuehu* and *kaīkū.*

ka'i ke'a. n. Station of the cross (Catholic); procession of the cross.

kai kī. n. Tide beginning to flow in. *Lit.,* shooting sea.

kāiki'alamea. A wasting disease, emaciation. (AP.)

kaiko. n. Policeman. *Rare.*

kai kō. n. Sea with a strong current.

kai ko'a.ko'a. n. 1. Fat sauce, as made from the liver of the parrot fish *(uhu)* and eaten with the flesh of the fish. 2. Watery fluid of the bowels.

kai.ko'eke. n. Brother-in-law or male cousin-in-law of a male; sister-in-law or female cousin-in-law of a female. Cf. *ko'eke. Kona kaiko'eke,* his *kaiko'eke.* (PPN *ta'okete.)*

kai ko'ele. n. Sea too shallow to float a canoe but good for seeking shellfish. *Lit.,* thumping sea, because the canoe thumps the coral.

kai kohola. n. Shallow sea within the reef, lagoon. *Lit.,* reef sea.

kā.ī koi. See *kāī.*

ka'i.kō.kō. nvs. One so old that he is carried in a net; bedridden (a favorite figure of speech; cf. *kani ko'o).*

ka'i komo. vi. To enter dancing, as in a hula.

kai ko'o. See *ko'o 3.*

kai.kō.wā. n. Straits. *Lit.,* space sea. *Ke kaikōwā o Pēlina,* Bering Straits.

kaī.kū. n. 1. Mid-tide. 2. Enema. Cf. *kaikea 4.*

kai.kua. nvs. Countryman; backwoodsman; sparsely inhabited place; countrified, rustic. *Lit.,* back person. Cf. *kua'āina.*

kai.kua.'ana, kai.ku'ana. n. Older sibling or cousin of the same sex; sibling or cousin of the same sex of the senior line, whether older or younger. (See *kua'ana.)* Cf. Gram. 2.7. **ho'o.kai.kua.'ana.** To claim a *kaikua'ana* relationship, to act as a *kaikua'ana,* to address and treat as *kaikua'ana;* to address a *kaikaina* as *kaikua'ana* as a means of showing great respect. (PCP *tuakana.)*

kai.kua.hine. n. Sister or female cousin of a male. (See *kuahine 1.)* **ho'o.kai.kua.hine.** To claim a *kuahine* relationship; to address and treat as *kaikuahine,* as from affection. (PPN *tuafafine.)*

kai.kuehu. n. Enema. Cf. *kaikea 4.*

kai.kunāne. n. Brother or male cousin of a female. (See *kunāne.)* Cf. Gram. 2.7. **ho'o.kai.kunāne.** To claim a *kaikunāne* relationship, to act as a *kaikunāne;* to address and treat as *kaikunāne,* as from affection. (PPN *tunga'ane.)*

kai kuolo. n. A rough sea with undercurrent, as pulling back and forth on a beach, undertow. Cf. *kuolo,* rub.

kai.kū.'ono. n. Guards posted at the entrance to the *hale nauā* enclosure (Malo 191.) Emerson (Malo 200) lists this as *kaikuone.*

kai kū.'ono. Same as *kū'ono,* inlet, bay.

kai.kuwa.hine. Var. spelling of *kaikuahine.* (Kin. 12.13.)

kai lalo. See *kai 1.*

kaila. n. Style, fashion; stylish. *Eng. Kū i ke kaila,* stylish, fashionable.

kai lā.nahu ahi. Very dark ocean water. (And.) *Lit.,* fire charcoal sea.

kai lawai'a. n. Fishing grounds. *Ke pono kai lawai'a,* rights to fishing grounds.

ka'i lewa. vt. To carry or go to and fro.

kā.ili. n. Runner on sweet potato vine; string of fish, string or fiber of any kind on which fish are strung. Also *kāī.*

kā.'ili. 1. vt. To snatch, grab, take by force, seize, abduct, usurp; to gasp, labor for breath. (See song, Elbert and Mahoe 58–9.) *Kā'ili malū,* to seize or abduct secretly, kidnap. *Moku kā'ili lā,* sun-snatching island [Lehua Island or sometimes Kaua'i, since they lie to the west]. *Ka wai kā'ili ao,* liquid that snatches away enlightenment [intoxicants]. **ho'o.kā.'ili.** To tug and pull as though to snatch, but not with great force, as in playing with a kitten; to cause a snatching, etc. (PCP *taakili.)* 2. vt. To cast for fish. 3. n. Fine net as used for *'ōpelu* fishing. (Malo 212.)

kā.'ili.'ili. Redup. of *kā'ili 1, 2;* snatching, pulling, especially of a newly carved canoe hauled from the mountains to the sea. Cf. *kaula kā'ili'ili.*

ka'i like. vt. 1. To march in step or proceed in unity, as soldiers; to lead together. 2. To divide. (Luke 22.17.)

kā.'ili.kū. vt. To plunder, rob, seize, as in premeditated violence. Cf. *kā'ili wale.*

kā.'ili.poni. vi. To die suddenly, as by stroke or accident. *Make kā'ilipono,* apoplexy.

Ka-'ili-'ula. n. Tutelary star of Ka'ū, Hawai'i.

kā.'ili wale. vt. To plunder, rob, seize, usually without premeditation. Cf. *kā'ilikū.*

Kai Loko 'Āina. n. Inland Sea (Japan).

kai lū he'e. n. Sea where octopuses are caught with lure. *Fig.,* the deep sea.

kaima. n. Thyme *(Thymus vulgaris)*, from southern Europe, a small plant with small leaves, in the mint family, used to flavor food. (Neal 734.) *Eng.*

kai ma ka lae. n. Sea at a point or cape.

kai make. n. 1. Low tide. 2. *(Caps.)* Dead Sea.

ka'i mali.hini. n. Corpus Christi procession, so called because first communicants march. *Lit.*, parade for-the-first-time.

kai malolo. n. Quiet sea, as in a calm cove; low tide.

kai malo'o. n. Low tide, as when much of the reef is exposed. *Lit.*, dry sea.

ka'i malū. vt. To abduct.

kai.mana, daimana. n. Diamond. *Eng.* See song, *hulali 1.*

Kai.mana-Hila. n. Diamond Head. *Lit.*, Diamond Hill *(Eng.).*

kai mau, kai mau.mau. n. Mid-tide.

ka'imi. n. A kind of Spanish clover, an erect fodder plant *(Desmodium canum)*, from the West Indies, a legume with three-parted leaves, pink flowers, and small, narrow, four-to-eight-jointed pods. (Neal 451.)

kai miki, kai mimiki. n. Receding sea, especially immediately before a tidal wave. *Lit.*, creeping sea.

kai.moku. Middle tide, when the tide begins to recede (And.); perhaps also similar to *kai'okia.*

kai.moni, daimoni. n. Demon. (Gr. *daimon.*)

kai.monio, daimonio. Same as *kaimoni.* (Gr. *daimonion.*)

kā i mua. nvt. Ceremony initiating boys, usually at age of six, after which they were permitted to wear a *malo* and join the men in the *mua*, men's house; henceforth they might not eat with women; to perform the ceremony. *Lit.*, thrust to the *mua* house.

kaina. 1. Same as *kaikaina*, most used as term of address. (PPN *t(e,a)hina.*) 2. n. Kind. *Eng. Kaina ho'okahi*, all of one kind; a set, as of dishes. *Kaina ho'okahi o nā mea inu ki*, tea set.

kā.ina. n. and interj. Hit, struck; strike! destroy (said by a sorcerer invoking eternal destruction upon a victim); incantation.

ka'ina. Same as *ka'i 1*; order, succession, sequence. *Ke ka'ina a'ela nā koholā*, the whales there are following in line. *Ho'ololiloli i ke ka'ina o nā hua 'ōlelo*, change the word order. (PPN *takinga.*)

Kai.nahai. Same as *Kanahai*, Shanghai.

kai.nakē. nvs. Hollow-head; brainless. *Kaua'i. Rare.*

kai.naliu. n. 1. Central part of a canoe, just aft of the point where the forward outrigger boom is attached to the hull (perhaps from *kā i nā liu*, bail the bilge). 2. *(Cap.)* Place name at Kona, Hawai'i, said to be the name of a canoe bailer for Keawe-nui-a-'Umi.

ka'i.napu. nvi. Graceful prancing motion; to toss, as a ship. *'Akahi ka nani ua 'ike 'ia, i ka holo ka'inapu a nā lio* (chant for Kuhiō), nothing as pretty has been seen, as the graceful running of the horses.

ka'ina wā.wae. n. Manner of walking, gait; pace, step. *Like ke ka'ina wāwae*, steps all alike and even, as of marching soldiers.

ka'i.nepu. Var. of *ka'inapu.*

kaini. n. Name of a mother *'ua'u*, bird.

kai niu. n. Coconut cream.

kai.nō, kai.noa. idiom. Why not; I thought, presumed, or assumed (but it was not so). (Gram. 4.6.) *Kainō ua hele 'oe*, I thought you had gone. *Kainō ho'i e hele mai 'olua?* Why don't you two come?

kai nui. n. High tide, big sea.

kai.nu'u. n. Possession of an altar by a god. **ho'o.kai.nu'u.** To take possession (referring to an action of a god). *E ala e ho'okainu'u, kaiao* (hula altar prayer), rise, take possession of the altar, bring light.

kai nu'u. n. High sea. *Kai nu'u aku*, ebbing sea. *Kai nu'u mai*, incoming tide.

ka'io. See *mai'a ka'io.*

Ka-'io. n. A *lua* fighting stroke; fish was taboo to learners. *Lit.*, the hawk. (Also without *Ka-*.)

kai.o'e. n. A plant mentioned in poetry, as *ka nani o ka*

pua kaio'e, the beauty of the *kaio'e* blossoms; a lizard god of the same name is associated with this plant.

kā.'io.'io. vi. To bear a second crop of sweet potatoes. (HP 148.)

kā.i'o.i'o. 1. vi. To grow irregular and scrubby, as unpruned *hau* trees. 2. n. *Panicum colliei. Ni'ihau.*

kai-o-kaua.kahi. n. Name of a long prayer in a temple service. (Malo 169.)

kai.oke, kaiote. n. Coyote. *Eng.*

kai.'okia. vi. Separated by sea, spared, set apart, separated (see *kānāwai*). *Ma ka inoa o kona kānāwai mau, kai'okia kānāwai, no laila, 'a'ole he luku hou 'ana a Lono-i-ka-makahiki* (For. 4:291), in the name of his customary law, sea-separation law, so there was no more destruction by Lono-i-ka-makahiki. *Ke hō'ike mai nei ke akua, ua kai'okia ka make o āu mau keiki*, the god reveals that your children are spared.

kai 'ō.lena. n. Water of purification composed of sea water or water with salt and *'ōlena* (turmeric root); to purify thus.

kai.'oloa. n. Ceremony of tying fine white tapa *('oloa)* as a *malo* on an image. (Malo 148, 154.)

kai.olo.hia. n. Calm, tranquil sea. (UL 207.) *Fig.*, peace of mind.

kai.o'o. Rare var. of *kai ko'o*, strong sea; to be such.

kai-o-pō-keo. Var. of *kai-a-pō-kea.*

kai 'ō.pū. n. Giblet gravy.

kai penu. n. Gravy. *Lit.*, sauce to sop up.

kai piha. n. High sea, high tide, full sea, spring tide.

kai pi'i. n. High or rising tide, high waves.

kai pili 'oai.kū. n. A churning, gasping sea.

kai po'i. n. Breaking waves or surf.

kai pū. n. 1. Sea where currents meet. 2. Mid-tide, quiet sea.

kā ipu. n. Hanger for *ipu*, calabashes.

kai pu'e.one. n. A sand-dune sea, said either of a sea at very low tide which leaves the sand exposed, or of a rough sea that washes up sand. *He lā kai pā, he kai pu'eone, ō e ho'iho'i nō ke kai i ke one . . . ma kona wahi kahiko* (Kep. 101), a day of a pounding sea, for the sea brings back the sand . . . to its old place.

kai puhi lala. n. Sea with meeting diagonal waves, said figuratively, of Pearl Harbor lochs. *Lit.*, sea blowing diagonally.

kai.puni, taifuni. n. Typhoon. *Eng.*

kai pupule. n. Crazy, restless, wild, agitated sea.

ka'i.pu'u. nvt. Division, portion; to divide into portions or heaps, apportion. *Rare.*

kai.ua. vi. 1. To continue, repeat. *E kaiua i ka ho'okahe i ka wai*, continue to irrigate. 2. Var. of *kaiue.*

kai.ue. 1. vi. To go back and forth, swing or move back and forth or up and down; to sway the hips in walking; to pitch, as of waves. *Ke lawe 'ia ala ka'u aloha e ka hope kaiue o ka Mauna Loa*, my love is carried away there by the pitching stern of the Mauna Loa [ship]. 2. vt. To hill up sweet potatoes. (Kep. 157, HP 148.)

Kai 'Ula. n. Red Sea.

kai ulu. n. Sea at full tide, mounting sea.

kai 'ū.poho. n. Breaking sea, breakers, whitecaps. *Lit.*, resounding sea.

kai 'uweke. Same as *kai kala.*

Kai Waena Honua. n. Mediterranean Sea. *Lit.*, sea middle earth.

kai wahine. n. Calm, gentle sea. *Lit.*, feminine sea.

Ka-iwi-po'o. n. See *iwi po'o, Kalewali.*

kaka. 1. vt. To rinse, clean. (PEP *tata.*) 2. vs. Arched; curving from end to end, as the top of a canoe. *Rare.* 3. Same as *kakaka 1. Kaka ihola 'oia i ka pua* (For. 4:35), he then shot the arrow. 4. Same as *kakaka 2.* 5. n. Cluster. *Rare.* 6. Also **gasa.** n. Gas. *Eng.*

kakā. nvi. Domesticated duck; to quack. *(Eng.)*

kā.kā. nvt. To strike, smite, dash, beat, chop; to thresh or beat out, as grain (Ruta 2.17); to kick and flail the arms as an angry child; to strike, as flint and steel; to hit broiled breadfruit with a stick to remove the blackened skin; slab. Cf. *kā 1, kākā pua'a. Pili kākā lalo*

(For. 5:131), to place bets. *Ke pau ka 'ai 'ana a ka moa, kākā i ka nuku,* when the chicken finishes eating, it shakes its beak. (PPN *taataa.*) **2.** vs. Odorous, either fragrant or otherwise; to make an odor. *Rare.* **3.** nvi. To excrete; dirty, excreta (a euphemism, taught to children). **4.** nvi. To fish, as for *uhu,* parrot fish, with a square net (FS 39) or *ulua* with hook and line but no pole; net or nets dropped in a semicircle in shallow water, as for mullets or *'ō'io.*

kaka'a. nvi. To roll, whirl, turn over; to revolve, as a wheel; to turn aside, deviate; rolling, turning, etc. See *maka kaka'a.* **ho'o.kaka'a.** To cause to turn, roll, etc.; to turn somersaults or cartwheels. (PPN *tataka.*)

kā.ka'a. vi. To shift or roll, as the eyes.

kā.kā.'āko. Dull, slow. (AP.)

kaka'a.lawa. vs. Far apart, not close. *Kanu kaka'alawa i ka huli,* to plant taro stalks sufficiently far apart.

Kā.kā-'au-kī. n. **1.** Name of a place at Kohala, Hawai'i, celebrated by name for the tests held there for the presence of sharks: ti stalks *('au kī),* whose bark had been beaten off *(kākā),* were thrown into the water; if the stalks were pulled under this was a sign of the presence of sharks and the natives climbed the steep cliff trail rather than swim. **2.** Name of a stroke in *lua* fighting.

kaka'a.wale. Redup. of *ka'awale.* **ho'o.kaka'a.wale.** Redup. of *ho'oka'awale.*

kakae. Spry, lively, quick; to run. (And.)

kaka'e. Similar to *hakaka'e,* transparent. *Rare.*

Kā.ka'e. n. Name of a star.

kakaha. Redup. of *kaha 1, 3. Kakaha nā maka o ka 'ilima,* the center of the *'ilima* flowers turn. (PPN *tataha.*)

kā.kaha. n. Strip of barren land near the sea shore; shoal.

kakahe. Redup. of *kahe 1. E kakahe mai noho'i nā kumu mua i ka wela loa o ke ahi* (2 Pet. 3.12), and the elements shall meet in the great heat of the fire. (PPN *tatafe.*)

kakahe.ā.wai. Similar to *kaheāwai.*

kaka.hele. To go quickly. (And.). **ho'o.kaka.hele.** To parade, as Lahaina-Luna students. (For. 6:531.)

kakahi. vs. Solitary, unique, outstanding. See *pākakahi. Kakahi Lahaina i ka malino* (chant for Ka-mehameha I), solitary Lahaina in the calm.

kaka.hiaka. n. Morning. *Kakahiaka nui,* early morning. *Kēia kakahiaka aku,* later this morning. (Cf. Tahitian *'a'ahiata,* dawn.)

kaka.hiki. Var. of *kakahili.*

kaka.hili. nvi. Idle chatter; to talk idly; to wander aimlessly. Cf. *hili,* to wander.

kā.kā.hou. **1.** vt. To torture to death by flaying or piercing. *Lit.,* strike poke. *Rare.* **2.** vs. Immature, unripe. *Rare.* Cf. *hou,* fresh.

kā.kai. nvt. Handle, as of a bucket, pot, basket, purse; strings by which a netted *(kōkō)* calabash is hung; woman's scarf (Ni'ihau); to tie on; to encircle with a band, specifically, to stretch the taboo cord before the entrance of a chief's house (this cord was said to fall of its own accord if a relative approached). *Kini kākai,* pail with a handle.

kā.kai-. See *kakaiawī, kākailena, kākaioiwi, kākaipū.*

kaka'i. nvt. To walk along with a group; to follow in line, as chickens after a hen; procession; litter, as of pigs. Cf. *kaka'i pali, ka'i. 'Oia nā hōkū he nui wale e kaka'i hele ana ma ka pōnaha lani* (Kep. 83), there are the many stars moving in groups in the firmament. *Kaka'i ka 'aha,* a prayer is rendered (same as *ka'i ka 'aha,* see *'aha 3).* **ho'o.kaka'i.** To lead, take along. (PPN *tataki.*)

kaka'i.ā.hele. vi. To go in file, wander. *Ke kaka'iāhele ala lākou,* they went in single file.

kaka'i.ā.hili. Var. of *kakahili.*

kaka'i.ā.lupe. Same as *kauālupe.*

kakai.ā.pola. n. Tail of a kite.

kā.kaia.wī. n. Ancient name of a disease, the symptoms of which suggest appendicitis in various stages.

kā.kai.ewa. vi. Long, fatiguing, as a trip. *Rare.*

Kā.kai.hili. n. Name of a star.

kaka'i.kahi. vs. Scarce, sparse, rare, few, uncommon; seldom, rarely; precious (in sense of rare, 1 Sam. 3:1). *Kaka'ikahi ka mau'u o kēia 'āina,* the grass on this land is sparse.

kā.kai.lena. Same as *kākaiawī.*

Kā.kā.ili. n. Name of a star.

kā.ka'i.hili. vs. Slow, slow moving.

kaka.'ina. n. Sequence, one of a series, branch, success. *'O nā kaka'ina ame nā loina li'ili'i 'ē a'e o ke 'ano ho'omana* (Kep. 19), sequences and various small rules of a religious nature. (PNP *tatakiina.*)

kā.kaio.iwi, kakai.owī. Var. of *kākaiawī.*

kaka'i pali. nvs. A series of precipices; consisting of such. *He ala kaka'i pali,* a road following cliff tops.

kā.kai pauka (pauda). n. Powder horn, cartridge box.

kā.kai.pū. n. A disease whose symptoms suggest appendicitis.

kakaka. **1.** nvt. Bow for shooting arrows; crossbow; the shooting of a bow; bent, as a bow; to shoot, as a bow. *Ua mākaukau lākou i nā kakaka* (1 Oihn. 12.2), they were adept at shooting bows. **2.** n. Deep-sea fishing with weighted line. **3.** Redup. of *kaka 1.* **4.** n. A sweet potato, usually qualified by the terms *'ili pahe'e,* smooth skin, or *'ili pohole o Keawe,* scraped skin of Keawe.

kaka.kaka. Redup. of *kaka 1.*

kaka.kau. Redup. of *kakau,* to place.

kā.kā.kau. **1.** Redup. of *kākau;* to reprint, to rewrite. *E kākākau ana kamali'i i ke kumu,* the children are writing to the teacher. *Kākākau ka 'āina i ka pali,* the scars are engraved on the cliff. **2.** n. A cuplike dish, usually of stone, used to hold tapa-printing or tattooing dye.

kaka.kē. vs. Poor quality, as of taro not fit for poi. *Rare.*

kaka.kī. **1.** n. Iron hoop, iron from a hoop. **2.** vs. Thin, stooped. *Rare.* **3.** n. Name given for a kind of *kala,* a fish. *Rare.*

kaka.kihi. vi. To step lightly or softly; to do quietly; to run lightly.

kā.kā.ki'i. vs. Clumsy, awkward-moving, gangling, blundering in speech, uncouth in manner and speech; rambling, as a road. *Rare.*

kaka.kō. n. Quail.

kā kā.kou. poss. Our, ours (*a*-form, plural, inclusive). (Gram. 8.4, 9.6.) (PNP *ta'a tatou,* PCP *taa taatou.*)

kakala. Redup. of *kala 1.* (PPN *tatala.*)

kā.kala. **1.** nvs. Knifelike cartilage near the tail of some fish, as surgeonfish; horn of a fish; cockspur; thorn; rostrum, as of a shrimp; caudal or anal horn, as of a caterpillar; sharp, rough, thorny, craggy; spines on fish fins. *Fig.,* rough, ill-natured, harsh. See *kala 3, 4; 'ōkala. Leo kākala,* harsh, grating voice. **2.** n. Octopus hook used with a stone sinker and a cowry shell. **3.** nvi. Surf comber; to form combers; to blow in gusts. **4.** vs. Mature, of a gourd, with a dry stem.

kā.kā lā.'au. nv. Spear fencing; to fence.

kakala.'ihi. Redup. of *kala'ihi. He mana kūkulu kakala-'ihi* (chant), power established oppressive.

kaka.lai.ō. nvi. Creepy sensation due to either cold or fright; to have goose flesh, shuddery feeling. *Rare.*

kā.kala.oa. **1.** vs. Thorny. (Kin. 3.18.) *Lei kākalaioa,* crown of thorns [as worn by Christ]. *Kū kākalaioa,* filled with thorns, wild, rude; to rage. **2.** n. Gray nickers *(Caesalpinia major,* misidentified locally as *C. crista),* a straggly bramble, a pantropical vine indigenous to Hawai'i, with thorny branches and leaf stems and with small yellow flowers. Within each large spiny pod are two or three gray marble-like seeds, which are used for leis, also powdered for medicine.(Neal 433.) Also *hihikolo.* **3.** n. Yellow nickers *(Caesalpinia bonduc),* today commonly called Hawaiian pearls, similar to the gray nickers, but with yellowish-gray instead of gray seeds. (Neal 433-4.) Also *hihikolo.* See *kinikini 3.*

kakala.keke, katarakete. n. Cormorant. (Kanl. 14.17.) (Gr. *kata(r)raktes.*)

kaka.lama, dagarama. n. Silver money.

kā.kala manini, kā.kala mani.nini. n. Half-grown *manini,* a fish.

kā.kā.lana. n. Proclamation. Cf. *kala 1.*

kā.kala-pī-ka-wai. n. Sharp spurs of a fighting cock.

kā.kala wela. 1. nv. Scar from burning; to scar. **2.** vs. Black with brown markings, of a pig. Cf. *kala wela.*

kakale. Redup. of *kale.* *'Ai kakale,* poi cocktail, thin poi. **ho'o.kakale.** To make soft or watery; soft, flexible, saggy, soft, limp; to dilute.

kaka.lema, sakarema. n. Sacrament. See *kakelema.*

kakali. Redup. of *kali 1.* (Isa. 64.4.) (PPN *tatali.*)

kaka.lina. n. Gasoline. *Eng.*

kā.kā.lule. vs. Uncertain, variable, equivocal.

kā.kā.maka. nvt. Raw salted meat; to cut raw meat into large pieces and salt it. *Lit.,* chop raw.

kaka.mina, katamina. n. Catmint, catnip. *Eng.*

kā.kā.mo'a. nvt. Hunks of cooked meat scored and salted for preservation; to prepare cooked meat thus.

kakana. vs. Harsh, rude, ungracious, surly.

Kā.kana, Satana. n. Satan. *Eng.*

kakana.i'i. Same as *kakana.*

kakana.kana. A grass. (And.)

kakana.li'i. vs. Stunted, wee. Also *'a'anali'i.*

kakana.lua. Redup. of *kānalua;* dubious.

kakane. nvi. Blight on plants; blighted. Cf. *kane.* **ho'o.kakane.** Caus/sim.

kakani. 1. nvi. Noisy; to make repeated noises, to talk incessantly; pealing, ringing, squeaking. Cf. *kani.* **ho'o.-kakani.** To make noises. (PPN *tatangi.*) **2.** n. A plant disease in hot areas, 1857.

kakano. Redup. of *kano 1,* hard; to persist, keep on. *Kakano hele,* to keep going on. **ho'o.kakano.** Caus/sim.

kaka'o. Same as *ka'oka'o 1-3. Kaka'o ka waha o ka ua, nahua i ka nahele,* lofty the mouth of the rain, pelting down in the forest.

kakā.ohi. Redup. of *kāohi.*

kā.kā.ola. 1. vt. To cut up alive. Cf. *kākāhou.* **2.** n. Visible spirit of a living person.

kā.kā.'ō.lelo. nv. Orator, person skilled in use of language; counselor, adviser; storyteller; oratory; to orate. *Lit.,* to fence [with] words.

kakapa. Redup. of *kapa,* edge, border. (Gram. 8.6.) *Ma kakapa o ka loko,* along the edges of the pond.

kā.kā pahi. nv. To fence with swords; fencing.

kā kā.pala. n. Dye container, probably so called because the edge of the container was hit *(kā)* with the bamboo stamp to dislodge excess dye before printing the tapa.

kā.kā pua'a. n. Slab of salted pork.

kaka.pila, katapila. n. Caterpillar (tractor). *Eng.*

kakau. Redup. and plural of *kau,* to place; to leave imprints; to stand out, as veins. (PCP *tatau.*)

kā.kau. 1. nvt. To write, sign; to print on tapa; to mark out for distribution, as land (Ios. 18:6, 8); writing. (Probably *kā-,* causative + *kau,* to place.) *Kākau wale,* to write carelessly, scribble. *Mea kākau,* writer, author. *Kākau 'ia mai,* written to us (as a report submitted). *Kākau 'ole,* unwritten. *Kākau 'āpuka,* forgery. (PPN *tatau.*) **2.** nvt. To tattoo; tattooing. (PPN *tatau,* PCP *taatau.*) **3.** n. Young but fully marked and fully developed fish.

kā kā.ua. poss. Our, ours (*a*-form, dual, inclusive; Gram. 8.4.1, 9.6). (PNP *ta'a taaua,* PCP *taa taaua.*)

kā.kau ali'i. n. Royal scribe; writer of chronology or history of chiefs.

kā.kau 'euane.lio (ewanelio). n. Evangelist.

kā.kā.uha. vi. Rigid, inflexible; stretched forth, as the arm (Puk. 6.6); oppressive; to display strength. **ho'o.kā.kā.uha.** To stretch forth (Puk. 7.5), to make rigid; to oppress; to flex muscles, as in desire to show off one's strength.

kā.kau hana. n. Recorder.

kā.kau ho'o.pa'a. vt. To register.

kā.kau inoa. nv. To sign a name, register, as for voting or as at a university; to endorse, enroll; sign, signature, autograph, registration, recorder. *E kākau inoa 'ia e ka Luna Kānāwai,* shall be signed by the Judge.

kā.kau kaha. nv. To make lines, print, mark, paint, tattoo.

kā.kau kā.ko'o. nv. To endorse; written support.

kā.kau kope. nv. Registration; to copy. *Mea kākau kope,* registrar.

kā.kau leka. nv. To write letters; correspondence.

kā.kau lima. nv. Handwriting, penmanship; written by hand.

kā.kau mo'o.lelo. n. Author, writer of stories; secretary or recorder.

kā.kau nū.pepa. nv. Reporter; to write for newspapers.

kā.kau 'ō.lelo. nv. Secretary, clerk, scribe; to act as secretary (Kel. 98).

kā.kau 'ō.lelo pō.kole, kā.kau pō.kole. Same as *kākau 'ōlelo;* stenographer, shorthand.

kā.kā.wahie. nvt. Solid tattoo pattern; to tattoo thus.

kā.kā.wahie. n. Moloka'i creeper *(Loxops maculata flammea);* the male is largely scarlet; the female and the immature male are brown with scarlet markings. *Lit.,* wood chopping. Also *'alauahio.*

kā.kawa.ū. Same as *nānawaū.*

kā.kā.wele.wele. Same as *kāwelewele. Rare.*

kake. 1. nv. Chants with mixed or garbled words, for and by chiefs, with inserted syllables and some secret words (as: *nohouwō o luhunā, nohouwō o lahalō,* for: *no'u 'o luna, no'u 'o lalo,* mine are the chiefs, mine are the commoners); to use this language; play language used for amusement and intrigue; code. *Hula kake,* hula danced to a garbled chant. **ho'o.kake.** To speak *kake;* to speak unclearly. Cf. *holokake, hōkake.* (PCP *tate;* cf. Marquesan *tate,* stammer.) **2.** vt. To slip back and forth; to mix, shuffle. **ho'o.kake.** Caus/sim.; to disturb. **3.** n. A native variety of sweet potato; the name may be qualified by the term *'ele'ele.* **4.** n. Cartridge. *Eng.* **5.** n. Jack (instrument). *Eng.*

Kā.kea. n. Name of a stormy wind. *He Kākea ka makani kulakula'i kauhale o Mānoa* [said of one who is excessively aggressive].

kake.kake. Redup. of *kake 1, 2;* to jerk, fidget, interfere; to shuffle, as cards. Cf. *hōkakekake. E holo kakekake ai ke aho i ka lima* (For. 6:411), the line runs and jerks in the hand. (PCP *tatetate.*)

kā.kē.kepa. Var. of *kākepakepa 1.*

kake.kimo. n. Catechism.

kā.keko. Powerful, strong. (And.)

kakeku.meno. n. Catechumen. (Gr. *katechoumenos,* Latin *catechismus.*)

kā.kela. 1. vt. To perform well. Cf. *kela,* to excel. *He kaka'ikahi loa nā kānaka 'ōpio i hiki ke lanakila maluna ona ma ke kākela 'ana ma kēia mau 'ike apau,* few young men could best him in clever performance of all these skills. **2.** n. Castle. *Eng.* **3.** Also **gazela.** n. Gazelle. *Eng.*

kā.kele. 1. vt. To rub with oil, to mix or stew with sauce or gravy. Cf. *kelekele,* greasy. *Lawe ipu kākele* (For. 5:81), bearer of ointment calabash. **2.** vt. To cast with hook and line, as for *ulua. Na'u e kākele a mau ia pua* (song), I will cast and get this flower. **3.** vi. To slide, skid, glide, to go rambling at will and hence to do as one pleases. *Kākele mai,* come on; act now. *Nana i kākele ke kaona lā* (song), she's the one to do the town.

kā.kele.kele. Redup. of *kākele 1-3.*

kake.lema, sakerema; kakele.meneka, sakereme-neta. n. Sacrament. (Latin *sacramentum* or Spanish and Portuguese *sacramento.*)

kā.kelo. Same as *hākelo.* Cf. *kelo.*

kā.kelo.kelo. vs. Slimy, as mucus; to hang, as mucus.

kā.kepa. Similar to common *kīkepa 2. Nā lei maile e kākepa ana ma ka 'a'ī ā ku'uwelo akula ma ka 'ao'ao, maile* leis crossing at the neck and hanging down on the side.

kā.kepa.kepa. vi. **1.** To cross the arms high in front, with hands on shoulders; to cross the hands behind the back (either was considered a curse and highly insulting). Same as *kākēkepa*. **2.** To think, ponder, consider. Cf. *kepakepa*, rhythmic recitation.

kake pauka (pauda). n. Cartridge box. *Eng.*

kaki. vs. Cross, irritable, petulant.

kāki. nvt. To charge, as a bill; a charge, bill. *Eng.*

kā.kī. nvs. Khaki. *Eng.*

kā.kia. 1. nvt. To nail down, to wedge or fasten tightly; nail, pin, wedge. See *kui kākia. Eia mai au o ʻuku liʻi, kākia kui nao a ke akamai*, here am I, so petite, skilled in hammering big nails. *Hale kākia kāmaʻa lio*, blacksmith shop. **2.** n. Cassia. *Eng.*

kaki.ana. n. Sergeant. *Eng.*

kaki.ana mekia. n. Sergeant major. *Eng.*

kā.kiʻi. vt. To strike at, aim at, smite (FS 89); to brandish threateningly, as a war club (FS 61).

kakili.leke, sakirilege. n. Sacrilege. *Eng.*

kaki.mea, kasimea. nvs. Cashmere. *Eng.*

kaki.nela, kadinela. n. Cardinal (Catholic Church). *Eng.*

kā.kini. n. **1.** Dozen; stocking, sock. *Eng. Lī kākini*, garters. **2.** Also **satini.** Var. of *kākīnia*.

kā.kī.nia. n. Sateen. *Eng.*

kā.kiʻo. n. Mange, impetigo, itch, itching pustules of the skin. (Kanl. 28.27.)

kā.kipi. Var. of *kāpiki*.

kā.kiwi. 1. vt. To strike *(kā)* with a side stroke or obliquely; to strike in order to ensnare or catch in a noose; crooked, bent, curved. *Pahi kākiwi*, sickle. **2.** nvt. To grow by ground layering; plant so grown. Cf. *laʻa. Fig.*, chain, succession: *ʻA ʻole i pau ʻia nei nā kākiwi a nā leo poloʻai i ke aliʻi*, the chain of voices summoning the chief was not ended.

kako. n. **1.** Also **sako.** Sage. *Eng.* **2.** Also **kado.** A liquid measure, about 42 pints.

kā.koʻi. nv. To make adzes; adze maker. (Malo 51.)

kā.kolea. nvt. To tie a slipknot securely, but so that it can be loosened with one jerk at the end of the rope; slipknot.

Kakō.lika, Katolika. nvs. Catholic. *Eng.*

Kakō.lika Helene. n. Greek Catholic.

Kakō.lika Loma (Roma). n. Roman Catholic.

kā.kolu. vs. Three-stranded.

kā.kona. vs. To stop, hinder, especially of a firebrand hurled in the old fire-throwing sport. *Kākona ke ahi, hāʻule wale iho nō*, the fire[brand] fails, it falls short.

kā.kona.kona. n. **1.** A native grass *(Panicum torridum)*, 30–70 cm. high, covered with silky, light-colored hairs, the cone-shaped flowering panicle 7.8 to 16 cm long, coated with silky hair. (Neal 73.) See *hākonakona*. **2.** A variety of sweet potato.

kā.kona.konā. Similar to *konā*. *Ka-la-ʻe peʻe kākonakonā*, Ka-la-ʻe hides and avoids contact [said of the timid *kauā*, outcasts, of Ka-la-ʻe, Molokaʻi].

kāko.ʻo. nvt. To uphold, support, favor, assist, prop up; to bind, as with a sash or belt; support, aid, recommendation, girdle. Cf. *koʻo*, support. *Mea kakoʻo*, sponsor. *Ā ʻo ka ʻoiaʻiʻo hoʻi ke kāko ʻo o kona kīkala* (Isa. 11.5), truth then is the girdle of his reins. **hoʻo.kā.koʻo.** Caus/sim. (PCP *taatoko*.)

kā.kou. pro. We (inclusive, three or more). *Kā kākou, kō kākou*, our, ours. (PNP *kita(a)tou*, PEP *taʻatou*, PCP *taatou*.)

kā.kū. 1. n. The barracuda *(Sphyraena barracuda)*, as long as 60 cm. Also *kūpala*. **2.** n. Gourd calabash, as used for fishing (HP 208). **3.** n. Weft strands of mat, so called because the strands are worked *(kā)* to run up *(kū)* from the worker. Cf. *kāmoe*. **4.** Short for *kākū ʻai*.

kā.kua. vt. **1.** To bind or fasten on, as a sarong or belt. Cf. *hahau kākua. Ka ʻohu kākua o Kī-lau-ea*, the mist that forms a sarong for Kī-lau-ea. (PCP *taatua*.) **2.** To worship the gods, especially by food offerings; to appeal to the gods.

kā.kū.ʻai. v. To sacrifice food (fish, bananas, kava) to the gods, as at every meal; to feed the spirits of the dead; to deify a dead relative by food offerings and prayer; to dedicate the dead to become family protec-

tors *(ʻaumākua)* or servants of *ʻaumākua* (Beckwith, 1970, p. 123); to transfigure, transfiguration (Kam. 64: 64, 91). (Contraction of *kākua ʻai*.) See *kino ahi*.

kā.kua-o-Hiʻi.aka. Same as *pāʻū-o-Hiʻiaka*, a beach vine.

Kakuke, Satude. n. Saturday. *Eng. Rare.*

Kaku.lena, Saturena. n. Saturn. *Eng.*

kala. 1. nvt. To loosen, untie, free, release, remove, unburden, absolve, let go, acquit, take off, undo; to proclaim, announce; to forgive, pardon, excuse; to substitute for (Kin. 22.13); counter-sorcery or sorcerer, proclamation, public crier, announcer; prayer to free one from any evil influence; to practice counter-sorcery. See *kala ʻōpelu, limu kala. E kala mai ia ʻu*, excuse me. *Kala ʻana*, forgiveness, absolution. **hoʻo.kala.** Caus/sim. (PPN *tala*.) **2.** n. Screwdriver. **3.** n. Surgeonfish, unicorn fish, Teuthidae; *Naso hexacanthus, N. unicornis, N. brevirostris*. Varieties are qualified by the terms *holo ihu loa* (long nose running), *lemu* (buttocks), *liʻiliʻi* (also *pahi kaua*), *lōlō, maoli, moe, palaholo*. See *hiʻikala. He kala iʻa i ʻoi ka hiʻu* (saying), *kala* fish with sharp tail [*fig.*, one who can defend himself]. (Probably PPN *talakisi*.) **4.** vs. Rough, as sharkskin. **hoʻo.kala.** To sharpen, grind (so called because things were formerly sharpened by rubbing against a rough surface); sharpener; to speak roughly or harshly (Ios. 10.21). *Hunahuna hoʻokala*, chips. (PPN *tala*.) **5.** vs. Same as *kākala 1–4*. **6.** vs. Long ago (usually followed by *loa, wale, kahiko*; when preceded by *aʻole, aʻoe*, or *eʻoe*, it means "quite a while ago," or, "for quite a long time." *E kala loa ka holo ʻana o ka moku*, the ship sailed long ago. *ʻA ʻole i kala ka noho ʻana o nā haole maʻaneʻi*, the white people lived here quite a time ago. **7.** Same as *hākala*, gable. (PPN *tala*.) **8.** Same as *pua kala*, prickly poppy. **9.** See *limu kala*, seaweeds. For a pun on *kala 8* and *9*, see Neal 367. **10.** n. A sweet potato. Kinds are qualified by the colors *keʻokeʻo* and *poni*. **11.** Same as *ʻākala*, a raspberry. **12.** Same as *pākalakala*, a tern. (PPN *tala*.) **13.** n. Collar. *Eng.* **14.** n. Color.

kā.lā, dala. nvs. Dollar, silver, money, price, currency, means, funds; moneyed. *Eng.* Cf. *kūkālā. Kālā ma ke kānāwai*, legal tender.

kala aloha. nv. Sorcery to free a victim from power of the *hana aloha*, love inducing sorcery. *Lit.*, to free love.

kala.ʻau. vt. To call, speak. *Kauaʻi.*

kāla.ʻau. 1. nv. Stick dancing; to stick dance; sometimes this term is applied to fencing instead of the more frequent *kākā lāʻau*. **2.** n. Mast. *Rare.*

kā.la.ʻe. 1. vs. Clear, calm, unclouded. **hoʻo.kā.laʻe.** To cause to clear; to become clear. **2.** n. Swelling, probably due to failing circulation.

kala.ʻea. vs. Rough, rude in speech. *He ʻōlelo kalaʻea wale nō kā Hākau iā ʻUmi*, Hākau spoke only roughly to ʻUmi.

kā.la.ʻe.la.ʻe. Redup. of *kālaʻe 1*.

Kā.laha. n. Stroke in *lua* fighting.

kala.hala. nvt. Atonement, remission of sins; to pardon, absolve from sin, ransom. *Lit.*, forgive sin. See *puʻukalahala.* **hoʻo.kala.hala.** Same as above. *Hoʻokalahala akula ʻo ʻAʻalona no lākou, i mea e huikala ai iā lākou* (Nah. 8:21), Aaron made an atonement for them to cleanse them.

kala hale. n. House gable; plaiting design, as in braids for hats.

-kalahē. hoʻo.kala.hē. Same as *hoʻokāluli*, to sway.

kala.hea. vt. To call out an announcement or proclamation, announce. *Kalahea i ka make*, announce the death.

kala hele. vi. To go forth issuing a proclamation or making an announcement. *Lit.*, traveling proclamation.

kala hewa.hewa. vt. To give away in an insane manner, as would a crazy person.

kala.hu.ʻa. n. Removal of taboo on fruits of land and sea, as during *makahiki* harvest ceremonies. (Malo 150, 155.)

kā.lai. vt. To carve, cut, hew, engrave, hoe; to divide, as land; to shape a canoe or *(fig.)* an enterprise or intellectual policy; to plan, formulate, budget *(kala 4 + -i,* transitivizer: Gram. 6.6.4). Cf. *kālai'āina, kālaimana'o, kālaimoku, kalakalaiaupuni, paiō kālaimana'o. Kālai 'ana o ke kuke,* tariff policy. **ho'o.kā.lai.** Caus/sim. (PPN *talai,* PEP *taalai.*)

kā.laia. Pas/imp. of *kālai.*

kalai.aha. n. Name of a bird (no data).

kā.lai.'āina. nvs. Political; politics; political economy. *Lit.,* land carving. *Kuhina Kālai'āina,* Minister of Interior.

Ka-la'i-ā.kea. n. Wind name. *Lit.,* the peace spread far. See chant, *hi'ia.* Cf. the island *Ra'i-atea.*

kala.'ihi. vi. Hard, rigid, stormy (see ex., *kūpiliki'i*); oppressive, as of either heat or cold or of an officious person who feels his importance. *Lā'au kala'ihi ia na ke anu* (song), it is a tree made rigid by the cold. *Kūkulu kala'ihi ka lā i Mānā* (saying), established [like] the sun's oppression at Mānā [of a boaster].

kā.lai hō. vt. To hoe.

kā.lai 'ino. v. To plot evil, concoct mischief, contrive secretly to destroy by witchcraft or treachery. *Lit.,* carve evil.

kā.lai ki'i. nv. Sculptor, wood carver; to make statues.

kā.lai lā.'au. nv. Woodcutter; to cut wood.

kalaima, karaima, nvs. Crime; criminal. *Eng. Hana kalaima,* criminal act.

kā.lai.mana'o. nv. Discussion; to discuss. See *paiō kālaimana'o. Ka'u mau kālaimana'o 'ana,* my thoughts, opinions.

kā.lai.moku. nvi. Counselor, prime minister, high official; to perform such office. *Lit.,* manage island.

kalaina. n. A carving, hewing. *Kalaina wāwae,* carved footprints, as in a rock.

kā.lai.'ō.lelo. n. Linguistics (a made-up word).

kā.lai.pā.hoa. n. Name of three woods *(kauila, nīoi, 'ohe)* believed to be the tree forms of two male gods (Kāne-i-kaulana-'ula and Ka-huila-o-ka-lani) and one goddess (Kapo); the wood was considered deadly poisonous at Mauna Loa, Moloka'i only; small pieces of the wood and roots were used in black magic. See *akua hānai.*

kā.lai pō.haku. nv. Stone cutter (2 Sam. 5:11); to carve or hew stone.

kalaiwa. nvt. To drive, as a car; driver; chauffeur. *Eng. Kalaiwa ka'a,* to drive a car; car driver.

kā.lai wa'a. nv. Canoe carver; to build a canoe.

kā.lai.wai.wai. vs. Financial, as a committee or bill.

kalaka. n. 1. Truck (vehicle). *Eng.* 2. Also **karata.** Carat. *Eng.*

kala kahiko. See *kala 6.*

kala.kala. Redup. of *kala 1, 4;* craggy, thorny, knotty. *Fig.,* rough in language, rude, harsh. (PPN *talatala.*)

kala.kalai. Redup. of *kālai;* to carve, cut, hew, hoe, etc., a little at a time; to whittle. See ex., *manumanu. Hana kalakalai,* trifling on inconsequential action, especially of a casual love affair. **ho'o.kala.kalai.** Caus/sim. (PNP *talatalai.*)

kala.kalai.au.puni. nv. Political activity; to do such.

kala.kala.'ihi. Redup. of *kala'ihi. Kalakala'ihi kaha ka lā ma ke kua o Lehua, lūlana ihola ka pihe a ke akua* (UL 238), the sun passes hot at the back of Lehua [Island], stilling the shouts of the gods.

kala.kala.'ula. v. To pick entangled debris, as brownish seaweed, from a fish net.

kā.lā ke'o.ke'o. n. Silver money.

kala.kia, garatia. n. Grace. Probably *Eng. He hō'ole i ke garatia,* denying the grace [of God].

kā.lā kini. n. Twenty dollar gold piece or (And.) silver money.

kala.koa. nvs. Calico; variegated in color, as of croton leaves, or of a pinto horse spotted with several colors; printed cotton cloth (modern); said also of scars left after impetigo. *Eng.*

kā lā.kou. poss. Their, theirs *(a-*form, plural; see Gram. 8.4, 9.6). (PNP *ta'a la(a)tou,* PCP *taa laatou.*)

kala.kū. 1. nvt. To proclaim, announce; announcer. *'O ke kalakū 'oia ka mea kala aku me ka leo nui* (Kep. 149), the *kalakū* is the one who announces in a loud voice. 2. vt. To release, undo, as evil by prayer. 3. vs. Chilled, shivering, bristling. *Fig.,* angry. Cf. *'ōkala. Kalakū Hilo i ka ua,* Hilo is shivering in the rain.

kala kua. 1. n. Sharp horn on dorsal fin. 2. vs. Long ago. See *kala 6,* long ago.

kala.kupua. nvs. Under control of a mysterious or supernatural power; magic. See *kupua.* **ho'o.kala.kupua.** Magic; to do wondrous acts; a magician, enchanter, witchcraft; extraordinary fisherman, elusive thief. *He ikaika ho'okalakupua,* extraordinary or supernatural strength. See *kupua.*

Ka-lā.lani-a-Maka.li'i. n. Star or stars, probably Pleiades. (Kuhelani.) See *Pleiades.*

kala.lau. n. A variety of taro; corm white, yielding gray poi; perhaps originated in Ka-lalau, Kaua'i.

Ka-lalau. n. A valley on northwest Kaua'i, uninhabited and difficult of access in 1977. *Hele i Ka-lalau,* go to Ka-lalau [go astray; see *lalau].*

kala.lea. vs. Prominent, protruding. *Fig.,* haughty, important. *Lālani kalalea,* protruding line [of dorsal fins of sharks above the water]. *Oni kalalea ke kū a ka lā'au loa,* the tall tree stands and projects prominently [of an important person].

kala.leka, kalareta. n. Claret. *Eng.*

kala.lī. nvi. To go quickly, briskly, without noticing anyone; to walk or talk in a brisk, haughty way; proud; such activity. *Noho ana ka makuahine i ka 'olu'olu, hele ke keiki i ke kalalī,* the mother stays in comfort, the child goes away with pride [a riddle: the answer is that the mother is the rough tip of a pandanus key, the child is the soft base made into a lei that is proudly worn]. **ho'o.kala.lī.** Caus/sim.; to hurry.

kala loa. n. Variety of *'ala'ihi,* a fish.

kala maka pi'i. Same as *mākole mākōpi'i* and *kalemakapi'i,* mosses.

kala.mā.lō. n. A grass once used for house thatch (For. 5:656). Also *'emoloa* and *kāwelu.*

kala.mania. vs. Level, even, smooth, as a cliff, calm sea, or sheer surface.

kā.lā maoli. n. Hard currency, real money.

kala.me'ula. Same as *humu'ula,* a stone.

kala.mela, karamela. n. 1. Caramel. *Eng.* 2. Carmelite. *Eng.*

kalamo. n. Calamus. (Mel. 4.14.) (Gr. *kalamos.*)

kala moe. A kind of *kala* fish. (And.)

kala.moho. n. 1. A kind of *awa,* a fish. 2. Cliffbrake *(Pellaea ternifolia),* a short, slender fern, the fronds with short, paired, narrow divisions. It grows in dry, sunny places, as at Kī-lau-ea Volcano. Also *kalamoho lau li'i.*

kala.mona. Same as *kolomona 1-4.*

kalana. 1. n. Division of land smaller than a *moku* or district; county. 2. nvs. Release, forgiveness, etc. Cf. *kala 1. Lā kalana ola,* life-giving sun.

kā.lana. Same as *kānana 1-4.*

kala.na'e. n. A person so lazy that he will work only when watched; to work only when watched. *He kalana'e ho'opau manawa,* one who works only when watched, a waster of time.

kā.lana kā.kau. n. Notebook, tablet.

kalana.kula, taranatula. n. Tarantula. *Eng.*

kala nao. n. Screwdriver.

-kalane'o. ho'o.kala.ne'o. Same as *ho'okanane'o.*

kā.lani, galani. n. Gallon. *Eng.*

kala.nia. vs. Smooth, as the sea.

kala nī'.au. n. A kind of *kala,* a fish.

kala.niā.'ula. Same as *humu'ula,* a stone.

Ka-lani-'ō.pu'u. n. 1. Name of a chief. 2. Var. of *Ka-'ā-wela,* a planet.

kalano.meka, karanometa. n. Chronometer. *Eng.*

kala ola. v. To save life by counter-sorcery.

kala 'ō.pelu. n. A *kala* fish staying in *'ōpelu* schools; when fishermen see it, they know *'ōpelu* are near.

kalapa, sarapa. n. Sulphur. *Eng.*

kā.lā pa'a. n. Coin, as distinguished from *kālā pepa.*
kala.paiki. n. Kind of stone used for octopus lures.
kala.pakī. Double-yolked egg. *Kaua'i.*
kala.pala. n. A kind of *Zebrasoma,* a fish. Cf. *lā 'īpala.*
kā.lā pepa. n. Paper money.
kala.pī. n. The introduced salsify or oyster plant *(Tragopogon porrifolius).* (Neal 860.) *Eng.*
kala poni. See *kala,* sweet potato.
kalapu, kalabu. 1. n. Club, society; club in a deck of cards. *Eng.* **2.** vt. To mop the floor, to club. *Eng. Rare.* **3.** nvt. To strap, tie; a strap. *Eng. E kalapu a'e ā pa'a ka 'ie,* strap the basket securely.
kalapu ho'o.hau.'oli. n. Social club.
kā.lau. To work inefficiently. (AP.)
kā lau. v. To thatch the inside of the house with leaves, especially pandanus leaves. *Lit.,* knot leaf.
kā lā.ua. poss. Their, theirs (*a*-form, dual; Gram. 8.4, 9.6). (PNP *ta'a laaua,* PCP *taa laaua*).
kalauae. Lazy. (And.)
kalau.ipo. n. A moss found in water.
kā.lā (dala) 'ula.'ula. n. Gold money. *Lit.,* red dollar.
kala uli. n. A variety of *kala,* a fish.
kalaunu (karauna). n. Crown, corona, diadem. *Eng.* Cf. also *pua kalaunu.*
kalaunu pī.hopa (bīhopa). n. Bishop's mitre. *Eng.*
kā.lawa. 1. n. Curve, as in the road or along a beach. Also *hālawa.* **2.** vi. To go from one side to another. *Ua kālawa a'ela ia mahope mai,* he went to the back side and back. **3.** n. Intermittent pains in the side of the neck, probably neuritis.
kala.wai. vt. To surround, go around. Also *pō'ai.*
kala wai. See *limu kalawai.*
kā.lā wai.wai. n. Property in terms of dollars, value of property in money.
Kā.lawa-kua. n. *Lua* fighting stroke from the back.
kā.lawa kua. v. To go around to the back from the side.
kā.lawa.lawa. Redup. of *kālawa 1, 2;* crooked, irregular. *Kanu kālawalawa,* to plant here and there.
kā.lawe. vt. To hold and carry, as a pail.
kala.weka. n. Cultivator. *Eng.*
kala wela. n. A black caterpillar with a red dot at the base of the head, probably the sweet potato sphinx moth *(Herse cingulata).* It is destructive, especially of sweet potato leaves.
Kala.wina. vs. Calvinistic, Congregational. *Eng.*
kale. vs. Watery, nearly liquid, as thin poi. Cf. *kakale, kalekale. Waha kale,* to drool at the mouth, talk excessively, gush. **ho'o.kale.** To make liquid (less used than *ho'okakale*). (Probably PCP *tale.*)
kā.lē. vs. Lazy, torpid, sluggish. *He aha ho'i kēia kālē nui wale?* What's the reason for this great disinclination to move about?
kalea. nvi. To choke; to whoop in coughing; whooping cough. Cf. *kunu kalea.* (PNP *kale.*)
kā.le'a. nvi. Prayer calling on the *'aumākua,* family gods, for help; to pray thus. Cf. *le'a,* successful, clear. *Ma nā pule kāle'a, he pule kāhea . . . i nā 'aumākua* (Kep. 55), and *kāle'a* prayers, prayers calling . . . the family gods.
kale 'ai. n. Watery residue on poi-pounding board, which was used to treat *kou* and *milo* wood to be made into utensils, as it was believed to draw out the acid remaining in wood after soaking in the sea; also used to massage babies' bodies lightly in order to strengthen them.
Ka-lehua-wehe. n. Name of a surf at Wai-kīkī. *Lit.,* the opening *lehua,* said to be so named when the taboo on surfing at Wai-kīkī was broken by a young chief from Mānoa who removed his *lehua* lei and gave it to the daughter of Chief Kā-kuhihewa, who had been the only one permitted to surf there; the taboo was broken when the princess accepted the lei.
kalē.huna. n. Root of *koali,* a vine.
Ka-lei-o-manu. n. A *lua* fighting stroke. (Also without *Ka-.*)
kale.kale. 1. Same as *kakale;* to gossip; garrulousness.
ho'o.kale.kale. To make watery or thin; to lie,

deceive; soft, spongy, sagging. **2.** n. Name of the fourth growth stage of the *'ōpakapaka,* a fish, about 60 cm long or more. *He i'a maika'i ke kalekale,* the *kalekale* is a good fish [said of a pleasant conversation, punning on *kūkalekale,* to chat].
kale.kana. n. A red- or yellow-flowered succulent *(Kalanchoe blossfeldiana),* a recent introduction. *Latin.* (Neal 378.)
Kaleke, Tarede. n. Thursday. *Eng. Rare.*
kale.kekona, kalekedona. n. Chalcedony. (Hoik. 21.19.) (Latin *chalcedonius.*)
Kale.kena, Sarekena. n. Saracen. *Eng.*
kale.kio, saredio. n. Sardius. (Puk. 28.17.) (Gr. *sardios.*)
kale.kona. n. Dragon. (Probably Gr. *drakon.*) Also *kelekona.*
kale.konuka, saredonuka. n. Sardonyx, onyx. (Probably Gr. *sardonyx.*)
kā.lele. nvt. Support, railing, arm of a chair; anything used to lean upon; stay (2 Oihn. 9:18); to lean upon, as a support, cane, staff; to trust, depend on, have faith in. **ho'o.kā.lele.** To cause to support; stress. See *hilina'i. Ka ho'okālele 'ana o ka leo maluna o kekahi hua 'ōlelo,* the stress of the voice on certain words.
kale.lē. n. Celery *(Apium graveolens).* (Neal 659.) *Eng.*
kale.lei. 1. vt. To turn toward, listen to, heed respectfully (probably *kā-,* causative + *lele,* 'leap' + *-i,* transitivizer; Gram. 6.6.4). *Kalelei i ka makua,* turn to the parent with respect. **2.** Beautiful, gracious, as a woman. (And.) (Perhaps PPN *lelei.*)
kā.lele kū. vt. To lean on in a rude fashion; to lean heavily; to press down hard.
kā.lele leo. n. Stress mark; stress, emphasis. See *kālele.*
kā.lele mana'o. vt. To stress, emphasize.
kā.lele.muku. vi. To lean back, to lean over the outrigger of a fast canoe to keep the canoe from capsizing. *Fig.,* to relax, lead an easy life.
kā.lele pono. Same as *lele pono.*
kā.lelewa. Redup. of *kālewa 1. 'A'ole na'e i kū ka moku, kālelewa wale nō,* but the ship did not anchor, it just lay off.
Kalema, Karema. n. Lent. *French.*
Kā.lema. n. Salem. *Eng.*
kale.maka.pi'i. Var. of *kala maka pi'i,* a moss. (Kam. 64:105, 115.)
kalena. 1. vt. To stretch, as the hide of an animal to be dried; taut. **2.** *(Cap.)* n. A *lua* fighting stroke.
kā.lena, talena. nvs. Talent. (Mat. 25.15.) *Eng.* See ex., *'ohina.*
kalene.kalio, kalenedario. n. Calendar. Cf. *'alemana-ka.* (Probably Latin *kalendarium.*)
kā.leo. n. Saying, expression.
kale.'oa, saleoa. vt. To sally over; to raise a bet, as in card games. *Eng.*
kalepa. 1. Same as *'ōkupe,* to stumble. **2.** n. Scraper. *Eng.*
kā.lepa. 1. nvt. Trader, merchant, salesman, peddler; to trade, sell as merchandise, peddle; mercantile. *Lit.,* to strike flag, so called because a salesman hoisted a small flag to show that poi or another article was for sale. *Moku kālepa,* trading ship. **2.** vi. To flutter, wave. *Rare.* **3.** Same as *pe'a,* canoe sail, as made of young pandanus leaves.
kā.lepa.lepa. Redup. of *kālepa 1-3;* to flap, wave, flutter, as sails of a ship; to luff.
kale.pona, carebona. n. Carbon. *Eng.*
Kale.poni. n. California. *Eng.* See *pāpale Kaleponi.*
kālewa. 1. vi. To move from place to place; to float or move with the wind, as clouds; to swing; to peddle (formerly of goods carried suspended and swinging on a carrying pole); to lie off, as a ship; unsettled, swinging, hanging, flying. *'Aho kālewa,* trolling line. *Kālewa mauka o Miki-lua* (song), [mist] drifting by the uplands of Miki-lua. (PCP *taalewa.*) **2.** n. Place near the *luakini,* temple, where the ruling chief and a few others stood apart from the multitude.

kale.wai. n. Kind of light-brownish tapa.

kā.lewa.lewa. Redup. of *kālewa.*

Kale.wali, Kalevari. n. Calvary. *Eng.* Cf. *iwi po'o.*

kali. 1. nvi. To wait, loiter, linger, tarry; loiterer; hesitant, slow. *Kali iki,* wait a moment, just a minute. *He kali ko'u waha, ā he kali ho'i ko'u elelo* (Puk. 4.10), I am slow of speech and slow of tongue. **ho'o.kali.** To cause to wait, delay; lingering, slow, as a disease. (PPN *tali.*) **2.** n. Vagina.

kā.lī. n. Spine, spindle, rod; string, as used to thread things upon, as flowers for a lei, or candlenuts for a torch; long vine or runner, as of sweet potato. Cf. *kāili. Kālī i'a,* string of fish.

kalia. 1. Pas/imp. of *kali 1.* **2.** n. A native tree *(Elaeocarpus bifidus),* with long-stemmed, ovate leaves and greenish flowers, formerly used for fire making and constructing grass houses, the bark for cordage. It belongs to the linden family. (Neal 545.) (PNP *tali(a,e).*) **3.** n. A variety of sweet potato.

kali.ali. A tree or plant used in medicine. (And.)

kā.li'i. vt. To hurl spears at a chief as he landed from a canoe, in order that he might exhibit his dexterity and courage in dodging them, almost a ritual.

kalika. n. **1.** Silk. *Eng.* **2.** Mulberry. **3.** A variety of sweet potato. The name may be qualified by *lau ke'oke'o,* white-leafed, and *'ula'ula,* red.

kā.lika, galika. n. Garlic. (Nah. 11.5.) *Eng.* See more common *'aka'akai pūpū.*

kali.kali. Redup. of *kali 1.* Cf. *pākalikali.* (PPN *talitali.*)

Kalika.maka. Same as *Kalikimaka.*

kā.liki. nvt. Corset, girdle, tight waist binder, suspenders; to tie, as a corset. *(kā- 2 + liki,* to tighten.) See ex., *pū'ali 2. Kāliki i pa'a ka pā'ele i ka wa'a* (For. 5:637), so the black paint will adhere to the canoe.

Kaliki.ano, Kristiano. nvs. Christian. (Probably Gr. *Christianos.*)

Kaliki.maka, Karikimaka. nvs. Christmas. *Eng. Mele Kalikimaka,* Merry Christmas.

kā.liki wai.ū. n. Brassiere, corset cover. *Lit.,* breast corset.

kaliko. 1. n. A wild, weedy euphorbia, or wild spurge *(Euphorbia heterophylla* var. *cyathophora),* a tropical American herb about 30 cm high, with green, oval leaves, but with floral leaves white or pink at the base; used medicinally as a purgative. (Neal 516.) **2.** See *hūpō kaliko.*

kaliko.lehua. n. A slow-growing sweet potato. (Kam. 76:27.)

kali.kone, karitone. n. Cretonne. *Eng.*

Kali.laia, Galilaia. n. Galilee. (Gr. *Galilaia.*)

kalili. Same as *nani Wai-'ale'ale.*

kā.lilo. vi. Dying, at death's door; to lie hovering between life and death. *(kā- 2 + lilo,* lost.) **ho'o.kā.lilo.** To cause death; to have the appearance of death.

kā.lilo.lilo. Redup. of *kālilo.* Also *kāninonino. Kālilolilo ho'i kēlā 'ano hānau 'ana,* at that kind of birth, life hangs in the balance. **ho'o.kā.lilo.lilo.** Caus/sim.

kalima. n. Cream. *Eng.*

kalima hamo. n. Face cream.

kalima wai.ū. n. Cream.

Ka-limu-kā-kanaka-o-Mahu.moku. n. A *lua* fighting stroke, named for a *limu* associated with Hanalei, Kaua'i (see *limu-kā-kanaka*). (Also without *Ka-.*)

kalina. n. A waiting. See *kali 1.*

kā.lina. n. **1.** Long vine, as of sweet potato. **2.** Sardine. *Eng. Rare.*

kalio. n. A gusty breeze, perhaps a proper name. (Ii 150.)

kalio.neke, kalionete. n. Clarinet. *Eng.*

kalipa. n. **1.** Caliph. *Eng.* **2.** Also **garipa.** Grippe. *Eng.*

kali.palaoa. n. Cauliflower *(Brassica oleracea* var. *botrytis).* Same as *kāpiki pua,* the common name. *Eng.*

Kalisto, Karisto, Kristo. n. Christ. (Gr. *Christos.*)

kalo. 1. n. Taro *(Colocasia esculenta),* a kind of aroid cultivated since ancient times for food, spreading widely from the tropics of the Old World. In Hawai'i, taro has been the staple from earliest times to the present, and here its culture developed greatly, including more

than 300 forms. All parts of the plant are eaten, its starchy root principally as poi, and its leaves as *lū'au.* It is a perennial herb consisting of a cluster of long-stemmed, heart-shaped leaves rising 30 cm. or more from underground tubers or corms. (Neal 157–60.) Specifically, *kalo* is the name of the first taro growing from the planted stalk; names of generations as listed for Hawai'i Island (Kep. 153) are (1) *kalo:* see ex., *palili,* (2) *'ohā* or *mu'u,* (3) *'a'ae* or *'ae,* (4) *'ōnihinihi,* (5) *kokole,* (6) *pahūpahū. Kō mākou kalo kanu o ka 'āina* (saying), our planted taro of the land [proud and affectionate reference to a chief]. (PPN *talo.*) **2.** Same as *kalokalo.* (PPN *talo.*)

kā.loa. n. **1.** Oval wooden dish or platter. **2.** *(Cap.)* Names of three nights of the month; see below. These nights were sacred to the god Kanaloa. *Kapu Kāloa* (Malo 35), monthly taboo nights of *'Ole Pau* and *Kāloa Kū Kahi.*

Kā.loa Kū Kahi. n. Twenty-fourth day of the Hawaiian month. *Lit., Kāloa* standing first.

Kā.loa Kū Lua. n. Twenty-fifth day of the Hawaiian month. *Lit., Kāloa* standing second.

Kā.loa Pau. n. Twenty-sixth day of the Hawaiian month. *Lit.,* last *Kāloa.*

kalohe. Rare var. of *kolohe.*

kalohi. n. Male sex organ. *Rare.*

kalo kala.koa. n. Caladium *(Caladium bicolor),* a tropical American herb, an aroid grown in gardens for the many color forms of its heart-shaped leaves. (Neal 160–1.) *Lit.,* calico taro.

kalo.kalo. nvi. Conversational prayer (informal appeal and not a memorized prayer or chant); to pray thus. (PPN *talotalo.*)

kalo.kalo leo. n. Best wishes. *Nā kalokalo leo 'ana no ke ola,* best wishes for health.

kā.loke. n. Carrot *(Daucus carota).* (Neal 660–1.) *Eng.*

kā.lole. 1. vs. Straight, of hair. **2.** n. Masseur, masseuse. (These services were usually performed by one of the opposite sex.) *Rare.* **3.** n. Ne'er-do-well, vagabond, one who could not support a wife and hence did not marry. (Malo 201.) **4.** vi. To change, as the voice. *Rare.* Cf. *lole,* to unfold.

kalo.line, kalorine. n. Chlorine. *Eng.*

kā.lolo. n. First liquor that runs off in distillation.

Ka-loloa-mai.au. n. A *lua* fighting stroke. *Lit.,* neat length. (Also without *Ka-.*)

kalo.mela. Calomel. *Eng.*

kā.lona. n. **1.** Old horse, old plug, slowpoke. **2.** *(Cap.)* Sharon. *Eng. Ka loke o Kālona,* the rose of Sharon.

kalo pa'a. n. Cooked unpounded taro. *Loa'a 'oe i ke kalo pa'a* (saying), you got hit by solid taro [i.e., you received a terrible blow].

kalo Pā.kē. Same as *'ili uaua,* a taro.

kā.lua. 1. vt. To bake in the ground oven; to burn brick or lime; baked. *(kā-,* causative + *lua,* pit). **2.** vs. Double, two-stranded. **3.** Same as *kāluālua.* **4.** n. Sinkhole, pit. *Rare.*

kā.lua.lua. Same as *'ālualua,* bumpy.

Ka-lua-o-ka-'ohe. n. Name of a star. *Lit.,* the pit of the bamboo.

Ka-lua-oka.oka. n. Name of a star. *Lit.,* the pit of dregs.

kā.lua pa'a. vt. To bake whole, as a pig. *Kālua pa'a 'ia 'oe e māua i ka imu* (Nak. 67), the two of us will bake you whole in the oven.

Ka-lu'e.lu'e. n. A *lua* fighting stroke. (Also without *Ka-.*)

kalu.hā. n. **1.** Papyrus *(Cyperus papyrus),* a large African sedge, growing in water. (Neal 183–4.) **2.** Some other large sedges (as species of *Scirpus*), if growing in water. **3.** Name of a fish (no data).

kā.luhā.luhā. nvs. Of the sedge family; sedge.

kā.luhe. vs. To droop, bend, vibrate as a leaf in the wind; to ogle, bend and twist, as a coquettish woman; to act the coquette. Cf. *luhe,* to droop. **ho'o.kā.luhe.** To pretend to droop, flirt, etc.; to cause drooping.

kalu.hea. vs. Fragrant.

kā.luheu'a. vs. Drooping with age, as of old ginger plants. (Kep. 93.)

kā.luhi. vs. Flexible, pliable; easily shaken, as a tree branch; easily scattered, as ripe fruit or withered leaves.

kalu.kalu. n. **1.** A fern somewhat like *palapalai*. **2.** A kind of rush or grass like *kaluhā* sedges, famous on Kaua'i. See ex., *kūmoena 2.* (PCP *talutalu*.) **3.** Fine gauze-like tapa made on Kaua'i, reserved for chiefs. *Pale kalukalu* (Isa. 3.19), muffler.

kā.luli. vi. To sway, bend. **ho'o.kā.luli.** To cause to bend and sway.

kaluna. n. Saloon. *Eng.*

kā.lunu. vi. To swell, as with moisture. *Pehu kālunu ka limu o Manu'akepa,* swollen with moisture is the moss of Manu'akepa.

Kalu.oka.oka. n. Unidentified star name, pronunciation uncertain. (Johnson and Mahelona 168.)

kā.lu'u. vi. To sweep and swerve, as a wind gust. *Pōhina luna i ke ao makani kālu'u,* gray above from the clouds swept by wind.

kaluulu. n. A land term of uncertain meaning and pronunciation commonly used in Kona, Hawai'i, in about 1848. Perhaps *ulu* is *'ulu,* breadfruit.

kama. 1. n. Child, person. Cf. *kama'āina. Kama 'ole,* childless, barren. *Kama 'oko'a,* unrelated child or person; offspring different from others in a family. **ho'o.kama.** To adopt a child or adult one loves, but for whom one might not have the exclusive care. (An older adult of either sex might be adopted thus. A child so adopted, termed *keiki ho'okama,* is somewhat comparable to a godchild. An adult so adopted might be called *kaikua'ana ho'okama, kaikaina ho'okama, kaikuahine ho'okama, kaikunāne ho'okama.*) Cf. *hānai, luhi.* (PPN *tama.*) **2.** nvt. To bind, tie, wrap. Used in *'anā'anā* sorcery, this term had three meanings: (1) to seize, bind, make fast; (2) name of a god to whom the appeal was made; (3) the victim. See *kama-i-kahuli-wa'a. Ua kama 'ia ka pū'olo,* the bundle was tied. *Ka make kama o nā kauā* (Kep. 145), the bound death of the outcasts [i.e., they were sacrificed on the altar]. (PCP *tama.*) **3.** n. Cavern, cleft, rock fissure. **4.** vi. To urinate. *Rare.* See *kamahānau.* **5.** Also **tama.** n. Nighthawk. (Oihk. 11.16.)

kā.ma'a. n. Shoe, sandal, slipper, boot; ti-leaf or tapa sandal; shoes. (*kā-,* causative + *ma'a,* to bind.) *Kāma'a 'ole,* barefoot, without shoes. **ho'o.kā.ma'a.** To put on shoes, furnish shoes. (PCP *ta(a)maka*)

kama 'aha. nv. To tie sennit, to bind securely, to form a loop to support a netted calabash; the loop itself; a belt.

kā.ma'a haka.haka. n. Openwork shoes, sandals. *Lit.,* shoes [with] spaces.

kā.ma'a hao. n. Horseshoe. *Lit.,* iron shoe.

kā.ma'a hā.wele. n. Sandal.

kā.ma'a holo pahe'e. n. Skates.

kā.ma'a 'ie. n. Braided sandals.

kā.ma'a 'ili. n. Leather shoes.

kama.'āina. nvi. Native-born, one born in a place, host; native plant; acquainted, familiar. *Lit.,* land child. *Ko'u kama'āina, ka'u malihini,* my host, my guest. *'O wai kou kama'āina o laila?* Who was your host there? *Mamua ke kama'āina, mahope ka malihini,* first the native-born, then the stranger [often said before legendary battles in deciding who was to strike the first blow]. *Ua kama'āina au i kō lākou 'ano,* I am accustomed to their ways. **ho'o.kama.'āina.** To become acquainted with. *E ho'okama'āina!* Make yourself at home [said to strangers].

kā.ma'a laho.lio. n. Rubber shoes, rubbers.

kā.ma'a lā.'T. n. Ancient sandal made of ti leaf, as used for crossing lava.

kā.ma'a loa. n. Runners of a *hōlua* sled. *Lit.,* long shoes.

kā.ma'a lō.'ihi. n. Boot, boots, hip boots. *Lit.,* tall shoes.

kama'a.lua. vt. Familiar with; well acquainted. *Ua kupa ā kama'alua i ke alo o nā haku,* well acquainted with and thoroughly accustomed to the presence of the chiefs.

kā.ma'a pale wā.wae. n. Slipper, slippers. *Lit.,* shoes to protect feet.

kā.ma'a puki. n. Boot, boots.

kā.mae. Same as *mae,* to wilt. (For. 6:369.)

kā.mae. vi. To feign friendliness and good will when there may be hatred; insincere, hypocritical. **ho'o.kā.mae.** Caus/sim.

kama.ehu. n. Strength, energy, firmness of resolution, fixedness of purpose. Cf. *ehuehu,* violence. *Kū kamaehu,* to stand firmly.

kama.'ehu. vs. Brownish, reddish-brown. *Ua 'ōmea 'ia ke kuahiwi, kū kama'ehu 'ōwela ulu wela ka lani* (For. 6:369), the hill is red-brown, the divine one is red-hot, hot waxing [in anger].

kama.'ele. Probably similar to *mā'ele,* numb.

kā.ma'e.ma'e. Redup. of *kāma'e.*

kama.ha'i.kana. Var. of *kāmeha'ikana.*

Ka-mā.hana. n. The constellation Gemini. *Lit.,* the twins. See *Māhana.*

kama.ha.nau. nvi. Urine; to urinate. *Rare.*

kama hā.nau. n. Husband or wife by whom one has had children; woman who has borne a child.

kama.ha'o. vs. Wonderful, astonishing, marvelous, wondrous, surprising, remarkable, incomprehensible. Cf. *pāha'oha'o.* **ho'o.kama.ha'o.** To be or do something wonderful; to take a new and more splendid form.

kama.hele. n. A far-reaching, strong or heavy branch, the main branch. *He lālā kamahele nō ka lā'au kū i ka pali* (saying), he is a far-reaching branch of the tree standing on the precipice [i.e., he is of very high rank because of inaccessibility].

kama hele. n. Traveler.

kama.hine. n. Girl. See *kaikamahine.* (PPN *tama'afafine.*)

kama.hoi. vs. Wonderful, marvelous, splendid; amazed, delighted. Cf. *hoi,* pleasure.

kā.ma'i. nvt. Place of prostitution, brothel; to prostitute. Cf. *kā-,* causative + *ma'i,* genital.

Ka-ma'i-'awa. n. A *lua* fighting stroke. *Lit.,* the bitter sickness. (Also without *Ka-.*)

kama-i-huli-pū. Same as *kama-i-kahuli-wa'a. Lit.,* tie for turning completely.

kama-i-kahuli-wa'a. n. The art of righting a capsized canoe; one man swims under the canoe with a line tied to the attachments of each outrigger boom *('iako)* and the outrigger *(ama);* he pulls on the line while others press down on the *ama* to bring it down under the canoe to right it; water remaining in the canoe is dashed out by jerking the canoe back and forth. *Lit.,* tie for turning canoe.

kama iki. Same as *kamali'i. Lit.,* small child. *Rare.*

Ka-maile Hope. n. Name of a star; probably this and *Ka-maile Mua* were a star pair, such as Castor and Pollux or Alpha and Beta Centauri. *Lit.,* the last *maile* vine.

Ka-maile Mua. See *Ka-maile Hope.*

kama.'i.lio. vi. To talk, converse; conversational. *Kama'ilio 'ana,* conversation. **ho'o.kama.'i.lio.** To talk and lead up to the subject one wishes to discuss.

Kama.'i.'o. n. Name of a star (no data).

-kāmaka. ho'o.kā.maka. Male homosexuality; to practice such. (Malo 67, Emerson note.) *Rare.*

kā.maka.'aha. Same as *kama 'aha. Pa'a i ke kānāwai kāmaka'aha,* bound by the belt law [a reference to the chastity belt of Lu'ukia].

kā.maka.hala. n. All species of a native genus *(Labordia)* of forest trees and shrubs. According to William Hillebrand, three species with orange flowers were used in leis for chiefs. See *nīoi kāmakahala.*

kā.maka.hala lau li'i. n. A native shrub *(Labordia waialealae)* with small leaves 1.3 to 2.6 cm long, found only on Mt. Wai-'ale'ale on Kaua'i. *Lit.,* small-leafed *kamakahala.*

kama kahi. n. Only child, single child.

kama.kama. Redup. of *kama 2.*

-kama.kama, **ho'o.kama.kama.** nvt. To prostitute; prostitute, prostitution, concubine. *Lit.,* to cause children.

kama.kama'i.lio. Redup. of *kama'ilio;* conversation, chitchat; to converse (Hal. 119.46).

kā.maka.maka. 1. vi. Fresh, alive, as of leaves or fresh fish; to lay green leaves on an oven (Kep. 163); mulch *(rare).* **2.** n. Prayer asking forgiveness. Cf. *maka,* fresh, raw, and *kalokalo.* **ho'o.kā.maka.maka.** To ask forgiveness, to seek restoration of friendship. **3.** vt. To tie securely with ropes. Cf. *kama 2.*

kama kāne. n. Son, boy, male child; masculine gender *(rare).*

Ka-maka-Unu.lau. n. Star name, perhaps same as *Unulau.*

kā make loa. See *kā 1.*

kā.maki. n. **1.** Garment. *Eng.* **2.** Also **damaki.** Damask. *Eng.*

kama.ki'i. vs. Lazy, shirking, indolent.

kama.ki'i.lohe.lohe. n. Name of the sacred sennit cord used in taboo services; name of this rigid taboo. *Lit.,* bind, tie, obey. *Hulihia pāpio a i lalo ke alo, hulihia i ka 'aha o kamaki'ilohelohe,* overturned with face down, overturned by the taboo cord *kamaki'ilohelohe.*

kama.kini. vi. To impose a general taboo. *Lit.,* to tie the multitude. *Kamakini ke kapu o ka ula,* a taboo was placed on lobsters.

kamako. n. Tomato *(Lycopersicon esculentum).* (Neal 747–8.) *Eng.* The word used today is *'ōhi'a.* See *'ōhi'a lomi.*

kā mā.koi. v. To fish with a pole. Also *kā mōkoi.*

kā mā.koi kanaka. n. A game in which one player lay rigid or limp on his back while the other player tried to lift him off the ground. *Lit.,* to fish with a human pole.

kamā.kou. Same as *pā'aila, kolī,* castor bean.

kā mā.kou. poss. Our, ours (*a*-form, plural, exclusive; Gram. 8.4, 9.6). (PNP *ta'a matou,* PCP *taa maatou.*)

kama.kū. n. Samshu, a Chinese liquor. *Chinese.*

kama-kū-i-kahi-lewa. n. The sky just below the zenith.

kā.mala. 1. nv. Crude, temporary shelter, hut, booth; stall, as for horses or cattle; to use such a shelter (Kin. 33.17). **2.** vt. To salt lightly to taste; to season.

Ka-malama. n. Name of a star. *Lit.,* the light.

kā.mala.mala. Redup. of *kāmala 2.*

kama.lani. nvs. Child of a chief; a petted child. *Fig.,* finicky, fussy. **ho'o.kama.lani.** To make a favorite of a person, to treat with indulgence, to pamper, spoil, or lavish with favors; to put on finicky airs and mannerisms.

Kama-lei. n. Name of a star.

kama lei. n. Beloved child.

kama lele. n. Orphaned child. (For. 6:393.)

kama.lena. nvs. Yellow, yellow-hued; tapa dyed yellow with *'ōlena.*

Ka-mā.lie. n. Name of a star. *Lit.,* the calm.

Ka-mā.lie Hope. n. Name of a star. *Lit.,* the last calm.

Ka-mā.lie Mua. n. Name of a star. *Lit.,* the first calm.

kama.li'i. n. Children, progeny (only used in the plural; sometimes used without the article *nā*). *Lit.,* small child. *E kōkōwē ana kamali'i i hea?* Where are the children running to? **ho'o.kama.li'i.** Childish. (PNP *tamariki.*)

kamā.li'i. n. Royal child. *(kama + ali'i.)*

kamā.li'i kāne. n. Prince.

kamā.li'i wā.hine. n. Girls, a group of girls.

kamā.li'i wahine. n. Princess (short for *kama ali'i wahine,* female, chiefly child).

kama.lino. n. A sweet potato.

Ka-malo-hei. n. A *lua* fighting stroke.

kama.lole. vt. To look over and reject, to examine and refuse to accept. *Kamalole 'oia i kā mākou 'ai,* he refused our food after looking at it.

kama.loli. n. Slugs and snails in general; *Eulota similaris,* a snail. *Lit.,* sea-slug child.

Ka-malo-o-Lī.loa. n. A *lua* fighting stroke. *Lit.,* the *malo* of Līloa. (This *malo,* of red feathers, is preserved in the Bishop Museum. Also without *Ka-.*)

kā.malū. vt. To do evil to another in secret; to forbid, warn in secret. Cf. *kā. Ua kāmalū mai 'oia iā māua 'a'ole make e hana,* he secretly warned us not to get the idea of doing [that].

kama lua. n. Two children reared together, two close companions.

kama.nā. n. Carpenter.

kama.nā kā.pili moku. n. Shipwright. *Lit.,* carpenter joining ships.

kā.mana.mana. n. A large-leafed weedy plant *(Adenostemma lavenia),* known in many tropical regions, belonging to the daisy family. Whitish flowers are borne in small round heads in open clusters. In Hawai'i, the leaves are used to treat fever. (Neal 829–30.)

kamani. 1. n. A large tree *(Calophyllum inophyllum),* at home on shores of the Indian and western Pacific Oceans, with shiny, oblong leaves to 20 cm long, white flowers much like orange blossoms, and globose green fruits about 2.5 cm in diameter. The wood is hard and was formerly made into calabashes. (Neal 585–6.) Also *kamanu, tamanu.* (PPN *tamanu.*) **2.** vt. Smooth, shiny, polished, as of *kamani* wood. *Kamani ke po'o,* baldheaded. **ho'o.kamani.** To act the hypocrite (Mat. 15.7); to deal falsely (Oihk. 19.11), to disguise oneself (1 Nal. 14.2), to pretend, be insecure; hypocrite; sham. *Ho'okamani 'ole,* honestly, unfeigned.

kama.niha. Same as *ho'okamaniha.* **ho'o.kama.niha.** Sullen, cross, resentful, hostile, uncivil. Cf. *'āniha, niha, maniha.*

kamani haole. n. The false *kamani* or tropical almond *(Terminalia catappa),* a tree from the East Indies grown widely in the tropics for ornament, shade, timber, and edible nuts. It thrives along sandy shores. (Neal 627.) *Lit.,* introduced *kumuni.*

kamani 'ula. Same as *kamani haole.*

kā.mano. n. Salmon. *Eng.*

kā.mano kini. n. Canned salmon.

kā.mano lomi. n. Salted salmon, mashed with onions and tomatoes and a little water.

kā.mano.mano. n. *Cenchrus agrimonioides,* a native grass bearing a spike of spiny flowers, related to *mau'u kukū.* The leaves used in love magic are called *ho'omano.*

kamanu. 1. Same as *kamani 1.* (PPN *tamanu.*) **2.** n. An amberfish or rainbow runner *(Elagatis bipinnulatus),* known also as sea salmon.

kā manu. v. To kill or snare *(kā)* birds. *Rare.*

kā.ma'o. n. Endemic and endangered Kaua'i thrush *(Phaeornis obscurus myadestina).* Kaua'i.

kama.pane. n. Champagne. *Eng.*

Kama-pua'a. 1. A pig demigod. (FS 196–249.) **2.** *(Not cap.)* n. A straggling native shrub *(Hedyotis fluviatilis* var. *kamapuaana),* found in Puna-lu'u Valley, O'ahu, where the pig god stole chickens (FS 197).

kama.puka. nvi. Gadabout who goes from house to house seeking favors, one who lives on others' favors; to do this. *Lit.,* door boy.

kā.mau. 1. vt. To keep on, continue, persevere, last, add a little more. See *kāmau ea, pili kāmau. Kahi pono e kāmau ai ke aho,* some goods to keep life going. *E kāmau iho i ka hoe,* keep paddling. **ho'o.kā.mau.** Caus/sim. (PPN *taamau.*) **2.** vt. and interj. To drink, especially intoxicants; to eat *(rare);* to your health (something like prosit). *Kāmau kī'aha i 'olu, i pahe'e i kō pu'u ke moni* (song), tip the glass and enjoy it, let it glide down your throat as you swallow. **ho'o.kā.mau.** Caus/sim.; to eat, as *'inamona* relish (For. 5:715). *E ho'okāmau mai 'oe,* add a little more. **3.** n. Small taro or sweet potato that serves as food until the major crop matures. **4.** nvt. Whist (card game), trumps; to trump.

kā mā.ua. poss. Our, ours (*a*-form, dual, exclusive; Gram. 8.4, 9.6). (PNP *taʻa maaua*, PCP *taa maaua*.)

kā.mau ea. v. To barely hold on to the breath of life, to endure unpleasant conditions in the hope of better to come; flickering of the breath. **hoʻo.kā.mau ea.** Same as above.

kā.mauli. n. Thank offering to the gods for abundant crops (Malo 199); ceremony to purify warriors returned from war. Cf. *mauli*, seat of life.

kā.mau.lia. Pas/imp. of *kāmau 1, 2.* (FS 87.)

kama.wae. vs. Selective, difficult to please. *Lit.,* person [who] chooses. *Keu kēlā a kahi kanaka kamawae,* what a finicky person that one is.

kama wahine. n. Female person, feminine gender.

kame. n. Chamois. *Eng.*

kā.mehaʻi. **1.** n. A portion of the body (nail, hair, etc., the "bait") of a person believed killed by sorcery, placed in a spot where the supposed murderer will contact it and be killed, as in a bathing place; also used in *kuni* sorcery. (Kam. 64:126–7.) **2.** vs. Unusual, surprising, astonishing. *He mea hou kāmehaʻi kēlā,* that is surprising news. **3.** n. Illegitimate child, since the identity of the father may be unknown.

kā.mehaʻi.kana. n. A multitude of descendants; one of the names for the wondrous *kāmehaʻi)* goddess Haumea, who presided over childbirth. She was thought to have borne numerous children to one husband, then to have gone to Kahiki, later returning as a young woman to bear numerous more children; she did this for many generations; hence her name is synonymous with prolificness. *He hanauna kāmehaʻikana lākou,* they are a generation extremely numerous.

kameki. nvs. Cement. *Eng. Puna kameki,* cement.

kame.leona. n. Chameleon (RSV), mole (KJV). (Oihk. 11.30.) Jackson's chameleon *(Chamaeleo jacksoni)* has been noted on Oʻahu since 1972, the green anole lizard *(Anolis carolinensis porcatus)* since 1950; this is also commonly called chameleon. (McKeown 28–33.) *Eng.* See ex., *kohu 1.*

kā.melo. n. Camel. (Gr. *kamelos*.)

kamelo.paki, kamelopadi. n. Cameleopard, giraffe. *Eng.*

kame.nā. Rare var. of *kamanā.* (Zek. 1.20.)

kameni. Rare var. of *kameki. Eng.*

kameo. n. Cameo. *Eng.*

kamila. n. Camellia. (Neal 583.) *Eng.*

kami.pulu. interj. Damn fool. *Eng.*

Kā.moa. **1.** nvs. Samoa; Samoan (old name was *Haʻamoa).* **2.** *(Not cap.)* n. A seashell, same as *moa.*

kamoe. See *pūpūkamoe.*

kā.moe. **1.** vi. To go straight ahead; to recline, lie flat; flattened. *Ke kāmoe aʻe o nā ao hāʻeleʻele* (Kel. 17), the flat-lying dark clouds. *Kāmoe ka waʻa i ka lae,* the canoe headed straight for the point. *Kāmoe kāna kākau ʻana,* he writes with a slanting hand. **2.** n. Recumbent weft of mat, so called because the strands lie horizontally *(moe);* overcasting stitches that lie neatly in the same direction. Cf. *lei kāmoe, kākū.*

kā.moena. Short for *kaʻa moena.* Rare.

kā.moko. vi. To start a fight or quarrel; to interrupt or interfere when others are speaking. *Inā paha ua lele kāmoko kēlā maluna ou,* he would have leapt aggressively on you.

kā.mō.koi. Same as *kā mākoi.*

kā.moku. vt. To break, cut, as land. **hoʻo.kā.moku.** Caus/sim.

kā.moku.moku. Redup. of *kāmoku.*

kā.mola. vt. To weave, entwine; to tie loosely, as twigs in a sluice gate. Cf. *mola,* to twist loosely.

kā.mola.mola. vi. To increase in numbers, as *ʻanae* fish in schools.

kamola.poki. n. Smallpox. *Eng.* Cf. *kapuahikuni.*

kā.mole. n. **1.** The primrose willow *(Ludwigia octivalvis* syn. *Jussiaea suffruticosa* var. *ligustraefolia),* a perennial herb .6 to 1.2 m high, distributed through the tropics in wet places. Its yellow flowers develop singly at the axils of the narrow leaves. Fruiting capsules are cylindrical, many-seeded. The plant is used medicinally. (Neal 648.) This name may be qualified by the terms *lau liʻi* and *lau nui.* See *alohalua.* **2.** A kind of knotweed *(Polygonum glabrum),* an American perennial herb 30 to 90 cm high, with narrow pointed leaves 5 to 25 cm long and many small flowers and fruits borne in terminal panicles. It belongs in the buckwheat family and grows in damp spots.

kamoli, kamori, samori. n. Psalms (1823 translation; see *halelū).* (Perhaps Eng. *psalmody*.)

kamu. n. Gum. *Eng.*

kā.mū. Rare var. of *mū,* silent.

kā.muku. **1.** vt. To diminish, decrease, lessen, use sparingly; less developed, decreased. **2.** *(Cap.)* n. A *lua* fighting stroke.

kā.muku.muku. Redup. of *kāmuku 1. Kāmukumuku ka ʻai a kākou,* our taro is growing less thriftily.

kamumu. nvi. Crunching sound, thud, thump, as of footsteps; rumbling, clatter; to crackle, crunch; roar, as of approaching rain; rustling, as wind (see ex., *aheahe).* Cf. *mumu.*

kā.mū.mumu. Redup. of *kamumu.*

kana. **1.** num. Tens (usually compounded with numbers from three to nine to indicate 30 to 90). (Gram. 10.3.) *Kanaiwa,* ninety. *Nā kana ʻekā* (Kep. 159), tens of banana hands. *ʻO ka waʻa kana koʻokahi* (Nak. 40), ten one-man canoes. **2.** Idiom that follows perfective verb marker *i* and poss. *o,* and is followed by directionals; it is preceded by negatives. Also see *kaʻe 2.* Extremely, beyond compare, without limit (in both favorable and pejorative senses). *ʻAʻohe i kana mai ka nui,* ever so huge. *ʻAʻole o kana mai kāu hana!* What a lot of work you have to do! There's no limit to your work! What dreadful things you do [in anger]. *ʻAʻole o kana mai ka uʻi!* How perfectly beautiful! **3.** n. Horizontal support in houses for carrying poles *(ʻauamo).* **4.** *(Cap.)* n. A stroke in *lua* fighting, for chiefs. **5.** *(Cap.)* A demigod (HM 464–77.) See *Kapuaʻi-o-Kana.* **6.** Rare var. of *pana,* to shoot. **7.** n. Ton. *Eng.* Also *kona.*

-kana. Nominalizer noted in *pale,* to ward off, and *palekana,* safety; *pili,* to cling, and *pilikana,* relative. (PPN *-tanga*.)

kāna. **1.** poss. His, hers, its (*a*-form; see Gram. 8.4, 9.6). (PNP *tana, taʻana;* PEP *taʻana;* PCP *taana.*) **2.** Also **Sana.** n. Saint (in proper names). Kāna Lui, Saint Louis. **3.** n. Canna. *Eng.*

kanaaho, kanaho. nvi. Relieved after a struggle; feeling of ease or relief after surviving sickness or danger; joy over escape; rest after violent exertion or danger; breathless arrival; refuge; one convalescing or resting after sickness or danger; to convalesce or rest; to find refuge. Cf. *aho,* breath, For. 4:71. *Wahi kanaaho,* sanctuary, place of refuge. *E kanaaho au ma ka hoʻomalu ʻana o kou mau ʻēheu* (Hal. 61.4), I find refuge in the shelter of your wings. **hoʻo.kanaaho.** Caus/sim.

Kana.ʻana. n. Canaan. (Heb. *Kenaʻana* or Gr. *Kanaʻan;* for Hawaiian glottal stop, Gram. 2.9.3.)

kā.naʻe. **1.** vs. Very fragrant, as of the *naʻenaʻe,* shrubby composites. *Kānaʻe hoʻi ke ʻala o ka pua,* the fragrance of the flower is very sweet. **2.** Var. of *kālaʻe,* clear.

kā.nae.nae. nvt. Chanted supplicating prayer; chant of eulogy or praise (the chanter hesitates at regular intervals to recover breath; tone variation is greater and pitch may be higher than in the *olioli);* to pray thus; to sacrifice; dedication. *He kānaenae aloha naʻu iāʻoe, ē Laka ē, ē Laka ē, e hoʻoulu ʻia* (hula prayer), this is a prayer I lovingly offer to you, O Laka, O Laka, inspire! (See similar ex., *ʻūlāleo.) Pule kāneanae ola,* prayer supplicating restoration of life.

kana.hā. **1.** num. Forty. **2.** *(Cap.)* n. Star name (no data). (Kuhelani.)

Kana.hai. nvt. Shanghai; to shanghai. *Eng.*

kana.haʻi. vt. To diminish, lessen. *Kanahaʻi anei ka inu lama?* Are fewer alcoholic drinks being drunk?

ho'o.kana.ha'i. Small, depressed, stunted, humble, cautious, moderate; to lessen.

kana.ha'u. Rare var. of *kanaha'i.* **ho'o.kana.ha'u.** Caus/sim.

kanahe. n. Porous coral.

-kanahē. ho'o.kana.hē. To drive or urge forward, accelerate, hurry, quicken.

kana.hiku. num. Seventy.

kanāho. See *kanaaho.*

kana.hua. vs. Humped up, bent, stoop-shouldered. Cf. *āhua,* heaped up. **ho'o.kana.hua.** To rise up, as a whale's back in the water; bent, humpbacked, disobedient; bend, crook.

kā.na'i. vs. Smooth, calm, of the sea. *Rare.*

kana.ie. Same as *ho'okanaie.* **ho'o.kana.ie.** Conceited, vain, overbearing.

kana.i'i. Same as *kā'i'ī. Kanai'i ka na'au,* hard-hearted. *Kanai'i noho'i ka leo,* what a harsh voice.

kanalo. n. A variety of taro.

kā.nai.oa. vs. Fierce, ferocious. *Rare.*

kana.iwa. num. Ninety.

kanaka. 1. nvs. Human being, man, person, individual, party, mankind, population; subject, as of a chief; laborer, servant, helper; attendant or retainer in a family (often a term of affection or pride); human sacrifice (FS 111); physique; human, manly, pregnant, inhabited; Hawaiian; private individual or party, as distinguished from the government. (Singular; cf. the plural, *kānaka.*) *Ko'u kanaka,* my helper, servant, etc. *Ka'u kanaka,* my man selected for a purpose. *Kanaka nō!* A real man! Well done! People have come. *Mahalo 'ia ke kāne i ke kanaka maika'i* (FS 205), the man was admired for his handsome physique. *He kanaka maoli,* a true human, a mortal. *I wawā 'ia nō he hale kanaka, na wai e wawā ka hale kanaka 'ole?* (name song for Ka'ahu-manu), the inhabited house sounds with voices, who would talk loud in an uninhabited house? **ho'o.kanaka.** Manly, human, courageous; to become a servant or helper; to assume human shape, as a child in the womb. See *ho'okanaka makua. E ho'okanaka, be a man. E ho'okanaka 'oukou, 'a'ole e ho'onāwaliwali kō 'oukou mau lima* (2 Oihn. 15.7), be strong, let your hands not be weak. (PPN *tangata.*) 2. n. After end of the float of a canoe. 3. n. Clitoris. 4. Also **Kanada.** *(Cap.)* nvs. Canada; Canadian. *Eng.*

kā.naka. Plural of *kanaka 1.* (PNP *taangata.*)

kanaka 'ē. Foreigner, outsider, stranger, heathen (Mat. 6.7).

kanaka hana. n. Worker, servant.

kanaka helu ukana. n. Shipping clerk.

kanaka ho'o.lewa. n. Undertaker.

kanaka lele. n. Angel. *Lit.,* flying person. *Rare.*

kanaka.loa. n. Name used by the medical *kahuna* for *'uhaloa,* a weed. *Lit.,* tall person.

Kana.kaloka. Santa Claus. *Eng.*

kana.kalū, kanagaru. n. Kangaroo. *Eng.*

kanaka.mai.ka'i. n. The *'ilima* flower used medicinally. (Neal 553.) *Lit.,* good person.

kanaka makua. nvi. Adult, mature person; to behave or speak as an adult; to become adult, or to obtain the strength and maturity of an adult. *Kanaka makua kēia keiki 'u'uku,* this little boy behaves as an adult. **ho'o.kanaka makua.** To act as an adult, to act mature. *Ko'u ho'okanaka makua 'ana,* my coming of age.

kanaka maoli. n. Full-blooded Hawaiian person.

kanaka noho meha.meha. n. Person living alone, hermit.

kana.kē. n. Candy. *Eng.*

kana.kē 'ele.'ele. n. Licorice. *Lit.,* black candy.

kana.kē pā.nini, kana.kē pī.lali. n. Cactus candy.

kana.kolu. num. Thirty.

kana.lani. num. In great numbers, numerous; abundance. (For. 6:398.) See ex., *'api'api 3.*

kana.le'o. vt. To deceive, mislead, feign, act the hypocrite; deceitful. **ho'o.kana.le'o.** Caus/sim.

Kana.lia. n. Star name (no data). (Kuhelani.)

kana.li'i. vs. Stunted, wee. Cf. *'anali'i.*

kana.lima. num. Fifty.

kana.li'o. vi. To stagger, zigzag, walk like a drunkard or very sick person.

Kana.loa. 1. A major god. (PPN *Tangaloa.*) 2. *(Not cap.)* n. A sea shell (Phasianelidae). 3. *(Not cap.)* n. Young stage of the *hou,* a fish. 4. n. A name for Kaho'olawe Island. (PH 75.) 5. *(Not cap.)* See *pahu kanaloa.* 6. *(Not cap.)* vs. Secure, firm, immovable, established, unconquerable. *Ua kanaloa ka nohona i kēia wahi,* residence is securely established at this place. 7. *(Not cap.)* n. Poetic term for food. *Rare.*

Kana.loa Kū Kahi. Same as *Kāloa Kū Kahi.*

kanalu. n. Priests of Kū serving in the *luakini* temple, said to be named for the first such priest. (And.)

kā.nalua. nvi. Doubtful, undecided, dubious, uncertain; to doubt, hesitate, distrust; reluctance, doubt, hesitation. Members of the Territorial legislature abstained from voting by saying, "kānalua." **ho'o.kā.nalua.** To cause doubt. *Ho'okānalu 'ole 'ia 'o kona 'oia'i'o,* there is no cause to doubt its truth.

Kana.me'e. n. Name of a star, said to be the tutelary star of Chief Ka-umu-ali'i of Kaua'i.

ka.nanā. n. An early growth stage of the fish *'ahi;* it is lighter in color. See *'ahi kananā, he aha sananā,* and *nanā.*

kā.nana. 1. nvt. Sieve, strainer; to strain, as kava in fibers; to filter, winnow (Ruta 3.2); to sift, as flour. Also *kālana.* 2. Writing paper, stationery. Also *kālana. Ua mākaukau ka 'īnika ame ke kānana,* the ink and writing paper are ready. 3. vt. To examine one's moral character. Same as *kālana* but more frequent. 4. See *iwi kānana.*

kā.nana 'ai. nvt. Poi strainer, cloth through which poi is strained; strained poi; to strain, as poi.

kā.nanana. Rare redup. of *kānana 1–4.*

kā.nana palaoa. nv. Flour sifter; to sift flour.

-kana.ne'o. ho'o.kana.ne'o. To disregard, as instruction, warning, danger, careless of danger, indifference to discomfort or health. See ex., *pu'umake. Ho'okanane'o ho'i ka hele i ka pō, ā la'a lā i ke anu,* insisting on going out at night against advice, then got a cold.

kana.nuha. vs. Stubborn, sulky. Cf. more common *nuha. Ke lilo nei Ha'i-kū 'ekalesia kananuha,* Ha'i-kū is becoming a stubborn church. **ho'o.kana.nuha.** To cause sulkiness; dull of hearing (Heb. 5.11).

-kana'ō. ho'o.kana.'ō. In doubt; to hesitate.

-kanao'e. ho'o.kana.o'e. Same as *ho'okanahē.*

-kana'oi. ho'o.kana.'oi. Conceited, feeling that one is superior to everybody else. Cf. *'oi,* best.

kana.ono. num. Sixty.

kana.papiki. interj. Son of a bitch. *Eng.*

kanapi. vi. To snap. *Eng.*

kana.pī. n. Centipede *(Chilopoda).*

kana.pu'u. vs. Uneven, as a surface of a table or road. Cf. *pu'u,* lump.

kā.nā.wai. nvs. Law, code, rule, statute, act, regulation, ordinance, decree, edict; legal; to obey a law; to be prohibited; to learn from experience. *Fig.,* ti leaves, as used in religious ceremonies as a plant respected by spirits. Since some early laws concerned water *(wai)* rights, some have suggested that the word *kānāwai* is derived from *wai,* water; this seems doubtful in view of the many ancient edicts of gods that have no relation to water (also cf. *wai 4* and derivatives). Perhaps the most famous *kānāwai* is the *kānāwai kai'okia* promulgated by the god Kāne after the flood of Kahinali'i, promising that ever afterwards the sea would be separated *('okia)* from the land (i.e., not encroach on the land). Persons swore oaths by this and other *kānāwai.* The *kānāwai* of Kū was that no one might lean backwards *(kīki'i)* during ceremonies; that of Kū-kaua-kahi that no one might bend forward *(kūpou);* that of Kānehe-kili, that no one might whisper *(hāwanawana)* during ceremonies; that of Ka-hō-ali'i, that the white *kā'upu* bird *(kā'upu kea)* must be used as his symbol during the *makahiki*. See below and Kam. 64:13–17 and note 9. *'Aha kau kānāwai*, legislature, law-making body. *Kānāwai (ho'opa'i) kalaima (karaima)*, penal code, criminal code. *Buke kānāwai ho'okahi*, sole statute law. *Kānāwai e pololei ai ka ho'okolokolo 'ana*, code of procedure; *lit.*, law which is correct in holding court. *Kānāwai o Pelekania (Beritania) i kākau puke 'ole 'ia*, British common law; *lit.*, law of Britain not written in a book. *Mamuli o ke kānāwai*, according to law; legal. *Ho'olilo i mea pono ma ke kānāwai*, to legalize, make lawful. *Ho'olohe 'ole i ke kānāwai*, lawless. *Ua kānāwai au i ka hele malaila*, I have learned not to go there. *E hele pū me ke kānāwai*, to go legally (with ti leaves). *Nā Kānāwai he 'Umi*, the Ten Commandments. *Kū 'ole i ke kānāwai*, illegal, contrary to law. **ho'o.kā.nā.wai.** To impose a law, especially to vow not to associate with certain persons or places until certain conditions are fulfilled. *Ho'okānāwai akula ia i kona wahi i hele ai, 'a'ole e hele hou; ho'okānāwai akula i nā makamaka*, he made a vow not to go again to that place; he made a rule not to associate with the friends.

kā.nā.wai hī.meni. n. Notes on the scale. *Rare.*

kā.nā.wai ho'o.pa'i kalaima. n. Penal code. *Lit.*, laws for punishing crime.

kā.nā.wai ho'o.pono.pono hou. n. Revised statute.

kā.nā.wai kai.'okia. See *kai'okia, kānāwai.*

kā.nā.wai kā.kau 'ole 'ia. n. Unwritten law, common law.

kā.nā.wai kī.wila. n. Civil laws or code.

kā.nā.wai koa. n. Military law, martial law.

Kā.nā.wai Kumu. n. Organic Act.

Kā.nā.wai Lua. 1. n. Book of Deuteronomy. *Lit.*, two laws, i.e., a repetition of the laws of Moses [the Hawaiian term is a translation of the Latin and Greek names for this book, *Deuteronomium* and *Deuteronomion*]. **2.** *(Not cap.)* Rules for *lua* fighting.

kā.nā.wai ma'a.mau. n. Common or customary law.

kā.nā.wai mana'o.'i'o. n. Article of faith, dogma.

kā.nā.wai mele. n. Musical notes.

kā.nā.wai 'ole. nvs. Lawless, anarchy.

kā.nā.wai pili lau.lā. n. Statute at large.

kana.walu. num. Eighty.

kana.wao. n. **1.** Small endemic trees *(Broussaisia arguta)*, with large, oval, toothed leaves, in the saxifrage family; the small flowers and berries are arranged in wide, convex clusters. The flowers of one form have bluish-green petals; of another, red, another white. An old belief was that eating the fruit helped in fecundity; the increase of chiefs was compared to a fruiting *kanawao*. (Neal 380.) Varieties are qualified by the colors *ke'oke'o* and *'ula'ula*. Also *kupuwao, piohi'a, akiahala, pū'aha nui.* **2.** Var. name for *nāwao I*, a taro. **3.** Hard, striped pebble, found in streams and used in slingshots and as sinkers. **4.** An insect.

kana.wao ke'o.ke'o. Same as *ha'iwale*, a shrub.

kā.nawe. vs. Poor, thin, just able to walk. Cf. *hīnawe*, feeble.

kane. Tinea, a fungus skin disease. Cf. *kakane.* (PPN *tane.*)

kāne. 1. n. Male, husband, male sweetheart, man; brother-in-law of a man; male, masculine; to be a husband or brother-in-law of a woman. See *kāne o ka pō. Pipi kāne*, bull. *Kai kāne* (Kep. 183), strong sea. *Hana keiki kāne*, man's work requiring strength. **ho'o.kāne.** To behave as a male; masculine; to adopt a man as a platonic friend, said of a woman (the relationship cements friendship between the relatives of both participants); to offer to become husband or sweetheart. Cf. *ho'owahine. Ua ho'okāne aku nei mākou nāu* (For. 4:59), we have obtained a husband for you. (PPN *ta'ane.*) **2.** *(Cap.)* n. The leading of the four great Hawaiian gods: see HM 42–66. (PCP *Taane.*) **3.** *(Cap.)* n. Name of the 27th night of the lunar month. *Kapu*

Kāne (Malo 35), monthly taboo nights of Kāne and Lono. **4.** *(Cap.)* n. Name of a sacred star, seen by priests as portending great misfortune, as the death of a chief; perhaps a variable like Mira or Algol, or even a nova. **5.** n. Name given at 'Ewa, O'ahu, for the Tahitian banana known as *polapola* and *hē'ī.*

kanea. nvs. Loss of appetite; to have no appetite; distaste for food. **ho'o.kanea.** To cause loss of appetite.

kane.ha'i. Var. of *kanaha'i*, to diminish.

kāne.hoa. See *pūkiawe*, native shrubs.

Kāne-hono-i-ka-pa'a. n. Name of the taboo imposed during the nights of Kāne. *Lit.*, Kāne bind firmly.

kāne ho'o.kāne. n. Platonic husband, an old Hawaiian relationship. Cf. *wahine ho'owahine. Lit.*, pretended husband.

kāne ho'o.moe. n. Husband acquired by matchmaking, not a love match.

kāne i ka 'ili. n. True husband. (FS 117.) *Lit.*, husband in the skin.

kane.ika.lau. n. Combination of the juices of *'ōlena* root and *mānienie* grass used medicinally.

Kaneka, Saneta. 1. nvs. Saint; holy. *Maria Saneta, makuahine o ka Akua*, Holy Mary, mother of God. *Eng.* **2.** *(Not cap.)* n. Garnet. *Eng.*

kane.kalū, kanegaru. n. Kangaroo. *Eng.*

kane.kanea. 1. Redup. of *kanea.* **2.** vs. Shaved smooth, as the head. Cf. *nea*, bare.

kā.neki. vi. Filled to overflowing, as with water. *Fig.*, anger. *Ua hele ka wai a kāneki wale i ka pua*, the water reaches the very flowers. *Kāneki i ka pilikia*, filled with trouble.

Kane.kopa. n. Vancouver. *Eng.*

kāne.kō.pā. n. A kind of foreign cloth.

kāne.kupua. n. Mock spear battle fought on arrival of chiefs.

kanela. n. Canal. *Eng.*

kāne make. nvs. Widowed; dead husband. *Wahine kāne make*, widow.

kāne makua. n. Elder brother or elder male cousin in the senior line of a woman's husband. Cf. *kāne 'ōpio.*

kāne male (mare). n. Married man, bridegroom, husband to whom a woman is legally married.

kāne manu.ahi. n. Common-law husband, lover.

kanene. vi. To fluff out the feathers, as birds do in hot weather. *Rare.* Cf. *nenene.*

Kāne-ne'e.ne'e. n. A place on the bird island Ka'ula and a name for the west. (Kam. 76:4–5.)

kane.nene. Redup. of *nene.* (Kep. 89.)

kāne noho pū. n. Common-law husband.

kāne.'ohe. n. A variety of sweet potato, named for the place on windward O'ahu. The name may be qualified by the colors *ke'oke'o* and *'ula'ula.*

kāne o ka pō. n. Spirit husband of the night (it was believed that a child born of such a mating might resemble an eel, lizard, shark, or bird, or might have supernatural powers; sometimes sickness or death followed his nightly visits: Nānā 120–2). Cf. *wahine o ka pō.*

kāne 'ole. nvs. Spinster, one without a husband; without a husband or lover.

kāne 'ō.pio. n. Younger brother or younger cousin in the junior line of a woman's husband. Cf. *kāne makua.*

kane.pa'a. vt. To hold a marble at a line just before shooting.

kāne.pa'ina. n. **1.** Click beetle or bug (Elateridae). **2.** *(Cap.)* Name of a god that sometimes took the form of a click beetle.

kāne wahine make. nvs. Widower. *Lit.*, man [with] dead wife.

kani. 1. nvi. Sound or noise of any kind; pitch in music; to sound, cry out, ring, peal, jingle, tinkle, toll, whir, resound, reverberate; roar, rumble, crow, resonance; to strike or tick, of a clock, to sing, as birds; voiced. Cf. *leokani. Ke kani 'ana o ka leo*, the sound or tone of the voice, intonation. *Kani nā pele* (song), jingle bells.

Kani ka pila, play music. *Kani 'ōkalakala,* screech. *Kani ka moa,* the rooster crows. *Kani ā hia'ā,* to grieve and moan so sorrowfully that one cannot sleep. *Kani ā 'u'ina,* a flash of lightning followed immediately by a peal of thunder. *Leo kani,* sweet or pleasant voice. *Mākaukau, kī, kani,* ready, aim, fire. *Kani ka papa wa'a,* the canoe floor sounds [a poetic expression applied to aged persons just before death, as the dead were sometimes laid in canoes which were placed in burial caves]. *'Umi minuke i koe, kani ka hola 'ewalu,* ten minutes before eight; *lit.,* ten minutes remaining strikes the hour eight. *Ua pūhā kēia lā'au, ke kani 'ia ala e ka manu* (Nak. 36), this tree is rotten, [it] is being made to sound by the bird [said of a tree not suitable for a canoe: see *'elepaio 1*]. **ho'o.kani.** To play a musical instrument or drum; to cause to sound, honk; to crack, as a whip; to ring up on the telephone. See ex., *pila 1.* *Ho'okani pono,* to tune, as a musical instrument. *Ho'okani pihe,* to shout, roar, wail, as by a crowd. (PPN *tangi.*) **2.** vs. Strong, hard, tough. Cf. *kani wahie, wīkani. He po'e lākou i kani a kani ā ua noho wahine ho'i,* they are a people whose bones have hardened and who are married to women. *Pūko'a kani 'āina,* a hard rock of land; *fig.,* a tough fighter. **3.** vt. To satisfy a need, particularly thirst; to drink. Cf. *Kani-lehua. Kani 'ai,* to eat. *E 'eleu lākou a'e kākou, e kani wai ā ho'i a'e* (chant for Ka-pi'o-lani), let's all hurry together, drink water and go home. (And.)

kani.a'ā. Same as *kaniā'au.*

kani.a'ā.hia. Pas/imp. of *kania'ā.*

kani.'ā.'au. vi. To mourn, grieve, moan, wail, cry; to wander about in grief and affliction. Cf. *kania'ā* and *'ā'ā 3.*

kani.'ahē. vi. To giggle or laugh softly, as with delight. (Kep. 93.) Cf. *hehē,* loud laughter. *Rare.*

kani.'ā.'ī. n. Adam's apple, larynx, trachea, neck, throat. *Lit.,* hard neck. *Ā 'o kō lākou kani'ā'ī he hale lua hāmama* (Hal. 5.9), their throat is an open sepulcher.

Kani.ha'a.lilo. n. Name of a star. *Lit.,* lost sound.

kani.hapa. n. Half-step interval in music, a minor second.

Kā.nihi. n. A stroke in *lua* fighting.

kani.hia. Pas/imp. of *kani 1. Ka po'e nāna ke ali'i e noho nei, e noho kanihia aloha a'e ana iā'oe* (chant for Kua-kini), the people whose chief is present express their great affection for you. (PPN *tangisia.*)

kani.kani. **1.** Redup. of *kani 1-3;* chattering, noisy, jingle. *Kanikani pihe akula ka 'aha,* the crowd shouted loudly. **ho'o.kani.kani.** Redup. of *ho'okani;* also a diminutive: *ka ho'okanikani mai o kēia leo 'ūlili li'ili'i (ka uē keiki),* the sobbing of the voice of the small tattler bird (a child's cry). (PPN *tangitangi.*) **2.** n. Jackknife, from the sound of opening and shutting *(rare);* knife made of hoop iron. **3.** Name of a particular famine. (And.)

kani.kani.'ā.'ula. **1.** n. Insomnia. **2.** vi. To mourn in chanting. *E 'ai aku 'oe i 'ole ho'i kēlā e kanikaniā'ula wale mai,* eat or he will mournfully chant. **3.** *(Cap.)* n. Name of a star.

kani.kani.hia. Pas/imp. of *kanikani.*

kani kanono. n. Sound of a loud explosion or blow; bang, as of a gun.

kani.kau. **1.** nvt. Dirge, lamentation, chant of mourning, lament; to chant, wail, mourn. *Ke Kanikau,* The Lamentations (Biblical). **2.** *(Cap.)* n. Name of a star (no data). (Kuhelani.)

kani.kē. nvi. Tolling of a bell, dingdong, sound of clashing objects; to toll, clang, clash. See ex., *kū'ikē. Kanikē kani kō ka pele,* the bell dingdongs, reverberates.

kani.kela, kani.kele. n. Consul. *Eng. Wahi noho o ke kanikela,* consulate.

kani kō. nvi. Long drawn-out peal of a bell; to ring thus, reverberate.

kani kohā. nvi. Sudden loud sound, as the report of a ri-

fle or pop of a paper bag, loud cry of a bird; to sound thus.

kani.kō.kō. Same as *ka'ikōkō,* probably by analogy with *kaniko'o.*

kani.ko'o. nvs. **1.** Aged person; aged, so old that one walks with a cane [a favorite metaphor]. *Lit.,* sounding cane. Cf. *ka'ikōkō.* **2.** *(Cap.)* n. Rain that accompanies the Ko'olau wind. (For. 6:474.) *Lit.,* cane-tapping.

kani ko'o.ko'o. Rare var. of *kaniko'o.*

kani.lā.hulu.hulu. n. Name of a temple prayer.

Kani-lehua. n. Name of a mistlike rain famous at Hilo. *Lit.,* [rain that] *lehua* flowers drink. [An alternate interpretation is "rain that makes *lehua* flowers rustle."] See ex., *pāwehi. Hilo Hanakahi, i ka ua Kani-lehua* (song), Hilo, [land of] chief Hanakahi and of the rain that gives drink to *lehua* flowers.

kani mo'o.puna. vi. To become a grandparent, the state of being a grandparent; grandchild's wail.

kanini. **1.** Rare var. of *konini.* **2.** To recover from sickness (And.), perhaps a var. of *kaninonino.*

kā.nino.nino. Same as *linolino 1* and *kālilolilo. Ihu kāninonino,* mercurial, changeable.

kā.ni'o. **1.** n. Rods supporting thatch purlins of a house. **2.** vs. Striped, streaked, usually crosswise rather than lengthwise, as of a brownish pig or dog with darker brown stripes. **3.** n. A striped watermelon. **4.** n. A striped *'o'opu,* a fish. **5.** n. A variety of taro. **6.** n. A variety of sugar cane.

kani.piha. n. Whole-step interval in music, a major second.

kani.puka. n. Door, gate, entrance. *Rare.*

kaniu. nvs. Lump under the skin; to raise a lump.

kani.'ū. nv. Groan, moan, grunt; to cause grunting, moaning, groaning, as from pain; to exclaim "mh" (a prolonged "m" sound) as in delight; such an exclamation; to cause such an exclamation.

kani.'uhū. nvi. Sigh, moan, sorrow, grief, complaint of troubles and pains; to complain, sigh, bemoan; to coo, mourn, as a mourning dove. *Lit.,* sound groan. *Kani'uhū a ho'omanoninia nō kō kākou lāhui, no ke emi 'ana mai,* grief and sorrow for the decreasing of our race.

kani.uli. vi. To purse the lips, as in disapproval or disagreement.

kani.'ū.'ū. **1.** Redup. of *kani'ū.* **2.** *(Cap.)* n. Star name (no data). (Kuhelani.)

kani wahie. n. Hard, ringing sound, as of a tree or log being struck. *Fig.,* hard wood.

kani.wā.wae. n. Infantryman, infantry. *Lit.,* sound of feet.

kano. n. **1.** Large, hard stem, as on a banana bunch, sweet potato, or pandanus fruit; shank of fishhook (Kam. 76:77); tool handle; crosspiece on a *lā'au kia,* bird-catching pole; bones of the lower arm or lower leg; male erection; stiffening, hardening; hard, stiff. **ho'o.kano.** To harden; to form a tuber, as of sweet potato. Cf. *kakano.* **2.** Same as *uma,* a wrestling game. **3.** Cubit (1941 Bible uses *kubita*).

-kano. **ho'o.kano.** Haughty, proud, conceited, rude, disdainful of others, insolent, vain; to act superior. *'Ai ho'okano,* proud eating; to eat food that one has not helped prepare.

kā.noa. n. Bowl, as for kava; hollow of land, pit *(rare);* circular. (PPN *taano'a.*)

kano.ā.lupe. Same as *ka'iālupe.*

Ka-noe-Maka.li'i. n. Name of a star. *Lit.,* the Pleiades mist.

kanoenoe. To blow, of the tradewind. (And.) Cf. *noe,* tradewind.

kano.kano. Redup. of *kano 1.*

-kanokano. **ho'o.kano.kano.** Redup. of *ho'okano.*

kano.kaomi. n. The shaft to which the presser foot is attached on a sewing machine.

kanono. **1.** vi. To whack, bang, smack, as of a blow; to receive such a resounding blow. *Kanono akula kou lae,* your forehead is smacked with a blow. *Kanono kona* *ho'opa'i,* he was lambasted a severe penalty; his punishment was a blow. **2.** n. Red chicken.

kā.nowa. Var. spelling of *kānoa.*

kanu. nvt. To plant, bury; planting, burial. *Fig.,* hereditary. *Mea kanu,* crops, plants. *Kanu papahu wili,* to set solidly into the ground by twisting in and then tamping with a post; *lit.,* plant stick twist. *He mo'opuna na kō lākou haku kanu,* he was a grandson of their hereditary lord. **ho'o.kanu.** To cause to plant or bury. (PPN *tanu.*)

kanū. vs. Sullen, sulky, stubborn.

kanu.'e'e.'ina. vi. To smooth down, as the wet, ruffled feathers of a bird; to preen; to tamp and smooth. *Rare.*

kanu.kanu. Redup. of *kanu. E kanukanu a'e ana au i nā nīoi a mākou.* I'm planting our chili peppers.

kā.nuku. n. Funnel (formerly made of gourd or coconut shell and used for filling water containers), spout, beaker. Cf. *nuku,* beak. *Kānuku 'aila,* oil can.

Ka-nuku-o-ka-puahi. n. Hyades. *Lit.,* the opening of the fireplace.

kanulu. nvi. Roaring, vibrating sound, as of distant thunder. *Kanulu ho'i ka leo o ka hekili,* the roaring sound of thunder. (PPN *ngulu.*)

kanunu. vs. Large physically, both tall and stout; husky. *Kanunu ho'i kēlā keiki,* how large that child is. *He he'e kanunu,* an enormous octopus.

kao. **1.** nv. Dart, fish spear, javelin; spike as on tail of a sting ray; skyrocket; firebrand thrown on grass houses in wars; to throw a spear, javelin, etc. *'O nā Pi'ipi'i nā po'e na lākou i kao i nā pua pana,* the Pi'ipi'i were the ones who hurled arrows. (PPN *tao.*) **2.** n. Snare of coconut midrib and fiber, used for *'a'ama,* a crab. **3.** See *Nā-kao,* a constellation. **4.** Interj. of surprise, as *kāhīhī.* **5.** n. Goat. (See saying, *'umi'umi 1* and Gram. 2.9.) *'A'ahu 'ili kao,* goatskin garment [said of shiftless people accused or sleeping under goatskins because they were too indolent to make tapa]. **6.** n. Scow. *Eng.*

kā o. The one of: *'O wau kā o kāua ke ha'alele iho ana iā'oe* (Kel. 60), I'm the one of the two of us to leave you. (This is probably short for *ka mea o;* Gram. 10.2.)

kā.ō. **1.** nvi. Crowd; to go together in a crowd; crowded. *Fig.,* in difficulties or trouble. **2.** n. Overripe pandanus fruit. **3.** Short for *kāohi. Rare.* **4.** vt. To bake in the oven without leaf wrapping, as taro, breadfruit. *Rare.*

ka'o. vs. Dry, arid, bare of vegetation, as of deserts (usually not used alone). Cf. *pōka'o, ka'oka'o.*

kao ahi. n. Firebrand.

kā 'oe. Rare var. of *kāu,* your, yours. (Gram. 8.4.) *Pio kā 'oe ahi, pau kā 'oe hana* (saying), your fire is out, your work is done [of old age]. (PCP *taa koe;* cf. Marquesan.)

Kao Ea. n. Name of a constellation said to preside over the destiny of Hanalei, Kaua'i (no data).

kao hele. n. Azazel (RSV), scapegoat (KJV). (Oihk. 16.8.) *Lit.,* goat going.

kā.ohi. vt. To hold back, detain, restrain, prevent, repress, withhold, check, try to hold back, control. See ex., *'uo'uo. Hiki 'ole ke kāohi,* unrestrained, uncontrollable. *Kāohi iāia iho,* to control himself. *E kāohi iho 'oe i kou mana'o kolohe,* repress your mischievous thoughts. *Kāohi nā ali'i iāia e noho, 'a'ole 'oia i 'ae mai,* the chiefs tried to make him stay but he didn't consent. *Ka pali kāohi kumu ali'i o 'Iao,* the cliff withholding chiefly origins of 'Iao [burial place of chiefs]. *Kāohi wa'a . . . kāohi aku* (FS 127), to hold a canoe in place with a paddle while others cast for bonito. (PPN *ta'ofi,* PNP *taa'ofi.*) **2.** nvt. Style of chanting in which prolonged vowels are cut off with glottal stops; to chant thus. *Rare.*

kao hihiu. n. Wild goat, gazelle, satyr (Isa. 13.21.)

kā 'ō.hiki. v. To catch *'ōhiki* crabs with a *nohu* blossom as bait. *Rare.*

kā.ohi.lani. nvs. Poetic name for the left hand, left. (UL 56.) Cf. *māhu'i lani.*

kā.ohi.ohi. Redup. of *kāohi.*

-kā'oi. ho'o.kā.'oi. To progress, go ahead, improve, better; progressive.

ka.'ō.ka'a. n. Game of spinning small gourds like tops.

kao kanaka. n. Satyr (1941 Bible has *kao hihiu*). *Lit.,* human goat.

kao.kao. n. Syphilis. Cf. *hākaokao.*

ka'o.ka'o. **1.** vs. High, lofty, prominent. *Fig.,* conceited. Also *kaka'o. Ka'oka'o ho'i kēlā hale e kau maila i ka pu'u,* how prominent is that house placed there on the hill. **2.** n. Rain cloud on the point of precipitation; first raindrops. (AP.) **3.** vs. Hard, arid, especially of red earth. *Rare.*

kao.kaomi. Redup. of *kaomi.*

kao keiki. n. Kid, young goat.

kā.oko. vs. Red-hot, as fire. Cf. *okooko. He ahi kāoko o nā ali'i,* red-hot fire of the chiefs.

kā.'oko'a. vs. Whole, entire; separated, independent, neutral, standing apart, definite. Cf. *'oko'a,* different, *kū'oko'a,* and *holo'oko'a,* entire. See *kū'ai. He 'uala kā'oko'a kāna,* he had a whole sweet potato. *Ua kā'oko'a nō kāna kalo mai kā mākou,* his taro was separated from ours. **ho'o.kā.'oko'a.** To separate from others, keep away, abstain.

kaola. n. **1.** Beam, bar, rail, shelf, railing; wall plate, in a house; stick or beam strengthening a rafter; ledge. **2.** Rare var. of *kaolo.*

kao lele. n. Dart, javelin, skyrocket, fireworks.

kaolo. n. Path, trail. *He ihona, he pi'ina, he kaolo* (saying), going down, going up, a path [life has its ups and downs].

ka'olo. n. Jowl, sagging chin, double chin; sagging part of the neck of an eel. Cf. *'olo,* sag.

kā 'olua. poss. Your, yours (*a*-form, dual: Gram. 8.4, 9.6). (PEP *taa koolua.*)

Kao-ma'ai.kū. n. Aldebaran, a star in the horns of the constellation Alpha Tauri.

Kao Maka.li'i. n. Makali'i's dart, a constellation. (Kep. 79.)

Ka-'ō.maka-o-ka-'ī.lio. n. A *lua* fighting stroke. *Lit.,* the foreskin of the dog. (Also without *Ka-.*)

kaomi. **1.** vt. To press down, squeeze with downward pressure; to massage by pressing firmly with the back of the palm of the hand; to suppress, as a thought or emotion; oppressive, as grief. *Kaomi maluna,* to force down, as medicine. *Kaomi moena,* to weigh down a partly finished mat. **ho'o.kaomi.** To add or feign pressing. (PPN *ta'omi.*) **2.** *(Cap.)* n. Northeast trade wind in some localities, as at Hāna, Maui.

kaomi lole. n. Pressure foot (part of a sewing machine).

kaomi waina. n. Wine press.

kaona. n. **1.** Hidden meaning, as in Hawaiian poetry; concealed reference, as to a person, thing, or place; words with double meanings that might bring good or bad fortune. *Kaona ho'o'ino'ino,* pejorative innuendo. *No wai ke kaona o kēlā mele?* Who is being referred to in veiled language in that song? **2.** Town. *Eng.*

Ka-'ō.nohi-ali'i. n. Star appearing in month of Kaulua, remaining visible through the month of Ikiiki. Cf. *Paumakua-lani.*

kā.o'o. **1.** vt. To bind, tighten, as a belt. **2.** Same as *kāō.* See ex., *kapakē. Ho'omoe wai kahi ke kāo'o,* forward together in unity. **3.** vi. To ebb, of the sea.

-kā.o'o. ho'o.kā.o'o. vi. To strut. *Rare.*

kā.o'o.loa. n. Ghost procession. *Rare.* Also *huaka'i pō.*

kā.'ope. n. Yellowish mother-of-pearl shell. *Rare.*

Ka'ō.pe'a-pani.pani. n. A *lua* fighting stroke. Perhaps *lit.,* the copulating scrotum. (Also without *Ka-.*)

kā 'ou.kou. poss. Your, yours (*a*-form, plural: Gram. 8.4, 9.6). (PEP *taa koutou.*)

kapa. n. **1.** Tapa, as made from *wauke* or *māmaki* bark; formerly clothes of any kind or bedclothes; quilt (various kinds are listed below). *'Elua kāua i ke kapa ho'okahi* (PH xiii), two of us in a single tapa [marriage]. (PCP *tapa.*) **2.** vt. To call, term, give a name to. *Kapa 'ia,* called, named. (PPN *tapa.*) **3.** loc. n. Edge, border, brim, boundary; side, as of a road; bank, as of a stream (often not preceded by *ke:* Gram. 8.6). *Kū ma kapa,* to stand on the edge; *fig.,* forbidding, unapproachable, unreceptive. *Keiki kapa aliʻi* (FS 115), child only one of whose parents was a chief. (PPN *tapa.*) **4.** n. Labia. (PCP *tapa.*) **5.** vi. To rustle, rattle, splash, as rain. **6.** Also **kaba.** n. Cab (a Hebrew measure). (Heb. *qab.*)

kā.pā. 1. Same as *puhi kāpā,* an eel. **2.** vt. To press, squeeze, as coconut flakes for cream; to strain. *Rare.*

kā.paʻa. vt. To hold, as a canoe on its course.

Ka-paʻa-heo. n. Name for the nether world, where ghosts of men strove to appease hunger by eating moths and lizards. (Malo 112, 114.)

kapa-aho. n. A tapa formerly made at Wai-mea, Kauaʻi. (GP 8.)

kā.paʻa.kai. n. Dish in which fish or meat is salted (short for *kāpī paʻakai*).

kapa ʻā.pana. n. Quilt with appliquéd designs. Also *kapa lau,* piece tapa.

kapa.ʻau. n. Raised place in the heiau where images and offerings were placed, and where the invisible gods were thought to dwell. Also *nuʻu* and *lananuʻu.*

Kapae. n. Star name (no data). (Kuhelani.)

kā.pae. 1. vt. To set aside, turn aside, deviate from, eliminate, discard, remove, lay aside, delete, omit, spare, stow away, cancel, be perverted from; to disqualify, suspend. See *noho kāpae* and ex., *pilipili 1. Hiki ʻole ke kāpae,* unavoidable. *Kāpae ʻia,* disqualified. *E kāpae aʻe ʻoe i kou manaʻo huhū,* put away your angry thoughts. *Ua kāpae ʻoia i ka ʻōlelo a ka makua,* he disobeyed his parent's teaching. *ʻAʻole e kāpae nei lāʻau iā ʻoe* (FS 95), this club will not spare you. *Kāpae i ka ihe,* set the spear down [do not fight any more, declare a truce]; throw a spear so that it will not strike a target, especially if the warrior wants to spare his foe's life. See Malo 203. **hoʻo.kā.pae.** To cause to turn off, push aside, parry, thrust away, refute an argument. **2.** *(Cap.)* n. Name of a trade wind at Hāna, Maui, and at Puna, Hawaiʻi. (PH 202.)

kapaea. n. Sapphire. *Eng.* See *kapeilo.*

kā.pae ʻō.lelo. v. To ignore a command; to change the meaning of a word from its original meaning.

kā.pae.pae. Redup. of *kāpae;* to hurry. *Kāpaepae akula ia no kauhale,* she hurried away to the household.

kapa.haʻi. n. Limit, border, as of land.

kapa hulu.hulu. n. Blanket.

kā.paʻi. 1. vt. To slap, pound, as the skin by a masseur; to shatter, as wood *(Maui).* **2.** n. Any kind of remedy for external use, especially a ball or pad of medicinal herbs for rubbing on the skin; poultice.

kapa ʻino.ʻino. n. Sackcloth, as worn by mourners in the Bible (Kin. 37.34). *Lit.,* despicable clothing.

kā.paʻi.paʻi. vs. Growing luxuriantly and thriftily, lush, flourishing. Cf. *lupalupa.*

kapaka. See *ʻōpae kapaka.*

kā paka. n. Container for tobacco, pipe, matches. Cf. *paka,* tobacco.

kapa.kahi. vs. One-sided, crooked, lopsided, sideways; bent, askew; biased, partial to one side; to show favoritism. *Lit.,* one side. Cf. *lawe kapakahi. Kū kapakahi ka lā ma Wai-ʻanae* (saying), the sun appears lopsided at Wai-ʻanae [said by the goddess Hiʻiaka while her lover was dallying with someone else, hence said of any unlawful dallying].

kapa kai. loc. n. Border of the sea, seashore, seaside, coast; sometimes interpreted as west or *komohana.* (Gram. 8.6.) (PCP *katai.*)

kapa.kaʻi. vs. To wait for. *Rare.*

kā.paka.kapa. n. Brief shower, scattered drops (used with *ua,* rain). (Perhaps *kāpakapaka.*)

kapaka.keʻu. Redup. of *kapakeʻu.*

kapa.kapa. 1. Plural of *kapa 3;* human crotch; *kilu* quoit shots that stray from the mark. (PPN *tapatapa.*) **2.** Redup. of *kapa 2;* to invoke, summon. *Inoa kapakapa,* nickname, fictitious name, pet name, pen name, alias, assumed name. (PPN *tapatapa.*) **3.**

Redup. of *kapa 5.* **4.** vs. Well-off, enjoyable. *Kapakapa ka nohona,* prosperous condition. **5.** *(Cap.)* n. Name of a star.

kapa.kapa.lili. Redup. of *kapalili.*

kapa.kapa.lulu. Redup. of *kapalulu.*

kapa.kē. vi. To splash, as raindrops on water. *Kāoʻo ihola ka ua o Kahana, kapakē aʻela ka wai ma Loʻi-keʻe* (chant), the rains gather at Kahana, splashing on the water of Loʻi-keʻe.

kapa.keʻe. vs. Lopsided. Cf. *keʻe,* crooked.

kapa.keʻu. vt. To complain bitterly, find fault. Cf. *keʻu.*

Kā.paki, Sabati. nvs. Sabbath. *Eng.*

kapa kila. n. Steel armor.

kapa komo. n. Clothing in general. *Lit.,* kapa to put on.

kapa.kū. vs. Overwhelmed, destroyed. *Hiki ke Kona, ka makani kūlaʻi kauhale, kapakū ka moku me ka ʻaina* (chant for Ke-kā-ulu-ohi), comes the Kona, the wind that pushes over houses, overwhelms the island and the land.

kapa kuʻina. n. Stitched tapas for bed covering. Cf. *kuʻinakapa.*

kapa.lā. Var. of *kopalā,* shovel. *Eng.*

kā.pala. 1. nvt. Printing, stamping, blot, daub, stain; to smear, smudge, blot, daub, dab, stain, spot; to paint or print a design, as on tapa; smudged, blurred; to spread, as butter on bread. *Kāpala ka leo,* blurred sound (as of a radio). *Kūlina kāpala me ka waiūpaka,* buttered corn. *Kāpala poʻomuku kona ʻike,* his is a short daub of knowledge. **2.** vi. Cabalistic. *Eng.*

kā.pala kiʻi. v. To daub designs, especially to fit ocherous earth in petroglyphs.

Kapala.kiko. n. San Francisco. *Eng.*

kā.pala.lū. vi. Indistinct, as mumbling; to mumble.

kā.pala.pala. Redup. of *kāpala.*

kā.pala poi. nv. To daub with poi. *ʻAhaʻaina kāpala poi,* poi-daubing party; a person daubed with a finger of poi had to provide an extra contribution to the feast; much amusement was afforded among the planners of the feast by attempting to daub one another. Cf. *ʻahaʻaina pi wai.*

kapa lau. n. **1.** Quilt with appliquéd designs. Also *kapa ʻāpana.* **2.** Leaf covering, as placed over a corpse in a pit.

kapa lau.ʻī. n. Plaited ti-leaf textile; ti-leaf covering.

kapa.lili. vi. Palpitating, as in fear or joy; trembling, twitching, fluttering, throbbing; waving; quivering, as a leaf in the wind; trilling, as *r*'s in some languages. *Kapalili ka houpo,* the heart is thrilled. *Lohe aku au i ka uwē kapalili,* I heard a terrified, quivering shriek.

kapa.lō. n. Tableau, pageant. *Eng.*

kapa.lulu. vi. Whirring, as of quail taking flight; buzzing; roaring, as of an airplane; crackling, as of a fire; to whiz. *Manu kapalulu,* quail. *Holo kapalulu,* to zoom. **hoʻo.kapa.lulu.** To crackle, roar, etc.

kapa moe. n. Blanket, quilt, bedspread (general name); sleeping tapa.

kapana. Same as *kapa 3.*

kā.pana. n. A slender native plant *(Phyllostegia grandiflora)* in the mint family, bearing paired ovate leaves and white flowers 2.5 cm long. (Neal 732.)

kapana.hā. n. Mild insanity. *Rare.*

Ka-pao. n. A *lua* fighting stroke.

Kā.pā.ōka. n. Sabaoth. *Eng.*

kapa olo.nā. n. Shroud. (Biblical.)

kā.papa. 1. Same as *hāpapa 1–3.* **2.** vi. Voracious in appetite, destructive. *Niuhi kāpapa o ka moana,* shark of the deep sea, voracious in appetite [an epithet for Ka-mehameha I]. **3.** nvi. Rhythmic tapping of canoe side with a paddle to drive fish into a net; to do so. *Kāpapa ulua,* to drive *ulua* thus; *fig.,* to obtain a human victim or sacrifice him (FS 143); priest who makes the sacrifice. **4.** vi. To do in unison, as of crowing cocks; all together. *Ā hiki i ka wanaʻao, kāpapa ana nā moa,* when morning arrived, the cocks crowed together. **5.** n. A variety of sweet potato (no data). (For. 5:664–5.)

kapa pa'ū.pa'ū. See *pa'ūpa'ū 2*, tapa.
kapa pe'a. n. Filthy rags; tapa worn by women in the menstruation hut *(hale pe'a)*. *Ke kapa pe'a lau'ī kolo hului ā kau ana i ke kua* (FS 161), a ragged garment of ti leaves used for a fish dragnet hanging on the back.
kapa pili. n. Lined quilt that is not padded, formerly used as a top sheet (old-time Hawaiians did not put a bottom sheet on top or vice versa, due to strict taboos concerning body contact). *Lit.,* clinging tapa.
kapa poho, kapa poho.poho. n. Patchwork or crazy quilt of varied color or design. *Lit.,* patch quilt.
kapa pulu. n. Padded quilt, comforter. *Lit.,* pad covering.
kapa ua. n. Raincoat.
kapa uhi lio. n. Horse blanket.
kapa.u'u. vs. Splashing, spattering, as fish being driven into a net; fluttering, flapping. *Fig.,* agitated, worried, disturbed (formerly said mostly on Kaua'i and O'ahu). Cf. *kāpeku. Ua kapau'u ka lani,* the high chief is greatly disturbed.
Ka-pawa. n. Name of a star. *Lit.,* the *pawa* or predawn hour.
Ka-pe'a. n. Southern Cross. *Lit.,* the cross. (PCP *Peka.*)
kā.pe'a. vt. To seize and hold a criminal; to knock down helter-skelter; to bring false accusation against an innocent person. *Kukulu 'ia mai nā pine, na ia nei e kāpe'a aku* (song), set up the pins, he'll knock them down. (PCP *taapeka.*)
kā.pe'a.pe'a. nvt. Barrier made of crossed sticks; barrier to progress; to cross one over another.
kape.au. vi. To go on hands and knees before high royalty; to act humbly. *Kō ia nei kapeau loa akula noho'i ia a hā'ule ihola, moe malalo o nā wāwae o Kūai-ka-ua-kama,* he crept up, fell down prostrate at the feet of Kūai-ka-ua-kama.
kā.pehe. 1. n. Fellow worker, associate, assistant. **2.** nvs. Soft, beguiling, gentle, quiet; soft and beguiling words. Cf. *waipehē. Hele kāpehe,* to go quietly. *Mai ho'olohe aku i kāna kāpehe,* do not heed his soft, beguiling words.
kā.pehi. vt. To throw at, pelt, strike.
kapeilo, sapeilo. n. Sapphire. (Gr. *sappheiros.*) (Mele 5.14.) Cf. *kapila.*
kā.peka. n. Carpet. *Eng.* Now called *moena weleweka.*
kapeke. 1. n. Kind of *malo* dyed one color on one side, and another color on the other side (the wind often blows and exposes *[kapeke]* the color on the reverse side). **2.** vi. Exposed, revealed; askew, out of joint; to slip to one side or out of joint, to miss in one's aim. *Kapeke ihola ku'u wāwae a 'eha ke ku'eku'e,* my foot slipped, hurting my ankle. **ho'o.kapeke.** To loosen, set askew; to tilt, as a canoe; to sit or loosen the clothing so as to cause indecent exposure.
kā.pē.ke'i. Var. of *kāpēke'u.*
kā.peke.peke. vi. To walk unsteadily, totter; insecure, unsteady. *Fig.,* doubtful, uncertain, vague, inconstant, fickle. *Pili kāpekepeke,* uncertain relationship. *E ka po'e mana'o kāpekepeke,* ye of little faith. *Pa'a kāpekepeke,* vaguely, incompletely recorded, as a legend. **ho'o.kā.peke.peke.** Caus/sim.
kā.pē.ke'u. vs. Quarrelsome, disagreeable, complaining, fault-finding. Cf. *ke'u.*
kā.peku. nvi. To splash the feet in the water, as in scaring fish; the person who splashes thus. *Fig.,* blustering, harsh. Cf. *kapau'u, peku. Kāpeku ka leo o ke kai, 'o ho'oilo ka malama,* blustering the voice of the sea, the month is winter.
kā.peku.peku. Redup. of *kāpeku.*
kā.pele. vs. Large, as an abdomen. *Rare.*
kā.pena. n. **1.** Captain. *Eng.* **2.** Cabin. *Eng.* Cf. *'ōhua kāpena.*
kā.pena.keoe. n. An introduced variety of sweet potato, probably named for a captain.
Kāpena Kuke. n. Captain Cook. *Eng.*
kā.pena.loke. n. Name of an introduced vine, the seeds of which are strung as leis, perhaps *lit.,* Captain Rhodes. *Kaua'i.*

kapene.kine, tapenetine. n. Turpentine. *Eng.*
kā.pī. vt. To sprinkle, as with salt; to salt; to scatter, as sand or salt. Also *kōpī. Mai kāpī mai 'oe i ke one,* don't throw sand at me.
kā.pi'i. nvs. Curly; person with curly hair, believed to be strong and hence a good warrior (Malo 201). *Fig.,* warrior, attendant to a chief.
kapi.kala. n. Capital, capitol (city, building). *Eng.*
kā.piki. n. 1. Poi made with an inferior grade of soggy taro. **2.** Cabbage *(Brassica oleracea* var. *capitata). Eng.*
kā.piki 'ai maka. n. Lettuce. *Lit.,* cabbage eaten raw. *Rare.* See *lekuke.*
kā.piki li'i.li'i. n. Brussels sprouts *(Brassica oleracea* var. *gemmifera). Lit.,* small cabbage.
kā.piki pua. n. Same as *kalipalaoa,* cauliflower. *Lit.,* flowering cabbage.
Ka-piko-o-Wā-kea. n. A *lua* fighting stroke. *Lit.,* the navel of Wā-kea. (Also without *Ka-.*)
kapila, sapira. nvs. Sapphire. (Ioba 28.6.) Cf. *kapeilo. Eng.*
kā.pili. vt. To build, put together, put on (as glasses), fit together, set (as precious stones), mend, fix, repair, shingle, join, plaster, unite, attach blame, shoe (as a horse). Cf. *pōhaku kāpili wa'a. Kāpili hou,* mend, fix, repair. *Ua popopo ke kia moku, ho'i hou 'oia e kāpili,* the mast was rotten, he returned to repair it. **ho'o.kā.pili.** Caus/sim. (PCP *taapili.*)
Ka-pili-mai.'u'u. n. A *lua* fighting stroke. *Lit.,* the clinging [to] fingernail. (Also without *Ka-.*)
kā.pili manu. nv. To catch birds with lime; one who does so.
kā.pili mekala. nvt. Solder.
kā.pili moku. nvt. Shipbuilding; shipbuilder, shipwright; to repair ships. (For. 5:479.)
kā.pili.pili. Redup. of *kāpili.* (Puk. 35.33.) (PCP *taapili-pili.*)
kā.pili wa'a. nv. Process of adding on canoe parts after the hull has been carved and rubbed smooth; to do so.
kā.pi'o. 1. nvt. Bird snare made by bending a sapling over and attaching a baited noose; the bird enters, dislodges a weight, the sapling straightens up and the noose tightens and catches the bird; to catch in such a snare. Also *pi'o 3. 'A'ohe manu noho i ka lipo e pakele i ke kāpi'o* (saying), no bird of the deep forest can escape the snare [of an expert lover]. **2.** nvs. Upright, as supporting corners in a house.
kapi.oka. n. Tapioca. *Eng.*
kā.pī.pī. Redup. of *kāpī.*
kā.pī pua'a. nv. To salt pork; one who salts pork. *Fig.,* dirty wretch.
-kāpō'ai. ho'o.kā.pō.'ai. To rotate, revolve, as in a hula. *Rare.*
Ka-pohā-kō.'ele.'ele. n. Unidentified star, no data. (Johnson and Mahelona 43.)
kā.pō.haku. n. Heap of stones, as thrown *(kā)* from a garden to make room for planting.
Ka-pola. n. Star name (no data). (Kuhelani.)
kā.pola. vt. To bind, wrap, bandage. *Rare.* (Perhaps PCP *taapola.*)
kapola.kā. vs. Mysterious, unfathomable. *No Kū, no Lono, no Kāne ma lāua 'o Kanaloa, no Papa nui āiwaiwa ā kapolakā* (old chant), in honor of Kū, Lono, Kāne and Kanaloa, in honor of great Papa, mysterious and unfathomable.
kapo.lena. n. Tarpaulin, canvas. *Eng.*
kapo'o. Same as *napo'o. Kani kapo'o,* loud echoing sound, as of a heavy object falling into water, or of waves booming.
kā.po'o.po'o. Redup. of *kapo'o;* to abound in ruts, as a highway.
kā.popo. See *kāhili kāpopo.*
kapou.lena. n. **1.** Jaundice. Cf. *lena,* yellow. **2.** vs. Lazy, idle, indolent. Cf. *lena,* lazy.
kapu. 1. nvs. Taboo, prohibition; special privilege or exemption from ordinary taboo; sacredness; prohibited, forbidden; sacred, holy, consecrated; no trespassing, keep out. **ho'o.kapu.** To make taboo, prohibit, sanc-

tify, consecrate, forbid. (PPN *tapu*.) **2.** n. Tub. *Eng.* **3.** n. *Cap. Eng.* See *pāpale kapu.*

kā.pua. See *mai'a kāpua.*

Ka-pua'a-kā-hulu.hulu. n. A *lua* fighting stroke. *Lit.,* the pig strikes body hair. (Also without *Ka-*.)

kapu.ahi. n. **1.** Fireplace, stove, furnace, heater, hearth; pan of a musket or gun; censer for sacrifice. **2.** Base of a fishhook point. **3.** *(Cap.)* Name of a star, perhaps the same as *Ka-nuku-o-ka-puahi.*

kapu.ahi 'aila māhu. n. Kerosene stove. *Lit.,* steam oil stove.

Kapu.ahi-a-Ku'i.a.lua. n. A *lua* fighting stroke. *Lit.,* fireplace of *Ku'ialua* [a god].

kapu.ahi ea. n. Gas stove.

kapu.ahi ho'o.hehe'e hao. n. Iron-melting foundry.

kapu.ahi ho'o.mahana hale. n. House heater, furnace.

kapu.ahi.kuni. n. **1.** Smallpox. Also *kamolapoki.* **2.** Small stone container in which the sorcerer burned his "bait" (hair, spittle, etc., of his victim).

kapu.ahi uila. n. Electric stove.

kapu.a'i, kapu.wa'i. n. **1.** Sole of the foot, footprint, footstep, tread, track; foot in measurement; paw of an animal. *Hele mai, ē Kāne, he kapua'i akua, he kapua'i kanaka* (ancient prayer), come, O Kāne, walk as a god, walk as a man. (PCP *tapuwae*.) **2.** Part of the canoe float where the outrigger boom *('iako)* is joined; the after one is the *kapua'i hope.*

kapu.a'i akua. n. Footprint of a god (see *kapua'i 1*). *Fig.,* foot of the rainbow.

kapu.a'i.hao lio. n. Horseshoe. *Lit.,* horse iron tread.

kapu.a'i hope. See *kapua'i 2.*

kapu.a'i-koloa. n. Design on tapa beater consisting of a series of Gothic arches. *Lit.,* wild duck tracks. Also *'aha.*

kapu.a'i kuea. n. Square foot.

kapu.a'i.lio. n. A modern Moloka'i name for the *pala* fern; the bases of the frond stems suggest a horse's hoof *(kapua'i lio).*

kapu.a'i mahele 'ia. vs. Cloven-footed.

Kapu.a'i-o-Kana. n. A *lua* fighting stroke, reserved for chiefs. *Lit.,* footprint of Kana, a stretching demigod. See *Kana 5.*

Ka-pua-lalo-ka-lani. n. Star name, no data. (Johnson and Mahelona 166.)

kapu ā noho. Same as *kapu noho.*

kā.pua.pua. Var. of *mai'a kāpua,* a banana.

kapu 'au.'au. n. Bathtub.

kā.puhi. n. Master of an animal; nurse or caretaker of a child; provider in general (named from the O'ahu custom of taming and feeding a particular eel *[puhi]* in the sea). **ho'o.kā.puhi.** Same as above; to feed an eel; to nurse or care for a child or person. *Fig.,* clever, smart. *Mai puni mai nā ho'okāpuhi,* don't be taken in by smart, wily folk. (PCP *ta(a)pusi*.)

kapu.hia. Pas/imp. of *kapu. He aha ka hala i kapuhia ai ka leo, i ho'okuli mai ai,* what was the wrong that silenced the voice and caused deafness? [Said of one who is silent.]

kapu.hili. n. **1.** The many taboos inherited from chiefly ancestors or from the gods; person with many taboos. **2.** A butterfly fish, *Chaetodon trifasciatus.* Cf. *lauhau.*

kapu holoi. n. Washtub.

kapu holoi maka. n. Wash basin.

kapu 'ili. n. A taboo on wearing another's clothing unless the relationship was very close. *Lit.,* skin taboo.

kapu kai. n. Ceremonial sea bath for purification, purification by sea water, as after contact with a corpse or by women after menstruation.

kapu.kapu. nvs. Dignity, regal appearance, noble bearing, entitled to respect and reverence, difficult of access because of rank, dignity, and station. *Ā kapukapu noho'i,* difficult to approach. **ho'o.kapu.kapu.** To impose a taboo, especially on something not previously taboo; to pretend a taboo that was not existent; to extol, praise, glorify. (PPN *taputapu*.)

kapu.kapu kai. Same as *kapu kai;* to purify by sprinkling with salt water *(kava,* ordinarily taboo to women,

might be made *noa* or free of taboo by sprinkling the place in this fashion; usually termed *pī kai).*

kapuka.wai. Handsome. (And.)

kā.puku. vt. To restore life. *Rare.*

kapu kū mamao. n. A taboo requiring lesser persons to keep their distance from a chief. *Lit.,* taboo stand far away.

kā.puku.puku. Same as *pukupuku;* shrunken object. *Make akula 'oe iā Ku'ika'a . . . ka mea e wali ai ia kāpukupuku* (GP 42), killed by Ku'ika'a . . . the thing that will smash this shrunken thing.

kapu lama. n. A ritual for the god Lono-i-ka-'ou-ali'i (Lono at the chiefly supremacy). (Kam. 64.7.) *Lit.,* torch taboo.

kā.pule. vs. Overripe, black or spotted, as a banana skin; fat, as a plover. See ex., *Ka'elo 1.* **ho'o.kā.pule.** To ripen, fatten.

Ka-pū.lehu. n. Star name (no data). (Kuhelani.)

kapu loa. vs. Strictly prohibited; inviolate (Catholic).

kapu loulu. n. A ritual for the god Lono-i-ka-'ou-ali'i. (Kam. 64.7.) *Lit.,* loulu palm taboo.

kā.pulu. vs. Careless, slovenly, unclean, gross, slipshod, untidy, disgusting, unkempt. *Kāpulu kāna humuhumu 'ana i kona lole,* she is careless in sewing her dress. *Hana kāpulu ka lima, 'ai kāpulu ka waha* (saying), unclean handling puts unclean food in the mouth [i.e., food should be prepared with cleanliness].

kā.pulu.pulu. Redup. of *kāpulu.*

kapu moe, kapu ā moe. n. Prostration taboo.

kapu noho. n. Taboo requiring everyone to sit in the presence of a chief, or when his food container, bath water, and other articles were carried by.

kapu.ō, kapu.wō. interj. and n. A cry proclaiming a taboo on the approach of a sacred personage or as part of a ceremony; the announcer of this taboo (Kep. 139) and the stick he bears (Ii 41). *Kapuō, e moe!* The taboo is on, prostrate!

kapu 'ō.hi'a kō. n. Sacred rituals for cutting an *'ōhi'a* log and dragging *(kō)* it to the coast to be made into a canoe. (Kam. 76:136-8; a note in Kam. 76:146 compares Kamakau's description with Malo's.) See *malu ko'i.*

kapu puhi kanaka. n. Taboo with the privilege of killing people. *Lit.,* taboo burn people. (Kam. 64:9.)

kapu wai. n. Washtub, water tub.

kapu.wa'i. Var. spelling of *kapua'i.*

kapu wohi. n. Taboo of *wohi* chiefs, including exemption from the prostration taboo.

kau. 1. vt. To place, put, hang, suspend, affix, gird on; to set, settle, perch, alight, rest, pose; to enact, impose, or pass, as a law; to levy, as a tax; to ride on or mount, as on a horse or in a car; to board, mount, get in or on; to rise up, appear, as the moon; to place in sacrifice, as a pig; to come to rest, as the setting sun; to arrive, come to pass; to hang up, as a telephone receiver. *Kau ka maka,* to set the eyes upon, as with desire or affection; to feast the eyes upon, to yearn to see. *Ka-lei-kau-maka* (name), beloved child to be looked upon with pride and love. *Kau ka mana'o,* to have an idea or thought, set the mind on. *Ka mea ho'i a ku'u mana'o i kau nui ai a hālāwai maka* (Laie 413), the one on whom my heart is set so keenly to meet face to face. *Pula kau maka 'ino loa,* a very bad mote in the eye [of a disliked person]. *Kau 'ino,* to slam or bang down [a telephone receiver]. *Nā kānāwai i kau nei,* existing statutes. *Kānāwai i kau 'ia,* laws passed. *Kau i ka uku pohō,* to assess damages. *E kau 'ia maluna ona ka ho'opa'i, 'a'ole e 'oi aku mamua o ho'okahi kaukani kālā,* liable to [*lit.,* set upon him] punishment not in excess of one thousand dollars. *Mai ka lā hiki a ka lā kau,* from the rising sun to its setting. *Kau ka makani,* the wind blows. *'Oi kau ka lā,* while the sun is up, i.e., while there is still time. *Ua kau ka waiū o Pō'ipe,* Phoebe's breasts contain milk. *Kau ka pilikia maluna o lākou,* they are in trouble. *Kau mai i luna,* to appear above. *Ua kau ka mālie,* the calm has settled. *Kau ka weli* (FS 93), full of fear. **ho'o.kau.** To put on, place on, lay on, as responsibility; to happen, come to pass. *Ho'okau hiamoe,* to fall asleeep. (PPN *tau.*) **2.** n. Period of time, lifetime; any season, especially summer; session of a legislature; term, semester; time of late night before dawn (Kep. 97). *Kau 'aha'ōlelo,* legislative session. *I ke kau i ke ali'i o Ka-mehameha,* in the time of the chief, Kamehameha. *Moe kau ā ho'oilo,* sleep summers and winters [a poetic expression of death]. *Kau ā kau,* season after season; *fig.,* always and forever. (PPN *ta'u.*) **3.** nvt. A sacred chant, as Hi'iaka's chants of affectionate greeting to persons, hills, and landmarks; a chant of sacrifice to a deity; to chant thus. See *kaukau 1. Kau akula ia i kēia kau ma ke oli* (FS 275), he offered this sacred chant in the chanted song. (PPN *tau.*) **4.** n. Wooden handle, as on stone chisels; perch; pole raised longitudinally over a canoe in stormy weather, on which mats were placed for protection. **5.** nvi. A method of feeding children or high-born persons as a special honor; the recipient held back his head and opened his mouth; the morsel of poi was dropped into his mouth; much enjoyed by children as a game. *'Ai kau,* to eat in this way. **6.** n. Center tapa under which the stone was hidden in the game of *pūhenehene.* **7.** n. Middle finger of the hand. **8.** n. Reason, cause. *'A'ohe kau e make ai,* no reason or cause to die. *Ua ha'alulu au i kau mea o ka maka'u i ka 'ino,* I trembled because of fear of the storm. **9.** Rare var. of *kākau 1. Lālā kau* (KL line 133), streaked fin. **10.** *(Cap.)* Name of a star in the northern sky that served as guide to mariners. **11.** *(Cap.)* The Milky Way. **12.** n. Depression between collarbone and neck. *Rare.* **13.** Part. indicating plural, much less used than *nā* and *mau* except in the compounds *kauhale, kaukolu, kauwahi.* See ex., *pā ipu 1,* Gram. 10.4. *Ua 'ike anei 'oe i kau pua'a a mākou?* Have you seen our pigs? (PCP *tau.*) **14.** Part. expressing superlative, preceded by *ho'i* or *mai ho'i.* (Gram. 7.5.) *He nani mai ho'i kau!* Oh, so beautiful! *He 'ono ho'i kau!* How very delicious! *E lohe mai auane'i kau i ka leo o ka makua,* won't listen at all to the parent's request. (*Kau* is sometimes replaced by *tau. He u'i ho'i tau!* How beautiful!) **15.** vt. To discuss. See *kaukau 1; kauoha.*

kāu. poss. Your, yours (singular, *a-*form; see Gram. 8.4, 9.6). *Ho'i nō kāu me 'oe,* [What] you [said] should go back to you [your curse will strike you; your bad words apply to you, take them back]. *'O kāu mai ā 'o ka'u aku,* your [turn] and then mine. (PNP *ta'au,* PCP *taau.*)

ka'u. poss. My, mine (*a-*form; see Gram. 8.4, 9.6). (PNP *ta'au.*)

-ka'u. Hesitation, fear. See *ka'uka'u, ka'unē, maka'u.* (PPN *-taku.*)

Ka'ū. n. Name of a district on Hawai'i. See epithets, *kua 1, Kuehu Lepo, mākaha 1, wehi 3,* and chant, *ki'eki'e.* (PNP *Takuu.*)

kaua. nvt. War, battle; army; war party; to make war, fight. (PPN *tau'a.*)

kau.ā, kauwā. n. Outcast, pariah, slave, untouchable, menial; a caste which lived apart and was drawn on for human sacrifices (these traditional meanings carried great opprobrium). Later it was used in the Bible and in formal correspondence to translate *servant.* Lesser chiefs who served higher chiefs were called *kauā maoli* (see *ali'i po'e kauā*). See *ha'alele loa 2, lau'ī pekepeke, makawela,* and below for insulting names for *kauā,* and pejorative *-ā* and Malo 68–72. *Kauā 'ai noa, kauā* who eats without observation of eating taboos. *Kauā kuapa'a,* hard-backed outcast. *Kauā make loa 'oe!* You are an outcast to be killed! I'll kill you. *Kauā a ke Akua,* servant of God. *'O wau kāu kauā,* I am, your servant [signature to a letter]. **ho'o.kauā.** To burden with work, make a servant of, enslave; to act as servant or outcast.

kā.ua. 1. vt. To detain, gently request to remain. *Ua kāua mai 'oia ia'u e noho iho ā li'uli'u me ia,* he politely asked me to stay a short time with him. **2.** pronoun. We, us (dual, inclusive). (Gram. 8.2.) *Mai kāua!* Come

to me. *Honi kāua,* kiss me. *Iā kāua,* us. *Aloha kāua!* Warm greetings [one person to another, as at the beginning of a letter]! (PPN *kitaua,* PNP *kitaaua,* PEP *taaua.*)

Ka-ua-hae. n. Wind name. *Lit.,* the raging rain. *Ē ka wahine noho i ka makani, i ka makani Ka-ua-hae, i ke ahi lele o Ka-maile* (chant), a lady dwelling in the wind, in the raging rain and wind, in the firebrands of Kamaile.

kau.ahe. Rare var. of *kauaheahe.*

kau.ahe.ahe. 1. vi. To look or move straight ahead; to gaze. *He aha kēia āu e kauaheahe nei?* What are you gazing at? *Kauaheahe ka holo 'ana o kahi ka'a o mākou,* our car went straight on and on. *Lele kauaheahe i luna lilo loa,* to fly on and on, way far up. **ho'o.kau.ahe.ahe.** To hover; to fly softly, gently, continuously, at the same speed. **2.** vs. Gentle, as a breeze; light. *Ka'ao kauaheahe,* light story. **3.** n. A variety of sweet potato.

kaua honua. n. World war.

kaua ho'o.kahuli au.puni. n. Revolutionary war.

kau.ā ho'o.luhi. n. Any type of *kauā* who works hard, vassal. *Lit.,* oppressed *kauā.*

kau ā.hua. See *āhua.*

Kaua'i. n. Kaua'i (name of one of the Hawaiian islands), Kaua'i person. (Perhaps *kau,* to place + *-a'i,* transitivizer; Gram. 6.6.4; possibly PPN *tauaki.*)

kaua.iki. n. First harvest of small sweet potatoes, others being left to grow larger.

kaua.kā. n. A boisterous person who speaks loudly and gestures wildly, making a spectacle of himself. *Rare.*

Kau-aka-pu'u. n. Name of a star associated with Kohala, Hawai'i.

kau.ā koni. n. *Kauā* branded with dot in the middle of the forehead. *Lit.,* dotted outcast. (Malo 70.)

kaua kio. n. Sham battle. See *kio 6.*

Ka-ua-Kī.pu'u.pu'u-o-Wai.mea. n. A *lua* fighting stroke.

kaua kū.loko. n. Civil war, internal war.

kau.ā lae puni. n. *Kauā* with tattooed label on temples. *Lit.,* outcast surrounded forehead. (Malo 70.)

kau.ala.kō. vt. To drag, pull along. Also *alakō.*

ka-ua-lau. See *mai'a-ka-ua-lau.*

Kau-ua-lē.hei-o-Maka.wao. n. A *lua* fighting stroke. (Also without *Ka-.*)

kau.ali'i. n. A commoner elevated to chieftainship.

kaua lio. n. Cavalry; cavalry war. *Lit.,* horse war.

kau.ā.lupe. vt. To carry a person supported by arms over the shoulders of two persons, as one drunk or sick, or for one person to half carry and half drag another person. *Lit.,* place like a kite.

Ka-ua-mea. n. A constellation, possibly Corona Borealis.

ka ua mea. See *mea,* cause.

kaua.moe. n. Ambuscade. *Lit.,* lying-down war.

kau.ana Lipo. n. The southern sky where the star Lipo may be seen; the rising of the star Lipo. Variants are *kauana Lepo, kauana Lewa,* and *kauana Liolio-iWawau.*

Kau-ano-meha. n. A star, possibly Sirius. *Lit.,* placed in holy stillness. Other names are *Kaulu-i-kua, Kau'ōpae, Ho'okele-wa'a, 'A'ā* and *'Ā-iki-kau-e-lono.* This star was used by navigators and fishermen.

kau anu. n. Winter, cold season.

kau 'apa.'apa. n. A single generation from father to son. (For. 6:269.) Cf. *'āpa'a 2.*

kau.ā pa'a.ua. nvi. Drudge; to be a drudge.

kaua paio. n. Combat, debate.

Ka-'ua'u-kaha. n. A *lua* fighting stroke. *Lit.,* the soaring petrel. (Also without *Ka-.*)

Ka-'ua'u-komo-hewa. n A *lua* fighting stroke. *Lit.,* the petrel trespasses. (Also without *Ka-.*)

Ka-ua-'ula. n. **1.** A strong mountain wind, often destructive, at Lahaina, Maui. *Lit.,* the red rain [referring to red soil washed away by a storm]. *Ke kukui pio 'ole i ke Ka-ua-'ula,* the light not extinguished by Ka-ua-'ula [in praise of Lahaina Luna school]. **2.** *(Not cap.)* Kind of soft, reddish porous stone used for polishing and smoothing and as a sinker for octopus lure.

Ka-'ua'u-lewa.lewa. n. A *lua* fighting stroke. *Lit.,* the swinging petrel. (Also without *Ka-*.)

kau.awe. Var. spelling of *kauwawe*.

kau 'eke.ke'i. vs. Too short, as a dress; to hang short.

kau.ele, kau.elu. Var. spellings of *kauwele* and *kau-welu*.

kau.'eli.'eli. vt. To dig up the past, to review the past. *'O ka'u ia e kau'eli'eli nei, e kaumo'o nei mamuli o kā Lono* (chant for Kua-kini), this is why I am reviewing the past, joining on to Lono's account.

kau.ha'a. vi. To move up and down as the waves, or as in dancing; to undulate. *Aia i Puna-lu'u ka'u aloha, i ke kai kauha'a a ka malihini* (song), my sweetheart is at Puna-lu'u, where the sea dances for visitors.

kau.hale. loc. n. Group of houses comprising a Hawaiian home, formerly consisting of men's eating house, women's eating house, sleeping house, cook-house, canoe house, etc. Term was later used even if the home included but a single house, and is sometimes used for hamlet or settlement. It is used without an article. (Gram. 8.6.) *Lit.,* plural house. *E ho'i kākou i kau-hale,* let's go home. *Kanaka hele i kauhale,* a person who goes from house to house; to gad.

kau.hale.lewa. n. Tabernacle. (Oihk. 23.34.) *Lit.,* movable house.

kau hapa. vt. Half-mast; to raise at half-mast.

kauhi. Same as *'ākia,* a shrub.

kau.hihi. vs. 1. Tangled, snarled, of vines. *Fig.,* in trouble. **ho'o.kau.hihi.** To entangle. 2. Lashing, as of thatching sticks to house post.

Kauhi.koa. n. Name of an unknown lazy man. *'A 'ohe hana a Kauhikoa* (Kel. 138), Kauhikoa has no work [of a lazy person].

kau.hilo. vt. To fasten horizontal thatching sticks and plates of a house with rope.

kau.hola. vi. 1. To open, unfold, as a tapa; to expand, as a flower in bloom. Cf. *hola.* 2. To lose consciousness, as in an epileptic seizure; heart attack, stroke.

kau.holo. vt. To pursue in order to harm, chase, to run after, run and fetch. *Kauholo aku 'oe iā La'a-kea,* run after La'a-kea and bring him back.

kau.hua. 1. n. Desire. *Ho'okahi . . . kauhua a ko'u pu'uwai* (Kel. 152), single desire of my heart. 2. n. State of pregnancy. **ho'o.kau.hua.** To cause pregnancy; gestation; pregnancy sickness; pregnancy craving [thought to indicate the character of the child in the womb]. *Makemake 'oia i ka he'e, he ho'okauhua paha,* she craves octopus, probably because of her pregnancy. *I ho'okauhua i ke kōlea, no kahiki ana ke keiki,* with a pregnancy craving for plover, the child will be a traveler. 3. nvt. Spelling, orthography; to write down, note. *Lit.,* place word.

kau hua. n. Fruit season.

kau.huhu. n. 1. House ridgepole. (PPN *ta'ofufu*.) 2. Edge of a precipice.

kau.hulu. n. Gathering of fish in schools near the surface of the sea. Cf. *pālauhulu. Ua 'ike au i ke kauhulu o ka i'a,* I saw the gathering of fish schools near the surface.

Ka-uhu-mā.ka'i.ka'i. n. A *lua* fighting stroke. Uhu-māka'ika'i was the name of the giant *uhu* fish that dragged Ka-welo for two days in his canoe from Wai-'anae to Ni'ihau and back to Wai-'anae (FS 42–49). (Also without *Ka-*.)

kau.ila, kau.wila. n. 1. A native tree in the buckthorn family *(Alphitonia ponderosa),* found on the six main Hawaiian islands, with alternating leaves, oblong to narrow and woolly below; its hard wood was used for spears and mallets. (Neal 541.) Its wood was one of three kinds from trees on Mauna Loa, Moloka'i, that were rumored to be poisonous from that location alone, and were used in black magic. The three trees were called *kālai pāhoa;* the others were *'ohe* and *nīoi.* 2. A native tree in the buckthorn family *(Colubrina op-*

positifolia), found only on O'ahu and Hawai'i, with opposite leaves, ovate and to 15 cm long. Its hard wood was valued for spears and tools, and was not reputed to be poisonous. (Neal 541.) Called *o'a* on Maui. Cf. *'ānapanapa.* 3. Taboo ceremony consecrating a temple; ceremonial readorning of images with feathers. 4. Hard, reddish rock resembling *'alā.* 5. A kind of black, tough sugar cane. Also *māikoiko, kō 'ele'ele.* 6. See *puhi kauila.*

kau.ila 'ā.napa.napa. Same as *'ānapanapa,* a scandent shrub.

kau.ila hulu.hulu. n. Temple ceremonies, during which images were readorned with feathers. (FS 139.)

kau.ila kukuku. Same as *kauila 'ānapanapa.*

kau.ila māhu. Same as *'ōlapa.*

kau.'ī.puka. nvi. To loiter about the door of a house as though desiring food gifts; one who does so. *Lit.,* placed [at the] door.

kauka. nvs. Doctor, physician; medical. *Eng.*

kauka ha'i.ha'i iwi. n. Chiropractor. *Lit.,* bone-breaking doctor.

kau.kahi. 1. vs. Standing alone, solitary, by oneself, lone; persevering, singleness of purpose, regularity. *Ma ke kaukahi kāna hana 'ana, 'a'ole ma ka lauwili,* his task was done with a singleness of purpose [or regularity], not with inconstancy. 2. n. Canoe with a single outrigger float. Cf. *kaulua.*

kauka holo.holona. n. Veterinary. *Lit.,* animal doctor.

kauka ho'o.hā.nau. n. Obstetrician.

kau.ka'i. nvt. To depend on; one depended on (*kau,* to place + *-ka'i,* transitivizer: Gram. 6.6.4). *Kauka'i au i kona hana mai i kā māua hana,* I depend on his doing our work. *'Ehia mea kauka'i ka pono iā'oe?* How many people depend on you for livelihood?

kauka kaha. n. Surgeon. *Lit.,* cutting doctor.

kauka lapa.'au. n. Medical doctor.

Kau-ka-li'a. n. Star name.

kauka lomi.lomi. n. Osteopath. *Lit.,* massage doctor.

ka'u.kama. n. Cucumber *(Cucumis sativus),* introduced. (Nah. 11.5; Neal 811.) Listed in Ellis 1825, p. 247.

ka'u.kama kai. Same as *loli. Lit.,* sea cucumber.

Kau-ka-malama. n. Name of a star that rises with Ka-welo-lani in the month of 'Ikuā.

kau ka mana'o. See *kau 1.*

kau kā.nā.wai. nv. To legislate, make or enact laws; legislator, lawmaker, legislation; legal.

kau.kani, tausani. num. Thousand. *Eng.*

kauka niho. n. Dentist. *Lit.,* tooth doctor.

kauka pale keiki. n. Obstetrician.

kau.kau. 1. nvt. Chant of lamentation, as addressing the dead directly; to advise, admonish, especially in a kindly or affectionate manner; to weigh in the mind, deliberate, reason with (Hal. 13.2), appeal to. Cf. *kau 3. He kaukau aloha na'u iā'oe,* a loving heart-to-heart talk with you. (PNP *tautau*.) 2. Redup. of *kau 1.* **ho'o.kau.kau.** To place, put, etc. 3. n. Heap of stones used as a temporary altar. Cf. *ahu.* 4. nvt. Bird snare; to set or fix a bird snare.

ka'u.ka'u. 1. nvi. To slow down, delay, procrastinate, hesitate, linger; inhibited, checked; reluctance. *He aha ka mea o ke ka'uka'u 'ana?* Why be hesitant? **ho'o.ka'u.ka'u.** To cause delay, linger. 2. n. Hemorrhoid or exterior obstruction to bowel evacuation.

kau.kau.ali'i. n. Class of chiefs of lesser rank than the high chief, the father a high chief and the mother of lower rank but not a commoner.(FS 159.) *Kona mau kaukauali'i* (Laie 475), his lesser chiefs.

kau.kau.kala.lē. nvi. Tap-tap, as of tattoo needle when it pierces the skin.

kau.kaula. n. Temporary rope fence.

ka'u.ka'u.lele. nvs. Nimbleness, joy; nimble, agile, active, joyful, as one leaping for joy. *Ke ka'uka'ulele a ka ua* (chant), the joyful leaps of the rain.

ka'u.ka'u.lī. Redup. of *ka'ulī. Ē Pele ē! Ka'uka'ulī* (FS 223)! O Pele! Shishing along!

ka'u.ka'u lua. Intensifier of *ka'uka'u. Ka'uka'u lua*

'ole, dauntless, quick, alert. *Ku'upau nā hana i ke ākea, ka'uka'u lua 'ole i ka lehulehu* (drinking song), unrestrained doings in public, unchecked by the crowd.

kau.kaunu. Redup. of *kaunu. Le'a ke kaukaunu i nā pua hala 'ai a ke kīna'u* (Kaua'i song), there is fun in loving the tip of the pandanus fruit of which *kīna'u* eels are fond [if these fruits fall into the sea they are said to be eaten by *kīna'u* eels].

kau kepa. vi. To fall or lie on a slant, as rain; slanting. *Mehe manu lā ka ua e kau kepa nei, e wili nei i luna o ka lā'au* (chant for Ka-Haku-o-Hawai'i), like a bird the rain falls slanting, whirling about on the tops of trees.

kau.kini, kausini. n. Cousin. *Eng.*

kau.ko'a. Short for *kau 'oko'a,* to place separately; to separate.

kau.koe. vt. To continue or persevere in a straight course. *E kaukoe aku 'oe i ka 'imi na'auao,* go on with your education.

kau.ko'e. See *kau'o'e.*

kau koho pā.loka. n. Election season, election.

kau.kolo. nvt. To creep on, as roots searching for moisture; to chase, follow; to persevere in making a request; creeping; petition. *E kaukolo aku ana au i ku'u akua, e kala mai i ku'u hewa iā'oe* (old prayer), I am pleading to my god, to forgive my wrongs to you.

kau.kolu. n. Triple, trinity, group of three (Kep. 27).

kau.ko'o. vt. To walk with a cane *(ko'o);* to lean on, rely on, depend on. *Fig.,* old and infirm. *ho'o.kau.ko'o.* To cause to walk with a cane; to walk thus. *Ua loa'a iā 'Alamila ke kuleana e ho'okauko'o aku ai maluna ona i nā lawelawe kōkua 'ana,* Almira obtained the right to depend on him for serving help.

kau.kukui. n. Candlestick, lamp stand. *Lit.,* place light.

kau.la. n. Rope, cord, string, line, strap, thong; lash or stroke, as of a whip (2 Kor. 11.24); arc of a circle in geometry; chain, as used by surveyors and engineers. (PPN *taula.*)

kā.ula. n. Prophet, seer, magician. (PPN *taula,* PNP *taaula.*)

Ka.'ula. n. **1.** A rocky islet off Ni'ihau. *Ke lei maila 'o Ka'ula i ke kai* (UL 56), Ka'ula wears the ocean as a lei. *'Ai lā 'oe i ka manu o Ka'ula* (FS 97), eat the birds of Ka'ula [Ka'ula was famous for its birds: see ex., *kē 1, kō'ala'ala 2, puaea*]. **2.** Name of a wind associated with Pōhaku-loa, Maui. (For. 5:101.) **3.** *(Not cap.)* A sea bird.

kaula ahi. n. Wick.

kau lā.'au. nvs. Growing in a tree; to be in a tree; all kinds of epiphytic plants. See ex., *'awa 1. Pīlali kukui kau lā'au* (song), candlenut gum on the trees.

kau.la'e.la'e. vs. Cloudless, standing out clearly, plainly seen.

kaula hao. n. Chain. *Lit.,* iron rope.

kaula hō.'ā. n. Fuse. *Lit.,* ignition rope.

kaula ho'o.he'e. Same as *kaula pahe'e.*

kaula ho'o.hei. n. Rope for lassooing or ensnaring.

kaula ho'o.lewa. n. Bracelets. (Kin. 38.18.) *Lit.,* dangling rope.

kaula ho'o.lu'u kapa. n. Cord for marking tapa.

kaula hope. n. Line from mast to stern.

kaula huelo. n. Tall strap.

kaula huki. n. Drawstring, rope or cord to pull on.

kaula huki pe'a. n. Halyard.

kau.la'i. vt. To hang up, as to dry in the sun. *(kau,* to hang + *la'i,* transitivizer: Gram. 6.6.4.) *Haka kaula'i,* drying rack or frame. *I'a kaula'i,* fish hung or spread for drying. (PPN *tauraki.*)

kaula ihu. n. Line from mast to bow *(ihu).*

kau.la'i iwi. v. To talk too much of one's family affairs or ancestors, to tell the cherished stories, and chants of one's ancestors (a taunt to those who reveal too much of the Hawaiian past). Cf. *kaula'i iwi. Lit.,* to dry out the bones, meaning to expose the bones of the ancestors, a crime.

ka'ula.iki. n. Type of pink, smooth, somewhat porous stone.

kau.la'i lā. nv. To sun, bleach in the sun; sun bath; to talk too much of family and ancestors (cf. *kaula'i iwi).*

kaula 'ili. n. Leather rope, lassoing rope, lariat, strap. *Mālama pono 'oe i ku'u kaula 'ili, o pa'a aku 'oe i ka ho'ohei 'ia* (song), watch out for my leather rope, or you'll be caught in my lasso.

kaula 'ila. n. Lariat of tanned leather.

kaula kā.'ili.'ili. n. Line from forward outrigger boom *('iako)* to prow to strengthen the boom in storms. Cf. *kā'ili'ili.*

kaula kā.liki. n. Lacings, cords as those by which the coconut knee drum *(pūniu hula)* was tied to the thigh of the player.

kaula kā.ohi. n. Reins, check line.

kaula kau.la'i lole. n. Clothesline. *Lit.,* line to dry clothes.

kaula kau.ō. n. Towline.

kaula kī. n. Swivel rope.

kaula kolo. n. Towline.

kaula kū.pe'e. n. Rope to tether, as horse, cow, or pig.

kaula lei. n. Cord on which flowers are strung into a lei; cluster of fruit or flowers growing together on a stem like a lei; streamer.

kaula lī. n. Lacing, as for shoes or corset.

kaula lī kā.ma'a. n. Shoelace.

kaula likini. n. Rigging.

kaula lio. n. Halter. *Lit.,* horse rope.

kaula lua.hine. n. Line running from the prow of a canoe to the after end, used to lash the *'ahu,* or mat, used for protection from high seas. *Lit.,* old woman line.

Ka'u-lama-'ā.kala. n. Name of a star.

kaula maka. n. Rope made of willow or other green bark or branch. (Lunk. 16.7.) *Lit.,* green cord.

kaula malina. n. Sisal rope.

kaula moku. n. **1.** Ship line of any kind. **2.** Broken rope, string.

kau.lana. **1.** nvs. Famous, celebrated, renowned, well-known; fame; to become famous. *Lā kaulana,* day of celebration or festivity, famous day. *ho'o.kau.lana.* To make famous; to spread a report concerning a person or thing. **2.** nvi. Resting place, place to put things, placement; restful, quiet *(kau,* to place + *-lana,* nominalizer: Gram. 6.6.2). (PPN *taulanga.*)

kau.lana 'a.ā. n. Heap of stones.

kau.lana 'āina. n. Land administrator. (For. 5:441.)

Kau.lana-a-ka-lā. n. Name of a star; a poetic name for the west.

kau.lana-a-Kāne. n. Resting place of Kāne, said to be on the islet of Ka'ula off Ni'ihau; also a poetic name for the west.

kau.lana.haka. n. Bridge, trestle.

kau.lana mahina. n. The position of the moon.

kau.lana.mū.he'e. n. A squid (family Sepiolidae), *Euprymna scolopes. Lit.,* resting *mūhe'e.* (Kam. 76:151.)

kau.lana.'ō.lelo. nv. Heir by word-of-mouth rather than by written will; to make a will verbally; a verbal will.

kau.lana wa'a. n. Place where canoes stop, as while fishing.

kau.lani. vi. To rely on the chief, to support the chief, to put confidence in the chief. *I ke kapu, 'a'ole e pono, 'o ka pono o ka 'āina e kaulani* (chant for Ke-kā-ulu-ohi), in the taboo there is no salvation, the salvation of the land is in upholding the chief.

kaula ō. n. Sprit line.

kaula 'ō.hi'a. n. Strong outrigger lashing used on deep-water canoes, probably so called because of the hardness of *'ōhi'a* wood.

kaula 'ō.pū. n. Saddle girth. *Lit.,* stomach rope.

kaula pa'a lima. n. Leash. *Lit.,* rope held hand.

kaula pae.pae. n. Sheet from boom to after outrigger boom *('iako hope).*

kaula pahe'e. n. Line, as to raise a sail. *Lit.,* sliding line.

kaula pā.'ū. n. Line holding in place the canoe *pā'ū,* cover.

kaula pū. n. Ship shroud.

kaula uaki. n. Watch chain.

kaula uea. n. Cable.

kaula uila. n. Streak of lightning.

kaula waha. 1. nv. Bridle, reins; to bridle. *Lit.,* mouth chain. **2.** n. Line extending from sail tip to the *'iako,* boom, on the edge of the canoe.

kāula wahine. n. Prophetess, priestess.

kau.lei. vi. **1.** Too high; too short, as a dress. *Fig.,* insecure, infirm. *He i'a pā kaulei,* a fish almost hooked. **2.** To rest, hang, be placed. *He aha lā kēlā mea e kaulei maila ma'ō?* What then is that resting over there?

kau lei. v. To sell leis; to hang leis. *Wahine kau lei,* lei seller. *Ua hele akula i ke kau lei,* having gone to sell leis.

kau.lei.lei. Redup. of *kaulei.*

kau.leina. n. Insecurity.

kau.lele. 1. vi. To take flight; soaring, on the wing. *Ahikaulele,* rocket. **2.** nvt. Exclamation, stress; to accent in music. *Kaulele ma ka pana malalo,* accent the down beat. *Kaulele iki,* secondary stress, in music. **3.** vs. Extraordinary, over and above the ordinary, extra, added on, additional, supplemental, random, excess. *He aloha kaulele iā'oe ē ka hoa luhi,* extra love for you, O fellow laborer. *Uku kaulele,* interest (money); extra charge. *Heluhelu kaulele,* read a little more, supplementary reading, read at random.

kaule.loa. n. An *'o'opu* fish found in brackish water. *Lit.,* the long penis.

kau.lelele. nvt. Insertion; to insert.

kau.leo. vt. To urge, exhort, enjoin, advise, command. *Lit.,* to place the voice. *E kauleo aku ana au iā'oe, ē ku'u kama, e noho mai kāua e pono ai,* I advise you, my child, it is better for you to remain with me.

kau lewa. vi. To hang, be suspended; unsettled. *Ua kau lewa ka 'umeke i luna,* the bowl is hanging above. *Kau lewa ka noho 'ana,* unsettled abode.

kau.lī. vi. To show off, play the dandy. **2.** vt. To lash.

ka'u.lī. vi. To creep along, move with a hissing sound, as fire. See ex., *ka'uka'ulī.*

kau.lia. 1. Pas/imp. of *kau 1, 2;* hung, suspended, hanging. (Gram. 6.6.3.) *Kaulia i ke ke'a,* crucify. (PNP *taulia.*) **2.** *(Cap.)* n. Name of a star called the chief of the month of Ikiiki because it appears in that month.

kau li'i.li'i. vt. To scatter here and there in small quantities; to divide or distribute small amounts.

kau.like. nvi. Equality, equation, equity, justice; equal, impartial, just, mutual, parallel; to balance evenly, make alike, be in a similar situation, treat fairly and impartially, dispense justice; to arrive at the same time (For. 4:293); par. *Pono kaulike,* equal rights and justice for all. *Kaha kaulike,* parallel line. *Helu kaulike,* even number. *Luna Kānāwai Ki'eki'e ā Kaulike,* Chief Justice. *Kaulike 'ole,* unjust, unreasonable, uneven. **ho'o.kau.like.** To equalize, balance. *Ho'okaulike ho'oka'a,* equalization of payments.

kau.liki. nvs. Southeast.

kau lio. nv. To ride horseback; horseback rider. *Koa kau lio,* cavalry.

Kau-lio.lio-i-Wawau. Probably same as *Liolio-i-Wawau,* a star name. (PPN *Wawa'u.*)

kau.loloa. vi. To ask frequently, tease; importunate, annoying. *Rare.*

kau.lona. vt. To observe closely, to direct attention to, aim at. *I luna nā maka o ke anaina kāhuna kahi i kaulona ai,* the eyes of the company of priests watched him with interest.

kaulu. n. **1.** Ledge, step, jog, as on a cliff. See ex., *pali. He kanaka no kaulu hānai* (saying), a man from the high cliff ledge [a prominent man]. **2.** *(Cap.)* Southern Cross. Also *Newe.* **3.** All species of an endemic genus *(Pteralyxia),* small trees related to *maile,* found only on O'ahu and Kaua'i, resembling *hōlei (Ochrosia)* with its shiny, oblong leaves. Fruits are paired, red, ovoid, and each contains one large winged seed. (Neal 684.) **4.** Same as *'ala'a (Planchonella),* a tree. **5.** Same as *āulu 5,* and *lonomea, Sapindus oahuensis,* a tree. **6.**

Neighborhood, locality, place. Cf. *kaiāulu.* **7.** Var. of *kaunu.*

Ka.ulu-. n. Names of several stars begin thus; see below.

kau.lua. 1. nvi. Double canoe, pair, span, yoke, two of a kind; to put together or pair, to yoke or harness together, to double in quantity; coupled. *Fig.,* two-natured. Cf. *kaukahi.* (PPN *talula.*) **2.** *(Cap.)* n. Name of a month. See Kep. 89. **3.** *(Cap.)* n. One of the many names for the star Sirius; according to some reports, a constellation. The name may be qualified by the terms *koko* (said to be Betelgeuse), *Lena* (Sirius), *Mōha'i* (or *Ha'i Mōha'i*), *Okaoka.* See *Wai-loa.* (PCP *Takulua.*)

ka'u.lua. nvi. Slackness, delay, procrastination, hesitation; to delay, stay, procrastinate; remiss in fulfilling a promise. **ho'o.ka'u.lua.** To cause delay, etc.

kau.lua lio. v. To harness or put two horses together.

kaulu 'anu'u. n. Ledge or terrace.

Ka-ulu-ho'i. n. Name of the Hawaiian newspaper printed by students of the Hawaiian language at the University of Hawai'i at Mānoa, begun in 1971. *Lit.,* the growing bitter yam [or happiness; see *hoi 1* and *2* for word play].

Kaulu-i-kua. n. Star name, perhaps same as *'A'ā,* Sirius.

Kaulu Ko'a.ko'a. Probably same as *'A'ā,* Sirius. (Cf. Maori *Te-Kokota;* the present Hawaiian form may have metathesized from an earlier *'Oka'oka;* Johnson and Mahelona 11.)

Kaulu Lena. Same as *'A'ā,* Sirius.

kaulu waha. Var. of *kaunu waha.*

kaulu.wehi. vi. To decorate, adorn, especially with greenery. Cf. *uluwehi.*

kaulu.wela. 1. vs. Glowing, bright-colored, colorful. **ho'o.kaulu.wela.** Caus/sim. **2.** vs. Swarming; innumerable. *Kauluwela ka moana i nā 'au wa'a kaua o Ka-lani-'ōpu'u; aia nā koa ke 'a'ahu lā i kō lākou mau 'ahu 'ula o nā waiho'olu'u like 'ole,* the ocean was swarming with the fleet of war canoes of Ka-lani-'ōpu'u; the warriors were wearing their feather cloaks of varied colors. **3.** n. Taboo ceremony in honor of the *akua loa,* long god, of the *makahiki* festival.

Kaulu-wena. n. Star name, no data. (Johnson and Mahelona 43.)

kau.maha. 1. nvs. Heavy; weight, heaviness. *Fig.,* sad, wretched, dismal, dreary, downcast, troubled, depressed; grief. *Mea kaumaha loa,* tragic event, tragedy. **ho'o.kau.maha.** To burden, load down, laden. *Fig.,* to oppress, cause sadness or grief; sorrowful, woeful, sorry, depressed, oppressive, burdensome. *Mea ho'okaumaha moku,* ballast. *Mai ho'okaumaha, don't worry.* (PPN *mamafa,* PCP *taumafa.*) **2.** nvt. Sacrifice, offering; to make a sacrifice or offering. See ex., *nikiniki 2. Kaumaha a'e ana iā Laka,* to offer to Laka. (PPN *taumafa.*)

kau.maha 'ai. n. Food offering to the gods. *Pule kaumaha 'ai* (Kep. 55), prayer before eating.

kau.maha lua. vs. Very heavily laden; bearing a heavy load, especially of one drenched with water. *Fig.,* extremely sad.

kau.mahana. n. Native mistletoes. Also *hulumoa.*

kau ma'i. n. Period or time of sickness.

kau.maka. Similar to *kau ka maka:* see *maka 2. Me ka pu'uwai i piha i ke kaumaka,* with his heart filled with loving thoughts.

kau maka 'iole. Var. of *haumaka'iole.*

kau.maka.nui. n. Ocean sunfish *(Mola mola). Lit.,* big eyes placed.

kau.malu.malu. vt. To overlook faults of others. *Lit.,* to place shade.

ka.'ū.mana. See *Makua-ka'ūmana,* a star.

kau.manu. n. **1.** Paper mulberry too old to be used for tapa. **2.** Method of catching birds by tying a caterpillar and a stick at one end of a string; when the bird swallows the caterpillar the stick lodges in his throat.

kau mau. n. Regular session, as of legislature.

kā 'umeke. n. Hanger for *'umeke,* bowls.

kau mele. n. Marks showing rhythm in songs. *Rare.*

kau mō.koi. n. Rack to hold fish poles.

kau.moli. n. Stick about 10 cm long with holes down its middle, used to hold gunwales in place while they are being sewed on with sennit.

kau.moʻo. **1.** nvt. To splice, mend a fracture with a splint; to fasten canoe gunwale; wooden canoe clamp. **2.** vs. Perched high. **3.** vs. Uncertain, hesitant. *ʻA ʻole i hoʻomau ʻia ka hana, kaumoʻo wale nō i ke akaaka ʻole,* work was not continued, just uncertainty with lack of clarity. **4.** v. To point out or determine boundaries of a *moʻo* land division.

kau.muku. **1.** vi. Too short; shrinking away, as in distaste. *ʻEʻeke ka piʻi pali o Mauna Hina, kaumuku ʻekekeʻi i ka wai o ka liko* (chant for Kua-kini), the climber of Mauna Hina cliff shrinks away, draws away, shrinks from the moisture of the leaf buds. **2.** n. Wind squall.

kauna. n. **1.** Placement, hanging, appearance. Cf. *kau 1.* (PPN *taunga.*) **2.** Count (title of nobility). *Eng.* **3.** Chanting. **4.** Voice used in choral singing, e.g. countertenor or alto. (Tatar, in Kanahele 87.)

kā.una. num. Four (formerly tubers were counted by fours; four was a formulistic number). (See *pākāuna.*) *Nā wahi kāuna ʻoʻopu* (Kel. 51), several foursomes of ʻoʻopu fish. *Ke kāuna hoʻokahi o ka huina o nā lā* (Kel. 47), a total of four days. *ʻEkolu kāuna,* twelve.

kauna.keke, kaunatese. n. Countess. *Eng.*

kauna.koma. n. Quotation marks.

kauna.lepo. Var. of *kaunalipo.*

kauna Lipo. Same as *kauana Lipo.*

kauna.loa. nvi. Perseverance; to persevere. *Kaunaloa i ka ʻimi naʻauao,* determined perseverance in seeking education.

kau.nana. Var. of *kaulana. Kaunana pālāmoa* (For. 6:472), dark clouds coming into the sky.

kau.nā.nā. To discover, perceive (Oih. 27.39).

kauna.ʻoa. n. **1.** A native dodder *(Cuscuta sandwichiana),* belonging to the morning-glory family, a leafless, parasitic vine, growing densely on other plants. The numerous, slender, orange stems are used for orange leis to represent the island of Lā-naʻi, as designated by the Territorial legislature in 1923. *Hihi kaunaʻoa, hihi Mānā, aloha wale ia lāʻau kumu ʻole* (saying), tangled parasite vine, tangled Mānā, pity for this vine without a trunk [of parasites or helpless folk]. (Neal 710-1.) **2.** A mollusk (Vermetidae). Also *kaunoʻa.* In adult stage it becomes solidly fixed to rocks; cuts resulting from stepping on it are considered deadly poisonous by Hawaiians. The mollusk was believed somehow related to the dodder. Also *kio, unaʻoa.* **3.** A coarse, tough seaweed *(Galaxaura rugosa),* calcified and inedible, resembling *kaunaʻoa 1* in being yellow to gold in color.

kauna.ʻoa kaha.kai. Same as *kaunaʻoa lei.*

kauna.ʻoa lei. Same as *kaunaʻoa 1.*

kauna.ʻoa malolo. Same as *kaunaʻoa pehu. Lit., mālolo* (flying fish) *kaunaʻoa,* so called because this plant was spread over *mālolo* caught in a canoe to keep them from escaping. Sometimes called *mālolo* or *pololo.*

kauna.ʻoa pehu. n. A greenish-yellow dodder vine *(Cassytha filiformis),* belonging to the laurel family, cosmopolitan in the tropics. It is coarser than the native orange dodder *(Cuscuta sandwichiana). Lit.,* swollen *kaunaʻoa.* Also *kaunaʻoa mālolo, kaunaʻoa uka.*

kauna.ʻoa uka. Same as *kaunaʻoa pehu. Lit.,* upland *kaunaʻoa.*

kauna wahine. n. Countess. *Lit.,* female count *(Eng.).*

kaʻu.nē. vs. Slow, lagging, delaying.

kau neʻi.neʻi. vi. To hang short. Cf. *neʻineʻi, ʻekekeʻi.*

kau.nihi.nihi. vi. Holding on precariously. *Lit.,* resting on the edges. Also *kaunukunuku.*

kau.noʻa. **1.** Var. of *kaunaʻoa 1-3.* (Niʻihau.) **2.** n. A rough seaweed *(Galaxaura rugosa).* Cf. *pākalakala.*

kaunu. **1.** nvi. To make love; to love; thrill of love, passion; to be fascinated, absorbed. *Ē ka hoa e kaunu pū nei ma kēia moʻolelo* (Kel. 38), O friend who is also ab-

sorbed in this story. **hoʻo.kaunu.** Caus/sim. **2.** Var. of *kaulu 6. Kaunu a nā lau,* a place of verdure, especially one frequented by birds. *Lit.,* place of leaves.

kaunuanalau. A large Hawaiian bird. (And.)

kau.nuku.nuku. Same as *kaunihinihi.*

kau.nunu. n. **1.** Pole set up as indicative of taboo. **2.** *(Cap.)* A *lua* fighting stroke.

kaunu waha. n. Insincere love-making.

kau.ō, kauwō. vt. To drag, haul, draw along, tow. *Kauō huluhulu,* to drag along roughly, as a canoe hull that is shredded *(huluhulu),* or a child who is bruised. *Kauō ka hiki,* possible to move by dragging. *Pipi kauō,* oxen. *Kauō ā lupe,* same as *kauālupe.* **hoʻo.kau.ō.** To cause to be dragged; to prolong vowels in chanting. **2.** n. Yolk or white of an egg. Cf. *kauō keʻokeʻo, kauō melemele.* **3.** n. Loud type of prayer, usually at *makahiki* festivals. Cf. *wōwō, hoʻokāwōwō.*

kau.ʻoʻe. An office in the king's train (And.); unarmed spy in enemy country (Malo 202, Emerson note; also *kaukoʻe*).

kau.oha. nvt. Order, command, demand, testament, decree, precept, will, message, statement; to order, command, direct, send for, subscribe, dictate, assign, decree, entrust, bequest, commit into the hands of; to summon, to order, as groceries or goods. *Kauoha ʻia,* entrusted, as to God's power. *Ma ke kauoha,* legal notice. *ʻŌuli kauoha,* sign of the imperative. *He kauoha na ka ʻaha,* a judicial decree. *Keʻehia i ka hoʻounauna, keʻehia i ke kauoha* (prayer), trample on the evil messenger, trample on the evil order. *Make kauoha ʻole,* die intestate, without a will. *Keiki kāne lawe kauoha,* messenger boy.

Kau.oha Hou. n. New Testament.

Kau.oha Kahiko. n. Old Testament.

kauo.kahiki. Same as *ʻōhiʻa hā.*

kau.ō keʻo.keʻo. n. White of an egg.

kau ʻokoʻa. vi. Placed, apart, separate.

kau.ō.lani, kauwolani. **1.** n. High shelf or place where chiefs hung or placed *(kau)* their clothes. Cf. *holopapa.* **2.** vt. To express admiration or praise of a chief, as in chant.

kau.ō lupe. Var. of *kauālupe.*

kau.ō mele.mele. Yolk of an egg.

Kau-ʻō.pae. n. Name for the star Sirius.

Kau-ʻō.pua. n. Name of a star.

kau.ō waʻa. v. To drag a canoe, especially if unfinished, from the mountain forest to the shore to be finished.

kau.pā. vi. To walk straight. *Rare.*

kau.paʻewa. vi. To appear irregular or crooked.

kau.paku. Common var. of *kaupoku.*

kau.pale. nvt. Boundary, barrier, partition; dam; to serve as a boundary; to thrust aside, parry, limit; to cover an oven, especially with rocks on its edge to keep earth out; to disown or sever relationship. *Lit.,* place ward off. *Ua kaupale mai kuʻu kaikamahine iaʻu,* my daughter disowned me. **hoʻo.kau.pale.** To cause a separation, barrier; to disown, disinherit.

kau.pale ʻana. n. Blockage, barrier, etc.

kau.pale ʻili. v. To draw the color line; to show race prejudice. *Lit.,* to make a skin boundary.

kau.palena. nvt. To limit, mark a border or boundary, restrict, moderate, set a deadline; limitation, deadline, ration. *Kaupalena ʻia,* limited (as an incorporated company). *Me nā kaupalena ʻole,* unconditional, without a deadline. *Ke kaupalena ʻana i ka manaʻo,* imposition of a condition. **hoʻo.kau.palena.** Caus/sim.

kau.palena hā.nau. n. Birth control.

kau.pale waena. n. Fence or boundary between one patch of land *(waena)* and another.

kau.paona. nvt. Scales, weight; to weigh. *Fig.,* to consider, judge, estimate. *Lit.,* place pound *(Eng.).* See ex., *puka 7. Luna kaupaona* (Isa. 33.18), receiver.

kau.papa. n. A generation back. Cf. *kau ʻapaʻapa.*

kaʻu.papā. vi. To limp. *Rare.*

kau.papa.loʻi. n. Molokai term for taro patch (D. Barrère).

kau.pau. n. An edible brown seaweed *(Chnoospora pacifica),* with many slender branches. Also *wāwahiwa'a.*

kau.pē. 1. vi. Humble, timid and cringing, crushed; to walk in a feeble, wobbly manner, as a sick or aged person. **2.** vt. To put forward, of a paddle. *E kaupē aku nō i ka hoe, e kō mai i ka hoe, o hoe,* put forward the paddle, draw the paddle toward you, paddle!

kau.pe'a. vi. Crisscross, interwoven. *Kī kaupe'a,* ti leaves crossed as a sign of taboo. *Hihia i loko o ke alohiki kaupe'a,* intermingled, mixed in a family united by several marriages. *Ua kaupe'a 'ia nā hae,* the flags are on crossed staffs.

kau.pili. n. Beloved wife or friend, beloved friendship united in such close relationship. *Lit.,* place clinging.

kau.pō. n. A variety of native bananas, perhaps named for the place on Maui. Also *waimūhea.*

kau.po'i. n. Median canoe-bow cover.

kau.poku. 1. nvs. Ridgepole, highest point, roof, ceiling, attic; to set up a ridgepole. *Fig.,* greatest. (Often used without *ke;* see ex., *home, 'ōlepe pū.*) *Ki'eki'e kaupoku o Hanalei,* the high ridgepole of Hanalei [said of conceited or willful persons; a pun on a place name at Hanalei]. *Kāhiko ka nani i Ka-ma'e, ke kaupoku lā o ke 'ala* (chant for Lili'u-o-ka-lani), beauty adorns Ka-ma'e, the greatest fragrance. **2.** vt. To thatch.

kau.poku.'iole. n. Second ridgepole placed above the main ridgepole. *Lit.,* rat ridgepole.

kau po'o.hiwi. nvt. Anything placed on the shoulder, as a cloak or musket; to place on the shoulders, to shoulder. *Hanohano O'ahu i ka 'ilima, kohu manu 'ō'ō kau po'ohiwi,* glorious is O'ahu with the 'ilima, like a [cape of] '*ō'ō* [feathers] on the shoulders.

ka'upu. 1. n. Perhaps Laysan albatross *(Diomedea immutabilis);* it breeds on the Northwestern Hawaiian Islands, Ni'ihau, and Moku Manu. See song, Elbert and Mahoe 65. *Ka'upu hehi 'ale,* billow-treading *ka'upu.* (PCP *takupu.*) **2.** n. A native rather narrow fern *(Polystichum hillebrandii)* with scaly stems, the fronds twice divided. Also *papa'oi.*

kau.pua. 1. Same as *'ōpua. Ke kaupua maila nā ao,* the clouds are gathering in banks. **2.** nvi. Sport: swimming or diving for half-submerged objects, formerly gourds, today *noni* or citric fruits or green coconuts or papayas; to play this game. (Malo 233.)

kau pua. v. To place flowers, especially on graves. *Lā Kau Pua,* Decoration Day.

kau.puka. n. Lasso suspended from bough or gate to trap cattle.

kauwā. Var. spelling of *kauā.*

kau waena. n. Arbitrator.

kau.wahi. paucal article and n. Some, a little, a few; something; some place. Cf. *kau 12; wahi; kekahi.* (Gram. 10.1.) *Na'u ho'i kauwahi i'a,* let me have a little fish. *Na'u ho'i kauwahi o ka i'a,* let me have a part of the fish. *Hiki akula au ma ke kauwahi, a moe ihola i loko o kekahi ana,* I went to a certain place and slept inside a cave.

kau wale. vt. To put or place for no reason; to ride free of charge; to ride bareback.

ka'u.wali. vi. To jiggle, joggle. *Kāua i ka holo ka'uwali* (song), we two joggling along.

kau.wawe, kauawe. n. **1.** Covering of ti leaves made with the stems tied together, and the leaves spread out fanwise, formerly used on the oven, replaced today by gunny sacks. Also *kauwewe, kawewe.* **2.** Ruffle for the neck, as worn by Elizabethans.

kau.weke. nvs. Southwest. *Eng.*

kau wela. n. Summer, hot season.

kau.wele. n. Grass, weeds hanging over fresh water.

kau.welu. Var. of *kauwele.*

kau welu. v. To hang conspicuously a tapa as a taboo sign; to hoist a tapa banner as indication that the *makahiki* ceremonies had begun (Kam. 64:19). *Lit.,* hang rag.

kau.wewe. Var. of *kauwawe.*

kau.wila. Var. spelling of *kauila.*

kau.wili. vt. To mingle, mix.

kauwō. Var. spelling of *kauō.*

kauwoha. Spelling used in letters by Queen Emma for *kauoha.*

kauwōlani. Var. spelling of *kauōlani.*

kauwō wa'a. Var. spelling of *kauō wa'a.*

kau.wowo. Var. of *kawowo.*

kawa. 1. n. Leaping place, as a precipice from which a swimmer leaps into a pool. *Ki'o kawa,* a pool below a precipice from which swimmers leap. **2.** vt. To assassinate, strike in the dark, kill and rob. **3.** *(Cap.)* n. Site of a jail in Ka-lihi, Honolulu. *Pa'a i Kawa* (Kel. 149), lock up in jail.

kā.wā. n. Distance between two points; length of time (Kel. 129). *Pehea ke kāwā mawaena o nā hale?* What's the distance between the houses? *'O ke ku'i kēia, 'o ka holo kēlā, moe kāwā, hāpala ka 'ele* (For. 4:57, *kōnane* chant), this is a stroke, that is a run, a space lies between, the black is blotted. *Kāwā loa ka mana'o o lāua,* their opinions are far apart.

kā.wa'a. 1. nv. To cast overboard from a canoe, as fish nets or as a victim to be executed at sea; a method of deep-sea fishing with nets. **2.** interj. Call of the curlew bird, believed to say: "*I kāwa'a, e holo, ua nui ke kai o ke aumoe,* let's do canoe net fishing, sail, the sea is high at midnight."

kā wa'a. nv. Canoe bailer; to bail a canoe.

kā.wae. 1. v. To bring up the foot, as in sitting cross-legged on a mat; to draw to one with the foot; to trip with the foot. *Rare.* **2.** Var. name for *pā'ao'ao,* a disease.

kā.wa'e. 1. vt. To treat in a mean way, to underrate others and treat them as of no value. **2.** *(Cap.)* Name of a star.

Ka.wa'e-kū. n. A *lua* fighting stroke.

kā.wa'e.wa'e. 1. n. Kind of stone or coral, as used in polishing canoes, or in rubbing off pig bristles. **2.** nvt. To pay out a fishline while deep-sea fishing; a binding line. *Rare.* **3.** See *Pulelehua Kāwa'ewa'e.*

Ka-wae.wae.wae-ka-hō.kū-ie-kau-i-luna-o-he-lani. n. Unidentified star, no data. (Kuhelani.)

kā.waha. nvs. Vacant; hollow; furrowed, as a sea with waves; hollowed, as a log; fissured; gap. Cf. *waha,* mouth, opening.

Ka-waha-o-ka-manō. n. A *lua* fighting stroke. *Lit.,* the mouth of the shark. (Also without *Ka-.*)

kā.waha.waha. Redup. of *kāwaha.*

kā.wai. 1. n. Last liquor run off in distillation, very thin and watery *(wai),* especially of brew made of ti root or cane; extremely weak and watery liquor. *'A 'ohe ikaika 'o kēia lama, he kāwai wale nō,* this rum has no strength; it is nearly all water. **2.** Same as *maniawai,* drowsy. **3.** *(Cap.)* n. Name of a navigation star (no data).

kā.wai hemo. ns. Extremely watery *kāwai. He kāwai hemo kēia,* this is just water, the very end of the brew.

kawa.kawa. 1. n. Bonito, little tunny *(Euthynnus yaito).* Sometimes called *pohopoho.* Growth stages are *kīna'u* (immature), *'āhua,* and *kawakawa* (adult). (PCP *tawatawa.*) **2.** vs. Dampish, saturated. *Ua kawakawa kahi moe i ka wai,* this sleeping place is saturated with moisture.

kawa.kawa.ū. Redup. of *kawaū.*

kā.wala. 1. vs. Scattered here and there, sparse, irregular, inadequate, insufficient; unintelligible, of speech. *ho'o.kā.wala.* To make sparse; to eat sparingly; to talk unintelligibly. **2.** vt. To throw with force. Cf. *wala,* to throw, tip. *Kāwala kua,* to strike from behind.

Kā.wala-ki'i. n. Upper stroke in club fighting (RC 59).

kā.wala.wala. Redup. of *kāwala. 'Ōlelo kāwalawala,* speech of which only a word here and there is understood. *He mā'ona kāwalawala,* insufficiently filled after eating.

kawa.lia. n. Cavalier. *Eng.*

kā.wao. 1. n. A variety of sweet potato. **2.** vi., interj. To work in unity; exclamation urging people to work together. *Rare.*

Kawa-o-Maka.li'i. n. Name of a constellation in the Milky Way. *Lit.,* precipice of Makali'i.

Ka-wao-nui-a-Ola. n. Name of a star appearing in the month of Hilina-mā. *Lit.,* the great forests of Life.

kawa.ū. vs. Damp, wet with cold, moist with fog, humid; wet, as in a cold sweat. Cf. *ū* (moist), *ma'ū, ko'ū.*

kā.wa'u. 1. Same as *wa'u,* to scrape. **2.** *(Cap.)* n. Name of a star. **3.** Same as *hea'e,* a variety of *Zanthoxylum dipetalum,* the wood of which was used for tapa-beating anvils. **4.** Same as *pūkiawe. Lā-na'i, Maui.* **5.** Same as *uhiuhi,* a tree. *Maui.* **6.** n. A native holly *(Ilex anomala),* a rather common shrub or tree, with shiny, oval leaves and panicles of small, white flowers and small, round, black fruits. (Neal 528.) Also *'aiea.* **7.** To detain, delay, keep back. (AP.)

kā.wa'u.pu'u. n. Type of stone from which sinkers for octopus fishing were made. (Malo 19.)

kawea. A kind of fish. (And.)

kawele. vi. To work or act slowly and in moderation, as in paddling a canoe or farming; slow, lingering, as disease.

kā.wele. 1. nvi. Kind of chant with clear, distinct pronunciation, somewhat like *kepakepa* but slower; to chant thus. **2.** nvi. A hula step: one foot makes a half circle forward and to the side without touching the floor; usually in combination with other steps as the *holo* or *'uwehe;* to do this step. Often called *'ai kāwele, kāwele* style. **3.** nvt. Towel, napkin, dishcloth; to wipe or dry with a cloth. *(Eng.,* towel.) *E kāwele mai i ke pā,* dry the dish. **ho'o.kā.wele.** To wipe, pretend to wipe.

kawele.'ā. n. *Sphyraena helleri,* a smaller relative of the *kākū,* a fish. See saying, *hauhili.*

kā.wele 'au.'au. n. Bath towel.

kā.wele holoi. n. Washcloth.

kā.wele.kā. Same as *kōwelokā.*

kā.wele pā. nv. Dish towel; to wipe dishes with a towel.

kā.wele wai. v. To mop or wipe with wet cloth or water.

kā.wele.wele. 1. nv. Ropes, especially those attached to *'iako,* outrigger booms, to assist in righting a capsized canoe; lines attached to a fish net; person or canoe at the head of a line being pulled. *Fig.,* to recall something almost forgotten; dim memory. Also *kākāwelewele. 'O Kama ka akua i ke kāwelewele,* Kama was the god [who held] the end of the rope being pulled. *Ā i loa'a ho'i ke kāwelewele, pono iki nō ia manawa,* when an almost forgotten thought is recalled, it helps a little for the time being. **2.** n. Goatee. **3.** Redup. of *kawele.* **4.** Redup. of *kāwele.*

kawelo. n. A variety of sweet potato.

Ka-welo Ali'i. n. Name of a star said to rise during the month of Hilinehu, and to be accompanied by the star Ka-malama. *Lit.,* the royal family.

kā.welo.kā. Var. of *kōwelokā.*

kawelo kupa. n. A variety of mountain sweet potato. It has heart-shaped leaves and hard tubers, and is very sweet.

Ka-welo Lani. n. Name of a star that rises with Kau-ka-malama in the month of 'Ikuwā and disappears shortly.

kā.welo.welo. vi. To flutter, whip, as a flag in the wind.

kā.welu. 1. n. A wind-blown grass *(Eragrostis variabilis),* famous in songs of Nu'u-anu *pali; E. niihauensis* on Ni'ihau. Also *kalamalō* and *'emoloa.* (Neal 64.) See song, *kehakeha.* **2.** nvi. A hula step, to do this step, which is said to be named for the grass: one foot taps time with the heel, the toes being stationary, while the other foot, flat, steps forward and then a little back, twice or more; the step is repeated reversing the feet. In English this is called the Ka-lā-kaua step because the step is used to begin the hula dedicated to Ka-lā-kaua: *Ka-lā-kaua nō he inoa, ka pua mae 'ole i ka lā,* a name chant for Ka-lā-kaua, the flower that wilts not in the sun. **3.** n. A seaweed, perhaps

Wrangelia penicillata, which resembles the flowering head of *Eragrostis variabilis.* **4.** n. A type of house thatching. **5.** vi. To hang loose, as long hair (Kel. 116).

Ka-weo. n. Name of a star (no data).

kawewe. 1. vi. To clatter, as dishes; to roar, as a sudden downpour; to snap or crackle; such a roaring, clatter, crackling. *Ke kawewe mai nei ka ua,* the rain suddenly pours down. **2.** Same as *kauwawe.*

kā.wī. vt. To press, wring out, squeeze out, as fruit juice. (Also *kōwī.* Cf. *'uwī.*)

kā.wili. vt. To mix ingredients, blend; to ensnare birds, as with lime; entwined, interwoven, interlaced. *Lepo kāwili,* clay, adobe. *Ka po'e kāwili manu 'ō'ō,* people who ensnared *'ō'ō.* **ho'o.kā.wili.** Caus/sim. *Rare.* (PPN *taawiliwili.*)

kā.wili kā.'ekā. vt. To entangle, involve, interweave, entwine, interlace.

kā.wili lā.'au. nv. To mix ingredients, drugs, medicine; pharmacist, druggist.

kā.wili manu. nv. Bird catcher or snarer; to snare birds.

kā.wili palaoa. nv. Flour mill; to grind flour. Also *ka'a palaoa.*

kā.wili.wili. Redup. of *kāwili.* (PPN *taawiliwili.*)

kā.wili.wili humu.humu. n. Sewing machine worked by hand rather than by a foot treadle.

kawoa. n. Savoy, common cabbage with curled leaves. *Eng.*

kawowo. nvi. Seedling; thrifty young plant; sucker, shoot from a parent stalk; to multiply and thrive, as a plant or people. *Fig.,* progeny. See *ho'ohua kawowo. Kāu mau kawowo hope loa* (FS 147), your most distant progeny. **ho'o.kawowo.** Caus/sim. *Rare.*

-kāwōwō. **ho'o.kā.wō.wō.** To roar, as a wind or waterfall. Cf. *wōwō,* roar.

kā.wō.wō.wō. Redup. of *-kāwōwō;* roar, as of thunder or earthquake. (For. 6:444, 445.)

ke. 1. definite article, same as *ka,* often translated "the." See Gram. 10.2. For use of *ke* as an alternant of *ka,* see *ka 1.* (PNP *te.*) **2.** Contraction of *ka mea e,* the one who will, should, or is; the thing that (or which) is, will, should. *'O wau ke hele a'e i ka hale,* let me go nearby to the house. *'O ka makuahine wale nō ke noho ana,* the mother was the only one staying. (Gram. 10.2.) **3.** conj. If, when (in the future; Gram. 11.1). *I kō mākou wā kamali'i, ke ho'olele aku i nā lupe, huhū maila nā kūpuna,* in our childhood, when we flew kites the grandparents scolded. *Ke hele 'oe, hele au,* if you go, I'll go. **4.** A particle connecting certain forms, as *hiki* and *pono,* with following verbs. (Gram. 5.4.) *Hiki ia'u ke hele,* I can go. *Pono ke hele,* right to go.

kē. nvt. Protest, complaint, criticism; critic, especially a hula critic; formerly a hula master who was invited by another hula master to criticize his class; to criticize; to push, shove, struggle against, oppose, shun, avoid, abstain from, refuse. *Kē 'ai,* to fast. *Nui ke kē o ka po'e i kēlā puke,* there was much protest by the people about that book. **ho'o.kē.** To crowd, elbow, push aside, jostle, struggle, oppress, shun, scorn, protest. *Fig.,* to beset with difficulties. *Ho'okē 'ai,* to fast. *Ho'okē ā maka,* to favor some at the expense of others, as relatives. *Ho'okē ihu,* to blow the nose. *Nā weliweli ho'okē,* oppressive terrors. *Ka'ula i ka ho'okē a nā manu* (saying), Ka'ula [Islet] is crowded with birds [of any crowded place]. **2.** vi. To clang, as a bell or gong; to dingdong, strike, as a clock. **3.** vi. To flatten out, adjust to a surrounding level, as in removing a heap of earth. *Rare.* **4.** n. Player of the *pūhenehene* game. *Ho'omau maila nā kē o kēlā 'ao'ao e koho i kahi i waiho ai ka no'a,* the players of that side continued to guess where the *no'a* was placed. **5.** Same as *kā,* the interj. (1 Kor. 15.36.) **6.** n. The letter "k." *Eng.*

-kē. Rare suffix. Here and there. See *holoholokē, holokē, lelekē.*

kea. 1. nvs. White, clear; fair-complexioned person, often favorites at court (Malo 201); shiny, white mother-of-pearl shell. Cf. *keakea, kekea, Mauna Kea.*

Po'o kea, towhead, gray-haired person. *One kea,* white sand [this is shortened to *ōkea* or *kea,* as in the expression *kea pili mai,* drift gravel [vagabond]. (PPN *tea.*) **2.** n. Breast milk. See *Nu'a-kea.* **3.** n. A variety of sugar cane, among Hawaiians one of the best-known and most-used canes, especially in medicine: clumps erect, dense, of medium height; pith white. (HP 223–5.) *Ua ola ā 'ō kō kea,* living until *kea* cane tassels [until the hair turns gray]. **4.** n. Name listed by Hillebrand for *kolomona (Mezoneuron kavaiense);* see *uhiuhi.* **5.** nvs. Share, as of stocks; stocks. *Ku'u kuleana kea,* my shared property. *Eng.* **6.** Also **dea.** n. Hart, male deer. (Kanl. 12.15.)

ke'a. 1. nvt. Cross, crucifix, any crossed piece; main house purlin; sticks connecting canoes of a double canoe. *Fig.,* to hinder, obstruct, intercept, block; obstruction, barrier; baffled *(fig.).* Used idiomatically like *kana 2* and *ka'e 1:* '*A 'ole i ke'a mai ka hahana wela o kēia lā* (Kel. 14), there was no limit to the stifling heat of this day. Cf. *ke'ahakahaka, ke'apa'a.* **ho'o.ke'a.** To cross, block, obstruct, hinder. (Probably PPN *teka.*) **2.** n. Hand, as of bananas. (FS 245.) **3.** nvt. Bow, dart; to shoot with bow and arrow (For. 4:259). (PPN *tika,* PCP *teka.*) **4.** n. Male animal reserved for breeding; virile male; sire. *Kū i ke ke'a,* like the sire [of a child]. **5.** Pleurisy. (AP.)

ke'a.awai.leia. n. Fishhook with more than one barb; small stick with hooks at each end and line in the middle, as used for small fish. *Rare.*

kē.'ae. vi. To saturate, soak in.

ke'a.haka.haka. n. **1.** Abdomen. (PPN *fatafata.*) **2.** Ladder with crosspieces, a poetic reference to the ladders used to scale Kaua'i precipices. *Rare.*

keahi. n. A native tree *(Nesoluma polynesicum),* with milky sap and oblong, alternate leaves.

Ke-ahi-lele. n. Name of a star that rises in the month of Welehu, accompanied by Ke-'alohi-lani. *Lit.,* the firebrand.

Ke-aho-lehi. n. A *lua* fighting stroke; fish was taboo to the learner.

ke'a ho'o.hano.hano. n. Honorary cross or medal.

kē 'ai. See *kē 1.*

keaka. 1. n. Theater, drama, theatrical. *Eng. Hale keaka,* theater building. *Hana keaka,* to act in the theater; show business; a play. *Mea hana keaka,* actor. *Wahine hana keaka,* actress. *Keaka lio,* horse show; circus. *Keaka nika,* minstrel show. **2.** *Eng.* Jack (in a deck of cards). *Eng.* **3.** vi. To chat, speak. *Eng.*

keaka hopena kau.maha. n. Tragedy.

kea.kea. n. Semen. *Fig.,* child, seed. *Pohō i ka mālama i kō ha'i keakea* (saying), bad luck from caring for the children of others [said in anger at a foster child].

ke'a.ke'a. Redup. of *ke'a 1;* to object, prevent, oppose; disputed. *Ke'ake'a 'ole,* unobstructed. *Ke'ake'a 'ia e nā au,* blocked by the currents [as a ship]. *E ke'ake'a ai i kā kāua ho'ohiki* (Laie 383), to circumvent our oath.

Ke-ake-o-Milu. n. A *lua* fighting stroke. *Lit.,* the liver of Milu. (Also without *Ke-.*)

kea.kula, teasura. n. Pine (RSV), box tree (KJV) *(Buxus sempervirens).* (Isa. 41.19, Neal 520.) (Heb. *teasur.*)

ke (verb) **ala.** Same as *ke* (verb) *lā,* but less common.

ke'a lā.'au. n. A stick game like peewee: one player pries a small stick up from the ground with a longer stick, hits it, and tries to run to a point and back before his opponent can catch it. *Lit.,* wooden cross.

Ke-ala-ka'a. n. Name of a star. *Lit.,* the rolling pathway.

Ke-ala-polo.hiwi-a-Kana.loa. Same as *Alanui-polo-hiwi-a-Kanaloa:* see *alanui.*

Ke-ala-polo.hiwi-a-Kāne. Same as *Alanui-polohiwi-a-Kāne:* see *alanui.*

Ke-ali'i-o-Kona-i-ka-lewa. n. The star Canopus. *Lit.,* the chief of the south in the heavens. Also *Ali'i-o-Kona-i-ka-lewa.*

Ke-'alohi. n. Name of a star that appears on the night of

Hoaka in the month of Ka'aona after the disappearance of Pau-ahi-lani; it in turn vanishes in Welehu. *Lit.,* the brightness.

Ke-'alohi-lani. n. A star that rises on the night of Mauli in the month of Welo and continues through the month of Māhoe Mua, when it vanishes on the night of Muku. A ring around it is said to portend a coming revolution. *Lit.,* the heavenly brightness.

-kēāmaka. ho'o.kē.ā.maka. Selfish, ungracious, as one eating in the presence of others; partial; partiality.

Ke-ā.mio. n. A *lua* fighting stroke. *Lit.,* the gusty one. (Also without *Ke-.*)

kea.nahā. n. A specially built place reserved for the high chief on the platform of a double canoe.

Ke-ao-lewa. Same as *Ke-ō-lewa.*

ke'a.pa'a. n. Human chest. *Lit.,* solid cross.

ke'a papa nu'u. n. Firmament. (Kam. 64:13.)

ke'a pua. v. To shoot or slide arrows made of the stems of sugar-cane tassels.

Ke'a 'Ula.'ula. n. Red Cross.

ke.au.mā.hina. n. A variety of sweet potato.

Keawe. n. Name of a southern star, said to be named for an ancient chief.

Ke-awe.awe-Maka.li'i. n. Perhaps the constellation Pleiades. (Kuhelani.)

ke'e. 1. nvs. Crookedness; fault, defect, flaw, deformity; crooked, bent, full of faults. *Nānā ke'e,* to look at with disfavor, look for faults. '*A 'ohe pu'u, 'a'ohe ke'e,* no physical defects, no flaws [common description of a handsome person]. *Noho ke'e,* to sit crookedly; in disagreement, opposition. **ho'o.ke'e.** To make a turn, as in cutting paper or cloth; to turn, as in walking; to bend, form an angle. *Ho'oke'e i ka wāwae,* to walk by crossing the feet one in front of the other, as in some kinds of square dancing. (PPN *teke.*) **2.** Same as *ke'ena;* nook. *Rare.* **3.** n. A stone used for adzes.

-kē.'ē. ho'o.kē.'ē. To shun, slight, avoid. Cf. *kē 1.*

ke'e.hana. n. Any footprint, footstool, footprint; ground or floor stamped on or trodden on. (Probably *kc'e + -hana,* nominalizer; *ke'ehi 1,* below, is probably *ke'e + -hi,* transitivizer. See *papa he'ehana* and Gram. 6.6.2.)

ke'e-. See *ke'ehana, ke'ehi.* (Probably PPN *teke.*)

ke'e.hana wā.wae. n. Footstool (Isa. 66.1), footrest.

ke'e.hau. vi. To farm at night, especially during the moonlight nights of Akua, Hoku, and Māhealani. *Rare.*

ke'ehi. 1. vt. To stamp, tramp, step, tread; to brace with the feet; to rebel against, repudiate; to strike against, to put foot into stirrup in mounting a horse; to trip; not to tolerate, to "put the foot down" in ending a situation; to get in by stepping up, as into a vehicle. *Ke'ehi akula ia i kekahi wāwae maluna o kekahi wāwae, ā hina ihola 'o Nūnū i lalo* (FS 147), tripping one foot over the other, Nūnū fell down. *Ke'ehi lō'ihi,* full pace; forward march. *Ke'ehi pōkole,* short step, half step; mark time. (PNP *takafi.*) **2.** n. Stirrup. **3.** n. Narrow space between top edges of house thatching.

ke'e.hia. Pas/imp. of *ke'ehi 1.* See ex., *kauoha.*

ke'ehi ka'a. Same as '*a'e ka'a.*

ke'ehi.lae. vs. Haughty, disdainful, assuming an air of superiority. *Lit.,* treading brow. *Rare.*

ke'e.hina. n. Footrest, footstool, position where one stands, stance, firm position, place.

ke'e.hina hana. n. Solution, remedy.

Ke-'ehu.hiwa. n. Name of a star visible on the night of Muku in the month of Hinaia'ele'ele, rising with Lua-ho'omoe.

ke'e.ke'e. 1. Redup. of *ke'e 1.* **ho'o.ke'e.ke'e.** Redup. of *ho'oke'e;* zigzag, angular; zigzag lines, as in a mat motif. (PPN *teketeke.*) **2.** Same as *kekē,* surly, cranky.

ke'e.ke'ehi. Redup. of *ke'ehi 1. E ke'eke'ehi kūlana i pa'a,* tread firmly in your stance.

ke'e.ke'e.hia. Redup. of *ke'ehia.*

ke'e.ke'e nuku. vt. To threaten, scold loudly.

ke'ele. vs. Great, excessive. *Ke'ele ka pī'ō'ō o ka ma'i,* the patient was greatly troubled. *Ke'ele ku'u aloha i ku'u kama,* great is my love for my child. *Ke'ele 'āwa'a ke ala,* the road has many gullies.

ke'e.moa. 1. vs. Sour, bitter, crabbed, surly, ill-natured, turning against friends (frequently follows *'ōpū,* disposition). **ho'o.ke'e.moa.** To behave thus. **2.** n. Rump bone of a chicken.

ke'ena. n. Office, room, booth, closet, stall, vault, studio, nook, cranny; drawer of a bureau *(rare);* department, board, bureau; memory *(fig.). Ke'ena pale ahi,* fireproof vault. *Pau ka mo'olelo kaulana o Ka-welo, a koe paha kekahi ma nā ke'ena 'ōpū o ka lehulehu* (FS 113), the famous story of Ka-welo is over, but some of it perhaps remains in the crannies of the hearts of the people.

Ke'ena Hā.lā.wai. n. Assembly Hall, where the Territorial House of Representatives met.

ke'ena hana. n. Place to work, workshop, office, laboratory.

ke'ena ho'o.nā. n. Office where land claims were adjudicated by the Board of Commissioners to Quiet Land Titles.

Ke'ena Ho'o.na'au.ao o ka Lehu.lehu. n. Department of Public Instruction.

ke'ena kā.kau kope. n. Recorder's office.

ke'ena kalaunu. n. Throne room.

ke'ena kapu. n. Taboo room; tabernacle (Puk. 25.9), sanctuary (Puk. 25.8), private room.

ke'ena koho pā.loka. n. Voting booth.

Ke'ena Kope. n. Bureau of Conveyances.

ke'ena noho. n. Apartment.

Ke'ena Uku Ho'o.mau. n. Pension Board.

ke'ena waiho. n. Closet.

ke'eo, ho'o.ke'eo. Same as *ka'eo.*

keha. nvt. Height, pride, dignity; lofty, high, prominent; majestic, dignified; to brag, boast, praise; to rise to the top. *Fig.,* head. *Ka lā e keha iho ai kō au hou* (Kel. 145), the day your new era boasts of. *Kau ke keha i ka uluna,* the head rests on the pillow [work is done]. *Ki'eki'e kau keha i luna,* high above it rests. *Moe keha,* to lie with the head on a pillow. *Ke keha nei 'oe i kō laki,* you are bragging of your luck. *La'i ke keha o ka nohona,* peaceful the dignity of life. *Ke kā'akepa ka 'ōlelo i Hīhīmanu,* toplofty and from side to side goes the talk at Hīhīmanu [said of a boaster who keeps repeating; Hīhīmanu is a Kaua'i peak]. **ho'o.keha.** To cause height, pride, boasting, etc. Same as *keha.*

kehaka, tehasa. n. Badger. (Hebrew *tahash.*)

keha.keha. Redup. of *keha;* to flaunt. *Kau kehakeha Nu'u-anu i ka makani, wehiwehi i ka holu a ke kāwelu* (song), proudly stands Nu'u-anu in the wind, adorned with the ripple of *kāwelu* grass. **ho'o.keha.keha.** To act proudly; to cause pride.

kē.hau. n. **1.** Dew, mist, dewdrop. See ex., *'ōpū 2.* **2.** *(Cap.)* Name of a gentle land breeze, as of West Hawai'i; Ka-pa'a, Kaua'i; Kula, Maui; Hālawa, Moloka'i and O'ahu. (For. 5:97.)

kē.hau anu. n. Cold dew, frost.

kē.hau.pa'a. n. Ice. (GP 20.)

kehe. Var. of *ke'e l. Ke-ala-kehe* (Kona place name), the winding path.

Kē.hela. n. Name of a star.

kehena. n. **1.** Place where refuse is thrown and burned, dump. **2.** *(Sometimes Cap.)* Gehenna, hell. (Hoik. 1.18.) *Eng.*

kē.hō.hō. interj. Bray, to bray, as a donkey.

Ke.ho'o.ea. n. Constellation name. See *Keoe.*

kēhu. Var. spelling of *ke ehu. Kāne ali'i i kēhu kai,* Kāne, chief in the sea spray.

kē.hue. vs. Yellowish, of soil.

kei. 1. nvt. To glory in, take pride in; dignified, proud, glorious; one's pride and glory. Cf. *ha'akei. Ē Ka-malama iki ku'u pōki'i, e kei ka noho* (FS 67), o little Ka-malama, my favorite younger brother, may you act with dignified pride. *E kei a'e ana au i ku'u keiki,* I'm glorying in my boy. *Kei ka nani o 'Iesū!* How glorious

is Jesus! **ho'o.kei.** Caus/sim. **2.** n. A hard rock from which adzes were made.

kē.ia. demon. This, this person, this thing; the latter. Cf. Gram. 8.3 For *kēlā mea kēia mea* see *kēlā . . . kēia. Kēia pule a'e,* next week. *A me nā pilikia o kēia,* and the troubles of the latter. *E hele ana kēia i ka hana,* this person is going to work; work; I'm going to work. [Note use of *kēia* for "I."] *Nā kānāwai . . . e ho'opau 'ia, a ma kēia ua ho'opau loa 'ia nō,* the laws . . . are to be revoked, and hereby are revoked. *Kēia mau mea,* these things. (PPN *ee,* PCP *teeia.*)

ke'ia. Var. of *kēia.*

kei.kei. Redup. of *kei. Keikei kūlana hale wili, 'a'ohe mea hana o loko* (chant), nice-looking spot has the sugar mill, but nothing doing inside. **ho'o.kei.kei.** Caus/sim.

keiki. 1. nvi. Child, offspring, descendant, progeny, boy, youngster, son, lad, nephew, son of a dear friend; calf, colt, kid, cub; worker; shoot or sucker, as of taro; to have or obtain a child; to be or become a child. Cf. *keiki kāne. Kāu keiki,* your son. *Keiki a ka pueo,* child of the owl [one whose father is not known]. *Keiki hānau o ka 'āina,* a native son, one born on the land. *Ua keiki kākou no ke Akua* (Rom. 8.16), we are the children of God. (PCP *t(a,e)iti.*) **2.** n. Gauge, as on a sewing machine. *Eng.*

keiki 'ai wai.ū. n. Suckling child. *Lit.,* child consume milk.

keiki ali'i. n. Prince, child of a chief.

keiki 'alu.'alu. n. A premature baby.

keiki hanauna. n. Nephew or niece.

keiki he'e wale. n. Miscarried foetus. *Lit.,* child slide without cause.

keiki hele kula. n. School child.

keiki hipa. n. Lamb. *Lit.,* sheep *(Eng.)* offspring.

keiki kame.ha'i. n. Illegitimate child whose father is not definitely known. *Lit.,* wonder child.

keiki kāne. n. Boy, lad, son.

keiki kao. Same as *kao keiki.*

keiki lawe nū.pepa. n. Paper boy.

keiki.mahine. An old spelling of *kaikamahine.*

keiki makua 'ole. n. Orphan. *Lit.,* child without parent.

keiki manu.ahi. n. Illegitimate child. *Lit.,* gratis child.

keiki mea makua. n. A child with parents who provide good care and affection; people who have important parents.

keiki papa. n. Native whose ancestors for several generations back were natives of the same place.

keiki papa.kema. n. Godchild. *Lit.,* baptismal *(Eng.)* child.

keiki pipi. Same as *pipi keiki.*

keiki po'o 'ole. n. Illegitimate child. *Lit.,* headless child.

keka, seka. n. Sex, gender. *Eng.*

kekahi. article. A, some, one, few, other, another, a certain; besides, too, also, including, moreover, likewise, someone, anyone, companion, fellow worker, spouse. *Kekahi lā,* some other day, a certain day. (Gram. 10.1.) *Kekahi kanaka,* someone else, someone, somebody. *Kekahi mea,* someone, else, something else, something. *Kekahi wā, kekahi manawa,* sometime, some other time. *Na'u kekahi,* give me some. *'O au kekahi e hele,* I'm going too. *'A'ole 'o au kekahi,* I'm not either. *Pehea kekahi o 'olua?* How's your companion (wife, colleague)? *'O ka i'a kekahi na ke akua,* the fish also for the god. *Eia kekahi,* moreover, furthermore, also. *I kekahi ā i kekahi aku,* to one or the other, alternatingly. *'O ka kama'ilio aku na moho kekahi me kekahi,* the candidates conversed with one another. (PEP *tetasi.*)

Ke.kahuna. n. The book Ecclesiastes.

Ke-kai-hili. n. Name of a southern star.

kē.kake. n. **1.** Donkey, jackass. *Eng.* Also *'ēkake, iākake.* **2.** Same as *piula,* a card game.

keka.kia, setadia, sedatia. n. Stadia, in surveying (RSV), furlong (KJV). (Hoik. 21.16.) *Eng.*

ke.kaloa-kā-maka.maka. n. A religious service, especially for dedication of timber for a temple building, or to dedicate a live chicken or pig to be killed for sacrifice. (Malo text, chapter 26, section 7.1.)

keka.mekele, dekametere. n. Decameter. *Eng.*

Ke-kau-hiwa-kā. n. Star appearing on the night of Hoaka in the month of Welehu and vanishing on the night of Muku in the same month. Other stars perhaps rising at about the same time are Hiʻi Lei, Hiʻi Kua, Pā-kōnane, and Kahuli-aliʻi.

keke. Same as *ʻakekeke*, turnstone.

kekē. 1. nvi. Scolding, shrieking angrily; exposure of the teeth, as in derision, anger, or hypocritical smiles; surly sharp-tongued, cranky; to crow, as a rooster. Cf. *kekē niho, kekē nuku.* **hoʻo.kekē, haʻa.kekē.** To scold, expose the teeth, etc. **2.** vs. Bony, skinny, thin. *Ua hele wale ā kekē nā iwi,* so thin that the bones show. **3.** Indecent exposure by a woman or girl; admonition to a female to sit properly. **hoʻo.kekē.** Caus/sim.

kē.kē. 1. nv. Distended, enlarged, as a stomach in pregnancy; big-bellied. Cf. *kekewe.* **2.** A kind of fish (And.), perhaps a variant name for *ʻoʻopu hue,* puffer fishes.

-kē.kē. hoʻo.kē.kē. Redup. of *hoʻokē. Ka hoʻokēkē o nā kānaka,* the shoving of the people.

kekea. n. Albino. Cf. *kea,* white. (PPN *tetea.*)

kekeʻe. 1. Redup. of *keʻe 1,* but more common; distorted, crooked, twisted. *Fig.,* unrighteous, erroneous, distorted. *Haʻina kekeʻe,* irregular verb. *E like me ke kekeʻe o ka lālā lāʻau, pēlā nō ke kekeʻe o kona aka* (saying), like the crookedness of the tree branch, so the crookedness of its shadow [like father, like son]. **hoʻo.-kekeʻe.** To crook, bend, twist out of shape, pervert. **2.** Same as *ʻaha,* a fish. (And.)

kē.kekaha. Same as *kīkahakaha.*

kekeko. vs. Small and ugly, with pug nose.

kekela. 1. Same as *kelakela.* **2.** Also *kedera.* Cedar. (Nal. 5.10.) *Eng.* **3.** Also **sekela.** n. Shekel. (Puk. 30.13.) *Eng.*

kekele, degere. n. Degree, as in latitude, music; an academic degree. *Eng. ʻElua kekele o ka pepehi kanaka,* second-degree murder. *Mea hōʻike kekele* (2 Nal. 20.11), sundial; *lit.,* thing showing degrees.

kekele hoʻo.hano.hano. n. Honorary degree.

Kē.kē.mapa, Dekemaba. n. December. *Eng.*

kekene. vs. Evilly disposed, jealous. *ʻŌpū kekene,* evil disposition.

kekē niho. vs. Surly, cross, cranky, violently rude, needlessly and unbearably insulting, snarling, often in the sense of making threats that may not be carried out; to shriek in anger.

kekē nuku. About the same as *kekē niho,* but with more verbalization and scolding; sharp-tongued. *Lit.,* scolding beak.

kekepa. Redup. of *kepa 1.*

kē.kē.pue. 1. vt. To shun others; to withdraw from others, as in shame. *(Cap.)* **2.** Name of a star.

kekē.ue, kekewe. vi. To gossip maliciously, slander, defame. *ʻŌpū kekēue,* evil-hearted, malevolent.

kē.kewe. vs. Bloated, swelled, as with dropsy; so fat that the stomach overhangs. Cf. *kēkē.*

keki.mala, dekimala. nvs. Decimal. *Eng.*

keko. n. **1.** Monkey, ape; said to be an ancient name for a small and ugly creature, especially with a pug nose. *Hana keko,* foolish or ugly behavior. **2.** Sago. *Eng.*

keko.keko. Same as *kekeko.*

Keko.kia, Secotia. nvs. Scotland; Scotch, Scottish. (*Eng.,* Scotia.)

keko.leka, setoreka. n. Stork. (Zek. 5.9.) *Eng.* Also *kikonia.*

kekona, sekona. Second (the time unit). (Hal. 30.5.) *Eng.*

keku. v. To repulse, shove away, nudge. **hoʻo.keku.** Caus/sim.

keku.keku. Redup. of *keku.*

kela. 1. vs. Excelling, exceeding, projecting beyond, reaching high above; to jut out, excel. Cf. *kākela, pākela, poʻokela* and ex., *ʻoi 2. Hanohano Hāʻupu kela*

i ka lani, glorious (Mt.) Hāʻupu reaching high in the sky. **hoʻo.kela.** To outdo, surpass, excel, exceed; to show off, try to excel, show preference; higher, superior, vain. **2.** Also **sela.** n. Sailor. *Eng.* **3.** n. Tailor. *Eng.* **4.** Also **gera.** n. Gerah. *Biblical. Eng.*

ke (verb) **lā.** Part. denoting present tense at a distance from the speaker. Cf. *ke* (verb) *nei* and Gram. 5.3, 8.3. (PCP *te* (verb) *laa.*)

kē.lā. demon. That, that one, he, she, it, that person or thing; the former. See *kēlā . . . kēia* below and Gram. 8.3. In connected discourse or narration, *kēlā* preceding a noun means "the" in the sense of aforementioned. *Kēlā mau mea,* those things. *Ua hele aku nei kēlā i ka hana,* he has just gone to work. *Ka mea kūpono i ka ʻike hapa o kēlā,* the proper thing for the limited knowledge of the former. *Kēlā pule aku nei,* last week. *Kēlā pule aku nei a ia pule aku,* week before last. *Kēlā Pōʻahā aku nei,* last Thursday. (PNP *teelaa.*)

kelaka, teraka. n. Tract. *Eng. Kō ʻAmelika ʻAhahui Kelaka,* American Tract Society.

kē.lā. . . . kē.ia. demon. This and that, all, every, everything, here and there; miscellaneous, various (*kēlā* always precedes *kēia:* see Gram. 11.2.) *ʻO kēlā aiʻole ʻo kēia,* this or that, alternating. *I kēlā me kēia lā,* daily. *I kēlā me kēia pule,* weekly. *I kēlā me kēia makahiki,* yearly. *I kēlā a me kēia ʻelua makahiki,* every other year. *Kēlā mahina kēia mahina,* every month, monthly. *ʻAʻohe pau pono o kāna pūlumi ʻana, o kēlā me kēia pau,* she did not sweep thoroughly, just here and there and finished, just a lick and a promise. *ʻO kēlā mea kēia mea e makemake ana i ka lio, e hele mai ʻoia,* whoever wants a horse, let him come. *Ua haʻi ʻia ka lono i kēlā mea a me kēia mea o lākou,* the news was told to all of them.

kela.kela. Redup. of *kela 1. Hōʻikeaʻe ʻoe i kou nani, ka mālamalama ʻoi kelakela* (*mele* for Ka-lā-kaua), reveal your glory, the light penetrating farthest. **hoʻo.kela.-kela.** To brag, show off, flaunt, display; disrespectful, overbearing, conceited. *Nā hana hoʻokelakela,* extravagant display. *Ua hoʻokelakela ka mea hewa i ka makemake o kona naʻau* (Hal. 10.3), the wicked one boasts of his heart's desire.

kelaki, keraki. n. Celery *(Apium graveolens)* (Neal 659.) *Eng.*

kela.kio, keratio. n. Carob tree *(Ceratonia siliqua),* somewhat like the algaroba; in Luke 15.16 Hawaiian *hua keratio* corresponds to English pods (RSV) or husks (KJV). (Neal 421.) (Gr. *keration.*)

kela.kona, deragona. n. Dragon. (Hoik. 12.3.) *Eng.*

kela (**tela**) **lole.** n. Tailor, dressmaker. *Lit.,* clothes tailor. *Eng.*

kelama, derama. n. Dram (the weight or coin). *Eng.*

kela.moku. 1. n. Sailor. *Lit.,* ship sailor (*Eng.*). **2.** n. Checkered jacket; the material from which it is made. **3.** nvi. A hula step invented by Hawaiian sailors: one foot swings alternately on ball and heel of foot, the other points with the toe front and back four times, then reversed; knees are bent, arms out, bent at elbows with hands up and fingers often snapping, swaying with the body; to dance thus.

kela.pima, serapima. n. Seraphim. (Isa. 6.2.) *Eng.*

kē.lau. vi. To put out first leaves. *Rare.*

kela.wini. n. Gale. *Lit.,* wind gale. *Eng.*

kele. 1. nvs. Watery, muddy, wet, swampy, greasy, fat, lush. *Fig.,* impurity. Cf. *kelekele, makele, ʻūkele. Wao kele,* forested uplands. *Moku kele,* district surrounded by water; submerged island. **hoʻo.kele.** Same as *hoʻokelekele.* (PCP *tele.*) **2.** nvi. To sail; reached by sailing; flight, sailing. Cf. *pōhaku kele. Awa kele,* harbor that may be reached by sailing. *He moku kele i ka waʻa,* an island reached by canoe. *Momoku ahi kele kahi,* firebrand lighted at one end only before being hurled over a cliff. *Momoku ahi kele lua,* firebrand lighted at both ends. **hoʻo.kele.** Steersman, helmsman, navigator; to sail or navigate, as the master of a ship; to steer; to drive, as a car. *Fig.,* to conduct any business. *Po'e ho'okele moku,* ship crew or navigators. *Ho'okele 'ino,* to speed, drive, sail recklessly. *Ho'okele-'ale,* name of a navigation star. *Ho'okele-wa'a,* the star Sirius. *Ho'okele ka'a,* chauffeur, driver; to drive a car. *Ho'okele wa'a lolo niu,* to sail coconut bloom sheaths as [toy] canoes. (PNP *tere.*) **3.** vt. To scrape cooked taro with *'opihi* shell or spoon after peeling is removed, to clean it in preparation for pounding. **4.** Var. of *kela 1.* **5.** n. A fresh-water weed. **6.** n. Any kind of wild taro. *Rare.* **7.** n. Jelly, jam. *Eng.*

-kele. ho'o.kele. Kind of stone found at craters, as Kīlau-ea, and used for adzes.

kelea. n. Process by which a priest cleansed himself of impurities *(kele)* from contact with the dead.

kele 'ai. Var. of *kale 'ai.*

kele.awe. nvi. General name for metals, as brass, copper, bronze, tin, steel, lead. *Ku'i keleawe,* metalsmith, one who makes brass, copper or tin articles; to work with these metals.

kele.kalama. nvt. Telegram; to send a telegram or cable. *Eng.*

kele.kalapa, kelekalepa, telegarapa. nvt. Telegraph; to send a telegram or cable. See song, Elbert and Mahoe 61.

kele.kele. 1. Redup. of *kele 1;* mud, mire, muck, slush, fat oil; muddy, oily, rich, greasy. *Nā kōhi kelekele o Ka-pu'u-kolu* (song), the fat delicious food of Thetriple-hills [descriptive of rich, sumptuous fare]. **ho'o.kele.kele.** To make muddy; to sprinkle; to soak material, as pandanus leaves, in water to make pliable for plaiting; to feed, fatten, especially with soft food or liquids. (PCP *teletele.*) **2.** Redup. of *kele 2.* **ho'o.kele.-kele.** Redup. of *ho'okele;* to steer, navigate or sail frequently; to manage; to cast, as for fish. *Ho'okelekele ka'a,* to drive a car; chauffeur.

kele.kona, delekona. n. Dragon. Also *kalekona.*

kelelo, kelero. n. A lot, in casting lots. *Biblical.* (Gr. *kleros.*)

kele lua. vs. Excessively damp, wet, muddy, greasy, fat, etc.

kelema, kerema. n. Consecrated oil and balm, as used in confirmation services; chrisom. (Gr. *chrisma.*) *Ke kopilimakio aku nei au ia 'oe me ke kerema o ke ola,* I confirm you with the chrisom of life.

Kele.mā.nia. 1. nvs. Germany; German. *Eng.* **2.** *(Not cap.)* n. Earthen crock as used for poi, said to have been introduced from Germany.

kele.mā.nia 'ai. n. Poi crock.

kele.moio. Same as *momona,* the cherimoya. Probably *Eng.*

kele.momeka, teremometa. n. Thermometer. *Eng.*

kele.pona, telepona. nvt. Telephone; to telephone. *Eng.*

Kele-wa'a. Var. of *Ho'okele-wa'a,* the star Sirius. See *kele 2.*

kele.wai. n. Coarse tapa, as made from *māmaki* bark or from the waste of better grade tapa.

kele wai. vs. Thin, as watery poi; muddy, as water. **ho'o.kele wai.** To use much water in mixing or pounding poi, or in irrigation.

kele waina. Grape jelly. *Eng.*

kele.wī, kele.wiki.ona. n. Television. *Eng.* Also *kīwī.*

keli.koli, teritori, teritore. nvs. Territory; territorial. *Eng.*

keli.liona, teriliona. num. Trillion. *Eng.*

keli.luma kelemana, deliruma teremana. n. Delirium tremens. *Eng.*

keli.uma, deliuma. Bdellium. *Eng.*

kelo. vs. Slimy, foul with snot; slippery, as thick mucus. Cf. *hākelo.*

kē.lō. Interj. Sail ho! *Eng.*

kelo.kelo. Redup. of *kelo.* Cf. *hākelo.*

keloko, keroko. n. Saffron. (Mele 4.14.) (Gr. *krokos.*)

kelo.kokile, kerokodile. n. Crocodile. *Eng.*

kelola, derora. n. Swallow (bird). (Sol. 26.2.) (Hebrew *deror.*)

kē.lou. nvt. Hook; to hook. Cf. *lou, kīlou.*

kē.lū, selu. n. Quail. (Puk. 16.13.) The usual name is *manu kapalulu.* (Heb. *selaw.*)

kelu.ika, deruida. n. Druid. *Eng.*

keluka, terusa. n. Thrush. *Eng.*

kelu.kake, kerusade. n. Crusade. *Eng.*

kelu.koliko, kerusolito. n. Chrysolite. (Hoik. 21.20.) (Gr. *chrysolithos.*)

kelu.kope.lako, kerusoperaso. n. Chrysoprase. (Hoik. 21.20.) (Gr. *chrysoprasos.*)

kelupa, keruba. n. Cherub. (1 Nal. 6.24.) *Eng.*

kelu.pima, kerubima. n. Cherubim. (Puk. 25.19.) *Eng.* See ex., *malumalu.*

keme.pulu. Var. of *kamipulu.*

kemika. nvs. Chemist; chemical. *Eng. Hana kemika,* chemistry.

kemo.kalaka, demokarata. nvs. Democrat; democratic. *Eng.*

kemu. 1. vt. To absorb, consume. *Kemu Wai-mea i ka ua kukupa'u o Hanakahi,* Wai-mea absorbs the pouring rain of Hanakahi. **2.** n. Game. *Eng. 'O ka'u kemu 'ike kēia, 'o ka ho'onoho papa kōnane* (hula song), this is the game I know, how to set the *kōnane* board.

kena. vs. **1.** Quenched; satisfied, of thirst. See ex., *puehu 1. Inu ā kena,* drink until satisfied. **ho'o.kena.** To satisfy thirst. **2.** Weary, as from heavy toil; grieved and distressed.

kē.nā. 1. vt. To command, order, give orders, summon, send on business. *Kēnā akula 'o Ka-mehameha i kona po'e kānaka e 'imi lā'au 'ala,* Ka-mehameha sent his people to look for sandalwood. **2.** demon. That (near the person addressed). Used disparagingly for "you." *He aha kāu, ē kēnā mo'o!* What's that to you, you reptile! Cf. *kēlā,* Gram. 8.3. (PPN *ena,* PNP *teenaa.*)

kena.kena. 1. Redup. of *kena 1, 2;* satiated, surfeit. **2.** n. Unpleasant stifling sensation of inhaling smoke; suffocation from smoke.

kēnā.kēnā. Redup. of *kēnā 1.* **ho'o.kenā.kenā.** To compel, order.

kenali, denari. n. Penny. (Eng. *dinar.*) (Mat. 20.2.)

ke (verb) **nei.** Part. denoting present tense near the speaker. Cf. *ke* (verb) *lā* and Gram. 5.3. *'O wau 'o Kamika, ke ho'ohiki nei au,* I, Smith, do hereby affirm. (PCP *te* (verb) *nei.*)

keneka. n. Cent, penny. *Eng.*

kene.kile, genetile. n. Gentile. *Eng.*

kene.koa. n. Senator. *Eng.*

kene.kulia, keneturia. n. Century. *Eng.*

kene.lala, genérala. n. General. *Eng. Hope kenelala,* adjutant general.

kenele. n. Canary. *Eng.*

Kene.maka. nvs. Denmark, Dane; Danish. *Eng.*

keni. 1. vi. To walk softly so as to make no noise. *Rare.* **2.** n. Change (money), small change. *Eng. He keni nō kāu?* Have you change?

kenika, tenisa. n. Tennis. *Eng.*

keni.keni. 1. vt. To assemble a complete outfit or set, as of furniture, food, fishing gear, clothing. *Rare.* **2.** n. Knife. *Rare.* **3.** n. Dime, ten cents, small change, means. (Eng. *ten.*) **4.** n. A variety of imported white sugar cane; also called lahaina cane.

keni.mekela. n. Centimeter. *Eng.*

ke.nola, tenora. Tern. *Eng.*

ke'o. 1. vs. White, clear. **ho'o.ke'o.** To whiten, bleach. **2.** n. Clitoris. **3.** vs. Proud, haughty. *Rare.* **4.** vi. To project. *Rare.* Cf. *pake'o.* (PCP *teko.*)

keoe. n. A sweet potato. **2.** *(Cap.)* Probably the constellation Lyra, including the star Vega. *Keho'oea* may be a variant.

ke'o.ke'o. 1. nvs. White, clear. *Kālā ke'oke'o,* silver money. *Ke ke'oke'o mai o ka nalu,* the whiteness of the (breaking) waves. *E 'ike ai ka mahi 'ai i ke ke'oke'o* (Kep. 91), the farmer sees clearly. **ho'o.ke'o.ke'o.** To whiten. (PCP *tekoteko;* cf. Marquesan *tekoteko.*) **2.** n. White muslin (usually followed by *maoli, pia,* or *wai*). **3.** vs. Proud. *Rare.* (PEP *tekoteko.*)

ke'o.ke'o maoli. n. Bleached muslin of good quality. *Lit.,* genuine whiteness.

ke'o.ke'o pia. n. Bleached muslin of inferior quality, so called because it was weighted down as though with starch *(pia);* it was used for underclothing.

ke'o.ke'o wai. n. Bleached muslin.

Ke-ola. n. Patron star of Lā-na'i. *Lit.,* the life.

Ke-ō-lewa. n. Star name, short for Ke-ao-lewa. (FS 65.) *Lit.,* the light [of the] atmosphere.

keoma. vs. Lazy. *Rare.*

Ke-omo-lewa. n. Old name for Vancouver.

keoni.mana. n. Gentleman. *Eng.* **ho'o.keoni.mana.** Gentlemanly conduct or etiquette; to act as a gentleman. *He mau lula no ka ho'okeonimana 'ana,* rules for gentlemanly etiquette.

ke.opu. vs. Lazy. *Rare.*

kepa. 1. nvt. Notched; cut or trimmed obliquely; to cut obliquely, notch; to turn to one side, to look sideways; to snap. *Ka'a kepa,* to roll diagonally. **ho'o.kepa.** To cut obliquely, snap, tear, rend. **2.** nvt. To catch bonito, so named because the fisherman's body turns as he snaps the fish from the sea into his craft; this kind of fishing. Also *kā'ili.* **3.** n. Wedge used in repairing wooden bowls, often hammered in obliquely in zigzag pattern. Also *kepakepa.* **4.** vt. To scrape, as dirt from a board. *Rare.* **5.** nvt. Contract labor (from *Eng.* "ship," so called because Hawaiians shipping out on whaling ships were under contract; the term was later applied to sugar contract laborers); to contract for such service. *Ua kepa 'ia ka po'e hana,* the laborers were under contract. **6.** n. Almond tree. (Kekah. 12.5.) See *'alemona.*

kē.pā. n. Spur, as used by horseback riders.

Kepa.honi. n. Cape Horn. *Eng.*

Kepake.mapa. n. September. *Eng.*

kepa.kepa. 1. Redup. of *kepa 1;* interruption; to interrupt; choppy, as the sea. See *'umeke kepakepa. Kepakepa 'ia ka i'a a lomi 'ia,* fish being cut in pieces and mashed. **2.** Same as *kepa 3.* **3.** nvt. Conversational chant, fast rhythmic chant or recitation, with every syllable clearly pronounced and without prolonged vowels and not requiring too much breath. The *paha* chants are in this style. To chant thus.

kepa.lō. Same as *kiapolō.* See *pua kepalō.*

kē.pama, sepama. n. Sperm. *Eng. Koholā kēpama,* sperm whale.

Kepa.nī. vs. Japanese. *Eng.* **ho'o.kepa.nī.** To act like or mimic Japanese.

Kepa.nia, Sepania. nvs. Spain; Spanish (Latin *Hispania.)* **ho'o.kepa.nia.** To act like or mimic Spaniards or Spanish.

Ke-pani-pa'a. n. Name of a star appearing in the month of *Māhoe Hope,* accompanied by Ka'a'ei.

Ke-pani-wai-o-loko-o-Kahiki. n. Star name (no data). (Kuhelani.) *Lit.,* the dam within Kahiki.

kē.pau. n. Lead, pitch, tar, resin, pewter; gum, as on ripe breadfruit; any sticky juice, as of *pāpala;* printers' type; sinker on a fishing line. *Hua kēpau,* type. *'Ōniu ho'olele hua kēpau,* to set type. *Kēpau ana hohonu,* lead for sounding depths.

kē.pau ka'a. n. Resin.

kē.pau kā.pili mekala. n. Solder.

kē.pau kā.pili pala.pala. n. Sealing wax.

kē.pau pō.kā. n. Lead, bullet lead.

kepela, sepela. 1. nvt. Spelling; to spell. *Eng. Puke a'o kepela,* spelling book. **2.** Also **zebera.** n. Zebra. *Eng.*

kepe.mineka, sepemineta. n. Spearmint *(Mentha spicata).* (Neal 734.) *Eng.*

kepena, gepena. n. Wild gourd. (2 Nal. 4.39.)

kē.pia. n. **1.** Dandruff. **2.** *(Cap.)* Name of a wind associated with Hilo. (Nak. 53.)

kepoa. Jerboa. *Biblical. Eng.*

kepola, zepora. n. Sparrow (RSV), bird (KJV). (Sol. 26.2.)

kepo.lō. Same as *kiapolō,* devil. *Eng.*

kē.pū. n. Zebu. *Eng.*

---

kepue. n. **1.** A kind of hard stone from which adzes were made. Also *humu'ula.* **2.** A bird (no data).

kē.puka. nvi. Sleight-of-hand trick; to play such tricks. Cf. *'apuka,* to cheat.

keu. vs. Remaining, excessive, additional, spare, surplus, extra, more, too much (often followed by *ā). Pākanahā ā keu,* forty and more. *He keu 'oe ā ke kanaka wahahe'e,* you're the greatest liar ever seen. *He keu ā ke kolohe!* Very, very mischievous! *He keu aku nō!* That's the limit! That's too much [said either in admiration or disapproval, indicated by voice tone]. (PNP *teu.*)

ke'u. vi. To croak, hoot, grunt; to protest, scold, snap at, contradict, find fault; to make the common Hawaiian exclamation of disapproval, *kā! chā! E ke'u 'oe, ē pueo ē* (Kep. 59), hoot, O owl. *Ka manu ke'u ahiahi,* the bird that croaks in evening [the *'alae,* said also of one who brings bad luck or talks of it].

kē.ue.ue. vt. To push against, oppose, seek to remove a person from his position. *Rare.*

keu.keu. Redup. of *keu,* remaining. (And.)

ke'u.ke'u. Redup. of *ke'u.*

kē.wā. 1. n. Far-off place inhabited by spirits. **2.** vt. To anticipate. *Ke kēwā nei i ka hō'ea mai o nā malihini,* anticipating the coming of the guests.

kē.wai. 1. vs. Watery, dripping, misty; damp, dewladen; spoiled, of eggs. See ex., *'ōmamaka. He makani kēwai,* a moisture-laden wind. **2.** *(Cap.)* n. Name of a Hilo wind.

kēwa.kēwai. Redup. of *kēwai.*

kewe. 1. vs. Convex, concave; crescent-shaped, as the moon; contorted, perverted. **2.** n. Boom, crane; beam from which a weight is suspended and swung to and fro; cable line, as on a cable car *(ka'akewe).* **3.** n. Stasis diffusion of lymph, said to be due to prolonged wetting of the feet, as in taro patch, sometimes called "Hawaiian elephantiasis," but no relation to elephantiasis as found in the South Seas.

kewe.kewe. Redup. of *kewe 1.* See song, *koheoheo 1.*

kī-. Same as **kī-.**

-kī. transitivizer. See *'iniki,* Gram. 6.6.4. (PPN *-ti.*)

kī. 1. n. Ti, a woody plant *(Cordyline terminalis)* in the lily family, native to tropical Asia and Australia. It consists of a branched or unbranched, slender, ringed stem, ending in a cluster of narrow-oblong leaves 30 to 60 cm long, from among which at times rises a large panicle of small, light-colored flowers. The leaves were put to many uses by the Hawaiians, as for house thatch, food wrappers, hula skirts, sandals; the thick, sweet roots were baked for food or distilled for brandy. (Neal 203–4.) Besides green-leaved tis, which rarely fruit, many ornamental varieties are grown in gardens, having leaves wide to narrow, large to small, the colors purple, crimson, scarlet, rust, pink, or green, striped or plain. Red tis may have red flowers and berries. Green ti leaves are still believed to afford protection from spirits and to purify a menstruating woman. (Nānā 190–2.) See *he'e 2, hōlua kī.* (PPN *tii.*) **2.** n. The Spanish needle *(Bidens pilosa),* a weed from tropical America, a kind of daisy with simple or compound leaves, small yellow flower heads, and narrow black bristle-tipped fruits. (Neal 844.) Also *kī nehe.* Cf. *ko'oko'olau.* **3.** vt. To shoot or aim, as with a gun; to squirt water, as with a syringe; to blow from the mouth, as a fisherman spitting chewed *kukui* nut on the sea to quiet it; to spit, as an angry cat; to travel fast, jet, hurry, especially on horseback *(Kaua'i).* Cf. *kai kī, kani.* **ho'o.kī.** Caus/sim.; to cause to shoot; to sick on, as a dog; to make a cat spit; to snort; emitted. (PCP *tii.*) **4.** nvt. Bundle of 40 pandanus leaves, sorted for size and length and set aside for plaiting; to sort leaves for such a bundle. **5.** Same as *'amakihi,* a bird. **6.** nvt. Key, latch; key, pitch, and clef in music; to lock, as a door; to wind or set, as a clock; to roll up, as a mat. *Eng. E kī aku i ka puka ā pa'a,* lock the door fast. **7.** n. Trigger of a gun. **8.** n. Tea. *Eng.* **9.** interj. Gee. *Eng.*

kī-. Intensifying prefix. Numerous examples follow, including *kīhelu, kīkaha, kīkākala, kīlaha, kīmanamana, kīʻoʻe, kīʻohuʻohu, kīʻōnaha.* (Gram. 6.3.3.)

-kī. Intensifying suffix. See *auwalakī, hilikī, kūpakakī, makakī, mōkākī, pūkalakī, walawalakī.*

kia. 1. n. Pillar, prop, post, pole; mast of a ship, spar; nail, spike; rod used in snaring birds with gum; one who so snares birds; fish trap. Cf. *kiaʻāina, kia hōʻailona, kia manu.* (PPN *tia.*) **2.** nvt. To concentrate or direct, especially in sorcery; evil force of black magic; a sorcerer might concentrate his prayers *(kia i ka pule)* to the destruction of an individual or object; to aim, as a gun. Cf. *kākia, mākia.* **3.** vt. To steer. *Eng.* **4.** Also **dia.** n. Deer, hart. *Eng.* **5.** Also **sia.** nvs. Dear. *Eng.*

kia-. A prefix to types of canoes. See *kialoa, kiapā, kiapoho, kiapoko.*

-kia. Pas/imp. similar to ʻia. See *holokia,* Gram. 6.6.3. (PPN -*tia.*)

kī.ʻā. Same as *pūʻā,* to feed from mouth to mouth. *Rare.*

kia.ʻāina. n. Governor; governorship. *Lit.,* prop [of the] land. *Koʻu hāpai ʻia ʻana i kiaʻāina,* my elevation to the governorship.

kī ʻaʻala. n. Sweet basil *(Ocimum basilicum),* an aromatic herb of the mint family, with small white to reddish flowers, the leaves used to flavor food. (Neal 735.) Also *kīpaoa. Lit.,* fragrant *kī.*

kia ao. n. Cloud pillar. (Nah. 12.5.)

kī.ʻaha. n. **1.** Cup, pitcher, basin, tumbler, mug. See ex., *kāmau* 2. *Lepo kīʻaha* (Isa. 45.9), clay vessel. **2.** *(Cap.)* The Big Dipper (modern).

kī.ʻaha.ʻaha. vt. To pour liquid out of a cup or container (*ninini* is now in common use).

kī.ʻaha ani.ani. n. Glass (for drinking). *Lit.,* glass cup.

kī.ʻaha inu waina. n. Wineglass.

kī.ʻaha kī. n. Teacup.

kiaha.manu. A fresh-water fish similar to *nāwao.* (And.)

kī.ʻaha ʻo.oma. n. Pitcher (*pika* is now in common use), vase. *Lit.,* concave tumbler.

kī.ʻaha pua.niki. n. Goblet. *Lit.,* holding cup.

kī.ʻaho. n. Cord or rope, as for hoisting a flag. *Rare.*

kia hō.ʻai.lona. n. Signpost, tall stop sign, any pillar or large object with a sign, or serving as a marker; image on the wall surrounding a temple. *Lit.,* sign pillar.

kia hoʻo.manaʻo. n. Monument, gravestone, memorial tablet, memorial, commemorative pillar.

kiaʻi. nvt. Guard, watchman, caretaker; to watch, guard, picket; to overlook, as a bluff. *Kiaʻi ʻai* (For. 5:479), food guardian. *Kiaʻi kupapaʻu,* funeral wake or gathering. **hoʻo.kiaʻi.** To post a watch. (PPN *tiʻaki.*)

kiʻai. Var. of *kiʻei.*

kiaʻi kai. n. Coast guard. *Lit.,* sea guard.

kiaʻi kino. n. Bodyguard. (Laie 499.)

Kī.ʻai.lana, Siailana. n. Sea Island, *Gossypium barbadense,* a variety of cotton grown in Hawaiʻi. (Neal 565.) *Eng.*

kiaʻi loko. n. Guard of a fish pond.

kiaʻi-ma-ka-lae. n. **1.** Beach plant like *kākalaioa,* but thornless. *Lit.,* guardian at the cape. **2.** Same as *mākoko,* a variety of taro.

kiaʻi ola. n. Lifeguard.

kiaʻi pō. n. Night watchman, night watch.

kiaʻi.poʻo. n. Bodyguard, security guard. *Lit.,* head guard.

kiaʻi puka. n. Guard at a gate or door, doorman, porter, gatekeeper.

kia kaʻa. n. Chauffeur, driver. *Lit.,* car steerer.

kia.kahi. nvs. Person of fixed purpose; with one accord or purpose; in unison, constant; alone, unique, supreme, only one. *ʻAkahi lani a ʻoukou e ʻike ai, he lani kiakahi ka lani o nā moku* (chant for Haku o Hawaiʻi), you know but one chief, a single supreme chief is the chief of the islands.

kia kahi. n. Sloop; one-masted vessel.

kia keiki. n. Fawn.

kia.kia manu. Redup. of *kia manu.*

kiʻaki.ʻena. n. Small cave, fissure, as used for burial. *Niʻihau.*

kia kolu. n. Three-masted vessel.

kia.kona, diakona. n. Deacon.

kia.kono, diakono. Var. of *kiakona.* (Roma 16.1.) (Gr. *diakonos.*)

kia.kula, tiasura. Same as *keakula.* (Isa. 60.13.)

kī ala.kaʻi. n. Tonic, keynote (music). *Lit.,* leading key *(Eng.).*

Kia-lehua. n. Niʻihau wind.

kī.ʻalo. vt. To dig out, as the eyes, to scoop out; to reach out with a scooping movement. Cf. *pōʻalo.*

kia.loa. n. **1.** Long, light, and swift canoe. *Fig.,* a tall, well-proportioned woman. **2.** Same as *kākā,* a kind of net fishing. **3.** Fishing grounds: also *pōhākialoa.* (Kam. 76:90.)

kia lua. n. Brig, two-masted vessel, two-masted schooner.

kia lua peʻa heke. n. Brig. *Lit.,* topsail two masts.

kia luna. n. Topmast.

kia manu. nvt. Birdcatcher, birdcatching by gumming; to catch birds by gumming. *Ea mai ke aliʻi kia manu, ua wehi i ka hulu o ka mamo* (hula chant for Ka-lā-kaua), the birdcatching chief arises, adorned with the feathers of the *mamo.*

kī.ʻamo. n. Plug, stopper; sanitary napkin or napkin of any sort; any nozzle inserted in the rectum *(ʻamo).*

kiana.pauka, giana pauda. n. Dynamite. *Lit.,* giant powder. *Eng.*

kiani. vt. To flick, flip, wave gently, as the hand overhead in a hula gesture; to wheel and dip, as a soaring bird; frisky. Cf. *ani,* to wave. *ʻAi kiani,* to nab at food.

kia nui. n. Mainmast.

kia.pā. n. Swift-sailing canoe; any vessel equipped with cross spars, bark.

Kia-paʻa.kai. n. North Star. *Lit.,* pillar of salt, so called because, like Lot's wife, it was immovable.

kia.pali. n. Term used in 1848 land claims, perhaps a steep hill.

kia.poho. n. A canoe with a deep, curving hull.

kia.poko. n. A short canoe with a rounded hull, as used for fishing near the shore.

kia.polō, diabolo. nvs. Devil; devilish. (Gr. *diabolos.*)

kī.ʻapu. nvt. Ti leaf folded into a cup and used for dipping water; the two hands rounded to form a cup for drinking water; to cup the hand; to catch with cupped hands, as tiny fish; ladle. Cf. *ʻapu,* cup. *Ua ʻike aku au i ka wai, me ka iʻa kīʻapu i ka lima* (chant for Ka-piʻo-lani), I saw the water, and the fish caught in cupped hands.

kī.ʻapu.ʻapu. n. A name for the curved portion of a canoe rim. (For. 5:612-3.)

kī.au. nvi. To gallop; to walk lightly and swiftly; fast movement. *Maʻō nō ka lio i kīau ʻe nei,* the horse just went trotting yonder.

kī.au.au. 1. Redup. of *kīau.* **2.** Interj. encouraging workers, as in drawing an unfinished canoe hull from the forest to the shed at the seashore where it was to be completed. *Pau kēia kīauau ʻana a ke keiki* (Nak. 62), after the boy's chant urging fast action. *Kīauau, kīauau, kīauau! holo auau, holo auau, holo auau!* (canoe-hauling chant), fast, fast, fast! run quick, run quick, run quick! **3.** vt. To smooth out wrinkles from tapa or clothes with light, deft touches.

kiawe. 1. n. Algaroba tree *(Prosopis pallida),* a legume from Peru, first planted in 1828 in Hawaiʻi, where, in dry areas, it has become one of the commonest and most useful trees (Neal 413-4.) **2.** nvi. A streak; to stream gracefully, as rain in the wind; to sway, as branches. *Ka ua kiawe i luna o ka lāʻau,* the rain streaming down on the tree. **hoʻo.kiawe.** Caus/sim.

kī.awe.awe. Redup. of *kiawe* 2.

kiawe ʻula. n. Faint streak of red, as in the rainbow or in the clouds.

ki'e. Same as *ki'eki'e.* **ho'o.ki'e.** Caus/sim. (PNP *tike.*)

kī.'e'ei. Redup. of *ki'ei.*

ki'ei. vt. To peer, peep, as through a door or crevice; to look at slyly; to protrude forth. *Kekē nā niho ki'ei,* the protruding teeth were exposed.

kī.'eke. n. Bag, satchel; basket. *Rare.* Cf. *'eke.*

ki'e.ki'e. nvs. Height, tallness, Highness; high, tall, lofty, exalted, majestic, superior, prominent; altitude. In 1845 the legislature conferred the title *Mea Ki'eki'e* upon the premier, probably best translated His Excellency. *Ka Mea Ki'eki'e, Kamāli'i wahine Luisa,* Her Highness, Princess Louise. *Ki'eki'e Ka'ū, kua makani, he umauma i pā 'ia e ke A'e Loa* (old chant of Ka'ū chiefs), majestic Ka'ū, wind [blown] back, breast blown upon by the A'e Loa tradewind breeze. *Kona ki'eki'e,* his rank. *Ki'eki'e loa,* maximum, highest, supreme. **ho'o.ki'e.ki'e.** To elevate, promote, lift up; proud, lording it over others, overbearing, disrespectful or disobedient to seniors, vain; promotion, elevation, conceit. (PCP *tiketike.*)

ki'e.ki'ena. n. Height, altitude, elevation, rise, tableland, bluff.

kiele. 1. n. Gardenia *(Gardenia augusta).* Originally Polynesian. (PPN *tiale.*) Cf. *nānū.* 2. vi. To emit fragrance; to perfume with *kiele,* as garments. 3. vt. To paddle. (UL 194.) *Rare.*

ki'e.lei. 1. vi. To squat on one's haunches; to straddle; to stand with legs far apart. Cf. Tongan *sike,* to squat on heels. 2. n. Type of hula in which the dancer danced in a squatting position. (Cf. UL 210.)

kī.'ele.lei. Redup. of *ki'elei.*

kī.'ene.nei. Var. of *kī'elelei.*

kiha. 1. n. Supernatural lizard (in such names as Kihalani-nui, Kiha-nui-lūlū-moku, and Kiha-wahine); reptile. (HM 125, 350.) 2. Var. of *kihe 1.*

kī.hā. 1. nvi. Belch, burp; to belch or burp. See ex., *pu'u ho'omaha.* **ho'o.ki.hā.** Caus/sim. 2. vi. To rise and pitch, as a canoe in heavy seas; to dive under water, as a porpoise. (Possibly PPN *tifa(a).*)

kī.hae. 1. vi. To tear or strip, as leaves; to remove thorns from pandanus leaves; to shred, as ti leaves for dance skirts. Cf. *hae,* to tear. See ex. *polapola 4.* (PCP *tiisae.*) 2. vs. Inspired with a wrathful spirit. Cf. *hae,* fierce.

kī.hae.hae. Redup. of *kīhae 1, 2.* (PCP *tiisaesae.*)

Kī.hae-lā.'ī. n. Breeze at Pu'u-'ōhua on the Hāmākua side of Hilo. *Lit.,* to shred ti leaves.

kī.haka.haka. vt. To force a wedge into an opening (formerly said of fighting).

kī.hala.lē. Perhaps intensifier *kī-* + *halalē.* (For. 6:412.)

kī.hamu. vt. To eat voraciously. Cf. *hamu.*

kī.hapa. vs. Incomplete, partly finished; half-covered, as with a shawl over one shoulder. *Kahi kīhapa,* to shave half of the head, as formerly in mourning.

kī.hā.pai. n. 1. Small land division, smaller than a *paukū;* cultivated patch, garden, orchard, field, small farm; parish of a church, diocese; department of a business or office; formerly various religious duties were divided into *kīhāpai,* as tending the altar, offering sacrifices. 2. Madagascar periwinkle *(Catharanthus roseus,* syn. *Vinca rosea),* a perennial herb or small shrub, from tropical America, grown for ornament; flowers rose-purple or white. (Neal 689.)

kī.hau. vi. Frugal, saving; sparingly; to ration carefully. *E 'ai kīhau kākou,* let's eat sparingly.

kiha.wahine. Same as *li'awahine,* blossoms of *kukui.*

kihe. 1. vi. Sneeze. Cf. *mauli ola, kiha.* (PPN *tise.*) 2. n. A small native fern *(Xiphopteris saffordii),* narrow, 4 to 14 cm high, the fronds somewhat notched. 3. A variety of sweet potato. 4. n. A red seaweed *(Chylocladia* sp.) with narrow cylindrical, branching stems. Also *akuila.*

kī.hē. 1. Var. of *kīhā 1, 2.* 2. Var. of *kīhae 1, 2.* (Kep. 157.)

kī.hea.hea. Similar to *āhea,* to blow.

kī.he'a.he'a. vs. Stained, streaked, especially with red or with blood; streak of fire, as seen in the wake of a fire-

brand sailing aloft. *Ua kīhe'ahe'a ihola ia papa pōhaku i ke koko o ke ali'i,* the stone floor was stained with the blood of the chief. *Nalohia nā 'ōahi i kīhe'ahe'a ao,* the rockets vanished in cloud colors.

kī.he'a.he'a pala.'ā. n. Coloring matter for tapa made from the *pala'ā* fern.

kī.he'e. vt. To pour.

kī.hē.hē. vi. To be or become deified; to pass into the air or to live invisibly there.

kī.hei. nvt. Shawl, cape, afghan; cloak of *makaloa* matting; rectangular tapa garment worn over one shoulder and tied in a knot; bed covering; to wear a *kīhei.* He *kīhei loloa,* a long *kīhei* [said of a gadabout].

kī.hei 'a'ahu no'e.no'e. n. Decorated cape. *Lit.,* colored garment cape.

kī.hei.hei. Redup. of *kīhei;* to wear a *kīhei.* See ex., *pā'ū heihei.*

kī.hei moe. n. Light bedspread.

kī.hei pili. n. Two sheets, as of printed percale or patchwork, sewn together at edges, used as bed covering over the sleeper and under the nicer quilt. In some, the lower edges are left open so that a blanket may be inserted. *Lit.,* clinging covering.

kī.hei pua. See *'uhane kīhei pua.*

kihe.kihe. Redup. of *kihe 1.*

kī.hele. nvt. Hook; to hook; to feed poi to a child on the finger, which is bent (like a hook) so as to dislodge the poi. *Kīhele ia ulu,* bail the center of a canoe [ambiguous expression: it may refer to the action of the hands in bailing].

kī.helei. Short for *ki'ihelei.*

kī.helu. vt. To scratch. Cf. *helu.*

kī.hene. n. Bundle or basket of ti or other leaves, as used to carry sweet potatoes, flowers, etc. *Nā wāhine kīhene pua,* women with baskets of flowers.

kī.heu. vt. To remove tiny weeds.

kihi. 1. nvi. Outside corner (cf. *kū'ono*), edge, tip, extremity; apex of an angle; sharp point of a leaf; to turn aside. *Maka kihi,* looking out of the corners of the eyes. *Kihi alanui,* street corner. *Kihi o ka pō,* beginning of the night. *Kihi o ka mahina,* way of fastening the *pā'ū* sarong; by knotting and tucking it in at each hip, but with one end tucked up cutting a corner; *lit.,* corner of the moon. *Pū kihi lua,* double-barreled gun. **ho'o.kihi.** To make a corner by overlapping, as in plaiting; to fold partially over; to turn aside, make a corner. (PCP *tifi.*) 2. n. A variety of sweet potato. Descriptive terms are *lau manamana, lau nui,* and *lau poepoe.* 3. n. Canoes guarding the sides of *mālolo* and *iheihe* fish nets. 4. vt. To plug or patch a calabash or canoe. *Rare.* 5. n. Kaua'i name for *'amakihi,* a bird.

kihi.kau. vt. To give lavishly. *Rare.*

kihi.kau.pe'a. Same as *kihikau.* Cf. *kīkaupe'a.*

kihi.kihi. 1. nvs. Corners, curves; angular, full of corners, zigzag. *Kihikihi nā po'ohiwi,* broad-shouldered. *Kālā kihikihi,* cornered money [gold coins of California gold-rush times brought to Hawai'i, so called because they were crescent shaped]. **ho'o.kihi.kihi.** To branch out, make corners, make irregular. (Probably PNP *tifitifi.*) 2. n. Moorish idol, a small, brilliantly colored fish *(Zanclus cornutus)* with black bands alternating with yellow. Varieties are qualified by the terms *lau nui* or *māne'one'o, alo 'ula, hālena,* and *pōhaka.* (PPN *tifitifi.*) 3. n. A variety of sweet potato. 4. Same as *kikihi 1-3.* 5. Same as *'amakihi,* a honeycreeper. *Kaua'i.*

kihi lau nui. n. 1. A sweet potato. *Lit.,* large-leafed *kihi.* 2. A taro.

kihi loa. vi. Crooked, twisted, angular; to turn aside; one who turns aside, as to avoid others.

kihi moe. n. Name of one of the places, as under a tapa, where the *no'a* stone was hidden in the game of *pūhene-hene.*

kihi po'o.hiwi. n. Points or edges of the shoulders; shoulder; shoulder of a mountain.

kihi puka. n. 1. Door corner. 2. Name of one of the

places under a tapa, where the *no'a* stone was hidden in the game of *pūhenehene.*

kī hō.'alu. n. Slack key (the first and last strings of the guitar are tuned to D, instead of E; the strings are picked individually and are not chorded).

kī.hoe. nvi. To lead a roving life, without fixed abode, wander; vagabond.

kī.holo. n. **1.** Large wood fishhook, as used for sharks and large fish. **2.** Large fish net about 20 fathoms long, held by a canoe at each end. **3.** Long ti-leaf food package, more commonly called *holo 'ai.*

kī.honua. n. Side or bank of a canal or ditch.

kī ho'o.ikaika. n. Staccato mark (music); small dot or wedge placed over a musical note.

kī ho'o.ku'u. Same as *kī hō'alu.*

ki'i. 1. n. Image, statue, picture, photograph, drawing, diagram, illustration, likeness, cartoon, idol, doll, petroglyph; features, as of a face; plans, as for a house; carved, as end of an *'auamo* pole. Cf. *akua kā'ai, hula ki'i, kaha ki'i, ki'i 'ōnohi, na'ana'a 1, pa'i ki'i.* *Kona ki'i,* his picture, statue (of him). *Kāna ki'i,* a picture (or statue) by him or owned by him. *Pepa ki'i,* joker, in deck of cards. *Ki'i maka nunui,* prominent, wealthy, or important person, VIP; *lit.,* big-eyed image. *Ki'i maka li'ili'i,* ordinary person; *lit.,* small-eyed image. *'O ke ki'i nō kēlā o ka makuahine,* he's the image of his mother. *He 'oko'a kona ki'i a me kona kūlana* (FS 279), her features and appearance were different. (PCP *tiki.*) **2.** vt. To fetch, get, procure, send for, go after, summon, attack; to seek for sexual ends. See *maka ki'i.* **ho'o.ki'i.** To send, have sent for; to take away (Isa. 34.4.) (PCP *tiki.*) **3.** vi. To try and, go and (idiomatic). See ex., *lolelole. E ki'i ā loa'a ā loa'a 'ole mai paha,* go and get or perhaps don't get. **4.** nvi. Hula step: one foot points to the side, front, and back; then the other foot does the same. Also *wāwae ki'i,* fetching step. **5.** Same as *'alani,* orange. **6.** n. Gesture, as in hula.

-ki'i. 1. See *hāki'i, hīki'i, mūki'i, nāki'i, nīki'i,* all meaning to tie, bind. (PCP *-tiki.*) **2. ho'o.ki'i.** Var. of *hōki'i,* thin, wasted. (Isa. 34.4.)

ki'i akua. n. Idol, image.

ki'i.hei. n. Lashing of wall plate to wall post.

ki'i.heke.kē. n. **1.** A variety of taro. **2.** A variety of sweet potato.

ki'i.hele. nvi. Gadabout, wanderer; to gad about, wander, on the move. Cf. *ki'inoho.*

ki'i.helei. vi. To stand, sit, or walk with legs wide apart, straddle; straddling.

ki'i ho'ā.kaaka. n. Illustration, picture. *Lit.,* clarifying picture.

ki'i hō.'aka.'aka. n. Cartoon. *Lit.,* picture to cause mirth.

ki'i ho'o.hehe'e 'ia. n. Molten or cast image.

ki'i ho'o.hene.hene. n. Caricature, mocking picture.

ki'i ho'o.laha. n. Poster. *Lit.,* advertising picture.

ki'i ho'o.lele. n. Enlargement of a picture.

ki'i ho'o.lele aka. n. Slide picture shown on a screen by a projector. *Lit.,* image enlargement.

ki'i ho'o.weli.weli. n. Scarecrow, terrifying image.

ki'i hua. nvi. To make gestures in the *hula pū'ili* and *hula 'ulī'ulī* imitative of the words of the chant; these gestures.

ki'i kā.lai 'ia. n. Carved image, graven image.

ki'i kapu. vt. To fetch something, as greenery for an altar, with observation of taboos.

ki'i.kau. n. Drifting clouds of different colors, including black and white.

ki'i.kea. n. Ointment made of breadfruit bark crushed with thin young coconut leaves.

ki'i.ki'i. 1. Redup. of *ki'i 2.* **ho'o.ki'i.ki'i.** To cause to fetch, fetch, take hold of, seize, get. **2.** Same as *kīki'i.*

kī.'iki.kī. Same as *kī. 'ililī 1.*

ki'i kino 'ie. n. John 'Ī'ī's name for *kā'ai,* casket. (Ii 155.) *Lit.,* image wicker body.

ki'i kuhi. nv. To make time-keeping hula gestures with

the left hand reaching forward and back to the front of the shoulder, while tapping the *'ulī'ulī* on the right lap; these gestures.

ki'i.lau. vi. To ramble in conversation. *Rare.*

kī.'ili.lī. vi. **1.** To squat on haunches; to perch. *Kī'ililī ka pua hau o Ka-lena,* the *hau* blossom of Ka-lena squats [said of beauties who squat but do no work; play on *lena,* lazy, in Ka-lena]. **2.** To trill, of a bird. Cf. *kī'ikikī, kū'ililī.*

ki'i.lua. nvi. Two-faced; liar, deceiver; to deceive. *Rare.*

ki'i maka manu. n. Bird's-eye view.

ki'i maka nunui. See *ki'i 1.*

ki'i.manana. vi. Enlarged, swollen, bloated, as of a rotting corpse.

ki'ina. Pas/imp. of *ki'i 2, 6;* war-club stroke. See Gram. 6.6.2. *I kāna ki'ina lā'au* (GP 66), his club stroke. *Ki'ina o ka leo,* voice intonation. *Ki'ina 'ōnohi maka,* glances of the eyes [*lit.,* fetching pupils of the eyes]. *Ki'ina 'ia aku nā paemoku,* search the archipelagoes.

ki'i.noho. nvi. Homebody; to remain at home constantly. Cf. *ki'ihele.*

ki'i 'oni.'oni. n. Moving picture, movie, cinema.

ki'i 'ō.nohi. n. Pupil of the eye. *Fig.,* beloved person. See ex., *ki'ina, loloku, walania.*

ki'i pā. nvi. In a hula, tapping the lap or left hand with the base of the *'ulī'ulī;* tapping the palm of the left hand, floor, back of left hand and right shoulder with end of *pū'uli;* both are now called in English "common motion"; to do so.

ki'i pala.pala. n. Printed picture, as in a newspaper.

ki'i pena. n. Painting. *Lit.,* painted picture. *Eng.*

ki'i pō.haku. n. Stone statue; petroglyph.

ki'i.pua. vi. To go about in idleness and mischief. [*Pua* was the name of a mischievous goddess of sorcery.]

kika. 1. vs. Slippery, slimy, as with mud. *E ua ana ka ua a kika malama, 'ōlali kika ana kikika i ka ua* (chant), the rain rains so that the month is slippery, bright, slippery, slippery in the rain. **2.** Also **tita.** n. Sister. *Eng.* **3.** Also **sida.** n. Cider. *Eng.* **4.** Also **tiga.** n. Tiger. *Eng.* **5.** Also **kida.** n. Cassia. *Eng.*

kikā. vs. Of humble position, lowly.

kī.kā. 1. n. *'Ōpelu* fish, when about the length of a finger. **2.** vs. Strong, energetic; having authority and force, as a magistrate. *Rare.* **3.** n. Guitar. *Eng.* **4.** n. Cigar. *Eng.* **5.** n. The cigar flower *(Cuphea ignea),* from Mexico, a small, smooth shrub with narrow, red, tubular, odorless flowers nearly 3 cm. long. The flowers are used for leis. (Neal 617–8.) Also *pua kīkā.*

kī.ka'ele.kē. vs. Frisky, restless; to jump here and there.

kī.kaha. vi. To soar, glide, poise, wheel, skim along, as a frigate bird; to turn aside, detour, veer, deviate; to maneuver, as fighting cocks; to walk along absent-mindedly, ignoring everyone. *Kīkaha ka 'iwa, he lā makani,* the frigate bird soars, it's a windy day [said of a beautiful woman or handsome man]. *Hele kīkaha a'ela ka ua,* the rain goes sneaking along [of one who goes out of his way to avoid an acquaintance]. (PCP *tiita(f,s)a.*)

kī.kaha.kaha. Redup. of *kīkaha.*

kī.kahō. vi. **1.** To splash. **2.** To speak or interrupt rudely.

kī.kakaha. Redup. of *kīkaha.*

kī.kā.kala. vt. **1.** To strike with spurs, as fighting cocks. **2.** To draw up with a hook, as in fishing octopus.

kī.kā.kapu. n. Various species of butterfly fishes of the genera *Chaetodon* and *Cheilodactylus.* Varieties are qualified by the terms *alo lua* and *ko'a.* See *hīlia, kī'oki, lauwiliwili.*

Kikako. n. Chicago. *Eng.*

kikala, tidara. n. Pine tree (RSV), fir tree (KJV). (Isa. 41.19.) (Heb. *tidhar.*)

kī.kala. n. **1.** Hip, coccyx bone; posterior; stern, as of a canoe. **2.** Same as *kīkala moa,* a seaweed.

kī.kala hā.ne'e.ne'e. n. Pyelitis, kidney disease; sacroiliac strain; lumbosacral slipped disks. *Lit.,* sliding hips.

kī.kala.kē. n. Kind of fishhook.

kī.kala moa. n. Name of a seaweed that irritates the throat if eaten alone.

kī.kala paʻa.kea. A rare idiom referring to hard-working tenant farmers in 1851.

kī.kala pai. n. Flat, thin buttocks.

kika.liki. n. Cigarette. *Eng.* See ex., *meʻomeʻo.*

kikama. n. White tapa made of *wauke.*

kī.kā.mū. vi. Suspicious, wary; gathering in silence, as fish about a hook they hesitate to bite. Cf. *mū,* silent.

kika.naine. n. Strychnine. *Eng.*

kikana.lei. vi. To sit on the heels, squat.

kika.ne. n. Jitney. *Eng. Kaʻa kikanē,* jitney carriage.

kī.kā.nia. n. 1. Weed (RSV), tares (KJV) (Mat. 13.25); zizania. *Gr.* See *pōpolo kīkānia.* 2. Cockleburs (*Xanthium* spp.), coarse herbs, bearing tenacious burs about 2.5 cm long. (Neal 838.) 3. Same as *kīkānia haole.*

kī.kā.nia haole. Same as *lāʻau hānō,* Jimson weed.

kī.kā.nia lei. n. A kind of nightshade *(Solanum aculeatissimum),* the round, scarlet fruits used in leis. (Neal 742-3.) Also *akaaka.*

kī.kā.nia pipili. n. Spanish clover *(Desmodium uncinatum),* a weedy, South American perennial herb with small clinging pods. (Neal 451.) Also *pua pilipili.*

kī.kanu. vt. To cover, bury.

kī kaola. n. Crossbar or beam used to close a door or gate. *Lit.,* wooden key.

kī.kā Puki.kī. n A mandolin, usually with 12 strings. *Lit.,* Portuguese guitar. *(Eng.)*

kī.kau. To give freely and with good will. (And.)

kī.kau.peʻa. Same as *kihikau.*

kika.wai.ō. n. A native fern *(Cyclosorus [Dryopteris] cyatheoides),* with pinnate fronds, 1 m high or more, used for food and medicine. Roots and young fronds eaten raw; the roots grated and salted to taste, slimy like okra. Also *pakikawaiō.* See ex., *kiʻoa.* Cf. *kupukupu makaliʻi.*

kika.wai.oa. Var. of *kikawaiō.*

kike. n. Kitty. *Eng.*

kī.kē. 1. vi. To rap, tap, knock; to break open, as with a hammer; to click glasses, as in drinking a toast. See ex., *māmane 1. Kīkē hala,* to break open pandanus fruit. 2.vi. To share. *E kīkē ka hānau ʻana me kuʻu punalua,* the children will share with my second wife.

-kī.kē. Back and forth. See *ʻōlelokīkē, walakīkē, pākīkē, kīkēʻōlelo.* Gram. 6.5. **hoʻo.kī.kē.** Ready with a rude retort.

kī.kē ʻalāna. nvi. Crashing sound, as of lava rock *(ʻalā)* smiting rock, or as made by an active *aa* lava flow (PH 38); to sound thus.

kī.keʻe. vi. To bend, crook; bending, zigzag; perverted. *Alanui kīkeʻe,* zigzag road. **hoʻo.kī.keʻe.** To go zigzag.

kī.keʻe.keʻe. Redup. of *kīkeʻe;* zigzag. *Alanui kīkeʻekeʻe,* road with many turns. **hoʻo.kī.keʻe.keʻe.** Caus/sim.

kī.kē.kē. vt. To knock, rap, tap, pound. Cf. *elelū kīkēkē* and *kīkoni,* to tap with a single knuckle.

-kī.kē.kē. Same as *-kīkē. ʻŌlelokīkēkē,* conversation, phrases.

kike.kikē. Redup. of *kīkē.*

kike.lona, kiterona. n. Citron *(Citrus medica).* (Neal 482.) *Eng.*

kī.kene.nei. vi. To contract, shrink; to crouch or squat.

kī.keke.ʻō.lelo. vt. To argue, talk back, banter.

kī.kepa. 1. n. Tapa or sarong worn by women under one arm and over the shoulder of the opposite arm. 2. vi. To lean over to one side, to cover one side; to turn to the side; to place in a one-sided manner; on the side, as a tapa or lei worn over one shoulder and under the opposite arm. *Kuʻu lei kīkepa kau poʻohiwi,* my lei over one shoulder and down on the opposite side. *ʻOki kīkepa,* to cut the hair on one side, as formerly in mourning. *ʻAko kīkepa,* to pluck on one side. *Kā kīkepa,* to strike on one side or glance off on a side; a

glancing blow. 3. vt. To bite sideways, snap. 4. n. Edge, rim, as of a canoe. 5. n. Pig of one solid color with a spot of another color on the shoulder.

kī.kepa.kepa. Redup. of *kīkepa 1-3.*

kī Kepa.nī. n. A weed *(Cassia leschenaultiana). Niʻihau. Lit.,* Japanese ti (its leaves were used for tea).

kikepe.pekia. n. Dyspepsia. *Eng.*

kiki. 1. nvt. A plug shaped like the *kepa* wedge but with the outer end longer, used in filling cracks in wooden bowls or canoes; to plug a hole, patch a canoe or calabash. (PEP *titi.)* 2. vt. To sting, as a bee; to peck, leap at, as a hen. *Fig.,* to make disagreeable remarks. 3. Same as *ʻūkīkiki,* a fish. 4. vt. To kiss. *Eng.* Rare.

kikī. 1. vi. To flow swiftly, spout; to spurt, as water from a hose (cf *kahe wai,* flowing water, as in irrigation); to eject, as octopus ink; to do swiftly. See *pau kikī. Kikī ka hou,* perspiration poured. *Holo kikī o ke kaʻa,* speeding of the car. **hoʻo.kikī.** To cause to flow, pour, etc. *Hoʻokikī kānāwai,* to enforce the law. (Perhaps PPN *titii.)* 2. n. Slimy liquid in the blossom of the mountain ginger.

kī.kī. 1. Redup. of *kī,* to shoot, as a gun; to incite or sick, as a dog; to spout. *Kīkī māka,* target shooting. *Kīkī manu,* to shoot birds. *Wai-kīkī* (name), spouting water [a reference to the many springs and streams in the Waikīkī *ahupuaʻa* that extended far inland]. **hoʻo.kī.kī.** Caus/sim. (PCP *tiitii.)* 2. vi. To do up the hair in a type of knot. 3. n. Crude temporary basket or bundle, as made of *ʻilima,* ti, or morning-glory plants and used to carry food. *Rare.* 4. n. A bird resembling the plover. 5. n. Name given a shellfish. (KL line 33.) 6. n. A seaweed.

-kikiʻa. hoʻo.kikiʻa. Same as *hoʻokiʻekiʻe.*

kī.kī.ʻalo. 1. Redup. of *kīʻalo.* 2. vi. To dodge quickly.

kī.kī.ao. n. Sudden wind gust, squall. *Fig.,* sudden burst of passion.

kikia.pali. Same as *kiapali.*

kikihi. 1. vs. Crescent-shaped; having corners like a cocked hat. 2. n. Doorframe, covering for doorframe; side posts of a door, house post on a heiau; door casing (cf. *kukuna).* Cf. *kihi.* 3. vi. To dodge or move about quickly, especially with quick turning of sharp corners; canoe sailing, to sail.

kikī holo. vi. To run fast, to grow fast. Cf. *holo kikī. Ma ia malama, ua pau ke kikī holo ulu haʻaheo ʻana o ka hoi* (Kep. 93), during this month, the fast proud growth of the *hoi* vine was finished.

kī.kiʻi. 1. vi. To lean back; to tilt, heel, as a ship; to stretch out, extend. See *kānāwai. No Kona ka makani he kulaʻi pau, kīkiʻi kapakahi ʻo ka ʻIwa-lani,* in Kona is the wind that pushes everything over, that heels the ʻIwa-lani to one side. **hoʻo.kī.kiʻi.** Caus/sim. *Noho hoʻokīkiʻi,* to sit up, as a dog; to sit leaning back. 2. n. Spiral fishhook with the end curled back fairly close to the shaft. (Malo 79.)

kikika. Redup. of *kika 1,* slippery. See ex., *kika 1.*

kikiki. 1. Same as *ikiiki,* stifling. 2. Short for *ʻūkīkiki,* a fish. 3. n. A bird. (KL line 313.) 4. Same as *ʻiʻiʻi* or *makaliʻi,* tiny. *He kanaka kikiki,* a small man. *ʻUpena kikiki,* small-meshed net. *Kikiki ka ʻai ʻana,* to eat very little. 5. n. Ticket. Also *likiki. Eng.* 6. nvt. Cheat; to cheat. *Eng.*

kiki.kiki. 1. vt. To mend, as a crack in a wooden bowl. 2. Redup. of *kiki 2,* to sting, peck.

kikiko. vt. Spotted, dotted, mottled, spattered; to make a dot; to print; to tattoo with dots and spots. *Ua kikiko ʻia kuʻu lole,* my dress is spotted, spattered [as with ink].

kiki.kō. interj. Cry of the *ʻōʻō* bird; to cry thus.

kī.kī.koʻele. vs. Done to completeness, perfection. *Ua hana kēlā mea kēia mea o kou alo aliʻi a kīkīkoʻele, ʻaʻohe mea koe,* every one of your royal retainers has done everything in proper order and to completion, nothing remains [undone].

kī.kī.koʻu. 1. n. Chirping or screeching, as of a flock of birds; deep tone in chanting; tapping noise. Cf. *koʻu,* to cluck. *He nahenahe ma kekahi wahi, ā he kīkīkoʻu ma kekahi wahi o ka mele,* soft in some places, deeptoned in other parts of the chant. **2.** Redup. of *kīkoʻu.*

kikila. n. Kettle. *Eng.*

kikila kī. n. Teakettle, teapot. *Eng.*

kikili. Redup. of *kili 1, 2.*

Kiki.lia, Sikilia. nvs. Sicily; Sicilian. *Eng.*

kikilo. nvs. Distant time, either in the remote past or future; far in time or distance. Cf. *kilo. I kikilo aku i nā mamo,* way in the future to the descendants.

kiki.loa. Var. of *kikilo.*

kī.kī.lona. vi. To incite. *Rare.*

-kikilua. hoʻo.kiki.lua. In the card game high-low-jack-and-the-game, to hide one's strength and then play a winning card.

kikima, sitima. n. Acacia (RSV), shittah (KJV). (Isa. 41.19.) (Probably Heb. *shittim.*)

kikimo. Redup. of *kimo 2.*

kikina. n. **1.** Urging, insistence. Cf. *hoʻokina. Kō kikina ua laki* (chant), your insistence has good luck. **hoʻo.ki.kina.** Redup. of *hoʻokina.* **2.** Season. *Eng.*

Kiki.nē, Sidine. Sydney. *Eng.*

kikiʻo. 1. nvi. Settling of water in pools or puddles; to settle. **2.** Redup. of *kiʻo 2.* (PNP *titiko.*)

kikipa. Redup. of *kipa 1, 2.*

kī.kī.pala.pala. n. A variety of taro.

kī.kī.pani. 1. n. Conclusion, last, end, every last one. **2.** nvi. Severe stomach pains that make breathing difficult; to endure such. *ʻA ʻole nō he nahu maoli o kona ʻōpū ā kīkīpani hoʻi i kona houpo,* it was not a normal ache in his stomach, but a pain that made breathing difficult. *E noho maila i loko o ka hauʻoli . . . ua wehe ʻia ke kīkīpani o ka makemake,* living happily . . . every desire satisfied.

Kī.kī-ʻula. n. Name of a star. *Lit.,* red emitting.

kikī wai. v. To shoot water with a hose or water pistol, to hose. Cf. *hoʻokahe wai,* to let water run in irrigation. *Pū kikī wai,* water pistol.

kikiwi. vi. Bent or curved, as a bird beak; humped; to bend or bow the head; to stagger forward, to weave along as a drunk. Cf. *ʻiʻiwi, kiwi. Ihu kikiwi,* hooked nose; curved beak.

kiko. 1. nvt. Dot, point, spot, speck of any kind; section of a story; cock or trigger of a gun (see ex., *ala 2*); punctuation mark; dot in music indicating time added to a note, also to repeat; dotted, speckled, spotted; to dot, mark, peck, hatch; to pick up food, as chickens; to injure fruit, as by a fruit fly; tattooed with dots on the forehead. *Ke aʻo ʻana i ke kau ʻana i nā kiko,* instruction in the placing of punctuation marks. **hoʻo.kiko.** To hatch. (PCP *tito.*) **2.** n. Taboo mark consisting of two crossed ti leaves held in place by a pebble. (PH 123.) **3.** vi. To draw or guess the winning number in *chee-fah,* a Chinese gambling game. *He aha ka hua i kiko mai nei?* What word was guessed correctly [in *chee-fah*]? **4.** n. Thin end of a fish pole.

kikoa. Pas/imp. of *kiko 1. Kikoa nā lae o nā kāne,* the foreheads of the men were tattoo-dotted.

kī.kohō. Var. of *kīkahō 1, 2.*

kiko hoʻ.ōho. n. Exclamation mark.

kiko hoʻo.maha. n. Punctuation mark indicative of a pause, as comma, colon, semicolon, period. *Lit.,* resting punctuation mark.

kī.kohu. nvt. Spots, stains, blemishes; to stain, spot [contraction of *kiko* and *kohu*]. *Kīkohu ʻia me ka ʻulaʻula,* spotted with red.

kiko hua. Same as *kikokiko hua.*

kī.kohu.kohu. Redup. of *kīkohu.*

kī.koi. vi. **1.** Rude, sarcastic. *I pane kīkoi mai ai* (FS 239), answered rudely. **2.** To do in irregular, haphazard fashion, as skipping about while reading; irregular. *Mahi kīkoi,* to farm scattered unsystematic patches, rather than a complete patch.

kiko kahi. n. Period mark in punctuation. *Lit.,* single dot.

kiko.kiko. nvt. **1.** Dotted, spotted, speckled, as a pig; to

dot frequently; to discolor with spots; to nibble, as fish at bait; to peck repeatedly, as a feeding hen. (PCP *titotito.*) **2.** To type.

kiko.kiko hua. nv. To typewrite; typist. Cf. *mīkini kikokiko hua.*

kiko.kikoi. Redup. of *kīkoi 1, 2.*

kiko koma. n. Semicolon. *Lit.,* dot comma. *Eng.*

kiko.lā. n. Timekeeper. *Lit.,* day marker.

kiko.luko. vt. Colored in stripes; to mark in long parallel lines in a variety of colors.

kī.komo. 1. vt. To inlay; to mix, as sap from tree-fern fronds *(palaholo)* and *māmaki* bark with *wauke* bark while beating tapa. **2.** n. Pole fishing in shallow sea.

kiko moa. nv. Term of reproach for commoners committing incest (perhaps a post-Christian term). *Lit.,* hatch like chickens.

kiko moe. n. Hyphen. *Lit.,* supine mark.

kikona, disona. n. Ibex (RSV), pygarg (KJV). (Kanl. 14.5.) (Heb. *dison.*)

kī.koni. nvt. Small adze used for smoothing and finishing a canoe; to smooth and finish a canoe; to soften *wauke* bark for tapa making; to pierce or lance a swelling; to peck; to blaze, as a tree; a piercing, peck, blaze; to rap on the forehead, usually with a single knuckle, especially as a gesture of rudeness or contempt, hence to treat contemptuously. Cf. *kīkēkē,* to rap with all the knuckles. *Ka ʻai kīkoni a nā manu,* peck eating of the birds.

kiko.nia. n. Stork. (Latin *Ciconia,* a genus.) Also *kekoleka.*

kī.koni.koni. Redup. of *kīkoni.*

kiko nī.nau. n. Question mark, interrogation point.

kī.koʻo. nvt. Span; extent; a measure from the end of the thumb to the end of the index finger; chord of an arc; a bent bow; a long surfboard, 3.7 to 5.5 m long; to stretch, reach or stick out; extend, as the hands, or as a bird its wings; to move; to shoot, as from a bow; to step in order to reach; to pay out money, disburse, draw money from the bank. Cf. *pana ʻiole. Palapala kīkoʻo, pepa kīkoʻo,* check or draft. *Lele kīkoʻo,* to take a flying leap with one foot first. *Pila kīkoʻo,* check, draft; bill. *ʻEhā kīkoʻo i koe o kō iala maikaʻi iāia nei* (Laie 363), that one's beauty is four times greater than this one's. (PCP *tiitoko.*)

kī.koʻo.koʻo. Redup. of *kīkoʻo.*

kī.koʻo.lā. n. **1.** Sarcastic, rude, tart, impertinent, insolent. **2.** Haphazard, miscellaneous; here, there, and everywhere; topsy-turvy; carelessly performed, entangled; of awkward shape, as a package. See *waiwai kīkoʻolā.*

kī.koʻo pā.naʻi. n. Bill of exchange. *Lit.,* exchange disbursement.

kī.koʻo pana ʻiole. See *pana ʻiole.* (FS 55.)

kī.koʻo pana.kō. n. Bank check.

kiko pū.ʻiwa. n. Exclamation mark.

kī.koʻu. vt. To cultivate with a hoe or digging stick; to rap or strike with a club; to tap.

kiko.waena. n. Center of a circle; headquarters; Central, telephone operator; bull's eye. See ex., *ʻohea.*

kī.kū. vi. To lean back firmly. *Niʻihau i ke kīkū* (saying), Niʻihau leans firmly back [the people of Niʻihau are independent].

kila. 1. nvs. High place; strong, stout, bold. *Rare.* Cf. *kilakila.* **2.** Also *sila.* nvt. Seal, deed, patent, brand; sealed; to fix a seal. See *palapala kila nui. Eng. Ua kila ʻia anei kāu palapala?* Was your document sealed? *Kēlā pūʻā kao . . . i hōʻailona ʻia me koʻu kila,* that flock of goats . . . marked with my brand. **3.** n. Steel, knife blade, chisel. *Eng. Puʻuwai hao kila,* a heart of steel [of courage]. **4.** nvt. Pen; to write with a pen. Probably Eng. *quill. Rare.* **5.** n. Earmark, as on cattle. **6.** *(Cap.)* Also *Sila.* n. Silas. *Eng.* **7.** Also *gila.* n. Gill, a small liquid measure. *Eng.*

kī lā.ʻau. n. Wooden key or latch, as in a gate.

kī.laha. vs. Broad, wide, ample, enlarged. Cf. *laha.*

kila.kila. vs. Majestic, tall, strong, imposing; having

poise that commands admiration. *Kilakila Hale-a-ka-lā, kuahiwi nani o Maui* (song), majestic Hale-a-ka-lā, beautiful mountain of Maui.

kila ʻoki pepei.ao. n. Steel for cutting ears [of cattle for identification].

kila.ʻo.oma. n. Lathe. *Lit.*, chisel steel.

kila paʻi puna. n. Trowel. *Lit.*, steel slap lime.

kila pao. n. Steel chisel.

kilape. n. Giraffe. *Eng.*

kī.lau. n. **1.** Bracken or brake *(Pteridium aquilinum* var. *decompositum),* a cosmopolitan, stiff, weedy fern, with creeping underground stems and long-stemmed, triangular fronds 60 or more cm long, much divided. (Neal 15–6.) Also *kīlau pueo, paiʻā.* **2.** Ti stalk with shredded leaves, as held by a fishing director *(kilo iʻa)* and used to guide the fishing canoes; ti stalk used to flip water of purification.

kī.lea. n. Small but conspicuous hill. *Rare.*

kileka, tireza. n. Holm tree (RSV), cypress (KJV). (Kanl. 44.14.) (Heb. *tirza.*)

kī.leo. n. **1.** Soft palate including uvula. (Ioba 29.10.) **2.** Trigger of a gun. **3.** Ring of ʻie, a vine, sewed to the top of a fish basket to hold fish in place.

kī.lepa. 1. vi. To float in the wind, to flutter, flap, flip. Cf. *lepa,* flag. **hoʻo.kī.lepa.** Caus/sim. **2.** vs. Irregular, uneven, of varying lengths. **3.** n. Rooster comb, wattle.

kī.lepa.lepa. Redup. of *kīlepa;* streamer, banner, tassel.

kī.lepa.lepa kō. n. Sugar-cane tassel.

kī.lepe. Rare var. of *kūlepe 1, 2.*

kili. 1. nvi. Raindrops; fine rain; to rain gently. *Fig.,* to go or move in a light, sprightly manner. See *kili hau, kilihune, kili nahe.* **hoʻo.kili.** To rain gently. **2.** nvi. Peal of thunder; to thunder. See *hekili.* **3.** *(Cap.)* nvs. Chile; Chilean. *Eng.*

kili.ani. Rare var. of *kiani.*

kili.ʻapu. nvi. A dipper or water carrier made of taro or ʻape leaf.

kili hau. nvi. Ice-cold shower; cold drizzle; to rain thus. *Fig.,* tipsy.

kili.hē. vi. Drenched, as by sea spray or fragrance. *Kilihē i ke kai melemele,* drenched by the sprays of the yellow sea.

kili.hea. Same as *kilihē. Puna paia ʻaʻala, kilihea i ke onaona* (Elbert and Mahoe 87), Puna's fragrant glades drenched with fragrance.

kili.heʻa. vi. Stained with color, as a sky at sunset.

kili.hē.hē. Obstinate, unmanageable. (AP.)

kili.huna. Var. of *kilihune.*

kili.hune. 1. vi. Fine, light rain, wind-blown spray, drizzle; to shower lightly. Cf. *hune.* **hoʻo.kili.hune.** Caus/sim. *He wahi lā hoʻokilihune ua kēia,* this is just a day of slight showers. **2.** n. A fine, delicate species of *Hypnea* (seaweed), probably *H. cervicornis.*

kili.hune.hune. Same as *kilihune 2.*

kilika. 1. nvs. Silk. *Eng.* **2.** n. The black mulberry *(Morus nigra),* introduced into Hawaiʻi in hopes of establishing a silk-producing industry. It is a low tree bearing juicy, sweet, red to black fruits and ovate leaves. The leaves are fed to silkworms. The tree comes from the Far East. (Neal 300.) *Lāʻau kilika* (2 Sam. 5.23), mulberry tree. *Eng.,* silk.

kili.kā. Short for *kilikaʻa 1.*

kili.kaʻa. 1. nvi. A passing, moving shower; to shower lightly and briefly. **2.** n. A kind of tapa, associated with Wai-piʻo, Hawaiʻi.

kilika lau. n. Brocaded silk.

kilika nehe. n. Taffeta. *Lit.,* rustling silk.

Kiliki.ano, Kiritiano. Var. of *Kalikiano,* Christian.

kili.kili. Redup. of *kili 1. Ka wai kilikili noe,* fine, misty rain water.

kili.kili hau. Redup. of *kili hau;* to sprinkle slightly.

kili.kili huna. Redup. of *kilihuna,* fine rain.

kili.kili.hune. Redup. of *kilihune.*

kili.kili.kā. Redup. of *kilikā.*

kili.kili.kaʻa. Redup. of *kilikaʻa.*

kili.kili.oe. Same as *kilikili noe,* misty, light rain. *Kilikilioe ka ua,* the rain falls in light mist.

kilina. n. **1.** Ceiling. *Eng.* **2.** Also **silina.** Shilling. *Eng.*

kili nahe. nvi. Light, soft, gentle rain; pleasant patter of gentle rain; to rain gently.

kili noe. nvi. Fine, misty rain, somewhat heavier mist than the *kili ʻohu. ʻO ka ua kili noe hau o Kēkē* (FS 249), the fine, cold, misty rain of Kēkē.

kili.oe. n. A vine with small elliptical leaves at internodes of 11.5 cm. According to C. S. Judd, this may be a native climbing shrub *(Embelia pacifica),* in the Myrsine family. (Neal 665.)

kili ʻohu. n. Fine rain and light mist.

kili.ona. num. Trillion. *Eng.*

kili.ʻo.ʻopu. n. **1.** Some small cosmopolitan weeds, grasslike sedges, as nut grass *(Cyperus rotundus);* also two others *(C. kyllinga* and *C. brevifolius);* the flower stalk with head is used for stringing small fish. (Neal 84, 86.) See *manunēnē.* **2.** *(Cap.)* Wind associated with Wai-heʻe, Maui, and windward Molokaʻi.

kili.ʻopu. 1. vi. Absorbed in an interesting, happy pastime, as love-making; contented. *Ua kiliʻopu māua i ka pō nei,* what pleasure was love-making for the two of us last night. **2.** vs. Graceful, as in running, jumping. **3.** *(Cap.)* Var. of *Kiliʻoʻopu,* a wind. **4.** Same as *lele ʻopu,* to dive.

Kili.paki, Gilibati. nvs. Gilbert Islands; Gilbertese. *Eng.*

Kili-poe. n. Name of wind.

kili.pohe. vs. Well-shaped and moist, as of a flower wet with dew or fine raindrops. *Kilipohe ka lehua i ka uka,* moist and of beautiful shape is the *lehua* flower of the uplands.

kili.poʻi.poʻi. 1. vi. To clap the hands with palms slightly cupped; to bring down the cupped hand. Cf. *poʻi,* to pounce. **2.** Same as *kīpoʻipoʻi,* to cover.

kili.pue. vt. To embrace tightly, hug ardently. *I kēlā wā i ala aʻe ai ua kanaka nei a ʻike ihola he pōhaku kā kāna e kilipue nei,* then the man awoke and saw that it was a stone he was embracing ardently.

Kili-ua. n. Wind associated with Wai-kāne, Oʻahu. (Nak. 57.)

kili.wehi. vi. To reverberate, rumble. *Nā leo hurō e kiliwehi ana,* the voices shouting hurrah reverberated.

kilo. 1. nvt. Stargazer, reader of omens, seer, astrologer, necromancer; kind of looking glass *(rare);* to watch closely, spy, examine, look around, observe, forecast. Cf. *hākilo* and below. *Kilo aupuni,* political expert. *Kilo ʻuala,* to examine sweet potatoes as in a new mound in order to thin. **hoʻo.kilo.** Caus/sim. (PPN *tiro.)* **2.** n. Kilo. *Eng.* **3.** Also **Silo.** *(Cap.)* n. Shiloh. (Heb. *shiloh.*) (Kin. 49.10 in the KJV, not translated in RSV.)

-kilo. hoʻo.kilo. Thin, wasted. Also *hōkilo.*

kī.loa. vt. To put away for safekeeping, as bundles on a shelf. *Rare.*

kilo.hana. 1. nvs. Name of the outside, decorated sheet of tapa in the *kuʻinakapa,* bed coverings; the four inner layers were white, contrasting with the decorated *kilohana.* Hence extended meanings: best, superior, excellent. *He aliʻi ke aloha, he kilohana e paʻa ai* (saying), love is like a chief, the best prize to hold fast to. **2.** n. Hillock, heap, lookout, top, view out, high point *(kilo + -hana,* nominalizer). (Probably PPN *tirofanga;* cf. Tongan *siofi, siofia* and Samoan *tilofia.*)

kilo heʻe. nv. One who fishes for octopus by looking through a glass-bottomed box; formerly the *kilo heʻe* spit chewed *kukui* nut on the sea to calm the water, then examined *(kilo)* the sea bottom for octopus; to fish thus. Also *ʻōkilo heʻe.*

kilohi. vt. To glance, gaze, as into a mirror *(kilo + hi,* transitivizer). (PPN *tirofi.)*

kilo.hia. Pas/imp. of *kilo.* (PPN *tirofia.)*

kilo hō.kū. nv. Astrologer, astronomer, astronomy; to observe and study the stars.

kiloi. vt. To throw away, discard, throw. **hoʻo.kiloi.** To feign throwing; to cause to throw; to attract someone's attention by throwing something at him, as a stone, leaf, flower.

kilo i'a. nv. A man who observes fish movements from a high place and directs fishermen; to so act.

kī.loi.loi. Redup. of *kiloi.*

kilo.kilo. Redup. of *kilo;* enchantment, magic, fortune telling; magical. (PPN *tirotiro.*)

kilo.kilo.hia. Redup. of *kilohia. Ua kilokilohia nā lae lā'au o Puna* (For. 6:390), the wooded cape of Puna was examined.

kilo.kilo pepa. Redup. of *kilo pepa.*

kilo lani. nv. Soothsayer who predicts the future by observing the sky; to do so; astronomer, astronomy, astrologer.

kilo makani. nv. One who observes the winds for purposes of navigation; to so observe.

kilo.mekele, kilo.metere. n. Kilometer. *Eng.*

kilo moana. nv. Oceanography, oceanographer; to observe and study the open seas.

kilo nā.nā lima, kilo.kilo nā.nā lima. nv. Palmistry, palmist; to predict on observation of the hand.

kilo pepa. n. One who tells the future by use of playing cards; to do so. Also *kilokilo pepa.*

kilo pō.haku. n. Stone placed under water to give a reflection, used as a mirror.

kī.lou. nvt. Hook; to catch with a hook. Cf. *lou,* hook.

kilo.ū. nvs. Quiet nook, lonely spot; silent (For. 6:386).

kilo 'uhane. nvt. Spiritualism, spiritualist; to communicate with spirits.

kī.lou.lou. Redup. of *kīlou. Ua kīloulou 'ia nā ma'awe koko ali'i lehulehu mai kēlā ā mai kēia mokupuni,* the many threads of royal blood are interwoven from one island to another.

kī.lou.lou.hia. Pas/imp. of *kīloulou.*

kilu. 1. nvt. A small gourd or coconut shell, usually cut lengthwise, as used for storing small, choice objects, or to feed favorite children from. Used also as a quoit in the *kilu* game: the player chanted as he tossed the *kilu* towards an object placed in front of one of the opposite sex; if he hit the goal he claimed a kiss; to play this game. (Malo chapter 42.) In the Bishop Museum are stone quoits labelled *kilu.* See ex., *eo* and FS 275-83. *Nā kilu a Lohi'au, kilu* hulas by Lohi'au [name of some hulas performed for the coronation of Ka-lā-kaua]. *Nā kilu a Pele, kilu* hulas by Pele [performed for the coronation of Ka-lā-kaua]. **2.** Same as *pūniu,* knee drum. **3.** n. Unpleasant musty odor, especially resulting from a cold in the nose. Also *i'akui, ihu kilu, ihu pilau.*

kī.lua. vi. To do with determination. *Kīlua ka po'e wa'a,* the canoe paddlers go on [implication they go ashore because of poor fishing].

kima.lola, kima rola. n. Steam roller. *Eng.*

kī.mana.mana. vs. Branching in various directions.

kime. n. Team. *Eng. 'A'ole 'oe pēlā mamua, he kime heihei no Kaleponi* (song), you weren't like that before, a racing team from California.

kimeki. nvs. Cement, concrete, asphalt. *Eng.*

kime.pala, kimebala. n. Cymbal. *Eng.* Also *kumepala.*

kime.pani. n. Chimpanzee. *Eng.*

kimo. 1. nvi. A game similar to jacks: a stone is tossed into the air by the player, who quickly picks another off the ground before he catches the other; jackstones; to play *kimo.* The players often chanted. **2.** nvi. To bob, as the head in watching the *kimo* stone; to bend or fall forward, nod with drowsiness; to go headlong, plunge; to dip, as a kite. (PCP *timo.*) **3.** *(Cap.)* n. James, Jim. *Eng.*

kī.mō. vt. To pound, bruise, mash, as with stick or stone; to smash, break into bits; to dub out the inside of a canoe log with an adze, tamping and smoothing the surface; to crack, as nuts. Also *kīpō.* **ho'o.kī.mō.** Caus/sim. *Rare.*

kimo.kimo. Redup. of *kimo 1, 2;* up-and-down motion, as of a trip hammer. (PCP *timotimo.*)

kī.moki.mō. Redup. of *kīmō. Rare.*

kī.mō.mō. Redup. of *kīmō;* to pound at a fast, steady rate.

kī.mo'o. 1. nvt. Neat bundles of stripped pandanus leaves ready for plaiting; to lay strips together and tie in long bundles, as of pandanus leaves or mulberry bark. **2.** Same as *kuamo'o. Rare.*

kī.mo'o.mo'o. Redup. of *kīmo'o.*

kīmo.pō. nvt. Night assassination, secret rebellion or coup; to waylay in the dark; to assassinate. *Fig.,* of any underhanded act.

kimo po'o. v. To bend down the head, bow; to go headlong as in diving.

Kina. nvs. China; Chinese. *Eng.*

-kina. ho'o.kina. (a) To persist, do continually; incessant. *Ua ho'okina,* continuous rain. *Ho'okina i ka inu,* to drink too much. (b) To urge, compel, add one burden or command to another. *Malia i ho'okina ai ku'u kāne ia'u i ka inu 'awa* (Laie 609), perhaps my husband urged me to drink kava.

kī.nā. nvi. Blemish, blotch, flaw, disfigurement or physical defect of any sort; blight; loss of crops due to any natural disaster, as drought, excessive rain, insects; sin, wickedness; disfigured, blemished, malformed, handicapped, imperfect, maimed; to mar, mutilate. **ho'o.kī.nā.** To cause defect, disaster, etc. (PNP *tiingaa.*)

kinai. 1. vt. To quench or extinguish, as fire; to put out, as a light; to suppress. *Mele kinai 'ona,* song to abolish intoxication [i.e., temperance song]. *Mai kinai i nā leo o nā hua palapala ma ka heluhelu 'ana,* don't lower too much your voice in reading the letters. *Kinai i ka hana a ke kiapolō,* put a stop to the work of the devil. (PNP *tinai.*) **2.** vi. To continue, persist. Cf. *-kina. 'O Hilo ia lā o ka ua kinai, kinakinai ka ua o Hilo, ka ua mao 'ole o Hilo* (chant), that is Hilo of the constant rain, the rains of Hilo go on and on, the rain of Hilo that never clears.

kinai ahi. nv. Fireman, fire extinguisher; to put out fires.

Kinai-lehua. n. Rain associated with Pana-'ewa, Hawai'i. *Lit.,* quenching *lehua* flowers.

kinaina. n. Extinguishing, putting out, snuffing out of life.

kina.kina. Redup. of *-kina.* **ho'o.kina.kina.** Redup. of *ho'okina. Ka ua ho'okinakina,* the continuous rain.

kina.kinai. Redup. of *kinai.* See ex., *kinai 2.*

kina.mona. n. Cinnamon *(Cinnamomum zeylanicum).* (Neal 362.) (Hoik. 18.13.) *Eng.*

kinamu. n. Gingham. *Eng. Pua kinamu,* flower appliquéd, as on quilt or cushion cover. *Kinamu Kekokia,* Scotch plaid gingham.

kī.nana. n. Mother hen or bird and her brood; a brooding place, chicken house. Cf. *'īnana.* (PNP *tinana.*)

kī.nana hale. n. Home, including the house grounds.

kina.nape. vs. Crammed, stuffed, as with food.

kina.na'u. Same as *kīna'una'u.*

kī.na'u. n. **1.** Stain, blemish, defect, minor flaw or imperfection, mistake, blunder. *'Ula kīna'u* (PH 39), red streaked with dark. **2.** An eel. See *puhi kīna'u.* **3.** Young of *aku* and *kawakawa.*

kī.na'u.na'u. Redup. of *kīna'u.*

kī nehe. n. The Spanish needle *(Bidens pilosa),* a lowland weed; young fresh plants are still brewed for tea *(kī).* Similar to *ko'oko'olau,* also used for tea. (Neal 844.) Also *kī, kī pipili, nehe.*

kineko. See *hua kineko.*

kine.mona. Var. of *kinamona.*

kini. 1. num. Multitude, many; forty thousand. *Ola nō ia kini i ka limu lomi lima o Kai-lua,* the crowd thrives on the hand-massaged seaweed of Kai-lua. (PEP *tini.*) **2.** n. King. *Eng. Kini peki,* king of spades. **3.** n. Kin, relatives. *Eng.* **4.** Also *gini.* n. Gin. *Eng.* **5.** Also *tini.* n. Tin, pail, can. *Eng. Kini kākai,* pail with a handle. *Hale ho'okomo kini,* cannery. *Pā kini,* tin plate. **6.** n. Marble (a child's best marble in the game; *kinikini* is more common). (Probably Eng. *tin*.) **7.** n. Zinc. *Eng.* **8.** n. Guinea (coin). *Eng.* **9.** n. Jean, Jane, Jennie. *Eng.*

kini ʻai. n. Pail for carrying poi (*ʻai*) or other food.

kini akua. n. The countless spirits and gods; the multitudinous spirits. (PCP *tini atua.*)

kini.hama. n. Gingham. *Eng.*

kini.hene. n. Guinea hen. *Eng.*

kini.holo. nvi. A ball game, something like playing catch on the run; to play the game.

kinika. n. Ginger. *Eng.* Cf. *ʻela kinika.*

kini.kini. 1. Redup. of *kini 1;* numerous, very many, multitudinous, myriad. (PCP *tinitini.*) **2.** nvi. Marble, game of marbles (formerly round pebbles or seeds); to play marbles. **3.** n. Niʻihau name for *kākalaioa 3,* yellow nickers.

Kini.kiu. n. Uncomplimentary name for Chinese, perhaps from English "Chink."

kini kohu. vs. Extremely well-suited, fine-looking. *Lit.,* many suitable. *Kini kohu ka hele ʻana o kahi leʻaleʻa o ke aliʻi,* going to the entertainment of the chief, [we will be] fine-looking.

kini lau. vs. Numerous, very many.

Kini-maka-lehua. n. Name of a mountain rain. *Lit.,* countless *lehua* blossoms.

kini ʻō.pala. n. Garbage or rubbish can.

kini.peki. n. Name of a game in which the stone called *hiu* was used.

kini pela. n. Pail. *Eng.*

kini.pō.pō. nvi. Ball, baseball; to play ball.

kini.pō.pō hī.naʻi. n. Basketball.

kini.pō.pō paʻi. nvi. Tennis. *Lit.,* ball to strike.

kini.pō.pō peku. nvi. Football. *Lit.,* kick ball. *Hoʻokū-kū kinipōpō peku wāwae,* football game.

kino. 1. nvs. Body, person, individual, self, main portion, physique, receptacle; form; fully formed, as a foetus; bodily, physical, material, nonspiritual; hull of a ship. Cf. *kino pālua, kinopāpālua* under *pālua, pāpālua.* Pili i ke kino, kō ke kino, carnal, bodily, corporal. *Kino lele* (For. 4:73), power to fly, flying form. *Ka poʻe e lawe ana i kou kino,* your subscribers [as of a newspaper]. *Nani ke kino o kēia kīhei,* the main part of this shawl is pretty. *Hoʻolako ma ke kino,* supply material (nonspiritual) needs. *ʻŌlelo pili kino,* material, personal or worldly talk (cf. *pili ʻuhane* under *ʻuhane*). *E lawe aku ʻoe i kēia ma kou kino lahilahi,* take this for your thin form [in the spare columns of a newspaper]. **hoʻo.kino.** To take shape, embody; to develop, as a puny infant; to take form, as a spirit. (PPN *tino.*) **2.** nvs. Person in grammar; personal. *Kino mua, kino kahi,* first person. *Kino lua,* second person. *Kino kolu,* third person. *Nā mea pili kino,* personal things. *Hoʻokō kino aku i kēia kono,* personally accept this invitation. *E hana mua i kā ke kino mamua o ka hana ʻana i kō haʻi,* do your personal work first before doing for others.

kino ahi. n. A "fire body": the bones of a deceased thrown into a fire pit so that the spirit of the deceased may be with and serve family relatives, of the Pele family. The bones of Mary Kawena Pukuiʻs great grandmother were thus buried. See *kākūʻai.*

kino aka, kino aka.kū. n. Spirit, especially of a living person.

kino ʻeʻepa. n. Spirit body, strange form.

kinohi. n. Beginning, origin, genesis. *Kinohi loa,* the very beginning. *Mai kinohi a Hōʻike ʻAna,* from Genesis to Revelations [from beginning to end].

kī.nohi. nvt. Decorated, spotted, ornamented; decoration, ornamentation. *Ua kīnohi ʻia ka pāpale me ka lipine ʻulaʻula,* the hat is trimmed with a red ribbon. **hoʻo.kī.nohi.** Caus/sim.

kī.nohi.nohi. Redup. of *kīnohi;* printed, as calico. See ex., *hoʻopukalia. He nani maoli nā kīnohinohi o kona lumi hoʻoluana,* very beautiful were the decorations of his reception room. *Ē ka honua ē, ē nahele lā, i kīnohinohi ē* (Kep. 31), O earth, O plants, be adorn-

ments. *Ka iʻa kīnohinohi pōhaku,* marine life that adorns rocks [periwinkles and nerita]. **hoʻo.kī.nohi.-nohi.** To adorn, add color. *Mea hoʻokīnohinohi,* decorations.

kino.hou. n. Beginning, first. *Lit.,* new body. *Pehea lā i loaʻa mai ai kēia hāʻawe i kinohou?* How was this burden obtained at first?

kino iwi. n. Skeleton.

kino kahi. See *kino 2.*

kino kanaka. n. Human form.

kino kau.lele. n. Apposition, in grammar. *Lit.,* enlarged form.

kino kolu. See *kino 2.*

kinola, kinora. n. Lyre (RSV), harp (KJV). (Hal. 57.8.) (Heb. *kinnur.*)

kino lau. n. Many forms taken by a supernatural body, as Pele, who could at will become a flame of fire, a young girl, or an old hag.

kino lepo. n. Earthly body.

kino lua. 1. See *kino 2.* **2.** vs. Dual-formed, dual-natured.

kino make. n. Corpse, dead body.

kino maoli. True form or body. *Ua hele kino maoli aku ʻo Ka-ʻai-aliʻi i mua o ke aliʻi,* Ka-ʻai-aliʻi went personally to the chief.

kino-o-Hau.mea. n. A type of low-lying breadfruit. (HP 187.)

Kino o ka Haku. n. Corpus Christi.

kino.ʻole. vs. Frail and thin (animate). *Ua hele kā hoʻi ʻo Iunia ā kinoʻole,* how frail and thin Eunice has become.

kinopu. n. A strong scent, as of tobacco.

kino wai.lua. n. Spirit of the dead; dead person, bodily remains, corpse. **hoʻo.kino wai.lua.** Caus/sim. (For. 6:452.)

kinu.wā. Hopscotch; to play hopscotch.

kio. 1. vi. To cheep, chirp. **hoʻo.kio.** Same as *hōkio,* a whistle. (PCP *tio.*) **2.** nvi. Projection, protuberance, bubo; to protrude. *ʻAʻohe kio pōhaku nalo i ke alo pali,* on the face of a cliff, not one jutting rock is hidden from sight [no use being secretive]. **hoʻo.kio.** To spread out, project. **3.** Same as *kaunaʻoa 2,* a mollusk. (PPN *tio.*) **4.** interj. Word used in reply to a question one does not care to answer, somewhat like rude English "What's it to you?" *E hele ana ʻolua i hea? Kio.* Where are you two going? *Kio.* **5.** n. Cords made of hibiscus bark used as drawstrings of a large net. **6.** n. Mock warfare, training in warfare by combat (And.); according to Malo 66 *kaua kio* is mock warfare with blunted spears. (Ka-welo's warriors greet him as he returns from fishing by hurling spears at him for him to dodge or parry: FS 52.) **7.** n. Mussels. See below. (PPN *kio.*)

kiʻo. 1. nv. Small pool for stocking fish spawn, as mullet, milk fish, tenpounder, usually attached to longer ponds; puddle, cistern, water sluice, dregs; to settle, as dregs; to deposit, especially of any element beginning with *kūkae,* as *kūkaehao, kūkaelā.* Cf. *kiʻo lepo, kiʻo wai. Kai kiʻo,* sea water remaining in rock hollows after the tide goes down. *Nā kiʻo wai o Kū-lani-hākoʻi,* pools of Kū-lani-hākoʻi [mythical spring in the sky; its overflow came to earth as rain]. **hoʻo.kiʻo.** To gather or settle, as water in a lake or pond; to cease flowing, of menstruation. *Lua hoʻokiʻo wai,* cistern. *Luawai hoʻokiʻo,* reservoir. **2.** vi. To excrete, evacuate, give birth to a child (often sarcastic). Cf. *kikiʻo, kiʻokiʻo, pākiʻokiʻo.* (PPN *tiko.*) **3.** n. Rootlet of sweet potato.

kiʻoa. Pas/imp. of *kiʻo.* **hoʻo.kiʻoa.** Same as *hoʻokiʻo. He ua nō, he kulu ua no ka liko . . . ke hoʻokiʻoa i nā kikawaiō* (chant for Ka-mehameha III), it is rain, raindrops for the buds . . . water settling on the *kikawaiō* fern.

kiʻo ahi. n. Fiery pit, place of torment, hell.

kī.oe. 1. n. Small surfboard. **2.** vi. To turn the head with a rotary motion, as of a bird watching its prey. Cf. *oeoe,* long neck.

kī.ʻo.ʻe. nvt. Ladle, dipper, cup; scoop or spoon made of coconut shell; dip, as of poi; arm or wrist motion in paddling or dipping; net-mending instrument; to skim, as cream from milk; to dip, ladle, scoop; to join nets together; to twist and snap, as breadfruit with a *lou* stick. Cf. *ʻoʻe,* to probe. *Ka ʻai kīʻoʻe lāʻau,* the food reached with a stick [breadfruit].

kio.ea, kiowea. 1. n. Bristle-thighed curlew *(Numenius tahitiensis),* large, dusky brown, migratory bird with a long, curved bill; the cry of this bird. See ex., *lawekeō.* **2.** nvi. Tall, long-legged, slender person; long; tall; standing high on long legs; to extend, stretch out. **3.** n. An extinct honeyeater *(Chaetoptila angustipluma).*

kio.ʻele. n. A small native shrub *(Hedyotis coriacea,* syn: *Kadua menziesiana),* belonging to the coffee family, a rare or extinct species.

kī.oe.oe. vs. Long, tall, as a ship mast or giraffe neck.

kī.ʻo.ʻe.ʻo.ʻe. Redup. of *kīʻoʻe.*

kī.ʻo.ʻe poi. n. Finger or single dip of poi.

kio.hoa. vi. Spoiling, as a flower too long in the rain. *Pala kiohoa i ka ua ka pua kou* (chant), yellowed, spoiling in the rain are the *kou* blossoms.

kio honua. n. Heap of food (For. 6:398), earth protuberance.

kī.ʻohu.ʻohu. nvs. Mist; misty; misty place. Cf. *kili ʻohu. Noho ana ke akua i ka nāhelehele i ālai ʻia e ke kīʻohuʻohu, e ka uakoko* (hula prayer), the gods dwell in the forest, hidden away by the mists and low-lying rainbow.

kī.ʻoki. nvs. Striped; creased with fat; stripes. *He kākau kīʻoki ʻōniʻo i ka lae, he kīʻoki ʻo ke kīkākapu, ʻo ka iʻa kapu* (chant), marked with bars and streaks on the forehead, the *kīkākapu* is [a fish] with bars [of color], a sacred fish.

kio.kio. Redup. of *kio 1, 2;* young, immature, as flora or fauna. Cf. *piopio, ʻōpiopio. Nā kiokio pōhaku,* rock heaps [or jutting rocks]. **hoʻo.kio.kio.** Redup. of *hoʻokio.* (PCP *tiotio,* to cheep.)

ki.ʻo.ki.ʻo. Redup. of *kiʻo;* variegated, as calm and unruffled spots in the sea.

kī.ʻoki.ʻoki. Redup. of *kīʻoki.*

kio.kiola. Redup. of *kiola.*

kio.kio pali. n. Cliff or ridge with irregular projections.

kiola. vt. To throw, toss; to deposit, as bones of the dead. *Kiola mai i ke kinipōpō,* throw me the ball. *Kiola ʻino,* to dash down, as in anger.

kī.ola.ola. 1. Redup. of *kiola;* tossing back and forth or up and down, as in juggling; to cast for fish; to sort and distribute, as sweet potato cuttings (For. 5:665). **2.** n. A form of black magic, by which a special stone was prayed over and hurled at a victim; it entered through the anus or mouth and destroyed the victim, and then returned to the magician.

kī.ola.ola hao lio. nv. Horseshoe pitching; to pitch horseshoes.

kī.ola.ola lina. n. Ringtoss.

kiola pō.kā. n. An old name for shot-put.

kio.lea. nvs. High, rickety or unsafe seat; high, long, rickety. *Aʻa kiolea* (FS 61), aerial roots, as of pandanus.

ki.ʻo.lei. Same as *kiʻelei,* to squat.

ki.ʻo.lena. nvt. Tapa-drying and bleaching place; to dry and bleach tapa; to dye tapa.

ki.ʻo lepo. n. Swamp, mire (2 Pet. 2.22), fen (Ioba 40.21); mud puddle, dirty pool.

kio.loa. 1. Same as *kialoa,* a long, narrow canoe. **2.** n. Long fishing line for deep-sea fishing.

kiolo.hia. Same as *puʻukaʻa,* a sedge.

kio.mana. vt. To ride or sit astride, as on a horse; to straddle. Cf. *kīhelei. Kiomana nā wāwae o ua keiki nei ma kēlā ʻaoʻao a me kēia ʻaoʻao o ua hā maiʻa nei,* then the legs of this child sat astride of each side of this banana trunk.

kī.ʻomo. Var. of *kīʻamo.*

Kiona, Ziona. n. Zion. *Eng.*

ki.ʻona. n. Dung heap, dump; privy, toilet. See ex., *lolena. Hale kiʻona* (2 Nal. 10.27), latrine (RSV), draughthouse (KJV).

kī.ʻō.naha. vs. Bent, crooked, curved. Cf. *ʻōnaha.*

kio naha.wele. n. A common mussel, probably *Brachidontes cerebristriatus.*

kī.ʻoni. n. Key to animate a toy.

kio-noho-one. n. Probably *Natica gualteriana. Lit.,* sand-dwelling *kio* (mollusk).

ki.ʻo.ʻohu. vt. To dip. *Ua kiʻoʻohu aʻela lākou i ka wai i loko o kekahi ʻumeke,* they dipped up water into a calabash.

ki.ʻo.ʻō.pae. n. Taro-leaf container as held in the mouth, so as to form a basket to hold shrimps *(ʻōpae)* while groping with the hands for shrimp. Also *pūʻolo ʻōpae.*

kī.ʻopa. vi. Lame; to limp. Cf. *ʻoʻopa.*

Kio-paʻa. n. North Star. *Lit.,* fixed projection.

kī.ʻope. 1. nvt. A bundle; to make a bundle. **2.** vt. To scatter a fire in order to put it out. (PH 119.) **3.** n. A fish resembling *kawakawa.*

kio poʻa.po.ʻai. Same as *poʻapoʻai 2,* a mollusk.

kio poi. Poi calabash. (And.)

ki.ʻo wai. nvi. Pool of water, water hydrant, water hole, fountain (Mele 4.12); to settle, as water.

Ki.ʻo-wao. n. Cool mountain rain accompanied by wind and fog, sometimes associated with Alakaʻi swamp on Mt. Wai-ʻaleʻale, Kauaʻi, as well as Nuʻu-anu Valley, Oʻahu. See chant, *kohāhā.*

kiowea. Var. spelling of *kioea.*

kipa. 1. vt. To visit, call. *Hale kipa,* guest house, inn (Puk. 4.24). *Ua kipa aʻe au i kō lākou hale,* I visited their house. **hoʻo.kipa.** To entertain, treat hospitably; hospitable; hospitality. **2.** vi. To turn aside; to turn from the direct path. Cf. *kepa.* (PPN *tipa.*)

kī.pā. nvi. Chinese gambling game *chee-fah;* to play this game. (Probably from Chinese: Gram. 2.9.)

kī.pae.pae. n. Stone pavement or steps for entering a house.

kipa hele. vi. To go visiting from place to place.

kī.pahulu. n. Place where soil is worn out *(pahulu)* from constant farming; worn-out soil.

kī.pa.ʻi. vt. **1.** To shoo away, as by clapping *(paʻi);* to drive away animals; to pat with the hands; to strike with the wings, as an angry bird. **2.** To cover or spread leaves.

kī.pai.pai. vt. To encourage, inspire.

kī.pa.ʻi.pa.ʻi. Redup. of *kīpaʻi.*

kī.paka.kē. Same as *pakakē,* gibberish.

kipa.kipa. Redup. of *kipa 2.* (For. 6:499.)

kipaku. vt. To send away, drive away, expel, discharge, banish, put out of the house, get rid of, rout, exile, evict.

kī.pala.he.ʻa. vs. Smeared, stained.

kī.pala.lē. nvi. Disorder, jumble, tumult; rapid flow, as of a swollen stream; disorderly, unsystematic, without method; to spread, extend in a disorderly fashion. *Kīpalalē ka ʻōlelo,* to talk in a rapid, incoherent manner.

kī.pala.pala.he.ʻa. Redup. of *kīpalaheʻa.*

kipao. Similar to *pao 1. I ke kipao ʻia e ke kai,* due to erosion by the sea.

kī paoa. Same as *kī ʻaʻala,* sweet basil.

kī.pao.pao. vt. To scoop out the earth from the side, as by the sea hammering on a coast.

kī.papa. 1. nvt. Pavement, level terrace; to pave, lay stones in pavement or terrace; to wall in, as with stones (GP 98). **2.** vi. To be close together, as clouds, or as taro neatly packed in a load; to shoot together (see *papa 3,* Kel. 45). **3.** n. A sweet potato. **4.** nvi. Prone position on a surfboard; to assume such.

kipa.pa.ʻi. Same as *kīpaʻipaʻi.*

kī.papala.lē. Redup. of *kīpalalē. Nā ʻōlelo kīpapalalē,* jumble of speech.

kī.pā.pali. nvs. Cliff brink, small cliffs; hilly.

kipa.pani. vi. To flock. *Kipapani ka noio e kīkīkoʻu i ke aku,* the *noio* birds flocked together to make a din over the bonito.

kipa.pau. Var. of *kipopou.*
kī.pau. vt. To overturn completely. *Rare.*
kipa.wale. n. A variety of sweet potato. (HP 142.)
kipa wale. vi. To call without being asked; to intrude; to happen in on a visit by chance.
kī.pē. 1. nvt. Bribe, bribery (Ioba 15.34); to bribe. Cf. *pē,* humbled, flattened. **2.** vt. To pelt with stones; to strike, as hail stones. **3.** n. A large ti-leaf bundle tied at one end. Also *wahī.*
kī.pe'a. vt. To cross sticks, as in building a temporary shelter.
kī.pe'a.pe'a. Redup. of *kīpe'a.*
kī.pehi. vt. To pelt, throw at. *Fig.,* to assail with rough language, speak harshly. **ho'o.kī.pehi.** Caus/sim.
kī.pē.pē. Redup. of *kīpē 2.*
kī.pē.pehi. Redup. of *kīpehi.*
kipi. 1. nvt. Rebellion, revolt, treachery, treason, uprising; rebel, seditious; to rebel, plot, revolt, resist lawful authority; to conspire against; to ram, as of a goat. *E kipi 'ia nō wau e 'oe* (FS 153), I have been conspired against by you. **ho'o.kipi.** To foment or act in revolt; rebellious. (PCP *tipi.*) **2.** n. Hilo name for mound taro patches. **3.** vt. To dig with a sharp tool. (PPN *tipi.*) **4.** n. O'ahu name for the *'akialoa* bird.
kipi.kelia, dipiteria. n. Diphtheria. *Eng.*
kipi.kipi. Redup. of *kipi 1, 3;* to hew, trim; little by little. (PPN *tipitipi.*)
kipi.kua. n. Pickaxe. *Lit.,* dig hew.
kī pipili. Same as *kī, kī nehe, nehe 3 (Bidens).*
kī.pō. 1. Var. of *kīmō.* **2.** n. Depot. *Eng.*
kī.pō.'ae'ae. n. Armpit *(pō'ae'ae)* and shoulder above it. *Pa'a a'e nā 'awe'awe ma kēlā a me kēia kīpō'ae'ae,* fastened the packs around each armpit and shoulder.
kī.poho. 1. n. Small, shallow pool, basin, or hollow in a rock, as where salt water collects; small container. **2.** vi. To dive, dip or pitch downward, as a kite.
kī.poho.poho. 1. Redup. of *kīpoho.* **2.** n. Small arable patch surrounded by lava beds, smaller than a *kīpuka.*
kī.po'i. vt. To cover, conceal, hide; to protest giving away objects to others. Cf. *po'i,* lid.
kī.po'i.po'i. 1. Redup. of *kīpo'i.* **2.** n. Sweet potato patch. (For. 5:115.)
kipoka, kipoda. n. Porcupine (Isa. 34.11); hedgehog (RSV), bittern (KJV) (Zep. 2.14); (Heb. *qippod.*) Cf. *pua'a 'ili 'oi'oi.*
kī pō.kā. v. To shoot.
kī.pola. nvt. Wrapper, such as ti leaves about fish; to wrap up, bundle up; to keep warm with wraps, as a sick person.
kī.pola.pola. Redup. of *kī.pola.*
kī.poli.poli. n. Nook and cranny. Cf. *poli,* bosom. *I loko o ka mahina me ka lā, i loko o nā ao 'ōpua o ka lewa a me nā kīpolipoli apau,* in the moon and sun, in the cloud banks of the firmament and in every nook and cranny.
kī.polo. n. Type of prayer used in black magic requesting that the victim be led to a place of death.
kī polo.lei. nvt. To shoot straight; sharpshooter.
kipona. 1. nvi. Intense; to intensify, usually but not always pejorative, often followed by a qualifier; translations vary greatly and depend on context; very common in Kelekona; distress, pain. *Ua hiki mai kona kipona huhū,* his worst of bad tempers is here; he has flown into a rage. *Malalo ho'i o nā kipona wela hahana a ka lā,* beneath the suffocating intense heat of the sun. *I loko o nā kipona o ka meha anoano 'e'ehia* (Kel. 6), in the distress of loneliness, solitude, fear. *Nā kipona o ka ma'i* (Kel. 6), the distress of sickness. *Nā kipona o nā 'ano hana hou,* the fascination of newly made kinds. *Mamuli o nā kokoina ho'omana'o i kipona 'ia e nā hāli'ali'a* (Kel. 3), because of the urging of memories intensified by recollections. *Ke anu 'iniki hō'eha o nā kipona wehe ka iao* (Kel. 21), the tingling painful cold of earliest dawn. **2.** vi. Own. *Nā kipona home o ka wahine 'oni 'o Hōpoe* (Kel. 3), the own home of the dancing woman, Hōpoe. **3.** vt. To make a hollow or round opening, like the eye socket; hollow. **4.** vt. Mixed, mingled; varying in color or texture, as of the sea; to add to, as something of different character, as ferns to a lei. *Ka wai kipona me ke kai,* water mixed with sea water. *Kipona paukū i ka laua'e, ka pua o ka 'ilima nono i ka lā* (chant for Ka-'iu-lani), add a section of *laua'e* fern [to] the flower of the *'ilima,* bright in the sunlight.
kī.pona.pona. 1. Redup. of *kipona 1-4.* **2.** n. A small, climbing, native shrub *(Phyllostegia racemosa)* in the mint family, with small, downy leaves, and small, purplish-white flowers in whorls.
kī.po'o.hiwi. Same as *kihi po'ohiwi. He kīpo'ohiwi i ke kīpo'ohiwi,* shoulder to shoulder. **2.** n. Gun.
kī.po'o.po'o. nvs. Indented, pitted with holes; pits.
kī.pō.pō. Redup. of *kīpō 1.*
kipo.pou. Redup. of *kīpou.*
kī.pou. vt. To drive down, as a stake into the ground; to go downward; descend; to lean, as a post.
kī.pū. 1. nvt. To hold back or brace, as a canoe on a wave with a paddle; to rein in, as a horse; to remain, as mist or rain; to fold tightly about one, as a blanket; steersman. *He mau ho'okele ā he mau kīpū noho'i* (For. 4:123), navigators and also steersmen. *Ā laila i kīpū auane'i lāua* (For. 4:123), then the two of them just braced [the canoe]. *Kīpū i ka mana'o, kīpū i ke kapa a ka noe; 'auhea wale 'oe ē ka 'ohu, kīpū maila i Ka'ala* (song), hold fast to an idea, hold fast to the tapa blanket of mist; listen here, O mist, nestling now on [Mt.] Ka'ala. **2.** n. Tranquillity. *Kīpū aheahe,* quiet peace. *Kīpū ahiahi,* tranquillity of eventide.
kī pū. v. To shoot, fire or discharge a gun. Cf. *laikini kī pū.*
kī.puka. n. **1.** Variation or change of form *(puka,* hole*),* as a calm place in a high sea, deep place in a shoal, opening in a forest, openings in cloud formations, and especially a clear place or oasis within a lava bed where there may be vegetation. **2.** Short shoulder cape; cloak, poncho. **3.** Loop, lasso; snare, as for catching owls (a rat was tied to a sharp stick in a net; the owl, pouncing on the rat, was pierced by this stick).
kī.pū.kai. n. Seaside heliotrope *(Heliotropium curassavicum),* a prostrate, perennial American herb 30 to 60 cm long, with narrow, hoary leaves, white or pale purple flowers, considered indigenous to Hawai'i. Formerly the plants were dried and brewed for tea used as a tonic. (Neal 718.) Also *nena* and *po'opo'ohina* or *lau po'opo'ohina* on Ni'ihau.
kī.puka 'ili. n. Leather lasso. *Nā keiki ho'olei kīpuka 'ili,* the boys who throw lassos.
kī.puka.puka. Redup. of *kīpuka.*
kī.pū lani. vs. Immobile, motionless in the sky, as clouds, stars; steadfast and loyal to one's chief.
kī.pulu. nvt. Fertilizer, mulch; to fertilize, mulch. **ho'o.kī.pulu.** To enrich or fertilize, as soil.
kī.pulu.pulu. Redup. of *kīpulu.*
kī.puni. vt. To gird, wrap around, surround. *Ua kīpuni 'ia mākou e ke aloha,* we are enfolded in love.
kī.pupū. Redup. of *kīpū 1;* to hinder, draw back; to jerk and start, as an automobile. Cf. *pupū,* to stall. **ho'o.kī.pupū.** Caus/sim.
kī.pu'u. Rare var. of *hīpu'u,* knot.
Kī.pu'u.pu'u. n. **1.** Name of a chilly wind and rain at Wai-mea, Hawai'i. *Hole Wai-mea i ke ahe u ka makani, hao mai nā 'ale a ke Kīpu'upu'u* (name song for Ka-mehameha I), Wai-mea is rasped by the blowing of the wind, billows of the Kīpu'upu'u wind ravage. *Kū i ka Kīpu'upu'u,* buffeted by the Kīpu'upu'u [of hurt feelings]. **2.** Name of a company of warriors from Wai-mea in Ka-mehameha I's time, named for the wind.
kipu.wē. vi. To keep away. *Eng.*
kiu. 1. nvt. Spy, scout; to spy, observe secretly. Cf. *ho'omakākiu.* *Māka'i kiu,* detective. *'Oihana kiu,* secret service. (PEP *tiu.*) **2.** *(Cap.)* Name of a strong, moderately cold northwesterly wind, known as *Mālualua, Mālua-ki'i-wai,* and *Ho'olua,* in some localities;

see also *Koholā Lele* and below. (PEP *Tiu.*) **3.** A fishhook. (And.) **4.** *(Cap.)* nvs. Jew; Jewish. *Eng.*

kī.'ū. n. Latch on sewing machine to which the bobbin is attached.

Kiu Anu. n. Wind associated with Ka-lā-heo, Kaua'i. (Nak. 59.)

kiu.ho'o.pulu. vt. To spy cunningly in order to entrap, perhaps by pretense of cultivating friendship.

Kiu Inu Wai. n. Name of a wind from the mountains, stronger and cooler than the Kēhau. *Lit.,* water-drinking Kiu. Also *Huehu.*

Kiu Kai Nui. n. Name of a wind associated with Ko'olau, Kaua'i. (For. 5:97.)

Kiu Ke'e. n. Name of a wind associated with Nā-wiliwili, Kaua'i.

kī 'ula.'ula. n. A red ti grown for ornament, long in Hawai'i but not native.

kiule, kiure. n. Jury. *Eng.*

Kiu Lehua. Probably same as *Kiu Wai Lehua.*

kiu.lela, kiurela. n. Squirrel. *Eng.*

kiule nui, kiure nui. Grand Jury.

Kiu Wai Lehua. n. Name of a cold wind. *Lit.,* Kiu of the *lehua* honey. *Ku'u hoa pili i ke anu o Kiu Wai Lehua* (For. 6:424), my close companion of the cold *Kiu-lehua*-honey wind.

kī.wa'a. 1. n. Name of a mythical bird. **2.** vt. To dredge. **3.** n. Stick formerly used as a vise to hold the canoe while attaching the gunwale strakes *(mo'o).* Also *mōlī.*

kī.wa'a.wa'a. 1. vs. Full of ruts and furrows, rough, rutty, uneven; broad-shouldered, muscular, as a strong man (so called because the muscular furrows suggest canoes, *wa'a).* **2.** n. Type of coarse, rough tapa.

kiwala.'ō. vs. Untidy, disorderly, unkempt; scrawly, as writing. *Kiwala'ō maoli nō kāu ho'onoho 'ana i ka wahie,* how carelessly you have heaped the wood.

kī.wala.wala. Same as *kiwala'ō.*

Kiwani. n. Kiwanis. *Eng.*

kī.wawā. n. **1.** Unintelligible sound of voices. **2.** Mulberry bark partly beaten into tapa.

kiwi. 1. nvi. Horn of an animal, antler; horn of the *kala,* a fish; curved object such as a sickle; curved, bent; to pull obliquely, as a fish on a line; to bend forward or sideways, as a sleepy person; to reel and stagger as in drunkenness; to fall or stumble head foremost. **ho'o.kiwi.** To curve, bend; to stagger, etc. **2.** Same as *kākiwi 2;* layering, plant grown from layering.

kī.wī. n. T.V. *Eng.*

kiwi.kiwi. Redup. of *kiwi.* **ho'o.kiwi.kiwi.** Caus/sim.

kī.wila, siwila. nvs. Civil, civic; civilian. *Eng. Hana kīwila,* civil service. *Hui Kīwila Hawai'i,* Hawaiian Civic Association. *Kānāwai kīwila,* civil laws, civil code. *Nā pono kīwila,* civil rights. *Po'e limahana kīwila,* civilian laborers.

kī.wini. vs. Brazen. Cf. *wini.*

kō. 1. n. Sugar cane *(Saccharum officinarum),* a large unbranched grass brought to Hawai'i by early Polynesians as a source of sugar and fiber. The thick stems are full of sweet juicy pulp. In time, many different kinds of cane were produced, with many different attributes and names. Cane yields one of the most valuable plant products known. For commercial purposes the yield has been increased by hybridizing with such success that the sugar industry was for many years the largest industry in Hawai'i. (Neal 77-9.) For. 5:582-9 lists types of *kō;* all are listed in the Dictionary except *kō malolo* (also known as *kō puhala* and *kō 'ailolo).* Cf. *kea 3. He 'oi kēlā 'o ke kanaka huhū . . . 'a'ohe pū kō momona iāia* (For. 5:209), he's a very angry man . . . no clump of sugar cane will sweeten him up [i.e., you can't mollify his anger]. *Kō 'eli lima a 'o Hālāli'i,* hand-dug sugar cane of Hālāli'i [famous in songs descriptive of Ni'ihau; its stalks grew in sand with only the leaves protruding]. (PPN *toro,* possibly PEP *toa,* PCP *too.*) **2.** nvi. Dragged, towed, wind-borne; long, as a vowel sound; to drag, push, prolong, tow, drawl; to hold a note for several beats in singing or chanting;

pull, tug, massage. Cf. *kani kō, lawai'a kō lau. Kō mai ana ke 'ala o ka pua o ka pīkake,* the fragrance of the jasmine flower is wind-borne. *I aloha i ke kō a ka wai, i ka 'ī mai "Anu kāua"* (chant), beloved is the [current] pulling in the stream, saying "we are refreshed." (PPN *toho.*) **3.** vi. To fulfill, come to pass, succeed, do, complete, foreclose; to win in dispute; to become pregnant; fulfilled. *Kō 'ole 'ia,* not done, accomplished; unsuccessful. *Ua kō ka'u ho'opi'i ma ke kānāwai,* I won the lawsuit. **ho'o.kō.** Executive; to fulfill; to carry out, as a contract; to enforce, execute, confirm, construe, interpret, decree; to award, as land; to probate, perform, satisfy; to transact, accomplish; to cause a conception; confirmation, award. *Luna ho'okō,* executive officer. *Luna ho'okō kauoha,* executor. *Ho'okō 'ana,* performance, accomplishment, achievement, carrying out. *Ho'okō kānāwai,* to enforce the law. *Ho'okō hana mamua o ka le'ale'a,* duty before pleasure. *Ka puke o ka pule 'ana a me ka ho'okō 'ana,* the book of prayers and the administration [of the sacrament]. (PPN *too.*) **4.** vt. To break up lumps in poi by pressing against the side of a container. **5.** n. Second note in musical scale, re. **6.** n. and interj. A call to pigs, fowl. Also *kolo, kolo, kolo.* **7.** prep. Of (*o*-form possessive; Gram. 8.4.1). Note idiomatic use with *ā,* as far as, plus a direction word: *kō ā uka,* those of the uplands; *kō ā mua,* those in the foreground; *kō ā hope,* those behind. *Kō kākou,* our (plural, inclusive). *Kō 'Ana hale,* Anna's house. *Kō ia,* of him, his, hers, its; belonging to him or her. *Kō laila,* of that place; belonging to that place, local. *Kō 'one'i mokomoko nui* (For. 5:411), the big fighter of this place. *Kō ka 'uhane,* spiritual things. (PNP *to'o.*) **8.** possessive. Your (of one person; singular possessed object; replacing both *kāu* and *kou,* often with affectionate connotation; see Gram. 8.4.1). (PCP *too.*)

koa. 1. nvs. Brave, bold, fearless, valiant; bravery, courage. Cf. *ho'onakoa, pu'ipu'i. A'o nō i ke koa, a'o nō i ka holo* (saying, Kel. 45), learn bravery, learn to run [be brave but prudent in war]. **ho'o.koa.** Brave; to cause bravery. (PPN *to'a.*) **2.** nvs. Soldier, warrior, fighter; military, hero, martial. *Kānāwai koa,* martial law. **ho'o.koa.** To act as a soldier; to cause to be a soldier. **3.** n. The largest of native forest trees *(Acacia koa),* with light-gray bark, crescent-shaped leaves, and white flowers in small, round heads. A legume with fine, red wood, a valuable lumber tree, formerly used for canoes, surfboards, calabashes, now for furniture and ukuleles. A small *koa* was sometimes added to the hula altar to Laka, goddess of the hula, to make the dancer fearless. (Neal 408-11.) The name *koa* may be qualified by the terms *kā, kū ma kua, kū mauna. E ola koa,* live like a *koa* tree [i.e. long]. (PPN *toa.*) **4.** *(Cap.)* n. Name of a wind at Mālei, Moloka'i. (For. 5:103.) **5.** n. Land crocodile (RSV), chameleon (KJV). (Oihk. 11.) (Pronunciation uncertain.)

ko'a. 1. nvs. Coral, coral head. Also *'āko'ako'a. Ke ko'a mokumoku o He'eia,* the broken coral beds of He'eia [an expression used in songs and chants referring to He'eia, O'ahu]. (PPN *toka.*) **2.** n. Fishing grounds, usually identified by lining up with marks on shore. **3.** n. Shrine, often consisting of circular piles of coral or stone, built along the shore or by ponds or streams, used in ceremonies as to make fish multiply; also built on bird islands, and used in ceremonies to make birds multiply.

kō.'ā. vs. Arid, barren, rocky and unfruitful; dry or tasteless, as overdone meat. *Fig.,* rude, nasty.

kō.'ā.'ā. Same as *kō'ā.*

koa 'awa.puhi. n. *Koa* with yellowish wood, regarded as female by Hawaiians. *Lit.,* ginger *koa.*

koa'e. n. **1.** The tropic or boatswain bird, particularly the white-tailed tropic bird *(Phaethon lepturus dorotheae),* which inhabits cliffs of the high islands. The red-tailed tropic bird *(P. rubricauda rothschildi)* is *koa'e 'ula;* the white is *koa'e kea. Ka pali lele koa'e,* cliff [where] tropic birds fly. (PPN *tawake.*) **2.** A variety of banana. (Neal 249.) Also *a'ea'e* and *manini*. **3.** A taro; varieties are qualified by the colors *'ele'ele*, *ke'oke'o*, *'ula'ula*. **4.** A snapper, probably *Etelis carbunculus*, an important commercial fish also known as *onaga* (Japanese). **5.** A variety of sweet potato.

koa.ea. vs. Rude, nasty.

koa'e.kea. vt. To adjust and fit canoe parts to the canoe body. *Rare.*

koa'e kea. See *koa'e 1.*

koa'e 'ula. See *koa'e 1.*

koaha. n. Young shoots of mulberry plant used for medicine; soft mulberry fiber used for making fine white tapa.

koa haole. n. A common roadside shrub or small tree *(Leucaena leucocephala)*, from tropical America, with pinnate leaves, round white flower heads, and long, flat, brown pods; closely related to the *koa*. The small brown seeds are strung for leis, purses, mats; plants used for fodder. (Neal 411–2.) *Lit.*, foreign *koa*. Also *ēkoa, lilikoa.*

kō.ahe. Same as *kōuheahe*. (Nak. 102.)

kō.ahe.ahe. vs. Blowing gently, as the wind. Cf. *kōaniani.*

koa hele wā.wae. n. Infantry soldier. *Lit.*, soldier goes afoot.

kō.'ai. vt. To stir with a circular motion of the hand; to wind around, creep around, as a vine; to gird around, as a *pā'ū* sarong; to brace with a paddle.

koai'a. Var. of *koai'e.*

kō.'ai.'ai. Redup. of *kō'ai.*

koai'e. n. A native tree *(Acacia koaia)*, much like the *koa* but smaller, the pods narrower and with seeds arranged vertically in the pod, rather than horizontally as in *koa*, and leaves averaging narrower; the wood is harder, formerly used for spears, fancy paddles, and for the *i'e* tapa beater; later for furniture. *Fig.*, person from the upland country. Also *koai'a*. Cf. *hu'e. Lau koai'e*, a *koai'e* leaf; *fig.*, anything from the upland country. (Neal 405.)

koaka. vs. Naked, exposed, of a male. *Fig.*, dissipated, debauchee (Laie 501), dissolute. See *kole koaka*. **2.** Quarter. *Eng.*

ko'a.kā. n. Coral shoal with rough sea where two or more opposing currents meet. *Fig.*, valiant. (1 Sam. 14.52.) *Lit.*, dashing coral.

koa ka'a kaua. n. War strategist. (Kep. 125.)

koa kahiko. n. Veteran; old soldier.

kō ā kai. n. Shore dweller; belonging to the shore or sea.

koa kaua lio, koa kau lio. n. Cavalry soldier.

koa kaua pū.ka'a. n. Cannoneer.

ko'a kea. n. White coral.

koa kelu.kake (kerusade). n. Crusader. *Lit.*, crusade *(Eng.)* soldier.

kō 'aki. n. Sugar cane (so called to distinguish from *kōpa'a* and *kōomoomo*).

koa kia'i. n. Military sentry, guarding soldier. *Nā Koa Kia'i Lāhui o ka Teritori*, National Guard of the Territory.

koa.koa. vs. Overbold, arrogant, daring, impudent. Cf. *koa*, brave. *Koakoa lapa*, fearless and mischievous.

ko'a.ko'a. 1. n. Coral. **2.** nvs. Scarred; rough scar. **3.** vs. Well-supplied, rich. *He nohona ko'ako'a kō lākou*, theirs is a contented, comfortable life. *Kai ko'ako'a*, rich, fat sauce as of the parrot fish; watery fluid of the bowels. **4.** vi. To stay or live in one place. *ho'o.ko'a.ko'a.* Caus/sim.

ko'a.ko'ai. Same as *kō'ai'ai.*

ko'a.ko'ana. Redup. of *ko'ana 1*; thrifty, saving; to have saved or accumulated.

ko'a.kole. n. Mushroom coral. *Lit.*, creased coral.

koa kumu 'ole. Var. of *koa makua 'ole*. *Lit.*, *koa* without trunk.

ko'ala. 1. Var. of *ko'ana 1, 2*. **2.** Coagulated mass of blood that fails to come away with afterbirth. (And.)

kō.'ala. 1. vt. To broil or barbecue (of meat, fowl, fish). Cf. *kunu, pūlehu*, and *ala*, fragrant. *Pipi kō'ala*,

broiled beef. **2.** vi. Fast, quickly. *Hao kō'ala ka makani lā, pau loa*, with one fast sweep of wind, all is gone.

kō.'ala.'ala. 1. Probable redup. of *ko'ana 1*, with *n* changed to *l*; food scraps. *'O ka ho'omakauli'i, loa'a nō nā wahi kō'ala'ala e ola ai ia mau lā nele*, by saving are obtained bits of food to survive on in these days of need. **2.** vi. Quickly. Cf. *ala-*, fast. *Hei kō'ala'ala ka manu o Ka'ula*, the bird of Ka'ula is quickly caught [perhaps as a sweetheart].

koa lau kani. n. A kind of *koa* tree regarded by Hawaiians as male. *Lit.*, strong *koa*.

koa lau nui. n. A variety of *koa*. *Lit.*, large-leafed *koa*.

koali, kowali. 1. n. Some kinds of morning-glory *(Ipomoea* spp.). The vines were used for swings and nets *(kōkō)*. (Neal 703–9.) **2.** nvi. Swing; to swing, twirl about, twine. *Lele koali*, to jump rope, to ride in a swing. **3.** n. A variety of sweet potato. **4.** See *puhi koali.*

koali 'ai. n. An African morning-glory *(Ipomoea cairica* var. *hederacea)*, with pink or purple flowers and five-to seven-lobed leaves; the long trailing stems were formerly used as cordage, the tuberous roots and main stems, though somewhat bitter, as famine food. (Neal 708.) Also *koali lau manamana* and *pa'ali'i*, and *koali 'ai'ai* on Ni'ihau.

koali 'awa. n. A morning-glory *(Ipomoea indica)*, a native of Pacific islands, with heart-shaped leaves, flowers opening blue in the morning and changing to pink later in the day. When pounded, the bitter-tasting stems and roots are used externally for bruises and broken bones, but are dangerous to take internally. (Neal 708.) Also *koali 'awahia* and *koali lā'au* on Ni'ihau.

koali kua hulu. n. A tropical American weedy vine *(Merremia aegyptia*, synonym, *Ipomoea pentaphylla)* with tawny-hairy stems and leaves, the leaves five-lobed, the flowers white. (Neal 709.) Also *kuahulu.*

koali lau mana.mana. Same as *koali 'ai.*

koali mā.hua, koali mā.kea. n. Kinds of morning-glory.

koali pehu. n. The moonflower *(Ipomoea alba)*, a morning-glory found in many tropical countries, with fragrant, white, night-blooming flowers, to 15 cm long, and heart-shaped, angled, or lobed leaves. Also, large form of *koali 'awa*. (Neal 705.)

koali poni. n. A kind of morning-glory.

koa makua 'ole. n. Famous legendary *koa* tree at Kahiki-kolo, Kaua'i, thought to have no roots or trunk, and to spread over the ground like a creeper (FS 232.) *Lit.*, *koa* without parent.

koa malina, koa marina. n. Marine (military). *Eng.*

koana. 1. n. Spacing, space, as between rows of stitching in a quilt; width of pandanus strips used in plaiting, weft. *He aha ke koana o ka mako o ka 'upena?* What's the width of the mesh of the net? **2.** vi. Bruised or parched spot on fruit, as breadfruit. *Rare.* **3.** See *mai'a koana.*

ko'ana. 1. nvi. Dregs, sediment, small fragments, particles; to settle, as dregs; to stay or settle in one place, as people. See *wai ko'ana waiūpaka. Ko'ana 'awa*, kava dregs; *fig.*, nursing of bitterness. *ho'o.ko'ana.* To settle, as dregs. *Fig.*, to put one's mind on a thing, concentrate upon. **2.** n. Bladder.

ko'ana mimi. n. Alkali in urine.

ko'ana wai. n. Small pool from which most of the water has evaporated. Cf. *ko'ana 1. E holoi 'ia mai ka pū niu, i ke ko'ana wai 'ākōlea* (hula chant), wash the coconut cup in the tiny pool amid the ferns.

kō 'ane'i. poss. The local, as *kō 'ane'i po'e*, the local people *(o*-class; cf. *kā 'ane'i).*

koani. 1. Same as *koali*. **2.** Same as *kōaniani.*

kō.ani.ani. vi. To waft, as a soft cooling breeze; to make a breeze with a fan; cooled by a breeze. Cf. *kōaheahe.*

kō.ano.ano. vs. Dark, gloomy, fearful.

koa.'ohā. Same as *koai'e.*

koa.paka. vs. Valiant, brave, especially in war. *Rare.*

kō ā uka. n. Upland dweller, belonging to the uplands.

koa wahine. n. Female soldier, Amazon.
koe. 1. nvs. To remain, exclude, exempt; remaining, left over, excessive, missing, spare; remainder, additional, surplus, excess; except; to be obtained; soon, about to; almost, but, only thing remaining, not yet. *Koe* is much used in idioms: *Koe aku ia,* except for this; this is not known or included; I don't know. *Koe kēia,* except for this, however, but, furthermore. *Koe 'ole kahi,* without a single exception. *'Umi minuke i koe, kani ka hola 'elima,* ten minutes before five [remaining ten minutes, sound the fifth hour]. *'A 'ohe hana a koe aku!* No work is left! Oh, what doings! *'A 'ohe huhū a koe aku!* [He] couldn't have been more angry! *Inā e mimi, 'a'ohe koe 'āina i ka lilo i ka wai* (For 5:139), if [he] urinates, there is no land that is not carried off by the water [i.e., all the land becomes water]. *He 'ai mai koe,* will soon be eating. *Hele maila nā koa . . . nānā 'ia aku, he hō'ea mai koe,* the soldiers are coming . . . look, they'll soon be arriving! *'O ka i'a koe,* the fish not yet gotten. *'O ka i'a i koe,* the fish that remain. *'Ane kipi wale aku nō koe o kēia keiki* (For. 4:260), this boy does everything but rebel. **ho'o.koe.** To save, reserve for later use, cause a remainder. *Nā koa i ho'okoe 'ia,* soldiers of the reserves. (PPN *toe.*) **2.** nvt. To scratch, claw, scrape; to strike, as a match; to card wool; to strip or split, as pandanus leaves; to clean off pulp, as of mulberry bark; to pull a stick with hooks through the water to impale fish; garden rake, wool carder; stripper for pandanus leaves, formerly a thorn, now either a board with razor blades and phonograph needles over which the leaves are drawn, or a stripping machine. (PCP *toe.*) **3.** To spit. (And.)
ko'e. n. Worm of any kind. *He ko'e ka pule a kāhuna,* the prayer of sorcerers is a worm [it moves like a worm to reach its victim]. (PPN *toke.*)
koea. vs. Scratched, eroded. Cf. *koe 2. Nihoa ka pali, kala lua i uka; koea a mania* (PH 206), notched cliff, very sharp in the mountain; eroded smooth.
koe.'ā. vs. Willful, obstinate, unsociable, taciturn.
ko'e.au. n. Design on a tapa beater or on tapa consisting of gently waving, delicate parallel lines (the waves are smaller and less jagged than those of the *hā'ao*). Cf. *pū'ili.*
ko'e.au hā.lu'a. n. *Ko'eau* design with one or more straight lines separating every two wavy lines.
kō.'eha.'eha. nvs. Heat, sultriness; sultry, uncomfortably hot. *Fig.,* physical or mental distress or discomfort; distressed. *Kō'eha'eha i ka lā,* uncomfortably hot in the sun. **ho'o.kō.'eha.'eha.** To cause heat. *Fig.,* to distress. *Ho'okō'eha'eha noho'i ka hana a keiki i ka makua,* how childish actions distress the parents.
ko'e.hana. 1. Warmth, heat; warm. (And.) **2.** Boxing ring, grandstand, booth. (AP.) **3.** Constant labor. (AP.)
koe.heke. interj. Go ahead! *Eng.*
koe.honua. 1. nvs. A large remainder, a balance, remnant; to be many remaining. *Koehonua ka 'uala,* plenty of sweet potatoes left. **2.** n. Two-pronged fishhook. *Rare.*
ko'e kai. n. Any sea worm, as the marine nematodes; roundworms or threadworms.
ko'eke. Same as *kaiko'eke,* most used as a term of address. (PPN *ta'okete.*)
koe.koe. Redup. of *koe 2;* to strum, as an ukulele.
ko'e.ko'e. vs. **1.** Cool, damp, chilled from wet and cold. **ho'o.ko'e.ko'e.** To make cold; to chill. (PCP *toke-toke.*) **2.** Tasteless; insipid, bland, as unsalted food or as too fresh poi; flat, unsavory, as warm food that has chilled.
kōe.koe aku. interj. Go away. *Eng.*
ko'e.ko'ele. Redup. of *ko'ele.*
koele. A tall man; equality; union. (And.)
ko'ele. nvi. Sound of tapping, as wood against wood; ticking, as of clock; thumping, trudging; rattling, as a window; crack of thunder; to tap, tick, thump, trudge, crackle, rattle; noisy, stormy. See ex., *pilina 2.* **ho'o.ko'ele.** Caus/sim. (PCP *to(o)kele.*)

kō.'ele. n. **1.** Small land unit farmed by a tenant for the chief; to be worked as a *kō'ele.* Also *hakuone.* **2.** Friday, so called because commoners worked on the chief's farm, called *kō'ele,* on this day. Any work for a chief. Also *lā kō'ele* and *lā pa'ahao. Kō'ele kālai wa'a,* canoe-making for a chief. **3.** Any variety of large, tough *'opihi* (the shells were used as scrapers and peelers). See *'opihi.* **4.** Same as *kō'ele'ele,* seaweeds. **5.** A small pond, reserved for a chief, where fish could be kept alive until required. **6.** Less desirable portions of meat or fish. *Rare.*
kō.'ele.'ele. 1. n. Small, edible red seaweeds (*Gymogongrus* spp.), with rather thick, flattened stems and branches. Also *'āwikiwiki, ēkahakaha 2, kō'ele, limu uaua loli, nei.* **2.** Redup. of *ko'ele. Kō'ele'ele ka haka ipu* (For. 6:490), the calabash shelf is rattling. *Pohā kō'ele'ele o 'Ikuwā,* the month of 'Ikuwā breaks forth in storm. *Hākā kō'ele'ele u'i 'o Lo'eau* (For. 6:383), the stalwart youth Lo'eau fights in a stormy valiant way.
kō 'ele.'ele. Same as *māikoiko,* a sugar cane.
kōo.ele.pā.lau. n. Pudding made by peeling and mashing cooked sweet potatoes, then adding coconut cream gradually. Also *pālau, poi pālau.*
ko'ele wā.wae. nvi. Sound of footsteps; to walk, trudge. *Mea 'ole ia loa i ke ko'ele wāwae 'ia,* this distance was as nothing when traveled on foot.
kō.elo. Var. spelling of *kōwelo.*
koena. n. **1.** Remainder, residue, remnant, surplus, scraps, leftovers, balance (in accounts), remains, ruins. Cf. *koe 1. Ke koe koena, na'u ia,* when leftovers remain, that's for me. (PPN *toenga.*) **2.** A scratching, raking.
koena 'oi. n. Difference, remainder, as in subtraction.
koene. vi. To edge away, back away, creep, move cautiously and carefully, as a frightened or feeble person. **ho'o.koene.** Caus/sim.; to endeavor to walk in spite of weakness; mentally at rest after mental agitation, calmed. *Ho'okoene kāna hele 'ana,* he goes slowly, cautiously.
kohā. nvi. Crack of a whip, report of a pistol, slapping sound, loud squeak; to resound thus, squawk, croak. *'Ōlelo kohā* (Kep. 127), rude or sarcastic remark. *Kohā pono maila 'oe i ka pa'i 'ia,* what a loud noise when you were slapped.
kō.hā. See *noio kōhā.*
kohā.hā. Redup. of *kohā. Kohāhā ka leo ka ua Ki'o-wao* (chant), loud sounds the rain Ki'o-wao.
kō.hā.hā. Same as *mōhāhā,* fully developed. (And.)
kō.hahe. vs. Desolate, destitute, uninhabited.
kohai. vi. To sway in the breeze, as a tree. *Ka waikekē 'olu kohai o Lādana,* the refreshing tipsy whiskey of London.
kō.hai.hai. Redup. of *kohai. Nā wai kōhaihai,* the liquor that makes [one] tipsy.
kō.ha'i.ha'i. Same as *kōnane 1.*
kohaka. Rare var. of *koaka 2.*
kohā.kohā. Redup. of *kohā.*
kohā lua. vi. To resound loudly, as poi being vigorously pounded.
kohana. vs. Nude, naked; bare, alone, by itself. *'Ai kohana,* to eat one thing only, whether flesh or vegetable. *Kū kohana,* to stand naked; to stand alone. *Hele kohana,* to go naked, empty-handed, or alone. **ho'o.-kohana.** To strip bare or naked. (Ier. 49.10.)
kō.hana.hana. vs. Warm, hot. Cf. *mahana.*
kohana.mimi. n. Taro growing in front of the door and about the house. *Lit.,* naked urine (so called because people urinated there). *Rare.*
kohe. n. **1.** Mortise; crease, as in the center of the crown of a hat; groove in wood; corner in a pandanus mat; fork at the lower ends of house rafters (the under side of the fork was cut back as far as the commencement of the fork or further to form the *'auwae*). Cf. *ko'a kohe.* **ho'o.kohe.** To fold pandanus matting to form a corner; to form a crease, groove, etc. **2.** Vagina. (PCP *to(f,s)e.*) **3.** Inside barb of a fishhook.

kohea. nvi. Warm, clear, serene weather; to be such.

kohe 'ako. n. Venereal disease of women. *Lit.,* itching vagina.

kō.he'e. vi. To train or practice, as for foot races. (Malo 219.)

kō.heheo. Var. of *kōheoheo.*

kohe.kohe. n. **1.** All species of a genus of sedges *(Eleocharis),* some introduced, some native. (Neal 87.) Also *pīpī wai.* See *'aoa 4.* **2.** Tonsillitis (used with *pu'u).* **3.** Same as *'ōkohekohe 2,* barnacle.

kohe.kohea. Redup. of *kohea.*

kohe.kohe papa. n. **1.** A variety of *kohekohe* plant. **2.** Bilateral tonsillitis.

kohe.lelewa. Same as *kohelewalewa.*

kohe.lemu. vs. Dull, inattentive, inactive.

kohe lemu. n. **1.** Division between the vagina and anus. **2.** Sodomy. *Lit.,* anus vagina.

kohe.lewa.lewa. n. A white *loli* that lives in the sand (perhaps *Holothuria arenicola). Lit.,* hanging vagina.

kohe lua. vs. Double-barbed, of a fishhook.

kohe lua pa'a. Same as *kohe lua.*

kohe.nalo. nvt. Corrugated stone used for smoothing wood or stone; to file or rasp with this stone.

kō.heo. **1.** vt. To show off, parade, strut. **ho'o.kōheo.** Caus/sim. **2.** Var. of *pōheo,* head of penis. **3.** Same as *kōheoheo 3.*

kō.heo.heo. **1.** vi. To fall, as through the air; to tumble. *'Ōpū nui kewekewe, pā i ka lani, kōheoheo!* (children's song ridiculing a fat stomach), big rounded belly, touch the sky and tumble down. *Lele kōheoheo i ka pali o Kapa'a-heo,* tumbling from the cliff of Ka-pa'a-heo [a "goner," play on *heo,* gone]. **2.** nvs. Poisonous. *He 'apu 'auhuhu kōheoheo,* a poisonous concoction of *'auhuhu; fig.,* a poisonous-natured person. **3.** n. Coattail. **4.** n. Stick or buoy that floats a fishhook. **5.** Redup. of *kōheo.* **6.** n. Nose flute *(hano* is more common).

kohe.popo. n. An ancient sickness characterized by ill-smelling vaginal discharge. *Lit.,* rotten vagina.

kōhi. **1.** nvt. To gather, as fruit; to break off neatly, as taro corm from the stalk with a stick or knife; to split, as breadfruit; to dig (For. 4:510); splitter, as stick, stone, knife. *Nā wāhine kōhi noni* (FS 217), the *noni*-gathering women [an insult to Pele, perhaps likening her disposition to sour *noni* fruit]. (PPN *tofi.)* **2.** nvs. Fat, rich, as food; fatness. *Nā kōhi kelekele o Kapu'u-kolu,* the rich foods of Ka-pu'u-kolu [Kaua'i, famous for abundance]. **3.** vt. To fill or heal, of a wound. *Ke kōhi maila ka 'i'o,* the flesh is beginning to heal. **4.** nvt. To hold back, check, restrain; to strain, especially as in childbirth, to travail; to hold or hold back by pressing a person's arm, as in withholding consent, or as in urging someone not to be generous; labor pains, travail. *Fig.,* agony, fear. Cf. *haukōhi, kāohi.* **ho'o.-kōhi.** Caus/sim. **5.** vs. Prolonged, as a sound; long. *He kōhi ka leo,* the sound is long.

kō.hia. Pas/imp. of *kōhi. Kōhia mai mākou e ka makani Moa'e* (chant), we were held back by the Moa'e wind. *Kōhia aku ka 'īlio,* hold back the dog.

kōhi 'ai. To separate taro corm from stalk; to pick taro.

kōhi.kōhi. Same as *kokōhi;* to cull, separate, grade, as fish or sweet potatoes.

kohi.kū. Same as *kokōhikū,* to lay waste.

kōhi.kōhi-kū-pala.lā. n. Children's guessing game, with an object hidden in the earth or sand.

kō.hina. n. Part of taro where the corm is cut away from the top; splitting of a breadfruit for cooking.

koho. **1.** nvt. Guess, election, choice, selection, interpretation; to choose, select, bid, guess, estimate, anticipate, decide on, pick, nominate, vote, elect, draw lots. *Lā koho,* election day. *Koho lā'au,* to draw straws. *Po'e i koho 'ia,* chosen representatives. *Mea koho,* bidder. *'O wai kāu moho i koho ai?* Which candidate did you vote for? *Po'e koho pāloka,* voters. *I ke koho 'ana o nā 'ao'ao,* at option of parties. **ho'o.koho.** To choose, elect, appoint. (Probably PPN *tofo.)* **2.** n. Tip of a paddle blade.

koho honua. vt. To choose at random, without thought or care, arbitrarily; to vote without forethought, or for the sake of voting.

kō.hoko. n. An infection, probably luetic.

koho.koho. Redup. of *koho 1.*

-koho.kola. ho'o.koho.kola. Same as *hō'aikola. Rare.*

kohola. **1.** n. Reef flats, bare reef. *Kai kohola,* lagoon. (PPN *tofola.)* **2.** The first law a chief promulgates, a strict law. (And.)

koho.lā. n. Humpbacked whale. (PNP *tafola'a,* PEP *tafola'a,* PCP *tofolaa.)*

Koho.lā Lele. n. Name of a wind blowing from east to west, associated with Hāmākua, Hawai'i, and Hāna, Maui. Also *Kiu* and *Koholā Pehu* (also of Kī-pahulu, Maui, Nak. 68). *Lit.,* leaping whale.

koho.lā.pehu. n. A scandent shrub, native to Kaua'i, in the composite family *(Dubautis latifolia),* with long branches, opposite, elliptical, pointed leaves, and small flower heads in large panicles.

Koho.lā Pehu. See *Koholā Lele.*

koho.lua. n. **1.** Lance for boils, sores, as of fishbone or a sharp stick; abortion stick; this term, like that referring to other sharp things (shark, sea urchin, eel) is applied to chiefs as indicative of the sharp defense of the chief against contact with his taboo person, or infringement of his taboos. *He koholua 'oi ke ali'i,* a sharp-pointed piercing instrument is the chief. **2.** A long shellfish *(Terebra* spp.)

koho mua. n. First choice, primary election, first guess; hypothesis. *Uku koho mua,* upset price, in public bidding.

kō honua.'ula. Same as *honua'ula,* a sugar cane.

koho pā.loka. nv. To cast a ballot, vote; voting, election, suffrage.

koho polo.lei. nvt. Right choice; to choose rightly; to vote a straight ticket.

koho wae moho. n. Primary election. *Lit.,* candidate-selection election.

kohu. **1.** nvs. Resemblance, appearance, likeness, match; suitable, agreeable, appropriate, matching, in good taste, attractive, becoming, pleasing, fit, like, resembling, alike, similar. See *kohu ali'i, kohu like, kohu pono. 'A'ohe kohu iki,* most inappropriate, unsuitable, in very bad taste, absurd. *Kohu kēnā pāpale iā 'oe,* that hat is becoming to you. *He kohu haole nō ke namu mai,* talks just like a white person. *'O kēlā kanaka, he kohu Pukikī 'oe ke nānā aku,* he looks just like a Portuguese. *Hiki i ke kameleona ke 'o'olopū i kona kohu 'ana, i hinahina, i 'ōma'oma'o, i 'ele'ele,* the chameleon can change his appearance to gray, green, black. *Ua kohu au me ia lā, me ka liko lehua o uka,* I'm a good match for her, for the *lehua* bud of the upland [a young girl]. **ho'o.kohu.** To assume a likeness to; to presume to; to make advances, perhaps hypocritically; to take a fancy to; to have a crush on; presumption, pretense. *Mea ho'okohu,* thing that matches, accessories. *Nānā aku 'oe i ka ho'okohu o mea iā Pole,* see how so-and-so is infatuated with Pole. *'A'ole ho'i i ka ho'okohu o ka make'e waiwai* (1 Tes. 2.5), nor a pretense of covetousness. *Ho'okohu ka ua i uka,* how fit and pleasing is the rain of the uplands. **2.** nvs. Sap, stain, blot; stained, discolored. *Mālama o kohu kō lole,* be careful or you'll stain your dress. *Wai i kohu i nā hua waina* (Nah. 6.3), liquor of grapes; *lit.,* liquid that is juice in grapes. *Kohu 'īnika,* ink blot. **3.** See *limu kohu.*

-koho.kohu. ho'o.kohu. To appoint, commission, authorize. *Ho'okohu 'ia 'o Keoni i kumu kula,* John was appointed school teacher. *Palapala ho'okohu,* certificate of appointment.

kohu ali'i. vs. Of chiefly bearing, stately, noble.

kohu.kohu. **1.** Redup. of *kohu 1. Kohukohu 'oe i ke kau lio,* attractive you are on horseback. **ho'o.kohu.kohu.** Redup. of *ho'okohu;* to pretend, impersonate, disguise, pose; affectation. *Ho'okohukohu kūlana māka-'iki'u,* impersonation of the office of detective. *He ho'okohukohu ho'ohanohano* (Kep. 105), a person pretending to honors not due. *Ho'okohukohu Akua,* to put on a show of serving God. *Ho'okohukohu ali'i,* to assume the manners of a chief. **2.** Redup. of *kohu 2.*

kohu kukui. n. Sap of *kukui* fruit stem used as a purge.

kohu like. vs. Exactly alike, uniform, consistent. See *kohu 1.*

kohu 'ole. nvi. Not matching, unsuitable, ill-suited, ridiculous, absurd, inappropriate, of poor taste, silly; nonsense.

kohu pono. vs. Decent, upright.

kohu wahine. vs. Effeminate.

koi. 1. nvi. To urge, implore, persuade, compel, require, insist on, ask insistently, demand, claim, pull; requirement. *Hana i ka mea a ke kānāwai i koi mai ai,* doing what the law commands. *Koi pohō,* claims for damage. *Pila koi,* requisition. *Mea koi,* claimant. **ho'o.koi.** Caus/sim. *Rare.* (PCP *toi.*) **2.** n. Fishing pole, pole fishing (same as the more common *mākoi*).

kō.ī. 1. Sharp, shrill, as a voice. **2.** nvi. To flow with force, as water over a dam. See *'enakōī. Kōī au,* a flowing current; *fig.,* a flow of eloquence. **3.** nvt. To string, as flowers for a lei or candlenuts on a coconut leaf midrib for a light; such a string. **4.** n. Sliding game; child's game with sticks dug into earth or sand while repeating a jingle (Malo 233). **5.** n. A small tree *(Coprosma kauensis),* a native of Kaua'i, related to the *pilo.*

ko'i. 1. nvs. Axe, adze; adzelike, sharp, projecting, as a forehead. See *malu ko'i, po'o ko'i.* (PPN *toki.*) **2.** n. Young stage of all *'ula'ula,* red snappers. **3.** Same as *ko'iko'i.* Same as *ho'oko'iko'i.*

kō ia. Same as *kona.* (Gram. 8.4.) *Kō ia,* his. (PCP *to(o) ia.*)

kō ia ala. poss. His, hers. Cf. *kō ia nei. He mana'o paha kō ia ala,* he may have an idea. *E 'ike i kō ia ala ho'opunipuni nui ia'u* (Laie 483), should see his great falseness to me.

koi.ala. Var. of *ko ia ala.*

kō ia nei. Similar to *kō ia ala,* but with idea of close by.

ko'i.awe. nvi. Light, moving rain; to shower. *É ka wiliwiliwai, ko'iawe i ka la'i* (song), O lawn sprinkler, light moving rain in the calm.

ko'i.awe.awe. Redup. of *ko'iawe. 'O ke kū a ka ua ko'iaweawe lā* (song), the column of light rain appears.

ko'i 'āwili. n. Socketed adze, as used for hollowing out the narrow bow and stern of a canoe hull.

kō.'ie. Similar to *kō'ie'ie 2. Kō'ie 'ia akula,* carried off by the current.

kō.'ie.'ie. 1. n. Plaything, toy, used in water. (FS 259.) **2.** nvi. Rapid current or what it carries; to rush, as water.

koi.ele. vi. To move to and fro restlessly, as the sea. *Ka nape koiele a ke kai,* the restless surge of the sea.

ko'i hole. n. Pig's jawbone used for grooving *(hole)* boards for making ribbed tapa. (Kam. 76:112.)

ko'i holu. n. Adze used to smooth a canoe.

koi.honua. 1. nvi. Genealogical chant; to sing such chants. **2.** vs. Presto (in music).

ko'i hō.'oma, ko'i hō.'o'oma. n. Chisel.

koi'i. vi. To diminish, decrease.

ko'i'i. 1. nvi. Fresh, as plants; erection of male genital. **2.** nvt. Desire; to desire. *I mau ai ke ko'i'i koi a loko* (song), to hold forever the insistent desire within.

ko'i kā.hela. n. Wood-working plane, carpenter's plane.

ko'i kahi. n. Carpenter's plane; scraper, as for *olonā* fiber. *Lit.,* shaving adze.

ko'i kā.holo. n. Planing adze. *Lit.,* smoothing adze.

ko'i kā.lai. n. Adze used for carving.

ko'i kā.pili. n. Joiner's adze. *Lit.,* adze for putting together.

koi.koi. Redup. of *koi 1.*

ko'i.ko'i. nvs. Weight, responsibility; stress, accent; heavy, weighty; prominent, prime, urgent, serious, influential; emphatic, stressed; harsh, severe. *Aia ke ko'iko'i ma kēia hua 'ōlelo,* the stress is on this word. *Maluna o'u kēlā ko'iko'i,* that responsibility is on me.

Ko'iko'i ka leo, loud, authoritative voice. **ho'o.ko'i.- ko'i.** To deepen the voice; to stress or emphasize in speech; to treat with severity, harshness, rigor; to burden, oppress. *Ho'ohana ihola kō 'Aikupika i nā mamo o 'Ikela'ela me ka ho'oko'iko'i* (Puk. 1.13), the Egyptians made the children of Israel serve with rigor. *Ho-'oko'iko'i pua ahi 'ole,* to practice trickery secretly, stealthily, without giving oneself away; *lit.,* to act emphatically without puffing fire [that will reveal the fire maker].

koi.koina. nvi. Urging; to urge. See ex., *kipona 1.*

ko'i.ko'ina. nvs. Stressing, accent; compulsive, compelling. *Mana'o ko'iko'ina* (Kel. 66), impelling thought. **ho'o.ko'i.ko'ina.** To stress; accent.

kō i kua. vi. To go behind one's back, to do in a person's absence what one would not do in his presence.

ko'i kū.kulu. n. Adze with straight edges, used to shave down the sides of a bowl or canoe.

koili. vi. To rest on, as the moon on the surface of the sea; to sink into, penetrate. Cf. *ili,* to land. *Kēlā kaha kūpā koili a ka lā i ke kula,* that place where the sun beats down on the plain. *Mokumokuāhua loko, kupā-kupā koili i ka 'ino,* heart torn with grief, penetrating, heart-rending tragedy.

ko'i lipi. n. Adze, axe, hatchet. *Lit.,* sharp adze. See ex., *hō 3.*

kō.ina. n. Urging, insistence; fine (as punishment). *Fig.,* firm attachment, as to a beloved child. Cf. *koi 1. Mai ho'olohe aku i kāna kōina,* don't listen to his insistence.

koine. To hasten, be quick. (And.)

ko'i nunu. Same as *ko'i kālai. Lit.* greedy adze. *Rare.*

kō 'i'o. vi. Accomplished, come to pass, come true, as a prophecy. *Lit.,* truly accomplished.

ko'i oma. n. Small, oval adze as used for finishing a canoe.

ko'i 'ō.wili. n. Gouge. *Lit.,* twisting adze. Also *ko'i wili.*

ko'i pā.hoa. n. Chisel, stone battle-axe. *Lit.,* dagger adze.

Koi-pali. n. Name of a wind associated with Hālawa, Moloka'i. (For. 5:103.)

koi pohō. vt. To sue for or claim damages.

koi.ū. n. Shoyu sauce. *Eng.*

kō.'iu. Same as *kō'iu'iu* (Kel.)

kō.'iu.'iu. vs. Distant, faraway, so high as to be barely visible.

ko'i.'ula. n. Rainbow-hued rain, mist, cloud. *Ua wili ko'i'ula ka lepo i ka lani mehe puahiohio lā* (FS 169), the dirt twirled into the sky like a red cloud in a whirlwind. *Hala i ke ala ko'i'ula a Kāne,* passed on along the rainbow-hued trail of Kāne [death].

kō iwi. See *iwi,* bone, for this idiom.

koka, koda. n. **1.** Soda. *Eng.* **2.** See *'aila koka.* **3.** Cord, as of wood. *Eng. Ho'okahi koka wahie,* one cord of firewood.

kō.kā. vi. **1.** To lash back and forth, as the tail of an animal. **2.** To gag, stuff the mouth.

kō.ka'a. nvs. Lean, of meat; dry, barren. Cf. *pāka'a.*

koka.hele. interj. Go to hell. (For. 5:427.) *Eng.*

Kokaka, Kosaka. nvs. Cossack. *Eng.*

koka.koka. Redup. of *kōkā 2.*

kō kā.kou. poss. Our, ours (o-form, plural, inclusive; see Gram. 8.4, 9.6). (PNP *to'o taatou,* PCP *too taatou.*)

kō.kala. n. **1.** Thorns on the edge of a pandanus or pineapple leaf; spines on a dorsal fin. *Maka kōkala;* thorny eyes, said (sometimes jestingly, For. 5:83) of the Puna people, who concealed the placenta of a newborn child in a pandanus tree, believing that the child's eyelashes would then grow long as the pandanus thorns, giving the child a bright, keen look. **2.** Porcupine fish *(Diodon hystrix, Diodon holocanthus, Cheilomycterus affinis);* both spines and flesh are regarded as poisonous; in some localities an *'aumakua.*

kokami, kokame. interj. God damn. (For. 5:427.) *Eng.*

kō kā.nā.wai. nv. Law enforcement; to enforce the law.

kō kāua. poss. Our, ours (*o*-form, dual, inclusive; see Gram. 8.4, 9.6). (PNP *to'o taaua*, PCP *too taaua*.)

-kō kauoha. ho'o.kō kau.oha. Executor of an estate (*o*-class).

koke. part. and n. Quick, near, quickly, soon, immediately, early; swift runner. Cf. *kokoke*, near; Gram. 7.1. *E hele koke 'oe*, go quickly.

kō.kē. vt. To strike, hit, punish. *Ka hana ia a ke akamai, ka 'ike i ke kōkē 'ulu* (song), that is what a clever one does, he knows how to hit the billiard ball. **ho'o.kō.-kē.** Caus/sim.

kō kea. See *kea 3*.

kō.keano. vs. Silent, deserted, uninhabited. Cf. *ano 1*.

kō.ke'e. vi. To wind, bend. *Rare*.

kō.kē.kō.kē. Redup. of *kōkē;* the noise of hitting.

koki. 1. vs. Snub-nosed, as of a bulldog. *'Īlio koki*, pug dog. **2.** Same as *'alae*, mudhen.

kokī. n. Settee, couch (formerly made of pandanus plaiting).

kō.kī. 1. n. Extremity, tiptop, topmost; upper limit. *'O ka pi'i nō ia a kōkī o Wai-lau* (saying), climbed to the very top of Wai-lau [i.e., has reached the peak of a career, has made a great achievement; Wai-lau is a very steep valley on Moloka'i]. *Nani-kōkī*, supremely beautiful [name of 'Umi's ivory pendant]. **2.** vi. To don a helmet. *Kākua nā pū'ali, hume nā malo, uhi nā 'ahu'ula, kōkī nā mahiole*, tighten the belt, don the *malo*, drape the feather cloak, put on the feather helmet.

kō.kia. Var. of *kōkī 1*.

koki.aka, zodiaka. n. Zodiac. *Eng*.

Kō.kia-Wai.lau. n. Stroke in *lua* fighting.

Kokika, Gotika. nvs. Gothic. *Eng*.

kō.kī.kī. nvs. Sagging, bending; place where a branch divides off.

kō.kikiu. vs. Away up high. *Fig.*, ambitious.

koki.koki. Redup. of *koki*.

kō Kina. n. A kind of sugar cane, 1857. *Lit.*, Chinese cane.

kō.kio. Same as *kio 4*. *E hele ana 'oe i hea? Kōkio!* Where are you going? Never you mind!

koki'o. n. **1.** A native shrubby hibiscus (*Hibiscus kokio*) with red flowers. The wood produced fine charcoal. (Neal 560-1.) Also *aloalo, mākū*. **2.** All species of a native genus (*Kokia*) of small trees related to the hibiscus, with red flowers, and round, leathery leaves with from three to seven shallow points. (Neal 567-8.)

koki'o kea. Same as *koki'o ke'oke'o*.

koki'o ke'o.ke'o. n. A native hibiscus, a small tree or tall shrub (*Hibiscus arnottianus*) with large, white, fragrant flowers. It is found chiefly on O'ahu; also a similar hibiscus (*H. waimeae*) from Kaua'i, with smaller leaves. (Neal 561.) Also *pāmakani, koki'o kea*.

koki'o 'ula'ula. n. *Hibiscus kokio*, a native red hibiscus. Also *koki'o, koki'o 'ula*.

koko. 1. nvs. Blood; rainbow-hued. See *koko pi'i, lana 1, pūkoko, waiwai koko*. *Ho'okomo koko*, blood transfusion. *Koko pau manō*, blood of a shark victim. *Uakoko*, rainbow-sparkling rain. *Kahe ke koko o ka ihu*, to have a nosebleed. **ho'o.koko.** To cause bloodshed; to blush *(rare). Fig.*, angry. Cf. *pi'i ka 'ula* under *pi'i*. (PPN *toto*.) **2.** Same as *'akoko*, shrubs and trees. **3.** Same as *limu kohu*, a seaweed.

koko. nvi. Crow, cackle, of chickens; to crow.

kō.kō. 1. n. A carrying net, usually made of sennit, as used for hanging calabashes; a string hammock, as formerly used for carrying the very old. *Kōkō pū'alu*, plain net carrier; *lit.*, slack net. *Kōkō pu'u*, a fine, knotted net carrier. *Ua ka'i kōkō*, carried about in a hammock [due to extreme old age]. (PCP *tootoo*.) **2.** nvt. To tie up strings, as of a calabash; lacings, as of sharkskin to a drum body. *Kōkō a'e i ka pū'olo a pa'a*, bring up the corners of the wrapper and tie together firmly in a bunch. **3.** Redup. of *kō 2;* to pull, jerk, drag, push, massage; to set a bone by applying pressure. Cf. *pale kōkō*. **4.** nvi. Pregnancy; pregnant,

heavy with child. *Nā malama o kō lākou kōkō 'ana* (Ioba 39.2), the months of their pregnancy. **5.** Redup. of *kō 3*, to fulfill. **6.** n. Cocoa. *Eng*. Also *kokoa*.

kokoa. Same as *kōkō 6 Rare*.

kokoe. Redup. of *koe 2*. *Kokoe maka*, to frown, cast shy glances. *Nānā kokoe*, to look with disapproval. *Kokoe akula nā maka i ka 'ike i kona 'enemi* (Laie 491), the eyes glared at seeing his enemies. **ho'o.kokoe.** Caus/sim. *Hō'inā'inau mea ipo i ka nahele, ho'okokoe ana ka maka i ka moani* (chant), lovers are wooing in the woods, casting shy glances at the wafted fragrance.

kokōhi. Redup. of *kōhi 1-4*. **ho'o.kokōhi.** Slow and stunted of growth; black and threatening, as clouds before a storm; forceful. Same as *ha'akokōhi 1, 2*.

kō.kō.hia. Pas/imp. of *kokōhi*.

kokōhi.kū. vt. To lay waste, especially to devastate crops. *Kokōhikū i nā kalo*, to lay waste the taro.

koko hō.wai. nvi. Anemia; to have such. *Lit.*, watery blood.

kokohu. Redup. of *kohu 2*.

koko hua waina. n. Wine. *Lit.*, blood of grapes. *Rare*.

kokoi. nvi. Jet, spurt; to flow, rush, as a torrent or crowd. *Kokoi hele nā kānaka i ke ki'i 'oni'oni*, the people rush in crowds to the movies. **2.** Redup. of *koi 1*.

kō.koia. n. Beating, as the heart.

Koko-iki. n. Star said to be named for Koko-iki, Kohala, Hawai'i, where it was first observed at the time of Kamehameha's birth. *Lit.*, little blood.

kokoi.na. n. Urging, insistence. See ex., *kipona 1*.

koko kahiki. n. A hairy cosmopolitan spurge (*Euphorbia hirta*), a small, weedy herb; leaves opposite, oblong, pointed at tip, oblique at base, with brownish spot near center, tiny flowers clustered at leaf axils. (Neal 516.) *Lit.*, foreign *koko*.

kokoke. vi. Near, close, adjacent, soon, shortly, immediately, friendly *(rare);* to draw near; almost, approximately. Cf. *koke*, fast. *Kahi kokoke*, nearby place, vicinity. *Kokoke lākou e loa'a i ka ulia*, they were almost in an accident. *Kokoke i ka hale*, near the house. **ho'o.kokoke.** To draw near, approach.

kokoki. Redup. of *koki 1*.

kō.kokī. Redup. of *kōkī 1, 2*.

kokoko. vs. Bloody; rare, as steak. *Fig.*, violently angry. (PPN *totototo*.)

koko.kohe. vt. To have intercourse with a menstruating woman. *Lit.*, vagina blood.

koko.komo. Redup. of *komo 1, 2*.

koko.ko'o.hā. n. Small, inferior, and sometimes soggy sweet potatoes.

koko lana. n. High blood pressure. See *lana 1*.

kokole. 1. Redup. of *kole 1*. (PPN *totolo*.) **2.** n. Taro of the fifth generation. (Kep. 153.) See *kalo* for names of generations. **3.** Any food crop stunted by weeds or drought. (AP.)

koko.leka. n. Chocolate. *Eng*.

kō.kō lele. See *ahahana*.

kokoli. Redup. of *koli 1*.

kō.kō.li'i. n. Thick black cloud. **ho'o.kō.kō.li'i.** To rise, as a thick black cloud.

kō.koli.koli. vs. Dark, burned, of a *kukui* nut candle.

kokolo. Redup. of *kolo*, to creep. **ho'o.kokolo.** Caus/sim. *Rare*. (PPN *totolo*.)

kokolo.lio. nvi. Sharp, swift wind gust; rapid flowing water; drafty; to blow in gusts, move fast.

kokolo.nahe. Redup. of *kolonahe*.

kokolo.wini. nvi. Sharp, penetrating, of wind; gust. *He makani kokolowini ka i hiki mai i ka pō nei*, swift, penetrating wind gust came last night.

kō.kō.mā.lei. Same as *'akoko*, shrubs and trees.

kokomi, sodomi. n. Sodomy. *Eng*.

kokomo. Redup. of *komo 1*. *Ke kokomo maila kēlā wa'a*, that canoe is filled [and about to sink]. *Kokomo akula ka wa'a i ka nalu*, the canoe is plunging through the waves.

kokona. nvi. Bleeding.

koko.nā. Same as *konākonā*, dislike.

kokoni. Redup. of *koni.*

kokono.iʻe. vi. To grow strong after a period of weakness. **hoʻo.kokono.iʻe.** To rouse, encourage, incite.

kō.koʻo. n. Partnership, partner, associate, companion (nearly always followed by a number designating the number of associated persons, as *kōkoʻolua, kōkoʻokolu.* (See *koʻo-,* Gram. 10.3.) *Nā lawaiʻa kōkoʻo o nā moku,* the associated fishermen of the islands.

kō.koʻo.hā. 1. n. Companionship, partnership, association of four persons; one of four associates. 2. Var. of *kokokoʻohā.*

kō.koʻo.hia. inter. How many? (Of associated persons.) (PPN *tokofiha,* PNP *tokofia,* PEP *tokofia.*)

koko-o-Kiawe. n. A variety of sweet potato.

kō.koʻo.kolu. n. Partnership of three, one of three associates. *Kō māua kōkoʻokolu ia,* he is a member of our partnership of three.

kō.koʻo.lau. Var. of *koʻokoʻolau,* beggar ticks.

kō.koʻo.lua. n. Companion, partner, associate, fellow worker, mate, partnership, second (in a dual), union (always of two). *Kona kōkoʻolua,* his companion.

kō.koʻo.ū. Redup. of *koʻoū.*

kokope. Redup. of *kope I;* to parry, defend.

koko piʻi. n. High blood pressure. *Lit.,* mounting blood.

kō.kō pū. n. Netted bag made of sennit with large plain mesh. *Lit.,* loose net. (For. 2:128–9.)

koko.puna. n. First menstruation. *Lit.,* spring blood.

kō.kō puʻu. n. Very fine *kōkō* net for a calabash carried by *kahu* of high rank with chief's food. (For. 2:130.) *Lit.,* knotted net.

kō.kō ʻula. n. Network of red color, as of a spreading rainbow.

kō.kō.wai.kī. n. Pith of banana stalk.

kō.kō.wē. Redup. of *kōwē,* to go away. *Eng.* See ex., *kamaliʻi.*

kō.kua. nvt. Help, aid, assistance, relief, assistant, associate, deputy, helper; Counselor (RSV), Comforter (KJV) in Ioane 14:26; co-operation, old term for lawyer before *loio* was used; to help, assist, support, accommodate, second a motion. *Mea kōkua,* helper, benefactor, useful, helpful. *Kōkua hewa,* partner in crime, accessory or accomplice; to aid in wrong doing. *Kōkua mamua i ka mea hewa mamua o ka hana hewa ʻana,* accessory to the offender before the commission of an offense. *Hui kōkua kūʻai home,* co-operative home purchasing society.

kō.kua.haʻina. Adverb. *Lit.,* aid in speaking.

Kō.kua Hou. 1. n. Counselor (RSV), Comforter (KJV). (Ioane 14.16.) 2. *(Not cap.)* nv. New help; to help again.

kō.kua kauka. n. Doctor's aide, intern.

kō.kua kumu. n. Assistant teacher, substitute teacher.

kō.kua luna kā.nā.wai kiʻe.kiʻe. n. Associate or deputy judge of the supreme court.

kō.kua maka.mua. n. Second team (horse or oxen following the lead team). See *makamua.*

kō kula kai. nvs. Lowland dweller; belonging to the lowlands.

kokuli. n. Earwax. Cf. *kuli,* deaf.

kola. 1. vs. Hard, rigid, sexually excited. *Maʻi kola,* sexually excited genital, a term of derision for an oversexed person. **hoʻo.kola.** To arouse sexual excitement, titillate. (PNP *tola.*) 2. vi. To spread out, as a turkey's tail. *Rare.* 3. Wedge, cleat. (AP.) 4. Also **kora.** Kor. *Eng.* (Ezek. 45.14.)

kō laila. nvs. Those of that place; local. (Isa. 34.4.)

kolaka, koraka. n. Raven. (1 Nal. 17.4.) (Gr. *korax.*)

kola.kola. Redup. of *kola I.* **hoʻo.kola.kola.** Caus/sim. *Rare.*

kō lā.kou. poss. Their, theirs (*o*-form, plural, Gram. 8.4, 9.6). (PNP *toʻo la(a)tou,* PCP *too laatou.*)

kolamu. n. 1. Column. *Eng.* 2. Also **koramu.** Quorum. *Eng.*

kō.lane. Same as *kōnane.*

kō.lani. n. Sitting hula in honor of a chief *(lani).* *Rare.*

kō lā.ua. poss. Their, theirs (*o*-form, dual, Gram. 8.4, 9.6). (PNP *toʻo laaua,* PCP *too laaua.*)

kole. 1. vs. Raw, as meat; inflamed; red, as a raw wound or as red earth. Cf. *hakukole, kolekole, mākole, ʻōkole kaʻaka, koaka. Kole ka ihu,* nose inflamed with cold. *Kole ka waha,* wrangling and quarrelsome. *Kole ke ahi,* fire that won't burn because of the dampness of the wood. *Kole ka ʻāina,* the land is bare and red. *Mālama o kole ka lae,* careful or your forehead will be skinned. **hoʻo.kole.** Same as *hoʻokolekole.* (PPN *tole.*) 2. n. Weak and spent, as an old plant. Cf. *ʻakole, mūʻokole.* 3. n. Surgeonfish *(Ctenochaetus strigosus). Kole maka onaona,* sweet-eyed *kole* [said of attractive people, as the eye of this fish is considered beautiful]. 4. nvt. Story; to tell stories, talk. *Eng.*

kō.lea. 1. nvi. Pacific golden plover *(Pluvialis dominica),* a migratory bird which comes to Hawaiʻi about the end of August and leaves early in May for Siberia and Alaska. *Fig.,* to repeat, boast; a scornful reference to foreigners (Kel. 70) who come to Hawaii and become prosperous, and then leave with their wealth, just as the plover arrives thin in the fall each year, fattens up, and leaves; a less common figurative reference is to one who claims friendship or kinship that does not exist; in some localities the *kōlea* is an *ʻaumakua;* to call *kōlea.* Cf. *hula kōlea* and saying, *kauhua 2.* Haole kī *kōlea,* plover-shooting white man [said in astonishment and horror at the white man's shooting of plovers, contrasting with the laborious Hawaiian methods of catching plovers, a way of saying that white people are strange and different]. *Kōlea ke kōlea i kona inoa iho,* the *kōlea* just says his own name [of a boaster]. (PCP *toolea.*) 2. n. Stepparent, as *makuahine kōlea, makua kāne kōlea.* 3. n. The mottled periwinkle, probably *Littorina pintado.* Also *ʻakōlea, kōlealea, kūkae kōlea, pūpū kōlea.* 4. n. Native species of trees and shrubs *(Myrsine [Rapanea, Suttonia])* with oval to narrow leaves more or less crowded at branch tips, small flowers, and small round fruits among or below the leaves. Uses: red sap and charcoal from the wood to dye tapa, wood for houses, logs for beating tapa. (Neal 664.) 5. *(Cap.)* nvs. Korea; Korean. *Eng.*

kō.lea lau liʻi. n. A native small tree or shrub with small leaves *(Myrsine sandwicensis).*

kō.lea lau nui. n. A native tree *(Myrsine lessertiana)* in the rain forests, with narrow to wide, large leathery leaves clustered at branch tips, bearing many small round red or black fruits usually just below the leaves. Wood is not very hard, but was formerly used for house posts and beams. (Neal 664.)

kō.lea.lea. 1. vt. To play with a child, as bobbing it up and down on one's leg and singing ditties with the refrain *kōlealea.* Cf. *kolekolea I.* 2. Same as *kōlea 3.*

kolea.moku. n. Heiau, temple, built by a chief after recovering from serious sickness, named in honor of the first man who learned the use of herbs in healing and who was deified after his death.

kole kaʻaka. n. Head of penis. Cf. *ʻōkole kaʻaka.*

kole.kole. Redup. of *kole I,* rawness. *Pipi moʻa kolekole,* beef cooked rare. *Kolekole ka maka,* pulling down the lower eyelid of an eye, an insulting gesture that might bring bad luck to the victim, especially if accompanied by the taunt: *Eia kāu, kolekole ka maka!* This is for you, a red eye! **hoʻo.kole.kole.** Caus/sim.; to cook rare; to skin, denude, bruise. *Hoʻokolekole maka,* to make the rude gesture. 2. Redup. of *kole 4;* Hawaiian pidgin "talk story."

kole.kolea. 1. nvi. To cry, of the *kōlea,* bird; to sing, of the *kāhuli,* land shell in Hawaiian belief. *Fig.,* a child that runs about wildly. 2. n. Variety of *moana,* goatfish, perhaps *Parupeneus chrysonemus. Rare.*

kole.kole.ʻā. n. Said to be Kauaʻi name for a large *kole,* the fish.

kole.kole.lehua. Same as *kolokolo kuahiwi.*

kolela, kolera. n. Cholera. *Eng.* See ex., *oneʻā.*

kole.neka, koreneta. n. Horn (RSV), cornet (KJV). (1 Oihn. 15.28.) *Eng.*

kole.nika, korenisa. n. Buzzard. (Kanl. 14.13.) (Latin *cornix,* crow.)

kole nuku heu. n. Variety of the fish *kole,* said to have fine hairlike growths around the mouth. *Lit., kole* with hairy mouth.

kolepa, golepa. n. Golf (the game). *Eng.*

kole.pana, korebana. Corban. (Mar. 7.11.) *Eng.*

kole.peia.'alu. vs. Old, wrinkled, bleary-eyed. *Rare.*

koli. 1. vt. To whittle, pare, sharpen, peel; to trim, as a lamp or the raveled edges of a dress; to shave, as hair (Oihk. 14.9). See *pa'i koli. Pahi koli,* carving knife. *Koli miki'ao,* to pare nails. *E lilo ana kā mākou mau keiki i ke koli kukui a maluhi,* our children are engrossed in lamp trimming until exhaustion [i.e., they are going on a night spree]. Cf. *kōkolikoli, kolikoli.* (PPN *toli.*) **2.** n. Meteor.

kolī. Same as *pā'aila,* castor bean or castor-oil plant. The name may be qualified by *ke'oke'o,* light-colored, and *'ula'ula,* red. *Ni'ihau.* See *castor bean.*

kolia. 1. Pas/imp. of *koli 1.* **2.** Pas/imp. of *kō,* to draw. *Hukia mai ke kaula i kūpono, kolia mai ke kaula i mālo'elo'e* (chant for Ka-lā-kaua), pull the rope till it fits right, draw the rope till taut.

koli.ana. n. **1.** Accordion. *Eng.* **2.** Also **koriana.** Coriander *(Coriandrum sativum;* Neal 659). (Puk. 16.31.) *Eng.*

koli.hana. vs. Straight, tall. *Oki kolihana ka pali o Wai-aloha,* very straight and tall is the cliff of Wai-aloha [admiration for a tall, well-formed person].

koli'i. 1. n. A native lobelia shrub *(Trematolobelia macrostachys)* to 1.8 m high, with several horizontal branches at the top when in flower, each branch bearing a long cluster of pink flowers, each flower 5 cm long; the narrow leaves to 30 by 2.5 cm. **2.** vi. To disappear gradually, as a ship on the horizon; to evaporate; to be barely visible, as the sun's first rays. **3.** n. *Luakini* dedication prayer. Also *koli'i maomao* (Kam. 64:27).

kō.liko. Same as *kōlikoliko.*

koli.koli. Redup. of *koli 1.*

kō.liko.liko. 1. vs. Swollen, enlarged, fat, greasy. **2.** n. Young *wauke,* bark.

koli.kukui. n. A variety of domesticated *'ilima* with bronze-red flowers. *Lit., kukui* candle.

kolila, gorila. n. Gorilla. *Eng.*

kō.lī.lā. vs. Thin, bony. Cf. *līlā,* thin. *Kōlīlā maila ke kino a hākau noho'i nā iwi,* the body was so thin that the bones stood out.

kō.lile.lile. vi. To glisten, sparkle, glitter.

kolili. 1. vi. To flutter, as a flag; to wag, as a dog's tail. Also *konini.* See *hula kolili.* **ho'o.kolili.** To flutter, wave. **2.** n. An *'ilima* rod, a fathom or so long, tipped with feathers and used as a wand in the *'ume* game. **3.** To rush out, as pent-up water; to flow swiftly, leak. (And.)

kō.lī.li'i. vi. Dwindling, diminishing, as of water in a stream or pool, or of something in the distance, or of pain; convalescing.

kō.lī.liko. Same as *'oliliko,* to sparkle.

kōli.lili. vi. To vibrate, as heat. Cf. *hulili.*

koli.li'u. Same as *kōli'uli'u.*

koli.neka, korineta. Var. of *koleneka.*

kō.li'u. Same as *kōli'uli'u.*

kō.li'u.li'u. vs. Dim, obscure, indistinct, as a distant object or sound. *Ka hānau 'ana ame ka wā kōli'uli'u o kō Ka-welo noho 'ana* (FS 33), the birth and dim distant time of Ka-welo's life. *'Ike kōli'uli'u,* to see faintly, to have slight knowledge.

kolo. 1. vi. To creep, crawl; to move along, as a gentle breeze or shower; to walk bent over as in respect to a chief or as indicative of humility. Cf. *kolo manu* and ex., *ua 1. Ahe kolo,* gentle-moving breeze. *Koa kolo,* a sprawling *koa* tree. **ho'o.kolo.** To cause to creep, crawl; to follow a trail, track, clue; to trace to a source. Cf. *ho'okolokolo.* (PPN *-tolo.*) **2.** vt. To pull, tow, drag, to pull a seine. *Moku kolo,* tugboat. **3.** n. Wagon tongue or shafts. Also *kolo ka'a.* **4.** vi. To grumble. **5.** interj. Call to fowl, pigs. *Kolo, kolo, kolo!* Come, come, come! **6.** Var. of *kono 2,* to attract birds. **7.** Also **koro.** Biblical liquid measure, about 420 pints.

koloa. n. Hawaiian duck *(Anas wyvilliana).* Also *koloa maoli,* native *koloa,* to distinguish it from migratory or introduced ducks, also called *koloa.* Formerly on all main islands except Lā-na'i and Ka-ho'olawe; in 1976 common only on Kaua'i; birds raised in capitivity and released have been seen on O'ahu and Hawai'i; considered endangered in 1978. *Koloa* birds protected a legendary blind giant, Ima-i-ka-lani, and quacked to warn him from which side he might expect an attack (FS 169). (PPN *toloa.*)

kō.loa. 1. n. Long cane with a crook. **2.** vi. To make a prolonged sound, roar. *'O Puna ia o ke kai kōloa i ka ulu mai,* this is Puna where the sea ever roars in the pandanus groves.

koloa maoli. See *koloa.*

koloa māpu. n. Pintail duck *(Anas acuta),* a common migrant to the Hawaiian Islands. *Lit.,* wind-blown duck.

koloa mohā. n. Shoveler or spoonbill *(Anas clypeata),* a migrant. *Lit.,* bright duck (said to be named for the dark glossy green head of the male).

Kolo-'ā.pu'u.pu'u. n. Name of a wind usually accompanied by rain, common at Wai-mea, Hawai'i. *Lit.,* rough creep.

kolo.au. vi. To stretch out; stretched out, long and thin. *Rare.*

kolo.hala. Pheasant *(Phasianus colchicus torquatus),* the showy ring-necked pheasant. *Lit.,* creep go on.

kolohe. nvi. Mischievous, naughty, unethical or unprincipled in any way, illegal, fraudulent, destructive; rascal, mischief-maker, scamp, rogue, prankster, comic, roughhouse, crook, vandal, lecher; to act in this fashion, misbehave, cheat, transgress, tamper; to violate, as a taboo. *Kolohe wale,* to be mischievous for no particular reason; to trifle. *Nānā 'ia ke kupu, ka 'eu, ke kolohe o kai,* look at the upstart, rascal, and mischiefmaker of the sea area. *Moekolohe,* adultery. *Hihia waiwai kolohe,* law suit or case involving smuggling; *lit.,* case for dishonest goods. *Kō lāua hui kolohe 'ana,* their adulterous union. *Waiwai loa'a ma ke kolohe,* ill-gotten gains. **ho'o.kolohe.** To do mischief, play pranks, etc.; to cause to be mischievous; to disturb, annoy; to do amusing things to create laughter; funny, humorous, comical, mischievous. *Ho'okolohe noho'i kāna hīmeni 'ana,* he sings in such an amusing manner.

kolo.hia. Pas/imp. of *kolo 1, 2, 4.*

koloka. n. Cloak, cape. *Eng.*

kolo ka'a. See *kolo 3.*

kolo.kē. n. Croquet. *Eng.*

kolo.kio. nvt. Method of catching birds by means of a long stick with a crosspiece at the end; flowers were attached and smeared with sticky juice to which the birds stuck. The birds were first attracted by whistling. A bird catcher; to catch thus. *Lit.,* creep whistle.

kolo.kolo. 1. Redup. of *kolo 1;* to track down, investigate, seek evidence. **ho'o.kolo.kolo.** To try in court, judge, investigate; judiciary; trial. *Ho'okolokolo moku,* admiralty cases. See *hale ho'okolokolo.* (PPN *tolotolo.*) **2.** n. Any creeping vine. **3.** vi. To gobble, rumble, grumble, scold. **4.** See *ānapanapa 2.*

kolo.kolo.hai. vs. Humble, modest, thoughtful, kind. Cf. *kolokolo,* creeping, as in respect to a chief, and *akahai,* modest. *Rare.*

kolo.kolo kaha.kai. n. The beach vitex *(Vitex ovata),* distributed from Hawai'i west to Japan and India, an aromatic, prostrate beach shrub, with downy, ovate leaves and small, blue, clustered flowers. (Neal 728.) *Lit.,* beach creeper. Also *mānawanawa, pōhinahina, pōlinalina.*

kolo.kolo.kio. Redup. of *kolokio.*

kolo.kolo kua.hiwi. n. Two loosestrifes *(Lysimachia daphnoides, L. hillebrandii),* small native shrubs with purplish flowers, the branches densely covered with narrow, pointed leaves. *L. daphnoides* is confined to the high bogs of Kaua'i. Lit., mountain creeper. Also *kolekole lehua.* Cf. *pua hekili.*

kolo.kolo lehua. Same as *kolokolo kuahiwi.*

kolo.kolo.nahe. Redup. of *kolonahe.*

kolo.kolo.pā. n. Tiny stage of the *kūmū, weke,* and other goatfish; other stages are *'āhuluhulu, kūmū a'e,* and *kūmū.* Also *mākolokolopā.*

kolo.lani. vi. To go away silently. *Niau kololani ka helena,* silently, quickly departed. *Ka uahi kololani,* the smoke that wisps away.

kolo.lio. 1. Same as *kokololio,* gust. **ho'o.kolo.lio.** Caus/sim. **2.** n. Wind associated with Moloa'a, Kaua'i (For. 5:97) and Kī-pahulu, Maui (Nak. 68).

-kololohe. ho'o.kolo.lohe. To delay maliciously, to loiter sullenly, to dillydally in order to annoy; to not cooperate, sulk.

kolo.lū. vi. Soft, weak and helpless, as a newborn baby or newly hatched bird; soft and not yet hardened, as a new growth of bone; easily influenced and impressed, as an unstable person.

kolo manu. Var. of *kono manu.* Cf. *'auli'i kolo manu,* daintiness that attracts birds.

kolo.meki. n. Third mate on a ship; the officer next to the second mate. *Eng.*

kolo.moku. nv. Tugboat; to tow a ship.

kolo.mona. n. **1.** A native shrub *(Cassia gaudichaudii)* with greenish-yellow flowers and thin flat pods. (Neal 427.) *Eng.* Also *kalamona.* **2.** A similar shrub *(Cassia surattensis* syn. *C. glauca),* with an Asian to Australian distribution, naturalized in Hawai'i and also grown ornamentally, with yellow flowers and flat pods. (Neal 427.) Also *kalamona.* **3.** A weedy shrub *(Cassia floribunda* syn. *C. laevigat),* from tropic America, with yellow flowers and cylindrical pods. (Neal 425.) Also *kalamona.* **4.** *Crotalaria incana, C. pallida, C. spectabilis* on Ni'ihau. **5.** Name listed by Hillebrand for *Mezoneuron kavaiense.* See *uhiuhi.* **6.** *(Cap.)* Also **Solo-mona.** Solomon. *Eng.*

kolona. n. **1.** Colon. *Eng.* **2.** Also **korona.** Crown, rosary. *Eng.* Cf. *lei kolona. Pule kolona,* prayer with beads. **3.** Solon. *Eng.*

kolo.nahe. vi. Gentle, pleasant breeze; gentle, mild; softly blowing. *Lit.,* gentle creeping.

kolone. n. Column, as military. *Eng.* See ex., *pili 1.*

kolo.nelo, koronero. n. Coroner (used with *kiure,* jury). *Eng.*

koloni.ala. vs. Colonial. *Eng.*

-kolono. ho'o.kolono. To pretend not to hear, to feign deafness; indifferent.

kolo.nuha. Same as *kananuha. Rare.* **ho'o.kolo.nuha.** Same as *ho'okananuha.*

kolo.pā. 1. vi. To fight, scream, kick, as children in tantrums; to jerk away from, as a runaway horse; to bolt. **2.** n. Crowbar. *Eng. 'A 'ole kēnā he kolopā* (song), that by you is not a crowbar.

kolo.pao. n. A bird (no data).

kolo.pe'e. vi. To skulk along.

kolo.poma. n. Chloroform. *Eng.*

kolo.pū. vs. Well-proportioned, of a large person whose flesh is evenly distributed; also said of a long *koa* tree trunk that grows straight without branching.

kolo.pua. vs. Fragrant, as air laden with the perfume of flowers, sometimes said of the breath. *Lit.,* creeping flowers. *Ua hala ku'u lehua, aia i Ko'oko'olau i ka nae kolopua,* my *lehua* blossom is gone to Ko'oko'olau to breathe perfume-laden air.

Kolo-pu'e.pu'e. n. Wind name.

kolo.pupū. vs. Old, infirm, of an aged person bent with age. *Lit.,* creep crouched.

kolo.'u'a. vs. Old, worn-out, of an old hag or old sow. Cf. *'u'a,* worn, faded.

kolo.waka. n. Soda water. *Eng.*

kolo.walu. n. Name of a law in the time of Kū-ali'i safeguarding the rights of commoners (For. 4:433.)

kolu. num. Three, third. (Gram. 10.3.) *Manawakolu,* eternal. (PPN *tolu.*)

kolū. n. **1.** Glue. *Eng.* **2.** A thorny, weedy shrub *(Acacia farnesiana),* widespread in the tropics. It is a legume with finely divided leaves and fragrant, round,

orange flower heads, used in the perfume industry. The bark yields a gum for glue; sometimes spelled *klu.* (Neal 406.) **3.** Bluing used in washing clothes. *Eng.* **4.** Same as *'iniko,* indigo plant, used for bluing. **5.** Screw. *Eng.*

kō.lū. nvi. To scatter; to drop, as bombs; bombing.

kō.lui.lui. n. Continued ringing sound. *Rare.*

kolu.kahi. n. Trinity.

Kolu.kahi Hemo.lele. n. Holy Trinity.

kolū keiki. n. Gauge screws.

kolu.keline, golukerine. n. Glycerine. *Eng.*

kō.lulu. vt. To defend, shield, ward off. *Rare.* Cf. *pālulu.*

Kom. Abbreviation for *komohana,* west.

koma. n. Comma. *Eng.*

kō.maka. See *nihokōmaka,* a fish.

komako. n. Tomato (generally called *'ōhi'a* or *'ōhi'a lomi). Eng.*

koma.koa, komadora. n. Commodore. *Eng.*

kō mā.kou. poss. Our, ours (*o*-form, plural exclusive; Gram. 8.4, 9.6). (PNP *to'o matou,* PEP *too maatou.*)

koma luna. n. Apostrophe, glottal stop. *Lit.,* comma *(Eng.)* above.

komana. n. Stone, as used with octopus lures. *Rare.*

kō mā.ua. poss. Our, ours (*o*-form, dual exclusive; Gram. 8.4, 9.6). (PNP *to'o maaua,* PCP *too maaua.*)

kome. n. Papyrus (RSV), bulrush (KJV). (Isa. 18.2.) (Heb. *gome.*)

kome.'ula.'ula. A variety of sweet potato.

kō.mi. vt. To press, bear down, rub, as in massage; to pull taut, as a fishline. Cf. *kaomi.*

kō.mike, komite. n. Committee, committee member. *Eng. Kōkime mau,* standing or permanent committee. *Kōmike kūikawā,* ad hoc committee.

kō.mike hui. n. Joint committee.

kō.mike komo 'ā.pana. n. Visiting committee.

kō.mike ola. n. Welfare committee.

kō.mike wae. n. Select committee.

komi.kina, komisina. nvt. Commissioner, commission; to commission. *Ali'i koa i komikina 'ia,* commissioned officer. *Uku komikina,* commission (pay).

Komi.kina Ho'o.nā 'Āina. n. Commissioners to Quiet Land Titles, a board set up by Ka-mehameha III to settle land claims; it served between 1846 and 1855 and heard more than 11,000 claims (Indices, VII-VIII).

komi.kina kū.i.ka.wā. n. Acting commissioner.

komi.kina palena 'āina. n. Land boundary commission or commissioner.

komi.kiona, komisiona. n. Commissioner.

kōmi.kōmi. Redup. of *kōmi.*

Komi.nika, Dominika. nvs. Dominican, dominical. *Eng.*

Komi.nika o ka 'Eha. n. Passion Sunday. (Catholic term.)

Komi.nika o nā Lā.lā Lā.'au. n. Palm Sunday. (Catholic term.) *Lit.,* dominical of the tree branches.

komo. 1. nvt, vs. To enter, go into, penetrate, include; to join, as a class or organization; to sink, as a heavily laden canoe; to entertain or feel, as an emotion; entered, filled, included; entrance. (Gram. 4.5.) *Komo 'ana,* access, admission, entry, entrance. *Haumana komo hou,* freshman, new pupil. *'Aha'aina komo,* initiation feast. *Komo mai!* Come in, welcome! *Mele komo,* welcoming song. *Komo mai e 'ai,* come in and eat. *Komo maila ka huhū,* filled with wrath. *Ua komo ka wa'a,* the canoe is filled [as with fish]. *Komo i ka hale,* enter the house. *E komo no ku'u ho'oilina ia 'īlio,* including for my heirs this dog. *Komo 'ole ka wai,* waterproof. *E nānā 'oe i kō lākou komo 'ana . . . a 'ike 'oe ua pau loa i ke komo . . .* (FS 111), watch them coming in . . . and when you see they are all in . . . **ho'o.komo.** To insert, put or let in, enter, pack, penetrate, import, sink into, deposit, install, admit. See *niho ho'okomo. Ho'okomo waiwai ho'opae mai,* entry of goods. *Ho'okomo makani, ho'okomo ea,* to ventilate. *Ho'okomo i ke kālā i ka panakō,* deposit money in the bank. (PPN *tomo.*) **2.** vt. To dress, put on, wear (any garment, formerly only lower garments). **ho'o.komo.** To dress another person. **3.** n. Ring, thimble, tenon.

komo 'āina. v. To take possession of a land; to acquire land, as by inheritance.

komo 'ā.pana. n. House visiting, as by a priest making the rounds of his district; visiting from district to district, as by a church committee. *Lit.,* enter district.

komo hale. nv. Housewarming; moving into a new house.

komo.hana. nvs. West, western, so-called because the sun "enters" *(komo)* the sea in the west. (*Komo,* to enter + *-hana,* nominalizer: Gram. 6.6.2.) (PEP *tomo-(f,s)anga.*)

komo.hana 'ā.kau. nvs. Northwest.

komo.hana hema. nvs. Southwest, southwestern.

komo hewa. vt. To trespass, enter by mistake or illegally, intrude; to put on in a wrong way, as clothes wrong side out.

komo.hia. Pas/imp. of *komo 1, 2.*

komo humu.humu. 1. n. Thimble. *Lit.,* sewing ring. **2.** vt. To put on clothing inside out. *Lit.,* wear seams.

komo.'i'i'i. vs. Very small, tiny, of small stature; also said of people of little consequence.

komo 'ino. vi. To enter wrongly, invade.

komo kau.hale. vi. To go from house to house, as a census taker or salesman. *Kōmike komo kauhale,* committee that pays visits to the houses of members, as of a church.

komo.komo. 1. n. Evil possession resulting from sorcery. Cf. *noho.* **ho'o.komo.komo.** To cause a spirit, usually evil, to possess; possession. **2.** vt. To fit a garment. **ho'o.komo.komo.** To dress, as children; to file, put in. (PCP *tomotomo.*)

komo lima. n. Ring, thimble *(rare).*

komo lole. vt. To dress, put on clothes.

komo mawaena. vi. To come between, intervene.

kō.mōmo. n. Candy. Also *kōomoomo.*

Kō-momona. n. Wind associated with Ka-hau-iki, Honolulu. (Nak. 57.) *Lit.,* sweat sugar cane.

komo 'oko'a. vt. To do with unanimity; to undertake a project wholeheartedly; to cooperate with enthusiasm. *Lit.,* to enter whole. *Komo 'oko'a akula mākou e kōkua,* we pitched in to help.

komo.pani. n. Term used in 1845 for a military company. *Eng.*

kō.mou. n. Prepared poi not yet mixed with water, softer than *pa'i 'ai.*

komo wale. vt. To enter without permission or ceremony, trespass, intrude.

komu.nio. n. Communion. (Latin *communio.*) *Ke komunio me ka po'e saneta,* the communion of saints.

Kona. 1. nvs. Leeward sides of the Hawaiian Islands; leeward (PPN *Tonga.*) **2.** nvi. A famous leeward wind; to blow, of this wind. Many names of Kona winds follow. See ex., *Kapakū.* **3.** n. Name of a star. **4.** *(Not cap.)* n. Also **tona.** Ton, tonnage. *Eng.* Also *kana.*

kōna. poss. His, her, hers, its (*o*-form; Gram. 8.4, 9.6.) (PNP *tona,* PEP *to'ona.*)

konā. vs. Hard, unyielding, unfriendly, contemptuous, brusque, haughty. Cf. *konākonā, laukōnā, mākonā.* **ho'o.konā.** Caus/sim. *Rare.*

konā.hao. vs. Strong, as the hand of a fighter.

konā.hau. vs. Cold, penetrating, damp, of wind.

Kona Hea. n. Name of a cold Kona storm. (Malo 14.) A var. name is *Kona Hea Puka.*

Kona Hili Mai'a. n. Name of a Kona wind with protracted rains, (Malo 14.) *Lit.,* Kona wind smiting bananas.

konā.hua. vs. Fat, grease; kidneys. (Puk. 29.13.)

kona.kona. 1. vs. Strong, bulging with muscles; rough and uneven, as a surface; hard. Cf. *pūkonakona.* **2.** n. A native tufted grass *(Panicum nephelophilum),* to 1.3 m high, with a large, open-flowering panicle to 35 by 25 cm. Cf. *kākonakona.*

konā.konā. vi. Dislike, contempt; disliked; to dislike.

kona.kū. n. Posts on each side of the two center posts at the back wall of a grass house.

Kona Kū. n. Name of a Kona wind with heavy rain. (Malo 14.)

Kona Lani. n. Name of a Kona wind with slight showers. (Malo 14.)

kō.nale. 1. Var. of *kōnane 1.* '*Ike kōnale mai,* to see clearly. **2.** vs. Quiet, tranquil, peaceful.

kō.nale.lewa. n. **1.** Variety of *'a'awa,* a fish. **2.** Same as *kohelelewa.* (Malo 46.)

kō.nale.nale. Redup. of *kōnale 1, 2.* See ex., *hulialana.*

kona.lewa.lewa. Same as *kōnalelewa 1, 2.*

Kona Mae. n. Name of a cold Kona wind. (Malo 14.) *Lit.,* withering Kona.

Kona-mau-kuku. n. Name of a star; probably short for *Kukui-a-kona-mau-kuku.*

Kona Moe. n. Name of a cold Kona wind and rain.

kō.nane. 1. nvi. Bright moonlight; to shine, as the moon; clear, bright. '*O ka pā kōnane a ka mahina,* the moon shines brightly. **2.** nvi. Ancient game resembling checkers, played with pebbles placed in even lines on a stone or wood board called *papa kōnane;* to play *kōnane.* Cf. *nane,* riddle; *mū, papamū.* **3.** n. Tapa-beater design.

kō.nane ho'o.pa'i. n. Tapa-beater design.

kō.nane pepehi. n. Tapa-beater design.

kō.nane pū.pū. n. A tapa-beater pattern; a *kōnane* checkerboard design with rounded pits *(pūpū)* in the middle of each square.

Kona-nui-a-niho. n. Name of a strong Kona storm. *Lit.,* great Kona that bites with teeth.

kona pā.keke. n. A variety of introduced sweet potato. *Lit.,* Kona packet *(Eng.)*

kona.pili.ahi. vs. Strong, powerful. *Keiki konapiliahi, lawakua, kino 'āwa'awa'a,* a youth, strong, powerful, [and with a] muscular body.

kone. n. Rock badger (RSV), coney (KJV) (Kanl. 14.7); described by Kep., perhaps a gony (gooney). *Eng.*

kō.nea. vs. Restored to health.

kō.nea.nea. Same as *konekonea 1, 2.*

koneka. n. Cornet. *Eng.*

koneko. n. Doughnut. *Eng.*

kone.konea. 1. Redup. of *kōnea;* convalescing. **2.** vs. Bald; hard, dry. Cf. *nea,* bare. *Rare.*

konela. n. 1. Colonel. *Eng.* **2.** Tunnel (also *konela puka*). *Eng.*

kone.lika, konerisa. n. Kite, a bird. *Biblical.*

kone.nea. Rare var. of *konekonea.*

kone.nene. Redup. of *konene 1, 2. Rare.*

koni. vi. To throb, pulsate, tingle, beat; to flutter, as the heart; to tug, as small fish on baited hook. '*Eha koni,* throbbing ache; *fig.,* pangs of love. *Koni au, koni au i ka wai, koni au i ka wai hu'ihu'i* (song), I throb, I throb for liquor, I am eager for cool liquor. **ho'o.ko.ni.** Caus/sim. (PNP *tongi.*)

konia. Pas/imp. of *koni.* (PNP *tongia.*)

koni.ā. vs. Stubborn, unyielding, sulky.

koni.aka. n. All kinds of asters. (Neal 833.)

koni.koni. Redup. of *koni;* to palpitate; passion. *He aloha hu'ihu'i konikoni ana i loko o'u,* a benumbing, tingling love within me.

koni loa. vi. To persist, keep on. *Koni loa maila kona holo 'ana ā loa'a 'o O'ahu* (Kep. 77), he kept on sailing until coming to O'ahu.

konini. vi. To wag, as a dog's tail; to flutter, wave, move to and fro. Also *kolili.* **ho'o.konini.** Caus/sim.

koni.niu. Var. of *kōniuniu.*

kō.niu.niu. vs. Dizzy. Cf. *pōniuniu.*

kono. vt. **1.** To invite, ask in, entice, induce, prompt. *Palapala kono,* (written) invitation. **ho'o.kono.** To invite (PCP *tono.*) **2.** To attract the attention of a bird, as by imitating its call, and then to snare it, as with gummed '*ie'ie* roots. *Ua'u* birds were snared thus. See *kono 'elepī, kono manu.*

kono.'ele. nvs. Darkness, as of a forest; said also of the inside of thighs thought to be darkened by the chafing of the *malo;* somewhat darker than *konouli.*

kono 'ele.pī. v. To catch black crabs (*'elepī*), as by tying *'opihi* limpets to a cord dangled above a rock fissure; the crab snatches the bait, the cord is drawn up and the crab seized. (Kep. 172.)

kono.hī. n. Chinese New Year. (Cantonese *kong-hee,* congratulations: Gram. 2.9.)

kono.hia. Pas/imp. of *kono 1.*

kono.hiki. n. Headman of an *ahupua'a* land division under the chief; land or fishing rights under control of the *konohiki;* such rights are sometimes called *konohiki* rights. (PPN *tongafiti.*)

konoki. n. Poker (card game). (Perhaps *Eng.,* knock.)

kono.kono. Redup. of *kono 1;* to require. **ho'o.kono.-kono.** To induce, entice, urge persistently, especially to urge someone to will him his property; to set dogs to fight.

kono manu. nv. To entice a bird, as by imitating its call, and then to snare it; a birdcatcher. Cf. *kono 2.*

kono.pue. vs. Short and plump.

kono.uli. Same as *kono'ele,* but perhaps less dark.

-konu. See *waenakonu,* center. (PPN *tonu,* true.)

kō.nui. Stricken with great heat, as by the sun's rays. (And.)

kō.nunu. vs. Rounded and well shaped, as a *lehua* flower. *Lehua maka kōnunu i ka wai, kōnunu, kōnunu, ō-hāhā, lehua* face rounded in the water, rounded, rounded, plump.

konu.waena. Same as *waenakonu.*

ko'o. 1. nvt. Brace, support, wand, prop, helper; small stalks to which feathers on large *kāhili,* standards, are tied, and which are attached to the main pole; pole as used in pushing a canoe; sprit of a canoe's sail; stick fastened across a small fish net near the meeting of the sticks *(kuku)* with a pole, prop; to uphold (Isa. 63.5). Cf. *kāko'o, kani-ko'o.* **ho'o.ko'o.** Prop with a pole, as a heavily laden banana plant, or a house to keep it from falling down; to pole, as a canoe.(PPN *toko.*) 2. n. Tail feathers, as of a cock, or as below the tail of the *mamo,* a bird. 3. nvs. Force, strength; strong, rough (rarely used except after *kai*). *Kai ko'o,* rough, strong sea. *Lilo a'ela ke ko'o makani o Lehua* (chant), the force of the wind of Lehua is spent. 4. vs. Larger, a trifle bigger. *A maluna mai o ka huli he wahi 'upena, ko'o a'e ia o ka maka,* and above the bag net is a small net with slightly larger meshes. 5. nvt. Loose, slack; to lay on in folds, as pleats in a dress; to loosen, slacken. 6. n. Light-green leaves near the center of a cluster of pandanus leaves. *'I'o ko'o,* leaves inside the *ko'o* [their base is white and the upper part dark green].

ko'o-. Same as *kōko'o,* but usually followed by a number; partner. (PPN *toko-,* PNP *toka-,* PEP *toko-.*)

ko'o.kā. 1. vt. To lambaste, buffet, hit. *He wa'a nahā i ko'okā kō kāne,* a smashed canoe that has been buffeted by your husband [overindulgence in sex leads to impotence]. 2. n. A variety of sweet potato.

ko'o.kahi. n. Canoe carrying only one person (a canoe carrying two persons was *ko'olua,* three was *ko'okolu,* etc.). (Malo 131.) See ex., *kana 1.*

ko'o.kapu. nv. Taboo with death as penalty for breaking; to lay such a taboo.

ko'o.kea. vs. To have gray or white hair.

ko'o.kolu. See *ko'okahi.*

ko'o.ko'o. 1. n. Cane, staff, rod; support, means of livelihood; staff in music. *He ko'oko'o haki wale,* an easily broken staff [a weak leader]. **ho'o.ko'o.ko'o.** To push, brace, resist, lean back and brace oneself. (PPN *tokotoko.*) 2. Var. of *kōko'o,* and likewise followed by numerals and *-hia.* 3. n. A prayer ending taboos. (Ii 60.)

ko'o.ko'o 'ā.mana. n. Cane with a handle. *Lit.,* tee-shaped cane.

ko'o.ko'o kā.lele. n. Crutch.

ko'o.ko'o.kolu. Same as *kōko'okolu.*

ko'o.ko'o.lau. n. All kinds of beggar ticks (*Bidens* spp.), most native, a few introduced, some used medicinally by Hawaiians, as a tonic in tea; the plants are still dried and used for tea, often in preference to tea bought in stores. (Neal 844.) Cf. *kī 2.* Also *ko'olau, kōko'olau.* 2. Ni'ihau name for *nehe, Lipochaeta perdita,* a hairy herb.

ko'o.ko'o.lau haole. n. An introduced coreopsis *(Coreopsis lanceolata),* with ray and central florets all yellow. (Neal 842–3.)

ko'o.ko'o.lua. Same as *kōko'olua.*

ko'o.ko'o.na. vt. To reach far for; to rest one hand for support *(ko'oko'o)* and reach out with the other. (FS 211.)

ko'o.ko'o 'oi.hana. n. Mace. *Lit.,* professional cane.

ko'o.ko'o.ū. Redup. of *ko'oū.* See *ko'ū.*

ko'o.kū. 1. vi. To swell out; stick out, as a ruffle. 2. n. Hillside, slope, mountain slope; hillside road or path.

ko'o lani. n. Help given to a chief. *'Awa ko'o lani,* kava that gives strength to a chief. *Ma'a ia i ke ko'o lani,* he is accustomed to giving all support to the chief.

Ko'o.lau. n. 1. Windward sides of the Hawaiian Islands. *He au Ko'olau aku ia,* that is the time of the Ko'olau [trouble]. (PPN *tokelau.*) 2. *(Not cap.)* Short for *ko'oko'olau.* 3. Wind between Ni'ihau and Kaua'i. (For. 5:95.)

ko'o.lau.loa. n. *Ulua* fishline 15 or so fathoms long. Rare.

Ko'o.lau-wahine. n. Breeze blowing from the north of Ni'ihau. *Lit.,* feminine windward. See ex., *pā kāhea.*

ko'o.lili. Same as *kolili 1–3.* Rare.

ko'o lima. nv. Push-up; to push up.

ko'o.loa kea. n. A native shrub with pale-pink flowers, otherwise like *ko'oloa 'ula.*

ko'o.loa 'ula. n. A native, hoary shrub *(Abutilon menziesii),* related to the hibiscus, with heart-shaped leaves 2.5 to 8 cm long, and dark-red flowers from which protrude many stamens borne on a central column. (Neal 550.)

ko'o.lua. 1. Var. of *kōko'olua.* (PPN *tokolua,* PNP *tokalua,* PEP *tokolua.*) 2. n. Canoe carrying two persons. 3. *(Cap.)* n. Star name (no data). (Kuhelani.)

kō 'olua. poss. Your, yours (o-form, dual; Gram. 8.4, 9.6). (PNP *to'o koulua,* PEP *too kolua.*)

Ko'o-makani. n. Wind associated with Mā-hā'ule-pū, Kaua'i. (For. 5:97.)

ko'o manu. n. 1. Support for birds; bird islet. 2. Long tail feathers.

ko'o moa. n. 1. Long tail feathers of a cock. 2. Support for chickens.

kō.omoomo, ko omōmo. n. Candy. *Lit.,* sucking cane. Also *kōmōmo.*

ko'ona. 1. Var. of *ko'ana,* dregs. 2. Same as *ko'o-ko'ona.*

ko'o.nā. n. The addressee, the one there. See ex., *ko'onei.*

ko'o.nei. n. The person here. *He pane ko'onei, he ho'olohe ko'onā,* the one here answers, you listen.

Ko'o.pali. n. Wind associated with Hālawa, Moloka'i.

ko'o.ū. Var. of *ko'ū.*

kō 'ou.kou. poss. Your, yours (o-form, plural; Gram. 8.4, 9.6). (PNP *too koutou.*)

kopa. 1. n. A native shrub *(Hedyotis [Kadua] glaucifolia),* found only on Kaua'i, with narrow, tubular, inconspicuous, pale-yellow flowers, and narrow-ovate to heart-shaped leaves; related to the *'uiwi.* 2. Also **sopa.** nvt. Soap; to cover with soap. *Eng. Kopa 'ala,* perfumed soap. *Kopa 'au'au,* bath soap. *Kopa holoi,* laundry soap. *Kopa pauka,* powdered soap.

kō.pa'a. n. Sugar. *Lit.,* hard sugar cane.

kō.pa'a hō.'ae, kō.pa'a hō.'ae'ae. n. Powdered sugar.

kō.pa'a ho.ke'o.ke'o. n. Refined sugar.

kō.pa'a mā.noa.noa. n. Coarse sugar.

kō.pa'a pu'u.pu'u. n. Lump sugar.

kō.pa'a 'ula.'ula. n. Brown sugar.

kopa.hela, gopahera. n. Gopher. *Eng.*
kō Pā.kē. n. A variety of sugar cane, probably imported by the Chinese.
kopako, topazo, topaza. n. Topaz. (Hoik. 21.20.) (Gr. *topazos.*)
kopala. n. **1.** Corporal. *Eng.* **2.** Copal. *Eng. Waniki kopala,* copal varnish.
kopa.lā. n. Shovel. *Eng.*
kō palani. See *palani 3.*
kope. 1. nvt. Rake, shovel (Nah. 4.14), dredge; to rake, scratch; scoop, as of a canoe paddle (For. 5:557). *Fig.,* to dislike, disregard. *Moku kope awa,* harbor dredge. (PPN *tope.*) **2.** n. Coffee, coffee beans. *Eng. Kope lā,* sun-dried coffee beans. *Kope wai,* fresh, undried coffee beans in the hull. **3.** nvt. Copy, duplicate; to copy or duplicate. *Eng.* Cf. *ponokope. Ke'ena kākau kope,* copyright office; office where deeds are copied.
kopea. Pas/imp. of *kope 1.*
kope ahi. n. Fire shovel, rake for ashes.
kope awa. n. Harbor dredge.
kope.kope. 1. Redup. of *kope 1;* to scribble. *'Ōpū kopekope,* ill-disposed. **2.** Redup. of *kope 3.*
kopela, kopera. n. Champhor tree and product.
kope lehu. n. Rake or shovel for ashes.
kopena. n. **1.** Hornet, wasp, scorpion (*kopiana* is the usual name for scorpion). **2.** Copy. *Eng. Ma ke kopena i ka puke, ua like, ma ka hapa ho'onui, ua 'oi* (hula song), according to the copy in the book, equal, according to the exaggerated portion, [one was] superior.
kō.pī. vt. To sprinkle, as salt, sand; to salt, as fish or meat. (FS 181.)
kopi.ana. n. Scorpion. *Eng.*
kō.piko. n. **1.** About 13 native species of trees belonging to the genus *Psychotria,* a member of the coffee family. Leaves are thick, leathery, blunt or pointed; flowers small, white, clustered at the ends of long stems at branch tips. Called *'ōpiko* on Hawai'i. (Neal 793–4.) **2.** Also **topido.** Torpedo. *Eng.*
kō.piko kea. n. A species of *kōpiko (Psychotria [Straussia] kaduana)* with short-stemmed, rather oblong leaves, small flowers in long drooping clusters, and with small fruits. The wood is orange.
kō.piko 'ula. n. A kind of *kōpiko (Psychotria [Straussia] hawaiiensis)* with large leaves to about 18 by 9 cm, on stems 2.5 cm long, with midrib reddish below; the flowers covered with reddish down.
kō.pili. n. **1.** Thin, transparent tapa made of mulberry bark. **2.** Small white tapa placed over images and altars during religious services; the ceremony; to perform the ceremony. Also *kōpilo nui.* **3.** Birthday gift to a child. (AP.)
kopili.makio, kopirimatio. Confirmation (Catholic term); to confirm. (Latin *confirmatio.*) See ex., *kelema.*
kopina. n. Coping on the top of a building. *Eng.*
kō.pī.pī. Redup. of *kōpī.*
kopola, kobora. n. Cobra. *Eng.*
kopo.lano, soporano. nvs. Soprano. *Eng.*
kopole. Same as *lāwalu,* a way to cook on coals. (And.)
kō pua 'ole. n. A variety of flowerless sugar cane.
kou. 1. n. A tree found on shores from East Africa to Polynesia *(Cordia subcordata),* with large, ovate leaves, and orange, tubular flowers 2.5 to 5 cm in diameter, borne in short-stemmed clusters. The beautiful wood, soft but lasting, was valuable to the early Hawaiians and was used for cups, dishes, and calabashes. (Neal 714–5.) (PPN *tou.*) **2.** *(Cap.)* n. Old name for Honolulu harbor and vicinity, famous rendezvous for *kōnane* checkers. *Hui aku nā maka i Kou* (saying), the eyes [friends] will meet at Kou. **3.** poss. Your, yours (*o*-form, singular; Gram. 8.4, 9.6). (PNP *tou,* PEP *to(o)u.*)
-kou. Indicator of plurality in the plural pronouns and possessives only *(kākou, mākou, 'oukou, lākou).* (PPN *-tolu,* PNP *-tou.*)
kō.ū. vi. To look about in all directions. *Rare.*

ko'u. 1. vi. To cluck. *Fig.,* to talk too much. *Waha ko'u,* gabbling mouth. *E nu'u a ko'u ka pu'u* (saying), pile on until the throat clucks [eat all one can]. **2.** nvt. Conception; male potency; to conceive. *Ua pau ke ko'u,* potency is over. *Ua ko'u ka moa kāne,* the rooster has mounted [a hen]. *Ua moe lāua a i laila ko'u,* they slept together and life came. **3.** poss. My, mine (*o*-form; Gram. 8.4, 9.6). (PNP *toku.*)
ko.'ū. vs. Damp, moist. *Fig.,* thriving, prosperous. **ho'o.ko'ū.** Caus/sim. (PCP *toku(u).*)
kou haole. n. The foreign *kou (Cordia sebestena),* a small tree, related to the *kou,* from which it differs in having stiff, rough, dark-green leaves, brighter red-orange flowers, and white, pulpy, instead of dry, fruits. (Neal 715.)
kou.kā, kouga. n. Cougar. *Eng.*
ko'u.ko'u. Redup. of *ko'u 1.*
ko'ū.ko'ū. 1. Redup. of *ko'ū. Ko'ūko'ū i ka wai a ka naulu,* damp from the water of the showers [drunk]. **2.** *(Cap.)* n. Stroke in *lua* fighting.
kow-, kōw-. Many words are spelled with and without -*w*- after -*o*- or -*ō*-, as *koali* and *kowali, kōelo* and *kōwelo.* In the dictionary the form without -*w*- is preferred unless the *w* is the initial of a base; cf. *wehe, kōwehe; welo, kōwelo;* cf. Gram. 2.1.
kō.wā. 1. nvs. Intervening space or time; channel, canal, strait, gulch; separated, as by a passage or channel. *Ke Kōwā o Pēlina,* Bering Straits. **ho'o.kō.wā.** To separate by a space. **2.** *(Cap.)* n. Star name (no data). (Kuhelani.)
kō wa'a. nv. Line used for towing a canoe, especially for dragging canoe hulls from the forest where they were hollowed out to the shore; to tow or drag a canoe.
kowa'e. Var. spelling of *koa'e,* tropic bird.
kowaha. Var. spelling of *koaha.*
kowa.kowa.ū. Redup. of *kowaū 1, 2.*
kowali. Var. spelling of *koali.*
kowa.ū. n. **1.** Fish eggs. **2.** Testicles.
kō.wō. vi. To go away. *Eng.*
kō.wehe. vi. To billow or flutter out, as a dancer's skirt. Cf. *wehe,* open. *Ua 'ike lihi aku nei au i ka lawe kōwehe a ka pā'ū* (song), I have just glimpsed the fluttering skirt.
kowela, towela. n. Tower. *Eng.* (The common term is *pū'o'a.*) *Ke Kowela o Lākana,* the Tower of London.
kō.welo, koelo. vi. To stream, flutter, wave; to trail behind, as the train of a gown. Cf. *welo 1. Kōwelo 'e'a,* dust streamer. *Kōwelo kō hae Hawai'i* (song), your Hawaiian flag waves.
kō.welo.kā. vi. To trail or drag, as a dress train. Also *kāwelokā.*
kō.welo.welo. Redup. of *kōwelo.*
kō.wī. Same as *kāwī,* to squeeze.
kō.wili. Var. of *kāwili.* Cf. *wili.*
kō.wili.wili. Redup. of *kōwili.*
kowo.wowo. vi. Noisy, as the sea dashing against the cliff. *Rare.*
Kp. Abbreviation used in surveying for *kapua'i,* foot.
Kristiano. Var. spelling of *Kalikiano.*
Kristo. n. Christ. (Gr. *Christos.*)
ku-. Var. of *kū-.*
kū. 1. vs. To stand, stop, halt, anchor, moor; to rise, as dust; to hit, strike, jab; to park, as a car; to alight, as a bird or plane on the ground; to land, as a plane or ship; to stay, remain, exist; to reach, extend, arrive; upright, perpendicular, steep, erect, standing, parked. See ex., *pololei 1. Kū* is used in some idioms in sense of "up, out": *Kū hele pēlā!* Get out! *Kū ā hele!* Go! Go away! *Kū!* Whoa! Stop! Halt! *Kū anahulu ka moku,* the ship anchors every ten days. *Mahea ke ka'a e kū ai?* Where will the car be parked? *Wai kū,* stagnant water. *Kai kū,* quiet sea, especially at mid-tide. *Ua ho'oholo 'ia ke kaula a kū ma'ō,* the rope was let out as far as over there. *E kū iho i ho'ike no'u,* stand as a witness for me. *Kū i ke kui,* pierced by the needle; punctured by a nail [as a tire]. *Kū i ka pōkā,* hit by a bullet. *Kū 'umi lau*

kānaka i ka make, ten four-hundreds of men were struck dead. *Nā kānāwai e kū nei,* existing laws. **ho'o.kū.** To set up, make stand, establish, as a society; to brace a canoe with a paddle while sailing or coasting over waves in order to steer and steady the canoe; to carry on, as a family name (Kanl. 25.7). *Ho'okū ākea,* to make known publicly. (PPN *tu'u.*) **2.** n. Stand, pedestal, base; stem, as of a goblet; frame of a bed, including footboard and headboard; end, as of a rainbow. Cf. *kūmoe.* **3.** vs. In a state of, resembling, like, due to, because of (often followed by *i* or *ā*). *Kū i ka pilikia,* to be in trouble, wrong. *Kū i ke kala,* to forgive. *A waiho kū ā ma'i maoli ihola ia,* he remained very sick. *I kū ka pōloli, eia nō ka 'ai,* when hungry, here's food. *Kū ā kahiko,* as of long ago. *Kū ka hakakā o kēlā po'e,* those people have long been fighting. *Kū nō i ka makuahine,* having the character or appearance of the mother. *Kū loa i ka leo,* exactly like the voice or tune, high fidelity. *Hele ā nui ka i'a, a kū ka hā'awi,* there were so many fish [they] gave [them] away. *Waiho wale mai nō ka limu, a kū ka pilau,* the seaweed lay there until it stunk. **ho'o.kū.** To produce a resemblance, likeness. *Na ia mea i ho'okū ā ma'i ia'u,* that thing made me ill. (PPN *tuu.*) **4.** vi. To appear, show, reveal; to start, go; to achieve; to change into, transform; beginning, appearance; arrival. *E noho ana nō māua a kama'ilio, a kū ana 'o Pele,* we were sitting talking when Pele suddenly appeared. *Ma ia malama e pono a'e ka pi'a kū* (Kep. 95), during this month it is right for the *pi'a* tuber to show above ground. *Nā hana kū i ke aloha,* deeds that show love. *Kū a kanaka a'ela ua mo'o nei,* the *mo'o* changed into a human. *Kū o pōhaku* (For. 4:61), to turn into stone. *Ma ke kū o ia malama e helu ai i ka makahiki hou,* with the coming of this month the new year will be counted in. **5.** vi. To run in schools, as fish; numerous, as octopus in season. *Nānā, he akule kū!* Look, the *akule* school is running! *Kai kū weli,* sea with phosphorescence. **6.** vs, vt. Suitable, proper, O.K., appropriate, fitting; ready, prepared; to fit, as clothes; merit, cause; to deserve. Cf. *kūpono. I kū nō ka hele i ka lako i ke kālā,* it is all right to go when supplied with money. *'E'oe kū ka hāuna lā'au a kāua i kō kāne* (FS 57), our club-thrusting technique is not suitable for your husband. **7.** vt. To rule or reign, as a land. *Ua kū 'o Lili'u i ka moku,* Lili'u is ruler of the land. **8.** vt. To soak, as clothes. **9.** vt. To post, as a bond. *Mea kū pona,* bondsman. **10.** *(Cap.)* n. Name for the third, fourth, fifth, and sixth days of the month, usually called respectively *Kū Kahi, Kū Lua, Kū Kolu, Kū Pau.* **11.** *(Cap.)* n. Ancient Hawaiian god of war. Prayers connected with this major god include *Kū-koli'i, Kū-lawa, Kū-lewalewa, Kū-papa'a, Kū-wā, Kū-wī.* Cf. *waipā.* (For. 6:21.) (PEP *Tuu.*) **12.** vi. To set apart a period for prayers for a special object; to pray for. *E kū ana au nou,* I will be praying for you. **13.** n. Months of pregnancy. *I ka hāpai 'ana a ka walu o ke kū, a laila ki'i i ka lā'au ho'opahe'e,* in the eighth month of pregnancy, get some slimy medicine. **14.** Part. qualifying verbs (Gram. 7.1). Abruptly, rudely, defiantly, unceremoniously, without observance of taboos or niceties, brusque. See *'ai kū, kuke kū. Ho'opuka kū,* to speak plainly, crudely, bluntly, without regard for feelings of others. *Kaha kū* (FS 235), to go anywhere one pleases. *Kā'ili kū,* to snatch away ruthlessly. *'Ako kū i ka pua,* to pick flowers without permission. *Moa'e kū,* strong Moa'e tradewind. **15.** nvi. Stew; to stew. *Eng. Moa kū,* stewed chicken. **16.** See *'ili kūpono.*

kū-. Qualitative and stative prefix. (Gram. 6.3.2.)

kua. 1. nvi. Back, rear, burden, windward; to carry on the back, as a child. See *'ōpe'a kua, paoa 2,* and saying, *pali. (Kua* refers to a husband: cf. *pilikua.) Ma ke kua,* behind. *Kahea kua,* to call from behind one's back. *Huli kua,* to turn the back on, as to insult; back wall of a house. *Pili ke kua me ke alo,* the back touches the front [of a thin person]. *He kua a kānāwai,* a back [guarded by] law [certain chiefs' backs were taboo and

such chiefs might not be approached from behind]. *Ka'ū nui kua makani,* great Ka'ū with windy back. *I kua na'u,* a burden for me [as a request to a dying person, asking for last instructions]. **ho'o.kua.** To persevere in work even when interest and pleasure have gone from it; burdensome. *He hana ho'okua nui,* it's a very burdensome job. (PPN *tu'a.*) **2.** nvt. To hew, chop, chip, hack, dub, strike, cut out; to fell, strike down, as an image (Oihk. 26:30); anvil, as of a blacksmith or for beating tapa; house used for beating tapa. See ex., *'auhau 3.* (PNP *tua.*) **3.** n. Beam, rafter. **4.** n. Yoke of a dress; back of a garment; ox yoke. **5.** n. Poles used in quilt making; the three unsewed quilt layers are placed on one another with the *kua,* poles, rolled into each end; the entirety is set over wooden horses and is stretched taut, so that the sewer may sew the layers together. **6.** Var. of *akua,* god, image, especially after *-a* (cf. *hoa kua*). Cf. also *Ke-ala-ke-kua* (place name), the pathway [of] the images. **7.** n. Midrib, as of pandanus leaf. **8.** n. Third brew from kava. Cf. *mahū, hope.* **9.** also *sua.* n. Sewer. *Eng.*

kua-. 1. Generations back, two (or sometimes today, one) more than the suffixed number; see *kuakahi, kualua, kuakolu, kuahā.* (PPN *tua-.*) **2.** Once, twice, three times, twofold, etc., depending on numeral suffix. *Rare.* **3.** Ridge, mountain. See *kuahiwi, kualapa, kualipi, kualono, kuamauna, kuanihi, kuaola.*

kū ā. vi. To turn into; to be similar to. (In some constructions this sequence is followed by particles or qualifiers and may be considered a verb compound; note *kūākanaka* and *kūāma'i* in Gram. 8.7.2.) See ex., *kū 4.*

kua.'ā. nvs. Severe taboo on approaching a chief from behind; having such a taboo. *Lit.,* flaming back, perhaps so called because infringement of the taboo was punished by death; a person with this taboo might not lend out any garment that had touched his back, or permit anyone to touch his back. Cf. *kuakapu, kualoi, kuapala. He ali'i kua'ā kēlā,* that is a chief with the back taboo.

kua.'a'ā. Var. of *kua'ā.* (Kep. 147.)

kua.'aha. n. Altar or place of worship in a private house. Cf. *ipu kua'aha.*

kua.'āina. nvs. Country (as distinct from the city), countryside; person from the country, rustic, backwoodsman; of the country, countrified, rustic, rural. *Lit.,* back land. **ho'o.kua.'āina.** To act like one from the country; countrified, rustic.

kua.aka. Var. spelling of *kuakā.*

kua.'ala. n. A kind of lichen *(Peltigera polydactyla* var. *dolichorhiza).*

kua.alo. Var. spelling of *kuālo.*

kua.'ana. n. **1.** Term of address for older sibling or cousin of the same sex, or cousin of the same sex of the senior line of a family; also sometimes used to replace the much more common *kaikua'ana* or *kaiku'ana.* (PEP *tuakana.*) **2.** First brewage of liquor; mixtures following are called *pōki'i,* little brother or sister.

kua.'au. n. Basin inside the reef; lagoon. *Kai kua'au o Hā'ena* (FS 237), lagoon sea of Hā'ena.

kua.auna. Var. spelling of *kuāuna.*

kua'e. n. Canoe keel.

kū.'ae'a. vi. To wander, stray. Cf. *'ae'a.*

kua.'ea. n. Same as *nēnē,* a variety of kava. *Lit.,* turtle back.

kua.'eho. n. Tumor. (Kam. 64:109.) Cf. *'eho 2.*

kua.ehu. vs. Silent, still, lonely. *'A'ohe mā'alo kanaka o Ho'okū ano, kuaehu, mehameha i ka wahine* (chant for Pele), no one passes at Ho'okū, awesome, silent, lonely because of the woman.

kū.'aha. Short for *kua'aha.*

kua.hā. 1. vs. Six generations removed. Cf. *kua-, kuakahi, kualua,* etc. **2.** num. Four times, fourfold. *Kaula kuahā,* four-strand rope.

kua.haka. vs. Surging, swelling, as waves. *Ke kai kuahaka o Ko'oko'olau* (chant), the surging sea of Ko'oko'olau.

kua hao. n. Anvil, as used by blacksmiths.

kua.haua. nvi. Proclamation, declaration; to proclaim, announce.

kua.hauli. n. Large *'ō'io,* ladyfish or bonefish.

kua.hea. nvt. Mountain area where trees are stunted as due to altitude.

kua.hele.mai. vs. Awkward.

kū-ā-hele-mai. Var. of *kū-hele-mai,* a gambling game.

kū.ā.hewa. nvs. Huge, vast; name of a farm inland from Kai-lua, Hawai'i, tilled by Ka-mehameha.

kū.ā.hewa.hewa. Redup. of *kūāhewa.*

kua.hilo. Same as *kuawili.*

kua.hilo.hilo. Redup. of *kuahilo.*

kua.hina.hina. vs. Gray-headed. *Moloka'i.*

kua.hine. n. **1.** Term of address for a male's sister or female cousin, sometimes replacing the more common *kaikuahine.* (PPN *tuafafine.*) **2.** (More commonly **Tuahine**). Name of a misty rain famous in Mānoa, O'ahu, named for Kuahine, who turned to rain after the murder of her daughter, Ka-hala-o-Puna; the rain is also in other localities. See ex., *ha'alulu, ha'a-nipo.*

kua.hiwi. n. Mountain, high hill. (PPN *tu'asiwi.*)

kua-honu. n. Name of a quilting design. *Lit.,* turtle back.

kua.honu. Same as *kūhonu,* a crab.

kuahu. n. Altar. *Kuahu 'ia* (FS 223), to be placed on an altar.

kua hua. n. Hunchback. *Lit.,* swollen back.

kū.ā.hua. nvs. Heap, pile; heaped or piled up; rising up, as a whale's back above water. *Lit.,* back heap *(āhua).*

ho'o.kū.ā.hua. Caus/sim.

kua.hui. n. **1.** Supporting rods for house purlins (Kam. 76:98), brace. Also *'aho pi'o kuahui.* **2.** vt. To cooperate, work together. *E kuahui a'e kākou i ka hana,* we are cooperating in the work.

kua.hulu. **1.** Same as *koali kua hulu,* a morning-glory. **2.** nvt. Any wild vegetable eaten in time of famine; to eat such.

kuai. vt. To scour, rub, polish, grind, scrape; to drag a scraping object; to mark a line from which marbles are shot. Cf. *kuakuai.* (PNP *tuai.*)

kua'i. vt. To remove internal organs of animals, disembowel; to clean, as chickens. *Mea kua'i 'i'o holoholona,* butcher. (PNP *tuaki.*)

kū.'ai. vt. To buy, barter. *Lit.,* to stand up food. Cf. *kūkālā. Kū'ai mai,* to buy. *Kū'ai aku,* to sell. *Mea kū'ai mai,* customer. *Kū'ai aku kū'ai mai,* buying and selling, trade. *Kū'ai nui, kū'ai kā'oko'a,* wholesale. *Mea nāna i kū'ai mai,* buyer. *Mea kū'ai,* purchase. *Hale kū'ai,* store. *Waiwai kū'ai,* goods for sale. *Kū'ai ho'opau,* close-out or clearance sale. *Kū'ai ho'ēmi, kū'ai emi,* reduction sale. *Kū'ai ho'ēmi kūikawā,* a special sale. *Kū'ai ho'olilo,* sale. *Kū'ai kūka'a,* wholesale buying. *Kū'ai li'ili'i,* retail buying or selling; *lit.,* little buying, selling. *Kū'ai malū,* to buy secretly, as contraband or as on a black market. *Kū'ai nui,* wholesale buying; *lit.,* big buying. *Po'e kū'ai,* merchants. *Mea kū'ai aku,* for sale. *Kū'ai hele,* to go shopping; to go about buying or selling; shopping. (In older usage directionals were not used with *kū'ai;* in such cases 'bargain' is a good translation.) *Kū'ai hō'ai'ē,* to buy on credit.

kua 'iako. n. Portion of boom *('iako)* lashed to the canoe.

Kua-'ie. n. Name of a star.

Kuai-he-lani. n. A famous legendary place in the high heavens, a home of the deified dead. (HM 78-80.) See ex., *'ehu 1, māpuna hoe.*

kū.'ai ho.'ōla. vt. To ransom. *Lit.,* to bargain to save life.

kū.'ai ho'o.lilo. n. Sale.

kua.'i'i. vt. To flatter, cajole with flattery. **ho'o.kua.'i'i.** Caus/sim.

kuai.kele. vt. To rub back and forth.

kua.ilo. vt. To give up, as a riddle; to be unable to answer; expression used in riddling. The person who can not guess a riddle says: *Kuailo!* I can't guess the answer, you tell me. If the riddler doesn't want to give

the answer, he may reply tartly: *'Eu nō ka ilo, make!* Maggots move! Defeated! *Kuailo 'ana,* answer. *Ā penei ke kuailo 'ana* (Kel. 90), this is the answer.

kū.ā.ilo. vi. To be devoured by worms *(ilo).*

kuaina. n. Twine, string. *Eng.*

kū.ā.'ino. vi. To turn from good to evil; wicked. **ho'o.kū.ā.'ino.** To influence one into bad behavior; evil.

kua.io. n. Border or bank as between taro patches or cultivated fields. Cf. *ioio.*

kua.'i'o. n. A strong brew of kava. Cf. *kua 8.*

-kuā.'i'o. ho'o.kuā.'i'o. Same as *ho'okū'i'o.*

kua.'iole. n. Upper ridgepole of a house above the lower ridgepole *(kauhuhu).*

kuaipa. n. Swipes, home-brew, as made of pineapples, mangoes, molasses, or watermelons. *Slang. Eng.*

kū'ai pohō. vt. To buy or sell at a loss or very cheaply.

kua.iwi. n. **1.** Long, straight, stone wall. *Ni'ihau.* **2.** Same as *kuāuna.*

kuaka. **1.** vs. Faded. **2.** Same as *akakū.* **3.** n. Cord, as of wood. **4.** n. Quart. *Eng.* **5.** n. Quagga *(Eng.),* zebra.

kū.akā. interj. Boom, boom! *'O ka 'ili kalakala, 'ili nākolokolo, kūakā ke kani, he kani kūpaukolo* (For. 6:412), a rough skin [of shark on a drum], a rumbling skin, a boom-boom sound, a rub-a-dub sound.

kua ka'a. **1.** See *lani kua ka'a.* **2.** n. Team (horse or oxen) closest to the pulled vehicle. See *makamua.*

kua.kahi. **1.** vs. Once, singly; first; single, unwedded, unmarried. Cf. *moa kuakahi. I hea 'oe i ka wā kuakahi o ku'u kino?* Where were you while I was single? **2.** vs. Three generations removed, as great-grandparent *(kupuna kuakahi)* and great-grandchild *(mo'opuna kuakahi),* as distinguished from a great-great-grandchild *(mo'opuna kualua)* and a great-great-grandparent *(kupuna kualua).* Sometimes today *kuakahi* denotes two generations removed. **3.** Unobstructed, unhampered, free from interference; straight to the point, without deviation, as a story. *E mihi mua i ka hewa, a wehewehe i nā ho'ohihia i kuakahi ka lā'au,* first repent of wrong doings, free [your mind] of problems, so the medicine will be free to work [common advice of old medical *kāhuna].* **ho'o.kua.kahi.** To remove obstruction, interference; to clear the way, free. **4.** *(Cap.)* n. Far mythical land, a rendezvous of spirits; homeland of the ancestors.

-kuaka'eo. ho'o.kua.ka.'eo. Var. of *ho'ohuake'eo.* (For. 5:561.)

kū.ā.kā.hili. n. One of high birth who stands by a *kāhili* feather standard, beside the high chief, in contrast to the *pa'a kāhili* who carries the *kāhili.*

kū.ā.kai.kai. Same as *kūhākakai. Rare.*

kua.kala. n. Medicine made of *pua kala* plant and taken as treatment for pyorrhea, neuralgia, stomach ulcers.

kūa.kali.kea. **1.** n. Kind of cloth with white on its edges. *Rare.* **2.** vs. Whorish [especially of Hawaiian women having love affairs with white men]. *Lit.,* becoming white vagina.

kua kapa. n. Tapa-beating anvil. **ho'o.kua kapa.** To make such an anvil.

-kūākapa. ho'o.kū.ā.kapa. To form a boundary. *Lit.,* make stand border.

kua.kapu. nvs. Taboo on approaching a chief from behind. *Fig.,* quiet, safe, peaceful, so called because of the protection and security afforded by the taboo. Cf. *kua'ā, kua liholiho, kualoi, kuapala.*

kua.kea. vs. Faded, bleached; white and encrusted, as salt deposits left by evaporated sea water; foamy; pale, as a person without a healthy color; to bleach white, fade; foam. Cf. *kea,* white; *po'o kuakea.* See ex., *hao 4, lōpā. Ke kuakea mai nei kō kuka,* your coat is fading. *Kahe ka wai 'ula, kuakea ka moana,* when the red waters run, the sea is white with foam. **ho'o.kua.kea.** To bleach or whiten. *E aloha a'e ana kēia i ka hau ho'okuakea 'ili* (song), this is a fond recollection of the snow that whitens the skin.

kū ā.kea. vi. To stand openly or in public; to take a public stand.

Kua.keahu. n. Distant legendary place, as the brink of the nether world into which spirits leaped. Also *Leina-a-ke-akua.* (Malo 112, Emerson note 114.)

Kua.ke.ao. Var. of *Kuakeahu. Lit.,* back of the light.

-kuake'eo. hoʻo.kua.ke'eo. Rare var. of *hoʻohua-ke'eo.*

kū.'aki. vs. Impatient, annoyed, irritated. (Nak.108.)

kū.ā.ki'i. vi. To stand with hands on hips or crossed in front, as suggestive of the stance of an image *(ki'i)* considered a sign of rudeness and an indication that one wants to lord it over others, or as a sign that one will not cooperate. *Kā! 'A'ohe kanaka kūāki'i noho wale o kahi o nā ali'i!* Ha! Nobody stands around with hands on hips doing nothing at the residence of the chiefs!

kua.kini. vs. Innumerable.

kū.ā.kino. n. Transformation, as from animal to human form. hoʻo.kū.ā.kino. To change form; transubstantiation.

kua.koko. nvi. Travail of childbirth, especially bearing-down pain; to suffer labor. *Fig.,* uncontrolled anger.

kua.kolu. 1. vs. Five generations removed, of a great-great-great-grandparent or great-great-great-grandchild, as *kupuna kuakolu, mo'opuna kuakolu;* for some speakers, four generations removed. **2.** vs. Thrice, three times. *I ka pō 'ana iho, a hiki i ka moa kuakolu,* after night fell, at the third cock [crowing].

kū.'akū. nvs. Sarcastic; sarcasm.

kua.kua. 1. Redup. of *kua 2.* **2.** n. Strip, especially space between lines of stitching in quilting; embankment between taro patches that was kept under cultivation (Malo 18, Emerson note); leaf midrib; narrow land strip; strip of fish netting; ridged cloth, as corduroy or piqué. ho'o.kua.kua. To heap up, as in banks; to make spaces between lines of stitching in quilting.

kua.kuai. Redup. of *kuai.* Cf. *moena kuakuai kāma'a.*

ku'a.ku'ai. Redup. of *kū'ai;* trade, exchange; for sale; to sell repeatedly; to give for the sake of receiving something in return. ho'o.ku'a.ku'ai. To trade, buy and sell.

kua.kua.kū. n. Newly made taro patch embankment; process of packing the earth for the banks and floor of a taro patch.

kua.kua.lau. Redup. of *kualau,* a shower.

kuā.kuā.nea. Redup. of *kuānea.*

kua.kuku. n. Wooden anvil, as used for beating tapa.

kua kū.pī. n. Abscess on the back.

kuala, kuwala. 1. nvi. Somersault; to fall backwards; to turn over and over or upside down; to fear somersaults; to toss with palm of hand up. *Kuala po'o,* to somersault. See *kūwalawala.* **2.** n. Interest, usury. See *puni kuala. He 'umi kālā ka uku kuala,* the interest was ten dollars. **3.** n. Cooked, unpounded taro (same as *kalo pa'a, nē'ū*). **4.** n. Pure white mother-of-pearl shell, much prized because of its rarity, as used for fishhooks or lures.

kua.lā. n. Dorsal fin.

kuala (kuwala) 'ano hui. n. Compound interest.

kua lā.'au. 1. nv. Hewer of wood, axman, feller of trees; wooden beam, log, anvil; to hew down a tree. **2.** n. Forest. *Rare.*

kuala (kuwala) ho.'ēmi. n. Discount on interest.

kuala (kuwala) ho'o.hui. n. Compound interest.

kuala.kai. 1. n. A sea creature, perhaps *Aplysia dactylomela* or *A. juliana.* **2.** vi. To quiver, quake, as jelly. *Hulihia ka moku, nakeke ka 'āina, kualakai, kūhulukū ka mauna* (old prayer), overturned is the island, trembling the land, quivering and quaking are the mountains. **3.** nvt. Raw fish mashed to a pulp; to be hand-fed this pulp by the *kau* method. **4.** n. Swelling, obesity. *Rare.*

kua.lā lalo. n. Ventral fin, anal fin.

kua.lana. vi. **1.** Lazy, indolent, bored, fatigued; roving about without a chief to support one, as a "floater" *(lana);* to wander. *Lilo 'oukou i ka 'ōlelo haole ā kualana mākou,* since you have all turned to speaking

English, we're bored. *Kualana ka 'ōpū,* very hungry. ho'o.kua.lana. Caus/sim.; to fail in strength. (For. 6:428.) **2.** To float on the back; buoyant.

kua.lana.puhi. n. Officer who watched over a sleeping or resting chief and waved the *kāhili,* feather standard.

kū.ā.lani. vs. Sour, especially of calabashes that have held poi and have not been soaked in the sun after washing.

kua.lapa. 1. n. Ridge. **2.** vi. To stretch out or project, as a cape.

kuala pa'a. Same as *kuala 3.* (FS 61.)

kuala pahi. n. Mumble-the-peg.

kua.pehu. n. Pugilist in the high chief's court, a muscular young man who might also be asked to massage a chiefess or have relations with her.

kua.lau. n. Shower accompanied by sea wind. (UL 258.) See ex., *pāuli. 'Auhea wale 'oe, ē ke kualau, ka ua nū hele ma ka moana* (chant), listen, o *kualau* shower, rain moaning over the open sea.

kū.ā.lau.wili. vi. Repetitious, confusing in talk and writing.

kua.lehe.lehe. nvi. A great talker; to talk verbosely. *Lit.,* lip chopping.

kua.lele. Short for *akua lele.*

kua.lena. vt. To stretch, as tapa to free from wrinkles; taut. *Fig.,* to concentrate the thoughts. *He manawa kēia a kākou e kualena ai i kō kākou mau no'ono'o,* this is the time to concentrate mentally.

kuali. vs. White, glistening, sparkling, shining. ho'o.-kuali. To whiten. Cf. *aliali,* clear.

kuali.ali. Redup. of *kuali.*

kua liho.liho. See *liholiho.*

kua.li'i. n. Dwarfed plant or animal.

kua.li'i.li'i. Same as *kualili'i.*

kua.lili'i. Redup. of *kuali'i;* to abate, slacken, diminish, grow less.

kua.lima. vs. **1.** Seven generations removed. Cf. *kua-, kuakahi, kualua,* etc. **2.** Five times, especially said of medicines given once a day for five days or five successive times morning and evening.

kua.lipi. n. Sharp mountain ridge.

kualo. 1. vt. To block, obstruct, hinder (less used than *ālai*). *He aha lā ho'i kāu i kualo mai nei?* Why are you standing in front of me? **2.** Also **sualo.** n. Swallow. *Eng.*

ku.ālo. n. Anal fin. Cf. *hakualo.*

kualo.hia. 1. Pas/imp. of *kualo.* **2.** n. Reported to be a kind of grass used in thatching.

kua.loi, kua.loi.loi. n. Taboo on approaching a chief from behind (same taboo as *kua'ā, kuakapu, kua liholiho, kuapala*). *Lit.,* critical back.

kū.ā.lole. vs. Faded.

kua.lono. 1. n. Region near the mountaintop, ridge. **2.** vt. To overturn, as an unfinished canoe. *Rare.*

kū.'alu. Same as *'alu.*

kua.lua. vs. **1.** Four generations removed, of a great-great-grandparent or great-great-grandchild, as *kupuna kualua, mo'opuna kualua;* for some speakers, three generations removed. **2.** Twice, second. *Kuakahi, kualua ko'u lohe 'ana, ua hiki mai kahi mokuahi* (song), once, twice I've heard, the steamship's come in.

kū.alu.'ula. n. Red cords used to decorate a chief's canoe. *Rare.*

kua maha. n. Back of the temple of the head.

kū ā maka.lau. vi. Having abundant offspring. *Lit.,* generation of many faces.

kuā.mano. vs. Innumerable.

kuā.mano.mano. Redup. of *kuāmano.* (Kam. 64:49.)

kua.mauna. n. Mountaintop.

kū.'ami.'ami. vi. Motions of turning hinges; motions of sexual intercourse; to turn on hinges.

kua.mo'o. n. **1.** Backbone, spine; road, trail, path (Mar. 1.3); custom, way (Mat. 10.5); canoe keel. Also *iwikuamo'o.* (PCP *tuamoko.*) **2.** Clamps used in making or repairing canoes.

kua.mo'o kaua. n. Main formation of an army. (FS 79.)

kua.mo.ʻo ʻō.le.lo. n. Continuous record, history, story, succession of events.

kua.mū. n. **1.** A variety of taro. Also *kuapapa.* **2.** *(Cap.)* Name of a wind accompanied by heavy rain. (PH 166.) **3.** *(Cap.)* Name of a goddess. **4.** A tapa used in sorcery ceremonies.

kū.amu.amu. vt. To revile, blaspheme, curse, swear, damn, insult; to chant a curse or reviling song. **ho.ʻo.kū.amu.amu.** Caus/sim.

kuana. n. Position, attitude; standing.

kua.naka. n. **1.** A shellfish, something like the *kuapoʻi.* **2.** Abscess in the back. **3.** Hard coral used for polishing. **4.** Ti-leaf sandals.

kuana.lio, kuana.lia. vt. Northern heavens and its stars. *Me ka liʻa lā i kuanalia, i kuanalipo ka newa ʻana* (chant), desire in the northern skies, dizzy in the southern skies.

kuana.lipo. Same as *kauana Lipo.*

kua nalu. n. Surf just before it breaks, wave crest (GP 8) (sometimes used without article).

kuā.nea. 1. vs. Lonely, forsaken, barren, desolate, dreary. *Fig.,* awkward, unintelligent, ignorant. Cf. *kuākuānea, nea, ʻōnea.* **ho.ʻo.kuā.nea.** To make lonely, barren. *Fig.,* to behave ignorantly; to cause boredom, dreariness; boring. *He hana hoʻokuānea,* a boring act. **2.** *(Cap.)* Star name (no data). (Kuhelani.)

kua.nihi. n. Steep ridge.

kua.niki, kuaniti. n. Quantity. *Eng.*

kū.ʻā.no.ʻa. vs. Parched.

kū.ano.ano. vs. Highly respected. (Malo text, chapter 16, section 15.)

kuā.noni. vi. To change, as color.

kua.no.ʻo. vs. Thoughtful, meditative, comprehending. **ho.ʻo.kua.no.ʻo.** To meditate, think deeply.

ku.ā.nue.nue. n. Boom connecting canoe hulls of a double outrigger.

kua.nui, ho.ʻo.kua.nui. To do a thing grudgingly; bored with a tedious task; tedious, boring; to struggle with a task, as one in which one has no interest.

Kua-nunu. n. Stroke in *lua* fighting.

kua.nu.ʻu. n. Kauaʻi name for *māono,* a basalt.

kua.ō.ʻa. vt. To fit in place. *Kuaōʻa ʻia nā ʻiako o ua waʻa nei,* the outrigger booms of this canoe were fitted in place.

kū.ʻao.ʻao. n. Attendant or witness at a wedding. *Lit.,* standing [at the] side. *Kūʻaoʻao o ke kāne,* best man. *Kūʻaoʻao o ka wahine,* bridesmaid, maid of honor.

kua.ola. n. Verdant mountain, where all thrives and grows. *E ō ē ka leo o ka ʻōʻū kani kuaola,* call in answer, voice of the honey creeper of the verdant mountain.

kua.pā. 1. vs. Dashing, slashing, as waves on a shore. **2.** n. Wall of a fish pond. *Loko kuapā,* fish pond made by building a wall on a reef.

kua.pa.ʻa. 1. nvs. Slave, bond servant; hard labor; oppressed, enslaved; slavish, back-breaking, servile, downtrodden. *Hana kauwā kuapaʻa,* slave labor. **ho.ʻo.kua.pa.ʻa.** To enslave, oppress. **2.** n. The chiton *(Acanthochiton viridis),* a small sea creature used in the *māwaewae* ceremony for babies. **3.** n. A variety of destructive caterpillar. **4.** vs. Parched and dried, as breadfruit. *Rare.*

kua.pala. n. **1.** A taboo chief who had the right to carry a *pala* fern in ceremonies. Cf. *kuaʻā, kuakapu, kualoi.* **2.** Sacrificial or offering stand for fruit. **3.** An inedible moss applied to sores (no data). **4.** Rare var. of *kākū,* barracuda. *Molokaʻi.*

kua.papa. 1. nvt. Heap, pile; to heap or pile up; heaped up; numerous. *He ʻohana ʻaiʻē nui kēia, ua hele a kuapapa nui ka ʻaiʻē,* a family with great debts, the debts are piled up. **2.** nvs. Peace, quiet, tranquillity; union under a single ruler; peace following a treaty, armistice; peaceful, secure (usually followed by *nui*). *A ʻo ka hope o ka maikaʻi, he kuapapa nui mau loa . . . e noho nō koʻu poʻe kānaka ma nā wahi kuapapa nui* (Isa. 32.17–18), and the effect of righteousness is quiet-

ness and assurance forever . . . and my people shall dwell in peaceful places. **3.** Same as *kuamū 1.* **4.** vs. Ancient, oldest. *Kauaʻi kuapapa,* Kauaʻi the oldest.

kua papa. v. To hew boards or planks; to hew out a poi-pounding board.

kua.papa lo.ʻi. n. Group of taro patches.

kua pipi. n. Ox yoke.

kuapo. 1. nvt. Belt; to put on a belt. Cf. *ʻili kuapo.* **2.** vt. To swap, exchange, trade. *Eng.*

kua.po.ʻi. 1. n. Weatherboard covering canoe top fore and aft. **2.** n. Shell on back of crab or turtle. **3.** Kneepan, patella; bone in arm or hand. **4.** vs. Full-fledged, feathered out. **5.** n. A sea mollusk, *Umbraculum sinicum.*

kua.po.ʻi.maka. n. Eyelid.

kua.pola. n. Taboo night proclaimed in month of ʻIkuwā during the *makahiki* festivals.

kua.pō.la.ʻo. n. Small tribute to a high chief. **ho.ʻo.kua.- pō.la.ʻo.** To assemble tribute for a high chief.

kuapo ʻō.pū. n. Belt.

kuapo pahu. n. Hoop.

kua.pu.ʻe. 1. n. Rage, fury, resentment. *E noho ana ke kuapuʻe i loko,* rage sits within. **2.** Deep-sea fishing grounds. (Kam. 76:78.)

kua puhi. n. Abscess on the back.

kuapu.iwi. n. Native land, homeland (same as *kulāiwi*).

kua.pu.ʻu. 1. nvs. Hunchback; hunchbacked; hump, as of a camel. See ex., *hahaʻi lua. He kuapuʻu nō ā he kuapuʻu, like ka ʻōlelo ʻana,* a hunchback and a hunchback, the same talk [equals speak the same language]. **ho.ʻo.kua.pu.ʻu.** Caus/sim. (PNP *tuʻapuku.*) **2.** n. Valve, as of clams.

kū.au. n. **1.** An endemic fern *(Asplenium kaulfussii)* with oblong fronds about 60 cm. long, with twelve or more pairs of narrow, pointed pinnae. **2.** A sea creature (perhaps *Aplysia* sp.).

kū.ʻau. n. Handle, stem, stalk, shaft, stick or mallet used in beating; shank limb of a fishhook. *Ka wai kūʻau hoe a ka lawaiʻa,* the water of the paddle handle of the fisherman [a famous trickling water on the cliffs along the Nā-pali coast, Kauaʻi; thirsty fishermen stuck the paddle handles into the cliff and let the water trickle down into their mouths]. See *Wai-kū ʻau-hoe,* Pukui, Elbert, and Mookini, 1974.

kuā.ua. nvi. Shower; to shower. *He ʻaloʻalo kuāua no kuahiwi,* facing the mountain showers [said of a brave person].

kuā.ua hope. n. Latter rain, spring rains. (Ioba 29.23.)

kū.ʻau.ʻau. vi. To tread water. *Lit.,* stand bathe.

kuau.hā. nvt. Advice, counsel; advised. *E kali ana au ā kuauhā ʻia mai,* I'm waiting to be advised.

kū.ʻau.hau. nvi. Genealogy, pedigree, lineage, old traditions; genealogist, historian; to recite genealogy.

kū.auʻi. According to Emerson (UL 95), same as *lūauʻi.*

kū.ʻau kui kele. n. Needle clamp on a sewing machine. *Lit.,* large needle shaft.

kua.ʻula. n. Ribbed or grooved tapa, as made with a grooved board.

kua.uli. n. Verdant countryside. *Lit.,* green back. *Hawaiʻi kuauli,* Hawaiʻi with its verdant country [poetic].

kū.ʻau lima. n. Arm below the elbow.

kū.ā.una, kuaauna. n. Bank or border of a taro patch; stream bank.

kū.ʻau.pa.ʻa. n. Bundle, as of *pololū* spears.

kū.ʻau wā.wae. n. Leg; shinbone. *Rare.*

kū.ʻau wili. n. Crank. *Lit.,* turning handle.

kuawa. n. **1.** Valley *(awaawa).* Used poetically, as follows: *Wai-luku i ka malu he kuawa,* Wai-luku in the shelter of the valley. Cf. *awaawa.* **2.** Guava *(Psidium guajava),* a low tree, native to tropical America, naturalized in Hawaiʻi; it bears lemon-sized fruits which are commonly made into jelly, jam, juice and sherbet. Hawaiians make a medicinal tea from leaf buds, which has an astringent effect. (Neal 632–3.) *Eng.*

ku.ʻā.wa.ʻa.wa.ʻa. vs. Hilly; filled with gullies.

kuawa keʻo.keʻo. n. A form of guava with white pulp *(Psidium guajava),* but otherwise like *kuawa lemi.* (Neal 632–3.)

kuawa lemi. n. Lemon guava *(Psidium guajava),* a form of guava with sour, pink pulp. *Lit.,* lemon guava. (Neal 632.)

kuawa momona. n. A form of guava *(Psidium guajava)* with sweet, pink pulp, thicker skin, and larger seeds than *kuawa lemi. Lit.,* sweet guava. (Neal 632.)

kua-wā.wae-nohu. n. A shrub in the carnation family *(Schiedea lychnoides),* endemic to Kauaʻi; leaves broad-ovate, 4 to 5 cm long, flowers many and small; said to be named for a place on Kauaʻi.

kua.wehi. n. **1.** Dark caterpillar resembling the *poko,* cutworm, about 5 cm or less in length; it feeds on grass and comes in great numbers. **2.** Overexposure to the sun; excessive ultraviolet rays.

kua.weli. vs. Dark in color. (Kam. 64:112.)

kua.wili. nvt. Long repetitious prayer said at *luakini* dedication ceremonies, hence repetitiousness in general; to repeat, wander, digress, perhaps senselessly. *Ā i ka pule ʻana, mai kuawili wale aku ʻoukou i ka ʻōlelo* (Mat. 6.7), but when ye pray, use not vain repetitions.

kue 1. interj. Call to attract *ʻuaʻu,* petrel birds, believed in imitation of their sound. **2.** n. Fishhook with point of hook curved inward almost to the shaft, used for large fish.

kuʻe. 1. vi. To push with the elbows, to elbow; to move back and forth, as a piston or as the action of the tide. Cf. *haʻakuʻe.* (PEP *tuke.*) **2.** vs. Deformed, malformed.

kū.ʻē. nvt. To oppose, resist, protest; opposite, versus, adverse, contrary, antagonistic, unwilling; objection. *Lit.,* stand different. *He manaʻo kūʻē,* an opposite meaning. *Kūʻē kānāwai,* unlawful, contrary to law, illegal, against the law. *Kūʻē aupuni,* opposed or disloyal to the government, rebel. *Hana kūʻē,* violation, opposition. *Mea kūʻē,* adversary, opponent. *Kūʻē i ka palapala kauoha,* to contest a will. *Kūʻē i kō haʻi manaʻo,* to oppose others' views; intolerant. *Nā kāhuna kūʻē i ka Pope,* ministers opposed to the Pope, Protestant ministers. *Kūʻē kumukānāwai,* unconstitutional. **hoʻo.kū.ʻē.** To cause opposition, to stir up resistance; to oppose, clash.

kuea. 1. n. Square. *Eng. Kamaki Kuea,* Thomas Square. *Kapuaʻi kuea,* square foot. **2.** vt. To swear. *Eng. ʻŌlelo kuea,* oath. **3.** n. Squad (military). *Eng.*

Kū.ea. n. Star name (no data). (Kuhelani.)

kū.ʻē.ʻē. 1. Redup. of *kūʻē;* disagreement, dissension, opposition, quarrel, bickering, animosity; to quarrel, bicker, disagree. **hoʻo.kū.ʻē.ʻē.** To stir up opposition or disagreement. **2.** n. Double canoe with one canoe longer than the other. (Malo 131.)

kuehu, kuwehu. vt. To shake, stir up, as dust; to knock a club from a foe's hands; to toss up, as spray; to brandish, wave; to clear or weeds; to drive off, especially evil spirits (tapa or ti leaves were torn into strips, blessed, and passed over a patient in order to exorcise spirits). Cf. *ehu,* spray. See *Kuehu Lepo. ʻO ka pali o Kīkī-ʻōpua i Hoʻomalele, e lele ana nā momoku kuehu pali* (For. 6:472), at the cliffs of Kīkī-ʻōpua at Hoʻomalele, firebrands leap spraying over cliffs.

kū.ehu.ehu. Redup. of *kuehu.*

Kuehu Kai. n. Name of a wind of Milo-liʻi, Kauaʻi. (For. 5:95.)

kuehu kapa. v. To shake a tapa in a way that seems innocent but that will bring a curse upon the person to whom the motion is directed. (Kam. 64:141.)

Kuehu Lepo. n. Name of a wind of Nā-ā-lehu, Kaʻū (For. 5:93) and Oʻahu (Nak. 56). *Lit.,* dust scatterer. *ʻO Kaʻū i ka makani, ka makani Kuehu Lepo* (song), Kaʻū in the wind, the dust-raising wind.

kueka. n. **1.** Sweater. *Eng.* **2.** *(Cap.)* Quaker. *Eng.*

kue.kaʻa. vt. To ransack, search. *Pau ka ukana i ke kuekaʻa ʻia,* the luggage was all ransacked.

Kue.kena, Suedena. nvs. Sweden; Swede; Swedish. *Eng.*

kue.kue. nvt. Sound of tapping, tap, as of a mallet on a tapa anvil; to tap-tap. *Kani kuekue a ka iʻe kuku,* thumping of the tapa mallet.

kuʻe.kuʻe. n. Elbow, wristbone, joint, knuckle. Cf. *kuʻekuʻe lima, kuʻekuʻe wāwae.* **hoʻo.kuʻe.kuʻe.** To elbow, push with the elbows. (PEP *tuketuke.*)

kū.ʻē.kū.ʻē. Same as *kūʻēʻē.*

kue.kuehu. Redup. of *kuehu.*

kuʻe.kuʻe lima. n. Elbow.

kuʻe.kuʻe.maka. n. Eyebrow. **hoʻo.kuʻe.kuʻe.maka.** To frown. *Hoʻokuʻekuʻemaka nui,* to frown severely, scowl.

kuʻe.kuʻena. vi. To push aside; to move back and forth, as a fan belt.

kue.kuene. Redup. of *kuene.* **hoʻo.kue.kuene.** Caus/sim. *Rare.*

kue.kueni. vi, vt. To shake, tremble, vibrate, swing back and forth, as a waving *kāhili,* feather emblem.

kue.kueʻo. vi. Able to move only slightly, as one hurt in an accident or as one near death.

kuʻe.kuʻe pipi. n. Beef joint or knuckle; soupbone.

kuʻe.kuʻe wā.wae. n. Ankle joint, heel.

kū.ʻele.kā. vi. Shiftless; to vagabond. *Rare.*

kuʻe lima. n. Elbow.

kuelo, kuwelo. n. Hard, cooked taro. Also *kūpuʻu.*

kuʻe.maka. n. Eyebrow. See ex., *nunu 2,* and saying, *ʻeaʻea.* **hoʻo.kuʻe.maka.** To frown, scowl. (PCP *tukemata.*)

kuʻe.maka pali. n. Brow of a cliff.

kue manu. v. To attract *ʻuaʻu,* petrel birds, to a net by imitating their call, *kue, kue, kue!*

kuemi. vi. To step back; to walk backward, as from the presence of a chief; to retreat; to shrink back, recoil, flinch, withdraw.

kū.ʻena. vs. Glowing, burning.

kuene. nvt. Waiter, steward, treasurer; to wait on table; to supervise, put in order, arrange; to lay out, as measurements for a building. *Kuene poʻo,* head waiter. *Kuene hale,* knowledge of house building, one skilled in house building; house waiter. *E kuene pono ai no kona kūlana* (GP 66), to keep up his reputation. *E kuene pono iho ana lā, i paʻa pono ke kaula waha* (chant for Queen Emma), all was fitted perfectly, so that the reins could be firmly held. **hoʻo.kuene.** Caus/sim.; all meanings. (Perhaps PCP *tuen(e,i):* cf. Marquesan *tueni,* servant.)

kuene kāne. n. Waiter.

kuene wahine. n. Waitress, stewardess.

kuene.nuʻu. vs. Completely stuffed, packed, as after overeating. *E ʻai aku i ka ʻulu a kuenenuʻu ka māʻona,* eat breadfruit until stuffed full, satiated.

kueni. Same as *kuekueni.*

kueʻo. nvi. Insecure, unsteady, unskilled. *Kū wale ana i ka hoka, kueʻo wale ana i ka mauna* (For. 6:376), in a state of being thwarted, insecure on the mountain. *Nā loea ame nā kueʻo,* the skilled and the unskilled.

kū.e.ʻo.eʻo. Redup. of *kueʻo.*

kuewa. nvi. Vagabond, exile, wanderer; wandering, friendless, homeless, unstable. *E lilo hoʻi ʻoe i kanaka ʻaeʻa a me ke kuewa wale maluna o ka honua* (Kin. 4.12), a fugitive and vagabond shalt thou be in the earth. **hoʻo.kuewa.** Caus/sim.

kū.ʻewa. vs. Askew, placed obliquely.

kuha. nvi. Saliva, spittle, sputum, expectoration; to spit, expectorate. (Ioane 9.6.) *Pakī ke kuha,* the saliva spatters [said of one who raves and rants, or spits constantly]. (PCP *tufa.*)

kū.haʻa.liki. vt. To brag, boast.

kuha.ʻeka. vs. Shabby, dirty.

kuhā.iki. vs. Narrow; in straitened circumstances.

kū.haka. vs. Of high position, as one possessed by the gods. *Lit.,* stand perch. *Kūlana kūhaka,* manner of one in high position.

kuha.hā.kakai. vs. Swollen, fat. *Rare.*

kuha.kuha. Redup. of *kuha.* (PCP *tufatufa.*)

kū.hala.hala. vt. To find fault with, criticize; dissatisfied. Also *hoʻohalahala.*

kū.hala.kai. Same as *kualakai.*
kū.hala.kau. n. Aerial tubers of *uhi,* yam, *hoi,* and related plants.
kū.haluka. vs. Many, numerous, as of a crowd; crowded, huddled together. Cf. *'aluka,* crowd. *Kūhaluka nā hale o kēia wahi,* the houses in this place are crowded close together.
kū.hana. n. Each of two gable posts in the old Hawaiian house.
kū.hana 'ole. nvs. Lazy, indolent, do-nothing. *Lit.,* condition of doing nothing. *Ma'a wale i ke kūhana 'ole,* just used to indolence.
kū.hanu. n. A mat motif consisting of red bands internally enhanced with a continuous row of white lozenges.
kū.ha'o. vs. Standing alone, independent. *Fig.,* unusual, extraordinary, as rain from a clear sky. *Nani wale 'o Mauna Kea, kuahiwi kūha'o i ka mālie* (song), beautiful is Mauna Kea, standing alone in the calm.
kū.hapa. vs. Resembling partially; of varying or unmatched size or appearance. *Lit.,* partly fit. *Ua kūhapa i ka makua kāne,* resembling somewhat the father.
kū.hapa.hapa. Redup. of *kūhapa.*
kū.hau. vs. Weak, tottering, feeble.
kū.ha'u. vi. To harangue, talk on and on urging a point but not saying much. Cf. *ha'u,* to puff.
kuhaua. Short for *kuahaua,* proclamation.
kū.hau.hau. Redup. of *kūhau.*
kū.ha'u.ha'u. Redup. of *kūha'u.*
kuhau.lua. n. Children of a high chief by a secondary wife or of second degree collaterality.
kuhe. 1. Same as *'ōkuhe,* a variety of *'o'opu,* a fish. **2.** vi. Of changed color, as of a bonito that is caught; black-and-blue, as after a bruise.
kū.hea. Var. of *kāhea,* to call.
kū.hea manu. nv. Bird imitator; fowler (Sol. 6.5).
kū.hē.kili. Same as *laukahi,* a weed.
kuhe.kuhe. Redup. of *kuhe 1, 2.*
kū.hela. 1. nvi. An unbroken swell of the sea, drifting in without breaking; to sweep along as the sea. **2.** n. Game played with sharp *'ūlei* sticks.
kū.hela.hela. vs. Weak, feeble. *Kūhelahela nā maka,* sickly weak eyes.
kū hele. vi. To get up and go. *Kū hele pēlā!* Get out! Get going! *Kū ā hele loa,* to go far without prospect of returning [as an exclamation: get out and don't come back!].
kū-hele-mai. n. Name of a gambling game.
kū.hepa. Same as *hepa,* moronic.
kū.hepa.hepa. Redup. of *kūhepa.*
kū.hewa. nvi. Sudden attack, stroke, as of heart failure; apoplexy; sudden wind gust; suddenly attacked by a stroke; hit without warning or in error; to strike. *Maka'u kūhewa,* sudden fear, panic. *Pilikia kūhewa,* sudden trouble, emergency.
kuhi. 1. nvt. To point, gesture, as in speaking, directing an orchestra, or dancing the hula; gesture, pointing. *Hula kuhi lima,* sitting dance with gestures of hands and swaying of torso. *Ka i'a kuhi lima o 'Ewa,* the gesturing sea creature of 'Ewa [the pearl oyster; it was taboo to talk while gathering them]. **ho'o.kuhi.** To teach the art of gesturing in the hula; to point, etc. (PPN *tusi.*) **2.** vi. To suppose, think, infer, presume, assume, expect, surmise, imagine. *He kuhi wale* (For. 6:523), a supposition. **ho'o.kuhi.** Caus/sim. *Rare.*
kuhia. Pas/imp. of *kuhi 1, 2.*
kuhi-'ai-ka-mo'o-wahie. n. An endemic lobelia *(Lobelia hypoleuca),* 60 to 120 cm high, with narrow, white-backed leaves 30 to 45 cm long, and bluish flowers in racemes. (Neal 815–6.) Also *liua, mo'owahie.*
kuhi 'alaea. nv. Certain priests of Lono who marked land boundaries with *'alaea* coloring; to mark thus.
kuhi 'ano. v. To explain a meaning. *E kuhi 'ano mai 'oe i kēia hua 'ōlelo,* explain the meaning of this word.
kuhi hewa. nvt. To suppose wrongly, err in judgment, give wrong directions; to mistake a person for someone else; erroneous supposition, illusion. See ex., *la'ahia.*

Mana'o kuhi hewa, delusion. *E ho'ā'o nō i pau kuhi hewa,* try to get rid of illusions.
kū.hihi. vt. To censure, condemn, especially of innocent persons; to involve, entangle, embroil. Cf. *hihia.*
kuhi.kau. vt. To point out, direct. *Ke kuhikau wale lā nā lima i ka hā'awi i ka hale makamaka,* the hand points out where to take the gifts to the house of friends.
kuhi.ke'e. vt. Blundering, off one's course; to give wrong directions.
kuhi.kuhi. 1. Redup. of *kuhi;* to show, demonstrate, designate, prescribe, teach, give orders; to direct heiau ceremonies; one always giving orders (Kep. 105); reference, direction, prescription, exponent; bossy. See *kuhikuhi hewa. Kuhikuhi o ka manawa,* time designation, chronology. *Kuhikuhi pono 'ia,* pointed out exactly and specifically. *Kuhikuhi i ka 'ao'ao,* page reference. *Nā kuhikuhi pono,* specifications. *Papa kuhikuhi,* index, contents, program. *Papa kuhikuhi uku,* salary schedule. *Palapala kuhikuhi,* chart. *Paniinoa kuhikuhi,* demonstrative pronoun. *Kuhikuhi i ke ke'a,* to make the sign of the cross. **ho'o.kuhi.kuhi.** Caus/sim. *Rare.* (PPN *tusitusi.*) **2.** vs. Sweet, tasty, fat. (PCP *tu(f,s)i.*)
kuhi.kuhi hana. n. Work program.
kuhi.kuhi hewa. Redup. of *kuhi hewa;* to misdirect, misinform.
kuhi.kuhina. n. Directing, pointing out, gesturing, reference, instruction, program, director. *Ma'ane'i ka maka, ma'ō ke kuhikuhina,* looking this way and gesturing that way. *Kuhikuhina a'o Hawai'i,* program of Hawaiian studies.
kuhi.kuhi.nia. Redup. of *kuhinia.*
kuhi.kuhi.pu'u.one. n. Seer, soothsayer, necromancer, especially a class of priests who advised concerning building and locating of temples, homes, fish ponds, hence a professional architect. *Lit.,* point out the sand dunes.
kuhi.lani. 1. nv. To point out and interpret signs in the sky; a reader of signs in the sky. **2.** vt. To keep others doing one's bidding, lord it over others, domineer, bossy.
kū.hili. 1. vt. To stain or dye by soaking in water containing mashed bark, as nets or mulberry bark before it is pounded into tapa. Cf. *hili,* bark dye. **2.** vi. To blunder. Cf. *na'au kūhili.*
kū.hilo. nvi. To wander about aimlessly; senseless digression.
kuhina. n. Minister, premier, regent, ambassador, secretary, diplomat, cabinet member; officer next to the king; officer in the king's guard (2 Sam. 23.23). Cf. *kuhi, 'aha kuhina, loio kuhina.* (Probably PNP *tusinga.*)
kuhina a'o pala.pala. n. Minister of (public) instruction.
kuhina hale leka. n. Postmaster general.
kuhina kā.lai 'āina. n. Minister of interior, in the days of the monarchy; secretary of interior.
kuhina kaua. Minister or secretary of war.
kuhina moku.'āina. n. Secretary of state.
kuhina noho. n. Minister resident.
kuhina nui. n. Powerful officer in the days of the monarchy. Ka-'ahu-manu was the first to have this title; the position is usually translated as "prime minister" or "premier," but according to Kuykendall (see Bibliography), carried greater power; the *kuhina nui* shared executive power with the king. The office was abolished in 1864.
kuhina o nā 'āina 'ē. n. Minister of foreign affairs.
kuhina wai.wai. n. Minister of finances.
kuhi.nia. vs. Fat, rich, satiated with rich or fatty food. (See *kuhikuhi 2* and *-nia;* Gram. 6.6.3.) *E 'ai iho 'oe ā kuhinia,* eat until satisfied with rich food.
kū.hinu. nvt. Greasy, oily, polished; to rub with oil, polish, grease; a name applied to women (except *kāhuna*) because they were not permitted to make offerings to the gods with their hands (Kep. 23).
kū.hipa. Var. of *kūhepa.*

kū.hipa.hipa. Redup. of *kūhipa;* to mutter indistinctly; unintelligible gibberish.

kū.hiwa. nvi. Special taboo made by a chief; to be subject to this taboo.

kuhō. nvi. To plop, splash, as a stone dropping into water, or as a leaping fish; sound of a deep cough. *Ke kuhō ʻana o ke kai* (Nak. 102), the splashing of the sea.

kū.hoe. n. Quartermaster of ship.

kū.hō.hō. nvs. Deep ravine; deep.

kū.hohonu. Same as *hohonu.*

kuhō.kuhō. Redup. of *kuhō.*

kū.honu. n. An edible spotted-back crab *(Portunus sanguinolentus). Lit.,* turtle back. Also *pāpaʻi kūhonu.*

kū.honua. 1. vi. Suddenly struck, as by disease. **2.** n. See *maile kūhonua.*

kū hou. vi. To rise again, recover from illness, resurrect. *Kū hou ʻana,* resurrection, recovery.

kū.hou poʻo. v. To dive headfirst.

kuhua. vi. To thicken, as scrambled eggs; to become pasty; to gel.

kuhue. Var. of *kuhua.* Cf. *lepo kuhue.*

kuhu.hua. Redup. of *kuhua.*

kuhu.kukū. n. Dove, turtledove (Kin. 15.9); cooing of a dove. *Ke leo o ke kuhukukū* (Mel. 2.12), the voice of the turtle.

kū.hulu.kū. n. Goose flesh, as from chill; quaking, as during an earthquake; agitated, disturbed. See prayer, *kualakai.*

kui. 1. vt. To string pierced objects, as flowers in a lei, or fish; to thread, as beads. Cf. *kui lima.* (PPN *tui.*) **2.** nvt. Needle, pin, spike, nail, screw, any pointed instrument of wood or metal; to sting. *Ē ka make, ai mahea kou kui?* O death, where is thy sting?

kuʻi. 1. vt. To pound, punch, strike, box, hit, hammer; to beat out, as metals; to churn, as butter; to boom or clap, as thunder; to smite, injure; to jar; to prod, as *ʻopihi* shells from rocks with a knife, formerly with sharp stones; to clash (as sound). See *hula kuʻi Molokaʻi.* *Piha kuʻi ka hale,* the house is jammed full. *Kuʻi palu,* to pound, as bait [to give a threshing]. With a fronted *n*-word, for emphasis, *kuʻi* is used as a stative: *ʻA ʻole naʻu ʻoe ā kuʻi, na kēlā wahi keiki . . . , nāna ʻoe e kuʻi* (Laie 387), I won't fight you, that little boy . . . will fight you. **hoʻo.kuʻi.** To hit, pound, collide, crash, bump. *Fig.,* to hurt the felings. *Hālāwai hoʻokuʻi,* collision; to collide. *Hoʻokuʻi i ka manamana,* stub the toe. (PPN *tuki.*) **2.** nvt. To join, stitch, sew, splice, unite; joined; seam. See *niho kuʻi.* *Hula kuʻi,* any interpretive hula, so called since the days of Ka-lā-kaua; *lit.,* joined hula, i.e., old and new steps were joined together. *Nā lā kuʻi o ke kapu akua,* days of godly taboo; *lit.,* days joined. *Aliʻi kuʻi,* the power behind the throne, the one who really holds the reins [often used in a derogatory way]. *E kuʻi ka māmā ā loaʻa ʻo Kaʻohele,* combine speeds and get Kaʻohele [a famous runner, Kaʻohele, could be caught only by relay runners; said of any cooperation]. **hoʻo.kuʻi.(a)** To join, connect, annex, weld, unite; to connect, as letters in forming a word; to spell; to dovetail, fit, splice; to add up, as numbers. *ʻAmi hoʻokuʻi,* joint. *Hoʻokuʻi nei kou alelo i ka hoʻopunipuni* (Hal. 50.19), thy tongue frameth deceit. **(b)** Zenith. *Mai ka hoʻokuʻi ā ka hālāwai,* from zenith to horizon. **3.** vs. Artificial. *Lauoho kuʻi,* wig or switch. *Niho kuʻi,* false teeth. *Wāwae kuʻi,* artificial leg. **4.** n. Back tooth, molar, tusk. **5.** vi. To disseminate news; to spread, as news. *Kuʻi ka lono i Pelekane,* the news spread to England. (PCP *tuki.*) **6.** n. Elbow of pipe. **7.** vs. Sheer, steep, tall. *Kuʻu kaikuaʻana o ka pali hiʻi, pali kuʻi o Ka-liu-waʻa* (chant by Kama-puaʻa), my older brother of the sheer cliff, steep cliffs of Ka-liu-waʻa. **8.** n. Move in the *kōnane* game. See For. 4:57.

kuʻia. 1. Pas/imp. of *kuʻi 1;* to meet an obstacle, stumble; to waver or be unsettled mentally; hit, hindered; attack, sudden blow (*loaʻa*-type word; Gram. 4.4).

Fig., disturbed or hurt mentally. Cf. *haʻakuʻia. He aha kō mea hele ʻole e kōkua iā lākou? ʻA ʻole, ua kuʻia au iā lākou!* Why don't you go and help them? No, they've hurt my feelings. *Ua kuʻia kona manaʻo no ka hilahila i kāna uku ʻole* (FS 103), his feelings are wounded from shame at having no pay. *Ke ʻole e kuʻia,* if there's no stumbling [i.e., if nothing prevents]. *Loaʻa kekahi kuʻia iāia,* he received a shock. **hoʻo.kuʻia.** Same as above; checks and balances, as in government. (PPN *tukia.*) **2.** n. Sharp, pointed stick, dagger, spear.

kuʻi ʻai. nv. To pound food, especially poi; one who pounds food, as poi.

Kūʻia-kā.naka-hele-o-ka-pō. n. A stroke in *lua* fighting. *Lit.,* people traveling at night are hindered.

Kuʻi-a-lua. n. God of trainees in *lua* fighting.

kuʻi a lua. nvi. Art of *lua* fighting; to fight thus.

Kuʻi-a-manini. n. Name of a wind of Weliweli, Kauaʻi. (For. 5:97.)

kuʻi.au.moe. n. Privileged and trusted persons in a chief's retinue. *Lit.,* join [at] late night.

kui.ʻē.ʻē. vt. To carry under the arm; to escort arm in arm. *Lit.,* string armpit.

kui hao. n. Nail, iron spike.

kuʻi hao. nv. To pound and shape iron; to forge; blacksmith.

kuʻi.hē. vs. Hesitating, uncertain, undecided, wavering; hurt in feelings.

kuʻi hekili. n. Peal of thunder, thunderclap.

kū iho.iho. n. Candlestick.

kui hou.hou. n. Awl, gimlet. *Lit.,* piercing sharp instrument.

kui hou lā.ʻau. n. Hypodermic needle.

kui humu.humu. n. Needle.

Kui-ʻilima. n. Name of a Honolulu rain.

kui iwi. n. Bone awl.

kuʻi.kā. vt. To pound smooth.

kuʻi.ka.ʻa. 1. vt. To swing and hit, as with a war club [this is the name of the club of the legendary hero, Ka-welo]. (FS 65.) See ex., *kāpukupuku.* **2.** To join together, splice.

kuʻi.kahi. nvs. Treaty, covenant, agreement, league, feeling of unity; united, unified; to agree. *Kuʻikahi like,* agreement, peace (Hoik. 6.4). *He mea anei ia e kuʻikahi ai?* Is it something to lead to peace or agreement? **hoʻo.kuʻi.kahi.** To unite, reconcile, agree, make a peace treaty or armistice; armistice. *Lā Hoʻokuʻikahi,* Armistice Day.

Kuʻi.kahi-a-Mē.hē.ʻula. n. Stroke in *lua* fighting. *Lit.,* Mēhēʻula's single blow.

Kuʻi.kahi Pā.na.ʻi Like. n. Reciprocity Treaty, by which Pearl Harbor was given to the United States as a coaling station. *Lit.,* treaty equal reciprocity.

kui kai.apa. n. Safety pin. *Lit.,* diaper pin.

kui kā.kia. n. Tack, small nail, wedge, plug.

kui kā.kia moena. n. Carpet tacks. *Lit.,* sharp instruments for nailing mats.

kui kala. n. Screwdriver. Commonly called *kala.*

kuʻi kā.lā (dala). nv. Silversmith; to weld silver.

kū.ika.wā. vs. Temporary, for the time being, ad hoc, transient, makeshift, occasional, provisional, special, acting; free and independent, not bound to a chief in opinion or course. *Lit.,* standing at the time. Cf. *pōpilikia. Kau kūikawā,* special session, as of a legislature. *Hōʻike kūikawā,* special or occasional report. *Komikina kūikawā,* acting commissioner.

kū.ʻike. 1. vt. To know by sight, to understand or know in advance or beforehand. *Ua kūʻike au i kēlā wahi,* I know that place by sight. *Aia a kūʻike au he pono ke hele, a laila hele,* when I know in advance it is proper to go, then I go. **hoʻo.kū.ʻike.** To show beforehand; to recognize at sight. **2.** n. Cash. *Uku kūʻike,* cash payment. *Kūʻike pau,* full payment.

kuʻi.kē. 1. vi. To toll or ring, as a bell. *Ke kuʻikē, kanikē maila nā pele,* the bells are tolling and ringing. **2.** vt. To pound smooth, level off, raze; to strike right and left indiscriminately; to destroy completely, as in war.

kui kele. n. Large needle, as for darning or on a sewing machine. *Lit.,* steering instrument.

ku'i kele.awe. nv. One who makes brass articles, metalsmith, tinsmith; to work with brass, copper, bronze; to pound brass.

kui kē.pā. n. Spikes on a spur.

ku'i.kepa. nvt. Sculpturing; to carve and shape an image; ceremonial making of the *makahiki* festival image, Lono-makua (And.).

kuiki. nvt. Quilting; to quilt. *Eng. Kuiki lala,* diagonal quilting. *Kuiki lau,* to follow designs in quilting; a kind of quilting that follows the design. *Kuiki maka moena,* quilting with squares formed by crisscrossing lines; to quilt thus; *lit.,* quilt with mat mesh. *Kuiki maka 'upena,* quilt design; *lit.,* net mesh quilt. *Kuiki pāpa'a pelena,* quilting with design of small squares inside larger ones and in parallel columns; *lit.,* whole cracker quilt. *Kuiki pūleholeho,* quilt design: vertical and horizontal lines form squares; wide arcs are drawn over every line, meeting at the corners; *lit.,* cowrie quilt.

Kuiki.lana. nvs. Switzerland; Swiss. *Eng.*

kui.kui. 1. Old form for *kukui,* candlenut, light (commonly used on Ni'ihau). **2.** Redup. of *kui 1.* (PPN *tuitui.*)

ku'i.ku'i. 1. Redup. of *ku'i 1;* boxing, prize fight; to box. See *Ulu-mano, wauke. Ku'iku'i aku me ka lima hana 'ino* (Isa. 58.4), smite with the hand of wickedness. *Ku'iku'i pu'upu'u,* fist fighting, prize fight, boxing. **ho'o.ku'i.ku'i.** Redup. of *ho'oku'i;* to jostle. *Ho'oku'iku'i ka mana'o,* crudely expressed thought. *Ho'oku'iku'i 'ōlelo,* to answer rudely, contradict. (PPN *tukituki.*) **2.** Redup. of *ku'i 2.* **ho'o.ku'i.ku'i.** Redup. of *ho'oku'i. Hiki iā La'a-kea ke ho'oku'iku'i i nā hua 'ōlelo,* La'a-kea can join words [in sentences]. **3.** Redup. of *ku'i 5.* **4.** n. Liquid medicine made of the sap of the *'akoko* tree.

ku'i.ku'ia. Redup. of *ku'ia 1. Ku'iku'ia mau, ha'aku'ia ka mana'o,* constant disturbance, wounded feelings.

kui.kui Pā.kē. n. Physic nut *(Jatropha curcas). Ni'ihau.* See *kuku'ihi.*

ku'i.ku'i.papa. n. Prayer closing *makahiki* festivals. (For. 6:45.)

kuila. n. Twill. *Eng.*

kui lā.'au. n. Wooden peg, especially as made of hardwood and used in mending bowls.

kui lā.'ī. n. Covering made of dried ti leaves attached to a netting of *olonā* fibers or hibiscus, and worn as a rain cape.

kui lau.oho. n. Hairpin.

Kui-Lehua. n. Name of a breeze blowing from the northwest of Ni'ihau. *Lit.,* strike Lehua (Island).

kui lei. nv. To string flowers, beads, seeds, shells into leis; a lei stringer.

kui lei 'ula. nv. One who decorates the chief in finest apparel; to decorate the chief thus; decorated elegantly. *Lit.,* string red leis.

ku'i lena. n. Molar tooth yellow with age; insulting reference to old person. *I ka 'awa mama a ke ku'i lena,* the kava chewed by old yellow tusks.

kuili. nv. Prayer committed to memory and recited in unison during *luakini* (temple) dedications (Malo 171); to repeat, pray.

kui lihi.lihi. n. Crochet hook.

kū.'ililī. Same as *kī'ililī 1, 2.*

kui lima, kui.kui lima. nv. To go arm in arm, to hold hands; arm in arm.

ku'i lima. nvt. Boxer, pugilist, pugilism; to strike with the fist.

ku'i.loko. n. Chief supporting a chief, a chief's mainstay. *Lit.,* inside joint.

ku'i lua. 1. Intensive of *ku'i 1, 2;* to add on, increase, punch doubly hard, etc. *E ku'i lua mai ka pōmaika'i iā lākou,* may their blessings be doubled. **2.** See *ku'i a lua.*

ku'i Molo.ka'i. See *hula ku'i Moloka'i.*

kuina. n. A stringing together, as of leis. (PPN *tuinga.*)

ku'ina. n. **1.** Blow, punch; peal, as of thunder. (PPN *tukinga.*) **2.** Joint, joining, seam, junction. *Fig.,* center, key. Cf. *ku'inakapa. Ku'ina wāwae,* ankle joint. **ho'o.ku'ina.** Same as above. *Ho'oku'ina 'ami,* hinge joint.

ku'ina.ho'ōla. Same as *ku'inakapa. Kaua'i.*

ku'ina.kapa. n. Tapa bed covering, consisting of five layers stitched together at one end; the inner four *(iho)* were white, the outer was designed *(kilohana).* Cf. *kapa ku'ina.*

kui nao. n. Screw, large nail.

ku'i.nō. nvi. Roaring, as of the sea; to roar.

ku'i.nehe. nvs. Quiet and still, without rustling; weird solitary quietness of a deep forest.

ku'i.neki. vi. Crowded, as a street.

kuini. n. Queen. *Eng. Ke kuini o Palani,* the queen of France.

kuini.keke, kuinikete. n. Quintet. *Eng.*

kū.'i'o. 1. nvs. Fact, a true statement; sincerity; true. *Lit.,* a state of truth. **ho'o.kū.'i'o.** Convinced; to prove, verify; to insist on the truth of a matter. **2.** vs. Fleshy, fat. *Lit.,* a state of flesh.

kui 'ō.mou. n. Stickpin, common pin; *lit.,* pin to attach.

kui 'onou. n. Thumbtack.

ku'i 'opihi. v. To pry *'opihi* limpets loose from a rock with a knife, formerly to hit a glancing blow with a sharp stone.

ku'i.pa'a. n. Lockjaw. *Lit.,* tight molar.

kui pahu. n. Thumbtack. *Lit.,* pushing nail.

ku'i pahu.pahu. n. Billiard cue.

ku'i palu. vt. To make *palu* relish or bait; to pound into fine pieces, to beat to a pulp, thresh, demolish.

kui.papa. nvt. Method of making a hat lei by sewing leaves and flowers to a pandanus strip; to make such a lei. *Lit.,* string on a base.

kui pā.uma. Large, curved needle as used in sewing gunny sacks.

ku'i pē. vt. To beat flat. *Lit.,* pound crush. *Ku'i pē 'ia e ka makani,* flattened by the wind.

ku'i.pehe. vs. Deflated. *Fig.,* discouraged. *Lit.,* punch swelling.

ku'i pehi. vt. To pummel, pound, abuse horribly. *Lit.,* pound pelt.

kui pi'o. n. Staple, as for wire. *Lit.,* bent nail.

ku'i.popo. n. A variety of sweet potato. *Lit.,* decayed molar.

kui ulana. n. Knitting needle.

kui 'ū.mi'i. n. Metal binder, as in a notebook.

kuiwa. An unknown word translated 'distribute' in For. 6:39.

kui wili lopi. n. Spindle. *Lit.,* instrument spin rope *(Eng.).*

kuka. n. Coat. *Eng.*

kū.kā. nvi. Consultation, discussion; to consult, confer, discuss, deliberate. Cf. *kākākūkā. 'Aha kūkā,* council, conference. *'Aha kūkā malū,* privy council.

kū . . . kā. Used only in the idiom *'o kū! 'o kā!* This originated in Wahine-'ōma'o's chant: *'O kū, 'o kā 'o Wahine-'ōma'o, wahine a Lohi'au-ipo* (PH 184), bam! boom! Woman-in-green, wife of Sweetheart-Lohi'au. Wahine-'ōma'o did not know how to dance or chant; her song was merely a rhythm beat to which she marched about comically. Hence the idiom has come to mean "a lick and a promise, do it as quickly as possible and get it over with."

kū.ka.'a. 1. nvt. Roll, bolt of cloth; rolled pack, as of pandanus leaves ready for plaiting; to roll up, as a bundle of cloth or tapa; to swell up. **2.** vs. Wholesale. *Lole kūka'a,* wholesale clothing.

kuka 'aila. n. Raincoat. *Lit.,* oiled coat, so called because early raincoats were made of oiled unbleached muslin.

kū ka'a.wale. vs. To stand apart, be entirely different, independent.

kū.ka'awe. nvt. Convoy, guard; safe, protected, convoyed; to place in custody for protection; to convoy, guard.

kū.kae. n. Excreta, dung, feces. See below for many compounds formed with *kukae; lepo,* dirt, is sometimes a euphemism. *Kūkae lio,* horse manure; *fig.,* common. *Kūkae lio kēlā mea ʻo ka pānini ma kō mākou ʻāina,* on our land cactus is as common as horse manure. *Kūkae ʻōhiki,* sand pellets as left on the beach by *ʻōhiki* crabs. (PEP *tuutaʻe.*)

kū.kae.akua. n. A brownish substance, sometimes noticed under trees in the shape of paste squeezed from a tube; if the substance contains reed, it is believed to be the excreta of the ghost of a dying person, and a sign that someone is dying. *Lit.,* ghost excrement. Also *huamai-lani,* fruit from the sky.

kū.kae.hao. nvs. Rust; rusty. *Lit.,* iron excrement. *Ua kiʻo kūkaehao,* it has become rusty; *lit.,* has excreted rust.

kū.kae.hipa. n. Spiny bur *(Acanthospermum australe),* a branching, prostrate tropical American weed, 10 to 60 cm long, bearing small star-shaped bristly fruits. (Neal 837.) *Lit.,* sheep dung. Also called *ʻihi kūkae hipa, pipili.*

kū.kae.hoki. n. A rattlepod *(Crotalaria incana),* an erect tropical American weed, about 94 cm high, with three-parted leaves, yellow flowers, and hairy, dark-brown pods, each pod 2.5 cm or more long and containing 20 or more seeds. (Neal 445.) *Lit.,* mule dung.

kū.kae.ʻiole. n. **1.** Small hard spots on an umbilical cord, the number of spots indicating the number of children the mother is to bear. *Lit.,* rat's dung. Cf. *piko pau ʻiole.* **2.** Taro found growing in inaccessible spots, as a tree crotch, believed carried there by rats. **3.** Insignificant trifles.

kū.kae.ʻiwa. n. A form of gourd having fruit green with white splotches, still grown on Molokaʻi and East Maui. *Lit.,* dung of *ʻiwa* bird. See *ipu.*

kū.kae.kō.lea. n. **1.** Same as *pūʻoheʻohe,* Job's tears. **2.** Same as *kōlea,* periwinkle.

kū.kae.koloa. n. A kind of grass.

kū.kae.lā. n. Eggs deposited by flies, as in meat. *Lit.,* sun excrement. *Ua kiʻo kūkaelā,* maggot eggs have been deposited.

kū.kae.lio. n. **1.** Toadstool, mushroom. **2.** A name for unidentified wild grasses growing where horses are pastured. (For. 5:641.) *Lit.,* horse dung.

kū.kae.loli. nvs. Mildew; mildewed. *Mālama o kiʻo kūkaeloli,* be careful of mildew. *Lit.,* sea cucumber dung.

kūkae manu. n. Bird dung, guano.

kū.kae.moa. n. A small tree *(Pelea clusiaefolia* subsp. *sapotaefolia* [synonym, *P. microcarpa]*) that grows at high altitudes on Kauaʻi. *Lit.,* chicken dung, named for the appearance of the seed capsules. Also *alani kuahiwi,* all species of *Pelea.* See also *mokihana kūkae moa.*

kū.kae.nalo. n. **1.** Mole on the body, believed to be deposits of flies during infancy. *Lit.,* fly dung. **2.** Beeswax. **3.** Unbleached muslin. *Lio keʻokeʻo kūkaenalo,* dusty white horse.

kū.kae.nēnē. Same as *ʻai-a-ka-nēnē. Lit.,* goose dung.

kū.kae-o-Kama.puaʻa. Same as *līpuʻupuʻu,* a seaweed.

kū.kae.paʻa. n. Constipation. *Lit.,* hard excreta.

kū.kae.pele. n. Sulphur, brimstone, match. *Lit.,* Pele's dung.

kū.kae pō.polo. n. Excreta after eating *pōpolo* greens, a term for a chief whose mother was said to be a commoner.

kū.kae.puaʻa. n. A weedy, creeping grass *(Digitaria pruriens),* native to Hawaiʻi; some introduced species of *Digitaria* are also sometimes called *kūkaepuaʻa,* as *D. sanguinalis* and *D. adscendens* (syn. *D. henryi);* a plant from the pig demigod Kama-puaʻa (Neal 72.) *Lit.,* pig dung. Cf. *mauʻu kūkaepuaʻa.*

kū.kae.puaʻa uka. n. Crab grass *(Digitaria violascens)* 30 to 60 cm tall, forming clumps. *Lit.,* upland *kūkaepuaʻa.*

kū.kae.pueo. n. **1.** A weed. **2.** A seaweed (And.)

kū.kae.ʻuaʻu. n. A medicinal plant (no data).

kū.kae ʻuaʻu. n. Excreta and scent of *ʻuaʻu* birds, as left in their holes.

kū.kae.uli. n. Ink squirted by octopus to discolor water. *Fig.,* prostitute, as in whalers' days, so called because of their alleged cleverness at escaping from precarious situations. *Lit.,* black excreta.

kū.kae weka. See *weka 3,* meconium.

kū.kaha. vi. To stand sideways, as in making room for another to pass.

kū.kahala.kē. vi. Scolding, raving and ranting in a fit of temper.

kū.kahe.kahe. vi. To while the time away in pleasant conversation, jesting, laughing, and telling anecdotes; pleasant conversation, chatting. *Lit.,* stand flowing.

Kū Kahi. 1. n. Name of the third day in the lunar month. Cf. *Kū Lua, Kū Kolu, Kū Pau.* **2.** *(Not cap.)* vs. Standing alone, outstanding, unique, first. *Ka wohi kū kahi,* outstanding one of *wohi* high rank [applied to Ka-lā-kaua in chants].

kū.kai. vs. Dipped frequently in the sea. *Oho kūkai,* hair immersed in the sea, as of a fisherman.

kū.kaʻi. 1. vt. To exchange, as greeting *(aloha),* conversation *(kamaʻilio),* letters *(leka).* *(Kū 1 + -kaʻi,* Gram. 6.6.4.) (PPN *tuʻutaki.*) **2.** vi. To appear. See ex., *ila.* **3.** vi. To stand guard as soldiers. **4.** Rope fastening fish nets together. (And.)

kū.kaʻi.kahi. Same as *kūkākaʻikahi.*

kū.kai.kea. vs. Faded, as cloth. *Fig.,* boring, dull, uninteresting.

kū.kaʻi leka. v. To correspond back and forth; to exchange letters.

Kū-kā.ʻili-moku. n. Kamehameha's war image.

ku.kaima. See *hua kukaima.*

kū.kaʻi makani. v. To attempt to induce the spirit possessing a person to talk through the person and reveal the reason for the possession. *Aia lākou i ke kūkaʻi makani ala i haʻi mai i ke kumu o ka pilikia,* there they are getting the spirit to tell the reason for the trouble.

kū.kaʻi ʻō.lelo. v. To converse, narrate; recount.

kū.kaka. Similar to *kaka 1,* translated 'purified' by Emerson (cf. Malo text, Chapter 26, section 36).

kū.kā.kaʻi.kahi. vs. Standing wide apart; scattered widely, as houses.

kū kā.kalai.oa. See *kākalaioa, 1.*

kū.kā kamaʻi.lio. nvt. Interview, conference; to hold such, negotiate. *Lit.,* confer chat.

kū.kake. n. Glib hanger-on, parasite; one who lives with others, depending on glibness of tongue; to be glib.

kū.kā.kā.kā. Redup. of *kūkā;* to discuss, negotiate.

kuka.kuka.ʻi. Redup. of *kūkāʻi.*

kū.kala. nv. To proclaim publicly, tell abroad, announce; herald. See *kūkala hewa. Kūkala ʻula,* to proclaim the day, as by sunrise glow. *Kūkala kaua,* to declare war.

kū.kā.lā, kudala. nvt. Auction; to sell at auction. *Lit.,* stand dollar *(Eng.). Kūʻai kūkālā,* auction sale. *Luna kūkālā,* auctioneer. *E kūkālā ʻia ana kēlā hale,* that house is being sold at auction.

Kū.kala-hale. n. Name of a rain and wind famous at Honolulu.

kū.kale.kale. n. False alarm.

kū.kale.kale. Same as *kūkahekahe.* Cf. *kalekale.*

kū.kaliki. nvi. Boasting; to boast. (See *liki 1,* Gram. 8.7.l.) *Kāu mau kūkaliki* (Kel. 135), your boasting. *Kēia mau mea nani e kūkaliki ai* (Kel. 136), these pretty things [you] are boasting about.

kuka.mino, sukamino. n. Sycamine, a tree mentioned by Jesus; according to *Harper's Bible Dictionary,* a mulberry, probably the black variety. (Luka 17.6.) (Gr. *sykaminos.*)

kū.kā moʻo. v. **1.** To study or consult genealogy. *Lit.,* confer lineage. **2.** To use enchantment (Oihk. 19.26). *Lit.,* consult *moʻo* spirits.

ku.kana.loa. n. A variety of banana.

Kū Kana.loa. v. To pray to the god Kanaloa, as on the *Kāloa* days of the month.

kū.kana.wao. n. General name for weeds. *Rare. Lit.,* resembling the *kanawao,* wild taro.

kukane. n. A rough lemon *(Citrus limonia),* liked for the fragrance of the skin, but too sour to eat. (Neal 482.) *Lit.,* having the nature of the *kane* skin fungus.

kū.kāne. nvs. Male. *He mau kūkāne kēia mau akua,* these gods are male. (Kep. 11.)

kū.kanono. vs. Excessive, more than usual. *Kūkanono ka wela a ka lā,* the heat of the sun is excessive.

kū.kapihe. n. 1. Lamentation. *Lit.,* the wail arises. 2. A strong purge made from bark of the shrub called *koko* and sap of the green *kukui* nut; it was administered only as a last resort and often resulted in death.

kū.kapu. nvs. Chastity; chaste; taboo-surrounded and unapproachable; in a state of taboo.

kuka ua. n. Raincoat.

Kū-kaua-kahi. n. Said to be an old name for the gods Kāne, Kū, and Lono. The theory of a trinity is believed due to remaking of Hawaiian legends by Kepelino, Kamakau, and Fornander to conform to the Bible. See Barrère 1969.

kū.kaula. n. Deep-water fishing with hook and line; fishing grounds at about 80 fathoms depth (Kam. 76:75).

kū.kau.lani. vs. With great care, with esteem, in chiefly fashion.

kuka waniki. n. Oilskin coat. *Lit.,* varnished coat.

kuka.weke. n. Raincoat (Perhaps *Eng.,* coat and [sou']wester.)

kū.kawowo. 1. vt. To care for young plants or seedlings. 2. vi. To spread, reach a goal (of a sorcerer's prayer). 3. vi. To rush or gurgle, as water. *Rare.*

kuke. 1. vt. To nudge, push, jostle. Cf. *kuke kū.* **ho'o.kuke.** To shoo, drive off, banish, expel, oust, evict, eject. (PEP *tute.*) 2. n. Thin type of adze (2.5 or 4 cm wide), as used for finer work in handicraft. Also *lipi kuke.* 3. nvt. Cook; to cook. *Eng.* 4. nvi. Customs, duty; to be on duty or watch (Kel. 115). *Eng. Hale kuke,* customhouse. *Uku i nā kuke,* pay duties. 5. Also **duke.** n. Duke. *Eng. Duke wahine,* duchess.

kuke.awa. n. Customhouse inspector, customs.

kuke awa. n. Harbor duty or tax.

kū.kēhu. Var. spelling of *kū ke ehu;* see *'ehu 1.*

kukeke, dukese. n. 1. Duchess. *Eng.* 2. Also *Tusede. (Cap.)* Tuesday. *Eng. Rare.*

kuke kū. vi. To push with elbows and shoulders, as forcing a way through a crowd; to blow violently, as wind, to bluster, rage, as waves or storm.

kuke.kuke. Redup. of *kuke 1.* (PCP *tutetute.*)

kū.kele. 1. vs, vi. Muddy, slippery; to slip, slide, as in mud. 2. vt. To sail, as a boat.

kuke wai.wai. n. Duty, tariff.

kuki. See *mea 'ono kuki,* cookie. *Eng.*

kū.kia. vi. Firm, steady, steadfast.

kū.kī.helei. vi. To straddle, stand with legs far apart.

kū.kila. Similar to *kūkilakila.*

kū.kila.kila. vs. Majestic.

kukima, dudima. n. 1. Mandrake (Mele 7.13.) (Heb. *dudha'im.*) 2. Also *dukima.* Bagpipe (RSV), dulcimer (KJV). (Dan. 3.5.) *(Eng.)*

kū.kini. 1. nvi. Runner, swift messenger, as employed by old chiefs, with a premium on their speed; to run swiftly, as of a messenger; to race. 2. vi. Close together, in great numbers, as plants. 3. n. Cushion. *Eng.*

kū.kini.kini. Redup. of *kūkini 2;* grouped together.

kū.ki'o. n. Small pool of water. *Lit.,* standing pool.

kuko. nvt. Strong desire, whether good or bad; lust, compulsion; to lust, desire; to think about, as approaching death (GP 56). *'Ano kuko,* of a lusty nature. *Kuko hewa, kuko 'ino, piha kuko,* lustful, lecherous, lewd, amorous, randy, "horny". *Kuko 'umi 'ole* (2 Tim. 3.3), unrestrained desire, incontinence. *Kuko makapehu,* gluttonous desire. *Nui ko'u kuko e loa'a*

ia'u ka na'auao, I have much ambition to attain education. (PCP *tuto.*)

kū.koa'e. n. 1. Temple for purification ceremonies (Malo 151–2, Emerson note 156), for prayers for food (Malo 188). *Kūkoa'e a hāwai,* ceremonial blessing of a stream so that water may continue flowing. 2. *(Cap.)* Name of a god appealed to in *'anā'anā,* evil sorcery.

kuko 'aihue. n. Kleptomaniac.

kuko.hia. Pas/imp. of *kuko.*

Kū Kolu. n. Name of the fifth day in the lunar month. Cf. *Kū Kahi, Kū Lua, Kū Pau.*

kuko.molea, sukomorea. n. Sycamore tree. (Isa. 9.10.) (Gr. *sycomorea.*)

kū.kona. vs. Unfriendly, cross, sullen. Cf. *konā,* haughty; *mākonā,* malevolent.

kū.kona.kona. Redup. of *kūkona.*

kū.konu.konu. vs. Excessive, overmuch, deep, profound, serious. *Ua 'ike kūkonukonu i nā 'ano 'ōlelo like 'ole,* having a profound knowledge of different languages. *He 'eha kūkonukonu ma ke po'o,* a serious head injury.

kuku. 1. vt. To beat, as tapa. (PPN *tutu.*) 2. n. Beam, as of a house; stick, as used to support and distend a net. (PCP *tutu.*)

kukū. 1. nvs. Thorn, barb, spine, bur; barbed, thorny, prickly, burry; jabbed, pricked, hurt by a thorn. *Lā'au kukū* (1 Sam. 13.6), brambles, thicket. *Uwea kukū,* barbed wire. 2. Redup. of *kū 1,* to hit; crowded. *Kō pāpālina e kukū nei* (song), your cheeks that stand firm. *Lihilihi kukū,* eyelashes that project. *Ua hele wale a kukū kānaka,* the people are standing close together. *Kukū mai nā ho'omana'o 'ana o ke au i hala aku,* crowding memories of the past.

kū.kū. 1. n. (Usually pronounced *tūtū.*) Granny, grandma, grandpa; granduncle, grandaunt; any relative or close friend of grandparent's generation (often said affectionately; apparently a new word as it has not been noted in legends and chants). 2. vi. To shake in jerks, bounce, trot, as on a horse; bumpy. *Hele kūkū,* to go jerkily, by fits and starts. *Holo kūkū,* to trot. **ho'o.kū.kū.** To cause to shake; to shake, bounce; uncomfortably full, as after overeating 3. nvt. Gourd beat; the gourd is thumped down on a pad three times, and on the third rise, it is slapped; to beat thus. Cf. *'ami kūkū, kāhela, pā 5.* 4. n. Sea gull (RSV), cuckoo (KJV). (Oihk. 11.16.)

-kūkū. ho'o.kū.kū. (a) Contest, game, match; to hold a contest, compete, compare; to place evenly, as canoes about to race *(ho'okūkū like i nā wa'a). Ho'okūkū hīmeni,* song contest. *Ka ho'okūkū 'ana,* the comparison. *Nānā a ho'okūkū,* to make comparisons. **(b).** To fit, as garment; a fitting. *'O ka ho'okūkū ka malo ali'i,* fitting the royal loincloth.

kukua. Faint, dizzy; to faint. (AP.)

kukua.'au. vi. To go smoothly. *Kaua'i. E holo ka lio ā kukua'au i ua mea o ka maika'i,* the horse ran smoothly along because everything was fine.

kū.kū.au. n. A large grapsid crab *(Metopograpsus thukuhar).*

kuku'e. n. Clubfoot; one with a twisted or deformed foot. Cf. *hapaku'e.* **ho'o.kuku'e.** To imitate the walk of a clubfooted person.

kū.kū.'ē.'ē. Redup. of *kū'ē* and *kū'ē'ē.* (For. 6:470.)

kukuhe. Redup. of *kuhe 2.*

kukuhi. Rare var. of *ukuhi,* to pour.

kuku.hilo. Redup. of *kūhilo.*

kukui. n. 1. Candlenut tree *(Aleurites moluccana),* a large tree in the spurge family bearing nuts containing white, oily kernels which were formerly used for lights; hence the tree is a symbol of enlightenment. The nuts are still cooked for a relish *('inamona).* The soft wood was used for canoes, and gum from the bark for painting tapa; black dye was obtained from nut coats and from roots. (Nuts were chewed and spat into the sea by men fishing with nets for parrot fish *(kākā uhu)* in order to calm the sea (FS 38–9): see ex., *pili 1).* Polished nuts are strung in leis; the silvery leaves and small white flowers are strung in leis as representative of Moloka'i, as designated in 1923 by the Territorial legislature. The *kukui* was named the official emblem for the State of Hawaii in 1959 because of its many uses and its symbolic value. *Kukui* is one of the plant forms of Kama-pua'a that comes to help him (FS 215). Called *kuikui* on Ni'ihau. (Neal 504-7.) See *lei kukui. He ali'i no ka malu kukui,* a chief of the candlenut shade [chief of uncertain genealogy]. **2.** Lamp, light, torch. *Fig.,* guide, leader. *Kukui ahi* (Dan. 10.6), lamps of fire. *E noho ana au ā puhi kukui,* I'll stay until the lights are lighted [until dark]. *Kukui 'ā i ke awakea,* torch burning in daylight [a symbol for descendants of a certain chief]. *Ua pio ke kukui,* the light is out [dead]. **3.** *(Cap.)* Star name (no data). (Kuhelani.)

kuku'i. Redup. of *ku'i 1, 2, 5;* to punch, join, spread news; fame. *No ke kuku'i o kō ikaika i Kaua'i* (FS 55), because of the fame of your strength on Kaua'i. *Kuku'i akula ka lono kaua puni ke ao,* news of the war went around the world. (PPN *tutuki,* to hit.)

Kukui-a-kona-mau-kuku. n. Name of a star.

kukui haole. n. General name for any nut not native to Hawai'i.

kukui hele pō. n. Lantern. *Lit.,* light [for] going [at] night.

kuku.'īhi. n. Physic nut *(Jatropha curcas),* a tropical American shrub or small tree with soft wood, milky juice, and very poisonous seeds. Like the *kukui,* it is in the spurge family. (Neal 512.) See *kuikui Pākē.*

kukui ho'o.lele aka. n. Projector, as for lantern slides; magic lantern.

kuku'i 'ō.lelo. nv. Storyteller; to recite, narrate, recount; to join words together coherently. *Lit.,* joining speech.

kukui pa'a lima. n. Flashlight. *Lit.,* light hold hand.

kukui pō.haku. n. Stone lamp burning sperm oil.

kukui uila. n. Electric light.

Kukui Wana.'ao. n. Morning Star. *Lit.,* early morning light.

kuku'i wana.'ao. n. Practice of telling stories all night, especially to a chief. *Lit.,* spreading tales dawn.

kū.kū (tūtū) kāne. n. Grandpa.

kukuku. 1. vs. Pimpled, pimply. **2.** n. Hawaiian soap plant *(Colubrina asiatica).* See *'ānapanapa.*

kuku.kū. 1. Redup. of *kukū 1. Kukukū mai auane'i nā wāwae o 'oukou,* your feet will likely be pricked by burs. **2.** nvi. Sound of boiling water; to sound thus; sputtering.

kū.kū.kū. Redup. of *kukū 2,* standing, rising up. *A'a kūkūkū,* varicose veins.

kuku.kuhe. Redup. of *kukuhe.* (For. 6:449.)

kuku.kukū. Rare var. of *kuhukukū,* dove.

kukula. Redup. of *kula,* school; to go to school. *Eng. I laila e kukula 'ia mai ai,* there to be schooled.

kukule. vs. Inactive, listless, unresponsive, dejected. *Ma'i kukule,* cholera, as of humans or chickens. **ho'o.-kukule.** Caus/sim.

kukuli. Redup. of *kuli;* knee; to kneel; to crouch or lie as an animal, with feet under the body (Nah. 24.9). *Noho kukuli,* to sit on bended knees, with the feet stretched backwards, with the front of the toes down. **ho'o.kukuli.** Caus/sim. (PCP *tu(u)tuli.*)

kukulu. Same as *kulukulu,* to leak. (PCP *tutulu.*)

kū.kulu. 1. n. Pillar, post, side, border, edge, horizon. Also *kūkunu. Nā kūkulu 'ehā,* four cardinal points (PCP *tutulu*). **2.** vt. To build, as a house; to construct, erect, establish, organize, set up; to put up, as a tent or as mast and sail; to heap up; to form, as a military unit; to found, as a society; to establish, as a game or dynasty; to lay, as an oven. *Kūkulu 'ana,* organization, arrangement, establishment, construction, formation. *Kūkulu kēpau,* to set type. *Kūkulu mana'o,* arrangement or presentation of a thought or idea. *Palapala 'ae e kūkulu,* building permit. *Ua kūkulu i luna kāu 'ōlelo i ka mea e hina ana* (Ioba 4.4), your words have upheld him that was falling. **3.** vt. To tie, tether (so called be-

cause formerly horses were tied to erected *[kūkulu]* stakes); to park. *Mahea 'oe i kūkulu ai i kō ka'a,* where did you park your car? *Kūkulu ihola lākou i nā hana le'ale'a apau loa* (F5:35), they exhibited all the sporting games. **4.** vi. To sit with one knee raised high towards the chin, considered bad form for women. **5.** n. Type of battle in which opposing forces were formally drawn up in line against each other; front, as in modern warfare. (Malo 196, 203.)

kukulu.ae'o. 1. nvi. Stilts; to walk on stilts. **2.** n. Hawaiian stilt bird *(Himantopus himantopus).* Also *ae'o. Fig.,* a thin, long-legged person.

kū.kulu kumu.hana. v. To pool thoughts and prayers to solving common problems, as during *ho'oponopono* (Nānā 78-80); to set up topics for discussion, as an agenda.

Kū.kulu-o-Kahiki. n. Pillars of Kahiki; it was believed that the sky was supported by a vertical wall along the horizon; the section of the wall over Kahiki (formerly Tahiti) was the *Kūkulu-o-Kahiki.* (UL 17.)

kū.kulu-o-ka-honua. n. Region just below the horizon where sea and sky meet. *Lit.,* pillars (or borders) of the earth. Cf. Isa. 45.22.

kū.kulu-o-ka-lani. n. Region just above the horizon where sea and sky meet. *Lit.,* pillars (or borders) of the sky.

kū.kulu papa. n. To pile in regular order; to arrange, classify, as plants, words. Less used than *ho'onoho papa.*

kukuma. n. A crab, often qualified by the terms *kea,* white, and *'ōhuluhulu,* hairy.

kukuna. n. Ray, as of the sun; radius of a circle; spoke of a wheel; antenna of a lobster; spike of *hā'uke'uke,* a sea urchin; feeler of any creature; pistil of a flower; gate, door, or gable post; end post of a Hawaiian house other than the main post and the corner posts (Malo 119). *Kukuna X,* x-ray.

kukuna-o-ka-lā. n. Mangrove *(Bruguiera gymnorhiza);* calyx of a mangrove, as used in leis. (Neal 626.) *Lit.,* ray of the sun.

kukuni. Redup. of *kuni,* to burn.

kū.kunu. Rare var. of *kūkulu,* pillar, border.

kū.kū.ohi. vs. Sharp, steep, conspicuous, as house roof.

kuku.pa'u. v. To do with great enthusiasm, with might and main. See ex., *kemu 1. E kukupa'u ana nō i kāna hana,* he's putting all he has into his work. *He kaua i kukupa'u 'ia,* a war fought with might and main.

kukupu. Redup. of *kupu,* to grow. See prayer, *hō'eu (a). He mau lā'au ho'olaha ali'i ke kukupu nei* (chant), these were trees from which chiefs were propagated, that put out new sprouts now.

kū.kū (tūtū) wahine. n. Grandma.

kula. 1. n. Plain, field, open country, pasture. An act of 1884 distinguished dry or *kula* land from wet or taro land. *Kō kula kai,* shore dweller. **2.** n. Source; container. See *kula kakalina, kula wai, kula waiwai. Kula kālā,* source of monetary income. *Kula loa'a,* source of profit or gain. **3.** n. Basket-like fish trap. *Rare.* **4.** nvi. School, academy; to teach school, go to school; to hold school or class sessions. *Eng. Kula 'ia,* to be educated in school, sent to school. Specialized schools are usually *kula a'o,* as *kula a'o hana lima,* manual training school, school of arts and crafts; *kula a'o hīmeni,* singing school; *kula a'o hulahula,* dancing school; *kula a'o humuhumu,* sewing school; *kula a'o kamanā,* carpenter's school; *kula a'o kuke,* cooking school. Cf. *kukula. Kumu kula,* school teacher. **5.** Also **gula.** nvs. Gold; golden. *Eng.*

kula'a. Rare var. of *hula'a.*

kula a'o kumu. n. Same as *kula kumu.*

kula a'o 'oi.hana. n. Trade school.

kula au.puni. n. Public school, government school.

kula hā.nai. n. Boarding school. *Lit.,* feeding school. Also *kula noho pa'a.*

kula hele lā. n. Day school. *Lit.,* school daily going. Also *kula lā.*

kula ho'o.polo.lei keiki kāne. n. Boys' reform school.

kula'i. vt. To push over, knock down, overthrow, shove, push to one side; to brush off, as a horse switches flies with its tail; to dash to pieces (Isa. 13.18); to hurl. See ex., *kūpahu.* (Probably *kū l + -la'i.*) *Kula'i pau,* to push completely over, as would a strong wind (see ex., *kiki'i l*). *Kula'i 'ohā,* to break off main parent taro and leave room for young shoots to grow. **ho'o.kula'i.** Caus/sim. *Na'u nō ia e ho'okula'i i ka pahi kaua* (Isa. 37.7), I, indeed, am the one to cause [him] to fall by the sword. (PPN *tulaki.*)

kulā.ia, ho'o.kulā.ia. nvi. Festive, festivities; festive. See *lā kulāia.*

kū.la.'i.la'i. Redup. of *kula'i.*

kula'i.lua. vt. To push, shove, etc., in two ways or with great force. *He 'e'epa ke aloha, he kula'ilua,* love is peculiar, it pushes in opposite directions [to love and be loved].

kula.'ina. nvi. Pushing over, flattening; overthrow, breakdown. *I kula'ina e ka wai o Hina, hina ke oho o ka hala* (chant), flattened by the water of Hina, the leaves of the pandanus fall.

kula'i wā.wae. n. Sport in which players attempted to unseat one another by pushing with their feet. *Lit.,* foot pushing.

kulā.iwi. nvs. Native land, homeland; native. Cf. *iwi, 'ōiwi. Ku'u home kulāiwi,* my own homeland.

kula kahuna pule. n. Theological seminary. *Lit.,* minister school.

kula kaka.lina. n. Gasoline drum, barrel, container.

kula kama.li'i. n. Primary school, kindergarten. *Lit.,* children's school.

kula Kā.paki (Sabati). n. Sunday school.

kula ki'e.ki'e. n. High school.

kula koa. n. Military Academy.

kula.kula. 1. Redup. of *kula l;* fields. (Gram. 8.6.) *Ua hiki aku kāua i kulakula,* we have reached the open fields [a place to stop]. *Kāpae a'e nō i kulakula,* just set aside in the fields [never mind, just put it aside, don't worry]. *Kū loa akula i kulakula,* stopped away up in the fields [stranded]. **2.** n. Game like ninepins.

kula.kula'i. 1. Redup. of *kula'i.* **2.** n. Chest-slapping game; the player attempts to push opponent out-of-bounds with his open palms.

kula kumu. n. Teachers' training school, normal school.

kula lā. n. Day school. Also *kula hele lā.*

kū.lā.lā. nvt. Plant propagated by slips or scions, formerly of pandanus aerial roots; to plant thus. *Lit.,* stand branch.

kula manu. n. Gathering place of birds, as near water or food; plain with birds; tree branch that is gummed or smeared to attract birds. **ho'o.kula manu.** To make into a bird place. *Ka wai e ha'akula manu, ka nahele o Kēhua i loa i ke kula o ho'okula manu* (PH 220), the water that attracted birds, the forest of Kēhua, far on the plains attracting birds.

kulana. vs. To tilt, rock, reel, sway, toss and pitch; wobbly, shaky, unsteady. *Fig.,* insecure, hesitant. *Kulana o ka noho paipai,* rocking of a rocking chair. **ho'o.kula-na.** Caus/sim., to cause insecurity.

kū.lana. nvs. Station, rank, title, condition, position, place, quality, grade, rating, reputation (see ex., *kuene),* stance, attitude, poise, carriage, posture, situation, patch, site; outstanding, prominent (*kū,* stand, + *-lana,* nominalizer). Cf. *kūlanakauhale. Mamule o ke kūlana,* by reason of position, ex officio. *Kūlana o ka nohona,* standard of living. *Kūlana ki'eki'e,* high position, rank, station. *Kūlana makahiki,* age. *Kūlana ipu,* melon patch. *Nā kūlana o kēia kū'ai ho'olilo,* the conditions of this sale. (PNP *tu'ulanga.*)

kū.lana.hale. Same as *kūlanakauhale;* house site.

kū.lana kai. Probably the same as *kūlana nalu. Aloha nā hoa o ka nalu mua kau, o kūlana kai o ke kaulua ē* (For. 6:292), greetings, friends of the waves first mounted, the breaking sea of the double canoe.

kū.lana.kau.hale. n. Village, town, city. *Lit.,* situation plural house.

kū.lana.lana. Redup. of *kulana;* unsteady, tottering, unsettled, wavering, wobbly, undecided, uncertain, fluctuating. (For. 4:271.) **ho'o.kū.lana.lana.** Caus/sim.

kū.lana nalu. n. Place where the waves swell up and the surf rider starts paddling and racing the wave, usually at the most distant line of breakers. (FS 153.) Also *kūlana he'enalu* (Laie 453).

kū.lana pa'a. n. Standard, as weight or money.

kū.lana pili.kia. n. Jeopardy.

kū.lana pule. n. Prayer meeting or other religious service.

kū.lana wae.wae. vs. Fussy, fastidious, choosy.

kū.lani. vs. Of chiefly nature.

Kū-lani-hā.ko'i. n. Mythical pond or lake in the sky; its overflow comes to the earth as rain. *Lit.,* like heaven agitated. See ex., *haukawewe, ki'o l.* '*Elo'elo i ka wai o Kū-lani-hāko'i,* drenched by the water of Kū-lani-hāko'i [soaked by a heavy rain].

kula noho pa'a. n. Boarding school. *Lit.,* school staying fixed. Also *kula hānai.*

kula.nui. n. University, college; formerly high school. *Lit.,* big school.

kū.lapa. 1. nvt. Earth piled on the sides of a ditch, as of a plowed furrow or as on the edge of a taro patch; to dig or plow and cast up earth or furrow. **2.** vi. To frolic, jump, or skip about in sport; to struggle, twist, turn, writhe.

kula.pepei.ao. n. **1.** Earring. *Lit.,* gold [for] ears. *Kulapepeiao hoaka,* crescent-shaped earrings. *Kulapepeiao kolū,* earrings held in place by a screw. *Kulapepeiao lewalewa,* dangling earrings. *Kulapepeiao 'ūmi'i,* earrings for unpierced ears; *lit.,* clamped earrings. **2.** Fuchsia *(Fuchsia magellanica),* an introduced plant so called because of resemblance of flower to an earring. (Neal 650.) **3.** Same as *aloalo ko'ako'a. Ni'ihau.* **4.** Modern name for cocoon. **5.** Same as *līpepeiao,* a seaweed.

kula pō. n. Night school.

kula uku. n. Private school. *Lit.,* paying school.

kula wae. n. Select school.

kula wai. n. Watering trough, water source.

kula wai.wai. n. Source of income or livelihood.

kule. 1. Same as *kukule,* inactive. (PPN *tule.*) **2.** Var. of *'ulae,* lizard fish. **3.** Var. of *akule,* scad.

kū.lē. vt. To seize, meddle in the concerns of others, oust, remove. *Rare.*

kū.le'a. vs. Successful, competent; happily. *Ua kūle'a kāna hana,* his work has been successful.

kule.ana. nvt. Right, privilege, concern, responsibility, title, business, property, estate, portion, jurisdiction, authority, liability, interest, claim, ownership, tenure, affair, province; reason, cause, function, justification; small piece of property, as within an *ahupua'a;* blood relative through whom a relationship to less close relatives is traced, as to in-laws. Cf. *'ākuleana. Kuleana lako,* supplies, equipment. *Kuleana pule,* necessary prayers, prayer responsibilities. *Ke kuleana o ke kanaka,* man's rights and privileges, human rights. *Kuleana wai,* water rights. *Ka ho'olimalima kuleana kū'ai,* rental with the right to buy. *Kō ha'i kuleana,* other persons' affairs or business. *Kuleana ala hele e hiki aku ai,* right of way of access. *Make wale nō lākou me ka hewa 'ole, a me ke kuleana 'ole no ka make* (Kep. 147), they were killed without having done wrong, and without justification for death. '*O Hina kō mākou kuleana, 'a'ole 'o ke kāne,* we are related through Hina, not through the husband. *Kuleana hapakolu o ka wahine kāne make,* dower right of a widow to a third of an estate. *Kuleana o ke kāne male,* estate by courtesy, of a husband's right in the estate of his wife. '*Elua lo'i 'ai, ua kuleana 'ia e a'u,* two taro patches claimed as *kuleana* by me [will]. **ho'o.kule.ana.** To entitle, give right to possess; to give a responsibility. *Palapala ho'okuleana,* patent, copyright.

kule.ana 'āina. n. Owned land (common term in wills of the 1860s).

kule.ana helu. n. Claim number.

kule.ana ho'o.pa'a, kule.ana koi. n. Lien.

kule.ana puka. n. Dividends. (Will 129, island of Maui, State Archives, 1856.)
kule.ana wai.wai like. n. Common ownership or interest. *He kuleana waiwai like kō mākou 'ohana i loko o ka 'āina mahi 'ai,* our family has a common ownership in the farm.
kū.leha. Same as *leha 1, 2.*
kū.lehu. Var. of *pūlehu.*
kule.kana, suletana. n. Sultan. *Eng.*
Kuleke, Tureke. nvs. Turkey, Turk; Turkish. *Eng.*
kule.kia, kuresia. n. Crusader. *Eng.*
kule.kule. vs. Secure, permanent. Cf. *kuleana.*
kū.lē.kū.kē. Redup. of *kūlē,* to seize.
kū.lele. vt. To scatter as does the wind. *Kūlele ke ehu kai i ka makani,* the sea spray is scattered by the wind. *Kūlele 'ula ke ehu wai,* the red tossing spray. (PCP *tuulele.*)
ku.lele.iwi. vs. Insecure, destitute. *Lit.,* wind-scattered bones.
kū.lē.lewa. Redup. of *kūlewa.*
kulepa, sulepa. n. Sulphur. *Eng.*
kū.lepe. 1. vt. Split open from head to tail, as fish prepared for drying and salting; to slit thus; to hew out roughly, as a canoe; to make a hole or dig out. *Kūlepe mai ka mahi 'ai i nā 'eka lepo* (For. 5:683), the farmer dug out blocks of earth [in a taro patch]. **2.** vi. To flap, flutter; strong, of wind. *Kūlepe nā pepa i ka makani,* the papers are flipped about by the wind. *Mai kūlepe i ka'u hana,* don't muss up my work. **3.** n. Harelip. (Less common than *'ūlepe.*)
kū.lepe.lepe. Redup. of *kūlepe 1, 2.*
kū.lewa. vs. Moving slowly through space, as clouds; swaying, dangling, hanging. *Fig.,* far away in space, as the ocean beyond sight of land or as its profound depths. (PCP *tuulewa.*)
kū.lewa.lewa. Redup. of *kūlewa.*
kuli. 1. n. Knee. (A mother would rap a disobedient child on the knee: see *ho'okuli;* knocking on the knee was also a sign of stinginess: the person referred to is deaf *(kuli 2)* to appeal for generosity.) (PPN *turi.*) **2.** nvs. Deafness, deaf person, noise, racket; deaf, noisy, loud. *Hana kuli,* noise, hubbub, cacophony; noisy. *Po'e kuli ā 'a'ā,* deaf-mutes. *Kuli 'oko'a,* stone deaf. *Mai hana kuli,* be quiet [politer than *kulikuli*] **ho'o.kuli.** Deaf; to feign deafness. *Fig.,* to disobey; disobedient. *Ho'okuli maila i ka waiwai* (For. 5:159), disregard or pay no attention to wealth. (PPN *tuli.*)
kū.lia. 1. Pas/imp. of *kū 1;* to stand, halt, etc. *Kūlia i ke ākea,* place before the public. *Ke kūlia nei ka lā i lalo,* the sun is setting. **2.** vt. To try, strive. *Kūlia i ka nu'u* (Queen Ka-pi'o-lani's motto), strive to reach the summit. *Kūlia i kō ikaika,* exert your strength. *Kūlia e loa'a kā na'auao,* strive to obtain wisdom. **ho'o.kū.lia.** Caus/ sim. **3.** vs. Outstanding, fortunate, lucky. *Kūlia i ka u'i,* outstanding beauty. *Lā kūlia,* lucky day.
kū.li'a. vt. To desire greatly.
kū.lihi. Var. of *kūnihi 1, 2;* grazed, as by a bullet; hit but not seriously hurt; hooked but escaped, as a fish.
kuli hia.moe. vi. To doze; too drowsy to hear (a deeper sleep than *kulu hiamoe*). *Lit.,* sleep deafly. *Rare.*
kū.lihi.lihi. Redup. of *kūlihi.*
kū.like. vt. Alike, identical, conforming, resembling; standing in similar fashion or in even rows. *Kūlike loa,* exactly similar, literal, precise. *Unuhi kūlike loa,* literal translation. *Kūlike 'ole,* different; to disagree. *Kūlike me ia,* in conformity with, according to. **ho'o.kū.like.** To conform, make alike. *Ka ho'okūlike a like i nā 'ao'ao a 'elua,* to balance the accounts.
kū.liki.liki. vs. Tight. See *liki 2.*
kuli.kuli. nvs. Noise, din; noisy, deafening, inharmonious; a noise. Be quiet! Keep still! Shut up! (PEP *tuli-tuli.*)
kuli.lipi. vs. Ridgelike, sharp. *Kua kulilipi,* razor back [as of a pig]. Cf. *lipi.*
kulima. Var. of *kalima,* cream. *Eng.*
kulina. n. Deafness, disobedience, noise. *Ka lono*

mamua, ke kulina mahope kulikuli wale i ka makani o Ka'ū (chant for Ka-umu-ali'i), hearing before, deafness afterwards, deafening in the wind of Ka'ū.
kū.lina, kurina. n. Corn, maize *(Zea mays).* (Neal 81-2.) *Eng.*
kū.lina 'ono. n. Sweet corn *(Zea mays).* (Neal 81-2.) *Lit.,* delicious corn.
kū.lina pohā.pohā. Popcorn. *(Zea mays).* (Neal 82.)
kū.lina wali. n. Cornmeal. *Lit.,* fine corn.
kuli.o'o. vs. Stingy, penurious.
kulipa. n. Tulip. *Eng.*
kuli.pa'a. vs. Stingy, penurious, niggardly, deaf. *Lit.,* solid deafness.
kuli.pe'e. vi. To creep along, as a sick person; to stumble awkwardly along; to walk as though weak-kneed. (PH 38.)
kū.lipo. vs. Dark, dank, deep, as a cave. *Fig.,* extremely, intense, much. Cf. *kumulipo, lipo.* **ho'o.kū.lipo.** Caus/sim.
kū.lipo.lipo. Redup. of *kūlipo.* *He 'eha kūlipolipo,* an intense pain.
kuli.pu'u. n. Design with zigzag stripes, in tapas, mats, and quilts. *Lit.,* bent knees. Also *niho-wili-hemo.*
kū.li'u. vs. **1.** Deep, as a voice; penetrating, profound, as thoughts; late, remote, of the distant past. *Kūli'u, sweetheart of the distant past. Kūli'u kona 'ike lapa'au,* his medical knowledge is profound. **2.** Same as *li'u 2.*
kū.lō. Same as *kūlō'ihi,* short for *kūloa.* *E kūlō a'e ana au i ku'u haku,* I am waiting long for my master.
kū.loa. Same as *kūlō'ihi, kūlō;* name of the lengthy ceremonies on the night before graduation day in hula; a "long waiting" with feasts and ceremonies lasting for hours; lengthy religious prayers, ceremonies. *He lā kēlā e kūloa ai i nā mea 'ai i ulu mai* (For. 6:125), that was the day for long prayers to get food to grow.
Kū-loa. Var. of *Hōkū-loa,* name of a star.
kū.loa'a. vs. Prosperous, well-supplied with needs. *Hānau ke kanaka ia lā, he kāne kūloa'a* (Kep. 107), a man born on this day is a prosperous man.
kulo.hia. vs. Languid, lounging about. *Lit.,* state of slowness. (PCP *tu(u)lohi.*)
kū.lō.'ihi. vt. To wait a long time; to stand long; to last long, endure; to take a long time. *E hana kūlō'ihi aku ana kēia,* this is work that takes a long time to do.
kū.loko. vs. Local, domestic. *Lit.,* state of being inside. *Kaua kūloko,* civil war. *Nā mea hou kūloko,* local news.
kū.loku. vs. Falling, flowing, as rain or stream; flattened, as plants by rain. *'O ka hoi, uhi, pia . . . ua nika nānawaū mai kō lākou ulu 'ana, ā ua kūloku loa ā make* (Kep. 93), the *hoi* vine, yam, arrowroot . . . are blackened and sickened in their growth, and flattened down [by bad weather] until dead.
kū.loku.loku. Redup. of *kūloku.* Also *kūnokunoku.* *Pakapaka ua, paka ua, kūlokuloku* (chant), rain of many drops, drops of rain, running, running in streamlets.
kulo.kulou. Redup. of *kūlou.*
kū.lola. vs. Helpless, inactive, due either to infirmity or laziness; sluggish. Cf. *kūlola.*
kū.lola.lola. Redup. of *kūlola.*
kū.loli. vs. Having no wife, children, or relatives (name derived from a lone mulberry tree growing in a cave at Kūloli, Kona, Hawai'i, which was known as *ka wauke kū kahi o Kūloli,* the lone mulberry tree of Kūloli); also said of any very young *wauke* plant.
kū.lō.lia. 1. Pas/imp. of *kūlō,* long waiting or enduring. *Ku'u hoa kūlōlia,* my companion of long years. **2.** vs. Of changed appearance, as of plants in different seasons (Kep. 89); grief-stricken, said to apply particularly to a mourner who wears a *malo* or *pā'ū* of the deceased about his neck as an expression of grief: he is breaking a taboo and has "changed" *(loli).*
Kū.lō.lio. n. Name of a wind at Hāmākua, Maui. (Probably a contraction of *kū kololio,* gusty state.)

kū.lolo. n. Pudding made of baked or steamed grated taro and coconut cream. Cf. *lololo 2, niu kūlolo.*

kū.lolo.hili. vs. Long in doing a thing; to tell a story with many unnecessary details; garrulous.

kū.lolou. Var. of *kūloulou.*

kū.loma. vs. Slow, dull, stupid, awkward, helpless.

kū.loma.loma. Redup. of *kūloma. Ua 'ane'ane e kūlomaloma ka 'emepera,* the emperor was almost helpless.

kū.lono. vs. **1.** Sheer, precipitous. *E pi'i kūlono i ke alo o ka pali,* climb straight up the face of the cliff. **2.** Leaky, as a calabash. Also *kūnono.* **3.** Insignificant, as an idea. *Rare.* Also *kūnono.*

kulo.pia. vi. To decay, as crops. (Malo 199, Emerson note.)

kū.lō pia. nv. The long process of sweetening arrowroot starch *(pia);* to do this.

kū.lou. vt. To bow the head, bend; to beckon with the head. Also *kūnou. Ua kulu ka pō* (Nak. 88), the night has passed. **3.** n. Timber used in houses, as sticks, posts; fuel sticks. Cf. *kūkulu,* to build a house. *Kūkulu ho'omoe mai nā kulu* (Kep. 163), to pile the sticks leaning against each other [of an oven]. **4.** vs. Drowsy (usually followed by *hiamoe*). Cf. *kuluhio.* **5.** vi. Swift. *Kaua'i. Kulu ke kī a ka lio,* swiftly runs the horse. **6.** n. Dysentery, gonorrhea. **7.** vs. To be late at night. *Kulu aumoe* is more common.

kulua. Pas/imp. of *kulu 1,* to drip.

kū.lua. n. Pairing off, as of mates; twins.

Kū Lua. n. Fourth day of the old lunar month; also, the name of the 17th day and second after the full moon (Malo 35).

kulu au.moe. n. Late night, midnight. *Hiki mai ke kulu aumoe,* the late night has come.

kulu hau pa'a. n. Icicle. *Lit.,* drop [of]hard dew.

kulu.hia. Pas/imp. of *kulu 1.*

kulu hia.moe. Similar to *kuli hiamoe.*

kulu.hio. vi. Wafted off to sleep.

kului. vi. **1.** To drip (*kulu 1 + -i,* transitivizer). *Hilo ua kului ua* (Nak. 28), Hilo with rain, dripping rain. (PPN *tulu'i.*) **2.** To be late at night. (For. 6:420.) Cf. *kulu 7.*

kulu.'ī. n. Endemic small trees and shrubs (*Nototrichium* spp.), with small more or less hairy leaves, and downy catkin-like flower spikes. (Neal 332.)

kului.kului. Redup. of *kului 2.* (For. 6:421.)

kulu.keoe. vs. Perfect, without error, as a prayer. *Kulukeoe kāna pule 'ana,* his praying is perfect.

kulu.kulu. Redup. of *kulu 1;* to drip, leak, drop; leaky. **ho'o.kulu.kulu.** Caus/sim; to cause to drip, distill. (PPN *tulutulu.*) **2.** vi. To multiply, become numerous. *Kulukulu ka hua o ka 'uala* (Kep. 109), the fruit of the sweet potatoes become numerous.

kulu.kulu.'ā. n. **1.** Sap from green *kukui* nuts, used to prevent infections in cuts and as a gargle for sore throat and thrush. **2.** *(Cap.)* Name of a legendary chief at Hilo. (FS 251.)

kulu.kulu.ae'o. Same as *ae'o 2,* stilt bird. (PNP *tuli,* PCP *tutul(i,u).*)

kulu.kulu au.moe. Same as *kulu aumoe.*

kulu.kuluna. n. Flowing, leaking, dripping.

kuluma. vs. Accustomed to, acquainted with, intimate with; customary, usual, chronic. *Ma'i kuluma,* chronic sickness. *'Akahi no ā 'ike, 'a'ole i kuluma,* we've just met and have not been acquainted.

kuma. 1. Var. of *hākuma 1, 2.* **2.** n. Cracking of the skin between fingers and toes, as with athlete's foot.

kū.mā-. Prefix to numbers as *'umi kūmākahi, 'umi kūmālua, iwakālua kūmākahi, kanakolu kūmālua,* etc. See Gram 10.3 and *kumamā-.*

kū.maha.kea. nvi. To work in gardens; such work. *Hele aku i ke kūmahakea,* gone to work in food patches.

kū.maka. nvs. Seen by the eye, seen, visible; eyewitness; associated with; to see for oneself. *Kuhina kūmaka,* associated councilor. *Kūmaka ka 'ikena iā Hi'ilawe i ka papa lohi a 'o Maukele* (song), see, indeed, Hi'ilawe and the sparkling flats of Maukele.

kū.maka.hiki. nvs. Annual, yearly; yearly contract (see ex., *lōpā 1*). *Pua kūmakahiki,* annual flower. *Hālāwai kūmakahiki,* annual meeting. *Hana kūmakahiki,* work on yearly contract.

kuma.kaia. nvt. Traitor, turncoat; traitorous; to betray; to abuse one who has been kind to one. **ho'o.kuma.kaia.** Caus/sim.

kū.makani. 1. nvs. Windbreak; wind-resisting. **2.** Same as *'a'ali'i,* a shrub or tree.

kū.mā.kena. vt. To lament, bewail, mourn loudly for the dead, grieve. Cf. *make,* death.

kū.makua. 1. Same as *'āhihi 2,* a lehua bush. **2.** *(Cap.)* n. Name of a strong wind.

kuma.kuma. Redup. of *kuma 1, 2.*

kū.mala.mala. Var. of *malamala,* see *mala.*

kuma.lau.ā, kumalauwā. vi. To rise above. *'Akahi, 'alua, 'akolu, ka heluna kupuna o lākou, 'a'e'a'e kumalauā i ka mo'o kanaka* (chant), once, twice, thrice the enumeration of their ancestors, stepping high over commoners.

kū.malolo. n. Reverential bowing during old prayers.

kū.malolo.hia. Pas/imp. of *kūmalolo.*

kuma.mā-. Same as *kūmā-* (rare in conversation, Biblical). The origin is uncertain. Ellis (1827:479) suggests that the old term may have been *kumu ma,* beginning and; perhaps *kumu* assilated to *kuma* before *mā. 'Umi kumamākahi,* eleven (Biblical).

kumano. To set in order, as in laying stones. (And.)

kū.mano. n. Water dam *(rare),* reservoir.

kū.manō. v. To catch sharks with bait and noose. (Malo 210, 213.)

kū.mano.mano. n. A bur grass *(Cenchrus agrimonioides).* Also *kāmanomano.*

kū.mau. 1. vs. Customary, usual, regular. See *pu'u kālā kūmau. Uku kūmau,* usual fees, taxes, dues. *Hālāwai kūmau,* regular meeting. **2.** n. Deep wooden bowl with a thick base, as for poi. *Nā kūmau palapa'a o Nā'ālehu, 'oia mau nō kā pāpa'a,* the thick-based calabashes of Nā'ālehu are always crusted [with dried poi; strict adherents to principles, are the thick-headed natives of Nā'ālehu; the old poi stays in the calabash]. **3.** *(Cap.)* n. North Star.

kū.maua. vs. Lazy, inactive. *Rare.*

kū.mau.mau. 1. Redup. of *kūmau 1.* **2.** Same as *maumau;* constant, continuous, together. *Hai kūmaumau ē, hai kuwā!* (chant for those carrying a log to shore to be made into a canoe), follow together, follow shouting!

kū.mauna. 1. Var. of *kūmau,* bowl. **2.** Same as *'alaea,* dye plant.

kume.heu. n. Path, trail, road.

kū.meka. n. Shoemaker. *Eng.*

kū.mene. vs. Blunt, flat, of the nose. **ho'o.kū.mene.** Caus/sim.

kume.pala, kumebala. n. Cymbal. *Kumepala wala'au* (1 Kor. 13.1), tinkling cymbal.

kumia. Same as *kualakai 1,* a sea creature.

Kumia, Tumima. n. Thummim. (Puk. 28.30.) (Heb. *tummim.*)

kū.mimi. n. Small crabs such as *Lophozozymus intonsus.* Varieties are *kūmimi māka'o (Petrolisthes coccineus)* and *kūmimi pua (Lybia tesselata).* Both were used in sorcery and are inedible.

kū.mī.mī. vs. Frail, feeble, blighted Cf. *mīmī, 'ōmīmī.*

kumino. n. Cumin (Isa. 28.25). *Kumino ʻeleʻele* (Isa. 28.25), dill (RSV), fitch [seed of a plant] (KJV). (Probably Gr. *kyminom*.)

kū.moana. n. Large deep-sea crab (no data).

kū.moe. Bedstead. *Lit.,* standing bed.

kū.moena. n. 1. Long strip commencement of a mat. 2. Pile of mats; spread out as a mat or landscape. *Kūmoena weuweu,* pile of mats with grass or leaves sandwiched between the upper and lower layers, used for sleeping out-of-doors. *ʻOia kūmoena kalukalu hoʻi o Ka-paʻa,* that expanse of *kalukalu* grass of Ka-paʻa.

kū.moho. vi. To rise, overflow, as water. *Kūmoho piha ke kahawai,* the stream water rose full.

kū.mole. vs. Smooth, slippery, sheer, steep, rounded. **hoʻo.kū.mole.** To smooth, make even, as stones in a wall.

kū.mole.mole. Redup. of *kūmole.*

kū.mololo. Var. of *kūmalolo. Rare.*

kū.momole. Same as *kūmolemole.*

kūmoʻo. n. Lineage, as of chiefs or priests.

kumu. n. 1. Bottom, base, foundation, basis, title (as to land), main stalk of a tree, trunk, handle, root (in arithmetic); basic; hereditary, fundamental. *Kumu pali,* base foot of a cliff. *ʻIke kumu,* basic, fundamental knowledge. *Aliʻi kumu,* hereditary chief. *Alanui kumu,* main street. *ʻAuikumu,* nominative case. *Kumu kāhili,* staff of a *kāhili. Kumu nalu,* source of waves, as where surfing starts. *Mai ke kumu ā ka wēlau,* from trunk to tip [all, entirely]. (PPN *tumu.*) 2. Teacher, tutor, manual, primer, model, pattern. *Kumu alakaʻi,* guide, model, example. *Kaʻu kumu,* my teacher. *Kumu hoʻohālike,* pattern, example, model. *Kumu hula,* hula teacher. *Kumu kuʻi,* boxing teacher. *Kumu kula,* school teacher. *Kumu leo mele,* song book. *Kumu mua,* first primer. 3. Beginning, source, origin; starting point of plaiting. **hoʻo.kumu.** To make a beginning, originate, create, commence, establish, inaugurate, initiate, institute, found, start. 4. Reason, cause, goal, justification, motive, grounds, purpose, object, why. *Kumu no ka ʻoki male,* grounds for divorce. *Kumu ʻole,* without reason or cause. *He aha ke kumu i ʻeha ai kou wāwae?* What is the reason for your foot hurting? 5. An article bought, sold or exchanged; price. Cf. *kumu kūʻai. Kumu lilo,* price paid, cost. *Kumu loaʻa,* selling price. 6. Herd, flock. Cf. *kumu hipa, kumu pipi.* 7. Tenon (RSV), socket (KJV). (Puk. 26.19.)

kū.mū. 1. n. Goatfish *(Parupeneus porphyreus).* The stages of growth are *kolokolopā, ʻāhuluhulu, kūmū aʻe,* and the adult *kūmū.* 2. vs. Good-looking, handsome, especially of a sweetheart. *Modern slang.* 3. n. A variety of red-stalked taro; varieties are qualified by the terms *ʻeleʻele, kea, kū loa poni, ʻulaʻula, welowelo lā.*

kumu ʻae.like. n. Conditions for agreement, stipulations. (For. 5:119.)

kumu aʻo. n. Teaching, source of learning, teacher, tutor.

kumu ʻea. n. Tortoise-shell handle as on a *kāhili* staff.

kū.mū.hā. Same as *kumu ʻūhā.*

kumu.haʻi. n. Subject of a sentence.

kumu.haka. n. 1. Shelf. 2. Same as *akua lele.* (Kam. 64:134.)

kumu.hana. n. Topic, subject (as topic of discourse or grammatical subject); matter. (*kumu 1* + *-hana,* nominalizer; Gram. 6.6.2.)

kumu.hele. n. 1. Crotch. *Lit.,* source of going. 2. Kind of lashing used on outrigger of a chief's canoe. (Malo 131.)

kumu hipa. n. Flock of sheep.

kumu.hoʻēmi. n. Minuend.

kumu.honua. n. Concoction made of gourd vine and *kukui* nuts.

Kumu-honua. n. Ancient ancestor. (Malo 3.)

kumu honua. n. Beginning of the world, creation, origin of the earth.

kumu hoʻo.hā.like ʻia. n. Example, pattern. (Heb. 8.5.)

kumu hoʻōla. n. Ransom. (Mat. 20.28.)

kumu hoʻo.laha. n. Means of propagation, source of progeny. *Hoʻōla i kumu hoʻolaha maluna o ka honua apau* (Kin. 7.3), to keep seed alive on all the earth.

kumu hoʻo.lale.lale. n. Incentive. *Lit.,* reason [for] encouragement.

kumu hoʻo.manaʻo. n. Reminder, cue.

kumu hoʻo.pai.pai. n. Incentive. *Lit.,* reason [for] encouragement.

kumu hoʻo.piʻi. n. Complaint.

kumu.ipu.kukui. n. Lamp, not including the chimney; candlestick (Puk. 25.34). *Lit.,* lamp base.

Kumu-kahi. n. Easternmost cape, Hawaiʻi. Kumu-kahi and the western extremity of the islands at Lehua are mentioned poetically *(welo 2, welona).*

kumu kahi. n. Origin, beginning.

kumu.kā.nā.wai. n. Constitution, law code, provision of law. *Lit.,* source of laws. See *kūʻē. Kū i ke kumukānāwai,* constitutional.

Kumu.kau.oha. n. Sovereign Pontiff. *Rare. Lit.,* teacher of testament.

Kumu.koʻa. n. Name of a star.

kumu kūʻai. n. Price, cost. *Kumu kūʻai nui,* high-priced, expensive, costly; big price.

kumu kuea. n. Square root.

kumu kula. n. School teacher.

kumu kule.ana ʻāina. n. Land title.

kumu.kumu. n. Truncated stumps, roots; stubs, as of cut grass or decayed teeth; stump, stubble, as of a beard.

kumu kupa (kuba). n. Cube root.

kumu.lā. Same as *kūlālā.*

kumu.lā.ʻau. n. Tree.

kumu.lani. n. Base of the sky; horizon.

kumu.lau. 1. nvs. Female who has produced young, as of horse, cow, pig, chicken; to have produced young, female; root with many sprouts, propagating plant *(rare);* major source. See ex., *ʻihīʻihī. Lio kumulau,* brood mare. *He kumulau hōʻilihune,* a major source of poverty. 2. n. Providers of ti leaves for *hukilau* seining.

kumu.lena. n. Name of a disease, perhaps jaundice.

kumu.lilo. n. Loss.

kumu.lipo. n. Origin, genesis, source of life, mystery; name of the Hawaiian creation chant (see Beckwith 1951 and Johnson 1981); written *kumu uli po* in Malo text, Chapter 1, section 11.

kumu.lī.poa. n. A crab *(Simocarcinus simplex)* commonly found in *līpoa* seaweed. *Lit.,* līpoa source. Perhaps also *makua-o-ka-līpoa.*

kumu.loaʻa. n. Gain, profit.

kumu.manaʻo. n. Topic, subject, essay, tract; text, as of a sermon; proposition, theory.

kumu.maʻo, kumu.maʻo.maʻo. n. Any type of green Hawaiian stone, as used for *maika* stones.

Kumu-maʻo.maʻo. n. Easterly wind at Ka-lua-koʻi, Molokaʻi and Ka-maile, Oʻahu (Nak. 57 and 70).

kumu.miki. n. A mat motif with a continuous row of red lozenges with their lateral angles touching.

kumumu. Rare var. of *kamumu,* to crunch.

kū.mū.mū. vs. Dull, blunt, obtuse.

kumumumu. Redup. of *kumumu. Iwi kumumumu,* cartilage, soft part of bone.

kū.mū.mū.mū. Redup. of *kūmūmū.*

kumu.niu. n. An endemic fern *(Doryopteris* spp.), with broadly heart-shaped fronds, spore-bearing on edges.

kumu niu. n. Coconut tree trunk. *Pehu kumu niu,* swelling of lower limbs. *Nui kumu niu,* body heavy-set from hip to feet, with thick ankles and legs; *lit.,* coconut-tree bigness.

kumu.noʻo.noʻo. n. Subject for thought.

kumu.nuʻa. n. Sleeping mat thicker at one end than the other, with the thicker end used as a pillow.

kumu.oka. n. Perhaps a net used in bag-net fishing. Also *oka.* (Kam. 76:63.)

kumu.ʻō.lelo. n. Subject of a sentence.

kumu.one. n. Sandbank; sandstone, used for *maika* stones. *Lit.,* sand base.
kumu.pa'a. n. 1. Principal, capital (contrasting with interest). 2. Firm foundation, ancient times, firmly established. *Kauā kumupa'a* (Kep. 101), outcasts from the earliest ancestors. 3. Family god (same as the much more common *'aumakua*). *Ma'i kumupa'a,* disease caused by offending a *kumupa'a.*
kumu pā.kō.lī. n. Staff or five lines on and between which music is written. Cf. *pākōlī.*
kumu pani haka.haka. n. Substitute teacher.
kumu pepei.ao. n. Mastoid process, ear bone.
kumu piha.piha. n. Base of fish gills.
kumu pipi. n. Herd of cattle (less common than *pū'ā pipi*).
kumu.pou. n. Kind of lashing on canoe outrigger. (Malo 131.)
kumu.pu'u.naue. n. Dividend.
kumu 'ū.hā. n. Groin, joining of leg and torso. *Lit.,* source of thigh. Cf. *kūmūhā.*
kumu wai. n. Source of a stream, spring.
kumu waina. n. Grapevine.
kumu wai.wai. n. Source of wealth; resources; capital.
kuna. 1. n. A variety of fresh-water eel. (PPN *tuna.*) 2. Same as *kunakuna 1.* 3. n. Schooner. *Eng.*
kū.na'au. vs. To have a grudge, bear ill will. *Rare. Lit.,* standing intestines.
kū.nae. Same as *nae,* short of breath.
kū.na'e. vi. To stand firmly against opposition; unyielding.
kū.na'e.na'e. Redup. of *kūna'e.*
kū.nā.helu. vs. Moldy smelling.
kū.nā.hihi. vs. Weak, as from shock; dismayed, numb, dazed, shocked, horrified. *Kūnāhihi ke kino i ke anu,* the body is numb with cold. *Kūnāhihi i ka lohe 'ana i ka mea hou kaumaha,* faint with shock at hearing the tragic news.
kū.nahua. Same as *kanahua,* bent.
kū.na'i. Same as *kūna'ina.* **ho'o.kū.na'i.** Caus/sim.
kū.na'ina. nvt. To conquer, push over; conquest. See *na'i 1.*
kuna.kuna. 1. nvt. Itch, scabies; scabby skin condition; to itch. 2. n. Doorposts. *Rare.* Also *lapauila.*
kū.nana. Var. of *kūlana,* position.
kū.nā.nā. 1. vs. Puzzled, stumped, at wit's end, hesitating, undecided, bewildered; uncertain. *Lit.,* stand look. *Kūnānā au i ka'u mea e hana ai,* I don't know what to do. **ho'o.kū.nā.nā.** Caus/sim. 2. n. Goat. 3. Same as *'ānaunau* and *naunau,* a plant.
kū.nana.hale. Same as *kūlanahale.*
kunāne. n. Brother or male cousin of a female, usually used only as term of address or as an affectionate variation of *kaikunāne.* (PPN *tu(o)nga'ane.*)
kū.napa. vs. Insecure, unsteady, as an infant or invalid.
kū.napa.napa. Redup. of *kūnapa.*
kū.nehi. n. Ocean sunfish (*Ranzania laevis, Mola mola, Masturus lanceolatus*). Also *'āpahu, mākua.*
Kuneke, Sunede. n. Sweden. *Eng. Rare.*
kū.neki. vi. Filled to overflowing; to flow away. *Kūneki nā kū'auhau li'ili'i, noho mai i lalo, ho'okahi nō 'o kō ke ali'i pi'i i ka 'i'o;* let the small genealogies flow away; keep [them] down; one indeed, the chief's who ascends. [Advice to youngsters to respect the senior line and not talk of their own relationship to it.]
kū.neu.neu. n. A kind of *loli,* sea cucumber, perhaps a *Stichopus.*
kunewa. nvi. Weariness, fatigue; to stagger, reel, totter with fatigue. (PCP *tunewa.*)
kū.newa. vs. To pass, of time; to age. *Ka lāhui 'ōpio e kūnewa a'e nei,* the young nation growing up now. *Aia i ke au kūnewa akula, ma ia wā i ho'omana 'ia ai ke akua 'o'opu* (For. 5:511), it was in past times, when the *'o'opu* fish god was worshiped.
kū.newa.newa. Redup. of *kunewa* and *kūnewa.* (PCP *tuunewanewa,* giddy.)
kuni. 1. nvt. To burn, blaze, kindle, scorch, sear, brand,

earmark (cattle); to etch, in leather; blaze, scar, brand. *Hao kuni,* branding iron. *Ma'i kuni,* fever. (PPN *tungi.*) 2. n. Postmark, seal; to stamp. 3. n. Type of black magic that results in the death of a sorcerer, achieved by burning an object taken from the corpse of the sorcerer's victim; to practice *kuni.* Pebbles and *kukui* nuts used for discovering the sorcerer were wrapped in tapa such as *'ae-o-kaha-loa, 'ēkaha-loa, 'ō'ū-holo-wai,* and *pua-kai.* (Malo, Chapter 28.) 4. vi. To pursue at full speed.
kunia. Pas/imp. of *kuni 1–3. Kunia iho a pa'a, ke aloha i ka pu'uwai* (song), branded until imbedded, love in the heart. (PPN *tungia.*)
kuni ahi. nv. Fire kindler; to kindle or light a fire.
kū.nihi. 1. vs. Steep, sheer, precarious. *Hele kūnihi,* to go with difficulty, as through a tight opening. 2. nvs. Ridge, as of a precipice; ridge of a feather helmet; ridge of uncut hair on the head; on edge; sideways; sheer; partly open, as a door. Cf. *nihi. Hoe ma ke kūnihi,* to paddle with the edge [of the paddle blade].
kū.nihi.nihi. Redup. of *kūnihi 1, 2. He nohona kūnihi-nihi kēia,* this is a precarious way of life.
kuni.kuni. Redup. of *kuni,* to burn. (PCP *tungitungi.*)
kuni.kuni.hia. Pas/imp. of *kunikuni.*
kū.nini. Rare var. of *kūnihi 1, 2.*
kuni 'ō. nvt. To heal one afflicted with illness from another's *'anā'anā.* (Kam. 64:119.)
kuni ola. nv. A type of *kuni* practiced while the sick person was still alive but showed symptoms of being prayed to death. It resulted in the death of the sorcerer and saved the life of the intended victim. To practice such. (Kam 64:36.)
kū.nī.nihi. Same as *kūnihinihi.*
kū.nipo.nipo. Var. of *kūlipolipo.*
kū.noku.noku. Var. of *kūlokuloku.*
kū.noni. vi. To progress or move slowly. *Ke kūnoni a'e nei i ke ala loa,* going slowly along on a long journey.
kū.nono. 1. vs. Red, bright red; fiery (see ex., *welo 3*). 2. vs. Stubborn, willful, headstrong. 3. Var. of *kūlono 2, 3.*
kū.nou. Var. of *kūlou.* (Oih. 24.10.)
kū.nou.nou. n. 1. A kind of *loli,* sea cucumber. Also *hulali.* 2. Name for *kūpoupou,* a fish.
kunu. 1. vt. To broil on coals, as of meat, fish. Also *kō'ala.* (PPN *tunu.*) 2. nvi. To cough; a cough. **ho'o.kunu.** To cause coughing; to pretend to cough. (PEP *tungu.*) 3. Same as *kunukunu 1.* 4. vi. To buck, as a horse.
kunu kalea. n. Whooping cough.
kunu.kunu. 1. vi. To grumble, complain; displeased, dissatisfied. 2. Redup. of *kunu 1, 2.* (PCP *tunutunu,* to broil, to cough.)
kununa. Same as *kunu 1. 'O ke kununa maila nō ia,* he's just been broiling food.
kū.ō, kū.wō. vi. To cry loudly, as with joy or pain; to howl, as a dog; to roar, as a lion. See *uō. Mele kūō,* lamentation. **ho'o.kū.ō.** Caus/sim.; to pretend to howl.
kū.o'e. vi. To saunter, trudge. **ho'o.kū.o'e.** Caus/sim. *Rare.*
kuoha. n. Love prayer used by a *kahuna hana aloha* to invoke love in one of the other sex. Cf. *oha.*
kū.'oha. n. Venereal disease of genitals, either sex. *Rare.*
kuoho. n. 1. A large cowry, probably *Cypraea reticulata.* (Malo 45.) 2. Kind of fishhook, said to resemble the top of a cowry shell.
kū.'oho. n. 1. A variety of taro; petiole is grass-green with darker shading midway, light above. *Hawai'i.* 2. Medium-sized, deep bowl.
-kū'oi. ho'o.kū.'oi. Similar to *'oi 2. 'O ka lani ho'okū'oi kapu* (chant), the superior sacred chief.
kū.'o'i. Same as *kūpā'o'i,* to limp. **ho'o.kū.'o'i.** Caus/sim.
kū.'o'ili. vi. Steep, difficult to climb; to climb with great difficulty. *Rare.*
kuo.keki.mala, duodekimala. vs. Duodecimal. *Eng.*

kū.'oko'a. nvs. Independence, liberty, freedom; independent, free. *Lā Kū'oko'a,* Independence Day. *Hō-'ike no ke Kū'oko'a,* Declaration of Independence. *Ka Nupepa Kū'oko'a,* The Independent Newspaper [name of a Hawaiian-language newspaper published in Honolulu 1861–1927]. **ho'o.kū.'oko'a.** To establish independence, make independent.

kuo.kuolo. Redup. of *kuolo 1, 2.*

kū.ola. vs. Alive and safe, as after escaping from danger.

kuolo. 1. vt. To rub, scrub, polish, scour, scratch. See *olo 1.* **2.** vi. To tremble, as the voice; to shake, as with palsy; to vibrate, resonate, as a chanting voice. See *hula kuolo. Kai kuolo,* sea with an undertow. **ho'o.kuolo.** Caus/sim. (PCP *tuolo.*)

kū.'olo. vs. Sagging, baggy, as clothes; old, as a person with sagging cheeks; to sag.

kuolo.hia. 1. Pas/imp. of *kuolo 1, 2.* **2.** n. Probably all endemic species of a genus of sedges *(Rhynchospora),* with tufted stems, numerous narrow leaves, and clusters of small brown flower spikelets.

kuolo.kani. n. Timbrel (Puk. 15.20), psaltery (Hal. 92.3).

kū.oloku. nvi. Trilling song of a bird; to warble, trill. *Kūoloku ka leo o ka manu kani le'a,* the voice of the bird singing joyfully is trilling.

kū.oloolo. Same as *kuokuolo.* Rare.

kuoni. vi. To walk gently, slowly, softly; to lag behind. **ho'o.kuoni.** Caus/sim.

kū.ono. 1. n. Nook, cranny, interior of a house opposite the door, inside corner of a house; gulf, bay, cove, indentation, cell (of a beehive). *'A'ohe mea koe ma kū'ono,* nothing left in the corners [of a generous person]. **ho'o.kū.'ono.** To indent, form a bay, cranny, or corner. **2.** vs. Deep, as a cave; deep down, profound.

kū.'ono.'ono. 1. vs. Well-off, comfortably situated, rich, wealthy, well-to-do, well-supplied. **ho'o.kū.-'ono.'ono.** To prosper. *'Āina ho'okū'ono'ono,* homestead land. *Po'e ho'okū'ono'ono,* homesteaders. **2.** Redup. of *kū'ono 2* (Kel. 76).

kū.o'o. vs. Serious, dignified, sedate, earnest, stern, solemn (1 Pet. 1.13).

kū.'ō.'ō. n. Broken fragments of sweet potato, as cut by *'ō'ō,* digging stick, or spade. See ex., *pūpū 5.*

kū.'ou. Possible var. of *kūlou.*

kū.'ou.lena. 1. A kind of coarse tapa. Also *akoa* (AP.) **2.** Listless, uninterested. (AP.)

kū.'ou.'ou. Redup. of *kū'ou.*

kupa. 1. nvi. Citizen, native; well-acquainted. *Kupa no ka 'āina 'ē,* alien. *Kupa 'Amelika,* American citizen. *Kupa 'ai au,* native-born long attached to a place; *lit.,* native eat long time. *Ua noho ā kupa i kou alo,* to have stayed and become accustomed to your presence. **ho'o.kupa.** To naturalize, make a citizen. *Palapala ho'okupa,* citizenship papers. **2.** n. Army worm *(Pseudaletia unipuncta).* Also *pe'elua.* **3.** n. A dark-red cowry shell, as used for octopus lures. **4.** nvt. Soup, stew; to boil, make soup or stew; boiled. *Eng.* See ex., *'āmikamika.* **5.** nvi. Cooper; to do the work of a cooper. *Eng.* **6.** Also **kuba.** n. Cube. *Eng.*

kū.pā. nvt. Swivel adze (said to be named for a god of canoe makers); to dig, scoop, hew, till.

kupa'a. nv. Steadfast, firm, constant, immovable; loyal, faithful; determined; loyalty, allegiance, firmness. See ex., *-hiki. Kūpa'a ka mana'o,* faithful in thought; settled in the mind. *Kūpa'a kākou mahope o ke ali'i,* we are loyal to the chief. **ho'o.kū.pa'a.** To remain loyal, firm, etc.; to persist, perform, make fast, strengthen, fortify, establish. *Ua ho'okūpa'a 'oe i nā kuli e hemo ana* (Ioba 4.4), you have strengthened feeble knees. *Ho'okūpa'a i ka 'ōlelo o kēia pelika* (2 Nal. 23.3), perform the words of this covenant.

Kū.pā-'ai-ke'e. n. God of canoe makers. (HM 176–7.)

kū.pā 'ai ke'e. n. Adze. See *kūpā.*

kū pa'a.kai. vt. To soak in brine, as meat.

kū.pa'a.kai. nvt. To eat poi or sweet potatoes with salt or relish such as *'inamona,* and without meat or greens; hence a place without fish or meat. Same as *pū pa'akai. Mai kākou e kūpa'akai,* come and let's have some poi with a little salt.

kupae. interj. Goodbye; to say goodbye. *Eng.* Rare.

kupa.'eli. vs. Slow-moving. *Kaua'i.*

kū.pa'ewa. vs. Imperfect. *Hakina kūpa'ewa,* improper fraction.

kū.pā.ho'o.ha'o. Same as *pāha'oha'o.* (Kel. 107.)

kū.pā.hoa. See *wa'a kūpāhoa.*

kū.pahu. vi. To brace oneself, as while being pushed; to hurl, as a spear. *Ua mana'o ai e kūpahu, a 'o 'oe e kula'i ia'u,* planning to brace when you push me.

kupai. Same as *kupae. Eng.*

kū.pa'i. nvi. Heap, pile, stack, lot; to pile, stack, heap up, as in a disorderly fashion. *Kūpa'i ke aloha nou, ē Kīna'u,* a great deal of love for you, O Kīna'u. *Kūpa'i ka ukana ma ka uwapo,* the freight is piled up on the wharf.

ku.pai.anaha. vs. Surprising, strange, wonderful, amazing, extraordinary, unaccountable, marvelous; astonishing situation. Also *kupanaha.* **ho'o.ku.pai.anaha.** Caus/sim.

kū.paka. vt. To kick, thrash, as one in anger or as a child having a tantrum; to writhe, twist, struggle (Isa. 21.3); contorted. *Ua hikiwawe kona make 'ana me ke kūpaka 'ole,* his death came quickly without a struggle.

kū.paka.kī. Intensive of *kūpaka.*

kupa.kako. n. Supercargo, bookkeeper, clerk, purser. *Eng.*

kupa.ke'e. vs. Crooked. *Fig.,* contrary.

kū.paku. vi. To recover, as from a nearly fatal illness, or as a dying plant *(rare);* resuscitation, as related in legends. (For. 5:188.)

kupā.kupā. Redup. of *kūpā.* See *koili.*

kū.pā.kū.pā. interj. Boom, boom, as of drums.

kū.pā.kū.pā.'o'i. Redup. of *kūpā'o'i.*

kū.pala. n. **1.** An endemic gourd *(Sicyos pachycarpa).* Cf. *'ānunu* and *pua-o-Kama.* **2.** Same as *kākū,* barracuda. **3.** A wild sweet potato or morning-glory with enlarged tuber, eaten in time of famine. Also *paha, 'uala koali.* (HP 214.) *Ka-ho'olawe 'ai kūpala,* Ka-ho'olawe, eater of *kūpala.* [*Kūpala* was eaten here for lack of other food.].

kū.palaha. n. **1.** Designation for a *koa* tree with a thick, straight trunk, perhaps flat on one side or leaning close to the ground, good for a canoe hull. **2.** Temporary heiau temple.

kū.pala.iki. nvt. To quiet, soothe; soothing. *Auwē ke kūpalaiki ua 'ainiha nei,* oh, the quieting of this bad temper.

kū.palaka. vs. **1.** Congested; blocked, as stagnant water. *Ua hoopiha ihola ā kūpalaka ka lua o ka inaina,* the pit of wrath is filled and congested [hunger is satisfied]. *Kūpalaka ka wai o Welokā,* the water of Welokā is stagnant [one inactive, uninterested, stagnating]. **2.** Too loose, large, as of a garment.

kū.pale. nvt. Defense; to defend, ward off. *'Ao'ao kūpale,* defense [as in a trial]. *Kūpale 'ana iā Honolulu,* defense of Honolulu. *Pona kūpale,* defense bonds.

kū.pali. vi. To pole fish from a rock or cliff; to stand on a cliff.

kupa.li'i. 1. Same as *'ala'ala wai nui,* forest herbs. *Hawai'i.* **2.** vs. Small, dwarfish, diminutive; humble, of low rank; of retarded growth. *Kupali'i 'aiau,* humble one who serves a chief a long time. **3.** n. A variety of kava with very small leaf.

kū.palina. Same as *kūpalaha 1, 2.*

kupa.loke. n. Tuberose *(Polianthes tuberosa),* popular in leis. (Neal 227.) *Eng.*

kū.palo.loi. vt. To vibrate, as the ruffle of a drum; to trill; to drum with the fingers. *Kūpaloloi ka leo o ka pahu,* the drum produces a vibrating sound.

kū.palu. vt. To stuff with food, fatten, hence to make a favorite; to attract fish by chumming, as with decayed pork; to mash to a pulp, sometimes said of tapa particles or cloth beaten into tapa as it is being prepared. Cf. *palu. Kūpalu manō,* to chum sharks; shark bait (said also of human taboo breakers thrown into the sea).

kū.palu.palu. Redup. of *kūpalu.* (For. 5:201.)

kupa.naha. Same as *kupaianaha.*

kū.pani. vi. Wind-blown, as of clothes against the body.

kū.paoa. n. **1.** Strong permeating fragrance, as of jasmine. *'O ke kūpaoa e ho'opē ana i ka 'uhane,* sweet perfume that softens the spirit. **ho'o.kū.paoa.** To emit fragrance; fragrant. **2.** Night cestrum *(Cestrum nocturnum)* and other strong-smelling plants; by some authorities *Peperomia* spp., *Railliardia* spp., and a plant used to scent tapa (see *pele 3).* Also *'ala aumoe, onaona Iāpana.* **3.** Stone from which octopus fishing sinkers were made. (Malo 19.)

kū.pā.'oi. vi. To speak well of one. *Rare.*

kū.pā.'o'i. vi. To limp; to travel slowly. Also *kū'o'i.*

kū.pā.pā. **1.** vi. To grope, feel, as when looking for flaws in a wooden bowl. **2.** nvi. Hand-to-hand fight, struggle; to fight thus. *I kō lāua kūpāpā 'ana, ua ho'onāueue 'ia nā kumu pali,* in their hand-to-hand struggle, the bases of the cliffs were shaken.

kū.papa.kū. nvi. Bedrock; to stand on bedrock; depths of the earth.

kū.papa.lani. n. Chief of the highest rank; state of heavenly foundation.

kū.papau. Same as *papau.*

kupa.pa'u. n. Corpse, cadaver, dead body, carcass. *Po'e nīnau kupapa'u* (Isa. 8.19), people with familiar spirits. (PEP *tupapaku.)*

kū.papa.ula. vi. To stand facing the wind, as a house; exposed to the wind. *Rare.*

kū.pau. vs. **1.** Entirely finished. **2.** Fearful, shrinking. *Rare.*

Ku Pau. n. Name of the sixth day of the lunar month, and last of the four taboo days of Kū.

kū.pau.kolo. vi. To reverberate. See ex., *kūakā.*

kupe. **1.** vi. To stumble, twist the ankle. *Fig.,* to misstep, err in conduct. Cf. *'ōkupe.* **ho'o.kupe.** Caus/sim. **2.** n. A hula step: with the feet still and the knees bent, the body swings three times quite low down to the right, over to the left, and up. **3.** Same as *'ōlepe kupe,* a bivalve. (PPN *tupe.)* **4.** nvt. To steer a canoe; canoe endpieces.

kū.pē.kū.pea. n. Two pairs, as in poker. *Eng.*

kū.pe'e. **1.** nvt. Bracelet, anklet; fetters, manacles, handcuffs; to put or tie on bracelets, anklets, fetters; to hogtie. *Kūpe'e houku,* bracelets as made of crescent-shaped hog's tusks. *Kūpe'e ho'okalakala,* bracelet of boar's tusks; *lit.,* sharp bracelet. *Kūpe'e palaoa,* bracelet of whale teeth, or a single pierced whale tooth on a string worn about the wrist. *Lā'au kūpe'e,* stocks. *I kō lākou kūpe'e 'ana i nā hoe* (Nak. 61), because they held back the paddles. **2.** n. An edible marine snail *(Nerita polita);* the shells were used for ornaments, the rare ones by chiefs. Varieties are qualified by the terms *ānuenue, 'ele'ele, kāni'o, mahiole, palaoa* (lit., ivory, rare), *puna* (rare), *'ula.*

kū.pe'e lima. n. Bracelet.

kū.pe'e niho 'Ī.lio. n. Dog-tooth anklets.

kū.pe'e pipi. v. To bind feet of cattle, especially with the lasso.

kū.pehe. vi. To walk slowly, unsteadily, as of a sick person. Cf. *pehe,* unsteady.

kū.pehi. vt. To pelt, throw at. Cf. *pehi,* to throw.

kupe.kala. n. An edible bivalve found at Pearl Harbor, possibly *Chama* species. (KL line 29.)

kū.pē.kia. vs. Nervously afraid. *Rare.*

kū.pele. **1.** vt. To knead, as bread dough or very hard fresh poi. **2.** vt. To dub out the inside of a log for a canoe hull; to scoop out, as a trench; to dig and plow, as a taro patch. **3.** n. Concoction of juices of herbs mixed with poi, tender taro leaves, coconut cream, mashed sweet potato, and other food. **4.** vt. To fatten. Cf. *pele 2.*

kupe.leko, kupereso. n. Cypress. (Probably Gr. *kyparissos.)*

kū.pele.leu. vs. Sprawling, occupying all the space so that others have no room; broad, as hips. *Kūpeleleu ke kīkala,* hips broad.

kū.pele.pele. Redup. of *kūpele 1, 2.*

kū.pelo, kupero. n. Camphire, camphor.

kū.pene. vi. Permanent, stationary; to reside long in one place. Cf. *pene. Kūpene ku'u nohona i laila,* I lived there permanently. **ho'o.kū.pene.** Caus/sim.

kū.penu. vt. To dip, to dye by dipping; to sop up; to dab as with a wet cloth; to plunge into water, immerse.

kū.penu.penu. Redup. of *kūpenu.*

kupe.'ulu. n. Canoe *manu* made of one piece. *Rare.*

kū.pī. **1.** Var. of *'ūpī.* **2.** n. Abscess. Cf. *kua kūpī.*

kū.pihi.pihi. vs. Tiny, small, insignificant; to become insignificant. *Kūpihipihi loa kahi koena 'opihi,* the remaining limpets have dwindled in size [finances have dwindled].

kū.pika, kubita. n. Cubit. *Eng. Iwi kūpika,* forearm bone.

kū.piki.'ō. vs. Agitated, raging, turbulent, as wind or storm. *Fig.,* mentally disturbed. **ho'o.kū.piki.'ō.** Caus/sim.

kū.piki.piki.'ō. Redup. of *kūpiki'ō.*

kū.pili.ki'i. nvs. Crowded, packed, distressed, severe; critical, as in a crisis; in dire trouble; difficulties. *Kūpiliki'i Hanalei lehua lā* (UL 210), the lehua of (beautiful) Hanalei are storm-buffeted. *He mea 'ē ka lele kūpiliki'i o kona kino 'oko'a i ke aloha i kēia wahine* (For. 5:579), his entire body suffered extraordinary agony for love of this woman. *Kūlana kūpiliki'i o ka waihona kālā,* critical financial situation. *Kala'ihi ka lani, kūpiliki'i ka honua,* stormy the sky, distressed the earth [an angry chief].

kū.pina, supina. n. Subpoena. *Eng.*

kū.pina'i. nvi. **1.** To echo, reverberate; to mourn, wail, lament. See ex., *laukanaka. Kūpina'i i ke alo o Haoa-loa,* echoing in the presence of Haoa-loa [of the din of shouting or of rushing water]. **2.** To crowd, throng; crowded.

kū.pina.pina'i. Redup. of *kūpina'i,* to echo.

kū.pipi. vs. Crowded, as people, stars, or *pipipi* shells.

kū.pī.pī. **1.** n. A reef fish *(Abudefduf sordidus).* Also *'ō'ō nui.* Cf. *'ao'ao-nui.* **2.** Rare var. of *kāpīpī,* to sprinkle; to dash, as spray.

kū.pipipi. Redup. of *kūpipi;* to throng. *Kūpipipi nā kānaka i kēlā 'aha kālai'āina,* the people at that political meeting were jam packed.

kū.pō. **1.** nvt. Long net stretched across the track of fish, one end anchored in deep water, the other in shallow (Malo 210, 212); to set a net at night. Cf. *ku'u 2.* **2.** Scoop net (AP.) Also *kūpo'o.*

kū.poe.poe. vs. Round; bundled up with clothes, as in cold weather.

kū.poho. vs. Calm.

Kū-po'i-lani-ua. n. Name of a star. *Lit.,* stands the rainy sky cover.

kū.poki. nvt. Plaiting process of turning a pandanus leaf back, thereby giving the product a neat edge; to plait thus. Also *hi'i.*

kū.pola. vt. To roll, wrap up, as a package; to wither and curl up, as a banana leaf. *Kūpola i kēia pū'olo,* tie up this package.

kū.polō. vs. Unresponsive, fatigued, exhausted, spiritless.

kū.polo.lū. vs. Vaulting on a long *pololū* spear.

kū.pō.lua. vs. Fragrance (similar to *kūpaoa).* *'O Puna kūpōlua i ke 'ala,* Puna, fragrant with perfume.

kū pona. v. To stand a bond. *Ka mea kū pona,* bondsman.

kū.pono. nvs. Upright, perpendicular, honest, decent, proper, appropriate, satisfactory, rightful, reliable, right, just, fair, qualified, suitable, advisable, advantageous, convenient, seemly, fit, natural, applicable, nearby; worth, merit, excellence. Cf. *huina kūpono.*

Mahope iho o ke kahuna imu e kūpono ana i ka loʻi, behind the cook house next to the taro patch. *Ka mea i ʻike ʻia he kūpono,* as is seen fit; as is deemed proper. *Ka hope kūpono i kāna hana ʻana,* the natural consequences of his acts. *Nā mea e kūpono ai nā lunamakaʻāinana,* qualifications of representatives. *Nā hua ʻōlelo kūpono i ka mea i oʻo, kūpono nohoʻi i nā keiki,* words referring to the middle-aged, also applicable to children. *Ua hoʻomāhuahua aku naʻe ka uku o nā kumu kula e like me kō lākou kūpono,* the pay of the teachers was increased according to their merit. *Kūpono lākou i waho o Hanamāʻulu* (FS 67), they were just outside Hanamāʻulu. **hoʻo.kū.pono.** To behave uprightly; to conform to; to go straight toward, face toward, proceed correctly.

kū.pono ʻole. vs. Unsuitable, improper, disqualified, ill-fitting, inauspicious.

kū.poʻo. Same as *kūpō 2.*

kū.popou. 1. Redup. of *kūpou 1. Kūpopou ana i ka pali o Keʻe,* going downhill at the cliff of Keʻe [word play on *ke,* to object, and *e,* against; of one who does not cooperate]. **2.** Similar to *kūpaʻakai. Kauaʻi.*

kū.pou. 1. vi. To go down, walk downhill fast, stagger; to bend far forward, as one reeling drunk. See *kānāwai.* **2.** n. Cigar wrasse fish *(Cheilio inermis).* Also *poupou.*

kū.pou.kia. n. Socket in canoe for mast. *Lit.,* stand mast pole.

kū.pouli. vs. Befuddled, stupefied, mentally clouded, dazed, carried away with emotion, stricken. *Kūpouli i ke kaumaha,* stricken with grief. **hoʻo.kū.pouli.** Caus/sim.; anguish (Kel. 22). *Hoʻokūpouli ka manaʻo* (Kel. 15), worried thoughts.

kū.pou.pou. 1. Redup. of *kūpou 1.* **2.** Same as *kūpou 2;* the name may be qualified by *lelo,* yellowish.

kupu. 1. nvi. Sprout, growth; offspring; upstart, as one rising suddenly and conspicuously to high position; to sprout, grow, germinate, increase; to occur. *Kupu wale,* to occur by chance or spontaneously; whimsical. *Ke kupu, ka ʻeu, ke kolohe,* the upstart, the rascal, the mischief-maker. *Na wai ke kupu ʻo ʻoe?* Whose sprout are you? **hoʻo.kupu.** To cause growth, sprouting; to sprout. (PPN *tupu.*) **2.** n. Spirit, supernatural being. (For. 4:161.)

-kupu. hoʻo.kupu. Tribute, tax, ceremonial gift-giving to a chief as a sign of honor and respect; to pay such tribute; church offering. (Ezera 6.8.)

kū.pū. vs. Thick, as gravy, or moisture-laden *lomi* fish; to jell. **hoʻo.kū.pū.** Caus/sim.; to thicken.

kupua. nvs. Demigod or culture hero, especially a supernatural being possessing several forms (as *Kama-puaʻa* and *Laenihi*); one possessing *mana;* to possess *kupua* (magic) powers. Cf. *kalakupua. Pōhaku kupua,* stones with *mana,* as to cure sickness or prolong life. (PPN *tupuʻa.*)

Kupua-lalo-o-ka-lani. n. Name of a star. *Lit.,* demigod beneath the heavens.

kupu.ʻeu. n. **1.** Rascal, scamp. **2.** Hero, wondrous one, so called because the hero of tales often as a youth was mischievous and fond of plundering taro or stealing chickens (as Kama-puaʻa), a means of showing his exemption from the taboos of ordinary men. (Laie 475.)

kupu.hia. Pas/imp. of *kupu. Kupuhia e ka limu* (For. 6:470), overgrown with moss.

kupu ʻino. n. Evil person. (Kel. 22.)

kū.puku. 1. vs. Clustered, thick, rank. *Kūpuku ka nāhelehele i ka pilipā,* the weeds grow rank along the fence. **2.** *(Cap.)* n. Name of a constellation of a cluster of seven stars. Cf. *Makaliʻi,* Pleiades.

kupu.pū. 1. Redup. of *kupu 1;* to surge forth, as lava. (For. 6:545.) See ex., *unu 2.* (PPN *tuputupu.*) **2.** n. General name for ferns on a single stem, such as *kupukupu 3. ʻAʻala kupukupu ka uka o Kāne-hoa,* fragrant with ferns is inland of Kāne-hoa. **3.** n. Sword fern *(Nephrolepis exaltata),* a long, narrow fern with many lateral divisions; it was sometimes added to the hula al-

---

tar to Laka, for knowledge to *kupu* (sprout). (Neal 14–5.) Also *niʻaniʻau* and *palapalai* on Niʻihau, and *ʻōkupukupu.*

kupu.kupu ʻala. n. Rose geranium *(Pelargonium graveolens),* flowers pink, leaves fragrant, used in leis with odorless flowers. (Neal 471.) Also *kupukupu haole* and *laniuma.* (Neal 471.)

kupu.kupu haole. Same as *kupukupu ʻala.*

kupu.kupu lau liʻi. n. Long, narrow fern *(Nephrolepis duffii),* with numerous short lateral divisions on the frond. (Neal 14–5.) *Lit.,* small-leafed fern.

kupu.kupu maka.liʻi. n. A fern *(Thelypteris boydiae,* synonym *Dryopteris cyatheoides* var. *depauperatum).* Cf. *kikawaiō.*

kupu.lau. n. Spring season. *Lit.,* leaf sprouting.

kū.pule. nvi. Days set aside for prayer; to set aside time for prayer. (Kep. 23.)

kupu.liʻi. Var. of *kupa liʻi 2.*

kupuna. n. **1.** Grandparent, ancestor, relative or close friend of the grandparent's generation, grandaunt, granduncle. **hoʻo.kupuna.** To take a person as a grandparent or grandaunt or granduncle because of affection; an adopted grandparent; to act as a grandparent. (PPN *tupuna.*) **2.** Starting point, source; growing.

kūpuna. Plural of *kupuna 1. Mai nā kūpuna mai,* from the ancestors, traditional. *Pili ma nā kūpuna,* related through a common ancestor. (PCP *tupuna.*)

kupuna.hine. Rare var. of *kupuna wahine.*

kupuna kāne. n. Grandfather, granduncle, male ancestor.

kupuna kua.kahi. n. Great grandparent, great grandaunt or uncle.

kupuna kua.kolu. n. Great-great-great-grandparent, aunt or uncle.

kupuna kua.lua. n. Great-great-grandparent, great-great granduncle or grandaunt.

kupuna wahine. n. Grandmother, grandaunt, female ancestor.

kū.puni. vt. To stand around, surround. Cf. *kaʻapuni.*

kupu.ohi. vi. To flourish, grow vigorously, mature early, as an adolescent.

kupu.ohi.ohi. Redup. of *kupuohi.*

kupu.puʻu. Redup. of *kūpuʻu. Mai kākou e kupupuʻu, maie ʻai,* come and have potluck, come and eat.

kū.puʻu. nvi. Taro or sweet potatoes eaten with no preparation other than scraping or baking, i.e., without being pounded into poi or mixed with coconut cream; to take food from the oven and eat it informally; to have potluck.

kupu.wao. n. An endemic genus of small trees *(Broussaisia),* with a few forms, in the saxifrage family. Cf. *kanawao. Lit.,* mountain sprout.

kuʻu. 1. nvt, vs. To release, let go, discharge, abandon, free, dismiss, give up, yield, slacken; to pay out, as a line or cable; to settle, as earth; to diminish, as stream water; to fail to help (Kanl. 31.6); to finish, as a chant; to adjourn, put down, subside. *Fig.,* to be at peace (see idioms that follow). *Kuʻu aku ʻoe,* relax. *Kuʻu i ka ʻuhane* (Kin. 35.29), to give up the ghost [die]. *Kuʻu ka hanu,* breath is abandoned [death]. *Kuʻu ka luhi,* to be freed from cares, to rest [die]. *Kuʻu ka nae,* to get one's breath, rest. *Kuʻu i ka luʻuluʻu,* put down the burden. *Ke kuʻu ākea ʻana i nā paʻahao,* parole of prisoners. **hoʻo.kuʻu.** To release, let go, put down, dismiss, send away, abandon, disperse, adjourn; to expel, as from school; to discharge, as from work; to free, acquit, let, permit, excuse, exempt, liberate; to settle, clear up; slope of a hill *(rare). Hīmeni hoʻokuʻu,* closing hymn. *Kī hoʻokuʻu,* slack key. *Hihia ua hoʻokuʻu ʻia,* case [of law] settled. *Hoʻokuʻu kāua,* let's stop [as a meeting]. *Hoʻoku ʻu ia mai ka hopu ʻia ʻana,* exemption from arrest. *Hoʻokuʻu maikaʻi,* honorable discharge. (PPN *tuku.*) **2.** nvt. Type of net let down from a canoe; gill net; to set or lower a net or catch in a net. Cf. *kūpō. E kuʻu ana ka iʻa* (FS 243), the fish were being netted. *Kuʻu ka* pua *'ama'ama mai ka loko i'a,* net young mullets from the fish pond. **3.** poss. My, mine (this form may replace both *ka'u* and *ko'u;* it is frequently used before *ipo* and *lei* and kinship terms and expresses affection (see ex., *kei 1*). (Gram. 8.4, 9.6.)

ku'ua. Pas/imp. of *ku'u 1.* See chant, *'alaneo 1.*

kū uaki, kū uwaki. nv. To stand a watch; watchman, sentinel, guard.

Ku'u.anu. n. Name of a wind associated with Ka-lā-heo, Kaua'i. (For. 5:97.)

ku'u.kino. See *palapala ku'ukino.*

ku'u kuli. v. To drop to one's knees; to bend the knees, as while genuflecting.

ku'u.ku'u. 1. Redup. of *ku'u 1;* to let down gradually, slack off a little at a time. See *ala ku'uku'u.* **ho'o.ku'u.ku'u.** Caus/sim.; lenient, permissive; to pay out, as a fishline. *Kī ho'oku'uku'u,* slack key, as on a guitar [*kī hō'alu* is more common]. *Ua ho'oku'uku'u loa na mākua i keiki,* parents are too lenient with children. (PPN *tukutuku.*) **2.** n. Small, short-legged spider, so called because it lowers itself *(ku'u)* on a single string fiber. *Ke alanui a ke ku'uku'u,* the path of the spider [a name for the Equator]. **ho'o.ku'u.ku'u.** Same as above. **3.** n. Boomerang.

kū.'ula. n. Any stone god used to attract fish, whether tiny or enormous, carved or natural, named for the god of fishermen; heiau near the sea for worship of fish gods; hut where fish gear was kept with *kū'ula* images so that gear might be impregnated with *kū'ula mana,* usually inland and very taboo. *Lit.,* red *Kū.*

ku'u.lala. vs. Unrestrained, promiscuous, wanton (Iak. 5.5); free to do as one wants, whether right or wrong.

ku'u.lia. Pas/imp. of *ku'u 2. Ku'ulia mai i ka 'upena,* let the net down.

kū.'ulu.kū. vs. Rough, high, as billows. *'Ino'ino ka moana uluulu kū'ulukū,* stormy the high seas, mounting billows.

kū.'ulu.lū. vs. Chilled, shivering with cold; shy, abashed. *Kū'ululū ka hulu o ka manu i ka ua pehia mai ma ka pali* (dance), feathers of the bird are chilled by the rain beating down on the cliff.

ku'una. 1. nvs. Slope of a hill; let down, descended. *Fig.,* traditional, hereditary. *Ma'i ku'una,* inherited disease. **2.** n. Place where a net is set in the sea; to let down a fish net. **3.** vs. Relaxed, relieved. *Ku'una ka na'au,* the heart is relieved.

ku'una hele.uma. n. Anchorage.

ku'u 'ō.lelo. v. To release a word, make known. *I hilahila au iā 'oe; i ku'u 'ōlelo 'ia mai nei au i ke kauwā* (FS

101), I am ashamed because of you; I am being publicized here as an outcast.

ku'u.pau. vi. To do with all one's might or strength, exert oneself;to go the limit; to release all checks, inhibitions, restraints. See ex., *ka'uka'u lua. Ku'upau ka hui kinipōpō peku,* the football team gave all.

ku'u.pau.lia. Pas/imp. of *ku'upau.*

kū uwaki. Var. spelling of *kū uaki.*

ku'u.welu. nvi. To hang loose, dangle, as a string; to droop, to float in the wind, flutter, swing; to fall, as ripened fruit; fringed; tassel, sarong. *Kihei ku'uwelu,* fringed shawl.

ku'u.welu.welu. Redup. of *ku'uwelu.*

kuw-. Considerable spelling variation exists between *kuw-* and *ku-,* as *kuwala, kuala; kuwelo, kuelo; kūwō, kūō.* Both variants are listed in the dictionary, but the definition follows the preferred form, which is usually *kū-* unless the remainder of the entry exists as a separate word, or begins with a long vowel. See Gram. 2.1.

kuwā. 1. vi. To make a din, talk loudly, resound. See *wā 3* and chant, *kūmaumau 3. He leo paha no ka 'i'iwi e kuwā nei,* perhaps voices of *'i'iwi* birds making a din. **2.** n. Prayer for special events, as trimming grass from over the door of a grass house, or completion of a new canoe or net. (Malo 184.) See *'eleao 3.*

kū.waho. vs. Outside, outer, foreign. *Nū hou kūwaho,* foreign news. **ho'o.kū.waho.** To stay or keep on the outside.

kuwai. Var. spelling of *kuai.*

kū.wai.ū. n. Sinker on an *'ōpelu* net.

kuwā.kuwā. Redup. of *kuwā 1.*

kuwala. Var. spelling of *kuala.* Note derivatives after *kuala.*

kū.wala.wala. Redup. of *kuwala* (and *kuala*); topsyturvy, handspring; to turn cartwheels.

kū.walu.walu. vi. Much, many. (KL line 541.) Cf. *makawalu, olowalu, walu 3.*

kuwehu. Var. spelling of *kuehu.*

kuwelo. Var. spelling of *kuelo.*

kū.welu. 1. n. Woody shrub with a long tail-like inflorescence resembling cockscomb, perhaps an amaranth. **2.** Same as *limu loloa 2.* **3.** Same as *ku'uwelu.*

kū.wili. 1. vt. To move restlessly, embrace, pet, caress; to spin in a dance. Cf. *kuili, wili 1.* **2.** n. Implement for piercing an ivory ornament.

kū.wili.wili. Redup. of *kūwili 1.*

kū.wō. See *uwō.* **ho'o.kū.wō.** Caus/sim.; to pretend to howl.

L

In some localities n *replaces more common* l; *some of the* n-*forms may be Hawaiian innovations. Cf. Gram. 2.8.2, Elbert 1982.*

-la. See *lā 6.*

lā. 1. nvs. Sun, sun heat; sunny, solar. See ex., *lolo,* brain. hoʻo.lā. To sun, put out in the sunlight. (PPN *laʻaa.*) 2. n. Day, date. *Kēia lā,* today. *Lāpule,* Sunday. *Ia lā aʻe, ia lā aʻe,* from day to day. *Ka lā i ala hou ai ka Haku,* the day the Lord rose; Easter (Protestant). *Poʻe Hoʻāno o nā Lā Hope Nei,* Latter-Day Saints; *lit.,* saint people of these last days. *Lā kākou i kēia lā,* we have much sun today. (PEP *laa.*) 3. n. A sail. (PPN *laa.*) 4. n. Fin. *Kua lā,* dorsal fin. Cf. *lālākea.* 5. n. Each of two cross sticks holding corners of the dip net called *ʻupena ʻakiʻikiʻi.* 6. Common demon. occurring after both nouns and verbs, and as the last part of the demon. *kēlā,* that (far, see table 12 in Gram. 7.2) and *pēlā,* like that; following directionals it is usually unstressed and written as the concluding part of the directional *(aʻela, akula, ihola, maila).* It occurs also in the sequence *ua* (noun) *lā,* that aforementioned. A var. is *ala 4.* (Gram. 7.4.) *He kanaka kēlā,* that's a human. *Maikaʻi pēlā,* [it's] good that way. *Hele maila ʻoia,* he came. *Ua kanaka lā,* that aforementioned person. (PNP *laa.*) 7. Part. expressing doubt, uncertainty. See Gram. 7.5. *Pehea lā!* How, I don't know. 8. n. The letter "l". *Eng.* 9. n. Sixth note on the musical scale, la. *Eng.* 10. interj. Common refrain in songs, as in Elbert and Mahoe 90.

lā-. 1. Short for *lau 1,* with *k-* of the following word omitted: *lā ʻalo* for *lau kalo,* taro leaf; *lā ʻī* for *lau kī,* ti leaf; *lā ʻō* for *lau kō,* sugar-cane leaf. Also *lā ʻie* for *lau ʻie, lākī* for *lau kī.* 2. Short for *lau 3.* Cf. *lā ʻā, lā ʻiki, lālahi, lānihinihi.* 3. Third person, in the dual and plural pronouns only, *lāua* and *lākou.* (PNP *kilaa,* PEP *laa-.*)

-lā. hoʻo.lā. (a) Parsimonious, miserly. (And.) (b) Gray tapa, tapa in general. *Kauaʻi.* (AP.)

laʻa. 1. vs. Sacred, holy, devoted, consecrated, set apart or reserved as for sacred purposes, dedicated. Cf. *laʻahia. Mea laʻa,* consecrated or holy one or thing. *Lāhui laʻa,* consecrated nation. hoʻo.laʻa. To consecrate, dedicate, sanctify, bless, hallow. *Ka hoʻolaʻa ʻana,* the consecration, dedication. (PCP *laka.*) 2. vs. Cursed, defiled (Kanl. 22.9), bound under an oath, doomed to death or destruction (FS 120-3), in great trouble. *E mālama hoʻi ʻoukou iā ʻoukou iho i nā mea i laʻa, o laʻa ʻoukou i ka ʻoukou lawe ʻana i nā mea laʻa, a hoʻolilo ʻoukou i ka ʻIseraʻela i mea laʻa, a hoʻopilikia hoʻi iā lākou* (Ios. 6.18), protect yourselves from accursed things, lest ye make yourselves accursed, when ye take of the accursed thing, and make of the Israelites a cursed thing, and indeed cause them trouble. *Ā laʻa, ā laʻa lā,* so you did get in trouble, hurt, serves you right! I told you so! *A laʻa kō kū i ke aʻu,* so you did get jabbed by a swordfish [get into trouble]. *A laʻa kō hāʻule lā,* there you did fall. 3. n. Time, season (perhaps short for *lāʻau* and a missionary introduction). Cf. *laʻa make, laʻa ua, laʻa ʻula, laʻa ulu.* 4. Same as *palai ʻula,* a fern. 5. To propagate plants by inarching. (AP.) Cf. *kākiwi.* 6. vs. Also, together with, so, besides, such as, like. *E laʻa me kēia,* besides this, like this, for instance, thus, such as this. *ʻO ka launa nui aku i ka wahine ʻē, e laʻa me ka wahine i ke kāne ʻē,* much association with a different woman, as well as the woman with a different man.

lā.ʻā. n. Width, breadth, as of cloth. Cf. *laulā.*

lā.ʻae.ʻoia. n. Past days of youth, strength, beauty, prosperity. *I nā lā ʻaeʻoia, ua hele wale ʻia nō kēia kai e aʻu,* in the good, long-ago days, the sea was often traveled by me.

lā.ʻaina. n. Feast day.

-laʻa hale. hoʻo.laʻa hale. Dedication of a house; to dedicate a house.

laʻa.hia. Pas/imp. of *laʻa 1, 2. ʻAʻohe kani leo o nā manu o Olaʻa, ua laʻahia au me ke kuhi hewa* (song), the voices of the Olaʻa birds sing no more, I am cursed by illusion [or: I have held myself apart for an illusion].

Lā ʻAi Pele.hū. n. Thanksgiving Day. *Rare. Lit.,* turkey-eating day.

laʻa kea. n. Sacred light, sacred things of day, as sunshine, knowledge, happiness. *Lit.,* light sacredness. Cf. *laʻa uli. E nānā ʻia ka pulapula i ka laʻa kea i ka laʻa uli,* may the descendants be cared for in times of light and times of misfortune. *ʻO Pele ia aliʻi o Hawaiʻi, he aliʻi no laʻa uli, no laʻa kea* (prayer), Pele is a chiefess of Hawaiʻi, chiefess of sacred darkness and of sacred light.

-laʻa.laʻa. hoʻo.la.ʻa.laʻa. Var. of *hoʻolāʻau.* See *lāʻau. Rare.*

laʻa.lā.au. n. Small sticks, twigs, herbs, shrubs, bush (Puk. 3.2). *Pā laʻalāʻau,* hedge.

lā.ʻalo. n. Mature taro tops too tough to eat, and good only for wrapping (contraction of *lau kalo,* taro leaf).

laʻa.loa. n. 1. Varieties of small, narrow-bodied kitchen roaches including the brown-banded cockroach *(Supella supellectilium)* and the German cockroach *(Blatella germanica* or *Symploce hospes).* Perhaps named for Olaʻa, Hawaiʻi. 2. Var. of *olaʻaloa,* a variety of hard taro.

Laʻa.lū.ʻau. n. Name of a legendary people who were said to worship images and not gods, in the time of Wākea or of Hawaiʻi Loa. (For. 6:266, 271.) Also *Lālālūʻau.*

laʻa make. n. Season when plants die or grow slowly, like autumn in cooler climates. *Lit.,* dead season.

laʻa.mia. n. Calabash tree *(Crescentia cujete),* introduced from tropical America, fruit used for hula rattle with *aliʻipoe* seeds. (Neal 771.)

lā ano.ano. n. Person presiding over the game of *kilu. Lit.,* quiet day. (Malo 217, Emerson note.)

lā.ʻau. 1. nvs. Tree, plant, wood, timber, forest, stick, pole, rod, splinter, thicket, club; blow or stroke of a club; strength, rigidness, hardness; male erection; to have formed mature wood, as of a seedling; wooden, woody; stiff, as wood. *Kumulāʻau,* tree. *Ua hele ke kino ā lāʻau,* the body is stiff in rigor mortis. hoʻo.lā.ʻau. To form mature wood, as of a shrub; to gather in trees, as birds. (PPN *raʻakau.*) 2. nvs. Medicine, medical. *Hoʻohuihui lāʻau, paʻipaʻi lāʻau,* chemistry. 3. nvi. Lump or knot in the flesh, as eased by the rubbing *kahi* massage; to feel such a knot or stiffness; cramp, Charley horse; to have a cramp. 4. n. Picture frame. 5. n. General name for canoe endpiece. See *lāʻau hope, lāʻau ihu.* 6. For nights of the moon beginning with *Lāʻau* see below and Malo 31, 35. (PEP *Laʻakau.*)

-lā.ʻau. hoʻo.lā.ʻau. To insist, urge persistently; continuously, persistently, endlessly. *Hoʻolāʻau ka ʻai ʻana a ka iʻa,* the fish ate ceaselessly.

laʻa ua. n. Rainy season.

lā.ʻau ʻai. n. Chopsticks.

lā.ʻau ʻaila. n. Castor-oil plant; *Lit.,* oil plant. Also *kolī, pāʻaila, kaʻapehā, kamākou.*

lā.ʻau ʻala. n. Fragrant wood, especially sandalwood.

lā.ʻau aliʻi. n. Children of chiefs by second matings; their children were termed *laʻa uli.* (Kam. 64:6.)

lā.ʻau ana. n. Yardstick, ruler, surveying rod, measuring stick.

lā.ʻau hamo. n. Salve, ointment. *Lit.,* rubbing medicine.

lā.ʻau hā.nō. n. **1.** Asthma medicine. **2.** Jimson weed *(Datura stramonium),* a cosmopolitan weed, related to *nānāhonua (Brugmansia candida),* a coarse annual herb with white or pale purple or blue trumpet-shaped flowers 5 to 10 cm long and spiny fruits about 5 cm long. The plant is strongly narcotic and poisonous. A drug called stramonium, extracted from dried leaves and flowering tops, is used to treat asthma. Also *kīkānia, kīkānia haole.* (Neal 750.)

lā.ʻau hihi. n. Vine.

lā.ʻau hili. n. Switch, club.

lā.ʻau hanu.hanu. n. Inhalant.

lā.ʻau hoʻo.hia.moe. n. Drug, narcotic, soporific, medicine to cause sleep, chloroform.

lā.ʻau hoʻo.ikaika. n. Tonic, any medicine that strengthens.

lā.ʻau hoʻo.kaʻa. n. Rolling pin, any wooden roller.

lā.ʻau hoʻo.kani pahu. n. Drumstick. *Lit.,* drum-playing stick. Cf. *ʻuha moa,* chicken drumstick.

lā.ʻau hoʻo.luaʻi. Same as *lāʻau hoʻopiʻi.*

lā.ʻau hoʻo.make mū. n. Insecticide. *Lit.,* medicine to kill insects.

lā.ʻau hoʻo.mā.lie.lie. n. Tranquilizer.

lā.ʻau hoʻo.malule kino. n. Narcotic, drug. *Lit.,* medicine to relax the body.

lā.ʻau hoʻo.moe. Same as *lāʻau hoʻohiamoe.*

lā.ʻau hoʻo.nahā. n. Cathartic medicine.

lā.ʻau hoʻo.noe.noe. n. Drug, as opium. *Lit.,* befogging plant.

lā.ʻau hoʻo.pā. n. Medicine to prevent fecundation.

lā.ʻau hoʻo.piʻi. n. Emetic. *Lit.,* medicine to make come up.

lā.ʻau hoʻo.piʻi.piʻi. Same as *lāʻau hoʻopiʻi.*

lā.ʻau hoʻo.polo.lei. n. Splint.

lā.ʻau hoʻo.wali ʻai. n. Implement for mixing poi or *poi palaoa.*

lā.ʻau hope. n. After endpiece of a canoe.

lā.ʻau hū. n. Any gum-producing tree or plant, as candlenut, spruce.

lā.ʻau ihu. n. Bow endpiece of a canoe.

lā.ʻau iki ʻai ʻia. n. Edible herb. Cf. Roma 14.2. *Lit.,* small eaten plant.

lā.ʻau kaʻa. n. Cypress (RSV), fir tree (KJV) (Zek. 11.2); terebinth (RSV), elm (KJV) (Hos. 4.13); conifer.

lā.ʻau kaha. n. Boom of a vessel. *Lit.,* turning stick.

lā.ʻau kā.hea. n. A type of faith healing of broken or crushed bones or sprains. *Lit.,* calling medicine.

lā.ʻau kahi hā. n. One-by-four lumber.

lā.ʻau kala.kala. n. Lantana. *Lit.,* thorny plant. See *lākana.*

lā.ʻau Kaliki.maka. n. Christmas tree.

lā.ʻau kā.pala.pala. n. Bamboo stamp for marking tapas. *Lit.,* printing stick.

lā.ʻau keʻa. n. Wooden cross or crucifix; bar to hold a gate shut, brace, bolt.

lā.ʻau kī. n. Bar to hold a gate shut, bolt. Cf. *kī,* key.

lā.ʻau kia. n. Stick for snaring birds. Cf. *kia manu.*

lā.ʻau kiʻi. n. Easel.

lā.ʻau kini.pō.pō. n. Ball bat of any kind.

lā.ʻau kū. n. House post, post, doorpost; mast. *Rare.* Cf. *pou. Lit.,* standing stick.

lā.ʻau kuʻi. n. Ladder, tree with crosspieces used as a ladder (PH 174). *Lit.,* joined wood.

lā.ʻau kuʻi kope. n. Coffee huller.

lā.ʻau kuʻi palu. n. Wooden *palu* pestle.

Lā.ʻau Kū Kahi. n. Eighteenth day of the lunar month.

Lā.ʻau Kū Lua. n. Nineteenth day of the lunar month.

lā.ʻau kumu ʻole. n. Parasite. *Lit.,* plant without foundation. A legendary *koa* tree with this name at Kahikikolo, Kauaʻi, was said to have only branches and no trunk.

lā.ʻau kū.peʻe. n. Stocks, wooden fetters, handcuffs. *Lit.,* bracelet sticks.

laʻa ʻula. n. Autumn. *Lit.,* red time [of leaves].

lā.ʻau lā.lau mea ʻai. n. Chopsticks.

lā.ʻau lalo. n. Boom of a vessel. Cf. *lāʻau kū. Lit.,* down stick.

lā.ʻau lapa.ʻau. n. Medicine. *Lit.,* curing medicine.

laʻa uli. n. Sacred or doomed darkness, ignorance, gloom, the unknown, misfortune. Cf. *laʻa kea, lāʻau aliʻi.*

lā.ʻau liʻi.liʻi. n. Small bush, plant, or stick.

lā.ʻau loke (rose). n. Rosewood.

laʻa ulu. n. Spring, time of growth. (Kep. 89.)

lā.ʻau lua hā. n. Two-by-four lumber.

lā.ʻau mā.kaʻi. n. Policeman's club.

lā.ʻau make. n. Poison.

lā.ʻau moe. Same as *lāʻau hoʻohiamoe.*

lā.ʻau moe.kū. n. Wooden bedstead.

lā.ʻau ʻō.hiki.hiki niho. n. Toothpick. *Lit.,* stick to pick teeth.

lā.ʻau ʻoʻoi. n. Bramble, briar, thorny tree.

lā.ʻau pae.pae. n. Boom of a vessel.

lā.ʻau paheʻe. See *paheʻe 3,* dart-throwing.

lā.ʻau pahu.pahu. n. Billiard cue. *Lit.,* billiard stick.

lā.ʻau paʻi kini.pō.pō. n. Ball bat, tennis racket, ping-pong paddle; any kind of paddle for slapping a ball. *Lit.,* stick for beating ball.

lā.ʻau pā.lau. n. Fighting club.

lā.ʻau palu.palu. n. Herbs, tender vegetables.

Lā.ʻau Pau. n. Twentieth day of the lunar month.

lā.ʻau pauka makika. n. Punk for mosquitoes. *Lit.,* stick mosquito powder.

lā.ʻau piʻi. Var. of *lāʻau hoʻopiʻi.*

lā.ʻau pili. n. Name of a gambling game. *Lit.,* betting stick.

-laʻa waʻa. hoʻo.laʻa waʻa. Blessing of a canoe launching; to dedicate a canoe.

lae. n. **1.** Forehead, brow. *Nalulu ka lae,* to have a headache. (PPN *laʻe*.) **2.** Cape, headland, point, promontory. (PEP *laʻe*.) **3.** Wisdom; mental or emotional qualities. Cf. *lae oʻo, lae paʻa, lae ʻula,* and idioms *pohā 1; poʻohū 1.* **hoʻo.lae.** To pretend to be wise; to act smart; pretentious. **4.** An insulting term, followed by qualifiers, referring to *kauā,* outcasts, who had dots tattooed on their foreheads (Malo 70–2). Cf. *lae kiko, lae mamo, lae puni.*

laʻe. Same as *laʻelaʻe 1;* pure in sentiment (Hal. 19.8). Cf. *kālaʻe.* **hoʻo.laʻe.** To clear up, brighten. (PCP *lake.*)

lae.hana. interj. Syllables repeated in chants at ends of verses to mark time and for gay effect, similar to *ehehene.*

lae.hao.kela. n. Unicorn, rhinoceros. *Lit.,* brow with protruding horn.

lae.hina. Same as *noio,* a tern. *Lit.,* white brow.

lae honua. vi. To bow low, as the head. *Lit.,* earthward forehead.

lae kiko. n. *Kauā,* outcast, with a dot tattooed on the forehead. *Lit.,* dotted forehead.

lae.koloa. n. Type of hard, red stone, as used for adzes. Also *humuʻula.*

lae lā.ʻau. n. Forested point, whether at sea or inland. See ex., *kilokilohia.*

laʻe.laʻe. **1.** vs. Bright, shiny, clear, serene, calm, pleasant. *Hoʻokuʻu laʻelaʻe,* set at liberty, freed [as after a verdict of "not guilty"]. **hoʻo.laʻe.laʻe.** Redup. of *hoʻolaʻe.* (PCP *lakelake.*) **2.** n. A variety of sweet potato. (HP 142.) **3.** *(Cap.)* n. Name of a star.

lae la lae. interj. Syllables repeated in songs at ends of verses to mark time and for gay effect, similar to *laʻehana.*

lā.ʻele. n. Old leaf, ready to fall or beginning to dry (a contraction of *lau ʻelemakule,* old leaf). *Fig.,* aged; old age. *Mai ka liko a ka lāʻele,* from leaf bud to old leaf.

lae.loa. n. A kind of wine-red cotton cloth. *Lit.,* long brow.

lae lua. vs. Prominent, as a ridge. *Lit.,* double brow.

lae mamo. n. *Mamo* (bird) brow, a derisive name for *kauā,* outcasts, perhaps because the *mamo,* like some *kauā,* has a black mark on its brow (the yellow feathers of the *mamo* were prized, not the black).

lae.nihi. n. Name applied to various high-headed labroid fishes of the genera *Hemipteronotus* and *Iniistius;* this name may be qualified by the terms *ʻeleʻele, kea, nēnē, pūkea. Lit.,* sharp forehead.

lae oʻo. n. An expert. *Lit.,* mature brow. Cf. *lae ʻula.*

lae paʻa. 1. vs. Hard headed, obstinate, stubborn, closed in mind and hostile to new ideas. *Lit.,* hard brow. 2. n. Term for *kauā,* outcast. *Lit.,* marked forehead, probably referring to tattoo marks on forehead.

lae puni. n. Term for *kauā,* outcast.

lae puʻu. n. Bulging forehead.

lae.ʻula. n. A well-trained, clever person; expert. *Lit.,* red brow [red being the sacred color]. Cf. *lae oʻo.*

laha. vs. Extended, spread out, broad, published, circulated, distributed, disseminated, promulgated, advertised, broadcast, widespread, increased, numerous, common, general, ordinary. See *laha ʻole. Ua laha nui ka pānini,* cactus grows far and wide. **hoʻo.laha.** To spread abroad, publish, advertise, broadcast, disseminate, distribute, circulate, make known, promulgate, increase, propagate; advertisement, propagation, publicity. *Hoʻolaha kūʻai, hoʻolaha hoʻolilo,* notice of sale. *Hoʻolaha lima hana,* help-wanted ad. *Hoʻolaha manaʻoʻiʻo,* propagation of the faith. (PPN *lafa.*) 2. n. Gourd calabash painted with patterns. (HP 208.) 3. n. A kind of yam with white flesh under the skin (HP 168), contrasting with those with purple-red flesh under the skin that were liked for medicine.

lā.hai. 1. vs. To poise aloft, as a kite. 2. Rare var. of *lēhei, lēkei,* to leap. 3. n. Short wing fence to guide cattle to a corral.

lahaina. n. 1. A variety of sugar cane, usually free tasseling, heavy stooling, and with rather semierect to recumbent growth; large, long heavy tops. (HP 222.) 2. A variety of sweet potato. (HP 142.) 3. Poising; leaping. See *lāhai 1, 2.*

laha.laha. Redup. of *laha 1;* also said of a hen covering her chickens with her wings. *Umauma lahalaha,* broad chest. **hoʻo.laha.laha.** Redup. of *hoʻolaha. Lele hoʻolahalaha,* to soar in the air with outspread wings; to hover without perceptible wing movement. (PPN *lafalafa.*)

laha.lahai. Redup. of *lāhai 1, 2.*

laha.lahaina. Redup. of *lahaina,* leaping.

laha.laha wai. n. Broad puddle, pool.

lahala.wai. Slippery, muddy. (And.)

laha.lile. n. 1. Dark navy-blue calico cloth with small white prints or polka dots. Also *laholile,* shiny scrotum. 2. A variety of sweet potato.

lā hana. n. Workday.

lā hā.nau. n. Birthday. *Hauʻoli lā hānau,* happy birthday.

laha ʻole. vs. Rare, choice, unique; not spread, not common.

lahe. Rare var. of *nahe,* soft.

lā.hea. nvs. Vile-smelling; stench; one of unsavory reputation. *Kū ka lāhea,* the stench rises.

Lā.hei. n. A *lua* fighting stroke.

lahi. 1. vs. Thin, frail, delicate. **hoʻo.lahi.** To cause thinness, frailty; thin, frail. 2. n. A variety of sugar cane; the yellow mutation of *laukona,* otherwise same as *laukona* without variegations and stripes and more robust in growth. Also *ʻuala lehu.* 3. n. A variety of banana.

lahi kaha.kaha ʻā.kala. n. A variety of sugar cane; a pink or light red, striped mutation of *lahi 2,* and otherwise same as *lahi.* (HP 223.) *Lit.,* pink-striped *lahi.*

lā hiki. nvs. Eastern sun, rising sun; eastern. *Mai ka lā hiki a ka lā kau,* from sunrise to sunset [a whole day or whole life span]. *Ka lā hiki ola,* the life-bringing sun.

lahi.lahi. 1. Redup. of *lahi 1;* weak, as coffee; flimsy.

Also *nahinahi. Kou pāpālina lahilahi* (song), your dainty cheeks. (PCP *la(f,s)ila(f,s)i.*) 2. vs. Single-flowering, as a hibiscus.

laho. n. 1. Scrotum; with qualifiers, a term of abuse. Cf. *hoʻolaholaho, laho kole, laho oʻo, laho paka, laho ʻula.* See saying, *ule 1.* (PPN *laso.*) 2. Male, as *pipi laho,* bull; *puaʻa laho,* boar (fig., promiscuous male).

Lā Hoʻā.loha.loha. n. Thanksgiving Day. *Lit.,* day for expression of affection.

lā hoʻāno. n. Holy day, day of worship.

lā.hoe. 1. Rare var. of *lāhai.* 2. n. Cactus. *Rare.*

laho heʻe. n. Hernia, rupture.

laho kole. n. Raw scrotum (an insulting reference to poverty).

laho.kū. n. Promiscuous male.

laho.laho. hoʻo.laho.laho. Miserly; to hoard.

laho.lena. vs. Lazy, indolent, idling. Cf. *lena 4. He aha kā ʻoukou e laholena nei?* Why are you idling?

laho.lile. See *lahalile.*

laho.lio. 1. nvs. Rubber; automobile tire; elastic, rubbery. *Lit.,* horse scrotum. *Laholio hoʻopaʻa,* rubber band. 2. n. India rubber *(Ficus elastica).* (Neal 312.)

laho.nua. Short for *ola honua.*

lā hoʻo.kaha.kaha. n. Holiday on which everyone dresses up, enjoys sports, parties. *Lit.,* display day.

Lā Hoʻo.mai.kaʻi. n. Thanksgiving Day. *Lit.,* day to bless.

lā hoʻo.malolo. n. Day of preparation (Mat. 27.62); day before the taboo day, hence Saturday. *Rare.*

lā hoʻo.manaʻo. n. Day of commemoration, anniversary day.

laho oʻo. n. Mature scrotum, said of a male who reaches maturity.

laho paka. n. Crinkled scrotum (implication that there has been excessive drinking of kava).

laho.pipi. n. Eggplant *(Solanum melongena).* (Neal 744.)

laho pipi. n. Bull scrotum, as eaten.

laho pō.ka.ʻo.kaʻo. n. Dry scrotum (an insult similar to *laho kole).*

laho ʻula. n. Red scrotum (an insult similar to *laho kole).*

lā.hui. 1. nvs. Nation, race, tribe, people, nationality; great company of people; species, as of animal or fish, breed; national, racial. *Lāhui kaua,* a warring people; a large company of soldiers *(rare). ʻAoʻao Lepupalika lāhui,* national Republican Party. *Lāhui ʻaeʻa,* nomadic people, gypsy. *Lāhui pua o lalo,* commoner. **hoʻo.lā.hui.** To form a nation, race, etc. 2. vi. To assemble, gather together. 3. vt. To prohibit, forbid, lay a taboo, proclaim a law (possibly *-i* as a transitivizer; cf. Gram. 6.6.4 and Samoan *lafu,* to prohibit). *Lāhui ʻia ka walaʻau e Pele,* loud talk was prohibited by Pele. **hoʻo.lā.hui.** To cause to be consecrated; to taboo. (PNP *lafu,* PCP *laafui.*)

lā.hui hui pū. n. United nation. *Nā Lāhui Huipū,* United Nations.

lā hui.kala. n. Day of purification ceremonies. Cf. *huikala.*

lā.hui kanaka. n. Nation, people, tribe, multitude; mankind, humanity.

lai. n. 1. Name applied to the species of *Scomberoides,* fish. (PPN *lai.*) 2. Also *rai.* Rye. *Eng.* Also *huapalaoa ʻeleʻele.*

laʻi. nvs. Calm, stillness, quiet, peace, contentment, tranquillity; solace; serene, as of sea, sky, wind; quiet, silent, peaceful, pacific, tranquil, contented; to find peace. See ex., *forecast. Pō laʻi, ʻihiʻihi ē,* silent night, holy. **hoʻo.laʻi.** To cause to be still; to poise aloft, as a bird; to quiet, as a mob; to cease talking; calm; peaceful, quiet.

-laʻi. Transitivizer, as in *kaulaʻi, kulaʻi, lualaʻi.* Cf. Gram. 6.6.4. (Perhaps PPN *-raki.*)

lā.ʻī. n. Ti leaf (contraction of *lau kī).*

laʻia. Rare var. of *laʻi. Nā kai laʻia* (chant), the tranquil seas.

lā.ʻie. 1. Short for *lau ʻie, ʻie* vine leaf. 2. *(Cap.)* n. Place name, windward Oʻahu. Mormon Temple and Brigham Young University-Hawaiʻi site.

laiki, raisi. n. Rice *(Oryza sativa).* (Neal 69–71.) *Eng.*

lai.kī. n. Litchi. *Eng.*

lā.'iki. vs. Tight, as a dress; painfully stuffed, as the stomach after overeating; narrow, as a gate opening (contraction of *lā'ā,* wide, and *iki,* small). *Lima lā'iki,* long, narrow sleeve.

laiki loloa. n. Long rice.

lai.kini. n. License. *Eng. Wahine laikini,* licensed prostitute.

lai.kini hahai holo.holona. n. Hunting license.

lai.kini ka'a. n. Auto or vehicle license.

lai.kini kalaiwa ka'a. n. Driver's license.

lai.kini kī pū. n. Firearms license.

la'i.kū. nvs. **1.** Great calm, quiet, peace, serenity; becalmed. **2.** *(Cap.)* Name of a wind associated with Hālawa, Moloka'i. (For. 5:103.)

laila. loc. n. There, then (usually pronounced *leila* or *lila;* Gram. 2.7, 8.6). *Laila* follows particles with varying meanings: *Ā laila,* then. *I laila,* there, at that place. *Mai laila mai ā hiki i keia mau makahiki,* from then until the present years. *Kō laila,* of that place, local. *He 'olu'olu kō laila po'e,* the people of that locality are kind. *Malaila,* there. *Mai laila,* from there, thence. *No laila,* therefore, for that reason, hence, consequently; belonging to that place. *O laila,* of that place. *'A'ohe a'u mea makemake o laila,* there is nothing I want there. (PEP *l(a,e)ila.*)

la'i.la'i. **1.** Redup. of *la'i;* light-hearted. **ho'o.la'i.la'i.** Caus/sim. **2.** n. A variety of sweet potato.

lai.mana. n. Layman. *Eng. Rare.*

laina. n. **1.** Hives, urticaria. **2.** Line, row, verse. *Eng.* **3.** Cane trash *(Eng.* rind), bagasse.

laina kaula waha. n. Reins, lines. *Lit.,* bridle (rope mouth) lines.

laina.kini. Same as *'ainakini,* navy blue cloth.

laina moku.ahi. n. Steamship line.

la'i-o-Kona. n. **1.** A variety of sweet potato. *Lit.,* calm of Kona. **2.** Design on a tapa beater.

lai.pala. Same as *laipila,* libel.

lā.'ī.pala. n. A bright-yellow reef fish *(Zebrasoma flavescens). Lit.,* yellow ti leaf. Also *lau'īpala, laukīpala.*

lai.pela, raifela. n. Rifle. *Eng.*

lai.pila. nvt. Libel; to libel. *Eng.*

la'i.pū. vs. To be peaceful.

laka. **1.** vs, vt. Tame, domesticated, gentle, docile; attracted to, fond of; to tame, domesticate, attract. See ex., *'ena 2. Nui ka laka o kēia keiki i ke kupuna,* this child is so fond of the grandparent. *Ē Laka ē . . . e laka i ka leo, e laka i ka loa'a, e laka i ka waiwai* (UL 34), O Laka, attract the voice, attract profit, attract wealth. *Mai 'ena i ke kanaka i laka aku,* don't shy away from a person attracted [to you]. **ho'o.laka.** To tame, domesticate; to treat with kindness, as a child or animal, so as to familiarize with one. (PPN *lata.*) **2.** nvt. Lock, padlock; to lock. *Eng.* **3.** n. Lark. *Eng.*

lā.kā. n. Lascar. *Eng.*

laka.heke. n. Loghead. *Eng.*

laka.laka. Redup. of *laka 1.* **ho'o.laka.laka.** Redup. of *ho'olaka.*

lā.kana. n. **1.** Lantana *(Lantana camara),* a thorny tropical American bush with variegated flower heads, yellow, orange, red, white, and pink. Also *lanakana* (Ni'ihau), *mikinolia hihiu, mikinolia hohono, mikinolia kukū.* (Neal 722-4.) **2.** *(Cap.)* Also **Ladana.** London. *Eng.* See song, *luala'i.*

Lā Kā.paki. n. Sabbath Day.

lā kau. n. Setting sun. See *lā hiki.*

Lā Kau Pua. n. Decoration Day. *Lit.,* day to place flowers.

lā.kea. vs. Fair, white, of complexion. *Rare.*

lā kea. n. White fin.

lā.ke'e. Var. of *lāpe'e.*

lakeke. n. Jacket, blouse. *Eng.*

lā.kewe. Same as *lāke'e,* bending.

laki. nvs. Luck, lucky. See ex., *keha. Eng.* **ho'o.laki.** To bring luck; lucky.

lā.kī. **1.** nvs. Ti leaf (short for *lau kī).* **2.** vs. Stunted, as of plants that have matured. *Lākī mai kō lāua ulu 'ana* (Kep. 93), their growth was stunted [of plants].

lakika, radika. n. Radix. *Eng.*

lā.kike, latike. n. Lattice. *Eng.*

laki.kū, latitu. n. Latitude. *Eng.*

Lā.kina, Latina. n. Latin. *Inoa Lākina,* Latin or scientific name.

lakio, ratio. n. Ratio. *Eng.*

lakio like. n. Proportion, equal ratio.

lakio like 'ano hui. n. Compound proportion.

lakio like huli hope. n. Indirect-inverse or reciprocal proportion.

lakio like kau.kahi. n. Simple proportion or ratio.

lakio like kū.pono. n. Direct proportion, equal ratio.

lako. nvs. Supply, provisions, gear, fixtures, plenty; wealth; well-supplied, well-furnished, well-equipped; rich, prosperous. **ho'o.lako.** To supply, equip, provide, furnish, enrich. (PCP *lato.*)

lā.kō. n. Sugar-cane leaf (same as *lā'ō,* contraction of *lau kō*).

lako hale. n. Furniture and fixtures for a house. Same as *pono hale.*

lako kā.kau. n. Stationery supplies.

lako kaua. n. War supplies, ammunition, munitions, armament. **ho'o.lako kaua.** To supply arms, arm, fortify.

lako ke'ena. n. Office supplies.

lako kula. n. **1.** School supplies. **2.** Also **lako gula.** Jewelry, especially gold.

lako.lako. Rare redup. of *lako.* **ho'o.lako.lako.** Redup. of *ho'olako.*

lako lawai'a. n. Fishing tackle.

lā.kou. pronoun. They, them (more than two). (Gram. 8.2.) See *ē lākou ala* and *ē lākou nei* for use of *lākou* as a third person plural vocative. *Lākou iho,* they themselves. *Kā lākou, kō lākou,* their (a- and o-forms). (PNP *kilaatou,* PCP *laatou.*)

lakua. To talk incongruously, mixing proper and improper talk. (And.)

lā kulā.ia. n. Day of celebration in honor of a chief.

lakuna, rakuna. n. Raccoon. *Eng.*

lala. **1.** nvs. Diagonal, slanting, oblique; diagonal surfing or surf. *Pā lala,* to blow at an angle, of the wind. *He'e ana i ka lala lā, ho'i ana i ka muku* (song for Ka-lā-kaua), surf out diagonally, come back on the crest. (Thrum's Annual, 1896, page 109, says that the *lala* is the seaward side of a wave building up to break; a third interpretation is that *lala* is a wave to the right, and *muku* a wave to the left.) **ho'o.lala.** To turn aside. (PCP *lala.*) **2.** vi. To warm, as over a fire, to warm oneself by a fire; to bask in the sun; to cook over a fire. Cf. *'ōlala 2.* (PPN *lala, rara.*) **3.** vs. Bright, shiny. (PPN *lala.*) **4.** vs. Thin. Also *'ōlala.* **5.** n. Cap visor. **6.** n. A small bait fish (no data). **7.** vt. To straighten. **8.** n. A style of diagonal quilting. **9.** The four corners of a house. (And.)

lā.lā. **1.** nvi. Branch, limb, bough, coconut frond; timber, as of outrigger boom or float; wing of an army; to branch out, form branches, diverge. *Lālā 'u'uku,* small branch, twig. *Lālā 'ole,* without branches; *fig.,* childless. *Lālā ola,* person with offspring. **ho'o.lā.lā.** To cause to branch out, as by topping; to branch out, to lay out land areas; to mark with lines; to plan, make plans or projects (see ex., *'ōhio*). (PPN *ra'ara'a.*) **2.** n. Member, as of a society. **3.** n. Term in fractions. **4.** n. Slip, as of hibiscus. Also *lālā ho'oulu.* **5.** n. Sweet potato produced on a branch vine. **6.** n. Barb or hook, as of bone or coconut shell, on a mother-of-pearl lure; bone point of a composite hook. **7.** n. Fins. See *lā 4.*

lā.la'au. vs. Rotten, as of eggs; disturbed, addled. *Rare.*

lā.laha. vs. Broad. *Lit.,* broad surface.

lala.hai. Same as *lahalahai.*

lā.laha.laha. vs. To rise and swell, of surf before it breaks; broad, as a surface.

lalahela. Lazy, sinful. (And.)

lā.lahi. vs. Thin, delicate. *Lit.,* thin surface.

lala.hiwa. vs. Dark, as of a cloud.

lala.hū. vs. Convex; swelling; increasing in size; erect, as male organ. **hoʻo.lala.hū.** To cause to swell.

lala.hua. Pas/imp. of *lalahū.*

lalaʻi. Redup. of *laʻi. ʻAuhea wale ʻoe, ē ke ānuenue e la-laʻi maila i Hale-ola* (chant), hearken to me, O rainbow, so serene at Hale-ola.

lā.lā kanu. n. A cutting (to plant).

lā.lā.kea. n. Whitetip shark *(Pterolamiops longimanus),* up to 4 m long. *Lit.,* white fins.

Lala.koʻa. 1. nvs. Rarotonga, Rarotongan. (Tahitian; the regular Hawaiian correspondent of Tahitian Raro-toʻa would have been Lalokona; the second *a* in Lalakoʻa probably assimilated to the preceding *a;* Gram. 2.9.4.) 2. *(Not cap.)* n. Prayer for *luakini* dedication. (For. 6:27.)

lā.lā.koʻa. vs. With strong limbs. *Lit.,* coral branch.

lā.lā.kukui. vs. Many. *Lālākukui akula ka manō o lalo* (For. 4:297), many sharks were below.

lalala. vi. To sun, bask; sunny. *He mau moʻo e lalala ana i ka lā,* several lizards basking in the sun.

lala.lawe. Similar to *lalawe.* (For. 6:523.)

Lā.lā.lū.ʻau. Same as *Laʻalūʻau.* (Kep. 19.)

lā.lama. 1. vs. Daring, fearless, clever, as of a climber of precipices or trees. 2. nvt. To pilfer, meddle, grope, reach here and there; to be scattered here and there, as houses (Kel. 119); pilfering. *He keu ka lālama o ka lima,* how the hands pilfer.

lalana. n. 1. Spider. Also *lanalana, nananana.* 2. Warming, as at a fire. Cf. *lala,* warm. 3. *(Cap.)* Old term for London.

lā.lani. n. 1. Row, rank, file, line; verse of poetry. *Hele lālani,* to march in line. **hoʻo.lā.lani.** To place in rows. 2. *(Cap.)* A name for the Milky Way (Kep. 81), and also of a single star. Cf. *Nā-lālani-a-pili-lua.*

lā.lani poe.poe. n. Curve, arc.

lalaʻo. Redup. of *laʻo 1. Lalaʻo ka ʻikena i ka manu* (song), see the bird all the time, as though in the eye.

-lalaʻō. hoʻo.lala.ʻō. To insist on accompanying. *Kaʻu poʻe moʻopuna he hoʻolalaʻō i ka hele me aʻu,* my grandchildren insist on going with me.

lalapa. Same as *lapalapa 1, 2.*

lalau. nvi. Mistake, blunder, going astray; to go astray, wander, blunder, err, gad about, have sexual affairs, miss the way. Cf. *maka lalau. Lalau ka noʻonoʻo,* to wander mentally. *Lalau wale,* to wander aimlessly. *Lalau ka ʻōlelo,* to talk nonsense or wander in talking. *He lalau!* Nonsense! *ʻO ia hele lalau wale iho nō e hele lalau ai!* Just wandering aimlessly and to no purpose! *Ke lalau wale lā ʻo Puna i Ka-lalau* (saying), Puna strays to The-stray [many puns illustrating a wandering mind refer to Ka-lalau, Kauaʻi: see Pukui, Elbert, and Mookini]. **hoʻo.lalau.** To cause to wander, lead astray; to procrastinate, dillydally, kill time; to digress or wander in speech, perhaps to avoid a subject; to deceive, as in actions to conceal what one is about; to divert, as a child from the matter he is crying about; roundabout.

lā.lau. vt. To seize, take hold of, grasp, reach out for, pick up, hold fast. **hoʻo.lā.lau.** To cause to seize, etc.; to tackle. (PCP la(a)*lau.*)

lā.lau.ahi. vs. Gray, stormy-looking, smoke-colored. *Makehewa iā kāua ke hele, ke lālauahi maila ʻo uka,* it would be a mistake for us to go, it's threateningly gray inland.

lalau hewa. vi. To wander in error, sin.

lā.lau ʻino. vt. To snatch away or grab roughly or ruthlessly.

lā.lau lima. vt. To grab in the hands, tackle, manhandle.

lā.lā.wai. vs. Prosperous, successful, well-to-do, rich.

lalawe. Redup. of *lawe,* to carry; thrilling, overwhelmed, transported with emotion; to itch. *Ka lalawe ninihi launa ʻole* (song) a quiet transport unsurpassing [love]. **hoʻo.lalawe.** To produce thrills, itching.

lale. 1. vi. To hasten, hurry, push on; to encourage, urge on, stir up to action. See ex., *ʻeka 2.* **hoʻo.lale.** To hasten, incite, propose, provoke, hurry; to urge, suggest strongly, encourage. *Ua hoʻolale mai ʻoia iaʻu e hele i*

Hilo, he suggested that I go to Hilo. 2. n. Legendary bird mentioned in old tales and songs as a sweet singer.

lā.lea. Buoy, beacon; prominent object or landmark ashore to steer by. (And.) Cf. *māka,* marker.

lā.lei. nvs. Cluster, bunch, as of bananas; assembled together, as flowers in a lei. *Rare.* **hoʻo.lā.lei.** To gather together, as flowers.

lale.lale. nvs. Redup. of *lale.* **hoʻo.lale.lale.** Redup. of *hoʻo-lale;* to inspire, incite, rouse.

lali. vs. Greasy, as pork fat; slippery and shiny, glittering, sparkling, bright; sticky. Cf. *ali, hulali. Lali ka ʻili i ka hou,* skin sticky with perspiration. **hoʻo.lali.** To cause greasiness, glitter. (PEP *lali.*)

lā.liʻi. vs. Detailed; to do detailed work, attend to small details.

lali.lali. Redup. of *lali. Lalilali ʻole ka ʻili o ke akamai* (UL 36), the skin of the skilled [surfrider] is not slippery [with water]. (PEP *rarirari.*)

lalo. loc. n. 1. Down, downward, low, lower, under, beneath, below, subordinate; depth, lowness, west (see ex., *naʻe 1*); hold of a ship (frequently preceded by prepositions, sometimes joined as single words). *I lalo, malalo,* below, underneath. *Kō lalo,* of or belonging to below or the south; the people from below; bottom. *Mai lalo,* from below. *No lalo,* from below, belonging to a lower or southern place. *O lalo,* from below, subordinate. *Kai lalo,* western sea, where the sun sets. *Lalo loa,* far down, below. *Lalo lilo,* very far below. (PPN *lalo.*) 2. Leeward, lee, southern.

lalo.lalo. vi. Of humble origin, lowly. (Malo 56.)

lalo.loa. n. A variety of sweet potato. (HP 142.)

lalu, laru. n. Name of a ravenous land bird, perhaps a gull (RSV); cuckoo (KJV). (Kanl. 14.15.) (Gr. *laros.*)

Lā Lū Pua. n. Decoration Day. *Lit.,* day to scatter flowers. Cf. *Lā Kau Pua.*

lama. n. 1. All endemic kinds of ebony *(Diospyros,* synonym *Maba),* hardwood trees with small flowers and fruits. (Neal 674.) Also *ēlama.* (PNP *lama.*) 2. Torch, light, lamp. *Lama* wood was used in medicine and placed in hula altars because its name suggested enlightenment; huts were built of *lama* wood in a single day during daylight *(lama)* hours, and the sick were placed inside them for curing. (PPN *rama.*) 3. Also **rama.** Rum; any intoxicating drink. *Eng. He kanaka inu lama,* a person fond of drinking; a drinker or heavy drinker.

lama hoʻo.hui.hui ʻia. n. Mixed alcoholic drink, cocktail, highball. *Lit.,* mixed rum.

lā maka kanaka. n. Holiday; festive day on which people gathered for parties and celebrations. *Lit.,* day of people's faces.

lama kea. n. A tree mentioned in a chant in Kam. 76:118.

lama.kū. n. 1. Large torch, formerly 60 to 90 cm tall, with the light coming from burning *kukui* nuts strung on a coconut midrib and wrapped in dried ti leaves and placed at the tips of bamboo handles; signal fires; lantern (Lunk. 7.16); sparks, as of a torch (Isa. 50.11). *Lamakū o ka naʻauao,* torch of wisdom [said of great thinkers]. 2. Name for a medicine applied to sores.

lama kuhi.kuhi. n. Beacon, signal light.

lama.lama. 1. nv. Torch fishing; torch; to go torch fishing. 2. vs. Fair-complexioned; bright-looking; animated; vivacious; to glow. *Lamalama ka ʻili,* to glow with health.

lama paʻi.paʻi ʻia. Same as *lama hoʻohuihui ʻia. Lit.,* mixed rum.

lamie, lamia. n. Ramie, an introduced plant *(Boehmeria nivea),* related to the *māmaki,* and yielding a strong fiber used for rope, paper, cloth. (Neal 318.) *Eng.*

lana. 1. nvs. Floating, buoyant; moored, afloat, adrift; to drift, lie at anchor, as a fishing canoe (For. 4:295); calm, still, as water; of *hālana, manaʻolana. Huki ka lana* (Nak. 87), pull in the anchor. *Lana ke koko,* buoyant blood [of youth]; to circulate, of blood; high blood pressure (Kam. 64:43). *Lana ka manaʻo,*

hopeful, without worry, thoughtful; to want. *Inā e ma'i kekahi kanaka, lana kona mana'o i ke kauka,* when a person is sick, he wants a doctor. *Lana mālie iho ho'i ka mana'o me ka nani lei 'awapuhi* (song), thoughts of the beauty of the ginger lei are serene. **ho'o.lana.** To cause to float, launch; to right a canoe. *Fig.,* to launch a project; cheerful, unworrying, hopeful; to cheer up, encourage (Mat. 14.27), be of good cheer; to lighten grief, as by taking a mourner on a trip and away from the grave of the one he mourns. *Home ho'olana ma'i,* convalescent home. *Ho'olana ma'i,* to ease the pain of sickness. *Ho'olana ka mana'o,* to have hopes. *Ho'olana kaumaha,* to ease grief, condolence. *Ho'olana i ka wai ke ola,* life barely surviving; semiconscious (Probably PPN *langa.*) **2.** n. Lowest floor of the oracle tower where offerings were placed. (Malo 176.) Cf. *lananu'u, mamao, nu'u.* **3.** vs. To be aware of noises as one wakes. *Lana ka hiamoe,* awakening from sleep. **4.** Also *rana.* n. Frog. (Latin *rana,* a genus.)
-lana. 1. ho'o.lana (a) Same as *lana 3.* **(b)** Disobedient, willful. *Ho'olana noho'i nā keiki,* the children are so willful. **2.** Nominalizing suffix, Gram. 6.6.2. Cf. *kaulana, kūlana, mana'olana.* (PNP *-langa.*)
lana.au. vi. To float or drift with the current; to look about in every direction, wander, ramble, drift aimlessly.
lana.ha'a.kei. vs. Haughty, superior-acting (Isa. 2.11). *Lit.,* proudly floating.
lana hele. vi. To drift, as a ship.
lana.hia. Pas/imp. of *lana 1.*
lana.hō! interj. Land ho! *Eng.*
lā.nahu. n. Charcoal, coal. *Lua lānahu,* coal mine. Also *nānahu.*
lana.hua. nvs. Crook, protuberance, hump; bent out, convex.
!ā.nahu pō.haku. n. Cinders.
lanai. Var. of *nanai,* stiff-backed.
lā.nai. n. Porch, veranda, balcony, booth, shed; temporary roofed construction with open sides near a house. *Lānai kaupoko 'ole,* terrace.
Lā-na'i. n. **1.** Lā-na'i Island. Perhaps *lit.,* day conquest. Also *Nāna'i.* **2.** *(Not cap.)* A variety of sweet potato. (HP 142.)
lanai.ea. Same as *nanaiea,* weak.
Lana-ka-malama. n. Name of a star. *Lit.,* the light floats.
lana.kana. See *lākana 1.*
lana.kea. Var. of *nanakea,* pale.
lana.kila. 1. nvt. Victory, triumph; to triumph, win, overcome, beat, prevail, outwit, conquer. *Mea lanakila,* winner, victor, champion. **ho'o.lana.kila.** To cause to triumph; overbearing or impudent, as of a spoiled child unafraid of punishment, or of a most privileged, unassailable person. (PCP *langatila.*) **2.** *(Cap.)* n. Wind, Hau-'ula, O'ahu. (Nak. 57.)
lana.koi. nvt. To ask for insistently; to desire greatly; great desire. Cf. *koi,* urge. *Mea 'ole ia anu i ka mana'o i ka lanakoi a ka makemake* (hula song), the cold is as nothing when the desire is so keen.
lana.lana. 1. Redup. of *lana 1.* **ho'o.lana.lana.** Redup. of *ho'olana.* (PPN *langalanga.*) **2.** n. Lashings, as of ornamental sennit binding the float *(ama)* to outrigger booms *('iako).* **ho'o.lana.lana.** To make lashings, to lash. **3.** n. Spider. (Isa. 59.5.) Also *lalana, nananana.* **4.** n. Ylang-ylang *(Cananga odorata).* (Neal 357-8.)
lana.lana.hia. Pas/imp. of *lanalana 1. Nānā i ka moku, ha'aha'a kilohana i lalo, 'imihia lanalanahia, lana* (For. 6:389), behold the island, magnificent far below, sought for, hoped for, hope.
-lanamana'o. ho'o.lana.mana'o. Hopeful, encouraging. (Kel. 15.) See *ho'olana* under *lana 1.*
lā.nana. Var. of *kānana,* to strain.
lana.nu'u. n. **1.** High frame where heiau images were placed. **2.** Same as *lananu'u mamao.* **3.** Image placed in front of a heiau (AP.)
lana.nu'u mamao. n. Oracle tower; the lowest floor was

the *lana,* the second and more sacred floor was the *nu'u,* and the top, where the high priest stood to conduct services was the *mamao.* (Malo 176.)
lanau. vs. Unfriendly, unsociable. Same as *nanau. Rare.*
lani. 1. nvs. Sky, heaven; heavenly, spiritual. *'Ai lani* (1 Kor. 10.3), spiritual food. *Mai ka lani nō ā ka honua,* from heaven to earth *(fig.,* suddenly, without rhyme or reason). (PPN *langi.*) **2.** nvs. Very high chief, majesty; host (Isa. 34.4); royal, exalted, high born, noble, aristocratic. This meaning is most common in personal names, as *Lei-lani,* royal child or heavenly lei; *Pualani,* descendant of royalty or heavenly flowers. Cf. *kamalani, kuhilani. Ka-lani-ana-'ole* (name), the incomparably exalted one. **ho'o.lani. (a)** To treat as a chief; to render homage to a chief; to act as a chief; to enjoy the position and prestige of a high chief. **(b)** Same as *ho'olanilani.* **3.** n. Kinds of flowers. See below.
lā.nia. vt. To warm, toast, or wilt over a fire, as young pandanus leaves. Cf. *'ōlala, 'ōlani.* (PPN *rara.*)
lani ali'i. n. **1.** Royal chief. **2.** Same as *nani ali'i,* shrubs.
lani ha'a.ha'a. nv. Low sky, of the low sky, a poetic reference to Hāna, Maui, and its rains.
lā.nihi.nihi. vs. Thin, narrow. *Lit.,* edge surface.
lani.ka'e. n. Individual privileged to sit with the chief while the latter ate; he might eat the remnants of the chief's food, thus preventing them from falling into the hands of a sorcerer. (Malo 61.) *Lit.,* chief at edge.
Lani-keha. n. Legendary part of heaven; frequent name for residences of high chiefs, as that of Ka-mehameha III at Lahaina, Maui. (Malo 104.) *Lit.,* lofty heaven.
lani kua ka'a. n. Poetic name for a very high chief or the highest heaven. *Lit.,* sky with rolling ridge [i.e., clouds].
Lani-kū-hana. n. Name of a star. *Lit.,* chief stands [at] work.
Lani-ku'u-wa'a. n. Wind of Ka-lalau, Kaua'i. (For. 5:95.) *Lit.,* heaven releasing canoe.
lani.lani. Redup. of *lani.* **ho'o.lani.lani. (a)** Redup. of *ho'olani;* to treat as a chief; to claim relationship to a chief, especially unwarranted. **(b)** To exalt, praise. (PPN *langilangi.*)
lani nu'u. n. Highest heavens, an epithet for royalty.
lani pa'a. n. Firmament. *Lit.,* solid heaven.
Lani-pa'ina. n. A rain known at 'Ulu-pala-kua, Maui.
lani.pili. n. See *ua lanipili.*
lani.pō. vs. Dense, dark, lush, as of plants; rain; said of luxuriant growth. *Ku'u haku i ka ua Lanipō-lua, mehe pō lā kā ke anu o ke Ko'olau* (chant for Bernice Bishop), my lord in the dark pouring rain like the night and the cold of the Ko'olau [the lord protecting one from darkness and cold]. *Maika'i ka pā hale i punia i nā pua nani, lanipō i nā mea kanu,* how fine the house yard bordered with beautiful flowers, dense with plants.
Lani.pō-lua. n. Rain name. See chant, *lanipō.*
lani.uma. n. Both flowering and aromatic-leaved pelargoniums, also called rose geraniums. Cf. *kupukupu 'ala.* (Neal 471.)
lani wai. n. Similar to *lemi wai,* a water lemon *(Passiflora foetida).* Ni'ihau.
lani wela. n. Canada fleabane *(Conyza canadensis),* a weedy composite herb from temperate North America, with long, straight hairy stem, hairy, narrow leaves, and clusters of small flower heads. (Neal 834.) Cf. *ilioha.* On Ni'ihau *Conyza bonariensis.*
lā noa. n. Weekday. *Lit.,* day without taboo.
lā.nui. n. Holiday, important or big day.
Lā-nui o nā Lima.hana. n. Labor Day. *Lit.,* holiday of the laborers.
lā.nu'u. Same as *lananu'u.*
la'o. 1. vi. Having something in the eye, as a mote or eyelash. *La'o ka maka,* the eye has something in it. **ho'o.la'o.** To get something in the eye. **2.** Same as *la'o-la'o 2, 3.* **3.** Var. of *'ōla'o,* to weed.
lā.'ō. 1. Same as *lau kō,* sugar-cane leaf. **2.** n. A bright-

colored greenish fish, about 1.3 cm long *(Halichoeres ornatissimus).*

laoa. Var. of *haoa,* eel-catching stick; to fish with this stick; to choke, as on a bone. (Var. pronunciations are *la'oa, haoa,* and *ha'oa.*) **ho'o.laoa.** To fish for eels thus. (Var. pronunciation is *ho'ola'oa.*) *Nui ka iwi, he ho'olaoa,* there are many bones, they cause choking. (PNP *laoa.*)

la'oa. 1. Pas/imp of *la'o 1, 2.* **2.** Same as *laoa.*

lao.lao. n. Deep booming sound, as of distant surf. *Rare.*

la'o.la'o. 1. Redup. of *la'o 1. La'ola'o ka maka i ka lihilihi,* to have an eyelash in the eye. *La'ola'o kanaka,* commoner. **2.** n. Lack of satisfaction, even discomfort, resulting from eating unaccustomed or foreign food. **3.** n. Kindling; small sticks placed at a break in a bank of a taro patch; trash. **4.** vs. Rough, pitted, calloused.

lapa. 1. nvs. Ridge, slope, steep side of a ravine; ridged. Cf. *kualapa.* **ho'o.lapa.** To form a ridge; ridge. **2.** nvs. Overactive, energetic, mischievous; gamboling and cavorting, as a young animal; roughhouse; to flash. Cf. *'ālapa, 'ōlapa. Ka puhi lapa i ke ale,* eel playing in the hollows. *Lapa kai,* restless, active sea. **ho'o.lapa. (a)** To rise up; to boil; to swell, as a blister; to spread or blaze, as fire or volcanic eruption; to excite or flare, as with passion; to animate; to cook by boiling. *Ho'olapa ka 'ōpū,* a disturbed stomach. *Ua wala kī'aha paha, ke ho'olapa mai nei,* the glass is tilted back perhaps, getting active. (PPN *lapa.*) **(b)** *(Cap.)* Wind famous at Ka'ū. **3.** n. Bamboo liners, for tapa printing. **4.** n. Orifice of the womb. Also *lapa pū'ao.* **5.** n. Clot, as of blood. **6.** n. A variety of sweet potato. **7.** n. A variety of taro. **8.** n. Male *mahimahi* fish. **9.** vt. To slacken off the lower section on an *'ōpelu* bag net; part of the catch remains in the water, and the top part only of the net is raised to the canoe and the catch taken; a large catch would be too heavy to bring up at once.

lā pa'a.hao. n. Days of labor required of tenants. Also *lā kō'ele.* See *pa'ahao 2.* (RC 378.)

lapa ahi. n. Flame, blaze.

lapa.'au. nvt. Medical practice; to treat with medicine, heal, cure; medical, medicinal. *Kauka lapa'au,* medical doctor. *Kahuna lapa'au,* medical priest or practitioner. *Lā'au lapa'au,* medicine. *Nā pono lapa'au,* articles used in curing disease. *E lapa'au ana ke kahuna i ke keiki,* the practitioner is treating the child. (PCP *lapakau.*)

lapa.iki. n. Small drum. (Ii 137.)

lā.paki. n. Rabbit, hare. *Eng. 'Iole lāpaki,* rabbit.

lapa koko. n. Blood clot.

lapa.kū. vs. Excessively active. *Lapakū i Hawai'i ka wahine, a'o Pele* (chant), the woman Pele is most active on Hawai'i.

lapa.lapa. 1. Redup. of *lapa 1;* steep-ridged, many-ridged. *Ihu lapalapa,* high-bridged nose. *Po'o lapalapa,* a square head. **2.** Redup. of *lapa 2;* to bubble, boil, blaze; to cavort. *Wai lapalapa,* boiling water. **ho'o.lapa.lapa.** To cause to blaze, boil, etc. *Ipu ho'olapalapa,* boiler. (PPN *lapalapa.*) **3.** vs. Clotted. Cf. *lapa koko.* **4.** n. Native mountain trees *(Cheirodendron),* in the panax family, conspicuous for the slender-stemmed leaves, each leaf with three to five, rarely six or seven leaflets that flutter *(lapalapa)* in the breeze. (Neal 652.) Also *ehu, kauila māhu, māhu, 'ōlapa, 'ōlapalapa.* See also *hū 'ōlapa.* **5.** n. Name for a large *mahimahi,* dolphin.

lapa pū.'ao. Same as *lapa 4.*

lā.pau.ea. Var. of *hāpauea,* aged.

lapa.uila, lapauwila. 1. Same as *kunakuna,* doorposts. **2.** n. Booms joining hulls of a double canoe, corresponding to *'iako* of a single canoe.

lapa uila. nv. Lightning flash; to flash, as lightning.

lapa.wai. n. Amniotic fluid.

lapa wai. n. Agitated fresh water, rippling water, cascading water; shining water, as in the sunlight.

lapa.wā.wae. n. Shin, shank. *Lit.,* leg ridge.

lā.pe'e. vs. Bent, crooked, doubled up; curled up, like the tail of a pig; coiled, flexed. Same as *lāke'e.* **ho'o.lā.pe'e.** Caus/sim.

lapi, rabi. n. Rabbi. (Mat. 23.7.) (Heb. *rabbi.*)

lā piha maka.hiki. n. Birthday.

lā.pika. Rare var. of *lāpaki.*

lā.pine. Same as *lūkini,* lemon grass.

lapu. nvs. Ghost (Isa. 34.14), apparition, phantom, specter; haunted; to haunt; to act as a ghost. *Ua lapu ke keiki a kāua ia'u* (For. 5:557), I have been haunted by our child. **ho'o.lapu.** To pretend to be a ghost, as children on Hallowe'en.

lapu.lapu. vt. To pick up, as sticks for fuel; to collect, gather; to handle, tie. **ho'o.lapu.lapu.** Caus/sim.

Lā.pule. n. Sunday. *Lit.,* prayer day.

lā.pu'u. vs. Bunched up, humped up, curled up; crooked, bent over, arched; head bent forward, as of a bucking horse. Also *nāpu'u.* **ho'o.lā.pu'u.** Caus/sim.

lapu.'una. n. A hump, crook, arch; a humping, arching.

lapu.wale. nvs. Vanity, foolishness, worthlessness; worthless, mischievous, of no value; wretch, scoundrel. See ex., *niho mole. Lapuwale o nā lapuwale,* vanity of vanities.

lau. 1. nvi. Leaf, frond, leaflet, greens; to leaf out. *Lau* is sometimes contracted to *lā-,* as *lā'ī, lā'ie, lā'ō.* **ho'o.lau.** To grow leaves; to leaf out. (PPN *lau.*) **2.** n. Dragnet, seine, so called because formerly made of ti leaves *(lau)* tied to a rope. Cf. *hukilau, lauahi, lau-'apo'apo, laukō.* **ho'o.lau. (a)** To use a *lau.* **(b)** A bundle of grass or ferns set in water to attract shrimps or *'o'opu* fish; a net is placed under this bundle, and the fish shaken into it. (PPN *rau.*) **3.** n. Sheet; surface; blade, as of grass. Cf. *lā- 2; lauahi, lauhoe, laulā, laumania, moena lau.* **4.** num. To be much, many; very many, numerous; four hundred. Cf. *kini, mano. Ahe lau makani,* gentle winds, caressing. *Lau ā lau nā hōkū o ka lani,* hundreds and hundreds of stars in the heaven. *Lau lena ka pua o ka māmane,* the māmane is yellow with blossoms. **ho'o.lau.** To make numerous; to assemble, as of numerous persons or animals; numerous. (PPN *rau.*) **5.** n. Pattern, as for quilts; design; print of a cloth. *Pāhoehoe lau,* brocaded satin. **6.** n. Thatched mountain hut, as used by farmers, canoemakers, birdcatchers. **7.** n. Tip, as of the tongue; top (probably related to *wēlau* and *'ēlau,* tip). *Lau make,* death-dealing tip, as of a weapon. *Moe . . . i ka lau o ka lihilihi* (Kep. 115), to doze; *lit.,* sleep by the tip of the eyelash. **8.** n. Sweet-potato slip or vine.

laua. vi. Not much remaining to do, progressing, nearly finished (commonly used after a negative). *Ke laua aku nei kāna hana,* his work is coming along. *'A'ohe i laua aku kā kāua hana,* there's a great deal for us both to do.

lā.ua. pronoun. They, them (dual). *Lāua 'elua,* both. (Gram. 8.2.) (See *ē lauala* for use of *lāua* as a second person vocative.) (PPN *kilaua,* PNP *kilaaua,* PEP *laaua.*)

lā.ua'a.ua. n. Counselor. *Rare.*

lau.a'e, lauwa'e. 1. n. A fragrant fern *(Phymatosorus scolopendria* syn. *Microsorium scolopendria;* when crushed, its fragrance suggests that of *maile;* famous for its fragrance on Kaua'i (see *laua'e 2).* Pieces were strung in pandanus leis between the keys. See chant, *punia.* (Neal 27.) **2.** nvs. Beloved, sweet, of a lover. *Ka ipo laua'e o Makana,* the sweet beloved of Makana [reference to the famous *laua'e* ferns of Makana, Kaua'i]. **ho'o.lau.a'e.** To cherish, as a beloved memory. *I ka make 'ana o kāna kāne, ua ho'olaua'e a'ela 'oia i ke aloha,* at the death of her husband, she cherished the loving memory. **3.** Same as *laua'e haole.* **4.** vt. To gather together, collect. **5.** *(Cap.)* n. Wind, Honopū, Kaua'i. (Neal 58.)

lau.a'e haole. n. A fern *(Phlebodium aureum),* hare's-foot fern, from tropical America, much like the *laua'e,* but with larger, dull light-green scentless fronds. First collected in Hawai'i in mountains of Kaua'i (August, 1909), probably as an escape. (Neal 26.)

lau.ā.hea. n. Rumor, hearsay.

lau.ahi. 1. nvt. To destroy, as by fire or lava flow. *Fig.*, quick, deft (as after *lima*); greedy, lecherous. See ex., *one 'ā, 'owāhi. Lauahi Pele i kai o Puna*, Pele's lava flows are devastating seaward of Puna. 2. n. Bag net used for fish, as *'ohua*.

lau 'ai. n. Salad. *Lit.,* edible leaves.

lau.ā.kea. nvs. Common; commoner. *Lit.,* much public.

lau.aki. vt. To cooperate, work together, as of experts; to concentrate on the same task; to pool talents.

lau alelo. n. Tongue tip.

lau.'alo. Contraction of *lau kalo,* taro leaf.

lau-'ama'u. n. Tapa-beater design. *Lit., 'ama'u* fern pattern.

lau.'apo.'apo. n. Type of *lau* fishing outside the reef, seine. *Lit.,* catching seine.

lau.'au'a. vi. To withhold; stingy. *Fig.* to withhold or conceal strength, as a warrior (Malo 196, 203) or gambler; this may refer to the common tale motif of the idol hero who enters the battle only after his confederates are losing, as of Ka-welo, Pele, Pana'ewa. Another figurative use concerns a woman unattractive to males, and (AP.) a lottery or game of chance. Cf. *'au'a.*

lau.'awa. n. Pagoda flower *(Clerodendrum buchananii* var. *fallax),* a low shrub with downy heart-shaped leaves and clusters of scarlet flowers, native to Java. (Neal 731.)

lau 'awa. n. 1. Kava leaf. 2. First two or three taro leaves, as offered with kava leaves with prayers for a good food supply.

Lau-'awa.'awa, Lau.'awa. n. A gentle wind and rain associated with Hāna, Maui.

lau.'ehu. n. A grass endemic to Ni'ihau, *Panicum niihauense*, red leaf.

lau.'eka. Same as *pālau'eka,* pittance.

lau.'ekī. n. Top, as of sugar-cane tassel or of shell ginger about to bloom. Cf. *'ekī.*

lau.ele. vi. To wander mentally, imagine. *Rare.* Cf. *-ele.*

lau.'ena. 1. vi. To glow with heat, anger, passion. 2. See *One-lau-'ena.*

lau hala. n. Pandanus leaf, especially as used in plaiting.

lau.hala.lana. n. Vagabond, drifter, one as useless as pandanus leaves adrift in the sea. *Lit.,* floating pandanus leaf.

lau.hā.papa. Same as *laupapa 1.*

lau.hau. n. Brightly colored butterfly fish *(Chaetodon quadrimaculatus* and *C. umimaculatus).* This name may be qualified by the terms *kapuhili, kīkākapu, maha uli, nuku 'i'iwi* or *nuku 'iwi,* and *wiliwili.* Cf. *kapuhili.*

lau hau. n. Leaf of *hau* tree.

lau.hele. Var. of *laulele,* weeds.

lau.hihi. n. Same as *'ilie'e,* plumbago. *Ni'ihau.*

lau.hoe. 1. n. Blade of a paddle. 2. vi. To paddle together and uniformly, either in the same or different canoes.

lau.hua. n. A kind of *'o'opu,* a fish.

lau.hue. n. 1. A variety of poisonous gourd; to spread, of this vine. *Ho'okahi nō Hāwa'e, lauhue 'o Kona,* only one Hāwa'e [and] Kona is covered with the poison gourd [Hāwa'e was an evil sorcerer who prayed many to death; one bad person can poison a whole area]. 2. Var. of *lauhua,* a fish.

lau.hu'e. vt. To clear, remove, as mulch.

lau.huki. 1. nvt. Tapa soaking, to soak tapa. 2. *(Cap.)* n. Name of a goddess worshiped by tapa makers.

lau.hulu. 1. nvt. Dry banana leaf; to wrap, as a bundle, with ti leaves inside and banana leaves outside. *Fig.,* outsider, one from another locality (sometimes said disparagingly). 2. vt. Fast, swift, as of destruction; to seize, as an *'ahi* seizes a hook.

lau.'ī. n. Ti leaf. Also *lā 'ī, lau kī.* See ex., *polopola 4.*

lau.ia. n. A parrotfish *(Scarus dubius).*

lau.'i'i. n. A native fern *(Doodia* spp.), somewhat like *kupukupu 3.*

lau.ili. Var. spelling of *lauwili.*

lau.'ī.pala. Same as *lā 'īpala,* a tang fish *(Zebrasoma flavescens).*

lau.'ī peke.peke. n. Short, stunted ti leaves; a term of opprobrium for the *kauā* (outcast), as such ti leaves were of less value than long leaves. Same as *lauwiliwili,* a fish.

lau'ī.wili.wili. Same as *lauwiliwili,* a fish.

lau.kahi. n. 1. Broad-leafed plantain *(Plantago major),* a Eurasian stemless weed, with thick broad leaves, 2.5 to 25 cm long, forming a rosette near the ground, and with tiny flowers developing in a cylindrical head at the tip of a slender stalk; used externally to ripen and heal boils, internally for diabetes and other ailments. (Neal 792.) *Lit.,* single leaf. Also *kūhēkili.* (Perhaps PCP *rautasi.*) 2. Marsh pennywort *(Hydrocotyle verticillata).* Ni'ihau. Cf. *pohe 2* and Neal 659.

lau.kahi kua.hiwi. n. Mountain *laukahi.*

lau.kahi lau nui. n. A species of *laukahi.* *Lit.,* big-leafed *laukahi.*

lau.kahi li'i.li'i. n. A native sword-shaped fern *(Elaphoglossum* sp.) *Lit.,* small *laukahi.*

lau.kahi nunui. n. 1. Native sword-shaped fern *(Elaphoglossum aemulum).* 2. Broad-leafed plantain. *Lit.,* large *laukahi.*

lau.kā.hi'u. n. A kind of shark, possibly thresher. *Lit.,* much hit tail.

lau.kala.koa. n. Snowbush *(Breynia disticha* syn. *B. nivosa)* from South Pacific islands. It has rounded-oval leaves, mottled green and white, or, in one variety, green, white, red, and pink. *Lit.,* calico *(Eng.)* leaf. (Neal 500.)

lau.kalo. Same as *pūnua,* fledgling.

lau kalo. n. Taro leaf.

lau.kamana, laudamana. n. Laudanum. *Eng.*

Lau-kamani. n. Wind associated with Hālawa, Moloka'i. (For. 5:103.) *Lit., kamani* leaf.

lau.kana. vs. Uninterested in religion, indifferent to religion. *Rare.*

lau.kanaka. nvt. Densely populated, having many people; many people; to populate. *I laukanaka au i nā leo kūpina'i* (Kel. 61), that I peopled with echoes.

ho'o.lau.kanaka. To have many people about one; to dispel loneliness with people. *Ka manu ho'olaukanaka, o ia uka 'iu ano* (song), the bird that dispels loneliness in that far, quiet upland.

-laukanea. Same as *ho'okanea. Ho'o-laukanea kēia piki ia'u no ka mea 'o ka puni kēia a ku'u mo'opuna,* I've lost appetite for this peach because it is my grandchild's favorite.

lau.kani. vs. Tough, hardy. (For. 6:392.)

lau.kanu. n. Planted sweet-potato vine. See *lau 8.*

lau.kapa.lala. n. Legendary name for broad leaves of the first taro, said to have been born of a woman. Cf. *lau kapalili 2.*

lau kapa.lili. 1. Same as *hukilau,* seine fishing, but reportedly used in deeper water and with yellowed ti or banana leaves. *Lit.,* trembling net. 2. n. Legendary name for trembling leaves of the first taro, said to have been born of a woman. (Malo 244.) Cf. *laukapalala.*

lau.kea. 1. n. A small tree or shrub *(Claoxylon sandwicense,* var. *tomentosum* and *degeneri; C. helleri)* on Kaua'i only, in the euphorbia family, having leaves to about 8 by 18 cm and small clustered flowers. Cf. *po'olā* (Neal 499.) 2. n. Hard gray stone, used for adzes. 3. vs. Gray with age or sickness; pale, as an invalid.

lau.kī. n. A cosmopolitan tropical weed *(Cassia leschenaultiana),* a small shrub with finely divided leaves, yellow flowers, and small narrow pods. (Neal 427.)

lau kī. n. 1. Ti leaf. 2. Tea leaf. Cf. *ko'oko'olau.*

lau.kī.pala. Same as *lā 'īpala,* a fish.

lau kī pala. n. Yellowed ti leaf.

lau.kō. n. Dragnet.

lau.koa. vi. To feather out, as young birds. **hoʻo.lau.koa.** Same as above. *I malumalu ai kāna pūnua i manaʻo ai e hoʻolaukoa* (chant for Ka-wānana-koa), to shelter their fledglings which they expect to feather out.

lau koa. n. Leaf of a *koa* tree.

lau.kona. n. A variety of sugar cane with green and yellow striped canes and leaves; used in sorcery, because of the meaning of *laukōnā,* to break the influence of the *hana aloha* love magic and change love into hatred. Also *manini.*

lau.kō.nā. vs. Hardhearted, merciless, heartless, unfriendly, implacable; furious, very angry. *Laukōnā au i kāna hana,* I'm furious about what he's done. *Laukōnā wale mai nō ke aloha* (prayer), may the love be turned to hate. **hoʻo.lau.kō.nā.** To treat cruelly, mercilessly; to oppress; to cause hatred.

lau.kona.kona. Same as *laukona.* (HP 225.)

lau.kona.konā. Redup. of *laukōnā.*

lau.kō pua. n. Fishing for young fish *(pua)* with fine nets.

Lau.kō-wai. n. Wind associated with Maui. (For. 5:101.) *Lit.,* water dragnet.

lau.kua. 1. vs. Confused, repetitious, mixed, incoherent, as speech; miscellaneous; irregular-shaped, as some leaves. 2. vt. To take or gather indiscriminately. Similar to *hāpuku.* 3. n. One skilled in many trades, a jack-of-all-trades. 4. Fish pond. (AP.)

lau.kū.kahi. n. A native fern *(Lindsaya macraena),* with narrow, divided fronds. *Hawaiʻi. Lit.,* leaf that is alone.

lau.lā. nvi. Broad, wide; liberal; width, breadth, extent; widely known; publicly. *Hele laulā,* to act with freedom or liberty, to go freely. *Inoa laulā,* name generally known, not taboo. *Maʻi laulā,* epidemic, contagious disease. *Manaʻo laulā,* broad-minded; liberal ideas. *ʻŌlelo laulā,* general conversation. *Unuhi laulā loa,* free translation. *Ua ʻōlelo laulā ʻia,* publicly stated. **hoʻo.lau.lā.** Same as *laulā;* to broaden, widen, extend. *Manaʻo hoʻolaulā,* consideration of many angles. *Hoʻolaulā i ka manaʻo,* to broaden the mind or thought.

lau.laha. vs. Spread far and wide, as news, widespread; circulated, publicized; of common or general knowledge; spread contagiously, as a disease. *Lit.,* much spread. *Nā mana laulaha o ke kiaʻāina,* general powers of the governor. **hoʻo.lau.laha.** To spread, circulate, publicize, make known.

lau.lahi.lahi. vs. Thin.

lau-lama. n. Design on a Niʻihau mat. *Lit.,* many torches or *lama* tree leaves.

lau.lau. 1. nvt. Wrapping, wrapped package; packages of ti leaves or banana leaves containing pork, beef, salted fish, or taro tops, baked in the ground oven, steamed or broiled; any cloth, net, or leaves used as a wrapper or carrier; to wrap or carry in such bundles. *Laulau moni* (Kin. 42.35), bundle of money. (PPN *laulau.*) 2. n. Hat rim. 3. vs. Pregnant. 4. n. Paddle blade.

lau.launa. Redup. of *launa;* sociable, friendly, gregarious, genial. *He ʻoluʻolu, he laulauna,* pleasant, sociable. *ʻA ʻohe laulauna wale mai,* not at all sociable. *Laulauna ʻole,* antisocial.

lau.lā.wili. Var. of *lauwili.* (And.)

lau.leʻa. nvs. Peace, happiness, friendship; restoration of a disrupted friendship; happy, glad, genial, courteous, peaceful. *Lauleʻa ʻole,* unsociable. *Lauleʻa ka nohona o nei kula,* life on this plain is happy. **hoʻo.lau.leʻa.** Celebration, festival, gathering for a celebration, large party; satisfaction; to hold a celebration, to celebrate; to reconcile, restore peace or friendship, appease (Kin. 32.20); to preserve friendship and good will; to be at peace with; to seek to please. *Ke hoʻolauleʻa nei anei au i kānaka, a i ke Akua anei?*

(Gal. 1.10), do I now persuade men or God? *Hāʻawi aku iā ʻoukou i nā hoʻolauleʻa ʻana ā nui wale ma ke kūʻai ʻana aku ma koʻu hale kūʻai,* to give you great satisfaction in making purchases at my store.

lau.lele. n. 1. Butterfly weed or milkweed *(Asclepias curassavica),* a tropical American perennial herb 60 to 90 cm high, with umbels of small orange and yellow flowers and pods full of tufted, wind-borne seeds; the leaves were eaten in time of famine; the Monarch butterfly feeds on the leaves. (Neal 697.) *Lit.,* flying leaf. Also *lauhele, pua ʻanuhe.* See also *hī laulele.* 2. Dandelion *(Taraxacum officinale).* See also *hualele.* (Neal 860.) 3. Net fishing with small nets as in shallow water (usually used with *lawaiʻa* or *papa*).

lā.uli. 1. nvs. Dark, overcast, shady; darkness. *Lit.,* dark sun. 2. A variety of *ulua,* a fish. *Lit.,* dark fin.

lau.lihi.lihi. n. A slender, prostrate shrub in the pink family *(Schiedea stellarioides),* endemic to Kauaʻi, with small, linear leaves, and large open panicles of small flowers. *Lit.,* bordered leaf. Also *māʻoliʻoli.*

lau liʻi. vs. Small-leafed; qualifying term for some plants, as *maile.* Cf. *ʻiʻo 3.*

lau.lima. nvi. Cooperation, joint action; group of people working together; community food patch; to work together, cooperate. *Lit.,* many hands. **hoʻo.lau.lima.** To get to cooperate.

lau.loa. n. 1. A variety of taro, said to be the original taro brought to Hawaiʻi. Sometimes poetically called *hāloa,* long stalk, because a god of that name was said to have been in the form of this taro. This name may be qualified by the terms *hāʻeleʻele* or *ʻeleʻele; ʻeleʻele ʻōmaʻo; ʻeleʻele ʻula* or *palakea ʻeleʻele; hāʻula, koko, ʻulaʻula,* or *palakea ʻula; uliuli* or *hāuliuli; keʻokeʻo; manini; ʻōniʻoniʻo; palakea* or *palakea papamū; pānaʻe; poni* (HP 33, TC 3). Cf. *hinapū.* 2. A variety of sugar cane. When young, yellow-green, striped with light yellow-brown; with exposure, a deep olive, striped with dark brown-red; broad, long, green leaves; large stalks. (HP 222, 225.) 3. Long wave or surf, as extending from one end of the beach to the other. Also *kākala.*

lau loa. 1. n. A long leaf. 2. nvs. Length; lengthwise. *Kā lau loa i ka ʻupena,* braid the net lengthwise.

lau lole. n. *Wauke* leaf. *Lit.,* clothing leaf.

lau.mā.ewa. vi. To sway with the movement of the wind, as leaves; to move to and fro, as algae in the sea; blown here and there, as sea spray.

lau.maʻewa. nvt. Insult, taunt, sneer, reproach, contempt; to insult, taunt, mock; taunting, mocking, sneering, derisive.

lau makani. n. Puff of wind.

lau.maki. 1. Var. of *laumeki 1–3.* 2. n. Low stroke in club fighting. (RC 59.)

lau.mana.mana. n. A variety of sweet potato.

lau mana.mana. n. A divided leaf; many leaves, many branches; descendants, as of a family.

lau.mania. vs. Smooth, sheer, steep, even. **hoʻo.lau.mania.** To smooth; to spread out smoothly and evenly; to free of bumps or lumps.

lau.manie. Var. of *laumania.*

Lau-maʻo. n. Wind, Puna-kou, Molokaʻi. (Nak. 69.) *Lit.,* green leaves.

lau-maʻu. n. Design on a tapa beater, said to suggest the *maʻu* leaf.

lau mauʻu. n. Blade of grass.

lau.meke. Var. of *laumeki 1–3. He koa ia e laumeke ai kahawai o Hilo,* a warrior who lessens the flow of Hilo streams [a mighty fighter].

lau.meki. 1. n. A kind of barbed spear. 2. vi. To recede, ebb, as the tide or flood waters. 3. vi. To wilt, as plants without water.

lau.milo. 1. vi. To writhe, turn, twist, squirm, torture, destroy. Cf. *ʻōmilomilo.* 2. n. A species of eel, so called because its color was thought to resemble a yellow *milo* leaf *(lau milo).*

launa. vs. Friendly, sociable; to associate with, meet with, fraternize with, visit, be sociable. Used idiomatically with *'a'ohe, 'a'ole, 'ole: 'A'ohe launa ka maka'u,* terrible fear; there's no limit to the fear; *lit.,* no meeting the fear. *'A'ole lihi launa mai o ka pilikia,* there's no end to the trouble. Cf. *hoalauna. Launa 'ana,* association, intercourse, connection. *Launa 'ōlelo,* dialogue, communication. **ho'o.launa.** To introduce one person to another; to be friendly. *Ho'olauna 'ana,* introduction. *Ke ho'olauna aku nei au i mua o 'oukou,* I introduce myself to you.

launa aloha. n. Friendly association, fellowship.

lau nahele. n. Plants, forest growth or leaves, herbs, greenery.

launa male (mare). n. Marriage relationship; marital rights (RSV), marital duties (KJV) (Puk. 21.10).

launa 'ole. vs. 1. Unequalled, incomparable, unsurpassed, superior (similar to *ana 'ole* and *lua 'ole*). See ex., *lalawe. U'i launa 'ole,* youthfully beautiful beyond compare. 2. Unsociable.

launa pala.pala. nv. Correspondence; to correspond.

lau.nea. vs. Bare, as of leaves. **ho'o.lau.nea.** Caus/sim.

lau.nie. Same as *launea.*

-launili. ho'o.lau.nili. Same as *luaiele.*

lau-niu. n. Design on a tapa beater.

lau niu. n. Coconut leaf, frond. (PPN *lau niu.*) See *hair.*

lau.nui. n. A variety of taro. (HP 33.) *Lit.,* large leaf, large design.

lau.'ō. n. 1. Sugar-cane leaf (same as *lau kō*). 2. Young white coconut leaves near the heart.

lau.o'e. Similar to *kūo'e,* to saunter.

lau.'oē. Var. spelling of *lau'owē.*

lau.oha. 1. n. Sail of a vessel. 2. vs. Dense, lush, of vegetation. Cf. *ohaoha.* 3. Variation in vision, depending on distance of the object seen. (AP.)

lau.oha.oha. Redup. of *lauoha 2.*

lau.oho. n. Hair of the head. *Lit.,* head leaf. (For types of hair see *hair.*) (PCP *lauo(f,s)o.*)

lau.oho ku'i. n. Hair switch, wig. *Lit.,* added hair.

lau.oho-o-Pele. n. 1. Pele's hair, volcanic glass spun out in hairlike form. 2. A fine, hairlike seaweed, found at Wai-kīkī.

lau.oho uli.uli. nvs. One with dark hair, brunette; dark hair.

lau 'oliwa. n. Olive leaves; perhaps formerly used fig. for letters. *Ka Lau Oliva* [The Olive Leaf], a monthly magazine edited by H. H. Parker 1871-3.

lau.one. n. Soil light, fertile, and easy to cultivate; alluvial soil, sandy soil. *Lit.,* sand surface.

lau 'ō.pae. n. Shrimp net, about a fathom long, placed around a heap of rocks called *ahu* or *imu* (fish and shrimp were prodded and frightened from the rock pile into the net); this type of fishing.

lau.'owē, lau.'oē. Intensive of *'owē,* murmuring.

lau.pa'a.pa'ani. vs. Merry, jolly, humorous, laugh-provoking, funny, playful, witty. *Lit.,* much playing.

lau.pa'e. n. First two leaves of a taro shoot (according to some, the first three leaves).

lau.pa'i. 1. Same as *laupa'e.* 2. nv. A great many, multitude, great quantity, heap; to increase, multiply; to have much of; well supplied with. *Ua laupa'i ka hana,* there was so much to do. *Laupa'i ka 'ohana,* a big family. **ho'o.lau.pa'i.** To make an abundance, supply, cause an increase, reproduce.

lau pala. n. Fading leaf turning yellow, red, or brown. *Fig.,* person failing in health. **ho'o.lau pala.** To show signs of fading, of a leaf; to show signs of failing health; also same as *lau pala.*

lau.palai. To shine, glitter, sparkle, as dew in the sun. (AP.)

lau.papa. n. 1. A broad flat, as of coral, lava, reef. *Ka-laupapa* (place on Moloka'i), the broad flat area. (PPN *laupapa.*) 2. Board, lumber. *Pā laupapa,* wooden fence.

lau.pau. A kind of fish. (And.)

lau po'o.po'o.hina. Same as *po'opo'ohina. Ni'ihau.*

lau.'ula.'ula. n. A kind of sweet potato. (HP 142.) *Lit.,* red leaf.

lau.'ulu. vs. Indistinct, as the voice of a sick person. *Rare.*

lau.wa'e. Var. spelling of *laua'e 1-4.*

lau wai. n. Stream or pond full of water; many streams; abundance of water.

lau.wī. Same as *'alauahio,* a bird.

lau.wili, lauili. vs. Circuitous, roundabout, indirect, turning, twisting, unstable, fickle, changeable, inconstant, double-tongued, variable. Cf. *wili. Pā lauwili,* to blow from various directions, of the wind. **ho'o.lau.wili.** To cause fickleness, change, twist. *Ho'olauwili i ka no'ono'o* (Kel. 56), to cause worry, concern, or consternation.

lau.wili.wili. 1. n. A butterfly fish *(Chaetodon miliaris).* 2. Redup. of *lauwili.*

lau.wili.wili nuku.nuku 'oi.'oi. n. Butterfly fishes *(Forcipiger longirostris* and *F. flavissimus). Lit.,* sharp-beaked *wiliwili* leaf.

lawa. 1. nvs. Enough, sufficient, ample; to have enough, be satisfied. *Lawa pono,* plenty, abundant, ample, adequate. *Lawa pono 'ole,* insufficient, deficit. *Ka'a i ka lawa,* to be enough. **ho'o.lawa.** To supply, apportion sufficiently, equip. *E ho'olawa mai 'oe i lau hala e pa'a ai kēia moena,* supply me enough pandanus leaves to finish this mat. (PNP *lawa.*) 2. vs. Possessed of enough or ample knowledge, hence wise, capable, competent. *Ua lawa ke 'ike,* knowing a great deal. *Ua lawa i ka hānai keiki,* wise in raising children. 3. vs. As soon as. *I lawa nō ā pau ka hana, ho'i kāua,* as soon as the work is finished, we'll leave. 4. nvs. Strong, husky; strong man, as in a king's retinue. Cf. *lawakua.* 5. vt. To bind, make fast, tie securely. (PPN *lawa.*) 6. vs. White, as of a cock or dog. *Moa lawa, moa lawa kea,* white cock. 7. A large shark fishhook. (AP.)

lawa.a'e.a'e. nvs. White mixed with a darker color, as of a chicken; dark hair streaked with gray; white chicken with sprinkling of red feathers. Cf. *a'ea'e.*

lawai'a. 1. nvi. Fisherman; fishing technique; to fish, to catch fish. *'O ka hī aku ka lawai'a nui a 'Umi-a-Līloa* (FS 173), casting for bonito was 'Umi-a-Līloa's principal means of fishing. (PCP *lawaika.*) 2. n. Cormorant. (Oihk. 11.17.) 3. *(Cap.)* n. Name of a group of seven stars.

lawai'a kō.kō. n. Fishing within the reef, as by women and children, with long bags of fine mesh into which fish were driven.

lawai'a kō lau. n. The old name for *hukilau* fishing.

lawai'a.manu. n. Birdcatcher, birdcatching with a net. *Lit.,* to fish birds.

lawa kea. Same as *moa 1.* See *lawa 6.*

lawa.kua. 1. vs. Strong-backed, muscular, of strong physique, bulging with muscles. See ex., *konapiliahi.* 2. vt. To bind or tie fast, as on the back. *Fig.,* to be a dear friend or companion. (PH 218.) *Ua lawakua i kō aloha* (dirge), bound to your love. 3. *(Cap.)* n. Name of a mountain wind at Nā-pali, Kaua'i. See ex., *noiele.* 4. *(Cap.)* n. A *lua* fighting stroke.

lawa.lawa. Redup. of *lawa 5.*

-lawalawa. ho'o.lawa.lawa. Redup. of *ho'olawa,* to supply. *Ua ho'olawalawa i ka 'ai,* supply all with enough food.

lawa.lawai'a. Redup. of *lawai'a;* to fish here and there. *Anu ke kupa lawalawai'a o Ho'olehua* (chant), cold are the native fishermen of Ho'olehua.

lawa.lawai.honua. n. Type of large wooden bowl.

lā.walu. nvt. Fish or meat bound in ti leaves for cooking; to cook thus. *Palaoa lāwalu,* dough cooked in ti leaves.

lawa lua. 1. vs. Very strong. 2. vt. To bind tightly.

lawa puni. vs. Enough for all, well-supplied or equipped. *Ua lawa puni kākou i ka i'a,* we all have enough fish.

lawe. 1. nvt. To take, transport, carry, bring, haul,

fetch, undertake, accept (as a duty), make off with, acquire; portable; bearer. Cf. *lalawe, lawe hānai. Lawe 'ana,* carrying, transportation. *Lawe aku,* take away. *Mea lawe,* bearer. *'O ka'u keiki . . . ke lawe ma ke 'ano mālama waiwai,* my son . . . shall serve as trustee. *Ka lawe 'ia 'ana,* the assumption [as of the Virgin Mary]. *He mea lawe nūpepa,* a newspaper subscriber; newspaper carrier, paper boy. *Lawe mai i ka puke,* bring the book. *Ua lawe mai au i ka 'ōlelo ho'ohiki,* I accepted the pledge. *Ua lawe nui au no loko a'e o kēia mau kānāwai,* from these laws I have borrowed largely. *Lawe i nā 'ōlelo ho'ohiki,* to take oaths. *Ka lawe kōwehe a ka pā'ū,* fluttering of the skirt. *Ua lawe ia i wahine no 'Aikiopa nāna* (Nah. 12.1), he took a woman from Ethiopia as his wife. **ho'o.lawe.** To cause to take, pretend to take, deduct, subtract; subtraction, deduction, minus. *E ho'olawe lua mai ka 'ewalu, a 'o ka ha'ina he 'eono,* take two from eight and the answer is six. (PPN *lawe.*) **2.** vs. Finally to become. See ex., *mikihilina. Ahonui 'ia, i lawe nō ā kau i ka hano,* be patient, and eventually you will be placed in a position of honor.

lawea. Pas/imp. of *lawe. Lawea mai ā pau pono nā 'ike kumu o Hawai'i* (chant for Ka-lā-kaua), bring every last bit of the original wisdom of Hawai'i.

lawe 'ai.'ē. vt. To borrow, take on credit.

lawe.ā.lani. n. Highest heavens. (For. 6:363.)

lawe.au. vi. To drift apart; to depart, as in death. *Mahope o ka make 'ana o ka luahine, ua laweau aku nā mo'opuna,* after the death of the old lady, the grandchildren drifted apart.

lawe hae. nv. To bear a flag; color bearer.

lawe.hala. nvs. Sin, sinner, delinquency, offense; evil, delinquent, sinful; to sin, transgress. *Keiki lawehala,* delinquent child. *Lawehala 'ōpiopio,* juvenile delinquency. **ho'o.lawe.hala.** Accusation; to accuse; to grow worse, of a sickness, especially an insignificant one. *He wahi 'eha wale nō kēia i ho'olawehala,* this is just a little pain that has become worse.

lawe.hana. nvs. Workman, laborer; industrious; to do labor, work. *Hoa lawehana,* fellow worker.

lawe hā.nai. vt. To adopt, as a child.

lawe hele. vt. To take here and there.

lawe kā.hili. n. Bearer of the feather standard of royalty *(kāhili).*

lawe kapa.kahi. vt. To act with partiality.

lawe.keō. interj. Cry of the *kioea,* curlew bird: *"Kioea, kioea, lawekeō, lawelawekeō."*

lawe.lawe. vt. **1.** To serve, work for, minister to, tend, attend to, do, perform, serve, transact; to treat, as the sick; to wait, as on tables; to handle. *Ka lawelawe 'ana,* the service, performance, procedure, execution, carrying out, administration. *Lawelawe ho'opi'i kalaima,* criminal procedure. *Kanaka lawelawe, mea lawelawe,* servant, waiter, steward [this term does not carry the opprobrium attached to *kauā*]. *Wahine lawelawe,* waitress, maid, stewardess. *Lawelawe 'oihana,* to conduct business. *'Ike pono i nā mea e lawelawe 'ia ana,* to see clearly what happened. *Ka loio nāna e lawelawe nei i ka hihia,* the lawyer who is handling the law case. *Ke lawelawe lā na'e ho'i; ā make akula 'oe iā Ku'ika'a* (victory chant of Ka-welo, FS 63), the [job] is being done; Ku'ika'a [the war club] slays you. (PPN *lawelawe.*) **2.** To pilfer, make off with. *Lima lawelawe,* pilfering hand.

lawe.lawe hana. n. Function, administration. *Kāna lawelawe hana 'ana,* his administration.

lawe.lawe iwi. n. One who cares for the bones of the dead.

lawe.lawe.keō. Redup. of *lawekeō.*

lawe.lawe kolohe. vt. To take illegally, without permission, tamper with.

lawe.lawe lima. nv. To carry in the hand; to pitch in and lend a hand, help; to assault, beat, tackle; anything carried in the hand. Cf. *lawelawe 2. I pono kēia hana i*

kona lawelawe lima maoli 'ana mai, this work is a success because he actually pitched in to help.

lawe leka. nv. Mail carrier, postman; to carry mail or letters.

lawe lima. vt. To carry by hand. *Puke lawe lima,* handbook.

lawe.lua. vt. To study both sides of a question; to act impartially. *Lit.,* take two.

lawena. n. Getting, acquiring, taking, carrying, acquisition; movement, as of dancing hands. *Pehea ka lawena a ka ipo?* (song), how to get a sweetheart? *Ka lawena ka maka,* flirtatious summons of the eye.

lawena 'ō.lelo. Same as *lawe 'ōlelo.*

lawe 'ō.hua. nv. Passenger carrier; to carry passengers.

lawe ola. nv. Manslaughter, homicide; to take a life; to take alive.

lawe 'ō.lelo. nv. Talebearer, tattle; gossip; to gossip, bear tales; microphone.

lawe pio. nvt. Conquest; to capture, take captive, abduct, conquer, take a prisoner, carry into captivity.

lawe wai. nvs. A great flow of water; water carrier; water-borne.

lawe wale. nvt. Extortion, seizure of property with the owner's knowledge; to extort, take without right.

lawewe. Var. of *lawelawe. Rare.*

lē. vs. To go about aimlessly, to do no work; listless, lazy. *Ua lē akula ka molowā,* lazy person just lounges about.

Lea. n. **1.** Goddess of canoe builders. **2.** Name of a star.

le'a. **1.** nvs. Joy, pleasure, happiness, merriment; sexual gratification, orgasm; pleasing, gay, delightful, happy, merry; delighted, pleased. Cf. *manawale'a.* **ho'o.le'a.** To cause pleasure, joy; to praise, please, delight, extol; praising, eulogistic. *Ha'i'ōlelo ho'ole'a,* eulogistic speech. *'Ehā kaukani ho'i i ho'ole'a iā Iēhowa me nā mea kani a'u i hana ai i mea ho'ole'a* (1 Oihn. 23.5), four thousand then praised Jehovah with the playing instruments I made as praising things. (PEP *leka.*) **2.** vs. Clearly, perfectly, thoroughly, successfully. Cf. *kāle'a, kūle'a. Ha'i le'a,* to describe fully and clearly; one skilled in clear, full explanation. *Holo le'a,* to progress smoothly, successfully. *'Ike le'a,* to see clearly. *Maopopo le'a,* obvious, clearly evident. *Mo'a le'a,* thoroughly cooked. **3.** *(Cap.)* n. The zenith star Arcturus. Also *Hōkū-le'a.*

le'a.le'a. **1.** Redup. of *le'a 1;* to have a good time; fun, gaiety (see ex., *henehene*), amusement. *Le'ale'a no'ono'o 'ole,* thoughtless gaiety, frivolous. *Puni le'ale'a wale,* fond of pleasure only, frivolity. *Nā mākua kāne le'ale'a o kāua* (GP 56), our uncles who have sported with us. **ho'o.le'a.le'a.** Redup. of *ho'ole'a;* to amuse oneself, have fun; amusement. *Po'e ho'ole'ale'a i kānaka* (Epeso 6.6), men-pleasers. (PNP *lekaleka.*) **2.** n. Name of a prayer to Kū, Kāne, Lono, and the *'aumākua* (family gods). (Kep. 23.)

le'e. See *'o'opu le'e.*

le'ema. n. Reem; wild ox (RSV), unicorn (KJV) (Nah. 24.8). (Heb. *reem.*)

le'e.nihi. Var. of *laenihi,* a fish.

leha. **1.** vt. To glance about, as with expectation or furtively. **2.** vs. Lazy, neglectful; to loaf. *Rare.* Cf. *palaleha.*

lē.hai. Rare var. of *lēhei.*

leha.lehai. Redup. of *lēhai.*

lē.hau. vs. Crowded, as with people. *Rare.*

lehe. **1.** n. Lip (used with complements, as *lehe luhe, lehe 'oi*). Cf. *lehelehe.* **2.** vs. Stretched, loose. (PEP *le(f,s)e.*) **3.** n. Deep-sea fish resembling *ulua,* perhaps *Caranx chelio.*

lē.hei. vi. To jump, hop, as a goat over a wall; to leap, start up and fly. *Lēkei* is a common variant. **2.** *(Cap.)* n. A rain associated with Maka-wao, Maui. **3.** *(Cap.)* n. A *lua* fighting stroke.

lehe.lehe. **1.** n. Lips; labia of vagina; language (Kin. 11.1; *rare*), mouth of the *iheihe* net. For fig. use cf.

lehelehe kiʻi, lehelehe nui, lehe ʻoi. **2.** Redup. of *lehe 2.*

lehē.lehē. vs. Fat, bulging with fat, unwieldy.

lehe.lehei. Redup. of *lēhei.*

lehe.lehe.ʻī.lio. Same as *lepe-o-Hina,* seaweeds.

lehe.lehe kiʻi. nvs. Indolent talker; to do nothing but talk. *Lit.,* image lips. **hoʻo.lehe.lehe kiʻi.** Caus/sim. *Kū hoʻolehelehe kiʻi i ka mahina ʻai a Nūkeʻe,* standing like a loose-lipped image in the garden of Twist-mouth [doing nothing but talk].

lehe.lehe.nui. n. A variety of sweet potato. (HP 142.)

lehe.lehe nui. n. Thick lips. **hoʻo.lehe.lehe nui.** Sullen, obstinate, sulky, pouting.

lehe luhe. n. Pouting lip.

lehe ʻoi. vs. Sharp-lipped, an epithet often applied to Pele because she devoured everything in her path; sharp-tongued, of one who makes cutting remarks.

lehia. vs. Skilled, expert, as in fishing; deft. Cf. *paulehia.*

lehiwa. nvt. Admirable, attractive; to admire. *Kuʻu pua lehiwa o ke kau* (song), my lovely blossom of the summer.

leho. **1.** n. General name for cowry shell; they were used as octopus lures. *Moe a leho,* lie still as a cowry shell, as to escape detection. (PPN *fole;* PCP *lefo.*) **2.** n. Callus, as on shoulders from carrying heavy loads. **3.** vs. Covetous. Cf. *maka leho.*

leho ahi. n. A species of cowry *(Cypraea mauritiana).* *Lit.,* fire cowry.

leho kō.lea. n. A species of cowry *(Cypraea maculifera, C. mauritiana). Lit., kōlea* bird cowry, perhaps so called because its brown streaks suggest the *kōlea* bird.

leho kupa. n. The serpent-head cowry *(Cypraea caput-serpentis). Lit.,* native cowry.

leho kū.peʻe lima. n. A species of cowry shell *(Cypraea caput-serpentis),* used for bracelets, *kūpeʻe lima.*

leho.leho. **1.** Redup. of *leho 2.* **2.** vs. Potbellied.

leho lei. Same as *leho puna,* sometimes used in leis.

leho maʻo. Same as *leho ʻōmaʻo,* a greenish cowry.

leho maoli. n. The common dotted, brown cowry. *Lit.,* genuine cowry.

leho nuku. n. A cowry with the extremities drawn out, a beaked cowry, such as *Cypraea cicercula* var. *tricornis;* sometimes used in leis.

leho ʻō.kala. n. A species of cowry *(Cypraea granulata). Lit.,* rough cowry.

leho ʻō.lū.palaha. See *ʻō.lū.palaha.* (Kam. 76:152.)

leho ʻō.maʻo. n. A greenish cowry (diseased cowries sometimes turn green).

leho ʻō.pule. n. A species of cowry *(Cypraea helvola). Lit.,* variegated cowry.

leho ʻō.puʻu.puʻu. Same as *leho ʻōkala. Lit.,* bumpy or rough cowry.

leho paʻa. n. A cowry of a solid color, as *Cypraea mauritiana.*

leho palaoa. Same as *leho puna,* but with a yellow hue. *Lit.,* ivory cowry.

leho pā.uhu. n. Cowries, as *Cypraea schilderdrum, C. carneola.*

leho pouli. n. A very dark-brown cowry *(Cypraea mauritiana).*

leho.pulu. n. Earth-clinging rainbow. Also *uakoko. Lit.,* wet cowry shell.

leho puna. n. A white money cowry *(Cypraea moneta). Lit.,* coral cowry.

leho ʻuala. n. A rare dark-yellow money cowry *(Cypraea moneta). Lit.,* sweet-potato cowry.

leho ʻula. n. The rare and highly prized red cowry, probably *Cypraea* sp.

lehu. **1.** nvs. Ashes; ash-colored or gray, as a chicken. See saying, *ash. Lehu ane,* fine ashes. *Pōpoki lehu,* gray cat. *Lā Hāpala Lehu,* Ash Wednesday. *Puhi lehu, hoʻolehu ʻia,* cremate. **hoʻolehu.** To reduce to ashes. (Perhaps PPN *refu.*) **2.** n. A variety of sugar cane, probably recently introduced, extensively planted by Hawaiians. The stunted mature stalks look dead except

for their green leaves. A gray to green-brown frosted-looking cane covered with hairs; pith green-white; both sides of leaves bearing long scattered hairs. (HP 224, 225.) **3.** num. The number 400,000; numerous, very many. Cf. *lehulehu,* Gram. 10.3.

lehua. **1.** n. The flower of the *ʻōhiʻa* tree *(Metrosideros macropus, M. collina* subsp. *polymorpha);* also the tree itself. The *lehua* is the flower of the island of Hawaiʻi, as designated in 1923 by the Territorial legislature; it is famous in song and tale. See *nāpolupolu, pōkiʻi 1, ʻūpolu. Fig.,* a warrior, beloved friend or relative, sweetheart, expert (see *lehua 9*). The plant has many forms, from tall trees to low shrubs, leaves round to narrow and blunt or pointed and smooth or woolly. The flowers are red, rarely salmon, pink, yellow, or white. The wood is hard, good for flooring and furniture, formerly used for images, spears, mallets. (Neal 637–8.) It grows abundantly in wet areas (see ex., *ʻūpolu).* It was believed that picking *lehua* blossoms would cause rain. For rain and wind names associated with *lehua* see *Kani-lehua, Kinai-lehua, Kini-moka-lehua, Kiu Wai Lehua, Līlī-lehua, Moaniani-lehua, Moe-lehua.* See also *lū lehua, Moaʻe Lehua, ʻōiwi Lehua* (chant). Cf. Marquesan *heʻua* (Lavondès, 1975, pp. 193–4.) **2.** vs. Laden, as a *lehua* tree with beautiful blossoms. *Ke hele lā ka papa ʻaina a ua aliʻi nei ā lehua,* the feast table of this aforementioned chief was beautifully supplied. **3.** n. Rainbow-colored mother-of-pearl shell used for fishing lure. **4.** n. A variety of taro, used for red poi. Cultivars may be qualified by the terms *keʻokeʻo* (white) or *maoli* (native). (TC 4.) **5.** n. Globe amaranth *(Gomphrena globosa).* Also *lehua mau loa, lehua pepa, leihua.* **6.** n. A variety of yam; the stem has red wings and the tuber has light pinkish flesh. (HP 168.) **7.** *(Cap.)* n. Name of the small island just west of Niʻihau. As the westernmost of the Hawaiian Islands (except for the Northwest Hawaiian Islands), *Lehua* is associated with a setting sun (see chant, *kalakalaʻihi*). In poetry, the extent of the Hawaiian Islands is shown by coupling Lehua Island and Haʻehaʻe and Kumu-kahi on East Hawaiʻi (see *welo 2, welona*). A breeze is named for this island. **8.** Pas/imp. of *lehu 1.* **9.** n. Expert, as in fishing. **hoʻo.lehua.** Swift, expert, strong.

lehua ʻā.hihi. n. A variety of *lehua (Metrosideros tremuloides),* noted in songs and chants of Nuʻu-anu Valley, Oʻahu. Also *ʻāhihi.*

lehua ʻā.pane. n. A kind of *lehua* tree bearing dark-red flowers.

lehua ʻele.ʻele. n. A variety of taro; corm white or slightly pink; may be a sport of a true *lehua. Lit.,* black *lehua.*

lehua haʻa.kea. Same as *lehua pua kea. Lit.,* white *lehua.*

lehua hā.mau. Poetic reference to the *lehua* tree. *Lit.,* silent *lehua,* so called because bird-catchers were silent when snaring birds on branches of this tree and this activity was taboo.

lehua haole. n. Red- or white-flowered species of *Calliandra* shrubs from various parts of America (Neal 404–5.) *Lit.,* foreign *lehua.*

lehu ahi. n. Ashes. *Lit.,* fire ash.

lehu kahiki. n. Clover. *Lit.,* foreign *lehua.*

lehua kea. Same as *lehua pua kea.*

lehua keʻo.keʻo. n. A variety of taro called *waiākea* in Kona, Hawaiʻi. *Lit.,* white *lehua.*

Lehua-kona. n. Star in the Milky Way, perhaps Antares. *Lit.,* south *lehua* flower.

lehua-kū-i-ka-wao. n. A variety of pink *lehua* taro. *Lit., lehua* standing in the uplands.

lehua-kū-kua.hiwi. n. A variety of taro. (HP 33.) *Lit.,* hill-standing *lehua* taro.

lehua-kū-ma-kua. n. A form of *lehua* with sessile cordate leaves.

lehua lau liʻi. n. A form of *ʻōhiʻa lehua* tree with very small leaves. *Lit.,* small-leafed *lehua.*

lehua maka ʻiʻi. n. A variety or taro. (HP 33.) *Lit.*, small-eyed *lehua.*

lehua maka noe. n. A small shrub *(Metrosideros pumila* var. *makanoiensis),* restricted to the high bogs of Kauaʻi, with leaves and flowers like those of *lehua.* (Neal 638.) Also *lehua neʻeneʻe. Lit., lehua* with misty face.

lehua mamo. n. A form of *ʻōhiʻa lehua* tree with yellow flowers. *Lit., mamo*-bird *lehua,* so called because the *mamo* has yellow feathers.

lehua mau loa. n. Globe amaranth *(Gomphrena globosa). Lit.,* everlasting *lehua,* so called because its flowers when used in leis do not wilt. Also *lehua pepa* and *leihua.* (Neal 334–5.)

lehu ane. n. Ash dust.

lehua neʻe.neʻe. Same as *lehua neneʻe, lehua maka noe. Lit.,* spreading *lehua.*

lehua ʻō.niʻo.niʻo. n. A variety of taro. (HP 33.) *Lit.,* spotted *lehua.*

lehua pala.ʻiʻi. n. A variety of taro, of common upland culture in Kona, Hawaiʻi. The plant is short to medium, slender, with lilac-purple corm flesh and dark green petioles; used for poi. Also *palaʻiʻi, ʻiʻi.*

lehua papa. n. A native shrub or small tree *(Metrosideros rugosa),* found in high forests of the Koʻolau Range, Oʻahu, and distinguished by its rounded, leathery, grooved leaves.

lehua pepa. Same as *lehua mau loa. Lit.,* paper *lehua,* so called because the texture of the flowers and the fact that they do not wilt suggest paper.

lehua pua kea. n. A form of *ʻōhiʻa lehua* tree with white flowers *(pua kea).* Also *lehua haʻakea, lehua kea.*

lehu.lehu. nvs. Multitude, crowd, great number, population, legion, the public; numerous, very many, innumerable, myriad. *No ka pono o ka lehulehu,* for the welfare of the public. **hoʻo.lehu.lehu.** To make a multitude; to increase into many.

lehu.liʻu. vs. White-hot, as oven stones.

lehu pele. n. Volcanic ash.

lehu.uila. nvi. Flashes of lightning; to flash.

lehu ʻula. n. Red ashes; reddish dust or dirt.

lei. **1.** n. Lei, garland, wreath; necklace of flowers, leaves, shells, ivory, feathers, or paper, given as a symbol of affection; beads; any ornament worn around the head or about the neck; to wear a lei; special song presenting a lei; crown; ring around a drake's neck; yoke, as for joining draft animals, especially oxen. *Fig.,* a beloved child, wife, husband, sweetheart, younger sibling or child, so called because a beloved child was carried on the shoulders, with its legs draped down on both sides of the bearer like a lei. Cf. *lei palaoa. Kāna lei,* his lei (to give away or sell). *Kona lei,* his lei (to wear). *Leilani* (name), royal child, heavenly lei. *ʻUhene ahahana kaʻu lei naʻu ia* (song), oh joy, oh boy, she's my darling. **hoʻo.lei.** To put a lei on oneself or on someone else; to crown. (PPN *lei.*) **2.** vi. To leap, fling, toss, spring forward; to rise, as a cloud. (Nah. 10.11.) Usually used with *hoʻo-.* **hoʻo.lei.** To cast, throw, heave, toss, pitch; to stretch, send. *Hoʻolei ukana,* to unload freight. *Ka hoʻolei wāwae ʻana,* marking time. *Hoʻolei wale,* to throw away wastefully, heedlessly, uselessly. *Hoʻolei wale nō i ke kālā i nā leʻaleʻa lapuwale,* merely throwing away money on worthless pleasures. *Ua hoʻolei mai me kō lākou waha* (Hal. 59.7), they belch out with their mouth. *Hoʻolei loa,* to throw completely away, to throw far. *Hoʻolei loa akula nā wāwae o Nā-maka-o-Kahaʻi ā pololei* (For. 4:69), Nā-maka-o-Kahaʻi stretched her legs out straight. *Hoʻolei pōpō,* name of an old ball game. *Pupuʻu hoʻolei loa,* to arrive with astonishing speed; to leave and arrive in no time at all; *lit.,* crouch fling far. *Hoʻōho hoʻolei,* far-flung shout. *Hoʻolei koke nō iāia mauka ma ka ʻāina,* quickly send him ashore. (PNP *lei.*)

lē.ʻī. vs. Crowded, full. Also *lēʻiwi.* See *ʻī 2, ipu lēʻī, lēʻia, mōʻī, pua lēʻī. Lēʻī Kohala, eia i ka nuku nā*

kānaka (FS 185), Kohala is crowded to the very mouth with people [a saying referring to the astonishment of Maui invaders of Kohala, Hawaiʻi, who, contrary to the report of their intelligence, found Kohala crowded with people; said of crowds of people anywhere].

leia. Pas/imp. of *lei 1, 2. Ke leia maila nō e Ka-piʻo-lani,* a lei is being worn by Ka-piʻo-lani.

-leia. Hoʻo.leia. (a) Name of a star. **(b)** *(Not cap.)* Pas/imp. of *hoʻolei.*

lēʻia. nvs. Abundance; full. Cf. *lēʻī. He moku lēʻia,* a district of abundance.

lei ʻā.ʻī. n. Any lei worn on the shoulders, as *maile;* necktie, scarf, neckerchief. *Fig.,* beloved person, especially child or mate. *Lit.,* neck lei. See *pōhākiʻikiʻi.*

lei aliʻi. n. Royal lei, chief's lei, crown (Hoik. 4.4), diadem.

lei.au. n. An ancient type of prayer. (For. 6:23.)

leʻie. Same as *hala pepe,* a tree.

lei haku. n. Braided lei, as of ferns and flowers.

lei.hala. n. A variety of eel. See *puhi lei hala.*

lei-hala. n. Plaiting and tapa designs consisting of a series of inverted triangles, suggestive of a *hala* lei.

lei hala. n. Lei made principally or solely of pandanus keys, sometimes considered bad luck because *hala,* pandanus, also means to pass away, to fail.

lei hili. n. A plaited lei, as of ferns and *maile* but without leaves.

lei hilo. Var. of *lei hili.*

lei hoaka. n. Necklace made of crescent-shaped *(hoaka)* hog's tusks, usually naturally so shaped, but sometimes carved; a pendant of a single crescent-shaped tooth.

lei.hua. Same as *lehua mau loa. Lit.,* fruit lei, so called because the flowers are round like a fruit.

lei hulu. n. Feather lei, formerly worn by royalty. *Fig.,* dearly beloved child or choice person.

lei humu.humu. n. Cloth lei.

lei kā.moe. n. Feather lei with feathers tightly folded together so that it suggests a rope, in contrast with the flat *lei papa.*

lei kā.wili. n. Same as *lei pāniʻo.*

lei.kini. Var. of *laikini. Eng.*

lei.kō. interj. Let go. *Eng.* Usually used as follows: *leikō ka ʻanakā,* let go the anchor.

lei kolona (korona). n. Rosary, prayer beads. *Lit.,* crown *(Eng.)* lei.

lei kui. n. A strung lei, as of plumeria.

lei kukui. n. *Kukui* nut lei. Cf. *ioio, ʻōmolemole, ʻōpaka.*

lei leho. n. Lei of cowry shells.

lei.lei. **1.** vt. To wear a lei or leis. *ʻO wai kēia e leilei maila?* Who is that wearing a lei there? **2.** Redup. of *lei 2.* **hoʻo.lei.lei.** Redup. of *hoʻolei;* to scatter, toss about, swing, dandle, as a baby; to juggle; juggling.

lei.leina. Redup. of *leina.* **hoʻo.lei.leina.** Redup. of *hoʻoleina.*

leina. n. Spring, leap, bound; place to leap from. *Leina-a-ke-akua,* place where the spirits leaped into the nether world; *lit.,* leap of the gods. *Leina-a-ka-ʻuhane* (a place name on every island), place where spirits leaped into the nether world; *lit.,* leap of the soul. **hoʻo.leina.** Same as *leina;* place to throw things, as a trash heap. *Ka-hoʻoleina-peʻa* (place on Kauaʻi), place where kites are flown. *Hoʻoleina moka* (Dan. 3.29), dung heap. (PCP *leina.*)

-leinamoa. hoʻo.leina.moa. Couch (probably from *hoʻoleina moe,* place to sleep).

-leinawao. hoʻo.leina.wao. A variety of wild taro. *Lit.,* thrown [into] wilderness.

lei.nekia, leinedia, leinadia. n. Reindeer. *Eng.*

lei niho ʻī.lio. n. Dog-tooth necklace.

lei niho palaoa. Same as *lei palaoa.*

lei.ʻō. Var. of *līʻō.*

lei.oa. vs. Tall, thin. (PH 83.) Cf. *paioa.*

lei.ʻoa. Var. of *leiʻō.*

lei ʻō.ʻā. See *ʻōʻā.*

lei-o-Hi'i.aka. n. A small native tree (*Pelea elliptica* and related species), related to the *mokihana.*

lei ole. n. **1.** Dog-tooth lei. **2.** Same as *'ana,* pumice stone used for medicine and for polishing.

lei.omano. n. A weapon, a large shark tooth set in a piece of wood about 6.4 cm long, with a string loop for attaching to the finger (probably from *lei o manō,* a shark's lei).

Lei-o-manu. See *Ka-lei-o-manu.*

lei 'oni. n. Lei with spirals of several colors, as the *kīkā* lei.

lei 'ō.pu'u. n. Whale-tooth pendant that tapers down to a point, rather than being hook-shaped, as the *lei palaoa;* especially worn by O'ahu chiefs. *Lit.,* bud lei.

lei.owī. n. Tuberculosis, consumption.

lei pā.laha.laha. Same as *lei papa.*

lei palaoa. n. Ivory pendant, originally probably whale's tooth, rarely of stone or wood, later also of walrus tusk; necklace of beads of whale's teeth; today, any pendant shaped like the old whale-tooth pendant, such as of beef bone. *Lit.,* ivory lei.

lei pā.ni'o. n. Lei of various colors, as feather leis. *Lit.,* spotted, motley lei.

lei papa. n. Flat lei, as for a hat; any lei on a flat surface, especially a feather lei. Cf. *lei kāmoe.*

lei pā.pahi. n. Leis of alternating groups of flowers and leaves, entwined leis of same or different flowers; adornment of several leis, usually both on head and around neck.

lei pā.pale. n. Hatband.

lei pau.kū. n. Lei with stripes or bands of varying colors. *Lit.,* link lei.

lei pau.kū.kū. Var. of *lei paukū.*

lei pā.wehe. Same as *lei paukū.*

lei piki. See *piki.*

lei pipi. n. Ox yoke.

lei pipipi. See *pipipi 1.*

lei poe.poe. n. Lei with flowers strung on stems or sides of flowers. See *lei waena.*

lei po'o. n. Lei worn on the head *(po'o).*

lei pū.pū. n. Shell lei, the most famous being from Ni'ihau, especially *kahelelani* and *momi.* These leis represent Ni'ihau in the leis of the islands, as designated in 1923 by the Territorial legislature.

lei pū.pū puka. n. Lei of white sea-perforated shells worn by men and women about the neck, popular in Hawai'i since the late 1960s. *Lit.,* perforated shell lei.

lei waena. n. Lei strung in the center of flowers. See *lei poepoe.*

lē.'iwi. **1.** Same as *lē'ī.* (For. 4:337, 339.) **2.** n. A kind of canoe with a flat *manu.*

lei wili. n. A lei that is not strung *(kui):* the leaves or flowers are entwined about each other, as *maile* leis.

lei wili.wili. n. Pendant carved of *wiliwili* wood; lei of *wiliwili* seeds.

leka. **1.** vs. Sticky, slimy, as mucus. Cf. *pīlalilali, pīlekaleka.* **2.** nvt. Letter; to write a letter. *Eng. Ua hō'ea mai ka'u leka,* my letter has come [either the one I wrote or the one received]. **3.** n. Leek *(Allium porrum).* (Neal 198, Nah. 11.5.) *Eng.*

leke. **1.** vi. Come. *E leke mai,* come. **2.** Also *lede.* n. Lady. *Eng.*

lē.kei. Var. of *lēhei.*

lekema, lesema. n. Jacinth (RSV), ligure (KJV). (Puk. 28.91.) (Heb. *lesem.*)

Lē.kē.mapa. n. December. *Eng.* Also *Kēkēmapa.*

leke.ona, legeona. n. Legion; a large number (Mar. 5.9, 15); used figuratively of one possessed by the devil or intoxicated. *Eng. Oia inu mai nō, ā noho 'ia e ka lekeona,* just drinking until possessed by a legion.

leki. n. Tape for dress trimming. *(Eng.,* lace.)

lekia. vt. To covet. *Ua lekia aku 'oia i kā ha'i wahine,* he covets someone else's wife.

leki.mana (regimana) koa. n. Regiment. *Eng.*

leki.ō. n. Radio. *Eng.*

lē.kō. n. Watercress *(Nasturtium microphyllum).* (Neal 372.)

lē.kō 'ele.'ele. n. A variety of watercress with dark stems and leaves. *Lit.,* black *lēkō.*

lē.kō ke'o.ke'o. n. A variety of watercress, said to be light green. *Lit.,* white *lēkō.*

lekue, legue. n. League. *Eng.*

lekuke. n. Lettuce *(Lactuca sativa).* (Neal 860–1.) *Eng.*

lele. **1.** nvi. To fly, jump, leap, hop, skip, swing, bounce, burst forth; to sail through the air, as a meteor; to rush out, as to attack; to get out of, as from a car; to dismount, as from a horse; to land, disembark, as from a canoe; to undertake; to move, as stars in the sky; to move, as in checkers; a jump, leap, attack. (For *lele* with emotional words, see ex., *hauli, kūpiliki'i;* also cf. *ha'alele.) Mea lele,* flyer. *Lele māmā,* fly swiftly, dart. *Mea lele mua,* aggressor. *Ka lele mua,* the first to play or speak [in a riddling contest]; the first sorcery victim (J. [Joseph] S. Emerson, 20). *Kanaka lele,* angel [old name]. *Lele maila ia uwē* (FS 57), tears poured forth. *Ua lele ka hanu o Moa,* Moa's breath has departed [he has died]. See also *'uhane. I hewa nō iā'oe i ka lele mua,* it is your fault for attacking first. *'Āmama, ua noa, lele wale* (For. 5:413), finished, free of taboo, fly on [of the taboo and prayer]. **ho'o.lele.** To cause to fly; to fly, as a kite; to disembark, to embark, as on a project; to palpitate, as the heart; to enlarge or project, as pictures. *Ho'olele leo,* radio broadcast, broadcaster, microphone, ventriloquism, ventriloquist. *Ho'olele hua kēpau,* to set type. *Ki'i ho'olele,* enlargement of a picture. *Mea ho'olele leo,* microphone. *Mea ho'olele ki'i,* picture projector. *E ho'olele mai i nā kānaka,* disembark the people. (PPN *lele).* **2.** vs. Contagious, as of disease. **3.** vi. Wind-blown, of the rain. Cf. *leleaka, lele ua. Ua lele ku'i lua,* hard-beating wind-blown rain. **4.** vs. Separate, detached, as a leaf separated from a plant for ceremonials. **5.** n. A detached part or lot of land belonging to one *'ili,* but located in another *'ili.* **6.** nvi. Hula step: the dancer walks forward, lifting up the rear heel with each step, with slight inward movement; sometimes with the *'uwehe* step with each foot forward. This can also be done backwards; to dance thus. **7.** n. An interval of music, the difference in pitch between two tones, always followed by a number from one to six, especially *lele kolu,* an interval of a third, as from C to E, or *lele lima,* an interval of a fifth. Minor intervals are followed by *hapa,* as *lele kolu hapa,* an interval of a minor third. *Lele* may also be followed by *pā-* and a number, to skip that number of notes. *Lele* in this sense also occurs as a verb, to sing thus. **8.** vi. To dry up, to have passed the menopause; to evaporate. *Ua lele ka waiū o Loika,* Lois' breasts have ceased to contain milk. *Ua lele ka wai nui o ka lepo* (Kep. 89), most of the water of the dirt evaporated. **9.** vi. To shrink, as clothes. **10.** n. Sacrificial altar or stand. **11.** n. A tall variety of wild banana *(Musa xparadisiaca),* formerly planted near the altar *(lele).* It was offered to the gods and used for love magic. Its essence was thought to fly *(lele)* to the gods. It was used for weaning (cf. *lele 8):* the banana was placed near the child with appropriate prayers in order to obtain the god's consent for weaning. This banana was taboo to women. **12.** n. Type of fish (no data). (KL line 161.) **13.** vt (followed by *hapa-* + digit). To count by _____ (digit). See below.

lelea. n. Prayer uttered by a priest as a chief drinks kava, so that the essence of the kava will fly *(lele)* to the gods. (PPN *lelea).*

lele.'ā. n. A marine creature (no data). (PH 121.)

lelea.aka. To hang, suspend, carry on the back, as a child or load. (And.)

lele.aka, lelele.aka. n. Light windblown rain or mist. *Rare.*

-leleaka. ho'o.lele.aka. To project, as magic lantern slides.

Lele-aka. n. Milky Way.
lele.aoa. vi. Flying away in groups, as migratory birds; to fly thus; to sail, as a canoe fleet.
lele 'ao.'ao. vi. To leap sideways; to shy, as a horse.
lele 'ē. vi. To speak prematurely or before one is spoken to; to jump to conclusions. *'A 'ole i pau ka'u wehewehe 'ana, 'o kou lele 'ē nō kā ho'i ia,* my explanation was not finished and there you had already leaped to a conclusion.
leleha. Redup. of *leha 1, 2.*
lele hapa.hā. vi. To count by fours.
lele hapa.kolu. vi. To count by threes.
lele hapa.lima. vi. To count by fives.
lele hapa.lua. vi. To count by twos.
lele hapa.'umi. vi. To count by tens.
lele hauli. See *hauli.*
lele ho'o.kau. n. **1.** Altar to place *(ho'okau)* things on, as sacrifices, especially a temporary altar. **2.** Peak, top of a peak.
lelehu. Same as *mōlelehu 1, 2.*
lele.hua. n. A good thinker, planner.
lele.huna, lelehune. nvi. Fine windblown rain spray, dust, mist; to fall as fine rain.
lele.'ino. vi. To spring or leap violently, as in an attack or fright; to rush violently, plunge. *Lit.,* to fly evil.
lele.iō. Same as *leleiona 2,* fidgety.
lele 'iomo. Same as *lele kawa.*
lele.iona. 1. n. Shark-sucker, remora (Echeneidae spp.); it clings to large fish, such as swordfish, marlin, bonito, shark. **2.** vs. Fidgety, foolish, restless. **3.** *(Cap.)* n. Milky Way.
lele.iwi. n. A kind of shark, possibly thresher, reported by Hyde (no data), perhaps the same as *laukāhi'u.*
lele kawa. vi. To leap feet first from a cliff into water without splashing or into (at Ka'ū) soft earth. *Papa lele kawa,* diving board. *Lele kawa o Kaumaea,* sport of leaping over earth banks, at Kaumaea, Ka'ū.
lele.kē. vi. To leap here and there. **ho'o.lele.kē.** A game of tossing ti leaves into Malama Crater at Puna, Hawai'i, and dedicating them to Ka-moho-ali'i.
lele.kepue. n. Hard volcanic rock, as used for adzes.
-lele kī. ho'o.lele kī. A game played only at Malama-kī, Puna, Hawai'i. A player would hold a ti leaf in his hand, chant *'O kēlā kī, 'o kēia kī, na Ka-moho-ali'i ka'u kī, lele!* That ti, this ti, my ti is for Ka-moho-ali'i, fly! If the wind was right and the chant correctly rendered, the ti would fly off and return to the sender. *Lit.,* make the ti fly.
lele koa'e. 1. nvi. Flight of tropic birds; to fly like a tropic bird. *Fig.,* sheer, steep. See *koa'e 1.* **2.** n. Name for *kauā,* outcasts.
lele koali. v. To swing; jump rope; swinging on a *koali* vine rope, an ancient sport.
lele koke. vi. To leap suddenly, immediately. *Fig.,* short-tempered, excitable, quick to fight.
lele kolu. See *lele 7.*
Lele-ku'i-lua. n. Name of a strong, wintry wind.
lele lā.'au. nv. Pole vaulting; to pole vault.
lelele. Redup. of *lele 1;* to beat swiftly, as the heart; to frisk, hop about, romp, caper; inconstant, promiscuous; at intervals, here and there. *Lelele i ka hau'oli,* to leap for joy. *Lelele ka 'ō'ili i ka mea hou,* the heart leaps at the news. *Holo lelele i ka lio,* to bounce, bump on a horse. *Lelele wāwae kahi,* to hop on one foot. **ho'o.lelele.** Caus/sim. (PEP *lelele.*)
lele.lele. Same as *lelele.* (PPN *lelelele.*)
-lele leo. See *lele 1.*
lele lima. See *lele 7.*
lele loa. vs. Completely severed, as a part of the body in fighting. (FS 99.)
lele lua. 1. vi. An interval of a second in music. Cf. *lele 7.* **2.** vi. To leap twice.
lele lupe. vi. To rise and fall, as the forepart of canoe outrigger *(lupe). Fig.,* the rise and subsidence of emotion.
-lele lupe. ho'o.lele lupe. To fly kites.

lelemu. nvs. A slowpoke; slow, sluggish, disinclined to get up. Cf. *lemu.*
lele.mū. vt. To seize victims for sacrifice.
lelena. Redup. of *lena 1, 3.* (PPN *rengarenga.*)
leleo. Redup. of *leo.*
lele.'oi. vi. Excessive, very great. *Lit.,* excessive leap. *Ua lele'oi ka loa'a mamua o ka mea i mana'o 'ia,* the gain went beyond expectations. *Ua lele'oi i kona na'auao i loko o ka papa,* his knowledge is way beyond that of the class.
lele 'ō.'ō. vi. To leap or plunge into water feet first. *Lit.,* piercing leap.
lele 'opu. v. To dive feet first into water without making a splash. Also *lele ā 'opu. Fig.,* unfavorable (For. 6:59).
lele.'opuhi. vi. To leap obliquely into the water from a height. (UL 192.) Same as *lele pāhi'a.* See *pāhi'a.*
lele.pā. nvt. One who jumps over a fence; to fence jump. *Fig.,* nonconformer; one who cannot be restrained, especially regarding the opposite sex; wanton; to hurdle. *'O kō pā lā, 'o lelepā* (FS 221), your sty there is one easily vaulted.
lele pā-. n. Singing intervals in music (*pā* is followed by a number). Cf. *lele 7.*
lele pahū. vi. To leap into water with a splash; as this was considered poor diving, the expression may refer figuratively to any poor performance; to leap and land with a thud.
lele pai.lani. vt. To praise, exalt, extol extravagantly or excessively (stronger than *pailani,* to praise).
lele pali. v. To leap or fall off a cliff; to practice the ancient sport of leaping from a precipice into water.
lele.pau. vt. **1.** To trust completely. **2.** To apply oneself to, concentrate wholly on.
lelepe. n. **1.** Toothed, sharp-pointed design, as in tapa. **2.** Same as *lepelepe 2,* wattles.
lele.pī. vi. To fly into a rage at the slightest provocation; to lose one's temper; hot-tempered. *Lit.,* jump [at a] drop.
lele pī.na'i. vi. To run with a rope around a coconut tree, and when going very fast, to lift the feet off the ground. *Lit.,* repeated leaps.
lele.pinao. vi. To swing on a *koali* vine. *Lit.,* dragonfly leap.
lele.pinau. Game said to resemble *kōnane.* (AP.)
lele pio. v. To run away in defeat; to avoid capture, as a thief. *Lit.,* to flee capture.
lele pi'o. vi. To fly or jump in a curve; to fly as a comet through the sky.
lelepo. 1. Same as *lepolepo,* dirty. **2.** n. Probably another species of *Padina,* similar in appearance to *'a'ala-'ula,* a seaweed.
lele.pō. n. A species of night-flying *(lele pō) mālolo,* flying fish.
lele.po'i.pū. vt. To pounce upon.
lele.poni. vi. To die suddenly, as by stroke or accident. Cf. *kā'iliponi.*
lele pono. vi. To jump carefully. *Fig.,* to live a happy life; to transact business justly; to rise rapidly to success.
lele.po'o. v. To dive headfirst.
lele.puni. n. **1.** A musical interval of an octave. Cf. *leo lelepuni.* **2.** A game said to resemble *kōnane.*
leleu. Name of a fruitful tree (no data). (And.)
lele.ū. Word said to describe sexual relations. (AP.)
lele ua. n. Windblown rain.
Lele-uli. n. Name of a gusty, wintry wind.
lele uli. v. To dispel darkness; to purify or cleanse, as in a religious ceremony.
lelewa. 1. Redup. of *lewa 2.* (PEP *lelewa.*) **2.** n. Hangers-on about a chief; parasitic persons. **3.** *(Cap.)* Var. of *lewalewa 3,* Gilbertese.
lele.wa'a. n. A shark listed by Kamakau, perhaps the friendly shark that was said to lean *(kālele)* on canoe outriggers for food and company.
lele wa'a. v. Transferring at sea from canoe to canoe or

canoe to surfboard for the sport of surfing to shore. *Lit.,* canoe leaping.

lele wai. v. To purge, cleanse, purify with water of purification.

lele wale. vi. To fly, jump, move of one's own accord or for no reason; in ancient prayers, to speed on, as a prayer to a god. *'Āmama, ua noa, lele wale* (For. 5:413), the prayer is finished, the taboo is lifted; go, prayer [or: the taboo is lifted and quite departed].

lele walo. nvi. Loud, distant cry; to call loudly.

lele wawalo. Redup. of *lele walo;* to reverberate, as an echo.

lele welu.welu. vs. Torn to shreds; broken up and scattered.

lelewi. n. Ornamental carved figurehead on a bowsprit; a canoe with such. (Malo text, chapter 34, section 35.) Pronunciation uncertain.

lelo. 1. n. Tongue (short for *alelo, elelo*). **2.** nvs. Yellowish, especially the hue imparted to a whaletooth pendant *(lei palaoa)* by smoking.

lelo.lelo. Redup. of *lelo 2.*

lelo pu'u. Same as *alelo pu'u.*

lemi. n. Lemon *(Citrus limonia),* lime *(C. aurantifolia).* (Neal 482–3.) *Eng. Wai lemi,* lemonade, limeade.

lemi wai. n. A kind of water lemon, sweet granadilla *(Passiflora ligularis),* a passion fruit with heart-shaped leaves; good-tasting fruits, 5 to 9 cm long, ovoid, orange to purplish. Also *lani wai, lemona.* (Neal 598.)

lemona. Var. of *lemi wai. Eng.*

lemu. 1. n. Buttocks (politer than *'ōkole*). *E 'eu ka lemu,* get moving. (PPN *lemu.*) **2.** vs. Slow-moving, sluggish; lagging.

lemu.'ā. n. Rubbish scattered by flood rains. *Rare.*

lemu.hao. n. Euphemism for *'ōkolehao.* (Ii 107.)

lemuku. vi. Broken off short, as a pole; to start out to do something and not finish it. *Hele akula kēia, a lemuku ihola,* he starts out and then cuts off [the project].

lemu.kū. nvi. One who sits around doing nothing, a term of reproach; also said to refer to a woman who is sexually unattractive. *Lit.,* standing buttocks.

lemu.lemu. Same as *lelemū, lemu 2.*

lemu.oma.kili. Same as *mohihihi,* a vine. (Kam. 64:103.)

lena. 1. nvs. Yellow, yellowish; jaundice; bile. (PPN *renga.*) **2.** n. Var. name for the *'ōlena* or turmeric plant. (PPN *renga.*) **3.** vi. To stretch out, as to dry; to draw tight, as a belt; to sight or aim; to bend, as a bow. *Lena ka maka,* to stare threateningly. *Lena nō lākou i kō lākou mau alelo, e like me kō lākou kakaka, no ka wahahe'e* (Ier. 9.3), they bend their tongues like their bows for lies. *ho'o.lena.* To stretch, pull back, as a bow. **4.** vs. Lazy, idle, indolent. Cf. *lē, lolena.* **5.** *(Cap.)* n. Name of a star, perhaps Sirius. **6.** *(Cap.)* n. Name of a yellow-tinted rain famous at Hanalei, Kaua'i, and on Maui.

lena.lena. Redup. of *lena 1.* Also *nenanena.* (PPN *rengarenga.*)

lene.kila, lenetia. n. Lentils *(Lens esculenta).* (Ezek. 4.9.) *Eng.*

leo. nvt. Voice, tone, tune, melody, sound, command, advice, syllable, plea, verbal message; to speak, make a sound. Cf. *leoleo, leo 'ole. Kona leo,* his voice. *Kāna leo,* his tune. *Ka leo o ke kai,* the sound of the sea. *Kū loa i ka leo,* exactly like the voice; high fidelity. *Nā leo a pau a kona kaikunāne* (FS 259), all commands of her brother. *I ali'i nō 'oe, i kanaka au, malalo aku au o kō leo* (hula song), you be the chief, I the servant, I shall be obedient to your command. (PPN *le'o.*)

le'o. 1. vs. Lofty, tall, high. Cf. *'ale'o,* turret. **2.** n. A variety of taro that cannot be eaten either cooked or as fresh poi without throat irritation. After fermentation, however, the poi is tasty.

leo ho'o.nani. n. Song of praise, hymn.

leo iki. nvi. A low voice; to speak softly.

leo kāne. n. Male voice, bass.

leo kāne ki'e.ki'e. n. Tenor. *Lit.,* high male voice.

leo.kani. n. Vowel. *Lit.,* voiced sound.

leo.kani.pū. n. Consonant. *Lit.,* sound said together [so called because a consonant in Hawaiian is pronounced with a following vowel].

leo ki'e.ki'e. n. High-pitched voice, falsetto.

leo.kū. n. Song sung to an audience. See ex. below. *Lit.,* standing voice.

leo.kū pā.hā. n. Quartet.

leo.kū pā.kahi. n. Solo. *Lit.,* single standing speech.

leo.kū pā.kolu, leo.kū pā.pā.kolu. n. Trio. *Lit.,* triple standing speech.

leo.kū pā.lua. n. Duet. *Lit.,* double standing speech.

leo kū.pina'i. n. Echo.

le'o.lani. nvs. Lofty, tall; chiefly height, rank.

leo lele.puni. n. A musical interlude of a full tone. Cf. *lelepuni 1.*

leo.leo. vi. To speak loudly, angrily, vociferously; to wail, as for the dead.

le'o.le'o. 1. n. Redup. of *le'o 1.* **2.** n. Children's leaping game. *Rare.*

-le'o.le'o. ho'o.le'o.le'o, hō.le'o.le'o. Agitated, stormy, tempestuous; rising and falling as waves; disturbing, confusing; uneven, as a pavement or a wrinkled mat.

leo.leo.ā, leo.leo.wā. vs. Speaking loudly; boisterous; to speak in a loud, noisy fashion.

leo lua. nvi. Duet; to sing in twos; two voices.

leo mana. n. Voice of authority. *E hele aku 'oe iā Palani, he leo mana kona,* go to Frank, his orders are heeded.

leo mele. n. Song tune; notes on the scale.

leo nui. nvi. Loud voice; to speak loudly.

leo 'oko'a. n. Sounds, as in a language. *Lit.,* separate speech.

leo 'ole. vs. Uncomplaining, agreeable; considerate of feelings of others; giving generously; noiseless, speechless, silent. See ex., *hale 2. Lit.,* no voice.

leo pa'a. n. Deaf-mute, dumb person. (Isa. 35.6.) *Lit.,* held voice.

leo.paki, leopadi. n. Leopard. (Ier. 5.6.) *Eng.*

leo pili aku. n. Active voice, in grammar. *Lit.,* voice referring elsewhere.

leo pili 'ia mai. n. Passive voice. *Lit.,* voice referred to.

leo uwō. n. Bass or baritone notes or voice; roar, as of a lion.

leo waena. n. Second treble, middle or alto voice.

leo wahine. n. Soprano, soprano voice, feminine voice, falsetto.

lepa. 1. n. Flag, ensign, place marked by a flag, tapa cloth on end of a stick, as used to mark a taboo area. Cf. *kālepa.* (PCP *lepa.*) **2.** Same as *lepe 1;* hem. (Puk. 28.33.) (PCP *lepa.*) **3.** Var. of *kepa,* notched. **4.** Rare var. of *lepe,* cockscomb.

lepa.hū. vi. To lose courage, give up (contraction of *lele,* to fly, and *pahū,* to thud). *Lepahū wale iho nō ka mana'o,* the idea was given up.

lepa.lepa. 1. Redup. of *lepa 1–3;* to hang in fringes or tatters. **2.** Same as *lepa 4.*

lepe. n. **1.** Hem or fringe, as of a garment; any loose attachment, as of torn cloth or torn flesh. *Nohae mai nei ku'u lole ā lepe,* my dress was torn and a piece hung loose. Cf. *lepa, 'ūlepe. ho'o.lepe.* To cut, tear; to stir, as water. (PEP *lepe.*) **2.** Rooster comb; turkey wattles. (PCP *lepe.*)

lepea. Pas/imp. of *lepe 1.*

lepe'a. vt. To twist, as the arm.

lepe-a-moa. n. Cockscomb *(Celosia argentea* var. *cristata),* an ornamental tropical herb, bearing flowers crowded either on narrow spikes or in large, plumed clusters, or in odd-shaped, crested combs, the colors including white, yellow, pink, and purple. (Neal 332–3.) *Lit.,* comb like that of a chicken.

lepeka, lepeta. n. Copper coin (RSV), mite (KJV). (Luk. 21.2.) (Gr. *lepeton.*)

lē.pela, lepera. nvs. Leprosy, leper; leprous (Oihk.

13.2). Formerly only *leprosy,* and not *leper.* (Eng. or Gr. *lepra.*)

lepe.lepe. 1. Redup. of *lepe 1;* fringed. (PEP *lepelepe.*) **2.** n. Wattles. **3.** n. Labia minor. (PCP *lepelepe.*) **4.** Same as *lepelepe-o-Hina.*

lepe.lepe-a-moa. n. *Selaginella arbusculla,* small club mosses; used for leis, braided with rosebuds. (Neal 3–5.)

lepe.lepe-o-Hina. n. **1.** Monarch butterfly *(Danaus plexippus);* Ka-mehameha butterfly. **2.** Nudibranchia. **3.** Same as *lepe-o-Hina 1,* a seaweed.

lē.pelo, lepero. Same as *lēpela* (formerly only *leper*).

lepe.lua. nvs. A turncoat; unfaithful. *Rare.*

lepe-o-Hina. n. **1.** A red seaweed *(Halymenia formosa)* with flat blades bearing fringed and irregular margins, with a variety of colors ranging from red to yellow; common allusion to swirling in water resembling movement of *pā'ū* in dancing. Also called *lehelehe'īlio, lepelepe-o-Hina, limu-pepe-o-Hina, pā'ū-o-Hi'iaka.* **2.** Same as *lepelepe-o-Hina,* a butterfly.

lepe.ulu. n. Split or crack in wood, running with the grain. *Rare.*

lepo. 1. nvs. Dirt, earth, ground, filth, rubbish, silt, soil, excrement; dirty, soiled. *Fig.,* common people (For. 6:391). See ex., *dust. Hana lepo,* stools, excreta; to excrete. **ho'o.lepo.** Caus/sim. (PEP *lepo.*) **2.** Var. of *lipo 1.*

lepo 'ae.'ae. n. Dust.

lepo hā.nai. n. Dirt; rubbish carried to a pit, as to a compost pit. *Lit.,* fed dirt.

lepo.hao. nvs. Rust; rusty. *Lit.,* iron dirt.

lepo kā.wili. n. Adobe; clay. (Isa. 41.25.) *Lit.,* mixed earth.

lepo kī.'aha. n. Potter's clay, clay vessel. *Lit.,* cup dirt.

lepo kuhue. n. Type of clay. *Lit.,* solidifying dirt.

lepo.lepo. vs. Dirty, turbid; contaminated, as water. (PCP *lepolepo.*)

lepo lo'i. n. Taro-patch mud.

lepo mā.noa.noa. n. Clay. *Lit.,* thick dirt.

lepo.nalo. n. 1. A euphemism for *kūkaenalo;* wax; mole (anatomical); muslin. **2.** A kind of seaweed.

lepo.nē.nē. Same as *'ai-a-ka-nēnē,* a plant.

lepo.pa'a. n. Hard earth; constipation.

lepo.pele. n. Match, sulphur (euphemism for *kūkaepele*). *Lit.,* volcanic dirt.

lepo pō. n. Night soil.

lepo pohō. n. Marshy ground, marsh, mire (Ioba 8.11).

lepo pō.polo. n. *Pōpolo* herb dirt, an uncomplimentary term for commoners. See *pōpolo.*

lepo 'ula.'ula. n. Red earth. *Fig.,* people interrelated for generations *(rare).*

lepo uli. n. Ashes of certain woods mixed with water, as for medicine. *Lit.,* dark earth.

lepu. n. Hare. (1843 Bible, Kanl. 14.7.) (Latin *lepus,* a genus.)

Lepu.palika, Repupalika. 1. nvs. Republican (political party). A newspaper, 1901–2, was entitled Home Rula Republalika. *Eng.* **2.** *(Not cap.)* n. Republic.

leu. n. Loins (rare, in a chant in Kam. 64:124).

leu.wī. n. Canoe with extra wide weatherboard; forepoint of a canoe where the two ends of the two weatherboards come together.

lewa. 1. n. Sky, atmosphere, space, air, upper heavens; aerial. *Ka'aahi kau i ka lewa,* elevated train. *He wai kau i ka lewa: he niu* (riddle), water perched in the sky: a coconut. *Mahele kaua lewa,* air force. **2.** vi. To float, dangle, swing, hang, oscillate; swinging, dangling, pendulous, afloat, unstable; limber-jointed, of admired hula dancers. Cf. *akalewa, ha'alewa. Halelewa,* tabernacle. *Hōkū lewa,* moving star, planet. *One lewa,* shifting sand. *Kai lewa,* deep sea out of sight of land. *Ka moana lewa loa,* the deep ocean. *Waiū lewa,* long, pendulous breasts. *E ola ana 'oia nei a lewa ke kanahiku,* he will live on to past seventy. **ho'o.lewa. (a)** To float, as a cloud; to lift up and carry, as on a stretcher; to sus-

pend. *Moe ho'olewa,* stretcher, hammock. *Nā mea ho'olewa,* peddlers [they carried their goods swinging on a carrying pole; cf. *kālewa 1*]. **(b)** To rotate the hips in dancing, sway. See song under Hopoe. *He aha ē ka hana a 'Ana-pau lā? Ho'olewa ka hana a 'Ana-pau lā* (song), what is the work of 'Ana-pau there? Rotating the hips is the work of 'Ana-pau there. (PNP *lewa.*) **3.** nvs. Homeless vagabond, wanderer; landless, homeless. *He lewa hele, 'a'ohe kahua pa'a,* a wandering traveler without fixed residence. *Po'e lewa* (1 Pet. 2.11), pilgrims. **4.** vi. To know thoroughly, as a type of work; to be thoroughly familiar with, as a place. *Ua lewa ia'u ka hana o ke kuiki kapa,* I'm thoroughly familiar with the work of quilting. *Ua hele au i kēia mau kuahiwi ā lewa,* I've gone to these mountains until I know every nook and corner. **5.** *(Cap.)* n. Name of a star.

-lewa. ho'o.lewa. Funeral. *Anaina ho'olewa,* funeral wake.

lewaa.lani. n. Part of a heiau temple where human sacrifices were offered.

lewaa.nu'u. n. Probably a part of the *lananu'u mamao* turret.

lewa ho'o.makua. n. Space just above the surface of the earth. (Malo 10.)

lewa lani. n. Highest stratum of the heavens.

lewa lani lewa. n. Lower atmosphere, just above the *lewa ho'omakua.*

lewa.lewa. 1. Redup. of *lewa 2;* oscillate. *Kulapepeiao lewalewa,* dangling earrings. *Keiki ma'i lewalewa,* boy before the age of puberty who did not wear a malo; *lit.,* child dangling genital. **ho'o.lewa.lewa. (a)** Same as *lewalewa;* to cause to dangle. **(b)** Kind of fish net suspended from a canoe in the deep sea. Also *maiewa.* (PNP *lewalewa.*) **2.** n. Unconcealed penis of a boy, usually called *ma'i lewalewa.* **3.** *(Cap.)* n. Nickname for Gilbertese, because their stretched ear lobes dangled.

lewa lilo loa, lewa luna lilo. n. Outer space, highest atmosphere.

lewa mawaho. n. Outer space.

lewa nu'u. n. Space in the heavens lower than the *lewa lani;* atmosphere reached by birds.

lewa.walo. vi. To run calling (probably a contraction of *lele wawalo*).

lewia.kana, leviatana. n. Leviathan. (Ioba 41.1.) *Eng.*

lewika, Levita. n. Levites. *Eng.*

lī. 1. nvi. Chills; to have chills; to tremble with cold; shuddery feeling of horror. Cf. *hulilī. Lī ka 'ili, lī ka 'i'o,* to have goose flesh. *Pi'i ka lī,* to get chills. **2.** nvt. Lace, as of shoes; to lace or tie. Cf. *lī kāliki, lī kāma'a. E lī mai i ke kāma'a o La'a-kea,* tie La'a-kea's shoes. **3.** nvt. To hang, gird; to furl or reef, as a sail. (PNP *lii.*) **4.** n. Third note in musical scale, mi.

lī-. A prefix to many kinds of seaweeds, short for *limu.*

lia. Var. of *liha 1.* (PNP *lia.*)

-lia. Pas/imp. suffix corresponding to 'ia. See *kaulia, kūlia* and especially Gram. 6.6.3. (PNP *-lia.*)

li'a. 1. nvt. Strong desire; yearning, amorous; to wish for ardently, crave. **2.** n. Fear, chills. (For. 5:585.) (PPN *lika.*)

lia.'aki.malala. n. Rear admiral. *Eng.*

Lī-anu. n. A wind reported at Hālawa, Moloka'i. (For. 5:103.)

lī anu. n. Cool chill.

lī.'apu. n. A variety of taro (no data). (HP 33.)

li'a.wahine. n. *Kukui* blossoms used as medicine, named for a woodland goddess. *Lit.,* female desire [or fear]. Also *kihawahine.*

liha. 1. n. Nit, louse egg. Also *lia.* (PPN *lisa.*) **2.** Same as *liliha;* dreadful, fearful.

liha.liha. 1. Same as *liliha 1. Lihaliha wale,* rich and oily; pitiful. *Lihaliha wale ke moni akula* (song about fish), so wonderfully rich to swallow. **2.** Redup. of *liha 1;* many nits.

liha.lihau. Redup. of *līhau 1. Makulu ka noe, lihalihau,* dripping fog, cool and damp.

lī.hau. 1. nvi. Gentle cool rain that was considered lucky for fishermen (UL 241); moist and fresh, as plants in the dew or rain; cool, fresh, as dew-laden air. *Onaona ke ʻala o ka maile i ka līhau ʻia e ka ua noe* (song), sweet fragrance of the *maile,* kept fresh and moist by the misty rain. *Līhau mai nei ʻoe,* you are freshly adorned as the cool dew-laden plants. **2.** n. A variety of sweet potato (no data). (HP 142.)

lihe. Rare var. of *liha 1.*

lihe.lihe. Redup. of *lihe.*

lihi. n. **1.** Edge, rim, border, boundary, margins, brim. Also *nihi.* See *nihi* for PPN. Cf. *kaunihinihi.* **2.** Small quantity, particle, a little bit, minutia; slight. *ʻIke lihi,* to glimpse. *Lihi kamaʻāina,* slight knowledge, casual acquaintance. *ʻA ʻohe ona lihi hoʻomaopopo iki,* he didn't in the least understand. *ʻA ʻole lihi launa o ka pilikia,* there's no end to the trouble. *ʻA ʻohe oʻu lihi hoihoi,* I haven't a particle of interest, not the slightest interest. *He lihi pili kō mākou,* we are remotely related. *Lihi launa ʻole,* not the slightest association. *ʻA ʻole e lilo kahi huna, ʻa ʻole hoʻi kahi lihi iki o ke kānāwai* (Mat. 5.18), not one jot, not one tittle shall in any wise pass from the law. **hoʻo.lihi.** Caus/sim.; to gird. **3.** Right or interest in property. *He lihi koʻu i laila,* I have an interest there. **4.** Point of fishhook. (Kam. 76:77.) **5.** Pearl-shell lure, as for *ʻōpelu* fish. **6.** Piece of land usually between two *ahupuaʻa* and of unestablished ownership.

lihili. vs. Confused, bewildered, unsuccessful. *Rare.* Cf. *hili, hilikau.*

lihi.lihi. 1. Same as *lihi 1–3.* **2.** n. Eyelashes, eyelid. See ex., *ʻeaʻea 1, lau 7. Lihilihi maka* (Ioba 16.16), eyelid. *Lihilihi maka kuʻi,* artificial eyelashes. *Lihilihi moku,* eyelash that breaks off and gets into the eye. *Lihilihi piʻi,* eyelashes that are long and curl upward. *Lihilihi ʻoʻoi,* long bristling eyelashes. *Moe i ka lau o ka lihilihi* (Kep. 115), to doze; *lit.,* sleep on the tip of the eyelashes. *ʻIke lihilihi* (Kam. 64:98), to observe critically. *Nā lihilihi o ʻĀwihi-ka-lani,* eyelashes of the blinking lord [a poetic reference to sleep]. **3.** n. Lace. *Kui lihilihi,* crochet needle or hook. **4.** vt. To crochet. *Ka hana lihilihi ʻana,* crocheting. **5.** n. Petals. **6.** n. A variety of sweet potato (no data). This may be qualified by the term *palu.*

lihi.lihi hana lima. n. Handmade lace; crocheting; any handmade trimming, as of knitting, tatting.

lihi.lihi kaka.hiaka. n. Hairy spurge *(Euphorbia hirta).* (Neal 516, 519.) *Niʻihau.*

lihi.lihi kui lau.oho. n. Maltese or hairpin lace.

lihi.lihi mō.lina. n. **1.** Lace edging. **2.** A variety of taro.

lihi.lihi ʻula. n. Narrow band of red, as on a skirt.

lihi lou. n. Tip of a barbless fishhook.

liho. vs. Choice, precious. *Rare.*

liho.liho. vs. Very hot, fiery, glowing. *Ka-lani-nui-kua-liholiho-i-ke-kapu* (name for Ka-mehameha II), the great chief with the burning back taboo [he could not be approached from behind].

liʻi. 1. vs. Small, tiny. (PPN *riki, liki.*) **2.** Short for *aliʻi,* chief, being especially common after *nā: nā liʻi,* the chiefs.

liʻi.li.liʻi. vs. Here and there, piecemeal, a little at a time; small, little, in bits, diminutive, infantile, few. Cf. *haʻāpuka. Mea liʻiliʻi,* trifle. *Kūʻai liʻiliʻi,* retail buying or selling. *Uku liʻiliʻi,* to pay in installments. *Lele liʻiliʻi,* to scatter or fall in every direction. *ʻOki liʻiliʻi,* to cut a little at a time. *ʻOki ā liʻiliʻi,* to cut into small bits. *Kau liʻiliʻi,* scattered or lying here and there. *Koʻu wā liʻiliʻi,* the time of my infancy. **hoʻo.liʻi.li.ʻi.** To decrease, lessen, make small. (PPN *likiliki.*)

liʻi.poe. n. Same as *aliʻipoe,* canna.

lika, lita. n. Liter. *Eng.*

līkā.kini. n. Garters. *Lit.,* tie stockings *(Eng.).*

līkā.liki. nv. Corset lace; to lace up a corset.

līkā.maʻa. nv. Shoelace; to lace shoes.

likā.nia, litania. n. Litany. (Latin *litania.*)

like. vs. Alike, like, similar, resembling, equal, same, uniform, mutual. Cf. *ʻālike, hālike,* and below. *Hana like,* to do together. *Mea like,* similar thing, copy. *Ola like,* living at the same time, contemporaneous; a similar way of living. *Nā mea like ʻole,* miscellany, assortment. **hoʻo.like.** Same as the more common *hoʻohālike;* to equalize, make alike, translate. (PEP *lite.*)

like ʻā like. vs. Equal, exactly alike.

like.like. Redup. of *like.* **hoʻo.like.like.** Redup. of *hoʻolike.*

like loa. vs. Exactly alike, identical.

like me. vs. Such as, according to, like. *He hale e like me kēia,* a house such as this.

like ʻole. vs. Various, all, different, not alike. *Nā pua like ʻole o Hawaiʻi,* the varied flowers of Hawaiʻi.

Like.pona, Lisebona. n. Lisbon. *Eng.*

like pū. vs. Just the same, alike, similar.

liki. 1. nvi. To boast, brag, exult; boaster. See *kūkaliki. Kū ka liki i Nuʻu-anu,* boasting like Nuʻu-anu [said of a boaster]. **2.** vt. To tighten, gird on; to pucker; stiff, as a limb. Cf. *kāliki, pūliki. E liki mai ʻoe ā pū ke kaula,* tighten the rope securely. **3.** n. Astringent, as medicine. **4.** n. A substance or glaze, such as juice of ti roots, that prevents colors from fading or mixing, a mordant.

likiki. n. Ticket, receipt. *Eng. Likiki hoʻokaʻa,* receipt; *lit.,* ticket for payment.

liki.liki. Redup. of *liki 2;* tight. Cf. *ʻalikiliki. Likiliki loa kēia lole,* this dress is too tight. **hoʻo.liki.liki.** To tighten.

likini. n. Rigging. *Eng.* See ex., *liolio.*

likini wā.wae. n. Leggings.

liki pahu. n. Iron hoop, barrel hoop. *Lit.,* barrel tightener.

liko. 1. nvi. Leaf bud; newly opened leaf; to bud; to put forth leaves. *Fig.,* a child or descendant, especially of a chief; youth. Cf. *ʻōhua liko. Liko aliʻi,* chief's child. (PPN *lito.*) **2.** vs. Shining, glistening, as with dew; sparkling, glowing; burning. *Ke liko aʻela ka ua i ke kai,* the rain sparkles on the sea. (PPN *lito.*) **3.** vs. Fat, fleshy. **4.** n. A Tahitian banana *(Musa troglodytarum).* **5.** vi. To burn. *Rare.*

liko.lehua. n. **1.** A variety of sweet potato. **2.** A kind of seaweed.

liko lehua. n. *Lehua* bud; red *lehua* leaves as used for leis or medicine; such a lei, as made in the Kī-lau-ea volcano area. See ex., *kohu 1* (the reference here is probably to a young and pretty girl).

liko.liko. Redup. of *liko 1–3;* fresh, young, oily. *He ahi likoliko o ka wela* (chant), glowing fire of heat. *Kai likoliko,* gravy full of fat or grease; oily sea water. (PPN *litolito.*)

likula, ligura. n. Ligure. (Puk. 28.19.) *Eng.*

lila, lira. 1. See *laila.* **2.** nvs. Lyre, harp (Kin. 4.21); lyric. *Lira kamaliʻi,* children's lyrics [a book of songs]. (Latin or Gr. *lyra.*)

lī.lā. vs. Spindly, undeveloped, as of plants; thin, as a line of words across a page. Cf. *ʻeʻa 2. He maiʻa līlā, ʻa ʻohe ʻiʻo,* a thin banana without substance [either fruit or plant]. (PPN *lila,* PCP *liilaa.*)

lilā.lilā. Redup. of *līlā.* (PPN *lilalila.*)

lile. vs. **1.** Bright, shiny, dazzling, sparkling. **2.** In unison, as chanting. *Rare.*

lī.lē. 1. Var. of *līlā.* **2.** n. Upland patch, as of *olonā.* (HP 199.) *Kauaʻi.*

lilei.uli. v. To cleanse, as of sin. *Rare.*

lile.lile. Redup. of *lile 1.*

lili. 1. nvs. Jealous; highly sensitive to criticism; jealousy, envy; anger and mental anguish felt if one's loved ones are criticized. *Lili punalua,* see *punalua.* **hoʻo.lili.** To provoke jealousy; jealous. (PPN *lili.*) **2.** vs. Blasted, as fruit.

-lili. hoʻo.lili, holili. Rippled surface of the sea, as caused by fish; undulation or vibration of light in the hot sun;

to ripple, vibrate, undulate; to close or blink the eyes in bright glare. Var. of *ha'alili. Ho'olili ka 'ōpelu*, the *'ōpelu* ripples [the sea]. (PPN *lili*.)

lī.lī. Redup. of *lī 1*. (PNP *liiiii*.)

lī.lia. n. Any kind of lily. *Eng.*

lī.lia-lana-i-ka-wai. n. Water lily (*Nymphaea* spp.) (Neal 348–51.) *Lit.*, lily floating on the water.

lī.lia-o-ke-awāwa. n. Lily of the valley *(Convallaria majalis)*. (Neal 209–10.)

lī.lia pala.'ai. n. Day lily (*Hemerocallis* spp.). (Neal 192–3.) *Lit.*, pumpkin lily.

liliha. 1. vs. Nauseated, nauseating, of rich or fatty foods only; very rich, of fatty, oily food, as of the *wolu*, a fish. *Fig.*, heartsick, as over a tragedy; revolted, disgusted, as by a hideous crime; dreadful, fearful. **2.** Redup. of *liha 1*; many nits.

lili.hua. vs. Prepared, supplied, outfitted. *Rare.*

lili'i. vs. Tiny, dainty, fine. *Lili'i wai lehua*, tiny drops of *lehua* honey.

liliko. Redup. of *liko 1, 2, 5*.

lili.koa. Same as *koa haole*, a shrub or small tree.

lili.ko'i. n. Passion fruit, purple water lemon, or purple granadilla *(Passiflora edulis)*, an American vine with three-lobed leaves and edible dull-purple fruits about 5 cm long, growing wild in many forests of Hawai'i; said to be named after Liliko'i, Maui, where it was first grown. The yellow-fruited *liliko'i (P. edulis* f. *flavicarpa)*, is similar but has yellow, better-tasting fruits; it is grown commercially in the Hawaiian Islands and used for desserts and beverages. (Neal 599.)

lī.lī.lā. Redup. of *līlā*.

lī.lī.lehua. n. **1.** The Texas sage (*Salvia coccinea)*, a weedy herb from southern United States, 30 cm high or more, with toothed, ovate leaves and red flowers, 2.5 cm long, borne in long narrow clusters. (Neal 736.) **2.** A variety of taro (no data).

lī.lī-lehua. n. Name of a wind and rain, famous at Pālolo, O'ahu, and Wai-ehu, Maui. *Lit.*, *lehua* chill.

lilili. Redup. of *lili*, often with meaning of petty jealousy.

lili.lili. Redup. of *lili*. (PPN *lililili*.)

lilina. n. Linen *(Eng.)*, flax, linseed *(Linum usitatissimum)*. (Neal 475.)

lilina pu'u mau'u. n. Grass linen. *Lit.*, grass-clump linen.

lili.noe. n. Fine mist, rain.

lilio. Redup. of *lio 2. Lilio ka pepeiao*, the ears are pulled back, as of a horse [also said of the frightened person]. *Maka lilio*, slant eyes, eyes with epicanthic fold.

lilipi. Redup. of *lipi*.

lili'u. 1. nvs. Scorching, burning, smarting, as salt in a raw wound or pain in the eyes. (Queen Lili'u-o-ka-lani was said to have been so named because at the time of her birth her foster mother's aunt, Kīna'u, was suffering with pain in the eyes.) *Lā lili'u*, burning sun. **ho'o.lili'u.** Caus/sim. *Ka ho'olili'u 'ana a ke aloha* (chant), the burning love. **2.** n. Ni'ihau name for *pua kalaunu*, crown flower.

lili.wai. n. A small native herb *(Acaena exigua)*, growing in bogs, only on top of West Maui and Kaua'i, the narrow, fernlike leaves forming a rosette. Also, *nani Wai-'ale'ale*.

lilo. 1. vs., vt. To accrue, be lost, gone, pass into the possession of; to relinquish; to become, turn into; to overcome; purchased, taken. (Gram 4.5.) *Lilo i ke aupuni*, accrue to the government. *Ke kālā e lilo ai*, expenses. *Lilo aku ka wa'a i ke kai*, the canoe was taken by the sea. *Kumu lilo*, cost, price. *'A'ohe wahi lilo o ke ali'i iā 'oe*, you are the perfect image of the chief; *lit.*, there is nothing in the chief that does not accrue to you. *Inā e mimi, 'a'ohe koe 'āina i ka lilo i ka wai* (For. 5:139), if [he] urinates, there is no land that does not turn into water [that is not flooded completely]. **ho'o.lilo.** To transfer, assign, as in legal transactions; to export; change, reduction, as in fractions. *Waiwai ho'olilo*, exports. *Ho'olilo 'ana*, loss, cession. *Ua ho'olilo 'ia i 'Amelika*, become Americanized. *Ua ho'olilo 'oia iāia*

iho i kanaka pono, he changed himself into a righteous man. (PPN *lilo*.) **2.** vs. Busy, absorbed, occupied, engaged, engrossed, devoted, dedicated. *Ua lilo loa au i ka heluhelu*, I'm completely absorbed in reading. *Lilo 'o Ka-welo i laila, hiki ua mau kānaka nei i Wai-kīkī* (FS 51), while Ka-welo was busy there, these aforementioned people came to Wai-kīkī. *No ka lilo loa o Lohi'au ipo i ka nani o Puna, ua lilo ka 'ai . . . i mea 'ole iāia*, because of sweetheart Lohi'au's fascination by the beauty of Puna, food became . . . as nothing [of no interest] to him. **3.** n. Expense, expenditure, outlay of money. *Nā uku makahiki a me nā lilo 'ē a'e*, annual salaries and other expenses. **ho'o.lilo.** Expense, expenditure; to spend; to lose; to buy or sell. *Nui ka ho'olilo*, great expense; very expensive. *Ka mea ho'olilo li'ili'i*, retail buyer. *Nui ka ho'olilo o ke aupuni no kēlā alanui hou*, the government spent much on that new road. **4.** vs. Far, distant, out of sight, completely, entirely (often follows a noun). *I luna lilo*, way up. *I waho lilo*, far outside, way out. *I ka moana lilo*, far out to sea. *Ua lawe a lilo 'ia ka ipo a ke kelamoku*, the sailor's sweetheart was swept completely off her feet.

Lī.loa. 1. n. Name of an early chief, the father of 'Umi. **2.** *(Not cap.)* A long time ago. *Rare.*

lilo.lilo. 1. vs. Openhanded, generous. **2.** vi. To break away again and again, as fish from a hook; to hover between life and death. Cf. *kālilolilo*.

lilo loa. vs. Completely engrossed, dedicated, absorbed; permanently lost, taken, or given; far.

lī lua. vs. Extremely chilly. Cf. *lī 1. Kau lī lua i ke anu Wai-'ale'ale* (UL 105), doubly chilled in the cold of [Mt.] Wai-'ale'ale.

lima. 1. n. Arm, hand; sleeve; finger. For types of sleeves see *'ekeke'i, lā'iki, loloa, pa'i 'ai, pihapiha, pōko'u, 'ūhā hipa*. See also *'eha. Kui lima*, to go hand in hand, arm in arm; to hold hands. *Hana lima*, handmade, hand work. *Hana lima 'ike*, expert craftsmanship. (PPN *lima*.) **2.** num. Five; fifth. (PPN *lima*.)

lima 'aina. n. Second finger. *Lit.*, eating finger.

lima 'ā.kau. nvs. Right hand; right-handed; dependable helper, right-hand man.

lima 'ā.pā. vs. Light-fingered, thieving.

lima.hana. nvs. Labor, laborer, worker, employee; industrious, busy. Cf. *hana lima* under *lima 1. Papa limahana*, labor board. *Komisina o nā limahana*, labor commission.

lima hehe'e. n. A thinning hand, of one whose poi thins and ferments quickly.

lima hema. nvs. Left hand; left-handed.

Lima-huli. n. Wind associated with Ha'ena, Kaua'i. (For. 5:97.) *Lit.*, turning hand.

lima ika. Same as *lima ikaika*.

lima ikaika. nvt. Strong hand or arm; power, strength; to handle roughly, assault, ravish, use force; strongarm.

lima iki. n. Small hand; little finger.

lima kā.kau. n. Handwriting; hand to write with.

lima koko. n. Assassin, murderer, shedder of blood, brute; bloody hand.

lima kuhi. n. Index finger; in printing, an index or hand calling attention to a note. *Lit.*, pointing hand.

lima kuhi.kuhi. n. Hands of a clock. *Lit.*, pointing hands.

lima.lau. Same as *laulima*, but some persons limit *limalau* cooperation to canoe and house building.

lima lawe.lawe. n. Pilferer, filcher. *Lit.*, handling hands.

lima lewa.lewa. n. Idler. *Lit.*, hanging hands.

lima.lima. 1. vt. To handle, use the hands; to pilfer, filch. **2.** vt. To hire. **ho'o.lima.lima.** To rent, hire, employ, lease, charter; paid, hired; a lease, rental. *Ho'olimalima hou*, sublease. *Ka mea ho'olimalima*, lessee, tenant. *'Āina ho'olimalima*, leased land. *Kanaka ho'olimalima*, hired man. *Ka'a ho'olimalima*, hired car, taxi. *Ho'olimalima manawa pau 'ole*, perpetual lease. *Ho'olimalima no ka manawa e ola ana*, life-time lease. *He hoʻolimalima makahiki haʻahaʻa,* minimum annual rent. **3.** vt. To massage. *Rare.* **4.** n. Prayer in which the priest gestured with his hands; the ceremony was called *hoʻopiʻi i nā ʻaha limalima,* the *limalima* assembly rises.

lima.lima pilau. n. One who handles dirty matter. *Fig.,* an immoral wretch, as a pimp.

Lima-loa. God of mirages.

lima loa. n. Grabber of other's property. *Lit.,* long arm.

lima.meke. Short for *lima ʻumeke,* index finger, so called because poi was dipped from the bowl *(ʻumeke)* with it.

lima miki. Index finger.

lī.mana.mana. n. A kind of seaweed. *Lit.,* branching seaweed.

lima.nui. vt. To attack violently, manhandle, assault, beat, roughhouse, administer a beating, take by force.

lima nui. n. Big hand; thumb. Cf. *lima iki.*

lima pili. n. Third or ring finger.

lima pū.haʻu.haʻu. n. Puffed sleeve, as sleeve gathered at shoulder and wrist.

lima ulu. n. A green thumb.

lima ʻumeke. See *limameke.*

lima.wī.wī. n. A variety of sweet potato. *Lit.,* thin hand.

limi. Same as *lumi 1. Rare.*

limi.limi. Redup. of *limi. Rare.*

lī.moa. Same as *hulu moa,* a seaweed.

limu. **1.** n. A general name for all kinds of plants living under water, both fresh and salt, also algae growing in any damp place in the air, as on the ground, on rocks, and on other plants; also mosses, liverworts, lichens. See saying, *hailepo. Ua ulu ka limu,* the seaweed (pubic hairs) are growing. (PPN *limu.*) **2.** vs. Tricky, deceiving, unstable (said to be named for the octopus' ability to change its color, and its waving of a tentacle to and fro like the motion of a seaweed in water). **3.** n. Wind gust. *Rare.* **4.** n. Coil, curl. *Rare.* **5.** n. Soft coral.

limua. vs. Overgrown or covered with moss, seaweed, or any *limu.* Cf. *ua limua.*

limu ahi. n. A tree moss or liverwort.

limu ʻahu ʻula. n. An upland moss.

limu alolo. n. A *limu, Potamogeton pectinatus* (pronunciation not certain). *Niʻihau.*

limu ʻele.ʻele. See *ʻeleʻele 3.*

limu haea. n. A lichen *(Sterocaulon* sp.), with erect, branching stalks.

limu hā.ʻula. n. A red seaweed *(Martensia fragilis).*

limu holo.ā.wai. n. A fresh-water moss.

limu ʻī.lio. Same as *hulu ʻīlio,* seaweeds.

limu kaha. n. A kind of liverwort.

limu kā-kanaka. n. A soft, sometimes gelatinous blue-green alga *(Nostoc commune)* sometimes covering the ground in the wet season as small slippery balls, especially at Hanalei, Kauaʻi. Also *limu kā-kanaka-o-Manuʻakepa. Lit.,* man-striking moss, so called because people are said to slip on it and fall.

Limu-kā-kanaka-o-Maha.moku. n. Stroke in *lua* fighting. (Also with *Ka-.) Lit.,* man-striking moss of Mahamoku.

limu kala. n. Common, long, brown seaweeds *(Sargassum echinocarpum),* their stems covered with short branches, bearing rather stiff, twisted, more or less toothed, narrow leaves. Rarely eaten raw because of toughness (though edible); used in ceremonies to drive away sickness and to obtain forgiveness (see *kala 1*). May be qualified by the terms *lau liʻiliʻi* or *lau nui.* Also *ʻākala.*

limu kala maka piʻi. See *kala maka piʻi.*

limu kala.wai. n. One or more kinds of dark green, slippery fresh-water algae (usually *Spirogyra* spp.) consisting of rows of cylindrical cells in unbranched filaments, common to fresh-water rivulets, dripping places, and taro patches. Also *pālāwai.*

limu kala.maka.piʻi. See *kalemakapiʻi.*

limu kau lā.au. n. All tiny ferns (such as filmy ferns), lichens, liverworts, and mosses growing on trees.

limu kele. n. Moss growing on trees in rain forests.

limu kohu. n. A soft, succulent, small seaweed *(Asparagopsis taxiformis),* with densely branched furry tops that are tan, pink, or dark red, arising from a creeping stem-like portion; one of the best-liked edible seaweeds, prepared in balls for market. Also *limu koko* and for some informants *līpehe, līpehu, līpaʻakai.*

limu koko. n. Same as *limu kohu. Lit.,* blood seaweed.

limu lana. n. Floating seaweed. *Fig.,* a drifter, vagabond.

limu.limu. Redup. of *limu 2–4.*

limu loloa. n. **1.** Several species of edible red seaweeds *(Gelidium),* cylindrical or flattened, more or less pinnately branched, texture firm and smooth. Also *ʻānapanapa, ʻēkahakaha, kūwelu.* **2.** A kind of edible red seaweed *(Pterocladia capillacea),* like *1* above but more finely divided.

limu lū.ʻau. n. A red seaweed *(Porphyra* sp.), growing in the winter on boulders in exposed places, with delicate, thin blades appearing in groups. Best known on Kauaʻi, but known on all the major islands. Also *paheʻe* or *paheʻeheʻe.*

limu-make-o-Hāna. n. A coelenterate *(Palythoa* sp.) containing a toxin, reported as deadly poisonous at Hāna, Maui. Also *limu-make-o-Muʻolea.*

limu-mā.kole-maka-ʻō.piʻi. Same as *mākole mākōpiʻi,* a moss.

limu manau.ea. See *manauea.*

limu moa. Same as *hulu moa,* a seaweed.

limu nehe. Same as *limu kalawai.*

limu paʻa.kai. n. *Limu* salted for indefinite storage without refrigeration. On Maui, usually *limu līpoa.* See *līpaʻakai.*

limu pae. n. Landed seaweed, said of a newcomer or in a bad sense of a drifter, vagabond, or *kauā* outcast.

limu pā.laha.laha. Same as *pālahalaha 2.*

limu pepei.ao. Same as *līpepeiao.*

limu-pepe-o-Hina. Same as *lepe-o-Hina,* a seaweed.

limu ua.ua loli. Same as *ʻēkahakaha 2,* a seaweed.

limu ʻula.ʻula. n. A red seaweed.

lina. **1.** vs. Soft; adhesive, sticky, clayey, gummy, tenacious; glutinous, as taro of poor quality. Cf. *nina, papālina, ʻūlika, ʻūlina.* **2.** n. Scar. Cf. *ʻālina.* *hoʻo.lina.* To scar. **3.** n. Ring *(Eng.),* hoop, race track. *Kuʻu lio kākele lina poepoe* (song), my racing horse [in the] round track.

lina.lina. Redup. of *lina 1, 2.*

lineka. n. Lynx. *Eng.*

lino. **1.** vs. Bright, shiny, shining with splendor, dazzling, brilliant. Cf. *linohau.* **2.** vt. To weave, twist, braid, tie. *ʻAʻohe ʻoe e pakele aku, ua lino ʻia i ka lino pāwalu* (song), you won't escape, you are bound with an eight-strand tie. **3.** Same as *linolino 2.* (PPN *lingo.*) **4.** vs. Taut.

linoa. Pas/imp. of *lino 2. Ua linoa ʻia a paʻa,* tied firmly.

lino.hau. vs. Dressed to perfection, beautifully decorated, ornamented. *Kū kilakila i ka noe, linohau i ka mālie* (song), standing majestic in the mist, beautifully attired in the calm.

lino.kaipa, linotaipa. n. Linotype. *Eng.*

linole.uma. n. Linoleum. *Eng.*

lino.lino. **1.** Redup. of *lino 1, 2.* **2.** vs. Calm, unruffled. (PPN *lingolingo;* see *malino.*)

linu. vs. Tight-fisted, ungenerous, heartless, ungracious. *Rare.*

lio. **1.** n. Horse (perhaps derived from *lio 2,* or, more likely, a shortening of *ʻīlio,* formerly a generic name for quadrupeds: Gram. 2.9.2). *Kona lio,* his horse. *Holo lio, kau lio,* to ride horseback. **2.** vs. Tight, taut, as a rope, or of hair or horse's ears pulled back tightly. Cf. *lilio.* **3.** n. Rope tied to the bottom of a large bag net.

liʻo. **1.** n. Same as *ʻaʻo,* a sea bird. **2.** Same as *liʻoliʻo 2,* the sound made by the *liʻo (ʻaʻo)* bird.

lī.ʻō. vs. To act wild, as a frightened animal; to open the eyes wide in terror; to quiver, leap away, shy, as a frightened horse. Also *leiʻō.* **hoʻo.līʻō.** To frighten, cause to shy, leap.

līʻoa. Pas/imp. of *līʻō.*

lio hei.hei. n. Race horse.

lio holo noho. n. Saddle horse.

lio huila māhu. n. Horse with a steam wheel, an old name for train. (Kel. 98.)

lio hulu ʻaeko. n. Dark-gray horse. *Lit.,* eagle feather horse.

lio kaʻa. n. Carriage horse.

lio kau. n. Riding horse.

lio keʻa. n. Stallion.

lio keiki. n. Colt.

lio lā.ʻau. n. Merry-go-round; horse on a merry-go-round; sawhorse; wooden horse, as used in quilting. *Holo lio lāʻau,* to ride on a merry-go-round. *I Ka-nēkina i ka holo lio lāʻau me ka ulua* (Elbert and Mahoe 78), riding the merry-go-round at Ka-nēkina with the *ulua* fish [man].

lio laho. n. Stallion. *Lit.,* testicle horse.

lio lawe ukana. n. Pack horse. *Lit.,* horse carry gear.

lio.lio. Redup. of *lio 2;* tense. *Ke liolio nei ke kaula likini,* the rigging lines are drawn tight.

liʻo.liʻo. 1. vs. Bright, dazzling, dazzled. Also *liko 2, lile 1, lino 1.* **hoʻo.liʻoliʻo.** Caus/sim. (PCP *likoliko.*) 2. Var. of *liʻo:* name of the sound made by the *ʻaʻo* bird; to call thus. 3. Redup. of *liʻo.*

Lio.lio-i-Wawau. n. Name of a star, and name for the southern sky. (PH 206; Wawaʻu is a widely distributed Polynesian place name: see Pukui, Elbert, and Mookini, 1974, p. 229.) (PPN *Wawaʻu.*)

liona. n. Lion. *Eng. Hui Liona,* Lions Club.

liona kai. n. Sea lion.

lio peki. n. Pacing horse.

lio poʻa. n. Gelding.

lio wahine. n. Mare.

līpaʻa.kai. n. *Limu* salted for indefinite storage without refrigeration; on Kauaʻi usually *limu kohu* from Niʻihau. Some consider *līpehe, līpehu,* and *līpaʻakai* as variants of *limu kohu.*

līpaha. Same as *līpahapaha,* a seaweed.

līpaha.paha. n. A general term for sea lettuce *(Ulva fasciata* and *Monostroma oxyspermum),* common green seaweeds with delicate broad blades, usually with wavy margins. Eaten as a minor element mixed with other tastier seaweeds. Also *ʻīliohaʻa, līpaha, līpālahalaha, pahapaha* (probably restricted to Kauaʻi), *pakaiea* (restricted to Hawaiʻi), and *pālahalaha* (Maui, Molokaʻi, and Oʻahu).

līpaheʻe. 1. Same as *pāheʻeheʻe,* a seaweed. Called *līpāhoe* on Maui. 2. Same as *limu lūʻau 1,* a seaweed. *Kauaʻi.*

līpā.heʻe.heʻe. Same as *līpaheʻe 1.*

līpā.hoe. Same as *līpaheʻe 1,* a seaweed. *Maui.*

lipaki, libati. n. Liberty. *Eng.*

līpā.laha.laha. Same as *līpahapaha,* sea lettuce.

līpā.lā.wai. Same as *līpālāwai,* fresh-water algae.

līpā.lā.wai. n. Edible, green, fresh-water algae, consisting of tufts of branching threads *(Pithophora* spp. and *Stigeoclonium* spp.), or of a network of threads *(Hydrodictyon),* or of simple threads *(Spirogyra* spp.). Also *līpalaʻō, nehe, palaʻō, pālāwai.*

līpalu. n. A seaweed much like *hulu ʻīlio 3,* and perhaps the same; edible, green, soft, slippery tufts.

lipano, libano. n. Frankincense. (Mat. 2.11.) (Gr. *libanos.*)

līpa.oa.oa. n. A seaweed. *Lit.,* fragrant seaweed. (GP 78.)

līpeʻe. Same as *līpeʻepeʻe.*

līpeʻe.peʻe. n. Some native species of a genus of edible red seaweeds *(Laurencia parvipapillata, L. dotyi, L. succisa),* short, with stiff, knobby branchlets, nestling especially in basaltic rock. Also *ʻāpeʻepeʻe, hoʻonunu, līpeʻe, peʻepeʻe.*

līpehe, līpehu. Same as *līpaʻakai,* salted *limu.*

lipe.lala, liberala, liberale. nvs. Liberal. *Eng. Ka*

ʻaoʻao lipelala, the liberal party. *Ka Liberale,* The Liberal [Hawaiian newspaper, 1892–3].

līpē.pē. Same as *līpeʻepeʻe. Niʻihau.*

līpepei.ao. n. 1. A seaweed. Also *limu pepeiao* and *limu kulapepeiao.* 2. A fresh-water moss, usually qualified by *wai.*

lipi. nvs. Adze, chisel; any sharp edge; sharp mountain ridge; sharp, tapering. (PPN *lipi.*)

lipi hoe.hoe. n. Adze or chisel with broad, flat blade. *Lit.,* paddle-like chisel.

lipi kā.hela. n. Adze or chisel with concave blade.

lipi kuke. n. Adze or chisel with thin, tapering blade.

lipi.lipi. Redup. of *lipi.* See *Poʻo-lipilipi.* (PPN *lipilipi.*)

lipina, ribina. Var. of *lipine. Lipina aliʻi,* royal ribbon or decoration.

lipine, ribine. n. Ribbon. *Eng.* See also below.

lipine hoʻo.kani. n. Tape, of a recorder.

lipine kiko.kiko. n. Typewriter ribbon.

li.pioma. n. Small rounded adze or chisel.

lipo. 1. nvs. Deep blue-black, as a cavern, the sea, or dense forest; dim, distant; grief (see ex., *haʻalipo*). See *kumulipo. Lipo lolohuamea,* the dark depths [the unfathomable mystery of the gods]. (Probably PPN *lipo.*) 2. *(Cap.)* n. Name of a star in the southern skies, and hence sometimes the name for the southern sky.

lipoa. Pas/imp. of *lipo 1. Ua lipoa wale i ka ua ka nahele,* forest dark with rain.

līpoa. n. 1. Bladelike, branched, brown seaweeds *(Dictyopteris plagiogramma* and *D. australis)* with conspicuous midrib on blade, unique aroma and flavor; highly prized on all islands. 2. Same as *līpoa kuahiwi.*

līpoa kua.hiwi. n. A nonedible mountain moss.

līpohā.pohā. Same as *pohāpohā 3,* a seaweed.

lipo.lipo. Redup. of *lipo 1.* See ex., *lūlana. Ka moana nui lipolipo,* the great blue ocean. *Ka uliuli lipolipo o nā lau nāhelehele,* the deep green of the forest leaves.

lipo wao nahele. n. Gloom and darkness of a great forest.

līpuʻu. Same as *līpuʻupuʻu.* (KL line 90.)

līpuʻu.puʻu. n. An edible green seaweed *(Valonia utricularis),* with turgid joints and short branches. Also *kūkae-o-Kamapuaʻa.*

liu. 1. nvt. Leakage, bilge water; to leak, of a canoe or ship. (PPN *liu.*) 2. Same as *liuliu.*

liʻu. 1. nvs. Slow, tardy, taking a long time; a long time. *Ala liʻu ka lā o Wai-ʻanae,* the Wai-ʻanae sun rises slowly. *ʻA ʻohe i liʻu iho kona hiki ʻana mai a hiki maila ʻoe,* he hadn't been here long when you arrived. 2. vs. Well-salted, salty, seasoned. 3. vs. Deep, profound, as of skill or knowledge. Cf. *kuliʻu, liliʻu, liʻua. Liʻu ka ʻike i ke kālai waʻa,* he's skilled in canoe carving. *Liʻu ka naʻauao i loko ona,* wisdom within him is profound.

liua. 1. Same as *niua, niniu,* dizzy, etc. (For. 6:295.) 2. Same as *kuhi-ʻai-ka-moʻo-wahie,* a lobelia.

liu.ā. Dissolute. (AP.)

liʻua. Var. of *liu 1, 2. ʻA ʻole i liʻua,* it wasn't long.

liʻu.lā. n. Twilight, dusk; mirage, hallucination. Cf. *poni liʻulā. Ka hulali a ka wai liʻulā,* the glitter of water in the mirage.

liu.liu. nvs. Prepared, ready; to make ready; preparations (Kel. 49.) **hoʻo.liu.liu.** To prepare.

liʻu.liʻu. Redup. of *liʻu 2;* to pass much time; to spend much time. *ʻA ʻole i liʻuliʻu ma Maui,* did not spend much time at Maui. *Liʻuliʻu nō nā lā i ua ai,* it rained many days. *Liʻuliʻu aku mahope* (2 Sam. 7.19), a great while to come. *E kali iho a liʻuliʻu,* wait a while. **hoʻo.liʻu.liʻu.** To cause a delay, prolong, procrastinate.

līwali. Soft, thin, as poi or dough. (And.)

liwele, livere. n. Book (French; seen in a Catholic publication but very rare).

L. K. Abbreviation for *luna kānāwai,* judge.

lō. n. 1. A black insect, earwig (Dermaptera). (PPN *loo.*) 2. Front half of the skull. (And.) 3. Lord. *Eng.* 4. *(Cap.)* A line of Oʻahu chiefs. (Kam. 64:5.)

lō-. Prefix, perhaps short for *lo‘o-*, to obtain; cf. *lōhai, lōkahi, lōkea, lōmilo, lo‘ohia, lo‘okahi, lōpi‘o, lōuhu.*

loa. 1. nvs. Distance, length, height; distant, long, tall, far, permanent. Cf. *loloa*, Gram. 8.7.5. *Mauna Loa* (name), long mountain. *Mea ‘ole ia loa,* this distance was nothing. *E loa ke ola,* may life be long. *Noho loa,* to stay permanently (cf. *noho lō‘ihi,* to stay a long time). *He aha ka loa o kēia pākaukau?* What's the length of this table? *Pau kukui pua i ka loa i lalo,* candlenut flowers blooming far down below. **ho‘o.loa.** To stretch, extend, prolong, lengthen. (PPN *loa.*) **2.** part. Very, very much, too, excessive, most. See *‘a‘ole,* Gram. 8.7.5. *Maika‘i loa,* very good. *Wela loa,* too hot. *Ma ke kūkala ākea i nā mea koho ki‘eki‘e loa,* at public auction to the highest bidders. (PCP *loa.*) **3.** conj. As soon as. *I loa no iāia e hala aku, ‘ō‘ili ana ka makua kāne,* no sooner had he gone, than the father appeared. **4.** n. Head tax officer; government tax as contrasting with king's taxes. **5.** n. A district (And.) or large section of it, contrasting with *poko.*

loa‘a. nvs. To find, get, obtain, discover, acquire, have, take, earn, gain, incur, locate, procure, reach, receive, catch, win, succeed; gain, earnings, profit, spoils, harvest, revenue, income, winnings, receipts, wealth, product, property, success, solution, answer; to have or beget a child; to be born; to find none to compare with; unequalled, incomparable, successful (often pronounced *lo‘a:* Gram. 2.7). This extremely common word is a model for *loa‘a*-stative verbs: Gram. 4.4. See *ha‘iloa‘a, huina loa‘a. Loa‘a ka hale i ke ali‘i,* the chief has a house. *Kanaka loa‘a ‘ole,* a person who gains little, has little. *He mea loa‘a wale nō kēlā iā mākou,* that's something we can easily get. *He mau maka loa‘a ‘ole,* eyes not easily obtained [said affectionately of a high chief not easily approached]. *Ua ‘ai au i kāna loa‘a,* I've eaten his earnings [said in pride by a parent who is cared for by a son or daughter]. *He mea pili o ka loa‘a* (Kep. 109), one to whom gain clings. *‘O ka‘u loa‘a nō kēia,* this is what I've gained. *Ka mea e loa‘a ana (ka mea e lo‘ana),* anything at all, whatever is to be had. *Ka manawa e loa‘a ana,* any convenient time. *‘O ‘oe ka mea e loa‘a ai a‘u wāhine, no ka mea ua pau ko ku‘u waiwai iā lāua, ‘a‘ohe na‘e he loa‘a iki* (FS 229), you're the one who can win my wives, because my wealth is entirely spent on the two without any success at all. *Loa‘a au i ke anu,* I caught a cold; *lit.,* the cold catches me. *Loa‘a Kāne-ālai, ke kupuna o lākou* (chant), their ancestor, Kāne-ālai, was born. *Ka‘u kāne i loa‘a ai ‘oe,* my husband by whom you were begot. *E nānā wāhine a‘e nō wau, ‘a‘ole ‘oe e loa‘a,* I look at all other women, there's not another your equal. *‘A ‘ole e loa‘a mai keiki o ke kaona* (song), none as fine as boys of the town. *Ma ka hīmeni, ‘a‘ohe ‘oe e loa‘a,* in singing you have no equal. **ho‘o.loa‘a.** To obtain, find, get; product, answer, etc. (PEP *loaka.*)

lo.‘a.‘ā. nvs. Rough jagged stone, either coral or lava; hence, hard, severe, as a taboo. *He kānāwai kū i ka lo‘a‘ā,* a cruel law.

loa‘a.hia. Pas/imp. of *loa‘a.*

loa‘a . . . kāu. idiom. You'll get what's coming to you (rude). *Ē Pi‘ikoi, he loa‘a iho kō kāu i ka huahua* (Nak. 24), say, Conceited, [they] will get you by the testicles.

loala. To praise, extol, as a chief (poetic). (And.)

loa.loa. Redup. of *loa 1;* elongated garden plot, as for sweet potatoes (so used in 1848 land claims).

lo‘a.lo‘a. Same as *‘alo‘alo‘a,* pitted, rough.

lo‘e. n. Curve of a fishhook.

loea. nvs. Skill, ingenuity, cleverness; expert, clever, ingenious, adept, deft, technical, skillful, dexterous, handy, skilled; skilled person. *‘Ike loea,* technical knowledge, knowledge of skills.

loea kā.lai.‘āina. nvi. Politician, politically expert.

loea kā.lai au.puni. n. Statesman.

lo‘e.lo‘e. Same as *mālo‘elo‘e,* aching.

lo‘ewa. Same as *pa‘ewa.*

loha. 1. vs. Drooping, wilting; hanging low, as a branch;

beaten down, as by rain. *Fig.,* sullen, spiritless, depressed, unsociable, subordinate, inferior. **2.** nvt. Trimmings of corners and ridge of a thatched house; to put on these trimmings (FS 25). **3.** Short for *aloha.* **4.** n. A variety of banana. **5.** A var. name for the *kilu* game (And.)

lō.hai. nvt. Lever or stick used in prying up or raising heavy articles; to lift thus.

loha.loha. 1. Redup. of *loha 1, 3.* **2.** Var. of *lohelohe 2.* **3.** n. Cocoon.

lohe. vt. To hear, mind, obey, listen; to feel, as the tug of a fishing line; obedient. See idiom, *a‘o 1. Lohe pono,* to listen carefully, attentive, to hear correctly. *Lohe mai i ke a‘o,* heed the teachings. *Lohe mai ke a‘o,* how terrible [in idioms]. *Lohe wale,* to hear vaguely, as rumors. *Pau ka ‘ike, pau ka lohe,* in a coma, unconscious. **ho‘o.lohe.** Caus/sim.; obedient; to mind, heed; attention (a military command). See *mea ho‘olohe. Ho‘olohe ‘ole,* inattentive, not heeding, unreceptive, unresponsive; to disobey. *He kanaka ho‘olohe i kauoha,* a person obedient to commands.

lohea. Pas/imp. of *lohe;* audible.

lohe.lau. 1. n. Wall and gable plates in house. **2.** vs. Exhausted, worn-out, dilapidated.

lohe lau ā.hea. See *āhea.*

lohe.lohe. 1. Redup. of *lohe;* to listen carefully, eavesdrop. *He ‘īlio lohelohe* (PH 75), a dog [sacrificed to obtain] obedience. **ho‘o.lohe.lohe.** Caus/sim. *Ho‘olohelohe ‘ōlelo,* to eavesdrop. **2.** n. Larvae of the dragonfly; this was used in hula ceremonies because *lohe* means to hear and obey. See *pua‘alohelohe.* Also *po‘olānui, lohaloha.* **3.** Poetic var. of *lohaloha 1. Lohelohe i honua,* poetic name for banana plant because its fruit droops *(loha),* to the ground *(i honua). Lohelohe pele-‘unu Mahiki i ka ua,* Mahiki is beaten down and made musty by the rain. **4.** n. Cocoon.

lohena. n. Hearing, obedience. Cf. *lohe. He lohena ka‘u i ka ‘olā‘olā* (chant), I heard a gurgling.

lohe ‘ō.lelo. n. Hearsay, gossip.

lohe pepei.ao. nv. Hearsay; to hear of. *He lohe pepeiao mai ko‘u, ‘a‘ohe he ‘ike maka,* I've just heard [about it], but have not seen for myself.

lohi. vs. **1.** Slow, tardy, late, retarded, backward, deliberate, gradual; to delay. *‘Ōlelo lohi,* speak slowly. *E hele, lohi!* Half step, march! **ho‘o.lohi.** To delay, make slow, detain; to go slowly, procrastinate, dillydally tag. (PCP *lo(f,s)i.*) **2.** Short for *‘alohi,* sparkle, shine. *I ka papa lohi a ‘o Maukele,* in the bright flats of Maukele. *Ka wai lohi o Maleka* (song), the sparkling water of America [alcoholic drink].

lohia. 1. Pas/imp. of *lohi 1, 2. Wai lohia,* sparkling water, intoxicating drink. **2.** Short for *lo‘ohia.* (Mat. 4.24.)

lohi.‘au. vs. Slow, retarded, backward, languid. *Lohi‘au Puna i ke akua wahine,* Puna is handicapped, retarded, set back, by the goddess. Cf. *Lohi‘au,* the unsuccessful suitor of Pele and Hi‘iaka.

lohi.lohi. Redup. of *lohi 1, 2.* **ho‘o.lohi.lohi.** Redup. of *ho‘olohi.* (Kel. 37.) (PEP *lo(f,s)ilo(f,s)i.*)

lohina. n. Delay.

loi. vt. To look over critically; to look at as though searching for flaws, scrutinize. (Probably PPN *loi.*)

lo‘i. n. Irrigated terrace, especially for taro, but also for rice; paddy.

loia. 1. Rare var. of *loea,* skill. **2.** Var. of *loio,* lawyer.

lo‘i ‘ai. n. Taro patch.

loia.like, roialiti. nvs. Royalist. *Eng.*

loie. Rare var. of *loina 1.*

lō.iele. 1. nvs. Sluggish, slow; slowness; to loiter, dillydally. Cf. *-iele. He aha ke kumu o kou lōiele?* Why are you so slow? **2.** n. Fool.

lō.‘ihi. 1. nvs. Length, height, distance; long. Also *lōkihi. Lō‘ihi ke ala,* the road is long. *Lō‘ihi a‘e nei ka manawa,* long time. **ho‘o.lō.‘ihi.** To lengthen, extend, prolong. **2.** *(Cap.).* Young undersea volcano 30 kilometers southeast of Hawai‘i Island.

loi.loi. Redup. of *loi;* to find fault, criticize.

loʻi.loʻi. 1. nvs. Pools of water; having many pools; taro patches. Cf. *hālo ʻilo ʻi, lo ʻi.* **2.** Same as *ʻālo ʻilo ʻi,* a fish. (KL line 157.)

loina. n. 1. Rule, custom, manners, code, precept, law; principle, as of a political party. **2.** Observation, scrutiny.

loio. 1. vs. Thin, spindly. **2.** Rare var. of *loea,* skill. **3.** nv. Lawyer *(Eng.),* attorney, counselor; to act the lawyer; to judge. *Loio o ka ʻao ʻao kūʻē,* lawyer for the opponent. *E loio ana i ke ʻano o kēlā kēia mo ʻolelo* (Kep. 131), judging the nature of all the tales. **hoʻo.loio.** To act the lawyer; to show off knowledge; to ask bewildering questions as a lawyer might.

loio hoʻo.kolo.kolo. n. Prosecutor.

loio kalana. n. County attorney.

loio kuhina. n. Attorney general.

loʻi paʻa.hao. n. A "prison" taro patch, meaning that if a tenant failed to pay for use of the land he was imprisoned.

loʻi Pō.ʻalima. n. A "Friday" taro patch, meaning one worked for the *konohiki* (supervisor), as Friday was the work day.

loka. n. 1. Also **roda.** Rod. *Eng.* **2.** Also **loga.** Log, Hebrew liquid measure (Oihk. 14.10).

-loka. See *maloka.*

lō.kahi. nvs. Unity, agreement, accord, unison, harmony; agreed, in unity. *Manaʻo lōkahi,* unanimous. **hoʻo.lō.kahi.** To bring about unity; to make peace and unity; to be in agreement.

lō.kā.lia. n. 1. Coral plant *(Russelia equisetiformis),* a Mexican low shrubby plant, 30 to 120 cm high, with many leafless, green, quadrangular branches, used for low hedges and in rock gardens; it bears bright-red flowers resembling small firecrackers. (Neal 757–8). *Eng.* **2.** *(Cap.)* Rosalie. *Eng.*

lō.kā.lio, rosario. n. Rosary. (Probably Latin *rosarium* or Spanish or Portuguese *rosario.*) Less common than *lei kolona.*

loke. nvs. 1. Rose; rosy. *Eng.* **2.** Also **roke.** Roast. *Eng. Pipi loke,* roast beef.

lō.kea. n. 1. Long European knife with a white handle. **2.** Child of a *nīʻaupiʻo, piʻo,* or *naha* chief, whose mother was related to him but of a junior line. (Kam. 64:5–6.)

loke Hawaiʻi. n. Double pink rose.

loke hihi. n. Climbing rose. (Neal 395.)

loke hui.hui. n. A pinkish-white rose, very fragrant and growing in a cluster; possibly the Duchess of Brabant, still common. (Neal 395.)

loke kūkae.pele. n. Sulphur rose. (Neal 395.)

loke lani, roselani. n. The common small red rose. It has been substituted for the pink rose, now rare, as the flower of Maui. (Neal 394.)

loke lau. n. Green rose *(Rosa chinensis,* f. *viridiflora).* (Neal 395.) *No ka pua loke lau ke aloha* (song), love for the green rose.

lokeli, loteri. n. Lottery. *Eng.*

lokema, rotema. n. Broom tree (RSV), juniper (KJV). (Hal. 120.4.) Cf. *nokema.* Heb. *rothem.*

loke-o-ka-lua-pele. n. A pink rose growing in the Kīlau-ea area, Hawaiʻi, commonly called volcano rose. (Neal 395.) *Lit.,* rose of the volcanic crater.

loke pihi. n. Tiny buttonhole roses *(Rosa chinensis* var. *minima).* (Neal 395.)

loke wai kā.huli. n. A kind of rose, red on the outside of the flower and pink in the center; used for hedges. (Neal 395.) *Lit.,* rose [with] changing color.

lokia. nvs. Roan, as a horse. *Eng.*

lō.kihi. Var. of common *lōʻihi.*

loko. 1. loc. n. In, inside, within; interior, mainland, inside; internal organs, as tripe, entrails (Gram. 8.6). *I loko,* into, inside, on or to the mainland. *I ka moe ʻana o loko o ka hale* (FS 259), while those in the house slept. *Ua lawe nui au no loko aʻe o kēia mau kānāwai,* I have taken much from within these laws. *Kō loko,* those inside. *Mea o loko,* things inside, contents. *ʻO ka*

inaina i loko o kekahi hana hewa, malice in respect to the commission of any offense. *Make na loko,* death caused by own relatives, or failure to observe one's taboo gods; *lit.,* inside death. **hoʻo.loko.** To insinuate, suggest, implant a thought, either good or bad. (PPN *loto.*) **2.** n. Character, disposition, heart, feelings. Cf. *loko hāiki, loko ʻino, loko liʻu, lokomaikaʻi.* (PPN *loto.*) **3.** n. Pond, lake, pool. **4.** n. Mainland of the United States (noted in a chant dated 1860, State Archives). *I loko aku nei au,* I've been to the mainland. **5.** n. In spite of, regardless. *I loko nō o ka waiwai, hana nō,* in spite of wealth, working anyway. **6.** n. By means of. *Loaʻa ka ʻāina iā mākou maloko o ka ikaika* (For. 4:47), we won the land by force.

loko hā.iki. nvs. Hardhearted, narrow-minded; tightfisted, parsimonious; such a person; ill will.

loko iʻa kalo. n. Combination fishpond and taro patch. (Summers, 1964:23.)

loko ʻino. nvs. Merciless, heartless, evil, malevolent, barbarous, cruel; such a person.

loko kai. n. Lagoon.

loko kuʻi. n. Man-made salt-water pond. *Lit.,* artificial lake.

loko liʻu. 1. n. Salt pond. **2.** nvs. Cross, embittered, sour in disposition; such a person.

loko.loko. n. Puddles, small pools. Cf. *hālokoloko.*

loko.maikaʻi. nvs. Good will, good disposition, generosity, grace; kind, humane, gracious, benevolent, beneficent, obliging. *Nā lā o ka lokomaikaʻi,* days of grace [time allotted for paying a bill].

Loko-paʻa.kai. n. Salt Lake City.

loko paʻa.kai. n. Salt pond or lake.

lokou, logou. n. Word, logos (Ioane 1.1).

loko ulu. n. Seedling bed. *Lit.,* inside growing.

loko ʻume iki. n. Shore fishpond with lanes leading in and/or out of the pond, used for trapping fish and probably only on Molokaʻi. (Summers, 1964:12–19, 24.) *Lit.,* small pond drawing in.

loko wai. n. Fresh-water pond or lake; fountain (Sol. 5.16).

loku. nvi. Downpour of rain; blowing of wind; to pour, of rain; to blow, as a gale; torrential. *Fig.,* to feel deep emotion, pain, sorrow; to weep profusely; intense. Also *noku. Ka ua loku,* the pouring rain. *Ke aloha loku i ka puʻuwai,* love surging in the heart. *Ke loku nei ka makani,* the wind is blowing in a gale. **hoʻo.loku.** To pour, as rain; to disturb; agitated.

lō.kū. n. A game, perhaps like *kilu* (FS 163); a place for indoor games; evening entertainment (Ii 63–4).

loku.loku. Redup. of *loku.* Cf. *haʻalokuloku, kaʻalokuloku.* **hoʻo.loku.loku.** Redup. of *hoʻoloku.*

lola. 1. vs. Drooping, hanging downward; droopy, sluggish, lazy, idle. *Lola moe hālau,* lazy one who sleeps in the workhouse [a lazy person]. **hoʻo.lola.** Caus/sim. **2.** n. A native fern *(Asplenium acuminatum),* with muchsubdivided fronds. **3.** n. A variety of taro. **4.** nvt. Roller, rolling pin; to roll. *Eng.*

lō.lā. vi. To sun. *Ke lōlā maila lākou,* they are sunning.

lola hoʻo.palaha. n. Roller. *Lit.,* flattening roller.

lola.lola. Redup. of *lola 1.* **hoʻo.lola.lola.** Caus/sim.

lola māhu. n. Steam roller.

lole. 1. nvt. Cloth, clothes, costume, dress, gown; to wear clothes. Cf. *ʻaʻa lole. Komo i ka lole,* to put on a dress. **2.** vt. To unfold, turn inside out, reverse; to strip or peel off, as bark; to skin, flay (Mika 3.3); to scalp; to handle, turn over with the hands. *Lole pipi,* butcher. *Hele akula ʻo ʻŌmaʻo-kāmaʻu . . . lālau ihola i ka ʻauwae (o Hākau) a lole aʻela i luna* (FS 141), ʻŌmaʻo-kāmaʻu went . . . grabbed (Hākau's) chin and yanked it up. **hoʻo.lole.** Caus/sim. (PCP *lole.*) **3.** n. Depigmentation, as of palm of hand or soles of feet.

lolea. vs. Worn smooth by friction, wear, or constant handling; turned inside out; weathered; skinned, flayed. Cf. *lole 2.*

lole ʻae.ʻae. n. Fine cloth, gauze.

lole ʻau.ʻau. n. Bathing suit.

lole hā.pai. n. Maternity dress.

lole.hau. vs. Limping, lame. *Rare.*

lole holoi. n. Laundry; soiled clothes ready to be washed, washing.

lole komo. n. Clothes, garments. *Lit.,* clothes to put on.

lole.lau. n. Thatching and trimming, of a house. *Lit.,* handle leaves.

lole lau.oho. n. Sackcloth of hair. (Hoik. 6.12.)

lole lepo. n. Soiled clothing, laundry.

lole.lole. Redup. of *lole 2. Mai ki'i 'oe e lolelole i ku'u ukana,* don't you go and go through my things. *'Ōlelo lolelole,* twisted, not straight-forward, roundabout speech. (PCP *lolelole.*)

lole.lua. nvs. Changeable, fickle, unstable, inconstant, inconsistent, variable; turncoat.

lole moe pō. n. Nightgown. *Lit.,* night-sleeping clothes.

lolena. 1. Nominalizing form of *lole 2. Palai lolena,* fern turned over. **2.** vs. Limp, flexible, as cloth; inefficient, unproductive, idle, sterile, barren, faded. *He u'i lolena kū i ki'ona* (saying), a stupid beauty fit for the dung hill. *'A'ohe lolena i ka wai 'ōpae* (saying), no slackers in water full of shrimps [there must be no slackers when work is to be done].

lole pai.kau. n. Marching garments, regalia, full regalia.

lole papa.mū. n. Checkered dress, especially gingham.

lole pia. n. Laundry washed, starched, and dried but not ironed. *Lit.,* starch clothes.

lole wai. n. Laundry washed and dried but not starched or ironed. *Lit.,* water clothes.

lole wā.wae. n. Trousers, pants, panties, slacks. *Lit.,* leg clothes.

lole wā.wae 'eke.ke'i. n. Shorts.

lole wā.wae 'epane. n. Overalls, coveralls. *Lit.,* apron trousers.

lole wā.wae loloa. n. Long trousers.

lole wā.wae moe pō. n. Pajamas. *Lit.,* trousers for night sleeping.

lole wā.wae pō.kole. n. Short trousers, shorts.

lole wā.wae pū.ha'u.ha'u. n. Bloomers. *Lit.,* puffed-up trousers.

loli. 1. vt. To change, alter, influence, turn, turn over. *Loli wale,* to change for apparently no reason or whimsically; variable. *Loli 'ana,* change, conversion, variation, evolution. *Loli a'e,* to vary, change. **ho'o.loli.** To change, convert, exchange, alter, transform, take a new form, amend; amendment, change. *Ho'ololi i ka lole,* change clothes. *Ho'ololi 'ōlelo,* amend, decline, conjugate. *Ho'ololi i ka mana'o,* to change the mind. *Ho'ololi mai i ka noi,* to amend a motion. *Ho'ololi kālā,* currency exchange. **2.** n. Sea slug, sea cucumber, beche-de-mer, trepang (*Holothuria* spp.); for some people an *'aumakua.* See *kūkaeloli* and saying, *'īloli.* (PPN *loli.*) **3.** vs. Spotted, speckled, daubed; to color in spots, as tapa. Cf. *'īloli 2.*

lolia. Pas/imp. of *loli 1.* **ho'o.lolia.** Caus/sim.

loli 'ano. n. Change of nature, as of words and their etymology.

lōli'i. v. Relaxed, at ease, without worry, carefree. *Moe lōli'i,* to lie at ease. *Ua noho 'o Maleka ā lōli'i* (song), America is well prepared.

loli ka'e. n. A variety of *loli,* sea slug.

loli kohola. n A variety of *loli (Holothuria),* black and cylindrical. *Lit.,* reef *loli.*

loli koko. n. A variety of *loli,* perhaps *Chirodota rigida. Lit.,* blood *loli.*

loli.loli. 1. Redup. of *loli 1;* changing, turning, changeable. **ho'o.loli.loli.** Caus/sim. See ex., *ka'ina.* **2.** vs. Soggy, gummy, tough and watery, as overripe taro.

loli.lua. Same as *lolelua.*

loli lū.'au. n. A variety of *loli (Holothuria). Lit.,* taro-tops *loli.*

loli mā.koko. n. A variety of *loli,* perhaps *Chiridota rigida. Lit.,* blood-red *loli.*

lolina. n. A change, alteration.

lolio. vs. Skinny, thin. Cf. *lio,* taut.

loli pua. n. A species of edible *loli (Holothuria). Lit.,* flower *loli.*

lolo. 1. n. Brains, bone marrow. *Kau ka lā i ka lolo,* the sun rests on the brains [it is noon; usually now without other connotation, but formerly believed a time with great *mana* as a man's *aka* (shadow, image) was no longer visible and was thought to have entered his sacred head—Nānā 123-4]. *Lolo 'eleu,* active mind or intelligence. (PPN *lolo,* oily; PEP brains; cf. *lololo 2.*) **2.** nvs. Religious ceremony at which the brain of the sacrificed animal was eaten (such ceremonies occurred at a canoe launching, start of journey, completion of instruction); to have completed the *lolo* ceremony, hence expert, skilled. *He lolo 'au moana,* seafaring expert. *A'o ihola 'o Hale-mano i ka hula . . . pau ke a'o 'ana, lolo ihola i ka pua'a* (FS 275), Hale-mano learned the hula . . . after learning, a pig was offered ceremonially. **3.** n. Pithy, white sponge in a sprouting coconut. Also *iho.* **4.** n. Long slender pole placed above the second ridgepole of a house, functioning as a batten for the attachment of additional layers of thatch. Also *lolo 'iole.* **5.** n. First brew made from ti root. **6.** Short for *hīnālea 'akilolo,* a fish. (PCP *lolo.*) **7.** Same as *holowa'a,* sheath covering coconut flowers. **8.** interj. Serves you right! I told you so!

lō.lō. vs. Paralyzed, numb, feeble-minded, crazy. *Lōlō moe hālau,* stupid one who sleeps in a workshop [a lazybones]. See *paka lōlō.* **ho'o.lō.lō.** To pretend paralysis, stupidity; to pretend to be asleep.

loloa. 1. Redup. of *loa 1. Lima loloa,* long sleeve. **ho'o.loloa.** To lengthen. (PPN *loloa.*) **2.** n. A seaweed (KL line 95), probably the same as *limu loloa.*

lolo'a. vs. Bleached, as a shell in the sea.

Loloa-mai.au. n. Same as *Ka-loloa-maiau.*

lolo.a'u. n. Flying gurnard, a fish (*Dactyloptena orientalis*). Also *pinao.*

loloha. Redup. of *loha,* to droop.

lolohe. 1. Redup. of *lohe;* to listen carefully, attentively, with good hearing. *He pepeiao lolohe,* an ear with good hearing. **ho'o.lolohe.** To iisten carefully; to strain the ear to hear. *He ali'i 'o ka lani, he mo'opuna na Lono, he hiapo na ke kini, ho'ololohe ua 'ana* (chant), the heavenly one is a chief, a descendant of Lono, the first-born of a multitude [of long lineage], a listener to the rain [unafraid of rain because of high rank]. **2.** vs. Stubborn; hard to move, as a rock. *Rare.* Cf. *ho'okololohe.* **ho'o.lolohe.** Caus/sim.

lolohi. Redup. of *lohi 1;* slowpoke. *Lolohi ke a'o 'ana,* slow in learning. **ho'o.lolohi.** Similar to *ho'olohi.* (For. 5:553.)

lolo.hili. Var. of *loloiāhili.*

lolo.hua. Same as *mīkololohua.*

lolo.huā, lolo.huwā. nvs. One who is jealous and constantly stirring up trouble; jealous.

lolo.hua.mea. 1. Same as *lolohua.* **2.** n. Variegated colors, as of the distant sea. See ex., *lipo 1.*

lolo.iā.hili. vs. To wander, as one lost; to stray, dilly-dally; to digress and wander in speech; roundabout. **ho'o.lolo.iā.hili.** Same as above. *Me ka ho'olololoiāhili 'ole aku,* without further digression.

lolō.iele. Redup. of *lōiele;* dull. **ho'o.lolō.iele.** Caus/sim. *Ho'olololoiele kāna hana 'ana,* he works so slowly.

lolo 'iole. Same as *lolo 4.*

lolo iwi. n. Bone marrow.

lolo.ka'a. nvs. Dizziness, with spinning head; dizzy. Cf. *niu loloka'a, pōniuniu.* See ex., *noiele.*

lolo.kia. n. Coconut stem.

loloku. Same as *lokuloku. 'O lili'u 'o loloku 'o walania i ke ki'i'ōnohi* (song), smarting, tearful, burning are the eyeballs.

lolo.kū. n. **1.** Midday. *Ke lolokū aku nei,* it is noon. Cf. *kau ka lā i ka lolo,* under *lolo 1.* **2.** Muscle on back of the head, probably the occipito-frontalis muscle; the nervous system. Also *molokū.*

lolo.kukui. nvt. To be raped, sexually molested or ravished; such a victim. *Ua lapa'au 'ia ka lolokukui,* the rape victim was treated. *Ua lolokukui 'ia ke keiki,* the child was sexually molested.

lō.lō.kuli. n. Deafness, as from disease. See ex., *'ā'ā 1.*

lololo. vs. **1.** Intelligent, brilliant; deep thinking. **2.** Tasty, rich, fat, as marrow. *Rare.* (PNP *lololo.*)
lolo.loa. Intensive of *loloa 1.*
lolo.lohe. Redup. and intensifier of *lohe,* to hear (said of a very keen ear). See ex., *'ā 'ā 1.*
lō.lolo.hua. Redup. of *lolohua.*
lolo.mū. vs. Unsuccessful, unlucky. *Rare.*
lolo.niu. n. Canoe hull made of coconut log. *Rare.*
lolo niu. n. Embryonic sponge in a coconut; coconut sheath. Cf. *haku 3, iho 2. Wa'a lolo niu,* coconut sheath used as a toy canoe.
lolo.pai.oa. Same as *lolopaioea.*
lolo.pai.oea. vs. Tall, spindly, thin.
lolo.pili. n. Name of a design used on Ni'ihau mats.
lolo.pio. vi. To die calmly and easily. (For. 6:297.)
lolo po'o. n. Brain. *Lit.,* head brain.
lolo.pua. n. Zenith. *Eia lā i ka lolopua o ka lani,* here is the zenith of the heavens.
lolo'u. Redup. of *lo'u.*
lolo uila. n. Computer. *Lit.,* electric brain.
lolo wa'a. nv. Canoe-launching ceremony; to perform the ceremony. See *lolo 2.*
loma. 1. vs. Lazy, indolent, slow, idle. Cf. *kūloma.* (PNP *loma.*) **2.** *(Cap.)* nvs. Rome; Roman. *Eng.*
loma.loma. Redup. of *loma 1.* See ex., *halalē.*
lomi. vt. To rub, press, squeeze, crush, mash fine, knead, massage, rub out; to work in and out, as claws of a contented cat. *Kāmano lomi, i'a lomi,* salmon or fish, usually raw, worked with the fingers and mixed with onions and seasoned. *Kanaka lomi,* masseur, masseuse. (PPN *lomi.*)
lomia. Pas/imp. of *lomi. Pēpē lomia e ka Inu-wai,* crushed and mashed by the water-drinking wind [as grass, but figuratively of lovers]. (PPN *lomia.*)
lō.milo. nvt. To spin with fingers; to twist, as thread in making rope or cord. Cf. *milo,* to twist.
lomi.lomi. Redup. of *lomi;* masseur, masseuse. (PPN *lomilomi.*)
lona. 1. Block of wood used to support a canoe out of water. Also *'aki.* **2.** Useless, vain. (And.) **3.** Straight, direct. (And.)
lona.lona. 1. Var. of *nonanona,* ant, gnat. **2.** Var. of *nonanona,* many. *Lonalona nā pu'u,* there are many, many hills.
loni.kū, lonitu. n. Longitude. *Eng.*
lono. 1. News, report, tidings, remembrance (Kanl. 32.26), rumor (sometimes formerly preceded by *ke*). *Ku'i ka lono,* the news spread. **ho'o.lono.** To listen, hear, obey; obedient, attentive. *Ku'i ka lono i Pele-kane, ho'olono ke kuini o Palani* (song), the news spread to England, the queen of France heard. (PPN *rongo.*) **2.** *(Cap.)* One of the four major gods brought from Kahiki. **3.** *(Cap.)* The 28th day of the lunar month. (PEP *Longo.*) **4.** *(Cap.)* Name of a star.
lono.ā, lonowā. nvt. Hearsay, rumor, gossip; to hear hearing, as rumor. Also *nonoā.*
lono.hi'i. vi. To cry to be carried, of an infant carried too much; to fret in a spoiled way to be carried. *Lit.,* hear carry. *Mai hi'i mau 'oukou o lonohi'i kēia keiki,* don't keep carrying this child or he'll want to be carried always.
lono honua. vt. To hear surprising or sudden news.
lono.kū. On the back; backward. (AP.)
lono.lau. n. Large-sized gourd. Also *nonolau.*
lono.lono. Redup. of *lono 1.* **ho'o.lono.lono.** Redup. of *ho'olono.* (PPN *rongorongo.*)
lono.lono.ā. Redup. of *lonoā.*
lono.lupe. n. A banner held up by two staffs. *Rare.*
lono.maka.ihe. n. Art of spear throwing, named for a god. *Ua 'o anei 'oe i ka lonomakaihe?* Have you learned the art of spear throwing?
Lono-makua. A legendary fire guardian and the name of the *makahiki* image.
lono.mea. n. A native tree *(Sapindus oahuensis),* to 10 m high, with ovate leaves 10 by 20 and 5 by 13 cm; it is found only on O'ahu and Kaua'i. *Kaua'i.* On O'ahu it is called *kaulu.* (Neal 533–4.) Also *āulu 5.*

lono.papa. 1. nvs. News spread far and wide; news so well bruited that everyone has heard repeatedly; spread far, of news. **2.** n. Name of an unknown disease or fever.
lono.pū.hā. n. **1.** Art of healing, especially of wounds, abscesses. *A'o i ka lonopūhā,* learn the healing art. **2.** A class of heiau, probably for healing.
lono.wā. See *lonoā.*
lonu. nvt. Cheat, liar, rogue; to cheat, lie. *Rare.*
lō.nū. vs. To swell up, as with disease. Cf. *ōnū.*
lo'o.hia. vs. Possessed, overwhelmed, overcome, stricken; to befall, happen. See ex., *hu'ahu'a 1. Ua lo'ohia i ka 'uhane 'ino,* possessed by an evil spirit. *Lo'ohia i ka nāwaliwali, lo'ohia i ke kaumaha,* overcome by weakness, overwhelmed by grief. *Ua lo'ohia mai lākou i kēia mau mea* (1 Kor. 10.11), these things happened to them. (PCP *roko(f,s)ia.*)
lō.'ohu. vi. To buck, of a horse. *Kaua'i.*
lo'o.kahi. Rare var. of *lōkahi.*
lō.pā. 1. nvs. One who farms under a tenant *(hoa 'āina),* peasant, farmer; shiftless. See *naunau 1* for an insulting epithet. *Lōpā iki hele wale,* little peasant who goes alone. *Lōpā ho'opili wale,* wretch entirely dependent on others for livelihood. *Lōpā kua kea,* lazy *lōpā* with untanned [lit., white] back. *E aho nō ke kūmakahiki i kō ka 'auana wale ā ho'opili mea 'ai paha ā noho lōpā wale iho nō,* it is better to have a yearly contract [as hired hand] than to vagabond and be dependent for food and live just as a shiftless tenant. (PCP *loopaa.*) **2.** An uncertain term in the phrase *ho'āo lōpā,* marriage with a relative 24 generations removed. (For. 6:268.)
lō.pā.lau.'eka. n. Worthless, shiftless squatter (contraction of *lōpā pālau'eka,* worthless *lōpā*).
lopi, ropi. n. Thread. *(Eng.,* rope.) (Lunk. 16.12.)
lopi ho'o.holo.holo. n. Basting thread.
lopi hulu.hulu. n. Worsted thread, yarn.
lopi humu.lau. n. Embroidery thread.
lopi kā.holo. n. Basting thread.
lopine. n. Robin. *Eng.*
lō.pi'o. vi. To bend over, as one nodding, sleeping.
lopu. n. Consecrated adze, as used in carving.
lou. 1. nvi. Hook; to hook, to fasten with a hook; to hook off, as with the *lou* pole. *Lou me ke alapi'i,* hook and ladder. *Lou ka i'a,* the fish is hooked. *Lou ka mana'o,* thoughts are hooked, as of two persons thinking of each other. **ho'o.lou.** To hook, catch with a hook; to put on a hook, as bait. *'O ka limu kala ka maunu e ho'olou ai i ka makau* (FS 143), *kala* (seaweed) was the bait placed on the hook. **2.** nvi. Very long fruit-plucking pole, with short sticks lashed obliquely near the end for plucking, as for breadfruit; to pluck. (PPN *lohu.*) **3.** n. Pain in the side, stitch. **4.** Same as *louulu.* **5.** n. Tache, clasp (Puk. 26.6).
lo'u. vi. To overhang, as a cliff; to bend over, as with grief or laughter; bent over, as a laden branch. Cf. *ha'alo'u, lo'u pali. Ko'i lo'u,* adze on bent haft. **ho'o.lo'u.** Caus/sim.; to droop. (Perhaps PPN *loku.*)
loua. 1. Pas/imp. of *lou 1. Loua mai,* hook and bring. **ho'o.loua.** Caus/sim. *Rare.* **2.** Var. of *laua. Loua 'ole aku ka hana,* much work to be done.
lō.uhu. Same as *uhu,* to bolt, strain. *Rare.*
lou.lou. 1. Redup. of *lou 1;* to link or hook together. (PPN *lohulohu.*) **2.** n. Finger-pulling contest: two players hook fingers and see who can keep his finger hooked the longest.
lo'u.lo'u. Redup. of *lo'u.* (Perhaps PPN *loku.*)
loulu. n. **1.** All species of native fan palms *(Pritchardia).* (Neal 97–9.) Hats are plaited of its leaves bleached white. Also *noulu.* Cf. *hāwane.* **2.** Umbrella, so called because the *loulu* palm leaf was formerly used as protection from rain or sun. **3.** *Alutera monoceros,* a fish, perhaps so called because its greenish-white skin resembled the *loulu* palm; used in sorcery to cause death because the name contains the word *lou,* to hook. **4.** Type of heiau said to be built for prevention of epidemics, famine, destruction; long rituals dedicating a temple including *kauila nui,* fetching of the *'ōhi'a*

logs for images *(haku 'ōhi'a), kuili,* and *hono* rituals (Ii 38).

lo'ulu. n. An endemic fern *(Coniogramme pilosa)* with leaves somewhat like those of the breadfruit tree *('ulu),* but the divisions narrower and deeper.

loulu hiwa. n. A small native fan palm *(Pritchardia martii),* with thick trunk to 1.9 m high. (Neal 97–9.) *Lit.,* dark *loulu.*

loulu lelo. n. A native fan palm *(Pritchardia hillebrandii),* with trunk to 6 m high. *Lit.,* yellowish *loulu.*

lo'u pali. n. Shelter formed by an overhanging cliff. (Malo text, chapter 33, section 3.)

louulu. n. Betrothal gift, as sent from one family to another. *Rare.*

lū. 1. vt. To scatter, throw, as ashes; to sow, broadcast; to shed, as a chicken its feathers or a tree its leaves; to push aside; to drip, as water; to shake; to cast off, as grief; to spend recklessly, squander, discard. *Pau ke kālā i ka lū 'ia,* all the money was squandered. (PPN *ruu.*) **2.** n. Seeds of the *pua kala,* prickly poppy. **3.** n. Gunshot, so called because the pellets suggested the *lū* seeds. **4.** n. Scalloped hat braid, as made of bamboo, sugar-cane stem, pandanus, or coconut.

lua. 1. n. Hole, pit, grave, den, cave, mine, crater. *Lua* is a hole that has bottom, contrasting with *puka,* perforation. *Ho'opiha i ka lua o ka inaina,* fill the pit of wrath [eat heartily]. **ho'o.lua.** To bake in the oven. Cf. *ho'olua* under *lua 3* and *kālua. Pua'a ho'olua,* pork and taro tops baked in ti leaves, called *laulau* today. (PPN *lua.*) **2.** n. Toilet, outhouse, bathroom, cellar. **3.** num. Two, second, secondary, twice, deuce, double; doubly, much, a great deal. *Ka lua kēia o ko'u hele 'ana mai,* this is the second of my trips here. *'O ka lua ia o nā keiki,* this is the second of the children. *Ka'uka'u lua,* to delay much. *Kaumaha lua,* extremely sad or heavy. *Konikoni lua i ka pu'uwai,* throbbing, throbbing in the heart. **ho'o.lua.** To do twice, repeat, do over again; to bake twice, as food in the oven. (PPN *rua.*) **4.** n. Equal, likeness, duplicate, copy, match. See *lua 'ole. Ōla'i ikaika loa i 'ike 'ole 'ia kona lua,* very strong earthquake, the like of which had never been seen before. **5.** n. Companion, mate. Cf. *kōko'o.* **6.** n. A type of dangerous hand-to-hand fighting in which the fighters broke bones, dislocated bones at the joints, and inflicted severe pain by pressing on nerve centers. There was much leaping, and (rarely) quick turns of spears. Many of the techniques were secret. *Lua* holds were named (see *fight*). *Lua* experts were bodyguards to chiefs. Also *ku'i a lua.* See *O'ahu.*

lua-. To enjoy oneself. Cf. *luakaha, luala'i, lualuana, luana.*

-lua. 1. Ho'o.lua. Name of a strong north wind associated with Makaiwa, Kaua'i; Hāna, Maui; and Hālawa, Moloka'i. At Hālawa the name may be qualified by Iho, Ka'i, Kele, Pehu, Wahakole (Nak. 69). *Ho'olua nui,* big Ho'olua wind; *fig.,* to talk loudly and to no purpose. **2.** *(Not cap.)* Dual number in pronouns and possessives, as *'olua, kāua, māua.* (PPN *-rua,* PNP *-lua.*)

lu'a. 1. vs. Old and wrinkled, worn and shabby with use, worn-out; sagging, hanging down, flimsy, soft, pliable. See *'ālu'a.* **2.** Same as *nu'a,* heap, pile.

-lu'a. ho'o.lu'a. (a) To bear many children. **(b)** To lay an egg, as of a chicken.

lua'a. vt. To pound poi. (For. 6:397.)

lua.ahi, luahi. 1. n. Victim, as of wrath. *Mai pa'akikī aku 'oe i ke anu, 'o ke kino mai nō ka luaahi,* don't persist in going into the cold, the body will suffer for it [*lit.,* be the victim]. *Akahele! He luaahi aku ia!* Be careful! There's a fire pit [Danger]! **2.** vs. Fearful, mighty. *Ka lima luaahi o ke koa,* fearful arm of the warrior.

lua ahi. n. Pit of fire; hell.

lua ahi ho'o.ma'e.ma'e. n. Purgatory. *Lit.,* cleansing fire pit.

lua.'ā.pana. nvs. Jester (For. 5:479); hilarity, sport; to laugh, jest, indulge in uproarious merriment.

lua.'ehu. vs. Many and colorful. *Lua'ehu ka i'a i loa'a*

mai i hei mai i ka 'upena (song), colorful and many are the fishes caught, snared in the net.

lua 'eli pō.haku. n. Quarry. *Lit.,* pit for digging stones.

lua 'eli wai.wai. n. Mine.

lua.haka. n. Outhouse.

lua.hele. nvt. Pitfall, seduction, deception; to lead astray, seduce, deceive.

luahi. See *luaahi.*

lua.hine, luwahine. 1. nvs. Old woman, old lady; to be an old woman. See saying, *hopena.* **ho'o.lua.hine.** To act or dress like an old lady; to try to be like one. (PEP *luafine.*) **2.** See *kaula luahine.*

lua.hoana. n. Halo or rainbow around sun or moon. *Lit.,* polished pit.

lua ho'o.ki'o wai. n. Cistern.

Lua-ho'o.moe. n. Name of a star, said to appear in the month of Hinaia-'ele'ele.

lua huna. n. Hidden or secret cave or pit, as where bones of the dead were hidden.

lua'i. nvi. Vomit; volcanic eruptions; to vomit, retch, erupt; to banish, expel, drive out, as people. (Probably PPN *lua,* to vomit + *-'i* or *-a'i,* transitivizers: Gram. 6.6.4.) Cf. *hīkākā, lua'i koko. Lua'i ā koko,* to vomit food until blood comes. *Lua'i pō,* outcasts, as wandering souls not accepted in the realm of the dead; *lit.,* night vomit. **ho'o.lua'i.** Emetic; causing vomiting; to cause a vomiting, to feign vomiting; to gag; to drive out people. (PPN *lua'aki.*)

lua.iele. vi. **1.** To live a dissipated life, reckless of health; to dissipate. See *-iele. Luaiele wale iho nō i 'ō i 'ane'i,* going here and there [as a fickle lover]. **2.** Swaying. *Nani ka 'ōiwi o ka lā'au i ka luaiele 'ia e ka makani,* beautiful the body of the tree swayed by the wind [some are handsome even in adversity or dissipation]. **ho'o.-lua.iele.** Caus/sim. *Ho'oluaiele i ka mana'o* (Cleghorn 59), distressing the thoughts.

lua'i koko. nv. Any kind of sickness with vomiting of blood; to vomit blood.

lua'i.kū. vs. Disgusting, nauseating, sickening. *'O kāna mau hana, he mea e lua'ikū ai,* what he does is disgusting.

lua'i pele. n. Volcanic eruption, lava, sulphur, brimstone (Hoik. 9.17).

lua.kaha. nvs. Enjoyable, pleasant, as a place to which one is attached; to while away the time enjoyably. *He luakaha kō mākou nohona i kēlā 'āina,* our stay at that land was comfortable and pleasant.

lua.kā.lai. Same as *luahoana. Lit.,* hewn pit.

lua.kā.lai. Same as *luakālai.*

lua.kele. n. Cave for concealing. For roots cf. *lua* (pit) and *hūnākele* (to bury).

lua.kini. nvi. Temple, church, cathedral, tabernacle; large heiau where ruling chiefs prayed and human sacrifices were offered; to perform temple work (For. 6:48).

lua ko'i. n. Adze quarry.

lua kupa.pa'u. n. Tomb, grave.

lua.la'i. Same as *luana.* (*Lua- + -la'i,* transitivizer: Gram. 6.6.4.) *E aha ana lā ku'u lani, e luala'i lā i Lākana* (chant for Ka-lā-kaua), what is my lord doing, enjoying life in London.

lua li'i.li'i. n. Outhouse, toilet. *Lit.,* small pit.

lu'a.loa. n. Large fishhook, as used for large fish or sometimes for bonito.

lua.lua. vs. Uneven, full of holes, rough, bumpy, as a road. **2.** Same as *luelue,* a fishing net.

lu'a.lu'a. Redup. of *lu'a;* aged.

lua.lua'i. 1. Redup. of *lua'i.* **ho'o.lua.lua'i.** Redup. of *ho'olua'i.* **2.** vi. To raise and chew the cud.

lua.lua.'ina. Var. of *luluā'ina 1, 2.*

lua.lua.na. Redup. of *luana.*

lua meki. n. Deep pit or cave. (Zek. 9.11.)

luana. vi. To be at leisure, enjoy pleasant surroundings and associates, live in comfort and ease, enjoy oneself, relax, be content. (See *lua-, -na.*) *He aha kō 'oukou e hana nei? E luana wale ana nō,* what are you all doing? Just enjoying ourselves. **ho'o.luana.** Caus/sim. Cf. *lumi ho'oluana.*

luana iki. vs. To pause a moment; to enjoy oneself a little. *Ma'ane'i kākou e luana iki iho ai no nā 'ōlelo e pili ana i ke ko'i* (FS 29), here we'll stop a moment for the story concerning the adze.

lua.nu'u. Dressed out in tapa, as temple images in Lono's temple on important occasions. (And.)

lua 'ole. vs. Superior, incomparable, unequalled, second to none, unique, unsurpassed (similar to *ana 'ole* and *launa 'ole*). See ex., *ka'uka'u lua.*

lua.'oni. n. Second person to fall in battle, the second victim.

lua 'ō.pala. n. Rubbish pit.

lua pa'a.hao. n. Dungeon. *Lit.,* jail pit.

lua pā.lolo. n. Clay pit.

lua pao. n. Burial cave. *Lit.,* cave pit.

lua.pa'ū. n. Refuse pit in the *luakini* or temple enclosure. *Fig.,* any place of destruction. *Lit.,* damp pit. *'O ka pākela inu lama 'o ka luapa'ū ia o ke kanaka,* excessive drinking of intoxicants is a cause of man's destruction.

lua pele. n. Volcano, crater. *Lit.,* volcanic pit.

lua.pō. n. Grave. (Hal. 88.3.) *Lit.,* night pit.

lua puhi. n. **1.** Blowhole. **2.** Eel hole.

lū.'au. n. **1.** Young taro tops, especially as baked with coconut cream and chicken.or octopus. (PPN *luu,* PNP *lu(u)kau.*) **2.** Hawaiian feast, named for the taro tops always served at one; this is not an ancient name, but goes back at least to 1856, when so used by the Pacific Commercial Advertiser; formerly a feast was *pā'ina* or *'aha'aina.* **3.** Greenish meat in a turtle, considered a delicacy; so named because the color of its meat suggested the color of taro tops. **4.** Same as *limu lū'au,* a seaweed. **5.** Kind of soft porous stone, as used in the ground oven. *Rare.*

lua.'uhane. n. The inner corner of each eye, next to the nose; tear duct. *Lit.,* soul-pit, so called because it was believed that the soul leaves and enters the body of sleeping persons at this point.

lū.au'i. n. True parent, as contrasting with foster parent or aunt or uncle *(makua).* See *moe lūau'i. Ku'u lūau'i makua kāne,* my true father.

lua unu. n. Refuse pit in a heiau.

lua.wai. n. Well, cistern (Isa. 36.16), pool, pond, reservoir. *Luawai aniani, luawai pipi'i,* artesian well. *Luawai pelapela,* cesspool.

lue, rue. n. Rue. (Luka 11.42.) *Eng.*

lu'e. vs. Loose, as a garment; hanging loose, long and flowing; loosened. **ho'o.lu'e (a)** To loosen, let down, as hair; to unfurl, as a flag; to hang down. **(b)** Same as *ho'olu'a.*

-lu'e. ho'o.lu'e. To shape a log for a canoe, as at bow and stern. *Rare.*

luea. n. Seasickness, nausea, dizziness. Cf. *poluea.*

luehu. **1.** vs. Easily scattered, dispersed, blown away; scaly, as skin. *Lit.,* scattered fine. **2.** n. Kind of soft, porous stone that breaks easily.

lue.lue. n. Bag net with meshes the width of a finger, as held open by a hoop of *walahe'e* wood and baited and lowered into the sea by four long cords.

lu'e.lu'e. **1.** Redup. of *lu'e.* **2.** n. Loose gown or robe, as of Biblical characters. **3.** *(Cap.)* Same as *Ka-lu'elu'e.*

Luha. n. Wind associated with Hanalei, Kaua'i. (For. 5:97.)

lū hau. nvi. Shaking down of dew or rain drops from tree boughs by a breeze; to fall thus; scattered dew, dew-laden.

Lū-hau-pua. n. A wind associated with Ōla'a, Hawai'i. *Lit.,* scattering dew and flowers.

luhe. vi. To hang down, overhang, sag, droop, wilt, wither. See saying, *droop.* **ho'o.luhe.** Caus/sim.

luhea. Pas/imp. of *luhe. Ka lau luhea o ka 'ōhai o Mānā,* the drooping leaves of the monkeypod of Mānā.

lū.he'a. nv. Fishing for octopus with line and cowry lure; the octopus lure; to fish thus.

lū hele.le'i. vi. To scatter, strew; to let hair hang loose and unbound. *Mai holo 'oe i waena o ke kaona me ka lū helele'i o kou lauoho,* don't ride through the midst of the town with your hair hanging loose.

luhe.luhe. Redup. of *luhe;* to sag with fat, overhang.

luhe.luhea. Pas/imp. of *luheluhe. Ka ua luheluhea i nā pali,* the [misty] rain hanging on the cliffs.

luhi. **1.** nvs. Weary, tired, fatigued; wearisome, burdensome, tiresome, laborious, tedious; burden, wearisome or tedious task; labor, work, pains, toil. *Ko'u luhi,* my fatigue. **ho'o.luhi.** To bother, disturb, trouble, wear out with work, overburden, inconvenience; nuisance, bother; burdensome, demanding. Cf. *hale ho'oluhi. Hana luhi,* boring or strenuous labor, toil. *Hiki anei ia'u ke ho'oluhi iā'oe,* may I trouble you [a polite preface to a request]. (PCP *lu(f,s)i.*) **2.** nvt. A child or other person tended and raised with devoted care; to care for and attend with care and affection; protégé. *Ka'u luhi,* the person I care for. *Luhi wahine 'ia,* to be cared for and raised by a woman. *'O La'a-kea, ka luhi a Nā-maka,* La'a-kea is devotedly cared for by Nā-maka. *Ua luhi ka makua kāne iāia,* the father cared for him with devotion and patience.

luhia. n. A variety of shark. (PPN *rufi.*)

luhi.ehu. vs. **1.** Beautiful, attractive, festooned. *Luhiehu ihola ka pua i Maile-huna* (UL 237), beautiful the flower at Maile-huna. **2.** Soft, cooked soft. (And.)

luhi hewa. vs. Tired without accomplishing anything; weary from efforts that bring no results. **ho'o.luhi hewa.** To oppress, harass, burden to no use.

luhi.luhi. Redup. of *luhi 1.* **ho'o.luhi.luhi.** To make tired, disturbed, etc.; to wear one down with work. Cf. *ho'oluhi.* (PEP *lu(f,s)ilu(f,s)i.*)

luhina. n. A laboring, wearying, caring for, etc.

lu'i. **1.** n. Imaginary or indistinct sound. *Rare.* **2.** vt. To abolish, nullify. *Rare.* (Oih. 5.39.)

luia. Same as *luhia.*

lu'i.lu'i. Redup. of *lu'i 1, 2.*

luina. n. Sailor. *Po'e luina,* sailors, crew.

luka, ruda. n. Rood, in surveying. *Eng.*

lū.kā. Var. of *mūkā,* to smack.

luka.luka. **1.** Var. of *lupalupa 1.* **2.** Same as *pālukaluka 1.* **3.** n. Tapa sarong, as worn by men. (Malo 182.)

lukā.nela, lutanela. n. Lieutenant. *Eng.*

luka.pia, rutabia. n. Root beer. *Eng.*

lukau. nvi. Lookout; to look out, be careful. *Eng.*

luke, lute. n. Lute. *Eng.*

lū.kē. vt. To prod open, as bivalves. *Rare.*

lū.kea. n. A kind of taro, probably Kaua'i name for *haokea.*

Lukela, Lutera, Lukelani, Luterano. nvs. Lutheran. *Eng.*

lukia. **1.** Short for *lu'ukia.* **2.** *(Cap.)* Also **Rusia.** nvs. Russia, Russian. *Eng.*

lū.kini. **1.** n. Perfume. **2.** *(Cap.)* nvs. Russian. *Eng.* Cf. *wai Lūkini.* **3.** n. Lemon grass *(Cymbopogon citratus),* a grass with fragrant leaves, lemony odor, edges sharp; the leaves are dried and used for tea. (Neal 79.)

lukipa, lucifa. n. Lucifer. *Eng. Ahikoe lukipa,* lucifer.

luku. nvt. Massacre, slaughter, destruction; to massacre, destroy, slaughter, lay waste, devastate, exterminate, ravage. *Mea luku wale,* vandal, one who destroys needlessly. *Hele luku,* go on a raid. *Wai-luku* (place name), waters [of] destruction. *Luku ho'opapau,* annihilate, destroy completely. (PEP *lutu.*)

lukua. Pas/imp. of *luku.*

luku lua. vs. Doubly destroyed, said of opposing forces despairing of victory and by mutual consent stopping fighting.

luku.lukua. Redup. of *lukua.* (For. 6:391.)

lukuna. n. Destruction, slaughter. (PCP *lutunga.*)

luku wale. nvt. Vandalism, useless slaughter or destruction; to destroy thus.

lula, rula. n. Ruler, tape measure; rules, manners, ethics, etiquette, regulations. *Eng.* See ex., *'a'ahu* and below. *Kū i nā lula maika'i,* with good manners, formal, ethical. *Kū 'ole i ka lula maika'i,* with bad manners, unethical. *Lula 'ole,* without manners, crude.

lū.lā. vi. Calm, windless, dead still; bored. *Lūlā au i ka ho'olohe i kāna ha'i'ōlelo,* I'm bored listening to his sermon.

lula hoʻo.keoni.mana. n. Rules of gentlemanly conduct, etiquette.

lula kumu. n. Fundamental or basic rule.

lū.lana. Same as *lūlā.* See ex., *kalakala ʻihi. Lūlana ihola ka pihe* (UL 288), the shouting quieted.*Kuʻu hoa lūlana i ka lipolipo,* my peaceful companion in the forest depth.

lula ʻole. vs. Disorderly, unruly, without manners, uncouth.

Lū-lau-kō. n. Name of a rain associated with Kauaʻi. *Lit.,* rain that scatters sugar-cane leaves.

lule. 1. vi. To quiver, as jello; to sag, as flesh of a fat person; weak, flexible. (PCP *lule.*) **2.** n. A variety of *pili* grass.

lū-lehua. n. A red tapa design.

lū lehua. v. To scatter *lehua* flowers, said poetically of rain.

lule.lule. Redup. of *lule 1.* (PCP *lulelule.*)

luli. vi. To shake, as the head in approval or disapproval; to pitch and roll, as a ship; to totter, be unsteady; to sway to and fro (Mat. 11.7), wag. *ʻOhe luli i ka makani,* bamboo swaying in the breeze. Cf. *ʻaluli.* **hoʻo.luli.** To rock, as a child; to shake, as a drink; to sway. Cf. *mōhai hoʻoluli.* (PCP *luli.*)

luli.luli. Redup. of *luli;* agitated. **hoʻo.luli.luli.** Redup. of *hoʻoluli;* to agitate. *Waiū hoʻoluliluli,* milk shake. (PCP *luliluli.*)

lulo. A rare word used to describe a fearless and physically perfect chief, used with *napa* and a negative. (For. 6:463, 488.) Pronunciation uncertain.

lū.lō. n. Lei of braided leaves or ferns. Cf. And.

luloni. To sleep soundly. (AP.)

lulu. nvi. Calm, peace, shelter, lee, protection, shield, cloak; to lie at anchor; to be calm; to shield. Cf. *lulu aliʻi, pālulu. E lulu hiwalani ana ʻoe* (chant), you are sheltering the royal favorite. *Lulu ʻia ke kai* (Nak. 72), the sea has calmed. **hoʻo.lulu. (a)** To lie quietly in calm water, as a ship in port; to be calm; to gather together, as objects, or to wait, as for transportation. See *kahua hoʻolulu. Kiʻi lāʻau hoʻolulu* (Kam. 64:18), fixed wooden images [as at Hale o Keawe]. *Hale hoʻolulu,* depot, waiting station. *Hoʻolulu lei,* to offer leis on an altar; the prayer uttered while making an offering of leis; *lit.,* to make leis repose in peace and quiet. (PPN *ruru.*) **(b)** To chum, for fish; this type of fishing and fisherman.

lū.lū. 1. Redup. of *lū 1;* to scatter, sow, as seeds; to fan, winnow; to shake, as dice or the hands, or as an earthquake. Cf. *haʻalulu. Hele akula kekahi kanaka lūlū hua e lūlū* (Mat. 13.3), a sower of grain went forth to sow. (PPN *ruuruu.*) **2.** nvt. Donation, offering, as in church; to make an offering. **3.** n. Raffle, lottery.

lulua.iele. Redup. of *luaiele.*

lulu.ā.ʻina. 1. n. Freckles. *Luluāʻina ʻole,* without a freckle, said of one well-cared for in childhood who grows up handsome, gracious, and agreeable. **2.** v. To pound ʻina and hāʻukeʻuke sea urchins for bait.

lulu aliʻi. n. Royal feather cloak *(rare);* chiefly protection.

lū.lū.heʻe. Redup. of *lūheʻe.*

luluhi. 1. Redup. of *luhi 1, 2. Ua luluhi nā maka,* the eyes are heavy with sleep. **hoʻo.luluhi.** To make sleepy; drowsy. *Mele hoʻoluluhi,* lullaby. **2.** Black and heavy, of clouds; overcast; threatening. (AP.)

lū.lū hua. nv. Sower; to sow seeds.

luluka. n. Peace, calm. *Rare.*

lū.lū lima. nv. To shake hands; handshake.

lululu. Redup. of *lulu;* dead calm, great calm; becalmed; hanging limp, as a sail in a calm.

lulumi. Redup. of *lumi 1;* crushed, crumpled, wrinkled. *E lulumi ana nā ʻale o Kaunā* (chant), the billows of Kaunā rush pell-mell. *Huki i ke kalo nui, lulumi i ka lepo ā popoʻi i ka mauʻu,* pull up the big taro, press the earth firmly and cover with grass.

luluʻu. Same as *luʻuluʻu 1;* said also of a tree laden with fruit, a person laden with leis. **hoʻo.luluʻu.** Same as *hoʻoluʻuluʻu;* to cause to bend down, to load heavily.

Pākaukau i hoʻoluluʻu pū me nā mea ʻai, tables laden down with food.

luma. Same as *lumaʻi.*

luma.haʻi. n. **1.** Certain twist of the fingers in making string figures, perhaps named for a place on Kauaʻi. **2.** A medicine. (Kam. 64:110.)

lumaʻi. vt. To douse, duck; to upset, tumble, capsize, as in the surf. *Fig.,* to destroy, overwhelm, as with trouble (*luma + -aʻi* or *-ʻi,* transitivizers: Gram. 6.6.4). *Lumaʻi ʻia ke kauā,* the *kauā* (outcast) was drowned. *Ua lumaʻi ʻia kona manaʻolana e nā pilikia,* his hopes were dashed by his troubles. *Lumaʻi ʻia e ka nalu,* rolled by the waves. (PCP *lumaki.*)

luma.ia. Pas/imp. of *lumaʻi;* capsized.

luma.ʻina. n. Drowning, etc. See *lumaʻi.*

luma.kika, rumatika. n. Rheumatism, arthritis, neuritis. *Eng.*

luma.lumaʻi. Redup. of *lumaʻi.*

lū.manawa.hua. nvi. Stomach disorder accompanied by gas and looseness of the bowels; to suffer thus. Cf. *manawahua.*

lumi. 1. vt. To crowd uncomfortably; to overturn, pound, crush, as the surf; to press; to be overwhelmed with trouble; to destroy by black magic. Cf. *lulumi.* **2.** Also *rumi.* n. Room, cell. *Eng. Nui ka lumi,* plenty of room.

lumia. Pas/imp. of *lumi 1. Lumia e ke kahuna ʻanāʻanā,* destroyed by an *ʻanāʻanā* sorcerer.

lumi ʻaina. n. Dining room.

lumi ʻau.ʻau. n. Bathroom. *Lit.,* washing room.

lumi hā.iki. n. Narrow room, cell.

lumi hoʻāhu. n. Storeroom.

lumi holoi. n. Laundry room.

lumi hoʻo.kipa. n. Parlor, living room, lobby. *Lit.,* entertaining room.

lumi hoʻo.luana. n. Lounge, reception room.

lumi hula.hula. n. Ballroom.

lumi kuke. n. Kitchen. *Lit.,* cooking room.

lumi.lumi. Same as *lulumi. Lumilumi ʻia lāua e ka ʻona o ka ʻawa,* they were overcome by the intoxication of the kava.

lumi moe. n. Bedroom. *Lit.,* sleeping room.

lumi waiho pā. n. Pantry. *Lit.,* room for leaving plates.

lumi waiho ukana. n. Storeroom. *Lit.,* room to leave goods.

luna. 1. loc. n. High, upper, above, over, up; on, in, to, into. *Luna* follows particles as *ā, i, kō, ma-, mai, no, o.* (Gram. 8.6.) *I luna o,* on top of, over, upon. *Kau i luna o ke kaʻa,* get into the car. (PPN *lunga.*) **2.** n. Foreman, boss, leader, overseer, supervisor, headman, officer of any sort, commissioner, superintendency, control, rule. *Ka mea iāia ka luna* (For. 6:4), the superintendency. **hoʻo.luna.** To appoint as foreman, officer, etc.; to act as officer. **3.** Chief piece in the *kōnane* game. (And.)

luna ʻae male. n. Officer who permits marriage (1851 term).

luna ʻaha.ʻaina. n. Toastmaster, director of a feast. (Ioane 2.8.)

luna ʻai. n. Food inspector.

luna ana ʻāina nui. n. Surveyor general.

luna ʻā.nela. n. Archangel. (Iuda 9.)

luna ʻā.pono. n. Censor, approving officer.

luna ʻau.hau. n. Tax collector (Luka 7.34), tax assessor, publican, master of tribute.

luna au.puni. n. Government official.

luna awa. n. Harbor master.

luna ʻekale.sia. n. Alderman, lay church official.

luna haʻi. n. Confessor, as Catholic priest. *Lit.,* speaking superior.

luna hale kiaʻi. n. Commander or chief guard of a fortress.

luna hana. n. Overseer, foreman, anyone in charge of work.

luna haneli. n. Centurion. (Oih. 10.1.) *Lit.,* overseer of hundred.

luna helu. n. Census taker. *Lit.,* counting supervisor.

luna helu kā.lā. n. Teller, as of a bank. *Lit.*, officer who counts money.
luna hoʻo.hana. n. Manager, administrative head, overseer. *Lit.*, supervisor to cause work to be done.
luna hō.ʻoia. n. Auditor. *Lit.*, proving officer.
luna hō.ʻoia.ʻiʻo pala.pala. n. Certifier of title. *Lit.*, officer who certifies the truth of document.
luna hoʻo.kō. n. Executive officer. *Lit.*, officer who accomplishes.
luna hoʻo.kō kau.oha. n. Executor.
luna hoʻo.luhi. n. Taskmaster. (Puk. 5.6.) *Lit.*, officer who makes weary.
luna hoʻo.malu. n. Chairman; speaker, as of the House of Representatives; presiding officer; comptroller.
luna hoʻo.nā. n. Commissioner who settles land claims.
luna hoʻo.pono.pono. n. Editor, supervisor, administrator, director.
luna hoʻo.pono.pono wai.wai. n. Executor, as of an estate; trustee.
luna hoʻo.puka. n. Publisher. *Lit.*, officer who makes appear.
luna.ʻike.hala. n. Conscience. *Lit.*, officer who knows wrong. (Oih. 23.1.) *ʻAʻole ʻāpono ʻo kuʻu lunaʻikehala i kēlā*, my conscience does not approve of that.
luna.kahiko. n. Elder (Puk. 3.16); elderly leader.
luna kā.kau kope o ke au.puni. n. Notary public. *Lit.*, officer who writes the government copy.
luna kā.lā. n. Comptroller.
luna kana.lima. n. Leader of fifty men. (2 Nal. 1.10.)
luna kā.nā.wai. n. Judge, magistrate; Book of Judges in the Old Testament; referee, as in a fight; judicial. *Lit.*, law officer.
luna kā.nā.wai ʻā.pana. n. District judge.
luna kā.nā.wai hoʻo.kō kau.oha. n. Probate judge.
luna kā.nā.wai hoʻo.malu. n. Police justice.
luna kā.nā.wai kaʻa.puni. n. Circuit judge.
luna kā.nā.wai kiʻe.kiʻe. n. Chief justice.
luna kā.nā.wai kō.kua. n. Associate justice.
luna kaua. n. War officer, captain, commander.
luna kau.kani (tausani). n. Officer in charge of a thousand or more men. *Lit.*, Officer of a thousand *(Eng.)*
luna kia. n. Upper part of a pillar, chapiter (1 Nal. 7.16).
luna kiaʻi. n. Supervisor; overseer of others; bishop (Pilipi 1.1).
luna kiʻe.kiʻe. n. High officer.
luna koa. n. Military officer. Cf. *aliʻikoa.*
luna koʻi.koʻi. n. Ambassador; important officer.
luna kula. n. School superintendent, schoolmaster, school committee (old term).
luna kula.nui. n. School superintendent (old term).
luna lawe hana. n. Chief servant, minister (Kol. 1.23). *Lit.*, officer undertaking work.
luna lawe.lawe no ke kene.lala. n. Aide-de-camp. *Lit.*, officer serving for the general.
luna leka. n. Postmaster. *Lit.*, letter officer.
luna.maka.ʻāi.nana. n. Representative in the legislature. *Lit.*, people's officer.
luna mā.kaʻi. n. District sheriff, chief of police.
luna mā.lama wai.wai. n. Trustee.
luna.manaʻo. Same as *lunaʻikehala.*
luna mele. n. Chorister. *Rare.*
luna nā.nā. n. Inspector; judge, as in song contests.
luna nā.nā helu. n. Auditor.
luna nā.nā koho. n. Election official.
luna noho. n. Chairman.
luna nui. n. Chief officer or foreman, especially head overseer of a sugar plantation, superintendent.
luna ʻohana. n. Head of a family; headman of a tribe. (1 Oihn. 9.34.)
luna ʻohi kā.lā ʻau.hau. n. Tax collector.
luna ʻohi kuke. n. Collector of customs.
luna.ʻō.lelo. n. Apostle; communication officer; proclaimer. (Oih. 1.2.)
luna pai. n. Officer who called warriors to battle. *Lit.*, urging officer.
luna.wae.manaʻo. n. Conscience. *Lit.*, officer that selects thoughts.

luna wai. n. Water master, one in charge of water distribution.
luna wehe pili.kia. n. Representative in the old Hawaiian parliament. *Lit.*, officer who removes trouble.
luni. vs. Limping, unsteady. *Rare.*
luni.hini. n. Perhaps a land shell. *Na ka lunihini leo leʻa* (For. 6:534), by the sweet-voiced *lunihini.*
lunu. Same as *nunu 1, 2.* Cf. *ʻalunu, ʻānunu.*
luʻoni. One who delivers a victim to the sacrificial altar; to so deliver. (AP.)
lupa. Same as *lupalupa.* Also *nupa.*
lupa.lupa. 1. vs. Flourishing, of luxuriant growth, lush, thriving. *Lupalupa ke oho o ka palai*, thriving fronds of fern. *hoʻo.lupa.lupa.* To cause to flourish; lush. See *nupanupa.* 2. nvi. Purifying ceremonies of various sorts, as to insure growth or to cleanse contaminated persons, as those who have buried the dead; prayer for the soul of one who has just died; to conduct such ceremonies.
lupe. n. 1. Kite. Cf. *kaʻiālupe. Hoʻolele lupe*, to fly a kite. Four types of *lupe* were said to exist; *lupe lā*, a round kite, *lit.*, sun kite; *lupe mahina*, kite with tapa covering cut in a crescent shape, *lit.*, moon kite; *lupe manu*, kite with wings on the side, *lit.*, bird kite; *lupe maoli*, kite suggestive of European kites in shape, *lit.*, genuine kite. (PPN *lupe*.) 2. Same as *hīhīmanu*, sting ray. 3. Flattened end of the forward end of the outrigger float outside of the joining of the outrigger boom to the float. 4. A kind of seaweed.
lupea. vs. Pleasing, attractive, as plants. *Lupea ka uka i ka palai*, the inland is lovely with ferns.
lupeʻa. vs. Drunk, intoxicated; to distress.
lupeʻa.keke. n. Hawaiian stormy petrel *(Oceanodroma castro cryptoleucura).* Also *oeoe.*
lupe.lupea. Redup. of *lupea. Lupelupea i ke ʻala*, attractive with perfume.
lupepa. n. 1. Rhubarb *(Rheum rhaponticum).* (Neal 328.) *Eng.* 2. Calomel and tartar emetic.
lupo. 1. Var. of *ulupō 3.* (PPN *lupo*.) 2. n. Wolf. (Latin *lupus* or Gr. *lukos*.)
lūpō. See *ulupō 3.*
Lū-pua. n. Wind name associated with Wai-niha, Kauaʻi. *Lit.*, flower scattering.
lū pua. v. To scatter flowers, as by a flower girl at a wedding; to decorate graves with flowers. *Lā Lū Pua*, Decoration Day.
luʻu. vi. To dive, plunge into water, immerse, duck; to dip in, as a shrimp net. *hoʻo.luʻu.* To dip, immerse, dye. *Hoʻoluʻu ʻili*, to tan hides. *hoʻoluʻu paʻakai*, basket for storing salt *(paʻakai);* to dye salt with ocherous earth. *Waihoʻoluʻu*, color dye. *Poʻe hoʻoluʻu*, dye makers. *Hoʻoluʻu lahilahi*, to dye lightly, tint. (PPN *ruku*.)
luʻua. Pas/imp. of *luʻu.* **hoʻo.luʻua.** Pas/imp. of *hoʻoluʻu. Pāʻū noʻeno ʻe i hoʻoluʻua*, dyed printed skirts.
luʻu ʻili. n. Tanner of skins and hides. **hoʻo.luʻu ʻili.** To tan skins.
luʻu.kia. nvt. Coconut fiber lashing; to lash thus. *Pāʻū-o-Luʻukia*, a kind of lashing, referring to a legendary woman's sennit chastity belt.
luʻu kimo. v. To dive headfirst.
luʻu.luʻu. 1. vs. Bent or bowed down, as with weight, sorrow, or trouble; painful, sorrowful, sad, wretched, woeful, depressed, downcast, toilsome, overladen. *Luʻuluʻu Hanalei i ka ua nui, kaumaha i ka noe o Alakaʻi*, Hanalei is downcast with great rains, heavy with mists of Alakaʻi [said in dirges to describe the weight of grief]. *Hala ka luʻuluʻu kaumaha*, the heavy sorrow is over. **hoʻo.luʻu.luʻu.** To cause sorrow, grief; to oppress, load down. (PPN *rukuruku*.) 2. Redup.of *luʻu;* to set a *hīnaʻi*, fish trap. **hoʻo.luʻu.luʻu.** Redup. of *hoʻoluʻu;* to set a fish trap.
luʻu poʻo. v. To dive headfirst.
luwa.hine. Rare spelling of *luahine.*
Luwele, Luvere. n. Louvre. *(French.)*

M

ma. prep. Indefinite locative, instrumental, manner. At, in, on, beside, along, through; by means of, because of, in behalf of, according to. This very common part. is perhaps more specific than the similar *i*, at, in; it is written in the dictionary as a part of the following words: *'ane'i, hea, hope, kai, laila, lalo, luna, muli, uka*. With meaning "because" it is frequently followed by *o*, of. (*Ma* is frequently pronounced *mā* before primary stress: Gram. 9.4.) *E noho ana ma Ulu-kou i Wai-kīkī* (FS 267), living at Ulu-kou in Wai-kīkī. *Ma'ane'i*, here. *Makai*, at the sea, seaward. *Mauka*, inland, at the mountains. *'A'ole au i hele mai ma ke 'ano ikaika, i hele mai au ma ka māka'ika'i* (For. 5:507), I didn't come in an aggressive way, I came to sightsee. *Ma o wai 'oukou i pili ai?* Through whom are you related? *Kona make 'ana ma o Ka-welo ala*, his death at the hands of Ka-welo there. *Ua hele mai au ma ona ala*, I came for his sake. (PCP *ma*.)

mā. 1. vs. Faded, wilted, stained, discolored, blushing; defeated; passed away, perished; to have lost a former attractiveness; to fade. *Mā wale*, to fade quickly, as earthly glory. *Ua mā ka mana'o kaumaha*, the sad thoughts have faded away. *ho'o.mā.* Caus/sim. (PPN *ma'a*.) 2. Part. following names of persons. And company, and others, and wife, and husband, and associates. (Gram. 8.7.5.) *Ke ali'i mā*, the chief and his retinue. *Hina mā*, Hina and the others; Hina and her husband, friends. *Mea mā*, they. (PNP *ma'a*.) 3. Same as *mākahakaha*, to clear. (Possibly PPN *ma'a*.)

mā-. 1. Short for *maka*, eye, as in *ho'omā'ē, mā'eo, mākahi, mākole*. 2. Short for *maka*, mesh, as in *māhā, mākahi, mākole*, etc. 3. Short for *make*, desire, as in *ho'omā'aka'aka*. 4. **mā-, ma-.** Stative prefixes indicating quality or state: *'alo, mā'alo; hai, māhai*. 5. Exclusiveness in first person dual and plural pronouns (*mākou, māua*) and possessives. (Gram. 8.2.) (PPN *ma(a)*.)

-mā. See *ko'i ho'omā*.

ma'a. 1. nvs. Accustomed, used to, knowing thoroughly, habituated, familiar, experienced; to adapt; custom, habit. Cf. *ma'ama'a, ma'amau. No kēia ma'a o ke ali'i*, because of this custom of the chief. **ho'o.ma'a.** To practice, gain experience or skill, become accustomed (less used than *ho'oma'ama'a*). 2. nvt. Sling, as made of coconut fiber, human hair, or aerial pandanus roots; to cast a stone in such a sling; string of a musical instrument *(rare)*. (PPN *maka*.) 3. vt. To tie. Cf. *kāma'a*. 4. n. Snapper at the end of a whip. Also *hu'a*.

mā.'ā. 1. vs. Bad-smelling. 2. Same as *mā'ā'ā*.

Ma'a. n. Name of a famous wind associated with Lahaina, Maui. Also *'A'a*. See ex., *waianuhea*.

mā.'ā.'ā. 1. vi. To reach out, as a baby or as an octopus. Cf. *'ama*. 2. nv. Goat's bleat; baa; to bleat.

Ma'a'a Kua Lapu. n. Wind at Kaha-lu'u, Hawai'i. (For. 5:93.)

ma'a.alai.oa. nvt. Slingshot; to shoot with sling *(ma'a). Rare*.

Ma'a'a Pa'i.malau. n. Wind name. *Lit.*, Portuguese man-of-war *Ma'a'a*.

mā.'ā.'ele. Same as *mā'e'ele*.

maahe. Var. spelling of *māhe*.

-mā'aka'aka. ho'o.mā.'aka.'aka.aka. Same as *ho'omāke'aka*, to cause laughter.

ma'a.kū. vt. To sling with a sling and stone. *Ua ma'akū aku lāua i ka manu*, they slung a stone at the bird with the sling.

ma'a.laea. nvs. Red color, red ocher color; stained red, as with ocherous earth; red, as earth.

ma'a.lahi. nvs. Contentment, simplicity, ease; to be easy, simple. *Ka maluhia a me ka ma'alahi*, peace and contentment.

ma'a.lea. nvs. Cunning, craft, trickery, deceit, guile; cunning, crafty, artful, deceitful, sly, shrewd; skillful; accustomed, skilled. (Ios. 9.4.) **ho'o.ma'a.lea.** Caus/sim.

ma'a.lea.lea. Redup. of *ma'alea*.

ma'a.lewa. 1. n. Aerial root or vine. (UL 63.) 2. vi. Surging, swinging.

mā.'ali. Same as *mō'ali*, furrow.

mā.'ali.'ali. Redup. of *mā'ali*, furrow.

ma'a.lili. vs. Cooled, of what has been hot, as food; abated, calmed, of anger, love, passion; blasted, of fruit (Am. 4.9). *Ka wā i ma'alili ai ka huhū* (Eset. 2.1), when wrath had been appeased. **ho'o.ma'a.lili.** To cause to cool; appease, soothe, quiet, pacify, assuage anger or grief (Sol. 16.14). (PPN *makalili*.)

mā.'alo. vi. To pass along, by, or alongside, as to overtake and pass a car; to transship; to pass through, as land; to pass away, as glory. (Dan. 4.31.) *Waiwai mā'alo*, transit goods. (PPN *maakalo*.)

ma'a.loa. n. A low native shrub *(Neraudia melastomaefolia)*, related to the *māmaki*, and like it, having strong bark formerly used for making tapa. Also *'oloa, ma'oloa*.

mā.'alo.'alo. Redup. of *mā'alo*, to pass to and fro, back and forth; to pass frequently. See ex., *pānoanoa*. (PNP *ma(a)kalokalo*.)

ma'a.lo'e.lo'e. Same as *mālo'elo'e*.

ma'a.ma'a. Redup. of *ma'a 1*; accustomed, experienced, used. **ho'o.ma'a.ma'a.** Same as *ho'oma'a*; to practice, become accustomed; to train, drill.

ma'a.ma'a.hia. Pas/imp. of *ma'ama'a*; familiar.

ma'a.ma'a.lea. Redup. of *ma'alea. He mau 'ōlelo ma'ama'alea*, crafty words.

mā.'ama.'ama. Same as *mālamalama*. (See Gram. 2.8.)

ma'a.mau. vs. Usual, customary, regular, habitual, ordinary, common. Cf. *'ama'amau. Uku ma'amau*, customary fee. *Hana ma'amau*, usual work. *'Ōlelo ma'amau*, common word. **ho'o.ma'a.mau.** To become accustomed, familiar.

mā.'ana. 1. n. Beginning. *Rare*. **ho'o.mā.'ana.** Beginning. (Kep. 175.) 2. Common colloquial pronunciation of *mā'ona*, full.

ma'a.ne'i. See *'ane'i*.

mā.ani.ani. 1. n. Gentle blowing of the wind. *Fig.*, tranquillity. 2. Var. spelling of *māniani*.

maao. Kind of fish. (And.)

-ma'au. ho'o.ma'au. To persecute, offend, injure, bully, tease, torment.

mā.'au. nvi. To sprout, germinate, spread, especially of useless weeds; weeds. *Fig.*, to go from place to place, gad about; rain belt in the upland forest (also, *ma'ū*). Cf. *ma'au'auwā. Ka wao mā'au kele* (KL line 618), the damp upland region.

mā.'aua. 1. Same as *'ā'aua*, coarse. 2. Pas/imp. of *-ma'au. Rare*.

ma'a.'au.'au. n. Poi calabash as used by poi peddlers. Cf. *mā'au*, going from place to place.

mā.'au.'aua. Redup. of *mā'aua*.

ma'au.'auā. nvt. Peddler, merchant; to sell, trade; to seige (GP 64). (An O'ahu term; Kam. [76:123] despised such people.)

-mā'auē. -mā'auwē. ho'o.mā'au.ē. To mimic speech in a nasty way, to mock, annoy thus.

ma'au.ea. Rare var. of *malauea*, lazy.

mā.'au.ea, mā'auwea. 1. Pas/imp. of *mā'aue. Ho'o-*

mā'aka'aka mā'auea (Laie 465), mocking laughter.
ho'o.mā.'au.ea. To laugh at, ridicule, mock; to disregard. **2.** Same as *manauea*, a taro. **3.** n. Plant listed by Kamakau as used for tapa.
ma'a.'ula.'ula. n. Red clay as used in coloring.
ma'aupopo. Thick. (And.)
-ma'auwē. See *mā'auē.*
mā'auwea. See *mā'auea.*
ma'awe. 1. nvt. Fiber, thread, rootlet (Kel. 121); wisp; strand, as of a spider web; faint footprint; to tread, track, follow, as a trail; small, narrow, thin, as of a fiber; weak, sickly. See ex., *puahilohilo. Ma'awe ala,* faint path or track; *fig.,* departure of the soul after death. **ho'o.ma'awe.** To make a tracing; footprint, track, slight path; to make small fibers or threads. (PNP *makawe.*) **2.** n. A variety of taro.
mā.'awe.'awe. Redup. of *ma'awe;* streaked, as with different colors.
ma'awe loloa. n. Lengthwise strand, warp (Oihk. 13.48). *Lit.,* long track.
ma'awe poko.poko. n. Transverse strand, woof (Oihk. 13.48). *Lit.,* short track.
ma'awe 'ula. n. A red track, as in well-trod red earth. *Ke alanui ma'awe 'ula a Kanaloa,* the red track pathway of Kanaloa [the western sky].
mae. vi. To fade, wilt, wither, droop; partially dry, as clothes; to fade away (Hal. 18.45); to pine away (Oihk. 26.39); to waste away, as with illness. *Noke i ka 'aka ā mae ka 'iwi'ao'ao,* kept on laughing until their ribs ached. **ho'o.mae.** To cause to wilt, fade; to fade. (PPN *mae.*)
-mā'ē. ho'o.mā.'ē. Short for *ho'omaka'ē.*
maea. vs. Stinking, as of unwashed bodies; malodorous, as a swamp; offensive-smelling, as vomit. (PPN *mae.*)
mā.ea. 1. vi. To rise to the surface. **2.** n. A variety of taro. *Hawai'i.*
mā.ea.ea. 1. Redup. of *maea* and *māea 1.* **2.** vt. To disregard.
mā.ea.lani. vi. To get up, rise. *E ala, e ho'okū, e māealani,* get up, stand, rise.
mā.'e'ele. nvs. Numb, as a foot that has "gone to sleep"; numb with cold or deeply moved by love; shocked, benumbed; stricken with fear, horror, grief; numb feeling during pregnancy. **ho'o.mā.'e'ele.** To cause numbness, shock, great love.
mā.'eha. Same as *'eha,* pain. **ho'o.mā.'eha.** Same as *ho'o'eha.*
mā.'eha.'eha. Redup. of *mā'eha;* much pain.
mā.'ele. Same as *mā'e'ele.* **ho'o.mā.'ele.** Caus/sim.
mae.mae. Redup. of *mae;* damp, as clothes suitable for ironing. *I'a maemae,* fish partially dried, much relished when cooked.
ma'e.ma'e. nvs. Clean, pure, attractive, chaste; cleanliness, purity. *Ma'ema'e 'ole,* unclean. *Ma'ema'e loa,* extremely clean, immaculate. *Ma'ema'e wale nō 'o Kaua'i, hemolele wale i ka mālie* (song), a perfect beauty is Kaua'i, flawless in the calm. **ho'o.ma'e.ma'e.** To clean, cleanse, purge, disinfect, purify. *'Ao'ao ho'o-ma'ema'e,* reform party.
mae.maea. Same as *māeaea.*
mā.'eno. Same as *'eno,* wild.
mā.'eno.'eno. Redup. of *mā'eno.*
mā.'eo. Same as *makā'eo.*
mā.'ewa. vs. Swaying, swinging, as something with an anchored base, as seaweed, hair, leaves; fluttering; wandering, unstable. See ex., *'ūki'ukiu 3. Māewa lani,* swinging in the air. *I hea 'oe i hele māewa aku nei?* Where did you go wandering?
ma'ewa. vs. Reproachful, scornful, mocking, mimicking in a nasty way, sneering; cruel; scorned, abused, desecrated, tousled. **ho'o.ma'ewa.** To reproach, sneer at, mimic, ridicule, desecrate, jeer, mock, scorn.
mā.ewa.ewa. Redup. of *māewa. Hulu māewaewa,* fluttering feathers.
mā.'ewa.'ewa. Redup. of *ma'ewa;* to treat roughly, beat; roughhouse. Cf. *mānewanewa.* **ho'o.mā.'ewa.-**

'ewa. Redup. of *ho'oma'ewa;* to purge oneself of the effects of black magic by performing a prescribed humiliating ceremony, as walking about naked.
maha. 1. n. Temple, side of the head. (Lunk. 4.21.) (PNP *mafa.*) **2.** n. Gill plate of a fish. **3.** n. Wings of a flying fish. **4.** n. Preputium, foreskin. **5.** n. Lower portion of a canoe *manu.* **6.** nvs. Rest, repose, vacation; freedom from pain; at ease, comfort. See *mahamaha 2.* **ho'o.maha.** Vacation; to take a rest or vacation; to retire, stop work; to obtain relief; to pause; rest in music (types are *ho'omaha po'o,* a whole rest; *ho'o-maha po'o'ele,* a quarter rest; *ho'omaha po'olima,* a half rest; *ho'omaha po'omana,* an eighth rest; *ho'omaha po'omanalua,* a sixteenth rest; *ho'omaha po'omanakolu,* a thirty-second rest). *Ua ho'omaha nā kula,* the schools are having a vacation. *Ho'omaha 'ia mai au i ku'u hā'awe,* I am relieved of my burden. *Ho'omaha ai ma nā kānāwai* (For. 6:159), to rest with the laws [obey them]. **7.** n. Severed portion Cf. *maha lā'au, mahamaha, maha 'ō'ō.* **8.** Same as *mahamoe 1.* **9.** Same as *māhana,* twin. *Maha pu'u,* twin hills. **10.** Rare var. of *mahamaha 3,* to show affection. **11.** n. Fishes. See *maha mea, maha 'ō'ō, maha wela.*
mā.hā. n. Net mesh large enough to admit the entrance of four fingers; net of such a mesh.
mahae. 1. vt. To tear, split, separate. *Mahae lua,* to split in two. *Ua mahae ka pili o kēlā pa'a male,* that couple has separated; *lit.,* the association of that married couple is split. (PPN *masae.*) **2.** n. A fish, said to belong to the *lā'īpala* group. (PCP *ma(f,s)ae.*) **3.** n. Net mesh, about 10 cm and above, between *māhā* and *mālewa.*
mā.hae.hae. Redup. of *mahae 1;* to tear to shreds. (PNP *masaesae.*)
mahaha. n. A surgeonfish (Acanthuridae).
mahāha. vs. Soft, tender, weak; soft and mealy, as a baked potato. **ho'o.mahā.ha.** To prepare soil for gardening, to make earth soft and fine.
mā.hā.hā. vs. Dry and hard, as poi made of poor quality taro.
-māhāhā. ho'o.mā.hā.hā. To place taro tops together until they begin to sprout and are ready for planting (perhaps a contraction of *ho'omaka hāhā,* to start stems).
mahaha.'ula.'ula. n. A variety of taro.
mahai. n. A variety of *ulua,* a fish.
mā.ha'i.ha'i. Same as *ha'iha'i,* brittle.
maha.kea. n. **1.** Once uncultivated land, as for bananas, sweet potato, taro; fallow land. Cf. *kūmahakea.* **2.** A variety of taro. **3.** A variety of kava, usually called *mā-kea.*
maha lā.'au. n. Clump or grove of trees. Cf. *maha 'ulu,* clump of breadfruit trees.
mahalo. nvt. **1.** Thanks, gratitude; to thank. *Mahalo nui loa,* thanks [you] very much. *'Ōlelo mahalo,* compliment. *Mahalo ā nui,* thanks very much. (PPN *masalo.*) **2.** Admiration, praise, esteem, regards, respects; to admire, praise, appreciate. *'O wau nō me ka mahalo,* I am, [yours] respectfully. *Ka mea i mahalo 'ia,* Mr. Pā-kī, the esteemed Mr. Pākī. (PEP *masalo.*)
maha.lua. Same as *maha'oi* but stronger: rude, disrespectful, saucy, overbearing; encroaching on the property or rights of others. *Lit.,* double temple.
maha.maha. 1. n. Gill plate. **2.** Redup. of *maha 6,* to rest, stop. (Laie 463.) **3.** vs. To show or feel pleasure, love, affection; affectionate. *Ka pili mahamaha,* affectionate relationship. **ho'o.maha.maha.** Caus/sim. **4.** Redup. of *maha 7.* **5.** n. A variety of taro, sometimes qualified by *ke'oke'o,* white.
maha.maha kea. vs. White-jowled, as of a pig or dog.
maha.maha.o'o. Redup. of *maha'o'o.*
maha.maha 'ō'ō. Redup. of *maha 'ō'ō.*
maha mea. n. Name of a deep-sea fish, said to be striped (no data).
maha.moe. 1. vs. Attractive, sleek, as a plump animal; smooth. *He kai mahamoe* (For. 6:297), a smooth sea. **2.** n. An edible bivalve (no data).

mahana. **1.** nvs. Warmth, heat; warm. Cf. *hahana, hanahana, mehana, pumehana.* **ho'o.mahana.** To warm, create warmth, heat. (PPN *mafana.*) **2.** n. Rest. Cf. *maha 6.* **ho'o.mahana.** Vacation, rest. **3.** Same as *mahina,* plantation. **4.** n. A class of chiefs.

mā.hana. **1.** nvs. Twins; double; having two branches or forks. *Māhana lua nā kukui* (UL 130), the torch lights are double [said of one drunk as with *kava*]. (PPN *maasanga.*) **2.** *(Cap.)* n. Castor or Pollux. The two together are called *Ka-māhana, Nā-hōkū-māhana, Nā-māhoe.* Individual names include *Māhoe Hope, Māhoe Mua, Nānā Hope, Nānā Mua.*

mā.hana.hana. **1.** Redup. of *mahana 1;* smarting, painful; unpleasant odor, as of flatulency; bad-smelling, lukewarm. *Ka pa'i māhanahana,* a slap that smarts. **ho'o.mā.hana.hana.** To make warm, heat. (PPN *mafanafana.*) **2.** Redup. of *mahana 2.* **ho'o.mā.-hana.hana.** To relax rigor of taboo during a long rigorous session. (Malo 160, 176.)

-māhanahana. **ho'o.mā.hana.hana.** To dedicate, as a temple (FS 117); to offer first fruits to the gods.

mā.hana.kana.loa. n. Name for large food calabash.

mā.hana pu'u. n. Double peak; twin peaks.

mā.hani. **1.** vi. Smooth. *Hahau ka wēlau kō, ā māhani 'āpa'apa'a,* the sugar-cane tops were beaten into the banks of taro patches smooth and compact. **2.** vs. Dull (not sharp). **3.** vi. To lessen, of heat. See *'ea māhani.* **4.** To vanish. (And.)

mā.hao. **1.** n. Pitch. **2.** vs. Rotten, hollow, as wood. *Rare.* Cf. *popopo.*

maha'o.ha'o. Same as *ha'oha'o,* strange.

maha.'oi. vs. Bold, impertinent, impudent, insolent, nervy, cheeky, rude, forward, presumptuous, saucy, brazen. *Lit.,* sharp temple. See ex., *'āhua.*

maha.o'o. nvs. Mature in wisdom; wise; wise person. *Lit.,* mature temple.

maha 'ō.'ō. n. **1.** A fish of the *'ahi* type. **2.** Piece of sweet potato broken off by the *'ō'ō,* digging stick. Same as the more common *kū-'ō'ō.*

maha pepe. vs. Broad-browed. *Lit.,* flat brow.

Maha-pili. n. Name of twin stars (no data).

maha 'ulu. n. Grove or clump of breadfruit trees.

maha wela. n. A variety of yam (no data). (Malo 46.)

maha.wele. Same as *nahawele,* a bivalve.

māhe, maahe. vi. To grow less distinct and fade out, as the sound of a voice or a wisp of smoke.

mahea. See *hea 5,* where.

mā.hea. vs. Hazy, as moonlight.

Mā.hea-lani. n. Sixteenth day of the lunar month, night of the full moon.

maheha. Same as *heha,* indolent.

mā.hela.hela. vs. Clearly showing, as grain of wood. (PPN *mafela.*)

mahele. **1.** nvt. Portion, division, section, zone, lot, piece, quota, installment, bureau, department, precinct, category, scene or act in a play; share, as of stocks; measure in music; land division of 1848 (the great *mahele*); part or organ, as of the body; section or wing (military, see *mokuna*); denominator, in fractions; to divide, apportion, cut into parts, deal. See *hele 7. Mahele lua,* to divide into two parts. *Hō'ailona mahele,* measure signature in music. *Mahele li'ili'i,* small portion, bit, fragment. **ho'o.mahele.** To have a division made, distribute, divide, etc. (PPN *masele.*) **2.** vt. To translate, interpret. **ho'o.mahele.** Caus/sim.

-māhele. **ho'o.mā.hele.** To lead conversation towards a topic. *'O 'Alamila e ho'omāhele ma kona kama'ilio 'ana no nā mea e pili ana no 'Enelani,* Almira in her chatting led the conversation to things pertaining to England.

mahele hana. n. Duty, work section, shift.

māhele.hele. Redup. of *mahele 1, 2.* (PPN *maselesele.*)

mahele kā.lā. n. Dividend.

mahele kaua lewa. n. Air force.

mahele koa. n. Military unit, squadron.

mahele lā.'au. n. Portion of medicine, dose.

mahele manawa. n. Division of time, as of a fiscal period.

mahele 'ō.lelo. nv. Interpreter, translator; to translate, interpret.

mahele wai.wai ho'o.puka. n. Share of profits, dividend.

mā.helu. vt. To dig, rake, scratch the earth; to spread loose soft earth over a taro patch after the bottom has been pounded hard to make it impervious. See *helu 4.* (Probably PPN *maselu.*)

mahena. n. Heap, pile, as of trash. *Rare.*

maheu. **1.** Rare var. of *meheu,* track. **2.** vt.. To dig and rake the earth, as for planting. *E maheu a'e ana i kēia pu'u e kanu 'uala,* preparing the soil in this hill for planting sweet potatoes. **3.** n. Kind of porous stone, used to rub, scour, polish, and as an octopus lure.

mahi. **1.** nvt. To cultivate, farm; a farm, plantation, patch. Cf. *mahi 'ai, mahi kō, mahikū, mahina, mahina 'ai.* **2.** vs. Strong, energetic, as a worker. Cf. *huliā-mahi. Moa mahi,* fighting cock. (PPN *mafi.*)

Mahi-'ai. n. Name of a star (no data).

mahi 'ai. nvt. Farmer, planter; to farm, cultivate; agricultural. *'Oihana mahi 'ai,* agricultural industry, farming.

mā.hie. vs. Delightful, charming, pleasant, handsome. **ho'o.mā.hie.** Delightful, charming; to cast shy glances, as of a coy child.

mā.hie.hie. Redup. of *māhie.* See song, *makalapua.*

mā.hihi. **1.** Same as *māihi,* to peel. **2.** Same as *mahimahi,* dolphin.

mahi.hiki. Redup. of *mahiki.*

mahi.'ili. vt. To plunder thoroughly; to take all, as a chief taking all the property of his subjects. *Lit.,* dig skin.

mahī.kā.kā. Same as *hīkākā,* to reel, stagger. *Rare.*

mahiki. **1.** vi. To jump, leap, hop, move up and down, vibrate; to spatter; to teeter, seesaw; to weigh, as on scales; a seesaw. **ho'o.mahiki.** To cause to leap, jump, etc. (PPN *mafiti.*) **2.** vt. To cast out spirits, exorcise, especially with *māhiki* shrimps; to treat in turn, as troubles in *ho'oponopono* family therapy (Nānā 75-7). *Mahiki ana i nā mea 'ino,* treating the deep troubles. **3.** n. Any kind of shrimp used ceremoniously. **4.** Same as *'aki'aki,* a grass used to exorcise evil spirits, especially when shrimps are not available. **5.** vt. To pry; peel off, as a scab; to appear. *Mahiki ka lā i ka 'ilikai,* the sun came forth on the horizon. **6.** Same as *'uku kai,* a sand hopper. **7.** n. A variety of taro.

mā.hiki.hiki. **1.** Redup. of *mahiki 1, 2, 5.* (PPN *mafitifi-ti.*) **2.** Same as *mahiki 4.* **3.** n. Stone, as used for adze. Also called *makai'a.*

mahi.kina lā. n. Crack of dawn.

Mahiki-o-ka-lua-kanaka. n. Stroke in *lua* fighting.

mahi kō. n. Sugar-cane plantation.

mahi.kū. nvt. To clear land for planting; plantation clearing not yet planted. *Rare.*

mahili. **1.** Same as *hili,* to deviate. *Mahili ho'i kāna mo'olelo,* how his story meanders. **2.** vt. To strip away property.

mā.hiloa. vs. Distant, far (perhaps contraction of *ma kahi loa,* at far place).

-māhilu. **ho'o.mā.hilu.** To beautify, adorn, bedeck. Cf. *hiluhilu.*

mahi.mahi. n. Dolphin *(Coryphaena hippurus),* a game fish up to 1.5 m long, popular for food. Cf. *lapalapa 5.* (PPN *masimasi.*)

mahina. n. **1.** Moon, month; moonlight. *Mahina meli,* honeymoon. (PPN *maasina.*) **2.** Crescent-shaped fishhook. **3.** Eye of the snail at the end of its horn. **4.** Farm, plantation, patch. **5.** A variety of onion, similar to silver onion. **6.** A variety of sweet potato.

mahina 'ai. Same as *mahi 'ai,* to farm; truck farm.

mahina hapa.lua hope. n. Waning of the moon. *Lit.,* last half of the moon.

mahina hapa.lua mua. n. Waxing of the moon. *Lit.,* first half of the moon.

mā.hina.hina. n. Pale moonlight.

mahina hou. n. **1.** New moon, new month. **2.** Church offering on the first Sunday of the month, of Congregationalists.

mahina.kē.hau. n. A variety of sweet potato.

mahina.lua. n. A small creeping native fern *(Grammitis tenella)*, with simple narrow fronds 5 cm long or longer, each bearing none to many round spots of spores.

mahina piha. n. Full moon.

mahina poe.poe. n. Full moon. *Lit.*, round moon.

mā.hinu. 1. Same as *hinu*, rubbed, anointed, polished. **2.** vs. Partly cooked, as Chinese vegetables; beginning to cook, as *lū'au* leaves that are getting greener and softer.

mahi.ole. nvt. Feather helmet, helmet; to wear a helmet. *'Oki mahiole*, a haircut with crest of hair left down the middle of the head.

mahi.ole haka. See *haka 3*.

mahi.'opu. 1. vs. Bold, rude. *Rare.* **2.** vt. To dig, as with a pickax. *Rare.*

mahi pua. n. Flower garden or patch; horticulture.

mahi waena. nv. Weed cultivator; to cultivate and weed. *Lit.*, weeding farm.

mahi waina. nv. Vineyard; grape raiser; to cultivate grapes.

mā.hoa. vi. To travel together in company, as canoes. *Nā wa'a e māhoa aku ana*, canoes traveling together. Cf. *hoa*, companion.

maho'a. vs. Thick, as a cloud. *Maui.*

mā.hoe. n. **1.** Twins. **2.** Two native trees *(Alectryon macrococcum* and *A. mahoe)*, related to the soapberry and the litchi; they have compound leaves and globose, brown, twinned or single fruits. (Neal 531.) Also *'ala'ala hua*. **3.** *(Cap.)* Names of months and stars. See *Māhoe Hope, Māhoe Mua*, and *Māhana 2*.

mā.hoe.hoe. Same as *mā'ohe'ohe*, tall. *Rare.*

Mā.hoe Hope. n. **1.** Star name, one of the twins, Castor or Pollux. *Lit.*, last twin. See *Māhoe Mua*. **2.** Month in the old lunar calendar, the eleventh (Hawai'i) or seventh (O'ahu, Kaua'i). Also *Hilina Mā*: see *month*.

Mā.hoe Mua. n. **1.** Star name, one of the twins, Castor or Pollux. *Lit.*, first twin. (Probably Pollux, the brighter of the two, that rises before Māhoe Hope, which is probably Castor: Johnson and Mahelona 15.) **2.** Month in the old lunar calendar, the tenth (Hawai'i) or sixth (O'ahu, Kaua'i). Also *Hilina Ehu*: see *month*.

mahola. vi. To spread out; to smooth out, as a cloth to dry; to extend, expand. See *hola 1* and ex., *he'e 1*. *Mahola a'ela ka 'ōpū o ka 'upena*, the bag of the net opened out. **ho'o.mahola.** Caus/sim.; to unroll. (PPN *mafola*.)

mā.hola.hola. Redup. of *mahola*. (PPN *mafolafola*.)

mahole. vt. To bruise, skin, scrape, as a flesh wound; to injure as the feelings. Cf. *hole*, peeled. (PPN *mafole*, cf. Nukuoro.)

mā.hole.hole. Redup. of *mahole*. (PPN *mafolefole*.)

Maho.meka, Mahometa. nvs. Mohammed; Mohammedan. *Eng.*

mahope. See *hope*, after.

-mahu. ho'o.mahu. To eat just a little to allay hunger, as while waiting for a feast.

māhu. 1. nvs. Steam, vapor, fumes; to steam, exude vapor. *Lola māhu hana alanui*, steam roller for streets. **ho'o.māhu.** To create steam; to cook or soften food by steam; to steam. **2.** Same as *'ōlapa*, trees.

mahū. vs. Weak, flat, as diluted kava or stale beer; insipid, as fresh poi kept too long in the icebox; quiet, peaceful, undisturbed. Cf. *mahūmahū*. (PPN *mafu(u)*.)

mā.hū. n. Homosexual, of either sex; hermaphrodite. **ho'o.mā.hū.** To behave like a homosexual or hermaphrodite. (PEP *maa(f,s)uu*.)

mahua. n. Mockery, derision, spying (rarely used without *ho'o-*). **ho'o.mahua.** To mock (Hal. 2.4); to spy, watch, as a cat watching a mouse. (PNP *masua*.)

mā.hua. nvs. Increase, growth; to increase, thrive, wax, accrue, multiply, flourish (less used than *māhuahua*). **ho'o. mā.hua.** To increase, expand, enlarge, multiply, grow. *Ho'omāhua i kona waiwai*, to increase its value, wealth. *Ho'omāhua ke aniani ho'onui 'ike i ka pūpū*, the microscope magnifies the shell. (PPN *masua*.)

mā.huā, māhuwā. Same as *huā*, envy, contempt. **ho'o.mā.huā.** To bring bad luck, misfortune; to annoy, distress, harm; adversity. *Ho'omāhuā i nā hoa noho*, to mistreat the people one lived with. *He hō'ailona ho'omāhuā ka makapa'a*, a one-eyed person is a sign of bad luck.

-mahuahana. ho'o.mahua.hana. vt. To disturb, bother.

mā.hua.hua. Redup. of *māhua*; to grow strong, as a ruler; to accrue, increase; productive, big. **ho'o.mā.hua.hua.** Caus/sim.; to enlarge. (PPN *masuasua*.)

mahua.kala. vs. Disbelieving, cynical, skeptical, as of religion; irreligious, atheistic. **ho'o.mahua.kala.** To show disbelief, skepticism; to ridicule, mock, as beliefs.

mahu'e. vt. To open, as a box; to take out, remove, as gear.

mahu.'ē. Same as *mahuka ē*, to flee beforehand.

māhu.ea. n. Gas.

mahu'i. nvt. To guess, suppose, surmise, expect, suspect, assume, imagine; clue. *'Ike mahu'i*, to catch a glimpse, have an inkling or hunch. *Lohe mahu'i*, to hear a hint or rumor without much detail; to have heard rarely. See ex., *ulua 1*. **ho'o.mahu'i.** Caus/sim.

mā.hu'i. vt. To imitate, ape, pattern after, do as, follow after. *Māhu'i lani* (UL 56), royal imitation, said of the right hand in dancing, as this hand always made movements first. **ho'o.mā.hu'i.** Caus/sim.; to mimic. *Po'e kumu lā, i ho'omāhu'i 'ia ai e kēlā po'e* (1 Pet. 5.3), teachers imitated by that people.

mā.hu'i.hu'i. Redup. of *mahu'i* and *māhu'i*.

mā.hu'i lani. See *māhu'i*.

mahuka. nvi. To run away, flee, escape, elope; fugitive. *Koa mahuka*, deserter soldier. **ho'o.mahuka.** To chase, drive away, assist or help to escape. (PPN *mafuta*.)

mā.huka.huka. Redup. of *mahuka*. **ho'o.mā.huka.huka.** Caus/sim. (PPN *mafutafuta*.)

mahu kai loloa. Same as *'a'au loa*. See *'a'au 2*. (Malo text, chapter 18, section 54.)

mahu kole, mahu kokole. Same as *mahumahu*.

mā.huli. Same as *huli*, to seek.

mahulu. Same as *pahulu 1*.

mahulu.kū. n. Aerial roots of pandanus or other trees, as banyans. See also *ule hala, uleule*.

mahu.mahu. 1. Rare redup. of *māhu 1*. *'O Kūmahumahu-kole, 'ōkole ka'aka* (FS 213), Kū-steaming-buttocks, wretched buttocks [Kama-pua'a insults his foe, implying flatulency]. **2.** Silent, weak, brittle. (And.)

mahū.mahū. Redup. of *mahū* (commonly said of tasteless poi).

mā.huna. 1. nvi. Scaly appearance of the skin, as resulting from excessive kava drinking; to scale thus. (PCP *ma(f,s)unga*.) **2.** n. Fine scented tapa dyed with *noni* bark, made under strict taboo and reserved for chiefs; used for the best *pā'ū* (sarongs) on Hawai'i. (FS 253.) **3.** Var. of *māhune 2*. **4.** n. A variety of taro.

mā.hune. 1. vs. Poor, destitute. **2.** nvs. Small particle, speck; fine. **3.** vi. Barely, with difficulty.

mā.hune.hune. Redup. of *māhune 1-3*. *Pakele māhunehune mai ka make mai*, barely escaping from death.

mā.hu.wā. Var. spelling of *māhuā*.

mai. 1. Directional part., towards the speaker, this way. (Gram. 2.7, 7.2; *mai* + directional *la* is written *maila* and often pronounced *meila* but not sung that way.) Come, come here, welcome; say, give (used idiomatically without preverb particles). *Hele mai*, come (cf. *hele aku*, go). *He mai* (Kel. 19)! Come! Welcome!

Hāʻawi mai, give me. *Mai hoʻi kauwahi wai,* do give me a little water. *Mai e ʻai,* come and eat. (PPN *mai.*) **2.** prep. From. Also *mai . . . mai:* see ex., *māhunehune.* (Gram. 9.8.) *Mai Hilo mai ka lei,* the lei is from Hilo. *Mai ʻō ā ʻō,* from there to there; from one point to another, everywhere. *Mai iā Maui,* from Maui. *Mai hea mai ʻoe?* Where did you come from? (PPN *m(a,e)i.*) **3.** Imminence-marking part. Almost, nearly, as though. (Gram. 5.4.) *Mai hoʻokuʻi ʻia au e ke kaʻa,* I was almost hit by the car. *Mai ʻike ʻole ʻia nō,* [he] was hardly seen at all (said sarcastically of a show-off). (PPN *mei.*) **4.** Preverb part. of negative command. Don't. (Gram. 5.4.) *Mai ʻai ʻoe,* don't eat.

mā.ī. nvt. To chew fine, soften, masticate; laceration in childbirth.

maʻi. nvs. **1.** Sickness, illness, disease, ailment, patient, sick person; sick, ill, menstruating. *Maʻi make,* fatal or terminal disease or sickness. *Maʻi na loko,* inside sickness [caused by family troubles]. *Maʻi na waho mai,* sickness from outside [caused by sorcery]. **hoʻo.maʻi.** To cause or feign sickness. (PNP *maki.*) **2.** Genitals, genital, genital chant. *Mele maʻi,* song in honor of genitals, as of a chief, as composed on his or her birth, rarely if ever composed for adults; usually gay and fast. See *ēhā. Maʻi* were commonly named, as *Hālala,* overly large, for Ka-lā-kaua, and *ʻAnapau,* frisky, for Liliʻu-o-ka-lani. *He maʻi no ka lani,* a genital song in honor of the royal chief. **3.** n. Tenon. Also *komo, ule.*

maiʻa. n. All kinds of bananas and plantains (for banana cultivation, see Kam. 76:37–9). Originally the banana was introduced by the Hawaiians, and native varieties were developed, some of which are still used. When the white man came, about 70 different kinds were known; today, only about half that number. These are mainly varieties of *Musa xparadisiaca,* especially the varieties *sapientum* and *normalis.* Some kinds are eaten raw, others cooked. (Neal 245–51.) Bananas were taboo to women except certain ones, as *maiʻa iho lena* and *maiʻa pōpō ʻula,* with yellow flesh. Bananas are not mentioned in songs because of unfavorable connotations: see *līlā, ʻolohaka.* It was considered bad luck to dream of bananas, to meet a man carrying bananas, or to take them in fishing canoes. *Pala ka maiʻa,* the bananas are ripe [a rude expression]. *Hoʻohui ʻāina pala ka maiʻa,* annexation is ripe bananas [no good for us]. (PEP *m(a,e)ika.*)

maiʻa ʻaʻao. n. Tall, wild bananas.

maiʻa aʻe.a.ʻe. Same as *maiʻa koaʻe. Lit.,* prematurely gray banana.

maʻi ʻaʻai. n. A spreading sore; cancer, infection.

maiʻa akua. n. Maui name for *maiʻa Polapola. Lit.,* god banana. (HP 177.)

maiʻa ʻano.ʻano. n. A variety of banana with seeds. *Lit.,* seeded banana.

maiʻa ʻau lena. n. An ancient variety of banana. *Lit.,* yellow-stem banana.

maiʻa ʻeka. n. A Hawaiian variety of banana; fruit with skin changing from red to green to yellow, edible when cooked. (HP 173.) *Lit.,* discolored banana.

maiʻa ʻeke ʻula. n. An ancient Hawaiian variety of banana.

maia ʻele.ʻele. n. A Hawaiian variety of mountain banana with black trunk, the skin of which is used to make designs in mats. The fruit has orange flesh, which is edible when cooked. Also *maiʻa hinu puaʻa, maiʻa poni, maiʻa Puna.* (HP 173.) *Lit.,* black banana.

maiʻa haʻa, maiʻa haʻa.haʻa. n. A Hawaiian variety of banana, with short trunk and leaves, but taller than *maiʻa Pākē.* The fruit is yellow, edible raw or cooked. (HP 175.) *Lit.,* low banana.

maiʻa hai.kea. n. A Hawaiian variety of banana that bears yellow fruit, edible raw or cooked. (HP 175.) *Lit.,* pale banana.

maiʻa hā.kea. Same as *maiʻa ʻohe.* (HP 177.) *Lit.,* whitish banana.

maiʻa hā.pai. n. A Hawaiian variety of banana of medium height, the fruit maturing within the trunk. The fruits are small, ten or fewer in a bunch, yellow, sweet, edible raw. (HP 175; Neal 250.) Also *maiʻa hua waena.*

maiʻa hē.ʻī. Same as *maiʻa Polapola.* (Neal 250–1.) *Fēʻī* is the Tahitian name.

maiʻa hila.hila. Same as *maiʻa iho lena.* (HP 175.) *Lit.,* bashful banana.

maiʻa hinu puaʻa. Same as *maiʻa ʻeleʻele.* (HP 173.) *Lit.,* hog's-grease banana.

maiʻa hua lua. Same as *maiʻa māhoe.* (HP 176.) *Lit.,* bearing two bunches, twin banana.

maiʻa hua moa. Same as *maiʻa moa.* (HP 176.) *Lit.,* egg banana.

maiʻa hua nui. n. A variety of banana. *Lit.,* big-fruited banana.

maiʻa hua waena. Same as *maiʻa hāpai.* (HP 175.) *Lit.,* central fruit banana.

maʻi ahu.lau. n. Epidemic, pestilence.

maʻi-ʻai-ake. n. Tuberculosis. *Lit.,* lung-eating sickness.

maiʻa iho lena. n. A Hawaiian variety of banana, popular and common. The trunk is green, purple, and pink. Fruits are salmon-pink, edible raw or cooked; one of the few bananas formerly permitted to women. Also *maiʻa hilahila.* (HP 175.) *Lit.,* yellow-cored banana.

maiʻa ʻū. n. A Hawaiian variety of banana, growing wild on Kauaʻi and Hawaiʻi, rarely cultivated. The fruit is yellow, edible only when cooked. (HP 175.) *Lit.,* snub-nosed banana.

maiʻa ʻili paka.paka. n. A kind of rough-skinned banana.

maiʻa kahiki. n. A variety of banana growing wild on Maui, rarely cultivated. The trunk is tall; the fruit long, skin yellow, flesh white and edible only when cooked. (HP 175.) *Lit.,* foreign or Tahitian banana.

maiʻa kahiki hae. n. A Hawaiian variety of banana, similar to *maiʻa kahiki,* but having a short trunk. (HP 175.)

maiʻa kahiki mā.lei. Same as *maiʻa mālei.* (HP 176.)

maiʻa kahiki mauki. n. A Hawaiian variety of banana with tall, green trunk. The fruit looks like *maiʻa kahiki.* (HP 175.)

maiʻa kahiki puhi. Same as *maiʻa puhi.* (HP 177.)

maiʻa kaʻio. Same as *maiʻa-pōpō-ʻulu.* (HP 177.)

maiʻa Kāne. n. An Oʻahu name for *maiʻa Polapola.* (HP 177.)

maiʻa kā.pua. Same as *maiʻa-pōpō-ʻulu-puapua-nui.* (HP 177.)

maiʻa-ka-ua-lau. n. A Hawaiian variety of banana. Fruit like that of *maiʻa maoli,* except that the young, dark-green fruit has light-green spots like raindrops; when ripe, yellow, waxy, with flesh light-yellow, good only when baked. (HP 175.) *Lit.,* many rain drops banana.

maiʻa Kau.pō. Same as *maiʻa wai mūhea.* (HP 177.)

maiʻa koaʻe. n. A Hawaiian variety of banana, beautifully striped leaves, trunk, and young fruit. Fruit is yellow and round; flesh yellow, edible cooked or raw. Also called *maiʻa aʻeaʻe, maiʻa manini.* (HP 177.) *Lit.,* tropic bird banana.

maiʻa koana. n. A Hawaiian seed-producing variety of banana. Also *ʻōpule.*

Maia.kū. n. Stars in the belt of Orion.

maiʻa lahi. n. An ancient Hawaiian variety of banana. *Lit.,* delicate banana.

maiʻa lele. n. A common wild Hawaiian variety of banana of the uplands; trunk tall, yellowish-green; fruit yellow; flesh pink, edible raw or cooked, good for *pie-piele,* eczema. Root of shoot used in medicine. The fruit was commonly offered to gods, the tree planted to shelter the altar. It was planted far from a dwelling house, for fear it would cause the occupants to *lele* (fly) elsewhere. (HP 176.) *Lit.,* altar banana.

maʻi aliʻi. n. Royal disease, leprosy (so-called because the first leper was said to have been a chief).

maiʻa liko. Same as *maiʻa Polapola.* (HP 177.) *Lit.,* bud banana.

maia.lile. vs. Quiet, calm, still. Same as *mālie. Rare.*

maiʻa loha. n. An ancient Hawaiian variety of banana; trunk and leaf like *maiʻa lele,* fruit like *maiʻa iho lena.* (HP 177.) *Lit.,* droopy banana.

maiʻa mā.hoe. n. A Hawaiian variety of banana, the stem bearing two bunches; fruit small, yellow, flesh light salmon and very palatable. Also *maiʻa hua lua, maiʻa mana lua, maiʻa pā lua.* (HP 176.) *Lit.,* twin banana.

maiʻa mā.lai ʻula. Same as *maiʻa mālei ʻula.* (HP 176.)

maiʻa mā.lei. n. A Hawaiian variety of banana; trunk green and pink, streaked with brown; fruit like *maiʻa puhi.* Also *maiʻa kahiki mālei.* (HP 176.)

maiʻa mā.lei ʻula. n. A Hawaiian variety of banana, common both cultivated and wild in the uplands. Fibers of the stalk are used for stringing flowers for leis with a coconut-leaf needle *(mānai).* Ripening fruit changes from maroon *(ʻula)* to green to yellow; the flesh is orange, edible only when cooked. Also *maiʻa mālai ʻula, maiʻa mānei ʻula, maiʻa mānai ʻula.* (HP 176.)

maiʻa mā.nai ʻula. Same as *maiʻa mālei ʻula.* (HP 176.)

maiʻa mana lua. Same as *maiʻa māhoe.* (HP 176.) *Lit.,* two-branched banana.

maiʻa manini. Same as *maiʻa koaʻe.* (HP 176.) *Lit.,* manini *(fish)* banana.

maiʻa maoli. n. A Hawaiian variety of banana, growing in uplands and lowlands. It has a green trunk, large leaves. The fruit is long, waxy-yellow, and has yellow flesh, edible raw or cooked. (HP 176.) *Lit.,* indigenous banana.

maiʻa moa. n. A Hawaiian variety of banana with a tall, yellowish-green trunk. The fruit is large, somewhat egg-shaped, and yellow; the flesh yellow, edible raw or cooked. Also *maiʻa hua moa.* (HP 176.) *Lit.,* chicken banana.

maiʻa noʻu. n. A Hawaiian variety of banana, usually cultivated; the trunk green, with pink and brown markings; fruit short, thick, yellow, the flesh cream-colored, edible raw or cooked. (HP 177.) *Lit.,* short banana or big-mouthful banana.

maiʻa Nuhō.lani. n. A variety of introduced banana cultivated by Hawaiians for many generations. The trunk is tall, green; the fruit yellow, edible raw or cooked. (HP 178.) *Lit.,* New Holland (Australian) banana.

Mai.ao. n. Name of a star used in navigation.

mai.ʻao. n. Nail of finger or toe; hoof of an animal; claw of a bird.

maiʻa ʻoa. n. Probably a distinct species of Hawaiian banana, according to W. T. Pope, being unique in producing fertile seeds. Trunk and leaves dull-green, tinted with bronze and purple; fruit inedible. (HP 177.) Also *hao, ʻoa, poni.*

maiʻa ʻohe. n. An ancient Hawaiian variety of banana. Also *maiʻa hākea.* (HP 177.) *Lit.,* bamboo banana.

maiʻa ʻō.pule. See *ʻōpule 3.*

maiʻa Pā.kē. n. Chinese banana *(Musa xnana,* syn. *M. cavendishii),* a stocky tree to more than 2 m high, a native of southern China, brought in 1855 to Hawaiʻi from Tahiti. (Neal 247–8.)

maiʻa pā.lua. Same as *maiʻa māhoe.* (HP 176.) *Lit.,* banana in pairs.

maia.pilo. n. A low, smooth shrub *(Capparis sandwichiana)* with vinelike branches, a member of the caper family, growing on some beaches and lava flows; leaves rounded-oblong; flowers white, pea-shaped, 5 cm long, with four petals surrounding a mass of long white stamens, open and fragrant only at night. (Neal 368–9.) Also *pilo, pua pilo.*

maiʻa Pola.pola. n. A species of banana *(Musa troglodytarum,* syn. *M. fehi)* recently introduced to Hawaiʻi, known in the South Pacific from Mangareva west to the Moluccas. It has a tall, black trunk and upright fruiting stalk bearing large fruits with reddish-orange skin, yellow flesh, edible when cooked, sometimes made into *poi maiʻa.* (HP 177.) Also *akua, maiʻa hēʻī, maiʻa akua, maiʻa Kāne, maiʻa liko. Lit.,* Borabora [i.e., Tahitian] banana. (Neal 250.)

maiʻa pō lua. An ancient Hawaiian variety of banana. (HP 177.)

maiʻa poni. Same as *maiʻa ʻeleʻele.* (HP 175.) *Lit.,* purple banana.

maiʻa pō.pō ʻulu. n. A Hawaiian variety of banana, with short, green trunk; one of two varieties not taboo to women in old times; the root of young plants used medicinally. Fruit is rounded and yellow, the flesh salmon-pink, edible raw but preferred baked. (HP. 177.) *Lit.,* breadfruit ball-like banana. Also *maiʻa kaʻio, pōpō ʻulu.*

maiʻa-pō.pō-ʻulu-ʻili-lahi. Same as *maiʻa-pōpō-ʻulu-lahi.* (HP 177.) *Lit.,* thin-skinned *pōpō ʻulu.*

maiʻa-pō.pō-ʻulu-pua.pua-nui. n. A Hawaiian variety of banana, resembling *maiʻa iho lena,* but the fruit broad-tipped. Also *maiʻa kāpua.* (HP 177.) *Lit.,* big-tailed *pōpō ʻulu* banana.

maiʻa pua.pua nui. n. A Hawaiian variety of banana. (HP 178.) *Lit.,* big-tailed banana.

maiʻa puhi. n. An ancient Hawaiian variety of banana with green and brown trunk. The fruit is twisted when young; when ripe long, thick, yellow, the flesh yellow and edible only when cooked. Also *maiʻa kahiki puhi.* (HP 177.)

maiʻa Puna. New name for *maiʻa ʻeleʻele. Lit.,* Puna banana.

mai.au. vs. Neat and careful in work; skillful, ingenious, expert; correct, careful, as in speech; thorough, meticulous, tidy, dainty. See ex., *pololei 2.*

maʻi ʻau.makua. n. Sickness caused by *ʻaumakua* as punishment for wrong doing, as eating the *ʻaumakua* animal form, or *kapu* plant or fish, or wearing forbidden clothing. (Kam. 64:95.)

maʻi.ʻawa. nvs. Sterile; sterility. *Lit.,* sour genitalia.

Maʻi-ʻawa. n. Same as *Ka-maʻi-ʻawa.*

maiʻa wai mū.hea. An ancient variety of Hawaiian banana. Also *maiʻa Kaupō.* (HP 177.) *Lit.,* insipid water banana.

mai.ele. 1. Same as *pūkiawe,* shrubs. **2.** nvs. Eloquence, skill in speech; eloquent; skilled in asking questions to puzzle and confuse. *Rare.*

maʻi ʻele.pani. n. Elephantiasis. *Lit.,* elephant *(Eng.)* sickness.

mai.ewa. 1. Same as *māewa.* **2.** n. Deep-sea fishing net. Also *maiʻolewalewa. Rare.*

maʻiha. vs. Energetic, persevering. *Rare.*

mā.ʻiha.ʻiha. Redup. of *maʻiha.*

maʻihe. Same as *ʻihaʻiha, puʻu mimi.*

maʻi Hepela (Hebera). n. Smallpox. *Lit.,* Hebrew disease.

mā.ihi. vt. To peel; strip, as bark. Cf. *ihi. Māihi ʻili,* to peel off the skin; *fig.,* to strip a person of all he has. *Māihi ola,* to escape by the skin of one's teeth; to barely escape; *lit.,* to scrape life. (PPN *maisi.*)

maʻihi. n. Dwarf.

maʻi hilo. n. Venereal disease, gonorrhea. *Lit.,* braiding disease.

maʻi hohola. n. Heart failure. *Rare.*

mai.hoʻi.kau. Intensifier of *hoʻikau* (usually written as three words).

maʻi.hole. n. A small holothurian. *Lit.,* pulled-back foreskin.

maʻi holu. Same as *ʻaʻawa,* a fish. *Rare.*

maʻi hoʻo.kaʻa.wale. n. Leprosy. *Lit.,* separation disease.

maʻi.hua. n. A variety of taro.

maʻi.huʻi keʻo.keʻo. n. A variety of sweet potato.

maʻi.huʻi ʻula.ʻula. n. A variety of sweet potato.

maʻi huki. n. Convulsion; fit. *Lit.,* pulling disease.

mai.huli. n. Presents made at the birth of a child. *Rare.*

mā.ʻiʻi. 1. Short for *māʻiʻiʻi.* **2.** vi. To sprout; to begin to open, as flower petals.

mā.'Ī.'Ī. n. Fatigue and backache. *Rare.*
mā.'i'i'i. n. **1.** A surgeonfish *(Acanthurus nigrofuscus).* **2.** A variety of taro.
mā.'Ī.'Ī.'Ī. Redup. of *mā'Ī'Ī. Rare.*
ma'i 'ino. n. Sinful disease, especially venereal disease.
maika. 1. n. Ancient Hawaiian game suggesting bowling; the stone used in the game; shot, shot-put. Cf. *'ulu maika.* **2.** n. Strengthening the body, as by athletics. Cf. *ika,* strong. **3.** vs. Tired, weary, lame. *Rare.* Cf. *mā'Ī'Ī, mālo'elo'e, mā'ulu'ulu.* **4.** vs. Tasteless, insipid. *Rare.*
mai.ka'i. nvs. Good, fine, all right, well; good-looking; handsome, beautiful; goodness, righteousness, benefit, well-being, morality; good looks, good health. See Gram. 2.7. *Pehea 'oe? Maika'i nō.* How are you? Fine. *He wahine maika'i loa ke nānā aku,* a woman very good to look at. *He maika'i 'ōlelo,* goodness in speech [with implication that actions are *not* good]. *E 'ai ā pau maika'i ka i'a,* eat until the fish is completely finished. **ho'o.mai.ka'i.** To thank, bless, render thanks, congratulate, make acceptable, praise, improve, perfect, correct; grateful, gratified, thankful. See *inu ho'omaika'i, palapala ho'omaika'i, pule ho'o maika'i. Ho'omaika'i!* Congratulations. *'Ōlelo ho'o-maika'i,* compliment, congratulations. *Ho'omaika'i 'ana,* congratulations, improvement. *Lā Ho'omaika'i,* Thanksgiving Day. *Mele ho'omaika'i,* song of praise; Doxology. *'O wau nō me ka ho'omaika'i,* I am very gratefully yours [in conclusion of a letter]. (PPN *ma'itaki.*)
mā.ikaika. Redup. of *maika 2.* Same as *ho'oikaika* but less common: to strengthen, etc. **ho'o.mā.ikaika.** Caus/sim.
ma'i kāne. n. Male sexual part. Cf. *ule 2.*
ma'i kau. n. Chronic or recurring disease or sickness. *Lit.,* placing sickness.
mā.'ike. vs. To know. *Rare.* **ho'o.mā.'ike.** To show.
mā.'ike.'ike. Redup. of *mā'ike.* **ho'o.mā.'ike.'ike.** To show, reveal, make known or comprehensible. *He ho'omā'ike'ike mai ka pō mai,* a revelation from the night [as in a dream]. *Mea ho'omā'ike'ike,* displayed object, curio.
ma'i keiki. n. Pregnancy sickness; child's disease. Cf. *ma'i o kamali'i,* children's disease.
mā.iki. 1. vs. Little, small, wee. **2.** n. An ancient type of tapa (no data).
ma'i kia'i kino. n. Illness due to natural causes rather than to sorcery or gods. (Kam. 64:96.) *Lit.,* disease guarding body.
ma'i kipa. n. Disease caused by an evil spirit. *Lit.,* visiting sickness.
maiko. n. A surgeonfish *(Acanthurus nigroris).* (PNP *ma'ito.*)
mā.iko.iko. n. **1.** A common variety of sugar cane relished for chewing, named for *maiko,* a fish; stems blackish; leaves light yellow-green tinged with red; pith dark-brown; seldom flowery. Also *'ele'ele, kō 'ele'ele, kauila, nika.* (HP 223, 224.) **2.** Same as *maiko.*
mā.iko.iko kaha.kaha. n. A variety of sugar cane, a buff-brown and striped maroon when young, becoming olive brown and very deep purple on exposure. Readily mutates to *māikoiko.* (HP 223.)
Mai.kone.kia, Maikonikia. nvs. Micronesia; Micronesian. *Eng.*
ma'i kukule. See *kukule.*
ma'i kumu.pa'a. See *kumupa'a.*
ma'i kuni. n. Typhus, fever. *Lit.,* searing disease.
maila. The directional *mai* plus *lā,* there, then. See Gram. 2.7, 7.2. *Hele maila ke ali'i,* the chief then came.
mā.'ila. 1. n. Light-brown skin, as of some part-Hawaiians. (Kep. 67.) **2.** vs. Clear, as the sea on a sunny day when the depths can be seen.
ma'i laha. n. Contagious or infectious disease.
mai laila. From there, thence, whence.
mai.lani. vt. To extol, praise, treat as a chief or great

favorite, indulge, spoil, favor. Also *pailani.* **ho'o.mai.lani.** Caus/sim. (FS 137.)
maile. n. **1.** A native twining shrub, *Alyxia olivaeformis.* St. John, 1975a, described four forms of *maile* based on leaf size and shape. They are believed to be sisters with human and plant forms and are listed below. They were considered minor goddesses of the hula. *Maile kaluhea* is also believed by some to be a sister. See *moekahi, māpu, palai 1,* and chants, *līhau* and *'ū 1.* The *maile* vine has shiny fragrant leaves and is used for decorations and leis, especially on important occasions. It is a member of the periwinkle family. Laka, goddess of the hula, was invoked as the goddess of the *maile,* which was one of five standard plants used in her altar. (Neal 690–1.) (PPN *maile.*) **2.** *Maile* sticks attached to the end of the *'auku'u* (pole) used for catching birds [the *maile* was gummed with lime, and birds perching on it were caught]; name of a snare used in catching plovers around the leg; rod or wand used in the games of *pūhenehene* and *'ume;* piece securing an ox's neck to the yoke.
maile ha'i wale. n. A variety of *maile (f. myrtillifolia) with small, rounded leaves. Lit.,* brittle *maile.* (St. John, 1975a: see *maile 1.*)
maile haole. n. The myrtle *(Myrtus communis),* an aromatic shrub from the Mediterranean region and western Asia, a favorite garden plant in many countries, and formerly used in Rome for wreaths to crown the victor. The leaves look like those of *maile* and formerly were used by Hawaiian for leis like *maile,* the bark being stripped from the stems in the same way, with teeth holding one end. (Neal 631.)
maile hohono. n. A tropical American annual composite *(Ageratum conyzoides* and *A. houstonianum),* both a weed and an ornamental. It is a hairy, branching, weak-stemmed herb, with light-blue (rarely white or pink) florets borne in small tufted heads. (Neal 830–1.) Also *maile honohono* and *maile kula.*
maile hono.hono. Same as *maile hohono.*
maile kā kahiki. Same as *maile pilau. Lit.,* foreign vine *maile.*
maile kalu.hea. n. A variety of *maile. Lit.,* sweet-smelling *maile.* See *maile 1.*
maile kū.honua. n. A *maile* seedling about 8 cm or less high, with two or three leaves.
maile kula. Same as *maile hohono.*
maile lau li'i. n. A variety of *maile* (f. *angusta),* with narrow pointed leaves. *Lit.,* small-leaved *maile.* (St. John, 1975a: see *maile 1.*)
maile lau nui. n. A variety of *maile* (f. *sulcata),* with large leaves. *Lit.,* big-leaved *maile.* (St. John, 1975a: see *maile 1.*)
ma'i lele. n. Contagious or infectious disease. *Lit.,* jumping disease.
ma'i lena. n. Jaundice. *Lit.,* yellow disease.
maile pā.kaha. n. A variety of *maile* (f. *rotundata),* with blunt ovate leaves. (St. John, 1975a: see *maile 1.*)
maile pilau. n. Stink vine *(Paederia foetida). Lit.,* stinking *maile.*
mā.'ili. 1. nvs. Pebble or stone, as used for making sinkers for squid fishing; pebbly, full of pebbles. Cf. *'ili,* pebble. **2.** n. Small arrowroot *(pia)* tubers, so called because they grow well in stones. **3.** n. Small taro, as found growing in weeds.
mā.'ili.hau. n. Cord made of inner *hau* bark. *Rare.*
mā.'ili.'ili. Redup. of *mā'ili.*
mā.ilo. nvs. Wasting away of the body; thin, emaciated, as with tuberculosis. **ho'o.mā.ilo.** To cause thinness. *He mea 'ino, ho'omāilo kino ka 'opiuma,* opium is a bad thing that causes the body to waste away.
ma'i lō.lō. n. Paralysis.
mā.'ilu. nvs. A trifle, pittance; insignificant.
mā.'ilu.'ilu. Redup. of *mā'ilu. He mā'ilu'ilu kona wahi uku,* his wage is a mere pittance.
mai . . . mai. See *mai 2.*

ma'i.ma'i. Redup. of *ma'i*, sick; chronically sick, ailing, sickly. **ho'o.ma'i.ma'i.** To pretend to be sickly.

maina. Same as *mine*.

maina ho'o.pahu. n. Explosive mine.

mai.naina. n. Anger, wrath. Cf. *inaina.* **ho'o.mai.- naina.** To cause anger; to anger.

maine. n. Mine. *Eng. Maine 'eli gula*, gold mine.

mā.ino. nvs. Cruelty, misery, harm; cruel, miserable, hurt. (Cf. *'ino* and note lack of glottal stop here.) **ho'o.mā.ino.** To treat cruelly, abuse, persecute; to cause misery and suffering. (PPN *'ingo.*)

ma'ino. Same as *mā'ino'ino.*

mā.ino.ino. Redup. of *māino. Hana māinoino i nā holoholona*, cruelty to animals. **ho'o.mā.ino.ino.** Caus/sim.; to torture; atrocity.

mā.'ino.'ino. vi. To deface, mar, spoil, ruin; defamed, defaced. *Mā'ino'ino ka helehelena i ka ma'i lēpela*, the face is disfigured by leprosy. **ho'o.mā.'ino.'ino.** To defame, slander, deface.

mā.io. vs. Furrowed, grooved, cut in ridges; very thin, wasted. Cf. *ioio*, groove, and *māilo*. **ho'o.mā.io.** To furrow, cut in ridges, cause thinness.

mā.i'o. Rare var. of *māilo*, thin.

mā.'i'o. 1. vt. To cut raggedly and unevenly, as cloth or hair; dented; chipped, as crockery. Cf. *'upena mā'i'o.* **ho'o.mā.'i'o.** Caus/sim. **2.** *(Cap.)* n. Name of a star. **3.** n. A variety of sweet potato. **4.** n. A variety of taro.

ma'i 'oā, ma'i 'owā. n. Slit genital, an insulting epithet for women.

mā.io.io. Redup. of *māio.*

mā.'io.'io. vi. To peep, chirp, as chickens. Cf. *'io'io.*

mā.'i.'i'o. Redup. of *mā'i'o.*

ma'i 'ō.ku'u. See *'ōku'u.*

Ma'i-ola. n. A god of healing. (Malo 82.)

ma'i ola. nv. To cure sickness; curable disease.

ma'i 'owā. See *ma'i 'oā.*

ma'i Pā.kē. n. Leprosy. *Lit.*, Chinese disease.

mai-poina-ia'u. n. Forget-me-not.

ma'i pū.hā. n. Ulcer, running sore.

ma'i pu'u.pu'u li'i.li'i. n. Smallpox. *Lit.*, disease with many little pimples.

ma'i pu'u.wai. n. Heart disease, heart attack.

ma'i 'uhola. n. Heart failure. *Rare.*

mā.'iu.'iu. vi. At a distance, out of sight. Cf. *'iu'iu.* **ho'o.mā.'iu.'iu.** To keep at a distance, avoid.

ma'i 'ula. n. Measles. *Lit.*, red sickness.

māi.'u'u. n. Toe- or fingernail, hoof, claw. See ex., *wawa'u.* (PNP *maikuku*.)

ma'i wahine. n. Female sexual part. Cf. *'auwae 2.*

ma'i wili. n. Incessant or recurring pain; venereal disease. *Lit.*, writhing sickness.

maka. 1. n. Eye, eye of a needle, face, countenance; presence, sight, view; lens of a camera. For idioms cf. *'ōnohi, pulakaumaka*, and the following. *Maka pōniuniu pōloli*, eyes faint with hunger. *Nānā maka*, to look, but not help. *Ho'okēamaka*, to be partial, show favoritism. *'Oi ka'aka'a ka maka*, while the eyes are open [and there is still life]. *'Ike maka*, to see for oneself. *Hō'ike ā maka*, to reveal in the light, as of something long hidden. *Ku'i ka hekili i ka maka o ka 'ōpua*, the thunder claps in the presence of the cloud bank. *Puka nā maka i ke ao*, the eyes appear in the light [said of birth]. *'A'ole e moe ku'u maka ā kō ku'u makemake*, my eyes won't sleep until my wish is accomplished [said with determination]. *'O nā maka wale nō kēia i hele mai nei*, only the eyes have come [said by one not bringing a gift, as was customary]. *Mōhala nā maka*, the eyes are open [a frank countenance]. (PPN *mata*.) **2.** n. Beloved one, favorite; person. Cf. *makamaka* (very common), *makana, pula, 'ōnohi.* The pig god was affectionately called *ku'u maka* (FS 199) by his grandmother, rather like "apple of my eye." *Kau ka maka*, to desire, to long to see, to think of fondly. *He kau maka 'oia na kona hoaloha*, he is the object of his friend's affection and respect. *Ka-lei-kau-maka*

(name), the beloved child. **3.** n. Point, bud, protuberance; center of a flower, including usually both the stamens and pistils; nipple, teat; sharp edge or blade of an instrument; point of a fishhook; beginning, commencement; source; any new plant shoot coming up. *Fig.*, descendant. *Ke 'au mahope a ka maka* (Lunk. 3.22), the haft after the blade. *Nā maka o Hā-loa i luna* (FS 39), descendants of Hā-loa above. *Maka mua o ka huaka'i* (FS 137), beginning of the procession. *Maka o ka makani*, beginning or origin of the wind. *'Ō maka kolu*, three-pronged spear. **ho'o.maka.** To begin, start, initiate; commence; to appear, of a child's first tooth; to put forth buds; to come to a head, as a boil. *Mea ho'omaka*, beginner. (PPN *mata*.) **4.** n. Mesh of a net, mesh in plaiting; stitch, in sewing. Cf. *maka 'aha, maka'opihi 2.* (PPN *mata*.) **5.** vs. Raw, as fish; uncooked; green, unripe, as fruit; fresh as distinct from salted provisions; wet, as sand. Cf. *kāmakamaka.* (PPN *mata*.) **6.** Probably same as *manu*, canoe bow and stern pieces. **7.** n. A seaweed. See *alani* and below. **8.** n. Varieties of sweet potato. See *maka kila, maka koali, maka nui.* **9.** n. Recognition token. (For. 5:171.)

māka. nvt. Mark, marker, blaze, target; to mark. *Eng. Ho'okīkī māka*, target shooting. *E māka mai 'oe ma'ane'i*, make a mark here.

mā.kā. n. A kind of stone (perhaps pronounced *māka*).

mā.ka'a. 1. nvs. Clear and open, as a view; a clearing. **2.** n. A faint green striped mutant of the sweet potato. (HP 221.)

maka.'ā. n. **1.** A fish *(Malacanthus hoedtii).* *Maka'ā hōlapu kāheka*, the *maka'ā* roils the pool [of a mischievous child]. **2.** A variety of sugar cane.

maka 'ā. n. Wide, staring eyes. *Lit.*, glowing eye.

maka.'a'ā. Redup. of *maka 'ā.*

maka.'ahə. n. **1.** Hammock, swinging netted bed. **2.** Skin eruption, itch.

maka 'aha. n. Sennit mesh; fairly fine mesh. *Uwea maka 'aha*, chicken-wire fence.

maka 'ā.hewa. nvs. Walleyed; cross-eyed. *Lit.*, eyes that err. Cf. *maka lalau.*

maka 'ai.au. nvt. Envious eye; to eye with envy.

maka.'āi.nana. n. Commoner, populace, people in general; citizen, subject. Cf. *lunamaka'āinana. Lit.*, people that attend the land. (PNP *matakainanga*.)

mā.ka'a.ka'a. Redup. of *māka'a.*

maka.'ā.kiu. Same as *makākiu.*

maka ala. n. Faint path or trail; beginning of a path.

maka.'ala. nvt. Alert, vigilant, watchful, wide awake; to attend to vigilantly. *Maka'ala i ka 'a'ahu o kāna kāne*, she tends carefully to her husband's clothes. *E maka'ala mai i ka hana!* Tend to the job!

maka.'alā. vs. Blind, but with eyes that look normal.

maka.'ā.loa. n. A small reddish crab *(Macrophthalmus telescopicus)* found on mud flats. *Lit.*, long, bright eyes. Also *'āloa.*

maka 'alo.'alo. nvs. Shifty-eyed. *Lit.*, dodging eye.

Maka-'ā.lohi.lohi. n. Name of a star. *Lit.*, bright eye.

maka.'ā.lua. Same as *makālua.*

Maka-'amo.'amo. n. Name of a star or constellation in the Milky Way. *Lit.*, twinkling eye.

maka.ani.ani. n. Eyeglasses, spectacles. *Lit.*, crystal eye. Cf. *'ūmi'i.*

maka.'aoa. Same as *'aoa*, a shellfish.

maka.au, makāu. nvi. To look around; a roving eye.

maka.'au. Var. of *makaau.*

-maka'au'a. ho'o.maka.'au'a. To hang moist, as undried tapa, over a line or drying rack *(haka)*, so that the edges will correspond and that a fixed crease will form.

maka.'ā.wela. n. Kind of soft, porous stone.

maka.'ē. vt. To look at with disfavor; to look askance. *Ua maka'ē aku au iā'oe*, I am against you. **ho'o.maka.'ē.** Caus/sim. *Ua ho'omaka'ē ka Haku i ka po'e hana hewa* (1 Pet. 3.12), the face of the Lord is against evildoers.

maka.'ele.'ele. vs. Chilled, frozen. *Fig.*, benumbing, intense, as emotion; exhausting, wearisome, of labor. *Rare.*

makā.'eo. vs. Angry-appearing (probably a contraction of *maka ke'eo,* angry eyes). **ho'o.makā.'eo.** To look at with anger, to avoid looking at because of anger; not to recognize because of anger.

maka 'eu. n. Mischievous or roving eyes, naughty eyes.

maka 'ewa.'ewa. See *'ewa'ewa 1.*

makaha. 1. Inflamed or swollen eye. (And.) **2.** Pig disease. (And.)

mā.kaha. 1. vt. Fierce, savage, ferocious; to seize property, to desolate, plunder, cheat. See *kaha 4. Ka'ū mākaha,* fierce Ka'ū [a description of the Ka'ū people, referring to their killing of several oppressive chiefs]. **2.** *(Cap.)* n. Name of a star; this star and Mākohi-lani were near the Pleiades, and were said to be patrons of fighters. **3.** Same as *mākahakaha.* **4.** vt. To speak disparagingly or insultingly of. *'O Hawai'i nō kēia i mākaha 'ia ai he palu lā'ī,* the people of [the island of] Hawai'i are spoken of derisively as lickers of ti leaves [so called because they were said to have done this at a feast in the time of Ka-mehameha where not enough food was provided].

mā.kā.hā. n. Sluice gate, as of a fish pond; entrance to or egress from an enclosure.

maka.hahi. Same as *makahehi. Ua haka mai lākou ia'u me ka makahahi* (Hal. 22.17), they stared at me with wonder.

maka.hai. vs. Hasty; active, as a child into everything.

Maka-hai-aku. Name of a star.

Maka-hai-wa'a. n. Name of a star. *Lit.,* eye following canoe.

mā.kaha.kaha. nvi. Clearing, as rain. **ho'o.mā.kaha.-kaha.** To show signs of clearing. *Ke ho'omākahakaha maila ka ua,* there are signs that the rain is clearing.

maka haka.haka. n. Sunken eyes, as of one long sick; deep pit or hollow; open space, as a clearing in a forest or clear space in a lava flow.

Mā.kaha Kona. n. Star name (no data). (Kuhelani.)

mā.kā.hala. n. Three shrubs in the tomato family: (1) wild tobacco or *paka (Nicotiana glauca),* from South America, with long, narrow, yellow flowers and ovate, blue-green leaves; (2) day cestrum *(Cestrum diurnum),* from the West Indies, with small, white, tubular flowers, fragrant by day; oval leaves; black berries; (3) orange cestrum *(Cestrum aurantiacum),* from Guatemala, with longer, narrow, orange flowers. (Neal 750–1.) On Ni'ihau, *Tecomaria capensis,* cape honeysuckle; cf. *'i'iwi haole.*

mā.kā.hala 'ula. n. A shrub similar to *mākāhala (3),* orange cestrum, except that the flower is bronze-red.

maka.hā.lili. n. A marine shell *(Peasiella tantilla).*

maka.hani. vt. To step lightly, touch lightly, to skim lightly. Cf. *hani, māhani.*

maka.hau.'iole. Rare var. of *haumaka'iole.*

maka.hehi. nvt. Admiration, desire for, wonder; amazement; attractive, entrancing; to admire; be entangled. *Nani e makahehi 'ia ai,* beautiful and alluring. *Ua holomua 'oia, ā he 'oihana noho'i ia nāna i makahehi nui,* he advanced, an employment indeed in which he was much admired. **ho'o.maka.hehi.** Caus/sim.

maka.hekili. n. Hailstone. *Lit.,* thunder eye. Cf. *huahekili.*

maka helei. n. Eye with lid drawn down; ectropion. Cf. *helei. Eia ka pua'a wāwae loloa, ua maka helei,* here is a pig with long legs [a human sacrifice] with drawn eyes [fat cheeks, fat].

makahi. A kind of fish. (And.)

mā.kahi. 1. vs. One-eyed (short for *maka kahi).* See chant, *mākole 1.* **2.** n. Net mesh large enough to admit the entrance of one finger; a net with such a mesh. *Mākahi 'oā, mākahi 'oene, mākahi hoene,* a mesh larger than one finger's width, but not large enough for two fingers *(mālua).*

maka.hia. nvi. Roving, unsteady, restless eyes; sleepless.

Ē Lono makahia, lele (Kep. 37), O Lono with the restless eyes, fly.

maka hia.moe. nvi. Sleepy eyes; sleepy, drowsy.

maka.hiapo. n. First-born child, oldest child. *Lit.,* first-born person. (PCP *mata(f,s)iapo.*)

maka.hiki. 1. nvs. Year, age; annual, yearly (sometimes written *MH.*) See *kūlana. 'Ehia ou makahiki?* How old are you? *Hō'ike makahiki,* annual report. *Hō'ike no 'elua makahiki,* biennial report. *Kēlā ma kēia lua makahiki,* every two years, biennial. *I ka makahiki,* in the year; yearly. *Nui nā makahiki,* many years; old, aged. (PEP *mata(f,s)iti.*) **2.** n. Ancient festival beginning about the middle of October and lasting about four months, with sports and religious festivities and taboo on war; this is now replaced by Aloha Week.

Maka.hiki Hou. n. New Year. *Hau'oli Makahiki Hou,* Happy New Year.

maka.hiki lā keu. n. Leap year. *Lit.,* extra-day year.

maka.hiki lele 'oi. n. Leap year. *Lit.,* year jump ahead.

maka hila.hila. nvs. Bashful eyes; bashful, timidly averting one's gaze.

maka.hinu. n. Kind of hard stone.

maka hinu. n. Bright face, cheerful look. **ho'o.maka hinu.** Caus/sim.; to conceal annoyance or anger by pretense of cheerfulness.

maka hī.'ō. n. Eyes that dart in every direction, as if looking for mischief; a mischievously alluring look.

mā.kahi 'oā. See *mākahi.*

Maka-holo-wa'a. n. Name of a star, perhaps variant name for the North Star. *Lit.,* sailing-canoe eye.

maka hou. n. Beginning, new start. **ho'o.maka hou.** To begin again.

maka.hune. n. Fine mesh or weft, as of net or mat.

makai. See *kai,* ocean.

mā.kai. Rare var. of *mānai,* needle.

mā.ka'i. nvt. Policeman, guard; to police, inspect, spy. Cf. *luna māka'i. Ua mau kānaka lā nāna i māka'i i ka 'āina* (Ios. 6.22), the aforementioned men who had spied in the country. **ho'o.mā.ka'i.** To act as a policeman; to appoint or invest as a policeman. (Probably PPN *mata + -ki,* transitivizer; PCP *maataki.*)

makaia. A rare term defined in For. 5:165 as a swift runner; probably *makai'a.*

mā.kaia. nvi. Revenge, vengeance, treachery, betrayal, traitor, betrayer, turncoat; treacherous. (Laie 513.) *Kū ho'i kāu hana i ka mākaia,* you've behaved treacherously.

maka.i'a. n. **1.** Whitened pupil of a blind person's eye, cataract. *Lit.,* fish eye. **2.** A kind of stone, used for adzes and poi pounders. Also *māhikihiki.* **3.** See *makaia.*

makaia.uli. n. A limpet, *Cellana exarata;* flesh within *'opihi* shells. (KL line 27.) See *'opihi.*

maka ihe. n. Spear point.

mā.ka'i ho'o.malu. n. Probation officer.

mā.ka'i ho'o.malu pō. n. Patrolling night police. *Lit.,* police making night peaceful.

maka ihu. n. Bowsprit of a canoe; sharp point at the bow. *Lit.,* bow point.

maka.ihu.wa'a. n. Phosphorescent light seen in water at night.

Maka-ihu-wa'a. n. Star name.

mā.ka'i.ka'i. nvi. To visit, see the sights; to stroll, make a tour, take a walk; to look upon (Puk. 3.4); spectator. *Māka'ika'i hele,* to stroll here and there. *Po'e māka'i-ka'i,* visitors, sight-seers, tourists, spectators. *Māka'i-ka'i 'ia,* visited. **ho'o.mā.ka'i.ka'i.** To take others on a visit; to show the sights; to escort. (PCP *maatakitaki.*)

maka 'ike. vt. To see clearly and with keen powers of observation; to see more than most, especially to see supernatural things or ghosts not seen by others; to have the gift of second sight. *Lit.,* seeing eye. Cf. *'ike maka.*

maka iki. n. Eye smaller than the other. *Lit.,* small eye.

mā.ka'i ki'e.ki'e. n. High sheriff.

Maka-iki-o-Lea. n. Wind name, probably at Kaua'i. *Lit.*, small eye of Lea.

mā.ka'i.kiu. n. Detective. *Lit.*, spying police.

mā.ka'i koa. n. Military police. *Lit.*, soldier police.

mā.ka'i kū huina. n. Traffic policeman. *Lit.*, policeman stationed at corners.

maka ila. n. A senile pigmentation caused by sunburn of the eye, as found among Hawaiians; person with such an eye (such persons were said to be observant and critical). *Lit.*, birthmark eye.

maka.ili. n. Rocky patches where sweet potatoes or taro were cultivated (For. 6:165); soil consisting of coarse sand, cinders, or gravel. Cf. *'ili*, pebble.

maka.ilo. n. Young shoot, as for transplanting.

Maka.'imo.'imo. n. Name of a constellation in the Milky Way. *Lit.*, blinking eyes, twinkling eyes.

maka.'ina. nvs. Guard; watchful.

maka 'ino. vt. To look at with hatred; to lose affection for one; one who looks with hatred. *'O ke kanaka palupalu . . . e maka 'ino aku ia i kona hoahānau* (Kanl. 28.54), the man that is tender . . . his eye shall be evil toward his brother.

mā.ka'i nui. n. Sheriff.

maka.'I.'ō. Same as *maka lī'ō*, wild eye.

Maka-'io-lani. n. Name of a star. *Lit.*, eye of the royal hawk.

mā.ka'i pō. n. Night watchman, night police.

maka.iwa. n. 1. Mother-of-pearl eyes, as in an image, especially of the god Lono. 2. (Cap.) Nine guiding stars. (Johnson and Mahelona 74.)

mā.ka'i wahine. n. Police matron.

maka.kā.'alā. Same as *maka keleawe*.

maka.kai. nvs. Sea-washed; spray. *Ea mai ka makakai he'e nalu* (UL 36), the spray of surfing rises. *Ua 'au'au akula 'oia i ka wai a pau ka makakai*, he bathed in fresh water so as to be rid of the spray.

maka kaka'a. nvs. Shifty eyes; to have such.

maka kanaka. n. Many people, crowds of people. *Lā maka kanaka*, day when many people gather, as a holiday.

maka.kē.hau. n. Heart's desire. *Lit.*, dew eye.

maka keleawe. n. Brazen look; horse eye of a whitish color, but with good vision. *Lit.*, brass eye.

maka.kī. vt. To look at with hatred. **ho'o.maka.kī.** To look at with hatred; to plan revenge or evil.

maka ki'e.ki'e. n. Proud look (Sol. 6.17); haughty air.

maka kihi. nvi. To look out of the corner of the eyes; eye drawn back at the corner.

maka.ki'i. n. Mask. *Lit.*, image face.

maka ki'i. nvi. Flirtatious eyes; to lure or attract with the eyes.

maka kila. n. 1. A name given to the *kala poni*, sweet potato. 2. Pen; steel point, as of a weapon. *Lit.*, steel *(Eng.)* point.

maka kilo. nvi. Observant, watchful eyes; to watch with great attention.

makā.kiu. nvs. Spy, detective, spying eye; watchful, vigilant, spying; to spy. **ho'o.makā.kiu.** To spy, watch, reconnoiter.

maka koa. nvs. Bold, unafraid, fierce. *Lit.*, brave eye. *He lāhui kanaka maka koa, 'a'ole e mālama mai i ka 'elemakule* (Kanl. 28.50), a nation of fierce countenance, which shall not care for the old. (PPN *mata to'a*.)

maka ko'a. n. Landmark for a fishing ground. *Lit.*, fishing-ground point.

maka koali. n. Wild sweet potato found in Puna, Hawai'i; it may have been eaten in famine times; fed raw to pigs.

maka kole. Same as *mākole*.

maka.kū. n. Creative imagination of an artist. *Rare.*

maka kui. n. Needle or nail point; stitch. Cf. *maka o ke kui*, eye of a needle.

maka.ku'i.ku'i. vt. To scowl, leer hatefully. *Lit.*, pounding eyes.

makala. 1. vs. To loosen, undo, untie, open a little, liberate or set at liberty; to remit, as a debt; to forgive; to free of defilement or uncleanness; to open or unfold, as a flower. Cf. *kala 1*. *Ua makala nā pua i ka ua*, the rain unfolded the flowers. **ho'o.makala.** Caus/sim. (PPN *matala*.) 2. n. A trail. (Malo 92.)

makāla. Short for *maka'ala. Rare.*

mā.kala. n. 1. Myrtle. *Eng.* 2. Marshal. *Eng.* 3. (Cap.) Marshall (Islands). *Eng.*

maka.lae. loc. n. Beach, shore, coast near a point *(lae)*. *Aia akula i makalae i ka paeaea*, there [he's] gone on the shore pole fishing.

makala.hia. 1. vs. Sleepless, awake. 2. Pas/imp. of *makala 1*.

mā.kala.kala. 1. Redup. of *makala. Mākalakala iāia nei a pau nā hihia i kauhale*, free him of all defilements at home. (PPN *makalakala*.) 2. Same as *makalahia*.

maka lalau. nvs. Cross-eyed, with eyes that seem to look inward. Cf. *maka 'ahewa*.

makala.pua. vi. Handsome, beautiful; to blossom forth. *'O makalapua ulu māhiehie* (Elbert and Mahoe 76), profuse bloom growing as a delight. *Nā hi'ona ua hele wale ā makalapua*, features handsome indeed. *Ke kau o makalapua* (Kel. 5), the spring season. *Nani ho'i nā lau nahele e 'ōmaka ana, e mōhala ana ā e makalapua ana*, beautiful indeed are the budding plants, opening and blossoming.

maka.lau. n. 1. Carbuncle, boil. 2. Cluster of spears. 3. Many buds, as on a pussy willow. *Fig.*, many offspring.

Maka-lau-koa. n. Rain name.

makāla ulua. n. *Ulua* fishermen; seekers of human victims for sacrifice. (Malo 92.) *Rare.*

maka launa. vs. Friendly, having many friends and associates; sociable. *Ua ma'a i ka maka launa*, used to being friendly.

maka.lē. n. Mackerel, canned sardines. *Eng.*

maka le'a. nvs. Twinkle-eyed, happy-eyed, mischievous.

maka.leha. vi. To look about as in wonder or admiration, to glance.

maka.leho. nvs, nvt. Covetous, lustful, wanton, lascivious; incontinence; to admire (Kel. 17), desire. *Lit.*, cowrie eye, perhaps so called because the octopus clings to the cowrie. *Hahai ana i ka makaleho* (1 Pet. 4.3), walked in lasciviousness.

maka lehua. nvs. *Lehua* flower petals. *Fig.*, attractive, as young girls. *Nā kini maka lehua o nā 'ōpio*, the many youths, lovely as *lehua* flowers.

mā.kā.lei. n. 1. Fish trap. 2. Name of a supernatural tree found on Moloka'i; portions of its root were placed by the gates of fish ponds, as they were thought to attract fish. 3. Same as *melomelo*, a stick lure.

maka.lele. n. Name of a major illness (no data).

maka.lena. n. Fine muslin cloth. *Eng.*

maka lena. 1. nvs. Unfriendly, suspicious glance from under the eyelid; to glance thus. *Lit.*, drawn eye. 2. n. Yellow center of a flower, as of a daisy. *Mehe ipo lā ka maka lena o ke Ko'olau* (chant), like a sweetheart is the yellow flower center of the Ko'olau.

maka.lena pu'u. n. Dotted swiss cloth. *Lit.*, lumped muslin.

makali. 1. Same as *mali*, to flatter. 2. vs. Barely cooked, underdone. *Rare.* 3. vs. Glowing, bright, as of fire. *He ahi makali ho'āli na ke kupa* (chant), a glowing fire stirred by the native son. 4. vt. To bait a hook. (PCP *matali*.)

maka.li'i. 1. nvs. Tiny, very small, fine, wee, smallmeshed; narrow wefts. *Makali'i 'ōhua*, tiny 'ōhua spawn; *fig.*, anything wee, tiny. (PPN *mataliki*.) 2. (Cap.) n. Pleiades; Castor and Pollux. See *Pleiades*. (PPN *Mataliki*.) 3. (Cap.) n. Hawaiian month name; the six summer months collectively.

maka.li'i.li'i. 1. Redup. of *makali'i. He i'e makali'ili'i* (For. 5:639), a tapa beater with closely spaced grooves.

maka.lika. n. Marguerite, daisy. *Eng.*

maka.like. nvs. Uniform, as in color, style, clothes. *Lit.*, similar face. *Pa'a lole makalike*, uniform, as of military.

maka lilio. n. Eyes with epicanthic fold.

maka.lio. vs. Taut, as a rope. *Lit.*, tight mesh.

maka.loa. n. **1.** A perennial sedge *(Cyperus laevigatus)*, found in or near fresh or salt water in warm countries. From a horizontal, creeping stem rise long, slender unbranched stems, each topped by a small inflorescence. Formerly the plants were valued in Hawai'i for making the fine Ni'ihau mats. (Neal 86.) Also *makoloa*. **2.** General name for shellfish with long sharp edges *(Thais intermedia, Drupa morum)*. Also *aupūpū, pūpū 'awa*. (KL line 30.) See also *'ōlepe makaloa*. **3.** A seaweed.

maka loa. vs. Very green, as a fruit; barely cooked, very raw.

maka loko.maika'i. n. Bountiful eye (Sol. 22.9); one who looks kindly, charitably, and with good will. *Lit.*, good-hearted face.

maka lole. n. Eyelid turned back, exposing the under side of the lid; an insulting term, as prisoners were tortured by tattooing the exposed eyelid. *Lit.*, turned eye.

maka lua. 1. vs. Two-face, double-edged; two-fold, as a plaited mat; hypocritical. **2.** n. Socket of the eyeball. *Fig.*, depths of the sea. **3.** n. Fishing net with mesh wide enough to admit two fingers. *Lit.*, double mesh.

mā.kā.lua. nvi. Hole for house posts or for planting, as taro; to dig such a hole.

mā.kā.lua kele. n. A large *mākālua* hole.

maka luhi. n. Tired eyes, tired people, especially those who have been working hard on a community project. Cf. *'aha'aina maka luhi*.

maka.luku. vt. To plan slaughter; to determine to destroy.

maka.mae. vs. Precious, of great value, highly prized, darling (Hal. 22.20). *Mea makamae*, precious object, treasure.

maka.maka. 1. n. Intimate friend with whom one is on terms of receiving and giving freely; pal, buddy; host. *Fig.*, anything very helpful, as education. Cf. *maka*, beloved. *Kona makamaka*, his friend. **ho'o.maka.- maka.** To befriend, be a friend to, make a friend, cause to be friends. Cf. *ho'okāmakamaka. Ho'omaka- maka wahine*, to make friends with a woman. **2.** Redup. of *maka*, raw, fresh. **3.** n. Buds, as forming on the corm of a taro. (HP 5.)

maka.maka hā.nai. n. Friend.

maka.maka helu.helu. n. Reader, as of a newspaper. *Lit.*, reading friend.

maka.maka nui. n. One with a host of friends because of a genial, kindly, or hospitable nature; many friends.

makame, madame. n. Madame. *Eng. Makame Pele*, Madam Pele.

maka mino. n. Indented, non-protruding nipple, as is difficult for a baby to grasp.

maka moena. n. Mesh in mat made by plaiting over one and under one; similar style in quilting; check plait. *Lit.*, mat mesh.

maka momi. See *momi 5*.

maka.mua. n. Lead horses or oxen in a team.

maka mua. n. First, beginning, commencement, first time; first child of a family. *Lit.*, first end. *Maka mua o ka huaka'i* (FS 137), beginning of the procession. *'O ka maka mua kēia o ko'u ho'ā'o 'ana i ka 'ōlepe*, this is the first time I've tasted an oyster.

makana. nvt. Gift, present; reward, award, donation, prize; to give a gift, donate. Cf. *maka 2. Kāna makana*, his gift [one that he gives or receives]. *Makana kā ho'i!* What a gift! [sometimes said sarcastically, indicating that a person is ungrateful].

makana.'ā. n. Plants growing on lava beds (probably a contraction or *maka i nā 'a'ā*, budding in the lava).

makana aloha. n. Gift of friendship or love; freewill offering.

makana.hele. vs. Wild, untamed; of the wilderness or forest. *Lit.*, forest person. *Pua'a makanahele*, wild pig. *Nohona makanahele*, living in the forest. *Mīkana ma-*

kanahele, papaya growing wild. **ho'o.makana.hele.** To let a garden grow wild; wild, untamed.

makana hele. n. Parting gift. *Lit.*, going gift.

makana.lau. Same as *makalau*.

maka.nau. n. Twinkling of eyes. *Rare.*

makani. 1. nvs. Wind, breeze; gas in the stomach, flatulent wind; windy; to blow. *Fig.*, anger, gossip; to show anger. Cf. *ani. Makani nui*, strong wind, gale. *Makani 'olu'olu*, fair wind. *Mai wala'au a'e ho'i o makani auane'i* (saying), don't talk too much or the wind will blow [gossip]. *Hāmau o makani auane'i*, be still or there will be anger. *Kali i ka makani 'ōahi*, wait for the firebrand wind. (PPN *matangi*.) **2.** n. Ghost, spirit. See *kahuna makani*. **3.** interj. Call of sentinel, similar to "all's well".

Makani-hā.nai-loli. n. Name of a gentle wind; it is said to permit *loli* to come out of their holes and feed. (UL 207.) *Lit.*, wind that feeds sea slug.

makani hau none. n. Ice-cold mountain wind. *Lit.*, icy, annoying wind.

makani holo 'ū.hā. n. Cold wind. *Lit.*, wind running [over] thighs. (PH 187.)

makani ka'a wili.wili. n. Tornado. *Lit.*, wind revolving twisting.

makani kama.'āina. n. Usual wind of a place.

makani kū honua. n. Sudden strong wind, gust. *Lit.*, wind arriving suddenly.

makani noho. n. Spirit that possesses a medium and speaks through him. *Lit.*, spirit that takes possession.

makani 'olu.'olu. n. Favorable or fair wind, refreshing breeze.

makani pā.hili. n. Cyclone, hurricane.

makani pū.kī.kī. n. Gust, strong wind.

makani uluulu, makani hele uluulu. n. Hurricane.

makani wili. n. Whirlwind, twisting wind.

maka nui. n. A variety of sweet potato. (HP 142.)

maka.nunui. vs. Widely spaced, as grooves on a tapa beater.

maka nunui. n. Big eyes. Cf. *ki'i maka nunui* under *ki'i 1*.

Makao. n. **1.** Star name (no data). (Kuhelani.) **2.** A city, governed by Portugal, near Hong Kong.

mā.ka'o. Same as *ka'oka'o 3*, arid. Cf. *kūmimi māka'o*.

maka 'oi. n. Piercing, penetrating, sharp eyes.

mā.ka'o.ka'o. 1. Var. of *mōka'oka'o*. **2.** nvs. High; height. *Māka'oka'o ke ahi 'au hau i ka pali*, high on the precipice are the firebrands.

maka ole. n. Eyetooth; point of a dog's tooth. *Fig.*, point of an *'ō'ō*, digging stick; sprouting plant.

maka onaona. n. A sweet, lovely, or tender expression of face or eyes; also said of the eyes of the *kole*, a fish. *Ā ua lilo ihola 'oia i mea ho'omakaleho mau 'ia e nā kaikamahine maka onaona o Kaua'i*, this became something much wanted by the fragrant-eyed girls of Kaua'i.

maka.'opihi. n. **1.** *'Opihi* scooped out of its shell. **2.** A fine pandanus mat, of 6 cm strands. *Lit.*, fine mesh.

maka.'ō.pi'i. Same as *mākole mākōpi'i*.

maka.'ō.pio. n. A variety of taro.

maka 'ou. n. Excelling eye, epithet for a councilor *(kā- laimoku)*, who had served under three rulers in three generations, and hence was regarded as full of wisdom.

maka.pā. 1. vs. Feeble, of light, as firelight in the daytime; shy, wild, as a bird. **2.** n. Stones that break in a fire, not desirable for the *imu*.

maka.pa'a. nvs. Person blind in one eye, one-eyed; blind in one eye (it was considered bad luck to meet such a person); blind (Oihk. 22.22). *Lit.*, closed eye.

maka pala. vs. Soft, ripe; ready to burst, of a boil.

maka.pā.pipi. n. Hollow worn in lava rock by the sea, where salt is collected, natural salt pan.

maka.pehu. nvs. Swollen; suffering from hunger; hungry person. *Ola ka makapehu i'a 'ole*, the suffering from lack of fish is over.

maka pela. n. Dirty face; sticky, dirty eyes. See ex., *hā- puku 1, 2*.

maka peni. n. Pen point.

maka.pepe. vs. Fine-meshed, as a mat of medium weft, as 1.5 cm.

maka pī. n. Running eyes, bleary eyes.

maka pia.pia. n. Eyes sticky with viscous matter; watery eyes; insulting epithet for one who does not find what he is looking for.

maka.pipipi. n. **1.** Small eyes; pregnant women were discouraged from eating *pipipi* shellfish lest their children be born with small eyes, hence the name. **2.** Tiny, twinkling stars.

maka.pō. nvs. Blindness, blind person; blind. *Lit.,* night eye. **hoʻo.maka.pō.** To cause blindness, to feign blindness, to blindfold. (PEP *matapoo.*)

maka pō.niu.niu. nvs. Dizziness, faintness, lack of courage; obscure, dizzy, faint (Lunk. 8.4). *Lit.,* dizzy eye.

maka.pō.uli. nvs. Dizziness; dizzy, faint. *Lit.,* black-night eyes.

-makapū. **hoʻo.maka.pū.** To frown, look with disapproval.

maka puaʻa. n. Breast nipple that stands out and is easy for a baby to take; pig nipple.

maka puhi. n. Fishhook with two opposite barbs, as used for eels. *Lit.,* eel point.

māka puke. n. Bookmark. *Eng.*

maka.puʻu. n. Variety of fish (no data). *Lit.,* bulging eyes, hill point.

makau. Fishhook. *Hilikau ka makau a ka lawaiʻa,* the fisherman's hook is snagged [said of disorder]. (PPN *maataʻu,* PCP *matau.*)

makāu. Var. spelling of *makaau.*

mā.kau. Same as *mākaukau.* The word is related to *ʻakau,* right hand. (PPN *mataʻu.*)

makaʻu. nvt. Fear; frightened, afraid, cowardly, timid, unsafe, dangerous. *Makaʻu ʻoia i ke kaua,* he is afraid of war. Cf. *makaʻuhia, makaʻulia.* **hoʻo.makaʻu.** To frighten, scare, terrify, make afraid; fear; to pretend to fear. (PPN *mataku.*)

makaua. **1.** nvi. Hardhearted, unfriendly; troubled, vexed. *Lit.,* tough face. **2.** vi. To increase, grow larger. **3.** n. A variety or taro.

mā.kaua. n. War dead (short for *make kaua*).

maka.ʻua. Pas/imp. of *makaʻu.* **hoʻo.maka.ʻua.** Caus/sim.; to frighten, scare.

maka.ua.ua. **1.** Redup. of *makaua.* **2.** vi. To toughen by drying, as hide. *Rare. Lit.,* tough face.

maka uhi. n. **1.** Face tattooed solid, without patterning. **2.** Tattooed eyelid, as a humiliating sign of a warrior's defeat. **3.** Downcast eyes. *Ke-au-hou maka uhi.* Ke-au-hou with downcast eyes [said of the people at Ke-au-hou who did not welcome visitors because of chiefly taboos].

makaʻu.hia. Pas/imp. of *makaʻu.*

mā.kau.kau. **1.** nvs. Able, competent, capable, handy, efficient, proficient, versed, adept, skilled, expert, qualified; prepared, ready; competence, proficiency, efficiency, aptitude, preparation; to know how, to know well. Cf. *ʻakau,* right. *Mākaukau ʻole,* unprepared, unskilled, unqualified, not ready. **hoʻo.mā.kau.kau.** To prepare, make ready. *Hoʻomākaukau ʻia ma kēia kānāwai,* provided for by this law. (PPN *mataʻu,* PCP *maatautau.*) **2.** *(Cap.)* n. Star name (no data). (Kuhelani.)

mā.kaʻu.kaʻu. Redup. of *makaʻu.* **hoʻo.mā.kaʻu.kaʻu.** To scare, frighten; scared, frightened. (PPN *matakutaku.*)

makaʻu kiʻi. n. Fear of images representing gods.

makaʻu kū.hewa. n. Sudden fear, panic.

makā.ula. Same as *kāula,* prophet.

maka ʻula.ʻula. n. Pinkeye; inflamed or bloodshot eye. *Lit.,* red eye.

maka uli. n. Black eye, as from a bruise.

maka.u.lia. Pas/imp. of *makaʻu.* (For. 6:299.) (PCP *matakulia.*)

makau.liʻi. vs. **1.** Saving, economical, thrifty, provident; miserly, avaricious, eager to own. **hoʻo.makau.liʻi.** To economize; thrifty, saving, economical, frugal; to desire, covet. See ex., *kōʻalaʻala. Poʻe hoʻomakauliʻi ʻāina,* people eager for land. *Ua hoʻokō ʻia ka hana hoʻomakauliʻi i loko o ke aupuni,* economies in government have been effected. **2.** Broad-backed, thick-shelled, of a turtle.

-makauliʻi. **hoʻo.makau.liʻi.** To seek every detail; to find out even the smallest things, scrutinize. Cf. ex., *kōʻalaʻala.*

Maka-ʻunu-lau. n. Name of a navigational star. *Lit.,* eyes drawing many.

maka.ʻuo. n. Gathering and tying, as *pala* fern for a heiau service. *Rare.*

makau pā.weo. n. Small shell hook, as used for ʻōpelu fishing. *Lit.,* hook to turn away.

maka.ʻū.pē. n. Grief. *Ka hale makaʻūpē, pā i ka ʻū lā* (Kep. 71), the sad house, touched by grief.

maka.ʻupena. n. Midriff, fat. *Makaʻupena e uhi ana i ka naʻau* (Oihk. 3.3), fat covering the intestines.

maka-ʻupena. n. Design, as carved on a tapa beater and used in quilting.

maka ʻupena. n. Net mesh. Cf. *ʻōpua maka ʻupena, uea maka ʻupena.*

makaʻu wale. nvt. Coward, cowardice; afraid for no reason, easily frightened.

makaʻu.wā.wae. n. **1.** Excrement lying exposed on the ground. *Lit.,* feared [by] feet. **2.** Anything on which one fears to tread.

maka.wai. n. Small outlets for water through banks of taro patches; small waterways; water sources.

maka wai. nvs. Watery-eyed; eyes welling with tears; tender-eyed (Kin. 29.17).

maka wai.ū. n. Nipple of the breast.

maka.walu. **1.** vs. Numerous, many, much, in great quantities (sometimes used with implication of chiefly *mana*). *Lit.,* eight eyes. Cf. *-walu. Nā wailele e iho makawalu mai ana,* waterfalls pouring down in quantity. *Ka iho makawalu a ka ua,* the great downpour of rain. *Makawalu nā moku,* many islands are scattered haphazardly. **2.** n. Type of fighting on plains covered with brush, with irregularly grouped warriors. (Malo 196, 203.)

maka.wela. **1.** nvs. Glowing, burning; full of hate, fury, anger. *Fig.* term for the despised *kauā,* outcasts. *Nā pōhaku makawela o Kī-lau-ea,* the burning lava rocks of Kī-lau-ea. *ʻŌlelo makawela,* words of hatred. **hoʻo.maka.wela.** To treat like a *kauā makawela.* **2.** n. Type of stone from which weights for cowry octopus lures were made. **3.** Same as *wela 3. Hele e kanu i ka makawela,* went to plant the land cleared by burning.

maka.wela.wela. Redup. of *makawela 1. Ua makawelawela wale mai nō ʻoia iaʻu,* he hated me for nothing.

maka weli. nvi. Glaring, threatening eyes; to glare, glower.

maka.wī. See *pahapaha 3.*

make. **1.** nvs. To die, perish; defeated, beaten, dead, killed, unfortunate; to faint (cf. *make loa,* definitely "to die"); death, fainting, danger of death, peril, destruction, misfortune; to kill, beat, execute; deathly, deadly, faint, deceased, extinct, late, obsolete, poisonous, venomous. (Gram. 4.5.) A pre-Christian concept was that *make* signified entry into the spirit world, and that *make loa* was the utter annihilation of the spirit, a kind of second death (cf. For. 5:581). *Make anu,* to die from the cold, freeze. *Make ʻole,* deathless, immortal. *Kona make,* his [own] death. *Kāna make,* his murder [of someone else]. *ʻAʻole kona he make maoli, he make na waho,* his was not a natural death, [but] a death by outsiders [sorcery]. *Nā-ʻehu i make aku nei,* the late Nā-ʻehu. *Makamaka make,* unresponsive friend. *Lawe i ka wā make,* taking at the time of death [a deceased might by his death remove taboos, curses, and sources of family discord: Nānā 137–8]. *Hele i ka make,* to pass away in death [common statement in wills]. *Emi maila ʻo Ka-malama, ā ʻaneʻane nō e make i nā wahi koa* (FS 85), Ka-malama fell behind and was almost killed by the warriors. **hoʻo.make.** To kill deliberately, execute; to pretend to be dead; to let die; to let diminish, grow faint. *Mai hoʻopae ʻoe, e hoʻomake ʻoe i kou nalu,* don't catch [the wave], let your wave get smaller. (PPN *mate*.) **2.** nvs. Desire, want; to want. Cf. *make ʻai, -mākeʻaka, make wai.* After *ʻaʻole, make* expresses a weak command, as "you better not." *ʻI mai nei ke aliʻi, ʻaʻole make kaha ka ʻōpū o ka puaʻa* (FS 205), the chief said, better not cut open the pig's stomach. *ʻAʻole make hana,* better not do it. *Mai make hele ʻoe!* Don't get the notion of going. (PCP *mate*.) **3.** n. Price, barter, exchange. Cf. *makehewa, makepono. ʻEhia hua moa make ka hapalua,* how many eggs for fifty cents? *Ā make na ʻIwa, na ke keiki ʻaihue a Kukui, ʻo ka waiwai o kuʻu waʻa* (FS 21), the reward for ʻIwa, Kukui's thieving son, is the value of my canoe.

mā.kē. n. Masthead. *Eng.*

makea. Pas/imp. of *make 1, 2.*

mā.kea. Same as *mahakea 1–3.*

make ʻai. vi. Hungry. *Lit.,* want food. (PCP *mate kai.*)

-mākeʻaka. **hoʻo.mā.keʻaka.** Witty, comic, funny, amusing; to cause laughter, exercise wit or humor. *Hana hoʻomākeʻaka,* funny antics; to do something to provoke laughter. *ʻŌlelo hoʻomākeʻaka,* joke, witticism. *Mea hoʻomākeʻaka,* joker, wit, clown.

make anu. vs. To be very cold, chilled, freezing.

Make.au.peʻa. n. Name of a star or constellation. See *Mekeaupeʻa.*

make ʻawa.hua iho. n. Death due to mental depression. (Kam. 64:44.) *Lit.,* bitterness within death.

makeʻe. vt. Covetous, greedy, desirous to have; to prize, have affection for. *He makeʻe keiki,* a great affection for children. *Ka mālama makeʻe loa* (Kel. 50), to preserve a desired object with great care. **hoʻo.makeʻe.** Caus/sim.

makeʻe kā.nā.wai. vs. Law-abiding.

mā.keʻe.keʻe. Redup. of *makeʻe.*

makeʻe kū.lana. nv. To desire to preserve the status quo; conservative.

makeʻe pono au.puni. vs. Patriotic; desirous for the welfare of the nation.

makeʻe wai.wai. nvs. Avarice, covetousness (Ier. 22.17); eagerness to acquire wealth.

mā.kē.hā. nvi. Shish, to shish, swish, especially accompanied by flash, as of skyrockets; flash, as of lightning; to flash. *Ka-uila-mākēhā-o-ka-lani* (name), flashing lightning of heaven.

make.hewa. nvs. Bad bargain, vain undertaking; in vain, useless, without profit. Cf. *makepono. ʻAʻa makehewa,* rash, desperate. *Makehewa ke kino uʻi, ʻo kēlā ke kāne,* the youthful beauty is wasted on a man like that.

make.hia. Pas/imp. of *make 2. ʻOnipaʻa ana ka pono, ʻonipaʻa me ka makehia* (song), let the right stand firm, stand firm because it is wanted.

make kaka ola. n. Death caused by capturing the spirit of a live person. (Kam. 64:43.) *Lit.,* death strike [the] living.

make.kau. vs. Warlike.

mā.keke. n. **1.** Market. *Eng.* **2.** Black mustard *(Brassica nigra),* a cosmopolitan herb, a weed in Hawaiʻi, but formerly cultivated for the seeds, which are the main source of table mustard. Small yellow flowers, and later erect seed pods, are borne on tall stems. *Eng. Hua mākeke* (Mat. 13.31), grain of mustard seed.

-mākeke ʻeo. **hoʻo.make.keʻeo.** Resentful.

mā.keke nui. n. Large market, supermarket.

makela, masela. n. Muscles. *Eng.*

makele. Same as *kele 1. Ka ulua makele,* the fat, large deep-sea *ulua,* a fish.

make.lia. n. Material. *Eng.*

makeli.monio, materimonio. n. Matrimony. *Eng.*

make loa. vs. To die (in contrast to *make,* which may mean "defeated, faint"). For a pre-Christian concept, see *make 1.*

make.make. **1.** nvt. Desire, want, wish; to want, like, prefer, favor, wish; willing (often replaced colloquially by *mamake*). See *make 2. E mālama ʻia Kou makemake,* may Thy will be done. **hoʻo.make.make.** To cause or feign desire. **2.** Redup. of *make 1;* defeated. (For. 6:371.) (PPN *matemate.*)

make.makika. n. Mathematics. *Eng.*

make.makika hoʻo.pili ʻia. n. Applied mathematics. *Lit.,* referred mathematics.

make.makika ʻokoa. n. Pure mathematics.

makena. **1.** nvi. Mourning, wailing, lamentation; to wail, lament, weep for joy. *Nona kēia makena e uwē ʻia mai nei* (For. 4.47), this wailing that is being sobbed forth here is for him. (PPN *matenga.*) **2.** n. Calm, of sea, atmosphere. Cf. *make,* dead.

mā.kena. vs. Many, numerous; often, much. *Mākena wale ua moa,* lots of chickens. *Mākena kā hoʻi koʻu hilahila iāʻoe,* how you humiliated me; you made me ashamed of you.

makena.wai. n. Place where a stream disappears in the ground.

mā.kē.neki. n. Magnet, magneto. *Eng.*

make pilau. nvs. Complete defeat, as in card games, to be completely defeated.

make pō.loli. nvi. To die of starvation; faint with hunger.

make.pono. nvs. Bargain; profitable, reasonable in price or in conduct. Cf. *makehewa.*

make ulu niu. nvs. Madness; to be mad. (Kam. 64:43.) *Lit.,* death [from] whirling. *Rare.*

make wai. nvi. Thirst; thirsty. See ex., *iho 7.* (PEP *mate wai.*)

make wale. vi. To die of itself, to die without cause, to die or wilt easily. *ʻO ka mea make wale* (Oihk. 22.8), that which dieth of itself.

māki. vi. To march. *Eng.*

mā.kī. vt. To roll, fold. *He aha ka mea i mākī ʻia ai kēia moena,* why was this mat rolled up?

mā.kia. **1.** nvs. Aim, motto, purpose; to aim or strive for, to concentrate on. *ʻOnipaʻa kā Liliʻu-o-ka-lani mākia,* stand firm was Liliʻu-o-ka-lani's motto. **2.** nvt. Pin, nail, wedge, spike, stake, bolt; to nail, bolt, crucify, pin; to establish, as a kingdom; to destroy by sorcery; to drive stakes, as in surveying; to fasten. *Mākia ʻia ma ka lāʻau keʻa,* nailed to the cross.

mā.kiʻa. conj. Maybe, perhaps, probably. *Mākiʻa o uhaele aku kāua,* we'll probably go.

maki.awa. n. Round herring *(Etrumeus micropus);* common in estuaries, as at Pearl Harbor. Also *miki-awa, ʻōmaka.*

makihi. *Cressa cretica* (Remy 19). Cf. Neal 701.

makiʻi.lohe.lohe. n. A service during *luakini* dedication. (For. 6:45.)

makika. n. **1.** Mosquito. *Eng.* In Puk. 8.16, *makika* translates "gnats" (RSV) and "lice" (KJV). In Hal. 105.31, *makika* is "swarm of flies" (RSV) and "divers sorts of flies" (KJV). **2.** Plant blight that attacked sweet potato, taro, and other food crops, believed caused by mosquitoes.

makiki. **1.** Same as *kiki,* to peck. *Makiki moa,* cockfight. **2.** n. Type of stone used as weights for octopus lures (Malo 19), and for adzes.

maki.koe. vs. Long, tall, slender, as a tree.

mā.kila. nvt. Maui name for *mānai,* needle; to string, as leis.

makili. vi. To crack, appear through a crack, show, come to light; to come off, as shingles; cracked, split open. *He lā makili loa ka uka* (For. 6:299), a sun just peering forth in the uplands. *Ua makili mai ka mālamalama ma ka hakahaka o ka puka,* the light shows through the open space of the door. **hoʻo.makili.** To open a crack; to crack. *Ho'omakili ka papa,* the board is cracked.

mā.kili. nvs. A drop; to drop, as water. Cf. *kilihau, kilihune,* Hal. 37.25. *He wahi mākili hou,* a drop of perspiration. *Mākili 'ai,* to eat just a little. *Mākili li'ili'i ka wai* (Kep. 165), add a little water [as in mixing poi].

mā.kili.kili. Redup. of *makili.*

mā.kilo. nvt. To eye wistfully, to look at longingly, to beg thus; beggar.

maki.maki. Similar to *'o'opu hue,* puffer. *(Arothron hispidus.)*

makini. 1. Uneven, as land. (And.) **2.** A kind of fish. (And.)

mā.kini. 1. n. Group of spears tied together, used as a battering ram in war (from *maka kini,* many points). **2.** nvs. Many deaths; death-inflicting, deathly (from *make kini,* many deaths). **3.** n. Gourd mask, as used by canoemen.

mā.kini.kā. 1. nvs. Monkey. *Fig.,* ugly person; ugly. **2.** *(Cap.)* n. Hawaiian whalers' name for Eskimo.

makini.kela. n. Martingale. *Eng.*

mā.kini.kini. nvs. Hilly; notched, as a ridge.

mā.kiu, ho'o.mā.kiu. Same as *makākiu, ho'omakākiu.*

mā.kō. 1. vs. Rough, rocky; large. *Mānoanoa mehe pali mākō* (chant), thick as a rock cliff. (PPN *mato.*) **2.** Similar to *mākonā,* mean. *Rare.*

makoa. 1. vs. Fearless, courageous, aggressive. Cf. *koa,* brave. **ho'o.makoa.** To act bravely. **2.** Similar to *mākonā. Pulu a'u lehua i ka makoa* (FS 87), my *lehua* trees are wet in the implacable [elements].

mā.ko'a. n. Coral head in the sea.

mā.ko.a.ko'a. Plural of *māko'a.*

mā.koe. To rake, strip, scrape away. Cf. *koe 2.*

mā.ko'e. Var. of *mākole 1.* (AP.)

mā.koe.ā. vs. Tedious, wearisome, difficult, as a task; hard to get along with, of a person. *Rare.*

mā.kohi. 1. Same as *kōhi 1,* to dig. (PPN *matofi.*) **2.** n. A red variety of taro, used for pink poi, sometimes qualified by the colors *'ele'ele* or *'ula'ula.* Also *mōkohi.*

Mā.kohi-lani. n. Name of a star. See *Mākaha 2.*

mā.koi. 1. nvt. Fishing pole; to fish with a pole (also *mōkoi*). Cf. *mākoi kanaka. Kā mākoi,* to fish with a pole. **2.** Same as *mākonā* (AP.) **3.** *(Cap.)* Also **Magoi.** n. Magi. **4.** n. Magician, enchanter.

mā.koi.ele. vi. To teeter, seesaw; to swing on a single rope. *Rare.*

mā.koi kanaka. n. A sport of strength; players lie on the ground, with bodies rigid. They are lifted up from the back and hoisted to their feet.

mā.koi.koi. Redup. of *mākoi 1.*

mā.ko'i.ole. vi. To hold the breath, of divers. *Rare.*

mā.koko. 1. n. Fresh-water leech or bloodsucker. Cf. *koko,* blood. **2.** vs. Reddish. Cf. *he'e mākoko, loli mākoko.* **3.** n. A variety of taro, used for red poi. (HP 22.) Also *nohu.*

mā.kole. 1. nvs. Inflamed or sore eye; bloodshot; red-eyed; red-hot; red or yellow, as dying leaves; red, as a tinted cloud. *Mākole, mākole 'akahi* (FS 223), so red-eyed, red-eyed [said tauntingly of Pele, referring to her fires]. **ho'o.mā.kole.** To cause redness or soreness of the eyes. **2.** nvi. Slightly decomposed pinkish octopus, relished by some; to turn pinkish, as octopus. Also *he'e pulu.* **ho'o.mā.kole.** To prepare octopus in this fashion. **3.** n. Rainbow. *Pō mākole,* night with a [lunar] rainbow. **4.** n. A small, smooth, succulent herb *(Nertera granadensis* var. *insularis,* commonly known as *N. depressa),* creeping on damp forest floors, a member of the coffee family with small ovate leaves and round, red to yellow, berry-like fruits. (Neal 794.) **5.** vt. To scrape. **6.** Same as *kahikole,* a time of day.

mā.kolea. vs. Bold, shameless. *Rare.*

mā.kole.kole. Redup. of *mākole 1–3. Ua mākolekole,* a rain with rainbow colors.

mā.kole lau. n. Leaf turning yellow or red, or drying.

mā.kole mā.kō.pi'i. n. A native moss *(Thuidium hawaiense),* the plants branching in one plane, looking like small ferns. Also *mākōpi'i, maka 'ōpi'i, limu-mākole-maka-'ōpi'i, kala maka pi'i.*

mā.koli. n. Fragment; tiny bit, as of small shavings. Cf. *koli,* to whittle. **ho'o.mā.koli.** To cut into small bits, to render small or fine.

makolo. Same as *kolo,* to creep.

mako.loa. Same as *makaloa,* a sedge.

mā.kolo.kolo. Same as *honohono,* the wandering Jew. *Lit.,* creeper.

mā.kolo.kolo.pā. Same as *kolokolopā,* young of goatfish.

mā.kolu. 1. vs. Thick, heavy, deep, as clouds; thick-coated, as dust; laden, as a high chief with taboo. (PPN *matolu,* PNP *maatolu.*) **2.** n. Net mesh large enough to admit the entrance of three fingers; a net with such a mesh; three-ply, as sennit. Cf. *mākahi, mālua.*

mā.kolu.kolu. 1. Redup. of *mākolu;* chubby. *He papa mākolukolu,* a thick plank. *Ka-lani-nui-mākolukolu-i-ke-kapu* (name), the great chief thickly surrounded by taboo. **2.** vs. Extremely, threefold. *Kuhikuhi mākolukolu* (Kel. 117), extremely savory. (PPN *matolutolu,* PNP *maatolutolu.*)

mā.kō.mako. Redup. of *mākō 1. Rare.* **ho'o.mā.kō.-makō.** Large, billowy; to increase, enlarge.

Makona, Masona. nvs. Mason. *Eng. Hui Makona,* Masons' Society.

mā.konā. nvs. Hard, mean, hard-hearted, malevolent, unyielding, arbitrary, implacable, nasty; evil disposition. Cf. *konā.* **ho'o.mā.konā.** To act mean, hard, etc.

mā.kō.pi'i. Same as *mākole mākōpi'i,* a moss.

makou. 1. n. All native and introduced species of buttercups *(Ranunculus),* coarse herbs with subdivided leaves and small yellow flowers. (Neal 351.) Also *'awa Kanaloa.* **2.** n. A native perennial herb *(Peucedanum sandwicense),* in the parsley family, with coarse leaves much subdivided and tuberous roots that were used medicinally. **3.** n. A native fern *(Botrychium subbifoliatum),* with fronds fan-shaped and lobed much like leaves of buttercups. **4.** nvi. To blush; red, as with sunburn; bloodshot. **5.** n. *Kukui* lamps, as burned all night while court retainers told stories to the chiefs; courtiers who told such stories; venerable statesmen who had served under three kings, presumably in three generations, perhaps so called because the *makou* torch consisted of three strings of *kukui* nuts.

mā.kou. pronoun. We, us (plural, exclusive; Gram. 8.2). (PPN *kimautolu,* PNP *kimaatou,* PEP *maatou.*)

mā.kū. 1. vs. Firm, hard; thick, stiff, as molasses; jellied, solidified; to gel, harden; to settle, as dregs; to thicken, as cream; dregs, sediment, lees. **ho'o.mā.kū.** To cause to harden, solidify, thicken, gel; to lower, as clouds. *Fig.,* to show off. **2.** Same as *koki'o,* a native hibiscus.

makua. nvs. Parent, any relative of the parents' generation, as uncle, aunt, cousin; progenitor; Catholic father; main stalk of a plant; adult; full-grown, mature, older, senior. *Fig.,* benefactor, provider, anyone who cares for one; the Lord (God). *Kamika Makua,* Smith Senior. *Ē ka Makua* (Ka Nonanona, beginning of a letter, Sept. 5, 1843), Sire. *Makua Laiana,* Father Lyons [the Hawaiians' name for the Rev. Lorenzo Lyons, 1807–1886]. *'O kō mākou Makua i loko o ka lani,* our Father who art in heaven. *'O ko'u makua aku ana kēia,* this one will be the one who cares for me in the future [may be said by a parent of his child]. **ho'o.makua.** To grow into maturity, mature; to act the part of a parent; to foster, adopt, as a child; to call or treat as a parent; to address as parent, aunt, or uncle one related by affection rather than by blood or adoption; to become established or permanent. *Ua ho'omakua aku au nona,* I became his parent or guardian. *'A'ole ho'i e ho'omakua aku 'oukou i kekahi kanaka*

(Mat. 23.9), and call no man your father. *'O kou ahonui ka i ho'omakua mai nei ia'u* (Hal. 18.35), your gentleness has made me great. (PPN *matu'a*.)

mā.kua. 1. Plural of *makua*. (Gram. 8.1.) (PNP *maatu'a*.) **2.** Same as *kūnehi,* sunfish.

mā.ku'a. Var. of *māku'e,* dark brown, dark red.

makua ali'i, makuali'i. n. Progenitor, patriarch, head of a tribe.

makua.hine, makuwahine. n. Mother, aunt, female cousin or relative of parents' generation. *Lit.,* female parent. *'Ōlelo makuahine,* mother tongue. **ho'o.makua.hine.** To act as or claim to be a *makuahine;* to treat as a *makuahine.* (PPN *matu'a fafine.*)

mā.kua.hine. Plural of *makuahine.* (Gram. 8.1.) (PCP *maatu'a wahine.*)

makua.hine hanauna. n. Female cousin of the parents' generation.

makua.hine kō.lea. n. Stepmother.

makua.hine makua. n. Aunt who is older sister or cousin of the father or mother. *Lit.,* older mother.

makua.hine 'ō.pio. n. Aunt who is younger sister of the father or mother. *Lit.,* young mother.

makua.hine papa.kema. n. Godmother.

makua.hō.nō.wai. Rare var. of *makuahūnōai.*

makua.hū.nō.ai, makahūnōwai. n. Parent-in-law; uncle- or aunt-in law; cousin of parent-in-law (sex may be designated by addition of *kāne,* male, or *wahine,* female). *Ho'ohoihoi makuahūnōai,* to please an in-law [of one whose first enthusiasm fades]. *Kona mau makuahūnōai* (Laie 613), his parents-in-law.

makua kāne. n. Father, uncle, male cousin of parents' generation. **ho'o.makua kāne.** To act as or claim to be a *makua kāne;* to address or treat as a *makua kāne.*

mā.kua kāne. Plural of *makua kāne.*

makua kāne hanauna. n. Male cousin of the parents' generation.

makua kāne kō.lea. n. Stepfather.

makua kāne makua. n. Uncle who is older brother or cousin of the father or mother.

makua kāne 'ō.pio. n. Uncle who is younger brother of the father or mother.

makua kāne papa.kema. n. Godfather.

Makua-ka'ū.mana. n. Name of a star, said to be in the Kaulua constellation.

makua.keahu. n. Spirit of a living person.

makua kō.lea. n. Stepparent.

mā.kua.kua. 1. Redup. of *makua;* aged, old. *Ua mākuakua kēlā kanaka,* that person is old. **2.** vs. Coarse, thick, as cloth; furrowed, as plowed land. **3.** n. A variety of grass. **4.** n. Young of *mākua,* a fish.

mā.ku'a.ku'a. Same as *māku'eku'e 1.*

makua.li'i. Same as *makua ali'i.*

makua lua. vs. Very old. (For. 6:400.)

makua mea keiki. n. A person who has children; mother and child.

makua-o-ka-limu-kohu. n. A seaweed. *Lit.,* parent of the *limu kohu.*

makua-o-ka-lī.poa. n. Sponge crab. Cf. *kumulīpoa.*

makua papa.kema. n. Godparent.

makua 'uhane. n. Spiritual father, Catholic priest.

makua wahine. Old spelling for *makuahine.* (FS 173.)

mā.ku'e. 1. nvs. Dark brown, any dark color. *Lole māku'e* (2 Oihn. 2.7), purple. *Poni māku'e,* dark purple. *'Ula māku'e,* dark or purplish red. *Kanaka 'ili māku'e o ka moana Pākīpika,* dark-skinned native of the Pacific Ocean. (PCP *matuke*.) **2.** nvi. Frown, scowl; to frown, scowl. **3.** n. A native fern *(Elaphoglossum hirtum* var. *micans),* with long, narrow, undivided fronds, which are coated on both sides with soft, brown scales.

mā.ku'e.ku'e. 1. Redup. of *māku'e 1.* **2.** n. Bunch grass. **3.** Same as *'ālinalina. Moloka'i.*

mā.ku'e lau li'i. n. A small native fern *(Grammitis hookeri),* with narrow, unbranched fronds 8 to 24 cm long, clothed with dark-red hairs. *Lit.,* small-leaved *māku'e.*

maku'i. n. Joint, joining. *Rare.*

maku.ika, makuisa. n. Marquis. *Eng.*

maku.kana. n. Boxfish *(Lactoria fornasini).*

mā.kū.koa'e. n. Tropic bird phantom, a poetic name for death and the spirit of death; to hover, of this bird; also similar to *akua ho'ounauna. Ua mākūkoa'e 'oia,* the tropic bird phantom hangs over him [he is dying or the victim of sorcery].

mā.kū.kū. Redup. of *mākū 1.*

Makula. n. Saturn.

makule. vs. Aged, elderly, old, of people. Cf. *'elemakule,* old man.

makulu. 1. Var. of *nakulu. Makulu ka noe i ka lehua,* the mist drips upon the *lehua* flowers. **2.** *(Cap.)* n. Saturn.

mā.kulu.kulu. 1. Redup. of *makulu 1.* **2.** *(Cap.)* n. Saturn.

mā.kuma. Same as *hākuma. Mākuma ke aloha,* love intense.

mā.kuma.kū. Redup. of *mākū;* thick, heavy.

mā.kuma.kuma. Redup. of *mākuma.*

maku'u. 1. n. Topknot of hair; pommel, horn, of a saddle; end pieces of a canoe; neck cut on the stern end of a canoe hull hewn in the mountains, to which a rope was fastened for dragging the canoe to the sea. **2.** n. Bundle, as of white tapa fastened to ridgepole during certain ceremonies. (Malo 171.) **3.** nvi. Uncontrollable bowel discharge, as after eating great quantities of *wolu (walu),* a fish; to have such discharge.

maku.wahine. Var. spelling of *makuahine.*

mala. 1. vs. Aching, as after unaccustomed exercise; stiff and sore, bruised. See *mamala.* **ho'o.mala.** To cause such aching. (PPN *mala*.) **2.** vs. Sour, as fermented sweet potatoes, insipid. See *mamala.* (PPN *mara.*) **3.** Same as *'āhui,* bunch, as of bananas.

māla. n. Garden, plantation, patch, cultivated field, as *māla 'ai, māla kalo, māla kō, māla kūlina.* (PPN *ma'ala.*)

māla 'ai. n. Taro patch, food garden or plantation.

Malae. nvs. Malaya; Malay. *Eng.*

-malae. ho'o.malae. To feign friendship.

mā.la'e. vs. Clear, calm; clear of weeds, as a field; serene, as a cloudless sky. Cf. *la'e, kāla'e.* **ho'o.mā.la'e.** To clear, explain clearly; to calm, cheer, dispel gloom; to clear away, as brush or weeds.

Malaea. Same as *Malaia.* (Kep. 67.)

māla.'ea. Pas/imp. of *māla'e.* **ho'o.māla.'ea.** Pas/imp. of *ho'omāla'e.*

mā.la'e.la'e. Redup. of *māla'e.* **ho'o.mā.la'e.la'e.** Caus/sim.

mā.lahi. Short for *ma'alahi.*

mala.hia. Pas/imp. of *mala 1, 2.* (PNP *ma(a)lasia.*)

malai. Var. of *palai 2.*

malaia. vs. **1.** Pas/imp. of *mala 2;* soured, a sour disposition, crosspatch. **2.** *(Cap.)* nvs. Malay, Malaya, Malaysia. *Eng.*

malaila. See *laila.*

mā.lai.lena. 1. nvs. Bitter, sour; sour or disagreeable disposition (For. 6:502). **ho'o.mā.lai.lena.** To cause sourness; to embitter. **2.** n. A kind of *'ahi,* a fish.

Malai.lua. 1. n. Name of a strong, blustering wind at Nu'u-anu; to blow, of this wind. **2.** *(Not cap.)* Hornless goat or cow (said to be named for a particular goat at Kona, Hawai'i). (AP.)

malai.oa. vs. Broken into small or minute particles, as dust. *Rare.*

malaka. nvs. Mulatto. *Eng.*

mala.keke. n. Molasses. *Eng.*

Malaki. n. March. *Eng.*

mala.kia. Rare var. of *malahia. 'Eha malakia ka 'ili i ka 'oli'oli* (chant), the skin is hurt, sore with joy.

mala.kile, maratire. n. Martyr.

māla lā.'au hua 'ai. Orchard.

mā.lalai.oa. 1. nvs. A thin person; thin. See ex., *wilimo'o.* **2.** n. Person skilled in trade or occupation. (Malo 194, 201.) *Rare.*

Mala.lei. n. Stroke in *lua* fighting.

malalo. See *lalo.*

mala lua. vi. Aching greatly.

malama. 1. n. Light, month, moon. (PPN *ma(a)rama, malama.*) 2. conj. Perhaps. *Malama ulu mai ka 'ano'ano,* perhaps the seeds will grow.

mā.lama. 1. nvt. To take care of, tend, attend, care for, preserve, protect, beware, save, maintain; to keep or observe, as a taboo; to conduct, as a service; to serve, honor, as God; care, preservation, support, fidelity, loyalty; custodian, caretaker, keeper. Cf. *makemake, mālama hale, mālama hele, mālama moku, mālama pū'olo, pālama 1. Mālama 'ana,* custody. *Mālama pono 'ia,* well cared for. *Mālama pono!* Be careful! Watch out! *Mālama makua,* one who cares for parents. *Mālama wahine,* caring for one's wife. *Mālama i kou makua kāne,* honor your father. *Mālama kauoha,* obey orders. *Mālama Lā Kāpaki,* keeping the Sabbath. *E ku'u Akua, e mālama au iā'oe ma ka no'ono'o,* O my God, let me serve you in thought. *O ka ho'olohe a me ka mālama pono i ke aupuni,* obedience and fidelity due the government. *Ka mālama 'ole i kō ha'i ola,* negligence of the lives of others. **ho'o.mā.lama.** (a) Caus/sim. (b) *(Cap.)* Star name. 2. n. Pancreas. 3. *(Cap.)* n. Stroke in *lua* fighting. See below.

mā.lama hale. n. Custodian of a house, janitor, housekeeper. *Kahu mālama hale,* housekeeper.

mā.lama hele. vt. To take constant care of. *E mālama hele i ka wahine* (For. 6:454), take constant care of the wife.

Mā.lama-i-hane'e.lekia. n. Unidentified star. (Johnson and Mahelona 44.)

Malamaiku. n. Unidentified star, pronunciation uncertain. (Johnson and Mahelona 44.)

Mā.lama-ka-'ō.pua-hiki. n. Stroke in *lua* fighting. *Lit.,* the rising cloud bank preserves.

Mā.lama-kū.'ē. n. Stroke in *lua* fighting. *Lit.,* watch opposition.

Mā.lama-kū.loko. n. A stroke in *lua* fighting. *Lit.,* watch within.

Mā.lama-kū.waho. n. A stroke in *lua* fighting. *Lit.,* watch without.

mala.mala. Redup. of *mala 1, 2.* **ho'o.mala.mala.** To leave so as to sour, as mashed sweet potato to be eaten as poi; to ferment.

mā.lama.lama. 1. Redup. of *malama 1;* light of knowledge, clarity of thinking or explanation, enlightenment; shining, radiant, clear. *Ka mālamalama o ka 'ākau,* northern lights. **ho'o.mā.lama.lama.** To cause light, brighten, illuminate, enlighten, inform, civilize. (PNP *malamalama.*) 2. *Coris ballieui,* a fish; the name may be qualified by the colors *'ula* and *uli.* 3. *(Cap.)* n. Star name, no data. (Kuhelani.)

Mā.lama.lama-iki. n. Wind associated with Ke-ālia, Kaua'i. (For. 5:97.)

mā.lama moku. n. Mate of a ship. *Mālama moku 'ekā-hi,* first mate.

mā.lama ola. nv. To support financially; means of livelihood. *Mālama ola ka'awale,* separate maintenance. *Ua ho'opi'i 'ia no ka mālama ola 'ole,* he was sued for nonsupport.

mā.lama pipi. nv. To work with cattle, as a cowboy; one who does so.

mā.lama puka. n. Doorkeeper, sergeant-at-arms.

mā.lama pū.olo. nv. Keeper of bundles, especially for objects used in sorcery; to keep such bundles. *Kanaka pupuka mālama pū'olo,* evil person who cares for sorcery objects in a bundle.

mā.lama wai.hona puke. n. Librarian.

mā.lama wai.wai. n. Trustee, executor. See ex., *lawe 1.*

malana. Same as *manana.*

mā.lana. 1. vs. Buoyant, light; to float, as canoes; to move together, as people; unsteady, shallow-rooted. **ho'o.mā.lana.** To make buoyant, lighten. (PPN *malanga.*) 2. *(Cap.)* n. Name of a star.

Mala.nai. n. Name of a gentle breeze associated with Kō-

loa, Kaua'i, Hāna, Maui (For. 5:97), and Kai-lua, O'ahu. (PPN *Malangai.*)

mā.lā.nai. 1. Similar to *pānānai,* shallow; undisturbed, serene. *Ua hui mālānai,* serene associations. *He ua mālānai wale iho nō kēia,* this is just a light rain. 2. vs. Loosely drawn, as a cord. (For. 6:481.)

mā.lana.lana. Redup. of *mālana 1.*

malana.'opi. vs. Unstable, about to collapse. *Rare.*

mā.lani. vs. Sketchy, not deep, superficial, as of knowledge, emotion, a sore; obvious or plain rather than profound; mild, as of sickness. *He 'ike mālani kona i ka hula,* he has a superficial knowledge of the hula.

mala'o. Same as *la'o 1;* aggravating, annoying. *Rare.*

malā.oa. vs. Sad, sorrowful; moping over one's woes. *Rare.*

mā.la'o.la'o. 1. Redup. of *mala'o.* 2. n. Twilight. *Rare.*

māla pua. n. Flower garden.

malau. 1. n. Canoe bait carrier, some two or three fathoms long, with holes pierced in the sides and bottom to admit water, as used for bonito fishing. *Ua huli ka malau,* the bait carrier is overturned [the project is completed]. 2. vs. Calm, as the sea. *Rare.* 3. vs. Spoiled, decomposed, as meat or fish. *Rare.*

-malau. **ho'o.malau.** Skeptical, unbelieving, irreverent. **malau.ea.** vs. Lazy. **ho'o.malau.ea.** Caus/sim.

mā.lau.lau. vt. To trade, peddle. *Rare.* Cf. *ma'au'auwā.*

malau.lau.ā, malaulauwā. Same as *ma'au'auā,* to peddle.

māla waina. n. Vineyard. *Lit.,* grape garden.

male. 1. n. Phlegm, mucus from lungs or throat. (PPN *male.*) 2. n. Young *uhu,* a fish. Also *'ōmale.* 3. Also **mare.** nvt. Marriage, matrimony, wedding; to marry, mate. *Eng. Male 'ole,* unmarried, single. *Kanaka i male 'ole,* bachelor. *Wahine i male 'ole,* spinster, old maid. *Male malū,* marry secretly, elope. *'Oki male,* divorce. *Wahine male hou,* bride. *Kāne male hou,* groom. *Male lehulehu,* polygamy, polyandry, bigamy. *Ua ho'opili 'ia ma ka perita ma'ema'e o ka male,* united in the clean bonds of matrimony. *Ua male 'ia lāua,* they were married. *Hele mai 'oe i kā māua male 'ana,* come to our wedding. **ho'o.male.** To perform the marriage ceremony, to marry off; to force into marriage. 4. n. A card game.

mā.lehu.lehu. Rare var. of *mōlehulehu,* twilight.

mā.lei. 1. Short for *mai'a mālei.* 2. *(Cap.)* n. Legendary fish guardian, Makapu'u to Hanauma, O'ahu.

malei.'ia. vi. To be decked with leis.

ma.leila. Common pronunciation of *malaila,* but not so written. (Gram. 2.7.)

mā.lei 'ula. Same as *mai'a mālei 'ula.*

Maleka, Mareka. n. 1. America. *Eng.* See ex., *lohi 2.* 2. Mars. *Eng.*

malela. vs. Lazy, idle.

malele. vs. Scattered here and there, spreading here and there, unsystematic, haphazard, irregular. *Kanu malele,* to plant in various places. *Leo malele,* far-reaching voice. **ho'o.malele.** To scatter, distribute. *Rare.*

mā.lena. 1. n. Ashes used as medicine, as of bamboo or makaloa reed. 2. vs. Tight, taut. 3. vs. Yellow. 4. Same as *'ōlena,* turmeric.

mā.lena.lena. Redup. of *mālena 2, 3.*

male 'ole. vs. Unmarried, single.

maleu.ō, maleuwō. vs. Rough, as the sea. *Rare.*

malewa. nvi. To sway, move to and fro, pass by; passerby.

mā.lewa. n. Net mesh wide enough for the entire hand to pass through. Cf. *māhā, mahae.*

mali. 1. vt. To flatter, soothe, persuade with soft words, cajole, speak gently (less common than *ho'omalimali*). *Ua puni au i kāu mali leo 'ana mai,* I believed your flattering words. 2. nvt. To tie, as bait to a hook, hook to a line, feathers to a lei, or the end of a rope so that it will not unravel; a string used for such purposes.

malia. 1. Pas/imp. of *mali 2. Ua pa'i i ka lino pāwalu i malia i ke aho makali'i* (chant for Ka-lā-kaua), made fast to an eight-ply line, bound on with fine-meshed string. **2.** conj. Perhaps, maybe (usually followed by *o* or *paha*). *Malia o hele au,* maybe I'll go. *Malia paha o lohe aku,* perhaps [they] will hear. *Malia o hā'ule aku,* apt to fall.

mā.lia. Rare var. of *mālie.*

mali'a. 1. Same as *malia 2.* **2.** vt. To recollect, recall. Cf. *hāli'a.*

mā.lie. vs. Calm, quiet, serene, pacific, still, silent, tranquil, gentle, gradual; calmly, slowly, softly, quietly. *Hele mālie,* go slowly, amble. *Noho mālie,* keep still, sit still, be quiet. *'Ai mālie,* to eat slowly. *Mālie ke kai me ka makani,* the sea and wind are calm. *Lana mālie ka mana'o,* to think quietly. **ho'o.mālie.** To calm, quiet, hush, soothe, lull, ease pain. (PPN *maalie.*)

mā.lie.lie. Redup. of *mālie.* **ho'o.mā.lie.lie.** To comfort one who is disturbed, to soothe; to slow down. *Ho'omalielie i ke kaumaha,* condolence.

-malihia. ho'o.mali.hia. Pas/imp. of *mali 2.*

mali.hini. nvs. Stranger, foreigner, newcomer, tourist, guest, company; one unfamiliar with a place or custom; new, unfamiliar, unusual, rare, introduced, of foreign origin; for the first time. *Malihini māka'ika'i,* sight-seeing visitor, tourist. *Akua malihini,* foreign or non-native god [an appellation for Pele since she came from Kahiki]. *Ka'u malihini,* my guest [cf. *ko'u kama'āina*]. *Lā'au malihini,* non-native or introduced plant. *Ka hele malihini 'ana mai kēia ao aku ā hiki i kēlā ao,* the first trip from this world to the other world [translation of "Pilgrim's Progress"]. *He mea malihini kēia i ku'u maka,* I've never seen that before; I've seen this rarely. **ho'o.mali.hini.** To be or act as a stranger, guest; to reveal that guests are coming, as by omens. *Ke ho'omalihini mai nei kahi moa a kākou,* our chicken reveals that guests are coming. (PCP *man(i,u)-(f,s)i(l,n)i;* PEP if Easter *manihini* is not a Tahitian loan.)

mā.li'i. Var. of *mālili.*

-maliko. ho'o.maliko. To refuse respect, discredit (AP.)

mā.liko. 1. vi. To bud, as leaves. **2.** vs. Transparent, as small fish of some species, as *manini;* a stage of growth of fish. Cf. *'ōhua liko.*

malila. 1. vs. Ghostly, shadowy. *'O ka malila mōhai a Ka-ulu-lani, nona ke aka ka hihi'o i ka pō nei* (chant for Kua-kini), the ghostly offering of Ka-ulu-lani, to him belonged the shadow, the fleeting dream of last night. **2.** Common pronunciation of *malaila,* there, but not so written.

mā.lili. 1. vs. Blighted, blasted, withered, stunted, as fruits. *Hua 'ai mālili* (Kanl. 28.22), blasted fruit. (PNP *ma(a)lili.*) **2.** Rare var. of *ma'alili,* cooled, calmed. **ho'o.mā.lili.** Caus/sim. *E ho'omālili ai ka 'ena'ena,* to appease the anger.

mali.mali. Same as *mali 1.* **ho'o.mali.mali.** To flatter (Hal. 78.36), wheedle; to mollify with soft words or a gift; to soothe, quiet. (PPN *malimali.*)

malina. 1. vs. Calming, soothing. See *mali 1.* **2.** n. Sisal *(Agave sisalana; Furcrae foetida* on Ni'ihau), a tropical American plant grown for its fiber; used for rope, twine, hula skirts. The plant forms a huge rosette of stiff, straight leaves (1.8 m by 15 cm). It is called *malina* because marine ropes were made from it; cf. *malina 4.* (Neal 224–5.) **3.** vt. To splice, as rope. **4.** Also **marina.** nvs. Marine. *Eng.*

malino. vs. Calm, quiet, peaceful, pacific, as the sea; smooth, as ironing nicely done or as a canoe with a smooth finish; unwrinkled. *Malino ke kai,* the sea is calm. (PNP *malino;* see *linolino 2.*)

mā.lino.lino. Redup. of *malino.*

mali'o. n. **1.** Dawn light, twilight, especially as it pierces the shadows of night. But cf. UL 63. *O ka mali'o o ke aka, 'o aka lei mali'o* (For. 6:381), the dawn light in the shadows, shadows thrown off by the dawning. (PPN *m(a,e)liko.*) **2.** *(Cap.)* A mythical woman. See *kahua o Mali'o.*

mā.lipo.lipo. nvs. Shady; deep, dark shade. *Ho'okaka'a*

'ia mai e ke ahe ka lau mālipolipo, moved by the breezes are the leaves that cast deep shade.

maliu. 1. vt. To heed, give attention, listen, look upon with favor, turn toward. *Maliu 'ana,* consideration. *E maliu mai i ka leo o ka makua,* heed the word of the parent. **ho'o.maliu.** To cause to heed, heed. *Ho'omaliu 'ia aku ke Akua,* God was entreated. (PPN *maliu.*) **2.** *(Cap.)* n. Name of a star.

mali'u. 1. vs. Well salted. *Fig.,* seasoned with wisdom. **2.** n. Depth of tone; deep tone or sound, of the human voice.

malo. n. **1.** Male's loincloth; chant in praise of a chief's loincloth. *Malo 'eka,* dirty *malo* [said of farmers in dry areas]. (PPN *malo.*) **2.** Leaf sheath that protects the young leaves of the breadfruit tree, sometimes called *malo 'ulu.*

malō. Var. of *malo'o.*

mā.lō. vs. Taut, firm, straight. *Kino mālō,* straight body. *Kū ā mālō,* stand straight. *Mālō pono,* taut. **ho'o.mā.lō.** To make straight, firm, as a cord or sail; to tighten. (Probably PPN *maaloo.*)

mā.lo'e.lo'e. vs. **1.** Tired, exhausted; stiff or aching, as from unaccustomed exercise. Also *lo'elo'e.* **ho'o.mā.-lo'e.lo'e.** Caus/sim. (Ier. 9.5.) **2.** Taut, firm, as a rope. See ex., *kolia 2.* **ho'o.mā.lo'e.lo'e.** To stretch, make taut.

malo.hā.hā. Same as *malo'ohāhā.*

malohi. vs. Drowsy, sleepy, sluggish. **ho'o.malohi.** Sluggish; to act drowsy, sleepy; to cause drowsiness, sleepiness. (PCP *malo(f,s)i.*)

mā.lohi.lohi. Redup. of *malohi.* (PCP *malo(f,s)i-lo(f,s)i.*)

mā.lo'i. vi. To well up, of tears in the eyes; to form puddles, pools.

maloka. vs. Skeptical, unbelieving. **ho'o.maloka.** Same as above. (1 Kor. 7.12.)

malo kai. nvs. Loincloth worn in the sea; to wear a loincloth in the sea, i.e., to go swimming or fishing; poetic name for the sea, which acts as *malo* for the bather. *E malo kai kākou i wahi mea e 'ai ai,* let's wet our loincloths so as to get something to eat [a circumlocution; to mention that one was going fishing was thought to bring bad luck].

malo kea. n. White loincloth, an epithet for a female priest enjoying masculine privileges and exemption from female taboos; in particular she might enter the heiau temple where female deities were worshipped.

malolo. 1. nvi. To rest, pause, adjourn; adjournment, pause. **ho'o.malolo.** To cease work for a time, recess; to adjourn temporarily. Cf. *lā ho'omalolo. Ho'omalo-lo kaua,* truce. (PPN *malolo.*) **2.** vs. Low, of a tide. **ho'o.malolo.** Caus/sim.

mā.lolo. n. **1.** General term for Hawaiian flying fishes *(Parexocoetus brachypterus* and others). This name may be qualified by the terms *'ēheu lā, 'ēheu 'ula,* and *hāpu'u. Fig.,* fickle person who leaps from mate to mate. Cf. *puhiki'i, wauke mālolo.* (PPN *maalolo.*) **2.** See *kauna'oa mālolo.* **3.** An ancient type of tapa (no data).

mā.lō.lohi. Same as *mālohilohi.*

mā.lolo.hia. Pas/imp. of *mālōlohi. Kū mālolohia Puna i ka ua 'awa,* Puna stands sluggish in the cold rain.

malo'o. nvs. Dry, dried up, evaporated, juiceless, desiccated; stale, as bread; drought, dryness. **ho'o.malo'o.** To dry out, dehydrate, blot; to season, as lumber; tracing, as of genealogy (FS 115). See *pepa ho'omalo'o 'īnika.*

malo'o.hā.hā. vs. Very dry, as some turkey meat; desiccated, arid. *Fig.,* cold, devoid of animation or expression.

Malo-o-Lī.loa. Same as *Ka-malo-o-Līloa.*

malo wai. n. A loincloth wet in fresh water; it was taboo to appear in a chief's presence in such disrespectful array, and death was said to be a penalty.

malu. 1. nvs. Shade, shelter, protection, peace, control, strength (Kanl. 33.25); shaded, peaceful, quiet, safe;

protected by taboo; reserved, held apart; taboo; the stillness and awe of taboo. *Kahua ho'omalu,* detention camp. *Ke'ena malu,* any private or restricted room. *Ma ka malu o kona 'ēheu,* within the shelter of his wings. *Ka'a i ka malu ō,* still being cherished, fostered. *No ka waiho wale 'ana nō ia mea ma kona malu,* for the retention of this thing for his protection. *He malu ka nohona,* life is protected, peaceful. *Ua malu neia kino mamuli o kō leo,* this person is set apart because of your wish. *Malalo o ka malu o kēia kūlanakauhale,* under the control of this city. **ho'o.malu.** To bring under the care and protection of, to protect; to keep quiet, still, as during taboos or (modern) for peaceful meditation during *ho'oponopono* family therapy; to restrict, confine, quarantine; to judge, rule over, govern, make peace between warring parties; to suspend, as a license; to preside, as at a meeting; to call to order; probation. Cf. *hale ho'omalu, luna ho'omalu. Ho'omalu ma'i,* quarantine. *Panakō ho'omalu 'ia,* security bank; *lit.,* protected. *Ho'omalu 'ia ka Hale,* the House was called to order. *Ua ho'omalu 'ia kākou e ke aupuni,* we are protected by the government. *Ho'omalu kaua,* armistice. *E ho'omalu kākou 'oiai e ho'omaka ana ka hālāwai,* let us be quiet while the meeting begins. *Ka po'e hewa i ho'omalu 'ia,* evildoers who were restricted. *'Aha ho'okolokolo ho'omalu,* police court. *Māka'i ho'omalu pō,* night-patrol police. *Ho'omalu i kou po'e* (1 Nal. 3.9), to judge thy people. (PPN *malu.*) **2.** n. Name recorded by Gosline for sidespot goatfish, *Parupeneus pleurostigma.*

malū. vs. Secretly, confidentially, clandestinely, illegally, stealthily, furtive. *Lawe malū,* to take secretly. *Ho'opae malū,* to bring ashore illegally, smuggle. (PPN *maluu.*)

mā.lua. 1. nvs. Net mesh large enough to admit the entrance of two fingers; a net of such a mesh; two-ply. Cf. *mākahi.* **2.** *(Cap.)* n. Sea breezes, famous in song. See ex., below. **3.** Depression or cavity, planting hole. (AP.)

malu.ā. Same as *moloā,* lazy.

Mā.lua Hele. n. Wind, well known on Kaua'i, said to blow from the northwest. *Lit.,* traveling *Mālua.*

Mā.lua Kele. n. Trade wind, as on north Kaua'i. *Lit.,* damp *Mālua.*

Mā.lua Ki'i Wai. n. Sea breeze accompanied by showers, known at Hilo. *Lit., Mālua* fetching water. Also *Huehu, Mālualua Ki'i Wai. Mālua Ki'i Wai ke aloha, ho'opulu i ka liko māmane* (song), greetings to the water-fetching Mālua breeze, bringing moisture to the *māmane* buds.

mā.lua.lua. 1. vs. Rough, bumpy, uneven, full of ruts or puddles. Cf. *lua,* hole. **2.** *(Cap.)* n. North wind, known at Maui, Moloka'i, and O'ahu. See ex., *pāhili.*

mā.lua.'ula. n. Type of tapa stained with dye made of *kukui* bark.

malu.hā. n. Mallow bush. (Ioba 30.4.)

maluhi. Same as *māluhiluhi;* dull, sleepy. Also *molohi.* **ho'o.maluhi.** Same as *ho'omāluhiluhi.*

malu.hia. nvs. Peace, quiet, security, tranquillity, serenity; safety; solemn awe and stillness that reigned during some of the ancient taboo ceremonies; peaceful, restful. *E ho'omaha me ka maluhia,* rest in peace. **ho'o.malu.hia.** To cause or give peace, protect; to arbitrate between warring parties.

mā.luhi.luhi. vs. Tired, weary; worn out; tiresome, wearisome, fatiguing. **ho'o.mā.luhi.luhi.** To cause fatigue, exhaust, tire; tiresome, exhausting, toilsome. *'A'ohe waiwai o ka hele 'ana, he ho'omāluhiluhi,* there's no use going, it wears one out.

Malu-ko'i. n. Name of a rain associated with Kaha-lu'u, O'ahu. (Elbert and Mahoe 61.)

malu ko'i. n. Services for consecrating *(malu)* adzes to be used for cutting *'ōhi'a* logs for images or canoes (also *malu 'ōhi'a*); people engaged in such services. (Kam. 76:146.) See *haku 'ōhi'a, kapu 'ōhi'a kō. Fig.,* shadow of death, deep gloom or shade (PH 25, FS 158–

9). *Lit.,* adze taboo. *Pi'i hou ka malu ko'i o nā kānaka* (For. 4:53), the image cutters of the people went up again.

Malu-lani. n. Name of a star. *Lit.,* celestial shade.

malule. vs. Limp, weak, flexible; soft and fragile, as some eggshells. Cf. *ha'i malule, hāpai malule.* **ho'o.malule.** To make lax, limp, weak; to relax, weaken, enfeeble; to shed a hard shell, as of a crab; to change from a caterpillar into a butterfly; to metamorphose. Cf. *lā'au ho'omalule kino. Wai ho'omalule,* water of relaxation [liquor].

mā.lule.lule. Redup. of *malule.*

malulu. Pool that never dries up. (AP.) Cf. *lulu,* sheltered.

malu make. n. Shadow of death. (Ioba 24.17.)

malu.malu. Redup. of *malu;* shelter or protection of any kind, often humble; shady. *Malumalu akua,* shelter or protection of the gods. *'A'ole maika'i loa 'o kēia hale akā he malumalu,* this house is not very good, still it is a shelter. *He malumalu hele lā,* it's protection [for] going in the sun. **ho'o.malu.malu.** To overshadow, cast a shadow; shade; darken, as by a cloud. *Nā kerubima nani e ho'omalumalu i ka noho aloha* (Heb. 9.5), the cherubim of glory overshadowing the mercy seat.

malu.malu.hia. Redup. of *maluhia.*

maluna. See *luna.*

malu 'ō.hi'a. n. Taboo ceremonies when an *'ōhi'a* tree was cut to be carved into images; the log itself. (Kam 76:136.) Cf. *malu ko'i.*

mama. vt. To chew, masticate (but not swallow; cf. *nau). Kona mau mama 'awa,* his kava chewers. (PPN *mama.*)

mā.mā. 1. vs. Fast, nimble, speedy of movement, quick, brisk, swift; to hasten, hurry. *Māmā i ka hele,* fast going, traveling far and fast; said also of an infant in the first stages of walking by himself. *Māmā i ka holo,* fast in running. **2.** vs. Light, of weight. *Fig.,* eased of pain, ache, or distress. *Eamāmā,* oxygen. *Akemāmā,* lungs. **ho'o.mā.mā.** To lighten, as a load; to ease pain; to cheer. *E ho'omāmā 'oe i kou kaumaha,* ease your grief. (PPN *ma'ama'a.*) **3.** n. Mama, mother.

mamae. Redup. of *mae;* sickly, listless; weakening or withering effect of pain; wan or pale, as after illness; crestfallen, as after enthusiasm is squelched. **ho'o.mamae.** Caus/ sim., to weaken. (PPN *mamae.*)

mama.iki. See *pūpū mamaiki.*

mamaka. 1. vi. To put forth buds, to bud; green. *Mamaka hou,* to bud anew. Cf. *maka,* bud. **2.** n. A variety of kava. (HP 202.)

mā.maka. 1. nvi. Horizontal carrying stick, borne over the shoulders; to carry this stick. *Ua māmaka lākou i ka huaka'i a ke ali'i,* they bore carrying sticks on the chief's journey. **2.** n. A game: one person grasps his own ankles from the back; others stick a *māmaka* pole between his arms and his back and carry him, as they would a bundle. A more difficult variant is that one person may attempt to carry two persons singlehanded. **3.**n. Bearer, traveler.

mā.maka.kaua. n. Company of warriors. *Lit.,* carriers of war. Cf. *'Ahahui Māmakakaua.*

mamaka.walu. Redup. of *makawalu. He mamakawalu lākou i loko o 'Ī* (chant), there are many in the 'Ī family.

mamoke. 1. Redup. of *make 1;* to die, of several; to wilt, wither, or fade, of plants. (PPN *mamate.*) **2.** Colloquial for *makemake,* to want, like.

mā.maki. n. Small native trees *(Pipturus* spp.) with broad white-backed leaves and white mulberry-like fruit; the bark yielded a fiber valued for a kind of tapa, similar to that made from *wauke* but coarser. Often misspelled *mamake.* (Neal 318–9.) Also *waimea.* See ex., *wale 1.*

mamala. Redup. of *mala 1, 2.* See ex., *pu'u lele.*

mā.mala. n. **1.** Fragment, splinter, chip, piece. *Nā māmala i koe* (Luka 9.17), fragments [of food] that remained. (PPN *mala.*) **2.** Stroke, as of paddle or of war club. *'Ehia māmala newa āu i hahau ai?* How many club blows did you strike? **3.** *(Cap.)* Old name of Honolulu harbor.

mamala.hia. vs. Sour, as poi.

Mā.mala hoa. Var. of *Māmala-hoe. Lit.,* club stroke.

Mā.mala-hoe. n. Name of a particular company of warriors of Ka-mehameha and the name of Kamehameha's famous law of the splintered paddle *(lit.,* paddle fragment) which guaranteed the safety of the highways to all, as women, children, sick, and aged; the law was so called because it was said to have been formulated after Ka-mehameha had been struck on the head with a paddle while his foot was trapped in a crevice. The law is often called *Māmala hoa.* According to one account (Thrum, 1906, 81-6) Ka-mehameha threw a stone at two attackers; it hit a *noni* tree, pierced one of the attackers and hit a precipice where it is still lodged. Ka-mehameha's supporters tortured and killed a "navigator" who had failed to guard Ka-mehameha properly by pulling a spear back and forth through his body. Ka-mehameha wept and formulated his law. *Lit.,* splintered paddle. Cf. Kam. 64:22.

mā.mala.'ō.lelo. n. Sentence, clause, phrase. *Lit.,* speech fragment.

mamali. 1. Redup. of *mali* 2. **n.** Young stage of *'ō'io,* a fish.

mamali.hini. Redup. of *malihini;* not well acquainted, somewhat unaccustomed to or unfamiliar with. See ex., *polepole* 2. *Mamalihini au i kēia hana,* I'm not too well acquainted with this work.

mā.malu. 1. Redup. of *malu;* protection, defense, shade, covering; protected, shaded. *Māmalu hale o Kū,* protection of the house of Kū. **ho'o.mā.malu.** To protect; to make shady; to cast gloom. **2.** n. Umbrella, parasol. **3.** n. Type of mushroom.

mama.make. Redup. and intensifier of *make 1,* to die, of very many, as in a disaster; more deaths than *mamake.*

mama.mala. vs. Small, little, especially of work. Cf. *māmala,* fragment. *He noho wale iho nō nā ali'i, he 'olu'olu, he mamamala, 'a'ole hana nui,* the chiefs live in an agreeable way, little work, not much work.

mamamo. Same as *mamo 3,* a fish.

mā.mane. 1. n. A native leguminous tree *(Sophora chrysophylla),* which thrives at high altitudes, up to the tree line, as on Mauna Kea and Mauna Loa. The leaves are narrow, compound, more or less downy, the flowers commonly yellow, the pods four-winged, yellowseeded. Hawaiians formerly used the hard wood for spades and sled runners. (Neal 442-3; Kep. 65.) See ex., *lau 4, Mālua Ki'i Wai. Uhiuhi lau māmane, kahi wai o Ka-pāpala,* covered with *māmane* leaves is the water of Ka-pāpala [any concealing, as of truth (Kel. 139) or scandal; *māmane* branches are said to have been tossed in this pool at Ka'ū to make the mud settle]. *Kīkē ka 'alā, uwē ka māmane,* rocks crash, the *māmane* tree weeps [someone weeps when there is a clash]. **2.** vs. Attractive, said of a person sexually appealing but not necessarily good-looking, perhaps so called because of the attractive flower of the *māmane* tree. **3.** n. A variety of taro. (HP 33.)

mamao. 1. nvs. Far, distant, remote, high in rank; distance. *Kū mamao,* far away, aloof. *Ka-'Ī-i-mamao* (name), the very highest 'Ī. **ho'o.mamao.** To keep away, keep one's distance; to go far; to remove someone to a distance. *Ho'omamao lani,* taboo of unapproachability, of some very high chiefs. (PPN *mama'o.)* **2.** n. Third or highest platform of the *lananu'u mamao* (oracle tower), where the high priest conducted services.

mama'o. 1. nvs. Greenish, light green. Cf. *ma'o,* green. **2.** Same as *mamo 3,* a fish.

mamau. Redup. of *mau 1-3.* See ex., *'i'ī 1. Ua mamau ka 'ai a ka i'a,* the fish are really biting. *Mamau nā ihu,* noses stuck together [said jokingly of long kisses]. **ho'o.mamau.** To cause to get stuck, to stall. (PPC *mamau,* fixed.)

mamaua. Redup. of *maua.*

mamau.ea. Same as *manauea 1, 2,* and *mā'auea.*

mamina. Same as *minamina* but less frequent. See ex., *pulakaumaka. Mamina au i ka lilo o ka wa'a,* I'm sorry the canoe is lost. *Mamina wale kā ho'i,* that's regrettable.

mā.mio. Same as *mio,* to disappear.

mamo. n. **1.** Black Hawaiian honey creeper *(Drepanis pacifica):* its yellow feathers above and below the tail were used in choicest featherwork. Formerly found only on Hawai'i, not seen since the 1880s. A Moloka'i species was *Drepanis funerea,* not seen since the 1890s; also *hoa* and *'ō'ō nuku mū.* **2.** Safflower or false saffron *(Carthamus tinctorius),* a branching annual, 30 to 120 cm high, from Asia, grown for its flowers, which are yellow, like the feathers of the *mamo* bird. (Neal 858.) **3.** A sergeant fish *(Abudefduf abdominalis),* to about 163 mm long. Also *mamamo, mamo pohole.* (PPN *mamo.)* **4.** Descendant, posterity. *Nā mamo o 'Ikera'ela* (Puk. 1.13), the children of Israel. *Nā mamo piha'ā o Ka-'alu'alu,* the driftwood descendants of Ka-'alu'alu [said derisively of a Ka'ū person with many children, because of the abundance of driftwood at Ka-'alu'alu, Ka'ū].

mamo ali'i. n. Descendant of a chief.

mamona. n. Mammon. (Mat. 6.24.)

Mā.mona. n. Mormon. *Ni'ihau.*

mamo pohole. Same as *mamo 3,* a fish.

mamua. See *mua 1.*

mamuli. See *muli.*

mana. 1. nvs. Supernatural or divine power, mana, miraculous power; a powerful nation, authority; to give mana to, to make powerful; to have mana, power, authority; authorization, privilege; miraculous, divinely powerful, spiritual; possessed of mana, power. Cf. *-āmana. Mana makua,* parental authority. *Leo mana,* voice of authority that is obeyed. *Mana kia'i,* guardian power. *Mana loa,* great power; almighty. *Noho mana,* to wield power, occupy a position of power. *Ke kumu . . . i mana ai ka 'ao'ao ali'i,* the reason for giving the chief's side power. *E mana ana nō i ke konohiki* (Kep. 159), it is the privilege of the landlords. *E mana nō ma ka lā 'umi,* effective on the tenth day [as a law]. **ho'o.mana. (a)** To place in authority, empower, authorize. *He bila e ho'omana ana i ke koho 'ia o nā luna māka'i,* a bill authorizing the election of district sheriffs. *'O nā kānāwai i ho'omana hou 'ia,* laws reenacted. **(b)** To worship; religion, sect. *Ho'omana Kepanī,* Buddhist; Buddhism. *Ho'omana ki'i,* idolatry, idol worship. *Ho'omana Na'auao,* Christian Science. *Ho'omana o Iesu Kristo o nā Po'e Ho'āno o nā Lā Hope Nei,* Church of Jesus Christ of Latter Day Saints. *Ho'omana Palani (Farani),* French religion; Catholicism. *Ho'omana Pīthopa (Bihopa),* Episcopalian religion; *lit.,* bishop's religion. *Ho'omana Pō'aono,* Seventh Day Adventist; *lit.,* Saturday religion.(PPN *mana.)* **2.** nvs. Branch, limb, crotch; crosspiece, as of the cross; a line projecting from another line; stream branch; road branch or fork, variant, version, as of a tale; to branch out, spread out. *Mana weu lani,* branch with divine foliage (a chief). (PPN *manga.)* **3.** n. Hook used in catching eels. **4.** n. Stage in growth of fish in which colors appear; stage of a foetus in which limbs begin to develop. **5.** n. A native fern *(Hypolepis punctata),* with large, much subdivided fronds. The dark-brown mature stems were used to plait the best hats, after being scraped to remove the pulp. Also *olua.* **6.** n. A variety of taro used in medicine; it propagates by branching from the top of the corm. (HP 23.) *Mana* may be qualified by descriptive terms, as listed below. **7.** n. A taboo house in a heiau. Cf. *'aha hele honua.*

-mana. ho'o.mana. Callus; callous. *Kaua'i.*

māna. 1. n. A chewed mass, as of kava for drinking, coconut flakes or *kukui* nut for medicine. *Māna pani* (Kam. 76:74), food taken after drinking kava [*lit.,* closing mouthful]. *Māna 'ai,* food chewed by adult for child; any mouthful of food. *Pehea ka ma'i? Ua komo kahi māna 'ai,* how is the patient? He has taken a little nourishment. (PPN *ma'anga.*) **2.** Trait believed acquired from those who raise a child. *Kū nō i ka māna a ke kahu hānai,* trait acquired from association with the one who raised the child. **3.** Short for *haumāna,* student. *'O ke kumu, 'o ka māna, ho'opuka 'ia,* the teacher, the pupil, come forth [challenge from pupil to teacher].

mā.nā. 1. vs. Arid; desert. Cf. *Mānā,* place on Kaua'i. **2.** n. A native fern *(Pteris irregularis),* with large, bright-green, much-subdivided fronds. Also *'ae, 'āhewa, 'iwa puakea.*

mana ala.nui. n. Road fork or branching.

manae. Probably same as *nae,* net.

mā.nae. Same as *nae,* shortness of breath.

mana'e. To the east (a direction, see *na'e 1).* (Nak. 121.)

mana 'ele.'ele. n. A variety of taro; petiole and leaf with red-black markings. (HP 23.) *Lit.,* black *mana* taro.

mana.halo. vi. To swim with paddling motions, as in learning to swim. *E manahalo a 'ike i ka 'au,* to paddle until knowing how to swim.

mana ho'o.kolo.kolo. n. Power of passing judgment, jurisdiction.

mana hua. n. A variety of taro (no data). (HP 33.)

mana.hu'a. Sad, grieving. (AP.)

mā.nai. nvt. Needle for stringing leis, formerly of coconut midrib, now of wire; to string leis. Also called *hānai* on Hawai'i, *mākila* on Maui, and *mōkila* on Kaua'i. *Mānai pua ana kākou,* we are stringing flowers.

manai.ea. Same as *manauea,* a seaweed.

mā.nai.nai. Redup. of *mānai.*

mā.nai.'ula. 1. Same as *mai'a mālei 'ula.* **2.** n. Marriage of close relatives.

mana.kā. vs. Boresome, tiresome, dull, monotonous, wearied (see ex., *kahiko 1),* wearisome, uninteresting; bored, uninterested. **ho'o.mana.kā.** Same as above; to cause boredom. *Mai hana ho'omanakā 'oukou,* don't work in a such a bored, indifferent fashion. (PCP *manataa;* cf. Rarotongan.)

mana Kahi.kolu Ki'e.ki'e. n. Power of the Holy Trinity. *Nonoi akahai a'e ana i nā mana Kahikolu Ki'eki'e loa* (Kel. 107), modestly beseech the powers of the most Holy Trinity.

mana kea. n. Same as *mana ke'oke'o.*

mana ke'o.ke'o. n. A native variety of taro; white corm; mainly used as table taro, a favorite for making *kūlolo;* consistency tough for poi. (HP 23.)

-manaki'i. ho'o.mana.ki'i. Idolatrous; to worship images.

mana.kō. n. Mango *(Mangifera indica),* a large, common fruit tree from India. Long, narrow leaves form a dense top, and large ovoid, juicy fruits develop usually between March and October. (Neal 521–3.) *Eng.*

mana.koho. n. Voter. *I nā manakoho,* to the voters.

mana.kō kāne. n. Mango chutney. Also *manakō kūkāne.*

mana.kō meneke. n. Variety of mango.

mana.kū. n. **1.** Humble commoner, used with *kanaka Rare.* **2.** *(Cap.)* Name of a star.

mana.kuke. n. Mongoose. *Eng.*

mana kū.kulu hema. n. A variety of taro, introduced from Samoa; chalky-white corm; a fair table taro. *Lit., mana* [from] southern border.

Mana Lani Kahi.kolo. n. Almighty Holy Trinity. (Kel. 18.)

mana lau loa. n. A native, large-leaved variety of taro, chiefly used as table taro; leaf stem pink and green below grading upward to light-green. *Lit.,* long-leaved *mana.*

māna.leo. n. Native speaker, a term invented by Larry Kimura and William H. Wilson in the late 1970s. *Lit.,* inherited language.

mā.nalo. 1. vs. Sweet, potable, of water that may be drunk but is not deliciously cool *(hu'ihu'i);* firm and tasty, as taro or sweet potato. *Wai-mānalo* (place name), potable water. *Mānalo iki kēia wai,* this water is drinkable, but perhaps a little brackish. **ho'o.mā.-nalo.** To remove bitterness or saltiness, as of overly salty salmon. (PNP *maangalo.*) **2.** nvs. Appeased, softened, mollified, as anger, curses, bad omens; safe from harm or danger; sweetness, appeasement. *'A 'ohe mea e mānalo ai ka huhū,* nothing will assuage the anger. *Mānalo ka moe* (Kep. 121), the dream is made harmless. *Mānalo ka heiau,* to sweeten a temple; to appease the gods, as by offering sacrifice. *Aukahi ka pua'a, mānalo ka wa'a,* perfect the [sacrificial] pig, safe the canoe. **ho'o.mā.nalo.** To appease, assuage, or mollify, as a god; to neutralize, as a curse. **3.** *(Cap.)* n. Name reported for both Venus and Jupiter. Also *Ho'omānalo.*

mana.loa. Same as *nenue,* pilot fish.

Mā.nalo Kai. n. Star name (no data). (Kuhelani.)

mā.nalo.nalo. 1. Redup. of *mānalo 1,* **2.** **ho'o.mā.-nalo.nalo.** Caus/sim. **2.** *(Cap.)* Same as *Mānalo 3.*

mana.lua. Same as *mai'a mana lua.*

mana lua. n. Two branches, fork, as in a road.

mana.mana. 1. Redup. of *mana 1.* **ho'o.mana.mana.** To impart *mana,* as to idols or objects; to deify; superstitious. (PPN *manamana.*) **2.** Redup. of *mana 2;* appendages, claws, branches, rays, forks; to branch out. *Lā manamana,* sun with rays. (PPN *mangamanga.*) **3.** n. Finger, toe. **4.** n. Third of three coconut husks tied to *'ahi* fishing line. Cf. *nuku* and *poli,* the first and second husks from the bottom. **5.** n. A variety of sweet potato with finger-like leaves, sometimes qualified by *ke'oke'o,* white. (HP 142.)

mana.mana iki. n. Little finger.

mana.mana kuhi. n. **1.** Index finger. **2.** Hand of a watch or clock.

mana.mana lima. n. Finger.

mana.mana lima nui. n. Thumb. *Lit.,* big finger.

mana.mana loa (loloa). n. Middle finger.

mana.mana miki. n. Index finger.

mana.mana nui. n. Big branch; big toe; thumb.

mana.mana pili. n. Third or ring finger.

mana.mana.'ula. n. A kind of seaweed. *Lit.,* red-branching.

mana.mana wā.wae. n. Toe.

mana mele.mele. n. A variety of taro. (HP 33.)

mana.moi. n. Medium-sized *moi,* a fish.

manana. 1. vi. To stretch out, as arms, fingers, feet; to spread out, as the tentacles of an octopus; to protrude, as ears; to distend, as nostrils while breathing hard; swelling, as with disease (Ii 164). **ho'o.manana.** To stretch out, extend; to loosen, as a grip. **2.** n. A variety of sweet potato.

mā.nana. Same as *mālana,* buoyant.

mana.nai. n. A pleasant breeze.

mā.nā.nai. Var. of *mālānai,* shallow.

mā.nana-kea. n. Star name (no data).

mana.na'o. Redup. of *mana'o;* opinions or viewpoints of several persons.

mana'o. nvt. Thought, idea, belief, opinion, theory, thesis, intention, meaning, suggestion, mind (Mat. 22.37), desire, want; to think, estimate, anticipate, expect (see ex., *lele'oi),* suppose, mediate, deem, consider (not the intellectual process of *no'ono'o).* See *mana'o nui. Kau nui ka mana'o,* think constantly, concentrate. *Eia ko'u mana'o iā'oe* (beginning of a letter), this is my thought for you. *Ka mea i mana'o 'ia,* the one thought of [the intended victim of sorcery]. *'O ka mea i ho'opi'i 'ia e mana'o 'ia nō, 'oia he kanaka maika'i nō,* the accused party shall be presumed a good man. **ho'o.mana'o.** To remember, recall, commemorate, reflect deeply on, meditate. See *'ōlelo ho'omana'o. Ho'omana'o aloha,* to remember with affection. *He ho'omana'o,* in memoriam. *Mea ho'omana'o,* souvenir, keepsake, reminder, memorandum. *Kia ho'omana'o,* monument, memorial tablet. *He mau 'ōlelo ho'omana'o,* notes. (PPN *manako.*)

mana'o aka.mai. n. Clever thought, wise thought; spirit of wisdom. (Puk. 28.3.)

mana 'oene, mana 'owene. n. A variety of taro, same as *mana 'ulu* except that the petiole is pinker. (HP 24.) This term may be qualified by the colors *ke'oke'o, lenalena, melemele, 'ula'ula.*

mana'o.ha'i. nvi. Something to say, thought to express, predication, theorem, problem; to predicate.

mana'o hā.iki. nvs. Narrow or intolerant mind; narrow-minded, intolerant.

mana 'ohe. n. A variety oof taro (HP 33.)

mana'o ho'o.hā.like.like. n. Comparison.

mana'o ho'o.mana.mana. n. Superstition.

mana'o ho'o.nalo.nalo, mana'o ho'o.nane.nane. n. Hidden or figurative meaning.

mana'o ho'o.pili.pili. n. Hidden or figurative meaning.

mana'o 'ino. nv. Evil thought or idea, hatred, ill feeling; to hate.

mana'o.'i'o. nvt. Faith, confidence; to have faith, confidence; to believe. *Kumu mana'o'i'o,* creed. *Pelika o ka mana'o'i'o,* covenant of faith. *Mana'o'i'o Nīkine,* Nicene creed. *Ua mana'o'i'o i ke Akua,* [he] believes in God.

mana'o kā.lā. vs. Money-minded, commercial.

mana'o ki'e.ki'e. n. Pride, conceit. *Lit.,* high opinion.

mana'o kipi. n. Rebellious thoughts; disloyal.

mana'o koho. n. Supposition, presumption.

mana'o.kō.kua. n. Hypothesis, lemma; thought to help. *'O ka mana'okōkua, 'oia kekahi mana'o a kumumana'o paha, i hō'oia 'ia i mea kōkua ma ka hō'oia 'ana i ka mana'oha'i nui a me ka wehe 'ana paha i ka nane-ha'i,* a hypothesis is a thought or proposition used as a demonstration and aid to proving a main predication [or theorem] or for the solution of a problem.

mana'o kū.pa'a. Same as *mana'o pa'a;* doctrine.

mana'o.lana. nvt. Hope, confidence, expectation; to hope (*mana'o + -lana,* nominalizer; Gram. 6.6.2).

mana'o lau.lā. nvs. Broad-minded, tolerant, tolerancy.

mana'o.lia. Pas/imp. of *mana'o.*

mana'o lō.kahi. vi. Unanimous.

mana'o maoli. n. Literal meaning; a real or true opinion.

mana'o.na'o. Redup. of *mana'o;* to meditate, ponder. (Hal. 63.6.)

mā.na'o.na'o. nvs. Horrible, dreadful, pitiful, horrifying, gruesome, shocking; shocked, horrified; heartsick, overcome with grief or horror; heartbreaking; grief. *Kona māna'ona'o* (Laie 591), his grief. *Māna'ona'o au i ka pepehi o ku'u keiki i kāna wahine,* I am horrified at the beating given his wife by my nephew. **ho'o.mā.-na'o.na'o.** To cause a sensation of horror, grief.

mana'o nui. nv. Important matter or idea, sense, signification; meaning *(Ni'ihau). Me ka mana'o nui,* with every consideration [formal ending of a letter]. *Mea mana'o nui 'ia,* person or thing constantly in mind.

mana'o 'ola.lau. n. Confused, erroneous thinking, hallucination.

mana'o.opa'a. nvs. Conviction, determination, firm intention; convinced, determined, resolute (Laie 591). *He mana'opa'a kona ua pono kāna hana,* he is convinced his conduct is righteous.

mana 'ō.pelu. n. A native variety of taro, named for a fish, *'ōpelu,* the corms of which were used as *'ōpelu* bait; the leaf stem is green with white streaks, becoming maroon above. (Whitney; HP 23.)

mana'o.pili. n. Corollary, as in mathematics.

mana'o poina. n. Postscript, afterthought, forgotten opinion.

mana'o ulu wale. n. Whim, fancy, impulse, notion, random thought, thought that has come for no particular reason.

mana'o wale. vt. To suppose, presume.

mana'o wehe.wehe. n. Explanatory thought, scholium, explanation.

mana 'owene. Var. spelling of *mana 'oene.*

mana piha. n. Supreme, absolute power.

mana piko. n. A native variety of taro, distinguished by purple on leaf center and extending on main veins; a fair table taro. (Whitney; HP 24.)

mana pipika. n. A variety of taro. *Lit.,* crinkled *mana.*

mana.pua. See *mea 'ono pua'a.*

mana ua.uahi. n. A variety of taro, the leaf stem mainly light green, the leaf blade with white leaf center, veins, and edges. (HP 24.) *Lit.,* smoky-gray *mana.*

manau.ea, manauwea. n. **1.** A small red seaweed *(Gracilaria coronopifolia),* with stiff, cylindrical, succulent stem and branches, a good alga for making food gels (KL line 53). The term may be qualified by *pala kea, pehu,* or *puakea.* Rarely *manaiea;* often called "short *ogo*" and "long *ogo*" (Japanese, dialectal). *Ogo* or long *ogo* is *G. bursa-pastoris.* **2.** A variety of taro.

mana 'uele, mana 'uwele. Same as *mana 'oene,* a taro.

mana 'ū.hā pua'a. n. A variety of taro.

mana 'ula'ula. n. A rare variety of taro, distinguished by its purplish-red flecked petioles; mainly used as table taro. (HP 24.) Also *mana hā'ula'ula.*

mana uli.uli. n. A variety of taro, introduced from South Seas; makes good poi of yellow color. The corms are tough and rubbery when cooked. Noted for prolific branching. *Lit.,* dark *mana.*

mana 'ulu. n. A native variety of taro distinguished by pinkish petioles. The corms have orange-yellow flesh when cooked (like fruit of breadfruit) and are used mainly as table taro. (Whitney 27; HP 24.) *Lit.,* breadfruit *mana.* Cf. *mana 'oene.*

manau.wea. Var. spelling of *manauea.*

manawa. 1. n. Time, turn, season, date, chronology, period of time. Cf. *ha'i manawa. No ka manawa,* for the time being, for a short time or while, temporary. *Ia manawa, ia manawa nō,* at this time, then, contemporary. *Nā manawa āpau loa,* always, all the time. *I ka manawa hea,* when. *'Elua manawa,* twice, two times. *No ka manawa pōkole,* for a short time or while, for awhile. *Mai kēia manawa aku,* henceforth, from now on. *Manawa iki,* a moment. *Manawa mau loa,* eternal; eternity. *Manawa 'ole,* in no time, instantly, immediately. *Manawa ua,* rainy season. *Ho'opaumanawa,* to waste time. *I kēlā manawa i kēia manawa,* now and then, from time to time. *'O kou manawa kēia,* this is your turn. *I ka manawa o Ka-mehameha,* in the time of Ka-mehameha. *Nā bona no ka manawa,* term bonds. **2.** vs. For a short time, infrequent. *Kū manawa ka moku,* the ship stops infrequently. **3.** n. Affections, feelings, disposition, heart, seat of emotions. Cf. *manawahuwā, manawa 'ino, manawale'a, manawanui. Hāli'ali'a mai ke aloha pili pa'a i ku'u manawa* (song), recalling love dwelling firmly in my affections. (PPN *manawa.*) **4.** n. Anterior fontanel in the heads of infants; top of the head of adults at position of the fontanel.

manawa.ea. 1. nvi. Hard breathing, panting for breath, from exertion; to pant thus, breathe. *Lit.,* rising breath. (PPN *maanawa.*) **2.** n. Infancy before the fontanel closes. *Lit.,* rising fontanel.

manawa hana. n. Working time or shift.

Mana-wahine. n. Name of a star, said to appear in the first night of the month *Nana* and to vanish after the night of *Muku. Lit.,* female power.

manawa.hua. 1. nvs. Discomfort of the stomach, or indigestion, with gas and often diarrhea, thought to be caused by wrong diet or by excessive handling of animals, such as kittens or puppies, which might also become sick; to suffer thus; great grief, as over the loss of a loved one; to grieve. *Lit.,* swollen stomach. Cf. *lūmanawahua. Manawahua kai ko'o,* great distress, pain; surging pain, distress [*lit.,* strong sea, stomach discomfort]. **2.** n. A native fern *(Doryopteris* spp.), about 30 cm high, with heart-shaped fronds divided into many long segments. Also *'iwa'iwa.*

manawa.huā, manawahuwa. nvs. Jealous, jealousy; to bear a grudge. *Ua manawahuā 'oia i nā hoahānau,* he bore a grudge against his brethren.

mana.wai. vs. Warped, depressed, bent in. *Rare.*

mana wai. n. 1. Stream branch. 2. A variety of taro. (HP 33.)

mana-wai-ke-'ohe. n. A variety of taro. (HP 33.)

manawa 'ino. nvs. Evil disposition, hard feelings, hardhearted, time of storm.

manawa ka'a.wale. n. Free time.

manawa.kolu. vs. Eternal. *Ola manawakolu,* life everlasting.

manawa kū.pono. n. Opportune time, appropriate time, opportunity, chance.

manawa.le'a. nvt. A generous heart, charity, alms, donation; to give freely and willingly; gratis, free, benevolent, beneficent. *Hui manawale'a,* relief society. *Ua manawale'a aku 'oia i nā hoahānau,* he gave willingly to the cousins. **ho'o.manawa.le'a.** Caus/sim.

manawa moe. n. Bedtime, time to sleep.

mā.nawa.nawa. Same as *kolokolo kahakai,* a beach vitex.

-manawanui. ho'o.manawa.nui. Patience, steadfastness, fortitude; to have patience, fortitude; patient, steadfast, courageous and persevering; to try one's patience. *E ho'omanawanui,* be patient. *He kanaka ho'omanawanui i ka lā a me ka ua,* a man who patiently endures the sun and the rain. *He nohona ho'omanawanui,* a way of life that tries one's patience. (PCP *manawanui.*)

mana weo. n. A variety of taro, probably the same as *weo;* distinguished by dark-purple petiole edges; a fair table taro.

mane. n. 1. Manna. (Puk. 16.31.) *Eng.* 2. Mina (RSV), maneh (KJV). (Ezek. 45.12.) *Eng.*

mā.nea. nvs. Hoof (Lunk. 5.22); claws; fingernails, toenails; ball of a foot; keel of a ship. *Fig.,* dependent, underling, inferior. *Mai ka piko o ke po'o a ka mānea o nā wāwae,* from the crown of the head to the balls of the feet. *Mānea 'u'uku o ka wāwae* (FS 91), toe of the foot. *He mānea 'o Ni'ihau, no Kaua'i,* Ni'ihau is a dependent of Kaua'i. **ho'o.mā.nea.** To harden, raise calluses; to strengthen, make steadfast.

mā.nei.'ula. Same as *mānai'ula.*

mā.nele. 1. nvt. Sedan chair, palanquin, litter, stretcher, bier (2 Sam. 3:31); to carry on a stretcher, bier, sedan chair. 2. Same as *a'e,* several trees.

mā.nele hu'a hiwa.hiwa. n. Litter with decorated sides on which a bride was carried to her groom's house. (Kam. 64:26.) *Lit.,* litter [with] festive sides.

manelo. Fissures, caves, as on ocean floor; free of stones, as land. (And.)

manena. n. A small native tree (several varieties of *Pelea hawaiensis*), with oblong leaves and four-parted fruit capsules; related to the *mokihana.*

manene. 1. nvi. Shuddery sensation of fear, as on looking over a precipice or if confronted by sudden danger; sensation of disgust, revulsion, or repugnance; sensation of inner quaking accompanying sexual desire; to shudder, quake. *Manene ka wāwae,* the feet shudder. *Manene ka pepeiao,* the ear shudders [as on hearing vile language]. 2. n. A kind of small plantain or *laukahi* (*Plantago grayana* var. *grayana* native to O'ahu and Kaua'i; *P. krajinai* native to Kaua'i).

mane'o. nvs. Itch; itchy; smarting, as the throat after eating raw taro or certain fish; prickly, as some clothes; sexually titillated; ticklish; tickling. *Nahele mane'o,* nettle. *Ke pi'i nei ko'u mane'o,* I am beginning to itch. **ho'o.mane'o.** To cause to itch; to tickle. (PNP *mangeo.*)

mā.neo.neo. 1. vs. Barren. *Rare.* Cf. *neo,* void. 2. n. Sailfish tang (*Zebrasoma veliferum*).

mā.ne'o.ne'o. 1. Redup. of *mane'o.* **ho'o.mā.ne'o.-ne'o.** Caus/sim.; to tickle, titillate. 2. n. An edible seaweed, *Laurencia nidifica.*

manewa. 1. Same as *mānewanewa.* **ho'o.manewa.** Same as *ho'omānewanewa.* 2. vi. To breathe, as a fish. *Rare.* 3. n. A kind of grass (no data).

mā.newa.newa. 1. nvi. Grief, sorrow, mourning; exaggerated expression of grief, as by knocking out teeth, cutting the hair in strange patterns, eating of filth, tattooing the tongue, removing the *malo* and wearing it about the neck; to do such. **ho'o.mā.newa.newa.** To display violent grief; to free oneself from black magic and regain health by extravagant conduct, as going nude or eating of filth or drinking *'auhuhu* juice. (PPN *manewanewa.*) 2. vs. Unkind. **ho'o.mā.newa.newa.** To treat unkindly. 3. Var. of *hīnawenawe, hīnewanewa,* weak, spindly. *'O ka hahu 'ape mānewanewa* (KL line 370), the weak young *'ape* plant. 4. n. Name given for a beach grass; used in leis on Lā-na'i.

mani. 1. vs. Dull, as a blade; slick; smooth, as a waterworn pebble. Cf. *hāmani.* 2. To cool off, of heat. (And.) *E mani ka umu,* let the oven cool.

mania. 1. nvi. Shuddering sensation as on looking down a great height, or hearing a saw filed; dizziness; dizzy; to shudder; to be contracted. *Mania ka niho,* the teeth are set on edge (as on eating certain green fruits). (PPN *mania.*) 2. vs. Inactive, drowsy, sleepy. **ho'o.mania.** To cause sleepiness, drowsiness. 3. Same as *mani 1.* (PCP *mania.*) 4. Same as *mani 2. Mai lohi 'olua o mania ka imu,* don't be slow or the oven will cool. 5. n. Lump, as on the skin. (Kel. 13.)

māni.ani. nvs. Acidity; tart, acid.

mā.nia.nia. Redup. of *mania.* (PPN *maniania.*)

mania.wai. vs. Drowsy, sleepy, especially after bathing.

manie. Var. of *mania.*

mā.nie.nie. 1. n. Bermuda grass *(Cynodon dactylon),* a fine-leafed, cosmopolitan grass, much used for lawns in Hawai'i. (Neal 67–8.) 2. Short for *mānienie 'aki'aki.* 3. vs. Bare, barren. 4. Same as *māniania.*

mā.nie.nie 'aki.'aki. n. 1. Seashore rush grass *(Sporobolus virginicus).* Also *'aki'aki, mānienie māhikihiki,* and *mānienie maoli.* (Neal 66–7.) 2. Buffalo grass *(Stenotaphrum secundatum),* a coarse-leafed grass from the southern United States, used for lawns in Hawai'i. Sometimes qualified by *haole* and also called *mānienie māhikihiki.* (Neal 72–3.)

mā.nie.nie ali'i. n. Wire grass *(Eleusine indica),* a weed in lawns and waste places, a strong, smooth, tufted grass, with pale-green, flattened stems. *Lit.,* chief *mānienie.* (Neal 67.)

mā.nie.nie haole. n. Bermuda grass *(Cynodon dactylon),* said to have been introduced by Dr. G. P. Judd about 1835; called *mānienie* because it creeps like buffalo grass (see *mānienie 'aki'aki*), which the Hawaiians originally called *mānienie.* (Neal 67.)

mā.nie.nie mahiki. *Cymbopogon refractus.* Ni'ihau. See Neal 79.

mā.nie.nie mā.hiki.hiki. Same as *mānienie 'aki'aki 1, 2. Lit., mānienie* for exorcising evil spirits.

mā.nie.nie maoli. Same as *mānienie 'aki'aki (Sporobolus virginicus). Lit.,* native *mānienie.*

mā.nie.nie 'ula. n. A small, stiff, weedy grass *(Chrysopogon aciculatus)* from southeastern Asia, found in some Pacific islands; it forms mats and bears a narrow head of reddish, barbed spikelets, which stick to animals' coats. Also *pi'ipi'i, pilipili 'ula.* (Neal 80.)

maniha. Same as *kamaniha,* sullen.

mani.he'u. Var. of *manuhe'u,* bruised.

manila. n. Manila hat, named for the city.

manīne. vs. Ashamed, humiliated. *Rare.*

manini. 1. n. Very common reef surgeonfish *(Acanthurus triostegus),* also called convict tang, in the adult stage. In legends *manini 'ele kuhō.* For younger stages see *'ōhualiko, 'ōhua kāni'o, palapōhaku,* and *kākala manini,* and *maninini.* (PPN *manini.*) 2. vs. Stingy. Cf. Fijian *manini-taka,* to hoard up like a miser. 3. n. A kind of banana generally eaten cooked; leaves and fruits green and white striped. Also *a'ea'e, koa'e.* (Neal 249.) 4. n. A variety of sugar cane, named for the fish. Also *laukona.* 5. n. A variety of dryland taro with striped petiole. The name may be qualified by the terms *'ele'ele, hā kikokiko, hā uliuli, kākau, kea, lau kikokiko, uliuli.* 6. n. A variety of sweet potato. 7. nvs. Wrath, anger; angry. 8. vi. To pour, spill; irrigated. *Manini aku a manini mai nā 'ōlelo 'ino,* evil words poured out, poured back and forth. 9. *(Cap.)* n. Hawaiian name of a well-known Spanish immigrant,

Francisco de Paula Marin, who knew Ka-mehameha for more than 25 years (Kuykendall 429.)

mani.nini. 1. n. Stage of *manini*, a fish, said to be larger than *'ōhua* and smaller than *manini*. **2.** Redup. of *manini*, to pour.

manini 'ō.pelu. n. A taro cultivar. (TC 4.)

manini 'ō.wali. n. A taro cultivar. (TC 3.)

manino. Var. of *malino*, calm. (PNP *malino*.)

mā.nino.nino. Redup. of *manino*.

mani.oka. n. The cassava or manioc *(Manihot esculenta)*, a bushy herb or shrub 1 to 2.8 m high, from Brazil, widely grown for its tuberous, edible roots, like sweet potatoes. The roots also yield a starch, tapioca. Cf. *pia manioka*. (Neal 513–4.) *Eng.*

mano. 1. num. Many, numerous, four thousand; thick. Cf. *kini, lau, lehu, manoa,* Gram. 10.3. *He lau ka pu'u, he mano ka ihona* (chant), many hills, numerous descents [of troubles]. **ho'o.mano.** To increase; to do repeatedly or persistently. *Koi ho'omano,* to keep asking and insisting. *Ka hahai e ho'omano ai* (For. 4:47), following persistently. (PPN *mano*.) **2.** vt. To throw, as a stone; to aim at and hit. *Rare.* **3.** *(Cap.)* Short for *Mano-ka-lani-pō.*

-mano. ho'o.mano. A name given to the *kāmanomano* plant when used in *hana aloha*, love sorcery.

manō. n. Shark (general name). Many kinds are listed below. Reef sharks may attain a length of 1.5 m. *Fig.,* a passionate lover. Sharks were *'aumākua* to some; they were said to have never harmed and frequently to protect those who fed and petted them. Cf. *'ai ā manō, hula manō, niuhi, pua 1. Manō i'a,* ordinary shark. *Manō hae,* fierce shark or fighter. *Manō kanaka,* shark thought to be born of a human mother and sired by a shark god, or by a deified person whose spirit possesses a shark or turns into a shark. *Manō ihu wa'a,* shark traditionally said to rest its head on the outrigger of a canoe, beloved by fishermen and fed; *lit.,* bow shark. *Pau pele, pau manō,* consumed by volcanic fire, consumed by shark [may I die if I don't keep my pledge]. **ho'o.manō.** To behave as a shark; to eat ravenously; to pursue women ardently. (PNP *mangoo*.)

māno. n. Dam, stream or water source, headwaters, place where water is obstructed for distribution in channels, channels (Isa. 8.7). Cf. *māno wai.*

manoa. vs. Numerous, very many. Cf. *mano 1. Manoa nā pua o kēlā pā,* there are many flowers in that lot. **ho'o.manoa.** To increase.

mā.noa. 1. nvs. Thick, solid, vast; depth, thickness. **ho'o.mā.noa.** To thicken. **2.** *(Cap.)* n. A large Honolulu valley.

mā.noa.noa. Redup. of *manoa* and *mānoa;* dull-witted, stupid, calloused, coarse, numbed, as the tongue from chewing kava. *Mānoanoa ke kapu o ke ali'i,* the chief has many many taboos [is of high rank]. *Lepo mānoanoa,* clay.

mano 'au wa'a. n. Large fleet of canoes.

mano.hā. Intensifier of *mano 1. Manomano, manohā nā li'i,* many, numerous the chiefs.

manō hi'u kā. n. Thresher shark *(Alopias vulpinus). Rare. Lit.,* tail-hitting shark.

mano'i. n. Coconut oil, perfume. (Perhaps from Tahitian; the Samoan cognate is *manongi,* and the normal Hawaiian equivalent would be *manoni:* Gram. 2.9.4.) *Kou mau mea mano'i* (Isa. 57.9), thy perfumes.

manō i'a. See *manō.*

Mano-ka-lani-pō. n. Name of a chief of Kaua'i. Kaua'i is sometimes referred to as *Kaua'i o Mano* (RC 194), *Kaua'i o Mano-ka-lani-pō* or *Manō.* (Elbert and Mahoe 21, 44, 63; HM366).

manō kanaka. See *manō.*

manō kihi.kihi. n. Hammerhead shark *(Sphryna zygaena). Lit.,* angular shark.

manō lā.lā kea. n. Shark, perhaps *Squalus fernandinus,* sometimes called dogfish; considered harmless. *Lit.,* white-fin shark.

manō lau kā hi'u. n. A shark, possibly thresher. *Lit.,* shark that frequently strikes tail.

manō lele wa'a. Cf. *lelewa'a.*

mano.mano. Redup. of *mano 1;* great; greatness; four thousand times four thousand; myriad. *Eia 'o ka lani, ka manomano, ka manomano heke o ke kapu* (chant), here is the heavenly chief, the great one, the very greatest of the taboo ones. *Ka manomano o kona ikaika* (Isa. 63.1), the greatness of his strength.

manoni. vs. Mixed feelings as of joy and sorrow, unhappiness. Cf. *noni 3.*

manoni.nia. Pas/imp. of *manoni.* **ho'o.manoni.nia.** Caus/sim. *Kani'uhū a ho'omanoninia no kō kākou lāhui, no ke emi 'ana mai,* grief and sadness for our race, for its decreasing.

manō niuhi. See *niuhi.*

manono. 1. vs. Red, as sunburn. Cf. *nono,* red. **2.** Redup. of *mano 1. Manono ho'i kēlā po'e e hele maila,* those people coming there are so numerous. **3.** Same as *nono;* to seep; to wane, as the moon. **4.** n. All species of an endemic genus *(Gouldia)* of shrubs or small trees belonging to the coffee family. (Neal 793.) **5.** n. Block set athwart a canoe to which *'iako* (outrigger booms) are lashed. **6.** vs. Laid across one another, as mats.

mano.noni. n. Young of the *kawakawa,* a fish.

manō pā.'ele. n. A shark. *Lit.,* black-smudged shark.

manō pahā.ha. n. A shark. *Lit.,* thick-necked shark.

manō 'ula. n. A shark. *Lit.,* red shark.

māno wai. Same as *māno. Fig.,* heart and circulatory system; source of water and of life.

manu. 1. n. Bird; any winged creature; wing of a kite. *Fig.,* person. *Ka nui manu,* the people, the many people. *He manu hulu,* a feathered bird [a prosperous person]. *He manu hulu 'ole,* a featherless bird [a poverty-stricken person]. *He aha kāu i pi'i aku nei i ka lapa manu 'ole?* Why did you climb the ridge without birds [go on a wild-goose chase]? *'Ai ka manu i luna,* the birds eat above [a poetic tribute to a handsome person, likened to an *'ōhi'a* tree with birds eating its *lehua* blossoms]. (PPN *manu.*) **2.** vs. Bruised, broken, scarred, injured. *Manu kinā,* bruised and injured. **3.** n. Ornamental elliptical expansions at the upper ends of the bow and stern endpieces, distinguished by *mua* and *ihu,* "forward" or "bow," and *hope,* "stern." (PPN *manu.*) **4.** Salty, pungent, acrid. (And.) **5.** n. Game similar to fox and geese. Also *punipeki.*

manua. 1. Pas/imp. of *manu 2.* **2.** Same as *mana kūkulu hema,* a taro. **3.** n. Manure *(Eng.);* any kind of fertilizer.

manu.ā, manuwā. 1. nvt. Wounded, bruised; to wound. *Manuā wale mai ana nō ia'u kō aloha,* your love keeps wounding me. **2.** n. Man-of-war, warship, battleship. *Eng.*

manu'a. vs. Piled, accumulated. *Hele ā manu'a ā 'eha, nui nā pilikia* (hymn), accumulated pains, much trouble.

manu.ahi, manuwahi. vs. Gratis, gratuitous, free of charge; adulterous. (This word is said to have originated from the name of a Hawaiian merchant famous for giving good measure with his sales.) *Keiki manuahi,* illegitimate child. *Wahine manuahi,* mistress, common-law wife.

manu 'ai.hue. n. Partridge. (Ier. 17.11.) *Lit.,* thieving bird.

manu-'ai-laiki. n. Ricebird *(Lonchura punctulata),* introduced from the Malay Peninsula in about 1865. *Lit.,* rice-eating bird.

manu-'ai-mī.kana, manu-'ai-papaia. n. Linnet, house finch, or papaya bird *(Carpodacus mexicanus frontalis),* introduced before 1870. *Lit.,* papaya-eating bird.

manu-'ai-pilau. n. Scavenger bird, mynah bird. *Lit.,* filth-eating bird. See *piha'ekelo.*

manu.ale. n. Manual. *Eng. Ka Manuale Kakolika,* the Catholic Manual.

manu aloha. n. **1.** Lovebird. **2.** Parrot, so called because it extends greeting *(aloha).*

mā.nu'a.nu'a. Rare var. of *māna'ona'o.*

manu.'awa. vt. To dislike, despise. Cf. *manu he'u, manumanu. Manu'awa ho'i 'oe ia'u,* you despise me.

manu.ea. 1. vs. Careless, blundering, slipshod, awkward. *Rare.* **2.** n. Center support of a house. *Rare.*

manu.hekili. n. Thundercloud. *Rare.*

manu-hele-kū. n. Penguin. *Lit.,* bird that walks upright.

manu heu. vi. To feather out, of young birds. *Fig.,* to leave home, as young people.

manu.heʻu. vt. Bruised, injured, damaged, dented; in bad condition, as an old building; to bruise, damage, injure, deface; to bite with the teeth and peel off, as bark. **hoʻo.manu.heʻu.** Caus/sim.

manu huhū. n. Wild, ravenous bird. (Isa. 46.11.) *Lit.,* angry bird.

manu humu.humu. n. Tailorbird.

manu ʻio.ʻio. n. Swallow. (Ier. 8.7, Isa. 38.14.) *Lit.,* chirping bird.

manu.kā. vs. Lagging, dilatory, slow, blundering. *Manukā nohoʻi kāna hana,* his work is certainly slow and careless.

manu kapa.lulu. n. California valley quail *(Lophortyx californicus californicus),* an early introduction, common in the 1890s. *Lit.,* whirr bird.

manu kū. n. Dove, including Chinese dove *(Streptopelia chinensis);* rock or wild pigeon *(Columba livia). Lit.,* coo *(Eng.)* bird.

manu.lele. n. A native variety of sugar cane, the stems green striped with yellowish and reddish brown, the pith brown, the leaves purplish. Used medicinally, also in love sorcery. See ex., *kāʻawe.* (HP 221; Neal 79.) *Lit.,* flying bird.

manu liʻi.liʻi. n. English sparrow; European housefinch *(Passer domesticus);* introduced before 1870; little bird. (Hal. 102.7.)

manu.manu. vs. Rough, irregular, nicked; dull, blunt, not sharp, as a knife; bruised; scarred, as by smallpox (Kam. 64:106). *Nui kalakalai, manumanu ka loaʻa,* much whittling, nicked product.

manu mele. n. Songbird, especially canary *(Serinus canaria).* Cf. *kenele.*

manu.nē.nē. n. Possibly a local name for a small sedge *(Cyperus brevifolius). Lit.,* goose bird. See *kiliʻoʻopu.*

manunu. 1. nvs. To creak or break, as bones; tremor, as of an earthquake. **2.** vs. Numb.

-manunu. hoʻo.manunu. To break out, as with a skin eruption. (Kam. 64:105.)

manu.nunu. Redup. of *manunu 1, 2.*

manu nū.nū. n. Dove. (Hal. 55.6.) *Lit.,* cooing bird.

manu-nū.nū-lawe-leka. n. Carrier pigeon. *Lit.,* dove carrying letters *(Eng.).*

manu-o-Kū. n. White tern, fairy tern, love tern *(Cygis alba rothschildi),* a small, friendly sea bird, pure white except for a black ring around the eye. *Lit.,* bird of Kū. Niʻihau.

manuʻu. 1. Same as *mānuʻunuʻu.* **2.** Sick, weak, in pain. (And.)

manu ʻū. n. Crane. (Ier. 8.7.) *Lit.,* groaning bird.

manu ʻula.ʻula. n. Cardinal, redbird. *Lit.,* red bird.

mā.nuʻu.nuʻu. vs. Vast, great, without measure, multitudinous. Cf. *nuʻu. Mānuʻunuʻu wale ka lokomaikaʻi,* very great is the kindness.

manu.wā. See *manuā.*

mao. 1. vs. Cleared, as rain; alleviated, assuaged, as grief; to clear up, as rain; to pass, as sadness. *Ua mao aʻela ke kaumaha,* the sadness has ceased. (PPN *mao.*) **2.** vi. To fade, as cloth. **3.** n. Type of fish. (KL line 158.) Cf. *maomao.*

ma o. Because of, due to, by means of, through. Cf. *ma,* at.

maʻo. 1. vs. Green. Cf. *mamaʻo, maʻomaʻo, ʻōmaʻomaʻo.* **2.** n. The native cotton *(Gossypium sandvicense),* a shrub in the hibiscus family, bearing yellow flowers and seed cases containing brown cotton. (Neal 566.) Also *huluhulu.* Cf. *pulupulu haole.* **3.** n. The hoary abutilon *(Abutilon incanum),* a small native, velvety shrub, in the hibiscus family, with small heart-shaped leaves, small pink and red flowers, and small dry fruits. (Neal 550.) **4.** n. The hairy abutilon *(Abuti-*

lon grandifolium), a weedy, hairy, South American shrub, with large, broad leaves, orange, *ʻilima*-like flowers, and ten-parted, black, dry fruits. When green and soft, these fruits are used in making *ʻilima* leis, one for each end of the lei. (Neal 550.) **5.** Same as *ʻōmaʻo,* thrush. (PCP *mako.*)

ma.ʻō. See *ʻō,* there.

maoa. vs. Chafing from friction, soreness from rubbing; to chafe, rub, become sore from rubbing. (PCP *maoa.*)

-maoe. hoʻo.maoe. To ask indirectly; to hint or suggest, as in asking; to imply, allude. *Ke nīnau hoʻomaoe nei nā kānaka i ke kumu o kona make ʻana* (Kep. 45), the people are now asking indirectly the cause of his death.

maʻoe.ā. vs. Lazy, uninterested in work. *Rare.*

maoha. Same as *maoa.*

maʻoha. vs. Grayish, especially when contrasted with black, as of bird feathers, cloud-capped mountains, graying hair. *Ka ʻiwa he manu nui ia, he ʻeleʻele kona hulu, he maʻoha kahi hulu,* the ʻiwa is a big bird, its feathers are black, some are gray.

mā.oha.oha. Similar to *ohaoha.*

maʻo hau hele. n. The native yellow hibiscus *(Hibiscus brackenridgei),* a small shrub with broad, lobed leaves and with large yellow flowers that turn green on drying. (Neal 560.) *Lit.,* green traveling *hau.*

mā.ʻohe.ʻohe. 1. vs. Tall and spindly, as trees in a dense forest that reach up for light, or as bamboo; straight and tall, as of a fine physique. Cf. *ʻohe,* bamboo. **2.** n. A variety of sugar cane.

mā.ohi.ohi. Same as *ohiohi 1;* to grow vigorously.

mā.ʻohi.ʻohi. n. A native mint *(Stenogyne rugosa),* found only on the island of Hawaiʻi, a shrub with smooth, ovate, toothed leaves and reddish flowers grouped in whorls of six to ten at leaf bases.

mā.ʻohu. vs. Misty. *Ka ua lei māʻohu o Wai-ānuenue,* rain of Wai-ānuenue that is like a wreath of mist.

mā.ʻoi. Same as *mahaʻoi,* bold. (2 Kor. 11.21.) **hoʻo.-mā.ʻoi.** To act bold, impertinent.

mā.ʻoi.ʻoi. 1. Redup. of *māʻoi.* **2.** vs. Uneven, notched, zigzag.

maoki. Var. of *maoli 1.*

maʻoki. nvi. Anything cut into pieces, streaked (less used than *māʻokiʻoki*). *Ua maʻoki ʻia kēia papa,* this board is cut into pieces.

mā.ʻoki.ʻoki. Redup. of *maʻoki,* sometimes with idea of small pieces. *Kaulana ʻo Kona i ke kai māʻokiʻoki.* Kona is famous for its streaked sea of various colors. **hoʻo.mā.ʻoki.ʻoki.** To make streaks, cut grooves.

maoli. 1. vs. Native, indigenous, aborigine, genuine, true, real, actual; very, really, truly. *Maikaʻi maoli,* very good indeed. *Kanaka maoli, ʻōlelo maoli,* Hawaiian native, Hawaiian language [so used in reports of 1852 legislative session]. *E puka ai ka makemake maoli o ka mea koho,* expressing the free will of the voter. (PPN *ma(a)ʻoli.*) **2.** n. A variety of *ʻahi,* a fish that may weigh about 90 kilos; it has light, slightly pinkish flesh. **3.** n. A native variety of banana, with tall, green trunk; the fruit forming large, compact bunches, having thick yellow skin and sweet yellow flesh; edible cooked or raw. (HP 176.) **4.** n. A variety of sweet potato.

maoli ʻili lahi.lahi. n. A native variety of banana. *Lit.,* thin-skinned *maoli.*

mā.ʻoli.ʻoli. 1. Same as *ʻoliʻoli,* joy. **2.** Same as *laulihilihi,* joy.

maʻo.loa. Same as *maʻaloa,* a shrub.

mao.loha. n. Large-meshed net used at *makahiki* ceremonies. It was filled with food and held at each of the four corners. The priest prayed, and the net was shaken. If the food did not fall out, the priest predicted famine. Perhaps this was named for a legendary net called *kōkō a maoloha.* During a famine Waia miraculously lowered this net from heaven and filled it with food. He shook the net, and food was scattered for the benefit of the starving people. (Malo 151, 155.)

mā.ʻolu. vs. Boggy, squashy; yielding to pressure, as a soft cushion. Cf. *ʻolu,* elasticity.

mao.lua. n. A kind of red tapa.

mao.mao. 1. n. Type of fish (KL line 158), perhaps same as *mamo, mamamo, mao.* **2.** Rare var. of *mamao,* far. **3.** vs. Calm, clear. *Rare.*

maʻo.maʻo. 1. nvs. Green, greenness. *ʻAno maʻomaʻo,* somewhat green, greenish. **hoʻo.maʻo.maʻo.** To paint green, make green. **2.** n. A green tapa, as of *māmaki* bark.

mao.mao pohole. n. Probably same as *maomao,* a fish.

mā.ʻona (usually pronounced but not written *māʻana*). vs. Satisfied after eating, full, satisfying; to have eaten, to eat one's fill. *Fig.,* intoxicated. For a rare use of *māʻona* as a noun, see *kuenenuʻu. Ua māʻona ʻoe?* Have you eaten? Have you had enough? Are you full? *Māʻona maikaʻi,* to have had enough to eat, but not to have overeaten. *Māʻona piha, māʻona loa,* completely full. *He lau māʻona* (For. 4:43), a leaf that gives plenty to eat. *Inu mai nei a māʻona, a laila hoʻohakakā,* drinking until drunk, then starting fights. *Māʻona ka ʻuhane i ka ʻōlelo a ke Akua,* the spirit is sustained by the word of God. **hoʻo.mā.ʻona.** To eat all one wants, to feed all that is wanted. (PPN *maakona.*)

mā.ono. n. A gray basalt, used for pounders. *Rare.* Also *kuanuʻu.*

maʻo.pa. Same as *māʻopaʻopa* (Nak. 75, 115).

mā.ʻopa.ʻopa. vs. Tired, aching, of legs; to limp. *Ua hele kuʻu mau wāwae ā māʻopaʻopa,* my legs are aching. **hoʻo.mā.ʻopa.ʻopa.** Fatiguing.

mao.popo. nvs. To understand, recognize, realize; clear; plainly, clearly; understanding. (Gram. 4.4.) *Ua maopopo iāʻoe?* Do you understand? *Ua maopopo iaʻu kou manaʻo,* I understand your idea. *Haʻi maopopo,* to tell clearly. *Maopopo ka ʻikena,* clearly seen or known. *Maopopo ʻole,* unintelligible, unaware, unaccountable. *Maopopo loa,* to understand clearly, definite, certain. *Maopopo maikaʻi, maopopo leʻa,* obvious, evident, clearly understood. **hoʻo.mao.popo.** To understand, make plain or clear, tell clearly, cause to understand, pay attention in order to understand; to certify, inform, remember, recollect, recall, think about, remind, believe in, realize, ascertain, take care of, recognize, discover. (Depending on context, many translations are possible; for substitution of *maopopo* for *hoʻomaopopo,* Gram. 4.4.) *Hoʻomaopopo ʻē,* to understand ahead, anticipate; inkling. *Hoʻomaopopo ʻole ia,* misunderstood, unintelligible, uncared for, unclear. *E hoʻomaopopo aku ʻoe, i ka hola ʻehia kākou e hele ai,* find out what hour we are going. *E hoʻomaopopo aku ʻoe e hele mai i kēlā ʻapōpō,* remind [him] to come tomorrow. *E hoʻomaopopo mai ʻoe i kēia mea e aʻo ʻia aku nei,* pay attention and comprehend these things being taught you.

maʻopu. Same as *ʻopu,* to dive. *Waiho akaaka ke kula o Kai-olohia, ka lele maʻopu a ka wai a ka nāulu* (chant), the Kai-olohia plain stays clear as the water of the *nāulu* shower leaps downward.

mā.pala. n. Marble *(Eng.),* granite. *Ipu hao māpala,* granite pot.

mā.pela, mabela. Var. of *māpala. Ma nā puka māpela* (hymn), at the marble gates.

mā.pele. n. **1.** Thatched heiau (temple) for the worship of Lono and the increase of food; the offerings were of pigs, not humans. (Malo 160.) **2.** A shrub, *Cyrtandra cyaneoidea.* (Kam. 76:125.) (Cf. For. 6:430, 444.)

mapū. Same as *pū,* rope tied to a canoe endpiece.

māpu. nvs. Fragrance, especially wind-blown fragrance; wafted; bubbling, splashing, as water; dipping, swooping. *Fig.,* surging, as emotion. *Ke māpu nei ke ʻala o ka maile,* the fragrance of the *maile* floating in the breeze. *Māpu mai kona aloha* (PH 30), her love pours sweetly forth. *ʻO ka uahi māpu kea,* white wafted smoke. *ʻO ka hinihini kani kua mauna, ʻo ka māpu leo nui, kani kohākohā* (PH 204), the land shell crying in the mountain ridge, loud voice carried in the wind, shrilly calling. **hoʻo.māpu.** Caus/sim. (Perhaps PPN *mapu.*)

-māpu. See *koloa māpu.*

mā.pū. n. Ape, baboon.

māpu.ana. Same as *māpu.* (Probably *māpu* + *-ana,* nominalizer: Gram. 6.6.2.) *Onaona māpuana o ka loke,* the soft wafted fragrance of the rose.

māpu.māpu. Redup. and intensifier of *māpu. ʻO ka ʻio lele māpumāpu* (For. 6:381), the hawk that flies swooping.

mā.puna. n. Bubbling spring; froth, as of a rough sea; source. *Fig.,* surging of emotion. *Wai māpuna,* spring water. *Mai ka māpuna hoʻokahi,* from the same source. (PPN *ma(a)puna.*)

mā.puna hoe. n. Dip of a paddle. *ʻElua nō māpuna hoe, kū ʻoe i Kuaihelani,* two paddle dips and you reach Kuaihelani.

mā.puna leo, mā.puna ʻō.lelo. n. Utterance, expression, wafted voice; few words. *Hoʻokahi nō māpuna leo a ke aloha,* a single expression by the lover.

mā.puna.puna. Redup. of *māpuna. Māpunapuna mai ana kō aloha iaʻu nei* (song), your love stirs and excites within me.

mau. 1. vs. Always, steady, constant, ever, unceasing, permanent, stationary, continual, perpetual; to continue, persevere, preserve, endure, last; preservation, continuation. *Mau loa,* eternal, everlasting, forever, endless. *Mai kēia manawa ā mau loa aku,* from now to eternity; from now on and forever. *Hana mau ʻia,* frequently done or used; common, as a word or custom; usual. *Ua mau ke ea o ka ʻāina i ka pono,* life of the land is preserved in righteousness [motto of Hawaiʻi]. *Mau maila kā Ke-aka kāhea me ka peʻahi* (For. 5:303), Ke-aka continued to call and wave. *ʻOia mau nō,* continuing all right; same as usual; just the same [often said in answer to *Pehea ʻoe?* How are you? *lit.,* this continuation indeed). **hoʻo.mau.** To continue, keep on, persist, renew, perpetuate, persevere, last. See *nuku hoʻomau. Hoʻomau ʻia,* continued. *E hoʻomau hou ʻia aku i ka laikini,* renew the license. (PPN *maʻu.*) **2.** vs. Stopped, as menstruation (FS 115); snagged, caught, as a fish or hook; retarded; grounded, as a canoe; set, as a wager; stuck or stalled, as a car. *Mau i ka palaoa* (FS 153), to wager a whaletooth pendant. *Mau ihola nā ihu,* a lingering kiss [*lit.,* noses caught]. **hoʻo.mau.** To make fast, as an anchor in sand; to snag; to cause to be retarded, grounded, wagered, stopped. (PPN *maʻu.*) **3.** vs. Conceived, as at the very moment of conception. **hoʻo.mau.** To mate for the purpose of having children. *Hoʻomau keiki,* to unite in order to conceive, as of ceremonial marriage of high chiefs for purpose of begetting children of high rank. **4.** n. Person who carried the wand and chanted in the *ʻume* game. (Malo 215.) **5.** Part. marking plural, used principally after the *k*-class possessives and demonstratives, numerals, and *he.* See Gram. 10.4. *Kaʻu mau puke,* my books. (PCP *mau.*)

-mau. hoʻo.mau. A variety of sweet potato.

maʻu. Same as *amaʻu,* a native genus of ferns.

ma.ʻū. 1. vs. Damp, wet, humid, moist, cool, refreshing. See ex., *huʻahuʻo kai. Maʻū ka lepo o kēia wahi,* the earth here is damp. *Wā maʻū,* cool time, as early morning. *Hele kākou ʻoi maʻū,* let's go while it's cool. *Maʻū aʻela ka ihu,* the nose is damp [as in a kiss]. **hoʻo.maʻū.** To dampen, moisten, irrigate, soak, saturate, baste; to shade, cool. (PCP *maakuu.*) **2.** Same as *māʻau,* to sprout. Cf. *wao maʻukele.* **3.** nvs. A little, of some little value, of slight use better than nothing. Cf. *maʻū wale, pohō maʻū. Maʻū nō ia,* it is better than nothing. *He maʻū ia ike ʻana iā Hawaiʻi,* this seeing of Hawaiʻi is better than nothing at all [at least it's something]. *Maʻū nō ka ʻole, maʻū nō ka nele,* nothing is better than that; that's worse than nothing.

maua. 1. nvi. Failure to give a return gift; to receive without giving in return; illiberal, ungrateful, close-fisted. Cf. *mamaua.* **2.** n. Native forest trees, *Xylosma hawaiiense.* See *aʻe 6.* (Neal 592.) **3.** n. A type of prayer for *luakini* dedication. (For. 6:23.)

mau.ā, mauwā. 1. vs. Lame, stiff, sore. **2.** n. Fallen tree or plant that sends up new branches; shoots from fallen trunks. See *ohiohi 1.*

mā.ua. pronoun. We, us (dual, exclusive). (Gram. 8.2.) *Kā māua,* belonging to us, our. (PPN *kimarua,* PNP *kimaaua,* PEP *maaua.*)

maʻuʻa. vs. Careless, as of clothing, mats, tapa, property. *I loko nō o ka hune, komo maʻuʻa nō i ka lole,* in spite of poverty, wearing clothes without taking care of them.

maua.ʻā.lina. vs. Powerful, strong, of superior strength, athletic; to exercise strength, to use force. *Rare.*

mau.ae. Var. spelling of *māwae,* crack. (Puk. 33.22.)

mau.ʻaʻe. nvt. To intrude, transgress, break taboo, interrupt, meddle in the concern of others; to step over; to flaunt, as authority; to override, as a veto; such action. Cf. *ʻaʻe,* to break taboo. *He hoʻokiʻekiʻe, he mauʻaʻe i ka ʻōlelo a ka makua,* proud and heedless of parental advice.

mau.ʻaʻe.ʻaʻe. Redup. of *mauʻaʻe;* lawless. *Mauʻaʻeʻaʻe ʻo Milu mā i ke kapu o Kāne* (Kep. 49), Milu and his companions broke the taboo of Kāne.

maua.kala. Var. of *mahuakala,* disbelieving. **hoʻo.-maua.kala.** Var. of *hoʻomahuakala. Rare.*

mā.ua.ua. vs. Tough, leathery, as skin of the old; old.

mau.ele, mauwele. vt. To clear, as brush.

maʻu.ele, maʻuwele. vs. Lazy, without energy.

mau.ele.kā, mauwelekā. vt. To clear, as brush; tangled, snarled. *Kā ke ala, mauelekā!* Cut a pathway! Cut and Clear!

maʻu.hā. vs. Weary, aching, tired. *E noke ana ua wahi keiki nei ʻo Māui i ka hoe a maʻuhā nā poʻohiwi,* the boy Māui kept plying the paddle until his shoulders ached.

mau.haʻa.lele. vt. To abandon, leave, as one's family; to cease, as sinning; to pass on, die. *He mau hōʻailono mauhaʻalele,* signs of death.

mau.haʻa.lelea. 1. Pas/imp. of *mauhaʻalele.* 2. n. A prayer to a forest god before cutting down a tree to be made into an image.

mau.haʻa.lina. 1. vs. Heavily burdened, weighted down. *Rare.* **hoʻo.mau.haʻa.lina.** To oppress, burden. *Rare.* 2. To bore, pierce, as a hole in a rock. (And.)

mau.hala. nvs. Grudge, resentment, spite; unforgiving, to nurse revenge. **hoʻo.mau.hala.** To bear a grudge, cherish revenge. *Kūʻē (kaua) hoʻomauhala,* feud. *Mai hoʻomauhala i nā keiki* (Oihk. 19.18), do not bear any grudge against the children.

mau.hili. vs. Entangled, snarled, interwoven. Cf. *hili. Keawe-a-mauhili* (name), Keawe entangled [in taboo] or interwoven [as chiefly blood].

Maui. n. 1. Name of one of the Hawaiian islands. Cf. Māui, the demigod. 2. *(Not cap.)* A variety of sweet potato.

Mā.ui. 1. n. The demigod and trickster who snared the sun. 2. n. Name of a star near the Pleiades. 3. *(Not cap.)* nvs. Sprain, bruise; sprained, bruised; pit-ripened, of bananas. See prayer, *nūpolupolu. Māui ka pua, uē ʻeha i ke anu,* bruised is the flower which weeps, hurt by the cold. **hoʻo.mā.ui.** To bruise, sprain, beat down, as by heavy rain or sea; to crush, as a leaf for a poultice; to cause a sprain; to ripen bananas by burying in a leaf-lined pit. (PNP *maaui.*)

mā.ui.ui. 1. vi. To ask continually, frequently. Cf. *ui.* **hoʻo.mā.ui.ui.** To ask over and over, mull over in the mind. 2. Redup. of *māui,* bruise. (PNP *maauiui.*)

mauka. See *uka,* inland.

ma.ʻuka. Same as *māʻukaʻuka.*

mau.kaʻa. Same as *milikaʻa.*

mā.ʻuka.ʻuka. nvs. Unskilled person; not adept, awkward, said derisively of an unsuccessful suitor. *Nā limahana māʻukaʻuka,* unskilled laborers.

Mau.kele. n. Place name at Puna, Hawaiʻi.

maʻu.kele. n. Rain-forest area.

mauki. Same as *maoli,* native.

mau.koli. 1. vt. To ration food or water, as in time of drought. 2. vs. Small, thin, fine, as a thread. 3. vs. Stilled, hushed, as worshippers. *E maukoli ke anaina,* let the assembly keep still. 4. vt. To offer to the gods, as

food. *Eia ka ʻawa, a nāu ponoʻī nō e maukoli aku i kō akua iā Kū-kāʻili-moku* (prayer), here is kava, for you indeed to offer to your god, Kū-kāʻili-moku. 5. vs. Constant, persevering. *Rare.*

Mau.kuku. n. Name of a star, perhaps related to Kona-mau-kuku.

mā.ʻula.ʻula. 1. Same as *ʻulaʻula,* red. 2. n. Red earth, as used in coloring.

maʻule. nvi. Faint, faint-hearted; dispirited, weak; fainting. **hoʻo.maʻule.** To cause fainting; to faint; to feign fainting. *Ā ua hoʻomaʻule hoʻi iā mākou no kō mākou mau hewa* (Isa. 64.7), and has consumed us because of our iniquities. *Hoʻomaʻule ka lemu* (For. 6:27), relax the buttocks [as during rituals].

mau.leho. vs. Calloused. Cf. *leho,* callus. **hoʻo.mau.-leho.** To cause calluses; to oppress, overwork.

mau.lele. n. Flotsam and jetsam. (For. 4:75.)

mā.ʻule.ʻule. Redup. of *maʻule.*

mauli. n. 1. Life, heart, seat of life; ghost, spirit. *Mauli hiwa,* choice or precious life. *Ā lele nui nā mauli o ua poʻe nei,* the spirits of these people have flown away together [death]. (PPN *maʻuri.*) 2. Fontanel. 3. *(Cap.)* Twenty-ninth of the old month. (Malo 32.) (PCP *mauli.*)

mā.uli. Same as *uli,* dark.

mauli.au.honua. nvs. Descendant of old chiefs of a land; established, ancient, as a family. *Ua kū kēia welo ā mauliauhonua,* this family is old and well established.

mauli.ʻawa. nvi. Hiccough; dying gasp; to hiccough, gasp in dying. *Mauliʻawa ke aho,* the breath has gasped; hiccoughed.

mau.lihi.lihi. vs. Hanging precariously, fastened slightly.

mau.lina. nvi. Failure; failing; to fail. *Rare.*

Mauli-ola. n. Place name at Kī-lau-ea Volcano, Hawaiʻi. (PH 94.)

mauli ola. n. Breath of life, power of healing. *Ka lā i ka mauli ola,* sun at the source of life. *Kihe a mauli ola,* sneeze and live [exclamation to one who has sneezed, to ward off ill effects].

mā.uli.uli. Redup. of *māuli,* dark.

mā.ʻulu. Same as *māʻuluʻulu.* See *puehu 1.*

mau.lua. vs. Difficult, hard.

mā.ulu.kua. n. Upland forest, said to be similar to *uka wao lāʻau. Mai ka uka māulukua ā hiki i ka pali kahakai,* from the upland forest to the shore cliff.

mā.ʻulu.ʻulu. vs. Lame, stiff, as from exercise; tired.

mau.mau. 1. Redup. of *mau 1,* frequent, often. *Kai maumau,* neap tide. *Maumau ʻole kāna ʻōlelo,* his words are inconsistent. **hoʻo.mau.mau.** Redup. of *hoʻomau. E hoʻomaumau i ka ʻikena* (song), continue seeing [one another]. 2. vs. Not sticky, not tenacious; of poi of medium texture, neither hard nor watery.

maʻu.maʻu. Same as *ʻamaʻumaʻu,* ferns. *Hale-maʻu-maʻu* (name of the pit at Kī-lau-ea Crater), *ʻamaʻu* fern house.

maʻū.maʻū. Redup. of *maʻū,* moist. **hoʻo.maʻū.maʻū.** Caus/sim. See ex., *mūkī.*

mau.maua. Pas/imp. of *maumau 1;* to do it continuously, repeat; repetitious; repeating (Kel. 59).

mau.mau.ae. Doubtful. (And.)

mauna. 1. nvs. Mountain, mountainous region; mountainous. *Mauna Loa* (name), Long Mountain. (PPN *maʻunga.*) 2. n. Kind of hard stone from which adzes were made.

mā.una. nvt. Waste; mistreatment; wasteful; injured; abusive; to waste, injure, mistreat. *Mai māuna wale i ka mea ʻai,* don't waste food unnecessarily. *Māuna ka ʻili i ka waʻuwaʻu ʻia,* the skin is injured in being scratched. *ʻO kēlā ke kāne, māuna ka ʻili,* with that man, (your) skin will be bruised [you will be beaten]. **hoʻo.mā.una.** To waste, spend carelessly, abuse; to help oneself lavishly, as to drinks. *Hoʻomāuna i ke kino,* to waste the body, as in dissipation.

Mauna Kea. n. The highest mountain on Hawaiʻi. *Lit.,* snow mountain.

mauna.loa. n. **1.** A sea bean, *Dioclea wilsonii,* a vine from Brazil growing wild in Hawai'i, the blue or white flowers used for leis, the beans for medicine. (Neal 463.) **2.** n. *Canavalia cathartica,* a vine from the Mascarene Islands, the white, lavender, pink, or reddish flowers commonly used for leis. (Neal 464.)

Mauna Loa. n. The second highest mountain on Hawai'i; a mountain and village on Moloka'i. *Lit.,* long mountain.

mā.unauna. Redup. of *māuna;* extravagant, wasteful, prodigal. **ho'o.mā.unauna.** To waste, squander.

Mauna Pō.haku. n. **1.** Rocky Mountains. **2.** Poetical name for Utah.

maunu. n. Bait; objects used in black magic, as hair, spittle, parings, excreta, clothing, food leavings. *Maunu 'ai 'ole,* bait that fish will not take. (PPN *maunu.*)

mā.unu. vi. To molt; to change skin, as of snakes; to change from a chrysalis state, as to a butterfly; to remove bristles, as of a pig for baking. Cf. *unuunu.*

mā.unuunu. 1. Redup. of *māunu.* **2.** *(Cap.)* n. Name of a strong, blustering wind associated with Wai-'alac and Pu'u-loa, O'ahu.

mau.ole. nvs. Teeth worn with age; aged, worn-out. Cf. *niho mauole.*

mau'u. n. General name for grasses, sedges, rushes, herbs; kava strainer; strand of pandanus plaiting, as in hat making. (PPN *mohuku,* PEP *mauku.*)

-mau'u. ho'o.mau'u. To give nothing of value (probably related to the fig. meaning of *mau'u Hilo.* '*O ka mea e ho'omanawale'a aku, ā momona ia, a 'o ka mea e ho'omau'u aku, e ho'omau'u 'ia mai 'oia* (Johnson 1976, p. 288), he who freely gives shall be enriched, and he who gives nothing of value shall receive nothing of value.

mā.'ū.'ū. 1. Same as *ma'ūma'ū.* *Mā'ū'ū ka pu'u i ka wai hu'ihu'i,* the throat is cooled by the cold water. **ho'o.mā.'ū.'ū.** To moisten, dampen, wet, as earth about plants. **2.** nvi. Gulping sound, stuttering; to make a gulping sound; to stutter.

mau'u 'aki.'aki. n. A sedge *(Fimbristylis pycnocephala).* *Ni'ihau.*

mau'u alo.alo. n. A grass *(Echinochloa colonum). Ni'ihau.*

mau'u haole. n. A grass *(Andropogon barbinodis). Ni'ihau.*

mau'u Hilo. n. Hilo grass *(Paspalum conjugatum),* a creeping perennial from tropical America. Though it is a coarse, weedy grass, it may serve as a lawn grass. It spreads rapidly and has become a pest because cattle do not eat it and it smothers slower-growing, desirable plants, especially in native forests. It first appeared in Hilo, Hawai'i, about 1840. (Neal 73.) For fig. use, see *he aha sananā* and *wēkenanā.*

mau'u hō.'ula 'ili. Same as *mau'u lā'ili,* a native iris. (Neal 232-3.) *Lit.,* grass reddening skin; see *mau'u lā'ili.*

mau'u hune.hune. n. McCoy grass *(Cyperus gracilis),* a small, fine-leafed sedge from Australia, used for lawns in Hawai'i. (Neal 85-6.)

mau'u Kale.poni. n. The yellow foxtail *(Setaria geniculata),* a weedy tropical American grass. The yellow or brownish, cylindrical flower heads are smooth and soft, and in Hawai'i are used for leis on hats. (Neal 75.) *Lit.,* California grass.

mau'u Kepa.nī. n. Velvet grass *(Zoysia tenuifolia),* a turf-forming lawn grass from the Mascarene Islands (Mauritius and Réunion). It is a dense, dark-green, fine grass, soon forming hummocks. *Lit.,* Japanese grass. (Neal 67.)

mau'u kū.kae pua'a. n. A kind of crab grass *(Digitaria pruriens),* used medicinally. *Lit.,* hog excrement grass. See *kūkaepua'a.* (Neal 72.)

mau'u kukū. Same as *'ume'alu,* bur grass. *Lit.,* prickly grass.

mau'u laiki. n. Rice grass *(Paspalum orbiculare),* a coarse, tufted, perennial grass, possibly native to Hawai'i. It was used like *pili* for thatching houses. (Neal 73.)

mau'u lā.'ili. n. **1.** A native iris *(Sisyrinchium acre),* with long grasslike leaves and small yellow flowers, found on Maui and Hawai'i between altitudes of 1,000 and 2,000 m. (Neal 232-3.) It grows in the Kī-lau-ea Volcano region, and formerly the sap was used to stain the skin so that travelers could prove to others at home that they had been to the volcano. Also *mau'u hō'ula 'ili.* **2.** Name of a kind of calico with tiny figures, so called because of resemblance to *mau'u lā'ili* stains.

mau'u lei. n. The swollen finger grass *(Chloris inflata),* an annual weedy grass from tropical America, 30 to 60 cm high. Two to eleven feathery, purplish flower spikes radiate from the top of the stem; they are used for hat leis. (Neal 69.)

mau'u mae. n. Wilted grass; name of a taboo on men, said to last ten days (sexual union was forbidden, and each man urinated in a particular spot only, where the grass wilted, hence the name of the taboo).

mau'u malo'o. n. Hay, straw, any dry grass.

mau'u mokae. n. A sedge. Same as *kili'o'opu.*

mau'u pili.pili. n. The bristly foxtail *(Setaria verticillata),* a hairy grass from Europe and Asia, growing like a weed in Hawai'i. The green, cylindrical flower heads are full of barbed bristles that cling to animals and clothing. *Lit.,* sticking grass. (Neal 75-6.)

mau'u pū.lumi. n. A grass *(Panicum maximum). Ni'ihau.*

mau'u pu'u.ka'a. Same as *pu'uka'a,* a sedge.

mau.wā. See *mauā.*

ma.'ū wale. vs. Profitless.

mau.wele. See *mauele.*

ma'u.wele. See *ma'uele.*

mau.wele.kā. See *mauelekā.*

mawa. Short for *manawa,* time. *Rare.*

mā.wae. 1. nvi. Cleft, fissure, crevice, crack, as in rocks; to crack, split, cleave. **ho'o.mā.wae.** To make a crack, furrow. **2.** vt. To separate, sort, select; to cleanse, as from defilement. Cf. *wae,* to select. (PPN *maawae.*)

mā.wae huna. n. Hidden cleft, as where things were hidden.

mawaena. See *waena.*

mā.wae.wae. 1. Redup. of *māwae 1, 2;* a ceremony for a child, held a few days after birth, during which the mother was given special food. **2.** n. A seaweed.

mā.wae.wae kili.hune. n. The name of a seaweed.

mawaho. See *waho.*

mā.wai. n. Cathartic medicine. *Rare.*

mā.wana.wana. Same as *kolokolo kahawai,* beach vitex.

mā.wao. Rare var. of *nāwao 1-3.*

mā.wehe. vs. Open, loose, separate, undone.

mā.weke. Var. of *māwehe.* (PPN *mawete.*)

me. prep. **1.** With. (Gram. 9.7.) *Ua hele au me ia,* I went with him. *A me,* and. *Ka puke a me ka peni,* the book and the pencil. *Ua noho 'oia me a'u,* he stayed with me. (PCP *me.*) **2.** Like, as. Cf. *mehe, me nei,* Gram. 9.7. *Like me 'oe,* like you. *Me 'oe pū,* same to you. *E kākau 'oe me nei,* write like this. (PCP *me.*)

mē. vt. To lap, as a dog. *E mē i ka wai,* to lap up water.

mea. 1. n. Thing, person, matter, stuff, object. Cf. *mea 'ole, what 3. Ka mea e loa'a ana,* whatever is gotten, found; anything. '*O wai ka mea e 'a'a e ha'i 'ōlelo?* Who will volunteer to make a speech? *Hā'awi mai i ka mea ke'oke'o,* give me the white one. *Nā mea āu i noi mai,* whatever you asked. *He aha ia mea?* What difference does it make? *Ka mea hea?* Which one? Which? Which person? *Nā mea 'elua,* two things, both. *Nā mea like 'ole,* varied things, miscellaneous. (PPN *me'a.*) **2.** n. Possessor or proprietor of. Cf. *mea 'āina, mea hale. He wahine mea kāne,* a woman with a husband. *He keiki mea kupuna,* a child with grandparents [as said of a child whose grandparents have made a great pet of him, said in admiration and praise of the grandchild, fortunate in having grandparents who love him]. **3.** n. Person or thing that does, is, did, or was. See *mea hula, mea kia'i, mea oli.* **4.** vt. To say. *Mea mai lāua,* they said. *Mai mea wale aku 'oe,* don't mention [it]. **ho'o.- mea.** To talk in a roundabout way, as to obtain information or conceal the truth; to hint at, trifle, joke, allude, pretend, act. *Hapai ho'omea a'e* (Kep. 159), to carry with pretended [groans from exertion]. *I ho'omea wale aku nei nō au,* I was just hinting, joking, talking generally. **5.** (Sometimes *cap.*) nvs. What-d'you-call-it, so-and-so (said when one is at a loss for a word or name); such and such. See ex., *pauaho.* *'O mea mā* (For. 4:47), so-and-so and the others. *I ka lā e mea,* on such and such a day. **6.** idiom. Cause, reason, purpose, means of, because (often used as *ua mea o* or *ka ua mea,* Gram. 7.4). *No ka mea,* because. *No ia mea,* therefore, for that reason. *Nui kō makou holo i ka ua mea o ka maka'u,* we ran fast because of fear. *Na wai 'ole nō ka nele i ka ua mea o ka piliwaiwai?* Who could help being poor because of the gambling? *Akamai kēlā Kepanī i nā hula Hawai'i, ā mea nō paha, hānai 'ia e nā Hawai'i,* that Japanese is clever in Hawaiian_hula, probably because he was raised by Hawaiians. *Ā mea lā ho'i ā hele mai e 'ike,* but because [one would think he would] come to see [said in disappointment or with hurt feelings]. *Mea* (or other word) following *ua* is sometimes deleted; the meaning then is something like 'aforesaid' (see *ua 2*). *Holo a'e nei na'e 'o ua o Wānu'a* (Nak. 42), now Wānu'a's canoe has just sailed on. *'O ka ua mua ia a Māui* (KL line 2000), this was the first [exploit] of Māui. **7.** vs. Reddish-brown, as water with red earth in it; yellowish-white, of feathers. *Wai-mea* (name), reddish water. (PPN *mea.*) **8.** vt. To bother, disturb. (Sol. 14.10.)

mea 'ai. n. Food, refreshment, groceries.

mea 'ai lau nahele. n. Vegetable. *Lit.,* forest leaf food.

mea 'ai mā.mā. n. Light refreshment.

mea 'ai momona. n. Dessert.

mea 'āina. n. Landowner.

mea akua. n. Godly or divine person; any person with a god to worship.

mea 'ala. n. Perfume, fragrance, incense.

mea aloha. n. Beloved or pitiful person or thing. See ex., *'ehia.*

mea ana 'āina. n. Surveyor.

mea 'ē. nvs. Extraordinary, unusual, strange, wonderful; unusual person; stranger, alien, one of another race; a wonder. *He mea 'ē ka 'eleu o nā mea apau* (Kep. 151), the energy of everyone was extraordinary. *He mea 'ē 'oia, 'a'ole he Hawai'i,* he is of a different race, not a Hawaiian.

mea 'eha, mea hō.'eha. n. Dangerous weapon.

mea hale. n. House owner; something belonging to a house.

mea hana lima. n. Handicraft, hand-made article.

mea hō.'ike.'ike. n. Display, exhibit, specimen.

mea ho'o.hana. n. Implement, tool.

mea ho'o.komo pepa. n. Folder, file.

mea ho'o.lohe. n. Hearing aid.

mea ho'o.pa'a. n. Brake, holder, fastener, cast.

mea ho'o.piha.piha. n. Stuffing.

mea ho'o.pono.pono. n. Manager, superintendent, editor.

mea hou. nvs. News, new. *He aha ka mea hou?* What's new?

mea hula. n. Hula dancer.

mea iki. n. Trifle, inconsequential thing. *He mea iki,* just a trifle, you're welcome [sometimes said in reply to "thank you"].

mea 'ino. n. Filth, sin, abomination (Mat. 24.15), deep trouble (see ex., *mahiki 2*), waste matter. *Lua o nā mea 'ino,* cesspool.

mea inu. n. Beverage, drink, potion.

mea kā.kau. n. Writer, author.

mea kanu. n. Plants, crops.

mea kaua. n. Weapon, warlike person, thing pertaining to war.

mea kia'i. n. Guard, preserver, protection. *Ka mea kia'i i nā kānaka* (Ioba 7.20), preserver of men.

mea kino. n. Tangible thing with form. (Kel. 123.)

mea kino ola. n. Physiology. *Lit.,* things [of the] live body.

mea koho. n. Voter.

mea kolo. n. Creeping insect.

mea kule.ana. n. One with a *kuleana;* claimant of a *kuleana. Mea kuleana i ho'okō 'ia,* confirmed claimant.

mea lele. n. Bird, flying insect.

mea make. n. Weapon, corpse.

mea mā.lama puke, mea mā.lama wai.hona puke. n. Librarian.

mea.mea. 1. Redup. of *mea 4, 7.* **ho'o.mea.mea.** Caus/sim.; to bluff, pretend, disguise. *Hā'awi ho'o- meamea,* to pretend to give [with the intention of taking back]. *He manu hulu meamea 'o Keawe,* a yellow- feathered bird is Keawe.

mea noi male. n. Suitor.

mea nui. n. Beloved person or thing; important person; thing of importance (sometimes said sarcastically). *Ma kona 'ano mea nui* (Laie 593), in his character as a person of importance. *He mea nui 'o La'a i kona makua- hine,* La'a is beloved by his mother.

mea ola. n. Live person, living being, survivor.

mea 'ole. nvs. Inconsequential, trifling, insignificant, unimportant, null and void; a mere nothing; trifle. *Mea 'ole ka pi'ina,* the climb was nothing at all. *He mea 'ole,* it doesn't matter, it's of no importance, never mind.

mea oli. n. Chanter of *oli;* one with an *oli* chant in his honor; *oli* chanter.

mea omo. n. Suction tube, drinking straw.

mea 'ono. n. Cake of any kind, pastry, dessert, cooky. *Lit.,* delicious thing.

mea 'ono kele. n. Jelly roll.

mea 'ono kihi.kihi. n. Square or rectangular pastry as made by Chinese. *Lit.,* cake [with] corners.

mea 'ono kuki. n. Cooky.

mea 'ono mo'a 'ole. n. Batter, uncooked cake.

mea 'ono 'ō.helo papa. n. Strawberry shortcake.

mea 'ono paona. n. Pound cake.

mea 'ono pua'a. n. Chinese pork cake. (Commonly called *manapua* today; cf. *pepeiao 7.*)

mea pā. n. Owner of a house lot.

mea pā.'ani. n. Recreation, game, sport.

mea paha. idiom. Perhaps. *Mea paha ua hele aku nei,* perhaps gone now.

mea pepehi kanaka. n. Weapon. Also *mea 'eha.*

mea ulu. n. Vegetable, growing plant.

mea 'ume. See *'ume 2.*

mea wa'a. n. Canoeman, canoe owner.

mea wehe kini. n. Can opener.

me'e. nvs. Hero, heroine; important person; favorite occupation; prominent, admired, heroic. *'O Ka-uahoa, 'o ka me'e u'i o Hanalei* (FS 97), Ka-uahoa, the handsome youthful hero of Hanalei.

me'ea. vt. To upturn, overturn, destroy. (For. 6:393.)

me'e.au. nvi. Itch, mange, ulcer; to itch, to afflict with blight; mangy, itching. *He 'īlio me'eau,* a mangy dog.

me'e.me'e. 1. Same as *me'e.* **2.** n. Halfbeak fish *(Hemir- amphus brasiliensis).* Also *iheihe.*

me'eu. vi. Rising up; to rise up, as from sitting; to start up, as a frightened bird; to rise, as hair in terror; startled. *Me'eu ka 'ili,* shuddering. *'Akahi au ā 'ike, ka me'eu ho'i o ku'u oho* (chant for Ka-lā-kaua), I've never felt my hair rise in terror like this before.

meha. Same as *mehameha.* (PCP *me(f,s)a.*)

-meha'i. See *kameha'i.*

mehame. 1. Same as *mehani 1.* **2.** Same as *hame 1,* trees. (Neal 500.)

meha.meha. nvs. Loneliness, solitariness, solitude, hushed silence; lonely, solitary; silent, as during the hush of taboo. *Hale mehameha,* lonely house. *Nohona*

mehameha, life of solitude and loneliness. *Pule mehameha,* silent prayer. **ho'o.meha.meha.** To cause silence, loneliness; to hush. (PCP *me(f,s)ame(f,s)a.*)

mē.hame.hame. n. A rare native tree *(Neowawraea phyllanthoides),* related to the *hame,* also has hard wood, ovate leaves, and red fruits, but the fruits are borne singly or few together. (Neal 504.)

Meha.meha-Pu'u.loa. n. A stroke in *lua* fighting. *Lit.,* Long-Hill (Pearl Harbor) loneliness.

mehana. Var. of *mahana. Ka mehana o ka lā* (Laie 613), the warmth of the sun.

mehani. 1. nvs. Hot, heat, but less hot than *'ena'ena;* unapproachable, as of a high taboo chief. 2. vs. Smooth, curved.

mehe. prep. Like, as though, as if (*me* + *he,* indefinite article; often written as two words). See Gram. 9.7 and ex., *maka lena* 2. *Mehe mea lā ua make,* as though dead. *Ua holo ia mehe lio lā,* he ran like a horse. *Mehe ala e 'ī mai ana, aia ka ua i ka nahele* (song), as though saying, there's the rain in the forest. (PCP *mese.*)

mehelu. Same as *māhelu. E mehelu i ka lepo i nenelu i 'ae'ae* (prayer to Kāne-pua'a), dig the soil and make it soft and fine.

meheu. 1. nvs. Track, footprint, tracing, trail, clue; trodden, beaten, as a path; walked on; to tread. **ho'o.me.heu.** To make a track; to follow a track, trail, trace; to lead up to deviously, as in asking a favor. 2. *(Cap.)* n. Wind associated with Ka-lihi-wai, Kaua'i. (For. 5:97.)

mē.heu.heu. Redup. of *meheu;* custom, beaten path. *'O ka mēheuheu nō ia mai nā mākua mai,* that was the customary way handed down from parents.

Mei. n. May. *Eng.*

meia. n. Mayor. *Eng.*

me ia. With him, her; like this, similar to this.

meka, mesa. n. Mass. *Pule meka,* mass. (French *messe.*)

mekala. n. 1. Also **medala.** Medal. *Eng.* 2. Also **metala.** Metal *(Eng.);* tag, as of a dog license.

mekala ho'o.hano.hano. n. Military or honorary medal.

meka.nika. n. Mechanic. *Eng.*

Meke.au.pe'a. Probably var. of *Makeaupe'a,* a star.

meke.kiko, metedito. n. Methodist. *Eng.*

mekele, metere. nvs. Meter; metric. *Eng.*

meke.leka, metereta. n. A measure said to equal about 20 liters. (Gr. *metretes.*)

meki. n. 1. Pit (often used with *lua.*) Cf. Hal. 88.12. (Possibly Heb. *michre.*) *Lua meki o Kehena,* pit of hell. 2. Ancient name for iron, as found on driftwood; nail, spike.

mekia. n. 1. Major (the military title). *Eng.* 2. Also **Mesia.** *(Cap.)* Messiah. (Gr. *Messias.*)

Mekiko. nvs. Mexico; Mexican. *Eng.*

mekila. vs. Handsome. Cf. *kilakila. Mekila ke ka'i a ka ua noe* (song for Lili'u-o-ka-lani), handsome the procession of misty rain.

Meko.kiko, Metodito. nvs. Methodist. *Eng.*

meko.pio, metopio. n. Galbanum. (Puk. 30.34.)

meku. vt. To scold, speak offensively; rude. *Rare.*

meku.lika, metulika. n. Methylated spirits. *Eng.*

mela.mela. vs. Lazy, indolent.

Mela.nikia. nvs. Melanesia; Melanesian. *Eng.*

mele. 1. nvt. Song, anthem, or chant of any kind; poem, poetry; to sing, chant (preceded by both *ke* and *ka*). Cf. *haku mele. Kāna mele,* his song [sung by him or composed by him]. *Kona mele,* his song [in his honor]. *Ke Mele a Solomona* (Biblical), the Song of Solomon. Cf. *oli,* a chant that is not danced to. *Mele 'oli,* gay song. **ho'o.mele.** To cause to sing or chant. (PNP *umele.*) 2. vs. Yellow. 3. vs. Merry. *Eng. Mele Kalikimaka,* merry Christmas.

mele ahi.ahi. n. Evening song, vesper.

mele au.puni. n. National anthem.

mele hai pule. n. Hymn, religious song.

mele hapa haole. n. Hawaiian type of song mostly with English words.

mele hei. n. Song sung while making a cat's cradle *(hei).*

mele ho'āla. n. Song to wake a sleeping child or person, especially one composed for a chief or favorite child and used thus. *Lit.,* awakening song.

mele ho'ā.loha.loha. n. Serenade.

mele ho'o.hia.moe keiki. n. Lullaby. *Lit.,* song to put children to sleep.

mele ho'o.ipo.ipo. n. Love song, serenade. *Lit.,* wooing song.

mele hō.'ole lama. n. Temperance song. *Lit.,* song refusing rum.

mele hō.'ole wai 'ona. n. Temperance song, *Lit.,* song refusing intoxicating liquor.

mele ho'o.nā.nā keiki. n. Lullaby, song to soothe children.

mele.huka. n. Sum total. *Ka helu a ka Hawai'i 'oia ho'i 'o ka lau, 'o ka mano, 'o ke kini a me ka lehu o ke akua, he melehuka kō lākou helu huina pau loa,* the counting of the Hawaiians, as follows: *lau, mano, kini,* and *lehu* of the Gods, all their total number is *melehuka.*

Mele.hune. Var. of *Menehune. Kaua'i.* See ex., *pā'ē'ē.*

mele inoa. n. Name chant, i.e., chant composed in honor of a person, as of a chief. Also *inoa.*

mele kā.hea. n. Chant for admittance to an old-time hula school. *Lit.,* calling song.

mele ka'i. n. Chant or song sung while dancers come out before the audience. *Lit.,* procession song.

mele ka'i ho'i. n. Chant or song sung while dancers leave the audience. *Lit.,* song for proceeding back.

mele ka'i kaua. n. Battle song. (PH 43.) *Lit.,* song to lead in battle.

Mele Kaliki.maka. interj. Merry Christmas. *Eng.*

mele kani.kau. n. Dirge, mourning song.

mele.kiana, merediana. n. Meridian. *Eng.*

mele kinai lama, mele kinai 'ona. n. Temperance song. *Lit.,* song abolishing rum, song abolishing drunkenness.

mele komo. n. Welcoming song.

mele kuahu. n. Altar chant, as before an altar in a hula school.

mele.kule. n. Pot marigold *(Calendula officinalis).* (Neal 855.) Other kinds of marigolds *(Tagetes)* are called *'ōkole'oi'oi.*

mele.kule wai kā.huli. n. An ornamental gaillardia *(Gaillardia pulchella)* from the United States mainland, both cultivated and wild in Hawai'i. The flowers are yellow and reddish. (Neal 847–8.) Also *waikāhuli.*

Mele.kulla, Merekuria. n. Mercury. (Probably Latin *Mercurius.*)

mele kū.ō, mele kūwō. n. Lamentation.

mele ma'i. See *ma'i,* genitals.

mele.mele. 1. vs. Yellow, blonde. **ho'o.mele.mele.** To color or paint yellow. 2. *(Cap.)* n. Star name. Melemele and Polapola were said to be twin stars, the former male and the latter female. (PNP *Melemele;* cf. Ka-pingamarangi.) 3. *(Cap.)* n. A mythical land. (Malo 6.)

mele.mele 'ili 'alani. nvs. Orange-yellow. *Lit.,* orange-peel yellow.

Mele.nekia. nvs. Melanesia; Melanesian. *Eng.*

mele.nio. n. Millennium. *Eng.*

mele pai.kau. n. A march; marching song.

mele ukali hua kumu. n. Alphabet song, as one repeating the vowels. *Lit.,* song following the basic letters.

meli. n. Bee, honey (Kin. 43.11). *Nalo meli,* bee. *Wai meli,* honey. *Pahu meli,* beehive. (Gr. *meli.*)

melia. n. All species and varieties of plumeria *(Plumeria)* or frangipani, small, broad-topped trees, from tropical America, grown ornamentally, the flowers being one of the commonest kinds for leis. The thick, stiff branches bear long leaves and many five-parted, tubular, fragrant flowers, which are white and yellow, pink to rose. Probably *Eng.* (Neal 688.)

meli.kiana, meridiana. n. Meridian. *Eng.*

melo.kia, melodia. n. Melody. (Latin *melodia.*)

melo.kiana. n. Melodeon. *Eng.*

melo.melo. n. Club used as lure; it was smeared with bait, such as roasted *'ala'ala he'e*, roasted coconut flesh, or various aromatic leaves; let down in the water, it was believed to attract fish to a net. Also *mākālei.* **ho'o.melo.melo.** To prepare this club; to use this club.

melu. 1. vs. Soft, decomposed, especially of fish; weakening. *'A 'ohe ma'i luku 'ē a'e nāna e melu a nome aku, 'o ka rama, moekolohe, like pū* (chant), no other destructive disease is as weakening and continuing as liquor, adultery, [and] such. **ho'o.melu.** To cause a decomposition, to leave (as fish) until decomposition begins. *I'a ho'omelu*, fish, such as *hīnālea*, slightly decomposed, then salted and seasoned with *kukui*-nut relish, chili peppers, etc. (PCP *melu.*) **2.** To pull out, as the beard. (And.)

melu.melu. Redup. of *melu 1.*

memeha. Same as *mehameha.*

memeki. nvs. Anger, wrath; angry. *Rare.*

memele. 1. Similar to *melemele*, yellow. *He memele maika'i kona 'ili* (For. 5:269), his skin was lightcolored and attractive. **2.** Redup. and plural of *mele*, to sing. *Nā po'e memele*, the singers. *Eia nā 'ānela ke memele nei*, here the angels sing.

memelu. Same as *melumelu.*

meme.mele. Same as *memele 1, 2.*

meme.ue. See *hāpaimemeue.*

mena. Var. of *mane 1.* (AP.)

mene. 1. nvs. Dullness, bluntness; dull, blunt, as a knife. Cf. *'ūmene. Ihu mene*, flat-nosed. *Ua mene ka ihu o ka wa'a*, the prow of the canoe is blunted. **ho'o.mene.** To make dull; dull. **2.** vi. To move back, step back, shrink. *E mene mai i hope*, step back. (PPN *mene.*)

Mene.hune. 1. n. Legendary race of small people who worked at night, building fish ponds, roads, temples; if the work was not finished in one night, it remained unfinished; also *Melehune*. See *'e'epa*. Luomala 1951 convincingly refutes the theory that Hawai'i was settled by *Menehune* before the arrival of the first Hawaiians. Cf. *hune 2.* (PCP *M(a,e)n(a,e)(f,s)une.*) **2.** *(Not cap.)* vt. To gather together to work and complete a task, as a band of *Menehune. E menehune mai kākou i ka hana*, let's get together and get the work done like *Menehune.*

me nei. Var. of *penei*, like this. *Me nei 'oe i hana ai*, do it this way.

meneke. See *manakō meneke.*

mene.mene. Redup. of *mene 1, 2;* to shrink from handling; hesitation (Nak. 118). *Fig.*, to feel sorry, compassionate, pathetic; compassion; to fear for a loved one. *Menemene au i ku'u mo'opuna*, I so do not want anything to happen to my grandson. *E menemene ana au i ka'u mea e menemene aku ai* (Rom. 9:15), I will have compassion on whom I will have compassion. **ho'o.-mene.menee.** Caus/sim.

mene'o. Var. of *mane'o.*

mene.ū. To double , as the arms at the elbows, or legs at the knees; foldedd, as a mat. (And.)

menui. vs. Contracted, shortened, blunted off.

me'o. 1. vt. To nag and tease, usually indirectly; to drool at the mouth while watching, as food being prepared; to linger about with greedy eyes; importuning. *Me'o maoli kēia kamali'i i ka mea 'ai*, these children are begging, watching, reaching for the food. **2.** vi. To sprout.

me'o.me'o. 1. Redup. of *me'o 1. Wahine momona waiū lewa, too muchee me'ome'o i ka'u sikaliki* (old hula song), fat woman with hanging breasts, always hanging around for my cigarette. **2.** Redup. of *me'o 2;* swelling as óf finger; to poke through, as body hairs through a hole in clothes.

meu. 1. vs. Blunt. **2.** To meet, touch, as persons kissing; to cohabit; to stitch together (And.). Cf. *peu.*

me'u. Same as *me'o 2;* to sprout, protrude.

meua. Pas/imp. of *meu 2.*

meu.keu. Knuckled, as of a doubled-up fist. (And.)

meu.meu. 1. Redup. of *meu 1, 2. Ihu meumeu*, flat nose. **2.** Kind of fish (no data.)

me'u.me'u. Redup. of *me'u;* same as *me'ome'o 2.*

MH. Year (abbreviation for *makahiki*).

mī. 1. vi. Urine; to urinate (less used than *mimi*). **2.** nvi. Dream; to dream. *He aha kāu mī?* What did you dream about? **3.** n. Seventh note in musical scale, ti. **4.** n. Me (in songs). *Eng.* **5.** n. Mister. *Eng. Mī Laiana*, Mr. Lyons.

mia. Pas/imp. of *mī 1.*

-mia. Pas/imp. suffix; *Gram.* 6.6. See *inumia.* (PPN *-mia.*)

mī.'ala. Same as *miki'ala.*

mī.ana. n. Place for urinating (formerly certain places outdoors were set aside for this purpose); urinal.

miha. vs. Silent, quiet. *Miha lanaau*, flowing quietly along, as a current. *'O Pele lā ko'u akua, miha ka lani, miha ka honua* (prayer), Pele is my god, silent the heavens, silent the earth. Cf. *hāmiha.*

miha.miha. Redup. of *miha.* (For. 5:329.)

-mihamiha. **ho'o.omihamiha.** To decorate, dot. *Kū-keao-ho'omihamiha-i-ka-lani* (Kam. 65:58), Kū-[in]-the-clouds-that-dot-the-sky [a Kū god].

mī.hau. n. Hau branch set up near the field of battle; as long as it stood upright, the nearby army was said to be winning. (Malo 199.)

mihi. nvt. Repentance, remorse; to repent, apologize, be sorry, contrite; to regret; to confess, as to a priest. *Mihi make*, death-bed repentance; to repent too late to remedy or prevent; tardy repentance. *Kāna mihi 'ana*, his confession. *E mihi 'oe iāia*, apologize to him. *Ua mihi au i ku'u hele 'ana*, I'm sorry about my going. (PNP *misi.*)

mihi.mihi. Redup. of *mihi.*

miho. vt. To pile up, place in a pile. *E miho ana 'oia i ka pōhaku no ke kūkulu pā*, he is piling up stones for fence building.

mi'i. 1. Short for *'ūmi'i*, clasp. **2.** vs. Attractive, fine-appearing, good-looking. *Mi'i noho'i 'o Nani*, Nani is certainly pretty.

mika. n. Mister. *Eng.*

mīka. n. Meter. *Eng.*

mī.kā. vt. To press, crush. *Rare.*

mika.mina. n. Misdemeanor. *Eng.*

mī.kana. n. The papaya *(Carica papaya*, a small tree, a native of tropical America, long popular in Hawai'i for its melon-like fruits. (Neal 600–1.) *Hawai'i.* Also *hē'ī, milikana, papaia.*

mika.nele. nvs. Missionary. *Eng.* Also *mikionali.* **ho'o.mika.nele.** To act as a missionary; to ape the missionaries; to be a goody-goody.

mike.lio, miterio. n. Mystery. (Gr. *mysterion.*)

mikepo, migebo. n. Goodly. (Puk. 39.28, KJV.)

miki. 1. nvs. Quick, active, nimble, prompt, alert, spry, sprightly, watchful, fast and efficient in work; speed, alertness. *He aha kāu 'o ka miki 'ana aku nei i laila?* Why were you so prompt in going there? **2.** vi. To suck in, dip in; to shrink, as clothes or as salt beef in boiling; to spring together, as sides of a steel trap; to draw in, as an octopus; to contract; to recede, as an undertow; to shrivel, as a leaf; to take up with the fingers, as poi; evaporated, as water by boiling. See *nalu miki. Miki poi*, dab of poi, as on the finger. *Miki pololei*, fresh poi, said to be so called because it wasn't tasty and one was content with a dab or two. (PPN *miti.*)

mikia. Pas/imp. of *miki 1, 2.*

miki 'ai. nv. Finger of poi,, a finger-dip of poi; to dip poi on the finger.

miki.'ala. vs. Alert, prompt; eaarly on hand. Cf. *'oihana miki'ala. E miki'ala mai i ke kakahiaka nui*, be here promptly in the early morning.

miki.'ao. n. Claw, nail, as of finger or toe. (PCP *miti-kao.*)

miki.awa. Var. of *makiawa*, a round herring.

miki.hilina. vs. Most beautiful, of dress, finery, ornaments. *Kāhiko ā oki ā pā'ihi'ihi, lawe ā linohau ā miki-hilina* (chant for Ka-lā-kaua), dressed in best, neatest finery, most fine and ornate.

miki.lana, misilana. n. The Chinese rice flower *(Aglaia* _odorata)_, a shrub or small tree in the mahogany family, from south China and Indo-China, grown ornamentally for the handsome leaves and fragrant flowers, which are tiny, round, and yellow; clusters of them are used for leis. (Perhaps Chinese _mei-sui-lan;_ Gram. 2.9.) (Neal 493.)

mikili. Var. of _nakili. Rare._

miki.lima. Short for _mīkini lima._

mī.kilolo.hua. Same as _mīkololohua._

miki.miki. 1. Redup. of _miki 1, 2;_ energetic. _Na ka mikimiki mua nō ka loa'a,_ for the most alert one the gains. **2.** vt. To talk in a friendly and ingratiating way, as to obtain a favor. **3.** n. A crape myrtle. (Neal 616–7.)

mikina. Same as _miki 'ana._ See _miki 1, 2._

miki.nalo. n. **1.** A sundew _(Drosera anglica),_ a small insectivorous bog plant found in the Hawaiian Islands only on Kaua'i in mountain bogs. The leaves bear stick glands to catch insects. (Neal 374.) _Lit.,_ to suck flies. **2.** Venus's-flytrap.

miki.nele. Var. spelling of _mikanele,_ missionary.

mī.kini. n. **1.** Machine _(Eng.),_ motor, engine. **2.** Mitten _(Eng.),_ glove.

mī.kini 'ai.ana. n. Clothes presser, mangle. _Lit.,_ ironing machine.

mī.kini 'apo leo. n. Recorder. _Lit.,_ machine that catches the voice.

mī.kini helu. n. Adding machine, comptometer.

mī.kini holoi. n. Washing machine.

mī.kini ho'o.ma'e.ma'e hale. n. Vacuum cleaner.

mī.kini ho'o.pa'a. n. Recording machine; any machine that binds.

mī.kini humu.humu. n. Sewing machine.

mī.kini kaomi. n. Press, as for clamping material, pressing clothes.

mī.kini kiko.kiko hua. n. Typewriter.

mī.kini lima. n. Glove, mitten. _Lit.,_ hand mitten _(Eng.)._

mī.kini nā.nā iā loko o ke kanaka. n. X-ray machine. _Lit.,_ machine inspecting innards of man.

mī.kini 'oki mau'u. n. Lawn mower. _Lit.,_ grass-cutting machine.

mī.kini pa'i nū.pepa. n. Printing press. _Lit.,_ machine to print newspapers.

mī.kini wili. n. Drill. See ex., _wili 1._

mikino.lia. n. Magnolia _(Magnolia grandiflora),_ a tree from southeastern United States, with large, white, fragrant flowers. _Eng._ (Neal 356.)

mikino.lia hihiu. Same as _lākana,_ wild magnolia.

mikino.lia hohono. Same as _lākana, mikinolia kukū. Lit.,_ bad-smelling magnolia.

mikino.lia kukū. n. Same as _lākana, mikinolia hohono. Lit.,_ thorny magnolia.

miki.oi. 1. vs. Dainty and neat in craftsmanship, or in doing anything; deft; excellently made, as result of workmanship. _Mikioi ka hana 'ia 'ana o kēla pākaukau,_ this table is neatly and skillfully made. **ho'o.miki.oi.** To do neatly; to work with skilled craftsmanship; to handle daintily. **2.** _(Cap.)_ n. Name of a strong, gusty wind of Ni'ihau (For. 5:95, UL 238). _Ka makani Mikioi o Lehua,_ the gusty Mikioi wind of Lehua Island. **3.** n. A native variety of sugar cane. (HP 225.)

miki.ona, misiona. n. Mission. _Eng._

mikio.nali, misionari. nvs. Missionary. _Eng._

mikio.neli. nvs. Missionary. _Eng._

miki.palaoa. Same as _'auko'i,_ a shrub.

miko. 1. vs. Seasoned with salt (Kol. 4.6); salted, tasty. Cf. _mikomiko._ **ho'o.miko.** To season, salt. _Ho'omiko ai me ka pa'akai_ (Oihk. 2.13), season with salt. **2.** nvi. To kink, snarl, become ensnared; kink, snarl. _Ua miko ka lopi,_ the thread has kinked.

mī.koho. vs. Good-looking, attractive, becoming. _Mikilima mīkoku,_ good-looking gloves.

mī.kohu.kohu. Redup. of _mīkohu._

mī.koi. vt. To nibble, eat in small pinches, as salt or _'inamona_ with poi. _Kāmano mīkoi,_ salmon eaten in small bits.

mī.koi.koi. Redup. of _mīkoi._

mīko.koi. 1. Redup. of _mīkoi._ **2.** n. A native variety of sugar cane; a lighter brown-red mutant of _manulele_ without purple cast to leaves and sheath. (HP 221.)

mī.kole. 1. vt. To eat fastidiously, in small portions; to nibble, as at salt or relish; to eat sparingly. **2.** vs. Persevering, continuing at a task little by little; working bit by bit. _'O kona mīkole nō ia ā hiki i ka wā e loa'a ai,_ he perseveres until he obtains.

mī.kolele.hua. Var. of _mīkololohua._

mī.kolo.hua. Same as _mīkololohua._

mī.kolo.hua. vs. Eloquent, fascinating in speech, moving, pleasing, delightful, entertaining. Cf. _miko 1._

mī.kolo.lia. vs. Changeable or varying in appearance, as the sea. _Rare._

miko.miko. Redup. of _miko 1;_ garnish; delicious; salted lightly; entertaining, instructive, as conversation. Cf. _mīkololohua._ **ho'o.miko.miko.** Caus/sim.

miko.mikoi. Redup. of _mīkoi._

mī.kua.kua. n. A medicinal plant (no data).

mila. n. Mill (tenth part of a cent). _Eng._

mile. n. **1.** Bunch of 40 loose, cleaned _olonō_ fibers. _Rare._ Also _'apana._ **2.** Mile, mileage. _Eng._

mileka, mileta. n. Millet. (Ezek. 4.9.)

mile loa. n. Nautical mile, knot. _Lit.,_ long mile.

mile.nio. n. Millennium. _Eng._

mili. vs. **1.** To handle, feel of, fondle, caress, as a beloved child; fondled, beloved. _Ka i'a mili i ka lima,_ the fish _['o 'opu]_ fondled in the hand [easily caught]. (PPN _mili.)_ **2.** Slow, inefficient in work. Cf. _mili 'apa, milimili. Nui ka mili o kāna hana,_ his work is very slow.

milia. Pas/imp. of _mili 1._ _Ka-pua-i-milia_ (name), the beloved flower or child.

mili.ame.kele, miliametere. n. Millimeter. _Eng._

mili.ani. vt. To fondle gently. _He pua ua miliani 'ia e ka Mālualua Ki'i Wai_ (song), she was a flower gently caressed by the water-fetching _Mālualua_ wind.

mili 'apa. vs. Slow, dilatory.

mili.ka'a. vt. To handle over and over, to do repeatedly; to keep doing something of little value; to repeat slowly; to fondle or caress over and over. _Ua milika'a 'ia e ka Inu-wai,_ caressed repeatedly by the Water-drinking wind.

mili.kana. Same as _mīkana._

mili.lani. vt. To praise, exalt; to give thanks; to treat as a favorite. _E komo 'oukou i loko o kona 'īpuka me ka mililani_ (Hal. 100.4), enter into his gates with thanksgiving.

mili.mili. 1. Redup. of _mili 1;_ toy, plaything; favorite, darling, pet, beloved; to examine with interest or curiosity and admiration. _Kō kino ē, ki'i milimili_ (song), your body, a beloved doll. (PPN _milimili.)_ **2.** Redup. of _mili 2._ _He keu noho'i kou milimili,_ how extraordinarily slow you are.

mili nanea, mili.mili nanea. nvt. Cherished person that absorbs and delights one; absorbed and charmed; to enjoy and take delight. _Mili nanea mau i kāna mo'opuna,_ constantly absorbed and delighted in his grandchild.

mili.ona. num. Million. _Eng._

mili.'opu. vs. Easy to catch with the hands, as some fish; easily handled. _Ka i'a mili'opu i ka lima_ (song), the fish caught in the hand.

milo. 1. n. A tree to 12 m high _(Thespesia populnea),_ found on coasts of the eastern tropics; used for shade, the wood for calabashes, other parts of the tree in many ways, as for medicine, dye, oil, gum. It is related to the _hau_ and resembles it somewhat. (Neal 563–4.) (PPN _milo.)_ **2.** nvt. Curl; to curl, twist, as sennit strands; to whirl, as water; to spin, as a tale; abortion. Cf. _'ōmilo. Milo li'i,_ fine twisting [as sennit]. _Milo 'ia ka mo'olelo,_ the tale was told. (PPN _milo.)_

milo lopi. nv. Distaff for spinning thread; to twist thread (written _milo lope_ in Sol. 31.19).

milo.milo. Redup. of _milo 2._

milu. 1. vs. Soft, rotten. **2.** _(Cap.)_ n. Underworld, ruler of underworld. (Kam. 64:51–60.)

milu.milu. vs. Gloomy, shady, solemn.

mimi. nvi. Urine; to urinate. *Mimi* beliefs (Nānā 181-2, 202): urine was sprinkled to repel evil; if an infant urinated on someone, that person might adopt the child. **hoʻo.mimi.** To cause urination; to help to urinate, as a child. (PPN *mimi.*)

mī.mī. Same as *ʻōmīmī.*

mimi ʻawa. nv. Bitter urine, said of vile-smelling urine; to urinate thus.

mimi ʻeha. vi. Painful urination; to urinate painfully.

mimi hele.leʻi. nvi. Involuntary urination, as caused by weakened bladder; to urinate frequently or without control.

mimihi. Redup. of *mihi.*

mimi hono. vi. To urinate repeatedly, as of untrained children. *Lit.,* bad-smelling urine.

mimi.ʻī.lio. n. Sand spurry *(Spergularia marina),* a weedy herb from Europe, with long narrow leaves grouped at intervals along the stem, growing on sand near beaches in Hawaiʻi. *Lit.,* dog urine, perhaps so called because of its unpleasant smell.

mimi.ʻiole. n. Wild taro on inaccessible cliffs believed carried there by rats. *Lit.,* rat urine.

mimiki. 1. Redup. of *miki 1;* to work with a will. *Pehea nō lā ʻoukou i mimiki aku nei maʻō?* What made you get there so quickly? **2.** Redup. of *miki 2;* to suck in, as a whirlpool (Malo 26). Cf. *one mimiki. Kai mimiki,* a roiling sea, as caused by an earthquake.

mimi kō. n. Diabetes. *Lit.,* sugar-cane urine.

mimilo. Redup. of *milo 2;* curly, kinky; whirlpool; to revolve or ripple, as water in a whirlpool; to roll, as to induce abortion. **hoʻo.mimilo.** To curl, twist. *Hao hoʻomimilo,* metal hair curler. *Hoʻomimilo i ka lauoho,* to have hair curled.

mimi.mihi. Same as *mihimihi.*

mimi.mio. Redup. of *mimio.*

mimino. Redup. of *mino;* to wither, as blighted fruit.

mimio. Redup. of *mio,* to disappear.

mimi paʻa. nvi. Inability to urinate. *Lit.,* closed urine.

mimo. vs. Gentle, of upright character, quiet; capable and deft but unassuming. *Rare.*

mimoka. n. Mimosa. *Eng. Biblical.*

mimo.mimo. Redup. of *mimo.*

mina. Same as *minamina, mamina.* (PCP *mina.*)

mina.mina. nvt. **1.** To regret, be sorry, deplore; to grieve for something that is lost; regret, sorrow. *Minamina nohoʻi,* too bad, what a shame. *Minamina au i kona puka ʻole ʻana mai ke kula mai,* I regret she did not graduate from school. **2.** To prize greatly, value greatly, especially of something in danger of being lost; to value, place great value on; value, worth. *He mea minamina ʻia ke keiki,* a child is to be prized. *ʻA ʻole minamina ʻo lākou i ke ola,* they do not set much value on human life. **3.** Saving, economical, miserly, ungenerous; covetous; of things that one values; economy, thrift. *Minamina au i kēia pepa,* I'm saving with this paper. (PCP *minamina.*)

minao. n. Minnow. *Eng.*

mine. n. Mine (for minerals). *Eng.*

mineka, mineta. n. Mint. (Mat. 23.23.) *Eng.*

mine.lala, minerala. n. Mineral. *Eng. Wai minelala,* mineral water.

mino. nvs. Dimple, depression, dent; crown of the head; dimpled, creased, wrinkled, withered, blighted, dented; shriveling, as fruit or grass.

mino.ʻaka. nvi. Smile; to smile. *Lit.,* laughing dimple. **hoʻo.mino.ʻaka.** To cause to smile; to smile a little.

minoi. vt. To pucker the lips; to suck, as of a child. *(mino + -i,* transitivizer; Gram. 6.6.4.) (Perhaps PNP *miinoi.*)

mī.noi.noi. Redup. of *minoi;* to fold and tie in a narrow space; to crowd, to swarm in one place *(rare).*

mī.nole. vt. To eat a very little, to pick at food without appetite or desire. Cf. *nīnole.*

mino.mino. Redup. of *mino;* wrinkled, as with age, mussed, as a dress.

minuke, minute. n. Minute. *Eng.*

mio. 1. nvi. To disappear swiftly; to move swiftly, as a stream of water; to make off with quickly; to steal; to wilt; to depart quickly; current. See *palamio. ʻIo o mio lani* (For. 6:395), hawk disappearing into the sky. *Ua mio ʻia aku nei ke kālā a Paulo,* Paul's money was quickly stolen. *Maʻō i mio aku nei,* went swiftly that way. *E holo pololei ai kona waʻa ma ka mio o ke kai* (Nak. 114), his canoe sails straight with the current of the sea. **2.** vs. Narrow, pointed, tapering.

mī.ʻoi. vs. Forward, aggressive, bold; advancing, outstripping others, as a racer; to move or progress fast; to shoot marbles by placing the hand on or in front of the line behind which the shooting is supposed to be done (a form of cheating). Cf. *mahaʻoi, māʻoi.*

mī.oi.oi. vi. To look through nearly closed eyes, as in facing a dazzling light; to wrinkle up the eyelids. Also *pīoioi.*

mī.ʻoi.ʻoi. Redup. of *mīʻoi;* upstart.

mio.mio. Redup. of *mio 1, 2;* pointed, narrowing, clearcut, precise, as carpentry; trim, neat; to dive into water without splashing. *E ʻopi aʻe a miomio,* fold neat and trim [as clothes]. *Kāmaʻa miomio,* shoe with pointed toe.

miona. n. **1.** Swift disappearance or movement. **hoʻo.miona.** Caus/sim. **2.** Crease, as in the buttocks; vent in a fish's stomach; division between the labia of the vagina. **hoʻo.miona.** Creased; to make a crease. *Hoʻomiona ʻia kēlā pāpale,* that hat is creased. **3.** Top, as of a hanging valley.

miu. vs. Attractive.

miula. n. Mule, ass (Kin. 36.24). *Eng.*

miu.lana. n. Orange and white champak *(Michelia champaca* and *M. longifolia),* tall trees with smooth gray trunks, from the Himalayas, related to the magnolia, bearing many-parted, orange or yellow flowers *(M. champaca)* or white flowers *(M. longifolia),* which are especially fragrant at night. (Neal 357.) The orange and white species may be distinguished by qualifying *miulana* with the colors *melemele* and *keʻokeʻo.* The Chinese name for the white species is *pak-lan,* but cf. *pakalana* (Gram. 2.9).

mō. Short for *moku 1, 2. Mō-kapu* (place name), taboo district. *Mō ka pawa,* day breaks. *Mō ka piko,* cut the navel cord [said also of related persons who sever relationship]. **hoʻo.mō.** Short for *hoʻomoku,* to cut, etc.

mō-. 1. Short for *moʻo,* succession. Cf. *moʻolelo,* story. **2.** Short for *moʻo,* lizard. *Mōʻiliʻili* (place name), pebble lizard. **3.** Var. of *mā-, ma,* stative prefixes, but less common. See *mōʻali, mōhai, mōhaʻi, mōʻiu, mōkila,* and others. (Gram. 6.3.3.)

moa. n. **1.** Chicken, red jungle chicken *(Gallus gallus),* fowl, as brought to Hawaiʻi by Polynesians; for some people, an *ʻaumakua. ʻO luna, ʻo lalo, ʻo uka, ʻo kai, ʻo ka moa kona ame Kākuhihewa* (For. 4:510), above, below, inland, seaward, the chicken is his and Kākuhihewa's [*moa* here probably represents supreme rule; cf. Ka-welo's chant: *He liʻi ka moa, kau ana ka moa i luna o ka hale* (FS 101), the chicken is a chief, the chicken perches at the top of the house]. (PPN *moa.*) **2.** A native banana fruit with large and plump skin and flesh yellow, edible raw or cooked, growing in a small bunch. Also *huamoa.* (HP 176.) (Probably PPN *moa.*) **3.** Tufted, green, leafless plants *(Psilotum nudum* and *P. complanatum),* about 30 cm long, with many slender branches, growing in most tropical countries, both on trees and on the ground. Hawaiians used them medicinally (the spore powder as a purge), and their children played a game with them. (Neal 1-2.) Sometimes called *moa nahele, pipi.* **4.** Children's game played with *moa* twigs; the tiny branches were interlocked, and the players pulled on the ends; the loser's twigs broke and the winner crowed like a rooster *(moa).* **5.** A dart, tapering at one end, usually 25 to 60 cm long, used in a sliding game on which bets were made. Cf. *paheʻe 3. Hoʻoholoholo moa,* to slide the *moa* dart. **6.** Var. of *pahu,* trunkfish *(Ostracion meleagris).* (PPN *moa.*) **7.**

Stone fastened to rope, used as a war weapon, said to be triangular in shape. **8.** A small gastropod mollusk. Also *kāmoa.*

mo'a. nvi. Cooked; burned, as by sun; cooking, cooked food; made brittle, as tobacco leaves over a fire. *Mo'a loa,* overcooked, well done, hard boiled. *Mo'a hapa,* partially cooked, soft-boiled. *'Ai i kalo mo'a* (FS 83), eat cooked taro [enjoy a life of ease, contentment]. **ho'o.mo'a.** To cook, bake. (PPN *moho.*)

moa 'alae. n. Completely black chicken, so called because the mudhen *('alae)* was black. *Moa 'alae hulu 'ula,* black chicken with red feathers at neck and rump.

mō.ae. Var. spelling of *mōwae.*

Moa'e. n. Trade wind. *Moa'e kū,* strong *Moa'e.* Also *Noe.* (Elbert and Mahoe 59.)

Moa'e Lehua. n. Trade wind.

moa ha'a. n. Bantam, any short-legged chicken.

mō.aho.aho. Var. spelling of *mōwahowaho.*

moa ho'o.moe. n. Broody hen.

moai. nvi. Bending over, arching, as a tree. *Rare.*

moaka. Same as *mōakaaka.* *'O moaka kū ke ao* (chant), the cloud stands clear.

mō.akaaka, moakaka. nvs. Clear, plain, intelligible, manifest; clarity. *'Ike mōakaaka,* to see clearly. Cf. *akaaka.* **ho'o.mō.akaaka.** Explanation, definition; to explain clearly, clarify, define.

moa kā.kala. n. Cock with sharp spurs. *Fig.,* warrior who is a good fighter.

moa kāne. n. Rooster, cock. *Lit.,* male chicken.

mo'a kole.kole. vs. Cooked rare, as beef.

moa kua.kahi. n. First cock crow. *Lit.,* chicken rising first. Also *moa kū kahi.* Cf. *moa kualua,* second cock crow.

moala. vt. To raise to the mouth, as poi, or as a Chinese feeds rice into his mouth. *Rare.* Cf. *ala,* to rise.

mo'ala. 1. n. An edible crab found in ponds and shallow water, probably *Podophthalmus vigil.* **2.** vi. To relish food, as after having lost the appetite. *Rare. Ke mo'ala maila ka 'ono o ka 'ai,* the savor of food has been renewed.

mō.'ala.'ala. vi. Going here and there, as one asking for handouts; to gad about. *Rare.* Cf. *kō'ala'ala,* quick.

mo'a le'a. vi. Well-cooked, as pig.

mō.'ali. nvs. Impression, trace, scar, mark, as left by a knife cut; furrow, rut, track, groove, thread, welt, strand; small, fine. See ex., *puahilohilo.* **ho'o.mō.'ali.** To make an impression; scar, tracing, groove.

mō.'ali.'ali. Redup. of *mō'ali.*

moa.mahi. vt. To cherish and cultivate. *Ua moamahi 'oia i ka na'auao,* he cherished and cultivated wisdom.

moa mahi. n. Fighting cock. *Fig.,* successful warrior.

mo'a maka. vs. Barely cooked. *Lit.,* cooked raw.

moa.moa. 1. vt. To act the part of a cock; to care for, attend to; to supply with food, as a child or ward. **ho'o.moa.moa.** To accompany, as a cock with hens; to care for, protect, cherish. **2.** n. Sharp point at the stern of a canoe. **3.** n. Paper nautilus. Also *'auwa'alālua, 'aumoana, moamoa wa'a.* **4.** Same as *pahu,* trunkfish. (PPN *moamoa.*)

moana. 1. n. Ocean, open sea, lake. (PPN *moana.*) **2.** n. Campground, consultation place for chiefs. **ho'o.-moana.** To camp, camp (see ex., *'īpuka*). *Hele akula lākou . . . ā ho'omoana ma 'Etama* (Puk. 13.20), they want . . . and encamped at Etham. **3.** vs. Broad, wide, extended, expansive, spread out. **ho'o.moana.** To spread down, as mats.

Moana Anu 'Ā.kau. n. Arctic Ocean.

Moana Anu Hema. n. Antarctic Ocean.

moa.naana. Redup. of *moana 3.*

moa nahele. See *moa 3.*

moana kai. n. Salt sea (Nah. 34.3), salt lake; deep sea.

moana pa'a.kai. n. Salt sea (Nah. 34.12), salt lake.

moana wai. n. Fresh-water lake; sea (Mat. 8.27).

moa nē.nē. n. Speckled chicken, so called because of resemblance to the *nēnē,* goose.

moani. nvi. Light or gentle breeze, usually associated with fragrance; wafted fragrance; to blow perfume. (See chant, *kokoe;* Mele 1.12.) *Moani ke 'ala o ka 'awapuhi,* wind-blown is the ginger perfume.

Moani 'Ala. n. Name of a land breeze that wafts out to sea at Puna, Hawai'i. *Lit.,* fragrant breeze, so named for the fragrance of pandanus.

moani.ani. Redup. of *moani.*

Moani.ani Lehua. n. Name of a rain or wind associated with Puna, Hawai'i. *Lit.,* wind that wafts the fragrance of *lehua* blossoms.

moano. 1. n. Goatfish *(Parupeneus multifasciatus).* The young are called *'āhua* or *'ōhua;* the red color was believed caused by eating *lehua* blossoms. The name may be qualified by the terms *'au kī, kea (P. chryserydros), pāpa'a, ukali, ukali ulua.* **2.** nvi. Pale red color, as of the *moano* fish. *Fig.,* to bloom. *Moano ka lehua* (For. 6:293), the *lehua* flowers become red. **3.** n. A native variety of sugar cane, named for the fish; a red cane becoming dark-purple; pith dark-brown. (HP 224.) **4.** n. A variety of taro. (HP 33.)

moano 'ā.hua. n. Young *moano,* goatfish.

moa pua hau. n. A chicken with yellow feathers. *Lit., hau-*flower chicken.

mo'au. vs. Stretched or spread out. *Moe mo'au ke kahaone,* the sandy beach lies stretched out.

Moa.'ula. n. Waterfall, Hālawa, Moloka'i, and wind there.

moa 'ula hiwa. n. Predominantly red chicken.

moa.uli. Short for *moana uli,* dark blue sea. *Kēlā 'āina i ka moauli* (Kep. 17), that land in the dark blue ocean.

moa wahine. n. Hen. *Lit.,* female chicken.

moe. 1. vi. To sleep, lie down; to lie in wait, ambush; to prostrate oneself, as before a chief; to lay down, as cards; to sit on eggs; horizontal, prone. See ex., *'oni, death. Kapu moe,* prostration taboo. *Hale moe,* sleeping house. *Moe kau a ho'oilo,* sleep summer to winter [the sleep of death]. *Moe ka ihu o ka pua'a,* the nose of the pig is down [a pig has been killed for ceremony]. *'A 'ohe e moe ku'u maka ā kō ku'u makemake,* my eyes shall not sleep until my desire is obtained. *Moe ke kanaka,* a human sacrifice was made. *Moe 'ia ka iwi 'ao'ao e ke kanaka 'ē* (For. 4:47), the rib bones will be laid to rest by strangers. **ho'o.moe.** To put to sleep, to lay down; to set, as a hen (Isa. 59.5) or fish net; to offer, as a sacrifice; to deposit, as in banks; to bring down, as a club (FS 241); to "drop" a matter; to defer, postpone, rest a while; to table, as a motion; to lay, as bricks or cement; to subscribe, as to a newspaper. As an epithet for Ka-lā-kaua, *moe* probably refers to the *kapu moe.* Cf. *ho'omoemoe. Ho'omoe kimeki,* to pave. *Koa ho'omoe,* reserve militia (term used in 1845). (PPN *mohe.*) **2.** nvt. To marry, mate with, sleep with, cohabit; marriage. *Moe i kā ha'i,* to sleep with the mate of another. **ho'o.moe.** To arrange a match. *Huaka'i ho'omoe wahine* (FS 157), trip to arrange for a bride. *Ho'omoe ā ipo,* to cause to take as a sweetheart or lover. **3.** n. Bed, sleeping place. **4.** n. Dream. *Ka mea nāna nā moe* (Kin. 37.19), dreamer. *He aha ka puana o ka moe?* What is the answer of the dream [what will the result be]? **5.** vs. Calm, as the sea. **6.** Same as *moea 2.* Cf. *kāmoe.* **ho'o.moe.** Caus/sim. See ex., *kāo'o.*

moea. 1. Pas/imp. of *moe 2, 3.* **2.** vi. To press onward, go straight toward. *Moea 'oe i Hawai'i nui,* go directly to great Hawai'i.

moe.ā.hua. n. **1.** A variety of sweet potato. **2.** *(Cap.)* Wind name, Ke-kaha, Kaua'i. (For. 5:95.)

moe ai.kāne. nv. Sodomy, sodomist; to commit sodomy (1 Kor. 6.9). *Lit.,* friend mating.

moe awa.kea. nvi. One who gets up long after sunrise; a late sleeper; to sleep late.

moe hā.lau. v. To sleep in the *hālau* (shed), sometimes said of a lazy, uncooperative person. See ex., *lola.*

moe.hewa. vi. To sleep restlessly; to fidget, talk, or walk in one's sleep; disturbed in one's sleep; nightmare; to have a nightmare. *Lit.,* wrong sleeping.

moe hili.na'i. nvi. Reclining chair, deck chair, chaise lounge; to sleep in a reclining position, as in such a chair.

moe ho'o.lana. vi. To doze.

moe 'ino. nvi. Nightmare; bad dream; to toss, turn while sleeping, have a nightmare.

moe ipo. nv. To have an affair; to sleep with a lover; to commit adultery; fornicator (1 Kor. 6.9). *Huaka'i moe ipo* (PH 16), a match-making mission, a mission for the purpose of arranging for a lover.

moe.ka'a. n. Trundle bed.

moe.kahi. 1. vi. To sleep alone. **2.** vi. To lie or incline in the same direction, of several; in order, sequence. *Moekahi ka hana,* the work is going ahead.**3.** n. A *maile,* before it forms branches.

moe.kā.hua. Same as *moe 'ino.*

moe kama.li'i. n. Child's crib or bed.

moe koke. vi. To go to bed early, to sleep quickly.

moe.kolohe. nv. Adultery; to commit adultery, fornicate; adulterous. *Lit.,* illegal mating. *Na'au moekolohe* (Ezek. 6.9), whorish heart. **ho'o.moe.kolohe.** To lead into adultery.

moe.kolu. vs. Striped, of three colors of about the same width and lying parallel. Cf. *moelua.*

moe.kū. n. Bed.

moe.kuhua. n. Viscous matter in the eyes. Cf. *hū'alu.*

moe.lawa. Same as *leleiona,* shark sucker.

moe lepo. nvi. Earth sleeper; to sleep in the earth. *Fig.,* the dead; dirty, shiftless individual.

Moe-lehua. n. Rain name.

moe lewa. n. Hammock, cradle. *Lit.,* swinging bed.

moe like. vi. To sleep in a similar way; parallel.

moe loa. vi. To oversleep, sleep a long time.

moe.lola. n. Striped tapa; an outer sheet *(kilohana)* for bed covers, as made by laying a red cloth or tapa over a white tapa in long panels with intervening white spaces, and then beating it into the tapa; striped. Cf. *pa'i'ula.*

moe.lua. vs. Striped, of two colors of about same width and lying parallel, as of tapa. Cf. *moekolu, weke.*

moe lū.au'i. nv. Mating of child with its parent, as by Wākea and Ho'ohoku-ka-lani; to mate thus.

moe luli.luli. n. Cradle. *Lit.,* rocking bed.

moe ma'i. nvi. To lie abed sick; bedridden; sickbed. *Ua lō'ihi ka moe ma'i o Koma,* Tom has been sick in bed for a long time.

moe make. vi. To lie at death's door; to be sick unto death; to lie in a dead faint.

moe mau. vi. To live with a mate out of wedlock; spouse. *Lit.,* constant mating. Cf. *moekolohe,* a short affair, and *noho manuahi.*

moe.moe. 1. nvi. Ambush, to lie in ambush; to lurk. **ho'o.moe.moe.** To cause to lie down; to hush or put to sleep; to arrange a match; to set a line or net; to pretend to sleep. Cf. *ho'omoe.* *'Upena ho'omoemoe,* net set in the sea. (PPN *mohemohe.*) **2.** vi. To sleep (a rare plural). *Iā moemoe a'e lāua* (GP 46), then the two slept together. **3.** Same as *hōlua,* sled.

moe.moe.ā. nvi. To dream or fancy; fantasy; dream of a cherished wish, whether good or bad.

moena. 1. n. Mat. Cf. *moe,* to lie down. (PPN *moenga.*) **2.** n. Couch, bed. **3.** n. Resting place, position of anything lying down; place for setting *(ho'omoe)* a fish net. *Na ka lawai'a e kuhikuhi i ka moena e ho'omoe ai i ka 'upena,* the fisherman points out the place to set the net. **4.** Same as *moe 6. Moena i mua,* to forge ahead.

moena 'ahu 'ao. See *'ahu 'ao.*

moena 'ahu li'i. n. Fine mat. *Lit.,* fine garment mat.

moe naha. See *naha 2.*

moena hī.nalo, moena hī.nano. n. Very fine mat made of the bracts of *hala* blossoms *(hīnalo).*

moena kau pā.kau.kau. n. Table mat, place mat.

moena kua.kuai kā.ma'a. n. Door mat.

moena lau. n. Mat made with wide wefts.

moena pā.wehe. n. Fine mat, woven in patterns, as on Ni'ihau.

moena pū.'ao. See *pū'ao.*

moena pulu niu. n. Door mat, foot mat, so called because its fibers suggested coconut husk *(pulu niu).*

moena wele.weka n. Soft carpet of any kind. *Lit.,* velvet *(Eng.)* mat.

moe.one. 1. n. Small worm that hides in the sand. **2.** Same as *pāki'i,* flounder. *Lit.,* sand lying.

moe 'opi.'opi. n. Folding cot or bed, camp bed.

moe pai.pai. n. Cradle. *Lit.,* rocking bed.

moe.pi'o. nvt. Union of brother and sister of high rank; to make such a marriage. (Malo 54.) *Lit.,* bent marriage, supposedly of a thing bent against itself. Also *pi'o 2.* Cf. *pi'o.*

moe.po'o. vs. Determined. *Lit.,* lay [the] head. *E moepo'o aku ana au ā hiki i ke kō 'ana o ko'u makemake,* I'll keep right on until my desire is fulfilled.

-moepū. ho'o.moe.pū. To place artefacts with the dead. *Mai lawe wale i nā mea i ho'omoepū 'ia,* don't wantonly take things placed with the dead. *Lit.,* put to sleep with.

moe.pū loa. vi. To offer oneself as a death companion. (Nānā 133.)

moe.pu'u. n. Victim slain at the secret burial of a chief, so as to reduce the number of witnesses; victim who commits suicide or has himself killed in order to show love for a dead chief; death. *Lit.,* lie [in a] heap. (Malo 226.)

moe.'uhane. nvt. Dream; to dream. *Lit.,* soul sleep.

moe.'uhane ho'o.pahulu. See *pahulu.*

moe 'u'uku. n. Cot, small bed, camp bed.

moe wa'a. nv. A dream of a canoe, formerly considered bad luck. *Fig.,* bad luck, disappointment; to dream thus or have bad luck.

mohā. vs. Bright, clear, shining. *Rare.*

mō.hā. 1. vs. Fully developed, as a flower; spreading widely, as plants; of fine physique, as a person. **2.** See *koloa mohā.*

mō.hā.hā. 1. Redup. of *mōhā 1. Mōhāhā kāna kalo,* his taros are well filled out. *E ulu ana me ka mōhāhā o kona mau lālā i nā lau uliuli,* growing with branches spreading wide with green leaves. **2.** Redup. of *mohā,* bright.

moha.hala. Same as *mōhalahala.*

mō.hai. nvt. Sacrifice, offering; to offer a sacrifice. Cf. *hai, haiau.*

Mō.ha'i. 1. n. Star name (KL line 1890), perhaps Sirius. **2.** *(Not cap.)* To break, as a stick. (And.)

mō.hai ahi. n. Burnt offering. (Puk. 29.25.)

mō.hai 'ai. n. Meat offering (Puk. 40.29); food offering. (Oihk. 2.4.)

mō.hai aloha. n. Free-will offering (Kanl. 12.6); love offering.

mō.hai hala. n. Trespass offering (Oihk. 7.37); sin offering, offering that a sin may be forgiven.

mō.hai ho.'āli. n. Wave offering. (Puk. 29.24.)

mō.hai ho'o.kō. n. Offering or sacrifice in fulfillment of a vow, or after a wish has been granted. (Nah. 15.3.)

mō.hai ho'o.luli. n. Wave offering.

mō.hai ho'o.malu. n. Peace offering. (Oihk. 3.3.)

mō.hai ka'i.ka'i. n. Priest's portion (RSV), heave offering (KJV). (Puk. 29.27.)

mō.hai kai.kea. n. Offering of fat, by fire. (Oihk. 10.15.)

mō.hai kala hewa. n. Expiatory offering to atone for sins. *Lit.,* offering for forgiveness of sins.

mō.hai kuni. n. Burnt offering. (Nah. 15.8.)

mō.hai lawe.hala. n. Sin offering. (Oihk. 4.3.)

mō.hai makana. n. Free-will offering (Puk. 25.2), gift offering.

mō.hai manawa.le'a. n. Free-will offering.

mō.hai mili.lani. n. Sacrifice of thanksgiving.

mō.hai ola. nv. Life sacrifice; to offer alive, to sacrifice one's life, as of Christ.

mō.hai pā.na'i. n. Substitute sacrifice, as *ulua* (a fish) instead of a human being.

mō.hai poni. n. Offering of consecration. (Oihk. 7.37.)

mō.hai puhi. n. Offering by fire. (Oihk. 2.3.)

mō.hai puhi ʻala ʻono. n. Sweet-smelling offering. (Oihk. 3.5.) *Lit.,* burnt offering tasty fragrant.

mohala. vs. Unfolded, as flower petals; blossoming, opening up; spread, as a turkey's tail; blooming, as a youth just past adolescence; shining forth, as a light; appearing clear, as a thought; evolved, developed; freed or recovered, as from fear, worry, illness. *ʻA ʻohe mohala pono ka manaʻo,* a thought not clearly stated or brought out. *Mohala ka helehelena,* pleasant, open features. **hoʻo.mohala.** To open, unfold, spread, recover, develop, evolve; development, etc. *Ua hoʻomohala ʻia kona naʻau kānalua,* his doubting heart began to feel courage.

mō.hala.hala. Redup. of *mohala.*

mō.hala.pua. n. Blossoming of flowers or youth. *Kona lā o ka mōhalapua,* his days of blossoming youth.

mō.halu. 1. vs. Loose, slack; at ease, unrestrained, at liberty; comfortable. *Hale mōhalu,* house of relaxation. **hoʻo.mō.halu.** To slacken, relax; to cause relaxation, ease. 2. *(Cap.)* n. Twelfth day of the month and first of the Kāne taboo, liked for planting flowers because it was believed the flowers would be round and perfect like the moon on this night. 3. vi. To open, unfold, as flowers. Also *mohala.*

mō.halu.halu. Redup. of *mōhalu 1, 3. Mōhaluhalu ka lihilihi o ka pua,* the petals of the flowers unfold in blossom. *Mōhaluhalu ka ʻai ʻana a ka iʻa,* the fish are opening [their mouths] to bite.

Moha.meka, Mohameta. nvs. Mohammed, Mohammedan. *Eng.*

mō.hihi. n. 1. A variety of sweet potato, sometimes qualified by the colors *keʻokeʻo* or *ʻulaʻula.* 2. A native mint *(Stenogyne scrophularioides),* more or less shrubby and climbing, leaves ovate, flowers reddish.

mohi.hihi. n. A herbaceous leguminous vine *(Vigna marina),* established on tropical shores of the world. Leaves are three-parted, the flowers yellow. (Neal 467–8.) Also *lemuomakili, nanea, ʻōkolemakili, pūhilihihi, pūlihilihi, wahineʻōmaʻo.*

mohi.hio. 1. Redup. of *mōhio. Mohihio hoʻi ka makani,* the wind is drafty. 2. Plant name. (And.)

mohi.hiʻo. Same as *moe hihiʻo:* see *hihiʻo.*

mō.hio. n. Draft, gust of wind. *Mōhio lū ʻopeʻope,* gust that scatters bundles; *fig.,* careless, heedless, impudent person.

mō.hio.hio. 1. Same as *mohihio.* 2. vs. Red, as from sunburn.

moho. 1. n. Candidate, as in politics; representative selected to participate in a race, wrestling, or betting contest, champion. 2. n. Hawaiian rail *(Pennula sandwichensis),* an extinct flightless bird. See ex., *pūhili 1.* (PPN *moso.*) 3. vi. To unfold, of leaves, especially upper leaf of a plant, as sugar cane, taro (PCP *mo(f,s)o.*)

-moho. **hoʻo.moho.** To stalk; to lie in wait, as a cat ready to pounce; to trail or follow behind, sneak. *Kaʻū.*

moho.ea. Same as *moho 2.*

mohola. Var. of *mohala. Heʻe mohola,* octopus lying flat on the sea floor with tentacles spread. Cf. *moho 3.*

mohole. Var. of *mahole.*

mō.hole.hole. Redup. of *mohole.*

moi. n. 1. Threadfish *(Polydactylus sexfilis).* Stages of growth: *moi liʻi,* little *moi,* 5 to 8 cm long; *pālāmoi* (Kauaʻi) or *manamoi* (Hawaiʻi), about 13 cm; *moi,* adult, 45 to about 97 cm. On Hawaiʻi the *pālāmoi* was about 30 cm. This fish was much esteemed for food. A large school was an omen of disaster for chiefs. See *ʻehu 1. Kō kuli ē, nuku moi oe* (song), your knees, like a *moi* fish nose. *He moi ka iʻa, ehu ka lani, moi* the fish, misty the sky [of easy victory]. (PCP *moi.*) 2. White birthmark. 3. A native variety of taro, with short, stocky growth, the leaf stems light green, the base pinkish, and base of leaf blade whitish; used for poi and table taro. Also *neʻeneʻe.* (HP 25; Whitney 69.) This name may be qualified by the colors *ʻeleʻele,*

keʻokeʻo, and *ʻula.* 4. A variety of sweet potato. (PCP *moi.*)

moʻi. vi. To remain long in one place. (Kam. 64:109.)

mō.ʻī. n. 1. King, sovereign, monarch, majesty, ruler, queen. (Perhaps related to *ʻī,* supreme. According to J. F. G. Stokes, the word *mōʻī,* king, is of recent origin and was first in print in 1832.) Temple image (Malo 162); lord of images (Malo 173); according to Kepelino and Kamakau, a rank of chiefs who could succeed to the government but who were of lower rank than chiefs descended from the god Kāne (For. 6:266). See *ikū nuʻu.* The term *mōʻī* was apparently not used in the Fornander legends collected in the 1860s nor in RC. 2. Same as *ʻawa mōʻī.*

mō.ʻike. nvt. To interpret dreams; dream interpreter. *Kauaʻi. E hele ana au e nīnau i ka mōʻike,* I'm going to question the dream interpreter.

mō.io.io. vs. Churning, roiled, as water.

mō.ʻiu. vs. Far, at a distance; venerated. Cf. *kōʻiuʻiu.*

mō.ʻiu.ʻiu. Redup. of *mōʻiu.* Cf. *kōʻiuʻiu.*

mō.ʻī wahine. n. Queen.

moka. n. Offal, waste matter, refuse, filth. *Hoʻoleina moka* (Dan. 3.29), dunghill.

mokae. 1. n. A plant resembling *kiliʻoʻopu,* a sedge. (KL line 246.) 2. Same as *mōkaekae.*

mō.kae.kae. vs. Gratifying to the taste, tasty, as mealy sweet potato. Cf. *kaekae.*

mokaika, mosaika. n. Mosaic. *Eng.*

mō.kā.kī. nvs. Scattered, littered, disheveled; disorder, untidiness, mess, chaos. **hoʻo.mō.kā.kī.** To litter, scatter, cause disorder or untidiness.

mokala. Var. of *makala.*

mō.kaʻo.kaʻo. vs. Hard and lacking moisture, as of tasteless bananas, taro, meat, poi.

-mokapu. **hoʻo.mokapu.** To separate by imposing a taboo.

Moke.kao, Mosekao. n. Moscow. *Eng.*

mokeko, moseko. n. Mosque. *Eng.*

mokī. vi. To spurt, shoot forth.

mō.kī. nvt. Bundle; to wrap in a bundle. *Rare.*

moki.awe. n. A variety of sweet potato.

mō.kiha. Short for *moʻo kiha.*

moki.hana. n. 1. A native tree *(Pelea anisata),* found only on Kauaʻi, belonging to the citrus family. The small, leathery, cube-shaped, anise-scented fruits, which change from green to brown, are strung in leis; they represent Kauaʻi in the leis of the islands, as designated in 1923 by the Territorial legislature. The large leaves are also fragrant. (Neal 478.) 2. A variety of kava famous on Kauaʻi; it has short, stubby internodes. It is named for the *mokihana* fruit because of its fragrance. 3. A native variety of taro. (HP 33.)

moki.hana kū.kae moa. n. A small native tree *(Pelea hawaiensis)* with red leaf stems; when bruised its leaves have a lemony odor; found on several islands. *P. h.* var. *gaudichaudii* is believed restricted to the Kī-lau-ea area. *Lit.,* chicken dropping *mokihana,* probably so called because of small black seeds falling from the fruit.

mō.kila. 1. Kauaʻi name for *mānai,* needle; to string, as leis. 2. Similar to *kilakila.*

mokī.mokī. Redup. of *mōkī.*

mō.kio. 1. vi. To pucker or contract, as the lips for whistling, or the nostrils after diving. 2. vi. To steal something and dash away; to head straight for a destination. *Mōkio pololei maila i Kauaʻi,* to go straight to Kauaʻi. 3. Also *motio.* n. Motion. (Latin *motio.*)

moki.weo. The name for *ʻaweoweo* seeds.

moko. 1. Same as *mokomoko.* (PPN *moto.*) 2. vs. Flooded, filled with water, as a taro patch. **hoʻo.-moko.** To flood, fill with water. 3. n. Lizard. *Rare.*

mokohi. Same as *lana,* to float. *Rare.*

mō.kohi. Same as *mākohi,* a taro.

mō.koi. Var. of *mākoi 1, 2.*

moko.kai.kala. n. Motorcycle. *Eng.*

mō.kole. Var. of *mākole.*

moko.moko. nvt. Rough, hand-to-hand fighting of any kind, whether boxing *(ku'i)* or free-for-all wrestling; prize fight; a fighter, pugilist, boxer; to box, fight. (PCP *motomoto.*)

moku. **1.** vs. To be cut, severed, amputated, broken in two, as a rope; broken loose, as a stream after heavy rains, or as a bound person; to punctuate. *Moku ka pawa,* dawn has broken. *Kai moku ka noho 'ana,* relations separated by the sea. **ho'o.moku.** To cut and divide; a cutting, division, separation. (PPN *motu.*) **2.** n. District, island, islet, section, forest, grove, clump, severed portion, fragment, cut, laceration, scene in a play. Cf. *mokupuni, momoku. Moku lehua,* lehua forest. **ho'o.moku.** To place one over a *moku,* district. (For. 6:377.) (PPN *motu.*) **3.** n. Ship, schooner, vessel, boat, said to be so called because the first European ships suggested islands. Many types are listed below. **4.** n. A stage of pounded poi (such poi sticks together as a mass and can be separated cleanly *(moku)* from the pounding board). (Kep. 165.)

mō.kū. **1.** vi. Remaining long in one place, stationary; tied to a stake, as in punishment; to hold in one place, as to drown; to be anchored or stationed, as ships in a harbor. **2.** nvt. Method of fishing *pāpa'i* crabs with bait and a net; to fish thus.

moku.ā.hana. nvi. Dividing into factions, strife, opposing sides; disagreement. **ho'o.moku.ā.hana.** To divide, alienate. *Ho'omokuāhana i kā lākou mau alelo* (Hal. 55.9), confuse their tongues.

moku.ahi. n. Steamship. *Lit.,* fire ship.

moku ahi. Same as *momoku ahi.*

moku.ahi lawe koa. n. Troop ship.

moku.ahi lawe 'ō.hua. n. Passenger ship.

moku.ā.hua. n. Grief, sorrow, pity, disappointment.

moku.'āina. n. State, as of the United States; district; island.

Moku.'āina-hui-'ia. n. United States.

moku.ā.wai. vi. To flow as a stream swollen by rain; to rush, as a crowd (2 Oihn. 23.12); multitudinous.

moku.ea. n. Airplane. *Lit.,* air ship.

moku 'eli awa. n. Harbor dredge.

moku hale. n. House set apart, as for training practitioners of sorcery or healing. (Kam. 64:106.)

moku hali.hali. n. Ferry.

moku hali.hali koa. n. Troopship.

moku hali.hali moku.lele. n. Aircraft carrier.

moku.hā.li'i. n. **1.** A medicinal plant. **2.** *(Cap.)* Name of a god of canoe makers.

moku hau. n. **1.** Clump of *hau* trees; *hau* thicket. **2.** Iceberg. *Lit.,* ice island.

moku.hia. Pas/imp. of *moku,* to cut. *Pa'a 'ole i ka mokuhia a ka waimaka* (chant), unchecked in the bursting forth of tears. *Mokuhia ka hī,* excessive discharge of feces. *'A 'ole pio ke aloha i nā wai he nui loa, 'a'ole ia e mokuhia e nā waikahe* (Mele 8.7), waters cannot quench love, nor can floods drown it. *Mokuhia mahope,* to run after. (PPN *motusia.*)

mō.kuhi.kuhi. vs. Sweet, as sugar.

moku holo ahi. n. Steamship.

moku kā.lepa. n. Trade ship, clipper ship.

moku kaua. n. Battleship, cruiser, warship.

moku kele. See *kele,* watery.

moku kia kahi. n. One-masted ship, sloop.

moku kia kolu. n. Three-masted ship, bark.

moku kia lua. n. Two-masted ship, as a schooner; brig.

moku kolo. n. Tugboat.

mō.kū.kū. Redup. of *mōkū 1, 2.*

moku lā.'au. n. Grove of trees.

moku lawe hae. n. Flagship.

moku lawe koa. n. Troopship.

moku lawe.lawe. n. Tender.

moku lawe leka. n. Mail ship, packet.

moku lawe 'ō.hua. n. Passenger ship.

moku lawe ukana. n. Freighter.

moku lehua. n. Solemn feast after the cutting *(moku)* of an *'ōhi'a* log for a temple image; cluster of *lehua* trees.

mokule.'ia. Same as *kāhala,* amberfish. *Rare.*

moku.lele. n. Airplane, flying ship. *Ma ka mokulele,* by air.

moku.lele holo kai. n. Hydroplane.

moku.lia. Pas/imp. of *moku,* to cut. *Pau ka limu i ka mokulia* (Kep. 105), all the seaweed is broken off.

moku li'i.li'i. n. Islet, small ship, small grove or cluster.

moku lua. n. Two adjacent islets.

moku.lu'u. n. Submarine. *Lit.,* diving ship.

moku.māhu. n. Steamship.

moku.moku. **1.** Redup. of *moku 1.* Cf. *palaoa mokumoku. Ko'a mokumoku,* broken coral bits. (PPN *motumotu.*) **2.** n. Kinds of fish.

moku.moku.ā.hana. Same as *mokumokuāhua.*

moku.moku.ā.hua. Redup. of *mokuāhua,* grief. *Ua mokumokuāhua kona manawa i kona kaikaina* (Kin. 43.30), his bowels did yearn upon his brother.

moku.moku hā nui. n. A damselfish. Also *hānui.*

moku.moku.mana.hua. Same as *mokumokuāhua.*

moku.moku waha nui. n. Name of a deep-sea fish (no data). *Lit.,* big-mouthed *mokumoku.*

mokuna. n. Division, boundary, border, as of land; severed portion, cut piece, part, severance; chapter, section, as of a book; platoon, as of soldiers (a *mokuna* may be divided into *mahele,* sections, and into *paukū,* squads). (PCP *motunga.*)

moku.'oi. vt. To scratch. *Ni'ihau.*

moku 'ō koho.lā. n. Whaling ship. *Lit.,* ship for piercing whales.

moku o loko. n. A district (as Kona), not an island. (Malo 16.)

moku pā.papa. n. Low reef island.

moku.pawa. vi. To break, come intermittently. Cf. *pawa 1. Ua like me ka 'eku 'ana a ka pua'a ka mokupawa o ka 'āina,* the breaking up of the soil is like a pig's rooting. *E mokupawa ai ka ua mahina 'ai,* the farming rains are intermittent.

moku pe'a. n. Sailing vessel, yacht.

moku popopo. n. Hulk, as of a rotted vessel.

moku pū. vi. Completely severed. (For. 5:705.)

moku.puni. n. Island. *Mokupuni pālahalaha,* low or flat island, atoll.

mola. vs. Turning, twisting, spinning; unstable. Cf. *kāmola. He huila nui e ka'a mola ana,* a big wheel revolving.

mō.la'e. vs. Clear, unobstructed; easily understood. *Mōla'e ke alo o ka pali,* the face of the cliff is clear. Also *māla'e.*

mō.la'e.la'e. Redup. of *mōla'e.*

mola.kea. nvi. Clear, clarity. *Ke pane aku nei au me ka molakea,* I hereby answer clearly.

molaki, moraki. n. Mortgage. *Eng. Mea pa'a molaki,* mortgagee.

molaki wai.wai lewa. n. Chattel mortgage.

molala, morala. nvs. Moral. *Eng.*

molale. vs. Clear, plain, unobstructed.

mō.lale.lale. Redup. of *molale.*

mola.mola. Redup. of *mola.*

mole. **1.** n. Tap root, main root; bottom, as of a pit or of a glass; ancestral root; foundation, source, cause. *'O ka puni kālā 'o ka mole nō ia o ka hewa* (1 Tim. 6.10), love of money is the root of evil. *Ho'i hou i ka mole,* return to the family, as after estrangement. (Perhaps PNP *mole.*) **2.** vs. Smooth, round, bald. **ho'o.mole.** To smooth. (PNP *mole.*) **3.** n. Name of the smooth, uncarved side of a tapa beater, as used at the end of the beating to smooth out the cloth. **4.** To linger, loiter, lag; backward. (And.) **ho'o.mole.** To cause delay; to delay. **5.** n. Bag in the *pāku'iku'i* net. See *'upena papa.* **6.** n. Mole. (Oihk. 11.29.) *Eng.*

molea. Pas/imp. of *mole 2. Fig.,* plain, homely.

mole.ana.honua. n. Geometry. *Lit.,* base for measuring land.

mole hā.lu'a. n. Stripes *(hālu'a)* on an otherwise smooth surface of a tapa beater; beater with one side smooth, and the other designed.

mole hā.lu'a pū.pū. n. Tapa beater with one side smooth, and another side with the design called *hālu'a pūpū.*

mole.hao. Same as *'ōkolehao,* a liquor. *Lit.,* iron bottom.

mō.lehu. nvs. Twilight, dusk; tipsy. Cf. *lehu,* ashes.

mō.lehu.lehu. Redup. of *mōlehu;* dim. (Laie 601.)

mō.lelehu. 1. n. Dusk. **2.** vs. Drowsy, sleepy. Also *lelehu, 'olelehu.*

mole.mole. Redup. of *mole 2.* **ho'o.mole.mole.** To smooth. (PPN *molemole, fakamolemole.*)

Mole.mona, Moremona. nvs. Mormon. *Eng.*

mō.lī. n. **1.** Laysan albatross *(Diomedia immutabilis).* (KL line 312.) **2.** Any straight line separating designs in tattoo pattern. **3.** Bone made into a tattooing needle, hence a tattooing needle. **4.** Same as *kīwa'a 3.*

mō.lia. vt. To set apart for the gods; to sacrifice or offer to the gods; to bless; to curse. *E mōlia mai e make,* curse so [he] shall die. (PNP *moolia.*)

mō.lia.ola. n. Sacrifice and prayer for life and safety; one who sacrifices himself that others may live, as Christ; passover; Easter (Oih. 12.4). *'Aha'aina mōliaola,* the feast of the Passover. *Ua mōhai 'ia 'o Kristo, kō kākou mōliaola no kākou* (1 Kor. 5.7), Christ our passover is sacrificed for us.

mō.lili. Same as *mālili.*

moli.molī. vt. To use the *mōlī* tattooing needle.

mō.lina. 1. nvt. Strip, as of cloth or wood, bias tape for trimming clothes; any border used for trimming; to trim the edge, as of a dress; trimmed (Kel. 135). **2.** n. Wing on stem of a plant, as of yam. (HP 167.) **3.** n. Any straight line separating designs in tattooing patterns. **4.** n. A variety of sweet potato. **5.** See *lihilihi mōlina.* **6.** n. Molding. *Eng.* **7.** n. Rim of a wheel.

mō.lio. vs. Taut, tight. Cf. *mo'olio.*

mō.lio.lio. Redup. of *mōlio.*

molo. vt. To turn, twist, spin; to interweave and interlace, as roots; to tie securely. *E molo mai 'oe ā pa'a pono kēia pū 'olo,* tie this so the bundle is quite secure.

molo.ā, molowā. vs. Lazy, indolent. *Moloā au i ka hele i laila,* I'm too lazy to go there. **ho'o.molo.ā.** To feign laziness; to waste the time of others; lazy.

molo.alo. n. Main stream into which branches enter. *Fig.,* of a chiefly lineage.

molo.hai. vs. Drowsy, sleepy. Cf. *malohi.*

molohi. Same as *molohai.* Cf. *lohi,* slow.

Molo.ka'i. 1. n. **1.** Name of a Hawaiian island. See song, *hapenuia.* **2.** *(Not cap.)* A variety of sweet potato.

molo.kala. Same as *makala.*

molo.kū. 1. Same as *lolokū 2.* **2.** vs. Of chiefly stock.

molola. vs. Tall, long. *Molola kēia keiki,* this child is tall.

molo.lani. 1. vs. Well-kept, well-nursed. *Rare.* **2.** *(Cap.)* n. Rain associated with Kaha-lu'u, O'ahu (Elbert and Mahoe 61); also a wind name.

molo.wā. See *moloā.*

molu. vs. Taciturn; to say little.

moluhi. Var. of *maluhi.*

molulo. 1. nv. Thief; to steal. *Rare.* **2.** vs. So fat that the flesh shakes when one walks. *Rare.*

mō.lulo.lea. n. Faint cry of one in distress, as of a shipwrecked person *('ōlulo),* or of a ghost. *Rare.*

mō.lulo.lulo. Redup. of *molulo 1, 2. Rare.*

moluna. nv. Thief, robber; to rob, plunder, take by force. *Rare.*

mome.neku, momenetu. n. Momentum. *Eng.*

momi. n. **1.** Pearl. (Mat. 13.46.) *Ku'u momi makamae,* my precious pearl [a beloved person]. *He momi waiwai nui,* Hawaiian translation of the title of the English book "A Pearl of Great Price" by Joseph Smith, the Mormon prophet. **2.** Ni'ihau name for *pūpū Ni'ihau,* a Ni'ihau shell used in leis; also *momi o kai.* **3.** Hard

center of eye, fish eyeball. **4.** Face of a watch. **5.** A fatty tissue between the cornea and the inner canthus of the eye, pinguecula. **6.** Same as *nuku momi,* a jackfish.

momi.momi. Redup. of *momi 1;* many pearls.

momio. Redup. of *mio,* narrow.

mōmo. Short for *omoomo,* to suck.

momoa. 1. Same as *moamoa 1.* **ho'o.momoa.** Same as *ho'omoamoa.* (Nak. 80.) **2.** n. Under part of the rear covered section of a canoe.

-momo'a. ho'o.momo'a. To cook.

momoe. 1. Redup. and plural of *moe 1;* to sleep. (PNP *momoe.*) **2.** Same as *kāmoe. Momoe aku i mua,* to push ahead with determination.

momoku. Redup. of *moku 1;* broken fragments, severed pieces; breaking forth, as of water from a dam. (PPN *momotu.*)

momoku ahi. n. Firebrand; charred wood. Cf. *kele 2.*

momole. 1. Same as *molemole. Pipi wahine momole,* hornless cow. **2.** Redup. of *mole 4.* **ho'o.momole.** Redup. of *ho'omole;* to hesitate; reluctant. *Ho'omomole ma ka hā'awi kālā 'ana,* slow about paying.

momō.lio. Redup. of *mōlio.* Cf. also *mo'olio.*

momomi. Same as *maomao,* a fish.

momo.moe. Same as *moemoe,* especially of many people.

momo.moni. Redup. of *moni 1.*

momona. 1. vs. Fat; fertile, rich, as soil; fruitful; soft, of wood *(rare).* **ho'o.momona.** To fatten, fertilize. *Ho'omomona lepo,* fertilizer; to fertilize the soil. (PPN *momona.*) **2.** vs. Sweet. **ho'o.momona.** To sweeten; candy. **3.** n. The cherimoya *(Annona cherimola),* a small fruit tree from tropical America, bearing large, heart-shaped, greenish fruits with white, pleasant-tasting pulp. (Neal 359.) Also *kelemoio.* **4.** n. A chicle or chico tree *(Manilkara zapota).* Ni'ihau. (Neal 668–9.)

momoni. Redup. of *moni 1. He 'ono ke momoni aku,* delicious to swallow.

momoua. vs. Far. *Rare.*

mona. Same as *momona 1, 2. Rare.* Cf. *'akimona, 'inamona.*

mō.nea. Same as *nea,* bare. (For. 6:390.)

mone.hā. vs. Far, distant. *Ua monehā ka wa'a i ke kai loa,* the canoe is away out at sea.

mō.neka. Monk. *Eng.*

Moneke, Monede. n. Monday. *Eng. Rare.*

mone.kekeli, moneseteri. n. Monastery. *Eng.*

Mone.lē. n. Monday. *Eng. Rare.*

mone'u. See *nuku mone'u.*

moni. 1. vt. To swallow, gulp down, absorb. *Moni ka hā'ae,* to swallow at the mouth, drool; *lit.,* swallow the saliva. *Moni kū,* to swallow defiantly, said by Kamehameha in contempt of a foe. *Ua moni mai au i kāna mau 'ōlelo apau,* I drink in all he says. **2.** n. Money. (Kin. 43.21.) *Eng. Waihona moni,* treasury, money depository.

monia. Pas/imp. of *moni 1. E monia i ka huhū,* swallow [control] your wrath.

monika, monita. n. Monitor. *Eng.*

moni.moni. Redup. of *moni 1.*

mō.noi.noi. Rare var. of *mīnoinoi.*

mono.kune, monosune. n. Monsoon. *Eng.*

monū. vs. Sulky, unsociable.

mo'o. 1. n. Lizard, reptile of any kind, dragon, serpent; water spirit. *Mea nānā mo'o* (Kanl. 18.10), enchanter. (PPN *moko.*) **2.** n. Succession, series, especially a genealogical line, lineage. Cf. *mo'o ali'i. Mo'o hihia* (For. 5:303), series of difficulties, troubles. **ho'o.mo'o.** To follow a course, continue a procedure. **3.** n. Story, tradition, legend (less common than *mo'olelo).* **4.** n. Narrow strip of land, smaller than an *'ili.* Also *mo'o 'āina.* **5.** n. Small fragment, as of tapa, not attached to a large piece. Cf. *mo'omo'o.* **6.** n. Narrow path, track; raised surface extending lengthwise between irrigation streamlets. **7.** n. Ridge, as of a mountain. *Moʻo muku,* ridge that is cut off. **8.** n. Young, as of pigs, dogs; grandchild. *Kuʻu moʻo lei,* my beloved grandchild. **9.** vs. Brindled, as a dog, favored for sacrifice to the *moʻo* spirits; streaked, tawny, as cattle; color of a tabby cat. Cf. *ʻīlio moʻo,* brindled dog, and *moʻo ʻīlio,* puppy dog. **10.** n. Side planks fitted to the middle section on each side of a canoe hull, technically termed gunwale strakes.

mooa. A faint path. (And.)

moʻo-ahi-lele, moahilele. n. Fiery flying dragon, as in European fairy tales. *Lit.,* flying fire lizard.

moʻo ʻāina. n. Land parcel.

moʻo akua. n. Legend or tale concerning the gods; godlike lizard.

moʻo ʻalā. n. Black lizard, gecko. *Lit.,* rock lizard. *Kaʻū,* Also *kaʻalā.*

moʻo.ʻali. Var. of *mōʻali.*

moʻo aliʻi. n. **1.** Genealogy of chiefs, history of chiefs, chiefly line of succession. **2.** Same as *moʻo kāula. Lit.,* royal lizard.

moʻo hele. n. Trail, road. *Kauaʻi. Lit.,* traveling land strip.

moʻo helu. n. Counting, enumeration, recitation.

moʻo.helu kā.lā. n. Budget, sum or list of expenditures or receipts. *Lit.,* money list.

moʻo huelo ʻawa. n. Scorpion (Hoik. 9.3), poisonous serpent. *Lit.,* lizard with bitter tail.

moʻo.kā. Same as *moʻo kaʻalā.*

moʻo kaʻa.lā. Same as *moʻo ʻalā.*

moʻo kaʻao. Same as *kaʻao,* tale.

moʻo kahuna. n. Genealogy of succession of priests; history of the priesthood.

moʻo kā lā.ʻau. n. Long-tailed lizard, found on trees. *Lit.,* lizard that strikes trees.

moʻo kanaka. n. List or succession of commoners, as for taxation. See ex., *kumalauā.*

moʻo kā.ula. n. A variety of gray lizard. *Lit.,* prophet lizard.

moʻo kiha. Same as *moʻo 1.*

moʻo.kiko. n. Epithet for a sorcerer who practices black magic. *Lit.,* pecking lizard.

moʻo Kū. n. Priests of the lineage of Kū, devoted to the worship of Kū.

moʻo kū.ʻau.hau. n. Genealogical succession, pedigree.

moʻo kupuna. n. Ancestral genealogy.

moʻo lani. n. Chinese dragon, as in a Chinese gambling game. *Lit.,* sky lizard.

moʻo lau. n. **1.** Many lizard gods, monsters, spirits, dragons. **2.** vs. Having many descendants (cf. *moʻo 8; moʻopuna*); female; woman. *Akua moʻo lau, ē, ʻo moʻo lau ke ala, ē* (PH 20), O goddess with many offspring, a path [beset by] many monsters.

moʻo lele. n. Flying serpent, dragon (Kanl. 32.33); viper (RSV), adder (KJV) in Kin. 49.17; great owl (Isa. 34.15); frog (old term).

moʻo.lelo. n. Story, tale, myth, history, tradition, literature, legend, journal, log, yarn, fable, essay, chronicle, record, article; minutes, as of a meeting. (From *moʻo ʻōlelo,* succession of talk; all stories were oral, not written.) *Puke moʻolelo aupuni,* public records. *hoʻo.-moʻo.lelo.* Caus/sim. (For. 6:523.)

moʻo.lelo ʻaha.ʻō.lelo lā.hui. n. Congressional record. *Lit.,* national legislative journal.

moʻo.lelo haku wale. n. Fiction; an invented story.

moʻo.lelo pō.kole. n. Short story, anecdote.

moʻo.lio. Same as *mōlio;* narrow, small, as a path where only one person can pass at a time.

moʻo lio. n. Sea horse. *Lit.,* horse reptile.

moʻo lono. nv. To hear report after report; succession of reports.

moʻo Lono. n. Priests of the lineage of Lono, devoted to the worship of Lono.

mō.ʻolu. **1.** Same as *ʻolu,* comfortable, cool. **2.** vs. Boggy; yielding, as a soft chair. *Rare.*

moʻo mahi. n. Small fish released in patches *(mahi)* to grow and multiply.

moʻo makā.ula. Same as *moʻo kāula.*

moʻo make. n. Deadly reptile; dead lizard; viper, adder (Hal. 91.13), asp (Isa. 11.8).

moʻo.moʻo. **1.** Same as *moʻo 5;* strips of *wauke* bast beaten together from which tapa sheets are to be made (Kam. 76:113). *hoʻo.moʻo.moʻo.* To beat raw bast into *moʻomoʻo.* **2.** n. Ridges (plural of *moʻo 7). Rare.* **3.** vs. Young, of animals.

moʻoni. n. Spiral design in featherwork. Cf. *ʻoni. Mehe lei moʻoni ʻula* (song), like a lei trimmed with a red spiral. See ex., *uhao.*

moʻo niho ʻawa. n. Scorpion (Scorpionida); viper, asp (Kanl. 32.33). *Lit.,* lizard with bitter tooth.

moʻo nui. n. Big lizard, dragon (Hal. 91.13), alligator, crocodile.

moʻo.ʻō.lelo. Same as *moʻolelo.*

moʻo.ʻō.mole. **1.** Same as *ʻōmolemole,* smooth. (And.) **2.** Bottle-shaped calabash used as a receptacle for fishing gear, larger than the *hue wai.* (AP.)

moʻo pekena, moʻo petena. n. Adder. See ex., *papani,* Hal. 58.4. (Heb. *pethen.*)

moʻo pepeiao hao. n. Adder (RSV), cockatrice (KJV). (Isa. 11.8.)

moʻo.puna. **1.** n. Grandchild; great-niece or -nephew; relatives two generations later, whether blood or adopted; descendant; posterity. *Kāna moʻopuna,* his grandchild. *Moʻopuna i ke alo,* beloved grandchild raised by a grandparent; *lit.,* grandchild in the presence. *hoʻo.moʻo.puna.* To claim a *moʻopuna* relationship; to address and treat as a *moʻopuna,* as from affection. (PPN *mokopuna*.) **2.** Short for *moʻopuna-a-ka-līpoa.*

moʻo.puna-a-ka-lī.poa. n. A fine red seaweed (*Griffithsia* sp.*),* consisting of branching hairlike tufts; edible. Common in Kaʻū and Kona, Hawaii. *Lit.,* grandchild of the *līpoa.* Also *aupūpū.*

moʻo.puna hanauna. n. Grandchild of a sibling or cousin. *Lit.,* generation grandchild.

moʻo.puna kāne. n. Grandson.

moʻo.puna kua.kahi. n. Great-grandchild, as distinct from great-great-grandchild; today a grandchild is sometimes called *moʻopuna kuakahi.*

moʻo.puna kua.kolu. n. Great-great-great-grandchild.

moʻo.puna kua.lua. n. Great-great-grandchild.

moʻo.puna wahine. n. Granddaughter.

moʻou. vs. Stretched. *Rare.*

moʻo.wā. nvs. Narrow or faint path, track.

moʻo waʻa. Same as *moʻo 10.*

moʻo.wahie. Same as *kuhi-ʻai-ka-moʻo-wahie,* a plant. *Lit.,* fragment of wood for burning.

moʻo.wai.wai. n. Account, as in a bank; inventory.

moʻo wili. n. Boa constrictor. *Lit.,* twisting lizard.

moʻo.wini. **1.** n. Small, fine, like the filaments of a spider web; tapering into a fine end, as a hair. **2.** nvs. Dim, as vision; partial blindness. *Ua loaʻa ka moʻowini i kekahi poʻe* (Rom. 11.25), blindness in part has happened to some people.

mō.pua. vs. Melodious, pleasant, of a voice. *Rare.*

mou. Var. of *mouo.*

mō.uki. vs. Vile-smelling, dirty. *Rare.*

mō.uki.uki. Redup. of *mōuki.* Cf. *ukiuki,* annoyed.

mouo. nvi. Buoy; float, as on a fishing net; board or anything to float on; a calm place in the sea where one may float; to lie at anchor.

mō.uo.uo. Same as *mouo.*

mō.wae, moae. Var. of *māwae.*

Mowaʻe. Var. spelling of Moaʻe.

mō.waho.waho, moahoaho. vs. Afar, very far. *Ua holo mōwahowaho ka waʻa,* the canoe sailed afar.

mū. **1.** n. General name for destructive insects that eat wood, cloth, or plants; cane borer, weevil, tamarind borer, moth (Mat. 6.19); caterpillar in the cocoon stage; germ, bug. (PPN *muu.*) **2.** vs. Silent; to shut the lips and make no sound. **ho'o.mū.** To sit in silence, to refuse to answer; speechless. (PPN *muhu*.) **3.** vi. Gather together, of crowds of people. Cf. *mui, mumulu. Kahi e mū 'ia ana e nā kānaka,* place where the people gathered. **ho'o.mū.** Same as above; multitude, crowd; to cause a gathering. *A pae a'e i Kai-mū, ho'omū nā kānaka* (chant), landing at Kai-mū, people gathered. **4.** n. A crab *(Dynomene hispida).* **5.** *(Cap.)* n. Legendary people of Lā'au-haele-mai, Kaua'i, often called *Mū 'ai mai'a,* banana-eating *Mū.* Cf. *Nāmū, Nāwao.* **6.** n. Bigeye emperor fish *(Monotaxis grandoculis),* perhaps named for the *Mū* people. (PNP *muu*.) **7.** n. Public executioner; he procured victims for sacrifice and executed taboo breakers; children were frightened by being told that the *mū* would get them. **8.** Var. name for the *kōnane* game. See *papamū.* **9.** n. Name of a small, yellow bird (no data). **10.** n. The letter "m".

mū-. Var. of *mā- 4,* prefix indicating quality or state, but less common. See *mū'ekeke'i, mūhea, mūhe'e, mūki'i, mūko'i, mūlehu, mū'olo,* and others.

mua. 1. loc. n. Before, ahead, forward, in advance, future, front, first, former, foremost, primary, principal; previously, beforehand; oldest, older brother or sister; senior branch of a family; leader, senior partner, senior; more than. (Gram. 8.6.) *I mua! Mamua!* Forward! *Holo i mua,* to progress, go forward. *Kēia mua iho,* the near future. *Kēia mua a'e,* fairly near in the future. *Kēia mua aku,* distant future. *Mamua aku nei,* some time ago. *Ua noho 'oia i mua o ke ali'i,* he stayed in the presence of the chief. *I mua ou,* before you. *I mua i hope,* back and forth. *'A'ole i . . . mamua,* never before. *'A'ole au i 'ike iāia mamua,* I've never seen him before. *'O kō mākou mua loa ia,* he is our eldest. *Na ka mua, na ka muli,* belonging to the older [sibling], belonging to the younger [sibling] [a way of describing the parentage of first cousins]. *Hele mua,* older brother or sister, senior branch of a family; to go ahead or first. *'Oi kēia mamua o kēlā,* this is better than that; *lit.,* superior this before that. **ho'o.mua.** To push forward, to do something first; to claim to be senior; to advance to seniority; to give the rights of seniority to a junior. (PPN *mu'a*.) **2.** n. Men's eating house.

mū.'ā. n. **1.** Feeding mouth-to-mouth. Cf. *kau, pū'ā. 'Ai ā kau, 'ai ā mū'ā* (KL line 472), fed in the mouth, fed mouth-to-mouth. **2.** Bottle-necked gourd, as used for drinking.

mū 'ai hea. n. A kind of caterpillar.

Mū 'ai mai'a. n. Name of a mythical people; they were not tiny like the *Menehune. Lit.,* banana-eating *Mū.* Also *Mū, Nāwao.*

mū 'ai palaoa. n. Rusty flour beetle *(Tribolium ferrugineum)* and its grub. *Lit.,* flour-eating borer.

mū 'ai puke. n. Bookworm.

mua.iwa. n. Crack or split in wood due to drying.

mua kau. n. First offering, as of fruit or fish. *Lit.,* first placing. *Ka mua kau kēia o ka mahina 'ai,* this is the first offering of the plantation.

mua.kua. Unfriendly, unsocial. (And.)

mua.mua. loc. n. Front, forward. *Kō a muamua,* those in front. **ho'o.mua.mua.** To push forward; to act as senior. (PNP *mu'amu'a*.)

mu'a.mu'a. Var. of *mu'emu'e.*

mu'e. vs. Bitter. **ho'o.mu'e.** To make bitter.

mū.'eke. vt. To shrink away, as in fear, pain, disgust. Cf. *'e'eke,* to shrink.

mū.'eke.ke'i. vs. Tight-fitting and short, as a dress; drawing upward, receding (probably *mū-* + a redup. of *'eke 2* + *-'i,* transitivizer: Gram. 6.6.4). Cf. *'ekeke'i,* short from the ground up.

mū.'eke.lei. Var. of *mū'ekeke'i.*

mu'e.mu'e. Redup. of *mu'e.*

mū.hea. vs. Tepid, lukewarm; insipid, tasteless.

mū.he'e. 1. nvs. Cuttlefish *(Sepioteuthus arctipinnis). Fig.,* fickle, changeable, unsteady, so called perhaps

---

because of the backward-forward movement of the cuttlefish. (PPN *nguufeke,* PCP *muufeke*.) **2.** n. Mother-of-pearl lure, usually qualified as below, perhaps so named because the colors of the shell suggested those of the cuttlefish.

mū.he'e 'ā.ko'a.ko'a. n. Pearl-shell lure named for the branching coral.

mū.he'e kā.'ope. n. Yellowish pearl-shell lure.

mū.he'e kī.kā.kapu. n. Pearl-shell lure spotted like the *kīkākapu,* a fish.

mū.he'e koa'e. n. Pearl-shell lure with three streaks like those in the tail of the *koa'e* bird.

mū.he'e lae.nihi. n. Pearl-shell lure with curves suggesting those on the head of the *laenihi* fish; considered a very fine lure.

mū.he'e mā.koko. n. Pearl-shell lure with reddish tinge suggesting the red of the *he'e mākoko,* a red octopus.

mū.he'e 'ō.hiki. n. Pearl-shell lure with streaks that suggested the legs of the *'ōhiki,* a sand crab.

mū.he'e pua hau. n. Pearl-shell lure with reddish tinge suggesting a fading *hau* flower *(pua hau).*

muhu. 1. Same as more common *mumuhu.* (PPN *musu*.) **2.** vi. To swarm, as insects or people. Cf. *mū 3, mumulu.*

mui. 1. nvs. Assembled, gathered together, an assembly *(mū 3 + -i,* transitivizer: Gram. 6.6.4). **2.** vs. Silent *(mū 1 + -i,* transitivizer: Gram. 6.6.4). *No'ono'o mui* (GP 38), meditate silently.

muia. Pas/imp. of *mui 1, 2.*

mu.ikiiki. vs. Cramped, as on a narrow seat; to crowd together.

mui.mui. 1. Redup. of *mui 1, 2.* **2.** Var. of *muli.* (PH 114, For. 6:493.) (PPN *muimui*.)

mui.muia. 1. Pas/imp. of *muimui. He kumu lehua muimuia i ka manu,* a *lehua* tree covered with birds [an attractive person]. **2.** vs. Inharmonious, of juxtaposed colors, as on tapa or quilt.

mui.mui i'a. n. Swarm of fish.

mui.ona. n. An annelid worm, resembling a centipede.

mū.kā. n. Sound of lips popped open; clicking sound, as in urging a horse to speed up; smack, as in eating. Cf. KL 205 line 687. *'Ai mūkā,* eat and smack the lips in appreciation, gobble. *He au pōhāhā wale i ka mūkā* (KL line 369), an era bursting forth with a pop. **ho'o.mū.kā.** Caus/sim.

mū.ka'e. n. Anything jutting or hanging over, as the brow of a precipice; rim (2 Oihn. 4.2), edge, as of a pit; circumference; bare toothless gums.

muka.kaka. Same as *nakakaka,* cracked.

mukā.mukā. Redup. of *mūkā.*

mu.kau. n. A fish of the family Bramidae.

mū.kei. vs. Silent.

mū.kekeke. vi. **1.** Chirping, as sparrows (perhaps related to *kekē,* scolding. Cf. *mūkā.* **2.** To thump. *Rare.*

mukeko. vs. Homely, monkey-like in appearance. Cf. *keko,* homely.

mū.kī. nvi. Sucking noise made by pursing the lips and expelling or drawing in the air, as in kissing; to play on the *hōkiokio,* wind instrument; to squirt water through the teeth; to suck into the mouth, as when lighting a pipe; to sip, as birds sip honey. Cf. *mūkā. Ka po'e mūkī* (Isa. 8.19), people that peep [as wizards]. *Lele aku ai e honi iāia, ā hā'awi i nā mūkī ho'oma'ūma'ū 'ana o ke aloha,* leapt up to kiss her and give moist smacks of love.

mū.ki'i. vt. To tie; tether. Also *nāki'i, hīki'i.*

mū.ki'i.ki'i. Redup. of *mūki'i.*

mū.kī.kī. Redup. of *mūkī. Mūkīkī wai lehua, nā manu o Pana-'ewa* (song), sipping *lehua* honey, the birds of Pana-'ewa. *Mūkīkī ka hua 'ōlelo o ka manu,* sucking water, the birds say [slang, let's get drunk].

muki.kiki. vi. To thump. *Rare.*

mukī.mukī. Redup. of *mūkī.*

mū.kini. Same as *nūkoki.*

mū.kī paka (baka). n. Pipe lighter, the one who attended to the chief's tobacco supplies and lit his pipe for him, a responsibility since the lighter put the pipe into his own mouth. (Kep. 131.)

mū.koʻi. vs. Sharp, projecting, of the forehead, not considered attractive. Cf. *koʻi 1.*

mū.koki. Same as *nūkoki.*

mū.kole. vs. Red, raw, galled, as an open sore; inflamed. Cf. *kole,* raw.

mū.kole.kole. Redup. of *mūkole.*

muko.mimi. n. A variety of *ʻōmilu,* a fish.

muku. 1. nvs. Cut short, shortened, amputated; at an end, ceased; anything cut off short; short, brief, quick *(rare). Ua muku koʻu lole,* my dress is shortened. *He kanaka wāwae muku,* a person with amputated foot. *Hoʻohuli muku aʻela nā waʻa,* the canoes turned sharply. (PPN *mutu.*) 2. n. A measure of length from fingertips of one hand to the elbow of the other arm, when both arms are extended to the side. 3. n. Broken section of a wave or crest. See *lala 1.* 4. *(Cap.)* Same as *Mumuku,* a wind. 5. *(Cap.)* n. Thirtieth night of the moon, when it has entirely disappeared *(muku).* (Malo 35.) 6. n. Starboard ends of *ʻiako* (outrigger booms), hence starboard sides of a canoe.

muku.ela, mutuela. n. Weasel. (Biblical: probably derived from the genus name *Mustela,* hence from Latin.)

muku.muku. Redup. of *muku 1.* (PPN *mutumutu.*)

muku.muku waha nui. n. Probably a kind of triggerfish (no data). *Lit.,* big-mouthed cut-short. (PPN *mutumutu.*)

mula, mura. n. Myrrh. (Mele 4.14.) *Eng.*

mule. 1. vs. Bitter, as herbs; insipid, warm. 2. Rare var. of *mumule.*

mulea. Same as *mule 1.* (Puk. 15.23.)

mū.lehu. 1. Rare var. of *mōlehu.* 2. *(Cap.)* n. One of three stars in a triangle, the others being Polo ʻUla and Polo Ahi Lani; they may be Alpha, Beta, and Gamma Cassiopeiae. In one account Mūlehu is a variant name for Venus.

mulei. 1. n. Bird name (no data). 2. Perhaps a transitive form of *mule 2,* silent.

muleko, mureto. n. Myrtle tree. (Zek. 1.8.) (Gr. *myrtos.*)

mule.lehu. Redup. of *mūlehu 1.*

mule.mule. Redup. of *mule. Fig.,* unpleasant person, one with a sour disposition. *Mea mulemule* (Puk. 12.8), bitter herbs.

muli. loc. n. After, behind, afterward, by and by; last, because, following behind; younger, youngest; follower; thin end of a pearl-shell shank; stern of a canoe, back. (Gram. 8.6.) *I muli,* afterwards. *Mamuli o kona akamai,* because of his cleverness. *Muli iho,* younger. *Muli loa,* youngest. *Mamuli o ka puke,* according to the book. *He muli pala kūkae,* excrement-smeared younger one, said in contempt by older brother or sister of a younger one, referring to the times he has helped to clean the youngest; also said contemptuously of one of a junior line. (PPN *muri.*)

muli hope. n. Youngest child; very last.

muli pō.kiʻi. n. Younger brother, sister, or cousin. *Fig.,* genitals.

muli.wai. n. River, river mouth; pool near mouth of a stream, as behind a sand bar, enlarged by ocean water left there by high tide; estuary. (PPN *muriwai.*)

mumu. n. Thud-like sound, as of footsteps. *Rare.* Cf. *kamumu.*

mū.mū. 1. vi. To rinse out the mouth, as with water; to swish water about in the mouth. **hoʻo.mū.mū.** Same as above. 2. vs. Silent, mum. *ʻAi mūmū,* to eat silently without smacking the lips; this was said of stingy people who ate silently so that others would not know they were eating and they would not have to share their food. *Mūmū ka ʻōlelo,* indistinct speech. (PPN *muhu-*

muhu.) 3. vs. Dull, blunt, rounded, as an axe. Same as *kūmūmū.*

mumuhi. nvi. Buzzing, as of mosquitoes, perhaps a higher tone than the *mumuhu.*

mumuhu. 1. nvi. Buzzing, humming sound, as of flies, perhaps a lower tone than the *mumuhi;* to swarm. *Rare.* Cf. *muhu.* (PPN *mumusu.*) 2. vs. Fat, very plump. *Rare.*

mumui. Rare var. of *muimui.*

mumuia. Pas/imp. of *mumui.*

mumuka. Same as *pupuka,* ugly.

mumuku. 1. Redup. of *muku 1;* amputated, mutilated, maimed; premature, as a baby. *Pau nā pepeiao ā mumuku* (For. 5:417), all the ears were cut off. **hoʻo.mumuku.** Caus/sim. 2. *(Cap.)* n. Name of a strong wind at Ka-wai-hae, Hawaiʻi.

mumule. vs. Speechless, silent, taciturn, mute, sullen, sulky. *Ua mumule loa au me ka leo ʻole* (Hal. 39.2), I was dumb with silence. **hoʻo.mumule.** Caus/sim.

mumulu. vi. To swarm, as flies, bees, mosquitoes.

mū.nā. Same as *muni 1. Rare.*

mūna.munā. Redup. of *mūnā.*

muni. 1. vt. To eat sparingly, as of an invalid. *Rare.* 2. vs. Indistinct. *Rare.* 3. n. Protuberance, hillock. *Rare.*

muni.muni. Redup. of *muni 1.*

munini. Same as *munimuni. Rare.*

mū.nō. vs. Of retarded or imperfect growth, as plants, hair; to weaken and die; dry rot.

munu. n. A goatfish *(Parupeneus bifasciatus).*

muʻo. nvi. Leaf bud; to bud, of a leaf; soft tip of aerial pandanus root; younger branch of a family. *Muʻo o ka lima* (Kep. 159), fingertips bunched together as though to form a bud. *I ka muʻo o ka lā* (For. 4:137), at the sun's rays. (PPN *muka.*)

muʻo hala. n. Pandanus budding leaf at the top of a bunch; tip of aerial pandanus root.

muʻo.iki. vi. Narrowing, tapering; to bud but a little, to cease budding. *Ulu akula ke kō a muʻoiki,* the sugar cane grew until it ceased budding.

mū.ʻokole, muʻomuʻokole. Same as *muʻoiki.*

muʻo koli. vt. To trim *(koli)* new buds and leaves; to pull, as hairs, as of human or pig.

mū.ʻō.lelo. vi. To speak constantly or in groups. *Mūʻōlelo ke kai,* the sea speaks on.

mū.ʻolo. 1. vi. To sag, hang down too long, hang loose, flop. Cf. *ʻolo 2. Papālina mūʻolo,* sagging cheeks. 2. n. Water gourd.

mū.ʻolo.ʻolo. Redup. of *mūʻolo 1.*

muʻo.muʻo. Redup. of *muʻo;* flower covered by the calyx. Cf. *ʻōmuʻomuʻo.* (Probably PPN *mukomuko.*)

muʻo.muʻo.iki. Redup. of *muʻoiki.*

mū.ʻou.ʻou. vs. Short, stubby, blunt, as a nose; fat and short. Cf. *pāpale mūʻouʻou.*

muʻu. 1. n. Second generation of taro. Same as *ʻohā.* See *kalo* for names of generations. *ʻO ke kalo ka mua, ā mahope ka muʻu, ā mahope loa ka ʻae* (Kep. 153), first the *kalo,* then the *muʻu,* and finally the *ʻae.* 2. vt. To miss, as in playing marbles.

mū.ʻululū. Same as *kū ʻululū,* chilled.

mū.ʻu.mō.kā.kī. vi. To collect or heap up untidily. *Muʻumōkākī maoli kēia lumi,* this room is heaped up in a most untidy way.

muʻu.mū.nā. vs. Insipid, tasteless.

muʻu.muʻu. 1. nvs. Cut-off, shortened, amputated, maimed; person with arms or legs missing, amputee. *Hula muʻumuʻu* (UL 213), a sitting dance. 2. n. A woman's underslip or chemise; a loose gown, so called because formerly the yoke was omitted (cf. *muʻumuʻu 1*), and sometimes the sleeves were short. Cf. *holokū.*

muʻu.muʻu moe pō. n. Nightgown. *Lit.,* slip for sleeping at night.

mū wā.wahi waʻa. n. Teredo, shipworm.

N

In more than 115 words n *and* l *are interchangeable. Usually the* l-*form is inherited and the* n-*form is an innovation. Usually the* l-*form is common and the* n-*form is spoken only in outlying areas. (See Elbert 1982: 513–514.)*

n-. 1. Initial in *no, na, noʻu, naʻu, nou, nāu, nona, nāna* with meanings 'for', 'by', 'of', 'from'. Gram. 9.11. (PCP *n-*.) **2.** Initial of words for soft sounds and movements. Cf. *nākuʻi,* to rumble; *nakulu,* to patter; *naue,* to vibrate; *nē,* to murmur; *nehe,* to rustle; *nei,* to rumble; *nēnē,* to chirp; *nenene,* to flutter; *nū,* to roar. Cf. Rennellese *ng-*. (PPN *ng-*.)

na. prep. By, for, belonging to (*a*-form; see *no* and Gram. 9.11). *Na wai ʻoe* (FS 117)? Who was your parent? (*Lit.,* by who you?) *Aloha ʻolua na Ka-wai,* greetings to you both from Ka-wai [close of a letter]. *He puke na Pua,* a book for Pua; a book by Pua [ambiguous]. (PCP *na(a)*.)

na-, nā-. Prefixes indicating a quality or state. See *nāhili, naholo, nakele, nākiʻi, nakulu* and others, and Gram. 6.3.2. (PPN *nga(a)-*.)

-na. 1. Common nominalizing suffix, sometimes with shortening of a long vowel in the base. See *haʻi, haʻina; hāpai, hapaina; kālai, kalaina, ʻohi, ʻohina; piʻi, piʻina* and others and Gram. 6.6.2. (PPN *-nga*.) **2.** Rare pas/imp. suffix. See *ʻaina, haʻina, kiʻina,* and Gram. 6.6.3. (PPN *-na*.) **3.** His, her (in poss. *kāna, kona*). (Gram. 8.2.) (PPN *-na*.)

nā. 1. vs. Calmed, quieted, pacified, assuaged, soothed; settled, as a claim. *E hoʻi, ē Pele, i ke kuahiwi, ua nā kō lili, kō inaina* (chant), return, O Pele, to the mountain; your jealousy, your rage are pacified. **hoʻo.nā.** To relieve pain, soothe, comfort, quiet, appease, lull, placate, make calm, pacify, console, find solace; to end, as a taboo; to settle a claim. *Hoʻonā wale,* to attempt to pacify without effect; to try vainly to assuage, allay pain, grief. *Poʻe hoʻonā kuleana ʻāina,* board of commissioners to quiet land titles. *Komikina Hoʻonā ʻĀina,* land commissioners who settle land claims. (PPN *naʻa*.) **2. vi.** To moan, groan, wail. *Nā ka ihu,* to snore with prolonged sounds. (PPN *ngaa*.) **3.** Plural definite article. (Gram. 10.2.) *Nā lani,* the chiefs. (PPN *nga(a)-*.) **4.** Demonstrative part. indicating the addressee, sometimes said disrespectfully and translated 'you'. Cf. *kēnā* and Gram. 8.3.2. *Ē nā keiki lapuwale,* O you worthless children. (PPN *naa*.)

naʻa. vs. Firmly seated. *Aia ā kīkoʻo nā wāwae maʻō ā maʻaneʻi, ā laila naʻa,* if the feet are stretched here and there, then [one is] firmly seated.

nā.ʻā. vs. Covered with ashes, as a fire. *Rare.*

-naʻaikola. hoʻo.naʻai.kola. Same as *hōʻaikola,* contemptuous, contemptuousness. (Kel. 26, 28.)

naʻa.naʻa. vs. 1. Potbellied, protruding. **hoʻo.naʻa.-naʻa.** To protrude. *I Pōkiʻi ke kiʻi, hoʻokikiʻi ke kiʻi, hoʻonaʻanaʻa ke kiʻi* (chant), the image is at Pōkiʻi, the image leans back, the image protrudes its belly. **2.** Confused, bewildered. Cf. *pōnaʻanaʻa.*

naʻa.naʻa. n. Small intestine.

Nā-ā.nue.nue-ʻewalu. n. Stroke in *lua* fighting. *Lit.,* the eight rainbows.

naʻau. n. Intestines, bowels, guts; mind, heart, affections; of the heart or mind; mood, temper, feelings. *Fig.,* child. Cf. *naʻau aliʻi, naʻauao, naʻau ʻino, naʻaupō.* *Helu naʻau* (name of an arithmetic book),

mental counting. *Pōkole ka naʻau,* short-tempered, cross. *Hoʻopaʻanaʻau,* to memorize. *Naʻau pōkole,* short-tempered; *lit.,* short intestine. (PPN *ngaakau*.)

Naʻau-ake-ʻai-haku. n. Name of a star. *Lit.,* heart eager to rule as a lord.

naʻau aliʻi. nvs. Kind, thoughtful, forgiving, loving, possessed of *aloha,* beneficent, benevolent, loving heart.

na.au aloha. nvs. Filled with *aloha,* beneficent, benevolent (similar to meanings of *aloha*).

naʻau.ao. nvs. Learned, enlightened, intelligent, wise; learning, knowledge, wisdom, science. *Lit.,* daylight mind. Cf. *ʻimi naʻauao. Naʻauao ʻike mua,* foresight. *Hoʻomana Naʻauao,* Christian Science. *Ka naʻauao loa ʻana,* the instruction, education. **hoʻo.na.au.ao.** To educate, instruct; educational, instructive, civilized. *Ua hoʻonaʻauao ʻia ʻoia,* he was educated. *Kuʻu home hoʻonaʻauao,* my home of learning.

naauau. Remission of a taboo. (And.)

na.ʻau.ʻau. Same as *naʻauʻauā.*

na.ʻau.ʻauā. nvi. Intense grief; anguish so great that it may lead to suicide; to mourn, grieve. *Naʻauʻauā hele,* to wander about in grief.

naʻau hoʻo.kiʻe.kiʻe. nvs. Conceited, proud, willful; proud heart.

naʻau ʻino.ʻino. nvs. Malicious, malevolent; evil or nasty heart, misanthrope. Also *naʻau ʻino.*

naʻau.kake. n. 1. Sausage, wiener. *Lit.,* sausage *(Eng.)* intestines. **2.** Same as *uahi-a-Pele 1,* a variety of sugar cane.

naʻau keʻe.moa. vs. Evil-hearted.

naʻau kō.kua ʻole. vs. Uncooperative, unaccommodating.

naʻau kope.kope. nvs. Of hateful or nasty nature, spiteful, surly, malevolent; sour or surly disposition, misanthrope.

naʻau kū.hili. vs. Blundering, careless, thoughtless.

naʻau.lau.wili. n. Name of an introduced flower (no data).

naʻau lua. vs. Doubtful, two-minded, undecided, indecisive.

naʻau.moa. n. Appendix. *Lit.,* chicken intestines. *ʻOki ʻia ka naʻaumoa,* the appendix was removed.

naʻau palu. palu. vs. Soft- or tender-hearted.

naʻau pē.pē. nvi. Modest heart; to have such; unpretentious.

naʻau.pō. nvs. Ignorant, unenlightened, uncivilized, benighted; ignorance, ignoramus. *Lit.,* night mind. Cf. *naʻauao. Holo naʻaupō,* run pellmell, wildly. *Inu naʻaupō,* to drink foolishly and to excess. *Naʻaupō ʻoukou i nā kūpuna o kākou* (1 Kor. 10.1), you are ignorant about our ancestors. **hoʻo.na.au.pō.** To cause or feign ignorance; ignorant.

naʻau pō.kole. See *pōkole.*

naʻau pono. nvs. Upright, just; right-minded; upright heart.

naʻau.wili. Same as *naʻaumoa.*

nae. 1. nvi. Shortness of breath; to pant or puff for breath, as a result of overexercise or asthma. *E noho iki iho a kuʻu ka nae,* stay a bit until the puffing for breath is over [i.e., rest a bit]. *Ke nae iki nei nō,* some breath remains [as of a dying person]. **ho'o.nae.** To cause shortness of breath. **2.** nvs. Fragrant, sweet-smelling; fragrance. *He 'ala ka nae o ka palai* (song), the perfume of the *palai* fern is sweet. **3.** n. Fishing net with small meshes; net structure to which feathers were attached for feather capes. Also *naepuni, puni, 'upena 'ōhua palemo.* **4.** To give or parcel out equally, as food. (And.)

na'e. 1. loc. n. Easterly, windward (used in some localities only, as on Moloka'i). See *a'e 2, 4. Mai na'e ā lalo* (For. 5:665), from east to west. **2.** conj. But, yet, furthermore, still, nevertheless. (Gram. 11.1.)

nae 'ā.'ī.kū. n. Croup. *Lit.,* gasping croup.

nā.eheehe. vs. Soft, thin.

nae kuku. n. Bag nets of fine-meshed *nae* (netting) consisting of rectangular pieces joined together; a stick *(kuku)* was used at each end of the foot or lower rope.

naele. 1. n. Rock crevice, as in the sea; full of holes, chinks. *Ka ula noho i ka naele* (FS 49), the lobster living in the crevices. **2.** vs. Stretched out of shape; yielding, soft, miry, spongy; misshapen; swamp, mire, bog; to stretch. **ho'o.naele.** Caus/sim.; to soften, as earth for planting.

nā.'ele. Same as *nā'ele'ele 1.*

naeleele. Redup. of *naele,* crevice. (And.)

nā.'ele.'ele. 1. Var. of *nāhelehele.* **2.** vs. Rotten, as timber. *Rare.*

nae.nae. Redup. of *nae 1. Ua naenae ko'u na'au* (Hal. 38.10), my heart pants. (PEP *ngaengae.*)

na'e.na'e. 1. n. All species of native genus in the daisy family *(Dubautia),* which are shrubs or small trees with narrow leaves and small yellow, orange, purple, or white flower heads borne in large cone-shaped clusters. (Neal 845.) Also *hanupaoa, hina-'ai-ka-malama, ne'ine'i.* **2.** vs. Fragrant, as the *na'ena'e* bloom. (But cf. *nae,* fragrant.) **3.** n. Design on outer sheet of a sleeping tapa. **4.** n. Fish of surgeon family *(Acanthurus olivaceus).* **5.** vs. Quick, alert.

nae.naele. Redup. of *naele 2.*

na'e.na'e pua kea. n. A kind of *na'ena'e (Dubautia paleata),* from Kaua'i, with large round flower heads, each head with 25 or more light yellow becoming purplish florets. *Lit.,* white-flowered *na'ena'e.*

na'e.na'e pua mele.mele. n. A kind of *na'ena'e (Dubautia laxa). Lit.,* yellow-flowered *na'ena'e.*

na'e.na'e 'ula. n. A kind of *na'ena'e (Dubautia raillardioides)* from Kaua'i, with white to purplish flowers. *Lit.,* red *na'ena'e.*

nae 'oai.kū. n. Severe asthma.

nae.'ō.pua.kau. n. A disease, accompanied by shortness of breath *(nae).* Cf. *wai'ōpua.*

nae 'owai.kū. Var. spelling of *nae 'oaikū.*

nae.puni. Same as *nae 3.*

nae wai.kū. Same as *nae 'oaikū.*

naha. 1. vs. Bent, curved, bowlegged. **2.** nvi. Union of a chief with his half-sister; their offspring was entitled to the *kapu noho;* to take part in such a marriage. (Malo, 55; Kamakau 64:9–10, 22.) Later *naha* was changed to mean what Malo calls *ho'i.*

nahā. 1. vs. Cracked, broken, as a dish; smashed to bits, as masonry; to act as a purgative; to split; loss of virginity. See ex., *ko'okā. Lā'au nahā* (FS 129), purgative. *'Aila nahā, 'aila ho'onahā,* castor oil. *Umauma nahā* (FS 195), hunger. **ho'o.nahā.** To smash, shatter, crack, split; to take a purgative (PEP *ngahaa.*) **2.** vi. To blot out from sight. *Holo akula lākou ā nahā nā moku o Hawai'i nei, ā nalowale ka 'āina* (For. 4:161), they sailed on until the islands of Hawai'i here were blotted out of sight and the land disappeared.

nahae. 1. vt. Torn, rent; tear; to rip or tear (said figuratively of emotions). See *hae 3.* (PCP *ngasae.*) **2.** vs. Branching out, as a family. *He nahae ali'i kēia,* this is a royal branch.

nā.hae.hae. Redup. of *nahae. Nāhaehae 'ana o ka 'uhane* (Isa. 65.14), vexation of spirit. (PCP *ngasaesae.*)

nā.hā.hā. Redup. of *nahā. Nāhāhā i ke ania e ka makani,* broken by the blowing by the wind.

naha.naha. Redup. of *naha 1.*

nāha.nahā. Redup. of *nahā.*

naha.nahae. Redup. of *nahae.*

nahana.wele. Rare var. of *nahawele 1.*

naha.wele. 1. n. A bivalve of the family Isognomonidae. Also *mahawele.* On O'ahu, the *Perna costellata, Atrina* sp. **2.** Same as *hulu 'īlio (Chaetomorpha antennina),* a seaweed.

naha.wele li'i.li'i. n. A shell *(Brachidontes crebristriatus). Lit.,* small *nahawele.*

nahe. Rare var. of *nahenahe.*

naheka, nahesa. n. Snake. *Naheka wela* (Kanl. 8.15), fiery serpent. (Heb. *nahas.*)

naheka (nahesa) huelo kani. n. Rattlesnake. *Lit.,* tail-sounding snake.

nahele. n. Forest, grove, wilderness, bush; trees, shrubs, vegetation, weeds. Cf. *ho'omakanahele. 'Upu mai ana ke aloha i ka uka nahele o Puna,* loving memory returns of the forest uplands of Puna. (PCP *nga(f,s)ele.*)

nā.hele.hele. Redup. of *nahele;* weeds, undergrowth. *Piha kēia māla i ka nāhelehele,* this patch is full of weeds. (PCP *ngaa(f,s)ele(f,s)ele.*)

nahele mane'o. n. Nettle. (Isa. 34.13.) *Lit.,* itching plant.

nahe.nahe. vs. Soft, sweet, melodious, as music or a gentle voice; soft, as fine cloth; softly blowing, as a gentle breeze; gentle-mannered, soft-spoken, suave. (PPN *ngasengase.*)

nahi. Var. of *lahi,* thin.

nāhi. 1. paucal article. Some, few, the, the little (contraction of *nā,* the, and *wahi,* little). See ex., *pōka'aka'a 2,* Gram. 10.4. *'Auhea akula nāhi keiki?* Where are the boys? (PPN *ngaafī.*) **2.** n. The fires (contraction of *nā ahi,* as in the name Nāhi-'ena'ena).

Nā-hiku. n. Constellation of the Big Dipper. *Lit.,* the seven.

nā.hili. vs. Blundering, confused, perplexed, wandering off the course; careless, awkward. *I hea aku nei lā i nāhili ai ka 'au wa'a?* Where did the canoe fleet wander off to? **ho'o.nā.hili.** To cause a blundering, wandering, as by misdirecting; to procrastinate, waste time through blundering.

nahi.nahi. Var. of *lahilahi.*

nahio.lea. n. A variety of taro.

naho. nvs. Hollow, as a cleft where fish hide; deepset, as eyes of a starving person; eye sockets.

nahoa. 1. vs. Bold, defiant, daring. Cf. *uahoa.* **ho'o.nahoa.** Caus/sim.; to challenge. *'A 'ohe wa'a ho'onahoa o ka lā 'ino,* no canoe defies a storm; *lit.,* no canoe defiant of a stormy day [do not venture in the face of danger]. **2.** nvi. Head wound; intense headache; mental agony; hit or wounded in the head. Cf. *hoa,* mallet, club. *Po'o nahoa,* fractured skull.

nā.hoa.hoa. Redup. of *nahoa 1, 2.*

Nā-hō.kū-mā.hana. See *Māhana.*

Nā-hō.kū-pā. n. Constellation of five stars forming a circle; they are said to be near *Nā-hiku,* the Big Dipper. *Lit.,* enclosure stars.

naholo. vi. To flee, of several; to run away; gone away (2 Sam. 23.9). *Pau nui nā koa i ka naholo,* every last one of the soldiers fled. **ho'o.naholo.** To chase, cause to run. (PPN *ngaasolo.*)

nā.holo.holo. 1. Redup. of *naholo.* (PNP *ngaasolosolo.*) **2.** *(Cap.)* n. Name of a star, perhaps Venus.

naho.naho. Redup. of *naho.*

nahu. 1. nvt. To bite; to have a tendency to bite, as a dog; to sting, as beating rain; pain, as of stomach-ache or of childbirth; bite. **ho'o.nahu.** To bite, cause a stomachache; to pretend to bite. **2.** n. Inexplicable bruise seen on the body, believed caused by the ghost of a living person who was about to die. Also *nahu akua.* (Nānā 156–7.)

nahua. 1. Pas/imp. of *nahu.* See ex., *'apoa. Loa'a akula i ka nahua a ka 'ino,* caught by the pelting of the storm.

2. *(Cap.)* n. Wind associated with Kā'ana-pali, Maui. (Nak. 68.)

Nā-hui.hui. n. The Pleiades. Also *Nā-huihui-a-Makali'i,* the clusters of Pleiades.

nahu kua.koko. n. Labor pains. (Mika 4.9.)

nahu.maka. n. Fattened, as a dog for offering.

nahuna. n. Bite.

nahu.nahu. Redup. of *nahu;* to suffer pangs of childbirth. *Pala nahunahu* (Kep. 93), partially ripe, of a fruit that can be bitten into, as a mountain apple. *Ka ua nahunahu,* the pelting rain.

nahu.nahu.ihu. n. Family discord, quarrel. *Lit.,* nose biting.

nahu.nahu.pū. vt. To bite into with relish. *Nahunahupū i ke alopiko,* bite the belly [of the fish] with relish.

na'i. 1. nvt. To conquer, take by force; conqueror. *'O Ka-mehameha ka na'i aupuni,* Ka-mehameha, the conqueror of the nation. (PCP *ngaki.)* 2. vt. To strive to obtain, endeavor to examine or understand. *Ua na'i 'oia i ka pono o nā keiki,* he does all he can for the well-being of the children.

-na'i. A rare transitivizer. Cf. *hili,* to wander, and *hilina'i,* to believe; *pī,* to sprinkle, and *pīna'i,* to fill a crack; Gram. 6.6.4. (PPN *-naki.)*

naia. vs. Insecurely tied. *Rare.*

na ia. Same as the poss. *nāna,* but rare. See ex., *kāpe'a,* Gram. 9.11.

nai'a. n. Porpoise, dolphin. (KL line 138.)

na'i.au. vt. To add to, join to. *Rare.*

nā.i'i. vt. To remove, take out. *Rare.*

nā.'ī.'ike. vt. To refuse to see, especially a relative or friend; to disown.

naika, naita. n. Knight. *Eng.*

nā.'ike. Same as *nā'ī'ike.*

nai.kola. Similar to *'aikola, ho'ona'aikola.* **ho'o.nai.-kola.** To show contempt, as by destruction. *'A'ohe koe i ka ho'onaikola 'ia e ka makani* (For. 4:476), nothing survived the contemptuous destruction by the wind.

na'īna. n. Conquering, endeavoring, etc. Cf. *na'i 1, 2.*

nai.nai. Rare var. of *nanai* and *nānai.*

na'i.na'i. 1. Redup. of *na'i 1, 2.* 2. vs. Crabbed, bitter, cross, of sour disposition; morose; ill-disposed; opposing. *Rare.* 3. vi. To shorten, to make short. *Rare.* 4. Similar to *pīna'i 1. Rare.* 5. n. Variety of fish (no data).

na'i.na'i mimi. n. Contest in urinating by small boys. *Lit.,* urine striving.

na'i.na'ina mimi. Same as *na'ina'i mimi.*

naio. n. 1. Pinworm, as in the rectum; white specks in feces; larvae, as of mosquitos; worm in dung or in taro. See *pala naio.* (PCP *ngaio.)* 2. Inferior taro left in the field after the crop is removed. 3. The bastard sandalwood *(Myoporum sandwicense),* a native tree, with hard, dark yellow-green wood, scented like sandalwood. Leaves are narrow-oblong, pointed, grouped at branch ends; flowers are small, pink or white; fruit, small, white, round. (Neal 791.) Cf. *'aka.* 4. Name of a seaweed.

naio 'ai kae. n. Dung-eating pinworm, said contemptuously of slanderers.

naio.ea. n. A native variety of taro, with long, blackish leaf stem; blades large, dark-green; grown in uplands, valued for its red poi. (Whitney 48; HP 25.) Also *'ele'ele* and also qualified by the colors *'ele'ele* and *'ula'ula.*

naio makika. n. Mosquito larvae.

naka. 1. nvi. To quiver, quake, tremble, shake, as jello or as with cold or fear; shaky, unsteady, shivering, shaking. *Ka naka o nā kuli* (Kel. 82), the shaking of the knees. 2. vi. To crack open, as earth from the heat; cracked and peeling, as the skin of one who has drunk kava to excess. 3. n. A land shell *(Thaumatodon nesophila).* 4. n. A sea creature. (Perhaps PPN *ngata.)*

Nā-kā-a-Maka.li'i. n. Pleiades. (Kep. 79.) *Lit.,* the bailers of Makali'i.

nakaka. Redup. of *naka 2.* **ho'o.nakaka.** Caus/sim.

naka.kaka. Redup. of *naka 2.*

naka kā.ni'o. n. A land shell *(Nesophila thaanumi). Lit.,* streaked *naka.*

naka kua mauna. n. A land shell *(Nesophila thaanumi, N. nesodonta). Lit.,* mountain-ridge *naka.*

naka kua po'i. Same as *'opihi kapua'i lio.*

Naka.like, Nazarite. n. Nazarite. *Biblical. Eng.*

naka.naka. Redup. of *naka 1, 2.*

Nā-kao. n. Belt and sword in the constellation of Orion. *Lit.,* the darts.

naka 'ō.ni'o.ni'o. n. A marine mollusc *(Pleurobranchus). Lit.,* mottled *naka.*

nakapa, natapa. n. Stacte. (Puk. 30.34.) (Heb. *nataph.)*

Na-ka-ui.lani-'elua. n. Star name (no data). (Kuhelani.)

nake. n. Name of a fish (no data). (KL line 142.)

nā.kea. n. Endemic fresh-water fish *(Awaous [Chonophorous] stamineus)* of the *'o'opu* or goby family, favorite for eating, sometimes 30 cm long. Also *nāwao, nōkea.* Cf. *'o'opu kumu iki, 'o'opu lehe.*

nakeke. 1. nvi. Rattling, as of a window; rustling, as of paper. **ho'o.nakeke.** To make a rattling or rustling noise. *'O wai kēlā e ho'onakeke maila i nā pā?* Who is that rattling the dishes? (PPN *ngatete.)* 2. n. A brown seaweed *(Hydroclathrus clathratus),* resembling *pūhā* and closely related to it, but the surface pierced with holes of different sizes; not eaten.

nake.keke. Redup. of *nakeke 1. He pili nakekeke,* a loose or uncertain relationship.

nakele. nvs. Soft, boggy, slippery, yielding, sinking in; a shallow boggy area. *Nakele 'ā,* fresh lava soft and not yet cold. **ho'o.nakele.** Caus/sim.

nā.kele.kele. Redup. of *nakele.* **ho'o.nā.kele.kele.** Caus/sim.

naki. Same as *nāki'i.* **ho'o.naki.** Caus/sim. (PNP *nati.)*

nā.ki'i. vt. To tie. Cf. *nīki'i. Nāki'i ā pa'a,* tie securely, tighten.

nā.ki'i.ki'i. Redup. of *nāki'i.*

nakili. vi. To glimmer through, as light through a small opening; to begin to open, as eyes of a young animal; to twinkle. *Rare.* Also *mikili.*

nā.kili.kili. Redup. of *nakili.*

naki.naki. 1. Redup. of *naki* (Hal. 105.22). 2. n. Difficult breathing, as during an asthma attack.

-nakoa. No vi. **ho'o.nakoa.** Brave, daring.

Nā-kō.kō-a-Maka.li'i. n. Probably Pleiades. (HM 368.) *Lit.,* the nets of Makali'i.

nako.kolo. Similar to *nākolokolo.* (For. 6:450.)

nā.kolo. 1. nvi. Rumbling, roaring, as of surf or thunder; reverberating. See ex., *'u'ina. Ua ha'alulu ku'u manawa, ua nei nākolo i ke aloha* (Laie 521), my heart trembles, reverberating sighs of love. 2. Redup. of *kolo,* to crawl (perhaps *nakolo).* (For. 6:450.)

nā.kolo.kolo. Redup. of *nākolo 1, 2.*

naku. 1. vi. To root, wallow, as a hog; to tread, trample, push, as through mud or grass; to struggle; to roil, as water; to delve, search. Also *haunaku.* See *'aka'akai* and ex., *oi 2. Naku li'i,* groveler. **ho'o.naku.** Caus/sim. (PPN *natu.)* 2. Same as *nānaku,* a bulrush. 3. n. A kind of red-skinned onion.

-nākū. **ho'o.nā.kū.** To suffer gas pains. *Ho'onākū nā mauna, ka'ahē nā mokupuni* (birth chant for Ka-māmalu), the mountains are in distress, the islands gasp for breath.

nakue. Active, diligent. (And.)

naku'e. 1. nvi. Elbowing; to elbow; piston-like motion. Cf. *ku'e,* to elbow. 2. Var. of *nāku'i.*

nā.ku'i. nvi. To rumble, roar, thump; rumbling; beating, as the heart; thrilled (perhaps *naku 1 + -'i,* transitivizer; Gram. 6.6.4). *Ka nāku'i o ka pū kuni ahi,* the roar of the cannon. **ho'o.nā.ku'i.** Caus/sim.

naku.lehu. n. A variety of white sweet potato.

-nakuli. **ho'o.nakuli.** Apathetic; lack of interest. *Rare.*

nakulu. nvi. Dripping, as water; patter, clatter, rattle, echo; rumbling, as the stomach; grumbling; vibrating, as thunder; to spread or circulate, as rumor. *Ua nakulu akula kēia lohe i ke alo ali'i* (Laie 599), this report reached the presence of the chief. **ho'o.nakulu.** Caus/sim. *Ke ho'onakulu nei i ku'u manawa; no ku'u ipo* *paha kēia wela* (Laie 487), causing my heart to pitter-patter; perhaps this warmth is from my lover.

nakulu.'ai. vs. Praiseworthy, upright. *Rare.*

nā.kulu.kulu. Redup. of *nakulu.*

naku.naku. Redup. of *naku 1.*

nala. 1. Var. of *ulana,* to plait. (PPN *(la)langa.*) **2.** n. A kind of fish (no data). (KL line 143.) **3.** n. A measurement of 6 cm. *Eng.,* nail.

Nā-lā.lani-a-pili-lua. n. Name of a constellation. *Lit.,* the lines of the clinging ones.

nale. 1. vs. Clear, bright. Cf. *kōnane, kōnale.* (PCP *ngale.*) **2.** Not fast; movable; independent. (And.)

naleko, naredo. n. Nard (RSV), spikenard (KJV). (Mele 4:13.) (Gr. *nardos.*)

nale.nale. Redup. of *nale 1, 2.*

nali. vt. To nibble, gnaw. (PPN *ngali.*)

nalili.ko'i. n. A variety of taro. (HP 33.)

nali.nali. Redup. of *nali.*

nalo. 1. vs. Lost, vanished, concealed, hidden, forgotten, missing; to lose, pass away, disappear (a *loa'a*-type word, see Gram. 4.4 and *pōnalo 2;* see ex., *'ikena*). *Nalo ka umu* (FS 133), the oven is covered. *'A'ole au e nalo iā'oe,* you will not fail to recognize me. **ho'o.nalo.** To cause to be lost; to conceal, secrete, put out of sight. (PPN *ngalo.*) **2.** n. The common housefly and other two-winged insects. See *pōnalo 1.* (PPN, PCP *lango;* note Hawaiian metathesis.)

nalo 'aki. n. Small stinging fly, as the stable fly *(Stomoxys calcitrans)* and horn fly *(Haematobia irritans);* gnat, hornet.

nalo.hia. Pas/imp. of *nalo 1.* See ex., *kīhe'ahe'a.* (PEP *ngalo(f,s)ia.*)

nalo hope 'eha. n. Hornet (Puk. 23.28) and other Hymenoptera. *Lit.,* fly with stinging posterior.

nalo kele.awe. n. A fly, perhaps the hover fly (Syrphidae). *Lit.,* brass fly.

nalo lawe lepo. n. Mud wasp, as *Sceliphron caementarium. Lit.,* dirt-toting fly.

nalo loa. vs. Lost forever, forever.

nalo meli. n. Honey bee *(Apis mellifera).* (Kanl. 1.44.) *Lit.,* honey fly.

nalo meli mō.'ī wahine. n. Queen bee.

nalo meli noho hale. n. Drone bee. *Lit.,* house-staying honey bee.

nalo meli pa'a.hana. n. Worker bee. *Lit.,* industrious honey bee.

nalo nahu. n. Stinging fly. *Lit.,* biting fly.

nalo.nalo. Redup. of *nalo 1.* **ho'o.nalo.nalo.** Hidden; to cause to disappear, camouflage. Cf. *mana'o ho'onalonalo, 'ōlelo ho'onalonalo. Kuhikuhi ho'onalonalo,* to speak in an enigmatic way or with hidden meaning so that only the confidant understands. (PPN *ngalongalo.*)

nalo paka. n. Tick (Hippoboscidae); ensign fly (Evaniidae). *Lit.,* lean fly.

nalo pilau. n. Bluebottle fly (Calliphoridae). *Lit.,* stink fly.

nalo.wale. vs. Lost, gone, forgotten, vanished, missing, hidden, extinct, disappeared (especially if unaccountably so); infinite (Gram. 10.3); to lose.

nalu. 1. nvi. Wave, surf; full of waves; to form waves; wavy, as wood grain. *Ke nalu nei ka moana,* the ocean is full of waves. **ho'o.nalu.** To form waves. (PPN *ngalu.*) **2.** vt. To ponder, meditate, reflect, mull over, speculate. Cf. Eset. 6.6. *Nalu wale ihola nō 'o Keawenui-a-'Umi i ka hope o kēia keiki* (For. 4:261), Keawenui-a-'Umi pondered about the fate of this child. (PPN *na(a)nunga.*) **3.** n. Amnion, amniotic fluid. (PPN, PCP *lanu;* note Hawaiian metathesis.)

nalu.ā, naluwā. vt. To nourish resentment, sulk.

nalu.ea. n. Nausea. Cf. *poluea.*

nalu ha'i lala. n. Wave that breaks diagonally.

nalu ho'o.kau.maha. vt. To ponder sadly, brood.

nalu.kai. vs. Weatherworn, as old canoes or persons who have weathered the storms of life. *Lit.,* ocean wave.

nalu kua loloa. n. Long wave.

naluli. vi. Shaky, unsteady, swaying (less common than *luli*).

naluli.luli. Redup. of *naluli.*

nalulu. nvi. Dull headache; dull pain in the stomach, queasy; to have such pains. *Nalulu ka 'ōpū,* uneasy stomach. **ho'o.nalulu.** To cause a pain in head or stomach. *Ho'onalulu ho'i keiki,* the children give [me] a headache. (PNP *nga(a)lulu.*)

nalu miki. n. Receding wave.

nalu muku. n. Broken section of wave.

nalu.nalu. vs. Rough, of a sea with high waves; to form high waves. (PPN *ngalungalu.*)

nalu pū kī. n. Wave that shoots high.

nalu.wā. Var. spelling of *naluā.*

Nā-mā.hoe. n. Castor and Pollux, Gemini. *Lit.,* the twins. Also *Māhana.*

namau.ahi. vs. Thinly scattered, few, of sparse growth. *Namauahi nā maile o kēia wahi,* the maile vines of this place are sparse.

namu. 1. nvt. Unintelligible muttering, gibberish; any foreign language, especially English; to speak gibberish or a foreign language, to mumble. *Namu haole,* English. *He aha ka namu?* What's the foreign term [What's the price]? *Ka mea namu li'ili'i* (Isa. 8.19), those that mutter. **ho'o.namu.** To pretend to speak in a foreign language, to mutter, mumble, speak gibberish. (PNP *nanu.*) **2.** vt. To nibble; to chew with closed mouth. *Ua namu ā pāhoehoe 'ia,* nibbled at and changed to pāhoehoe lava. (PPN *lamu.*) **3.** n. Name of a fish. (no data).

Nā.mū. n. Legendary little people. *Lit.,* the silent ones. Cf. *Nāwā,* the noisy ones.

namu.namu. Redup. of *namu 1, 2;* to grumble, complain, mumble, babble.

namu pa'i 'ai, namu pa'i kalo. n. Pidgin English. *Lit.,* hard-poi gibberish, hard-taro gibberish.

nana. 1. Var. of *ulana 1. E nana moena ana,* plaiting mats. **2.** Short for *'īnana.* Cf. *kīnana, pūnana.* (PPN *langa.*) **3.** *(Cap.)* n. Name of a star or taro. **4.** *(Cap.)* n. Name of a month. See *'e'eleku, month.* **5.** n. A variety of taro. **6.** Similar to *manana;* to spread. **7.** n. A variety of fish (no data). (KL line 141.)

nāna. *n*-poss. For him, her, it; by him, her, it; belonging to him, her, it, whose (cf. *nona, a*-form, Gram. 9.11). (PCP *naana.*)

nanā. vs. Snarling; to strut or provoke, as one looking for a fight, as a threatening boaster, or stiff-legged dogs ready to pounce on each other; sexually excited, of males; to stretch, as muscles. *Ihu nanā,* snarling nose; *fig.,* quarrelsome, aggressive. **ho'o.nanā.** Aggressive, looking for a fight, threatening; to antagonize.

nā.nā. 1. vt. To look at, observe, see, notice, inspect; to care for, pay attention to, take care of. Cf. *kūnānā, nānā 'ole. Mai nānā i kāna 'ōlelo,* don't pay any attention to what he says. *He keiki nānā mākua,* a son who cares for his parents. *Nānā ma ka 'ākau,* dress right [military command]. *Maika'i ke nānā aku,* goodlooking. *Nānā i nā puke,* to audit accounts. *Nānā a'ela ia ma nā ki'i maka nunui, koe nō nā ki'i maka li'ili'i,* he caters to the important people, and leaves out the ordinary folk. *Hiamoe wale ke kāne, nānā wale ka wahine,* the husband just sleeps, the wife looks about but has nothing. **ho'o.nā.nā.** To cause to look, show. *Ho'okūkū ho'onānā, nānā kō maka i ka mahina* (children's game chant), stand about, look, let your eyes see the moon. **2.** nvi. Quiet restful. Cf. *nā 1,* calmed. *Kau i ka nānā ka moe* (For. 6:396), sleep in peace. *Hula ho'o-nānā* (UL 244), a hula for amusement. (PPN *ngaangaa.*) **3.** n. Goat. Cf. *kao 5.*

nana'a. Var. of *na'ana'a.*

nā.nā ao. nv. Cloud interpreter, one who observes the clouds; to observe omens in the clouds; seer, forecaster. *'A'ole ho'i e nānā ao* (Oihk. 19.26), nor practice witchcraft (RSV), nor observe times (KJV).

nana.au. Var. of *lanaau.*

nanae. 1. Redup. of *nae 1.* **2.** vs. Potbellied, fat. *Rare.*

nana'e. n. Small piece of land. *Rare.*

nana.hā. Redup. of *nahā.*

nanahe. 1. Same as *nahenahe.* **2.** Weak, as from not eating; thin, as silk.

nana.hea. vs. Animated, as birds; lively. *Rare.* Cf. *'īnana.*

nana.hili. Redup. of *nāhili.*

nanaho. Redup. of *naho.*

nā.nā.honua. n. A tropical American shrub *(Brugmansia candida),* known as the angel's trumpet; it bears white, trumpet-shaped, pendent flowers to about 25 cm long. Though flowers and leaves are poisonous to eat, the plant is grown for its high ornamental value. (Neal 748–9.) *Lit.,* earth-gazing. Cf. *lā'au hānō.*

Nā.nā Hope. n. Pollux. Cf. *Māhana, Nānā Mua.*

nanahu. Redup. of *nahu.*

nana.hū. vs. Bent out of shape, crooked, as a stick.

nā.nahu. 1. Var. of *lānahu. Nānahu pikimana,* coal; *lit.,* bituminous *(Eng.)* charcoal. **ho'o.nā.nahu.** To turn into charcoal, as burnt wood. (PEP *ngaalafu;* cf. Métraux p. 236.) **2.** n. A native variety of sugar cane, the red mutant of *'akilolo 'ula'ula.* (HP 220.)

nana.hua. 1. Same as *nanahu;* ill-feeling, bitterness. **2.** n. A post temporarily set up in the back of the *mana* house in the heiau enclosure; later a *haku 'ōhi'a* image was installed in this place (Malo 166); name of the two posts at the entrance of a temple to which the *'aha* (taboo cord) was fastened.

nana.huki. vs. To pull away from; contrary, disdainful (perhaps from *nanā,* surly, and *huki,* pull).

nanai. 1. vs. Difficult to climb, as a cliff; stiff-backed; to walk with stiff back; to strut, act the dandy; to lean back stiffly or haughtily; stiff-backed; humped over as a result of stiffness. Also *lanai.* **2.** Swift. (AP.)

nā.nai. 1. Same as *pānānai,* shallow. **2.** vi. Empty, as a taro patch. *Rare.* **3.** vi. Taking an uneven course, as a canoe in a rough sea, or a kite. *Rare.*

nana'i. vi. To spread, as a topped tree. *Rare.*

nā.na'i. Var. of *Lā-na'i,* island name. (For. 6:493.)

nanai.ea. vs. Weak, feeble, frail.

nā.naina. n. General appearance, view, aspect, panorama, sight, scenery, scene.

nanaka. Redup. of *naka 1, 2;* marked in sections, as a turtle's back or breadfruit skin. **ho'o.nanaka.** Caus/sim.

nana.kea. vs. Pale, wan. (FS 199.)

nā.nā ke'e. See *ke'e.*

nanaki. Redup. of *naki.*

nā.nā kokoe. See *kokoe.*

nā.naku. Same as *'aka'akai,* great bulrush *(Scirpus validus).* (Neal 88–9.) (PEP *nga'atu;* cf. Easter *nga'atu* and Emory 1972, p. 62.)

nana.kuka, nanasuka. n. Nainsook. *Eng.*

nā.nā.kuli. vt. To look at but not respond when spoken to; to see but pay no attention, ignore. For the O'ahu place of this name, see Pukui, Elbert, and Mookini, 1974.

nanala. Redup. of *nala,* to plait. (PPN *lalanga.*)

nā.nā.lā. n. Sunflower *(Helianthus annuus).* Also *pua nānā lā.* (Neal 840.) *Lit.,* sun-gazer.

nanali. Redup. of *nali.*

nā.nā.lia. Pas/imp. of *nānā.*

nā.nā maka. vt. To look at without helping; indifference to one in trouble; heartless. *Ua nānā maka 'oia i kona makuahine,* he was indifferent to his mother.

nanamu. Redup. of *namu;* to grumble.

Nā.nā Mua. n. The star Castor. Cf. *Māhana, Nānā Hope.* According to some, both were the names of a single star. *Lit.,* look forward.

nanana. 1. vi. To flutter, as wings. Cf. *nana 2.* **ho'o.nanana.** Caus/sim. *Ho'onanana ka manu e lele,* the bird flutters its wings to fly. **2.** Redup. of *nana,* to plait. (PPN *lalanga.*) **3.** Same as *nananana 1,* spider. **4.** n. Swelling, as in dropsy. *Rare.*

nana.nai. Redup. of *nanai 1.*

nana.nai.ea. Redup. of *nanaiea.*

nanana.kea. Redup. of *nanakea.*

nana.nana. 1. n. Spider *(Araneida);* today this is the house spider, formerly the outdoors spider. Cf. *pe'epe-'emakawalu.* **2.** Var. of *lanalana 1, 2.*

nanana.nai.ea. Same as *nananaiea.*

nana.napa. Redup. of *napa 1–3. Rare.*

nanani 'ele.'ele. n. A variety of sweet potato.

nanani ke'o.ke'o. n. A variety of sweet potato.

nā.nā-nu'u. n. Design on Ni'ihau mats consisting of alternating solid and white triangles.

nana.nu'u mamao. Same as *lananu'u mamao.*

nanao. Redup. of *nao 1, 2.* (PPN *nanao.*)

nā.nā 'ole. nvi. Disregard, heedless disregard; oblivious; to pay no attention. *Nānā 'ole i kō ha'i ola,* heedless disregard for the lives of others. *Me ka nānā 'ole, pehea kāna hana, ua makemake 'ia nō,* regardless of the quality of her work, she's liked anyway.

nana.pau. A tree. (And.)

nana.piko. n. A native variety of taro.

nā.nā pono. vt. To watch carefully, pay particular attention to, note carefully, stare at, observe, scrutinize.

Nā.nā-pua. n. Said to be a name for Eromanga Island in the southern New Hebrides; Boki sailed for here in 1829 to get sandalwood; his ship disappeared. (RC 293.) *Lit.,* look at flowers. See *'Āina-wohi.*

nanau. 1. Redup. of *nau,* to chew. **2.** vs. Unfriendly, bitter, crabbed, estranged; to pay no attention to a call; to ignore, as former friends. Also *lanau. Rare.*

nanauha. Same as *kākāuha,* rigid. **ho'o.nanauha.** Caus/sim.

nanauki. Same as *nāukiuki.*

nā.nā uli. nv. To study the sky, as for omens; one who does so.

nanawa. Same as *nanau 2.* (And.)

nā.nā wale. vt. Just to look, especially to look on without helping.

nāna.waū. vs. Weakened, unhealthy, as plants; sickly. See ex., *kūloku.* **ho'o.nāna.waū.** To cause to be weak and unhealthy.

nane. 1. n. Riddle, puzzle, parable, allegory; to riddle, speak in parables (Mar. 4.2). See *kōnane 2.* **ho'o.-nane.** To make riddles, speak in parables. (Perhaps PCP *nane.*) **2.** Rare var. of *nini 3,* fence.

nanea. 1. nvs. Of absorbing interest, interesting; fascinating, enjoyable; repose, leisure, tranquility; relaxed, at ease, at leisure, amused, engaged with, busy with; to have a good time. *He hana nanea ke kui lei,* lei making is pleasant. **ho'o.nanea.** To pass the time in ease, peace, and pleasure; to relax, lounge, repose; absorbed, contented. *He hana ho'onanea ka ho'okani pila,* playing a musical instrument is pleasant. (PNP *nanea.*)**2.** Same as *mohihihi,* a vine. **3.** n. A seaweed *(Hypnea nidifica).*

nane.ha'i. n. Problem, riddle to be solved. *Lit.,* telling riddle. See ex., *mana'okōkua, wehe 'ana.*

nane huna. n. Hidden riddle, conundrum.

naneki. n. Nankeen, denim. *Eng.*

nane.nane. Redup. of *nane 1.* **ho'o.nane.nane.** Same as above; puzzling, riddling; figurative. See *'ōlelo ho'onanenane.*

nani. 1. nvs. Beauty, glory, splendor; beautiful, pretty, glorious, splendid. *Nani makamae,* precious, exquisite. **ho'o.nani.** To beautify, adorn, trim, decorate, glorify, honor, exalt, praise, adore; decorative, glorifying. *Nā mea ho'onani,* decorations of any kind. *Ho'onani kākou iā Ia* (hymn), let us adore Him. *Mea ho'onani kino,* any bodily adornment, as jewelry. **2.** n. Beautiful flower (sometimes followed by *-o-* + place name: see below. **3.** n. Good thing (idiom). *He nani nō ia,* it's a good thing. **4.** conj. Since, because. *Nani ho'i ua ki'i 'ia maila e make, he aha lā ho'i . . .* (Kel. 37), since [I] am indeed summoned by death, what of it . . . *Nani nō ia e hele ana 'oe i ke kula, e ho'o'oikaika i ka ha'awina,* since you are going to school, work hard on the lessons. **5.**

interj. How much, how. *Nani ka maika'i,* how fine. *Nani ka pupuka,* how very ugly. *Nani 'ino ku'u make-make,* how much I want it. (*He* may precede *nani* in these sentences.)

nani ahi.ahi. n. The four o'clock *(Mirabilis jalapa),* from tropical America, a shrubby herb with fragrant, red, white, yellow, or striped flowers, opening in late afternoon, and used by Hawaiians for leis in the evening. The plants have medicinal properties. (Neal 335–6.) *Lit.,* evening beauty. Also *pua ahiahi.*

nani ali'i. n. Allamandas with large yellow flowers (*Allamanda cathartica* and some varieties), from Brazil, ornamental climbing shrubs. Also *lani ali'i.* (Neal 687.) *Lit.,* chiefly beauty.

naniha. n. An indigenous *'o'opu* fish, *Awaous genivittatus.*

nani mau loa. n. An everlasting or strawflower *(Helichrysum bracteatum),* from Australia, an annual, 30 to 90 cm high. The conspicuous parts of the daisy-like flowers are the many overlapping white or yellow to red scaly bracts, which are long lasting. *Lit.,* everlasting beauty. Also *pua pepa.* (Neal 836–7.)

nani.nani. 1. Redup. of *nani 1.* **ho'o.nani.nani.** To beautify, adorn. 2. Same as *nalinali,* to gnaw.

nani.nui. Soft stone used in making *lūhe'e,* squid-fishing sinkers. (Malo 19.)

nani-o-Hilo. Same as *wilelaiki. Moloka'i.*

nani-o-Ola'a. A kind of *Torenia (T. asiatica),* a blue-flowered ornamental annual, belonging to the snapdragon family, used in leis. (Neal 759.)

nani Wai-'ale-'ale. n. A native violet *(Viola kauaensis)* found only in high bogs on Kaua'i and on O'ahu. The plants are 10 to 20 cm tall, with few broad leaves and one or two white or pale-blue fragrant flowers. *Lit.,* Wai-'ale'ale beauty. Also *kalili, liliwai, pohe hiwa.* (Neal 591.) See *waioleka.*

nano. Var. of *nalo 1.*

nanō. Var. of *nonō.*

nano'o. n. A dark-red or purple seaweed, said to be same as *nanea.*

nano.wale. Var. of *nalowale.*

nanu. Var. of *nalu,* wave.

nā.nū. n. Native species of gardenia, shrubs and trees with broad leaves and tubular, white single flowers. (Neal 800.) Also *nā'ū.* Cf. *kiele.*

nanue. 1. Var. of *nenue,* a fish. See *hoe nanue.* (PNP *nanue.*) 2. n. An edible seaweed.

nā.nue. Same as *'ōlanalana,* nauseating.

nanuha. Stingy. (And.)

nanulu. 1. Var. of *nalulu.* 2. vi. Rising, as smoke. *Rare.*

nao. 1. nvs. Ripple; ridge, as of twilled cloth or a tapa beater; groove; streak on tapa; grain of wood or stone; thread of a screw; crevice, as in rocks; grooved. See *nao-ho'opa'i. Kui nao,* screw; *lit.,* nail with thread. 2. vt. To thrust the hands into an opening, as in fishing; to probe. (PPN *nao.*) 3. Intensifying idiom following *'a'ole* or *'a'ohe* and usually followed by words expressing damage, havoc, distress, pain. (Gram. 4.6.) See ex., *pāpa'a 1. 'A'ohe nao ka pilikia!* How very much trouble! *'A'ohe nao i ka ua!* What didn't the rain do! *'A'ohe nao ka 'eha!* Terrible pain! 4. nvs. Dark-red dye; red. 5. n. A variety of taro. (HP 33.)

na'o. nvs. Spittle, phlegm, mucus; slimy. (PPN *ngako.*)

naoa. 1. Pas/imp. of *nao 1, 2.* 2. n. Loss of appetite, sick at the sight of food. Cf. more common *kanea.* 3. vs. Chilled, chilling, as water. *Pulu i ka wai naoa a ke kēhau,* wet in the chilly water of the dew.

nao-hā.lu'a. n. 1. A tapa pattern with lines. 2. n. Curly grain, as in *koa* wood.

nao-ho'o.pa'i. n. Tapa beater pattern. *E 'ike auane'i 'oe i ka nao-ho'opa'i a Malailua, ka lā'au e wali ai kō papa 'auwae* (FS 63), you will soon know the tapa-beater pattern of Malailua, the club that will soften your lower jaw.

nao.maka.lua. n. 1. Fish-basket trap made of *'inalua* vines, used for small fish. *Lit.,* double-meshed groove. 2. Two-edged adze.

na 'olua. poss. For you, belonging to you, by you (dual, *a*-class).

nao.nao. 1. n. Ants, Formicidae. Also *'ānonanona, nonanona.* 2. Redup. of *nao 1–3. Ua pohihihi naonao,* extremely puzzling. (PPN *naonao.*)

na'o.na'o. Redup. of *na'o.* (PPN *ngakongako.*)

nao.nao lele. n. Termite. *Lit.,* flying ant.

nao 'ohi.'ohi. n. Prominent grain in wood. *Lit.,* picked grain.

nao-ua-hā.'ao. Same as *hā'ao 3,* a tapa pattern.

nao-ua-nana.huki. n. Name of a tapa design.

na 'oukou. poss. For you, belonging to you, by you (plural, *a*-class).

nao.wili. n. A bit for a drill. *Lit.,* twisting thread.

napa. 1. vs. Uneven, bent, crooked, out of shape; warped. 2. vs. Flexible, springy, elastic; tremulous, as air under a hot sun. 3. nvi. Delay, procrastination; to delay, procrastinate. **ho'o.napa.** To cause delay. 4. n. Type of fish. (KL line 143.)

nā.pai. Same as *napa 1, 2. Nāpai ka papa i ka waiho 'ia ka lā,* the board warped from being left in the sun.

nā.pana. n. Socket. *Rare.* Cf. *pona.*

napa.napa. 1. Redup. of *napa 1, 2;* to writhe and twist, as an eel. See ex., *lulo.* 2. Same as *napenape.*

nape. 1. vs. Bending and swaying, as coconut fronds; surging, as the sea; to rise and fall, as the chest in breathing; yielding, springy. Cf. *holu nape. Nape ka hanu i ka houpo,* palpitating the breath in the chest. *Nani wale ke kai o Mamala, ke nape maila i ka makani,* beautiful sea of Mamala, rising, falling in the wind. **ho'o.nape.** Caus/sim. 2. Var. of *napo.*

Nā.pē.hā. n. 1. Name of a star. 2. Name of a pool on O'ahu over which the chief Kuali'i was said to have leaned to drink.

napele. vs. Soft, as overripe fruit; bruised, broken, crushed; soggy, swampy; crumbly, as a cliff; wounded in spirit. **ho'o.napele.** Same as above; to wound, to make soft; to digest, as food.

nā.pele.pele. Redup. of *napele.*

nape.nape. Redup. of *nape 1;* fluttering, flickering, flexible.

nā.pili. n. Kind of endemic *'o'opu* or goby *(Sicydium stimsonii);* so called because it is said to cling *(pili)* to stones; used in weaning and housewarming ceremonies so that luck will cling *(pili).* Called *nōpili* on Kaua'i.

napo. vs. Mashed soft, as finely pounded poi that is free of lumps; glutinous, gluey; dented, as by hammering.

napolo. Straightened. (And.)

napo.napo. Redup. of *napo.*

napo'o. nvi. Cavity, hollow, rut, depression; armpit; hollow at the juncture of the wing with the body of a fowl; to sink, go down, set (of the sun), to enter or sink into out of sight. Cf. *po'o,* depression. *Ua napo'o ka lā,* the sun has set. *Ua napo'o ka 'iole i loko o ka lua,* the rat has gone down the hole.

napo.'ona. n. Setting, entering. *Napo'ona lā,* sunset.

nā.po'o.po'o. Redup. of *napo'o.*

napu. Var. of *nape 1.*

nā.pu'u. 1. Var. of *lāpu'u,* bunched up. 2. nvt. Knot; to tie.

nā.pu'u.pu'u. Redup. of *nāpu'u 1, 2;* to tie, as in a bundle.

nau. nvt. To chew, munch, masticate, gnash the teeth; grinder, as of a sugar mill; feed dog on sewing machine that holds cloth at the needle. *Fig.,* surly, full of hatred, as eyes. Cf. *mama,* to chew without swallowing, as *kava. Nau kamu,* to chew gum. *Nau paka,* to chew tobacco. *Paka nau,* chewing tobacco. (PPN *ngau.*)

nāu. n-poss. Yours, belonging to you, for you, by you (singular, *a*-form; Gram. 9.11). *Nāu mai ā na'u aku,* your turn and then mine. *Nāu anei?* Is [it] yours? Was it you? (PCP *naau.*)

na'u. n-poss. Mine, belonging to me, for me, by me (singular, *a*-form; Gram. 9.11). *Na'u ka pua'a,* give me the pig. (PCP *na(a)ku.*)

na'ū. vi. To come, go. *Rare.*

nā.'ū. 1. Same as *nānū.* 2. nvs. Pale yellow, as the gardenia; a yellow gardenia. 3. n. A variety of sweet potato. (HP 142.) 4. vi. Sighing deeply; to prolong the breath, especially in a children's game at Kona: children would make a prolonged *u*-sound just at sunset, believing that the sun would not set as long as they held their breath; to play *nā'ū. Hā'ule naoa ka wai a ke kēhau, ke nā'ū lā nā kamali'i* (chant for Ka-mehameha II), the water of the *kēhau* mist falls rippling as the children play *nā'ū.* 5. n. Variety of fish (no data).

naua. 1. Pas/imp. of *nau.* 2. vs. Aloof, not cordial, distant, unaccommodating. 3. vs. Slow, tardy. *Naua ho'i kāu hele 'ana,* how slowly you walk. 4. n. A variety of taro.

nau.ā, nauwā. n. A secret society formed or revived by King Ka-lā-kaua for the study of the ancient Hawaiian religion and manner of living. *Hale nauā,* a place where genealogy was scanned to see whether applicants were related to the high chief and therefore eligible to become members of the royal household. Emerson says *nauā* was the word of challenge addressed to those applying for admission. (Malo 191–2, Emerson note 199–200.)

na'u.ā, na'uwā. n. Noon. *Rare.*

Naua-a-ke-au-haku. n. Name of a star or constellation in the Milky Way.

nau.ane! interj. On the way! Moving along! (This exclamation is reported to have been said by priests as they carried the images; it is used alone or with the imperative *e* preceding.)

naue, nauwe. vi. To move, shake, rock, sway, tremble; to quake, as the earth; to vibrate; to march; loose and insecure, as a tooth; revolving, as hips in a hula. *Naue i mua,* forward, march. ho'o.naue. To cause to shake, revolve, sway, rock; to disturb. *Ka ua hō'oni, ho'onaue i ka pu'u ko'a,* the rain sways in a dance and shakes the coral pile. *No ke aha lā 'oe i ho'onaue mai ai ia'u?* (1 Sam. 28.15), Why have you disquieted me? Cf. *ue 1.* (PPN *ngaue.*)

nā.ue.ue, nauweuwe. Redup. of *naue.* ho'o.nā.ue.ue. To cause to sway back and forth.

naue.wai. n. A variety of sweet potato.

nā.'uke. n. To search for lice, as in hair of person or fur of animal.

nauki. vs. Impatient, irritable, cross, vexed. *Mai nauki mai 'oe,* don't be irritable. ho'o.nauki. Causing irritation; aggravating, annoying, exasperating, provoking.

nā.uki. Intensive of *nauki;* vexation, anger; to harass. ho'o.nā.uki. Caus/sim.

nau.kilo. n. Nautilus. *Eng.*

nā.uki.uki. Redup. of *nauki.* ho'o.nā.ukiuki. Redup. of *ho'onauki;* to provoke, annoy.

naule. Same as *pua kala;* prickly poppy. *Rare.*

nau.lia. Pas/imp. of *nau.* (For. 6:400.)

nā.ulu. 1. nvs. Sudden shower; showery; to shower. See ex., *haehae 2. Ka ua nāulu o Ka-wai-hae,* the sudden shower of Ka-wai-hae. *He ao nāulu,* a shower cloud. 2. *(Cap.)* n. Sea breeze at Ka-wai-hae, Hawai'i; Wai-mea, Kaua'i; and Kanaloa, Maui (UL 100.) 3. vs. Vexed, angry, irritated by being teased or nagged. Cf. *uluulu,* frayed, angry. ho'o.nā.ulu. To provoke to anger by taunting and teasing.

nā.ulu.ulu. Redup. of *nāulu 1, 3.*

nau.nau. 1. Redup. of *nau;* to munch one's words and speak indistinctly, mumble. *Naunau lepo,* dirt muncher [insulting term for *lōpā,* tenant farmers]. (PPN *ngau-ngau.*) 2. Same as *'ānaunau 2.* 3. n. Shellfish such as *Cymatium muricinum, C. gemmatum, C. pileare, Bursa granularis.* Also *'ānaunau.*

nau.paka. n. Native species of shrubs *(Scaevola)* found in mountains and near coasts, conspicuous for their white or light-colored flowers that look like half flowers. (Neal 819–21.) (PCP *naupata.*)

nau.paka kaha.kai. n. The beach *naupaka (Scaevola taccada),* a spreading, succulent shrub found on coasts of tropical Asia and some islands of the Pacific. Flowers are white and may be streaked with purple. The ber-

ries are white and about 1.3 cm long, looking like hailstones. (Neal 820–1.) Also *huahekili; aupaka (Niihau).*

nau.paka kai. Same as *naupaka kahakai.*

nau.paka kua.hiwi. n. All mountain species of *naupaka.* (Neal 819–20.) Cf. *'ohe naupaka.*

nau.wā. Var. spelling of *nauā.*

na'u.wā. Var. spelling of *na'uā.*

nauwe, nauweuwe. Var. spelling of *naue.*

nā.wā. n. 1. Babbling; loud, confusing talk. 2. *(Cap.)* Legendary little people. Cf. *Nāmū,* the silent ones.

Nā-wā.hine-a-Maka.li'i. n. Pleiades. (Kep. 79.) *Lit.,* the wives of Makali'i.

nā.wali. vs. Weak, feeble, infirm, limp, frail; weakness, feebleness. *Hā'wali.* ho'o.nā.wali. To cause weakness; to enfeeble; to feign weakness. *'O ke anu ka mea ho'onāwali i ke kino,* cold is what weakens the body. (PPN *ngawari,* PCP *ngaawali.*)

nā.wali.wali. Redup. of *nāwali,* weak. ho'o.nā.wali.-wali. Caus/sim. (PPN *ngawariwari.*)

nā.wao. 1. n. A domesticated taro that has gone wild in the forest *(wao).* (Ka'ū name.) A native taro cultivated in Puna. *Hui aku, hui mai, hui kalo me ka nāwao,* mixed here, mixed there, mixed wild taro with tame taro [utter confusion]. 2. Same as *nākea,* a fish. 3. *(Cap.)* Same as *Mū 'ai mai'a,* a mythical people.

nawe. 1. Var. spelling of *naue. Ua nawe pakika* (Kep. 87), moving slippery rain. 2. vi. Panting for breath, as after exercise or from illness. *Rare.*

nā.wele. nvs. Fine, threadlike, small; weak, thin; soft, gentle; tracery; softness, gentleness, as of a voice. *He 'ike nāwele,* seeing just a little; a slight knowledge. *Hele maila nō ke 'ala o ka hala, māpu maila nō me ke onaona o ka maile, nāwele pū maila nō me ka hu'ihu'i o ka lehua,* there comes the fragrance of the pandanus, wafting thither with the soft sweetness of the *maile,* and with them a trace of the coolness of the *lehua.* ho'o.nā.wele. Same as above. *Ma ke kama'ilio ho'o-nāwele 'ana,* by speaking softly.

nā.weo. Same as *weo,* red. *Rare.*

nawewe. Var. of *nāueue.*

nē. 1. vi. Fretting, teasing or nagging for something; murmuring, as the sea; returning persistently, as a thought or desire. *Nē ho'ohune,* to wheedle. *Nē hone ka leo o ka waiolina,* sweet, teasing appeal in the sound of the violin. ho'o.nē. Teasing, fretting, appealing. 2. Short for *nele. E nē ka lā, ka malama,* without [light] the sun, the moon. 3. n. A seaweed. (KL line 101.)

nea. Same as *neo, 'ōnea.* (PCP *nea.*)

nea.nea. Same as *neoneo, 'ōneanea.*

neau. Var. of *niau.*

ne'e. vi. Moving along little by little or by fits and starts; to step, march, creep, hitch along; to push along, as work; to squirm. *Ma ka 'ākau ne'e,* to the right, march. *Ua ne'e lāua mai Liliha a Wai-kīkī,* they moved from Liliha to Wai-kīkī. *Oia ne'e aku i ka hana a pau ke aho,* just pushing ahead the work until exhausted. ho'o.ne'e. To cause to move, shift, hitch along, push ahead. *Ho'one'e ikaika,* to push on vigorously. (PNP *neke.*)

ne'e he'e. vi. To creep along, as a child or octopus. *Lit.,* octopus hitch.

ne'e hope. vi. To retreat, move backward; to back up, as a car (less used than *peki*). ho'o.ne'e hope. To back up, as a car. *Ho'one'e hope i ke ka'a,* back up the car.

ne'e i mua, ne'e mua. vi. To advance, go forward, progress. ho'o.ne'e mua. To cause progress. *Nā hana ho'one'e mua,* improvements [as to property].

ne'ena. n. Movement, moving.

ne'e.ne'e. 1. Redup. of *ne'e. Ne'ene'e ā pili,* to move close by, snuggle. ho'o.ne'e.ne'e. Caus/sim. (PNP *nekeneke.*) 2. n. A native variety of taro. Also *moi.* (HP 33, Whitney.) 3. n. A variety of sweet potato.

ne'e.ne'eu. 1. Redup. of *ne'eu.* See ex., *wahi 2.* 2. Stative verb showing superlative or comparative degree. *Ua ne'ene'eu a'e ka nui o kēia i'a i kēlā,* this fish is somewhat larger than that one.

ne'e.papa. vs. To move as a whole or unit; moving or working together in unison; spreading all over, as a lava flow or vine; combined, united; swarming; flank movement. *Ne'epapa ka hana,* joint action. *Ne'epapa ka ulu 'ana o ka maunaloa,* the *maunaloa* vine spreads everywhere. *Ne'epapa ka naonao,* swarming ants. *He hō'ike ne'epapa,* a joint report.

ne'e.pū. vi. **1.** To move together. **2.** Sitting with one leg crossed the other, as in certain ancient religious ceremonies. *Rare.*

ne'eu. vi. To move, budge. *'A 'ohe ne'eu mai ke kāhea 'ia aku,* doesn't budge when called. *A kahi ho'i ka ne'eu o ko'u oho* (song), never before has my scalp had such a creepy sensation.

nehe. 1. vi. To rustle, as leaves or the sea; rumbling; groping with the hands, as in searching. *Nehe lani,* rumbling of thunder in the sky. **2.** n. Taffeta, so called because it rustles *(nehe). Nehe lau,* brocaded taffeta. **3.** Same as *kī nehe (Bidens pilosa);* young plants, just before flowering, are cooked for tea. Also *kī, kī pipili.* Cf. *ko'oko'olau 2.* **4.** n. Native shrubs and herbs *(Lipochaeta* spp.) in the daisy family, with yellow flowers. (Neal 840.) **5.** n. Some kinds of pond scums *(Spirogyra* spp.), fine fresh-water algae, consisting of rows of single-celled filaments, each cell containing ribbonshaped spirals. Also *limu kala wai, līpala'ō, līpālāwai, pala'ō, pālāwai.*

nehe.kū. nvi. Gaseous condition of the digestive tract, occasionally audible; to belch.

nehe.nehe. Redup. of *nehe 1.*

nehe.nu'u. n. Sound of lightning striking. *Rare.*

nehi. vs. Rotten, moldy, spoiled, as food.

nehine.hā.uli. n. Mouse-eared chickweed, a small-leafed weedy herb *(Cerastium vulgatum),* from Europe. *Lit.,* dark *nehine.*

nehi.nei. loc. n. Yesterday (usually preceded by locative particle *i* and not an article; Gram. 8.6). *I nehinei a i kēia lā aku,* day before yesterday.

nehiwa. nvi. Play language, and to use the play language with order of syllables of most words reversed, as *nehiwa* from *wahine,* or as in this example: *'ohe u'o kemakema iā e'o,* for *'a'ohe o'u makemake iā 'oe,* I don't like you. Also *wehiwa.*

nehoa. Var. of *nahoa.*

nehu. n. Anchovy, a fish *(Stolephorus purpureus),* used for eating and to chum bonito. This name may be qualified by the terms *kū lani, maoli, pāki'i, pala.* See ex., *pō'ie'ie.*

nehu.nehu. Same as *lehulehu.*

nei. 1. nvi. To rumble, as an earthquake; sighing, soughing, as of the wind; indistinct sound, as of distant shouting. See ex., *nākolo. Nei akula ka 'aha le'ale'a no kēia po'e wāhine, no ke 'ano 'ē o kō lākou kapa* (Laie 491), the pleasure gathering was in an uproar about the women and the strangeness of their tapa. **ho'o.nei.** Caus/sim. **2.** Same as *kō'ele'ele,* a seaweed; according to Reed 116, same as *limu uaua loli.* **3.** Demon. occurring in several positions with several meanings. *Nei* may be considered a part of the present tense verb marker *ke* (verb) *nei* (see *ke . . . nei* and Gram. 5.3), and of the sequence *ua* (noun) *nei,* this aforementioned noun (see *ua . . . nei* and Gram. 8.3.4). After directionals and some nouns, *nei* may indicate past time (Gram. 7.2, 8.3.2): *hele mai nei nō 'oia,* he came here. *I ka pō nei,* last night. *Kēia pule aku nei,* last week. Following nouns and pronouns, *nei* means 'this' and may indicate affection, as in the common sequences *Hawai'i nei,* this [beloved] Hawai'i, and *e ia nei* or *e i nei,* you [beloved] who are here. Preposed *nei* seems to carry both favorable and pejorative emotional connotations: *nei 'āina,* this [fine] land, *nei ma'i 'o ka lepela,* this [horrible] disease, leprosy. (Gram. 8.3.2.) (PPN *ni,* PNP *nei.*)

ne'i. 1. Rare var. of *ne'e.* **2.** loc. n. Here, this place, local (often preceded by *i, ma, o;* cf. *'ane'i, 'one'i,* Gram. 8.6). *Nā kānaka lawai'a o ne'i nei,* the fishermen of this

place; the local fishermen. *No ne'i ka'u huaka'i,* my journey will be to this place.

neia, nē.ia, ne'ia. Demon. similar to *kēia,* this, but mostly Biblical. (Gram. 8.3.5.) *O neia manawa,* of this time.

ne'i.kū. n. Avalanche, rapid fall with great momentum. *He ikaika hiliau ka lani o ka ne'ikū* (For. 6:381), the royal chief is strong in devious ways, swift in movement.

nei.nei. Redup. of *nei 1,* to rumble, quake.

ne'i.ne'i. 1. Same as *ne'ene'e 1. Rare.* **ho'o.ne'i.ne'i.** Caus/sim. **2.** vs. Short, small, as clothes; low-lying, squatting; crowded; to shrink, a small bit. *Ke hele ne'ine'i ka,* walking with very short steps. *Ne'ine'i ka hanu,* short of breath. *Ne'ine'i ka mea i loa'a,* not much obtained. **ho'o.ne'i.ne'i.** Caus/sim. **3.** Same as *na'ena'e 1,* shrubs or small trees.

neke. 1. n. A fern *(Cyclosorus interruptus)* found in many tropical countries, somewhat like the *kikawaiō,* but only half as large. **2.** Rare var. of *nakeke.*

Nekelo, Negero. n. Negro. *Eng.*

neki. 1. n. Great bulrush. Also *'aka'akai, nānaku.* (Neal 88.) **2.** vs. Full, crowded, packed. *Rare.* **3.** vs. Awkward, unskillful, ignorant. *Rare.*

neko. vs. Dirty, filthy; vile-smelling, as perspiration. Cf. *'eko, weko.* **ho'o.neko.** To make dirty, soil.

neko.neko. Redup. of *neko.*

neku'e. vi. To rub back and forth, as the elbow *(ku'eku'e);* angry *(rare).* Cf. *naku'e.*

nele. nvs. Lacking, destitute, deprived, needy, wanting, deficient, without; to need; deficit (sometimes followed by a negative without change of meaning: *nele nā kānaka i ke kumu 'ole,* the people lack a teacher [*lit.,* the people are lacking because no teacher]). Cf. *hakanele, kā 1,* and ex., *goose. He nele 'āina auane'i kākou, e nānā aku ai i kāna,* so we'll be lacking land and have to pay attention to what he says [sarcastic]. **ho'o.nele.** To deprive, make destitute; to deny, impeach. *Ka ho'onele i ke kanaka i kekahi mau pono,* the forfeiture by the individual of some rights. *Ho'onele 'ia lāua i ka 'ai* (Nak. 102), they lacked food. (PEP *ngele.*)

nele.au. n. The native Hawaiian sumach *(Rhus sandwicensis,* synonyms *R. semilata* var. *sandwicensis* and *R. chinensis* var. *sandwicensis)* a shrub or small tree, with light, soft, tough wood. (Neal 525-6.) Also *neneleau.*

nelu. Same as *nenelu.*

nelu.nelu. Same as *nenelu.*

nema. nvt. Criticizing; critical; to criticize, find fault, censure. Cf. *ka'anema.* **ho'o.nema.** Same as above.

nema.nema. Redup. of *nema;* to belittle. See *hula nemanema.*

nemo. vs. Smooth, smoothly polished, slick; rounded smooth, bare. **ho'o.nemo.** To polish, smooth. *Ho'onemo ka wai i ka pōhaku,* the water wears the stone smooth.

nemo.nemo. Redup. of *nemo;* sleek. *Nemonemo ka pua'a i Hā'upu, e ha'i mai ana he lā mālie* (chant), bare of clouds is Hā'upu, telling us it is a calm day.

nena. Same as *kīpūkai,* a prostrate herb.

nena.nena. Var. of *lenalena. Nenanena 'auwae,* yellowed jaws (insult to old men).

nene. 1. vi. To stir, show animation, move, as a fledgling. Cf. *nenene.* **ho'o.nene.** Caus/sim. **2.** Var. of *manene 1. Wai-o-ka-nene* (name of a stream at Wai-'anae, O'ahu), water of the cooling sensation. (PCP *nene.*) **3.** n. A kind of shellfish.

nē.nē. 1. nvi. To chirp, as a cricket; to croak, as a mudhen; crying, as in distress; whimpering, as a sleeping infant; rumor, gossip; to be attracted to; to cherish, think of, as with affection. Cf. *hōnēnē; nē,* fretting; *nēnē hiwa. 'O nā kānaka Hawai'i, he po'e make'e haku, he po'e nēnē 'ili kapu,* the Hawaiian people are people who cherish their lords, people constantly thinking of the sacred skin [of chiefs]. **ho'o.nē.nē.** Same as above. *Ho'onēnē kaua* (FS 139), rumors of war, talk or threats of war. **2.** n. Hawaiian goose *(Nesochen sandvicensis),* protected and rare on Maui and in Hawaiʻi uplands (down to 40 at one time and about 1,000 in 1978). **3.** n. Mat pattern: two vertical rows of triangles, with the bases below, and the apices touching the bases above. **4.** n. A variety of *ʻawa,* stems green with dark-green spots. Also *kuaʻea.* **5.** Same as *ʻai-a-ka-nēnē,* a plant. (Neal 803.) **6.** Probably same as *nēnē ʻau kai.*

nē.nē ʻau kai. n. Sea gull, rarely seen, so named because of its resemblance to the Hawaiian goose, *nēnē. Lit.,* sea-travelling goose. *Na ka Pueo-kahi ke aloha, nēnē ʻau kai o Maui* (song), greeting to the Pueo-kahi [ship], seafaring gull of Maui.

nenea. Var. of *nanea.*

neneʻe. Redup. of *neʻe,* but less used than *neʻeneʻe;* low-growing, spreading, creeping, as a ground vine.

nenehe. Redup. of *nehe 1.*

nē.nē hiwa. vs. Prized, beloved, precious. *He nēnē pūlama ʻia, he nēnē hiwa i ka manaʻo* (chant), a cherished beloved one, precious to think of.

nene.hū. vs. Warped, bent out of shape. Cf. *hū,* swollen.

Nē.nē.hua-ka-wā.wae. n. Star name (no data). (Kuhelani.)

Nē.nē.hua Kea. n. Star name (no data). (Kuhelani.)

Nē.nē.hua Uli. n. Star name (no data). (Kuhelani.)

nenei. Same as *nanai.*

neneke. 1. vs. Shuffling, scratching, thumping sound; to sound thus. **2.** Same as *nanaka.*

nē.nē.leʻa. n. Joyous, gladness.

nenele.au. Same as *neleau.* (KL line 102.)

nenelu. nvs. Flabby fat; soft, as fine, worked-up soil (see ex., *mehelu*); boggy, marshy, springy, swampy; mire, bog, marsh; soft plumpness.

nenene. 1. nvi. Fluttering the wings; contracting the muscles, flexing the muscles, as preparing for exercise. **2.** Redup. of *nene 2.*

nene.nepu. Plural of *nenepu.*

nenepu. Redup. of *nepu.*

nenewa. Redup. of *newa.*

nene.wai. n. A variety of sweet potato.

nenewe. Redup. of *newe.*

neno. vt. To question repeatedly.

nenu. Var. of *nūnū 3.*

nenue, nenuwe. n. **1.** Chub fish, also known as rudder or pilot fish *(Kyphosus bigibbus, K. vaigiensis).* This name may be qualified by the terms *eleʻele, kea, pāʻīʻiʻi, pākiʻikiʻi, uli.* Also *nanue, enenue, manaloa.* See *hoe nenue.* (PNP *nenue.*) **2.** Var. of *nanue,* seaweed. **3.** A paddle with a broad blade. *Rare.*

neo. nvs. Empty, bare, desolated; nothing, naught; failing, getting nowhere. *Ahu ka neo!* A heap of nothing! Nothing gained or worth anything at all. *Kahi a ka neo,* place of nothing [nothing gained, obtained]. **hoʻo.neo.** To lay waste, devastate, make destitute; desolation; turning to naught.

neo.neo. Redup. of *neo;* to ravage; chaos. **hoʻo.ne-o.neo.** Redup. of *hoʻoneo.* (Oihk. 26:32) *Aia ʻike ʻoukou i ka mea ʻino e hoʻoneoneo ai* (Mat. 24.15), when you see the abomination of desolation.

nepu. vs. Plump, full and round in flesh, bulging; swollen, as a stream. Cf. *nenelu.* **hoʻo.nepu.** To cause plumpness, swelling; plump.

nepue. Var. of *nepu.*

nepu.nepu. Redup. of *nepu;* chubby. *Nui nepunepu,* large and plump.

nē.ʻū. n. Cooked and unpounded taro; also *kalo paʻa, kuala, kūpuʻu.*

neʻu.neʻu. Same as *nepunepu. Rare.*

newa. 1. n. War club, cudgel, policeman's club; fluted stone, as held in the hand as a stone club; fluted stone inserted in one end of a war club or dagger, as the *pāhoa.* **2.** nvi. To reel, stagger; dizziness, vertigo; dizzy. **hoʻo.newa.** Caus/sim. (PCP *newa.*) **3.** *(Cap.)* A constellation, probably the Southern Cross.

newa.newa. Redup. of *newa 2.*

newe. 1. vs. Plump; filled out, full, as a pregnant

woman; billowy, as a cloud; moving, as a current. **2.** *(Cap.)* Var. of *Newa 3.*

Newe.newe. Same as *Newa 2.* (PCP *newenewe.*)

newe.newewe. 1. Redup. of *newe 1.* **2.** Exclamation of *maika* players as they cheer the rolling stone. **3.** n. A kind of fish (no data).

newewe. Same as *newenewewe.*

nia. vs. Smooth, round, bald; calm, as a smooth sea. *Poʻo nia,* bald head. **hoʻo.nia.** To make smooth and even, as in carving; to remove all vestige of vegetation. (PCP *nia.*)

-nia. pas/imp. suffix. See *ʻaihuenia, kuhinia, manoninia, walania,* Gram. 6.6.3. (PPN *-ngia.*)

niʻa. nvt. Malicious gossip or accusation; slanderous; to accuse falsely or by trapping, malign.

Nia.kala, Niagara. n. Niagara. *Eng.*

nia.nia. Redup. of *nia.* **hoʻo.nia.nia.** Caus/sim.

niʻa.niʻa. Redup. of *niʻa. E ʻimi ana e hopu i kekahi mea no loko mai o kona waha, i niʻaniʻa ai lākou iāia* (Luka 11.54), seeking to catch something from within his mouth with which they might accuse him.

nia.niape. 1. Redup. of *niape.* **2.** vs. Bending, arching.

nia.niau. Var. of *niniau.* **hoʻo.nia.niau.** Var. of *hoʻoniniau. Hoʻonianiau i ka naʻauao,* quiet, persistent pursuit of knowledge.

niʻa.niʻau. Same as *kupukupu. Niʻihau.* Cf. *ʻōkupukupu,* ferns.

nia.niele. Var. of *nieniele.*

nī.ao. 1. n. Edge, as of a canoe (FS 143); groove; rim, as of a bowl. (PCP *ni(i)ao.*) **2.** nvi. Mewing, purring. **3.** nvi. Stretching up, as by one standing on tiptoe. **4.** n. Sharp edge of a knife blade.

niape. vs. Long, extended, as a pole. *Rare.*

niau. vi. Moving smoothly, swiftly, silently, peacefully; flowing or sailing thus; to pass on, glide. *He ʻale niau,* a moving billow. *Niau aku nei ma ka Penekia* (chant), swiftly sailing away on the Benicia. *Ua niau ke kapu,* the taboo has passed. **hoʻo.niau.** Following swiftly and silently; continuing; prolonging; copying, imitating. *Hoʻoniau akula ka makāula i kāna pule ʻana,* the prophet continued on and on with his prayer.

nī.ʻau. n. 1. Midrib of coconut leaf or frond; rib of an umbrella; coconut-leaf midrib or *ʻilima* rod used as a taboo marker at end of a *hālau;* groove. *Fig.,* tall, thin person. Cf. *akenīʻau.* (PCP *niikau.*) **2.** Ramrod. **3.** Billow. *Rare.* **4.** Diseases. See below.

nī.ʻau hō.lua. n. Name of a disease (no data).

nī.ʻau kā.hili. n. Broom made of coconut-leaf midribs tied together at one end. Also *pūpū nīʻau.*

nī.ʻau kani. n. A true jew's harp, made of a thin strip of wood, about 10 cm long and 2.5 cm wide, with a coconut midrib *(nīʻau)* or bamboo strip lashed lengthwise; played something like the *ʻūkēkē.* Ka-mehameha's return from Oʻahu to Hawaiʻi was called *ka nīʻau kani* because of the sound of the wind rustling the feathers of the many *kāhili* escorting him. Cf. *ʻūkēkē. Lit.,* sounding coconut midrib.

nī.ʻau.piʻo. n. Offspring of the marriage of a high-born brother and sister, or half-brother and half-sister. *Lit.,* bent coconut midrib, i.e., of the same stalk.

nī.ʻau pū.lumi. n. Broom straw. *Lit.,* broom *(Eng.)* coconut-leaf midrib.

nī.ʻau ʻū.kē.kē. Same as *nīʻau kani.*

nī.ʻau wā.wae kahi. Same as *kākaiawī,* a disease.

nie. 1. Short for *nīele. Nie au, Moala, ʻehia inu ʻawa* (PH 121)? I asked with curiosity, Moala, how many kawa drinkers? **2.** Var. of *nia.*

nī.ele. nvs. To keep asking questions; inquisitive, curious, plying with frivolous questions (often used in pejorative sense, as of a busybody asking things that do not concern him); to quiz, pump; question. As an exclamation of annoyance: you are too inquisitive! Who cares to answer your questions! **hoʻo.nī.ele.** Questioning, especially by leading up indirectly rather than directly; quizzing; curious; curiosity.

nie.nie. vs. Sheer and smooth, as a cliff. *Ka piʻina nienie o Haʻaheo,* the sheer ascent of Haʻaheo.

nie.niele. Redup. of *nīele;* to investigate.

niha. Same as *kamaniha,* cross.

niha.niha. Redup. of *niha.*

nī.heu. n. Fancy or unusual style of hair dressing.

nihi. 1. nvs. Edge, brink, rim, border; sideways, on edge, steep. Also *lihi.* Cf. *kūnihi.* (PPN *nifi.*) **2.** vs. Stealthily, quietly, softly, unobtrusively, carefully; creeping silently and softly, as on tiptoe; difficult or precarious of passage, as a trail along a precipice; circumspect, prudent, with careful observance of taboos, with discrimination. *Hele nihi,* to proceed with caution and diplomacy. *Noho nihi,* to act with caution, diplomacy. *E nihi ka hele i ka uka o Puna, mai ʻako i ka pua, o lilo i ke ala o ka hewahewa* (PH 31), circumspect (or prescribed) the voyage inland of Puna, do not pick flowers or be led to the paths of wrongness. (PCP *nifi.*) **nihia.** Pas/imp. of *nihi 2.*

nihina. Same as *nihi 1, 2. Nihina ka hele a ka makani,* the wind goes quietly.

nihi.nihi. Redup. of *nihi 1, 2;* fastidious, overly strict, finicky, decorous, dainty. Also *lihilihi.* See ex., *noho lihilihi. Lā nihinihi,* very severe taboo day. **hoʻo.nihi.-nihi.** Caus/sim. *ʻAi hoʻonihinihi,* to pick at food, as a finicky person; to eat with careful observance of taboos.

nihi.pali. n. A kind of fish (no data).

niho. 1. nvs. Tooth; toothed; nipper, as of an insect; octopus beak; Aristotle's lantern, of a sea urchin; claw, as of crab; tusk; stones set interlocking, as in a wall; biting, of the teeth; cog. See *niho-manō. Mai hana wale aku ʻoe iā Keʻoi, he niho,* don't act indiscriminately toward Keʻoi, he has teeth! [He is dangerous, as in sorcery.] *Nā niho o kāna pale kaua* (Ioba 15.26), the bosses of his bucklers. *Puka ka niho o Laʻa-kea,* Laʻa-kea is getting his teeth. *Hoʻonoho niho ʻia,* the stones are set [as in a fence]. **hoʻo.niho.** To lay stones interlocking; to set stones, as in a fence. (PPN *nifo.*) **2.** n. Tapa or mat patterns, always followed by qualifiers; see below.

nihoa. 1. Pas/imp. of *niho;* toothed, serrated, notched, jagged, sharp; firmly imbedded and interlocked, as stones in a fence. *Nihoa ka pali,* toothed is the cliff. **2.** *(Cap.)* n. Name of an island between Kauaʻi and Midway. See saying, *pākū.*

niho ʻaki. n. Front teeth, incisors; nippers of insects. *Lit.,* biting teeth.

niho ʻawa. n. Poisonous fang or tooth, as of a centipede.

niho ʻele.pani. n. Elephant tusk, ivory (Hoik. 18.12).

niho hoʻo.komo. n. False tooth. Also *niho kuʻi.*

niho huʻi. nvs. Toothache; having a toothache.

niho kahi. nvs. Single-toothed, having one tooth remaining; a general term for old age.

niho kaʻi. n. **1.** Aching tooth or teeth. *Lit.,* leading tooth, i.e., it draws the attention. **2.** Stones set in a row, as in a fence.

niho keu. n. Protruding, uneven tooth. *Lit.,* extra tooth.

niho kī.lou. n. Claws of a crab. *Lit.,* hook tooth.

niho.kō.maka. n. A kind of fish (no data).

niho kuʻi. n. False tooth. Also *niho hoʻokomo.*

niho lena. nvs. Yellow tooth; yellow-toothed, said derisively of the old.

niho-liʻi.liʻi. n. A tapa design. *Lit.,* small teeth or notches.

niho-manō. n. A tapa design. *Lit.,* shark tooth.

niho mau.ole. n. Worn teeth, a figurative term for a chief who has outlived his usefulness. (Malo 201, Emerson note.) A class of chiefs. (AP.)

niho mole. nvs. Gap in a row or series, as left by a missing tooth; notch; worn smooth, as teeth of a saw. *He iʻa lapuwale, he pāpaʻi niho mole* (hula song), a worthless sea creature, a crab with missing claw.

niho naue. n. Loose tooth.

niho.niho. nvs. Set with teeth, as a saw; toothed, notched, jagged, serrated; scalloped, as lace; scalloped,

as potatoes; scallops, notches. Cf. *huila nihoniho.* **hoʻo.niho.niho.** To make into a toothed, scalloped, notched design; to make teeth; to carve an irregular notched edge. (PPN *nifonifo.*)

niho ʻoki. n. Shark's-tooth knife, as used for wood carving and cutting hair. *Lit.,* cutting tooth.

niho palaoa. n. Whale tooth, whale-tooth pendant, a symbol of royalty.

niho peku. n. New tooth appearing in the gums; bud shooting from the ground (Malo 199).

niho pō.haku. n. Interlocking stones (see *niho*). *Pau i ka nōhāhā nā niho pōhaku i pani ʻia* (For. 5:513), the interlocking stones that had dammed [the stream] were torn apart.

niho.popo. n. A variety of sweet potato.

niho popo. n. Decayed tooth.

niho puaʻa. n. Pig tusk, especially that worn as an ornament. *Fig.* young ʻawa sprout.

niho.puʻu. n. A taro cultivar. (TC 4.)

niho puʻu. n. Buckteeth.

niho-wili-hemo. n. Design on Niʻihau mats consisting of a series of pointed notches, called *kulipuʻu* elsewhere. *Lit.,* twisting loose tooth.

niʻi. vs. Salt-encrusted, as one exposed to sun and sea. Cf. *uāniʻi.*

Niʻihau. n. **1.** Name of one of the Hawaiian Islands; an inhabitant of Niʻihau Island. See saying, *kīkū.* **2.** *(Not cap.)* A variety of *uhi,* yam.

nika. 1. nvs. Nigger, black, blackness, blackened; a term of derision for a marble player who misses a shot. *Eng.* See ex., *kūloku. Keaka nika,* minstrel show. **2.** Same as *māikoiko,* a variety of sugar cane. **3.** n. A variety of sweet potato; sometimes qualified by the terms *ʻeleʻele, keʻokeʻo, nui.* Also *pāʻele.*

nike.lake, niterate. n. Nitrate. *Eng.*

niki. 1. Var. of *ʻiniki,* to pinch. **2.** Same as *nīkiʻi.*

nī.kiʻi. vt. To tie, as a rope or knot (For. 4:259). Also *hī-kiʻi, hīkiʻikiʻi, mūkiʻi, mūkiʻikiʻi, nākiʻi, nākiʻikiʻi, niki, nikiniki.*

nī.kiʻi.kiʻi. Redup. of *nīkiʻi,* to tie.

Nī.kine. n. Nicene. *Eng.* See ex., *manaʻoʻiʻo.*

niki.niki. 1. Redup. of *niki 1, 2.* **2.** n. Membrane binding the intestines, peritoneum. Cf. *maka ʻupena. He mōhai i kaumaha ʻia ma ke ahi iā Iēhowa, ka maka ʻupena e uhi ana ka naʻau, a me ka nikiniki apau ma ka naʻau* (Oihk. 3.3), an offering made by fire to Jehovah, the fat that covers the intestines, and all the membrane with the intestines.

niki o na ʻaka. n. Jester, clown; clowning.

niki.paʻu. vs. Wilted, scorched, as with heat. *Rare.*

niku. 1. vs. Dirty, smelly, filthy. **hoʻo.niku.** To soil, make dirty. *He keu ʻoe a ke keiki hoʻoniku ʻaʻahu,* never was a child like you for getting clothes dirty and smelly. **2.** Also **nisu.** n. Hawk. (Oihk. 11.16.)

niku.niku. Redup. of *niku 1.*

nilea. Same as *nīnole.*

nile.kai, nilegai. n. Nilgai, antelope. *Eng.*

nilu. nvs. Admirable, fine. *He nilu ke ʻikena aku,* admirable to behold.

nina. 1. Same as *lina 1. Waha nina,* soft mouth [said of a finicky eater]. **2.** n. A variety of taro. (HP 33.)

nina.nina. Redup. of *nina 1.*

nina.ninau. Redup. of *nīnau;* to examine.

nī.nau. nvt. Question; to ask a question, inquire, interrogate; interrogation, query. Cf. *noi,* to ask for something. *He nīnau wāhi pūniu,* a question that cracks the skull [a difficult question]. **hoʻo.nī.nau.** To ask a question; to have questions asked; to ask indirectly.

nī.nau.ele. Same as *nīele. Rare.*

nī.nau hoʻi. n. Cross-examination, as of a witness. *Lit.,* return question.

nī.nau hō.ʻike. n. Interrogation, usually oral; quiz, examination; catechism. *Lit.,* revealing questions.

nī.nau kupa.paʻu. n. One who consults the dead or familiar spirits (Isa. 8.19); necromancer. *Lit.,* corpse question.

nī.nau pili hoʻo.mana. n. Catechism (Protestant). *Lit.,* questions concerning religion.

nī.nau ʻuhane. nv. One with familiar spirits, necromancer; to speak through familiar spirits (Oihk. 19.31). *Lit.,* soul asking.

nini. 1. nvt. Ointment, balm; to apply ointment; to pour, spill. (PPN *lingi.*) **2.** Same as *lili,* jealous. **3.** n. Fence, line of stones; pavement. Cf. *pānini.* **4.** Same as *ninini,* to pour. (PPN *lingi.*)

ninia. Pas/imp. of *nini 1.*

nini.au. 1. Redup. of *niau. Niniau ke kahe o ka wai,* swiftly silent flowing of the water. **hoʻo.nini.au.** Redup. of *hoʻoniau. Ka hoʻoniniau ʻana iā Lohiʻau,* pursuit of Lohiʻau. **2.** vi. To droop, as a flower. *Niniau, ʻeha ka pua o ke koaiʻe* (UL 68), the *koaiʻe* flower droops, injured.

niniha. Redup. of *niha.*

ninihi. Same as *nihinihi. Ka lalawe ninihi launa ʻole* (song), quiet taking over, unsurpassed.

nini.hua. nvs. Resentment; resentful. **hoʻo.nini.hua.** Caus/sim.

nī.nika. 1. Same as *pūkāmole.* **2.** Same as *ʻīnika,* a plant.

nini.kea. n. White tapa, as worn by priests during ceremonies.

niniki. Redup. of *niki 1. Ka niniki makani o Kāne-hoa* (chant), the wind piercing of Kāne-hoa.

ninini. Redup. of *nini 1, 2;* to cast, as a solid from liquid (1 Nal. 7.37). *Ninini wai,* to water. (PPN *lilingi.*)

nini.nia. Pas/imp. of *ninini.*

nini.nini. Redup. of *nini 1.*

niniʻo. Same as *ʻōniʻoniʻo,* spotted, streaked. **hoʻo.nini.ʻo.** Caus/sim.

nini.ole. n. A fish. (And.; cf. Malo text, chapter 15, section 8.)

ninipo. Redup. of *nipo 1, 2. Nipo ninipo i ke aloha lā, ka wuhine huʻulewa, huʻulewa i ke kai* (song), yearning, longing for love is the woman swaying, swaying by the sea.

nini.polo. Redup. of *nīpolo 1, 2. Rare.*

niniu. Redup. of *niu 2;* to spin; worried, sad; dizzy; dizziness, vertigo, unclear or blurred vision; blurred, indistinct. *Niniu hele,* to spin forward, as a *kilu* piece. *Niniu Puna pō i ke ʻala,* Puna is dizzy and thick with fragrance. **hoʻo.nini.niu.** To cause dizziness; to spin, as a top. (PPN *liliu.*)

nī.nole. 1. vs. Weak, as an infant; swaying, bending, as a plant; pliable. Cf. *mīnole. ʻO ka haki pua nīnole* (song), breaking the pliant flower. **2.** n. Name of a crustacean said to resemble lobster (no data).

nio. Same as *kē,* to criticize. (Malo 140.)

niʻo. 1. nv. Highest point, pinnacle; to reach the summit. Cf. *noho niʻo. ʻO ʻoe a ʻo wau kau i ka niʻo,* you and I shall reach the highest point. *Kū i ka niʻo,* to reach the pinnacle, as of achievement or accomplishment. **2.** n. Altar, as for hula. See *kuahu.* **3.** n. Doorway or threshold of a house, very taboo in ancient times. (Kep. 137.) **4.** Same as *ʻōniʻo,* spotted, streaked.

nī.oi. n. 1. Any kind of red pepper *(Capsicum annuum).* (Neal 741–2.) *Fig.,* a controversial or important problem. **2.** A tree *(Eugenia* sp.). Its wood was said to be poisonous only from trees at Mauna Loa, Molokaʻi. See *kālai pāhoa, kauila.*

nī.oi ʻalu.ʻalu. Same as *nīoi pūhaʻuhaʻu. Lit.,* loose.

nī.oi kā.maka.hala. n. A chili pepper *(Capsicum annuum* cv. *ʻabbreviatum')* that is nearly round and about 2.5 cm in length. (Neal 742.)

nī.oi lei. n. A kind of red pepper, with red, cherry-shaped fruits, used for leis. Possibly some kind of cherry pepper *(Capsicum annuum* cv. *ʻcerasiforme').* (Neal 742.)

nī.oi līpoa. n. A small variety of hot chili pepper. *Lit.,* seaweed *nīoi.*

nī.oi loloa. n. The long, narrow, hot chili pepper. *Lit.,* long *nīoi.*

nī.oi niho puaʻa. n. A chili pepper about 8 or 10 cm long and curved like a hog's tusk. *Lit.,* hog-tusk *nīoi.*

nī.oi nunui. n. Large peppers, much liked by Hawaiians in relishes. *Lit.,* big *nīoi.*

nī.oi pekela (betela). n. Betel nut. *Eng.*

nī.oi pepa. n. Chili pepper *(Capsicum annuum* cv. *ʻlongum'),* grown for its hot, peppery-tasting fruits, which are red, narrow, 7.5 cm long or more. (Neal 742.)

nī.oi pū.ʻalu.ʻalu. Same as *nīoi pūhaʻuhaʻu.*

nī.oi pū.haʻu.haʻu. n. The bell or sweet pepper *(Capsicum annuum* cv. *ʻgrossum')* with large mild-flavored fruits which are eaten when green. (Neal 742.) *Lit.,* puffed. Also *nīoi ʻaluʻalu, nīoi pūʻaluʻalu.*

nioke. n. Ebbing, receding, of the tide. (Kep. 103.)

niole. vi. To eat without relish; to pick at food without appetite. *Rare.* Cf. *mīnole.*

nī.ʻole. vs. Toothless. *(Nī* is short for *niho.)*

niolo. vs. **1.** Upright, straight; stately; tall and straight as a tree without branches; sharply peaked, as mountains. *Fig.,* righteous, correct. **2.** Drowsy, sleepy.

niolo.pua. 1. vs. Handsome. *He kanaka niolopua,* a handsome person. **2.** *(Cap.)* n. The god of sleep. *Fig.,* sleep. See ex., *ʻoni 1. Ua laʻi me Niolopua,* peaceful with Niolopua [sleep]. *Ua kui lima akula au me Niolopua,* I went off hand-in-hand with Niolopua [went to sleep]. *Hoʻi akula e moe i ka moe a Niolopua,* return to sleep the sleep of Niolopua [death].

nī.peʻa. vt. To tie or bind together. *Kauaʻi.*

nipo. vs. **1.** To yearn for; to be in love with; to love, desire, long for. See ex., *ninipo.* **hoʻo.nipo.** To make love, court, woo, yearn for. *ʻO ka holu nape a ka lau o ka niu, hoʻonipo ana lā i ke ehu kai* (song), swaying dipping of the coconut leaves, making love in the sea spray. **2.** Drowsy, languid, sleepy. **hoʻo.nipo.** To cause sleepiness, make drowsy. *E hoʻonipo ʻia ana e ka hiamoe iki,* made drowsy by a light sleep.

nipoa. 1. Pas/imp. of *nipo 1, 2. He iʻa ua nipoa i ka ʻauhuhu,* a fish drugged by *ʻauhuhu* poison [a victim of sorcery]. **2.** *(Cap.)* nvs. Nippon; Japanese.

nī.polo. 1. vt. To drum and chant at the same time. *Rare.* **2.** vs. Sick, weak. *Rare.* Cf. *nipo 2.*

Nī.pona. nvs. Nippon; Japanese. *Eng.*

nipo.nipo. Redup. of *nipo 1, 2.*

nī.puʻu. Same as *hīpuʻu,* to tie knots. *Nīpuʻu paʻa ʻia me ʻoe, ke aloha o kāua* (song), bound fast to you is our love.

nī.puʻu.puʻu. Redup. of *nīpuʻu;* knotted, knotty.

niu. 1. n. The coconut *(Cocos nucifera),* a common palm in tropical islands of the Pacific and warm parts of eastern Asia; coconut meat or oil. Hawaiians used all parts of the tree.(Neal 119–21.) Coconut water and coconut cream (the white liquid squeezed from ripe-grated coconuts) were both called *wai niu* and *wai o ka niu.* In For. 5:596 *niu ā wali* was translated 'milk of the coconut'. *Niu moe o Kala-pana,* the supine coconut palm of Kala-pana. [Young trees went bent over and made to grow crookedly, in order to commemorate great events; two of such trees were at Kala-pana in 1950.] *Ē niu, ē kūlolo,* O coconut, O coconut pudding [said of one who talks too much; see *niu kūlolo*]. (PPN *niu.*) **2.** vs. Spinning, whirling, dizzy. Cf. *niniu, niua, niuniu,* make ulu niu. (PPN *liu.*)

niua. Pas/imp. of *niu 2,* with connotations of *niuniu, niniu. Ua niua nā maka,* eyes were fascinated (also used unfavorably in 2 Pet. 2.14: *Ua niua nā maka i nā wāhine moekolohe,* eyes made dizzy [or shocked] by adulterous women). **hoʻo.niua.** To cause to spin, whirl, stir. *He kaʻao hoʻoniua puʻuwai no Kamiki,* a heart-stirring story about Kamiki. (PPN *liua.*)

niu ʻā.kaʻa. Var. of *niu ʻōkaʻa.*

ni.ua.ua. vs. Somewhat dizzy; sad, unlucky. Cf. *niua.*

niu haku. n. Sprouting coconut.

niu hao.hao. See *haohao 2.*

niuhi. n. Man-eating shark, *Carcharodon carcharias;* any Hawaiian shark longer than 3.5 m is probably a *niuhi.* Catching *niuhi* was the game of chiefs; it was a dangerous sport and special techniques were used. Its flesh was taboo to women. See ex., *holopapa 2, kāpapa 2.* (PPN *n(a,e)ufi,* PEP *niufi.*)

niu hiwa. n. A variety of coconut, with husk of fruit dark green when mature and shell black. Used ceremonially, medicinally, and for cooking. (HP 190.) *Lit.,* dark.

niu hua lau. n. A variety of coconut, with very numerous small, sweet fruits. *Lit.,* coconut with many fruit.

niu ka'a. Same as *niu 'ōka'a.*

niu kahiki. n. Date palm. *Lit.,* foreign coconut.

niu kuli. n. A disease characterized by loss of hearing and dizziness, perhaps Ménière's disease. *Lit.,* dizzy [and] deaf.

niu kū.lolo. interj. Stop talking! See *niu 1. Lit.,* coconut-pudding.

niu lelo. n. A variety of coconut with fruit reddish and shell yellow, used in many ways, but not ceremonially or medicinally. (HP 190.) *Lit.,* yellow coconut.

niu lolo.ka'a. 1. Same as *niu 'ōka'a.* **2.** n. Dizziness.

niu malo'o. n. Copra, dry coconut meat.

niu.niu. 1. vs. Rich, oily, as fat food. **2.** Same as *niniu;* unlucky, unfortunate. *He niuniu ka'u i nehinei,* I had bad luck yesterday. *Ua ho'omā'ona wau i nā 'uhane apau i niuniu* (Ier. 31.25), I have replenished every sorrowful soul.

niu 'ō.ka'a. n. Shriveled, dry coconut meat separated from the shell; a nut with loose meat. *Lit.,* rolling coconut.

niu Pola.pola. n. A variety of coconuts with large nuts. *Lit.,* Borabora or Tahitian coconut.

no. prep. Of, for, because of, belonging to, in behalf of, honoring, to, for, from, resulting from, concerning, about. See *na* and Gram. 9.11. *He mele no ka lani,* a song for the chief. *He lio no Pua,* a horse for Pua. *No laila lākou?* They are from there? (PCP *no(o).*)

nō. 1. nvi. Seepage; to leak, ooze, seep, sink. **2.** n. Fifth note on the musical scale, so. **3.** intensifying part. Very, quite, fairly, anyway. (Gram. 7.5.) *Maika'i nō,* quite good, very good, fairly good. *'Oia nō,* so that's it; that's so. *Ua 'ike nō 'oe,* you do know. *Inā maopopo 'ole, kākau nō,* if [you] don't understand, write anyway. (PCP *noo.*)

nō-, no-. Stative prefixes. Gram. 6.3.2.

noa. 1. nvs. Freed of taboo, released from restrictions, profane; freedom. *Lā noa,* weekday. *He ali'i noa au loa,* a chief who frees [his people] from taboo for a long time. **ho'o.noa.** To cause to cease, as a taboo; to free from taboo; to repeal, revoke; to adjourn, as a meeting; to prostitute, as one's daughter (Oihk. 19.29). *Ua wehe 'ākea 'ia ka noa o nā wahi apau o ke kūlanakauhale,* the restrictions on all parts of the city were opened up completely. (PPN *noa.*) **2.** n. Commoner; formerly, the offspring of the marriage of a *pi'o, naha,* or *nīaupi'o* aristocrat with a person without rank or possibly of *papa* rank.

no'a. 1. n. Stone or small piece of wood used in the games of *pūhenehene* and *no'a.* **2.** nv. A game in which the *no'a* was hidden under bundles of tapa and the players guessed where it was; to play this game. *Fig.,* secret thoughts or plans. (Malo 225–6.) **3.** vs. Colored, as color streak in pearl shell. Cf. *no'eno'e.*

nō.'ā. vs. Constantly burning, of fire; unquenchable, as a volcano; dried up, as land in drought. See ex., *no'ao. Ke nō'ā lā i ka uka o Hāmākua* (FS 285), raging fire inland of Hāmākua. **ho'o.nō.'ā.** To cause a burning.

noa.noa. Same as *noa 2. Kahuna noanoa,* a priest not of high rank.

-noanoa. ho'o.noa.noa. To free from taboo.

no'ao. nvs. Fiery, hot; heat. *'O Kauhola-nui ke kapuahi no'ao, nō'ā wela i ke kapu* (chant), Kauhola-nui the hot fire place, burning hot with taboo.

no'a pahe'e. n. Game in which *no'a* pebbles were pitched as quoits. *Lit.,* sliding *no'a.*

noe. 1. nvi. Mist, fog, vapor, rain spray; to form a mist; to settle gently as mist (poetic); misty. *Ua noe,* misty rain. *Noe ke 'ala o ka lehua,* misty is the fragrance of

the *lehua. Noe wale mai nō ke aloha i ku'u lei a'u i haku ai,* love alights like mist over the lei I have woven. (Perhaps PEP *ngo'e;* cf. Easter *ngo'e.*) **2.** *(Cap.)* n. A rare name for the northeast tradewind *(Moa'e).*

no'e. Same as *no'eno'e.*

no'e.au. vs. Clever, skillful, dexterous, wise, artistic, talented, expert, technical. *'Ōlelo no'eau,* wise or entertaining proverb, saying. *He wahine no'eau i ka haku lei hulu,* a woman skillful at making feather leis.

no'e.au ho'o.kele. n. Management, administrative skill.

no'e.au ho'o.kele wai.wai. n. Estate management, economics.

noe kolo. n. Creeping mist.

Noela. n. Noel. *Eng.*

noelo, nowelo. vt. To delve, seek, as for knowledge. *Noelo i ka pili 'ao'ao* (song), seeking ways and means of being at [her] side. *Nāu i noi'i noelo aku, pau nā pali pa'a i ka 'ike 'ia* (chant for Ka-lā-kaua), you sought and searched for wisdom, all the solid cliffs were seen.

noe.noe. Redup. of *noe;* gray-haired; to feel foggy due to intoxication, befogged. *Ua pā kī'aha paha lā, ke noenoe mai nei,* maybe he's touched a glass, the one here who is so befogged. **ho'o.noe.noe.** Redup. of *ho'onoe.* Cf. *lā'au ho'onoenoe.*

no'e.no'e. vs. **1.** Printed, of tapa; colored. Cf. *kīhei 'a'ahu no'eno'e.* **2.** Quiet, sedate. *Noho mālie, like me ka hilu, he i'a no'eno'e,* sitting quietly like the *hilu,* a quiet fish.

nō.eo. Var. spelling of *nōweo,* bright.

noe.uahi. n. Haze, as after a volcanic eruption. *Lit.,* smoke mist.

noe 'ula. nvs. Pink mist, as that about the rainbow; redor sore-eyed, as from going in the sea. *Ka maka noe 'ula i ke kai,* eyes reddened by the sea.

nohā. Var. of *nahā.*

nohae. Var. of *nahae.*

nō.hae.hae. Var. of *nāhaehae.*

nō.hā.hā. Var. of *nāhāhā.* See ex., *niho pōhaku. Nōhāhā li'ili'i,* broken into bits.

nohea. nvs. Handsome, pretty, lovely, of fine appearance; a handsome or fine looking person. *He nohea 'oe i ku'u maka* (song), you are lovely in my eyes. (PPN *ngose.*)

no hea. interj. From where, whence.

nohe.nohea. 1. Redup. of *nohea* (UL 41). **2.** Same as *noenoe. I pō i ka uahi nohenohea i ka nahele* (prayer), darkened by the smoke spreading like fog in the forest.

nohe'o. Mischievous, mischief; rascal. (And.)

nohi. vs. Bright-colored, vivid, as the rainbow. Cf. *kīnohi.*

nohili. vs. Tedious, slow. Cf. *hili 2.*

nohi.nohi. Redup. of *nohi.*

noho. 1. n. Seat, chair, stool, bench, pew, saddle. *Noho kula,* golden throne. **2.** vt. To live, reside, inhabit, occupy (as land), dwell, stay, tarry, marry, sit, be in session; to be, act as; to rule or reign (usually but not always followed by a qualifier, as *noho moku,* to rule a district). *Noho 'ia,* inhabited. *Noho malihini,* to sojourn. *Ua noho ka 'aha,* the court is in session. *Noho me ka hau'oli,* to be happy. *Noho mālie,* to keep quiet, remain still. *Noho like,* to live in unity, with equal rights. *Noho 'olu'olu,* to live comfortably. *'O 'Olopana ke ali'i o ia wā e noho ana ma O'ahu nei* (FS 197), 'Olopana was the chief of this time ruling here on O'ahu. **ho'o.noho.** To take up residence; to install, establish, provide, seat, locate, arrange, pack, regulate, convey, carry, appoint; to place in authority; to set, as type. *Ho'onoho kahu,* installation of a pastor. *Ho'onoho i ka pākaukau,* to set a table. *Ho'onoho kēpau,* to set type. *Ho'onoho iwi,* to set bones; a bone setter. *Ho'onoho 'alu,* cf. *'alu. Mīkini ho'onoho hua pa'i palapala,* linotype machine. *He kānāwai e ho'onoho ana i aupuni,* an act to provide a government. (PPN *nofo.*) **3.** nvt. Possession of a medium by a spirit or god; possessed; to possess. *Akua noho,* god that possesses. *Ua noho ʻo Pele i luna o ʻAne,* Pele possessed Annie. **hoʻo.noho.** To summon a spirit to possess. (PPN *nofo.*) **4.** vs. A strong negative following *mai. Mai noho ʻoe ā kolohe i kaʻu mea hana,* don't you dare disturb my work.

-noho. hoʻo.noho. Bone hooks lashed together. (Malo 79.)

noho aliʻi. nvt. Throne, reign, chieftainship, tenure as chief, rule; to reign, act as chief.

noho aloha. nvs. Mercy seat (Heb. 9.5); on friendly terms; dwelling at peace; friendly relationship.

noho ʻā.mana. n. Pack saddle. *Lit.,* y-shaped crosspiece saddle.

noho ʻana. n. Conduct, bearing, deportment, treatment, condition, way of life, term of office, stay. *Kona noho ʻana,* his stay. *Pēlā nō ka noho ʻinoʻino ʻana o Hākau iā ʻUmi* (FS 125), such was the cruel treatment of Hākau to ʻUmi. *E holo ʻoe i Hawaiʻi e nānā ai i ka ʻāina, i ke kanaka, a me kō laila noho ʻana* (FS 183), go to Hawaiʻi, examine the land, the people, and the local way of life.

noho.anu. n. Native geraniums (*Geranium* spp.), shrubs and small trees found only at high altitudes in Hawaiʻi. They have small, ovate, green or silvery leaves, edged or tipped with teeth, and reddish or white flowers. *Lit.,* cold dwelling. Cf. *hinahina 4.*

noho au.puni. nvt. To rule; a reign, ruler. (FS 169.) *Nā lā o kona noho aupuni ʻana,* the days of his reign.

noho hale. nv. House occupant, owner, sitter, appointee, legatee; to act in such capacity; *fig.,* ashes. See ex., *ʻimi hale 1.*

noho hana ʻole. vi. To be unemployed, inactive; to sit alone.

noho hele. nvi. To sojourn briefly and then go on elsewhere; to travel with brief stopovers (FS 173).

noho hiki.kiʻi. n. Chair that tilts backward. (Kel. 136.)

noho hoʻo.hihi. n. Possession by a spirit that has taken a fancy (*hoʻohihi*) to the recipient, perhaps causing him to act strangely.

noho hoʻo.kolo.kolo. n. Judgment seat.

noho huila. n. Wheel chair.

nohoʻi. intensifying part. *(nō + hoʻi).* (Gram. 7.5.) *Auē nohoʻi,* Oh oh. *ʻO au nohoʻi,* really me.

noho kaʻa.wale. v. **1.** To live apart. See also *plural.*

noho ʻie. n. Wicker chair.

noho kai. nvi. Dweller on the seashore; to live by the sea.

noho kā.lele. n. Armchair.

noho kanaka. v. To serve under. *Ua nui ka poʻe Kauaʻi i hoʻopaʻa mai iā lākou iho e noho kanaka aku no Pākaʻa* (Nak. 27), many Kauaʻi people bound themselves as subjects of Pākaʻa.

noho kāne. v. To marry, of a woman; to live with a man.

noho kā.pae. nvi. Sidesaddle; to ride sidesaddle. *Fig.,* to have an illicit love affair. See also *kāpae.*

noho kapa.kahi. n. Sidesaddle.

noho keiki. v. To be a child.

noho kū. n. Straight chair.

noho lihi.lihi, noho ʻana nihi.nihi. nv. Strict way of life, rigid observance of taboos; rigid way of sitting during ceremonies; genteel deportment, etiquette; to observe proper decorum, circumspect conduct. (Kep. 125, 141.)

noho lio. n. Saddle.

Noho-loa. n. North Star.

noho loa. nvi. To remain long, permanently.

noho lō.ʻihi. 1. n. Bench, settee. **2.** vi. To stay long.

noho male. nv. To be married; wedlock.

noho male ʻole. nv. To remain unmarried; spinsterhood, bachelorhood.

noho.mā.lie. n. The yellow oleander or be-still tree (*Thevetia peruviana*), an ever-blooming shrub or small tree from tropical America, with long narrow leaves and yellow funnel-shaped flowers. All parts of the plant are poisonous to eat. (Neal 693.) *Lit.,* be still.

noho mā.lie. See *mālie.*

noho moe. n. Couch, divan.

nohona. n. Residence, dwelling, seat, mode of life, existence, relationship. *Nohona kuhina,* residence of the minister; embassy. *Nohona waʻa,* canoe thwart, seat. *Ua laʻi ka nohona,* life is peaceful. *He nohona kūʻēʻē kō ka makua kāne me ke keiki,* there is a strained relationship between father and son. (PEP *nofonga.*)

noho niʻo. n. A pretense to knowledge or skill; bluff, false front. Also *poupou noho niʻo,* which Emerson (Malo 73) translates 'tale-bearing'.

noho.noho. Redup. of *noho 2, 3.* **hoʻo.noho.noho.** Redup. of *hoʻonoho;* to pretend to be possessed by a spirit; to arrange, classify, organize. *Hoʻonohonoho hou,* to reorganize, rearrange. *Hoʻonohonoho papa,* to classify. *Hoʻonohonoho i nā noho,* to arrange the chairs. *Papa hoʻonohonoho kūlana hana,* classification board of positions. *Hoʻonohonoho ʻana,* arrangement, system. *Hoʻonohonoho hoʻolilo,* to plan or budget expenses. (PPN *nofonofo.*)

-nohonoho. hoʻo.noho.noho. A variety of yam *(uhi)* having tuber with white flesh and red skin; vine and its wings green, petiole red, veins of blade red and green.

-nohonoho helu. hoʻo.noho.noho helu. To calculate, compute, figure.

noho.noho.puʻu.one. Same as *hinahina 3.* Niihau.

noho ʻoi.hana. See *ʻoihana 1.*

noho ʻopi.ʻopi. n. Folding chair.

noho paʻa. vi. To live permanently; to settle down; to be established. **hoʻo.noho paʻa.** Caus/sim.

noho pai.pai. n. Rocking chair. *Hoʻoluli noho paipai,* to rock the rocking chair.

noho papa. 1. vs. Arranged in order, as feathers in a hatband, shingles on a roof; placed in rows or regular formation, as soldiers. **hoʻo.noho papa.** To arrange, put in order. *Hoʻonoho papa i ka ʻōlelo,* a talk thoroughly covering an entire subject. **2.** vi. To dwell in one place for generations.

noho poka.ʻa. n. Swivel chair.

noho polo.lei. vi. To sit properly, straight. *Noho pololei ʻole,* to sit improperly, slouch.

noho pono. nvi. Sitting properly, behaving well; moral deportment; morality.

noho.pū. vi. To live together, especially out of wedlock; to cohabit.

noho pū. vi. To sit quietly or dejectedly.

noho uka. nvi. Upland dweller; to live inland.

noho wahine. v. To marry, of a man; to live with a woman.

noho wale. vi. To do nothing; to be idle or inactive; to sit alone.

nohu. n. **1.** Scorpionfish (*Scorpaenopsis cacopsis* and other scorpaenids) with poisonous spines. The fish is edible. (PPN *nofu.*) **2.** A prostrate, hairy perennial *(Tribulus cistoides),* found on coasts of tropical regions around the world. It has spiny dry fruits, yellow five-petaled flowers; each leaf has about twelve leaflets. (Neal 477.) Also *nohunohu.* **3.** A native variety of taro. Also *nohu ʻeleʻele, mākoko.* See ex., *hanoa.* **4.** Soft, porous stone, used in scouring.

-nohu. hoʻo.nohu. (a) To scowl, frown. **(b)** To reef, as the sails of a ship. (AP.)

nohu.nohu. Same as *nohu 1, 2, 4.*

nohu ʻoma.kaha. n. Variety of *nohu (Scorpaenopsis diabolus).*

nohu pinao. Variety of *nohu. Lit.,* dragonfly *nohu.*

nohu poʻo lā.ʻau. n. Variety of *nohu;* it was believed that its eggs hatched into sharks. *Lit.,* wooden-headed *nohu.*

noi. nvt. To ask for something, request, solicit, appeal, apply, make a motion, move, propose, plea; proposal, request, petition, motion (in documents of the 1860s, often preceded by the article *ke*). Cf. *nīnau,* to ask a question, *noinoi, nonoi. Ka mea noi,* the applicant, petitioner. *Ma ka noi a Mr. Mahelona,* on motion of Mr. Mahelona. *Ke noi aku nei au i kou ʻoluʻolu,* I am asking a favor of you. *Noi haʻahaʻa,* to beg humbly, implore. *Noi mau,* to ask constantly, nag, importunate. ho'o.noi. Caus/sim. (PPN *no'i.*)

no'i.au. Var. of *no'eau. No'iau ka hoe a Ka-moho-ali'i* (PH x), skillful was the paddling of Ka-moho-ali'i

noi.ele. vs. Shaken, beaten, as by wind. *I noiele, i kā 'ia e ka Lawakua, niua loloka'a ke po'o o Hanalei* (chant), shaken, beaten by the Lawakua wind, the head of Hanalei [Valley] reels with dizziness.

noi hele. vi. Going about asking or begging from place to place.

noi'i. vi. To seek knowledge or information; to investigate; investigation, examination, research, searching for even the smallest detail. *'Auhau noi'i,* a tax on every last item. *Kōmike noi'i,* reference committee.

noi.'ina. n. Investigation, search, etc.

noi kū. vt. To ask rudely, abruptly, point-blank.

noili. Same as *no'eau. Rare.*

noi male (mare). nvt. Proposal of marriage; to propose marriage.

noi.noi. Redup. of *noi.*

no'i.no'i. 1. n. Young of *kawakawa,* bonito. Usually called *kīna'u.* **2.** vs. Small, dwarfish, stunted. *Rare.*

noio. n. Hawaiian noddy tern *(Anous tenuirostris melanogenys),* smaller than noddy tern; subspecies is widespread in the Central Pacific. Also *'eki'eki, laehina.* (PCP *noio.*)

noi'o. Var. of *noi'i.*

noio kō.hā. n. Noddy tern *(Anous stolidus pileatus),* larger than the tern, *noio;* sooty, except top of head, which is light gray. The name is possibly from *noio kōhāhā,* plump *noio.*

noka, nota. n. Note. *Eng.* Also *noka kālā, nota dala.*

nō.kali, notari. nvt. Notary; to notarize. *Eng. Nōkali no ka lehulehu,* notary public.

no ka mea. idiom. Because, whereas (in legal documents), thereby; in informal correspondence, introducer of paragraphs with little meaning. (Gram. 9.11.) *Lit.,* because of the thing. (PCP *no te mea.*)

nō ka 'oi. This common sequence can only *follow* nouns, as in *Maui nō ka 'oi,* Maui indeed is the best. See *'oi 2.*

noke. nvt. To persist, continue, repeat, persevere, keep on; perseverance, persistence. See ex., *'e'elekū. E noke kāua i ka hana, a pau kēia,* let's persist in the work until this is finished. *Noke i ka nuku,* keep on scolding. ho'o.noke. Caus/sim.

nokea. Pas/imp. of *noke.*

nō.kea. 1. Var. of *nākea,* a goby. **2.** vs. White-spotted, as the *nākea,* a fish.

noke'a. vs. Overstuffed with food; filled, as a cup to the brim; packed full. *Rare.*

no ke aha? idiom. Why? See *aha.* (Gram. 9.11.) (PEP *no te afa.*)

noke.kula, noketura. n. Water hen (RSV), swan (KJV). (Kanl. 14:16.)

nō.kele, notere. Same as *nōkali. Eng.*

nokema, notema. n. Juniper roots.

noke.noke. Redup. of *noke. Nokenoke i ke 'aki i ke ku'i,* continued grinding of the teeth.

nō.kī. vs. Deep. *I loko nōkī o ka 'ōpū, wāwahi hua o ka lani* (chant), though deep within the womb, a high chief would break forth. *Kau nōkī ka mana'o,* concentrate deeply.

noko.noko. nvi. Nervous anticipation and sensation that one is going to cough; to have such.

noku. Var. of *loku.*

nokule. 1. vs. Numb. *Noho i ka wai a nokule ka 'ili,* staying in the water until the skin was numbed. **2.** Same as *kukule,* listless. *Rare.*

noku.noku. Var. of *lokuloku.*

nō.la'e.la'e. Same as *māla'ela'e,* clear. (For. 6:378.)

no laila. See *laila.*

nole. 1. vs. Sickly, unhealthy. *Rare.* Cf. *mīnole, nīnole.* **2.** vt. To annoy by overfamiliarity. *Rare.* Cf. *hole, pīhole.*

-nole. ho'o.nole. Awkward, without skill. *Rare.*

Nole.wai, Norewai. nvs. Norway; Norwegian. *Eng.*

Nole.weke, Noreweke. nvs. Norwegian. *Eng.*

noliki. nvs. Northeast. *Eng.*

nō.lino.lino. Var. of *'ōlinolino,* shiny. *'Ano nōlinolino ka 'i'o kanaka i ke ahi* (chant), human flesh is somewhat shiny in the fire [light].

nolo. 1. vs. Filled full, crowded. *Nolo ka wa'a i ka i'a; nolo ka 'īlio i ka 'uku,* the canoe is full of fish; the dog is full of fleas. **2.** Same as *nonō.*

nolo.nolo. Redup. of *nolo.*

nolu. 1. vs. Springy, elastic, soft, yielding, boggy. Cf. *holu. Nolu ka ihu o Hōpoe i ka makani,* yielding is the nose of Hōpoe [rock] to the wind [of a balancing rock]. ho'o.nolu. Caus/sim. **2.** vt. To cheat, deceive. *No ke aha lā 'oukou e nolu mai ai ā puni mākou* (Ios. 9.22), why have you beguiled us? (PEP *ngolu.*)

nolu.ā.kaua. Traitor; one born under one chief who fights for another. (And.)

nolu ehu. vs. Softened and wet with mist and rain, as upland ferns. *Nolu ehu luhe i ka palai* (song), a soft mist dripping on drooping *palai* fern.

nolu.nolu. Redup. of *nolu. 1, 2. Mau'u nolunolu kohu lole weleweka,* soft grass like velvet cloth.

-nolunolu. ho'o.nolu.nolu. A name for the straight portion of a canoe rim. (For. 5:612–3.)

nolu pē. vs. **1.** Graceful bending, swaying, as of shrubs. **2.** Drenched. *Ohaoha pua i ka wai, i ka nolu pē i ka ua* (song), flowers thrive in the water, softened and drenched by the rain.

nome. vt. To eat a little at a time for a long time, as horses eating grass; to munch along; revolving or rolling along, as a wheel. See chant, *melu 1. 'Ūhī'ūhā mai ana eā, ke nome a'ela iā Puna eā* (song for Pele), shish shish here [the fires of Pele], eating munching along through Puna. ho'o.nome. To cause to munch, move along.

nomea. Pas/imp. of *nome.*

nome.nome. Redup. of *nome.* ho'o.nome.nome. Redup. of *ho'onome;* to move the lips silently, as though speaking to oneself. *E ho'onomenome 'oe i kō waha ā hiki i ka wā e pau ai ku'u oli 'ana,* mouth your words until I finish my chant.

nona. n-poss. His, hers, its, for him, for her, for it (o-form, Gram. 9.11). *Ke kanaka nona ka pāpale i lawe 'ia,* the man whose hat was taken. (PCP *nona.*)

nona.nona. n. **1.** Ant (same as more common *naonao). Ka-nonanona,* (Hawaiian newspaper 1841–5), the ant (see *'ānonanona*). **2.** Gnat. **3.** Many, a great many. *Nonanona kānaka i kahaone* (Kel. 141), crowds of people on the beach.

none. vs. **1.** Slow, tedious, time-consuming. ho'o.none. To work slowly and with disinterest; to be a slowpoke. **2.** Patience-trying, teasing, annoying, fretting; to tease, nag.

nonea. Same as *none 1, 2. He nonea kēia 'ano hana,* this kind of work is tedious, annoying.

none.ā. n. Distaste for food that one has had too much of, as fats; surfeit. (Gram. 6.5.)

none.nea. Same as *nonenonea.*

none.none. Redup. of *none 1, 2.*

none.none. Redup. of *none.*

noni. 1. n. The Indian mulberry *(Morinda citrifolia),* a small tree or shrub in the coffee family, a native of Asia, Australia, and islands of the Pacific. Leaves are large, shiny, deep-veined. Many small flowers are borne on round heads, which become pale-yellow unpleasant-tasting fruits. Formerly Hawaiians obtained dyes and medicine from many parts of the tree. (Neal 804.) See *kōhi 1, pūhai.* (PPN *nonu,* PCP *nono,* but Marquesan *noni.*) **2.** vs. Troubled, agitated, perplexed, confused. ho'o.noni. To create a disturbance, cause trouble, incite. **3.** Same as *'ānoni,* to mix. Cf. *manoni. Rare.* **4.** nvi. Poor appetite, as of an invalid; to take food unwillingly. *Rare.*

noni kua.hiwi. n. Native trees *(Morinda trimera* and M.

sandwicensis), related to the *noni,* but having smaller leaves and fruits, the fruits being only 2.6 cm in diameter. *Lit.,* hill *noni.*

noni.noni. Redup. of *noni.*

noni.nui. n. Soft, pinkish porous stone, as used in polishing.

nono. vs. **1.** Red, redness; rosy-cheeked; red-faced, as from sunburn; sunburned, bronzed. *Nono 'ula,* to flush, blush. Cf. *pūnono.* **2.** Full of holes, perforated, moth-eaten; oozing, seeping out, as water in the sand; seepage. Cf. *hānonono.*

nonō. vi. To snore, gurgle. **ho'o.nonō.** Caus/sim.

nono.ā, nonowā. Var. of *lonoā,* rumor.

nō.noe.noe. Same as *noenoe.*

nonohe. vs. Attractive, beautiful. *Lehua, 'o ka lehua maka noe, ua nonohe wale i Haua'iliki* (chant for Haku-o-Hawai'i), *lehua,* misty-faced *lehua,* beautiful at Haua'iliki.

nonohi. Redup. of *nohi.*

nono.hia. Pas/imp. of *nono 1.*

nono.hina. n. Blossoms of the *olopua,* a tree.

nonoho. Redup. and plural of *noho. Ke nonoho like maila nā ao 'ōpua,* the cloud banks are sitting together. (PPN *nonofo.*)

nonohu. Same as *'o'ohu,* stooped.

nono.hua. nvi. Diarrhea; to have symptoms of diarrhea; disgust; to be vile. *'Oia ia mau 'ōpala o ka mana'o nonohua* (Kel. 26), such was the rubbish of vile thoughts.

nono.huā, nonohuwā. nvs. Jealous; jealousy, quick-tempered jealousy. **ho'o.nono.huā.** To nurse jealousy and ill will; to hate.

nonoi. Redup. of *noi. Nonoi no ka manawa,* ask for temporarily, borrow. (PEP *nono'i.*)

nono.i'i. Same as *no'ino'i,* stunted.

nono.kea. See *puhi nonokea.*

nono.lau. Var. of *lonolau.*

nonolo. **1.** Redup. of *nolo;* purring. **2.** Defeated in war. (AP.)

nonolu. Redup. of *nolu.*

nonome. Redup. of *nome. Ho'ohie ka mana'o no ka huila, ka nonome ho'ola'i i ka 'ilikai* (song), thinking with happy pride of the wheel [of the vessel], rolling quietly along on the surface of the sea.

nono.mea. vs. Reddish.

nono.nea. vt. To redden, as the cheeks with *'ōlena* or *'alaea.*

nononi. Redup. of *noni.*

nonono. Redup. of *nono 1, 2.*

nono.noā. Redup. of *nonoā.*

nono.noho. Redup. of *nonoho. Nononoho a moe nā keiki* (chant for Kua-kini), dwelt together and mated were the children.

nono.noke. Redup. and plural of *noke.*

nono'o. Var. of *no'ono'o.*

nono.papa. nvs. Invalid, sick. *Rare.*

nono.wā. Var. spelling of *nonoā.*

nonu. Var. of *nolu.*

no'o. Same as *no'ono'o. Rare.*

no'oa. Pas/imp. of *no'o.*

no'olu. Same as *'olu'olu. Rare.*

no 'olua. poss. For you, belonging to you (dual, *o*-class).

no'o.no'o. nvt. Thought, reflection, thinking, meditation; to think, reflect, meditate, concentrate; to consider; as a case at law; thoughtful, mental. Cf. *mana'o, no'ono'o 'ole. No'ono'o makua,* to be thoughtful and considerate of parents and elders, filial. *No'ono'o pono,* to think carefully, meditate, concentrate. *No'ono'o mua,* to anticipate, estimate (see *'ōlelo no'ono'o*). *No'ono'o hāiki,* narrow-minded; a narrow mind. *No'ono'o laulā,* broad-minded. *No'ono'o nui,* to think much, concentrate, meditate; meditation. **ho'o.no'o.no'o.** To cause to think, reflect; reminiscent, recalling to mind, remembering. Cf. more common *ho'omana'o.*

no'o.no'o 'ole. nvs. Thoughtless, irresponsible, heedless, unconcerned, without thinking, carefree, careless; thoughtlessness. Also *'a'ohe no'ono'o. Ua hele aku au me ka no'ono'o 'ole i ka hopena,* I went without considering the consequences.

no'o.no'o ulu wale. n. Imagination, impulse. *Lit.,* thought growing by itself.

no 'ou.kou. poss. For you, belonging to you (plural, *o*-class).

nopa. **1.** vs. Lazy, slow. *Rare.* **2.** Crooked. (And.)

nopa.nopa. Redup. of *nopa 1.*

nō.pili. Var. of *nāpili,* a fish.

nō.polo. Same as *nīpolo. Rare.*

nopu. **1.** nvs. To swell; sprouting, plump. *Fig.,* to spring up in the mind, as a thought or desire. See ex., *'ae 3. Nopu maila ka mana'o e hele aku i ou lā,* the thought has come to go to you. **2.** vs. Hot, as from the sun or fire. *I ka lā ikiiki nopu i ke one* (song), in the hot sun warming the sand.

nopue. Var. of *nopu 1.*

nopu.nopu. Redup. of *nopu.*

nopu'u. n. Child. *Ni'ihau.*

nou. **1.** nvt. To throw, pelt, cast, pitch, hurl; buffeting, throwing; pitcher. *'O ka ho'oili i ka ihu o ka wa'a a nou i ke kai* (chant), to conduct the prow of the canoe until it beats into the sea. *Lehua maka nou i ke ahi* (chant by Hi'iaka), *Lehua* face pelted by the fire. **ho'o.nou.** To throw, pelt; to put forth physical effort; to strain; to pretend or cause to throw. Cf. *ha'anou.* **2.** *n*-poss. For you, yours, in your honor (*o*-form, singular; Gram. 9.11). (PCP *no(o)u.*)

no'u. **1.** nvs. Short, thickset, plump but not tall (said more often of plants than of humans). A short, stocky *koa* tree suitable for a wide, short canoe was also called *no'u.* **2.** n. A native variety of banana, bearing small bunches of thick, round fruit, eaten raw or cooked, the skin yellow, the flesh cream-colored. **3.** vi. To eat greedily with great mouthfuls, even when no longer hungry. Cf. *nu'u.* **4.** *n*-poss. For me, mine, in my honor (*o*-form, Gram. 9.11). *No'u kēlā,* give that to me. (PCP *no(o)ku.*)

-no'u. See *ha'ano'u.*

no'ū. vs. Suffused with water; drenched, as with rain; moist and fragrant, as a flower in the rain or dew.

noua. Pas/imp. of *nou 1.*

noulu. Var. of *loulu,* a palm.

nou.nou. Redup. of *nou 1.*

no'u.no'u. **1.** Redup. of *no'u 1, 3.* **2.** n. A variety of gourd with a short *(no'u)* fruit. Also *pāha'aha'a, pākākā.*

nou.nou pū.niu. n. Game of throwing tapa balls at suspended coconut shells.

noweke. n. Northwest. *Eng.*

nowelo. Var. spelling of *noelo.*

Nowe.mapa. n. November. *Eng.*

nō.weo. vs. Bright, shiny. *'Ula nōweo ka lā i ka pua 'ilima* (song), the sun is bright and scarlet on the *'ilima* blossom.

Nō.weo-'ula. n. Rain name associated with Nā-pili, West Maui.

nū. **1.** nvi. To cough; to roar, as wind; grunting, as of pigs; cooing, as of doves; patter, as of rain; groaning, deep sighing, moaning; mentally agitated, worried, grief-stricken. *Ka ua nū hele ma ka moana,* the rain coming pattering over the open sea. **ho'o.nū.** To moan, groan, sigh, hum, roar, etc. *Ka ua 'awa'awa e ho'onū lā i uka,* the bitterly cold rain pattering in the uplands. (PPN *nguu.*) **2.** Short for *nuku,* beak. *'alae nū kea.* **3.** Same as *lū 1,* to scatter, etc. **4.** n. The letter "n". **5.** n. News. *Eng.* See *nū hou.* **6.** n. Gnu. *Eng.* **7.** n. A crescendo followed by a decrescendo in music.

nu'a. **1.** nvs. Thick; piled one on top of the other, as leis, mats, or ocean swells; heaped; lush, thick-growing; much traveled, as a road; multitude, as of people, mass. Also *hānu'a. Moena kumu nu'a,* a sleeping mat made thick at one end to serve as a head rest; *lit.,* mat piled beginning. *Nu'a moena,* a heap of mats. *Nu'a kanaka,* many people. *Haki nu'a ka uahi i ke kai,* the spray breaks in masses in the sea. *Ka nu'a o ka palai,* the thick clump of *palai* ferns. **ho'o.nu'a.** To heap up; to give generously and continuously; to indulge, as a child; surging, rising in swells, as the sea. **2.** n. A kind of seaweed.

nū.'ai.hea. n. Name of a destructive caterpillar. *Rare.*

Nu'a-kea. n. A goddess of lactation.

nu'a.lia. Pas/imp. of *nu'a l.*

nu'a.nu'a. Redup. of *nu'a;* large, soft, fleshy. *Pā nu'anu'a,* to blow strongly, as to make large sea waves. *Nu'anu'a nā lei i ka 'ā'ī o ka malihini,* the leis were piled about the neck of the visitor. **ho'o.nu'a.nu'a.** Redup. of *ho'onu'a. 'Ula Ka-lae-loa i ka lepo a ka makani, ho'onu'anu'a i ka lepo* (chant), Ka-lae-loa is red with the wind's dirt, encrusted with dirt.

nu'ao. n. Porpoise.

nuha. vs. Sulky, sullen, peeved, peevish, stubborn; to sulk, balk. Cf. *nunuha.* **ho'o.nuha.** To cause to sulk; to sulk.

nuha.nuha. Redup. of *nuha.* **ho'o.nuha.nuha.** Redup. of *ho'onuha.*

nuhe. 1. Rare var. of *nuha.* **2.** Var. of *'enuhe,* caterpillar.

nuhi. Same as *unuhi. Rare.*

nuhō.lani. 1. Same as *'eukalikia, palepiwa,* eucalyptus. (Neal 640–2.) *Lit.,* New Holland (old name for Australia). *Eng.* **2.** n. Introduced Brazilian banana.

nū hou. n. News, recent or late news or information, tidings. *Nū hou kūloko,* local news. *Nū hou kūwaho,* foreign news. *Nū hou noho'i kāu hana,* how strangely you act. *Ka Nū Hou Hawai'i,* The News [of] Hawai'i [a Hawaiian-language newspaper].

nuhu. Same as *nūnū 3,* trumpet fish.

nui. nvs. Big, large, great, greatest, grand, important, principal, prime, many, much, often, abundant, bulky; plenty, a lot, maximum, most, size, number, amount, bulk, volume, magnitude, quantity, dimension, extent, area, entirety, greater part, enough, sufficiency. Before a noun, *nui* may mean 'group', as *nui manō,* group of sharks, or *nui manu,* flock of birds. Cf. *'ano nui, ha'anui, hapa nui, mea nui, nui kino. Nui loa, nui 'ino, nui hewahewa,* very much or many, abundant, too much, very large, immense, huge. *Aloha nui loa, aloha ā nui,* very much *aloha* [common salutations to letters]. *Leo nui,* loud voice, loud. *Nui nā hewa,* many mistakes. *Nui lua 'ole,* immeasurably large, tremendous. *Nui iki,* a trifle larger. *Nui a'e,* larger. *Ka nui mai auane'i kona kino,* what a large body he has. *Nui 'ino lākou,* they were very many. *Ua hele nui aku nei i kahakai,* the many of them went to the beach. *Ua ho'i aku nei ka nui kamali'i,* the great part of the children have returned. *Ua nui kēia,* this is enough. **ho'o.nui.** To enlarge, increase, multiply, magnify, exaggerate, add to; dilate; multiplication; to increase in volume, of music; crescendo mark in music. *Ho'onui leo,* loud speaker. *Ho'onui 'ōlelo,* wordy, verbose, padded, prolix; to exaggerate, boast, enlarge on the truth; to talk excessively. (PNP *nui;* cf. Nukuoro.) **2.** *(Cap.)* n. Name of a star (no data).

nū.ia. n. New Year. *Eng.* See *hapenuia.*

nui kino. n. Whole body.

-nuinui. ho'o.nui.nui. To use threatening language, usually without carrying out the threat; to exaggerate, stretch the truth, talk verbosely. *Mai nānā 'oe, he ho'o-nuinui wale nō,* don't pay attention, [he's] just exaggerating.

Nui.oka. n. New York. *Eng.*

nuka. vs. Large, plump, fat and sleek, stout.

nuka.nuka. Redup. of *nuka.*

nū.kea. 1. Same as *'alae kea.* **2.** vs. White-beaked, as the *nūkea* bird; white around the mouth or snout, as an aging animal. *'O ka lani ka hiapo kama kapu, ka hānau mua i Hawai'i, ka 'īlio nūkea ma ka lani* (chant), the

chief is a sacred first-born one, the first born in Hawai'i, the white-mouthed dog in the heavens [probably clouds indicative of a chief].

nū.ke'e. vs. Awry; twisted to one side, as a mouth; crooked, as a bill. See ex., *ho'olehelehe ki'i.* **ho'o.nū.-ke'e.** To twist the face to one side.

Nuki.lani. n. New Zealand. *Eng.*

nū.koki. vs. Snub-nosed, homely, of facial features; pugnosed. Cf. *kokikoki, mūkoki.*

nuku. 1. n. Beak, snout, tip, end; spout, beak of a pitcher; mouth or entrance, as of a harbor, river, or mountain pass or gap. See idioms, *hapahapai* and *huapala 2. Nuku awa,* entrance to a harbor. *Ka nuku o ka ule hala,* tip of aerial pandanus root. *Ka nuku kaulana o Nu'u-anu,* the famous Nu'u-anu gap. *Pu'u ka nuku,* to protrude the lips. (PPN *ngutu.*) **2.** nvs. Scolding, raving, ranting, grumbling; to nag. (PNP *ngutu.*) **3.** n. Series of hooks attached to a line (Malo 79); first coconut husk attached to an *'ahi* fishline, the others being *poli* (bosom), and *manamana* (fingers). *Ka nuku o ka pua'a,* poetic name for deep-sea *ulua* fishing line; *lit.,* the pig snout. **4.** n. See below for *nuku* sequences as names of taros, a legume, sweet potatoes, jackfish, and birds.

nuku.ā.'ula, nukuwā'ula. n. Type of fishing net, with mesh so fine that only the very tip *(nuku)* of the finger could be inserted.

nuku 'e'ehu. n. A native variety of taro. (HP 33.) *Lit.,* red beak.

nuku 'ehu. Same as *nuku 'e'ehu.*

nuku ho'o.mau. nvi. Constant scolding, grumbling, chitchat; harangue.

nuku 'i'iwi. n. A woody, climbing legume *(Strongylodon ruber)* native to Hawai'i. It has leaves with three leaflets, and scarlet flowers shaped like narrow beaks, hanging in narrow clusters. Also *kā 'i'iwi.* (Neal 461.)

nuku.kau. vs. Thick-lipped.

nuku kau. n. **1.** A variety of taro. (HP 34.) **2.** A variety of sweet potato.

nū.kuke. vs. Silent, refusing to speak.

nuku lehu. n. A variety of sweet potato.

Nuku.loa. n. Star name (no data). (Kuhelani.)

nuku.mane'o. n. A malignant *'unihipili,* spirit. *Lit.,* itching grumbler.

nuku manu. n. **1.** Bird's beak. **2.** A variety of taro. The corm is pointed like a bird's beak. Used on Kaua'i only.

nuku momi. n. A variety of jackfish *(Caranx melampugus).* Also *momi.*

nuku mone'u. n. A variety of jackfish, probably same as *nuku momi.*

nuku.nuku. 1. Redup. of *nuku;* to scold, nag. **2.** vs. Short, broken off short, blunt. *Nukunuku ho'i kēia wahi lou,* this fruit-picker is too short. **3.** n. Butterfly fish *(Forcipiger longirostris).*

nuku.nuku.ā.'ula. Same as *nukuā'ula.*

nuku peu. n. Name of a bird (no data); perhaps same as *nuku pu'u.*

nuku pueo. n. Large bottle gourd used for water.

nuku pu'u. 1. n. Group of Hawaiian honey creepers *(Hemignathus lucidus lucidus, H. l. hanapepe* [endangered sp.], *H. l. affinis* [endangered sp.]) with long curved upper mandible and shorter lower mandible of the beak, with subspecies on Kaua'i *(hanapepe),* O'ahu *(lucidus),* and Maui *(affinis),* and a closely related endangered species *(Hemignathus wilsoni)* on Hawai'i. Plumage is brownish-green on the back, yellow-green below. The Hawai'i species is also called *'akihi po'o lā'au.* Cf. *'akialoa, 'i'iwi. Lit.,* hunched beak. **2.** nvi. Protruding lips; to pout the lips. *Fig.,* to speak evil of others, then them evil.

nuku wai. n. Stream mouth.

nuku.wā.'ula. Var. spelling of *nukuā'ula.*

nulu. vi. To rise up, as smoke or steam.

nulu.nulu. Redup. of *nulu.*

numela, numera. n. Numeral. *Eng.*

numi. vi. To subside gradually, as tears, laughter, emotions. *Numi maila kona kaumaha,* his sorrows gradually ebbed away. (PCP *numi.*)

numo.nia. n. Pneumonia. *Eng.*

nuna. 1. Rare var. of *luna,* above. **2.** n. Nun. *Eng.*

nuna.nuna. Same as *nupanupa.*

nū.nē. nvi. Speculation; to wonder, speculate, discuss and wonder about. *Ia wā noho ihola lākou me ka nūnē aku a nūnē mai,* then they sat and asked wondering questions of each other.

nū.nea. Same as *nūnē.*

nunele, nunere. n. Nunnery, convent. *Eng.*

nunoi. n. According to Emerson, the "posterior fontanelle" of Haumea from which Hiʻiaka was born as a clot of blood. (PH X.)

nunu. 1. nvt. Greed; to covet, extort, take property by force. Cf. *ʻālunu, ʻānunu, lunu.* (Perhaps PPN *-nu;* cf. Tongan *mānu-,* to be always wanting.) **2.** vt. Swollen, puffed up; to swell up; to swathe or roll up, as an article in tapa; to fold, bind. *Ua hoʻomaka naʻe ke ʻano nunu mai o nā kuʻemaka* (Kel. 18), the eyebrows began to be puffed up [raised]. (PPN *ngungu.*)

-nunu. hoʻo.nunu. A seaweed *(Laurencia obtusa* var. *racemosa).* Cf. *līpeʻe.*

nū.nū. 1. n. Introduced rock pigeon or wild pigeon *(Columba livia);* dove (Mele 2.14). See saying, *dove.* **2.** nvi. Moaning, groaning, cooing, grunting; to do so. (PPN *nguungu.*) **3.** n. Trumpet fish *(Aulostomus chinensis).* Also *nuhu.*

nunuʻa. vs. Crowded, confused, clustering, swarming, assembling promiscuously.

nunuha. Redup. of *nuha;* sulky, moody, morose.

nunuhe. Redup. of *nuhe 1.*

nunui. Plural of *nui 1.*

nunuki. vi. To rise and fall, as the sea. *Rare.*

nunulu. vi. To growl or snarl, as a dog; warbling, as a bird; reverberating. (PPN *ngungulu.*)

nupa. 1. Var. of *lupa.* **2.** n. A deep cave or chasm; gloominess, as in a cave. **3.** vs. Enlarged, swollen. *Rare.*

nupai.kini. vs. New-fashioned. *Eng.*

nupa.nupa. Redup. of *nupa 1–3.* Also *lupalupa.* Cf. *hānupanupa.* **hoʻo.nupa.nupa.** Same as *hoʻolupalupa. Ua piha kā kākou mau mele me nā hoʻonupanupa ʻana a ia mea, he aloha,* our songs are filled with lush [descriptions] of that thing, *aloha.*

nū.pepa. n. Newspaper *Eng.*

nū.pepa puka lā. n. Daily newspaper.

nū.polu.polu. vs. Scattered, thick, as flowers. *ʻO aʻu lehua i ʻaina e ka manu a mā.ui i ke kai, nūpolupolu akula i ke kai o Hilo* (prayer to Kapo), my *lehua* blossoms picked by the birds and bruised by the sea, scattered there on the sea of Hilo.

nū.ponuponu. Var. of *nūpolupolu.*

nuʻu. 1. nvs. Height, high place, summit, crest, elevation; the second platform in the *lananuʻu mamao,* oracle tower on a heiau; stratum; piled high. *Fig.,* great. *Ka ua nuʻu,* torrential rain. *ʻEkolu mau nuʻu pō* (Kep. 49), three strata of night. *Ua hiki aku i ka nuʻu ka mana o Roma,* the power of Rome reached its culminating point. (PPN *nuku.*) **2.** Same as *hoʻonuʻu.* **hoʻo.nuʻu.** To eat heartily (see saying *koʻu 1*).

nuʻu.anu. n. Name of a card game. (Ii 127.)

Nuʻu.anu. n. Place name and star name. *Lit.,* cool heights.

Nuʻu.hiwa. 1. nvs. Marquesas Islands; Nukuhiva Island in the Marquesas; Marquesan. **2.** *(Not cap.)* n. A variety of banana, mistakenly called in English the New Zealand banana.

nuʻu.kole. Same as *hiʻukole,* a fish.

nuʻu mamao. Same as *lananuʻu mamao.*

nuʻu mao.mao. Rare var. of *nuʻu mamao.*

nuʻu.mela. Same as *laulele,* milkweed.

nuʻu.paʻa. Same as *pokipaʻa.*

nuʻu.pē. nvs. A fat person; fat. *Ua hoʻi mai nei paha kuʻu nuʻupē,* perhaps my fat [friend] has come home.

O

O *and* ʻo, ō *and* ʻō *are followed by predictable and nonphonemic* w-*glides before* a, ā, e, ē, i, *or* ī. *This* w-*sound need not be written unless a* w-*sound introduces a recognizable base, as* ʻō + wela, *hottish; it is preferable to write this* w. *Spellings with and without* w *are given in the Dictionary, with the definition following the preferred spelling, and with a cross reference to the other form.*

All words beginning with o *or* ō *may be preceded by the article* ke *unless otherwise stated.*

o. 1. prep. Of. (Gram. 9.6.) This *o* forms part of the possessives, as *koʻu, kou, kona, kō laila.* Note idiomatic use, as below. *ʻAʻohe mea o loko,* nothing inside. *ʻA ʻole ʻili o ka puke,* the book has no cover. *Ma o kō ke Akua aloha,* because of God's love. (PPN *(ʻ)o.*) **2.** conj. Or, lest, if. (Gram. 11.1.)

ō. 1. nvi. To answer, reply yes, agree, say, talk; halloo, yes (in reply); tinkling, tolling, or chime of a bell; resonance, as generated by the thumping of a gourd drum on a pad; sound of whistling *(Kauaʻi);* sound of peacocks; to make such sounds. *Kou inoa, e ō mai* (FS 199), your name chant, answer. *E uhaele kākou i kahakai. Ō, e uhaele ʻiʻo aku kākou.* Let's go to the beach. Yes, let's do go. (PPN *oo.*) **2.** vi. To remain, endure, survive, continue, go on, exist; continuing. See *oia, oia mau nō, malu. A pēlā paha i kō ai ke ō ʻana o kona inoa,* probably thereby assuring the perpetuation of his name. *Ke ō nei nō kēlā mele,* that song still survives now. **3.** n. Food provisions for a journey, especially at sea; sea rations. **hō.ʻō.** To provide food for a journey. (PPN *ʻoho.*) **4.** n. Sprit of a sail or spar. **5.** Short for *one,* sand, in place names, as Ke-ō-kea, the white sand. **6.** Imperative marker, sometimes less emphatic than the more common *e.* See ex., *ʻī 1. Ō hele kāua,* let's go. *Ō uhaele mai,* won't you come. **7.** Short for the part. *iō,* as after prepositions. *Holo akula ʻoia mai ō lāua nei aku* (Laie 603), he ran from the two of them. *Kiʻi mua akula ʻoia ma ō Kapa-hai-haoa* (Laie 595), he first looked for Kapa-hai-haoa.

ʻo. Part. marking the subject, being especially common before names of people, the interrogative *wai,* and the pronoun *ia.* (Gram. 9.2.) *ʻO* also marks apposition (Gram. 9.13). *ʻO au nō,* it's I. *Me kāna wahine ʻo Hina,* with his wife, Hina. *ʻO hea?* Where? *Make nō ʻoia iaʻu,* I killed him (*lit.,* died indeed subject-he by-me). (PPN *ko.*)

ʻo-. Same as *ʻō-* (cf. *ʻolalau*); pronounced *ʻow-* before *e* (*ʻoehuehu*); the *-w-* need not be written unless the following vowel is the initial sound of a recognizable base, as *ʻowala,* to turn over (cf. *wala,* to tilt). (PCP *ko(o)-.*)

ʻō. 1. loc. n. There, yonder, beyond (usually visible or pointed to; cf. *laila,* usually invisible and anarphoric; often following *ma-, i, mai,* Gram. 8.6). *I ʻō i ʻaneʻi,* here and there, to and fro. *Maʻō aʻe nei,* nearby, not far. *Mai ʻō ā ʻō,* everywhere. *I ʻō, i ʻō,* this way and that way. *Noho maʻō,* sit over there. *Maʻō loa aku,* far beyond. *ʻAlawa nā maka o ka ʻaihue i ʻō i ʻō,* the eyes of the thief glanced this way and that. *I ʻō i ʻō aʻe,* from that point to yonder point. *Nā ʻōlelo pili i ʻō i ʻaneʻi,* general provisions; *lit.,* words referring to there to here. *Mai ʻō a ʻō,* from that point to that point [all over, everywhere]. *E ulu mai ka puka o ke dālā maʻō nā pakeneka ʻaʻole e ʻoi aku maʻō o ʻelima pakeneka o ka makahiki,* the interest on the money grows because of the percentage of not more than five percent yearly. (PPN *koo.*) **2.** nvt. Any piercing instrument, fork, pin, skewer, harpoon, sharp-pointed stick, pitchfork, fishing spear; coconut husker; sharp darting body pain; to pierce, vaccinate, prick, stab, thrust; to flash, as lightning; to extend; to dip in, as the finger; to reach, to appear; to force a way out; to fall into, tumble out; to tassel, as sugar cane. Cf. *ʻōahi, ʻō lima. Ua ʻō kō kea,* the white sugar cane has tasseled [to gray with age]. *Ka ʻō ʻana o ka uila,* the flash of lightning. *He ʻō ʻia ka mea hāwāwā i ka heʻe nalu,* one unskilled in surfing is given a tumble. *ʻŌ aku ʻoia i kona mau lima i ka poʻe nele* (Sol. 31.20), he extended his hands to the needy. **ho.ʻō.** To cause to enter, put or dip in, thrust in, insert; to reach in. *Hoʻō ʻoma,* to put in an oven. *Hoʻō poʻo,* to rush headlong regardless of consequence. *Hoʻō akula ʻo Hiku i ka ʻuhane o Ka-welu ma nā wāwae* (For. 5:189), Hiku caused Ka-welu's soul to enter at the feet. (PNP *koso,* PCP *koo.*) **3.** Similar to *kuni ola* but with less elaborate ceremony. (Kam. 64:37.) **4.** n. A hula step in which the hip is quickly thrust (*ʻō*) outward; similar to the *kāwelu* except that the foot pivots while turning to the opposite direction. **5.** nvi. To hail, whoop, a hail; (commonly preceded by *ke*). *Kani ke ʻō, he ihona pali,* a whoop going down hill [an easy task]. **6.** vt. To fly, as a kite. **7.** n. The letter "o." *Eng.*

ʻō-. Similitude prefix sometimes translated somewhat, -ish: cf. *aʻa,* fibrous, *ʻōaʻa,* somewhat fibrous. *ʻŌ-* is pronounced *ʻōw-* before *a* (*ʻōaʻa*) and *i* (*ʻōiwi*) but *-w-* need not be written unless the following vowel is the initial sound of a recognizable base, as *ʻōwili,* bundle (cf. *wili,* to roll up). (Gram. 6.3.1.) (PCP *ko(o)-.*)

oʻa. n. 1. House rafter; timbers in the side of a ship; sides of a rock wall. (PPN *hoka.*) **2.** Gill of a fish; mouth of an eel. **3.** Maui name for *kauila (Colubrina oppositifolia),* a tree. (Neal 541.)

ʻoa. See *maiʻa ʻoa, Uluʻoa.*

ʻoā, ʻowā. 1. vi. Split, cracked, burst, grooved; to split, crack. *Fig.,* bereaved, forsaken. *ʻAʻohe pono ka nohona o nā keiki ʻoā makua ʻole,* the life of forsaken, parentless children is not good. **hō.ʻowā.** To cause to split, crack. **2.** See also *ʻowā 1–5.*

ʻoʻa. See *puhi ʻoʻa.*

ʻō.ʻā. vs. Mixed, as of colors in a lei or as blood. *He lei* *kolohala uliuli i 'ō'ā 'ia me ke ke'oke'o,* a dark pheasant feather lei mixed with white. *He Hawai'i 'oia akā ua 'ō'ā 'ia me ke koko Pākē,* he's Hawaiian, but there is a little strain of Chinese also. **ho'ō.'ā.** To mix.

'ō.a'a, 'ō.'a'a'a, 'ō.a'a.'a'a. Somewhat fibrous. Cf. *'a'a'a.*

'ō.ahe.ahe. To blow gently, as a breeze. Cf. *aheahe.*

'ō.ahi. n. 1. Rocket, fireworks; clot of burning lava, as from an eruption; hurling firebrands, as from a cliff for ancient Kaua'i spectacle; flashing lightning. *Lit.,* projecting fire. See ex., *kīhe'ahe'a. Nā pali 'ōahi o Makana,* the cliffs of Makana, where fire was hurled forth. **2.** Rough stone or pumice, as used for polishing surfboards or bowls, or for scraping bristles of a pig (a specimen in the Bishop Museum was made of coral).

O'ahu. n. Name of the most populous of the Hawaiian Islands and the seat of Honolulu. The name has no meaning (see Pukui, Elbert, and Mookini, 1975, 262). See saying *kau po'ohiwi,* and epithets, O'ahu (English-Hawaiian).

'oai, 'owai. 1. vt. To entwine, twine; to stir round and round, as a liquid; to go round and round. **hō.'oai.** To cause to entwine; to twist, entwine. **2. n.** Bubo, swelling. *Rare.* **3. n.** Porous stone, as used for polishing canoes and calabashes. *Rare.*

'o ai. Var. spelling of *'owai:* see *wai,* who.

'oai.kū, 'owai.kū. n. Gasping for breath, as during an attack of asthma; shortness of breath accompanied by a churning, heaving motion as by one attempting to breath. *Kai pili 'oaikū* (Kep. 183), a churning, gasping sea.

'oai.'oai. Redup. of *'oai 1.*

'oaka, 'owaka. 1. Same as *hoaka 5,* to open. *'Oaka a'ela kona waha, a'o maila 'oia iā lākou* (Mat. 5.2), he opened his mouth instantly and taught them. **hō.'oaka.** Caus/sim. **2. vi.** To sprout, as sweet potatoes. *Waiho ā 'owaka like ka ulu o ka lau 'uala,* left until the sweet potato leaves all grow and sprout. **3.** Var. spelling of *'owaka,* to flash.

'oa.kaaka, 'owa.kaaka, 'owaka.waka. Redup. of *'oaka 1.*

'Oā.ki'i.ala, 'Owā.ki'i.ala. n. A stroke in *lua* fighting.

oala. A kind of fish. (And.)

'oala. Var. spelling of *'owala.*

'oā.laala, 'owā.lala. nvi. Rising of the wind; to rise, as wind; to occur, as a thought. Cf. *-alaala. He 'oālaala makani iki nō* (Kep. 103), a slight rise of the wind.

'ō.ali, 'ō.wali. 1. n. Cretan brake, a fern *(Pteris cretica),* widely distributed in warm parts of the world, growing wild in Hawai'i. Long-stemmed, ovate fronds rise about 60 cm from creeping underground stems, and each frond has four to six pairs of long narrow divisions. (Neal 17.) **2.** Var. spelling of *'ōwali 1.*

'oā.li'i, 'owā.li'i. n. Maidenhair spleenwort, a fern *(Asplenium trichomanes)* found on high mountains of Hawai'i and also present in many temperate regions of the world. Wiry-stemmed, narrow fronds grow in dense tufts 10 to 30 cm high, the fronds consisting of numerous small, round divisions on two sides of the stem.

'oā.li'i maka.li'i. n. A native fern *(Schizaea robusta).* Called *haili-o-Pua* on Hawai'i.

oalu. n. A variety of taro. (HP 34.)

oalu nui. n. A variety of taro. (HP 34.)

'oama, 'owama. n. Young of the *weke,* goatfish. (PCP *koama.*)

o'a moku. n. Ship's spar.

'ō.ana, 'ō.wana. n. Small taro peeled, wrapped in ti leaves, and baked in the ground oven.

'ō.ani.ani. nvi. Very slight stir of air, a breeze; to blow slightly. Cf. *ani. He kai mehana no ke 'ōaniani makani 'ole* (Kep. 101), it is a very warm sea where there is no breeze stirring.

oa.oa. Same as *ohaoha.* (AP.)

'oā.'oā, 'owā.'owā. 1. Redup. of *'oā.* **2.** A variety of taro.

'o'ā.'o.'ā. Same as *'olā'olā,* to gurgle. (And.)

'oā.'oaka. 1. Redup. of *'oaka.* **2.** Var. spelling of *'owa'owaka 1.*

'oala. Var. spelling of *'owala.*

'oā.'oala. Var. spelling of *'owā'owala.*

o'a pe'a. n. Spar for a sail.

o'a pō.kole. n. Ledger line in music.

'oau, 'owau. 1. n. O'ahu and Maui name for a freshwater *'o'opu* fish *(Eleotris sandwicensis)* called *'ōkuhe* elsewhere. See *'ōkuhe* for other names. The name *'oau* is said to be so called because of a tale: a fisherman caught a lot of these fish, but they disappeared; the fisherman called for them and a voice answered " '*o au, 'o au*'' (it's me, it's me) and the fish turned into lizards and scampered off. **2. nvi.** A cat, so called because of its cry: to mew. *Mikimiki mai ka 'owau lā, no ka hemahema o ia ala* (song of the 1880s), the cat is on the alert, when someone is careless. **3. n.** A variety of taro. **4. n.** A moss.

'o au, 'o wau. See *au 14.*

'ō.au.au. vi. To go faster. See *au 3. He 'oālaala makani, he 'ōauau* (Kep. 103), it's a rising wind, one blowing faster.

'oā.ulu.niu. n. A variety of taro (no data).

'oawa. Var. spelling of *'ōawaawa* and *'owāwa,* valley.

oe. nv. Prolonged sound or thing; sound of chanting, vibration, whistle of a train; whistling of a bull-roarer; drawn out wail of an infant; long, prolonged. *Fig.,* to assume a superior air. (Preceded by *ke.) Nānā aku 'oe, ke kūkulu maila ke oe,* look, acting superior there.

'oe. 1. idiom. Resembling, like. *Ke pinana kēlā keiki i ke kumulā'au, 'oia nō 'oe 'o ke keko,* when that child climbs the tree, he's just like a monkey. *'Oia nō 'oe 'o ke kaimana,* just like a diamond. *He nuku moi 'oe,* like a *moi* [fish] beak. **2.** pronoun. You (singular), thou. (Gram. 8.2.) *'Oe pono'ī, 'oe iho,* you yourself. (PPN *koe.*) **3. idiom.** Much, indeed (sometimes following *nō* or connecting enumerations). *Ua nui ka mea 'ai, 'o ka pua'a 'oe, 'o ka lū'au 'oe, 'o ka limu 'oe,* there was much food, pork, taro greens, and seaweed. *I laila nō 'oe, pau ka hoihoi,* no more fun there at all.

'oē. Var. spelling of *'owē.*

'o'e. nvt. To probe upward, prod, pry, prick, jab, poke, gore; sharp darting pain; jagged, spiked. See ex., *'owala.* **hō.'o'e.** To probe, prick, jab, etc.

Oea. n. Star name (no data). (Kuhelani.)

'oe.ha'a. nvi. Crooked, distorted, deformed; to walk in an ungainly manner, swaying the shoulders; to waddle. *Fig.,* deceitful; trick. Cf. *'ōpae 'oeha'a.* **hō.'oe.ha'a.** To cause to walk in a crooked way or be crooked; to pretend such.

'ō.ehe.ehe. Var. spelling of *'ōwehewehe.*

'oehu, 'owehu. vt. To romp, gambol, prance, leap; blustery, gusty, as a storm or angry person; to head straight for, as a canoe. Cf. *ho'ēhu.*

'oehu.ehu. Redup. of *'oehu.* Cf. *ehuehu. He aha kēia 'oehuehu nei, pi'i 'ōkala o ka hulu* (song), what is this disturbance, this bristling of the fur?

'oeke. Var. spelling of *'oweke.*

'oene, 'owene. n. 1. Mesh size between one and two fingers. **2.** Last taro taken from a crop; small-sized taro.

'o'eno. Twill plaiting, as in hats, mats. Cf. *'ahu 'o'eno, ho'ohewahewa.*

oe.oe. 1. Redup. of *oe;* whistle, as of steamer or train, siren; bull-roarer, as made of *kamani* seed or coconut shell on a long string; long, tall, tapering, towering; a long object, pillar (preceded by *ke). Pe'a oeoe,* a long sail. *Kani oeoe ke oeoe,* the bull-roarer whistles. **ho.'ōe.oe.** To stretch out, as the neck; to reach high; to prolong, as a sound; to toll; to yodel. *Uwē ho'ōeoe,* prolonged wailing. **2.** Same as *lupe'akeke,* a bird. **3.** *n.* Temporary booth occupied by priests during taboo days of a heiau. (Malo 163.)

'oe.'oe. Young stage of the *kawakawa,* bonito.

'o'e.'o'e. Redup. of *'o'e. I ho'i iho au e moe, 'o'e'o'e ana kō ia lā kuli* (song), I went back to sleep, but his knees kept prodding. *Kino 'o'e'o'e* (Malo 46), body with spiked protuberances, as of a fish.

oe.oe ha'ina pō.pili.kia. n. Siren warning of disaster.

'oē.'oene, 'owē.'owene. Redup. of *'oene 2*.

'ō.eo.eo. n. Tall and slender, as trees growing without sunlight.

'oeo.wewe. vs. Fluttering. *He lau 'oeowewe*, a fluttering leaf.

oha. 1. vs. Spreading, as vines; thriving; to grow lush. **2.** nvt. Affection, love, greeting; to greet, show joyous affection or friendship, joy. Cf. *aloha*. (PPN *'ofa*.)

'ohā. n. Taro corm growing from the older root, especially from the stalk called *kalo;* tender plant (Isa. 53.3), shoot, sucker, branch (Isa. 11.2). *Fig.*, offspring, youngsters (FS 235; cf. *'ohana*). Also *mu'u*. See *kalo* for names of generations. *Kai 'ohā*, sea with small waves.

'ō.hā. n. Native lobelias. Also *ālula, hāhā, 'ōhāhā, 'ōhā wai*. (Neal 815-8.)

ō.hā.hā. 1. vs. Flourishing, fully developed, plump, healthy. See ex., *konūnū. Ōhāhā ka ulu 'ana o kēia kalo*, this taro's growth is thrifty. *He hua ali'i ōhāhā*, a flourishing royal offspring. **2.** n. Distinct, clear sound or voice. *Rare.*

'ō.hā.hā. Same as *'ōhā*, lobelia. (Neal 815-8.)

'ō.hā.hā wai nui. Same as *'ōhā kēpau*.

'ohai. n. **1.** Monkeypod or rain tree *(Samanea saman)*, a large leguminous tree from tropical America, grown in Hawai'i for shade and street planting; flowers pink, tufted. (Neal 401-3.) See saying, *luhea*. (PCP *koofai*.) **2.** n. A native legume *(Sesbania tomentosa)*, a low to prostrate shrub with hairy, pale leaves and red or orange flowers about 2.5 cm long. (Neal 450.) (PCP *koofai*.) White monkeypod *(Albizia lebbeck)* on Ni'ihau. Cf. Neal 403.

'ō.ha'i. vs. Imperfectly healed, as a broken limb. Cf. *ha'i 1*. *'A'ohe ikaika kēia lima, he lima 'ōha'i*, this arm isn't strong, it's imperfectly healed.

'ohai ali'i. n. The pride of Barbados *(Caesalpinia pulcherrima)*, an ornamental leguminous shrub with red and orange flowers. One variety has yellow flowers. (Neal 432.) *Lit.*, royal *'ohai*.

ohai.kau. Name given to a kind of sled obtained from Captain Cook; it is said to have had supernatural qualities. (And.)

'ohai ke'o.ke'o. n. The sesban *(Sesbania grandiflora)*, a leguminous tree from tropical Asia with pea-shaped flowers about 7.5 cm long and pods to 60 by 1.3 cm. (Neal 449-50.) *Lit.*, white *'ohai*. (PCP *koofai*.)

'ohai 'ula. n. The royal poinciana *(Delonix regia)*, a legume from Madagascar, one of the showiest ornamental trees in Hawai'i because of its bright-red canopy of flowers, which are common and prolific in early summer. One form has yellow flowers. (Neal 430-2.)

'ohai 'ula.'ula. n. The red-flowered variety of *'ohai ke'oke'o (Sesbania grandiflora* var. *coccinea)* (Neal 450.) *Lit.*, red *'ohai*.

'ō.haka. Same as the more common *'olohaka*.

'ō.hā.kā.lai. To polish lightly, as a spear; a stick for polishing. (And.)

'ō.hā.pa'a. n. A native lobelia *(Clermontia hawaiiensis)*, a shrub or small tree; the gum was used to catch birds which yielded feathers for featherwork. (Neal 816-7.) *Lit.*, gum *'ōhā*. Also *'ōhāhā wai nui, 'ōhā wai nui*.

'ohā.kia. Probably same as *'ohā* (perhaps a pas/imp., Gram. 6.6.3). *'O 'oe ia ē ka 'ohākia* (Ii 175), you are the one, o tender plant.

'ohā.kula'i. Same as *pu'uhau. Rare.*

'ō.hala. vs. Green, immature, as fruit. *Rare.*

'ō.hala.hala. 1. Same as *halahala 1;* to grumble. **2.** Redup. of *'ōhala. Rare.*

'ohana. n. **1.** nvs. Family, relative, kin group; related. *'Ohana holo'oko'a, 'ohana nui*, extended family, clan. **2.** vi. To gather for family prayers (short for *pule 'ohana*).

O-hana-ke-ke'a-ua-mai.ka'i. n. Name of a stroke in *lua* fighting. *Lit.*, make the cross, is good.

'ohana manu. n. Brood.

'ō.hani. vt. To stir, as fire, or earth in a garden. *Rare.*

'ō.hao. 1. nvs. Swelling, dropsical condition; swollen. **2.** n. Dog's neck. *Rare.* **3.** nvt. To tie, especially a dog by the neck, or *lau* nets together. *Rare.* Cf. *'ōhao 'īlio*.

'ō.ha'o. Rare var. of *'ōla'o*, to weed.

'ō.haoa. Same as *haoa*, scorched.

oha.oha. Redup. of *oha 1, 2;* delight. *Ohaoha launa 'ole nā pua ma ka hikina* (song), the flowers [maidens] in the east are incomparably friendly; the flowers in the east thrive without rival. (PPN *'ofa'ofa*.)

'ohao.hala. 1. nvi. A half-truth, exaggeration; to enlarge on certain points; to exaggerate the arguments on one side, but overlook conflicting evidence; dichotomized thinking. *Rare.* **2.** vs. Rank, of lush growth. *Rare.* **3.** Soft, sweet, of melody. (And.)

'ō.hao.hao. Same as *'ōhao 1*.

oha'o.ha'o. n. A fresh-water alga reported on Maui.

'ō.hao 'i.lio. n. Insulting term for *kauā*, outcasts; they were likened to dogs *('īlio)* tied *('ōhao)* and waiting to be baked; similarly *kauā* wore small gourd pendants as insignia that they were to become human sacrifices.

'ō.hā pali. n. A kind of lobelia. *Lit.*, cliff *'ōhā*.

oha.pueo. n. A fruit tree listed by Thrum (no data).

'ō.hā.wai. n. Water dripping down a cliff as to a pool.

'ō.hā wai. Same as *'ōhā*, native lobelias.

'ō.hā wai nui. n. A native lobelia *(Clermontia arborescens)*, similar to *'ōhā kēpau*.

'ohe. n. **1.** All kinds of bamboo; reed (Mat. 27.48); flute; pipe, hose, tube; bamboo tube for preserving fish. *Puhi 'ohe*, to play a wind instrument; player of a wind instrument. *Hula 'ohe* (UL 135), dance to the music of the nose flute. (PPN *kofe*.) **2.** A coarse, jointed, native grass *(Isachne distichophylla)*, to 190 cm high, with stiff, pointed leaves and open flowering panicle. **3.** A native bamboo-like plant *(Joinvillea ascendens)*, with stem about 3 m high, 2.5 cm or less in diameter, unbranched; leaf blades 60 to 90 cm by 8 to 13 cm, pointed and plaited; flowering panicle about 30 cm long. (Neal 166.) **4.** A native tree *(Reynoldsia sandwicensis)*, an araliad, with leaves about 30 cm long, each leaf with seven to eleven broad leaflets with scalloped edges. (Neal 652.) The wood of this kind of tree growing at Mauna Loa, Moloka'i, was reputed to be poisonous, was used for making poison images, and is the tree form of Kapo, a goddess. (Neal 652.) This tree growing elsewhere was not considered poisonous and was used for making stilts, hence it was also called *'ohe kukuluae'o* or *'ohe-o-kai* or *'ohe-ma-kai*. **5.** A native variety of taro, thriving at altitudes above 450 m; leaf stem light-green, tinged with reddish-brown (perhaps like some variety of bamboo); the corm pink-tinted, making excellent poi. (Whitney 58.) The term may be qualified by the colors *ele'ele, kea* or *ke'oke'o, 'ula'ula*. *Lele nō ka 'ohe i kona lua*, the 'ohe leaps into its hole [a legendary reference; each in his own place]. **6.** Variety of fish (no data).

'ō.hea. vs. **1.** Drowsy, apathetic, as after eating a big meal. *Fig.*, weak, ineffective. *He pua 'ōhea kēnā, kū 'ole i ke kikowaena* (song), a weak arrow that of yours, it doesn't hit the bull's eye. **2.** Warm, tasteless, as water exposed to the sun.

'ō.hea.hea. Redup. of *'ōhea 1, 2. 'Ōheahea ho'i kēia lā*, today is drowsy, sleepy.

'ohe 'ala. n. Sweet cane (Isa. 43.24).

'ō.he'e. Same as *alahe'e*, a small tree.

'ō he'e. nv. Octopus spearing; to spear octopuses.

'ō.heha. vs. Somewhat lazy. See *heha, maheha*.

'ohe hano ihu. Same as *hano*, nose flute.

'ohe Hawai'i. n. Native bamboo *(Schizostachyum glaucifolium)* with long green joints, and large leaves. Wood soft, makes best *pū'ili*, rattles; formerly made into straw for hats. (Neal 62.)

'ohe ho'o.nui 'ike. n. Microscope. *Lit.*, tube magnifying vision.

'ohe kā.'eke.'eke. See *kā'eke'eke.*

'ohe Kahiki. n. Bamboo with short, green joints and large leaves. Wood hard, used for knives, fishing poles, house construction. Introduced from Tahiti. (HP 213.)

'ohe kani. n. Flute. *Lit.*, playing bamboo.

'ohe kā.pala, 'ohe kā.pala.pala. n. Piece of bamboo carved for printing tapa; bamboo stamp. *Lit.*, printing bamboo.

'ō.heke. vs. Somewhat modest, shy. Cf. *heke.* *He 'ōheke wale kō ke kua'āina kānaka,* country people are rather shy. *ho'ō.heke.* To cause shyness, to be modest.

'ohe kiko'o.lā. n. A native tree *(Tetraplasandra waimeae),* found only in forests of Kaua'i above Waimea; about 9 m tall, with few branches, the leaves about 30 cm long, each leaf with five to thirteen large, oblong leaflets, and like some other araliads, with many flowers in umbels. *Lit.*, straggly bamboo.

'ohe kukulu.ae'o. Same as *'ohe 4.*

'ō.hela.hela. Similar to *helahela.*

'ohe lau li'i.li'i. n. Small-leafed bamboo.

'ohe li'i.li'i. n. Dwarf bamboo.

'ō.helo. 1. n. A small native shrub *(Vaccinium reticulatum),* in the cranberry family; it has many branches with many small, rounded, toothed leaves, and bears round, red or yellow berries, which are edible raw or cooked for sauce. Formerly sacred to Pele, to whom offerings were made by throwing fruiting branches into the fiery pit at Kī-lau-ea. Wind-dried leaves are still used for tea. (Neal 662–3.) 2. nvi. To move rapidly this way and that or back and forth, as a stick poking an oven; to ram; ramrod. See *helo 1, ōno'unou, pae 1.* 3. n. A hula dance; the dancer leans over on one side, supporting himself with one hand, and with the opposite foot and arm making a sawing motion; many *mele 'ōhelo* have sexual import. Also *hula helo.* 4. n. General name for *Vaccinium* spp., found on all islands but not common around Kī-lau-ea Crater. Fruits are edible but smaller than *'ōhelo 1.*

'ō.helo 'ai. Same as *'ōhelo 1.* *Lit.*, edible *'ohelo.*

'ō.helo ele.'ele. n. Blackberries.

'ō.helo.helo. vs. Pink, rosy, of the color of *'ōhelo* berries. *He aloha nō nā pua, nā pua 'ōhelohelo,* beloved the blossoms, the pink blossoms. *ho'ō.helo.helo.* To color pink.

'ō.helo hui.hui. n. Name of a seaweed.

'ō.helo huki manu. n. Flexible gummed rod used for extracting *'ua'u* fledglings from their holes. *Lit.*, rod for pulling birds.

'ō.helo kai. Same as *'ae'ae,* a shrub.

'ō.helo kau lā.'au. n. A native bush *(Vaccinium calycinum)* related to the *'ōhelo 1* but taller and having larger leaves and less palatable fruit. *Lit.*, *'ōhelo* placed on trees.

'ō.helo papa. n. A native strawberry *(Fragaria chiloensis* var. *sandwicensis)* growing on Hawai'i and Maui between altitudes of 1,050 and 1,800 m, and closely related to varieties from Alaska and Patagonia. The whole plant, except the upper side of the leaves, is silky-hairy. Fruits ripen from June to September, and are red. Other cultivated species and varieties, with larger fruits, are grown in Hawai'i. (Neal 393.)

'ohe mauka. n. A small native tree *(Tetraplasandra oahuensis),* found only on O'ahu; much like its relative, the *'ohe-o-kai,* but having oblong, entire leaflets. *Lit.*, upland *'ohe.*

'ō.hemo. 1. vs. Weak, as resulting from dysentery. *ho.'ō.hemo.* To cause weakness; to pretend weakness. 2. Rare var. of *ho'ohemo.* See *hemo.* *He ukuhi 'ōhemo nā keiki,* children completely weaned.

'ō.hemo.hemo. Redup. of *'ōhemo.*

'ohe nā.nā. n. Spyglass, telescope, microscope. See ex., *'ōhuna. Lit.*, tube for looking.

'ohe nau.paka. n. A native *naupaka (Scaevola glabra* and *S. kauaiensis),* a shrub or small tree of the moun-

tains, with yellow, curved, tubular flowers, about 2.5 cm long.

'ohene. Same as *'Olu-'Ekeloa-ho'oka'a-moena,* but a guardian of the opposite sex of the high chief or chiefess whose sleeping place was guarded.

ohe.ohe. vs. Tall and straight, as a tree; precipitous, steep. See *Liliko'i ē, oheohe i luna lā,* the rain at Liliko'i, so steep and high.

'ohe.'ohe. n. 1. Tall native trees *(Tetraplasandra kavaiensis* and varieties), closely related to the *'ohe mauka,* and found on all Hawaiian Islands. (Neal 652.) Also *Reynoldsia sandwicensis* (Niihau). 2. Same as *pū'ohe-'ohe,* Job's-tears. 3. A variety of sweet potato.

'ohe-o-kai. Same as *'ohe kukuluae'o.*

'ō.hepa. vs. Moronic. See *hepa.*

'ohe pi'o. n. Siphon. *Lit.*, bent bamboo.

'ohe puhi ahi. n. Bamboo fire-blowing tube.

'ohe puluka. n. Flute. *Lit.*, flute *(Eng.)* bamboo.

'ō.heu. vt. To sprout, as young seedlings or as a young man's beard; to weed fine young seedlings.

'ō.heu.heu. Redup. of *'ōheu;* fuzzy.

'ō.hewa. vs. Delirious, incoherent, as a drunkard. *ho.'ō.hewa.* To bring on drunkenness; drunk, incoherent.

'ō.hewa.hewa. Redup. of *'ōhewa;* psychotic. *'Ōhewahewa 'ōpulepule,* delirium tremens. *'Ōhewahewa ka maka,* bleary eyed, glazed eyes. *ho.'ō.hewa.hewa.* Redup. of *ho'ōhewa.*

'ohe wai. n. Water pipe, hose; bamboo water container.

ohi. 1. nvs. Young animal, usually female; maiden just entering womanhood; youth; youthful growth. See *pua'a ohi, wohi. Ohi moa,* pullet. *Pipi ohi* (Isa. 7.21), young cow, heifer. (PPN *osi.*) 2. vt. To peel, as bark. *Rare.* 3. n. Shoots from roots, as of the *wauke* plant. See *wohi. 'O ka huli maika'i, 'oia ka wauke i pau i ke kua 'ia mamua, ā 'o ka wauke i ulu a'e mahope he 'ae ia, ā me ohi; ua ulu a'e ka wauke hou ma ke a'a a ma ka weli o ka wauke kahiko,* the best planting slips were from the mulberry which had been cut back before; the mulberry that grew back afterward were the *'ae* and the *ohi* shoots; the mulberry grew again from the roots and the main root of the old mulberry.

'ohi. 1. nvt. To gather, harvest, cull, pick, select; to collect, as wages or taxes; to take away or usurp, as land; to draft, as soldiers; to buy; gathering, selection; bundle, as of taro leaves. *Nā mea 'ohi,* gleanings. *Mea 'ohi kālā,* cashier, money collector. *Ua 'ohi 'ia nā kia'i,* the guards were selected. *Ka-'ohi-nani* (street name, Honolulu), the beautiful gathering [said to refer to bountiful harvests]. *'Ohi mai noho'i 'o Iēhowa ia'u* (Hal. 27.10), the Lord has taken me up. (PCP *ko(f,s)i.*) 2. vi. To gush, chatter aimlessly and ramblingly, gabble. See *hāpuku 2; 'ohikui, pua'ohi, waha'ohi.*

'ohia. Pas/imp. of *'ohi 1. 'Ohia mai ā pau pono nā 'ike kumu o Hawai'i* (chant for Ka-lā-kaua), gather up every bit of the basic knowledge of Hawai'i.

'ō.hi'a. 1. n. Two kinds of trees: see *'ōhi'a 'ai* and *'ōhi'a lehua.* (PCP *k(a,o)(f,s)ika.*) 2. n. Tomato. See *'ōhi'a lomi.* 3. n. A native variety of sugar cane: deep-red and green striped cane when young, becoming bronze-red and yellow-brown on exposure (like leaves and flowers of the *'ōhi'a 'ai,* the source of its name); leaves somewhat variegated. (HP 222, 225.) 4. n. A variety of taro. 5. n. A red birthmark, said to be caused by the pregnant mother's longing for mountain apples *('ōhi'a 'ai)* and eating them. 6. vs. Tabooed, as food patches during famine, so-called because people did not eat from their taro patches, but from upland *'ōhi'a 'ai,* ti, and sweet potatoes (Ii 77).

'ō.hi'a 'ai. n. The mountain apple *(Eugenia malaccensis),* a forest tree to 15 m high, found on many islands of the Pacific. It belongs to the myrtle family, has large oval leaves, tufted flowers growing from trunk and branches, and cerise, apple-like fruits. Formerly Hawaiians prepared the fruit, splitting and drying it in the sun. (Neal 636.) *Lit.*, edible *'ōhi'a. 'Ōhi'a noho i ka malu,* 'ōhi'a staying in the shade [of flawless beauty; this tree grows in forests].

'ō.hi'a 'ā.hihi. See 'āhihi 1.

'ō.hi'a 'ai ke'o.ke'o. n. A rare form of 'ōhi'a 'ai (Eugenia malaccensis f. cericarpa) with white blossoms and white fruit.

'ō.hi'a 'ā.pane. Same as 'ōhi'a lehua except that the blossom is dark-red. Perhaps the name refers to the redness of the 'apapane, a bird.

'ō.hi'a hā. Same as hā 7, a native species of Eugenia (E. sandwicensis, Neal 635), reported by Thrum as kauokahiki and by Rock as pā'ihi (Maui).

'ō.hi'a hā.kea. Same as 'ōhi'a kea.

'ō.hi'a hā.mau. Same as lehua hāmau.

'ō.hi'a haole. n. Tomato. See 'ōhi'a lomi.

'ō.hi'a kea. n. An 'ōhi'a 'ai or 'ōhi'a lehua with white blossoms.

'ō.hi'a kō. n. 'Ōhi'a log dragged (kō) from the uplands to the sea to be made into a canoe.

'ōhi'a kū. n. A native filmy fern (Mecodium recurvuum) with narrow, subdivided fronds, to 30 cm long, growing on trees in damp forests. Lit., standing [on] 'ōhi'a.

'ō.hi'a kū ma kua. Same as 'ōhi'a lehua.

'ō.hi'a Laka. n. A legendary 'ōhi'a tree that bore only two flowers, a red one on an eastern branch and a white one on the western branch; the wood was believed endowed with mana.

'ō.hi'a lehua. See lehua.

'ō.hi'a lehua pua.kea. n. An 'ōhi'a lehua with white flowers.

'ō.hi'a leo. n. A poetic name for 'ōhi'a 'ai. Lit., voice 'ōhi'a, so called because these fruit trees were not taboo. Cf. lehua hāmau.

'ō.hi'a loke. n. The rose apple (Eugenia jambos), a tree from tropical Asia, to about 9 m high, bearing round, crisp, edible fruits 2.5 cm or more in diameter, which are yellowish and pink and have a roselike odor. (Neal 635.) Lit., rose (Eng.) 'ōhi'a.

'ō.hi'a lomi. n. The common table tomato (Lycopersicon esculentum var. commune), sometimes used for lomi salmon. (Neal 747–8); called 'ōhi'a on Ni'ihau.

'ō.hi'a ma ka nahele. n. The currant tomato (Lycopersicon pimpinellifolium), resembling the common table tomato but with small round red fruits only about 1.3 cm in diameter. A native of Peru, it has long been growing wild in Hawai'i. Lit., 'ōhi'a in the brush. (Neal 478.)

'ō.hi'a 'ula. n. An 'ōhi'a 'ai with red fruit.

'ō.hi'a 'ula.'ula. n. Similar to 'ōhi'a lehua puakea but with red flowers. (For. 5:623.)

'ohi hā.puku. See hāpuku 2.

'Ohi'i.kau. n. A hold in lua fighting.

'ohi.kau. nvi. To listen in order to gossip; to gossip; a gossip.

'ō.hiki. 1. vt. To probe, pry, pick out; to prod, as the earth with a digging stick; to shell, as peas; to pick, as the teeth or nose; to clean out, as the ears. 2. n. Sand crab, probably Ocypode ceratophthalma and O. laevis. Lua 'ōhiki (For. 6:80), sand crab hole [said of a house improperly placed and open on all sides to attack, as a crab hole, by sickness or misfortune]. 3. n. Tapa design.

'ō.hiki 'au moana. n. Crabs found in the open ocean, possibly of the genera Planes or Pachygrapsus (P. marinus). Lit., ocean-swimming 'ōhiki.

'ō.hiki.hiki. Redup. of 'ōhiki 1; to pry into the past, especially an unsavory past. Cf. lā'au 'ōhikihiki niho.

'ō.hiki maka loa. n. 1. A variety of edible crab (no data). Lit., long-eyed 'ōhiki. 2. (Cap.) Name of a stroke in lua fighting.

'ō.hiki niho. n. Toothpick.

'ohi.kui. vi. To talk ramblingly.

'ō.hila. vs. Somewhat ashamed, shy. See hila.

'ohi loa'a. nv. To collect revenue; revenue collection.

'ohina. n. Gathering, collecting; selection. Cf. 'aupapa and 'ohi, to pick. Ho'okahi nō 'ohina, piha ku'u 'eke

kālena (old sailor's song), only one collecting, my coin purse is full.

'ō.hinu. 1. nvs. Shiny, greasy; piece of roasted meat; roast; grease. Ka 'ōhinu lele uahi manu ē (chant), the grease coming from the bird smoke. 2. vt. To roast or broil lightly. (For. 5:277.)

'ō.hinu.hinu. Redup. of 'ōhinu.

'ō.hio. vi. Gusty, windy; to let wind. Fig., uncertain, vague, flighty. Cf. hihio. 'O ka mea i ho'olālā 'ia, ke 'ōhio nei nō, the plan is still vague.

ohi.ohi. 1. nvi. To grow vigorously, flourish; young shoots, as of wauke (Kam. 76:110) or from natural layering of olonā branches on fallen trunks. Ulu ohiohi nā lehua o Pana-'ewa i ka mili 'ia e ka ua Kani-lehua (song), the lehua of Pana-'ewa grow splendidly, constantly fondled by the lehua-drinking rain. Ua like nō ke kanu 'ana (o ke olonā) me ke kanu 'ana o ka wauke, he ohiohi kekahi, he mauwā kahiko kekahi; he pālaha na'e kona i lalo, a ma ka lālā e ulu kākiwi a'e ai, the planting (of olonā) was like the planting of wauke, some (slips) were young shoots, some (from) fallen trunks; but they spread downward, and from the branches layerings grew. 2. vs. To show, of wood grain.

'ohi.'ohi. Redup. of 'ohi 1, 2. (PCP ko(f,s)iko(f,s)i.)

'ohi.'ohia. Redup. of 'ohia.

'ō.hi'o.hi'o. 1. vs. Tipsy. Cf. kāhi'o. 2. n. A seaweed.

'ō.hipa. Var. of 'ōhepa.

'ohi.pua. Same as pua'ohi, to chatter.

'ō.hi'u. 1. Same as 'ōhiki; to dig up the past, especially past sins of others. 2. nvt. Stick used as a needle in thatching; to thatch thus.

'ō.hi'u.hi'u. 1. Redup. of 'ōhi'u. 2. Var. name for blue uhu, parrot fish, so called at Ka-wai-hae, Hawai'i.

'ō.hi'u niho. n. Toothpick. Lit., probe tooth.

'ohi wauke. n. Bundle of wauke bark.

oho. nvi. 1. Hair of the head; leaves of plants; fronds of ferns (see ex., 'ūpalu); to leaf out, sprout. Cf. lauoho. Oho kā ho'i ka ulu 'ana o ka palai, the ferns are growing and sending out leaves. 2. To call out, cry, yell; outcry; to leap up, as startled birds. Ke oho 'ālana (For. 6:377), the proclaimed offering. ho.'ō.ho. To exclaim, cheer, shout, halloo. (Puk. 24.3.) Cf. ho'ōhooho below and kiko ho'ōho. 'Ōlelo ho'ōho, interjection, exclamation, whoop. (PPN ofo.)

oho.hia. Pas/imp. of oho 2; enthusiasm; enthusiastic, delighted, pleased; enthusiastic acclaim.

oho.ku'i. n. Wig, switch. Lit., added hair.

ō.hole.hole. Same as āholehole, a fish. Rare.

'ō.holi. Same as holi 1, 2.

oho lupa.lupa. 1. vs. Abundant, luxuriant, as plants or hair tresses; lush. 2. n. Name of a tapa design.

'ō.homa. Same as homa 1–3.

'ō.hono.hono. nvs. Slightly offensive odor, as of bog, marsh. Cf. honohono.

ohooho. Redup. of oho 2; to acclaim. ho.'ō.hooho. Redup. of ho'ōho. (Hal. 41.11.) (PPN ofoofo.)

'ō.hope.hope.ke'a. vi. To begin to form, of tubers (Kep. 87). Rare.

'ohu. nvs. Mist, fog, vapor, light cloud on a mountain; adorned as with leis. Hui 'ia ke 'ala me ke onaona i lei 'ohu nou, ē Ka-lani (name song for Lili'u-o-ka-lani), combined are fragrance and sweetness into a lei to adorn you, O Queen. hō'ohu. To form mist; misty, etc. (PNP kofu.)

'ō.hū. nvi. Swelling, as of the sea, especially a small comber that rises without breaking, but of sufficient strength to speed a surfboard; protuberance, bump on the head; hillock, knoll, elevation; to swell, rise in a lump, protrude; to rise, of a wave before it breaks. hō.'ō.hū. Caus/sim.

'ō.hua. 1. n. Retainers, dependents, servants, inmates, members (of a family), visitors or sojourners in a household; passengers, as on a ship. 2. n. Young of such fish as hīnālea, humuhumu, kala, kūpou, manini, pualu, uhu; also the ornate wrasse (Halichoeres orna-

tissimus). Cf. *'āhua.* **3.** vi. To slide, slip, ricochet, glance, as an arrow.

'ō.hua hā.'eka.'eka. Same as *palapōhaku,* young of *manini.*

'ō.hua kala. n. Young of the fish *kala.*

'ō.hua kā.ni'o. n. Second growth stage of *manini,* with stripes. *Lit.,* striped young.

'ō.hua kā.pena. n. Cabin *(Eng.)* passenger.

'ō.hua kū.kae pua'a. n. Young of the fish *humuhumu.* *Lit.,* pig excrement young; said to be so called because of the tale that the demigod Kama-pua'a disguised himself as one of a school of *humuhumu;* when Pele's family caught some of the *humuhumu* he appeared as a human and taunted them as grasping his excrement.

'ō.hua liko. n. Earliest growth stage of *manini,* which is transparent.

'ō.hua lī.poa. n. Young fish feeding on *līpoa,* a seaweed.

'ō.hua niho nui. n. Young, probably of *'āwela,* a fish. *Lit.,* big-toothed young.

'ō.hua 'oneki. n. Deck passenger.

'ō.hua pa'a.wela. n. Young, probably of *'āwela,* a fish.

'ō.hua pala.pō.haku. See *palapōhaku, manini* young.

'ō.hua palemo. n. Young of *uhu,* parrot fish. *Fig.,* a clever person who gets away with mischief. *Lit.,* slippery young.

'ō.hua unahi nui. Same as *'ōhua palemo. Lit.,* big-scaled young.

'ō.hu'i. vt. To twist, as in pulling out a tooth; to extract, pull out. *Rare.*

'ō.hu'i.hu'i. **1.** vs. Somewhat cool. See *hu'ihu'i.* **2.** Redup. of *'ōhu'i.*

'ō.huku. Same as *huku. 'Ōhuku 'ale,* rising billow, swell.

'ō.hule. nvs. **1.** Bald; bald person. **ho.'ō.hule.** To cause baldness; to shear the hair completely. **2.** Defeated without getting a single score, whitewashed, skunked; loser in the card game build. **ho.'ō.hule.** To whitewash, defeat.

'ō.hūle. n. Meeting point of receding and incoming waves. *Rare.*

'ō.hulu. vi. To feather out; to grow, especially of vines growing from discarded or broken bits of sweet potato; watery and of poor quality, as such potatoes.

'ō hulu. nv. Seal hunter; to spear seals. *Lit.,* spear fur.

'ō.hulu.hulu. vs. Hairy (of body hair), shaggy.

'ō.humu. nvt. To grumble, complain, find fault, conspire, plot; conspiracy. Cf. *'ōhumuhumu. 'O ka 'ōhumu e make ke ali'i,* the plot to kill the king. *'Ōhumu kini,* constantly complaining. (PCP *koo-(f,s)umu.)*

'ō.humu.humu. Redup. of *'ōhumu;* to relate one's woes, as to a sympathetic friend. *Ku'u hoa 'ōhumuhumu,* the friend to whom I may unburden myself. (PCP *koo(f,s)umu(f,s)umu.)*

'ō.humu kipi. n. Conspiracy or plot to rebel.

'ō.huna. **1.** n. Secret, hidden thing. See *huna 2. He 'ōhuna nalo 'ole kāu i ka 'ike a ku'u 'ohe nānā* (song), yours is a secret that cannot be hidden from my telescope. **2.** Same as *'ōhune 1, 2.*

'ō.hune. **1.** n. Skin rash. **2.** n. Small goby. See *'ōlohe 6.* **3.** Same as *hune,* tiny. **4.** n. A kind of seaweed.

'ō.hune wela. n. A heat rash, prickly heat. *Pi'i ka 'ōhune wela,* to get a heat rash.

'ohu.'ohu. **1.** Redup. of *'ohu. 'Ohu'ohu i nā lei,* decked with leis. **2.** n. White tapa with black dots and figures.

'ohū.'ohū. Redup. of *'ōhū.*

oi. **1.** vi. To move; to turn sideways, as contemptuously; to slouch along, gyrate along; to pull away, as in anger; motion of leisurely swaying (less common than *oioi).* Cf. *-oio, oioi. Mai oi aku 'olua a kokoke* (FS 49), don't you two move up too close. *Pau ke oi 'ana o kō lāua mau kino,* their bodies stopped slouching about [in anger]. (PNP *oi.)* **2.** Same as *ō 2, oia. 'Oi noke, oi huli, oi naku, oi huli nā kānaka, 'a'ole loa'a iki,* the people kept persevering, kept hunting, kept delving, kept hunting, without any success at all.

oī. Var. spelling of *ōwī 1–3.*

'oi. **1.** nvs. Sharp, acute; sharpness; a sharp sign in music which raises the pitch of the following note a semitone. *I laila ka 'oi kepa lua o Hina-moe* (For. 6:373), there the sharp double snapping [tusks] of Hina-moe. **hō.'oi.** To sharpen. (PPN *kohi.)* **2.** nvs. Best, superior, superb, main, prominent, exceeding; to exceed, excel; left-over, extra, remaining, above, odd. *Maui nō ka 'oi,* Maui indeed is the best. [Note that *nō* in this sentence qualifies *Maui. Nō ka 'oi* without a preceding noun is ungrammatical.] *Mea e 'oi a'e,* what is best, advantage. *A 'oi, emi mai,* more or less. *Hola 'elua ā 'oi,* two o'clock or a little after. *'Oi aku ka 'ino,* worse. *'O ka lehua ka 'oi kela o nā pua, lehua* is the best of flowers. *'Oi loa,* superlative, the very best. **hō.'oi.** To excel; best. *Hō'oi i ka pili,* to raise a bet. *Nā pono kaulele hō'oi* (song), the gains over and above. [In divination, a priest may put two piles of pebbles under a tapa; then he counts the pebbles in each pile by twos; if none are left over in the would-be thief's pile this is called even *(pahu);* this means bad luck for the thief if his would-be victim is odd. If both piles are odd, or both piles are even, this, too, is indicative of failure. Having an odd number is good if the victim has an even number. (For. 6:73.)] **3.** Same as *oiai 1, 2* but rare.

'o'i. vi. To limp. **hō.'o'i.** To cause to limp, pretend to limp. (PEP *koki.)*

oia. Same as *ō 2* and *oi 2;* to keep doing, persevere, continue. See *ne'e, oia mau nō.*

'oia. **1.** nvs. Truth; true. Often used idiomatically to mean this, namely this, namely, thus, that's it, that's right, go ahead; start, begin, go (as shouted by referee at beginning of games). See *'oia ana. 'Oia nō!* Yes, that's so; that's right, really. *'Ā 'oia,* certainly, that's right, really. *'Oia 'ea!* Is that so! So that's it! *'Oia ho'i! So it is! That's so! Namely . . . , as follows . . . 'Oia paha,* maybe so, all right (as in reluctant acquiescence). *Maka-pu'u lā a 'oia mai,* just this side of Maka-pu'u. *Ke nānā aku 'oe i kēlā keiki, 'oia nō 'oe 'o ke keko,* when you look at that child, [he's] just like a monkey. *'Oia noho'i hā kona meu i hele ai,* so that's why hc went; no wonder he wcnt. *E hele mai ā 'ike he 'oia ka'u,* come and see the truth with me. **hō.'oia.** To confirm, affirm, guarantee, audit, verify, profess (Kanl. 26.17). *Luna hō'oia,* auditor. **2.** Part. *'o + ia 1.*

'o . . . ia. Idiom indicating recent action. Just, just now. (Gram. 9.2.) *'O ka 'ai 'ana ihola nō ia o lākou, ā hele aku nei,* they had just eaten, and then went. *'O ka make nō ia o ke ali'i,* the chief has just died.

'oia ana! interj. Let me see! Show me! I dare you (sarcastically)! (Usually shortened to *'olana* or *'oliana.)*

'oia ana nō. idiom. It's the same result; regardless.

'oia 'ane'i! interj. Is that so! So that's it!

'oia ho'i hā! interj. All right, then; so that's it after all. (About the same as *'oia ho'i:* see *'oia 1.)*

'oi.ai. conj. **1.** While, meanwhile, during. (Gram. 11.1.) *'Oiai au i ke kula,* while I was at school. *'Oiai i ke au o Ka-mehameha,* during the time of Ka-mehameha. **2.** Although. *Ua hō'eha 'oia 'oiai nō 'a'ohe ona lima,* he was hurt, but not his hands.

'oia.'i'o. nvs. True; truth, fact; truly, firmly, certainly, genuine, real, sure, verily, authentic; faithfulness (Hal. 92.2). Cf. *'i'o, palapala hō'oia'i'o. 'O au nō me ka 'oia'i'o,* I am, sincerely; yours truly. *Nā mea 'oia'i'o,* facts, true items. *'Oiu'i'o, he 'oia'i'o* (Ioane 16.20), verily, verily. *'Oia'i'o kā ho'i,* is that so, so [as in surprise, anger]. **hō.'oia.'i'o.** To verify, certify, check, convince, make sure, prove; to acknowledge, as a title; deed, proof, verification. *Hō'oia'i'o 'ana,* acknowledgments. *Ma laila i hō'oia'i'o ai lāua i kō lāua mau minute 'olu'olu* (Laie 581), there they fulfilled their minutes of pleasure.

oia mau nō. idiom. Same as ever, continuing the same, just the same (often said in answer to *Pehea 'oe?* How are you?) See *ō 2; oia.*

'oiana. See *'oia ana.*

'oia noho'i hā. Same as *'oia ho'i hā.* See ex., *'oia 2.*

'oia paha. See 'oia.

'oi.hana. 1. nvs. Occupation, trade, job, employment, position, career, service (as religious or military), ministry, rite, industry, business, bureau, customs, activities, department, agency, office; Biblical book of Acts; professional. *Noho 'oihana,* office or job holder; to stay in an office or job. *'Oihana mahi 'ai,* agricultural industry. *'Oihana mākaukau loa,* speciality. *Ma o ka 'oihana,* ex officio. *'Ike pili 'oihana,* professional knowledge. *'Oihana 'oko'a o nā hua 'ōlelo,* function of words. 2. n. Tools, utensils. (Puk. 38.3.)

'oi.hana ali'i. n. 1. Duty or office of chief or king. 2. *(Cap.)* Book of Chronicles (Old Testament).

'oi.hana hana kā.lā (dala). n. Mint. *Lit.,* moneymaking department.

'oi.hana hana lima. n. Trade.

'oi.hana hemo.lele. n. Clergy. *Lit.,* pure profession.

'oi.hana ho'o.na'au.ao. n. 1. Educational system, profession. 2. *(Cap.)* Department of Instruction.

'oi.hana hui malū. n. Society of Masons.

'oi.hana kahuna. n. 1. Priesthood, office and duties of a priest, minister, or sorcerer. 2. *(Cap.)* Book of Leviticus in the Old Testament.

'oi.hana kā.kau kope. n. Registration office. *Lit.,* copyrighting office.

'oi.hana kā.lā, 'oi.hana 'imi kā.lā. n. Finance.

'oi.hana kā.lai.'āina. n. Department of Interior, in the days of the monarchy.

'oi.hana kā.lepa. n. Commerce, mercantile profession.

'oi.hana kā.nā.wai. n. Judicial department.

'oi.hana kinai ahi. n. Fire department; job of putting out fires. *Lit.,* fire-extinguishing job or department.

'oi.hana kiu. n. Secret service, department of secret police.

'oi.hana koa. n. Military service.

'oi.hana kū.'ai 'āina. n. Real estate business.

'oi.hana leka. n. Postal department.

'oi.hana miki.'ala. n. Manufacturing. *Rare.*

'oi.hana moku.lele. n. Aviation.

'oi.hana wai. n. 1. Water works. 2. *(Cap.)* Department (or Board) of Water Supply.

'oi ho'i hā. Same as *'oia ho'i hā.*

'ō.iho.iho. vi. To go downwards, as deep sweet potatoes. (For. 6:125.)

'ō.iki. vs. Somewhat small, narrow.

'ō.ikiiki. vs. Somewhat hot, warm. Cf. *ikiiki.*

oi.kū. vi. To heave the shoulders, as during an attack of asthma; to wallow, strain; spasm of pain. *Eia Hawai'i nui o Keawe, ke oikū nei me ka 'eha'eha* (chant for Kapi'o-lani), here is great Hawai'i of Keawe, heaving spasms of pain.

'o'i.lepa. Short for *'ō 'ili lepa,* a fish.

'ō.'ili. 1. nvi. To appear; come into view; appearance. *'Ō'ili ka maka,* to come up, as seeds, bulbs; to sprout. See ex., *pulelo.* 2. n. Heart (of emotions). *Ku'u 'ō 'ili ke lele wale nei* (For. 5:307), my heart throbs with strong emotions. *'Apo'apo a'ela kona 'ō'ili* (Mat. 2.3), troubled, agitated. 3. n. Filefish, including *Cantherhines dumerili;* see below. (PEP kookili.)

'ō.'ili.'ili. Redup. of *'ō'ili;* appearing here and there, once or successively. *Ua 'ō'ili'ili* (Kep. 184), rain that comes and goes. (PCP kookilikili.)

'ō.'ili lepa. n. Squaretail filefish *(Cantherhines sandwichiensis);* black with reddish-yellow fins. *Lit.,* flag appearing, so called because of top fin.

'ō.'ili lua. vs. Prominent, conspicuous, clearly seen. *'Ō'ili lua kēlā hale e kū maila i ka pu'u,* that house on the hill is very conspicuous.

'ō.'ili oe.oe. Said to be same as *'ō'ili 'uwī'uwī. Lit.,* long-necked *'ō'ili.*

'ō.'ili 'uwī.'uwī. n. Fantail filefish *(Pervagor spilosoma);* yellow with black dots on its body, a diagonal stripe on head; the tail is orange; this fish is seldom seen but occasionally appears in great numbers and by some is considered an omen of the future death of royalty; sometimes they are washed ashore; seldom eaten but sometimes the dried fish are used for fuel. *Lit.,* squealing *'ō'ili,* so called because of the noise it makes.

'ō.'ili wale. vi. To appear for no apparent reason, especially of premature birth.

'ō.ilo. 1. nvi. Seedling; to germinate, sprout. 2. n. Young, as of *'ō'io* or of eel. (PEP koo'ilo.)

'oi lua. vs. Two-edged, as a dagger.

oio. Name given for a section of a canoe rim, pronunciation unknown. (For. 5:612–3.)

'oio. Rare var. of *noio,* a tern.

-'oio. hō.'oio. To show off, boast; to assume an air of superiority, as a child who cuts capers; conceited; affectation, conceit. Cf. *'oi. Hō'oio le'a,* to show off with delight.

'oi'o. n. Procession of ghosts of a departed chief and his company. More commonly called *huaka'i pō.*

'ō.'io. n. 1. Ladyfish, bonefish *(Albula vulpes).* Stages of growth are: *pua 'ō'io,* finger length; *'āmo'omo'o,* forearm length; *'ō'io,* adult, 60 to 90 cm long. See ex., *halalē.* 2. Soft jelly-like coconut flesh, so called perhaps because of its resemblance to mashed *'ō'io.* 3. Kind of braid or plaiting, as in hat bands, so called because it was thought to resemble the backbone of the *'ō'io.* 4. Stone used for polishing and as octopus lure. 5. Long bundle of salt or fish. (And.)

'ō 'i'o. n. Fork (Puk. 38.3), flesh hook.

oi.oi. Redup. of *oi 1;* to squirm.

o'i.o'i. vi. To rest. (For. 5:499.) Cf. *o'io'ina.* (PPN okioki.)

'oi.'oi. 1. Redup. of *'oi 2;* superior; a superior person. *He 'oi'oi nō Maui Hikina* (FS 299), East Maui is prominent indeed [said of a superior thing, as of feminine beauty]. hō.'oi.'oi. To show off, act superior or aggressive, flaunt; pretentious, obtrusive; upstart. *Hō'oi'oi 'ole,* unobtrusive, modest. *Hahaki i ke kānāwai me ka hō'oi'oi mai,* blatant law breaker. (PPN kohikohi.) 2. nvi. Full of sharp points, pointed, sharp; thorn; to protrude, stick or jut out. *Pā lā'au 'oi'oi* (Mika 7.4), thorn hedge. hō.'oi.'oi. To sharpen, make sharp points. (PCP koikoi.)

'o'i.'o'i. Redup. of *'o'i,* to limp.

oi.oi.kū. Redup. of *oikū.*

'oi.'oina. n. Point, peak, cape, promontory, headland.

o'i.'oina. nv. Resting place for travelers, such as a shady tree, rock (PH 20); to rest. *Kahi o'io'ina* (Kin. 42.27), inn.

'ō.'io.'io. vi. To chitchat, chirp. Cf. *'io'io.*

-'oiole'a. hō.'oio.le'a. Conceit; to show off.

'ō.iwi. 1. nvs. Native, native son. Cf. *iwi,* bone; *kulāiwi.* *Hui 'ōiwi,* society of native sons. ho.'ō.iwi. To pass oneself off as a native son; like a native son. (PCP kooiwi.) 2. nvi. Physique, appearance; to appear. *Lamalama ka 'ōiwi,* a physique glowing with health. *Maika'i ho'i kō ia ala 'ōiwi kino,* he certainly has a fine physique. *Nani ka 'ōiwi o Hilo i ka lehua* (chant, For. 5:305), Hilo appears beautiful with *lehua.* 3. n. Self; own. See ex., *pūpū 5.*

oka. 1. n. Dregs, crumbs, sediment, hulls, grounds, small bits or pieces. Also *'āoka.* 2. Var. of *kumuoka,* net.

'oka. n. 1. Oak. *Eng.* 2. Also ota. Oats. *Eng.* 3. See *'oka kilika.*

'ō.kā. 1. vs. Overcome by emotion, as fear; speechless with emotion. *Fig.,* destroyed *(rare).* 2. vt. To set a decoy. *Rare.*

'ō.ka'a. nvi. To revolve, spin; to roll, as a mat; a top; a roll; a dry coconut whose meat has detached itself so as to make a rattling sound. *'Ōka'a lau hala,* roll of pandanus leaves.

o ka'e. Same as *o kana* (always used with *'a'ole*).

'ō.kai. Same as *'ōkaikai. Ka 'ōkai makani* (For. 4:591), the rough wind.

'ō.ka'i. 1. n. Large night moth. See ex., *'aolo.* 2. nvi. Tendrils of a plant; to grow, interlock, interweave, as tendrils. Cf. *wili'ōka'i.* 3. Same as *ka'i,* procession. See ex., *'e'a 1*. **4.** n. Blossom container of bananas. Cf. *'e'a 2*. **5.** n. Cords on the mouth of a fish net, as for *iheihe* fish. **6.** Small oblong net connecting two larger fish nets. (AP.)

'ō.kai.kai. nvs. Rough, as the sea; angry, bad-tempered; rough seas (sometimes preceded by *ke*). *Ka lua o nā lā 'ōkaikai* (Kep. 105), second of the days with rough sea. *Ke mau ala nō ke 'ōkaikai ma Rusia* (a newspaper headline), rough seas continue for Russia.

'Okaka. n. A particular company of soldiers belonging to Ka-mehameha.

'ō.kā.kai. Same as *hūkākai*, insipid.

'ō.kā.ka'i. n. Follower, as in a retinue.

'ō.kakala. Redup. of *'ōkala 1, 2*. *Pi'i maila ka 'ōkakala*, goose flesh comes.

'okaka.lika 'akika, okasalika asida. n. Oxalic acid. *Eng.*

'oka kilika. n. The silky or silver oak *(Grevillea robusta)*, a large tree from Australia, used for reforesting in Hawai'i. The leaves are subdivided like some ferns; the orange flowers are abundant in early summer. (Neal 320–1.) *Lit.*, silk oak. *Eng.* Also *ha'ikū ke'oke'o* and on Ni'ihau, *'oka.*

'Oka.kopa, Okatopa. n. October. *Eng.*

oka kope. n. Coffee grounds.

'ō.kala. **1.** nvi. Goose flesh, creepy or shuddery sensation; to bristle, stand up, as hair. See ex., *'oehuehu.* **2.** vs. Rough, coarse, as cloth, shark skin. **3.** See *leho 'ōkala.* **4.** Same as *'ōkole 2*, a sea creature. **5.** n. A rather small red seaweed *(Galaxaura rugosa)*, regularly and densely branching, the branches hollow and marked with rings; not edible. Also *pākalakala (Galaxaura* spp.*)*

oka lā.'au. n. Wood shavings, sawdust.

'ō.kala.kala. **1.** Redup. of *'ōkala 1, 2*; rough, boisterous in manner. See *kani 1*, bristle. *'Ōkalakala kāna pane*, his reply was gruff. *Pi'i a'ela kona huhū ā ke po'o 'ōkalakala* (For. 5:409), his anger flashed up to his bristling head. *'Ōkalakala koke a'ela 'o 'Ai-wohikupua e hele e māka'ika'i i ka 'aha mokomoko* (Laie 383), 'Ai-wohi-kupua bristled with eagerness to visit the boxing arena. **2.** vt. To undo evil influence by prayer.

'ō.kale.kale. vs. Watery, as inferior poi.

o kana. See *kana 2*.

'okana. n. **1.** District or subdistrict, usually comprising several *ahupua'a*; portion, as of food. See *'oki*, to cut. **2.** Organ. *Eng. 'Okana wili lima*, hand organ.

'oka.naki, oganadi. n. Organdy. *Eng.*

'oka.nika. vs. Organic (said of the Organic Act). *Eng.*

oka.oka. Redup. of *oka. Ua nau 'ia ka niu e ka pua'a a okaoka*, the coconut was chewed by the pig into small particles. **ho.'ōka.oka.** To pulverize, cut into little pieces. (PPN *'ota 'ota*.)

'oka.'oka. n. A bad odor, as of garbage.

'oka'o.kai. vs. Insipid, tasteless, especially of freshly pounded poi.

oka palaoa. n. Chaff. *Lit.*, wheat sediment.

'oka pua 'ula.'ula. Same as *kāhili, ha'ikū*, gingers. *Ni'ihau.*

'okawa, otava. n. Octave. (MK 7.) *Eng.*

'oke. vs. Rotten, as wood, cloth. *Rare.*

ō.kea. **1.** n. White sand or gravel (contraction of *one*, sand, and *kea*, white). Cf. *Ke-ōkea*, a place name. *Ōkea pili mai*, drift gravel, said disparagingly of persons who attach themselves to others for support; parasite. *Lit.*, gravel clinging. **2.** vs. Hot, as stone heated to whiteness. **3.** n. A bird (KL line 432, no data).

'ō.ke'a. nv. To place cross sticks, as to block an entrance; cross sticks.

'ō.ke'a. vi. To veer, as the wind; to change, as direction; to eddy.

'okeke.lika, oseterika. n. Ostrich. *Eng. 'Akolika* is more common.

'okele, okere. n. Ocher. *Eng.*

ō.kele.kele. vs. Muddy.

'okele.kelika. n. Ostrich. *Eng.*

'ō.keni. Same as *kenikeni*, small change. *Ua loa'a nā wahi 'ōkeni a nā limahana*, the workers received some small change.

'oke.'oke. Redup. of *'oke. Rare.*

'oke.pela, osepera. n. Osprey. (Oihk. 11.13.) *Eng.*

'okepe.laka, oseferaga, osiferaga. n. Vulture (RSV), ossifrage (KJV). (Oihk. 11.13.)

oki. vi. **1.** To stop, finish, end. Cf. *uoki. He i'a anei kō ka mākeke? 'A'ole, he oki loa!* Is there fish at the market? No, all gone. *Ua oki nā 'ōlelo a kāua no ka mea ke oki mai nei ka 'ona o ka 'awa ia'u* (Laie 377), our talk stopped because the intoxication of the kava for me became extraordinary. **ho.'ōki.** To put an end to, terminate, conclude, annul, finish, stop; end. (PPN *'oti*.) **2.** vs. Extraordinary, wondrous, superlative, much (usually but not always in an unfavorable sense, sometimes with idea: not at all, none, all gone). See ex., *kolihana, oki 1. Oki pau*, extraordinary. *Pehea kou makua kāne? Ua oki loa!* How's your father? Much worse! *Ua hele ke kino ā oki*, his body is wasted [by disease]. *Ua hele 'oe ā oki loa i ka lepo!* You're filthy with dirt! *Kāhiko ā oki a pā'ihi'ihi*, dressed in best finery, so attractive. *Oki noho'i ka hana a ka Hawai'i 'imi loa*, wondrous indeed are the deeds of deep-seeking Hawai'i. *Oki pau ka hana a ka huila*, wondrous the doings of the wheel. **3.** vi. To take effect, as *'awa* intoxication. See ex., *oki 1*.

'oki. nvt. To cut, especially the hair (see below); to sever, shear, snip, slit, trim, hew, mow, fell, separate, annul, cancel, divorce; to cut, as cards; to operate, amputate; to excommunicate; a cut, division, limit, operation, amputation; stanza (called *paukū* today). *'Oki i nā aumākua*, to separate oneself from pagan worship of *'aumākua* gods. *'Oki i ka moe'uhane*, cancel the dream [end bad effects of a dream by Christian prayer]. *'Oki ā lele ke po'o*, behead. *'Oki ka lauoho*, to have a haircut. **hō.'oki.** To pretend to cut short, to cause to cut, cut, divorce, dismiss, cancel, excommunicate. (PPN *koti*.)

'okia. **1.** Pas/imp. of *'oki*. See *kai'okia.* **2.** *(Cap.)* n. Wind name, Hālawa, Moloka'i. (For. 5:103.)

'ō.kihi.kihi. vs. Angular, slanting. *'Ōkihikihi nā po'ohiwi*, angular, squared shoulders. *'Ōkihikihi ka ua ke nānā aku* (chant), rain appears slanting.

'oki huelo. vt. To cut only the ends of the hair. *Lit.*, cut tail.

'oki 'ino. vt. To mutilate.

'okika. n. Orchid. *Eng.*

'okika hono.hono. n. An orchid *(Dendrobium anosmum)*. (Neal 281–2.)

'oki.kene, okigene. n. Oxygen. *Eng.*

'oki kū.mā.kena. vt. To cut the hair on one side of the head, formerly a sign of mourning.

'oki.lipi. n. A variety of sweet potato.

'ō.kilo. Same as *kilo.*

oki loa. See *oki 2.*

'oki mahi.ole. vt. To cut the hair leaving a strip down the middle. *Lit.*, helmet cut.

'oki male (mare). nvt. Divorce; to divorce. *Lit.*, cut marriage.

'oki mau'u. v. To mow the grass. *Mīkini 'oki mau'u*, lawn mower.

'okina. n. **1.** Cutting off, ending, severance, separation. (PPN *kotinga*.) **2.** Glottal stop.

'oki.'oki. Redup. of *'oki;* to cut into pieces, prune, chop, slash, carve. *Pai wela me nā mea 'ai 'oki'oki 'ia*, hot mince pie; *lit.*, hot pie with cut up food. (PPN *kotikoti*.)

'oki pahu. vt. To bob the hair. *Lit.*, smooth cut.

oki pau. See *oki 2.*

'oki poe. vt. To bob the hair. *Lit.*, round cut.

'oki poe.poe. nvt. Subincision, to subincise; circumcision, to circumcise (a Biblical euphemism, Kin. 17.10; the Hawaiian terms were *kahe ule* and *kaha ule*). *Lit.*, cut roundness.

'oki pohe. See *pohe 1.*

'oki po'o. nv. To behead.

'oki.pu'u. n. Forest clearing (term noted in O'ahu land records).

'oki pu'u. nv. To cut the throat; cutthroat.

oko. vi. To move ahead of others; to try to be better than others, surpass. *He aha kēia e oko a'e nei,* why this pushing ahead of others.

'oko'a. vs. **1.** Different, separate, unrelated, another; whole; entirety; a whole note in music; entirely, wholly, completely; altogether, fully, independently, exclusively. Cf. *ha'ina 'oko'a, holo'oko'a, ka'a'oko'a, kū'oko-'a.* See ex., *kuli 2.* *'Ai 'oko'a,* cooked unpounded taro; *lit.,* whole food. *No ke kōkua 'ole 'ia mai, hana 'oko'a ihola nō wau,* because of not being helped, I worked independently. *He ho'okuli 'oko'a iho nō.* (FS 217), a pretense of being stone deaf. *Moe 'oko'a* (FS 149), to lie down and stay, as of one exhausted. *Holo 'oko'a,* to run far away. *Ha'awipio 'oko'a,* to give up completely; unconditional surrender. **hō.'oko'a.** To make different, to set apart, distinguish, separate, cause to differ, discriminate. Cf. *ho'oka'a'oko'a.* **2.** To be early or continuing, of time of day. *I ka lā 'oko'a* (FS 31), while still daylight; in broad daylight.

'ō.kohe. vs. To form a scab, as a sore; swollen, as tonsils. **ho.'ō.kohe.** To cause a scab to form, etc.

'ō.kohe.kohe. 1. Redup. of *'ōkohe. Pu'u 'ōkohekohe,* swollen tonsils. **ho.'ō.kohe.kohe.** Redup. of *ho'ō-kohe.* **2.** n. Barnacle, such as adhere to rocks, ship bottoms, floating timber.

'ō.koholā. n. A variety of sweet potato, said to have been introduced during whaling days.

'ō koholā. nv. Whaling; to whale, harpoon whales. *Lit.,* pierce whale. Cf. *moku 'ō koholā.*

'ō.koho.lua. n. Two-pronged post-European fishing spear.

'Okoi.kua. n. Stroke in *lua* fighting.

okoko. Var. spelling of *okooko.*

'oko.komo. vs. Filled, as a canoe.

'ō.kole. n. **1.** Anus, buttocks (less polite than *lemu*). *'Ōkole maluna,* Hawaiian translation of English toast "bottoms up" [this expression is condemned by older Hawaiians as vulgar and indecent because of the sacredness of the human body in old belief]. (PCP *kootole.*) **2.** A sea creature, eaten cooked, perhaps a sea anemone. **3.** A kind of birthmark; round, black, and raised higher than the surface of the skin; believed caused by the mother's eating an annelid when pregnant.

'ō.kole emi.emi. n. A sea anemone. *Lit.,* shrinking *'ōkole.*

'ō.kole.hao. n. **1.** Liquor distilled from ti root in a still of the same name; later, a gin as made of rice or pineapple juice. *Lit.,* iron bottom. **2.** Iron try-pot still.

'ō.kole hā.wele. Same as *'ōkole emiemi. Lit.,* tied *'ōkole.*

'ō.kole ka'aka. n. Rascal anus, an insult chanted by Kama-pua'a. (FS 213.) Also *kole ka'aka.*

'okole.kē. n. A play language something like pig Latin. Example: *e hesele ana 'outou sele ihesele,* for *e hele ana 'oukou i hea?* Where are you going? [*sele* is added at random.]. See *language.*

'ō.kole.makili. Same as *mohihihi,* a vine. *Lit.,* cracked buttocks.

'ō.kole.oi.oi. nvi. To turn one's back on someone who has aroused one's anger; to walk to and fro with back towards the object of anger; to scorn; one who does this. *Lit.,* moving buttocks.

'ō.kole.'oi.'oi. n. Marigolds (*Tagetes* spp.). (Neal 849.) *Lit.,* jutting buttocks. Cf. *melekule.*

'ō.kole.pu'u. n. Bustle-style dress. *Lit.,* humped buttocks.

'ō.kolo. Same as *kolo.*

'ō.komo. vt. To insert, include; to calk, as a ship; to inlay. **ho.'ō.komo.** Caus/sim.

'ō.komo.komo. Redup. of *'ōkomo.* **ho.'ō.komo.komo.** Redup. of *ho'ōkomo.*

'okomo.pila. n. Automobile. *Eng.*

okooko, okoko. nvs. Red hot, blazing hot; burning, smarting, as an itch. *He 'ula okooko,* fiery red. *I loko 'oia o ke okooko o ke kaua,* he was in the heat of battle. *Waha okooko,* venemous, slanderous mouth.

'ō.kū. 1. nvt. To stand erect, protrude, emerge, hold upright (Nak. 79); to wield with vigor, as paddles. *Ke kanaka 'ōkū mai i ka hoe* (Kel. 46), the man working hard with the paddles. *Aia ma'ō e 'ōkū maila,* there it is, standing over there. **2.** vs. Thunderstruck, taken aback, horrified, agitated. *'Ōkū ho'i au i kō ia ala hō'ino,* I was horrified by his cursing. **3.** n. Young stage of *kūmū,* smaller than the *'āhuluhulu* stage. **4.** nv. Live bird used as decoy; to decoy. *Rare.*

'ō.ku'e.ku'e. n. Knuckles. See *ku'eku'e. Ka 'ōku'eku'e o ka pua'a,* pig knuckles.

'ō.kuhe. n. A fresh-water *'o'opu (Eleotris sandwicensis),* a fish. Called *'oau* on O'ahu and Maui. Also *'akupa, 'apohā, kuhe.*

'ō.kuhe.kuhe. n. Young *'ōkuhe,* after the *hinana* stage.

'ō.kuhe mele.mele. n. *'Ōkuhe* with yellow tinge.

'ō.kū.kū. 1. Redup. of *'ōkū 1, 2. 'Ōkūkū ihola mākou e nānā i ka i'a o ka loko,* we stood looking at the fish in the pond. *'Ōkūkū ka noho o ka humuhumu i ka 'ilikai,* the noses of the *humuhumu* rise above the surface of the sea. **2.** Same as *'ōkū 3.*

'ōku.kuli. vs. Filled to satiety, as with fat or sweet food; rich, fat. *Rare.*

'oku.kupu. Redup. of *'ōkupu.*

'oku.ku'u. n. Plural and frequentative of *ōku'u 1. 'Oku-ku'u ka noe i ka mauna,* the mist settles on the mountain.

'ō.kule.kule. vs. Somewhat *kukule,* listless.

'ō.kuli.kuli. Same as *'okukuli.*

'ō.kuma. vs. Rough, coarse, as scarred or pitted skin; close together; dark and lowering, as clouds. Cf. *kumakuma, hākumakuma. Maka 'ōkuma i ke kapu, 'o ke kapu o ka haku* (name chant for Ke-kā-ulu-ohi), face encrusted with taboo, taboo of the lord.

'ō.kuma.kuma. Redup. of *'ōkuma..*

'ō.kumu. 1. n. Pommel; canoe end-piece. Cf. *maku'u.* **2.** nvs. Stump; stumpy, blunt, cut off short, coarse. *'Ōkumu lau,* stump sending out shoots. (PEP *kootumu.*)

'ō.kumu.kumu. Redup. of *'ōkumu 2;* stumps here and there; uneven, as stubble.

'ō.kunu.kunu. vs. To have a cough, to cough constantly.

'okū.'okū. Redup. of *'ōkū;* to pitch, as a canoe tossed by waves; to rear and pitch, as a horse.

'ō.kupe. 1. nvi. A method of digging holes with a stick, prodding the earth to one side, as for taro (Kep. 153); to dig thus. **2.** vi. To trip in walking, stumble, make a false step; to err in conduct, go astray morally. **ho.'ō.-kupe.** To trip someone; to stumble or pretend to stumble. **3.** n. A bivalve *(Spondylus tenebrosus).*

'ō.kupe.kupe. Redup. of *'ōkupe 1, 2.*

'ō.kupu. vi. To sprout, as seeds; to send out shoots, as ti plants; to come forth, as clouds; sprouting, stubbles.

'ō.kupu.kupu. Redup. of *'ōkupu.* **2.** Same as *kupukupu, ni'ani'au;* any fern growing on a single stem, as the sword fern *(Nephrolepis exaltata).*

'ō.kupu.kupu lau.'i'i. n. A fern *(Doodia kunthiana)* much like *Nephrolepsis exalata, 'ōkupukupu,* but hairy. Cf. *lau'i'i.*

'ō.ku'u. 1. vi. To squat on the haunches, crouch, sit hunched up; to perch, as a bird; to settle, as mist. **ho.'ō.ku'u.** To cause to squat, crouch, perch; to crouch, perch. **2.** n. Disease at time of Ka-mehameha I, perhaps cholera, and perhaps so called because it was dysenteric, and people were squatting *('ōku'u)* much at stool. **3.** vt. To swing in *aku* (fish) on a line so they fall from the lure directly into the canoe. **4.** n. A method of catching birds by gumming artificial *lehua* blossoms made of *le'ie* to a tree.

'ō.ku'u lepo hehe'e. Same as *'ōku'u 2. Lit.,* running excrement *'ōku'u.*

ola. nvs. Life, health, well-being, living, livelihood, means of support, salvation; alive, living; curable, spared, recovered; healed; to live; to spare, save, heal, grant life, survive, thrive. (See Gram. 4.4.) *Ola loa,* long life, longevity. *Ola 'ana,* life, existence. *Mālama ola,* financial support, means of livelihood. *Nā kālā no ke ola o ka nūpepa,* money for the support of the newspaper. *'O nā lā apau o kona ola 'ana,* all the days of his life. *Makamaka ola,* a live friendship; a friend who extends hospitality and appreciation. *I ola 'ole nei keiki,* this (beloved) child did not survive. *Ua loa'a ke kāne a ku'u hānai, a ua ola nā iwi o ke kahu hānai,* my foster child has found a husband, and the foster parent will enjoy peace and comfort in life and the body will be preserved after death; *lit.,* the bones will live, i.e., they will not fall into an enemy's hands. *Ola ka inoa,* the name lives on, said of a child bearing the name of an ancestor. *Ola ka pōloli,* hunger is satisfied. *Ola ke Akua, God save the king. *E ola au i ke Akua,* may God grant me life; so help me God. *E ola au iā 'oe,* save me, spare my life. **ho.'ōla.** To save, heal, cure, spare; salvation; healer; savior. *Po'e i kū'ai ho'ōla 'ia* (Isa. 35.10), ransomed people. (PPN *ola*.)

-ola. hō.'ōla. Small piece of tapa; tapa in general *(Kaua'i).*

'olā. nvi. Gurgling; to gurgle. **hō.'olā.** Same as *hō'olā-'olā.*

ō.lā. n. A weedy raspberry *(Rubus rosaefolius)* native to southeastern Asia. (Neal 391.) Also *'ākala, 'ākalakala.*

ola'a.loa. n. A variety of hard taro. Also *la'aloa.*

'ō.lā.'au. v. To strike with sticks, as beaters driving fish.

'ō.lae. n. Small cape, promontory.

'ō.lae.lae. 1. Redup. of *'ōlae;* a number of small capes, promontories. Also *'ālaelae.* **2.** nvs. Bitter, acrid; a bitter gourd *(rare).*

ola honua. nvi. Earthly life, life on earth; to live. *He mea ia e pono ai kēia ola honua 'ana,* that is something to help in this earthly life. *'Oi ola honua,* while there is life on earth; *fig.,* while there is time. *E a'o mai 'oe i ke oli 'oi ola honua,* learn the chant while there is opportunity.

ola hou. nvi. To revive, recover, restore to health, resuscitate, save a life; resurrected; resurrection. **ho.'ōla hou.** To restore to life, revive, resurrect.

ola'i. Bible spelling for *ola + ai.*

ō.la'i. n. **1.** Earthquake, tremor. See ex., *lua 4.* **2.** Light porous stone or pumice, as used for polishing canoes or for scraping off hair of pig or dog to be roasted.

ola.kino. n. State of health, constitution. *Mea olakino,* things necessary for life, as food. *Kāne olakino maika'i,* able-bodied male.

'ō.lala. 1. vs. Lean, thin; stunted, as plants. **2.** Same as *lala 2;* to wilt, as pandanus leaves over a fire for plaiting. *'Ōlala ia i kona kino i ka lā,* he laid down his body in the sun.

'olala.hina. vs. Frail, delicate. *Rare.*

'ola.lala. Redup. of *'ōlala 1, 2.*

'ola.lau. vi. Somewhat *lalau;* wrong, incorrect; mistakenly. See *mana'o 'olalau. Kaha 'olalau i ke kaha pe'a,* to mark an X incorrectly [as on a ballot].

'ō.lali. 1. vi. To glide smoothly along, as a ship on the sea or as a fish slipping through one's hand. *Ma ia mau alanui malihini āu i 'ōlali ho'okahi ai* (chant for Ka-lā-kaua), these unfamiliar paths you travel all alone. **2.** vs. Bright, shiny, glistening; brightness. **3.** n. Skilled person. **4.** n. Young stage of *hou,* a fish. *O'ahu.*

'ō.lali.lali. Redup. of *'ōlali 1, 2.*

ola loa. nvs. Long life; completely cured or recovered.

ola mau. vs. Immortal; to live long.

'ō.lana.lana. nvs. Nauseating; seasick; nausea.

'ō.lani. 1. vt. To toast over a fire, broil, warm in sunlight. (PPN *lani, rara.*) **2.** Var. of *'ōlali 4.*

'ō.la'o. vt. To weed and work the soil, to hoe; to gather, as *'opihi* shells; to extract.

'olā. Redup. of *'olā.* See ex., *lohena. 'Olā'olā ka ihu,* to snore with short puffs. **hō.'olā.'olā.** To cause gurgling; to gargle. *E hele e hō'olā'olā i ka pu'u,* go and gargle for your throat.

'ō.la'o.la'o. vt. To weed, dig, as with an *'ō'ō* or spade. *'A'ole ia e pa'ipa'i 'ia, 'a'ole ho'i e 'ōla'ola'o 'ia* (Isa. 5.6), it shall not be pruned, nor dug.

'ola'o.lapa. Redup. of *'ōlapa 1.*

'ō.lapa. 1. vi. To flash, as lightning; to blaze suddenly, flare up; to rumble uneasily, as a queasy stomach. *'Ōlapa ka hoe a ka lawai'a, he 'ino,* the fisherman's paddle flashes, a storm [of haste]. **2.** n. Several native species and varieties of forest trees *(Cheirodendron),* with opposite leaves, each leaf divided palmately into three to five (rarely six or seven) leaflets, and with flowers borne in umbels. (Neal 652.) Also *ehu, kauila māhu* (on Maui), *lapalapa, māhu, 'ōlapalapa.* Cf. *hū 'ōlapa.* **3.** n. Dancer, as contrasted with the chanter or *ho'opa'a* (memorizer); now, any dance accompanied by chanting and drumming on a gourd drum. **4.** n. Name for the *āholehole* (fish) used as sacrifice for love sorcery *(hana aloha),* or for sorcery that sends a bad spirit to plague another *(ho'ounauna),* probably so called because of the desired rapidity of the spirit's actions. **5.** Same as *'ōlapalapa 3.*

'ō.lapa.lapa. 1. Redup. of *'ōlapa 1.* Pi'i *'ōlapalapa kona inaina me ka huhū,* his wrath flared forth angrily. **2.** Same as *'ōlapa 2.* **3.** vs. Full of ravines, projections, cornices, ridges.

ola pā.na'i. vs. Redeemed, ransomed, saved; to redeem. **ho.'ōla pā.na'i.** To redeem, ransom; redeemer (Isa. 41.14).

'ō.lapu. Rare var. of *hōlapu.*

'Ō-lau-niu. n. Name of a wind (For. 5:93) on Hawai'i (Nak. 55) and at Ka-pālama, Honolulu (Nak. 57). *Fig.,* promiscuous. *Lit.,* coconut-leaf piercing.

ole. 1. n. Eyetooth, fang. *Lei ole,* dogtooth lei. **2.** Same as *hole,* to squirm.

'ole. 1. nv. Not, without, lacking; to deny; zero, nothing, nought, negative; nothingness, nobody; im-, in-, un-. Cf. *'a'ole, mea 'ole, 'ole loa. Maika'i 'ole,* not good; bad. *Pa'a ka 'ole i ka waha,* holds "no" in the mouth. *Na wai e 'ole ka ho'ohihi i ka nani o Leahi?* Who can help taking a fancy to the beauty of Diamond Head? *'A'ohe āna hana, hana 'ole,* there is no work he won't do. *E 'ole nō 'oe,* if it weren't for you; [sarcastically] you think you are indispensable! *Na wai 'ole nō ka nele i ka ua mea o ka piliwaiwai?* Who could help being poor with so much gambling? *'Ole wale,* useless. *'A'ole e 'ole,* undoubtedly, of course. *Ua a'e 'o 'ole wale mā,* here come Mr. and Mrs. Nobody [insulting]. *'A'ole e 'ole kona hele i kēia lā,* there's no doubt of his going today. *He 'ole manawa 'ino* (FS 245), don't be cruel. **hō.'ole.** To deny, refuse, reject, veto, contradict, prohibit, protest, nullify, disclaim, renounce, repudiate; refusal, denial, negative. *Hō'ole loa,* to deny or refuse absolutely. *Hō'ole 'ino,* to spurn. *Hō'ole Akua,* to deny the existence of God; atheist. *Hō'ole lama,* temperate; teetotaler. *Hō'ole wai 'ona,* prohibition of intoxicants. *Hō'ole Pope,* Protestant; *lit.,* deny Pope. *Hō'ole pule,* to deny authority to act as a priest. *Hō'ole 'ana,* waiver. (PEP *kole.*) **2.** *(Cap.)* For nights of the moon beginning with *'Ole* see below and Malo 31, 32, 35. Collectively these nights were called *nā 'Ole;* they were considered unlucky for fishing, planting, or beginning any important activity because *'ole* also means nothing. *Eia kākou i nā 'Ole,* here we are at the *'Ole* nights [a time of poor luck]. (PEP *Kolekole.*)

'olē. 1. n. Conch shell *(Charonia tritonis),* trumpet; cro-chet pattern with a design suggestive of a trumpet. Cf. *'olē'olē. 'Olē leo nui,* foghorn. **2.** vi. To talk indistinctly or garrulously. **3.** n. Tapa beater. (Kam. 76:109.)

'ole.ana. Same as *'oliana 2.*

-olea'i. hoolea'i. Old spelling for *hō'ole + ai.*

'ō.leha. vs. Dazzled, bleary-eyed, as one ill or drunk; dazzling.

'olē.hala. n. Cheerful singing, as of birds in treetops. *Rare.*

'ō.leha.leha. Redup. of *'ōleha.*

'Ole Kū Kahi. n. Seventh and twenty-first nights of the month. (PEP *Kolekole Tuu Tahi:* cf. Marquesan.)

'Ole Kū Kolu. n. Ninth night of the month. (PEP *Kolekole Tuu Tolu.*)

'Ole Kū Lua. n. Eighth and twenty-second nights of the month. (PEP *Kolekole Tuu Lua.*)

'Ole Kū Pau. n. Tenth night of the month.

'ole.lehu. vs. Drowsy, sleepy. Cf. *mōlelehu.*

'ole.lepa. Same as *'ō'ili lepa,* a fish.

'olele.pā. Same as *lelepā. He ke'a pua'a maka 'olelepā,* a boar with unrestrained eyes [a fierce warrior].

'ō.lelo. nvt. Language, speech, word, quotation, statement, utterance, term, tidings; to speak, say, state, talk, mention, quote, converse, tell; oral, verbatim, verbal, motion (in early House of Nobles regulations). Cf. *ho'onui 'ōlelo, hua 'ōlelo, ku'u 'ōlelo, luna 'ōlelo, mahele 'ōlelo, pili'ōlelo, uwea 'ōlelo. 'Ōlelo a nā hō'ike,* evidence, as in court; *lit.,* word of the witnesses. *'O John Owen i 'ōlelo 'ia,* the aforesaid [or alleged] John Owen. *I kekahi manawa i 'ōlelo 'ia,* at a specified time. *'A'ohe 'ōlelo 'ana,* not worth mentioning. *'Ōlelo mai nā kūpuna mai,* tradition, traditional lore. *'Ōlelo 'ia maluna a'e,* above-mentioned. *Inā 'oe e makemake i ke kō, 'a'ohe 'ōlelo 'ana, na'u e ki'i,* if you want some sugar cane, don't say anything about it; I'll get some. (PEP *koolelo.*)

'ole loa. nvs. Not at all, void, not in the least, none whatsoever; of no value, worthless. *He like me ka 'ole loa kā kekahi, he 'oia'i'o kā kekahi* (Kep. 9), those of some are as though of no value at all, those of others true. *'Ole loa aku 'oe, he 'ōpiopio* (FS 37), you are so young that you are worthless. *He 'ole loa,* nothing doing. *He 'ole loa ka loa'a i ka 'ō he'e,* nothing at all was gotten in octopus spearing.

'ō.lelo 'ae.like. n. Resolution, joint resolution.

'ō.lelo a'o. nvt. Counsel, advice, precept, instruction; to advise, counsel.

'ō.lelo 'ē. n. Foreign language, incomprehensible lingo; mention of a matter other than the subject under discussion.

'ō.lelo ha'i mua. n. Foreword, preface. *Lit.,* word told first.

'ō.lelo hewa. n. Mistaken word, slip of the tongue.

'ō.lelo ho.'ā.hewa. nvt. Accusation; to accuse, charge.

'ō.lelo hō.'eu.'eu. n. Encouraging word, slogan.

'ō.lelo hō.'ike. n. Affidavit; testimony, as of a witness; evidence.

'ō.lelo hō.'ino. nvt. Curse, defamation; to curse, revile. *'Ōlelo hō'ino ho'onalonalo,* veiled insult, slur.

'ō.lelo ho'o.hā.like.like. n. Comparison, simile.

'ō.lelo ho'o.hiki. n. Oath, vow, promise, pledge.

'ō.lelo ho'o.holo. n. Verdict (as of a jury), judgment, decision, resolution, conclusion. See saying, *hehikū. 'Ōlelo ho'oholo hilina'i,* vote of confidence. *'Ōlelo ho'oholo hui,* joint resolution. *'Ōlelo ho'oholo 'ia,* enacting clause.

'ō.lelo ho'o.kō. n. Judgment.

'ō.lelo ho'o.laha. n. Advertisement, ad, notice.

'ō.lelo ho'o.mai.ka'i. n. Acknowledgment.

'ō.lelo ho'o.mā.ke'aka. n. Joke, witticism.

'ō.lelo ho'o.mana'o. n. Reminder, cue.

'ō.lelo ho'o.nalo.nalo. nvt. Figurative language; obscure speech with puns and poetic references; to speak thus.

'ō.lelo ho'o.nane.nane. n. Figurative speech, riddle.

'ō.lelo ho'o.pa'a. n. Stipulation. See *'ōlelo pa'a.*

'ō.lelo ho'o.pi'i. n. Accusation.

'ō.lelo ho'o.puka. n. Comment.

'ō.lelo ho'o.weli.weli. nvt. Threat; terrifying talk; to threaten.

'ō.lelo hou. vt. To speak again, repeat.

'ō.lelo huna. n. Secret language, speech with hidden meaning.

'ō.lelo kaki. vi. To speak in irritation, sharply, curtly; to snap.

'ō.lelo kau.oha. nvt. Decree, order, commandment; to order, decree.

'ō.lelo kē.nā. n. Mandate.

'ō.lelo.kī.kē. nvt. Dialogue, repartee, conversation; to engage in such. Cf. *kīkē'ōlelo.*

'ō.lelo.kī.kē.kē. Same as *'ōlelokīkē.*

'ō.lelo kū.kā. nvt. Consultation, discussion; to discuss, consult, deliberate.

'ō.lelo kū.kae manu. n. A play language originated by Hawaiian guano *(kūkae manu)* diggers in the South Pacific to keep their bosses from understanding; this speech has substitution of forms as well as transpositions. *E hele mai kāua ma'ane'i* (let us come here) might be rendered: *i hile mia kua mu 'enu'e.* Cf. *kake, nehiwa, 'okolekē.*

'ō.lelo kumu. n. Term once used (and rarely) for a "language" containing words known only to a few, perhaps priests; not the same as *kake;* basic or original language.

'ō.lelo kū.pa'a. n. Ordinance, legal decree, judgment, statute.

'ō.lelo lalau. See *lalau.*

'ō.lelo maika'i. n. Good word, gospel.

'ō.lelo makua.hine. n. Mother tongue. (This name is often used for the Hawaiian language.)

'ō.lelo mua. n. Introduction, preface.

'ō.lelo nane. n. Riddle, parable, allegory.

'ō.lelo no'e.au. n. Proverb, wise saying, traditional saying.

'ō.lelo no'o.no'o mua. n. First estimate. *'Ōlelo no'ono'o mua o ke dālā e lilo ai,* preliminary estimate of expenses.

'ō.lelo pa'a. n. Precept, command, vow, promise, oath, statute (Hal. 119.117).

'ō.lelo pā.'ani. n. Joke, jest, banter.

'ō.lelo pa'i 'ai. n. Pidgin English, pidgin Hawaiian. *Lit.,* hard-taro speech.

'ō.lelo pai.pai. n. Word of encouragement, exhortation, commandment (Mal. 2.1).

'ō.lelo pā.ku'i. n. Appendix, supplement, added words, postscript, addendum.

'ō.lelo pale. nv. Defense, as in a trial; to defend.

'ō.lelo uea 'ole. n. Wireless message.

'ō.lemu. Same as *lemu 1, 2.*

'ō.lemu hue. n. Base section of a gourd.

'ō.lemu.ka'a. n. Vagabond, rover. *Lit.,* rolling backsides.

'ō.lena. 1. n. The turmeric *(Curcuma domestica,* also incorrectly called *C. longa),* a kind of ginger distributed from India into Polynesia, widely used as a spice and dye in foods, to color cloth and tapa, and medicinally for earache and lung trouble. A cluster of large leaves rises from thick, yellow underground stems, which are the useful part of the plant, either raw or cooked. (Neal 255–6.) (PPN *renga.*) 2. Same as *lena,* yellow. 3. Also **orena.** n. Ash tree. (Heb. *oren.*) 4. n. A small mountain tree on Kaua'i *(Coprosma waimeae),* with yellow wood.

'ō.lena.lena. 1. n. Yellow, sallow. See *lenalena.* 2. n. Dye made of *'ōlena* plant.

ole.ole. n. Rack or branched post on which wooden bowls or netted calabashes were hung; a coat tree.

-'ole'ole. hō.'ole.'ole. To deny repeatedly. (PCP *korekore.*)

'olē.'olē. 1. n. A small conch shell. Cf. *'olē 1.* 2. Redup. of *'olē 2;* to rant. *Kani 'olē'olē ka waha o ka uila,* the mouth of the lightning makes an incessant noise [of a garrulous person]. 3. nvs. Wide-mouthed grin, as of an idol; to grin thus.

'olē.'olē.hala. Redup. of *'olēhala. Rare.*

ole.ole kau ipu. Same as *oleole.*

ō.leo.leo. nvt. To quarrel or speak noisily, raise a din.

ō.le'o.le'o. vs. Stormy, tempestuous, agitated.

'Ole Pau. Same as *'Ole Kū Pau.*

'ō.lepe. 1. nvt. To turn, as on hinges; to shut and open, as Venetian blinds; to peel off, as shingles in a gale; to upset, overturn, tear asunder. **ho.'ō.lepe.** To cause to turn, shut, etc. (PCP *koolepe.*) 2. n. Any kind of bivalve, as a mussel or oyster. See below and ex., *maka* *mua.* **3.** n. Garden balsam or impatiens *(Impatiens balsamina),* from southeastern Africa, an annual to about 90 cm tall, grown ornamentally for its pink, red, yellow, white, or spotted flowers. (Neal 539–40.)

'ō.lepe kupe. n. Bivalve, possibly *Codakia punctata* and *Ctena bella.* Cf. *kupe, 'ōkupe.*

'ō.lepe.lepe. Redup. of *'ōlepe 1;* shutters, Venetian blinds, lattice work (Mele 2.9); diaphragm between chest and stomach *(rare).* See *hula 'ōlepelepe.* **ho.'ō.lepe.lepe.** Redup. of *ho'ōlepe.*

'ō.lepe maka.loa. n. A kind of *'ōlepe 2 (Martesia striata);* also *makaloa.*

'ō.lepe nui. n. Any large bivalve, *Tridacna.*

'ō.lepe pā.paua. n. A kind of *'ōlepe 2 (Barbatia (Acar) divaricata).* See *pāpaua.*

'ō.lepe pū. vt. To overturn completely. Cf. *'ōlepe.* *'Ōlepe pū 'ia kaupoku e ka makani,* the roofs were ripped off by the wind.

'ō.lepe waha nui. n. A rock borer *(Gastrochaena cuneiformis). Lit.,* big-mouthed *'ōlepe.*

'ō.lepo. Rare var. of *'ōlepolepo.*

'ō.lepo.lepo. vs. Somewhat dirty, murky, sullied; to sully. *Fig.,* to offend. *A kāhiko noho'i nā maka'āinana i 'ole e 'ōlepolepo nā maka o ke ali'i ke nānā mai* (Kep. 165), the commoners were dressed up so as not to offend the eyes of the chiefs who might look upon them. *'Ōlepolepo ka 'ōpū,* the stomach is out of order, needs cleansing.

'ole.pū. vt. To discard. *E 'olepū ana i nā mea kūpono 'ole o kēia mo'olelo,* discarding all that is valueless in this story.

'ō.lewa. vs. Swinging. *Fig.,* fickle, changeable, not firmly established or fixed, variable.

'ole wale! nvi. Not at all! Of no interest, value, use. *'O 'ole wale mā!* Those nobodies! *He 'ole wale,* nothing doing.

'ō.lewa.lewa. Redup. of *'ōlewa. Fig.,* hungry.

oli. nvt. Chant that was not danced to, especially with prolonged phrases chanted in one breath, often with a trill *('i'i)* at the end of each phrase; to chant thus. *Ke oli,* the chant. *Mea oli,* chanter. (PNP *oli.*)

'oli. nvs. Joy, happiness, pleasure; happy, joyful, gay. Cf. *hau'oli. Wai-'oli* (place name), happy water. **hō.'oli.** To give joy, make happy. (PEP *koli.*)

'oli.ana. **1.** n. A common ornamental shrub *(Nerium oleander* and var. *indicum),* native from south Europe to Japan. Its flowers may be single or double, white, pink, or red. (Neal 695.) *Eng.* Also *'oliwa.* **2.** n. A variety of sugar cane, like lahaina in type of growth and color, but the pith dark-brown and the leaf sheath covered with red-brown hairs. *(Eng.,* Oriental.) Also *'oleana.* **3.** interj. Let me see! Show me! Also *aliana, inane, 'oia ana.*

'olia.paha. Same as *'oia paha,* maybe so. *Rare.*

'ō.liha.liha. vs. Somewhat *liliha.*

'oliko. vs. Shiny, sparkling, bright. *Ka ua 'oliko i ka lani,* the rain sparkling in the sky.

'ō.liko. vi. To bud. Cf. *liko.* **2.** n. A small tree, possibly *Rapanea helleri, Myrsine hosakae* (syn. *M. angustifolia, Suttonia angustifolia),* a kind of *kōlea.*

'ō.liko.liko. Redup. of *'ōliko 1.*

'ō.lile.lile. vs. Somewhat *lile.*

'olili. vs. Shiny, sparkling, shimmering, as moonlight. Cf. *hulili.*

'ō.lili. vs. Withered, stunted, poor, as fruit. Cf. more common *mālili.*

'oli.liko. Redup. of *'oliko* and *'ōliko 1;* shimmering. *Ka 'oliliko wai a ka ua,* liquid sparkling of the rain.

'ō lima. n. Arm vaccination. *Lit.,* arm piercing.

'olina. vs. To make merry; joyous, rejoicing, merry-making.

'olina.kio, orinatio. n. Ordination. *Eng.*

'ō.lino. **1.** nvs. Bright, brilliant, dazzling, gleaming; brightness, glare. *He 'ōlino aloha kēia iā'oe ē* (chant of Hi'iaka), this is a bright ray of love for you. **2.** vs. Parched, dry.

'ō.lino.lino. Redup. of *'ōlino 1, 2;* shining, radiant. (2 Sam. 22.13.) *E lilo nō ka lepo 'ōlinolino i wai 'au'au* (Isa. 35.7), the parched ground shall become a bathing pool.

oli.oli. Redup. of *oli;* chanter. *Kau akula 'o Hale-mano i kēia kau olioli* (FS 277), Hale-mano then sang this chanting song. (PNP *olioli.*)

'oli.'oli. Redup. of *'oli;* delight, enjoyment. See ex., *malakia.* **hō.'oli.'oli.** Caus/sim. (PNP *kolikoli.*)

'ō.li'o.li'o. vs. Somewhat *li'oli'o,* dazzling.

'Oli.ona, Oriona. n. Orion. (Ioba 9.9.) *Eng.*

'ō.li'u.li'u. vs. **1.** Blurred, indistinct. Cf. *kōli'uli'u, li'ua. 'Ōli'uli'u ke ala e ma'awe nei* (KL line 496), indistinct the path tread here. **2.** Brackish.

'oliwa, oliva. n. **1.** The olive tree *(Olea europaea),* from the Mediterranean region, a small tree grown only ornamentally in Hawai'i, where it rarely flowers or yields fruit. (Neal 677–8.) *Eng.* See *lau 'oliwa.* Called *'oliwa haole* on Ni'ihau. **2.** Same as *'oliana,* oleander.

'oliwa kū kaha.kai. n. Air plant *(Kalanchoe pinnata,* also *Bryophyllum pinnatum),* a succulent growing wild and cultivated in Hawai'i and other tropical countries. New plants develop along the edges of the thick scalloped leaves. The tubular green and red flowers hang lantern-like. The Hawaiian name was given because the first plants seen in Hawai'i grew near the beach. (Neal 376–8.) *Lit.,* beach-standing olive.

olo. **1.** nvi. To rub back and forth, grate, saw; a saw (also *pahi olo).* Cf. *hale olo papa.* (PPN *holo.*) **2.** vi. To resound, sound long. Cf. *olo 'awa, olo pihe. Olo ke kani o ka pila,* the instruments sounded together. *Ua olo pawa ke kani nei ka moa,* the dawn sounds are here, the cocks crow. (PPN *olo.*) **3.** n. Long surfboard, as of *wiliwili* wood. (Laie 449.) **4.** n. Hill *(rare* now except in place names, as *Olo-ku'i,* tall hill; *Olo-mana,* divided hill; *Olo-walu,* many hills). (PPN *olo.*) **5.** n. Shelf. *Rare.* Cf. *olo'ewa, olohaka.* **6.** n. Large foreign glass beads, said to be so called from a Hawaiian name given to the British ship, Queen Charlotte Mary, which came in 1786 under the command of Captain Dixon; this ship is said to have introduced the beads. *Rare.*

'olo. **1.** n. Long gourd container used as a receptacle, as for kava or water; long body of a gourd used as a hula drum (cf. *heke, ipu).* Cf. *'olo 'awa.* **2.** nvi. Double chin, sagging skin, jowls, calf of leg; scrotum; wattles of a turkey; fat part under the jaws of an eel; pendant; pendulous; to roll with fat; to sag, hang down.

'olo-. See *'olomeka, 'olomene.*

'oloa. **1.** Same as *ma'aloa, ma'oloa,* a shrub. **2.** nvt. Fine white tapa, said to have been placed over an image during prayers (Laie 467); perhaps a verb to make *'oloa* tapa (For. 6:444). (PPN *koloa.*) **3.** n. Gift to a child at birth.

olo'a. n. Reported as a bird name (no data).

'olo.'ā. vi. Splashing on rocks, as a rough sea.

olo.alu. Var. spelling of *olowalu.*

olo 'awa. n. An address to a deity accompanied by an oblation of kava.

'olo 'awa. n. Coconut shell cut lengthwise as a cup for kava.

olo.'ewa. n. Shelf.

olo.haka. n. Shelf.

'olo.haka. nvs. Empty, sunken, hollow, as eyes or cheeks; emptiness, deficiency, deficit. *Po'o 'olohaka,* numskull, empty head, dunce. *He pū mai'a, he 'olohaka o loko,* a banana tree, hollow inside [said of one lacking strength]. *Ka 'olohaka o ka waihona,* deficit in the treasury.

olo.hana. *Rare* var. of *'olohani.*

'olo.hani. nvi. To strike, quit work; mutiny, riot (said to be from *Eng.* "all hands"). **hō.'olo.hani.** To cause or foment a strike or mutiny.

olo.hao. n. Cannon. *Lit.,* iron noise. *Rare.*

'ō.lohe. **1.** vs. Bare, naked, barren; hairless, as a dog; bald; destitute, needy. *Ka lua 'ōlohe o ke ālialia,* the barren pit of the salt marsh. **ho.'ō.lohe.** Caus/sim. **2.**

nvs. Skilled, especially in *lua* fighting, so called perhaps because the beards of *lua* fighters were plucked and their bodies greased; bones of hairless men were desired for fish hooks because such men were thought stronger; also said of hula experts; skilled fighter (Kel. 115). **3.** vs. Pale. *'Ōlohe nā maka* (Ier. 30.6), pale faces [in a later edition of the Bible this was changed to *nananakea*]. **4.** vs. Sick, as after childbirth. **5.** n. Ghost; image, as in clouds. **6.** n. A small salt-water *'o'opu*, a fish, found with the *'ōhune*.

'ō.lohe.lohe. Redup. of *'ōlohe 1.* *'Ōlohelohe ke ku'emaka,* eyebrows very sparse. *He 'ano 'ole ka honua, ua 'ōlohelohe* (Kin. 1.2), the earth was without form and barren. *Ua nele mākou i kekahi mau mea e pau ai ke 'ōlohelohe o kō mākou kino,* we have nothing to cover the nakedness of our bodies. ho.'ō.lohe.lohe. Caus/sim.; to denude.

'olo.hewa. vs. Demented, deranged; delirious, incoherent. *Kāhea pau ahi 'olohewa,* false fire alarm.

olo.hia. Pas/imp. of *olo 1, 2. Kai-olohia* (place name), fluctuation [or sounding] sea.

'ō.lohi.lohi. Same as *'ālohilohi.*

olo.hio. vi. To move quickly, as a gust of wind. *Rare.*

olo.hi'o. vt. To cultivate, weed. *Rare.*

'olo.hū. Same as *'ulu maika.* (For. 4:259.)

'olo.hua. Same as *hua pōpolo,* fruit of the *pōpolo.*

oloi. vt. To rub, grate, run aground, run over (*olo 1 + -i,* transitivizer: Gram. 6.6.4). *Rare.*

'olo.'io. vi. To move swiftly. *Ke olo'io nei nā pōkā kila,* the steel bullets dart swiftly.

'olo.kā. vi. To shake or quiver, as flesh of a fat person. *Rare.*

'olo.ka'a. 1. vt. To roll along, as a wheel; to remove; to transfer, as a debt. Cf. *paukū 'oloka'a. Ua 'ā uahi Puna, 'o ka 'oloka'a pōhaku 'ia i ka hūnā pa'a 'ia e ka Wahine* (PH 34), Puna burns and smokes, rocks roll over it and it is buried solidly by the Woman. **2.** n. Stake to which a live rat was tied as a decoy in an owl-catching trap. *Rare.*

olo kani. vi. To sound. *Ka nākolo o nā pū, kōwelo nā hae, olo kani nā pele, hone ana nā pila* (name song for Ka-lā-kaua), guns rumbled, flags fluttered, bells pealed, and stringed instruments played sweetly.

olo.kē. vs. Clamorous, incoherent, excited in speech or sound. Cf. *holokē. Olokē, ooolokē, pi'oloke ka leo o ka palila,* agitated, agitating, frightened the cry of the *palila* bird.

'olo.ke'a. nvs. Cross, gibbet, gallows (Eset. 5.14), scaffolding; ladder made of sticks tied horizontally; crisscross, crossed; bones of a corpse buried with knees tied to breast. *Fig.,* contrary, antagonistic. *Ua hana nā kamanā i mau 'oloke'a lā'au ā puni ka hale pele,* the carpenters built a wooden scaffolding around the belfry. ho.'olo.ke'a. To crisscross; to cross.

olo.kele. 1. Same as *'i'iwi,* honeycreeper. *Kaua'i.* **2.** n. A kind of tapa associated with Nā-pali, Kaua'i. (GP 8-9.)

'olo.kele. n. Bog, swamp.

olo.kele hō.ki'i, olo.kele pō.polo. n. Immature *olokele,* bird.

olo.kī.kī. vi. To slide, skid; to saw, rub fast. *Rare.*

'olo.kū. Same as the more common *'o'olokū. 'Olokū wale i ka pilikia,* disturbed by trouble.

'olo.lā. 1. vs. Broad. Cf. *'ololī. Hānau kāne iā wai 'ololī, 'o ka wahine iā wai 'ololā* (KL line 34), man is born for narrow stream, woman for broad stream. **2.** n. A small flying fish resembling the *puhiki'i.*

'olo.laiki. interj. All right. *Eng.*

olo.lani. 1. vs. Acclaimed, as a chief. **2.** n. Poetic for coconut tree. (Kam. 76:118.)

'olo.lī. vs. Narrow. See ex., *'ololā. He ala 'ololī kō nā kāhuna* (saying), priests have a narrow path.

'ō.loli.loli. vs. Somewhat soggy, as taro.

olōlo. Var. spelling of *oloolo.*

'olo.lū. 1. vs. Dejected, downcast. *Rare.* **2.** (*Cap.*). n. Name of a star (no data).

'olo.mana. n. Old man. *Eng.*

olo.ma'o. n. The endangered Lā-na'i thrush (*Phaeornis*

obscura lanaiensis), and Moloka'i thrush (*Phaeornis obscura rutha).*

olo.mea. 1. n. A native shrub or small tree (*Perrottetia sandwicensis*) with ovate, red-veined leaves, and many tiny greenish flowers and red fruits borne in panicles. The wood is hard and formerly was used with soft *hau* wood to produce fire by rubbing. It is one of the plant forms of the pig god Kama-pua'a. (Neal 530.) Also *waimea;* see also *pua'a olomea.* **2.** vs. Brown, with darker stripes or spots, of pig or dog. **3.** n. Kind of *wauke* tapa dyed with *'ōhi'a* bark, *hōlei,* and coconut water.

olo.mehani. n. Dumping ground, refuse or rubbish dump. (For. 6:373.) *Rare.*

'olo.meka, olomeda. n. Old maid. *Eng.*

'olo.mene. n. Old man. *Eng.*

olo.mio. vi. Tapering, narrowing; to start to form a crust, as a wound; to go quickly, vanish.

'olo.mua. n. Foreskin (Ier. 4.4; changed to *'ōmaka* in later editions of the Bible).

olo.mu'o. nvs. Uncircumcised; prepuce or foreskin cut off in circumcision; bud.

olo.nā. n. A native shrub (*Touchardia latifolia*), with large, ovate, fine-toothed leaves, related to the *māmaki.* Formerly the bark was valued highly as the source of a strong, durable fiber for fishing nets, for nets (*kōkō*) to carry containers, and as a base for ti-leaf raincoats and feather capes. See *ōpuhe* and ex., *kaekae 1.* (Neal 319-20, Kam. 76:44-7, 52-5.) Cord of *'olonā* fiber; flax (Sol. 31.13), hemp, linen; muscle ligament, sinew (Kol. 2.19). *Olonā i hilo 'ia* (Puk. 28.15), fine twirled linen.

oloolo, olōlo. 1. Redup. of *olo 1, 2;* to saw back and forth; corrugated; roiled, as streams. **2.** vs. Long and narrow, as a head; elongated, oblong, oval. ho'o.oloolo. Caus/sim.; to elongate. **3.** n. A variety of watermelon, and covered over as the surface of a washboard. **3.** vs. Rough, as the surface of a washboard.

'olo.'olo. 1. Redup. of *'olo 2;* to hang too low, as a petticoat; to hang loose and long; to hang (as coconuts). *Waiū 'olo'olo,* sagging breasts. **2.** vi. To overflow, flood, as streams. See *hā'olo'olo.* **3.** vi. To loiter, lag. *'Olo'olo aku nō i hope, kū i ke a'u* (saying), lagging behind, struck by a swordfish. hō.'olo.'olo. To delay, cause to loiter.

oloolo hio. n. Type of weeded taro patch. (For. 5:681.)

'olo.'olo.kā. Redup. of *'oloka.*

'olo.'olo.ka'a. Redup. of *'oloka'a.*

oloolo.kē. Redup. of *olokē.*

oloolo.nā. Redup. of *olonā;* fibrous, tough; cords, muscle, ligaments.

'olo.'olōna. nvs. Sagging under a weight, overladen, loaded down; a burden. *Rare. 'O ka'u 'olo'olōna kēia i kauoha 'ia mai ai,* this is the load required of me.

'olo.'olo wā.wae. n. Calf of the leg. Also *'olo wae.*

'olo.pā. Same as *'ulupā.*

'olo.pala. n. Old fellow. *Eng. Ho'okolohe lua nei mau 'olopala,* these old fellows are very, very mischievous.

olo papa. v. To saw wood.

olo.pē. nvt. Falling; ruin, overthrow, demolition, humiliation; to overthrow, fall. *Rare.*

'ō.lope.lope. n. Larvae of dragonfly.

'olo.pī. Same as *pī'ao 1. Rare.*

olo pihe. vi. To cry out, shout, wail.

'olo.pū. nvs. Inflated, billowed out, as a sail in the wind; puffed out, as cheeks of one eating; blistered, as hands from work; mouthful of food or water. hō.'olo.pū. To dilate, inflate, blister. (PCP *kolopupuu.*) **2.** n. A native shrubby violet (*Viola chamissoniana*). **3.** n. Adze for cutting *'ōhi'a* logs for images. (Ii 42.)

olo.pua. 1. n. A large native tree (*Osmanthus sandwicensis*), to 19 m high, in the olive family. It bears narrow or oblong leaves, yellowish flowers, and blue 1.3 cm-long fruits. The hard wood, dark-brown with black streaks, was used for spears, adze handles, and digging sticks. Cf. *nonohina.* Also *pua, ulupua.* (Neal 676-7.) **2.** vs. Lovelorn, heartbroken. (Laie 521.)

olo.'ū. vt. To strike, as the forehead. *Rare.*

'olouha. vs. Overstuffed with food, an insulting epithet. *Lit.,* sagging intestine.

olo.wā. n. Space. *Rare.*

'olo.wa'a. Var. of *holowa'a. Ka 'olowa'a 'auwai o Roma,* the water aqueduct of Rome.

'olo wae. n. Calf of the leg. Also *'olo'olo wawae.*

olowa.hia. n. *Pāwehe* mat pattern listed by Brigham.

'olo wai. n. Gourd water container.

olo.walu, oloalu. 1. nvi. Joint action; simultaneous sounds; din of many voices, sounds, as of horns or roosters; to rush or attack in concert; a group, as of hills *(olowalu pu'u).* Cf. *makawalu, -walu. Olowalu a'ela nā moa,* the cocks crowed. *Ka 'alo 'ana o ke olowalu ihe* (For. 4:269), dodging the onslaught of spears. 2. n. Storehouse, as for chief's property. *Rare.*

olo.wī. Var. of *oloĪ.*

'olu. nvs. Cool, refreshing; soft, supple, flexible, pliant, elastic, slack, springy; pleasant, comfortable, at ease; polite, kind, courteous; coolness; softness, grace, slackness; comfort, amenities; courtesy, kindness. Cf. *'olu'olu. Ka 'olu o ka noho 'ana* (Kep. 97), the amenities of life. *'Olu kona kino i ka hula,* her body is supple in the hula. **hō.'olu.** To make soft, limber, pleasant, cool, comfortable; to comfort, please, satisfy, pacify. (PCP *kolu.*)

ō.lū. vs. Soft-shelled, as of a crab *(pāpa'i)* or lobster *(ula).*

olua. Same as *mana 5,* a fern.

'olua. pronoun. You two. *Kō 'olua,* your, yours (of two). (PPN *kimoura,* PNP *koulua,* PEP *kolua.*)

ō.lū.au. Short for *'ao lū'au.*

'olu.ea. nvi. To slacken, ease. *Fig.,* mental relaxation. **hō.'olu.ea.** To slack. *Hō'oluea Mauna Kapu a ha'aha'a, a laila 'oe 'ike i ka nani o Puna* (chant for Ka-umu-ali'i), ease and lower the mount of taboo, then appreciate the beauty of Puna.

'Olu-'Eke.loa-ho'o.ka'a-moena. n. Guardian of the sleeping place of the high chief or chiefess (said to be an expert *lua* fighter and of the same sex as the chief or chiefess). *Lit., 'Ekeloa* breeze coolness that rolls mats. Cf. *'ohene.*

'ō.luhe.luhe. vs. Sagging, drooping, as a potbelly; limp; flabby; soft, as a crab that has shed its shell. **ho.'ō.luhe.luhe.** To cause limpness, etc.

'ō.lule.lule. Same as *lulelule.* Cf. *hōlule.*

'ō.lule.lulea. Pas/imp. of *'olulelule.*

'ō.lulo. 1. nvs. Castaway; shipwrecked; storm-beset at sea. 2. Similar to *hōlū* and *'ōlū,* soft. 3. n. Gourd container, as for bamboo stamps used for marking tapas. 4. Statue, figure, idol. (And.)

'ō.lulo.lulo. Var. of *'olulelule.*

'ō.lulu. n. A lobelia *(Brighamia insignis).* Also *pū aupaka.* Cf. *ālula* and Neal 816.

'ō.lū.lū. nvs. To shake *(lūlū)* with fat; one who so jiggles.

'olu.'olu. Redup. of *'olu;* pleasant, nice, amiable, satisfied, contented, happy, affable, agreeable, congenial, cordial, gracious; please. *E 'olu'olu 'oe e hele mai,* please come here; *lit.,* be kind to come here. *E 'olu'olu 'oe i ko'u mana'o,* please do me a favor. *'Olu'olu 'ole,* unpleasant, impolite, uncomfortable. *'A 'ole o lākou 'olu'olu i 'elua dālā,* they are not satisfied with two dollars. *Mo't 'olu'olu,* gracious majesty. *'Olu'olu nō iāia iho,* satisfied with himself, complacent. *'A 'ahu 'olu'olu,* comfortable, casual, informal wear. *Ke noi aku nei au i kou 'olu'olu,* I am asking a favor of you. *E 'olu'olu i ka mea i loa'a,* be satisfied with what you have got. **hō.'olu.'olu.** Redup. of *hō'olu;* to satisfy, alleviate, allay, console; to retire to rest, to seek rest; parade rest, at ease (military commands). *E hō'olu'olu mai i kō 'oukou mau na'au* (2 Tes. 2.17), comfort your hearts.

olu.walu. n. Name reported for a minor illness (no data).

'ō.lū.palaha. n. Cowrie shell used as an octopus lure.

oma. 1. vi. To strike with the hands and arms, as in swimming. *Rare.* 2. n. High officer of the chief. *Rare.* 3. n. Variety of *mahimahi,* a fish (no data).

'oma. 1. nvt. Oven, baking pan; to roast, bake; roasted. *Fig.,* sacrificial victim. *Pelehū 'oma,* roast turkey. 2. vt. To open the mouth, as though to speak, or as a child about to nurse at the breast; to ask indirectly. *Rare.* 3. n. Female *mahimahi* fish; but cf. *oma 3.* 4. Same as *'o'oma,* concave. **hō.'oma.** Same as *ho'o'oma. Ko'i hō'oma,* chisel. 5. Small adze. (And.) 6. Space between opposing armies where sacrifices were offered; preparations for war; first men killed in war. (And.)

'ō.ma'i. vs. Sickly, weak, ailing, not well.

'ō.ma'i.ma'i. Redup. of *'ōma'i;* chronic sickness.

'ō.maka. 1. nvi. Budding; beginning; source, as of a stream; to leaf out or bud; to nip off; rising of the sun: See ex., *welo 2. 'Ōmaka a'ela ka huli, 'ōmaka pū noho'i ka nahele* (Kep. 153), the taro top leafs out, the plants too leaf out. 2. n. Nipple. *Ka pēpē 'ana o kou mau 'ōmaka* (Ezek. 23.21), the crushing of your breasts. 3. n. Foreskin. (Ier. 4.4.) 4. n. Hilo name for the *makiawa,* herring. 5. n. Belted wrasse fish *(Stethojulis balteata).*

'oma.kaha. See *nohu 'omakaha.*

'ō.maka.maka. Redup. of *'ōmaka 1;* to leaf out or bud afresh.

'Ō.maka-o-ka-'Ī.lio. Same as *Ka-'ōmaka-o-ka-'Īlio.*

'ō.maka wai. n. Stream source, headlands.

'ō.maka wai.ū. n. First liquid in the breast before the milk begins to flow.

'ō.male. Same as *male,* the young *uhu,* a fish.

'ō.male.male. Same as *'ōmale.*

'ō.mali. nvs. Weak, infirm, puny, shriveling, wilting, as of unripe fruit; weakling.

'omali.ō. nvs. Broad, extended, extensive, flat, as land; a wide athletic field of ancient times. *Rare.*

'ō.malu. vs. Cloudy, overcast, shady. **ho.'ō.malu.** To cast a heavy shade; overcast.

'ō.malu.malu. Redup. of *'ōmalu.* **ho.'ō.malu.malu.** Redup. of *ho'ōmalu.*

ō.mamaka. Same as *'ōmakamaka. Nā 'ōmamaka kēwai o nā paka ua,* the liquid beginnings of raindrops. **ho.'ō.mamaka.** Caus/sim.

'oma.male. Same as *'ōmale.*

'oma.malu. Redup. of *'ōmalu.*

'ō.ma'o. 1. nvs. Green, as plants. 2. n. A bundle wrapped in green leaves, as of ti, for carrying food. *Rare.* 3. n. Hawai'i thrush *(Phaeornis obscurus obscurus).* (PCP *koomako.*) 4. n. Greenish tapa. 5. Rare var. of *'ōme'o 2.* 6. *(Cap.)* n. Star name (no data).

'oma.'oma. Redup. of *'oma 2.* **ho.'oma.'oma.** To cause to open the mouth, speak, etc. *Hō'oma'oma i ka waha,* to open the mouth; to work the mouth but not sing with others, to pretend to sing.

'ō.ma'o.ma'o. 1. Redup. of *'ōma'o 1;* an emerald (Puk. 28.18). *'Ano 'ōma'oma'o,* greenish. **ho.'ō.ma'o.ma'o.** To make green, paint green. 2. n. Name of a seaweed.

'ō.ma'o.ma'o mae wale. n. Name of a seaweed. *Lit.,* seaweed that wilts easily.

'oma Pukikī. n. Dome-shaped cement or stone outdoor oven, as used by the Portuguese *(Pukikī)* for bread.

'ō.mau. 1. nvt. To pin on, fasten (same as *'ōmou*); to gird or bind on, as a sword (Lunk. 3.16); to tuck in, as a sarong; to sew (RSV) or baste together; a doubling over, tuck. 2. n. Loom (RSV), pining sickness (KJV). (Isa. 38.12.) 3. n. A barbless fishhook. Cf. *mau,* to hold fast. 4. nvi. A brief love affair; to have such an affair. *Rare.*

'ō.mea. 1. vs. Reddish; murky. *Ua 'ōmea 'ia ke kuahiwi* (For. 6:369), the hills are reddish. 2. n. Beloved, respected person. *Ua hehi ka lā iā Hawai'i, he 'ōmea Pele no Hi'iaka* (prayer), the sun has trod upon Hawai'i, Pele is loved of Hi'iaka. 3. vt. To sun. *E 'ōmea aku i ka moena,* put the mat in the sun. 4. Same as *'ōuli. Rare.*

'ō.mea.lani. n. Variety of sweet potato.

'ō.mea.mea. Redup. of *'ōmea 1.*

'omeka, omega. n. Omega. (Hoik. 1.8.) *Eng.*

'omela, omera. n. Omer. (Puk. 16.16.) *Eng.*

'ō.me'o. 1. vi. To bud, to unfold, as a blossom; to come into view; to sprout. Cf. *me'o 2.* **2.** Same as *me'o,* nagging.

'ō.me'o.me'o. Redup. of *'ōme'o.*

'omī. vi. To wither, droop; to burn weakly, as a candle. Cf. *hōmī.*

'ō.miko. vs. Saline, salty, as soil near the sea. Cf. *miko 1.*

'ō.milo. nvt. To twist, turn, curl; to shape, as a canoe hull; to taper, as a baby's fingers by rolling the tips between thumb and index finger; to spin, as thread; to produce abortion, destroy; abortion, foeticide, drill. Cf. *milo 2.*

'ō.milo.milo. Redup. of *'ōmilo.* Cf. *train 1.*

'ō.milu. 1. n. Kind of *ulua,* a fish, probably *Carangoides ferdau, C. gymnostethoides, C. ajax.* **2.** nvs. A trifle, mere nothing; insignificant. *'A 'ohe 'ano o ia mea, he 'ōmilu,* this thing has no significance, it's a mere trifle.

'ō.milu.milu. Same as *'ōmilu.*

'ō.mī.mī. Redup. of *'omī.*

'omi.mino. Redup. of *'ōmino.*

'omimo. vs. Naked, nude. *Rare.*

'ō.mino. vs. Wrinkled, withered, shriveled, stunted; sickly and constantly crying, as an unhealthy child. See ex., *'alalehe.*

'ō.mino.mino. Redup. of *'ōmino.*

'omī.'omī. Redup. of *'omī,* to wither.

'ō.mio.mio. Same as *olomio.*

omo. 1. nvt. To suck, absorb; suckling; to gasp (Kep. 116); to evaporate, as water; absorbent; suction tube, rubber nipple. *Keiki omo waiū* (Nah. 11.12), suckling child. *'Ili omo wai,* suction tube. **ho.'ōmo.** Caus/sim.; to draw in, as a wave. (PEP *'omo.*) **2.** nvi. Sport of leaping from heights into water without a splash; to leap thus. **3.** n. Remora, sucking fish. (KL line 155.) **4.** n. Gourd, as used for a container. **5.** Same as *alaia,* type of surfboard. *Rare.*

'omo. n. Lid, cover, plug, cork, as of a calabash; lamp chimney. (PEP *komo.*)

omō.hā. n. Tapa design. Cf. *mōhā,* migratory duck.

'ō.mohe.mohe. Same as *'ōmolemole.*

'omo ipu.kukui. n. Lamp chimney.

omoki. Var. of *omo 1, 2.*

'omoki. Var. of *'umoki,* stopper.

omo koko. nv. Bloodsucker, leech; to suck blood.

'ō.mole. 1. n. Bottle, jug, jar. *'Ōmole 'aila,* cruse of oil. **2.** vs. Bare, smooth, hairless.

'ō.mole hā.nai wai.ū. n. Nursing bottle.

'ō.mole 'ie. n. Jar or bottle bound with rope or wicker, demijohn.

'ō.mole waha nui. n. Large-mouthed bottle or jar.

'ō.mole.mole. Redup. of *'ōmole 2. Kukui 'ōmolemole,* a *kukui* nut finished for a lei, but smooth and without design, less choice than the *ioio* or *'ōpaka.*

omo liu. nv. Ship's pump; to suck up bilge.

omoomo, omomo. Redup. of *omo 1.*

'omo.'omo. n. Loaf; any long, oval body, as balls of arrowroot; a mold or molded thing, as adobe bricks. **hō.'omo.'omo.** To mold, shape. *Hana ihola 'o Kū, 'o Kāne, 'o Lono i ka lepo kele, hō'omo'omo ihola a pa'a* (Kep. 33), Kū, Kāne, Lono made muddy earth, molded it firm.

'ō.mo'o.mo'o. 1. Same as *'omo'omo;* ridge, crest, as of mountains. **2.** n. Bits and pieces, trifles. Cf. *mo'o 5.*

'omo.'omo palaoa. n. Loaf of bread.

'ō.mo'o.mou. Redup. of *'ōmou.*

'ō.mou. vt. To pin on, attach, fasten securely, as a brooch. See *pōkē 'ōmou. Kahi 'ōmou,* comb to hold the hair in place or for ornamentation. *Kui 'ōmou,* stick pin, common pin. *Pine 'ōmou,* brooch. *Pua 'ōmou,* corsage. **ho.'ō.mou.** To cause to pin, to pin, to pretend to pin.

omo wai.ū. nv. Nipple for a milk bottle; to suck a nipple.

-'omu. hō.'omu. A calabash for fish. *Rare.*

'omua. n. Whiplash used to throw a *ke'a,* dart, as of *olonā* fiber.

'ō.mu'a. Var. of *'ōmu'o.*

'ō.mu'a.mu'a. Redup. of *'ōmu'a.*

'ō.mu'e. vs. Bitter.

'ō.mu'e.mu'e. Redup. of *'ōmu'e.*

'ō.muku. nvi. Stump, projection, pommel of a saddle; to project; to cut off short.

'ō.mu'o. nvt. Bud, budding; to have buds; to nip off, as a leaf bud; to circumcise; to bring to a point; to be cut off, stopped; sharpened. See *mu'o, mu'omu'o. 'Ōmu'o 'ia a'e ia hana i ka wā kūpono loa,* that project was nipped in the bud at the proper time.

'ō.mu'o.mu'o. Redup. of *'ōmu'o;* tapering off, dying. *Ke ulu 'ōmu'omu'o nei ke kō,* the cane growth is petering out.

'ō.mu'u. Var. of *'ōmu'o.*

ona. 1. n. Mite, louse. **2.** vt. Infatuated, attracted. Cf. *onaona. Eia mai au 'o Mākālei,lā'au ona mau 'ia e ka i'a,* here am I, Mākālei, wood always attractive to fish. *No ke aha lā e ona 'oe?* (Sol. 5.20). Why should you be infatuated? **3.** For *ona* in an idiom, see *ua ona o,* aforementioned. **4.** poss. His, hers, its (*o*-form, zero class; Gram. 8.4). (PPN *ho'ona.*) **5.** Plural marker preceding the last of two or more things (goods, not people) and usually preceding *mau.* And, and also. *Kalakoa me ona mau lipine,* calico and also ribbons. *Lawe mai i puke, i pepa, a me ona mau peni,* bring books, paper, and also pencils. (Gram. 10.4.)

'ona. 1. nvs. Drunk, dizzy and unsteady; intoxicating; intoxication. *Wai 'ona,* intoxicating liquor. *Mea 'ona,* drug, intoxicant, narcotic. **hō.'ona.** Intoxicating. See more common *hō'ona'ona.* (PPN *kona.*) **2.** nvt. Owner, possessor, proprietor; to own. *Eng.* Cf. *'ona miliona. E 'ona 'ia ana e a'u,* owned by me.

'ō.naha. vs. Bowlegged, bent over, stooped, bent, arched; curved, crescent-shaped, as the moon; pigeon-toed. **ho.'ō.naha.** To cause to be stooped, bent, bowlegged; to imitate the walk of a bowlegged person.

'ō.naha.naha. Redup. of *'ōnaha.*

ō.naha.naha.ia.ua. n. Fertile spot in a lava bed. *Rare.*

'ona.kaka. Same as *nakaka.* (PH 34.)

'ona lama. nvs. Drunk on rum or any alcoholic liquor; drunkenness; alcoholic.

'ō.nalu.nalu. vs. Somewhat rough, as the sea; to be forming waves of some size.

'ona mau. vs. Constantly drunk, alcoholic.

'ona mili.ona. n. Millionaire. *Lit.,* owner [of a] million. *Eng.*

ona moa. n. Chicken lice or mites.

'onana. vs. Weak, awkward, unskilled. Cf. *'īnana, kīnana.*

onaona. nvs. Softly fragrant; soft fragrance or perfume, aroma; gentle and sweet, as the eyes or disposition; inviting, attractive, alluring, lovely. Cf. *maka onaona, friend. Kole maka onaona,* sweet-eyed *kole* (a fish), [said of a person with alluring eyes]. **ho'ō.naona.** To impart fragrance; attractive, sweet, alluring. *Ho'ōnaona i ka i'a,* to attract fish, as with the *melomelo,* baited stick. *Ho'ōnaona ho'i nā maka o kēia keiki,* what attractive, sweet eyes this boy has.

'ona.'ona. vs. **1.** Faint, dizzy, punch-drunk. **hō.'ona.-'ona.** To cause intoxication or dizziness, to feign intoxication or dizziness; intoxicating. **2.** Bad-smelling, as stagnant water; unpalatable.

onaona lā.pana. Same as *'ala aumoe* and *kūpaoa,* the night cestrum. *Lit.,* Japan fragrance.

'onaulu loa. n. A wave of great length and endurance. (UL 35.)

'ona wai.wai. n. Rich person.

'ō.nā.wali. Same as *'ōwali,* weak.

'ona.wali.wali. Redup. of *'ōnāwali.*

'ona.wele. Same as *nāwele.*

one. nvs. Sand; sandy; silt; poetic name for land (cf. *one hānau*). *One maka,* wet sand. *Ke one 'ai ali'i o Kākuhihewa,* the chief-destroying sands of Kākuhihewa [said of O'ahu because of the prophecy made by Ka'ōpulupulu about the death of the O'ahu chiefs upon the coming of foreigners]. **ho.'ōne.** Pumice; to rub and polish with sand. (PPN *'one*.)

'ō.nea. Same as *nea*, desolate. **ho.'ō.nea.** To cause desolation; to desolate.

one.'ā. nvs. Afflicted, affliction. *I ka hiki 'ana mai o ke kolela, ho'okahi helena o kō mākou one'ā,* when the cholera came, all at once we were all afflicted.

one 'ā. nvi. Black sand or gravel made of *'a'ā* lava; volcanic cinder; to form such; gunpowder. *Lauahi Pele i kai o Puna, one 'ā kai o Malama* (chant), Pele swept her many fires down to Puna; seaward of Malama is a cinder heap.

'ō.nea.nea. Redup. of *'ōnea*. See ex., *desolate*. **ho.'ō.-nea.nea.** Redup. of *ho'ōnea*.

one.hahi. n. Menstrual blood.

One-hali. n. Name of a Kaua'i wind. *Lit.,* sand carrying.

one hali. n. Sand carried away by the sea.

one hā.nau. n. Birthplace, homeland. Cf. *kulāiwi. Ē Hawai'i ē, ku'u one hānau ē, ku'u home kulāiwi nei* (song by L. Lyons), O Hawai'i, sands of my birth, my (beloved) native home.

'ō.nehe.nehe. Same as *nehenehe*, rustling.

'one'i. loc. n. Here, local. See ex., *'ane'i 1. Kō 'one'i keiki,* the local youngsters.

'oneki. n. Deck. *Eng.*

One-lau-'ena. n. Legendary homeland of the god Kāne, a land of plenty.

one mimiki. n. Quicksand.

onena. vs. Sandy; pale. *Rare.*

'ō.nē.nē. 1. vs. Fretful, fussy. Cf. *nē.* **ho.'ō.nē.nē.** Caus/sim. 2. Rare var. of *nūnē*, speculation.

one.one. 1. vs. Sandy, gritty, grainy. (PPN *'one'one*.) 2. n. Name of a seaweed.

one.one-i-honua. n. Name of a death-bringing prayer or for a heiau dedication (For. 4:148–9, 6:119).

one.pohō. n. Quicksand.

one.'ula. vs. Vast, great, without bounds.

one wai. n. Sand near outlet of fresh-water springs; *pokipoki*, sand crabs, are said to be found here.

oni. vi. To appear, reach out, jut or extend out. *Hala a'e ka lae o Ka-lā'au, oni ana Moloka'i mamua* (name chant for Ka-mehameha V), passing Ka-lā'au Point, Moloka'i appears ahead.

'oni. 1. nvi. To move, stir, shift, fidget, squirm, wiggle; to take to court, as land matters; movement, motion. *'Oni ā puhi,* to squirm like an eel. *'Oni 'ino,* to jar, shake badly. *'Oni 'ole,* immovable, steady. *Ka moe 'oni 'ole a Niolopua,* the sleep without movement of Niolopua [death]. *'Oni hikiwawe,* sudden movement, jolt. *Ua 'oni ke keiki,* the child has moved [the fetus]. *E 'oni ana nā keiki i ka 'āina o ka makua kāne,* the children are taking the matter of the father's land to court. **hō.'oni.** To bestir, cause to move, shake, disturb, jiggle. See ex., *wilimo'o. Mai noho 'oe ā hō'oni i ka wai ua lana mālie* (hula chant), do not stay to disturb the water floating peacefully. *He mo'olelo hō'oni pu'uwai,* a heart-stirring story. (PNP *koni*.) 2. n. Spirals of several colors in composite leis.

'onia. Pas/imp. of *'oni*.

'ō.nihi.nihi. n. Small taro shoots, as of the fourth generation. (Kep. 153). See *kalo* for names of generations.

'ō.niho. vs. Toothed, sharp-edged, tooth-edged, serrated.

'ō.niho.niho. 1. Redup. of *'ōniho*. 2. n. Variety of *'ulae*, lizard fish.

'onika. n. Onyx. (Kin. 2.12.) *Eng.*

'ō.niki. 1. nvt. A pinch, bit, as of *lū'au* (taro tops); to pinch off. 2. vs. Flat, smooth, level. *Rare.*

'ō.niki.niki. Redup. of *'ōniki 1, 2*.

'onina. n. Moving, etc. See *'oni*.

'ō.nina.nina. vs. Yielding, soft, as fat cheeks. Cf. *lina, nina, papālina.*

'ō.nini. 1. nvi. A slight breeze, puff of wind; to gasp for breath, blow softly, blink. *Na ka 'ōnini lākou e lawe*

---

aku (Isa. 57.13), a breath will take them away. 2. Similar to *hulili*, dazzling; vibration. 3. n. A kind of surfboard difficult to manage, used by experts. *Rare.*

'oni.nihi. Same as *'ōnihinihi*.

'oni.niki. vt. To pick at food with no appetite, as would a sickly child. Cf. *mīnole*.

'Ō.nini-pua-'i'o. n. Sea rain at Hāna, Maui.

'ō.nino. Var. of *'ōlino 1.*

'ō.nino.nino. Redup. of *'ōnino*.

'ō.ni'o. vs. Spotted, streaked with various colors, as a pig, or as tapa prints. **ho'ō.ni'o.** To spot or print with colors, as tapa.

oni.oni. Redup. of *oni. Pu'u-onioni* (place name), extending hill.

'oni.'oni. Redup. of *'oni 1, 2*; to wag; striped. *Ki'i 'oni'oni,* moving picture, movie. **hō.'oni.'oni.** Redup. of *hō'oni*. (PNP *konikoni*.)

'ō.ni'o.ni'o. Redup. of *'ōni'o*; embroidered *(Biblical);* mottled. **ho'ō.ni'o.ni'o.** Caus/sim. *E ho'ōni'oni'o 'oe i ka pālule olonā . . . a e hana 'oe i ke kā'ei, he humuhumu 'ōni'oni'o* (Puk. 28.39), you shall weave the coat in checkerwork of fine linen . . . and shall make a girdle embroidered with needlework.

'oni.pa'a. vs. Fixed, immovable, motionless, steadfast, established, firm, resolute, determined (this was the motto of Ka-mehameha V and of Lili'u-o-ka-lani. *Lit.,* fixed movement. See ex., *makehia.* **hō.'oni.pa'a.** To fix, establish firmly. *E hō'onipa'a loa wau iā 'oukou* (Ier. 42.10), I will plant you securely.

'ō.niu. 1. nvt. A spinning top; to spin a top; informal game with dancing and top spinning; spinning, whirling. *Ke 'ala 'ōniu,* dizzy fragrance. **ho'ō.niu.** To spin, as a top; to cause to whirl. *Ua ho'ōniu aku 'oia i kona hoa hulahula,* he whirled his dancing partner. 2. See *'ami 'ōniu,* a hula step. 3. vt. To set, as type. *'Ōniu huakēpau,* to set type. 4. n. Coconut-husking stick.

'ō.niu lā.'au. v. To ward off clubs, as in mock warfare.

ono. 1. n. Large mackerel type fish *(Acanthocybium solandri),* to 1.5 or 1.8 m in length; choice eating. Known in Florida and the West Indies as the wahoo. (PPN *'ono*.) 2. num. Six; sixth. (PPN *ono*.)

'ono. nvt. Delicious, tasty, savory; to relish, crave; deliciousness, flavor, savor. Cf. *mea 'ono. 'Ono ka pu'u,* tasty to the palate; *lit.,* the throat craves. *He 'ono 'i'o nō* (song), how delicious. *Ho'omanawanui i ka 'ono,* wait patiently and you'll have what you crave. *Hana 'ia maila ka wai ā 'ono* (Puk. 15.25), the waters were made sweet. **hō.'ono.** To tempt the appetite; to make tasty, season. (PCP *kono*.)

'ō.nohi. n. 1. The eyeball; center; setting, as of a ring. *Fig.,* eyes. See ex., *hehelo. 'Ōnohi kaimana,* set diamond. *'Ōnohi kau maka,* beloved one; *lit.,* eyeball placed in the eye. *'Ōnohi uliuli,* dark pupil of the eye. *Kahi mea iāia ka 'ōnohi o ka pahu hula,* the one who has the central [role] among hula drummers. *He pa'akai poepoe li'ili'i, he 'ōnohi awa ka inoa,* small round-grained salt is called milkfish eyeball. (PNP *kanofi,* PCP *ko(a)nofi*.) 2. Patch or fragment of a rainbow. (Laie 351.)

'ō.nohi.ā.i'a. n. Cataract of the eye. *Lit.,* eyeball like fish, so called because of alleged similarity of a cataract to a fish eye.

'ō.nohi.awa. n. Black moss found in fresh water (no data). *Lit.,* eyeball of the fish, *awa.*

'Ō.nohi-ka'i-'ole-pohi.hihi-ka-lawai'a-o-ka-lā-'ino. n. Stroke in *lua* fighting. *Lit.,* rainbow patch that does not move, puzzling the fisherman on a stormy day.

'ō.nohi.lehua. n. A mother-of-pearl lure that was said to catch fish by day or night without fail.

'ō.nohi maka. n. Pupil of the eye.

'ō.nohi.nohi. 1. Same as *'ōlohilohi, 'ālohilohi*. 2. n. A variety of sweet potato.

'ōnohi 'ula. n. Red eyeball; red rainbow segment; cloud with red hues of rainbow; variety of red tapa; *fig.,* fury, anger.

ono mā.lani. Variety of *ono*, a fish.

'ō.noni.noni. Similar to *noninoni*, agitated, and *'ānoninoni*, mixed. See ex., *wehiwa 2*.

'ono.'ono. Redup. of *'ono*. hō.'ono.'ono. To make tasty, flavor, create a desire. *Hō'ono'ono 'ai*, appetizer, condiment, dressing, relish, hors d'oeuvre. *Hō'ono'ono lau 'ai*, salad dressing. (PCP *konokono*.)

'ō.no'o.nou. Redup of *'onou;* to force upon. *Ka ho'opiha 'ia 'ana o nā pū me ka pauka a me ka 'ōno'onou 'ia 'ana me nā 'ōhelo loloa*, guns filled with powder rammed in with long ramrods. *'A 'ohe ia he kāne na'u i makemake, nāna ka 'ōno'onou*, he was not the husband I wanted, she forced him on me. ho.'ō.no'o.nou. Caus/sim.

'onou. vt. To shove, push, force into, thrust on; to persuade; to give secretly or underhandedly; to offer in secret. See *kui 'onou*. *Piha 'onou*, full to the cramming point. *Ua 'onou 'oia i ka pepa i ku'u lima*, he thrust the paper into my hand. *'Onou ihola ka huli* (Kep. 153), to shove in the taro shoots. hō.'onou. Caus/sim.

'ono.'ū. Same as the bird, *'ō'ū*.

'onou po'o. v. To shove or push into something headlong, regardless of consequence. *Lit.*, shove head.

'ono wai. v. Thirsty; to crave water.

'ō.nū. nvi. A swelling, protuberance, hill; rising of the surface; buckling; erection of the male member; to swell. *Pipi ōnū*, bucking cow. ho.'ō.nū. To cause to swell, expand. *Ho'ōnū a'ela ka 'ale o ke kai*, the billow of the sea was swollen.

'ō.nuhe.nuhe. vs. Tainted, unsavory.

'ō.nuhe.nuhea. Pas/imp. of *'ōnuhenuhe. He 'ōnuhenuhea kahi mea haole* (Kep. 161), white man's things [food] are unsavory.

o'o. nvi. Matured, ripe, as fruit; of mature age, middle-aged, elderly; to mature, ripen, or grow old; an adult human, maturity (see ex., *'e'elekū*). Cf. *o'o 'ole*. *Moloka'i pule o'o*, Moloka'i [of the] potent prayers [*fig.* reference to Moloka'i's fame in sorcery]. (PCP *oko*.)

'o'ō. vi. To crow, as a rooster; cock-a-doodle-doo. *Komo ka 'uhane a loko o ke kino ā ka umauma, ā ka pu'u, 'o'ō moa a'ela 'o Ka-welu* (For. 5:189), the soul entered within the body, up to the chest, to the throat, and then Ka-welu crowed like a chicken [a sign that she had been resuscitated]. (PPN *kokoo*.)

'ō.'ō. 1. Redup. of *'ō 1;* to pierce, lance, poke, put in, insert; to pierce the fetus in the womb with a sharp instrument in order to practice infanticide; to abort; to cut, as to let blood; to hurl, as a spear. *Lele 'ō'ō*, to leap into the water feet first, without splashing. *'Ō'ō he'e pali* (Kep. 103), to poke out tiny octopuses from cracks. hō.'ō.'ō. To insert, put in, pierce, cause to pierce. 2. n. Digging stick, bucking implement, spade. (PCP *kookoo*.) 3. n. A black honey eater *(Moho nobilis)*, with yellow feathers in a tuft under each wing, which were used for featherwork; endemic to island of Hawai'i, now extinct. *M. bishopi*, endemic to Moloka'i, possibly also extinct. *M. apicalis*, the extinct O'ahu species. The Kaua'i species was called *'ō'ō 'ā'ā*. See *'ē'ē 2, pīpī 3*. (PPN *koo*.) 4. n. A type of fish, perhaps a swordfish.

'ō.'ā.'ā. n. The endangered Kaua'i species of *'ō'ō*, honey eater *(Moho braccatus);* on Hawai'i, said to be the name for the male *'ō'ō. Lit.*, dwarf *'ō'ō*.

'ō.'ō.ahi. 1. Redup. of *'ōahi*. 2. nv. Fire poker or shovel; to poke the fire.

'o'o'e. Redup. of *'o'e. Rare*.

'ō.'ō halo. n. Harrow. *Lit.*, harrow *(Eng.)* digging implement.

'ō.'ō hao. n. Iron tool for digging, plow.

'ō.'ō hou. n. Plow. *Lit.*, new digging implement, or poking, digging implement.

'o'ohu. vs. Stoop-shouldered, bent, as with age. hō.-'o'ohu. To walk stooped; to cause to stoop; to imitate a stooped person.

'ō.'ō.hū. Redup. of *'ōhū*, swelling.

'o'oi. 1. Redup. of *'oi;* prickly; sting, as of scorpions

(Hoik. 9.10); to protrude, as eyelashes. *Nahele 'o'oi* (2 Sam. 23.6), thorns. 2. n. An inedible seaweed. Also called *popohe makali'i*.

'ō.'ō ihe. nv. To hurl spears or javelins; sport of spear throwing.

'o'oki. 1. Redup. of *'oki*. (PPN *kokoti*.) 2. vs. To take effect, as intoxication. *'O'oki maila ka 'ona o ka 'awa* (FS 135), the intoxication of the kava took effect.

'ō.'ō kila. n. Steel spade.

'ō.'ō kope. nvt. A rake; to rake. *Lit.*, scratching digging implement.

'ō.'ō kū.pī.pī. n. A name for the female *'ō'ō*, honey eater. *Hawai'i*.

'o'o.lā. 1. Short for *'o'olapū*. 2. Same as *'o'olōlā*, young of fish.

'o'olo.pū. Rare var. of *'olopū*, inflated.

o'ole. Var. spelling of *o'o 'ole*.

'o'o.le'a. nvs. Hard, stiff, strong, inflexible, rigid, harsh, rough; rigor, strength, hardness. *Fig.*, strenuous, severe, strict, stubborn, obstinate; obstinacy. *Lauoho 'o'ole'a* (Kep. 67), coarse hair. *'O'ole'a nā lālā*, strong of limb. *'O'ole'a ke a'a koko*, hardening of arteries. *'O'ole'a nā 'ami*, stiff joints. *'O'ole'a nā 'ōlelo*, harsh of speech. *'Ā'ī 'o'ole'a*, stiff-necked; *fig.*, disobedient, heedless. *Hana 'o'ole'a*, hard physical labor. *Ka lokomaika'i a me ka 'o'ole'a o ke Akua* (Rom. 11.22), the kindness and the severity of God. hō.'o'o.le'a. To harden (Ezek. 3.8), stiffen, resist, strengthen. *Hō'o'ole'a kino*, to strengthen the body, as with physical exercise; calisthenics.

'o'olo.hua. Same as *'olohua*.

'o'olo.kū. nvs. Boisterous, stormy, blustering, disturbed; upset, as stomach; fury, rage. (Kep. 175.)

'o'olo.lā. n. Young of fish. *Rare*.

'o'olo.lī, 'o'olo.li'i. Redup. of *'ololī*, narrow.

'o'olo.ma'o. n. Variety of bird, perhaps the *ma'o*, thrush.

'o'olo.pū. Redup. of *'olopū;* to change, as appearance. See ex., *kohu 1*.

'o'olu. 1. n. Two edible, fragile, red seaweeds *(Champia* sp. and *Chondria tenuissima)*. They melt in fresh water, hence must be cleaned in sea water. 2. vs. Thin, feeble. 3. Rare frequentative of *'olu*. 4. n. A variety of taro.

'o'oma. nvs. Concave; concavity, spout, gouge, flare of a bonnet; oval-shaped chisel; large sharp nose. Cf. *pāpale 'o'oma. Kī'aha 'o'oma*, vase. *Kī'aha 'o'oma wai* (Luka 22.10), pitcher. hō.'o'oma. To shape concavely; to turn down the rim of a hat on both sides of the face so that the front is like the flare of a bonnet.

'o'oma noho. n. Leather covering of stirrups.

'o'o.moa. Same as *moa 3*.

'ō.'ō.nui. Same as *kūpīpī*, a fish.

'ō.'ō nuku mū. Same as *mamo*, a honey creeper. *Lit.*, *'ō'ō* with sipping beak.

o'o.'o. 1. vs. Parsimonious, careful of one's property. 2. n. A small dipper for bailing, as a coconut shell.

'o'o.'ō. Redup. of *'ō'ō*, to crow.

'o'o 'ole. vs. Immature, minor.

'o'o.'o'ō. Same as *'o'o'ō*.

'o'opa. nvs. Lame, crippled; a cripple, lame person; to limp, be lame. *Ua 'o'opa ma kona mau wāwae* (2 Sam. 4.4), he was crippled in his feet. hō.'o'opa. To cause lameness, to feign lameness. (PCP *kokopa*.)

'ō.'ō pā.laha.laha. n. Trowel. *Lit.*, flat digging instrument.

'ō.'ō palau. nvt. A plow; to plow. *Lit.*, plow *(Eng.)* digging implement. *E ku'i lākou i kō lākou mau pahi kaua i 'ō'ō palau* (Isa. 2.4), they shall beat their swords into plowshares.

'o'ope. Redup. of *'ope*. (For. 5:665.)

'ō.'ō.pē. n. Spade. *Lit.*, spade *(Eng.)* digging implement.

'o'opu. n. 1. General name for fishes included in the families Eleotridae, Gobiidae, and Blenniidae. Some are in salt water near the shore, others in fresh water, and some said to be in either fresh or salt water. Varieties include bluespotted goby *(Quisquilius eugenius)* and indigo hover goby *(Ptereleotris heteropterus)*. *'O'opu 'ai lehua,* poetic description of *'o'opu* found in upland streams where *lehua* flowers drop into the water; *lit., lehua*-eating *'o'opu. Kau ke alapi'i a ka 'o'opu,* the *'o'opu* fish form a stairway [*'o'opu* are said to jump over rocks from pool to pool]. See also *alamo'o, naniha, 'ōkuhe, 'oau 1.* (PCP *kokopu.*) 2. *(Cap.)* Name of a wind associated with Wai-he'e, Maui. (For. 5:101.)

'o'opu haole. n. Name for black bass, introduced in 1901. *Lit.,* foreign *'o'opu.*

'o'opu hā.pu'u. n. A variety of large deep-sea fish said to be related to the *'o'opu. Lit., 'o'opu* of the *hāpu'upu'u* [family].

'o'opu hi'u kole. n. A variety of fresh-water *'o'opu. Lit.,* red-tailed *'o'opu.* It is believed that this fish drives other fish away, and hence must be thrown out of a net with an exclamation of disgust.

'o'opu hi'u 'ula. Same as *'o'opu hi'u kole.*

'o'opu.hue. n. Strong concoction made of green gourd and *kukui* nut, used as an enema.

'o'opu hue. n. Swellfishes, puffers, balloon fishes, globefishes *(Arothron meleagris* and *Chilomycterus affinus);* not related to *'o'opu;* these fish contain poison which is sometimes removed by those who like the flesh, especially the Japanese; the poison is sometimes fatal; considered by some an *'aumakua. Lit.,* gourd *'o'opu.* Also *makimaki.*

'o'opu kā.ha'i.ha'i. Same as *piliko'a,* a fish.

'o'opu.kai. n. A native variety of taro, so named as the leaf stem is similar in coloring to the salt-water *'o'opu* (the fish), being yellow-green with dark-purple markings. The corms are used mainly as table taro, the leaves often for *lū'au.* Grown chiefly in uplands of Kona, Hawai'i. The name may be qualified·by the colors *ke'oke'o* and *'ula'ula.*

'o'opu kai. Same as *po'opa'a,* a fish.

'o'opu kai nohu. n. Var. of *'o'opu,* a fish.

'o'opu kana.ni'o. Var. of *'o'opu kāni'o.*

'o'opu kā.ni'o. n. A brackish-water *'o'opu. Lit.,* striped *'o'opu.*

'o'opu kau.ila. n. A variety of *'o'opu.*

'o'opu kawa. Same as *'o'opu hue.*

'o'opu kui. Same as *'o'opu 'umi'umi. Lit.,* spiked *'o'opu.*

'o'opu kukū. n. An introduced fresh-water black fish with sharp spines near the gills, said to have been introduced from China. *Lit.,* spiny *'o'opu.*

'o'opu kumu iki. n. Female *nākea* variety of the fish *'o'opu. Lit.,* small source *'o'opu.*

'o'opu le'e. Same as *'o'opu lehe.*

'o'opu lehe. n. Large male of the *nākea* variety of *'o'opu,* so called because its lip *(lehe)* is said to show when it hides in the mud.

'o'opu mā.kole. n. A variety of *'o'opu. Lit.,* red-eyed *'o'opu.*

'o'opu maoli. n. A variety of *'o'opu. Lit.,* indigenous.

'o'opu mo'ala. n. A variety of *'o'opu* smaller than the *kāni'o,* perhaps named for the *mo'ala,* a crab.

'o'opu moana. n. A variety of *'o'opu. Lit.,* ocean.

'o'opu nā.kea. Same as *nākea.*

'o'opu nā.pili. Same as *nāpili.*

'o'opu nō.kea. Same as *nōkea.*

'o'opu nō.pili. Same as *nāpili. Kaua'i.*

'o'opu 'ō.kala. n. Spiny puffer fish, *Diodon holocanthus.*

'O'opu-ola. n. A stroke in *lua* fighting; fish was said to be taboo to those learning the stroke. *Lit.,* alive *'o'opu.*

'o'opu pili.ko'a. Same as *piliko'a.*

'o'opu po'o.pa'a. Same as *po'opa'a,* a fish. *Lit.,* hardheaded.

'o'opu puhi. A variety of *'o'opu. Lit.,* eel.

'o'opu 'umi.'umi. Same as *i'a Pākē,* an introduced *'o'opu. Lit.,* bearded *'o'opu.*

o'ou. vs. To hail, halloo. *Rare.*

o'ou.mamā.'au.wele. n. A fish *(Stethojulis albovittata),* evidently of the *'ōmaka* type.

'opa. Same as *'o'opa, mā'opa'opa.* (PCP *kopa.*)

'ō.pā. 1. vt. To press, squeeze, knead, as in massaging or in working dough. *'Ōpā pū 'ia ke kanaka mawaena o nā ka'a,* the man was crushed between the cars. **hō.'ō.pā.** To cause to squeeze. **2.** vi. To ache, as from sitting in a cramped position. **hō.'ō.pā.** To cause such aching.

'ō.pae. n. General name for shrimp. For some persons, *'ōpae* were *'aumakua.* See ex., *lolena 2, panau.* (PNP *pae.*)

'ō.pae hua. n. A shrimp *(Palaemon).*

'ō.pae huna, 'ō.pae hune. n. An indigenous shrimp, *Palaemon debilis,* almost transparent, found in brackish ponds. *Lit.,* small shrimp.

'ō.pae kai. n. Any sea shrimp.

'ō.pae kā.kala. n. A spiked shrimp.

'ō.pae-kala-'ole. n. Species of fresh-water shrimp, *Atya bisulcata.* Also *'ōpae kuahiwi,* mountain shrimp, and *'ōpae kolo,* crawling shrimp.

'ō.pae kapaka. n. A shrimp (no data).

'ō.pae kolo, 'ō.pae kua.hiwi. See *'ōpae-kala-'ole.*

'ō.pae lō.lō. n. Brackish-water shrimp or prawn *(Penaeus marginatus).*

'ō.pae lua.hine. n. A variety of salt-water shrimp.

'ō.pae oe.ha'a. n. **1.** Clawed shrimp *(Macrobrachium grandimanus),* found in inland streams and taro patches, perhaps endemic. *Lit.,* crooked-walking shrimp. See ex., *'īnana.* **2.** An indigenous crab *(Matapograpsus thukuhar,* not *M. messor).*

'ō.pae 'ō.hune. Same as *'ōpae huna.*

'ō.pae 'ō.lulo. n. A variety of soft *('ōlulo)* fresh-water shrimp.

'ō.pae 'ula. n. Small, endemic reddish shrimp used for *'ōpelu* bait.

'ō.paha. nvs. Lopsided, flattened on one side, dented, bent in, caved in, misshapen; dent, cavity. **ho.'ō.paha.** To make lopsided; misshapen.

'ō.paha.paha. Redup. of *'ōpaha.* **ho.'ō.paha.paha.** Redup. of *ho'ōpaha.*

'ō.pa'i.pa'i. 1. vi. To flap, as wings; to shake, tremble, as the earth. *Fig.,* feeble. **2.** n. A sea gull (very rarely seen).

'ō.paka. 1. nvs. Cut in evenly matched vertical facets, often eight, as of a bowl, spittoon, *kukui* shell in a lei; facet, prism. See *'umeke 'ōpaka.* **ho.'ō.paka.** To cut in *'ōpaka* fashion. **2.** n. Mountain ravine. (PCP *(k)o(o)pata;* cf. Marquesan *opata.*)

'ō.paka.paka. 1. n. Blue snapper; *Pristipomoides sieboldii, P. microlepis, Aphareus furcatus, A. rutilans;* the four stages of *'ōpakapaka* were *'ūkīkiki, pākale, 'ōpakapaka, kalekale.* **2.** Redup. of *'ōpaka 1.* **3.** vs. Rough, as breadfruit skin; crinkled, as crepe; wrinkled.

'opa.kuma. n. Opossum. *Eng.*

'ō.pala. nvs. Trash, rubbish, refuse, litter, waste matter, junk, garbage, muck; littered (said also of "trashy" people); riff-raff. *Ahu 'ōpala,* junk heap, garbage pile. **ho.'ō.pala.** To litter, make rubbish, strew, soil, make untidy.

'ō.pala.pala. Redup. of *'ōpala;* bits of trash and rubbish.

'ō.pala.pala unu. n. Trashy pebbles. *Fig.,* persons of no account.

'ō.pali.pali. nvs. A place with many precipices; having many cliffs, cliffed; mountainous, hilly.

'ō.palu.palu. Similar to *palupalu.*

'opa.'opa. Redup. of *'opa.*

'opā.'opā. Redup. of *'ōpā 1, 2.*

'ō.papa. vs. Smooth, floorlike, as *pāhoehoe* lava. *Rare.*

'opā.pali. Same as *'ōpalipali.*

'ope. nvt. Bundle, package; to tie in a bundle (sometimes preceded by *ke*). **hō.'ope.** To tie a bundle. *Ā laila hō'ope 'ia maila ā pa'a i ka 'ope,* then it was bundled up securely in a bundle. (PNP *kope.*)

'ō.pē. nvs. Feeble; feebleness. See pē 1. He 'ōpē wale nō kō 'olua hele 'ana, your walk is quite feeble.

'ō.pe'a. 1. nvt. To twist, bind, or cross the hands, as behind the back; to throw over the shoulder, as a shawl; to overturn, overthrow; to evict, as a tenant; to trip, as with a spear thrust between the legs. Fig., to deceive, trick, treat treacherously; treachery. Ka 'ōpe'a aku i ka mea pono ma ka ho'okolokolo 'ana (Sol. 18.5), to trip up the righteous man in trial. ho.'ō.pe'a. Treacherous, overturning; to cause to twist, cross, etc. 2. n. Scrotum. 3. n. Small boom or spar to extend and elevate the sails of a canoe.

'ō.pe'a kua. v. To cross the hands behind the back, a gesture considered rude because it was thought to bring bad luck to a fisherman or one beginning a venture. It signified: "May your disappointment be so great as to weigh down your back."

'ope.'alu. vs. Baggy and ill-fitting, as clothes; loose, sagging. Lit., slack bundle.

'Ō.pe'a-pani.pani. Same as Ka-'ōpe'a-panipani.

'ō.pe'a.pe'a. n. 1. General name for starfish. 2. Bat. Lele 'ōpe'ape'a, to fly like a bat, i.e., to flutter wings, as would a frightened bird. 3. Half-leaf, said of a taro plant remaining on the stalk after the top half has been removed for cooking; so called because its form suggests that of a bat. 4. Window shutters, Venetian blinds. 5. See iwi 'ōpe'ape'a. 6. Canoe sails. Rare.

'opeha. n. A native fern (Elaphoglossum aemulum variety), a small variety of 'ēkaha 'ula.

'ope.kama, opesama. n. Opossum. Eng.

'ō.pele. vs. 1. Swollen. 2. Protected by taboo, so named for 'Ōpele, the patron of the fish 'ama'ama, who lived near Kolekole Pass, Wai-'anae, and who called 'ama'ama by prayer to certain places where they would be protected from fishermen by taboo for several months. Rare.

'ō.pele.pele. Redup. of 'ōpele 1.

'ō.pelu. n. 1. Mackerel scad (Decapterus pinnulatus and D. maruadsi); an 'aumakua for some people. See kala 'ōpelu, pepenu. 'Ōpelu ana, a satisfied (ana) 'ōpelu that has escaped after eating the bait. (PCP koopelu.) 2. A variety of taro. 3. Lobelia hypoleuca, a plant named for the supposed resemblance of its leaf to the fish of the same name.

'ō.pelu haole. n. A variety of taro.

'ō.pelu kā.kala lei. n. A variety of small deep-water 'ōpelu. Lit., rough 'ōpelu with leis.

'ō.pelu kala.moho. n. A variety of large 'ōpelu.

'ō.pelu kī.kā. n. Young stage of 'ōpelu, about the length of a finger. Lit., strong 'ōpelu.

'ō.pelu pā.kā. Same as 'ōpelu palahū.

'ō.pelu pala.hū. n. Variety of 'ōpelu.

'openi, ofeni. n. Offense. Eng. See ex., paha 6.

'ope.'ope. 1. Redup. of 'ope; bundles, packages, baggage; to fold, as clothes (Ioane 20.7); pillow (Kaua'i). See ex., palale. Eia a'e ua keiki 'ope'ope nui nei o Ka-lua-ko'i (Nak. 100), here's the Ka-lua-ko'i boy with the big bundle [said of persons with big bundles, referring to Kū-a-Paka'a's bundle of rocks carried aboard a canoe]. hō.'ope.'ope. Redup. of hō'ope. (PEP kope-kope.) 2. Same as 'ōpe'a. 'Ope'ope Kohala i ka makani, Kohala is buffeted by the wind.

'ope.'ope kau. n. Bundle that is hung, as bones of a relative.

'opi. nvt. Fold, crease; wrinkled; bend of a wave; sunken, as the jaw of a toothless person; to fold, crease. See 'opi wai. (PNP kopi.)

'ō.pī. 1. Rare var. of 'ūpī. 2. Short for 'ōpili. 'Ōpī i ka ua, cramped and chilly because of rain.

'ō.piha. Same as 'ōpihapiha.

'ō.piha.piha. nvs. Uncomfortable fullness after overeating; gaseous; somewhat full, as a pool.

'opihi. n. 1. Limpets. Hawaiians recognize three kinds: kō'ele (Cellana talcosa, the largest), 'ālinalina (C. sandwicensis), makaiauli (C. exarata). Scientists also recognize C. melanostoma. (Kay 43–46.) Also kā'ala. For some persons, 'opihi are an 'aumakua. Cf.

maka'opihi. 2. Salted and dried abalone from the mainland. Also 'opihi malihini. 3. Design for tapa and mats consisting of small triangles, probably named for the limpet.

'opihi 'ā.lina.lina. n. Yellow-meated 'opihi. Lit., scarred 'opihi. See 'opihi māku'eku'e.

'opihi 'awa. n. Small bitter 'opihi, perhaps Cellana sandwicensis, nonedible, used in sorcery, perhaps hoofshells. Lit., bitter 'opihi.

'opihi kapu.a'i lio. n. Limpet, umbrella shell (Siphoneria sp.). Lit., horseshoe 'opihi [this name postdated arrival of horses in Hawai'i]. Called naka kua po'i in some areas.

'opihi kō.ele. See kō'ele.

'opihi makaia.uli. See makaiauli.

'opihi mā.ku'e.ku'e. Same as 'opihi 'ālinalina. Moloka'i.

'ō.pihi.pihi. 1. nvs. A mere trifle, small thing; tiny, trifling, as a fish or worthless sweet potato. 2. n. Kind of mat, as used for sails.

'Opi.kana. Short for 'Opikanalani or 'Opikananu'u. Ē ka lewa nu'u, ē ka lewa lani, ka 'Opikana (FS 211), O high atmosphere, O heavenly atmosphere, the faraway place.

'Opi.kana.lani. n. Name of a mythical faraway place, higher than 'Opikananu'u.

'Opi.kana.nu'u. n. Name of a mythical, faraway place. Cf. 'Opikanalani.

'ō.piki. Same as more common 'ūpiki, trap.

'ō.piki.piki. nvs. Anxiety, mental disturbance; agitated, as the sea. Cf. pikipiki'ō.

'ō.piko. 1. Same as kōpiko, a native genus of trees. Hawai'i. 2. Same as 'ōpikopiko 1.

'ō.piko.piko. 1. vs. Spotted, dotted, as with tattoo marks; stained, as by the grip of an octopus tentacle. Cf. 'āpikapika. 2. n. A form of syphilis, in which the skin is said to be spotted.

'ō.pili. nvs. Cramped or numbed, as by cold or sitting long in one position; aching; clamped together, as leaves of a sensitive plant when touched; a cramp; to clamp or close together. Cf. 'ūpili. 'Ōpili a'ela ia i kona mau wāwae maluna o kahi moe (Kin. 49.33), he drew up his feet into the bed. ho.'ō.pili. To cause a cramp, numbness, etc.

'ō.pilo. 1. Same as 'ōpilopilo. 2. vs. Sick, especially when suffering a relapse; breaking out afresh, as a sore. Rare.

'ō.pilo.pilo. 1. nvs. Bad-smelling, as stagnant water; a marshy odor; halitosis. 2. n. Scraps, fragments. Cf. pilo, any kind.

'opina. n. Fold, bend, crease. Cf. 'opi.

'ō.pio. n. Youth, juvenile; youngster; young, junior. Cf. pio 3. Kale 'Ōpio, Charles, Junior. ho.'ō.pio. To make young, freshen, refresh, rejuvenate; to act young. (PCP ko(o)pio.)

'opi.'opi. 1. Redup. of 'opi; to fold; folding. Moe 'opi'opi, folding cot or bed. Pākaukau 'opi'opi, folding table. 2. n. A seaweed.

'ō.pio.pio. nvs. Young, immature, juvenile; unripe; fresh, as a dress nicely laundered; youth, young person. One 'ōpiopio (UL 203), clean, newly washed fresh sand. Ao 'ōpiopio, white cloud. ho.'ō.pio.pio. Redup. of ho'ōpio.

'opi.uma. n. 1. Opium. Eng. See ex., māilo. 2. The Manila tamarind (Pithecellobium dulce), from tropical America, both cultivated and wild in Hawai'i. It is a medium-sized tree, a legume, with long slender branches, four-parted leaves, whitish flowers in small round heads, and red, twisted pods. Round, flat, black seeds embedded in white, edible pulp were thought to resemble commercial opium, hence the name. (Neal 399–401.)

'opi wai. n. Stream embankment. (UL 155.)

'opo. vt. To lay a foundation, as of stones; to dam up, as water. Rare. Also hau'opo.

'opu. 1. nvi. To dive into the water, feet first, without making a splash, an ancient sport (used only with lele or *lele a*); one so skilled. Cf. *ma'opu*. **2.** Rare var. of *'upu*.

ō.pū. 1. n. Clump, as of sugar cane, bananas, kava; cluster. Cf. *pū 4*. See ex., *'ahu'awa*. **2.** vi. To open, as a flower; to rise, as water; to swell, as waves; to grow, as a foetus; to sit with knees gathered up. *'O Ka'ala, kuahiwi mauna kēhau, ke ōpū maila lā i Kama-oha* (PH 100), Ka'ala, mountain hill with cool rain, rising there perhaps at Kama-oha. **3.** nvi. To rest, hover, live idly or lazily, exist; existence, rest. *'O ke ōpū wale iho nō kā mākou* (For. 4:171), ours is a bare existence. **4.** n. A tower in a heiau. See drawing, Ii 57.

'ō.pū. n. Belly, stomach, abdomen, tripe, giblet; bag, as of a net (see ex., *mahola*); gizzard, bladder, crop of a bird (Oihk. 1.16), maw of an animal, womb; disposition. *Kai 'ōpū*, giblet gravy. *'O ku'u 'ōpū, 'o ku'u 'ōpū! Ua ho'oka'awili 'ia au ma ku'u na'au* (Ier. 4.19), my bowels, my bowels! I am pained at my heart. (PPN *koopuu*.)

'ō.pua. nvi. Puffy clouds, as banked up near the horizon, often interpreted as omens; cumulus or billowy cloud, cloud bank; to form such clouds. See sayings, *clouds, proud. 'O Kona kai 'ōpua i ka la'i, 'ōpua hīnano kau i ka mālie* (chant), Kona with its cloud billows and sea in the calm, puffy clouds white like *hīnano* blossoms resting in the quiet. (PEP *ka(a)pua*.)

'ō.pua-. See *nae'ōpuakau, wai'ōpua*.

'ō.pū aho.nui. nvs. Patient; patience; a patient person. *Lit.*, disposition of great breath.

'ō.pū 'ai. Same as *'ōpū 'ai'ai*.

'ōpū 'ai.'ai. n. Stomach; craw, as of a bird.

'ō.pua ki'i. n. Cloud bank containing images.

'ō.pū ali'i. Same as *na'au ali'i*.

'ō.pua maka 'upena. n. Mackerel sky with cloud flakes; cirro-cumulus clouds. *Lit.*, net-mesh cloud bank.

ō.pū ao. n. Cluster of clouds.

'ō.pū.ao. Same as *na'auao*.

'ō.pū 'ā.pika.pika. n. Beef tripe. *Lit.*, spotted stomach.

ō.pū hale. n. Hut, as in a forest.

'ō.pū hana.wai. n. Bladder (euphemism for *'ōpū mimi*).

'ō.pū ha'o. n. Hunger pains. *Lit.*, stomach longing for or missing something.

ō.puhe. n. Three species of endemic trees *(Urera)*, related to the *olonā*, the bark of which was also formerly used for fishing nets. (Neal 320.) See also *hona, hōpue*.

ō.pū.hea. nvs. Quiet, tranquil, calm, disinclined to work, lazy; tranquillity. Cf. *'ōhea*.

ō.pū.heha. Same as *ōpūhea*.

'ō.puhi. Same as *'awapuhi*, a kind of ginger.

ō.pū.hue. n. Round, low calabash. *Lit.*, calabash clump.

'ō.pū huli. n. A "turned stomach," believed caused by falls, especially of small children, resulting in a kink or turning of the stomach, with attendant vomiting; a symptom is said to be a shortening of one leg; the cure is massage and binding of the stomach; this diagnosis and treatment are said to have been learned from the Portuguese.

'ō.pū hulu.hulu. n. Beef tripe. *Lit.*, hairy belly.

'ō.pū 'ino, 'ō.pū 'ino.ino. Same as *na'au 'ino*.

'ō.pū.ka'e.moa. Rare var. of *'ōpūke'emoa. Lit.*, chicken-edge stomach.

opu.kea. n. A large, strong, superior variety of sugar cane, the stalks yellow, sometimes rose-flushed, the pith white. (HP 223.)

'ō.pū.ke'e.moa. vs. Hardhearted, mean. *Lit.*, chicken crookedness gizzard.

'ō.pū kope.kope. Same as *na'au kopekope*.

'ō.puku.puku. vs. Frowning, wrinkled; lowering, as clouds. Cf. *pukupuku, pupuku. 'Ōpukupuku ke ao melemele* (birth chant for Ka-mehameha III), yellow clouds are lowering.

'ō.pū.lau.oho. n. **1.** Case and larva of case moth *(Tineola uterella)*, found on cement walls of basements or in caves, so called perhaps because the interior of the case is sometimes lined with hair. *Lit.*, head-hair womb. *Pūlauoho* is a short variant. **2.** A strange mala-

dy, the only symptoms of which were fine tracings of blood vessels on the stomach at birth which vanished shortly afterward. One with such tracings would grow up to be sterile, if a male, or if a female, would not have a child that lived more than a few months.

'ō.pule. 1. Same as *'ōpulepule 2*. **2.** n. A wrasse *(Anampses cuvier, A. godeffroyi)*; the name may be qualified by the terms *lā uli* and *uli*. (Malo 46.) **3.** Same as *mai'a koana*.

'ō.pule-kai. n. Stroke in *lua* fighting.

'ō.pule.pule. 1. vs. Moronic, somewhat crazy, psychotic. See *pule* and ex., *'ōhewahewa*. **ho.'ō.pule.-pule.** Caus/sim. **2.** vs. Spotted, speckled, mottled. **3.** n. A spotted land moss.

'ō.pū makani. n. Bellows. *Lit.*, wind belly.

'ō.pū maka 'upena. n. Beef tripe. *Lit.*, net mesh belly.

ō.pū malu.malu. n. Shady clump; a humble way to refer to one's house.

'ō.pū mimi. n. Bladder. *Lit.*, urine belly.

'ō.pū nā.hele.hele. n. Cluster or clump of any growth; thicket.

'ō.pū nini. vs. Jealous. *Lit.*, jealous disposition.

'ō.pū nui. nvs. Corpulent, large-bellied; corpulency; big belly.

'ō.pū 'ō.hao. n. Disease in which the abdomen becomes enlarged and hard, while the limbs are enervated; dropsy. Cf. *'ōhao 1*.

'ō.pū 'opi.'opi. n. Beef tripe. *Lit.*, folding belly.

'opu.'opu. 1. vs. To belch; filled, as a calabash. **2.** Redup. of *'opu 2*. **hō.'opu.'opu.** To think, surmise, want. *'Eā, ua pi'o ka uahi lepo i ka lani, ke hō'opu'opu lā kō ia ala kupa* (chant), oh, the dusk cloud bends in the sky, the native son is speculating.

'ō.pū pa'a. nvi. The ability to go a long time without eating; to fast for a long time; one who can go long without eating. This was believed due to a belated dropping off of the umbilical cord in infancy. *Lit.*, solid stomach.

'ō.pū pala.'ai. vs. Potbellied, pumpkin-bellied.

'ō.pū palula. vs. Idle, indolent, eating food without working; potbellied. *Lit.*, sweet-potato-leaf stomach; said to be so called because it took little effort to cook sweet potato leaves.

'ō.pū pipi. n. Beef tripe.

'ō.pū pua'a. n. Pig intestine; tripe.

'ō.pū puna.lua. See *punalua*.

'ō.pu'u. 1. nvi. A bud, the budding breasts of a girl, the budding spur of a young cock; to bud; a child; a geometric cone. *Na 'ōpu'u maka mo'a me ke ahi* (Oihk. 2.14), fresh ears [of grain] parched with fire. *He 'ōpu'u 'oe, he kākala kēlā* (FS 95), you have young spurs, that one [a cock with old] spurs. **2.** n. A whale-tooth pendant, not tongue-shaped like the *lei palaoa*. See ex., *hulali 1*. Ka-lani-*'ōpu'u* (name of a chief), the whale-tooth pendant high chief. **3.** n. A large surf, swell. (UL 36.)

'ō.pu'u kai.mana. n. A cut diamond, as for a ring.

'ō.pu'u 'uku.'uku. vs. Of limited ability, importance, or strength, as once said of women and children. *Lit.*, small disposition.

'ō.pu'u mai'a. n. The root bud and buds of a banana plant, and the sheaths enclosing them.

'ō.pu'u.pu'u. 1. vs. Lumpy, bumpy, hilly, rough, as cloth or a road. **2.** n. Knuckle, as on fingers, wrist. **3.** n. Shore fish listed by Malo (no data). (Malo 46.)

ō.pū weu.weu. n. Clump of grass, a polite depreciatory way to refer to one's home, however magnificent it may be. *'Oku'u wahi ōpū weuweu lā, nou ia*, my little clump of grass shelter is for you.

ou. 1. n. Float, as on a net. *Rare*. **2.** vs. To lean on something, hide. *Rare*. **3.** poss. Your, yours (*o*-form, zero-class, singular; Gram. 8.4). (PPN *(')o'ou*.)

o'u. 1. n. A fish (no data). **2.** poss. Mine, my, of me (*o*-form, zero-class; Gram. 8.4). (PPN *ho'oku*.)

'ou. 1. nvs. Sharp, protruding, piercing; to protrude, project, jut out, pierce, puncture; to reach out for; to stretch out; to sound sharply; pinnacle, high peak;

royal; sharp sound as of knee drum or of tapa anvil. *Kāne-i-ka-ʻou-aliʻi* (Kep. 15), Kāne-of-the-royal-supremacy [a name]. *ʻOu ka leo o ka pahu,* the voice of the drum sounds. (PCP *kou.*) **2.** n. Bulwer's petrel *(Bulweria bulwerii),* a small sea bird; for some people, an *ʻaumakua.* Also *ʻouʻou.*

ō.ʻū. 1. vt. To pinch or nip off, as a bud. *ʻAko poʻo ʻōʻū,* to cut off all the hair at the back of the head and leave hair only in front. *E ʻōʻū i ka maka o ka wauke ʻoi ʻōpiopio,* pinch off the bud of the *wauke* plant while it is young [nip it in the bud; teach while young]. **2.** vi. To perch, as on a tree. *Fig.,* lazy. *ʻŌʻū ō loa nā manu o Kaupeʻa* (chant), the birds of Kaupeʻa [sing] long as they perch. **hō.ʻō.ʻū.** To cause to perch. **3.** n. A finch-like Hawaiian honey creeper *(Psittirostra psittacea),* with an almost parrot-like bill, endemic to the main Hawaiian Islands, but becoming very rare. Its green feathers were used for making cloaks and leis. See ex., *kuaola.* Cf. *ʻōʻū lae oʻo, ʻōʻū poʻo lapalapa. ʻAuhea wale ʻoe, ē ka manu ʻōʻū ʻoe o ka nahele* (song), listen, O bird, you honey creeper of the forest. **4.** vi. To hump up, as an octopus out of its burrow.

ʻoua. Var. of *ʻouo. ʻOua niu,* small, immature coconut.

o ua o. Same as *ua ona o.* (Gram. 8.3.4.)

ō.ua.ua. vs. **1.** Showery, somewhat rainy. **2.** Somewhat tough, rubbery.

ō.ʻū-holo-wai. n. Same as *ʻōʻū-holo-wai-o-Laʻa.* (For. 5:565.)

ō.ʻū holo wai. n. Kauaʻi *ʻākepa (Loxops coccinea caeruleirostris),* a bird.

ō.ʻū-holo-wai-o-Laʻa. n. A well-known kind of tapa said to have been associated with the goddess Laka and to be used in *kuni* ceremonies. (FS 253.)

ou.kou. pronoun. You (plural), ye. *Kā ʻoukou,* your (*a*-form). *Kō ʻoukou,* your (*o*-form). (Gram. 8.2.) (PNP *koutou.*)

ou.kuʻu. Rare var. of *ʻaukuʻu,* a heron.

ō.ʻuku.ʻuku. 1. n. A small *oʻu,* a fish. **2.** vs. Small, petite.

ō.ʻū lae oʻo. n. A variety of *ʻōʻū,* a bird similar to *ʻōʻū poʻo pāpale. Lit.,* mature-headed *ʻōʻū.*

ou.lana.kana, ouranatana. n. Orangutan. *Eng.*

ō.uli. n. Sign, omen, portent, prognostication, nature, symptom, character; mood in grammar. Also *aouli, ʻōmea. Haʻi ōuli,* to prognosticate, declare the future according to signs; to interpret omens.

ō.uli.haʻi. n. Indicative mood.

ō.uli hiki. n. Symptom, prognostication.

oulu. n. Growth.

ʻou.mua.mua. n. Leader, as in battle or other activity; scout.

ō.unauna. Same as *unauna,* hermit crab.

ʻouo, ʻouwo. nvs. Young animal, plant or person; young woman, pullet, cock, youth; youthful, sprightly; immature, as a coconut.

ō.ū.ʻole. Fearless, courageous. (And.)

ʻou.ʻou. 1. Redup. of *ʻou 1. Nuku ʻouʻou,* long protruding nose, as of a swordfish [sometimes said of gossips]. *I ka lālā wēkiu ka pua o Lono, i ka ʻouʻou o nā lani nui (kāhili* chant), in the topmost branch of the flowers of Lono, among the highest of the high chiefs. **hō.ʻou.ʻou.** To jut, project, cause to puncture, etc. **2.** nvi. A sharp sound, as of a tapa mallet or of a tapping knee drum; to sound thus. **3.** Same as *ʻou 2.* (PCP *koukou.*)

ō.ʻū.ʻō.ʻū. Same as *ʻōʻū 3.*

ō.uo.uo. vs. Growing thriftily, as plants.

ʻou.pē. 1. vs. Beaten down, as by storm (UL 79); to cast down (2 Oihn. 25.8). *Pēpē Hilo nāwali i ka ua, ʻoupē i ke anu a ka makani,* Hilo is crushed weak by the rain, beaten in the coldness of the wind. **2.** n. Extreme lower end of a canoe paddle. *Rare.*

ō.ʻupē. 1. vt. To deceive, fool, vex, trouble. **2.** vs. Limber, flexible; to tilt as a canoe in the water.

ō.ʻupē.ʻupē. Redup. of *ʻōʻupē.*

ō.ʻū poʻo lapa.lapa. n. A variety of *ʻōʻū,* a bird. *Lit.,* square-headed *ʻōʻū.*

ō.ʻū poʻo pā.pale. n. Variety of *ʻōʻū,* a bird. *Lit.,* head-crested *ʻōʻū.*

ouwa. Person living with strangers. (And.)

ʻowā, ʻoā. 1. vi. To talk loudly back and forth, roar. *Rare.* Cf. *wā 3.* **2.** nvi. Cry of the *ʻaukuʻu,* heron, which suggests *ʻowā;* to cry thus. **3.** vi. To retch, gag. **hō.ʻowā.** Same as above; to vomit. **4.** n. A measurement equal to half the width of a finger, of fishing nets. Cf. *wā 4. Mākahi a ʻowā,* the width of one and a half fingers. **5.** n. In music, one of the five lines of the staff. **6.** Var. spelling of *ʻoā 1.*

owaawa. Same as *awaawa.*

ʻō.waʻa.waʻa. Same as *ʻawaʻawaʻa.*

ō.wae. vi. To crack, fissure, split open, as dry ground; cracked, fissured, gullied. Cf. *māwae.*

ō.wae.wae. Redup. of *ʻowae. Nā ʻowaewae pali o Unu-lau* (PH 101), the cliffed gullies of Unu-lau.

ō.waha.waha. vs. Grooved, furrowed. Cf. *waha 1.*

ʻowāhi. Same as *wāhi. Ua namu a pāhoehoe ʻia apau, i ʻowāhi, kaʻa lauahi ʻia ke one* (chant), all is chewed up to smooth lava, sand rolled over, broken through.

ʻowai. Var. spelling of *ʻoai 1–3.*

ʻo wai. See *wai,* who.

ʻowai.kū. Var. spelling of *ʻoaikū.*

ʻowaka. 1. Same as *hoaka 3.* Cf. *waka 2. Ka ʻowaka o ka lani* (PH 195), lightning flash of heaven. **hō.ʻowaka.** Caus/sim. **2.** Var. spelling of *ʻoaka 1, 2;* to open; to sprout.

ʻowa.kaaka, ʻowaka,waka. Var. spelling of *ʻoakaaka.*

ʻOwā.kiʻi.ala. Var. spelling of *ʻOākiʻiala.*

ʻowala, ʻoala. vi. To gambol, buck, rear, turn over, somersault; to brandish a club with a twirling motion; bucking, rearing, brandishing. Cf. *wala,* to tilt. *He aha ka hana a Pāwela? ʻO ka ʻoʻe, ʻo ka ʻowala* (Kaʻū song), what does Pāwela [a cow] do? She hooks and bucks. **hō.ʻowala.** To cause to buck, somersault, etc.

ʻowā.lala. Var. spelling of *ʻoālaala.*

ʻo.wali, ʻo.ali. 1. Weak, sickly, puny. Cf. *wali, nāwali.* **2.** Var. spelling of *ʻoali 1.*

ʻowā.liʻi. Var. spelling of *ʻoāliʻi.*

ʻowama. Var. spelling of *ʻoama.*

ō.wana. Var. spelling of *ʻoana.*

ʻowā.ʻoā. Var. spelling of *ʻoāʻoā.*

ʻowā.ʻowaka, ʻoā.ʻoaka. 1. n. A bivalve, perhaps one of the Isognomonidae. **2.** Var. spelling of *ʻoāʻoaka 1.*

ʻowā.ʻowala. Redup. of *ʻowala. Owāʻowala lua nā hala o Naue i ka makani* (hula chant), the *hala* of Naue caper in the wind. **hō.ʻowā.ʻowala.** Redup. of *hōʻowala.*

ʻowau. Var. spelling of *ʻoau 1–4.*

ʻo wau. See *au,* I.

owāwa, oawa. Same as *awaawa,* valley, gulch. *Owāwa o nā waimaka,* vale of tears.

ō.wā.wā. Redup. of *ʻowā 6.* . . . . *i ʻōwāwā ai ka hā o ka ʻape* (For. 5:563), and so the stalk of the *ʻape* became grooved.

ʻowē, ʻoē. nvi. Murmuring, rustling, soughing, whining, as of surf, leaves, water, wind, a bullet; to pitter patter, as rain; to sound thus; sound of tearing, as of cloth; buzzing of insects. Cf. *wewe 2. Ka ʻowē nahenahe a ka wai,* the soft murmur of the water. **hō.ʻowē.** To cause such a sound.

ō.wehe.wehe. vi. To open partly, as the clouds.

ʻoweke, ʻoeke. Rare var. of *ʻuwehe, ʻuweke.*

ʻowehu. Var. spelling of *ʻoehu.*

ō.wela. vs. Hottish, warm, feverish; burned and blistered, as by sun; glowing, bright, as feather cloaks and helmets of an army; heat. See ex., *kamaʻehu.*

ō.wela.wela. Redup. of *ʻōwela.*

ō.welo. vs. Waving slightly, streaming. Cf. *kōwelo.*

ʻŌ.welo-ka-huelo-kū. n. A *lua* fighting stroke. *Lit.,* the upright tail waves [perhaps referring to the tail of the *malo*].

ō.wena. n. A faint glow *(wena). Ke ʻā maila i Kī-lau-ea, ke ahi ʻōwena i ka lani* (prayer), burning at Kī-lau-ea, the fire glowing in the sky.

ō.wena.wena. Redup. of *ʻōwena.*

'owene. Var. spelling of *'oene 1, 2.*

'ō.weo. nvs. Red; to redden. See ex., *pūnoni.*

'owē.'owē. Redup. of *'owē.* **hō.'owē.'owē.** Redup. of *hō'owē.*

'owē.'owene. Var. spelling of *'oē'oene.*

ō.wī, oī. 1. n. A weedy kind of verbena *(Verbena litoralis),* from tropical America, with square stems 30 cm to 2 m high, toothed oblong leaves, and narrow flower spikes bearing tiny blue flowers. Hawaiians use it for cuts and bruises, applying the juice externally and later sprinkling the affected area with powdered *pia* root. Also *ha'uōwī.* (Neal 721–2.) **2.** n. The Jamaica vervain *(Stachytarpheta jamaicensis),* another kind of weedy verbena also from tropical America, similar to the above, but with oval toothed leaves, and tiny blue flowers borne on longer, narrower spikes. It is not used medicinally by Hawaiians. (Neal 725.) **3.** nvi. Cry of the bird *'ō'ū;* to cry, of the *'ō'ū.*

'ō.wili. 1. nvt. Roll, bolt, as of cloth or paper; scroll of binder, as of a sewing machine; skein, coil; to roll up, twist, coil, wave; to fold, as the arms. *'Ōwili palapala* (Ier. 36.2), scroll. *Ke oho 'ōwili* (Isa. 3.24), well-set hair. *Ko'i 'ōwili, ko'i wili,* gouge-like adze. **2.** n. Surfboard of *wiliwili* wood. **3.** n. Powder horn. See *holowa'a 'ōwili.*

'ō.wili.'ō.ka'i. Same as *wili'ōka'i 1,* cocoon.

'ō.wili.wili. Redup. of *'ōwili 1. 'Ōwiliwili me ka uila,* electrically waved [permanent wave, as of hair].

P

pā. 1. nvi. Fence, wall, corral, pen, sty, enclosure, court-yard, patio, arena, (house) lot, yard, extremity; to build a fence, enclosure. Cf. *pānini, Pā-lama* (place name), fence built of *lama* wood. *Mai kēlā pā o ka honua, a mai kēlā pā o ka lani mai* (Mar. 13.27), from that end of the earth and from that end of the heavens. (PPN *paa.*) 2. n. Dish, plate, pan; elongated food bowl used for meat or fish; flat basin; phonograph record, disk (preceded by *ke*). Cf. *halepā.* 3. n. Mother-of-pearl shell *(Pinctada margaritifera)*; pearl-shell lure; fishhook (cf. *pā ʻiʻo, pā kau ulua*). Both *ke* and *ka* are used with *pā* 3. *Pā ā eo,* a successful *pā* lure. *Pā hau,* shell with white on inside. *Pā mae,* variegated shell; *lit.,* faded shell. (PPN *paa.*) 4. nvs, nvi. A broadly used *loaʻa*-type word (Gram. 4.4), said of drinking, hearing, feeling, and activity of wind, sun, moon; also used as a noun with similar meanings (see ex., *pualalea*). To touch, get, contact, reach, gain control of, hit, experience; to blow (as wind), shine (as moon or sun), hear, drink. Cf. *pā kāhea, pā wai. Ua pā maila kuʻu lima iāʻoe,* you touched my hand. *Pā kanaka,* to have sexual experience; *lit.,* touch someone. *Pā ka ʻai,* to taste food. *Pā kīʻaha,* to touch a tumbler; to sip intoxicants. *Pā i ka leo,* to be struck by a voice, i.e., to be told something that hurts the feelings, to be rebuked. *Mālama o pā,* watch or you'll be hurt. *Pā nō lilo,* touch and gone [of a stolen object]. *Mālama o lilo i ka lima ā pā,* watch out or [it] will disappear into [someone's] hands and be taken away. *Pā ka ʻāina iāʻoe* (FS 133), you'll get control of the land. *Ka pā ʻana a ka lā,* sunshine. *ʻO ka pā kōnane a ka mahina* (song), the bright touch of the moon. *Pā i ka ʻupena,* touched by a net [said of a fish that has escaped a net and is wary]. *Pā i ka makau,* touched by a hook [said of a fish that has been hooked and then, having escaped, is very wary]. **hoʻo.pā.** About the same as *pā* 4; to touch; to try out, test. *E hele aku ʻoe e hoʻopā i ke kahuna pule,* go and see if you can get the minister to help, put a "touch" to him. *Pōhaku hoʻopā,* touchstone. *Hoʻopā iki,* to touch lightly or cautiously; to eat or drink sparingly. (PPN *paa.*) 5. nvi. A sound; to sound; beat, rhythm, as of a dance; stroke, as of an instrument; thump of a gourd down on a pad, with one quick slap of the fingers as the gourd is raised; signal to begin a dance or drumming. *Pā maila ka leo hone o ka waiolina,* the sweet sound of a violin reached here. 6. vs. Barren, as a female; to have ceased bearing; parched, as land. *ʻO Kila pā wahine,* Kila, the last born of the woman. **hoʻo.pā.** To procure barrenness, as by prayer or medication. (PPN *paʻa.*) 7. n. Flat top of a hat. 8. n. Lowest and highest note in the musical scale, do. 9. vs. Temporary, fleeting. *He nohona pā wale,* temporary residence. 10. n. Section of net attached to a bag in certain types of fishing.

pa-, pā-. Prefix to many bases, with general meaning of "in the nature of, having the quality of." Cf. *pāheahea, pahemo, pāhemahema, pāhaʻohaʻo,* etc. (Gram. 6.3.2.) (PPN *pa-.*)

pā-. Prefix to numerals: at a time, at once, number of times; to divide by. Cf. *lele* 7. (Gram. 10.3.) *Pālua,* doubly, by twos, two at a time, twice; to divide in two shares. *Miki pālua,* to eat poi with two fingers. *Pālua i ka iʻa,* divide the fish in two shares. **hoʻo.pā-.** Caus/sim. Cf. *hoʻopālima.*

paʻa. 1. nvs. A common and broadly used *loaʻa*-type word (Gram. 4.4); many meanings depend on qualifying words. Firm, solid, tight, solidified, adhering, durable, fast, fixed, stuck, secure, closed, jelled, con-gealed, frozen, hard, sound (as wood), busy, occupied, engaged, definite, steadfast, permanent; finished, completed, whole, complete, learned, memorized, mastered, retained, kept permanently; stubborn, determined, constipated, solid or fast, as colors; sturdy, as cloth, furniture; strong and vigorous; versed in, learned in; one who holds, a bearer; to hold, bear, keep, detain, withhold; a solid, as in geometry; to wear well, as clothes; to look well or not show age, of a person. See *paʻa kāhili. Mea paʻa ipu hao,* a pot holder. *ʻAila paʻa,* thick grease. *Paʻa ā paʻa,* held fast. *Paʻa i ka ʻole,* to deny persistently. *Paʻa mele,* one versed in songs. *Paʻa maila ʻo uka i nā kānaka* (FS 71), the shore was packed solid with people. *Paʻa ka wai ā lilo i hau,* water solidified into ice. *Paʻa ʻoia ma ka pono,* he is steadfast in righteousness. *Paʻa ka manaʻo,* determined in thought; to have made up one's mind. *Ua paʻa kaʻu haʻawina,* my lesson is learned. *Mea paʻa molaki,* mortgagee. *Paʻa ka hale hou,* the new house is finished. *Hana paʻa,* steady work. *Uku paʻa,* fixed salary. *Noho paʻa,* permanent residence. *Paʻa i ka ʻūkele,* stuck in the mud. *Kanu paʻa,* to bury whole, as a body. *Paʻa ke kelepona,* the telephone line is busy. *Paʻa i ka hana,* very busy working. *Paʻa ka puka,* the door is closed. *Mai paʻa ʻoe iaʻu,* don't detain me. *E paʻa ā paʻa ʻolua i ke kaula,* hold fast to the rope. *Hoʻonoho ihola lākou iāia ma kahi paʻa* (Nah. 15.34), they put him in custody. *Ua paʻa iāia ka waha o ka poʻe Sadukaio* (Mat. 22.34), he had silenced the mouths of the Sadducees. *Paʻa mai me ona lole ʻauʻau,* bring some bathing suits too. *Mai paʻa i ka leo, he ʻole ka hea mai* (hula pass-word), do not withhold the voice, or refuse to call to us [said by one wishing permission to enter a hula]. *I paʻa ke kino i ka lāʻau,* that the body be strengthened by medicine. *Nā lole i paʻa mua,* ready-made clothes. *E loaʻa ai ke anapaʻa o nā paʻa,* obtaining the cubic content of a solid. **hoʻo.paʻa.** To make fast, firm, hard, tight, solid; to bind, attach, moor, snub, hold fast to, hold back, keep, restrain, confine, detain, withhold, reserve, close, catch; to learn, memorize, master, study, complete, fix; to record, as music; to plug or seal, as a hole; to subscribe, as to a newspaper; to order, reserve, register; to insist on, persist; to insure; to bolt, as a door; to muzzle (Kanl. 25.4); drummer and hula chanter (the memorizer); insurance. Cf. *hoʻopaʻa haʻawina, mea hoʻopaʻa, ʻōlelo hoʻopaʻa. Hoʻopaʻa kuleana,* to copyright, establish ownership. *Hoʻopaʻa o hana,* apprentice. *Hoʻopaʻa inoa,* to register, enroll. *Hoʻopaʻa i ka hau,* to freeze (i.e., ice solidifies). *I hoʻopaʻa mai iā lākou iho* (Nak. 27), to bind themselves [as under contract to a chief]. *Hoʻopaʻa hao,* to weld. *Hoʻopaʻa leho,* to get calluses from work. *Hoʻopaʻa manawa,* to make an appointment. *Hoʻopaʻa ola,* life insurance. *Uku hoʻopaʻa,* insurance premium. *Leka i hoʻopaʻa ʻia,* registered letter. *Hoʻopaʻa ihola lāua ā ʻelua i berita* (Kin. 21.27), the two together sealed a covenant. *Mea hoʻopaʻa,* stopper. *Hoʻopaʻa moʻolelo,* to keep the minutes; to record a story. *Ua hoʻopaʻa au i mau noho no māua i ka ʻaha mele,* I reserved some seats for us at the concert. *Hoʻopaʻa i kāna ʻae,* holding back his consent. 2. n. Pair, couple; couplet. Cf. *paʻa kāmaʻa, paʻa lio, paʻa male.* 3. n. Suit of clothes. *Nā paʻa kapa* (Lunk. 14.12), garments. 4. n. Stratum, foundation, especially *paʻa-i-lalo,* earth, and *paʻa-i-luna,* heavens. 5. n. Extremity, border. 6. n. Type of sweet potato, pronunciation not certain. (For. 5:664-5.)

pā.ʻā. 1. Same as *paʻaʻā* 1, 2. 2. vs. Dry and rocky. *He ʻāina pāʻā,* a dry, rocky land.

pa'a.'ā, pā.'ā. n. **1.** Fiber, as of sugar-cane stalk or of banana sheath (probably a contraction of *pa'a*, solid, and *'a'a*, fiber). **2.** Var. of *pāpa'a 3*.

pā.'ā.'ā. n. **1.** First stage of growth of the fish *akule*, 6 or 7 cm. long. Cf. *halalū*. **2.** Inferior tapa made from small lengths of bark.

pa'a 'ahu, pā 'ahu. n. A carrier of mats (Kep. 129), a heap of mats.

pa'a.'āina. nv. Landholder; to hold land.

pa'a.aloha. Same as *pa'aloha*.

-pa'a ha'awina. ho'o.**pa'a ha'a.wina.** To study the lesson; studious.

pa'a.hana. 1. nvs. Industrious, busy, hard-working; workman, laborer, worker, industry. **2.** n. Implement, tool, utensil, furnishings (Nah. 7.1). *Mea pa'ahana,* tool, workman.

pa'a.hao. 1. nvi. Prisoner, convict; to be imprisoned. *Hale pa'ahao,* prison, jail. ho'o.**pa'a.hao.** To make a prisoner. *Ho'opa'ahao pono 'ole,* false imprisonment. **2.** n. Proceeds (as pigs, sweet potatoes or taro) paid to holders of land on which tenants worked; penalty for failure to pay was imprisonment. Cf. *lā pa'ahao, lo'i pa'ahao.*

pā ahi. n. Shovel (RSV), fire pan (KJV) (Ier. 52.19.) (Preceded by *ke*.)

pa'a.hia. Pas/imp. of *pa'a 1*.

pa'a.hihi. vs. Spread here and there.

pa'a.hiku. n. Heptagon.

pa'a.hono. Same as *pāhono*.

pā 'ahu. Var. of *pa'a 'ahu*.

pā.'aila. n. The castor-oil plant *(Ricinus communis)*, an introduced shrub with large lobed leaves and dry prickly seed cases. The seeds contain a dangerous poison. The Hawaiians use the leaves, rubbed on the face, to relieve fever. (Neal 509–10.) Also *ka'apehā, kamākou, kolī, lā'au 'aila*.

pa'a-i-lalo. n. The earth below.

pa'a.'ili. n. A solid, usually with number of sides following, as *pa'aili hā*. *Lit.,* surface solid.

pa'a.'ili hā. n. Four-sided solid (this term was said to be used formerly for a pyramid).

pa'a.'ili hā like. n. *Pa'a'ili* with equal sides.

pa'a.'ili iwa.kā.lua. n. A twenty-sided solid.

pa'a.'ili kau.like hiō. n. Oblique parallelepiped. *Lit.,* solid leaning similarly.

pa'a.'ili kū.pono. n. Cube or rectangular parallelepiped. *Lit.,* straight solid.

pa'a.'ili ono. n. Six-sided solid, cube; cubic. See ex., *iā*, yard.

pa'a.'ili ono like. n. Cube. *Lit.,* equal six solid.

pa'a.'ili 'umi kuma.mā.lua. n. A twelve-sided solid.

pa'a-i-luna. n. Heavens above.

pa'a ipu kuha. n. Bearer of the chief's spittoon.

pa'a kā.hili. nv. Bearer of the royal feather standard; to carry a *kāhili*.

pa'a.kai. n. **1.** Salt; encrusted discharge in the inner corners of the eyes, as after sleeping. Types of salt are *pa'akai lele wai,* very fine, dried salt; *pa'akai walewale,* slimy salt; *pa'akai pu'upu'u,* coarse salt; *pa'akai lepo,* salt mixed with earth; *pa'akai 'ula'ula,* salt mixed with ocherous earth. Cf. *alaea 1. Loko-pa'akai,* Salt Lake City. (Perhaps PNP *pakatai;* cf. East Futuna.) **2.** A variety of taro, usually grown in the uplands, the plant short and stocky; petioles dark-green, edged with red; corm flesh white, used chiefly for poi. **3.** Same as *līpa'akai,* a seaweed.

pa'a.kai hao. n. Copperas. (Hae Hawaii, May 13, 1857.)

pa'a.kai.hele.le'i. n. A fish, said to be one of the Hemiramphidae. *Lit.,* scattered salt.

pa'a.kai holoi. n. Lye (RSV), nitre (KJV) (Ier. 2.22.) *Lit.,* washing salt.

pa'a.kai ho'o.hanu.hanu. n. Smelling salts.

pa'a.kai hū. n. Effervescent solution.

pa'a.kai inu. n. Epsom salts. *Lit.,* drinking salt.

pa'a.kai miko.miko. n. A variety of taro.

pa'a.kai mu'e.mu'e. n. Alum. *Lit.,* bitter salt.

pa'a kā.ma'a. n. Pair of shoes.

pa'a.kea. n. Limestone, coral beds, as found on the leeward sides of the islands. *Lit.,* white hardness.

pa'a.kikī. vs. Hard, tough, unyielding; arbitrary, inflexible, compact, difficult, stubborn (Kanl. 9.27), obstinate. *Mai pa'akikī aku 'oe i ke anu,* don't be so obstinate about going out in the cold. ho'o.**pa'a.kikī.** Same as *pa'akikī;* to cause hardness, obstinacy; to pretend to be hard, stubborn.

pa'a.kō. n. Dry lowland plain. (Kep. 87.)

-pa'a.kope. ho'o.**pa'a.kope.** Copyright; to copyright.

pa'a.kū.kū. vi. To jell, set firmly, congeal; to clot, as blood; to stiffen, as hard poi; avaricious. *Koko pa'akūkū,* blood clot. ho'o.**pa'a.kū.kū.** To cause to clot, congeal, etc.

pā akule. n. Fish pond for trapping *akule,* fish.

-pa'a kuleana. ho'o.**pa'a kule.ana.** nvt. Copyright; to copyright.

pa'a.lā. n. **1.** Smooth, water-worn *'alā* rock. (FS 153.) **2.** *(Cap.)* A Maui wind.

Pa'a.la'a. Same as *pa'alā 2*. See chant, *ka'alani*.

pa'a.lalo. n. Attendants of a chief; bridal attendants.

pa'a lau. nv. Those holding a *lau,* dragnet; to hold the *lau*.

pa'a.lia. Pas/imp. of *pa'a 1*. *Eia 'o Hawai'i ua ao, pa'alia i ka pono i ka lima* (name song for Lili'u-o-ka-lani), here is Hawai'i, enlightened, held by justice in the hand.

pa'a.li'i. Same as *koali 'ai,* a morning-glory, when used as a medicine.

pa'a.lima. n. Pentagon.

pa'a lima. nvs. Held in the hand; handle. *'Auhea ku'u 'eke'eke pa'a lima?* Where is my handbag?

pa'a lio. n. Team of horses.

pa'a.loha. n. Keepsake, memento, souvenir. Also *pa'aloha*.

pa'a.lole. n. Suit of clothes. Also *pa'alole komo*.

pa'a.lole maka.like. n. Uniform, as of military.

pa'a.lua. n. **1.** A variety of banana. **2.** Deuce.

pa'a luhi. vs. Overcome with weariness.

pa'a.lula. nvs. Formal, according to rule, decorous; to observe rules, as of etiquette; one who observes such rules. *Pa'alula 'ole,* one with poor manners, uncouth.

pa'a male. n. Married couple.

pa'a male hou. n. Bridal couple.

pa'a mana'o. vs. Firm in one's memory; memorized. ho'o.**pa'a mana'o.** To keep a memorandum, make a record of thoughts, memorize.

pa'a mau. vs. Regular, customary, usual. *Lit.,* continually fixed. *Hālāwai pa'a mau,* customary or regular meeting. *Manawa pa'a mau,* usual or regular time.

pa'a mau no'o.no'o. nvs. A keepsake, memento; to keep a thought of something. *Lit.,* hold continued thinking.

pa'a mo'o.lelo. nvs. Versed in lore, legends, history, tradition; documented in such; one so versed.

pa'a.mua. 1. nvs. Gaseous condition of the bowels, to have such. **2.** n. Dam, windbreak. **3.** nvs. Steadfast in prayer for the welfare of the family, one so steadfast. *Rare.*

pa'a mua. vs. Ready-made, as clothes.

pa'a.nā. Same as *pa'apa'anā 1, 2*.

pa'a.na'au. vs. Memorized, remembered. *Lit.,* fixed intestines. ho'o.**pa'a.na'au.** To memorize.

pa'a.nehe. Same as *palanehe. Rare.*

pā.'ani. nvt. Play, sport, game, amusement, joke; joking, playing, amusing, playful; to play, sport. *Pā'ani kinipōpō,* to play ball; ballplayer. *Pā'ani pepa,* to play cards. *Mea pā'ani,* toy, plaything. *Pā'ani hewa,* foul. *Pā'ani lapa,* frolic. Cf. *ho'okani,* to play music. ho'o.**pā.'ani.** To make sport, cause to play, joke, playful. *He mea ho'opā'ani,* a game.

pā.ani.ani. Var. spelling of *pāniani 1, 2*.

pā ani.ani. n. Glass dish (preceded by *ke*).

pā.'ani koho.koho. nv. Guessing game, puzzle; to play such games.

pā.'ani lā.'au. n. Any stick game.

pā ā.nue.nue. n. Pearl-shell lure named for the rainbow *(ānuenue)*.

Pā.'ao. n. Name of a star, said to be one of a large group resembling a double canoe. *Pā'ao* was a famous priest said to have conveyed a colony from Central Polynesia to Hawai'i.

pā.'ao.'ao. 1. vs. Sideways, one-sided. *Kau pā'ao'ao,* to place on the side. 2. n. Latent childhood disease, with physical weakening; a general term for ailments. *Rare. Kahuna hāhā pā'ao'ao,* practitioner who felt *(hāhā)* infants to see if they had *pā'ao'ao* disorders.

-pa'aola. ho'o.pa'a.ola. Life insurance; to get life insurance.

pa'a.oloulu. n. Young *loulu* palm leaves, as used in making hats.

pa'a.ono. n. Hexagon.

pa'a.pa'a. 1. n. Dispute, argument, quarrel. **ho'o.pa'a.-pa'a.** To argue, dispute; argument, quarrel. 2. Same as *pāpa'a 1. Ua pa'apa'a kō lākou alelo i ka make wai* (Isa. 41.17), their tongues burned with thirst. (PCP *pakapaka.*) 3. n. A fish *(Dascyllus albisella).* 4. n. A kind of sugar cane. Also *ho'opa'apa'a.*

pa'a.pa'a.'ina. 1. nvs. Brittle, crisp, crackling; to snap, crackle. *Ka pa'apa'a'ina o nā kākalaioa* (Kekah. 7.6), the crackling of thorns. **ho'o.pa'a.pa'a.'ina.** To make a crackling sound, etc. 2. n. A variety of taro. 3. n. A variety of sweet potato.

pa'a.pa'a.kai. vs. Salt-encrusted.

pa'a.pa'a.nā. 1. vt. To ease, as pain; to soothe; to entertain, amuse. *Pa'apa'anā mai i ua wahi 'eha nei ona,* easing his little pain. **ho'o.pa'a.pa'a.nā.** To cause pain to be soothed; to entertain. 2. vi. To hurry, hasten. *Rare.*

pa'a.pa'ani. vt. Playful, to play frequently. Cf. *pā'ani.*

pa'a.pa'ina. Redup. of *pa'ina. Nā leo hurō e pa'apa'ina i ka lewa,* the sounds of hurrah burst forth in the air.

pa'a.pani. Rare var. of *papani.*

pa'a poe.poe. n. Globe, circular solid, sphere. *Lit.,* round solid.

pa'a.pū. vs. Covered with, solid with, teeming with, crowded, congested, as people, fog, or clouds; dense, impervious, nonporous; stifling, stuffy, as a room; thick or coarse, of banana fruit peeling (HP 173). (Ioba 7.5.) *Pa'apū o loko,* tense, repressed. *Pa'apū i ka ulu lā'au,* forested, wooded. *Pa'apū ka umauma,* the chest is stifled [as from a severe attack of asthma]. **ho'o.pa'a.pū.** To make crowded, covered with, stifling, etc. *Ua ho'opa'apū lākou i kō waena ou me ka haunaele* (Ezek. 28.16), they filled those around you with violence.

pa'au. Rare var. of *pa'a'ā.*

pa'a.ua. nvi. Hard physical labor or drudgery; a drudge (perhaps contraction of *pa'a,* hold, and *uaua,* tough); to work hard. **ho'o.pa'a.ua.** To enslave, overwork, treat as a drudge.

pa'au.hau. n. A variety of sweet potato.

pa'a uma. nv. A type of hand wrestling in which each player tried to push his opponent's hand back to his chest *(uma);* to wrestle thus. *Pahi pa'a uma,* draw knife.

pa'a.waha. nv. Gag; to gag the mouth (Hal. 39.1). *Lit.,* make the mouth solid.

-pa'a waiwai. ho'o.pa'a wai.wai. To insure property; property insurance.

pa'a walu. n. Octagon.

pa'a.wela. nvt. A burned area; a scar from burning; to burn. *Ma kahi maika'i e pa'awela ana nō* (Isa. 3.24), instead of beauty, burning. 2. n. Probably a wrasse fish.

pae. 1. nvs. Cluster, row, group; margin or bank, as of a taro patch; level, as of a platform. Cf. *pae 'āina, pae kō, pae moku. I ka hele 'ana o ka imu ā 'ena'ena, ua 'ōhelo noho'i ka lā'au ulu imu a nonoho a pae like,* when the oven is red-hot, the oven-poking stick is pushed around so that [the stones] are in even levels.

ho'o.pae. To build up an embankment, row, cluster. (PNP *pae.*) 2. vi. To land, disembark, come ashore; to mount or catch a wave, as of a surf rider; washed or drifted ashore. *Niho pae,* a loose tooth. *Manu pae,* a bird that lands from afar, as a migratory bird. *Palaoa pae,* whale washed ashore. *Pae i ka nalu,* to ride a wave into the shore. *Po'e pae mai,* immigrants. *'A 'ole e pae nā wa'a o ke ali'i iā'oe* (Nak. 56), the chief's canoes cannot land because of you. *E 'ai kākou. Mahalo, ua pae kēia wa'a.* Let's eat. Thanks, this canoe has landed [i.e., I have eaten]. **ho'o.pae.** to cause to land, reach shore. *Ho'opae malū,* to smuggle, bring in secretly. *Waiwai ho'opae malū 'ia,* smuggled goods. (PPN *pae.*) 3. n. Type of sweet potato, pronunciation uncertain. (For. 5:664-5.)

pa'ē. vs. To strike the ear, as a distant sound. *Pa'ē mai ana ka leo o ke kai,* the sound of the sea strikes the ears.

pā.'ē. nvt. To peel, as bark; a bunch of cleaned bark, as of *olonā. Rare.*

paea. n. Flint *(Eng.,* fire.) *Pōhaku paea,* flint (Isa. 50.7); agate, carbuncle (Isa. 54.12).

pa'ea. n. A variety of taro.

paea.ea. nvi. 1. To fish with a light pole offshore; pole-fishing. *Kanaka paeaea,* fisherman. *Hele kākou i ka paeaea,* let's go pole-fishing. 2. nvi. A chant of supplication; to chant thus, perhaps so called as a means of "fishing" for something. (PH 149.)

pā.ea.ea. 1. vs. Smooth, calm, as the sea. 2. n. A variety of fish mentioned as having sharp protuberances (Malo 46). 3. vt. To signal with the arms. *Rare.*

paea.ea 'a.ama. n. A method of catching *'a'ama* crabs with a coconut fiber snare on a coconut midrib; it is looped over the crab's eye and jerked upward; to crab thus.

paea.ea 'ō.hiki. nv. A method of catching *'ōhiki* sand crabs, with a blossom, usually *nohu,* tied to the end of a line as bait; to crab thus.

pae 'āina. n. Group of islands, archipelago.

pā.'ē.'ē. vs. 1. Here and there, everywhere but the right place. *Kuhi pā'ē'ē,* to misdirect, mislead, give inaccurate information. **ho'o.pā.'ē.'ē.** To cause to go astray, mislead, misrepresent. 2. Supernatural. *Ka lāhui kino pā'ē'ē i kapa 'ia he Melehune,* a people with supernatural bodies, called Melehune.

pae.heu. n. Large bundle. *Rare.*

pae hewa. vi. To stray.

pae.hi'a. vt. To fasten *'aho* sticks to thatching, of a house.

pae.humu. n. 1. Taboo enclosure about a chief's house or about a heiau (Kep. 137). *Mālama o pā ka 'auwae i ka paehumu* (saying), be careful or the chin will rest on the taboo enclosure [you will get into serious trouble]. 2. Bannister.

pa'eke. n. Pocket. *Eng.*

pā 'eke. n. Small corral.

pae.ki'i. n. Row of clouds, as on the horizon. *Lit.,* row of images.

pae kō. n. Cultivation of sugar cane growing along a border.

pā.'ele. nvt. Negroid, dark, black; to blacken; to tattoo solid black without design; to paint black, as a canoe; to blot. *Pā'ele i ka 'alaea a me ka nānahu* (FS 259), paint black with red coloring and charcoal. **ho'o.pā.'ele.** To blacken, etc. 2. *(Cap.)* n. Negro, Black. 3. n. A variety of sweet potato. Also *nika.*

pā.'ele-hili-mā.noa.noa. n. A variety of taro. *Lit.,* thick-barked blackness.

pā.'ele hili mā.noa.noa. n. A variety of sweet potato.

pā.'ele kū.lani. n. Solid tattooing of one side of the body; Ka-hekili, chief of Maui, was said to have been tattooed thus. *Lit.,* chiefly darkening.

pā.'eli. vt. To dig the earth, as to plant in a taro patch. **ho'o.pā.'eli.** to cause such digging.

pā.'eli'eli. Redup. of *pā'eli.* **ho'o.pā.'eli.'eli.** Redup. of *ho'opā'eli.*

Pae-loa-hiki. n. Name of a star or for the Milky Way. *Lit.,* eastern long row.

pae moku. n. Group of islands, archipelago. *Lit.,* cluster of islands.

pae moku.puni. n. Archipelago.

paena. n. Landing place, as of canoes *(paena wa'a)* or of waves *(paena nalu);* landing. Cf. *pae 2.* (PCP *paenga.*)

pae niho. n. Row of teeth.

pae.pae. 1. nvt. A support, prop, stool, pavement, house platform; plate of a house on which the rafters rest; block to keep an outrigger float off the ground; log or wooden horse that supports a seesaw; to support, hold up, sustain; rows. *Loina paepae āhua,* customs that add prestige; *lit.,* elevated mound customs. *E paepae mai i ka uluna ā ki'eki'e,* pile the pillows high. *Paepae 'o'opu,* old term for a built-up pool for keeping *'o'opu* fish. **ho'o.pae.pae.** To build up a *paepae* (platform) or a taro embankment; to finish a space in quilting. (PPN *paepae.*) 2. Redup. of *pae 2.* **ho'o.pae.pae.** Redup. of *ho'opae.* 3. n. Boom of a ship. Cf. *kaula paepae.* 4. Same as *iwi 'ao'ao.*

pa'ē.pa'ē. Redup. of *pa'ē;* to publicize. **ho'o.pa'ē.pa'ē.** To be noisy, as a distant sound; to talk loudly.

pae.pae kī. n. Ti-stalk fence (the stalks are crossed and a stick put into the notches made by the crossings).

paepae komo huila. n. Axle of a wheel (1 Nal. 7.33). *Lit.,* support where wheel enters.

pae.pae puka. n. Threshold (Isa.6.4). *Lit.,* door platform.

pae.pae puka.ani.ani. n. Window sill.

pae.pae wā.wae. n. Footstool. (Iak. 2.3.)

pa'ē pū. nvi. To sound together, a deafening roar.

pae pu'u. n. Row or cluster of hills.

pa'ewa. nvs. Crooked, misshapen, bent, uneven, odd, imperfect; wrong, incorrect; error, mistake. *Helu pa'ewa,* odd number. Cf. *'auipa'ewa.* **ho'o.pa'ewa.** To cause to be crooked, wrong, etc.

pā.'ewa.'ewa. Redup. of *pa'ewa;* biased, partial, unfair, prejudicially. *E 'imi pono me ka pā'ewa'ewa 'ole,* investigate carefully and impartially. **ho'o.pā.'ewa.-'ewa.** Redup. of *ho'opa'ewa.*

paha. 1. nvt. To improvise a chant; an improvised or conversation chant, as the *kepakepa.* (PCP *pa(f,s)a.*) 2. n. Uncooked young taro leaves. (PH 74.) Cf. *lū'au, pē'ū.* 3. Same as *kūpala,* a plant. 4. n. A kind of surfboard. *Rare.* 5. Short for *pahāha. Rare.* 6. Part. Maybe, perhaps, probably, possibly, may, might (very common, used to make speech less blunt and more conciliatory, something like English use of the conditional mode; it frequently follows *'a'ole* and *pēlā,* and never occurs after a pause). (Gram. 7.5.) *'A'ole paha,* maybe not, possibly not, likely not, probably not. *Pēlā paha,* maybe so. *Ā . . . paha,* or. *'Elua ā 'ekolu paha* (For. 4:259), two or three. *'O ka po'e kōkua i hana i kekahi hewa 'ofeni, ā ua noho paha malaila,* the people who help in the committing of an offense, or are present there. *Hele paha,* [I] may [or might] go. (PCP *pa(f,s)a.*)

pā.hā. vt. By fours, four at a time, four times; to distribute to four; to divide by four.

pā.ha'a. vs. Short in stature.

pā.ha'a.ha'a. 1. Redup. of *pāha'a.* 2. Same as *no'uno'u,* a gourd.

pahaha. n. Young stage of the mullet, also called *kahaha.* (KL line 173.)

pahāha. vs. Swollen, as the neck or the cheeks of one with mumps; to strut, walk proudly. *Rare.* Cf. *'auwaepahāha, manō pahāha.* **ho'o.pahāha.** To cause swollenness; to hoist the shoulders; to strut.

paha.kū. n. Name of a design on Ni'ihau mats consisting of squares with corners touching and forming a line.

pā.hala. n. A method of making mulch soil by placing pandanus *(hala)* branches and leaves in holes in rocky soil containing mulch, and then burning the *hala* for fertilizer.

-pāhala. ho'o.pā.hala. Sceptical. *He kanaka ho'opā-*

hala, he mana'o'i'o 'ole (Kep. 107), a skeptical person of no faith.

pā hale. n. House lot, yard, fence.

pā hali.hali. n. Tray (preceded by *ke*). *Lit.,* plate for carrying.

pā.haneli, pāhaneri. nvt. A hundredfold, by the hundred; to distribute to a hundred.

pā hao. n. 1. Iron fence. 2. Iron dish, pan (preceded by *ke*).

pā.ha'o. 1. About the same as the more common *pāha'oha'o.* 2. n. Name of a guessing game. *Rare.*

pā.ha'o.ha'o. vs. Mysterious, puzzling, incomprehensible; transfigured. **ho'o.pā.ha'o.ha'o.** To mystify, bewilder, cause wonder, puzzle; transfigured. *Ho'opā-ha'oha'o 'ia ihola ia i mua o lākou* (Mat. 17.2), he was transfigured before them.

-pahaola. See *akepahaola.*

paha.paha. 1. Redup. of *paha 1, 5.* (PCP *pa(f,s)apa-(f,s)a.*) 2. Same as *līpahapaha,* sea lettuce. 3. n. O'ahu name for a kind of stone used for poi pounders. Called *makawī* on Kaua'i.

paha.paha kua.hiwi. n. A liverwort *(Dumortiera* sp.).

paha.paha-o-Poli.hale. n. A kind of *pahapaha* said to be found only at Poli-hale, Kaua'i; after drying it was believed to revive when immersed in sea water; it was made into leis. (FS 103.)

paha.paha wai. n. A sea lettuce *(Ulva* sp.) with narrow frond. Found where sea and fresh water meet.

pā.hau. 1. n. Striped flatfish. (KL line 156.) 2. nvs. Person who cared for chief's food and clothes; well-cared for, as clothes. *Rare.* 3. vt. To filch. *Rare.*

pā hau. n. 1. Enclosure or fence of *hau* trees. 2. White pearl-shell lure or shell.

pahē. vs. Soft-spoken, soft-mannered; soft and about to spoil, as fruit; pulp, of fruit. See the more common *waipahē.*

pā.hea.hea. nvt. To call, especially to invite someone to eat; hospitality.

pahe'e. 1. vi. Slippery, smooth, as a surface; soft, satiny; to slide, slip, skid; sliding, slipping. Cf. *holo pahe'e, pakika, pōhaku pahe'e 'ānai.* *Lole pahe'e* (Hoik. 18.12), silk. *'Ōlelo pahe'e,* fluent speech; glib or cunning tongue. **ho'o.pahe'e.** To cause to slip, slide; to make smooth, slippery; to smooth with oil, as the hair; to lubricate. See ex., *kū 13.* (PPN *paseke.*) 2. n. Cleared area, bare dirt. 3. n. Spear throwing (FS 114–5); dart-throwing; sport of sliding a stick over a smooth surface; the dart itself. Buck describes the darts as from 34.5 to 67 inches (about 85 to 170 cm) long, tapering at one end, with the greatest diameter of from 1 to 1½ inches (2.6 to 3.9 cm). Cf. *moa 5.* 4. n. Shallow hole or grave, as for flexed burial. (For. 5:571.) 5. Same as *pāhe'ehe'e,* seaweed.

pā.he'e.he'e. 1. Redup. of *pahe'e 1. Wahi pāhe'ehe'e* (Hal. 73.18), slippery places. **ho'o.pā.he'e.he'e.** Caus/sim. (PPN *pasekeseke.*) 2. n. A green cushion-shaped solid seaweed *(Porphyra* sp., formerly *Dictyosphaeria).* Also *līpahe'e, līpahe'ehe'e, līpāhoe, pahe'e.*

pahe'e 'ulu. nv. To bowl; bowling.

pahele. n. A snare, noose, trap; to ensnare, trap; deceit, treachery. *'Ōlelo pahele,* deceitful speech. *I pahele a i 'ūpiki no ka po'e* (Isa. 8.14), a trap and a snare to the people. **ho'o.pahele.** To cause to be ensnared; to ensnare, deceive. 2. Same as *mānai,* needle.

Pahele-hala. n. Wind off Wai-'anae, O'ahu (PH 161), and associated with Naue, Kaua'i (For. 5:97). *Lit.,* pandanus ensnarement.

pā.hele.hele. Redup. of *pahele,* snare. *He pāhelehele puhi no Hāmākua,* an eel snarer from Hāmākua. *He pāhelehele 'ōpae* (Nak. 85), a snarer of shrimps.

pahelo. 1. Var. of *pakelo.* **ho'o.pahelo.** Var. of *ho'opakelo.* 2. vt. To peel, as taro. *Kaua'i.*

pā.hema.hema. About the same as *hemahema:* awkward, unskilled. *Pāhemahema i ka ho'onohonoho 'ana i nā hua 'ōlelo,* awkward in the arranging of words, as of one speaking brokenly. **ho'o.pā.hema.hema.** Same as *pāhemahema;* to cause awkwardness, to fake lack of skill.

pahemo. nvs. About the same as *hemo;* loosened, slipping off; to loosen, get loose; weakening, as a voice. *Iwi pahemo,* dislocation. *Ua pahemo ka hō mai ke kū'au,* the hoe slipped off the handle. **ho'o.pahemo.** To cause to slip, slacken, loosen, etc.

pā.hemo.hemo. Redup. of *pahemo. Pa'a pāhemo-hemo,* to remember here and there, imperfectly, as a song. **ho'o.pā.hemo.hemo.** Redup. of *ho'opahemo.*

pā.hene.hene. vt. To ridicule, laugh at, make fun of, mock, scoff. **ho'o.pā.hene.hene.** Caus/sim.

pahe.pahē. Redup. of *pahē.*

pā.heu.heu. n. A fish (no data).

pahi. **1.** nvt. Knife, flint; to skin, as cattle. (PCP *pa(f,s)i.*) **2.** To stand on edge. (And.)

pā.hia. inter. How many to each? How many in a group?

pā.hi'a. nvt. A slipping, falling down; oblique cut; obliquely, as of clipping, cutting, falling; to miss. *Kū pāhi'a ku'u pua i ke kaha,* my arrow slipped to one side of the mark. *Lele pāhi'a,* leaping sideways into water without a splash, as in the *lele kawa* sport. (PCP *paasika.*)

pā.hi'a.hi'a. Redup. of *pāhi'a.* (PCP *paasikasika.*)

pā hī'aku. n. Bonito hook.

pahi hahau. n. Cleaver, chopping knife. *Lit.,* striking knife.

pā.hihi. vi. To spread, as vines; to stream, as water over a cliff.

pahi kā. n. Cane knife, machete. *Lit.,* striking knife.

pahi kahi. n. Razor. Cf. more common *pahi 'umi'umi. Lit.,* shaving knife.

pahi kā.kiwi. n. Sickle, scythe, cutlass. *Lit.,* bent knife.

pahi kani.kani. n. Knife made of a piece of hoop iron. *Lit.,* sounding knife.

pahi.kaua. **1.** Same as *kala li'ili'i,* a fish (see *kala 3*). **2.** n. A long narrow bivalve, possibly the Pinna shells (Pinnidae).

pahi kaua. n. Sword. *Lit.,* war knife.

pahi kaua pā.laha.laha. n. Cutlass. *Lit.,* flat war knife.

pahi keke'e. n. Sickle.

pā.hiki. vi. To pass quietly, go lightly, touch gently.

pahi koli. n. Carving knife.

pā.hiku. vt. Sevenfold, by sevens; seven times; to distribute to seven or divide by seven.

pā.hila. vi. To stagger. Cf. *hilala.*

pahi.lau. vs. Untrue, false; untruth (contraction of *pāhili,* variable, and *lau,* much). Cf. *'alapahi.* **ho'o.pahi.lau.** To tell lies.

pahili. vt. To braid. *Fig.,* to confuse, entangle, deceive.

pā.hili. vi. To blow strongly, as a wind, especially of a veering wind; to lash, as a storm. *Makani pāhili,* strong wind, cyclone, hurricane. *Ka pāhili 'ia o ka 'ama'u e ka Mālualua,* the lashing of the *'ama'u* fern by the Mālualua wind. **ho'o.pā.hili.** To cause such a wind; to blow, as such a wind, etc.

pahilo. Same as *puāhilo.*

pahi lole pipi. n. Sharp knife used for dressing beef. *Lit.,* knife for skinning beef.

pahi.lolo. vs. Proud, strutting. *Rare.*

pahi maka lua. n. Double-edged sword or knife.

pahinu. vs. About the same as *hinu. Kāma'a pahinu,* patent-leather shoes; *lit.,* shiny shoes. **ho'o.pahinu.** To make shiny, etc.

pahi.ō. vi. Leaning, slanting, stooping; tall, slender (And.). See *hiō.*

pahi 'ō. n. Dagger. *Lit.,* piercing knife.

pahi 'oki.'oki. n. Carving knife.

pahi 'oki.'oki pipi. n. Butcher knife.

pahi 'oki pepa. n. Paper knife.

pahi olo. nvt. A saw; to saw.

pahi olo lua. n. Whipsaw.

pahi olo poe.poe. n. An unknown type of saw mentioned in wills during the 1850s.

pā hipa. n. Sheepfold.

pahi pa'a uma. n. Drawknife. *Lit.,* knife solid [at] chest.

pahi.pahi. nvi. To slap hands; to play "peas-porridge-hot"; this game; a game formerly played by children: a rotten object was buried in the sand and others were asked to dig for it, while the leader said *"kōhi kōhi kūpā, no wai, no wai ka lima i hawahawa,"* gather, gather, dig, whose hands, whose hands are dirtied.

pahi pa'i.pa'i. n. Pruning knife.

pahi pā.kā.kā. n. Chopping knife of any kind.

pahi pelu. n. Jackknife, penknife, folding knife.

pahi po'o muku. n. Short-bladed knife. *Lit.,* cut head knife.

pā.hi'u.hi'u. **1.** nvt. A game: throwing darts at a target, or pushing a stone with sharp sticks to a goal; to play this game. *Hele ana 'oe i hea? Hele ana i ka pāhi'ihi'u.* Where are you going? To play *pāhi'uhi'u* [to pry into others' affairs, snoop]. **2.** n. A type of sorcery. (Kam. 64:131, 140.)

pahi 'ume. n. Drawknife.

pahi 'umi.'umi. n. Razor. *Lit.,* beard knife.

pā.hiwa. nvs. Dark, to darken (note that *hiwa* is a sacred, desirable black that contrasts with *uli*). *Lau pāhiwa* (KL line 280), dark leaf. *Ka lani nui pāhiwa* (chant), the sacred, dark, heavenly one. **ho'o.pā.hiwa.** Caus/sim.

pahi waka.waka. n. Flaming sword (Kin. 3.24); saw, sword. *Lit.,* shining knife.

pahō. Var. of *pohō.*

pā.hoa. n. Short dagger; sharp stone, especially as used for a weapon; Moloka'i name for stick for beating clothes; taboo sign. *Ko'i pāhoa,* stone battle-axe. *Kūkulu i ka pāhoa,* to set up a taboo sign.

pā.hoe. nv. To paddle; to drive fish into a net by beating the paddles rhythmically against the canoe; paddler. Cf. *homa 3, kāpapa. E pāka'au 'ia nō i nā pāhoe āpau* (Nak. 106), 40 [fish] for each paddler.

pā.hoe.hoe. **1.** nvt. Smooth, unbroken type of lava, contrasting with *'a'ā;* to turn into *pāhoehoe* lava (see ex., *namu 2*). **2.** n. Satin. *Pāhoehoe lau,* brocaded satin. **3.** Redup. of *pāhoe. Ha'a ke akua i ka la'i o Mahiki, pāhoehoe i luna o ka Pu'u-lena* (chant), the goddess does a bent-knee dance in the calm of Mahiki, paddling above the Pu'u-lena breeze.

pā.hoe.hoe.pele. Hooks used in catching sea turtles. (And.)

pā hohonu. n. Soup plate, deep dish (preceded by *ke*).

pā.hola. vt. **1.** To spread about, extend, diffuse; spread too thin, dissipated. Cf. *hohola. E pāhola mai i kou aloha maluna o mākou* (prayer), spread forth your love to us. **ho'o.pā.hola.** To cause to spread, have spread. **2.** To stupefy fish by drugging with *'auhuhu,* the poison spreading *(pāhola)* through the water.

pā.hola.hola. Redup. of *pāhola 1, 2.*

pahole. Same as *pohole.*

pahole.hole. Redup. of *pahole.*

pā.hō.lei. n. Legendary name for kava. (For. 5:607.)

pā.holo. vi. To appear in great numbers, as octopuses. *Rare.*

pā holo.holona. n. An enclosure for animals, as a dog pound.

pā.hono. n. Wash pan or basin (preceded by *ke*).

pā.hono. vt. To mend, sew up a tear, patch, darn, repair. **ho'o.pā.hono.** To have mended, etc.

pā.hono.hono. Redup. of *pāhono.* **ho'o.pā.hono.hono.** Redup. of *ho'opāhono.*

pā ho'o.kani. n. Phonograph record.

paho'o.lā. n. Torn tapa. (And.)

pā ho'o.lapa.lapa. n. Saucepan (preceded by *ke*). *Lit.,* boiling pan.

pā ho'o.puni. n. Central corral.

pā.hou.hou. Same as *pā'ou'ou,* young of the fish *hou.*

pahu. **1.** n. Box, drum, cask, chest, barrel, trunk, tank, case, ship binnacle, collection box, keg, ark, coffin, dresser, bureau, cabinet; bald heads were sometimes ridiculed as drums. Cf. *hulipahu, pahu pāpale. Hula pahu* (UL 103), dance to drum beat, perhaps formerly called *'ai ha'a.* (PPN *pasu,* PEP *pahu.*) **2.** n. Stake, staff, stick, post, pole. Cf. *pahu hope, pahu hopu, pahukū.* **3.** vt. To push, shove; to thrust or hurl, as a spear or javelin; to pierce with a sharp instrument, as in letting blood; to fall overboard (For. 5:123). *Fig.,* to bruise the feeling of others. *Wai-pahu* (place name), pushing water, said to be named for water that forced its way out of the earth at Wai-pahu, O'ahu, said to have been formerly called Wai-pahū (see *pahū*). **ho'o.pahu.** To cause to push, etc. (PPN *pasu.*) **4.** vt. To cut off short; odd-numbered. Cf. *'āpahu, 'oi 3, pahupū. I pahu kō 'oukou 'ao'ao* (For. 6:53), if your side is odd-numbered. **5.** n. Trunkfishes, boxfishes, cowfishes *(Ostracion).* Malo says that *pahu* were taboo to women (Malo 29). Also *moa.* **6.** n. Name of a region below the *'ilima* and above the *kula.* **7.** n. Gill net used in shallow water. (Malo 213, Emerson note.)

pahū. nvi. To explode, burst; explosive, blast, thud; outburst. Cf. *pōkā pahū.* See ex., *walawala.* **ho'o.pahū.** To explode, set off, as dynamite or firecrackers; to blast, blow up. *Mokulele ho'opahū nui,* large bomber. (PPN *pasuu.*)

pahua. 1. Pas/imp. of *pahu 3.* See *hula Pahua,* a spear dance. (UL 183.) **2.** vs. Downtrodden, as grass where cattle have stamped. *Rare.*

pahu'a. nvs. Unsuccessful, ineffective, ruined, spoiled; lack of success. *Ka pahu'a o ka 'awa i ke keiki,* the lack of effect of the kava on the child. *Ua pahu'a ia mea he "maka 'ewa'ewa,"* this thing "crooked eyes" [said insultingly of O'ahu] doesn't amount to anything. **ho'o.pahu'a.** To spoil, wreck.

pā.hu'a. Similar to *kīpuka 1,* said especially of clear areas in pastures where it is easy to rope cattle.

-pāhua. ho'o.pā.hu'a. To move sideways; to sail to windward. *Rare.*

pahu ani.ani. n. Glass box, especially a glass-bottomed box for fishing; glass case, as in a museum.

pahu hae. n. Flagpole.

pahu hao. n. Safe, strong box. *Lit.,* iron box.

pahu hau. n. Icebox, refrigerator.

pahu hei.au. n. Temple drum.

pahu hō.'ike. n. Ark of the testimony. *Lit.,* testifying box. *E kau ana i mua o ka pahu hō'ike, i mua ho'i o ka noho aloha e kau ana maluna o ka pahu kānāwai* (Puk. 30.6), put it before the ark of the testimony before the mercy seat that is over the testimony.

pahu hope. n. Final goal or stake.

pahu hopu. n. Final goal. *Lit.,* catching goal.

pahuhu. n. Young of the fish *uhu.*

pā.hū.hū. vi. To gush, ooze forth, as blood. **ho'o.pā.-hū.hū.** To cause to gush forth.

pahu hula. n. Hula drum.

pahu i'a. n. Small aquarium box for fish.

pā.hu'i.hu'i. Var. of *pāhi'uhi'u,* a game.

pahu.ka'a. n. Juice extracted from a green gourd by pounding, said to be used in an enema.

pahu.kaina. n. Ashes. Also *lehu, noho hale.*

pahu.kala. n. 1. Sham battle with sharp weapons. (Malo 66.) **2.** Herald who announces *(kala)* war.

pahu kā.lā. n. Safe-deposit box.

pahu kala.loa. n. Prayer drum (perhaps from *pahu kala loa,* drum proclaiming to a distance).

pahu kā.nā.wai. n. Ark of the testimony. *Lit.,* legal box. Cf. *pahu hō'ike.*

pahu kani. n. Drum; tabret (Kin. 31.27), eardrum (Kel. 115; translation from Eng.). *Fig.,* bald head. *Lit.,* sounding drum.

pahu kapu. n. A stake beyond which it was taboo to pass; sanctuary. *Lit.,* taboo stake.

pahu.kū. 1. n. Goal or stake at the starting place of a race. **2.** n. Reserve of an army, especially a rear guard. **3.** vt. To repel, as in war.

pā.huku. Same as *pōhuku.*

pahu kui. nv. Hypodermic injection; to be injected. *Lit.,* needle piercing.

pahu kupa.pa'u. n. Coffin. *Lit.,* corpse box.

pā hula. n. Hula troupe, hula studio, place reserved for hula dancing.

pahu lole. n. Clothes chest or trunk.

pahulu. 1. nvs. Nightmare (named for a chief of evil spirits on Lā-na'i who was killed by Ka-ulu-lā'au; his spirit enchanted certain fish, especially goatfish *(weke);* if a *weke* head is eaten near bedtime, nightmares are said to result; the closer to Lā-na'i the *weke* is caught, the worse the nightmare); ghost; haunted; unlucky. *He hale pahulu,* a haunted house. *Pō nā maka i ka noe, i ka pahulu i ke ala loa,* eyes blinded by the mist, by the haunts of the long road. **ho'o.pahulu.** to have a nightmare; nightmare; to haunt; to bring bad luck; unlucky. **2.** nvs. Exhausted, worn-out, of over-farmed soil; such soil. **ho'o.pahulu.** To exhaust the soil; to let the land rest and lie fallow. **3.** n. Volunteer sweet potatoes, sweet potatoes of the second growth.

pahulu.hope. vs. Demented, to behave as if crazy.

pahu.lulu. vs. Somewhat rainy, showery. *Rare.*

pahu mana.mana. n. Intersection, crossroads. *Lit.,* branching stake.

pahu meli. n. Beehive.

pahuna. n. A pushing, thrust, hurling, piercing, etc., as of an *ihe* spear. Cf. *pahu 3. Ho'okahi nō ia pahuna, 'o ka hā'ule nō ia,* but a single thrust and he fell.

pahu noho. n. Box, as at a theater.

pahu 'ō.lelo. n. Phonograph. *Lit.,* speaking box.

pahu pā. n. Meat safe, cupboard. *Lit.,* dish box.

pahu.pahu. 1. Redup. of *pahu 3. Ua pahupahu 'oia i kāna kaikaina,* he bruised the feelings of his younger brother. (PPN *pasupasu.*) **2.** nv. Billiards, pool; to play billiards or pool. **3.** Redup. of *pahu 4;* blunt, dull.

pahū.pahū. 1. Redup. of *pahū;* firecrackers. **ho'o.-pahū.pahū.** Redup. of *ho'opahū;* to drum or stamp with force; to squeeze certain types of small fish so they burst. (PPN *pasuupasuu.*) **2.** Same as *kā'eke'eke.* **3.** n. Tiny and worthless taro offshoot from an offshoot of several generations. (Kep. 153.) See *kalo.*

pahu pa'i. n. Small sharkskin hula drum. *Lit.,* beating drum.

pahu.pa'i.ki'i. n. Camera, kodak. *Lit.,* box for printing pictures.

pahu paka. n. Tobacco box or container.

pahu pala.pala. n. Writing desk; formerly a container for the coloring liquid used in printing tapa. *Lit.,* document box.

pahu pā.nā.nā. n. Binnacle.

pahu pā.pale. n. Hatbox; wooden block upon which a hat is plaited; such hats are called *pāpale pahu.*

pahu pelika (berita). n. Ark of the covenant (Ios. 3.3). *Lit.,* covenant box.

pahu po'o li'i.li'i. n. Keg. *Lit.,* small-headed barrel.

pahu.pū. vs. Cut in half, cut in two, severed, cut short, chopped off. *Nui pahupū,* of uneven size; poorly proportioned, as overly large buttocks, shoulders; unsymmetrical. *E 'oki 'o mua me hope o ka wa'a ā pahupū* (FS 187), sever the bow and stern of the canoe, completely sever.

pahu puke. n. Bookcase.

pahu 'ume. n. Drawer, bureau, buffet.

pahu wai. n. Water barrel, tank.

pahu waiho lole. n. Clothes chest or trunk.

pahu wai.hona. n. Chest of drawers, cabinet, bureau.

pai. 1. vt. To urge, encourage, rouse, stir up, excite. **ho'o.pai.** To encourage, cause to rouse, etc. **2.** vt. To raise, lift up, increase. (PCP *pai.*) **3.** vt. To laud, praise, exalt. Cf. *pai ali'i.* **4.** vt. To pamper, spoil, as a favorite child; to make a pet of. *I kū nō ka ho'oki'eki'e i ka pai 'ia e ke kupuna wahine,* the willfulness is due to being pampered by the grandmother. **5.** n. A funnel-shaped wicker basket used for catching shrimps and small fish, so called because it was lifted *(pai)* from the water. Also *'apai, 'āpua.* **6.** n. A native fern *(Adenophorus hymenophylloides)* with clustered, narrow, pinnate fronds, 5 to 13 cm long, growing on trees at rather high altitudes. Also *huna palai, palai huna.* **7.** n. A kind of snail shellfish said to be poisonous to touch (no data). **8.** Same as *pānānai. Rare.* See *kīkala pai.* **9.** n. Pie, tart. *Eng.* (1 Sam. 17.18.)

pa'i. 1. nvt. To slap, spank, beat, hit, clap; to print, publish; to snap, as pictures; to break, as a taboo; a slapping, slap, stamping, printing (several old types of tapa begin with *pa'i: pa'ipa'inahā, pa'iua, pa'i'ula;* preceded by *ke).* Cf. *pa'i ā pa'i, pa'i ki'i, pa'i puna. Pa'i 'ana,* printing, edition, impression. *Pa'i ipu,* to beat a gourd drum. *Ke kolu o ke pa'i 'ana,* third edition. **ho'o.pa'i. (a)** To slap, hit, punish, chastise, fine, pay back, seek revenge; punishment, revenge, fine, penalty. *'Ōlelo ho'opa'i,* sentence (penalty). *Ka mea ho'opa'i koko* (Ios. 20.9), avenger of blood. **(b)** Design with 12 to 18 ruled parallel lines on a tapa beater. *Ho'opa'i hālu'a,* sets of parallel lines on a beater at right angles. (PPN *paki.*) **2.** nvs. To tie; a draw; equal; to make an agreement (said to be so called because champions slapped each other's open palms after they had agreed on the terms of a match or race, and with a draw it was as though they had no more than concluded the terms). Cf. *pa'i ā pa'i. Inā e pa'i ana e koho ana 'oia,* if it's a tie, he will vote. **3.** vt. To mix, as ingredients; to mingle. **4.** To put clothes to soak, as in soapy water. **5.** nvt. A bundle, package, especially of food; to tie up such a bundle; bunch, cluster, as of grapes (preceded by *ke).* Cf. *pa'i a'a, pa'i 'ai, pa'i palaoa, pa'i 'uala; pa'i waina. Kū ke pa'i,* what a load [of work to do]. **6.** Rare var. of *pa'ipa'i;* to strip, as bark. **7.** nvt. Lining, as of pandanus or sugar-cane leaves, inside thatching of *pili* grass; to line thus. **8.** vs. Decaying, of fruits or plants; blight. *Rare.* Cf. *kāpa'i,* poultice. **9.** Short for *pa'i malau.* **10.** n. A heap. **11.** vt. To evict, as from land. *'O ka pa'i 'ana o 'Ai-kanaka i nā mākua . . . ma kēia pa'i 'ana a 'Ai-kanaka i nā mākua* (FS 47), as for Man-eater's eviction of the parents . . . in this eviction by Man-eater of the parents [from their land] (note possessive prepositions *o* and *a* in similar environments).

paia. nvs. Wall, side of a house, clearing in a forest (often translated *bower*); walled in, as by vegetation. *Paia 'ala i ka hala,* forest bower fragrant with pandanus [also said of grass houses with *hīnano* bracts stuck in the walls so that all might enjoy the fragrance].

pai.'ā. n. Bracken, a fern *(Pteridium aquilinum* var. *decompositum).* Also *kīlau, kīlau puoe.* (Neal 15–16.)

pa'ia. vs. Temporarily deaf, as from ascending to a high altitude. *Ua pa'ia hinihini,* heard indistinctly.

pā 'ia. v. Fenced in; struck. Cf. *pā 1, 4.*

pa'i a'a. n. Root system, rootlets, small branches. *Pa'i a'a koko,* small arteries or veins.

pa'i.aha. n. A variety of taro.

pai.ā.ha'a. 1. vs. Short, dumpy, as a person or animal. **2.** vi. Dancing, surging, undulating, as the sea; tossing, as a canoe in a rough sea.

pa'i 'ai. n. Hard, pounded but undiluted taro; heavy, as poorly made cake. *Lima pa'i 'ai,* loose-flowing sleeve. *'Ōlelo pa'i 'ai,* English or pidgin Hawaiian.

pa'ia kuli. vs. Deafening.

pai.ā.lewa. vt. Tossed here and there, as by a rough sea; to carry back and forth, to and fro, up and down, as a boat or kite; to tote. (For. 5:548.) *Lit.,* lift unto space.

pai ali'i. v. To laud or praise a chief; to elevate one's own ego by recounting one's association with chiefs; name-dropping.

Pai-alo-pā-'owā. n. Wind inland of Hāna, Maui.

pa'i 'ana. n. Printing, edition.

pa'i ā pa'i. vs. Equal, as of two persons; to tie, have a draw. Cf. *pa'i 2. Ua pa'i ā pa'i lāua ma ka na'auao,* they are equals in wisdom. **ho'o.pa'i ā pa'i.** To make similar; to copy the clothing or manners of another, to ape, mimic, imitate.

pai 'ā.pala. n. Apple pie. *Eng.*

pa'i.ā.uma. v. To slap the chest, as in grief. *Fig.,* to show grief, wail in lamentation. Gram. 8.7.2. *Pa'iāuma wale aku nō i ke aloha i nā kāne,* just showing great grief from love for the husbands.

pai.'ea. n. An edible crab, found where the *'a'ama* is found, but with a harder shell and shorter legs fringed in front with short, stiff hair; perhaps one of the grapsids; one of the names of Ka-mehameha I. *Fig.,* a star athlete. (PPN *pa'ikea.*)

pa'iha. Same as *'iha'iha. Pa'iha 'oukou i ke ala, e 'āpu'e* (For. 6:294), you are strained on the path, struggle.

pai.ha'a. Var. of *paiāha'a 1, 2.*

pa'i haka.haka. n. Printing, as contrasted with handwriting *(kākau);* form, questionnaire; blank, as on a questionnaire. *Lit.,* space printing.

pa'i hale. v. To thatch or line a house. See *pa'i 7.*

pa'i hewa. nvt. Misprint, typographical error; to make such an error. *Lit.,* mistaken printing.

paihī. n. Trickling water, as down the face of a cliff. *Rare.*

pa'ihi. vs, vt. Clear, bright, cloudless; neat, tidy, well dressed in one's best; to honor; set, as a ship's sails (often preceded by *hao ā). Hō'ike ka nani o ka wahine, a i kō lā nui hao ā pa'ihi* (name song for Ka-pi'o-lani), the beauty of the woman shows, and on your important day dress in your best. *Kūlana hanohano i pa'ihi 'ia aku maluna ona,* an honor conferred upon him. (PCP *paki(f,s)i.*)

pā.'ihi. n. **1.** A small weed *(Nasturtium sarmentosum),* related to watercress; used medicinally and as a tapa dye. (Neal 372.) Cf. *'ihi kū kēpau.* (PPN *pakisi.*) **2.** Maui name for *'ōhi'a hā.*

pā.'ihi.'ihi. 1. Redup. of *pa'ihi.* See ex., *mikihilina, oki 2.* **2.** Same as *pā'ihi 1, 2.*

paiho. 1. vi. To project, as a bone through flesh. *Rare.* **2.** vi. To make hand signals. *Rare.* **3.** vs. Peeled, as skin. **ho'o.paiho.** To peel. *Rare.*

pai.hō. n. Flapping, of a malo. *Rare.*

pai hua. n. Custard pie, egg pie, fruit pie.

pa'i hua. n. **1.** Bundle of fruit; fruit cluster, as of grapes. **2.** Bulge, as in canoe sides. *Rare.*

pa'i hua piku (fiku). n. Cake of figs. (1 Sam. 25.18.)

pa'i hua waina. n. Cluster of grapes. (1 Sam. 25.18.)

pā'ī.'i'i. See *nenue.*

pai.'i'i.hā. n. A small, light-green, oblong fern *(Dryopteris dentata),* tapering at both ends and divided into many long, narrow divisions, widely distributed in woods of temperate and tropical countries. In Hawai'i it also volunteers in gardens. (Neal 20–1.)

pa'i.'ina. Redup. of *pa'ina.*

paika. nvt. Fight; to fight. *Eng.*

pai.kano. vt. To make a great pet of; to treat with great favor. *E paikano nui ana nō 'oia i ke ali'i,* he treated the chief with great favor.

pai.kau. vi. To march, drill, parade, pass to and fro; to practice firearms. *He kumu paikau no nā koa hele wāwae,* manual of arms for infantry soldiers. **ho'o.pai.kau.** Caus/sim.

pa'i kau. vs. Equal. *Rare.*

pai.kau.hale. vt. To go gadding about from house to house.

Pai-kau.hale. n. Name of a star. See *Au-haele.*

pai.kau.lei. Rare var. of *pakaulei.*

pai.kau.leia. Pas/imp. of *paikaulei.*

paiki. n. Bag, suitcase, satchel, pocketbook, purse. *Eng.*

pā.iki. 1. n. Hollow of the hand. *Rare.* **2.** vs. Cramped, pressed close, crowded. *Rare.*

pa'i ki'i. nv. To take pictures, photographs; photographer. *Lit.,* snap pictures. Cf. *pahu pa'i ki'i, pepa pa'i ki'i.*

pai.kikala. n. Bicycle (usually follows *ka'a,* vehicle). *Eng.*

pai.kini. n. Fashion, style. *Eng.*

pa'i kini.pōpō. nv. Baseball bat, tennis racquet; to hit a ball.

paiki pa'a.lima. n. Handbag.

pa'i koli. vt. To trim, cut short.

pa'i kukui. n. A kind of dark tapa cloth dyed with juice from *kukui* bark, said to be from Hālawa, Moloka'i (Ii 83). According to Andrews, a pale yellow tapa made on Moloka'i. Also *pa'ipa'i kukui.*

pai.kuli. Those in charge of a chief's property. (And.)

pai.kumu. vs. To have connections with important or influential persons. *Rare.*

paila. nvt. **1.** Pile, heap; to heap up. *Eng. Kū ka paila,* a big pile [work to do]. **2.** Also **baila.** To boil, percolate. *E paila aku i ka 'i'o pipi,* boil the beef.

pai.laka, pailata. nvt. Pilot; to pilot. *Eng. Iesū, e pailaka ia'u* (hymn), Jesus, pilot me.

pai.lani. Similar to *mailani,* to praise, but often pejorative; to spoil. **ho'o.pai.lani.** Caus/sim.

pa'i.lau.'ula. n. Dry pandanus leaves still clinging to the tree. *Lit.,* cut red leaves. *Rare.*

paila wahie. n. Woodpile, pile of firewood.

pā.'ili. n. Swelling, as of newly made tattooing. *Rare.*

pā 'ili. v. To touch the skin. *Ka i'a pā 'ili kanaka o Waimea,* the fish that touches the skin of the people of Wai-mea [said of great schools of *hinana,* fish].

pā ilina. n. Cemetery, graveyard. See ex., *wailua 1.*

pai.loka. Same as *pailaka,* pilot.

pai.lolo. n. **1.** A variety of sugar cane. Also *hou, pakaweli.* **2.** *(Cap.)* Name of the channel between Moloka'i and Maui.

pai.lua. nvs. Nausea; nauseating, abominable. **ho'o.-pai.lua.** To cause nausea, vomiting; nauseating, sickening, revolting, disgusting, loathsome. *Nā mea lele 'ē a'e apau e kolo ana, me nā wāwae 'ehā, he mea ia e ho'opailua 'ia e 'oukou* (Oihk. 11.23), all other flying things that creep, which have four feet, shall be an abomination unto you.

pa'i.malau. n. **1.** Portuguese man-of-war *(Physalia).* **2.** A fleet of canoes fishing for *aku* with the *malau,* bait carrier.

paina. 1. *-Na* form of *pai 2;* to lift; lifting, swelling or breaking, as waves. **2.** n. Fine cloth like serge. **3.** n. Pine trees and all kinds of conifers; ironwood; cedar (RSV), ash (KJV) (Isaia 44.14). *Eng.* **4.** n. Pint. *Eng.*

pa'ina. 1. nvi. To crackle, snap, click, tick, pop, resound; crackling, etc; brittle, easily torn. Cf. *kānepa'ina, 'u'ina. Pā pa'ina,* to click, ticktack. (PEP *pakinga.*) **2.** n. Hawai'i Island name for *pohā 2,* cape gooseberry.

pā.'ina. nvt. Meal, dinner, small party with dinner; to eat a *pā'ina.*

pā.'ina ahi.ahi. n. Evening meal, dinner, supper.

paina kaha.kai. n. French tamarisk *(Tamarix gallica),* shrub or small trees. *Ni'ihau.* Cf. Neal 587.

Pa'ina-kuli. n. A stroke in *lua* fighting. *Lit.,* deafening crackle.

pā.ina male. n. Wedding feast or reception.

pā.'ina poi. nv. Poi lunch or supper.

paina pupupu. Same as *paina kahakai. Ni'ihau.*

pai.niki. vt. To dress in tight-fitting garments; buttoned up tightly. Cf. *niki,* to tie.

pai niu. n. Coconut pie.

pa'i.niu. n. **1.** Some native Hawaiian lilies *(Astelia* spp.) with long, narrow, silvery or tan leaves forming rosette-shaped plants growing either on the ground or perching on trees. Small yellow or greenish flowers develop in a panicle on a stalk shorter than the leaves. Formerly, Hawaiians braided hat leis out of the shiny outer layer of the leaves and wore them as a sign that they had visited Kī-lau-ea Volcano, where one species is common. (Neal 192.) Also used, rarely, for house thatch (For. 5:655).

pa'i-niu. n. A very thin type of tapa.

pai.nu'u. vt. **1.** To carry on the hip or back, as a heavy child; to lug, as a heavy object that must be hitched up now and then. *Ahonui kēia kaikamahine i ka painu'u i ke kaikaina,* this girl is so patient in lugging about her little sister. **2.** To boast. See ex., *'ēkā.*

paio. nvt. To quarrel, argue, fight; combat, argument, conflict, strife, battle, struggle; to contend, as conflicting winds. *Hoa paio,* opponent, enemy. *'Ahahui paio,* debating club. *Ha'a nā makani, pā e paio nei, paio i ke alo o makani pā lua* (For. 6:299), moving low are the winds, striking as they contend here, blustering before the strong-blowing winds. **ho'o.paio.** Caus/sim. (For. 6:487.)

pā 'i'o. nvt. Fishhook baited with flesh; to remove flesh from bones, as of fish. Cf. *pā 3.*

pai.oa. vs. Tall, slim. Cf. *leioa.*

paio.ea, paio.wea. n. A variety of sweet potato.

pai 'ō.hua. n. Basket trap for fishing *'ōhua.* Cf. *pai 5.*

paio kā.lai.mana'o. n. Debate, argument.

pā 'iole. n. Food left for rats on a tray *(pā).*

pai.onia. nvs. Pioneer. *Eng.*

pai 'o'opu. n. Basket trap for fishing *'o'opu.* Cf. *pai 5.*

pai.pai. Redup. of *pai 1, 2;* to lobby; to rock. See *noho paipai.* **ho'o.pai.pai.** Redup. of *ho'opai;* to promote, cheer, lobby; promotion, agitator.

pa'i.pa'i. 1. Redup. of *pa'i 1;* to applaud, clap; applause; to sprinkle coloring matter (as charcoal or red cloth) on tapa and beat it in. **ho'o.pa'i.pa'i.** Redup. of *ho'opa'i. Ho'opa'ipa'i 'aumakua,* sickness or trouble due to the displeasure of the *'aumakua,* family god. (PPN *pakipaki.*) **2.** Redup. of *pa'i 3;* mixed, diluted. *Lama pa'ipa'i 'ia,* mixed alcoholic drink, cocktail. *Waiū pa'ipa'i,* diluted milk. **3.** vt. To trim, prune, cut, clip, as a plant or the hair; to strip off, as leaves. See ex., *'ōla'ola'o. Lauoho pa'ipa'i,* trimmed hair.

pai.pai.e'e. Same as *pepeie'e.*

pa'i.pa'i 'iole. See *papa'iole.*

pa'i.pa'i kukui. Same as *pa'i kukui.*

pa'i.pa'i lima. nv. To clap, applaud; applause, clapping.

pai.pai mana'o. n. Memorial, revived memory (Puk. 30.16).

pa'i.pā.'ina. Redup. of *pā'ina.*

pa'i.pa'i.nahā. n. Tapa cloak worn over the shoulder like a cape.

Pai.pala, Baibala. n. Bible; Biblical. *Eng. Wehe i ka Paipala* (Nānā 204), open the Bible [at random, select a passage and interpret this as help or solution to a problem].

pai pala.'ai. n. Pumpkin pie.

pa'i palaoa. n. Cakes of fine flour. (Nah. 6.15.)

pa'i pala.pala. nv. Printing press; to print.

pai pelena (berena). n. Loaves. (1 Sam. 25.18.)

paipu. n. Pipe, faucet. *Eng. Paipu lawe 'ino,* sewage system. *Ke kī o ka paipu,* faucet key.

pai pū. n. Pumpkin pie.

pā ipu. 1. n. Calabash, wooden dish in general, cooking utensil, bowl (Ier. 52.18) (preceded by *ke*). Cf. *waihona pā ipu. Lawea mai i kau pā ipu a kākou,* bring our dishes, cooking utensils. **2.** nv. To beat a gourd drum; the drum itself and accompanying chant and sitting dance by the chanter; also *hula kuolo.*

pa'i puna. v. To whitewash, plaster. *Lit.,* to slap coral.

pa'i.puna.hele. nv. To fete a favorite *(punahele),* especially by composing songs in his honor, and staging dances and feasts for him; an expression of love for a favorite. *He pa'ipunahele kēlā nā ke kupuna i ke keiki,* that is the grandparent's expression of affection for the child.

pa'i.ua. n. Fine, white tapa.

pa'i 'uala. n. Cooked and compressed sweet potatoes allowed to ferment slightly and used as a substitute for poi when poi was scarce. Also *poi 'uala* by analogy with poi.

pa'i.'ula. 1. n. Tapa made by beating red rags or tapa pieces to form a mixture of white and red (as outer or *kilohana* sheet for bedcovers). Also *welu 'ula.* Cf. *moelola.* **2.** Calabash receptacle for sarongs. (AP.)

pa'i uma.uma. n. Chest-slapping hula. (PCP *paki umauma;* cf. Marquesan *pakiuma.*)

pā.iwa. vt. Nine times, nine at a time, to divide by nine or distribute to nine.

pa'i waina. n. Cluster of grapes.

pa'i wale. nv. A draw or tie; to have a draw or tie. Cf. *pa'i 2.*

paka. 1. vt. To remove the dregs, such as fibers, from herbs used for medicine; to strain. **2.** vt. To criticize constructively, as chanting; to look for flaws in order to perfect; to teach, correct. **3.** n. Raindrops, patter of rain, especially of big drops. *'O ka ua paka kahi, paka lua, pakapaka ua, paka ua, kūlokuloku* (chant for

Kua-kini), the rain falling in single drops, in double drops, the many drops, raindrops, rain in streams. *Hana ka uluna i ka paka o ka ua,* work the pillow during the dropping of rain [i.e., might as well rest when it's raining]. (PCP *pata.*) **4.** Same as *kākala,* cartilage. **5.** n. Ka'ū name for *'ōpakapaka,* a fish. **6.** n. Tobacco *(Nicotiana tabacum),* a hairy annual herb from tropical America, which may grow nearly 2 m high, introduced to Hawai'i in about 1812. It was tried out unsuccessfully from 1908 to 1929 as a possible industry. Plants are now growing both wild and cultivated. (Neal 752.) Wild tobacco *(Nicotiana glauca).* (Neal 751.) **7.** n. Butter (usually follows *waiū). Eng.* **8.** Also **bata.** n. Curds. (Kin. 18.8, KJV.) *Eng.* **9.** n. Bugger. *Eng.*

pāka. 1. n. Park. *Eng.* **2.** vt. To park, as a car. *Eng.*

pā.kā. 1. Var. of *pāka'a 1. 'I'o pākā,* lean meat. **2.** vt. To cut in long slices, to hack, as pig or fish for salting; to cut back, as a plant. **3.** vt. To scramble, as eggs. *Hua pākā,* scrambled eggs, omelet. **4.** vi. To surf, as with canoe, board, or body; to skim, as a surfing canoe; to skip stones. **5.** n. Sinker on a fish line for deep-sea fishing. (For. 4:293.) **6.** vt. To fish with hook and line but no pole, as *ulua.* Also *kākā.* **7.** Var. of *pākākā 1.* **8.** vs. Wrinkled. *Rare.* Cf. *pākāeaea, pakalua.* **9.** Same as *hoka,* to strain. *Rare.*

pā.ka'a. 1. vs. Lean, as meat. **2.** Var. of *'āka'a.* **3.** vt. To converse, tell interesting tales or anecdotes. *Rare.*

pā.ka'au. vt. Forty at a time; to divide by forty or distribute to forty. See ex., *pāhoe.*

pā.ka'a.wili. Same as *pāka'uwili, ka'awili;* spiral. *Ke ahi e pāka'awili ana iāia iho* (Ezek. 1.4), the fire enfolding itself.

pā.kā.ea.ea. vs. Wrinkled. Cf. *pākā 3. 'Ai ka lani iā Hawai'i, kau ka pākāeaea i luna* (For. 6:386), the heavenly chief rules Hawai'i, [he] is covered with wrinkles.

pakaha. n. A native herb *(Lepechinia [Sphacele] hastata)* found only at altitudes of 600 to 1800 m on East Maui. It is a mint, 1 to 1.5 m high, more or less downy, with large leaves and clustered, narrow red-violet flowers. (Neal 732.)

pā.kaha. 1. vt. To cheat, fleece, plunder, rob, raid; robbery, raid, etc. See song, *'ānulu. Pākaha mai ka lewa,* air raid. **ho'o.pā.kaha.** To cause to cheat. **2.** n. A kind of shell, perhaps a conch. See *maile pākaha.*

pā.kaha.kaha. n. A native fern *(Pleopeltis thunbergiana),* with related forms in Asia and Africa, common on forest trees. A creeping, underground stem bears erect, short-stemmed, narrow fronds 15 to 30 cm long. (Neal 25.) Also *'ēkaha 'ākōlea, pua'akuhinia.*

paka hanu.hanu. n. Snuff. *Lit.,* inhaling tobacco.

pā kā.hea. nv. Welcoming call; to call in welcome. *Lohe mai i ka pā kāhea a ke Ko'olau-wahine,* hear the call of Ko'olau-wahine (a wind).

pā.kahi. vt. Singly, once, one at a time, one by one, respectively, separately, apiece, individually; to distribute one at a time or one apiece. *Miki pākahi,* to dip in succession for poi; to eat poi successively.

paka honi.honi. n. Snuff. *Lit.,* smelling tobacco.

pakai. 1. n. Spleen amaranth *(Amaranthus dubius),* a coarse, erect, spineless, weedy, tropical herb; it looks much like spinach, and the young plants are similarly used. **2.** Slender amaranth *(Amaranthus viridis),* resembling the spleen amaranth and used for greens. It differs in its habit of spreading close to the ground. (Neal 334.) Called *'āheahea* in some localities and *pakapakai* on Ni'ihau.

pakai.ea. n. **1.** Same as *līpahapaha,* sea lettuce. *Hawai'i.* **2.** Same as *halāli'i,* a variety of sugar cane; named for the seaweed. **3.** A variety of taro. **4.** *(Cap.)* Name of a wind at Wai-'anae, O'ahu. **5.** Name of a type of wave at Kai-mū, Hawai'i. (FS 255.)

pakai.ele. n. Young of the *hou,* a fish.

pā.kai.kai. 1. vt. To pound, as with a pestle, especially small fish for bait. **2.** Same as *pakai 1, 2.* **3.** Same as *pakaiea 1–5.*

pā.kai.kā.wale. n. A fish, perhaps an *'ōpakapaka.*

pakai kukū. n. Spiny amaranth *(Amaranthus spinosus),*

a widespread, weedy herb, 30 to 70 or 80 cm high, with many branches bearing narrow or ovate leaves, each leaf with a pair of spines at the base, and male flowers in long spikes. (Neal 333–4.)

pā.kā.kā. 1. nvs. Low and broad, especially of a wooden bowl or door; a low, wide wooden bowl, according to Buck the largest ever made. *Puka pākākā* (FS 119), low side door in a house, not the main door, through which one must stoop to enter. *Nīnau pākākā,* leading question. **ho'o.pā.kā.kā.** To shape into a low, wide door or bowl. **2.** n. A variety of gourd: squatty, small, used for meat and fish *(ipu kai).* (HP 208.) Also *no'uno'u.* **3.** Redup. of *pākā 2, 3, 4;* slab, as of salted pork. **4.** vt. To inflate, blow up, as a balloon with air.

pā.kaka'a. vi. To roll one at a time. Cf. *kaka'a.* **ho'o.pā.kaka'a.** Caus/sim.; to mill around.

pā.kakahi. vt. To distribute one at a time to several; scattered, here and there, as light rain. Cf. *kakahi, pākahi,* Gram. 10.3. *E pākakahi aku i ka i'a i kamali'i,* giving the children fish one each, or one at a time.

paka.kē. nvi. Gibberish, garbled speech, jibber jabber; to jabber. **ho'o.paka.kē.** To talk thus.

paka.keha. n. Mat spread across a door for privacy. *Rare.*

paka.ke'u. vt. To scold excessively.

paka.kī. 1. vt. To talk irrationally, loudly, or contentiously. **2.** To skim over the water, as a flying fish.

paka.kū. vi. To fall; falling in heavy splotches, as rain. (Kep. 37.)

pā.kala. 1. n. Young of the *kala,* a fish. **2.** vs. Rough, as skin of *kala,* a fish. **3.** Also **bakala.** n. Buckle. *Eng.*

pākala lā.hui. n. National park.

pā.kala.kala. 1. n. Gray-backed tern *(Sterna lunata),* also called the bridled, spectacled, or gray wide-awake tern. The forehead is white, as is a broad stripe over the eye; the nape, the top of the head and a stripe through the eye are black; the upper parts are dark ashy, with white beneath. **2.** Same as *pākala 1, 2.* **3.** n. A coarse, nonedible seaweed *(Galaxaura* spp.). Cf. *kauno'a, 'ōkala, pākolekole, piliko'a.*

paka.laki. nvs. Bad luck, unlucky. *Eng.* **ho'o.paka.laki.** To cause bad luck.

paka.lana. n. The Chinese violet *(Telosma cordata),* which has yellowish-green flowers. (Neal 700–1.) Cf. *miulana.*

pā.kale. n. Second growth stage of the *'ōpakapaka,* a fish.

pā.kali. 1. vt. To dole out little by little; to decoy fish by doling out bait little by little; a decoy. Cf. *kali,* to wait. **2.** Also **batari.** n. Battery. *Eng.*

paka.lia. Pass/imp. of *paka 1, 2.*

pakali.ao. n. Codfish. *Portuguese.*

pā.kali.kali. Redup. of *pākali 1. Uku pākalikali,* to pay on the installment plan, little at a time. *Hā'awi pākalikali,* to pay in irregular installments, to give piecemeal.

paka.liona, bataliona. n. Battalion. *Eng.*

paka lō.lō. n. Marijuana, "pot," "grass" *(Cannabis sativa).* Also *pakalōlō,* numbing tobacco.

paka.lua. vs. Wrinkled, coarse, as skin or bark; encrusted, as with grime or rust.

paka.nā. n. Partner. *Eng.*

pā.kana. n. Waist, shirtwaist, blouse; pattern. *Eng.*

pā.kana-. Same as *pāpākana-.*

pā.kanaka. vs. Tame, accustomed to people, unafraid of people; to know a man carnally; concerning humanity; commoner. *Ka'ina mai ke akua pākanaka, he akua kanaka, ua wale wale, he akua kanaka, 'o 'oe ia, ē ka lani* (chant for Ka-lā-kaua), coming along is the god who knows mankind, a human god who pleases himself, a human god, such are you, O heavenly one.

pā.kana.loa. 1. Same as *pakaiele.* **2.** n. A kind of banana.

paka nau. n. Chewing tobacco.

paka.neo. vs. Destitute, poverty-stricken. **ho'o.paka.neo.** To bring destitution or poverty. *He mea ho'opakaneo ka piliwaiwai,* gambling causes poverty.

paka.nika. n. Parsnip *(Pastinaca sativa).* (Neal 659.) *Eng.*

pā kanu. n. Garden, cultivated field. *Lit.,* planting enclosure.

pā.kaʻo. Similar to *pōkaʻo. Rare.*

paka.paka. 1. Redup. of *paka 3.* **2.** vs. Many, numerous. *Pakapaka ka iʻa a Paulo,* Paul has a great lot of fish. **3.** Same as *ʻōpakapaka 2, 3;* wrinkled; scaly. Cf. *pakalua.*

paka.pakai. 1. n. Young *pakai* seedlings. **2.** See *pakai 2.* **3.** Same as *ʻāheahea 2. Niʻihau.*

pā kā.pili moku. n. Dock.

paka puhi. n. Smoking tobacco.

pā.kau. nvt. To place; table, stand. See *pākaukau. Fig.,* beloved. *Hoa pākau nohoʻi i ke aloha,* companion upon whom [my] love rests.

paka ua. n. Raindrops. See ex., *ʻōmamaka.*

pā kaua. n. Fortress, stronghold; palace (Neh. 1.1). *Lit.,* war enclosure.

pakau.ʻaʻaka. vs. Cranky, cantankerous. Cf. *ʻaʻaka,* cranky. *Rare.* **hoʻo.pakau.ʻaʻaka.** Same as *pakau-ʻaʻaka;* provocative of crankiness.

pakaua.helo. Rare var. of *pakauhelo.*

pā.kau.ā.keʻe. Same as *kīkeʻekeʻe;* crooked, bent, curled; dishonest. *Rare.*

pakau.ele. n. General name for small fish that are easily caught by hand, as *manini, lauhau, pāoʻo.*

pakaue.loa. Var. name for young stage of *hou,* a fish.

pakau.helo. vi. To live as a vagabond, wander. *Rare.*

pā.kau.kani. vt. By thousands, thousandfold; to distribute to thousands or divide by thousands.

pā.kau.kau. 1. n. Table, counter, stand, booth, desk; formerly a long mat on which food was placed *(kaukau)* (occasionally preceded by *ke).* **2.** vt. To sell, as over the counter (said also of wanton women).

pā.kau.kau ʻaina. n. Dining table.

pā.kaukau ʻopi.ʻopi. n. Folding table.

pā.kau.kau uai i ka loa. n. Table that can be lengthened by adding new leaves. *Lit.,* table with movable length.

pā.kaula. n. Rigging. *Rare.*

pakau.lei. vi. To gad about as a vagabond, to live without care or responsibility, carefree; to live wantonly with one mate after another. **2.** Same as *kaulei,* too high or short.

pā.kā.una. vt. Four at a time. (Nak. 106.)

pā kau ulua. n. Hook for *ulua,* fish. *Rare.*

pā.kaʻu.wili. Same as *pākaʻawili.*

paka.weli. n. **1.** A variety of sugar cane, with different names on different islands. A deep purple-red and green striped cane resembling *ʻakilolo* but the leaves somewhat variegated; also producing mutants of solid yellow and red, like *nānahu, pilimai.* Also *hou, pailolo.* **2.** A fish (no data).

pake, pate. n. Putty. *Eng.*

pakē. 1. vs. Brittle; weak, of health *(rare).* **hoʻo.pakē.** To cause to be brittle, weak. **2.** n. A variety of sugar cane. **3.** n. Plain undyed tapa. *Rare.*

Pā.kē. nvs. China, Chinese (noted in documents in the State Archives dated 1854, but possibly of earlier introduction) Also *Kina.* See *maʻi Pākē, maiʻa Pākē. ʻĀina Pākē,* China. **hoʻo.pākē.** To imitate or act like a Chinese. (Chinese *pak ye,* father's older brother.)

pā.kea. 1. vs. Pale, gray, as the face of a sick person. Cf. *kea 1. Rare.* **2.** n. White inner sheets of sleeping tapa. **3.** n. Kind of mat made of *makaloa* rush, without design. Cf. *hoehoe-pākea. Rare.* **4.** n. Type of stone (no data). *Rare.* **5.** n. A variety of taro.

pake.ʻai. Short for *pākela ʻai,* to eat to excess.

pā.keke. n. **1.** A variety of sweet potato. *Eng.* **2.** Also **bakete.** Bucket, pail. *Eng.* **3.** Pocket. *Eng.* See *ʻinipākeke. Kauoha Hou Pākeke,* pocket-sized New Testament. **4.** Also **pakete.** Packet (a ship). *Eng.*

pakeko. n. Small slimy discharges, as of diarrhea.

pā.kela. nvs. Excess; excessive, surpassing, intemperate; to exceed, surpass, excel; exceedingly; great person who excels. Cf. *kela,* to exceed. *Pākela inu,* drink to excess, heavy drinker. *Pākela nani* (2 Kor. 3.10), glory that excelleth. **hoʻo.pā.kela.** To cause to exceed. *Na ia mea i hoʻopākela aku i kona ʻike,* it was this thing that made his knowledge great.

pā.kela ʻai. nv. To eat to excess; gluttonous; gluttony, glutton. *He kanaka pākela ʻai, pākela inu waina* (Mat. 11.19), a man gluttonous, and a winebibber.

pakele. vt. To escape, be exempt. *I pakele mai au i ka nui manu* (song), I escaped from the many birds. *Pakele mai ka hopu ʻia,* freedom from arrest. *Na wai, na wai nō ʻoe aʻe pakele aku* (song)? Who, who can escape you? *Ka poʻe pakele i ka ʻauhau,* people exempt from taxes. **hoʻo.pakele.** To rescue, save or deliver from danger, free; to protect; to help escape. *Hana kinai ahi hoʻopakele,* fire-protection work.

pakele-a-waʻa. n. An edible seaweed. Also *huluhulu waena.*

pakelo. 1. vi. To slip out, as an animal from a trap or a fish from the hand; slippery, slick, slipping, sliding; to thrust, as a spear. See ex., *uhu 1. ʻŌlelo pakelo,* to talk in a wily, slippery fashion. **hoʻo.pakelo.** Caus/sim. (PCP *pa(a)telo.*) **2.** n. A purgative in which a slimy substance made of *hau* bark is drunk. **3.** n. A seaweed.

pakelo.kelo. Redup. of *pakelo 1.*

pake.lona, paterona. n. Patron, patron saint. *Eng.*

pakemo. Same as *pakelo.*

pake.neka. n. Per cent, percentage. *Eng.*

pakeʻo. vi. To project, stick out, as the tongue tip (a gesture of contempt); slipped, escaped by slipping. **hoʻo.pakeʻo.** To thrust out, slip out, etc.

pā.keo.keo. People who might eat with the chief. (And.)

pā.kepa. n. Extravagant mourning behavior, as knocking out the teeth, cutting the hair, destroying property.

pakē.pakē. 1. Redup. of *pakē 1;* friable. **2.** n. A seaweed. Also *pakūpakū.*

pā.keu. vt. Excessive, over and above; to surpass. *Ua pākeu aku kō ʻAu-kele lele i kō nā kaikoʻeke* (For. 4:79), ʻAu-kele's flying surpassed that of the brothers-in-law. **hoʻo.pā.keu.** To increase, exceed. *Ua hoʻopākeu ʻia aku nā keneka o ka waiwai kūʻai,* more cents were added to the sales value.

pā.keu.pali. vs. Excessively great, greatly exceeding. *Ka pākeupali aku o ke kuko,* the excessiveness of the lust.

pakī. vs. To splash, spatter, squirt, spurt; splashing, spattering, squirting. *Ka ʻauwai pakī,* the ditch [that is but a] splatter. *Nānā nō a ka ʻulu i pakī kēpau,* look for the breadfruit spattered with gum [mature; *fig.,* a man of substance]. **hoʻo.pakī.** To splash, spatter, etc. (PCP *patii.*)

pāki. n. **1.** Barge. *Eng.* **2.** Also **padi.** Paddy. *Eng.*

pā.kī. 1. vt. To smash, crush, pound, dash to pieces, flatten, throw; worn-out, driven to death, as an abused horse. Cf. *pākī ʻai, pākī lio.* **hoʻo.pā.kī.** To smash, etc. **2.** vs. Numerous, overplentiful, surfeit, so many of a thing that it is sold cheaply; well-equipped, abundant, well-supplied, well cared for. *Pākī ka hahalalū i ka mākeke,* the *hahalalū* [fish] were so numerous that they were sold cheaply in the market. **hoʻo.pā.kī.** To act as though one has plenty, to show off, as by spending in a flashy way.

pā kī.ʻaha. v. To hold a glass, as to make a toast. *Nā ʻano wai pā kīʻaha like ʻole,* all kinds of alcoholic drinks.

pā.kī.ai. vs. Over-sexed, sensual. *Lit.,* excessive copulation.

pā.kī.ʻai. 1. vs. Scorched, burned, parched, as land by the sun in hot months; sunburned. (Kep. 91.) *Lit.,* excessively eaten. **2.** vi. To break up cooked taro with a pounder in first stage of poi making.

pā kiaʻi. n. Watchman's stand, as in an enclosure or on a wall.

pā.kiʻa.kiʻa. vs. Wanton.

pā.kiʻi. 1. vs. Flat, fallen flat, spread out flat, flattened. *Ihu pākiʻi,* flat-nosed. *Moe pākiʻi,* to lie sprawled. **hoʻo.pā.kiʻi.** To flatten out. **2.** n. Various flatfishes *(Bothus mancus).* The name may be qualified by the terms *ha'awale* and *moana*. (PCP *paatiki*.) **3.** vs. Broiled, as puppies that were split and laid flat.

pā.ki'i.ki'i. 1. Redup. of *pāki'i 1.* **ho'o.pā.ki'i.ki'i.** Redup. of *ho'opāki'i.* **2.** n. Small dip net used in fishing in shallows.

pakika. vs. Slippery, smooth; to slip, slide. *He pakika, he pahe'e i ke ala* (song), slipping, sliding on the road. **ho'o.pakika.** To make smooth, as by polishing; to make slippery, as by greasing; to cause to slip and slide. **pā.kika.kika.** Redup. of *pakika.* **ho'o.pā.kika.kika.** Redup. of *ho'opakika.*

pakika.wai.ō. Same as *kikawaiō.*

pā.kī.kē. nvt. To answer saucily or rudely; rude, sarcastic, insolent, saucy, impudent; rudeness. Cf. *-kīkē, 'u'u. Pākīkē 'ia* (For. 4:291), insulted, taunted, jeered at. **ho'o.pā.kī.kē.** Caus/sim.

pā.kī.kē.kī.kē. Redup. of *pākīkē.*

paki.kī. Redup. of *pakī.* **ho'o.paki.kī.** Caus/sim.

pā.kiki. Same as *pāki'i 2.*

pā.kī.kī. 1. Redup. of *pākī 1;* to crush, as pandanus aerial roots with a stone in order to obtain fibers for kava strainers. **ho'o.pā.kī.kī.** Redup. of *ho'opākī.* (PCP *paatiitii*.) **2.** n. A variety of poisonous crab, said to be the same as *kūmimi.*

pā.kiko. nvi. Temperate, abstemious, frugal, economical, skimpy; temperance (sometimes preceded by *ke*). *'Ai pākiko,* eat sparingly; continence. *Inu pākiko,* drink temperately. *He pono ke pākiko mamua o nā hana ho'okelakela wale aku,* it is better to be economical than to [indulge in] extravagant display. **ho'o.pā.- kiko.** Caus/sim.

pā.kī.kō. n. Stone adze.

pā.kī.ko'ele. nvi. A rolling, rumbling sound; to rumble.

pā.kiko.kiko. 1. Redup. of *pākiko.* **ho'o.pā.kiko.kiko.** Caus/sim. **2.** vs. Scattered, dotted, spotted.

pā.kī lio. v. To ride a horse until it is exhausted or dead.

pā kini. n. Tin pan, pan, basin (preceded by *ke*). *Pā kini holoi,* wash pan.

pā.ki'o. vi. To settle in pools, as rain water; to drizzle; to evacuate the bowels.

pā.ki'o.ki'o. Redup. of *pāki'o;* to leave excreta here and there, as an animal. *Ua pāki'oki'o,* short showers; to rain often and clear between showers.

pā.kipa. n. Barkeeper. *Eng.*

pakī.pakī. Redup. of *pakī.* **ho'o.pakī.pakī.** Caus/sim.

pakipa.kika. Redup. of *pakika.* **ho'o.pakipa.kika.** Redup. of *ho'opakika.*

Pā.kī.pika, Fatifika. nvs. Pacific. *Eng.*

pā.kī pō.haku. v. To throw stones.

pako, baso. n. Bass. *Eng.*

Pakoa. n. Catholic term for Easter, Passover. (Gr. *Pascha* or possibly Portuguese *Pascoa* or Spanish *Pascua*.)

pā koa. n. Barracks.

pako (bato) 'aila. n. Measures of oil. (Luka 16.6.) (Gr. *batous*.)

pako.hana. Same as *kohana;* bare. *'Au pakohana i Wai-niha, nā lehua o Lulu'u-pali* (song), swimming naked at Wai-niha, are the *lehua* blossoms of Lulu'u-pali.

pakoke. Rare var. of *pakeko.*

pā.kole. 1. Var. of *pōkole,* short. **ho'o.pā.kole.** Var. of *ho'opōkole.* **2.** n. A fish (no data). **3.** vs. Uncertain. *Rare.*

pā.kō.lea. vt. **1.** To train to grow straight, as an infant's crooked limb; to train to grow in a desired shape, as a plant. **2.** To tie or fasten, as a canoe mast. **3.** To gather information about one's relatives.

pā.kole.kole. 1. Same as *pākalakala,* a seaweed. **2.** Redup. of *pākole.*

pā.kolo.kolo. n. Probably a weir (term used in land claims of the 1840s).

pā.kō.līī. n. Musical scale, named for the first three notes of the scale.

Pā-kolo.lio-kai.ā.ulu. n. Wind associated with Ke-ālia, Maui.

pā.kolu. vt. By threes, three at a time, three times, threefold; to distribute by threes, to divide by three, treble.

pā.konā.konā. Similar to *konākonā,* contemptuous. (For. 6:454.)

Pā-kō.nane. n. Name of a star said to appear on the night of Hilo in the month of Hinaia-'ele'ele.

pā kō.nane. vi. To shine brightly, of the moon.

pā.koni. vi. To throb, ache, as teeth.

pā.ko'u. Rare var. of *pōko'u,* short.

paku. vt. To send away, expel; to unite portions of tapa by beating. *Rare.* Cf. *kipaku.* (PEP *patu*.)

pakū. vi. To burst out, break open; squeeze out; crushed. See ex., *au 4.* **ho'o.pakū.** To burst, etc.

pā.kū. n. Curtain, screen, partition, veil; partitions before openings of deep-sea bag nets. *Fig.,* shield, defense. *Iēhowa kō mākou pākū* (Hal. 89.18), the Lord our defense. *Kū pākū ka pali o Nihoa i ka makani* (saying), the cliff of Nihoa stands as a bulwark against the wind [said of one bravely facing misfortune]. (PCP *paatuu*.)

pā.kū.ā, pā.kū.wā. vs. Commonplace, trite, ordinary. **ho'o.pā.kū.ā.** To do over and over; to render commonplace or trite, as a song.

pā kū.'ai. n. Public mart (term found in laws 1845–7).

pā kua.lau. n. Pearl-shell lure that is dark-colored inside. *Lit.,* showery lure.

pā.kū.'ei. vi. To do hurriedly and without thoroughness, to skimp. *Rare.*

pā kuhi.kuhi manawa. n. Sundial. *Lit.,* flat surface telling time.

pā.ku'i. 1. nvi. To splice or add on, append, annex, supplement, engraft (Rom. 11.17); graft; suffix, prefix, affix; extension, wing of a house; additional. See *'ōlelo pāku'i. Lumi pāku'i,* additional room. *Mea pōmaika'i pāku'i,* fringe benefits. *Hō'ike pāku'i,* rebuttal. **2.** vt. To beat, pound, oppose, oppress. *Ua pāku'i ka makani mamua o lākou* (Mar. 6.48), the wind beat ahead of them. **ho'o.pā.ku'i.** To beat, cause to beat. (PCP *paatuu*.) **3.** vs. Heavy scented, whether sickly sweet or foul. *Ua ho'opailua loa mākou i kēia kālā, ua pāku'i,* we are sick of this money, [it's] foul smelling. *Pāku'i lua nā pali o Pelekunu* (saying), doubly foul-smelling are the cliffs of Musty [said of vile-smelling places]. *Ua ana pāku'i lā i ke aloha* (chant), satiated with the aroma of love.

pā ku'i a lua. n. Arena where *lua* fighting was taught. *Lit.,* striking in *lua* style enclosure.

pakui.kui. Var. of *pākukui 1, 2.*

pā.ku'i.ku'i. 1. Redup. of *pāku'i 1, 2;* to splash by beating the water; disjointed, as a poorly constructed story. (2 Sam. 22.43.) **ho'o.pā.ku'i.ku'i.** Redup. of *ho'opā-ku'i. Ua ho'opāku'iku'i 'ia mai kō lāua noho 'ana ma-laila e nā kānaka,* their way of life there received blow after blow from the people. (PCP *paatukituki*.) **2.** vt. To argue, contradict. **ho'o.pā.ku'i.ku'i.** Caus/sim. **3.** n. A long fishing net; Emerson specifies a net laid in coral reef, into which fish were driven by beating the water (Malo 212, Emerson note); the joining together of long nets. Also *'āku'iku'i.* **4.** n. A surgeonfish (*Acanthurus achilles*), good eating. (PEP *paatuki*.)

pā.ku'i.pai. n. Shrimp net. Also *pāloa.*

pakū.kū. Redup. of *pakū. He hehi 'ia . . . a pakūkū ka waina,* the grapes were tramped on and crushed. *Pakūkū ahi ka makani* (For. 6:387), the wind breaks forth like fire.

pā.kukui. 1. nvi. Shiftless, vagabond; to wander; to play the wanton; to nibble but not take the hook, of fish. **2.** n. A method of enriching the soil for taro plantings by use of *kukui* leaves, which in rocky areas were covered with dirt in order to make soil. *Lit.,* candlenut enclosure. (Kep. 153.)

pā.kule. Var. spelling of *pā akule.*

pā.kū makika. n. Mosquito net or netting.

paku.paku. Rare var. of *pokopoko,* short.

pakū.pakū. 1. Redup. of *pakū.* **ho'o.pakū.pakū.** Redup. of *ho'opakū,* to pop, as a Portuguese man-of-war that is stepped upon on the beach. **2.** n. A seaweed. Also *pakēpakē.*

pā kupa.pa'u. Same as *pā ilina.*

pā.kū pouli. n. Window shade. *Lit.*, dark-night curtain.

pā.kū puka.ani.ani. n. Window curtain, drapes.

pā.kū.wā. Var. spelling of *pākūā*.

pala. 1. vs. Ripe, mellow; yellow, as leaves; soft, as an infected boil; rotten, as taro corm. Cf. *huapala, pala 'ehu, pala hehe'e, pala lau hala. Pala 'e'ehu ka lau o ka 'ulu,* the breadfruit leaves are reddish-yellow. **ho'o.-pala.** To ripen, turn yellow. *Ho'opala mai'a,* to ripen bananas [as by burying in a pit]. (PPN *pala.*) **2.** n. Daub, smear, smudge, blot; dab of excreta (cf. *pala kūkae*). Cf. also *'ai pala maunu, hāpala, kāpala, pala niho, pala 'ole.* **ho'o.pala.** To daub, besmear. **3.** vs. Underdone. *Pupuhi ka umu, mo'a pala ka 'ai,* the oven smokes, food is underdone. **4.** vs. Coated, as the tongue. Cf. *waha pala.* **5.** n. A form of gonorrhea. **6.** n. Intoxicating drink made of watermelon juice. **7.** n. A native fern *(Marattia douglasii),* with a short trunk and large, long-stemmed, much divided, dark-green fronds. In time of famine, the thick, starchy, hoof-shaped bases of the frond stems, which cover the short trunk, were eaten after being baked in an *imu* over night. The mucilaginous water resulting from slicing and soaking the raw stems in water was used medicinally. Pieces of the fronds mixed with *maile* leis enhanced their fragrance. The fern was used also in heiau ceremonies. (Neal 6, 7.) (PNP *pala.*) **8.** n. A variety of sweet potato. **9.** n. A variety of taro. **10.** n. Seaweeds or scum. **11.** n. Parlor. *Eng.*

pala.'ā. 1. n. The lace fern *(Sphenomeris chinensis* syn. *chusana),* a common wild fern in Hawai'i; also known in other parts of Polynesia and in Asia. Long, slender stems support smooth, ovate, pointed fronds, about 30 cm long, which are subdivided three times. Formerly a brown dye was extracted from the fronds. Also *palapala'ā* and *pā'ū-o-Pala'e.* (Neal 15, 16.) **2.** n. A tapa of *māmaki* bark dyed brownish-red with *pala'ā* fern, of silky quality. **3.** vs. Brownish-red. **4.** n. Type of stone, used for sinkers for octopus fishing.

pala.'ai. 1. n. Original name for pumpkin *(Cucurbita pepo),* as well as squash, named for their resemblance to a long-extinct gourd of the same name. See also *pū.* **2.** nvs. Fat, as animals. *'Ōpū pala'ai,* potbellied, a term of ridicule.

pala 'ai. n. A daub of food, especially the film of poi that adheres to the walls of the container after the mass has been eaten.

pā.lā.'au. vt. To heal, as with herbs. *'O Hi'iaka ke kāula nui, nāna i hana, nāna i pālā'au i nā ma'i apau* (prayer), Hi'iaka the great priest, she acts, she treats all ailments.

pā lā.'au. n. **1.** Wooden fence, hedge. *Pā lā'au 'oi'oi* (Mik. 7.4), thorn hedge. **2.** Wooden dish or tray (preceded by *ke*).

pala'e. 1. Short for *pā'ū-o-Pala'e.* **2.** n. Scar or lump, as left by a disease of glands in the neck (usually follows *'ā'ī,* neck). Cf. *'ala'ala.*

pala.e'a. Var. name for young stage of *hou,* a fish.

pala 'ehu. vs. Reddish-yellow.

pā.la'e.la'e. vs. Bright, as the sun.

pala.'ewa. vs. Oblique.

palaha. vi. To slip and fall, stumble; smooth, slippery, slick. **ho'o.palaha.** To cause to fall, trip, push over; to fall.

pā.laha. 1. vs. Spread out, extended, flattened, wide, broad, broadened. *Hina pālaha,* to fall sprawling. *Pālaha akula ka ua ma ka 'āina,* the rain spread over the land. **ho'o.pā.laha.** To spread, extend, flatten; leveling, flattening. *Ke ho'opālaha maila ka moa maluna o nā hua,* the hen spreads out over the eggs. (PCP *pa(a)lafa*.) **2.** vi. To broil, of flattened-out flesh on coals. **ho'o.pā.laha.** Transitive of above. **3.** n. A kind of small *'ahi,* a tuna *(Germo alalunga).* **4.** n. Ti-leaf sandals. *Rare.*

pala hā.'ama. vs. Yellow but not dead ripe, of bananas; half ripe.

pala.hai.kala. Old name of an illness (no data). Cf. *haikala.*

pā.laha.laha. (sometimes shortened to *pālālā*). **1.** Redup. of *pālaha 1. Ma'i pālahalaha,* contagious disease, epidemic. **ho'o.pā.laha.laha.** Redup. of *ho'opālaha 1. Ua ho'opālahalaha mai ke Akua ia'u* (Kin. 41.52), God has caused me to be fruitful. (PCP *paalafalafa.*) **2.** Same as *līpahapaha,* a seaweed.

pā.laha.laha lau. vs. Having many leaves, but little fruit.

pala hao. n. A form of gonorrhea. *Lit.,* hard rottenness.

pala.hē. vs. Fragile, easily torn, as rotting cloth; pulverized, smashed. *Mo'a palahē,* overcooked to the point of falling apart, as meat. *Pōluku 'ia a palahē ke kino,* a body pounded and mashed.

pala.he'a. vs. Stained, smeared, bedaubed. **ho'o.pala.-he'a.** To stain, besmear. *Ā ho'opalahe'a nō wau i ko'u 'a'ahu apau* (Isa. 63.3), I shall stain all my raiment [with blood].

pala.he'a.he'a. Redup. of *palahe'a.* **ho'o.pala.he'a.-he'a.** Redup. of *ho'opalahe'a.*

pala.he'e. 1. vs. Overripe, as fallen fruit. **2.** vi. To flee in fear. *Rare.* **ho'o.pala.he'e.** To cause to flee, chase.

pala he'e. nvs. A running boil; to run, of a sore.

pala.heha. vs. Lazy, negligent. Cf. *maheha.*

pala.hē.hē. n. Pus. *Pakū ka palahēhē,* the pus breaks out.

pala hehe'e. n. Abscess, running sore.

palahe.'ī. n. Region below *kualono. Rare.*

pala.hemo. Similar to *pahemo,* loose, easily untied. *Rare.*

pala.heo. vs. Not clear, as the speech of some old persons. Perhaps Wai-mea, Hawai'i.

pala.hī. nvi. Diarrhea, liquid bowel evacuations; to have diarrhea.

pala.hi'a. vi. To glide. Cf. *pāhi'a. 'O ka lua o ka ihe ua palahi'a wale akula nō,* the second spear glided along.

pala hinu. vs. Polished, bright.

pala.hō. nvs. Rotten, putrid, decayed, corrupt; rot. **ho'o.pala.hō.** To cause to rot, etc.

pala.ho'a. n. Young *'ama'u* fern fronds cut to be made into *palaholo* paste.

pala.hoana. See *puhi palahoana.*

pala.holo. 1. n. Rolled-up frond of the *'ama'u* fern; paste made of sap from the fronds, used in welding strips of tapa together. Tapa made with old torn pieces added to new pieces was also called *palaholo* (For. 5:641). **2.** Same as *palahuki.*

pala.hū. 1. nvs. Rotten; to spoil, rot; overripe. **2.** n. Same as *pelehū,* turkey. **3.** n. A kind of *'ōpelu,* a fish.

pala.huki. vs. Rotten, as a banana stump; overripe, as banana fruit with juice dripping and black skin, as used in medicine.

pala.huli. vi. To turn over, fall over. *Palahuli i lalo ka waha 'ai ai* (saying), the food-eating mouth is fallen over [said of one in serious trouble]. **ho'o.pala.huli.** To cause to turn over, fall.

palai. 1. n. A native fern *(Microlepia setosa),* growing wild and cultivated, 95 to 130 cm high. The lacy, ovate fronds look much like those of the *pala'ā* but are somewhat hairy instead of smooth. (Neal 12.) The *palai* was one of the important plants placed on the hula altar to Laka, goddess of hula; it is named in song (see *wilia*). Also *palapalai.* See ex., *popohe.* **2.** vi. To turn the face away, as in embarrassment, confusion, humility; bashful; to conceal one's true feelings; to cloak dissatisfaction or feign friendship; hypocritical (Kel. 130) (often used with *maka*). *Hūnā palai iki ke akamai,* to hide and conceal somewhat the cleverness. **ho'o.palai.** To have turned the face away, to cause to turn away; ashamed, confused, etc. *E hilahila auane'i, a e ho'opalai maka ho'i ka po'e* (Isa. 41.11), the people shall be put to shame and confounded. **3.** Also **parai, farai.** vt. To fry; frying, fried. *Eng. Palaoa palai,* pancake.

palai ali'i. n. A variety of *palai,* a fern.

pala.'ie. 1. vs. Flexible, inconstant, changeable. **2.** nvi. To play the game of loop and ball; the game itself: a flexible stick made of braided coconut leaflets with a loop at one end and a tapa ball on a string attached below the loop, the object being to catch the ball in the loop; this game was often played to a chant.

palai hihi. n. A native filmy fern *(Vandenboschia davallioides),* climbing on trees in damp forests, with narrow dark-green fronds, 13 cm long or more, divided three times. *Lit.,* creeping *palai.*

palai hina.hina. n. A native filmy fern *(Sphaerocionium lanceolatum),* climbing on trees, with narrow fronds 5 cm long or longer, divided three times, edged with red hairs. *Lit.,* white-haired *palai.*

palai huna. Same as *pai,* a native fern.

pala.'i'i. Same as *lehua pala'i'i,* a variety of taro.

palai kaha.wai. Same as *hihiawa,* a fern.

pala.iki. nvi. Sound of a stone falling into water; to fall with a sound; plump. *Rare.*

pala ila. vs. Overripe, as bananas that have turned black. *Lit.,* spotted ripening.

palai lā.'au. n. A small native fern *(Adenophorus pinnatifidis),* with narrow fronds 10 to 40 cm long, having many short side lobes; they hang down on forest tree trunks. *Lit.,* plant *palai.*

palai.lai. n. Young of the *lai,* a fish.

palai lau li'i. n. A small native filmy fern *(Sphaerociomium obtusum),* growing on forest trees, 2.5 to 6 cm long, with oblong, much-divided fronds. *Lit.,* small-leafed *palai.*

pala.'ī.loli. vs. Discolored, as of pandanus fruit that darkens; to assume a softer, darker color.

palai maka. See *palai 2.*

palai moe anu. n. A variety of stunted fern.

palaina. 1. nvi. Turning away in embarrassment, confusion, or humility, concealment of true feelings. Cf. *palai 2.* **2.** vt. To smooth, as fresh cement with a trowel. **3.** n. A word said in card games (no data).

palaina kimeki. nv. Cement; to cement. Cf. *palai 2.*

palaina puna. nv. Whitewash; to whitewash. Cf. *palai 2.*

palai 'ula. n. Dark-stemmed form of *palai.* Also *la'a.*

palaka. 1. nvs. Indifferent, inactive, uninterested, lax, listless, apathetic, oblivious, careless or negligent in doing something, as going to church; disinterest, indifference. (FS 111.) Cf. *kūpalaka. Palaka ka na'au* (Mat. 13.15), the heart has grown dull. **ho'o.palaka.** To feign indifference; indifferent, etc. (Isa. 6.10.) **2.** n. A fish (no data). **3.** n. A checkered shirt, usually blue and white, of block-print cloth; in the 19th century, a coarse work shirt worn by males, known then in English as a "frock", mentioned frequently in the literature and especially in Peter Ka'eo's letters in 1873–4 to his cousin, Queen Emma (Korn 1976, pp. 14–38), and hence probably from English "frock" rather than from "block". **4.** n. Block, as block and tackle. *Eng.*

palaka aloha. n. Aloha shirt.

pala kā.'ao. vs. Ripe, as pandanus.

-palaka'eo. **ho'o.pala.ka'eo.** Peeved, resentful. *Rare.* Cf. *ka'eo.*

palaka.hē. Short for *palakāhela 1.*

pala.kā.hela. vs. **1.** Overripe, spoiled; yellowed and falling, as leaves. *Palakāhela 'ai ka Maka-'Ūkiu* (chant), the food crops of Maka-'Ūkiu are spoiled. **2.** Curved, bent; stooped, as one lifting a weight to one's back. **ho'o.pala.kā.hela.** To curve, bend, stoop.

palaka.huki. Same as *palahuki;* overcooked to the point of falling apart, as meat (less common than *mo'a palahē).*

pala.kai. vs. Sickly, withered, stunted, puny, as unhealthy plants or people.

pala kaia. n. A variety of sweet potato.

pala.kaiko, paradaiso. n. Paradise. (Luka 23.43.) (Gr. *paradeisos.*)

pala.kama, balasama. Balsam. *Eng.*

pala.kē. vs. Soggy and watery, as taro or sweet potatoes of poor quality.

pala.kea. 1. n. A variety of taro, tall and stocky, distinguished by the black edge of the petiole; corm white, less acrid than most taros, used chiefly as a table taro,

also medicinally. The name may be qualified by the colors *'ele'ele* and *ke'oke'o.* Also *lauloa hā'ele'ele, lauloa palakea.* **2.** vs. Soft, white, clear, unclouded.

pala.kei. n. Rocky patch, as for planting. *Rare.*

Pala.keliko, Paradelito. n. Counselor (RSV), Comforter (KJV). (Ioane 14.16.) (Gr. *paracletos.*)

palaki. 1. nvt. Brush; to brush. *Eng.* **2.** vs. Black, as skin. *Eng.* **3.** Also *barati.* n. Ballast. *Eng.* **4.** n. Flush, in poker. *Eng.*

pala.kī. n. Small daubs of soft excrement, so called because bowels were loosened during time of famine by eating ti root. *Lit.,* ti daubs.

palaki 'ā.nai. n. Scrubbing brush.

pala.kiko. Petty pilfering; to pilfer little by little. (AP.)

palaki lau.oho. n. Hairbrush.

palaki niho. n. Toothbrush.

pala.ki'o. n. A venereal disease.

pala.kiu. vs. Rotted, as taro corm in cold, wet weather.

pala.kū. vs. Ripe to perfection, as of bananas that drop when touched; to ripen uniformly. (PPN *palatu'u.*)

pala.kua. Var. of *palakū.*

pala kū.kae. n. Residue of excreta that remains to be wiped off. *Lit.,* excreta daub. *Ahu ka pala kūkae,* a heap of excreta daub [an expression of contempt].

palala. n. Barrel. *Eng.*

pala.lā. n. A low or rumbling sound (similar to *palalū).* Cf. *kōhikōhi-kū-palalā.* (PPN *palalaa.*)

pā.lala. 1. nvi. Gift or tax given to a chief at the birth of a child; to honor a child with a gift; house-warming feast; to have such a feast. (Laie 445.) *'Aha'aina pālala,* feast, as in honor of a child. **2.** vs. Clear. *Rare.* (PCP *paalala.*)

pā lala. vi. To strike obliquely, as wave or wind.

pā.lā.lā. Same as *pālahalaha.*

pala.laha. Same as *pālahalaha 1.*

pā.lala.huki. Same as *palahuki.*

pā.lala.ka'i.moku. Plain, cape, land jutting into the sea. *Fig.,* kingdom. (AP.)

pala.lalo. n. **1.** Gonorrhea. **2.** Soft, rotten. (And.)

pala lau hala. vs. Yellow as a pandanus leaf, said of the very old.

pala.lē. 1. nvi. To speak imperfectly, as of one with a foreign accent or speech defect; to work in a disorderly, slipshod way; confusion. Cf. *hiohio haole, kīpalalē.* **ho'o.pala.lē.** Caus/sim. **2.** vi. To drip, spatter, spill, fart. *He mau 'ōhua lemu kaumaha, he mau 'ope'ope palalē* (For. 4:577), heavy-butted passengers, farting bags.

pala.leha. vs. Indifferent, careless, slack, neglectful of duty. Cf. *paleha.* **ho'o.pala.leha.** Caus/sim.; to neglect. *'O ka lima ho'opalaleha, he mea ia e 'ilihune ai* (Sol. 10.4), he becometh poor that dealeth with a slack hand.

pala.lehe. Var. of *palaleha.* **ho'o.pala.lehe.** Var. of *ho'opalaleha.*

pala.lei. n. Uncut tapa fringe. *Rare.*

pala.lī. nvs. Any flutelike, shrill, or high sound; to sound thus; sound of flatulency.

pala.loa. 1. Same as *pālala 1.* (Malo 199, Emerson note.) **2.** nvi. A circuit of the island by the high chief, building heiaus (Malo 189); to make such.

pala.loli. Same as *pala'īloli.*

pala.lū. 1. nvi. A low rolling or rumbling sound, as cooing of a dove or low blare of a trumpet; sound of the *moho,* wingless rail; to make such. **ho'o.pala.lū.** To sound thus. **2.** vs. Weak, nervous, with shaking limbs. **ho'o.pala.lū.** To cause nervousness, weakness.

pala luhi.ehu. nvs. Golden yellow, a beautiful yellow.

palama. n. **1.** Plum. *Eng.* **2.** Plumber; plumbing. *Eng.*

pā.lama. 1. nvi. A sacred and taboo enclosure, especially for royal women placed under taboo; to place under taboo. (For. 5:387.) *Lit., lama* wood enclosure. *Kapālama* (place name), the sacred *lama* enclosure. *Ua pālama 'ia ke keiki,* the child is under taboo. *Ke 'ī a'e nō wau, 'o ka 'oi o ka pālama, mālama 'ia kō kino* (song), I do say, the best of the sacred enclosures is to care for your body. **hoʻo.pā.lama.** To guard, protect, as a taboo princess in a *pālama*. **2.** n. Palm. *Eng.*

pala mahiki. n. **1.** A variety of taro. **2.** A variety of sweet potato.

pā.lama.lama. Redup. of *pālama 1.*

palama wai.ū. n. Madagascar olive, a rare evergreen (*Noronhia emarginata,* Neal 677).

pala.mea. 1. vs. Plump. *Rare.* **2.** n. Clear atmosphere. *Rare.*

pala.mimo. vi. To pilfer quickly, as of a skilled pickpocket; to move easily and noiselessly; to do or act deftly; neatly; swift, neat. *Palamimo ka lima i ka ulana,* the hand is deft in plaiting. *Palamimo ka hoʻonoho ʻana i ka ukana,* the gear is packed neatly.

pala.mio. Same as *palamimo.*

pā.lā.moa. n. **1.** Thick, dense, as clouds. See ex., *kaunana.* **2.** A grass. (UL 124.)

pā.lā.moi. n. Second growth stage of the *moi,* a fish, about 13 cm long *(Kauaʻi);* third growth stage, about 30 cm long *(Hawaiʻi).*

Palana.heika, Faranaheita. Fahrenheit. *Eng.*

pā.lā.nai. Same as *pānānai,* flat.

pā.lana.iki. nvs. Small, compact; slim and trim figure.

pala naio. n. Pinworm daub, a term of contempt something like "not worth a daub of excreta," so called because *naio* were believed to get into the bowels of children and cause itching. *He aha kāna pala naio?* What in blazes is he good for?

pala.nehe. vs. Noiseless, quiet, dainty, deft; to move in a dainty fashion. *Kō wāwae, kiʻi palanehe* (chant), your feet, dainty fetching. Also *paʻanehe.*

palani. 1. n. A surgeonfish *(Acanthurus dussumieri),* famous for a strong odor. (PPN *palangi*.) **2.** nvi. To stink, smell sour or rancid; a detested person; a *kauā,* outcast. **hoʻo.palani.** To cause to go sour, rancid. **3.** n. A variety of sugar cane, short, purple with deep olive-green cast when young, changing to reddish-yellow on exposure, pith dark. Probably the parent of *ʻakoki.* Sometimes qualified by *hao* or *ʻula* (For. 5:585). **4.** n. A variety of sweet potato. **5.** Also **barani.** n. Brandy. *Eng. ʻUla palani,* brandy red. **6.** *(Cap.)* Also **Farani.** nvs. France; Frenchman; French; Frank. *Eng. Hula Palani* (UL 203), same as the *paʻi umauma* hula. **7.** n. Bran. *Eng.*

pā.lani. vi. To skim lightly; to paint or daub lightly, especially to paint tapa in light shades. Cf. *mālani.*

pala niho. n. Tartar of the teeth. *ʻAi pala niho,* food remnants; to eat food remnants; an eater of food scraps left by others [a term of reproach].

palani.oa. vs. Sour or rancid smelling, especially of an improperly washed or insufficiently sunned food container.

palaʻo. n. **1.** Walrus. Also *waleluka, wolu.* **2.** *(Cap.)* Also **Parao.** Pharaoh. *Eng.*

pala.ʻō. Same as *līpālāwai,* fresh-water algae.

palaoa. n. **1.** Sperm whale; ivory, especially whale tusks as used for the highly prized *lei palaoa;* whale-tooth pendant. *Makau palaoa,* fishhook made of whale ivory. (PCP *pala(a)oa*.) **2.** Flour, bread, wheat *(Biblical). Eng.* Cf. *lāwalu.*

palaoa hoʻo.pā.paʻa. n. Toast.

palaoa hoʻo.wali ʻia. n. Dough.

palaoa hulu.hulu. n. Barley *(Hordeum* spp.) (Puk. 9.31). *Lit.,* hairy flour.

palaoa kuʻi. n. Whale-tooth pounder or pestle, as for crushing medicine, a highly valued chief's possession.

palaoa liʻi.liʻi. n. Roll, biscuit.

palaoa lina.lina. n. Thin pancake made without baking powder.

palaoa lū.lū. n. Dumpling (some localities), Hawaiian-style mush *(Hawaiʻi).*

palaoa maka. n. Flour.

palaoa moku.moku. n. Dumpling.

palaoa palai. n. Pancake. *Lit.,* fried flour.

palaoa pā.paʻa. n. Toast. *Lit.,* crisp bread. Cf. *pāpaʻa palaoa.*

palaoa pū.lehu. n. Toast.

pā.laʻo.laʻo. 1. Same as *laʻolaʻo,* mote. **2.** n. A fish (no data).

pala ʻole. vs. Perfect, flawless, consummate. *Lit.,* without a daub. *He ʻike pala ʻole,* a perfect knowledge.

Pala-ʻole. n. Name of a *lua* stroke.

pala.paʻa. n. Any wooden calabash with a thick base. See ex., *kūmau 2.*

pala.pala. 1. nvt. Document of any kind, bill, deed, warrant, certificate, policy, letter, tract, writ, diploma, manuscript; writing of any kind, literature; printing on tapa or paper; formerly the Scriptures or learning in general; to write, send a written message. **2.** n. Maui name for *pualu,* a fish. (KL line 147.) **3.** n. Var. name for *maomao,* a fish. (Malo 211.)

pala.pala.ʻā. Same as *pala ʻā,* lace fern.

pala.pala ʻae. n. Permit, license. *Lit.,* agreeing document. *Palapala ʻae e komo mai,* entrance permit. *Palapala ʻae e holo,* passport.

pala.pala ʻae.like. n. Written contract, as for labor; treaty, agreement. *Palapala ʻae mamuli o nā kumu,* conditional permit.

pala.pala ʻai. Redup. of *pala ʻai 2.*

pala.pala ʻai.ʻē. n. Note (to pay money), bond. *Lit.,* debt document.

pala.pala.ʻāina. n. Map. *Lit.,* land document.

pala.pala ʻalo.kio (alodio). n. Alodial title, fee simple title.

pala.pala haʻa.lele. n. Letter of resignation. Also, *palapala waiho ʻoihana.*

pala.pala haʻi ā kuhi.kuhi hewa. n. Writ of error. *Lit.,* document reporting error.

pala.pala haʻi hewa. n. Writ of error. *Lit.,* document reporting error.

pala.pala hā.nau. n. Birth certificate.

pala.pala.hē. Redup. of *palahē.*

Pala.pala Hemo.lele. n. Holy Scriptures.

pala.pala hoʻ.ai.ʻē. n. Promissory note.

pala.pala hoʻ.ā.loha.loha. n. Written condolence.

pala.pala hoʻ.ā.mana. n. Power of attorney. *Lit.,* document giving power.

pala.pala hoʻ.ā.pono. n. Any document granting permission, as a passport.

pala.pala hoʻ.ike. n. Affidavit, report, certificate. *Lit.,* reporting document.

pala.pala hoʻ.ike manawa. n. Chronology, timetable.

pala.pala hoʻ.ike no ke ola. n. Bill of health. *Lit.,* document reporting concerning the health.

pala.pala hoʻ.ike pili.kino. n. Identification papers. *Lit.,* document telling about self.

pala.pala hoʻ.ike ukana o ka moku. n. Bill of lading. *Lit.,* document reporting cargo of the ship.

pala.pala hoʻ.ike wai.wai. n. Report of finances.

pala.pala.honua. n. Map (less used than *palapala ʻāina). Lit.,* land document.

pala.pala hoʻo.hano.hano. n. Honorary diploma or document of any kind.

pala.pala hoʻo.hiki. n. Adoption paper; certificate that a child is legally adopted; a written oath.

pala.pala hoʻo.hiki ʻia. n. Affidavit.

pala.pala hoʻo.hui. n. Charter. *Lit.,* association-forming document.

pala.pala hoʻ.oia. n. Certificate.

pala.pala hoʻ.oia.ʻiʻo. n. Voucher, certifying document.

pala.pala hoʻ.oia kula.nui. n. Collegiate certificate; college diploma.

pala.pala hoʻ.oia mā.kau.kau. n. Professional certificate.

pala.pala hoʻo.ilina. n. Last will and testament. *Lit.,* document to convey inheritance.

pala.pala hoʻo.kaʻa. n. Receipt, as for paying a bill.

pala.pala hoʻo.kō. n. Verdict, decision (written); award; certificate of title; warrant. *Lit.,* accomplishing document.

pala.pala hoʻo.kohu. n. Certificate of appointment; power of attorney.

pala.pala hoʻo.kohu hui, pala.pala hoʻo.kumu. n. Charter.

pala.pala hoʻo.kule.ana. n. Patent, copyright. *Lit.,* document granting ownership.

pala.pala hoʻo.kuʻu. n. Certificate of release; pass, as for soldiers; discharge, as from the army.

pala.pala hoʻo.launa. n. Letter of introduction.

pala.pala hoʻo.lilo. n. Quitclaim; deed, as of transference sale; assignment, transfer.

pala.pala hoʻo.lilo wai.wai. n. Inheritance deed.

pala.pala hoʻo.lima.lima. n. Lease.

pala.pala hoʻo.mai.kaʻi. n. Graduating diploma; letter of commendation, certificate of merit. *Lit.,* congratulatory document.

pala.pala hoʻo.malu. n. An uncertain legal term placing restrictions on ownership of land, as a lien or easement.

pala.pala hoʻo.nā. n. Certificate of title. *Lit.,* satisfying document.

pala.pala hoʻo.paʻa. n. Bond, insurance policy.

pala.pala hoʻo.piʻi. n. Warrant, as for arrest; claim, indictment, petition, application.

pala.pala hoʻo.piʻi kipaku. n. Document for ejection.

pala.pala hopu. n. Warrant of arrest, summons.

pala.pala hui.kala. n. Written pardon.

pala.pala huli. n. Search warrant.

pala.palai. n. 1. Same as *palai,* a fern. 2. A Niʻihau name for *niʻaniʻau* and *kupukupu.* 3. Niʻihau name for gold fern, *Pityrogramma calomelanos* (syn. *P. chrysophylla).* (Neal 20.)

pala.palai-a-Kama.puaʻa. n. A native fern *(Dryopteris globulifera),* 45 to 120 cm high, the frond 15 to 45 cm wide, and pinnate to almost bipinnate. *Lit.,* fern of Kamapuaʻa.

pala.palai au.makua. n. A native fern *(Dryopteris crinalis* var. *tripinnata),* 60 to 120 cm high, with broad, much-subdivided fronds.

pala.palai lau liʻi. n. A native fern *(Diellia pumila),* 10 to 30 cm high, with narrow, pinnate fronds. *Lit.,* small-leaved fern.

pala.pala ʻini.kua. n. Insurance policy.

pala.pala kā.koʻo. n. Letter of recommendation or support.

pala.pala kala.hala. n. Indulgence (Catholic). *Lit.,* forgiving document.

pala.pala kau.oha. n. Last will and testament. *Lit.,* commanding document.

pala.pala kau.oha pā.kuʻi. n. Codicil to will.

pala.pala.kea. Redup. of *palakea 2.*

pala.pala kē.nā. n. Summons, subpoena.

pala.pala kiʻi. n. Summons, process, writ, warrant, subpoena. *Lit.,* document for fetching.

pala.pala kī.koʻo. n. Check, draft, warrant (for drawing money).

pala.pala kila (sila). n. Deed, patent. *Lit.,* seal document.

pala.pala kila nui. n. Royal patent (in times of monarchy).

pala.pala kilo.kilo hō.kū. n. Horoscope.

pala.pala kipa. n. Calling card.

pala.pala koi pala.pala pā.pā aku. n. Mandamus. *Lit.,* document urging forbidding document.

pala.pala komo. n. Pass to enter.

pala.pala kono. n. Invitation.

pala.pala kū.ʻai. n. Deed or bill of sale.

pala.pala kū.ʻē. n. A written protest.

pala.pala kuhi.kuhi. n. Chart; statement, as of an account.

pala.pala kuhi.kuhi hewa. n. Writ of error.

pala.pala kuhi.kuhi kino. n. A certificate of identification, as a passport.

pala.pala kumu. n. Original or basic document.

pala.pala kumu kule.ana ʻāina. n. Land claim or title of ownership.

pala.pala kuʻu.kino. n. Writ of habeas corpus. *Lit.,* document releasing body.

pala.pala lima. n. Billet; any handwritten manuscript or document.

pala.pala loaʻa. n. Receipt.

pala.pala mā.kaʻi.kaʻi. n. Calling card.

pala.pala male (mare). n. Marriage license or certificate.

pala.palani. Redup. of *pālani.*

pala.pala noi. n. Written petition, application.

pala.pala noho. n. Residency permit (for foreigners in 1852).

pala.pala pī.ʻā.pā. n. Speller, alphabet book.

pala.pala pona (bona). n. Bond.

pala.pala puka (mai ke kula mai). n. Diploma for graduation (from school).

pala.pala ui. n. Catechism.

pala.pala.ulu. vs. Colorful. *Palapalaulu i ke kanaka,* colorful with people.

pala.pala waiho ʻoi.hana. n. Letter of resignation.

pala.pala.weka. Redup. of *palaweka.*

pala.pī. vs. Wet, as green wood, said to be so called because green wood sputters *(pī)* on the fire. *Lit.,* sputtering daub.

pala.pō. nvs. Dark, darkness. *Lit.,* black smudge.

pala.pō.haku. n. Third stage of *manini* fish, so called because they are said to feed on *pala pōhaku.*

pala pō.haku. n. A kind of fine, slippery brown alga forming a thin layer on stones in ocean pools. Eaten by small fish but not by people. *Lit.,* rock slime.

pala.pole, parabole. n. Parable. *Eng.*

pala.pū. nvs. Wound, flesh injury; soft, as a boil ready for lancing. *Ma kona mau palapū ua hoʻōla ʻia mai kākou* (Isa. 53.5), with his stripes we are healed.

palau. 1. nvs. Betrothal; betrothed, engaged. hoʻo.palau. To betroth in marriage; engaged. 2. nvt. Plow; to plow. *Eng.* Cf. *ʻōʻō palau.*

pā.lau. 1. vt. To tell tall tales, exaggerate, talk. hoʻo.pā.lau. Same as above; to cause to tell tall tales. (PPN *pa(a)lau).* 2. n. War club; wooden implement with convex cutting edges, for cutting off ends of taro corm for planting (also *pālau kōhi);* knife. 3. n. Mat, wrapper. Cf. *pālau kea, pālau moena, pālau ʻula. Pālaulau* is commoner. 4. Short for *kōʻelepālau,* a pudding of sweet potatoes and coconut cream. *Kīʻoʻe pālau,* a spoon used for stirring and dipping *pālau* pudding. 5. n. A variety of *hīnālea,* a fish. 6. n. Maui name for yam. 7. n. A variety of taro.

palau.alelo. nvs. Lazy, idle, especially of a verbose person; such a person; lazy windbag, a do-nothing. *Lit.,* tongue lying.

pā.lau.anahu. Same as *ʻae-o-kaha-loa,* a tapa.

palau.ea. 1. Same as *malauea,* lazy, listless. 2. *(Cap.)* n. Place name, East Maui.

pā.lau.eka. Var. spelling of *pālauweka.*

pā.lau.ʻeka. nvs. A mere trifle, pittance; worthless, trifling; vagabond, shiftless neʻer-do-well. *Kumu kūʻai pālauʻeka,* a pittance of a price. *Hoʻi pālauʻeka ʻole,* come back without even a trifle.

palauha. vs. Very lazy.

pā.lau.hala. Var. of *pūlauhala. Rare.*

pā.lau.hulu. vt. To take all of a fish catch for a chief instead of dividing it. *Ua pālauhulu ʻia ka iʻa na ke aliʻi,* all of the fish were taken for the chief alone.

pā.lau leo. n. Mat of light pandanus leaves, with meshes about .6 to 1.1 cm wide. *Lit.,* white mat.

palauki. n. Blouse. *Eng.*

pā.lau kōhi. See *pālau 2.*

pala ʻula. n. A seaweed.

pā.lau.lau. 1. Redup. of *pālau 3;* broad, flat, extended; a wrapper, especially apron or skirt used as a conveyor; to carry in a wrapper. *He aha kā ʻoukou pālaulau? He lāʻī nō!* What's your wrapper? Just ti leaves. hoʻo.pā.lau.lau. Caus/sim. 2. n. Broad, flat part of a paddle or tool, as of a pickaxe, hoe. 3. n. A kind of red fish resembling the *ʻūʻū* (no data).

pā.lau.lau moena. Same as *pālau moena.*

pā.lau.lau paʻa.kai. n. Thick, coarse mat on which salt is dried.

pala.uli. vs. Dark, as the skin, clouds.

pā.lau moena. n. Ordinary floor mat.

pā.lau 'ula. n. Thick mat of reddish-brown pandanus leaves with meshes about 4 to 5 cm wide.

pā.lau.weka. Same as *palaweka.*

pala.wai. n. 1. Athlete's foot. 2. Bottom lands. *Penei ke 'ano o ka mahi 'ai 'ana o ka palawai,* this is how the bottom lands were cultivated.

pā.lā.wai. Same as *limu kala wai,* pond-scums.

pā.lawa.iki. vs. Neat, tidy, dainty, fastidious; having good taste in clothes and the like.

pala.weka. vs. Dim, obscure, indistinct, hazy, as moonlight. Cf. *palauweka, pāpalaweka, palapalaweka.*

pala.wili. vt. To twist, turn. *Moe kahuli, hī'ō i ka nahele i ka palawili 'ia e ka noe,* land shell lying down, restless in the forest as it is twisted by the mist.

pale. 1. nvt. To ward off, thrust aside, parry, fend off, bar, shield, defend, protect; to ignore a command or law, make void, nullify, prevent, repulse, resist, break, avoid, not adhere to; protection, defense, barrier, warding off, guard; curtain (Puk. 26.4); bib, partition, bar, railing, bulwark, shield, sheath, outer garment; division, canto of a song, scene of a play, division of song in a hula (preceded by both *ka* and *ke). Pale lua* (Heb. 9.3), second veil or partition in the temple of Solomon. *Pule pale* (Kep. 57), prayer asking for protection. *Pale 'ōlelo,* disobey. *'Ili pale o kāma'a,* sole of shoes. *Pale hewa i ke kuke,* avoid the duty, smuggle. *Nīnaninau pule,* cross-examination. *Mea pale,* defendant. *Pale ka 'a'aka,* crosspatch, cantankerous person; *lit.,* cranky one who shoves. *Ua pale ka pilikia,* the trouble is thrust aside, finished, over. *Pale kauoha,* to ignore, fail to carry out a command. *Pale i ke a'o a ka makua,* to thrust aside the teaching of the parent. *Pale ka leo* (Kel. 61), voice is silenced [in death]. *He lā ikaika 'ole o ke au i ke pale* (For. 5:561), a day when the head current was not strong. **ho'o.pale.** To fend or ward off; to separate, partition off; to defend in court; to disown. *Ma ka 'ao'ao ho'opale,* on the side of the defendant. (PPN *pale).* 2. vt. To deliver, as a child. 3. nvt. Lining, as of a garment; leaf lining of a ground oven; flap of a *malo;* to cover, overlay, line; to form a barrier. See *pale hou.* 4. n. Gunwale lashed to a canoe. 5. n. An interval of time in music, a bar in music which separates the staff into measures. See below. 6. n. Presser foot on a sewing machine. 7. n. Apron, bib. 8. Also *bale, bare.* n. Barley (*Hordeum* spp.), bran. *Eng. Hua pale,* grain of barley.

palea. Pas/imp. of *pale 1.*

pale.'a'ahu. n. Underclothes, underwear. (Kel. 105.)

pale ahi. n. Fire protection; fireproof.

paleha. vs. Loose, slack, sagging; shaking, as a loose object. Cf. *palaleha.*

pale hā.li'i moena. n. Coarse mat covering, as spread on the ground; insulting epithet for worthless, low person.

pale hā.nai. n. Child's bib.

pale hau.hana. See *hauhana.*

palehe. Rare var. of *paleha.*

pale hope. n. 1. After part of a canoe. 2. Bearers of the after part of a canoe. Cf. *pale wa'a.*

pale hou. n. Sweatband, in a hat; protection from perspiration.

pā.lehu. n. Ash tray (preceded by *ke).*

pale.hui. n. Brace or bar, in punctuation. *Lit.,* joining border.

pale huila. n. Fender, as of a car. *Lit.,* wheel guard.

pale.'ili. n. Undershirt. *Lit.,* skin protector. Cf. *palema'i.*

pale.'ili o lalo. n. Underdrawers. (Kel. 105.)

pale.'ili o luna. n. Undershirt. (Kel. 105.)

paleka, bareka. n. Carbuncle. (Puk. 28.17.) (Heb. *barakath.)*

pale ka'a. n. Car bumper.

pale kai. n. Breakwater; any wall or embankment that protects the land from the sea, levee; taffrail of a vessel; railing of a vessel. *Lit.,* sea guard.

pale.kaiko, paredaiso. n. Paradise. (Probably Gr. *paradeisos.)*

pale.kalapa, paregarapa. n. Paragraph. *Eng.* Also *paukū.*

pale kalu.kalu. See *kalukalu.*

pale.kama, balesama. n. Balsam. (Ezek. 27.17.) *Eng.*

pale.kana. nvs. Safe, saved, rescued; convalescent; to ward off, brush aside, rescue, protect; to recover from illness; defense, savior, safety, security. *E ho'oikaika mai 'oe ia'u ā laila palekana wau* (Hal. 119.117), strengthen me, then I am saved. (*Pale 1* + *-kana,* nominalizer: Gram. 6.6.2.) **ho'o.pale.kana.** To save, rescue.

pale kaua. n. War defense, shield (Kin. 15.1), defensive armor.

pale kau.oha. v. To break or ignore a law.

pale ke'ehi. n. Stirrup shield.

pale keiki. nv. To deliver a child; midwife (Kin. 38.28). *Kauka pale keiki,* obstetrician.

paleki. n. Brake. *Eng.*

pale.kikena, paresidena. Var. of *pelekikena,* president. *Eng.*

pale kiko. n. Repeat mark in music.

pale kila. n. Armor. *Lit.,* steel shield.

pale kō.hina. n. Boundary left by cutting; division between taro patches.

pale.koki. n. Petticoat, skirt. *Eng.* Cf. *pūheheo.*

pale kō.kō. n. In music, vertical row of dots which forms a repeat mark. *Lit.,* prolonging bar.

pale kolo. n. Horse or ox next to wagon tongue.

pale.kona, falekona. n. Falcon. (Oihk. 11.14.)

palela. 1. vs. Lazy, indolent, slow-moving; to saunter along as though bored. (Puk. 5.17.) **ho'o.palela.** To cause laziness; same as above. 2. Var. of *palala,* barrel. *Palela li'ili'i,* small barrel, keg.

pale lā. n. Awning. *Lit.,* sun protection.

pale lau.ī. n. Ti-leaf covering; said also to be a prayer asking for release from a taboo that prevents one from leaving a taboo spot.

pale.lē. To deliver, as of *palalē 1, 2.*

pale.lei. n. Head covering of tapa wrapped over the head with the ends hanging down in front. *Rare.*

pale lima. n. A shield, worn on the arm; armguard.

pale lio. n. Saddle blanket. *Lit.,* horse guard.

pale.lona, farelona. n. Furlong, in surveying. *Eng.*

pale lua. n. Double bar in musical notation.

pale lua 'ele.'ele. n. Heavy black bar in musical notation.

pale.ma'i. n. Underdrawers; sometimes used for undershirt (Kel. 45). *Lit.,* genital protection.

pale.ma'i o lalo. n. Underdrawers.

pale.ma'i o luna. n. Undershirt.

pale maka. n. Veil that conceals the face, especially as worn by Arab women.

pale makani. n. Windshield.

palemo. 1. vi. To sink, be sunk, slip away, vanish; drowned. *Hoku palemo,* the full moon *(hoku)* that vanishes at sunup. **ho'o.palemo.** To drown, plunge into water, sink. (PPN *m(a,e)lemo,* PCP *palemo).* 2. vs. Promiscuous. *He nohona palemo,* a promiscuous way of living. *He kāne palemo,* a temporary male lover. 3. n. Young of *uhu,* a fish.

pale moe. n. Bed sheet.

pale mua. n. 1. Fore part of a canoe. 2. Bearers of the fore part of a canoe. Cf. *pale wa'a.*

palena. n. 1. Boundary, limit, border, margin, juncture, separation, partitioning; terms of a fraction. Cf. *kaupalena. 'O ka ho'ohelu a me ka mahele pū, ua kapa 'ia lāua 'elua, 'o nā palena o ka hakina,* the numerator and denominator together, are called the terms of the fraction. **ho'o.palena.** Caus/sim.; to confine. 2. Also **ba.rena.** Var. of *pelena,* crackers.

palena 'āina. n. Land boundary.

palena 'ole. vs. Boundless, without limit, vast. *He palena 'ole ka 'ike,* unsurpassed knowledge.

pale noho. n. Seat cover.

pale nui 'ele.'ele. n. Heavy black bar in musical notation.

pā.leo. nvi. To converse, chat; to talk loudly; chatting.

Cf. *pā 4* for *pā i ka leo. 'O ko'u makemake iā'oe, 'o ka pāleo iki aku* (song), my desire with you, is to chat a little.

pā.leo.leo. Redup. of *pāleo.*

pā.leo.leo.ā. nvi. To talk loudly and unpleasantly; a din; loud reviling talk. (Gram. 6.5.)

pale.'ō.pua. vt. To pardon offenses, as by a priest's offering, in pagan times only. *Rare. Lit.,* ward off billowy clouds.

pale pā.kau.kau. n. Table cloth.

pale pā.kau.kau 'aila. n. Oilcloth.

pale.pale. 1. Redup. of *pale 1-3;* to parry, as in boxing. *Palepale ke kapa o ka wahine hele ua o Ko'olau* (For. 6:476), protecting the tapa of the woman going into the Ko'olau rain. (PNP *palepale.*) **2.** Same as *pale 4.*

pale pā.pale. n. Hat lining.

pā.lepe.lepe. n. Young cactus leaf.

pale.piwa. n. All species of eucalyptus trees. *Lit.,* prevent fever, so called because the leaves were used as fever medicine, and in the *pūlo'ulo'u* steam bath. Also *'eukalikia, nuhōlani. 'Aila palepiwa,* eucalyptus oil.

pā lepo. n. **1.** Adobe wall. **2.** Clay dish, soiled dish.

pale po'o.hiwi. n. Shoulder pads or protection.

pale puka.ani.ani. n. Window curtain, drapes.

pale uhi. n. Veil, covering.

pā.leu.leu. vs. Old, worn-out, as tapa, mats, or clothing. Cf. *'āleuleu.*

pale uluna. n. Pillowcase. *Lit.,* pillow guard.

pale uma.uma. n. Breastplate, as in armor. (Isa. 59.17.) *Lit.,* chest shield.

pale uma.uma unahi. n. Brigandine (Ier. 46.4), coat of mail. *Lit.,* scales chest shield.

pale 'umeke. n. Dish towel. *Lit.,* bowl protection, so called because dish towels were tied about poi bowls to prevent dust or insects from falling in.

pā.lewa. n. Low wooden bowl.

pale wa'a. n. Persons who protect *(pale)* a log canoe being carried from the forest to the sea. Those in front were *pale mua,* those aft were *pale hope.*

pale wai. n. Breakwater.

pale wai.ū. n. Brassiere. *Lit.,* breast guard.

pale.wā.wae. n. **1.** The joy weed *(Alternanthera amoena),* a small herb from Brazil, used as a low border for paths and flower beds. It has red, branching stems and variegated red, green, and yellow, small oval leaves. (Neal 334.) **2.** Small, fan-shaped brown seaweeds (two species of *Padina* [*P. commersonii,* light-brown, and *P. vickersiae,* larger, darker-brown]), common on the reef, each fan more or less split and curled. Not eaten.

pale wā.wae. n. Foot covering or protection; house slipper or sandals (also *kāma'a pale wāwae*); leather part of stirrups covering the rider's feet. *He pale wāwae ko'u 'ili nona* (For. 5:547), my skin is [something] for her feet to walk upon.

pali. nvs, nvi. Cliff, precipice, steep hill or slope suitable for *olonā* or *wauke;* full of cliffs; to be a cliff. *Fig.,* an obstacle, difficulty; haughty or disdainful. See ex., *pu'upu'u 1* and saying, *ha'akoa'e. E pali paha wau?* Shall I become [magically] a cliff? *He pali lele koa'e* (poetic), a cliff where tropic birds fly [i.e., very high]. *Pali kaulu 'ole ka lani,* the cliff without a jog [of very high rank]. *Pali ke kua, mahina ke alo,* the back is a cliff, the front a moon [said of handsome persons]. *Pali mai nā maka o ka hoa* (song), the companion's eyes are a haughty cliff. (PCP *pali,* possibly PEP.)

pā.lia.lia. Var. of *ālialia.*

pā lihi. vi. To touch lightly, graze.

pā li'i.li'i. n. Small dish; saucer (preceded by *ke*).

palika. 1. Also **barika.** n. Carbuncle. (Heb. *barakath.*) **2.** *(Cap.)* Also **Parisa.** nvs. Paris; Parisian. *Eng.*

pali kā.moe. n. Low hillock, terrace.

pali.nau. n. A sweet potato.

Pali.kū. n. **1.** Initial point of a genealogy line. (Malo 2.) **2.** Priests of Lono (Malo 159); ancient order of priests (AP.)

pali kū. n. Vertical cliff.

pali ku'i. n. Notched, toothed cliff; joined succession of cliffs.

palila. n. An endangered gray, yellow, and white Hawaiian honey creeper *(Psittirostra bailleui, P. kona);* endemic to the island of Hawai'i. Its bill is especially suited for opening *māmane* tree pods. Its only home is on Mauna Kea, Hawai'i. See ex., *olokē, pi'oloke.*

palile. Same as *lile. Rare.*

pā.lī.lea. vs. Inactive, sluggish.

palili. n. Small weak taro shoot (preceded by *ke*). *He make nō ke kalo, ā ola nō i ke palili* (saying), the old taro stalk is dead, but survives in the shoots [the ancestors are dead, but survive in their offspring].

Pali-loa. n. Rain name.

pali loa. nvs. Distant or tall cliff. *Fig.,* distant, aloof, disdainful; aristocratic, regal.

palima. nvt. Primer; to study a primer. *Eng.*

pā.lima. 1. vt. Five times, in fives, fivefold; to divide in fives or distribute in fives. *Hānau pālima,* quintuplet birth. **ho'o.pā.lima.** To divide in fives; same as above. **2.** n. Temporary booth occupied by priests during taboo days of a heiau.

pā.lina. Rare var. of *papālina.* Cf. *puhi pālina.*

pali.pa'a. n. Cliff.

pali.pa'a maoli. n. Base of a cliff. *(Thrum's Annual, 1925, p. 68.)*

pali.pali. vs. Precipitous, full of cliffs and steep hills. **ho'o.pali.pali.** Caus/sim. *E 'eku i ka moku e kupu ā pu'u, e ho'opalipali ana ke kua, ho'opalipali ke alo* (KL lines 488–9), root up the land that it may grow high, build cliffs in back, build cliffs in front. (PCP *palipali.*)

Pali-uli. n. A legendary land of plenty and joy, said to be on Hawai'i, where chiefs' children were raised; now a place name on several islands. *Lit.,* green cliff. See chant, *pulelo* and saying, *glory. Hanohano Pali-uli i ka ua noe,* majestic is Pali-uli in the misty rain [said in admiration of a person].

palo. n. **1.** Revelation, as from the gods. *Rare.* See For. 6:4. **2.** Parlor. *Eng.*

palō, ho'o.palō. vi. **1.** To feign ignorance. **2.** To act the goody-goody.

pā.loa. 1. Same as *pāku'ipai;* long seine, as used for mullet. (PCP *paaloa.*) **2.** n. A fish (no data).

pā loa. n. Long fence or enclosure, long wing fence to guide cattle to corral.

pā.loka, balota. n. Ballot, poll, vote. *Eng. Koho pāloka,* to vote. *Po'e koho paloka,* voters. *Ka pāloka a Kū,* the ballot cast by Kū. *Ka pāloka o Kū,* the vote for Kū. *Hā'awi i ka pāloka,* to cast a ballot.

paloke. vs. Broken.

pā.loke. Same as *pālokeloke.*

pā.loke.loke. vs. Loose-fitting, as a peg or key; not solid, wobbly, as a table.

palola, parola. n. Parole. *Eng.*

pā.lola. vs. Helpless, blundering, awkward. *Rare.*

pā.lola.lola. Redup. of *pālola,* helpless.

palolo. vs. Glib-tongued, garrulous; gossiping, as maliciously. *Palolo lua,* very gossipy, glib. **ho'o.palolo.** To cause garrulousness; same as above.

palolo hua. vs. Glib in speech, garrulous.

pālo.lolo. Redup. of *pālolo;* claylike, sticky.

pā.lolo. n. Clay; hard, sticky mud; mortar (Puk. 1.14).

palo.meka, barometa. n. Barometer. *Eng.*

pā.lona, barona. n. Baron. *Eng.*

pā.lo'o. Rare var. of *pāmalo'o.*

palu. 1. vt. To lick, lap. (Nah. 22.4.) **ho'o.palu.** To cause to lick, to lick. (Perhaps PPN *palu.*) **2.** n. A relish made of head or stomach of fish, with *kukui* relish, garlic, chili peppers; fish bait made of fish head or stomach, also used for chumming. See *ku'i palu* and ex., *'u'u. Kā palu,* a bailer with *palu* bait in it [said deprecatingly of ordinary food]. *Ahu ka 'ala'ala palu,* a heap of octopus liver bait [not worth anything at all]. (PPN *palu.*) **3.** Same as *palupalu.*

palū. n. Flu, influenza. *Eng.*
pā.lua. vt. Two by two, double, twofold, dual, twice; to distribute two at a time. *Kino pālua,* one with a dual character or body. *Makani pālua,* wind blowing in various directions. *Hui pālua,* coupled, joined. *Pālua hou a'e ka nui o kēia mamua o kēlā,* this is twice as big again as that. **ho'o.pā.lua.** To divide in two parts; double; pair.
palu.'ai. n. Vegetable food. *Kaua'i.*
palu.hē. nvs. Reduced to pulp, as *palu;* cooked to a pulp; cooked to the point of falling apart, as meat. *Paluhē ka palu,* the bait is pulverized; *fig.,* a meek, humble or abused person. **ho'o.palu.hē.** To make soft, pulpy; to reduce to pulp, cook until soft.
palu.he'e. Var. of *paluhē.* **ho'o.palu.he'e.** Var. of *ho'opaluhē.*
paluhi. Same as *luhi. Rare.*
palu.hia. Pas/imp. of *palu 1. Pau ka hale i ka paluhia e ke ahi,* the house was consumed by being licked up by fire.
pā.luka.luka. 1. nvi. Looseness of the bowels, with slimy, greenish stools; to have such. 2. n. Redlip parrot fish *(Scarus rubroviolaceus).*
pā.luku. vt. To beat, pommel, hit hard, thrash, pound, destroy. Cf. *pōluku.* **ho'o.pā.luku.** Caus/sim.
pā.luku.luku. Redup. of *pāluku.*
palula. n. Cooked sweet-potato leaves.
pā.lū.lā. vs. Tranquil, serene, calm.
palu lā.'ī. nv. Ti-leaf relish, a term of derision for the people of Hawai'i, because at a feast for Ka-meha-meha I on O'ahu there was not enough food, and the late-comers were said to have had to lick the ti-leaf food wrappings.
palule. n. Commoner. *Rare.*
pā.lule. n. Shirt. See ex., *'oni'oni'o. Eng.,* blouse.
pā.lulu. nvt. Screen, shield; shade, window blind, protection of any kind from the elements, as a windbreak, windshield, sun visor, curtain; to screen, shield. *Lit.,* sheltering wall. (PCP *paalulu.*)
pālulu 'ao.'ao. n. Curtain; as about a shower. *Lit.,* side screen.
pā.lulu kukui. n. Lamp shade.
pā.lulu maka. n. Eye shade.
pā.lulu makani. n. Windbreak.
pā.lulu puka.ani.ani. n. Window screen, shade.
pā.luna, baluna. n. Balloon. *Eng.*
palunu 1. n. A creeping plant (no data). 2. nvi. A dull thud; to thud. *Rare.*
palu.palu. vs. Weak, soft, limber, flexible, supple, fragile, flimsy, feeble, frail, tender. *Na'au palupalu,* softhearted. *Maka palupalu,* tender-eyed (as pretty girls). *'Ōlelo palupalu,* soft-spoken, gentle in speech, easy to understand. *Ka 'ao'ao palupalu* (Kel. 85), the weaker sex. **ho'o.palu.palu.** To soften, weaken, mollify, make pliant or flexible; to feign softness. (PCP *palupalu.*)
palū.palū. n. A kind of yellow tapa.
pāma. n. 1. Palm (Puk. 15.27); date palm *(Phoenix dactylifera)* . (Neal 125–7.) *Eng.* See *hua pāma.* 2. Also **bama.** Balm. *Eng.* 3. Sperm. *Eng. Pāma 'aila,* sperm oil.
pā mae. n. Pearl-shell lure with variegated colors, as of red, white, blue. *Lit.,* fading pearl-shell lure.
Pā.mā.'ele. n. Name of a star said to appear on the night of Hoku in the month of Welehu.
pā.ma'i. vs. Susceptible to sickness, sickly, proneness to catching every possible contagious disease; qualmish. *Lit.,* touching sickness.
pā.makani. n. 1. Same as *koki'o ke'oke'o,* a native hibiscus *(Hibiscus arnottianus).* (Neal 561.) 2. A native violet *(Viola chamissoniana),* a shrub 92 to 150 cm high, bearing pale-purple flowers.
pā makani. vi. To blow, of the wind; wind-blown.
pā.makani haole. n. The white thoroughwort *(Eupatorium adenophorum),* from Mexico, a branching herb, much like *maile hohono,* bearing many small white flower heads, which produce tiny, hair-tipped fruits. It

is a serious pest, first becoming common on Maui. (Neal 831.)
pā.makani mā.hū. n. A native shrub *(Phyllanthus sandwicensis),* 30 to 92 cm high, with small, alternate, narrow or ovate leaves, small flowers and fruits; a member of the euphorbia family.
pā.make. vs. Fatal, of disease; to be near death. *Lit.,* touch of death. Cf. *pāola.*
pā.malō. 1. vs. Dry, rainless. 2. vi. To thunder without rain. 3. vs. Expressionless, without animation or facial expression; dull, as a party.
pā.malo'o. Var. of *pāmalō 1–3.*
pā.moho. n. A creeping fern *(Asplenium unilaterale),* found in tropical Polynesia, Asia, and Africa, 35 to 105 cm high, the fronds about 5 or more cm wide, pinnate, with 15 to 30 pairs of oblong, blunt pinnae, their upper edges more or less indented.
pamo.moa. n. A fish (no data).
pana. 1. nvt. To shoot, as marbles, arrows, bow; bow and arrows; to snap, as with fingers and thumb to punish a child; to flip. Cf. *pana 'iole. Pua pana,* arrow. *Kāu mau pana* (Kin. 27.3), thy weapons. **ho'o.pana.** Caus/sim. (PPN *fana,* PEP *pana;* the meaning 'bow, arrow' is noted only in Marquesan *pana* and Hawaiian; see Green, p. 24.) 2. nvi. Heartbeat, pulse; beat in music; to beat time, pulsate, throb. *Nānā i ka pana,* to take the pulse. (PCP *pana.*) 3. nvi. Celebrated, noted, or legendary place; to be such. 4. n. Pan. *Eng. Kū pana,* stew pan. 5. n. Bung.
pāna, bana. n. Band, orchestra. *Eng.*
pā.na'au. Short for *pa'ana'au.* (For. 5:551.)
pā.na'e. vs. Short, broad, as a leaf. *Rare.*
Pana-'ewa. n. Place name in the Hilo District, famous in legend and song (see *huluhulu 4, mūkīkī*); place names also on other islands.
pā.nai. Same as *pānānai,* flat.
pā.na'i. 1. nvt. Revenge, vengeance, reciprocity, substitute, reward; to revenge, pay back, reward, reciprocate, whether good or bad; to replace, substitute (probably *pana 1* + *-'i,* transitivizer: Gram. 6.6.4). Cf. *Ku'ikahi Pāna'i Like, uku pāna'i. Po'e pāna'i* (Oihn. 25.24), hostages. *Ho'ōla pāna'i,* ransom, redeemer (Isa. 41.14). *Pāna'i like,* equal give-and-take, reciprocity; mutual; to pay back equally. *'O wau nō ka pāna'i nona* (Kin. 43.9), I will be surety for him. *'A 'ohe lokomaika'i i nele i ka pāna'i,* no kind heart lacks a reward. **ho'o.pā.na'i.** 1. To seek revenge, reward, etc. 2. vt. To fit one on to another, splice, graft, lengthen.
pana i'a. nv. Fishing spear shot by a how; to shoot fish thus.
pana.iki. Diagonal. (And.)
pā.nai.nai. Var. of *pānānai.* (For. 5:385.)
pā.nai'i.na'i. Redup. of *pāna'i 1, 2.*
pana 'iole. nv. To shoot rats or mice with bow and arrow, an ancient sport; bow and arrow. (Malo 233.) *I ki'i mai nei au i kekahi mau kīko'o pana 'iole a kāua* (FS 59), I have come to fetch some rat-shooting arrows and a bow for us.
pana kai. 1. v. To flip, as salt water with finger or fingers during a purification ceremony. 2. vs. To heel over, as a vessel. *Rare.*
pana.kalupa. vs. Bankrupt. *Eng.*
pana.kō, banako. n. Bank. *Eng.* See ex., *komo.*
pana.lā.'au. n. Colony, dependency, territory, province (Ezera 4.15); colonist. In early times Hāna, Maui, was a *panalā'au* (dependency) of Hawai'i. *Hui panalā'au,* society of colonizers. *Panalā'au o Hawai'i,* Territory of Hawai'i [name used in 1900]. *Nānā 'o Ka-mehameha i kona aupuni, ā e 'ai i kona panalā'au,* Ka-mehameha attended to his kingdom and ruled his dependency.
pana.le'a. vs. Dexterous, gleeful, quick, as in danger. *Rare.*
pana.nā. nvs. Weak, tottering; such a person.
pā.nā.nā. 1. nvi. Compass; pilot; to row here and there irregularly. Cf. *pahu pānānā. Aia i hea? Aia i ka 'au-*

wa'a i pānānā. Where [is he]? With a fleet of straying canoes [anywhere, a way of avoiding the question]. **2.** n. Possibly a local name of the Jacobean lily *(Sprekelia formosissima),* a kind of amaryllis from Central America, cultivated in Hawai'i since about 1850. The flowers are red, 8 to 10 cm long, irregularly funnel-shaped, usually single on a long stem. The plant is named for a chiefess, the wife of Samuel Parker, owner of the Parker Ranch. (Neal 223.)

pā.nā.nai. vs. Flat, shallow, as a dish; slim of physique. Also *pālānai*

pā.nana.iki. Same as *pālanaiki.*

pana.pana. Redup. of *pana 1, 2;* to strike gently, as the butt of a coconut midrib used as a pole for catching crab. Cf. *panapana nī'au.* (PPN *fanafana,* PCP *panapana.)*

pana.pana nī.'au. v. To shoot a coconut leaf midrib (the leaf was bent like a bow and released so that it sprang away).

pana.pana.puhi. A kind of shellfish. (AP.)

pana.panau. Redup. of *panau.* **ho'o.pana.panau.** Redup. of *ho'opanau.*

pana po'o. v. To tap or snap the head (it was rude or provocative to tap another's head, as the head was sacred).

pana pua. nv. To shoot with bow and arrow; archer, archery.

pāna puhi 'ohe. n. Band (wind instruments).

panau. nvi. To move up and down as a seesaw; to flip along, as a lobster; restless, uneasy, always on the move; to gad about; pulsating motion of male organ; a vulgar or contemptuous gesture signifying the latter, made with the fist of one hand, while the other hand grasps the elbow joint, jerking the forearm and clenched fist upwards. *Panau ka 'ōpae,* the shrimp moves with a flip [of a gadabout]. **ho'o.panau.** To cause to seesaw, wander, etc.; to make the vulgar gesture. (PCP *panau.)*

pā.nau.ea. vs. Thin, weak, feeble, slow. Cf. *hāpauea.*

pā.nau.nau. **1.** Redup. of *panau. Rare.* **ho'o.pā.nau.-nau.** Redup. of *ho'opanau.* **2.** n. A native plant *(Lobelia yuccoides),* 1.2 to 1.8 m high, with a slender, unbranched trunk tipped with a crown of narrow, white-backed leaves about 30 cm long, from which rises a flower spike 0.6 to 1 m long crowded with 200 to 400 narrow blue flowers.

pane. **1.** nvt. Answer, reply, response; to answer, speak. *Pane 'ole,* not answering, unresponsive. *Ā hua ā pane,* it has been spoken, now answer (said after a riddle is told). **ho'o.pane.** Caus/sim. **2.** n. Hind part of the head; top or summit, as of a mountain (preceded by *ke).* (PCP *pane.)* **3.** vt. To pull. *Kaua'i.*

panea. Pas/imp. of *pane 1.*

pane'e. **1.** vi. To move along, bring, push along a little; pushed forward. *Pane'e i mua,* to progress. *Ua pane'e maila kekahi mau mea 'ai,* some food was served. **ho'o.pane'e.** Caus/sim. **2.** nvi. Delayed, postponed; delay, postponement; to do in installments, as to serialize a novel in a newspaper. *Uku pane'e,* interest on money. *He 44 hola ka pane'e 'ana mai,* a delay of 44 hours. **ho'o.pane'e.** To postpone, delay, put off, defer (Kin. 34.19), procrastinate. **3.** vs. Old, worn-out. *Kaua'i. Rare.*

pane'e.hā. vt. To drag, haul. *Rare.*

pā.ne'e.ne'e. Redup. of *pane'e;* to move on little by little, slowly. **ho'o.pane'e.ne'e.** Redup. of *ho'opane'e;* to keep putting off, etc.

pane'e.'ū.piki. n. Clamp feed, of sewing machine.

pane.hū. vs. Quick. *Rare.*

paneka, paneta. n. Panther. *Eng.*

pane.kai. vi. To move in, of the tide. *Ua panekai 'ole ia pō ā hiki aku i ke kakahiaka* (Kep. 101), that night the tide did not move in until morning.

pane.kalupa, banekarupa. vs. Bankrupt. *Eng.*

pane.kana. Var. of *palekana.*

pā.neki, panesi. n. Pansy *(Viola tricolor* var. *hortensis).* (Neal 592.) *Eng.* Also *po'okanaka.*

---

panena. n. Answer. *Ua pau ka panena a ka leo,* the answering by voice is over.

pane.pane. vt. To retort, talk back. **ho'o.pane.pane.** To cause controversy by arguing; same as above.

pane.po'o. n. Pinnacle, summit; topmost, most important (preceded by *ke).* Lit., hind part [of] head.

pā.newa.newa. nvt. Mourning, grief; to mourn. *Nā lā pānewanewa o ke ali'i,* the days of mourning for the chief.

pani. **1.** nvt. To close, shut, block (For. 5:460–1), dam (For. 5:509), dike, substitute, replace, represent, fill a breach or vacancy; closure, stopper, valve, cork, plug, lid, cover, gate, blockade, door, agreement (GP 14), substitute, vice- (sometimes preceded by *ke).* Cf. *pani hakahaka. Pani 'ino,* to slam or close forcefully. **ho'o.pani.** To cause a closing, pretend to close. (PCP *pani.)* **2.** n. Final bit of food closing a period of treatment by a medical practitioner, commonly but not always sea food; final gift in a *ho'okupu* ceremony. Cf. *aeāea, 'akilolo 1.* **3.** n. Odd-shaped pandanus key that fits like a keystone at the bottom of a pandanus cluster; when this is knocked out, the others fall easily. **4.** n. The bottom of a coconut when cracked off by blows around the base of the nut; it fits like a lid *(pani).* **5.** n. Disease with severe pain at the solar plexus and choking. **6.** n. Pan. *Eng. Rare.*

pania. Pas/imp. of *pani 1. Pania mai ka waimaka* (Laie 523), the tears are stopped.

pani.ana, baniana. n. Banyan *(Ficus* spp.) *Eng.*

pāni.ani, paaniani. **1.** n. Spanner, an instrument for making rope of hair or yarn; spun yarn. *Rare.* **2.** vs. Clear. *Rare.*

pānie. v. To lessen. *Kaua'i.*

pani haka. Same as *pani hakahaka. Lit.,* closing breach.

pani haka.haka. nv. To substitute, fill a vacancy, replace; substitute, replacement, successor, deputy, proxy. *'O wau nō anei ka pani hakahaka no ke Akua* (Kin. 30.2)? Am I in the place of God? *'O Kū kona pani hakahaka,* Kū is his replacement. *Ua pani hakahaka 'ia,* [he] is replaced. *Pani hakahaka kūikawā,* alternant, temporary replacement.

pā nihi. Var. of *pā lihi.*

pā.niho.loa. n. One of the wrasses *(Thalassoma trilobata),* 45 cm long, red body with green rectangular spots. *Lit.,* long-toothed shell.

pani.inoa. n. Pronoun. *Lit.,* name substitute.

pani.inoa huli 'aui.kumu. n. Reflexive pronoun (a concept not used in present-day Hawaiian grammars). *Lit.,* pronoun reverting to the subject case.

pani.inoa kā.lele mana'o. n. Emphatic pronoun (a rarely used concept). *Lit.,* pronoun that supports thought.

pani.inoa kuhi.kuhi. n. Demonstrative pronoun. *Lit.,* directing pronoun.

pani.inoa kuhi lau.lā. n. Indefinite pronoun (a rarely used concept). *Lit.,* pronoun pointing widely.

pani.inoa nina.ninau. n. Interrogative pronoun.

pani.inoa pelu hope. n. Reflexive pronoun. *Lit.,* pronoun folded back.

pani.inoa pili.kino. n. Personal pronoun.

pani kai. n. Levee, dike, sea wall or any protection against the sea.

paniki. Coloring matter, as for tapa. (And.)

pā.niki. nvt. **1.** To press or pinch the hand or arm, as to attract attention; punch as for paper. *Eng.* **2.** To punish; punishment. *Eng.*

pani.kū. vt. **1.** To slam shut, as a door, to close abruptly, as in slamming a door in one's face; to foreclose, as a mortgage. **2.** To pound, break. *Rare.*

panina. **1.** nvs. End, closing, closure, very last, conclusion, finish, cessation, breaking off or cutting short; definitive, classic. **2.** n. Plump cheeks. *Rare.* Cf. *papālina.*

pā.nini. n. **1.** The prickly pear *(Opuntia megacantha),* a Mexican branching cactus about 4.5 m high, with a cylindrical trunk, and green, succulent, flattened, oblong to ovate joints, from which protrude many spines about 2.5 cm long. Flowers are yellow or orange, large; the fruit is ovoid, about 8 cm long, yellow or purple, spiny. This cactus is a weed in Hawai'i; the fruits are eaten or made into liquor. *Lit.,* fence wall. (Neal 607–8.) In some localities called *pāpipi.* **2.** A variety of sweet potato.

pā.nini 'awa.'awa. n. The true aloe *(Aloe vera* syn. *A. barbadensis),* a rosette-shaped plant from Africa and the Mediterranean region, with narrow, thick, pale-green leaves, 30 cm long or longer, with prickly edges. The leaves yield a medicine used to treat some kinds of blisters or burns. (Neal 196–7.) Also *'aloe.*

panini.kū. n. The name of a seaweed.

pani.ni'o. Same as *nini'o,* spotted. **ho'o.pani.ni'o.** Same as *ho'onini'o.*

pā.nini-o-Ka-puna-hou. n. The night-blooming cereus *(Hylocereus undatus),* a Mexican cactus with succulent, green, jointed, three-winged stems that climb on trees and walls. About 1830 it was brought to Hawai'i, where during summer and fall it bears large numbers of large white flowers which open in the evening and last only until the next morning. (Neal 609–11.) A famous hedge is at Puna-hou School (formerly called Ka-puna-hou). *Lit.,* Ka-puna-hou cactus. Also *pāpipi pua.*

pani'o. vs. Smooth.

pā.ni'o. Same as *ni'o.* **ho'o.pā.ni'o.** Same as *ho'oni'o,* streaked.

pani.ola. Late var. of *paniolo,* cowboy.

pani.'ole. n. **1.** A variety of sweet potato. **2.** A variety of taro.

pani.olo. nvs. **1.** Cowboy (sometimes called *paniolo pipi* to distinguish from *paniolo 2.* **ho'o.pani.olo.** To be like a cowboy or pretend to be a cowboy. **2.** *(Cap.)* Spaniard, Spain; Spanish. (Spanish, *español.*)

pani 'ō.mole. n. Bottle stopper, cork.

pā.ni'o.ni'o. Redup. of *pāni'o.*

pani.pani. **1.** Redup. of *pani,* to close. **2.** nvt. Coition, or to practice such (vulgar). **3.** n. Small outrigger canoe. *Rare.*

pani.pipi. n. Cat's-eye. *Lit.,* shell closure.

pani.po'o. Var. of *panepo'o.*

pani.pū. n. Plug or wad of a gun. *Rare.*

pani puka. n. Door, gate; cover of an opening; beggar sitting near a doorway.

pani pū.pū. n. A cat's-eye, operculum, valve or round substance that closes a shell. *Lit.,* shell closure.

pani wai. n. Dam, sluice, levee, dike.

pano. nvs. Dark, as clouds; obscure, black, shiny-black, deep blue-black. *Fig.,* unapproachable as the unknown, said of very high chiefs believed to be of divine descent. Cf. *pano pa'u. He pano ke ali'i, he weo ke kanaka* (saying), the chief is obscure, the commoner is scarlet [in the sunlight, obvious]. **ho'o.pano.** To cause darkness; to make mysterious, unknown, unfathomable; same as above. (PCP *pango.*)

panoa. vs. Barren, arid, desert, dry, hot, parched. Also *'anoa. Ko'a panoa* (For. 6:501), dry coral bank, as at low tide. *Panoa e like me ka wao akua* (Zep. 2.13) a dry waste like the wilderness. **ho'o.panoa.** Caus/sim.; to cause barrenness.

pā.noa. **1.** vs. Easily taken, of a woman at the beck and call of any man. *Lit.,* touch freely. **2.** n. Lightweight wood. *Rare.*

panoa.noa. Full of holes, cracked. (And.)

pā.noa.noa. **1.** Redup. of *panoa.* **2.** vs. Scarce, very rare. *Pānoanoa ka mā'alo'alo 'ana a ka i'a,* fish rarely passed there.

pāno.ea. Same as *pānauea. Rare.*

pano.hi'i.aka. n. A bird (no data).

pā.noho.noho. n. **1.** The young of the *nenue,* a fish. **2.** A seaweed.

pano.nono. vs. Full of holes, cracks; cracked. *Rare.*

pā.no'o. Same as *pao'o,* fish. (PCP *panoko.*)

pā.no'o.no'o. **1.** Same as *ho'omana'o.* **2.** Same as *pānoanoa.* **3.** n. A seaweed.

pano.pano. Redup. of *pano. Ao panopano,* thick cloud. *'O pano ia, 'o panopano 'o Kāne i ka pō panopano i*

hānau (KL line 386–7), a darkness, a dark darkness, Kāne born in the deep dark night. **ho'o.pano.pano.** Redup. of *ho'opano. 'Ele'ele Hilo ē, ho'opanopano i ka ua,* Hilo is black, darkened in the rain. (PCP *pango-pango.*)

pano pa'u. vs. Glossy, glistening black, sooty-black; black streaks in grain of wood.

pano.pa'ū. vs. Somewhat wet. *Rare.*

pā.no'u.no'u. vs. Short, stumpy, thick.

pā.no'ū.no'ū. vs. Somewhat wet. *Rare.*

pā.nuhu. **1.** Probably same as *pānuhunuhu 1.* **2.** vs. Thrifty, as of plants. *Rare.*

pā.nuhu.nuhu. **1.** n. Stareye parrot fish *(Calotomus sandvicensis),* said to be second growth stage of *uhu.* Also *pōnuhunuhu, pāuhu.* **2.** Same as *pānuhu 2.*

pā.nū.nū. Perhaps the same as *pānuhunuhu,* or a different type of *uhu.*

panunu.kua.hiwi. n. A native member of the gourd family *(Sicyos cucumerinus),* a more or less climbing herb with variable leaves, which range from entire and rounded to many-lobed. The fruit is narrow, about 2.5 cm long, grooved, one-seeded.

pā.nu'u. Same as *pānuhu 1, 2. Rare.*

pao. **1.** vt. To scoop out, dub out, as a log for a canoe, or as of the action of the sea on the coast; to peck, chisel out, gouge, undermine, erode, bore. *Fig.,* blunt, cruel, harsh in speech; to rebuke; digging, scooping, etc. (preceded by *ke*). Cf. *paoke'e, paokoke, paomoni. Pōhaku pao,* stone chisel. *Ua pao 'ia 'o Pua e ka hoahānau,* Pua was rebuked by the cousin. *Pao ka lima, 'ae ka waha,* the hand bores from below, the mouth says yes. (PEP *pa'o.*) **2.** vt. To insert, stick in, as wood into a fire; to stoke, as coal into a furnace. Cf. *imu pao, pao ahi.* **3.** n. Cave, pit, cavern. *Lua pao,* pit cave, as for burial. **4.** n. Arch of a bridge, bridge.

paoa. **1.** nvs. Strongly odoriferous; a strong odor, whether pleasant or unpleasant. *Paoa ke 'ala o ka na'ena'e* (song), the perfume of the *na'ena'e* is strong. *Iwi paoa,* lucky; *lit.,* fragrant bones. [But cf. *paoa 2*]. *'O ka hana ia a ka lawai'a iwi paoa,* that is the way of the lucky fisherman. **2.** nvs. Unlucky, unsuccessful, as in fishing or sex; bad luck. [But cf. *iwi paoa* under *paoa 1.*] *Na wai e 'ole ka paoa, ua kāhea kua 'ia,* who can help having bad luck, when called from behind the back. **3.** vt. To have a taste or desire for (usually used with *waha,* mouth). *Paoa ka waha i ke kanaka,* the mouth loves the taste of man [said of a shark]. **4.** Rare var. of *pawa,* predawn. See ex., *alaula.*

pā.oa. n. The divining rod by which Pele tested the suitability of areas for excavation on the island of Nihoa, at various places on O'ahu (Salt Lake, Punchbowl, Diamond Head, Maka-pu'u), and on Maui. Finally she planted the staff at Pana-'ewa, Hawai'i, and it became a tree. (PH x-xii.)

pao ahi. nv. To stoke a fire; stoker. *Lit.,* fire inserter.

pā.o'i.o'i. vs. Imperfect, as in speech. *Rare.*

pā.'o'i.'o'i. vi. To limp.

paoka, paoda. n. Powder. *Eng.*

pao.ke'e. nvt. To slander, betray, defame; slanderer, traitor.

pao.koke. vt. To betray one's relatives or those close *(koke)* to one.

pā.ola. nvs. Quick recovery from sickness; quick healing; to recover or heal quickly. Cf. *pāmake. Rare.*

pā.'olo. Rare var. of *pū 'olo.*

pao.moni. vt. To contend with, make war on. *Rare.*

paona. n. Pound *(Eng.),* balance, scales, weight. Cf. *kaupaona. Mea 'ono paona,* pound cake. *Ho'onui nā paona,* to gain weight.

paona kau.like. n. Balance, scales. *Lit.,* equally placed poundage.

paona keiki. n. Baby scales.

pā.oni. nvt. Disagreement, argument, contention; to argue, quarrel; envy *(Biblical).* **ho'o.pā.oni.** To cause quarrel, strife; to argue.

pā.oni.oni. Redup. of *pāoni.* **ho'o.pā.oni.oni.** Redup. of *ho'opāoni.*

pā.ono. vt. By sixes, sixfold; to divide by sixes; to have six or distribute to six. **ho'o.pā.ono.** Caus/sim.

pāo'o. n. Name for several varieties of *'o'opu*, especially *Istiblennius zebra, Entomacrodus marmoratus* (marbled blenny); also called rockskippers because of their ability to leap across stretches of rocky shoreline. The name may be qualified by the terms *kauila* (*Exallias brevis*, shortbodied blenny), *luahine, puhi. Pāo'o* figure prominently in legends and for some are *'aumākua.* See ex., *ha'apupū.* Also *pāno'o.* (PEP *paoko.*)

pā.'ō.'ō. n. Broken or discarded portions of sweet potatoes; sprouting bits of these fragments.

pao.pao. Redup. of *pao 1, 2. Ua paopao 'ia 'oia no kō kākou hala,* he was wounded for our transgressions. *Paopao noho ni'a,* blunt or proud speech [caused by] slander. (PEP *pa'opa'o.*)

pa'o.pa'o, ulua pa'o.pa'o. n. A species of *ulua*, a fish *(Caranx speciosus);* green and yellow with vertical green bands; considered one of the best fishes for eating raw.

Pā-'ō.pua. n. Name of a star (no data).

pā.'ou.'ou. n. Name given to young of the *hou*, a fish.

papa. 1. nvs. Flat surface, stratum, plain, reef, layer, level, foundation, story of a building, floor, class, rank, grade, order, table, sheet, plate, shelf *(rare)*, face (of a watch); flat, level; to be a great many. Cf. *ali'i papa, noho papa 1, papa ali'i. Kui papa,* to make overlap on a lei, as feathers. *Helu papa,* to recite in consecutive order. *Ne'e papa,* to move in rank. *Kūkū papa,* to stand in ranks, as an army. **ho'o.papa.** To place in rank or file; to put in order, to put in layers, overlay, as shingles; to make a shelf; to pack neatly. (PPN *papa.*) 2. nvs. Native-born, especially for several generations (see *noho papa 2*); offspring of the mating of an individual of *pi'o, naha,* or *nī'aupi'o* rank, with one of *kaukauali'i* rank; the lowest ranking aristocrat. 3. vs. Set close together, thick together, as of growing plants; in unison, all together. Cf. *holopapa, kāpapa, ne'epapa, papapū. He kāhili papa iki,* a feather standard with small feathers. 4. nvs. Board, lumber; wooden. 5. n. A variety of kava. The name may be qualified by the colors *'ele'ele, kea.* 6. n. Middle portion of a fishing net, bag net. 7. *(Cap.)* n. Wind associated with Honua-'ula, Maui. (For. 5:101.) 8. n. Stone used as sinker for *lūhe'e,* octopus lure. (Malo 19.) 9. n. Wafer. (Puk. 29.2.)

-papa. ho'o.papa. Purification of woman after childbirth, involving medicinal herbs bound to the abdomen, and a taboo on sex relations. (Malo 138.)

papā. vi. To blow, as the wind; to sound, echo; to shine, as sun or moon. Cf. *pā 4. Papā ka leo o ke kai,* the voice of the sea sounds.

pā.pā. 1. vt. To forbid, prohibit, taboo. *Pāpā 'ana,* prohibition. *Waiwai i pāpā 'ia e ke kānāwai,* contraband goods; *lit.,* goods forbidden by the law. *Ua pāpā au iāia, 'a'ole e hele,* I forbid him to go. 2. vt. To touch, as of two objects; contest (same as *ho'opāpā [a]*). **ho'o.pā.pā.** (a) To touch repeatedly; to feel one's way, as a blind person does; a contest in wit (as riddling) or strength; to hold such a contest; repartee, banter; to endeavor to find out something or obtain something by indirect methods, by feeling out the person indirectly; to debate, argue. (b) A style of guitar playing in which one person strums, and the other touches the strings of the same guitar to produce certain effects; to play thus. (PPN *paapaa.*) 3. n. A small, active green-colored crab, perhaps *Percnon planissimum.* 4. n. Papa (introduced by white missionaries, who thought it rude for children to call father by first name). Eng.

pā.pā-. Redup. of *pā-*, preceding numerals. (Gram. 10.3.) *Hūnā pāpākanalima a'e iā lākou i loko o ke ana* (1 Nal. 18.4), hid them by fifties in a cave. *Ua pāpāono lākou i nā 'ēheu* (Hoik. 4.8), each of them had six wings. **ho'o.pā.pā-.** Redup. of *ho'opā-.* Rare.

papa'a. Redup. of *pa'a 1;* tight, secure, especially of a walled stronghold; to hold back. *Hale papa'a,* store-

house. *Nā kūlanakauhale papa'a oo Solomona* (2 Oihn. 8.6), the store cities of Solomon. *E 'ae ho'i 'oe e hā'awi mai i kahi keiki no māua, papa'a mai nei ho'i 'oe,* why not agree to give us two a child, you are just holding back.

pā.pa'a. 1. nvs. Cooked crisp, as pig; overdone, burned, parched; scab, of a sore; crust. Cf. *palaoa pāpa'a, pāpa'a palaoa* and saying, *kūmau 2. 'Ili pāpa'a lā,* sunburned or tanned skin. *'A'ohe nao 'ai i ka pāpa'a,* what a calamity to eat the burned food [a calamity]. **ho'o.pā.pa'a.** To make crisp, brittle; to burn, scorch. *Ho'opāpa'a palaoa,* to toast bread. *Palaoa ho'opāpa'a,* toast. Also *pa'apa'a.* (PEP *paka.*) 2. n. Slice, as of bread; uncut piece. Cf. *pāpa'a hao, pāpa'a lepo, pāpa'a palaoa, pāpa'a pelena.* 3. n. Cluster of tiny red and yellow feathers tied together fanwise, as presented to a chief to be used for featherwork. Also *pa'a'ā.* 4. n. A red sugar cane with light-brown fibers; it has an odor similar to burnt sugar, hence its name. 5. n. Bark, as of trees. 6. Same as *pāki'i 2,* fish. 7. *(Cap.)* n. Wind names. See below.

pā pa'a. 1. n. A sturdy mother-of-pearl; a strong *pā.* 2. vs. Securely closed, fastened. *Pā pa'a ka pu'u* (Nak. 106), the throat is shut tight [of one who can eat no more].

pā.pa'a hao. n. Scrap iron.

pā.pa'a.hekili. Same as *huahekili uka,* a shrub. See *pūailewa.*

pā.pa'a.hū.pē. n. Dried nasal mucus.

papa 'ai.ana. n. Ironing board.

papa 'aina. n. Dining table; eating mat, as laid on the floor; meal, dinner, mess.

pā.pa'a.'ina. nv. To crackle, snap; crackling, snapping; sharp crack, as of something breaking, or of crackling sound of feet walking over a crusty surface; to crack, as joints; brittle, easily broken. Cf. *'u'ina.*

Pā.pa'a Inu Wai. n. A gentle Kaua'i wind with rain that reaches Ni'ihau.

pā.pa'a kai. nvs. Salt-encrusted; salt; coated by sea spray, as plants near the sea.

pā.pa'a kao. n. Slabs of salted and dried goat meat.

pā.pa'a.kea. 1. Same as *pa'akea,* limestone. 2. n. A seaweed *(Liagora valida),* related to *puakī.*

pā.pa'a.koali. A sweet potato.

pā.pa'a.kō.nā.hua. n. Entrails, as of a pig. *Rare.*

pā.pa'a kukui. See *pāpa'a 6.*

pā.pa'a lā. vs. Sunburned, tanned; parched, dried up by the sun.

Pā.pa'a Lā. n. A wind similar to Pāpa'a Inu Wai except that it blows in sunny weather, noted at East Maui.

pā.pā.'ale. nvt. Agreement; to agree. *Ka'ū. Ua pāpā'ale lāua i ka hana,* they agreed on the work.

pā.pa'a lepo. n. Clod of dirt. (Ioba 7.5.)

papa ali'i. n. One of the chiefly class; chiefly class. Cf. *ali'i papa.*

pā.pa'a.nā. Same as *pa'apa'anā 1, 2. E pāpa'anā mai 'oe e kōkua mai ia'u,* haste thee to help me.

pā.pa'a palaoa. n. Slice of bread. Cf. *palaoa pāpa'a.*

pā.pa'a pelena (berena). n. A whole, unbroken cracker; crust of bread; wafer (Oihk. 8.26).

pā.pa'a piele. n. Crusty scalp due to eruption of matter.

papa a po'o. Same as *papa po'o.*

pā.pa'a.pū. vs. Cooked to a crisp, burned; crusty, heavily encrusted.

papa.'aua. Redup. of *pa'aua.*

papa.'au.wae. n. Lower jaw. See ex., *nao-ho'opa'i.*

pā.pa'a wela. nvs. A burn; burned; scorched; hardened, as breadfruit on one side.

Papa E'e Moku. n. Board of Immigration.

papa 'ele.'ele. n. 1. Blackboard. 2. See *papa 1.*

pā.pā.hā. Redup. of *pāhā.*

papa hana. n. 1. Work method, plan, stratagem, policy, program, agenda, project; workbench. *'O ka papa hana kēia i Kua'ua'u,* this is Kua'ua'u's method [that of a famous medical practitioner]. 2. Ceremony for the gods, as in offering kava.

pā.paha.paha. n. An edible seaweed, *Ulva fasciata.* Also *līpahapaha, pahapaha, pālahalaha, pakaiea.* For other variants, see *līpahapaha.*

papa.hā.puʻu. n. A fish, possibly a *hāpuʻu* (no data).

papa heʻe nalu. n. Surfboard. *Lit.,* board [for] sliding waves. *Hāʻawi papa heʻe nalu,* to give with the understanding that the object will be returned [surfboards were loaned rather than given].

papa hehi. n. Footboard, used for dancing; treadle. *Lit.,* board to step on.

papa.hele. n. Floor, deck. *Lit.,* walking board.

papa.hele o luna. n. Upper floor, upstairs.

papa helu. n. Table, list, enumeration, scoreboard, statistics.

pā.pahi. nvt. To decorate, honor, confer honors; adornment, decoration. Cf. *lei pāpahi.*

pā.pā.hiku. Redup. of *pāhiku. Hoʻokomo pāpāhiku ʻo Noa iā lākou* (song), Noah put them in by sevens.

papa hī.meni. n. Choir, choral group.

papa hō.ʻike. n. Program, timetable, index, schedule, sign, bulletin board, sign board.

papa.hola. n. 1. Face of a clock or watch. 2. Level pavement beside a heiau. (Malo 162.) 3. Priests who prohibited noise during taboo. 4. Division of spoils among the victors. *Rare.*

papa hola.hola kā.nā.wai laʻa. n. Universally sacred decree. (Kam. 64:11.)

papa hole. n. Smooth, planed lumber; grooved board for making ribbed tapa.

papa.holo. n. Lattice. (2 Nal. 1.2.)

papa holoi. n. Washboard.

papa hō.lua. n. Sled composed of two narrow runners, 2 to 6 m long, as used for the *hōlua* sport.

papa honua. n. Foundation of the earth.

papa hoʻo.holo. n. Slide plate on a sewing machine.

papa hoʻo.laha. n. Billboard.

papa hoʻo.lewa.lewa. Same as *papa lewalewa.*

Papa Hoʻo.paʻa. n. Board of Education.

Papa Hoʻo.paʻa Inoa. n. Board of Registration. *Lit.,* board to affix names.

papahu. Same as *pahu,* stake; to push. See ex., *kanu.*

papa hulei. n. Seesaw, teeter.

papa huli honua. n. Experts who determined land boundaries.

papa hulu.hulu. n. Rough lumber.

papa hului. 1. n. Pile, as of winnings, objects. Cf. *hului 2.* 2. n. A fishing net. (Malo 210.)

pā.pai. Same as *pōʻou,* fishes.

papaʻi. 1. Redup. of *paʻi 1-5.* hoʻo.papaʻi. Redup. of *hoʻopaʻi;* to move the stomach muscles, as in certain hula dances. (PPN *papaki.*) 2. See *hale papaʻi.*

pā.paʻi. n. 1. General name for crabs. (PPN *papa,* probably PCP *paapaka.*) 2. Small temporary hut or shelter. See below.

papaia. Same as *mīkana,* papaya. *Eng.*

pā.pa.ia. n. An offering or place for offering, as of kava.

pā.paʻi ʻai. n. Cookhouse.

papai.ā.ulu. vi. To blow, rise, as a breeze. *Aia ka papaiāulu makani ke kū maila,* there's the breeze coming up over there.

pā.pai.ʻawa, pā.pāia ʻawa. nvi. Ceremonial offering of kava, especially to free one from the necessity of completing an oath or vow; to perform such a ceremony. (Laie 475.)

pā.paʻi iwi pū.pū. n. Hermit crab. Also *unauna, ʻōunauna. Lit.,* bone shell crab.

pā.paʻi kahu. n. Cookhouse. *Lit.,* baking shed.

pā.paʻi kilu. n. Shed where *kilu,* a game, was played. (For. 6:197.)

pā.paʻi kua lena.lena. n. Yellow-backed crab. *Fig.,* experienced warrior.

pā.paʻi kua loa. n. The crab commonly called "Kona crab" *(Ranina ranina). Lit.,* long-backed crab.

pā.paʻi kū.honu. Same as *kūhonu,* a crab.

papaʻi kukui. Same as *paʻi kukui.*

pā.paʻi Lā.naʻi. n. A kind of crab. (Malo 45.)

pā.paʻi lawaiʻa. n. Fisherman's hut.

papa ʻili.ʻili. n. Arrangement of pebbles in the form of a man used for instruction by a *kahuna hāhā.* (Kam 64:108.)

pā.paʻi limu. n. A species of crab, probably *Simocarcinus simplex. Lit.,* seaweed crab.

pā.paʻi lī.poa. Same as *pāpaʻi limu. Lit., līpoa* (seaweed) crab.

papai.lua. Redup. of *pailua.* hoʻo.papai.lua. Redup. of *hoʻopailua;* beginning to be nauseated, first symptoms of nausea.

pā.paʻi mahi ʻai. n. Temporary hut of a farmer near plantations.

papa inoa. n. List or catalogue of names, register.

papai.ō. n. Sacrifice; propitiatory offering or food offering.

papai.oa. n. Long reef. *Kū ka hālelo, ʻaʻaka ka papaioa* (chant), the jaggedness appears, the coral reef is cracked.

papa.ʻiole. n. Irregularly cut, of hair, said to be named for an irregular haircut given to Pīkoi-a-ka-ʻalalā (a demigod born of a crow father, who sometimes appeared as a rat) by his rat sisters, and short for *paʻipaʻi ʻiole,* rat haircut.

papa ipu. n. Shelf for food containers.

pā.pā.iwa. Redup. of *pāiwa.*

pā.pā.kahi. Redup. of *pākahi. Miki pāpākahi,* to dip up poi with one finger.

papa kahuna. n. Priestly class.

pā.pā kai. vi. Shoved, pounded by the sea.

papa kā.kau. n. Slate, writing board.

pā.pā.kana-. Prefix to numbers from *kolu* (three) to *iwa* (nine); see *pāpā-.*

papa kaua. n. Division of an army; group of men armed with *pololū,* spears, surrounding the king (Malo 204, Emerson note).

papa kau.kau. Same as *pākaukau.*

papa kea. n. 1. White stratum, sand beach. 2. See *papa 5,* a variety of kava.

papā.kea. nvs. White spray, as of sea; to rise in spray; white caps.

papa keʻe.hana. Var. of *papa keʻehina.* (1 Nal. 6.30.)

papa keʻe.hina. n. Floor. *Lit.,* trampled stratum.

papa.kema, bapatema. n. Baptism. *Eng.* Also *papekema. Makua papakema,* godparent. *Keiki papakema,* godchild.

pā.pā.kiʻi. vi. To sit flat, as on the floor. *Rare.*

papa koa. n. 1. Board of wood of *koa,* a tree. 2. Group or band (Oih. 10.1) of soldiers; rank or company of an army.

pā.pā.kole. n. Hip, hipbone, buttocks. (For. 4:293, Dan. 5.6.) *He pili pāpākole,* related to in-laws *(lit.,* back-sided relationship; rude because of implication that one is not a true relative).

papa kō.lea. n. Plover flats.

papā.kolea. vi. To break, of waves. *Rare.*

pā.pā.kole-kā-waʻa. Same as *pāpākole koaʻe.*

pā.pā.kole koaʻe. n. A variety of taro, grown chiefly in Kona, Kaʻū and Puna, Hawaiʻi; plant stocky, petioles red-striped, corm white, used especially for table taro. Cf. *koaʻe 3,* a taro.

pā.pā.kolu. Redup. of *pākolu.*

Papa Komi.kina. n. Board of Commissioners.

papa-kō.nane. n. A mat design.

papa kō.nane. n. Stone on which the checkerlike game *kōnane* was played.

papa.kū. 1. n. Foundation or surface, as of the earth; floor, as of ocean; bed, as of a stream; bottom. *Papakū kia,* slab holding a canoe mast. 2. vs. Upright (this is said in answer to the question *"pehea ʻoe?"* and means "I'm fine"). Cf. *papa moe.* 3. n. A disease with severe constipation (AP) or accompanied by vomiting, back pains, belching, red eyes (*Ka Leo o ka Lahui,* Feb. 7, 1893).

papa kuhi.kuhi. n. Table of contents, index, schedule,

directory, program, timetable. *Lit.*, pointing-out stratum. *Papa kuhikuhi i ka poʻe koho,* instructions to voters.

papa kuhi.kuhi manawa. n. Schedule, as of ship arrivals and departures.

papa kuhi.kuhi mea ʻai. n. Menu, bill of fare.

papa kuʻi. n. Jawbone, lower plate.

papa kuʻi ʻai. n. Poi-pounding board.

papala. Redup. of *pala 1.* (PPN *papala.*)

pā.pala. 1. n. All species of a native genus *(Charpentiera),* shrubs and small trees, belonging to the amaranth family. Formerly on the north coast of Kauaʻi, Hawaiians used the wood, which is light and inflammable, for fireworks, throwing burning pieces from cliffs. (Neal 332.) **2.** n. Firebrand, as hurled from the cliffs in the famous Kauaʻi sport, so called because *pāpala* wood was often used. *Ke ahi pāpala welo i Makua* (chant), the streaming *pāpala* firebrand at Makua. **3.** nvs. Haze, fog; hoarse, as the voice. *Rare.*

papa lā.ʻau. n. Board, plank, any large wooden platter, lumber.

pā.pā lā.ʻau. vt. To fence, to hit repeatedly with sticks.

papa lā.ʻau mā.noa.noa. n. Plank. *Lit.*, wide wooden board.

pā pā.laha.laha. n. Platter (preceded by *ke*). Lit., flat plate.

pā palai. n. Frying pan (preceded by *ke*).

Pā.pala-kā.ʻili-ʻū. n. Name of a *lua* fighting stroke, perhaps from *pāpala kāʻili ʻula,* red snatching firebrand.

pā.pala.kea. n. A variety of taro.

pā.pala kē.pau. n. Three native species of trees in the four-oʻclock family, belonging to the genus *Pisonia.* (Neal 335.) *Lit.*, gum *pāpala;* the gum was used for bird catching. See also *āulu 3.*

pā.pala.lē. Redup. of *palalē 1, 2.*

pā.pala.lī. Redup. of *palalī.*

papa lalo. n. Lower floor of a house, valley bottom, lower stratum.

pā.pala.lū. Redup. of *palalū 1, 2.*

pā.pala.moa. Same as *pālāmoa.*

papa lani. n. Heavenly stratum, heaven and all the spiritual powers; upper regions of the air, upper heavens, firmament.

pā.pala.oa. Same as *pāpala 3. He ao pāpalaoa no ke kuahiwi* (chant), a misty cloud for the hill.

papa.lau.lele. n. Small net, as for fishing in shallow water.

pā.pala.weka. Same as *palaweka.*

papale. Redup. of *pale,* to ward off. (PNP *papale.*)

pā.pale. nvt. Hat, head covering; crest, as of a quail; chapter on top of a column (2 Oihn. 3.15); to put on a hat, wear a hat; to overshadow. *Poʻo pāpale,* crested head. *Pāpale i ka pāpale,* to put on or wear a hat. *Komo i ka pāpale,* to put on a hat [new form]. *Ua ulu kou nani ā pāpale maluna o kou kaikuaʻana,* your beauty has increased so it overshadows that of your sister. (PPN *pale.*)

pā.pale aliʻi. n. Crown.

pā.pale hai.nikā. n. Mitre. (Puk. 28.4.)

pā.pale.lehu. vt. To count by four hundred thousands, four-hundred-thousand-fold. (KL line 1773, Gram. 10.3.)

pā.pale ʻie. n. Hat made by plaiting a long strip, as of coconut or bamboo, which was then sewn into a hat. Some of the braids were *alahaka-o-Nuʻalolo, ʻekeʻeke, iwi-puhi, kala hale, lū, haka-o-Hale-a-ka-lā.* *Lit.*, basket hat, so called because the narrow strip is similar to that used in making the basket *ʻie.*

pā.pale kahuna. n. Mitre, priestly hat. (Oihk. 8.9.)

pā.pale Kale.poni. n. Felt hat. *Lit.*, California *(Eng.)* hat.

pā.pale kapu. n. Cap. *Lit.*, cap *(Eng.)* hat.

pā.pale laʻa. n. Holy crown or head covering. (Puk. 39.30.)

papa lele kawa. n. Springboard for diving.

pā.pale mū.ʻou.ʻou. n. Poke bonnet. *Lit.*, blunt hat.

papa.lena. n. Fending off, warding off, pushing aside. Cf. *papale.*

pā.pā.leo. Same as *pāpāʻōlelo.*

pā.pale ʻo.ʻoma. n. Bonnet, sunbonnet. *Lit.*, flared hat.

pā.pale pahu. n. Hat plaited on a *pahu pāpale.*

pā.pale wai.okila. n. Panama hat.

papa lewa.lewa. n. Net used in deep water with the *melomelo* club. *Rare.*

papali. n. Small cliff or slope, as along a ravine.

papa like. vs. Of the same species, class, rank.

pā.pā.lima. 1. Redup. of *pālima 1.* **2.** vs. Confirmed, as an agreement by striking hands. *hoʻo.pā.pā.lima.* To touch hands as in making an agreement.

papa lima.hana. n. Labor board.

papā.lina, pā.pā.lina. n. Cheek, cheeks. See ex., *lahilahi 1. Papālina nui,* big cheeks, flabby fat flesh in general. (PEP *pa(a)paalinga.*)

papa loio. n. Legal profession. *Hoa o ka papa loio,* member of the bar.

pā.pa.lole. vs. Sluggish, indolent. *Rare.*

papalu. Same as *palupalu.*

pā.palu. nvt. Apron, covering, as to conceal nakedness; to cover. *Kui ihola lāua i nā lau piku a paʻa, i mau pāpalu no lāua* (Kin. 3.7), they sewed fig leaves together, and made themselves aprons.

papa lua. n. Second floor or story, second class.

pā.pā.lua. Redup. of *pālua;* twice as much, very much, doubly, couple. *ʻAno pāpālua,* dual natured. *ʻIke pāpālua,* to have the gift of second sight. *Kino pāpālua,* to have a dual form, as the demigod Kama-puaʻa, who could change from man to hog. *Miki pāpālua,* to eat poi with two fingers. *Pāpālua aku ke kolohe,* twice as much mischief. *Ua pāpālua ka nui o kēlā ma mua o kēia,* there's twice as much of this as of that.

papa lua hā. n. Two by four lumber.

Papa Luna Kiaʻi. n. Board of Supervisors.

Papa Mahi ʻAi ame Ulu Lā.ʻau. n. Board of Agriculture and Forestry.

papa mana.mana. n. Grate, grating. *Lit.*, branching flat surface. *Papa manamana pukapuka keleawe* (Puk. 27.4), grate of network of brass.

papa manawa. Same as *papahola.*

pā.pā.mano. vt. To count by four thousands, four-thousand-fold. (KL line 1773, Gram. 10.3.)

papa mā.noa.noa. n. Plank.

papa moe. n. Horizontal stratum. *Fig.*, sick. Cf. *papakū.*

papa.moʻi. Same as *moʻi.*

papa.mū. n. **1.** Stone on which the checkerlike game, *kōnane,* was played; plaid; checkered, as gingham; checkerboard. Cf. *mū 8.* **2.** A variety of taro.

papāna. Same as *papā.*

papane. Redup. of *pane 1.*

papani. Redup. of *pani 1;* interception, shutting off, as from view; to block. *Holo papani ka ʻeha,* the pain shuts off of breath. *Ka moʻo pekena kuli i papani i kona pepeiao* (Hal. 58.4), the deaf adder that has stopped up her ear. (PCP *papani.*)

papa niho. n. Row of teeth, set of teeth; jaw, bridge for false teeth.

pā.pani.pani. Redup. of *panipani 1.*

papano. Redup. of *pano,* dark.

papa.noa.noa. Redup. of *panoa. Rare.*

papa noho. n. Bench.

papao. Same as *paopao.*

papa.ohe. n. Young of *akule,* a fish.

papa ʻohi. n. Draft board, selection board.

papa.ʻoi. Same as *kaʻupu,* a fern.

pā.pā.ʻō.kole. Same as *pāpākole.*

Papa Ola. n. Board of Health.

pā.pā.ʻō.lelo. nv. To converse, talk; conversation. *E pāpāʻōlelo kāua, ʻoiai ka manaʻo i ʻaneʻi* (chant), let's converse while the desire is here.

papa 'ō.lewa.lewa. Same as *papa lewalewa*. (Malo 212, Emerson note.) *Rare*.
Papa o nā Kahu Kula o ke Kula.nui. n. Board of Regents of the University.
pā.pā.ono. Redup. of *pāono*. *Ā 'o ua po'e mea ola lā 'ehā, ua pāpāono lākou i nā 'ēheu* (Hoik. 4.8), and the four beasts had each of them six wings.
papapa. n. Young stage of *nenue*, rudder fish.
papa.pā. Redup. of *pā l*.
pā.papa. 1. vs. Low, flat, as a reef. Cf. *hāpapa*. 2. n. Beans, peas, lentils; the hyacinth bean *(Dolichos lablab)*, from tropical Asia, a long vine somewhat like the Lima bean and having edible seeds, growing wild in Hawai'i. Also *pī*. (Neal 468.) *Ka pāpapa maka a me ka pī a me ka pāpapa pāpa'a* (2 Sam. 17.28), beans and lentils and parched pulse.
papa pa'a.kai. n. Salt flat. *Fig.*, sour disposition.
papa pa'i. Reduplication and frequentative of *pa'i l*.
papa pa'i. n. Printing press. *Ka mana o ka papa pa'i*, the power of the press.
papa pā.'ina. n. Table for eating.
papa palaoa. n. Breadboard; cake (Ier. 7.18); pancake, wafer *(rare)*.
papa pala.pala. n. Writing desk, board, or flat surface where writing is done.
papa.papa. Same as *papa l*. *Rare*. *I ka papapapa ka nalu o O'ahu* (chant), the waves of O'ahu on the flat reefs. (PPN *papapapa*.)
papa.pau. Redup. of *papau*; everyone. *A no ka hewa 'ana o Kumu-honua mā, papapau ai kānaka i ka make* (Kep. 49), because of the sin of Kumu-honua, everybody died. ho'o.papa.pau. Redup. of *ho'opapau*.
papa pelena (berena). n. A flat cake. *Biblical*.
papa pō.haku. n. 1. Row or tier of stones. 2. Slate, stone tablet. 3. Stone table, stone flat, or stone surface, as for pounding.
papa po'o. n. The leading division, class, rank, especially the first company of warriors sent out to plunder in order to provoke war. *Lit.*, head rank.
papa.pū. 1. n. Row or tier of guns, class of guns. 2. vs. Completely covered, as rocks by shellfish. *Papapū ka pōhaku i ka 'opihi*, the rock is covered with limpets.
papa.pueo. n. A variety of taro, grown on Maui; petioles deep-pink at base, grading to light-pink and green with white edge; corm used for poi. *Lit.*, owl flat.
papa pu'u.kani. n. Choir, choral group.
papau. vs. Deeply engaged, as in an activity; finished; engrossed, absorbed, united; all, all together. Cf. *pau*. *Ua papau ku'u no'ono'o i ka hana*, my entire thoughts are absorbed in the work. *Papau pū lākou i ka 'eha*, they were all hurt. ho'o.papau. To devote oneself, to make an effort to finish up, to concentrate.
pā.pa'u. nvs. Shallow, shoal. *Pāpa'u ka 'ike o kēlā kanaka*, that man's knowledge is shallow. (PNP *papaku*.)
pā.paua. n. A bivalve *(Isognomon)*, clam. (KL line 25.) But cf. *'ōlepe pāpaua*.
pā.paua momi. n. A bivalve (said to be *Chama iostoma*).
papa uhi wa'a. n. Board used to cover space forward of the forward outrigger boom.
papa.'ula. n. A mat motif consisting of a row of opposing triangles with their apices touching.
pā.pā.uli. Redup. of *pāuli*. *E ho'omaka mai ai ka 'ino ka pāpāuli makani, ua, a me ke kai* (Kep. 93), beginning the storm, wind bringing clouds and dark seas, rain, and sea.
papau make. nvi. To die, of many; complete annihilation; cemetery *(rare)*.
pā.pā.'umi. Redup. of *pā'umi*.
papa.'unu. vt. To fill up, cram.
papa waena. n. Middle floor or story; middle class or layer.
papa waha nui. n. Large baglike net used for *akule* fish.
Papa-wai. n. Rain name associated with Olowalu, West Maui.

pā.pā.walu. Redup. of *pāwalu*.
papa wili. n. Mixing board or tray.
papa wili 'ai. n. Mixing board, food trough, board for kneading poi, kneading trough (Puk. 12.34).
pape.kema, bapetema. nvt. To baptize, baptismal; baptism. Also *papakema*. Cf. *keiki papakema, papakema*.
Pape.kike, Bapetite. n. Baptist. *Eng*.
pape.kiko, bapetiso. 1. nvt. To baptize; baptismal. 2.*(Cap.)* nvs. Baptist.
pā pepa. n. Paper plate or dish (preceded by *ke*).
Papine. n. Baffin. *Eng. Kai o Papine*, Baffin Bay.
pā.pine. n. Pen where oxen were yoked together, corral.
pā.pio. 1. Same as *pāpiopio*, a fish. (PCP *papio*.) 2. vt. Pressed down, flat, especially of a woman's *pā'ū*, skirt; furled, as a flag, or as the *makahiki* banner; to hold flat; to tuck under, as a hen with chicks; sideways. *Noho pāpio*, to sit properly with knees together and feet to one side, of women. *Pāpio i ka palekoki*, to hold the skirt flat down [as in a strong wind]. *Ka-malo-pāpio* (name), the *malo* [-flap] held down.
pā.pi'o. nvi. To form an arch; to arch; an arch.
pā.pio.pio. n. The young stage of growth of *ulua*, a fish.
pā.pipi. Same as *pānini*, cactus. *Lit.*, cattle fence.
pā.pipi pua. Same as *pānini-o-Ka-puna-hou*.
pā pō.haku. n. Stone wall.
Pā.polo.hiwa. n. Name of a star observed by priests.
pā.po'o. v. To dive to the opening of a *papa* (net) in fishing. *Lit.*, head touching.
pā.pū. 1. n. Fort, fortress. *Lit.*, gun enclosure. *Alanui Pāpū*, Fort Street. 2. nvs. A plain, clear piece of ground; clear, unobstructed, visible, in plain sight, directly confronting. *Pāpū like* (For. 5:649), level, even. *Kū pāpū mai ka pali i mua o ka hale*, the cliff stood directly visible in front of the house. (PCP *paapuu*.)
pā.pua. nv. To shoot with bow and arrow; archery.
pā.pū.hea. n. Dead calm.
pā.puhene. Same as *pūhenehene*, the game.
pā.pū lewa. n. Flying fortress, battleship.
papulo, papuro. n. Papyrus, rush (Ioba 8.11). (Gr. *papuros*.) See *kaluhā*.
pā.pulō, bafulo. n. Buffalo. *Eng*. Cf. *pūpalō*.
papuna, babuna. n. Baboon. *Eng*.
pā puni. n. Circular enclosure, surrounding wall, as about a fishpond.
pau. 1. vs. Finished, ended, through, terminated, completed, over, all done; final, finishing; entirely, completely, very much; after; all, to have all; to be completely possessed, consumed, destroyed. (Used in *loa'a*-type constructions, Gram. 4, as: *E pau nō kēia hana iā kākou*, we will finally finish this work; also an intensifier before verbs: see *pau 'eka, pau kilo, pau lehia, pau 'ono, pau pā'ele*. *Pau* or *pau ā* precedes some words with meaning of "very, very much." Cf. *pau ma'alea, pau 'ole, pau 'ono*. Cf. also *apau, kū'ike, pau a pau, pau loa, pau nui, -pau pilikia*. *Pau ka ha'awina*, the lesson is finished. *Pau ke ka'a i ka nāhāhā*, the car was completely destroyed. *Pau 'eka*, very dirty, filthy. *Oki pau ka hana a ka huila*, extremely wonderful is the doing of the wheel. *Pau nā luna i ka 'eha*, all the officers were injured. *Pau i ka lilo*, all sold, gone, taken, consumed. *Ka pau 'ana ihola nō ia o ka'u ha'awina*, my lesson is just finished. *Pau Pele, pau manō*, consumed by Pele, consumed by a shark [an oath meaning "may I be destroyed if I have not spoken truth"]. *Pau po'o, pau hi'u*, consumed head, consumed tail [total destruction]. ho'o.pau. To put an end to, finish, get rid of, suppress, terminate, conclude, annul, stop, cancel, revoke, repeal, abolish, consume; to dismiss or discharge, as from work; to use too much, waste; cancellation, finishing; completely, all. Cf. *ho'opau manawa*. Ho'opau 'ana, abolition, cancellation, revocation. *Ho'opau ho'o'ino 'ia aku*, dishonorably discharged [as from the armed services]. *Ho'opau 'ai*, to waste food, said figuratively of one not worth his food. Ho'opau

wale, nolle prosequi. *E ho'opau 'oe i kāu uwe 'ana,* stop your crying. *E ho'opau 'ia ā ma kēia ke ho'opau loa 'ia nei ke kānāwai,* the law shall be and hereby is revoked. *Ka ho'opau 'ana o ka 'aelike,* cancellation of contract. *Ua ho'opau 'ia kō Haua'īliki na'au 'e'ehia, ala a'ela ia ā holo wikiwiki akula* (Laie 457), Haua'īliki's heart was completely filled with terror, he jumped and ran swiftly away. (PNP *pau*.) **2.** idiom. Said to be (used in special idioms, unfavorably). *Hele akula i kauhale e kama'ilio ai, i laila pau ko'u hiamoe nui, ka hana 'ole,* going to houses of others and chatting, there saying that I'm sleeping all the time, doing no work. *Pau kona lapuwale i nā hoahānau,* said by his cousins to be worthless.

pa'u. nvs. **1.** Soot, smudge; ink dregs; ink powder; ink used for tattooing made of burned *kukui* shells; tar-colored excrement as resulting from hemorrhage; sooty. **ho'o.pa'u.** To soil, smudge, make sooty. **2.** Drudgery, slaving; tedious and laborious work, toil; toilsome. **ho'o.pa'u.** To treat as a drudge, overwork, oppress with tedious labor.

pa'ū. vs. Moist, damp, soaked, drenched, moldy. Also *ma'ū.* See *Pa'ū-pili.* **ho'o.pa'ū.** To soak, moisten, dampen.

pā.'ū. 1. nvt. Woman's skirt, sarong; skirt worn by women horseback riders; to wear a *pā'ū.* Fig., the sea (UL 36). Cf. *pā'ū halakā. Pā'ū hula,* any kind of dance skirt. *Pā'ū lā'ī,* ti-leaf skirt. *Pā'ū-o-Lu'ukia,* ornamental sennit lashing of canoe float to outrigger boom, said to have been named for the chastity belt worn by Lu'ukia (Malo 134, Emerson note). **ho'o.pā.'ū.** To put on a *pā'ū.* **2.** n. Mat covering for a canoe, sometimes with crew sticking their heads out through holes in the mat. (Malo 135, Emerson note.) **3.** n. Red feathers bound to base of yellow feathers in an *'uo,* bunch.

paua. 1. Same as *pāpaua,* a clam. (PPN *paasua,* PCP *pa(a)(s)ua.*) **2.** n. A rare crab. **3.** n. A variety of taro, extinct in Kona and Kā'ū, Hawai'i; petiole dark-green, becoming whitish above; corm white, long-keeping. *E 'ai ana 'oe i ka poi paua o Ke-āiwa,* you are eating the *paua* poi of Ke-āiwa [the very best; said also of ardent lovers].

pauā.'ā.lina. vs. Heavy, burdensome. *Rare.*

pau ahi. nv. Destruction by fire, burned; to put out a fire. *'Inikua pau ahi,* fire insurance. *Kāhea pau ahi,* fire alarm.

Pau-ahi. n. Name of a star of astrologers, said to rise in the early morning during the month of Kaulua.

pa'u ahi. n. Soot, black cindery sand or ash. *Lit.,* fire soot.

Pau-ahi-lani. n. Name of a star, said to appear early on the night of Muku.

pau.aho. vs. Out of breath, breathless, gasping for breath, panting, worn out. *Fig.,* discouraged, faint-hearted, despairing, desperate, weary, exhausted; to die. *Pauaho mai 'o Mea i kēia ola 'ana,* so-and-so has departed this life. **ho'o.pau.aho.** Caus./sim.; to cause shortness of breath, panting, despair, etc. *Ho'opauaho lākou iā lākou iho i ka 'imi i ka puka* (Kin. 19.11), they wearied themselves to find the door.

pau.'aka. 1. vs. Grotesque, odd. *Ua kālai pau'aka 'ia ke po'o o ke ki'i,* the head of the image is carved grotesquely. **ho'o.pau.'aka.** To make grotesque, odd. **2.** vt. Damaging; unreliable, deceitful; to disturb. *Mai pau-'aka mai 'oe i ka hana a mākou,* don't you disturb our work. **3.** vs. Of no use, fruitless, unproductive, without reward or profit, discouraging. **ho'o.pau.'aka.** Same as above. **4.** n. Quail, so called because of its song. *Rare.* See *manu kapalulu.*

pau.'aka. 1. Redup. of *pau'aka 1-3.* **2.** Same as *maku'u 1* and *moamoa 2.* **3.** n. Neck in a house rafter. (Malo 120.)

pau.'ali. vs. Crooked, perverse. *Rare.*

pau ā ne'i.ne'i. Same as *ne'e,* to move.

pau.ā.nihi. Same as *paunihinihi.*

pau ā pau. n. Everyone, all the people (as with the idea

of participating in a previously stated act). *I ka poni mō'ī 'ana, pau ā pau,* at the coronation, everyone [was there]. *Inā he kōkua no ka hale pule, pau ā pau,* if it is for help for the church, everyone [helps].

pā uea (uwea). n. Wire fence.

pā uea (uwea) kukū. n. Barbed-wire fence.

pā uea (uwea) maka 'aha. n. Chicken-wire fence. *Lit.,* sennit-mesh wire fence.

pā uea (uwea) maka 'upena. n. Chicken-wire fence. *Lit.,* net-mesh wire fence.

pā uea (uwea) poe.poe. n. Smooth-wire fence. *Lit.,* round-wire fence.

pau 'eka. vs. Very dirty. See *'eka 1.* **ho'o.pau 'eka.** To soil, make dirty.

-pauhā. ho'o.pau.hā. Similar to *ho'opaumanawa.*

pā.'ū hala.kā. According to Emerson, shielding of one's modesty with the hand; also said of the sea. (UL 124.)

pa'u hana. nvs. Constantly at work, drudgery; tedious, prolonged work.

pau hana.nu'u. vs. Plump, waddling.

pā.'ū hei.hei. n. A *pā'ū* festooned with leaf or ferns tied about; a sarong made of such leaves. *Nā wāhine kīheihei, pā'ū heihei o uka* (PH 170), women with shawls, leaf-draped sarongs of the uplands.

pā.uhi. n. A mother-of-pearl bonito hook used when the sun was bright and high. *Lit.,* covering lure.

pa'u.hia. vi. Overcome with sleep; overwhelmed with desire; overtaken by evil or calamity. **ho'o.pa'u.hia.** To cause to fall into a deep sleep, as a drug.

paūhu. vs. Small, narrow-chested. *Rare.*

pā.uhu. 1. See *leho pāuhu.* **2.** Same as *pānuhu 1.*

pau.hū. Same as *pānuhu. Rare.*

pā.uhuuhu. n. A kind of *uhu,* a parrot fish that is red and brown in color.

pau.'iole. n. A variety of taro.

pauka, pauda. 1. nvt. Powder; to powder. Also *paula. Eng.* **2.** See *kake pauka.*

pau.ka.'a. vs. All taken, consumed. *Rare.*

pauka kī pū. n. Gun powder.

pau kaua. n. Armistice, truce. **ho'o.pau kaua.** To make a truce or armistice.

pau.ke.aho. Same as *pauaho. I paukeaho a'e 'oe* (chant), you were breathless.

Pau-ke-aho. n. One of the Line Islands where Hawaiians dug guano, perhaps Baker Island. *Lit.,* exhausted. See *Pua-ka-'ilima.*

pau.ke'e. vs. Curved. *Fig.,* dishonest, deceitful.

pau.kī. Same as *paukikī.*

pau.kikī. nvs. Fast, speedily; speed; to do with great speed. *Paukikī ka holo 'ana o ke ka'a,* the car has speeded along.

pau kilo. Intensifier of *kilo,* to see. *Pau kilo i ka hana a ke ali'i,* to observe intently what the chief does.

pau.kū. 1. nvs. Section, link, piece; stanza, verse, as in the Bible; canto; article, as of law; paragraph; to section off, cut in sections, slice in sections; to make a lei with sections of different colors, as feathers, or roses and begonias; land section smaller than a *mo'o* (*Thrum's Annual,* 1925, p. 68); a unit of measurement; a squad (military; see *mokuna*); jointed, linked. *E paukū ana nō ka hala me ka lehua* (PH 27), pandanus and lehua sections being made into a lei. **2.** n. Root of the *kā'e'e* vine, used medicinally. **3.** Same as *'ōpū 'ōhao,* a disease.

pau.kua. Pas/imp. of *paukū 1.*

pau.kū kino. n. Body trunk, torso.

pau.kū.kū. Redup. of *paukū 1.* See *lei paukūkū. Ko'i paukūkū,* an adze used for cutting sections in a canoe log that is to be made into a canoe.

pau.kū manawa. n. Portion of time, era.

pau.kū 'olo.ka.'a. n. Cylinder. *Lit.,* revolving section.

pau.kū pā.laha.laha lahi.lahi. n. Slab. *Lit.,* thin flat portion.

paula. n. Powder. *Eng.* Also *pauka. Eng.*

pā.'ula. vs. Darkened, of mature wood. *Lit.,* red-touched.

pau.lā.'ī. vi. To walk over the sea or fire, as a god.

pau.lehia. vs. To be overwhelmed (Kel. 107); completely, totally immersed, absorbed. *Paulehia i ka hiamoe,* fast asleep. Also *paulehua.*

pau lehia. vs. Expert; to be such.

pau.lehua. Same as *paulehia.*

pau.lele. nvt. Faith, confidence, trust; to have faith, confidence, to believe implicitly; to lean against, rely on. *Paulele 'ia,* trusted, trustworthy. *'A 'ole au i 'ike i ka paulele nui* (Luka 7.9), I have not seen so great faith.

pā.uli. nvs. Dark, as sea or skin; gloom, darkness. *Ua ho'i ka pāuli makani kualau* (For. 5:91), the gloomy wind showers have gone. *He pāuli hiwa na ka ua haoa,* deep gloom of the pelting rain.

pau.lia. Pas/imp. of *pau l. Rare.*

Pā.uli-kū-ali'i. n. A star observed by priests in the month of Ikiiki. *Lit.,* chief-like darkness.

-paulina. ho'o.pau.lina. Same as *ho'opaulinalina.*

pau.lina.lina. vi. To gird the waist tightly, to stretch, make taut.

-paulinalina. ho'o.pau.lina.lina. To waste time on trivials, to take life easy, relax.

pā.uli.uli. Redup. of *pāuli.*

pau loa. vs. All, everything, to have all. Cf. *pau. Pau loa iāia ka 'ike,* he has all the knowledge.

pau.lua. See *wa'a paulua.*

pā.'ulu.'ā. vt. To abuse, mistreat, knock around; to beat carelessly, as poi that one does not pound until all the lumps are removed.

pauma. vt. Pump; to pump. *Eng.*

pā.uma. 1. n. Large curved needle, as used in sewing gunny sacks. **2.** vs. Curved, bent, as a needle. **3.** n. Breastbone, as of a chicken. **4.** vi. To turn, move along, push; to turn into the wind, to face the wind, as a ship, bird. *Pāuma wāwae,* tread of feet. *Kīkaha koa'e, lele pāuma ka hulu māewaewa* (PH 206), the tropic bird soars, the tousled feathers beat against the wind. **5.** vi. To slosh a canoe back and forth, so as to empty it of water. *Rare.*

pā uma. nv. Standing wrist wrestling: the players face each other, and each grasps the other's right thumb, and tries to force the opponent's hand to his chest; to wrestle thus. *Lit.,* chest touching.

pau ma'a.lea. Intensive of *ma'alea.*

pau.mā.'ele. vs. Dirty, defiled, sordid, unclean. *Ua paumā'ele kō 'oukou mau lima i ke koko* (Isa. 59.3), your hands are defiled with blood. **ho'o.pau.mā.'ele.** To soil, make dirty, smear, pollute, befoul, defile.

Pau.maka. n. A star in the month of Ikiiki, an omen for chiefs.

pau.mā.kō. nvt. Grief, mourning, lamentation; to weep loudly. *I ka paumākō o ko'u na'au* (Hal. 61.2), when my heart is overwhelmed. **ho'o.pau.mā.kō.** To cause great grief, lamentation; to pretend grief.

pauma.kō.kō. Redup. of *paumākō.*

Pau-makua. n. A small bright star that appears on the night of Hilo in the month of Welo and stays all the month.

Pau-makua-lani. n. A star observed by priests, in the month of Kaulua and visible through the month of Ikiiki. Cf. *Ka-'ōnohi-ali'i.*

-pau manawa. ho'o.pau manawa. To waste time; not worth doing, undesirable, unnecessary, waste of effort.

pā uma.uma. vi. See *pa'iāuma.*

pau.mau.no'o.no'o. n. Keepsake, memento. *Rare. Lit.,* all continuing thoughts.

pauma wai. n. Water pump.

pā.'ume.'ume. 1. nvi. Tug-of-war game; to play such a game, in land or sea. Also *hukihuki.* **2.** nvt. Contentious, quarreling, contending, fighting.

pā.'umi. vt. Ten times, tenfold, by tens; to divide by tens or distribute by tens; decimal.

pau.ne'i.ne'i. Excited; to cry out, as in excitement. (And.)

pau.nihi.nihi. n. Small, worthless taro shoots.

pau nui. vi. All (followed by qualifying verb or noun). *Pau nui nā koa i ka nāholo,* all the soldiers fled. *Pau nui mai nei ke kalo i ka 'ai 'ia,* all the taro has been eaten. *Ua pau nui ka hana,* all the work is finished.

pau.oa. n. A fern *(Dryopteris squamigera)* to 90 cm or more high, the stem clothed with tan scales, the frond triangular to ovate and two or three times pinnate.

pā.'ū-o-Hi'i.aka. n. **1.** A native beach vine *(Jacquemontia sandwicensis),* in the morning-glory family, with pale blue or white flowers and small rounded leaves. *Lit.,* sarong of Hi'iaka, so named because the goddess Pele, on returning from a long morning's fishing trip, found that this little vine had spread itself over her baby sister, Hi'iaka, whom she had laid on the beach, and had protected the baby from the sun. (Neal 710.) Also *kākua-o-Hi'iaka.* **2.** A kind of red seaweed with wide, thin thallus. Perhaps same as *limu hā'ula.* **3.** Same as *lepe-o-Hina,* a seaweed. **4.** A variety of taro: petiole and leaf have smoky look; corm white, used to make good, gray poi. **5.** A variety of sweet potato.

pau 'ole. vs. Endless, unceasing, always. *Me ke aloha pau 'ole,* with love forever.

pā'ū-o-Lu'u.kia. See *pā'ū l.*

pau 'ono. vs. Very delicious, etc. Cf. *'ono.*

pā.'ū-o-Pala'e. Another name for the *pala'ā* fern. Pala'e was a servant of Pele and a companion of Hi'iaka.

pau pā.'ele. vs. Very black, dirty. See *pā'ele.*

pau.pau. Same as *papau. Ke kū lā nā ki'i 'elua i ka paupau make* (For. 6:369), the two images stood there in the slaughter of all.

pa'u.pa'u. Redup. of *pa'u l, 2.*

pa'ū.pa'ū. Redup. of *pa'ū.* **ho'o.pa'ū.pa'ū.** Redup. of *ho'opa'ū.* **2.** n. Overlaid tapa (Kam. 76:115) said to be so called because it was wet during its manufacture; sometimes worn by dancers.

pau.pau.aho. Redup. of *pauaho.* See ex., *kahiko l.*

pa'u.pa'u.hia. Redup. of *pa'uhia.* **ho'o.pa'u.pa'u.hia.** Redup. of *ho'opa'uhia.*

pā.'upena. n. A series of network of pens or corrals.

Pa'ū-pili. n. Rain name associated with Lahaina, Maui. *Lit.,* rain that moistens *pili* grass. *Ua 'ike 'ia 'oe e Rain Pa'ū-pili* (song), you are seen by Pa'ū-pili rain.

-pau pilikia. ho'o.pau pili.kia. To attend the calls of nature. *Lit.,* to put an end to trouble. *Wahi ho'opau pilikia,* toilet, outhouse.

pau pono. vs. Completely finished, terminated.

pau pū. vs. All together, including all; completely demolished, etc. Cf. *pau. Pau pū kākou i ka huhū 'ia e ke kumu,* every one of us was scolded by the teacher.

pā.'ū.'ū. 1. Redup. of *pa'ū,* soaked. **2.** n. Second stage in the growth of *ulua,* a fish. Cf. *pāpio, ulua.* **3.** n. A variety of sweet potato.

Pau.wala. n. A star that appears in the night of Muku in the month of Māhoe Mua, and remains visible through the month of Māhoe Hope; it follows the star Ulu-loa, and was considered the latter's "servant."

pā uwea. Var. spelling of *pā uea.*

pawa. 1. n. The darkness just before dawn, predawn. See *mokupawa. Moku ka pawa,* the predawn darkness is breaking. *I ka moku 'ana o ka pawa* (1 Sam. 11.11), in the morning watch. **2.** vs. Smooth, fat and sleek. *Rare.* **3.** n. Custom. *Rare.* **4.** *(Cap.)* n. Name of a star (no data).

pā.wā. Same as *oeoe,* bull-roarer.

pā.wa'a. Untamed, unruly, uncivil, bad-mannered. (AP.)

pā wa'a. n. Canoe enclosure; touching of canoes.

pā.wai. Same as *limu kala wai,* pond scums.

pā wai. 1. n. Water trough or container. (Kin. 30.41.) (Preceded by *ke*). (PCP *paa wai.*) **2.** v. To have water, take a sip or drink.

pā waina. n. Vineyard.

pā.wale. n. Native dock *(Rumex giganteus* and *R. skottsbergii),* a coarse erect or vinelike plant with ovate or oblong leaves, and topped with panicles of tiny flowers, belonging to the buckwheat family. Also *uhauhakō.* See also *hu'ahu'akō.*

pā.wali. vi. To talk soothingly, softly, sweetly, sometimes to flatter or deceive. *Lit.,* touch smoothness.

pā.walu. By eights, eightfold; to divide by eights, to have eight, distribute to eight, eight times. See *pāpāwalu;* song, *lino 2;* and chant, *malia 1.*

pā.wao. vi. To see indistinctly, uncertainly. *Rare.*

pawa.pawa. Redup. of *pawa 2. Rare.*

pā wā.wahi pipi. n. Pen or corral for separating cattle.

pā.wehe. nvt. Generic name for colored geometric motifs, as on *makaloa* mats made on Ni'ihau, bowls, and gourds; to make such designs.

pā.wehe pū.pū. n. Tapa beater design.

pā.wehi. vt. To beautify, adorn. Cf. *wehi 1. Ua Kanilehua i pāwehi ho'oipo 'ia . . . me ka lehua,* Kanilehua rain lovingly adorned . . . with *lehua.*

pā.wela. nvs. Overcooked, scorched, burned; a burn.

pā.welu. vs. Old, worn, ragged. *Fig.,* worthless.

pā.weo. vi. To turn away the face, as in order to avoid seeing someone. *Maka pāweo,* to avert the eyes. *Ā he aha kāu hana e pāweo nei, ē ka makani Pu'u-lena* (song), why are you turning away, O Pu'u-lena wind. **ho'o.pā.weo.** To cause to turn away, snub, etc.

pā wili 'ai. Same as *papa wili 'ai.* (Puk. 8.3.)

pē. prep. Like, resembling. (Gram. 9.12.) *Pē kēia,* like this, thus. (PPN *pehee,* PNP *pe.*)

pe-, pē-. Like, resembling (in the demonstratives *pēia, pēlā, pēnā, penei* and *pehea*). (Gram. 8.3.) (PPN *pehe-.*)

pē. 1. vs. Crushed, flattened; humble, low, modest. *Na'au pē,* modest heart. *Kani pē,* a hollow flat sound. **ho'o.pē.** To crush, break fine, mash, pulverize; to cringe, assume a humble or fearful attitude. See ex., *kūpaoa.* (PPN *pe'e.*) **2.** vs. Perfumed, sweet with fragrance. *Nolu pē i ke onaona* (song), softly fragrant with perfume. **ho'o.pē.** To perfume, anoint. **3.** vs. Drenched, soaked (often following *pulu* or *nolu;* sometimes *drenched* and *perfumed [pē 2]* are combined). *Pulu pē nei 'ili i ka ua,* this skin is drenched and soaked by the rain. (PEP *pe'e.*) **ho'o.pē.** To drench, soak. **4.** vt. To bribe. Cf. *kīpē.* **ho'o.pē.** Caus/sim. **5.** nvt. Pay; to pay. *Eng.*

pea. 1. Also **fea.** n. Fair, carnival, exhibit. *Eng.* **2.** n. Pear, avocado *(Persea americana).* (Neal 363–4.) *Eng.* **3.** Also **bea.** n. Bear. *Eng.*

pe'a. 1. nvs. A cross (X-shaped); cf. the Christian cross, *ke'a*); to cross, as the hands or arms; to cross and tie; to turn and go. *Pe'a a'ela nā lima i ke kua,* crossed the hands on the back [a sign of grief (FS 285), anger, danger, or an insulting way to wish bad luck on another]. **ho'o.pe'a.** To cross and tie; *fig.,* to persecute. *No ka huāhuā i ho'ope'a aku ai lākou iāia* (Mat. 27.18), for envy they had bound him. (PCP *peka.*) **2.** n. Bat. Cf. more common *'ōpe'ape'a. Hanalei . . . 'āina a ka pe'a i noho ai* (FS 95). Hanalei . . . land where the bat lived. (PPN *peka.*) **3.** n. Starfish, various species of Asteroidea. (KL line 18.) Also *ke'ape'a, hōkū kai.* **4.** n. Sail, as of a canoe. **5.** n. Forks or branches made of stalks of feathers bound at their bases with *'ie'ie* roots, coming together to form the *ko'o* (stalk) which in turn is attached to the *kāhili* staff. **6.** n. Boundary, edge, border, as of land. *Mai kēlā pe'a ā kēia pe'a,* from that border to this. *E kau mai ana 'o Hala-'ani'ani ma ka pe'a o ka nalu* (Laie 509), Hala-'ani'ani landed on the edge of the wave. **7.** vs. Menstruating, unclean, tattered (FS 167); to menstruate. *Hale pe'a,* menstrual house. *Kapa pe'a* (Isa. 64.6), filthy cloth. **8.** n. Kite. **9.** n. Tileaf thatch bundle. **10.** n. Base of a leaf. *Rare.* **11.** n. Sacred house.

pe'a heke. n. Triangular sail set above the gaff; topsail. Cf. *kia lua pe'a heke.*

pe'ahi. 1. nvt. Fan; to fan, brush, wave, signal, beckon, winnow. *Ka mea i pe'ahi 'ia i ka pe'ahi* (Isa. 30.24), which has been winnowed with the fan. **ho'o.pe'ahi.** To beckon or wave, pretend to wave, etc. (PCP

peka(f,s)i.) **2.** n. The open hand, bones of the hand. *Kou pe'ahi 'ākau, a me kou lima* (Hal. 44.3), your right hand and your arm. **3.** n. A native fern *(Microsorium spectrum* syn. *Polypodium spectrum)* about 30 cm high, the fronds broad, pointed, commonly three-lobed. (Neal 26.) **4.** n. A dark-colored stone with grain said to suggest the fingers of a hand. *Rare.*

pe'ahi lima. nv. The open hand, a hand's breadth (Ezek. 40.5); to beckon or wave with the hand.

pe'ahi uila. n. Electric fan.

pe'a hope. n. Mainsail.

pe'a ihu. n. Jib sail. *Lit.,* bow sail.

pe'a.kua. n. A trusted relative of a chief who attends to his personal needs. *Lit.,* back-cross, so called because such a person might go behind the back of the chief. **-pe'a kua. ho'o.pe'a kua.** To cross the hands behind the back. See *pe'a 1.*

pe'a nui. n. Mainsail. *Lit.,* big sail.

pe'a oe, pe'a oe.oe. n. A long sail.

pe'a.pe'a. 1. Redup. of *pe'a 1;* crossing. *Fig.,* entangled, perplexity. **2.** n. Hawaiian bat *(Lasiurus cinereus).* Also *'ōpe'ape'a, 'āpe'ape'a, pe'a.* (Probably PPN *pekapeka.*) **3.** n. Small *pe'a,* starfish. (KL line 18.) **4.** Redup. of *pe'a 7;* filthy, unclean; slime. (KL lines 589–92.) **5.** See *pe'ape'a pōhaku.*

pe'a.pe'ahi. Redup. of *pe'ahi 1.* **ho'o.pe'a.pe'ahi.** Redup. of *ho'ope'ahi.*

pe'a.pe'a pō.haku. n. Heap of pebbles, as at the opening of an octopus burrow.

peawa, beava. n. Beaver. *Eng.*

pea.wini. n. Fair wind. *Eng.*

pe'e. vi. **1.** To hide oneself; hiding, clandestine. Cf. *hūnā,* vt, to hide an object. *E pe'e ana au iā La'a-kea,* I'm hiding from La'a-kea. **ho'o.pe'e.** To hide or pretend to hide. (PCP *peke;* cf. Maori *whakapeke.*) **2.** vs. Coarse, thick. *Rare.* Cf. *pe'ekue.*

pe'e-. See *pe'elua, pe'epe'emakawalu.*

Pe'e-hala. n. Name of a wind associated with Hāmākua, Hawai'i. Cf. *Pe'e-pū-hala-hīnano.*

pe'e.kue. Same as *pepe'ekue.* Cf. *honu pe'ekue. 'O ke kā pe'ekue, 'o ke kā lahilahi* (For. 5:89), the thick bailer, the thin bailer.

pe'e.lua. 1. n. Caterpillar (2 Oihn. 6.28; KL line 287); army worm *(Cirphis unipuncta).* Also *kupa.* **2.** vs. Brindled, striped: see *pōpoki.*

pe'e.lue. Var. of *pe'elua.*

pe'e.lulu. nvs. Confusing; confusion. *Rare.* **ho'o.pe'e.lulu.** To create confusion; confusion; confusing.

pe'e.one. n. Sand crab that buries itself backwards in wet sand *(Hippa pacifica). Lit.,* sand hiding.

pe'e pao. nv. One who hides in a cave; to hide in a cave; secret cave; term of contempt for vagabonds or cowards.

Pe'e-pā-pō.haku. n. Name of a rain associated with Kau-pō, Maui. *Lit.,* hide [at the] stone wall.

pe'e.pe'e. 1. Redup. of *pe'e 1. Pe'epe'e pueo,* to hide like an owl, i.e., in a tree. **ho'o.pe'e.pe'e.** Redup. of *ho'ope'e;* camouflage. **2.** Same as *līpe'epe'e,* a seaweed. *Maui.* **3.** n. Name of an ancient illness (no data).

pe'e.pe'e akua. Same as *pe'epe'e kua.*

pe'e.pe'e kua. nv. The game of hide-and-seek; to play the game (short for *pe'epe'e akua,* hiding ghost).

pe'e.pe'e.kue. Redup. of *pe'ekue.*

pe'e.pe'e.maka.walu. 1. n. Large house spider. Cf. *hula pe'epe'emakawalu.* **2.** vs. Alert.

pe'e poli. vs. To hide in one's bosom, as a secret; secretive. *Ka lei pe'e poli* (Kel. 2), child cherished in the heart.

Pe'e-pū-hala-hī.nano. n. Rain name. Cf. *Pe'e-hala.*

pehe. n. Owl snare. *Rare.* **2.** Same as *mehe,* like. *Pehe ua lā,* like rain. **3.** vs. Unsteady. *Rare.*

-pehe. See *kāpehe 2; waipehē.*

pehē. vt. To peel off, pare, strip; to remove skin or bark.

pehea. inter. How? What? How about it? (Gram. 8.3.) *Pehea 'oe?* How are you? What about you? *Pehea lā!* I don't know how! *Pehea ho'i!* How, I don't know! Who knows? *Pehea ʻoe i kēia pālule?* What do you think of this shirt? *Pehea ka luhi, hana nō,* whatever the tiredness, just keep working. *Pehea nohoʻi inā maʻaneʻi* (song), how would it be if [you looked] here. (PNP *pefea.*)

pehemo, behemo. n. Behemoth. (Ioba 40.15.) *Eng.*

pē.heu. 1. Same as *ʻeheu 1-4.* **hoʻo.pē.heu.** Same as *hoʻeheu.* (PCP *pe(e) (f,s)eu,* wing; cf. Marquesan *peheu.*) **2.** vs. Soft, flabby, sagging, as fat flesh; swelling or protuberance, as on cheeks or neck.

pē.heu.heu. Redup. of *pēheu 1, 2. ʻUmiʻumi pēheuheu,* sideburns. **hoʻo.pē.heu.heu.** Redup. of *hoʻopēhue.*

pehi. nvt. To throw, throw at, pelt; an overhand throw, as in throwing the *ʻulu.* Cf. *kīpehi, kūpehi, pepehi.* **hoʻo.pehi.** To cause to throw or pretend to throw. (PNP *peesi.*)

pehia. Pas/imp. of *pehi. I ka pehia mau a ka ua,* in the constant pelting of the rain.

pehina. n. Throwing; pelting, as of rain (Kel. 17).

pehu. 1. nvs. Swollen, distended; swelling; to swell; dropsy, edema. *Fig.,* swollen with pride or conceit; longing to eat, hungry (short for *makapehu,* eyes big with hunger). Types of *pehu,* dropsy, were qualified by the terms *ale ʻai,* food gulping; *kāla ʻe,* clearing. See *wāwae pehu* and below. *Kai pehu,* surging sea. *Maʻi pehu,* dropsy. *Moaʻe pehu,* a strong *Moaʻe* wind. *A loaʻa i ke kanaka ka pehu ʻana, ma ka ʻili o kona ʻiʻo, ā ʻo ka pehu pala paha* (Oihk. 13.2), when a man shall have in the skin of his flesh a rising, or a scab. *He kuleana pehu, ka hoʻokaʻa pehu* (For. 6:402), a business of swelling in pride, a prideful paying of debt. *Hō mai he iʻa na ka pehu o uka* (PH 29), give some fish for the big [-eyed] hungry ones ashore. **hoʻo.pehu.** To swell, cause to swell, brag, boast. (PCP *pe(f,s)u.*) **2.** n. A variety of sweet potato. **3.** n. A kind of seaweed.

pehua. 1. Pas/imp. of *pehu 1.* **2.** n. A variety of taro.

pehu-a-koa. n. Tapa colored with an infusion made of *koa* bark. *Lit., koa* swelling.

pehu.ea. nvi. To increase in volume, of the wind; such an increase. *He makani pehuea ia no lalo* (chant), this is a rising wind from the south.

pehu holo.kū. n. Swelling of entire body. (Kam. 64: 108.)

pehu kumu niu. n. Swelling of lower limbs. (Kam. 64:108.) *Lit.,* coconut tree swelling.

pehu pala. n. Scab (Kanl. 28.27), scurvy.

pehu.pehu. Redup. of *pehu 1.* **hoʻo.pehu.pehu.** Redup. of *hoʻopehu;* to brag; braggadocio; swollen, billowy, as a cloud.

pei. vs. Bent. *Rare.*

pē.ia. 1. demon. Thus, like this, this way (less definite than *penei*). (Gram. 8.3.) **2.** vt. To say. *Pēia mai ʻoia iaʻu,* thus he spoke to me.

peka. 1. Same as *pekapeka. Holo peka,* to run and tattle. *Kolo peka,* to sneak and tattle. **2.** Also **beka.** n. Bekah (ancient Hebrew unit of weight). (Puk. 38.26.) *Eng.*

pē.kaʻa. n. **1.** Sap of the green *kukui* nut, formerly rubbed over the tongue with the finger as a remedy for coated tongue or sore throat; very bitter. **2.** Seed of the *kāʻeʻe* vine. *Rare.*

pekala.kelia, pesalateria. n. Harp (RSV), psaltery (KJV). (2 Sam. 6.5.) *(Eng.* or Gr. *psalterium.)*

pekale. n. Peccary. *Eng.*

pekana, pegana. nvs. Pagan, heathen. *Eng.*

peka.peka. nvt. To tattle, tell tales, act as stool pigeon; tattler, stool pigeon.

pē.kau. vt. To place. *He pōhaku pēkau,* a placed stone.

peke. nvs. Dwarf, brownie, elf, goblin, midget; dwarfish, minute; short, as steps or stitches; tiny.

peke.keu. Same as *ʻekekeu,* wings.

peke.kue. vs. Blunt.

pekela, betela. See *nīoi pekela.*

peke.lala, federala. vs. Federal. *Eng.*

pekena, petena. See *moʻo pekena.*

peke.peke. 1. Redup. of *peke.* See *lauʻī pekepeke. Pekepeke ka humu,* the stitches are small. **2.** n. Ridge (?).

Nā ʻalu ame nā pekepeke o laila (chant), the ravines and ridges (?) of the place.

pē.keu. 1. Same as *pēheu 1, 2.* **hoʻo.pē.keu.** Same as *hoʻopēheu.* (PCP *peekeu,* wing; cf. Marquesan *pekeheu.*) **2.** n. Method of trapping owls by gumming ropes on an upright stick. *Rare.* **3.** n. Stirrups. *Rare.*

pē.keu.keu. Redup. of *pēkeu 1.*

peki. 1. nvi. Pace; to move along step by step, to tread along, trudge along, jog. *Eng. Kuʻu lio holo peki,* my pacing horse. **2.** vi. To back up, as a car. *Eng. E peki mai ʻoe i hope,* back up. **hoʻo.peki.** Caus/sim. **3.** n. Spade, as in playing cards. *Eng.*

peki.kini, petikini. vt. To present, as arms *(petikini i nā pū). Eng.*

pē.koi. Rare var. of *pīkoi.*

peku. nvt. A kick; to kick; to ward off, as a spear. *Kinipōpō peku,* football. **hoʻo.peku.** To have kicked, cause to kick, feign kicking, kick.

pekua. Pas/imp. of *peku.*

pekula. n. Picul, as used for the sale of sandalwood. *Eng.*

pekuna. n. A kick.

peku.nia. n. Petunias *(Petunia* x*hybrida),* garden herbs grown for their bright, attractive, funnel-shaped flowers of various colors. (Neal 739.) *Eng.*

peku.peku. Redup. of *peku;* to flick out, as bark while scraping *olonā* (Kam. 76:45).

pela. 1. Same as *pelapela;* fertilizer, any decomposed material, especially decayed flesh and intestines removed from a corpse; the bones were buried secretly, and the flesh *(pela)* thrown into the sea (cf. *kapa lau*). (PPN *pela.*) **2.** nvs. Spelling; to spell. *Eng. Pehea e pela ai kou inoa?* How is your name spelled? **3.** nvt. Bale; to bale; mattress, cushion; package, as of hard poi. *Eng. Pela mauʻu maloʻo,* bale of hay. **4.** Also **bela.** nvt. Bail; to bail. *Eng.* **5.** n. Pail. *Eng.*

pē.lā. 1. demon. In that way, like that, thus, so, that way. (Gram. 8.3.) *Pēlā anei?* Is that the way it is? Is that so? *Pēlā ʻea?* Is that how? So thatʻs it! Isnʻt it? *Pēlā iho!* Wait! Wait a minute! *Pēlā ʻiʻo nō,* thatʻs right, thatʻs certainly it. *Pēlā nō,* thatʻs so, thatʻs it, thatʻs how it is, exactly. *Ā pēlā aku,* and so forth, thereby. *Pēlā paha,* maybe so, perhaps, probably so [very common]. *Hele pēlā!* Get out! Go away! Begone! *Pēlā iho ā hina leʻa mai ka makani,* wait a moment until the winds blow fair. (PNP *peelaa.*) **2.** vi. To say. *Pēlā aku ʻo Ka-malama,* Ka-malama said.

pela.kano, pelatano. n. Plane tree (RSV), chestnut (KJV). (Ezek. 31.8.) *(Gr. platanos.)*

pela.mika, pelamida. n. Pyramid. *Eng.*

pela moe. n. Mattress.

pelane. n. Plane tree (RSV), chestnut (KJV) (Kin. 30.37.) *Eng.*

pela.pela. vs. Filthy, dirty, nasty, indecent, unclean, vulgar, lewd, obscene. **hoʻo.pela.pela.** To befoul, make dirty or filthy, soil, pollute. (PPN *pelapela.*)

pela uea (uwea). n. Bedsprings (later replaced by *pilina*). *Lit.,* wire bale. *Eng.*

pela uluna. n. Pillow.

pele. 1. nvs. Lava flow, volcano, eruption; volcanic (named for the volcano goddess, Pele). See ex., *kūkaepele, lepopele, manō. ʻA pele,* lava rock of any kind. *Hū ka pele,* lava pour forth, to erupt. **2.** vs. Soft, swollen, fat; pounded or kneaded soft, as poi or dough. Cf. *hāpele, kāpele, kūpele, napele. ʻŌpū pele,* fat stomach. **hoʻo.pele.** To knead. **3.** n. Choice Kauaʻi tapa (FS 252-3), scented with *maile* and *kūpaoa,* said to be gray and dyed with charcoal made of burned sugar cane mixed with coconut water (preceded by *ke*). *Pele ʻiliahi* (GP 8), *pele* tapa scented with sandalwood and associated with Kahana, Kauaʻi. **4.** vs. A term qualifying *koʻi* (adze), similar to *kūpele.* **5.** Also **bele.** n. Bell. *Eng. Hale pele,* belfry. *Pele ʻaina,* dinner bell. **6.** *(Cap.).* Volcano goddess.

pele.au. Same as *pele 2.*

pele.hū. n. **1.** Turkey *(Meleagris gallopavo). Lit.,* swollen swelling. Also *pōkeokeo. Wahine hulu pelehū,* turkey-feathered woman [said of women with mercenary interest in white men; the call of turkey hens *(pelehū)* is *pōkeokeo,* cluck, cluck, which also means prosperous]. **2.** Same as *pele 3.*

pele.hū kāne. n. Turkey gobbler.

Pelei.ake, Peleiade. n. Pleiades. (Ioba 9.9.)

peleka. n. **1.** Also **pereka, perka.** Perch, in surveying. *Eng.* **2.** Also **peleta.** Spelt (RSV), fitch (KJV). (Ezek. 4.9.) (Latin *spelta,* a species.)

pele.kana. n. Pelican. *Eng.*

Pele.kane. nvs. Britain, British, England, English, Englishman. *Eng. 'Ōlelo Pelekane,* English language.

Pele.kane Nui. n. Great Britain.

Pele.kania, Beretania. nvs. Britain; British. *Eng.*

peleke. Same as *peleki. Eng.*

Pele.kepuli.kano, Pereseburitano. nvs. Presbyterian. *Eng.*

peleki. nvt. Brake; to apply brakes. *Eng. E pa'a ana ka huila mua o ua ka'a lā mehe peleki ho'opa'a lā,* the front wheel of the car there was stopped as though stopped by brakes. **ho'o.peleki.** Caus/sim.

Pele.kia, Peresia. nvs. Persia; Persian. *Eng.*

pele.kikena, peresidena. nvs. President; presidential. *Eng.* Cf. *aupuni.*

Pele.kiuma, Belegiuma. nvs. Belgium; Belgian. *Eng.*

pele.kona, peresona. n. Person. *Eng.*

pele.kunu. n. **1.** Musty, moldy, or rank odor. **2.** *(Cap.)* Wet valley, north Moloka'i. See ex., *pāku'i 3.*

pele.leu. 1. nvs. Extended, either longitudinally or horizontally; long, broad, wide, as a nose; spreading, extending; extension, projection. See *huinakolu peleleu, huina peleleu. Wa'a peleleu,* a very large canoe type, sometimes a double canoe. *Kīkala peleleu,* wide, spreading hips. *I 'Īnia aku nei au i ke kau 'elepani ihu peleleu* (song), I was in India riding long-trunked elephants. **ho'o.pele.leu.** To cause to spread, extend; same as above. **2.** Same as *lanai. Rare.*

Pele.lina, Berelina. n. Berlin. *Eng.*

pele.makani. n. Propeller, as of an airplane. *Ni'ihau.*

pelena, berena. n. Crackers, biscuit, bread (Kin. 18.5). *Eng.* See *pa'i pelena. Pelena hū 'ole,* unleavened bread. *Pelena hō'ike* (Puk. 25.30), shewbread, bread of the Presence. *Pelena mo'a 'ole,* bread dough; *lit.,* uncooked bread. *'Aha'aina Pelena,* Holy Communion. *Lāpule 'Ai Pelena,* Communion Sunday.

pelena pa'a. n. Hardtack.

pelē.pelē. n. Boxing, fighting for sport. *Eng., play.*

pele.pulu. vs. Soaked, drenched, as by rain.

peleu. Same as *peleleu.*

pele.'ū. vs. Mildewed; wet, rotting, and vile-smelling, as of clothes. Cf. *pelekunu.*

pele.'unu. Var. of *pelekunu.* See ex., *lohelohe 3.*

peli.ala, feriara. n. Friar. *Eng.*

peli.hele, perihele. n. Periphery. *Eng.*

pelika, berita. n. Covenant, bond (formerly said of matrimony). (Heb. *b'rith.) Pahu pelika* (Heb. 9.4), ark of the covenant. *Pale pelika* (2 Tim. 3.3), truce-breakers. *Pelika o ka pelika'o'i'o,* creed, covenant of faith. *Ka pelika ma'ema'e o ka male,* the pure bonds of matrimony. *Eia ka'u pelika me lākou* (Isa. 59.21), here is my covenant with them.

peli.kana. n. Pelican. (Kanl. 14.17.) *Eng.*

Pē.lina. n. Bering. *Eng. Ke kai kōwā o Pēlina,* Bering Straits.

pelio, perio. vs. Counterfeit. *He kālā pelio ka'u,* I have counterfeit money.

pelo. vt. To flatter, tell tall tales, lie. (Nak. 31.) **ho'o.-pelo.** Caus/sim. (PNP *pelo.*)

peloka, peroka. n. Perch, rod, pole. *Eng.*

peloni, feloni. n. Felony. *Eng.*

pelo.pelo. Redup. of *pelo.* **ho'o.pelo.pelo.** Caus/sim.

pelu. 1. vi. To fold, turn over or under, bend. Cf. *alelo pelu, pahi pelu. Pelu 'ia,* bent. *Pū'ao pelu,* fallen womb. *Pelu ka huelo o ka 'īlio i ka maka'u,* the dog folded in his tail in fear. **ho'o.pelu.** To fold, turn, etc. (PNP *pelu.*) **2.** nvi. A hem, tuck, as in a dress; to take a

tuck, hem. *E ho'oku'u mai i ka pelu o ka lole,* let down the hem of the dress. **3.** vi. To turn and go. *Pelu mai i hope,* turn back.

pelua. Pas/imp. of *pelu 1-3. Pelua ihola ka makani,* the wind turned.

pē.lu'e. vs. Feeble, weak. *Rare.* Cf. *lu'elu'e.*

pelu.hā.'ele. n. A variety of taro.

Pelu.kia, Perusia. nvs. Prussia; Prussian. *Eng.*

pelu.kia 'akika, perusia asida. n. Prussic acid. *Eng.*

pelu.kua. vi. To turn about; to turn and go back.

peluli.ahi. n. A type of *kīhei* shawl dyed with sandalwood. (GP 16.)

pelulo, berulo. n. Beryl. (Hoik. 21.20.) (Gr. *beryllos.*)

pelu.luka. vs. Rotting, of crops (Malo 199, Emerson note); to soak and squeeze, as in preparing *pia. Rare.*

pelu.pelu. 1. Redup. of *pelu 1-3.* (PPN *pelupelu.*) **2.** Same as *pepelu,* repetitious.

pena. 1. nvt. Paint; to paint. *Eng. Pena 'ia,* painted. **2.** n. Package. *Rare. Pena ahipele,* package of matches. **3.** vs. A Maui word for *nīele,* curious.

pē.nā. demon. Like that; to do or say like that. *Rare.* (Gram. 8.3.) (PPN *pehena,* PNP *peenaa.*)

pena hale. nv. House paint; house painter; to paint a house.

pena ki'i. nv. To paint pictures; picture painter; water colors.

pena miki.'ao. n. Fingernail polish.

pene. vi. To reside a long time in one place. *Ka'ū.* Also *kūpene. Ua noho a ua pene i kēia wahi,* staying and living long in this place.

penei. demon. This way, like this, for instance, so, thus, as follows; to be thus (more definite than *pēia*). (Gram. 8.3.) *Penei ke 'ano,* like this, this way, such and such. *Pehea ke ki'ina a ka ipo? Penei iho, penei a'e, penei nō* (song), how to get a sweetheart? Thus, thus, so thus. (PPN *peheni,* PNP *pe(e)nei.*)

pe neia. Same as *pe kēia* and *penei.*

Pene.kekoka, Penetekota. nvs. Pentecost; Pentecostal. (I Kor. 16.8.) *Eng.*

pene.kine, benezine. n. Benzine. *Eng.*

pene.kū. vi. To reside at a place for several generations.

pene.kuina, peneguina. n. Penguin. *Eng.*

peni. n. **1.** Pen, pencil. *Eng. Maka peni,* pen point. **2.** Penny. *Eng.*

peni.kala. n. Pencil (sometimes preceded by *ke*). *Lit.,* sharpening pen.

peni.kenia, penitenia. n. Sacrament of confession. (Eng. *penitence.*)

peni.kila. n. Painkiller. *Eng.*

peni kila. n. Steel pen. *Eng.*

peno. vt. Soaked, drenched; to soak. Cf. *penopeno, pepeno.*

peno.peno. Redup. of *peno;* dirty, smutty.

penu. vt. To sop up, as gravy; to dunk; to dab up, as tears. Cf. *pepenu. Mea penu 'īnika,* blotter. **ho'o.-penu.** To cause to sop, dunk; to dunk. (PPN *penu.*)

penu.penu. Redup. of *penu.* **ho'o.penu.penu.** Redup. of *ho'openu.* (PNP *penupenu.*)

peo. 1. n. Vagina. **2.** vs. Round, globular. *Rare.*

peo.peo. Redup of *peo 2.*

pepa. 1. n. Paper; card, playing cards; to play cards. *Eng. Pā'ani pepa,* to play cards. *'Eke pepa,* paper sack. *Lei pepa,* paper lei. *Kāwele pepa,* paper napkin or towel. *Pu'u pepa,* deck of cards. **2.** n. Black or white pepper, produced from the fruit of a climbing Oriental shrub *(Piper nigrum).* (Neal 291.) *Eng.*

pepa hahau. n. Playing cards. *Lit.,* striking cards.

pepa hale. n. Wallpaper.

pepa hā.leu. n. Toilet paper. *Lit.,* cleansing paper.

pepa ho'o.kē. n. Kleenex or paper handkerchief. *Lit.,* nose-blowing paper.

pepa ho'o.loli ka'a. n. A transfer authorizing change from one vehicle to another. *Lit.,* paper for changing cars.

pepa ho'o.nani hale. n. Wallpaper.

pepa ho'o.malo'o 'Ī.nika. n. Blotter.

pepa kaha.kaha. n. Scratch paper.

pepa kala.kala. n. Sandpaper. *Lit.,* rough paper.
pepa.kene. n. Cayenne pepper *(Capsicum annuum* cv. *'longum').* (Neal 742.) *Eng.*
pepa ki'i. n. Joker, in a deck of cards. *Lit.,* picture card.
pepa kī.ko'o. n. Check or draft for paying money. *Lit.,* withdrawing paper.
pepa kī.ko'o kā.lā. n. Money order.
pepa kope. n. Carbon paper, xerox.
pepa lahi.lahi. n. Tissue paper, thin paper.
pepa lei. n. Crepe paper, as used in lei making. *Lit.,* lei paper.
pepa mā.noa.noa. n. Cardboard. *Lit.,* thick paper.
pepa.mina. n. Peppermint *(Mentha piperita).* (Neal 734.) *Eng.*
pepa 'omo 'ī.nika. n. Blotter.
pepa pa'i ki'i. n. Photographic film.
pepa po'o.leka. n. Postcard.
pepa wahī. n. Wrapping paper.
pepe 1. vs. Flat, as a nose; low, squatty. Cf. *mene, 'ūmene, 'ūpepe.* **2.** vs. Small, fine-meshed, as of a mat. *Pepepe* is more common. **3.** n. Perhaps short for *pepeiao 6;* Emerson however gives "canoe seat" (UL 194) and "chock on which a canoe rests" (PH 114).
pē.pē. 1. Redup. of *pē 1. Na'au pēpē* (Kep. 75), modest spirit. *Hanapēpē* (place name), crushed bay [perhaps so called because of landslides]. *He pēpē 'ōmaka no Hilo, pā i ka pa'akai, uāni'i,* a crushing of the fish *'ōmaka* from Hilo, touched with salt, stiffens [of a weakling]. **ho'o.pē.pē, hō.pē.pē.** Redup. of *ho'opē;* to flatten; humble. (2 Sam. 22.43.) (PPN *pee.*) **2.** n. Baby. *Eng.* **ho'o.pē.pē.** To act like a baby; infantile.
pepe'e. 1. nvs. Twisted, crooked, deformed, misshapen, out of shape; deformity. **ho'o.pepe'e.** To bend, twist, etc. (Kep. 159.) **2.** n. Young fern leaves, as of *hāpu'u, hō'i'o,* and *'ama'u,* that are rolled up, sometimes suggesting a question mark. **3.** See *pepe'e paka.*
pepe'e.kua. Var. of *pepe'ekue.*
pepe'e.kue. vs. Coarse, as lace or hair; thick; clumsy, lumbering, as a puppy's feet. See ex., *pupuka.*
pepe'e paka. n. Tobacco plug.
pepehi. 1. vt. To beat, strike, pound, kill. *Pepehi ā make,* to beat to death, kill. *Pepehi i ka mana'olana,* to dash hopes. *Pepehi i nā mū, pepehi mea 'ino,* disinfect. *Mea pepehi kanaka,* weapon. *Pepehi ā 'oki'oki holoholona,* to butcher animals. **ho'o.pepehi.** To cause to beat, strike, kill; to pretend to beat. (PNP *pepesi.*) **2.** n. Surface of a tapa beater formed by deep grooves with the wide ridges (up to 14) rounded off in the form of an inverted *U;* sometimes the beater itself was so called. Cf. *hoahoa, hohoa.*
pepe.hia. Pas/imp. of *pepehi 1.* (For. 5:509.)
pepehi kanaka. nv. Murder, murderer, manslaughter; to commit murder.
pepehu. Redup. of *pehu 1.* **ho'o.pepehu.** Redup. of *ho'opehu;* to flex the muscles or make them bulge.
pepe.hua. Pas/imp. of *pepehu.*
pepe.hue. Var. of *pepehua.*
pepei. Rare var. of *paipai,* to encourage.
pepei.ao. 1. nvi. Ear; to hear *(rare).* Cf. *līpepeiao. Lohe pepeiao,* hearsay, to have heard only. *Pepeiao manana,* protruding ears. *Pepeiao pili,* ears pressing close to the head. *Pepeiao pilau,* infected ear. *E heluhelu ma nā pepeiao o nā kānaka* (Puk. 24.7), read in the audience of the people. **2.** n. Cotyledon, as of beans. **3.** n. Stipule, as of *noni,* a tree. **4.** n. Scallops in lace. **5.** n. Lugs or blocks inside a canoe hull to which the *'iako,* booms, and perhaps the mast (For. 5:633) are fastened. **6.** n. Comb cleats for canoe thwarts or seats. **7.** n. Chinese cake stuffed with meat, named for a resemblance to an ear. Cf. cup-shaped *mea 'ono pua'a.* **8.** n. Long nets 30 to 37 m deep, attached at each side of the *'upena kolo,* bag net. **9.** n. Valve of the heart. **10.** Same as *pepeiao akua.*
pepei.ao akua. n. Tree fungus, the Jew's-ear *(Auricularia auricula).* Also *akua pepeiao.*
pepei.ao 'eha. n. Earache.
pepei.ao.hao. n. Horn of an animal; trumpet or horn

made of an animal's horn. (Hal. 118.27.) *Lit.,* iron ear.
pepei.ao hohono. n. Infected ear; said derisively of farmers with reference to the smoky odor *(hohono)* of their fires.
pepei.ao kuli. n. A deaf ear, deafness, disobedience, refusal to listen to advice.
pepei.ao lā.'au. Same as *pepeiao akua,* tree fungus. *Lit.,* tree ear.
pepei.ao pulu.'aha. See *pulu'aha.*
pepei.e'e. n. Overripe breadfruit or banana kneaded with coconut cream, wrapped in ti leaves, and baked in the oven. This could be preserved for a season. Also *paipaie'e.*
pepela. 1. Same as *pelapela,* filthy. **2.** Redup. of *pela,* to spell. *Eng.*
pepele. Same as *pele 3,* a tapa.
pepelo. Same as *pelopelo,* to lie. (PNP *pepelo.*)
pepelu. Redup. of *pelu 1–3;* repetitious in speech. (PPN *pepelu.*)
Pepe.luali. n. February. *Eng.*
pepe.lu'e. Redup. of *pēlu'e.* Rare.
pepena. Redup. of *pena 1,* to paint. *Eng.*
pepeno. Redup. of *peno.*
pepenu. Same as *penupenu.* *'O ka 'ōpelu e pepenu ana lā* (song), the *'ōpelu,* the fish that is dunked [in sauce].
pepe-o-Hina. Same as *lepe-o-Hina,* a seaweed.
pepepe. Redup. of *pepe 1, 2. Maka pepepe,* small mesh. (PCP *pepepe(pe),* low.)
pepeu. Redup. of *peu 1, 2.*
pepeua. Hard, thick, disobedient. (And.)
pepeue. Redup. of *peue.*
peu. 1. vi. To thrust up, push up, uproot, prod, bunt, root, nudge upward, elbow upward, pout, jostle with the feet as to attract attention; to rise up, as grass that has been trod upon; to thrust, as a male in coition. **ho'o.peu.** To thrust up, etc. **2.** nvi. A vulgar gesture, in which the fist is doubled and jerked upward; to make the gesture. **3.** n. Cartilage of a pig's nose. **4.** n. Point at canoe bow.
pe'u. Same as *pelu. Moloka'i.*
pē.'ū. n. Cooked taro leaves. (PH 74.) Commonly called *lū'au.*
peua. Pas/imp. of *peu 1, 2.*
peue. vs. Dull, blunt. *Fig.,* stupid, dull. *Ka peue, pepeue, ho'owalea o loko o ka hale* (For. 6:402), the stupid ones, the stupid, stupid ones, passing the time within the house.
peu.peu. 1. Same as *pepeu.* **2.** Same as *peue.*
pewa. 1. n. Tail of fish, shrimp, lobster. Cf. *hi'u.* **2.** n. Rectangular patch or wedge used for mending bowls, perhaps so called because of a resemblance to a fishtail. **3.** Rare var. of *pawa 1,* usually following *huli. 'Elua wale nō huli pewa 'ana o ka piha makahiki* (Kel. 10), after the dawning of just two years. (Also Kel. 61.) **4.** n. Clump or group, as of trees near a forest. *'Ōhi'a uliuli i ka ua i moku pewa 'ia* (PH 33), *'ōhi'a* trees darkened by the rain and cut off as a clump.
pewa.pewa. 1. Pectoral fins of a fish; to move or vibrate these fins. **2.** Redup. of *pewa 4. I ka pewapewa lā'au mauka o Pu'u-lele* (song), the tree clump inland of Pu'u-lele.
pī. 1. nvs. Stingy, miserly, niggardly; stinginess (sometimes preceded by *ke*). **ho'o.pī.** Stingy, extremely economical, frugal; to skimp. **2.** nvi. Sputtering, smoldering, as green wood that burns poorly; to snort, as a horse; to sniffle or have difficulty breathing due to a congestion in the nose, as caused by a cold; to break wind with a slight sputtering sound. See *maka pī. Pī ka 'amo,* the anus sputters [to work hard like a slave]. *'O ke kāne kēnā, pī ka 'amo,* if he's your husband, you'll know plenty of drudgery; *lit.,* the anus will give a *pī* sound. **3.** vt. To sprinkle, as water with the fingers. (PPN *pihi.*) **4.** n. Peas, lentils (2 Sam. 17.28); a kind of bean; hyacinth bean *(Dolichos lablab)* or Lima bean. *Eng.* Called *pāpapa* in some localities. **5.** n. The letter "p." *Eng.*

pia. 1. n. Polynesian arrowroot *(Tacca leontopetaloides,* formerly known as *T. pinnatifida),* an herb known in the eastern tropics, formerly cultivated in Hawai'i for the starchy tubers, which were used for medicine and food. In spring or summer, a few leaves rise on long stems from a tuber and die back in the winter. The blades are much divided, about 30 cm wide, somewhat like papaya leaves in shape. Cf. *mā'ili 2.* (HP 212, Neal 228–9.) (PPN *pia.*) 2. n. General name for starch; starch made from arrowroot is called *pia Hawai'i* to distinguish from other starches; *pia* is used in *haupia* pudding, as medicine, and as talcum powder. *Pia kūlina,* cornstarch. *Lole pia,* starched clothes. 3. vs. Pale yellow. Cf. *hala pia,* a pandanus, and *hēpia,* of the *'ilima* flower. 4. n. A variety of taro. (HP 34.) 5. n. A variety of sweet potato. (HP 142.) 6. n. A kind of stone, as used for adzes. 7. Also **bia.** n. Beer. *Eng. Bia nui,* lager beer. *Bia wei,* weiss beer. 8. n. Stork.

pi'a. n. A kind of yam *(Dioscorea pentaphylla),* a climber with lobed leaves known throughout Pacific islands and in tropical Asia. It bears small aerial and subterranean, edible tubers. (HP 215, Neal 230–1.)

pī.'ā. n. 1. Cluster, as of bananas, grapes. *Rare.* 2. Measure of one hand's distance. (For. 5:645.)

pia.ea. n. Small fish, as *'ōhua manini. Ku'u piaea,* to scoop up *piaea,* as with a mosquito net or skirt.

pia Hawai.'i. See *pia 2.*

pi'a Hawai'i. n. Same as *pi'a.*

pī.'ai. 1. Same as *pī'ao 1. Kaua'i.* 2. n. Any berry-like fruit, as of *māmaki, olonā, 'ōhelo. Rare.*

pia.ia. n. Young *manini* fish. *Ni'ihau.*

pī.'alu. nvs. Wrinkled with age, as with sagging eyelids or jowls; a term of reproach for a man who has lost his sexual potency; an impotent male.

pia maka hinu. n. A type of stone used for adzes. See *pia 6.*

pia mani.oka. n. Starch made from manioc.

piano. n. Piano. *Eng.*

pī anu.hea. Same as *pī wai anuhea,* sweet pea.

pī.'ao. 1. nvt. To fold ti leaves into a cuplike package, as for dipping water or for baking food in the oven; such a package. **ho'o.pī.'ao.** To make such a package. (PCP *pi(i)kao;* cf. Marquesan *pikao.*) 2. vs. Curling or shriveling, as of leaves in the heat; crumpling up, as of meeting waves. (Isa. 25.5.)

pī.'ā.pā. n. Alphabet; name of an early spelling book; this word is said to have derived from the method of teaching Hawaiians to begin the alphabet *"b, a, ba."* The Hawaiians pronounced *"b"* like *"p"* and said *"pī 'ā pā."* See ex., *puana 2.*

pia.pia. 1. nv. The encrusted white matter in the eyes, as from sleeping or sore eyes, "sand" in the eyes; to get such matter in the eyes; an abusive epithet applied to one who was unwashed, said to refer to genitals. *Maka piapia,* eyes with white matter, said insultingly of one who does not see what he ought to see (For. 5:219). (PPN *piapia*.) 2. n. A variety of taro. 3. n. A variety of sweet potato. (HP 142.)

pie. Var. of *piele 1. Rare.*

pī.'ei. Rare Kaua'i var. of *ki'ei,* to peer.

piele. 1. nvi. Mattery eruptions or eczema on the scalp; to have such eruptions. 2. nvt. To trade, peddle; trader, peddler. 3. n. Pudding of grated taro, sweet potato, yam, banana, or breadfruit, baked in ti leaves with coconut cream.

pieleele. Redup. of *piele 1–3.*

piena. vs. Offensive to smell, stinking. *Rare.*

pī.'ena. vs. Fiery-tempered; to shy, of a horse. Cf. *'ena.* **ho'o.pī.'ena.** To cause anger; to cause shy; to feign anger.

pī.ena.ena. Redup. of *piena. Rare.*

pī.'ena.'ena. Redup. of *pī'ena.*

pie.pie. Redup. of *pie. Rare.*

pie.piele. 1. Redup. of *piele 1–3.* 2. vi. To do small favors in order to receive greater ones; to flatter or fawn in order to receive something.

pie ue.ue. n. Eczema, a name for *kauā,* outcasts.

piha. nvs. Full, complete, filled, loaded; full-blooded; completion, capacity, fullness; pregnant. Cf. *piha makahiki, pihapiha, piha pono. Piha loa,* stuffed full. *Ho'oka'a piha,* to pay in full. *Piha maika'i,* well-filled, filled just right. *Hawai'i piha,* pure Hawaiian. *Ho'i mai nō ke kai i kona piha 'ana* (Puk. 14.27), the sea returned to its wonted flow. *Iā lākou e piha ana ma Pā-'auhau* (For. 5:411), while they crowded about at *Pā-'auhau.* **ho'o.piha.** To fill, complete, pervade, stuff, eat one's fill, cram; to fill out, as a growing child; to breed, as of a female animal; to impregnate; to fill, as a tooth; to load, as a gun; to thread, as a needle. *Ho'opiha 'ia i ka pulupulu,* stuffed with cotton. *Moa ho'opiha 'ia me ka laiki,* chicken stuffed with rice.

pī.hā. 1. n. Material of any sort carried by flood waters or sea, flotsam and jetsam, driftwood, floating debris. 2. n. A round herring *(Spratelloides delicatulus);* the largest is about 8 cm long; preferred dried and salted. 3. vi. To belch. 4. Poi pounder. (AP.)

piha.'ā. 1. Same as *pīhā 1. Koa piha'ā,* a fallen *koa* tree suitable for a canoe, so called even though it was not driftwood. *Hana a ka wai nui, piha'ā o kai,* when the waters are great, the shorelands are littered with jetsam [said of a person who talks foolishly]. See also *mamo 4* and Hal. 102.3. *Hu'ea i kai nā piha'ā moe wai o uka,* washed to the sea is debris of upland streams. 2. Same as *pīhā 2.*

piha.'ekelo. n. Mynah bird *(Acridotheres tristis),* introduced from India in 1865. *Lit.,* full of *'ekelo* sound. Also *'ekelo.*

piha 'eu. vs. Spirited, enthusiastic.

piha.ku'i. vs. Brimful, jammed full, packed tight, crowded.

piha lima. n. Handful. *Nā piha lima o ka pale* (Ezek. 13.19), the handfuls of barley.

piha maka.hiki. nvs. Yearly anniversary; to have an annual anniversary. See ex., *pewa 3. Lā piha makahiki,* birthday, anniversary day. *'Aha'aina piha makahiki,* feast to celebrate an anniversary.

pihana. nvs. Fullness, filling up, completion. See ex., *heana 2. Pihana kanaka,* a crowd or gathering of people. *Pihana-ka-lani* (place name), gathering place [of] high supernatural beings.

pihano. vs. Silent, weak-voiced. *Nona ka hale i Kaumai-lani, no Kāka'e no ka leo pihano* (chant for Kuakini), his is the house at Kau-mai-lani, for Kāka'e, the weak-voiced.

piha.piha. 1. vs. Full, complete; filled; full and flowing, as a garment; filed, as cards; completed, as a questionnaire. **ho'o.piha.piha.** To fill, complete; to file, as cards; frame, questionnaire, any kind of form to be completed. *Ke ho'opihapiha maila ke kino o ke keiki,* the body of the child is filling out. *Aia 'o mea ma'ō, ke ho'opihapiha maila,* so-and-so is over there, stirring up hard feelings with tales. (Cf. *ho'opihapiha 'ōlelo.*) 2. n. Gills of a fish. *Kūkū ka pihapiha a pi'i ka lena,* the gills stand out and the bile rises [of anger]. 3. n. Ruffle, fringe, as on a dress. (Nah. 15.38.) *Lima pihapiha,* ruffled sleeve. **ho'o.piha.piha.** To make a ruffle; ruffler, as on a sewing machine. 4. Var. of *'ōpihapiha.*

piha.piha 'ā.'ī. n. Ruff.

piha.piha 'ō koho.lā. n. Pleated ruffle. *Lit.,* whaler's ruffle, so called because such ruffles were stylish in whaling days.

-pihapiha 'ōlelo. ho'o.piha.piha 'ō.lelo. To stir up dislike for another, to turn against another, as by telling tales or gossip.

piha pono. vs. Completely full, complete. *'A'ole piha pono,* incomplete. *Piha pono ka manawa,* to mature [of bonds]. *Piha pono ka mana'o,* completely clear and intelligible idea. **ho'o.piha pono.** To complete, make completely full, clear, intelligible.

piha pū. vs. Completely filled.

piha puna. n. Spoonful.

piha.'ū. vs. Jam-packed, packed tight, full, crammed. *Ho'okēkē a piha'ū nā alanui,* the streets were jammed and packed.

piha.weu.weu. 1. n. Temporary bed made of dry *'ilima* branches, dried banana leaves and grasses, over which a mat or two were spread. **2.** vs. Full of grass, but thin, said of a grass-eating animal that does not put on flesh.

pī.hā.weu.weu. n. A fish (no data).

pihe. nvi. Din of voices, crying, shouting, wailing, lamentation; to mourn, shout, etc. *Kani ka pihe,* a shout is heard. *Kū ka pihe,* a shout or lamentation arises. (PCP *pi(f,s)e.*)

pihea. Pas/imp. of *pihe. Ka wawā pihea a nā manu* (chant), the loud din of the birds.

pī.heka. vs. Inflamed, of eyes. Cf. *heka. Mākole, mākole ā kahi, hele i kai o Pīheka* (chant), sore-eyed, sore-eyed as no one else, go to the sealand of Inflamed-eye [Kama-pua'a taunts the goddess Pele].

pī.heka.heka. Redup. of *pīheka.*

pī.hele.hele. vs. Grated, mashed, pulverized; to grate.

pihi. 1. n. Scab, scar. **2.** n. Button, badge; to button (preceded by *ke*). Cf. *huka pihi, pihi pūlima. Pihi mākaʻi,* police badge. *Pihi 'ūmi'i,* snap fastener. (PCP *pi(f,s)i;* cf. Marquesan *pihi.*) **3.** vs. Blunt, dull, as a wooden digging stick. *Rare.* **4.** n. Fish. *Eng. Ua loa'a mai ka pihi nui* (song), got the big fish.

pihi.pihi. 1. Redup. of *pihi 1;* scarred. **2.** Redup. of *pihi 2;* any small objects shaped like buttons, as washers (preceded by *ke*). **3.** nvt. To skip stones on the surface of the water; stone skipping. **4.** Redup. of *pihi 3. Rare.*

pihi pū.lima. n. Cuff button.

pihō. 1. nvs. Swamp, mire; swampy. **2.** Var. of *piholo,* to swamp, as a canoe. (For. 5:541.) **hoʻo.pihō.** Caus/sim.

pihoa. Dizzy. (And.)

pī.hō.hō. Same as *pihōpihō.*

pī hohono. Same as *'aukoʻi,* a plant.

pī.hoi. Same as *pīhoihoi.*

pī.hoi.hoi. nvs. Disturbed, excited, worried, agitated, alarmed, perturbed, upset, uneasy, astonished, emotional; worry, anxiety, astonishment. (Dan. 5.6.) *Hana pīhoihoi,* exciting event, adventure. *Ka pīhoihoi o ka na'au* (Kanl. 28.28), astonishment of heart. **hoʻo.pī.-hoi.hoi.** To cause anxiety; to worry, excite, astonish.

pī.hole. vi. To fidget, as a child; to paw, as a drunk; to squirm, flirtatiously sidle up to a man; restless.

piholo. vi. To sink, founder, drown, be swamped, shipwrecked. **hoʻo.piholo.** To sink, drown.

pī.holo.holo. 1. Redup. of *piholo.* **2.** vs. Watery, as poi. *Rare.*

pī.hopa, bihopa. nvs. Bishop; Episcopalian. *Eng. Hoʻo-mana Pīhopa,* Episcopalian religion.

pihō.pihō. Redup. of *pihō;* to bob up and down or swamp, as a canoe.

pihulu. vs. Hairy, fuzzy. *'Eki pihulu,* ace of spades.

piʻi. 1. vi. To go inland or overland (whether or not uphill), to go or walk up, climb, ascend, advance, mount, rise; to grow up, as a child; to fall, as one shadow on another. See *ihu piʻi. Piʻi kuahiwi,* mountain climber; to climb mountains. *Piʻi ke kai,* the sea rises [the temper flares]. *Maloʻo ka wai, piʻi ka lepo,* the water dries up, the dirt comes up [reasoning and understanding are gone, only invective is left]. **hoʻo.piʻi.** To cause to rise, promote, mount, come up, raise up, bring forth, utter; to turn unto the wind; promotion. See ex., *limalima 4. Me ka hoʻopiʻi aku ma ka inoa o kō kākou Haku,* and call forth the name of our Lord. (PEP *piki.*) **2.** vi. To experience personally, or appear, as heat, cold, emotion. See ex., *maneʻo. Hānau ka piʻi 'awaʻawa, he 'awaʻawa kona* (KL line 520), are born those of bitter disposition, theirs is bitterness. *No kona huhū, piʻi ka 'ōlelo 'ino,* because of his anger, evil words come forth. *Ke piʻi nei ka manaʻo,* the idea comes now. *Piʻi ka makemake,* the desire comes. *Piʻi ke anu,* to get chills. *Piʻi ka huhū, piʻi ka 'ena, piʻi ka heu,* to get very angry, heated, bristling. *Piʻi ka wela,* to get a fever; to feel the heat of anger. *Piʻi ka 'ōhune wela,* to get prickly heat. *Piʻi ka 'ula,* to blush. **hoʻo.piʻi.** Same as *hoʻopiʻipiʻi.* **3.** Same as *piʻipiʻi 3,* curly. (PEP *piki.*) **4.** Same as *pipiʻi,* expensive. **5.** nvt. Intercourse; to practice inter-

course; to mount, as of male animals. **hoʻo.piʻi.** To cause to mount, as of male animals; to breed, impregnate. **6.** n. Triangular piece inserted in a *holokū* skirt to add width, or inserted at the base of the legs of bell-bottom trousers. (PPN *piki.*) **7.** n. Taros. See below.

-piʻi. hoʻo.piʻi. To sue (see ex., *mālama ola*), bring suit, bring a complaint to one in authority, accuse in court, prosecute, petition; appeal, lawsuit, court case, petition. Cf. *palapala hoʻopiʻi. Mea i hoʻopiʻi 'ia,* accused. *Hoʻopiʻi 'āina,* to have a suit over land matters. *Poʻe (mea) hoʻopiʻi,* plaintiff. *Poʻe (mea) hoʻopiʻi 'ia,* defendant, accused party. *Hoʻopiʻi pohō,* suit for damages.

piʻia. Pas/imp. of *piʻi 1. Ke āhua i piʻia e ke keiki,* the mound climbed by the child.

piʻi.aliʻi. n. A native variety of taro, one of the oldest varieties grown in Hawaiʻi; formerly known as one of the royal taros and desirable as an offering to the gods; today, an important wet-land poi taro. Leaves and corm are tinged with pink. (HP 28, Whitney.) This name may be qualified by the colors *'eleʻele, keʻokeʻo, 'ulaʻula.* See ex., *hanoa.*

piʻi aliʻi. v. To claim chiefly blood, whether or not it exists. **hoʻo.piʻi aliʻi.** Caus/sim.

piʻi.hā.lā.wai. n. A variety of taro. (HP 34.)

piʻi kea. vi. To become light, as the day; to begin to gray, of hair.

piʻi.koi. vt. To claim honors not rightfully due, to seek preferment, to aspire to the best or to more than is one's due; to claim to be of higher rank than one is. See ex., *loaʻa . . . kāu. Mai piʻikoi i ka 'amaʻama,* don't strive for the *'amaʻama* [this fish was very choice; the meaning is: be satisfied with what you have, why aim for the moon].

piʻi.kū. 1. nvi. To climb a steep slope; to climb, as a coconut palm by grasping the trunk with the hands and walking up with the feet; a steep climb. **2.** n. A medicine made of the sap of young *kukui* nuts, used as a gargle for sore throat and thrush; if swallowed it causes nausea and looseness of the bowels. **3.** n. Transpiration, water drops on leaves of plants. *Rare.* Cf. *wai hua.*

piʻi.kuma. n. A type of ancient prayer. (For. 6:23.)

piʻi.lae. vs. Haughty, proud. *Lit.,* forehead rising. *Rare.*

piʻina. n. Climb, ascent, rise, incline, etc. Cf. *piʻi 1.* **hoʻo.piʻina (a)** Same as above. **(b)** Quilting in a direction away from the quilter. Also *hoʻopiʻipiʻi.* (PEP *pikinga.*)

piʻi pā.walu. n. Octave. *Lit.,* eightfold ascent.

piʻi.piʻi. 1. Redup. of *piʻi 1;* bubbling forth, as water (Kanl. 8.7); to overflow, as charged water; effervesce. *Wai piʻipiʻi,* charged water or liquid. *Piʻipiʻi akula nā 'ale* (Hal. 107.25), lifting the waves up [of a wind]. **hoʻo.piʻi.piʻi. (a)** Redup. of *hoʻopiʻi;* to sail, beat, or tack against the wind; to regurgitate. *Lā'au hoʻopiʻi-piʻi,* emetic, medicine to cause vomiting. **(b)** Same as *hoʻopiʻina (b).* (PCP *pikipiki.*) **2.** Redup. of *piʻi 2.* Cf. *piʻipiʻi kai, piʻipiʻi 'ōlelo.* **hoʻo.piʻi.piʻi.** To stir up ill feelings, to rouse anger; jealousy. **3.** vs. Curly, curled, wavy. *Piʻipiʻi lau nui,* wavy, of hair. *Piʻipiʻi Pukikī,* kinky, of hair. (PEP *pikipiki.*) **4.** Same as *pipiʻi,* expensive. **5.** Redup. of *piʻi 5.* **6.** Same as *mānienie 'ula,* a grass.

piʻi.piʻi aliʻi. Redup. of *piʻialiʻi.*

piʻi.piʻi kai. vi. To rise, of a strong sea. *Fig.,* to flare, as anger.

piʻi.piʻi.lau.mana.mana. Same as *'analiʻi,* a fern.

piʻi.piʻi 'ō.lelo. n. Words of anger, emotion, controversy. **hoʻo.piʻi.piʻi 'ō.lelo.** To cause controversy, words of anger, etc.

pika. 1. n. Short for *pīkaʻo 2. Rare.* **2.** n. Pitcher *(Eng.),* vase. **3.** n. Beet *(Beta vulgaris).* (Neal 331.) *Eng.* **4.** n. Picul; half. *Eng.* **5.** vs. Hot, as peppery food (said in pidgin Eng.).

pī kai. v. To sprinkle with sea water or salted fresh water to purify or remove taboo, as formerly done after a death or after a boy's subincision. (Nānā 179–82.) *Pī kai kea,* to sprinkle with white sea [from waves, and not with salted fresh water].

pī.kai.kai. Redup. of *pī kai.*

pī kai 'ō.lena. v. To sprinkle with sea water or salt water, with a bit of *'ōlena* root, to purify or remove taboo.

pī.kaka. 1. vs. Smooth, polished. *Rare.* 2. Same as *pīka'o 1.* (UL 96.) *Rare.*

pī.kā.kā. Var. of *pākākā.*

pika.kani. n. A rattlebox *(Crotalaria pallida,* formerly known as *C. mucronata),* known in many tropical countries, a small, weedy, shrubby legume with three-parted leaves, yellow flowers striped with red, and many-seeded pods to 5 cm long. (Neal 443, 445.)

pika.ka'o. Redup. of *pīka'o 1.* (UL 96.)

pī.kake. n. 1. The Arabian jasmine *(Jasminum sambac),* introduced from India, a shrub or climber, with rounded, dark-green leaves and small, white, very fragrant flowers used for leis. Since Princess Ka-'iu-lani was fond of both these flowers and her peacocks *(pīkake),* the same name was given the flowers. (Neal 680.) 2. Peacock, peafowl *(Pavo cristata),* said to have been introduced to Hawai'i about 1860. They are wild on Ni'ihau and at Wai-'anae, O'ahu.

pī.kake hihi. n. A creeping *pīkake.*

pī.kake hohono. n. A low shrubby plant *(Clerodendrum philippinum),* from China, a weed with broad, downy leaves and white or pink, scented, double flowers. (Neal 731.) *Lit.,* bad smelling. *Hawai'i.* Also *pīkake wauke.*

pī.kake hō.kū. n. The star jasmine *(Jasminum multiflorum),* a shrubby, somewhat downy vine, from India. Leaves are ovate or cordate; flowers white, 2.5 cm wide, starlike, with four to nine lobes. (Neal 679–80.)

pī.kake lahi.lahi. n. The single-flowered form of *pīkake.*

pī.kake mele.mele. n. The yellow jasmine *(Jasminum humile),* a shrub from tropical Asia. It has compound leaves and yellow flowers about 2.5 cm wide. (Neal 681.)

pī.kake pupupu. n. The double-flowered form of *pīkake.*

pī.kake wauke. Same as *pīkake hohono. O'ahu.*

pī.kala. n. Pickle. *Eng.*

pī.kale. nvs. Sticky, as water on a poi board after poi has been pounded on it; the watery residue.

pī.kale.kale. Redup. of *pīkale.*

pīka.nalā. Var. of *pīkananā.*

pīka.nanā. vs. Quick-tempered, snappish, cross; raging, storming.

pī.kanele. vs. Small, very little. *Rare.*

pika.nika, picanica. Var. of *pikiniki,* picnic.

pika.nini. Small (slang, from *pickaninny).*

pī.ka'o. 1. nvs. Dehydrated food, as yam cooked, grated, dried, packed in banana fiber, used on long sea voyages; dried up, juiceless, parched (applied jestingly to old hags). (For. 6:386.) Cf. *pōka'o.* 2. n. Canoe hold under both the foreward cover and aft cover. *Piha noho'i ka wa'a mai ka pīka'o mua a ka pīka'o hope,* the canoe was filled from within the bow to within the stern.

pika.pika. 1. n. Suction cups on octopus tentacles. 2. n. A kind of lava rock with points said to resemble the suction cups of an octopus. 3. vs. Variegated, spotted; of varying colors, as the ocean.

pika pua. n. Flower container, vase. *Lit.,* flower pitcher.

pika.wai. vt. To pick up, as a rooster picks up food. *Rare.*

pika wai. n. Water pitcher.

pike.kakio, pisetakio. n. Pistachio *(Pistacia vera).* (Neal 524.) *Eng.*

pī.kela. n. Name of a skin eruption.

pikele. n. Pitcher. *Eng. Rare.*

pī.kele. Same as *pīkanele. Rare.* **ho'o.pī.kele.** To dole out in small quantities.

pī.kele.kele. Redup. of *pīkele. Rare.*

piki. 1. vs. Shrunk, shortened, irregular. *Lei piki,* lei made of feathers of uneven length that protrude unevenly, as of *mamo* feathers. **ho'o.piki.** To shorten, shrink; to make, as a *lei piki.* (PCP *piti;* cf. Marquesan.) 2. n. The peach *(Prunus persica),* possibly a native of China, introduced to Hawai'i but not common. (Neal 395–6.) 3. n. Beet. *Eng.* Also *pika.*

Pī.kī. 1. nvs. Fiji; Fijian. *Eng.* 2. Also **P.K.** n. Provisional Government. *Eng.*

pikiki. Redup. of *piki 1. Rare.*

piki.mana. nvs. Bituminous; coal. *Eng. Lānahu pikimana,* bituminous coal.

piki.neki. n. Business. *Eng. 'A 'ohe ou pikineki malaila,* you have no business there.

piki.niki. n. Picnic. *Eng.*

piki.piki. 1. vi. To pinch or squeeze, as in milking. *Rare.* Cf. *'ūpikipiki.* (PCP *pitipiti;* cf. Marquesan.) 2. Same as *pikipiki'ō.*

piki.piki.'ō. vs. Rough, stormy, choppy, as the sea. *Fig.,* agitated in spirit.

piko. n. 1. Navel, navel string, umbilical cord. *Fig.,* blood relative, genitals. Cf. *piko pau 'iole, wai'olu. Mō ka piko, moku ka piko, wehe i ka piko,* the navel cord is cut [friendship between related persons is broken; a relative is cast out of a family]. *Pehea kō piko?* How is your navel [a facetious greeting avoided by some because of the double meaning]? (PPN *pito.)* 2. Summit or top of a hill or mountain; crest; crown of the head; crown of the hat made on a frame *(pāpale pahu);* tip of the ear; end of a rope; border of a land; center, as of a fishpond wall or *kōnane* board; place where a stem is attached to the leaf, as of taro. 3. Short for *alopiko. I ka piko nō 'oe, lihaliha* (song) at the belly portion itself, so very choice and fat. 4. A common taro with many varieties, all with the leaf blade indented at the base up to the *piko,* junction of blade and stem. (HP 29.) 5. Design in plaiting the hat called *pāpale 'ie.* 6. Bottom round of a carrying net, *kōkō.* 7. Small *wauke* rootlets from an old plant. 8. Thatch above a door. *'Oki i ka piko,* to cut this thatch; *fig.,* to dedicate a house.

piko 'ele.'ele. n. A native variety of taro, with dark-purple petioles; common poi and table taro; the leaves are good for *lū'au.* Also *helemauna.*

piko.holo. n. Slipknot. *Lit.,* loop rope-end.

pī.koi. n. 1. Core, as of breadfruit or pandanus. Also *'īkoi.* 2. A tripping club, as of wood or stone, with a rope attached; this was hurled at the foe to encircle his arms or legs and render him helpless. (FS 95.) Also *'īkoi.* 3. Wooden floats attached to upper or head cord of gill nets. Cf. *'alihi pīkoi. Ka i'a pīkoi 'o Kālia, he kanaka ka pīkoi, he kanaka ka pōhaku,* Kālia is a fishing net with human floats, human sinkers.

pī.koi.koi. 1. Var. of *pīkokoi.* 2. nvi. Onanism, masturbation; to practice onanism or masturbation; one who does so. *Fig.,* to work hard with little produce. (PCP *piitoitoi.)*

pī.koi lua. n. A type of dagger, perhaps used by *lua* fighters.

pī.koka. Rare var. of *pīkake,* peacock. (1 Nal. 10.22.)

piko kea. n. A native variety of taro widely planted; an important poi taro, especially on O'ahu, distinguished by whitish *piko* and by leaf stems light-green with pinkish base. Also *piko ke'oke'o.*

pī.kokoi. vi. To swarm, as small fish coming to the surface with open mouths.

piko lehua 'ā.pi'i. n. A native variety of taro, with leaves dark-green and crinkled below; the corms with lilac-purple flesh, yielding the popular *lehua* red poi; the leaves good for *lū'au. Lit.,* curly red *piko* taro.

piko lua. n. Double crown of the head, a sign that a child will be persevering and determined.

pī.koni. n. 1. Cord attaching floats to a fishing net. 2. Same as *pīkoi 1. Kaua'i.*

pī.konia. n. Begonia (garden variety). *Eng.*

piko-o-Hale-a-ka-lā. n. Type of braid used in the *pāpale 'ie.*

piko-o-Wā-kea. n. **1.** Equator. **2.** Same as *Ka-piko-o-Wā-kea.*

piko pau 'iole. n. Rat-taken navel cord, i.e., a chronic thief. It was believed that one became a chronic thief if his navel cord was stolen by a rat. Rats were famous for thieving.

piko.piko. Same as *pikapika 1, 3.*

piko ua.ua. n. A native variety of taro, one of the hardiest *piko* taros and perhaps the only kind common in upland culture; yields good grade light-colored poi; distinguished by dark-green leaf stems with a pinkish base.

piko 'ula.'ula. n. A native variety of taro, distinguished from *piko lehua 'āpi'i* by having leaves smooth below; corms yield red poi of good grade.

piko uli.uli. Same as *haehae 3,* a taro.

piku, fiku. n. Fig *(Ficus carica).* (Neal 309–11.) *Eng.* See ex., *pāpalu.*

piku.mena. Same as *pikimana,* bituminous; coal. *Eng. Lua pikumena* (Kin. 14.10), slime pit.

pila. 1. n. Any string instrument, formerly the fiddle; violin. *Eng. Ho'okani pila,* to play music. **2.** Also **bila.** nvt. A bill; to make out a bill. *Eng.* **3.** Also **fira.** n. Fir. *Eng. Lā'au fira* (Mele 1.17), fir. **4.** nvt. To build, in a card game. (Eng. *pile.*)

pila 'aha. n. String musical instrument.

pila (bila) 'ai.'ē. n. Voucher.

pila (bila) ha'a.wina. n. Appropriation, allotment bill.

pila hāpa. n. Autoharp. *Lit.,* fiddle harp. *Eng.*

pī.lahi. vs. Thin, slim, frail, delicate.

pī.lahi.lahi. Redup. of *pīlahi.*

pī.laho. Short for *'ūpī laho.*

pila (bila) hō.'ai.'ē. n. Promissory note. *Lit.,* bill to extend credit.

pila kī.ko'o. n. Check, draft, bill.

pila kī.ko'o hale leka. n. Money order. *Lit.,* post-office draft.

pila kī.ko'o ho'o.hui.hui 'ia. n. Blanket warrant.

pila koi. n. Requisition.

pila kuolo. n. Violin. *Lit.,* rubbing fiddle.

pī.lalahi. Redup. of *pīlahi.*

pī.lali. nvs. Hardened sap *(kohu)* of the *kukui* tree, gum; resin, birdlime; wax; honey in a banana blossom; gummy, sticky. *Kanakē pīlali,* cactus candy. *Pīlali kukui kau lā'au* (song), *kukui* gum on the trees. *Pīlali pālolo,* wax. *Pipili ka pīlali i ke kumu kukui,* the gum sticks to the *kukui* tree [a person who stays close]. **2.** n. White and black feathers under the tail of the *'ō'ō,* a bird; used for *kāhili,* feather standards. **3.** n. A seaweed.

pī.lali.lali. vs. Sticky, gummy, slimy, greasy.

pī.lali mai'a. n. Honey in a banana blossom, fed to small children.

pī.lali mea 'ala. n. Camphor. *Lit.,* fragrant gum.

pī.lali.'ohe. vs. Thin, delicate, rickety. *Rare.*

pī.lali pā.nini, pī.lali pā.pipi. n. Dried juice of prickly pear chewed as candy.

pila pā.'ume.'ume. Var. of *pila 'ume 'ume.*

pila.pilau. vs. Somewhat bad-smelling, not quite spoiled. **ho'o.pila.pilau.** To allow to spoil, as fish or meat. Cf. *ho'omelu. I'a ho'opilapilau,* slightly tainted fish eaten raw with salt and *kukui* relish.

pila puhi.puhi. n. Harmonica, mouth organ. *Lit.,* blowing fiddle.

pilau. nvs. Rot, stench, rottenness; to stink; putrid, spoiled, rotten, foul, decomposed. Cf. *pilo, popopo. Kū ka pilau,* the stench rises. *Maka pilau,* rotten eyes, one with rotten eyes, a ghost. *Make pilau,* complete defeat in a game. **ho'o.pilau.** To cause a stench. (PPN *pilau.*)

pila 'ume.'ume. n. Accordion. *Lit.,* tugging fiddle.

pila.wai.wai. n. Account, reckoning, as of an estate; invoice.

pī.leka.leka. nvs. Gummy, sticky, gluey, moldy; mold.

pili. 1. nvi. To cling, stick, adhere, touch, join, adjoin,

cleave to, associate with, be with, be close or adjacent; clinging, sticking; close relationship, relative; thing belonging to. Cf. *'auipili, pili wale. Pili 'ana,* connection. *Pili maika'i,* fitting nicely, compact. *Hoa pili,* intimate friend. *Ko'u pili* (Laie 483), my partner [in a *kilu* game]. *Kolone pili,* column at close intervals [military]. *E pili kāua,* let's be together. *Hehi i ka pili, wehe i ka pili,* to abolish relationship. *Maka pili,* squinting eyes that seem almost closed. *Pili hukihuki,* clashes between close associates, a bickering relationship. *He pili wehena 'ole,* an unseverable relationship. *Pili i ka hewa,* to be found guilty. *Pili ke kua me ke alo,* the back and front meet [said of a thin person]. *Ke kukui ka pili ia o ka uhu,* the *kukui* is the thing pertaining to the parrot fish; the *kukui* is related to the parrot fish (see *kukui 1).* **ho'o.pili.** To bring together, stick; to attach oneself to a person; united, as friends; to mimic, imitate; to claim a relationship; to put together, as parts of a puzzle. Cf. *ho'opili wale. Ke 'ano a me ka ho'opili 'ia 'ana o nā helu,* the nature and application of numbers. *Ua ho'o-pili 'ia ma ka perita ma'ema'e o ka male,* united in the pure bonds of matrimony. (PPN *pili.*) **2.** n. A grass *(Heteropogon contortus)* known in many warm regions, formerly used for thatching houses in Hawai'i; sometimes added to the hula altar to Laka, for knowledge to *pili* or cling; thatch (preceded by *ke).* (Neal 80.) *Hale pili,* house thatched with *pili* grass. *Lei kōkō 'ula i ke pili* (song), red network *lei* [rainbow] on the *pili* grass. *Hū wale aku nō ka waiwai i ke pili* (Kep. 119), the wealth overflowed on the *pili* grass [of great quantities]. **3.** vt. To refer, concern, relate, pertain, apply. **ho'o.pili.** Caus/sim. **4.** n. Shingles, so called because they replace the *pili* grass of the roofs of the old houses (preceded by *ke).* **5.** nvt. A wager, bet, stake; to bet, wager. See *piliwaiwai.* **6.** n. Border, edge of time units, especially of late night. *Pili aumoe,* the late night. *Ka pili o ka wana'ao* (Laie 469), at the approach of dawn. *Ka pili o ke ahiahi* (Laie 457), at the end of the evening, nightfall. **7.** n. Uncolored sheets in a *ku'ina,* sleeping tapa. **8.** n. Lining of a quilt under the layer of cotton or wool. **9.** n. First stage of poi-pounding, with taro beginning to stick. **10.** n. A narrow or precarious pass. *Rare.* **11.** Same as *'ume,* the game, so called because the wand touched *(pili)* the players. (Malo 215.) *Rare.* **12.** Same as *'ōpili,* numb. (UL 61.)

pilia. Pas/imp. of *pili 1, 3. Pilia i ke 'ala,* clinging to the fragrance. (PNP *pilia.*)

Pili-'ā. n. Rain name, Kani-kū, Hawai'i. (For. 5:93.)

pili.ā.'ai.kū. Var. of *pili'aikū. Rare.*

pili.'ai.kū. vs. Cramped, stiff, numb. *Rare.*

pili.'āina. n. Shore; interisland. *Hui Moku Holo Pili'āina,* Interisland Steam Navigation Company.

pili.alo. nvi. Bosom friend, beloved wife. Cf. *pilikua.*

pili.aloha. nvi. Close friendship, beloved companionship, beloved relative; loving association; to have a loving or tender relationship, to be in a bond of love, romance.

pili ā mo'o. vi. To cling like a lizard, as on a cliff.

pili 'ana wā anō. n. Present participle.

pili 'ana wā hala. n. Past participle.

pili 'ano. v. To resemble in character or nature.

pili.'ao.'ao. n. Mate, spouse, common-law mate with whom one lives.

Pili-hala. n. Wind associated with Ka-'awa-loa, Hawai'i. (For. 5:93.) *Lit.,* near pandanus.

pili hale. n. House shingle (preceded by *ke).*

pili hao. n. Corrugated iron, as used for roofing (preceded by *ke). Lit.,* iron shingles.

pili hihia. vi. To become involved in gambling, usually disastrously; in the old days, to bet one's life or wife; to be involved in an entangling affair of any sort.

pili ho'o.ipo.ipo. n. Love affair.

pili.hua. vs. Sad, sorrowful, dejected, astonished, confused (Ier. 14.9), bewitched (Oih. 8.9); weary. *Ā pilihua ku'u nui kino* (chant), and my entire body is weary. *I* **ho'o.pili.hua.** To cause sorrow, astonishment, etc. *I* *ho'opilihua ai 'oia iā lākou i ke kilokilo 'ana* (Oih. 8.11), he had bewitched them with sorceries.

pili.kaha.kai. nvs. Shore, especially the area between high and low tides; near the shore.

pili.kai. n. **1.** A vine *(Stictocardia tiliaefolia)* in the morning-glory family, native from India eastward, possibly into Polynesia, long known in Hawai'i, as on roadsides and rocky shores. Flowers are funnel-shaped, rose-purple, about 5.1 cm in diameter, the leaves heartshaped. (Neal 702.) **2.** The wood rose *(Merremia tuberosa),* another kind of morning-glory, with deep yellow flowers and five- to seven-lobed leaves, grown ornamentally in Hawai'i for its dry, brown, rose-shaped fruit. (Neal 709.)

pili kā.mau. n. Relationship by friendship rather than by blood or adoption. *Lit.,* added-on relative.

pili.kana. n. Relation, relationship, kin, family. (Probably *pili,* to cling, + *-kana,* nominalizer; Gram. 6.6.2.) (PCP *pilitanga.*)

pili.kia. nvi. Trouble of any kind, great or small; problem, nuisance, bother, distress, adversity, affliction, accident, difficulty, inconvenience, perturbation, tragedy, lack; in trouble, troubled, bothered, cramped, crowded (2 Nal. 6.1), unsafe. Cf. *-pau pilikia, wahi ho'opau pilikia. 'A 'ole pilikia,* no trouble, no problem. *Ke noho kāua a pilikia 'ia au* (Kel. 60), when we live together and I get into difficulties. **ho'o.pili.kia.** To cause trouble, bother, disturb, inconvenience; to lead into difficulty, get into trouble, meddle. *Hō'ailona ho'opilikia,* inauspicious omen. (Possibly PNP *pilitia;* cf. Rennellese *pigitia.*)

pili.kino. vs. Personal, private, subjective, worldly. *Kākau 'ōlelo pilikino,* private secretary. *Paniinoa pilikino,* personal pronoun.

pili.ko'a. n. **1.** Hawkfish *(Paracirrhites forsteri, Cirrhitops fasciatus, Amblycirrhites bimacula),* 18 cm or less in length and light-pink in color. *Lit.,* coral clinging. Also *Cirrhites pinnulatus* and *Oxycirrhites typus.* **2.** A native variety of sugar cane named for the fish; stems yellow-green, with pale brown-red stripes when young, changing to bronze-yellow with darker brown-red stripes. **3.** A stiff kind of *pākalakala,* a seaweed *(Galaxaura lapidescens).*

pili koke. vs. To be closely related; to be very close, intimate.

pili koko. nvs. Blood relationship, blood relative; related by blood.

pili.kua. **1.** nvs. Giant, large strapping fellow, country person, one living in the country; countrified. **2.** n. Beloved husband. Cf. *pilialo.* **3.** vi. To fight in single combat. *Rare.*

pili kua. vi. To cling to the back.

pili lā.'au. n. **1.** Wooden house shingle. **2.** Edge of a forest.

pili.lā.'ele. n. Dark green pandanus leaves with white bases, above the *lā'ele,* old leaves.

pili lau.lā. vs. Of wide application, of broad or general interest.

pili lima. nv. A guessing game: to guess the contents of another's folded hand. *Lit.,* wager hand.

pili loko. nvs. A close relative, closely related; concerning local places.

pili lua. nvi. A close companionship of two; to associate, of two; related in two ways.

Pili-lua. n. Name of a pair of stars, said to bring *'ōpelu* fish.

pili.mai. n. **1.** A native variety of sugar cane, a yellow-green mutant of *'akilolo;* used in *hana aloha,* love sorcery, with the prayer for love to cling and hold fast. **2.** A variety of taro. **3.** A variety of sweet potato.

Pili-mai.'u'u. n. Same as *Ka-pili-mai'u'u,* a stroke in *lua* fighting. *Lit.,* clinging to fingernail.

pili.mea.'ai. Same as *ho'opilimea'ai. Lit.,* close association [for] food. **ho'o.pili.mea.'ai.** (a) To attach oneself for personal gain, as to a chief (often said disparagingly); to fawn; to support, especially one in the wrong. *He kaikamahine mana'opa'a nō, 'a'ole e ho'opilime-*

a'ai (Laie 591), a resolute girl, not fawning. **(b)** Perjury; to commit perjury. *He hewa ho'opilimea'ai,* perjury.

pili-moe. n. Name of one of the tapas in the game of *pūhenehene.*

pili.mua. n. Article, the part of speech: *ke, ka, he, nā. Pilimua maopopo,* definite article. *Pilimua maopopo 'ole,* indefinite article.

pili mua. n. Elder relative; preferred friend or companion; former associate.

pilina. n. **1.** Association, relationship, union, connection, meeting, joining, adhering, fitting. Cf. *pili 1. He pilina wehena 'ole,* an unseverable relationship. *Ua 'ewa ka pilina a ka nihoniho,* the toothed edges do not fit perfectly [said of anything that is unsuitable or in poor taste]. (PEP *pilinga.*) **2.** Springs, as of a mattress, watch, car. *Eng. He mana'o ko'u i ke kano ko'ele; ua haki ka pilina a 'o luna iho* (song), my thought is of the snapping affair; the upper springs [of the automobile] were broken.

Pili-nahe. n. Rain name.

pilina moe. n. Bedsprings.

pilina 'ohana. n. Kinship.

pili nohona. n. Family or social structure.

pili.'oki, bilioki. n. Billiards. *Eng.*

pili 'ole. vs. Unrelated, not concerned with.

pili.'ō.lelo. n. Grammar, word or sentence structure.

pili.pā. loc. n. Alongside a fence or enclosure; hedge (Luk. 14.23). See ex., *kūpuku.*

pili pa'a. vs. To stick firmly, associate constantly; to live in harmony; to fit closely, tenacious.

pili papa. n. Shingle roofing.

pili.pili. **1.** Redup. of *pili 1;* any sticky matter, adhesive; pasty, gluey, viscid. *He mea 'ai 'ia kahi pilipili maunu kāpae 'ia,* the bit of bait set to one side is edible still [one who has been the mate of another can still be a good mate]. **ho'o.pili.pili.** Redup. of *ho'opili;* to court, woo, make advances (FS 155); to associate in close friendship; to claim relationship, especially if unwarranted. *'Ōlelo ho'opilipili,* figurative language, simile (cf. *ho'opilipili 'ōlelo,* below). (PPN *pilipili.*) **2.** Same as *pipili 2,* an herb.

pili.pili 'āina. vs. Close to land. *'A 'ohe pilipili 'āina mai,* not anywhere near land [far off].

-pilipili ali'i. ho'o.pili.pili ali'i. To claim relationship to a chief, as of one only remotely related, or of one desirous of favors.

pili.pili he'e. n. **1.** Thin ends of octopus tentacles, as braided together when dried. **2.** Octopus or squid ink sac *('ala'ala)* molded about a fishhook for bait.

pili.pili.kana. Redup. of *pilikana.*

pili.pili.ko'a. Same as *piliko'a 3.*

-pilipili 'ōlelo. ho'o.pili.pili 'ō.lelo. Word play, punning; to illustrate a point with parables, stories, anecdotes.

pili.pili.'ula. n. A close blood relationship to one of high rank; this was said by persons entering the *hale nauā,* desirous of asserting their royal blood. (Malo 199, Emerson note.) *Lit.,* red relationship [red was a sacred color].

pili.pili 'ula. Same as *mānienie 'ula,* a grass; also *Desmodium uncinatum* on Ni'ihau.

Pili.pino, Filipino. nvs. Philippines; Filipino. *Eng.*

pili piula. n. Corrugated iron roofing.

pili.pō.haku. n. A fish (no data).

pili poli. vs. To be close to the bosom or heart (affectionate).

pili pono. vs. Well-suited, well-matched; close-fitting, as clothes; to refer exactly or concisely. *Mana'o pili pono,* literal meaning. *Ā ua pili pono nā 'ōlelo e like me ka mea hiki,* and as concise in language as possible.

pili pū. vi. To unite, join, cling to; hard-pressed, as in danger. *Pili pū ka hanu,* hardly able to breathe; to hold the breath, as in astonishment or fear. *Pili pū i ka paia,* backed up against the wall, hard-pressed. *Ua pili pū ko'u mau iwi me ko'u 'i'o* (Hal. 102.5), my bones cleave to my flesh. *Pili pū ka pilina,* the springs are broken; *lit.,* packed down.

pili.puka. n. **1.** The period between midnight and dawn. *Lit.*, near appearance [of the sun]. **2.** One of the tapa covers in the *pūhenehene* game, which were named for different parts of the night.

pili 'uhane. vs. Spiritual.

pili uka. n. A stiff, tufted, native grass *(Trisetum glomeratum)*, 0.3 to 0.9 m high, with leaves 10.2 to 25 cm long and flowers crowded in narrow spikes; a good forage grass, growing only at rather high altitudes. On Hawai'i this is apparently called *he'upueo.*

pili.wai.wai. nvs. Gambling, betting, gambler; to bet, gamble. *Lit.*, to wager wealth.

pili wale. vi. To cling, etc., for no reason or cause; often used in unfavorable sense of living off other people. **ho'o.pili wale.** Caus/sim. *Nohona ho'opili wale,* living as a dependent.

piliwi. vt. To believe. *Eng. 'A 'ole i piliwi 'ia* (song), [it] was not believed.

pilo. 1. nvs. Swampy, foul odor, as of a swamp; halitosis; polluted. **ho'o.pilo.** To cause a bad odor. (PPN *pilo.*) **2.** n. Some species of native shrubs, in the coffee family *(Hedyotis [Kadua]),* the leaves bad-smelling when crushed. See also *kōī (Coprosma kauensis)* and *au 13.* **3.** n. All Hawaiian species of *Coprosma,* a genus of shrubs and small trees belonging to the coffee family, with narrow to rounded leaves, tiny greenish flowers, and yellow, red, or black berries. **4.** Same as *maiapilo (Capparis sandwichiana).* **5.** idiom. Any kind, any whatsoever (used with *'a'ohe). 'A 'ohe pilo uku,* any pay at all is all right; any pay whatsoever. *I lei paha no kākou, 'a'ohe pilo lei,* let's wear leis, any kind of leis. *'A 'ohe pilo 'ō'ō* (Kep. 159), any kind of digging stick.

pilo kea. n. A small native tree or shrub *(Platydesma spathulata),* in the orange family; leaves large, thick, oblong, more or less pointed; flowers few, cream-colored; fruits small, dry, four-lobed.

pilo kea lau li'i. n. A native shrub *(Platydesma rostratum),* with long, narrow leaves, clustered, axillary flowers, and beaked, four-lobed fruits.

pī.loli. vs. Weak, small. *Rare.*

pilo.pilo. Redup. of *pilo 1. Wai puna pilopilo* (Sol. 25.26), polluted water. (PCP *pilopilo.*)

pilu. vi. To shake, quiver, vibrate. *Rare.*

pilu.pilu. 1. Redup. of *pilu. Rare.* **2.** vi. Overdressed, richly and elaborately overdressed, perhaps in a ridiculous way. *Rare.*

pima, bima. n. Beam, as for scales. *Eng.*

pime.neko, pimeneto. n. Pimento *(Capsicum annuum). Eng.*

pina. Rare var. of *pine.*

-pī.na'au. See *Holoholo-pīna'au.*

pī.na'i. 1. nvs. Again and again, repeatedly; to come or do repeatedly, constant; to wear out a welcome by repeated visits; close together, crowded. Cf. *kūpina'i, lele pīna'i. 'O ka pīna'i iho nō, e pīna'i ai,* just repeating, repeating a visit and wearing out one's welcome. *Mai pīna'i i ke aloali'i,* don't stay constantly in the presence of the chief. *Pīna'i kāna 'ai 'ana,* he eats all the time. **2.** vt. To patch, fill up a crack or hole, as in wood.

pinana. nvi. To climb; a climb. See ex., *'oe 1. Pinana ka ihu,* to elevate the nose, as in scorn. **ho'o.pinana.** To elevate, cause to climb.

pīnana.ea. Same as *pīnauea 1, 2. Rare.*

pina.na'i. Var. of *pinapina'i.*

pina.na'i.ea. vi. To turn aside, as the head, or as the bow of a ship when struck by a large wave. *Rare.*

pinao. 1. n. Dragonfly. (KL line 290.) Cf. *lelepinao.* (PCP *pingao.*) **2.** n. Flying gurnard, a fish *(Dactylopterus orientalis).* Also *loloa'u.* **3.** vs. Blurred, as eyes of a drunkard. Similar to *pōnalo 2.* **4.** n. Broad jump. **5.** n. Perhaps a swing. (For. 6:374.)

pī.nao.nao. Redup. of *pinao 3.*

pinao 'ula. n. A variety of dragonfly. *Lit.*, red *pinao.*

pina.pina'i. Redup. of *pīna'i. Kani pinapina'i o nā pū kuni ahi,* successive booms of the cannons.

pinau. vi. **1.** To recoil, snap, as a rope. *Rare.* **2.** See *lelepinau.*

pī.nau.ea. vs. **1.** Weak; of dim vision, as of an aged person. **2.** Short and skimpy, as a skirt or *pā'ū. Rare.*

pine. 1. nvi. Pin, compass needle, peg, bolt, picket; stanchion to hold animal's head with yoke and pin; to pin. *Eng. Kui pine,* common pin. **2.** n. A tame bullock tied to a newly captured wild cow or bull. When released it would lead the wild animal to a pen. *Ke pine,* the tame bullock. (Larry Kimura, personal communication.)

pī.nē. nvi. Falsehood, lie; liar; to lie. *Rare.*

pine hoaka. Same as *pine niho pua'a. Rare. Lit.,* crescent pin.

pine kai.apa. n. Safety pin. *Lit.,* diaper pin.

pine kau.la'i. n. Clothespin. *Lit.,* hanging pin.

pineki. n. Peanut *(Arachis hypogaea).* (Neal 450-1.) *Eng. 'Aila pineki,* peanut oil.

pī.nē.nē. n. Vagina. *Rare.*

pine niho pua'a. n. Hog's tooth pin. Formerly also called *pine hoaka. Lit.,* pig tooth pin.

pine 'ō.mou. n. Stickpin, brooch.

pine pā. n. Fence picket.

pine.pine. vs. Frequent; often, many times, frequently. (PNP *pine.*)

pine uma.uma. n. Breast pin, brooch.

pinika. n. Vinegar; an intoxicating drink made of fermented molasses and water. *Eng.*

pino. Var. of *pilo 1, 2.*

pino.pino. Var. of *pilopilo.*

pī nū.nū. n. Pigeon pea *(Cajanus cajan).*

pio. 1. nvs. Captive, prisoner, victim, prey; conquered, captured, made prisoner; game of tag; to play tag. **ho'o.pio.** To conquer, subdue, defeat, make prisoner, capture, overcome. **2.** vs. Extinguished or out, as a fire or light (used in pidgin English); disappeared, as a ship at sea; to have gone out of sight; to die down, as a wave. *Pio loa,* to vanish. **ho'o.pio.** To put out, extinguish, as a light or fire. *Ho'opio mana'olana* (Kel. 14), sinking hopes. (PCP *pio.*) **3.** nvi. To peep, chirp; to whistle with fingers on the mouth; to pipe on any flute-like instrument; peeping, peep. *Kani ka pio hone i ke kula* (song), a sweet whistle sounds on the plains. **4.** n. A measure of three *iwilei* (yards), especially of cloth.

pi'o. nvs. **1.** Arch, arc; bent, arched, curved; to arch, of a rainbow. *Ka-pi'o-lani* (name), the heavenly arch. *Ka pi'o mau o ke ānuenue i luna o ia wahi* (FS 127), the constant arching of the rainbow above this place. **ho'o.pi'o.** To arch, bend, curve, crook. (PPN *piko.*) **2.** n. Marriage of full brother and sister of *nī'aupi'o* rank, presumably the highest possible rank. Their offspring had the rank of *naha,* which is less than *pi'o* but probably more than *nī'aupi'o.* Later *pi'o* included marriage with half-sibling. Cf. *moe pi'o.* (Malo 54.) **3.** Same as *kāpi'o 1.*

pi'o.ā.'ea. vs. Tactless. *Ka'ū.*

pī.'oe. n. General name for barnacles. (KL line 24.)

pio.ea. Same as *pīnauea 1.*

pī.oe.oe. vs. Long and sharp, as a pin; long and thin, spindly. *He wahine pīoeoe, wīwī, lō'ihi,* a thin woman, bony, tall.

pī.'oe.'oe. Same as *pī'oe. Pipili mau 'ia e ka pī'oe'oe,* always clung to by barnacles [one constantly pursued by those of the opposite sex].

pi'o.hi'a. Same as *kanawao 1,* small trees.

pi'oi. n. **1.** Kaua'i name for *hoi,* the bitter yam *(Dioscorea bulbifera).* **2.** Hawai'i name for edible fruit of the *lama (Diospyros* spp.) or perhaps *kukui.*

pī.oi.oi. vs. Half-shut, as eyes; to look with half-closed eyes.

pi'o.lepo. n. Column of dust, cloud of dust. *Lit.,* dirt arch.

piolo. vt. To rub back and forth, saw; to pucker and unpucker the lips. *Fig.,* to go over and over in the mind, to mull over, think. Cf. *olo.*

pi'olo. Short for *pi'oloke.*

pi'o.loke. nvs. Alarmed, startled, perturbed, vexed, disturbed, confused and excited, agitated, harassed; in noisy consternation; confusion, alarm (sometimes preceded by *ke*). *Pi'oloke ka leo o ka palila,* frightened is the voice of the *palila* [bird]. *Ua pi'oloke loa ko'u 'uhane* (Hal. 6.3), my soul is sore vexed. **ho'o.pi'o.- loke.** To cause confusion, consternation, vexation. *E ho'opi'oloke au i ka na'au o nā kānaka* (Ezek. 32.9), I will vex the hearts of the people.

pi'olo.kū. Intensifier of *pi'olo*.

pio.loolo. 1. Redup. of *piolo*. *Rare.* **2.** Same as *'apu,* medicinal concoction; to feed such a concoction. *Rare.*

pī.'ō.'ō. 1. Same as *pi'oloke.* See ex., *ke'ele.* **ho'o.pī.- 'ō.'ō.** Same as *ho'opi'oloke. He mea hou ho'opī'ō'ō,* disturbing news. **2.** Same as *pioloolo 2. Rare.*

pi'o.o.loke. Redup. of *pi'oloke.*

pio.pio. 1. Redup. of *pio 1–3. Piopio moa,* chicken at about the fryer stage; little chick (see ex., *'īnana*). **ho'o.pio.pio.** To pipe on a flute-like instrument. **2.** Same as *pāpiopio,* a fish. **3.** interj. Call to chickens.

pi'o.pi'o. Redup. of *pi'o 1.* **ho'o.pi'o.pi'o.** Redup. of *ho'opi'o;* a form of imitative magic in which the practitioner, while concentrating, touched a part of his own body, thereby causing injury to his victim's body in the same place, as a chest pain or headache. If the intended victim saw the gestures, he might imitate them and thereby send the black magic back to the original practitioner. Both practices were *ho'opi'opi'o.* (PPN *pikopiko*.)

pī.pā. 1. nvi. Alongside, as of a road, sidewalk, or river; to go along the side, turn to the side, dodge; sidewalk. *Ma ka pīpā kahawai,* along the stream. *Ma nā pīpā alanui,* along the roadside. **2.** n. *Kā'e'e* bean and purgative made from it; the bean is also strung in leis. **3.** Precipice, cliff. (And.) **4.** *(Cap.)* n. Star name (no data).

pī.pā.pī.pā. Redup. of *pīpā 1.*

pipi. n. **1.** Hawaiian pearl oyster *(Pinctada radiata);* in songs this is known as the *i'a hāmau leo o 'Ewa,* 'Ewa's silent sea creature [it was believed that talking would cause a breeze to ripple the water and frighten the *pipi*]. (PPN *pipi*.) **2.** Feelers of an insect, as of an ant. **3.** Same as *moa 3 (Psilotum).* **4.** A kind of tapa. **5.** Body depression; eyeball. *Rare.* **6.** Lower part of an adze. (Malo 51.) *Rare.* **7.** Also **bipi.** Beef, cattle, ox. *Eng.* See *pipi kāne, pipi wahine. 'I'o pipi,* beef meat.

pipī. Redup. of *pī 2;* squinting; twinkling, as stars. *Fig.,* barely surviving. *Pipī ka ihu,* the nose sniffles and is stopped up. *Inā i kanu mau ā mahi mau ke kauwahi 'āina, ulu pipī wale nō ia lau kanu,* if certain lands have been continually planted and farmed, the plants grow feebly. *Pipī ka wahie, ho'onui ka pulupulu,* if wood smolders, add more tinder. **ho'o.pipī.** Caus./sim.; to smoke, as ham. *Kinai i ka 'uwiki e ho'opipī ana* (Mat. 12.20), quench a smoldering wick.

pī.pī. 1. Redup. of *pī 1,* stingy. **2.** Redup. of *pī 3;* to urinate *(Eng.) A Inā e pīpī 'ia ke koko ona ma ke kapa komo* (Oihk. 6.27), when there is sprinkled of the blood thereof upon any garment. *Pīpī holo ka'ao,* sprinkled, the tale runs [a phrase used at the end of tales]. **ho'o.- pī.pī.** To cause to sprinkle, urinate. (PPN *piipii*.) **3.** n. Female *'ō'ō,* a honey eater.

pipi 'au.amo. n. Ox yoke.

pipi'i. Same as *pi'ipi'i 1–5;* the commonest meaning is "expensive, high-priced." *Wai pipi'i,* bubbling water, charged water, fountain. **ho'o.pipi'i.** Same as *ho'opi'i-pi'i;* to set a high price. *Wai ho'opipi'i,* charged water.

pipika. vi. To draw away, shrink away, as an octopus tentacle on a fire; to crinkle up, contract; to turn aside so as not to meet, avoid. *Pipika a'ela ia ma ka pā pōhaku* (Nah. 22.25), he drew up against the wall. **ho'o.pi.pika.** Caus./sim.

pipi kāne. n. Bull. *Lit.,* male beef.

pipi kaula. n. Jerked beef (beef salted and dried in the sun, broiled before eaten). *Lit.,* rope beef.

pipi kauō. n. Ox. *Lit.,* dragging beef.

pipi keiki. n. Calf. *Lit.,* child beef.

pipiki. vs. Shrunk, crinkled; tight, cramped. Cf. *piki 1, pipika, 'ūpiki.* **ho'o.pipiki.** To cause to shrink, clamp.

pipi kō.'ala. n. Broiled beef, steak.

pipi kolo. n. Yearling cow or bull.

pipi kū. n. Stew beef, beef stew.

pipi kua.pu'u. n. Bison. *Lit.,* beef [with] humped back.

pipi laho. n. Bull.

pī.pī.lani. n. Some kinds of green seaweeds (species of *Enteromorpha). Maui.* Also *'ele'ele.*

pipili. 1. Same as *pilipili;* tenacious. *Lepo pipili,* sticky earth. *Pipili me nā hoa lapuwale,* associating with worthless companions. **ho'o.pipili.** Same as *ho'opili-pili;* to paste, glue, stick. *Mea ho'opipili,* paste. (PNP *pipili*.) **2.** n. Drymaria *(Drymaria cordata),* a slender, weedy herb, with rounded leaves, tiny flowers, and tiny one-seeded dry fruits with sticky stems, which catch on passersby. It is a tropical shade-dwelling plant. (Neal 345.) Also *pilipili.* **3.** Same as *'ihi kūkae hipa, kūkaehipa,* a weed.

pipili.kia. Redup. of *pilikia.*

pipilo. Redup. of *pilo 1.* (PCP *pipilo*.)

pipi loke (roke). n. Roast beef. *Eng.*

pipina. Var. of *pipine.*

pipine. nvs. Promiscuous; promiscuous person.

pī.pine. vs. Miserly, stingy. *Lit.,* stingy often.

pī.pī.noke. vi. To rain continuously; to jibber jabber, talk and argue continuously. *Lit.,* constant sprinkling. *Rare.*

pī.pī.nola. n. A kind of squash with edible shoots and fruit, commonly fed also to pigs, called chayote and pipinella by Neal 813, and *Sechium edule.* (Probably Portuguese *pepineiro*.)

pipio. Redup. of *pio 1–3.*

pipi'o. Redup. of *pi'o 1. He kanaka kua pipi'o,* a stoop-shouldered or hunchbacked person.

pipi ohi. See *ohi 1.*

pipi'o.lepo. Redup. of *pi'olepo.*

pipi Pā.kē. n. Water buffalo, carabao. *Lit.,* Chinese beef.

pipi palai. n. Beefsteak. *Lit.,* fried beef.

pipipi. 1. n. General name for small mollusks, including *Theodoxus neglectus.* (KL line 32.) *Lei pipipi,* lei of *pipipi* shell, a new type of lei; formerly *kūpe'e* ornaments were called *lei pipipi* because of a superficial resemblance. (PCP *pipipi*.) **2.** vs. Small and close together, as stars or *pipipi* shells; small, squinting, as eyes. **ho'o.pipipi.** To put close together; to squint. *Kanu ho'opipipi i nā 'ano'ano,* plant the seeds close together. **3.** See *pipipi.*

pipipi 'ā.kō.lea, pipipi kō.lea. Same as *'ākōlea 2.*

pipipi 'ā.kō.lea ihi.loa. n. A mollusk *(Planaxis labiosus). Lit.,* long-necked gourd *'ākōlea* shell, so called because of its shape.

pipi.pi'i. Redup. of *pi'i 1–5. 'O Pi'i-lani, 'O Pi'i-kea, 'o Lono-a-Pi'i, pipipi'i i ka 'ako'ako nā li'i nui* (chant for Kua-kini), Pi'i-lani, Pi'i-kea, Lono-a-pi'i, the great chiefs climbing to the crest [note fondness for repetition].

pipipi kō.lea. n. Periwinkle *(Littorina pintado, L. scabra). Lit.,* kōlea-bird shell, perhaps so called because of its color. Also *pūpū kōlea.*

pipipi kō.lea ihi.loa. n. Periwinkle *(Planaxis labiosus).*

pipi po'a. n. Steer. *Lit.,* castrated beef.

pipi pulu. n. Bull. *Lit.,* bull beef. *Eng.*

pipi wahine. n. Cow. *Lit.,* female beef.

pī.pī.wai. n. All species of a genus of sedges *(Eleocharis).* (Neal 87.) Also *kohekohe.*

pī.pī wai. v. To percolate, ooze, of water; to sprinkle water.

pipi wai.ū. n. Milk cow.

pī Poko.liko. Same as *pī nūnū. Lit.,* Puerto Rican pea.

piuka. n. Pewter. (Nah. 31.22.) *Eng.*

piuke, biute. n. Beauty. *Eng.*

piula. 1. n. Mule, donkey *(Moloka'i).* **2.** n. A card game; the player must follow suit in discards, and if he cannot, he draws from a pack; the object is to play all of one's cards, and the player left with a card at the end is the *piula.* Also *kēkake.* **3.** vs. Tired, exhausted, worn-

out. *Slang.* **4.** n. Pewter, tin (Nah. 31.22), corrugated iron as used for roofing; any metal suggesting pewter. *Eng.* See *pili piula. Wai piula,* water from a faucet.
piula wai. n. Faucet, water tap, hydrant. *Lit.,* water metal.
pī ulua. v. To fish *ulua* from the shore with a line but no pole.
piwa. n. **1.** Also **fiwa.** Fever. *Eng. Pi'i ka piwa,* to have a temperature or fever. **2.** Also **biwa.** Beaver. *Eng. Pāpale piwa,* beaver hat.
piwa 'ele.'ele. n. Black plague.
piwa ha'i.ha'i iwi. n. Dengue fever.
piwa haka. n. Beaver hat. *Eng.*
piwa ho'o.nā.wali.wali. n. Typhoid fever. *Lit.,* weakening fever.
pī.wai. n. **1.** A variety of wild duck. **2.** A type of hard rock used for adzes.
pī wai. v. To sprinkle water. See *'aha'aina pī wai.*
pī wai anu.hea n. Sweet pea *(Lathyrus odoratus).* Also *pī anuhea.* (Neal 455.) *Lit.,* cool, fragrant pea.
piwa lena.lena. n. Yellow fever. *Ua loa'a i ka piwa lenalena,* gotten the yellow fever [lazy; a pun on *lena* meaning "yellow" and "lazy"].
piwa 'ula.'ula. n. Scarlet fever.
po-. Same as *pō-.* See *poale, pohole, poka'i, poluhi.*
pō. 1. nvs. Night, darkness, obscurity; the realm of the gods; pertaining to or of the gods, chaos, or hell; dark, obscure, benighted; formerly the period of 24 hours beginning with nightfall (the Hawaiian "day" began at nightfall, cf. *ao 1.*) *Fig.,* ignorance; ignorant. Cf. *Halāli'i, Pō'akahi, Pō'alua. Hō'ike a ka pō,* revelation from the gods [as in dreams or omens]. *Inoa pō,* name suggested for a child in a dream. *Mai ka pō mai,* from the gods; of divine origin. *Kāne o ka pō, wahine o ka pō,* husband of the night, wife of the night [spirit lover: it was believed that a child born of such a mating might resemble an eel, lizard, shark, or bird, or might have supernatural powers; sometimes death or sickness followed nightly visits]. *Nā pō o ka mahina,* days [*lit.,* nights] of the month. *Pō 'ahia kēia?* What day of the week [or month] is this? *Pō nui ho'olakolako,* the great night that supplies [the gods revealed their will in revelations and dreams at night]. *Pō pouli 'a'aki,* a night so dark it bites with the teeth. *Pō i ka lā'au,* darkened by the tree. *Ua pō,* it's late [not necessarily night, but usually said if one is in danger of not being home by dark]. *Ua hana māua ā pō ka lā,* we worked until night; *lit.,* until the day darkened. *Ua hana māua ā ao ka pō,* we worked until daylight; *lit.,* until the night lighted. *Kēlā pō ā ao a'e i nehinei,* night before last; *lit.,* that night until dawned yesterday. *Kēia pō,* tonight. *Ka pō nei,* last night. *'O ke kumu o ka pō i pō ai* (KL line 8), the source of the night that was dark. *Ua hiamoe akula kona pō* (FS 99), he spent the night sleeping. *Kou pō ua moe 'ia, 'o ko'u nei lā, 'a'ole* (song), you slept during the night, but not I. *Iho i ka pō, ā i ke kolu o ka pō, ola hou mai,* descended into hell, the third day rose again from the dead. *He aha ka puana a ka pō?* What declares the night [any revelation from the gods? what is to happen in the future?]? *'O 'akahi ka pō, 'o 'alua ka pō . . . lele wale ka pō* (FS 47), one night spirit, two night spirits . . . the night spirits fly off. **ho'o.pō.** To behave in an ignorant manner, perhaps purposely; to keep out of sight, to stay in the dark; ignorant. (PPN *poo.*) **2.** vs. Thick, dense, of flowers or heady fragrance; to issue perfume. See ex., *niniu. Ma'ema'e Līhau pō i ka lehua* (song), lovely Līhau dense with *lehua. E pō puni ana ke 'ala o ka hala,* the fragrance of pandanus spreads everywhere and is overpowering.
pō-. Time of, state of. See below, especially *pō'ele'ele, pōhae, pōhihi, pōhina, pō'ino, pōka'a, pōka'o, pōlena, pōlewa, pōluku, pōmaika'i, pōnalo, pōniho, pōniu, pōpilikia, pōule.* Also *po-.* (Probably PCP *po(o)-.*)
pō.ā, pōwā. nvt. Robber, pirate; to rob, plunder. See ex., For. 5:489. *E pōā wale ka hele aku ā kō ha'i 'āina,*

make (For. 4:47), like a robber to go on the lands of others, death.
po'a. 1. nvs. Castrated, emasculated; eunuch. Cf. *lio po'a, pipi po'a. Ka luna o ka po'e i po'a 'ia* (Dan. 1:3), the chief eunuch. (PPN *poka.*) **2.** nvi. A sudden sound, as of flapping wings of a rooster, or of the thumping sound of the palms of the hands pressed together with fingers locked, or of hands striking the surface of the water; to make such sounds. **3.** vt. To dig under, undermine.
po'a.'aha. 1. Redup. of *pō'aha 1.* **2.** n. The same as *wauke,* but the leaves commonly smaller, entire, and rounded. The leaves of *wauke* are commonly lobed.
po'a.'ala. vi. To thump, as a drum with the base of the hand. *Rare.*
poa'e. Same as *poahi 1, 2. Rare.*
pō.a'e.a'e. Redup. of *poa'e.*
pō.'ae.'ae. n. **1.** Armpit. **2.** Axil of coconut frond. (For. 5:595.)
pō.'aha. n. **1.** Circle, as of flowers; ring, as of tapa about a sore that prevents friction; a round support for a calabash made of pandanus or ti leaves wrapped into a ring and bound with a cord. *Pō'ai 'ia ka pō'aha a puni i ka pōhaku,* the circle was completely encircled by stones. **2.** General name for trailing plants.
Pō.'ahā. n. Thursday; Congregational church meetings held weekly on Thursdays. *Lit.,* fourth day.
pō.'aha mā.lama.lama. n. Halo. *Lit.,* light circle.
poaha.nui. Hollyhock. (And.)
poahi. 1. vs. Dim, obscure. **2.** vi. To revolve, spin, go around; to rotate, of hips in a hula. *Rare.*
pōahi.ahi. Redup. of *poahi 1, 2.*
pō.'ai. nvi. Circle, circuit, hoop, girdle; group, as of friends; to go around, make a circuit, encircle, girdle, coil, wind up; circulating; encircled, surrounded. Also *pōhai.* See ex., *pō'aha 1. Pō'ai a'ela ka huaka'i a puni 'o Hākau* (FS 141), the procession completely surrounded Hākau. **ho'o.pō.'ai.** To encircle, surround, besiege, etc. (PCP *pookai.*)
pō.'ai.'ai. Redup. of *pō'ai.*
pō.'ai.'ā.lunu. n. Monopoly. *Lit.,* greedy circle.
Pō.'ai-anu 'Ā.kau. n. Arctic Circle. Lit., north cold circle.
Pō.'ai-anu Hema. n. Antarctic Circle. *Lit.,* south cold circle.
pō.'ai haele. vt. To go around, make a circuit, circumnavigate. *Ke pō'ai haele nei 'oukou i ke kai a me ka 'āina* (Mat. 23.15), you traverse sea and land.
Pō.'ai-hala. n. A rain famous at Kaha-lu'u, O'ahu. *Lit.,* surrounding pandanus.
Pō.'ai-hale. Var. of *Pō'ai-hala. Lit.,* surrounding house.
pō.'ai hapa.lua. n. Semicircle, half circle.
pō'ai hele. Same as *pō'ai haele.*
pō.'ai.lani. n. Horizon. *Lit.,* sky circle.
pō.'ai.lewa. n. Firmament. *Lit.,* air circuit.
pō.'ai lō.'ihi. n. Ellipse, oval. *Lit.,* long circle.
Pō.'ai-'olu 'Ā.kau. n. Tropic of Cancer. *Lit.,* northern cool circle.
Pō.'ai-'olu Hema. n. Tropic of Capricorn. *Lit.,* southern cool circle.
pō.'ai puni. vt. To travel around, circumnavigate, go completely around, encircle, besiege.
pō.'ai puni maka.pō. n. Blindman's bluff. *Lit.,* circle surrounding blind.
pō.'ai-waena-honua. n. Equator. *Lit.,* circle middle earth.
po'aka. n. Scar; mark, as of tattooing or tapa design.
Pō.'akahi. n. Monday. *Lit.,* first day.
Pō.'akolu. n. Wednesday. *Lit.,* third day.
Pō.'akolu Kau Lehu. n. Ash Wednesday.
pō.'ala. 1. Same as *pōka'a.* **2.** vi. To sail off and on, as a vessel. *Rare.* **3.** vt. To gargle. See *'ai pō'ala.*
pō.'ala.'ala. Redup. of *pō'ala 1–3.*
po'a.lani. n. A variety of fish (no data).
poale. vs. Deep, open, as a hole or sore; absorbent. Cf. *ale 2.*

pō.ale.ale. Redup. of *poale;* pierced; wound. Cf. *aleale.*

pō.ʻali. Same as *mōʻali.*

Pō.ʻalima. 1. nvs. Friday. *Lit.,* fifth day. **2.** nvi. Work on the chief's plantations, so called because this work was done on Fridays; the chiefs' plantation where the people worked on Fridays; to work thus (For. 5:709). *ʻAʻole i Pōʻalima ʻia mamua,* not used as a *Pōʻalima* before.

Pō.ʻalima Hemo.lele. n. Good Friday.

Pō.ʻalima Mai.ka.ʻi. n. Good Friday.

pō.ʻalo. vt. To gouge out, scoop out, pluck, extract; to shell, as beans; to reach up at.

pō.ʻalo maka. nv. To gouge out the eyes; an eye gouge for torturing criminals. *Fig.,* an ungrateful person who repays kindness by unkindness, especially by stealing a mate.

Pō.ʻalua. n. Tuesday. *Lit.,* second day. See *ʻauhau Pō-ʻalua.*

po.ʻana. 1. Same as *poʻa 3. Kai poʻana,* eroding, undermining sea. **2.** vs. Weary, sore, lame, fatigued. *Rare.*

pō.ʻana.ʻana. Redup. of *poʻana 2. Rare.*

Pō.ʻaono. n. Saturday. *Lit.,* sixth day. *Hoʻomana Pō-ʻaono,* Seventh Day Adventist religion.

po.ʻa.po.ʻai. 1. Redup. of *pōʻai.* **2.** n. A worm shell, a marine mollusk of the family Vermetidae. Also *kio poʻa-poʻai, pōhakupele, pohokūpele.*

po.ʻa.po.ʻala. Redup. of *pōʻala 1-3.*

po.ʻa.po.ʻa.pō.lā. vi. To gad about from house to house, especially of persons who eat constantly at houses of others. *Rare.*

poe. 1. vs. Round; rounded. **hoʻo.poe.** To round; to form into a round shape, as a loaf of bread. *Pipi hoʻo-poe,* meat ball. *ʻOki hoʻopoe,* to cut the hair evenly on all sides. **2.** n. A sweet potato. **3.** n. Stone poi pounder. *Rare.* **4.** n. A fish (no data). **5.** Also **boe.** n. Boy. *Eng. He poe mai au no Hawaiʻi* (song), I'm a boy from Hawaiʻi. **6.** n. Buoy. *Eng.*

po.ʻe. 1. n. People, persons, personnel, population, assemblage, group of, company of. (Gram. 10.4.) *ʻEwalu ka poʻe kaua* (FS 97), eight groups of warriors. **2.** Plural marker. (Gram. 10.4.) *Ka poʻe wāhine,* the women. *Poʻe hale,* houses. *Poʻe nalo meli* (Lunk. 14.8), swarm of bees. **3.** Var. of *poʻi 5.* (Kep. 157.) **4.** n. A native purslane *(Portulaca sclerocarpa),* with narrow, succulent leaves which have many hairs in their axes and white flowers.

poea. Same as *poe 1.*

po.ʻea. Same as *poʻe 2.*

po.ʻē.ʻē. Same as *pōʻaeʻae.* (Ier. 38.12.)

poehi. Var. spelling of *powehi.* **hoʻo.poehi.** Caus/sim.

poehi.ehi. Var. spelling of *pōwehiwehi.*

poeko, poweko. vs. Fluent, eloquent, clever and able in speaking.

po.ʻe kū.ʻai. n. Merchants.

pō.ʻele. nvs. Black, dark; dark night. *Fig.,* ignorant, benighted. (PCP *po(o)kele;* cf. Maori *pokele.*)

pō.ʻele.ʻele. Redup. of *pōʻele. Pōʻeleʻele e nalo ai ka ʻili o ke kanaka,* darkness in which the skin of man vanishes.

poe pele. n. Bellboy. *Eng.*

poe.poe. 1. nvs. Round, rounded, circular; compact, compressed; full, as the moon; sphere, globe; to gather together in a circle. *Uea poepoe,* smooth wire [contrasting with barbed]. *E ʻaiana i nā kāwele i poepoe,* iron the towels so they will be compact. *Nele i ka mea poepoe,* lacking round things [i.e., dollars]. **hoʻo.poe.poe.** Redup. of *hoʻopoe.* (Oihk. 19.27.) **2.** n. A euphemism for penis in the phrase *ʻoki poepoe,* subincision, circumcision.

po.ʻe.po.ʻe. Redup. of *poʻe 2.*

poe.poe.hā.wa.ʻe. n. Flat sphere; oval. *Lit.,* sea-urchin round.

poe.poe honua. n. Globe of the earth.

po.ʻe.po.ʻele. Same as *pōʻeleʻele. Ua poʻepoʻele Hilo,* Hilo is darkened.

poe.poe.pī.koi. n. Oval; sphere. *Lit.,* core roundness.

pohā. 1. nvi. to burst, crack, break forth, crash, pop, bang; to ferment (of poi); bursting, cracking, as of explosives or of a whip; flashing of light, breaking of bubbles. *Ua pohā ka ʻai,* poi is bubbly [in fermentation]. *Ua pohā ka male,* the phlegm has come up into the mouth. *Mālama o pohā ka lae,* watch out or [you] will crack [your] forehead [get into trouble; be shocked at the high prices]. **hoʻo.pohā.** To cause to break, burst; to crack, as a whip. *Hoʻopohā maila hoʻi ka mea kiʻekiʻe loa i kona leo* (2 Sam. 22.14), the most high uttered his voice. (Probably PCP *pofa(a).*) **2.** n. The cape gooseberry *(Physalis peruviana),* a South American perennial herb in the tomato family, growing wild. Flowers are yellow; round, orange, many-seeded fruits develop singly within the heart-shaped, papery, enlarged calyxes; they are edible raw and are also cooked for jam. (Neal 740-1.) Called *paʻina* on Hawaiʻi. **3.** Same as *pohāpohā,* a seaweed.

pō.hā. Short for *pōhaku,* stone.

pō.hae. vs. Torn, easily torn, fragile. **hoʻo.pō.hae.** To tear, as a hole in cloth.

pō.hae.hae. Redup. of *pōhae.*

pō.haha. Same as *poʻaha 1. Rare.*

pō.hā.hā. Redup. of *pohā 1;* volcanic ejecta of any kind. See ex., *mūkā. Ke pōhāhā mai nei ka lā,* the sun is breaking forth.

pō.hā.hā ahi. n. Fireball.

pō.hā.hā wai. n. Bubble. *Lit.,* water bursting.

pō.hai. nvi. Circle, group, as of people, trees (For. 5:287); gathering; to gather about in a circle. Also *pōʻai. Pōhai-nani* (name of a retirement home, Oʻahu), beauty surrounded. *He pōhai aliʻi,* a group or circle of chiefs, people constantly in a chief's circle of companions. *Pōhai ʻula,* red cloud, as of dust.

pō.haka. n. Splotch, spot, dot; small area, as a bald spot; a spot in a design. *Pōhaka keʻokeʻo,* white splotch, as of tinea, a skin disease.

pohā ka.ʻa. n. Rolling stone; thunder, peal of thunder, so called because thunder was believed caused by the gods hurling stones in the heavens. *Kāne-i-ka-pohā-kaʻa* (a name for the god Kāne), Kāne of the rolling stones.

pō.haka lā. n. Sunbeam.

pō.hā.kau. n. **1.** Anchor. *Rare.* **2.** Stone that travelers rest on. *Rare.*

pohā kea. nvi. Bursting forth of light, as dawn.

pō.hā kea. n. White stone, as limestone.

pō.hā.kia.loa. n. Stone used as a landmark, as of a land boundary, or for locating a fishing ground; stone with a knob at the top, used as a weight for deep-sea fishing; fishing grounds about 260 m deep (Kam. 76:75, 90).

pō.hā kī.helei. n. Balancing stone, said to be the name of a water game, in which one person sank with a stone in his hand and tried to pull others down.

pō.hā.kiʻi.kiʻi. vt. To carry on the shoulders, as a favorite child who holds on to the head, with legs dangling down in front. See *lei ʻāʻī.*

pō.hā.kio.loa. Var. of *pōhākialoa.*

Pohā-kōʻele.ʻele. Same as *ʻIkuwā,* a month of storms; also said to be the name of a rain occurring in that month (For. 5:663). *Lit.,* break forth in storms.

pō.hā.koʻi. n. Firm rock or obstruction; prominent cliff. *Rare.*

pō.hā.kō.ʻī. n. Rock avalanche. *Rare.*

pō.haku. 1. nvs. Rock, stone, mineral, tablet; sinker (see ex., *pīkoi 3);* thunder; rocky, stony. See *haku 3. Mauna Pōhaku,* Rocky Mountains. *Ke kaʻa maila ka pōhaku,* the thunder peals. *Ke kaʻa maila, as lava;* to petrify; hard. *Fig.,* stubborn. (PPN *fatu,* PCP *poo-fatu.*) **2.** vs. Weighted with rocks, hence stationary, not moving. *Pōhaku kaomi moena,* a stone weighing down a mat, said of a homebody. *Pōhaku ʻau waʻa lā leʻaleʻa i kai nei* (chant), fleet of canoes at anchor, happy here at sea. **hoʻo.pō.haku.** To stay at home in one place; to stay at home. *E hoʻopōhaku, e noho mālie* (chant), stay, rest quietly. **3.** n. Type of crab. See below.

pō.haku ʻā.nai. n. Stone rubber.

pō.haku ʻā.nai puaʻa. n. Stone for rubbing off singed hair of pigs.

pō.haku 'au.makua. n. Stone believed possessed by an *'aumakua* god.

pō.haku 'eho. See *'eho.*

pō.haku hali. n. A species of crab, perhaps one of the Leucosiidae, as *Nucia* sp. *Lit.,* stone-fetcher.

pō.haku hā.nau. n. Stones at Kū-kani-loko, O'ahu, and Holoholokū, Kaua'i, against which chiefesses rested as they gave birth, hence called birth stones. *He kapu nā pōhaku hānau ali'i,* the royal birth stones are taboo.

pō.haku hekau. n. Stone anchor.

pō.haku hele. Var. of *pōhaku hali.*

pō.haku ho'o.ikaika. n. Stones for weight lifting, weight lifting.

pō.haku ho'o.kala. n. Stone to sharpen tools, as adzes.

pō.haku ho'o.kumu. n. Foundation stone. (Ier. 51.26.)

pō.haku ho'o.pā. n. Touchstone.

pō.haku ka'a. n. Millstone, rolling stone. *Pōhaku ka'a palaoa* (Lunk. 9.53.), millstone.

pō.haku kani. Same as *pōhaku kīkēkē;* also said to refer to rumbling thunder (For. 6:449).

pō.haku kā.pili wa'a. n. Stone hammer used to tap chisels in making lashing holes in canoe parts.

pō.haku kele. n. Flat stone used for skipping.

pō.haku ke'o.ke'o. n. Marble. (Hoik. 18.12.) *Lit.,* white stone.

pō.haku kihi. n. Cornerstone. (Ier. 51.26.)

pō.haku kī.kē.kē. n. A kind of large stone that is resonant when struck. *Lit.,* knocking stone.

pō.haku kī.kē mo'o wa'a. n. Stone for tamping canoe gunwale strakes.

pō.haku kōhi. n. Stone breadfruit splitter.

pō.haku kuai kua. n. Bath rubber. *Lit.,* stone for rubbing back.

pō.haku ku'i 'ai. n. Poi pounder. *Pōhaku ku'i 'ai puka,* poi pounder with a hole in the center of the handle, through which the fingers are put, used on Kaua'i. Also *pōhaku puka.*

pō.haku ku'i nā.nahu. n. Stone muller for charcoal.

pō.haku ku'i palaoa. n. Whale-tooth pounder.

pō.haku ku'i poi. Same as *pōhaku ku'i 'ai.*

pō.haku ku'i wa'a. n. Stone canoe breaker used in warfare; it had deep grooves in the middle, in which ropes were placed, and was hurled into opposing canoes and hauled back with the rope so as to be thrown again.

pō.haku lana. n. Mooring rock for anchoring canoes, said to float, perhaps of pumice or mythical. (For. 4:295.) *Lit.,* floating stone.

pō.haku lepo. n. Adobe, brick (Puk. 1.14). *Lit.,* dirt rock.

pō.haku lū.'au. n. Fine-grained dark *'alā* stone, as used for adzes; water-worn basalt. *Lit.,* cooked-taro green rock, so called perhaps because of the dark color.

pō.haku lū.he'e. n. Stone weight fastened to the octopus lure, *lūhe'e;* general name for soft or porous stone.

pō.haku mai.ka'i. n. Precious stone. (Hoik. 18.12.) *Lit.,* good stone.

pō.haku maka.mae. n. Gem, precious stone.

pō.haku mole. n. Perforated stone tied to the end of the bag in the *pāku'iku'i* net to hold it in place. *Lit.,* base rock.

pō.haku o Kāne. n. Stone monuments that were places of refuge *(pu'uhonua)* where families made offerings, such as pig, red fish, kava, and tapas, to atone for wrong-doing. (Kam. 64:32–3.) *Lit.,* stone of Kāne.

pō.haku 'oki 'āina. n. Land-dividing rock.

pō.haku 'ō.ma'o.ma'o. n. Emerald. (Hoik. 4.3.) *Lit.,* green stone.

pō.haku pa'a. n. Firm, solid rock, basalt; general name for hard rocks, such as were used for adzes. Cf. *pōhaku lūhe'e.*

pō.haku paea. n. Firestone, flint, agate. (Ezek. 3.9.)

pō.haku pahe'e 'ā.nai. n. Stone rubber.

pō.haku pao. n. Stone chisel.

pō.haku.pele. Same as *po'apo'ai 2. Lit.,* volcanic rock.

pō.haku pele. n. Any lava rock, especially rock containing olivine crystals.

pō.haku pō.polo. n. Same as *pōhaku lū'au. Lit.,* pōpo-

lo berry stone, so called perhaps because of the dark color of these berries.

pō.haku puka. Short for *pōhaku ku'i 'ai puka* (see *pōhaku ku'i 'ai).*

pō.haku puna. n. Round coral piece, as used for polishing or rubbing; concrete.

pō.haku 'ula. n. Brick, tile (Ezek. 4.1). See ex., *inā 1. Lit.,* red stone.

pō.haku wai.kī. n. Bullets or pellets from bursting bullets. *Lit.,* gun stone.

pō.haku wā.wahi wa'a. n. Stone hammer used under water to break enemy canoe hulls in war.

pohala. 1. nvi. To revive after fainting, recover consciousness; to recover from sickness; relieved of worry; relief, rest, recovery. ho'o.pohala. To revive, etc. 2. vi. To open, as flower petals. ho'o.pohala. To clarify. 3. Same as *ho'opāhala.* ho'o.pohala. To discredit, not believe, depreciate. *Rare.*

pō.hala.kē. vs. Full, uncomfortably filled, as one who has overeaten. Cf. *kēkē.*

pohale. Same as *poale.* Cf. *halehale.*

pō.hale.hale. Redup. of *pohale.*

pohalu. Var. of *puhalu 1.*

pō.hā.nō. Wheezy. *Rare.*

pohā.pohā. 1. Redup. of *pohā,* to burst, pop. Cf. *kūlina pohāpohā.* ho'o.pohā.pohā. Redup. of *ho'opohā. Ho'opohāpohā nō ia i ka hohonu, mehe ipu hao lā* (Ioba 41.31), he makes the deep to boil like a pot. (Cf. Marquesan *pohapoha.)* 2. n. A kind of passion flower, called running pop *(Passiflora foetida),* a tropical American weedy vine, the hairy leaves commonly three-lobed; the fruit, enclosed in lacy bracts, is round, red or yellow, popping when crushed. (Neal 599.) 3. n. A non-edible, green seaweed *(Dictyosphaeria cavernosa),* small, round, hollow, that bursts with a pop when stepped on. Also *līpohāpohā, pohā.*

poha.pohaka. Redup. of *pohaka.*

pohe. 1. Same as *popohe. 'Oki pohe,* to cut off the hair only at the top of the head, as formerly by one in mourning. 2. n. The marsh pennywort *(Hydrocotyle verticillata),* a small weed known in many parts of the world, the stem creeping, leaf blade round, scalloped, attached near its center to the stem. (Neal 659.) Also *pohepohe.*

pō.he'e.pali. vi. Killed by a fall from a precipice. *Fig.,* to die mysteriously or by accident.

pō.he'e.ua. Landslide caused by rain; to slip or fall due to rain. (And.)

pohe haole. n. The nasturtium *(Tropaeolum majus* hybrids), a smooth, succulent, creeping herb, grown for its bright-colored flowers, the leaf blade round and attached near the center to the stem. (Neal 474.) It grows wild at middle elevations.

pō.heheo. Same as *pūheheo.*

pohe hiwa. Same as *nani Wai'-ale'ale,* a native violet.

poheke. vs. 1. Forced out, squeezed. ho'o.poheke. To squeeze out. 2. Same as *pōhekeheke.*

pō.heke.heke. vs. Plump.

pohe kula. n. The Asiatic pennywort *(Centella asiatica),* a small, weedy creeper, with round, scalloped leaves indented at the base, and white flowers and seeds. (Neal 660.)

pō.heo. n. Knob or knoblike object; head of a penis (insulting if said of a male; see *heoheo).*

pō.heo.heo. n. Knob; any round, smooth, knoblike object; head of a rafter; nail, pin; rounded top of a poi pounder, rounded head of a cane. ho'o.pō.heo.heo. To round, smooth, or shape into a knob (insulting: see *pōheo).*

pohe.pohe. 1. Redup. of *pohe 1.* 2. Same as *pohe 2.*

pohe.ue. n. Nether region, place of torment. *Rare.*

pohī. vi. To sink, settle, ebb. *Rare.*

pō.hihi. 1. Same as *pohihihi.* Cf. *hihi.* 2. n. Ancient name of a plant used for medicine (no data).

pohi.hihi. nvs. Obscure, entangled, mysterious, intricate, confused, confusing, bewildering, baffling, complex; mystery, obscurity. Cf. *hihi. I 'ole e pohihihi i nā kānaka maoli,* so as not to confuse the native peoples. *Ka mea pohihihi o Kristo* (Kol. 4.3), the mystery of Christ. **hoʻo.pohi.hihi.** To confuse, bewilder, puzzle, make mysterious.

pohi.hiu. vs. Evasive, obscure, difficult to grasp or comprehend.

pō.hina. 1. vs. Gray, misty, foggy, dimly visible, hazy. See ex., *kāluʻu. Pōhina i ka uahi,* hazy with smoke. **2.** vi. To fall prone, topple. *Pōhina-ka-honua* (personal name, For. 4:167), the land topples. **3.** *(Cap.)* Same as *Polo Ahi Lani,* a star. **4.** n. A variety of sugar cane, red or brown, similar to *uahi-a-Pele* but less vigorous, dying back after tasseling. (HP 223, 225.) **5.** n. A variety of taro. **6.** n. A variety of sweet potato.

pō.hina.hina. 1. Redup. of *pōhina 1.* **2.** Same as *kolokolo kahakai,* beach vitex.

poho. 1. n. Hollow or palm of the hand, hollow of the foot, depression, hollow; container, receptacle, pouch, as for tobacco; box, as for matches; hollow of a canoe, divided into three parts *(mua, waena, hope).* See ex. below. *Poho kai,* hollow where sea remains at low tide. (PCP *po(f,s)o.)* **2.** nvt. Mortar; to knead, as bread or poi (Kep. 165). *Poho ʻinamona,* stone mortar for grinding cooked *kukui* nuts and salt into a relish; to mix the relish. **hoʻo.poho.** Caus/sim. **3.** nvt. Patch, as in clothes; a wooden patch inserted into a calabash, as to mend a break; to patch, mend. **4.** vt. To belly out, puff out, as clothes on a line or a sail; to hollow or dub out, as a wooden container. *Poho pono nā peʻa i ka makani* (song), the sails are well filled with wind. **5.** n. Chalk, chalky white earth, as of limestone. **6.** n. A unit of measure equal to half a span *(kīkoʻo). Rare.* **7.** n. A bundle of tapa pieces *(moʻomoʻo). Rare.*

pohō. nvs. **1.** Loss, damage; out of luck; vain. See ex., *keakea. Koi pohō,* to sue for damages. *ʻO ka puka a me ka pohō ma nā hana kālepa,* profit and loss in merchandising affairs. *Pohō ka manaʻolana,* hopes in vain, lost, blasted. *Pohō wale,* useless, in vain, without profit. **hoʻo.pohō.** To cause a loss, fail; to sell at a loss. **2.** Bog, swamp, mire, slough; sunken, sinking; to settle, as earth. Cf. *onepohō. Lepo pohō,* marshy earth, swamp, bog.

poho ahi. n. Matchbox. *Lit.,* fire container.

poho aho. n. Container for fishing lines.

poho ʻāina. n. Land basin.

poho ani.ani. n. Glass container or jar.

poho holo.waʻa. Same as *holowaʻa.*

poho hō.lua. Same as *paheʻe 4.*

poho hoʻo.luʻu. n. Cup of coconut shell, gourd, or stone, containing dye for tapa.

poho kaha paʻa.kai. n. Rock with a depression or dish in which salt was extracted from sea water. *Lit.,* saltplace receptacle.

poho.kano. n. Hollow stone containing *kukui* oil used as a lamp (Malo 63); palm of the hand (stingy).

poho kā.pala.pala. n. Container for tapa dye.

poho kukui. n. Stone lamp.

poho kuni ʻanā.ʻanā. n. Small cup-shaped stone used for sorcery.

poho.kū.pele. Same as *poʻapoʻai 2.*

poho.lalo. vt. Underhanded, deceitful, dishonest; to come up from below, as an undercut blow; to undermine, dig under, burrow beneath, filch, deal dishonestly; to reach up from under the crotch. *Nā hana poholalo a nā mākaʻi,* deceitful activities of the police. *E poholalo aʻe ana o ʻAi-wohi-kupua i kāna puʻupuʻu* (For. 5:411), ʻAi-wohi-kupua dealt his undercut blow.

poho.lawa. vs. Somewhat rotten, decayed. *Rare.*

pohole. 1. nvs. Bruised, skinned, scraped; peeled, as cooked taro; slipped back, as the skin of the sex organ of a man or dog; bruise, sore. **hoʻo.pohole.** To bruise, skin, peel, etc. Cf. *hole 1.* **2.** n. Maui name for *hōʻiʻo,* a native fern, but larger and coarser on Maui.

pō.hole.hole. Redup. of *pohole 1. Ua pōholehole ka ʻili* (FS 109), the skin was bruised.

pohole.lua. vs. Slow, as a vessel; unskilled, bungling, as in mechanical work. *Rare.*

poho lima. n. Palm or hollow of the hand; handful.

poholo. vi. To sink, slip into easily, plunge out of sight, vanish; to miscarry.

pō.holo.holo. Redup. of *poholo;* loose fitting. *Pōholoholo maikaʻi ke kāmaʻa,* the shoe is comfortably loose.

poholo.pū. vs. To slip through; too large, as a hat.

poho.lua. 1. vi. To billow out, as sails. *Poholua nā peʻa i ka makani* (song), the sails billow out in the wind. **2.** n. Cavity of anus or vagina. *Lit.,* pit hollow. **3.** vi. To lie to, as a ship. *Rare.*

pohō maʻū. nvi. A complete loss; to be such. *Pohō maʻū wale nā puaʻa,* the pigs were completely lost.

poho mea kanu. n. Flower pot.

poho-mō.koi. n. A mat design. *Niʻihau.*

pohona. nvi. Sinking in, caving in, hollowing, as cheeks of an aged person; settling; bend, as in a U-shaped fishhook.

poho paʻa.kai. n. Saltcellar, salt shaker, any salt container.

poho paka. n. Tobacco pouch, as a tin, coconut shell, or wooden container.

poho pā.pale. n. Inside of crown of hat.

poho pauka. n. Powder container, compact, vanity case.

poho pō.haku. n. Stone bowl.

poho.poho. 1. Redup. of *poho 2, 3;* patched. *Kapa pohopoho,* crazy or patchwork quilt. **2.** Same as *kawakawa,* a fish, so called because of black patch-like dots on its belly. **3.** vi. To stick out the buttocks, as in bending over to pick up something, or as a sign of contempt. **hoʻo.poho.poho.** Caus/sim.

pohō.pohō. Redup. of *pohō 2.*

poho.poho.lalo. Redup. of *poholalo.* (Kep. 87.)

poho ʻulu. n. A sinkhole of breadfruit trees, as on Niʻihau, where breadfruit trees were planted in holes.

poho.waʻa. Same as *poho holowaʻa.*

poho wā.wae. n. Hollow of the foot, instep.

pohu. 1. nvs. Calm, quiet; calmed, quieted, soothed; to calm down, become quiet. Cf. For. 5:93. *Lilo i ka pohu,* becalmed, of a ship. *Pohu loa na makani,* the wind has calmed. **hoʻo.pohu.** To calm, quiet; to bring into a calm, as a ship. *Hoʻokō i nā kuko haumia apau a kona naʻau e hoʻopohu ai* (Kep. 67), satisfy all the filthy lusts of his heart so they are calmed. **2.** *(Cap.).* n. A wind associated with Kona, Hawaiʻi. (Nak. 55.)

pō.hue. n. **1.** General name for gourd plant (also *ipu).* See saying *poʻohū 1. ʻUmeke pōhue,* gourd bowl. *Hale pōhue,* storehouse for gourds. *Ihu pōhue,* gourd-nosed [stupid]. (PCP *poofue.)* **2.** Earthen vessel (RSV), potsherd (KJV). (Sol. 26.23.) **3.** A climbing legume *(Canavalia sericea)* native to central and southeastern Pacific Islands, now established in Hawaiʻi. Each leaf has three silky-hairy, rounded leaflets; flowers are rose-colored; and the flat, tan pods contain three or four seeds apiece. (Neal 464.)

pō.hue.hue. n. **1.** The beach morning-glory. *(Ipomoea pes-caprae* subsp. *brasiliensis),* a vine strong found on sandy beaches in the tropics, the smooth, broad leaves notched at the tip; the flowers pink, bell-shaped; a white-flowered form is rare in Hawaiʻi; the fruits small, dry, round, four-seeded. Hawaiians still use the vines to drive fish into nets. Roots, stems, and seeds were used for medicine, the flowers poisonous in large amounts. (Neal 709.) *E kā i ka pōhuehue,* strike with the *pōhuehue.* [One hit the sea with this vine to make a rough sea for surfing, or to kill an enemy who was in the sea.] **2.** Poetic name for a fisherwoman's skirt, so called because the goddess Haumea draped *pōhuehue* vines about herself as she fished. **3.** A variety of yellow sweet potato. **4.** A kind of stone used for polishing canoes.

pō.hue.hue uka. Same as *pōniu 3.*

pō.hū.hū. vs. **1.** Smoky, dusty, filled with spray. **2.** Unusually large or big. *Ua pōhūhū maikaʻi ka lau,* the leaves were well formed and very large.

pohu.huku. Same as *pōhukuhuku.*

pō.huku. vs. Swollen; protruding, especially of a round object; piled up, as a coil of hair on the head; heaped. Cf. *'ōhuku, pāhuku.*

pō.huku.huku. Redup. of *pōhuku;* rising up and spreading, as smoke or clouds; overflowing; increasing in prosperity or number.

pō.huli. nvi. Sucker, sprout, shoot; to sprout, usually of bananas. See Neal 246. *E kanu ai i nā mea kanu maika'i, a e pōhuli i nā lālā waina* (Isa. 17.10), plant good plants, so that grapevine branches will sprout.

poi. n. **1.** Poi, the Hawaiian staff of life, made from cooked taro corms, or rarely breadfruit, pounded and thinned with water. Cf. *kalo. Poi 'ili,* portion of a taro between the center *(hē)* and the peel. *Poi 'awa'awa,* sour poi [an unpleasant disposition]. (PPN *po'oi,* PCP *po(po)i.*) **2.** Also **boi. Boy.** *Eng.*

po'i. 1. nvt. Cover, lid; to cover (preceded by *ke.*) Also *'ūpo'i. Hana Hilo i ke po'i a ka ua,* Hilo works under cover of the rain [much rain at Hilo]. **ho'o.po'i.** To cover. (PCP *poki.*) **2.** nvi. Top or crest of a breaking wave; to break, of waves. *Inā e lawe 'ia au a ke po'i 'ana o ke kai, make au* (FS 15), if I am carried off by the breaking sea, I die. **3.** n. Container, basin, as for liquids. **4.** vt. To catch between cupped hands, as a small bird or butterfly; to pounce, as a cat on a mouse; to snatch. *Po'i moa,* chicken-catching hawk [a thief]. (PPN *pō.*) **5.** vt. To mound up, hill up.

po'ia. Same as *po'i 1. Pu'ia i ke po'i,* cover with the lid.

pō.'ie.'ie. vs. Tired, weary, worn-out. *Pō'ie'ie ka lawai'a a nehu o Wai-ākea, i ka ua, i ke anu, i ka ua, i ke anu* (chant), the *nehu* fishers of Wai-ākea are weary of the rain, the cold, of the rain, the cold.

poi hē. See *hē 6.*

po'i kalo. n. Mulch for dry-land taro. *Lit.,* taro cover.

pō iki. n. Early in the morning. *Ala i ka wā pō iki* (chant), rise in the early morn.

po'i.kū. vs. Overpowering, as love.

po'i lani. n. High heavens (preceded by *ke*).

poi mai'a. n. Mashed ripe bananas and water.

po'i.malau. n. Portuguese man-of-war *(Physalia).* Also *pa'imalau.*

poina. vt. To forget; forgotten. *Mai poina 'oe ia'u,* don't forget me. *Poina wale,* forgetful, absent-minded. *Poina ka no'ono'o,* forgetful; amnesia, dim memory. *'A 'ole 'oe e poina i ke ali'i* (For. 5:125), the chief will not forget you. **ho'o.poina.** To cause to forget; same as above. *Ua ho'opoina 'oe i ke Akua* (Isa. 17.10), you have forgotten God. (PCP *poina.*)

po'ina. Same as *po'i 2,* but usually used as a noun. *Po'ina kai,* cresting of the sea, place where the sea crests and breaks.

Poi.nikia. nvs. Phoenicia; Phoenician. *Eng.*

pō.'ino. nvs. Misfortune, ill luck, affliction, distress, disaster, calamity, danger, misery, ill fate, damage, injury, peril, disaster; unfortunate. *Lit.,* evil time. Cf. *pōmaika'i. Pō'ino no ke Akua mai,* act of God. *Nui nā ola i pō'ino, ā 'o ka nui o nā pohō o nā waiwai i pō'ino,* many lives lost, and much loss of property through devastation. **ho'o.pō.'ino.** To harm, injure, distress, devastate; to cause misfortune, distress, damage. *Ho'opō'ino malū,* secret bringing of misfortune, sabotage. *Hale e hiki 'ole ai ke ho'opō'ino 'ia e ke ahi,* fireproof houses.

poi palaoa. n. Flour poi, made by stirring flour in hot water, eaten alone or mixed with taro poi.

po'i pō. nvt. Night attack or ambuscade; to attack thus.

po'i.po'i. Redup. of *po'i 1, 4, 5;* to conceal, as property that one does not want to share with others, or as a secret; to cover up, as the truth; to smother, as a fire; to hush the wailing of a child. **ho'o.po'i.po'i.** Caus/sim. (PCP *pokipoki.*)

po'i.pū. 1. nvt. To cover over entirely, as of clouds or engulfing waves; to attack, overwhelm; onslaught, attack (For. 4:53). *Ua po'ipū i ka mana o ke kahuna,* entirely under the influence of the priest. **2.** n. A kind of tapa.

po'iu. vs. Afar, very high, of high rank, glorious, sacred.

poi 'uala. Same as *pa'i 'uala.*

po'i 'uhane. nv. Soul snatching; to snatch or capture the souls of either the dead or of living persons, as by sorcery.

pō.'iu.'iu. Redup. of *po'iu.*

poi 'ulu. n. Breadfruit poi.

po'i wai holoi. n. Washbasin, finger bowl. *Lit.,* water container for washing.

poka. Same as *moka,* offal.

pō.kā. n. Bullet, cannon ball, shot, shell, pellet; ball at the end of a prisoner's chain. *Pōkā ua hekili,* hailstones; *Lit.,* thunder-rain ball.

pō.ka'a. nvt. Ball, coil, roll, reel, spool, as of twine; dried pandanus leaves being kept for plaiting; to wind, roll, coil, as into a ball; to revolve, go around, gyrate. Cf. *ka'a,* turn.

pō.ka'a.ka'a. 1. Same as *pokaka'a;* overwhelmed and confused as by too much work. **ho'o.pō.ka'a.ka'a.** Same as *ho'opokaka'a;* to overwhelm, bewilder with a succession of tasks. **2.** Redup. of *pōka'a. E pōkā'aka'a mai 'oe i nāhi lau hala,* wind up some pandanus leaves.

pō.ka'a kaula. n. **1.** Ring, as used in a game of ringtoss. *Kiloi pōka'a kaula,* to toss rings in a game of ringtoss or quoits. **2.** Coil or roll of rope.

pō.ka'a lopi. n. Spool of thread.

pō.ka'a pī.lali. n. Bobbin winder, of a sewing machine.

pō.ka'a.wili, pō.ka'u.wili. Similar to *ka'awili. Ahi poka'uwili,* pinwheel (fireworks).

poka'i. vi. To go along, as wind-blown smoke. *Rare.*

pokaka, potasa. n. Potash. *Eng.*

poka.kā. Short for *pokaka'a. Ua lohi nā pokakā o kona mau ka'a kaua* (Lunk. 5.28), the wheels of his war chariot were slow.

poka.ka'a. Redup. of *pōka'a;* revolving, gyrating, whirling, spinning; wheel, as on a pulley or cart, swivel. **ho'o.poka.ka'a.** To spin, roll, coil, revolve; to repeat the same story over and over.

poka.ka'o. Redup. of *pōka'o.*

pokake. nvs. Mushroom-shaped; head of the penis.

pō.kala.kala. Same as *pua kala,* the beach or prickly poppy.

pō.kā lū. n. Buckshot, grapeshot, grapeshot. Cf. *lū.*

pō.kano. vs. Very dark.

pō.ka'o. vs. Barren; dry and tasteless, as flavorless meat; naked, destitute. *Fig.,* boring, lacking in humor. Cf. *ka'o, pīka'o.*

pō.ka'o.ka'o. Redup. of *pōka'o.* Cf. *laho pōka'oka'o.*

pō.kā pahū. nvs. Bomb, bullet, mine, bombardment; to bomb, shoot. *Lit.,* bursting bullet.

pō.kā pō.pō ahi. n. Incendiary bomb.

pō.kā pū. n. Bullet for gun or pistol.

pō.kā pū kuni ahi. n. Cannon ball. *Lit.,* bullet from the fire-burning gun.

pō.kā ukali. n. The wadding discharged from a weapon, such as rifle or cannon; the weapon is muzzle-loaded with powder secured by wadding followed by a projectile in the form of a ball or small shot.

poke. nvt. To slice, cut crosswise into pieces, as fish or wood; to press out, as the core of a boil (Kam. 64:105) or the meat of an *'opihi* shell; section, slice, piece. *Poke he'e,* a severed portion of octopus; *fig.,* a chubby person. *Poke 'ina,* the tongue-like meat found in the *'ina,* sea urchin; to remove this meat.

pō.kē. nvt. Bouquet; to make a bouquet. *Pōkē 'ōmou,* corsage. *Eng.*

pokea. Pas/imp. of *poke.* (For. 6:401.)

Poke.kona. n. Boston. *Eng.*

pokela, potera. n. Potter; pottery. *Eng. Ka 'āina o ka potera* (Mat. 27.10), the potter's field.

poke'o. 1. nvs. Child, childhood; preadolescent. **2.** Rare var. of *pake'o.* **3.** n. A type of ancient prayer. (For. 6:17.)

pō.keo.keo. 1. nvs. Turkey gobble, turkey, sound of a turkey hen's cluck. *Ni'ihau.* More commonly called *pelehū.* **2.** vs. Plump. **3.** nvs. Prosperous, well-to-do; prosperity, a large sum of money. Also *po'okeokeo.* **4.** vs. Drenched. *Rare.*

poke.poke. Redup. of *poke;* to chop.

poke.pokea. Pas/imp. of *pokepoke*. (For. 6:401.)

poke.pola, posepora. n. Phosphorus. *Eng.*

poki. 1. vs. Fine, as stitches or mesh; small, dainty, close together. **2.** *(Cap.)* n. General name for supernatural dog after the time of Ka-mehameha I, said to have been taken from the name of Ka-mehameha's favorite dog, Boss *(Eng.)*, which was deified and worshipped; name of a supernatural dog on Kaua'i, said to have owned land at Lāwa'i and Wahi-awa (Beckwith, 1970, p. 573). According to some, any supernatural animal. **3.** See *hale poki*. **4.** Also **bosi.** boss. *Eng.* **5.** n. Boat. *Eng. Ipu poki*, oval dish. *Huelopoki*, whaleboat.

pokia. n. Pole smeared with gum so that birds lighting on it will be caught.

pō.ki'i. n. **1.** Younger brother or sister or closely related younger cousin, often spoken affectionately. *Pōki'i ka ua, ua i ka lehua*, the rain a younger brother, raining on the *lehua* flowers [the rain and *lehua* are dear to each other]. **ho'o.pō.ki'i.** To claim a *pōki'i* relationship; to behave as a *pōki'i*. (PEP *pootiki*.) **2.** Second or final brewing, as of ti root or sugar cane. **3.** Name of the canoe of the owner of the net used in *mālolo* or *iheihe* fishing. *Rare.*

pō.ki'i kaina. n. Younger sibling of one's own sex.

pokiko, potiko. n. Portico. *Eng.*

pō.kina.hua. n. Assembly honoring a chief. *Rare.*

pokini. n. Boatswain. *Eng.*

pō kini.kini. n. A dark night; many nights.

poki.pa'a. vt. To bind together, as the bones of a chief for preservation and honoring. Cf. *poki 1.*

poki.poki. n. **1.** A parasitic isopod found clinging to the skin, gills, fins, mouths, and tails of fish. **2.** A gray hard-shelled box crab *(Calappa hepatica)*, not liked as food. **3.** Sow bug, pill bug (Isopoda). **4.** Redup. of *poki 1.* (PCP *potipoti*.)

poki.poki 'au moana. n. A kind of deep-water crab. *Lit.*, sea-swimming *pokipoki*.

poki.poki kua pa'a. Same as *pokipoki 2. Lit.*, hard-backed *pokipoki*.

Pokiu.lai. n. Fourth of July. *Eng.*

poki.wai. n. A drink of either warm or cold water, with sugar and cream.

poko. 1. Short for *pōkole. Ao poko*, small cloud. *Ko'o-lau Poko* (place name), short Ko'olau. *Keiki haehae poko o Nā-'ā-lehu*, the lad of Nā-'ā-lehu who tears into bits [admiration for a fierce warrior]. **ho'o.poko.** Short for *ho'opōkole*. (PNP *poto*.) **2.** n. Greasy cutworm, such as *Agrotis ypsilon* and *Lycophotia margaritosa*, the variegated cutworm; caterpillar (Hal. 78.46). **3.** n. Small division of a district, sometimes the personal lands of a chief. See *akua poko.*

pokoa. Same as *poko 1. Rare.*

pō.kohu.kohu. n. Dye made of *noni* root.

pokoke. n. Kidney disease, urinary leakage. *Rare.*

pō.kole. nvs. Short, brief; shortage, shortness. Cf. *'eke-ke'i*, and Ke'ehi *pōkole*, short stride; halfstep [military]. *Pōkole ka na'au*, quick-tempered. **ho'o.pō.kole.** To shorten, cut short, abbreviate; contraction. *Ho'opōkole 'ana*, abbreviation.

Poko.liko, Poto Riko. nvs. Puerto Rico; Puerto Rican. *Eng.*

poko.poko. Redup. of *poko 1.* (PCP *potopoto*.)

pō.ko'u. vs. Short. *Lima pōko'u*, short sleeve.

pō.kū. 1. Same as *paukū. Moloka'i.* **2.** vi. To cry out in the night, as to create disturbance. *Rare.*

Poku.kala, Potugala. n. Portugal. *Eng.*

pola. n. **1.** Flap, as of a loincloth or sarong; tail of a kite. *Lawai'a pola malo* (Malo 211), fisherman who tucks away his fishing tackle in the flap of his *malo. Kani ka pola o ka malo*, the flap of the loincloth snaps [of speed in running]. (PPN *pola*.) **2.** Platform or high seat between the canoes of a double canoe. (PH XI.) **3.** Blossoms and sheath of a banana. **4.** Rare var. of *kākala*, spines on fish. **5.** Also **bola.** Bowl, cup, mug (preceded by *ke*). *Eng.*

pola.lau.ahi. n. Haze, as during a volcanic eruption. *Rare.*

pō.lale. vs. Clear, bright. *Rare.*

pō.lalo.uli. n. Depth of night. *Rare. Lit.*, night below darkness.

pō.lani. 1. vs. Handsome, beautiful, clean, pure. **2.** *(Cap.)* nvs. Poland, Pole; Polish. *Eng.*

pola.pola. 1. nvi. Recovered from sickness; well, after sickness; to get well, convalesce; filling out, as after loss of weight; sprouting, as a bud. *Polapola iki*, a little better. **ho'o.pola.pola.** To cure, make get well; to fill out, as after sickness. **2.** *(Cap.)* nvs. Tahiti, Borabora; Tahitian. *'Ōlelo Polapola*, Tahitian language. (PCP *Pola-pola*.) **3.** Same as *hē'ī*, the Tahitian banana. **4.** Redup. of *pola 1*; flapping. *Lālau koke a'ela i ka lau'ī, 'awa-puhi, kīhae ihola a polapola ihola ma ka 'ā'ī* (Kep. 95), quickly grabbing ti leaves, ginger, tearing and flapping them about the neck. **5.** *(Cap.)* n. Star name, paired with the star Melemele.

pole. Rare var. of *pale.* (AP.)

pō.lea. vs. **1.** Sunken in, as the lips and cheeks of a toothless person. *Rare.* **2.** Blurred, as eyes of a diver. *Rare.*

pō.lehe.lehe. vs. Insecurely bound, as a bundle. *Rare.*

pō.lehu.lehu. n. Twilight, dusk. **ho'o.pō.lehu.lehu.** Beginning of dusk; to become dark.

poleke. vs. To have lost property by authority of a chief. *Rare.*

poleko. Same as *poeko*, fluent. (And.)

polemo. Var. of *palemo.*

pō.lena. 1. vs. Yellowish, as bird feathers or muddy water. Cf. *'i'iwi pōlena. Lena, pōlena, ā kī lena*, yellow, yellowish, and yellow ti. **2.** nvs. Bowline; furled, as sails; tightly bound. *Eng. Pōlena pa'a 'ia iho ke aloha, i kuleana like ai kāua* (song), love knotted tightly so we two have equal rights.

Pole.nekia. nvs. Polynesia; Polynesian. *Eng.*

pole.pole. 1. Rare var. of *palepale*, to ward off. **2.** n. A child's game. The children put their clenched fists on top of each other; each child makes a wish or suggests a game to play, and sings a chant such as the following: *Polepole ka mamalihini, ka'a mai ka'a mai i kou, i kou kauhale 'ou'ou; ke 'ākia nei ku'u piko e kaulele lā e kō lā ē*, ward off the strangeness, roll here, roll here the *kou* wood, for a *kou* house, a high house; there's a nip at my navel to make an effort to accomplish.

pō.lewa. vs. Loose, swaying, unsteady, flowing.

poli. n. **1.** Bosom, breast; depression; (poetic) heart, arms. Cf. *poli lima, poli wāwae. Ma ka poli iho nei, ho'onanea* (song), in the arms, relax. (PCP *poli*.) **2.** Instep. (Short for *poli wāwae*). **3.** Coconut husk attached to a fishing line. Cf. *nuku.*

pō.lia. Pas/imp. of *pō 1. Rare.* (Gram. 6.6.3.)

poli.'ahu. vt. To caress. *Rare.*

Poli-'ahu. n. Snow goddess of Mauna Kea. *Lit.*, Bosom goddess.

poli 'ai. nv. To nurse at the breast; a nursing breast. *Lit.*, eating breast.

poli 'awa. n. A bitter breast. *Fig.*, one who has lost several mates in death.

polie. Shining, gleaming; a gleam, flash of light. (And.)

poli.kia. nvs. Tied tightly, not easily unfastened. *Fig.*, severe suffering. *Rare.*

poli.kika. vs. Political. *Eng.*

poli.kua. n. The dark, invisible beyond, as on beyond the horizon or in the upper stratum. (KL line 263.) *Lit.*, back bosom. *Polikua puhohō*, wind-blown deep beyond. *Hala a'ela ua makahiki nei a kapo'o akula 'oia i loko o ka polikua o nā manawa hiki 'ole ke ho'i hou mai i hope nei*, this year has passed and descended within the deep beyond of times that cannot return back here. *E unaue koko'olua ana i ke ala hele polikua a Kāne* (Kel. 61), sadly move as two on the road to Kāne's invisible beyond.

poli lima. n. Center of the palm *(poho)* of the hand.

poli make. n. Dead breast. *Fig.*, see *poli 'awa.*

polina. nvs. Resplendent, shiny black. *Rare.*

poli.nahe. vs. **1.** Soft and gentle, as low music or a breeze. **2.** Slim-waisted and broad-shouldered.

pō.lina.lina. Same as *pōhinahina,* a beach shrub. *O'ahu.*

pō.lio. nvs. Dark, dismal, gloomy; place of torment. *Rare.*

poli.poli. 1. n. A soft, porous stone as used for polishing or for octopus lure sinkers. 2. vs. Rounded, of an adze. (Malo 51.)

pō.liu. vs. Dark, mysterious.

pō.liua. Same as *polohiwa. Rare.*

pō.liu.kua. Same as *polikua. Lit.,* back mystery.

pō.li'u.li'u. Same as *kōli'uli'u,* far, dimly seen.

poli.wai.ū. n. Wet nurse. *Lit.,* milk bosom.

poli wā.wae. n. Hollow of the foot, instep.

polo. 1. vs. Large, thick, plump. *Polo hana 'ole,* fat one who does no work [especially one depending on his mate]. 2. vt. To poke, stab. 3. n. Special prayer offered to the spirits of the dead. (Kep. 23.) 4. Var. of *pololei 2,* and also usually followed by the epithet *kani kua mauna.* 5. n. Polo. *Eng.* 6. *(Cap.)* n. Star names. See below.

polo-. An initial part of certain words referring to pandanus: *polohīnano, polokā, polope'a, polopoloua.*

Polo Ahi Lani. n. Name of a star, said to be associated with Mūlehu. Also *Pōhina, Polohilani, Polo 'Ula, Polo Wehi Lani.*

polo.'ai. vt. To summon, command to appear, invite; to proclaim publicly.

polohi. vs. Smooth, as of skin. *Ka-'ili-polohi-lani-o-Lo'eau* (name), the smooth royal skin of Lo'eau.

Polohi.lani. Var. of *Polo Ahi Lani,* a star.

polo.hina. nvs. Gray, misty, smoky. *Fig.,* affectionate grief, pity. *Noe polohina no ke aloha i ku'u hoa* (chant), gray pitying mist for the love of my companion.

polo.hī.nano. n. White male pandanus bloom *(hīnano)* with its stem.

polo.hiwa. vs. Dark, glistening black, as clouds or tapa. (Kep. 175.) *Ua hala i ke ao polohiwa a Kāne,* passed to the dark clouds of Kāne [death].

polo.hua. Same as *'olohua,* berries of *pōpolo. Rare.*

polo.huku. 1. vs. Large, plump, swelling; bulging; rich, prosperous. 2. n. Boat hook. *Eng.*

poloka. n. 1. Frog, toad, bufo. *Eng.* 2. Also **boroka.** Broker. *Eng.* 3. Also **borota.** Broth. *Eng.* 4. Canna *(Canna indica).* (Neal 263–4.) Also *ali'ipoe.*

polo.kā. n. Ripe pandanus fruit.

polo.kake. nvs. Slippery; wobbly; saturation. *Ka polokake wai ua o Ko'olau,* the saturation of rain water at Ko'olau.

poloka (poroka) kuea. n. Square pole, in surveying.

polo.kalama. n. Program, a term invented in the mid-1970s for the Hawaiian language radio program. *Eng.*

polo.kā.wa'e. n. 1. Fish spear. *Rare.* 2. Pining, wasting sickness. *Rare.*

poloke. vs. Broken; broke, without funds (slang). *Eng.* ho'o.poloke. Caus/sim. *Ho'opoloke i ka mana'o,* to change the mind.

polo.kē. n. Fresh poi. *Rare.*

pō.loke. Var. of *pāloke,* wobbly. (FS 213.)

polo.kika, polotika. nvs. Political; politics. *Eng.*

polo.lei. 1. vs. Straight, upright, direct, correct, right, O.K., accurate, all right; eyes front [military command]. Also *pololoi.* *Kū pololei,* to stand straight, sheer, perpendicular, vertical. *E pololei ana ke kua,* the back will be straightened. ho'o.polo.lei. To straighten, correct, reform; to aim, as a gun; to be partial and treat with favoritism. *Kula ho'opololei keiki kāne,* boys' reform school. 2. n. A land shell *(Lamellaxis),* frequently followed poetically by the epithet *kani kua mauna,* singing in the mountain ridges. *'O ka maiau pololei kani le'ale'a* (PH 204), the land-shell neatness singing gaily. 3. n. Fresh poi. *Kaua'i.* 4. n. An adder's-tongue fern *(Ophioglossum concinnum),* a small native fern with single narrow-oblong blade, which supports one narrow spore-bearing spike about 2.5 cm long.

pō.loli. nvs. Hunger, famine; hungry. *Make pōloli,* starved to death. ho'o.pō.loli. To deprive of food, starve, cause hunger; to fast. (PCP *pololi.*)

polo.lia. n. Jellyfish.

pololo. vs. Talkative; to talk without tact. *Pololo ka waha,* to talk abusively.

pō.lolo. Same as *kauna'oa pehu,* one of the dodders *(Cassytha filiformis).*

polo.loa. vs. Blundering, awkward; to go astray. *Rare.*

pololo.hua. Same as *pololo.* Cf. *mīkololohua.*

pō.lolo.hua.mea. vs. Dark, dense, distant. *Rare.*

polo.loi. Var. of *pololei 1.*

polo.lū. n. Long spear.

polona. Same as *polopolona.*

polo.pe'a. n. Thick stem of a pandanus fruit.

polo.peka. nvs. Professor; professorial; to be a professor. *Eng.*

polo.polo. Same as *pōpolo,* the plant.

polo.polona. n. Musty odor; rancid, moldy odor, as of mildewed clothes; stuffy or stale smell of a room long closed.

polo.polo.ua. n. Unripe, growing pandanus fruit.

Polo 'Ula. Same as *Polo Ahi Lani,* a star.

polo wai. n. Water polo.

Polo Wehi Lani. Same as *Polo Ahi Lani,* a star.

polu. Rare var. of *'ūpolu,* wet.

polū. vs. Blue, as of clothes or Euro-American objects and not of sea or sky. *Eng.* Cf. *uliuli.*

polu.ā, poluwā. n. Nausea, retching. Cf. *poluea.*

pō.lua. 1. vs. Dark, stormy. *Ku'u hoa pili o ka ua lani pōlua,* my constant companion in the rains from the deep dark heavens. 2. n. Disturbances produced by conflicting currents, as of air, water, tides, winds.

polu.ea. nvs. Nausea, dizziness, seasickness; hangover; seasick, qualmish, dizzy. (Cf. *-ea.*) *'O Ka'ala, kuahiwi mauna kēhau . . . poluea ihola i lalo o Hale-'au'au* (PH 100), Ka'ala, hill mountainous and dew-covered, dizzy [to gaze] below at Hale-'au'au.

poluhi. vs. Dull, sleepy. Also *malohi.*

pō.luhi. n. Long spear. *Rare.*

pō.luhi.luhi. Redup. of *poluhi.* Also *mālohilohi.*

pō.luku. vt. To pound, as poi (Kep. 163); to destroy, slaughter, overthrow, pound to pieces. See ex., *palahē.* Cf. *pāluku.*

pō.luku.luku. Redup. of *pōluku.*

polu.luhi. 1. Redup. of *poluhi. Ho'omamalu ē, malu ka lani, poluluhi kaumaha ka honua* (chant), casting gloom, gloomy is the sky, the earth is heavy with drowsiness. 2. vs. Cloudy, misty, shady. *Rare.*

pō.lumi.lumi. vs. Packed, crushed together, as in a crowd.

pō.lumu. n. General name for trailing plants. *Rare.*

pō.lunu. vs. Chubby, plump, and short. *Rare.*

pō.lunu.lunu. Redup. of *pōlunu,* chubby, short.

polu.polu. vs. Flabby, fat.

poma. Same as *'āpala,* apple *(Pyrus malus).* (Neal 388.) (French *pomme.*)

pō.mai.ka'i. nvi. Good fortune, blessedness, blessing, profit, prosperity; prosperous, fortunate, beneficial, blessed, lucky; good luck, improvement (of property), welfare, benefits. Cf. *pō'ino. Pōmaika'i 'ole,* unfortunate, unlucky. *Pōmaika'i au,* blessed am I. *He pōmaika'i 'ia mai ke Akua* (Kel. 38), a blessing from God. *E pili mau nā pōmaika'i me 'oe,* may you always have good fortune [a way to say 'best wishes']. ho'o.pō.-mai.ka'i. To cause good fortune; to bless, improve, ask grace; blessing.

pō.mano. n. Dam. *Rare.*

pō mano. nvs. Many nights; very dark.

pō mano.mano. Redup. of *pō mano.*

pomei.kalana. n. The pomegranate *(Punica granatum),* an ornamental and fruit-bearing shrub from Persia. *Eng.* Also *pomelaike, pomekelane, pomeraite.* (Neal 620–2.)

pomeke.lane, pomegerane. n. Pomegranate. *Eng.* (Kanl. 8.8.) See *pomeikalana.*

pome.laike, pomeraite. n. Pomegranate. *Eng.* See *pomeikalana. Kīhāpai pomeraite* (Mel. 4.3), orchard of pomegranates.

pona. 1. n. Socket; eyeball, eye socket; joint of sugar-cane stalk, bamboo; hollow, as left after a sweet potato vine has been dug. Cf. *puna.* (PPN *pona.*) **2.** vs. Spotted, as the sea with various shades, variegated. Cf. *kipona.* **3.** Also **bona.** n. Bond. *Eng.*

pō.na'a.na'a. vs. Confused, bewildered; tumult. **ho'o.-pō.na'a.na'a.** To confuse, bewilder.

pō.naha. 1. Same as *pō'aha 1.* Cf. *pōnaha lani.* *'O ka pōnaha iho a ke ao, ka pipi'o mālie maluna* (UL 169), circling of clouds, arching calmly on high. *Pōnaha ke one,* the sand is circular; *fig.,* bloated, as the stomach. **2.** n. Round swelling in the body. (Kam. 64:108.)

pōna.hai.ā.ua. Circular. (AP.)

pō.naha lani. n. Firmament. (Kep. 83.) See ex., *kaka'i.*

pō.naha.naha. Redup. of *pōnaha.*

pō.naha wai. n. Small, circular water pool.

pō.naho. vs. Dark, gloomy.

pō.naho.naho. Redup. of *pōnaho.*

pona kū.pale. n. Defense bonds.

pō.nalo. nvs. **1.** Plant louse, gnat, small fly, such as *Drosophila;* blight; shriveled, as by blight; swarming, as with gnats. See ex., *uluulu 1.* **ho'o.pō.nalo.** To cause blight. **2.** Dim, blurred, obscure; misfortune, distress, death (probably *pō-* + *nalo 1*). Also *pinao. Ke uhai mai nei ka pōnalo iā kāua, 'alua paha auane'i keiki a kāua e make* (For. 4:145), misfortune seems to be pursuing us and perhaps two of our children will die.

pō.nalo.nalo. Redup. of *pōnalo 1, 2;* swarming with gnats. **ho'o.pō.nalo.nalo.** Caus/sim.

pona.nā. vs. **1.** Dry, arid. *Rare.* **2.** Lame, stiff, sore, as legs. *Rare.*

pō.nano.nano. Var. of *pōnalonalo.*

pona.pona. Redup. of *pona 1, 2;* jointed. (PPN *ponapona.*)

pona.wa'a. n. Circle of canoes. (For. 6:298.)

pone. n. Pony. *Eng.*

pō nei. n. Last night.

pō.neko. vs. Dirty, filthy. **ho'o.pō.neko.** To soil, besmirch.

pō.neko.neko. Redup. of *pōneko.*

pō.neo.neo. Similar to *neoneo;* barren.

poni. 1. nvt. To anoint, consecrate, oil, crown, ordain, appoint, inaugurate; to daub; ointment. *Ha'i'ōlelo poni a ke kia'āina,* governor's inaugural address. *Ipu 'alapaka poni* (Luka 7.37), alabaster box of ointment. *'Oia ka lā poni mō'ī, i poni 'ia ai nā ali'i,* that was the coronation day on which the monarchs were crowned. **ho'o.poni.** To anoint, crown, ordain, consecrate, inaugurate. (PPN *pani.*) **2.** nvs. Purple, any purplish color (a color associated with the first glimmer of dawn). Cf. *poni li'ulā, poniponi. He poni uliuli ā he poni 'ula-'ula kō lākou lole* (Ier. 10.9), dark-purple and reddish-purple were their clothes. **3.** n. A variety of taro, used as medicine. The term *poni* may be qualified by the colors *'ele'ele* or *uliuli, kea, 'ula'ula.* **4.** Same as *mai'a 'oa,* a banana. **5.** n. A variety of sweet potato. (HP 142.) **6.** n. A variety of yam. (HP 169.)

-poni. Suddenly, without warning, as death. Cf. *kā'iliponi, leleponi,* Gram. 6.5.

ponia. Pas/imp. of *poni 1. Ē ka lani i ponia,* O crowned majesty. (PPN *pania.*)

poni.aka. n. Poniard. *Eng.*

pō.niho. vi. To bare, as the teeth; to expose, as the sea floor; to bristle, as sea urchins; thorny, as cactus. *Pōniho 'ino ka lae o Pipa, ahuwale ka 'ina uli, ka 'ina 'ele'ele,* Pipa point is bristling with sea urchin [or is greatly exposed], plainly seen is the dark sea urchin, the black sea urchin.

poni li'u.lā. n. Early glimmer of dawn.

poni mā.ku'e. nvs. Dark purple.

poni.mō.'ī. n. The introduced carnation or pink *(Dianthus caryophyllus),* a plant widely cultivated for its attractive and spicy-fragrant flowers, one of the commonest flowers used for leis. The Hawaiian name resulted from confusing the English name with "coronation." (Neal 345–6.)

poni mō.'ī. nv. Coronation; to crown a king or queen.

poni.mō.'ī li'i.li'i. n. The sweet william *(Dianthus barbatus),* a relative of the carnation, grown in gardens for its abundance of small, bright-colored flowers. (Neal 346.)

poni.niu. Redup. of *pōniu.* See *puka poniniu.*

poni.poni. Redup. of *poni 2. Kakahiaka poniponi,* purple morning [before dawn]. (PPN *pongipongi.*)

pō.niu. 1. nvs. Dizzy, giddy; dizziness; to rotate, whirl, spin, revolve, gyrate. *Ke aloha pōniu 'ailana,* dizzy with love and compassion. **ho'o.pō.niu.** To revolve, spin. **2.** Same as *lolo,* coconut sponge. **3.** n. The balloon vine or heartseed *(Cardiospermum halicacabum),* a slender, herbaceous, tropical vine, with finely subdivided leaves, small white flowers, and 2.5 cm-wide balloon-like fruiting capsules, each with three seeds (black with a white heart-shaped scar). Hawaiians formerly used the whole plant as a magic remedy for dizziness, wearing it as a lei and eating a little, before throwing it away into the ocean. (Neal 532.) Also *halea-ka-i'a, 'inalua, pōhuehue uka.*

pō.niu.niu. Redup. of *pōniu 1;* grief-stricken (Kel. 57). *Maka pōniuniu pōloli,* eyes giddy or faint with hunger. **ho'o.pō.niu.niu.** Caus/sim.

pono. 1. nvs. Goodness, uprightness, morality, moral qualities, correct or proper procedure, excellence, well-being, prosperity, welfare, benefit, behalf, equity, sake, true condition or nature, duty; moral, fitting, proper, righteous, right, upright, just, virtuous, fair, beneficial, successful, in perfect order, accurate, correct, eased, relieved; should, ought, must, necessary. *Pono 'ole,* unjust, unrighteous, dishonest, unprincipled, unfair, wrong. *No kou pono,* in your behalf. *Ka pono o ka lehulehu,* public welfare. *Nā pono lāhui kānaka,* human rights. *Nā pono o nā wāhine,* women's rights. *Ka pono kahiko,* the old morality or moral system. *Pono i ke kānāwai,* legal, legality. *Pono 'ole ka mana'o,* disturbed, worried, upset. *Me ka pono,* respectfully [complimentary close in letters]. *Nā mea e maopopo ai kona pono,* proofs in his own favor, his defense. *Kōkua no ka pono o ka lehulehu,* help for the public welfare. *Ka no'ono'o e pono ai kēia hana,* the study necessary for this work. *Loa'a ka pono i ka lāhui mamuli o ke ahonui o ka 'elele,* the people were benefited by the patience of the delegate. *E pono iā 'oe ke hele,* you should go. *Pono 'o 'oe ke hele,* you should be the one to go. *Pono i ke keiki e hele,* the child ought to go. *Ke ui mai nei 'oe, 'a'ohe a'u pono,* when you turn to me, I have no rights. *E 'eha nō a e pono, no ka pinana nō i ke kumulā'au,* serves you right to be hurt, since you climbed the tree. *Aia ka pono, 'o ka pae aku,* what is necessary is to reach shore. *Pono e pili pa'a loa,* inalienable rights. **ho'o.pono.** Righteous, respectable, correct, upright; to behave correctly. *Ho'opono 'ole,* unjust, dishonest. (PCP *pono.*) **2.** vs. Completely, properly, rightly, well, exactly, carefully, satisfactorily, much (an intensifier). *Pau pono,* completely finished. *Piha pono,* completely filled; complete, as a thought; clear. *Nānā pono,* look or examine carefully. *A'o pono 'ia,* well-taught. *Ua loa'a pono 'o Lawa mā e 'aihue ana,* Lawa and others were caught in the act of stealing. *I luna pono o ka pu'u* (For. 5:61), at the very top of the hill. **3.** n. Property, resources, assets, fortune, belongings, equipment, household goods, furniture, gear of any kind, possessions, accessories, necessities. **4.** n. Use, purpose, plan. *Ē ku'u haku, pale ka pono! 'A'ohe pono i koe, ho'okahi nō pono 'o ka ho'i wale nō koe o kākou, ka'uka'i aku nei ho'i ka pono i kō kaikuahine muli lā ho'i . . .* (Laie 419); priest is advising his lord to give up quest of Lā'ie and depend on his sister's help), my lord, set aside the plan; there is no hope left; the only hope is for us to go back and depend on your youngest sister . . . *Nā 'āpana 'āina aupuni no ka pono home noho wale nō,* government land parcels for the upkeep of dwelling houses only. **5.** n. Hope. See ex., *pono 4. Ua pau ka pono a ke kauka,* the doctor has lost hope. **6.** vs. Careless, informal, improper, any kind of (preceding a stem). *Pono 'ai,* to eat in any way or anything, take potluck. *Pono hana,* to work any way that suits one. *Pono nō i ka noho,* living any old way, shiftless. *Pono lole,* any kind of clothes. *Mai pono hana 'oe, akā e hana pono,* don't work carelessly, but work carefully.

pono hale. n. Furniture, household goods.

pono hana. n. Tools. See also *pono 6.*

pono.huku. Var. of *polohuku 1, 2.*

pono.'ī. nvs. Self, own; private, personal; directly, exactly. *'O wau pono'ī,* I, myself. *Kona pono'ī,* his own. *Hawai'i pono'ī,* Hawaii's own [own people]. *No'u pono'ī kēia,* this is my own. *I mua pono'ī,* directly in front. *'I'o pono'ī,* own flesh and blood. *Kona mana'o pono'ī,* his personal opinion. *Nā hana loio nona pono'ī iho,* attorney's private practice.

pono kai lawai'a. n. Fishing rights.

pono.kalapa, ponogarapa. n. Phonograph. *Eng.*

pono kau.like. n. Equal rights.

pono kī'.wila. n. Civil rights.

pono koho pā.loka. n. Right of suffrage.

pono.kope. nvt. Copyright; to copyright; to copy in any way, not necessarily properly.

pō.nolu. vs. Carelessly, unceremoniously. *Rare.*

pono pa'a mau. n. Fixtures.

pono pili.kino. n. Private rights.

pono.pono. 1. vs. Neat, tidy, in order, arranged, cared for, attended to, administered. **ho'o.pono.pono. (a)** To put to rights; to put in order or shape, correct, revise, adjust, amend, regulate, arrange, rectify, tidy up, make orderly or neat, administer, superintend, supervise, manage, edit, work carefully and neatly; to make ready, as canoemen preparing to catch a wave (For. 5:127). Cf. *luna ho'oponopono, mea ho'oponopono. Ho'oponopono 'ole,* slovenly untidy, disorderly, careless, thoughtless, uninhibited, blunt, reckless. *Ho'oponopono hou,* to revise, reorganize, re-edit. *Noho ho'oponopono 'ole,* sitting in a careless or indecent way. *Kāna ho'oponopono 'ana i ka 'āina* (Laie 495), his apportioning of the land [on becoming chief]. *Ka ho'oponopono waiwai 'ana* (For. 5:129), the financial arrangements, adjustments. *Ho'oponopono waiwai,* administrator or executor of an estate; to administer an estate. *Hale ho'oponopono,* administration building. *Ka ho'oponopono 'ana,* regulation. *Kānāwai ho'oponopono 'ia,* revised law. **(b)** Mental cleansing: family conferences in which relationships were set right *(ho'oponopono)* through prayer, discussion, confession, repentance, and mutual restitution and forgiveness (Nānā 60). **2.** Redup. of *pono 1.* **3.** vs. Comfortably well off, wealthy. *Ponopono ka nohona,* comfortably well-to-do.

pono 'uhane. n. Spiritual welfare.

pono wai. n. Water rights.

pō.nuhu.nuhu. Var. of *pānuhunuhu.*

pō.nulu. vs. **1.** Bulky, loose, as a bundle. *Rare.* **2.** Rising and floating off, as smoke, clouds. *Rare.* **3.** Short, stumpy. *Rare.*

ponu.lulu. Redup. of *pōnulu 1-3. Rare.*

pō.nulu.nulu. Redup. of *pōnulu 1-3. Rare.*

ponunu. Var. of *ponululu.*

po'o. 1. n. Head, summit, head or director of an organization, executive, principal; end, as of a rope, leaf, pole, cane, *kōnane* board; head of a penis or boil; headline, heading, title; father (see *po'o lua, po'o 'ole*); hair in such expressions as *po'o hina, po'o kea* (preceded by *ke*). See saying, *pau 1. Po'o mai'a,* upper part of a banana stalk. *Ke po'o o nā moku,* the head of the islands [Hawai'i]. *Nā po'o 'oihana,* executive departments. *'A'ohe mea nāna e pa'i i ke po'o,* no one can slap his head [he has no superior, especially in knowledge]. *Moe po'o ā hi'u,* to lie from head to tail [in trouble]. **ho'o.po'o.** To appoint a head or leader; to go ahead; to be brave. *Lele ho'opo'o a'ela ka ua* (For. 6:240), the rain falls headlong. (PEP *'upoko.*) **2.** n. A whole note (music). Cf. *po'o'ele, po'olima, po'omana,*

po'omanakolu, po'omanalua. **3.** nvt. Depression, cavity; to dip, scoop, hollow out, dub, erode, dig; to splash, as water by scooping the base of the palm; to make a squeaky sound by placing one hand against the armpit of the opposite arm, and pressing that arm against the hand; to make a noise by snapping the lips with the fingers. Cf. *kapo'o, napo'o.* **ho'o.po'o.** To dig, dub out. (PPN *poko.*)

po'o.'ele. n. Quarter note (music). *Lit.,* black full note.

po'o.hala. vt. To carry on the virtues, arts, and skills of the family. *Lit.,* passing on the head.

po'o hina. vs. Gray- or white-haired; ash-colored. (PH 34).

po'o.hiwi. n. **1.** Shoulder. *Ua lawa pono nā po'ohiwi,* shoulders are very strong. (PCP *pokofiwi.*) **2.** Wing of the body *(manu)* of a kite.

po'o ho'o.lewa. n. A very taboo chief whose shadow might not fall on himself or on any other person; he was carried about at night. *Lit.,* carried head.

po'o hou. n. Symbol of a paragraph. *Lit.,* new heading.

po'o.hū. nvs. **1.** Wound, swelling, as on the head. *Po'ohū ka lae,* his forehead is bruised [he has paid dearly]. *Po'ohū ka lae i ka 'alā,* lumps in the forehead from the hard volcanic rock (a large fee). *Po'ohū ka lae, kahi i ka pohue,* lumps in the forehead, rub with a gourd [get the remedy for trouble]. **2.** Prolonged resonance, as of a gong or as heard after striking a certain kind of stone. *Rare.*

po'o hua'i. n. Splitting headache. *Po'o hua'i lama,* a splitting headache or hangover caused by liquor.

po'o huku. n. Top point of a hill, ridge; sharp tips of ridges of a file or rasp. *Lit.,* protruding head.

po'o hulu. n. Chief featherworker for a chief, a hereditary office.

po'o huna. vs. Hidden, mysterious, invisible, as the gods. *Po'o huna i ke ao uli,* godheads hidden in the dark clouds.

po'o.ka'eo. vs. Bent over, as in carrying a heavy load. *Rare.*

po'o.kanaka. n. **1.** A variety of watermelon. *Lit.,* human head. **2.** Kohala name for pansy. See *pāneki.*

po'o kanaka. n. Human head, skull. Cf. *heiau po'o kanaka.*

po'o kea. Same as *po'o hina.*

po'o.kela. nvi. Foremost, best, superior, prime, outstanding, greatest, supreme, utmost, superlative; champion; to excel. *E ho'oha'aha'a 'ia nō kō 'olua mau po'okela* (Ier. 13.18), your principalities shall come down.

po'o.keo.keo. Same as *pōkeokeo 3. I ku'u 'ike 'ana i ka po'okeokeo 'ana o ka po'e hewa* (Hal. 73.3), when I saw the prosperity of the wicked.

po'o ke'o.ke'o. nvs. White-haired; platinum blonde.

po'o kepa. n. Hair cut in an extraordinary manner, as of one in mourning in the old days, with only part of the hair cut. *Lit.,* sideways head.

po'o.ki'e.ki'e. n. High heads, a name for the great gods, Kāne, Kana, and Lono. (Kep. 19.)

po'o kihi.kihi. vs. Cocked, as a hat; angular, as a head.

po'o.ki'i. n. Mask, jack-o'-lantern. *Lit.,* image head.

po'o.koi. vs. Envied. *Rare.*

po'o.ko'i. n. Sorcerer.

po'o ko'i. nvs. Adze-headed, a term of ridicule for one with a sharp or projecting forehead; also an insulting term for evil sorcerers, so-called because they were "frequently" beheaded (Kam. 64:123).

Po'o.kole. n. Rain said to occur in the month of Welo. (For. 5:665.)

po'o kua.kea. vs. Gray-haired. *Lit.,* bleached head.

po'o kumu. n. School principal. *Lit.,* teacher head.

po'o.lā. n. **1.** Stevedore. *Lit.,* sun head. **2.** The few Hawaiian varieties of small native trees *(Claoxylon sandwicense),* in the euphorbia family, with soft wood, large oblong, toothed leaves, small clustered flowers, the fruit a three-parted capsule. (Neal 499.) **3.** See *'ama'ama 1, laukea 1.*

po'o.lā.nui. n. Young stage of dragonfly, between the larval stage *(lohelohe)* and adulthood *(pinao);* beggarticks. *Lit.*, great sun head.

po'o.lā nui. n. A native species of *ko'oko'olau (Bidens cosmoides),* on Kaua'i only, with yellow flowers 5 cm across.

po'o lau. n. Leaf base; butt end of a leaf.

po'o.leka. n. Postage stamp. *Lit.*, letter head. See ex., *'ili'ili.*

po'o.leka kaua. n. War-savings stamp. *Lit.*, war stamp.

pō.'ō.lelo. Short for *po'o'ōlelo.*

po'o.lima. n. A half note (music). *Lit.*, arm note.

Po'o-lipi.lipi. n. A rain associated with Ka-lihi, O'ahu, and Hilo, Hawai'i (For. 5:119). *Lit.*, adzelike head, said to be so called because this heavy rain forced the people to spend so much time sleeping that their heads were sharpened as though by an adze.

pō.'olo.pū. nvi. Blister; to billow out, as wind-filled clothes.

po'o lua. nvi. Child sired by other than the husband, but accepted by both husband and sire; this acceptance increased the number of relatives of the child who gave their loyalty to him as kinsmen; it thus fostered the prestige of children of chiefs; translated "adulterous" in the 1843 Bible (Mar. 8.38), but changed in later editions. *Po'o lua 'ia* (Ii 152), to be doubly fathered.

po'o luluhi. Same as *poluluhi. Lit.*, tired head.

po'o.mahi.ole. n. Crest, as of a bird. *Lit.*, helmet head.

po'o.mana. n. An eighth note (music). *Lit.*, branching note, named for the stem mark.

po'o.mana.kolu. n. A thirty-second note (music). *Lit.*, triple branching note.

po'o.mana.lua. n. A sixteenth note (music). *Lit.*, doubly branching note.

po'o.mana'o. n. Topic, title, theme, heading, headline; subtitle, as of law. *Lit.*, thought heading.

po'o maunu. n. Bait remainder. *Ola nō ka lawai'a i kahi po'o maunu,* the fisherman can live on leftover bait.

po'o.muku. vs. Cut off, severed, shortened. See ex., *kāpala.*

po'o niu.niu. n. Dizzy head. Same as *pōniuniu.*

po'o no'o, po'o no'o.no'o. n. A thinker, a thoughtful head.

po'o.nui. 1. n. A variety of *'ahi,* tuna fishes, with a short body and thin tail. **2.** vs. Top-heavy, as a house. (Kam. 76:97.)

Po'o-nui. n. Name of a cold, continuous rain. (Kep. 97.)

po'o nui. nvs. Hangover, worried head, worry; to be a "headache" or source of trouble (Kel. 45).

po'o ole. vs. Illegitimate. *Lit.*, no head.

po'o.'ō.lelo. n. Title, as of an article; text, as of a sermon. *Lit.*, speech heading.

po'o 'ō.pae. n. Shrimp head, an opprobrious term because the shrimp's excretory organs are said to be in its head.

po'o.pa'a. n. Hawkfish *(Cirrhites pinnulatus),* about 10 to 22cm long with large scales on body and small scales on face, colored in blotches of blue, brown, and red with white vertical bars; eaten raw, broiled, or salted and dried. *Lit.*, hard head. Also *'o'opu kai, 'o'opu po'opa'a, piliko'a.* See ex., *hōkai.*

po'o pa'a. vs. Hardheaded, stubborn, obstinate, unreasonable, set in one's ways.

po'o.palaoa. n. A kind of white shell (no data). *Lit.*, ivory head.

po'o.pao'o. n. Name for highest tip of the canoe endpiece.

po'o.pā.pale. n. A drooping crest, as of some birds. *Lit.*, hat head.

po'o pepe. n. Flathead, a name for lesser gods. (Kep. 19.)

po'o.po'o. Redup. of *po'o 3;* sunken, as eyes of a sick person; indented, deep (as a bay penetrating the coastline); nook, cranny. *'A'ohe 'oe i 'ike i ko'u po'opo'o,* you did not know my nooks and crannies [about my family and background]. *Ua 'eli ihola 'oia i ka lua a*

po'opo'o (Hal. 7.15), he dug the pit deep. **ho'o.po'o.-po'o.** Redup. of *ho'opo'o.* (PPN *pokopoko.*)

po'o.po'o.hina. Same as *kīpūkai,* seaside heliotrope. Also *lau po'opo'ohina.* Both names on Ni'ihau.

po'o.pua'a. n. **1.** Head pupil in a hula school. *Lit.*, pig head, so named because the head pupil provided a pig or pig-head offering. Cf. UL 29. **2.** Image of a pig, carved of wood such as *kukui,* placed on the stone heap marking the boundary of an *ahupua'a* land division. **3.** Offering. See ex., *pua'a 1.*

po'o.pū.'ali. n. Any depression in the head, as a sunken temple.

po'o pu'u. n. Bulging head; hilltop. *Fig.*, sullen, unsocial person.

po'ou. n. **1.** Wrasse *(Cheilinus rhodochrous).* Varieties are qualified by the colors *kea* and *'ula.* **2.** Same as *'a'awa,* wrasse.

po'o.uli. n. Honeycreeper *(Melamprosops phaeosoma),* discovered in 1973 by Tonnie Casey and James Jacobi, upper Hāna rainforest, Maui, named by Kawena Puku'i. *Lit.*, black head.

po'o wai. n. Water source or head, dam. Cf. *'iole po'o wai.*

pō.pahi. Small, of man or woman. (And.)

Pope. 1. nvs. Pope; papist, Catholic. *Eng. Hō'ole Pope,* Protestant; *lit.*, deny Pope. *Ho'omanapope,* Catholic religion. **2.** *(Not cap.)* n. Poppy. *Eng.*

popela. n. Poplar. (Kin. 30.37.) *Eng.*

pō.pili.kia. n. Trouble, distress, tribulation, straits, disaster, calamity, ordeal, hardship, adversity, misfortune. *Ulia pōpilikia,* crisis, emergency. *Ke'ena o nā pōpilikia kūikawā,* industrial accident board. **ho'o.pō.-pili.kia.** To cause distress, harm, trouble; to afflict.

popo. Same as *popopo. Ua 'ai 'ia e ka popo kō 'oukou kula, a me kō 'oukou kālā, he hō'ike ka popo o ia mau mea* (Iak. 5.3), your gold and silver are cankered, and the rust of these things shows. (PPN *popo.*)

pō.pō. 1. nvt. Ball, round mass, wad; cluster, bunch, as of flowers; to shape or wad up into a ball or bundle; baskets of *'ie'ie* vine as used by *nehu* fishermen to collect *nehu* (For. 6:481). Cf. *kinipōpō, Pōpō-kapa, Pōpō-ua.* **ho'o.pō.pō.** To shape or wad into a ball. (PCP *poopoo.*) **2.** Short for *'apōpō,* tomorrow.

pō.pō.ahi. n. Fireball.

pō.pō 'ai. n. Ball of poi or other food.

pō.pō 'au.huhu. n. Ball of pulverized *'auhuhu* as inserted in coral to poison fish. *Fig.*, poison, danger, venomous attack. *Mālama pono 'oe i kānā pōpō 'auhuhu,* watch out for a venomous attack from him.

popoe. Redup. of *poe 1.*

pō.pō.hau. n. The hydrangea *(Hydrangea macrophylla),* an eastern Asiatic shrub, grown for the large, rounded or flat-topped clusters of pink, white, or blue flowers. In Hawai'i it succeeds at high, cool altitudes. (Neal 381.)

pō.pō hau. n. Snowball, ball of snow.

pō.pō-hau-o-Ni'i.hau. n. A large sedge with edible seeds.

popohe. nvs. Round, shapely; neat and trim, as flowers; roundness, a round or clean-cut object. *Ka popohe lau o ka palai,* the dainty leaf roundness of the *palai* fern. **ho'o.popohe.** Caus/sim.

popohe maka.li'i. Same as *'o'oi,* a seaweed.

popo.iwi. n. Inside corner. Cf. *kihi. Ma ka popoiwi o ka pā* (2 Oihn. 26.9), at the turning of the wall.

pō.pō iwi. n. Bundle of bones, as preserved of beloved relatives.

Pō.pō-kapa. n. Rain name. *Lit.*, tapa bundle, so-called because people bundled up tapa during rains to keep it from becoming wet. Also *Pōpō-ua.*

pō.pō kā.pa'i. n. Ball of medicinal herbs used for massage.

popoke. Var. of *pokepoke.*

popoki. 1. Var. of *pokipoki 1, 2;* short, thick. (FS 235.) **2.** *(Cap.)* n. Name of a *lua* fighting stroke, said to be used by women as well as men.

pō.poki. n. Cat (noted in Arago's 1819 vocabulary; said

by some to be derived from English "poor pussy").
Pōpoki kī, a spitting cat [a spiteful, malignant person].
Pōpoki lehu, Maltese cat; *lit.,* ash cat. *Pōpoki nāwali-wali,* weak cat [a weakling]. *Pōpoki pe'elua,* gray cat with darker markings, as a tabby cat; *lit.,* caterpillar cat.

pō.pō lā.'au lapa.'au. n. Medicine wrapped in leaves.

pō.pō.lehua. n. An ixora *(Ixora casei)* from Kosrae (Kusaie Island), a shrub grown ornamentally for its large round clusters of red flowers, which are used for leis. Each flower has a narrow red tube about 5 cm long, tipped with four short lobes. (Neal 802.)

popoli. vs. Arched, curved, warped. *Rare.*

pō.pō limu. n. Ball of seaweed, cleaned and salted, as sold for food.

pō.polo. n. **1.** The black nightshade *(Solanum nigrum,* often incorrectly called *S. nodiflorum),* a smooth cosmopolitan herb, .3 to .9 m high. It is a weed with ovate leaves, small white flowers, and small black edible berries. In Hawai'i, young shoots and leaves are eaten as greens, and the plant is valued for medicine, formerly for ceremonies. (Neal 744.) Also *polopolo.* The fruit is *hua pōpolo, 'olohua, polohua, pū'ili.* Because of its color, *pōpolo* has long been an uncomplimentary term: see *lepo pōpolo.* In modern slang, Blacks are sometimes referred to as *pōpolo.* See *pōpolohua.* (PPN *polo,* PEP *poopolo.*) **2.** An endemic lobelia *(Cyanea solanacea),* a shrub to 2.5 m high; in young plants the leaves are large, sinuate, thorny on both sides; in mature plants the leaves are unarmed; flowers 5 cm long, light-colored; fruit a large orange berry. **3.** The native pokeberry. See *pōpolo kū mai.* **4.** Same as *maiko,* a fish. *Ni'ihau.*

pō.polo-'ai-a-ke-akua. n. A shrub or small tree from Kaua'i *(Solanum kauaiense),* without thorns and with large ovate or oblong, sinuate leaves, densely downy on the under side. Cream- and purple-colored flowers less than 2.5 cm in diameter are borne in erect clusters. The fruit is a berry. *Lit., pōpolo* eaten by the god.

pō.polo hiwa. vs. Very dark, as *pōpolo* berries.

pō.polo.hua. vs. **1.** Purplish-blue, as the sea; dark, as a bruise. *Kai pōpolohua mea a Kāne,* the purplish-blue reddish-brown sea of Kāne. **2.** Same as *pōpolo 1* on Ni'ihau.

pō.polo kī.kā.nia. n. Apple of Sodom, yellow-fruited or thorny *pōpolo (Solanum sodomeum),* from the Mediterranean region, a small, thorny, somewhat shrubby weed, with lobed leaves, violet flowers, and yellow or orange fruits resembling small tomatoes. The plant is slightly poisonous. (Neal 743-4.)

pō.polo kū mai. n. **1.** The native pokeberry *(Phytolacca sandwicensis),* a small shrub with rather large, ovate leaves, many small flowers borne in long, narrow racemes, and dark-purple berries. The berries may have been used for dye. (Neal 340.) **2.** A low shrub *(Solanum incompletum var. mauiense),* a native of Maui, with large, ovate, sinuate, downy, uneven-sided leaves. The plants are somewhat thorny, the flowers purplish-white, the fruits orange berries.

popolo.lei. Same as *pololei 1.* **ho'o.popolo.lei.** Caus/sim.

pō.polo.lū. vs. Courageous, bold. *Rare.*

popo.lona. Var. of *polopolona.*

popo'o.hina. Redup. of *po'o hina. Ua kū kepakepa ka maka o ka lehua, ua popo'ohina i ka wela a ke akua* (chant), the faces of the *lehua* are snipped, gray ash in the heat of the god.

popo'o.kea. Redup. of *po'o kea.*

pō.pō paka (baka). n. Wad or plug of tobacco.

pō.pō palaoa. n. Round loaf of bread. *Pōpō palaoa hū 'ole* (Oihk. 8.26), unleavened bread.

pō.pō pelena (berena). n. Loaf of bread. *Pōpō pelena ho'oluli* (Oihk. 23.17), wave loaf. *Pōpō pelena i hamo 'ia i ka 'aila* (Oihk. 8.26), cake of oiled bread.

popopo. nvs. Rot, as of wood or cloth; decay, as of

teeth; moth-eaten; worm offal; rust *(Bible);* rotten, decayed. Cf. *pilau. Maka popopo,* rotten eye [of a ghost]. (PPN *popo.)*

popo.pono. Redup. of *pono,* goodness.

pō.pō pulu. nvt. A wet bundle, as of laundry; to wrap up wet, as laundry that is not allowed to dry.

Pō.pō-ua. n. Name of a rain. (PH 109.) Also *Pōpō-kapa.*

pō.pō uahi. vs. Dense, gray, puffy, as smoke, fog. *Lit.,* smoke ball. *Pōpō uahi ka wai kilikili noe,* dense as smoke is the misting fine rain.

pō.pō.'ulu. Same as *mai'a pōpō 'ulu.*

pō.pua.ki'i. n. Clusters of cloud banks.

pō.pu'ali. To girdle, tie tightly or constrict in the middle. (AP.)

poro.poleme. n. Problem. *Eng. He Mau Poropoleme,* Some Problems [book title, Judd, Bell, and Murdoch 222].

pou. 1. n. Post, pole, pillar, shaft. (PPN *pou.)* **2.** n. Ridge, as of nose; lump (Kam. 64:108). **3.** n. Mast of canoe. **4.** n. Machine gun. **5.** n. Part of snood lashing on composite hook, as for bonitos; sometimes shaft of a hook is so called. **6.** n. Spool pins on a sewing machine. **7.** Same as *poupou 1.* **8.** n. A canoe, broad for its length and wide and blunt at the ends, used for baggage. **9.** n. An internal hardening or tumor.

po'ū. Same as *pa'ū,* drenched.

pou alo. n. House wall posts, front row of posts.

poua.manu. Var. of *pouomanu.* (FS 205.)

pou.hana. n. Post set in the middle of each end of the house, supporting the ridgepole. *Fig.,* support, mainstay, as of a family. (PPN *pou + -sanga.)*

pou.hana.nu'u. vs. Short, stout. Var. of *pau hananu'u.*

Pou-hā.nu'u. n. Name of a star. *Lit.,* low post.

po'u.hia. Var. of *pa'uhia.*

pou hiō. n. Bent corner post, probably as supporting the ridgepole of a canoe house.

pou ho'o.pa'a lio. n. Hitching post.

pō.uhu. 1. Var. of *pāuhu,* a cowry. **2.** vs. Homely, ugly. *Rare.*

pouka, pouda. Var. of *pauka,* powder. Cf. *paula.*

pou kihi. n. Corner post.

pō.uki.uki. vs. Mildewed, moldy, musty. *Rare.*

pou.kū. n. Cleats supporting canoe seats.

pou kua. n. House wall posts, back row of posts.

pou kukuna. n. Gable post. See *kukuna.*

pō.ule. n. Male flower of the breadfruit. Cf. *ule,* penis.

pouli. 1. nvs. Dark; darkness, dark night. *Fig.,* ignorance. *He 'ano ē ka pouli nui,* how strange is deep ignorance. Cf. *kūpouli. ho'o.pouli.* To darken, make dark, blind, mislead; to pretend to be ignorant or not know. *Mai ho'opouli mai 'oe, ē ka hoa, 'o wau nō kēia 'o ka 'ano'i* (song), do not feign ignorance, O companion, this is I, the lover. (PPN *po'uli.)* **2.** n. Eclipse. *Pouli ka mahina,* eclipse of the moon. *Pouli holo'oko'a 'ana a ka lā,* total eclipse of the sun.

pō.uli.uli. Redup. of *pouli 1;* murky, gloomy. **ho'o.pō.-uli.uli.** Redup. of *ho'opouli;* blackout. (PNP *poo-'uli'uli.)*

pō.'ulu. n. **1.** Bark of tender breadfruit shoots, as used for less fine tapa. **2.** Euphemism for *pōule.*

pou lua. n. Shaft of the *lūhe'e,* octopus lure, perhaps so called because one side has a stone attached, with a cowry on the other side. *Lit.,* double shaft.

pouna. Var. of *paona,* pound. (Luka. 19.13.) Cf. *paona, paona kaulike.*

pou nana.hua. See *nanahua 2.*

pouo.manu. n. House post; post designating place of human sacrifice, said to be named for an ancient deity.

pou.ono. n. Fishing net. (Malo 212.)

pō.uo.uo. n. Bag net with meshes two fingers wide, similar to but larger than the *luelue.*

pou.pou. 1. vs. Short and stocky, stout, thickset. Cf. *noho ni'o.* **ho'o.pou.pou.** To shorten, stoop. **2.** Same as *kūpou 2,* a fish.

pou.pou noho ni'o. Same as *noho ni'o.*

pō.wā. Var. spelling of *pōā*.

powehi, pō.wehi.wehi. vs. Dim, obscure, indistinct, vague, faint, unclear. (KL line 135.) **ho'o.powehi.** Caus/sim.

poweko. Var. spelling of *poeko*.

pū. 1. n. Large triton conch or helmet shell *(Charonia tritonis)* as used for trumpets; any wind instrument, as horn, trumpet, cornet. The instrument may be distinguished from other *pū* by the qualifier *ho'okani,* sounding. *Nā pū kiwi hipa 'ehiku* (Iosua 6.4), seven trumpets of rams' horns. (PPN *puu.*) **2.** n. Gun, pistol. Cf. *pū aloha. I lalo pū,* order arms [military command]. **3.** n. General name for pumpkin or squash. Also *ipu pū, pala'ai.* **4.** n. Tree, cluster of several stalks, as of bananas, pandanus, or kava; clump, as of sugar cane (always precedes a noun). Also *ōpū.* (PCP *puu.*) **5.** n. Head of octopus or squid. **6.** n. Canoe endpiece, both fore and aft. **7.** nvt. Coil of hair, topknot of hair; rope or line, as attached to sticks in an *'ōpelu* net; rope attached to the front of an unfinished canoe to haul it to the shore; *olonā* string used in the game *pū kaula;* snotter holding the end of the sprit of a sail; to coil; to gather in, as sails; to form a topknot. *Pū i ka wa'a,* ceremony during which a head craftsman prayed that the gods would protect the newly carved canoe hull as it was drawn from the forest to the sea; to attach a line to a canoe; such a line. *Kaula pū* (For. 6:483), drag or towline. *Pū i ka lauoho,* to form the hair in a topknot. **8.** vi. To divide by lot: pebbles or seeds were placed under a tapa, and divided unseen into heaps, and the players drew to get the largest heaps. **ho'o.pū.** Caus/sim. **9.** vi. To eat a little, share potluck, said in a humble invitation, as *Mai kākou e pū 'ai,* come and have a little food with us [take potluck]. *Mai kākou e pū pa'akai,* come and share a little salt with us [said disparagingly of the meat]. **10.** n. A variety of sweet potato. **11.** vs. Inactive, sluggish, quiet, dejected, bored (often following *noho*). (Gram. 7.1.) *'Oia noho pū wale ihola nō 'o ke ali'i,* the chief just sits quietly. *'Ōku'u pū,* to crouch dejected. *Kai pū,* sea without animation; sea at midtide. **ho'o.pū.** To crouch, sit dejected and silent. **12.** part. Together, entirely, completely, also with, together with. (Gram. 7.1.) *'Ula pū,* entirely red. *Me 'oe pū,* same to you [as in reply to a good wish]. *Like pū,* exactly alike. *Noho pū,* to live together, as without benefit of clergy. *'O au pū,* me too. *'O kāua pū,* so will I; you and I both. *Moku pū,* broken completely. *Pau pū kāua i ka ho'opa'i 'ia,* we'll be punished together. (PPN *puu.*) **13.** Probably a rare var. of *puoho,* startled. (GP 66.)

pū-. 1. Short for *puna.* See *pūhau.* **2.** Also *pu.* A simulative prefix to a great many roots with similar meanings, as *'alu, pū'alu; hano, puhano; ha'u, puha'u; hemo, puhemo; hene, pūhene; hili, pūhili; hole, puhole; ko'a, pūko'a; koko, pūkoko; lama, pūlama; lawa, pūlawa; lewa, pūlewa; liki, pūliki; mehana, pumehana.* (Gram. 6.3.2.) (PPN *puu-, pu-.*)

pua. 1. nvi. Flower, blossom, tassel and stem of sugar cane; to bloom, blossom. *Pāpale pua, pāpale pua kō,* hat made of stem of sugar cane. *Pua ka wiliwili, nanahu ka manō,* the wiliwili tree blooms, the sharks bite [a blossoming girl is desired by males; sharks are believed to mate when the *wiliwili* blooms and to be especially ferocious]. *E hau'oli ho'i ka wao akua, ā e pua mai ho'i* (Isa. 35.1), the wilderness shall be glad and blossom too. (PPN *pua.*) **2.** vi. To issue, appear, come forth, emerge, said especially of smoke, wind, speech, and colors, hence to smoke, blow, speak, shine. Cf. *pua ahi, pua ehu, pua 'ehu, pua 'ena, pua hina, puana, puka. Pua ka uahi,* the smoke rises. *E pua ana ka makani,* the wind rises. *Kapu ka nū, ka 'ī, i ka pua o ka leo,* forbidden to groan, to speak by sound of voice. *A 'ike pua iki aku nō 'oe iā Ka'ula,* you barely see Ka'ula. **ho'o.pua.** Caus/sim. *Mai ho'opua 'oe,* do not say a word. (PCP *pua.*) **3.** nvi. Progeny, child, descendant, offspring; young, spawn, fry, as of *āholehole,*

'ama'ama, 'anae, awa, kāhala, 'ō'io, uouoa; to produce progeny or young. *Pua ali'i,* descendants of chiefs, royal progeny. *Pua 'ūhini,* young *'ūhini,* a grasshopper. *Kāna mau pua,* his descendants. *Pua i'a,* baby fish, fish fry. *Lau kō pua,* netting drive for young fish. *Ua pau, ua hala lākou, a koe nō nā pua* (song), they are gone, passed away, and the descendants remain. **4.** n. Arrow, dart, sometimes made from flower stalks of sugar cane. **5.** Same as *olopua 1,* a tree. (Perhaps PPN *pua.*) **6.** n. Float, buoy. *Rare.* **7.** Short for *'ōpua,* a cloud bank. **8.** *(Cap.)* A Moloka'i sorcery goddess. **9.** A fishhook for turtles. (And.)

pu'a. 1. Same as *hōkiokio,* a whistle. *O'ahu.* **2.** vi. To excrete. See *pu'a hana lepo, pu'a ki'o, pu'a mimi.*

pū.'ā. 1. nvi. Flock, herd, drove; to flock. *Pū'ā hipa,* herd of sheep. **2.** nvt. Sheaf, bundle, as of grain or fuel that is not wrapped; binder, bunch, package; clump, as of sugar cane (Kel. 116); to tie in bundles, bind. *Pū'ā 'i'o,* bundle of flesh. *I ka pū'ā 'ana a kākou i nā pū'ā* (Kin. 37.7), we were binding sheaves. **3.** vt. To feed by passing directly from mouth to mouth, as of masticated food such as fish or poi; infants and the aged were fed thus. **4.** vt. To cut crosswise. **5.** vt. To besiege. *(Pua* in 2 Sam. 11.1 of the 1843 Bible was changed to *pue* in later editions; cf. *pu'e.*)

pua'a. n. 1. Pig, hog, swine, pork. Cf. *hula pua'a, wilipua'a, ulepua'a.* Gram. 2.7. Many references to *pua'a* are to Kama-pua'a and his plant forms (FS 215, 229). *Pua'a 'imi ali'i* (FS 127), a chief-seeking pig [a priest after proper prayers would release a pig, which would then approach a chief that the priest was to serve]. *Pua'a nui huelo huluhulu,* great pig with hairy tail [a name given to the horse on Lā-na'i]. *Moe ka ihu o ka pua'a,* the snout of the pig has been laid down [entire pig sacrifice is offered]. *Iā'oe ke po'opua'a a kākou,* you are in charge of our offering of pig [*lit.,* pig head]. (PPN *puaka.*) **2.** Formerly a general name for introduced quadrupeds; see below and Gram. 2.9.2. **3.** Banks of fog or clouds, often as gathered over a mountain summit, a sign of rain and believed to be the cloud forms of Kama-pua'a. *Mehe ao pua'a lā, ke aloha e kau nei,* like a cloud resting on the mountain is the love alighting here.

pū.'ā.'ā. 1. vs. Scattered, dispersed; to flee in disorder and fright. Also *pūkākā. Holo pū'ā'ā,* to scatter in excitement, stampede. **ho'o.pū.'ā.'ā.** To put to flight, drive in confusion. **2.** Redup. of *pū'ā 2, 5;* bundles, sheaths; to tie many; to besiege frequently.

pua'a 'ehu.'ehu. n. Red pig, a poetic name for *'āma'uma'u,* ferns. The demigod Kama-pua'a took this form when he ran from Pele to the forest of *'ama'u* ferns and turned into a fern himself.

pua'a hame. n. Ham.

pua'a he'a. n. Blood-stained pig, hence a sacrificed pig, also said of human sacrifice.

pua ahe.ahe, pū.ahe.ahe. vi. To blow gently; light, as work.

Pua-ahi. n. Name of a star. *Lit.,* fire flower.

pua ahi, puahi. vi. To glow like fire. For figurative use see *ko'iko'i. Lohi mai 'Āpua, 'anapa i ka lā, pua ahi ka lā i ka papa o Maukele* (chant), 'Āpua sparkles, glistens in the sun, the sun shines like fire on the flats of Maukele.

pua ahi.ahi. Same as *nani ahiahi,* the four-o'clock flower.

pua'a hinu. n. Greasy pig. *Fig.,* human sacrifice.

pua'a hiwa. n. A solid-black pig, much desired for sacrifice.

pua ā.hole.hole. n. Young *āholehole.*

pua'a holo honua. n. The Tahitian name for horse, perhaps used at one time in Hawai'i. *Lit.,* pig runs [on the] ground.

pua'a hulu 'ole. n. Hairless pig, a figurative name for taro leaves, since they might sometimes replace pig as sacrifice.

pua'a 'ili 'oi.'oi. n. Porcupine (Isa. 34.11), hedgehog

(Zep. 2.14) (RSV); in KJV, both references, bittern, heron. *Pua'a 'ili 'oi'oi* of the 1843 Hawaiian Bible was changed in later editions to *kipoda*.

pua'a.inaka. n. An endemic long-branched plant *(Stenogyne rotundifolia)* in the mint family, found only on Mount Hale-a-ka-lā; the 2.5 cm long flowers woolly, purple-tinted, in whorls of six; the leaves round and rough.

Pua'a-kā-hulu.hulu. n. Same as *Ka-pua'a-kā-huluhulu.*

pua'a kai. n. Certain fish (as *āhole, 'ama'ama, 'anae, humuhumunukunukuapua'a, kūmū, pualu*) used as substitute for pig offering. *Lit.,* sea pig.

pua'a kāne. n. Boar.

pua'a kau. n. Hog offered as sacrifice.

pua'a.kuhi.nia. Same as *pākahakaha,* a fern.

pua'a.kukui. n. Carved log of *kukui* wood placed with hard taro *(pa'i 'ai)* on the altar marking boundary of *ahupua'a.* (Malo 163.)

pua'a kumu.lau. n. Sow, pig who has borne young.

pua 'ala. Same as *ālula,* lobelia. *Moloka'i. Lit.,* fragrant flower.

pua'a laho. n. Boar; term of reproach for a lecherous male, named for the pig demigod, Kama-pua'a. *Lit.,* scrotum hog.

pua'a lau. n. Name for plants that might replace pig in some sacrifices, a favorite being young taro leaves. Others were *'ama'u, hāpu'u, kūkaepua'a, kukui, olomea,* and *'uhaloa.* They were considered the plant forms of the pig demigod, Kama-pua'a. *Lit.,* leaf pig.

pua ali'i. n. Descendant of a chief.

pua alo.alo. n. Hibiscus flower. See *aloalo.*

pua'a.lohe.lohe. n. Larvae of dragonfly *(lohelohe)* used ceremonially as an offering.

pua'a mā.iki. n. Small pig.

pua.ane.ane, puane.ane. n. Extremity of life, extreme old age. *Kau i ka puaaneane,* to reach a stage of advanced old age.

pua 'anuhe. Same as *laulele,* butterfly weed *(Asclepias). Lit.,* caterpillar flower.

pua'a huelo hulu.hulu. n. Horse (old name, *Lā-na'i). Lit.,* big animal hairy tail.

pua'a ohi. n. A young female pig that has not borne young.

pua'a 'ō.kala.kala. n. Hedgehog. *Lit.,* rough pig.

pua'a olo.mea. n. 1. A striped pig. 2. Poetic name for the *olomea,* a tree. Kama-pua'a took this form when pursued by Pele.

pua 'ā.piki. n. A name for the *'ilima* flower. See *āpiki.*

pua'a pipi. n. Early name for cattle when brought to the islands by Vancouver. *Lit.,* beef *(Eng.)* pig.

pua'a pū.ko'a. n. Spotted pig. *Lit.,* coral head pig.

pua'a ū.kō. n. Pig offering at the death of a chief as a plea to the *'aumākua* gods to receive the spirit of the departed. *Lit.,* fulfillment pig.

pua.'awa.'awa. n. Great hunger. *Rare. Lit.,* issuing sourness.

pua'a wahine. n. Sow.

pua'a wā.wae loloa. See saying, *maka helei.*

pua.ea. vi. To expire, breathe one's last. *Puaea ka manu o Ka'ula i ke kai,* the bird of Ka'ula expires at sea [utter destruction, as of birds dropping dead while flying overseas].

pua ehu. vi. To blow spray or dust. *Pua ehu akula ka moana,* the ocean spray flies.

pua 'ehu. vi. To shine brightly, as reddish flowers. *Pua 'ehu maila uka* (For. 6:545), the uplands sparkled with red color.

pua 'ena. vi. To glow brightly.

pua.hala. n. 1. A medium-sized bowl, as used for serving poi, named for a supposed resemblance to a pandanus key *(pua hala).* 2. A variety of sugar cane.

pua-hala. n. Design in tapa and patchwork quilts.

pua hala. n. Bright yellow base of a pandanus *(hala)* key that may be used for leis.

pu'a hana lepo. Same as *pu'u ki'o.*

pū.'aha.nui. Same as *kanawao 1,* small trees.

pua hau. 1. n. Blossoms of *hau,* a tree. **2.** vs. Yellow, as a *malo. Moa pua hau,* chicken with yellowish feathers at neck and flanks.

puahe.ahe. Var. spelling of *pua aheahe.*

pua.hekili. n. One of the native loosestrifes *(Lysimachia hillebrandii). Lit.,* thunder flower. Cf. *kolokolo kuahiwi.*

puahi. 1. Var. spelling of *pua ahi.* **2.** Same as *puahia,* spry, quick. **ho'o.puahi.** Caus/sim.

pua.hia. vs. **1.** Spry, quick. *Holo puahia i ka wao o lehua,* swiftly running in the *lehua* forest. **2.** Hazy, gray.

puahi.ahi. Var. spelling of *pua ahiahi,* a flower.

pua.hia.hia. Redup. of *puahia 1, 2.*

pua hila.hila. n. The sensitive plant *(Mimosa pudica* var. *unijuga),* a low, spreading American plant, with round pink flower heads. The leaves, compound, with many small leaflets, droop and close when touched. (Neal 412.) *Lit.,* bashful flower.

puā.hilo. 1. vs. Fine, slender, frail as a spider's web, delicate. **2.** vi. To chap, peel, crack, as skin.

pua.hilo.hilo. Redup. of *puāhilo 1, 2. Hilo, he puahilo-hilo ke 'ano, no ka mea 'a'ole i aka loa a'e kona nui, akā ua mō'ali ma'awe ke'oke'o iki wale nō* (Kep. 99), the lunar night of Hilo, the name of the moon is a narrow sliver, because its full size has not been made clear, but is just a small white fibrous strand.

pua.hina. vs. Gray. *Ka lani pua hina o ka ho'oilo,* the gray skies of winter.

pua.hio. vi. To come and go swiftly, as a puff or gust of wind.

pua.hio.hio. 1. Redup. of *puahio;* whirlwind, gust. *Fig.,* worthless talk. See ex., *ko'i'ula,* For. 5:93. *E lawe aku 'o Iēhova iā 'Elia i ka lani ma ka puahiohio* (2 Nal. 2.1), Jehovah was to take Elijah up to heaven by a whirlwind. (PPN *'asiosio.*) **2.** *(Cap.)* n. Wind, Nu'uanu, O'ahu. (Nak. 57.)

pua hipa. n. Lamb. Also *hipa keiki.*

pū.'ā hipa. n. Flock of sheep.

pua hō.kū. n. A tropical American herb *(Laurentia [Isotoma] [Hippobroma] longiflora),* 30 to 60 cm high, with few or no branches, with long, narrow, lobed leaves, and starlike flowers with 7.5 cm long tube. The plant is related to the lobelias. It is poisonous, especially to stock. (Neal 818.) *Lit.,* star flower.

pua hō.kū hihi. n. The waxflower *(Hoya bicarinata),* an ornamental vine from Samoa, Tonga, and Fiji, in the milkweed family. Leaves are thick, broad-oval, paired, at their bases bearing short clusters of waxy, fragrant, white and pink, star-shaped flowers used for leis. (Neal 700.) *Lit.,* entangled star flower.

puā.hole. Var. spelling of *pua āhole,* young of *āhole.*

pua.huku. n. A term of contempt; perhaps literally rising octopus head; said also to refer to erections not followed by satisfaction. *Rare.*

pua.hulu. Same as *pupuāhulu.*

pua'i. vi. To flow out, as water; to bubble or gurgle, boil; to vomit; to appear, as a color; to utter, as speech (probably *pua 2 + -'i,* Gram. 6.6.4). (Mar. 7.15; Ier. 6.7.) *Pua'i wai,* fountain. *'A'ohe pua'i leo mai,* no word uttered. *Pua'i mai ka 'ula mai loko mai o ka 'ele'ele,* the red shows through the black. **ho'o.pua'i.** To cause to flow, show, etc. (PPN *pu'aki.*)

pū 'ai. v. To share a little food, take potluck. See *pū 9.*

pū.'ā.'ī. n. Adam's apple (probably from *pu'u 'ā'ī,* neck lump).

pua i'a. n. Fish spawn.

pū.aia.lewa. Same as *pūailewa.*

pua 'i'i. n. Tiny fry of fish.

pua'i.leho. Same as *puleileho.*

pū.ai.lewa, pū.aia.lewa. 1. vs. Suspended in the air, as clouds. **2.** vi. To breathe with difficulty, gasp. **3.** n. Name of a drastic remedy made of *pāpa'ahekili* bark. *Rare.*

pua 'ilima. n. *'Ilima* flower; eaten as a mild cathartic, especially by children.

pua.'ina. n. Flowing, bubbling, boiling, etc. See *pua'i. Pua'ina waimaka,* flow of tears.

pua.inā.wele. vs. Thin, weblike, weak. *Makali'i puaināwele ke kai o Ke-one-'ō'io,* the sea of Ke-one-'ō'io is like a fine-meshed web [one who considers himself too good for his associates]. *Lohe kōli'uli'u puaināwele mehe leo lā no ka hinihini,* to hear faintly, weak, like the voice of the land shell.

puai.nea. Same as *puanaiea.*

puai.ohi. n. Small Kaua'i thrush *(Phaeornis palmeri).*

pu'aka. 1. vt. To bind, tie. *Rare.* **2.** vi. To work hard without reward or appreciation. *Rare.*

pū.'aka.'aka. Redup. of *pu'aka 1, 2.*

pua ka'a.ona. n. Dart made of the stem of sugar-cane tassel smoked reddish-brown *(ka'aona).*

pua kā.hala. n. Small *kāhala,* a fish.

pua.kai. 1. Same as *pūkai 1.* **2.** nvs. Red of tapa or *malo* dyed with *noni* juice (Malo 49); a red tapa used in *kuni* ceremonies. See *wauke puakai.*

Pua-kai.ā.ulu. n. Rain name. Probably same as Kaiāulu.

Pua-ka-'ilima. n. Howland Island, a name used by Hawaiian guano diggers there in about 1856. *Lit.,* the *'ilima* flower. See song, Pukui and Korn 80-2.

pua.kala. 1. v. To assume the appearance of *kala* seaweed, said of octopus in the sea. **2.** n. A kind of crab.

pua kala. n. **1.** The beach or prickly poppy *(Argemone glauca),* a Hawaiian species closely related to a southern United States species, a gray, prickly plant with stiff, lobed, toothed leaves and fragile, white-petaled flowers. Formerly, Hawaiians used the yellow juice to relieve pain. *Lit.,* thorny flower. Also *kala, naule, pōkalakala.* See *lū 2,* Neal 367. **2.** A native prickly lobelia *(Cyanea solenocalyx),* a shrub with large ovate or oblong, prickly leaves and hairy, purple flowers, found in gulches of Moloka'i. **3.** The spear thistle *(Cirsium vulgare),* a coarse, prickly European weed, 60 to 150 cm high, with large, spiny, lobed leaves, and dark-purple, spiny flower heads about 5 cm. (Neal 857.)

pua kalaunu. n. The crown flower *(Calotropis gigantea),* a large shrub, native from India to the East Indies, belonging to the milkweed family. The crown-shaped flowers, white or lavender, are commonly used for leis, and the plants for hedges in dry areas. (Neal 698-9.) Called *lili'u* on Ni'ihau.

Pua-ka.uahi-hae.hae-ka-manu. n. A *lua* fighting stroke. *Lit.,* the smoke blows, the birds rage.

pua.kauhi. Same as *'āwikiwiki,* a vine. *Kaua'i.*

pua.ka.wai.hae. n. **1.** A variety of taro. (HP 34.) **2.** A variety of sweet potato.

pua.kea. 1. nvs. Pale-colored, especially a tint between white and pink, as sunset clouds; the color of a buckskin horse. Cf. *na'ena'e pua kea. 'Ilipuakea,* white person [a poetical name]. *Ku'u lio puakea,* my buckskin horse. **ho'o.pua.kea.** To appear bright, shine. **2.** vi. To spread, as a ship's sails or as fog.

pua-Kele.kino. n. A spiny climbing vine *(Caesalpinia sepiaria)* from India, first grown in Ka'ū, Hawai'i, by Father Celestino. (Neal 434.) *Lit.,* Celestino flower.

pua keni.keni. n. A shrub or small tree *(Fagraea berteriana),* from the South Pacific, grown ornamentally for foliage, flowers, fruit. The flowers are 5 cm long, white, changing to orange, fragrant, and used for leis. The 2.5 cm-wide berry is orange or red. (Neal 682.) *Lit.,* ten-cent flower, so-called because at one time the flowers are said to have sold for ten cents each.

pua kepa.lō. n. Bougainvillea. *Lit.,* devil flower [so-called because of thorns]. *Hawai'i.* Cf. *pukanawila.*

pua.kī. 1. Same as *puaki'i 1.* **2.** n. A young eel. **3.** n. A red seaweed *(Liagora decussata),* somewhat calcified but flexible, branched; not edible; related to *pāpa-'akea.*

pua kī. n. Flower of the ti.

pu'aki. 1. vs. Stingy; antisocial, suspicious and distrustful of others *Rare.* **2.** n. Lines meeting on a mast. *Rare.*

pua.kiawe. Same as *pūkiawe.*

pua.ki'i. 1. vs. Thin, skinny. Cf. *hōki'i.* **2.** vt. To take, as without permission. *Rare.*

pua ki'i. Same as *'ōpua ki'i.*

pua kī.kā. n. Cigar flower. See *kīkā.*

pu'a ki'o. Same as *pu'u ki'o. Moloka'i.*

pua kō. n. Stem and tassel of sugar cane (the stem was used in making hats). *Pāpale pua, pāpale pua kō,* hat made of sugar-cane stem.

pua.koali. n. A tapa colored by beating in sandalwood. (Kam. 76:157.)

pua.kō.'ula. vs. Red, as *lehua* blooms. *'A'ala lau lehua ka wao o Puna, puakō'ula i ka mau'u Ko'o-lihilihi* (chant), fragrant with many *lehua* is the upland of Puna, red in the grass at Ko'o-lihilihi.

pua kukui. Blossoms of *kukui.*

pū.'ala. 1. Same as *pū'ā,* sheath. **2.** vs. Overcooked, as taro. *Rare.*

pū.'ala'a. Short for *pu'u 'āla'a,* heap of small taro tubers.

pua laha 'ole. n. A choice and rare flower. *Fig.,* a beloved person. *Lit.,* flower not widespread.

pua lahi.lahi. n. Single flowering. *Lit.,* thin flower.

pū.'ala.lā. vi. To scream, shriek, cry out, bleat; to cry loudly like a baby. See ex., *'uwī'uwī 5.*

puala.lea. vs. Clear, bright. *Pualalea Mauna Loa i ka pā a ka lā* (chant), Mauna Loa is bright with the touch of sun.

pua lani. n. Descendant of a chief.

pua.lau. vt. To carry on the hip, as a child. *Rare.*

pu'ala.wāhi. vt. To divide. *Rare. Lit.,* bundle split.

pua lei. n. Flowers for leis; cherished blossom or child.

pua lē.'ī. n. Flower that attracts many *(lē'ī),* as a *lehua* that attracts birds.

pua.lele. n. **1.** The sow thistle *(Sonchus oleraceus),* a weedy herb in the daisy family, from Europe. It is 30 cm tall or more, the leaves narrow, lobed, toothed, the flower heads clustered, yellow, about 3 cm in diameter. The light seeds are tipped with hairy tufts. The plant is sometimes fed to pigs and the leaves eaten by people during famine. (Neal 860.) **2.** A weed *(Emilia fosbergii,* misidentified as *E. javanica).* Ni'ihau. Cf. Neal 854-5.

pua.lena. 1. nvs. Yellow color; to appear yellow, as said of dawn or muddy water. *Ka wā e pualena ana 'o ke ao* (Puk. 14.27), the time when the light appears yellow at dawn. **2.** vi. Lazy; to loll about.

pua.lewa. nvs. Unsettled, unfixed, always on the move; upset stomach.

pū.'ali. 1. n. Warrior, soldier, so called because Hawaiian fighters tied *(pū'ali)* their *malos* at the waist so that no flap would dangle for a foe to seize; army, host, multitude. Various types of military formations are listed below. *Kona pū'ali apau* (Puk. 14.4), all his host. *Pū'ali 'ānela,* host of angels. **2.** nvt. To gird tightly about the waist, as of *malo-*clad warriors, or as corseted women; compressed, constricted in the middle; grooved, notched; irregularly shaped, as taro; notch; tight belt (see *kōkī* for example). *Ua kāliki 'ia ā pū'ali ke kino o ka wahine,* the body of the woman is corseted and pulled tight. *'Eono pū'ali o kānā lā'au pālau* (For. 5.221), his war club has six notches. *Pū'ali ka hau nui i ka hau iki* (Nak. 108), the big *hau* tree is grooved by the small *hau* [a child annoying an adult; a small warrior harassing a big one]. **hopū.'ali.** To gird, compress; grooved. **3.** n. Isthmus. **4.** n. Slender abdominal stalk on a wasp's body. **5.** n. In music, a decrescendo followed by a crescendo. **6.** n. Irregularly shaped ravine. **7.** n. A vague term for an adopted man or boy who had no servants. (Ii 38.)

pū.'ali.'ali. Redup. of *pū'ali 2;* of varying thickness, as a cord or *'ilima* lei not carefully woven.

Pū.'ali Ho'ōla. n. Salvation Army. *Lit.,* saving army.

pua.li'i. 1. Var. spelling of *pua ali'i.* **2.** n. Kind of tapa used for loincloths and sarongs.

pū.'ali inu wai. n. Temperance league. *Lit.,* water-drinking host.

pū.'ali kaua ka'i wā.wae. n. Infantry. *Lit.,* war army proceeding afoot.

pū.'ali kaua lio, pū'ali kau lio. n. Cavalry.

pū.'ali koa. n. Armed forces, troops, regiment, brigade, corps.

pū.'ali koa ho'o.hano.hano. n. Honor guard.

pū.'ali koa lio. n. Cavalry. *Lit.,* horse-soldier army.

pualo.alo. Short for *pua aloalo.*

pū aloha. n. Gun salute.

pualu, puwalu. 1. n. A species of surgeonfish *(Acanthurus xanthopterus* and *A. mata),* up to 15 and 20 cm in length and brown or dull-gray in color. It resembles the *palani* in tough skin and strong smell but may be distinguished from the latter by a blue line across the soft part of the fin. 2. Var. spelling of *puwalu 1.*

pū.'alu. vs. Loose, slack; crumpled, crinkled, as ruffles. Cf. *'alu.*

pū.'alu.'alu. Redup. of *pū'alu.*

pua maka.hiki. n. Annual flower.

pua maka nui. Same as *aka'aka'awa,* a begonia. *Lit.,* large-eyed flower.

pua male. n. A kind of vine *(Stephanotis floribunda),* in the milkweed family, from Madagascar. It has oval, leathery, paired leaves and clustered, fragrant, white, tubular flowers, which are sometimes worn by brides in Hawai'i. (Neal 699–700.) *Lit.,* wedding flower.

pua.mana. n. Caret sign of omission.

pua mana. n. Same as *ilioha,* horseweeds.

pua melia. See *melia,* plumeria.

pu'a.mimi. Same as *pu'u mimi. Moloka'i.*

puana. 1. nvt. Attack or beginning of a song; in music, the tonic or keynote; to begin a song; summary refrain, as of a song, usually at or near the beginning of a song; theme of a song. See ex., *pō 1. Ka puana a ka moe,* revelation or message of a dream. *Ha'ina 'ia mai ana ka puana,* tell the summary refrain [this line followed by the refrain is at the end of many songs or precedes the name of the person in whose honor the song was composed]. *Puana 'ia* (Kel. 111), sung for the first time. *E puunu mai 'oe i ka puana,* start the summary refrain of the song. 2. n. Pronunciation, utterance. *E ho'opuka pololei ana ka haumāna i ka puana pololei o ia mau hua pī'āpā,* the student was saying the pronunciation of the letters of the alphabet well. 3. vt. To surround, encompass, crowd. *'O ka puana 'ana aku i kēlā ulu lehua,* crowding about that *lehua* grove. *Ā puana maila lākou iāia ā puni* (2 Oihn 18.31), they completely surrounded him.

pū.'ana.'ana. Same as *pū'ali'ali.*

puana.'ī. n. Front of the neck and throat. *Kā'awe i ka puana'ī,* hang by the neck.

pua.nai.ea. vs. Weak, sickly. *Puanaiea ke kanaka ke hele i ka li'ulā,* the one going after a mirage becomes weak [don't try for the impossible].

Puana-kau. n. The star Rigel, tutelary star of West Maui.

pua nā.nā honua. n. A tree *(Solanum auriculatum* syn. *S. carterianum)* native to Madagascar and tropical Asia, related to the tomato, having large, downy, oblong leaves, and blue flowers clustered at branch tips. *Lit.,* flower looking [at] earth.

pua nā.nā lā. n. The common sunflower *(Helianthus annuus),* a coarse annual herb, 1 to 4.5 m high, from the western United States. It is a member of the daisy family and has flower heads from 8 to 35 cm across, the yellow ray florets surrounding a brown-purple center. (Neal 840.) *Lit.,* flower looking [at] sun.

Pua-nau.ane. n. Name of a star.

-puananu. ho'o.pua.nanu. To rise as a wave. *Ua ho'opuananu 'ia kou umauma,* your breast rises and falls like a wave [grief].

pua.nea. vs. Mournful. *Puanea ka hele 'ana a Kristo* (chant), how mournful was Christ's going.

puane.ane. Var. spelling of *puaaneane.* See ex., *kāhoahoa.*

puani.ea. Rare var. of *puanaiea.*

pua.nihi. Young taro, taro tops. (AP.)

pua.niki. 1. vt. To bind tightly. *Kī'aha puaniki,* goblet. 2. n. Small wooden bowl, as for an individual serving of poi.

pua.niu. n. A tapa dyed with coconut, probably oil; a tapa dye (Kam. 76:109).

pua niu. 1. n. Coconut flower. *Hale pua niu,* house where offerings of bananas, coconuts, kava were kept, said to be offered in order to deify a deceased person and make him into a lizard god. 2. vs. Color of the coconut flower; ivory-colored.

pū.anu.anu. nvs. Cold, chilly, damp and shivering. *Pūanuanu ka hale,* the house is chilly [of a house where a loved one has died; apology for not serving alcoholic drinks].

pua.'ō. nvs. Bluster, onslaught, as of high wind or dashing waves; rude, abrupt speech; to speak thus.

pū.'ao. n. 1. Mesh about 0.5 to 1.3 cm wide, of mats. 2. Womb. Cf. *lapa pū'ao. Pū'ao pelu,* fallen womb.

pua.'ohi. nvi. To chatter, gush, ramble verbally; chattering, chatterbox.

pua-o-ka-lani. n. False daisy *(Eclipta alba).* (Neal 838.) *Lit.,* flower of the chief [or heaven].

pua-o-Kama. n. A gourd *(Sicyos niihauensis),* first collected and identified by H. St. John. Cf. *kūpala* and Neal 808.

pua 'ole. n. Same as *'āwela,* a flowerless *(pua 'ole)* sugar cane.

pua Pā.kē. n. A genus *(Chrysanthemum)* in the daisy family, including many species of ornamental annual and perennial herbs, with small to large flower heads, which are white to red, yellow, or purple. Most species are from the Eastern Hemisphere. (Neal 850–1.) Cf. *haleloke, wailuku.*

pua Pā.kē pihi. n. Dwarf *pua Pākē.*

pua pepa. n. 1. The everlasting or straw flower. *Lit.,* paper flower. Also *nani mau loa.* 2. Bougainvillea *(Bougainvillea spectabilis). Ni'ihau.*

pua pihi. n. All kinds of zinnias, especially one *(Zinnia elegans),* a Mexican annual grown ornamentally for the flowers. The flower heads are 5 to 13 cm across, single and daisy-like, or double and somewhat round, and of various colors. In Hawai'i is also found a wild species *(Z. pauciflora),* from Mexico and South America, with 2.5 cm-wide, single flower heads, the central florets yellow, the rays yellow, red, or purple. (Neal 838.) *Lit.,* button flower.

pua pili.pili. n. The Spanish clover *(Desmodium uncinatum),* a South American herb, long established in Hawai'i. It is good fodder. The plant is 30 to 90 cm high, each leaf having three ovate leaflets with a light area along the midrib. Flowers are small, pink or whitish, pea-shaped. Pods are narrow, flattened, chainlike, 2.5 to 5 cm long, clinging to clothing and animals. (Neal 451.) Also *kīkānia pipili.* See *pilipili 'ula.*

pua pilo. Same as *maiapilo,* a plant.

pū.'ā pipi. n. Herd of cattle.

pua.po'o. n. Comb or crest of a bird, as of a chicken. *Lit.,* head issue.

puapu. Same as *apuapu,* file.

pua.pua. 1. n. Tail feathers, as of a cock; rump, as of a chicken; streamer; coattails; this word is used as a means of avoiding answering questions: *Aia 'oia i hea? Aia i ka puapua.* Where is he? Gone to get tail feathers. *Kuka puapua,* swallow-tailed coat. 2. Redup. of *pua 2.* ho'o.pua.pua. Redup. of *ho'opua;* to appear again and again. (PCP *puapua.)* 3. n. Spike in the back of sphinx moths. 4. Same as *pupua 3.* 5. n. A variety of banana. 6. Same as *'āpua 2,* fishhook shank.

pu'a.pu'a. vs. Tasteless; not tasty.

pu'a.pū.'ā. Redup. of *pū'ā 1, 5.*

pua.pua'a. Plural of *pua'a 3. Mehe ao puapua'a lā ke aloha e kau nei* (Laie 605), like cloud banks is the love settling here.

pua pua'a. n. Piglet. *Kaka'i ka pua pua'a i ka mālie, he 'ino,* when the little pigs follow in the calm, it is bad weather [pun on *puapua'a* clouds piling up in the sky].

pua.puahi. Redup. of *puahi 1, 2. Puapuahi ka pahapaha o Poli-hale,* gray is the seaweed of Poli-hale.
pua.pua'i. Redup. of *pua'i;* to pour continuously or often. *E puapua'i mai anei ka wai 'ono?* (Iak. 3.11), does sweet water pour forth?
pu'a.pu'ala. Redup. of *pū'ala 1, 2.*
pua.pua.moa. n. **1.** Long-tailed dinner coat. Also *pupuamoa.* **2.** A kind of adder's-tongue fern *(Ophioglossum pendulum),* found in Polynesia westward into Madagascar, commonly growing on trees. It has ribbon-like fronds, erect or bent and hanging, 60 cm long or less, some bearing short, narrow, spore-filled spikes.
pua.pua moa. n. Tail feathers of a chicken.
pua.pua.nui. n. A variety of banana.
pua pupupu. n. Double flowering.
pū.'au. n. Ti-leaf blossom stem. (HP 206.) *Rare.*
pua.'ula. n. Young *kūmū* or *'āhuluhulu,* fish.
pua 'ula.'ula. n. Natal grass *(Rhynchelytrum repens),* grown for forage; highly ornamental. (Neal 74.)
pū aupaka. Same as *'ōlulu.*
pua.'u'u. nv. Masturbation; to masturbate. *Lit.,* to pull issue.
puawa. **1.** Same as *pua awa,* young *awa,* fish. **2.** Same as *kuawa,* guava. *Ni'ihau.*
pū.'awa. **1.** n. Young white pandanus leaves that are good for plaiting. **2.** nvs. Bitter; bitterness.
pū 'awa. n. Kava plant or root portion, formerly used as offerings: see *'ike 1.*
pū.'awa.'awa. Redup. of *pū'awa 1.*
pu'a.wai. n. Spittle, slobber; spray. *Rare.*
puawe. Same as *awe,* thin, soft. *Rare.*
pū.awe.awe. Redup. of *puawe. Rare.*
pue. vi. To huddle or sit crouched, as with cold. **ho'o.-pue.** Caus/sim. *'O ka pua 'ilima i kui 'ia, ka'u e ho'o-pue nei i ka poli* (song), the *'ilima* blossoms strung in a lei, that I press to my heart. *Ho'opue au i ke ko'eko'e,* I sit huddled up with cold. **2.** n. Feathers on the back of a bird above the *puapua,* tail feathers.
pu'e. **1.** nvt. Hill, as of sweet potatoes; dune; to hill up. Cf. *pu'e one.* (PPN *puke.*) **2.** vt. To attack, force, ravish, rape, compel. *Keiki pu'e,* boy or youth who ravishes women. (Puk. 22.16.) (PPN *puke.*) **3.** n. A lobelia *(Lobelia gaudichaudii* var. *kauaensis)* found only in mountains of Kaua'i. The stem, 1 to 2 m high, bears a tuft of narrow leaves 15 cm long, and three or four racemes of large flowers, whitish streaked with purple.
pu.'e.'eke. vi. To shrink away from; to shorten, contract; to grimace. **ho'o.pu.'e.'eke.** Caus/sim.
pu.'e.'ena. vs. Glowing, as fire. *Pu'e'ena maila ka lua i ke akua* (chant of Ka'ū chiefs), the pit glows because of the goddess.
puehu. **1.** vs. Scattered, dispersed, routed, gone, tousled; fine, crumbling; every which way, as hair in the wind. *'Ai ā lawa, inu ā kena, puehu 'oe,* eat until satisfied, drink until replete, all gone! *Ua puehu ka hulu o ka manu,* the feathers of the bird have scattered [said of one who has left in a hurry]. *No Hanamā'ulu ka ipu puehu,* an empty calabash at Hanamā'ulu [no hospitality at Hanamā'ulu, probably a play on *mā'ulu,* tired]. **ho'o.puehu.** To scatter, disperse, rout, blow away, whisk, crumble; blown away, fluff; gone. (PCP *pu(u)efu.*) **2.** vi. Peeling, as human. **3.** nvi. Remainder, remnant; to remain. *'Elua ā puehu,* two and a little over. *Ā 'o ka puehu ka mea i puehu aku o nā pale o ua uhi lā, ā ka hapalua o ka pale puehu, e kau nō ia ma ke kua o ka halelewa* (Puk. 26.12), and the remnant that remained of the curtains of the tent, the half of the remaining curtain, it shall hang at the back of the tabernacle.
pū.ehu.ehu. Redup. of *puehu 1–3;* tousled; flaky. *Hau pūehuehu,* snowflake. *Māhuna ka 'ili, nakaka pūehuehu 'ino'ino loa ke nānā aku,* the skin is flaked, cracked and peeling, unpleasant to look at. *Pūehuehu ka lā, komo 'ino'ino* (Malo 216), the sun is routed, storms enter. (PCP *puuefuefu.*)
pū.'eke. Same as *pūliki,* to gird.

puela. nvs. A long tapa strip, as used for a marker or banner; narrow, thin, as a banner.
pueo. **1.** n. Hawaiian short-eared owl *(Asio flammeus sandwichensis),* regarded often as a benevolent *'aumakua* (HM 124). *Keiki a ka pueo,* child of an owl [one whose father is not known]. **2.** vs. Short (perhaps so called because the owl's neck was short). Cf. *hue nuku pueo. 'Oki pueo 'ia ka lauoho,* hair cut short. **3.** Same as *'aho pueo,* main purlin of a house. *Ku'u manu noho pū me ke kanaka: pueo* (riddle), my bird living with people: owl [pun on *'aho pueo*]. **4.** vt. To rock a child on the foot; while doing this one amused the child by chanting *pūeoeo.* **5.** n. Shroud of a ship or canoe. **6.** See *papapueo,* a taro. Other names recorded (HP 34) are *pueo hālenalena* and *pueo ke'oke'o.* **7.** n. House lashing. (Kam. 76:97.)
pū.eo.eo. Redup. of *pueo 4;* to rock a child.
pu'e one. n. Sand dune, sand bar. *Ku'u ipo i ka he'e pu'e one* (song), my sweetheart surfing [over the] sand bar [referring to the old sport of surfing up into the very mouth of a stream].
pue.pue. Redup. of *pue 1.*
pu'e.pu'e. Redup. of *pu'e 1, 2.* (PPN *pukepuke,* to hold; PCP *pukepuke,* hills.)
pue.puehu. Same as *pūehuehu.*
puewa. nvi. To float, drift, as carried by wind or tide; a vagabond. *Rare.*
pu'e.wai. n. Agitated water, as under a waterfall or at the meeting of stream and sea. Cf. *he'e pu'ewai.*
pu'e wale. vt. To force, attack, rape. *Ē ku'u kaikunāne, mai pu'e wale mai 'oe ia'u* (2 Sam. 13.12), my brother, do not force me.
pū.hā. **1.** nvi. Abscess, burst sore, ulcer; to break, burst. *Ua pa'apū ko'u kino i ka ilo a me ka pāpa'a lepo, a laila pūhā hou a'ela* (Ioba 7.5), my body is covered with worms and filthy clots and then breaks out afresh. **2.** n. Hollow, as a tree. *Noho ihola lākou maloko o nā pūhā lā'au* (Laie 431), they then lived within hollow trees. **3.** vi. To belch, burp, clear the throat, hawk up phlegm. **ho'o.pū.hā.** Caus/sim. (PCP *pu(u)fa(a).*) **4.** vi. To breathe air, as a sea turtle. *Pūhā hewa ka honu i ka lā makani,* the turtle breathes at the wrong moment on a windy day [one who says the wrong thing]. (PCP *pu(u)-(f,s)a(a).*) **5.** n. A brown seaweed *(Colpomenia sinuosa),* cushion-shaped, hollow, surface smooth and uneven; not eaten. Cf. *nakeke.*
pū.hā.'ā. nv. Spots, as uncooked spots in taro; light spots on a cowry shell; to burst forth, as light. *Rare.*
puhaakakaiea. Malo's spelling of *pūhakakaiea.* (Malo 40.)
pū.hā.hā. Redup. of *pūhā 4. Fig.,* to speak loudly, harshly, or evilly of others.
puha.halu. Redup. of *puhalu.*
pū.hai. vs. Shallow, of roots. *He noni no Ka-ua-lehu, he pūhai a'a,* a *noni* tree of Ka-ua-lehu [a rocky place at Ka'ū Hawai'i] whose roots are in shallow ground [one with superficial knowledge].
puhai.nā.nā. To stare without replying, as to a question. (And.)
pū.haka. **1.** n. Loins, waist. *Ka mea ma nā pūhaka, a me ka 'a'a o ke au ma ke akepa'a* (Oihk. 3.4), the thing by the flanks and the caul of the bile at the liver. **2.** Same as *hakahaka,* empty. *Rare.*
pū.haka.haka. Redup. of *pūhaka 2. Rare.*
pū.haka.kai.ea. Same as *noio,* a sea bird. *Rare.*
pū hala. n. Pandanus tree. See *hala. Kumu pū hala,* pandanus tree. *Ulu pū hala,* pandanus grove. (PPN *fala,* PCP *puu fala.*)
pū.hā lā.'au. n. Hollow in a tree.
pū.hala.hio. vi. To run away, dash by, whiz by. **ho'o.-pū.hala.hio.** To chase off, help escape.
pū.hala.kē. Same as *pōhalakē. Rare.*
pū.hala.lū. **1.** vs. Large, flabby, fat, bloated, obese. **ho'o.pū.hala.lū.** To fill with air, inflate. **2.** vi. To cry out, as a bird. *Rare.*
pū.hali. **1.** n. A kind of fragile sea shell, possibly *Janthina* or *Argonauta. Lit.,* carried shell. **2.** Stingy. (And.)

puhalu. 1. vs. Soft, flabby, loose, sagging, sunken, deflated; to loosen, deflate, sink, sag. *Fig.*, unenthusiastic, relaxed, weak. Also *halu, uhalu. Ua puhalu ka pāluna,* the balloon collapsed. *Puhalu ka ihu, nānā i ke kā'ao,* stretch the nostrils, see overripe pandanus fruit [one doesn't see the pandanus until the fruit has fallen and scattered its scent; one appreciates people after they are gone]. ho'o.puhalu. Caus/sim.; to pulverize or loosen, as the soil. **2.** To stare wide-eyed. (AP.)

pū.halu.halu. Redup. of *puhalu 1, 2.*

pū.hano. vt. To beautify, glorify. *Rare.* Cf. *hano, hanohano.*

pū.hanu. vi. To catch the breath after exertion. Cf. *hanu.* ho'o.pū.hanu. Caus/sim.

pū.hau. n. Cool spring.

puha'u. vi. To puff out, billow out, swell out. Cf. *ha'u.*

pū.ha'u.ha'u. Redup. of *puha'u.* Cf. *lima pūha'uha'u, lole wāwae pūha'uha'u. Palekoki pūha'uha'u,* large gathered skirt.

pū.he'e. vi. To flee. Cf. *he'e 2. Pūhe'e nā ali'i,* the chiefs fled.

pū he'e. n. Octopus head; figurative name for a small fontanel (cf. *wāwahi*).

pū.he'e.miki. vt. To steal or filch and run away.

pū.heheo. vs. Round and swirling, as a full skirt or *pā'ū* with many folds. Also *pōheheo.* Cf. *heo 1.*

puhemo. vs. **1.** Loose, set free, released, taken off. Cf. *hemo 1.* ho'o.puhemo. To loosen, release. **2.** Weak, listless.

pū.hene. 1. vt. To tease, giggle. *Rare.* Cf. *hene 3.* **2.** n. A crude basket, as for carrying food. *Rare.* **3.** Same as *pūhenehene.*

pū.hene.hene. nvt. To play a game: a stone or piece of wood called *no'a* was hidden on the person of a player, and the other players tried to guess on whom it was hidden; the game itself (Malo 218; For. 6:197–9), sometimes accompanied by gambling (Kam. 64:128–9).

pū.heo.heo. 1. n. A whistle sometimes blown during the game of *pūhenehene;* the answer of the players when addressed by the guesser in the game of *pūhenehene* (Malo 218) and perhaps also in the game of *kilu.* **2.** Same as *pūheheo.*

pū.heu. Same as *'ena'ena 2,* cudweeds. *Ni'ihau.*

puhi. 1. vt. To burn, set on fire, bake (preceded by *ke*). Cf. *hale puhi palaoa. E puhi ana kēia kūlanakauhale o kākou i ke puhi 'ana i ke ahi,* this town of ours will be burned completely in the fire. *Puhi mana'o 'ino,* arson, to burn maliciously. **2.** nvi. To blow, puff; blowhole; spouting, as by a whale; to smoke, as tobacco. Cf. *puhi 'ole. Noho i ke puhi,* to stay in the blowhole [jail]. ho'o.puhi. To cause to blow, blow. *Fig.,* to steal. (PPN *pusi.*) **3.** vt. To extract, as water from steam; to distill, brew. *Ipu hao puhi,* still. **4.** n. Eel (see below). A hitherto undescribed eel was identified in 1978 as *Gymnothorax ruepelliae.* Some persons considered *puhi* as *'aumākua.* Cf. *wa'a puhi* and saying, eel. *Puhi niho wakawaka,* sharp-toothed eel [fierce warriors]. *'Oni ā puhi ka mana'o i ka pilikia,* the thoughts squirm like an eel because of the trouble. (PNP *pusia.*) **5.** Same as *mai'a puhi,* a banana. **6.** n. Sticks supporting a *pāku'iku'i* net, called the *puhi nui* and the *puhi 'u'uku* (or *puhi iki*). Nets forming the *'upena papa* had the same names. **7.** n. Uncircumcised foreskin. **8.** See *kua puhi, puhi kaokao.*

puhia. Pas/imp. of *puhi 1–3. Wai-puhia* (original name for the Upside Down Falls, O'ahu), blown water. *Mehe mea i puhia ā wela e ka papa* (chant), like something burned and heated by the foundation. (PPN *pusia.*)

puhi ahi. nv. To burn, set on fire, cremate; arson, fireman who tends to the fire of a steam engine. See *wahi puhi ahi.*

puhi ao. n. An eel *(Muraena pardalis).* Also *puhi kauila.*

puhi 'apo. n. Barred moray eel, *Gymnothorax ruepelliae* (formerly *G. petelli*); the Hawaiian name was coined in 1978 by Mary Kawena Pukui.

puhi hā.pala. n. An eel, *Gymnothorax pictus.*

pū.hihio. vi. **1.** To whirl, blow, as wind; gusty. **2.** To

break wind noiselessly. *'Ai pūhihio,* same as *'ai pūhi'u* (see *pūhi'u 2*).

puhi hoana. Same as *puhi palahoana,* a fish.

puhi ho'o.lā.'au. n. A variety of eel. *Lit.,* stick-like eel.

puhi iki. See *puhi 6.*

puhi 'ini.'iniki. n. Infant eels, about the size of a lead pencil; catching infant eels with the hands. *Lit.,* pinching eels.

puhi kai. n. Blowhole.

puhi kao.kao. n. Active venereal sore.

puhi kā.pā. n. An eel called by some voracious and fierce, perhaps *Echidna nebulosa.*

puhi kā.pa'a. n. A species of eel *(Gymnothorax pictus),* or perhaps a variant of *puhi kāpā.*

puhi kā.pī.pī. n. A variety of eel. *Lit.,* salt lightly eel.

puhi kauila. n. Same as *puhi ao,* an eel.

puhi.ki'i. n. According to some, young of all flying fish; according to others, same as *mālolo.*

puhi kī.na'u. n. A variety of small, white eel, mentioned in chants as eating fallen pandanus keys.

puhi kō. nvt. To burn cane trash or a cane field; burning cane.

puhi koali. n. A variety of white eel. *Lit.,* morning-glory eel.

puhi.kole. nvs. Poor, destitute; poverty.

puhi kumu.one. n. A variety of sand-colored eel. *Lit.,* sandstone eel.

puhi lā.'au. n. A variety of eel *(Myrichthys maculosus). Lit.,* wood eel.

puhi lau milo. n. A variety of eel *(Lycodontis undulatus),* highly relished. *Lit.,* milo leaf eel.

puhi lehu. vt. To cremate, burn and reduce to ashes.

puhi lei hala. n. A variety of eel. Its coloring suggests a lei of pandanus keys. *Lit.,* pandanus-lei eel.

pū.hili. 1. vi. To veer, as the wind. Cf. *hili 2. Ke pā pūhili nei ka makani,* the wind is blowing every which way. ho'o.pū.hili. To blow in gusts from varying directions. *'A'ohe mea nāna e ho'opūhili, he moho no ka lā makani,* there is none to blow [him] aside, for he is a wingless rail [or candidate] of a windy day [admiration for one who lets nothing stop him from carrying out a task]. **2.** vs. Confused, thwarted, frustrated, set to naught. ho'o.pū.hili. To confuse, thwart, frustrate. **3.** Same as *pūhilihili, a vine.*

pū.hili.hili. Same as *mohihihi,* a vine.

puhina. Same as *puhi 1–3;* blowhole (preceded by *ke*).

puhi nanaka. n. A black and white eel that attacks and bites. *Lit.,* cracked eel.

puhi nau 'ai. n. A variety of eel. *Lit.,* food chewer.

puhi nono.kea. n. A variety of eel.

puhi nui. See *puhi 6.*

puhi nuku 'ula. n. A variety of eel. *Lit.,* red-mouth eel.

puhi 'o'a. n. A brightly colored eel *(Muraena pardalis)* up to 60 or 90 cm long. Cf. Marquesan *puhi a'oa, 'o'oa* (Lavondès).

puhi 'ohe. v. To play a wind instrument; a player of a wind instrument; a flute. *Hui puhi 'ohe,* band.

pū.hio.hio. Same as *pūhihio.*

puhi 'ō.ilo. n. Infant eel.

puhi oka.oka. n. A name applied to priests versed in all branches of the profession, as divining, meteorology, healing. (For. 6:59.) Probably *lit.,* to blow to bits.

puhi 'ō.lohe. n. An eel mentioned by Kepelino (no data). *Lit.,* bare eel.

puhi 'ō.mole. n. A variety of eel. *Lit.,* smooth eel.

puhi.'ō.ni'o. vt. To paint in spotted colors, as tapa.

puhi 'ō.ni'o. n. Whitemouth moray eel, *Lycodontis meleagris,* 50 cm in length. *Lit.,* spotted eel.

puhi 'ō.pule Same as *puhi pule.*

puhi 'ou, puhi 'ō.ū. n. A variety of eel *(Gymnothorax petelli).*

puhi paka (baka). nv. To smoke tobacco; one who smokes; smoking.

puhi paka. n. One of the commonest of the larger eels, *Lycodontis flavimarginatus,* perhaps up to 1.2 m long, considered dangerous by some. Cf. Marquesan *puhi pata* (Lavondès).

puhi pala.hoana. n. A shallow-water fish *(Brotula multibarbata).* Also *puhi hoana, palahoana.*

puhi.pala.lā. vs. Tall, thin, emaciated. *Rare.*

puhi palaoa. n. Baker.

puhi pā.lina. n. A variety of eel (no data).

puhi pā.paʻa. n. A variety of eel (no data). *Lit.,* burned eel.

puhi pau. vt. Blown away; completely burned; to blow or burn away. *Puhi pau ʻia nā mea huna,* all the secrets were blown away [revealed].

puhi.puhi. Redup. of *puhi 2,* to blow. (PPN *pusipusi.*)

puhi.puhi ahi. Redup. of *puhi ahi. Fig.,* short-tempered.

puhi pule. n. A small, spotted eel. *Lit.,* eel variegated in color.

pū.hiʻu. vi. 1. To break wind audibly (cf. *hio 3*), considered rude; to cause failure by audible flatulency; a term of contempt for show-offs. *Ua pūhiʻu ʻia ka hālāwai,* the meeting failed because of [a member's] flatulency (a belief). *Puʻu pūhiʻu,* flatulency difficult to suppress. **hoʻo.pū.hiʻu.** Caus/sim. *Lāʻau hoʻopūhiʻu,* a medicine for relief of gas pains by flatulency. 2. Irreverence; rude. *ʻAi pūhiʻu* (Malo 30), to eat without observance of taboos, especially of men who prepared food for chiefesses and who were allowed to eat in their presence.

puhi ū.hā. n. A variety of eel *(Conger cinereus),* mustache conger. It has a white ventral side and darker dorsal side and is nearly 1 m in length; greatly favored by some to eat.

puhi ū.hā kala.koa. n. A variety of eel (no data). *Lit.,* calico *(Eng.) ūhā* eel.

pū.hiʻu.hiʻu. Redup. of *pūhiʻu 1, 2.*

Puhi-ʻula. n. Name of a legendary eel; according to one authority, a *Conger cinereus* eel. *Lit.,* red eel.

puhi ʻuʻuku. Same as *puhi 6.*

puhi wela. n. A variety of eel (no data). *Lit.,* warm eel.

pū.hō. Same as *pūhā 1.*

puho.hō. vi. Windy; to blow strongly, as through an aperture; a sweep of wind. See ex., *polikua.*

puhole, hoʻo.puhole. Same as *pohole, hoʻopohole.* Cf. *hole 1.*

pū.holo. vt. To steam, especially by stuffing flesh, as of pig, with hot rocks and placing in a sealed calabash; to take a sweat bath; to steam a corpse so that the flesh *(pela)* will separate from the bones.

pū.holo.holo. Redup. of *pūholo.*

pū hoʻo.kani. n. Conch trumpet; any wind instrument, as trumpet, cornet, saxophone. *Lit.,* sounding triton shell.

puhue.hue. Var. of *pōhuehue,* morning glory. (And.)

pū.huli. vi. To grow thick, of *huli,* taro shoots.

pū.hulu.hulu. 1. vs. Hairy, shaggy, downy, hirsute, bushy. *ʻUmiʻumi pūhuluhulu,* bushy beard. 2. Same as *hulu ʻīlio 1, 2,* seaweeds.

puʻi. Same as *puʻipuʻi.*

puīa. vs. Sweet-smelling, diffused, as fragrance; permeated with perfume, fragrant. *Ka puīa ʻala o ka hanu* (song), the fragrant issue of the breath. **hoʻo.puīa.** To perfume.

puihe. Same as *iheihe,* a fish.

pū.ʻika.ʻika. vs. 1. Difficult to acquire or do. *Pū ʻikaʻika ke komo aku i kēlā kula,* difficult to enter that school. *Pū ʻikaʻika ka loaʻa mai ʻo kahi kālā,* difficult to get money. 2. Packed, crowded. *Piha pū ʻikaʻika,* crowded full.

puiki. Same as *puhikiʻi,* young flying fish.

pū.ʻiki. Var. of *pūliki 1.*

pū.ʻili. 1. n. Bamboo rattles, as used for dancing. 2. vt. To clasp, hold fast in the hand, embrace, grasp firmly. *Pū ʻili mai ʻoe ā paʻa,* hold tight. 3. n. A type of tapabeater pattern: tips of zigzag ridges in adjacent surfaces meet and form sunken lozenges. Cf. *koʻeau,* in which the ridges are parallel. 4. n. Berry of the *pōpolo* plant. Also *ʻolohua.* 5. A game played with sugar-cane flowers. *Rare.*

pū.ʻili-hā.luʻa. n. *Pū ʻili* design with one or more *hāluʻa* ridges or strips between the panels of the beater.

pū.ʻili.ʻili. 1. Short for *puʻu ʻiliʻili.* 2. Similar to *pū ʻuluʻulu;* to collect.

pū.ʻili-koʻe.au. n. *Pū ʻili* and *koʻeau* designs combined.

puʻi.puʻi. vs. Plump, stout, stocky, heavy-set, sturdy, husky. *Puʻipuʻi ka ua Waʻahila o Mānoa* (song), stocky the Waʻahila rain of Mānoa. *He poʻe puʻipuʻi wale nō; ua koa nō lākou āpau* (Lunk. 3.29), they were strong, able-bodied people; all were soldiers. **hoʻo.puʻi.puʻi.** To grow or increase in weight.

pui.puia. Redup. of *puīa.*

pū.ʻiwa. nvs. Startled, surprised, astonished, aghast, frightened; surprise, amazement, fright. **hoʻo.pū.ʻiwa.** To startle, astonish, etc. *Me nā mea kani e hoʻopūʻiwa iā ʻoukou* (2 Oihn. 12.12), with the instruments to startle you.

pū.ʻiwa.ʻiwa. Redup. of *pūʻiwa;* to shy, as a horse; excitable, as a horse that is easily frightened.

puka. 1. n. Hole (perforation; cf. *lua,* pit); door, entrance, gate, slit, vent, opening, issue. Cf. *pukaihu, puka kui, lei pūpū.* *Ka puka kahiko,* the ancient hole [the anus]. **hoʻo.puka.** To perforate, puncture, make a hole or opening. (PCP *puta.*) 2. vi. To pass through, appear, emerge, come out, get out of, issue, come into sight; to rise, as the sun. *Kua puka,* a sore on the back, as a saddle sore on a horse's back. *Puka mau,* to appear frequently, as a newspaper. *Puka lā,* daily issue. *Puka mahina,* monthly issue. *Puka makahiki,* annual issue. *Puka wā,* to appear irregularly, as a paper. *Puka ka niho,* to teethe. *Puka kinikini, kinikini, ʻaʻohe ona puka e puka aku a* (riddle), many many holes, many many holes, no hole to go out through [answer: a fish net]. *Puka mai ka lā,* the sun rises. *Puka ka niho o ke keiki,* the child gets his teeth. **hoʻo.puka.** To issue, as a permit; to acquit, as a defendant in court; a chant to which dancers issue. *Hoʻopuka ʻana,* edition. *Hoʻopuka mua,* first edition. *Ua hoʻopuka ʻia paha mamuli o ka palapala hoʻopiʻi kūpono,* acquitted after a proper indictment. *Hoʻopuka i kai ka lā i Unulau,* let the sun rise at the sea at Unulau. (PCP *puta.*) 3. vi. To graduate. **hoʻo.puka.** To graduate. *E hoʻopuka ʻia ana ka papa i kēia makahiki,* the class will be graduated this year. 4. vi. To say, utter, speak. *Puka maila kāna ʻōlelo,* he spoke (*lit.,* his word came out). **hoʻo.puka.** To proclaim, speak, say, pronounce. *Hoʻopuka ʻana,* pronunciation. *Hoʻopuka manaʻo,* to suggest, comment. *Hoʻopuka hewa,* to speak out of turn, make a slip of the tongue. *Hoʻopuka ʻino, hoʻopuka pono ʻole,* to insult, slur, say evil or blasphemous things. *Hoʻopuka kū,* to speak rudely, uncivilly, bluntly. *He wahi manaʻo hoʻopuka,* a modest comment. *Kou naʻau e hoʻopuka aku i kekahi mea* (Kekah. 5.2), your heart to say something. 5. nvi. To gain, win, profit; to draw interest; winnings, gain, profit. *Puka o ke kālā,* interest. *Puka nui,* large profit or gain. *Puka a me ka pohō,* profit and loss. **hoʻo.puka.** To invest; to make a profit; profitable. Cf. *waiwai hoʻopuka.* 6. n. Trap, snare. Cf. *kīpuka.* 7. idiom. Almost. *Nā anana ʻeono ā puka hiku,* six and a fraction fathoms. *Kaʻu kaupaono, ua puka haneli,* my weight is almost one hundred.

pū kaʻa. n. Mounted cannon, artillery. *Lit.,* rolling gun. *Nā mahele koa pū kaʻa,* artillery divisions.

puka.ʻaki. To distribute evenly, as a fish catch. (And.)

pukaa.maka. vi. To seal an affinal relationship by the birth of a child. *Lit.,* appear to eye. (Gram. 8.7.2.) *Ua pukaamaka mākou me kēlā poʻe,* our relationship with those people is sealed by the birth of a child.

puka ʻana. n. Exit, Exodus (in the Bible). *Ka puka ʻana o ka lā,* sunrise.

puka.ani.ani, pukāni.ani. n. Window. *Lit.,* transparent opening.

puka hale. n. Door of a house; window (Isa. 60.8). *Kau i ka puka hale,* placed in the doorway (of a beggar).

pū.kahi. Same as *pūpūkahi;* sometimes said of the three Hawaiian gods, Kū, Kāne, and Lono.

puka.hipa. n. Sheep market. (Ioane 5.2.)

puka hoʻo.komo iho. n. Socket. *Lit.,* hole for entering core.

pukai. A kind of fish. (And.)
pū.kai. **1.** nvt. Lime bleach for hair; to bleach. *Oho pūkai,* hair dyed brown with lime. **2.** n. Salty tears. *Rare. E loku ai ka maka i ka pūkai* (chant), eyes that well with salt tears.
pū ka'i. n. Trumpet leading an army.
puka.ihu. n. Hole in pearl-shell shank.
puka ihu. n. Nostril. *Lit.,* nose aperture. *I ka ho'ohanu 'ana o kou mau puka ihu* (Puk. 15.8), with the blast of your nostrils.
pū.ka'i.ka'i. vt. To lift, as the feet in dancing; to swing on the foot, as a child. *Rare.*
pukaka, busada. n. Buzzard. *Eng.*
puka.kā. vi. To cackle, cluck.
pū.kā.kā. vi. To flee, as in fright; scattered. *Pūkākā nā lehua o Mānā,* the warrior flowers of Mānā are routed.
puka kahiko. n. Anus opening. *Lit.,* ancient hole.
puka.kala. Rare var. of *'ōkalakala.*
puka.kū. vi. To gush forth, ramble. *Rare.* **ho'o.puka.-kū.** To speak plainly, frankly, bluntly, crudely, without regard to feelings of others.
puka kui. n. Eye of a needle.
puka kui kele. n. Needle slot of a sewing machine.
puka kū.kae. n. Anus aperture (vulgar).
puka lā. vi. To appear daily; daily.
pū.kala.kī. vs. Rough, boisterous, as wind; ruffled, mussed, tousled, disheveled, uncombed, as hair. *Fig.,* bad temper; gruff.
pū.kala.lī. Same as *kalalī.*
-pu.kalia. ho'o.puka.lia. To bring forth. *Ē ke ao uli, ho'opukalia mai kīnohinohi* (Kep. 29), O blue heavens, bring forth beauty.
puka lou. n. Hook hole, noose, loop. *Puka lou lole uliuli ma ke kihi o kekahi pale* (Puk. 26.4), loops of blue cloth on the edge of one curtain.
puka makani. n. Opening for ventilation, window (1 Sam. 19.12); anus. *Lit.,* wind hole.
puka mā.lama.lama. n. Skylight.
pū.kā.mole. n. A low, shrubby plant (*Lythrum maritimum*) native to Peru, with slender branches and small narrow leaves. Sometimes the bark is stripped off and wound around leis for its mild fragrance and small pink flowers. It belongs to the crape myrtle family. (Neal 617.) Also *nīnika.* Some persons qualify the name by *lau li'i* and *lau nui.*
pukana. n. **1.** Outlet, exit, issue, exodus, descendant. **2.** Keepsake, memento, remembrance, souvenir.
pukana aloha. n. Souvenir of a beloved, gift from a loved one, keepsake.
pukana lā. n. Sunrise. *He hālāwai pukana lā,* a sunrise service.
pukana wai. n. Source of water, especially from the ground.
pukana.wila. n. Large woody vines (*Bougainvillea* spp.) from Brazil, bearing during their long flowering time masses of bright-colored bracts, which accompany small hidden flowers. Flower bracts are purple-red, rose-red, brick-red, and orange to whitish. (Neal 337–8.) *Eng.* Also *pua kepalō.*
pū.kani. **1.** n. Fine white leaves in the center of a cluster of pandanus leaves; fine soft sleeping mats made of these leaves. **2.** Rare var. of *wīkani.*
pū kani. n. Trumpet (1 Oihn. 13.8), any wind instrument. *Lit.,* sounding horn.
pukāni.ani. Var. spelling of *pukaaniani.*
pū.kani lua. vt. To oppose; strong; intensive of *pūkani 2.*
puka niho. n. Tooth cavity.
puka nui. **1.** n. A large opening or hole. **2.** Var. of *'āpua;* basket of *'ie'ie* vine aerial roots for carrying fishing gear.
puka pā. n. Gate. (Ier. 17.24.) *Lit.,* fence opening.
puka.pa'a. n. Osseous vagina. *Lit.,* closed opening.
puka pā hale. n. Gate of a city or house lot. *Lit.,* house enclosure hole.
puka.pai. vt. To rebuke mildly, as because of affection. *Pukapai a'ela kahi luahine makuahine: "Ē ku'u keiki,*

kanaka maika'i, 'a'ole noho'i e akahele ka le'ale'a 'ana.'' The motherly old woman mildly rebuked: "My child, handsome person, why not be prudent in your amusements.''
puka pā.kā.kā. See *pākākā 1.*
puka.pakī. n. A pore, as in the skin. *Lit.,* dripping hole.
puka pihi. n. Buttonhole.
puka po.niniu. n. Turnstile. *Lit.,* turning door.
puka.puka. **1.** Redup. of *puka 1;* many holes, filled with holes, chinks, cracks; pock-marked, as due to smallpox; porous, as stone; cells, as in honeycomb. See ex., *papa manamana.* ho'o.puka.puka. Caus/sim. (PCP *putaputa.*) **2.** Redup. of *puka 2–4.* ho'o.puka.puka. To keep talking, issuing, etc. (PCP *putaputa,* hole.) **3.** Redup. of *puka 5.* ho'o.puka.puka. Redup. of *ho'o.-puka;* to invest, speculate, search for profit. *Ho'o-pukapuka hewa,* to seek profit by fraudulent means; profiteer. *Ua lilo nā koa i pio no nā po'e ho'opukapuka hewa,* the soldiers became victims of profiteers.
pū.kaua. n. General, war leader, champion; second in command; fortress.
pū kaua. n. Artillery.
puka uahi. n. Smokestack, chimney.
puka uai. n. Sliding door or gate, movable door, turnstile.
pū.kaula. n. A bag or bundle carried on the back. *Rare.*
pū kaula. n. An old guessing game: a knot was tied in a cord and the two ends given to two persons to hold; the onlookers guessed and wagered whether the knot could be loosened by pulling on the ends of the string. This game was sometimes called in English slip trick. Many kinds are listed by Dickey.
pū kau po'o.hiwi. n. Gun carried on the shoulder.
puka wā. See *puka 2.*
puka wai. n. Water outlet; eye of a coconut.
puke, buke. n. Book, volume (in a series). Types of books are listed below. *Eng.*
pū.kē. nvt. To strike, hit, beat. (Dan. 5.6.) *I ka pūkē iki, i ka pūkē nui* (PH 195), by the small onslaught, by the great onslaught. *Pau akula kēlā lā'au i ka pūkē 'ia,* that tree is all beaten down.
pū.kea. **1.** Same as *'ainakea,* a sugar cane. **2.** See *laenihi,* a fish.
puke a'o. n. Text book, instruction book.
puke a'o kepela. n. Spelling book.
puke helu. n. Accounts book.
puke helu.helu. n. Reader, book or magazine to read.
puke ho'āhu. n. Savings bank book.
puke hō.'ike hana. n. Catalogue.
puke ho'o.komo pepa. n. Folder, paper holder.
puke ho'o.mana'o. n. Memorandum, memoirs, diary, journal.
puka inoa. n. Book listing names, directory of names.
puke kā.lā (dala) hale leka. n. Postal savings deposit book.
pū.kē kī.'aha. v. To touch glasses, as before drinking.
puke kuhi.kuhi. n. Manual, book of directions.
pū.kela.'ai. Same as *pūkele'ai.*
puke lawe lima. n. Handbook.
pū.kele. **1.** Var. of *'ūkele,* muddy. **2.** n. Bushel. *Eng.*
pū.kele.'ai. n. Small package of unmixed poi. (*Pa'i 'ai* is larger, and *holo 'ai* still larger.)
puke nā.nā mea kū.'ai. n. Catalogue.
puke pakeke. n. Pocketbook. *Eng.*
puke pala.'āina. n. Atlas.
puke wehe.wehe 'ō.lelo. n. Dictionary. *Lit.,* book to explain words.
puki. **1.** n. Boot. *Eng.* **2.** vs. "Broke," out of funds (probably from *Eng.* boot).
pū.kī. **1.** Same as *kōkō,* a carrying net. **2.** vt. To check, curb, pull back, as an unruly horse.
pū.kiawe. n. **1.** The black-eyed Susan (*Abrus precatorius*), a slender climbing legume, long known in the tropics, respected for its small round red and black seeds, which are used for leis, rosaries, and costume jewelry. Though the seeds are edible when cooked, when raw and broken they are poisonous. Flowers are

small, light-colored; leaves small, compound. (Neal 455–6.) Also *pūpūkiawe, pūkiawe lei,* to distinguish from *pūkiawe 2* and *pūkiawe 'ula'ula* on Ni'ihau. **2.** Native shrubs and small trees *(Styphelia [Cyathodes],* all species and varieties), 1 to 2 (rarely 4.5) m high, common near Kī-lau-ea Volcano, bearing narrow leaves 1.3 cm long, tiny whitish flowers, and many round red to white fruits .6 cm in diameter. The leaves were used medicinally for cold or headache. (Neal 663–4.) Also *'a'ali'i mahu, kānehoa, kāwa'u, maiele, pūpūkiawe.*

pū.kiawe lena.lena. n. *Abrus precatorius* f. *lutiseminalis. Ni'ihau.*

pū kihi lua. See *kihi.*

pū.kiki'i. A variety of flying fish.

pū.ki'i 1. vt. To tie. For variants see *nīki'i. Pūki'i wa'a,* clamps for binding down the canoe gunwale strake *(mo'o)* while it was being secured to the canoe. **2.** Same as *puhiki'i.*

Puki.kī. 1. nvs. Portuguese. *Eng. Pukikī 'ele'ele,* dark-skinned Portuguese. *Palaoa Pukikī,* Portuguese sweetbread. *Pi'ipi'i Pukikī,* kinky hair. **2.** n. A tight-waisted dress, supposedly worn once by Portuguese.

pū.kī.kī. vs. Strong, boisterous, stormy, as wind.

pū kī lū. n. Shotgun. *Lit.,* gun that shoots gunshots.

pū.kini. n. Pudding. *Eng.*

pū.kipa. n. Bookkeeper. *Eng.*

pū kī wai, pū kī.kī wai. n. Water gun, squirt gun. *Lit.,* gun shooting water.

pū.kō. Same as *pua'ō;* driven away. *Ho'okahi nō peku 'ana a ka moa mahi, pūkō ana* (FS 63), a single kick of the chicken champion, driven off.

pū kō. n. Clump of sugar cane. *Cf. pū kō ko'o. 'A'ohe pū kō momona* (For. 5:407), there is no clump of sugar cane that can sweeten him [said of a great warrior who has no worthy foe, of one in great anger, or of a dreadful situation].

pū.ko'a. 1. n. Coral head. *Pūko'a wāwahi wa'a,* a coral head that wrecks canoes. *Pūko'a kani 'āina,* a reef that makes the land ring [a great and invulnerable fighter]. **2.** vs. Spotted, as in several colors. *Cf. pua'a pūko'a.* **3.** vi. To rise, blow, as smoke. *Ua pūko'a a'ela ka uahi* (Hal. 18.8), the smoke rose. **4.** Same as *pu'uka'a,* a plant.

pū.ko'a.ko'a. 1. Redup. of *pūko'a 1, 2. Hina-ka-'ōnohipūko'ako'a* (name), Hina the many-colored rainbow bit. **2.** n. A somewhat calcified green seaweed *(Halimeda* sp.), erect but not stiff, about 10 cm high, branching and spreading in fan shape, with round to triangular, flattened joints. Used medicinally, pounded up with *laukahi (Plantago)* and applied as a poultice to boils. The name may be qualified by the terms *lau li'i* and *lau nui.*

pū.kohu.kohu. vs. Red, of tapa, as dyed with *noni* juice (Malo 49). (FS 252–3.)

pū.kō.ke'e. n. The lashing that holds the canoe spreader *(wae)* in place on a canoe. *Pūkōke'e, 'oia ke kaula e hīki'iki'i ai i ka wae,* the *pūkōke'e* ties down the canoe spreader.

pū.koko. vs. To appear red, as sunset glow or blood. *E pūkoko ana ka lā i ke kai* (chant), the sun shines red in the sea. (PCP *puutoto.)*

pū.kō.kō. vi. To cackle, coo; cackling, cooing. See more common *kokō.*

pū kō ko'o. n. Sugarcane clumps held up with sticks to prevent the long stems from falling down and taking root. *Also pū kō ko'o.*

pū.kolo. n. Team, as of oxen or mules pulling a plow.

Pū.kō.loa. n. Name of a star.

pū.kolu. 1. n. Trio, triplet. *Ua hānau pūkolu 'ia,* born as triplets. **2.** Triple canoe. (Laie 461, Malo 131.)

pū.kona.kona. vs. Strong, husky, muscular, virile, tough, mighty. *Cf. konakona.*

pū ko'o. Same as *pū kō ko'o.*

puku. 1. vi. To gather together, pucker; shrunken, contracted. *Cf. pukupuku, pupuku, hāpuku. Ua puku 'ia nā lau lā'ī,* the ti leaves have shriveled up. (PPN *putu.)* **2.** nvt. Final offering; to end. *Puku 'awa,* final kava

offering. Property given by a chief into the care of his servants. (And.)

pukua. Pas/imp. of *puku 1* and *puku 2;* to offer, as a fish.

pū kua.lau. n. Winter crookneck squash *(Cucurbita moschata).* (Neal 813.)

pū.ku'i. 1. vi. To collect, assemble, as people, things *(puku + -'i,* transitivizer: Gram. 6.6.4). **ho'o.pū.ku'i.** To collect, assemble. **2.** n. Council, assembly, as of chiefs or gods, especially of the major gods, Kāne, Kū, Lono, and Kanaloa *(pūku'i akua).* (PPN *pu(u)tuki.)* **3.** vi. To sit doubled up, as for protection from the cold; to nestle together, as in embrace; to hug, huddle. *Ho'i mai ke anu o ka ho'oilo, pūku'i aku au ma kō poli* (song), the cold of winter returns, I nestle close within your arms. **ho'o.pū.ku'i.** Caus/sim. **4.** n. Hub, as of a wheel. *Uhi pūku'i,* hub cap.

pū.ku'i.ku'i. Redup. of *pūku'i.* **3.** *Piha pūku'iku'i,* crowded, packed full.

puku kā.lina. n. Collected sweet-potato vines. Poetical, a stormy or whirling wind.

puku.ku'i. 1. Redup. of *pūku'i 1, 3. Pukuku'i lua i ke ko'eko'e* (song), embracing tightly in the cold. **2.** n. A fish (no data).

puku.lia. Pas/imp. of *puku 1. Na Māui i pukulia i nā moku,* the islands were pulled together by Māui.

puku.moa. vs. Saving, miserly. *Rare.* **ho'o.puku.moa.** Saving, miserly. *Rare.*

pū kuni ahi. n. Cannon. *Lit.,* gun burning fire. See ex., *nāku'i.*

puku.puku. Redup. of *puku 1;* wrinkles, crumples, frowning; to wrinkle, frown, purse, as the lips. *Pukupuku mai* (slang), to fetch, bring. *Pukupuku ku'emaka,* wrinkled brow. **ho'o.puku.puku.** Same as above and transitive. (PPN *putuputu.)*

pula. 1. nvi. Particle, as dust; particle in the eye, mote, speck; to have something in the eye. *Cf. pulakaumaka. E 'au mālie i ke kai papa'u, o pakī ka wai ā pula ka maka,* swim quietly in a shallow sea, lest it splash into the eye [be careful!]. (PCP *pula.)* **2.** n. Leafy branch, as of coconut, pandanus, or *'ilima,* used as a broom to drive fish into a net and to poke into reef crevices in order to frighten out the fish. **3.** nvt. Kindling; to start a fire with kindling. **4.** n. A fish, perhaps *Pempheris mangula.* **5.** Also *pura.* n. Pur (see M. S. Miller and J. L. Miller, *Harper's Bible Dictionary).* (Eset. 3.7.)

pū la.'ī. n. Ti-leaf whistle.

pula.kamaka. n. A variety of sweet potato. (HP 142.)

pula.kau.maka. n. A person one thinks of constantly, either because of affection or from a desire to injure or take revenge on; obsession, fixation. *Lit.,* mote resting eye [one is as conscious of the individual as of a mote in the eye]. *'O ka pulakaumaka ia, walania ke ki'i 'ōnohi,* that is the one constantly in mind like a particle in the eye, smarting the eyeballs. *Kēia kumuhana pili ho'ōla lāhui, ke kumuhana i lilo i pulakaumaka mamina nui 'ia i ka 'elele,* this topic concerned with the nation's welfare, a topic that became the desired ever-present goal to the delegate. **ho'o.pula.kau.maka.** To cherish.

pula lā.nahu. n. Cinder, as in a fire.

pū.lale. 1. v. To hurry, rush; to hasten, as to touch, possess. *Cf. lale 1. Mai pūlale mai 'oe,* don't hurry here. **ho'o.pū.lale.** To stir up to action, hurry. **2.** Same as *pula 2.*

pū.lale.lale. Redup. of *pūlale.*

pū.lama. 1. n. Torch. **2.** vt. To care for, cherish, treasure, save. *He waiwai nui ke aloha, 'o ka'u nō ia e pūlama nei,* love is of great value, it is what I do cherish.

pula maka wela.wela. n. Object of hatred. *Lit.,* hot mote in eye. *Cf. pulakaumaka.*

pū.lana. nvi. To float; a floating object.

pū.lapu. vt. To bluff, as in poker; to fool. *Eng. Pūlapu i ka wahine,* to fool the woman.

pula.pula. 1. n. Seedlings, sprouts, cuttings, as of sugar cane. **ho'o.pula.pula.** (a) To start seedlings or cuttings; to multiply, procreate. (b) To rehabilitate; rehabilitation. *Hoʻopulapula lāhui,* rehabilitation of the nation. *ʻĀina hoʻopulapula,* homesteading lands, especially for rehabilitation of Hawaiians. *Nā hana hoʻopulapula ma Iāpana,* rehabilitation acts in Japan. (PPN *pulapula.*) **2.** n. Descendant, offspring. *Huli mai, nānā i ka pulapula* (prayer to family ʻaumākua), turn, behold your offspring. **3.** nvi. Annoyance, an offense to the eyes; to offend (used with *maka*). Cf. *pulakaumaka. He mea ia e pulapula ai ka maka o ka ʻaoʻao kiʻekiʻe o nā aliʻi* (Kep. 133), this is a thing that offends the eyes of high-ranking chiefs.

pū.lau.hala. n. Many. Cf. *pūliʻuliʻu 2.*

pū.lau.oho. Same as *ʻōpūlauoho 1.*

pū.lawa. vs. **1.** Foggy, cloudy. *Rare.* **2.** Enough, ample, well-supplied. *Rare.* **3.** Firm, tightly bound, as a thatched house; strong. *Rare.*

pū.lawa.lawa. Redup. of *pūlawa 1-3.*

pule. **1.** nvt. Prayer, magic spell, incantation, blessing, grace, church service, church; to pray, worship, say grace, ask a blessing, cast a spell. (Probable derivatives are *pulepule, pupule,* and *ʻōpulepule.*) Many types of prayer are listed below. *Lāpule,* Sunday; *lit.,* prayer day. *Kahuna pule,* minister. *Pule a ka Haku,* the Lord's prayer. *Iāʻoe ka pule a kākou,* will you say grace; pray. *Ua hele anei ʻoe i ka pule?* Did you go to church? To cause to pray, to feign praying. (PPN *pule.*) **2.** n. Week. *Kēlā pule, kēia pule,* weekly. *Puka pule,* weekly issue. *Ma ka pule,* weekly. *Kēia pule aʻe,* next week. *Kēia pule aʻe a ia pule aku,* week after next. *Kēlā pule aku nei,* last week. **3.** Same as *ʻōpule 1.*

pule ʻaha. Same as *ʻaha 3.*

pule ʻanā.ʻanā. See *ʻanāʻanā.*

pule hai. n. Sacrificial prayer.

pule hā.mau. n. Silent prayer.

pule hana aloha. See *hana aloha.*

pū.lehe. vs. Loose, insecure. *Rare.*

pule heʻe. n. An octopus prayer: according to Emerson (Malo 111), such prayers were said to an octopus lying spread on the ocean floor *(heʻe mahola)* while it was being tempted with a cowry hook; the octopus once caught was offered to a deity for the curing of a patient; the prayer might also be said over the patient. Emerson gives such a prayer.

pule.heke. vi. To gather together, as canoes. *Rare.*

pū.leho. n. An elongated type of cowry *(Luria isabella);* worn in leis. *Rare.*

pū.leho hō.lei. n. A yellowish *pūleho* cowry. *Lit., hōlei* tree cowry, so named for the yellow dye extracted from the *hōlei* bark and root.

pū.leho kā.niʻo. n. A streaked *pūleho.*

pū.leho.leho. n. **1.** A small *pūleho.* Cf. *kuiki.* **2.** A callus, as from carrying burdens on the shoulders.

pule hoʻo.kuʻu. n. Closing prayer, as in Christian service or in *hana aloha* sorcery.

pule hoʻōla. n. Prayer to heal life.

pule hoʻo.laʻa. n. Dedicatory prayer.

pule hoʻo.mai.kaʻi. nvt. Prayer of thanks, benediction, grace; to say grace, to offer a prayer of thanks.

pule hoʻo.mau. n. Same as *pule hoʻouluulu ʻai;* to continue praying. (Malo 177.) *Lit.,* continuation prayer.

pule hoʻo.noa. n. Prayer to lift or free from taboo.

pule hoʻo.noho. n. Prayer calling on a god to possess an individual or a hula altar.

pule hoʻo.pō.mai.kaʻi. nvt. A blessing; to ask a blessing, grace.

pule hoʻo.ulu.ulu ʻai. n. Prayer to insure good crops. (Malo 177.) *Lit.,* prayer to make food grow.

pule hoʻo.una.una. n. Prayer sending gods or spirits of deified persons on errands of destruction. *Lit.,* sending prayer.

pule hoʻo.wili.moʻo. See *wilimoʻo.*

pū.leho palaoa. n. An ivory-colored *pūleho.*

pū.leho ʻula. n. A red *pūleho.*

pū.lehu. **1.** vt. To broil, as sweet potatoes, breadfruit or bananas placed on hot embers. Cf. *kōʻala,* to broil flesh. **2.** n. Waterspout. *Rare.* Cf. *waipuʻilani.* (PCP *puulefu.*)

pule.hua. vt. To gum *lehua* flowers for the purpose of catching birds.

pule hui. n. **1.** A prayer in unison. **2.** Short for *pule huikala.*

pule hui.kala. n. A purification prayer. (Malo 97.)

pule hula.hula. See *hulahula.*

pū.lehu.lehu. **1.** n. Dusk, twilight. Cf. *mōlehulehu.* (PCP *puule(fu)lefu.*) **2.** nvs. Many, numerous, miscellany. **hoʻo.pū.lehu.lehu.** To collect, bring many things together. *Rare.*

pulei.leho. nvs. A storm at sea; rough, as the sea. *Puleileho ka moana,* the sea is stormy.

pule ipu. n. Gourd prayer offered during ceremonies, accompanying removal of a boy from his mother to the men's eating house; the sacrificed pig's ear was placed in a gourd hanging about the neck of an image of Lono; the child was referred to in the prayer as a gourd.

pulei.pulu. vs. Rancid, musty. *Rare.*

pule kā.hea. n. Prayer calling on family gods.

pule kā.hiu. n. A prayer for victory in battle.

pule kā.hoaka. See *kāhoaka.*

pule kā.holo. n. A fast prayer spoken in a moderate or natural voice. (Kam. 64:140.)

pule.kakoli, puregatori. n. Purgatory. *Eng.*

pule kala. n. Prayer of protection from any evil, as of hula teachers before a program. Cf. also Malo 113. *Lit.,* removal prayer.

pule kame.haʻi. n. A black magic prayer, as to destroy a victim.

pule.kina, buletina. n. Bulletin. *Eng.*

pule kuili. See *kuili.*

pule kuni. n. Prayer uttered as a part of *kuni,* black magic.

pū.lele. n. Scrofulous neck sore.

pule.lehua. **1.** n. Butterfly, moth, the Ka-mehameha butterfly *(Vanessa tameamea).* (KL line 288.) See ex., *ʻāolo.* **hoʻo.pule.lehua.** To act the butterfly, to talk much but say little; frivolous. (PCP *puurere(f,s)ua.*) **2.** vi. Blown in the air, as spray. **hoʻo.pule.lehua.** To blow.

Pule.lehua Ka.waʻe.waʻe. n. Var. name for *Pulelehua Kea.*

Pule.lehua Kea. n. The Greater Magellanic Cloud. *Lit.,* white butterfly.

Pule.lehua Uli. n. The Lesser Magellanic Cloud. *Lit.,* dark butterfly.

pulelo. vi. To float, wave, rise, as a flag or fire (often used in sense of triumph after *ʻōʻili*). *ʻŌʻili pulelo ke ahi o Ka-maile* (chant), the fire of Ka-maile rises in triumph. *ʻŌʻili pulelo ʻo ka Puna-hou,* Puna-hou triumphs. *Ka mea nani kai Pali-uli ʻeā, ke pulelo aʻela i nā pali ʻeā* (chant), the beauty at Pali-uli, oh, rising fine on the cliffs, oh [of Pele's fires].

pule.lua. **1.** vi. To hurry. *Rare.* **2.** Same as *punalua. Rare.*

pule mahiki. n. Prayer to cast out spirits. See *mahiki.*

pule.mika. n. Pyramid. *Eng. Puʻu pulemika o ʻAikupika,* Egyptian pyramid.

pule ʻohana. nvi. Family prayer; to pray, of a family.

pule pale. n. Prayer to ward off evil influence. *Lit.,* protecting prayer.

pū.lepe. vt. To turn over, reverse. *Rare.*

pule.pule. **1.** Same as *pupule.* **2.** vs. Spotted, speckled with various colors, as a chicken. (PPN *pulepule.*)

pule ʻumi. n. A black magic prayer which was uttered without drawing breath. *Lit.,* throttled prayer.

pū.lewa. **1.** vs. To float back and forth; unstable, varying, changeable; swinging, as a ship at anchor. *He pūlewa ka ʻāina* (chant) the land is unstable (PCP *puulewa.*) **2.** vs. Weak, hungry, feeble. **3.** Same as *hālili,* sun-dial shell. **4.** n. A kind of stone from which sinkers were made for octopus hooks. (PEP *puurewa.*)

pū.lewa.lewa. Redup. of *pūlewa 1, 2.*

pule wī. n. A prayer for life of the chief and of the assemblage. (Kep. 25.) *Lit.,* famine prayer.

pū.lihi. vi. Light, as wind. *Rare.*

pū.lihi.lihi. Same as *pūhilihili*. (AP.)

puli.kana, pulitano. n. Puritan. *Eng.*

pū.liki. 1. vt. To embrace, hug; to gird on, as armor or a corset; to grip tightly. Cf. *liki 2. Pūliki 'ia i ka 'ēpoda olonā* (1 Sam. 22.18), did wear a linen ephod. *He he'e ka i'a, he pūliki ka lani,* an octopus, the marine creature [seen by the seer in the clouds], the heavens are clutched [a fierce battle]. **ho'o.pū.liki.** To gird on. **2.** n. Vest.

pū.liki kaua. n. Suit of armor, coat of mail, habergeon (2 Oihn, 26.14). *Lit.,* war vest.

pū.liki koa. n. Same as *pūliki kaua.* (Neh. 4.16.)

pū.liki.liki. Redup. of *pūliki.*

pū.liki wai.ū. n. Brassiere.

pū.liko. vs. Having many shoots, as a plant. **ho'o.pū.liko.** To bud, form shoots.

pū.liko.liko. Redup. of *pūliko.*

pū.lima. 1. n. Wrist, cuff. *Pihi pūlima,* cuff button. **2.** vt. To clasp the hands. *Pūlima a'e ia i kona mau lima,* he clasped his hands. **3.** n. Handwriting, signature. **4.** A fire to cure the sick. (And.)

pū.lima kā.kau. n. Handwriting, signature.

pū.limu. n. A ceremonial cleansing for the sick: taboo food articles were burned. (Malo 110.)

pū.lina. Var. of *pūkini. Eng.*

pū.li'u.li'u. 1. Same as *pū'ulī'ulī.* **2.** n. Innumerable, many. *Pūli'uli'u ā pūlauhala ua mea he 'Ilikini,* innumerable and many were these Indians.

pulo. 1. Short for *pūholo. 'Elua pōhaku wela e pulo ai,* steam with two hot stones. **2.** Also **buro.** n. Bureau, agency. *Eng.*

pū.lō. vi. To pass by, especially of one alone; lonely. *Rare.*

pū loa. n. Species of octopus that comes out at night, with longer head *(pū)* and tentacles than those of the common octopus; it is used for bait rather than for food.

Pulo (Buro) E'e Moku. n. Bureau of Emigration. *Lit.,* bureau for boarding ships.

pulo (buro) ho'o.kipa mali.hini. n. Visitor's bureau.

pulo (buro) ho'o.kō. n. Executive board. *Lit.,* accomplishing bureau.

Pulo (Buro) Ho'o.laha I'a. n. Bureau of Fisheries.

pū.loku. vs. **1.** Comely (Ier. 6.2), tender (Isa. 47.1), as of a virgin. (PCP *pulotu.*) **2.** Bright, sparkling, as sun or dew.

pū.lō.lia. Pas/imp. of *pūlō.*

pū.lo'u. 1. nvt. To cover the head; head covering. *Pūlo'u ihola ia i ke kapa,* he covers his head with tapa. *Pūlo'u ihola ia i kona maka* (2 Sam. 19.4), he covered his face. **ho'o.pū.lo'u.** To blindfold, veil. (PPN *puulou.*) **2.** n. Rainbow that arches but with ends that do not touch the earth. **3.** n. A black tapa made of *wauke,* same as *'ō'ūholowai* (but Kamakau says this was made of *māmaki* bark). (Malo 48.)

pū.lo'u.lo'u. 1. Redup. of *pūlo'u.* **2.** n. A tapa-covered ball on a stick *(pahu)* carried before a chief as insignia of taboo. **3.** n. A steam bath, as for certain illnesses. **ho'o.pū.lo'u.lo'u.** To take a steam bath.

pulu. 1. vs. Wet, moist, soaked, saturated. *Pulu au i ka huna kai,* I am soaked by spray. **ho'o.pulu.** To wet, soak, moisten, saturate. *Nā paipu ho'opulu pāka,* park sprinkler system. (PCP *pulu.*) **2.** n. A soft, glossy, yellow wool on the base of tree-fern leaf stalks (*Cibotium* spp.). It was used to stuff mattresses and pillows and at one time was exported to California. Hawaiians stuffed bodies of their dead with *pulu* after removing vital organs. **3.** nvt. Any greenery or underbrush cut to be used as mulch, as well as the mulch itself; coconut husk, coconut fiber, raw cotton, tapa pulp; cushion; fine linen; tinder, kindling; soft, padded; to kindle, as fire (preceded by *ke*). See ex., *'ē 1. Kapa pulu,* quilt. *Pau napu i ka kanu* (saying), mulch is gone, no [taro] leaves to plant [all is destroyed]. **ho'o.pulu.** To mulch, fertilize with compost. (PPN *pulu.*) **4.** n. Low branch, as of certain trees such as *'ohai, koa, 'ōhi'a.* **5.**

Also **bulu.** n. Bull. *Eng. Keoni Pulu,* John Bull. *Ua holo 'o Hanalē, komo mai 'o Keoni Pulu,* Henry has run off, John Bull has come in [said when one is full: hungry (which sounds like "Henry") has gone, and John Bull (which sounds like "full") has come]. **6.** nvt, nvs. To fool; fooled; fool. *Eng.* Cf. *kamipulu.* **ho'o.pulu.** To act the fool.

pū.lua. n. Two persons together, as for mutual help. *Ku'u hoa pūlua 'alo 'īnea,* my companion who endures hardships with me.

pulu.'aha. n. A snare used to catch shrimps and small fish, made of sennit and coconut midrib. *Lit.,* sennit husk. *Pepeiao pulu'aha,* a snare ear [an ear used for carrying a snare rather than for hearing and obeying, a term of contempt].

pulu.ea. nvs. Odor of perspiration combined with dirt, body odor; to have such. **ho'o.pulu.ea.** To cause body odor; to sweat offensively. *He ma'i ho'opuluea po'o,* a disease to make the head sweat [of trouble].

pulu 'elo. vs. Drenched, soaked.

puluhi. vi. Drenched. (Perhaps *pulu 1* + *-hi,* transitivizer.)

puluka. n. Flute. *Eng. Rare.*

pulu.kā. vs. Soaked, drenched.

pulu.kene. Same as *pulukā.*

pulu kui. n. Pin cushion.

pū.lū.lū. Same as *pūhalalū 1.*

pulu.luhi. vs. Hazy, foggy, cloudy. *Fig.,* befogged, as with sleep.

puluma. n. Plum. *Eng.*

pulumi. n. Flume, as for cane; gutter, as on a house. *Eng.*

pū.lumi. 1. Also **burumi.** nvt. Broom; to sweep; to sweep away, as foe (For. 5:721). *Eng.* **2.** Also **bulumi.** n. Boom, as of a ship. *Eng.*

pū.lumi ehu lepo. n. Whisk broom, dust broom.

pū.lumi hale. nvt. To sweep a house; janitor.

pū.lumi nī.'au. Same as *pūpū nī'au.*

puluna. 1. n. One's child's parents-in-law or aunts and uncles by marriage; *kāne,* male, and *wahine,* female, may follow. *Kona puluna kāne,* his child's father-in-law (in Hawaiian sense of father, which includes uncle, foster father). *Kona puluna wahine,* his child's mother-in-law (in Hawaiian sense of mother, which includes aunt, foster mother). *Inoa puluna,* one's child's aunts and uncles by marriage. (The term *puluna* is used by the child's parents.) **2.** n. Prune. *Eng.*

pū.luna.luna. vs. Scattered, blown helter-skelter.

pulu niu. n. Coconut husk or fiber.

pulu pē. vs. Thoroughly drenched, soaked, saturated. *Fig.,* drunk. *Pulu pē nei 'ili i ke anu, ā he anu mea 'ole i ka mana'o* (song), drenched this skin in the cold, cold that is nothing to the thought.

pulu.pulu. 1. Redup. of *pulu 1, 2;* tinder, to form kindling or ignitable material, as while rubbing sticks for fire. (FS 229.) *Pipī ka wahie, ho'onui i ka pulupulu,* if wood burns slowly, add more tinder. **ho'o.pulu.pulu.** Redup. of *ho'opulu;* to make compost. *Ho'opulupulu pa'ū,* to rot by wetness. (PCP *pulupulu.*) **2.** n. Cotton, as for quilt padding; fine linen (2 Oihn. 2.14). (PPN *pulupulu.*) **3.** Same as *pulupulu haole.* **4.** n. Coition. *Rare.* **5.** To keep warm, as a bird on its nest. (And.)

-pulupulu. ho'o.pulu.pulu. To protest, deceive; hypocrite. (And.)

pulu.pulu ahi. nvi. Fire kindling; to kindle fire. *Fig.,* hot-tempered.

pulu.pulu haole. n. The cotton plant *(Gossypium barbadense),* a shrub in the mallow family, from tropical America. The leathery seed cases contain black seeds, which yield a valuable oil, and masses of white cotton fiber, used for cloth. (Neal 565.) Also *pulupulu.*

pulu.pulu kanaka. n. Common people. *Lit.,* human mulch.

pulu.wai. n. Land patch. *Rare.*

puma. n. Small opening or door, as in a chief's sleeping house. *Rare.*

puma.hana. Var. of *pumehana.* (Ioba 31.20.) **ho'o.-puma.hana.** Var. of *ho'opumehana. Ā ho'opumahana iā lākou iho* (Ioane 18.18), warming themselves.

pū mai'a. n. Banana stalk. *Nui pū mai'a,* large as a banana stalk [a weakling]. *He wa'a pū mai'a,* a canoe with straight, rounded hull. *'I'o pū mai'a,* straight grain [as in wood].

pū makani. **1.** Same as *pūhi'u. Lit.,* wind horn. **2.** n. Air gun.

pū mana.mana. n. Stalk with many branches, said of a person with many descendants.

pume.hana. nvs. Warm, warm-hearted; warmth, affection. *Me ke aloha pumehana,* with warm *aloha.* **ho'o.-pume.hana.** To warm, heat.

pumi, bumi. n. Boom or spar, as of a ship. *Eng.*

pū mī.kini. n. Machine gun.

puna. **1.** n. Spring (of water). Cf. *pūnāwai. Puna-hou* (place), new spring. *Wai puna,* spring water. (PPN *puna.*) **2.** n. Coral, lime, plaster, mortar, whitewash, calcium; coral container, as for dye, coral rubber. *E lawe 'oia i ka puna hou e hamo i ka hale* (Oihk. 14.42), and he shall take new plaster and plaster the house. (PPN *punga.*) **3.** n. Section between joints or nodes, as of bamboo or sugar cane. **4.** n. Cuttlebone, as of octopus. **5.** Short for *kupuna* as a term of address. **6.** Short for *punalua.* **ho'o.puna.** Same as *ho'opunalua.* **7.** vi. To paddle with the hands, as to start a surfboard on its way to catch a wave. *Rare.* **8.** n. Spoon (preceded by *ke*). *Eng. Ke iho ihola ke puna,* the spoon is let down [the lower lip, of a pouter].

-puna-. See *kapuna, mo'opuna, punahele, punalua.*

puna hamo. n. Mortar. *Lit.,* plastering coral.

puna.hele. nvs. A favorite or pet; to treat as a favorite (children were often treated as favorites; they might be carried on the grandparent's shoulders, and songs were composed for them); favoritism. (This word may have the *loa'a*-type of construction; see Gram. 4.4.) *No kēia punahele o 'Au-kele i kō lākou makuakāne,* because their father made a favorite of 'Au-kele. **ho'o.puna.-hele.** To treat as a favorite, make a favorite, indulge. *Hō'ike ka makua i kona ho'opunahele i kāna wahine* (Kep. 165), the parent showed how he treated his wife as a great favorite. (PCP *(f,s)ele.*)

puna.helu. vs. Moldy, mildewed. *Ua 'I'ī, ua punahelu o loko* (chant), sour, moldy within. **ho'o.puna.helu.** To grow moldy, musty; to cause mildew.

puna kameki. n. See *kameki.*

puna.kea. n. A barely visible rainbow. (GP 8.)

puna kea. n. White coral, as cast ashore by the sea. (GP 16.)

puna kī. n. Teaspoon.

puna kī.'o'e. n. Ladle. *Lit.,* dipping spoon.

puna.lua. n. Formerly, spouses sharing a spouse, as two husbands of a wife, or two wives of a husband; also, wives of brothers, husbands of sisters (no sexual privileges); sister-in-law (Ruta 1.15). *Kona punalua,* his punalua. *Lili punalua,* bitter jealousy of a rival. *'Ōpū punalua,* evil disposition; hating, malevolent, hateful. **ho'o.puna.lua.** To attain or have the *punalua* relationship, to pretend to be a *punalua.* (PCP *punalua.*)

pū.nana. **1.** nvs. Nest, gathering place, shelter, hive; to nest. *Fig.,* home. *Pūnana ka manu i Haili,* the bird nests at Haili. *E make auane'i au i loko o ku'u pūnana* (Ioba 29.18); I shall die within my nest. *He aikāne, he pūnana na ke onaona,* a friend is a nest of fragrance. **ho'o.pū.nana.** To make a nest, to settle in a nest or over young; to sit on eggs, as a hen; to take shelter. *Ho'opūnana ka mana'o,* to set the mind on, plan, focus attention on. **2.** n. A variety of sweet potato. **3.** n. A process of making women's *pā'ū;* white tapa.

puna.nā. Same as *nanā,* surly.

pū.nana ke'o.ke'o. n. White tapa used for making *pā'ū.*

pū.nana.manu. n. A fern *(Asplenium caudatum),* 60 cm high or more, known from Polynesia west into Africa. It resembles the *kupukupu,* but the narrow-oblong divi-

sions of the frond taper to sharp points, and the spores are borne in oblique lines, not in dots. *Lit.,* bird nest.

pū.nana meli. n. Beehive.

pū.nanana. n. **1.** Same as *nananana,* a species of spider. **2.** Spider's web.

puna nui. n. Large spoon, serving spoon (preceded by *ke*).

puna pō.haku palu.palu. n. Gypsum.

puna.puna. **1.** vs. Mealy, firm, not soft or soggy, as taro or sweet potato. **2.** Redup. of *puna 3;* jointed. *He punapuna noho'i e like me ke kō* (For. 5:607), jointed too, like sugar cane [of kava]. (KL line 60.) **3.** vs. Scattered, wind-blown, pulverized. *Rare.*

pū.naue. Short for *pu'unaue.*

pū.nā.wai. n. Water spring. *He pūnāwai e inu 'ia* (FS 229), a spring with potable water. (PPN *pu(u)naawai.*)

Pū.nā.wai-ea. n. Rain name. *Lit.,* spray [of] rain.

pū.nā.wele. vs. Fine, as a spider's web; thin.

pū.nā.wele.wele, punawelewele. n. Cobweb, spider web; spinning spider. *Kāhihi ka puka o ka hale i ka pūnāwelewele,* the door of the house is tangled with cobwebs [the house is vacant]. (PPN *kalewelewe,* PCP *puungaawelewele.*)

pū.ne'e. **1.** n. Movable couch; pew *(rare),* table (Mar. 7.4). Cf. the immovable *hikie'e.* **2.** vi. To crawl or move humbly, as formerly towards a high chief; to move along, as fine rain.

pū.ne'e.ne'e. Redup. of *pūne'e 2.*

pū.neki. vi. To cluster, as leaves. *Rare.*

punelu. Same as *nenelu. Rare.*

pū.nē.nē. Same as *'ai-a-ka-nēnē,* a plant.

puni. **1.** vs. Surrounded, controlled; overcome, as in battle or by emotion; to pervade, gain control of; to enclose (*loa'a*-type construction; Gram. 4.4). *Puni i ka maka'u,* overcome with fear. *Ulu puni i ka huhū,* to grow extremely angry. *Ka wā e puni ai 'o Hawai'i iā 'Umi* (FS 125), the time that 'Umi would control all Hawai'i. **ho'o.puni.** To surround, enclose, get control of, besiege. *Ho'opuni akule,* to drive *akule* fish into nets by surrounding them. *Ua ho'opuni 'ia 'o Ka-welo i ka weliweli* (FS 93), Ka-welo was filled with terror. (PPN *puni.*) **2.** nvt. To be fond of, desire, covet, like, be partial to; devoted; a favorite thing, delight, love. Cf. *puni 'ai, puni kālā, puni kaua, puni koko, puni le'ale'a, puni nani, puni waiwai.* **ho'o.puni.** To be charmed by, desire greatly. **3.** vs. Deceived, deluded; to believe a lie. Cf. *puni wale. Mai noho 'oe ā puni . . . ,* don't you believe . . . **ho'o.puni.** To deceive, fool, delude. **4.** nvs. Completed, terminated, as a period of pregnancy; completely, all. *Ua hāpai, kokoke nō i puni* (1 Sam. 4.19), to be with child, nearing completion. *Ua pōholehole ka 'ili a puni* (FS 109), the skin was completely covered with bruises. *Ka puni 'ana o ka haneli makahiki,* centennial. **5.** n. A fine-meshed net. Also *nae, naepuni.* **6.** nv. An even number; to be such. See *'oi 3.*

punia. **1.** Pas/imp. of *puni 1-4. Ke 'ala o ka laua'e, punia ai ka nahele* (chant), the fragrance of *laua'e* fern permeates the forest. *Aloha wale ku'u kaikunāne ē, ua punia au* (dirge), alas for my brother, I am overcome with grief. **2.** n. Head cold. **3.** n. A kind of coconut, the husk of which is chewed for its sweet juice.

puni 'ai. nvt. Fond of eating; glutton.

puni.hai. vs. Fearful, afraid; to run off in fear.

pū.niha.niha. Same as *ho'okamaniha.*

puni.hei. vs. Ensnared, entangled, caught, as in a trap; gullible, easily tricked; captivating, fascinating, entrancing. *Mo'olelo punihei,* fascinating tale. *Punihei aku nei au i ka nani o ia pua* (song), I was captivated by the beauty of that flower. **ho'o.puni.hei.** To fascinate, charm, captivate, ensnare, decoy, trap.

puni hele. vs. Fond of going about from place to place, addicted to travel.

pū.nihi. vs. Lofty, majestic, dignified. *Rare.*

pū.niho. vi. To bristle, as sea urchins. *Rare.*

puni ho'o.pa'a ha'a.wina. vi. Studious, fond of study.

pū.nika, pū.nika.nika. vs. Black-skinned, Negroid. Cf. *nika,* nigger.
puni kā.lā. vs. Avaricious, mercenary, commercial-minded. *E noho ʻoukou me ka puni kālā ʻole* (Heb. 13.5), keep your life free from love of money.
puni kaua. v. Militaristic, warlike, fond of war.
puni.kihi. n. A game. *Rare. Lit.,* surround corner.
puni koko. v. Bloodthirsty.
puni kuala. nvs. Usurious; usurer; extortion.
puni leʻa.leʻa. v. Pleasure-loving, fond of fun.
puni nani. v. Fond of beauty, beauty-loving, fond of adorning self.
pū.nini. vi. To tack, as a ship; to float here and there, drift. **hoʻo.pū.nini.** Caus/sim. *Ke hoʻopūnini maila ka iʻa,* the fish are drifting here.
-pūnini. hoʻo.pū.nini. To demonstrate pleasure at seeing one, as a child or dog; to cling to as with delight, frisk about happily; to perform ritual with the object of pleasing the gods *(rare).*
puni.peki. n. A game similar to fox and geese (the name is said to come from *Eng. Bonaparte*).
puni.puni. Redup. of *puni 3;* lie, to tell a lie, cheat; liar. **hoʻo.puni.puni.** To lie, liar; to deceive, deceitful, false. *Kālā hoʻopunipuni,* counterfeit money.
pū.niu. 1. n. Polished coconut shell or bowl. *ʻUmeke pūniu,* coconut-shell calabash, as for poi. 2. n. Small knee drum made of a coconut shell with fishskin cover, as of *kala.* 3. n. Human skull. *I holo mua nō i ka pūniu,* to go ahead indeed because of one's skull [intelligence]. See also *nīnau.* 4. n. Small fontanel of an infant. 5. vi. To spin, as a top; dizzy.
pū.niu hui. n. Place at the top of the skull where the bones unite, skull joint, bregma. *Lit.,* joining skull.
puni wai.wai. v. Avaricious, covetous, desirous of wealth.
puni wale. vt. Gullible, easily deceived, swayed, influenced. See also other meanings of *puni.* **hoʻo.puni wale.** To fool, deceive easily.
pū.nohu. 1. nvi. To rise, as smoke, mist; to billow out, as a ship's sail; to spread out, as a shrub with low branches or as a cloud, to whiffle; such rising. *Pūnohu ʻula, i ke kai* (song), red rising mist on the sea. (The connotation of redness is sometimes present even without *ʻula.* Cf. *ua pūnohu.*) *Nā ao ʻeleʻele, maluna aʻe o nā ao polohiwa i mau ao uli, a me nā pūnohu huna one, i mau ao uli* (Kep. 175), black clouds above the solid black clouds to dark clouds, and small sandlike rising clouds to rain clouds. Cf. also Lunk. 20.40. 2. n. Rainbow lying close to the earth. (UL 99.) 3. n.Slate pencil sea urchin. Also *hāʻueʻue.*
pū.nohu ʻā.lewa.lewa. n. Smoke, clouds rising and spreading.
pū.nohu.nohu. Redup. of *pūnohu 1.*
pū.nolu.nolu. vs. Affable, good-natured.
pū.noni. nvs. Red dye from *noni*-root bark; red, as tapa dyed thus. *Lehua pūnoni ʻula ke kai o Kona, ke kai pūnoni ʻula i ʻōweo ʻia* (chant), *lehua* flower that colors red the sea of Kona, the sea dyed red with scarlet. **hoʻo.pū.noni.** To dye red with this dye.
pū.nono. vs. Gorgeously red, filled with sunshine, everbeautiful; flushed red, as the skin; glowing. *Mau loa nō koʻu mahalo nui i ka nani pūnono o Kahana* (song), my great admiration for the gorgeous beauty of Kahana remains always. **hoʻo.pū.nono.** To make attractive with bright or red colors, to dress or appear gorgeous.
pū.nonohu. Redup. of *pūnohu 1.* *Ulu pūnonohu,* to grow round and full at the base, rather than tall and spindly. *Ka ua pūnonohu ʻula i ka nahele* (UL 110), the rising red rain in the forest. **hoʻo.pū.nonohu.** Caus/sim.
puno.nono. Redup. of *pūnono.*
pū.nonu, pū.nonu.nonu. vs. Spoiled, rotten, as eggs.
pū.nua. n. Young bird, fledgling. *Fig.,* young child or sweetheart. *Ka pūnua peʻe poli,* fledgling hiding in the bosom [a young sweetheart]. (PPN *punua.*)
pū.nuhu. Rare var. of *pūnohu 1.*
pū.nuku. nvt. Muzzle, halter; to muzzle; muzzled. *Ke*

hemo ka pūnuku, when free of the halter [when at liberty].
puō, puwō. nvi. To roar, wail, howl; muffled sound, as of clapping.
puʻō. Same as *puaʻō;* to blaze up, as fire; to bend, as coconut fronds in a wind; to lift up; to bloom. *Puʻō ke ahi,* the fire blazes up. **hoʻo.puʻō.** Caus/sim.
puoʻa. n. Thicket. *Rare.*
puʻoa. Pas/imp. of *puʻō. Mehe kapa kea lā ka ʻale o ka moana, ka puʻoa a ke kai i nā moku manu* (chant), like white tapa are the billows of the ocean, as the sea lashes against the bird islands.
pū.ʻoʻa. n. Tower, steeple, pyramid, peak; house for depositing a corpse; peaked hut, lean-to, tent. *Pūʻoʻa o ka nalu,* crest of the wave. *Pūʻoʻa pele,* belfry. *Nā pūʻoʻa kiʻekiʻe o nā hale pule,* the tall steeples of the churches.
pū ʻohai. n. *ʻOhai* tree or shrub. See *ʻohai 1.*
pū.ʻohe.ʻohe. n. Job's-tears *(Coix lachryma-jobi),* a coarse, branched grass closely related to corn, growing in many tropical regions, either wild or cultivated. It is an annual, .3 to 1.8 m high, with long, pointed leaves, and, at stem tips, hard, round, beadlike seeds—black, gray, or white—which are used for leis, mats, food, medicine. (Neal 80–1.) Also *kūkaekōlea, ʻoheʻohe, pūpū kōlea.*
puoho. nvi. Startled; to cry out in alarm; fright, shock; to explode, as a lava flow; to wake suddenly; sudden appearance, as a burst of fragrance. *Puoho ʻo Lono ma ka hoʻāla o kona akua,* Lono was startled and awakened by his god. **hoʻo.puoho.** Caus/sim. (PCP *puoho.*)
puoko. vi. To rage, burn hot.
puoko.oko. Redup. of *puoko.*
puo.lani. v. To place high, or in a lofty or sacred place. *Rare.*
pū ʻolē.ʻolē. n. Conch horn.
pū.ʻolo. nvt. Bundle, bag, container, parcel, packet; bale, as of hay; to tie up in a bundle. Cf. *kiʻoʻōpae, mālama pūʻolo. Kaʻu wahi pūʻolo,* my small bundle; *fig.,* message, topic. *Hoʻi pūʻolo,* to return home with a bundle, especially a gift (cf. *hoʻina*). *ʻO ka iliau loha i ka lā, pūʻolo hau kakahiaka* (For. 4:283), the *iliau* plant drooping by day, the carrier of morning dew.
puolo.olo.heʻe. A kind of grass. (And.)
puoni. To save, preserve. (And.)
pū.ʻō.niʻo.niʻo. n. A shell *(Partridge tun).*
puʻō.pu.ʻō. Redup. of *puʻō;* to blaze up and die down; to bob up and down, as a canoe in the waves. **hoʻo.puʻō.-pu.ʻō.** Redup. of *hoʻopuʻō.*
pū paʻa.kai. See *pū 9,* to eat a little. **hoʻo.pū paʻa.kai.** To gather salt; salt gatherer. *Kaʻū.*
pū pā.ʻani. n. Toy gun, popgun.
pū.palō, bufalo. n. Roebuck (RSV), fallow deer (KJV). (1 Nal. 4:23.) *Eng.* Cf. *pāpulō.*
pū.pana.pana. n. Pistol. *Lit.,* snapping gun, revolver.
pupo, bubo. n. A kind of small owl. (Kanl. 14.16.) (Latin *bubo*).
pū pō.kole. n. Blunderbuss. *Lit.,* short gun.
pupo.nika, bubonika. vs. Bubonic. *Eng.* See ex., *hoene.*
pū poʻo.hiwi. n. Musket. *Lit.,* shoulder gun.
pupu. Probably similar to *pupupu 3. Kuʻu wahi pupu* (Nak. 96), my small shelter. *ʻO kahi pupu mamua o kuʻu wahi waʻa lā, ʻo Pākaʻa nō ia* (Nak. 119), the one in my shelter for my small canoe is Pākaʻa.
pupū. vi. 1. To stall; to move slowly and with difficulty, as a canoe or invalid; to remain near; stuck, blocked. *Pupū ke kaʻa,* the car is stalled. *Aʻo pupū,* to learn slowly. *Kō lākou mau kaʻa kaua, i hele pupū ai lākou* (Puk. 14.25), their war chariots, so that they drove heavily. *Pupū ke kai i ka ʻalalauā,* blocked is the sea by the fish *ʻalalauā* [of any difficulty; an omen of the death of royalty]. **hoʻo.pupū, hō.pupū.** To stall; cause to get stuck *(transitive);* to balk, resist, hold back; bumpy, rough, as a road. Also *haʻapupū.* 2. Same as *kolopupū. Kuʻu wahi pupū ʻelemakule* (For.

5:121), my poor feeble old man. *Kahi pupū* (For. 5:133), an old man.

pū.pū. 1. n. General name for marine and land shells; beads, snail (Biblical). *Lei pūpū o Ni'ihau*, shell beads of Ni'ihau. See *lei pūpū. Mehe pūpū lā e hehe'e ana* (Hal. 58.8), like the snail that dissolves [into slime]. (PCP *puupuu*.) **2.** n. Any circular motif, as in tapa. *Kōnane pūpū*, checkerboard pattern [with rounded pits on each square, as on tapa]. **3.** nvt. Relish, appetizer, canapé, hors d'oeuvre; formerly, the fish, chicken, or banana served with kava; to eat a *pūpū*. Cf. *pū 9. Ā pūpū i ka 'anae* (For. 5:491), and mullet as appetizer. (PPN *puupuu*.) **4.** nvi. Bunch, tuft, bundle, as of grass; bouquet; to be bundled up; three or four *'uo* tied together, to be used for featherwork. Cf. *pūpū weuweu. Pūpū pili*, bundle of *pili* grass. *Pūpū husopa* (Puk. 12.22), bunch of hyssop. **ho'o.pū.pū.** To arrange in bunches. (PPN *puupuu*.) **5.** nvt. To draw or gather together; to draw tight, as a fishing net. Cf. *pūpū lauoho, pūpū weuweu. Pūpū wahi kū'ō'ō ka mahi 'ai o uka; ola nō ia kini he mahi 'ai na ka 'ōiwi*, the upland farmer gathers the small injured sweet potatoes; the multitudes find life, when the farmer farms for himself [though the potatoes may be small, the independent farmer supplies his kin]. **6.** See *'upena papa*.

pupua. 1. Var. of *puapua 1. 'Eu'eu kōlea i ka pupua* (FS 81), the plover stirs with his tail feathers. **2.** n. Tuft of dried ti leaves on end of an octopus lure. **3.** Redup. of *pua 1, 2;* to blossom, as a tree covered with blossoms.

pupu.ā.hilo. Redup. of *puāhilo.*

pupu.ā.hulu. vs. To hurry, hasten; in a hurry; to make a careless mistake.

pū.pū 'ai. v. To eat *pūpū;* to eat a little. *E pūpū 'ai kākou*, let's eat a little.

pū.pū 'alā. n. Cone shell (*Conus* sp.). *Lit.,* volcanic rock shell.

pū.pū ala.pa'i. n. A marine shell, *Epitonium* sp.

pupua.moa. n. Dress suit, tails.

pū.pū au, pū.pū 'awa. n. A marine shell, *Drupa ricinas, Purpura aperta. Lit.,* bitter shell. Cf. *makaloa.*

pupue. 1. vi. To crouch, as a cat about to pounce; to draw up the legs, as for warmth. **2.** *(Cap.)* n. Name of a star in the constellation Kaulua.

pupu'e. Redup. of *pu'e;* to attack, force (either often or by many persons).

Pupū-hale. n. Rain famous at Hāmākua, Hawai'i. *Lit.,* [rain] remaining [near] house.

pupuhi. Redup. of *puhi 1–3;* to spit. *Fig.,* to abolish, as taboo (Kep. 143); to be blown away, flee. *Pupuhi kukui i ka lani, mālamalama ka honua* (chant for Kamehameha V), blow out the lights in the heavens, the earth is lighted. *Pupuhi ka i'a o 'Uko'a*, the fish of 'Uko'a have vanished [of one who flees; 'Uko'a is at Wai-a-lua, O'ahu]. *Pupuhi ka 'ulu o Ke'ei*, the breadfruit of Ke'ei have disappeared [a reference to a legendary stealing of breadfruit at Ke'ei, Kona, Hawai'i; this may be said of any strange disappearance]. *Pupuhi kukui o Pāpala-ua*, light the candle of Pāpala-ua [of Pāpala-ua, Moloka'i, where there was little sun]. *Lālau akula 'o Ka-welo i ke kukui, mama ihola ā pupuhi i ke kai i malino* (FS 39), Ka-welo took the candlenut, chewed, and spit [it] into the sea to calm [it]. (PPN *pupusi*.)

pū puhi. n. Trumpet, horn, conch shell trumpet.

pū.pū hoaka. Shell bracelet. (And.)

pū.puhu. Plump. (And.)

pupu'i. Same as *pu'ipu'i.*

pupuka. vs. Ugly, unsightly, unseemly, unattractive, homely, wicked (frequently *pūpuka* for emphasis; if said with a friendly or admiring intonation among friends, it meant the opposite, i.e., beautiful, attractive; this was due to reluctance to express admiration for fear a sorcerer would in jealousy bewitch the admired person; it is also said in answer to the question *pehea 'oe*, how are you, with meaning that one is improving but hesitates to say he is well for fear of bad luck). *Pupuka pepe'ekue*, grotesque. *Pupuka 'ino, pupuka ha'alele*

loa, extremely ugly, hideous. *'O ka mea e hā'ili'ili aku i kona hoahānau, e, pupuka! e lilo ia i mea no ka 'aha ho'okolokolo* (Mat. 5.22), the one who reviles his cousin, you fool! shall be liable to judgment. *He kanaka u'i, akā he pupuka nā hana*, a handsome person, but wicked in deeds. **ho'o.pupuka.** To make ugly, disfigure, deform. (PCP *puputa*.)

pū.pū.kahi. vi. United, as in harmonious co-operation. *I mua, i mua, e nā hoa, a e pūpūkahi i loa'a ai ka holomua a me ka pōmaika'i*, forward, forward, companions, unite to obtain progress and good fortune.

pū.pū.kamoe. Perhaps a Kaua'i var. of *pūpū kani oe.* (Kel. 61.)

pū.pū kani oe. n. A land shell *(Partulina physa). Lit.,* shell that sounds long, so called because of the belief that land shells sing.

pū.pū kea. n. A stone used as an octopus lure.

pū.pū.kiawe. Same as *pūkiawe 1, 2*, plants.

pū.pū koa'e. n. A rare land shell *(Succinea olaaensis). Lit.,* tropic-bird shell.

pū.pū kō.lea. 1. Same as *pū'ohe'ohe*, Job's-tears. **2.** Same as *kōlea*, periwinkle.

pū.pū kō.lea uka. n. A land shell *(Partulina confusa). Lit.,* inland-plover shell.

pupuku. Same as *pukupuku. Pupuku ka lae*, to frown. **ho'o.pupuku.** Same as *ho'opukupuku.* (PNP *puputu*.)

pū.pū kua.hiwi. n. Land shell.

pū.pū kua mauna. n. A land shell *(Lamellaxis oparanum).* Also *pololei. Lit.,* mountain ridge shell.

pū.pū kui. n. A marine shell *(Natica gualteriana). Lit.,* pin shell.

pū.pū kupa. n. A marine shell *(Trachycardium orbita, Periglypta reticulata). Lit.,* native shell.

pū.pū lau.oho. n. Topknot.

pupule. vs. Crazy, insane, reckless, wild (sometimes *pūpule* for emphasis; probably derived from *pule*, prayer: see *haihaiā, 'ōpulepule*). Cf. *hilo pupule. Pupule ka moa, 'a'ohe puka mimi*, the chicken is crazy, it has no urine vent [the vulgar latter part of this saying is sometimes omitted]. **ho'o.pupule.** To make insane; to drive crazy; to act crazy, pretend to be crazy.

pū.pū leho.leho. n. A cowry shell *(Cypraea moneta). Lit.,* cowry or calloused shell.

pū.pū lei. n. A bead of any kind, a shell for a shell lei.

pū.pū lei 'aha.'aha. n. A marine shell *(Mitra litterata).*

pū.pū lei hala. n. A marine shell *(Hydatina amplustre, Bursa granularis). Lit.,* pandanus-lei shell.

pū.pū lo'i. Same as *pūpū Pākē. Lit.,* irrigated-terrace shell.

pū.pū loloa. n. Auger shell. *Lit.,* long shell.

pupulu. 1. Same as *pulupulu. Mai Maui a Hawai'i ka wahine 'o Pele i hi'a i kāna ahi i pupulu, kukuni ā wela 'o Kahiki* (chant), from Maui to Hawai'i, the woman Pele who lighted her fire, kindled it, burned and heated Kahiki. **2.** Same as *mumulu*, to swarm. *Rare.*

pū.pū mahina. n. A marine shell *(Turbo sandwicensis). Lit.,* moon shell, so called because the operculum is round like the moon.

pū.pū maka 'aha. n. A marine shell *(Rhinoclavis sinensis, Cerithium nesioticum). Lit.,* sennit-mesh shell.

pū.pū maka 'awa. n. A marine shell *(Morula granulata). Lit.,* sour-faced shell.

pū.pū makua. n. A marine shell *(Turbo sandwicensis).*

pū.pū mama.iki. n. A marine shell *(Strombus maculatus).*

pū.pū momi. n. A small mother-of-pearl shell *(Spondylus tenebrosus). Lit.,* pearl shell.

pū.pū mo'o. n. A chiton mollusk. *Lit.,* lizard shell.

pupuni. Redup. of *puni 1–4.* **ho'o.pupuni.** Caus/sim.

pū.pū nī.'au. n. Broom made of coconut midribs tied together at one end. A later name is *pūlumi nī'au.*

pū.pū Ni'i.hau. n. Small shells, especially *Columbella* and *Leptothyra* used in Ni'ihau shell leis; known as *momi* or *momi-o-kai* on Ni'ihau.

pū.pū noho. n. A marine shell (no data). *Lit.,* sitting shell.

pū.pū nuku loa. n. A shell *(Fusinus nicobarus, Latirus nodatus). Lit.*, long-beaked shell.

pū.pū-o-Hā.'upu. n. A shell *(Trochus histrio). Lit.*, Hā'upu-hill shell.

pū.pū 'ō.kole 'oi.'oi. n. Trochidae shell. *Lit.*, sharp-buttocks shell.

pū.pū 'olē. n. A marine shell *(Terebra maculata, Pyramidella sulcata).*

pū.pū 'olē kiwi. n. A marine shell *(Cymatium muricinum).*

pū.pū 'ō.lepe. n. A marine shell *(Tapes japonica). Lit.*, bivalve shell.

pū.pū 'ō.nohi awa. n. A marine shell *(Haminoea sp.). Lit.*, milkfish-eyeball shell.

pū.pū Pā.kē. n. An introduced edible shellfish (perhaps *Viviparus* sp.), found in taro or rice patches; Chinese snail. Also *pūpū lo'i.*

pū.pū pani. n. A marine shell *(Janthina fragilis). Lit.*, cork shell.

pū.pū pe'e.lua. n. A marine shell *(Acanthochiton viridis);* used in *māwaewae* ceremonies for first-born babies. *Lit.*, caterpillar shell. Also *kuapa'a.*

pū.pū pō.niu.niu. Var. of *pūpū 'alā. Lit.*, dizzy shell, perhaps so called because they were considered poisonous.

pupupu. 1. vs. Numerous, crowded, thick, teeming, congested. 2. vs. Double-flowering, as hibiscus, hollyhock, *pīkake.* 3. n. Temporary hut, as for shelter from the sun for beating tapa; hovel; covering. 4. n. White tapa.

pupu.pua. Redup. of *pupua 2.*

pupu.pue. Redup. of *pupue 1.*

pupu.puhi. Same as *pupuhi.*

pū.pū puhi. n. 1. Sundial shell *(Solarium* sp.). Called *hālili* in some localities. 2. Conch shell. *Lit.*, shell to blow. *Kona.*

pupu'u. vi. To double up, draw the limbs together; foetal position, hence, *fig.*, the womb; position of an infant able to get up partially on its knees. *Moe pupu'u,* to sleep curled up. *Pupu'u anu,* to curl up or huddle because of cold. *Pupu'u ho'olei loa,* quick as a flash. *Pupu'u ho'olei loa, kū ana ke kūkini i ke alo o ke ali'i,* quick as a flash the messenger stood in the presence of the chief. *Mai loko mai o ka pupu'u ho'okahi,* from within the same womb.

pupu'u ho'o.lei loa. See *pupu'u.*

pupu'u.lia. Pas/imp. of *pupu'u. Ē Kaulu ē, pupu'ulia* (For. 4:527), O Kaulu, double up.

pū.pū waha loa. n. A shell *(Bulla* sp.). *Lit.*, long-mouthed shell.

pū.pū weu.weu. n. 1. Clump of grass; clump of greenery, especially as placed on the hula altar to the goddess Laka. 2. A chant prayer to Laka after a period of training in the hula to free the taboo.

pu'u. 1. n. Any kind of a protuberance from a pimple *(pu'u 2)* to a hill: hill, peak, cone, hump, mound, bulge, heap, pile, portion, bulk, mass, quantity, clot, bunch, knob; heaped, piled, lumped, bulging; pregnant; to pucker. *Fig.*, obstacle, burden, problem, discomfort, trouble, sorrow. Cf. *alelo pu'u, 'ōkolepu'u, pu'u kālā. Pu'u kaimana,* diamond setting. *Lae pu'u,* prominent or bulging forehead. *Pu'u kānaka,* group of people, mass of people. *Pu'u ka leo,* paralyzed tongue with resulting speech defects. *Pu'u ka nuku,* protruding the lips, as in anger; to eat until satiated, or to be unable to eat all one has. *Pu'u kapu,* a forbidden or taboo place. *Eia ka pu'u nui mawaho nei, he ua, he 'ino, he anu* (chant), here is the burden of discomfort outside, rain, storm, cold. *ho'o.pu'u.* To heap up, collect in heaps; to frown; resentment. Cf. *ho'opu'ukahua.* (PPN *puke.*) 2. n. Any of various round parts or protuberances of the body, as pimple, wart, mole, callus, lump, Adam's apple, throat (see ex., *burn*), larynx, tonsils, heart, stomach, fist, knuckle, ankle joint; gizzard, as of chicken; hard stomach, as of some fish. Cf. *pu'u kohekohe, pu'upu'u, pu'upu'u lima, pu'upu'u wāwae, pu'uwai. Mau nā pu'u,* stuck together, of dogs occasionally in coition. *Pu'u 'eha,* sore throat. 'A'ī

pu'u, calloused neck. *Pu'u 'ōkohekohe,* swollen tonsils. *'A'ohe pu'u, 'a'ohe ke'e,* no pimples, no crooks [commonly said in tales of flawless persons]. *He ma'ū i ka pu'u ke moni* (song), refreshing to the throat to swallow. *Ka pu'u o Abesaloma* (2 Sam. 18.14), the heart of Absalom. 3. n. A desire, need, as for evacuation (used with *hī, ki'o, mimi, pūhi'u). Hae ka pu'u i ka 'ai,* fierce is the craving for food. 4. n. Any earth bug, beetle, especially as found in dry earth; rose beetle, Olinda beetle, stinkbug, ground beetle. 5. n. Hand of cards, stack of cards, deck or pack of cards. Cf. *pu'u pepa.* 6. n. Stack, shock, as of grain. (Lunk. 15.5.) *Nā pu'u hua palaoa* (Puk. 22.6), stacks of grain. 7. nvi. Head, as of cabbage or lettuce; to form a head, sprout. *Kupu ā pu'u* (KL line 487), to grow and sprout. 8. n. Dress material such as dotted swiss that has raised dots. 9. n. Fancy knot or mesh, as in *kōkō,* net. 10. vt. To cast or draw lots, as with a knotted string, or by heaping up pebbles under a tapa, and guessing the number in each heap, or calling one heap positive and the other negative, with the answer to the question provided by the heap with the greatest number of pebbles. *Pu'unaue i ka 'āina ma nā pu'u e ili ana* (Nah. 34.18), divide the land by lot for inheritance. 11. n. Hinge of pearl oyster. 12. n. A method of catching plover: a sharpened bone was half buried and anchored on a string tied to a rock. The bone would become lodged in the throat *(pu'u)* of a plover attempting to eat it, which was then held by the string. 13. n. Sixth stage in the growth of taro. See *kalo* for names of generations. (Kep. 153.) *Rare.* 14. n. A kind of fish. Also *ehe-'ula. Rare.* 15. 'O'opu young about 5 or 10 cm long. *Rare.* 16. n. A hard, white variety of sweet potato. Also *pu'u ke'oke'o.*

pu'ua. 1. vs. Choked, suffocated, strangled; to choke, strain. *Fig.*, disturbed mentally. *Pu'ua keiki,* a baby that is not born at the proper time and must be removed by surgery. *A pu'ua i ka hānau keiki 'ana* (Kin. 35.16), travail in childbirth. *ho'o.pu'ua.* To choke. 2. n. A surfboard. *Rare.*

pu'ua.ahi. n. Bonfire.

pu'u.'ai. Same as *pu'u'ai'ai.*

pu'u.'ai.'ai. n. Stomach, gizzard. *Lit.*, eating round organ.

pu'u 'ai loke. n. Rose beetle *(Adoretus sinicus). Lit.*, rose-eating *pu'u.*

pu'u 'ako. n. Throat inflammation.

pu'u.alu. vt. To carry on the hips or back, as supporting by the arms.

pu'u 'eha. n. Sore throat.

pu'u.haku. vs. Protruding, bulging, irregular; to bulge. Cf. *haku,* lumpy.

pu'u hā.nau. n. Hillock or obstacle encountered while hauling a new canoe from the forest to the shore.

pu'u.hau. n. A hard lump growing on the joints or in the groin, consisting of calcium deposits. *Rare.* Also *haupu'u, 'ohākula'i.*

pu'u hī. n. A desire to evacuate when bowels are loose. Cf. *wai hī. Rare.*

pu'u holo. n. Mobile lump. (Kam. 64:108.)

pu'u.honua. 1. nvi. Place of refuge, sanctuary, asylum, place of peace and safety. *Kūlanakauhale pu'uhonua* (Nah. 35.11), cities of refuge. 2. n. A level area, as used for game sites; also used for grave plots in Puna.

pu'u ho'o.maha. n. A resting place for travelers; easement, relief; to find such. *He aha ka pilikia o ke kīhā, 'oiai he pu'u ho'omaha ia,* what's wrong with belching, for it is a source of physical relief.

pu'u i'a. n. 1. A heap of fish; a string of fish, as on a ti leaf. 2. The hard rounded stomach of some fish, as mullet.

pu'u.ili. n. A fish related to the 'aha and iheihe.

pu'u 'ili.'ili. n. A pile of pebbles, as used in drawing lots or in divination.

pu'u.ka'a. n. A coarse native sedge *(Cyperus ferax* var. *auriculatus),* growing in marshes. It has long narrow leaves, and many tiny flowers are borne at the top of a stem .6 to 1 m high, in a large ray-shaped head. Formerly, when *'ahu'awa* was not available, the fibers of this sedge were used for straining kava. Also *mau'u pu'uka'a, pūko'a, pu'uko'a.* Cf. *kāhili kāpopo, kiolohia. C. trachysanthos* on Ni'ihau.

pu'u.ka'a haole. Same as *'ahu'awa haole.*

Pu'u-Ka'ala. n. Wind, Mt. Ka'ala, O'ahu. (Nak. 57.)

-pu'ukahua. ho'o.pu'u.kahua. Same as *huahua;* to ridicule, belittle, taunt.

pu'u kā.lā. n. Sum of money. See ex., *a'e 5.*

pu'u.kala.hala. n. Redeemer, safeguard, one who helps in time of trouble; remission of sins, absolution (Kam. 64:119). *Lit.,* hillock erases sins. *'O Iesu kō kākou pu'ukalahala,* Jesus is our redeemer.

pu'u kā.lā kū.mau. n. Perpetual endowment.

pu'u.kani. nvi. Sweet-voiced, as in singing; sweet-toned, as music; a singer. *E mele mai ana nā pu'ukani kaulana,* the famous singers will sing.

pu'u.kani.lua. vs. Taut. *Rare.*

Pu'u-ka-pele. n. Same as *Pu'u-pele,* the name of a wind at Mānā, Kaua'i.

pu'u.kaua. n. Fort, fortification, stronghold (Lunk. 6.2). *Lit.,* war hill.

pu'u ke'o.ke'o. Same as *pu'u 16.* (HP 143.)

-pu'ukie, ho'o.pu'u.kie. To ensnare, entrap. (And.)

pu'u ki'o. nvi. The urge to evacuate the bowels; to evacuate. Also *pu'a hana lepo, pu'a ki'o.*

pū.'uki.'uki. vi. Crowded, packed tightly, difficult. *Pū'uki'uki i ka pilikia,* beset by trouble. *Ku'u hoa o ka ua pū'uki'uki o ka mauna* (chant), my companion of the cold unpleasant rain of the mountain.

pu'u.ko'a. n. 1. Same as *pu'uka'a,* a sedge; *fig.,* one of low rank (Ii 150). *Hihia aloha ke oho o ka pu'uko'a* (chant), the leaves of *pu'uko'a* entwined affectionately. 2. A reddish-brown tapa.

pu'u.ko.ā.maka. n. A law or taboo pertaining to the god Ka-hō-āli'i only; the one breaking the law was said to have his eye scooped out and devoured by the god.

pu'u kohe.kohe. n. Enlarged or swollen tonsil, tonsillitis. *E hō'olā'olā me ke kohu kukui no ka pu'u kohekohe,* gargle with candlenut juice for enlarged tonsils.

pu'u.kohu.kohu. n. A gray tapa, Wai-pi'o, Hawai'i.

pu'u koko. n. Clot of blood; heart; blood-clot foetus, in which shape the heroes of some of the tales are born.

pu'u.kole. n. 1. Mons pubis. 2. Upper part of paddle blade joining the handle.

pu'u.kō.lea. n. 1. Sweet potato tubers that form on old vines. 2. *(Cap.)* Wind associated with Kapa'au, Hawai'i.

pu'u.kole.lei.loa. n. An unknown minor illness.

pu'u.kō.nane. n. A little-known variety of taro.

pu'u.kū. n. Treasurer, steward (1 Nal. 16.9).

Pu'u-kū-'akahi. n. The hill that stands alone, name of the tarrying place of souls, where souls of living persons might obtain reconciliation with an estranged *'aumakua* god.

pu'u.kukui. n. Tapa colored with dye made of breadfruit blossom and *kukui* tree bark.

pu'u.ku'ua. n. Stone used for octopus lure. (Kam. 76:169.)

pū.'uku.'uku. vs. Wee, tiny, small.

pū.'ula. A seaweed. (And.)

pū.'ulau. vi. To increase rapidly in number. *Pu'ulau keiki,* to have many children.

pū.'ula.'ula. 1. n. Red hill, earth bank (short for *pu'u 'ula'ula*). 2. vs. Red.

pu'u lehu. n. Ash or tuff cone.

pu'u.lele. n. Rupture, hernia. *Lit.,* falling round organ.

pu'u lele. v. To remove a lump. *Mamala 'eha'eha o ka lani, i ke ko'i pu'u lele, hana 'oi, pu'u lele, hana 'oi* (chant), the chief is sore and aching due to the adze removing lumps, a knife, removing lumps, a knife.

Pu'u-lena. n. Name of a famous cold wind at Kī-lau-ea, Hawai'i and at Puna. See ex., *ahe, pahoehoe 3, pāweo. Ke ano la'i aloha a ka Pu'u-lena* (chant), the peaceful loving mystery of the Pu'u-lena wind. *Ua hala ka Pu'u-lena, aia i Hilo, ua 'imi akula iā papa lauahi* (saying),

the Pu'u-lena wind has gone away, there [it] is at Hilo looking for lava flats [off one's course]. Cf. For. 5:581 for nuance of sadness.

pu'u-lepo. n. A reddish-brown tapa.

pu'u lepo. n. Earth mound or heap; earth target for archery *(pāpua).*

pu'u lima. n. Wrist joints, knuckles, fist.

pū.uli.uli. nvt. Dark; to paint or stain dark.

pū.'ulī.'ulī. n. A variety of small gourd, as used for making feather gourd rattles *('ulī'ulī),* medicine cups *('apu),* and individual poi containers. *Ka lonolau nō i ka lonolau, ka pū'ulī'ulī nō i ka pū'ulī'ulī,* large gourds to large gourds, small gourds to small gourds [chiefs seek the society of chiefs, commoners seek the society of commoners; in battle chief against chief and commoner against commoner].

pū.'ulu. nvi. Group, crowd, army, party, gang, retinue; to form a group, crowd; to crowd, throng, assemble. *Pū'ulu ali'i* (Kep. 141), chiefly retinue, band. *Nā pū'ulu kīwila,* civilian groups. *Ka pū'ulu ha'aha'a iho o nā koi,* lower group requirements. ho'o.pū.'ulu. Caus/sim.

pū.'ulu kaua. n. Army, fighting band, division, phalanx.

pū.'ulu.'ulu. Redup. of *pū'ulu;* to collect.

pu'u makani. n. 1. Gaseous stomach, biliousness. 2. Windy hill.

pu'u.make. n. Dire threat, mortal danger. *Mai ho'okanane'o aku i ke anu, he pu'umake kēnā,* don't persist in going into the cold, it will be [your] death.

pu'u.mana. n. 1. A caret sign of omission. 2. A new mesh added in the enlargement of a net. *Lit.,* branching knot.

pu'u.mimi. n. Bladder.

pu'u mimi. n. Desire or need to urinate. Cf. *'iha'iha.*

pu'u.momoni. Same as *pu'umoni.*

pu'u.moni, pu'u.moni.'ai. n. Throat. *Lit.,* swallowing throat, food-swallowing throat.

Pu'u-nahele. n. Wind associated with Wai-pā, Kaua'i. (For. 5:97.) *Lit.,* forested hill.

pu'u.naue, pu'u.unauwe. nvt. To divide, share; division. *Pu'unaue aku i ka waiwai pio* (Puk. 15.9), divide the spoils.

pu'u.naue loa. n. Long division.

pu'u.naue pō.kole. n. Short division.

pu'u.nohu. Same as *pūnohu.*

pu'u.'o'a. Same as *pū'o'a. Rare.*

pu'u 'oi.'oi. n. Sharp point, peak, summit.

pu'u o'i.o'ina. n. A roadside resting place *(o'io'ina)* consisting of a hillock, heap of stones, rock, mound.

Pu'u-o-Kona. n. Wind associated with Kuli-'ou'ou, O'ahu. (Nak. 56.)

pu'u.ō.la'i. n. The sharp-nosed puffer fish *(Canthigaster rivulatus). Lit.,* volcanic cone, earthquake hill.

pu'u.one. n. 1. Divination. See *hale pu'uone, pu'upu'uone.* 2. Pond near the shore, as connected to the sea by a stream or ditch.

pu'u one. n. Sand dune or heap.

pu'u.one.one. Redup. of *pu'uone 1.*

pu'u 'ō.pala. n. Trash heap, garbage pile.

pu'u.pā. 1. nvi. Obstacle, struck object; to be struck. *Pu'upā Ni'ihau na ka Unulau* (chant) Ni'ihau is struck by the Unulau wind. *He pu'upā hiolo wale nō i ka leo,* an obstacle that can be upset by the voice [by gentle speech]. 2. n. A stone used for *maika* stones. *Rare.* 3. *(Cap.)* n. A *lua* fighting stroke. 4. vt. To give and receive freely. *Rare.*

pu'u.pa'a. n. 1. Virgin, virginity. *Lit.,* firm mound. *'A'ole i loa'a ia'u he pu'upa'a* (Kanl. 22.14), I did not find virginity. 2. Kidneys. *Fig.,* affections, emotions. (Oihk. 3.4.) *Na ke Akua pono i ho'ā'o nā na'au a me nā pu'upa'a* (Hal. 7.9), the righteous God will try the minds and hearts.

pu'u.pale. n. Defense, shield.

pu'u.pau. n. Sore throat with swelling on sides of the neck; throat cancer. *Lit.,* destroyed throat.

pu'u pa'u lena. n. Hill of yellow soot (a term of reproach, especially for *kauā* outcasts, usually followed by *i ka uahi*, in the smoke).

Pu'u-pele. Same as *Pu'u-ka-pele.*

pu'u pele. n. Volcanic mound, heap, hill.

pu'u pepa. n. Deck of playing cards; stack of playing cards; hand of cards; pile of paper.

pu'u.po'o.lā. n. Biliousness, gastric discomfort. *Rare.*

pu'u pū.hi'u. n. Urge or need to break wind.

pu'u.pu'u. 1. Redup. of *pu'u 1;* full of protuberances, lumps; lumpy, piled in heaps; heaped up, swollen up. *'A 'ā pu'upu'u,* water-worn gravel or stones. *Poi pu'u-pu'u,* lumpy poi, *fig.,* an unsocial person. *Pu'upu'u lei pali i ka 'ā'ī,* an irregular or imperfect [*lit.,* lumpy] lei is a cliff on the neck [a lei is beautiful when worn]. *ho'o.*-**pu'u.pu'u.** Redup. of *ho'opu'u;* a mound, to mound up. (PCP *pukupuku.*) **2.** Redup. of *pu'u 2;* knuckles, joints; clenched fist, blow with the fist; pimply, full of blotches; skin eruptions, scurvy (Oihk. 21.20). *ho'o.*-**pu'u.pu'u.** To clench the fist, to shake the fist threateningly. **3.** Redup. of *pu'u 9;* knotty. **4.** n. Eyes at a joint, as of sugar cane or kava. **5.** n. Capital, as of a candlestick. (Puk. 25.31.)

pu'u.pu'ua. Redup. of *pu'ua 1.*

pu'u.pu'u hala. n. Lumps or growths on the trunk of a pandanus tree.

pu'u.pu'u.kaua. Same as *pu'ukaua.*

pu'u.pu'u koko. Same as *pu'u koko;* tumor (1 Sam. 5.9).

pu'u.pu'u kula (gula). n. Gold nuggets.

pu'u.pu'u lā.'au. n. Knot, lump, as on a tree trunk; knothold.

pu'u.pu'u laina. Same as *laina,* hives.

pu'u.pu'u li'i.li'i. nvi. Smallpox; to have smallpox. *Lit.,* small lumps.

pu'u.pu'u lima. n. Clenched fist, knuckles, blow of the fist.

pu'u.pu'u mane'o. n. Itching skin irritation or eruption.

pu'u.pu'u niu. n. Coconuts right after blossom stage.

pu'u.pu'u.one. n. **1.** A beach hut, as for fishermen or for teaching and practicing the divination called *pu'u-one* or *kuhikuhipu'uone.* **2.** A game in which small stones were hidden in mounds of sand.

pu'u.pu'u wā.wae. n. Ankle bones, ankles. *Nā pu'u-pu'u wāwae ona* (Oih. 3.7), his ankles.

pu'u.wai. n. **1.** Heart. Use of *pu'uwai* as a center of emotions (instead of *na'au, 'ōpū,* or *loko*) is probably a Western concept, but was noted in a chant dated 1853: *Ke hō'eu'eu nei i ka pu'uwai,* stirring now the heart. *Pu'uwai 'ele'ele,* scoundrel, rogue; black-hearted. *Pu'uwai hāmama,* generous, openhearted. *Pu'uwai hao kila,* heart of steel, courageous. *Pu'uwai Ho'āno,* Sacred Heart. *Pu'uwai kapalili,* fluttering heart. **2.** A heart-shaped locket, as of gold *(kula)* or silver *(kālā).* **3.** Small suckers on a taro plant (probably from *pu'u uai,* lumps removed, since these shoots were broken off so that the tuber might grow larger). *Rare.* **4.** Wrapped packages of vegetable food. *Rare.*

Pu'u.wai La'a.hia. n. Sacred Heart.

pu'u.wai.ū. n. Breast. *Ua nui nā pu'uwaiū* (Ezek. 16.7), the breasts were large.

pu'u welu. n. A heap of rags. *Fig.,* straggler, as a *hau* tree growing apart from a *hau* clump. *Hānau ka pu'u welu, he weluwelu kona* (KL line 529), the stragglers are born, they are despised.

Pu'u.wepa. n. Name of a star (no data). Also *Pūwepa.*

pu'u wini.wini. n. Sharp-pointed hill.

pū.wā. vi. To shine, glitter, reflect brightly, as a night fire. *Ua pūwā ka 'ili o kona maka* (Puk. 34.30), the skin of his face shone.

pū.wa'a.wa'a. vs. Stupid.

pū.waha.nui. n. A medicinal plant (no data).

pū.wai. n. A sentinel's call of alarm, a trumpet call, as in war. (Ioela 2.1.)

pū wai. n. Water gun, squirt gun.

pū wai.kaua. n. War alarm. (Ioela 2.1.)

puwalu, pualu. 1. vs. All together, in unison, united, co-operative. (Cf. *-walu,* many, as in *makawalu, olowalu.*) *Hīmeni puwalu,* choral singing. *Heluhelu puwalu,* reading in unison. **2.** Var. spelling of *pualu,* a surgeonfish. **3.** n. Flag, as on a pole or canoe sail.

pū.wela.wela. vs. Warm, hot.

Pū.wepa. Var. spelling of *Pu'uwepa.*

pū.weu.weu. 1. Same as *pūpū weuweu. E noho iho i ka pūweuweu, mai ho'oki'eki'e,* in the grass clumps, do not be conceited. **2.** Same as *pūhuluhulu 1, 2.*

pū wili. n. An old type of gun, sometimes called Maxim gun.

puwō. Var. spelling of *puō.*

puwō.puwō. Var. spelling of *puōpuō.*

R

All loan words from English sometimes spelled with initial r- *are entered under* l-. *For example:* raisi, *see* laiki, *rice;* ropi, *see* lopi, *rope;* rumi, *see* lumi, *room.*

S

All loan words from English sometimes spelled with initial s- *are entered under* k-. *For example:* Sabati, *see* Kāpaki, *Sabbath;* sopa, *see* kopa, *soap.*

T

All loan words from English sometimes spelled with initial t- *are entered under* k-. *For example:* tausani, *see* kaukani, *thousand;* tiga, *see* kika, *tiger.*

U

The words sometimes spelled uwē, 'uwī, *and* uwō *or with initial* uwa, uwe, *or* uwi *are written in the Dictionary* uē, 'uī, uō, ua-, ue-, *and* ui-, *with cross references from the spellings containing the predictable* w-*glides. The initial* w *of root words, however, is written after* u-: *see* wā, uwā; wa'a, uwa'a, *and others.*

u-. 1. Prefix to some words to denote plural, as *uhaele, ulawai'a, unoho, unonoho.* (This *u-* is sometimes written as though forming a word with a preceding *o,* imperative marker, as *ou haele oukou* (Mat. 2.8), you go. (Gram. 6.3.3.) *E uhaele 'olua,* you two go. *O u'ai like,* eat together. **2.** Prefix to many words with meanings 'quality or state'; there is variation in some words of *u-, 'u-,* and *'ū,* especially in rare words. See *uahi, uhaki, uhemo, 'uhene, uhinu, 'ūlika, 'uwa'a,* and others; see also Gram. 6.3.2.

-u, Second person singular poss. suffix in *kāu* and *kou,* your. (Gram. 8.2.) (PPN *-u.*)

'u-. See *u- 2.*

-'u. First person singular poss. suffix in *ka'u, ko'u,* and *ku'u,* mine, my. (Gram. 8.2.) (PPN *-ku.*)

ū. 1. n. Breast, teat, udder. Cf. *waiū.* (PPN *huhu.*) **2.** vs. Moist, soaked; to drip, drizzle, ooze; impregnated, as with salt. Cf. *kawaū, ko'ū, ma'ū. Ū ke kapa i ka ua,* the tapa was wet by the rain. **ho'o.ū, hō.'ū.** To moisten, soak, wet.

ū-. Rare var. of *u- 2.* Cf. *ūkō, ūpē.* (Probably length of *ū-* was due to assimilation of the long vowel in the base.)

'ū. 1. vi, interj. To grunt, groan, moan, sigh, hum, coo, mourn, grieve, complain; grief, sorrow; an exclamation of delight or assent; to exclaim thus; to grunt 'yes, yes (saying that you are listening)!' *Noho 'ū,* grief; grief-stricken. *Pā i ka 'ū lā* (Kep. 71), touched by grief. *Pōmaika'i ka po'e e 'ū ana* (Mat. 5.4), blessed are the people that mourn. *'Ū ke kai o 'Ewa i ke 'ala o ka maile,* the lowlands of 'Ewa exclaim over the perfume of the *maile* vine. *E 'ū hele ana* (Hal. 38.6), to go mourning. **ho'o.'ū, hō.'ū.** To grunt and strain, as with physical exertion (Kep. 159); to mourn. (PCP *kuu.*) **2.** vi. To hold the breath. *'A'ole i 'ū,* in no time at all; *lit.,* in not even time to take a breath. Cf. *'upu.* **3.** vs. Snub-nosed (used with *ihu*). **4.** n. Short for *'ulu,* breadfruit, as in the place name *Ka-'ū-pūlehu.* **5.** n. The letter "u."

'ū-. See *u- 2.*

ua. 1. nvi. Rain; to rain; rainy. See **rain.** Rain was beloved as it preserved the land; it was called *kāhiko o ke akua,* adornment of deity. For symbolic connotations of rain cf. *wai 1, rain,* and Elbert 1962. Many rains are named and associated poetically with particular places. Many rain names refer to the action of rain on plants, as *Hehi-pua-hala, Kani-lehua, Kinai-lehua, Lū-lau-kō, Moaniani-lehua, Moe-lehua, Pō'ai-hala.* Other names show the supposed effects of rain on people or their possessions, as *Po'o-lipilipi, Po'o-nui, Popo-kapa, Pupū-hale.* See *hikiki'i 1, lehua,* Hilo. Rains are often referred to with *ua* preceding a base, as *ua Kuahine.* They are entered in this dictionary without initial *Ua. (Ua-* is retained before prepositions, as *Ua-ma-ka-laukoa.*) *Ua li'ili'i,* light rain, drizzle. *Kā hewahewa, he ua* (FS 37), hit wildly, it's raining [let's get going, let the fight begin]. **ho'o.ua.** To cause rain. *Ē ka 'ohu kolo ē, ho'oua 'ia mai i ulu ka 'awa,* O creeping mist, make it

rain so that the kava will grow. (PPN *'uha.*) **2.** demon. Aforementioned, the one talked of. *Ua* is often followed by a noun and *nei,* here, or *lā,* there, and is used idiomatically (see *ua o, ua ona o, mea 6,* and Gram. 8.3.4.). (PCP *taua.*) **3.** Common part. preceding verbs and denoting completed or recently completed action; to become. (Gram. 5.2.) (PPN *kua.*)

-ua. Indicator of the dual number in first and third persons of pronouns and poss. only *(kāua, māua, lāua).* Cf. *-lua 2* and Gram. 8.2. (PPN *-ua.*)

'uā. Var. spelling of *'uwā.*

'u'a. 1. vs. Useless, unproductive, vain, to no profit, good-for-nothing, worn-out; completely unattractive. Cf. *kolo'u'a, ma'u'a. Luhi 'u'a,* vain effort. **2.** n. A coarse mat or tapa.

Ua-a-ka-lī.poa. n. Name of a fine, cold rain. *Lit.,* rain by the *līpoa* seaweed.

ua 'awa. n. Cold, bitter, drizzling rain. *Fig.,* hard experience.

ua-hā.'ao. Same as *hā'ao 3,* a tapa pattern.

ua hā.nai. n. Rain that nurtures the earth.

uahi, uwahi. nvs. Smoke; smoked; dustlike, spraylike; dust, spray, wisps. Cf. *auahi. Pipi uahi,* smoked beef. *Ola i ka 'ai uahi 'ole ke kini o Mānā,* the multitudes of Mānā live on smokeless food [they were said to trade fish and gourds for cooked food]. *I ke kau uahi o ke ao* (For. 5:715), at the coming of the wisps of dawn. **ho'o.uahi.** To smoke, emit smoke, cure by smoking. (PPN *'ahu,* PEP *auafi.*)

uahi-a-Pele. n. **1.** A native variety of sugar cane, heavy-stooling, light red-purple, the nodes hairy-fringed, the internodes sausage-shaped. (HP 223, 225.) Also *na'aukake.* **2.** Several varieties of taro described at Puna, Wai-pi'o, and Kona, Hawai'i. (HP 30.) **3.** A variety of sweet potato. **4.** A tree *(Pelea barbigera),* endemic to Kaua'i, with opposite, elliptical leaves, conspicuous for their smoky-gray color. It is related to the *mokihana.* **5.** *(Cap.)* A wind associated with Kī-lau-ea, Hawai'i. (Nak. 55.)

uahi 'awa. n. Pungent sulphur smoke, as from a volcano. (For. 6:478.) *Lit.,* bitter smoke.

uahi lepo. n. Dust wisps. *Ua pi'o ka uahi lepo i ka lani* (chant), the dust wisps bend in the heavens.

uahi wai. n. Mist, spray, steam. *Lit.,* liquid spray.

ua.hoa. vs. Hard, severe, harsh, indifferent to the distress of others. *Nā-maka-uahoa* (name), the hard eyes.

uai, uwai. vt. To move, as an object; to push aside; to move from place to place, as a tethered animal; sliding, as a door; opening and shutting; to be dislocated, as a joint. Cf. *pākaukau uai i ka loa, puka uai. Uai ka mana,* to lie down to sleep in security; *lit.,* the *mana* is set aside. **ho'o.uai.** Caus/sim. (PCP *uai.*)

u'ai. Plural of *'ai,* to eat.

ua.iki. n. Offspring of a chief and a mother of no rank. (Malo 55.) *Lit.,* little rain.

ua.kaha. Same as *uauakaha.*

ua.kea. 1. n. Mist (famous at Hāna, Maui). *Lit.,* white rain. **2.** vs. White as mist, mist-white, white as breaking surf or snow. *Moa uakea,* white chicken, as used in offering. *Ē Kāne uakea, eia ka 'ālana, he moa ualehu, he moa uakea, he moa 'ula hiwa* (Malo 180), O Kāne white as mist, here is the offering, an ashy-gray chicken, a mist-white chicken, a black-red chicken. *Na Kahiko ka nalu uakea i hānau* (chant), Kahiko gave birth to the mist-white waves.

ua.ke'e. n. Bend, crook, as in a path.

uaki, uati, uwaki, waki. n. Watch, clock; a watch, as of a sailor. *Eng.* See *kū uaki.*

uaki pū.āla. n. Alarm clock.

uaki pū.lima. n. Wrist watch.

ua.koko. n. **1.** A low-lying rainbow. *Lit.,* blood rain. See ex., *kī'ohu'ohu.* **2.** A rain so heavy that it turns stream waters red-brown with the wash of the hillside. **3.** Reflection of rainbow colors in the clouds.

'uala, 'uwala. n. **1.** The sweet potato *(Ipomoea batatas),* a perennial, wide-spreading vine, with heart-shaped, angled, or lobed leaves and pinkish-lavender flowers. The tuberous roots are a valuable food, and they vary greatly in many ways, as in color and shape. Though of South American origin, the plant has been a staple food since ancient times in many parts of Polynesia, as well as in some other regions. (HP 131–66, Neal 706–7.) (PEP *kumala;* cognates elsewhere in Polynesia may be borrowings from PEP.) **2.** A variety of sugar cane, a yellow mutant of *'akoki* with large stalks; often called *pilimai* and similar to it but stronger. (HP 221, 225.) **3.** See *uhi 'uala,* a variety of yam *(Dioscorea alata).* **4.** Large muscles of the upper arm, biceps, brachii. **5.** A kind of cowry shell (no data).

'uala 'awa.'awa. n. Sweet-potato beer.

'uala hē.'ī. n. A variety of sweet potato.

'uala ho'o.mala.mala. n. Mashed sweet potato, slightly fermented and eaten as poi.

'uala hū.pē. n. Madeira vine *(Boussingaultia gracilis.)* (Neal 344.) *Lit.,* mucus sweet potato.

'uala kahiki. n. The white or Irish potato *(Solanum tuberosum),* a weak-stemmed herb about .9 m high, with lobed leaves. The white, starchy, underground tuber is a valuable food in many countries. A native of the Andes, it was introduced to Hawai'i in the early 1800s. (Neal 745.) *He Hawai'i 'uala kahiki,* an Irish-potato Hawaiian [one who apes white men instead of appreciating his own culture]. *Lit.,* foreign sweet potato.

'uala koali. Same as *kūpala 3,* a wild sweet potato.

'uala.lehu. n. A name later applied to yellow bamboo. (HP 222.)

'uala lehu. 1. Same as *lahi,* a variety of sugar cane. (HP 222.) **2.** n. A variety of sweet potato. (HP 225.)

'uala nika. n. A variety of introduced sweet potato.

ua lani.pili. n. A heavy rain, as one lasting for days and days, or a cloudburst.

'uala pilau. n. Turnip *(Brassica rapa). Lit.,* smelly potato.

'uala 'ula kī.na'u. n. A variety of red sweet potato.

ua.leha. vs. Lazy. Cf. *palaleha.*

ua.lehe. 1. vs. Loose, loose-fitting, as a dress; sitting with the knees wide apart; stretching the mouth, as in a grimace. **hō.'ua.lehe.** Caus/sim. **2.** vs. Wary of a hook, as a fish once caught and having escaped. *Rare.* **3.** vt. To oust a tenant from his land and deprive him of the fruit of his work; to evict.

Ua-lē.hei. Short for *Ka-ua-lēhei-o-Makawao.*

ua.lehu. 1. vs. Gray, ashy-gray. See ex., *uakea 2.* **2.** n. A variety of taro. **3.** *(Cap.)* n. Wind name, Hālawa, Moloka'i.

ua.lei. vt. To spread out, as a fish net.

ua limua. n. A period of constant rain. *Lit.,* moss-growing rain.

ualo. Var. spelling of *uwalo.*

Ua-ma-ka-lau-koa. n. Name of a rain at Nu'u-anu, O'ahu. *Lit.,* rain amid the *koa* tree leaves.

ua mea. See *mea 6.*

ua.nana.huki. n. Tapa beater. (Kam. 76:109.)

ua (noun) **nei.** See *ua 2.*

ua.ne'i. Short for *auane'i 2,* probably not, especially after words ending with *-a.* Cf. Oih. 5.39. *E mana'o ana he 'oia'i'o ka 'ōlelo a nā 'elemākule, 'a'ole kā uane'i* (FS 139), it was thought that the word of the old men was true, but it was not.

uā.ni'i, uwāni'i. nvs. Stiff, as salted fish; stiffness. See ex., *pēpē 1., uwa'uwali.* **ho'o.uā.ni'i.** To stiffen. *Ua ho'ouāni'i i kona kino me ka 'o'ole'a loa,* stiffened his body with all his might.

ua noe. n. Misty rain, fog.

ua o. Same as *ua ona o,* aforementioned. (Gram. 8.3.4.) *Mehameha nā hale ua o Ka'ōleiokū* (FS 133), the aforementioned houses of Ka'ōleiokū are deserted.

'uao, 'uwao. nvt. To intercede, arbitrate, reconcile, mediate; referee, umpire, conciliator, arbitrator, peacemaker. *E 'uao ana nō lākou* (Heb. 7.25), to make intercession for them.

ua ona o. idiom. Aforementioned (often before names of people). *Ua hānau 'ia ua ona o Meipala i Kahiki,* the Mabel we've been talking of was born in Tahiti.

ua.oa. n. Light rain, mist. *Rare.*

uapo, uwapo. n. Wharf, pier, quay, dock, bridge. *Eng. Nā loa'a mai nā uapo mai,* revenues from wharves.

ua pū.nohu. n. A red rain in the sunshine.

ua'u. Var. spelling of *uwa'u* and same as *wa'u,* to grate.

'ua'u, 'uwa'u. n. Dark-rumped petrel *(Pterodroma phaeopygia sandwichensis),* an endangered sea bird, considered by some an *'aumakua.* See *kaini.*

ua.ua. 1. nvs. Tough, sinewy, glutinous, viscid, leathery; not easily broken, as cord. *Fig.,* hardheaded, willful, obstinate, tough-minded. *'Ā 'ī uaua,* stiff neck. (For a rare use of *uaua* as a noun, see *'īlio-holo-i-ka-uaua.*) **ho'o.ua.ua.** To toughen; tough, stubborn. (PPN *uaua.*) **2.** n. A variety of taro. The name may be qualified by the terms *'ele'ele, ke'oke'o, mōlina, piko.* (HP 29, 30, 34.)

'uā.'uā. Var. spelling of *'uwā'uwā.* Redup. of *'uā.*

u'a.u'a. n. A tapa dyed as with *'ōlena* (turmeric) or *noni.* **'u'a.'u'a.** Redup. of *'u'a.*

ua.uahi. nvs. Smoky-gray color, as of tapa; gray quality, as of a whitened sugar-cane leaf; smoky, hazy; a reddish-blue tapa (Kam. 76:157).

ua.ua.hoa. Redup. of *uahoa.*

ua.uai. Redup. of *uai.*

ua.ua.kaha. nvs. Stiffness of the cords of the neck.

'ua.'uala, 'uwa'uwala. nvi. Sour odor as of fermenting or decaying sweet potatoes; to smell thus.

ua.'uali. Var. spelling of *uwa'uwali.*

ua.ua loli. See *limu uaua loli.*

'Ua'u-kaha. Same as *Ka-'ua'u-kaha.*

'ua'u kani. n. Wedge-tailed shearwater or moaning bird *(Puffinus pacificus chlororhynchus). Lit.,* calling *'ua'u.* Also *hō'io.*

'ua'u kē.wai. n. A variety of *'ua'u.* (Malo text, chapter 13, section 23.)

'Ua'u-komo-hewa. Same as *Ka-'ua'u-komo-hewa.*

'Ua'u-lewa.lewa. Same as *Ka-'ua'u-lewalewa.*

uau.o'a, uauwo'a. n. Distant sound, as of blended voices.

ue, uwe. 1. vt. To jerk, pull, twist, pry, turn, sway. Cf. *naue. Ka ue 'ana, 'o ka ue 'ana ia o ka mahi kalo i nā 'ohā ulu mua* (Kep. 157), the pulling away, this is a pulling away in the taro plantation of the first growing shoots. (PPN *ue.*) **2.** nvi. A hula step: the caller announces the step to drummer (who changes the beat) and dancers by calling *e ue (e* imperative and *ue).* The right foot is extended forward with toes pointing, while both arms are brought forward to chest level with hands crossed and fingers tipped upward; the left hand stays up, while right arm and foot swing back in an outward arc. Then the right arm and foot are moved forward, and the step is repeated to the left. Then three short steps are taken forward. In the last step the left hand is forward, and the right foot and arm back. To do this step. **3.** vs. Tall, far apart. Rare except in proper names. *Ka-pali-ue-loa* (name of a chief), the very tall cliff. **4.** A kind of mat made without stripping the pandanus leaves. (And.)

uē, uwē. nvi. To cry, weep, lament, mourn; a cry, lamentation, weeping; to salute (Mat. 5.47). Cf. *auē*, *ha'uha'u uē*. *Uē wale*, to cry for no reason; crybaby. **ho'o.uē.** To cause weeping, make someone cry.

uea, uwea. n. Wire. *Eng.* See *pā uea.*

uea haka.haka. n. Wire screen; screen, as on windows. *Lit.*, space wire.

uea kele.pona. n. Telephone wire.

uea kukū. n. Barbed wire.

uē (uwē) ala.lā. vi. To wail loudly, yelp.

uea maka 'upena. n. Chicken wire. *Lit.*, net-mesh wire.

uea moana. n. Undersea cable.

uea 'ole. n. Wireless.

uea 'ō.lelo. n. Telegraph wire. *Lit.*, speaking wire.

uea poe.poe. n. Smooth wire. *Lit.*, round wire.

uē.'ehene, uwē'ehene. Same as *ehehene.*

'uehe. Var. spelling of *'uwehe.*

uē helu. nvi. A wailing call of grief and love, recounting deeds of a loved one and shared experiences; to weep and speak thus. *Lit.*, enumerating weeping.

uē 'ino. nvi. To cry loudly; tantrum.

ueka. Var. spelling of *uweka*, dirty.

uē kani.kau. vi. To wail; wailing prayer.

'ueke. Var. spelling of *'uweke.*

ueko. Var. spelling of *uweko.*

ueko.eko. Var. spelling of *uwekoweko.*

uē leo nui. vi. To cry loudly, bawl.

uene, uwene. 1. vi. To move back and forth, oscillate. *Uene ke kolopā*, the crowbar lifts [of success]. **2.** vi. To break wind slightly. **3.** n. Name of a string figure.

uepa, uwepa. 1. n. Wafer. *Eng.* **2.** n. Whip. *Uepa kiani*, a flexible hand whip. *Eng.* **3.** nvt. Wax seal, as used on envelopes; to seal.

ue.ue, uweuwe. Redup. of *ue 1*; to wriggle, squirm. (PPN *ueue*.)

uē.uē, uwēuwē. Redup. of *uē*. **ho'o.uē.uē.** Caus/sim.; to imitate wailing; a wailing dirge.

ue.ueko. Var. spelling of *uweuweko.*

'ue.'uele, uwe'uwele. vs. Wet (used with *kēhau*, dew).

uha. n. Large intestine, alimentary canal, colon. Cf. *uhahemo, uhalehe, uhalena, uhanui, uha'ula*. See saying, *kāhela 1.*

ū.hā. Same as *puhi ūhā*, an eel.

'uha. nvt. Wasteful, extravagant; waste, extravagance; to waste.

'ū.hā. 1. n. Thigh, lap, shoulder; hindquarters, as of a horse, beef, or pig. *'Ūhā moa*, drumstick of a chicken. (PCP *kuu(fs)aa*.) **2.** n. Foster parent of a chiefly child, or guardian, so-called because he might hold the child on his lap (*'ūhā*). **3.** Var. of *pūhā 1–4.* **4.** Rare var. of *hāhā*, to grope.

'uha. nv. To waste food or anything; to squander; extravagant; extravagance. (The old Hawaiians did not waste food.)

uhae. Same as *hahae.*

uhaele. Plural of *haele*, to go, come. See ex., *māki'a. O uhaele mai*, won't you (plural) come.

'ū.hā hame. n. Leg of ham. See *hame.*

'ū.hā heke. Emerson (Malo 201) correction of *'ūhā kākau.*

uha.hemo. n. Hemorrhoids.

'ū.hā hipa. n. Leg of mutton. *Lima 'ūhā hipa*, leg-of-mutton sleeve.

'ū.hā hope. n. Hindquarters, as of horse, beef, pig.

uhai. Same as *hahai. Ka uhai manu* (Kep. 89), the bird hunter.

uha'i. 1. Same as *uhaki*, to break. *E uha'i ia i ko lākou mau iwi* (Nah. 24.8), he shall break their bones. **2.** n. Covering for door opening, doorway frame. *Lele kāhili, holo ka uha'i, uhi kapa*, feather standards sway, the door opening is moved into place, the tapa covers [the chief sleeps]. **3.** Similar to *'alu.*

uhai.ā.holo. vt. To pursue or run swiftly; to pass swiftly, as time. *E uhaiāholo ana i ka lei aloha* (Kel. 61), following quickly after the beloved child [in death].

'ū.hā kā.kau. n. Subjects of the high chief. (Malo 194.) *Lit.*, tattooed thighs.

'ū.hā kapu. n. A taboo lap, said of persons unable to raise children successfully, believed due to jealousy of an *'aumakua* (family god); a person with the taboo lap. (It was believed that children of the *'ūhā kapu* would die unless reared by relatives.)

uha.kē. Same as *hakē*; broad, wide. *Uhakē nā iwi pāpā-kole*, the hip bones are broad.

uha.ke'e. vs. Crooked, as a road.

uhaki. Same as *hahaki*, to break.

uha.kole. vi. To strain in an effort to evacuate the bowels. *Fig.*, disobedient, stubborn. *Lit.*, red colon.

uhaku. vt. To put together, roll up.

uhala.lē. vs. Obese. Cf. *halalē. Rare.*

uha.lehe. Same as *wahalehe.*

uha.lei. Same as *helei.*

uha.lena. vs. Lazy, overstuffed with food. *Lit.*, lazy colon.

'uha.loa. n. A small, downy, American weed *(Waltheria indica* var. *americana)*, with ovate leaves and small, clustered yellow flowers. Leaves and inner bark of root are very bitter and are used for tea or chewed to relieve sore throat. (Neal 575–6.) One of the plant forms of the pig demigod Kama-pua'a (FS 215). Also *'ala'ala pū loa, hala 'uhaloa, hi'a loa, kanaka loa.*

uhalu. Same as *puhalu 1, halu;* to deplete. *Uhalu ka waihona aupuni no ia mau loa'a*, deplete the national treasury of these revenues.

uhalu.halu. Redup. of *uhalu.*

uha.lula. 1. Same as *hālula*, a sea urchin. **2.** vs. Lazy.

'ū.hā mua. n. Shoulder, as of a cow, horse, pig.

'uhane. nvs. Soul, spirit, ghost; dirge or song of lamentation *(rare)*; spiritual. *'Uhane 'ole*, without a soul; shameless, like a beast. *Lele ka 'uhane*, the soul leaves [death]. *Ku'u i ka 'uhane* (Kin. 35.29), to give up the ghost. *Pili 'uhane*, spiritual. *'Uhane 'ololī*, thin, shriveled soul or ghost. (PEP *ku(f,s)ane*.)

'uhane hau.ka'e. n. Wandering, friendless spirits.

'uhane hele. n. A traveling spirit, usually of a living person.

'Uhane Hemo.lele. n. Holy Ghost, Holy Spirit.

'uhane 'ino. n. Unclean or evil spirit *(Biblical)*, demon.

'uhane kia'i. n. Guardian spirit.

'uhane kī.hei pua. n. A spirit partially controlling a person and giving him strength, animation, or talents. *Lit.*, flower-mantle spirit.

'uhane noho. n. A spirit possessing a person completely and talking through him. Also *akua noho.*

uha.nui. vs. Fat, weak. *Rare. Lit.*, big colon.

uhao. 1. Same as *hao 3, 4.* **2.** n. Cone-shaped base from the *kāhili* staff to the first feathers, formerly of feathers, later also of silk or ribbons. *'O ka mo'oni 'ula ka uhao ma ke kumu, i hana 'ia i ka hulu lena 'ō'ō (kāhili* chant), the cone-shaped base forms a red spiral at the staff, made with yellow *'ō'ō* feathers. **3.** n. Tenderloin. *Rare.*

'ū.hā pua'a. n. Ham.

uhau. Var. of *hahau.* (Neh. 3.2.) *Uhau i ke kau*, to present a chant; to strike, as in sorcery or as a blow (GP 66). *Uhau akula ia i ka pua'a ma ke alo o 'Iwa* (FS 21), he laid a pig down before 'Iwa. *'Ehia āu manawa i uhau ai iāia?* How many times did you hit him?

uhā.uhā. vi. To pant, puff, as a dog or as the wind (For. 4:77).

'uha.'uha. Redup. of *'uha;* prodigal, wastrel; to squander, debauch, dissolute. *'Uha'uha wale*, wanton. *Ka pa'ani, ua 'uha'uha, a me ka ho'ohiki 'ino*, gaming, waste, and blasphemy. *Ka 'uha'uha a me ka lapuwale* (Kekah. 1.17), madness and folly.

uhau.hakō. Same as *pāwale*, a plant; used as medicine the name may have been *uhau*. (Kam. 64:141.)

uhau.hala.lē. Redup. of *uhalalē. Rare.*

uhau.hau. Redup. of *uhau.*

uha'u.ha'u. Same as *ha'uha'u.*

uhau hili kini.pō.pō. n. Batter (in baseball).

uhau.hui. nvt. Presentation of a prayer, especially in *'anā'anā* sorcery; to present such a prayer.

uhau.humu. vt. To sew together, as sails; to lay together, as stones in a wall; to interlock. *Rare.*

uha.'ula. vs. Lazy, good-for-nothing. *Rare.*

uhau 'upena. v. To strike with a net, as a bird-catching net on a long handle.

uhe. nv. Offering place for fish on a heiau; to offer, as fish. *Rare.*

'uhē. vs. Chilly, wet and cold. *Ua uhi mai ka hau o nā kuahiwi; he manawa kēwai ia o ka mauna a me ka 'uhē* (Kep. 97), the dew of the hills settles down; it is a wet time in the mountains and uncomfortably cold.

uhe'e. Plural of *he'e 2–4.*

uhe.heu. vi. To fly or hurry as though on wings *(ēheu).* (Kep. 95.)

'uheke. vs. Plump, fat-cheeked, fleshy.

'ū.heke.heke. Redup. of *'uheke.*

uhele. 1. Plural of *hele*, to go. 2. Rare var. of *helehele*, to cut, skin, strip off bark or rind.

uhe.lehe. vs. Sulky, annoyed, vexed. *Rare.*

uhe.lei. Same as *helei.*

uhemo. Same as *hemo.*

'uhene. nvt, interj. To play a merry tune, converse quietly and romantically, tease coquettishly; exclamation of exultation, as in songs; happy or joyous sound. Cf. *henehene. Ua 'uhene maila lākou i ka mele,* they played a merry tune. *'Uhene ahahana ka'u lei, na'u ia* (song), oh joy, oh boy; she's my darling.

'uhene.hene. Same as *henehene.* **hō.'uhene.hene.** Same as *ho'ohenehene.*

'uhē.'uhē. 1. Redup. of *'uhē.* 2. Interj. similar to *'uhī-'uhā,* ha ha!

'uhe'u.hene. Redup. of *'uhene;* tra-la-la.

uhe.ule. vs. Weak, imbecilic, impotent (an epithet applied to men). *Rare.* Cf. *ule,* penis.

uhi. 1. nvt. Covering, cover, veil, film, lid, solid tattooing, tent (Puk. 26.12); to cover, spread over, engulf, conceal, overwhelm; to don, as a feather cloak. *Fig.,* to deceive, hide the truth. *Kākau uhi,* to tattoo solidly. *Uhi mai ka lani pō,* the night sky spreads forth [ignorance]. *Ua uhi 'ia kō lāua mau mana'o i ke aloha* (For. 4:67), their thoughts were overwhelmed with love. *Uhi i ka moe,* to make a bed. **ho'o.uhi.** Caus/sim. (PPN *'ufi.*) 2. n. Large, bluish-brown birthmark. 3. n. The yam *(Dioscorea alata),* from southeast Asia, a climber with square stems, heart-shaped leaves, and large, edible, underground tubers. The plant is widely distributed through islands of the Pacific, where it is commonly grown for food. (HP 166–172, Neal 230.) Also *pālau, ulehihi.* In the past botanists have applied the name *uhi* incorrectly to the *hoi kuahiwi.* (PPN *'ufi.*) 4. n. Mother-of-pearl bivalve, mother-of-pearl shank. (PPN *'ufi.*) 5. n. Turtle shell piece used for scraping *olonā.* 6. n. Mark made by the gall of raw *pūpū 'awa* (a shellfish) on tapa or on the skin as an ornament. (PCP *u(f,s)i.*)

uhia. Pas/imp. of *uhi 1.* (PPN *'u(u)fia.*)

uhi 'ā.lela. n. A variety of yam, the tuber having white flesh and skin; grown in Puna, Hawai'i. (HP 168.)

uhi.'ā.pana. vt. To debate, argue. *Rare.*

uhi 'ā.pana. n. Patchwork cover or spread.

uhi ho'o.noho.noho. n. A variety of yam. See *-nohonoho.*

uhi kala.koa. n. A variety of yam, the tuber with mottled red and white flesh and white skin; grown at Hā-'ena, Kaua'i. (HP 168.) Also *uhi 'ōni'oni'o.*

uhi ke'o.ke'o. n. A variety of yam, grown throughout the islands; tuber with white flesh and skin. (HP 168.)

uhi.kino. n. Body covering, garment, shield. *Pale kaua a me ka uhikino* (Hal. 35.2), shield and buckler.

uhi laha. See *laha 3.*

uhi lehua. n. A variety of yam, grown in Kona, Hawai'i,

having a tuber with pinkish flesh, the vine stem with red wings. Perhaps the same as *uhi 'ula'ula* (HP 168.)

uhi maka. n. Veil, mask.

uhi moe. n. Bedspread.

uhina. n. Covering; throw or cast net.

'ū.hini. 1. n. Long-horn grasshopper (Tettigoniidae); cricket (Grillidae); locust (Mat. 3.4). *'Ūhini pua,* young *'ūhini,* especially before wing development. 2. vs. Fine, weblike, tapering into a fine point; slender. 3. Short for *'uhinipili 1–3.* 4. n. Carob, an evergreen *(Ceratonia siliqua).* Ni'ihau.

'ū.hini 'ake.lika (akerida). n. Grasshopper. (Oihk. 11.22.) (Gr. *akrida.*)

'ū.hini hulu.hulu. n. Cankerworm. (Ioela 1.4.) *Lit.,* hairy grasshopper.

'ū.hini hulu 'ole. n. Palmer worm, caterpillar. (Ioela 1.4.) *Lit.,* hairless grasshopper.

uhi Ni'i.hau. n. A variety of yam, the tuber with pink flesh; grown in Kona, Hawai'i (HP 168.)

'ū.hini lele. n. Beetle, cricket. (Oihk. 11.22.) *Lit.,* flying grasshopper.

'ū.hini pa'a.wela. n. An edible locust. *Lit.,* seared locust.

'uhini.pili. 1. n. Same as *'unihipili.* 2. vs. Thin, tapering, feeble, weak. 3. vs. Flexed position in which Hawaiians were often buried.

'ū.hini pua. n. Young *'ūhini* (locusts) as found on *'ilima* bushes; they were eaten.

'ū.hini wā.wae hā. n. Bald locust. (Oihk. 11.22.) *Lit.,* four-legged grasshopper.

uhinu. Same as *hinu, hinuhinu.*

uhi 'ō.ni'o.ni'o. Same as *uhi kalakoa.*

uhi.pa'a. n. Mother-of-pearl hook that might be used at any time of day. *Lit.,* solid cover.

uhi pā.kau.kau. n. Tablecloth.

uhi pela. n. Bed sheet, mattress cover.

uhi poni. n. A variety of yam, the tuber with red skin and red and white flesh; grown on the island of Hawai'i. (HP 169.)

uhi.pū. n. Apoplexy. *Rare.*

uhi pū.ku'i. n. Hub cap.

uhi 'uala. n. A variety of yam, the tuber like a sweet potato; grown on the island of Hawai'i. (HP 169.)

'ūhī.'ūhā. vi. Sonorous puffing and blowing sounds, as accompanying the surging of volcanic fires; to puff or blow thus; shish-shish. See as *, nome.*

uhi.uhi. 1. Redup. of *uhi 1.* (PPN *'ufi'ufi.*) 2. n. An endemic legume *(Mezoneuron kauaiense),* a tree with pink or red flowers and thin, broad, winged pods (Neal 435). The wood is hard and heavy and formerly was used for *hōlua* (sleds), spears, digging sticks, and house construction. Also *kawa'ū, kea, kolomona,* and the weedy herb *Phaseolus lathyroides* (Niihau). **ho'o.uhi.-uhi.** To prepare *uhiuhi* wood for house posts (GP 8).

'uhī.'uhī. nvi. Whine, as of a child; to whine.

uhi 'ula, uhi 'ula.'ula. n. A yam, probably the same as *uhi lehua.*

uhi.wai. n. 1. Heavy fog, mist. *Lit.,* water covering. *Nae iki 'Iao i ka uhiwai,* [Mount] 'Iao is barely breathing in the heavy mist [one in dire distress]. 2. Type of tapa.

uho.ho'i. Plural of *hoho'i.*

uho'i. Plural of *ho'i,* to leave.

'uhola. Same as *hola,* to unfold, spread. *Fig.,* receptive and open, as the mind. Cf. *ma'i uhola.*

uhole. Plural of *hole;* to strip, as tough skin of fish such as *manini, humuhumu.*

uholo. Plural of *holo,* to run. *'O ka uholo ihola nō ia ā nalowale loa,* they hurried off and disappeared.

uhoni. Plural of *honi.*

uhu. 1. n. The parrot fishes, of which *Scarus perspicillatus* is among the most abundant and largest; *uhu* are plant eaters, the teeth are strong and beaklike, well fitted for clipping off food from coral. The name may be qualified by the terms *a'a, 'āhiuhiu, 'ahu 'ula* or *'ula, 'ele'ele, halahala, kuwalakai* or *pālukaluka, lā uli, pānoa, piko 'ula,* and *uliuli.* Names of growth stages are '*ōhua* (very young), *pānuhu* or *pōnuhunuhu* (medium), and *uhu* (mature). Variant names are *male* and '*ōmale* for a young stage. The colors of this fish are so pretty that it is sometimes compared to a sweetheart: *Momomi wale ku'u 'ono i ka uhu mā'alo i ku'u maka*, my craving makes my mouth water for the parrotfish passing before my eyes. *Uhu-māka'ika'i* (FS 45), name of a fish killed in the Kawelo legend, said to be a designation for all *uhu; lit.*, traveling *uhu*, perhaps so called because they follow one another in line. '*A 'ohe e loa'a, he uhu pakelo*, not to be caught, a slippery parrot fish [a wily person]. (PPN *'ufu*.) **2.** n. A variety of sugar cane. **3.** vt. To bolt, break away, as a horse; to pull, strain, chafe under restraint; willful, headstrong. *Uhu ka mana'o e hele*, straining, frantic to go. Also *lōuhu*.

'**uhū.** vi, interj. To sigh, moan, groan; to grunt as a pig (often used after *kani*); interj. of scorn (Kel. 20), huh! *Kani 'uhū a'e ana i ke aloha 'ole o ku'u kaikamahine*, sighing over the heartlessness of my daughter.

uhu.ao. Rare var. of *'uao.*

-uhuhī, ho'o.uhu.hī. To tease, annoy, vex, nag. *Rare.*

uhuki. Same as *huhuki*. (Am. 9.15.)

'**uhuku.** Var. of *'ōhuku.*

Uhu-mā.ka'i.ka'i. Same as *Ka-uhu-māka'ika'i.*

Uhu-maka.li'i. n. A stroke in *lua* fighting.

uhu pā.kali. n. An *uhu* fish used as a decoy. *Fig.*, to deceive.

uhu pā.nuhu.nuhu. n. Same as *pānuhunuhu.*

'**uhū.'uhū.** Redup. of *'uhū*; to neigh (Ier. 8.16), bray, cough, hem; to hawk, as in clearing the throat.

ui. **1.** nv. To ask, question, appeal, turn to for help or advice, query; question, catechism. *He ui, a he nīnau kēia* (chant), a query, a question this. **ho'o.ui.** To cause a question to be asked, to ask. (PPN *'ui*.) **2.** v. To stir up, activate. *Rare.* **ho'o.ui** To bestir, hurry, surge. *Rare.* **3.** Rare var. of *uhi 1.*

ūi. interj. Halloo.

u'i. nvs. Youthful, youthfully stalwart, heroic, handsome, pretty, beautiful, vigorous, youth; youthful vigor and beauty; youthful hero, beautiful young woman. *Ka wā u'i*, youth; age of youthful vigor, grace, and beauty; age of greatest physical beauty. *Nā po'e u'i*, young people, as in the late teens and early twenties. **ho'o.u'i.** To beautify, make beautiful.

'**ui.** Var. spelling of *'uwī 1, 2.*

uia. n. A variety of taro. (HP 34.)

uifi. n. Whiff. *Eng.*

ui.hā. vs. Weary, tired, bored, tiresome, burdensome.

'**uiki, 'uwiki. 1.** vi. To glimmer, especially of a light through a hole, crack, or narrow opening; to twinkle faintly; the opening through which light shines. **hō.'uiki.** To open a crack or sliver; to cause to gleam. *Hō'uiki mai i ka maka*, to open the eyes just a slit. **2.** n. Piping, as used for dress trimming. **3.** n. Wick. *Eng.* **4.** n. Whist. *Eng.*

ui kula Sā.bati. n. Sunday school catechism.

uila, uwila. nvs. Lightning, electricity; electric. *Ka'a uila*, electric bus. *Kapuahi uila*, electric stove. *Kukui uila*, electric light. *He nuku uila*, a lightning snout [an incessant talker]. **ho'o.uila, hō.'uila.** To flash, as lightning. (PPN *'uhila*.)

ui.lani. vs. To chafe under control, fret; restless, irritated by restraint; constantly seeking pleasure, spirited, flighty. *Uilani noho'i ka na'au*, the mind is restless.

uilo. n. Square-shaped braid, as in *lei palaoa* cord.

'**u'ina. 1.** nvi. Sharp report, as crack of a pistol; to crack, snap, crackle, creak (as joints); to make a splashing sound. Cf. *'a'ina, 'e'e'ina, pāpa'a'ina.* '*U'ina ka pu'u*, sound of swallowing. '*U'ina pōhaku a Kāne*, crackling rocks of Kāne [thunder]. *He 'u'ina, he nākolo ka wai o Nā-molo-kama* (song), the water of Nā-molo-kama makes a splashing and rustling sound. (PCP *ku(u)-kina*.) **2.** n. Glottal stop.

'**u'ina.kolo.** nvi. Rustle, roar; to rustle (*'u'ina* and *nākolo*). *I ka ua nui hō'eha 'ili, i ka wai 'u'inakolo*, in

the rain whose cold penetrates the skin with the rumble of roaring water.

uini.hapa. Var. spelling of *winihapa*, brick.

ui.ui. Redup. of *ui 1, 2.* **ho'o.ui.ui.** Caus/sim. *Ho'ola'i nā manu ke 'ike i ka wai ho'ouiui kino* (chant), the birds are calmed when they see the liquid that excites the body.

-u'iu'i. ho'o.u'i.u'i. To beautify, make attractive. *Mea ho'ou'iu'i*, cosmetics.

'**uī.'uī.** Var. spelling of *'uwī'uwī.*

'**ui.'uiki, 'uwi'uwiki.** Redup. of *'uiki 1.*

ui.ui.lani. Redup. of *uilani.*

'**u'i.'u'ina.** Redup. of *'u'ina.*

'**uiwi.** n. A small endemic undershrub *(Hedyotis cookiana)* with narrow leaves and slender branches. Cf. *kopa.*

uka. loc. n. Inland, upland, towards the mountain, shoreward (if at sea); shore, uplands (often preceded by the particles *i, ma-* [usually written *mauka*], or *o*). (Gram. 8.6.) *Uwā 'o uka* (FS 259), those inland shouted. *Kō uka*, those belonging to the uplands; mountain folk. *Hele i uka*, go inland; go ashore [if at sea]. *Uka manu*, uplands where birds are found. (PPN *'uta*.)

-uka. Cf. *ukana*. **ho'o.uka. (a)** To load, as cargo or freight; to put on, as gear on a horse; to send, as a letter (2 Sam. 11.14). *Ho'ouka pū nā wāwae*, to cross the legs. (PPN *uta*.) **(b)** To rush on, as in battle; to attack, raid. *Ho'ouka kaua*, to attack, battle, wage a military campaign. Cf. *kahua ho'ouka.*

'**uka. 1.** n. Wrinkles. **2.** vs. Good-for-nothing, worthless. Cf. *'ala'uka, ma'uka.*

'**ukā.** interj. A word used in calling hogs; to gobble noisily, as a pig; to eat loudly, smack. *Mai, mai, 'ukā, 'ukā*, come, come, gobble, gobble [calling pigs].

uka'a.wale. Plural of *ka'awale.*

'**ū.ka'e.** vs. Having no teeth; sloppy and smeary in eating, as one without teeth. Cf. *mūka'e.*

ū.kā.kā. n. Female of '*ō'ō* and '*ō'ū*, birds.

'**uka.kai.** Same as *'u'ulukai.*

uka lā.'au. n. Forested uplands.

ukale.kale. vs. Watery, fluid. *Fig.*, deceitful.

ukali. 1. nvt. To follow, come after, succeed, attend, accompany, escort; follower, attendant, complement; as in grammar; reserve. *Ukali o ke kia'āina*, governor's aide. *Lede ukali*, lady in waiting. *Ali'i ukali* (FS 163), attendant chief. *Nā ukali pa'a male*, attendants of a bridal couple. *Nā ali'i koa ukali*, reserve officers. **ho'o.ukali.** To cause, pretend, or try to follow, accompany, attend, etc. **2.** *(Cap.)* Same as *Ukali-ali'i.*

Ukali-ali'i. n. The planet Mercury. *Lit.*, following the chief [i.e., the sun].

ukali ha'i.'ano. n. Adjective complement.

ukali ha'i.inoa. n. Noun complement.

ukamu. n. Oakum. *Eng.*

ukana. n. Baggage, luggage, freight, cargo, supplies. *Ka'a ukana*, baggage car, baggage or freight vehicle. *Ke mālama nei au i ka ukana a ke aloha* (chant), I preserve the love carried [by me]. **ho'o.ukana.** To bundle up, pack up, load, as freight. (PCP *utanga*.)

-ukauka. ho'o.ukauka. Redup. of *ho'ouka.* See *-uka.*

'**ukā.'ukā. 1.** Redup. of *'ukā.* **2.** v. Rolling up of waves. *Rare.*

ukau.kai. vs. Fat, feeble. *Rare.*

'**ukē. 1.** vi. To swing, sway, as breasts of a large-busted woman or as a pendulum. **2.** nvi. Sound of a thud, collision, tick, tap; to thud, tick, rap, tap. *Rare.* Cf. *kē.*

'**ū.ke'e.** vs. Twisted, crooked, as the mouth. **hō.'ū.ke'e.** To screw or twist the mouth to one side, as in disapproval or dislike.

'**ukeke. 1.** Same as *'ukekeke, 'akeke'e*, a bird. **2.** Same as *ha'ukeke*, to quiver. *Rare.*

'**ū.kē.kē.** nvt. A variety of musical bow, 40 to 60 cm long and about 4 cm wide, with two or commonly three strings drawn through holes at one end. The strings were strummed. According to Roberts (see Bibliography), the old experts made no sound with the vocal cords, but the mouth cavity acted as a resonance chamber. The resulting sound suggested speech and trained persons could understand. It was sometimes used for love making. To play the *'ūkēkē.* Cf. *nī'au kani.*

'ū.kē.kē hahau. n. Jew's-harp. *Lit.,* striking musical bow.

'ū.kē.kē hao. n. Jew's-harp. *Lit.,* metal musical bow.

uke.keke. n. Same as *'ukeke, 'akeke'e,* a bird.

'ū.kele. nvs. Muddy; oily; slush. *Lepo 'ūkele,* mud. *Waha 'ūkele,* drooling mouth.

'ū.kele.kele. Redup. of *'ūkele.*

'ukemu. Same as *kemu 1,* to absorb, consume.

'ukeni. n. Small change. *Eng. Ka'ū.*

'ukē.'ukē. Redup. of *'ukē 1, 2. 'Ukē'ukē a'ela ka ho'o-kele i kāna hoe ma ka 'ao'ao o ka wa'a,* the steerer rapped his paddle on the side of the canoe.

'uke'u.kele. Redup. of *'ūkele.*

uki. Same as *ukiuki. Rare.* **ho'o.uki.** Same as *ho'ouki-uki. Rare.*

'uki. n. Coarse native sedges of several genera. See *'ahaniu.*

'ukī. n. An unpleasant odor, as halitosis. *Rare.*

'ū.kī. Same as *'uwī,* to wring.

'uki haole. n. All cultivated forms of *Gladiolus (*as *G. blandus),* ornamental plants in the iris family, with sword-shaped leaves and one-sided sprays of large colorful flowers. (Neal 235.)

'ū.kihi. 1. nvi. Cold sores, any sores about the corners *(kihi)* of the mouth; to have such. *Fig.,* to talk too much. 2. n. Name of a bird (no data). (KL line 314.)

'ukiki. 1. vs. Thin, puny, small, stunted, sickly. Cf. *'aki-ki, hukiki.* 2. Same as *'ūkīkiki 1.*

uki.ki'i. vt. To fetch, of several. Cf. *ki'i,* to fetch.

'ū.kī.kiki. 1. n. Early stage of both *'ōpakapaka* and *'ula-'ula,* fish, less than 30 cm long. Also *'akiki, kiki, ko'i, 'ukiki.* 2. Redup. of *'ukiki 1.*

uki.one. n. Extreme unction.

'ū.kiu. 1. Same as *'ūkiukiu.* 2. *(Cap.)* nvi. Name of a chilly north wind associated with Maka-wao, Maui; to blow, of this wind. 3. Same as *'uki'ukiu 1.*

uki.uki. nvt. Anger, resentment (FS 129); angry, annoyed, offended, vexed, displeased (2 Sam. 6.8), irritated, peeved; to hate (Kin. 50.15); fierce, adverse, as a wind; petulant. **ho'o.uki.uki.** To provoke, offend, displease, irritate. (PCP *utiuti.*)

'uki.'uki. n. *Dianella sandwicensis,* a native member of the lily family, with a short stem and long, narrow leaves, from among which arises a cluster of white or bluish flowers. The attractive fruits are blue, long-persistent berries formerly used to dye tapa. (Neal 191–2.)

'ukī.'ukī. Redup. of *'ukī.*

'Ū.kiu.kiu. n. Perhaps the same as *'Ūkiu,* but a rain associated with Hikilei, Kaua'i. (For. 6:454.)

'ūki'u.kiu, 'ū.kiu.kiu. 1. n. Broken *kukui* nut shells, as after the kernel has been extracted. Also *'ākiu.* 2. Same as *palakiu,* rotted. 3. *(Cap.)* n. Diminutive *'Ūkiu* wind; to blow gently, as this wind. *Māewa ana ka 'Ūkiukiu o Honokoa* (For. 5:57), the gentle breeze of Honokoa flutters.

ū.kō. vs. Fulfilled. *Fig.,* pregnant. See *pua'a ūkō* and Gram. 6.3.2.

'uko. n. Use (often used with *'ole*). *Eng. Hana 'uko 'ole* (For. 5:521), useless, improper, unseemly activity. *Na'u e mālama i kēia? I ka 'uko!* May I keep this? Of what use is it!

uko.kole. 1. vs. Sore, inflamed, as eyes. 2. Same as *mū-'okole,* to stop budding. *Rare.*

uko.komo. vi. To enter together. See *komo.*

ukole. Same as *kole,* a fish.

ukole.kole. Same as *ukokole 1, 2.*

uko'o. n. A human sacrifice or pig substitute, as made after a chief was a victim of sorcery, in order to protect the living.

'uko 'ole. vs. Useless, of no use.

uku. 1. nvt. Pay, payment, wages, fee, fare, toll, commission, reward, recompense, compensation, remit-

tance, tuition, prize, fine, tax, installment, tribute; to pay, remunerate, compensate, repay, revenge. Many types of *uku* are listed below. *Na'u e uku,* I'll pay; my treat. *Kou uku,* your pay, wages (paid to you). *Kāu uku,* your pay, wages (paid to someone else). *Ka hila-hila i kāna uku 'ole e uku ai iā 'Ai-kanaka* (FS 103), shame for his lack of reward for recompensing 'Ai-kanaka. **ho'o.uku.** To make someone pay; to levy a tax, fine, assess, charge. (PPN *utu.*) 2. n. A deep-sea snapper *(Aprion virescens).* (Probably PPN *'utu.*)

uku-. See *ukuhi.* (PPN *'utu.*)

'uku. 1. n. Louse, flea. (PPN *kutu.*) 2. vs. Small, tiny (less used than *'u'uku*).

uku 'ē.kena (egena). n. Agent's fee, commission.

'uku.'ele. n. Name given for a sea creature (no data).

uku hala. nv. Penalty for wrongdoing; to pay for wrong done, as damages. Sugar cane, as *halāli'i,* used in ceremonies for the remission of sins might be so called.

uku hana. nv. Wages, salary, pay for work; to pay wages.

uku hapa. nv. Installment payment; to pay in part.

ukuhi. vt. To pour out, dip, as water; to wean, as a child (*-hi* is a transitivizer and a reflex of PPN *-fi;* cf. Tongan *'utu,* to pour, and Gram. 6.6.4). *'O ka mea ukuhi ka i 'ike i ka lepo o ka wai, 'o ka mea inu 'a'ole 'oia i 'ike,* he who dips is the one who knows how dirty the water is, but he who drinks does not. (PPN *'utufi.*)

uku.hia. Pas/imp. of *ukuhi.*

uku.hina. n. A pouring out, dipping, weaning.

'uku hipa. n. Tick, mite (Acari).

uku ho'ēmi. n. Cheap or reduced price, discount.

uku ho'o.mau. n. Pension, alimony. *Lit.,* permanent pay.

uku ho'o.pa'a. n. Premium, as insurance; down payment, deposit. *Lit.,* payment [to] solidify.

uku ho'o.pa'i. n. Fine, forfeit.

uku ho'o.pane'e. nvt. Interest, usury; to pay interest.

uku ka'a. n. Carfare, transportation charge.

'uku kai. n. A sand hopper, probably an amphipod. Also *mahiki.*

uku kā.ko'o. n. Subsidy, monetary aid, grant-in-aid.

'uku kapa. n. Body louse *(Pediculus humanus humanus). Lit.,* tapa louse.

uku kau.lele. n. Interest on principal, premium, extra or overtime pay. *Lit.,* payment added on. *Me kō lākou ho'ouku kaulele pū 'ia he 10 keneta o ke dālā,* together with interest of ten cents a dollar.

uku keu. n. Extra pay, bonus, left-over pay.

uku kī.pē. nv. Bribe, to bribe.

uku ko'a.ko'a. n. Coral polyp.

uku komo. n. Entrance fee.

uku komo.kina. n. Commission (pay).

ū.kū.kua. vs. Besieged, pressed with work, crowded.

uku.kuhi. Redup. of *ukuhi.*

uku kū.'ike. n. Cash payment.

uku kula. n. School tuition.

uku kū.mau. n. Customary or usual fees; dues, taxes.

uku kuwala. n. Interest payment, bounty.

'uku lā.'au. n. Wood-eating beetle.

uku lawe.lawe. n. Tip, gratuity, service charge. *Lit.,* service pay.

uku leka, uku leta. n. Postage, postage stamp.

'uku.lele. n. Ukulele. *Lit.,* leaping flea, probably from the Hawaiian-nickname of Edward Purvis, who was small and quick and who popularized the instrument brought to Hawai'i by the Portuguese in 1879. (Elbert and Knowlton, 1957.)

'uku lele. n. Flea (Siphonaptera). *'A'ohe 'uku lele nāna i 'aki,* not a flea to bite [perfect comfort].

'uku li'i. nvs. Tiny, small, petite; wee; small flea or louse.

uku li'i.li'i. n. Installment payment, small payment.

'uku limu. n. Sand hopper, an amphipod. *Lit.,* seaweed bug.

'uku lio. n. Bed bug *(Cimex lectularius). Lit.,* horse louse.

uku maka.hiki. n. Annual payment or salary, annuity.

uku makana. n. Tip; gift payment, bonus.

uku male (mare). n. Dowry; marriage fee, as to the minister. *Lit.*, marriage payment.

uku manawa. nvi. Installment payment; to pay on time.

uku moku. n. Steamship fare.

uku.pa'a. Same as *ukupau.*

uku palu. n. A variety of *uku*, a fish. *Lit.*, soft *uku.*

uku pā.na'i. nvt. Refund, redemption, ransom, reward; to redeem, refund.

uku pane'e. Same as *uku ho'opane'e.*

'uku papa. n. Crab louse *(Phthirus pubis). Lit.*, surface louse.

uku.pau. nvt. Piece labor, pay by the job rather than according to time, as on sugar plantations; used in pidgin for any work that everyone should pitch in gladly to finish; contract labor. *Lit.*, finished pay.

'uku pepa. n. Book louse *(Atropus divinatoria). Lit.*, paper louse.

uku pohō. nvt. Damages; to pay damages.

'uku po'o. n. Head louse *(Pediculus humanus capitus).*

'uku pua'a. n. Pig louse *(Haematopinus suis).*

'uku.'uku. Same as *'u'uku.*

uku.wai. n. **1.** Place in the grass house where host and guests visited, between the sleeping place and the door. **2.** Name for that portion of a canoe between forward and after outrigger booms.

ula. **1.** n. Spiny lobster *(Panulirus marginatus* and *P. penicillatus).* Varieties are qualified by the terms *hiwa, koa'e,* and *poni.* (PPN *'ura.)* **2.** nvi. A flame; to flame, blaze.

'ula. **1.** nvi. Red, scarlet; brown, as skin of Hawaiians; to appear red. *Pi'i ka 'ula,* to blush, flush. *A 'ula! 'Ula ka maka!* Red! Red-eyed! [a rude remark, often said while drawing down an eyelid, a way of wishing ill luck]. Cf. *'ula'ula.* **hō.'ula.** To redden, make red. (PPN *kula.)* **2.** n. Short for *koa'e 'ula,* red-tailed tropic bird. **3.** nvs. Sacred; sacredness; regal, royal (probably so called because red was a sacred color). Cf. *'aha 'ula, 'ūlāleo. Ka makani 'ula,* the sacred spirit. **4.** n. Blood. *He 'ula waiwai,* blood of great value, as royal blood. **5.** n. Agate. (Puk. 30.12.) **6.** Same as *'ula 'ai hāwane.* **7.** n. A ringing in the ears, as due to rising in altitude, believed by some to be a sign that one is being talked of. *Ke kani mai nei ka 'ula o ko'u pepeiao,* [I] hear my ear ringing. **8.** n. Ghost, spirit. Cf. *'ūlāleo. Kapua'i-ka-'ula* (O'ahu place name), footprint [of] spirits.

'ula'a. Var. of *hula'a, kula'a. He hina nō ka 'a'ali'i kū makani, he 'ula'a pū me ka lepo,* the wind-resisting *'a'ali'i* falls, [but] is uprooted together with the dirt [said of a strong warrior].

ula ahi. n. Fire flames.

'ulaa.hiwa. Same as *'ula hiwa.*

'ula-'ai-hā.wane. n. A small red Hawaiian honey creeper, with black crown, wings and tail and gray neck *(Ciridops anna),* formerly endemic to the island of Hawai'i, probably now extinct. *Lit.*, red bird eating *hāwane* fruit.

'ula ali'i. n. Chiefly blood.

'ulae. n. Lizard fishes of the family Synodontidae, *Synodus* spp., *Saurida gracilis,* common reef fishes. Varieties are qualified by the terms *niho 'ā, 'ula,* and *uli.*

'ula.hea. vs. Faded red.

ulā.heo. To appear and disappear quickly, as steam. *Rare.*

'ula hiwa. nvs. Purplish red, dark red, as of a Rhode Island Red chicken; a red cock; formerly, a black cock with red neck feathers and red rump feathers. See ex., *uakea 2.*

ulaia. Same as *'ūlala.*

'Ula-ka-maka-iā-Kui.kui-pahu. n. A stroke in *lua* fighting. Cf. *'ula 1.*

'ula kī.na'u. nvs. Red streaked or dotted with dark, said of red feathers and a type of red feather cloak; to be such.

ulako.lako. Plural of *lakolako.*

'ū.lala. vs. Crazy, mad, demented, harmlessly deranged,

silly. **ho'ū.lala.** To behave as one crazy; to cause craziness.

'ula lele. n. Disembodied spirit. *Fig.*, esteemed favorite.

'Ula-lena. n. A reddish-hued rain associated with Ha'ikū, Maui, and Mt. Ka'ala, O'ahu. Also a wind at Pi'iholo, Maui (Nak. 68). *Kapu ka luna o Ka'ala i ka ua 'Ula-lena* (chant), the uplands of Ka'ala mountain are sacred with the red-yellow rain.

'ula lena. nvs. Yellowish-red.

'ū.lā.leo. n. An intense emotional appeal to the gods, as in chant; a voice from the spirits. *Eia nō ka 'ula lā, he 'ūlāleo, he kānaenae aloha iā 'oe, ē Laka* (chant), here is a sacred thing, a calling appeal, a chant of affection for you, O Laka. See *inoa 'ūlāleo.*

'ulā.li'i. n. **1.** Measles; red spots of measles. **2.** Dotted swiss or other cloth with red spots; red spots.

'ula mā.ku'e. nvs. Dark or purplish red.

ulana. **1.** vt. To plait, weave, knit, braid; plaiting, weaving. Also *unala, nala, unana. Mea ulana 'ia,* plaited or woven material, textile. *Mea ulana lole,* weaver (Isa. 38.12), loom. (PPN *langa.)* **2.** vs. Still, calm. Cf. *lana 1.* **3.** nvt. Prophecy of a seer *(kilokilo);* to prophesy.

'ula.'ō.koko. vs. Blood-red.

'ula.pa'a. n. A girl of preadolescent age prior to the time of menstruation. *Lit.*, held redness. Cf. *pu'upa'a.*

'ula palani. vs. A bright-red percale; a vivid red, brandy red.

ula pā.papa. n. A gray crayfish *(Parribacus antarcticus). Lit.*, flat *ula.*

'ula.'ula. **1.** Redup. of *'ula 1;* bay, as a horse. *'Ula'ula o ke ahi,* the red of fire; *fig.*, a flush of intoxication, newly distilled liquor. *'Ili 'ula'ula a na'au 'ula'ula,* venom-tongued and heart filled with hate. **hō.'ula.'ula.** To redden, make red. *Mea hō'ula'ula lehelehe,* lipstick. *Mea hō'ula'ula papālina,* rouge. (PPN *kulakula.)* **2.** n. Various red snappers of the family Lutjanidae as *Etelis marshi.* Varieties are qualified by the terms *hiwa, koa'e* (tropic bird, perhaps named because of the long streamer on the fish's tail thought to resemble the bird), *maoli, 'ōpūlauoho.* **3.** n. A native variety of taro, with red or purple petioles, small leaf blades with purple *piko,* reddish flowers, the corms used for both poi and table taro, grown in wetland and upland culture. (Whitney 50–52.) *'Ula'ula* may be qualified by the terms *kumu, moano,* and *poni.* **4.** The cardinal, Kentucky cardinal *(Cardinalis cardinalis),* established in about 1930. **5.** n. Blood. **6.** n. A red tapa. **7.** n. A variety of sugar cane. (HP 222, 225.)

'ula'u.la'a. Redup. of *'ula'a.*

'ula.'ula hā.'ula, hā.'ula.'ula. nvs. Dark red, formerly said of dark bay horses.

'ula.'ula.ila. n. A child whose sire was a chief and whose mother a commoner. *Lit.*, birthmark red.

-'ula'ula lehelehe. See *'ula'ula 1.*

-'ula'ula papālina. See *'ula'ula 1.*

ula.wai'a. vt. To fish, of many persons or often.

'ula waina. nvs. Wine-red.

'ula wena. nvs. A glowing red, as from fire.

'ula weo. nvs. Dark-red.

ule. **1.** n. Penis. For imaginative compounds see *'a'awa 1, 'aweule, ulehala, ulehole, ulepa'a, ulepua'a, ule'ulu. Kū ka ule, he'e ka laho,* the penis is upright, the scrotum runs away [refers to breadfruit: when the blossom *(pōule)* appears erect, there will soon be fruit. (PPN *ule.)* **2.** n. Tenon for a mortise; pointed end of a post which enters the crotch of a rafter (also called *ma'i kāne).* **ho'o.ule.** To form a tenon or post for the crotch of a rafter. **3.** v. To hang.

ule.hala. n. Aerial pandanus roots. Also *uleule hala.*

ulehe. Same as *ulehelehe.*

ulehe.lehe. vs. Unbound, unfastened, not tied, as a bundle; open, as a wound.

ule.hihi. Same as *uhi,* yam. *Rare.*

ule hilo. n. Gonorrhea.

ule.hole. n. Channel markers in a harbor.

ule hole. n. Pulled back penis (an insulting epithet for men).

ulei. Same as *hulei. Ulei 'ia akula ua paukū laholio nei,* this rubber was stretched.

'ū.lei. n. **1.** A native spreading shrub *(Osteomeles anthyllidifolia),* closely allied to other species found on some other islands of the Pacific. It has compound leaves, small white roselike flowers, small round white fruits. The wood is tough and formerly was used for digging sticks, fish spears, and the *'ūkēkē* (musical bow). (Neal 387.) Also *eluehe.* **2.** Digging stick of *'ūlei* wood. See ex., *wali.*

ule kahe. n. Subincised or circumcised penis. See *kahe ule.*

ulele. 1. nvi. To leap at, get into action, do quickly, do at once; one moving swiftly. *He ulele Kū mai ka lani* (For. 4:395), Kū moving swiftly from the heavens. **2.** vt. To set, as type. *Nā keiki ulele kēpau,* the typesetter boys.

ule.'ohi'u. n. A type of sugar cane, unknown in 1978, once used as a salve (For. 5:585); perhaps the same as *'āwela melemele* and *uluhui.* (HP 225.)

ule.pa'a. nvs. A male who has not known a woman; not to have or have had relations with a woman. *Lit.,* bound penis.

'ū.lepe. 1. n. Harelip. Also *kūlepe.* **2.** vi. Erect, as a cock's comb; to stand erect; to bristle with anger.

ule.pua'a. Same as *wilipua'a. Lit.,* pig penis.

'uleu. Same as *'eleu. E wiki mai 'oe e 'uleu* (song), hurry and be spry.

ule.ule. 1. vs. Pendulous, hanging. (PCP *uleule.*) **2.** n. Sty, as on the edge of the eyelid.

ule.ule hala. Same as *ule hala.*

'uleu.lele. vs. Spry, active, nimble. *Rare.*

'ule'u.leu. Redup. of *'uleu. Ke 'ule'uleu nei nā manu inu wai lehua o Pana-'ewa* (song), the birds that sip *lehua* honey at Pana-'ewa are lively now.

ule.'ulu. n. Male breadfruit flower. *Lit.,* breadfruit penis. Also *pōule* and *pō'ulu.*

uli. 1. nvs. Any dark color, including the deep blue of the sea, the ordinary green of vegetation, and the dark of black clouds; the black-and-blue of a bruise. Some song composers avoid this word because connotations of evil or misfortune are associated with darkness and because Uli is a goddess of sorcery (see *uli 2*). Also *uli-uli. Kai uli,* the deep blue sea. *Nuku uli,* dark lips. *Nā pali uli,* the green cliffs. *Uli māhole ka 'ili* (song), the skin is bruised black-and-blue. *Uli ka maka,* a black eye. **ho'o.uli.** To darken, to make blue, green, etc.; to make the skin black and blue; to bruise. (PPN *'uli.*) **2.** *(Cap.)* n. Name of a goddess of sorcery, said to have come from Kahiki. See HM 574, PH 144-7. *E Uli ē, ē Uli nānā pono, ē Uli nānā hewa, ē Uli i uka, ē Uli i kai* (prayer), O Uli, O Uli observe good, O Uli observe evil, O Uli inland, O Uli seaward. *'O 'oe kā ia, ē ka lāuli pali o Uli* (chant by Hi'iaka), it is you then, O cliff darkness of Uli. **3.** n. Early stage in the development of a foetus, as the body begins to form. **4.** n. Name given by Malo for subjects of the chief; Emerson says they are black-haired persons. (Malo 194, 201.) **5.** nvt. To steer; steersman. *Uli hou 'o 'Iwa* (For. 5:287), 'Iwa again steered. (PPN *'uli.*) **6.** n. Short for *'ōuli,* omen. *'O ka nānā uli, 'o ka nānā 'ana nō ia i nā uli o ke kanaka, inā he kanaka waiwai, a inā he kanaka 'ilihune* (For. 6:85), the study of omens, is a study of the omens regarding a person, whether [he will become] a person of wealth or a poor person. **7.** n. Crowing of a cock. *Rare.* **8.** n. Type of sweet potato (no data). (For. 5:664-5.)

'ulī. vi. To rattle, especially of seeds in the *'ulī'ulī,* gourds; to gurgle.

ulia. nvs. Accident; sudden; to come upon suddenly. *Ulia ka'a,* auto accident. *Ulia pōpilikia,* emergency. *He ulia pōmaika'i,* sudden good fortune. *He ulia pō'ino,* sudden trouble, unfortunate accident. (PPN *ulia.*)

uli.'eo. nvs. Fitness, aptitude; preparedness, as for running. *Rare.*

ulihi. 1. n. A small endemic shrub *(Phyllostegia glabra* and varieties), in the mint family. Leaves are ovate, 7

to 15 cm long; flowers are small, white, tubular, abundant, in racemes. **2.** vs. Feebleness, of old age. *Rare.*

'ū.li'i. vs. Tiny, wee, petite.

'ū.lika. vs. Soft, sticky, claylike, glutinous, adhesive, gluey. *Kalo 'ūlika,* taro that is so glutinous, especially when cold, that it takes much water to grind it by machine, as of the delicious *kāī* taro.

'ū.lika.lika. Redup. of *'ūlika. Lepo 'ūlikalika,* clay. Cf. *pālolo.*

uli koa. Bruises or wounds of a warrior.

'ū.lili. 1. nv. Wandering tattler *(Heteroscelus incanum),* a slender regular winter migrant to Hawai'i, slaty above and white with dusky bars and streaks beneath. It breeds in Alaska and the Yukon. The cry of the bird; to cry thus. **ho'ū.lili.** To act like the tattler bird. (PPN *ku(u)lili.*) **2.** n. Police whistle; ancient type of bamboo whistle; sound of these whistles. The whistles are said to be named for the cry of the tattler. **3.** n. A bamboo tube used for blowing on a fire; to use this tube. **4.** n. A musical instrument consisting of three gourds pierced by a stick; a whirring sound is made by pulling a string, thus twirling the gourds. **5.** n. Hula step similar to *'uwehe,* except that only one heel at a time is raised; this step has a distinctive beat. **6.** Same as *hū,* small gourd used as a spinning top; to spin this top. **7.** vs. Steep, as a mountain road. **8.** vs. Firm. *Kaula 'ūlili,* strengthening cords holding the canoe cover (*'ahu uhi wa'a)* in place. See *wai 'ūlili.* **9.** n. A religious ceremony in *'anā'anā,* sorcery. **10.** Var. of *hulili. Ku'u 'ia maila kekahi ānuenue i 'ūlili 'ia* (Laie 581), let down a rainbow that sparkled. (PCP *kulili,* cf. Marquesan *ku'i'i.*) **11.** n. Poles separating bannisters, as on stairs; rails of *hōlua* sleds.

'ū.lili wā.wae. n. Flooring inside a *peleleu* canoe where paddlers might rest their feet.

Ulima, Urima. n. Urim. (Heb. or Eng.) (Puk. 28.30.)

'ū.lina. vs. Soft, rubbery, plastic. Cf. *papālina.*

'ū.lina.lina. Redup. of *'ūlina.*

uli.uli. 1. Same as *uli 1. He lole uliuli* (Puk. 25.4), blue clothing. *'Ili uliuli,* brown skin. *Uliuli mau,* evergreen. **ho'o.uli.uli.** Same as *ho'ouli.* **2.** n. A kind of rock from which adzes were made. (Malo 19.) **3.** *(Cap.)* n. Name of a star (no data).

'ulī.'ulī. nvi. A gourd rattle, containing seeds with colored feathers at the top, used for the *hula 'ulī'ulī* (at one time there were no feathers); to rattle. **hō.'ulī.'ulī.** To shake the *'ulī'ulī;* to rattle.

Uli.uli-ka-pali-o-Kahiki-nui. n. A stroke in *lua* fighting. *Lit.,* the cliffs of great Tahiti are green.

'ū.li'u.li'u. 1. Rare variants for *'ūlili 3, 7.* **2.** Same as *pū-'ulī'ulī,* a gourd.

'ū.lō.lohi. Same as *lohi,* slow. *Ua 'ūlōlohi loa kāna hele 'ana,* his going was very slow.

'ulono. nvt. To cry out, as a prayer or lamentation; such crying. *Ka 'ulono 'ana o ka po'e ha'aha'a* (Hal. 9.12), the cry of the humble.

'ulono.kū. n. A prayer as to a god not an *'aumakua,* family god.

ulu. 1. nvi. To grow, increase, spread; growth; increase or rising of the wind; to protect (PH 116, For. 6:474). Also *unu.* Cf. *mea ulu. Ka ulu o ka lā,* the rising of the sun. *Kai ulu,* sea at full tide. *Ulu ehuehu,* to grow fast, as a child. *Mauka 'oe e hele ai, ma ka ulu o ka makani* (PH 213), go inland where the wind blows. **ho'o.ulu.** To grow, sprout, propagate; to cause to increase, as the surf. Cf. *mea ho'oulu,* growth, crop. *Ho'oulu mea kanu,* horticulture. *Mea ho'oulu pilikia,* troublemaker, agitator. *Ho'oulu lāhui,* to increase and preserve the nation [said to be the aim of King Ka-lā-kaua]. *Pule ho'oulu 'āina,* prayer for the increased productivity of the land. **2.** vi. Possessed by a god; inspired by a spirit, god, ideal, person, as for artistic creation; stirred, excited; to enter in and inspire. Also *unu. Mana'o ulu wale,* a thought entered of its own accord, hence fancy, impulse, imagination. *E ulu, e ulu kini o ke akua, ulu ō Kāne me Kanaloa* (prayer), enter and inspire, may myr-

iads of spirits enter and inspire, including Kāne and Kanaloa. *Ua ulu a'e ia mamuli o ka mahele lua o ke ko'iko'i,* this occurred because of the division of the responsibility. **ho'o.ulu, ho.'ūlu.** To stir up, inspire, excite, taunt. *Pule ho'oulu,* prayer for inspiration. *Oli ho'oulu,* taunting chant, as before combat. *Ka ho'oulu hakakā,* stirring up fights. *Ho'oulu haunaele,* stirring up a mob, agitator. (PPN *huru.*) **3.** n. Grove (see *ulu kanu, Ulu-kou, ulu kukui, ulu lā'au, ulu niu*); assemblage, collection, or flock, as of stars *(ulu hōkū),* birds *(ulu manu),* ships *(ulu moku),* canoes *(u!u wa'a).* (PPN *'ulu.*) **4.** Same as the more common *uluulu 3.* **5.** nvt. Stick used in spreading hot oven stones; to spread the stones. **6.** n. Kind of tapa made at Wai-pi'o, Hawai'i; name of a quilt design. **7.** n. Center, as of a canoe or net. Cf. *uluna 3. Kīhele ia ulu,* bail out the center. **8.** n. A name used repeatedly in For. 5:703–9 for Ka-welo's warriors whose names begin with Ka-ulu (Ka-ulu-kauloko, Ka-ulu-kau-waho). *Ua po'e ulu nei* (For. 5:709), these *ulu* people. *Ka nui ulu,* the many warriors.
ulu-. See *uluna 1.* (PPN *'ulu.*)
'ulu. n. **1.** The breadfruit *(Artocarpus altilis),* a tree perhaps originating in Malaysia and distributed through tropical Asia and Polynesia. It belongs to the fig family, and is grown for its edible fruits, sometimes for ornament. The leaves are large, oblong, more or less lobed; fruits are round or oblong, weighing up to 4.5 kilos, when cooked tasting something like sweet potatoes. (Neal 302–4.) See ex., *pakī,* and saying *ule 1. 'Ulu hua i ka hāpapa,* breadfruit that bears fruit on the flats [of the famous Ni'ihau breadfruit growing in the sand dunes]. (PPN *kulu.*) **2.** Round, smooth stone as used in *'ulu maika* game; bowling ball; bell clapper; dice. *Ka iki 'ulu kēia o Kanēkina e kōkē ai nā pine,* a small [fellow] is this bowling ball of Kanēkina that knocks down the pins [boast of a small fellow who can do much]. **3.** Muscles in calf of leg. **4.** Name for *kōnane* stone.
ulua. 1. n. Certain species of crevalle, jack, or pompano, an important game fish and food item. Cf. *ulua aukea, ulua 'ele'ele,* and *pa'opa'o.* Unidentified *ulua* are qualified by the terms *kaha uli, kihikihi* (or *kihi* or *huli pū*), *lā uli, mahai, moha'i* (AP), *nuku momi, uli.* Growth stages are *pāpio* (or *pāpiopio), pā'ū'ū,* and *ulua,* the last attaining a length of 1.5 m and a weight of over 45 kilos. This fish was substituted for human sacrifices when the latter were not available, probably because of word magic and the meaning of *ulua 2.* Since an *ulua* replaces a man, *ulua* also means "man, sweetheart," especially in love songs (see ex., *wewehi).* *Huki i ka ulua,* pull in the *ulua; fig.,* get your man. *'A 'ole nō wau i mahu'i mua, e lilo ana 'oe i ulua na'u* (song), I never thought before that you'd be my sweetheart. (PPN *'ulua.*) **2.** Similar to *ulu 1, 2.*
ulu.'ā. Similar to *pā'ulu'ā.* Rare.
'ulua. 1. Same as *'ulu'ulu.* **ho'o.'ulua.** To assemble. **2.** Same as *'unua.*
ulua au.kea. n. A variety of *ulua,* probably *Caranx ignobilis,* one of the largest of *ulua.* Also *ulua kea.*
ulua 'ele.'ele. n. A variety of dark-skinned *ulua,* probably most commonly *Caranx melampygus.* Lit., black *ulua.*
ulu.ā.hewa. 1. nvs. Mania, delusion, craziness; deranged; somewhat crazy, sometimes believed due to possession by a spirit. **2.** nvi. Overgrowth; to grow wild and lush; bushy.
-ulu 'ai. ho'o.ulu 'ai. To grow food plants; a prayer to bless crops. *Heiau ho'oulu 'ai,* temple where first crops were offered. *Kahuna ho'oulu 'ai,* a priest who made such offerings, agricultural expert.
ulua kā.ni'o. Same as *ulua pa'opa'o.* Lit., striped *ulua.*
ulua kihi.kihi. n. A variety of *ulua, Alectis* sp.
ulua kū.kae.nalo. n. Probably a species of *'ōmilu,* a fish. Lit., beeswax *ulua.*
ulu.'ā.lana. n. Offering, especially as made to priests for them to offer to the gods.
ulua.lono. n. Genealogist in the *hale nauā.* (Malo 200.)

ulua.mahi. n. Officer in the *hale nauā.* (Malo 200.)
ulu.ā.o'a. nvi. **1.** Confusion, mob, disturbance, riot; tumult; gathered in excitement and confusion. *'A 'ole na ke Akua mai ka uluāo'a* (1 Kor. 14.33), confusion is not from God. **ho'o.ulu.ā.o'a.** To create confusion, excitement; to incite, stir up bedlam, cause trouble. **2.** Jungle; growing in wild profusion. *Uluāo'a ka lau o ke kāhili i kapa 'ia ai ka inoa o Hawai'i-loa* (kāhili chant), bristling is the top of the feather standard of royalty that is called by the name of Hawai'i-loa.
ulua 'ō.milu. n. Probably same as *'ōmilu,* a fish.
Ulu-au. n. A wind associated with Wai-ākea, Hawai'i (Nak. 53.)
Ulu-au-nui. n. Name of a stormy Maui wind.
ulua pa'o.pa'o. See *pa'opa'o.* Also *ulua kāni'o.*
ulu.eki. n. Brush, undergrowth, forest. Rare.
ulu.'eo. n. Name recorded by Thrum for a tree with hard wood.
ulu.ha'e.ha'e. Same as *ha'eha'e,* intense feeling.
ulu.haka. n. Elevated place in the high chief's house where those of rank might rest. (For. 6:418.)
'ulu.haku. vs. Lumpy, as of poi; knotty, bumpy, pimply. Cf. *'u'uluhaku.*
ulu hale. Same as *moku hale.* (Kam. 64:106.)
ulu hā.nau. vs. Of the same age group, contemporary. Lit., birth growth. *Ho'okahi o mākou ulu hānau,* we are of the same age.
ulu.ha'o. vs. Rough, jagged, as rocks. Cf. *hāo'eo'e.*
ulu.ha'o.'a. Same as *ulu ha'o.*
uluhe. n. All Hawaiian species of false staghorn fern (formerly known as *Gleichenia* spp., now listed under three genera: *Dicranopteris, Hicriopteris, Sticherus),* weedy, creeping, branching ferns, forming dense thickets. (Neal 9.) Also *uluhe.* (PPN *hulufe.*)
uluhe lau nui. n. A large species of false staghorn fern *(Hicriopteris pinnata,* formerly known as *Gleichenia glauca).*
ulu.hia. Pas/imp. of *ulu 1, 2. Po'e i uluhia e nā daimonio* (Mat. 4:24), people possessed by devils. (PPN *hurufia.*)
ulu hō.kū. n. Constellation.
ulu.hua. vs. Vexed, annoyed, discouraged, displeased (1 Nal. 20.43), harassed, weary, offended, angry. **ho'o.-ulu.hua.** To annoy, weary, vex.
ulu.hui. See *'āwela melemele* and *ule'ohi'u.*
-ulu i'a. ho'o.ulu i'a. To cause fish to be numerous, as by prayer.
ulu imu. Same as *ulu 4;* to stir up an oven. (For. 4:259.)
ulu.kai. n. Water chestnut. Lit., sea growing.
ulu.kake. Var. of *hōkake,* to disturb.
'ulu kani. n. Clapper of a bell.
ulu kanu. n. Garden patch.
ulu kau. n. Unexplained acquisition of prophetic and interpretive powers without visible possession by a god. Lit., placed inspiration.
-ulu kauō. ho'o.ulu kau.ō. To inspire canoe haulers by chant and prayer.
Ulu-koa. n. Name of a star. Also *Ulu'oa.*
ulu koko. n. First victim slain in battle.
Ulu-kou. n. **1.** Site of the Moana Hotel, Wai-kīkī, Honolulu. **2.** An old name for Howland Island. Lit., *kou* tree grove.
ulu.kū. nvs. Disturbed, upset, restless, depressed, nervous, agitated, perturbed; nervousness, agitation; to disturb. See ex., *hana aloha. Ulukū o ka no'ono'o,* frustrated. **ho'o.ulu.kū.** Caus/sim.
ulu.kua. Same as *ulukū.*
ulu kukui. n. Candlenut grove.
ulu.lā. n. Ostrich (RSV), owl (KJV). (Kanl. 14.15.) (Lat., *ulula).*
ulu lā.'au. n. Forest, grove of trees. *Ulu lā'au makai,* forest by the sea; *fig.,* a fleet at sea.
-ulu lā.hui. See *ulu 1.*
ululele. A chief's favorite. (AP.)
Ulu-loa. n. Name of a star, said to appear on the night of Muku in the month of Māhoe-Mua. Cf. *Pauwala.*

ulūlu. Var. spelling of *uluulu.*

ulu.mā.hie.hie. vs. Festive, attractively adorned and arrayed; to make a fine appearance, decorated, pleasing. *Ka lā ho'omana'o ulumāhiehie o ka na'i aupuni,* the festive commemorative day of the conqueror. **ho'o.ulu.mā.hie.hie.** To adorn, decorate attractively.

'ulu maika. nvt. Stone used in *maika* game; to play the *'ulu maika* game; bowling, bowling ball.

Ulu-mano. n. A strong wind blowing from a given direction in each locality, as a strong southeast wind in Ka'ū and Puna, Hawai'i, and at Kāne-'ohe, O'ahu. Also *'Ao'aoa. Lit.,* blowing hard. *'Eha i ke ku'iku'i a ka Ulu-mano,* pained by buffets of the Ulu-mano wind.

ulu manu. n. Flock of birds.

ulu.moku. Same as *ulupō 2.* (Kam. 64:91.)

ulu moku. n. Fleet, collection of ships.

uluna. **1.** nvi. Pillow, cushion, formerly made of pandanus; to use as a pillow (Kin. 28.18). See ex., *welehu 2.* Also *ununa.* (PPN *'ulunga;* cf. PPN *'ulu,* head.) **2.** n. Upper part of the arm. **3.** n. Center part of a net, as of a large *'upena iheihe* (net used for *iheihe* fish). Cf. *ulu 7.*

ulu.nahele. n. Wilderness, place of wild growth.

ulu niu. n. Coconut grove.

ulu.o'a. vs. Upright, erect. *Rare.*

Ulu.'oa. n. Var. of *Ulu-koa.* (See Gram. 2.9 for alternation of glottal stop and *k.*)

'ulu.pā. vt. To break to pieces, burst forth, dash to pieces (Hal. 2.9), raze to the ground, destroy, beat; to rage, as a storm; to slam shut, hurl down.

'ulu pa'a. n. Cooked but unpounded breadfruit.

ulu pali. n. Talus slope, transitional slope between cliffs and base.

ulu.pau. vi. To gather together; to go everywhere. See ex., *holokahiki. Ua ulupau lākou i ka hana,* they all worked.

ulu.pē. Same as *pulu pē;* intoxicated.

ulu.pi'i. vi. To shiver, shake, tremble, as with cold or fright.

'ulu pilo. n. Rotten breadfruit, a term of abuse for *kauā* (outcasts) at Puna, Hawai'i, since they were said to live in caves and hollows, as breadfruit fallen on the ground to rot.

ulu.pō. **1.** vs. Dark or dense as growth. *Kona, mauna uliuli, mauna ulupō,* Kona, green mountain with dense flora. **2.** n. Sudden sickness or stroke, the sign of which is a cock crowing at untimely hours; such crowing was also believed to indicate the arrival of visitors or a ship. (Kam. 64:91.) **3.** n. A fish said to resemble the *pāpiopio.* Also *lūpō.*

'uiu pohole. n. Bruised breadfruit; *fig.,* bruised, buffeted.

ulu pono. vs. To grow well; progressive, thriving, successful. *Rare.* **ho'o.ulu pono.** Caus/sim; to make grow well, thrive.

ulu.pua. Same as *olopua,* a tree.

ulu pua. n. Flower garden, growth of flowers. *Ka pua o ke Ko'olau i ka ulu pua* (chant), the flower of the Ko'olau in the flower garden.

'ulu pū loa. n. A variety of breadfruit with oval, rather than round fruit.

ulu.puni. vs. Overcome by emotion, hysteria, passion, or an occult influence. *Ulupuni ihola kō Mose huhū* (Puk. 32.19), Moses' anger waxed hot. **ho'o.ulu.puni.** To cause passion, possession, etc.

uluulu, ulūlu. **1.** Redup. of *ulu 1;* growing things. *Pōnalo ihola ka uluulu,* the growing plants swarmed with flies. **2.** Redup. of *ulu 2.* **ho'o.uluulu.** Caus/sim. *Ho'o-uluulu a'ela 'o Ka-welo i nā akua ona* (FS 63), Kawelo appealed to his gods. **3.** vs. Tangled, snarled, snagged, mussed, ruffled, frayed; angry, violent, agitated. See ex., *kā'ulukū.* **ho'o.uluulu.** To wrangle, snarl, snag, taunt, rouse to anger, excite. *Mea ho'ouluulu,* one who stirs up trouble or excites others, activist. (PCP *uluulu.*) **4.** Same as *ununu 1,* to singe. **5.** n. Diving or scoop net, its mouth being held open with two

sticks. (Malo 213.) **6.** n. Sea cavern. *Rare.* **7.** To munch. (AP.)

'ulu.'ulu. n. Collection, gathering, assembly. **hō.'ulu.-'ulu.** To collect, assemble, gather together, compile; addition, to add; collection. *Hō'ulu'ulu pōkole,* brief summary, resumé, synopsis.

uluulu lei. n. Leis offered to the gods. **ho'o.uluulu lei.** Hula altar where fresh leis were placed during hula instruction.

ulu wa'a. n. Fleet of canoes. See ex., *honu pe'ekue.*

ulu wale. vi. To grow easily or without care; spontaneous. See *ulu 1, 2.*

ulu.wehi. nvs. Lush and beautiful verdure; a place where beautiful plants thrive;festively adorned. *Lit.,* decorative growth. Cf. *uluwehiwehi.* **ho'o.ulu.wehi.** To bedeck with plants; to adorn, bedeck, decorate.

ulu.wehi.wehi. Redup. of *uluwehi. Uluwehiwehi mai ka mana'o,* the thoughts were delighted, filled with enthusiasm. **ho'o.ulu.wehi.wehi.** Caus/sim.

ulu.wela. Same as *kauluwela.*

uma. **1.** nvt. Hand wrestling: each tries to force his opponent's hand to the mat; to push, press, grip; to pry, as a lever. **2.** n. Stern of a canoe. *Rare.* **3.** n. Curve. *Rare.* Cf. *pā uma. Hanauma* (place), curved bay.

'umaka. Same as *māmaka 1,* carrying pole. *Rare.*

'umala. Same as *mala,* aching.

uma.lei. n. **1.** Apoplexy, stroke. *Rare.* **2.** Same as *umaumalei,* a fish.

'ū.malu. nvi. Brow of a hill or cliff; shade under cliff or hill; to frown, cast shade. *Maka 'ūmalu,* eyes with heavy upper lids. **ho'o.'ū.malu.** To cast a shadow, overshadow, frown.

uma.uma. n. Chest, breast. *Fig.,* heart, character. *Umauma nahā,* very hungry. *Ho'okahi ka umauma!* United, all as one! *He aha ka hua i ka umauma?* (PH 42), what is the thought in the heart? *E wehe i ka umauma i ākea,* open the chest wide [be generous, kind]. *'Au umauma 'o Hilo i ka wai,* Hilo swims breasting the water [travel regardless of obstacles; Hilo district had gulches and streams hard to cross]. (PPN *uma,* shoulder; PCP *uma,* chest.)

uma.uma.lei. n. A fish similar to but darker than the *palani* or *pualu.* It has bright orange-red spots around the gills and side fins and at the base of the caudal fin where the spike is set. *Lit.,* lei [for the] chest.

ume. n. Same as *kala,* a fish. (PPN *'ume.*)

'ume. **1.** nvt. To draw, pull, attract, entice; attractive, alluring; attraction. (Mele 1.4.) *'Ume i ka ihu,* to pull on the nose, as with a handkerchief or with the fingers, causing the nose to discharge, said of one who weeps in sorrow. *Pahu 'ume,* drawer, bureau. (PEP *kume.*) **2.** nvt. A sexual game for commoners, the counterpart of *kilu,* the chiefs' game. (Malo, chapter 41.) It was called *'ume,* to draw, because players of opposite sex were drawn to one another. To pair off in the game. *Mea 'ume, anohale,* master of ceremonies in the game of *'ume. Ua 'ume 'ia a'e nei kāua e ka mea 'ume o ka 'aha le'ale'a* (Laie 483), we hav been paired off by the master of ceremonies of this merry throng. **3.** nvt. Fermata in music, hold, pause; to lengthen, as a sound. **4.** An overlaid or braided thatching used on corners and ridges of a house. (AP.)

'ume.'alu. n. Bur grass *(Cenchrus echinatus),* a weedy grass bearing round burs, which stick to passersby. (Neal 76–7.) Also *mau'u kukū.*

'ume.kau.maha. n. Gravity. *Lit.,* weight attraction.

'umeke. n. Bowl, calabash, circular vessel, as of wood or gourd. *'Umeke kā'eo,* a well-filled calabash [a well-filled mind]. *'Umeke pala 'ole,* calabash without a dab [empty bowl, empty mind]. **ho'o.'umeke,** **hō.'umeke.** To assume the shape of a bowl; to assume the shape of fruit, to bear fruit. *Fig.,* to hav enough to eat. *E pua ana ka 'ōhi'a 'ai a hō'umeke i ka malama o Hinaia'ele'ele* (Kep. 93), the mountain apple blooms and fruits form in the month of Hinaia'ele'ele. (PPN *kumete.*)

'umeke 'ai. n. Poi bowl. *Fig.*, source of food, of the uplands.

'umeke ipu kai. n. Bowl, as for serving meat or salty meat.

'umeke kepa.kepa. n. Bowl with horizontal flat panels. *Lit.*, wedged bowl.

'umeke lā'au. n. Wooden bowl.

'umeke māna 'ai. n. Very small bowl, as formerly used for poi by favorite children. *Lit.*, poi mouth-fed bowl.

'umeke 'ō.paka. n. Bowl with vertical panels with vertical edges between them. See *'ōpaka 1.*

'umeke pala.pa'a. n. Thick-bottomed wooden calabash. *Lit.*, firm-dabbed bowl, perhaps so called because dabs of poi are held firm in this type of calabash that does not upset.

'umeke pā.wehe. n. A decorated gourd bowl, as made on Ni'ihau.

'umeke pō.hue. n. Gourd calabash.

'ume launa. n. The attraction that draws two solids and makes them one.

'ume lau.oho. n. The attraction that draws liquids up through narrow tubes, capillary action; siphon. *Lit.*, hair attraction.

'ū.melu. vs. Somewhat decomposed, as fish. Cf. *melu.*

'ume mā.kē.neki (mageneti). n. The attraction or pull of a magnet.

'umena. n. An attraction, pulling. See *'ume 1.*

'ū.mene. Same as *'ūpepe.*

'ume.'ume. Redup. of *'ume 1-3.* (PCP *kumekume*, to pull.)

'umi. 1. vt. To strangle, choke, suffocate, stifle, throttle, smother, suppress; to repress, as desire. *E 'umi i ka waimaka*, hold back the tears. (PPN *komi*, PCP *kumi*.) 2. num. Ten, tenth (num. from 11 to 19 are listed below). (PPN *kumi*.)

'umia. Pas/imp. of *'umi 1. 'Umia ka hanu!* (a war cry), hold the breath! Be patient, persist!

'umi.hau. n. Offering of pig between two armies before starting battle. (Malo 197.)

'ū.mi'i. nvt. Clamp, clip, clasp, staple, clutch, buckle, vise, trap; to pinch, clip, clasp, clamp, squeeze; sharp body pain, pang, or cramp, as in the side. Also *'umiki. Makaaniani 'ūmi'i*, spectacles held on the nose with clips, and without supporting handles on the ears; pince-nez. *Mea ho'opa'a 'ūmi'i*, stapler. *Ka 'ūmi'i 'ana i ka wāwae*, binding of feet (as formerly of Chinese women).

'ū.mi'i 'iole. n. Rattrap, mousetrap.

'umi'i.kō. n. Introduced sugar-cane leafhopper *(Perkinsiella saccharicida).*

'ū.mi'i kuapo. n. Belt buckle.

'ū.mi'i kukui haole. n. Nutcracker.

'ū.mi'i lau.oho. n. Hair clasp.

'ū.mi'i pepa. n. Paper clip, clamp, staple.

'umi kama.li'i. Same as *'umi keiki.*

'umi keiki. nv. Infanticide; to strangle infants; foeticide.

'umiki. Same as *'ūmi'i.* Cf. *'Ulu'oa.* ho'o.*'umiki.* Caus/sim.; to shape a gourd for a drum, as by tying.

'ū.miki.miki. Redup. of *'umiki;* to crumble.

'umi kū.mā-. An element compounded with numbers from one to nine to indicate 11 to 19. See Gram. 10.3. Cf. *'umi kumamā.*

'umi kū.mā.hā. num. Fourteen.

'umi kū.mā.hiku. num. Seventeen.

'umi kū.mā.iwa. num. Nineteen.

'umi kū.mā.kahi. num. Eleven.

'umi kū.mā.kolu. num. Thirteen.

'umi kū.mā.lima. num. Fifteen.

'umi kū.mā.lua. num. Twelve.

'umi kuma.mā-. Same as *'umi kūmā-.* Numbers one to nine are suffixed to this also. *Biblical.*

'umi kū.mā.ono. num. Sixteen.

'umi kū.mā.walu. num. Eighteen.

'umina. n. Strangling, choking, etc. See *'umi 1.* (PNP *kominga*.)

'umi.'umi. 1. n. Whiskers, beard, goatee, mustache; ten-dril; barbel or feelers on lower jaw of a fish; suckers that fasten bivalves such as the *nahawele* to rocks; rope used for hauling unfinished canoe hull from the forest to the shore. *Ē! 'umi'umi kao!* Say! Goat's beard! [a taunt of one child to another child who has been scolded, sometimes accompanied by goat-like bleating and tugging on an imaginary beard]. (PPN *kumikumi*.) 2. Redup. of *'umi 1.* (Possibly PNP *kumikumi*, PCP *kumikumi*.)

'umi.'umi-o-Dole. Same as *hinahina 2*, Florida moss. *Lit.*, Dole's whiskers.

'umi.'umi pē.heu.heu. n. Sideburns.

'umi wai. v. To flush, of a toilet.

umo. nvi. To moo, bellow; to bark, of seals; mooing.

'umoki. 1. nvt. Cork, stopper, plug, bung; to cork, stop up; wad of a gun; partitions in bamboo water containers; to shoot an arrow so that it hits a mark squarely. See *wili wehe 'umoki.* 2. vt. To plant taro shoots in small holes made by a stick. (Kep. 153.)

'umo'u.moki. Redup. of *'umoki 1, 2;* to puff at a pipe or cigar, so called because of the movement of the cheeks.

umu. n. Oven, furnace (Ezek. 22.20); a heap of rocks placed in the sea for small fish such as the *manini* to hide in: this was surrounded by a net and the fish were caught. More commonly called *imu.* ho'o.umu. To make an *umu;* to pile in a heap. (PPN *'umu.*)

umu ahi. n. Fire pit. *Ka umu ahi e pūnohu ana* (Kin. 15.17), a smoking furnace.

umu.akua. Same as *waiakua*, aloof.

umu lepo. n. Earth oven.

umu loa. Same as *imu loa.*

'ū.mu'o. Var. of *'ōmu'o*, to nip.

umu pao. Same as *imu pao.*

una. 1. n. Shell of turtle or tortoise, carapace. (PPN *una*.) 2. Same as *haha kā 'upena* (net gauge or spacer) so called because some were made of turtle shell. 3. Var. of *une.* 4. n. Dice.

-una. ho'o.una. To send, transmit, send on an errand, command, put to work; to mail; to send spirits on an errand, especially of destruction. See *hoa una. Ho'ouna na ka mokulele*, to send by air mail. (PPN *unga*.)

unā. vs. Fatigued, weary (Lunk. 4.21). Cf. *nā 1.* ho'o.-unā. To cause weariness.

'unae. 1. n. The lumpy sea cucumber *(Stichopus chloronotes).* 2. vs. Worn thin and lumpy, as a mattress, or formerly, the dried leaves under the sleeping mat.

unahe. 1. Same as *nahe;* light breeze. *Unahe ka pā o ka makani*, the wind blows gently. *Ho'olele lupe i ka unahe* (Kep. 115), fly kites in a light breeze. 2. A foliose lichen *(Parmelia perlata).*

unahe.nahe. Same as *nahenahe*, soft.

unahi. nvs, vt. Scales of a fish; scaly; to scale. (PNP *'unafi*.)

unahi kala.kala. n. Rough scales, especially from midbody to tail of certain fishes; scute.

unahi.nahi. Redup. of *unahi;* many scales.

unahi.pi'i. vs. Cracked and peeling, of the soles or heels of the feet.

unahi.pipi. n. Young *pipi* shellfish.

unahi pō.haku. n. Lichen growths on stones. *Lit.*, stone scales.

unahi.uhu. n. A variety of sweet potato.

unala. Var. of *ulana 1-3.*

unana. 1. Var. of *unala*, to plait. 2. vs. Wee, tiny. *Rare.* 3. n. A bird (no data). (KL line 321.) 4. n. A plain. *Rare.*

una.'oa. Same as *kauna'oa*, a mollusk. (PPN *'ungakoa*.)

unaue. Plural of *naue.* See ex., *polikua.*

una.una. n. Hermit crabs in general. Also *pāpa'i iwi pūpū.* (PPN *'unga*.)

-unauna. ho'o.una.una. Redup. of *ho'ouna;* sorcery. (PNP *ungaunga*.)

unā.unā. Redup. of *unā.*

unau.nahi. vt. To scale, of fish.

une. nv. Lever; lever on a sewing machine that raises or lowers the presser foot; to pry. *Fig.*, to urge, disturb, harass. **hoʻo.une.** Caus/sim.

unea. n. Nausea, exhaustion (Nak. 103).

unea.nea. Redup. of *unea.*

une kī. n. Shift lever for bobbin winder of a sewing machine.

unele. nvi. Honk of a goose; to honk. *Unele! unele! wahi a ka nēnē*, honk! honk! says the goose [of failure or lack; pun on *nele*, loss, deprived].

ʻunelu.nelu. Same as *nenelu*, marsh.

une.une. Redup. of *une.*

une.unea. Same as *uneanea*, nausea.

une.une ʻū.hā. n. A kind of sitting wrestling with thighs of contestants shoved back and forth. *Lit.*, prying thigh.

ʻunia. n. Adult *ʻūhini*, locust; cricket.

uni.hapa. Same as *uwinihapa.*

ʻū.nihi. Var. of *ʻūhini 1, 2.*

ʻunihi.pili. n. **1.** Spirit of a dead person, sometimes believed present in bones or hair of the deceased and kept lovingly. *ʻUnihipili* bones were prayed to for help, and sometimes sent to destroy an enemy. Also *ʻuhinipili.* **hō.ʻunihi.pili.** Caus/sim.; to deify. **2.** Same as *ʻuhinipili 2.*

uni.kalio, unitario. n. Unitarian. *Eng.*

ʻū.niki. nvi. Graduation exercises, as for hula, *lua* fighting, and other ancient arts (probably related to *niki*, to tie, as the knowledge was bound to the student).

ʻū.nina. Var. of *ʻūlina.*

ʻū.nina.nina. Redup. of *ʻūnina.*

uni.ona. n. Union, labor union. *Eng.*

ʻuniu. Same as *manu 3*, canoe projections.

unoʻa. Var. of *unoʻo.*

unoho. Plural of *noho 2, 3.*

ʻunoko. Same as *kōʻeleʻele*, seaweeds. *Hawaiʻi.*

uno.noho. Plural and frequentative of *noho 2, 3.*

uno.noke. Redup. of *noke. ʻUnonoke ihona i ke ʻāʻumeʻume*, persist in the struggle.

unoʻo. vs. Scorched, partly consumed by fire, inflamed. (Probably PPN *ʻunoko.*)

unou.noʻo. Same as *unoʻo. Unounoʻo Puna i ke kua wahine*, the goddess scorched Puna.

unu. **1.** n. Small stone, pebble, stone chip; wedge, prop. Cf. *unu pehi ʻiole. Kohala i ka unu paʻa*, Kohala with the solid stone [firmness]. **hoʻo.unu.** To place stones; to pave, macadamize. **2.** n. Altar, heiau, especially a crude one for fishermen or for the god Lono. *Unu kupukupu* (PH 31, 202), an agricultural heiau. **3.** Rare var. of *inu*, to drink (PNP *unu*; cf. Nukuoro.) **4.** Rare var. of *ulu 1, 2. E ka unu me ka ua Kīpuʻupuʻu* (song), by the stirring [of the wind] and the Kīpuʻupuʻu rain. **5.** n. Name given for a section of canoe endpiece. (For. 5:612–3.) Cf. *ulu 7.*

ʻunu. vt. To shorten, hoist, jerk upwards; to pull or draw together, as the hair. **hoʻo.unu.** Caus/sim.; to massage with the palm of the hand and with quick movements rather than gentle pressure.

ʻunua. Pas/imp. of *ʻunu.*

unuhe. Same as *uluhe*, ferns.

unuhi. vt. To take out, withdraw, as money from a bank, or a drawer from a desk; to unsheath, extract; to take off, as a ring; to translate, interpret. *Mea unuhi*, translator, interpreter. **hoʻo.unuhi.** To have something translated, withdrawn, etc. (PPN *unusi*, which is PPN *unu* + PPN *-si.*)

unu.hia. Pas/imp. of *unuhi.*

unuhi kū.like loa. nvt. Literal translation; to make such.

unuhi lau.lā loa. nvt. Free translation; to make such.

unu.hina. n. Translation.

unuhi ʻō.lelo. nv. To translate or interpret; translator, interpreter.

unuhi pili. nvt. Close, literal translation; to make such.

Unu.lau. n. **1.** A wind famous in song noted on Kauaʻi, West Maui, and Niʻihau; according to Emerson (UL 196), the trade wind. See ex., *puka, puʻupā, wiliʻōkaʻi 2.* **2.** Name of a star.

ʻunu.loa. n. **1.** Kauaʻi name for *nāpili*, a fish. **2.** *(Cap.)* A wind, Puna, Hawaiʻi.

ununa. Var. of *uluna 1–3.*

unūnu. Var. spelling of *unuunu.*

unu pehi ʻiole. n. Rat-pelting pebble, insulting epithet for a person of no consequence.

unuunu. **1.** vt. To singe, as the feathers of a chicken before dressing it, or the hairs of a pig or dog by rolling it over hot oven stones; to pluck, as feathers from a fowl. Also *uluulu.* (PCP *(u)ngu(u)nu.*) **2.** Var. of *uluulu 3*, tangled. **3.** Stick erected as a taboo sign. (AP.) **4.** Young *ʻōhiʻa* timber, as used in making images. (AP.)

ʻunu.ʻunu. Redup. of *ʻunu.* **hō.ʻunu.ʻunu.** To pleat, overlap in sewing; to pull up, as a sagging petticoat.

unuunu hoʻo.ulu ʻai. n. Agricultural heiau.

ʻuo, ʻuwo. **1.** nvt. A group of feathers tied together in a small bunch, to be made into a feather lei or cloak; to tie thus; to tie into a lei; to string on a needle; to splice, interweave, as strands of a rope; seizing turns in lashing. *Ke ʻuo lā i ka mānai* (PH 191), threading [flowers] on the needle. *ʻUo ʻia i ka mānai hoʻokahi*, strung on the same lei needle [married]. (PCP *kuo.*) **2.** Same as *ʻuoʻuo 1.*

uō, uwō. vi. To bellow, roar, shout loudly, howl. See *kūō, leo uō. Pule uō* (Kep. 57), loudly chanted prayer.

uoa. **1.** Same as *uouoa*, a fish. **2.** n. Name given for an unknown disease, characterized by aching shoulders.

uoi. vi. To move along, of many; to slouch along together. *I ka hele ua o Manuʻa-kepa uoi aku i ka loa o Koʻi-ālana* (song), the rain journey of Manuʻa-kepa, moving at random along the length of Koʻi-ālana. **hoʻo.uoi.** Caus/sim.

uoki, uwoki. Idiom used only in commands. Stop it! Quit! Don't touch! Be careful (see ex., *hāmama*)! (PPN *ʻoti.*)

uolo. nvi. To call out; a loud calling. *I kaʻu uolo ʻana aku e lohe mai iaʻu* (Hal. 4.1), when I call out, listen to me.

uoʻo. vs. Tough. *He pū hala uoʻo*, a tough old pandanus [a tight-fisted person, named for Pū-hala-hua, a Hawaiian noted for thrift].

uō.uō, uwō.uwō. Redup. of *uō. Uōuō leo*, shouting voices, especially said of noisy pickers of mountain apples *(ʻōhiʻa ʻai)*, contrasting with the silent people snaring birds on the branches of the *ʻōhiʻa hāmau* trees. **ho.ʻūouo.** Caus/sim.

ʻuo.ʻuo. **1.** vs. Adhesive, sticky, but without lumps, as good poi; tough, strong. *Ka poi ʻuoʻuo o kāohi puʻu*, sticky poi that settles nicely down the throat. **2.** vt. To string, as leis.

uou.oa. n. A fish *(Neomyxus chaptalii)*, known as the false mullet or false *ʻamaʻama*, distinguishable from the true mullet by its narrower and tapered mouth and creamy rather than silvery pectoral fins. The head, when eaten, was supposed to cause sleeplessness and nightmares. *Ua hopu hewa i ka uouoa*, accidentally caught an *uouoa* [in trouble, play on *uō*, to howl].

ʻuo.ʻulea. Shadows and gloom of a forest; weird, ghostly, fearsome. (AP.)

ʻū.pā. nv. Any instrument that opens and shuts, as shears, scissors, tongs, bellows, carpenter's compass; to beat, as the heart; to open and shut, as the mouth champing food; to slam, bang, as a door. *Fig.*, a furious attack, onslaught.

ʻū.pā ahi. n. Tongs for picking up hot coals.

upaʻa.paʻani. vt. To play together.

upai. Tall, thin. (And.)

ʻupaʻi. vi. To flap, as wings, clothes in the wind; to bend in the wind, as a branch; to walk with a flapping movement. *Mehe ʻupaʻi na ke koaʻe lā* (PH 101), like the flapping of a tropic bird's [wings].

ʻupaʻi.paʻi. Redup. of *ʻupaʻi*; to hover.

ʻū.pā koli kukui. n. Candle snuffers. *Lit.*, scissors cutting off candlenut.

ʻū.palu. **1.** vs. Gentle, mild, soft-spoken, soft, tender, fragile, languid. *Ua ʻūpalu wale ke oho o ke kupukupu*, the *kupukupu* fern fronds are soft. **2.** n. A soft-bodied holothurian *(Opheodesoma spectabilis),* sea cucumber. **3.** n. A bird (no data).

'ū.palu.palu. 1. Redup. of *'ūpalu 1.* **2.** nvt. According to Malo, a type of fishing; translated by Emerson as "ordinary angling." (Malo 210, 213.)

'ū.pā makani. n. Bellows.

'ū.pā mau'u. n. Grass shears.

'ū.pā miki.'ao. n. Fingernail or manicure scissors.

'ū.pā nui. n. Shears.

'ū.pā 'oki niho.niho. n. Pinking shears. *Lit.,* shears for cutting points.

'upā.palu. 1. Same as *'ūpalupalu 1.* **2.** n. The larger cardinal fishes, *Apogon* spp., *Apogonichthys perdix, Foa brachygramma.* A var. name is *'upāpalu maka nui.*

'ū.pā 'ume. n. Nippers.

'ū.pā 'ū.mi'i. n. Pliers.

'upa.'upā. Redup. of *'ūpā;* to rub clothes up and down a washboard.

ū.pē. vs. Crushed, flattened; humble, bashful; dry and juiceless, as sugar cane. Cf. Gram. 6.3.3. *Hale maka ūpē,* humble-appearing house. **ho'o.ū.pē.** To crush, belittle, flatten, treat contemptuously (Kep. 107).

'upe. 1. Same as *io,* a rib on a paddle. **2.** n. Spear point. *Pa'a loa i loko o ka 'upe o ka ihe* (For. 4:469), firmly stuck within the spear point.

'ū.pē. n. Mucus. *Fig.,* tears, grief. Also *hūpē. Kahe ka 'ūpē,* mucus flows. *He 'ūpē, he waimaka, he waimaka aloha* (PH 139), the nose runs from weeping, tears, tears of love. *Mai ho'omakamaka wahine, he 'ūpē ka loa'a,* don't make a pal of a woman, nose running in grief is the outcome. *Ē kēnā wahi keiki 'ūpē kole* (GP 24), O you little mucus-laden red [nosed] boy. (PPN *isupe'e,* PEP *supe'e;* PCP supe, suupee.)

'ū.pehu.pehu. vs. Swollen, bloated; inflammation. Cf. *pehu 1.*

'upena. n. Fishing net, net, web. *Fig.,* trap. (PPN *kupenga.*)

'upena ahu.ulu. n. Same as *'upena uluulu.*

'upena 'ā.ki'i.ki'i. n. Dip net. Cf. *lā 5.*

'upena 'akuku. n. Net held open by supporting stick. Cf. *kuku, puhi.*

'upena 'alihi. n. Name given for a net spread over a patient by a medical *kahuna* in order to catch evil spirits.

'upena 'apo.'apo. n. Gill net.

'upena-hā.lu'a. n. Tapa-beater design.

'upena-hā.lu'a-niho-manō. n. Tapa-beater design, with stripes and shark-teeth motifs.

'upena ho'o.hei.hei. n. A type of net or snare (no data).

'upena ho'o.lei. n. Throwing net.

'upena ho'o.lewa.lewa. n. Gill net stretched at high tide across fish runs in shallow water. *Lit.,* suspended net.

'upena ho'o.moe.moe. n. Set net.

'upena hō.una. n. Net made of fibers of *hau* and *'ahu-'awa. Lit.,* scoop net.

'upena 'iao. n. Net for *'iao,* bait fish.

'upena kahe. n. Net similar to the *pāku'iku'i. Lit.,* flow net.

'upena kā.he'e. n. Scoop or hand net. See *kāhe'e.*

'upena kā.'ili. n. A type of net or seine (no data).

'upena kā.kā uhu. See *kākā 4.*

'upena kā.wa'a. n. Net about forty fathoms long used in deep-sea fishing with canoes.

'upena kiloi. n. Throwing net.

'upena kiola. n. Throwing net.

'upena kō lau. n. Seine. Also *hukilau. Lit.,* rope-pulling net.

'upena kolo. n. Immense bag net said to be from sixteen to twenty-four fathoms deep. *Lit.,* towing net.

'upena ku'u. n. Gill net, set net.

'upena lau.oho. n. Hair net.

'upena lu'u.lu'u. n. Small net, baited, weighted down, and set on the sea floor; fishermen dived *(lu'ulu'u)* to bring it up.

'upena mā.'i'o. n. Net made of *hau* fiber. *Lit.,* jagged net.

'upena mā.kini. n. A net used for destruction, as by robbers to snare victims.

'upena mao.mao. n. A large net used in deep water with the *melomelo* lure. *Lit.,* far net.

'upena mō.kū. n. Net that is baited and left in the sea, as for *pāpa'i,* crabs.

'upena nana.nana. n. Spider web.

'upena 'ō.hua palemo. n. Net used for young *palemo,* a fish. Also *nae.*

'upena pā.ki'i.ki'i. n. Same as *'upena 'āki'iki'i.*

'upena papa. n. Bag net, said to be a combination of three nets, with the *puhi nui* at the opening (meshes two or more fingers in width), then the *puhi iki* (meshes half as large), and at the end the *pūpū,* which was also called the *mole. Lit.,* stratum net.

'upena pā.pa'i. n. Net for catching *pāpa'i,* crabs. Also *'upena mōkū.*

'upena pili. n. Two nets attached to either side of the opening of the *pāku'iku'i. Lit.,* joining net.

'upena po'o. n. Bag net. *Lit.,* head net.

'upena pū.nā.wele.wele. Same as *'upena nananana.*

'upena-pupu. n. A tapa-beater design with net meshes enhanced with small circles.

'upena uluulu. n. A scoop net with two parallel sticks for a frame. Probably *lit.,* frayed net. *Ka 'upena uluulu noho i ka hāpapa* (song), the *uluulu* net in the shallows.

ū.pē.pē. Redup. of *ūpē.*

'ū.pepe. vs. Flat-nosed. Also *'ūmene, kūmene.*

'upe.pehu. Same as *'ūpehupehu.*

'ū.pī. nvt. Sponge; syringe, enema; to squirt, squeeze, spray through an orifice; to squish-squash, as the noise made by walking with shoes full of water; to extract by pressing and wringing; to express; to give an enema.

upi'i. Plural of *pi'i,* to go up.

'ū.piki. 1. nvt. Trap, snare, clamp; treachery; to snap or clamp together, as a trap, the jaws, or a bivalve; to shut or close, as a flower; to pinch, as with pressure of thumb and fingers. Same as *'ōpiki.* See ex., *pahele.* **2.** A tapa stamp.

'ū.piki 'iole. n. Rattrap, mousetrap.

'ū.piki lima. n. Handcuff.

'ū.piki.piki. Redup. of *'ūpiki 1.*

'ū.pī laho. nv. Testicle squeezing, said of male homosexuality.

'ū.pili. vs. Cramped, crowded, packed tight. Cf. *'ōpili. Maka 'ūpili,* tightly closed eyes.

'upi.'upī. Redup. of *'ūpī;* to soften an octopus, as by holding the head and working the tentacles up and down in a container with salt.

'ū.poho. 1. nvi. Same as *poho;* the sound produced by clapping the body with cupped hands. Cf. *kai 'ūpoho.* **2.** n. Bagpipe.

'ū.po'i. Same as *po'i 1–5;* to move, as a bird its wings. (Isa. 10.14.)

'ū.po'i maka. n. Eyelid.

'ū.po'i.po'i. Same as *po'ipo'i. 'Ō'ili maila 'o 'Ai-ohi-kupua a ma ke alo o Ihu-anu kū ihola, a ua 'ūpo'ipo'i nā lima* (For. 5:409), 'Ai-ohi-kupua appeared before Ihu-anu and stood there and slapped his cupped hands against his body [to resound defiantly].

'ū.polu. vs. Moist. *Ka maka 'ūpolu o ka lehua i ka ua,* the soft petals of the *lehua* wet by the rain.

'upu. nvt. Recurring thought, desire, attachment, hope, expectation; to desire, long for, covet, keep thinking of with anticipation. Cf. *hā'upu'upu, nahele. E 'upu a'e ka mana'o e 'ike i ka nani* (song), thinking and longing to see the beauty. *'A'ole nō i 'upu iho, komo mai ana ka mō'ī wahine,* in a moment, the queen entered [*lit.,* not indeed a thought given]. Cf. *'ū 2.* (PPN *kupu.*)

'ū.puku. Rare var. of *'īpuka.*

upu.pā. n. Sandpiper; lapwing (KJV), hoopoe (RSV) (Oihk. 11.19).

'upu.'upu. Redup. of *'upu. 'A'ole i 'upu'upu,* in hardly any time. **hō.'upu.'upu.** To recall to someone else, remind; to terrify someone by repeating an unpleasant impending event, especially that one is to be the victim of sorcery; to harp on impending doom. Cf. *hā'upu-*

'upu, to recall without this pejorative connotation. (PNP *kupukupu*.)

'u'u. nvt. To strip, as leaves or *maile* bark; to draw in, as a line on a ship; to draw out, unsheath, as a sword; to draw back, as the fist preparing to strike, or as the foot about to kick; to hoist, as a sail; to practice masturbation; to answer back sharply or rudely; to pour suddenly, as rain. *'U'u ke kuāua,* down came the shower. *'O ka 'u'u maila nō ia i ka pākīkē,* it was a snapping forth rudely. *He po'e 'u'u maunu palu 'ala'ala no kekahi po'e lawai'a,* a people who draw out the octopus ink sac bait preparation for other fishermen [those who do the dirty work from which others reap the benefit]. (PPN *kuku*.)

'ū.'ū. 1. Redup. of *'ū 1;* to stutter, stammer. *Ka 'ū'ū 'ana o nā mamo o 'Isera'ela* (Puk. 6.5), the groaning of the children of Israel. (Possibly PPN *kuukuu*.) 2. Redup. of *'ū 2;* impregnated partially, as fish with salt. (*Ho'oma'ū* is used today for soaking.) 3. n. All soldier-fishes of the genus *Myripristis;* some were considered *'aumākua. Ua loa'a akula ka i'a 'o ka 'ū'ū'* the soldier-fishes have (just) been caught [one has cause to sigh or grieve, a play on *'ū,* to sigh]. 4. *(Cap.)* n. Star name (no data).

'ū.'ua, 'ū'uwa. vs. Slippery, slimy.

'u'u.'ina. Redup. of *'u'ina 1.*

'u'uku. vs. Tiny, small; few. See *'uku. 'U'uku iho,* undersized, smaller. ho'o.'u'uku. To make small, reduce, lessen.

'u'ulu.haku. vs. Lumpy, bumpy, coarse, said of some skin diseases. Cf. *'uluhaku.*

'u'ulu.kai. vs. Bloated, swollen, dropsical.

'u'umi. Redup. of *'umi 1,* to strangle. See ex., *auka.* (PNP *kokomi,* PCP *kukumi.*)

'u'umuiku. Short, deficient, defective. (AP.)

'u'unu. Redup. of *'unu.*

'u'u.peku.peku. vi. To sway, teeter, as the mast of a ship at sea.

'u'u'u. Redup. of *'u'u.*

'ū.'u'u. Same as *'ū'ū 1. Ka po'e 'ū'u'u* (Isa. 32.4), the stammerers. *Ua 'ū'u'u noho'i kona leo* (Mar. 7.32), an impediment also in his speech.

'ū.'uwa. Var. spelling of *'ū'ua.*

'uwā. nvt. To shout, cry out, yell, sound loud, shout, racket. See *wā,* noise. *'Uwā ho'ohilahila,* to hoot at, shout at in derision. ho'o.uwā. Caus/sim.

'uwa'a. vt. To dig or dredge a trench or furrow. Cf. *wa'a,* trench.

uwahi. Var. spelling of *uahi.*

uwai. Var. spelling of *uai.*

ū wai. vs. Water-soaked, soggy.

uwaki. Var. spelling of *uaki.*

'uwala. Var. spelling of *'uala.*

uwali. Same as *wali,* soft, smooth. Cf. *uwa'uwali.*

uwalo, ualo. nvt. To call out, as for help; to resound; a call. Cf. *walo. Ke akua uwalo i ka la'i* (chant), the god calling out in the calm.

'uwalu. Same as *walu,* to claw. *'Eha ka pōhaku i ka 'uwalu a ke ahi* (PH 202), the stone suffers as it is clawed by the fire.

uwā.ni'i. Var. spelling of *uāni'i.*

'uwao. Var. spelling of *'uao.*

uwapo. Var. spelling of *uapo.*

uwa'u, ua'u. Same as *wa'u,* to grate.

'uwa'u. Var. spelling of *'ua'u,* petrel.

'uwā.'uwā. Redup. of *'uwā.*

uwau.wai. Var. spelling of *uauai.* See *uai.*

uwa'u.wali. vs. Soft, limp, weak. *Lilo kō lāua uāni'i i mea uwa'uwali wale nō,* their stiffness will become just limpness.

uwe. Var. spelling of *ue.*

uwē. Var. spelling of *uē.*

'uwehe, 'uehe. 1. vt. To open, uncover, reveal, untie; to pry open, as a bivalve; to remove evil influence, as by prayer. Cf. *wehe.* 2. nvi. Hula step: one foot is lifted with weight shifting to opposite hip as the foot is lowered; both knees are then pushed forward by the quick raising of the heels, with continued swaying of the hips from side to side (a difficult step); to do this step.

uwē.hehene. Same as *ehehene.*

uweka, ueka. vs. Dirty, bleary, as the eyes. Cf. *weka.*

'uweke. Same as *'uwehe 1, 2.* ho'o.uweke. Caus/sim.; to open a little.

uweko, ueko. vs. Bad-smelling, musty. Also *weko.*

uweko.weko, uekoeko. Redup. of *uweko.*

uwene. Var. spelling of *uene.*

uwenewene. Unclean in habits. (AP.)

uwepa. Var. spelling of *uepa 1–3.*

uwē.uwē. Var. spelling of *uē.*

uweu.weko, ueueko. Redup. of *uweko.*

'uwe'u.wele. Var. spelling of *'ue'uele.*

'uwī, 'uī. 1. nvi. To squeak, squeal; to gnash, as teeth; such sounds. Cf. *wī. Mea 'uwī,* wringer. ho'o.uwī. Caus/sim. 2. nvt. To twist, squeeze, wring, grind; to express, as juice from fruit; to milk, as a cow. hō.'uwī. Caus/sim.

'uwia. 1. Pas/imp. of *'uwī 1, 2.* 2. n. A split in a tree.

'uwiki. 1. Var. spelling of *'uiki 1–4.*

uwila. Var. spelling of *uila.*

uwini.hapa. Var. spelling of *winihapa.*

'uwī.'uwī, 'uī'uī. 1. Redup. of *'uwī 1, 2.* ho'o.uwī.'uwī. Redup. of *hō'uwī.* 2. n. A variety of triggerfish (family Balistidae), so called because it is said to make a squeaky sound. Also *humuhumu.* 3. vi. A ceremony to insure sharp teeth for infants: after an infant's tooth is pulled, it is passed under the knee of the child while chanting: *'Uwī'uwī ka niho o ke kanaka no ka 'iole, ka niho o ka 'iole no ke kanaka, e 'oi ka niho o* [name of the child], grind the tooth of the person for the rat, the tooth of the rat for the person, so the tooth of [name] will be sharp. The tooth is thrown away so that a rat will find it and grant the sharpness of its own teeth to the new tooth that will grow in the child's mouth. To perform this ceremony. 4. n. Fermented liquor, swipes. 5. Same as *ilioha,* horseweeds; to use as a switch; to beat. *'Uwī'uwī aku au iā'oe a pū'alalā,* I'll take a switch to you until [you] bawl.

'uwi'u.wia. Var. spelling of *'ui'uwī 4.*

'uwi'u.wiki. Var. spelling of *'ui'uiki.*

'uwī.'uwī lua. n. A variety of *'uwī'uwī,* triggerfish.

'uwī wai.ū. v. To milk, as a cow. *Hui 'uwī waiū,* dairy.

uwō. Var. spelling of *uō.*

'uwo. Var. spelling of *'uo 1, 2.*

uwoki. Var. spelling of *uoki.*

uwō.uwō. Var. spelling of *uōuō.*

'uwo.'uwo. Var. spelling of *'uo'uo.*

V

For words sometimes spelled with initial v-, *see* w-. *For example:* vabine, *see* wāpine, *verbena;* vinega, *see* wīneka, *vinegar;* vito, *see* wiko, *vito.*

W

Initial w *is sometimes omitted in spelling before* -a *or* -o, *as in* wai, *who;* Polo-wahi-lani, Wākea, wānini, wau, wohi. *Cf. also reconstructions for* wahī, wauke, wāwae. *For loan words sometimes spelled with initial* w, *see* u- *or* ʻu-, *as in* uapo, *wharf, and* ʻuiki, *wick.*

wā. 1. n. Period of time, epoch, era, time, occasion, season, age. *I ka wā o,* at the time of, during. *I ka wā mua, i ka wā mamua,* before, in past times, formerly. *I ka wā hea,* when. *I ka wā i hala,* before. *Wā mahope,* future. *Ia wā,* then, at that time. *Wā kamaliʻi, wā liʻiliʻi,* childhood. *Wā uʻi,* age of youth and beauty. *Mai kēia wā aku,* from this time forth, henceforth. *Mai kēlā wā mai,* from that time on. *I ka wā pau ʻole, i ka wā mau loa,* forever, eternity. *Wā huli i luna ke alo,* the time the belly turns up [infancy]. *Nā wā me nā kau,* seasons, chronology. *ʻA ʻohe wā,* almost, no time. *ʻA ʻohe nohoʻi he wā, hoʻokuʻi ʻia e ke kaʻa,* in no time at all, hit by the car; almost hit by the car. (PPN *wahaʻa.*) **2.** n. Tense, in grammar. Cf. *wā ʻanō. Wā i hala,* past tense. *Wā e hiki mai ana,* future tense. **3.** vi. To make a noise, roar, din; noisy, loud; to talk much, as of gossip: to talk loudly back and forth; to reason. Cf. *wawā. Wā ihola lākou iā lākou iho* (Mat. 16.7), they reasoned among themselves. **hoʻo.wā.** To make a sound, roar; to cause gossip, talk. See ex., *haʻanou. Kai hoʻowā,* roaring sea. (PPN *waa.*) **4.** n. Space, interval, as between objects or time; in music, one of the four spaces of the staff; channel. Cf. *kōwā.* (PPN *waa.*) **5.** n. Fret of an ukulele, guitar, or similar instrument.

-wā. hoʻo.wā. To retch. See ex., *haʻanou.*

waʻa. n. 1. Canoe, rough-hewn canoe, canoemen, paddlers; a chant in praise of a chief's canoe. *Waʻa kome* (Puk. 2.3), basket [RSV], ark [KJV] of bulrushes. **hoʻo.waʻa.** To make or shape a canoe. (PPN *waka.*) **2.** Trench, furrow, receptacle. *Fig.,* a woman. (PCP *waka-.*) **3.** Moving masses of liquid lava, so called because of similarity to a moving canoe. *Rare.* **4.** Same as more common *waʻawaʻa 3,* stupid.

waʻa ʻā.kea, waʻa kea. n. Starboard hull of a double canoe.

waʻa ʻau.hau. n. Tribute canoe; a basket filled with food and set adrift during the *makahiki* ceremonies, said to represent the canoe in which Lono returned to Tahiti (Malo 151).

wā.ʻae.ʻoia. Same as *lāʻaeʻoia.*

Waʻa-hila. n. A rain in Nuʻu-anu and Mānoa Valleys and the name of a ridge separating Mānoa and Pālolo Valleys. See saying, *puʻipuʻi. Ola ke kai o Kou i ka ua Waʻa-hila* (saying), the land of Kou [Honolulu] lives by the Waʻa-hila rain.

waʻa holo hau. n. Sleigh. *Lit.,* canoe running on snow.

waʻa honua. n. A wide canoe.

waʻa kai like. n. A canoe with little sheer. *Lit.,* equal-sea canoe.

waʻa kau. n. Head fisherman's canoe.

waʻa kaua. n. War canoe; an army formation (Malo 197).

waʻa kau hī. n. Canoe for fishing *aku.*

waʻa kau.kahi. n. Single canoe, as contrasted with the *kaulua. Lit.,* single-placed canoe.

waʻa kau.lua. n. Double canoe. *Lit.,* double-placed canoe.

waʻa kea. 1. n. Unpainted canoe set to sea after the taboos were lifted during the *makahiki* harvest festivals. (Malo 151.) *Lit.,* white canoe. **2.** Same as *waʻa ʻākea.*

waʻa kome. n. Vessel of papyrus (RSV), bullrush (KJV).

waʻa kū.pā.hoa. n. A long, thin canoe. *Rare.*

waʻa lau kī. n. Toy canoe made of ti leaves.

-waʻalia. hoʻo.waʻa.lia. Pas/imp. of *hoʻowaʻa,* to dig a trench.

waʻa lolo niu. n. Toy canoe made of coconut sheath.

wā ʻā.nō. n. Present tense.

waʻa.pā. n. Skiff, rowboat; ferryboat (2 Sam. 19.18). *Lit.,* board canoe.

waʻa pā.hoa. Same as *waʻa kūpāhoa. Rare.*

waʻa pau.lua. n. Said to be a large or double canoe with three *ʻiako.*

waʻa puhi. n. A small, slim canoe used for surfing. *Rare.*

waʻa ʻula. n. A chief's canoe with red sails.

waʻa.waʻa. 1. Redup. of *waʻa 2;* full of gulches, gullies, grooves; gullied, furrowed, grooved. (PCP *wakawaka.*) **2.** nvs. Muscular, one whose back bulges with muscles. (PPN *wakawaka.*) **3.** nvs. Stupid, ignorant; ignoramus, simpleton, fool. Cf. *hāwāwā. Waʻawaʻa-iki-na-ʻaupō,* ignorant stupid one [name of a legendary simpleton]. **hoʻo.waʻa.waʻa.** To act the fool. **4.** n. Upper end of a lobster's leg. **5.** n. U-shaped canoe spreader. **6.** vs. Desolate, uninhabited. *Waʻawaʻa kō kāua hale, ʻaʻohe kānaka* (a dirge), our house is desolate without people.

waʻa.waʻa.hia. Pas/imp. of *waʻawaʻa 1. Ka ua waʻawaʻahia o Wai-piʻo,* the furrow-cutting rain of Wai-piʻo.

waʻa.waʻa iki. n. Same as *waʻawaʻa 3.*

waʻa.waʻa.lia. Same as *waʻalia.* **hoʻo.waʻa.waʻa.lia.** Caus/sim.

wae. 1. nvt. To choose, select, pick out, sort, discriminate, separated, cull, nominate; to draft, as soldiers; to preen, as of a chicken; finicky, fussy; to reflect, meditate; appointment. *Hīmeni wae,* selected hymn or anthem. **hoʻo.wae.** To choose, pretend to choose; finicky. (PPN *wahe.*) **2.** n. U-shaped canoe spreader. See ex., *pūkōkeʻe.* **3.** n. Leg. *Rare.* See *wāwae.* **4.** n. Rib of a ship.

-wae. See *māwae, ʻōwae.*

waʻe. Same as *ʻaʻae,* third generation taro.

wae ʻana. n. Selection, choice.

wā e hiki mai ana. n. Future tense or time.

waele. vt. To weed, clear, remove grass or weeds. *Nāna i waele ke ala, mahope aku mākou,* he opened up the path, we followed [respect the older sibling]. (PEP *waele.*)

waena. 1. loc. n. Middle, between, center, central, intermediate, medial (often preceded by *i, ma-, mai*), mean, average. Cf. *leo waena, paʻapū.* (PEP *waenga.*) **2.** n. Cultivated field, garden, vegetable plot. *Nā mea kanu o ka waena* (Kin. 3.18), the herb of the field.

waena.konu. loc. n. Center, middle, midway. *I waena-*

konu o ke kai (Puk. 14.29), in the midst of the sea. (PEP *waenga* + PPN *tonu*.)

waena moku. loc. n. Amidships.

wae wa'a. Same as *wae 2.*

wae.wae. Redup. of *wae 1;* selective. See *kūlana waewae.* (PPN *wahewahe*.)

wa'e.wa'e. n. **1.** Cloven hoof, as of cattle, goats, and deer. *Kaua'i. Rare.* **2.** Head fisherman in charge of *kū-'ula,* stone gods.

waha. 1. n. Mouth, opening, inner surface of a bowl, open top of a canoe, muzzle of a gun, oral, one who talks too much (see *ex., hewa 4*). See *kaka'o, waha wale, wahāwahā. Ma ka waha,* oral. *Waha nui, waha kani,* garrulous. *Kā i ka waha,* smite the speaker [said disparagingly of one who does himself what he has condemned others for doing]. *Mai lawe mai i kāna 'uala, he waha,* don't bring his sweet potato, [he] talks too much. **ho'o.waha.** To talk excessively; to make faces; to make an opening or furrow; to dub out a canoe, hew. (PEP *fafa,* PCP *wafa;* cf. Marquesan *fafa.*) **2.** n. Neck of a dress. *Mu'umu'u waha nui,* gown *(mu'umu'u)* with a low neck. **3.** nvt. To carry on the back, as a child; a load so carried. **ho'o.waha.** Caus/sim. (PPM *fafa,* PCP *wafa.*) **4.** n. Square notch cut in the upper part of house posts, in which the wall plates *(lohelau)* were placed; tenon (For. 5:651).

waha 'ā. vs. Sharp-tongued, rude; to speak heatedly and rudely. *Lit.,* burning mouth.

waha 'awa. n. A bitter *('awa)* and sadistic person who makes impulsive vindictive statements about the one he hates, attempting to strike at his weaknesses or guilts, and usually predicting misfortune that often comes true. (Nānā 197–200.)

waha hau.ka'e. nvs. Smeared mouth; smutty-mouthed, evil-tongued.

waha.he'e. nvi. To lie; lying, deceitful, false; a lie, liar. *Lit.,* slippery mouth. See ex., *keu. Kapa wahahe'e 'ana,* false impersonation.

waha kale. nvi. To drool at the mouth, talk excessively, gush; one who does so.

waha kole. nvi. Garrulous, noisy, boisterous and obstreperous in speech; such a person; to rant.

waha ko'u. nvi. Garrulous, clucking mouth; to gabble.

wā hala. n. Past tense.

waha lapa.lapa. nvt. To scold, utter scathing remarks; one who does so. *Lit.,* blazing mouth.

waha.lehe. vs. Wide open, as a door; too large, as the neck of a dress. *Fig.,* to exaggerate. *Lit.,* wide mouth. Also *uhalehe.* **ho'o.waha.lehe.** To stretch the mouth with fingers; to stretch out of shape, as the mouth.

waha lina. nvs. Finicky, of eating. *Lit.,* tight-mouthed; such a person.

waha.mana. n. Screen, shutter. *Rare.*

waha mana. 1. n. Voice of authority, person in authority. *Lit.,* powerful mouth. **2.** nvi. One who digresses from subject to subject; to digress. *Lit.,* branching mouth.

wā.hane. n. Same as *hāwane,* seed of the *loulu.*

waha nui. nvi. A big mouth; to talk too much; tattle; tattler.

waha.'ohi. nvi. To talk in a foolish, silly, senseless manner; such talk; such a talker.

Waha-o-ka-manō. n. See *Ka-waha-o-ka-manō.*

waha 'ō koko. v. To slander one's own blood. *Lit.,* mouth that pierces blood.

waha 'ō.lelo. n. Spokesman, mouthpiece, herald; speaking mouth.

waha.pa'a. vt. To goad, tease, banter; argumentative. *Lit.,* hard mouth.

waha pala. n. A coated mouth, said in derision of an ignoramus, especially one who does not know the chants honoring his chief.

waha pilo. n. Halitosis; foul mouth.

waha pio. To be unable to speak; not to dare to speak, speechless. *Lit.,* imprisoned mouth.

waha pu'u. n. Protruding lips; unintelligible speech, as of one who has had a stroke. *Lit.,* lumpy mouth.

waha.'ula. vt. To nibble and pick at food without appetite. *Lit.,* red [sore] mouth.

wahā.wahā. vt. To treat with contempt, scorn, despise, abhor, ridicule; be disgusted, defy. **ho'o.wahā.wahā.** Caus/sim. Cf. *waha 1. Ho'owahāwahā i ka 'aha,* contempt of court. (PCP *wafa(a)wafa(a).*)

waha.wai. vt. To talk glibly, brag. *Lit.,* watery mouth.

waha wale. vs. Deceitful, lying. *Lit.,* slimy mouth.

waha wali. vs. Glib-tongued.

wā he'e. n. Time when *he'e* (octopus) abound.

wā heu 'ole. n. Time of beardless youth, preadolescence. *Lit.,* time without whiskers.

wahi. 1. n. Place, location, position, site, setting. *(Ka wahi* contracts to common *kahi.) Ma kekahi wahi,* somewhere. *Kēlā wahi kēia wahi,* everywhere. *Ma ia mau wahi,* hereabouts, thereabouts. *Ma nā wahi āpau,* everywhere, wherever, universal. *Ua hele akula lāua ia wahi a'e, ia wahi a'e,* they went everywhere. *Iā 'oe ia wahi,* none of your business [rude]; it's your turn [polite]. (PPN *fa'asi,* PCP *wa(a)si.*) **2.** Paucal article. Some, a little, a bit of. (Gram. 10.2.) *Ho wahi makana kēia wai,* please a little water. *He wahi makana kēia,* this is just a little gift. *'A 'ohe wahi ā ne'ene'eu mai,* does not bestir at all. (PCP *wa(a)si.*) **3.** idiom. To say, according to (usually followed by the possessive *a* or by a zero-class possessive and not preceded by either verb or noun particles). *Wahi a wai?* Who said so? *Wahi a ke ali'i,* the chief said. *Wahi a kahiko,* according to the ancients.

wahī. nvt. Wrapper, envelope, case, covering, sheath; a ti-leaf bundle; to wrap, cover, bundle up, fold up, roll up, swathe; to dress, as a wound. Cf. *'ili wahī, kīpē. Wahī makaaniani,* glasses case. *Ā wahī ihola 'oia i nā papa i ke gula* (Puk. 36.34), and he overlaid the boards with gold. (PEP *fa'asi,* but cf. Marquesan *fafi, vahi* [long vowels are not marked].)

wāhi. vt. To cleave, split, burst through, break through; to change, as money; to have sex relations with a virgin, deflower. Cf. *wāwahi. O wāhi mai, ē Lono, o wāhi 'o luna, o wāhi 'o lalo, o wāhi ka uka, o wāhi ke kai* (prayer to Lono for rain), break through, O Lono, break through above, break through below, may the uplands break through, may the lowlands break through. *E wāhi mai i ka berena e ola ai* (hymn), break the bread of life. **ho'o.wāhi.** Caus/sim. (PNP *fa'asi,* PCP *waasi.*)

wāhia. Pas/imp. of *wāhi. Ka hūlili pa'a 'a'oe e wāhia* (chant for Ka-lā-kaua), the strong bridge that cannot be broken. (PCP *wafia.*)

wā hia.moe. n. Time to sleep, bedtime.

wahie. 1. n. Fuel, firewood; to serve as firewood. (PPN *fafie,* PCP *wafie.*) **2.** n. Stroke in spear or club fighting.

wahie-'eke.'eke. n. Upper stroke in club fighting. (RC 59.)

wahī 'eha. n. Bandage.

wahie-o-ke-ola. n. Lignum vitae *(Guaiacum officinale),* a small tree from tropical America, with heavy, hard wood, useful for many purposes. The resin yields medicine and stain. The tree is also ornamental, each leaf with two or three pairs of rounded leaflets, the flowers blue and clustered, the fruits yellow and heart-shaped. (Neal 476.)

wahi hana. n. Workshop, place to work.

wahi hā.nai holo.holona, wahi hā.nai pipi. n. Cattle ranch.

wahi hila.hila. n. Private parts.

wahi ho'āhu 'ō.pala. n. Dump, garbage pile.

wahi ho'o.malu. n. Shelter.

wahi ho'o.pau pili.kia. n. Toilet, rest room.

wahi ka'a.wale. n. Vacant place, vacancy.

wahi kia'i. n. Lookout.

wahi kū moku. n. Anchorage.

wahī lawe pepa. n. Brief case.

wahī leka. n. Envelope.

wahi lulu. n. Shelter.

wahī maka.ani.ani. n. Glasses case.

wahi mā.lama pipi wai.ū. n. Dairy.
wahi moe. n. Bed (Hal. 132.3), place to sleep.
wahi nānā. n. Lookout.
wahine. 1. nvs. Woman, lady, wife; sister-in-law, female cousin-in-law of a man; queen in a deck of cards; womanliness, female, femininity; feminine; Mrs.; to have or obtain a *wahine;* to become a woman, as an adolescent. In some chants, as those about Pele, the word *wahine* has a connotation of goddess (see ex., *ʻolokaʻa*). Cf. *wāhine. Kai wahine* (Kep. 183), a gentle sea. *Kamika wahine,* Mrs. Smith. *Pipi wahine,* cow. *A laila wahine ʻoe* (Laie 493), then you will have a wife. *Kāna wahine maikaʻi,* his good wife. *Kona wahine maikaʻi,* her good-looking femininity. **hoʻo.wahine.** To behave like a woman, effeminate, feminine; to imitate the ways of a woman; to grow into womanhood; to have the manners and ways of a lady; to become a wife; to obtain a wife *(rare);* to take a wife. *ʻIke ʻoia i ka wahine maikaʻi o Ka-maile, ʻo ka hoʻowahine ihola nō ia* (For. 5:607), he saw the beautiful womanliness of Ka-maile, [and] took her as wife. *Ua wahine ʻoe* (GP 12), now you have a woman. (PPN *fafine,* PCP *wafine.*) **2.** n. Plant names. See below.
wā.hine. Plural of *wahine. Nā wāhine,* the women. (Gram. 8.1.) (PPN *fafine,* PNP *faafine,* PCP *waafine.*)
wahine hana. n. Female servant.
wahine hiʻu iʻa. n. Mermaid. *Lit.,* fish-tail woman.
wahine hoʻo.wahine. n. Platonic wife, an old Hawaiian relationship. Cf. *kāne hoʻokāne. Lit.,* pretended wife.
wahine kāne make. n. Widow. *Lit.,* woman with dead husband.
wahine kāne ʻole. n. Spinster, woman without a husband, single woman.
wahine kapu. n. Taboo woman, goddess (specifically Pele—not a woman who might not have sex relations, as some believe, Nānā 200–3).
wahine kāpulu. n. Untidy woman, slattern.
wahine kaua. n. Fighting woman, woman in the armed services, Amazon.
wahine mai.kaʻi. n. A gray lichen.
wahine makua. n. Older woman; older sister-in-law or female cousin-in-law of a man.
wahine mā.lama kapa. n. Wardrobe mistress.
wahine male (mare). n. Married woman, bride, wife.
wahine noho kula. n. An endemic shrub *(Isodendrion hawaiiense)* in the violet family, having the petals equal and without spurs. *Lit.,* woman dwelling [on the] plains. Cf. *aupaka.*
wahine noho mauna. n. An endemic fern *(Adenophorus tamariscinus),* with finely subdivided narrow-elliptical fronds 10 to 40 cm long, growing on trees and on the ground. *Lit.,* mountain-dwelling woman.
wahine o ka pō. n. Wife of the night. Similar to *kāne o ka pō* but less common.
wahine ʻole. nvs. Without a wife or sweetheart; bachelor.
wahine ʻō.maʻo. n. Same as *mohihihi,* a vine.
wahine ʻō.pio. n. Young woman; younger sister-in-law or female cousin-in-law of a man.
wahi noho. n. Dwelling place, address.
wahi pana. n. Legendary place.
wahi puhi ahi. n. Crematory, incinerator.
wahi waiho lole. n. Clothes hamper.
waho. loc. n. Outside, beyond, out, outer, outward, exterior (frequently preceded by particles *ʻo, ma-, mai*). See ex., *make 1. Mawaho o Hanalei* (FS 45), off Hanalei [as a ship]. *Mawaho aku ʻolua!* Go out, you two! *Mawaho aku o ka poʻina nalu,* beyond the breakers. *He make na waho,* death by outside [sorcery, not a natural death]. *E ʻimi i ke ola mawaho,* seek help outside [consult a *kahuna*]. (PPN *fafo,* PCP *wafo.*)
wahu. To take without consent, as food at a feast; to ensnare, trap. (AP.)
wahulu. Same as *ahulu,* overcooked.
wahu.wahū. To interlock arms, as while walking. (AP.)

wai. 1. nvs. Water, liquid or liquor of any kind other than sea water (see ex., *koni*), juice, sap, honey; liquids discharged from the body, as blood, semen; color, dye, pattern; to flow, like water, fluid. *Wai o ke kāne,* semen. *Wai o ka wahine,* menstruation or other discharge. *Wai o kaunu,* thrilling discharges of love. *Komo wai ē ʻia,* foreign liquid has entered [of a child conceived by other than the married husband]. *I wai noʻu,* give me some water [let's have a contest or fight]. *Wai ihola ke koko,* the blood flowed. *Wai o ka lehua,* lehua flower honey. *Hoʻokahi wai ʻo ka like,* the sameness of a single dye [unity]. *E wai kahi ka pono i mānalo,* better sweeten with a single color [unity to find serenity]. *Ua hewa i ka wai,* great quantities of water. *Hoʻolana i ka wai ke ola,* life floats on water [near death]. *Paʻihi ʻoe lā, lilo i ka wai, ʻaʻohe ʻike iho i ka hoa mua,* well-adorned are you, carried to water [wealth], not knowing former friends. (PPN *wai.*) **2.** *(Cap.)* n. Place names beginning with *Wai-,* river, stream. Nā Wai-ʻehā, the four waters, a poetic name for Wai-luku, Wai-ehu, Wai-heʻe and Wai-ka-pū, Maui. **3.** n. Grain in stone. **4.** vi. To retain, place, leave, remain, earn, deposit (see more common *waiho, waihona, waiwai,* and less common *wailana; waina 2, wai ʻūlili). Hale wai,* prison. (PCP *wai.*) **5.** (Also spelled *ai.*) interr. pronoun. Who, whom, whose, what (animate antecedents).(Gram. 8.5.) *ʻO wai? Who? ʻO wai kou inoa?* What is your name? *ʻO wai ia?* Who is he? (angrily) Who does he think he is? *Kō wai, kā wai?* Whose? *No wai?* For or in honor of whom? *Na wai?* By whom? *Kō wai kaʻa kēlā?* Whose car is that? *Iā wai ʻoe i kamaʻilio ai?* To whom did you speak? *Na wai nō i ʻōlelo iāʻoe e hele malaila?* Who told you to go there? (PPN *hai.*) **6.** n. Type of house with thatch purlins separated by a width of two fingers. (For. 5:645.)
waʻi. vi. Same as *wāhi,* to break, end. *Kauaʻi. Lā-waʻi* (place name), day to end [fishing taboo].
waia. 1. nvs. Disgraced; shame, dishonor. *Waia nohoʻi ka inoa o ka ʻohana,* the name of the family is disgraced. **hoʻo.waia.** To disgrace, put to shame. **2.** *(Cap.)* n. Name of a star.
wā iʻa. n. Season in which fish are numerous.
wai.ʻaʻa. Same as *wai ʻaʻapu.*
wai ʻaʻapu. Rare var. of *wai ʻapo.*
wai.ahu. Same as *waiehu.*
wai ahu. n. Pool of water.
wai aka. n. Water showing a reflection; name of a Nuʻu-anu pool.
wai.ā.kea. Same as *lehua keʻokeʻo,* a taro.
wai ʻakika. n. Acid.
wai.akua. Var. Distant, aloof, unsociable, exclusive, as of a chief too high to mingle with others. *Lit.,* godly blood.
wai ʻala. n. Perfume, cologne, toilet water. *Lit.,* fragrant liquid.
Wai-ʻale.ʻale. n. Name of the highest mountain on Kauaʻi.
wai ʻale.ʻale. n. Rippling water, artesian water.
wai aliʻi. n. Chiefly water; royal liquor, gin (in Kalākaua's song, *Koni au*).
wai.ani.ani. n. A variety of Molokaʻi sweet potato.
wai ani.ani. n. Crystal-clear water, artesian water.
wai.anu.hea. Same as *anuhea.* See *pī waianuhea. Waianuhea ke ʻala o ka ʻawapuhi,* the cool fragrance of ginger. **hoʻo.wai.anu.hea.** To cool, make fragrant and cool. *Na ka Maʻa ʻa i hoʻowaianuhea ā ʻolu wale,* cooled by the Maʻaʻa wind so as to be pleasant.
wai anu.hea. n. Tepid water, neither hot nor cold.
waia.nuʻu.kole. n. Name of a soft porous stone, as used in medicine or for octopus sinkers. (Malo 19.) Rare.
wai ʻapo. n. Water caught in a taro leaf, often used in ceremonies as it was regarded as pure in not having touched the ground. *Fig.,* a beloved mate, spouse. *Lit.,* caught water.
wai au. n. Swirling water of a current.
wai ʻau.ʻau. n. Bath water; bathing place or pool. A figurative use follows: *he wai ʻauʻau ia nona* (FS 51), it

was like bath water for him [of heroes dodging spears or engaged in fights; the hail of spears is as pleasant as splashing water].

wai ʻawa. nvs. Poisoned or bitter water; bitter. *Fig.,* same as *poli ʻawa.*

wai ʻawa.ʻawa. Redup. of *wai ʻawa. Imua ē nā pōkiʻi ā inu i ka wai ʻawaʻawa,* forward, young ones, and drink the bitter water [exhortation of Ka-mehameha to his warriors at the battle of ʻĪ-ao; i.e., face danger!].

wai.awī. n. The yellow strawberry guava *(Psidium cattleianum* f. *lucidum),* a small tree, like the *waiawī ʻula-ʻula* in many ways but bearing larger, yellow fruit. (Neal 634.)

wai.awī ʻula.ʻula. n. The purple strawberry guava *(Psidium cattleianum),* a small tree from Brazil, with smooth bark, smooth, shiny, obovate leaves about 5 cm long. The purplish-red fruit is round, about 2.5 cm in diameter, and has white pulp, good to eat raw or made into jam or jelly, tasting like strawberries. (Neal 633–4.)

wai ea. n. **1.** Aerated water. **2.** Small house at the entrance of a heiau temple, where the ceremonial *ʻaha* (cord) was stretched. (Malo 162.) **3.** Sea water used for purification. *Lit.,* water of life.

wai.ehu. n. A file; formerly a rough stone used to grind and polish.

wai ehu. n. Spraying water.

wai.ʻele. **1.** n. Black tapa dye; tapa so dyed. **2.** vt. To drug fish with *ʻauhuhu.*

wai.ʻele.ʻele. n. **1.** Black dye. **2.** Ink. **3.** A dark-skinned person.

wai ʻeli. n. Well water, well. *Lit.,* dug water.

wai.hā. n. Water upon which the breath *(hā)* of the priest has been expelled in order to impart mana; to give mana by breathing upon an image or person; to request earnestly in prayer. See ex., *waipā.*

wai.hae. n. Agricultural land term commonly used in the 1840s, especially on Maui; meaning unknown.

wai hā.nai. n. Small well from which brackish water was taken and poured into shallow pools called *wai kū;* this water later was placed into shallower pools and allowed to evaporate, leaving the salt. *Kauaʻi.*

wai.hau. **1.** n. A heiau where hogs, bananas, and coconuts were sacrificed, but not human beings; a heiau for *moʻo* spirits. **2.** nvt. A small, tight bundle; to do up in such a bundle. *Rare.*

wai hau. n. Ice water.

wai hī. n. Water oozing as from a precipice or trickling down. *Lit.,* purging water.

wā.ʻihi. Short for *wai ʻihi.*

wai hili. n. Water obtained by shaking the dew or rain drops from the leaves of plants or trees, as was said to have been done in dry areas. *Lit.,* hit water.

waiho. nvt. To leave, lay or put down, place before, present, refer, submit, place in nomination, file, deposit, set aside, exclude, evacuate, abdicate, desist, cease, stop, omit, quit, resign, abandon, remain; to table, as a motion; a leaving, depository, etc. (Coalescence of *wai* 4 and the directional *iho.)* Cf. *palapala waiho ʻoihana, waihona, waiho wale* and Gram. 2.7. *Waiho make,* to be left as though dead; to be faint; unconscious. *Waiho ʻaoʻao,* to lie on the side; heeled over, as a ship. *ʻO ka waiho haʻahaʻa ʻana aku,* respectfully submitting. *Waiho i kahi moe,* lie sick in bed, bedridden. *Ua pani ʻia ka waiho ʻana aʻe i nā inoa,* the nominations were closed. *Waiho akula ʻoia i kāna puʻupuʻu,* he laid to with his fists. *ʻAʻole au e waiho iāʻoe, e ʻeha ana ʻoe iaʻu,* I won't spare you, I will inflict punishment on you. *Ka waiho helahela mai o nā Koʻolau,* the panoramic view of the Koʻolaus. *Waiho ʻai,* to fast. *ʻO ka waiho ʻana o ka ʻāina* (old land claim), the lay of the land. *Waiho ʻia,* left, entrusted. **hoʻo.waiho.** To leave, abandon, ignore, shun; to expose or leave naked. *Ua hoʻowaiho maila ia i ka pōkiʻi,* he shunned the younger brother. (PCP *waifo.)*

wai.hoa. Pas/imp. of *waiho.*

wai hō.ʻa.ala. n. Toilet water, liquid spice, scented extract. *Lit.,* liquid that perfumes.

waiho akaaka, waiho.kāka. vt. To lie or place in full view; easily seen, obvious.

wai hoʻāno. n. Holy water.

waiho kā.hela. vi. To lie widespread before one.

waiho loa. vt. To abandon completely, give up.

wai.holo.moku. n. Flood. *Ua kahe nohoʻi ka waiholomoku* (Hal. 124.5), the waters have gone over.

waiho mahi ʻole. vi. To lie fallow.

waiho maʻi. vi. To lie sick, remain sick.

wai.hona. nvs. Depository, closet, cabinet, vault, file, receptacle, savings, place for laying up things in safekeeping; internal organs of the body, funds, treasury; fiscal. *(Wai* 4 + *iho,* directional, + *-na,* nominalizer.) Numerous types of *waihona* are listed below. *Hale waihona puke,* library. *Hana waihona kālā,* fiscal service. *Waihona nui o ka Teritori,* general fund of the Territory. *Waihona o ka naʻauao,* repository of learning [a learned person].

wai.hona ʻāina. n. Position of the land, lay of the land, position of the earth, landscape, panorama, scenery, topography.

wai.hona hoʻo.manaʻo. n. Memory.

wai.hona hoʻo.nanea. n. Playroom, parlor; private rooms of the captain of a ship.

wai.hona ʻike. n. Intelligence.

wai.hona ipu. n. Cupboard, place to keep food containers; bases supporting bath basins in Solomon's temple (1 Nal. 7.35).

wai.hona kā.lā (dala). n. Treasury, money depository, fund; fiscal. *Lit.,* dollar depository. See ex., *kūpilikiʻi.*

wai.hona keiki. n. Womb.

wai.hona kukui. n. Candlestick, lamp stand. *Waihona kukui gula* (1 Oihn. 28.15), candlesticks of gold.

wai.hona kupa.paʻu. n. Burial vault.

wai.hona lako kaua. n. Arsenal, arms depository. *Lit.,* war goods depository.

wai.hona lā.nahu. n. Coalbin.

wai.hona mea laʻa. n. Place for sacred objects; treasure (Neh. 7.70).

wai.hona meli. n. Honeycomb. (1 Sam. 14.27.)

wai.hona moni. n. Place for keeping money, treasury. *Rare.*

wai.hona noʻo.noʻo. n. Mind, mentality.

wai.hona ʻō.pala. n. Dump, garbage container.

wai.hona pā ipu. n. Cupboard.

wai.hona pala.pala kahiko. n. Archives. *Lit.,* depository of ancient documents.

wai.hona pana.kō. n. Bank account, depository.

wai.hona puke (buke). n. Library.

wai.hona wai.wai. n. Treasury, depository for goods, property; treasurer. (2 Oihn. 5.1.)

wai hoʻo.heheʻe. n. Digestive juice.

wai hoʻo.hui. nvs. Water color.

waiho ola. v. To spare the life, to remain living.

wai.hoʻo.luʻu. nv. Color, dye, coloring liquid; to impart scent. *Paʻa i ka waihoʻoluʻu,* dyed, colored. *He aha ka waihoʻoluʻu o kēlā pua?* What is the color of that flower?

wai hoʻo.maʻe.maʻe. n. Disinfectant; any kind of cleaning liquid, cleansing liquid, liquid soap.

waiho wale. vt. To leave without reason; to leave about carelessly; to set aside as useless; to neglect, to expose to view. *Lumi waiho wale,* room left unused. *Mai waiho wale i kō puke o lilo i ka ʻaihue,* don't just leave your book around or a thief will take it.

wai hū. n. Gushing spring, overflowing water.

wai hua. n. Water-drop caught as in a taro leaf, much liked for purification and medicine, as it has not touched the earth. Also called *wai ʻapo.*

wai hui.kala. n. Water for purification.

wai ʻihi. n. Sacred blood, as of royalty. *Fig.,* prominent, royal.

wai.iki. n. A kidney disease that impedes urination. *Lit.,* little water.

wai inu. n. Drinking water, potable water.
wai.kahe. nvi. Stream (Hal. 124.4); to flow, overflow, as a stream. *Lit.,* flowing water. See ex., *mokuhia. Waikahe nui,* torrent. (PPN *waitafe.*)
wai kahi. vs. United, of one dye. See ex., *kāoʻo.*
wāi.kāhuli. 1. n. A calliopsis *(Coreopsis tinctoria),* an annual ornamental herb, in the daisy family, from central United States, the ray flowers yellow with dark-red at the base. (Neal 842.) *Lit.,* change [of] color. **2.** See *aloalo,* hibiscus. **3.** See *melekule wai kāhuli.*
wai kai. n. Brackish or salty water.
wai.kā.lā (dala). nvs. Quicksilver, mercury; silver, silver-colored. *Lit.,* silver liquid.
wai.kanaka. vs. Having ways of ordinary folk. *Rare. Lit.,* human pattern.
wai.kaua. 1. n. A war temple. **2.** Same as *waiwai kaua.*
wai.kea. n. Juice of fresh *kukui* nuts, as mixed with fresh or brackish water and used as an enema. *Lit.,* white liquid.
wai.kekē. Same as *wekekē,* whiskey.
wai keʻo.keʻo. n. Leucorrhea. *Lit.,* white liquid.
wai.kī. 1. n. Gun. *Rare.* See *pōhaku waikī.* **2.** Enema of a concoction consisting of the juice of the poisonous gourd, water, salt, and other matter, drastic and painful. Cf. the more mild *waikea.* **3.** Gonorrhea, of males; painful urination, perhaps due to cystitis. *Rare. Koko waikī,* blood discharge in urine. **4.** One whose father was a chief but whose mother was not, a term of contempt. *Rare.* Cf. *ʻahunāliʻi.*
wai kī. n. Water in which tea has been brewed, tea.
Wai-kī.kī. n. Place name used as a direction marker in Honolulu. *Lit.,* spouting water. *Ma ka ʻaoʻao Wai-kīkī,* on the Wai-kīkī side.
wai kō. n. **1.** Water with a strong current. **2.** Sugary water.
wai koʻana wai.ū paka. n. Buttermilk.
wai.kō.ʻihi. n. Waterspout. Cf. *waipuʻilani.*
Wai-kō-loa. n. Cold wind blowing with Mt. Kaʻala, Oʻahu, and the nearby place of the same name (FS 282).
wai.koʻo.lihi.lihi. n. Tears that seem to cling to eyelashes. *Lit.,* liquid supporting eyelashes. *Poetic.*
wai.kū. Same as *nae waikū.* (For. 6:451.)
wai kū. See *wai hānai.*
wai kula (gula). vs. Gold-colored.
wai.kū.lono.ʻako.a.koʻa. n. An old name for syphilis.
wai.kulu. n. Alcohol.
wai.kū.oa. n. Dart, as for war. *Rare.*
wai lā.ʻau. n. **1.** Sap of plants. **2.** Liquid medicine.
wai.lana. 1. nvs. Calm, quiet, as the sea; still water. **2.** nvs. Banished, as for unworthy conduct; exile. (Perhaps *wai 4,* to leave, + *-lana,* nominalizer; Gram. 6.6.2.) **3.** n. A prayer uttered to free a taboo period.
wai lani. n. Rain water, especially as used for medicine and purification. Cf. *wai hua.*
wai.lau. 1. n. Large leaf bundles of food, as poi, for carrying. **2.** An ancient variety of tapa. (For. 5:112.)
Wai-lau. n. Place names on Hawaiʻi, Kauaʻi, and Molokaʻi.
wai lau.lau. n. Water carried in folded taro leaves.
Wai.leia. n. Name of a morning star.
wai.lele. n. Waterfall, cataract, cascade. *Lit.,* leaping water. (PCP *wailele;* cf. Marquesan *vaiʻeʻe.*)
wai lemi. n. Lemon juice, lemonade, limeade.
wai.lena. n. Bile. *Lit.,* yellow water.
wai.lewa. n. Coconut water. *Lit.,* hanging water. See riddle, *lewa 1.*
wai.liʻi.liʻi. n. A decorated tapa. *Lit.,* small colors.
wai.liʻu. Same as *wailiʻulā. Aloha i ka wailiʻu o ka ʻāina* (PH 116), greeting to the mirage of the land.
wai.liʻu.lā. 1. n. Mirage. **2.** nvs. Of changing color, as taffeta or a stone; taffeta.
Wai-loa. n. Name of a star near the Pleiades, said to be a member of the group called *Kaulua.* It is also said to be a name of an ancient chief. *Lit.,* long stream.
wai.lua. n. **1.** Spirit, ghost; remains of the dead. *Hoʻi-*

hoʻi ʻia aku kona kino wailua ā hoʻomoe ʻia maloko o ka pā ilina, his remains were taken and laid away in the cemetery. (PEP *wailua.*) **2.** An ancient variety of sweet potato, presumably introduced from Wai-lua, Kauaʻi.
wai Lū.kini. n. Perfume. *Lit.,* Russian liquor, so-called because musk was obtained from Russians in early days, the wet product being perfume. Cf. *hualūkini,* For. 5:656.
wai.luku. 1. n. Name reported for an *ulua* fishing line. **2.** Same as *haleloke,* a chrysanthemum.
Wai-luku. n. A West Maui city, site of a late eighteenth century battle. *Lit.,* destructive water.
wai.mā.hoe.hoe. vt. To strip the flesh from bones, as for burial.
wai.maka. n. Tears. *Lit.,* eye water. See ex., *pania.* (PEP *waimata.*)
wai.maka-ia-kohi. n. Name of a minor illness (no data).
wai.maka lehua. n. Waterdrops from the *ʻōhiʻa lehua* tree; euphemism for menstruation. Also *waimaka-o-lehua.*
wai.maka.nui. n. **1.** An endemic fern *(Thelypteris keraudreniana),* with large, broad, pale, subdivided fronds, the last divisions triangular or oblong, the spores arranged in small dots scattered on the frond back. Also *alaʻalai.* **2.** A native fern *(Pteris excelsa),* with large, broad, bright-green, subdivided fronds, in general like *waimakanui 1,* but the last divisions longer and subfalcate, and the spores arranged in a line under the curled frond margin.
wai-maka-o-Pele. n. Pele's tears.
wai-maka-ua. n. Services to get rain. (For. 6:153.)
wai.mano. 1. Stone from which octopus sinkers were made. (Malo 19.) **2.** Adobe. (AP.)
wai.mea. n. **1.** Maui name for *olomea,* a shrub. **2.** Kauaʻi name for a kind of *māmaki,* having leaves with red veins and stems resembling those of the *olomea.*
Wai-mea. n. A place name. *Lit.,* reddish water. See ex., *pā ʻili.*
wai mea ʻino. n. Slop.
wai meli. n. Honey. *Lit.,* bee liquor.
wai mimi. n. Urine. (2 Nal. 18.27.)
wai momona. n. Soda water, sweet water.
wai.mū.hea. n. Same as *kaupō,* a native banana.
waina. n. **1.** Place with water. **2.** Depository. See *wai 4. Pū-o-waina* (Hawaiian name for Punchbowl, Honolulu), hill of deposits [human sacrifices]. **3.** Pyorrhea, bleeding gums. **4.** Wine. *Eng.* See *pā waina.* **5.** Isabella grape *(Vitis xlabruscana),* a strong-climbing vine, bearing blue, loose-skinned fruits. This is a hybrid that succeeds best of any grape introduced to Hawaiʻi; little interest has been shown in the past in the grape industry. (Neal 542-3.) See *hua waina.*
Wai-naku. n. Star name, sometimes called the patron star of Hilo.
waina maloʻo. n. Raisins. *Lit.,* dry grapes.
wai niu. n. Coconut water or cream (the distinction was not clear; cf. *kai niu, wailewa). Wai o ka niu,* coconut cream.
wai.nohia. 1. Probably similar to *waipahē. Nanea wainohia no Maka-kēhau,* [a] pleasant [and] agreeable [story] about Maka-kēhau. **2.** Safe, safety. (And.)
wai nui. nvi. A large flow of water; excessive flow of saliva; to flow in great quantities, juicy.
wai.oha. Same as *ohaoha,* joy.
wai.ʻō.hiʻa. n. A variety of sugar cane.
wai ʻō.hiʻa. n. Juice or cider of mountain apples; cider in general; tomato juice.
wai.ohinu. n. All kinds of cultivated dahlias *(Dahlia* spp.), named for a town on Hawaiʻi where the plant was first grown. (Neal 843-4.) *Pika waiohinu,* vase or pitcher of dahlias [name of an old quilt design showing a pitcher containing dahlias].
wai.okila. See *pāpale waiokila.*
wai.oleka. n. Fragrant cultivated violets (as *Viola odorata).* (Neal 591.) *Eng.* See *nani Wai-ʻaleʻale* (native violets).

wai.olina. n. Violin. *Eng.* See ex., *nē.*
wai.olina kū. n. Cello.
wai.olina kū nui. n. Bass viol.
Wai-olo.hia. n. A Kauaʻi wind. (For. 5:97.)
wai.olono. vs. Careful, cautious about what one says. *Rare.*
wai.ʻolu. vs. Cool, pleasant, attractive, soft, gentle, pleasing. *Kou piko waiʻolu* (song), your pleasant private parts.
wai ʻona. n. Intoxicating liquor or spirits. *Hōʻole wai ʻona,* prohibition of intoxicants.
wai ʻono. n. Honey, sweet liquid.
wai-ʻoʻopu. n. Type of tapa.
wai.ʻō.pua. n. 1. A disease similar to pulmonary consumption. 2. Leucorrhea.
Wai-ʻō.pua. n. Name of a pleasant breeze at Wai-lua, Kauaʻi. (For. 5:97.) *Lit.,* water of cloud banks.
wai.ʻō.upe. n. Mirage. *Lit.,* deceiving water.
wai.pā. n. Request, prayer, as to the gods. *Pēlā kaʻu waihā me kaʻu waipā aku iāʻoe, ē ke akua,* such is my request and prayer to you, O god.
wai.paʻa. n. Ice. (Ioba 6.16.) *Lit.,* hard, solid water.
wai paʻa.kai. n. Salty water, brine.
wai.pahē. vs. Courteous, gentlemanly, polite, modest, gentle, good-natured, easygoing, agreeable, complacent, gracious. This word is usually used in a favorable sense, but occasionally pejoratively: *he wahine waipahē wale ma nā mea ʻano ʻino,* a woman complacent indeed in the ways of sin.
wai.pahū. n. Gunpowder. *Lit.,* explosive liquid.
wai pahū. n. Spouting water, geyser.
wai paʻi.paʻi. n. Mixed liquid, solution, or drink of any kind (*lama paʻipaʻi* is more common for alcoholic drinks).
wai.palu.palu. n. Name recorded for a variety of sweet potato.
wai-palu.palu. n. A kind of tapa. *Lit.,* soft dye or pattern.
Wai-paoa. n. Cool breeze famous at Wai-mea, Kauaʻi. *Lit.,* scooped water.
wai.pehē. Var. of *waipahē.*
wai piʻi. nvi. Rising water, overflow of water, flood (Ier. 46.7); to flow, overflow.
wai piʻi.piʻi, wai pipiʻi. Redup. of *wai piʻi;* charged water, bubbling water.
wai piula. n. Water from a faucet.
wai.pū. n. Gunpowder. *Rare.*
wai pua. n. Honey from flowers.
wai puhia. n. Wind-blown water or spray, as of a waterfall; name of the "upside-down" waterfall in Nuʻu-anu Valley.
wai.puʻi.lani. n. Waterspout (perhaps from *wai puhi lani,* heaven-blown water). *I ka halulu mau ʻana o kou waipuʻilani* (Hal. 42.7), at the noise of thy waterspouts.
wai puna. n. Spring water. *Fig.,* a sweetheart. (PPN *wai puna.*)
wai pū.ʻolo. n. Water in leaves, as of taro, that could be carried; coconut water. *Lit.,* bundled water.
wai pū.ʻolo i ka lau lā.ʻau. n. An ancient name for ice. *Lit.,* water in a package of tree leaves, so called because ice was said to be brought down from the mountains in leaves. (Malo 241-2.)
wai.ū. n. Milk; a wet nurse; breast. *Lit.,* breast liquid. *Kau ka waiū,* breasts filled with milk. *Keiki waiū,* nursing child. *Hoʻokau i ka waiū,* to perform ceremonies to make the breasts fill with milk. *Lele ka waiū,* breast milk has ceased to flow. *Hoʻolele i ka waiū,* to perform ceremonies to make the breast cease flowing. *He ʻāina e kahe ana ka waiū a me ia meli* (Nah. 14.8), a land which flows with milk and honey. (PNP *waiuu.*)
wai ua. n. Rain water.
wai.ū haki. n. A breast that sags, but not long or pendulous. *Lit.,* broken breast.
wai.ū.haku.haku. n. Clabbered milk, cottage cheese. *Lit.,* lumpy milk.
wai.ū heʻe.heʻe. n. Caked breast.

wai.ū hoʻo.hui.hui. n. Milk combined with other ingredients, as for a baby or person on a liquid diet; formula. *Lit.,* mixed milk.
wai.ū kahe. n. Flowing breast or milk.
wai.ū kau. n. Breast filled with milk.
wai.ū kia. n. Condensed milk. *Lit.,* deer milk, so called because the first cans of condensed milk had a picture of deer on the label.
wai.ū kini. n. Canned milk.
wai.ū.ko.a. n. A breast that has milk from the beginning of pregnancy to long after weaning.
wai ʻula. n. Red liquid, blood, menstrual flow; rain run-off red with soil.
Wai-uli. n. Name of a wind, Honolua, Maui. (For. 5:101.)
wai ʻū.lili. vt. To fix firmly. Cf. *ʻūlili 8. ʻO kēia mau mea auaneʻi apau aʻu e ʻōlelo aku nei iāʻoe lā, e waiʻūlili aʻe ʻoe a paʻa i loko o kou nāʻau,* all these things I will tell you, you should fix them firmly in your mind.
wai.ū luli.luli. n. Milk shake.
wai.ū.paʻa. n. Cheese. (1 Sam. 17.18.) *Lit.,* solidified milk.
wai.ū paʻi.paʻi. n. Diluted milk.
wai.ū.paka, waiu bata. n. Butter.
wai.ū.paka.paʻa. n. Cheese. *Lit.,* solidified butter.
wai.ū puʻu. n. Budding breast, as of a young girl.
wai.wai. nvs. Goods, property, assets, valuables, value, worth, wealth, importance, benefit, estate, use; useful, valuable, rich, costly, financial. (Probably related to *wai 4,* to retain, rather than to *wai 1,* water.) See *kumu waiwai, waiwai ʻole. Waiwai i hao ʻia,* booty, spoils, goods of any kind seized or appropriated. *Waiwai kī-koʻolā,* miscellaneous valuables. *Hoʻoponopono waiwai,* administrator of property or of an estate. *Waiwai loaʻa ma ke kolohe,* ill-gotten gains. *Kōmike waiwai,* financial committee. **hoʻo.wai.wai.** To enrich, bring prosperity.
wai.wai hapa ʻumi. n. Tithe, tithing. *Lit.,* one-tenth property.
wai.wai hoʻo.ilina. n. Inherited property, heritage, estate.
wai.wai hoʻo.lilo. n. Exports.
wai.wai hoʻo.paʻa. n. Security, fixed assets. *Lit.,* solid property.
wai.wai hoʻo.pae mai. n. Imports.
wai.wai hoʻo.pae malū. n. Smuggled goods.
wai.wai hoʻo.puka. n. Profits.
wai.wai hui. n. Assets. *Lit.,* combined wealth.
wai.wai inoa. n. Par value, as of stocks. *Lit.,* name value.
wai.wai ʻiʻo. n. True worth, as of heirlooms; marked value, as of stocks.
wai.wai kā.lepa. n. Merchandise.
wai.wai kaua. n. War goods, spoils.
wai.wai kau.like. n. Par value, just value.
wai.wai koko ola. n. Wealth taken to cause by sorcery the death of an innocent person—this was punishable by the sorcerer's own death. (Kam. 64:120.) *Lit.,* live blood goods.
wai.wai koko pī.lau. n. Wealth taken to cause by sorcery the death of a sorcerer who had prayed others to death. (Kam. 64:120.) *Lit.,* foul blood goods.
wai.wai komo. n. Imports.
wai.wai kū.ʻai. n. Investments. (Will 129, 1856, State Archives.)
wai.wai lewa. n. Movable or personal property; liquid assets; chattel. *Moraki waiwai lewa,* chattel mortgage.
wai.wai maloko. n. Tribute or wealth from the uplands.
wai.wai nui. n. Great wealth, fortune.
wai.wai ʻole. vs. Worthless, useless, of no use or value, good-for-nothing.
wai.wai paʻa. n. Real estate, property that cannot be moved.
wai.wai pio. n. Booty, plunder, spoils (Puk. 15.9).
wai.wai puka aku. n. Exports.

wai wela.wela. n. Warm or hot spring.
waka. 1. vs. Sharp, protruding. **2.** Same as *'owaka, wawaka,* to flash.
wā kahiko. n. Ancient times, antiquity.
wā kama.li'i. n. Childhood. Also *wā li'ili'i. Ko'u wā kamali'i,* my childhood.
waka.waka. 1. Redup. of *waka 1;* serrated, pointed, sharp, as a rake's prongs or the spikes of a sea urchin; hilly. *Puhi niho wakawaka,* sharp-toothed eel [a mighty warrior]. *Hāmākua i ka wakawaka,* Hāmākua with the sharp hills. **2.** Redup. of *waka 2.*
Wā-kea, Ā.kea. n. The mythical ancestor of all Hawaiians. (Kep. 61-7.)
wā keiki. n. Childhood.
wā keiki kāne. n. Boyhood.
waki. Var. spelling of *uaki,* watch.
waki kia'i hale. n. House guard.
Waki.kana, Vatikana. n. Vatican. *Eng.*
Wakine.kona, Wakinetona. n. Washington. *Eng.*
wā.kiuma. vt. To vacuum. *Eng.*
wala. vi. To tilt, lift backwards, fall backwards; to throw backwards, as with a backhand flip. *Wala kī'aha,* to tip the glass in drinking, tipple. *Ua wala 'ia mai au i ka pahi,* a knife was thrown at me.
wala.'au. vi. To talk, speak, converse; formerly, to talk loudly, shout. See saying, *makani 1. Hoa wala'au,* person to speak with. *Wala'au wale,* to talk for the sake of talking, chatter; talkative, garrulous. *Wala'au ka waha,* to speak too much. *Kumepala wala'au* (1 Kor. 13.1), tinkling cymbal. **ho'o.wala.'au.** To cause talk, start talk or conversation. (PNP *walakau.*)
wala.he'e. Var. spelling of *alahe'e,* a shrub or small tree.
wala.he'e haole. Var. spelling of *alahe'e haole,* mock orange.
wala.kī.kē. vt. To toss, hurl back and forth, as spears in battle.
wala kua. vi. To fall over backward; to throw or stab at the back; to turn a somersault backwards; to rear, as a horse.
wā.lana. Var. of *wānana.* (For. 6:489.)
wala.nia. nvs. Anguish, hurting pain, woe, torment; anguishing, smarting. See ex., *loloku. Walania ke ki'i-'ōnohi,* smarting eyeballs. *Nā 'eha walania o ka make mau loa,* the agonizing pain of eternal death. **ho'o.-wala.nia.** To cause pain, wound.
wala.nuka, walanuta. n. Walnut. *(Juglans* spp.) (Neal 296.) *Eng.*
wala.wala. 1. Redup. of *wala;* to tilt, as a canoe in waves. *Walawala pahū,* to fall backwards and land with a thud. **2.** *(Cap.)* n. Rain name.
wala.wala.'au. Redup. of *wala'au. Rare.*
wala.wala.kī. vi. To fall back; to plummet to the ground.
wala.wala.nia. Redup. of *walania.*
wale. 1. n. Slime, mucus, phlegm; sticky sap, as from cuts in tree ferns and *māmaki* wood that is mixed with bark in making tapa. Cf. *waha wale.* (PEP *wale.*) **2.** A common part. that always follows modified words and has many meanings, as: only, just, very; alone; without pay, payment, reward, cause, reason; easily; gratuitous, free, casual. See *hele wale, hikiwale, mea wale (mea 4), wale nō. 'Ai wale,* to eat without pay or reason; to eat alone. *Hana wale,* to do or act without justification, cause, reward. *Ho'i wale,* to go back empty-handed. *Huhū wale,* quick-tempered, angry without cause. *Loa'a wale,* easily obtained. *Maika'i wale 'o Kaua'i* (song), how beautiful is Kaua'i. (PPN *wale.*) **3.** *(Cap.)* n. Wales, Welshman; Welsh. *Eng. Ke keiki ali'i o Wale,* the Prince of Wales.
walea. 1. Same as *nanea.* See ex., *pākanaka. E walea, nanea ana paha i ka leo nahenahe o nā manu* (song), relaxing at ease with the gentle voices of the birds. **ho'o.-walea.** Caus/sim. See ex., *peue.* (PCP *walea.*) **2.** vs. Accustomed; so familiar that one does a thing without effort, as a dance; adept; to do well and effortlessly, as an acquired skill. *Ua hana ā walea,* done until automat-

ic. *Ua walea i ka pena ki'i,* an experienced and perfect painter.
wale.'ā. Same as *wele'ā,* a fish.
wale hau. n. Sap in *hau* tree blossoms, chewed and swallowed to relieve constipation, and given to women before labor; slimy liquid obtained by immersing *hau* bark in water, drunk as a laxative. **ho'o.wale hau.** Unreliable, fickle, unstable; slippery and amusing, as in speech.
wale kea. n. White mucus, as in the eyes.
wale.luka, walerusa. n. Walrus. *Eng.* Also *wolu.*
wale.nia. Var. of *walania.*
wale nō. part. Only, just, all, very. (Gram. 7.5.) *'Elua wale nō,* only two. *He po'e wāhine wale nō,* just women, only women. *He maika'i wale nō kāu mau kūkaliki* (Kel. 135), your boasting is quite okay. *Maika'i wale nō Kaua'i* (Elbert and Mahoe 75), so very beautiful is Kaua'i.
wale.waha. vs. To know a thing so well that it can be spoken without thought; letter-perfect; to know by rote or as a mother tongue. *Ha'i walewaha mai,* to recite perfectly, by memory. *Ua lilo ia i mea walewaha iāia,* this has become known to him letter-perfect.
wale wai. vs. Slimy with saliva. *Fig.,* to talk too much.
wale.wale. 1. Redup. of *wale 1.* **2.** vs. Deceived. *Rare.* **ho'o.wale.wale.** To tempt, decoy, lead astray, beguile, fool, entice, take advantage of; tempter, temptation. *Ho'owalewale i nā naheka,* to charm snakes. *Walewale moekolohe,* libidinous soliciting, adulterous tempting. *Ho'owalewale hewa,* to seduce, lead into sin. **3.** Same as *wale 2,* just, only, etc. (Nal. 1:22–34.)
wale.wale keiki. n. Discharge following childbirth.
wale.walena. n. Slimy discharge.
wali. vs. Smooth, thin, as poi; fine, mashed, soft, powdery, supple, limber, as a dancer's body. Cf. *nāwaliwali, niu 1, 'ōnāwali, 'ōnāwaliwali.* **ho'o.wali.** To make soft, smooth, as soil, to mix, as poi or dough; to digest. *'Aila ho'owali pena,* paint thinner. *'Uala ho'owali 'ia,* mashed sweet potatoes. *Nā lio ka'inapu ho'owali lua* (chant), graceful, doubly supple horses. *Nā mea ho'owali o loko,* digestive organs. *'Ūlei ho'owali 'uala,* digging stick of *'ūlei* wood that softens [the earth for] sweet potatoes [sexual reference]. (PCP *wali.*)
wā li'i.li'i. See *wā kamali'i.*
walina. n. Softness. Cf. *wali.*
wali.wali. Redup. of *wali;* gentle, easygoing, good-natured, smooth. Cf. *nāwaliwali. He waliwali kāna 'ōlelo,* he speaks gently, softly. *Aloha nō au i kou maka, kou ihu waliwali ka'u i honi* (song), I love your eyes, your soft nose I kiss.
walo. Same as *uwalo,* to call, resound. *Kani ka pio, walo i ke kula,* the whistle sounds, carries across the plain. (PPN *walo.*)
walo.hia. Pas/imp. of *walo;* pathos; touching, pathetic. See ex., *ha'alipo. Mo'olelo piha walohia,* tale full of pathos.
walo.ina. Same as *walo,* to call.
walo.walo. Redup. of *walo.* (PPN *walowalo.*)
walu. 1. vt. To claw, scratch, rub, grate, rasp, scrape. Also *'uwalu, wa'u.* (PPN *waru.*) **2.** n. Oilfish *(Ruvettus pretiosus),* caught in deep water; large, much prized for eating and used as a cathartic. See ex., *maku'u 3.* (PPN *walu.*) **3.** num. Eight, eighth *(walu* and other multiples of four are formulistic numbers; cf. *-walu). Hapawalu,* one eighth. *Kanawalu,* eighty. (PPN *walu.*)
-walu. Many. Cf. *kūwaluwalu, makawalu, olowalu, puwalu.* (Eight being a sacred number may have led to this extension of the meaning.)
wā.lua. 1. vt. To carry on a pole on the shoulders, of two. **2.** n. Middle, interior. (Mele 3.10.)
walu.hia. 1. Pas/imp. of *walu 1.* **2.** n. Bird name (no data).
waluna. n. Clawing, scratching. Cf. *walu 1.*
wā.luna. n. Prophecy. (And.)
walu.walu. Redup. of *walu 1.*
wā mamua. n. Formerly, old times.

wana. 1. n. A sea urchin, as *Diadema paucispinum* and *Echinothrix diadema,* considered by some an *'auma-kua.* (PPN *wana.*) **2.** nvs. Sharp-pointed, as sea-urchin spines; jagged, sharp; spike. **3.** n. A long spike or streak of light, as at dawn; to appear, as a ray of light. Cf. *wana'ao. Wana kau lani,* a streak in the heavens, as of light or cloud. (PCP *wana.*)

wana.'ao. nvi. Dawn; to dawn.

wana hina. n. Streak of gray, as in hair.

wana kau.ila. n. A *wana* with dark spikes. *Lit., kauila* wood *wana.*

Wana.koua, Vanakoua. n. Vancouver. *Eng.*

wā.nana. nvt. Prophecy; to prophesy, predict, prognosticate, foresee, foretell. *Ka-wānana-koa* (name), the brave prophecy. *Wānana i ke au o ka manawa,* weather forecast. Also *wālana.* (PEP *waananga.*)

wana.o'a. vs. Projecting in every direction, as the spines of a sea urchin; sharp-edged and projecting; to bristle, radiate.

wana.wana. Redup. of *wana 2;* spiny, thorny, as cactus; spiked, pointed; sharp, as jagged cliffs, spine, quills. *He wana ka i'a, wanawana ka lani,* sea urchin the sea creature, thorny the heavens [a fierce battle]. (PPN *wanawana.*)

waniki. nvt. Varnish; to paint (Kel. 135). *Eng.* See *kuka waniki.*

wanila. nvs. Vanilla. *Eng.*

wā.nini. Var. spelling of *ānini,* a plant.

wao. n. A general term for inland region usually forested but not precipitous and often uninhabited. See ex., *puahia* and below. (PPN *wao.*)

wao akua. n. A distant mountain region, believed inhabited only by spirits *(akua);* wilderness, desert. See ex., *panoa, pua 1. Wao akua nui o Sahara,* great Sahara desert.

wao.'eiwa. n. An inland region.

wao.hua. vi. To plot to trap. *Rare.*

wao 'ilima. n. An area at a lower altitude than that called *wao 'ama'u;* also *'āpa'a.* See *'ama'u 2.*

wao kanaka. n. An inland region where people may live or occasionally frequent, usually considered below the *wao akua.*

wao kele. n. Rain belt, upland forest. *Ka 'uhane i ka wao kele* (FS 273), the soul in the rainy depths.

wao koa. n. Inland region where *koa* trees grow.

wao lā.'au. Same as *wao nahele.*

wao lani. n. Mountain area believed occupied by gods.

wao lipo. n. Inland region, said by Kamakau to be between the *wao'eiwa* and the *wao nahele. Lit.,* dark *wao.*

wao ma'u kele. Same as *wao kele.*

wao nahele. n. Inland forest region, jungle, desert (Hal. 107.4).

wao one. n. Desert.

wā o'o. n. Maturity.

wā 'ō.pio, wā 'ō.pio.pio. n. Youth (time of).

wā.pine, vabine. n. The lemon verbena *(Aloysia triphylla),* a South American shrub, with rough lemonscented, narrow leaves, and small white or lavender flowers in spikes. Formerly the plant was a favorite in Hawaiian gardens, and was used in leis. (Neal 724.) *Eng.*

wau. Var. of *au,* I. (PPN *au.*)

wa'u. nvt. To grate, scrape, scratch, rasp, claw, wear away by friction; grater, scraper, as of cowry or other shell. Also *uwa'u, walu.* (PPN *waku.*)

wā ua. n. Rainy season.

wau.'aha. n. Prayer for deliverance or thanksgiving.

wā u'i. n. Youth, time of physical perfection.

wauke. n. The paper mulberry *(Broussonetia papyrifera),* a small tree or shrub, from eastern Asia, known throughout the Pacific for its usefulness. It belongs to the fig or mulberry family. The bark was made into tough tapa used for clothing, bed clothes; it lasted longer than *māmaki* tapa. (Neal 301.) Cf. *po'a'aha 2.* (PCP *(w)aute.*)

wauke ku'i.ku'i. n. Bast from fully mature *wauke* that required more beating *(ku'iku'i)* than younger *wauke (wauke ohiohi).* (Kam. 76:40.)

wauke mā.lolo. n. A *wauke* that was used medicinally, perhaps as a substitute for the *mālolo* (flying fish) often used in sacrifices.

wauke pua.kai. n. *Wauke* bast dyed red for use as coloring material in tapa. (Kam. 76:114.)

wa'u niu. nv. Coconut grater; to grate coconut.

wā 'u'uku. n. Childhood. *Lit.,* small time. See ex., *hiwahiwa.*

wau.wau, wau.au. vi. To travel off the path or crookedly. *Rare.*

wa'u.wa'u. Redup. of *wa'u. Pōhaku wa'uwa'u 'ili,* stone that claws the skin [name of a stone offshore at Wai-ka-puna, Ka'ū; formerly persons would entice a would-be lover to this stone and scratch his or her skin as an indication of sexual possession]. (PPN *wakuwaku.*)

wawā. Redup. of *wā 3, 4;* tumultuous; racket, loud talk, echo, sound of distant voices, roar; rumored, talked about, resounding, repeating (see *hānau wawā*). *Ua wawā 'ia e kaua ana nā aupuni 'elua,* it is rumored that the two governments are going to battle. *Ahu wawā ka nahele,* a mass of sound in the forest [of rumor, gossip]. *Ka wawā lapuwale* (1 Tim. 6.20), profane babblings. **ho'o.wawā.** Caus/sim. (PPN *wawaa.*)

wā.wae. 1. nvs. Leg, foot, paw; upper leg of a crab; foot of a rainbow; trousers *(rare);* afoot, on foot; to walk. See *hele wāwae. Lole wāwae,* trousers. *Wāwae olonā* (Puk. 28.42), linen breeches. *Kinipōpō peku wāwae,* football. *Pōhaku 'ai wāwae o Malama,* feet-eating rocks of Malama [of sharp *aa* lava]. *Pua'a wāwae loloa,* long-legged pig [human sacrifice]. (PPN *wa'e,* PCP *wae(wae);* cf. Tahitian *'aavae.*) **2.** n. Hula step (general name).

wā.wae huki. n. Cramps in foot or leg, charley horse.

wā.wae.'iole. n. A cosmopolitan tropical club moss *(Lycopodium cernuum),* a far-creeping mosslike plant, growing .3 to 1.5 m high. Its stems and many branches are covered with short, narrow-pointed leaves, and are made into Christmas wreaths. Eight other species of club mosses also bear this name. (Neal 2–3.) Other analysts call *wāwae'iole, Codium edule,* and list *'a'ala-'ula* and *'ala'ula* as variant names. Some equate *huluhulua-'iole* and *hulu'iole* with *wāwae'iole.*

wā.wae ki'i. Same as *ki'i 4,* and *wāwae 2,* a hula step.

wawaele. Redup. of *waele. Nāna i wawaele i ke ala, mahope aku kākou,* he cleared the way, we came later [respect is due an older sibling].

wā.wae pehu. n. Gout, swollen legs or feet.

wawaha. Redup. of *waha 1;* to storm, rave, rant.

wā.wahi. Redup. of *wāhi;* to tear down, shatter, wreck, dash to pieces, break into, demolish; to break, as a law or a twenty-dollar bill; to cause disorder. Cf. *pōhaku wāwahi wa'a* and Gram. 6.2.1. *Mīkini wāwahi pōhaku,* rock crusher. *Wāwahi i ka hua,* to break the egg. *Wāwahi pu'upa'a,* to ravish a virgin. *Wāwahi pā hula,* to disturb a hula show by presenting a rival show. *Wāwahi i ka manawa,* to keep open an infant's fontanel by applying crushed *pōpolo* berries; it was believed that an infant might be fed through the fontanel. (PCP *waawasi.*)

wā.wahia. Pas/imp. of *wāwahi. Ua wāwahia, ua nāhāhā, ua helele'i ka papa* (chant), split, shattered, crumbled foundation. (PCP *waawa(a)sia.*)

wā.wahi hale. nv. Burglary, housebreaking; to break and enter.

wā.wahi panakō. v. To break the bank, as in chee-fah or other games.

wā.wahi wa'a. 1. n. Borer that bores into canoe hulls, a teredo. *Lit.,* canoe breaker. **2.** Same as *kaupau,* a seaweed.

wawai. vs. Watered well, watery. (PPN *wawai.*)

wawaka. Same as *wakawaka,* flashing. See *'ea wawaka.*

wawala.nia. Same as *walawalania,* pain.

wawali. Same as *waliwali*, smooth.

wawalo. Redup. of *walo*. *Kohā ka leo o ka wai kini, ua la'i eā, ka wawalo i ka 'ohu noe i nā mauna eā* (song), The roaring voice of the many waters is calm, tra-la, the roaring in the misty clouds in the mountains, tra-la. (PPN *wawalo*.)

wawalu. Redup. of *walu 1*, to scratch.

wawana. Redup. of *wana 2*, sharp. (PCP *wawana*.)

Wawau. See *Liolio-i-Wawau*, a star.

wā.wau. n. Name recorded as an insulting term similar to dumb brute. *Rare*.

wawa'u. Redup. of *wa'u*. *Fig.*, ill-natured, quarrelsome. *'O nā 'ao'ao apau o ua wahi mokupuni pōhaku lā, he mania pū e hiki 'ole ai i nā māi'u'u o ke kanaka ke wawa'u aku ā kau i luna*, all the sides of this rocky island are slippery and men cannot claw with their fingernails to rest on top. (PPN *wawaku*.)

wawe. vs. Quickly; fast. *Hikiwawe*, quickly or easily done. (PPN *wawe*.)

wā.wena. nvs. Heat; hot. *Nui ka wāwena o kēia lā*, this sun is very hot.

wē. 1. vt. To sift. *Rare*. 2. n. The letter "w."

we'a. 1. Same as *we'awe'a 1*. *Kāu e we'a mai nei ia'u*, what you tempt me to. 2. n. A red dye; to print or color red.

we'a.we'a. 1. nvt. To help, abet, or tempt, especially in love affairs; accomplice; accessory in crime; one who aids or incites but does not share; procurer, pimp; to procure. *'O wai ka we'awe'a o kēia mea?* Who is the accomplice in this affair? 2. Same as *'āwe'awe'a*, trace, streak, spot.

wehe. 1. vt. To open, untie, undo, loosen, undress, uncover, unfasten, unlock, unfurl, unsheath, unwrap, unhook, exorcise; to take off, as clothes; to take apart, as a machine; to unfix, as a bayonet; to tip, as a hat; to solve, as a problem; to cleanse of defilement, remove, forgive, satisfy (see ex., *kīkīpani 1*). See ex., *alaula*. *Wehe 'aha mele*, to hold a concert. *Wehe ā kohana*, to strip naked. *Wehe i ka pihi*, unbutton the buttons. **ho'o.wehe.** To cause to open, undo, etc. (PCP *we(f,s)e*.) 2. vi. To go away. *Ua weheke akule i ka hohonu*, the *akule* [fish] has fled to the depths. *Wehe pau ka pāpale*, the hat is removed [the person has left]. (PCP *we(f,s)e*.)

wehea. Pas/imp. of *wehe 1*.

wehe 'ana. n. Opening, untying, etc. *Ka wehe 'ana i ka naneha'i*, the solving of the problem.

wehe hala. nv. To remove a personal transgression by prayer, with or without offering; remission of sins; name for sugar cane used in such ceremonies.

Wehe-lau-niu. n. Wind name associated with Māla, Maui.

wehena. n. 1. Opening, unfastening, taking off; solution, as of a problem. *Wehena 'ole*, closely related, as of blood kin. *Pili wehena 'ole*, inseparable association, close relationship. *Ka wehena o ke ao*, the opening up of light [daybreak]. 2. n. Difference (with *'a'ohe*). *'A'ohe wehena iki aku 'o ke ali'i ia'oe*, there is no difference between you and the chief.

wehe.wehe. 1. vt. To explain. Cf. *puke wehewehe 'ōlelo*. *Wehewehe 'ana*, explanation, definition. 2. Redup. of *wehe*; to unsaddle or unharness, as a horse; to pull growing taro stalks slightly apart so as to strengthen the corm. 3. *(Cap.)* n. Name of a star (no data).

wehe.wehe 'ano. nv. Analysis; to define, analyze.

wehe.wehe hala. Redup. of *wehe hala*.

wehi. 1. nvt. Decoration, adornment, ornament; to decorate. Cf. *pā wehi*. **ho'o.wehi.** To beautify, decorate, adorn. (PCP *we(f,s)i*.) 2. n. A song composed as an adornment, a song honoring someone. *Ha'ina kou wehi*, sing the adornment, your song. 3. vs. Dark. *Ka'ū malo 'eka, kua wehi*, Ka'ū of dirty *malo* and black back [due to working in the sun].

wehiwa. 1. n. A variety of taro. Also *wewehiwa*. 2. vs. Dark. *Hakuko'i uli ka lani, 'ononinoni ke ao, wehiwa hāpokopoko ka 'ōpua* (name song for Queen Emma),

agitated dark the heavens, disturbed the clouds, short dark cloud patches. 3. nvs. Choice, prized; a choice object. 4. A variety of sweet potato. 5. n. A secret play language used on Hawai'i to prevent others from understanding; *u* was substituted for vowels: *U hulu unu ūkua ūhua* for *E hele ana 'oukou i hea?* Where are you going. Cf. *kake*.

wehi.wehi. 1. Redup. of *wehi*; festive. Cf. *wewehi*. **ho'o.wehi.wehi.** Redup. of *ho'owehi*. (PCP *we(f,s)i-we(f,s)i*.) 2. n. Type of *pā'ū*.

weka. n. 1. Ink discharged by squid or octopus. 2. Dark organs of an *'opihi*, a limpet. 3. First dark excreta of an infant, meconium. (PCP *weta*.) 4. Mucus in the eyes. Also *pīheka*. 5. Also **weta.** Weight. *Eng. Teroe weta*, troy weight.

weka.weka. 1. Same as *weka 1–4*. 2. n. A foul stomach. 3. vs. Hardhearted; stingy.

weke. 1. nvt. Crack, narrow opening; to open a crack, as a door; to separate, loosen, free. **ho'o.weke. hō.weke.** To open. (PPN *wete*.) 2. n. Certain species of the Mullidae, surmullets or goatfish. All *weke* have large scales and are usually found in reefs, sometimes in deep water. Both red and light-colored *weke* were popular as offerings to the gods to turn away curses: see *weke 1*. For the connection of *weke* with nightmares, see *pahulu 1*. Unidentified varieties of *weke* are qualified by the terms *koa'e, lā'ō, moelua*. See also *weke 'ā* or *weke ke'oke'o, weke ahulu* or *weke pahulu* or *weke pueo, weke nono, weke 'ula*. (PPN *wete*.) 3. Rare variant of *waka*, to flame, flash.

wekea. 1. Pas/imp. of *weke 1*. *Rare*. 2. n. Midday; zenith. *Rare*.

weke 'ā, weke 'a'ā. n. A fish (*Mulloidichthys samoensis*). *Lit.*, staring *weke*.

weke ahulu. Same as *weke pahulu*.

weke.kē. n. Whisky. *Eng.*

weke ke'o.ke'o. Same as *weke 'ā*. *Lit.*, white *weke*.

wē.kena.nā, wēsenanā. Same as *he aha sananā*, frequently followed by *mau'u Hilo*, a pest. *Wēsenanā, he mau'u Hilo!* Who cares! Just Hilo grass. No good!

weke nono. n. Name given for a red *weke* identified as *Upeneus*. *Lit.*, red *weke*.

weke pahulu. n. A *weke* (*Upeneus arge*) named for a god on Lāna'i. *Lit.*, nightmare *weke*. Also called *weke ahulu* and *weke pueo*. See *pahulu 1*.

weke pueo. n. A *weke*, probably the same as *weke pahulu*. *Lit.*, owl *weke*, probably so called because of similarity of stripes on the tail and the bars of the Hawaiian owl's feathers.

weke 'ula. n. A species of *weke* (*Mulloidichthys vanicolensis*). The color effect of a school of *weke 'ula* is not red but yellow. They show themselves red when taken out of the water. *Lit.*, red *weke*.

weke.weke. 1. Redup. of *weke 1*; to open, as a crack. (PPN *wetewete*.) 2. Redup. of *weke 3*, to flame.

weke.wekea. Pas/imp. of *wekeweke 1*; pried open, loosened.

wē.kiu. nvs. Tip, top, topmost, summit, peak; of the highest rank or station. *Ka-wēkui-lani*, the royal height [a name of Princess Ka-'iu-lani].

weko. Same as *uweko*, bad-smelling, musty.

weko.weko. Redup. of *weko*.

wela. 1. nvt. Hot, burned; heat, temperature. *Fig.*, lust, passion; to feel such. (*Wela* may refer to the fiery heat of taboo, an epithet applied to Ka-lā-kaua.) *Ua wela kekahi i kekahi* (Kep. 97), one lusted for another. *Wela ka hao!* The iron's hot [now is the time for fun! Whoopee! Hurray! (see also *'alu*). *Wela ka hao i nā kaikamāhine home lula!* Hurray for the home rule girls. **ho'o.wela.** To beat, burn, arouse passion. (PPN *wela*.) 2. Same as *puhi wela*, an eel. 3. n. A new field, as of sweet potatoes; a piece of land cleared for planting by burning. Also *makawela*. *He wela he kauwahi e mahi 'ai*, a *wela* is a certain place to be cultivated.

wela ahi. vs. Scald, burned.

wē.lau. n. Tip, top, extremity, end, pole (not necessarily high or lofty, as *wēkiu*); extremes, as in fractions. Also *ʻēlau. Wēlau o ka make,* point of death. *Mai ke kumu a ka wēlau,* from base to tip.

Wē.lau ʻĀ.kau. n. North Pole.

wē.lau alelo. n. Tip of tongue.

Wē.lau Hema. n. South Pole.

wela.wela. Redup. of *wela 1.* Cf. *makawelawela.* (PPN *welawela.*)

wele. 1. Same as *waele. Wele i luna ka māla lani a ka ua, ke pulu ʻino i ka hiō a ka makani* (chant), the heaven's rain garden is cleared above, the rotten mulch by the slanting blowing of the wind. (PNP *wele.*) **2.** vs. Suspended, hanging; fine, thin, as thread. Cf. *nāwele, pūnāwelewele.*

wele.ʻā. n. A lizard fish *(Trachinocephalus myops).*

wele.hia. Pas/imp. of *wele 1, 2.*

welehu. n. **1.** A deep sea fish resembling the *hāuliuli.* **2.** *(Cap.)* Ancient Hawaiian month, corresponding approximately to November. See **month**. *Kau ke poʻo i ka uluna, ʻo Welehu ka malama,* rest the head on the pillow, Welehu is the month [a stormy month and little could be done except stay at home and sleep; said of one who may rest since his work is done].

wele.lau. Same as *wēlau;* to touch the tip, as of a spear (FS 55).

wele.nia. Same as *walania.*

wele.weka. 1. nvs. Velvet. *Eng. Moena weleweka,* carpet. **2.** n. The coleus *(Coleus blumei),* an ornamental perennial herb or small shrub, from Java. The leaves are ovate, toothed, variegated with red, yellow, green, purple. Small blue flowers are borne in spikes. (Neal 734.)

wele.wele. Redup. of *wele 1. Mai ka uluulu ā ka welewele* (KL line 585), from the tangle to the clearing.

wele.wele iwi. v. To strip the bones of flesh, as for burial. *Fig.,* to criticize or slander one's kin.

wele.wele.lau. n. Very end of the tip.

weli. 1. nvs. Fear, terror, dread; fearful, afraid. *Kau ka weli, kū ka weli,* full of fear; terror-stricken. *Ua kau koʻu weli i ka luaʻi pele,* I was filled with fear of the lava eruption. **hoʻo.weli.** To frighten, terrify, arouse fear. (PPN *weli.*) **2.** n. A holothurian. (KL line 19.) **3.** n. Scion, sucker, shoot, as from a root; spreading root. **4.** n. Phosphorescent light on water, believed caused by a ghost that was interfering with fishing. See ex., *kū 5.* **5.** Same as *welina. E weli hoʻi iāʻoe* (For. 4:163), greetings to you.

welina. nvt. A greeting of affection, similar to *aloha;* a salutation in a letter, in longer form as follows: *me ʻoukou ka welina o ke aloha,* to you an expression of affection [or love]; to greet.

weli.weli. 1. Redup. of *weli 1;* violent, dreadful, horrible, fearful, ferocious; revered; respectful, as of the word of a chief; full of awe. See ex., *puni 1.* **hoʻo.weli.weli.** Redup. of *hoʻoweli;* to threaten; terrible, fierce. **2.** n. A small *weli,* holothurian. (KL line 19.) (PPN *weli.*) **3.** Redup. of *weli 3;* numerous, immense, prolific. *Ua ʻapo ʻia mai ʻo Ka-welo e nā kukuna weliweli o kō Ka-uahoa kūlana uʻi* (FS 93), Ka-welo was caught by the numerous terrible rays of Ka-uahoa's reputation as a youthful stalwart. *Weliweli ka pua,* many flowers. *Weliweli ka nui o kēlā ʻelepani,* the size of that elephant is immense.

welo. 1. vi. To flutter, float, or stream, as in the wind. *Welo kīhei i ke Aʻe Loa,* the shawl streams in the Aʻe Loa wind [said of a swift runner]. **2.** vi. To set, of the sun. *Mai ka ʻōmaka ʻana o ka lā ma Kumu-kahi ā ka welo ʻana a ka lā i Lehua* (Kel. 85), from the rising of the sun at Kumu-kahi to the setting of the sun at Lehua. (Probably PPN *welo.*) **3.** n. Progeny, ancestry, breed, family trait or strain, group custom, heritage, characteristic. *He welo huhū,* a family trait of quick tempers. *Ka poʻe o ʻEnelani Hou he welo holomoku,* the people of New England have the trait of seafaring. *Ua kapa ʻia kō mākou ʻohana ka welo kūnono o Wai-ka-puna,* our family is called the fiery breed of Wai-ka-puna. **4.**

(Cap.) n. Name of a month in the lunar calendar. See **month. 5.** *(Cap.)* n. Name of a star used by navigators. **6.** n. A strong purge made of the juice of the bitter gourd or seeds of *kāʻeʻe.*

welo.kā. n. Thrashing, smiting, as a fishtail.

welo.kike, welosite. n. Velocity. *Eng.*

welona. Same as *welo 2. Mai ka piʻina a ka lā i Haʻehaʻe ā ka welona a ka lā i Lehua,* from the rising of the sun at Haʻehaʻe [East Hawaiʻi] to the setting of the sun at Lehua Island [a poetic reference to all Hawaiʻi].

Welo ʻUla. n. A star name, perhaps same as *Welo 5.*

welo.welo. Redup. of *welo 1, 2;* flying streak, as of the tail of a comet or of a firebrand. Cf. *hōkū welowelo.* (PNP *welowelo.*)

welo.welo-lā. Same as *ʻala-o-Puna,* a taro. (HP 31, 34.)

welu. 1. nvs. Rag, ragged fragment; ragged, frayed, tattered. *He ʻīlio welu moe poli,* a tattered dog sleeping on the bosom [a pampered person]. (PCP *welu.*) **2.** n. Straggling clump, as of trees.

welu ahi. n. Ball of tapa cord used to carry fire.

welu ʻula. n. Red rag; tapa made of pieces of red tapa beaten up with other tapa. Also *paʻiʻula.*

welu.welu. 1. Redup. of *welu;* shredded to bits. (PCP *weluwelu.*) **2.** Same as *kāwelu,* a seaweed.

wena. 1. nvs. Glow, as of sunrise or fire, red. *Wena ʻula,* red glow. *Hōʻike ʻo Pele i kona nani, ka ʻula wena i ka maka o ke ao* (song), Pele reveals her beauty, the rosy glow in the countenance of the cloud. **2.** n. A close relationship, blood relative. *He hoahānau kēnā e loaʻa ai ka wena,* that is a cousin in whom there is a close blood tie.

wena.wena. Redup. of *wena 1.*

Wenuka, Venuke, Venuse. n. Venus. (Laie 599.) *Eng.*

weo. 1. nvs. Red, redness; to blush. See ex., *pano.* (PCP *weo.*) **2.** n. Dried banana bark, perhaps so called because of a reddish color. **3.** n. A variety of taro. Also *mana weo* (PCP *weo.*)

weʻo. Same as *ʻaho kopekope.*

weo kanaka. See *pano, weo 1.*

weo.weo. 1. Redup. of *weo 1.* (PCP *weoweo.*) **2.** Same as *ʻāweoweo,* fishes. **3.** n. A type of tapa.

wepa. Var. spelling of *uwepa.*

wepele, vepere. n. Vesper. *Eng.*

weu. Same as *weuweu.* (PCP *weu.*)

weu.weu. nvs. Herbage, grass, greenery; bushy or fuzzy, as a beard; fluffy. Cf. *holoholona ʻoi weuweu, kūmoena, pūpū weuweu, pūweuweu. Hele ana i ka ʻohi weuweu,* going to gather herbs [often said when going fishing, which it was bad luck to mention]. *Nalo i loko o ka weuweu,* lost in the herbage [sometimes said of a love affair]. **hoʻo.weu.weu.** Caus/sim.; fluff. (PCP *weuweu.*)

wewe. 1. Same as *ʻiewe,* navel string. **2.** Same as *kawewe* and *hawewe,* to clatter, roar, pour. (PCP *wewe.*)

wewehe. Same as *wehewehe. Rare.*

wewehi. Same as *wehiwehi. Onaona i ka ihu ke honi iho, ka wewehi i ka maka o ka ulua* (chant), fragrant is the nose that is kissed, lovely in the eyes of the jackfish [the lover].

wewe.hiwa. Same as *wehiwa,* a taro.

wewehe. n. Prayer for *luakini* dedication. (For. 6:25.)

wewela. Same as *walawela.* (PNP *wewela.*)

weweli. 1. vs. Somewhat afraid (less strong than *weliweli*). **2.** Same as *weliweli 3. Ka wahine weweli wale* (KL line 691), the woman of many offspring.

wewelo. Same as *welowelo. Mea hoʻowewelo,* streamer. (PCP *wewelo.*)

wewena. Redup. of *wena 1. Wewena ʻula ke kai,* red glowing sea.

wewenoe. Same as *weoweo.*

wewe.weke. Same as *wekeweke 1, 2.*

wī. 1. nvi. Famine; to suffer a famine. **2.** To squeal (For. 4:457), squeak, tinkle; the sound of wind, of gnashing teeth; any high shrill sound. Cf. *pule wī. Wī ka niho o ke kolohe lā,* the rascal's teeth are gnashing [he is getting his just merits]. *Wī mai nei hoʻi kou leo,* how shrill your voice is. **3.** n. The *wī* tree *(Spondias dulcis),* a smooth, gray-barked tree in the mango family, from islands of the South Pacific. The round or ovoid orange fruits, called *wī* apples, are 2.5 or more cm in diameter, have apple-flavored, yellow pulp surrounding a core with a few seeds. (Neal 523.) (PPN *wii.*) **4.** n. The tamarind *(Tamarindus indica),* a large leguminous tree from tropical Africa and possibly Asia, grown for shade and ornament, and for the wood and fruit. The brown pod contains a few seeds embedded in sticky, brown, acid pulp, which is eaten or made into a drink. (Neal 417.) Sometimes called *wī 'awa'awa.* (PPN *wii.*) **5.** See *hīhī wai 1,* a grainy snail. **6.** n. A female *kīkī,* a bird.

wihi. Same as *'āwihi,* to wink.

wī.kani. vs. Strong, hard, rigid, inflexible. *Wīkani nā a'ahuki,* hard tendons.

wī.ka'o. Same as *wīkani;* dry. *Rare.*

wikeke, wiseke. n. Whiskey. *Eng.*

wiki. vs. To hurry, hasten; quick, fast, swift. See *ala-wiki. Hele wiki,* quick time, quick step. *E wiki 'oe, mai lohi* (FS 111), hurry, don't delay. (Probably PEP *witi,* although Easter Island *viti* may be a Tahitian loan.) **ho'o.wiki.** To hurry, hasten.

wiki.lia, vigilia. n. Vigil. (Latin *vigilia.*)

wikili.ola, vitiriola. n. Vitriol. *Eng.*

wiki.wama. n. Wigwam.

wiki.wiki. 1. Redup. of *wiki,* fast, speedy. (PEP *witi-witi,* but see *wiki.*) **2.** *(Cap.)* n. Star name (no data). (Kuhelani.)

wiko, vito. nvt. Veto; to veto. *Eng.*

wiko.lia. n. **1.** A fine lawn used in dresses; victoria lawn. **2.** *(Cap.)* Victoria. *Eng.*

wile.laiki. n. The Christmas-berry tree *(Schinus terebin-thifolius),* a rather small tree, from Brazil, the leaves compound, each leaf having about seven leaflets, the flowers whitish, small, in large bunches, the small red fruits of the female tree abundant, resembling those of the *pūkiawe.* Named for Willie Rice, who during political campaigns wore a hat lei of the red berries. (Neal 525.)

wili. 1. nvt. To wind, twist, writhe, crank, turn, screw, drill, bore; to dial, crank, or ring up, as on the telephone; to roll up, as a mat; crank, coil, lock, as of hair. See *ma'i wili, wili lauoho. Wili mawawo,* whip [on a sewing machine]. *Wili Ko'olau,* Ko'olau whirlwind [careless, hurried work]. *Ma ka 'ākau, wili,* right, turn. *Ua wili 'ia kou niho me ka mīkini wili,* your tooth was drilled with the drill. **ho'o.wili.** To wind, coil, twine, drill, turn; to mill about, as a school of fish. (PPN *wili.*) **2.** n. Mill, drill, wrench, bit; various implements or machines used for turning are listed below. Cf. *hale wili. Nā mea wili* (Nah. 11.8), mills. **3.** n. Spirals of several colors in composite leis, as of the cigar flower *(kīkā).* **4.** n. A bird (no data). (KL line 420.)

wilia. Pas/imp. of *wili 1. Ka liko o ka palai i wilia me ke 'ala* (name song), the young fern frond is interwoven with fragrance.

wili 'ā.'ī. v. To twist the neck; bulldog.

wili.au. vi. To stir, circulate, move in eddies; mixed currents and eddies; turbulent. See ex., *īkā 1.*

wili.kā.'ekā. vs. Snarled, tangled, as hair.

wili kā.hei. n. Bit for boring, drilling. *Lit.,* circling drill.

wili.kī. nvs. Engineer, turnkey; engineering. *Lit.,* turn key.

wili.kī kī.wila. n. Civil engineer.

wili.kina. n. Sister, nun (Catholic). *Eng.* virgin.

Wili.kine, Virigine. n. Virgin. *Eng.* See ex., *epukane.*

wili kō. nv. Sugar mill, sugar grinder, to grind sugar cane.

wili.kō.ī. n. Dust or trash blown by the wind. *Rare.*

wili kope. n. Coffee mill, coffee grinder.

wili lau.oho. n. Locks of hair (Mele 5.2); false human hair twisted to fall down from the back, like a hair switch, described by Samwell of the Cook expedition (J. C. Beaglehole 1967, Part 2:1179; Buck 562–3).

wili makani. n. Windmill.

wili.mo'o. vi. To turn, twist, writhe, as a reptile. **ho'o.-wili.mo'o. (a)** Same as above. *Lele mai ke kanaka mā-lalaioa me ka ho'owilimo'o, me ka hō'oni puhi 'ana o kona kino,* the tall slim man leaped in with a twist and turn, his body moving like that of an eel. **(b)** Ceremony during *luakini* or war temple dedication. For a *pule ho'owilimo'o* see Malo 185. **(c)** Quadrille dance.

wili.nau. vi. To writhe, twist, wriggle.

wili nui. n. Auger.

wili ohi 'ili kope. n. Mill for peeling coffee beans.

wili 'ō.hiki kulina. n. Corn sheller or husker.

wili oho. n. Coil or strand of hair, as in a *lei palaoa* necklace. *Ka wili oho o ka lani nui* (For. 6:413), the hair dresser of the great chief.

wili.'ō.ka'i. 1. n. Chrysalis of night moth *('ōka'i),* cocoon. Also *'ōwili'ōka'i.* **2.** nvi. To whirl, bluster, as wind. *Ka wili'ōka'i a ka Unulau,* the whirling turning of the Unulau wind.

wili papa. n. Planing mill.

wili peahi. n. Fan, as for cleaning seeds.

wili.pua'a. n. Corkscrew, hand drill, gimlet, screw auger (a euphemism for *ulepua'a).*

wili.wai. n. Eddy, whirlpool. *Ua ka'aniniau i ka wiliwai,* tossed in the whirlpools [of love].

wili wehe 'umoki. n. Corkscrew.

wili.wili. 1. Redup. of *wili 1. Pā wiliwili,* blowing of wind in all directions. **ho'o.wili.wili.** Redup. of *ho'o-wili;* to swirl, circle. *Ho'owiliwili ka ua i ka 'ino,* the rain swirls in the storm. *Ho'owiliwili ka i'a,* the fish swim in circles. (PPN *wiliwili.*) **2.** n. A Hawaiian leguminous tree *(Erythrina sandwicensis,* formerly called *E. monosperma),* found on dry coral plains and on lava flows, somewhat spiny, with short thick trunk. Each leaf has three ovate leaflets; flowers are clustered near branch ends and range in color from red to orange, yellow, white; pods contain red, oblong seeds, used for leis. The wood is very light and formerly was used for surfboards, canoe outriggers, net floats. (Neal 458–60.) See ex., *pua 1.*

wili.wili haole. n. The tiger's-claw *(Erythrina variegata* var. *orientalis,* synonym *E. indica),* distributed from India to southern Polynesia, resembling the native *wili-wili* in many ways but larger and commonly grown ornamentally in Hawai'i for its large, bright-red flowers. (Neal 460.)

wili.wili.wai. n. Lawn sprinkler. See song, *ko'iawe.*

wī.lou. n. Willow. (Isa. 44.4.) *Eng.*

wī.lou loha.loha. n. Weeping willow. *Lit.,* drooping willow.

wilu. Same as *weko,* stink, stench.

wilu.wilu. Redup. of *wilu.*

wī.neka, vinega. n. Vinegar. *Eng.*

wini. 1. vs. Sharp, as a point. *Fig.,* impudent, nervy. Cf. *'auwiniwini. Ua wini kākala,* the spurs are sharp [said of a youth who has reached manhood]. *Wini 'i'o nō!* How sharp! [Such boldness, nerve!] **ho'o.wini.** To sharpen, make a point. **2.** n. Wind. *Pea wini,* fair wind.

wini.hapa, uinihapa, uwinihapa. n. Brick, named for Captain Winship, said to have brought the first bricks to Hawai'i.

wini.wini. Redup. of *wini 1;* tapering, ridged. *Ihu wini-wini,* sharp nose.

wiola, viola. n. Viol. (Am. 6.5.) *Eng.*

wiola 'umi, viola 'umi. n. Instrument of ten strings (Hal. 92.3), psaltery (Hal. 81.2). *Lit.,* ten viol.

wi'u. 1. vi. To smart with pain. **ho'o.wi'u.** To cause to smart. **2.** vs. Dirty, filthy. **ho'o.wi'u.** To besmear, soil. **3.** vs. Entangled, as a kite. **ho'o.wi'u.** To entangle.

wi'u.wi'u. n. Redup. of *wi'u 1–3. Wi'uwi'u loko i ke aloha,* heart painful with love; heart entangled with love. **ho'o.wi'u.wi'u.** Redup. of *ho'owi'u.*

wī.wī. 1. vs. Thin, lean, slender, bony, skinny, rickety, emaciated. See ex., *pīoeoe. Pā wīwī,* rickety, insecure fence. **ho'o.wī.wī.** To make thin, slenderize; to diet in order to lose weight; to reduce. (PPN *iwiiwi*.) **2.** Redup. of *wī 2*, to squeal.

wiwini. Same as *winiwini*, sharp.

wiwo. vs. **1.** Fearful, bashful, modest, afraid, timid, shy. *Ua hilahila wau, ua wiwo hoʻi, ke nānā aʻe koʻu mau maka iāʻoe, ē kuʻu Akua* (Ezera 9.6), I am ashamed and blush to lift up my face to thee, my God. (PCP *wiwo*.) **2.** Obedient; to mind, obey.

wiwo ʻole. vs. Fearless, brave, bold, courageous, dauntless, intrepid. *Hana wiwo ʻole,* bold or brave deed, adventure. *Mea wiwo ʻole,* intrepid person, adventurer.

wiwo.wiwo. Redup. of *wiwo 1, 2*.

woa. vs. Calm. *Ke kai koʻo me ke kai woa* (chant), the strong sea and the calm sea.

wohi. **1.** n. One whose parent was of *piʻo, naha,* or *nīʻaupiʻo* rank, and the other parent of second degree collaterality. A *wohi* chief was exempt from the prostration taboo *(kapu moe);* he preceded the king on public occasions to see that others prostrated themselves; he was generally a near relative. *ʻAi-wohi-kupua* [name], semidivine *wohi* ruler. Rare, *ohi,* as in the spelling *ʻAi-ohi-kupua* (For. 5:411). See saying *kū kahi.* **2.** Var. spelling of *ohi 1, 2*.

wolu. **1.** Same as *walu,* a fish. *Kaʻū* and *Puna, Hawaiʻi.* **2.** n. Walrus. *Eng.* Also *waleluka.*

wō.wō. vi. To bellow, roar.

Wule.kake, Vulegate. nvs. Vulgate. *Eng.*

wule.kula, vuletura. n. Vulture. *Eng.*

Z

Loan words from English sometimes spelled with initial z- are entered under k-. *For example:* zebela, *see* kepela, *zebra;* zizania, *see* kīkānia.

ENGLISH-HAWAIIAN

A

a. 1. *The letter.* 'Ā. *Key of A,* 'o 'ē ke kī. *A-minor,* hapa. *A-flat,* emi. 2. *Article.* He, kekahi, ho'okahi.
aa. 'A'ā. *See saying,* **wāwae.**
abacus. Helu hō'ike.
abalone. 'Ōpihi malihini.
abandon. Ha'alele, ha'alele loa, waiho, ho'oku'u, ku'u, mauha'alele.
abashed. Hilahila.
abate. Akaku'u, emi. *Also:* kualili'i, kāha'u.
abbreviate. Ho'opōkole.
abbreviation. Hua hō'ailona, ho'opōkole 'ana.
abdicate. Ha'alele, waiho. *Abdicate a throne,* ha'alele noho ali'i.
abdomen. 'Ōpū; *lower —,* ke'ahakahaka. *See* **stomach.**
abdominal aorta. Ēwe.
abduct. Kā'ili, lawe, ka'i malū, pio, 'aihue kanaka.
abet. Kōkua; we'awe'a, we'a *(in doing wrong).*
abhor. Ho'okae 'ino, wahāwahā, ho'owahāwahā, inaina.
abide. Noho.
ability. Hiki. *Of limited ability,* kaupalena 'ia ka mea hiki iāia, 'ōpū 'uku'uku *(fig.). According to his ability,* like me kona hiki, like me ka mea hiki iāia.
abject. Ha'aha'a loa.
ablative. 'Auihele.
able. 1. *Can.* Hiki. 2. *Capable.* Mākaukau, mākau.
able-bodied. Olakino maika'i.
abnormal. 'E'epa, 'ano 'ē.
aboard. Maluna. *Go aboard,* e'e.
abode. Wahi noho. *Abode of gods or spirits,* wao akua, kaha akua.
abolish. Ho'opau. *Also:* pupuhi, lu'i. *Abolish a relationship,* wehe i ka pili, mō ka piko.
abolition. Ho'opau 'ana.
abominable. Ho'opailua, 'ino loa.
abomination. Mea 'ino, mea haumia, mea ho'opailua.
aboriginal. Maoli, kupa maoli.
abort. 'Ō'ō, 'ōmilo, ho'ohemo.
abortion. 'Ōmilo, milo, milomilo, hoene, ho'ohemo keiki 'ana. *Instrument for abortion,* ā 'ō'ō, koholua. *Potion to cause abortion,* lā'au ho'ohemo keiki.
about. 1. *Concerning.* E pili ana no, no. *About him,* e pili ana iāia; e pili ana nona. 2. *See* **almost.** *About ten feet,* ma kahi o 'umi kapua'i.
about-face. E huli loa.
above. Maluna, i luna. *Also:* nuna, kumalauā. *Above the house,* maluna o ka hale.
above-mentioned. 'Ōlelo 'ia maluna a'e.
abroad. Ma ka 'āina 'ē *(in foreign lands).*
abrupt. Kū, honua.
abscess. Pala he'e, kūpī, pūhā, pūhō, puhi kaokao; kua puhi, kuanaka *(on back);* 'a'ī 'ala'ala *(on neck).*
absence. Hele 'ole mai.
absent. Ma kahi 'ē, ma kahi 'oko'a, ka'a, 'a'ole i hiki mai.
absent-minded. Poina wale, aia i kahi 'ē ka no'ono'o, ho'omaopopo 'ole.
absolute. Holo'oko'a. *Absolute power,* mana piha.
absolution. Huikala, kala 'ana, pu'ukalahala.
absolve. Huikala, kalahala, kala, ho'okala, ho'okalakala.
absorb. Omo, moni, monimoni, momomoni, momoni, kemu, ale, hei.
absorbed. 1. *Imbibed.* Omo 'ia. 2. *Occupied.* Lilo loa, papau. *Pleasantly absorbed,* mili nanea, nanea, milimili nanea; kili'opu *(as in love-making).*
absorbent. Omo i ka wai; poale *(rare).*
abstain. Kē, ho'okā'oko'a. *To abstain from voting,* kānalua.
abstemious. Pākiko. *See* **refrain.**
abstract. Mo'olelo i ho'opōkole 'ia *(summary).*
absurd. Kohu 'ole, 'a'ole kohu iki, 'āpiki.
abundant. Nui, nui 'ino, lawa pono, nui hewahewa. *Also:* 'ena, lē'ia, pākī, 'api'api, kanalani.
abuse. Hana 'ino, hō'ino, ho'o'ino, ho'omāino. *Also:* hainā, ho'omāuna, pā'ulu'ā, ku'i pehi, pololo ka waha.
abused. Ho'oma'ewa 'ia, hō'ino 'ia. *See saying,* **bait.**
abusive. Hō'ino. *Also:* māuna, 'a'ana.
abutilon. Ma'o.
Abyssinia. 'Apikinia, Abisinia; 'Apukinia, Abusinia.
acacia. Koa, koai'e, kikima.
academy. Kula, 'ahahui 'imi na'auao; hale hō'ike'ike *(for exhibits).*
accelerate. Ho'ohikiwawe, ho'oholo 'āwīwī; ho'okanahē *(rare).*
accent. 1. *Speech.* Hopuna. *To speak imperfectly, as with foreign accent,* palalē. 2. *Stress.* Kaulele leo, ho'oko'iko'i, ko'iko'ina. 3. *Diacritical mark.* Kaha, kiko.
accept. 'Āpono, ho'āpono, 'ae, lawe.
acceptable. 'Āpono 'ia.
acceptance. 'Āpo. *See* **accept.**
access. *Way.* Ala e hiki ai, komo 'ana.
accessories. Mea ho'okohu, pono.
accessory. Kōkua. *Accessory in crime,* kōkua hewa, we'a, we'awe'a.
accident. Ulia, pilikia. *Auto accident,* ulia ka'a.
accidental. Ulia, pō'ino hiki wale.
accident insurance. 'Inikua ulia.
acclaim. Ohohia, ohooho, ololani. *See* **praise.**
accommodate. Kōkua.
accompany. Hele pū, ukali, 'alo, hahai. *To insist on accompanying,* ho'olala'ō. *One accompanying a messenger,* hoa una.
accomplice. Hoa hana, kōkua; we'awe'a, we'a, kōkua hewa *(in wrongdoing).*
accomplish. Ho'okō, holo pono.
accomplishment. Ho'okō 'ana.
accord. Lōkahi, hui kahi, 'ae like, kiakahi.
according to. Like me, ma, mamuli o, wahi a.
accordion. Pila'ume'ume, koliana, 'akoleana.
account. Pilawaiwai, helu; mo'owaiwai *(rare). Bank account,* waihona panakō.
accrue. Lilo, māhuahua, māhua, ho'omāhuahua.
accumulate. Ho'āhu, hō'ili'ili, ho'ākoakoa, manu'a.
accumulation. Nā mea i ho'ākoakoa 'ia, nā mea i hō'ili'ili 'ia.
accurate. Pololei, pono.
accursed. Kūamuamu 'ia, hā'ili'ili 'ia.
accusation. 'Ōlelo ho'opi'i, 'ōlelo ho'āhewa, ho'olawehala, ni'a.
accusative case. 'Auialo.
accuse. Ho'āhewa, ho'olawehala, ho'opi'i, ni'a.
accused. Mea i ho'opi'i 'ia. *See ex.,* **presume.**
accustomed. Ma'a, ma'ama'a, ma'ama'ahia, ho'oma'a, ho'oma'amau, walea. *Also:* kuluma.
ace. 'Eki.
ache. 'Eha, hu'i. *Also:* mala, mālo'elo'e, mā'opa'opa, 'ōpā, nalulu, hōka'a, pākoni, 'ōpili, ma'uhā, 'ainā. *See* **toothache.**
achieve. Ho'okō, kū.

achievement. Hoʻokō ʻana, kū i ka niʻo.
acid. ʻAkika, ʻawaʻawa, wai ʻakika; māniani. *See* **carbolic acid.**
acknowledge. Hōʻoiaʻiʻo, ʻae, mahalo.
acknowledgment. Hōʻoiaʻiʻo ʻana, ʻōlelo hoʻomaikaʻi.
acne. Huehue. *See* **pimple.**
acquaint. Hōʻike, hoʻolauna.
acquaintance. Hoalauna.
acquainted. Kamaʻāina. *Also:* kamaʻalua, kuluma. *Not well acquainted,* mamalihini.
acquire. Loaʻa, lawe. *To acquire land,* komo ʻāina.
acquisition. Loaʻa ʻana, lawena.
acquit. Hoʻokuʻu, kala, hoʻopuka.
acquittal. Hoʻokuʻu.
acre. ʻEka, ʻakele.
acrid. Hohono, ʻōlaelae.
across. Ma kēlā ʻaoʻao.
act. 1. *To do.* Hana. *To act as,* noho. *Act of God,* pōʻino no ke Akua mai. **2.** *Theatrical.* Mahele *(of a play).* *To act in a play,* hana keaka. **3.** *Law.* Kānāwai. **4.** *To pretend.* Hoʻomeamea, hoʻomea.
acting. E hana ana, kūikawā. *Acting officer,* hope.
acting commissioner. Komikina kūikawā.
action. Hana. *Joint action,* huki like ʻana, olowalu. *To get into action,* hiu, ʻaʻako. *To stir up to action,* hoʻoulu, lale, hoʻolale. *See saying,* **crab.**
activate. Hoʻolale, ui.
active. ʻEleu, miki, kāʻeuʻeu, ʻālapa, hālapa, lapakū. *Also:* kaʻukaʻulele, ʻākepa, ʻakeu, hīʻō, makahai, ʻuleulele. *Active mind,* lolo ʻeleu.
active voice. Leo pili aku.
activist. Mea hoʻouluulu. *See* **agitator.**
activity. Hana, ʻoihana. *Come to activity,* ʻīnana.
actor. Mea hana keaka.
actress. Wahine hana keaka.
Acts. ʻOihana.
actual. Maoli, ʻoiaʻiʻo.
actually. ʻIʻo.
acute. 1. *Pointed.* ʻOi. *Acute angle,* huina ʻoi. **2.** *Of pain.* Huʻi. **3.** *Of mind.* ʻAʻapo.
adamant. Paʻakikī, ʻakama.
Adam's apple. Puʻu, pūʻāʻī, kaniʻāʻī. *Hollow at meeting of bones below Adam's apple,* waʻawaʻa.
adapt. Maʻa aku.
add. Hōʻuluʻulu, hoʻohui, pākuʻi, kuʻi lua, hoʻonui; hoʻokuʻi *(as numbers);* kipona *(as ferns to a lei);* hoʻoholo *(as water to poi). Also:* naʻiau. *Add two and two,* hoʻohui ʻelua me ʻelua.
addendum. ʻŌlelo pākuʻi.
adder. Moʻo make, moʻo lele, moʻo pekena, moʻo pepeiao hao.
adder's-tongue fern. Puapua moa.
adding machine. Mīkini helu.
addition. Hōʻuluʻulu. *Addition to a house,* hale pākuʻi.
additional. Koe, keu, pākuʻi, kaulele.
address. 1. *Speech.* Haʻiʻōlelo. *To make an address,* haʻiʻōlelo. **2.** *Residence.* Wahi noho, kahi noho.
addressee. Ka mea nāna ka leka.
adept. Mākaukau loa, noa. *Also:* walea, lolo, ʻailolo, hei. *Not adept,* ʻaʻole mākaukau, māʻukaʻuka.
adequate. Lawa pono.
adhere. Pipili, pili, hoʻopili, pilipili, hoʻopilipili, hoʻopipili.
adhering. Pilina, paʻa.
adhesive. Pilipili, lina, ʻūlika, ʻuoʻuo, aweawea.
ad hoc. Kūikawā.
ad interim. No ka manawa, kūikawā.
Adirondack. ʻAkilonakaka, Adironadaka.
adjacent. Kokoke, pili.
adjective. Haʻiʻano. *Verbal adjective,* haʻina pili haʻiinoa.
adjective complement. Ukali haʻiʻano.
adjoin. Pili. *Adjoining,* e pili mai ana.
adjourn. Hoʻomalolo, malolo, kuʻu, hoʻokuʻu, hoʻonoa.
adjournment. Hoʻomalolo.
adjudication. Hoʻokolokolo.

adjust. Hoʻoponopono.
adjustment. Hoʻoponopono ʻana.
adjutant. Hope, ʻakukana.
adjutant general. Hope kenelala.
administer. Hoʻoponopono, hoʻohana, hoʻoholo.
administered. Hoʻoponopono ʻia.
administration. Hoʻoponopono ʻana, lawelawe hana, lawelawe ʻana, hoʻohana.
administration building. Hale hoʻoponopono, hale mana hoʻokō.
administrative head. Luna hoʻohana.
administrator. Luna hoʻoponopono, kahu, kahu hoʻoponopono; hoʻoponopono waiwai *(of an estate);* kaulana ʻāina *(of land).*
admirable. Kū i ka mahalo. *Also:* lehiwa, nilu.
admiral. ʻAkimalala. *See* **rear admiral.**
admiration. Mahalo, makahehi. *To glance about, as in admiration,* maka leha.
admire. Mahalo. *Also:* makahehi, hiʻilani, hoʻohihi, lehiwa. *See* **akena, makaleho, praise.**
admired. Mahalo ʻia.
admission. Hoʻokomo ʻana, ʻapo.
admit. 1. *Allow to enter.* Hoʻokomo, ʻae. **2.** *See* **acknowledge.**
admonish. Aʻo, hoʻoponopono.
adobe. Lepo kāwili, pōhaku lepo, ʻakopie. *Adobe house,* hale lepo.
adopt. 1. *As a child.* Hānai, lawe hānai; hoʻokama *(as a child or adult one adopts because of affection but does not rear);* hoʻomakua *(as a parent).* **2.** *To approve.* ʻĀpono.
adopted. Hānai. *Adopted brother or sister,* kaikuaʻana hānai, kaikaina hānai, kaikuahine hānai, kaikunāne hānai. *Adopted child,* hānai, keiki hānai. *Legally adopted child,* hānai, keiki hānai hoʻohiki. *Siblings in the* hoʻokama *relationship may speak of* kaikuaʻana in the hoʻokama, *etc. (see* **kama***).*
adoption. Lawe hānai.
adoption paper. Palapala hoʻohiki.
adoration. Hoʻonani.
adore. Hoʻonani, hoʻomana *(worship).*
adorn. Hoʻohiwahiwa, hoʻonani, hoʻokāhiko, hoʻowehi, hoʻoulumāhiehie, hoʻouluwehi. *Also:* hoʻomāhilu; kauluwehi *(as with greenery).*
adorned. Uluwehiwehi, uluwehi, ulumāhiehie; ʻohuʻohu *(with leis).*
adornment. Wehi, wehiwehi; pāpahi *(rare).*
Adriatic. ʻAkiliakika, Adiriatika.
adrift. Lana, lana hele, lanaau.
adult. Makua, makua makua, oʻo. *To act as an adult,* hoʻokanaka makua. *To become an adult,* kanaka makua.
adulterous. Moekolohe, noho manuahi.
adultery. Moekolohe, hana i ka hewa; ʻakulekele *(rare).*
advance. Holo i mua, neʻemua, hoʻomua. *In advance,* ʻē, mua. *Advance in office,* piʻi hou aʻe. *To make advances,* hoʻopilipili, hoʻokohu.
advancement. Holo i mua.
advantage. Mea e ʻoi aʻe. *Take advantage,* hana i ka wā kūpono *(as of a benefit);* kolohe, hoʻowalewale, kāhina *(deceive).*
advantageous. Kūpono, mea e kūpono ai.
advent. Hikina.
Adventist. Hoʻomana Pōʻaono.
adventure. Hana hoʻopīhoihoi, hana wiwo ʻole.
adventurer. Mea wiwo ʻole, mea ʻaʻa.
adverb. Haʻinaleʻa, kōkuahaʻina. *Directional adverb,* haʻinaleʻa kuhikuhi.
adversary. Hoa paio, mea kūʻē.
adverse. Kūʻē; ukiuki *(as wind).*
adversely. Kūʻē, ʻēʻē.
adversity. Pilikia, pōpilikia. *To bring adversity,* hoʻomāhuwā.
advertise. Hoʻolaha.
advertisement. Hoʻolaha, ʻōlelo hoʻolaha. *Advertisement, for sale,* hoʻolaha kūʻai, hoʻolaha hoʻolilo. *Ad-*

vertisement, for rent, ho'olaha ho'olimalima. Advertisement, help wanted, ho'olaha limahana.
advice. 'Ōlelo a'o, a'o, leo, a'oa'o, kuauhā. To give advice, ha'i a'o. Refusal to listen to advice, pepeiao kuli.
advisable. Kūpono.
advise. A'o, 'ōlelo a'o; kauleo.
adviser. Hoa kūkā, kākā'ōlelo.
advisory council. 'Aha kūkā.
advocate. 1. See **urge**. 2. See **lawyer**.
adze. Ko'i (see Haw.-Eng. entry and entries that follow it), lipi (for various kinds, see Haw.-Eng. entry). Also: kūpā, kūpā 'ai ke'e, lopu, pākīkō, iwiole, kīkoni, ko'i paukūkū, nao-maka-lua, 'olopū. To make adzes, kāko'i. Adze-headed, po'o ko'i (term of ridicule). Adze handle, 'au ko'i.
adze maker. Kāko'i.
aerated waters. Wai ea.
aerial. Pili ana i ka lewa, lewa. Radio aerial, uea radio. Aerial tuber, kūhalakau (as of yam). See **root**.
afar. Mamao. Rare: po'iu, 'iu'iu, mōwahowaho.
affable. 'Olu'olu; pūnolunolu.
affair. Hana, mea, kuleana. Love affair, moe ipo, hana kalakalai, 'ōmau. Affairs of others, kō ha'i kuleana.
affect. Ho'ololi, ho'ohuli.
affectation. Hō'oio, ho'okohukohu.
affection. Aloha, aloha pumehana, 'ena aloha, ho'oheno. Also: oha, make'e, ha'eha'e, mahamaha. See **endearing.**
affectionate. Aloha, ho'oheno; mahamaha. Affectionately, me ke aloha.
affidavit. Palapala hō'ike, palapala ho'ohiki 'ia, 'ōlelo hō'ike.
affinal relative. Inoa. Cf. **in-laws.**
affinity. Pili.
affirm. Hō'oia.
affix. 1. Place. Kau. 2. Word portion. Hua pāku'i.
afflict. Ho'opōpilikia, ho'eha'eha.
afflicted. Pilikia, one'ā.
affliction. Pilikia, pō'ino.
afghan. Kīhei.
Afghanistan. 'Apekanikana, Afeganitana.
afloat. Lana, lewa.
afoot. Wāwae, hele wāwae.
aforementioned. Ua . . . nei, ua . . . lā, ua ono o. Gram. 8.3.4. This aforementioned person, ua kanaka nei. That aforementioned person, ua kanaka lā.
aforesaid. I 'ōlelo 'ia. The aforesaid John Owen, 'O John Owen i 'ōlelo 'ia.
afraid. Maka'u, weli, weliweli, wiwo, 'e'ena; kūpēkia (rare). Afraid for no reason, maka'u wale, maka'u honua. To make afraid, ho'omaka'u, ho'omāka'uka'u. He is afraid of war, maka'u 'oia i ke kaua.
Africa, African. 'Apelika, Aferika.
African Gold Coast. Kapakai Kula 'Apelika, Gula Aferika.
aft. Hope.
after. Hope, mahope, muli, mamuli, pau. After school, pau ke kula, mahope o ke kula.
afterbirth. Ēwe, 'iewe, 'iawe, wewe.
afterglow. Akaakalani, akalani.
afterlife. 'Ao'ao mau o ka honua.
afternoon. 'Auinalā. Late afternoon, ahiahi, 'āluna ahiahi.
afterthought. Mana'o poina.
afterward. Hope, mahope, mahope iho, mamuli iho.
again. Hou. To do again, hana hou.
against. Kū'ē. Against the law, kū'ē kānāwai, 'a'e kānāwai.
agate. Pōhaku paea, 'ula, 'akake.
age. 1. Period. Au, manawa, wā. 2. Age of a person. Kūlana makahiki, makahiki. See **old age**. To age, kahiko, kūnewa. What is your age? 'Ehia ou makahiki? Seven years of age, nā makahiki 'ehiku.
aged. Nui nā makahiki, makule. Rare: 'āpela, lā'ele, mauole, kaikapū, mākuakua. See sayings, **old age**.

Aged man, 'elemakule. Aged woman, luahine. Aged animal, nūkea.
agency. Pulo, 'oihana, ke'ena.
agenda. Papa hana. See **kukulu kumuhana.**
agent. Hope, 'ākena, 'ēkena.
agentive case. 'Aui'ia. The common agentive preposition is e. (Gram. 9.9.)
aggravate. Ho'onāukiuki, ho'olawehala, nui a'e; mala'o (rare).
aggressive. Hō'oi'oi. Also: nanā, ho'onanā, makoa, mī'oi'oi. See saying, **Kākea.**
aggressor. Ka mea lele mua.
aghast. Pū'iwa, kākāhā i ka 'ino.
agile. 'Eleu. Rare: ka'uka'ulele, 'ele'io.
agitated. Pīhoihoi, pi'oloke. Also: ho'oluliluli, kūpiki-'ō, hō'ale'ale, 'akūkū, kōkūkū, pikipiki'ō, 'āpikipiki, 'ōpikipiki, 'āwili, uluulu, ho'oloku, noni, ānoni, ānoninoni, ānononi, 'ōnoninoni, ho'ole'ole'o, 'ōle'ole'o, hakuko'i, hāko'i, hāko'iko'i, 'ō'ili, 'ō'ili'ili, 'ōkū, ulukū, hōkūkū, aukūkū, 'ele'elepī, kapau'u, nū, 'apo'apo, kūhulukū. See saying, **olokē**.
agitator. Mea ho'oulu pilikia, ho'oulu haunaele, ho'ohaunaele, ho'opaipai.
ago. Mamua aku nei, wā i hala. A while ago, aku nei. A long time ago, kala loa, kala wale, kala kahiko, hala kahiko, kala kua, 'a'ole i kala, 'e'oe i kala, līloa, iō kikilo. A few days ago, kēia mau lā aku nei.
agonize. Hō'eha'eha.
agony. 'Eha'eha, kōhi.
agree. 'Ae, 'aelike, lōkahi. Also: ku'ikahi, ō, 'eo, pāpā'ale.
agreeable. 'Olu'olu, launa 'olu'olu, waipahē, leo 'ole, 'inā'inau.
agreement. 'Aelike, palapala 'aelike, lōkahi, hui kahi, ku'ikahi like, pāpā'ale; 'ae waha (oral). To confirm an agreement by touching hands, pāpālima. To make an agreement, pa'i.
agricultural. Mahi 'ai. Agricultural heiau, heiau ho'oulu 'ai. Agricultural industry, 'oihana mahi 'ai. Agricultural expert, kahuna ho'oulu 'ai.
agriculture. 'Oihana mahi 'ai.
aground. Ili, ilihia, mau, ho'omau, oloi.
ah! 'Ā! Kāhāhā. Cf. Gram. 12. To oh and ah, āhē, kāhāhā.
aha! Āhā! Ahahana!
ahead. I mua, mamua aku.
aid. Kōkua, kāko'o. Also: we'awe'a, we'a (in wrongdoing).
aide. Ūkali. Governor's aide, ukali o ke kia'āina.
aide-de-camp. Ali'ikoa lawelawe no ke kenelala.
ailing. 'Ōma'ima'i, ma'ima'i.
ailment. Ma'i, 'eha, pā'ao'ao.
aim. 1. As a gun. Mākia, kia, kaulona, ho'opololei, kāki'i. Also: hikia, lena, mano. 2. Intention. Mana-'opa'a, mākia.
aimless. Lalau wale, lanaau.
air. Ea, eaea, lewa. Upper regions of the air, papa lani. Rarefied air, ea māmā. By air, ma ka mokulele.
air base. Kahua kaua lewa.
aircraft carrier. Moku halihali mokulele.
air current. Eaea; holouka (rare).
air force. Mahele kaua lewa.
air gun. Pū makani.
air hole. Puka makani.
air mail. Ma ka mokulele.
airplane. Mokulele, mokuea.
airplane carrier. Moku halihali mokulele.
air plant. 'Oliwa-ku-kahakai.
airport. Kahua ho'olulu mokulele; kahua kaua lewa (military).
air raid. Pākaha mai ka lewa.
airy. Holomakani.
aisle. Kahi hele mawaena o nā noho.
akimbo. 'Ekemo.
akin. Pili.
Akron. 'Akelona, Akerona.

-al. Kū. *See* constitutional.
Alabama. 'Alapama, Alabama.
alabaster. 'Alapaka.
alarm. Kāhea. *See* alarmed. *Fire alarm,* kāhea pau ahi. *False alarm,* kūkala hewa.
alarmed. Pi'oloke, hopohopo, pīhoihoi.
alas. Aloha 'ino. Auē! Auē noho'i ē! *Alas for us!* Auē kākou!
Alaska. 'Ālaka; Alakeka, Alaseka.
albacore. *Same as* tuna.
Albania. 'Alepania, Alebania.
Albany. 'Alapani, Alabani.
albatross. Ka'upu, mōlī.
albino. Kekea.
Albuquerque. 'Alepukaka, Alebukaka.
alcohol. 'Alekohola, waikulu.
alcoholic. 'Ona mau, 'ona lama, 'alekohola.
Aldebaran. 'Au-kele, 'Au-kele-nui-a-Iku(?), Kao-ma'aikū.
alderman. Luna 'ekalekia (ekalesia).
ale. 'Ela.
alert. Maka'ala, miki'ala, 'eleu, 'eu'eu. *Also:* miki, ka'uka'u lua 'ole, alawiki, pe'epe'e makawalu, hāna, na'ena'e.
Alexandria. 'Alekanekalia, Alekanedaria.
alfalfa. Mau'u 'alapapa, mau'u 'alafafa.
alga. Limu *(see Haw.-Eng. entry and entries that follow it). See* lichen, moss, sea lettuce, seaweed. *Some fresh-water algae:* nehe, limu kalawai, līpala'ō, līpālā-wai, pala'ō, pālāwai, pāwai, hulu 'īlio, ha'ulelani, oha'oha'o.
algaroba. Kiawe.
algebra. Hō'ailona helu.
Algeria. 'Alekelia, Alegeria.
algum. 'Alekuma.
alias. Inoa kapakapa.
alien. Kupa no ka 'āina ē.
alienate. Ho'ohuli kū'ē, ho'omokuāhana.
alight. Kū *(as a bird or plane on the ground);* kau *(as a bird on a branch).*
alike. Like, like pū, likelike, kohu like. *Also:* 'ālike, kūlike, kaulike, hālike, hālikelike. *Just alike,* like loa, like ā like, kūlike loa.
alimentary canal. Uha.
alimony. Uku ho'omau mahope o ka 'oki male 'ana.
alive. Ola, kūola, kāmakamaka. *To take alive,* lawe ola.
all. Āpau, pauloa, pau, papau, like 'ole, puni, holo-'oko'a, paunui. *All the people,* nā kānaka apau loa, pau apau. *All over,* mai 'ō ā 'ō. *All things,* kēlā mea, kēia mea. *All together,* pau pū. *Not at all!* 'Ole wale! 'A'ole loa!
alkali. Ko'ana mimi *(in urine).*
allamanda. Naniali'i, laniali'i.
allay. Ho'ēmi, hō'olu'olu.
allege. Hō'ike. *The alleged,* ka mea i 'ōlelo 'ia.
Allegheny. 'Ālekani, Alegani.
allegiance. Kūpa'a. *Pledge of allegiance,* ho'ohiki kūpa'a.
allegory. Mo'olelo e a'o ana i ka hana pono loa; 'ōlelo nane, nane.
allegro. 'Ai ha'a.
alleviated. Hō'olu'olu 'ia, mao.
alley. Ala 'ololī. *Bowling alley,* kahua 'olohū, ala maika.
alliance. Hui.
allied. Ho'ohui 'ia.
allies. Aupuni kāko'o.
alligation. 'Āwili.
alligator. Mo'o nui, 'ālikekoa.
allot. Hā'awi.
allotment. Ha'awina.
allow. 'Ae, ho'oku'u.
allowance. Ha'awina. *To make allowances for,* ho'oku'u.
alloy. Mea ho'ohuihui.
all right. Hiki, hiki nō, pololei, 'oia paha, maika'i. *All right, then,* 'oia ho'i hā. *It's all right,* 'oia a'e lā nō.

allspice. 'Alakapaika.
allude. Ho'omea, ho'omaoe, 'ōlelo ma ke 'ano ho'ona-lonalo.
alluring. Nani e makahehi 'ia ai, 'ume, onaona, ho'ō-naona.
ally. Hoa kāko'o.
Alma Mater. 'Alemamaka.
almanac. 'Alemanaka.
almighty. Mana loa.
almond. Kamani haole, 'alemone, kepa.
almost. Kokoke, 'ane'ane; 'ānihaniha *(rare). Almost dead,* mai make. *Almost seven fathoms,* nā anana 'eono ā puka 'ehiku. *Almost hit by a car,* 'a'ohe noho'i he wā, ho'oku'i 'ia e ke ka'a.
alms. Kōkua, laulima.
alodial. 'Alolio, alodio, 'alokio. *Freehold less than alo-dial,* kuleana malalo o ke 'ano 'alolio. *Alodial title,* 'alolio, palapala 'alolio.
alodium. 'Alokio, 'ano 'alokio.
aloe. Pānini 'awa'awa, 'aloe.
aloft. I luna, maluna.
aloha. Aloha.
alone. Ho'okahi wale nō, wale, ho'okahi, kohana, kiakahi. *See saying,* aka 1. *To live alone,* noho ho'okahi. *To go alone,* hele ho'okahi.
along. Ma.
alongside. Ma ka 'ao'ao, pilipā, pīpā.
aloof. Kū mamao, kū ho'okahi, ihu pi'i, waiakua, umu-akua, naua, pali loa.
aloud. Leo nui.
alpaca. 'Alapaka.
alpha. 'Alepa.
alphabet. Pī'āpā, hua kumu, 'alepapeka. *Alphabet song,* mele ukali hua kumu.
Alps. 'Alepa.
already. 'Ē.
also. Ho'i, kekahi, kahi, eia kekahi, la'a, ho'oiho. *I also,* 'o au pū.
Altair. Humu, Ho'ohumu.
altar. Kuahu, lele, lele ho'okau, ahu, kū'ula, ahupua'a, ni'o, unu, unu kupukupu. *Also:* hāunu kupukupu, ho'ouluulu lei, hūlili, kua'aha, hanoalewa, ka'ānani'au, uhe. *Altar platform,* haka lele.
alter. Ano'ē. *See* change.
alteration. Lolina.
alternate. 1. *Following by turns.* 'O kēlā ai'ole 'o kēia. *Alternate Sundays,* he lāpule ā he lapule 'alo. 2. *Substitute.* Pani hakahaka kūikawā.
alternately. I kekahi ā i kekahi aku.
alternative. 'O kēlā ai'ole 'o kēia.
although. 'Oiai.
altitude. Ki'eki'e, ki'eki'ena.
alto. 'Aeko, 'aleko, leo waena.
altogether. 'Oko'a, holo'oko'a. *All of us together,* kā-kou pū.
alum. Pa'akai mu'emu'e.
always. Nā manawa apau loa, mau, pau 'ole, kau ā kau.
am. *See* be. *I am, yours respectfully,* 'o au iho nō, me ka mahalo.
amaranth. Pakai, 'āheahea, pakai kukū; kūwela *(possibly). Amaranth seedlings,* pakapakai.
amateur. Hōlona, mea 'akahi akahi.
amaze. Ho'okupaianaha, kamahoi.
amazement. Pū'iwa, kupaianaha, kupanaha, kāhāhā, makahehi, kamahoi. *See* astonishment.
Amazon. Wahine kaua, koa wahine *(female warrior).*
ambassador. 'Elele aupuni, kuhina. *Rare:* 'emepakekoa, luna ko'iko'i.
amber. 'Amepela, amebera.
amberfish. Kamanu.
ambergris. Hūpē koholā.
amberjack. Kāhala (mokule'ia), āmuka.
ambition. 'Onipa'a e loa'a ka mea 'i'ini, 'i'ini, kuko kōkikiu.
amble. Hele mālie; haki'opa *(rare).*
ambulance. Ka'a lawe ma'i.

ambuscade. Hālua, kauamoe; po'i pō *(night).*
ambush. Hālua, ho'ohālua, moe, moemoe.
amen. 'Āmene.
amend. Ho'oponopono, ho'ololi.
amendment. Ho'ololi 'ōlelo pāku'i.
amenities. 'Olu o ka noho 'ana.
America. 'Amelika; Maleka *(rare).*
American. 'Amelika, haole. *American citizen,* kupa 'Amelika.
Americanized. Ho'ohaole 'ia, ho'olilo 'ia i 'Amelika.
American Tract Society. Kō 'Amelika 'Ahahui Kelaka.
amethyst. 'Ameki, 'amekukeke.
Amherst. 'Amehaka, Amehasa.
amiable. 'Olu'olu, waipahē.
amid. Mawaena.
amidships. Waena moku; ukuwai *(of canoes).*
amiss. Pilikia, pono 'ole.
ammonia. 'Amonia.
ammunition. Lako kaua.
amnesia. Poina ka no'ono'o.
amnion. Nalu.
amniotic fluid. 'Ina'ina, lapawai.
amomum. 'Amomo.
among. Mawaena, i waena.
amorous. 'Ano kuko, li'a, ake ho'oipoipo.
amount. Heluna, huina, nui.
amphibious. Holo 'āina holo kai.
amphipod. 'Ami kai.
ample. Lawa pono. *Also:* ka'aka'alawa, pūlawa, kīlaha.
amputate. Moku, momoku, mokumoku, muku, 'oki.
amputated. Mu'umu'u, mumuku, muku, 'oki 'ia.
amputee. Mu'umu'u.
Amsterdam. 'Amekekama, Ametedama.
amuse. Ho'ole'ale'a, ho'okolohe, ho'ohoihoi; pa'apa'anā *(rare).*
amused. Hoihoi, nanea.
amusement. Ho'ole'ale'a, le'ale'a, pā'ani.
amusing. Mea ho'ole'ale'a, ho'omāke'aka, pā'ani, hū'eu, ho'owale hau.
an. *See* **a.**
analysis. Wehewehe 'ano.
analyze. Wehewehe pono, wehewehe 'ano.
anarchist. 'Anakia.
anarchy. 'Anakia, kānāwai 'ole.
anatomy. 'Anakomia. *Ancient method of teaching anatomy,* ho'onoho i ka 'ili'ili.
ancestor. Kupuna; 'eleua *(rare). Related through a common ancestor,* pili ma ka hanauna, pili ma nā kūpuna. *See* 'iewe.
ancestors. Nā kūpuna. *To talk too much of ancestors,* kaula'i iwi.
ancestral. Pili i nā kūpuna.
ancestry. Hanauna, kupuna, welo.
anchor. Heleuma, hekau; kū *(verb). Also:* 'anakā, pōhākau, pōhaku hekau. *To weigh anchor,* huki i ka heleuma. *To lie at anchor,* lana, lulu, mouo, mōuouo.
anchorage. Wahi kū moku, awa kū moku.
anchored. Kū, hekau.
anchovy. Nehu.
ancient. Kahiko; mauliauhonua *(rare). Ancient times,* wā kahiko, kumupa'a, kuapapa.
and. Ā *(usually preceding verbs);* a me *(usually preceding nouns);* eia ho'i.
andante. Ho'āeae.
Andes. 'Aneke, Anede.
andiron. Hao ho'opa'a wahie ma ke kapuahi.
Andover. 'Anekowela, Anedovera.
and so forth. Ā pēlā aku.
anecdote. Mo'olelo pōkole. *To illustrate with anecdotes,* ho'opilipili 'ōlelo; pāka'a *(rare).*
anemia. Koko hōwai, kaiaka ke koko; 'īkoko *(rare).*
anemone. 'Ōkole emiemi, 'ōkole hāwele *(kinds of sea anemones).*
anew. Hou.
angel. 'Ānela, hemolele, kanaka lele. *Guardian angel,* 'ānela kia'i.

angel's trumpet. Nānāhonua.
anger, angry. Huhū, ho'ohuhū, inaina, ukiuki, uluhua, nāuki. *Also:* ho'omainaina, uluulu, laukōnā, kahu ka 'ena, 'āniha, ioiole'a, manini, makā'eo, memeki, makani, nāulu, 'ōkaikai, ho'okuake'eo, 'ōnohi 'ula, neku'e, ho'okoko, 'ā, 'a'ā, 'ena, ehuehu, hōkūkū, kalakū. *See sayings,* **hālelo, hao 4, hao'e, kō 1, pihapiha 2, molar.** *Very great anger,* huhū wela loa, huhū loa, hū'ena, hahana ka wela, kokoko. *Anger without cause,* huhū wale. *Uncontrolled anger,* huhū kāohi 'ole, kuakoko. *Quick anger,* huhū hikiwawe. *Slow to anger,* ka'alolohi. *Words of anger,* pi'ipi'i 'ōlelo. *Interjections of anger:* kāhūhū, kāhōhō, chā. *To arouse anger,* ho'oinaina, ho'opī'ena, ho'opi'ipi'i, hō'ena'ena, ho'ohae. *To become angry,* pi'i ka huhū, pi'i ka heu, pi'i ka 'ena.
angle. Huina; 'anekelo *(rare). Acute angle,* huina 'oi. *Obtuse angle,* huina peleleu. *Right angle,* huina kūpono. *To cut at an angle,* ka'akepa.
angler. Kanaka kā makoi.
Anglican. 'Anekalikana.
angry. *See* **anger.**
anguish. Na'auauā, walania, walawalania, walenia, wawalania, welenia; 'awa'awa *(Ioba 7:11),* ho'okūpouli.
angular. Hiwi, hiwihiwi, kihi loa, kihikihi, 'ōkihikihi, ho'oke'eke'e.
animal. Holoholona. *Young animal,* ohi, 'ouo. *Pet animal,* hānai ā huhu.
animate. Hō'eu, hō'eleu, ho'olapa, ho'oikaika, hō'īnana.
animated. 'Eu'eu, 'īnana, 'eleu, ehuehu, lamalama, nanahea.
animation. 'Eu, 'eleu, ehuehu, lamalama, nene.
animosity. Kū'ē'ē. *See* **hate.**
ankle. Ku'eku'e wāwae, 'ami wāwae; ku'ina wāwae *(joint);* pu'upu'u wāwae, pu'u *(bone).*
anklet. Kūpe'e.
Ann Arbor. 'Ane Apa, Ane Aba.
annex. Pāku'i, ho'ohui, ho'oku'i. *Annex to a house,* hale pāku'i.
annexation. Ho'ohui 'āina.
annihilation. Papau make, luku ho'opapau.
anniversary. Piha makahiki, lā ho'omana'o.
announce. Hō'ike, kūkala, kalakū, kala, kalahea, kuahaua.
announcer. Kala, kalakū. *Radio announcer,* mea ho'olaha, leo kala.
annoy. Ho'onaukiuki, ho'okolohe, ho'ouluhua, hōkake, hana wale. *Also:* ho'omāhuā, ho'omā'auē, nole.
annoyance. Ho'onaukiuki, pulapula, mala'o, none. *Interjections of annoyance:* kā! kaī! i ka ī!
annoyed. Ukiuki, uluhua, kū'aki. *Rare:* uhelehe.
annual. Makahiki, kūmakahiki, ma ka makahiki. *Annual flower,* pua makahiki. *Annual issue,* puka makahiki. *Annual report,* hō'ike makahiki. *Annual salary,* uku ma ka makahiki.
annuity. Uku makahiki, 'anuiki.
annul. Ho'opau, ho'ōki.
annunciation. Ha'i 'ana.
anoint. Poni, ho'oponi, hamo, ho'opē, kāhinu.
anointed. Hamo, poni 'ia, māhinu.
anon. Auane'i.
anonymous. 'A'ohe i hō'ike 'ia ka inoa.
another. Kekahi, ha'i, 'oko'a, 'ē a'e. *Another day,* kekahi lā. *Another person,* kekahi mea, ha'i.
answer. Pane, panena, ō, eō; 'ī mai *(cf. Gram. 7.2);* ha-'ina *(as to a riddle);* hua loa'a, ha'iloa'a *(as to a problem);* pākīkē, ho'okīkē, 'u'u *(rude);* 'āpa'apani *(clever). To answer briefly,* 'ekemu. *To refuse to answer,* mū.
ant. Naonao, 'ānonanona, nonanona, lonalona.
antagonist. Hoa paio.
antagonistic. Ho'onanā, 'imi hakakā, ho'okū'ē; 'oloke'a *(rare).*
antarctic. 'Anealika, anearika.
Antarctic Circle. Pō'ai-anu-hema.

Antarctic Ocean. Moana-anu-hema.
Antares. Kao, Hōkū-'ula, Melemele, Auhaele, Welehu, Lehua-Kona(?).
antelope. 'Anekelopa, nilekau, pipi hihiu.
antenna. Kukuna.
anthem. Mele hīmeni. *National anthem,* mele aupuni.
anthropology. Huli kanaka.
antichrist. 'Anikaliko 'anikelikeko.
anticipate. No'ono'o i ka mea e hiki mai ana, no'ono'o mua, ho'omaopopo 'ē, koho, kau nui ka mana'o; kēwā *(rare).*
antics. Hana ho'omāke'aka.
antique. Kahiko, mea kahiko.
antiquity. Ka wā kahiko.
antisocial. Laulauna 'ole; pu'aki *(rare).*
antler. Kiwi.
anus. 'Ōkole, poholua. *See* **buttocks.** *Anus opening,* 'amo, puka makani, puka kahiko, puka kūkae. *Sputtering anus,* pī ka 'amo *(of an overworked drudge).*
anvil. Kua, kua hao, kua lā'au; kua kuku, kua kapa *(for tapa).*
anxiety. Hopohopo, pīhoihoi, 'ōpikipiki, no'ono'o 'iha'iha.
any. Kekahi. *Any kind, any whatsoever,* 'a'ohe pilo. *See* **pono 6.**
anybody. *See* **anyone.**
anyhow. *See* **however.**
anyone. Kekahi, kekahi mea, 'o ka mea nō e. *Who will go? Oh, anyone.* 'O wai ka mea e hele ana? 'O ka mea e hiki ana nō ke hele.
anything. Ka mea e loa'a ana.
anyway. *See* **however.**
anywhere. Aia nō i kahi e hele ai; ma nā wahi like 'ole. *Just anywhere,* aia i ka 'auwa'a i pānānā.
aorta. Ēwe.
apart. Ka'awale. *To stand apart,* kū ka'awale. *Placed apart,* kau 'oko'a.
apartment. Ke'ena noho. *Apartment building,* hale papa'i.
apathetic. Kukule, palaka, ho'onakuli, 'ōhea.
ape. 1. *Monkey.* Keko, māpū. 2. *To imitate.* Māhu'i, ho'opa'i ā pa'i. *To ape a white person,* ho'ohālike me ka haole, ho'ohaole.
apex. Kihi.
aphid. 'Eleao.
apiece. Pākahi.
Apocrypha. 'Apokelupo.
apologize. Mihi, mimihi, mimimihi.
apoplexy. Ma'i kūhewa, make kā'iliponi; umalei *(rare).*
apostate. 'Apokaka.
apostle. Luna'ōlelo, 'apokolo, 'apokekolo.
apostolic. 'Apokolika.
apostrophe. Koma luna.
apothecary. Kāwili lā'au.
apparatus. Mea pa'ahana.
apparent. Mōakaaka.
apparition. Akakū, lapu, hoaka, mea 'ike 'ia 'ana.
appeal. Noi, nonoi; ho'opi'i *(legal). Also:* ui, 'ūlāleo, kāhoahoa, kākua.
appealing. Makahehi; hone *(of sound). See* **attractive.**
appear. Puka, kau, hiki, ho'omaka, kū, 'ō'ili, 'ōiwi, oni, pua, ho'omahiki; pua'i *(as color);* wana *(as a ray of light);* hala'o'a *(dimly). Also:* 'ōme'ume, 'ō'ili wale, ulāheo. *To appear for no reason,* 'ō'ili wale. *To cause to appear,* ho'ohiki. *To appear angry,* pi'i ka huhū.
appearance. 1. *Resemblance.* Hi'ona, 'ōiwi, kū, kohu, hālina, hālinalina, nānaina. *See ex.,* **'ōiwi.** 2. *Arrival.* Kauna, 'ō'ili. *Appearing here and there,* 'ō'ili'ili.
appease. Ho'onā, ho'omānalo, ho'oma'alili, ho'olaule'a.
appeased. Mānalo, akaku'u.
appeasement. Ho'omānalo 'ana.
append. Ho'ohui, pāku'i.
appendages. Manamana.
appendicitis. Ma'i o ka na'aumoa. *Symptoms of some*

ancient diseases, perhaps appendicitis: hoaka, kākaiawī, kākaipū.
appendix. 1. *Anatomy.* Na'aumoa, hoaka *and below. See also* **kākaiawī, kākaipū** *(none of these meanings are certain).* 2. *Supplement.* 'Ōlelo pāku'i hou.
appetite. 'Ono ka 'ai, hia'ai'ono. *Lack of appetite,* kanea, kanekanea, naoa, kaea, niole, noni, uanaoa. *Ravenous appetite,* 'aiāmanō. *He has a good appetite, his food is appetizing,* 'ono kāna 'ai 'ana.
appetizer. Pūpū, hō'ono'ono 'ai.
applaud, applause. Pa'ipa'i lima, pa'ipa'i.
apple. 'Āpala, poma.
apple of Sodom. Pōpolo kīkānia.
applicable. Kūpono.
applicant. Mea noi.
application. Palapala noi, palapala ho'opi'i.
apply. 1. *Adhere.* Pili, ho'opili. 2. *Petition.* Noi. 3. *Concentrate.* No'ono'o pono, kau ka mana'o, lelepau.
appoint. Ho'onoho, ho'okohu, ho'okoho, poni.
appointment. 1. *Engagement.* Ho'opa'a manawa. *Have you made an appointment?* Ua ho'opa'a 'oe i kou manawa? 2. *Nomination.* Wae, ho'okohu.
appointment certificate. Palapala ho'okohu.
Appomattox. 'Apomakoka, Apomatoka.
apportion. Mahele, māhelehele, kā'ana; ka'ipu'u *(rare).*
apposition. Kino kaulele *(in grammar).*
appraise. Ho'oholo, ho'oholo waiwai.
appreciate. Ho'omaika'i, mahalo, maopopo loa ka waiwai; poma *(rare).*
apprentice. Haumāna a'o 'oihana, ho'opa'a a'o hana, haumāna.
approach. Ho'okokoke, hiki, hō'ea'ea.
approaching. Eia a'e, eia aku, a'e.
appropriate. 1. *Set aside.* Ho'oka'awale, hā'awi. 2. *Suitable.* Kūpono, kohu, kū.
appropriation. Ha'awina, pila ha'awina; alāiki *(taking by force).*
approval. Ho'āpono, 'ae.
approve. Ho'āpono, 'ae, 'āpono.
approved. Holo, 'ae.
approximately. Kahi, kokoke. *Approximately ten feet,* ma kahi o 'umi kapua'i.
apricot. 'Apelekoka.
April. 'Apelila.
April Fools' Day. Lā 'Epa o 'Apelila.
apron. 'Epane, pāpalu, pale, pālaulau.
apt. 1. *Clever.* 'A'apo. 2. *Likely.* Malia. *Apt to fall,* malia o hā'ule aku.
aptitude. Mākaukau; uli'eo *(rare).*
aquarium. Hale hō'ike'ike i'a, pahu i'a.
aqueduct. Hā wai.
Aquila. *Probably* Humu, Humu-mā, Ho'ohumu.
Arabia, Arabian. 'Alapia, Arabia.
Aragon. 'Alakona, Aragona.
Ararat. 'Alalaka, Ararata.
arbitrary. 1. *Inconsiderate.* Pa'akikī, mākonā. 2. *Without reason.* Hana kumu 'ole.
arbitrate. Ho'omaluhia, 'uao.
arbitrator. 'Uao, kau waena.
Arbor Day. Lā Kanu Lā'au.
arc. Pi'o, kaula, lālani poepoe.
Arcadia. 'Akakia, Akadia.
arch. Pi'o, pāpi'o, hoaka; pao, lapu'una. *Arch of a foot,* poho wāwae. *Arch over a door,* hoaka, hoakake'a. *Arch of rainbow,* pi'o ke ānuenue.
archaeologist. Mea 'ike hana lima o ke au i hala.
archaeology. Noi'i 'ike hana lima o ke au i hala.
archangel. Ali'i 'ānela, luna 'ānela.
archbishop. 'Akipihopa.
arched. Pi'o, lāpu'u, 'ōnaha, kaka, popoli.
archer, archery. Pana pua, pana 'iole, pāpua.
arching. Pipi'o, nianiape, moai.
archipelago. Pae 'āina, pae moku.
architect. Kaha ki'i hale; kuhikuhipu'uone.
archives. Waihona palapala kahiko.
arctic. 'Ālika, arika.

Arctic Circle. Kā'ei-anu, Pō'ai-anu-'ākau.
Arctic Ocean. Moana-anu-'ākau.
Arcturus. Hōkū-le'a *(probably)*.
Arden. 'Alakena, Aradena.
ardent. 'I'ini nui, ake nui. *Ardent love-making,* ho'okela o ka ho'oipoipo, hiu ā wela.
are. 1. *See* **be. 2.** *Unit of measurement.* 'Ale.
area. Nui, 'ili, 'alea.
arena. Kahua, pā. Lua *fighting arena,* pāku'i a lua.
Argos. 'Alekoka, Aregosa.
argue. Ho'opa'apa'a, ho'opāpā, paio, pāku'iku'i, pāoni, ho'opāoni, kīkē'ōlelo, ho'opanepane, hākā 'ōlelo; uhi'āpana *(rare)*.
argument. Paio, pa'apa'a, pāoni, ho'opa'apa'a, hakakā 'ōlelo.
argumentative. Wahapa'a, puni ho'opa'apa'a.
arid. Mānā, 'āpa'a, panoa, anoa, ka'o, ka'oka'o, kō'ā, malo'ohāhā, ponanā.
Aries. Hipa-kāne.
arise. Ala, hiki.
aristocracy. Ali'i.
aristocratic. Ali'i, lani.
Aristotle's lantern. Niho.
arithmetic. Huina helu, helu, 'alimakika. *Mental arithmetic,* helu na'au. *Children's arithmetic,* helu kamali'i.
Arizona. 'Alikona, Arizona.
ark. Hale lana, wa'a kome, pahu.
Arkansas. 'Akanaka, Akanasa; 'Alekaneko, Arekaneso.
ark of the covenant. Pahu pelika.
ark of the testimony. Pahu kānāwai, pahu hō'ike.
arm. *Anatomy.* Lima; kālele *(as of a chair); upper part of* —, uluna, ununa. *Arm below elbow,* kū'aulima. *Arm in arm,* kui lima, kuikui lima, kui'ē'ē. *To swing the arms,* kāia.
armament. Lako kaua.
armchair. Noho kālele.
armed. Lako i nā mea kaua. *Armed division,* papa kaua.
armed forces. Pū'ali koa.
Armenia, Armenian. 'Alemenia, Aremenia.
arm guard. Pale lima.
armistice. Ho'opau kaua, ho'oku'ikahi, ho'omalu kaua; ho'okuapapa *(rare)*.
Armistice Day. Lā Ho'opau Kaua, Lā Ho'oku'ikahi.
armor. 'A'ahu kaua, pale kila, kapa kila, pūliki kaua.
armorer. 'Āmala.
armory. Hale koa, hale ho'olako kaua.
armpit. Pō'ae'ae, kīpō'ae'ae, napo'o, 'ē'ē, po'ē'ē.
arms. 1. *Anatomy.* Nā lima; poli *(fig.).* **2.** *War.* Lako kaua. *Manual of arms,* he kumu lako kaua. *Carry arms!* Hāpai pū! *To supply arms.* Ho'olako i nā mea kaua.
army. Pū'ali, kaua, pū'ulu, pū'ulu kaua. *Army unit,* kaua, huna kaua, papa kaua, papa koa, pū'ulu; honua, kuamo'o kaua *(main);* hunalewa, papa po'o *(van);* hunapa'a *(rear). Army disposition in battle,* kahului.
army worm. Kupa, pe'elua.
aroma. 'A'ala, onaona, 'aloma. *See* **smell.**
around. Puni. *To go around,* ka'apuni, pō'ai, anapuni, kalawai. *"Around the island" hula,* ka'apuni.
arouse. Ho'āla, pai, ho'opaipai, hō'eu, ho'ā, ho'ohana; ho'okola *(sexual).*
arrange. Ho'onoho, ho'onohonoho, ho'onoho papa, ho'oponopono, kūkulu papa, haku, hakuhaku, kuene. *Arrange flowers,* ho'onohonoho pua.
arrangement. Ho'onoho 'ana, kūkulu 'ana, ho'onohonoho 'ana.
arrayed. Ulumāhiehie, ho'ouluwehiwehi 'ia, kāhiko 'ia.
arrears. Ka'a hope.
arrest. 1. *Seize.* Hopu, hopuna. *Warrant of arrest,* palapala hopu. *Freedom from arrest,* pakele mai ka hopu 'ia. **2.** *Check.* Ke'ake'a, ke'a, ho'oke'a.
arrive. Hō'ea, hiki, kū, kau.
arrogant. *See* **proud.**
arrow. Pua, pua pana; kaha kuhi *(reference mark). To shoot with an arrow,* pana.
arrow case. 'A'a pua.
arrowroot. Pia. *Arrowroot starch,* pia. *Process of sweet-*

ening arrowroot starch, kūlō pia. *To place arrowroot in packages,* 'a'aho. *Small arrowroot tubers,* mā'ili. *Arrowroot balls,* 'omo'omo, pia.
arsenal. Waihona lako kaua.
arsenic. 'Alakenika.
arson. Puhi ahi, puhi mana'o 'ino.
art. Hana no'eau.
art academy. Hale hō'ike'ike.
artemisia. Hinahina.
artery. A'a.
artesian water. Wai aniani, wai 'ale'ale.
artesian well. Luawai aniani, luawai pipi'i.
artful. Ma'alea.
arthritis. Lumakika, hu'i o ka 'ami o ke kino.
article. 1. *Object.* Mea; kumu *(rare).* **2.** *Essay.* Mo'olelo. **3.** *Grammatical.* Pilimua. *See* **definite article, indefinite article. 4.** *Section.* Paukū, ha'awina.
artificial. Ku'i *(as a leg);* ho'ohālike *(as flowers). See* **plastic.**
artillery. Pū kaua, pū ka'a.
artist. Kaha ki'i.
artistic. No'eau, 'ike hana no'eau.
as. 1. *Resembling.* Me, like me. *As though,* mehe. *As follows,* penei; 'oia ho'i. *As if,* mehe mea lā. *As far as,* ā, ā hiki i. **2.** *See* **because.**
ascend. Pi'i.
ascent. Pi'ina, alapi'i.
ascertain. Ho'omaopopo.
ash. Lehu, pa'u ahi.
ashamed. Hilahila, 'ōhila, ho'opalai, manīne. *To make ashamed,* ho'ohilahila.
ash-colored. Lehu, po'o hina.
ash dust. Lehu ane.
ashes. Lehu, lehu ahi, lehu ane, lehu 'ula, lehu pele, pa'u ahi. *Rare:* lepo uli, mālena, pahukaina, noho hale. *Ashes of the fireplace scatter in all directions,* puehu li'ili'i ka lehu o kapuahi *(of violent temper).*
ash-gray. Ualehu.
ashore. I uka. *To go ashore,* hele i uka. *Washed or drifted ashore,* pae. *To put ashore,* lawe i uka, ho'oīkā.
ash tray. Pā lehu.
ash tree. 'Ōlena; paina *(KJV).*
Ash Wednesday. Lā Hāpala Lehu, Pō'akolu Kau Lehu.
Asia, Asian, Asiatic. 'Ākia, Asia.
Asia Minor. 'Ākia 'U'uku.
aside. Ma ka 'ao'ao, ma kahi ka'awale. *To set aside,* ho'oka'awale.
ask. 1. *To question.* Nīnau, ui. *To ask insistently,* koi. *To ask indirectly,* ho'ohuahualau, ho'omaoe. *To keep asking,* nīele, ho'omāuiui, kauloloa. **2.** *To request.* Noi, nonoi. **3.** *To invite.* Kono.
askance. Me ka ho'owahāwahā. *Eyed askance,* maka 'ewa'ewa 'ia. *To look askance.* maka'ē.
askew. Kapakahi, kapeke, kū'ewa. *To set askew,* ho'okapeke.
asleep. Hiamoe. *Fast asleep,* pa'uhia i ka hiamoe, hiamoe pa'a loa, kāia i ka hiamoe. *To pretend to be asleep,* ho'ohiamoe, ho'olōlō.
asp. Mo'o make, mo'o niho 'awa.
aspect. Hi'ohi'ona, nānaina.
asphalt. Kā, kimeki. *Asphalt surface,* kā hāli'i.
ass. *See* **donkey.**
Assam. 'Akama, Asama.
assassin. Lima koko.
assassinate. Ho'omake. *Rare:* kīmopō, kawa.
assault. Limanui, lima ikaika, lawelawe lima. *Assault and battery,* hoana e hō'eha.
assemble. 1. *To meet.* Hui pū, anaina, 'ākoakoa, ho'ākoakoa. *Also:* pūku'i, pū'ulu, lāhui, ho'olau, 'āpo'epo'e, ho'ulu'ulu, nunu'a. **2.** *To collect.* Hō'ili'ili, hō'ulu'ulu, ho'opili.
assembly. Anaina, 'aha *and entries that follow it. Rare:* mui, 'ulu'ulu, pōkinahua. *See* **meeting.** *National assembly,* 'aha 'ōlelo lāhui.
Assembly Hall. Ke'ena Hālāwai.
assess. Helu, ho'ouku.

assessment. 'Auhau.
assets. Waiwai, waiwai hui, waiwai lewa, pono.
assign. Kauoha, hā'awi ha'awina, kuhikuhi i ka ha'awina e hana ai, ho'olilo.
assignee. Hope waiwai.
assignment. Palapala ho'olilo, ha'awina.
Assisi. 'Akiki, Asisi. *Francis of Assisi,* Palakiko o 'Akiki.
assist. Kōkua, kāko'o.
assistant. Hope, kōkua, kāpehe.
assistant teacher. Kōkua kumu, hope kumu.
associate. 1. *To join.* Launa, hui, pili. **2.** *Partner.* Hoa, hoalauna, hoahui, kōko'o, pili pa'a, kāpehe, kūmaka. *See* **justice.**
association. Launa 'ana, pilina *and below,* 'ahahui, hui, 'ahahuina; — *of two,* kōko'olua; — *of three,* kōko'okolu. *Loving association,* pilialoha.
assort. Wae.
assortment. Mea like 'ole, 'ano like 'ole. *See* **collection.**
assuage. Ho'oma'alili, mānalo, ho'onā.
assuaged. Nā, mao.
assume. Kuhi, mahu'i, kainō.
assumed. Kuhi. *Assumed name,* inoa kapakapa.
Assumption. Lawe 'Ia 'Ana *(as of the Virgin Mary).*
Assyria. 'Akulia, Asuria.
aster. Koniaka *(all kinds).*
asterisk. Kaha kuhi.
astern. I hope.
asteroid. Hōkū li'ili'i.
asthma. Hānō; nae 'oai kū *(rare).*
astonished. Pū'iwa, ho'opū'iwa, ha'oha'o, pīhoihoi, kāhāhā, hauli, pilihua.
astonishing. Ha'oha'o, kamaha'o, ho'okāhāhā, kāmeha'i.
astonishment. Kāhīhī 'ana, ha'oha'ona. *See* **amazement.**
astray. 'Auana, lalau, hō'aiā, pololua. *See saying,* **Kalalau.** *To lead astray,* ho'olalau, ho'ohili, luahele, hō'aiāhua.
astringent. Liki.
astrologer. Kilo hōkū, kilo, kilo lani.
astronomer, astronomy. A'o hōkū, kilo hōkū, kilo lani.
asylum. Pu'uhonua.
at. Ma, i, iā. *Look at him,* nānā iāia.
Athabasca. 'Akapakeka, Atabaseka.
atheist. Hō'ole Akua, mahuakala.
Athens. 'Akenai, Atenai.
athlete. Mea i ma'ama'ahia i nā pā'ani ho'oikaika kino, 'ālapa; pai'ea *(rare).*
athlete's foot. Palawai, kuma.
athletic. Pili ho'oikaika kino, 'ālapa; maua'ālina *(rare).*
athletic contest. Ho'okūkū ho'oikaika kino; kahului.
athletic field. Kahua pā'ani. *Rare:* 'aha maha, 'omaliō.
Atlantic. 'Akelanika, Atelanika.
atlas. Puke palapala'āina.
atmosphere. Lewa *and entries that follow it. Cf.* **halalani.** *Lower atmosphere,* lewa ho'omakua. *Next lower atmosphere,* lewa lani lewa. *Clear atmosphere,* palamea *(rare).*
atoll. Mokupuni pālahalaha.
atomic. 'Akomika.
atonement. Kalahala, huikala.
atrocity. Ho'omāinoino nui.
attach. Ho'opili, ho'opa'a, 'ōmou.
attachment. Ho'opili, 'upu.
attack. Ho'ouka kaua, pu'e, po'ipū, po'i pō, lele, ku'ia, limanui, 'aki, ki'i, olowalu, pōpō 'auhuhu, 'ūpā. *See* **heart attack.**
attempt. Ho'ā'o.
attend. 1. *Escort.* Ukali, 'alo. *To attend a meeting,* hele i ka hālāwai. **2.** *Execute.* Lawelawe, mālama, moamoa, momoa, ho'omoamoa.
attendant. Kahu *and entries that follow it,* lawelawe, ukali, 'aialo; kāpi'i *(fig.). See* **bridal attendants.**

attention. Nānā, maliu; —, *as a military command,* ho'olohe. *To pay attention,* nānā, maliu, kaulona, ho'omaopopo.
attentive. Ho'olohe, ho'olono, lohe pono.
attic. *Same as* **upstairs.**
attire. 'A'ahu.
attitude. Kūlana, kuana.
attorney. Loio. *Power of attorney,* palapala ho'āmana. *County attorney,* loio kalana.
attorney general. Loio kuhina; kōkua *(old term).*
attract. 'Ume, ala'ume, hōnēnē, kā'ana, ho'ōnaona. *To attract with the eyes,* makaki'i. *To attract the attention of a bird,* kono, kolo *(by imitating its call).*
attracted. 'Ume 'ia, nēnē, ona, laka.
attraction. 'Ume, 'ume launa, 'ume mākēneki; 'ume lauoho *(siphon);* 'umena.
attractive. 1. *As a magnet.* 'Ume. **2.** *As a person or scene.* Hie, makahehi, ma'ema'e, nonohe, lehiwa, 'ume, onaona, wai 'olu. *Fig.:* maka lehua, maka onaona, maka palupalu, māmane, kohu, mi'i, kaekae, ka'aona, miu, alokele, luhiehu, mahamoe, lupea, mīkohu. *See saying,* **hā'ale.**
Auckland. 'Aukelana.
auction. Kūkālā.
auctioneer. Luna kūkālā.
auction sale. Kū'ai kūkālā.
audible. Hiki ke lohe 'ia, lohea.
audience. Anaina. *Royal audience,* anaina 'ike ali'i.
audit. Hō'oia.
auditor. Luna hō'oia, luna nānā helu.
auger. Wili nui.
August. 'Aukake.
aunt. Makuahine, makuahine hanauna, 'anakē; makuahine 'ōpio *(younger sister or cousin of a parent);* makuahine makua *(older sister or cousin of a parent).*
aunt-in-law. Makuahūnōwai.
Australia. 'Aukekulelia, Auseturelia; Nuhōlani *(old name).*
Austria. 'Aukekulia, Auseturia.
authentic. 'Oia'i'o.
author. Mea kākau, kākau mo'olelo, haku mo'olelo, haku puke.
authority. Mana, kuleana, mea 'ike; kīkā *(rare). Voice of authority,* leo mana, leo hano, waha mana, leo ko'iko'i.
authorize. Ho'āmana, ho'omana, ho'okohu.
auto. Ka'a.
autocrat. Ali'i kū'oko'a.
autograph. Kākau inoa, hapapūlima.
autoharp. Pila hapa.
auto license. *See* **license plate.**
automatic. Hana nona iho, holo nona iho. *Done until automatic,* ua hana ā walea. *Automatic machine,* mīkini hana nona iho.
automobile. Ka'a, ka'a 'okomopila, otomobila. *Automobile insurance,* 'inikua ka'a.
autumn. *See* **fall 3.**
avalanche. Hehe'e, he'ehe'e, 'aholo, pōhākō'ī.
avarice. Make'e waiwai.
avaricious. Puni waiwai, puni kālā. *Also:* makauli'i, pa'akūkū.
avenge. Ho'opa'i, kū ka mākaia, ho'oka'a. *Avenger of blood,* mea ho'opa'i koko.
avenue. Alanui ākea.
average. 'Awelika, waena.
avert. Pāweo. *To avert the eyes,* pāweo maka.
aviary. Hale manu.
aviation. 'Oihana mokulele.
aviator. Pailata mokulele.
avocado. Pea.
avocation. Hana ho'onanea.
avoid. 'Alo, hō'alo, kē, ka'akepa, pāweo, ho''ē'ē, ho'okē'ē, mā'iu'iu, pipika.
avoirdupois. 'Awakupoi.
'awa. *See* **kava.**
await. Kali, kakali.

awake. Ala, makalahia. *To awake from sleep,* lana ka hiamoe. *To awake suddenly,* puoho.

awaken. Ala, hoʻāla, hoʻālahia.

awakening. Alana.

award. Haʻawina, palapala hoʻokō, hoʻokō, makana.

aware. Hoʻomaopopo, ʻike.

away. Aku, ʻē, ma kahi ʻē, lilo. *Go away!* Hele ma kahi ʻē! Hele pēlā! *Six miles away,* ʻeono mile ke kaʻawale. *Away down,* i lalo lilo.

awe. ʻEʻehia, ano, hoʻāno, anoano, malu. *Stricken with awe,* ilihia.

awe-inspiring. ʻEʻehia.

awe-stricken. ʻEʻehia.

awful. Weliweli.

awhile. Manawa pōkole, liʻuliʻu iki.

awkward. Hemahema, pāhemahema, hāwāwā, māʻukaʻuka, kūloma, kuāhea, ʻonana, nāhili. *Rare:* manuea, neki, pololoa, pālola, hoʻonole, kākākiʻi. *Of awkward shape,* kīkoʻolā.

awl. Kui houhou, kui iwi.

awning. Pale lā, ʻanini.

awry. Keʻe, ʻewa, nūkeʻe.

axe. *See* **adze**.

axiom. ʻAkioma.

axis. Iho.

axle. Iho, paepae komo huila.

axman. Kua lāʻau.

aye. ʻAe.

Azores. ʻAkole, Azore.

B

b. *No Hawaiian term.*

baa. Mā'ā'ā.

babbling. Nāwā, hauwala'au, hauwalawala'au, hauka'e, namunamu.

Babel. Papela.

baboon. Māpū, papuna.

baby. Keiki, pēpē, kama. *Fig.:* lei, hāpu'u. *Premature baby,* keiki 'alu'alu. *Suckling baby,* keiki 'ai waiū. *Baby so young that it lies on its back.* keiki huli i luna ke alo (*see* **huli**). *To act like a baby,* ho'opēpē.

bachelor. Wahine 'ole, kanaka i male 'ole; ha'aiwi *(rare).*

bachelorhood. Noho male 'ole.

back. 1. *Anatomy.* Kua. *See* **taboo.** *Back of the neck,* hono. *To cling to the back,* pili kua. *To go behind one's back,* hele i hope o ke kua, kō i kua. *To call from behind one's back,* kāhea kua. *To turn the back on,* huli kua *(insult). Back wall of a house,* paia o hope, huli kua. *Stiff-backed,* nanai, lanai. *Burning back taboo,* kua'ā, kua liholiho, kualoi, kualoiloi. **2.** *Behind.* Hope, muli. *At the back,* i hope, mahope. *To back up or away,* peki, emi hope, ne'e hope, ho'one'e hope, koene. *Back and forth,* i mua i hope, ha'aku'e, helo. *To back water with a canoe,* ho'ēmi hope i ka wa'a, *Backed up against the wall (hard-pressed),* pili pū i ka paia.

backache. 'Eha o ke kua; mā'ī'ī *(rare).*

backbiter. 'Alapahi, mea paoke'e, 'aki.

backbone. Iwikuamo'o, kuamo'o.

backbreaking. Kuapa'a.

background. Kahua. *One without background,* kahua 'ole. *Background in quilt design,* honua.

backpack. 'Awe, 'awe'awe.

backslide. Ho'i hope.

backward. 1. *Rearward.* I hope. *To go backward,* emi hope, emi kua, peki, ne'e hope, emiemi. *To fall backward,* wala. **2.** *Stupid.* Lohi, lolohi, lohi'au. *Backward in learning,* lolohi ke a'o 'ana.

backwoodsman. Kua'āina, kaikua. *To act like a backwoodsman,* ho'okua'āina.

bacon. 'I'o pua'a uahi.

bad. Maika'i 'ole, 'ino, kolohe. *See* **breath, smell, temper.** *Too bad!* Minamina noho'i! Aloha 'ino. Auē! *Bad debt,* 'ai'ē pohō, 'ai'ē uku 'ole, 'ai'ē pono 'ole. *Bad luck,* po'ino, pakalaki.

badge. Pihi, hō'ailona. *Police badge,* pihi māka'i.

badger. Kehaka.

Baffin. Papine, Bafine. *Baffin Bay,* ke kai kū'ono o Papine.

baffled. Ke'a, ho'opohihihi, hoka.

bag. 'Eke, 'eke'eke. *Also:* 'a'a, kī'eke, pūkaula, hakai. *Netted sennit bag,* kōkō pū'alu. *Bag for carrying birds,* 'a'a manu. *Bag for carrying fire-making implements,* 'aahi.

bagasse. 'Aina kō, laina.

Bagdad. Pakekaka, Bagedada.

baggage. Ukana, 'ope'ope. *Baggage car,* ka'a ukana. *To carry baggage,* hali ukana.

baggy. 'Ope'alu, kū'olo.

bag net. *See* **net.**

bagpipe. 'Ūpoho, kukima *(RSV).*

Bahama. Pahama, Bahama.

bail. 1. *As a canoe.* Kā. *To bail a canoe,* kā wa'a. **2.** *Legal.* Pela.

bailer. Kā, o'o'o. *Canoe bailer,* kā wa'a.

bait. Maunu. *Also:* palu; pilipili he'e *(octopus or squid ink sac molded around a fishhook for bait);* hi'ukā *(rare). Leftover bait,* po'o maunu. *Bait container,* ipu holoholona. *Canoe bait carrier,* malau. *Bait stick,* lā'au melomelo. *To make* palu *bait,* ku'i palu. *The bait is pulverized,* paluhē ka palu *(of one meek, humble, abused).*

bake. Kālua, ho'omo'a, 'oma, ho'o'oma, puhi, ho'olua, kāō. *Baked pumpkin or squash,* ipu kālua. *To bake in ground oven,* kālua. *To bake whole, as a pig,* kālua pa'a.

baker. Kanaka puhi palaoa, puhi palaoa.

bakery. Hale puhi palaoa, hale kū'ai palaoa.

baking powder. Ho'ohū.

balance. 1. *Weigh.* Kaulike, ana paona, paona, paona kaulike. *See* **kūlike.** *To balance evenly,* ho'okaulike. **2.** *Remainder.* Koena, koehonua, hakina.

balcony. Lānai.

bald. 'Ōhule. *Also:* po'o nia, nia, mole, molemole, molea, pahu, pahu kani, kamani ke po'o, konekonea. *See sayings,* **goat, moon.** *Bald spot,* pōhaka.

bale. Pū'olo nui, pela. *Bale of hay,* pū'ā, pela mau'u malo'o.

balk. Nuha, nuhanuha, nunuha, ho'opupū.

Balkans. Palekana, Balekana.

ball. 1. *Sphere.* Kinipōpō. *Also:* pōpō, pōka'a, pōkā. *Ball of poi or food,* pōpō 'ai. *Ball for bowling,* 'ulu maika. *Tapa-covered ball (insignia of taboo),* pūlo'ulo'u. *Ball game,* pā'ani kinipōpō; kiniholo *(rare). Cannon ball,* pōkā pū kuni ahi. *Ball bat,* lā'au pa'i kinipōpō, lā'au kinipōpō. *Ball and socket joint,* 'ami ho'okuina lewa. *Ball of the foot,* mānea o ka wāwae. *To play ball,* kinipōpō, pā'ani kinipōpō. *To shape or wad into a ball,* ho'opōpō. **2.** *Dance.* 'Aha hulahula, anaina hulahula, hulahula.

ballast. Palaki, mea ho'okaumaha moku.

balloon. Pāluna.

balloon fish. 'O'opu hue.

balloon vine. Pōniu, hale-a-ka-i'a, 'inalua.

ballot. Pāloka. *To cast a ballot,* koho pāloka. *To count ballots,* helu pāloka.

ballroom. Lumi hulahula.

balm. Lā'au hamo, pāma; nini *(rare).*

balsam. Palamana, palekana, balesama, 'ōlepe.

Baltic. Palakika, Balatika. *Baltic Sea,* Kai Balakika.

Baltimore. Palakimoa, Balatimoa.

bamboo. 'Ohe *(various kinds, see* **'ohe***);* 'ualalehu. *Bamboo musical pipes,* kā'eke'eke, pahūpahū. *Bamboo rattles,* pū'ili. *Bamboo fire-blowing tube,* 'ohe puhi ahi, 'ūlili. *Bamboo water container,* 'ohe wai. *Bamboo stamp for marking tapa,* lā'au kāpalapala.

banana. Mai'a *(for various kinds and unfavorable connotations, see Haw.-Eng. entry and entries that follow it). Also:* a'ea'e, āewa, 'eka, hualau, lahi, maoli-'ili-lahilahi, pākanaloa, nu'uhiwa; lohelohe i honua *(poetic),* kahiki, kahiki hae, kahiki mauki, kahiki puhu, kūkanaloa. *See ex.,* **'e'a 2,** *ripe. Banana blossoms and sheath,* pola. *Dry banana leaf,* lauhulu. *Banana bunch,* 'āhui mai'a. *Hand, as of banana,* 'ekā, kē'a. *Banana bark,* weo. *Banana stalk,* pū mai'a. *Mountain banana patch,* 'e'a. *Unhealthy condition of banana fruit,* hākonakona. *Mashed ripe bananas and water,* poi mai'a. *Banana pudding,* pepeie'e, paipaie'e, piele. *A banana tree, hollow inside,* he pū mai'a, he 'olohaka o loko *(of a weakling). Big as a banana stalk,* nui pū mai'a *(of a weakling).*

band. 1. *Span.* Apo. *Iron band,* apo hao. *Gold band,* apo kula. *Yellow band (as on a fish),* haili. **2.** *Music.* Pāna puhi 'ohe, hui puhi 'ohe. *Band leader,* alaka'i pāna. **3.** *Group.* Hui, po'e.

bandage. Wahī 'eha; kāpola *(rare). To bandage,* wahī.

bandstand. 'Ale'o puhi 'ohe.

bang. Pohā *(as a gun);* kanono *(blow). Also:* haluku, 'a'ina; kani kanono; kani kohā *(as of a gun);* ūpā *(as of a door);* kau 'ino *(as of a telephone receiver).*

Bangkok. Panekoka, Banekoka.

Bangor. Panekola, Banegora.

banish. Kipaku, ho'okuke, wailana.

banished. Kipaku 'ia, wailana.

banishment. Kipaku i nā 'āina 'ē.

bank. 1. *Border.* Kapa, ka'e. *Earth bank,* āhua lepo, pū-'ula'ula. *Bank of a taro patch,* kuaauna, kuāuna, kaikā. *Bank between fields,* kuaio. **2.** *Finance.* Panakō. *Bank check,* kīko'o panakō. *Bank savings book,* puke ho'āhu. *Bank discount,* ho'ēmi panakō.

bankrupt. Panakalupa, panekalupa.

banner. Kīlepalepa. *See* **flag.**

bannister. Paehumu.

banquet. 'Aha'aina.

bantam. Moa ha'a.

banter. 'Ōlelo pā'ani, wahapa'a, ho'ohenehene, ho'opāpā, kīkē'ōlelo.

banyan. Paniana, baniana.

baptism. Papakema, bapatema; papekema, bapetema; hānau hou.

baptismal. Papekiko, bapetiso. *See* **baptism.**

Baptist. Papekike, Papekiko.

baptize. Papekema, papekiko, ho'ohānau hou. *See* **baptism.**

bar. 1. *Barrier.* Kaola, lā'au kī, lā'au ke'a, paukū, pale. *To bar,* ālai, pale, ho'oka'awale. *See* **sand bar. 2.** *Long object.* 'Aukā. *Soap bar,* 'aukā kopa. *Gold bar,* 'aukā kula. **3.** *For drinking.* Wahi inu lama, pākaukau. **4.** *Music.* Pale, pale lua, pale nui 'ele'ele. **5.** *Punctuation.* Palehui. **6.** *Legal.* Papa loio.

barb. Kukū *(thorn);* lala, kohe, 'ie'iea *(of a fishhook). See* **fishhook.**

Barbados. Palepakoa, Barebadoa; Papekoka, Babedosa.

barbarian. Kanaka na'aupō.

barbarous. Hana loko 'ino.

barbecue. Kō'ala; 'aha'aina me ka pipi kō'ala 'ia.

barbed. Kukū, 'ie'iea. *Barbed-wire fence,* pā uea kukū. *Barbed spear,* ihe laumeki.

barbel. 'Umi'umi.

barber. Kanaka 'ako lauoho, kahi 'umi'umi.

Barcelona. Pakelona, Baselona.

bare. 1. *Without covering.* Kohana; — *of leaves,* launea, ananea. *Also:* neo, nea 'ōnea, mōnea, ānea, 'ōlohe, 'ōlohelohe, mānienie. *See* **barren, naked. 2.** *Mere.* Wale nō.

barefoot. Kāma'a 'ole. *To go barefoot,* hele wāwae.

barely. Wale nō; māhune *(rare).*

bargain. Makepono, ho'ēmiemi i ke kumu kū'ai; *bad —,* makehewa, pohō.

barge. Pāki, pāki lawe ukana.

baritone. Leo uō.

bark. 1. *Of a tree.* 'Ili, 'ili lā'au; pāpa'a *(rare);* hili *(for dyeing);* hā'ana'ana *(waxed);* pā'ē *(olonā);* weo *(banana). Outer bark,* 'ili luna. *New bark,* 'ili hou, 'ili lua. **2.** *Of an animal.* Hae, haehae, 'aoa; *seal —,* umō. **3.** *Ship.* Moku kia kolu, kiapā.

bark cloth. *See* **tapa.**

barkeeper. Pākipa.

barking. Haena.

barley. Palaoa huluhulu, huapale, pale.

barn. Hale holoholona, hale lio.

barnacle. Pī'oe, pī'oe'oe, 'ōkohekohe *(see saying,* pī-'oe'oe). *Cf.* **shell.**

barometer. Palomeka.

baron. Pālona.

barracks. Hale koa, pā koa.

barracuda. Kākū, kūpala *(Sphyraena barracuda,* up to

nearly 2 m long); kawele'ā *(S. helleri,* up to 0.6 m long).

barred. Apo, 'aukā.

barrel. Pahu, palala, palela. *Small barrel,* palela li'ili'i, pahu po'o li'ili'i. *Water barrel,* pahu wai.

barren. 1. *Bare.* Panoa, anoa, 'ōlohe, 'ōlohelohe, kō'ā, mānienie, ka'o, pōka'oka'o, pōka'o, neo, neoneo, pōneoneo, māneoneo. *See* **bare. 2.** *Without offspring.* Kama 'ole, pā, lolena, hoki.

barrier. Pale, ke'a, mea ke'ake'a, kaupale, kāpe'ape'a.

barter. Kū'ai. *Rare:* hailawe, make.

basalt. Pōhaku pa'a; *waterworn —,* 'alā, pōhaku lū'au; *coarse vesicular —,* 'elekū, māono, kuanu'u.

base. 1. *Foundation.* Kumu, kahua, kū. *Base of a breaker,* honua nalu. *Base or butt end of a leaf,* po'o lau; pe'a *(rare). Base of the sky,* kumulani. *Base, as of a triangle,* 'ao'ao moe. **2.** *Vile.* Haumia. **3.** *Mole (word root).*

baseball. Kinipōpō. *To play baseball,* pā'ani kinipōpō.

basement. *See* **cellar.**

bashful. Hilahila, maka hilahila, wiwo, ūpē, ho'opalai, palai.

bashfulness. Hilahila.

basic. Kumu, honua. *Basic knowledge,* 'ike kumu.

basin. 1. *Container.* Ipu, po'i; pā *(flat);* kīpoho, ipu holoi, po'i wai, pā holoi, pā kini. *See* **washbasin. 2.** *Land.* Poho 'āina, kīpoho; kua'au *(inside reef).*

basis. Kumu. *Basis for work,* kahua hana.

bask. Lalala, lala.

basket. 'Eke, 'ie, hīna'i, hīna'i poepoe. *Also:* kīhene, hene, pai, hopai, pūhene, kī'eke, kīkī, 'api.

basketball. Kinipōpō hīna'i.

basket grass. Honohono, honohono kukui.

bass. 1. *Music.* Leo kāne, leo uō, pako. *Bass fiddle,* waiolina kū nui. **2.** *Fish.* 'O'opu haole *(black).*

bass fiddle, bass viol. Waiolina kū nui.

bast. Kae.

bastard. Keiki manuahi. *Rare:* keiki po'o 'ole, hua hā-'ule, kāmeha'i.

baste. 1. *Sewing.* Ho'oholoholo, kāholo, 'ōmau. **2.** *Cookery.* Ho'oma'ū.

basting. Holoholo, humu ho'oholoholo, kāholo. *Basting thread,* lopi kāholo, lopi ho'oholoholo.

bat. 1. *Mammal.* 'Ōpe'ape'a, pe'a, pe'ape'a, 'ape'ape'a. *To fly like a bat,* 'ōpe'ape'a. **2.** *To strike.* Hili, hahau. **3.** *Bat for ball.* Lā'au kinipōpō, lā'au pa'i kinipōpō.

Batavia. Pakawia, Batavia.

bath. 'Au'au. *Steam bath,* pūlo'ulo'u. *To take a bath,* 'au'au. *To give a bath,* hō'au'au. *It is bath water for him,* he wai 'au'au nona *(of a hero who enjoys war or spear dodging).*

bathe. 'Au'au. *Sea bathing,* 'au'au kai.

bathhouse. Hale 'au'au.

bathing suit. Lole 'au'au.

bathroom. Lumi 'au'au, lua. *See* **toilet.**

bathtub. Kapu 'au'au.

Baton Rouge. Pakona Luka, Batona Rusa.

battalion. Pū kaliona.

batten. 'Aho lolo.

batter. 1. *As in baseball.* Mea hili kinipōpō, uhau hili kinipōpō. **2.** *Cookery.* Mea 'ono mo'a 'ole. *To mix batter,* ho'ohuihui mea 'ono mo'a 'ole.

battering ram. Hipa kāne wāwahi.

battery. 1. *Artillery.* Huina pū kuni ahi. **2.** *Electric.* Pākali, iho uila. **3.** *Assault.* Hō'eha 'ana. *See* **assault.**

battle. Kaua, ho'ouka kaua, paio. *See sayings,* **pūliki 1, wanawana.** *Formal battle lines,* kūkulu. *Sham battle,* kānekupua, pahukala, kaua kio. *Type of battle formation,* kahului. *Battle unit,* huna kaua. *Battle song,* mele ka'i kaua.

battle-axe. Ko'i pāhoa *(stone).*

battlefield. Kahua kaua.

battleground. Kahua ho'ouka kaua.

battleship. Moku kaua, pāpū lewa, manuā.

Bavaria. Pawalia, Bavaria.

bawl. 'Alalā, uē leo nui.
bay. 1. *Geographic.* Kū'ono, kai kū'ono; Hono-, Hana- *(only in place names).* **2.** *Color.* 'Ula'ula, hulupala, apowai.
bayonet. 'Ēlau waikī, 'ekī, 'ēlau.
bdellium. Keliuma.
be. *There is no verb "to be" in Hawaiian. The copula may be entirely omitted, or represented by verb markers* (ua, e . . . ana, ke . . . nei, i, e) *or by* he. *I am well,* ua maika'i au. *I was well,* ua maika'i au. *I will be well,* e maika'i ana au. *You are happy,* hau'oli 'oe. *You were happy,* hau'oli 'oe. *He is going,* e hele ana 'oia, ke hele nei 'oia. *To be with (accompany),* 'alo. *To be happy,* noho me ka hau'oli. *To be chief,* noho ali'i. *To be in a state of,* hele ā, ka'a. *She is a teacher,* he kumu 'oia.
beach. Kahakai, kahaone, papa kea, makālae.
beachcomber. 'Ae'a hauka'e. *See* **vagabond.**
beach poppy. Pua kala, pōkalakala; naule *(rare).*
beach vitex. Kolokolo kahakai, māwanawana, pōhinahina, hinahina kolo.
beacon. Lama kuhikuhi.
Beacon Hill. Pikina Hila, Bikina Hila.
bead. Pūpū lei. *Glass bead,* hua aniani; olo *(rare). Prayer beads,* lei kolona. *String of beads,* akalei.
beak. Nuku, ihu; nū *(rare).*
beaker. Kānuku, nuku *(of a pitcher).*
beam. 1. *Bar.* Kaola, kuku, kua, kua lā'au; kī kaola *(to close a door).* **2.** *Ray.* Kukuna.
bean. Pāpapa, pī. *See* **sea bean.**
bear. 1. *Carry.* Hāpai, hi'i, hali, pa'a; hā'awe *(on the back);* — *down,* kaomi, kōmi. **2.** *Reproduce.* Hānau, hāpai, hua, ho'ohua. *Bear fruit or seed,* ho'ohua. **3.** *See* **turn. 4.** *See* **endure. 5.** *Animal.* Pea. *Bear baiting,* ho'ohaehae pea.
beard. 'Umi'umi; hulu weuweu *(poetic);* hulu pua'a *(of male turkeys).*
beardless. Heu 'ole, 'umi'umi 'ole. *Beardless youth,* wā heu 'ole.
bearer. Pa'a, mea lawe, lawe, māmaka. *Bearer of a feather standard,* pa'a kāhili; lawe kāhili; ha'akoni *(rare). Spittoon bearer,* pa'a ipu kuha. *Bearer of canoe bow,* pale mua. *Bearer of canoe stern,* pale hope.
bearing. 1. *Carrying.* Hapaina. **2.** *Mien.* 'Ano, hālina. *Noble bearing,* kohu ali'i. **3.** *Position.* Kūlana o ka moku *(of a ship).*
beast. Holoholona.
beat. 1. *Strike.* Pepehi, ku'i, pa'i, hahau, uhau, hau, hauhia, pāku'i, pā, hāku'i. *Also:* 'uī'uī, koni, lawelawe lima, limanui, kākā, ho'ohāhā, 'ulupā, pāluku, pūkē, pana; —, *as the heart or pulse,* pana, 'api, 'ūpā, lelele; *to* —, *as tapa,* kuku, 'akuku; *to* —, *as water in fishing,* pāku'iku'i, 'ōlā'au; *to* —, *as paddle on canoe side,* homa, kāpapa; *to* —, *as lumpy poi,* pāku'iku'i, pā-'ulu'ā. *See* **drum.** *To beat to death,* pepehi ā make. *To beat to a pulp,* ku'i palu. *To beat flat,* ku'i pē. **2.** *In music.* Pana. **3.** *Defeat.* Make. *You beat me,* make au iā'oe; eo au iā'oe. **4.** *Sail to windward.* Ho'opi'ipi'i; ho'opahu'a *(rare).*
beaten. 1. *Hit.* Pepehi 'ia. *Beaten down,* meheu, loha, ho'omāui, 'oupē, noiele. **2.** *Defeated.* Make.
beater. Hohoa, hoahoa. *See* **tapa** *for* **tapa beater.** *Knee-drum beater,* kā.
beautiful. Nani, u'i, maika'i. *Also:* makalapua, pōlani, nonohe, hiluhilu, luhiehu, mikihilina *(as dress, finery, ornaments);* pa'anehe *(as work). Supremely beautiful,* keu ā ka u'i; nani kōkī.
beautify. Ho'onani, ho'onaninani, ho'ou'i, ho'ou'iu'i, ho'owehi, ho'ohiehie, ho'ohilu, ho'ohiluhilu, ho'omāhilu, pūhano.
beauty. Nani; u'i *(youthful);* piuke *(rare). Beauty-loving,* puni nani. *Poetic tributes to beauty:* 'ai ka manu i luna; pali ke kua, mahina ke alo; 'a'ohe pu'u, 'a'ohe ke'e; ke kumu lehua muimuia a ka manu; hā'ale i ka wai o ka manu. *See also* **kī'ilili, lā'ae'oia, manu,**

'ōhi'a 'ai, mulberry. *In poetry, beauty is shown by references to nature, especially to the sea and rain.*
beaver. 'Īlio hulu pāpale, piwa. *Beaver hat,* pāpale piwa, piwa haka.
becalmed. Lululu, lilo i ka pohu, la'ikū.
because. No, no ka mea, ma, i, ma o, muli, mamuli. *Also:* nani, ho'ohua, kū.
beche-de-mer. Loli *(for various kinds, see Haw.-Eng. entry and below). See* **sea cucumber.**
beckon. Ani, -ali, pe'ahi, ho'āni; — *with the hand,* ani pe'ahi; — *with the head,* kūlou, kūnou.
become. Lilo, hele . . . ā, ua *(Gram. 5.2),* lawe. *He will become a doctor,* e lilo ana 'oia i kauka. *He has become angry,* ua hele 'oia ā huhū. *He has become tired,* ua māluhiluhi 'oia.
becoming. 1. *Attractive.* Kohukohu, hiehie, mīkohu. *See* **attractive. 2.** *Befitting.* Kūpono.
bed. Moe, moena, moekū, kahi moe, wahi moe. *See* **cot, sheet.** *Temporary leaf and grass bed,* pihaweuweu. *Bed in a grass house,* ka'anu'a. *To go to bed,* moe. *To make a bed,* uhi i ka moe. *Stream bed,* kahua, kahena wai papakū.
bedaubed. Kāpala, palahe'a, loli, 'īloli. *See* **daub.**
bed bug. 'Uku lio.
bed covering. Kīhei, kīhei pili, ku'inakapa. *See* **bedspread.**
bedeck. Ho'ouluwehi, ho'ouluwehiwehi, ho'omāhilu, ho'ohiluhilu; — *with leis,* 'ohu'ohu.
bedfellow. Hoa moe.
bedridden. Moe ma'i, ka'ikōkō, waiho i kahi moe, ka'a moena.
bedrock. Kūpapakū.
bedroom. Lumi moe.
bed sheet. Uhi pela.
bedspread. Kapa moe *(general name);* hāli'i moe, uhi moe.
bedsprings. Pilina moe, pela uea.
bedstead. Kūmoe; lā'au moekū *(wooden).*
bedtime. Wā hiamoe, manawa moe.
bee. Meli, nalo meli *(honey bee). Queen bee,* nalo meli mō'ī wahine. *Drone bee,* nalo meli noho hale. *Worker bee,* nalo meli pa'ahana.
beef. Pipi. *Beef meat,* 'i'o pipi. *Beef stew,* pipi kū. *Roast beef,* pipi loke. *Dried or jerked beef,* pipi kaula. *Beefsteak,* pipi palai, pipi kō'ala.
beehive. Pahu meli, pūnana meli.
beer. Pia, bia. *Lager beer,* bia nui. *Weiss beer,* bia wei. *Sweet potato beer,* 'uala 'awa'awa.
beer parlor. Hale inu pia.
beeswax. Kūkaenalo, leponalo.
beet. Pika.
beetle. Pu'u, ane, 'ūhini lele, mū. *Rose beetle,* pu'u 'ai loke. *Flour beetle,* mū 'ai palaoa. *Wood-boring beetle,* 'uku lā'au. *Olinda beetle,* pu'u.
befall. Lo'ohia, hekau.
befit. Kohu pono.
befogged. Noenoe, pululuhi.
before. Mua, 'ē, alia, i ka wā mamua. *Ten minutes before five,* 'umi minuke i koe, kani ka hola 'elima.
beforehand. Mua, 'ē. *To show beforehand,* ho'okū'ike, hō'ike 'ē.
befoul. Ho'opaumā'ele, ho'opelapela, ho'ohaumia.
befriend. Ho'omakamaka, ho'ohoaloha, ho'ā'ikāne.
befuddled. Kūpouli.
beg. Mākilo; *humbly* —, noi ha'aha'a. *See* **beggar, entreat.** *To beg from place to place,* noho'ana.
beget. Loa'a. *Jacob begot Joseph,* na Iakopa 'o Iokepa.
beggar. Mākilo, 'ai pala maunu, 'auhaupuka, pani puka, kanaka kua-i-ka-puka-hale.
beggar ticks. Po'olānui; ko'oko'olau *(all kinds).*
begin. Ho'omaka, ho'okumu; 'oia *(as a race). To begin again,* ho'omaka hou. *To begin work, as a job,* komo i ka hana.
beginner. Mea ho'omaka. *Also:* 'akahi akahi, hōlona.
beginning. Ho'omaka 'ana, maka, maka mua, kinohi,

kinohou, kumu, kumu kahi, 'ōmaka, mā'ana; kāhoa *(as of a chant). The very beginning,* kinohi loa. *Beginning of the world,* kumu honua.
begone. Hele pēlā, hele i kahi 'ē.
begonia. Aka'aka'awa, pua maka nui, pīkonia.
begrudge. 'Au'a wale.
beguiling. Ho'owalewale, ho'ohei mana'o, kāpehe.
behalf. Ma, no, pono. *In your behalf,* no kou pono.
behave. Hana, noho. *Behave well,* noho pono, hilu. *Behave wickedly,* kolohe, 'eu, lapuwale, hana 'ino, hana pono 'ole. *Behave reasonably,* aokanaka.
behavior. Hana.
behead. 'Oki ā lele ke po'o, 'oki po'o.
behemoth. Pehemo.
behind. Hope, muli, ma ke kua; mahope *(referring to both time and place);* i hope *(does not refer to time). To fall behind (as in learning),* hā'ule hope.
behold. Aia ho'i, eia ho'i. *See* **see.**
being. Mea *(person, thing);* kanaka *(human). See* **legendary being.**
belch. Kīhā, 'opu'opu, pīhā, pūhā.
Belfast. Pelepake, Belefase.
belfry. Hale pele, pū'o'a pele.
Belgian, Belgium. Pelekiuma, Belegiuma.
belief. Mana'o.
believe. Mana'o'i'o, hilina'i, piliwi; — *implicitly,* paulele. *He believes in God,* ua mana'o'i'o 'oia i ke Akua.
belittle. Ho'oha'aha'a. *Also:* ho'oūpē, huahua, ho'opu'ukahua, ho'ohenehene, pāhenehene, ho'opāhenehene, nemanema.
bell. Pele. *See* **scrotum.** *Dinner bell,* pele 'aina. *Bell clapper,* 'ulu, 'ulu kani.
bellboy. Poe pele.
bellow. Uō, wōwō, kūō, umō.
bellows. 'Ūpā, 'ūpā makani, 'ōpū makani.
bell pepper. Nīoi pūha'uha'u, nīoi pū'alu'alu, nīoi 'alu'alu.
belly. 'Ōpū, hakualo; alopiko, alapiko *(of fish). See* **kōheoheo 1.** *To belly out, as clothes on a line or a sail,* poho.
belong. No, na. *This belongs to me,* na'u kēia, no'u kēia.
belonging. Kō, kā, no, na. *Belonging to that place,* no laila. *The hat belonging to Pua,* kō Pua pāpale.
belongings. Pono.
beloved. Aloha 'ia, mea aloha, milimili, milia, mili, maka, hiwahiwa, nēnē hiwa, 'ōmea, 'ano'i, mea nui, hiwa lani, kaupili. *Fig.:* laua'e, lei, pākau, 'ōnohi kau maka, ki'i 'ōnohi.
below. Lalo, i lalo, malalo, iho.
belt. Kuapo, 'ili kuapo, kaula 'ōpū, apo, kā'ai, kā'ei. *Also:* kama 'aha, kāmaka'aha, 'a'a, 'a'a pūhaka. *To belt on,* kākua, ka'ako'o.
bemoan. Kani'uhū i ka pōpilikia.
Benares. Penale, Benare.
bench. Noho, noho lō'ihi, papa noho. *Workbench,* papa hana. *Judge's bench,* noho ho'okolokolo.
bend. Pelu; pe'u *(Moloka'i),* ho'opi'o, ho'oke'e, ho'okeke'e. *Also:* 'alu, hō'alu, nīnole, 'a'apu, kāluli, ha'i, ho'oholu, nape, nolu pē, 'upa'i, ho'opepe'e, kīke'e, uake'e, kōke'e, 'opi; — *down,* 'aui, 'auina; — *over,* lo'u, 'ekepue, lōpi'o, ha'alo'u; — *forward,* kimo, kūpou; — *the neck,* kūlou; — *the head,* kimo po'o, kikiwi, ha'inau, hakinau. *See* **bent, curved.** *To bend, as a bow,* lena. *To sit on bended knees,* noho kukuli.
bends. Holoā i'a *(caisson disease).*
beneath. Lalo, malalo, i lalo.
benediction. Pule ho'omaika'i.
benefactor. Mea kōkua.
beneficent. Lokomaika'i, manawale'a, na'au aloha, na'au ali'i.
beneficial. Pono, pōmaika'i.
beneficiary. Ka mea i ho'opōmaika'i 'ia, mea ho'okahu 'ia.
benefit. Pono, maika'i, waiwai.

benevolent. *See* **beneficent.**
Bengal. Penekala, Benegala.
benighted. Na'aupō, pō, pō'ele.
bent. Pi'o, pelu 'ia, ke'e, lāke'e, lāpe'e, kapakahi, kiwi, kikiwi, kākiwi, pa'ewa; lu'ulu'u *(as in grief);* 'anake'e, palakāhela; manawai *(rare);* — *out,* lanahua; — *over,* lāpu'u, 'ōnaha, lo'u, po'oka'eo; hanunu *(rare);* — *out of shape,* nenehū, nanahū; —, *as with age,* 'o'ohu; —, *as as bow,* lena, kakaka. *Also:* napa, nāpai, kanahua, ho'okanahua, pāuma, naha, kī'ōnaha, pei, pākauā-ke'e, pe'u, lāpu'u, napu'u.
bent grass. He'upueo.
benumbed. Lōlō, mā'e'ele. *Also:* huehu, hau'oki, maka'ele'ele.
benzine. Penekine.
bequeath. Ho'īli, ho'oili, kauoha.
bequest. Kauoha, ho'oili.
bereaved. Lu'ulu'u, kaumaha no ka mea i hala aku, 'oā.
Bering. Pēlina, Berina.
Bering Straits. Ke kōwā o Pēlina, ke kai kōwā o Pēlina.
Berlin. Pelelina, Berelina.
Bermuda grass. Mānienie haole.
berry. Hua li'ili'i.
beryl. Pelulo.
beset. Ho'opilikia, ho'ohei; ho'okē *(fig.).*
beside. Ma, ma ka 'ao'ao.
besides. Koe, ho'i, kekahi, kahi, la'a. *Besides this,* aia kēia. *Besides that,* koe kēlā, e la'a me kēlā, ho'oiho, ho'īho.
besiege. Pō'ai puni, ho'opuni; ūkūkua *(as with problems);* pū'ā *(rare).*
besmear. Hāpala, ho'opala, ka'e, ho'oka'e, ho'ohauka'e, hamo, ho'owi'u.
besmirch. Ho'ohauka'e, ho'ohaumia, ho'opōneko.
best. 'Oi, 'oi loa, maika'i a'e, po'okela, kilohana, hō'oi, 'ī, helu 'ekahi, heke, paua. *Maui is the best,* Maui nō ka 'oi (no ka 'oi *without a preceding noun would mean 'for the best person' but would be rarely if ever said).*
be-still tree. Nohomālie.
bestir. Ho'oni, hō'eu'eu, ho'oui.
best man. Kū'ao'ao o ke kāne *(at a wedding).*
bet. Pili, piliwaiwai. *To bet disastrously,* pili hihia, pili pohō. *To raise a bet,* hō'oi i ka pili, kale'oa.
Betelgeuse. 'Aua, Kaulua-koko, Koko; Kā'elo *(possibly).*
betel nut. Nīoi pekela.
Bethany. Pekania, Betania.
Bethel. Pekela, Betela.
Bethlehem. Pekelehema, Betelehema.
Bethsaida. Pekekaika, Bctesaida.
betray. Kumakaia. *Also:* paoke'e; paokoke *(one's relatives or those close to one);* 'ōpe'a.
betrayal, betrayer. Mākaia.
betroth. Ho'opalau.
betrothal. Palau, ho'opalau.
betrothed. Palau, ho'opalau 'ia.
better. Maika'i a'e, aho, ahona, ho'okā'oi. *Better not,* 'a'ole make. *That is better,* e aho ia.
betting. Piliwaiwai, pili.
between. Waena, mawaena, i waena.
beverage. Mea inu. *Cold beverage,* mea inu ho'ohu-'ihu'i.
bewail. Kūmākena, auē, uē, kanikau, uē helu.
beware. Akahele, mālama, ao.
bewilder. Ho'opohihihi, ho'opōna'ana'a, ho'opāha'oha'o.
bewildered. Pohihihi, kūnānā, pōna'ana'a. *Also:* na'ana'a, lihili, hihipe'a.
bewitched. Mea i ho'ohei 'ia ka no'ono'o, hana 'ia e ke kahuna; lihua *(rare).*
beyond. Waho, ō. *Far beyond,* ma'ō loa aku. *The dark, invisible beyond,* polikua, pōliukua.
biased. *See* **partial.**
bib. Pale, pale hānai.
Bible. Paipala, Baibala. *Holy Bible,* Paipala Hemolele.

Biblical. Paipala; Baibala.
bibliography. Papa kuhikuhi o nā puke i heluhelu 'ia.
bicentennial. Ka puni 'ana o 'elua haneli makahiki.
biceps, brachii. 'Uala.
bickering. Kū'ē'ē, ho'opa'apa'a. *Bickering relationship,* pili hukihuki.
bicycle. Paikikala, ka'a paikikala, ka'a hehi wāwae.
bid. Koho *(as at an auction);* kauoha, kēnā *(command). Bid good-by,* hā'awi i ke aloha.
bidder. Mea koho. *Highest bidder,* mea koho ki'eki'e loa.
bidding. Koho, kauoha. *Do one's bidding,* ho'okō kauoha.
biennial. Kēlā me kēia lua makahiki. *Biennial report,* hō'ike no 'elua makahiki.
bier. Mānele. *To carry on a bier,* mānele.
big. Nui, nunui, hālala, māhuahua; *impressively—,* ka'a-peha.
bigamy. Male punalua.
big-bellied. 'Ōpū nui, kēkē, 'ākēkē.
Big Dipper. Nā-hiku, Ki'aha.
bigeye tuna. 'Āweoweo; 'alauā, 'alalauā *(young stage).*
bigger. Nui a'e, kā'eu'eu.
bile. Au, lena, wailena.
bilge. Liu. *Bilge pump,* omo liu.
biliousness. Pu'u makani; pu'upo'olā *(rare).*
bill. 1. *Document.* Pila; kāki *(charge);* palapala *(document);* pila kīko'o *(draft). Bill of exchange,* kīko'o pāna'i. *Bill of health,* palapala hō'ike no ke ola. *Bill of lading,* palapala hō'ike ukana o ka moku. *Bill of sale,* palapala kū'ai. *Bill of fare,* papa kuhikuhi mea 'ai. *To bill,* ho'ouku. 2. *See* **beak.**
billboard. Papa ho'olaha.
billet. Palapala lima.
billfold. 'Eke'eke kālā.
billiard cue. Lā'au pahupahu, ku'i pahupahu.
billiards. Pahupahu, pilioki. *To play billiards,* pahupahu.
billion. Piliona.
billow. 'Ale, 'aui, 'aui 'ale; nī'au *(rare);* 'ōhuku 'ale *(rising);* — *out,* puha'u, pō'olopū, pūnohu; 'olopū, poholua *(as sails);* kōwehe *(as a dress).*
billowy. Ho'omākōmakō, ho'opehupehu *(as a cloud);* newe *(rare). See* **billow.**
billy. Lā'au māka'i.
bind. *See* **tie.** *Also:* pū'ā, kāo'o, ho'ohīpu'u, hauhoa, hauhō, hāwele, nīpe'a, awaiāulu, pu'aka, kāpola; — *tightly,* lawa lua, kama 'aha, pūlawa, pōlena, puaniki; — *up,* nunu; — *on,* 'ōmau, hume; — *beforehand,* hele honua; — *the hands,* 'ōpe'a; — *together, as bones of a chief for preservation,* pokipa'a; —, *as a sarong,* kākua; —, *as with a sash or belt,* kāko'o; —, *as a book,* humu, humuhumu.
binder. Ho'ohui, pū'ā, ho'opa'a. *Metal binder,* kui 'ūmi'i. *Machine binder,* mīkini ho'opa'a. *Tight waist binder,* kāliki.
binding. 'Ili *(as a book cover);* hīki'i, hoana.
binnacle. Pahu pōhaku pānānā.
biology. 'Ike no'eau e pili ana no nā mea ola.
bird. Manu *(fig., people; for various kinds and sayings, see Haw.-Eng. entry that follow it). Migratory birds,* manu pae, manu o kahiki. *Native birds,* manu kama'āina. *Introduced birds,* manu lawe 'ia mai, manu malihini, manu mai nā 'āina 'ē. *Legendary birds:* 'ā 'aia, Halulu. *Bird islet,* moku manu, ko'o manu. *Plains with birds,* kula manu. *Birds whose feathers were used in leis:* mamo, 'ō'ō, 'i'iwi, 'apapane, 'ō'ū. *When even the birds of Ka'ula are wild, a day of storm,* 'āhē nō ka manu o Ka'ula, he lā 'ino *(trouble).*
bird catcher. Kia manu, kia, kono manu, kolokio, lawai'amanu. *God of bird catchers,* Ha'ina-kolo.
birdcatching. Kia manu, kaumanu, kāpili manu, kono manu, 'ōku'u, kahekahe, lawai'amanu, kolokio. *Birdcatching pole,* lā'au kia, kia, alakō, 'auku'u, hāpapa, pokia.

bird dog. 'Īlio hahai manu.
birdhouse. Hale manu.
birdlime. Pīlali.
bird's-eye view. Ki'i maka manu.
bird's-nest fern. 'Ēkaha, 'ēkahakaha, 'ākaha.
Birmingham. Paminahama, Baminahama; Peleminahama, Bereminahama.
birth. Hānau, hanauna, ho'ohānau; ki'o *(often sarcastic). Premature birth,* hānau ēwe. *Peculiar or unusual birth,* hānau 'e'epa. *Quintuplet birth,* hānau pālima.
birth certificate. Palapala hānau.
birth control. Kaupalena hānau.
birthday. Lā hānau, lā piha makahiki. *Happy birthday,* hau'oli lā hānau, hānau.
birthmark. Ila. *Kinds of birthmarks:* humuhumu, moi, 'ōkole, 'ōhi'a; uhi.
birth pebbles. 'Ili'ili hānau.
birthplace. 'Āina hānau, one hānau. *Also:* ēwe, kulaiwi, ōpū 'ahu'awa hānau. *See* **residence.**
birth stones. Pōhaku hānau.
biscuit. Pelena; *ship —,* 'ao.
bisect. 'Oki ā ka'awale, pālua, pahupū.
bishop. Pīhopa, luna kia'i, 'epikopo.
Bishop Museum. Hale Hō'ike'ike o Ka-mehameha.
bison. Pipi kuapu'u.
bit. 1. *Small amount.* Wahi, hunahuna, mahele li'ili'i, 'ōniki. 2. *Tool.* Wili, wili kāhei, nao wili. 3. *Part of a bridle,* Hao, hao waha, hao kaula waha.
bitch. 'Īlio wahine. *See* **son of a bitch.**
bite. Nahu, nanahu, 'aki, 'a'aki, 'akina; — *on a hook,* 'ai, 'a'ai; — *sideways,* kīkepa; — *with relish,* nahunahupū; — *with the teeth and peel off, as bark,* 'aki.
Bithynia. Pikunia, Bitunia.
biting. 'Akina, niho.
bits. Li'ili'i, oka, hunahuna, hunehune. *Bits of news,* nā hunehune mea hou.
bitter. 'Awa, 'awa'awa. *Also:* wai'awa, 'awa'awahia, 'awa'awahua, mu'e, mu'emu'e, mu'amu'a, 'ōmu'e, 'ōmu'emu'e, mule, mulemule, haoa, haua'īliki, malailena, 'ōlaelae; pēka'a *(very bitter),* halahala, pū'awa. *These words mean bitter to the taste, and figuratively of disposition. Other words for bitter disposition:* ke'emoa, na'ina'i; nanau, lanau *(rare). Bitter cold, bitter to taste,* 'āmu'emu'e. *Bitter rain,* ka ua 'awa *(of disaster, hardship). Kī-lau-ea overturned, darkened with smoke, lost in bitterness (PH 197),* hulihia Kī-lau-ea, pō i ka uahi, nalowale i ke 'awa *(disaster).*
bitter gourd. Hue 'awa'awa.
bittern. Kipoka, pua'a 'ili 'o'oi *(KJV).*
bitterness. 'Awa'awa, 'awa'awaina, 'awa'awahia, ko-'ana 'awa, nanahua. *Remove the bitterness,* hulialana.
bitter yam. Hoi.
bituminous. Pikimana. *Bituminous coal,* lānahu pikimana.
bivalve. 'Ōlepe *(for various types, see entry Haw.-Eng.),* 'owā'owaka, kupekala, 'ōkupe, papaua, papaua momi, pahikaua. *Muscle attaching a bivalve to rock,* hulu.
blabber-mouth. 'Ele'elepī ka waha.
black. 1. *Color.* 'Ele'ele, 'ele, pō'ele, pā'ele, 'ene'ene; uliuli *(sometimes pejorative);* 'ele hiwa, hiwa pa'a *(usually desirable);* 'ele hiwa, 'elekū *(all black);* pano, hākuma, ho'okokōhi, polohiwa *(as clouds). Grayish black,* 'eleuli. *Blue-black,* 'ele'ī. *Glossy black,* pano pa'ū. *Very black,* pau pā'ele. *Also:* 'e'ele, palaki, nika, polina. *Black dye for tapa was obtained from* kukui *nuts, bark, and roots.* 2. *Person.* Pā'ele, nekelo, nika; pōpolo *(slang).*
black-and-blue. Uli; kuhe, kuhekuhe, kukuhe *(as after a bruise).*
blackberry. 'Ōhelo 'ele'ele.
blackboard. Papa 'ele'ele.
"black coral." 'Ēkaha kū moana.
blacken. Hō'ele'ele, pā'ele, ho'opā'ele.
blackened. Hō'ele'ele 'ia, ho'opā'ele 'ia, 'e'elekū.

black eye. Maka uli.
black-eyed Susan. Pūkiawe.
blackish. Hāʻeleʻele, hāuli, hāuliuli.
black magic. *See* **sorcery.**
black market. Makeke mawaho o ke kānāwai. *To buy, as on a black market,* kūʻai malū.
blackout. Hoʻopōuliuli.
Black Sea. Kai-ʻeleʻele.
blacksmith. Kuʻi hao, ʻamala.
blacksmith shop. Hale kuʻi hao, hale ʻāmala, hale kākia kāmaʻa lio.
bladder. ʻŌpū mimi, ʻōpū hanawai, puʻumimi, koʻana, koʻala.
blade. 1. *Of grass.* Lau. **2.** *Of instrument. No general name. See* **paddle.** *Sharp edge of blade,* nīʻau. *Tip of blade,* maka.
blame. ʻĀhewa, ʻimi hala, hoʻāhewa, hoʻohewa, kāpili.
bland. Hūkākai, koʻekoʻe.
blank. Hakahaka; paʻi hakahaka *(as on a questionnaire).*
blanket. Kapa moe, huluhulu, kapa huluhulu. *Saddle blanket,* pale lio. *To cover with a blanket,* ʻaʻahu.
blaspheme. Kūamuamu, hāʻiliʻili, hoʻohiki ʻino.
blast. Pahū.
blasted. Pahūpahū; maʻalili, mālili, lili *(as fruit).*
blaze. 1. *Fire.* Lalapa, lapalapa; ʻā, ʻaʻā, ula, hulili, ʻulili, haulalapa; *sudden —,* ʻōlapa. *Eyes blazing with wrath,* hulili ka maka i ka huhū. **2.** *Mark.* Kīkoni, kuni, māka, kahakuhi.
bleach. Hoʻokeʻokeʻo, pūkai, kuakea, hoʻokuakea, loloʻa; hālena *(as tapa).*
bleached. Kuakea. *Bleached muslin,* keʻokeʻo wai; keʻokeʻo maoli *(good quality);* keʻokeʻo pia *(inferior quality).*
bleary. ʻŌleha, ʻōlehaleha, ʻōhewahewa. *See* **blurred.**
bleat. ʻAlalā, ʻalalāna, pūʻalalā, heehe, māʻāʻā.
bleed. Kahe koko.
bleeding. Kahe koko, kokona. *Bleeding heart,* hōʻeha puʻuwai. *Bone instrument for bleeding, lancing,* ā, ā ʻōʻō.
blemish. Kīnā, kīnaʻu, kīnaʻunaʻu, ʻālina, kīkohu.
blend. Hui pū, kāwili.
blenny. Pāoʻo (pānoʻo).
bless. Hoʻomaikaʻi, hoʻopōmaikaʻi, mōlia. *The Lord bless you and keep you (Nah. 6:24),* na Iēhowa ʻoe e hoʻomaikaʻi mai, ā e mālama mai.
blessed. Pōmaikaʻi. *See ex.,* **spirit.**
blessing. Pōmaikaʻi, pule, pule hoʻopōmaikaʻi, haʻawina. *Blessing of a house,* hoʻolaʻa hale. *Blessing of a canoe,* hoʻolaʻa waʻa. *To ask a blessing,* hoʻopōmaikaʻi.
blight. ʻEleao. *Also:* kakane, pōnalo, kīnā, aʻe, kūmīmī, mālili, mōlili, makika, meʻeau, mino, mimino, paʻi.
blind. Makapō, makaʻalā; — *in one eye,* makapaʻia; *partially —,* hāpōpō, moʻowini. *To pretend to be blind,* hoʻomakapō.
blindfold. Hoʻomakapō.
blindman's buff. Pōʻai puni makapō.
blinds. Pālulu pukaaniani, ʻōpeʻapeʻa, ʻōlepelepe.
blink. ʻIʻimo, ʻōnini, hoʻolili, haʻalili.
blister. Pōʻolopū, hōʻolopū, ʻolopū, ʻōwela.
bloated. ʻAlakai, ʻuʻulukai, hūkākai, kēkewe, pūhalalū, ʻūpehupehu, hoʻoʻihaʻiha; kiʻimanana *(as a corpse);* hakakai *(rare).*
block. 1. *Obstruct.* ʻĀkeʻakeʻa, keʻakeʻa, keʻa, paʻa, ālai, ānai, ʻāpani, papani a paʻa, kualo, pupū, kūpalaka. **2.** *Piece of wood.* Palaka; — *in hat plaiting,* iho; — *to support canoe or outrigger float,* paepae, lona. *Block-print cloth,* palaka. *Children's blocks,* huinahā pāʻani.
blockade. Pani, kaupale ʻana, ālai, ānai.
blockage. Pani paʻa.
blonde. Oho hākeakea, lauoho melemele. *Platinum blonde,* poʻo keʻokeʻo.
blood. Koko; — *red,* heʻa. *Also:* wai, wai ʻula, ʻula, ʻulaʻula. *Royal blood,* koko aliʻi. *Flow of blood,* kahe

koko, heʻe koko. *Blood clot,* puʻu koko, koko paʻakūkū. *Menstrual blood,* hanawai; waimaka o lehua, onehahi *(rare). Sacred blood,* wai ʻihi, wāʻihi. *Shedder of blood,* lima koko. *Blood relative,* ʻiʻo pono, pili koko. *Mixed blood,* hapa, hapa haole, koko ʻānoni, koko ʻāwili. *High blood pressure,* koko piʻi, koko lana. *To shed blood,* hoʻokahe koko. *My blood pressure is high,* he koko piʻi koʻu. *See* **ʻea kū manawa.**
bloodhound. ʻĪlio hanu kanaka.
bloodshed. Hoʻokahe koko. *To cause bloodshed,* hoʻokoko.
bloodshot. Mākole, makou, maka ʻulaʻula.
bloodsucker. Omo koko, mākoko.
bloodthirsty. Puni koko, haekoko.
blood vessel. Aʻa koko.
bloody. ʻĀkokoko, kokokoko, kāheʻa.
bloom. Pua, moano, mōhala.
bloomers. Lole wāwae pūhaʻuhaʻu.
blossom. Pua. *Cherished blossom,* pua lei. *To blossom forth,* makalapua, ʻōmeʻo, mōhala, mohahala, mōhalahala, mōhola.
blot. Hāpala, kāpala, pala, kohu. *Ink blot,* kohu ʻīnika. *To blot,* pāʻele, hoʻopāʻele, hōkaʻe, hoʻomaloʻo; holoi ā nalo *(remove blot);* — *out,* ʻānai; hoʻohōkai *(memory).*
blotch. Kīnā.
blotter. Pepa hoʻomaloʻo ʻīnika, pepa ʻomo ʻīnika, mea penu ʻīnika.
blouse. Palauki, lakeke, pākana.
blow. 1. *As air current.* Puhi, pā, papā, pā makani, ulu, unu *(wind);* pūhihio, makani, pua; — *softly,* ani, aniani, ʻōaniani, māaniani, hiohio, ʻōnini, pua aheahe, ahe, kōaheahe, ʻōaheahe, papaiāulu; — *in gusts,* hio, kākala; — *strongly or in a gale,* pāhili, loku, kuke kū; — *in a straight course,* hina; — *at an angle,* pā lala; — *favorably,* hinaleʻa; — *away,* puhi pau, pupuhi, luehu, hoʻopuehu; —, *as a cool breeze,* hau; — *spray or dust,* pua ehu, pulelehua, laumāewa; — *smoke,* pūkoʻa; — *a Kona wind,* Kona; — *in a current or draft,* āmio; — *helter-skelter,* pūlunaluna; — *up,* pākākā *(as a balloon);* pahūpahū, pahū, hoʻopahūpahū *(explode);* — *from the mouth,* kī, puhi; — *sonorously,* ʻūhīʻūhā *(as accompanying volcanic surging). Cf.* **ulu 1, wind 1.** *Blow the nose,* hoʻokē ihu. **2.** *Strike.* Haua, hāuna, hahau, hauhāuna, uhau, kuʻia, kuʻina, lāʻau; *undercut —,* poholalo; *underhanded —,* huʻalepo; *glancing —,* kā kīkepa; — *of fist,* puʻupuʻu lima; — *of a club,* lāʻau. *To hurl a blow by swinging from the shoulders,* hahau kākua. *To deliver a blow of the fist,* hao mai i ka puʻupuʻu; hāneoʻo *(rare). To receive a resounding blow,* kanono. *Loud sound, as of a blow,* kani kanono. *A single blow of the youth,* hoʻokahi lāʻau o ka uʻi *(boast of a fighter who fells a foe with a single blow).*
blowhole. Lua puhi, puhi, puhi kai, puhina.
blue. *No exact equivalent;* uli, uliuli *(of deep sea);* polū *(of clothes, eyes); dark —,* hāuliuli; — *black,* ʻeleʻī; *deep — black,* lipo; *purplish —,* pōpolohua *(as the sea or a bruise). See* **black-and-blue.** *Blue eyes,* maka ʻalohilohi, maka polū. *A pale blue dye for tapa was obtained from* ʻukiʻuki *berries.*
bluebottle fly. Nalo pilau.
blue jeans. ʻĀhina, ʻāhinahina.
bluff. 1. *Height.* Kiʻekiʻena, ʻoiʻoina. **2.** *Pretense.* Hōʻano, hoʻomeamea. *Also:* pūlapu *(as in card game);* noho niʻo, poupou noho niʻo; hāwale *(rare).*
bluing. Kolū *(used in laundering).*
blunder. Lalau, hewa, kīnaʻunaʻu, kinanaʻu. *Also:* hōʻāʻā, nāhili, hoʻonāhili, kūhili, naʻau kūhili, hāwāwā, hōkai, manukā, manuea, pālola, pololoa, kākākiʻi.
blunderbuss. Pū pōkole.
blunt. Kūmūmū. *Also:* mūmū, ʻamumū, ʻakumu, ʻōkumu, ʻoi ʻole, manumanu, mūʻouʻou, mene, kūmene, meu, nukunuku, pahupahu, pekekue, pihi, peue. *Blunt in speech,* hoʻopuka kū, ʻōlelo hoʻoponopono ʻole, ʻōkalakala, paopao.

blurred. 1. *As vision.* 'Ōli'uli'u, niniu; haumaka'iole *(of the very old). Also:* pinao, pōnalo, pōlea. *See* **bleary. 2.** *As sound.* Huikau, kāpala, hānuna.
blush. Pi'i ka 'ula, weo, nono 'ula, makou, mā, 'āpane, ho'okoko.
bluster. Pua'ō, kuke kū, wili'ōka'i, 'o'olokū, kāpeku, 'oehu.
boa constrictor. Mo'o wili.
boar. Pua'a laho *(an insult).*
board. 1. *Lumber.* Papa, papa lā'au, laupapa. *See* **surfboard.** *Breadboard,* papa palaoa. *Poi pounding board,* papa ku'i 'ai. *Mixing board,* papa wili, papa wili 'ai. *Rough unfinished board,* papa huluhulu. *Ironing board,* papa 'aiana. *Grooved board for making ribbed tapa,* papa hole. Kōnane *board,* papamū. *Center of a* kōnane *board,* piko. *Board to float with,* mouo, mou. **2.** *To go on board.* Kau, e'e. *To board a ship,* e'e moku. **3.** *To feed.* Hānai, 'ai. **4.** *Council.* Papa, ke'ena. *Labor board,* papa limahana. *Draft board,* papa 'ohi. *Executive board,* pulo ho'okō.
boardinghouse. Hale 'aina.
boarding school. Kula hānai, kula noho pa'a.
Board of Agriculture and Forestry. Papa Mahi 'Ai a me Ulu Lā'au.
Board of Education. Papa Ho'ona'auao.
Board of Commissioners. Papa Komikina.
Board of Commissioners to Quiet Land Titles. Komikina Ho'onā 'Āina.
Board of Health. Papa Ola.
Board of Immigration. Papa E'e Moku.
Board of Regents of the University. Papa o nā Kahu Kula o ke Kulanui.
board of registration. Papa ho'opa'a inoa, 'aha 'uao.
Board of Supervisors. Papa Luna Kia'i.
Board of Water Supply. 'Oihana Wai.
boast. Kaena, ha'anui, liki. *Also:* hō'oio, akena, ākenakena, keha, ha'akoi, ha'ano'u, ha'aliki, kūha'aliki, ha'i liki, ho'oheo, ho'opehu, painu'u, kōlea. *To boast of courage that is lacking,* hō'a'ano. *To boast of one's association with chiefs,* pi'i ali'i. *Stylized boasts and taunts anciently preceded combat. See proud sayings of a boaster:* **'a'ali'i, kamahele, 'ula'a, 'ulu, blow, bowl, wave.** *See sayings derisive of a boaster:* **kala-'ihi, kaupoku, keha, kōlea, liki.**
boat. Moku, poki. *Rowboat,* wa'apā. *Steamboat,* mokuahi.
boat hook. Polohuku, ponohuku.
boatswain. Pokini.
boatswain bird. Koa'e.
bob. E'ea; kimo *(as the head in watching the* kimo *game);* pihōpihō *(as a canoe);* 'oki pahu, 'oki poe *(as hair).*
bobbin winder. Pōka'a pīlali.
bode. Hō'ailona. *Bode well,* hō'ailona pōmaika'i. *Bode ill,* hō'ailona pō'ino.
bodily. Kino. *Bodily remains,* kino wailua, kupapa'u.
body. Kino; paukū kino *(torso); soft parts of —,* 'api; *whole —,* nui kino; *— depression,* pipi *(rare); long, oval —,* 'omo'omo.
body-building. Ho'oikaika kino.
bodyguard. Kia'i kino, kia'ipo'o; 'ūhā heke *(fig.). King's bodyguard,* kau'o'e.
body hair. Hulu, huluhulu.
body louse. 'Uku kapa.
body odor. Hohono.
body surfing. He'e umauma, kaha nalu.
bog. Pohō, naele, nenelu, 'olokele.
boggy. Mā'olu, nolu, nakele, hāwali, nelenu; mō'olu *(rare). See* **bog.**
boil. 1. *As water.* Paila, kupa; *— over,* hū. *Also:* pua'i, ho'olapa, huahua'i, hua'ina. *Ancient method of boiling by placing hot stones in a bowl containing water,* hākui, puholo. **2.** *Carbuncle.* Ma'i hēhē, makalau; maka pala, palapū *(ready to burst). Running boil,* pala he'e.

boiled. 1. *As vision.* Kupa. *Soft-boiled,* mo'a hapa. *Hard-boiled,* mo'a loa.
boiler. Ipu ho'olapalapa, ipu māhu. *Sugar boiler,* ipu ho'omo'a kō.
boiling. Pua'ina; kukukū *(sound). Boiling house (of sugar mill),* hale puhi kō.
boisterous. 'O'olokū, 'ōkalakala, leoleoā, waha kole.
bolas. Pīkoi, 'īkoi.
bold. Koa, maka koa, wiwo 'ole, 'a'a, maha'oi. *Also:* 'āwini, nahoa, mī'oi, mī'oi'oi, kila, pōpololū, mahiopu, mākolea. *To act bold,* ho'omā'oi, hō'a'ano.
bolt. 1. *Lock.* Lā'au ke'a, lā'au kī; ho'opa'a. **2.** *Pin.* Mākia, pine. **3.** *Quantity of cloth.* Kūka'a, 'ōwili, 'āpā. **4.** *See* **run.**
bomb. Pōkā pahū. *Incendiary bomb,* pōkā pōpō ahi.
bombardment. Pōkā pahū.
bomber. Mokulele ho'opahū nui.
bombing. Kōlū, pōkā pahū 'ana.
bond. Pona, palapala pona, palapala ho'opa'a, palapala 'ai'ē, hīpu'u. *Mature bond,* pona piha pono. *Term bond,* pona no ka manawa. *To stand a bond,* kū pona.
bondage. Luhi. *House of bondage (Puk. 13:3),* hale ho'oluhi.
bond servant. Kuapa'a.
bondsman. Mea kū pona.
bone. Iwi *(for various kinds and idioms, see Haw.-Eng. entry and entries that follow it). Also:* 'aulima, kuapo'i, pe'ahi, iwi kūpika, iwi hope, kano, 'au, huamoa, huapo'o, 'auwāwae, kā. *Union of molar or cheekbone with temporal bone,* apo. *Small bone of deceased beloved,* heia. *Bone fishhook,* makau iwi. *Bone needle,* mōlī. *Bundle of bones, as of relatives,* pōpō iwi. *Corpse bones in flexed position,* 'oloke'a. *Bones of chiefs as receptacles of mana were preserved in sennit caskets in houses called* hale poki. *These bones will survive,* ola nā iwi *(said also of one cared for in old age). Act for your own bones,* hana nō i kā kō iwi *(take care of yourself and your own interests).*
bonefish. 'Ō'io *(for growth stages, see Haw.-Eng. entry); large —,* kuahauli.
bonfire. Pu'uahi.
bonito. Aku, kawakawa (pohopoho) *(for growth stages, see Haw.-Eng. entries);* no'ino'i, 'oe'oe *(young). Bonito lure,* pāhī aku, kaiānoa.
bonnet. Pāpale 'o'oma. *Poke bonnet,* pāpale mū'ou'ou.
bonus. Uku keu, uku makana.
bony. Iwiiwi. *Also:* hiwi, hiwihiwi, kōlīlā, kekē.
booby. 1. *Bird.* 'Ā; 'a'ā *(probably).* **2.** *See* **fool.**
book. Puke *(for various kinds, see Haw.-Eng. entry and entries that follow it),* liwele *(French origin, very rare). Instruction book,* puke a'o. *Spelling book,* puke a'o kepala.
bookbinding. Humuhumu puke. *Bookbinding paper,* humuhumu puke 'ili pepa. *Bookbinding cloth,* humuhumu puke 'ili lole.
bookcase. Pahu puke, pahu waiho puke.
bookkeeper. Kupakako, pūkipa.
book louse. 'Uku pepa.
bookmark. Māka puke.
bookstore. Hale kū'ai puke.
bookworm. Mū 'ai puke.
boom. 1. *Spar.* Pumi, pūlumi, kewe, lā'au kaha, lā'au lalo, lā'au paepae, paepae; *outrigger —,* 'iako, ekea; *— connecting hulls of double canoe,* kuānuenue, lapauila; *inboard part of outrigger —,* kua 'iako; *— for canoe sail,* 'ōpe'a. **2.** *Noise.* Ku'i, kani; kūpākūpā *(as of drums);* laolao *(rare). Boom, boom!* Kūakā! 'O kū 'o kā!
boomerang. Ku'uku'u.
boot. Puki, kāma'a puki, kāma'a, kāma'a lō'ihi.
bootblack. Mea ho'ohinuhinu kāma'a.
Boötes constellation. Hōkū-'iwa.
booth. Lānai, pewa, hale lālā lī'au, hale kāmala; pākaukau *(in a market); temporary —,* kāmala, pālima, hale pu'uone *(as in a luakini temple enclosure);* oeoe.

booty. Waiwai pio, waiwai i hao 'ia.

Borabora. Polapola.

border. Palena, līhi, nihi, kapa, peʻa, kaʻe. *Also:* hulilau, huʻa, paʻa, mōlina, haʻi, kuaio, kūkulu, pili, mokuna. *Border of the sea,* kapa kai. *Border of a land,* palena, piko, kapahaʻi. *Border of a mat,* alahiʻi. *Border of a garment,* huʻa lole. *Taboo border,* huʻa kapu. *To mark a border,* kaupalena.

bore. 1. *Tool.* Wili, hou, hou puka, pao. **2.** *See* **boring.**

borer. Mū, wāwahiwaʻa. *Wood-eating borer,* huhu-ʻailāʻau, huhu-pao-lāʻau.

boring. Hoihoi ʻole, manakā, hoʻomanakā. *Also:* kuanui, hoʻokuanui, kualana, hoʻokuānea, pū, kūkaikea, pōkaʻo, uihā, lūlā. *A boring task,* he hana hoʻokuānea. *Don't work in such a bored fashion,* mai hana hoʻomanakā ʻoukou.

born. Hānau, loaʻa. *Born with strange sign or mark,* hānau ʻeʻepa. *Hina was born,* hānau ʻia ʻo Hina.

borrow. Hōʻaiʻē, nonoi no ka manawa, lawe ʻaiʻē.

bosom. Poli.

boss. Luna, haku hana, poki. *To boss,* noho haku.

bossy. Hoʻohaku, kuhikuhi, kuhilani.

Boston. Pokekona, Posetona.

botany. ʻIke noʻeau i nā lāʻau like ʻole.

both. Lāua ʻelua, nā mea ʻelua. *You and I both,* ʻo kāua pū.

bother. Pilikia, hoʻopilikia, hana luhi, hoʻoluhi. *Also:* hōkai, hoʻohōkai, kaiele. *May I bother you?* Hiki iaʻu ke hoʻoluhi iāʻoe?

bottle. ʻŌmole, hue wai. *Nursing bottle,* ʻōmole hānai waiū.

bottom. Kumu, mole, kō lalo loa, papakū, kahi malalo. *Bottom of a carrying net,* piko. *Valley bottom,* papa lalo. *Inside bottom (as of a calabash),* kaʻele, ʻele. *"bottoms up."* Huli pau; ʻōkole maluna *(vulgar).*

bougainvillea. Pukanawila, pua kepalō; pua pepa *(Niʻihau).*

bough. Lālā.

boulevard. Alanui ākea.

bounce. Lele, lelele, kūkū, hoʻokūkū; — *back and forth,* lāʻukeʻukē.

bound. 1. *Leap.* Lele, leina. **2.** *See* **bind.**

boundary. Palena, mokuna, ʻaoʻao, kapa, lihi. *Also:* anapuni, hulilau, peʻa, huʻa, kaupale, kaha kaupale, kaupale waena. *Land boundary,* palena ʻāina. *Boundary between taro patches,* pale kōhina. *To form a boundary,* hoʻokuākapa. *To set a boundary,* kaupalena.

boundless. Palena ʻole, ana ʻole, oneʻula.

bounty. Uku kuwala.

bouquet. Pōkē, pōkē pua, pūpū.

Bourbon. Pulepona, Burebona.

bow. 1. *Obeisance.* Kūlou, kūnou, kūʻou, kimo poʻo; — *low,* lae honua; *reverential* —, kūlou haʻahaʻa; kūmalolo *(rare).* **2.** *Forward part of vessel.* Ihu, ihu waʻa. **3.** *Weapon.* Pana, pana ʻiole, kīkoʻo, kakaka, keʻa. *To shoot with bow and arrow,* pana, pāpua, keʻa. **4.** *Musical.* ʻŪkēkē.

bowed down. Luʻuluʻu.

bowels. 1. *Evacuation.* Kiʻo, kākā, pākiʻo; hana lepo *(euphemism).* *See* **excrement, feces.** *Have your bowels moved?* Ua kiʻo ʻoe? Ua hana lepo ʻoe? Ua hoʻopau pilikia? **2.** *Innards.* Naʻau, ʻōpū.

bower. Paia.

bowl. 1. *Vessel.* ʻUmeke *(for various types, see Haw.-Eng. entry and entries that follow it);* ipu, pola; *kava* —, kānoa, kāʻava; *low, broad wooden* —, pākākā; *stone* —, poho pōhaku; *medium-sized* —, puahala; *small wooden* —, puaniki; *medium-sized deep* —, kūʻoho; *large wooden* —, lawalawaihonua; *elongated* —, pā; *low wooden* —, pālewa; *cooking* —, pā ipu; *poi* —, ʻumeke poi, ʻumeke ʻai, kūmau, kumauna; — *of polished coconut shell,* pūniu. *Rim of a bowl,* nīao. *See* **finger bowl** *and chant,* **hana 1. 2.** *Game.* ʻUlu maika, maika, paheʻe ʻulu, ʻolohū. *Bowling ball,* ʻulu, puʻupā.

See **alley.** *The little fellow, he is a master bowler (For. 5:441),* ʻo ka iki, makua ia o ka ʻulu *(good in small packages).*

bowlegged. ʻŌnaha, naha.

bowline. Pōlena.

bowling. *See* **bowl.**

bowsprit. Ihu waʻa, maka ihu.

bowwow. ʻAoa.

box. 1. *Receptacle.* Pahu *(for various kinds, see Haw.-Eng. entry and entries that follow it);* oblong —, holowaʻa, holoaʻa; poho. **2.** *Fight.* Kuʻikuʻi, kuʻikuʻi puʻupuʻu, mokomoko, pelēpelē. *See* **fight.**

box crab. Pokipoki.

boxer. Kuʻi lima, mokomoko.

boxfish. Makukana, pahu.

boy. Keiki, keiki kāne, kama kāne, poe, poi. *O boy!* Auē!

boyhood. Wā keiki kāne. *See* **childhood.**

boy scouts. No equivalent; sometimes heard: pūʻali kamaliʻi kāne.

brace. Koʻo, hoʻokoʻokoʻo, lāʻau keʻa, kīpū; palehui *(in punctuation);* hoʻokū *(as a canoe with a paddle);* kuahui, ʻīlio *(in house construction);* kūpahu, keʻehi.

bracelet. Kūpeʻe *(for various kinds, see Haw-Eng. entry);* kūpeʻe lima, apo, apo lima. *Gold bracelet,* apo kula. *Bracelet of tusks of hog or dog,* kūpeʻe hoʻokalakala, hoakakala, hūlili.

bracken. Kīlau, kīlau pueo, paiʻā.

bracket. Kahaapo, kahahui.

brackish. Wai kai, wai ʻawaʻawa, ʻawaʻawa, kai, ālia, ālialia, hukahūkai, hūkai, hūkākai, ʻoliʻuliʻu, halahala.

brag. Kaena, akena, haʻakoi, hoʻokelakela. *Also:* hoʻopehu, hoʻopehupehu, wahawai, haʻanui, liki, haʻaliki, kūhaʻaliki, ākenakena, keha. *See sayings,* ʻēkā, **boast.** *Bragging and wheedling,* ke ā nui, ke ā iki.

braid. Haku, hilo, hili, pahili, ulana, lino, hōʻaha, ʻie, kaʻa. *For hat braids, see* **pāpale** ʻie. *Wispy end of a braid,* hiʻuhiʻu. *Some types:* hili kolu, hili pā kolu, hili hā, hili pā hā, uilo, ʻōʻio, piko-o-Halc-a-ka-lā, alahaka-o-Nuʻalolo.

brain. Lolo, lolo poʻo. *See sayings,* **hāwaʻe, lolo.**

brake. 1. *Retard.* Paleki, peleki, mea hoʻopaʻa. **2.** *Fern.* Kīlau, kīlau pueo, paiʻā.

bramble. *See* **briar.**

bran. Palani. *Rice bran,* pale laiki.

branch. Lālā, mana, ʻohā; *main* —, manamana nui, kamahele; *small* —, paʻi aʻa; *low* —, pulu. *Stream branch,* mana wai. *Place where a branch divides off,* kōkīkī *(rare).* *Branch with divine foliage (a chief),* mana weu lani. *To branch out,* mana, manamana, hoʻokihikihi.

branches. Manamana; mana lua *(two, as in a road);* lau manamana *(many).* *Branches forming "Y,"* ʻāmana. *Branches of a road,* mana alanui. *Various branches of the priesthood,* kēlā a me kēia kakaʻina o ka ʻoihana kahuna.

branching. Hāmana, manamana, kīmanamana, hanahihi; alau *(as of winds and lineages).*

brand. 1. *As cattle.* Kuni, hao, kila. **2.** *See* **kind 1.**

branding iron. Hao kuni.

brandish. Kuehu; ʻowala *(as a club);* hoaka *(as a spear);* hoana *(as a whip);* — *threateningly,* kākiʻi.

brandy. Palani.

brass. Keleawe. *To work with brass; one who makes brass articles,* kuʻi keleawe. *To cut or engrave in brass,* kaha keleawe.

brassiere. Pale waiū, pūliki waiū, kāliki waiū.

brave. Koa, hoʻokoa, wiwo ʻole. *Also:* ʻā, ʻaʻa, hoʻonakoa, hoʻomakoa, haʻalokuloku; koapaka. *See saying,* **kuāua.**

brawl. Haunaele, hakakā, ʻāpuni.

bray. Haʻu, haʻuhaʻu, ʻuhūʻuhū, hohō, kēhōhō.

brazen. Mahaʻoi, māʻoi, kīwini, hilahila ʻole. *Brazen look,* maka keleawe.

Brazil, Brazilian. Palakila, Barazila.
breach. Haka; haka'ano *(rare).*
bread. Palaoa, pelena. *See* **dough.** *Unleavened bread,* pelena hū 'ole. *Slice of bread,* pāpa'a palaoa. *Loaf of bread,* 'omo'omo palaoa, pōpō pelena. *Round loaf of bread,* pōpō palaoa. *Pilot bread,* 'ao. *Shewbread, bread of the Presence,* pelena hō'ike.
breadbasket. 'Ie palaoa, imu ō nui.
breadboard. Papa palaoa.
breadfruit. 'Ulu, kino-o-Haumea. *See sayings,* kī'o'e, pakī, ule, 'ulu. *Cooked but unpounded breadfruit,* 'ulu pa'a. *Breadfruit pudding,* paipaie'e, pepeie'e, piele. *Rotten breadfruit,* 'ulu pilo. *Male breadfruit flower,* ule'ulu, pōule, pō'ulu. *Bark of tender breadfruit shoots,* pō'ulu. *Breadfruit core,* pīkoi, 'īkoi, pīkoni, iho. *Markings on breadfruit skin,* nanaka. *To hit broiled breadfruit with a stick to remove blackened skin,* kākā.
breadth. Laulā, ākea, lā'ā.
break. *There is no general term; the main usages follow.* **1.** *As a stick or bones broken in two.* Ha'i, haha'i, uha'i, haki, hahaki, hakihaki, uhaki; *manunu; break easily,* ha'i wale. **2.** *As a flat surface split or broken into pieces.* Wāhi; wāwahi *(for various uses, see Haw.-Eng. entry and entries that follow it);* wāhia, 'ulupā. **3.** *As a string that is severed.* Moku, momoku, mokumoku, mō. **4.** *As a dish.* Nahā. **5.** *General.* Ho'opilikia *(damage); — open or burst,* pohā, moku; *— open, as a nut,* kīkē, kīpō, kīmō; *— or pluck, as flowers,* 'ako, 'ako'ako; *—, as waves,* po'i, popo'i, haki; *— apart, as taro from stalk,* kōhi; *—, as lumps,* kō; *—, as taboo,* 'a'e, 'a'e kū, hehi, mau'a'e, hō'a'e, hehikū; *—, as law,* wāwahi, pale, ha'iha'i; *—, as a horse,* ho'olakalaka. *See* **break wind, broken, daybreak.** *To break without permission or recklessly,* hahaki kū. *To break and enter a house,* wāwahi hale. *To break the Sabbath,* hehi Sabati.
breaker. Po'ina nalu, kai 'ūpoho. *Base of a breaker,* honua nalu.
breakfast. 'Aina kakahiaka.
breakfast food. Mea 'ai no ke kakahiaka.
breakwater. Pale kai, pale wai.
break wind. Hi'u, ho'āni, makani, palalē; *— audibly,* pūhi'u; *— silently,* hio, 'ōhio, pūhihio; *— sputteringly,* pī; *— foully,* 'enakōī; *— slightly,* uene. *Urge or need to break wind,* pu'u pūhi'u. *Sound of breaking wind,* palalī.
breast. Ū; waiū *(for various types, see Haw.-Eng. entry and entries that follow it);* pu'uwaiū *(female);* poli, umauma; *budding —,* 'ōpu'u; *nursing —,* poli 'ai. *See idioms,* **poli, poli 'awa, poli make.** *Hard core in a breast,* waiū. *First liquid before milk begins to flow,* 'ōmaka waiū. *A breast disease,* he'ehe'e. *Breast stroke,* 'au umauma.
breastbone. Iwi umauma; iwi pāuma, pāuma *(as of a chicken).*
breastplate. Pale umauma.
breath. Hanu, aho, ea, eaea. *Breath of life,* mauli ola, ane. *Last breath,* hanu pau *(as one dying). See ex.,* ka'apā. *Bad breath,* hanu pilo, 'alaea. *Deep breath,* hanu nui. *Out of breath,* pauaho, paupauaho, 'api'api, 'oaikū, kā'ili, ka'ahē, ka'ahili, manawaea. *To hold the breath,* 'umi i ka hanu. *Old breath-holding game,* 'ū, nā'ū. *To catch breath after exertion,* pūhanu. *To draw in the breath and expel it with whistling sound,* hoe.
breathe. Hanu, aho. *Also:* hā, haha, manawaea, pūailewa, haluhalu, haluna, hapaipū, hapahapai, ehaha, hō, hohō, nae'ōpuakau, nakinaki. *See* **pant.** *Shortness of breath, difficult to breathe,* pa'apū ka hanu, hanu pa'a. *To breathe gently,* ahe. *To breathe air, as turtle or fish,* pūhā, 'api, ho'omanewa. *To cause to breathe,* ho'ohanu.
breathless. Pauaho, paupauaho.
breed. **1.** *Variety.* Lāhui. **2.** *To engender.* Ho'opi'i, ho'opiha. **3.** *Descent group.* Welo.
breeze. Ahe, aheahe, makani, ani, aniani, makani aniani, ane, ea; *gentle —,* makani aheahe, 'ōnini, kolonahe, hinihini, 'ōaniani, ahe kolo, nahe, unahe; *cool —,* hau; *fragrant —,* moani, moaniani. *See* **wind.** *Wisp of breeze,* 'ēlau makani. *To blow, rise, as a breeze,* ani, papaiaūlu.
breezy. Holomakani, ania, kōaniani.
bregma. Pūniu hui.
Bremen. Pelemena, Beremena.
Brest. Pelekeka, Bereseta.
brew. Puhi. *Stages of brew:* kū, hāwai, pōki'i, kua'ana. *See* **home-brew, swipes.**
brewery. Hale hana pia.
briar. Lā'au 'o'oi, lā'au kukū.
bribe. Uku kīpē, kīpē, pē.
brick. Winihapa, winihepa, pōhaku lepo, pōhaku 'ula.
bricklayer. Hamo puna.
bridal attendants. Ukali pa'a male, pa'alalo, kū'ao'ao.
bride. Wahine male hou, wahine mare; wahine ho'āo *(rare).*
bridegroom. Kāne male hou, kāne mare; kāne ho'āo *(rare).*
bridesmaid. Kū'ao'ao o ka wahine, kaikamahine hoa wahine.
bridge. Uapo, pao, hūlili; *wooden —,* ala holo papa; *plank —,* alahaka, kaulanahaka. *Bridge of nose,* pou iwi. *Bridge for false teeth,* papa niho.
bridle. Kaula waha.
brief. **1.** *Short.* Pōkole, muku. **2.** *Summary.* Palapala ho'opōkole 'ia.
brief case. 'Eke pa'a lima, 'eke'eke pa'a lima, wahī lawe pepa.
brig. Moku kia lua, kia lua pe'a heke.
brigade. Pū'ali koa.
brigandine. Pale umauma unahi.
bright. 'Alohi, 'ālohilohi, kōnane, 'ōlino, 'ōlinolino, 'ōninonino, la'ela'e. *Also:* pāla'ela'e *(as sun);* lala, nale, pualalea, 'ōliko, a'ia'i, 'a'ai, pūloku, akaaka, huali, kauluwela, nohi, hinuhinu, pala hinu, 'ōlali, lali, hehelo, li'oli'o, lino, huaka, hoaka, 'ama, lile, nōweo; pa'ihi *(cloudless);* 'ōwela *(as feather cloaks);* pōlale, makali, mohā, mōhāhā. *See ex.,* '**ōlino.** *Bright-looking,* lamalama.
brighten. Ho'omālamalama, ho'ola'e, ho'ā'ia'i.
brilliant. 'Alohi, 'ālohilohi, lino, a'ia'i, 'ōlino, 'ōlinolino; lololo *(intellect).*
brim. Ka'e, nihi, lihi, kapa, nīao.
brimful. Pihaku'i.
brimstone. Kūkaepele, lua'i pele.
brindled. Pe'elua, mo'o *(of a dog).*
brine. Wai pa'akai. *To soak in brine,* kū pa'akai.
bring. Lawe mai, hō mai, pane'e mai; *— together,* ho'opili; *— up,* ho'āla *(as a topic);* hānai *(as a child); — down,* ho'omoe, hahau *(as club);* kilipo'ipo'i *(as cupped hand).*
brink. Nihinihi. *See* **brim.**
brisk. Maka'ala, 'eleu, 'uleu, māmā, ioiole'a. *To walk, talk in a brisk manner,* kalalī.
bristle. Wanao'a, 'ōkala; pōniho *(as sea urchins); — with anger,* pi'i ka heu, 'ūlepe; pūniho *(rare). Chin whiskers bristle,* 'ōkalakala nā hulu 'auwae *(of ranting).*
bristle worm. 'Aha huluhulu, huluhulu.
bristling. Kalakū, huhulu, huluhulu, huluhulu weo, i'i.
Britain, Britannia, British. Pelekane, Pelekania, Beretania.
British Columbia. Kolumepia Pelekania.
Brittany. Pilikane, Biritane.
brittle. Pa'ina, pāpa'a'ina, pa'apa'a'ina, pakē, ha'iha'i, ha'i wale.
broad. Laulā, ākea. *Also:* laha, lālaha, lālahalaha, pālaha, kīlaha, pālaulau, peleleu, moana, moananaka; 'omaliō *(as land);* kūpeleleu *(as hips). Rare:* 'ololā; pāna'e *(as a leaf). Low and broad, as a door or bowl,* pākākā.
broad-browed. Maha pepe.
broadcast. Laha, ho'olaha, ho'olele leo, lū. *See* **radio broadcast.**

broaden. Hoʻolaulā.
broad jump. Pinao.
broad-minded. Manaʻo laulā, noʻonoʻo laulā, ākea ka noʻonoʻo.
broad-shouldered. Kīwaʻawaʻa, kihikihi nā poʻohiwi, polinahe.
brocaded silk. Kilika lau.
broil. Pūlehu *(on coals);* lāwalu *(in leaves);* alehu, kōʻala, kunu, ʻōlani, pālaha, ʻōhinu, pākiʻi.
broke. See **break.** Puki, poloke *(out of funds, slang).*
broken. See **break.** *Also:* poloke, paloke, ʻinoʻino, napele, nāpelepele, mokulia, manu, lemuku, ʻakumu. *Broken English or other language: see* **speak.**
broker. Poloka.
bronze. Keleawe.
brooch. Pine umauma, pine ʻōmou.
brood. 1. *Of birds.* ʻOhana manu. *Mother hen and brood,* kīnana. 2. *Mull over.* Nalu hoʻokaumaha.
broody. Moa hoʻomoe *(of a hen).*
brook. See **stream.**
Brooklyn. Pulukelina, Burukelina.
broom. Pūlumi, pūpū nīʻau, nīʻau kāhili.
broomstraw. Nīʻau pūlumi.
broom tree. Lokema, nokema, iunipela *(RSV).*
broth. Kai.
brothel. Hale hoʻokamakama, kāmaʻi.
brother. Kaikuaʻana, kuaʻana *(older sibling of same sex);* kaikaina, kaina *(younger sibling of same sex);* kaikunāne, kunāne *(of a female);* mua, hānau mua, hele mua *(older sibling);* hānau hope, hele hope *(younger sibling);* hoahānau kāne *("brother" in the church);* pōkiʻi, muli pōkiʻi *(youngest sibling).* Cf. **sister.** *They are brothers,* ʻo lāua, he kaikuaʻana a he kaikaina. *They are brother and sister,* ʻo lāua, he kaikunāne a he kaikuahine. *Kuaʻana, kaina, and kunāne are often used as terms of address.*
brotherhood. Aloha hoahānau.
brother-in-law. Kaikoʻeke, koʻeke *(of a male);* kāne *(of a female; this term might be qualified by* makua *as indicative of the elder brother or older male cousin in the senior line of a woman's husband, or by the term* ʻōpio *as indicative of a similar relative in the junior line).* Koʻeke *is used as a term of address.*
brow. Lae; — *of a cliff or hill,* hono, kuʻemaka pali, kaʻe, ʻūmalu, hanahanai.
brown. *No exact English equivalent:* uliuli, kamaʻehu, ʻaʻula *(reddish-brown);* makuʻe *(dark);* olomea *(with darker stripes or spots, of pig or dog);* hulupala, ʻea, ʻea mālani *(light brown). Brown skin,* ʻili ʻula, ʻili ʻulaʻula, ʻehu. *Brown hair,* lauoho hāʻehuʻehu. *Brown eyes,* maka uliuli. *Brown shoes,* kāmaʻa ʻili ʻulaʻula. *Brown sugar,* kōpaʻa ʻulaʻula. *Dyes from which brownlike colors are named:* hilihili, palaʻā.
brownie. *No equivalent.* See **legendary beings.**
bruise. Pohole, hoʻopohole, māhole, mōhole, mōholehole, hāuli, hoʻouli, māui, hoʻomāui, māuiui, mala, manu, manumanu, manuheʻu. *Also:* maniheʻu, nahu, palapū, kīmō, kīpō, napele, hoʻokolekole, koana, manuā; paopao, pahu *(feelings).*
brunette. Lauoho uliuli.
brush. 1. *Instrument.* Palaki, hulu. See **toothbrush.** *Scrubbing brush,* palaki ʻānai. *Scrubbing or painting brush,* hulu ʻānai. *Hairbrush,* palaki lauoho. *To brush,* palaki. 2. See **forest.** 3. *To graze.* Peʻahi, kāhili. 4. *To brush aside.* Pale, palepale.
brusque. Konā, kū, kala, kākala, kalakala. See **abrupt.** *To speak brusquely,* kuaʻō.
Brussels. Palukela, Barusela.
Brussels sprouts. Kāpiki liʻiliʻi.
brutal. Lima loko.
brute. Holoholona, kanaka loko ʻino.
bubble. Huʻa, pōhāhā wai, puaʻi, lapalapa. *Water bubble,* huʻa o ka wai. *Soap bubble,* huʻa o ka kopa.
bubbling. Huʻahuʻa, puaʻina, piʻipiʻi, māpu.
bubo. ʻAwaiāhiki, ʻaukoʻi, ʻauwaihiki, ʻāwai, ʻēwai, hahaʻi, ʻanakoʻi, kio, ʻowai, ʻoai.

bubonic. Puponika.
buck. ʻOwala, ʻoala, lāpuʻu, hoʻolāpuʻu, ōnū, ʻanapuʻu, kunu, lōʻohu.
bucket. Pākeke.
Buckingham. Pakinihama, Bakinihama.
buckle. ʻŪmiʻi; ʻūmiʻi kuapo *(belt);* pākala.
buckshot. Pōkā lū.
buckskin. Lio puakea.
buckthorn. Kauila.
bucktooth. Niho puʻu.
buckwheat. Huʻahuʻakō *(— family).*
bud. Liko, ʻōpuʻu. *Also:* muʻo, olomuʻo, ʻōmuʻo, ʻōliko, māliko, hāliko, ʻao, maka, mamaka, ʻōmaka, hoʻopūliko, hāpuʻu, ʻomeʻo. *To bud just a little, to cease budding,* muʻoiki, mūʻokole, muʻomuʻokole. *Young plant bud,* niho peku.
Buddhism. Hoʻomana Buda.
buddy. Makamaka.
budge. Neʻeu, neʻeneʻeu.
budget. Moʻohelu kālā, hoʻonohonoho hoʻolilo. *To plan a budget,* hoʻolālā i ka hoʻolilo ʻana.
buds. Makamaka, makalau *(many, as pussy willow).* To put forth buds, mamaka.
buffalo. Pāpulō. *Water buffalo,* pipi Pākē.
buffalo grass. ʻAkiʻaki haole, mānienie ʻakiʻaki.
buffet. 1. *Hit.* Hahau, nou, koʻokā. 2. *Sideboard.* Pahu ʻume.
bufo. Poloka.
bug. Mū, puʻu.
bugger. Paka.
buggy. Kaʻa.
bugle. Pū.
build. Kūkulu, hana, kāpili; hahau *(as with bricks);* hoʻopae, hoʻopaepae *(as an embankment or platform);* pila *(in card games).*
building. Hale. *Building with many stories,* halekuʻi. *Building permit,* palapala ʻae e kūkulu.
bulb. Hua kanu *(plant). Electric light bulb,* aniani kukui uila.
Bulgaria, Bulgarian. Pulukalia, Bulugaria.
bulge. Puʻu. *Also:* hakū, hakē, nepu, puʻuhaku, polohuku, hūkeu, hūhū; paʻi hua *(as in canoe sides).*
bulk. Nui, puʻu.
bulky. Nui, nunui; pōnulu *(rare).*
bull. Pipi kāne, pipi laho, pipi pulu, pulu.
bulldog. ʻĪlio pulu. *To bulldog, as a cowboy,* wili ʻāʻī.
bullet. Pōkā, pōhaku waikī. *Bullet for gun or pistol,* pōkā pū. *Bullet lead,* kēpau pōkā.
bulletin. Palapala hoʻolaha, pulekina, buletina.
bulletin board. Papa hōʻike.
bull-roarer. Oeoe, pāwā.
Bull Run. Pulu Lana, Bulu Rana.
bull's eye. Kikowaena.
bully. ʻAʻano, hoʻomaʻau.
bulrush. Nānaku, naku, ʻakaʻakai, ʻakaʻakainaku, neki; kome *(KJV).*
bulwark. Pale, pale kai.
Bulwer's petrel. ʻOu, ʻouʻou.
bump. Puʻu, ʻanapuʻu, ʻōhū; — *against,* hoʻokuʻi.
bumper. Pale kaʻa, pale huila.
bumpy. Anapuʻu, ʻāpuʻupuʻu, hāpuʻupuʻu, ʻōpuʻupuʻu, ʻuluhaku, ʻuʻuluhaku; kūkū; lualua, kālualua, ʻālualua, mālualua, hoʻopupū, ʻakūʻakū *(as a road);* holu *(as an airplane ride);* kūkū *(as on a horse).*
bunch. ʻĀhui, mala *(as of bananas);* hui, huihui, huhui, ʻāwai, puʻu, pūpū, paʻi, pūʻā, apoapo; pūpū *(as of flowers);* lālei *(rare);* — *up,* lāpuʻu; — *together,* hōʻili.
bunch grass. Mākuʻekuʻe.
bundle. Pūʻolo, ʻope, ʻopeʻope, pūʻā, wahī, paʻi; *long —,* holo; *large ti-leaf —,* kīpē; hīpuʻu. *Also:* kīʻope, kūʻaupaʻa, wailau, ʻio, makuʻu, ʻāwai, mōkī, paeheu, pūkaula, kīkī, poho, ʻōmaʻo, waihau; pūpū *(as of grass);* kīhene, ʻohi *(as of leaves).* See *saying,* **pūʻolo.** *Bundle of hard poi,* paʻi ʻai. *Bundle of wauke bark,* ʻohi wauke. *Bundle of fruit,* paʻi hua. *Food bundle,* holo ʻai. *Bundle of stripped pandanus leaves,* kī-

moʻo. *To bundle up,* pūʻolo, ʻopeʻope, ʻope, wahī, hoʻoukana, hīpuʻu, kīpola, kīʻope, kūpoepoe.

bung. Popoʻi, ʻumoki, pana.

bungling. Hemahema, kāpulu; poholelua *(rare).*

bunt. Peu.

buoy. Poe, mou, mouo, ʻīkoi; pua *(rare).*

buoyant. Lana, ʻalana, mālana, mānana, kualana, ʻālewalewa. *To make buoyant,* hoʻomālana. *Buoyant blood,* lana ke koko *(of youth).*

bur. Kukū, kūkaehipa, pīpili, ʻihi kūkae hipa, hua kalakala.

burden. Luhi, haʻawina; hāʻawe, hōʻawe, ʻawe *(carried on back);* amo, ʻauamo *(carried on shoulders). Also:* kua, ʻoloʻolōna, puʻu; hoʻomauhaʻalina, mauhaʻalina *(heavily burdened). To burden,* hoʻokaumaha, hoʻokoʻikoʻi, hoʻoluhi, hoʻoluhi hewa, hoʻopuʻu, hoʻokina, hoʻokauā. *Race with burden on the back,* heihei hāʻawe.

burdensome. Hoʻokaumaha, hoʻoluhi, hoʻokua; pauāʻalina *(rare).*

bureau. 1. *Office.* Keʻena, ʻoihana, mahele, pulo. **2.** *Chest of drawers.* Pahu ʻume.

Bureau of Conveyances. Keʻena Kope.

Bureau of Emigration. Pulo Eʻe Moku.

Bureau of Fisheries. Pulo Hoʻolaha Iʻa.

burglary. Wāwahi hale, ʻaihue.

bur grass. Mauʻu kukū, ʻumeʻalu, kūmanomano.

burial. Kanu, kanu ʻana. *Burial place where bones of chiefs were hidden,* awaloa *(rare).*

burlap. ʻEkemauʻu.

Burma. Pulema, Burema.

burn. ʻĀ, ʻaʻā, hōʻā, puhi, kuni, puhi ahi; — *intensely,* hāʻena, hūʻaʻā, puoko; — *weakly,* ʻomī, ʻomīmī, mīmī; —, *as with anger,* ʻā. *Also:* pāwela, kā liliko, liko, likoliko, kūʻena, makawela, pāpaʻa wela, hoʻowela, liholiho, nōʻā. See **back, smart,** *and saying,* ʻaʻā **1.** *To burn cane,* puhi kō. *Scar from burning,* paʻawela. *To burn maliciously,* puhi manaʻo ʻino. *The throat burns,* ʻaʻā ka puʻu *(great thirst).*

burned. Pau ahi, wela, welawela, pāpaʻa, kunia; — *completely,* puhi pau; —, *as a* kukui *nut candle,* kōkolikoli. *Also:* pāwela, pāpaʻapū, pāpaʻa wela. See **sunburned.**

burnt offering. Mōhai kuni.

burp. Pūhā, kīhā.

burrow. *See* **dig.**

burry. Kukū.

burst. Pahū, pakū, pohā, pūhā, ʻoū, ʻowā; — *through,* lele, wāhi; — *forth,* pohā kea, ā, pūhāʻaʻā, lele, ʻulupā *(as light).*

bury. Kanu; kanu paʻa *(whole, as a body);* kīkanu; kākāhou *(just buried, rare).*

bus. Kaʻa ʻōhua; kaʻa uila *(electric).*

bush. 1. *Shrub.* Lāʻau liʻiliʻi, lāʻau haʻahaʻa, laʻalāʻau. **2.** *Vegetation.* Nahele.

bushel. Pūkele.

bushy. Uluāhewa, pūhuluhulu, weuweu.

business. ʻOihana, hana, kuleana, pikineki. *Official or government business,* hana o ke aupuni. *To transact business,* hoʻoholo i ka hana, lawelawe ʻoihana. *None of your business!* Iāʻoe ia wahi! *You have no business there,* ʻaʻohe ou kuleana malaila. *What business is this of yours?* He aha ia iāʻoe? He aha kāu?

bustle. 1. *To move.* Holo hele, ʻeleu, kalalī. **2.** *Dress style.* ʻŌkolepuʻu.

busy. Paʻahana, paʻa i ka hana; paʻa *(as telephone);* lilo, limahana. *Happily busy,* nanea, walea.

busybody. Nīele. *See* **gossip.**

but. Akā, ā, naʻe, aia naʻe, eia (nō) naʻe, koe, koe kēia, ka mea ʻāpiki. *But withal,* eia kekahi.

butcher. Mea lole pipi, mea kūʻai ʻiʻo holoholona. *To butcher,* pepehi ā ʻokiʻoki holoholona.

butcher knife. Pahi ʻokiʻoki pipi.

butler. ʻĀʻīpuʻupuʻu.

butter. Waiūpaka, paka.

buttercups. Makou, ʻawa Kanaloa.

butterfly. Pulelehua. *Monarch butterfly,* lepelepe-o-Hina.

butterfly fish. Kīkākapu, nukunuku, lauhau, lauwiliwili.

butterfly weed. Laulele, pua ʻanuhe. *Seeds of butterfly weed,* hualele.

buttermilk. Wai koʻana waiūpaka.

buttocks. Lemu, ʻōkole, pāpākole, ʻelemu, hope; kīkala *(side);* hena; *cheek of —,* hūkeu; *thin or flat —,* kīkala pai. *To bare the buttocks in bending over, a sign of contempt,* pohopoho, hoʻopohopoho. *Fig. idioms, see* **anus, vagabond.**

button. Pihi. *See* **cuff button.**

buttonhole. Puka pihi.

buttonhole stitch. Humu puka pihi.

buttonhook. Huka pihi.

buy. Kūʻai, kūʻai mai, ʻohi, hoʻolilo; — *cooperatively,* huihui. *Buy wholesale,* kūʻai nui, kūʻai kūkaʻa. *Buy retail,* kūʻai liʻiliʻi. *Buy and sell,* kuʻakuʻai.

buyer. Mea nāna i kūʻai mai, mea kūʻai mai. *Retail buyer,* ka mea hoʻolilo liʻiliʻi.

buzz. Muhu, mumuhi, mumuhu, kapalulu, auwēuwē, halahī, ʻowē.

buzzard. Pukaka, kolenika.

by. E, na, ma, i. *By me,* naʻu. *By him, her, it,* nāna. *By you,* nāu.

by-and-by. Mahope, mamuli, auaneʻi.

C

c. *No Hawaiian term.*
cab. 1. *Taxi.* Ka'a ho'olimalima. **2.** *Hebrew measure.* Kapa, kaba.
cabalistic. Kāpala.
cabbage. Kāpiki, kākipi, kawoa.
cabin. Kāpena, hale 'u'uku.
cabinet. 1. *Furniture.* Waihona, pahu waihona. **2.** *Political.* 'Aha kuhina.
cabinet member. Kuhina.
cable. Kaula uea. *To cable,* kelekalapa. *Undersea cable,* uea moana.
cable car. Ka'a kewe.
cableline. Kewe.
cackle. Pūkōkō *(as in alarm);* kokō *(as after laying an egg);* pukakā.
cacophony. Hana kuli.
cactus. Pānini, pāpipi; lāhoe *(rare). Cactus candy (made of dried juice),* kanakē pānini, pīlali pānini, kanakē pīlali.
cadaver. Kupapa'u.
Caesarian. Kaha 'ia no ka ho'ohānau.
café. Hale 'aina.
cage. Pahu manu, pahu holoholona.
cairn. Ahu.
Cairo. Kailo, Kairo.
caisson disease. *See* **bends.**
cajole. Ho'omalimali, mali, mali leo; kua'i'i *(rare).*
cake. Mea 'ono *(for various kinds, see Haw.-Eng. entry and entries that follow it). Chinese meat cake,* pepeiao. *Fig cake,* pa'i hua piku. *Flour cake,* pa'i palaoa.
calabash. 'Umeke, ipu, pā ipu, hōkeo, hue, hulilau, ōpū hue, ipu pāwehe. *Also:* mā'au'au, palapa'a, kākū, māhanakanaloa. *See sayings,* '**umeke.** *Netted calabash carrier,* kōkō, 'a'aha. *Strings by which a netted calabash is hung,* kākai. *To tie up a calabash,* hō'aha.
calabash tree. La'amia.
caladium. Kalo kalakoa.
Calais. Kalei.
calamity. Pōpilikia, pō'ino. *See ex.,* **pāpa'a 1.** *Overtaken by calamity,* pa'uhia.
calamus. 'Ohe 'ala, kalamo.
calcium. Puna.
calculate. Ho'onohonoho helu.
Calcutta. Kalekuka, Kalekuta.
Caledonia. Kalekonia, Kaledonia.
calendar. 'Alemanaka, kalenekalio.
calf. 1. *Animal.* Pipi keiki. **2.** *Anatomy.* 'Olo, 'olo'olo wāwae, 'olo wae.
calico. Kalakoa; mau'u lā'ili *(a kind of).*
California. Kaleponi.
caliph. Kalipa.
calisthenics. Ho'oikaika kino, hō'o'ole'a kino.
calk. 'Ōkomo.
call. 1. *To speak out.* Hea, kāhea; —, *as in welcome,* heahea, pā kāhea, pāheahea. *Also:* kūhea, oho, eō, kalahea, walo, uwalo, uolo, waloina, walowalo, wawalo, kala'au. *Call the roll,* hea inoa. *Call to eat,* kāhea 'ai. *Call loudly,* kāhea leo nui. *Call over and over,* heahea. *Call the first lines of a stanza by the dancer as a cue to the chanter,* kāhea. *A call to pigs,* kolo, kolo, kolo! *A call to petrel birds,* kue, kue, kue! **2.** *To give a name.* Kapa. **3.** *To visit.* Kipa.
called. Kapa 'ia *(named).*
calling. Hea, kāhea, heahea. *Calling card,* palapala kipa, palapala māka'ika'i.
calliopsis. Waikāhuli.

calloused. Mauleho, pu'u, leho, mānoanoa; ho'omana *(rare). Calloused neck,* 'ā'ī pu'u. *Calloused skin,* 'ili mānoanoa.
callus. La'ola'o, leho, pūleholeho, pu'u. *To get calluses,* ho'opa'a leho, ho'omānea.
calm. Mālie, la'i, hāla'i, kāla'e, māla'e, malino, manino, linolino, lana, wailana, lulu, lululu, lūlā, lūlana, hālūlā, pohu. *Also:* la'ela'e, moe, pāpūhea, malina, nia, makena, ōpūhea, ulana, kūpohu, pāeaea, pālūlā, 'alaneo, āniania. *Rare:* kāna'i, maomao, luluka, ho'ohaha, malau, hāmiha, woa. *Calm place in the sea,* mouo, mōuouo. *Great calm,* la'ikū. *The sea and wind are calm,* mālie ke kai me ka makani. *To make calm,* ho'omālie, ho'onā. *To grow calm,* akaku'u. La'i *frequently has sexual connotations: see* **passion.** *Other ex.,* **peace.**
calmed. La'i, mālie, nā, akaku'u, ma'alili, ho'okoene. *See* **calm.**
calomel. Kalomela. *Calomel-and-tartar emetic,* lupepa.
Calophyllum inophyllum. Kamani, kamanu, tamanu.
Calvary. Kalewali, Kaiwipo'o.
Calvinistic. Kalawina.
Cambridge. Kamepelika, Kameberiga.
camel. Kāmelo.
camellia. Kamila.
camelopard. Kamelopaki, kamelopadi.
cameo. Kameo.
camera. Pahupa'iki'i.
camouflage. Ho'ope'epe'e, ho'onalonalo.
camp. Kahua, ho'omoana. *To make a camp, to camp,* ho'okahua, ho'omoana.
campaign. Ho'ouka kaua *(military);* paipai kalai'āina *(political).*
camp bed. Moe 'u'uku, moe 'opi'opi.
campground. Kahua ho'omoana.
camphor. Kūpelo, kopela, pīlali mea 'ala.
can. 1. *Able.* Hiki. *I can go,* hiki ia'u ke hele. *It can be done,* hiki nō. **2.** *Tin.* Kini. *To can,* ho'okomo iloko o ke kini.
Canaan. Kana'ana.
Canada, Canadian. Kanaka, Kanada.
canal. Alawai, 'auwai, 'auwaha, kōwā, kanela. *Panama Canal,* ke Kōwā o Panamā. *Side of a canal,* ka'e o ke alawai, kīhonua.
canapé. Pūpū.
canary. Manu mele, kenele.
cancel. Ho'opau, kāpae, 'oki, hō'oki.
cancellation. Ho'opau 'ana.
cancer. Ma'i 'a'ai; — *of the throat,* pu'upau.
cancerous. 'A'ai.
candidate. Moho.
candle. Ihoiho, ihoiho kukui. *Kukui-nut candle,* ihoiho kukui.
candlenut. Kukui; kuikui *(Ni'ihau). Candlenut lei,* lei kukui. *Smooth candlenuts used in leis,* kukui 'ōmolemole. *Candlenuts carved in ridges,* kukui ioio. *Candlenuts cut in facets,* kukui 'ōpaka. *Relish of cooked candlenut,* 'inamona, 'akimona. *Concoction of gourd vine and candlenut,* kumu honua. *Candlenut blossom used as medicine,* li'awahine, kihawahine. *Sap of green candlenut,* kohu kukui, pēka'a. *Candlenut branches are heaped up,* ahu a lālā kukui *(of untidiness). See another saying,* **a'ea'e.**
candlenut tree. Kukui, lā'au hū.
candle snuffer. 'Ūpā koli kukui.
candlestick. Ipukukui. *Also:* kū ihoiho, kaukukui,

kumuipukukui, waihona kukui. *Capital of a candlestick,* puʻupuʻu.
candy. Kanakē. *Also:* kōomoomo, kō omōmo, kōmōmo, hoʻomomona.
cane. 1. *See* **sugar cane. 2.** *Staff.* Koʻokoʻo, kōloa. *See* **kanikoʻo.** *Head of cane,* pōheoheo. *Cane with a handle,* koʻokoʻo ʻāmana. *To lean on a cane,* kālele.
cane knife. Pahi kā.
cankerworm. ʻŪhini huluhulu.
cannas. Aliʻipoe, kāna, poloka.
cannery. Hale hoʻokomo kini. *Pineapple cannery,* hale hana hala kahiki.
cannibal. ʻAi kanaka.
cannon. Pū kuni ahi; olohao *(rare)*. *Cannon ball,* pōkā pū kuni ahi. *Mounted cannon,* pū kaʻa.
canoe. Waʻa *(fig., woman); for various types, see Haw.-Eng. entry and entries that follow it. For sayings, see* **hoe 1, kani 1, dream.** *See also* **ihu nui, kaukahi, kaulua, kiapā, kialoa (kioloa), kiapoho, kiapoko, koʻokahi, koʻolua, koʻokolu, kūʻēʻē, lēʻiwi, leuwī, malau, panipani, peleleu, pou, pūkolu, crew.** *To lean over outrigger to counterbalance canoe in rough seas,* kālelemuku. *To paddle a canoe,* hoe waʻa. *To right a canoe,* hoʻolana waʻa. *To steer or navigate a canoe,* hoʻokele waʻa, uli, kupe. *Toy canoes,* waʻa lau kī, waʻa lolo niu. *Canoe guarding fish net,* kihi.
canoe bailer. Kā.
canoe ceremony. Pū i ka waʻa.
canoe dedication. Hoʻolaʻa waʻa.
canoe enclosure. Pā waʻa.
canoe fleet. ʻAu waʻa, mano ʻau waʻa.
canoe house. Hālau.
canoe landing. Paena waʻa.
canoe maker. Kālai waʻa, kahuna kālai waʻa; aukukui *(apprentice)*.
canoeman. Mea waʻa, waʻa.
canoe owner or crew member. Mea waʻa.
canoe paddler. Hoe waʻa, mea waʻa, waʻa ʻīhoe *(rare)*.
canoe parts:
bilge, hold: liu, pikaʻo.
boom: ʻiako, lāʻau kaha, lāʻau lalo, muku, ʻopeʻa, ʻekea.
bow, prow: ihu, peu, ʻeku.
connectors (of double canoe): keʻa, kuanuenue.
covers: kupoʻi, papa uhi waʻa.
edge: niao.
endpieces or parts thereof: manu, makuʻu, kupe, pū, ʻōkumu, lāʻau, lāʻau ihu, lāʻau hope, kupeʻulu, maha, poʻo pāoʻo, unu.
float or part thereof: ama, kapuaʻi, kanaka.
gunwale strakes: pale, pale mua, pale hope, moʻo waʻa.
hollow: poho, poho mua, poho waena, poho hope.
house on platform: hale lanalana.
keel: kuamoʻo.
lashings: lanalana, pāʻū-o-Luʻukia.
mast: kia, lāʻau kū, pou.
platform: pola, keanahā.
rigging, lines: kaula, kaula likini, kaula kāʻiliʻili, hoa waʻa.
sail: lā, peʻa, ʻōpeʻapeʻa.
seat: nohona waʻa.
stern: muli, hope; moamoa, momoa *(points at end of stern)*.
thwart: wae waʻa, nohona waʻa.
other parts: ʻākea, hākaokao, holo, honua, kainaliu, kaumoli, kūpoukia, manono, paʻi hua, papakū kia, pepe, pepeiao, ulu.
canoe race. Heihei waʻa.
canoe rest or support. Loha, hakalauluha.
canoe shipmate. Hoa waʻa.
can opener. Mea wehe kini.
Canopus. Ke-aliʻi-o-Kona-i-ka-lewa.
canʻt. ʻAʻole hiki, hiki ʻole. *I canʻt go,* ʻaʻole hiki iaʻu ke hele.
cantaloupe. Ipu, ipu ʻala, ipu pāʻina.

cantankerous. Huhū wale, ʻaʻaka, pale ka ʻaʻaka.
Canterbury. Kanakupele, Kanekapuli, Kanatubere, Kanetaburi.
canto. Pale mele, paukū mele.
Canton. Kanakona, Kanatona.
canvas. Kapolena; ʻie *(rare)*.
cap. Kapu, pāpale kapu.
capable. Mākaukau, lawa.
capacity. Ka nui e lawa ai. *Capacity for crime,* kū i ke kalaima.
cape. 1. *Geographical.* Lae, ʻōlae, ʻoiʻoina. *A place with many capes,* ʻōlaelae, ʻālaelae. **2.** *Garment.* Kīhei, ʻahu, kīpuka, koloka; *feather —,* ʻahu ʻula; *decorated —,* kīhei ʻahu noʻenoʻe; *tapa —,* paʻipaʻinahā.
Cape Fear. Lae-Makaʻu.
cape gooseberry. Pohā, paʻina.
cape honeysuckle. ʻIʻiwi haole; mākahala *(Niʻihau)*.
Cape Horn. Kepo-honi, Kepa-honi, Lae-Hao.
Cape of Good Hope. Lae-Manaʻolana.
caper. Lelelele, lelele, ʻowāʻowala, hōʻanapau.
capillary action. ʻUme lauoho.
capital. 1. *City.* Kapikala. **2.** *Wealth.* Kumu waiwai, kumupaʻa. **3.** *See* **candlestick.**
capital letter. Hua palapala nui.
capital punishment. Hoʻopaʻi kū i ka make.
capitol. Kapikala, hale poʻo ʻoihana aupuni.
Cappadocia. Kapakokia, Kapadokia.
caprice. *See* **whim.**
capsized. Kahuli, luma ʻia.
capstan bar. ʻAukā.
captain. Kāpena, luna kaua, kāpena aliʻikoa.
Captain Cook. Kapena Kuke, Lono.
captivate. Lawe pio *(capture);* hoʻopunihei *(charm)*.
captive. Pio.
capture. Lawe pio, hopu. *To avoid capture,* lele pio.
car. Kaʻa. *To ride in a car,* kau kaʻa, holo kaʻa. *Pleasure ride,* holoholo kaʻa. *To drive a car,* kalaiwa kaʻa. *To park a car,* kū ke kaʻa, pāka ke kaʻa. *To get in a car,* kau i ke kaʻa. *To get out of a car,* lele mai ke kaʻa. *He sits in a car,* noho ʻoia i luna o ke kaʻa.
carabao. Pipi Pākē.
caramel. Kalamela.
carapace. Una *(turtle);* kuapoʻi *(turtle or crab)*.
carat. Kalaka.
caravan. 1. *Travelers.* Huakaʻi *(Biblical).* **2.** *See* **trailer.**
carbolic acid. ʻAkika kapolika.
carbon. Kalepona.
carbon paper. Pepa kope.
carbuncle. Paleka, palika. *See* **boil.**
carcass. Kupapaʻu, heana; iwi *(as bones of a chicken)*.
card. 1. *Paper.* Pepa. *Names of card games:* kāmau, ʻuwiki, piula, konoki, kēkake, hai-lo-keaka, male. *To build in a card game,* pila. *To tell the future by cards,* kilokilo pepa. *See* **cards. 2.** *To comb.* Koe *(as wool)*.
cardboard. Pepa mānoanoa.
cardinal. 1. *Of the church.* Kakinela. **2.** *Bird.* Manu ʻula-ʻula, ʻulaʻula.
cardinal fish. ʻUpāpalu.
cards. Nā pepa, pepa hahau *(playing)*. *Stack, deck, or pack of cards,* puʻu pepa. *Hand of cards,* haʻawina pepa. *To play cards,* pāʻani pepa. *See* **card, game.**
care. 1. *To care for.* Mālama, nānā. *Also:* pūlama, luhi, luhina, momoa, moamoa, hoʻomoamoa, aumoa *(rare)*. *To care for well, as a pet,* hānaiāhuhu. *Person cared for,* luhi. *Well cared for,* mālama pono ʻia, pākī. *To not care for, see* **neglect. 2.** *See* **like.** *I donʻt care,* ʻaʻohe oʻu nānā; he mea ʻole. *What do you care?* He aha ia mea iāʻoe?
career. ʻOihana.
carefree. ʻAʻohe noʻonoʻo, ʻaʻohe hoʻokaumaha, ʻaʻohe pīhoihoi, pakaulei, lōliʻi.
careful. Akahele, nānā pono, mālama pono. *Also:* akanahe, ao, maiau, lukau, waiolono. *See saying,* **pula 1.** *Be careful,* nānā pono. *Be careful or (you) will be hurt,* mālama o pā.

carefully. Pono, nihi, aka-. *Look carefully,* nānā pono. *Go carefully in the uplands of Puna; pick no flowers lest you be lost on the path of error,* e nihi ka hele i ka uka o Puna; mai ʻako i ka pua, o lilo i ke ala o ka hewahewa.

careless. Kāpulu, palaka, kīkoʻolā, hoʻoponopono ʻole, hoʻohemahema, palaleha. *Also:* naʻau kūhili, nāhili, mōhio, mōhiohio, mohihio, maʻuʻa, hīlea, manuea, pōnolu. *See sayings,* **hīlea, mōhio, wili 1.** *To eat in a careless way,* pono ʻai. *To sit carelessly,* noho hoʻoponopono ʻole.

caress. Hamo, hoʻoheno, hole, kūwili; poliʻahu *(rare). To caress repeatedly,* milikaʻa.

caret. Puamana, puʻumana.

caretaker. Kahu *(for various kinds, see Haw.-Eng. entry and entries that follow it);* kahu mālama, mālama, kiaʻi; hānai *(rare);* land —, hoaʻāina; — *of images,* kahuna kiʻi; — *of bones of dead,* lawelawe iwi; — *of chief's food and clothing,* pāhau. *See* **kāpuhi.**

carfare. Uku kaʻa.

cargo. Ukana.

Caribbean. Kalepiana, Karebiana; Kalipia, Karibia.

caricature. Kiʻi hoʻohenehene.

Carmelite. Kalamela.

carnal. Kō ke kino. *Carnal desire,* kuko. *To know a man carnally,* pākanaka.

carnation. Ponimōʻī.

carnival. Hana hōʻikeʻike, pea.

carnivorous. ʻAi ʻiʻo.

carob. Kelakio.

Carolina. Kalolaina, Karolaina.

carp. Iʻa ʻulaʻula uli.

carpenter. Kamanā.

carpet. Moena weleweka, kāpeka.

carpetbagger. *See* **plover.**

carpet tacks. Kui kākia moena.

carriage. 1. *Vehicle.* Kaʻa lio, hale kaʻa. *To ride in a carriage,* holo kaʻa. **2.** *Stance.* Kūlana.

carriage horse. Lio kaʻa.

carrier. Lawe, hapaina.

carrier pigeon. Manu nūnū lawe leka.

carrot. Kāloke.

carry. Lawe, hāpai, hali, halihali. *Ways to carry:* amo, ʻauamo *(on shoulders);* lawe lima *(in hands);* hāʻawe, hōʻawe, waha *(on back);* painuʻu *(on hips);* kauālupe, kaʻiālupe *(suspended between others); also:* hiʻilawe, ʻawe, ʻāhaʻi, wālua, hiʻi, hiʻilei, hiʻikua, pōhākiʻikiʻi, kālawe, puʻualu, pualau, hāpai pū, kuiʻēʻē. *To carry to and fro,* kaʻi lewa, kaʻikaʻikū, halihali, hauhauhali, hali hele, paialewa. *To cause to carry,* hoʻohali. *To carry on command,* hoʻomau, hoʻokū *(as a name).*

carrying. Hapaina, lawena, kaʻikaʻina. *Carrying pole,* māmaka, ʻauamo.

carry out. 1. *See* **carry. 2.** *To perform.* Hoʻokō, hoʻohana.

cart. Kaʻa, kaʻa huila lua. *See* **handcart.**

cartilage. Iwi kamumu, iwi kumumumu; paka, kākala *(near the tail of some fish);* peu *(of pig snout).*

cartographer. Mea kaha palapalaʻāina.

cartoon. Kiʻi hōʻakaʻaka.

cartridge. Kake. *Cartridge box,* kake pauka, kākai pauka.

cartwheel. Hoʻokakaʻa, kūwalawala.

carve. Kālai, kalakalai; kuʻikepa *(as wood);* ʻokiʻoki *(as meat). To carve figures in the* iʻe *tapa beater,* hole iʻe.

carving. Kalaina. *Carving expert,* kahuna kālai. *Shark's tooth used for carving,* niho ʻoki.

carving knife. Pahi ʻokiʻoki, pahi koli.

cascade. Wailele.

case. 1. *Container.* Pahu, wahī. **2.** *Court case.* Hihia, hihia kalaima, hihia waiwai. *Admiralty case,* hoʻokolokolo moku. **3.** *Situation.* Kūlana. *Serious case,* kūlana pilikia loa, kūlana kūpilikiʻi. *In case of trespassing,* a ma kahi o ke komohewa. *The first case known,* ka maka mua i ʻike ʻia. **4.** *Grammatical.* ʻAui. *See the fol-*

lowing cases: **ablative, accusative, agentive, dative, genitive, nominative, possessive, vocative.** *These names were introduced by Andrews 1854 but have been rarely used.*

cash. Kālā kūʻike.

cashier. Mea ʻohi kālā.

cashmere. Kakimea.

cash payment. Uku kūʻike.

cask. Pahu.

casket. Pahu, pahu kupapaʻu. *Sennit casket for bones of chiefs,* kāʻai. *See* **kāʻai, kiʻi kino ʻie.**

Caspian. Kakepiana, Kasepiana.

cassava. Manioka.

cassia. Kākia, kika. *Many kinds are described in Neal 421–8.*

cast. 1. *To throw.* Hoʻolei, nou, kiola, lū. *To cast a shadow,* ili ke aka. *To cast a stone in a sling,* maʻa. *Cast down (sad),* luʻuluʻu, ʻoupē, kaumaha. **2.** *To cast for fish.* Kākele, kāʻili, hī, hoʻokelekele, kīolaola. **3.** *To cast metals.* Hoʻoheheʻe, ninini. **4.** *Medical.* Mea hoʻopaʻa.

castanet. Mea hoʻonakeke i ka lima. *See* **pebble.**

castaway. ʻŌlulo.

castle. Kākela, hale pūkaua.

Castor. Nānā-mua. *Castor and Pollux,* Nānā-mua, Nānā-hope, Māhana, Ka-māhana, Nā-hōkū-māhana, Māhoe, Nā-māhoe, Māhoe-hope.

castor bean. Pāʻaila,kolī, kaʻapehā, kamākou, lāʻau ʻaila.

castor oil. ʻAila hoʻonahā, ʻaila nahā, ʻaila nohō, ʻaila kolī.

castor-oil plant. *Same as* **castor bean.**

castrate. Poʻa.

casual. Wale. *Casual acquaintance,* he lihi kamaʻāina. *Casual knowledge,* ʻike mālani. *Casual wear,* ʻaʻahu ʻoluʻolu.

cat. Pōpoki, ʻoau, ʻowau. *Maltese cat,* pōpoki lehu. *Tabby cat,* pōpoki peʻelua.

catalogue. Puke nānā mea kūʻai, puke hōʻike hana. *Catalogue of names,* papa inoa.

cataract. 1. *See* **waterfall. 2.** *Disease.* Makaiʻa, ʻōnohiāiʻa. *Remove a cataract,* kā.

catch. Hopu *(grab);* ʻapo *(as a ball);* ʻapoʻapo; hei *(in a net);* loaʻa, hoʻopaʻa; hupu; poʻi, kīʻapu *(between cupped hands);* miliʻopu, hāhāmau *(as fish with the hands). To catch a cold,* loaʻa i ke anu. *Catch the dog,* hopua mai i ka ʻīlio.

catching. ʻĀpona, hopuna.

catechism. Kakekimo, nīnau hōʻike, ui, palapala ui; nīnau pili hoʻomana *(Protestant);* ui kula Sabati *(Sunday School).*

catechumen. Kakekumeno.

category. Mahele, ʻano.

caterpillar. 1. *Insect larva.* Peʻelua, ʻenuhe, nuhe, ʻanuhe, poko. *Also:* hē *(tiny);* ʻūhini hulu ʻole; lohaloha, lohelohe, mū *(in cocoon). Kinds:* kalawela; ʻenuhe *(hawk or sphinx moths);* kuawehi *(dark);* kuapaʻe *(destructive). First appearance of young caterpillars on vines,* kāhē. *To metamorphose from a caterpillar into a butterfly,* hoʻomalule. *Infested with caterpillars,* ʻanuhe, ʻānuhenuhe. **2.** *Machine.* Kakapila.

cathartic. Lāʻau hoʻonahā. *See* **medicine.**

cathedral. Luakini, hale nui pule nui.

Catholic. Kakōlika, Kakōlika Loma *(Roman);* Kakōlika Helene *(Greek). Catholic religion,* Hoʻomanapope.

Catholicism. Kakōlika, Hoʻomana Palani, Hoʻomanapope.

catmint, catnip. Kakamina.

cat's cradle. Hei.

cat's-eye. Pani-pūpū.

cattle. Pipi, puaʻa pipi; pipi kāne *(bull);* pipi wahine *(cow);* pūʻā pipi, kumu pipi *(herd). See* **steer.** *To bind the feet of cattle,* kūpeʻe pipi. *To work with cattle, especially as a cowboy,* mālama pipi. *Cattle herdsman, owner,* kahu pipi. *Cattle roundup, to drive cattle,* hoʻohuli pipi, hoʻā pipi.

Caucasian. Haole. *See* white man.
caudal fin. Hiʻu.
caught. Hopu ʻia, ʻapo ʻia, helea, heia; mau *(as a fish or hook).*
caul. ʻAʻa.
cauliflower. Kāpiki pua, kalipalaoa.
cause. Kumu, mole, mea, ka ua mea, kuleana, kau, kū.
cautious. Akahele, hoʻokanahaʻi; waiolono *(rare). See* **carefully** *and saying,* tongue.
cavalier. Koa kawalia.
cavalry. Pūʻali kaua lio, pūʻali kau lio, pūʻali koa lio, kaua lio, koa kau lio. *Cavalry soldier,* koa kaua lio. *Cavalry war,* kaua lio.
cave. Ana, lua, pao; lua pao *(burial);* luakele *(concealing);* nupa *(deep);* peʻe pao, lua huna *(hidden);* ʻaʻaʻā *(lava). To hide in a cave,* peʻe pao.
caved in. ʻŌpaha, pohona, hāneʻe.
cavern. Ana.
cavernous. Halehale.
caviar. Kowaū.
cavity. Poʻo, napoʻo, ʻāpoʻopoʻo, ʻōpaha, mālua. *Tooth cavity,* puka niho.
cavort. Lapa, hōʻanapau, hulahē.
caw. ʻAlalā, ʻaua.
cease. Pau, hoʻopau, oki, hoʻōki, waiho, hoʻomalolo, akakuʻu.
ceaseless. Pau ʻole, mau.
cedar. Kekela, ʻaleka, paina.
Cedar Hill. Kila-hila.
ceiling. Kaupaku, kaupoku, kilina.
celebrate. Hoʻolauleʻa. *Also:* hoʻokulāia, hoʻokahakaha. *Come to the house to celebrate Christmas,* e hele mai i ka hale e hauʻoli Kalikimaka ai.
celebrated. Kaulana; — *place,* pana.
celebration. Hoʻolauleʻa; hana hoʻohiwahiwa *(as to honor an individual).*
celebrity. Kanaka kaulana.
celery. Kelaki, kalelē.
celestial. ʻAno lani.
cell. Lumi hāiki; kūʻono; pukapuka *(of a beehive). Prison cell,* lumi paʻahao, keʻena paʻahao.
cellar. Lumi hoʻāhu malalo o ka hale. *Wine cellar,* wahi hoʻāhu waina.
cello. Waiolina kū.
cement. Kameki, kimeki, palaina kimeki, puna kameki. *To smooth fresh cement with a trowel,* palaina.
cemetery. Ilina, pā ilina, pā kupapaʻu; papau make *(rare). Plot in a cemetery,* pā ilina.
censer. Ipu ahi, ipu kuni ʻala; kapuahi *(for sacrifice).*
censor. Luna ʻāpono.
censure. ʻĀhewa, nema, kūhihi. *See* blame.
census. Helu, helu kanaka. *Census taker,* luna helu. *To take a census,* helu, helu kanaka.
cent. Keneka. *Ten cents,* kenikeni.
centennial. Ka puni ʻuwa o ka haneli makahiki.
center. Waena, waenakonu, konuwaena, kikowaena. *Also:* ʻōnohi, kuʻina; maka *(of a flower or cloud);* ulu *(as of a canoe or net);* piko *(of a kōnane board).*
centimeter. Kenimekela.
centipede. Kanapī.
central. Waena; kikowaena *(telephone operator).*
Central America. ʻAmelika Waena.
centurion. Luna haneli.
century. Kenekulia.
cephalopod. *See* cuttlefish, squid.
cereal. *See* breakfast food.
cerebral hemorrhage. Aʻa moku i ke poʻo. *Cf.* stroke 3.
ceremony. Hana hoʻohanohano. *See* canoe. *Religious ceremony,* hana pili haipule. *Ancient ceremonies:* ʻaha hele honua, hehu, hoʻohāpai, hoʻowilimoʻo, kā i mua, kaiʻoloa, kāmauli, kekaloakāmakamaka, lolo waʻa, hono, loulu, kauila, kuili, lupalupa, māwaewae, ʻoki poepoe, papa hana, ʻūlili, ʻuwīʻuwī, ʻiui.
cereus. *See* night-blooming cereus.

certain. 1. *Particular.* Kekahi. **2.** *Positive.* Maopopo loa. *Certain knowledge,* ʻike pono.
certainly. Hiki, hiki nō, ā ʻoia, pēlā nō, ʻoiaʻiʻo, pēlā ʻiʻo nō. *Certainly not!* ʻAʻoleʻloa!
certificate. Palapala *(for various kinds, see Haw.-Eng. entry and entries that follow it);* palapala hōʻoia, palapala hōʻike. *Certificate of identification,* palapala kuhikuhi kino. *Birth certificate,* palapala hānau. *Certificate of merit,* palapala hoʻomaikaʻi. *Certificate of appointment,* palapala hoʻokohu. *Certificate of clearance,* palapala hoʻokuʻu. *Counselor's certificate,* palapala hōʻoiaʻiʻo a ke kanikela. *Certificate of title,* palapala hoʻokō.
certifier of title. Luna hōʻoiaʻiʻo palapala.
certify. Hōʻoiaʻiʻo, hoʻomaopopo. *Certified true,* hōʻoia ʻia ka ʻoiaʻiʻo.
cessation. Panina, pau ʻana, oki.
cession. Hoʻolilo ʻana.
cesspool. Lua o nā mea ʻino, luawai pelapela.
cestrum. Mākāhala, kūpaoa.
Cetus. Hōkū-pā *(head of constellation).*
Ceylon. Kilona.
chafe. Maoa *(from friction);* uhu, uilani *(rebel).*
chaff. Oka palaoa, ʻaʻa, ʻaʻaʻa, hāʻaʻa.
chagrin. Hoka. *To cause chagrin,* hoʻohoka.
chain. Kaula, kaula hao. *Watch chain,* kaula uwaki.
chair. Noho. *Kinds:* noho aliʻi *(throne);* noho huila *(wheel);* noho ʻie *(wicker);* noho kū *(straight);* noho moe *(divan);* noho ʻopiʻopi *(folding);* noho paipai *(rocking).*
chairman. Luna hoʻomalu, aliʻi hoʻomalu, luna noho, ikū haʻi.
chaise lounge. Moe hilinaʻi.
chalcedony. Kalekekona.
Chaldea. Kalekea, Kaledea.
chalk. Poho.
challenge. Hōʻaʻano, ʻaʻa. *Also:* hoʻohoa, hoʻonahoa; ʻaʻahuā *(jealous). To accept a challenge,* ʻaʻa.
chamber pot. Ipu lepo, ipu mimi, ipu hana lepo, ipu hanawai.
chameleon. Kameleona.
chamois. Kame.
champagne. Kamapane.
champak. Miulana.
champion. Mea lanakila, poʻokela, pūkaua, moho.
chance. Manawa *(opportunity). Take a chance,* hoʻaʻo.
chancellor. Poʻo nui.
change. 1. *Transformation.* Loli, hoʻolilo, hoʻololi, huli, hoʻohuli. *Also:* kāhuli, lolina; kuanoni *(as color);* hulihia *(complete);* ʻoʻolopū *(rare);* mīkololia *(as appearance);* ʻōkeʻe *(direction);* kaʻa mea *(as the wind, or an idea);* — *into,* lilo. *Time of change,* huliau. *To change form,* hoʻokūākino. *To change skin from chrysalis state,* māunu. *Changes of instrument,* hoʻololi ʻana maloko o ka palapala *(legal). To cause or induce change,* hoʻohuli. *To change clothes,* hoʻololi i ka lole. *Change the mind (of someone else),* hoʻohuli manaʻo. **2.** *Money.* Kenikeni, keni; wāhi *(to change, as a hundred dollar bill); small* —, ʻōkeni, mea heleleʻi. *Have you change?* He keni nō kāu?
changeable. Loliloli, lolelua, lauwili. *Also:* pūlewa, palaʻie, ihu kāninonino; mūheʻe, ʻōlewa.
channel. Kōwā. *Also:* alawai, wā, ʻauwaha, awa, māno; āmio *(narrow). Channel markers,* ula huna.
chant. Oli *(not for dancing);* hula *(for dancing);* mele *(general name for chants and songs; for various kinds see Haw.-Eng. entry and entries that follow it). Kinds of chants:* ʻalalā, haʻanoʻu, haʻi kupuna, hea inoa, helu, heʻu, hoʻāeae, hoʻāla kuahu, hoʻi, hoʻopuka, ʻiʻi, inoa, kāhea, kaʻi, kake, kakekake, kanikau, kāohi, kau, kaukau, kāwele, kepakepa, kūʻauhau, malo, nīpolo, paeaea, paha, waʻa. *See Elbert and Mahoe 6–7 for a classification of chants. Humming sound of chanting,* hano.
chanter. Mea oli, mea olioli, hoʻopaʻa.

chaos. Neoneo, pō.
chap. Kaʻaka. *Old chap,* ʻelekule.
chapel. Hale pule.
chapiter. Luna kia.
chapter. Mokuna; pāpale *(architectural).*
character. 1. *Nature.* ʻAno. *Also:* ʻōuli, loko, umauma. **2.** *Symbol.* Hōʻailona. **3.** *See* **person.**
characteristic. ʻAno, welo, kū i ke ʻano.
charcoal. Lānahu, nānahu.
charge. 1. *Levy a price.* Hoʻouku, uku. *Transportation charge,* uku kaʻa. *Free of charge,* manuahi. **2.** *Defer payment.* Hōʻaiʻē, kāki, ʻauhau. **3.** *Accusation.* ʻŌlelo hoʻāhewa, ʻāhewa, hoʻopiʻi. **4.** *In battle.* Hoʻouka. **5.** *Command.* Kauoha. *To be in charge of,* kaʻa, kuleana.
charged water. Wai pipiʻi, wai piʻipiʻi.
chariot. Hale kaʻa; kaʻa kaua *(war).*
charitable. Lokomaikaʻi, aloha.
charity. Aloha, manawaleʻa.
Charleston. Kalekona, Kaletona.
Charley horse. Wāwae huki, lāʻau.
charming. Māhie, hoʻomāhie, hoʻopunihei, hoʻohoihoi.
charred wood. Momoku ahi.
chart. Palapala kuhikuhi.
charter. Palapala hoʻohui, palapala hoʻokumu, palapala hoʻokohu hui; hoʻolimalima *(rent).*
chase. Alualu, hahai, uhai, ʻāhaʻi. *Also:* naholo, hoʻonaholo, kaukolo, kauholo. *Chase off,* kipaku, hoʻopuhalahio, hoʻopalaheʻe, hoʻomahuka.
chasm. Nupa. *See* **ravine.**
chaste. Maʻemaʻe, kūkapu.
chastise. Hoʻopaʻi.
chastity belt. *See* **luʻukia.**
chat. Kamaʻilio hoʻonanea, keaka. *Also:* pāleo, hūhā.
chattel. Waiwai lewa.
chatter. Puaʻohi, ʻohi, ʻohi hāpuku, ʻohipua, ʻohikui, walaʻau wale, hauwalaʻau, kūkahekahe, kakahili.
chatterbox. Puaʻohi.
chauffeur. Kalaiwa, hoʻokelekele kaʻa, hoʻokele kaʻa, kia kaʻa.
cheap. Emi, makepono.
cheapen. Hoʻēmi i ka waiwai ʻiʻo.
cheat. ʻĀpuka, pākaha, kikiki, kolohe, ʻaihue, hoʻopunipuni. *Also:* kaha, hōʻepa, ʻapuhi, hōʻiole, lonu. *See* **ratlike.** *Gross cheat,* ʻimi loaʻa ma ka hoʻopunipuni.
check. 1. *Bank.* Pila kīkoʻo, pepa kīkoʻo, palapala kīkoʻo. **2.** *To restrain.* Keʻakeʻa, kāohi, hoʻālia. *Also:* kōhi, kaʻukaʻu, ʻaʻa, pūkī. *Checks and balances, as in government,* hoʻokūʻia. **3.** *To mark.* Kaha. **4.** *To verify.* Nānā pono i nā hewa, hōʻoiaʻiʻo.
checkerboard. Papa kōnane, papamū.
checkered. Papamū *(as gingham).*
checkers. Kōnane. *Also:* kōlane, papamū, mū, hiua. Kōnane *stone,* hiu, ʻulu; ʻiliʻili kea *(white);* ʻiliʻili ʻeleʻele *(black). See ex.,* **Kou.** *To move, as in checkers,* kaʻi hele, kuʻi. *To lose in checkers, as a stone or game,* holo. *To play* kōnane, kōnane.
check line. Kaula kāohi.
checkmark. Kaha.
chee-fah. Kīpā.
cheek. Papālina, pāpālina. *Rosy cheeks,* papālina ʻulaʻula, nono, nononea. *Plump cheeks,* papālina ʻuheke. *Soft cheeks,* papālina lahilahi. *Long cheeks,* papālina loloa. *Cheek of the buttocks,* hūkeu.
cheekbone. Ā; *high —,* kekē nā iwiiwi papālina.
cheeky. Mahaʻoi.
cheep. Kio, ʻioʻio. *See* **chirp.**
cheer. 1. *Encourage.* Hoʻolana, hoʻopaipai. *Also:* hoʻomālaʻe, hoʻomāmā. **2.** *Shout.* Hoʻōho, hulō.
cheerful. Hoihoi, hauʻoli mau, hoʻolana. *Cheerful look,* maka hinu.
cheerleader. Alakaʻi hoʻopaipai.
cheers. Hipahipa, hulō.
cheese. Waiūpaʻa, waiūpakapaʻa; *cottage —,* waiūhakuhaku.

chemical. Kemika.
chemise. Muʻumuʻu.
chemist. Kemika. *See* **chemistry.**
chemistry. Hana kemika, paʻipaʻi lāʻau, hoʻohuihui lāʻau.
cherimoya. Momona, kelemoio.
cherish. Pūlama, hoʻoheno; haʻaheo *(with pride). Also:* nēnē, hoʻolauaʻe, hoʻomoamoa, hoʻopulakaumaka; hōkeo *(secretly);* moamahi.
cherished. Pūlama ʻia, mili nanea, milimili nanea.
cherub. Kelupa.
cherubim. Kelupima.
chest. 1. *Anatomy.* Umauma, keʻapaʻa, houpo. *Narrow-chested,* umauma hāiki; paūhu *(rare). Broad-chested,* umauma lahalaha. **2.** *Container.* Pahu, holoaʻa.
chestnut. Pelakano, pelane *(KJV).*
chest-slapping game. Kulakulaʻi.
chest-slapping hula. Paʻi umauma.
chew. Mama *(without swallowing);* nau, namu *(with closed mouth). To chew gum,* nau kamu. *To chew the cud,* hoʻolualuaʻi. *Chewed food (as kava,* kukui *nut for medicine),* māna ʻai.
chewing tobacco. Paka nau.
Cheyenne. Kene.
Chicago. Kikako.
chick. *See* **chicken.**
chicken. Moa; moa hiwa, moa ʻalae *(black);* moa lawa, moa uakea *(white);* moa ʻula hiwa *(black with red at neck and rump);* moa nēnē *(speckled);* moa pua hau *(yellow);* piopio *(at about the fryer stage). The chicken is a chief, the chicken sits on top of the house,* he liʻi ka moa, kau ana ka moa i luna o ka hale *(FS 101). Chicken house,* hale moa. *Little chicken,* moa keiki, ʻioʻio moa, kīnana. *Little chicks, bristling down (FS 81),* moa keiki, kukū ka heuheu *(fear of a great warrior). Scatter everywhere peeping chicks in the forest, chilled and fleeing (FS 81),* ʻauheʻe liʻiliʻi, ʻioʻio moa o ka nahele, i ka lī a ke ʻauheʻe nui *(defeat in war).*
chicken pox. Maʻi puʻupuʻu liʻiliʻi.
chickweed. Nehinehāuli.
chief. Aliʻi, lani. *See sayings,* **ʻawaʻahia, kalo, leo, mana 2, uhaʻi 2, chicken, cliff.** *Tenure of a chief,* noho aliʻi. *To claim relationship to a chief,* hoʻopilipili aliʻi, piʻi aliʻi. *To boast of association with a chief so as to enhance one's glory,* pai aliʻi. *Offspring of a chief,* hua lani, mamo aliʻi, pua aliʻi, kama lani. *Chief of an island or district,* aliʻi ʻai moku, aliʻi kū i ka moku, aliʻi noho moku. *To make a chief,* hoʻāliʻi. *Epithets for an exalted chief:* lani aliʻi, ēwe lani, hiwa lani, mana weu lani, lani kua kaʻa, aliʻi pūʻō lani, koholua. *Peace is a chief, the lord of love,* he aliʻi ka laʻi, he haku na ke aloha *(poetic). In poetry, the presence of a chief may be signified by references to rain, mist, rainbow, hawk, cliff, or great height.*
chiefess. Aliʻi wahine, aliʻi.
chief justice. Luna kānāwai kiʻekiʻe a kaulike.
chiefly. Lani, leʻolani, kūlani, aualiʻi, papa aliʻi. *See* **chief.**
chief of police. Luna mākaʻi.
chieftainship. Noho aliʻi.
Chihuahua. Kihuahua.
child. Keiki, kama; nōpuʻu *(Niʻihau). Also:* lei, pua, liko, ʻōpuʻu, hāpuʻu, hānau, pokeʻo. *See* **orphan.** *Beloved child,* kama lei, pua lei, lei kau maka, keiki punahele. *Only child,* kama kahi, hua kahi, hānau kahi *(see saying,* **ʻaʻo**). *Oldest child,* makahiapo, hiapo, hānau mua. *Youngest child,* keiki hope loa, muli hope. *Royal child,* keiki aliʻi, kama lani, lei lani, pua lani. *Adopted child,* keiki hānai, keiki hoʻokama. *Illegitimate child,* keiki manuahi, hua hāʻule. *One who tends a child,* kahu keiki. *Mischievous child,* keiki kolohe, kolekolea. *Child who stays near a parent,* hiʻialo. *To carry, and care for, a beloved child,* hiʻialo, hiʻipaka, hiʻipoi, hiʻilei. *To bear a child,* hānau, hua, keiki, loaʻa. *Cere-*

mony for first-born child, māwaewae. *Child's disease,* ma'i keiki, 'ea. *To instruct a child,* hi'ipaka.

childbearing. Hānau kama.

childbirth. Hānau, hānau keiki 'ana, ho'ohānau. *See* **discharge.**

childhood. Wā kamali'i, wā keiki, wā li'ili'i, wā 'u'uku. *Also:* poke'o. *Childhood playmate,* hoa kamali'i.

childish. Ho'okamali'i.

childless. Kama 'ole, keiki 'ole, lālā 'ole. *Cf.* **barren.**

children. Kamali'i; 'ohā *(fig). Two children reared together,* kama lua. *Children who leave home,* hi'ikua. *Children of Israel,* mamo o 'Ikela'ela. *To bear many children,* hānau kama, ho'olu'a.

Chile, Chilean. Kili, Kile.

chili peppers. Nīoi *(for various types, see Haw.-Eng. entry and entries that follow it).*

chilly. Hu'ihu'i, lī, ko'eko'e, make anu, anuanu. *Also:* pūanuanu, lī lua, naoa, maka'ele'ele, hau'oki, mū'ululū, kū'ululū, kalakū, 'uhē. *See* **cold.** *To get chilly,* pi'i ke anu.

chime. Ō.

chimney. Puka uahi; aniani ipu kukui, 'omo, 'omo ipu kukui *(lamp).*

chimpanzee. Kimepani.

chin. 'Auwae. *Also:* ka'olo, 'olo; 'ā'ī 'olo'olo *(double). Mature chin,* 'auwae o'o *(unsocial, unfriendly). Yellowed chin,* 'auwae lenalena *(of old age).*

China. 1. *The country.* Pākē, Kina, 'Āina Pākē; 'āina pua *(poetic).* 2. *(Not cap.) Crockery.* Pā a me nā pola like 'ole.

Chinese. Pākē, Kina; Kinikiu *(uncomplimentary name).*

Chinese banana. Mai'a Pākē.

Chinese New Year. Konohī.

Chinese rice flower. Mikilana.

chink. 'Akaka. *Chinks,* pukapuka.

chip. Māmala, hunahuna ho'okala *(as of wood);* unu *(of stone);* mā'i'o *(crockery).*

chiropractor. Kauka ha'iha'i iwi.

chirp. 'Io, kio, 'ō'io'io, mā'io'io, pio, nēnē, hānēnē; hae *(noisily);* mūkekeke, kīkīko'u.

chisel. Pao, kila, ko'i pāhoa, lipi; 'o'oma *(gouge);* pōhaku pao *(stone);* kila pao *(steel);* ko'i hō'oma.

chitchat. 'Ō'io'io, kamaka'ilio, nuku ho'omau.

chiton. Kuapa'a.

chlorine. Kaloline.

chloroform. Lā'au ho'ohiamoe, lā'au moe.

chocolate. Kokoleka.

choice. 1. *Selection.* Koho, wae 'ana. *First choice,* koho mua. *Right choice,* koho pololei. *Choice song,* mele koho 'ia. 2. *Of high quality.* Laha 'ole, mea laha 'ole, hiwa; 'ele'ī *(fig).*

choir. Papa hīmeni.

choke. Laoa, pu'ua, kalea *(intransitive);* 'umi *(transitive);* kāhihi *(as by weeds);* ha'u *(as with sobs). Choking sensation,* kā'awe'awe.

choking. 'Umina.

cholera. Kolela, ma'i kukule.

choose. Koho, ho'okoho, wae, ho'owae, waewae. *To choose rightly,* koho pololei. *To choose arbitrarily, at random,* koho honua.

choosy. Waewae, kamalani, kūlana waewae.

chop. Kua, kākā, 'oki'oki, 'āpahu, pokepoke; 'āpana *(as of lamb). Chopped off,* pahupū.

choppy. 'Ahulu, hānupa; kepakepa, pikipiki'ō, hao'a.

chopsticks. Lā'au 'ai, lā'au lālau mea 'ai.

choral group. Papa hīmeni.

choral singing. Hīmeni puwalu.

chord. Kīko'o *(of an arc);* hua māhoe *(in music).*

chorus. Hui, mele hui *(of a song). See* **choral group.**

chrisom. Kelema.

Christ. Kristo, Karisto. *Jesus Christ,* Iesu Kristo.

Christian. Kalikiano, Kristiano, Kilikiano, Kiritiano.

Christian Endeavor Society. 'Ahahui Hō'ikaika Kalikiano. *See* **Young People's Christian Endeavor Society.**

Christianity. Ho'omana Kalikiano.

Christian Science. Ho'omana Na'auao.

Christmas. Kalikimaka, Kalikamaka.

Christmas-berry tree. Wilelaiki; nani-o-Hilo *(Moloka'i).*

Christmas Eve. Ahiahi Kalikimaka.

Christmas tree. Lā'au Kalikimaka.

chronic. Ma'amau, kuluma. *Chronic illness,* ka'a ma'i, ma'i kuluma, ma'ima'i, ōma'ima'i.

chronicle. Mo'olelo.

Chronicles. 'Oihana Ali'i *(Biblical).*

chronology. Manawa, hō'ike manawa, palapala hō'ike manawa, kuhikuhi o ka manawa.

chronometer. Kalanomeka.

chrysalis. Wili'ōka'i, 'ōwili'ōka'i *(of night moth).*

chrysanthemum. Pua Pākē; pua Pākē pihi *(dwarf). Varieties:* haleloke, wailuku.

chrysolite. Kelukoliko.

chrysoprase. Kelukopelako.

chubby. Nepunepu, mākolukolu; pōlunu *(rare). See* **idiom, octopus.**

chuckle. 'Aka iki.

chum. 1. Makamaka. 2. *For fish.* Kūpalu, ho'olulu.

church. Hale pule, luakini, pule; 'ekalekia, ekalesia *(the organization, not the building). Church census,* helu 'ekalekia.

Church of Jesus Christ of Latter-Day Saints. Ho'omana o Iesu Kristo o nā Po'e Ho'āno o nā Lā Hope Nei.

churn. Ipu ku'i waiūpaka, ku'i.

chutney mango. Manakō kāne, manakō kū kāne.

cider. Kaika, kika, wai 'ōhi'a.

cigar. Kīkā.

cigarette. Kikaliki.

cigar flower. Kīkā, pua kīkā.

cinder. 'Ākeke, pula lānahu, lānahu pōhaku; hunaahi *(live);* one 'ā *(volcanic).*

cindery. 'Ākeke, makaili.

cinema. Ki'i 'oni'oni.

cinnamon. Kinamona.

circle. Apo, pō'ai, pōhai, ho'owiliwili; pō'aha *(as of flowers);* — *of canoes,* ponawa'a *(rare); circumference of a —,* kahapō'ai; *radius of a —,* kahahānai; *tangent of a —,* kahapili.

circuit. Ka'apuni, apo, pō'ai, puni.

circuit court. 'Aha ka'apuni, 'aha ho'okolokolo ka'apuni.

circuit judge. Luna kānāwai ka'apuni.

circuitous. Lauwili, lauwiliwili, ka'awiliwili.

circular. Poepoe.

circulate. Ho'olaha, ho'olaulaha, wiliau; nakulu *(as a rumor),* lana *(as blood);* holo ka'apuni.

circulated. Laulaha, laha.

circulatory system. Māno wai.

circumcise. Kahe, kahe ule, 'oki poepoe. *Also:* kaha ule, ōmu'o. *See* **subincise.** *Circumcised penis,* ule kahe.

circumference. Anapuni, kahaapo; kahapō'ai *(of a circle).*

circumnavigate. Holopuni, pō'ai haele, pō'ai puni.

circumspect. Me ke akahele, nihi, nihinihi.

circumstance. 'Ano. *Under these circumstances,* malalo o kēia mau 'ano.

circumvent. Ke'ake'a. *See* **prevent.**

circus. Hō'ike'ike; keaka lio *(horse show).*

cirro-cumulus clouds. 'Ōpua maka 'upena, kaha'ea.

cistern. Luawai, ki'o, lua ho'oki'o wai.

citizen. Kupa, maka'āinana. *Fellow citizen,* hoa maka-'āinana.

citizenship papers. Palapala ho'okupa.

citron. Kikelona.

city. Kūlanakauhale, kūnanakauhale, kūlanahale, kūnanahale. *City of refuge,* pu'uhonua.

civic. Kīwila, siwila.

civil. 1. *See* **polite.** 2. *Pertaining to citizens.* Kīwila, siwila.

civil case. Hihia waiwai.

civil code. Kānāwai kīwila.
civil engineer. *See* **engineer.**
civilian. Kīwila, siwila.
civilian laborers. Poʻe limahana kīwila.
civilization. Ka nohona mālamalama o ka lāhui, aokanaka.
civilize. Hoʻomālamalama.
civilized. Hoʻonaʻauao ʻia.
civil laws. Kānāwai kīwila.
civil rights. Pono kīwila.
civil service. Hana kīwila.
civil war. Kaua kūloko.
clabbered milk. Waiūhakuhaku.
claim. Palapala hoʻopiʻi; palapala kumu kuleana ʻāina, kuleana *(for land);* koi. *Claims for damage,* koi pohō.
claimant. Mea nāna ke kuleana, mea e koi ana, mea koi.
claim number. Kuleana helu.
clam. ʻŌlepe, pāpaua, paua.
clammy. ʻĀlikalika.
clamorous. ʻIkuwā, olokē, ʻuwā nui.
clamp. ʻŪmiʻi, ʻumiki, ʻūpiki; ʻūmiʻi pepa *(paper). Needle clamp on a sewing machine,* kūʻau kui kele. *Clamps for canoe,* pūkiʻi waʻa, kuamoʻo.
clan. *No Hawaiian term in the anthropological sense; see* **family, ʻalaea, ʻohana.**
clandestinely. Malū, peʻe.
clang. Kē, kanikē.
clap. Paʻi, paʻipaʻi, paʻipaʻi lima; kuʻi *(as of thunder). To clap the hands against the body,* ʻūpoʻipoʻi. *To clap the hands with the palms slightly cupped,* kilipoʻipoʻi.
clapper. ʻUlu, ʻulu kani *(bell).*
claret. Kalaleka.
clarification. Hoʻākaaka.
clarify. Hoʻākaaka, hoʻomōakaaka, hoʻopohala, hoʻaʻiaʻi.
clarinet. Kalioneke.
clarity. Mōakaaka, moakāka, moaka, aliali, ali, mālamalama.
clash. 1. *Sound.* Kuʻi, kanikē. **2.** *Conflict.* Hoʻokūʻē.
clasp. Miʻi, apo, lou, pūʻili, pūliki; pūlima *(hands);* ʻūmiʻi; ʻūmiʻi paʻa *(firmly).*
class. Papa. *Chiefly class,* papa aliʻi. *Leading class,* papa poʻo. *Middle class,* papa waena. *Second class,* papa lua. *Commoner class,* hū, makaʻāinana, noanoa.
classic. Panina.
classification board. Papa hoʻonohonoho.
classify. Hoʻonohonoho, hoʻonohonoho papa, kūkulu papa.
classmate. Hoa kula.
clatter. Kamumu, kāmūmumu, haukamumu, haluku, hālukuluku, hawewe, haukawewe, kawewe, nakulu, nākulukulu; hāʻukēʻukē *(in swinging back and forth).*
clause. Māmalaʻōlelo.
claw. Mikiʻao, mānea, maiʻao, māiʻuʻu *(bird);* niho, niho kīlou *(crab). To claw,* koe, walu, ʻuwalu, waluhia, waluwalu, waʻu, uwaʻu, waʻuwaʻu, wawalu.
clawing. Waluna.
clay. Pālolo, lepo kāwili, lepo mānoanoa, lepo ʻūlikalika. *Kinds:* lepo kuhue, maʻaʻulaʻula, lepo kīʻaha. *Clay pit,* lua pālolo. *Clay dish,* pā lepo. *Clay pot,* ipu lepo. *Clay vessel,* lepo kīʻaha.
claylike. Pālololo, ʻūlika, lina.
clean. Maʻemaʻe; pōlani *(rare). To clean,* hoʻomaʻemaʻe, holoi, hoʻoholoi, kaka; kuaʻi *(as a chicken);* ʻōhiki *(as ears).*
cleaning fluid. Wai hoʻomaʻemaʻe.
cleanliness. Maʻemaʻe. *See saying,* **kāpulu.**
cleansing. Hoʻomaʻemaʻe ʻana. *Also:* wehe, wehewehe, lele wai, lele uli, māwae, mōwae, mōae, lileiuli; *ceremonial —,* huikala; pūlimu *(for the sick);* kelea *(for a priest); mental —,* hoʻoponopono; *— fluid,* wai hoʻomaʻemaʻe.
clear. Mōakaaka, akaaka, akāka, mālaʻe, kālaʻe, mālamalama. *Also:* kōnane, kōnale, mā, laʻelaʻe, mōlaʻelaʻe, hoʻolaʻe, nōlaʻelaʻe, kaulaʻelaʻe, kānaʻe, mōhala, mōhola, mōhalahala, aniani, aliali, hoʻāliali, aʻiaʻi,
hoʻāʻiaʻi, alenale, nale, molale, pualalea, kea, palakea, paʻihi, māhelahela, ʻalaneo, leʻa, māʻila, keʻo, keʻokeʻo, aukahi, pāniani, miomio, hahu, pālala, molakea, pōlale, ōhāhā, palamea, maomao, mohā, mahikū, huaka. *To clear off (as weather),* mao, hoʻokuʻu. *To clear, as brush,* waele, wawaele, wele, welewele, welehia, kā, hoʻokuakahi, kuehu, mauele, mauwele, mauwelekā, lauhuʻe, kāheu. *To clear, as the throat,* pūhā, ʻuhūʻuhū. *To see clearly,* ʻike maopopo, maopopo ka ʻikena, ʻike leʻa. *Clearly thought,* piha pono ka manaʻo. *Hale-a-ka-lā is clear,* akaaka wale ʻo Hale-a-ka-lā *(of anything clear).*
clearing. Paia, mākaʻa, pāpū; kāhanahana *(as in a forest). See* **clear.**
cleats. Poukū *(supporting canoe seats).*
cleave. Māwae, mōwae, wāhi.
cleaver. Pahi hahau.
clef. Hōʻailona mele, kī. *Tenor clef,* kahahui.
cleft. Māwae, mōwae, kama.
clergy. ʻOihana hemolele. *See* **minister 1, priest.**
clerk. Kākau ʻōlelo, kupakako.
Cleveland. Kaliwalana.
clever. Akamai, noʻeau, loea. *Also:* lae ʻula, hoʻokāʻau, hoʻokāpuhi.
click. Hāʻukēʻukē, mūkā, kīkē, paʻina. *Click glasses,* kīkē kīʻaha.
click beetle, click bug. Kānepaʻina.
cliff. Pali, palipaʻa. *Tall or distant cliff,* pali loa. *Towering cliff,* pali halehale, pali hiʻi. *Sheer sea cliff,* hulaʻana. *Vertical cliff,* pali kū. *Base of cliff,* palipaʻa maoli. *Small cliff or slope,* papaʻi. *Small cliffs,* kīpāpali. *Notched cliff,* pali kuʻi. *Series of cliffs,* pali kuʻi, kakaʻi pali. *To stand on or fish from a cliff,* kūpali. *A cliff where tropic birds fly,* he pali lele koaʻe *(sheer, tall). Back a cliff, front a moon,* pali ke kua, mahina ke alo *(of handsome persons). Poetic references to* pali *may signify a handsome physique, a chief, or hardships, difficulties, and disdain.*
cliffbrake. Kalamoho, kalamoho lau liʻi.
cliffed. ʻŌpalipali.
climb. Piʻi. *Also:* piʻikū, pinana, piʻina, eʻe, kūʻoʻili. *To keep climbing,* eʻeʻe. *To climb mountains,* piʻi mauna, eʻe kuahiwi. *A place to climb with ropes,* ala kuʻukuʻu.
climber. Piʻi mauna, eʻe mauna, piʻi kuahiwi *(in mountains);* piʻi.
cling. Pili, pili pū; *— to the back,* pilikua. *Cling like a lizard,* pili ā moʻo. *Cling for no reason,* pili wale.
clip. ʻAko, paʻipaʻi, ʻūmiʻi, ʻumiki. *See* **paper clip.**
clipper ship. Moku kālepa.
clitoris. Keʻo, ʻiʻoʻiʻo, kanaka.
cloak. Koloka, kīpuka, kīhei, ʻahu, lulu; holokū *(Biblical);* paʻipaʻiniahā. *Feather cloak,* ʻahuʻula, hulu aliʻi.
clock. Uaki. *See* **hand, o'clock, time.** *Alarm clock,* uaki hoʻāla. *Face of a clock,* papahola.
clod. Pāpaʻa lepo, puʻu lepo *(of dirt).*
close. 1. *Near.* Kokoke, pili. *Also:* aukukū, papa, ʻōpili, pilipili, ʻōkuma, kūkini, pipipi, pīnaʻi. *Close friend,* hoa aliʻi. **2.** *Stuffy.* Paʻapū, ikiiki. **3.** *To shut.* Hoʻopaʻa, pani, panipani, panikū, ʻūpiki. **4.** *To finish.* Hoʻopau. *Close-out sale,* kūʻai hoʻopau.
closed. Paʻa. *Closed mind,* lae paʻa, poʻo paʻa.
closet. Waihona, keʻena waiho.
closing. Panina.
closure. Pani, panina.
clot. Puʻu. *Blood clot,* koko paʻakūkū, lapa koko.
cloth. Lole. *Also:* ʻaʻa, ʻaʻa lole. *Kinds of cloth: see* **calico, cashmere, coconut, corduroy, cotton, denim, dotted swiss, flannel, khaki, linen, muslin, sateen, satin, silk, taffeta, wool.** *Also:* ʻainakini, ʻalapia, lainakini, palaka, hōlei, kaha, kānekopa, kūakalikea, kuaʻula, laeloa, lahalile, nanakuka, paina, ʻulāliʻi. *Diaphanous cloth,* ʻaʻamoʻo. *Narrow cloth strip,* kahakahana. *Protective cloth,* kāʻai.
clothe. ʻAʻahu, hōʻaʻahu, hoʻokomo lole; ālaulau *(rare).*
clothes. Lole, ʻaʻahu, kapa komo, lole komo; ālaulau

(rare). Old clothes, lole kahiko, 'āne'ene'e. *Suit of clothes,* pa'a, pa'a lole. *Ready-made clothes,* lole i pa'a mua.

clothesline. Kaula kaula'i lole.

clothespin. Pine kaula'i.

clothes presser. Mīkini 'aiana.

clothing store. Hale kū'ai lole.

clotted. Lapalapa.

cloud. Ao; 'ōpua *(banks, billows). See* pua'a 3. Ao *is often followed by epithets, as* ao akua *(godly);* ao ho'opehupehu *(billowy);* aokū *(rain);* ao loa *(long, high, stratus; fig., distinguished);* ao 'ōnohi *(with rainbow colors);* ao 'ōpiopio *(white);* ao panopano *(thick);* ao 'ele'ele, lalahiwa, kōkōli'i *(black);* ao pōpolohua *(purplish-blue). Other names:* kaupua, 'ohu, 'īlio; ko'i-'ula; 'ōnohi 'ula *(rainbow-tinted);* paeki'i *(row);* ōpū ao, pōpuaki'i, ao pua'a *(banks or clusters);* 'ala'apapa *(long formation);* pālāmoa, kaha'ea *(in a mackerel sky);* ki'ikau *(variegated);* Pulelehua-Uli *(Lesser Magellanic);* Pulelehua-Kea *(Greater Magellanic);* pōhai 'ula *(red);* ka'apeha *(large mass). Cloud interpreter,* nānā ao, kilo lani. *See sayings,* **forecast, proud.** *Cloud pillar,* kia ao. *Opening in clouds,* 'ena. *Knowledge is built in cloud billows,* kūkulu ka 'ike i ka 'ōpua *(clouds were observed for signs).*

cloudburst. Ua lanipili.

cloudless. Kaula'ela'e, māla'e, pa'ihi. *See* **clear.**

cloudy. 'Ōmalumalu, hea, pululuhi, 'e'a'e'a, poluluhi, pūlawa.

cloven-footed. Kapua'i mahele 'ia.

clover. Lehua kahiki, ka'imi, pua pilipili, kīkānia pipili *(Spanish).*

clown. Mea ho'omāke'aka, niki o nā 'aka. *See* **jester.**

club. 1. *Organization.* Hui, 'ahahui *(for various kinds, see Haw.-Eng. entry and entries that follow it);* kalapu. *Also:* 'ahahui paio *(debating).* 2. *Weapon.* Lā'au, lā'au pālau, lā'au māka'i, pālau, newa; pīkoi, 'īkoi *(tripping);* hoa *(for striking). The reach of the club,* ka hu'a o ka lā'au. *To strike, as with a club,* hahau, ho'omoe, uhau, hau, hoa. *To wield a war club,* ka'a lā'au.

clubfoot. Kuku'e, 'aku'e.

club-lure. Melomelo.

club mosses. Wāwae'iole, lepelepe-a-moa.

cluck. Ko'uko'u, ko'u, pōkeokeo *(of a turkey hen). See saying,* **ko'u.**

clue. Māheu, meheu *(trace);* mahu'i *(faint inkling). To follow, as a clue,* ho'okolo.

clump. Ōpū, maha, moku, pewa. *Clump of grass,* ōpū weuweu, ōpū nāhelehele.

clumsy. Hemahema, pepe'ekue, hāwāwā, kākāki'i.

cluster. 'Āhui, huihui. *Also:* hui, huhui, huina, pae, ōpū, pōpō, pa'i, 'āwai, pī'ā, lālei, pūneki, kaka. *Cluster of grapes,* pa'i waina, huhui waina, pa'i huawaina, huina waina. *Cluster of fruit or flowers,* kaula lei.

clutch. 'Umiki, 'ūmi'i, lālau.

coach. 1. *Vehicle.* Ka'a. 2. *Advise.* A'o; kumu *(noun).*

coachman. Kahu ka'a, kahu lio.

coal. Lānahu, nānahu, pikimana. *Bituminous coal,* lānahu pikimana. *Coalbin,* waihona lānahu.

coal-black. 'Ele'ele pa'a, 'ele hiwa, hiwa pa'a.

coarse. Mānoanoa, pepe'ekue, 'ōkumu, hākuma, mā'aua, 'ā'aua, pakalua. *Also:* mākuakua, hūnunu, 'u'uluhaku, pa'apū, pe'e.

coast. Kapakai, makālae.

coast guard. Kia'i kai.

coat. Kuka, 'ahu; puapuamoa *(long-tailed dinner coat). Coat of arms,* hō'ailona no ke kūlana. *Coat of mail,* pale umauma unahi. *Coat tree,* oleole.

coated tongue. 'Ea.

coattail. Kōheoheo, puapua.

cob. Iho. *See* **corncob.**

cobra. Kopola.

cobweb. Pūnāwelewele, hihi pūnāwelewele.

coccyx. Kīkala.

Cochin China. Kokinakina.

cock. 1. *Fowl.* Moa kāne, 'ouo; moa mahi *(fighting);*

moa kākala *(with sharp spurs). See saying,* **pūkō.** *Sharp spurs of a fighting cock,* kākala, kākala-pī-kawai. *To act the part of a cock,* momoa, moamoa. *When the cock's spur is sharp and the comb red, then (he) gets on the perch,* a wini kākala a 'ula ka lepe o ka moa, a laila kau i ka haka *(of youth).* 2. *Gun part.* Kiko. *To cock a gun,* ho'āla i ke kiko.

cock-a-doodle-doo. 'O'ō.

cockatrice. Mo'o pepeiao hao.

cocked. Po'o kihikihi *(as a hat).*

cockfighting. Hakakā-a-moa, hākā moa, ho'ohākā moa.

cockleburs. Kīkānia.

cockroach. 'Elelū *(for various kinds, see Haw.-Eng. entry and entries that follow it).*

cockscomb. Lepe-a-moa.

cockspur. Kākala.

cocktail. Lama ho'ohuihui 'ia, lama pa'ipa'i, lama pa'ipa'i 'ia. *Poi cocktail,* 'ai kakale.

cocoa. Kōkō; kokoa *(rare).*

coconut. Niu *(for various kinds, see Haw.-Eng. entry and entries that follow it);* pu'upu'u niu, punia, 'ōka'a. *Parts:* nī'au, hā niu, wai niu *(coconut water or cream);* 'a'a, 'a'a'a, hā'a'a, 'a'amo'o, 'a'a niu, 'a'a lole *(cloth);* puka wai, hipahipa *(eye);* 'a'a puhi niu *(husk or fiber);* pua niu *(flower);* lau niu *(leaflet or frond);* lau'ō *(leaves near heart);* pō-'ae'ae *(axil of frond);* iwi pūniu *(shell);* lolo, lolo niu, iho, haku *(sponge);* lolo, holoa'a (holowa'a) *(sheath);* kumu niu *(trunk);* niu lolokia *(stem);* niu malo'o, niu 'ōka'a, 'ilikole, 'ō'io, haohao *(flesh);* wai niu, wai o ka niu, wailewa, wai pū'olo *(water);* kai niu, niu wali *(cream). For uses of coconut, see* **copra, pudding.** *Coconut drum,* pahu, pūniu. *Coconut grove,* ulu niu. *Coconut husking stick,* 'ōniu. *Polished coconut shell or bowl,* pūniu, 'a'apu. *Game of throwing tapa balls at suspended coconut shell,* nounou pūniu.

cocoon. Wili'ōka'i, 'ōwili'ōka'i, lohaloha, lohelohe. *Caterpillar in cocoon,* mū.

code. Kānāwai, kumu kānāwai, puke kānāwai, loina. *See penal. Code writing,* hua 'ālualua.

codfish. Pakaliao.

codicil. Palapala kauoha pāku'i.

cod-liver oil. 'Aila koka, 'aila.

coffee. Kope. *Coffee beans,* kope, kope lā *(sun-dried);* kope wai *(fresh undried). Cf.* pilo 2, 3, pino.

coffee grinder. Wili kope.

coffee grounds. Oka kope.

coffeehouse. Hale inu kope.

coffee huller. Lā'au ku'i kope.

coffee mill. Wili kope.

coffee senna. 'Auko'i.

coffin. Pahu, pahu kupapa'u. *Also:* holoa'a (holowa'a).

cog. Niho.

cohabit. Moe, ai, noho pū, meu.

coil. 'Ōwili, pō'ai, pōka'a, lāpe'e; pōka'a kaula *(of rope);* pū *(as sails);* wili, wili oho *(as of hair).*

coin. Kālā pa'a.

coition. Ai, ei; panipani *(vulgar);* pulupulu. *Spirit who brought dreams of coition,* Kaha'ula.

cold. 1. *Not warm.* Anu, anuanu; ko'eko'e, hu'ihu'i *(chilly). Also:* pūanuanu, konāhau *(of wind);* hau'oki, haua'īliki, 'āmu'emu'e, 'uhē *(bitter). To be very cold,* make anu. *To shiver, as with cold,* lī, ulupi'i. *Cold are nights without a mate,* ko'eko'e ka pō hoa 'ole *(of loneliness). For symbolism, see* **cool.** *Cold and chilly (see* **chicken)** *may also signify emotions, as of fear, sorrow.* 2. *Disease.* Anu. *Head cold,* hanu pa'a, punia. *To have a cold,* anu. *To get a cold,* loa'a i ke anu. *Frequent colds,* 'ea hanu pa'a.

cold sore. 'Ūkihi.

collapse. Hāne'e, hiolo; 'ananu'u *(as a balloon);* malana'opi *(rare).*

collar. 'Ā'īkala, kala, 'ā'īkala kū; 'ā'īkū *(high or stiff);* apo 'ā'ī 'īlio *(dog).*

collarbone. Iwilei; kau *(depression near collarbone).*

colleague. Hoa hana.
collect. 'Ohi, ho'ākoakoa, ho'āhu, ho'ili, hō'ili'ili, hāpuku, hō'ulu'ulu; 'ohi loa'a *(revenue). Also:* ākuli, ho'āuna, 'i'i, lapulapu, pūku'i, laua'e, ho'opūlehulehu. *To collect taxes,* 'ohi 'auhau. *To collect untidily,* mu'umōkākī.
collected. 'Ākoakoa, 'ohi 'ia. *See* **collect.**
collection. Ho'āhu, hō'ili'ili; lūlū *(church). Also:* huhui, huihui, ulu, hō'ulu'ulu, 'ulu'ulu, 'ohina, ahu, hupu. *To take up a collection,* 'ohi i ka lūlū.
collection box. Pahu.
collector. Mea 'ohi; luna 'auhau *(tax);* luna 'ohi dute *(customs).*
college. Kulanui.
collide, collision. Hālāwai ho'oku'i, ho'oku'i.
cologne. Wai Kolona.
colon. 1. *Anatomy.* Uha. **2.** *Grammar.* Kolona, kiko ho'omaha.
colonel. Konela.
colonial. Koloniala.
colonist, colony. Panalā'au.
color. Waiho'olu'u, kala. *Also:* wai, 'ano; muimuia *(inharmonious);* 'a'ai *(bright, contrasting);* pa'a *(solid);* hulu *(rare);* streaked with —, 'ōni'o; *variegated* —, kalakoa, pikapika, kuhe; *mixing of a brilliant with a lighter* —, a'ea'e; *to assume a softer, darker* —, pala'īloli; *to print with* —, *as tapa,* ho'ōni'o. *See* **sea.** *To sprinkle coloring matter on tapa and beat it in,* pa'ipa'i. *To draw the color line,* kaupale 'ili.
Colorado. Kololako, Kolorado.
color-bearer. Lawe hae.
color detachment. Huina lawe hae.
colored. Pa'a i ka waiho'olu'u, no'eno'e; nohi *(brightly). See* **black 2.**
colorful. Nui nā waiho'olu'u. *Also:* kauluwela, lua'ehu; palapalaulu *(rare).*
colt. Lio keiki.
colter. Hō *(of a plow).*
Columbia. Kolumepia, Kolumebia.
column. Kolamu.
coma. *Same as* **unconscious.**
comb. Kahi; — *of a bird,* puapo'o; — *of a rooster,* lepe, hoahoaka, kīlepa.
combat. Paio, kaua paio, hakakā. *To fight in single combat,* pilikua.
comber. Kākala *(surf).*
combination. Hui 'ana; hua ho'one'e *(of a safe).*
combine. Hui, hui pū, ho'ohui, ala pū, ne'epapa. *See saying,* **ku'i 2.**
combustible. 'A'ā koke.
combustion. 'Ā; 'ā wale *(spontaneous).*
come. Hele mai; mai *(in commands);* hiki mai; haele mai; uhaele mai *(plural);* — *out,* puka mai; — *back,* ho'i mai; — *back again,* ho'i hou mai; — *forth,* puka, pua, 'ōkupu; — *far or permanently,* hele loa mai; — *repeatedly,* hikihiki; — *accidentally,* hikiwale; — *swiftly,* hele koke mai, puahio; — *to pass,* kō 'i'o; — *forward,* ala mai; — *into view,* makili, 'ōme'o; — *up, as plants,* 'ō'ili ka maka; — *upon,* hihiki, —, *of many people,* hihihiki. *Also:* kākele mai, hē, leke, na'ū. *I'll come later,* mahope aku au. *So you have come,* eia kā 'oe. *The thought comes,* ke pi'i nei ka mana'o.
comely. Pūloku, 'ūpalu. *See* **pretty.**
comet. Hōkū welowelo, hōkū puhipaka.
comfort. 'Olu, ho'olu, maha, ho'onā. *Place of comfort,* kahua o Mali'o *(poetic). In poetry, coolness and rain may signify comfort. See saying,* **'uku lele.**
comfortable. 'Olu'olu, hō'olu, mōhalu, mōhaluhalu, mō'olu.
Comforter. Kōkua, Kōkua Hou; Palakeliko *(Catholic). See* **cheer.**
comic. Kolohe, ho'omāke'aka, hō'aka'aka.
comical. Ho'okolohe, hū'eu.
comma. Koma, kiko ho'omaha.
command. Kauoha, kēnā, ho'ouna. *Also:* 'ōlelo pa'a, leo, kauleo. *By command of,* ma ke kauoha o.

commander. 'Alihikaua *(in war);* ali'i, luna kaua.
commandment. 'Ōlelo kauoha, 'ōlelo paipai. *Ten Commandments,* nā Kānāwai he 'Umi.
commemorate. Ho'omana'o.
commemorative monument or pillar. Kia ho'omana'o.
commence. Ho'omaka, ho'okumu.
commencement. Maka mua, ho'omaka 'ana; hō'ike, puka *(school).*
commend. 'Āpono, ho'āpono.
commendation. Ho'omaika'i. *Letter of commendation,* palapala ho'omaika'i.
comment. Mana'o ho'opuka; wahi mana'o ho'opuka *(modest);* 'ōlelo ho'opuka. *No comment,* 'a'ohe mana'o. *I have just a small comment,* he wahi mana'o ho'opuka ko'u. *To make a comment,* hō'ike i ka mana'o.
commerce. 'Oihana kālepa.
commercial. Pili i ka 'oihana kālepa, 'imi kālā, puni kālā, mana'o kālā. *Commercial traveler,* kālepa ka'ahele.
comminuted. 'Ae *(as dust or powder).*
commission. Komikina *(board);* uku, uku 'ēkena, uku komikina *(pay);* ho'okohu, ho'āmana *(appointment).*
commissioned officer. Ali'ikoa, ali'ikoa i komikina 'ia, ali'i maoli *(old term).*
commissioner. Komikina, luna. *Board of commissioners,* papa komikina.
Commissioners to Quiet Land Claims. Komikina Ho'onā 'Āina.
commit. Hana, ho'okō. *In such phrases as the following, commit is usually not translated: commit perjury,* hō'ike wahahe'e; *commit adultery,* moekolohe. *I did not commit myself,* 'a'ole i 'ae, 'a'ole i hō'ole; 'a'ole i hō'ike i ka mana'o.
committee. Kōmike.
commodore. Komakoa.
common. Hana mau, ma'amau, laha, lauākea, laulaha. *Not common,* laha 'ole. *Common sense,* no'ono'o pono. *Common word,* hua 'ōlelo hana mau 'ia. *Common ownership,* kuleana waiwai like. *See* **common law, manure.**
commoner. Maka'āinana, kanaka, noa, 'ino, hū, noanoa, la'ola'o, lāhui pua o lalo, pulupulu kanaka, lepo, lepo pōpolo. *See saying,* **fish.**
common law. Kānāwai kahiko 'ole 'ia, kānāwai ma'amau. *Common-law husband,* kāne manuahi, kāne noho pū. *Common-law mate,* pili'ao'ao.
common noun. Ha'iinoa laulā.
commonplace. Pakuā, pakuwā.
commonwealth. Aupuni maka'āinana.
commotion. Haunaele, pi'oloke.
communicate, communications. Launa 'ōlelo. *See* **officer.**
communion. Komunio. *Holy Communion,* 'Aha'āina a ka Haku, 'Aha'āina Pelena. *Communion of saints,* komunio me ka po'e saneta. *Communion Sunday,* Lāpule 'ai Pelena.
communist. *No Hawaiian term:* po'e hilina'i na ke aupuni nā kuleana apau *(lit., people believing all powers are for the government).*
community. Wahi noho like o ka po'e.
compact. 1. *Agreement.* 'Ōlelo 'aelike. **2.** *Condensed.* Pa'a, pili maika'i, pa'apū, poepoe. *Also:* lawa pono, 'akipohe, pālanaiki. **3.** *Vanity case.* Poho pauka, poho ho'onaninani.
companion. Hoa *(for various kinds, see Haw.-Eng. entry and entries that follow it);* kekahi, kōkō'o. *Also:* kahi; lua, kama lua, pili lua *(of two).*
companionship. Pilialoha; pili lua, kōkō'olua *(two);* kōkō'okolu *(three);* kōkō'ohā *(four).*
company. Hui, 'ahahui *(association);* malihini, 'ōhua *(visitors). Army company,* papa koa, pū'ali koa, papa po'o, māmakakaua. *Trading company,* hui kālepa. *To move in a company,* ka'i, ka'i 'āuna. *Hofgaard and Company,* Hapakole Mā.
comparative degree. 'Anu'u waena, ne'ene'eu.

compare. Hoʻohālikelike, hoʻokūkū. *See* **incomparable.** *Beyond compare,* launa ʻole.
comparison. ʻŌlelo hoʻohālikelike, hoʻohālikelike, hoʻokūkū ʻana, manaʻo hoʻohālikelike.
compass. Pānānā, ʻūpā. *Compass needle,* pine.
compassion, compassionate. Aloha, menemene.
compel. Hoʻokina, koi, puʻe, hoʻokenākenā.
compensate. Uku.
compensation. Uku. *See saying,* **eat.**
compete. Hoʻokūkū.
competent. Mākaukau, mākau, lawa ka ʻike, kūleʻa.
compile. Hōʻuluʻulu, hōʻiliʻili.
complacent. ʻOluʻolu nō iāia iho, waipahē.
complain. Hoʻohalahala, namunamu, ʻōhumu, ʻōhumuhumu. *Also:* ʻū, kunukunu, kapakeʻu, kani ʻuhū.
complaint. Kumu hoʻopiʻi. *See* **complain.**
complement. Ukali *(as in grammar). Adjective complement,* ukali haʻiʻano.
complete. Piha pono, pau pono, hoʻopau, hoʻopaʻa, hoʻokō pono; holoʻokoʻa. *Also:* piha, hoʻokō, paʻa, paʻa pono, hoʻoholopau, hemolele, kaʻaoki, holopapa, kīkīkoʻele.
completion. Piha, pihana.
complex. Pohihihi, ʻano huikau.
complexion. ʻIli. *Dark complexion,* ʻili hāuli. *Fair complexion,* ʻili kea.
complicate. Hoʻohuikau, hoʻohihia.
compliment. ʻŌlelo hoʻomaikaʻi, ʻōlelo mahalo. *With compliments (as at end of a letter),* me ka mahalo.
compose. Haku; haku mele *(song or chant);* haku moʻolelo *(story).*
composer. Haku mele, haku leo mele.
composite number. Helu hana ʻia.
compost. Pulu, hoʻopulupulu, pākukui (kukui *leaf for taro beds).*
compound. Hoʻohui, ʻano hui. *Compound words,* nā hua ʻōlelo hoʻohui ʻia. *Compound proportion,* lakio like ʻano hui.
comprehend. Hoʻomaopopo, kuanoʻo.
compressed. Pūʻali, poepoe.
compromise. ʻAelike hoʻokuʻu ma kahi.
comptometer. Mīkini helu.
comptroller. Luna kālā, puʻukū, luna hoʻomalu.
compulsion. Kuko ā hoʻokō.
compute. Helu.
computer. Lolo uila, kamepiula. *Cf. page* x.
comrade. Hoa.
concave. ʻOʻoma, kewe; — *surface,* ʻili poʻopoʻo.
conceal. Hūnā *(transitive);* peʻe *(intransitive). Also:* uhi, poʻipoʻi, kīpoʻi, palai, palaina, nalohia, hūnākele. *Attempt to conceal,* ʻāpoʻipoʻi.
concealed. Nalo, nalowale. *See* **conceal.**
conceited. Hoʻokano, hoʻokiʻekiʻe, hoʻoio, hoʻokelakela. *Also:* ʻieʻie, hōʻieʻie, hoʻokanaʻoi, hoʻokanaie, kanaie, kaena, kaʻokaʻo, haʻikū.
conceive. Koʻu, mau, hāpai *(as a child);* haku *(invent);* hoʻomaopopo *(understand).*
concentrate. Kau nui ka manaʻo, noʻonoʻo pono, hoʻopapau; hoʻohui ʻoia *(bring together). Also:* kia, lelepau, lauakī, mākia, hoʻokō ʻana, kualena ka manaʻo, hāmauāua, ʻakipohe.
conception. Manaʻo *(thought);* koʻu *(becoming pregnant). To cause conception,* hoʻohāpai, hāpai ʻana, hoʻokō. *Medicine for women to induce conception,* hoʻohua kawowo.
concern. Kuleana, pono *(affair). To concern,* pili i, no.
concert. ʻAha hīmeni, ʻaha mele.
conch shell. Pū, ʻolē; ʻolēʻolē *(small). Conch horn,* pū ʻolēʻolē. *Other kinds:* pūpū puhi, makaloa, kanaloa. *Conch for rallying warriors,* pū waikaua.
conciliator. ʻUao.
concise. Pili pono ā kūlike, wehewehena kūpono a pōkole, ʻakipohe.
conclude. Hoʻopau, pau, hoʻoki; hoʻoholo *(decide).*
conclusion. Panina manaʻo, hopena, hope, panina,

ʻōlelo hoʻoholo, kīkīpani. *To jump to a conclusion,* lele ʻē.
concrete. 1. *Cement.* Kimeki, pōhaku puna. 2. *See* **specific.**
concubine. Haiā wahine *(Biblical),* hoʻokamakama.
concupiscent. Puni ai.
condemn. Hoʻāhewa, ʻāhewa, hoʻohewa, kūhihi.
condemnation. ʻĀhewa. *To seek condemnation,* ʻimi hala.
condensed milk. Waiū kia.
condescend. Hoʻohaʻahaʻa aku i kekahi.
condiment. Hōʻonoʻono ʻai.
condition. Kūlana, ʻano.
conditional. Mamuli o nā loina, koe nā loina. *Conditional permit,* palapala ʻae mamuli o nā kumu.
conditions. Nā mea ʻaelike *(terms).*
condolence. Hoʻolana kaumaha, hoʻomālielie i ke kaumaha. *Letter of condolence,* palapala hoʻālohaloha.
conduct. 1. *Deportment.* ʻAno o ka hana ʻana, noho ʻana. 2. *To lead.* Alakaʻi, hoʻokele, mālama, lawelawe, hana *(as a class).*
conductor. Alakaʻi. *Orchestra conductor,* alakaʻi o ka pāna.
conduit. ʻAuwai paʻa.
cone. Puʻu, ʻōpuʻu.
coney. Kone *(bird).*
confederation. Aupuni hui.
confer. Kūkā, kūkākūkā. *One with whom one confers,* hoa kūkā, hoa kūkākūkā. *To confer honors,* hoʻohanohano, pāpahi.
conference. ʻAha kūkā, kūkā kamaʻilio.
confess. Mihi, hōʻike i ka hana i hana ʻia. *Also:* mimihi, mihimihi, mimimihi, haʻi, haʻina.
confession. Haʻina; penikenia *(sacrament).*
confessor. Luna haʻi.
confide. Hōʻike i ka manaʻo huna. *See* **confidence.**
confidence. Hilinaʻi, manaʻoʻiʻo, paulele. *This is between the two of us,* mawaena wale nō kēia o kāua *(in confidence).*
confidential. Hūnā, malū, paulele ʻia. *Confidential friend,* hoa hilinaʻi, hoa ʻōhumuhumu.
confine. Hoʻomalu, hoʻopaʻa, hoʻopalena.
confines. Palena.
confirm. Hōʻoia, ʻāpono, ʻae; kopilimakio *(sacrament). One who confirms,* hōʻike paʻa.
confirmation. Kopilimakio *(religious);* hōʻoia, hoʻokō, ʻae.
confirmed. Hōʻoia ʻia, ʻāpono ʻia, ʻae ʻia, pāpālima.
confiscate. Lawe ma ke ʻano kāʻili; alāiki *(rare).*
conflict. Kūʻē, hakakā, paio.
conform. Kū, hoʻokūlike, hoʻokūpono.
conformity. Kūlike.
confound. Hoʻokahuli, hoʻohuikau.
confront. Kū he alo he alo, pāpū, kū i ke alo.
confuse. Hoʻopohihihi, hoʻohuikau. *Also:* hōkai, hoʻopōnaʻanaʻā, hoʻaleʻale, hoʻopūhili, pahili, hoʻoleʻoleʻo, hōleʻoleʻo, nāwā, kūālauwili, peʻelulu.
confused. Huikau, pohihihi, pōnaʻanaʻā. *Also:* hili hewa, hauhalakī, pōkaʻakaʻa, ʻānoni, piʻoloke, hoʻopalai, nunuʻa, laukua, noni, pilihua, pūhili, hāʻekā, naʻanaʻa, nāhili, lihili. *See sayings,* **huikau, nāwao 1.**
confusion. Huikau, haunaele, pōnaʻanaʻa, piʻoloke. *Also:* hōkai, hili hewa, palalē, uluāoʻa, peʻelulu. *Mental confusion,* hili hewa ka noʻonoʻo. *To look about or search in confusion,* hōʻāʻā. *To turn the face away in confusion,* palai, palaina.
congeal. Paʻakūkū, paʻa.
congenial. ʻOluʻolu *(kind).*
congested. Paʻapū, kūpalaka, pupupu.
congratulate. Hoʻomaikaʻi.
congratulations. Hoʻomaikaʻi ʻana, ʻōlelo hoʻomaikaʻi.
congregate. Hoʻākoakoa, hui.
congregation. Anaina; ʻaha pule, anaina hoʻomana *(for worship).*

Congregational. Kalawina; 'Ahahuina *(rare).*
congress. 'Aha'ōlelo lāhui *(as of the United States);* 'aha'ōlelo nui.
conifer. Paina, lā'au ka'a.
conjecture. Mana'o wale, haku wale. *Also:* nalu, nūnē.
conjugate. Hō'aui, ho'ololi 'ōlelo.
conjugation. Hō'aui 'ana, ho'ololi 'ōlelo.
conjunction. Huipū *(part of speech).*
connect. Ho'oku'i, ho'ohui.
Connecticut. Konekikuka, Konetikuta; Konekikaka, Konetikata.
connection. Pili, pili 'ana, pilina, hui 'ana, launa.
conquer. Lanakila, lawe pio, na'i, kūna'ina.
conquered. Pio. *See* eo.
conqueror. Na'i.
conquest. Lanakila, lawe pio 'ana, kūna'ina, na'ina.
conscience. Lunawaemana'o, luna'ikehala.
conscientious. Ho'opono i ka hana.
conscious. 'Ike ho'omaopopo.
consciousness. 'Ike ho'omaopopo. *To lose consciousness,* pau ka 'ike, pau ka lohe; kauhola. *To regain consciousness,* pohala, ao.
conscript. 'Ohi *(soldiers).*
consecrate. Ho'ola'a, ho'okapu, poni, ho'oponi.
consecrated. La'a, la'ahia, kapu, ho'ola'a, ho'olāhui. *Consecrated nation,* lāhui la'a.
consecration. Ho'ola'a 'ana.
consecutive. Kekahi mahope aku o kekahi. *In consecutive sequence,* moekahi, pili aku nō ā pili aku nō. *Report consecutively,* hō'ike papa. *Count consecutively,* helu papa.
consent. 'Ae, 'āpono, ho'āpono.
consequence. Hopena, hope. *Of no consequence,* 'ano 'ole; komoi'i'i *(people).*
consequently. No laila.
conservative. Make'e kūlana.
conservatory. Hale ho'oulu mea kanu.
consider. No'ono'o pono, mana'o, kau paona, kākepakepa. *Cf.* meditate.
considerate. Leo 'ole, no'ono'o. *Considerate of parents,* no'ono'o makua.
consideration. Maliu 'ana. *In consideration for,* no, mamuli o.
consign. Ho'oili.
consignment. Waiwai ho'oili 'ia.
consolation. Hō'olu'olu 'ana, 'olu'olu.
console. Hō'olu'olu, ho'onā.
consolidate. Ho'ohui ā ho'opa'a.
consonant. Leokanipū, hua palapala leo hui, hua leo hui.
conspicuous. Ahuwale, 'ō'ili lua, 'ike wale 'ia.
conspiracy. 'Ōhumu, 'ōhumu kipi, 'ōhumu 'ino.
conspire. 'Ōhumu. *To conspire against,* kipi, 'ōhumu kipi.
constant. Mau, kūpa'a. *Also:* kiakahi, kūmaumau, maukoli, maumau, pīna'i.
Constantinople. Konakinopela.
constellation. Huihui, ulu hōkū. *See* planet, star, Aquila, Big Dipper, Boötes, Corona Borealis, Gemini, Hyades, Leo, Lyra, Orion, Pleiades, Southern Cross. *For some unidentified constellations, see* Hakamoa, Kao Ea, Kao Makali'i, Kawa-o-Makali'i, Keho'oea, Lawai'a, Maka-'imo'imo, Makaiwa, Makeaupe'a, Mekeaupe'a, Nā-hōkū-pā, Nā-lālani-a-pili-lua, Naue-a-ke-au-haku.
consternation. Pi'oloke.
constipation. Kūkae pa'a, lepo pa'a, papakū; kā'ana-'ana *(rare).*
constitution. Kumukānāwai *(document);* olakino *(bodily).*
constitutional. Kū i ke kumukānāwai.
constitutional convention. 'Aha 'elele hana kumukānāwai.
constrain. Kāohi.
constricted. Pū'ali.
construct. Kūkulu, hana.

consul. Kanikela, kanikele.
consulate. Wahi noho o ke kanikela.
consult. Kūkā, kūkākūkā, 'ōlelo kūkā.
consultant. Hoa kūkā, hoa kūkākūkā, kumu kūkā.
consultation. Kūkā 'ana, kūkākūkā. *Consultation place,* wahi kūkākūkā *(for chiefs).*
consume. 'Ai, ho'opau, kemu, hamu.
consumed. 'Aina; pau, pauka'a *(completely).*
consummate. Hana'i'o *(finish);* pala 'ole *(unblemished).*
consumption. *See* tuberculosis.
contact. Pā, ho'opili 'ana.
contagious. Lele. *Contagious disease,* ma'i lele, ma'i pālahalaha. *Contagious skin disease,* 'ili e'e.
contain. Aia maloko, kō loko. *Containing a book,* he puke kō loko.
container. Ipu, pū'olo, po'i, kā, poho, kula, hōkeo, hakai; *large —,* ipu nui; *small —,* kīpoho; *coral —,* puna; *gourd —,* 'ōlulo. *Containers for various purposes:* 'olo wai, 'ohe wai, hue wai pū'ali, hue wai, hue wai 'ihi, hue wai 'ihi loa, hano, kula kakalina, ipu 'au-'au, hue'ili, 'ōka'i, poho kāpalapala, ipu lei, ipu 'ala, pika pua, poho ho'olu'u, kā paka, 'io pa'akai, poho kaha pa'akai, ipu kua'aha, 'a'aho, poho aho, ipu mimi, hōkelo, hē.
contaminate. Ho'ohaumia.
contaminated. 'Ino, haumia, lepolepo, 'ino'ino.
contemplate. No'ono'o nui, nalu.
contemporaneous. Ulu hānau like, ola hanauna like.
contemporary. Hanauna like, o kēia wā.
contempt. Ho'owahāwahā, ho'okae, konākonā, 'a'ahuā. *Also:* ho'oūpē, kīkoni, helei, mahua, lauma'ewa. *See* helei 2, buttocks. *Contempt of court,* ho'owahāwahā i ka 'aha, ho'ohaunaele i nā 'aha ho'okolokolo. *To stick out the tongue in contempt,* ho'opake'o.
contemptible. Hō'aikola, 'ino loa. *See* wretch.
contemptuous. Ihu pi'i, ihu kū, konā.
contend. 'Ā'ume'ume, pā'ume'ume; paomoni *(rare).*
content. 'Olu'olu, hau'oli, luana.
contented. La'i, la'i ka nohona, 'olu'olu, luana, kili-'opu, 'ai i kalo mo'a.
contention. Paio, pāonioni, 'ā'ume'ume.
contentious. Pā'ume'ume, ho'opa'apa'a wale, hakakā wale, pāoni.
contents. Mea o loko. *Table of contents,* papa kuhikuhi.
contest. Ho'okūkū, ho'opāpā, pāpā; kahului *(athletic). Place used for competitive contests,* kahua ho'ouka. *To contest a will,* kū'ē i ka palapala kauoha.
contestant. Hoa pāonioni, moho, hoa paio.
contest song. Mele ho'okūkū.
contiguous. Pili loa, kokoke, a'e.
continence. Pākiko.
continent. 'Āinapuni'ole.
continual. Mau, kūmaumau, ho'okina.
continue. Ho'omau. *Also:* ō, kāmau, mau, ho'olā'au, noke, kaukoe, hele, ho'ohuelo, 'oi, ho'oniau, kinai, kaiua, mīkole, ho'omo'o. *See* hoe.
continued. Ho'omau 'ia.
contorted. Kewe, kūpaka, ho'o'i'ika.
contraband. Waiwai i pāpā 'ia e ke kānāwai. *To buy, as contraband,* kū'ai malū.
contraceptive. Mea e hāpai 'ole ai.
contract. 1. *Agreement.* 'Aelike, kepa, palapala 'aelike, ukupau. *Contract labor,* limahana malalo o ka 'aelike, kepa. 2. *Shrink.* Mimiki, miki, 'i'ika, ho'ohāiki. *Also:* mania, puku, nenene, ho'o'i'ika, kīkenenei, mōkio, pu'e'eke, pipika, menui.
contraction. Ho'opōkole 'ana.
contradict. Ho'oku'iku'i 'ōlelo, hō'ole, pāku'iku'i, ho'opāku'iku'i. *Also:* ke'u, āke'uke'u.
contrary. Kū'ē, pa'akikī. *Also:* nanahuki, 'ē'ē, 'oloke'a, kupake'e.
contrast. Ho'ohālike, ho'ohālikelike; 'oko'a *(noun). Contrasting colors,* nā waiho'olu'u 'oko'a.
contribute. Hā'awi.

contribution. Ha'awina.
contrite. Mihi.
control. Kāohi. *Also:* ho'omalu, holopapa, monia. *Control yourself,* kāohi iho. *Control the temper,* 'u'umi i ka inaina; kāohi i ka lelepī. *Under control of a supernatural power,* kalakupua. *To gain control,* pā.
controversy. Pi'ipi'i 'ōlelo, ho'opa'apa'a. *To cause controversy by arguing,* ho'opanepane.
conundrum. Nane huna, 'ōlelo nane.
convalesce. Polapola, palekana, konekonea, konenea, kōlili'i.
convalescent home. Home ho'olana ma'i; hale pipipi *(ancient kind).*
convene. Ho'ākoakoa, kāhea.
convenient. Kūpono.
convent. Nunele, kula Kakōlika.
convention. 'Aha, 'ahahui, hō'ike.
conversation. Kama'ilio 'ana. *Also:* pāpā'ōlelo, kūka'i kama'ilio, 'ōlelokīkē, 'ōlelokīkēkē; 'ōlelo laulā *(general).* See **chat, talk,** *and saying* **kalekale.**
converse. Kama'ilio, wala'au, kamakama'ilio, pāpā-'ōlelo. *Also:* kūka'i 'ōlelo, pāleo; 'uhene *(quiet, romantic);* paka'a.
conversion. Loli 'ana, huli 'ana, ho'ohulihuli 'ana.
convert. Ho'ololi, ho'ohuli mana'o, ho'ohulihuli. *He is a convert,* ua huli 'oia.
convex. Lalahū, kewe, lanahua.
convey. Lawe, halihali, ho'onoho.
conveyance. Ka'a. *Passenger conveyance,* ka'a hali 'ōhua. *Freight conveyance,* ka'a hali ukana.
convict. **1.** *Find guilty.* 'Āhewa, ho'āhewa. **2.** *Prisoner.* Pa'ahao.
conviction. **1.** *Found guilty.* 'Āhewa 'ia. **2.** *Belief.* Mana'opa'a.
convince. Hō'oia'i'o.
convinced. Mana'opa'a, ho'okū'i'o. *He is convinced his conduct is righteous,* he mana'opa'a kona, ua pono kāna hana.
convoy. Kūka'awe.
convulsion. Huki, ma'i huki.
coo. Nū, nūnū, 'ū, palalū.
cook. Ho'omo'a, kuke; 'ōlala, lala *(over a fire);* kahu, kahuna *(at an oven);* kahu 'ai *(taro or vegetable food).* See **bake, boil, broil, fry, roast.**
cooked. Mo'a; pāpa'a, pāpa'apū *(to a crisp);* pala, mo'a hapa, mo'a iki, mo'a kolekole, mo'a maka, māhinu *(underdone);* mo'a le'a *(thoroughly);* kokoko *(rare).* See **overcooked.**
cookhouse. Hale imu, hale umu, hale kāhumu, pāpa'i kahu, pāpa'i 'ai, kāhuna imu *(pre-European);* hale kuke *(modern).*
cooking school. Kula a'o kuke.
cooky. Mea 'ono, mea 'ono kuki.
cool. 'Olu'olu *(pleasantly);* hu'ihu'i *(chilly);* ma'ū *(damp). Also:* anu, anuanu, ho'ānu, hau, 'olu, ko'e-ko'e, aniani; anuhea; waianuhea *(as in mountains);* wai'olu, hauhau, ho'oma'alili, mō'olu, līhau, ho'ānu. *Cool chill,* lī anu. *To cool off,* hō'olu'olu, mani. *Poetic references to coolness may signify comfort, happiness, and sexual passion. See* **cold.**
cooled. Ma'alili; ma'ū'ū; kōaniani *(by a breeze).* See **cool.**
cooper. Kupa.
cooperate. Ho'olaulima, kōkua, huki like, kāko'o, alu, alu like, hana like. *Also:* lauaki, komo 'oko'a, kā'eu-'eu, puwalu, huliāmahi, kuahui, huihui ā kōlea. *To not cooperate,* hukikū.
cooperation. Laulima, kōkua, hana laulima. *See saying,* **ku'i 2.**
cooperative company. Hui laulima.
coot. 'Alae kea.
copal. Kopala. *Copal varnish,* waniki kopala.
Copenhagen. Kopenahakena, Kopenahagena.
coping. Kopina.
copper. Keleawe. *To engrave in copper or brass,* kaha keleawe.

copperas. Pa'akai hao.
coppersmith. Kaha keleawe, ku'i keleawe.
copra. Niu malo'o.
copse. Ōpū nāhelehele.
copulate. See **sexual intercourse.**
copy. Ho'ohālike; kope, kopena, mea like, kākau kope, lua, ponokope; ho'opa'i ā pa'i, ho'oniau.
copyright. Palapala ho'okuleana, ho'opa'akope, ponokope. *Copyright office,* ke'ena kākau kope. *To copyright,* ho'opa'a kuleana.
coquette. Wahine ho'oha'i; kāluhe *(rare).* See **flirt.**
coquettish. 'Ano ho'oha'i.
coral. Puna, ko'a, ko'ako'a. *Also:* 'āko'ako'a, hāko-'ako'a. *Kinds:* 'āko'ako'a kohe, 'ēkaha kū moana, kanahe, ko'a kea, kuanaka, limu, pa'akea, pā'eke, puna kea. *Coral head,* pūko'a, ko'a, māko'a, 'āko'ako'a. *Coral plant,* lōkālia. *Coral sea cavern,* hālelo. *Coral shoal,* ko'akā. *Coral flat,* 'āpapa, pāpapa, hāpapa, laupapa. *Coral reef,* kohola *(outer).*
corban. Kolepana.
cord. Kaula *(for various kinds, see Haw.-Eng. entry and entries that follow it);* aho, olonā; piko *(umbilical). Also:* 'aea, 'aha, 'aha'aha, 'ahakū, 'alihi, 'alihi kēpau, 'alihi pīkoi, 'alihi pōhaku, 'auku'u, kī'aho, kio, kūalu-'ula, mā'ilihau, 'ōka'i, pīkoni; kuaka, koka *(of wood).*
cordial. 'Olu'olu, hō'olu'olu, pumehana.
cordially. Me ka ho'omaika'i *(ending to letter).*
Cordova. Kokowa, Kodova.
corduroy. Kuakua, 'ie.
core. Haku, 'īkoi, pīkoi, iho. *Hard core in a breast,* haku waiū. *Very core of one's being,* iwi hilo. *Core of a speech,* iwi ha'i a'o.
coreopsis. Ko'oko'olau haole.
coriander. Koliana.
cork. 'Umoki, 'omo, pani, pani 'ōmole *(stopper). (No name for the material.)*
corkscrew. Wili wehe 'umoki. *Also:* wilipua'a, ulepua'a.
corm. 'Ohā *(of taro growing from older root),* 'ilikana *(under peeling, as of taro). The taro has formed a corm,* ua 'i'o ke kalo.
cormorant. Manu lawai'a; kakalakeke, katarakete *(Biblical).*
corn. Kūlina; kūlina 'ono *(sweet);* kūlina pohāpohā *(pop).* Mānoanoa ka 'ili *(calloused skin, corn on toe).*
corncob. Iwi kūlina.
corner. Huina; kū'ono *(inside);* kihi *(outside);* kohe *(mat);* huina alanui *(street);* hio. *Corner post,* pou kihi. *Looking out of the corners of the eyes,* maka kihi. *To make a corner in plaiting by overlapping,* ho'okihi.
corners. Kihikihi. *Full of corners,* kihikihi. *To make corners,* ho'okihikihi.
cornerstone. Pōhaku kihi.
cornet. Koneka, pū, pū ho'okani.
cornice. Mōlina. *Full of cornices,* 'ōlapalapa.
corn meal. Kūlina wali.
cornstarch. Pia kūlina.
Cornwall. Konewala.
corollary. Mana'opili *(as in mathematics).*
corona. Kalaunu.
Corona Borealis. Ka-ua-mea (?).
coronal suture. Hoai manawa.
coronary. A'a e hele ana i ka pu'uwai.
coronation. Poni mō'ī.
coroner. Kolonelo. *Coroner's inquest,* 'aha nīele kumu make.
coronet. Koleneka.
corporal. **1.** *Military.* Kopala. **2.** *Bodily.* Pili i ke kino, kō ke kino.
corporation. Hui, 'ahahuina.
corps. Pū'ali koa. *Marine Corps,* Pū'ali Koa Malina.
corpse. Kupapa'u, kino wailua, kino make, heana.
corpulent. 'Ōpū nui, momona loa. *Also:* hōlūlū, hīwa'awa'a; ka'apeha *(in a distinguished manner).*
Corpus Christi. Kino o ka Haku. *Corpus Christi procession,* ka'i malihini.

corral. Pā, pā ʻaʻaho. *Various types:* pā ʻeke, pā hoʻopuni, pā loa, pā pine, pā ʻupena, pā wāwahi pipi.

correct. Pololei, pono. *To correct,* hoʻopololei, hoʻopono, hoʻoponopono, hoʻomaikaʻi. *Also:* niolo, maiau.

correspond. Launa palapala, hololeka, kūkaʻi leka *(write letters);* pili, like me.

correspondence. Launa palapala.

correspondent. Kākau leka.

corrode. Popo, popopo, ʻaʻai. *Bitter sad thoughts that corrode,* manaʻo ʻaʻai ʻawa kaniʻuhū.

corrugated. Oloolo. *Corrugated iron,* pilihao, piula.

corrupt. Haumia, haukaʻe, pono ʻole, palahō, ʻapakeʻe.

corsage. Pōkĕ ʻōmou, pua ʻōmou.

corset. Kāliki. *Corset cover,* kāliki waiū.

Corsica. Kokika, Kosika.

cosmetic. Mea hoʻouʻiuʻi.

Cossack. Kokaka.

cost. Kumu kūʻai, kumu lilo. *Cf.* **price.**

costly. Pipiʻi, nui ka hoʻolilo, waiwai, kumu kūʻai nui.

costume. ʻAʻahu, lole.

cot. Moe ʻopiʻopi, moe ʻuʻuku.

cottage. Hale ʻuʻuku.

cottage cheese. Waiūhakuhaku.

cotton. Pulu, pulupulu, maʻo. *Also:* huluhulu, pulupulu haole, ʻie, kīʻailana *(variety grown in Hawaiʻi).*

cotyledon. Pepeiao.

couch. Hikieʻe *(large);* pūneʻe *(movable);* kokī, noho moe, moena; hoʻoleinamoa *(rare).*

cougar. Koukā.

cough. Kunu, ʻehē, ʻahē, ʻahēʻahē, kalea. *Also:* ʻuhūʻuhū, nokonoko, kuhō, ʻōkunukunu. *See* **whooping cough.**

council. ʻAha kūkā, pūkuʻi. *Privy council,* ʻaha kūkā malū. *Council of state,* ʻaha kūkā o ke aupuni. *Council of chiefs,* ʻahaʻula.

councilor. Kahuna nui; maka ʻou *(rare).*

counsel. Aʻo, aʻoaʻo, ʻōlelo aʻo, kuauhā, loio.

counselor. Loio, kākāʻōlelo, hoa kūkā, hoa kūkākūkā, kālaimoku, pohokano; lāuaʻaua, Palakeliko *(KJV).*

count. 1. *Number.* Helu, heluhelu, heluna. *To count ballots,* helu pāloka. *To count in order,* helu papa. *Counting game with chants,* helu pāʻani. **2.** *Title of nobility.* Kauna.

countenance. Maka, helehelena.

counter. Pākaukau.

counteract. Keʻakeʻa; ʻōkalakala *(evil by prayer).*

counterfeit. Hoʻopunipuni, ʻāpuka, ʻoiaʻiʻo ʻole, pelio. *Counterfeit money,* kālā hoʻopunipuni. *Counterfeit resemblance,* hoʻohālike kolohe.

counter sorcery or sorcerer. Kala.

countess. Kauna wahine, kaunakeke.

counting. Helu, moʻo helu. *Counting game,* helu pāʻani.

countrified. Kuaʻāina, hoʻokuaʻāina, pilikua, kaikua.

country. ʻĀina *(land);* kuaʻāina *(as distinct from the city);* kahiki *(any foreign country). Country person, see* **countrified.**

countryside. Kuaʻāina, kuauli.

county. Kalana.

couple. Lua, paʻa, papa lua. *Married couple,* paʻa male. *Bridal couple,* paʻa male hou.

coupled. Hui pālua, kaulua.

coupon. *No general word; see* **certificate, paper.**

courage. Koa, wiwo ʻole, hoʻāho. *Lack of courage,* hāʻawipio ka manaʻolana, lepahū. *See* **courageous.**

courageous. Makoa, hoʻokanaka, manawanui; ʻahi kananā *(idiom);* puʻuwai hao kila *(fig.);* pōpololū. *See* **courage.**

course. Ala, alanui, kahua. *Sea course,* ala kai. Holua *course,* holo holua. *Of course,* ʻoia, ʻoia hoʻi, hiki nō, ʻaʻole e ʻole. *In the course of events,* i ka hala ʻana o nā mea i hana ʻia. *In due course,* i ka wā kūpono. *Course in a meal, not known. To hold a canoe on course,* homa. *To turn off one's course,* kahakū, kuhikeʻe, halakī, hū ā puaʻa.

court. 1. *Legal.* ʻAha *(for various kinds, see Haw.-Eng. entry and entries that follow it). To accuse in court or take to court,* hoʻopiʻi, ʻoni. *To defend in court,* hoʻopale.* **2.** *Royal.* Aloaliʻi. *Members of the court,* aloaliʻi, kaʻalani. **3.** *To woo.* Hoʻoipo, hoʻoipoipo, hoʻonipo, hoʻopilipili. **4.** *See* **courtyard.**

courteous. ʻOluʻolu, waipahē, waipehē, ʻolu.

courthouse. Hale hoʻokolokolo.

court-martial. ʻAha hoʻokolokolo koa.

courtship. Hoʻoipoipo ʻana.

courtyard. Pā, kahua.

cousin. Hoahānau, kaukini. *Male cousin of the parents' generation,* makua kāne, makua kāne hanauna. *Female cousin of the parents' generation,* makuahine, makuahine hanauna. *Male cousin of parent-in-law,* makuahūnōai kāne. *Female cousin of parent-in-law,* makuahūnōai wahine. *Terms for brother and sister are commonly used for cousin of one's own generation.*

cousin-in-law. Kaikoʻeke *(of same sex). Female cousin of a male,* wahine; wahine makua *(older);* wahine ʻōpio *(younger). Male cousin of a female,* kāne; kāne makua *(older);* kāne ʻōpio *(younger).*

cove. Kūʻono, awa; hahape *(Kauaʻi).*

covenant. Pelika, berita, kuʻikahi. *Ark of the covenant,* pahu pelika. *Covenant of faith,* pelika o ka manaʻoʻiʻo.

cover. Uhi, pani, pale, wahī. *Also:* ʻili *(as of a book);* hoʻouhi, ʻomo; kaupale *(as an oven);* ʻaʻahu *(as with a blanket);* kīpaʻi, pāpalu, kīkanu, kīpoʻi, kilipoʻipoʻi, kīpoʻipoʻi, papapū, paʻapū; poʻipū *(cover entirely). Mattress cover,* uhi pela. *Cover of an opening,* pani puka. *Patchwork cover,* uhi ʻāpana. *Seat cover,* pale noho. *Hard cover (of a book),* ʻili paʻa.

coveralls. *Same as* **overalls.**

covering. Wahī, uhi, pale uhi, uhina. *Also:* hāliʻi, māmalu, pupupu, pāpalu; *doorframe —,* kikihi; *head —,* pāpale, pūloʻu, palelei; *ti-leaf —,* kui lāʻī, pale lauʻī.

covert. Hūnā. *See* **hidden.**

covet. Puni. *Also:* ʻālunu, ʻānunu, nunu, lunu, makeʻe, kuko, makauliʻi, hoʻomakauliʻi, minamina, ʻupu, leho, maka leho, lekia. *To covet wealth,* puni waiwai, makeʻe waiwai.

cow. Pipi wahine, pipi waiū; pipi kolo *(yearling).*

coward. Hōhē, hoʻohē, makaʻu wale; peʻe pao *(contemptuous).*

cowboy. Paniolo; paniola *(later variant);* keiki hoʻolei kīpuka ʻili.

cowfishes. Pahu.

cowhide. ʻIli pipi.

cowry shell. Leho *(for various kinds, see Haw.-Eng. entry and entries that follow it). Also:* kuoho, kupa, ʻōlūpalaha; pāuhu *(singly);* pūlehu, pūleholcho, pūleho hōlei, pūleho kāniʻo, pūleho ʻuia, pūleho palaoa, pūpū leholeho, ʻuala. *Wonderful how octopus notices little cowries,* nani ka ʻike o ka heʻe i nā pūleho liʻiliʻi *(of an older man eyeing young beauties).*

coy. Hoʻomāhie, palai maka, hōʻeno, hani.

coyote. Kaioke.

cozy. ʻOluʻolu.

crab. Pāpaʻi *(general name, for various kinds see Haw.-Eng. entry, also entries to follow; alternate names are in parentheses). See sayings,* **ʻeleʻelepī, niho mole.** *Crab claws,* niho kīlou. *Crab with yellow back,* pāpaʻi kua lenalena, ʻaʻama kua lenalena *(warrior). Corpse-eating black crab,* ʻalamihi *(ʻai kupapaʻu (of scavengers). Crab claws are spread,* kekē ka niho o ka pāpaʻi *(talk—but not action).*

COMMON KINDS: ʻaʻama, ʻalaʻeke, ʻelemihi (ʻalamihi, ʻeleʻelepī, ʻelepī), kūhonu (kuahonu), moʻala, ʻōhiki.

OTHER KINDS: ʻalakuma, ʻeʻeke, ʻelekuma, hīhīwai, kūkūau, kukuma, kūmimi, kūmoana, kumulīpoa, makaʻāloa (ʻāloa), makua-o-ka-līpoa, mū, ʻōhiki-ʻaumoana, ʻōhiki-maka-loa, paʻiwa, pākīkī, pāpā, paua, peʻeone, pōhakuhali, pokipoki (pokipoki-kua-paʻa), pokipoki-ʻau-moana, unauna (ōunauna, pāpaʻi-iwi-pūpū).

crabbed. *See* **bitter.**

crab grass. Kūkae-puaʻa-uka, mauʻu kūkae puaʻa.

crab louse. 'Uku papa.
crack. **1.** *Aperture.* Māwae. *Also:* nakaka, 'owā, 'owā'owā, weke, wekeweke, 'akaka, 'ōwae, ho'onahā, makili; puāhilo *(skin);* lepeulu, muaiwa *(in wood). To crack,* kīkē, kīmō, kīpō *(as nuts);* naka *(as earth).* **2.** *Noise.* 'U'ina *(as a gun);* kani 'a'ina, ko'ele *(as thunder);* kohā, ho'okani *(as a whip);* pāpa'a'ina *(as joints).*
cracked. Nahā, naka, makili; unahipi'i *(feet).*
cracker. Pelena. *Whole unbroken crackers,* pāpa'a pelena.
crackle. Pāpa'a'ina, kani 'a'ina, 'u'ina. *Also:* pa'ina, pa'apa'a'ina, 'e'e'ina.
cradle. Moe luliluli, moe paipai.
craft. **1.** *See* **handicraft.** **2.** *Boat.* Moku li'ili'i.
craftsmanship. 'Ike hana lima.
crafty. Ma'alea, 'āpiki.
craggy. Kākala, 'āpali, 'ōwa'awa'a, 'āwa'awa'a.
cram. 'Onou ā piha ku'i, ho'opiha nui, piha'ū. *Also:* papa'unu, hakē, kinanape.
cramp. Huki, lā'au; 'ūmi'i *(as in side);* wāwae huki; haikala *(severe);* haikala muku *(less severe).*
cramped. 'Ōpili, pipiki, muikiiki, pilikia. *Also:* 'ūpili, pāiki, pili'aiku.
cranberry. 'Ōhelo *(Hawaiian).*
crane. **1.** *Bird.* Manu 'io'io *(RSV),* manu 'ū *(KJV).* **2.** *Machine.* Kewe, hāpuku.
crank. Wili, kū'au wili. *Hand crank,* wili lima.
cranky. 'A'aka, kekē, kekē niho, 'eke'eke, ho'oke'eke'e. *Also:* pale ka 'a'aka, papaka'a'aka, malaia.
cranny. Ke'ena, po'opo'o, kū'ono, kīpolipoli.
crape myrtle. Kāhili, mikimiki.
crash. **1.** *Hit.* Ho'oku'i. **2.** *Sound.* Pohā, pahū; kīkē 'alāna *(as of rocks).*
crater. Lua, lua pele.
crave. 'I'ini, li'a; 'ono *(food).*
craw. 'Ōpū 'ai'ai *(of a bird).*
crawl. Kolo. *Also:* kokolo, makolo, nakolo, 'eu, 'e'eu, pūne'e.
crawl stroke. 'Au kolo *(swimming).*
crayon. Pena me nā waiho'olu'u like 'ole.
crazy. Pupule, lōlō, hehena, hewahewa. *Also:* 'ūlala, uluāhewa, 'ōpulepule, pahuluhope. *Cf.* **feeble-minded.**
crazy quilt. Kapa pohopoho.
creak. 'E'e'ina, 'u'ina; manunu *(as bones).*
cream. Kalima, kalima waiū; kalima hamo *(face). See* **coconut, ice cream.**
crease. Mino, 'opi *(as in clothes or paper);* kohe *(as in a hat). Also:* mimino, minomino, miona *(as in the buttocks). Creased with fat,* kī'oki. *To form a crease, as in a hat,* ho'okohe.
create. Hana, ho'okumu.
creation. Kumulipo, kumu honua.
creative. No'ono'o hana.
creator. Ka mea nāna i hana.
creature. Mea ola *(living);* holoholona *(animal);* manu *(bird);* mea kolo *(creeping);* holoholona lele *(flying);* i'a *(fish, mollusk).*
credentials. Palapala ho'āpono, hō'ailona.
credit. Hō'ai'ē; hua, heluna *(as for a university course). Buy on credit,* kū'ai hō'ai'ē. *Ask for credit,* hō'ai'ē. *Give him credit for working hard,* e ho'omaika'i iāia no kona hō'ikaika 'ana.
credit union. Hale hō'ai'ē kālā.
creed. Kumu mana'o'i'o, pelika o ka mana'o'i'o.
creek. Kahawai.
creep. Kolo. *Also:* kokolo, makolo, kaukolo, kō'ai, 'akolo, koene, ilo, hihi, nihi, kulipe'e, ne'e, ne'e he'e, nene'e, ka'uli'; 'e'eu *(as an insect). To creep with age,* kaikapū. *Creeping rain,* ua nihi. *Creeping mist,* 'ohu kolo.
creeper. 'Āhihi *(vine);* kākāwahie *(bird).*
cremate. Puhi ahi, puhi lehu, ho'olehu.
crematory. Wahi puhi ahi.
crepe. Pepa lei *(paper). Black crepe worn for mourning,* 'ele'ele kanikau.

crescendo. Ho'onui, nū *(in music).*
crescent. Hoaka.
crescent-shaped. Kikihi, kewe *(as the moon),* 'ōnaha. *Crescent-shaped design at base of temple drum,* hoaka.
crest. Wēkiu, wēlau, piko, nu'u; po'omahiole, pāpale, hulukoa, po'opāpale, puapo'o *(bird);* hoaka *(helmet);* 'ōmo'omo'o *(mountain);* 'ale, 'ako'ako, pū'o'a, hokua *(wave);* po'i, muku *(breaking wave). See* **top.** *Family crest,* hō'ailona kū'auhau.
crestfallen. Kū i ka hoka, mamae.
cresting. Po'ina *(of sea).*
Crete. Keleke, Kerete.
cretonne. Kalikone.
crevalle. Ulua *(for various types, growth stages, fig. meanings, see Haw.-Eng. entry and following entries).*
crevice. Naele, nao, māwae. *See* **crack.**
crew. Po'e ho'okele moku, po'e luina *(ship);* mea wa'a *(canoe).*
crib. Moe kamali'i.
cricket. 'Ūhini, 'ūhini lele, 'unihi; 'unia *(adult).*
crier. Kala, leo kala, luna kala *(public).*
crime. Kalaima, hewa.
criminal. Kalaima. *See* **penal code.** *Criminal case,* hihia kalaima. *Criminal procedure,* lawelawe ho'opi'i kalaima.
crimpy. 'Āpi'ipi'i.
cringe. Ho'opē, 'e'eke, 'eke, kaupē, ka'apē.
crinkled. Pipiki, pū'alu, pipika, 'ōpakapaka.
cripple. 'Ō'opa, hapaku'e.
crisis. Ulia pōpilikia *(emergency);* akaaka 'ole ka pono a me ka pono 'ole *(as of sickness, lit., not clear the well or the not well).*
crisp. Pa'apa'a'ina.
crisscross. Kaha pe'a, 'oloke'a, hō'oloke'a, kaupe'a, kahahiō *(mark).*
critic. Mea loi i ke 'ano; kē *(especially a hula critic).*
criticize. Loiloi, kē, paka *(often constructively);* ho'ohalahala *(faultfinding). Also:* kūhalahala, nio, āke'uke'u, welewele iwi, 'ainemanema, 'a'anema, nema, 'ākē.
croak. Ke'u, kohā, he'u, nēnē.
crochet. Lihilihi hana lima. *Crochet hook,* kui lihilihi. *To crochet,* hana lihilihi.
crock. Kelemania.
crocodile. Mo'o nui, kelokokile.
crook. **1.** *Bend.* Kīke'e, lanahua, lapu'una, ho'okeke'e, ho'okanahua, uake'e. *See ex.,* **pimple.** **2.** *Cheat.* Kanaka pale kānāwai.
crooked. Kapakahi, keke'e, kīke'eke'e, hapaku'e, nanahū, uke'e. *Also:* lāpe'e, lāpu'u, 'anake'e, napa, nāpai, kupake'e, hō'ewa, kihi loa, 'oeha'a, pākauāke'e, uhake'e, kālawalawa, nūke'e, 'ewa, pau'ali, pepe'e, pa'ewa, 'ehipa, kī'ōnaha, 'ūke'e, kākiwi.
crop. **1.** *Harvest.* Mea ho'oulu, mea kanu; 'a'ae *(third crop, as of taro).* **2.** *Of a bird.* 'Ōpū.
croquet. Kolokē.
cross. **1.** *Of disposition.* 'A'aka, nauki, ka'e, kekē niho, niha. *Also:* na'ina'i, kaki, pīkananā, kamaniha, ho'okamaniha, 'ainiha, kūkona, loko li'u, pōkole ka na'au. **2.** *Overlap.* Ke'a, pe'a. *Also:* kaha pe'a, ho'oke'a; lā'au ke'a, 'oloke'a *(wooden). Cross sticks,* 'ōke'a, lā. *Station of the cross,* ka'i ke'a. *To cross the hands,* 'ōpe'a; 'ōpe'a kua, ho'ōpe'a kua, kākepakepa *(behind the back). To cross the legs,* ho'ouka nā wāwae. *To cross one over another,* kāpe'ape'a. *To cross sticks,* kīpe'a. *To make the sign of the cross,* kuhikuhi i ke ke'a. *To cross the street,* hele ma kēlā 'ao'ao o ke alanui.
crossbar. Kī kaola.
crossbow. Kakaka.
cross-examination. Nīnau ho'i, ninaninau ho'ohuahualau, ninaninau pale.
cross-eyed. Maka 'āhewa, maka lalau.
cross-legged. 'Aha'aha; ne'epū *(rare).*
crosspatch. *See* **cranky.**
crosspiece. Mana, 'āmana.

crossroads. Huina, huina alanui, pahu manamana.
cross-stitching. Humukā, kā.
crotch. Kumuhele; kapakapa *(human)*; mana.
crouch. 'Ōku'u, ho'opū. *Also:* kīkenenei, ho'ōku'u, 'āpo'ipo'i, 'ekepue, pupue.
croup. 'Ā'īkū, nae 'ā'īkū.
crow. 1. *Bird.* 'Alalā *(see saying).* **2.** *Sound.* 'O'ō, kokō, kani, kekē. *Also:* 'o'o'ō, 'o'o'o'ō, uli. *First cockcrow,* moa kuakahi.
crowbar. Kolopā *(for a song, see Haw.-Eng. entry).*
crowd. Lehulehu, pihana kanaka, pū'ulu, anaina kanaka. *Also:* ho'okē, mōnoinoi, mīnoinoi, haluku, muikiiki, kūpina'i, kāō, puana, 'āluka, ho'omū, haiamū, lumi, maka kanaka. *See also* **nonanona, lē'ī.** *To move in great crowds,* kaheāwai *(fig.).*
crowded. Pa'apū, pihaku'i. *Also:* haluku,kukū, nunu'a, hālo'alo'a, kūhaluka, kāō, kūpiliki'i, 'ūpili, pupupu, kūpipi, pū'ika'ika, pilikia, pū'uki'uki, ūkūkua, aukuku, ku'ineki, piha pū'ika'ika, piha pūku'iku'i, ne'ine'i, hakakē, lēhau. *See sayings,* **kē 1, lē'ī.**
crown. Kalaunu, kolona, pāpale ali'i, lei ali'i. *Holy crown,* pāpale la'a. *Crown of a hat,* ipu, piko. *Crown of the head,* piko, mino. *Crown lands,* 'āina lei ali'i. *Crown prince or princess,* ho'oilina mō'ī. *Crown of thorns,* lei kākalaioa. *To crown a king,* poni mō'ī. *To crown with a lei,* ho'olei.
crown flower. Pua kalaunu.
crucifix. Ke'a.
crucifixion. Kaulia 'ia 'ana i ke ke'a.
crucify. Kaulia i ke ke'a, mākia.
crude. 1. *Harsh.* Lula 'ole, ho'oku'iku'i, hanahihi. **2.** *Raw.* Maka.
cruel. Loko 'ino, māino, hana 'ino, ho'omāinoino, ho'olaukōnā, hainā; pao, houhou *(in speech, fig.).*
cruelty. Hana 'ino, māinoino, ho'omāinoino, hana māino.
cruise. Holoholo moku, holo moana.
cruiser. Moku kaua.
crumb. Huna. *Bread crumb,* huna palaoa. *Crumbs,* hunahuna, oka.
crumble. 'Ūmikimiki, hehelele'i, lulumi, puehu, napele.
crumple. Pū'alu, lulumi, lumilumi, 'oupē, pī'ao.
crunch. Kamumu, haukamumu. *Crunching sound,* kāmūmumu.
crusade. Kelukake.
crusader. Koa kelukake, kulekia.
crush. Lomi, ho'oūpē, ho'opē, ho'omāui, 'ōpā, pākī, mīkā; pākīkī *(as pandanus aerial roots to make kava strainers).*
crushed. Ūpē, kaupē, lulumi, lumilumi, lumi, pē, pēpē, pakū, napele; pōlumilumi *(as in a crowd).*
crust. Pāpa'a. *Crust of bread,* pāpa'a o ka palaoa. *To begin to form a crust, as a wound,* olomio.
crusted. Pāpa'a. *See ex.,* **kūmau 2.**
crusty. Pāpa'apū.
crutch. Ko'oko'o kālele.
cry. Uē, uwē *(weep);* — *out,* kani, oho, 'uwā; puoho *(in alarm);* olo pihe, kāhea, huene, pū'alalā, pūhalalū. *Also:* hauwene, kaniā'au, 'ōmino *(weep). See* **onomatopoeia, shout.** *Teasing cry,* uē ho'ohune. *To cry loudly,* uē hāmama, pū'alalā, lele walo, kūō, kūwō, kani kohā.
crybaby. Uē wale.
crying. Uē, auēuē, nēnē. *See* **cry.**
crystal. Pōhaku a'ia'i.
cub. Keiki. *Lion cub,* liona keiki.
Cuba, Cuban. Kupa, Kuba.
cube. Pa'a'ili ono, pa'a'ili ono like, kupa.
cube root. Kumu kupa.
cubic. Pa'a'ili ono. *Cubic yard,* iā pa'a'ili ono.
cubit. Kūpika, kano.
cuckoo. Kūkū.
cucumber. Ka'ukama.
cud. Lualua'i. *To raise and chew the cud,* lualua'i.
cudgel. Newa. *See* **club.**
cudweeds. 'Ena'ena.

cue. 1. *Billiards.* Lā'au pahupahu. **2.** *Reminder.* Kumu ho'omana'o, 'ōlelo ho'omana'o. *To recite the first lines of a stanza as a cue to the chanter,* kāhea.
cuff. Pūlima.
cuff button. Pihi pūlima.
cull. Wae, 'ohi, kōhikōhi.
cultivate. Mahi. *Also:* olohi'o; kīko'u *(with a hoe or digging stick).*
cultivation. Mahi 'ai 'ana.
cultivator. Kalaweka.
culture. 1. *Customs.* Nā 'ike a me nā hana. *See also* **versed. 2.** *Agriculture.* Ho'oulu.
culture hero. Kupua.
Cumberland. Kumepelana.
cumin. Kumino.
cumulus cloud. 'Ōpua, kaha'ea.
cunning. Ma'alea, 'āpiki; 'ōlelo pahe'e *(speech).*
cup. Pola, ipu, kī'aha, kī'o'e; 'apu *(coconut shell);* 'auhuhu *(poison);* 'āpikapika *(suction);* pī'ao *(made of folded ti leaves);* dye —, kākākau. *Kava cup,* 'apu 'awa, 'olo 'awa. *Cup-shaped,* 'apu'apu, 'a'apu. *To cup the hand,* kī'apu. *To fold a leaf into a cup, form a cup of the hollow of the hand,* hō'a'apu.
cupboard. Pahu pā, waihona pā ipu, waihona ipu, halepā.
cup of gold. Ipu kula, 'āhihi.
curb. 1. *Street curb.* Ka'e. **2.** *To restrain.* Kāohi.
curds. Paka, bata *(Kin. 18.8, RSV).*
cure. Ho'ōla, lapa'au, ho'opolapola.
cured. Ola loa *(completely).*
curing medicine. Lā'au lapa'au.
curio. Mea ho'omā'ike'ike.
curiosity. Nīele.
curious. 1. *Strange.* 'Ano 'ē, kupanaha, kupaianaha, ho'onīele. **2.** *Inquisitive.* Nīele.
curl. Milo. *Also:* milomilo, 'ōmilo; pī'ao *(as leaves in heat);* kūpola; limu *(rare). To curl, as hair,* ho'omimilo. *To curl over, as a breaker,* huli.
curled. Pi'ipi'i; pākauāke'e *(rare);* — *in,* menui; — *up,* lāpu'u, lāpe'e. *To sleep curled up,* moe pupu'u.
curlew. Kioea *(fig., tall).*
curly. Pi'ipi'i *(as hair). Also:* pi'i, 'āpi'i, kāpi'i, mimilo, 'ānu'unu'u.
currency. Kālā, kālā aupuni.
current. 1. *Moving water.* Au, kai *(in the sea);* kai holo, wai kō; wiliau *(mixed);* aumiki *(outgoing); rapid* — *or what it carries,* kō'ie'ie. *Sea with a strong current,* kai kō. *To float or drift with the current,* lanaau. *Flowing current,* kōī au *(eloquence). Strong current,* au kanai'i, aukana. **2.** *Contemporary.* O kēia au, o kēia manawa.
currycomb. Kahi lio.
curse. Kūamuamu, amu, 'ānai, 'ōlelo hō'ino, hā'ili'ili, mōlia, heoheo, kā i ka 'ino.
cursed. Kūamuamu 'ia, hā'awi 'ia i ke akua, 'ānai 'ia.
curtail. Ho'oli'ili'i, ho'ohāiki; ho'oemi *(as expenses).*
curtain. Pākū, pale, pālulu, pālulu 'ao'ao. *Window curtain,* pākū pukaaniani, pale pukaaniani.
curve. Pi'o, kālawa, hālawa, hālawalawa, uma, ho'okiwi, lālani poepoe. *See* **curved.**
curved. Pi'o, kiwi, pāuma, kākiwi, kihikihi. *Also:* kikiwi, hualala, 'a'api, kī'ōnaha, mehani, naha, 'ōnaha, pauke'e, palakāhela, popoli. *Curved beak,* ihu kikiwi. *Curved over,* kiwi.
cushion. Kūkini, uluna, pulu, pela.
custard pie. Pai hua.
custodian. Mālama, kahu mālama; mālama hale *(of a house).*
custody. Mālama 'ana; ho'opa'ahao 'ana *(prison).*
custom. Nā hana i kuluma, loina, mea ma'a. *Also:* kuamo'o, welo, mēheuheu, pawa.
customary. Ma'amau, pa'a mau, kūmau, kuluma, laha.
customer. Mea kū'ai mai.
customhouse. Hale kuke, hale dute aupuni. *Customhouse officer,* luna kuke.
customs. Kuke, dute. *See* **custom.** *Customs duty,* kuke. *To pay customs,* uku i nā kuke.

cut. 'Oki, hō'oki, moku, mō, mokumoku, momoku, mokuhia, kālai, kaha; kua *(as a tree);* mahele, 'ako, 'ai kepa, ho'olepe; pa'ipa'i *(as a plant or the hair);* 'ō'ō *(as in bloodletting);* ka'akepa *(at an angle);* 'ōpaka *(in evenly matched vertical facets);* pāhi'a *(obliquely);* kahe, kahi *(longitudinally);* 'āpahu, ka'āpahu *(squarely off);* pa'i koli *(short);* mā'i'o *(raggedly);* kalakalai *(a little at a time);* ka'āpahu, pū'ā *(crosswise);* — *apart,* hele *(rare);* — *up,* helehele; — *off,* mu'umu'u, 'akumu, po'omuku, 'ōmu'o; — *off short,* 'ōmuku, 'ōkumu, pahu; — *up alive,* kākāola; — *into pieces,* ma'oki, ho'omākoli, 'oki'oki, paukū; — *in short pieces,* 'āpoke, poke, pokepoke; — *in half,* pahupū; — *in long slabs, as pig or fish for salting,* pākā; — *back, as a plant,* pākā. *To cut cards,* 'oki pu'u pepa. *To cut in copper or brass,* kaha keleawe. *To cut stone,* kālai pōhaku. *A cut portion,* mokuna.

cute. *No exact equivalent:* nani, 'auli'i.

cutlass. Pahi kākiwi, pahi kaua pālahalaha.
cutting. 1. *Plant.* Lālā kanu, kā, ēulu. **2.** *See* **cut.**
cuttlebone. Puna.
cuttlefish. Mūhe'e. *The cuttlefish, a sea creature running two ways,* 'o ka mūhe'e ka i'a holo lua *(of duplicity and fickleness).*
cutthroat. 'Oki pu'u.
cutworm. Poko.
cycle. 1. *Period.* Au, wā. **2.** *Wheel.* Huila.
cyclone. Makani pāhili.
cylinder. Paukū 'oloka'a.
cymbal. Kimepala, kumepala.
cynical. Ho'omahuakala.
cypress. Kileka, kupeleko, lā'au ka'a.
Cyprus. Kupelo, Kupero.
Cyrene. Kulene, Kurene.
czar. Kā.

D

d. *No Hawaiian term.*

dab. Kāpala, kūpenu, hauka'e. *Cf.* **daub.** *Dab of poi,* pala poi. *To dab up, as tears,* penu.

da capo. Hele mua, mua loa, mamua.

dagger. Pāhoa, pahi 'ō, ku'ia, pīkoi lua; kaha kuhi *(reference mark in writing).*

dahlia. Waiohinu.

daikon. Ananū pilau.

daily. I kēlā me kēia lā; puka lā *(as a newspaper).*

dainty. Mikioi, maiau, 'auli'i, palanehe, nihinihi, lili'i, poki, pa'anehe.

dairy. Hale 'uwī waiū, hui 'uwī waiū, wahi mālama pipi waiū.

dais. 'Anu'u, 'āwai.

daisy. Na'ena'e *(for various types, see Haw.-Eng. entry and entries that follow it),* nehe, makalika.

Dakota. Kakoka, Dakota.

Dalmatia. Kalemakia, Dalematia.

dam. Pani wai, kaupale, māno, ākuli, pa'amua, kūmano, pōmano, pāni, hau'opo.

damage. Pohō, pō'ino, ho'opō'ino, hō'ino'ino, ho'o-'ino; nao *(always with* 'a'ole, *or* 'a'ohe). *See* **damages.** *To damage,* hō'ino, manuhe'u, pau'aka.

damaged. 'Ino'ino, manuhe'u.

damages. Uku pohō. *To pay damages,* uku pohō. *To sue for damages,* koi pohō, ho'opi'i pohō.

Damascus. Kamakeko, Damaseko.

damask. Damaki.

damn. Hō'ino wale, kūamuamu. *See* **God damn.**

damn fool. Kamipulu.

damp. Ma'ū. *Also:* kawaū, kēwai, pa'ū, ko'ū, ko'eko'e; kele lua *(excessively),* maemae, pūanuanu, kawakawa; konāhau *(of wind).*

dampen. Ho'oma'ū, ho'omā'ū'ū.

damselfish. 'Ā ('a'ā), mokumoku hā nui (hānui), 'alo-'ilo'i (lo'ilo'i). *Cf.* **'ala'ihi.**

dance. Ha'a: *with bent knees, formerly only in religious rituals, with leg and body motives, performed by gods (as Pele), nature, and men; called* hula *after mid-nineteenth century; previously* hula *was only for entertainment. See* **Kaeppler.**

dancer. Mea hula, 'ōlapa.

dancing. Hulahula *(ballroom). Place reserved for dancing, dancing troupe,* pā hula.

dancing school. Kula a'o hulahula.

dandelion. Laulele.

dandle. Ho'oleilei.

dandruff. Kēpia.

dandy. Kanaka ho'okahakaha. *To act the dandy,* ho'o-kahakaha, kaulī, ho'opulelehua.

Dane, Danish. Kenemaka.

danger. Mea pō'ino, maka'u; — *of death,* make; *mortal* —, pu'umake. *See sayings,* **nahoa 1, wai 'awa'awa.**

dangerous. Maka'u loa, weliweli 'ia, pō'ino.

dangle. Lewa, ku'uwelu, kūlewa, lewalewa.

Danube. Kanupe, Danube.

Danville. Kanewile, Danevile.

Dardanelles. Kakanele, Dadanele.

dare. 'A'a, 'ā, ho'ohoa, hō'a'ano.

Darien Sea. Kai-o-Kaliana, Dariana.

daring. 'A'ano, lālama, koakoa, ho'onakoa, nahoa, ho'ohoa, 'a'a.

dark. Pō'ele, pō'ele'ele, 'ele'ele, pā'ele, uli, uliuli, āuli, hāuli, hāuliuli, lāuli, māuli, pouli, pohohiwa, 'āhiwa, pahiwa, pōuliuli, pō, pōliu, pōlua, kuaweli; māku'e *(any dark color);* kōkolikoli *(of a kukui nut candle);* pōpolo hiwa *(as pōpolo berries);* pano, 'e'elekū, hākuma, mākuma *(as clouds);* — *brown,* māku'e; — *purple,* poni māku'e. *Also:* ulupō, 'elewawā, kono'ele; 'elemoe *(as forest);* pōnaho, pōkano, pō mano, konouli, 'eleua, lanipō, palapō, kōanoano, ila, pāuli, palauli, lalahiwa, wehi, wehiwa, kūlipo, kūlipolipo, kūniponipo, mālipolipo, 'a'aki, pahiwa, pōlio, pōlolohuamea, 'elekū. *See* **black.** *Dark-complexioned,* 'ili uliuli, 'ili pala uli, 'ili māku'e, 'ili kou, pā'ele; pōpolo *(slang). Dark-skinned native,* kanaka 'ili māku'e. *Until dark,* ā pō ka lā. *To become dark,* hō'ele'ele. *Dark-red bark,* 'ili māku'aku'a.

darken. Ho'ouli, ho'opouli, ho'oahiahi, pahiwa *(rare),* hō'ele'ele.

darkened. Pō'ele'ele. *Also:* kā'ele, 'e'a'e'a; pā'ula *(of matured wood).*

darkness. Pō'ele'ele. *Period of darkness,* 'eleau. *See* **dark.** *Sacred darkness,* la'a uli. *To dispel darkness,* lele uli.

darling. Makamae, hiwahiwa, milimili, lei; eia nei *(vocative). See* **endearing.**

darn. Pāhonohono, humuhumu ulana.

dart. Ihe, ihe 'ō, kao. *Also:* moa, pua, kao lele, pahe'e, ke'a, pāhi'uhi'u, panapana nī'au; waikūoa; pua ka'aona *(of sugar-cane tassel). To dart,* lele māmā, holohi'a. *Dart game,* ke'a pua.

dash. 1. *Run.* Holo māmā, heihei, pūhalahio. **2.** *Strike.* Kā, kākā, kuapā; — *down,* kiola 'ino, ulupā, kula'i; — *to pieces,* wāwahi, pākī; kā make loa *(to death).* **3.** *Punctuation.* Kaha maha.

data. Nā mea like 'ole i pili i ke kumuhana.

date. 1. *Time.* Manawa, lā, makahiki **2.** *Fruit.* Hua pāma. **3.** *Engagement.* Ho'opa'a manawa no ka launa pū.

date palm. Pāma, niu kahiki.

dative case. 'Auipa'ewa.

daub. Pala, hāpala, kāpala, poni. *See* **bedaubed, dab.** *Daub of food,* pala 'ai. *Daub of turmeric or ochre with salt water,* īhe'ekai *(used by priests). To daub designs,* kāpala ki'i.

daughter. Kaikamahine.

daughter-in-law. Hūnōna wahine.

dauntless. Wiwo 'ole, maka'u 'ole, ka'uka'u lua 'ole.

dawn. Ao, wana'ao, kaiao, moku ka pawa. *Fig.:* 'ehu kakahiaka, Iao. *See* **daybreak, morning,** *and sayings,* **kaiao, kipona 1.** *Darkness just before dawn,* pawa, paoa. *Until dawn,* ā pō ka ao. *Dawn glow,* alaula. *Red streaks at dawn,* kāhe'a. *Period between midnight and dawn,* pilipuka.

day. Lā, ao. *Weekday,* lā noa. *Day of worship,* lā ho'āno. *School day,* lā kula. *Workday,* lā hana. *Any possible day,* lā lā e hiki mai ana. *From day to day,* ia lā a'e, ia lā a'e. *To become light, as the day,* pi'i kea. *Day set aside for prayer,* kūpule. *Period of ten days,* anahulu. *For days of the month, see* **month.**

daybreak. Hiki mai ka wana'ao, moku ka pawa, wehe mai ke alaula, wehe kaiao. *See* **dawn.**

dayflower. Honohono, makolokolo.

daylight. Ao.

day school. Kula lā, kula hele lā.

Dayton. Kekona, Detona.

daze. Kūnāhihi, kūpouli, heihei, aia i kahi 'ē ka no'ono'o.

dazzling. 'Ōlinolino, lino, hulili, 'ulili, 'ōlehaleha, 'ōnini, li'oli'o; 'ōli'oli'o *(somewhat);* huaka, lile.

deacon. Kiakona, kiakono.

dead. Make, make loa, moelepo. *See* **kukui, death.** *Dead body,* kino make, kino kupapaʻu. *War dead,* mākaua. *To pretend to be dead,* hoʻomake.
dead-end road. Ala muku.
deadline. Kau palena. *To set a deadline,* kaupalena, hoʻokaupalena.
deadly. Make. *Deadly weapon,* nā mea pepehi kanaka.
Dead Sea. Kai-make.
dead shot. Kā make loa.
deaf. Kuli, hoʻokuli, pepeiao kuli. *Also:* pāʻia *(temporarily);* aʻalolo kuli, lōlōkuli. *Deaf person,* kuli. *Stone deaf,* kuli ʻokoʻa. *To pretend to be deaf,* hoʻokuli, hoʻokolono.
deafening. Kulikuli, pāʻia kuli.
deaf-mute. Leo paʻa, aʻalolo kuli. *Deaf-mutes,* poʻe kuli a ʻāʻā.
deal. 1. *Apportion.* Mahele; hāʻawi, haʻawina *(as cards).* 2. *Agreement.* ʻAelike, ʻaelike i loko o ka ʻoihana. 3. *Act.* Hana, hoʻohana.
dear. 1. *Beloved.* Aloha. *Dear Mr. Smith,* iāʻoe ē Kamaka, aloha kāua. 2. *Costly.* Pipiʻi. 3. *Exclamation.* Auē, auwē!
death. Make, make loa. *Some fig. and poetic expressions for death follow:* hiamoe loa, hāʻule, lele ka ʻuhane, lele ka hoaka, ala hoʻi ʻole mai, mākūkoaʻe, waiho nā iwi, moe kau ā hoʻoilo, ā lele nui nā mauli, kani ka papa waʻa, ʻaoʻao mau o ka honua. *See sayings,* **ala 1, koʻiʻula, Niolopua 2, pupū, wai 1, die, weariness.** *Shadow of death,* malu make. *His death,* kona make. *Sign of death,* hōʻailona make. *Near death,* kālilo, kaʻahē. (Make *as a noun is commonly preceded by a k-word: afraid of death,* makaʻu i ka make.)
deathless. Make ʻole.
deathly. Make, hana make, mākini.
debase. Hoʻohaʻahaʻa, kāwaʻe.
debate. Kaua paio, paio kālaimanaʻo, hoʻopāpā; uhiʻāpana *(rare). Debating club,* ʻahahui paio.
debauch. ʻUhaʻuha, koaka.
debilitated. Hākalalū, hīnawenawe.
debit. Ka ʻaoʻao ʻaiʻē *(in bookkeeping);* pōkole ke kālā *(shortage of funds).*
debris. *See* **flotsam.**
debt. ʻAiʻē. *To pay a debt,* hoʻokaʻa.
decameter. Kekamekele.
decay. Palahō; popopo *(wood, teeth);* kulopia, hākaokao, paʻi, poholawa.
deceased. Make, mea make.
deceit. ʻImi ʻepa, ʻapaʻapa, nolu. *See* **deceive, deceitful.**
deceitful. Hoʻopunipuni, hoʻopuni, ʻāpiki, wahaheʻe, waha wale, haku ʻepa, ʻeʻepa, poholalo, elelo lua. *Deceitful speech,* ʻōlelo pahele. *Rare:* holo lua, paukeʻe, ukalekale, kaʻalalo, ʻoehaʻa, kanaleʻo, pauʻaka, alapahi, ʻapakeʻe. *See* **deceive.**
deceive. *See* **deceitful.** *Also:* hoʻopunipuni, hoʻopahele, hōʻepa, ʻapuhi, kalekale, pāwali, luahele, ʻōʻupē, kanaleʻo, kahina, kiʻilua. *Fig.:* uhi, pahili, uhu pākali, ʻōpeʻa.
deceived. Puni, puni wale; walewale *(rare).*
December. Kēkēmapa, Lēkēmapa, Dekemaba.
decent. Kūpono, kohu pono, hoʻopono.
decide. Hoʻoholo, holo manaʻo, koho.
decided. Holo.
decimal. Kekimala, pāʻumi. *Circulating decimal,* kekimala kaʻapuni.
decision. Hoʻoholo, ʻōlelo hoʻoholo, manaʻo hoʻoholo. *Written decision,* palapala hoʻokō.
deck. 1. *Platform.* ʻOneki, papahele. 2. *Of cards.* Puʻu pepa. 3. *Adorn.* Hoʻokāhiko, hoʻohiluhilu, hoʻowehiwehi, hoʻonani.
decked. ʻOhuʻohu, ulumāhiehie, hoʻouluwehi.
declaration. Kuahaua, haʻina; — *of principles,* kahua *(fig.). Declaration of Independence,* Hōʻike no ke Kūʻokoʻa.
declare. Haʻi, hoʻolaha, wahi, ʻī, ʻōlelo, hōʻike. *To declare war,* kūkala kaua.

declension. *See* **conjugation.**
decline. 1. *Descending slope.* ʻAui, ʻauina. 2. *Refuse.* Hōʻole.
decomposed. Pilau, pela, ʻūmelu, melu, malau.
decorate. Wehi, wehiwehi, hoʻowehi, hoʻowehiwehi, hoʻouluwehi, hoʻouluwehiwehi, hoʻoulumāhiehie, kauluwehi, hoʻohiwahiwa, hoʻokāhiko, hoʻohiluhilu, pāpahi, hoʻonani, hoʻoheno. *One who decorates the chief in finest apparel,* kui lei ʻula.
decorated. Kīnohi, linohau, kui lei ʻula, ulumāhiehie, kāhiko ʻia.
decoration. Wehi, wehiwehi, mea hoʻohanohano, hōʻailona hoʻohanohano. *Also:* kīnohi, pāpahi, kāhele.
Decoration Day. Lā Kau Pua, Lā Lū Pua.
decorous. Hilu, nihinihi, paʻalula, akahai.
decoy. Pākali, kaʻana, ʻapi, hoʻowalewale, hoʻopunihei.
decrease. Emi, koiʻi, hoʻoliʻiliʻi, kāmuku.
decree. Kauoha, ʻōlelo kauoha, kānāwai. *Legal decree,* ʻōlelo kūpaʻa.
decrepit. Kolopupū, kaʻikōkō, pala lau hala.
decrescendo. Pūʻali.
dedicate. Hoʻolaʻa, hoʻomāhanahana; hoʻāu *(rare). See ex.,* **essence.** *Dedicate a house,* hoʻolaʻa hale, ʻoki i ka piko. *Dedicate a canoe,* hoʻolaʻa waʻa.
dedicated. 1. *Consecrated.* Laʻa, hoʻolaʻa, laʻahia, kānaenae. 2. *Devoted.* Paʻa ka manaʻo, lilo loa. *Man is dedicated to love, caught by love (FS 231),* e laʻa ke kanaka i ke aloha, ua loaʻa i ke aloha.
dedication. Hoʻolaʻa ʻana, hoʻowilimoʻo.
deduct. Hoʻolawe.
deed. 1. *Act.* Hana. 2. *Document.* Palapala, palapala hoʻolilo, palapala kila, hōʻoiaʻiʻo, kila. *Deed of sale,* palapala kūʻai.
deem. Manaʻo.
deep. Hohonu, kūhohonu, kūʻono, kūlipo *(as a cave);* poale *(as a hole or sore). Also:* ʻeleʻeli *(as a taboo or its removal);* kūhohō, kūkonukonu, auwaea, honu, nōkī. *Deep tone or sound of the human voice,* maliʻu, kūliʻu, leo halulu. *Deep shade,* mālipolipo. *Deep-set, as eyes,* poʻopoʻo, nuku. *Not deep,* mālani.
deepen. Hoʻohohonu, hoʻohonu.
deer. Kia. *Fallow deer,* pūpalō.
deface. Hōʻinoʻino, māʻinoʻino, manuheʻu, hōʻaliʻali.
defaced. Māʻinoʻino, haukaʻe.
defamation. ʻŌlelo hōʻinoʻino.
defame. Hōʻino. *Also:* māʻinoʻino, hakukole, ʻalapahi, kekēue, kekewe, hāpala, paokeʻe.
defamer. Hakukole. *See saying,* **wood borer.**
defeat. Make, hoʻopio, holopapa, hoʻāʻeʻe, lilo, hāʻule, eo. *See ex.,* **chicken.** *Complete defeat, as in card games,* make pilau, hoʻōhule. *To run away in defeat,* lele pio.
defeated. Make, pio, mā, hiolo, lilo, hāʻule, hoʻauheʻe, eo.
defecate. *See* **excrete.**
defect. Kīnā, kīnaʻu, kīnaʻunaʻu, hewa, keʻe.
defection. Kipi, haʻalele, hapakuʻe.
defective. Hemahema, kīnā, hapakuʻe.
defend. Pale, kūpale, ālai; ʻōlelo pale, hoʻopale *(in court);* kokope, kōlulu *(rare).*
defendant. Hoʻopale, mea pale, poʻe (mea) hoʻopiʻi ʻia.
defense. Pale, kūpale, palekana. *Also:* puʻupale, ʻalama, māmalu, pākū. *Defense, as in trial,* ʻōlelo pale, ʻaoʻao kāpae *(legal);* pale kaua *(in war). Defense bonds,* pona kūpale.
defer. 1. *Postpone.* Hoʻomalolo, hoʻomoe, hoʻopaneʻe. 2. *Yield.* Maliu.
defiant. Nahoa, hōʻaʻano. *Also:* hoʻohoa, ʻaʻana. *Defiant of the law,* hoʻowahāwahā i ke kānāwai. *Do not use defiant language,* mai ʻaʻana mai ʻoe.
deficient. Nele, hemahema, ʻolohaka.
deficit. Lawa pono ʻole, nele, ʻaʻole piha pono, ʻolohaka.
defile. Hoʻohaumia, hoʻopaumāʻele, hāpala.
defiled. Haumia, hawa, paumāʻele, hauʻeka, haukaʻe.
define. Wehewehe ʻano, wehewehe pono.

definite. Pa'a, maopopo, kā'oko'a.
definite article. Pilimua maopopo.
definition. Wehewehe 'ana.
definitive. Panina.
deflate. Ho'opuhalu.
deflated. Puhalu, halu, uhalu, 'ananu'u, ku'ipehe. *Somewhat deflated,* hahalu.
deflower. Wāhi, nahā.
deformed. Pepe'e, kīnā, hapaku'e, ku'e, 'oeha'a, 'anahua.
deformity. Kīnā, pepe'e, ke'e.
defraud. 'Āpuka. *See* **cheat.**
deft. Loea, no'eau, mikioi, 'ike hana lima, palanehe, lehia, lauahi, pa'anehe, mimo.
defy. 'A'a, 'ā, hō'a'ano, kū'ē akena.
degenerate. Emi ke kūlana a ka ha'aha'a loa; mea ha'aha'a ha'alele loa.
degraded. Ho'oha'aha'a 'ia, 'ālina.
degree. Kekele. *Honorary degree,* kekele ho'ohanohano. *See* **comparative, superlative.**
dehydrate. Ho'omalo'o. *Dehydrated food,* pīka'o.
deify. Ho'ākua, ho'omanamana, hō'unihipili, kīhēhē. *To deify a dead relative by food offerings and prayer,* kākū'ai.
dejected. Kaumaha, pilihua, pū, noho pū, kukule; 'ololū *(rare).*
Delaware. Kelawea, Delawea.
delay. Lohi, kali, ho'okali, 'apa. *Also:* 'emo, pane'e, ho'opane'e, ho'ohākālia, ho'olohi, ka'unē, kā'ele, hō'olo'olo, napa, ho'onapa, 'āpa'apāna, ho'omole, ka'uka'u, ka'ulua, kāwa'u. *Without delay,* 'emo 'ole. *To delay maliciously,* ho'okololohe.
delegate. 'Elele. *To delegate responsibility,* 'ākuleana. *To delegate to another,* ho'oili iā ha'i.
delete. Kāpae.
deliberate. 1. *Confer.* Kūkākūkā, 'ōlelo kūkākūkā, no'ono'o pono, kaukau. *One with whom one confers and deliberates,* hoa kūkā, hoa kūkākūkā. 2. *Slow.* Lohi, hō'apa'apa.
delicate. Lahi, lahilahi, lālahi, pīlahi, hunehune, hune, hini, puāhilo, 'olalahina, pīlali'ohe.
delicious. 'Ono, mikomiko; lihaliha *(and oily). Very delicious,* 'ono loa.
delight. Hau'oli, 'oli'oli, hau'oli'oli, hoihoi, ho'ohoihoi, puni, ohaoha. *To delight in,* hia, puni, milimili nanea, hia'ai, ho'ohia'ai.
delighted. Ohohia, kamahoi, hia'ai, hia'ai'ono, hiala'ai
delightful. Māhie, ho'omāhie, ho'ohie, le'a, mīkilolohua, mīkolohua, mīkolelehua, hia'ai; *most —,* hia'ai'ono.
delinquency. Lawehala. *Juvenile delinquency,* lawehala 'ōpiopio.
delirious. 'Olohewa, 'ōhewahewa, 'ōhewa, 'auana hewa o ka no'ono'o.
delirium tremens. Keliluma kelemana, 'ōhewahewa 'ōpulepule.
deliver. Hā'awi, lawe, ho'opakele. *To deliver a child,* pale, pale keiki, ho'ohānau. *Deliver us from evil (Mat. 6:13),* e ho'opakele nona'e iā mākou i ka 'ino.
deliverer. *See* **savior.**
delouse. Nā'uke, hā'uke, hā'ule.
deluge. Kai a Kahinali'i.
delusion. Uluāhewa, mana'o kuhihewa.
delve. 'Eli; noi'i, nowelo *(as for knowledge).*
demand. Koi, kauoha. *Supply and demand,* ka nui a me ka makemake 'ia.
demanding. Ho'ohaku, ho'okina, ho'oluhi. *See* **bossy.**
demented. Pupule, 'ā'ā, 'a'aia, 'ūlala, 'a'alaioa, 'olohewa, hewahewa, uluāhewa, pahuluhope. *See* **psychotic.**
demigod. Kupua.
demijohn. Hue'ie, 'ōmole 'ie.
democracy. Aupuni a ka lehulehu.
Democrat. Kemokalaka.
demoiselle fish. *See* **damselfish.**
demolish. Wāwahi, ho'ohiolo, ku'ipalu, nāhāhā, olopē.

demon. Kaimoni, kaimonio, kiapolō, 'uhane 'ino.
demonstrate. Hō'ike maopopo aku, kuhikuhi.
demonstration. Hō'ike'ike, wehewehe 'ana.
demonstrative pronoun. Paniinoa kuhikuhi.
den. Ke'ena, lua.
dengue. Piwa ha'iha'i iwi.
denial. Hō'ole.
denim. 'Āhina *(blue),* naneki.
Denmark. Kenemaka, Denemaka.
denomination. 'Ano, mahele, 'ao'ao; inoa papa *(arithmetic).*
denominator. Mahele.
denounce. Ho'opi'i, ho'āhewa, hō'ino.
dense. Pa'apū, lanipō, pōpō uahi; pōlolohuamea *(rare); — vegetation,* lauoha, ulupō; *—, of flowers or fragrance,* pō.
dent. Mino, mimino, minomino, 'ōpaha.
dented. 'Ōpaha, manuhe'u, mā'i'o, napo.
dentist. Kauka niho.
denude. Ho'ōlohelohe; hō'ilikole *(of property).*
deny. Hō'ole, 'ole, ho'onele; hō'ole'ole *(repeatedly). Deny persistently,* pa'a i ka 'ole.
depart. Hele i kahi 'ē, ha'alele, waiho; *— in haste,* heo, mio. *Also:* alaheo, hū, laweau.
department. Mahele, ke'ena, 'oihana; *— of a business or office,* kīhāpai.
Department of Education. 'Oihana Ho'ona'auao, Papa Ho'ona'auao.
Department of Instruction. 'Oihana Ho'ona'auao.
Department of Interior. 'Oihana Kālai'āina.
Department of Public Instruction. Ke'ena Ho'ona'auao o ka Lehulehu.
Department of Water Supply. 'Oihana Wai.
depend. Kauka'i, kauko'o, kālele. *That depends on you,* aia nō ia iā 'oe.
dependency. Panalā'au *(colony).*
dependent. Mea kauka'i ka pono, 'ai'ai, 'ōhua, 'alopalopā. *See ex.,* **mānea.** *Living as a dependent,* nohona ho'opili wale.
deplete. Puhalu, uhalu.
deplore. Minamina *(regret);* ho'ohalahala *(criticize).*
deportment. *See* **conduct.**
deposit. Ho'okomo, waiho; uku ho'opa'a *(as on a purchase). Deposit money in the bank,* ho'okomo i ke kālā i ka panakō.
deposition. 'Ōlelo hō'ike i kākau 'ia *(written testimony).*
depository. Waiho, waihona, waina.
depot. Hale ho'olulu, kīpō.
depraved. Lilo loa i ka hewa.
depreciate. Ho'ēmi *(as money);* hō'ino *(disparage).*
depressed. 1. *Sad.* Kaumaha, lu'ulu'u. *Also:* ulukū, ho'okanaha'i, loha, manawai, make 'awahua iho. 2. *See* **sunken.**
depression. 1. *Land.* Poho, 'āpoho, 'alu, 'a'alu, hō'alu, po'o, po'opo'o, napo'o. *Also:* 'ali, 'a'ali, ioio, mino, mimino, poli, uha'i, pipi. 2. *See* **depressed** 1. 3. *Business.* Au nele.
deprive. Ho'onele. *To deprive utterly,* ho'onele loa, kā i ka nele loa, 'elehe'u.
depth. Hohonu. *Depth sounding,* ana i ka hohonu.
depths. Hohonu, lalo; *— of the earth,* kūpapakū.
deputation. Po'e i wae 'ia.
deputy. Hope, kahu aupuni, pani hakahaka.
deranged. *See* **demented.**
deride. *See* **jeer.**
derision. 'Ōlelo ho'ohenehene. *Terms of derision:* O'ahu maka 'ewa'ewa *(see* **'ewa'ewa***),* Moloka'i pule o'o *(see* **o'o***),* po'o hakahaka *(empty heads, Maui),* unahi pikapika he'e *(scalers of octopus suction cups, Kula, Maui),* 'ai loli *(Kau-pō, Maui),* Lā-na'i puhi kūkae *(burner of feces, referring to a Lā-na'i sorcerer's burning of the feces of Lani-kāula and thereby causing his death),* palu lā'ī *(Hawai'i),* maka lepo *(dirty eyes,* Ka'ū*). See* **insult, scale** 2.
descend. Iho, hele iho, ho'oihona, hele i lalo, kīpou.
descendant. Mamo, pua, mo'opuna, keiki, pulapula,

pukana; hele mua *(of an older brother or sister);* hele hope *(of a younger brother or sister). Also:* maka, liko, liko ali'i, lei, hauloli'i. *Descendant of a chief,* pua ali'i, pua lani, mamo ali'i, mauliauhonua. *Many descendants,* lau manamana, mo'o lau, pū manamana.

descended. Ku'una, iho.

descent. Ihona, ho'oihona, 'auina, 'āluna; 'alu *(as a trail). Descent of water,* iho wai. *Genealogical descent,* papa kū'auhau.

describe. Hō'ike 'ano, ha'i 'ano, ho'ākaaka, hoakaka; — *fully;* huliko'a.

description. Hō'ike 'ano, huliko'a.

desecrate. Ho'ohaumia i ka mea la'a, ho'oma'ewa, hehi.

desecration. Hehi 'ana.

desert. 1. *Arid or unoccupied region.* Wao one, wao akua, panoa, ānoa, mānā *(terms used by Bible translators; Hawai'i has no deserts as occur in the Holy Land).* **2.** *Abandon.* Ha'alele; mahuka *(flee).*

deserter. Mea ha'alele. *Soldier deserter,* koa mahuka.

desertion. Ha'alele.

deserve. Pono, kū.

desiccated. Malo'o, malo'ohāhā; konene *(rare).*

design. Lau, ana, ki'i kaha i hō'ike 'ano. *For designs, see* **hat, mat, spiral, tapa.**

designate. Wae, koho, kuhikuhi.

desire. Makemake, 'i'ini, 'ano'i, hia, make, ake, puni, 'upu. *Also:* 'i'i, kuko, makahehi, ha'eha'e, mana'o, kauhua, nipo, ninipo, pu'u, ko'i'i, 'īloli, ho'omakauli'i, ha'e. *To desire greatly,* kūli'a, li'a, 'ena aloha, lanakoi. *Overwhelmed with desire,* pa'uhia. *Cessation of desire,* kaea. *To feign or cause desire,* ho'omakemake. *To stare, as in desire,* 'a'ā maka.

desirous. Make'e. *Desirous for the welfare of the nation,* make'e pono aupuni.

desist. Waiho, ho'opau, uoki.

desk. Pākaukau, pākaukau hana. *Rare:* papa palapala, pahu palapala.

Des Moines. Kemoine, Demoine.

desolate. Nea, kuanea, 'alaneo, neoneo, 'ōneanea, 'ōnea, ho'ōnea, ho'oneanea. *Also:* kaha, aukaha, kōhahe. *The end, desolation,* ka pau, 'o ka 'ōneanea.

despair. Hā'ule ka mana'olana, ku'ihē ka na'au, paupauaho. *See* **desolate, hopeless.**

desperate. Kū i ka hō'ā'ā, 'a'a makehewa.

despise. Ho'okae, ho'owahāwahā, manu'awa.

dessert. Mea 'ai momona, mea 'ono.

destination. Kahi e hele aku ai.

destiny. Hopena, hope.

destitute. Nele loa, hune, 'ilihune, māhune. *Also:* pakaneo, puhikole, akakole, 'akole, 'ilikole, kuleleiwi, pōka'o, 'ōlohe, 'ōlohelohe, ka'a ka lolo, 'aupapa, hemahema, auwalakī, ho'oneo, kōhahe. *To make destitute,* ho'onele, kā i ka nele loa.

destroy. Luku, ho'opau, hana make. *Also:* 'ai, pāluku, pōluku, luma'i, kāpapa, apu, apakaū, 'aihumuhumu, humuhumu, 'ānai, hamu, me'ea, 'ulupā, 'ōmilo, laumilo, 'ōkā, ho'okae. *See sayings,* **manō, pau 1, pulu 3, tail.** *Destroy completely,* luku ho'opapau, ho'opau, ku'ikē. *Destroy by fire or lava,* lauahi, pau ahi, he'a. *Determine to destroy,* makaluku.

destruction. Luku, lukuna, make. *See sayings,* **destroy.** *Any place of destruction,* luapa'ū.

detach. Ho'oka'awale, wehe.

detachment. Mahele, huina; pū'ali *(military).*

detailed. Piha pono, lāli'i *(rare). See* **minutia.** *Detailed report,* hō'ike piha pono.

details. *See* **data.**

detain. Kāohi, 'au'a, pa'a, ho'olohi. *Also:* kāua, kāwa'u.

detective. Māka'ikiu, makākiu.

detention camp. Kahua ho'omalu.

detention home. Home ho'opa'a, home ho'opa'a 'au'a 'ia.

deteriorate. 'Ino mai ke kūlana, ho'īno a'e.

determine. Holo mana'o, holo, ho'oholo, mana'o pa'a.

determined. Mana'o pa'a, pa'a ka mana'o, kūpa'a, moepo'o, 'onipa'a, kīlua.

detest. Ho'okae, ho'opailua. *Detested person,* palani.

detour. Ala kāpae; kaha loa *(long);* ho'oke'e i ke ala 'oko'a.

Detroit. Kekoloike, Detoroite.

deuce. Lua, pa'alua.

Deuteronomy. Kānāwai Lua.

devastate. Luku, ho'oneo, ho'opō'ino, ho'okae; kokōhikū *(crops).*

develop. Ho'omōhala; hana *(as a photograph);* ho'okino *(as an infant).*

developed. Mōhala, mohahala, mōhalahala, mōhola; — *fully,* mōhā, mōhāhā, ōhāhā, hōpoe.

development. Ho'omōhala.

deviate. 'Aui, huli, kīkaha, kaka'a, hili, auhili, mahili, 'auana, kāpae.

deviation. 'Aui 'ana. *Without deviation,* kuakahi.

devil. Kiapolō, kepolō, akua.

devilish. Kiapolō.

devious. Keke'e, ka'awili, lauwili, like 'ole.

Devon. Kewona, Devona.

devoted. Aloha, la'a, la'ahia, puni, lilo, pili aloha *(loving);* ho'opapau. *A child devoted to parents,* he keiki aloha mākua. *A man devoted to his wife,* he kanaka aloha wahine.

devour. Hamu. *See* **eat.**

devoured. 'Aina, 'ai 'ia, pau.

devout. Haipule, piha haipule.

dew. Kēhau, hau. *Collection of dew,* huawaimaka. *Scattered dew,* lū hau.

dewdrop. Kēhau.

dew-laden. Kēwai, lū hau.

dexterous. No'eau, loea, 'eleu; panale'a *(rare).* **Diabetes.** Mimikō. *See also* **'ea houpo lewalewa.** *Diabetes medicine.* Laukahi.

diadem. Lei ali'i, kā'ei po'o, kalaunu.

diagnose. Nānā ā loa'a ke 'ano o ka ma'i *(of sickness). See also* **'alawa, hāhā 1.**

diagonal. Lala, ka'akepa, hiō; — *surf or surfing,* lala.

diagram. Ki'i.

dial. Wili *(as on a telephone).*

dialect. 'Ano 'ōlelo o kekahi 'āina a i 'ole kekahi 'ano kanaka.

dialogue. 'Ōlelokīkē, 'ōlelo kīkēkē, launa 'ōlelo.

diameter. Anawaena.

diamond. Kaimana. *Cut diamond,* 'ōpu'u kaimana. *Diamond setting,* pu'u kaimana.

Diamond Head. Kaimana Hila, Lē'ahi, Lae-'ahi. *Beautiful Diamond Head, a thing to see for those from afar,* nani Lē'ahi, he maka no kahiki.

diaper. Kaiapa.

diaphanous. 'A'amo'o *(cloth).*

diaphragm. Houpo; 'ōlepelepe *(rare).*

diarrhea. Hī, palahī, nonohua; pakeko *(small, slimy discharges). See* **dysentery.**

diary. Puke ho'omana'o. *To keep a diary,* ho'opa'a mana'o, ho'opa'a puke ho'omana'o.

dice. Una pili'aiwai, 'ulu. *Shake dice,* lūlū una.

dictate. Kauoha *(order);* ha'i aku ā na ha'i e kākau *(for writing).*

dictator. Po'o nāna ka mana āpau loa.

dictionary. Puke wehewehe 'ōlelo.

did. *See* **do.** *The one who did,* ka mea i, ka i. *He did go,* ua hele nō 'oia.

die. 1. *Decease.* Make, make loa *(contrasted to make, which may mean "defeated, faint"). Also:* moe i ka make, hala, hā'ule, hā'ule'ule, hā'ulehia, mauha'alele, pauaho, hele, kālilo, kālilolilo, kāninonino, 'ōmu'omu'o, āmio, ku'u i ka 'uhane, ku'u ka hanu, ku'u ka nae, ku'u i ka luhi; — *prematurely,* 'a'aiole; — *mysteriously or by accident,* pōhe'epali *(rare);* — *suddenly,* leleponi, kā'iliponi; — *without cause,* make wale; — *calmly and easily,* lolopio, make wale. *See sayings,* **ku'u 1,** *and death. To weaken and die,* mūnō. *To let die,* ho'omake. *To die, of several,* mamake, papau make; mamamake *(of very many, as in a disaster). That which dieth of itself,* 'o ka mea make wale. **2.** *Molding device.* Ana.

diet. Ho'ēmi i ke kino; mea 'ai e pono ai ke kino.

difference. Mea 'oko'a. *It makes no difference,* he mea 'ole; he aha ia mea.

different. 'Ē, 'ē a'e, 'ano 'ē, 'oko'a, like 'ole, kūlike 'ole, ka'awale. *Entirely different,* kū ka'awale.

differentiate. Maopopo ka loina e 'ike 'ia ai ka 'oko'a o kekahi me kekahi.

difficult. Hana nui, pa'akikī. *Also:* 'o'ole'a, maulua, pū-'uki'uki, 'āpu'epu'e, mākoeā. *See* ala *'ololī,* pū'ika-'ika.

difficulties. He mau pilikia, hihia, kūpiliki'i. *See* trouble *and saying* 'alauā. *To beset with difficulties,* ho'o-hei. *To get into difficulties,* ho'ohihia. *Poetic references to rain and cliffs may signify difficulties.*

diffidence. Hilahila, ho'okano 'ole. *With unfeigned diffidence,* me ka hopohopo ho'okamani 'ole.

diffuse. Pāhola, hohola.

dig. 'Eli; — *with a sharp tool,* kipi; — *holes with a stick,* 'ōkupe; — *with a spade or an* 'ō'ō, 'ōla'ola'o; — *food crops,* kā'ai; — *a trench, ditch, or furrow,* uwa'a, 'awa'a; — *often,* 'eli'eli; — *under,* poholalo, po'a; — *up,* hehu, hua'i. *Also:* pā'eli, 'ali, kūpā, po'o, kūpele, kōhi, mākohi, kau'eli'eli, ho'owa'a, ho'owa'alia, māhelu, maheu, mahi'opu.

digest. 1. *As food.* Ho'owali, ho'owali 'ai, ho'onapele. **2.** *Summary.* Huina mana'o, hō'ulu'ulu mana'o.

digestive juice. Wai ho'ohehe'e.

digging place. Wahi 'eli, 'ekulēkū.

digging stick. 'Ō'ō; 'ō'ō hao *(iron);* 'āla'a. *God of makers of digging sticks,* Kū-ka-'ō'ō.

dignified. Hanohano, kūo'o, kei, 'ihi, keha. *Rare:* hako, pūnihi.

dignify. Ho'ohilu, ho'ohanohano.

dignitary. Kanaka ma ke kūlana ki'eki'e.

dignity. Hanohano, kapukapu, hie, hiehie, keha, kapukapu lani.

digress. 'Auana, ho'olalau. *Also:* 'aui, hūhewa, loloiāhili, kuawili, waha mana.

digression. Kaha loa; *senseless —,* kūhilo.

dike. Pani kai, pani wai, pani.

dilapidated. Helele'i, 'alu'a, hāpa'upa'u, lohelau.

dilate. Ho'onui, hō'olopū; enene *(as nostrils).*

dilatory. Hākālia, ho'ohākālia, lolohi, lōiele, mili 'apa, manukā.

diligent. Huli hana, hana mau, pa'ahana.

dill. 'Aneko, kumino 'ele'ele.

dillydally. Ho'olohi, loloiāhili, lōiele, hō'apa'apa, ho'olalau, 'e'elo.

dilute. Ho'okakale, pa'ipa'i. *Diluted milk,* waiū pa'ipa'i. *Diluted fluid,* kaiaka.

dim. Poahi, kōli'uli'u. *Also:* palaweka, pālauweka, lipo, 'āhiahia, 'awe'awe'a, haili, pōnalo, poehi, pōwehiwehi, pōhina, mo'owini, pinauea, mōlehulehu.

dime. Kenikeni.

dimension. Nui.

diminish. Emi, ho'ēmi, ho'oiki, akaku'u, ho'ohapa; —, *as stream water,* ku'u. *Also:* kāmuku, kāha'u, kualili'i, kuali'ili'i, kōlīli'i, koi'i, kanaha'i, kaneha'i.

diminutive. Li'ili'i, kupali'i, iki, 'u'uku.

dimple. Mino.

din. Kulikuli, hana kuli, wā, wawā, ahu wawā, 'ikuwā, olowalu, ōleoleo, pāleoleowā; pihe *(of voices); confused, excited —,* hauwalao'a, haualao'a. *To make a din,* kuwā, 'ikuwā.

dingdong. Kanikē, kē.

dingy. Hāpa'upa'u, 'āpulu.

dining room. Lumi 'aina, ke'ena 'aina.

dining table. Papa 'aina.

dinner. 'Aina ahiahi, papa 'aina, pā'ina. *Dinner party,* 'aha'aina.

diocese. Kīhāpai.

dip. 1. *To plunge or immerse.* Kūpenu, ho'olu'u, lu'u; *to —, as with a cup,* kī'o'e, ukuhi; *to —, as the head or a*

kite, kimo, kīpoho; *to —, as an oar,* māpuna; *to —, as to insert,* 'ō, ho'ō, miki. *Also:* māpu, kūkai, po'o. *A dip of water,* ukuhina wai. *Two dips of the paddle,* 'elua nō māpuna hoe. **2.** *Depression.* Hālua.

diphtheria. Kipikelia.

diphthong. Leo hui o nā hua palapala 'elua.

diploma. Palapala. *High school diploma,* palapala puka, palapala ho'omaika'i. *University diploma,* palapala hō'oia kulanui.

diplomacy. Kūkā 'ana mawaena o nā aupuni, ka hele nihi, noho nihi.

diplomat. 'Elele, kuhina.

dipper. Kī'o'e, ipu kī'o'e, o'o'o; — *made of ti leaf,* kī'apu; — *made of taro or 'ape leaf,* kili'apu. *See* Big Dipper.

direct. 1. *Oversee.* Alaka'i, kuhikuhi, kauoha, ka'i; kia *(especially in magic);* kuhikau *(rare).* **2.** *Straight.* Pololei.

direction. 1. *See* direct. *Wrong directions,* kuhi hewa, kuhike'e. **2.** *Compass direction.* 'Ao'ao.

directions. Kuhikuhi *(instructions).*

director. Po'o, alaka'i, kuhikuhina, luna ho'oponopono. *Acting director,* hope po'o.

directory. Papa kuhikuhi, puke inoa.

direct proportion. Lakio like kūpono.

dirge. Kanikau, mele kanikau, ho'ouwēuwē; 'uhane *(rare).*

dirt. Lepo, lepo hānai, 'e'a, 'eka. *Red dirt,* lehu 'ula, lepo 'ula'ula. *Clod of dirt,* pāpa'a lepo. *To scatter, stir up dirt or dust,* kaiehu, kuehu.

dirty. Lepo. *Also:* lepolepo, paumā'ele, 'eka'eka, 'eka, hā'eka'eka, kuha'eka, wi'u, pelapela, neko, pōneko, niku, hau-, kākā, penopeno, uweka, moelepo; mōuki. *See saying,* hua'i. *Somewhat dirty,* 'ōlepolepo. *Very dirty,* pau pā'ele, pau 'eka. *To make dirty,* ho'olepo, hō'eka, ho'oniku, ho'opau 'eka.

dis-. 'Ole, 'a'ole.

disability. Hiki 'ole, kīnā.

disagree. Kū'ē'ē, hukihuki, kūlike 'ole, lōkahi 'ole.

disagreeable. 'Olu'olu 'ole, kahakā, kāpēke'u; 'a'aka *(cranky);* 'awa'awa, 'awa'awahia, mālailena *(bitter);* kiki.

disagreement. Kū'ē'ē, hukihuki, mokuāhana, pāoni. *In disagreement,* noho ke'e. *To stir up disagreement,* ho'okū'ē'ē.

disappear. Nalo, nalowale, nalohia, pio, hanini, 'āha'ikapupuhi, uholo; — *swiftly,* mio, miona; ulāheo *(rare);* — *gradually,* koli'i.

disappoint. Ho'ohoka.

disappointment. Hoka, mokuāhua, homa. *See* dream *and saying,* sea cucumber. *To cause disappointment,* ho'ohoka.

disapprove. 'Āpono 'ole. *See* exclamation.

disarrange. Ho'omōkākī, waiho huikau, waiho kapakahi, 'apakau.

disaster. Pōpilikia, pō'ino, ulia weliweli. *See* bitter. *To cause disaster,* ho'opōpilikia, ho'opō'ino. *Disaster area,* wahi i ho'opō'ino 'ia. *To predict disaster,* ho'oiloilo.

disbelief. Hilina'i 'ole, mana'o'i'o 'ole. *Interj. of disbelief or disapproval,* kāhīhī, kā, chā, sā.

disbelieve. Hilina'i 'ole, mana'o'i'o 'ole, mahuakala, ho'opohala.

disburse. Uku, ho'oka'a, kīko'o.

discard. Kiloi, kiola, kiolaola, ho'olei, kāpae, ha'alele, 'olepū.

discharge. 1. *Dismiss.* Ho'oku'u, ho'opau, kipaku, lū, kaiehu. *Discharge, as from army,* palapala ho'oku'u loa. *Dishonorable discharge,* ho'opau ho'o'ino 'ia aku. *Discharge of seamen,* ho'oku'u i nā luina 'a. **2.** *See* unload. *Permit to discharge, as cargo,* palapala 'ae e ho'opae. **3.** *Flow.* Ho'okahe, walewale, walewalena; hehe'e *(as of pus);* 'ina'ina *(reddish, preceding childbirth);* piapia, pa'akai *(of the eyes).* **4.** *Fire, as a gun.* Kī pū.

discharged. Ho'opau 'ia, hemo, ho'oku'u 'ia.

disciple. Haumāna, haumana.
discipline. Aʻo ikaika, aʻo ʻoʻoleʻa.
disclose. Hōʻike, huaʻi.
discolored. Mā, kohu, kāpala. *Also:* ʻahulu, palaʻīloli.
discomfort. ʻOluʻolu ʻole, noʻonoʻo ʻihaʻiha, ʻīnea, ʻiha-ʻiha, puʻu; ikiiki *(acute);* hōkūkū *(preceding bowel discharge);* hoʻīloli *(of pregnancy). See saying,* **puʻu 1.**
disconcerted. Hōʻāʻā.
disconnect. Hoʻokaʻawale, hoʻohemo, kala.
discount. Uku hoʻēmi, hoʻēmi. *Bank discount,* hoʻēmi panakō.
discouraged. Pauaho. *Also:* paupauaho, ʻauwaepuʻu, uluhua, ʻaikena, kuʻipehe, pauʻaka. *See* **dispirited.**
discourse. Kamaʻilio, hoʻokamaʻilio, haʻi a ʻo, ʻōlelo, ʻōlelo kūkā.
discover. ʻImi ā loaʻa, ʻike mua, loaʻa, hōʻike. *Rare:* hoʻomaopopo, kaunānā.
discoverer. ʻImi ā loaʻa.
discredit. 1. *Disbelieve.* Manaʻoʻiʻo ʻole, hilinaʻi ʻole; hoʻopohala *(rare).* **2.** *Disgrace.* Waia, hoʻohilahila, hoʻomaliko.
discrimination. Wae, hōʻokoʻa, hoʻokaʻawale. *Race discrimination,* hoʻokae ʻili, kaupale ʻili.
discuss. ʻŌlelo kūkā, kūkā, kūkākūkā, kālaimanaʻo, hoʻokamaʻilio, kau. *To discuss and wonder about,* nūnē.
discussion. ʻŌlelo kūkā, kūkā, kūkākūkā, kālaimanaʻo.
disdainful. Hoʻokano, ihu piʻi, pali, pali loa, nanahuki, keʻehilae. *Interj. of disdain,* kā, chā.
disease. Maʻi. *See* **ailment, sickness.** *Contagious disease,* maʻi lele, maʻi laulā, maʻi pālahalaha. *Chronic disease,* ʻōmaʻimaʻi. *Recurring disease,* maʻi kau. *Fatal disease,* pāmake. *Various little understood ancient diseases or combinations of diseases:* aʻakū, ʻea, hoaka, pani.
disembark. Lele, pae.
disembowel. Kuaʻi i ka naʻau.
disfavor. Hoihoi ʻole. *To look at with disfavor,* nānā me ka hoihoi ʻole, nānā keʻe, maka ʻewaʻewa, makaʻē.
disfigure. Hōʻinoʻino, hoʻopupuka, hoʻokīnā.
disfigured. Kīnā, ʻanahua, ʻālina.
disgrace. Waia, hoʻohilahila, ʻālina.
disgraceful. Hoʻowaia, hoʻohilahila.
disguise. Hoʻomeamea, hoʻokohukohu, hoʻonalonalo i ke kūlana, hūnā, hoʻololi i ke ʻano, hoʻohūnāhūnā i ke ʻano.
disgust. Hoʻopailua, hoʻowahāwahā. *To shrink away in disgust,* mūʻeʻeke.
disgusted. Ana. *See* **disgust.**
disgusting. Hoʻopailua, kāpulu, luaʻikū, nonohua.
dish. Pā, ipu; pā ipu *(wooden dish in general). Oval wooden dish,* kāloa. *Oval dish,* ipu poepoe, ipu poki. *Glass dish,* pā aniani. *Iron dish or pan,* pā hao. *Paper dish,* pā pepa. *Wooden dish or tray,* pā lāʻau. *Small dish,* pā liʻiliʻi. *Deep dish,* pā hohonu. *Dish containing liquids,* pā hōwai. *Clay or soiled dish,* pā lepo. *To dish up,* hao.
dishcloth. Kāwele pā. *To wipe or dry with a dishcloth,* kāwele.
dishevelled. Pūkalakī, mōkākī.
dishonest. Hoʻopono ʻole, pono ʻole, hoʻopunipuni, ʻāpiki, paukeʻe, ʻapakeʻe. *Also:* ʻepa, poholalo, pākauākeʻe. *See* **cheat.**
dishonor. Waia, ʻālina, hōʻino.
disinfect. Hoʻomaʻemaʻe, pepehi i nā mū, pepehi mea ʻino.
disinfectant. Wai hoʻomaʻemaʻe.
disinherit. Kāpae mai ka hoʻoilina ʻana, kaupale.
disinter. Huaʻi.
disinterest. Manakā, hoihoi ʻole, palaka.
disinterment. Wehe hou ʻana i ke kino kupapaʻu.
disjointed. Pākuʻikuʻi *(as a poorly constructed story). Disjointed vertebra,* ʻanuʻu.
disk. Pā *(phonograph). See* **slipped disk.**
dislike. Makemake ʻole, hoihoi ʻole. *Rare:* manuʻawa, kope, hoʻāhu. *Strong dislike,* hoʻokae, konākonā. *To stir up dislike,* hoʻopihapiha ʻōlelo, hoʻohaunaele.

dislocated. Hemo, uai. *Dislocated knee,* kuli hemo.
dislocation. Iwi pahemo.
disloyal. Manaʻo kipi, kūʻē aupuni, ʻāpua.
dismal. Kaumaha, hoʻokaumaha; pōlio *(rare).*
dismayed. Pīhoihoi, kāhāhā, kuʻihē, kūnāhihi.
dismiss. Hoʻokuʻu, kuʻu, hoʻopau, kipaku.
dismount. Lele mai i lalo.
disobedience. Lohe ʻole, hoʻokuli. *Also:* pepeiao kuli, kūlina, ʻaʻī ʻoʻoleʻa, hoʻokanahua.
disobey. Hoʻolohe ʻole, pale ʻōlelo, hoʻokuli; *willfully* —, hoʻolana. *Rare:* ʻaʻī ʻoʻoleʻa, ihumaʻa, uhakole, hanaea, ʻāpua.
disorder, disorderly. Mōkākī, hoʻoponopono ʻole, lula ʻole, lauhili, kīpalalē, hōkaʻi, kiwalaʻō; ʻano ʻino *(of conduct). See saying,* **makau.** *To work in disorderly fashion,* palalē.
disown. Kaupale, hoʻopale, nāʻīʻike.
dispatch. Hoʻouna hikiwawe.
disperse. Hoʻi, hoʻi nui *(intransitive);* hoʻokuʻu *(transitive). See* **scatter.**
dispirited. Kaumaha, hoihoi ʻole, maʻule, māʻuleʻule, wiwo. *See* **discouraged.**
displace. Lawe i kahi ʻē, ʻapakau, hoʻoneʻe.
display. Hōʻike, hōʻikeʻike, hoʻokahakaha, hoʻokelakela; mea hōʻikeʻike.
displease. Hoʻoukiuki, hoʻonāukiuki, hoʻouluhua.
displeased. Ukiuki, uluhua, hoʻohuakeʻeo, nauki, nāuki, nāukiuki, kunukunu.
displeasing. Kū ʻole i ka hoihoi.
displeasure. Ukiuki. *To exhibit wrath or displeasure due to jealousy,* kahalili.
dispose. Hoʻonohonoho, hoʻolilo.
disposition. ʻAno, loko, manawa, naʻau, ʻōpū. *See* **honey creeper, salt.** *Sour disposition,* naʻau ʻawaʻawa, ʻawaʻawahia, loko liʻu, keʻemoa, malaia, mālailena, naʻinaʻi. *Evil disposition,* mākonā, manawa ʻino, ʻōpū kekene. *Good disposition,* lokomaikaʻi, ʻōpū aliʻi, naʻau aliʻi, ʻoluʻolu.
dispute. Hoʻopaʻapaʻa, paʻapaʻa, hakakā ʻōlelo, ʻāpuni.
disqualified. Kūpono ʻole, kāpae ʻia.
disqualify. Kāpae, ʻapono ʻole.
disregard. Nānā ʻole. *Also:* hoʻokuli, hoʻokananeʻō, māeaea, noʻomāʻauea, kope. *See* **neglect.** *To disregard the rights of others,* hehikū.
disrespectful. ʻAʻe kū, hoʻowahāwahā, hoʻokiʻekiʻe, hoʻokelakela, mahalua.
dissatisfied. Kūhalahala, hoʻohalahala, loiloi, kunukunu; hala iwi nui *(fig.).*
dissect. ʻOkiʻoki liʻiliʻi.
dissemble. *See* **disguise.**
disseminate. Laha, hoʻolaha. *To disseminate news,* kuʻi ka lono.
dissension. Hukihuki, kūʻēʻē.
dissipate. ʻUhaʻuha. *Also:* luaiele, hoʻomāuna, haulani, pāhola, koaka.
dissolute. *See* **dissipate, lecherous.**
dissolve. Hoʻoheheʻe.
distaff. Milo lopi.
distance. Mamao, lōʻihi, loa, analipo; — *between two points,* kaʻawale, kōwā, kāwā. *Six-mile distance,* ʻeono mile ke kaʻawale. *At a distance,* mamao, mōʻiu, mōʻiu-ʻiu. *Turn and then go straight for a long distance,* kaha loa. *To keep a distance,* hoʻokaʻawale, hoʻomamao, ʻāloaloa.
distant. Mamao, lilo, loa, haʻalilo. *Also:* lipo, māhiloa, monehā, naua, auwaea; ʻiuʻiu *(distant realm, as of the gods);* māʻiuʻiu, kōʻiuʻiu, ai loa, aia i loa; waiakua, pali loa *(fig., aloof);* pōlolohuamea. *Distant traveler,* ʻimi loa. *Any distant land,* kahiki. *Distant time,* wā mamao, wā mamua, wā i hala, io, kikilo. *The distant seas were traveled on,* ua ʻau ʻia nā kai loa.
distasteful. Makemake ʻole, hoihoi ʻole. *Distaste for food,* kanea, noneā.
distend. Kēkē, pehu, hoʻopehu, manana.
distill. Puhi.
distinct. Akaaka, mōakaaka.
distinction. Kaulana, hanohano, poʻokela. *Person of*

distinction, kanaka po'okela, mea hanohano, 'iele. *To keep a distinction,* ho'oka'awale. *To conduct oneself with distinction,* ho'ohanohano.

distinguish. Ho'oka'awale, wae, hō'oko'a, ho'omaopopo i ka like 'ole. *To distinguish oneself,* ho'okaulana, ho'ohanohano. *Fig.:* ao loa.

distinguished. Hanohano, hie, ho'ohie, ho'ohiehie, hāweo. *See* **cloud.**

distort. Ho'opa'ewa.

distorted. 'Oeha'a, keke'e.

distraught. Ulukū. *See* **nervous.**

distress. Pilikia, pōpilikia, pō'ino, ho'opō'ino, 'īnea, ho'īnea, 'eha, hō'eha'eha. *Also:* ho'okō'eha'eha, kūpiliki'i, ho'omāhuwā, manawahua kai ko'o, kipona, pōnalo. *See saying,* **uhiwai.** *Distress signal,* hō'ākaaka no ka wā pilikia.

distribute. Ho'omāhelehele, ho'olaha; ho'omalele *(rare).* *Distribute small amounts,* kau li'ili'i. *Distribute one at a time,* pākahi. *Distribute one at a time to several,* pākakahi. *To mark out for distribution, as land,* kākau.

district. 'Āpana, 'okana, moku, mō, moku'āina, moku o loko.

district court. 'Aha 'āpana, 'aha ho'okolokolo 'āpana.

distrust. Ho'ohuoi, kānalua, hilina'i 'ole.

disturb. Ho'oluhi, ho'opilikia. *Also:* pau'aka, hōkai, ka'ahōkai, kaiele, ulukū, hōlapu, hailapu, ho'okolohe, hō'oni, ho'oloku, ulukake, hōkake, wāwahi, ho'ohaunaele, une, ho'onaue.

disturbance. Haunaele, uluāo'a. *Constant disturbance,* ku'iku'ia mau. *To create disturbance,* ho'ohaunaele, ho'ononi.

disturbed. Ho'oluhi 'ia, pono 'ole ka mana'o, pīhoihoi, pīhoi, pi'oloke. *Also:* hakuko'i, ulukū, 'olokū, 'o'olokū, kūhulukū, ho'ole'ole'o, ha'aku'ia ka mana'o, ku'ia, kūpiki'ō, 'ōpikipiki, pu'ua. *Disturbed in sleep,* moehewa.

ditch. 'Auwaha, hā, 'āwa'a. *Water ditch,* 'auwai, 'auwai pa'a, holowai.

divan. *See* **couch.**

dive. Lu'u. *Also:* omo, miomio, kīpoho, lele 'opu, kili-'opu, lele'opuhi, lele pahū; kūhoupo'o, kūlou po'o, lelepo'o, lu'u kimo, lu'u po'o *(headfirst);* lele kawa, lele pāhi'a, lele 'ō'ō *(feet first);* kīhā *(under water as a porpoise).* *Dive down and come up,* lu'u aku ā aea mai *(see* **aea***).* *Sport of diving for gourds,* kaupua.

diverge. Lālā.

divert. Ho'olalau *(as a child).*

divide. Mahele, pu'unaue, 'oki'oki, helehele, ka'ana, kālai. *Rare:* ka'ipu'u, pu'alawāhi. *Divide in two,* pālua, ho'opālua. *To divide equally,* ka'i like, ho'oka'ana. *To divide by lot,* hailona, pū. *To divide small amounts,* kau li'ili'i. *To divide into factions,* mokuāhana.

dividend. Mahele kālā, waiwai ho'opuka, kuleana puka *(payment);* kumupu'unaue *(division).*

divination. Hailona, pu'uone. *Gourd used in divination,* ipu 'ōlelo. *See* **'oi 2.**

divine. Akua, ho'ākua, 'ano akua.

diving board. Papa lele kawa.

division. 1. *Section.* Mahele, pale, mokuna, ka'ipu'u. *Army division,* papa kaua. **2.** *Arithmetic.* Pu'unaue. *Long division,* pu'unaue loa. *Short division,* pu'unaue pōkole. *Division sign,* kaha pu'unaue.

divisor. Helu komo.

divorce. 'Oki, hō'oki, 'oki male.

divorced. 'Oki male 'ia, 'oki 'ia, hemo.

dizzy. Pōniu, pōniuniu, niniu, niua, niu, liua. *Also:* kōniuniu, pūniu, niuaua, maka pōniuniu, makapouli, newa, ka'a ka lolo, niu loloka'a, ānewa, ānewanewa, mania, ka'akua, kā'ihi, loloka'a, hōka'a, 'ona, 'ona-'ona, luea, poluea. *Dizzy, with loss of hearing,* niu kuli. *Nauseous and dizzy,* aneane.

do. 1. *Verb.* Hana, lawelawe; ho'okō *(complete).* *See* **done.** *There is no Hawaiian equivalent for the English auxiliary. Do you like this?* Makemake 'oe i kēia? *Yes, I do,* 'Ae, makemake nō. *How do you do?* Pehea 'oe? **2.** *Note in music.* Pā.

docile. Akahai, laka.

dock. 1. *Wharf.* Uapo, pā kāpili moku. **2.** *Vine.* Pāwale, hu'ahu'akō, uhauhakō.

doctor. Kauka. *Medical doctor,* kauka lapa'au, kahuna lapa'au. *Doctor's aide,* kōkua kauka.

doctrine. Mana'o'i'o kūpa'a, kahua.

document. Palapala *(for various kinds, see Haw.-Eng. entry and entries that follow it).*

dodder. Kauna'oa *(for various kinds, see Haw.-Eng. entry and entries that follow it).*

dodge. 'Alo, 'alo'alo, hō'alo, ho'ohala; — *quickly,* kikihi, kīkī'alo.

does. *See* **do.** *One who does,* ka mea e, ka e, ke.

dog. 'Īlio *(for various kinds, see Haw-Eng. entry and entries that follow it);* 'apowai; *supernatural* —, poki. *See* **bracelet** *and saying,* **welu.** *Dog-tooth anklet,* kūpe'e niho 'īlio. *Dog-tooth lei,* lei niho 'īlio. *Dog-tooth necklace,* lei ole, lei niho 'īlio. *Dog collar,* apo 'ā'ī 'īlio. *Tied dog,* 'ōhao 'īlio *(insulting name for outcasts).*

dogfish. Manō lālā kea.

dogma. Kānāwai mana'o'i'o.

dole. Ho'opīkele; pākali *(little by little).*

doleful. *See* **sad.**

dolichocephalic. Po'o oloolo.

doll. Ki'i, ki'i pēpē.

dollar. Kālā.

dolphin. 1. *Fish.* Mahimahi, oma *(rare); large* —, lapalapa. **2.** *See* **porpoise.**

dolt. Lolohi ka no'ono'o.

dome. Pū'o'a.

domestic. 1. *Native or pertaining to the household.* Kūloko. **2.** *See* **servant.**

domesticate. Ho'olaka.

domesticated. Laka.

dominate. Ho'ohaku, ka'aluna, kuhilani.

Dominican. Kominika, Dominikana.

dominion. Aupuni, lāhui.

donate. Hā'awi wale, makana, hā'awi manawale'a.

donation. Lūlū, ha'awina, makana, manawale'a.

done. Hana 'ia, pau. *See* **do.** *Thy will be done,* e mālama 'ia kou makemake.

donkey. Kēkake, 'ēkake, iākake; piula *(Moloka'i).*

do-nothing. Palaualelo, kūhana 'ole, lemukū.

don't. 1. *Negative command.* Mai, uoki. **2.** *Negative.* 'A'ole.

doomed. La'a i ka pō'ino, la'ahia, hopena pō'ino; —*darkness,* la'a uli.

door. Puka, puka hale, puka komo, 'īpuka, pani puka; *low side* —, pākākā; 'eleua, 'eleao *(ancient). Thatch above a door,* piko. *Door casing,* kikihi. *Door corner,* kihi puka. *Sliding or movable door,* pani uai, puka uai. *Door covering,* uha'i. *Arch over door,* hoaka.

doorframe. Kikihi, uha'i.

doorkeeper, doorman. Kia'i puka, mālama puka.

door mat. Moena kuakuai kāma'a.

doorpost. Lā'au kū, kukuna; lapauila, kunakuna *(rare).*

doorstep. Alapi'i.

doorway. Puka komo, ni'o. *Doorway covering,* uha'i.

Dorchester. Kolekeka, Doreseka.

dormitory. Hale moe.

dorsal fin. Kualā.

dose. Mahele lā'au.

dot. Kiko, pōhaka; — *in music,* kiko. *To make a dot,* kiko, kikiko.

dote on. Puni.

dotted. Kiko, kikokiko, kikiko; 'ōpikopiko *(as with tattoo marks);* pākikokiko.

dotted swiss. Pu'u, 'ulāli'i *(rare).*

double. Pālua, pāpālua, ho'opālua, kālua, lua like, lua, kaulua, 'āpipi, māhana. *Double number,* helu lua. *Double thickness,* ihe māhana; pāpālua ka mānoanoa, ahue. *Double-tongued,* elelo lua, lauwili. *Double-edged,* maka lua, 'oi lua. *Double canoe,* kaulua, wa'a kaulua. *Double bone of arm or leg,* iwi pili. *Double-flowering,* pupupu. *Double-barbed,* kohe lua *(of a fishhook).* *To double up,* meneū, lāpe'e, pupu'u.

doubly. Lua, pālua, pāpālua.
doubt. Kānalua. *Also:* hopo, hopohopo, 'āpaha; lā, ho'i *(particles). There is no doubt of his going,* 'a'ole e 'ole kona hele *(see* **'ole***). To evoke or produce doubt, fear, anxiety,* ho'okānalua, ho'ohopohopo.
doubtful. Kānalua, na'au lua, kāpekepeke, auane'i, 'ānoni.
douche. Hālalo, hoene.
dough. Palaoa ho'owali 'ia, pelena mo'a 'ole.
doughnut. Koneko.
douse. Luma'i, lu'u, hō'au.
dove. Manu kū, manu nūnū, nūnū, kuhukukū. *Ringneck dove,* 'ehakō. *Cooing of a dove,* kuhukukū. *Softeyed dove,* nūnū maka onaona *(endearing term).*
dovetail. Ho'oku'i.
down. 1. *Below.* Lalo, i lalo, iho. *To go down,* iho, kūpou. *To knock down,* kula'i, ho'ohina, hina, kāhina. *Down there,* ai lalo, aia i lalo. *Far down,* i lalo lilo. 2. *Feathers.* Heu, heuheu, 'ae, 'ae moa, hulu weuweu. *See ex., chicken.*
downcast. Lu'ulu'u, kaumaha; 'ololū *(rare).*
downhill. I lalo. *Go or walk downhill,* iho, hele iho.
down payment. Uku ho'opa'a.
downpour. Loku, ua lanipili, ho'olokuloku, ha'alokuloku, kūlokuloku, noku, nokunoku, kūnokunoku, 'iliki. *See rain for symbolism.*
downtrodden. Hehi 'ia, ho'opa'aua, ho'okuapa'a; pahua *(rare).*
downward. Lalo, iho, ihona.
downy. Heu, heuheu, pūhuluhulu, hulu weuweu, 'ae, 'ae'ae.
dowry. Uku male a ka wahine.
Doxology. Mele Ho'omaika'i.
doze. Moe ho'olana; kuli hiamoe. *See saying,* **lau 7.**
dozen. Kākini, 'umi kūmālua, 'umi kumamālua.
draft. 1. *Current of air.* Hihio, mōhio; holouka *(rare). See* **gust.** 2. *See* **draw, write.** 3. *Selection.* 'Ohi, wae. *Army draft,* kāhea e komo i ka 'oihana kaua. *Draft board,* papa 'ohi. 4. *Money order.* Palapala kīko'o, pepa kīko'o, pila kīko'o.
drag. Kauō, alakō. *Also:* kaualakō, kōkō, kolo, kuai, ka'ihuluhulu, pane'ehā. *To drag a canoe,* kauō wa'a.
dragged. Kō.
dragnet. Lau, laukō, 'alihilele.
dragon. *No Hawaiian term; the closest is perhaps* mo'o. *From English are* kalekona, kelekona. *Also:* mo'o lele, mo'o kiha, mo'o nui, mo'o ahi lele. *Chinese dragon,* mo'o lani.
dragonfly. Pinao, pinao 'ula. *Larvae of dragonfly,* lohelohe, lohaloha, pua'alohelohe, 'olopelope. *Young stage of dragonfly,* po'olānui.
drain. Ho'okahe, ho'omalo'o.
drama. Hana keaka.
drape. Kau.
drapes. Pale pukaaniani, pākū pukaaniani *(window).*
draw. 1. *Sketch.* Kaha. *To draw a picture or plan,* kaha ki'i. 2. *Pull, extract.* 'Ume, huki, 'u'u; *to — in,* miki; *to — up,* hulei; *to — towards,* ala'ume; *to — back,* ho-'ēmi, kīpupū; *to — away,* 'eke, pipika; *to — together,* pūpū, 'unu, hupua; *to — in the breath,* hiohio; *to —, as money,* kīko'o. *To draw water,* huki wai. *To draw a winning number,* kiko. 3. *Tie.* Pa'i, pa'i wale, pa'i ā pa'i.
drawer. Pahu 'ume.
drawing. 1. *Picture.* Ki'i, ki'i i kaha 'ia, kahana. 2. *Pulling.* 'Ume 'ana, kō; — *up,* mū'ekeke'i.
drawknife. Pahi pa'a uma, pahi 'ume.
drawn. Kaha 'ia, huki 'ia; huki, 'i'ika *(face). See* **draw.**
dread. Weli, weliweli. *Stricken with dread,* ilihia.
dreadful. Weliweli, māna'ona'o.
dream. Moe'uhane, moe; *recollected* —, haili moe; — *while dozing,* hihi'o; *erotic —,* moe kaha'ula, aikaha-'ula, kaha'ula. *Rare:* moemoeā, mī, ha'awina. *See* **mai'a.** *Name that came in a dream,* inoa pō. *To interpret dreams,* wehewehe moe'uhane, mō'ike. *To dream of canoes,* moe wa'a *(bad luck, disappoint-*

ment). Man's privilege is to dream, 'o ke kanaka ke kuleana o ka moe. *There is no truth in dreams (FS 273),* 'a'ole ka 'oia'i'o i loko o ka moe.
dreamer. Ka mea nāna nā moe.
dreary. Kuanea, kaumaha.
dredge. Kope, uwa'a, kīwa'a.
dregs. Oka, ko'ana, ko'ala, ki'o, mākū. *See* **ahu 'awa.** *Dregs of society,* 'ala'uka. *To remove dregs from medicinal herbs,* paka.
drenched. Pulu pē, pē. *Also:* pa'ū, po'ū, no'ū, kilihē, 'e'elo, hō'e'elo, 'elo'elo, pulu 'elo, pulukā, pelepulu, nolu pē, peno, pōkeokeo.
dress. 1. *Garment.* Lole, 'a'ahu. *To dress,* komo, komo lole, hō'a'ahu. *To dress others,* ho'okomo. *Types of dresses:* holokū, mu'umu'u, pukikī, 'ōkolepu'u. *To dress up, as in one's best,* kāhiko, linohau, pa'ihi, hao ā pa'ihi, haukalī. *Have you dressed yet?* Ua komo mai nei 'oe i kou 'a'ahu? 2. *To wrap a wound.* Wahī. 3. *As a fowl.* Unuunu *(pluck);* kua'i *(disembowel).* 4. *Military command.* Left, dress, nānā i ka hema.
dresser. Pahu waihona *(furniture).*
dressing. Kai, hō'ono'ono 'ai. *See* **stuffing.** *Salad dressing,* ho'ono'ono lau 'ai.
dress suit. Pupuamoa, puapuamoa.
dried. Malo'o. *Also:* konene, nō'ā. *See* **dry.** *Dried up by the sun,* pāpa'a lā.
drift. Lana wale, lana hele. *Also:* lanaau, au, auhele, 'auana *(wander);* ka'alewa, laweau, īkā, ho'oīkā, puewa, pūnini.
drifter. 'Ae'a wale. *See* **vagabond.**
driftwood. Pīhā, piha'ā. *See saying,* **mamo 4.**
drill. 1. *Tool.* Nao wili, wili, 'ōmilo. *To drill a hole,* hou puka, wili puka. 2. *Military.* Paikau. 3. *Practice.* Ho'oma'ama'a.
drink. 1. *Verb.* Inu, inumia, pā; kani, unu *(rare). For drinking songs, see* **kāmau 2** *and Elbert and Mahoe 68 (chorus), 83. To drink intoxicants,* inu lama, pā kī'aha, ho'okāmau. *To drink until satisfied,* inu ā kena. *To drink excessively,* pākela inu, ho'okina i ka inu. *To drink sparingly,* inu li'ili'i, ho'opā iki. *To drink temperately,* inu pākiko. *To give to drink,* ho'īnu, ho'ōhā-inu, hāinu, ho'okāmau. 2. *Noun.* Mea inu. *Mixed drink,* mea inu ho'ohuihui, mea inu kāwili. *Iced or chilled drink,* 'awa, aumiki, pokiwai. *Intoxicating drink,* lama, wai 'ona. *Let's have a drink,* e kāmau kī'aha kākou.
drip. Kulu, kulukulu. *Also:* lū, he'e, kēwai, nakulu, palalē, ū.
drive. 1. *As cattle.* Ho'ohuli, hō'ā; pāhoe *(fish).* 2. *To drive away.* Kipaku, ho'okuke, ho'omahuka. *Also:* ho-'ēhu, hehu, ho'ohemū, ho'ohū, hoaka, kuehu, ho'oka'a, kīpa'i, pūkō. 3. *As a car.* Kalaiwa, ho'okele. *To drive a carriage,* ho'oholo ka'a, ka'i i ke ka'a. *To go for a drive,* holoholo ka'a. *To take someone for a drive,* ho'oholoholo ka'a. *To drive hard, as a horse,* pākī. 4. *As nails.* Kākia, mākia, kīpou.
driver. Kalaiwa, ho'okele ka'a, kia ka'a *(as of a car).*
driver's license. Laikini kalaiwa ka'a.
drizzle. Ua li'ili'i, ua kilihune, kili hau.
drone bee. Nalo meli noho hale.
drool. Hā'ae, kahe ka hā'ae, moni ka hā'ae. *Also:* waha kale, waha 'ūkele, ka moe.
droop. Luhe, loha, ho'olo'u, ku'uwelu, kūwelu. *Also:* kāluhe, kāluheu'a, 'ōluheluhe, lola, emi, niniau, 'omī, mīmī, mae. *Drooping over Pā-'ie'ie pool,* luhe i ka wai o Pā-'ie'ie *(intoxicated).*
drop. 1. *Trickle.* Kulu, kahe, mākili. *Drop of rain,* paka ua. *Drop of water,* kulu wai. *Drop of perspiration,* mākili hou. 2. *Let fall.* Hā'ule, hā'ule'ule, hā'ulehia, ho'ohā'ule, ha'ulena. *To drop dead,* hina moe, hina make. *To drop, as bombs,* ho'oku'u e hā'ule, kōlū. *To drop a matter,* ho'omoe. *To set a drop net,* hō'au.
dropsy. Pehu *(for various kinds, see Haw.-Eng. entry and entries that follow it),* ma'i pehu. *Also:* 'ōhao, 'ōpū'ōhao, 'alaneo, 'u'ulukai.

drought. Wā maloʻo; nōʻā *(rare).*
drove. Pūʻā *(noun). See* **drive.**
drown. Piholo, hoʻopiholo, hoʻopalemo, holoāiʻa.
drowsy. Maka hiamoe, kulu, kulu hiamoe. *Also:* mania, hoʻomania, malohi, hoʻomalohi, maniawai, heha, kāwai, molohai, niolo, mōlelehu, ʻolelehu, nipo, hoʻoluluhi, ʻōheahea, kuli hiamoe. *Wai-piʻo is drowsy in the mist (saying),* heha Wai-piʻo i ka noe.
drudge. Paʻu, paʻaua, kauā paʻaua. *See saying,* **anus.** *To treat as a drudge,* hoʻopaʻu, hoʻopaʻaua.
drudgery. Paʻu hana.
drug. Lāʻau hoʻomalule kino, lāʻau hoʻonoenoe, lāʻau hoʻohiamoe, lāʻau moe, mea ʻona. *Cf.* **marijuana, opium, medicine.** *Plants used to drug fish:* ʻauhuhu, hola, ʻauhola. *A drug on the market (plentiful),* pākī. *To mix drugs,* kāwili lāʻau.
drugged. Malule mahope o ka inu lāʻau ʻana.
druggist. Mea kāwili lāʻau.
drug store. Hale kāwili lāʻau, hale kūʻai lāʻau.
drum. Pahu, ipu *(for various kinds, see Haw-Eng. entry and entries that follow it);* pūniu *(knee drum). Also:* pahu hula, pahu kani, pahu paʻi, pahu kanaloa, pā ipu. *See* **kāʻeke, kāʻekeʻeke** *and saying,* **goat.** *Gasoline drum,* kula kakalina. *Drum house,* hale pahu. *Ruffle of drums,* kāʻeleloi. *To drum,* paʻi ipu, hoʻokani pahu; pahūpahū *(with force);* kūpaloloi *(with fingers);* nīpolo *(rare),* ʻeʻekeloi. *Drumbeats:* pā *(general term; a particular beat);* kūkū, kāhela *(particular beats).*
drummer. Mea hoʻokani pahu, paʻi ipu, hoʻopaʻa.
drumstick. Lāʻau hoʻokani pahu *(drum beater);* ʻūhā moa *(chicken leg).*
drunk. ʻOna. *See* **intoxicated.**
drunkard. ʻOna mau, ʻona lama. *See saying,* **hū 4.**
dry. Maloʻo. *Also:* ʻāpaʻa, ʻāpaʻapaʻa, kaulaʻi, kōkaʻa, pāmalō, mae, māhāhā, anoa, panoa, ūpē, ʻeʻe, ʻōlino, wīkaʻo, ponanā, konekonea, mōkaʻokaʻo, maloʻohāhā, malōhāhā, pīkaʻo, pokaʻo, kaʻo, kōʻā. *Rack for drying,* haka kaulaʻi. *Dry rot,* mūnō, alapuka. *Dried up,* kaʻeʻe, pīkaʻo, hōmī; lele *(breasts). To dry out,* hoʻomaloʻo. *To wipe dry, as dishes,* kāwele, kaʻa maloʻo.
dual. Pālua. *Dual form,* kino pālua, kino lua, kino pāpālua. *Dual natured,* kino pālua, kino lua. *Dual number (in grammar),* helu lua.
dub. Pao. *Also:* poho, poʻo, kua, kūpele, hoʻowaha, kīmō.
dubious. Kānalua, kakanalua.
Dublin. Kupelina, Dubelina.
duchess. Kukeke, kuke wahine.
duck. 1. *Bird.* Kakā *(domesticated);* pīwai *(wild);* Hawaiian —, koloa, koloa maoli; *pintail* —, koloa māpu. 2. *To plunge or bow.* ʻAlu, lumaʻi, luʻu.
due. Manawa kūpono. *The debt is due,* hiki mai ka manawa uku. *To aspire to more than is oneʻs due,* piʻikoi.
duel. Hakakā, pepehi lua; hakakā pahi *(sword);* hakakā pūpanapana *(pistol).*
dues. Uku kūmau.
duet. Leo lua, leokū pālua.
due to. *See* **because.**
duke. Kuke, duke.
dulcimer. Kukima.
dull. 1. *Not sharp.* Kūmūmū, mūmū, ʻoi ʻole. *Also:* ʻamūmū, manumanu, haumanumanu, pahupahu, māhani, mene, kaʻakumu, pihi, peue, mani, hāmani. 2. *Slow-witted.* Lolohi, maluhi, molohi, poluhi, kūloma,

kohelemu, lolōiele, mānoanoa. 3. *Uninteresting.* Hoihoi ʻole, manakā, leʻaleʻa ʻole, pāmalō, kūkaikea.
dumb. Leo paʻa, mūmule, ʻāʻā. *Struck dumb,* hakanū.
dump. Kahua waiho ʻōpala, waihona ʻōpala, kiʻona. *Also:* wahi hoʻāhu ʻōpala, hoʻoleina moka, ahu kūkae, kehena, olomehani.
dumpling. Palaoa mokumoku, palaoa lūlū.
dumpy. Poupou, paiāhaʻa.
dunce. Poʻo ʻolohaka.
dune. Puʻe. *Sand dune,* puʻe one, puʻu one.
dung. Kūkae; kūkae manu *(bird).*
dungarees. ʻĀhina, ʻāhinahina.
dungeon. Lua paʻahao.
dung heap. Kiʻona, hoʻoleina moka, ahu kūkae.
dunk. Penu, pepenu, hoʻopenu.
duodecimal. Kuokekimala, duodekimala.
duplicate. Lua, lua like, kope.
duplicity. Hana maʻalea, hoʻopunipuni. *See* **deceitful** *and saying,* **cuttlefish.**
durable. Paʻa, mau.
Durham. Kulahama, Durahama.
during. ʻOiai, ʻoi, i ka wā o.
dusk. Mōlehu, mōlehulehu, mōlelehu, pōlehulehu, pūlehulehu, liʻulā; ʻehu ahiahi *(fig.).*
dust. Ehu lepo, kuehu, ehu, ʻehu, uahi, lelehuna, lepo ʻaeʻae. *Dust of morning,* ehu kakahiaka. *Dust of evening,* ehu ahiahi. *Dust streamer,* kōwelo ʻeʻa. *Dust particle,* huna lepo. *Dust cloud,* ʻeʻa. *Dust column or cloud,* piʻolepo. *Red dust,* alaʻula. *Wind-blown dust,* ʻeʻa; wilikōī *(rare). To scatter dust,* huʻalepo, kaiehu. *To dust, as furniture,* kāwele, kāhili lepo. *You are dust, and to dust you shall return (Kin. 3:19),* he lepo nō ʻoe, ā e hoʻi hou aku ʻoe i ka lepo.
dusty. Ehu, ehu lepo, ʻeʻa; pōhūhū *(rare).*
dusty miller. Hinahina ʻaʻala.
Dutch. Hōlani.
duty. 1. *Obligation.* Pono, hana, mahele hana. *Duty before pleasure,* hoʻokō hana mamua o ka leʻaleʻa *(see* **hoʻokō**). 2. *Customs.* Kuke. *To pay duty,* uku i ke kuke.
dwarf. Peke, ʻāʻā, haʻa. *Also:* kualiʻi, haʻakualiʻi, kupaliʻi, ʻiʻi, ʻakiki, noʻonoʻi, ʻanini, maʻihi *(these are terms for short people; there may have been no dwarfs in ancient Hawaiʻi; cf.* **ʻĀʻāhualiʻi,** *HM 338).*
dwell. Noho.
dweller. Mea noho. *Shore dwellers,* nā kānaka o kai, noho kai, kō kula kai.
dwelling. Nohona, noho ʻana. *Dwelling house,* hale noho. *Dwelling place,* wahi noho, kahi noho. *Dwelling in peace,* noho aloha.
dwindling. Emiemi, kōlīliʻi.
dye. Wai, waihoʻoluʻu, wai ʻele, wai ʻeleʻele. *Also:* weʻa, hili, kūhili; kūpenu *(by dipping);* kiʻolena, hōlei, kīheʻaheʻa palaʻā. *Dye colors:* ʻōlenalena *(yellow);* puakai *(red);* pōkohukohu *(made of* noni *root);* ʻakala *(raspberry or thimbleberry juice). Dye cup,* kā kāpala; kākākau, pahu palapala *(rare). To extract dye colors,* hoʻawa.
dyehouse. Hale hoʻoluʻu.
dye plant. ʻAlaea, kūmauna.
dynamite. Kianapauka.
dysentery. Hī, kulu. *Bloody dysentery,* hī koko. *A disease with characteristics of dysentery,* ʻōkuʻu, ʻokuʻu lepo heheʻe. *Weak from dysentery,* ʻōhemo.
dyspepsia. Kikepepekia.

E

e. 'Ē.
each. Kēlā mea kēia mea, pākahi.
eager. Ake, 'i'ini.
eagle. 'Aeko. *Golden eagle,* 'aeko kula.
ear. Pepeiao; 'e'eiao *(rare); piko (tip). For inner ear, see* **niu kuli.** *Protruding ears,* pepeiao manana. *Ears pressing close to the head,* pepeiao pili. *Infected ear,* pepeiao pilau, pepeiao hohono. *Ear bone,* kumu pepeiao. *Ear drum,* pahu kani. *Ear of corn,* hua kūlina.
earache. Pepeiao 'eha.
earl. *Same as* **count.**
early. Koke, mua, hiki mua, miki'ala. *Early morning,* kakahiaka nui.
earmark. Kila, kuni.
earn. Loa'a.
earnest. Kūo'o. *To take things in earnest,* hō'i'o.
earnings. Loa'a.
earring. Kulapepeiao *(for various kinds, see* **kulapepeiao**). *Also:* apo, apo pepeiao *(hoop-shaped).*
earth. 1. *World.* Ao, honua, 'āina, pa'a-i-lalo. *Foundation of the earth,* papa honua. *Globe of the earth,* kāhonua. *Origin of the earth,* kumu honua. **2.** *Dirt.* Lepo; 'alaea *(soluble);* lepo pa'a, kahua pa'a *(solid);* lepo 'ula'ula, mā'ula'ula *(red);* kūlapa *(piled on side of ditch). To come out of the earth, as a spring,* hū honua. *To soften the earth, as for planting,* 'eku'eku. *Earth oven,* umu lepo. *Earth protuberance,* kio honua. *Earth ridge,* iwi. *Earth pot,* ipu lepo. *The earth-devouring woman,* ka wahine 'ai honua (Pele).
earthquake. 'Ōla'i.
earwax. Kokuli.
earwig. Lō.
ease. Maha, nanea, walea, 'oluea, pu'uho'omaha. *See saying,* **taro.** *To ease pain,* ho'omāmā, ho'onā, ho'omālie; pa'apa'anā *(rare). To ease your grief,* ho'omāmā i kou kaumaha. *To do with ease, as of long custom,* hana walea. *At ease,* 'olu, hālūlā, lōli'i, mōhalu, mōhaluhalu; hō'olu'olu *(military command).*
eased. Pono, nā, māmā *(of pain, ache, or distress).*
easel. Lā'au ki'i.
easement. *See* **palapala ho'omalu.**
easily. Hikiwale, wale, ma'alahi. *Easily handled,* mili'opu.
east. Hikina; 'elelani, 'eleiālani *(priests' names). To the east,* mana'e, ma ka hikina.
Easter. Ka lā i ala hou ai ka Haku *(Protestant);* Pakoa *(Catholic);* mōliaola.
eastern. Hikina, lā hiki, na'e. *Eastern Hemisphere.* 'Ao-'ao Hikina. *Eastern sun,* lā hiki.
East Indian. 'Inia.
East Indies. 'Inia Hikina.
Eastport. 'Ikepoka.
easy. Hikiwale, ma'alahi. *See sayings,* **'ama'ama, hāhāpa'akai, girl.** *To lead an easy life,* 'ai ali'i, 'ai i kalo mo'a, kālelemuku, ho'opaulinalina.
easygoing. Waipahē, 'olu'olu, hilu, waliwali, wawali. *Cf.* **worry.**
eat. 'Ai, 'ai iho, amu, ho'opiha; — *heartily,* ho'omā'ona, ho'onu'u, nu'u, no'u, hiala 'ai, kīhamu, haupa; — *much,* 'ai nui, 'ai ā hewa ka waha, 'ai lau, pākela 'ai, pake'ai *(see* **stuffed** *and sayings,* **ko'u, lua, lip**); — *enormously,* 'ai ā manō; — *greedily,* 'ai ā pua'a; — *little, without relish,* pū, pūpū 'ai, mīnole, ho'omahu, ho'opā iki, niole, māna 'ai, muni; — *fastidiously or slowly,* mīkole, 'oninini, aka'ai. *Longing to eat,* puni 'ai, pehu. *Ways to eat (other);* hamu, nome, 'ai kau, 'ai 'uha'uha, 'ai noa, 'ai kapu, kūpa'a-kai; 'ai kohana *(alone);* mīkoi, miki pāpālua, miki pālua, kūpu'u, 'ōpū palula, 'ūka'e, halalē; 'ai pilau, 'ai pala mauna *(of sorcerers). A call to eat,* kāhea 'ai. *Eat all you want,* 'ai ā mā'ona. *An invitation in chant or song to eat:* 'ai ā hewa ka waha, 'o ka leo ka uku! *Eat until the mouth can have no more, [my] reward, [your] voice!*
eaten. 'Ai 'ia, 'aina. *Fig. expressions for one who has eaten much:* **kāhela, lua, pae.** *Have you eaten?* Mā-'ona 'oe?
eating. 'A'ai *(as a sore).*
eating companion. Hoa 'ai.
eating house. Hale 'aina.
eavesdrop. Ho'olohelohe 'ōlelo, ho'olono.
ebb. Emi, emiemi. *Also:* laumeki, hanu'u, kāo'o, nioke; pohī. *Ebbing sea,* kai ho'i, kai emi.
ebony. Lama, 'ēponi; ēlama *(rare).*
eccentric. 'Ano 'ē.
Ecclesiastes. Kekahuna.
echo. Kūpina'i, leo kūpina'i, nakulu, papā, hāku'i, wawā.
eclipse. Pouli. *Lunar eclipse,* pouli ka mahina. *Solar eclipse,* pouli holo'oko'a 'ana o ka lā *(total). Partial eclipse,* pouli hapa.
economical. Makauli'i, minamina, pākiko; ho'opī *(extremely).*
economics, economy. No'eau ho'okele waiwai.
economize. Ho'omakauli'i.
Ecuador, Ecuadorian. 'Ekuakola, Ekuadora.
eczema. Piele *(on the scalp).*
eddy. Au, wiliau, wiliwai, 'oke'e.
edema. 'Ālaneo, pehu.
Eden. 'Ēkena, Edena. *Garden of Eden,* Kīhāpai o 'Ēkena, mahina 'ai ma 'Ēkena.
edge. Ka'e, kapa, kihi, lihi, nīao, maka, nihi, kūkulu, hu'a, pe'a, ha'i, kīkepa, muka'e; kauhuhu, hanahanai *(of a precipice, rare). Water's edge,* 'ae kai. *Edge of time units, especially of late night,* pili. *Forest edge,* pili lā'au. *Two-edged,* maka lua. *To edge away,* ne'e aku, koene. *Teeth set on edge,* mania ka niho.
edible. Hiki ke 'ai 'ia. *Edible herb,* lā'au iki 'ai 'ia.
edict. Kānāwai.
Edinburgh. 'Ekinapolo, Edinaboro.
edit. Ho'oponopono.
edition. Pa'i 'ana, ho'opuka 'ana. *First edition,* ho'opuka mua. *Second edition,* ho'opuka 'elua. *Third edition,* ke kolu o ka pa'i 'ana.
editor. Luna ho'oponopono.
educate. Ho'ona'auao.
educated. Ho'ona'auao 'ia.
education. A'o palapala, ho'ona'auao. *See* **Board of Education, Department of Education.** *To seek education,* 'imi na'auao.
educational. Ho'ona'auao. *Educational system,* 'oihana ho'ona'auao.
eel. Puhi *(for various kinds, see* **puhi** *and following entries);* kuna, i'a; puhi 'īni'iniki *(infant);* 'au'aukī, puakī, 'ōilo *(young). Eel-catching stick,* haoa puhi. *Eel hole,* lua puhi. *Eel tentacle,* 'awe puhi. *An eel of the billows, the sagging chin protrudes,* ka puhi o ka 'ale, ahu ke 'olo *(of a wealthy person).*
effect. Hopena, ho'okō, hua. *Take effect,* ka'a *(as medicine);* 'o'oki *(as kava intoxication).*
effeminate. Kohu wahine, hō'owahine.
effervesce. Huahua'i, pipi'i, pi'ipi'i, hū.
effervescent solution. Pa'akaihū.
efficiency. Mākaukau, miki, mikimiki.

effort. Hoʻāʻo, hoʻāho. *To make a great effort,* hoʻoikaika, hōʻikaika.
effortless. Walea.
egg. Hua, hua moa *(chicken);* kalapaki *(double-yolked);* huamakani *(yolkless);* huaʻaluʻalu *(with a very soft shell).* See **yolk.** *Hard-boiled egg,* hua moʻa loa. *Soft-boiled egg,* hua moʻa hapa. *Scrambled egg,* kai hua, hua pākā. *Fried egg,* hua palai. *Rotten egg,* hua āelo. *White of an egg,* ēwe o ka hua moa, kauō keʻokeʻo; ēwe *(rare). Eggs deposited by flies,* kūkaelā. *Fish eggs,* kowaū. *To lay an egg,* hoʻoluʻa. *To lay many eggs,* huahua.
eggplant. Lahopipi.
egotism. *See* **proud.**
Egypt, Egyptian. ʻAikupika, Aigupita.
eight. ʻEwalu, walu, ʻawalu. *Eight times,* ʻewalu. *To divide by eight, eightfold, to have eight,* pāwalu. *Eight o'clock,* kani ka hola ʻewalu. *Hina's pig child has eight eyes (FS 197),* ʻewalu maka o ke keiki puaʻa a Hina *(eight was a sacred or formulistic number).*
eighteen. ʻUmi kūmāwalu, ʻumi kumamāwalu.
eighth. Walu. *Eighth part, one eighth,* hapawalu.
eighty. Kanawalu.
eighty-eight. Kanawalu kūmāwalu, kanawalu kumamāwalu.
eighty-five. Kanawalu kūmālima, kanawalu kumamālima.
eighty-four. Kanawalu kūmāhā, kanawalu kumamāhā.
eighty-nine. Kanawalu kūmāiwa, kanawalu kumamāiwa.
eighty-one. Kanawalu kūmākahi, kanawalu kumamākahi.
eighty-seven. Kanawalu kūmāhiku, kanawalu kumamāhiku.
eighty-six. Kanawalu kūmāono, kanawalu kumamāono.
eighty-three. Kanawalu kūmākolu, kanawalu kumamākolu.
eighty-two. Kanawalu kūmālua, kanawalu kumamālua.
either. Kekahi. *I don't either,* ʻaʻole ʻo au kekahi. *Either Kū or Hina,* Kū aiʻole Hina.
eject. Kipaku, hoʻokuke; kikī *(as octopus ink).*
ejection. Kipaku. *Document for ejection,* palapala hoʻopiʻi kipaku.
elapse. Hala, pau.
elastic. Laholio, ʻolu, nolu, napa, ʻapiʻapi; ʻapeʻape.
elbow. Kuʻekuʻe, kuʻekuʻe lima, kuʻe lima; kuʻi *(as of a pipe). To elbow,* hoʻokuʻekuʻe, kuʻe, hoʻokē, nakuʻe.
elder. Kahiko aʻe; kaikuaʻana *(sibling of the same sex);* lunakahiko *(church). Elder relative,* pili mua.
elderly. ʻĀoʻo, oʻo, makule.
eldest. *See* **elder.** *Eldest child,* makahiapo, hiapo.
elect. Koho, hoʻokoho.
election. Koho, koho pāloka. *Election day,* lā koho. *Election season,* kau koho pāloka. *Election teller,* helu pāloka. *Primary election,* koho wae mua, koho mua.
electors. Poʻe koho.
electric. Uila, uwila. *Electric bus,* kaʻa uila. *Electric stove,* kapuahi uila. *Electric light,* kukui uila. *Electric light bulb,* amani kukui uila. *Electric fan,* peʻahi uila.
electricity. Uila, uwila.
eleemosynary. ʻImi i ka pono o ke kanaka.
elegant. Hoʻohiehie, hīhīmanu, hiluhilu.
elementary. Kumu mua.
Eleotridae fishes. ʻOʻopu *(for various kinds, see Haw.-Eng. entry and entries that follow it).*
elepaio. *See* **flycatcher.**
elephant. ʻElepane, ʻelepani. *Elephant tusk,* niho ʻelepani.
elephantiasis. Kewe, maʻi ʻelepani. *Cf.* pehu kumu niu.
elevate. Hāpai, hoʻokiʻekiʻe, hōʻiu, hiu, hoʻopinana. *To elevate oneself by boasting of chiefly associates,* pai aliʻi.
elevated. Hoʻokiʻekiʻe; kaʻanuʻa *(place). Elevated train,* kaʻaahi kau i ka lewa.
elevation. Kiʻekiʻena, huku, nuʻu; ʻōhū *(hill).*
elevator. ʻEleweka.

eleven. ʻUmi kūmākahi, ʻumi kumamākahi.
elf. *See* **legendary beings.**
eligible. Kūpono, kohu.
eliminate. Kāpae, hoʻopau, hoʻokaʻawale.
elk. ʻEleka.
ellipse. Pōʻai lōʻihi.
elm. Lāʻau kaʻa. *(KJV.)*
elongate. Hoʻolōʻihi, hoʻooloolo.
elongated. Oloolo.
elope. Mahuka e male, male malū.
eloquent. Mīkololohua, mīkolohua, mīkolelehua, maiele, poeko. *See idiom,* **current.**
else. ʻĒ aʻe. *Someone else,* kahi, kekahi, haʻi. *Or else,* iʻole. *What else?* He aha hou aʻe?
elsewhere. Ma kahi ʻē, ʻē.
elude. ʻAlo, pakele aku.
emaciated. Wīwī loa, iwiiwi, hakahaka. *Also:* ʻamopuʻu, māilo, hōmale, hōmali, puhipalalā.
emasculated. Poʻa.
embalmed. Iʻaloa. *Embalmed body,* iʻaloa.
embankment. Hoʻāhua. *Also:* ʻopi wai; kāhonua *(dirt);* pale kai, kuakua. *Embankment newly made,* kuakuakū. *To build an embankment,* hoʻopaepae. *Process of packing earth to make an embankment,* kuakuakū.
embark. Eʻe, hoʻoili.
embarrass. Hoʻohilahila, palai.
embarrassed. Hilahila, hoʻopalai, palaina.
embassy. Nohona kuhina, ʻemepake.
embezzlement. ʻĀpuka, ʻaihue i ka waiwai i hāʻawi ʻia mai e mālama ʻia.
embitter. Hōʻawaʻawa, hoʻomālailena.
embittered. ʻAwaʻawahia, loko liʻu.
emblem. Hōʻailona.
embody. Hoʻokino.
embrace. Pūʻili, pūliki, pūlikiliki, pūʻiki, pili koke, ʻāpona, kūwili, apo; — *tightly,* kilipue, pukukuʻi.
embroider. Humulau, ʻoniʻoniʻo.
embroil. Kūhihi.
embryo. Aka *(at the moment of conception);* hāuli, ʻele. *Embryo of Kū (said of a child born on the night or day of Kū),* ʻele Kū.
emerald. ʻEmelala, ʻōmaʻomaʻo, pōhaku ʻōmaʻomaʻo.
emerge. Puka, pua; ʻōkū, hoʻāpuka *(rare).*
emergency. Ulia pōpilikia, pilikia kūhewa.
emetic. Lāʻau hoʻopiʻi, lāʻau hoʻopiʻipiʻi, hoʻoluaʻi.
emigration. Poʻe hele mai ka ʻāina aku. *See* **Bureau of Emigration.**
eminent domain. Lawe ʻana i ka waiwai no nā hana o ka lehulehu.
emir. ʻEmila.
emitted. Hoʻopuka, hoʻokī.
emotion. *No general term, but emotions may be described by descriptive words following* puʻuwai, naʻau, *or* puʻupaʻa *(rare), or* piʻi ka, *as* puʻuwai hauʻoli, *happiness,* piʻi ka huhū, *to be angry;* pīhoihoi, hoʻolokuloku, piʻoloke, mālani, auālipo; kipona *(strong);* uluhua, mokuāhua, pilihua *(as grief, sorrow, anger);* ulu; hakukoʻi; olokē *(as speech);* hōpūpū *(of hate, love, lust). See idioms,* **hauli, outrigger float.** *Words of emotion,* piʻipiʻi i ʻōlelo. *Transported with emotion,* lalawe ke kino. *To feel emotion of love,* hū aʻe ke aloha.
emotional. Pīhoihoi, pono ʻole ka manaʻo. *Emotional crisis,* kipona koʻikoʻi loa. *Emotional disturbances,* ʻīloli, hoʻīloli. *Emotionally excited, as with hate, love, lust,* hōpūpū.
emperor. ʻEmepela.
emphasize. Hoʻokoʻikoʻi, kālele leo, kālele manaʻo.
emphatic. Koʻikoʻi.
empire. Aupuni ʻemepela, ʻemepaea.
employ. Hoʻohana *(use);* hoʻolimalima, hai *(hire). He employs six servants,* ʻeono āna kānaka hana.
employed. Paʻa i ka hana; kaʻakaʻahiki *(rare).*
employee. Poʻe hana, limahana.
employer. Haku, haku hana. *Female employer,* haku wahine.
employment. Hana, ʻoihana, hoʻohana. *Steady employ-*

ment, hana pa'a. *Employment committee,* kōmike 'imi hana. *To accept employment,* lawe i ka hana. *To begin employment,* komo i ka hana.

empower. Ho'omana, ho'āmana.

empress. 'Emepela wahine.

emptiness. Hakahaka, 'alaneo.

empty. Hakahaka, haka, 'olohaka. *Also:* nea, neanea, neoneo, 'ōnea, 'ōneanea, neo; ka'ele *(as a bowl).* An *empty house,* he hale noho 'ole 'ia. *To go empty-handed,* hele wale. *To slosh a canoe back and forth so as to empty sea water,* pāuma.

enact. Ho'oholo, kau, ho'omana. *Enacting clause,* 'ōlelo ho'oholo.

enacted. Holo, ho'oholo 'ia. *Be it enacted,* e ho'oholo 'ia.

enamel. 'Enamela.

enchant. Ho'okalakupua, ho'ohia'ai, ho'ohei mana'o, heihei, ho'oheihei.

enchanted. Heihei.

enchanter. Ho'okalakupua; mea nānā mo'o, kilo, kilo-kilolani; mākoi *(Biblical).*

enchantment. Kilokilo. *To use enchantment,* ho'okalakupua, kūkā mo'o.

encircle. Pō'ai, anapuni, 'aipuni, ka'apuni, kā'ai, kākai.

enclose. Puni, ka'apuni.

enclosure. Pā. *Enclosure for animals,* pā holoholona. *Canoe enclosure,* pā wa'a. *Circular enclosure, as about a fishpond,* pā puni. *Taboo enclosure,* pālama, paehumu.

encompass. Ka'apuni, 'aipuni, puana.

encore. Hana hou.

encourage. Ho'opaipai, paipai, ho'opai, pai, hāpai, ho'oikaika, hō'ikaika, ho'olana, hō'eu, hō'eu'eu, ho'okā'eu'eu, ho'ohana, ho'ohoihoi, lale, ho'olale, kī-paipai, ho'okokonoi'e, ha'inole.

encouragement. 'Ōlelo paipai.

encrusted. Pāpa'apū; ni'i *(with salt);* pakalua *(as with grime or rust).*

encyclopedia. Puke hō'ike pōkole no kēlā me kēia mea.

end. Pau 'ana, panina, hope. *To end,* ho'opau, ho'ōki. *Also:* nuku, wēlau, 'ēlau, welelau, welewelelau, kīkī-pani; kiko *(as of a fish pole);* po'o *(as of a cane, rope, or pole);* wāwae *(as of a rainbow);* puku *(rare). See* pīpī **2.** *At an end,* muku. *End of knots in plaiting,* hi'uhi'u. *There's no end,* 'a'ohe lihi launa mai.

endearing. 'Ālohaloha. *Endearing terms:* nūnū maka onaona *(see* **dove***);* kole maka onaona *(see* **kole***);* kūmū *(slang);* milimili, lei, aloha, ku'u 'ōnohi, hiwa-hiwa, pua mae 'ole, aloha makamae. *The singular possessives* ku'u, *my, and* kō, *your, are endearing, and the inclusive pronouns* kāua *and* kākou, *as well as the demon.* nei, *as in* Hawai'i nei, *my [beloved] Hawai'i. Cf.Gram. 12.*

endeavor. Ho'ā'o, ho'oikaika, 'imi pono, na'i. *See* **Christian Endeavor Society.**

endeavoring. Na'ina.

ended. Pau.

ending. Hopena, 'okina, panina, pau 'ana.

endless. Pau 'ole, mau loa, ho'olā'au.

endorse. 'Āpono, kākau kāko'o; kākau inoa *(as a check).*

endow. Ho'olako, ho'oili.

endowment. Pu'u kālā kūmau.

endpiece. *See* **canoe.**

endure. Ho'omanawanui, ahonui, mau, 'alo, ō, kāmau ea, kūlō'ihi.

enema. 'Ūpī, hano, hahano, waikī, hoene. *Kinds:* pahu-ka'a, kaikea (kaikuehu, kaīkū), 'o'opuhue, waikea. *To give an enema,* hālalo.

enemy. Hoa pa'io, hoa kaua, hoa pāonioni, 'enemi. *To make an enemy,* hō'enemi.

energetic. 'Eleu, 'ele'eleu, hō'ele'eleu, 'uleu, mahi, mikimiki, lapa. *Also:* kīkā, ma'iha, kamaehu. *Not energetic,* ma'uwele.

enfeeble. Ho'onāwali, ho'omalule.

enfold. Ka'awili, pāka'awili, pāka'uwili.

enforce. Ho'okō, ho'oholo. *To enforce the law,* ho'okō kānāwai; ho'oholo i ke kānāwai.

engaged. 1. *Occupied.* Pa'a, lilo; walea, nanea, luana *(usually in a pleasant way); deeply —,* papau. **2.** *Betrothed.* Palau, ho'opalau.

engine. 'Enikini, 'enekini, mīkini. *Locomotive engine,* ka'aahi. *Fire engine,* ka'a kinai ahi, ka'a wai, ka'a pauahi.

engineer. Wilikī. *Civil engineer,* wilikī kīwila, 'enekinia kīwila.

engineering. Wilikī.

England. Pelekane, 'Enelani.

English. Pelekane, Pelekania, Beretania, haole. *English language,* 'ōlelo Pelekane, 'ōlelo haole, namu haole.

Englishman. Pelekane, haole.

engraft. Pāku'i.

engrave. Kaha, kālai. *To cut or engrave in copper or brass,* kaha keleawe.

engraver. Kaha mekala, kaha keleawe.

engrossed. Lilo, lilo loa, papau.

enjoin. Kauoha, kauleo.

enjoy. Luana, walea, nanea, ho'ohoihoi, 'oli'oli, le'a. *To enjoy a life of ease: see* **taro.**

enjoyable. Nanea, ho'onanea, walea, le'ale'a, kapakapa, luakaha.

enjoyment. 'Oli'oli, hau'oli, hoihoi. *My enjoyment is completely gone (UL 251),* pau ai ko'u lihi hoihoi.

enlarge. Ho'onui, ho'omāhua, ho'omāhuahua, ho'omākōmakō; ho'olele *(as a picture).*

enlarged. Ho'onui 'ia. *Also:* kēkē, kōlikoliko, ki'imananana, kīlaha, nupa.

enlargement. Ki'i ho'olele *(of a picture).*

enlighten. Ho'omālamalama, kaiao.

enlightened. Na'auao, ao.

enlightenment. Aokanaka, mālamalama.

enlist. Komo no ka makemake.

enmity. Inaina. *To feel enmity,* hō'enemi, 'enemi.

enormous. Nui hewahewa.

enough. Lawa, nui, lawa puni, ka'aka'alawa, ana, pūlawa. *To be enough,* ka'a i ka lawa.

enraptured. Ho'ohihi, ho'ohei.

enrich. Ho'owaiwai, ho'olakolako.

enroll. Kākau inoa, ho'opa'a inoa.

ensign. Lepa.

enslave. Ho'okauā, ho'okuapa'a, ho'opa'auā.

ensnare. Ho'opunihei, hei, ho'oheihei, ho'okāhihi, huahualau, pahele; kāwili *(as birds).*

ensnared. Punihei, heia, miko.

entangle. Hihi, ho'ohihi, hei. *Also:* kūhihi, kauhihi, ho'okāhihi, hehei, kāwili, kā'ekā, hauhilikī, ho'owi'u, pahili. *To be involved in an entangling affair of any sort,* pili hihia.

entangled. Hihia, kāhihi, hihipe'a, hakakē, punihei, hauhili, hauhauhili, hili hewa, pohihihi, hilikau, mau-hili, kā'ekā, auwalakī, kīko'olā, heheia, heia, pe'ape'a; wi'u *(as a kite).*

entanglement. Hihia. *Also:* hihi, hihina, kāhihi, hili hewa. *To cause entanglement,* ho'ohihi.

enter. Komo, ho'okomo; ukokomo *(together),* ulu, unu. *To enter by mistake,* komohewa. *To enter without ceremony or permission,* komo wale.

entertain. Ho'okipa, ho'ohale kipa, ho'ohau'oli, ho'ohoihoi. *Also:* komo *(as an emotion);* pa'apa'anā, ho'opa'apa'anā.

entertainer. Mea ho'ole'ale'a. *See* **musician.**

entertaining. Hoihoi. *Also:* ho'okā'au, mīkololohua, mīkolelehua, mīkolelehua, mikomiko.

entertainment. Mea ho'ohau'oli, hō'ike'ike ho'ohau'oli.

enthrall. Heihei.

enthusiasm. 'Oli'oli nui, ohohia. *To do with enthusiasm,* kukupa'u.

enthusiastic. Piha 'eu, kā'eu'eu, ohohia.

entice. Kono, ho'okonokono, 'ume, ho'ohahai, ho'owalewale. *To entice a bird,* kono manu.

entire. Holoʻokoʻa, kāʻokoʻa.
entirely. Holoʻokoʻa, āpau, pū, ʻokoʻa, pau, lilo.
entirety. Nui, ʻokoʻa.
entitle. Hoʻokuleana.
entity. Holoʻokoʻa. *To establish as a seperate entity,* hoʻokaʻawale.
entrails. Naʻau, loko; papaʻakōnāhua *(rare). Cord made from the entrails of an enemy,* ʻahamoa.
entrance. 1. *Opening.* Komo ʻana, puka, ʻīpuka, nuku. *Entrance fee,* uku komo. *Entrance permit,* palapala ʻae e komo mai. 2. *To charm.* Hoʻohiaʻai, hoʻohoihoi, punihei, makahehi.
entrap. Hoʻoheihei, hoʻokāhihi. *See* **trap.**
entreat. Koi ikaika.
entrusted. Kauoha ʻia, waiho ʻia. *One entrusted to speak for another,* hoʻoilina ʻōlelo. *See* **trust.**
entry. Hoʻokomo ʻana. *Inward entry of goods,* hoʻokomo waiwai hoʻopae mai.
entwine. Hoʻohihi, ʻāwili, kāwili, kāmola, ʻoai, ʻowai, hōʻoai.
enumerate. Helu.
enumeration. Helu, helu papa, moʻohelu.
enunciation. Hopunaʻōlelo.
envelop. Hoʻopuni.
envelope. Wahī, wahī leka; ālaulau *(rare);* ʻaʻa *(for a foetus).*
environ. ʻAipuni.
environment. ʻAno o ka nohona, nā mea e hoʻopuni ana. *See* **place.**
envoy. ʻElele.
envy. Lili, pāoni, huā; hoʻōioi *(arouse);* poʻokoi *(rare).*
ephah. ʻApa, ʻepa.
ephod. ʻĒpoka.
epicanthic fold. Maka lilio.
epidemic. Maʻi laulā, maʻi ahulau, ahulau, maʻi pālahalaha.
epidermis. ʻIli luna.
epileptic seizure. Kauhola.
Epiphany. ʻEpipania.
Episcopal. ʻEpekopala.
Episcopalian. ʻEpekopala, hoʻomana Pīhopa.
epistle. ʻEpikekolo, ʻepikekole, episetole.
epithet. ʻŌlelo kaena *(lit., word of praise). See also* **taunt.**
epoch. Au, wā, auhonua.
epsom salts. Paʻakai inu.
equal. Like, like ā like, lua, kaulike, paʻi; paʻi ā paʻi *(as two persons);* paʻi kau *(rare). Without equal,* ana ʻole; lua ʻole; launa ʻole; ʻaʻohe mea nāna e paʻi i ke poʻo *(see poʻo). Equal ratio,* lakio like, lakio like kūpono. *See saying,* **kuapuʻu.**
equality. Kaulike.
equalize. Hoʻokaulike, hoʻolike, hoʻohālikelike.
equally. Like ā like.
equation. Kaulike.
equator. Pōʻai-waena-honua, ke alanui a ke kuʻukuʻu, alanui, piko-o-Wākea.
equip. Hoʻolako, hoʻolawa. *Well-equipped,* hoʻolako maikaʻi ʻia, pākī, lawa puni, koʻakoʻa.
equipment. Kuleana lako, lako, pono.
equity. Pono, kaulike.
equivocal. Kākālule.
er. Mea, ʻā *(as a speaker at a loss for words).*
-er. 1. *Agent in Hawaiian is expressed in several ways. See* **driver, leader, paddler** *(agent same as act performed);* **actor, dancer, rider, translator** *(act performed preceded by* mea *or* kanaka*);* **teacher** *(term other than the action).* 2. *Comparative degree.* Aʻe. *(Gram. 7.2.)* Ikaika aʻe, *stronger.*
era. Wā, paukū manawa, au, auau, auhonua.
erase. Holoi.
eraser. Mea holoi.
erect. Kū, kūkulu. *Also:* ʻūlepe *(as a cock's comb);* lāʻau, kano, kuʻiʻi, ōnū, lalahū *(as male organ);* uluoʻa *(rare). Cf.* **puahuku.** *To become erect,* kū, ea.
Erie. ʻElie.

eroded. ʻAi, ʻai ʻia, ʻaʻai, pao, poʻo, koea.
Eromanga. Nānā-pua *(name told to Boki in 1829).*
erosion. ʻAʻai.
err. Hewa. *Also:* hana hewa, hele hewa, lalau, halahū, kekeʻe; kupe, ʻōkupe *(as in conduct);* kuhihewa *(in judgment).*
errand. Hana.
error. Hewa, hala, paʻewa; ʻanuʻu *(fig). See sayings,* **carefully, reflect.** *Typographical error,* paʻi hewa. *To wander in error,* lalau hewa.
erudition. ʻIke. *To display erudition,* hoʻākamai.
eruption. Luaʻi, pele, hū ka pele, luaʻi pele *(volcanic);* puʻupuʻu maneʻo, pīkela, huhune *(skin). Mattery eruption on the scalp,* piele.
escalator. Alapiʻi lawe ʻōhua.
escape. Pakele. *Also:* hoʻāho, hōʻalo, mahuka; māihi ola *(barely);* ʻākelekele *(from danger or sickness). See sayings,* **akule, ʻāpua** 2. *Narrow escape,* pakele mai make. *To help escape,* hoʻopakele, hoʻopūhalahio.
escort. ʻAlo, ukali, hoʻoholoholo; huakaʻi hoʻohanohano *(honor). To escort arm in arm,* kuiʻēʻē.
Eskimo. ʻEkekemō, Mākinikā.
especially. *See* **exceedingly.**
essay. 1. *Composition.* Moʻolelo, kumumanaʻo. 2. *To try.* Hoʻāʻo.
essence. Aka, ʻiʻo. *Yours the essence, ours the flesh,* ʻo ke aka kā ʻoukou, ʻo ka ʻiʻo kā mākou *(dedication to the gods at feasts).*
Essex. ʻEkeka, Eseka.
-est. *Superlative degree. No Hawaiian equivalent other than* loa, nui loa. *Bravest,* koa loa.
establish. Hoʻokahua, hoʻokumu, hoʻokū, hoʻokūpaʻa, hoʻonoho, kūkulu; mākia *(as a kingdom).*
established. Noho paʻa, ʻonipaʻa, kumupaʻa *(firmly);* hoʻomakua; mauliauhonua *(rare).*
establishment. Hale ʻoihana *(business);* ka poʻe e loaʻa ʻo ka mana *(those with power).*
estate. Kuleana, waiwai; waiwai hoʻoilina *(inherited). See* **noʻeau hoʻokele waiwai.**
esteemed. Iliwahiwa, aloalo, mahalo ʻia, hulu; ʻala *(fig.). Esteemed chief,* hiwa lani. *Esteemed name,* inoa ʻala. *The esteemed Mr. Smith,* ka mea i mahalo ʻia, Mī Kamika.
estimate. Koho, manaʻo, kau paona.
estranged. Hoʻokaʻawale ʻia; nanau, lanau *(rare).*
estray. Holo lalau, ʻaeʻa.
estuary. Muliwai.
etch. Kaha; kuni *(in leather).*
eternal. Mau loa, manawakolu, i ka wā pau ʻole. *Eternal sleep,* hiamoe loa.
eternity. Wā (au) pau ʻole, wā (au) mau loa.
ethical, ethics. Kū i nā lula maikaʻi.
Ethiopia. ʻAikiopa.
ethnology. Noiʻi pono ʻana o ke kūlana o ke kanaka.
etiquette. Lula, lula hoʻokeonimana, noho nihinihi. *One who observes etiquette,* paʻalula.
eucalyptus. Palepiwa, ʻeukalikia, nuhōlani. *Eucalyptus oil,* ʻaila palepiwa.
Eucharist. ʻEukalikia.
eulogistic. Kaena, kānaenae, hoʻoleʻa.
eunuch. ʻEunuha.
euphorbia. Poʻolā, hame, mehame, haʻā; kaliko *(a wild kind).*
euphoric. Piha hauʻoli, piha ola kino maikaʻi. *Legendary place of euphoria,* kahua o Maliʻo.
Europe, European. ʻEulopa, Europa.
Europeanized. Hoʻohaole ʻia.
evacuate. Haʻalele, waiho; kiʻo *(bowels).*
evade. ʻAlo.
evaluate. Ana.
evangelical. ʻEuanelio.
evangelist. ʻEuanelika, kākau ʻeuanelio, haʻi ʻeuanelio.
evangelistic. ʻEuanelio.
evaporate. Maloʻo wale ka wai, omo, lele; koliʻi.
evaporated. Maloʻo, miki, kaʻeʻe.
evasive. ʻAloʻalo, pohihiu.

even. Aulike, kaulike; pāpū like *(flat)*. *Also:* aukahi; alania, laumania; kalamania *(as a calm sea or cliff);* paʻi ā paʻi *(evenly matched, as in a contest).* *Even number,* helu kaulike. *Even numbers, totals,* helu ʻano like. *Even so,* pēlā ʻiʻo nō.

evening. Ahiahi, hōʻahiahi. *Early evening,* ʻāluna ahiahi. *Good evening,* aloha ahiahi. *To spend an evening,* hōʻahiahi. *Overtaken by evening,* ahiahihia.

Evening Star. Hōkū-kau-ahiahi. *See* **Venus.**

event. Hanana.

ever. Mau. *Forever and ever,* ā mau loa aku. *Did you ever go to California?* ʻAʻole loa anei ʻoe i hele i Kaleponi?

evergreen. Uliuli mau.

everlasting. Mau loa, pau ʻole.

everlasting flower. Pua pepa, nani mau loa.

every. Kēlā . . . kēia, āpau. *Every two hours,* nā ʻelua hola āpau.

everybody, everyone. Ka poʻe āpau, pau āpau, papapau.

everything. Nā mea āpau, pau loa, kēlā mea kēia mea, ʻaupapa, ulupau.

everywhere. Ma nā wahi āpau, mai ʻō ā ʻō; ia wahi aʻe, ia wahi aʻe; kēlā wahi kēia wahi, holopuni, holopapa, hele, ulupau.

evict. Kipaku, hoʻokeke, hehu, ʻōpeʻa, ualehe.

evidence. ʻŌlelo hōʻike, ʻōlelo a nā hōʻike. *To seek evidence,* kolokolo.

evident. Akaaka, maopopo maikaʻi. *Cf.* **obvious.**

evil. Loko ʻino, lawehala, ʻino. *Also:* kahaʻino, hoʻokūā-ʻino. *See ex.,* **deliver, storm.** *Evil-hearted,* naʻau ʻino, manawa ʻino, naʻau keʻemoa, ʻōpū kekēue. *Overtaken by evil,* paʻuhia i ka ʻino. *To plot evil,* kālai ʻino. *To speak evil of,* hōʻino. *To undo evil by prayer,* kalakū. *To tell evil of relatives,* holehole iwi, kaulaʻi i nā iwi o nā kūpuna. *To turn from good to evil,* kūāʻino. *To do evil to others in secret,* kāmalū.

evolution. Loli ʻana. *Theory of evolution,* kumumanaʻo o ke kinohi o ke ao nei.

ewe. Hipa wahine.

ex-. Mua. *See* **ex-wife.**

exacting. *See* **demanding.**

exactly. Pono, ponoʻī. *To refer exactly,* pili pono. *Exactly that,* pēlā ʻiʻo, pēlā nō.

exaggerate. Hoʻonui, hoʻonuinui, hoʻonui ʻōlelo, pālau, hoʻopālau, haʻanui, haʻanoʻu, wahalehe. *Rare:* uhalehe, ʻohaohala.

exalt. Hoʻonani, hoʻohanohano, hoʻokiʻekiʻe. *Also:* hoʻolanilani, mililani, hiʻilani, hoʻomailani, hoʻohilu, pai, lele pailani, hilaʻi.

exalted. Kiʻekiʻe loa, lani.

examination. Haʻawina hōʻike, nīnau hōʻike, noiʻi; hōʻike kula *(school).* *Examination board,* papa ninaninau.

examine. Ninaninau, kilo, hākiu; kānana, kālana *(moral character).* *To examine with interest, curiosity, or devotion,* milimili. *To examine sweet potatoes,* kilo ʻuala.

examined. Kilohia, kilokilohia.

example. Mea hoʻohālikelike, hōʻike ʻano, kumu hoʻohālike, kumu alakaʻi.

exasperate. Hoʻonāuki, hoʻohae, hoʻouluhua. *See saying,* **ʻea 3.**

excavate. ʻEli.

exceed. Hoʻokela, ʻoi, pākela, hoʻopākeu, pākeupali.

exceeding. Kela, ʻoi.

exceedingly. Pākela, loa, haʻalele loa.

excel. Kela, hoʻokela, poʻokela, ʻoi, hōʻoi, pākela. *To try to excel,* hoʻokela; oko *(rare).*

excellence. Maikaʻi loa, pono loa, kūpono.

excellency. Ka mea hanohano, poʻokela, ʻoi. *His Excellency the Governor,* ka mea Hanohano ke Kiaʻāina.

excellent. Kilohana, maikaʻi loa, ʻaʻole o kana mai ka maikaʻi. *Excellently made,* mikioi.

except. Koe. *Except for this,* koe kēia.

exceptional. Poʻokela, ʻoi.

excess. Pākela, koe, kaulele, ʻuhaʻuha. *To drink to excess,* pākela inu. *To eat to excess,* pākela ʻai, pakeʻai.

excessive. Pākela, koe, loa, keu, pākeu, hū ā keu, keʻele, leleʻoi, kūkonukonu, kūkanono, pākeupali.

exchange. Kūkaʻi, kuʻakuʻai, pānaʻi, hoʻololi, kuapo; hailawe. *To exchange conversation,* kūkaʻi kamaʻilio. *To exchange greetings,* kūkaʻi aloha. *To exchange letters,* kūkaʻi leka.

excise tax. ʻAuhau helu waiwai.

excitable. Pūʻiwaʻiwa, lele koke.

excite. Hoʻopīhoihoi, hōʻeuʻeu, hoʻolalelale, hoʻoouluulu. *Also:* hoʻolapa, pai, hoʻopai, hoʻoouluāoʻa, nanā.

excited. *See* **emotion, emotional.**

exciting. ʻEuʻeu, hoʻopīhoihoi.

exclaim. Hoʻōho, ʻū, āhē, kaniʻū *(as in delight);* kaulele.

exclamation. Hoʻōho. *Exclamations of surprise, scorn, dismay:* auē, kāhūhū, kāhīhī, kāhōhō, kā, kaī, ʻī, i ka ʻike, ʻaikola, aī, āhā, kao. *See also Gram. 12.*

exclamation mark. Kiko pūʻiwa, kiko hoʻōho.

exclude. Koe, pale, waiho aku.

exclusive. Helu ʻole ʻia *(excepting);* noho kaʻawale, launa ʻole, waiakua; mā- *(of pronouns and possessives).* *See* **plural.**

excommunicate. ʻOki, ʻoki mai ka hale pule aku.

excrement. Kūkae, kae; lepo, hana lepo *(euphemism);* honowā, paʻu *(tar-colored, as due to hemorrhage);* palakī *(small dabs);* makuʻu *(uncontrollable).* *See* **diarrhea.** *Watery excrement,* hī, palahī, kai koʻakoʻa, pālukaluka. *Excrement that remains to be wiped off,* pala kūkae. *Excrement lying exposed on the ground,* makaʻuwāwae. *Daubed with excrement,* hawa. *Person who cared for the chief's excrement,* kahu moka, kahu poka.

excreta. Kūkae, kākā, hana lepo; weka, wekaweka *(of an infant).* *Dab of excreta,* pala. *To leave excreta here and there, as animals,* pākiʻokiʻo.

excrete. Kiʻo, kākā, hana lepo. *Need to excrete,* puʻu kiʻo, puʻakiʻo. *Discomfort preceding excreting,* hōkūkū.

excursion. Huakaʻi mākaʻikaʻi; holoholona *(rare).* *To take someone out for an excursion,* hoʻoholoholo.

excuse. 1. *Pretext.* ʻŌlelo hōʻaloʻalo. 2. *Pardon.* Kala, huikala, hoʻokuʻu. *Excuse me,* kala mai iaʻu.

execute. 1. *Perform.* Hoʻokō. 2. *Kill.* Hoʻomake, make.

executioner. Ka mea nāna e hoʻomake, mū.

executive. Hoʻokō, poʻo. *Executive officer,* luna hoʻokō, ilāmuku. *Executive council,* ʻaha hoʻokō.

executor. Kahu waiwai, luna hoʻoponopono waiwai, mālama waiwai, luna hoʻokō kauoha.

exemplify. Hoʻohālikelike.

exempt. Koe, hoʻokuʻu, pakele.

exercise. Hoʻoikaika kino *(bodily);* haʻawina hoʻomaʻamaʻa *(lesson);* kāholoholo hoʻoikaika *(as a horse);* haʻihaʻi *(limbering).*

exert. Hoʻoikaika, kuʻupau.

exhale. Hanu, hanu i waho, hā.

exhaust. Hoʻomāluhiluhi. *Exhaust fumes,* hoʻopuka ea.

exhausted. Paupauaho, pauaho, māloʻeloʻe; piula *(slang).* *Also:* aneane, auka, kūpolō, ʻaikena, lohelau; pahulu *(of over-farmed soil);* ʻainea *(by strain or trouble);* ʻākaʻakaʻa *(fig.).* *See saying,* **Hilo** (Eng.–Haw.).

exhausting. Hoʻopauaho, hoʻomāluhiluhi. *Rare:* makaʻeleʻele, ʻaiea.

exhibit. Hōʻikeʻike, hōʻikeʻike, mea hōʻikeʻike.

exhibition. Hōʻikeʻike. *Art exhibition,* hōʻikeʻike kiʻi. *Exhibition hall,* hale hōʻikeʻike.

exhort. Kauleo.

exhortation. ʻŌlelo paipai.

exhume. Huʻe.

exile. Wailana, kuewa, kipaku.

exist. Kū, ō, ʻōpū, ola. *Existing laws,* nā kānāwai e kū nei.

existence. Nohona, ola ʻana. *Existence is peaceful,* laʻi ka nohona. *Ours is a bare existence,* ʻo ke ʻōpū wale iho nō kā mākou.

exit. Puka ʻana, pukana, ʻīpuka.

exodus. Puka ʻana, pukana.

ex officio. Mamuli o ke kūlana, ma o ka ʻoihana.

exorcise. Mahiki, hoʻomahiki, wehe.

expand. Hoʻonui, hoʻomāhua, hoʻomāhuahua, māhola, mōhala, hoʻōnū; kauhola *(bloom)*.
expect. Mahuʻi, kuhi, manaʻolana, kakali, manaʻo.
expectorate, expectoration. Kuha.
expedient. Pono.
expedite. Hoʻohikiwawe.
expel. Kipaku, hoʻokuke, paku, luaʻi, hulā; hoʻokuʻu *(as from school)*.
expend, expenditure, expense. Lilo, hoʻolilo.
expensive. Pipiʻi, piʻipiʻi, kumu kūʻai nui, piʻi, nui ka hoʻolilo.
experience. ʻIke; piʻi *(as heat, cold, emotion)*; pā, hoʻomaʻa; nā mea ʻike ʻia.
experienced. Maʻa.
experiment. Hoʻāʻo.
expert. Kahuna *(for various kinds, see Haw.-Eng. entry and entries that follow it)*; akamai, ʻailolo, lolo, noʻeau, loea, mākaukau. *Also:* lehia, lae oʻo, lae ʻula, ʻeʻea, kāʻeʻaʻeʻa, ihupani, hiapaʻiʻole, maiau, lehua. *See saying,* **kāʻeʻaʻeʻa.** *Extremely expert,* pau lehia.
expire. Pau, make, puaea.
explain. Wehewehe, hoʻākaaka, hōʻike; hoʻomōakaaka, hoʻomālaʻe *(clearly).* *To explain a meaning,* wehewehe manaʻo, kuhi ʻano.
explanation. Wehewehe ʻana, hoʻākaaka, haʻina, hoʻomōakaaka, manaʻo wehewehe.
explode. Hoʻopahū, pahū, puoho, pohā.
explore. ʻImi loa, huli.
explorer. ʻImi loa.
explosion. Halulu; kani kanono *(loud sound). See* **explode.**
explosive. Hoʻopahū, mea pahū.
export. Waiwai hoʻolilo i kō nā ʻāina ʻē; hoʻolilo. *Fraudulent exporting,* hoʻoili kolohe.
exports. Waiwai hoʻolilo, waiwai puka aku.
expose. Hōʻike ākea, hoʻowaiho, waiho wale, hoʻohāmama, huʻe; pōniho *(as the sea floor, rare).*
exposed. Ahuwale, kapeke; koaka *(of a male);* hoʻohena, kekē *(of a female);* kūpapaula *(to the wind, rare). Exposed teeth,* niho kekē.
exposition. Hōʻikeʻike.
express. 1. *To state.* Hoʻopuka, haʻi, hoʻākaaka, hōʻike. 2. *To extract.* ʻUī, ʻūpī *(by squeezing).* 3. *Company.* Hui hali ukana.
expression. Kāleo, māpuna leo, māpuna ʻōlelo. *A sweet, lovely expression of face or eyes, also said of the* kole, *a fish,* maka onaona. *A single expression by the lover,* hoʻokahi nō māpuna leo a ke aloha.
exquisite. Nani makamae, ʻauliʻi.
extend. Hoʻoloa, hoʻolōʻihi, kīkoʻo; — *out, as land,* oni, ʻau, hāpapa. *Also:* kū, ʻō, hoʻoākea, hoʻolaulā, kīkiʻi, māhola, pāhola, hoʻopālahalaha, hoʻopālaha, hohola, hoʻomanana, halaʻoʻa.
extended. Hoʻolōʻihi ʻia. *Also:* peleleu, moana, moananaana, laha, pālaha, pālaulau; ʻomaliō *(as land);* niape.
extension. Peleleu, pākuʻi.
extensive. Laulaha, nui; ʻomaliō *(as land).*
extent. Kīkoʻo, laulā, nui.
exterior. Waho.
exterminate. Luku ā pau.

extinct. Make, pio, nalowale.
extinguish. Hoʻomake, hoʻopio, kinai *(as a fire).*
extinguished. Pio.
extinguishing. Kinaina.
extol. Kaena. *See* **praise.**
extortion. Pākaha, lawe wale, lawe waiwai ma ke ʻano kolohe. *Also:* puni kuwala, nunu.
extra. Keu, ʻoi, kaulele. *Extra charge,* uku kaulele.
extract. Pōʻalo, ʻōlaʻo; puhi *(as water from steam);* ʻūpī *(by squeezing);* unuhi; ʻōhuʻi *(rare).* *Difficult to extract,* ʻiʻī.
extramarital lover. Ipo manuahi.
extraordinary. Kupaianaha, kupanaha, mea ʻē, hoʻākua, kaulele, ʻeʻepa, oki, oki pau, ʻeʻena.
extrasensory perception. ʻIke pāpālua. *See* **premonition.**
extravagant. ʻUhaʻuha, ʻuha, ʻuha ʻai, māunauna.
extreme. Wēlau, ʻēlau, welelau, palena, ʻoi loa aku. *Extreme unction,* ukione.
extremely. ʻAʻohe i kana mai, ʻaʻole o kana mai, haʻalele loa, naonao; kūlipo *(fig.).*
extremity. Wēlau, ʻēlau, welelau, welewelelau, kihi, pā, kōkī, paʻa.
exult. *See* **brag.**
ex-wife. Wahine i kaʻawale aku *(separated),* wahine ʻoki male ʻia *(divorced).*
eye. Maka; ʻōnohi *(fig.). Kinds:* mākole, pīheka, noeʻula, maka pili. *See* **maka, cross-eyed, epicanthic fold, inflamed, pinkeye, tooth.** *Eyes at a joint,* puʻupuʻu. *Coconut eye,* puka wai. *Mother-of-pearl eye,* makaiwa. *Needle eye,* maka, maka kui, puka kui. *Snail eye,* mahina. *Eye pigmentation,* maka ila. *Black eyes,* maka ʻeleʻele *(as of Hawaiians). Brown eyes,* maka uliuli. *Blue eyes,* maka polū, maka ʻālohilohi. *Black eye (bruised),* maka uli. *One-eyed,* maka paʻa, mākahi. *One eye smaller than the other,* maka iki. *Flirtatious eyes,* maka kiʻi. *Staring eye,* maka ʻā, hoʻā maka. *Bashful eyes,* maka hilahila. *Roving eye,* maka ʻeu, makaau, makāu, makaʻau. *Dark pupil,* ʻōnohi uliuli; kahiwa *(rare). Encrusted white matter in the eyes,* maka piapia *(insult);* paʻakai. *Viscous matter in the eye,* moekūhua. *Fatty tissue between cornea and inner canthus,* momi. *Membrane covering the eye,* hūʻalu. *Inner corner of each eye,* luaʻuhane. *Eye inflammation,* helei. *Having something in the eye, as a mote or eyelash,* pula, laʻo. *To look wistfully,* mākilo. *To look with half-closed eyes,* pīoioi, mīoioi. *To open the eyes,* kaʻakaʻa. *Eyes, front,* pololei.
eyeball. ʻŌnohi, haku ʻōnohi, pona; momi *(of fish);* pipi *(rare). See* **ʻaʻa 3.** *Red eyeball,* ʻōnohi ʻula. *Membrane over eyeball,* hūʻalu.
eyebrow. Kuʻemaka, kuʻekuʻemaka, hulu kuʻemaka.
eyeglasses. Makaaniani.
eyelashes. Lihilihi.
eyelid. ʻŪpoʻi maka, kuapoʻimaka, lihilihi; maka lole *(turned back; an insult).*
eyesight. ʻIke maka. *Poor eyesight,* ʻike pōwehiwehi, hāpōpō.
eye socket. Pona, naho, maka lua.
eyetooth. Ole.
eyewitness. ʻIke maka, kūmaka.

F

f. *No Hawaiian term.*

fa. Hā.

fable. *Fables in the Aesop sense do not exist in Hawaiian. A possible definition of fable in Hawaiian is* moʻolelo pōkole e hōʻike i ke ʻano o ka noho pono ʻana ʻana *(lit., short story showing how to live righteously).*

fabricate. 1. *Falsehood.* Haku wale, haku ʻōlelo, haku ʻepa, hoʻopunipuni. **2.** *See* **build.**

face. Maka, helehelena, alo; — *of clock or watch,* papa, momi. *See* **about-face, grimace, scowl.** *Bright face,* maka hinu. *Dirty face,* maka lepo. *Face cream,* kalima hamo. *Face to face,* he alo ā he alo, hulina alo. *To face death,* huli ke alo i ka make. *Face the facts,* nānā pono i ka ʻoiaʻiʻo. *Face the wall,* huli ke alo i ka paia. *To make faces,* haikaika, hoʻowaha, ʻeʻewa.

facet. ʻŌpaka, ʻaukā.

facing. Hulina alo.

fact. Mea kūʻiʻo, mea ʻoiaʻiʻo.

faction. ʻAoʻao, mahele. *Dividing into factions,* mokuāhana.

factor. Heluhana *(arithmetic);* ʻākena, hope *(agent).*

factory. Hale hana.

faculty. 1. *Academic.* ʻĀuna kumu kula, pūʻulu kumu kula. **2.** *See* **ability.**

fade. Mae, hoʻomae *(as flowers);* heheʻe *(as clothes);* hākea, hākeakea, kuakea, ākeakea, kūkaikea *(as in the sun).* *Also:* mao, hiahia, ahia, ʻāhiahia, kuaka, kūālole, lolena; ʻāhiehie *(especially gray);* ʻalaʻihi *(any faded color);* māhe *(as a voice).*

Fahrenheit. Palanaheika.

fail. Pohō, hoʻopohō; hāʻule *(as in school);* emi mau ke olakino *(of health).* *Also:* hāʻuleʻule, hāʻulehia, neo, kāhewa, halahū, maulina, haho. *Three people in the class failed,* ʻekolu poʻe i hāʻule i ka papa.

failure. Holomua ʻole, holo leʻa ʻole, hāʻule. *See sayings,* ʻelepaio 1, unele, goose.

faint. 1. *Lose consciousness.* Maʻule, hoʻomaʻule, make. *Faint from hunger,* make pōloli. *To grow faint,* hoʻomake. *To feign fainting,* hoʻomaʻule. *To lie in a dead faint,* moe make. **2.** *Weak, dizzy.* Makapōuli, maka pōniuniu, ʻanaʻona, aneane, hemoʻē. **3.** *Difficult to see.* ʻĀweʻaweʻa, ʻehu, pōehiehi, poehi.

faint-hearted. Pauaho, maʻule.

fair. 1. *Just.* Kūpono, pono, kaulike. *Fair wind,* peawini, makani ʻoluʻolu. **2.** *Complexion.* ʻIli kea, ʻili māʻila, lākea, hākeakea, halakea, aʻiaʻi, lamalama. **3.** *Exhibit.* Pea, hōʻikeʻike. **4.** *Somewhat good, pretty good.* ʻAno maikaʻi.

fairly. ʻAno, kokoke, ʻaneʻane, nō.

fairy. *No general term; see* **legendary being.**

fairy story. Kaʻao no nā poʻe kupua.

faith. Manaʻoʻiʻo, paulele. *To have faith,* kālele. *Covenant of faith,* pelika o ka manaʻoʻiʻo.

faithful. Manaʻoʻiʻo, kūpaʻa. *See* **faith.** *Oh come, all ye faithful,* e hele mai ʻoukou, ka poʻe manaʻoʻiʻo.

faith healing. Hoʻōla maʻi me ka pule, lāʻau kāhea.

falcon. Palekona, ʻaekelona.

fall. 1. *From a height.* Hāʻule *(a solid object; sometimes said of rain);* helelei, heleleʻi, hoʻoheleleʻi *(as leaves, rain).* *Also:* hāʻuleʻule, hāʻulehia; pakakū, kūloku *(as rain);* hāʻule, heleleʻi *(as fruit);* kōheoheo *(as through the air);* hāʻulepio *(surrender);* palaiki. **2.** *Topple.* Hina; — *prone,* hina pālaha, moe pākiʻi, pōhina; — *backwards,* kuwala, wala, wala kua, walawala pahū, walawalakī; — *sideways,* hiō; — *forward,* kimo; — *over,* palahuli; —, *as a building,* hiolo, hāneʻe; *cause to* —, hoʻohina, hoʻohihina; — *in (military),* kaʻa malalo;

— *down or off,* ʻakaʻa; — *and roll,* kaʻahina; — *head foremost,* kiwi; — *upon, as sorrow,* ili. *Also:* pāhiʻa, olopē; piʻi *(as shadows);* hihina, hinahina. *See* **stumble. 3.** *Autumn.* *No Hawaiian word; terms sometimes used:* hāʻule lau, laʻa make, laʻa ʻula, ke kau o hāʻule lau.

falling. Haʻulena. *See* **fall.**

fallow. Mahakea, waiho mahi ʻole, hoʻopahulu.

false. Hoʻopunipuni, wahaheʻe. *Also:* ʻolohewa, pahilau. *False fire alarm,* kāhea pau ahi ʻolohewa. *False imprisonment,* hoʻopaʻahao pono ʻole. *False teeth,* niho kuʻi, niho hoʻokomo. *False witness,* hōʻike hoʻopunipuni. *To bring false accusation,* hoʻāhewa kumu ʻole, kāpeʻa.

falsehood. *See* **false.** *Rare:* ʻalapahi, pīnē.

false mullet. Uouoa, uoa.

falsetto. Leo kiʻekiʻe; leo wahine *(old term).* *See* **Kanahele 525.**

fame. *See* **famous.** *Also:* kukuʻi.

familiar. Kamaʻāina, walea, maʻa, maʻamaʻahia, kamaʻalua.

family. ʻOhana; pilikana. *Old family,* ʻohana kupa *(several generations in a place);* ʻēwe, ʻohana ʻāpaʻakuma *(for centuries in a place).* *Family line,* iwikuamoʻo, āewa. *Extended family,* ʻohana holoʻokoʻa. *Family trait or custom,* ʻēwe, welo. *Family name,* inoa ʻohana. *Family discord,* nahunahu ihu. *To carry on family virtues and skills,* poʻohala.

famine. Wī, wā wī. *For fig. and other names, see* **kaha lelelepō, hī laulele.**

famished. Hae i ka pōloli.

famous. Kaulana. *Famous day,* lā kaulana. *To make famous,* hoʻokaulana. *To become famous,* kaulana.

fan. Peʻahi. *To fan,* peʻahi, ani peʻahi; kōaniani *(as a breeze);* lūlū. *Electric fan,* peʻahi uila. *Fan me,* peʻahi mai.

fan belt. ʻIli.

fancy. Manaʻo ulu wale, moemoeā. *Take a fancy to,* hoʻohihi, hoʻokohu.

fang. Ole, niho ʻawa.

fan palm. Loulu, loulu hiwa, loulu lelo, noulu. Loulu *nut,* hāwane, wāhane. *Young loulu leaves,* paʻaoloulu.

fantastic. Āiwaiwa.

fantasy. Nā mea kupanaha i haku ʻia ma ka noʻonoʻo ʻana, moemoeā.

far. Mamao. *Also:* lilo loa, loa; — *away,* maʻō loa aku, kūlewa; — *and small,* halalī; ʻāloaloa, māhiloa, hala loa, haʻalilo, mōwahowaho, kikilo, monehā, momoua. *Far-reaching,* hāloa. *As far as,* ā, ā hiki i. *Not far,* maʻō aʻe nei. *To go far,* hele loa, ʻau i ke kai loa, hiʻikua. *Far-off place inhabited by spirits,* kēwā, ʻOpikana. *Far, paradisiacal, and venerated,* ʻiuʻiu, mōʻiuʻiu, mōʻiu, kōʻiuʻiu. *Far from land,* ʻaʻohe pilipili ʻāina mai.

fare. 1. *Pay.* Uku. **2.** *Happen.* Holo. *To fare well,* holo leʻa. *To fare badly,* holo pono ʻole. *How did your trip fare?* Pehea aku nei kāu huakaʻi? *How did his work fare?* Pehea ka pono o kāna hana? Pehea ka holo ʻana o kāna hana? **3.** *Food.* ʻAi. *Bill of fare,* papa kuhikuhi mea ʻai.

farewell. Aloha. *To bid farewell,* aloha.

farewell gift. Hoʻina.

farm. Mahi ʻai, mahi, mahina ʻai; *small* —, kīhāpai; *to* — *at night,* pelika o ka hana.

farmer. Mahi ʻai. *See saying,* ʻaluʻalu. *Tenant farmer,* lōpā. *Derisive names:* malo ʻeka, naunau lepo, pepeiao hohono.

farming. Mahi 'ai 'ana.
far-sighted. 'Ike mamao.
fart. Palalī. *See* **break wind.**
farther. Mamao a'e, mamao aku, mamao mai, ma'ō aku. *A little farther,* mamao iki aku.
farthing. 'Akalio.
fascinate. Ho'opunihei, ho'oheihei, punihei, ālai maka, nanea, walea. *Fascinating speech,* mīkololohua, mīkolelehua.
fashion. Paikini, 'ano, kaila. *Chiefly fashion,* kūkaulani.
fashionable. Kū i ke kaila.
fast. 1. *Quick.* 'Āwīwī, wikiwiki, wiki, māmā, holo, 'ino. *Also:* ala-, alamimo, alapine, alawiki, wawe, miki, 'akī, kikī, paukikī, 'emo 'ole; pu'upu'u ho'olei loa; kō-'ala, lauhulu. *See* **lei 2, speed,** *and saying,* **'ōlapa.** *To run fast,* holo 'ino, holo kikī. *To move or progress fast,* kāholo, mī'oi, kokololio. **2.** *Fixed.* Pa'a; —, *of colors,* pa'a. *To make fast,* ho'opa'a, lawakua, lawa, hīki'i, hekau. **3.** *Not eat.* Ho'okē 'ai, ho'opōloli, waiho 'ai. *Ability to fast,* 'ōpū pa'a.
fasten. Ho'opa'a, hana pa'a; — *loosely,* maulihilihi. *Also:* hākia, mākia, kākia, 'ōmau, pākōlea, paehi'a, hīpu'u *(as a knot);* 'ōmou *(as a brooch);* awaiāulu *(as marriage tie).*
fastener. Mea ho'opa'a. *Snap fastener,* pihi 'ūmi'i.
fastidious. Kūlana waewae, nihinihi.
fat. 1. *As a human.* Momona. *Soft and fat,* pele, 'olo, polupolu, nenelu, 'uheke, 'a'alina, hīwa'awa'a. *Shaking with fat,* 'ōlūlū, hōlule. *Rare:* mona, hakakai, mumuhu, lehēlehē, molulo, nuka, nanae, uhanui, ukaukai, hoko, mū'ou'ou, pawa, kāpele, pūhalalū, kūhākakai, hūhā, kū'i'o. *See* **plump.** *Overhanging fat belly,* 'ōpū nui, 'ōpū kēkewe. *Fat person, "fatty,"* nu'upē. **2.** *Animal fat, food.* Momona *(uncooked);* kelekele *(cooked);* kuhikuhi. *Also:* kōnāhua, niuniu, kōhi, kuhinia, liko, kōlikoliko, lololo, halalē, kāhā, kaikea, 'okukuli.
fatal. Ma'i make, pāmake.
fatalism. *No Hawaiian term; the idea is expressed in the idioms and saying:* hopena 'elemakule, *the result of being an old man;* hopena luahine, *the result of being an old woman.* 'A'ole hiki ke alo a'e, *can't be helped. See also* **kaolo.**
fate. Hopena, hope. *Ill-fated,* kūlana pō'ino.
father. Makua kāne, makua. *See* **stepfather.** *Spiritual father, ecclesiastical father,* makua 'uhane. *The same father,* ho'okahi nō makua kāne. *To act, claim, or treat as a father,* ho'omakua kāne. *Father Lyons,* Makua Laiana.
father-in-law. Makuahūnōai kāne.
fatherland. 'Āina makua.
fathom. Anana, ana.
fatigue. Māluhiluhi, luhi. *Also:* unā, ho'omā'opa'opa, kunewa, kualana, kūpolō, po'ana, 'aikena, mā'ī'ī, kākaiewa. *To cause fatigue,* ho'omāluhiluhi.
fatten. Ho'omomona, kūpele, hānai i momona, kūpalu, ho'okelekele; nahumaka *(rare). Fatted calf (Luka 15:23),* keiki pipi i kūpalu 'ia.
Fatu Hiva. Hakuhiva, Pakuhiva.
faucet. Piula wai, paipu. *Faucet key,* kī o ka paipu. *Water from a faucet,* wai piula.
fault. Hewa, hala, ke'e. *To find fault,* ho'ohalahala, nemanema, nema, 'ōhumuhumu, 'ōhumu, kūhalahala, 'imi hala, nānā ke'e, loiloi, ke'u, kapake'u, kāpēke'u. *Correct a fault,* paka.
faultless. Hewa 'ole, kīnā 'ole, hemolele.
faulty. Hape. *See* **fault.**
favor. Hana lokomaika'i; kāko'o, makemake *(prefer). To lavish with favors,* ho'okamalani; paikano *(rare). To do small favors in expectation of greater ones,* piepiele. *To go about asking for favors,* pakaulele. *Please do me a favor,* e 'olu'olu 'oe i ko'u mana'o.
favorite. Punahele, milimili. *Also:* hiwahiwa, maka, hulu manu. *Royal favorite,* hulu ali'i, hiwa lani. *Favorite child,* hiwa lani. *Favorite grandchild,* mo'opuna i ke

alo. *To make or treat as a favorite,* ho'opunahele, ho'ohiwahiwa, mililani, mailani, ho'omailani, ho'opailani.
favoritism. Ho'okē ā maka, kapakahi, ho'opololei, mailani loa. *See* **favorite.**
fawn. 1. *Young deer.* Kia keiki. **2.** *To cringe and flatter.* Piepiele, ho'opilimea'ai, ka'apē.
fear. Maka'u. *Also:* weli, weliweli, 'e'ehia, kōhi. *Sudden fear,* maka'u kūhewa. *Intense fear,* kipona maka'u. *Shuddery fear,* manene i ka maka'u. *To cause fear,* ho'omaka'u, ho'ohihiu, ho'ohopohopo. *To flee in fear,* palahe'e. *Startled in fear,* pū'iwa.
fearful. Maka'u loa, wiwo, hopohopo, weliweli, kau ka weli. *Also:* 'eno, luaahi, liha, liliha, kōanoano, kūpau, punihai.
fearless. Maka'u 'ole, wiwo 'ole, koa. *Also:* makoa, ka'alokuloku, lālama; koakoa lapa *(and mischievous).*
feast. 'Aha'aina *(for various types, see Haw.-Eng. entry and following entries);* lū'au, pālala, 'aipo'olā; pā'ina male *(marriage);* moku lehua. *Feast of unleavened bread,* 'akima.
feast day. Lā 'aha'aina.
feasting. Haupa 'ana.
feather. Hulu. *See* **bird.** *Wing feathers,* hulu 'ekekeu. *Tail feathers,* puapua, analio; hulu ko'o *(long). Feathers above tail feathers,* pue. *Downy chicken feathers,* 'ae moa. 'Ō'ō *bird feathers:* pīlali *(white and black under tail);* 'ē'ē *(yellow under wing). Clusters of feathers used in featherwork,* pāpa'a, pa'a'ā, pā'ā. *Small bunch of feathers,* 'uo. *Fork or branches made of stalks of feathers, attached to* kāhili *staff,* pe'a. *Feather top of* 'ulī'ulī *gourd rattles,* heke. *To sew feathers for a hatband,* hakupapa. *To feather out,* 'ōhulu, manu heu, laukoa, kuapo'i. *To plait feathers,* haku hulu.
feather cloak. 'Ahu 'ula. *See saying,* **'e'a 1.** *Net foundation of cloak,* nae.
feather helmet. Mahiole.
feather image. Akua hulu.
feather lei. Lei hulu.
feather standard. Kāhili.
featherworker. Haku hulu. *Chief featherworker,* po'o hulu. *God of featherworkers,* Kū-huluhulu-manu.
feathery. Huluhulu, 'ahulu.
features. Hi'ohi'ona, helehelena *(human).*
February. Pepeluali, Feberuari.
feces. Kūkae, 'aukā. *See* **mokuhia, excreta.**
federal. Pekelala, federala.
fee. Uku. *Entrance fee,* uku komo. *Agent's fee,* uku 'ēkena. *Marriage fee,* uku male. *Usual fee,* uku kūmau.
feeble. Nāwaliwali, hāpauea, nāwali, palupalu. *Also:* pānauea, aneane, 'ōpē, 'ōpa'ipa'i, kūhelahela, kūhau, hōmī, hīnawenawe, hini, pūlewa, nanaiea, hākupe, hemo, hemo'ē, ka'ahē, 'o'olu, 'uhinipili, 'unihipili, kūmīmī, ulihi, ukaukai, pēlu'e.
feeble-minded. Hepa, lōlō.
feed. Hānai, hānai 'ai, hō'ai, ho'omā'ona. *To feed mouth to mouth,* mū'ā, pū'ā, kī'ā. *Also:* ho'okelekele, haumāna, 'ai kau.
feed dog. Nau *(of sewing machine).*
feel. 1. *Grope, touch.* Hāhā, hāhā hele, hāpapa, ho'opāpā, pā, mili, kūpāpā. **2.** *As emotion.* 'Ike, lohe, komo, loku; 'o'oki *(as intoxication). To feel angry,* pi'i ka huhū.
feeler. 'Umi'umi, kukuna, pipi *(as of insect).*
feelings. Na'au, loko, ha'awina; manawa *(poetic). Hurt feelings,* 'eha'eha ka na'au, ku'ia ka na'au, ku'ia o loko, ha'aku'ia, ho'oku'ia, halupu'ia, hili a ka leo. *Hard feelings,* manawa 'ino. *To stir up ill feelings,* ho'opi'ipi'i haunaele. *To conceal feelings,* hūnā i ka mana'o, pe'e poli, palai, palaina.
fee simple. 'Āina kū'ai, 'ano 'alokio, 'ano 'alolio, 'ano alodio.
fee simple title. Palapala 'alokio, palapala 'alolio, palapala alodio.
feet. *See* **foot.**

feign. *See* pretend; *also* ho'o-, faint, friendship, indifference.
felicitate. Ho'omaika'i.
fell. Kua, 'oki. *See* fall.
fellow. Hoa, kōko'olua; ka'aka *(slang).*
fellow chief. Hoa ali'i.
fellow citizen. Hoa maka'āinana.
fellow laborer. Hoa lawehana.
fellow man. Hoa kanaka.
fellow partaker, fellow receiver, fellow sharer. Hoa loa'a.
fellowship. Launa aloha.
fellow soldier. Hoa kaua.
fellow traveler. Hoa hele.
fellow worker. Hoa hana, hoa pa'ahana, hoa lawehana, hoa luhi, kāpehe.
felony. Peloni.
felt. Mānoanoa *(as cloth). Felt hat,* pāpale Kaleponi. *See* feel.
female. Wahine. *Also:* -hine, kama wahine, mo'o lau, kumulau.
females. Wāhine.
feminine. *See* female.
femur. Iwi hilo, 'auhau.
fen. Ki'o lepo *(KJV).*
fence. 1. *Barrier.* Pā; kaupale waena *(between land patches). Picket fence,* pā pine. *Wooden fence,* pā lā'au, pā laupapa. *Iron fence,* pā hao. *Stone fence,* pā pōhaku, nini, niho, niho ka'i. *Rail fence,* pā 'a'aho. *Ti-stalk fence,* paepae kī. *Wire fence,* pā uea. *Barbed-wire fence,* pā uea kukū. *Chicken-wire fence,* pā uea maka 'aha, pā uea maka 'upena. *Smooth wire fence,* pā uea poepoe. **2.** *With swords or sticks.* Kākā pahi, kākā lā'au, pāpā lā'au.
fender. Pale huila *(of a car).*
fend off. Pale, papalena.
fermata. 'Ume.
fermented. Hū, ho'ohū, 'awa'awa; pohā (poi); ho'omalamala, 'ākia, hanoa, hanowa. *Fermented liquor,* 'uwī'uwī.
fern. Kupukupu (ōkupukupu, *general name for ferns growing on a single stem, also a specific kind). According to Neal 6, 16 families, 40 genera, and 200 species grow in Hawai'i, native and introduced. Young fern leaves and rolled un fronds,* pepe'e. *Young fern fronds,* palaho'a. *Paste made of sap from fronds,* palaholo. *Poetic name for ferns,* pua'a'ehu'ehu.
COMMON KINDS INCLUDE *(alternate names are in parentheses):* bird's-nest fern, 'ēkaha ('ākaha, *see* 'ēkaha *and entries that follow it);* bracken, kīlau (kīlau pueo, pai'ā); lace fern, pala'ā (palapala'ā, pā'ū-o-Pala'e); maidenhair ferns, 'iwa'iwa *(see Haw.-Eng. entry and entries that follow it);* staghorn fern (false), uluhe, unuhe; sword ferns, hi'ui'a, kupukupu *(see Haw.-Eng. entry and entries that follow it);* tree ferns, 'ama'u ('āma'uma'u, ma'u, ma'uma'u), hāpu'u *(see Haw.-Eng. entry and entries that follow it); some edible ferns,* hō'i'o (pohole), hō'i'o kula, kikawaiō (pakikawaiō); *a common fragrant fern,* laua'e, laua'e haole.
ADDITIONAL FERN NAMES *(alternate names are in parentheses):* 'āhina kuahiwi (kā'ape'ape), 'ākōlea, ala'a-lai, 'anali'i, 'apu'u, haili-o-Pua, hihiawai, hohiu, 'i'i, 'i'o nui, 'iwa ('alae), kalamoho, kalukalu, ka'upu (papa'oi), kihe, kūau, kumuniu, lau'i'i, laukūkahi, lola, lo'ulu, mahinalua, makou, māku'e, mana (olua), mānā ('ae, 'āhewa, 'iwa puakea), manawahua, neke, 'ōali, 'ōhi'akū, 'opeha, papi (hunapalai, palaihuna), pai'i'ihā, pākahakaha ('ēkaha 'ākōlea, pua'akuhinia), pala *(and below),* palai (palapalai), palai 'ula (la'a), pāmoho, pauoa, pe'ahi, pololei, puapuamoa, pūnanamanu, wahine-noho-mauna, waimakanui.
ferocious. Hae, weliweli, mākana, kanaloa.
Ferris wheel. Huila pōniuniu, ka'a pōniuniu.
ferry. Moku halihali, wa'apā.

fertile. 1. *Of soil.* Momona; *rare:* mona, 'ōnahana-haiaua. **2.** *Of people.* Hānau, hānau kama.
fertilize. Ho'omomona, kīpulu, ho'opulu.
fertilizer. Ho'omomona lepo, kīpulu, pela, manua.
festering. 'A'ai *(as a sore).*
festival. Ho'olaule'a, manawa ho'olaule'a, lā kulāia, anaina ho'olaule'a. *An ancient fall festival was the* makahiki, *with the bringing of produce to chiefs, games, and the suspension of wars and taboos.*
festive. Hiwahiwa, ulumāhiehie, ho'owehiwehi, kulāia. *Festive day,* lā ho'ohiwahiwa.
festoon. Hei, heihei; luhiehu *(rare).*
fetch. Ki'i, lawe. *Also:* ho'oki'iki'i, hali, hiki, hikihiki, ukiki'i; pukupuku mai *(slang).*
fete. Ho'okipa, ho'ohiwahiwa, pa'ipunahele.
fetters. Kūpe'e. *Wooden fetters,* lā'au kūpe'e.
feticide. 'Umi kamali'i, 'umi keiki, 'ōmilo, 'ōmilomilo.
fetus. 'Alu'alu. *Also:* uli, kaha, mana. *Envelope for fetus,* 'a'a. *Blood-clot fetus,* pu'u koko. *Fetus lost through miscarriage,* hua hā'ule.
feud. Kū'ē ho'omauhala, kaua ho'omauhala.
fever. Piwa, ma'i kuni. *Dengue fever,* piwa ha'iha'i iwi. *Scarlet fever,* piwa 'ula'ula. *Typhoid fever,* piwa ho'onāwaliwali. *Yellow fever,* piwa lenalena. *To get a fever,* pi'i ka wela.
feverish. 'Ōwelawela.
few. Kaka'ikahi, wahi, kekahi, 'u'uku, li'ili'i. *Also:* helu, huahelu, kauwahi, 'ehia, nāhi, namauahi.
fiber. Ma'awe. *Types of Hawaiian fibers:* olonā *(a shrub);* pa'a'ā, pā'ā *(as of sugar cane);* 'a'a *(from coconut husk);* heu *(of fruits). Rare:* mile, hāpue. *Waste fiber of* olonā, huna olonā, kae.
fibrous. 'Ōa'a, 'a'a'a, hā'a'a, 'ōa'a'a.
fickle. Lolelua, lolilua, lauwili, 'ōlewa, kāpekepeke, ho'owale hau. *See* mālolo *and sayings,* luaiele, cuttlefish.
fiction. Ka'ao, mo'olelo haku wale.
fiddle. Pila.
fidelity. Mālama pono, kū loa. *High fidelity,* kū loa i ka leo.
fidget. Hole, pīhole, 'oni. *Also:* kakekake, moehewa, leleiona.
field. Kīhāpai, kula; *cultivated —,* māla, waena, pā kanu. *See* athletic field.
fierce. Hae, ho'oweliweli. *Also:* mākaha, maka koa, uki-uki, kānaioa.
fiery. 'Ā, ahi, liholiho, no'ao. *Fiery pit,* lua ahi, ki'o ahi. *Fiery surface,* 'ili ahi.
fifteen. 'Umi kūmālima, 'umi kumamālima.
fifth. Lima, hapalima. *The fifth time,* ka lima o ka manawa.
fifty. Kanalima.
fifty-eight. Kanalima kūmāwalu, kanalima kumamāwalu.
fifty-five. Kanalima kūmālima, kanalima kumamālima.
fifty-four. Kanalima kūmāhā, kanalima kumamāhā.
fifty-nine. Kanalima kūmāiwa, kanalima kumamāiwa.
fifty-one. Kanalima kūmākahi, kanalima kumamākahi.
fifty-seven. Kanalima kūmāhiku, kanalima kumamāhiku.
fifty-six. Kanalima kūmāono, kanalima kumamāono.
fifty-three. Kanalima kūmākolu, kanalima kumamākolu.
fifty-two. Kanalima kūmālua, kanalima kumamālua.
fig. Piku.
fight. Hakakā, paio, kaua; mokomoko *(general free-for-all, including wrestling and boxing);* pā'ume'ume. *Also:* kūpāpā, kolopā, paika, hu'alepo, makawalu, pilikua. *See sayings,* helu 4, wai 'au'au, fighter, cockfighting, wrestling. *Specialized types include:* ku'iku'i *(boxing);* pa'a uma *(hand wrestling);* lua, ku'i-a-lua *(bone-breaking, spear thrusting, noosing, leaping). Quick to fight,* lele koke. *To set to fight, as dogs,* ho'okonokono.
Following are about 90 names of lua *fighting strokes*

obtained from a newspaper (Ka Nupepa Kuokoa, April 27, 1865), or from Fornander. The names have little to do with fighting. Many are folkloristic and poetic, with names of things important in the old culture. Initial Ka (the article) on some names is optionally omitted.

NAMES OF STROKES CONTAINING NAMES OF SUPERNATURALS AND CHIEFS: Haehae-ka-manu-o-Kāne-aloha, Ka'a-'ē-nā-ali'i, Ka-ihu-o-ka-pua'a *(probable reference to Kama-pua'a),* Ka-malo-o-Līloa, Kana, Ka-piko-o-Wākea, (Ka)-pua'a-kā-huluhulu (Kama-pua'a), Kapu-ahi-a-Ku'ialua, Kapua'i-o-Kana, Ke-ake-o-Milu.

CONTAINING PLACE NAMES: E-ho'i-ka-u'i-o-Mānoa-ua-ahiahi, Hāmākua-i-ka-paia-'ala-i-ka-hala, Ka-ua-Kīpu'upu'u-o-Wai-mea, Ka-ua-Lēhei-o-Maka-wao, Kokia-Wai-lau, Mehameha-Pu'u-loa, Uliuli-ka-pali-o-Kahiki-nui.

CONTAINING REFERENCES TO OCEAN DWELLERS: Alapi'i-a-ka-ōpae, (Ka)-i'a-ho'opāpā-'ili-kanaka, (Ka)-limu-kā-kanaka-o-Mahamoku, (Ka)-hau-palemo, (Ka)-waha-o-ka-manō, Mahiki-o-ka-lua-kanaka, 'Ōhi-ki-maka-loa, 'O'opu-ola, 'Ōpule-kai, Uhu-makali'i.

CONTAINING REFERENCES TO BIRDS: Au-koa'e-ua-mā-lie, Hakakā-a-moa, (Ka)-'ēheu, (Ka)-'io, (Ka)-'ua'u-kaha, (Ka)-'ua'u-komo-hewa, (Ka)-'ua'u-lewalewa, Pua-ka-uahi-haehae-ka-manu.

CONTAINING ANATOMICAL REFERENCES: 'Ai-lima-iki, Iwi-ko'o, (Ka)-'auwae-lewa, Kālawa-kua, (Ka)-'ōma-ka-o-ka-'īlio, (Ka)-'ōpe'a-panipani, (Ka)-pili-mai'u'u, 'Ōwelo-ka-huelo-kū.

CONTAINING REFERENCES TO ARTEFACTS: (Ka)-'ahu-'ula, (Ka)-lei-o-manu, Ka-malo-hei *(see also under supernaturals).*

NAMES OF OTHER STROKES: 'Ahamaka, 'Aho-lehia, Hana-ka'i-luna, Hana-kau-luna, Hanu-i-pi'i, (Ka)-hau-komo, (Ka)-hau-palemo, Ka-he'e-pālaha, (Ka)-hili-kolo, ([Ka]-hihi-kolo), Kahului, Kākā-'au-kī, Kālaha, Kalena, (Ka)-loloa-maiau, (Ka)-lu'elu'e, (Ka)-ma'i-'awa, Kāmuku, Kānihi, Kau-nunu, Kawa'e-kū, (Ke)-aho-lehi, (Ke)-āmio, Ko'ūko'ū, Kua-nunu, Kū'ia-kānaka-hele-o-ka-pō, Ku'ikahi-a-Mēhē'ula, Lāhei, Lēhei, Malalei, Mālama, Mālama-ka-'ōpua-hiki, Mālama-kū'ē, Mālama-kūloko, Mālama-kūwaho, Nā-ānuenue-'ewalu, 'Oā-ki'i-ala, O-hana-ke-ke'a-ua-mai-ka'i, Ohi'ikau, 'Okoikua, 'Ōnohi-ka'i-'ole-pohihihi-ka-lawai'a-o-ka-lā-'ino, Pa'ina-kuli, Pala-'ole, Pāpala-kā'ili-'ū, Popoki, Pu'upā, 'Ula-ka-maka-iā-Kuikui-pahu.

fighter. Pūkaua, mokomoko, koa, kā'e'a'e'a; 'ōlohe (lua *fighter).* Fig., ahi-ka-nanā, moa kākala, pūko'a kani 'āina, manō hae. See **warrior.** *God of lua fighters,* Ku'i-a-lua.

figurative. See **meaning.**

figure. 1. *Number.* Huahelu, helu, hua. 2. *Human figure.* Kino.

figure-eight hula. Hula 'ōniu.

figurehead. Ki'i, leleiwi *(on a canoe).*

Fiji, Fijian. Pīkī.

filch. 'Aihue. *Also:* hue, huhuhue, poholalo, pāhau, lima 'āpā, lima lawelawe, limalima.

file. 1. *Rasp.* Apuapu, apu, waiehu, waiahu. See **grate.** *To file,* hole, kohenalo. *Fishhook file,* apuapu 'ānai makau. 2. *Row.* Lālani. *To go in file,* kaka'i ā hele. 3. *Collection.* Waihona (palapala). *To file papers,* ho'opi-hapiha waihona pepa; ho'okomokomo, waiho.

filefish. 'Ō'ili *and entries that follow it.*

filial. Aloha makua, no'ono'o makua.

Filipino. Pilipino.

fill. Ho'opiha; papa'unu *(rare);* — *a vacancy,* pani, pani hakahaka; — *a crack or hole,* pīna'i.

filled. Piha, pihapiha. *Also:* 'aki, kūneki, 'okokomo, komo, 'opu'opu, kāneki, 'okukuli, 'api'api, nolo, newe, noke'a. See **full.** *Completely filled,* piha pono, piha pū.

fillet. 'Aukā.

filling. Pihana.

film. 1. *Photography.* Pepa pa'i ki'i. *Roll of film,* 'ōwili pa'i ki'i, pōka'a pa'i ki'i. 2. *Thin covering.* Uhi. See **slime.**

filter. Kānana, kālana. See **strain.**

filth. Haumia, lepo, pelapela, 'eka, 'eka'eka, mea 'ino, moka, hauka'e. *Also:* hau'eka, pe'ape'a, pōneko, neko, niku, hawa, wi'u, pau 'eka.

filthy. See **filth.**

fin. Lā. *Anal fin,* kuaalo. *Caudal fin,* hi'u, pewa. *Dorsal fin,* kualā. *Pectoral fin,* 'ēheu, pewapewa. *Ventral fin,* hakualo, kuālo. *Base of caudal fin,* akahi'u. *Fin near gill plate,* halo. *Motion of fins,* halo.

final. Hope loa, pau, panina.

finance. 'Oihana kālā, 'oihana 'imi kālā. *Minister of finance,* kuhina waiwai.

financial. Waiwai. *See ex.,* **kūpiliki'i.**

financier. Kanaka loea ma ka 'imi waiwai.

finch. Manu-'ai-mīkana, manu-'ai-papaia, hōpue.

find. Loa'a; — *enough,* hulilawa *(rare);* — *out even smallest things,* ho'omakauli'i. *Find fault, see* **fault.**

fine. 1. *Minute.* Hune, hunehune; makali'i *(as mats, mesh);* nāwele, māhune, 'ae'ae, puehu, lili'i. *Also:* huhuhune, mō'ali, mo'o'ali, pūnāwele, puāhilo, wele, welehia, pokipoki, poki, hīnau, 'ūhini, mo'owini, wali, waliwali, wawali, maukoli, nilu. 2. *Excellent.* Maika'i nō, maika'i loa, pono, papakū. *Fine-looking,* maika'i ke nānā aku, nohea, mi'i, kini kohu. 3. *Penalty.* Uku ho'opa'i, uku, kōina. *To fine,* ho'opa'i, ho'ouku.

fine-meshed. Makapepe, makali'i, makahune.

finery. Mea kāhiko. *War finery,* kāhiko kaua.

finger. Manamana lima. *Cf.* **thumb.** *Index finger,* manamana kuhi, manamana miki, lima 'umeke, limameke, lima 'aina. *Middle finger,* manamana loa, kau. *Third or ring finger,* manamana pili. *Little finger,* manamana iki. *(In the above,* manamana *is sometimes replaced by* lima). *Finger of poi,* miki 'ai. *Fingerpulling contest,* loulou.

finger bowl. Ipu holoi lima, po'i wai holoi.

fingernail. Miki'ao, mai'ao, mā'i'u'u. *Fingernail polish,* pena miki'ao, ho'ohinuhinu miki'ao. *Fingernail of deceased relative,* heia.

finicky. Kamalani, ho'okamalani, wae, ho'owae, waewae, nihinihi, waha lina.

finish. Ho'opau, oki, ho'ōki; panina *(noun);* kaekae *(rub smooth);* ka'aoki. *To make an effort to finish,* ho'opa-pau.

finished. Pau, pa'a, 'anakoe. *Partly finished,* kīhapa, laua, hapapū. *Completely finished,* pau pono, kūpau.

Finland, Finnish. Pinilana, Finilana.

flr. Lā'au ka'a, pila, 'aleka.

fire. Ahi. *Also:* 'a'ā, 'ā; ho'opau *(discharge). See saying,* **ho'oko'iko'i.** *The fires,* nāhi. *Pit of fire,* lua ahi. *Fire builder,* kahu ahi. *Bag for carrying fire-making implements,* 'aahi. *To fire a gun,* kīpū. *Ready, aim, fire,* mākaukau, kī, kani. *To light or kindle a fire,* ho'ā ahi, kuni ahi; kaihu *(for an oven);* hi'a *(with fire plow). To put out a fire,* ho'opau ahi, kinai ahi. *Gods of fire,* Pele, Lono-makua, 'Ai-lā'au.

fire alarm. Kāhea pau ahi.

firearms. Pū. *To practice firearms,* paikau.

firearms license. Laikini kī pū.

fireball. Pōpōahi, pōhāhā ahi.

fire-blowing tube. 'Ohe puhi ahi, 'ūlili.

firebrand. Momoku ahi, ahi lele, pāpala, kao, ahi 'au hau. *The firebrands of Ka-maile rise in triumph,* 'ō'ili pulelo ke ahi o Ka-maile *(of triumph, see* **pulelo***).*

fire bucket. Pākeke kinai ahi.

firecracker. Pahūpahū.

fire department. 'Oihana kinai ahi.

fire engine. Ka'a kinai ahi, ka'a pau ahi, ka'a wai.

fire extinguisher. Kinai ahi.

fire fountain. Ahi lele.

fire insurance. 'Inikua pau ahi.

fireman. Kinai ahi.

fire pit. Umu ahi, lua ahi.

fireplace. Kapuahi.
fire-plow. 'Aunaki. *Stick held in hand and rubbed on,* 'aunaki, 'aulima. *To make fire with fire-plow,* hi'a.
fireplug. Wahi ho'okomo 'ili kinai ahi.
fireproof. Pale ahi. *Fireproof vault,* ke'ena pale ahi.
fire protection. Hana kinai ahi ho'opakele, pale ahi.
fire station. Hale kinai ahi.
firestone. Pōhaku paea.
firewood. Wahie.
fireworks. Kao lele, ahikao, 'ōahi.
firm. 1. *Solid.* Pa'a, kūpa'a, 'onipa'a. *Also:* kūkia; mālō, mālo'elo'e *(taut);* mākū; mānalo, punapuna *(as taro, sweet potato);* ha'apapa'a, pūlawa, kamaehu, 'ūlili. *See* **motto.** *To make firm,* ho'opa'a, hō'onipa'a, ho'okūpa'a, ho'omālō, wai'ūlili. *Firmly established or imbedded,* pa'a loa, ho'ohonua, nihoa. 2. *Company.* Hui. *Mercantile firm,* hui kālepa.
firmament. Lani pa'a, papa lani, aouli, pōnaha lani, pō'ailewa, ke'a papa nu'u.
first. Mua, mua loa, 'akahi . . . ā. *Also:* kinohou, kuakahi, kū kahi. *First time,* maka mua, malihini, 'akahi nō . . . ā. *First-born,* hiapo, makahinau, hānau mua. *To have the privileges of a first-born, treat or act as a first-born,* ho'ohiapo. *To go for the first time,* hele malihini. *This is the first time I've seen Hilo,* 'akahi nō au ā 'ike iā Hilo.
fiscal. Waihona kālā.
fish. I'a; pihi *(rare); to fish,* lawai'a, ulawai'a. *See* **fishing grounds, fishhook, fishing rights, net, seine, trap, and names of individual fish.** *Some fish names vary according to islands, and all fishermen do not agree. Some fish have special names for growth stages. General names for young growth stages, applied to several fish:* aka *(newly hatched),* mana, hāuli, kākau; pua *(common name),* pua i'i; 'o'ololā *(rare). Fish raised in ponds,* i'a loko. *School or run of fish,* i'a kū, kahe i'a, kū, kauhulu. *Season of abundant fish,* wā i'a. *Fish accompaniment to poi,* i'a, 'īna'i. *Shrine for fish offerings,* kū'ula, heiau ho'oulu i'a, ko'a i'a. *Fish substitute for pig offerings,* pua'a kai. *String of fish,* kāili i'a, kāili, pu'u i'a. *Ways to fish:* kā makoi (mokoi), paeaea, kīkomo, koi, kūpali *(with pole);* hī, kā'ili, kepa *(casting);* pākā, kākā, kūkaula *(with hook and line but no pole);* laulele *(with net);* lamalama *(with torches);* pana i'a *(with bow and spear);* ho'okāholoholo *(skittering);* pākali, kūpalu *(decoy by doling out bait or chumming);* hāhāmau, hāhā *(with hands);* 'auhuhu, pāhola, hola *(stupefy with drugs);* ho'ā, aupula, pula *(driving);* kakaka, kūkaula *(deep-sea, rare);* koe *(pulling stick with hooks through water),* 'ūpalupalu. *Fish caught in hands,* i'a mili lima; pakauele *(rare). A small fish cannot swallow a big fish,* 'a'ole hiki i ka i'a li'ili'i ke ale i ka i'a nui *(of a commoner).*
fish eggs. Kowaū.
fisherman. Lawai'a, kanaka paeaea, wa'ewa'e. *See saying,* **'ea'ea 1.**
fishery. Kai lawai'a.
fishhook. Makau *(for various kinds, see Haw.-Eng. entry and following entries);* pā, pāuhi, uhipa'a, pā ānuenue, pā hau, pā mae, mūhe'e *(for various kinds, see* **mūhe'e** *and following entries),* kaiānoa, lihi, 'ōnohilehua *(pearl-shell lures);* pā hī aku *(bonito lure);* kīki'i, kue *(rotating hooks);* makau manō, lawa, kīholo *(shark hooks);* 'auku'u, hi'ikala, hiohio; huikala *(with inside and outside barbs);* hulu *(with outside barb);* hululua *(with two barbs);* kaiānoa *(two small barbless hooks);* kākala *(octopus lure);* ke'aawaileia, kīkalakē, koehonua; kohe lua (kohe lua pa'a) *(with two barbs);* kue, kuoho, lu'aloa; mahina *(crescent point);* makau pāweo, anea; 'ōmau *(no barb);* ho'onoho *(two points on one shank);* nuku *(series of hooks on one line);* maka puhi *(for eels). Eel gorge,* haoa puhi. *Parts of a fishhook:* ka'ā, ka'i *(snood);* kū'au, pou *(shank);* kohe *(inside barb);* lo'e, pohona *(bend);* lihi *(portion just below point);* lihi lou *(point of barbless hook);* lālā *(bone*

or shell point of two-piece hook); maka *(point). Parts of pearl-shell lure:* ihu *(head);* muli *(tail);* pukaihu *(hole in head for snood);* pou *(snood);* 'uo *(seizing);* hulu *(hackle);* lālā *(point);* kapuahi *(base of point);* humu *(hole in point);* hāmama *(gape of point);* 'auwae *(portion of point which overhangs the shank). Fishhook container,* waihona makau; ipu lē'ī *(rare). To make a fishhook,* kā makau.
fishing. Lawai'a. *See saying,* **'elepaio, weuweu.** *To avoid saying one was going fishing (considered bad luck), some said:* hele i uka *(go inland);* malo kai *(wear a malo in the sea);* hele 'auana *(go wandering).*
fishing grounds. Ko'a, kai lawai'a, āukauka, ka'aka'a, ko'a hohonu, kuapu'e, kūkaula, pōhākialoa. *(Fishing stations at sea were identified by citing landmarks and were often named.)*
fishing pole. Mākoi, koi, mōkoi.
fishing rights. Konohiki, pono kai lawai'a.
fishline. Aho. *Also:* kioloa, ko'olauloa, wailuku. *Snell of a fishline,* ka'ā. *Fishline container,* poho aho, hōkeo.
fish net. 'Upena. *See* **net.**
fishpond. Loko i'a, loko kuapā.
fish run. I'a kū, i'a kahe.
fishtail fern. Hi'ui'a.
fish trap. *See* **trap.**
fissure. Māwae, mōwae, 'ōwae, ki'aki'ena, kama, kāwaha.
fist. Pu'upu'u lima, pu'u, pu'u lima, pu'upu'u.
fit. 1. *Suitable.* Kohu, kū, kūpono; ho'okūkū, komokomo *(as a garment). To fit closely,* pili pa'a, pili pono. *To fit loosely,* pālokeloke. *Not at all fitting,* 'a'ole kohu iki. *My shoes don't fit,* 'a'ohe kū ko'u kāma'a. 2. *Seizure.* Huki, ma'i huki, 'apo'apo. 3. *To join.* Ho'oku'i, pāna'i, kāpili; kuaō'a *(rare).*
fitches. Peleka, kumino 'ele'ele.
fitting. Pilina, pono, ho'okūkū. *See* **fit.** *Clothes fitting,* ho'okūkū lole.
five. Lima, 'elima, 'alima. *Five times, by fives, fivefold; to divide in fives,* pālima. *Five times,* kualima. *To count by fives,* helu pālima.
five cents. 'Elima keneka. *See* **nickel.**
fix. Ho'opa'a, kāpili hou, hana ā maika'i, hō'onipa'a.
fixation. Pulakaumaka.
fixed. Pa'a, 'onipa'a.
fixtures. Pono pa'a mau, lako.
flabby. 'Alu'alu, nenelu. *Also:* 'aluhe'e, pūhalalū, puhalu, halu, uhalu, peheu, 'ōluheluhe, homa, polupolu.
flag. Hae, lepa. *Also:* alia, puwalu; lonolupe *(rare).*
flag-bearer. Lawe hae.
flagpole. Pahu hae, kia hae.
flagship. Moku lawe hae.
flagtail. Āholehole, āhole, 'apo'apo.
flail. Kākā.
flame. Ula ahi, ula, lapa ahi. *To flame,* ula. *Also:* weke, wekeweke, wawaka, 'owaka, wakawaka, hoaka, 'oaka. *See* **blaze.**
flank. 'Ao'ao. *Flank movement,* ne'epapa.
flannel. Huluhulu.
flap. 1. *Motion.* 'Upa'i, 'ōpa'ipa'i, kūlepe, hulei, kālepalepa, kīlepa, kapau'u. *Also:* mū'olo, ho'ēheu, paihō. 2. *End.* Pola *(as of a malo).*
flare. Ho'olapa, 'ōlapa, pi'ipi'i kai, hōlapu; 'o'oma *(of a bonnet).*
flash. 'Ōlapa, lapa, lapa uila. *Also:* ōahi, 'oaka, 'ō, huaka, waka, 'owaka, wawaka, weke, 'anapa, hālapa, lehuuila, pohā, mākēhā.
flashlight. Kukui pa'a lima.
flask. Hue, 'ōmole.
flat. 1. *Level.* Pālahalaha. *Also:* 'iliwai, pānānai, pālānai *(as a dish);* pānai, pāki'i, kāhela, pāpio, pālaulau, 'omaliō, 'ōniki. *See* **flat-nosed.** *Flat tire,* hemo ke ea o ka laholio. 2. *A plain.* Papa, laupapa; 'āpapa, pāpapa *(as coral).* 3. *Tasteless.* Ko'eko'e, pau ka 'ono; mahū *(as poi). Also:* pōka'o, kāhalahala. 4. *In music.* Emi.

flatfish. Pāki'i ha'awale, pāki'i moana, pāhau. Cf. Titcomb, 1972, paki'i.
flathead. Po'o pepe *(a name for lesser gods).*
flat-nosed. 'Ūpepe, 'ūmene, kūmene, pepe, 'ū, ihu pāki'i, ihu mene.
flatten. Ho'opālahalaha, ho'oūpē, pākī, ho'opēpē, ho'opālaha, pāki'i. *Also:* ho'ohāne'e, ho'okūmene, kē, kula'ina.
flattened. Pē, pālaha. *Also:* ūpē, kāmoe, kūloku, 'ōpaha, he'a, ku'i pē.
flatter. Ho'omalimali. *Also:* malimali, mali, hamo, makali, piepiele, pelo, pāwali, kua'i'i.
flatulent. Makani, palalī. *See* **break wind.**
flaunt. Ho'okelakela, hō'oi'oi. *Also:* ho'okeha, mau'a'e.
flavor. 'Ono, hō'ono'ono. *What flavor?* Ke 'ano hea?
flavorless. 'Ono 'ole, ko'eko'e, pau ka 'ono. *See* **flat.**
flaw. Kīna'una'u, ke'e, kīnā. *To seek flaws,* paka, 'ainemanema. *No flaws,* 'a'ohe ke'e, kīnā 'ole, pala 'ole; hemolele.
flawless. *See* **flaw.**
flax. Olonā.
flay. Lole; kākāhou *(rare).*
flea. 'Uku lele, 'uku.
fleabane. Laniwela.
fledgling. Pūnua, laukalo.
flee. He'e, 'auhe'e, mahuka. *Also:* 'āha'i, hō'auhe'e, nāholo, pūhe'e, 'io, pū'ā'ā, pūkākā, palahe'e, pupuhi, pūhalahio. *See saying,* **pupuhi.**
fleece. Hulu hipa, huluhulu.
fleet. 1. *Naval.* 'Au moku, 'au wa'a, ulu moku, ulu wa'a; pa'imalau *(rare). See* **forest. 2.** *Fast.* Holo. *See* **fast.**
flesh. 'I'o. *To strip flesh,* holehole, hole, pūholoholo, waimāhoehoe, pā'i'o.
flesh food. I'a.
fleshpot. Ipu i'a.
fleshy. 'I'o nui, hō'i'o, nu'anu'a, 'uheke. *Also:* kū'i'o, liko, hahei, hoko. *See* **fat.**
flex. Ho'okākāuha, nenene.
flexed. Lāpe'e, 'uhinipili *(as for burial).*
flexible. 'Olu, napenape, holuholu. *Also:* hōlule, napa, hō'alu'alu, malule, lule, 'ō'upē, pala'ie, kāluhi, ho'okakale, 'ape'ape, lolena.
flick. Kiani, pekupeku.
flicker. Napenape.
flies. Pōnalonalo, pōnanonano.
flight. Lele. *See* **flee.** *To take flight,* lele, kaulele. *To put to flight,* ho'ohe'e, hō'auhe'e, hehu, ho'opū'ā'ā. *Flight of birds,* lele manu, aulia manu.
flighty. Hī'ō, uilani, 'ōpulepule.
flimsy. Palupalu, lahilahi, ikaika 'ole, lu'a.
flinch. 'E'eke, kuemi.
fling. Kā, hiu, ho'olei. *See* **throw.**
flint. Paea, pōhaku paea; pahi *(knife).*
flip. Pana. *Also:* kiani, wala, kīlepa, panau.
flipper. Hui, 'ēheu.
flirt. Ho'oha'i, ho'oha'i wale, ho'oha'ilua; ho'oheihei *(to ensnare). Also:* ho'okāluhe, hani.
flirtatious. *See* **flirt.** *Flirtatious eyes,* maka ki'i.
float. 1. *Not sink.* Lana, lanalana. *Also:* mālana, lewa, ho'olewa, au, aumiha, 'ālana, 'ālewalewa, pūlana, pūlewa, nananana, ho'oīkā, lanaau, welo, kālewa, pulelo, kīlepa, ku'uwelu, puewa, pua, kualana, pōnulu, pōnululu, pōnununu. **2.** *Of a net.* Mouo, pīkoi, haukoi, 'īkoi, ou. *Cord attaching float to net,* pīkoni. **3.** *Of a fishhook.* Kōheoheo. **4.** *See* **outrigger float.**
flock. Pū'ā, 'āuna, ho'āuna, ulu. *Also:* haiamū, kipapani, kumu. *To move in a flock,* ka'i 'āuna.
flood. Wai hālana, wai pi'i. *Also:* waiholomoku, 'olo'olo, kai a ka Hinali'i.
floor. Papahele, papa ke'ehina, papa; papakū *(as of ocean).*
flooring. Holopapa. *See* **floor.** *Canoe flooring,* 'ūlili wāwae.
flop. Mū'olo.

Florence. Pololena, Folorena.
Florida. Pololika, Folorida.
Florida moss. 'Umi'umi-o-Dole, hinahina, 'āhinahina.
flotsam and jetsam. Pīhā, piha'ā, īkā, maulele.
flounder. Moeone, pāki'i.
flour. Palaoa maka, palaoa. *Cakes of flour,* pa'i palaoa.
flourish. Lupalupa, hālupa, lupa. *Also:* māhuahua, māhua, ohiohi, kupuohi, ōhāhā, kāpa'ipa'i.
flour mill. Hale wili palaoa, kāwili palaoa.
flow. Kahe; — *swiftly,* kikī, kīpalalē; — *in spurts,* hanu'u *(see* spurt*). Also:* kulu, hī, holo, kukulu, kulukulu, kāhele, kūneki, kūloku, niau, hu'ena, aukahi, pōlewa, pua'ina, he'e, pua'i, kōī, waikahe, kokoi, mokuāwai, īhe'ehe'e.
flower. Pua. *Center of flower,* maka. *Single-flowering,* pua lahilahi. *Double-flowering,* pua pupupu. *Flower covered by calyx,* mū'olo'olo, mu'omu'o. *Flower that attracts,* pua lē'ī. *Rare choice flower,* pua laha 'ole. *Flower that never fades,* pua mae 'ole *(of a sweetheart).*
flowing. Kahena, aulia. *See* **flow.**
flu. Palū.
fluctuate. Hanu'u, kūlanalana. *To mark fluctuation,* kaha i ka hanu'u.
fluent. Poeko, 'ōlelo pahe'e.
fluff. Ho'opuehu, ho'oweuweu; kanene *(rare).*
fluffy. Weuweu.
fluid. Wai, hehe'e. *Also:* kaiaka, ukalekale. *Amniotic fluid,* lapawai, 'ina'ina.
flume. Hā wai, pulumi, 'auwai papa, haka lā'au.
flush. 1. *Show red.* Pi'i ka 'ula, nono 'ula, 'āpane. *See* **blush. 2.** *To wash out.* Ho'oholo i ka wai. *Flush the toilet,* ho'oholo wai i ka lua, 'umi wai. **3.** *In poker.* Palaki.
flute. 'Ohe kani, puhi 'ohe, 'ohe puluka, puluka. *See* **nose flute.**
flutter. Kōwelo, kapalili, kolili, konini, welo, konikoni. *Also:* kāwelowelo, napenape, kālepalepa, kālepa, kūlepe, kīlepa, ku'uwelu, kōwehe, ho'okolili, koni, nini, konini, hāku'i, kapau'u; hulahula *(as eyelid);* māewa, nenene, 'oeowewe. *Carried away with a fluttering,* 'āha'i i ka welowelo *(of speed and a kite).*
fly. 1. *As a bird.* Lele. *Also:* kālewa, ka'ale, uheheu, 'alelele, holohu'a, lelele, aulele, ho'okauaheahe. *To fly, as a kite,* ho'olele; 'ō *(rare).* **2.** *Insect.* Nalo *(for various types, see Haw.-Eng. entry and entries that follow it),* pōnalo; makika *(Hal. 105.31). See* **flies.**
flycatcher. 'Elepaio, 'āpekepeke.
fly eggs. Kūkaelā.
flying fish. Mālolo *(fig., fickle, perhaps due to continual leaping);* puhiki'i, puiki *(young);* lelepō, 'ololā, pūkiki'i.
flying gurnard. Loloa'u, pinao.
flywheel. Huila nui.
foam. Hu'a, hehu. *Sea foam,* hu'ahu'a kai, 'ehu kai, huna kai, hune kai, kaikea, 'ae'ae.
foamy. Kuakea, 'ahulu. *See* **foam.**
fog. 'Ohu, noe, ua noe, uhiwai. *See* **mist.** *Also:* 'awa, pāpala, pululuhi, pōhina, pūlawa. *Fog signal,* ho'ākaaka no ka pa'a i ka noe.
foghorn. 'Ole leo nui.
foiled. *See* **thwarted.**
fold. 'Opi, pelu, ho'opelu, pelupelu, pe'u, 'opi'opi, 'ōwili. *Also:* ho'okihi, nunu, mākī, ka'apeha, ahue, kīpū, hakuhaku, mōnoinoi, mīnoinoi.
folder. Mea ho'okomo pepa, puke ho'okomo pepa.
folding chair. Noho 'opi'opi.
folding cot. Moe 'opi'opi.
folding table. Pākaukau 'opi'opi.
folds. 'Ā'īlepe, ko'o.
follow. Hahai, ukali, alualu, ma'awe, kaukolo, hai, haihai. *As follows,* penei. *To follow in line,* kaka'i. *To follow a course,* ho'omo'o.
follower. Ukali, muli, 'ōkā'i, haiā; haialo, hukailoloa *(of a chief).*
foment. Ho'okipi, ho'ohaunaele *(revolt, riot).*

fond. Puni, laka, aloha. *See* **like, love.**
fondle. Milimili, milika'a, miliani, mili, hamo, ho'o-ka'awili.
fontanel. Manawa, mauli, pūniu *(of an infant);* pū he'e *(fig.).*
food. 'Ai, mea 'ai; 'īna'i *(eaten with poi);* ō *(for a journey);* kā palu *(deprecatory);* palu'ai *(vegetable);* pīka'o *(dehydrated);* pani *(medicinal);* pala 'ai *(daub);* pā'iole *(left by rats).* *Food package,* laulau, holo 'ai, 'io, kīholo. *Food gift,* ho'ina. *Food trough,* papa wili 'ai. *Food guardian,* kia'i 'ai. *Food inspector,* luna 'ai. *Food provider,* hānai 'ai. *Food scraps,* 'ai pala niho, kō'ala'ala. *To offer food and prayers,* kahukahu.
fool. 1. *Simpleton.* Hūpō. *Also:* hawāwā, 'āna'anea, hāpuku. *See* **crazy.**
foolishness. Hūpō, lapuwale, na'aupō.
foot. 1. *Anatomical.* Wāwae. *Ball of foot,* mānea. *Hollow of foot, instep,* poli, poli wāwae,poho wāwae. *To trip with the foot,* kāwae. *Foot-binding,* 'ūmi'i 'ana i ka wāwae. **2.** *Twelve inches.* Kapua'i.
football. Kinipōpō peku.
football game. Ho'okūkū kinipōpō peku.
footboard. Papa hehi *(used in hula).*
footprint. Kapua'i wāwae, meheu wāwae. *Also:* ke'ehana, ma'awe.
foot race. Heihei kūkini.
footrest. Ke'ehana, ke'ehina, ke'ehana wāwae, hehina, hahina.
footstep. Kapua'i wāwae. *Sound of footsteps,* ko'ele wāwae.
footstool. Ke'ehana, ke'ehina, ke'ehana wāwae, paepae wāwae.
for. No, na, i, iā. *For me,* no'u, na'u. *For you,* nou, nāu. *For him, her, it,* nona, nāna. *Look for him,* 'imi iāia.
forbid. Pāpā, ho'okapu, hō'ole. *Also:* kāmalū, lāhui.
forbidden. Kapu, pāpā 'ia.
force. 1. *Strength.* Ikaika; ko'o *(rare).* **2.** *To use force.* Ha'akoi, pu'e, pu'e wale, hao, hu'e. *Also:* 'onou, 'ōno'onou, 'ō, ka'ihuluhulu, maua'ālina, lima ikaika, hikipua.
forceful. Ikaika loa, ho'okokōhi.
ford. Hele mai kekahi 'ao'ao ā kekahi 'ao'ao, ala'au.
Ford Island. Poka 'Ailana.
forecast. Wānana. *See* **cloud.** *Forecast weather,* wānana i ke au o ka manawa. *Kona seas with cloud billows that forecast peace (UL 117),* Kona kai 'ōpua i kala i ka la'i.
forecaster. Nānā ao *(cloud observer);* kilo. *See* **seer.**
foreclose. Panikū, ho'okō.
foreclosure. Panikū. *Foreclosure notice,* ho'olaha panikū, ho'olaha mana'o panikū.
forehead. Lae *(for fig. meanings, see Haw.-Eng. entry).* *Bulging forehead,* lae pu'u. *Forehead bone,* iwi kānana, kālana.
foreign. Mai ka 'āina 'ē mai, 'ē, haole; kūwaho *(not domestic);* malihini *(of foreign origin).* *Foreign land,* 'āina 'ē; 'āina haole *(of white people);* kahiki *(any foreign country).*
foreigner. Kanaka 'ē, haole, malihini, mea mai ka 'āina 'ē.
foreman. Luna, luna hana, luna nui.
foremost. Mua loa, po'okela, heke, hiapa'i'ole.
foresee. 'Ike 'ē, wānana, kilokilo, kilo, ho'okilo.
foresight. Na'auao 'ike mua.
foreskin. 'Ili 'ōmaka, 'ōmaka, 'olomua. *Foreskin cut off in circumcision,* olomu'o. *Uncircumcised foreskin,* puhi. *Slipped back, of foreskin,* pohole.
forest. Ulu lā'au, nahele. *Also:* moku, mō, kua lā'au, ulueki. *Forest clump,* maha lā'au. *Rain forest,* ma'ukele. *Uplands forest,* wao kele, māulukua. *Edge of forest,* pili lā'au. *Forest of the sea,* ulu lā'au makai *(of a fleet at sea).*
forested. Pa'apū i ka ulu lā'au.

foretell. Wānana, ha'i 'ōuli. *See* **predict.**
forever. Mau loa, i ka wā pau 'ole, kau ā kau, nalo loa.
foreword. 'Ōlelo ha'i mua.
forfeit. Uku ho'opa'i, kā'ihi.
forge. Ku'i hao.
forgery. 'Āpuka, kākau 'āpuka. *Forged document,* palapala 'āpuka.
forget. Poina. *See* **forgotten.**
forgetful. Poina wale, poina ka no'ono'o.
forget-me-not. Mai-poina-'oe-ia'u.
forgive. Kala, huikala. *Also:* wehewehe, wehe, makala, mokala, kū i ke kala. *See ex.,* **trespass.**
forgiveness. Kalana. *See* **forgive.** *To ask forgiveness,* noi e kala 'ia, ho'okāmakamaka.
forgiving. Na'au ali'i. *See* **forgive.**
forgotten. Nalo, nalowale, nalohia, poina, poina 'ia.
fork. Mana *(branching);* 'ō *(eating);* hāmana; kohe *(at lower ends of house rafters).*
forked. Hāmana. *Cf.* **manamana.**
form. Kino. *Printed form,* pa'i hakahaka, ho'opihapiha. *Shadowy form,* haili aka. *To have a dual form,* kino pāpālua. *To take form,* ho'okino; 'ōhopehopeke'a *(of tubers, etc.).*
formal. Kū i nā lula, pa'alula. *Formal party,* 'aha'aina pa'alula. *Formal attire,* 'a'ahu i kau lula 'ia, 'a'ahu ho'ohiwahiwa.
formation. Kūkulu 'ana, ho'okumu 'ana, noho papa *(military).*
former. Mua, kēlā.
formerly. Wā mamua.
formulate. Kālai *(a policy, plan).* *See* **plan.**
fornicate, fornicator. Moekolohe, moekolohe male 'ole 'ia, ai; moe ipo *(Biblical).*
forsake. Ha'alele.
forsaken. Ha'alele 'ia, kuānea, 'owā.
fort. Pāpū, hale pūkaua, pu'ukaua, hale kaua, hūlili.
forth. I mua, aku. *And so forth,* ā pēlā aku, ā pēlā wale aku.
fortify. Ho'oikaika, ho'okūpa'a, ho'olako i nā mea kaua.
fortitude. Manawanui. *See* **courage.**
fortress. Pāpū. *Flying fortress,* pāpū lewa. *See* **fort.**
Fort Street. Alanui Pāpū.
Fort Sumter. Pāpū Kumeka, Pāpū Sumeta.
fortunate. Pōmaika'i, ahona, kūlia.
fortune. Pono, holo 'ana; waiwai nui *(wealth).* *See* **fare, rain.** *Good fortune,* pōmaika'i, ulia pōmaika'i. *Fortune-telling,* kilokilo, kilo nānā lima, kilokilo pepa.
forty. Kanahā. *Also:* ka'au, 'iako.
forty-eight. Kanahā kūmāwalu, kanahā kumamāwalu.
forty-five. Kanahā kūmālima, kanahā kumamālima.
forty-four. Kanahā kūmāhā, kanahā kumamāhā.
forty-nine. Kanahā kūmāiwa, kanahā kumamāiwa.
forty-one. Kanahā kūmākahi, kanahā kumamākahi.
forty-seven. Kanahā kūmāhiku, kanahā kumamāhiku.
forty-six. Kanahā kūmāono, kanahā kumamāono.
forty thousand. Kini.
forty-three. Kanahā kūmākolu, kanahā kumamākolu.
forty-two. Kanahā kūmālua, kanahā kumamālua.
forward. Mua, i mua; maha'oi, mī'oi, 'āwini *(rude).* *Forward, march!* naue i mua! ke'ehi lō'ihi! *Forward!* I mua! Mamua!
foster. Hānai, ho'omakua, hi'i, mālama, kōkua. *Foster child,* keiki hānai *(see saying,* **keakea***).* *Foster parent,* kahu hānai, makua hānai, makua kōlea; 'ūhā *(chiefly).*
foul. 1. *Filthy.* Pilau, 'eka, kelo, 'ino'ino, 'iku'iku. **2.** *In sports.* Hewa *(e kū 'ole i nā kānāwai).*
found. Ho'okahua *(establish);* kūkulu *(as a society);* ho'okumu. *See* **find.**
foundation. Kahua, kumu, papa, mole, kumupa'a. *Also:* pa'a, honua. *House foundation,* kahua hale. *Foundation of the earth,* papa honua, papakū. *Foundation principles,* kahua hana. *To lay a foundation,* ho'okahua, hau'opo, 'opo.
founder. 1. *See* **sink.** Piholo. **2.** *See* **establish.** *Founder*

of, mea nāna i hoʻokumu. *Group of founders,* poʻe nāna i hoʻokumu.
foundry. Wahi (kapuahi) hoʻoheheʻe hao.
fountain. Puaʻi wai, wai pipiʻi.
four. ʻEhā, hā, ʻahā, kāuna. *By fours,* pāhā. *Four times,* ʻehā, ʻahā, kuahā.
fourfold. Kuahā *(rare).*
four hundred. ʻEhā haneli (hanele), lau.
four oʻclock. Hola ʻehā; nani ahiahi, pua ahiahi *(flower); pāpala kēpau (trees).*
foursome. Kāuna.
fourteen. ʻUmi kūmāhā, ʻumi kumamāhā.
fourth. Hā, hapahā. *The fourth time,* ka hā o ka manawa.
Fourth of July. Lā ʻEhā o Iulai, Pokiulai.
four thousand. ʻEhā kaukani, mano.
fowl. Moa, manu.
fowler. Alualu manu, uhai manu, hahai manu, kāwili manu, laukia manu, kūhea manu, kono manu.
fox. ʻAlopeke.
fox and geese. Punipeki, manu *(game).*
foxtail. Mauʻu pilipili, mauʻu Kaleponi.
fraction. Hakina *(for various types, see Haw.-Eng. entry and entries that follow it),* hakihana, ʻano pili, hapa. *Terms of fractions,* lālā, palena.
fracture. Haʻi. *Fractured skull,* poʻo nahoa.
fragile. Haki wale, palupalu, ʻūpalu, palahē, pōhae.
fragment. Hapa, hunahuna, hakina, hakihana, moku, mahele liʻiliʻi. *Also:* ʻāpana, ʻāpaʻapana, mō, momoku, welu, huhuna, māmala, mākoli, ʻōpilopilo. *Food fragment,* hakina ʻai, hamu.
fragrance. ʻAʻala, ʻala, onaona, anuhea; moani *(wafted). See* hala 3, pō 2, smell, sweet, *and saying,* friend.
frail. Nāwaliwali, palupalu. *Also:* lahilahi, lahi, kūmīmī, hakakaʻe, pīlahi, nanaiea, kinoʻole, puāhilo, ʻolalahina.
frame. Haka kaulaʻi, hakakū *(for drying); haka ipu (for hanging calabashes); lāʻau (picture frame); holopapa (for tapa); oʻa (of ships); kū (of a bed). Frame a picture,* hoʻopaʻa i ka lāʻau kiʻi.
France. Palani, Farani.
frangipani. *See* plumeria.
frank. Hunāhunā ʻole.
Frankfort. Palanipoka, Faranifota.
frankincense. Lipano.
fraternity. Hui malū *(society);* aloha i ka hoa kanaka *(love of fellow man).*
fraternize. Launa aloha.
fraudulent. ʻĀpuka, kolohe.
frayed. Weluwelu, welu, uluulu, huluhulu.
freak. ʻAno ʻē, ʻeʻepa.
freckles. Luluāʻina.
free. 1. *State.* Kūʻokoʻa, kuakahi, kuʻu ʻia; manuahi, manawaleʻa *(gratis);* noa, kaʻanīʻau *(of taboo);* mokala, makala *(of defilement);* mōhala, mōhalahala *(as from fear). See* translation. *Free time,* manawa kaʻawale. **2.** *To free.* Hoʻokuʻu, hoʻokuʻu laʻelaʻe, kala, weke, hoʻohemo; hoʻopakele *(save);* molokala, hoʻokuakahi, hoʻomānewanewa; hoʻonoa *(taboo).*
freedom. Kūʻokoʻa, noa. *Freedom of speech,* pono kūʻokoʻa nō ka ʻōlelo, lanakila o ka ʻōlelo. *Freedom from arrest,* pakele mai ka hopu ʻia.
freely. ʻAno kūʻokoʻa. *To give freely,* hāʻawi hemolele. *To go freely,* hele laulā, hele wale, kahakū.
freeze. Make anu, hoʻopaʻa i ka hau, makaʻeleʻele.
freight. Ukana. *Freight conveyance,* kaʻa hali ukana.
freighter. Moku lawe ukana.
French, Frenchman. Palani.
frequent. Pinepine, mau, maumau, alapine.
fresh. Hou. *Also:* maka, makamaka hou *(as fish);* līhau *(as moist plants);* koʻiʻi, kāmakamaka, ʻōpiopio.
freshman. Haumāna komo hou.
fret. 1. *Complain.* Nē, hoʻonē. *Also:* none, hauwene, loloā, uilani, ʻōnēnē, ʻalalehe. **2.** *Of ukulele.* Wā.
friable. Palahē, pakēpakē.

friar. Peliala.
friction. 1. *Rub.* ʻĀnai. *Fire by friction,* hiʻa ahi. **2.** *Disagreement.* Hukihuki, kūʻē.
Friday. Pōʻalima; kōʻele.
fried. Palai. *Fried chicken,* moa palai.
friend. Hoaloha, hoaaloha, makamaka *(o-class);* aikāne *(a-class);* hoa pili *(intimate, personal);* hoa. *Also:* hoalauna, makamaka hānai, ʻaikapa, pilialo, pili mua, lawakua, lehua, hale aikāne, ʻau koʻi, pili. *See saying,* kou 2. *My friend,* koʻu hoaloha, koʻu makamaka, kaʻu aikāne. *Friend as close as a relative and treated as such,* hale aikāne. *To make friends,* hoʻohoa, hoʻāikāne, hoʻohoaloha. *A friend, a nest of fragrance,* he aikāne, he pūnana na ke onaona *(poetic).*
friendless. Makamaka ʻole, kuewa.
friendly. Hoʻālohaloha, hoʻohoaloha, laulauna, maka launa, heahea, hoʻolauna. *Also:* launa, noho aloha, kāʻēʻē.
friendship. Pilialoha, lauleʻa, ʻimi hale. *See* friend. *To feign friendship,* palai, hoʻokāmaʻe, hoʻomalae, hoʻokamani.
frigate bird. ʻIwa *(see sayings,* ʻiwa 1).
fright. Pūʻiwa, hopohopo, makaʻu, puoho, hikilele. *See* fear.
frighten. Hoʻomakaʻu, hoʻoweli. *Also:* hoʻopūʻiwa, hoʻohihiu, hoʻoliʻō, hoaka, aulau, hoʻēno, hoʻolele hauli. *To stare as to frighten,* ʻaʻā maka.
fringe. Kaʻe, palena *(edge);* kuʻuwelu *(on a shawl);* lepe *(tear);* palalei *(tapa). Fringe benefits,* mea pōmaikaʻi pākuʻi.
fringed. Kuʻuweluwelu, kuʻuwelu.
frisky. Lelele, ʻanapau, kiani, kīkaʻelekē.
frivolous. Puni leʻaleʻa wale, leʻaleʻa noʻonoʻo ʻole, hoʻopulelehua.
frock. Palaka *(Korn, Oceanic Linguistics* 15:14–38.)
frog. Poloka, lana, moʻo lele luʻeluʻe.
frolic. Lapa, kūlapa, pāʻani lapa, ʻanapau.
from. Mai, mai . . . mai, no. *From Honolulu,* mai Honolulu, mai Honolulu mai, no Honolulu. *From there,* mai laila.
frond. Lau, oho, lālā.
front. Alo, mua.
frontage. Alo.
frost. Hau, hauʻoki, kēhau anu.
froth. Huʻahuʻa, huʻa; ʻaeʻae, māpuna *(of the sea). Froth at the mouth,* kahe ka huʻa o ka waha.
frown. Hoʻomakaʻu, pupuku, hoʻomakaʻeku, hoʻomakaʻekuʻemaka. *Also:* pukupuku, ʻōpukupuku, hoʻopukupuku, pupuku ka lae, hoʻonohu, ʻūmalu, hoʻoʻūmalu, ʻiʻī, hoʻomakapū, mākuʻe.
frugal. Hoʻomakauliʻi, hoʻopī, pākiko, kīhau. *See* thrifty.
fruit. Hua, huaʻai; pīʻai *(berry-like fruit, rare). Small or inferior fruit,* hua liʻi, hua iki. *Blasted fruit,* hua ʻai mālili, hua lili. *Fallen fruit,* hua hāʻule. *Having many leaves but little fruit,* pālahalaha lau. *To bear or form fruit,* hua, hoʻohua, hōʻumeke, hoʻoʻumeke, hōʻiʻo.
fruitful. Hua nui, huahua, momona.
fruitless. Hua ʻole; pauʻaka, ʻuʻā *(unproductive).*
frustrate. Hoʻohoka, hoʻopūhili.
frustrated. Pūhili, ulukū o ka noʻonoʻo, hoka.
fry. 1. *Cook.* Pua, pua ʻiʻi. **2.** *Small fish.* Pua, pua ʻiʻi. *Cf.* fish.
frying oil. ʻAila palai.
frying pan. Pā palai.
fuchsia. Kulapepeiao.
fuel. Wahie.
fugitive. Mahuka.
fulfill. Kō, hoʻokō.
full. Piha; poepoe *(as the moon);* māʻona, piha ka ʻōpū, pōhalakē *(from eating; see saying,* pulu 5); pihapiha, ākea *(as a garment);* ʻeo, kāʻeo *(as a calabash). Also:* ʻōpihapiha, nokeʻa, nolo, lēʻia, lēʻī, hūalakē, hāʻale, hoʻokūkū, newe, nepu, neki. *See saying,* lua 1. *Completely full,* piha pono, pihaʻū, piha pū. *Full-blooded,* piha. *Nights of full moon,* Hoku, Māhea-lani. *Full tide,* kai piha, kai nui.

full-grown. Makua.
fullness. Pihana, piha, 'ōpihapiha.
fully. 'Oko'a. *See* **entirely.**
fume. Māhu, ea. *Tobacco fumes,* ea paka.
fumigate. Pepehi mea 'ino, ho'ouahi mū.
fun. Le'ale'a, ho'ole'ale'a. *See sayings,* **Halāli'i, wela.**
function. Kuleana, lawelawe hana, hana.
fund. Waihona kālā.
fundamental. Kumu, honua. *See* **Pentecost.** *Fundamental knowledge,* 'ike kumu.
funds. Kālā. *Out of funds,* 'a'ohe kālā; puki, poloke *(slang).*
funeral. Ho'olewa. *See* **wake.**
funeral feast. 'Aha'aina make.
funeral parlor. Hale ho'olewa.
fungus. Akua, pepeiao, pepeiao akua; kane *(tinea);* unahi pōhaku *(on stones).*
funnel. Kānuku.
funny. Ho'omāke'aka, kū i ka 'aka, ho'okolohe. *Also:* hū'eu, laupa'apa'ani, ho'okā'au.
fur. Hulu, huluhulu, huhulu, hulu kupu, 'ili holoholona.
furious. Hae, pi'i ka huhū wela loa. *Also:* ehuehu, iō'ena, laukōnā, pūkīkī. *See* **angry.**

furl. Lī, 'ākī, pōlena, pāpio.
furlong. Palelona, kekakia.
furnace. Kapuahi, umu.
furnish. Ho'olako. *Well-furnished,* lako.
furniture. Lako hale, pono hale. *Also:* kāhiko o ka hale, pa'ahana.
furrow. 'Auwaha, wa'a, wa'awa'a, mō'ali, mā'ali, hālua, holowa'a, mo'o'ali.
furrowed. 'Au'auwaha, wa'awa'a, wa'awa'ahia, 'āwa'awa'a, 'ōwahawaha, kāwaha, māio, 'ānuhenuhe, mākuakua.
furthermore. Koe kēia, aia kēia, eia hou ho'i, eia nō na'e, aia na'e, na'e, eia kekahi, ho'oiho.
furtive. Malū, hialele.
fury. Huhū wela loa, maka welawela, hae. *Also:* 'a'ā, ehuehu, 'ōnohi 'ula, 'o'olokū, kuapu'e.
fuse. Kaula hō'ā *(as on firecracker);* iho uila *(electric).*
fuss. Ka'e, hauwala'au, hauwalawala'au.
fussy. Kamalani, 'ōnēnē, 'eke'eke, waewae.
future. Mua, ka wā mahope. *See* **tense.** *Near future,* kēia mua iho. *Distant future,* kēia mua aku.
fuzz. Hulu weuweu, heu.
fuzzy. Weuweu, pihulu, 'ōheuheu.

G

g. *No Hawaiian term.*

gabble. Hauwala'au, hauwalawala'au, 'ohi. *Gabble mouth,* waha ko'u.

gable. Hākala, kala hale. *Gable post,* kuhana.

gadabout, gad about. Ki'ihele, hele kauhale, 'ae'a wale, lalau. *Also:* 'anau hele, 'āpo'o, po'apo'apōlā, kamapuka, mā'au, pakaulei, paikaulei, paikauhale, kīhei. *See* **vagabond** *and sayings,* **kīhei, panau.**

gag. Pa'awaha, ho'opa'a i ka waha, 'owā, hō'owā, lua'i, kōkā; ho'olua'i *(make vomit).*

gaiety. 'Oli, le'ale'a. *To cause gaiety,* ho'ohau'oli.

gaillardia. Melekule wai kāhuli.

gain. Loa'a, puka, kumuloa'a.

gait. Ka'ina wāwae, ke 'ano o ka hele 'ana.

gale. Makani nui, kelawini.

Galilee. Kalilaio, Galilaio; Kalilaia.

Galipoli. Kalipoli.

gall. Au *(for idioms, see* **au***);* au 'awa *(bitter).*

gall bladder. Au. *The gall bladder has burst, yellowness spreads,* pohā ke au, ke pi'i nei ka lena *(of ill will).*

galled. Mūkole.

gallinule. 'Alae *(for various types, see Haw.-Eng. entry and entries that follow it);* nūkea.

gallon. Kālani.

gallop. Holo nui, kīau, holo'anai.

gallows. 'Āmana, 'oloke'a.

Galveston. Kalewekekona, Galavesetona.

gamble. Piliwaiwai. *Gambling games:* pili kālā, pili hihia, lā'au piti, kū-hele-mai, kīpā. *See* **bet.**

gambol. 'Owala; 'oehu, lapa.

game. *No distinction was made between game, sport, and recreation, all of which might be* mea pā'ani. *See* **Mitchell.** *Eng.-Haw. entries:* **archery, bowling, box, cartwheel, checkers, cock-fighting, dive, fence, gamble, guess, hide-and-seek, hopscotch, jacks, juggle, kite, marbles, mumble-the-peg, pole vault, quoits, race, ring and ball game, ringtoss, shot-put, somersault, stilt, string figure, swing, tag, top, tug-of-war, wrestling.** *For game chants, see* **holohi'a, punikihi.** *Complete defeat in a game,* make pilau. *Place for indoor games,* lōkū.

GAMES OF STRENGTH: hā'awe, honuhonu, hukihuki, kā mākoi kanaka, kano, kula'i wāwae, kulakula'i, māmaka, pā uma, pā'ume'ume, uma.

GAMES WITH STONES, STICKS, CLUBS, SPEARS: āneo, holoholo, ho'olei pōpō, ka'ōka'a, kaupua, ke'a lā'au, ke'a pua, kiniholo, kinipeki, kūhela, kulakula, lā'au pili, lele puni, no'a, 'ō'ō ihe, pahe'e, pahe'e 'ulu, pāhi'uhi'u, pala'ie, pōhā kīhelei, pūhenehene *(cf.* **kihi moe, kihi puka**), pū'ili, pu'upu'uone.

CARD GAMES: hai-lō-keaha, kāmau, kekake, konoki, male, nu'uanu, piula.

SEXUAL GAMES: kilu, 'ume, pili, loku.

MISCELLANEOUS GAMES: aho loa, honohono, ho'olelekē, kōhikōhi-kū-palalā, kōī, kū-hele-mai (kū-ā-helemai), le'ole'o, loulou, mimi ho'okahekahe wai, moa, moa nahele, na'ina'i, nā'ū, paha'o, pahipahi, pili lima, pinao, pio, polepole, pūkaula, punikihi, punipeki.

gang. Pū'ulu, po'e.

gap. Hakahaka, kāwaha, niho mole *(aperture);* nuku *(mountain).*

gape. Hāmama.

garage. Hale ka'a.

garbage. 'Ōpala. *Garbage pile,* pu'u 'ōpala, ahu 'ōpala. *Garbage can,* kini 'ōpala. *Garbage container,* waihona 'ōpala.

garble. Kake *(chant);* ho'okake, pakakē.

garden. Māla, māla pua, māla 'ai. *Also:* kīhāpai, pā kanu, ulu kanu, ulu pua, waena, kā'ao'ao, laulima. *See* **Eden.**

gardenia. Kiele, nā'ū, nānū.

gargle. Hō'olā'olā, 'alalā *(rare),* pō'ala.

garland. Lei.

garlic. 'Aka'akai pilau, 'aka'akai pūpū, kālika.

garment. 'A'ahu *(for various kinds, see Haw.-Eng. entry and entries that follow it);* lole komo, kāmaki; uhikino, pale *(outer).* *Full and flowing garment,* pihapiha. *Garments,* pa'a kapa.

garnet. Kaneka, ganeta.

garnish. Mikomiko. *To garnish,* ho'omikomiko.

garrison. Nā koa o ka pā kaua, hūlili.

garrulous. Waha nui, waha, wala'au wale, waha kani, waha ko'u, waha kole, kūlolohi, kanikani ka waha, palolo, palolo hua. *See* **talk** *and sayings,* 'alalā, 'olē'olē.

garters. Lī kākini.

gas. 1. *A fluid.* Ea, ea'a'ā, eamāmā, māhuea, kaka. **2.** *Of the stomach.* 'Ōpihapiha. *Also:* ho'onākū, nehekū, makani, pa'amua.

gasoline. Kakalina, 'ailaea, 'ailea, ahimakani.

gasp. Hanu pa'a, pauaho, paupauaho, kā'ili'ili, mauli'awa, omo. *Also:* 'ā'ili, ka'ahili mauli'awa, hikilele, pūailewa, pūaialewa, 'oaikū, hemo'ē, 'ōnini.

gate. Puka, pani, pani puka, kukuna. *Sliding or movable gate,* puka uai.

gatekeeper. Kia'i puka.

gateway. 'Īpuka, puka pā.

gather. 1. *Collect (mostly transitive).* 'Ohi *(pick);* ho'āhu, hō'ili'ili *(collect);* ku'i, 'ōla'o *(as 'opihi shells).* *Also:* 'i'i, hō'ulu'ulu, lapulapu; hukihuki *(as taro);* kōhi *(as fruit);* aulau *(as leaves);* laua'e. **2.** *Assemble (mostly intransitive).* Ho'ākoakoa. *Also:* mū, haiamū, mui, hāpuku, lāhui, pūpū, laukua, puku, huihui ā kōlea; 'ohana *(for family prayers);* pū *(as sails);* hō'alu-'alu *(as in sewing).* puleheke.

gatherer. Hō'alu'alu *(as on a sewing machine).*

gathering. 1. *Collecting.* 'Ohina, 'ulu'ulu, maka'uo. **2.** *Assembly.* Anaina, 'aha, pihana kanaka. *Also:* pōhai, hono, kīkāmū, ikāmū. *See* **gather.** *Gathering place of birds,* kula manu.

gathers. Hō'alu'alu; 'ā'īlepe *(as about the neck of a garment).*

gaudy. 'A'ai loa kohu 'ole *(pejorative);* ho'ohiehie launa 'ole, hine *(usually not pejorative).*

gauge. Ana; keiki *(on sewing machine);* una, haha kā 'upena *(net);* ana ua *(rain).*

gauge screw. Kolū kēpau.

gauze. 'A'amo'o, lole 'ae'ae loa.

gay. 1. *Cheerful.* Hau'oli, hau'oli'oli, 'oli'oli, le'ale'a. **2.** *See* **homosexual.**

gaze. Kauaheahe, haka, hālalo. *See* **stare.**

gazebo. 'Ale'o.

gazelle. Kao hihiu, kākela, kea, 'anekelopa.

gear. Pono, lako *(goods).*

gecko. Mo'o 'alā, mo'okā, mo'o ka'alā, 'anaka.

Gee! Kī!

Gehenna. Kehena, Gehena.

gel. Mākū, kuhua.

gelding. Lio po'a.

gem. Pōhaku makamae.

Gemini. Ka-māhana, Nā-māhoe. *See* **Castor, Pollux.**

gender. Keka.

genealogist. Mea pa'a mo'o kū'auhau; ipu wai 'au'au *(fig).*

genealogy. Kū'auhau, mo'o kū'auhau, mo'o ali'i, mo'o kupuna, mo'o kahuna, ikū pau. *See* **ipu wai 'au'au.**

Genealogy chant, koʻihonua. *Versed in genealogy,* paʻa kūʻauhau. *To recite genealogy,* haʻi kupuna, koʻihonua. *To discuss genealogy,* kūkā moʻo. *Place where genealogies were studied,* hale nauā. *To possess a genealogy,* āewa.

general. 1. *Army.* ʻAlihikaua, pūkaua, kenelala. **2.** *Widespread.* Laulaha, laulā, laha. *General name,* inoa laulā, inoa nui. *General provisions,* ʻōlelo pili i ʻō i ʻaneʻi.

generation. Hanauna. *Relative or one of the same generation,* hanauna like, hoa hanauna. *A single generation,* kau ʻapaʻapa. *A generation back,* kaupapa. *Relative of the parent's generation,* makua. *Three generations removed.* kuakahi. *Four generations removed,* kualua. *Five generations removed,* kuakolu. *Six generations removed,* kuakā. *Seven generations removed,* kualima. *To live in one place for generations,* noho papa.

generous. Manawaleʻa, puʻuwai aloha, lokomaikaʻi; lilolilo, kahiau *(rare). See sayings,* **kūʻono 1, umauma.**

genesis. Kinohi, kumulipo.

genial. ʻOluʻolu, laulauna, lauleʻa, heahea.

genital. Maʻi, piko. *Also:* muli pōkiʻi; ule, ʻamokiʻi, anakiʻi, anakiʻu, anamiʻu *(male). Genital chant,* mele maʻi. *Slit genital,* maʻi ʻoā *(insult for women).*

genitive case. ʻAuiiki. *See* **possessive case.**

Genoa. Kenoa.

genteel. Kūlana nihinihi, nihinihi.

Gentile. Kō nā ʻāina ʻē, kenekile.

gentle. Akahai, mālie, laka, waipahē; —, *as a breeze,* kauaheahe, kolonahe, nahenahe, ʻālaʻi, ānea, aheahe. *Also:* waiʻolu, akanahe, wawali, waliwali, kāpehe, nāwele, ʻūpalu.

gentleman. Keonimana. *Act as a gentleman,* hoʻokeonimana, waipahē.

genuine. Maoli, ʻiʻo, oiaʻiʻo.

geography. Hōʻike honua.

geology. Huli honua, ʻike noʻeau i nā pōhaku.

geometry. Anahonua, moleanahonua.

Georgia. Keokia, Geogia.

gerah. Kela.

geranium. Nohoanu, laniuma, hinahina, kupukupu ʻala.

germ. Mū, ʻeleao, ʻanoʻano.

German, Germany. Kelemānia.

germinate. Ilo, kupu. *Also:* ōilo, māʻau, hoʻoheu.

gestation. Hoʻokauhua.

gesture. Kuhi. *Vulgar or contemptuous gestures:* hōʻauwaepuʻu, panau, hoʻopanau, hoʻohuahua, hoʻopuʻukahua, hoʻopohopoho, hoʻokolekole maka, hoʻohelei maka, peu, kū ʻahaʻaha, kūākiʻi, ʻōpeʻa kua, hoʻopakeʻo. *To teach hula gestures,* hoʻokuhi.

gesturing. Kuhikuhina.

Gesundheit! Kihe a mauli ola!

get. Loaʻa, kiʻi, hoʻokiʻikiʻi, pā; — *up,* ala, māealani; — *out of,* lele; *to* — *on,* kau, eʻe. *Get out!* Kū hele pēlā! Kū ā hele loa! Hele i kahi ʻē! Hele pēlā! *Disinclined to get up,* lelemu. *Get to work,* hele e hana, hoe aku i ka waʻa. *Get angry,* piʻi ka huhū. *Get me some poi.* Lawe mai he poi.

Gethsemane. Kekekemane, Getesemane.

getting. Lawena, loaʻa ʻana.

geyser. Wai pahū.

ghost. Lapu, akua lapu, akua, ʻuhane. *Also:* mauli, wailua; maka pilau, haili, makani, ʻōlohe, ʻula, hoaka, akalau. *See* **Holy Ghost.** *Ghost procession,* huakaʻi pō, ʻoiʻo, kāoʻoloa. *To give up the ghost,* kuʻu i ka ʻuhane.

ghostly. Hanehane, auakua, pahulu, malila. *See* **ghost.**

giant. Pilikua.

gibberish. Hīkapalalē, pakakē, kīpakakē, namu, hiohio, kūhipahipa.

gibbet. ʻOlokeʻa.

giblet. ʻŌpū. *See* **gravy.**

Gibraltar. Kipalaleka, Gibaraleta.

giddy. Hānewanewa, pōniu, pōniuniu.

gift. Makana, haʻawina; wainohia *(rare). Farewell gift,* hoʻina, makana hele. *Ceremonial gifts,* pālala (palaloa), ʻoloa, louulu, pani. *Gift of second sight,* haʻawina ʻike pāpālua. *Failure to give a return gift,* maua.

giggle. Hene ka ʻaka, ʻaka iki, hene iki, henehene. *Also:* uwēʻehene, ehehene, kaniʻahē, pūhene.

Gilbertese. Kilipaki, Gilibati. *Also:* Lelewa, Lewalewa.

Gilbert Islands. ʻĀina Kilipaki.

gill. Pihapiha, ʻapi, oʻa; hāʻali *(rare). Gill plate,* maha, mahamaha. *Depression under gills,* ʻaʻali. *Base of gills,* kumu pihapiha. *Gill net,* ʻupena ʻapoʻapo.

gimlet. Kui houhou, wilipuaʻa, ulepuaʻa.

gin. Kini, wai aliʻi.

ginger. ʻAwapuhi *(for various kinds, see Haw.-Eng. entry and entries that follow it),* kāhili, ʻamomo, kinika. *Slimy liquid in blossoms of* ʻawapuhi kuahiwi, kikī.

ginger ale. ʻEla kinika.

gingham. Kinamu. *See* **lole papamū.** *Scotch plaid gingham,* kinamu Kekokia.

giraffe. Kilape, kamelopaki, kamelopadi.

gird. Lī, kāʻai, pūliki. *Also:* pūʻali, ʻaʻa, hoʻopūʻali, kau, paulinalina, liki, kōʻai, ʻōmau, kīpuni; hume *(of a malo).*

girdle. Kāʻai. *Also:* kākoʻo, ʻaʻa, ʻaʻa pūhaka, kāliki, apo, pōʻai.

girl. Kaikamahine, kamahine; *preadolescent* —, ʻulapaʻa. *See saying,* **shark.** *Group of girls,* kamaliʻi wāhine. *Girl's task,* hana kaikamahine *(easy work).*

girl scout. *No equivalent; sometimes heard:* pūʻali kamaliʻi wahine.

girth. Kaula ʻōpū *(of a saddle).*

gist. ʻIʻo, manaʻo nui.

give. Hāʻawi. *Also:* hō, kaʻa aku. *Give birth,* hānau. *Give food,* hānai ʻai. *Give gladly,* hāʻawi manawaleʻa, manawaleʻa, hoʻonuʻa, puʻupā, kahiau. *Give me,* mai, naʻu, hāʻawi mai. *Give for the sake of receiving a return gift,* kuʻakuʻai, hāʻawi papa heʻe nalu. *Give lavishly,* hoʻonuʻa, kihikau. *Give up,* hāʻawipio, kuʻu, haʻalele, lepahū; kuailo *(as a riddle).*

gizzard. ʻŌpū, puʻu, puʻuʻaiʻai.

glad. Hauʻoli, lauleʻa, kāʻēʻē. *I'm glad to meet you,* hauʻoli ka hui ʻana me ʻoe.

gladiolus. ʻUki haole.

gladness. ʻOliʻoli, nēnēleʻa. *See* **glad.**

glance. ʻAlawa, ʻalaʻalawa, kilohi, leha, maka leha, maka lena, kokoe maka, kiʻina ʻōnohi maka. *Glance off,* holohuʻa, kā kīkepa, ʻōhua.

glare. Maka weli, ʻaʻā maka; hulili, ʻōlinolino *(of sun).*

glass. Aniani; kīʻaha *(for drinking). Glass dish,* pā aniani. *Glass-bottom box,* pahu aniani. *To touch glasses, as in drinking,* pūkē kīʻaha. *Volcanic glass in hairlike form,* lauoho-o-Pele.

glasses. Makaaniani *(spectacles). Glasses case,* wahī makaaniani.

Glauber salts. Hauʻeli.

glazed. ʻŌhewahewa *(eyes).*

gleam. ʻAnapa, ʻōlino, huali.

glean. Hōʻiliʻili. *(Luka 2:2.)*

gleanings. Mea ʻohi.

glede. Kolenika.

gleeful. Piha ʻoli; panaleʻa *(rare).*

glib. Palolo, palolo hua, wahawai, waha wali, ʻōlelo paheʻe, kūkake.

glide. Kīkaha. *Also:* kākele, niau, palahiʻa, ʻōlali, ʻōhua.

glimmer. ʻUiki, ʻamo, nakili.

glimpse. ʻIke mahuʻi, ʻike lihi, ʻaweʻaweʻa.

glisten. Liko, ʻōlali, kuali, kōlilelile.

glitter. ʻĀlohi, ʻālohilohi, ʻanapa. *Also:* lali, hulali, hūlalilali, huali, hinuhinu, hoaka, ʻoaka, kōlilelile, kuali, ʻōlali, liko, ʻā, pūwā.

gloat. Haʻanui. *Gloat over misfortunes of others,* ʻakola, ʻaikola.

globe. Paʻa poepoe, poepoe, hulipoepoe, poepoe honua, kāhonua.

globe amaranth. Leihua.

globefish. 'O'opu hue.
globular. Poepoe.
gloom. Pōuliuli. *Also:* pāuli, la'a uli, malu ko'i, milu-milu, 'e'elekū, kōanoano, pōnaho, nupa, pōlio; *forest* —, lipo wao nahele. *To cast gloom,* ho'omāmalu. *To dispel gloom,* ho'omāla'e.
Gloria Patri. Ka Ho'onani 'Ana i ke Akua.
glorify. Ho'onani, ho'ohanohano, ho'okapukapu, kaena; pūhano *(rare).*
glorious. Hanohano, nani, kei, po'iu.
glory. Hanohano, nani, kei; hoaka *(rare). Glory, glory,* nani, nani. *The glory of Pali-uli is the misty rain,* hanohano Pali-uli i ka ua noe *(of a handsome person).*
glossy. Hulali, hūlalilali, hinuhinu; pano pa'u *(black).*
glottal stop. 'Okina, 'u'ina; koma luna *(apostrophe).*
glove. Mīkini lima, mikilima.
glow. 'Ena, 'ena'ena, 'a'ā. *Also:* 'ōwena, 'ōwela, hāweo, huluhulu weo, liko, lamalama, makawela, maka weli, kū'ena, pua'ena, lau'ena, kauluwela, pua ahi, pu'e-'ene, liholiho, makali. *Sunset or dawn glow,* alaula.
glue. Kolū, mea ho'opipili.
gluey. 'Ūlika, 'ūlikalika, pilipili. *Also:* aweawe, ka'aka'alina, pīlekaleka, hulina, napo, lina.
glutton. Pākela 'ai, puni 'ai. *Lazy glutton,* lomaloma 'ai halalē. *Desires of a glutton,* kuko makapehu.
glycerine. Kolukeline.
gnash. 'Uwī, nau *(as the teeth). Sound of gnashing,* wī.
gnat. Nalo 'aki, nonanona, lonalona, pōnalo; makika *(RSV).*
gnaw. Nali, nalinali, naninani.
gnu. Nū.
go. Hele, hele aku, haele, uhaele, haeleele, uhele; — *down,* iho, hele iho, kīpou; napo'o *(as the sun);* — *up,* pi'i, pi'i aku, ea; — *inland,* pi'i aku, hele i uka; — *back,* ho'i, ho'i hou, ho'i hope; — *backward,* emi hope; — *forward,* ne'emua, hele i mua; — *ahead,* holo i mua, hoe aku i ka wa'a, hoea, ho'okā'oi; — *on, continue,* ho'omau, ō, 'oia; — *by, pass,* ma'alo, ka'a, kaha; — *into,* komo; — *out,* puka, puka i waho; — *aboard,* e'e; — *with,* hele pū, 'alo, hahai; — *around,* ka'apuni, pō'ai, pō'ai haele, 'aipuni, 'oai; — *far,* ho'omamao, hele loa, hele wale, hi'ikua; — *for,* ki'i; — *fast,* holo, hele kikī, kalalī; — *on foot,* hele wāwae; *turn and* —, kaha, pe'a, pelu; — *back and forth,* ka'i lewa; — *from house to house,* hele kauhale, pakaulele; — *from place to place,* mā'au; — *astray,* hele hewa; — *permanently,* hele loa, ho'i loa; — *for the first time or as a stranger,* hele malihini; — *headlong,* hele — *riding,* holoholo, holoholo ka'a; — *to and fro together,* haeleele. *Ready, set go!* 'Oia! *Go away!* Hele ma kahi 'ē! Hele pēlā! Kū ā hele! Kū ā hele loa! Kōekōe aku! *To go asking questions,* nīnau hele. *To go asking for something,* noi hele. *For rather rare expressions see* **akauahelo, 'ele'io, hālawa, hele honua, hele kūkū, hihihiki, kahakū, kaha loa, kaiue, kaka'iāhele, kālawa, kalawai, ki'ipua, koeheke, kololani, kōwē, kōkōwē, kukua'au, mō'ala'ala, moe, moea, momoe, na'ū, 'ōauau, olomio, pāhiki, poka'i, wehe.**
goad. Ho'okikina, wahapa'a. *See* **tease, urge.**
goal. Pahu hope, pahu hopu, pahukū; kumu *(objective).*
goat. Kao. *Also:* kūnānā, nānā. *Cf. Gram. 2.9.2.* Wearer *of goat hides,* 'a'ahu 'ili kao *(of one so shiftless that he sleeps on smelly goat hides instead of mats). The drum sounds, the goat flees,* kani ka pahu, holo ke kao *(of a bald head likened to a goatskin drum cover).*
goatee. 'Umi'umi, kāwelewele.
goatfish. *Three adult stages are* kūmū, weke, *and* moano; *see Haw.-Eng. entries. Also:* kolekolea, malu, munu.
Goat Island. Mokupuni Kao.
gobble. 1. *Eat noisily.* 'Ai mūkā, 'ai halalē, 'ukā, hūkā. 2. *As turkeys.* Pōkeokeo, kolokolo.
gobbler. Pelehū kāne, pōkeokeo kāne.
goblet. Kī'aha puaniki.
goblin. *No general term. See* **Menehune, peke.**

goby. 'O'opu *(for various kinds, see Haw.-Eng. entry and entries that follow it),* nōkea, nākea, nāpili, 'ōhune, aualaliha, kāni'o.
god. Akua *(both Christian and pre-Christian; for various types, see* **akua** *and below);* Makua *(in Christian prayers); stone fishing* —, kū'ula; *family or personal* —, 'aumakua, kumupa'a, 'ao'ao. *See* **legendary beings, life, prayer.** Akua *is usually preceded by* ke: *God is love,* aloha ke Akua. *Abode of gods:* pō, 'āpapa lani, kaha akua, Kahiki. *One who cared for gods and images,* kahu akua. *So help me God,* e ola au i ke Akua. *Great gods,* po'o ki'eki'e. *Names of the great gods:* Kāne, Kū, Lono, Kanaloa. *The gods,* nā hoa ali'i. *In poetry, references to rain, rainbow, and mist may signify the gods.*
godchild. Keiki papakema, keiki ho'okama.
God damn. Kokame, kokami.
goddess. Akua wahine, akua.
godless. 'Aiā, 'aiāhulu.
godfather. Makua kāne papakema, makua 'uhane.
godlike. 'Ano akua, akua, ho'ākua. *Godlike companion,* hoa kua.
godmother. Makuahine papakema.
godparent. Makua papakema.
going. Helena, hele. *Going and asking,* noi hele. *See* **go.**
goiter. 'Ā'ī 'olo'olo.
gold. Kula, gula. *Gold money,* kālā 'ula'ula. *Gold jewelry,* lako kula. *Gold nuggets,* pu'upu'u kula. *Five-dollar gold piece,* hapahā kini. *Ten-dollar gold piece,* hapalua kini. *Gold-colored,* wai kula.
golden. Kula, gula. *Golden finery,* ho'ohiluhilu kula.
Golden Gate. 'Īpuka Gula.
golden eagle. 'Aeko kula.
goldfish. I'a 'ula'ula. *White-marked goldfish,* i'a 'ula'ula lā kea.
golf. Kolepa, golepa.
golf course. Kahua kolepa.
gone. Nalowale, lilo, hele i kahi 'ē. *Also:* ka'a, alaheo, pu-ehu. *All gone,* pau i ka lilo. *Gone a long time or distance,* hala loa. *Several days gone by,* he mau lā i ka'a a'e.
gonorrhea. Pala, pala hao, pala lalo, waiiki.
good. Maika'i. *No good,* 'a'ole maika'i. *Good fortune,* pōmaika'i. *Very good,* maika'i loa.
good afternoon, good evening. Aloha ahiahi.
good-by. Ā hui hou aku *(lit., until meet again),* aloha; kupae, kupai *(rare, Eng.).*
good-for-nothing. Lapuwale, mea waiwai 'ole. *Also:* 'u'a, 'uka, uha'ula. *See* **useless, vagabond.**
Good Friday. Pō'alima Hemolele, Pō'alima Maika'i.
good-looking. Maika'i, maika'i ke nānā aku; kūmū *(slang). Rare:* mi'i, mīkohu.
good morning. Aloha kakahiaka.
good-natured. Waipahē, 'olu'olu. *Also:* wawali, waliwali, pūnolunolu.
goodness. Pono, maika'i, hemolele; kā, auē *(exclamations).*
good night. *See* **greeting.**
goods. Waiwai, pono, mea.
good will. Lokomaika'i.
goody-goody. Ho'opalō, ho'omikanele.
gooney. Kone *(probably).*
goose. Nēnē. *See saying,* 'ala'ala pū loa. *We heard the goose,* lohe mai nei mākou i ka nēnē. *The goose honks unele unele (this suggests nele, nothing, hence failure, nothing gotten).*
gooseberry. Pohā, pa'ina.
goose flesh. 'Ōkala, 'ōkakala, lī ka 'ili, lī ka 'i'o. *Also:* kūhulukū; kakalaiō *(rare).*
gopher. Kopahela.
gorge. Haoa puhi *(for catching eels).*
gorgeous. Pūnono, ho'ohiehie loa.
gorilla. Kolila.
gospel. 'Euanelio, 'ōlelo maika'i. *To preach the gospel,* ha'i 'euanelio.
gossip. Lawe 'ōlelo, lawena 'ōlelo, holoholo 'ōlelo, 'imi 'ōlelo, lohe 'ōlelo, ho'owā, hauwala'au. *Also:* ili 'ōle-

lo, lonolonoā, nonoā, nonononoā, hoʻopihapiha ʻōlelo, ʻohikau, nuku ʻouʻou, niʻa; hunehune *(small talk);* nēnē, wā, kalekale, ʻioʻiolepo, kekēue, hauhauhali. *See sayings,* **hapuku 2, hū 2, huʻea, makani, ʻouʻou 1, wawā, heron.**

got. Loaʻa. *See* **get, have.** *He has got five cars,* loaʻa iāia ʻelima kaʻa.

Gothic. Kokika.

gouge. Pōʻalo, hao, pao; koʻi ʻōwili, hōʻoʻoma *(carpenter's). Eye gouge, to gouge out eyes,* pōʻalo maka *(fig., ungrateful; one who steals a spouse).*

gourd. Ipu *(term used for both the gourd plant and the hula drum made of two gourds sewed together, played by chanters; various types,* **ipu** *and below;* hue *(various types,* **hue** *and below);* pōhue, ʻumeke pōhue. *Other kinds:* hue ʻawaʻawa *(bitter);* hulilau *(fig., woman, wife, mother);* ihiloa, ʻio, ʻiole-holo-kula, kepena, kūkaeʻiwa; kūpala, lauhue, mūʻolo, noʻunoʻu, nukupueo, ʻōlaelae, pāhaʻahaʻa, pākākā, palaʻai, panunu kuahiwi; pūliʻuliʻu, pūʻulīʻulī, ʻulīʻulī *(for rattles). Stem of gourd leaf,* hā ipu. *Upper part of gourd,* hū pā ipu. *Juice of a green gourd,* pahukaʻa. *Gourd with hourglass shape,* ipu pueo. *Large gourd,* hulilau *(fig., woman);* lonolau, nonolau. *Bottle-necked gourd,* mūʻā. *Gourd containers:* hōkeo *(fig., a trifle);* omo, ʻolo, hue wai, ipu ʻaumakua, laha. *Cord support for gourds,* ʻaha hāwele. *Cord with which cracks in gourds were sewn together,* ʻahamaka. *Gourd hanger,* haka ipu, kā ipu. *Gourd drums:* ipu hula, ipu paʻi, ipu heke, ipu heke ʻole, ipu wai. *Top gourd in drum,* heke. *Gourd drumbeat,* pā, kāhela, kūkū. *Gourd hula,* hula kuolo *(large gourd);* hula ʻulīʻulī *(rattle). Gourd whistle,* ipu hoehoe, ipu hōkiokio. *Gourd for fishing,* kākū. *Gourd for kilu game,* kilu. *Concoction made of gourd fruits and kukui nuts,* kumuhonua. *Pōhue gourd nose,* ihu pōhue *(stupid). The gourd bottle gurgles when not filled,* i ʻolāʻolā nō ka hue wai i ka piha ʻole *(of ignorant talk). See saying,* **haumanumanu.**

gout. Wāwae pehu.

govern. Hoʻomalu, noho aupuni, noho aliʻi, noho.

government. Aupuni. *Government business,* hana o ke aupuni. *Government building,* hale aupuni. *Colonial government,* aupuni koloniala. *Federal government,* aupuni pekelala.

governor, governorship. Kiaʻāina.

gown. ʻAʻahu, lole; *loose —,* holokū, muʻumuʻu, luʻeluʻe. *Evening gown,* ʻaʻahu hoʻohiwahiwa. *Train of a gown,* huʻa.

grab. Kāʻili, ʻapo. *Grab roughly,* lālau ʻino.

grabber. Lima lālau, mea kāʻili, lima loa.

grace. Aloha *(mercy, compassion);* lokomaikaʻi *(kindness);* ʻolu *(as in a dance);* pule hoʻomaikaʻi i ka papa ʻaina *(before a meal);* kalakia *(Catholic). For a preChristian grace, see* ʻ**aumakua 2.** *To ask grace,* pule hoʻopōmaikaʻi. *The grace of God,* ke aloha o ke Akua. *Hail, Mary, full of grace,* aloha ʻoe, ē Mālia, piha ʻoe i ka maikaʻi.

grace note. Hua liʻiliʻi, hua kōkua.

gracious. Lokomaikaʻi, ʻoluʻolu, waipahē.

grade. 1. *Rank, class.* Kūlana, papa. *Sixth grade,* papa ʻeono. *Highest grade,* papa kiʻekiʻe loa, hulinuʻu. 2. *Evaluation.* Heluna, kaha. 3. *To level.* Hōʻiliwai.

gradual. Mālie, liʻiliʻi, lohi.

graduate. Puka, hoʻopuka.

graduation exercises. ʻŪniki.

graduation feast. ʻAhaʻaina ʻūniki, ʻahaʻaina puka.

graft. 1. *To connect.* Pākuʻi, pānaʻi. *Grafted hibiscus,* aloalo hoʻokuʻi pākuʻi. 2. *Dishonest dealing for profit.* Hana ʻaihue i ʻuhi ʻia.

grain. 1. *Small particle.* Huna. 2. *In wood, stone.* ʻIʻo, wai, nao, au, nao ʻohiʻohi. *Curly grain,* nao hāluʻa. *Yellowish grain in wood,* ʻiʻo lau maiʻa. *Black streaks in grain,* pano paʻu. 3. *See* **seed.** *For small grains see* **barley, oats, rye, wheat.**

grainy. Oneone.

gram. Huna.

grammar. Piliʻōlelo, hōʻike ʻōlelo. *To study grammar,* aʻo piliʻōlelo.

grammatical. Like me nā lula piliʻōlelo.

Granada. Kalenaka, Garenada.

granadilla. Lilikoʻi, lemi wai.

grand. Maikaʻi loa *(fine);* hanohano *(glorious);* nui *(large, important).*

grandaunt. *Same as* **grandmother.**

grandchild. Moʻopuna. *Grandchild of a sibling or cousin,* moʻopuna hanauna. *To have a grandchild,* kani moʻopuna *(poetic). To carry a grandchild in the arms,* hiʻi moʻopuna.

granddaughter. Moʻopuna wahine.

grandfather. Kupuna kāne, tūtū, kūkū, kūkū kāne.

grand jury. Kiule nui, ʻaha kiule kiʻekiʻe.

grandma. *Same as* **grandmother.**

grandmother. Kupuna wahine, tūtū, kūkū, kūkū wahine.

grandpa. *Same as* **grandfather.**

grandparent. Kupuna; hulu kupuna *(poetic). To be or become a grandparent,* kani moʻopuna, hiʻi moʻopuna.

grandson. Moʻopuna kāne.

granduncle. *Same as* **grandfather.**

granite. Māpala.

granny. Tūtū, kūkū.

grant. Hāʻawi *(give);* haʻawina *(appropriation);* ʻae, ʻāpono *(approve).*

grant-in-aid. Haʻawina kākoʻo, uku kākoʻo.

grape. Hua waina, waina. *Cluster of grapes,* paʻi waina, paʻi hua waina, huihui waina. *Grape jelly,* kele waina. *Grape raiser,* mahi waina.

grapefruit. *No known Hawaiian name.*

grapeshot. Pōkā lū.

grapevine. Kumu waina.

grasp. Hopu, ʻapo, hao, lālau; haika *(rare). Fail to grasp,* ʻapo hewa, hala ka lālau ʻana, hūhewa. *To grasp the meaning quickly,* ʻaʻapo.

grasping. Hopuna, ʻāpona. *See* **grasp.**

grass. Mauʻu *(for various kinds, see Haw.-Eng. entry and entries that follow it),* weuweu. *Other kinds:* ʻakiʻaki, honohono, honohono kukui, hoʻomanewa, hulukoaʻe, kākonakona, kalamālō (ʻemoloa, kāwelu), kauwele, kauwelu, kiliʻoʻopu, konakona, kualohia, kūkaekōlea, kūkaepuaʻa *(crab),* kūmanomano; lāpine, lūkini *(lemon);* lule, mākuakua; mānienie *(for various kinds, see Haw.-Eng. entry and entries that follow it),* mānewanewa; mauʻu Kepanī *(velvet);* mauʻu kukū, ʻumeʻalu *(bur);* mauʻu mokae *(nut);* mauʻu laiki *(rice);* ʻohe, pālāmoa, pili, pilipili ʻula. *Blade of grass,* lau mauʻu. *Clump of grass,* pūpū weuweu, ōpū weuweu. *Wilted grass,* mauʻu mae. *Full of grass,* pihaweuweu *(rare).*

"grass." Paka lōlō.

grasshopper. ʻŪhini, ʻūhini akelika.

grass house. Hale pili, hale weuweu.

grass linen. Lilina puʻu mauʻu.

grate. Walu, waʻu (uaʻu), olo *(verb);* hao manamana, papa manamana *(noun). Also:* pīhelehele, ʻānai, ʻuwalu, waluhia, wauhalu, uwaʻu, waʻuwaʻu, wawaʻu, wawalu. *To grate coconuts,* waʻu niu.

grateful. Hoʻomaikaʻi. *Grateful heart,* naʻau hoʻomaikaʻi. *I am grateful for your help,* hoʻomaikaʻi au i kou kōkua mai. *I am very gratefully (yours),* ʻo wau nō me ka hoʻomaikaʻi.

grater. Waʻu. *Also:* uwaʻu, waʻuwaʻu, wawaʻu. *See* **grate.** *Coconut grater,* waʻu niu.

gratification. Mahalo; leʻa *(sexual).*

grating. Papa manamana, hao manamana.

gratis. Hāʻawi wale, manuahi, manuwahi, manawaleʻa, hāʻawi hemolele.

gratitude. Hoʻomaikaʻi, mahalo.

gratuitous. Manuahi, hāʻawi me ka uku ʻole.

grave. 1. *Burial.* Hē, lua kupapaʻu, ilina. *Also:* hale lua, luapō, hē kupapaʻu, hale kupapaʻu, paheʻe. *To decorate, as graves,* kau pua, lū pua. 2. *Serious.* Koʻikoʻi, kūoʻo.

gravel. 'Ili'ili makali'i; one 'ā (black lava); ōkea (white); 'a'ā pu'upu'u.
graven image. Ki'i kālai 'ia.
gravestone. Kia ho'omana'o.
graveyard. Pā ilina, pā kupapa'u.
gravity. 'Umekaumaha.
gravy. Kai, kai penu, kai likoliko. Giblet gravy, kai 'ōpū. To stew or mix with gravy, kākele.
gravy boat. Ipu kai.
gray. 'Āhinahina, hinahina, 'āhina, hina; po'o hina (of hair). Also: hiahia, 'āhiehie, lehu, lālauahi, ualehu, uauahi, pōpō uahi, pua hina, puahia, polohina, pōhina, pākea, laukea, noenoe, ko'okea; po'o kea, po'o kuakea, kuahinahina (of hair). To gray (of hair), hina ulu, pi'i kea, a'ea'e. For sayings honoring gray hair, a'ea'e, 'ō 2.
grayish. Hinahina, ma'oha.
grayish-black. 'Eleuli.
graze. Ho'ohani, hani, pā lihi (touch lightly); kūlihi (as a bullet); 'ai mau'u (eat grass).
grease. 'Aila, 'aila hamo, hinu, 'ōhinu, kōnāhua. Thick grease, 'aila pa'a.
greasy. Same as grease. Also: kele, kelekele, kele lua, hinu, hinuhinu, lali, pīlalilali, kūhinu, kōlikoliko.
great. Nui, nunui. Also: manomano, mānu'unu'u, 'ī, ke'ele, one'ula, ho'ikau, pākeupali. See greatest. Very great, nui loa, lele'oi, 'oi aku ka nui.
great-aunt. See grandaunt.
Great Britain. Pelekane Nui.
greatest. Nui, po'okela, heke, hapa nui, hapa loa, kaupoku. See great.
great-grandchild. Mo'opuna kuakahi.
great-grandparent. Kupuna kuakahi.
great-great-grandchild. Mo'opuna kualua.
great-great-grandparent. Kupuna kualua.
great-great-great-grandchild. Mo'opuna kuakolu.
great-great-great-grandparent. Kupuna kuakolu.
great-nephew. Same as grandson.
greatness. Nui, manomano.
great-niece. Same as granddaughter.
great-uncle. See granduncle.
Greece, Grecian, Greek. Helene.
greed. 'Ālunu, lunu, nunu, 'ānulu, 'ānunu, make'e. Also: no'u, lauahi, hulipeua, 'a'ao.
green. 'Ōma'oma'o, 'ōma'o, ma'oma'o, ma'o, uliuli (vegetation); maka (as fruit). Also: mama'o, mamaka, 'ōhala. See thumb. To make or paint green, ho'ōma'oma'o.
greenery. Lau nahele; lau ho'ohiwahiwa (for decorations); weuweu (in chants). See rain.
greenhouse. Hale ho'oulu mea kanu.
greenish. 'Ano 'ōma'oma'o, mama'o.
Greenland. 'Āina 'Ōma'oma'o.
green rose. Loke lau.
greens. Lau; lau 'ai 'ia (edible). Edible greens: lū'au (taro); palula (sweet potato); pōpolo, hinihini, pualele, pakai ('āheahea), hō'i'o, kikawaiō (eaten raw or cooked). See spinach, watercress.
greet. Aloha, aloha aku. Old forms: weli, welina, 'ano'ai. Also: kāhea, oha, 'ike. See greeting.
greeting. Aloha. The old greetings were: aloha, 'ano'ai, welina me ke aloha. Post-missionary greetings include: aloha kakahiaka, good morning; aloha ahiahi, good afternoon, good evening. The farewell greeting was ā hui hou aku or aloha. These were said also for good night, as for leaving a meeting, but not within the home. To extend greeting, aloha aku, kāhea, oha, e'e, a'a. To press noses in greeting, honi.
gregarious. Laulauna.
greyhound. 'Īlio hahai.
gridiron. Hao manamana (grate); kahua pā'ani (arena).
grief. Kaumaha, kani'uhū, kūmakena, 'ū. Also: 'ūpē, maka'ūpē, mānewanewa, ho'omānewanewa, pānewanewa, māna'ona'o, ho'omāna'ona'o, mokuāhua, mokumokuāhua, paumākō, hihipe'a, ikiiki, polohina, na'auauā, manawahua. To lighten grief, ho'olana. For

poetic expressions of grief, see hanane'e, lu'ulu'u, 'ū'ū 3, tear 1. In poetry, grief may be represented by heavy rain (ua).
grief-stricken. Noho 'ū, pā i ka 'ū, nū, ho'onū, mā'e'ele, kūlōlia.
grieve. See grief. Also: auē, aumihi, minamina, kaniā'au.
grill. Hao manamana, hao hakahaka.
grimace. Ho'owaha; haikaika, ho'ohaikaika (defiance, contempt); ualehe, pu'e'eke.
grin. 'Olē'olē (wide mouthed, as of an image). See smile.
grind. Wili, 'uwī, ho'okala, 'ānai, kuai, hoana. See ground. Grind sugar cane, wili kō. Grind flour, kāwili palaoa.
grinder. Nau.
grindstone. Hoana, hoana ka'a.
grip. See grasp. Also: uma, pūliki.
gripe. Kalipa, garipa.
gritty. Oneone.
groan. Nā, 'ū, 'uhū, kani'ū. Also: 'uhū'uhū, auē, nū, nūnū, ho'onū, 'i'i'ī.
groceries. Mea 'ai.
grocery store. Hale kū'ai mea 'ai.
groin. Kumu 'ūhā; pani kai (sea wall); hola (rare). Swelling in the groin, 'ēwai, 'awaiāhiki ('āwai), 'auko'i, haha'i.
groom. Kahu lio. See bridegroom.
groove. Nao, hālua, 'a'ali. Also: 'ali, mo'o'ali, mō'ali, 'auwaha, ioio, nī'au, kohe. To make grooves, hole, ho'oioio.
grooved. See groove. Also: ioio, 'ali'ali, pū'ali, 'ōwahawaha, māio, wa'awa'a, wa'awa'ahia.
grope. Hāhā. Grope here and there, hāhā hele, hilihua. Grope as a blind person, ho'opāpā. Also: hāpapa, kūpāpā.
gross. Kāpulu (coarse). Gross profit, huina loa'a.
grotesque. Pupuka pepe'ekue, pau'aka.
grotto. Ana.
ground. 1. Earth. Lepo. 2. See grind. Ground round steak, 'i'o pipi i wili 'ia.
grounded. Ili, mau.
grounds. Oka (dregs); kahua (site); kumu (cause). See fishing grounds. Grounds for divorce, kumu no ka 'oki male.
group. Pū'ulu, 'ao'ao. Also: 'au, 'āuna, pōhai, pō'ai, pewa, pae. See cluster, flock. Group of islands, pae 'āina.
grouper. Hāpu'u; young stage: hāpu'upu'u ('āpu'upu'u).
grove. Ulu, ulu lā'au, maha lā'au, moku lā'au, nahele. Coconut grove, ulu niu.
groveler. Naku li'i.
grow. Ulu, ho'oulu, kupu; — wild and lush, uluāhewa, uluāo'a, kupuohi, pūhuli, oha; — easily, wild, ulu wale; — thriftily, kā'aha'aha, 'ōuou; — fast, ulu 'āwīwī, kikī holo, ahuahu; — by layering, kākiwi; — irregularly, kāi'oi'o; — thick, hō'i'o; —, as a fetus, ōpū; —, as tendrils, 'ōka'i; — low, nene'e. Also: āulu, ululu, 'ōhulu, ohiohi, māohiohi, heu, ho'oheu. To train to grow as desired, pākōlea. To fill out in growing, ho'opiha.
growing. Kupuna. See grow.
growl. Nunulu, hae.
growth. Ulu, kupu. Also: 'oulu, 'i'o ulu, māhua, ohi. Slow growth, kupu lohi, mūnō, kupa li'i, ho'okokōhi. Forest growth, lau nahele. In poetry, rain and mist may signify growth and greenery (see weep). Young growth stages of some fish are reduplicated bases, as 'a'ala'ihi, 'aha'aha, 'āholehole, a'ua'u, halahala, hāpu'upu'u, 'ōkuhekuhe, pākalakala, pālailai.
grudge. Mauhala, 'au'a. To bear a grudge, ho'omauhala, manawahuā, 'eleiki, kūna'au. To do grudgingly, kua nui, ho'okua nui.
gruesome. Māna'ona'o, weliweli.
gruff. 'Ōkalakala, pūkalakī.
grumble. 'Ōhumu, 'ōhumuhumu, namunamu, kunu-

kunu, 'ōhalahala, nuku, nuku ho'omau. *Also:* nakulu, helu, kolo, kolokolo.

grunt. Hū. *Also:* ke'u, nū, 'ū, ho'o'ū, hō'ū, kani'ū, 'uhū, nūnū, hō'i'ī.

guano. Kūkae manu.

guarantee. Hō'oia.

guard. Kia'i, mea kia'i. *Also:* māka'i, maka'ina, pale, kūka'awe, ho'opālama; *rear* —, hunapa'a; *king's* —, apo hao. *To stand guard,* kū uwaki. *Citizens' guard,* pū'ali kia'i māka'i.

guardian. Kahu. *Also:* 'ohene; 'ūhā *(of a chiefly child).* *See also* **kaikū'ono, 'ohene, 'Olu-'Ekeloa-ho'oka'a-moena.** *Royal guardian,* kahu ali'i. *Guardian angel,* 'ānela kia'i.

Guatemala. Kuakemala.

guava. Kuawa *(for various kinds, see* **kuawa** *and below); strawberry* —, waiawī.

guess. Koho, koho wale, mahu'i. *See* **riddle.** *Guessing game,* pā'ani koho. *Guessing contest,* ho'opāpā. *Some guessing games:* no'a, pūhenehene, pu'upu'uone, pili lima. *I can't guess.* Kuailo.

guest. Malihini kipa, mea i kono 'ia. *My guest,* ka'u malihini. *To be a guest,* ho'omalihini. *Be my guest,* ke kono aku nei au iā'oe. *Guest for a day,* he malihini no ka lā ho'okahi *(a newcomer, as though on a honeymoon, is not criticized; later he is to do his share of work).*

guesthouse. Hale kipa.

guffaw. Hehē ka 'aka, hū ka 'aka.

guidance. Alaka'ina.

guide. Alaka'i, hō'ike; kukui *(poetic).* *My guide of the eight seas,* ku'u hō'ike o nā kai 'ewalu *(in praise of a leader).*

guile. Ma'alea.

guilt. Hewa.

guilty. Hewa. *To find guilty,* ho'āhewa. *Found guilty,* pili i ka hewa. *Found not guilty,* ho'āpono. *He is guilty,* kū ka hewa iāia.

guinea. Kini *(coin).*

guinea hen. Kinihene.

guinea pig. 'Iole pua'a.

guitar. Kīkā. *See* **slack key.** *To play the guitar,* ho'o-kani kīkā; ho'opāpā *(a certain way).*

gulch. Awāwa, kahawai, 'oawa, kōwā, 'ōawaawa.

gulf. Kai kū'ono, kū'ono.

Gulf of Darien. Kai-o-Kaliana (Dariana).

Gulf of Mexico. Kai-kū'ono-o-Mekiko.

gull. 'Ōpa'ipa'i, nēnē 'au kai *(sea gull).*

gullible. Punihei, puni wale. *See idiom,* **'ama'ama.**

gullied. Wa'awa'ahia, ku'āwa'awa'a, 'ōwae.

gully. 'Āwa'a. *See* **gulch.**

gulp. Ale, alapoho, moni. *Also:* momoni, momomoni, monimoni, 'ai pō'ala. *Gulping sound,* mā'ū'ū.

gum. Kamu *(for chewing);* pīlali, hū, kēpau *(as on a ripe breadfruit).* *Gum-producing tree,* lā'au hū. *To chew gum,* nau kamu. *To gum lehua trees for catching birds,* kāpili manu, pulehua.

gumboil. 'I'o kupu.

gummy. Pīlalilali, pīlekaleka, lina, loliloli. *See* **gluey, sticky.**

gums. 'I'o pale niho. *Toothless gums,* ka'e, mūka'e.

gun. Pū; waikī *(rare).* *Machine gun,* pū mīkini. *Toy or popgun,* pū pā'ani. *Water or squirt gun,* pū kī wai, pū wai. *Double-barreled gun,* pū kihi lua. *Gun carried on shoulders,* pū kau po'ohiwi. *Maxim gun,* pū wili. *Cock of a gun,* kiko. *Gun bayonet,* 'ēlau waikī. *Gun salute,* pū aloha. *Row or tier of guns,* papapū. *To load, as a gun,* ho'opiha.

gunny sack. 'Eke huluhulu, 'ekemau'u.

gunpowder. Pauka kī pū. *Also:* waipahū, one 'ā, waipū.

gunshot. Lū, pōkā lū.

gunwale. Pale.

gunwale strakes. *See* **canoe.**

gurgle. 'Ōlā'olā. *Also:* hohō, nonō, pua'i, 'ulī, kūkawo-wo. *See ex.,* **gourd.**

gurnard. Pinao, loloa'u.

gush. 1. *Of water.* Huahua'i, hua'ina, hū, pāhūhū. **2.** *Of speech.* Pua'ohi, waha kale, 'ohi, hūlani, ha'ano'u.

gust. Kokololio, makani pūkīkī, puahio. *Also:* kololio, kokolowini, hio, hihio, mōhio, mōhiohio, mohihio, pūhihio, 'ōhio, kākala, āmio, āmiomio, makani kū honua, 'oehu, 'ale.

guts. Na'au.

gutter. 'Auwaha *(ditch);* 'alu *(ravine);* pulumi *(as on a house).*

guttural. Pili i ke kani'ā'ī. *Guttural quality in chanting,* 'i'i.

guzzle. Hūkā.

gymnasium. Wahi no nā pā'ani ho'oikaika kino.

gypsum. Puna pohaku palupalu.

gypsy. Lāhui 'ae'a, mea 'ae'a.

gyrate. Pokaka'a, pōniuniu, oi.

H

h. Hē.
habeas corpus. Palapala ku'ukino *(writ of).*
habit. Hana ma'a, 'ao'ao, ma'a, mea hana ma'a.
habitual. Ma'amau.
habituated. Ma'a, ma'ama'a, ma'ama'ahia.
hack. 1. *To cut.* Kā, kua, pākā. 2. *Carriage.* Ka'api'o.
hackle. Hulu.
had. *See* have.
Hades. Pō, Kehena, Gehena.
hag. Luahine pī'alu, luahine 'ālu'a, kaikapū, kolo'u'a. *Dried-up hag,* luahine pīka'o.
Ha Ha! 'Ūhē'ūhē!
hail. 1. *Greeting.* 'Ō, aloha; o'ou *(rare).* 2. *Frozen rain.* Huahekili.
hailstone. Makahekili, pōkā ua hekili.
hair. Lauoho, oho *(head);* hulu, huluhulu, huhulu *(body). See* gray, haircut, Pele's hair, topknot. *Coarse hair,* lauoho 'o'ole'a. *Wavy hair,* pi'ipi'i lau nui, lauoho pipi'i. *Kinky hair,* lauoho pi'ipi'i Pukikī. *Straight hair,* lauoho kālole. *Long hair,* lauoho loloa. *Short hair,* lauoho pōkole, lauoho 'ekeke'i. *Hair in curls,* lauoho mimilo. *Person with curly hair,* kāpi'i. *Reddish hair,* lauoho 'ehu. *Hair black at the roots that shades out to reddish,* 'ehu kumu uli. *Body hair,* hulu. *Piece of hair of beloved deceased,* heia.
hairbrush. Palaki lauoho.
hair clasp. 'Ūmi'i lauoho.
hair curler. Hao ho'omimilo.
haircut. 'Oki ('ako) ka lauoho. *See* barber, bob. *To trim, cut only the ends,* 'oki huelo. *Mourning haircut,* 'oki kūmākena. *Kinds of mourning haircuts:* 'oki mahiole, 'ako po'o 'ō'ū, papa'iole, pa'ipa'i'iole, po'o kepa, 'oki kīkepa. *Shark's tooth for hair cutting,* niho 'oki. *"Crew" haircut,* 'oki pohe.
hair dresser. Wili oho.
hairless. Heu 'ole, 'ōmole, 'ōmolemole; 'ōlohe *(as a dog).*
hair net. 'Upena lauoho.
hairpin. Kui lauoho.
hairpin lace. Lihilihi kui lauoho.
hair switch. *See* switch.
hairy. Huluhulu, 'ōhuluhulu, pūhuluhulu, pihulu.
Haiti, Haitian. Haiki.
hale. Ikaika, olakino maika'i, pa'a.
half. Hapalua, pika. *Half-covered,* kīhapa. *Half dollar,* hapalua. *Half flower,* naupaka. *Half step (interval in music),* kanihapa. *Half-past five o'clock,* hapalua hola 'elima.
halfbeak. Iheihe.
half-mast. Kau hapa.
Halifax. Halipaka, Halifaka.
halitosis. Hanu pilo, pilo, waha pilo, 'ōpilopilo, 'alaea. *See saying,* hīnālea 1.
hall. Holo, hale. *Meeting hall,* hālau, ke'ena hālāwai.
hallelujah. Haleluia.
halloo. 'O, ho'ōho, ūi, hui, o'ou.
hallow. Ho'ola'a. *To hallow,* hō'ihi, ho'ola'a. *Hallowed,* ho'āno *(see ano).*
hallucination. Mana'o 'olalau, li'ulā, akakū, kūaka.
halo. Pō'aha ōlamalama. *Halo around sun or moon,* luahoana, lua kālai lani.
halt. Kūlia, kū.
halter. Kaula lio, pūnuku.
halyard. Kaula huki pe'a.
ham. Pua'a hame, 'ūhā pua'a, hame, 'ūhā hame. *To smoke, as a ham,* ho'opipī.
Hamburg. Hamepuka, Hamebuga.

hamburger. 'I'o pipi i wili 'ia.
hamlet. Kauhale.
hammer. Hāmale. *See* adze. *To hammer,* ku'i, hāmale. *Stone hammer for canoes,* pōhaku kāpili wa'a.
hammerhead shark. Manō kihikihi.
hammock. Moelewa, moe ho'olewa, maka'aha, 'ahamaka. *String hammock,* kōkō.
hamper. 1. *Clothes container.* Wahi waiho lole. 2. *Hinder.* 'Ala'alai, ālai, ānai, ho'opilikia.
hampered. Hihia.
Hampton. Hamekona, Hametona.
hamzah. *See* glottal stop.
Hāna. *See* rain.
Hanalei. Hanalei *(lit., bay that is a lei). See sayings,* lu'ulu'u, FS 97.
hand. Lima; manamana, lima kuhikuhi, manamana kuhi *(of a clock);* 'ekā, ke'a *(of bananas);* ha'awina *(of cards). To hand,* hā'awi, hō mai *(towards speaker). Hollow of the hand,* poho lima; pāiki *(rare). A hand's breadth; to beckon or wave with the hand,* pe'ahi lima. *To form a cup of the hollow of the hand,* hō'a'apu. *To hold hands, go hand in hand,* kui lima, kuikui lima. *To cross the hands behind the back,* ho'ope'a kua. *On the other hand,* ma kekahi 'ao'ao, akā. *Thinning hand (of one whose poi thins and ferments quickly),* lima hehe'e.
handbag. 'Eke'eke pa'a lima, 'eke pa'a lima, paiki pa'a lima.
hand basket. 'Eke pa'a lima, 'eke'eke pa'a lima.
handbook. Puke lawe lima.
handcart. Ka'a huki. *See* pushcart.
handcuffs. 'Ūpiki lima, kūpe'e, lā'au kūpe'e.
hand drill. Wilipua'a, ulepua'a.
handful. Piha lima, poho lima. *Rare:* haona, haohana.
handicapped. Kīnā. *Handicapped in work,* pilikia i ka hana.
handicraft. Nā mea hana lima.
handkerchief. Hainakā, hinakā. *Pocket handkerchief,* hainakā pa'eke, hainakā pakeke. *Paper handkerchief,* hainakā pepa.
handle. 1. *Touch.* Lawelawe, limalima, lole, lapulapu, mili; — *over and over,* milika'a; —, *as a court case,* hana. *Easily handled,* mili'opu. *One who handles filth,* limalima pilau. 2. *Shaft.* 'Au, kū'au, pa'a lima, kano, kau; kākai *(as of a bucket),* 'āpua, kumu. *Adze or axe handle,* 'au ko'i.
handmade. Hana lima.
handshake. Lūlū lima.
handsome. U'i, nohea, maika'i. *Also:* niolopua, makalapua, pōlani, mekila; huapala, kūmū *(slang). See sayings,* 'io, 'iwa, Pali-uli, cliff, glory, pimple.
handspring. Kūwalawala.
hand wrestling. Uma, pā uma, huinalima.
handwriting. Kākau lima, lima kākau, pūlima kākau, pūlima, hapapūlima.
handy. Mākaukau, loea, no'eau.
hang. Ho'olewalewa, lewalewa, lewa, kau, kau lewa. *Also:* 'alu, kaulei, kā'awe, lī; — *up, as telephone,* kau; — *down,* mū'olo, he'e, mū'olo, 'olo, luhe; — *loose,* mū'olo, ku'uwelu, 'olo'olo; — *short,* kau ne'ine'i; — *up, as to dry,* kaula'i. *To hang leis,* kau lei. *He hanged himself until dead,* ua kā'awe 'oia a make.
hanger. Kā. *Hanger for gourds,* kā ipu. *Hanger for bowls,* kā 'umeke.
hanging. Kālewa, kūlewa, kaulia, kauna, uleule, lola, lu'a, wele, welehia, mūka'e; — *precariously,* makalihilihi; — *low,* loha.

hangover. Poʻo huaʻi lama, poʻo nui, poluea.

Hanover. Hanowa, Hanova; Hanowela, Hanovera.

haphazard. Huikau. *Also:* malele, kīkoʻolā, kīkoi.

happen. 1. *Occur.* Hana, loʻohia. *Also:* hekau, holo ʻana. *The thing that happened,* ka mea i hiki mai; ka mea i loʻohia. *What happened?* He aha ka mea i hana ʻia? I aha ʻia? *Happened to fall,* ʻo ka hāʻule wale ihola nō ia. *What will happen?* E aha ʻia ana? **2.** *By chance.* Kupu wale, hiki honua.

happening. Hana, haʻawina.

happiness. Hauʻoli, ʻoli, ʻoliʻoli. *Also:* lauleʻa, hoihoi, leʻa, hauʻoliʻoli, kūleʻa. *To cause happiness,* hoʻohauʻoli. *Place of happiness, comfort, pleasure,* kahua o Maliʻo *(poetical). In poetry, coolness, fragrance, and rain may signify happiness.*

happy. *See* hoi 1 *(saying) and* happiness. *To be happy,* noho me ka hauʻoli. *Happy-eyed,* hauʻoli nā maka. *Happy birthday,* hauʻoli lā hānau; hānau *(in toasts). Happy New Year,* Hauʻoli Makahiki Hou *[a partial translation from English],* Hapenuia.

harangue. Nuku hoʻomau, kūhaʻu.

harass. Hoʻonāukiuki, hoʻouluhua, hoʻouluulu, hoʻopiʻoloke.

harbor. Awa, awa kū moku.

harbor dredge. Moku kope awa, kope awa.

harbor master. Luna awa.

hard. 1. *Not soft.* ʻOʻoleʻa, paʻa. *Also:* ʻeʻe, kaʻeʻe, kani, kani wahie, wīkani, mākū, kalaʻihi, wīkaʻo; pāpaʻa wela *(as adhering on one side);* konakona, konekonea, mōkaʻokaʻo. *See* **hardhearted.** *Fig. words for severe, hard:* konā, mākonā, uahoa; loʻaʻā *(as taboo);* kāʻiʻī; akaoʻo *(miserly). Hard labor,* hana ʻoʻoleʻa; kuapaʻa. **2.** *Difficult.* Paʻakikī, hana nui, maulua. *Hard times,* au nele.

hard-boiled. Moʻa loa.

harden. Hoʻopaʻa, hōʻoʻoleʻa; hoʻopōhaku *(as lava). Also:* hoʻomānea, hoʻohāhā, mākū, hoʻokano. *Hardening of the arteries,* ʻoʻoleʻa keʻa koko.

hardheaded. Poʻo paʻa, poʻo paʻakikī, lae paʻa, uaua.

hardhearted. Mākonā, laukōnā, loko ʻino. *Also:* kāʻiʻī, kanaiʻi ka naʻau, manawa ʻino, makaua, ʻāniha, ʻōpūkeʻemoa, wekaweka. *See* **hard.**

hardly. *See* almost.

hardness. ʻOʻoleʻa, lāʻau.

hardship. Pōpilikia, ʻīnea, hoʻīnea. *In poetry, heavy rain* (ua) *sometimes represents hardships. See sayings,* ʻeʻelekoa, Hilo *(Eng.-Haw.).*

hardtack. Pelena paʻa, ʻao.

hardware. Mea hao.

hardware store. Hale kūʻai o nā mea hao.

hardy. Ikaika, ulu nui, ulu maikaʻi.

hare. Lepu, hale, lāpaki, ʻiole lāpaki. *See* rabbit.

harelip. Kūlepe, ʻūlepe.

harem. Hālema.

hare's-foot fern. Lauaʻe haole.

harlot. *See* prostitute.

harm. Hoʻopōpilikia, hoʻopōʻino, hoʻopilikia. *Also:* hoʻoʻino, ʻino, pōʻino, māino, hoʻomāhuā, āulu.

harmonica. Pilapuhipuhi.

harmony. 1. *Agreement.* Lōkahi, maikaʻi, laʻi ka nohona. **2.** *Musical.* Ka hui maikaʻi ʻana o nā leo mele.

harness. ʻIli kaʻa, ʻili; kaulua lio *(two horses);* kāhiko *(Ier. 46.4).,*

harp. Lila, kinola, hāpa. *See* autoharp. *To harp on a subject,* hōʻupuʻupu.

Harper's Ferry. Hapa Pele, Hapa Fere.

harpoon. ʻŌ; ʻō koholā *(for whales);* hāpuna.

harrow. Halo, ʻōʻō halo.

harsh. ʻOʻoleʻa, kanaiʻi, uahoa, ʻawaʻawa. *Also:* koʻikoʻi, hoʻokoʻikoʻi, kāpeku, kala, kakana, kakanaiʻi, kalakala, kākala.

hart. Kea *(Biblical).*

Hartford. Halakepoka, Haratefoda.

Harvard. Hawaka, Havada.

harvest. Loaʻa, wā ʻohi *(season). See* gather, pick. *To harvest,* ʻohi.

hasten. Hoʻohikiwawe, ʻāwīwī, māmā. *Also:* wiki, wikiwiki, lale, hoʻolale, pūlale, kāholo, holo, hoʻāuau, makahai, ʻakūʻakū, ʻālulu, pūpuahulu, paʻapaʻanā.

hasty. Kāholo, makahai. *See* hurry.

hat. Pāpale *(for various kinds, see Haw.-Eng. entry and entries that follow it). Hat made of sugar-cane stem,* pāpale pua, pāpale pua kō. *Hat made of a long plaited* ʻie strip, pāpale ʻie. *Hat plaited on a wooden block,* pāpale pahu. *Wooden block for plaiting hats,* pahu pāpale. *Manila hat,* pāpale manila. *Panama hat,* pāpale waiokila. *Beaver hat,* pāpale piwa, piwa haka. *Crown of a hat,* piko. *Flat top of a hat,* pā. *Hat rim,* laulau, ʻēheu. *Hat designs:* piko, kala hale. *To tip the hat,* wehe i ka pāpale. *To wear a hat,* pāpale, pāpale i ka pāpale.

hatband. Lei pāpale, apo pāpale, kāʻei pāpale.

hatbox. Pahu pāpale.

hatch *(verb).* Kiko, hoʻokiko, kiko ka hua *(of little chickens).*

hatchet. Koʻi lipi.

hate. ʻIno, manaʻo ʻino, puʻuwai ʻeleʻele. *Also:* inaina, hoʻononohuā. *See* malice. *Full of hate,* makawela, nau. *Look at with hate,* maka ʻino. *Object of hate,* pula makawelawela. *Words of hate,* ʻōlelo makawela.

haul. Kauō, lawe, paneʻehā; — *in,* hōlina. *To haul energetically with rope,* hiu.

haughty. Hoʻokano, hukikū, haʻakei, haʻaheo, heo, konā. *Also:* lanahaʻakei, haha, kaha, haʻikū, keʻo, piʻilae, keʻēhilae. *Fig.:* kalalea, ihu piʻi, ihu kū, pali. *Haughty air,* maka kiʻekiʻe. *To walk or talk in a haughty or brisk way,* kalalī.

haunt. Lapu, hoʻopahulu.

haunted. Lapu, auakua, pahulu. *Haunted house,* hale hoʻopahulu.

have. 1. *To possess. No word in Hawaiian; commonly expressed by* he *followed by a possessive: I have a car, I had a car,* he kaʻa koʻu. *See* got. **2.** *Necessity.* Pono. *I have to go,* pono au e hele. **3.** *Verb auxiliary.* Ua *or unexpressed. I have gone,* ua hele au; hele au.

Hawaiʻi. Hawaiʻi. *See* kuauli, righteousness. *This name occurs in many parts of Polynesia (Havaiki: New Zealand, North Marquesas; ʻAvaiki: Cook Islands; Savaiʻi: Samoa). In some areas, but not in Hawaiʻi, it is the name of the homeland, or of the underworld to which the dead went. Epithet, island of Hawaiʻi: great Hawaiʻi of Keawe (a chief),* Hawaiʻi nui a Keawe.

Hawaiian. Hawaiʻi. *Hawaiian person,* Hawaiʻi, kanaka Hawaiʻi. *To act as Hawaiian, to ape or imitate Hawaiians,* hoʻohawaiʻi.

Hawaiian Civic Association. Hui Kīwila Hawaiʻi.

Hawaiian Historical Society. ʻAhahui Moʻolelo Hawaiʻi.

Hawaiian Islands. Kō Hawaiʻi Pae ʻĀina.

Hawaiian Sugar Planters' Association. ʻAhahui Kanu Kō Hawaiʻi.

hawk. 1. *Bird.* ʻIo, ʻio lani, ʻio mea, niku. *The* ʻio *symbolized royalty because of the great height at which it flew, hence the name* ʻIo-lani. *I am a hawk, no branch that (I) may not light upon,* he ʻio au, ʻaʻohe lālā kau ʻole. *For other connotation and saying, see* māpu-māpu, poʻi 4. **2.** *To clear the throat.* ʻUhūʻuhū, pūhā.

hawkbill turtle. ʻEa.

hawkfish. Pilikoʻa, hilu pilikoʻa, poʻopaʻa.

hay. Mauʻu maloʻo, mauʻu hē, hē. *Bale of hay,* pela mauʻu maloʻo.

hazardous. Makaʻu.

hazel tree. ʻAlemone.

hazy. Noeuahi, uauahi *(as during a volcanic eruption). Also:* pululuhi, māhea, pōhina, palaweka, pālauweka, hiahia, puahia, pāpala, polalauahi.

he. ʻOia, ia, ʻoia nei, ʻoia ala. *While he, as soon as he, at the time that he,* iāia.

head. Poʻo, keha *(fig.). Human head,* poʻo kanaka. *Head bone,* iwi poʻo. *Crown of head,* piko. *Side of head,* huapoʻo. *Hind part of head,* pane, panepoʻo. *Bulging head,* poʻo puʻu *(fig., sullen, unsociable). Head* *of male organ,* pōheo, heo, pokake, kole keaka. *Head of octopus,* pū. *Head of cabbage,* pu'u kāpiki. *Head of water,* po'o wai, māno wai. *Head of an organization,* po'o, alaka'i, ikū lani. *Head of a tribe,* makua ali'i. *Acting or deputy head,* hope po'o. *Head covering,* pāpale; pūlo'u, palelei *(as of tapa).* *To head straight for,* hele pololei, mōkio, 'oehu. *To raise, as the head,* aea.

headache. 'Eha ke po'o. *Also:* 'aki, nahoa; nalulu, nanulu *(dull);* po'o hua'i *(splitting);*'ea kū manawa.

heading. Po'o, po'omana'o.

headland. Lae, 'oi'oina.

headline. *See* **heading.**

headlong. Kimo po'o *(as in diving).* *To run headlong,* holo kikī.

headman. Ali'i, po'o, luna; konohiki *(of an* ahupua'a).

headquarters. Kikowaena.

headstrong. Po'o pa'akikī. *Also:* uhu, ho'ohuki, ho'ohuhuki, hukihuki, kūnono, kā'ape.

headwaiter. Kuene po'o.

headwaters. Māno wai, 'ōmaka, 'ōmaka wai.

heal. Lapa'au, ola, ho'ōla, lonopūhā; 'aki, kōhi *(as a wound);* pāla'au *(as with herbs).* *See* **faith healing.** *Healed imperfectly,* 'ōha'i. *Power of healing,* mauli ola. *To heal quickly,* pāola. *A god of healing,* Lonopūhā.

healer. Ho'ōla, kahuna lapa'au.

health. Olakino, ola pono, ola. *See* **Board of Health.** *Public health,* ola o ka lehulehu. *Good health,* olakino maika'i; ahuahu, ehuehu, e'ehu, hāehu, kā'ala'ala, ōhāhā. *Poor health,* nāwaliwali ke kino, halalū, lau pala, pakē. *To glow with health,* lamalama ka 'ili. *A god of health,* Mauli-ola.

health certificate. Palapala hō'ike ola.

heap. Pu'u, ahu, kūāhua, āhua, kuapapa, anu'a, nu'a, lu'a, ho'onu'a. *Also:* 'āluka, pa'i, laupa'i, kūpa'i, paila, huku, kilohana, mahena. *Heap of food,* pu'u 'ai, kio honua. *Heap of stones,* pu'u pōhaku, kaulana 'a'ā. *Heap of pebbles,* pu'u 'ili'ili, pe'ape'a pōhaku. *Sand heap,* pu'u one. *Earth heap,* pu'u lepo. *Volcanic heap,* pu'u pele. *Heap of rags,* pu'u welu. *Trash heap,* pu'u 'ōpala. *Heap of mats,* pa'a 'ahu. *Heap of goods,* ahu waiwai. *To heap up,* ho'āhu, kūkulu, ho'okuakua. *To heap up untidily,* mu'u mōkākī.

heaped. Āhua, ahulau, kūāhua, ahuwale, pu'u, pu'upu'u, pōhuku (pāhuku), 'ākoakoa.

hear. Lohe, ho'olono. *Also:* pā, pā'ia. *To pretend not to hear,* ho'okuli, ho'okolono.

hearing. Lohe 'ana, lohena. *Keen hearing,* lolohe. *Loss of hearing and dizziness,* niu kuli.

hearing aid. Mea ho'olohe.

hearken. Ho'olohe, hāliu.

hearsay. Lohe lauāhea. *Also:* lohe pepeiao, lohe 'ōlelo, lonowā, lonoā, lonolonoā, nonoā.

hearse. Ka'a ku'ʌpua'u.

heart. Pu'uwai; iho *(as of celery, core);* 'i'o *(as of wood, central part);* haka *(in deck of cards).* *Fig.:* na'au, loko, poli, umauma, manawa. *Also:* pu'u, pu'u koko, mauli, 'ō'ili. *See* **apoplexy, heart ailment, heart attack, overwhelm.** *Valve of the heart,* pepeiao. *Heartbeat, pulse,* pana. *Heart and circulatory system,* māno wai. *Generous heart,* manawale'a. *Heart's desire,* 'i'ini o ka na'au, makakēhau.

heart ailment. Ma'i pu'uwai, 'apo'apo.

heart attack. Ma'i hohola, houpo 'ume pau, ma'i 'uhola, kūhewa; kauhola *(fatal).*

heartbreaking. Hō'eha'eha i ka na'au. *Also:* māna'ona'o, olopua.

heartburn. Haoa.

hearth. Kapuahi.

heartless. Laukōnā, loko 'ino. *Also:* nānā maka, hainā, linu.

heartseed. Pōniu.

heartsick. Māna'ona'o, hō'eha'eha i ka pu'uwai.

heart-stirring. Ho'oniua pu'uwai.

heat. Wela, hahana, ikiiki. *Also:* welawela, wewela, 'āwela, 'ōwela, mahana, mehana, mehani, no'ao, kō'eha'eha, wāwena. *See ex.,* **okooko, hot, warm.** *To heat,* ho'opumehana, ho'omāhanahana, ho'omahana, hō'ena'ena, ho'okō'eha'eha, ho'olala. *In heat (of a bitch),* kahe.

heater. Kapuahi, mea ho'omahana.

heathen. Pekana, kanaka 'ē.

heat rash. 'Ōhune wela.

heave. Ho'olei, pākī, 'oaikū; — *shoulders,* oikū. *See* **throw.**

heaven. Lani, papa lani, lewa, aouli, pa'a-i-luna. *Highest heaven,* apo-a-lewa, lewa lani, lani kua ka'a *(poetic).* *Space in heavens,* lewa nu'u. *Heaven above, earth below,* he lani i luna, he honua i lalo *(of one owning his property, security).*

heavenly. Lani.

heavy. Kaumaha. *Also:* ko'iko'i, mākolu; pauā'ālina *(rare).* *Heavy with child,* kaumaha keiki; kōkō. *Heavyset,* pu'ipu'i.

Hebrew. Hepela, Hebera.

Hebron. Helepona, Herebona.

hedge. Pā lā'au, pā la'ala'au, pilipā. *Thorn hedge,* pā lā'au 'o'oi. *Trimmed hedge top,* ēulu.

hedgehog. Pua'a 'ōkalakala, pua'a 'ili 'oi'oi, kīpoka.

heed. Maliu, ho'omaliu, ho'olohe, mālama. *Heed the word of the parent,* e maliu mai i ka leo o ka makua.

heedless. Nānā 'ole, no'ono'o 'ole. *Fig.:* mōhio, mohihio, mōhiohio. *See ex.,* **mau'a'e.**

heehaw. Hohō.

heel. Ku'eku'e wāwae *(human);* hila *(shoes).* *Low heels,* hila ha'aha'a. *High heels,* hila 'auli'i. *To heel, as a ship,* waiho 'ao'ao, kīki'i; pana kai *(rare).*

heiau. Heiau *(for various kinds, see Haw.-Eng. entries and entries that follow).* *Also:* ewe'ai, haiau, hale heiau, hale poki, hale 'ope'ope, hale hau, hale la'a, hale lau, hale lama, hale pipipi, hale o Papa, hale o Lono, ipu-o-Lono, unu, alaō, kūkoa'e, koleamoku, kūpalaha, lonopūhā, loulu, luakini, māpele, waihau, waikaua; pu'uhonua *(place of refuge);* kū'ula, ko'a *(fishing shrines);* mua *(men's eating house).* *See* **altar, oracle tower, prayer, shrine.** *Parts of heiau:* paehumu, pā *(enclosure);* kahua *(area within enclosure);* kīpapa *(pavement);* papahola *(outside pavement);* ahu, kuahu, lele *(altar);* lananu'u, kapa'au *(place for images and offerings);* nanahua *(posts);* luapa'ū, lua unu *(refuse pit);* hale pahu, hale pu'uone, hale umu, hāwai, mana, oeoe, pālima, wai ea *(houses or booths within heiau).* *To direct, as heiau ceremonies,* kuhikuhi. *Circuit of the island by a chief to build heiaus,* palaloa. *To build heiaus,* kūkulu heiau. *Place where dignitaries stood near heiaus,* kālewa.

heifer. Pipi ohi.

height. Ki'eki'e, ki'eki'ena, loa, lō'ihi, nu'u, keha. *Also:* ho'okeha, 'aki, māka'oka'o. *Poetic references to height may signify royalty; see* **hawk, high, lofty, top.**

heir. Ho'oilina, ho'īlina. *Heir to the throne,* ho'oilina mō'ī. *Heir by word-of-mouth,* kaulana 'ōlelo.

heirloom. Waiwai i ho'oilina 'ia, mea ho'oilina.

held. *See* **hold.**

Heligoland. Helikolani, Heligolani.

heliotrope. Heliokalope, hiliokalupa. *Seaside heliotrope,* kīpūkai (nena). *Native heliotrope,* hinahina.

hell. Kehena, lua ahi, ki'o ahi, pō.

Hellespont. Heleponeko, Heleponeto.

Hello! Aloha! *See* **halloo.**

helm. Hoe uli.

helmet. Mahiole; 'a'ahu a po'o *(head shield).* *Crested feather helmet,* haka. *To don a helmet,* kau i ka mahiole, kōkī.

helmet shell. Pū, 'olē.

helmsman. Ho'okele.

help. Kōkua; kōkua mai, hōlina! *Also:* lawelawe lima; ko'o lani *(given a chief).* *To refuse help,* huli kua, kā'i'ī. *Help wanted (advertisement),* ho'olaha limahana.

helper. Kōkua, hoa lawehana, kanaka, ko'o. *Dependable helper,* lima 'ākau. *Helper to priest,* helē.
helpful. Kōkua nui, kā'eu'eu.
helpless. Nāwaliwali. *Also:* kūlola, kololū, kūloma, pālola. *See saying,* **kauna'oa.**
helter-skelter. I 'ō ā i 'ane'i, ka'a i 'ō ā i 'ane'i, holokē.
Helvetia. Helewekia, Helevetia.
hem. Pelu. *Also:* lepa, lepe, hu'a, alahi'i. *To hem,* humuwili. *Let down the hem of the dress,* e ho'oku'u mai i ka pelu o ka lole.
hemisphere. 'Ao'ao.
hemorrhage. Kahe koko, he'e koko.
hemorrhoids. Uhahemo, ka'uka'u, hī koko.
hemp. Olonā.
hen. Moa wahine. *Hen and brood,* kīnana.
hence. No laila, no ia mea.
henceforth. Mai kēia wā aku, mai kēia manawa aku.
hepatitis. 'Ea 'ōlena.
heptagon. Huinahiku.
her. 1. *Possessive. Same as* **his.** 2. *Pronoun. Same as* **him.**
herald. Kūkala, waha 'ōlelo. *Also:* helela, 'io. *Herald who announces war,* pahukala.
herb. Lau nahele. *Also:* lā'au palupalu, la'alā'au, mau'u. *Edible herb,* lā'au iki 'ai 'ia, lau nahele 'ai 'ia. *Bitter herbs,* lau mulemule. *Ball of herbs used for massage,* pōpō kāpa'i. *Decoction of herbs,* hālalo po'i. *To heal, as with herbs,* pāla'au.
herbage. Weuweu.
herbarium. Wahi mālama mea ulu.
herbivorous. 'Ai weuweu.
herd. Pū'ā, kumu. *Herd of cattle,* pū'ā pipi. *To move in a herd,* ka'i 'āuna. *To herd,* ho'opū'ā, hō'ā.
herdsman. Kahu pipi.
here. Ma'ane'i, eia nei. *Also:* i ne'i, ne'i, 'one'i, 'ane'i; inā *(rare). Here!* Eia! 'Ei'a! *Here is, here are,* eia. *Here, close by,* eia a'e. *The one here,* e i nei, e ia nei. *Here it is,* eia lā, ei ne'i, eia i 'ane'i, ai'a, 'ei'a. *Well, here you are,* eia 'oe. *Here and there,* i 'ō i 'ane'i, kēlā . . . kēia, pākakahi, pā'ē'ē, li'ili'i, hele, lelele, kiko'olā. *The here and the hereafter,* ke eia me ke eia aku.
hereafter. Mahope aku.
hereby. Ma kēia.
hereditary. Mai nā kūpuna mai, welo; kanu *(fig.);* ku'una. *Hereditary trait,* kū i ka welo.
Hereford. Helepoka, Herefoda.
herein. Maloko nei.
heretic. Helekika.
heritage. Waiwai ho'oilina, ho'oilina.
hermaphrodite. Māhū. *Also:* 'alaneo, papa pae māhū *(legendary).*
hermit. Kanaka noho mehameha, 'elemika.
hermit crab. Pāpa'i iwi pūpū, unauna, 'ōunauna.
hernia. Pu'ulele, hualele, laho he'e.
hero. Me'e. *Also:* kupu'eu, koa, kā'e'a'e'a. *Youthful hero,* u'i. *Hero of a story,* ka mea nona ka mo'olelo. *See saying,* **wave 1.**
heroic. Me'e, u'i.
heroine. Me'e wahine. *See* **hero.**
heron. 'Auku'u, 'auku'u kāhili (kōhili), 'alekea, pua'a 'ili 'oi'oi. *Pond-watching heron,* 'auku'u kia'i loko *(of a spy). Croaks the voice of the heron,* kohā ka leo o ka 'auku'u *(of gossip).*
herring. Makiawa, pīhā, mikiawa, 'ōmaka.
herringbone design. 'Eke'eke.
hers. *Same as* **his.**
herself. *Same as* **himself.**
hesitate. Kali, kūnānā, kānalua, ho'ohākālia, ka'ulua. *Also:* ku'ihē, ka'uka'u, menemene, ho'omomole, ho'ēmiemi, hakupehe, hākupe.
hesitation. Kānalua.
hew. Kua, kālai, kūpā, 'oki, kipikipi, ho'owaha. *To hew down a tree, hewer of wood,* kua lā'au. *To hew boards or planks or a poi-pounding board,* kua papa. *To hew a little at a time,* kalakalai. *To hew stone,* kālai pōhaku.
hewing. Kalaina, kua.

hexagon. Pa'aono, huinaono.
hibiscus. Aloalo, hae Hawai'i, koki'o (mākū), koki'o ke'oke'o (koki'o kea), koki'o 'ula'ula, ko'oloa 'ula, hau hele 'ula, pāmakani, ma'o hau hele. *Hibiscus flower,* pua aloalo, pualoalo.
Hibiscus tiliaceus. Hau *(for various kinds, see Haw.-Eng. entry and entries that follow it).*
hiccough. Mauli'awa.
hidden. Huna, nalowale, nalonalo, nalohia, nalo, ho'onalonalo. *Also:* 'ōhuna, po'ohuna, uhi 'ia. *Hidden meaning, see* **meaning.**
hide. 1. *Conceal.* Hūnā, ho'ohūnā *(transitive);* pe'e *(oneself, intransitive). Also:* kīpo'i, palai, 'āpo'o, ou. *To hide in one's bosom, as a secret,* pe'e poli. *To hide like an owl (in a tree),* pe'epe'e pueo. *To hide in a cave,* pe'e pao. 2. *Skin.* 'Ili. *To stretch the hide of an animal,* kālena.
hide-and-seek. Pe'epe'e kua, pe'epe'e akua, haupe'e-pe'e.
hideous. Pupuka 'ino, pupuka ha'alele loa.
high. Ki'eki'e; —, *as waves,* nalunalu, halehale, hahale, amoamo, kū'ulukū. *Also:* luna, hā'iu'iu, ka'oka'o, kiolea, le'o, le'ole'o, kahakea, keha, māka'oka'o, hakalī. *See* **height.** *Away up high,* luna lilo, ki'eki'e loa, 'iu'iu, kōkikiu. *High cliff,* pali ki'eki'e, pali lele koa'e. *Perched high,* kaumo'o. *High point,* nu'u, ni'o, kila, kilohana, wēkiu. *Too high,* kaulei, pakaulei. *High chief,* ali'i nui, lani, wohi, pali kaulu 'ole ka lani *(see* **pali***). High rank,* kūlana ki'eki'e loa, wēkiu, po'iu, kūhaka. *Highborn,* lani, kūākāhili. *High blood pressure,* koko pi'i, koko lana.
highball. Lama ho'ohuihui 'ia, lama pa'ipa'i 'ia.
higher. Ho'okela, 'oi aku ke ki'eki'e.
highest. Ki'eki'e loa.
high-low-jack-and-the-game. Hai-lō-keaka.
highness. Ki'eki'e. *His Highness,* ka mea ki'eki'e.
high priest. Kahuna nui.
high school. Kula ki'eki'e.
high sheriff. Māka'i ki'eki'e.
highway. Alanui, alaloa, ala hele.
hike. Hele wāwae mamao.
hilarity. Piha le'ale'a, ho'omāke'aka, lua'āpana.
hill. Pu'u, kuahiwi *(high);* pu'e *(as of sweet potatoes). Also:* ōnū, olo, hila, kīlea, apoapo; *to — up,* pu'e, po'i. *Volcanic hill,* pu'u pele. *Row or cluster of hills,* pae pu'u. *Red hill,* pu'u 'ula'ula.
hillock. Pu'u. *Also:* pu'uhānau, pali kāmoe, āhua, 'ōhū, kilohana, muni.
hilltop. Piko, po'o pu'u.
hilly. Kuahiwi nui, 'ōpalipali. *Also:* 'āpali, ku'āwa'awa'a, mākinikini, 'ōpu'upu'u, wakawaka.
Hilo. Hilo, *the city and district (also the name of a famous Polynesian navigator and of the first night of the new moon), perhaps mentioned in chant and saying more than any other single place in the Hawaiian Islands: see* **'A'ala honua, hālau 1, holowa'a 1, ka'ele 1, kinai 2, laumeke, 'ōiwi 2, po'i 1, umauma, rain, storm,** *UL 104. All of these refer to rain and its rich symbolism. Lehua blossoms and Chief Hanakahi are also associated with Hilo. Exhausted by the many streams of Hilo, many hills, countless descents . . . cliffs of windward the upright cliffs of Hilo (PH 32), pau ke aho i ke kahawai lau o Hilo, he lau ka pu'u, he mano ka ihona . . . he pali no Ko'olau kā Hilo pali kū (of trial and hardship). Voice with many tears of Hilo (FS 225), ka leo waimaka nui o Hilo.*
Hilo grass. Mau'u Hilo.
him. Ia, iāia. *To him,* iāia. *For him,* nona, nāna. *By him,* nāna.
Himalayas. Himela.
himself. 'Oia iho, 'oia pono'ī *(subject);* iāia iho *(object). For himself,* nona iho, nāna iho. *By himself,* nāna iho, 'oia ho'okahi.
hin. Hina.
hinder. Ālai, ke'a, ke'ake'a, ho'oke'a. *Also:* ala'alai, 'āke'ake'a, kualo, kākona, kīpupū, āke'uke'u.
hindquarters. 'Ūhā, 'ūhā hope.

Hindu. Hinekū.

hinge. 'Ami; pu'u *(of pearl oyster)*. *Door hinge,* 'ami puka. *Hinge joint,* ho'oku'ina 'ami. *To turn on hinges,* kū'ami'ami.

hint. Ho'ohelehele 'ōlelo, ho'ohele 'ōlelo, ho'omaoe, ho'omea, hani, ho'ohani. *A hint,* he 'ōlelo ho'ohali.

hip. Kīkala, pāpākole. *Wide hips,* kīkala peleleu. *To rotate or sway, as hips,* ho'olewa, kaiue, 'oni'oni.

hipbone. Iwi hua, pāpākole.

hip, hip, hurray. Hipahipa.

hippopotamus. Hipopokamu.

hire. Limalima, ho'olimalima, hai.

hirsute. Pūhuluhulu.

his. 1. *Singular possessed object.* Kona *(o-class);* kāna *(a-class);* kō ia, kā ia *(o- and a-class forms).* *His house,* kona hale. *His child,* kāna keiki. 2. *Plural possessed objects.* Ona *(o-class);* āna *(a-class).* *For other uses of k-less (zero-type) possessives, Gram. 9.6.3.*

hiss. Hī, hīhī; ka'ulī *(as fire).*

historian. Ho'opa'a mo'olelo o ka wā kahiko, ho'opa'a kū'auhau, kākau mo'olelo o ka wā kahiko *(ancient);* kākau mo'olelo ali'i *(of chiefs).*

history. Mo'olelo, mo'o'ōlelo, kuamo'o 'ōlelo. *History of the priesthood,* mo'o kahuna.

hit. Ku'i, ho'oku'i, pa'i, ho'opa'i, hahau, kū, ku'ia, kā, pā. *Also:* hau, hauhau, hauhia, uhau, kukū, kōkē, pūkē, ko'okā, kāina. *To hit hard,* ku'i ikaika, pāluku. *To hit by mistake or without warning,* kūhewa, kāhewa. *To hit lightly,* kūlihī. *To hit carelessly, at random,* hilikū. *Hit by a bullet,* kū i ka pōkā. *To fail to hit,* holohu'a. *Hitting noise,* kōkēkōkē.

hitch. 1. *To move with jerks.* Ne'e. 2. *See* **tie.**

hitching post. Pou ho'opa'a lio.

hither. Mai, i 'ane'i, i kēia wahi.

hive. Pūnana meli, pahu meli.

hives. Laina.

hoard. Ho'āhu; ho'olaholaho *(as a miser).*

hoarse. Hā, leo hā, hano, hanopilo; pāpala *(rare).*

hobble. Haki'opa. *See* **limp.**

hobby. Hana punahele, hana ho'onanea, hana ho'ohala manawa.

hockey. Holohau *(ice).*

hoe. Hō, kālai, 'ōla'o.

hog. Pua'a. *Words used in hog calling:* 'ukā, hūkā.

hogfish. 'A'awa.

hogtie. Kūpe'e *(as cattle).*

hoist. Hāpai, huki i luna. *Also:* 'unu, 'u'u, hiu.

hold. 1. *Grip.* Pa'a, ho'opa'a; 'ai *(lua fighting, see* **fight***);* — *back,* kāohi, kīpū, kōhi, ho'opa'a, papa'a; — *up,* paepae *(intransitive);* — *fast,* ho'opa'a, ho'opa'a ā pa'a, lālau; — *in the arms, as a child,* hi'i; —, *as a pail,* kālawe; — *on course,* kāpa'a; — *down, as to drown,* make; — *precariously,* kaunihinihi, kaunukunuku; — *a note,* kō. *One who holds,* pa'a. *Hold in music,* 'ume. *To hold in the hand,* pa'a lima. 2. *Of a ship.* O lalo.

holder. Mea pa'a.

holds (lua). *See* **fight.**

hole. Puka *(usually of a perforation);* lua *(with a bottom);* haka *(breach). Also:* mākālua, mākālua kele *(for planting);* pukaihu *(as in pearl-shell shank);* holo *(in canoe edge);* hākaokao *(for inserting mast in canoe);* hiana *(underwater depression). Full of holes,* pukapuka, haka, ho'ohaka, lualua, hālua, nono, panonono.

holiday. Lānui. *Also:* lā maka kanaka, lā ho'okahakaha.

holiness. Hemolele, ano. *To feign holiness,* ho'ohemolele.

Holland. Hōlani.

hollow. Pūhā, māhao *(as a log);* hakahaka, 'olohaka *(as a surfboard);* po'opo'o, 'āpo'opo'o, hālua, napo'o, kānoa *(as in earth);* poho, pāiki, ka'ele, kāwaha, homa *(as of the hand or of a bowl). Hollow-eyed,* hakahaka nā maka, naho nā maka, po'opo'o nā maka. *Hollow of the back,* kīkala. *Hollow bone, eye socket,* iwi pona. *Hollow where sea remains at low tide,* poho kai. *Hollow, as worn in lava rock, where salt collects,* makapāpipi.

hollowing. Pohona *(as cheeks of an aged person). See* **hollow.**

hollow out. *See* **dub.**

holly. Kāwa'u, 'aiea.

hollyhock. Halehaka. *Double form of hollyhock,* halehaka pupupu.

holothurian. *See* **sea cucumber.**

holy. Hemolele, ho'āno, kapu, la'a, la'ahia, 'ihi'ihi, Kaneka, Saneta. *Holy one,* mea la'a. *Holy day,* lā ho'āno. *Holy Week,* Hepekoma Hemolele. *Holy water,* wai ho'āno. *To make holy,* ho'ohemolele. *Holy, Holy, Holy (Hoik. 4:8),* Ho'āno, Ho'āno, Ho'āno.

Holy Communion. 'Aha'aina a ka Haku, 'Aha'aina Pelena.

Holy Ghost. 'Uhane Hemolele.

Holy Land. 'Āina Ho'āno, 'Āina Hemolele.

Holy Mary. Maria Saneta, Maria Hemolele.

Holy Roller. Holelola.

Holy Spirit. 'Uhane Hemolele.

Holy Trinity. Akua Kahikolu, Kolukahi Hemolele, Mana Kahikolu.

homage. Mahalo, ho'omaika'i; ho'olani *(to a chief or king).*

home. Home, kauhale; ōpū malumalu, ōpū weuweu *(humble expressions). Also:* kīnana hale *(including house grounds). To remain constantly at home,* ki'inoho.

homebody. Ki'inoho. *See* **pōhaku** 2.

home-brew. Kuaipa.

homeland. One hānau, 'āina hānau, kulaiwi; kuapuiwi *(rare). Homeland of ancestors,* kuakahi; ēwe 'āina o ke kupuna *(see* **ēwe***).*

homeless. Kuewa, lewa, home 'ole.

homely. Pupuka. *Also:* 'ala'uka, mukeko, mūkoki, nūkoki, mūkini, molea; pōuhu *(rare).*

homeopathic. Homeopakika, homepakika.

homesick. Aloha kaumaha i ka home.

homestead. 'Āina ho'okū'ono'ono, home ho'okū'o-no'ono. *Homestead land,* 'āina ho'okū'ono'ono; 'āina ho'opulapula *(rehabilitation). To homestead,* ho'oka-hua.

homesteaders. Po'e ho'okū'ono'ono.

homicide. Lawe ola.

homosexual. Māhū, ho'okāmaka. *Cf.* **ūpī laho** *(male). To practice homosexuality,* moe 'aikane, ho'okāmaka *(male).*

honest. Pono, kūpono, ho'okamani 'ole.

honey. Meli, wai meli, wai pua, hone; pīlali, pīlali mai'a *(in a banana blossom).*

honey bee. Nalo meli, meli.

honeycomb. Waihona meli.

honey creeper. *(Species and subspecies may vary on different islands. Some are presumed extinct and many are endangered. Var. names are in parentheses.)* 'I'iwi (olokele), mamo (hoa), 'ō'ū; palila *(see saying,* **olokē***),* 'akeke'e, 'akikiki, 'apapane *(apakane, 'āpane, nukupu'u, 'akihi po'o lā'au), 'anianiau, 'alauahio, 'ula-'aihāwane (ula), 'amakihi (kihi), 'ākepa, 'akepeu'ie, 'akialoa ('akihi loa, kipi), po'ouli. Sour 'amakihi, 'amakihi 'awa'awa (of a sour disposition).*

honey eater. 'Ō'ō, 'ā'ā *(male);* 'ākohekohe; 'ō'ō 'ā'ā *(Kaua'i);* hulimai'a. *Honey eater singing with gay voice in the forest (FS 287),* ka 'ō'ō kani leo le'a i ka nahele.

honeymoon. Mahina meli. *See saying,* **guest.**

honeysuckle. Honekakala.

Hong Kong. Honokaona.

honk. Kani, uhene *(of goose).*

Honolulu. Honolulu *(lit., sheltered bay). Section of Honolulu near the harbor,* Kou. *Honolulu harbor entrance,* Māmala.

honor. Ho'ohanohano, hanohano. *Also:* ho'onani, ho'ohiwahiwa, pāpahi, mālama, pa'ihi, hano hāweo. *Honor guard,* pū'ali koa ho'ohanohano. *A great honor,* he ho'ohanohano nui. *Honor your father,* mālama i kou makua kāne. *Placed in a position of honor,* kau i ka hano. *To claim honors not rightfully due,* pi'ikoi.

honorable. Hanohano; hako *(rare)*. *To the honorable speaker,* i ka mea hanohano, ka luna hoʻomalu *(see* **hanohano***)*. *Honorable discharge,* hoʻokuʻu maikaʻi.

honorarium. Haʻawina hoʻohanohano.

honorary. Hoʻohanohano. *Honorary degree,* kekele hoʻohanohano. *Honorary diploma,* palapala hoʻohanohano.

honoring. No. *A song honoring the chief,* he mele no ka lani.

hoof. Maiʻao holoholona, mānea, māiʻuʻu; waʻewaʻe *(rare)*.

hook. Lou, loulou; kīlou *(as on a door);* kēlou, huka. *See* **fishhook**. *To hook,* kīlou, kēlou, kīhele. *To draw up with a hook, as in fishing octopus,* kīkākala. *Hooked, but escaped, as a fish,* kūlihi. *Hooked finger (for feeding poi),* kīhele.

hooked. Kikiwi *(as nose)*.

hoop. Apo, pōʻai, lina, kuapo pahu, hupa. *Iron or barrel hoop,* apo hao, liki pahu, kakakī.

hoot. Keʻu, heʻu *(as owl),* ʻeu.

hop. Lele. *Also:* mahiki, lēhei; — *about,* lelele, lehelehei. *Hopping on one foot,* lelele wāwae kahi.

hope. Manaʻolana, ʻupu, pono, lana ka manaʻo. *To dash hopes,* pepehi i ka manaʻolana.

hopeful. Lana ka manaʻo, hoʻolana, hālana ka manaʻo.

hopeless. ʻAʻohe manaʻolana i koe, ʻaʻohe pono i koe; pau ka pono.

hopscotch. Kinuwā. *To play hopscotch,* kinuwā.

horizon. ʻIlikai, hālāwai, ʻalihi lani, ʻalihi moana. *Also:* pōʻailani, kumulani, ʻalihi, Kahiki Moe, kūkulu. *See ex.,* **hālāwai**. *Region below horizon,* kūkulu-o-ka-honua. *Region just above horizon,* kūkulu-o-ka-lani.

horizontal. ʻIlikai, moe. *Horizontal stratum,* papa moe.

horn. 1. *On animal.* Kiwi, hao, pepeiaohao; kākala *(as of fish or caterpillar).* *See* **powder horn**. 2. *See* **saddle horn**. 3. *Wind instrument.* Pū, pū puhi.

"horny." *See* **randy**.

hornet. Hopeʻō, kopena, nalo ʻaki, nalo hope ʻeha.

horoscope. Palapala kilokilo hōkū.

horrible. Weliweli, mānaʻonaʻo, ʻino loa.

horrified. Mānaʻonaʻo, māʻeʻele, kūnāhihi, kāhāhā i ka ʻino, ʻōkū.

Horrors! Kāhīhī!.

hors d'oeuvre. Pūpū, hōʻonoʻono ʻai.

horse. Lio; puaʻa nui huelo huluhulu *(old Lā-naʻi name).* *See Gram.* 2.9.2. *Race horse,* lio heihei. *Pack horse,* lio lawe ukana. *Pacing horse,* lio peki. *Old, worn-out horse,* kālona. *Dark-gray horse,* lio hulu ʻaeko. *Bay horse,* lio hulupala. *Wooden horse,* lio lāʻau. *Team of horses,* paʻa lio. *Horse-drawn vehicle,* kaʻa lio. *To ride a horse until it is exhausted or dead,* pākī lio.

horseback. Kau lio. *To ride horseback,* kau lio, holo lio, holoholo lio. *To ride horseback wearing a pāʻū,* holo pāʻū.

horseman. Mea kau lio, kanaka holo lio.

horsepower. Ikaika lio.

horse race. Heihei lio.

horseshoe. Kāmaʻa hao, kapuaʻihao lio. *Horseshoe pitching,* kīolaola hao lio.

horseweeds. Ilioha, pua mana.

horticulture. Hoʻoulu mea kanu, mahi pua.

hosanna. Hōkana.

hose. 1. *See* **stocking**. 2. *Conveyor.* ʻIli. *Water hose,* ʻiliwai. *To hose,* kikī wai.

hospitable. Hoʻokipa aloha, hoʻohale kipa, heahea, makamaka nui, hale. *Also:* pāheahea, kāʻēʻē.

hospital. Hale maʻi, haukapila, hale lapaʻau.

hospitality. Hoʻokipa, pāheahea. *See sayings,* **hewa 4, welcome**.

host. 1. *As at a party.* Haku hale, mea hoʻokipa, ka mea nāna ka ʻahaʻaina, ka mea nona ka hale, kamaʻāina. *Also:* makamaka, hale, lani. 2. *Crowd.* Lehulehu.

hostage. Poʻe pānaʻi.

hostess. Haku hale wahine.

hostile. Paio, kamaniha, hoʻokamaniha, ʻāniha, loko ʻino, hōʻauwaepuʻu.

hot. Wela, hahana; ikiiki *(stifling).* *Also:* wewela, welawela, ʻāwela, pūwelawela, hoʻowela, ʻōwelawela, panoa; ʻānia *(as an oven);* noʻao; nopu *(as from sun or fire);* hanahana; wāwena *(rare).* *See* **pika, warm**. *Red-hot,* ʻena, ʻenaʻena, okooko, liholiho. *White-hot,* ahuliʻu. *Uncomfortably hot,* kōʻehaʻeha. *Hot-tempered,* pulupulu ahi, lelepī *(see* **quick-tempered***).* *Hot spring,* wai welawela. *Hot-water bag,* ʻeke wai wela.

hotel. Hōkele.

Hottentot. Hokenekoka.

hottish. ʻŌwela.

hour. Hola.

hourglass. Ana hola.

house. Hale *(for various kinds, see Haw.-Eng. entry and the many entries that follow it),* kauhale. *Two-story house,* hale i luna a i lalo. *House trailer,* kaʻa hale. *Ancient types of houses:* mua *(eating, for men);* hālau *(for canoes, hula instruction);* kua *(for beating tapa);* peʻa *(menstrual);* pūʻoʻa *(for corpses);* hāwai *(for purification ceremonies);* ʻeleua *(new);* moku hale *(ulu hale) (set apart, as for instruction);* wai ea, haʻi. *(See also* **heiau***.) Humble references to houses,* ōpū malumalu, ōpū weuweu. *House parts:* kahua *(platform, foundation);* paepae puka, niʻo *(threshold);* paia *(wall, side);* hākala, kala *(end, gable); also:* holo, hoʻoholo, lolo, kana, uluhaka, ukuwai. *See also* **post, purlin, thatch**. *House site,* kahua hale. *House adornments and furniture,* pono hale, kāhiko o ka hale. *House dedication,* hoʻolaʻa hale, ʻoki i ka piko. *To have a house,* hale. *To go from house to house,* komo kauhale. *House visiting,* komo ʻāpana. *To receive in a house,* hoʻohale. *House lot, yard, fence,* pā hale. *House dweller,* noho hale. *House owner,* haku hale, mea hale, noho hale. *See fig. meaning,* **welcome**.

houseboat. Hale lana.

housebreaking. Wāwahi hale.

housefly. Nalo.

household. ʻOhana *(family);* kauhale *(houses occupied by a family).*

housekeeper. Mālama hale, kahu mālama hale.

House of Nobles. Nā Aliʻi o ka Hale ʻAhaʻōlelo.

House of Representatives. Hale o nā Lunamakaʻāinana.

house sitter. Noho hale.

housewarming. Komo hale.

housewife. Wahine mālama hale.

hovel. Pupupu hale. *Cf.* **hut**.

hover. Hoʻokauaheahe, hoʻolahalaha, ōpū, lāhai. *To hover between life and death,* kālilolilo.

how. Pehea, pehea lā; nani *(rare).* *How?* Pehea? *How are you?* Pehea ʻoe? *How about it?* Pehea? *So how!* Pehea lā *(in answer to a question with* pehea *that one cannot or does not wish to answer)! How many? How much?* ʻEhia? ʻAhia? *How many (of associated people)?* Kōkoʻohia? *How many (to a group)?* Pāhia? *How beautiful!* Auē ka nani! Kai ka nani!

however. Akā, koe kēia, eia naʻe, ka mea ʻāpiki.

howl. Uō, puō, kūō.

Howland Island. Ulu-kou.

hub. Pūkuʻi. *Hubcap,* uhi pūkuʻi.

hubbub. Haunaele, hauwalaʻau, hauwalawalaʻau, hana kuli.

huddle. Pūʻuluʻulu, pūʻulu, pūkuʻi, hoʻopūkuʻi, pue; hāpue *(rare);* — *together,* kūhaluka.

hug. Pūliki, pūkuʻi, apo; — *ardently,* kilipue.

huge. Nui loa, nui hewahewa, kūāhewa.

Huguenot. Hukuenoka.

huh! ʻUhū.

hula. Hula *(for various kinds and references, see Haw.-Eng. entry and entries that follow it). Also:* ʻōlapa, ʻulīʻulī, paʻi umauma, kuʻi Molokaʻi, hula noho, hula pahu, papa hehi, ʻālaʻapapa, hue, kiʻelei, ʻōhelo, kālāʻau, pahua, kōlani. *See* **dance, sitting hula**. *Americanized hula,* hula hapa haole. *Hula by many persons,* huhula, huhuhula, hulahula. *Hula dancer,* hula, mea

hula. *Hula leader,* 'alaka'i hula. *Hula teacher,* kumu hula. *Hula troupe,* pā hula. *Assistant leader in a hula troupe,* iwi 'ao'ao. *Assistant to head student,* paepae, iwi 'ao'ao. *Head student,* po'opua'a. *Graduating exercises for hula,* 'ūniki, hu'elepo. *Hula steps:* 'ai, 'ami, 'ami kūkū, 'ai 'ami, 'ai ha'a, ha'a, kāwele, 'ai kāwele, kāwelu, 'ami kāhela, 'uwehe, 'ō, kāholo, ki'i, wāwae ki'i, wāwae, lele, 'aui, kelamoku, 'ūlili, ka'apuni, hela, huki, kupe, ue, holo. *Hula gestures,* ki'i kuhi, ki'i hua. *Hula altar,* kuahu, ni'o. *Hula goddess,* Laka. *Hula rattle,* 'ulī'ulī. *Feathered top of hula rattle,* heke. *To dance the hula,* hula. *To undulate the arms in a hula, imitating the flight of a bird,* ho'ēheu. *To move the stomach as in certain hula dances,* papa'i. *To twist and turn with rapid hip movements,* hō'anapau. *To sway the hips,* ho'olewa. *Dare to hula, leave shyness at home,* 'a'a i ka hula, waiho i ka hilahila i ka hale.
hulk. Moku popopo *(of a ship).*
hull. Ka'ele. *Also:* 'ele, 'a'a, kino; ama *(of a double canoe).*
hulls. Oka.
hum. Hū, 'ū, hamumu, hamumumu, muhu, mumuhu, auēuē. *Humming top,* hū oeoe.
human. Kanaka, ho'okanaka. *Human sacrifice,* kanaka, heana kanaka, i'aloa. *Human form,* kino kanaka. *Human bone,* iwi kanaka. *To assume human shape (as a child in the womb),* ho'okanaka.
humane. Lokomaika'i, kū'ē i ka ho'omāinoino.
Humane Society. 'Ahahui Kū'ē i ka Ho'omāinoino.
humanity. Lāhui kānaka. *Concerning humanity,* pākanaka.
human rights. Nā pono o ka lāhui kanaka, nā kuleana o nā kānaka.
humble. Ha'aha'a, ho'oha'aha'a, pē, pēpē, ūpē. *Also:* ka'apē, kupali'i, kaupē, kolokolohai, 'ālo'ilo'i, ho'okanaha'i, lalolalo, kapeau, kikā. *See saying,* bait.
humbug. 'Āpiki, hamapaka.
humerus bone. Iwi uluna, 'auhau.
humid. Kawaū, ma'ū; ikiiki *(and hot).*
humiliate. Ho'ohilahila, ho'oha'aha'a. *Also:* ho'okūlou, manīne, olopē. *See* mākena.
humility. Ha'aha'a. *See* humble. *To turn away in humility,* palai, palaina.
humor. Ho'omāke'aka, piha 'eu.
humorous. *See* funny.
hump. Pu'u, lapu'una, lanahua. *Also:* 'anapu'u. *Humpbacked,* kuapu'u, ho'okanahua.
humped. Lāpu'u, kikiwi, hūnunu, āhua, kanahua, nanai, lanai. *Sit humped,* ho'okuapu'u.
hunch. 'Ano 'ike mahu'i.
hunchback. Kuapu'u. *Also:* kua hua, kanaka kua pipi'o. *The hunchback island (Maui),* ka mokupuni kuapu'u.
hundred. Hanele, haneri. *By the hundred, hundredfold,* pāhanele. *Hundredth part,* hapahaneli. *The year 1900,* ka makahiki 'umi kūmāiwa hanele.
hung. Kaulia. *See* hang.
Hungarian, Hungary. Hunekali, Hunegari, Hunakalia, Hunagaria.
hungry. Pōloli, make 'ai. *Also:* pehu, makapehu, hanalē *(in a saying),* hemo'ē, pūlewa, hahalu, 'ōlewalewa, ho'ohaka, kualana ka 'ōpū, umauma nahā, halehale, houpo lewalewa, pua'awa'awa. *See ex.,* houpo, makapehu. *Hunger pains,* 'ōpū ha'o, ho'īlewa. *Hunger is satisfied,* mā'ona, ola ka pōloli. *My day of hun-*

ger *survives through your love,* ku'u lā pōloli, ā ola i kou aloha.
hunt. Hahai, imi, hahai holoholona.
hunter. Kanaka hahai holoholona.
hunting dog. 'Īlio hahai holoholona.
hunting license. Laikini hahai holoholona.
hurdle. Lelepā.
hurl. Nou, kūpahu, kā. *Also:* walakīkē; 'ō'ō, pahu *(as a spear);* kā 'alā *(as stones with a sling);* — *down,* kiola 'ino. *See* throw.
hurling. Pahuna *(as of a spear);* kāhei. *See* hurl.
Huron. Hulona, Hurona.
hurrah. Hulō.
hurricane. Makani pāhili, makani uluulu, makani hele uluulu; Ka-ua-'ula *(Lahaina).*
hurry. 'Āwīwī. *Also:* āwiki, wiki, ho'owiki, wikiwiki, alawiki, elewiki, māmā, pūlale, ho'opūlale, lale, ho'olale, ho'ohikiwawe, uheheu, ho'okalalī, ho'okāholo, pupuahulu, kī, kāpaepae, au, ho'āuau, ho'okanahē, ho'oui, pa'apa'anā, pākū'ei, pulelua. *See sayings,* puehu 1, wili 1. *To hurry from place to place,* holo 'āwīwī, 'alakē.
hurt. 'Eha. *Also:* hō'eha, 'ino, māino, ho'ohuake'eo. *Easily hurt,* 'eha wale. *Hurt by a remark,* pā i ka leo. *To hurt for no reason,* 'eha wale. *Hurt in feelings,* ku'ihē, hailuku, ho'oku'i, pahu.
husband. Kāne. *Also:* pilikua, kāne i ka 'ili; lei *(affectionate);* ali'i kāne *(polite, not said of one's own husband).* *To be a husband,* kāne. *To offer to become a husband,* ho'okāne. *Husband acquired by matchmaking,* kāne ho'omoe. *Her husband,* kāna kāne.
hush. Hāmau, ho'ohāmau, ho'omālie. *Also:* ho'omoemoe; maukoli *(rare).*
husk. Pulu; 'a'a *(coconut).* *To husk,* wehe i ka pulu. *Husking stick,* 'ōniu.
husker. 'Ō.
husky. Pūkonakona, lawa, pu'ipu'i; kanunu *(rare).*
hut. Pupupu hale, pāpa'i, hale kāpi'o 'ili lā'au, kāmala. *Thatched hut,* hale pili. *Beach hut,* pu'upu'uone. *Hut for fish gear,* kū'ula. *Fisherman's hut,* pāpa'i lawai'a. *Farmer's hut,* pāpa'i mahi 'ai. *Peaked hut,* pū'o'a *(rare).*
hyacinth. Haikina.
hyacinth bean. Pāpapa, pī.
Hyades. Ka-nuku-o-ka-puahi.
Hyde Park. Haika Paka, Haida Paka.
hydrangea. Pōpōhau.
hydrant. Piula wai, ki'o wai.
hydroplane. Mokulele holo kai.
hyena. Hiena.
hymn. Hīmeni, leo ho'onani, mele haipule, mele ho'omaika'i. *Selected hymn or anthem,* hīmeni wae. *Closing hymn,* hīmeni ho'oku'u.
hyoid bone. Iwi elelo.
hyphen. Kiko moe, kahamoe.
hypocrite. Ho'okamani, kanale'o, hūpō kaliko, holo lua, kāma'e, maka lua. *See* palai 2. *Hypocritical smile,* kekē niho.
hypodermic injection. Pahu kui.
hypodermic needle. Kui hou lā'au.
hypotenuse. 'Ao'ao loa.
hypothesis. Koho mua, mana'okōkua.
hyssop. Hukopa, 'ae'ae.
hysteria. Ulupuni.

I

i. 1. *The letter.* 'Ī. 2. *(Cap.) Pronoun.* Au, wau, 'o wau, 'o au.

ibex. 'Ipeka.

ice. Hau, kēhaupa'a. *Also:* hau'oki, waipa'a, wai pū'olo i ka lau lā'au. *Ice age,* ka wā i uhi 'ia ai ka 'āina e ka hau.

iceberg. Haulana, moku hau.

icebound. Pō'ai 'ia ā pa'a i ka hau.

icebox. Pahu hau.

icecap. Haukōhi, 'eke hau.

ice cream. Haukalima, 'aikalima.

iced. Hau. *Iced beverage,* mea inu ho'ohu'ihu'i. *Iced tea,* kī i ho'okomo 'ia ka hau.

icehouse. Hale hau.

Iceland. 'Āina Hau.

ice plant. 'Ākulikuli lei.

ice skate. Holo hau.

ice skates. Kāma'a holo hau.

ice water. Wai hau.

icicle. Kulu hau pa'a.

icing. Mea momona e uhi 'ia ai maluna o ka mea 'ono.

iconoclast. Mea wāwahi ki'i ho'omana, ho'omahuakala.

Idaho. 'Ikahō.

idea. Mana'o; mana'o 'ino *(evil);* mana'o nui *(important). Completely clear and intelligible idea,* piha pono ka mana'o.

ideal. Kūpono ma nā 'ano apau *(perfect);* mea i kuko 'ia, mea i mana'o nui 'ia *(thing desired).*

identical. Like loa, kūlike, like ā like.

identification papers. Palapala kuhikuhi kino, palapala hō'ike pili kino.

identify. Hō'oia, hō'oia 'ike maka, ho'omaopopo.

identity. 'Ike e ho'omaopopo ai.

idiom, idiomatic. 'Ikeoma.

idiot. Lōlō, hūpō, hepa, hipa; 'āna'anea *(rare).*

idle. Moloā, molowā, noho wale. *Also:* lena, lenalena, lolena, malela, laholena, kapoulena, lola, loma, hāloli'ili, malela, 'ōpū palula, palaualelo, lima lewalewa. *See* **indolent, lazy.**

idol. Ki'i akua, akua. *See* **image.**

idolatry. Ho'omana ki'i.

if. Inā, nō. *Also:* aia nō, i, ke *(Gram. 11.1). If you go,* inā 'oe e hele. *Only if you come,* aia nō i kāu hele 'ana mai. *If there were much money, the work would progress,* inā he nui ke kālā, inā ua holomua ka hana.

ignite. Ho'ā, hō'a'ā.

ignoble. 1. *Not noble.* Kūlana ha'aha'a. 2. *Vile.* Haumia.

ignoramus. Na'aupō. *Also:* wa'awa'a, Wa'awa'a-ikina'a-po, kahua 'ole, hu'ahu'a lani.

ignorance. Na'aupō; pō, pōuli, la'a uli. *See sayings* **uhi 1, scale 2, sea cucumber.** *To feign ignorance,* ho'opalō.

ignorant. Na'aupō, hūpō, ho'ona'aupō, 'ike 'ole. *Also:* pō'ele, kuānea, wa'awa'a, neki. *To behave ignorantly,* ho'okuānea. *Ignorant talk or behavior, see* **gourd.**

ignore. Nānā 'ole, kāpae 'ōlelo, huli kua. *Also:* nānākuli, ho'owaiho, nanau, lanau.

il-. 'Ole.

ill. Ma'i, 'ōma'ima'i, nāwaliwali.

illegal. Kū 'ole i ke kānāwai, mawaho o ke kānāwai, kū'ē kānāwai, kolohe.

illegally. *See* **illegal.** *To bring in illegally,* ho'opae malū, komohewa.

illegitimate. Manuahi, po'o 'ole, mawaho o ke kānāwai, kāmeha'i. *Illegitimate child,* keiki po'o 'ole, keiki ma-nuahi, keiki kāmeha'i, hua hā'ule; ua iki *(offspring of chief and commoner).*

ill-fated. Kūlana pō'ino.

ill-feeling. Mana'o 'ino, 'ōpū kopekope, na'au kopekope. *Also:* nanahua, wawa'u, ke'emoa, kākala, na'ina'i.

ill-fitting. Kūpono 'ole, 'aluhe'e, 'ewa; 'ope'alu *(as clothes).*

ill-gotten. Loa'a me ka hewa. *Ill-gotten gains,* waiwai loa'a me ke kolohe.

illicit. Kū 'ole i ke kānāwai. *Illicit cohabitation,* moekolohe. *To live together illicitly,* nohona 'āpono 'ole 'ia, noho kāpae.

Illinois. 'Ilinoe.

illiterate. 'Ike 'ole i ka heluhelu.

ill-natured. Wawa'u *(fig.). See* **ill-feeling.**

illness. Ma'i. *See* **disease, sickness.**

illogical. Kū 'ole i ka mea i no'ono'o pono 'ia.

ill-omened. Pono 'ole nā 'ōuli, hō'ailona pōpilikia, 'āpuni.

ill-suited. Kohu 'ole.

illuminate. Ho'omālamalama.

illusion. Kuhi hewa, 'ike 'ōhewahewa. *Try and end illusion,* e ho'ā'o nō i pau kuhi hewa *(saying).*

illustrate. Kaha ki'i; ho'ohālikelike *(exemplify). Illustrated newspaper,* nūpepa hō'ike'ike ki'i.

illustration. Ki'i, ki'i ho'ākaaka; hō'ike 'ano *(example).*

ill will. Loko 'ino. *See sayings,* **au, gall bladder.**

im-. 'Ole.

image. Ki'i, akua, ki'i akua, kia hō'ailona, 'ano; ki'i kālai 'ia *(carved);* ao *(exact);* haku 'ōhi'a *(of 'ōhi'a wood);* aka *(reflection);* mō'ī *(temple);* ki'i ho'oweliweli *(terrifying);* 'ōlohe *(as in the clouds);* akua kā'ai *(carved on a tall spearlike stick). Caretaker of images,* kahuna ki'i, kahu akua. *Lord of images,* mō'ī. *Exclamation said by priests as they carried images,* nauane! *In his image (Kin. 1:27),* ma kona 'ano. *This boy is the exact image of his father,* 'a'ohe wahi ka'awale o kēia keiki i ka makua kāne; kū loa kēia keiki i ka makua kāne.

imagination. No'ono'o ulu wale, mana'o ulu wale; makakū *(rare).*

imagine. Kuhi, mahu'i; lauele *(rare).*

imbecile. 'Īhepa, hepa.

imbibe. Inu, kāmau.

imitate. Ho'opili, ho'o-. *Also:* mahu'i, ho'omahu'i, ho'ohele; ho'omā'auwē *(to ridicule by mimicking);* ho'oniau. *Imitate birds,* kūhea manu. *He imitates Hawaiians,* ho'ohawai'i 'oia.

immaculate. Ma'ema'e loa, hemolele.

immature. O'o 'ole, 'ōpiopio, holina.

immeasurable. Ana 'ole.

immediate. Koke, hikiwawe, wawe.

immediately. Koke, emoole, 'emo 'ole.

immense. Nui loa, nui hewahewa, nui 'ino.

immerse. Ho'olu'u, kūpenu.

immigrant. E'e moku.

immigration. Po'e pae mai. *See* **Board of Immigration.**

immobile. 'Oni 'ole.

immoral. 'Ino, hewa haumia.

immortal. Ola mau, make 'ole.

immortality. Ola mau.

immovable. Kūpa'a, 'onipa'a; lolohi *(rare).*

impartial. Kaulike, lawelua. *To treat fairly and impartially,* kaulike.

impatiens. 'Ōlepe.

impatient. Nauki, kūʻaki, ahonui ʻole.
impeach. Hoʻopau mai ka ʻoihana aku. *Impeach a high officer,* hoʻopiʻi luna nui.
impediment. *See* **block.** *Speech impediment,* hāpuʻupuʻu, hapakuʻe ka ʻōlelo.
imperfect. Kīnā, hemahema, ʻaʻole i ponopono loa, paʻewa, ʻewa, kūpaʻewa, paoʻioʻi.
imperial. ʻImepeliala.
impersonate. Hoʻohālikelike, hoʻokohukohu.
impersonation. Hoʻohālikelike ʻana.
impertinent. Mahaʻoi, hoʻomaʻoi, kīkoʻolā; ʻāpali *(fig.).*
impervious. Paʻapū.
impetigo. Kākiʻo.
impious. ʻAiā, hoʻomaloka.
implacable. Laukōnā, mākonā.
implement. Paʻahana, mea hoʻohana.
implore. Koi, noi haʻahaʻa.
imply. Hoʻomaoe.
impolite. ʻOluʻolu ʻole. *See* **rude.**
import. 1. *Bring in.* Hoʻokomo. *See* **imports.** 2. *Meaning.* Manaʻo nui.
importance. ʻAno nui, waiwai. *Thing of importance,* mea nui. *Limited importance,* ʻōpū ʻukuʻuku, kaupalena ʻia.
important. Nui, ʻano nui; *most —,* panepoʻo. *See* **kalalea.** *Important person,* kaʻapeha, kiʻi maka nunui, meʻe.
imports. Waiwai hoʻopae mai, waiwai komo.
importunate. Kauloloa, meʻo, noi mau.
imposing. Kilakila, mōkila.
impossible. Hiki ʻole, ʻaʻole hiki. *See* **saying, puanaiea.**
impotent. Pau ka hiki. *Also:* pīʻalu, uheule. *See* **saying, koʻokā 1.**
impoverish. Hoʻohune, hoʻoʻilihune.
impregnate. Hoʻopiha, hoʻopiʻi.
impregnated. Hoʻopiha ʻia, mau; ʻūʻū, ū *(as with salt).*
impression. Paʻi ʻana, mōʻali, moʻoʻali. *See* **opinion.**
impressive. ʻIkena hoʻopoina ʻole, kilakila; ʻeʻena *(in speech).*
imprint. Paʻi, heʻaheʻa. *To leave imprints, as of feet,* kākau.
imprison. Hoʻopaʻahao.
improper. Kūpono ʻole; pono *(preceding a modified word).*
improve. Holomua, hoʻomaikaʻi, hoʻokāʻoi.
improved. Ahona.
improvement. Hoʻomaikaʻi ʻana, holomua, hana hoʻoneʻemua; pōmaikaʻi *(as to property).*
improvise. Haku wale; paha *(a chant).*
impudent. Mahaʻoi, ihumaʻa. *Also:* wini, koakoa, hoʻolanakila, honekoa; mōhio *(fig.).*
impulse. Manaʻo ulu wale, noʻonoʻo ulu wale. *Act impulsively,* lele ʻē.
impute. Hoʻopiʻi.
in. I. *Also:* ma, i loko, maloko, i luna, maluna. *In the house,* maloko o ka hale. *In the car,* i luna o ke kaʻa. *In the canoe,* maluna o ka waʻa.
in-. ʻOle.
inability. Hiki ʻole.
inaccessible. Hiki ʻole ke hoʻokokoke aku, kahakea.
inaccurate. Hewa, ʻapakeʻe, hape.
inactive. Noho wale, noho hana ʻole. *Also:* kukule, kūlola, pālīlea, pū, palaka, mania, kūmaua.
inadequate. Lawa pono ʻole, kāwala.
inalienable. Pili paʻa loa. *Inalienable rights,* pono e pili paʻa loa.
inappropriate. Kohu ʻole. *Most inappropriate,* ʻaʻohe kohu iki.
inattentive. Hoʻolohe ʻole.
inaugural address. Haʻiʻōlelo poni.
inaugurate. Poni, hoʻoponi, hoʻokumu.
inauspicious. Hōʻailona hoʻopilikia, kūpono ʻole nā ʻōuli, ʻāpuni.
incantation. Pule hoʻokalakupua.
Incarnation. ʻEnekelea *(Catholic).*

incense. Mea ʻala. *Incense burner,* ipu kuni ʻala.
incentive. Kumu hoʻolalelale, kumu hoʻopaipai.
incessant. Hōʻoki ʻole, hoʻokina. *Cf.* **constant.**
incest. Moe ʻohana pili pono'ī, moe lūauʻi. *Marriage of close relatives, as of brother and sister (or half-brother or -sister) of very high chiefs,* moe piʻo, moe naha, hoʻi; mānai ʻula *[poetic]*) *was a means of preserving the family line and was not considered incestuous; commoners had no such marriages; see* **kiko moa.**
inch. ʻĪniha.
incident. Hanana, mea hiki wale mai, hana.
incinerator. Wahi puhi ahi.
incisors. Niho ʻaki.
incite. Hoʻoālaala, hoʻolale, hoʻouluāoʻa, hoʻolalelale. *Also:* hōʻeu, hoʻononi, kīkī, kīkīlona, hoʻokokonoiʻe, hoʻā, haʻinole.
incline. Piʻina, ihona, hiō. *Also:* hāliu; ʻāluli *(incline the head),* moekahi.
inclose. Hoʻopuni.
include. Helu, hoʻokomo pū, hoʻohui pū, pau pū, ʻōkomo. *Including women,* a me nā wāhine.
inclusive. Kā- *(of pronouns and possessives). See* **plural,** *Gram., p. 107.*
incoherent. ʻŌhewa, hoʻōhewa, ʻolohewa, laukua, olokē.
income. Loaʻa mai. *Annual income,* loaʻa makahiki.
income tax. ʻAuhau maluna o ka loaʻa.
incomparable. Ana ʻole, lua ʻole, ʻaʻole o kana mai, launa ʻole.
incompetent. Mākaukau ʻole, hemahema, hāwāwā.
incomplete. ʻAʻole piha pono, hapapū, kīhapa.
incomprehensible. Maopopo ʻole. *Also:* kamahaʻo, hōʻeʻepa, ʻeʻepa, pāhaʻohaʻo, āiwaiwa.
inconsequential. Mea ʻole. *Inconsequential deeds,* hana hope ʻole. *Inconsequential thing,* mea iki. *Trifling or inconsequential action, as a casual love affair,* hana kalakalai.
inconsistent. Lolelua, lolilua, maumau ʻole, kūlike ʻole.
inconstant. Lolelua, lelele, lauwili wale, kāpekepeke, palaʻie.
incontinence. Kuko ʻumi ʻole, maka leho. *See* **lecherous.**
inconvenience. Pilikia, hoʻopilikia, hoʻoluhi.
incorporated. Hui ʻia.
incorrect. Pololei ʻole, paʻewa, pāʻewaʻewa, hewa, hape, ʻewa, ʻolalau.
increase. Hoʻonui, hoʻomāhuahua, māhua, māhuahua, hoʻomāhua. *Also:* ulu, hoʻolaha, laha, lalahū, hoʻomano, hoʻomanoa, makua, hoʻomākōmakō, kupu, kuʻi lua, hoʻopākeu, laupaʻi, paʻi, hoʻolaupaʻi; puʻulau *(rapidly);* kāmolamola *(in numbers).*
incur. Loaʻa, loʻohia.
incurable. Hiki ʻole ke hoʻōla, ola ʻole.
indecent. Haumia, pelapela, kūpono ʻole.
indecisive. Naʻau lua. *See* **fickle.**
indeed. Hoʻi, nohoʻi, nō.
indefinite. Maopopo ʻole, akaaka ʻole. *Indefinite time,* akaaka ʻole ka manawa.
indefinite article. Pilimua maopopo ʻole. *The indefinite article is* he.
indefinite pronoun. Paniinoa kuhi laulā.
indented. Poʻopoʻo. *Also:* kīpoʻopoʻo, maka mino.
independence. Kūʻokoʻa, ea. *Independence Day,* Lā Kūʻokoʻa. *To establish independence,* hoʻokūʻokoʻa.
independent. Kūʻokoʻa, kūhaʻo, kū kaʻawale, kāʻokoʻa, kaʻaʻokoʻa. *See* **saying, kīkū.**
index. Papa kuhikuhi, papa hōʻike. *Index finger,* lima kuhi.
India. ʻInia.
Indian. ʻInikini, ʻIlikini *(American),* mea ʻInia *(from India);* ʻIniana *(as Indian Ocean).*
Indiana. ʻInikiana, Inidiana.
Indian mulberry. Noni.
Indian Ocean. Moana ʻIniana.
India rubber. Laholio.
indicate. Hōʻike.

indicative mood. 'Ōuliha'i.
indictment. Palapala ho'opi'i, palapala ho'opi'i ho'āhewa. Indies. 'Inia.
Indies. 'Inia.
indifference, indifferent. Ho'omaopopo 'ole, palaka, nānā 'ole. *Also:* ho'okanane'o, nānā maka, ho'okolono, palaleha. *To feign indifference,* ho'opalaka, ho'opalai maka.
indigenous. Maoli.
indigestion. Manawahua, nahu ka 'ōpū.
indignant. Huhū, ukiuki, ka'eo.
indigo. 'Inikō, inikoa. *Indigo plant,* kolū, 'inikō.
indirect. Lauwili; hiliau *(rare). Indirect-inverse proportion,* lakio like huli hope. *Indirect questioning,* nīnau ho'ohele, ho'ohuahualau, nīnau ho'omaoe. *To endeavor to find out something or obtain something by indirect methods,* ho'opāpā.
indiscriminately. Wae 'ole, hāpuku.
indistinct. 1. *Of vision.* Pāpalaweka, palaweka, palapalaweka, pālauweka, poehi, pōwehiwehi, kōli'uli'u. *Also:* 'ōli'uli'u, kāpala, haili, niniu. 2. *Of speech.* Akaaka 'ole, huikau ka leo, 'olē, nei, hepa. *Also:* ho'okake, naunau, kāpalalū, mūmū, hemuwā, hinihini; lau'ulu.
individual. Kanaka.
indolent. Moloā, lena, kapoulena. *Also:* hāloli'ili, heha, maheha, kaialile, palela, ahio, loma, kamaki'i, kualana, melamela, kūhana 'ole, 'ōpū palula, pāpālole. *See* idle, lazy.
induce. Ho'o-, ho'okonokono, kono.
indulge. Ho'opunahele, palani, mailani. *See* spoil.
indulged. Pailani loa, ho'opunahele 'ia, ho'onu'a.
indulgence. Palapala kalahala *(Catholic). See saying,* ko'okā 1.
industrial school. Kula a'o hana lima.
industrious. Pa'ahana, lawehana, limahana.
industry. 1. *Diligence.* Pa'ahana. 2. *Trade.* 'Oihana.
ineffective. Holo le'a 'ole, pahu'a, 'ōhea.
inefficient. Hemahema, lōlena, mili. *See saying,* hīlea.
inevitable. Hiki 'ole ke 'alo a'e.
inexperienced. 'Akahi akahi, hemahema, ma'a 'ole. *See* novice.
inexpert. Hemahema.
inexplicable. Āiwaiwa, āiwa, hiki 'ole ke wehewehe pono.
infancy. Wā li'ili'i, wā 'u'uku, manawaea, wā huli o ke alo i luna.
infant. Keiki li'ili'i, kamali'i *(plural);* 'awa *(premature). See* baby. *The sound "ay" made by infants calling for attention,* 'a'aea.
infanticide. 'Umi kamali'i, 'umi keiki.
infantile. Ho'opēpē, li'ili'i, 'ano pēpē, 'ano kamali'i, hana kamali'i.
infantry. Pū'ali kaua ka'i wāwae, koa hele wāwae, kaniwāwae.
infatuate. Ho'ohei, ho'ohei mana'o, li'a nui.
infatuated. Ona. *Infatuated with desire,* ulupuni i ka makemake.
infection. Ma'i lele, ma'i laha, ma'i 'a'ai; kōhoko *(probably syphilitic).*
infer. Kuhi. *See* imply.
inferior. 'A'ohe maika'i loa, ha'aha'a, emi iho; holina, 'a'aiole *(of fruit). Rare:* huelo, mānea, loha.
infinite. Palena 'ole, nalowale.
infirm. Nāwaliwali, palupalu, nāwali. *Also:* kolopupū, kauko'o *(of an aged person);* kaulei, 'ōmali. *See* feeble, old age.
inflame. Hō'ā, ula.
inflamed. Ula. *Also:* kole, mūkole, heka, hekaheka, he'a, uno'o; pīheka, uikokole, mūkole *(eyes).*
inflammable. 'A'ā koke.
inflammation. 'Ūpehupehu; pu'u 'ako *(throat).*
inflate. Ho'ohū, ho'olopū. *Also:* pākākā, ho'opūhalalū.
inflation. Emi ka waiwai o ke kālā *(financial).*
inflexible. 'O'ole'a, 'olu 'ole, pa'akikī. *Also:* wīkani, kākāuha, wīka'o.

influence. Ho'ohuli mana'o, ho'ololi. *To influence to bad behavior,* ho'okūā'ino.
influenced. Ho'ohuli 'ia. *Easily influenced,* puni wale, kololū.
influential. Ko'iko'i, mana ko'iko'i, ka'apeha.
influenza. Palū.
inform. Hō'ike, ho'omaopopo.
informal. Kāpae i nā lula 'o'ole'a. *To eat informally,* 'ai kū. *Informal attire,* 'a'ahu ·'olu'olu, 'a'ahu nō e holo ana i ka mana'o.
information. Nū hou, hō'ike. *To obtain information by roundabout methods,* ho'ohuahualau. *To gather information about one's relatives,* pākōlea.
infrequent. Kaka'ikahi, no ka manawa. *See* seldom. *The ship stops infrequently,* kū manawa ka moku.
-ing. Ana, 'ana. *His going,* kāna hele 'ana. *He is going,* e hele ana 'oia. *Repetitive action is also shown by reduplications.*
ingenious, ingenuity. Loea, maiau.
ingrate. Mea mahalo 'ole, mea aloha 'ole, pō'alo maka.
ingratiate. Ho'omalimali, mikimiki.
ingratitude. 'Awahua, ho'omaika'i 'ole. *See* idiom, au 4.
inhabit. Noho.
inhabitant. Kanaka, kama'āina; po'e *(plural). See* citizen.
inhabited. Noho 'ia. *Also:* aukanaka, kanaka. *Sparsely inhabited,* noho kaka'ikahi 'ia, kaikua. *Densely inhabited,* noho nui 'ia.
inhalant. Lā'au ho'ohanuhanu. *To administer an inhalant,* ho'ohanu.
inhale. Hanu, hanu i loko.
inharmonious. Kūlike 'ole; muimuia *(of colors);* kulikuli *(of sounds).*
inherit. Ili. *Inherited land,* 'āina ho'oilina. *I inherited that land,* ua ili mai kēlā 'āina ia'u.
inheritance. Ho'oilina, ho'īlina, waiwai ho'oilina, ili. *To seek and establish inheritance for one's children,* 'imi hale.
inheritance deed. Palapala ho'olilo waiwai.
inhibited. Kāohi mana'o, ka'uka'u. *See* uninhibited.
initial. Mua. *Initial letter,* hua mua.
initiate. Ho'omaka, ho'okumu; ho'olilo i lālā *(to membership).*
initiation. Ho'okumu 'ana e lilo i lālā, kā i mua. *Initiation feast,* 'aha'aina komo.
inject. Hou, hano.
injection. Hoene, pahu kui *(hypodermic). Injection needle,* hou kui.
injure. 'Ino, ho'o'ino, hana 'ino, ho'opō'ino. *Also:* ho'oma'au, ku'i, māuna, māhole, māholehole, mōhole, mōholehole, āulu, manuhe'u.
injured. 'Ālina, māuna, 'eha, manuhe'u, manu, pala pū. *Bruised and injured,* manu kīnā.
injustice. Kaulike 'ole, pololei 'ole, hana pono 'ole, hana pā'ewa'ewa.
ink. 'Īnika, wai 'ele'ele. *Ink squirted by octopus,* kūkaeuli, weka, wekaweka. *Ink sac in octopus or squid,* 'ala'ala. *Ink used for tattooing,* pa'u. *Ink dregs or powder,* pa'u.
ink blot. Kohu 'īnika.
inkling. Ho'omaopopo 'ē, 'ike mahu'i.
inkstand, inkwell. Ipu 'īnika.
inland. Uka, mauka, āuka, i uka; wao *(see Haw.-Eng. entry and following entries),* āukauka. *To go inland,* pi'i, hele i uka.
Inland Sea. Kai Loko 'Āina.
in-laws. 'Ohana pili ma ka male 'ana, inoa, alohiki; pili pāpākole *(disrespectful). Parents-in-law of one's child, or their relatives of the same generation,* puluna.
inlay. 'Ōkomo, kīkomo.
inlet. 'Ōkomo.
inmate. 'Ōhua.
inn. Hōkele, hale kipa, hale ho'okipa, kahi o'io'ina.
inner. Loko.
innkeeper. Haku hale kipa.

innocent. Hala ʻole, hewa ʻole.

innuendo. Kaona hoʻoʻinoʻino *(pejorative).*

innumerable. Hiki ʻole ke helu, nui hewahewa, lehulehu, kinikini, kini lau ā mano. *Also:* kuakini, kuāmano, kuāmanomano, kauluwela, pūliʻuliʻu. *See* **kini, lau, mano.**

in order to. E, i, no, i hiki ai ke. *Cf.* **because.** *In order not to,* i ʻole e, o.

inquest. ʻAha nīele. *Coroner's inquest,* ʻaha nīele kumu make. *Fire inquest,* ʻaha nīele pau ahi.

inquire. Nīnau.

inquisition. ʻAha nīele, ʻinekuikikio.

inquisitive. Nīele.

insane. Pupule, ulala, hehena; kapanaha *(rare).*

insatiable. Ana ʻole.

insect. Mea kolo *(creeping);* holoholona lele; mū *(destructive);* huhu *(wood-boring). Feelers of an insect,* pipi. *Insect-eaten,* ane, huhuhu, ʻai ʻia.

insecticide. Lāʻau hoʻomake mū, mea pepehi mea kolo.

insecure. Paʻa ʻole ke kahua. *Also:* naue, pūlehe, kāpekepeke, kauleina, kuleleiwi, kueʻo, kūnapa, kaulei, kulana.

insert. Hoʻokomo. *Also:* ʻōkomo, hoʻō, ʻōʻō, hōʻōʻō, hahao, pao, kaulelele. *Inserted word,* hua ʻōlelo puʻumana ʻia.

inside. Loko.

insight. ʻIke kūhohonu, ʻālawa maka.

insignia. Hōʻailona, mea hoʻohanohano *(of royalty).*

insignificant. Mea ʻole. *Also:* ʻano ʻole, aʻe nei, māʻilu, ʻōmilumilu, ʻōmilu, kūpihipihi, kūlono, kūnono.

insincere. ʻOiaʻiʻo ʻole, kū ʻole i ka ʻoiaʻiʻo, hoʻokamani, hoʻokāmaʻe.

insinuate. ʻŌlelo kāpilipili ʻino; hoʻoloko *(rare).*

insipid. Hūkākai, ānea, āneanea, koʻekoʻe, mūhea, mule, mulea. *Also:* hukahūkai, ʻokaʻokai, ʻōkākai, kai, heahea, ʻāheahea, muʻumūnā, ʻaʻalakai, mala, kāhalahala, maika, mahū. *See* **tasteless.**

insist. Koi, hoʻolāʻau, hoʻopaʻa, haʻakoi, hoʻohuʻa. *Insistent urge,* koi hoʻokina, koi huhuki.

insistence. Kōina.

insolent. Mahaʻoi, pākīkē, kīkoʻolā, hoʻokano.

insomnia. Hiaʻā, hoʻālahia, kanikaniāʻula, moe ʻole.

inspect. Nānā, mākaʻi.

inspector. Luna nānā.

inspiration. Mea hoʻoulu i ka manaʻo, ulu, aʻo loko.

inspirational meeting. Hālāwai hōʻeuʻeu.

inspire. Ulu *(see ex.,* **ulu***),* hoʻoulu, hoʻolalelale, kīpaipai.

inspired. Ulu *(by a spirit, ideal, person);* kīhae *(with a wrathful spirit).*

install. Hoʻokomo, hoʻonoho.

installment. 1. *Payment.* Uku, mahele uku. *Installment payments,* uku liʻiliʻi, uku manawa, uku hapa, uku pākalikali. **2.** *Portion.* Mahele, hapa, ʻāpana.

instance. Mea hoʻohālike. *For instance,* penei; e laʻa me kēia.

instant. Manawa pōkole loa. *Instant coffee,* kope hikiwawe.

instantly. Manawa ʻole, ʻemo ʻole.

instead. Ma kahi o.

instep. Poli, poli wāwae, poho wāwae.

instinct. ʻIke hānau.

institute. 1. *See* **institution. 2.** *To begin.* Hoʻokumu.

institution. Hui hoʻohana ʻimi naʻauao *(scholarly);* hui, hale. *See* **eleemosynary.**

instruct. Aʻo, hoʻonaʻauao; hiʻipaka *(as a child).*

instruction. Aʻo, ʻōlelo aʻo, aʻo palapala, kuhikuhina. *Instruction house,* hālau.

instructive. Hoʻonaʻauao.

instrument. Mea paʻahana; pila *(musical). See* **musical instrument.**

insufficient. Lawa ʻole, kāwala.

insult. Kūamuamu ʻia, hoʻoʻino, hoʻopuka hewa, hoʻopuka pono ʻole. *Hawaiian is rich in insults. Some refer to body parts:* ʻauwiniwini; kole kaʻaka, ʻōkole kaʻaka, kolekole ka maka *(see* **kolekole***);* eia kāu, ʻo

ka heoheo *(see* **heoheo***);* ihu papaʻa, laho kole, laho paka, laho pōkaʻokaʻo, laho ʻula, maʻi ʻoā, maka lole, maka piapia, ʻolouha, poʻo koʻi, ule hole. *Others concern excrements:* ahu ka pala kūkae, aweawe poi, hele i ka ʻenakōī *(see* **ʻenakōī***);* naio ʻai kae, pala kūkae, pala naio. *A few others:* kamipulu, kanakapika, koko moa, moe hālau, ʻōhao ʻīlio, unu pehi ʻiole. *See also* **adze, beggar, boar, derision, dog, eye, eyelid, farmer, genital, gesture, mat, pebble, penis, pinworm, shrimp, slur, taunt.**

insulted. Kūamuamu ʻia, hōʻino ʻia.

insurance. Hoʻopaʻa, ʻinikua *(for various kinds, see* ʻinikua *and following entries). Also:* hoʻopaʻa ola *(life),* ʻinikua pau ahi *(fire),* hoʻopaʻa waiwai *(property),* hoʻopaʻa. *Insurance policy,* palapala hoʻopaʻa, palapala ʻinikua. *Insurance company,* hui hoʻopaʻa.

insure. Hoʻopaʻa, ʻinikua. *Insure property,* hoʻopaʻa waiwai.

intelligence. Waihona ʻike.

intelligent. Akamai, naʻauao, lololo.

intelligible. Akaaka, mōakaaka. *To make intelligible,* hoʻākaaka.

intemperate. Pākela. *Intemperate drinker,* pākela inu lama. *Intemperate eating,* pākela ʻai.

intend. Manaʻopaʻa.

intense. ʻIno *(after the modified word, as* nui ʻino*);* nui loa, ikaika loa, koʻikoʻi. *Fig.:* hākuma, mākuma, kūlipo, loku, makaʻeleʻele.

intensifier. ʻŌlelo hoʻokoʻikoʻi i ka manaʻo. *Examples:* hoʻi, nō, nohoʻi, kipona.

intention. Manaʻo. *Lawless intention,* manaʻo kūʻē kānāwai.

intercede. ʻUao, ʻuwao, kāhoahoa.

intercept. Keʻa.

interception. Papani.

intercourse. Launa ʻana. *See* **sexual intercourse.**

interest. 1. *Concern.* Hoihoi, kuleana, pili laulā *(broad, general). See saying,* **bone.** *I haven't the least interest,* ʻaʻohe oʻu lihi hoihoi. *Of no interest,* ʻole wale, hoihoi ʻole. *Lack of interest,* hoihoi ʻole, ʻonakuli. **2.** *On principal.* Kuwala, kuala, puka, puka o ke kālā, uku paneʻe, uku hoʻopaneʻe, uku kaulele; kuwala ʻano hui, kuwala hoʻohui *(compound). Discount on interest,* kuwala hoʻēmi. *Rate of interest,* helu kuala. *Interest payment,* uku kuala. *To draw interest,* puka.

interested. Hoihoi.

interesting. Hoihoi, nanea, walea.

interfere. ʻĀkeʻakeʻa, kakekake, komo kuleana ʻole, hōkake, hōkai, kāmoko. *Free from interference,* kuakahi. *To remove interference,* hoʻokuakahi.

interior. Loko, wālua. *Minister of the Interior,* Kuhina Kālaiʻāina.

interisland. Piliʻāina.

Inter-Island Airways Company. Hui Mokulele Piliʻāina.

Inter-Island Steam Navigation Company. Hui Moku Holo Piliʻāina.

interjection. ʻŌlelo hoʻōho. *(Gram. 12.)*

interlace. Kāwili, molo.

interlocked. ʻŪmiʻi paʻa. *Also:* nihoa, niho, ʻokaʻi; uhauhumu *(rare).*

intermarry. Male ʻohana, male nō iā loko iho. *Rare:* hoʻi, hihi ka lani. *See* **incest.**

intermediate. Mawaena, i waena, waena.

intermingle. Hihi, hui.

intern. Kōkua kauka *(medical).*

internal. Loko.

international. O nā ʻāina ʻē, kō nā ʻāina like ʻole.

interpret. Unuhi, unuhi ʻōlelo, hoʻomahele, mahele ʻōlelo. *To interpret dreams,* wehewehe moeʻuhane, mōʻike.

interpretation. Wehewehe ʻana, koho.

interpreter. Mea unuhi, unuhi ʻōlelo, mahele ʻōlelo; nānā ao *(clouds);* mōʻike *(dreams).*

interrogate. Nīnau, ninaninau.

interrogation. Nīnau, nīnau hōʻike; huahualau *(to incriminate). Interrogation point,* kiko nīnau.

interrogative pronoun. Paniinoa ninaninau.
interrupt. Kahamaha, kepakepa, mauʻaʻe, kāmoko, kīkahō *(rudely)*.
intersection. Huina, pahu manamana.
intertwine. ʻĀwili, hihi, ʻānoni.
interval. Wā; pale, ʻanuʻu, lele *(in music)*. *To take interval (military command),* kaʻawale.
intervene. Komo mawaena; komo kuleana ʻole *(without right)*.
interview. Kūkā kamaʻilio. *To hold an interview,* kūkā kamaʻilio.
interweave. Kāwili, ʻāwili, kāʻekā, molo, ʻānoni, ʻōkaʻi, ʻuo, ʻuwo.
interwoven. Hihia, mauhili, kaupeʻa.
intestines. Naʻau; naʻanaʻau *(small)*; uha *(large)*.
intimate. Pili koke, kuluma. *Intimate friend,* hoa pili.
into. I loko. *Into the house,* i loko o ka hale.
intolerant. Kūʻē i kō haʻi manaʻo, manaʻo hāiki.
intonation. Kiʻina o ka leo, ke kani ʻana o ka leo.
intoxicant. Lama, wai ʻona; mea ʻona *(drug). Fig. names:* wai lohia, wai hoʻonoenoe, wai hoʻomalule, wai kulu; wai kāʻili ao *(see* **kāʻili***). See* **swipes.** *Various intoxicants:* ʻōkolehao *(ti-root);* pinika *(molasses and water);* pala *(watermelon juice).*
intoxicated. ʻOna. *Fig. names:* ulupē, pulu pē, kili hau, noenoe, lupeʻa, māʻona, māʻona loa, hoʻōhewa, kāhiʻo, ʻōhiʻohiʻo, mōlehu, mōlehulehu. *See sayings,* **heha, koʻūkoʻū, māhana, mūkīkī, noenoe, droop.** *To weave along, as one intoxicated,* kikiwi.
intoxicating. ʻOna, hōʻona. *Intoxicating liquor,* wai ʻona.
intoxication. ʻOna. *The intoxication of the ʻawa sank in (FS 135),* ʻoʻoki maila ka ʻona o ka ʻawa.
intransitive. *See* **verb.**
intrepid. Wiwo ʻole, ʻaʻa, kaʻalokuloku.
intricate. Pohihihi.
introduce. Hoʻohui, hoʻolauna *(as people)*.
introduced. Hoʻolauna ʻia *(as people);* malihini *(as plants). See* **plant.**
introduction. Hoʻolauna ʻana *(as people);* ʻōlelo mua.
intrude. Komo wale, komohewa, kipa wale, mauʻaʻe.
invade. *See* **attack.**
invalid. 1. *Ill.* Mea nāwaliwali, mea ʻōmaʻimaʻi; hāpai kanaka *(fig.);* nonopapa *(rare).* **2.** *Not valid.* Mana ʻole, waiwai ʻole.
invasion. Komo ʻino, hoʻouka wale.
invent. Haku wale. *Invented story,* moʻolelo haku wale.
invention. Hana mea hou i hana mua ʻole ʻia.
inventory. Helu, helu waiwai, moʻowaiwai.
inverse. Huli hope.
invest. Hoʻopuka, hoʻopukapuka.
investigate. Kolokolo, hoʻokolokolo, noiʻi.
investigation. Huli, noiʻina, noiʻi.
investment. Waiwai no ka hoʻopukapuka ʻana, waiwai kūʻai. *Investment business,* ʻoihana mahele kumupaʻa.
invincible. Pio ʻole, hiki ʻole iā haʻi ke lanakila.
inviolate. Kapu loa.
invisible. ʻIke maka ʻole ʻia, poʻo huna. *To live invisible in the air,* kīhēhē.
invitation. Kono, palapala kono *(written)*.
invite. Kono, hoʻokono, poloʻai.
invoice. Pila waiwai, pepa hōʻike waiwai.
invoke. Kāhea, kapakapa.
involuntary. Me ka ʻae ʻole. *Involuntary servitude,* hoʻohana me ka ʻae ʻole.
involve. Hihia, kūhihi, kāwili kāʻekā.
involved. Hihia, kāhihi. *To become involved in gambling, in an entangling affair of any sort,* pili hihia.
involvement. Hihia, kāhihi.
Iowa. ʻIowa.

Iran. ʻIlana, Irana.
Iraq. ʻIlaka, Iraka.
Ireland. ʻIlelani, Irelani.
iridium. ʻIlikiuma.
iris. Mauʻu lāʻili.
Irish. ʻAiliki, ʻIlelani.
Irish potato. ʻUala kahiki.
iron. Hao; kakakī *(hoop);* meki *(Biblical);* pāpaʻa hao *(scrap);* ʻaiana *(for pressing clothes);* pilihao, piula *(corrugated iron roofing). See sayings,* **ʻalu, wela.** *Iron pan, dish, fence,* pā hao. *Iron pot,* ipu hao. *Iron spike,* kui hao.
ironing board. Papa ʻaiana.
ironwood. Paina.
ironworks. Hale hana hao.
irony. *See* **sarcasm.**
Iroquois. ʻIlokuoa.
irregular. E like ʻole me ka mea mau, loli ke kūlana, pololei ʻole. *Also:* malele, ʻewaʻewa, manumanu, haumanumanu, kālawalawa, kīlepa, puʻuhaku, āmokemoke, piki. *To make irregular,* hoʻokihikihi. *Irregular-shaped,* laukua. *Irregular verb,* haʻina kekeʻe.
irreligious. ʻAiā, ʻaiāhua, ʻaiāhulu, hoʻomahuakala; laukana *(rare).*
irresponsible. Noʻonoʻo ʻole, ʻaʻole e ʻimi pono i ka mea ʻoiaʻiʻo, pakaulei. *See* **vagabond.**
irrigation. Hanawai.
irritable. Nauki, hoʻonauki, nāukiuki, hoʻonāukiuki, ʻaʻaka, huhū koke.
irritate. Hoʻoukiuki, hoʻouluhua.
irritated. Ukiuki, nāulu, kūʻaki, uilani.
irritation. Ukiuki, ʻena, hoʻopehu ʻana; puʻupuʻu maneʻo *(skin)*.
is. *See* **be.** *He is sick,* maʻi ʻoia, ua maʻi ʻoia.
ischium. Iwi kā.
-ish. ʻAno, hoʻo-, haʻa-, ʻō-, pā-. *Gram. 6.3.*
island. Moku, mokupuni, mokuʻāina, mō, ʻailana; moku kele *(submerged);* moku pāpapa *(low reef)*.
islands. Pae ʻāina. *Hawaiian Islands,* kō Hawaiʻi pae ʻāina.
Isle of Wight. Mokupuni-o-Waika.
islet. Moku, moku liʻiliʻi. *Abounding in islets,* ʻāmokumoku.
isn't. ʻAʻole. *Isn't it?* ʻaʻole anei? *He isn't going,* ʻaʻole ʻoia e hele ana.
isolate. Hoʻokaʻawale.
isolated. Hoʻokaʻawale ʻia, noho kaʻawale.
isopod. Pokipoki.
isosceles triangle. Huinakolu ʻelua ʻaoʻao like.
Israel, Israeli. ʻIkelaʻela, Iseraela, Israeli.
issue. Puka, hoʻopuka, pukana.
isthmus. Pūʻali.
it. Ia, ʻoia, kēlā; akua *(in game of tag). This word is frequently omitted. It is said,* ua ʻōlelo ʻia. *It was a big house,* he hale nui ia.
italics. Hua palapala hiō.
Italy, Italian. Ikalia, Italia.
itch. Maneʻo, āneʻoneʻo. *Also:* kākiʻo, lalawe, ʻako, makaʻaha, kunakuna, meʻeau. *To cause to itch,* hoʻomaneʻo. *I am beginning to itch,* ke piʻi nei koʻu maneʻo.
itching. Puʻupuʻu maneʻo, meʻeau.
item. ʻIkamu.
itinerary. Ala hele.
its. *Same as* **his.**
it's. *See* **it, be.**
itself. ʻOia nō, ʻoia iho, ʻoia ponoʻī. *By itself,* nāna iho, kohana.
ivory. Palaoa *(as whale);* niho ʻelepani. *Ivory-colored,* pua niu. *Ivory pendant,* lei palaoa.
ixora. Pōpōlehua.

J

j. *No Hawaiian term.*
jab. 'O'e, hou, houhou.
jabbed. Kū, kukū, hou 'ia.
jabber. Ā, ā wale, ho'ā, wala'au wale, pakakē, 'ohi, 'ohi'ohi, hiohio, laukua, 'ai kepakepa.
jacinth. Huakineko.
jack. 1. *Instrument.* Lā'au hāpai huila ka'a, kake. **2.** *(Cap.) Male name, knave in a deck of cards.* Keaka.
jackal. 'Īlio hae, iākala.
jackass. *Same as* **donkey.**
jacket. Iakeke. *Checkered jacket,* kelamoku.
jackfish family. 1. *Caranx sp.:* nuku momi (momi), nuku mone'u. **2.** *Kuhlia sp.:* 'āholehole, āhole, 'apo'apo.
jackknife. Pahi pelu; kanikani.
jack-of-all-trades. Mea mākaukau i nā hana like 'ole, laukua.
jack-o'-lantern. Po'oki'i, po'oki'i pala'ai.
jacks. Kimo *(game).*
Jacksonville. Iakekonawili, Iakesonavili.
jackstones. Kimo.
Jacobean lily. Pānānā.
jagged. Nihoniho, nihoa. *Also:* hālelo, hālelolelo, wanawana, wawana, 'o'e, 'anapu'u, 'a'anapu'u, 'ana'anapu'u, uluha'o, uluha'o'a, hao'e, hao'eo'e, hao'a, hao'ao'a.
jaguar. Iākua.
jail. Hale pa'ahao, hale wai. *See saying,* **puhi 2.** *To jail,* ho'opa'ahao.
jailer. Kia'i hale pa'ahao.
jam. Kele *(jelly).* *See* **crowd, crush.**
Jamaica. Iāmeka, Iamaika.
jammed. Pihaku'i, piha'ū. *See* **crowded.**
janitor. Mālama hale.
January. Ianuali, Ianuari.
Japan. Iāpana, 'Āina Kepanī.
Japanese. Kepanī. *Also:* Nipoa, Nīpona.
jar. 1. *Container.* 'Ōmole waha nui; poho aniani *(glass).* **2.** *Move.* Ku'i, 'oni 'ino, 'anu'u.
jargon. 'Ōlelo 'ē, 'ōlelo hilikau.
jarred. 'Anu'u.
jasmine. Pīkake *(for various types, see Haw.-Eng. entry and entries that follow it).*
jasper. Humu'ula, kalama'ula, kalaniā'ula, iākepi.
jaundice. Ma'i lena. *Also:* lena, kapoulena, 'ea 'ōlena, kumulena.
Java. Iawa.
javelin. Kao lele, kao, ihe. *To throw a javelin,* kao, 'ō'ō ihe, pahu ihe.
jaw. Ā, papa niho; papa 'auwae *(lower jaw).* *See* **jabber, wheedle.** *To open and shut, as jaws,* hā'upā, 'ūpā.
jawbone. Iwi ā, papa ku'i.
jealous. Lili, nini, 'ōpū nini, manawa huā, huā, huāhuā, 'a'ahuā, lolohuā, nonohuā, kekene.
jealousy. *See* **jealous.** *Also:* 'ōpi'ipi'i. *To show jealousy and anger,* kahilili. *To burn, as with jealousy,* 'ā.
jeer. 'Aka henehene, 'a'ahuā, ho'ohenehene. *See* **taunt.** *Jeered at,* ho'omā'ewa'ewa, ho'omā'ewa, pāhenehene.
Jehovah. Iēhowa, Iehova.
Jehovah's Witnesses. Nā Hō'ike o Iēhowa.
jell. Pa'akūkū, kūpū, pa'a.
jelly. Kele; hu'ahu'a *(rare).*
jellyfish. Pololia.
jeopardy. Kūlana pilikia.
jerboa. Kepoa.
Jericho. Ieliko, Ieriko.
jerk. Huki 'ino. *Also:* 'unu, ue, uwe, kakekake, 'a'ili, kolopā, ho'ānu'unu'u, helo, hukihuki. *To jerk and

start,* kīpupū, 'āne'e, hele kūkū. *Jerked beef,* pipi kaula.
Jerusalem. Ielukalema, Ierusalema.
jest. 'Ōlelo pā'ani; lua'āpana *(rare).*
jester. Lua'āpana *(rare).*
Jesuit. Iēkuiko, Iesuito, Iesuita.
Jesus. Iesū.
jet. Kī; kokoi *(rare).* *Jet-propelled,* ho'one'e i mua ma ke kī 'ana i ka māhu.
jet-black. 'Ele hiwa.
jetsam. *See* **flotsam and jetsam.**
jetty. Uapo, uwapo, pani kai.
Jew. Kiu, Iukaio.
jewelry. Lako kula, mea ho'onani kino, ho'ohiluhilu kula.
Jewish. Iukaio.
Jew's-ear. Pepeiao akua, akua.
jew's harp. 'Ūkēkē hahau, 'ūkēkē hao, nī'au kani.
jibber jabber. Hiohio, ā, pakakē; pīpīnoke *(rare).*
jib sail. Pe'a ihu.
jiggle. Hō'oni'oni, hō'oni, 'oni'oni; ka'uwali *(rare).*
Jimson weed. Lā'au hānō, kīkānia haole.
jingle. Kanikani. *Jingle bells,* kani nā pele.
job. 'Oihana, hana.
job holder. Noho 'oihana.
Job's-tears. Pū'ohe'ohe, 'ohe'ohe, kūkaekōlea, pūpū kōlea.
jock strap. 'Eke ho'opa'a laho.
jog. 1. *Run slowly.* Peki. **2.** *Cliff ledge.* Kaulu, 'anu'u.
join. Pili, pili pū, hui, ku'i; komo *(enter, as a class).* *Also:* kāpili, kuku'i, ho'oku'i, pāna'i, pāku'i, ku'i-ka'a; kī'o'e *(as nets);* hū, na'iau.
joined. Ku'i, hui 'ia, huia, huihui, 'āpipi. *See* **join.**
joining. Pilina, hoana, hono, ku'ina. *Rare:* hoai, maku'i. *See* **join.**
joint. 1. *Anatomical.* Ku'eku'e, 'ami ho'oku'i, 'ami, ha'i; ku'ina, hua, maku'i *(general);* pona *(as of sugar-cane stalk or bamboo).* *Hinge joint,* ku'ina 'ami. *Ball-and-socket joint,* 'ami ho'oku'ina lewa. *To slip out of joint,* kapeke. **2.** *United.* Hui 'ia. *Joint report,* hō'ike ne'epapa. *Joint action,* ne'epapa ka hana, hana laulima, olowalu.
jointed. Ponapona, punapuna, paukū.
joints. Pu'upu'u, aka. *See* **joint.**
joke. 'Ōlelo pā'ani, pā'ani, mea ho'opā'ani, ho'omea, 'ōlelo ho'omāke'aka.
joker. Mea ho'omāke'aka; pepa ki'i *(in a deck of cards).*
joking. Pā'ani, ho'opā'ani.
jolly. Le'ale'a, laupa'apa'ani.
jolt. Lūlū, lū, 'oni hikiwawe.
jolting. 'Akūkū, lū, lūlū. *Sudden jolting,* 'oni hikiwawe.
jostle. Ku'iku'i, kuke, ho'okē.
jounce. Holo kūkū.
journal. Mo'olelo, mo'o'ōlelo, puke ho'omana'o.
journey. Huaka'i.
jowl. Ka'olo, 'olo.
joy. Hau'oli, 'oli, 'oli'oli, le'a, le'ale'a. *Also:* hau'oli'oli, hoihoi, waioha, ohaoha, kā'ē'ē, kā'eu'eu, ka'uka'ulele, nēnēle'a, a'a. *To give joy,* hō'oli, ho'ohau'oli. *The heart leaps for joy,* lele ka houpo i ka 'oli'oli.
joyful, joyous. Piha hau'oli.
joyweed. Palewāwae.
Juan Fernandez. Huana Pelenana, Huana Ferenana.
Juarez. Hualeke, Huarese.
jubilee. Iupilē.
Judea. Iukea, Iudea.
judge. Luna kānāwai. *(For various kinds, see Haw.-Eng.*

entry and entries that follow it.) Also: luna nānā *(as of song contests);* loio, hoʻomalu. *To judge,* hoʻokolokolo; loi *(as contests).*

judgment. ʻŌlelohoʻoholo, ʻōlelohoʻokō, ʻōlelo kūpaʻa, hoʻoholo.

judgment seat. Noho hoʻokolokolo.

judiciary. Hoʻokolokolo.

jug. ʻŌmole.

juggle. Hoʻoleilei, kīolaola.

juice. Wai; pahukaʻa *(of green gourd).*

juiceless. Maloʻohāhā, pīkaʻo.

juicy. Wai nui.

July. Iulai.

jumble. Kīpalalē, ʻōlelo kīpalalē, huikaʻi, huikau.

jump. Lele, lelele. *Also:* lēhei, lēkei, mahiki, kūlapa, ʻalakē, ʻalelele. *To jump rope,* lele koali. *To swing a rope (for jumping),* kā i ke kaula. *To jump from shock,* hikilele. *To jump for joy,* lelele me ka ʻoliʻoli, hulahē. *To jump here and there,* kīkaʻelekē.

junction. Huina, kuʻina.

juncture. Palena, huina, kuʻina, pilina. *Word juncture,* hoʻohuina ʻōlelo.

June. Iune.

jungle. Wao nahele, uluāoʻa, hihipeʻa.

junior. ʻŌpio. *Charles, junior,* Kale, ʻōpio.

juniper. Iunipela, lokema, rotema *(KJV).*

juniper roots. Nokema.

junk. ʻŌpala.

Jupiter. Iupika, Ao-hōkū, ʻIao, ʻIkaika, Ikiiki, Ka-lua-i-hai-mohai. *Names reported for both Jupiter and Venus:* Ka-ʻā-wela, Mānalo.

jurisdiction. Kuleana, mana hoʻokolokolo.

jury. Kiule, kiure. *Grand jury,* kiule nui.

just. 1. *Fair.* Pono, kūpono, kaulike, naʻau pono, ʻewa-ʻewa ʻole. **2.** *Recently.* ʻAkahi, ʻānō iho nei; ʻo . . . ia. **3.** *Quite.* Wale, wale nō, nō, aʻe nei, auaneʻi. *This is just as good as that,* like ka maikaʻi o kēlā me kēia.

justice. Kaulike. *Chief justice,* luna kānāwai kiʻekiʻe ā kaulike. *Police justice,* luna kānāwai hoʻomalu. *Associate justice,* luna kānāwai kōkua. *Obstruct the course of justice,* hoʻokāpae i ka hoʻoponopono ʻana o ke kānāwai.

justification. Kuleana, kumu.

justify. Hoʻāpono, ʻāpono, pono, kū i ka pono.

jut out. Kela, oni, ʻou, ʻoiʻoi, hōʻouʻou, ʻau, huku, hoʻohuku.

juvenile. ʻŌpio, ʻōpiopio.

K

k. Kē.

kāhili. 1. See **standard. 2.** See **ginger. 3.** See **crape myrtle.**

kāhili flower. Ha'ikū.

Ka-ho'olawe. Ka-ho'olawe; Kanaloa *(ancient name).*

kangaroo. Kanakalū, kanagaru, kanekalu, kanegaru.

Kansas. Kanekaka, Kanesasa.

Ka'ū. Ka'ū. *Epithets:* kua makani, *wind-blown back; see* **mākaha.**

Kaua'i. Kaua'i. *Epithets:* Kaua'i o Mano, Mano-kalani-pō.

kava. 'Awa *(for various kinds, see Haw.-Eng. entry and entries that follow it). Also:* kupali'i, nēnē (kua'ea), mākea (mahakea), mamaka, mo'ī, mokihana, papa, papa 'ele'ele, papa kea; paholei *(legendary). Kava plant or root portion,* pū 'awa. *Young kava plant,* 'awalau. *Kava stalk or slip,* aka. *Kava drinker,* inu 'awa. *Kava dregs,* ko'ana 'awa. *Kava cup,* 'apu 'awa, 'olo 'awa. *Kava mixing bowl,* kānoa. *Kava strainer,* hoka 'awa. *Brews of kava,* hope, kua. *Strong kava brew,* kua'i'o. *The bird that carries Puna kava slips (PH 30),* ka manu 'āha'i lau 'awa o Puna *(Puna was famous for kava believed planted by birds in trees). Copious drinking of kava is said to have induced sleep—never boisterousness.*

keel. Iwi ka'ele. *Also:* iwi kele, kua'e, mānea, kuamo'o.

keep. Mālama, pa'a. *See ex.,* **bless.** *To keep away,* ho'omamamao, ho'ē'ē, ho'okā'oko'a. *To keep on doing,* ho'omau, 'oia, noke, kakano. *To keep the Sabbath,* mālama Lā Kāpaki. *To keep sorcery bundles,* mālama pū'olo. *Keep out,* kapu. *Keep still,* kulikuli, noho leo 'ole *(silent);* noho mālie *(don't move).*

keeper. Kahu, mālama *(for various kinds, see* **kahu,** **mālama** *and following entries).*

keepsake. Mea ho'omana'o. *Also:* pa'aloha, pa'a aloha, pukana, pukana aloha, paumauno'ono'o.

keg. Pahu, pahu po'o li'ili'i, palela li'ili'i.

Kensington. Kenikikona, Kenisitona.

Kent. Keneke, Kenete.

Kentucky. Kenekuke, Kenetuke.

Keokuk. Keokuka.

kept. Mālama 'ia, pa'a.

kernel. 'Ano'ano.

kerosene. 'Ailahonua, 'aila māhu.

kettle. Ipu hao, kikila.

key. Kī *(latch or music);* ha'iloa'a *(to a problem);* ku'ina *(fig.). Wooden key,* kī lā'au. *Key to animate a toy,* kī 'oni.

keynote. Kī alaka'i, puana 1.

Key West. Kī-komohana.

khaki. Kākī.

kick. Peku, pekuna, kūpaka; kolopā *(in tantrums). To kick and flail, as the arms,* kākā.

kid. Kao keiki.

kidnap. 'Aihue kanaka. *See also,* **abduct.**

kidnapper. 'Aihue kanaka.

kidneys. Pu'upa'a, kōnahua. *Diseases of kidneys,* ma'i pu'upa'a, kīkala hāne'ene'e, 'alaneo, waiiki.

kill. Pepehi ā make, ho'omake, make, hana make. *To kill a pig ceremonially,* hulahula.

killed. Make.

kilo. Kilo.

kilometer. Kilomekele.

kin. 'Ohana, pili koko, pilikana, kini, 'ewe, ēweewe, 'i'o 'alaea. *See* **welewele iwi,** **relative.** *To speak ill of kin,* holehole iwi.

kind. 1. Sort. 'Ano; kaina, hulu *(rare). That kind of person,* kēlā 'ano kanaka. **2.** *Not cruel.* 'Olu'olu, 'olu, lokomaika'i, aloha, na'au ali'i, akeake, hulu, kolokolohai.

kindergarten. Kula kamali'i.

kindle. Hō'a'ā, kuni.

kindling. Pulu, pulupulu, pulupulu ahi, pula, mea hō-'a'ā ahi; la'ola'o *(rare).*

kindness. See **kind.** *See saying,* 'ena 2. *Treat with kindness,* aulike, aloha aku, ho'olako.

king. Mō'ī, ali'i kāne, kini.

kingdom. Aupuni mō'ī.

kingly. Ali'i, ho'āli'i.

Kings. Nā Ali'i *(Biblical).*

Kingston. Kinikaona, Kinitaona.

kink. Miko, wahi hihia.

kinky. Pi'ipi'i Pukikī, mimilo, 'āpi'ipi'i.

kinship. Pilina 'ohana. See **relative.**

Kirtland. Kekalana, Ketalana.

kiss. Honi. *Also:* kiki, ihu, hō mai i ka ihu. *See ex.,* **mau 2, ma'ū 1** (mau *and* ma'ū *plus* ihu *are both possible, but with different translations). To kiss repeatedly,* honihoni. *To cause or pretend to kiss,* ho'ohoni.

kitchen. Lumi kuke.

kite. Lupe. *Also:* pe'a, hānai. *See saying,* **flutter.** *Kite parts:* manu, po'ohiwi; kakaiāpola, pola, puapua *(tail). String of a kite,* aho. *To fly a kite,* ho'olele lupe. *To fly steadily, as a kite,* ho'okauaheahe. *A god who sometimes assumed the shape of a kite,* Lōlupe, Ololupe.

kite bird. Koleneka, konelika.

kitty. Pōpoki keiki, kike.

Kiwanis. Kiwani.

Klamath. Keamolewa. See **salmon.**

Kleenex. Pepa ho'okē.

kleptomania, kleptomaniac. Kuko 'aihue.

knapsack. 'Eke lawe ukana, 'awe.

knead. Kūpele, kūpelepele, ho'opele, lomi, pele, poho, ho'opoho, 'ōpā, ka'awili.

knee. Kuli. *To bend the knees, to drop to one's knees,* ku'u kuli.

kneecap. Iwi po'i, kuapo'i.

knee drum. Pūniu, kilu.

kneel. Kukuli.

kneepan. See **kneecap.**

knickknack. Kēlā mea kēia mea 'u'uku.

knife. Pahi *(for various kinds, see Haw.-Eng. entry and entries that follow it);* niho 'oki, lōkea, pālau, kenikeni. *See* **drawknife.** *Knife blade,* kila.

knight. Naika.

knit. Kā, ulana.

knitting needle. Kui ulana.

knob. Pōheo, pōheoheo, heo, heoheo, pu'u, 'āpua.

knock. Kīkēkē. *To knock down,* kula'i, kāhina, kāpe'a. *To knock around,* pā'ulu'ā.

knoll. 'Ōhū, āhua, 'ōhuku.

knot. 1. Tied. Hīpu'u, hīpu'upu'u, kīpu'u, nīpu'u; *fancy —,* pu'u; *— in a fish net,* a'a pu'upu'u. *See* **slipknot, topknot.** *To knot the meshes of a net,* hi'a. **2.** *In a tree.* Kīnā o ka lā'au. **3.** *In flesh.* Lā'au. **4.** *Nautical.* Mile loa.

knothole. Pu'upu'u lā'au. *Full of knotholes,* 'ālualua.

knotty. Nīpu'upu'u, hīpu'upu'u, kalakala, 'uluhaku.

knotweed. Kāmole.

know. 'Ike; mā'ike *(rare). To know well, thoroughly,* walewaha, makaukau, ma'a, lewa, hani. *To know by sight,* kū'ike. *To know definitely,* 'ike pono. *To know sexually,* 'ike; pākanaka *(know a male sexually). Not to know well,* 'ike hemahema, 'ike pāhemahema. *I don't know,* 'a'ole au i 'ike; pehea lā; pehea ho'i. *Be still and* *know that I am God (Hal. 46.10),* e noho mālie, a'e 'ike ho'i ē, 'o wau nō ke Akua.

knowing. 'Ikena, ma'a.

knowledge. 'Ike, na'auao, 'ikena; la'a kea *(rare). See sayings,* **kāpala 1, cloud.** *Deep knowledge,* 'ike kūhohonu. *Unsurpassed knowledge,* palena 'ole ka 'ike. *Common knowledge,* 'ike laulaha. *Seeker of knowledge,* 'imi 'ike, 'imi na'auao, 'imi loa, akeakamai. *Limited knowledge,* 'ike hapa, hi'u kahi. *One without knowledge,* he mea kahua 'ole. *One with wide knowledge,* he 'umeke kā'eo *(fig). With knowledge!* I ka 'ike *(said in scorn of pretense to knowledge)!*

known. 'Ike 'ia; laulaha, laulā *(widely). To make known,* hō'ike, ho'olaha; ku'u 'ōlelo *(rare).*

knuckle. Ku'eku'e, 'ōku'eku'e, pu'upu'u, pu'u, 'ōpu'upu'u, aka. *Pig's knuckles,* 'ōku'eku'e o ka pua'a.

Kodak. Pahupa'iki'i.

Kohala. Kohala. *Epithets: Kohala, cherished land,* Kohala, 'āina ha'aheo. *See* **hakahaka, lē'ī.**

Kona. Kona. *See* **'ōpua, pūnoni, peace, sea,** *and saying,* **forecast.** *Greetings, Kona, my land in the calm (PH 69),* aloha, Kona, ku'u 'āina i ka pohu.

kōnane. *See* **checkers.**

kor. Kola.

Korea, Korean. Kōlea, Korea.

kukui. *See* **candlenut.**

Kyoto. Kioko, Kioto.

L

l. Lā.

la. Lā.

labia. Kapa, lehelehe. *Division between labia,* miona.

labial. Hui puana 'ia me nā lehelehe.

labia minor. Lepelepe.

labor. Hana, limahana, lawehana, luhi, pa'aua, 'a'aka, pa'u. *See* **labor pains.** *Hard labor,* hana 'o'ole'a.

laboratory. Ke'ena hana, ke'ena 'imi na'auao.

labor board. Papa limahana, papa luna 'oihana.

labor commission. Komisina o nā limahana.

Labor Day. Lānui o nā Limahana.

laborer. Limahana, lawehana, pa'a hana. *Fellow laborer,* hoa lawehana.

laboring. Luhina.

laborious. Pa'ahana, luhi, pa'u.

labor pains. Nahu kuakoko, nahunahu, hō'i'ī, kōhi. *Medicine for women in labor,* hau'oki.

labroid fishes. Laenihi.

lace. 1. *Needlework.* Lihilihi, lihilihi hana lima. *Lace edging,* lihilihi mōlina. *Maltese or hairpin lace,* lihilihi kui lauoho. *Scallops in lace,* pepeiao. 2. *Cord.* Lī. *Shoelace,* lī kāma'a. *Corset lace,* lī kāliki.

lace fern. *See* **fern.**

laceration. Moku, pohole; māī *(rare).*

lacing. Kaula kāliki, kaula lī, kōkō.

lacking. Nele, 'ole, hemahema.

lactation. Kau ka waiū, hānai waiū. *Goddess of lactation,* Nu'a-kea.

lad. Keiki, keiki kāne.

ladder. Alapi'i, alahaka, haka; haka 'ūlili, hūlili *(as a rope ladder).* *Rare:* alahaki, 'oloke'a, ke'ahakahaka.

laden. Kaumaha lua, ho'okaumaha, lulu'u, lehua, mākolu, ho'olu'ulu'u.

ladle. Kī'o'e, kī'apu.

lady. Wahine, haku wahine; leke *(title of nobility);* old —, luahine, 'elehine; — *in waiting,* leke ukali.

ladyfish. *Same as* **bonefish.**

lag. Ho'olohi, hō'apa'apa, ho'ēmiemi, emiemi, 'olo'olo, hākālia, ho'ohākālia, manukā, lemu, ka'unē, kuoni. *Lag behind,* hā'ule hope.

lagoon. Kai kohola, loko kai, kua'au.

Lahaina. Lahaina. *Ancient names:* Lele, Lā-hainā. *Epithet: breadfruit-sheltered land of Lele, ever-burning torch not darkened by the Ka-ua-'ula gales,* ka malu 'ulu a'o Lele, kukui 'a'ā mau pio 'ole i ke Ka-ua-'ula.

laid. Ho'omoe 'ia, ho'owaiho 'ia; manono *(rare).* *See* **lay.**

lake. Loko. *Also:* loko wai, loko pa'akai, moana, moana wai, moana pa'akai.

Lake Erie. Moana Wai 'Elie.

Lake Huron. Moana Wai Hulona.

Lake Michigan. Moana Wai Mikikana.

Lake Ontario. Moana Wai 'Onekalio.

Lake Superior. Moana Wai Nui.

lamb. Keiki hipa, hipa keiki, pua hipa.

lambaste. Hahau ikaika, ko'okā. *See* **hit.**

lambdoidal suture. Hoai kala.

Lambeth. Lamapeka, Lamabeta.

lame. 'O'opa, kī'opa, mā'ulu'ulu. *Rare:* mauā, ponanā, po'ana, maika, lolehau. *See* **limp.**

lament. Uē, uwē, uē helu, kanikau, makena, kūmākena, kūpina'i.

lamentation. Uē, uwē, uē helu, kanikau, makena, paumākō, ho'opaumākō, 'aoa, 'ao'aoa, pihe, kūkapihe, pa'iāuma, 'uhane.

lamp. Kukui, ipukukui. *Also:* kukui pōhaku, pohokano, poho kukui, lama, makou, kumuipukukui. *Lamp*

chimney, 'omo ipukukui. *Lamp shade,* pālulu kukui. *Lampstand,* kaukukui, waihona kukui.

Lā-na'i. Lā-na'i, Nāna'i.

Lancaster. Lanakeka, Lanaseta.

lance. 1. *Spear.* Ihe pakelo. 2. *Surgical instrument.* Ā, ā 'ō'ō, koholua.

land. 1. *Ground.* 'Āina, honua; one *(poetic);* puluwai *(rare).* *See* **legendary place.** *Native land,* 'āina hānau, kulāiwi, one hānau. *Land one has lived on for a long time,* 'āpa'a. *Once uncultivated land, fallow land,* mahakea. *Foreign land,* 'āina haole, kahiki. *Land rights,* konohiki. *Fee simple land,* 'āina kū'ai, 'alolio, alodio. *Land anciently exempt from rent and taxes,* 'āina kūpono. *Land inheritance,* ili 'āina. *Land grant,* hā'awi 'āina. *Crown lands,* 'āina lei ali'i. *Land boundary,* palena 'āina. *To establish or to act as land,* ho'ohonua. *Place where land and sea meet,* 'ae kai. *Altar marking land division,* ahupua'a, ka'ānani'au. *Ancient land units, in approximate order of size:* moku, kalana, ahupua'a, 'ili, 'ili pa'a, 'ili kūpono, 'ili lele, lele, mo'o, mo'o 'āina, paukū, kīhāpai, kō'ele, kuleana; *also:* 'okana, 'āpana, ahunāli'i, hakuone, kuakua, nana'e. *Land areas,* wao *(see Haw.-Eng. entries and entries that follow it),* 'ilima, kalulu, kualono, kula, palahe'ī, poko. 2. *Debark.* Pae, lele, hō'ili, ho'oili.

land commissioner. Komikina ho'onā 'āina.

land ho! Lanahō!

landholder. Pa'a 'āina, mea kuleana.

landing. Paena, pāhonua. *Canoe landing,* paena wa'a. *Wave landing,* paena nalu.

landlady. Haku hale wahine.

landless. 'Āina 'ole.

landlord. Haku 'āina, haku hale.

landmark. Hō'ailona 'āina. *Landmark for fishing grounds,* hō'ailona ko'a, māka ko'a.

landowner. Haku 'āina, mea 'āina.

landscape. Hi'ohi'ona 'āina, waihona 'āina, ka moena 'ana o ka 'āina. *Landscape gardener,* mea ho'oulu ho'onani. *To landscape a garden,* ho'onani kīhāpai.

land shell. Pūpū kuahiwi *(for various kinds, see Haw.-Eng. entry and entries that follow it).* *Also:* hinihini, hinihini konouli, hinihini kua mauna, kāhuli, naka, naka kāni'o, naka kua mauna, pololei *(see saying),* pūpū kani oe. *Listen to the voice of the land shell* (UL 120), ho'olono aku i ka leo o ke kāhuli.

landslide. Hāne'e ka mauna, hehe'e, hiolo, holo, 'aholo.

land title. Kumu kuleana 'āina, palapala kumu kuleana 'āina.

lane. Ala ololī.

language. 'Ōlelo. *Also:* alelo, elelo, lehelehe *(rare).* *Foreign language,* 'ōlelo o nā 'āina 'ē, 'ōlelo 'ē. *European language, especially English,* 'ōlelo haole. *Pidgin,* 'ōlelo pa'i 'ai. *Threatening language,* ho'onuinui. *Rough in language,* kalakala. *Play languages,* 'ōkoleke, 'ōlelo kūkae manu, nehiwa. *Secret language,* 'ōlelo huna, memene.

languid. Lohi'au, 'ūpalu, 'ūpalupalu. *Also:* kolohia, nipo.

languish. Ka'ahea.

lantana. Lākana, lā'au kalakala, mikinolia hohono, mikinolia kukū; lanakana *(Ni'ihau).*

lantern. Ipukukui hele pō, kukui hele pō, lamakū.

lap. 1. *Anatomy.* 'Ūhā. 2. *Lick.* Mē, palu, paluhia. 3. *Overlap.* Ho'opapa.

Lapland. Lapelana.

lapwing. Upupā.

larceny. 'Aihue.

lard. 'Aila pua'a.

large. Nui, nunui. *Also:* hālau, hālala, pūhalalū, halakau, nuka, nu'anu'a, kāhā, 'a'alina, 'a'alakai, aka-'ika'i, polohuku, mākō, ho'omākōmakō, polo, mākōmakō. *Too large,* kūpalaka, poholopū, wahalehe, uhalehe. *Impressively large,* ka'apeha. *To go at large,* hele laulā.

larger. Nui loa, kā'eu'eu, ko'o, nui a'e, 'oi aku ka nui.

lariat. Kaula 'ili.

lark. Laka.

larvae. Naio. *Dragonfly larvae,* 'ōlopelope, pua'alohelohe, lohelohe, lohaloha.

larynx. Kani'a'ī, pu'u, ana.

lascar. Lākā.

lascivious. Kuko hewa, maka leho, kuko 'ino. *See* **pig.**

lash. **1.** *Whip.* Kaula, hahau, hilikua, kōkā, kaulī. *To lash, as a storm, wind,* pāhili. **2.** *Tie.* Hāwele, ho'olanalana, hauhana, hauhoa, hauhō, lu'ukia, hele.

lashing. Aho, aho kā, lu'ukia. *Types of house lashings:* kauhihi, aho pueo, aho 'ōwili, ki'ihei, kauhilo. *Types of canoe lashings:* kāholo, kumuhele, lanalana, kumupou, pā'ū-o-Lu'ukia. *Adze lashing,* hauhana. *Net lashing,* hāwele.

lass. Kaikamahine.

lasso. Ho'ohei, kaula ho'ohei, kaula 'ili, kīpuka, kīpuka 'ili, kaupuka.

last. **1.** *Most recent.* Hope, muli, nei, aku nei. *Very last,* hope loa, muli hope. *Last night,* i ka pō nei. *Last week,* kēlā pule aku nei. *Last-born,* hānau hope. **2.** *Continue.* Kāmau, ho'omau, mau, kūlō'ihi. **3.** *Conclusion.* Hopena, panina, kīkīpani.

latch. Kī. *Wooden latch,* kī lā'au. *Latch on sewing machine,* kī'ū.

late. Lohi, hope, mahope, kūli'u. *Late at night,* aumoe. *Late sleeper,* moe awakea. *The late Nā-'ehu,* Nā-'ehu i make aku nei.

lately. Nei, 'ānō iho nei, 'ānō wale iho nei nō.

later. Mahope aku. *A little later,* ā 'oi. *A little later than two o'clock,* hola 'elua ā 'oi. *Later today,* kēia lā aku. *I'll come later,* mahope aku au.

lathe. Ka'awili lā'au, kila 'o'oma.

lather. Hu'ahu'a kopa *(soap).*

Latin. Lākina.

latitude. Lakikū, latitu.

latrine. Ki'ona *(Biblical). See* **toilet.**

latter. Kēia, hope a'e, hope iho.

Latter-Day Saints. Po'e Ho'āno o nā Lā Hope Nei.

lattice. 'Ōlepelepe, papaholo, lākike.

laud. *See* **praise.**

laugh. 'Aka, 'aka'aka, hō'aka, hō'aka'aka. *Rare:* kani-'ahē, ehehene, lua'āpana. *Laugh-provoking,* ho'omāke'aka, laupa'apa'ani. *To laugh at,* henehene, ho'ohenehene, pāhenehene, ho'omā'auea.

laughter. 'Aka, hō'aka, 'aka'aka. *Burst of laughter,* hehē, hā loa. *Provoke laughter,* hō'aka, hō'aka'aka, ho'omāke'aka.

launch. **1.** *Vessel.* Wa'apā. **2.** *Set afloat.* Ho'olana; ho'okumu i ka hana *(fig.).*

laundry. Lole lepo, lole holoi, mea holoi, lole pia, lole wai, hale holoi lole. *Laundry room,* lumi holoi.

laurel tree. Hōlio.

lava. 'Ā, 'a'ā, 'ā pele *(rough lava);* pāhoehoe *(smooth). Also:* lua'i pele, 'ōahi, 'alā *(hard). Lava flow,* 'ā pele, pele; wa'a *(rare). Lava cave,* 'a'a'ā. *Open place (often with vegetation) surrounded by lava,* kīpuka, kīpohopoho.

lavender. Kai 'ina. *See* **purple.**

lavish. Nui loa, 'a'ole laua a'e, hīhīmanu.

law. Kānāwai *(for various kinds, see Haw.-Eng. entry and entries that follow it). Code of law,* kumukānāwai. *Lawmaking body,* 'aha'ōlelo kau kānāwai. *Law of the splintered paddle,* Māmala-hoe, Māmala hoa. *Other ancient laws:* 'aumoana, kai'okia, kolowalu. *To impose a law,* ho'okānāwai. *To enforce a law,* ho'okō

kānāwai. *To obey a law,* mālama kānāwai, ho'olohe kānāwai. *To violate a law,* a'e (a'e kū) kānāwai, pale kauoha, uhaki kānāwai.

law-abiding. Mālama kānāwai, make'e kānāwai.

law enforcement. Ho'okō kānāwai.

lawful. Kū i ke kānāwai.

lawless. Ho'olohe 'ole i ke kānāwai, 'a'e kānāwai, hehi kānāwai, kānāwai 'ole, mau'a'e'a'e.

lawmaker. Mea kau kānāwai.

lawn. **1.** *Grass.* Pā mau'u. *Lawn mower,* mīkini 'oki mau'u. *Lawn sprinkler,* wiliwiliwai. **2.** *Linen.* Wikolia.

lawsuit. Ho'opi'i, hihia.

lawyer. Loio; kokua *(old term).*

lax. Ho'omalule; —, *as in work,* palaka, palaleha.

laxative. Lā'au ho'onahā. *See* **purgative.** *Kinds:* kukui *(nuts and flowers),* koali *(leaves and flowers),* pua aloalo, pua 'ilima, kanakamakika'i ('ilima *flower used medicinally),* wale hau.

lay. Waiho, moe, ho'omoe; — *aside,* kāpae, ho'oili; — *before,* hau, uhau, hahau; — *away,* ho'āhu; — *waste,* luku, *also:* 'ānai, kohikū, kohikūhū, ho'oneo, ho'oneoneo; — *out,* kuene; ho'olālā *(as land areas);* kīpapa *(as stones). Rare:* uhauhumu, 'opo, hau'opo. *Lay of the land,* waihona 'āina, waiho 'ana o ka 'āina. *See* **laid.** *To lay eggs,* hānau i ka hua, hā'ule hua, ho'olu'a hua, huahua. *To lay bricks,* ho'omoe uwinihapa. *To lay an oven,* kūkulu imu.

layer. Papa. *Put in layers,* ho'opapa.

layering. Kākiwi.

layman. Laimana.

lazy. Moloā. *Also:* molowā; palaualelo *(and verbose);* kālē, palauha, heha, maheha, 'oheha, palaheha, malauea, ma'auea, melamela, malela, ma'uwele, lena, pualena, kapoulena, uhalena, uhalula, ualeha, ōpūhea, ōpūheha, palela, lola, laholena, kūhana 'ole, kualana, loma, kaialile, kamaki'i, ahio; 'ō'ū *(fig.);* keoma, keopu, kūmaua, ma'oeā, lē, leha, nopa, uha'ula, kalana'e. *See* **Kauhikoa, loma, idle, indolent,** *and sayings,* **kī'ililī 1, lōlō, piwa lenalena.** *Lazy weather,* 'ōheahea ho'i kēia lā.

lazybones. Lola moe hālau.

lead. **1.** *Mineral.* Kēpau, kēpau pōkā. **2.** *Guide.* Alaka'i, ka'i, ka'ika'i. *To lead against the will or without permission,* ka'ika'ikū. *Lead astray,* ho'ohala, ho'ohili, ho'olalau, ho'owalewale.

leader. Alaka'i, mua, ali'i, luna; kukui *(fig.). See sayings,* **ko'oko'o 1,** *guide.* *Battle leader,* ali'i kaua, 'alihikaua, 'oumuamua. *Acting leader,* hope po'o. *Leader of fifty men,* luna kanalima. *Song leader,* alaka'i mele, alaka'i hīmeni. *Hula leader,* alaka'i hula. *Bandleader,* alaka'i pāna.

leadership. Alaka'ina.

leading. Ka'ika'ina.

leaf. Lau; lā- *(in contractions, as* lā'alo *[taro leaf];* lā'ī *[ti leaf];* lā'ie ['ie'ie, 'ie *leaf];* lā'ō *[sugar-cane leaf]). Also:* 'ao, loho, oho, 'ao kahi. *See* **pandanus.** *Leaf turning red,* mākole lau *(rare). Leaf fading or withering,* lau pala, lau palakāhela, lā'ele. *Small-leafed,* lau li'i *(qualifier of some plants, as* maile, 'ohe). *Large-leafed,* lau nui. *Long-leafed,* lau loa. *Thin-leafed,* lau lahilahi. *Divided or incised leaf,* lau manamana. *Parts of leaves:* 'auwiniwini, kihi, piko, pe'a; po'o *(butt); see* **midrib, tip.** *Leaves strung at end of seines,* 'aulau. *Having many leaves but little fruit,* pālahalaha lau. *Young loulu palm leaf,* pa'aoloulu. *Young fern leaves,* pepe'e. *To leaf out,* ho'alau, ho'alau, oho, 'ōmaka; kēlau *(rare). Leafless,* ananea.

leafhopper. 'Ūmi'ikō.

league. **1.** *Union.* Hui, ku'ikahi. **2.** *Measure of distance.* Lekue.

League of Nations. Nā Aupuni Hui 'Ia.

leak. Kulu, kulukulu, liu, nō, kūlono, kūnono.

leaky. Kulukulu, kūlono, kūnono.

lean. **1.** *Thin.* Wīwī. *Also:* 'ōlala, 'ā'aua, 'aua, 'amopu'u. *See* **thin.** **2.** *Not greasy.* Pākā, pāka'a, kōkaʻa. *Lean beef,* ʻiʻo pipi momona ʻole, ʻiʻo pākā, ʻiʻo pākaʻa. **3.** *Incline.* Hiō, hiōhiō, pahiō, kahiō; — *back,* hoʻokīkiʻi, hikikiʻi, kīkū, nanai, hoʻokoʻokoʻo; — *on,* kaukoʻo, kālele, hilinaʻi; — *against,* paulele; — *over,* hoʻohina, hoʻohilala; ou *(rare).* *Also:* hilala, kīkepa, kīpou.

leaning. Hiō, hiona, pahiō.

lean-to. Pupupu hale, hale kāpiʻo, pūʻoʻa.

leap. Lele; — *at,* kiki, ulele; — *away,* līʻō; — *suddenly,* lele koke; — *into water,* ʻiamo, lele ʻōʻō, lele kawa; *take a flying —,* lele kīkoʻo; — *on a spear,* kūpololū. *Also:* leina, lei, mahiki, lelekē, huhuhulei, lahaina, ʻanapau, ʻoehu, oho.

leap year. Makahiki lele, makahiki lā keu.

leap year's day. Lā kaulele.

leaping. Lele kawa, lele pahu.

leaping place of spirits. Leina-a-ka-ʻuhane, Leina-a-keakua.

learn. Aʻo *(for various subjects, see Haw.-Eng. entry and entries that follow it);* hoʻopaʻa, ʻimi naʻauao. *To learn quickly,* ʻaʻapo. *To learn slowly,* aʻo pupū.

learned. Naʻauao, paʻa. *See saying,* **waihona.** *Learned persons,* poʻe ʻimi naʻauao, ipu o ka ʻike. *One learned in songs,* paʻa mele.

learning. Aʻo, naʻauao, palapala, ʻike. *Learning very fast,* hikiwawe ka ʻike. *Source of learning,* kumu aʻo. *Depository of learning,* ka waihona o ka naʻauao *(of a learned person).*

lease. Hoʻolimalima, palapala hoʻolimalima. *Conditional lease,* hoʻolimalima ma ke ʻano ʻalolio. *Perpetual lease,* hoʻolimalima manawa pau ʻole.

leash. Kaula paʻa lima.

leather. ʻIli, ʻili holoholona, lapaʻau ʻia, ʻili pipi. *Thick leather,* ʻili mānoanoa. *Thin leather,* ʻili lahilahi.

leathery. Uaua, māuaua.

leave. Hoʻi, haʻalele, waiho. *Also:* hohoʻi, hohohoʻi, hoʻia, mauhaʻalele, hoʻowaiho. *To leave home, as young people,* manu heu *(fig.).*

leaven. Hū, hoʻohū.

leaves. *See* **leaf.**

Lebanon. Lepanona, Lebanona.

lecherous. Kuko ʻino, kuko hewa, piha kuko, puaʻa laho, kola; lauahi *(fig.).* *See* **pig.**

lecture. Haʻiʻōlelo, haʻi aʻo.

ledge. Kaulu, kaunu, kaulu ʻanuʻu, ʻanuʻu, kaola, lihi kaola, niao, holopapa.

ledger line. ʻOwā pōkole.

lee. Lulu. *Lee side of the island,* ʻaoʻao Kona o ka moku, lalo.

leech. Mākoko, omo koko.

leek. Leka.

leer. Nānā ma ke ʻano kuko hewa; makakuʻikuʻi, makaleho.

leeward. Lalo, alo, Kona 1. *See* **lee.** *Sail to leeward,* kaʻalalo.

left. **1.** *Sinister.* Hema; kāohilani *(poetic).* *Left, face,* ma ka hema, huli. **2.** *Remain.* Koe. *Left over,* koe. *Leftovers,* koena. *There is no room left in this box,* ʻaʻohe wahi kaʻawale o kēia pahu. **3.** *Departed.* Haʻalele.

leg. Wāwae; kūʻauwāwae *(rare).* *See* **drumstick.** *Leg of ham,* ʻūhā hame. *Leg of mutton,* ʻūhā hipa. *Leg-of-mutton sleeve,* lima ʻūhā hipa. *Lobster leg,* waʻawaʻa. *Upper leg of crab,* wāwae; hē *(rare).*

legacy. Hoʻoilina, hoʻīlina.

legal. Kū i ke kānāwai, pono i ke kānāwai, kau kānāwai, kānāwai. *Legal notice,* ma ke kauoha. *Legal profession,* papa loio. *Legally adopted child,* keiki hānai hoʻohiki.

legality. Pono i ke kānāwai.

legalize. Hoʻolilo i mea pono ma ke kānāwai.

legatee. Noho hale *(for a house).*

legend. Moʻolelo, kaʻao. *Also:* moʻoʻōlelo, moʻo, moʻo kaʻao. *Legend concerning the gods,* moʻo akua.

legendary beings. Poʻe o nā moʻolelo. *Legendary beings include* akua *(gods);* kupua *(demigods);* ʻaumākua

(family gods); akua lapu *(ghosts);* poʻe ʻeʻepa *(mysterious beings);* moʻo, kiha *(water lizards);* koa *(warriors).* *See HM.* *No concepts were comparable to European fairy, brownie, elf; supernatural beings looked like people. Some little people:* Menehune, Melehune, Mū, Nāmū, Mū-ʻai-maiʻa, Nāwā, Nāwao, peke. *Other beings:* ʻaʻāhualiʻi, ʻaʻaia, ʻaʻai anuhea a Kāne, ʻalaneo, ʻEleʻū, Hā-loa, Hānai-a-ka-malama, Hiʻiaka, Hilo, Hina-ʻai-ka-malama, Holu, Hoʻohoku-i-ka-lani, Hōpoe, Kahaʻula, Kahinaliʻi, Kaioʻe, Kama-puaʻa, Kanaloa, Kāne, Kāne-paʻina, Kiha, Kiha-wahine, kīwaʻa, Kū, Kuamū, Kuʻi-a-lua, Kulukuluʻā, Laʻalūʻau, Laenihi, Laka, lale, Lani-kāula, Lima-loa, Lohiʻau, Lono-pūhā, Mālei, Maliʻo, Māui, Mauli-ola, Mokuhāliʻi, Nuʻa-kea, Pele, poki, Poli-ʻahu, Pua, Wākea.

legendary place. Wahi pana. *Legendary places:* ʻāpapa lani, Haka-lau-ʻai, Hōlani-kū, Kahiki-kū, Kahiki-moe, Kāne-hūnā-moku (Ulu-koa), Ka-paʻa-heo, Kuai-helani, Kuakahi, Kuakeahu, Kūkulu-o-Kahiki, Kū-lanihākoʻi, Lani-keha, Melemele, Milu, One-lau-ʻena, ʻOpikana, ʻOpikanalani, ʻOpikananuʻu, Pali-uli, Pihana-ka-lani.

legendary trees. Lāʻau o nā moʻolelo. *Names of legendary trees:* kālai-pāhoa, koa mākua ʻole, mākālei.

leggings. Likini wāwae.

Leghorn. Lekahone, Legahone *(city and chicken).*

legion. Lekeona, lehulehu.

legislate, legislation. Kau kānāwai.

legislator. Lālā o ka ʻahaʻōlelo, kau kānāwai.

legislature. ʻAhaʻōlelo, ʻahaʻōlelo kau kānāwai, ʻaha kau kānāwai. *Session of the legislature,* ʻaha kau kānāwai, kau ʻahaʻōlelo.

legitimate. Kū i ke kānāwai.

lehua. **1.** *Flower of Hawaiʻi.* Lehua. *Scarlet lehua, twisted by fire (UL 88),* lehua ʻula, i wili ʻia e ke ahi. *Great Kauaʻi, island of lehua (FS 75),* ʻO Kauaʻi nui moku lehua *(warriors).* **2.** *(Cap.) Island west of Niʻihau.* Lehua. *Epithet:* sun-snatching island, moku kāʻili lā *(the west).*

lei. Lei *(for various kinds, see Haw.-Eng. entry and entries that follow it).* *See saying,* **puʻupuʻu 1.** *Feather lei,* lei hulu. *Any lei for the neck,* lei, lei ʻāʻī. *Head lei,* lei poʻo. *Flat lei,* lei pāpale. *Flat lei, as for a hat,* lei papa. *Shell lei,* lei pūpū. *"Puka shell" lei,* lei pūpū puka. *To wear a lei,* lei, leilei, lei pāpahi. *Decked with leis,* ʻohuʻohu. *Lei seller, to sell leis,* kau lei. *Spirals of several colors in composite leis,* ʻoni, wili. *To string a lei,* kui lei. *To braid a lei,* haku lei. *To make a lei with sections of different colors,* paukū. *To slip flowers from stringing needle to string,* kāheʻe. *Method of making a hat lei,* kuipapa. *Old (but not ancient) leis of the islands:* ʻilima *(Oʻahu);* kukui *(Molokaʻi);* lokelani *(Maui);* kaunaʻoa *(Lā-naʻi);* hinahina *(heliotrope or its substitute, Florida moss, Ka-hoʻolawe);* lehua *(Hawaiʻi);* mokihana *(Kauaʻi);* pūpū *(Niʻihau).* For songs about lei see Elbert and Mahoe.

lei day. Lā o ka lei.

Leipzig. Lipekika, Lipesiga.

leisure. Manawa nanea, manawa walea, wā kaʻawale. *At leisure,* luana, walea, nanea.

lemma. Manaʻokōkua.

lemon. Lemi, kukane, lemiwai, laniwai, lemona.

lemonade. Wai lemi.

lemon verbena. Wāpine.

lend. *No exact equivalent:* hāʻawi no ka manawa.

length. Lōʻihi, loa, loloa, lololoa, lau loa. *Of varying length,* kīlepa.

lengthen. Hoʻolōʻihi, hoʻololoa, hoʻohuelo. *To lengthen by grafting or splicing,* pānaʻi. *To lengthen a sound,* hoʻokō i ka leo, ʻume. *To lengthen, as a speech or story,* hoʻolōʻihi; hilohilo *(rare).*

lengthwise. Lau loa.

lenient. Hoʻokuʻukuʻu. *See* **easygoing.**

Lent. Kalema, Karema.

lentils. Lenekila, pī, pāpapa.

Leo. Hōkū-pā *(constellation).*
leopard. Leopaki.
leper. Lēpela.
leprosy. Maʻi lēpela, lēpela, maʻi Pākē, maʻi aliʻi, maʻi hoʻokaʻawale.
leprous. Lēpela.
less. Hapa iki, hapa ʻuʻuku, hapa ʻuku, emi iho, hapa. *To grow less,* kualiliʻi, kualiʻiliʻi.
lessee. Mea hoʻolimalima.
lessen. Hoʻēmi, hoʻohapa, hoʻoiki, hoʻoliʻiliʻi, hoʻo-ʻuʻuku. *Also:* kāhaʻu, kāmuku, kualiliʻi, kualiʻiliʻi, kanahaʻi, hoʻokanahaʻi, māhani, pānie.
lessened. Akakuʻu, emi mai.
lesson. Haʻawina. *Review lesson,* haʻawina hoʻi hope.
lessor. Mea hoʻolimalima aku.
lest. O.
let. ʻAe, hoʻokuʻu, e. *To let down,* kuʻukuʻu, kuʻuna, hoʻoluʻe. *To let go,* kala, kuʻu, hoʻokuʻu, leikō. *To let in,* hoʻokomo. *Let's go,* e hele kākou; ikū, inā *(rare). Let me see,* ʻoia ana, ʻoliana, aliana, inane. *Let me in,* hoʻokuʻu iaʻu e komo aku; ʻae mai iaʻu e komo.
letter. **1.** *Missive.* Leka, palapala, ʻelele waha ʻole. *Registered letter,* leka i hoʻopaʻa ʻia. **2.** *Character.* Hua palapala, hua; hua nui *(capital);* hua iki, hua liʻi *(small). Names of the letters of the Hawaiian alphabet:* ʻā, ʻē, ʻī, ʻō, ʻū, hē, kē, lā, mū, nū, pī, wē; ʻokina *(glottal stop).*
letter-perfect. Walewaha.
lettuce. Lekuke; kāpiki-ʻai-maka *(rare).*
let wind. *See* **break wind.**
leucorrhea. Wai keʻokeʻo, waiʻōpua.
levee. Pale kai, pani kai, pani wai.
level. ʻIliwai, ʻiliwai like, pālahalaha. *Also:* kalamania, ʻōniki, pāpū like. *Carpenter's level,* ʻiliwai. *To level,* hōʻiliwai, hiʻohiʻolani, kuʻikē.
lever. Une, lōhai.
Leviathan. Lewiakana.
Levites. Lewika.
Leviticus. ʻOihana Kahuna.
levy. Kau, hoʻouku, ʻauhau.
lewd. Pelapela, haumia, kuko ʻino.
Lewiston. Luikini.
Lexington. Lekinekona.
liability. Kū i ka hana hewa, kumu ʻaiʻē, kuleana.
liar. Wahaheʻe, hoʻopunipuni, punipuni. *Also:* haku ʻepa, pelo, kiʻilua, lonu, pīnē. *See saying,* **octopus.**
libation. Mōhai inu.
libel. Laipila.
liberal. Ākea, manaʻo laulā, lipelala. *See* **generous.**
liberate. Hoʻokuʻu, makala, hoʻohemo.
Liberia. Lipelia.
liberty. Kūʻokoʻa. *Also:* mōhalu, mōhaluhalu, lipaki. *To set at liberty,* hoʻohemo, hoʻokuʻu, makala, hoʻokuʻu laʻelaʻe.
librarian. Kahu puke, mea mālama puke, mea mālama waihona puke, mālama waihona puke.
library. Hale waihona puke, waihona puke.
lice. ʻUku, ona; makika *(KJV). See* **louse.** *Chicken lice,* ona moa. *Search for lice,* hāʻuke, hāʻule, nāʻuke.
license. Laikini *(for various kinds, see Haw.-Eng. entry and entries that follow it);* palapala ʻae. *Licensed prostitute,* wahine laikini.
license plate. Laikini kaʻa *(automobile).*
lichen. Limu, wahinemaikaʻi, kuaʻala, haea.
lick. Palu, paluhia. *"A lick and a promise",* ʻo kū, ʻo kā (kū . . . kā); *also see* **kēlā . . . kēia.**
licorice. Kanakē ʻeleʻele.
lid. Pani, poʻi, uhi, ʻomo.
lie. **1.** *Recline.* Moe; hina moe, waiho *(rare). Lie at ease,* hiʻolani. *Lie sick,* moe maʻi, waiho maʻi. *Lie down in pain,* kaʻakua, kaʻakukua. *Lie sprawled,* moe pākiʻi, kāhela, waiho kāhela. *Lie on the side,* waiho ʻaoʻao. *Lie in ambush,* moemoe. *Lie in wait,* hālua, hoʻiole *(fig.);* moe. *Lie low, as smoke,* hina moe. *Lie in same direction,* moekahi. *Lie to, as a ship,* kālewa, poholua. **2.** *Falsify.* Hoʻopunipuni, punipuni, hoʻopuni, waha-

heʻe, waha wale. *Also:* hoʻopelo, pahilau, hoʻopahilau, pahili, haku ʻepa, alapahi, ʻapuni, hoʻokalekale, pelo, hāwale, pīnē, kaʻalalo. *See* **liar.**
lien. Kuleana koi, kuleana hoʻopaʻa. *See* **palapala hoʻo-malu.**
lieutenant. Lukānela.
lieutenant governor. Hope kiaʻāina.
life. Ola *(as opposed to death);* nohona, noho ʻana *(way of life). Also:* ea, mauli, iwi *(fig.),* hā. *His life,* kona ola ʻana. *Long life,* ola loa, ola lōʻihi. *Happy life,* nohona hauʻoli. *Breath of life,* mauli ola. *Extremity of life,* puaaneane. *Seat of life,* mauli. *Source of life,* kumulipo. *Full of life,* ʻeuʻeu, hōʻeuʻeu, ʻeleʻeleu, ʻeu, hōʻeu, hōʻeleʻeleu. *Life span,* ka lā hiki ā ka lā kau *(see* **lā hiki***). Sacrifice and prayer for life,* mōliaola. *Earthly life,* ola honua. *May God grant me life,* e ola au i ke Akua. *While there is life on earth,* ʻoi ola honua. *To save a life,* hoʻopakele ola. *To come to life,* ʻīnana. *To give life to,* hoʻōla, hoʻīnana; hane *(rare). Life-bringing sun,* ka lā hiki ola. *To take a life,* lawe ola. *Life is in Tahiti,* aia ke ola i Kahiki *(with the gods). In poetry, rain and mist may signify life (see saying,* **weep***).*
lifeboat. Waʻapā hoʻopakele ola.
lifeguard. Kiaʻi ola.
life insurance. ʻInikua ola, hoʻopaʻa ola.
lifesaving. Hoʻopakele ola.
lifetime. Ka wā e ola ana.
lift. Hāpai. *Also:* hiʻilawe, aukū, hulei, wala, pūkaʻikaʻi; — *up,* hoʻokiʻekiʻe, kaʻikaʻi, pai, hāpai; — *off,* huʻe; — *from beneath,* hālalo; — *again and again,* hiuhiu. *Lift weights,* hāpai mea kaumaha, amo. *Game of lifting a person holding his body rigid,* mākoi kanaka, hāpai malule.
lifting. Hapaina, huhuhulei.
ligament. Aʻa puʻupuʻu, olonā, oloolonā.
light. **1.** *Illumination.* Ao, lama, malama, kukui. *Electric light,* kukui uila. *Daylight,* ao, ʻeleao. *Faint streak of light,* hilo. *Dazzling light,* hulili. *Light with a torch,* aulama. *Light color, fair,* halakea. *Light of knowledge,* mālamalama, ʻama, māʻamaʻama. *Sacred light,* laʻa kea. *To cause light,* hoʻomālamalama. **2.** *Ignite.* Hōʻā, hōʻaʻā. **3.** *Not heavy.* Māmā, mālana. *Also:* hani, ʻālana. *Light work,* hana māmā, pua aheahe. *Light refreshment,* mea ʻai māmā. *Light rain,* kilihune, kili nahe. *Light wind,* kauaheahe; pūlihi *(rare).*
lighten. Hoʻomāmā, hoʻomālana.
light-fingered. Hue, lima ʻāpā.
lighthearted. Naʻau kaumaha ʻole, leʻa ka naʻau.
lighthouse. Hale ipukukui.
lightning. Uila, ahi. *Flash of lightning,* lapa uila, lehu-uila. *The lightning flashes,* ʻōlapa ka uila. *Streak of lightning,* kaula uila. *Lightning followed by thunder,* kani ā ʻuʻina. *Sound of lightning striking,* nehe, nehenehe, nehenuʻu. *Snout of lightning,* nuku uila *(of too much talk; see saying,* **ʻōlēʻolē***).*
lightning bolt. Lapa uila.
ligure. Lekema, likula.
like. **1.** *As.* A, me, like me, kū, kohu, mehe, mehe mea, pe, hele ā, laʻa, ʻoe. *Like this,* penei, pe kēia, pēia, ʻano like me kēia, e laʻa me kēia. *Like that,* pēlā. *Exactly like, just alike,* kohu like, like ʻālike. *What is it like?* Pehea kona ʻano? **2.** *Wish.* Makemake, mamake, puni, ʻiʻini; ʻono *(food).*
likely. Paha.
likeness. Kohu, kohu like, ʻano, kiʻi, aka, lua. *To assume a likeness,* hoʻokohu, hoʻokū.
likewise. Kekahi, nohoʻi, pēlā hoʻi.
liking. ʻIʻini.
lilac. Hueloʻīlio.
lily. Lilia. *Day lily,* lilia palaʻai. *Water lily,* lilia-lana-i-ka-wai. *Lily of the valley,* lilia-o-ke-awāwa. *Kinds:* ʻukiʻuki, paʻiniu.
limb. Lālā, mana. *With strong limbs,* lālākoʻa.
limber. Palupalu, wali, hōʻolu, ʻōʻupē, ʻapeʻape. *Limber-jointed,* lewa.
lime. **1.** *Fruit.* Lemi. **2.** *Calcium oxide.* Puna. *Lime hair*

bleach, pūkai. *To burn lime in a pit*, kahu. **3**. *See* **bird-lime**.
limeade. Wai lemi.
limestone. Hauone, paʻakea, pāpaʻakea, pōhā kea. *Limestone house*, hale puna.
limit. Palena, kaupale, ʻoki. *To limit*, kaupalena. *Land limit*, palena ʻāina, kapahaʻi. *Off limits*, kapu, hoʻokapu ʻia, pāpā ʻia. *Without limit*, ana ʻole, palena ʻole, ʻaʻole o kaʻe mai, ʻaʻole o kana mai, ʻaʻohe launa. *Limited*, kaupalena ʻia *(limits set)*; hui ʻia *(incorporated)*.
limitation. Kaupalena, hāiki.
limp. **1**. *Lame*. ʻOʻopa, ʻopa. *Also:* māʻopaʻopa, hakiʻopa, kīʻopa, ʻoʻi, hāʻoʻi, kūʻoʻi, kūpāʻoʻi, hakupeʻoʻi, pāʻoʻiʻoʻi, kaʻupapā, lolehau, luni. *See* **lame**. **2**. *Weak, soft*. Malule, nāwali, nāwaliwali. *Also:* uwaʻuwali, haʻimalule, hōlule, hoʻokakale, ʻōluheluhe, lolena. *Hanging limp, as a sail*, lululu.
limpet. ʻOpihi *(for various types, see Haw.-Eng. entry)*; kāʻala. ʻOpihi *scooped out of its shell*, makaʻopihi. *To gather* ʻopihi, kuʻi (ʻōlaʻo) ʻopihi. *A cliff-clinging limpet*, he ʻopihi kau pali *(of a parasite)*.
limu. *See* **alga, lichen, moss, seaweed**.
line. **1**. *Cordage*. Kaula *(for various kinds, see Haw.-Eng. entry and entries that follow it)*; aho. *Names of lines used on canoes and boats*, ʻalihi pāʻū, hāunu, kō waʻa, heʻe, hekau, kaula, pūkōkeʻe; puʻaki *(rare)*. *Fishing line*, aho. *Trolling line*, aho kālewa, aho kākele. *Ulua line*, Hawaiʻi-loa. **2**. *Geometric*. Lālani, laina, kaha, kahahiō, mana, kahakahana. *To mark with lines*, hoʻolālā, kākau kaha. *To march in line*, hele lālani, kaʻi, kaʻina. *Lined paper*, pepa kahakaha. *Lines, as in the face*, kahakahana, ʻaluʻalu, ʻalu, *Lines on the stomach*, alawela. *Line of stones*, nini. *Line of surf*, kūlana nalu, iwi. *To draw a color line*, kaupale ʻili. **3**. *To cover*. Pale. *To line or thatch a house*, paʻi hale.
lineage. Lālani ʻohana, kūʻauhau, welo, ēwe kapu, āewa, ēweewe, kūmoʻo. *Chiefly lineage*, kūʻauhau aliʻi, moloalo. *Lineage kin*, ēwe.
linen. Lilina, pulu, pulupulu, olonā, ʻie. *See* **grass linen**.
liner. Lapa *(for tapa)*.
linger. Kali, ʻapa, kaʻukaʻu; — *with greedy eyes*, meʻo. *See* **loiter**.
linguistics. Kālaiʻōlelo.
lining. Pale *(of a garment)*; paʻi *(thatch)*.
link. Paukū, loulou, hoʻohui, hoʻokuʻi. *Link of chain*, paukū kaula hao.
linnet. ʻAimīkana, manu-ʻai-mīkana, manu-ʻai-papaia.
linoleum. Linoleuma.
linotype. Linokaipa, mīkini hoʻonoho hua paʻi palapala.
linseed. Lilina.
lintel. Hoakakeʻa.
lion. Liona. *Sea lion*, liona kai. *Lion's Club*, Hui Liona.
lioness. Liona wahine.
lip. Lehe, lehelehe. *See* **idiom, sharp**. *Thick lip*, lehelehe nui, nukukau. *Protruding lip*, waha puʻu, puʻu ka nuku. *Pouting lips*, lehe luhe. *To move lips silently*, hoʻonomenome. *Eat until the lips protrude*, ʻai ā puʻu ka nuku *(eat much)*.
lipstick. Mea hōʻulaʻula lehelehe.
lipstick plant. ʻAlaea lāʻau.
liquefy. Hoʻoheheʻe.
liquid. Wai, ʻae. *Nearly liquid, as thin poi*, kale.
liquor. Wai; wai ʻona, kulu *(intoxicating)*. *See ex.,* **hoʻomalule, intoxicant**. *First and last distillations of liquor*, kālolo, kāwai. *Tī-root liquor*, ʻōkolehao.
Lisbon. Likepona.
list. Helu, papa helu. *See* **heel**. *List of names*, papa inoa.
listen. Lohe, hoʻolohe, hoʻolono. *Also:* lolohe, lohelohe, maliu, ʻauhea, ʻohikau, kālelei. *Listen*, ʻauhea wale ʻoe *(common in beginnings of songs)*.
listless. Palaka. *Also:* kukule, ʻōkulekule, puhemo, mamae, hoʻopuhemo, ʻea kāmoloa, nokule, lē.
litany. Likānia.
litchi. Laikī. *Cf.* **māhoe**.

liter. Lika.
literal. Pili pono, kūlike loa. *See* **meaning, translation**.
literate. Hiki ke heluhelu puke.
literature. Moʻolelo; palapala *(written only)*.
litter. **1**. *Trash*. ʻŌpala, mōkākī, hoʻōpala, hoʻomōkākī. **2**. *Stretcher*. Mānele.
little. Iki, liʻi, liliʻi, liʻiliʻi. *Also:* huahelu, hukuliʻi, huna, hune, ʻōhune, māiki, mamamala, pīkanela. *A little*, iki, wahi, kauwahi, nāhi, maʻū. *Little bit*, lihi. *To eat very little*, kikiki ka ʻai ʻana.
little people. *See* **legendary beings**.
live. **1**. *Exist*. Ola. *The name lives on*, ola ka inoa. *Live idly*, ōpū. *Live in comfort*, luana. *Live off others*, pili wale. *Living as a dependent*, nohona hoʻopili wale. *Live a happy life*, noho hauʻoli; lele pono *(fig.)*. **2**. *Dwell*. Noho. *Live alone*, noho hoʻokahi. *To live together*, noho pū, pili paʻa. *To live with a man*, noho kāne. *To live with a woman*, noho wahine. *To live cautiously*, akahele ka noho ʻana, akanoho. *To live permanently*, noho paʻa. *To live by the sea*, noho kai. *To live inland*, noho uka. *Let us live together*, hoʻokahi kō kāua noho pū ʻana.
livelihood. Ola, pono. *Means of livelihood*, mālama ola, koʻokoʻo. *To earn a livelihood*, ʻimi i ola. *Deprivation of livelihood*, hoʻopilikia i ka nohona, hana kaha ea.
lively. ʻEleu, ʻeuʻeu, ʻakeu, ʻeleʻeleu, ioioleʻa, nanahea. *To act lively*, ʻīnana.
liver. Ake, akepaʻa. *Raw liver*, ake maka. *Octopus liver bait*, pilipili heʻe.
Liverpool. Liwapula.
liverwort. Limu, limu ahi, limu kaha, pahapaha kuahiwi.
livery stable. Hale lio hoʻolimalima.
livestock. Holoholona hānai *(i ka mahina ʻai)*.
living. Nohona, ʻaoʻao *(way of life)*; ola *(life)*. *Still living, not dead*, e ola ana nō, ʻaʻole i make.
living room. Lumi hoʻokipa.
lizard. Moʻo, mō, moʻokiha; moko *(rare)*. *Big lizard*, moʻo nui. *Long-tailed lizard*, moʻo kā lāʻau. *Black lizard*, moʻo alā, moʻokā, moʻo kaʻalā. *Common lizard*, moʻo kāula, moʻo makāula. *Supernatural lizard*, Kiha. *Lizard god*, Kaioʻe. *Godlike lizard*, moʻo akua. *Many lizard gods, monsters, spirits, dragons*, moʻo lau.
lizard fish. ʻUlae, kule, ʻōnihoniho.
lo! Aia hoʻi! Eia hoʻi!
load. Hāʻawe. *See* **burden**. *To load*, hoʻohāʻawe, hoʻokaumaha, hoʻīli, hoʻouka, hoʻoukana. *To load a gun*, hoʻopiha. *Neatly arranged load*, kīpapa. *I have a heavy load*, luʻuluʻu loa au.
loaded. Piha, piha ukana; ʻoloʻolōna *(rare)*.
loaf. **1**. *Ovate body*. ʻOmoʻomo. *Loaf of bread*, ʻomoʻomo palaoa, paʻi pelena, pōpō palaoa. **2**. *Idle*. Hoʻohala manawa. *See* **lazy**.
loan. Hāʻawi no ka manawa, hōʻaiʻē. *Cf.* **lend**.
loathe. *See* **hate**.
loathesome. Hoʻopailua.
loaves. Paʻi pelena. *See* **loaf**.
lobby. **1**. *Foyer*. Lumi hoʻokipa. **2**. *Political*. Hana hoʻopaipai, paipai.
lobelia. ʻŌhā, ʻōhāhā, pua ʻala. *Various kinds:* ʻalula, ʻōhā wai, ʻōhā kēpau, ʻōhā pali, hāhā, hāhā-ʻai-a-kamanu, hāhā lua, hāhā nui, pānaunau, puakala, puʻu, liua, ʻakū, ʻakūʻakū, kuhi-ʻai-ka-moʻo-wahie, pōpolo, koliʻi.
lobster. Ula. *Varieties are qualified by* hiwa, koaʻe, poni; *also:* ʻāpaʻapaʻa; hāwaʻewaʻe *(small)*; nīnole *(?)*. *Upper leg of lobster*, waʻawaʻa. *The lobster is the creature living in coral beds*, he ula ka iʻa noho i ka hāpapa *(of shy persons)*.
local. Kūloko, kō laila, neʻi, ʻoneʻi. *See* **place**. *Local people*, kō ʻoneʻi poʻe. *Concerning local places*, pili loko.
locality. *See* **place**.
locate. Hoʻonoho, loaʻa.
location. Kahua, wahi, kahi.
locative case. ʻAuimoe.

lock. 1. *Latch.* Kī, laka. *Lock the door,* e kī aku i ka puka ā paʻa. **2.** *Tress.* Wili, wili lauoho.
locked. Paʻa i ka laka ʻia.
locket. Puʻuwai *(heart-shaped).*
lockjaw. Kuʻipaʻa.
locomotive. Kaʻaahi.
locust. ʻŪhini; *edible* —, ʻūhini paʻawela; *bald* —, ʻūhini wāwae hā; *adult* —, ʻunia. *To catch edible locusts,* kāhau.
lodge. 1. *House.* Hale. *To lodge in a house,* hoʻohale. **2.** *Fraternal or secret society.* Hui malū.
lodginghouse. Hale kipa, hale hoʻokipa, hale me nā lumi hoʻolimalima.
lofty. Kiʻekiʻe, i luna, luna lilo, luna loa. *Rare:* ʻiu, ʻiuʻiu, hōʻiu, kaʻokaʻo, keha, leʻo, leʻolani, pūnihi.
log. 1. *Portion of tree.* Paukū kumulāʻau, kua lāʻau. *Carved log on land boundary,* puaʻakukui. *Log cabin,* hale kua. **2.** *Hebrew measure.* Loka. **3.** *Ship's record.* Moʻolelo.
logarithm. Huhui helu.
loghead. Lakaheke.
logic. Kūkulu manaʻo ʻana.
logos. Lokou.
loincloth. Malo, malo kai, malo kea, malo wai. *Also:* ʻaʻahu makaloa, kapeke. *The loincloth of the handsome one . . . tie on the loincloth curved like the moon, the sea loincloth, loincloth of the chief. Stand, gird on your loincloth (UL 35–36)!* Ka malo a ka māhiehie . . . o kākai malo hoaka, ʻo ka malo kai, malo o ke aliʻi. E kū, e hume ā paʻa i ka malo!
loins. Pūhaka, leu. *Part covered by the malo,* humena.
loiter. Kali. *Also:* kauʻīpuka, ahio, lōiele, ʻoloʻolo, hoʻokololohe, ʻeʻelo. *See* **linger.**
loiterer. Kali, kauʻīpuka.
loli. *See* **sea cucumber.**
loll. Pualena. *See* **lazy.**
London. Lākana, Lalana, Ladana.
lone. Hoʻokahi, kaukahi, noho hoʻokahi.
loneliness. Mehameha. *See* **alone** *and saying,* **cold.**
lonely. Mehameha. *Rare:* kuānea, kuaehu, pūlō.
long. Loa, loloa *(usually spatially);* lōʻihi *(also figuratively);* kō *(as a sound);* — *and oval,* ʻomoʻomo; — *and narrow,* oloolo; — *and sharp,* pīoeoe. *Also:* lōkihi, oe, oeoe, kīoeoe, makikoe, hāloa, peleleu, koloau, holowī, niape. *Long-legged,* wāwae loloa, kioea. *Long-limbed,* ʻau loa. *Long hair,* lauoho loloa. *Long time,* manawa lōʻihi. *Long ago,* i ka wā kahiko, mamua loa, kū ā kahiko, kala kahiko. *Long trip,* huakaʻi lōʻihi; kākaiewa *(rare).* *To take a long time,* lōʻihi ka manawa, kūlolohili.
longevity. Ola loa. *See saying,* **koa 3.**
long for. *See* **want.**
longitude. Lonikū.
long rice. Laiki loloa.
look. Nānā, kilo; — *for,* ʻimi, huli, nānā; — *around,* makaau, makaʻau, makāu; — *longingly,* mākilo, ʻaiau; — *like,* kūlike me; — *sideways,* ʻalawa; — *out of the corners of the eyes,* maka kihi, nānā kihi; — *without helping or responding,* nānā maka, nānā kuli; — *heavenward,* kilo lani, hikaʻa lani; — *with favor,* maliu; — *with disapproval,* maka kokoe, nānā kokoe, makakīʻi, hoʻomakapū; — *straight ahead,* nānā pono, kauaheahe; — *with nearly closed eyes,* pīoioi, mīoioi. *Also:* hākiu, hāliu, aua, mākaʻikaʻi. *See* **gaze, peep, stare.** *Look out!* Nānā pono! Mālama pono!
looking. Nānā ʻana, nānaina. *Good-looking,* maikaʻi ke nānā aku.
looking glass. Aniani, aniani kilohi, aniani nānā, aniani kū, kilo.
lookout. Wahi nānā, wahi kiaʻi, ʻaleʻo. *Also:* kilohana, ʻīmaka, lukau, hālona.
loom. Mea *(weaving),* mea ulana lole. *See* **plait.**
loop. Puka lou, kīpuka, kama ʻaha, apo.
loop and ball. Palaʻie, hoʻolei pōpō.
loose. Hemo, puhemo, ʻaluʻalu, hōʻaluʻalu, pūʻalu. *Also:* ʻopeʻalu, ʻaluheʻe, holokake, hūalakē, hōloke-

loke, koʻo, lehe, luʻe, māwehe, māweke, mōhalu, puhalu, halu, uhalu, paleha, pōlewa, naue, kaʻamola, palahemo, pūlehe, pōnulu, pōnulunulu, pōnununu, kūpalaka. *Loose attachment,* lepe. *Loose-jointed,* hoʻohaʻilua, ʻaluheʻe. *Loose-fitting, as clothes,* poholo, pōholoholo, haloke, hālokeloke, ualehe, pūʻalu, pūʻaluʻalu. *To prod loose,* kaiehu.
loosen. Hoʻohemo, pahemo, hoʻopahemo, hōʻalu, hoʻopuhemo, puhalu, wehe, weke, hoʻokapeke, hoʻoluʻe, kala, makala, mokala, molokala, hoʻomanana, koʻo.
loosening. Hemohemo, ʻāluna.
loosestrifes. Puahekili, kolokolo kuahiwi, kolokolo lehua.
loot. Waiwai pio; *to* —, hao.
lopsided. Kapakahi, kapakeʻe, ʻōpaha, ʻanahua.
lord. Haku; lō *(rare).* *To seek a lord,* ʻimi haku *(as for privileges, possessions, security, matrimony; cf. Sahlins, as p. 36).* *Lord Jehova,* ʻO Iēhowa ka Haku. *My Lord,* kuʻu haku. *To lord it over others,* hoʻohaku, hoʻokiʻekiʻe, kuhilani.
Lord's Supper. ʻAhaʻaina a ka Haku.
lose. Hoʻolilo, nalo, nalowale.
loser. Mea i pohō, eo; ʻōhule *(in card games, slang).*
loss. Emi, pohō; pohō maʻū *(complete);* kīnā *(of crops).* *To refuse to pay for losses or forfeit, as in a game,* kāʻihi. *To sell at a loss,* hoʻopohō.
lost. Lilo; lilo loa *(permanently);* nalo, nalowale, nalohia, nano. *Rare:* ʻiʻī, poleke.
lot. 1. *Quantity.* Nui, nui ʻino, nui loa; kūpaʻi *(heap);* mahele *(portion).* *See* **hewa 4. 2.** *Land.* Pā, pā hale, ʻāpana. **3.** *Chance.* Hailona, hōʻailona, kelelo. *To draw lots,* hailona, hōʻailona, puʻu. *To divide by lot,* pū, hailona.
lotion. Lāʻau wai hamo. *Skin lotion,* lāʻau hoʻopalupalu ʻili.
lots. *See* **lot.**
lottery. Lūlū, lūlū me ke ʻano piliwaiwai, lokeli, leʻaleʻa ulia.
loud. Wā, wawā, nāwā, āwā, ʻuwā, hana kuli. *Loud noise,* halulu. *Loud-voiced,* leo nui, ʻikuwā.
loud-speaker. Hoʻonui leo.
Louisiana. Luikiana, Luisiana.
Louisville. Luikiwila, Luisivila.
lounge. 1. *See* **couch. 2.** *Parlor.* Lumi hoʻoluana. **3.** *Relax.* Hoʻonanea, hōʻoluʻolu i ke kino, kulohia, hiʻolani.
louse. ʻUku, ʻuku liʻi; ona; ʻuku poʻo *(head);* ʻuku kapa *(body);* ʻuku puaʻa *(pig);* ʻuku papa *(crab);* ʻuku pepa *(book);* ʻeleao, pōnalo *(plant).* *See* **delouse, lice.** *Louse egg,* liha, lia.
Louvre. Luwele, Luvere.
lovable. Hoʻālohaloha, hoʻoheno, henoheno, hoʻohenoheno, aloha.
love. Aloha, ʻanoʻi, nipo, kaunu, hoʻoipoipo, hoʻoheno, puni, oha, mahamaha. *See sayings,* **ana 2, ʻeha, hākoʻī, hāloa, hilo 1, kilohana, kulaʻilua, lalawe, lomia, mākuma, ʻōlino, wiliwai, wiʻuwiʻu, dedicated, expression, hungry, mist, overwhelm.** *Gods of love:* Lono-i-ke-aweawe-aloha, Makani-ke-oe, Laukapalili, Hono-a-lele. *Deep love,* kipona aloha, halehale ke aloha. *Loved one,* mea aloha, aloha. *With love,* me ke aloha. *Insincere love-making,* kaunu waha. *An expression of love for a favorite,* paʻipunahele. *Love song,* mele hoʻoipoipo. *Love magic,* hana aloha *(see* **āhole***).* *To cherish secretly, as love,* hōkeo. *To be in a bond of love,* pilialoha. *To make love,* hoʻoipo, hoʻoipoipo, hōʻaloha, hoʻonipo, hōʻināʻinau, kaunu, kaululu. *No man who does not suffer in love (UL 82),* ʻaʻohe kanaka ʻole i ke aloha i ke kino. *Mist, rain, spray, and coolness may represent love in poetry.*
love affair. Pili hoʻoipoipo. *To have a love affair,* hana. *Casual love affair,* hana kalakalai, ōmau.
lovebird. Manu aloha.
lovelorn. Maʻi aloha; ʻeha i ka ʻeha lima ʻole *(see* **lima***);* olopua *(rare).*
lovely. Nohea, onaona.

love magic. Hana aloha.

love pangs. Koni, konikoni lua, 'eha konikoni lua i ka pu'uwai.

lover. Ipo, aloha, huapala. *Also:* ipo ahi *(ardent),* ipo laua'e *(sweet-natured),* hoa kaunu, 'ano'i; kūmū *(slang),* kāne palemo *(temporary),* ipo mā'uka'uka *(unskilled),* hauhole *(over-persistent),* kāne manuahi *(common-law husband),* ipo manuahi; manō *(fig.).* See **sweetheart** *and sayings,* **ha'u, kāpi'o 1, lomia, paua.** *Spirit lover,* kāne o ka pō *(male),* wahine o ka pō *(female). To sleep with a lover,* moe ipo. *A lover for the late night,* he hoa kaunu no ke aumoe.

loving. Aloha, ālohaloha, ho'ālohaloha, na'au ali'i, 'ōpū ali'i, pu'uwai aloha.

low. Lalo, ha'a, ha'aha'a, pē, pēpē, emi; pāpapa *(as a reef). See* **tide.** *Low and broad, as a door or bowl,* pākākā. *Low-growing,* nene'e. *Low-lying,* ne'ine'i.

lower. Lalo, lalo iho, emi, ho'oha'aha'a; ku'u *(as a net);* ho'ēmi, emiemi, ho'ēmiemi *(price);* ho'omākū, 'ōkuma, 'ōpukupuku *(as clouds).*

lowland. Kai; ipu kai *(fig.). Of the lowland,* o kai. *Lowland dweller,* kō kula kai.

lowly. Ha'aha'a, lalolalo, kikā.

lowness. Lalo, ha'aha'a.

loyal. Kūpa'a, ho'okūpa'a. *Steadfast and loyal to one's chief,* kīpū lani, kūpa'a mahope o ke ali'i.

loyalty. Kūpa'a, mālama.

lua. *See* **fight.**

lubricate. Ho'opahe'e, ho'opahe'ehe'e, 'aila, 'aila hamo.

lubrication. Lā'au ho'opahe'e, lā'au ho'opalupalu, 'aila, 'aila hamo.

Lucerne. Lukene, Lusene.

lucifer. *See* **match.**

luck. Pōmaika'i, laki. *See* **dream** *and sayings,* **hīhīwai 1, ke'u, mud hen.** *Bad luck,* pō'ino, pohō, pakalaki, moe wa'a *(fig.),* nā 'ole, niuniu, paoa *(see also* **'ula 1).**

lucky. Laki, pōmaika'i, kūlia. *See saying,* **hīhīwai 1.** *Lucky day,* lā pōmaika'i, lā kūlia.

luff. Ho'opi'i i ka makani, kālepalepa.

lug. Pai̇nu'u.

luggage. Ukana, ukana pilikino.

lukewarm. Māhanahana, mūhea, 'ala'alae, 'ano 'ōwelawela.

lull. Ho'onā, ho'omālie.

lullaby. Mele ho'ohiamoe keiki, mele ho'onānā keiki, mele ho'oluluhi.

lumbago. Hu'i ma ka pūhaka, 'ea kakua.

lumber. Papa, papa lā'au, laupapa. *Rough lumber,* papa huluhulu. *Planed lumber,* papa hole.

lumbering. Pepe'ekue *(as a puppy's feet).*

luminous. Akaaka. *See* **bright.**

lump. Pu'u, haku, huku, lā'au, pou; —, *as left by disease of glands in the neck,* pala'e; — *under the skin,* pu'u, kaniu; — *on joints or in the groin,* pu'u, pu'uhau. *See* **sugar.** *Lumps on neck,* 'ā'ī pu'u.

lumpy. Pu'upu'u, hakuhaku. *Also:* 'āpu'upu'u, 'ōpu'upu'u, 'anapu'u, hākuma, hūnunu, 'u'uluhaku; hakukele, 'uluhaku *(as of poi);* 'alo'alo.

lunatic. Hehena.

lunch. 'Aina awakea. *Poi lunch,* pā'ina poi.

lung. Akemāmā, akemakani, akepāhola, akepahaola.

lunge. Lele i mua, lele'ino.

lunkhead. Ihu papa'a.

lure. **1.** *Attract.* 'Ume, ho'owalewale; maka ki'i *(with the eyes);* ho'ōnaona. **2.** *See* **fishhook.**

lurk. Ho'ope'e ma kahi kokoke, moemoe, nihi ka hele.

luscious. 'Ono.

lush. Uluwehi, uluwehiwehi, ulu nui, lupalupa, oho lupalupa, lupa, nupa. *Also:* nu'a, lauoha; kele *(moist);* nupanupa, ho'olupalupa, ho'onupanupa, lanipō, kāpa'ipa'i, ohaohala.

Lusitania. Lukikania.

lust. Kuko, 'a'ako, 'ako, wela. *See saying,* **cowry.**

lustful. Kuko hewa, kuko 'ino, maka leho. *See* **randy.**

lustrous. Hinuhinu.

lute. Luke.

Lutheran. Lukelano, Lukela.

luxuriant. *See* **lush.**

luxury. Mea e ho'ohiwahiwa ai ka noho 'ana.

lye. Pa'akai holoi.

Lynchburg. Linepuka, Linebuga.

lynx. Lineka.

Lyra. Ke-ho'oea, Keoe *(probably).*

lyre. Līla.

lyric. Lila.

M

m. Mū.
macadamize. Ho'ounu. *See* pave.
mace. Ko'oko'o 'oihana.
Macedonia. Makekonia, Makedonia.
machete. Pahi kā.
machine. Mīkini.
machine belt. 'Ili.
machine gun. Pū mīkini, pou.
mackerel. Makalē. *Mackerel scad,* 'ōpelu *(for various kinds, see* 'ōpelu *and entries that follow it).*
mackerel sky. Pālāmoa.
macron. Kahakō.
mad. 1. *Insane.* Hehena, 'ūlala, pupule, make ulu niu. *Mad running,* holo pupule. 2. *Angry.* Huhū.
Madagascar. Makakakeka, Madagaseka.
madam. Makame.
Madeira. Makela, Madera.
Madeira vine. 'Uala hūpē.
madness. Hehena.
Madras. Makalaka, Madarasa.
Madrid. Makelika, Maderida.
maestoso. Ha'aheo akā me ka hanohano.
magazine. Puke heluhelu.
Magellanic Clouds. Pulelehua Kea, Pulelehua Kāwa'e-wa'e, Pulelehua Uli.
maggot. Ilo. *See* kūkaelā.
maggoty. Iloilo.
Magi. Mākoi, Magoi.
magic. Ho'okalakupua, ho'opi'opi'o *(imitative).* *See* sorcery.
magician. Kahuna, kāula, ho'okalakupua; mākoi.
magic lantern. Kukui ho'olele aka.
magistrate. Luna kānāwai.
magnet. Mākēneki, hao mākēneki. *Attraction of a magnet,* 'ume mākēneki.
magnetism. 'Ume mākēneki.
magneto. Mākēneki.
magnificent. Hanohano, nani loa, hīhīmanu, uluwehi-wehi, kāhiko.
magnify. Ho'onui, ho'omāhua, ho'omāhuahua.
magnifying glass. Aniani ho'onui 'ike.
magnitude. Nui.
magnolia. Mikinolia.
maid. 1. *Servant.* Wahine lawelawe, kauā wahine. *Maid of honor,* kū'ao'ao o ka wahine. 2. *Girl.* Kaikamahine, ohi.
maidenhair fern. 'Iwa'iwa *(for various kinds, see Haw.-Eng. entry and entries that follow it).*
mail. 1. *Letters.* Leka. *To carry mail,* lawe leka. *To mail letters,* ho'okomo i ka leka *(put in box);* ho'ouna i ka leka *(send).* 2. *Armor.* Pūliki kaua, pūliki koa.
mailbag. 'Eke leka.
mail carrier. Lawe leka.
maile. Maile *(for various types, see Haw.-Eng. entry and entries that follow it);* maile haole, kāhili *(crape myrtle);* mākala, hakaka, muleko, moekahi. Laka, *the hula goddess, was invoked as the goddess of* maile. *Four varieties of* maile *are named for four demigoddess sisters* (maile pākaha, maile kaluhea, maile lau li'i, Kahala-o-māpuana). *They possessed the fragrance of* maile.
mail pouch. 'Eke leka.
maimed. Mu'umu'u, mumuku, kīnā, 'ālina.
main. 'Ano nui, 'oi.
Maine. Maine.
mainland. 'Āina makua, 'āina nui, loko, 'āina haole. *To go to the mainland,* hele i loko.

mainmast. Kia nui.
mainsail. Pe'a hope, pe'a nui.
maintain. 1. *Support.* Mālama. 2. *See* affirm.
maintenance. Mālama 'ana. *Maintenance of life,* mālama ola.
maize. Kūlina.
majestic. Kilakila. *Also:* mōkila, 'iu'iu, 'ihi'ihi, 'ihi, keha, ki'eki'e, pūnihi.
majesty. Lani, mō'ī; ehuehu *(rare).* *Your majesty,* ē ka lani ē; ē ke ali'i. *His majesty,* ka lani.
major. 1. *See* majority. 2. *Military.* Mekia.
majority. Hapa nui, hapa loa.
majority rule. Hapa nui o ka mana.
make. Hana; — *known,* hō'ike, ho'olaha; — *fast,* ho'o-pa'a, ho'omau, hele, hekau; — *up, invent,* hakuwale; — *off with,* lawe, mio; — *faces,* haikaika; — *sturdy,* ho'oikaika, ho'opa'a, hāluapou; — *ready,* ho'o-mākaukau. *See* build, compel, earn. *Make love, see* love. *Make merry, see* merry.
maker. Mea nāna i hana.
makeshift. Kūikawā. *Makeshift house,* hale pupupu.
Malacca. Malaka.
malady. *See* disease.
Malaya. Malae, Malaia.
Malaysia. Malaia.
male. Kāne, kūkāne; laho *(vulgar);* ke'a *(virile).* *See* masculine. *To behave as a male,* ho'okāne. *Male animal reserved for breeding,* ke'a.
malevolent. Na'au 'ino, loko 'ino. *Also:* na'au kope-kope, mākonā, 'ōpū kekēue. *See* sorcerer.
malformed. Ku'e, kīnā.
malice. Inaina *(legal term).*
malicious. *See* malevolent. *Malicious gossip,* lawena 'ōlelo hō'ino, haku 'epa, ni'a, 'io'iolepo. *Malicious burning,* puhi mana'o 'ino. *Malicious injury,* hana 'ino ma ke 'ano kolohe.
malign. Hō'ino, ho'o'ino. *Also:* a'ana, 'a'anema, 'aki, 'aki'aki, ni'a, ni'ani'a.
malignant. 'A'ai.
mallet. Kū'au, hāmale, hāmale lā'au.
mallow. Maluhā.
malo. *See* loincloth.
malodorous. *See* smell.
malt. Hua mea ulu (huika, pale).
Maltese cat. Pōpoki lehu.
mama. Māmā. *See* mother.
mammon. Mamona.
man. Kanaka *(human being),* kāne *(male);* ulua *(fig.).* *Old man,* 'elemakule. *Fellow man,* hoa kanaka. *To become an old man,* 'elemakule. *Get your man,* huki i ka ulua *(slang).* *Be a man,* e ho'okanaka.
-man. Mea, kanaka. *See* horseman, oarsman.
mana. Mana. *To impart mana,* ho'omanamana.
manacle. Kūpe'e, hao ho'opa'a lima.
manage. Ho'oponopono, ho'oholo, ho'ohele, ho'o-hana, ka'a, ho'okele.
management. Ho'oponopono 'ana, ho'oholo 'ana, ho'ohele 'ana; ho'okele 'ana.
manager. Haku nui, luna ho'ohana, mea ho'opono-pono. *To act or serve as manager,* noho ho'ohana.
manapua. Mea 'ono pua'a.
Manchester. Manakekeka, Manakeseta.
Manchuria. Manakulia.
mandamus. Palapala koi, palapala pāpā aku.
mandarin. 'Alani Pākē.
mandate. 'Ōlelo kēnā.
mandolin. Kīkā Pukikī.

mandrake. Kukaima, hua kukaima, hua kudaima.
mane. Hulu 'ā'ī.
man-eater. 'Ai kanaka.
maneh. Mane.
maneuver. Ka'a kaua *(war);* kīkaha *(as fighting cocks).*
mange. Kāki'o, me'eau.
mangle. 1. *See* **mutilate. 2.** *Ironing machine.* Mīkini 'aiana.
mango. Manakō. *Varieties:* manakō kāne, manakō meneke.
mangrove. Kukuna-o-ka-lā.
mangy. *See* **mange.**
manhandle. Limanui, lālau lima.
mania. Uluāhewa.
maniac. Hehena.
manifest. 1. *Evident.* Mōakaaka, moakaka, akaaka, akaka, moaka. **2.** *Document.* Pepa helu waiwai, pepa hō'ike ukana, pepa hō'ike 'ōhua.
Manila. Manila.
manioc. Manioka.
mankind. Lāhui kanaka.
manly. Kūlana o nā kāne.
manna. Mane.
manner. 'Ano.
manners. Lula, loina, 'ano launa. *Without manners,* lula 'ole. *Genteel manners,* ka noho 'ana nihinihi.
man-of-war. Manuwā, manuā. *See* **Portuguese man-of-war.**
man-of-war bird. 'Iwa.
manslaughter. Pepehi kanaka, lawe ola.
manta ray. Hāhālua. *Cf.* **ray 2.**
mantle. 'A'ahu. *Cf.* **kīhei.**
manual. 1. *Directory.* Kumu, a'o, manuale. *Manual of punctuation,* a'o kiko. *Catholic Manual,* Manuale Kakōlika. *Manual of directions,* puke kuhikuhi. *Manual of arms,* kumu paikau. **2.** *By hand.* Hana lima. *Manual training school,* kula a'o hana lima.
manufacture. Hana mīkini; 'oihana miki'ala *(rare).*
manure. Kūkae lio *(horse);* manua.
manuscript. Palapala.
many. Nui, nunui, lau, mano, manomano, lehu, lehulehu, kini, kinikini. *Also:* kini lau, kūhaluka, 'āluka, makawalu, manoa, mānoanoa, nonanona, lonalona, hewahewa, mākena, kūwaluwalu, hikuhiku, pūli'uli'u, pūlauhala, pakapaka, lālākukui, manohā, weliweli, pulehulehu. *How many?* 'Ehia? *Many times,* pinepine. *Very many,* nui 'ino, nui hewahewa. *Many and colorful,* lua'ehu.
map. Palapala'āina, palapalahonua.
mar. Ho'okīnā, hana 'ino.
marble. 1. *Mineral.* Māpala, māpela, pōhaku ke'oke'o. *At the marble gates,* ma nā puka māpela. **2.** *See* **marbles.**
marbles. Kinikini, kini. *Cf.* **nika 1.** *To shoot, as marbles,* pana.
march. 1. *Action.* Naue, ka'i huaka'i, ka'i like, paikau, hele lālani, ne'e, māki. *Marching to war,* naue kaua. **2.** *Music (military).* Mele paikau. **3.** *Month.* Malaki.
mare. Lio wahine.
margin. Kae, lihi, palena, pae.
marguerite. Makalika.
marigold. 'Ōkole'oi'oi. *Pot marigold,* melekule.
marijuana. Paka lōlō.
marine. 1. *Of the sea.* Kai, malina. *Marine animal,* i'a. *Marine railway,* alahukimoku. **2.** *Military.* Koa malina.
Marine Corps. Pū'ali Koa Malina (Marina).
marital. Launa male; — *rights,* launa male *(RSV);* — *duties,* launa male *(KJV).*
mark. Kaha, kahakaha, kiko, kākau, kākau kaha, māka; mō'ali, ho'omō'ali'ali *(scar);* heluna *(grade);* hō'ailona *(distinguishing);* kahahiō *(crisscross);* kālele leo *(stress);* kahakuhi *(reference, as asterisk).* *High mark (grade),* kaha ki'eki'e. *Low mark,* kaha ha'aha'a. *To mark with lines,* ho'olālā. *To mark parallel lines,* kikoluko. *Marks of worry, as on the face,* kahakahana

kaumaha. *To mark time,* ke'ehi pōkole, ho'olei wāwae 'ana. *To give a mark or grade,* kaha.
marked. Kaha 'ia, kuni 'ia. *Also:* 'a'ali; nanaka *(in sections).*
marker. Māka; ulehole *(harbor).*
market. Mākeke; mākeke nui *(large);* pukahipa *(sheep, Biblical).* *Market value,* waiwai 'i'o.
markings. Kahakahana.
marlin. A'u, a'ua'u; a'ukī.
Marquesan, Marquesas. Nu'uhiwa.
marquis. Makuika.
marriage. Male 'ana, moe, noho pū 'ana, ho'āo. *Marriage relationship or rights,* launa male. *Marriage proposal,* noi male. *Marriage license,* palapala male. *Marriage fee,* uku male. *Marriage records,* puke i kākau 'ia ka po'e male. *To perform the marriage ceremony,* ho'omale. *Families united by marriage,* alohiki.
married. Male 'ia; noho wahine, mea wahine *(of a male);* noho kāne, mea kāne *(of a female).* *See saying,* **'uo 1.**
marrow. Lolo, lolo iwi.
marry. Male, moe, ho'āo, noho; noho kāne *(of a woman);* noho wahine *(of a man).* *See* **ho'i 4.** *To marry off,* ho'omale. *Married couple,* pa'a male. *They were married,* ua male 'ia lāua.
Mars. Hōkū-'ula, Maleka, Mareka. *Perhaps:* Holoholopīna'au, 'Aukele-nui-a-Iku ('Aukele).
marsh. Lepo pohō, 'unelunelu, nenelu, 'alē, naele.
marshal. Ilāmuku, mākala.
Marshallese. Mākala, kanaka Mākala.
Marshall Islands. Mākala 'Ailana, Mākala.
marshy. Nenelu, 'unelunelu, 'alē. *Also:* nakele, napele, nāpelepele, naele, ho'onaele, naenaele.
Martha's Vineyard. Pā-waina-o-Mareta.
martial. Koa. *See* **court-martial.**
martial law. Kānāwai koa.
martingale. Mākīnikela.
martyr. Malakile.
marvel. Ha'oha'o, ha'o, ho'oha'oha'o.
marvelous. Kupaianaha, kupanaha, kamaha'o, ho'ā-kua, āiwaiwa, pāha'oha'o, pāha'o.
Maryland. Melelana, Merelana.
mascot. Mea ho'olaki.
masculine. Kāne, ho'okāne.
mash. Ho'owali, lomi, ho'opē, ku'i ā 'ae'ae. *Also:* kīmō, pīhelehele, kūpalu.
mashed. Wali, waliwali, wawali, 'ae'ae, 'ae, pīhelehele; palu *(fig.);* napo *(soft).* *Mashed potatoes,* 'uala kahiki ho'owali 'ia.
mask. Makaki'i, po'oki'i, uhi maka; mākini *(gourd).*
mason. Makona. *See* **bricklayer.** *Masons' society,* hui Makona, hui malū.
masonic. Hui malū.
mass. 1. *Quantity.* Pu'u, anu'a, anu'a, ahu. **2.** *Ritual.* Meka, pule meka.
Massachusetts. Makakukeka, Masakuseta.
massacre. Luku, lukua, lukuna, lukuwale. *See* **destroy.**
massage. Lomi, lomilomi, kō, 'opā'opā, kōkō, kaomi, ho'o'unu, au; 'a'e *(the back with feet);* limalima *(rare).*
masseur. Kanaka lomi, lomilomi; kālole *(rare).*
mast. Kia *(ship);* pou *(canoe). Rare:* lā'au kō, kāla'au.
master. Haku; kahu, kāpuhi *(of an animal).* *See* **learn.** *His master,* kona haku. *Hula master,* kumu hula.
mastered. Pa'a, loa'a.
masthead. Heke o ke kia, mākē.
masticate. Nau ā wali, nau, naunau, nanau; mama *(but not swallow);* māī *(raw).*
mastoid. Kumu pepeiao *(process);* — *infection,* hōkale.
masturbate. 'U'u, pua'u'u. *See* **onanism.**
mat. Moena, 'ahu, pālaulau *(for various kinds, see Haw.-Eng. entries and entries that follow them).* *Also:* ālaulau, 'āne'ene'e, ao, 'apeu, 'āpeupeu, 'āleuleu, kumunu'a, maka'opihi, 'ōpihipihi, pālau; pākaukau, papa 'aina *(for food);* pā'ū, 'u'a, pakakeha, pākea. *Coarse mat,* moena lau. *Mat with medium weft,* moena makapepe. *Mat with finger-sized mesh,* moena pu'ao, moena makali'i. *Pile of mats,* hu'a moena, kūmoena,

pa'a 'ahu, pā 'ahu. *Long strip mat commencement,* kūmoena. *Mat designs:* 'eke'eke, hale, hoehoe-pākea, hōkū-helele'i, ho'oke'eke'e, honu, humuniki, kūhanu, kumumiki, lau-lama, lolopili, nānā-nu'u, nēnē, nihowili-hemo, olowahia, 'opihi, pahakū, papa-kōnane, papa-'ula, pāwehe, poho-mōkoi, pua-hala. *Coarse mat covering,* pale hāli'i moena *(worthless person).*

match. 1. *Contest.* Ho'okūkū; kahului *(rare).* **2.** *Equal.* Lua, kohu like, like 'ālike, like, like loa, like pū, likelike, kohu. *To match,* ho'ohālikelike, ho'olikelike, ho'ohālike. *To arrange a match,* ho'omoe, ho'omoemoe *(marriage).* *Well-matched,* pili pono. *To match coins,* pili kālā. *Women are looked at—you are not matched [i.e. equal],* e nānā wahine a'e nō—'a'ole 'oe e loa'a. **3.** *Lucifer.* Kūkaepele, ahi, ahikoe. *Also:* ahipele, lukipa, lepopele. *Package of matches,* pena ahipele.

matchbox. Poho ahi.

matching. Kohu.

matchless. Lua 'ole, ana 'ole, launa 'ole. *See ex.,* **match.**

mate. 1. *Companion.* Hoa, koko'olua, lua. *See* **spouse** *and saying,* pilipili. *To mate,* moe, male, ho'omau, ho'omau keiki, ho'āo. **2.** *Of ships.* Mālama moku, kahu moku. *See* **shipmate.** *First mate,* mālama moku 'ekahi. *Second mate,* kahu moku, hulipahu. *Third mate,* kolo meki.

material. Kino, makelia. *To supply material needs,* ho'olako ma ke kino. *Dress material,* lole, 'āpā lole.

maternal. Makuahine.

maternity. Kūlana makuahine. *Maternity dress,* lole hāpai.

mathematics. Makemakika. *Applied mathematics,* makemakika ho'opili 'ia. *Pure mathematics,* makemakika 'oko'a.

matrimony. Male, makelimonio. *United in the pure bonds of matrimony,* ua ho'opili 'ia ma ka pelika ma'ema'e o ka male.

matter. 1. *Thing,* Mea; kumuhana *(topic). Important matter,* mea nui, mana'o nui. *What's the matter?* He aha lā ka pilikia? *What's the matter with you?* He aha nō lā kou 'ano? *It doesn't matter,* he mea 'ole. *No matter how much,* 'ehia. **2.** *To be important.* 'Ano nui, mana'o nui. **3.** *Secretion.* Piapia, pa'akai, piele, pieleele, piepiele. *See* **pus.**

matter-of-fact. Ka mea 'oia'i'o.

mattress. Pela, pela moe. *Mattress stuffing,* pulu. *Mattress cover,* uhi pela, hāli'i pela.

mature. Makua, kanaka makua, o'o. *Also:* mahao'o; laho o'o *(male);* kākala *(gourds);* piha pona *(bonds). To mature,* ho'omakua, o'o, kupuohi. *Your gentleness has matured me,* 'o kō ahonui ka i ho'omakua mai nei ia'u. *See saying,* pakī.

maturity. Wā o'o, ka piha o ka manawa.

Maui. 1. *The island.* Maui. *Epithets: Maui is the best,* Maui nō ka 'oi. *Great Maui of Kama,* Maui nui a Kama *(short for Kama-lālā-walu, a famous chief).* Nā Hono-a-Pi'i-lani *(see* **Hono-***). The hunchback island,* ka mokupuni kuapa'a. **2.** *Name of a demigod.* Māui.

mausoleum. Ilina. *Royal mausoleum,* ilina o nā ali'i. *Famous ancient mausoleums:* hale o Līloa, hale o Keawe.

maw. 'Ōpū *(of an animal).*

maximum. Nui.

may. 1. *Possibility.* Paha. **2.** *Permission.* Hiki. **3.** *(Cap.) Month.* Mei.

maybe. Paha *(not used alone);* pēlā paha, malia paha, malia, mali'a. *Also:* māki'a, 'āpaha. *Maybe so,* pēlā paha, 'oia paha, 'oliapaha. *Maybe not,* 'a'ole paha.

mayhem. 'Elehe'u *(rare). See* **maimed.**

mayor. Meia.

maze. Ala pāka'awili, ala ka'awili.

McCoy grass. Mau'u hunehune.

me. A'u, ia'u, i o'u, mi. *To me,* ia'u, i o'u. *By me,* na'u. *Of me,* a'u, o'u. *For me,* na'u, no'u. *Fan me,* pe'ahi mai.

meadow. Kula mau'u.

meager. Lawa 'ole, 'u'uku.

meal. 'Aina, pā'ina, papa 'aina; 'ai māmā *(light).*

mealy. Punapuna.

mealybug. Ana 'uku.

mean. 1. *Cruel.* Mākonā. *Also:* kāwa'e, 'ōpūke'emoa, mākō. *See* **malevolent. 2.** *Average.* Waena. **3.** *Signify.* Mana'o, hō'ailona.

meaning. Mana'o, mana'o nui, 'ano. *Literal meaning,* mana'o maoli, mana'o pili pono. *Hidden, figurative meaning,* kaona, mana'o ho'onalonalo, mana'o ho'onanenane, mana'o ho'opilipili *(see ex.,* **kolopā, 'ōhea 1**). *Principal meaning,* mana'o nui.

means. 1. *Resources.* Ola, mālama ola, kālā, kenikeni. *He has limited means,* kaupalena 'ia kāna wahi loa'a. *I have no means,* 'a'ohe a'u kenikeni. **2.** *Agency.* Mamuli o, i, ma o, ma, loko, mea. *Means of transportation,* ala hele.

meantime. Ia wā nō, ia manawa.

meanwhile. 'Oiai, 'oi.

measles. 'Ulāli'i, ma'i 'ula.

measure. Ana, ho'oana, ho'āna. *See* **mesh.** *Ancient measures were of made objects, as of net meshes (not of land):* 'owā, mākahi, mākahi hoene, 'oene, kīko'o, poho, pī'ā; muku, ha'ilima *(elbow to end of fingers),* iwilei *(collarbone to end of fingers),* anana *(between fingertips, arms extended),* kahakū *(2.5 or 4.5 m). Measure of cloth,* pio. *Liquid measures:* ana waina, kako, kolo, mekeleka, pako 'aila. *Cubic measure,* anapa'a. *Measuring stick,* lā'au ana. *Measuring cord,* 'ahakū. *Measure in music,* mahele. *Measure signature in music,* hō'ailona mahele. *Metric measure,* ana mekele.

measureless. Ana 'ole, palena 'ole, mānu'unu'u.

measurement. Ana; ana loa, lō'ihi, lōkihi *(length);* ana piha *(capacity);* anakahi *(unit);* 'aha *(of an edge or border).*

measuring worm. 'Ami.

meat. 'I'o, 'i'o holoholona; 'i'o pipi *(beef);* 'īna'i, i'a *(anything eaten with poi). Meat ball,* pipi ho'opoe. *Meat dish,* ipu i'a, ipu kai.

Mecca. Meka.

mechanic. Mekanika, hana mīkini.

meconium. Kūkae weka, weka, nalu.

medal. Hōkai. *Military or honorary medal,* medala ho'ohanohano. *Honorary cross or medal,* ke'a ho'ohanohano.

meddle. Hōkai, ho'opilikia. *Also:* lālama, mau'a'e.

medial. Waena.

mediate. 'Uao, uwao.

medical. Lā'au, kauka. *Medical doctor,* kauka lapa'au, kahuna lapa'au. *Medical practice,* lapa'au.

medicinal. Lā'au, lapa'au.

medicine. Lā'au, lā'au lapa'au, wai lā'au, hālalo. *Various kinds of medicine:* 'apu, lā'au hānō, lā'au mae, lā'au ho'omoe, lā'au ho'ohiamoe, lā'au ho'onahā, lā'au ho'opūhi'u, hālalo po'i, 'aikūpele, ehu, hau'oki, hoene, ho'ohua kawowo, kāpa'i, kāhili kāpopo, kuakala, ku'iku'i, pi'ikū, pīpā, pūailewa, pūailewa, pioloolo. *To mix medicine,* kāwili lā'au. *Commonly used medicinal plants (Blaisdell):* 'a'ali'i, *leaf used for rash, insomnia, asthma;* 'āheahea, 'āweoweo, *leaves used for wounds and as tonic;* 'ahu'awa, *powder of stem and flower for skin lesions;* 'ākia, *leaf for asthma and as a cathartic;* 'ala'ala wai nui *(succulents), bud to treat asthma, leaf for ear infections and as a tonic;* 'aloe, pānini *'awa-'awa, leaf for burns, wounds, arthritis, dermatomycosis, and as a cathartic;* 'awa, *root as narcotic for pain, insomnia, anxiety;* 'awapuhi kuahiwi, *leaf for lacerations, root for toothache and abdominal pain;* hala, *seed and flower as cathartic, aerial root as tonic;* hau, *bud and bark as cathartic, bark for fever and as demulcent in childbirth;* 'ilima, *flower as cathartic, leaf shoot for asthma and as tonic, root bark for asthma;* ipu *'awa'awa (gourd), shoot and leaf as sedative and ca-*

thartic and to treat skin lesions; kā'e'e *(sea bean), seeds as cathartic;* kaliko, *a cathartic;* kalo *(taro), root as tonic and cathartic, leaf for skin infections, stem for stings;* kī *(ti), flower for asthma, leaves* (lā'ī) *for headache, fever, and as bandages;* kō *(sugar cane), shoot for lacerations, juice as herb sweetener;* koali 'awa *(morning glory), whole plant for fractures, wounds, joint pain, poultice for infection, cathartic;* ko'oko-'olau *(beggars tick), leaf as tea tonic and for asthma, flower for heartburn and fever;* kuawa *(guava), seeds and leaf for diarrhea, fruit rind as cathartic;* kukui *(candlenut), nut and bark as cathartic, leaf for wounds, sap to treat thrush;* laukahi *(plantain), leaf as poultice for infections, sap to arrest bleeding;* mai'a *(banana), fruit for abdominal pain and asthma and as a cathartic, bud sap to treat thrush;* māmaki, *berry to treat thrush and as laxative and tonic, root for childbirth;* moa, *stem for tea, as cathartic, and to treat thrush;* naupaka, *leaf for lacerations, bark for skin lesions, diarrhea;* nīoi *(pepper) for muscle and joint pain;* niu hiwa *(a variety of coconut), young shoot for lacerations, dry meat for oil for skin and hair and to use for massage, water for eye disorders;* noni *(Indian mulberry), fruit for lacerations and as poultice, leaf and bark as tonic and for urinary disorders and muscle and joint pain;* 'ōhi'a 'ai *(mountain apple), bark for mouth lesions and lacerations, bark, leaf, and bud as tonic;* 'ōhi'a lehua, *flower for childbirth, leaf bud as tea tonic;* 'ōlena *(turmeric), bulb for earache, nose and throat discomfort;* palepiwa (nuhōlani) *(eucalyptus), leaves for sweat bath, pain, fever, respiratory congestions;* pia *(arrowroot), tuber for diarrhea and as tonic;* pilikai, *as cathartic;* pōhuehue *(morning glory), seed and stem as cathartic, leaf in childbirth;* pōpolo *(black nightshade), leaf for wounds, cough, and tonic, berry as cathartic and to treat thrush;* pua kala *(poppy), sap and seed* (lū) *for toothache and pyorrhea and skin itch, root for warts;* 'uala *(sweet potato), root for asthma and as emetic, leaf* (palula) *as tonic, to aid lactation;* 'uhaloa, hi'aloa, 'ala'ala pūloa, kanakaloa, *roots for sore throat, leaves as poultice for infections;* 'ulu *(breadfruit), sap for lacerations and skin infections. Some of these are post-European.*

Medina. Mekina.
mediocre. 'A'ole maika'i loa.
meditate. Nalu, no'ono'o pono. *Also:* ho'okuano'o, wae, waewae.
meditative. Kuano'o. *See* **meditate.**
Mediterranean Sea. Kai-waena-honua.
medium. 1. *Intermediate.* Waena. **2.** *Spiritualist.* Haka, haka 'ōlelo.
meek. Akahai, ha'aha'a. *See saying,* **bait.**
meet. Hui, hālāwai, meu. *Until (we) meet again,* ā hui hou aku. *To meet an obstacle,* ku'ia. *I'm glad to meet you,* hau'oli kēia hui 'ana o kāua.
meeting. 'Aha *(for various kinds, see Haw.-Eng. entry and entries that follow it);* hālāwai, pilina. *To arrange a meeting,* ho'ohālāwai. *Regular meeting,* hālāwai pa'a mau. *Meeting place,* kahua ho'olulu.
meetinghouse. Hale hālāwai.
megaphone. Mea ho'onui leo.
Melanesia, Melanesian. Melanikia.
Melbourne. Melepona, Melebona.
mellow. Pala.
melodeon. Melokiana.
melodious. Honehone, nahenahe; mōpua *(rare).*
melody. Leo, melokia.
melon. Ipu. *See* **cantaloupe, watermelon.** *Pulp and seeds of a melon,* haku ipu. *To burst, as a ripe melon,* 'a'aka.
melt. He'e, hehe'e, ho'ohehe'e, kahe.
member. Lālā *(as of a society).*
membrane. Nikiniki, 'ili lahilahi.
memento. Mea ho'omana'o, pa'aaloha, pa'aloha, pa'a mau no'ono'o, pukana, paumauno'ono'o.
memoirs. Puke ho'omana'o.

memorandum. Mea ho'omana'o, puke ho'omana'o. *To keep a memorandum,* ho'opa'a mana'o.
memorial. Mea ho'omana'o.
Memorial Day. Lā Kau Pua, Lā Lū Pua.
memorize. Ho'opa'ana'au, ho'opa'a, ho'opa'a mana'o.
memorized. Pa'ana'au, pa'a, pa'a mana'o.
memory. Ho'omana'o 'ana, waihona ho'omana'o, hali'a. *Dim memory,* mana'o pōehiehi, mana'o pōwehiwehi, mana'o kāwelewele. *Cherished memory,* hali'a aloha. *In memory,* he ho'omana'o.
Memphis. Memapika, Memapisa.
men. Kāne *(males),* kānaka *(human beings),* po'e, nā kānaka, ka po'e kānaka.
menace. *See* **threat.**
mend. Hono, pāhono, pāhonohono, poho, hana hou, kāpili. *Also:* kikikiki, hāuna, hauhāuna, kaumo'o; ho'oheihei *(a net).*
menial. Ha'aha'a loa, kauā.
menopause. Ho'oki'o, lele, mau.
menstrual flow. *See* **menstruate.**
menstruate. Hanawai, kahe, pe'a; hiua *(rare). Menstrual house,* hale pe'a. *Taboo on menstruating women,* kahapouli.
menstruation. Hanawai, he'e koko, wai, wai 'ula, wai o ka wahine, waimaka lehua; *first —,* kokopuna; *to have ceased —,* ho'oki'o, mau, lele.
-ment. 'Ana, -na. *(To manage,* ho'oponopono. *Management,* ho'oponopono 'ana.)
mental. No'ono'o. *For mental qualities, see* **lae o'o, lae pa'a, lae 'ula.**
mental arithmetic. Helu na'au.
mentality. Waihona no'ono'o.
mention. Ha'i, 'ōlelo. *Don't mention it,* mai ho'opua a'e *(see* **welcome**). *Not worth mentioning,* 'a'ohe 'ōlelo 'ana, he mea 'ole.
menu. Papa kuhikuhi mea 'ai.
mercantile. Kālepa.
mercenary. Puni kālā.
merchandise. Waiwai kālepa.
merchant. Kālepa, ma'au'auwā.
merchant marine. 'Au moku kālepa.
merchants. Po'e kū'ai, po'e kālepa.
merciless. Aloha 'ole, laukōnā, loko 'ino.
mercurial. Pili kāninonino.
mercury. Waikālā; *— on back of a mirror,* heu.
Mercury. Ukali-ali'i, Melekulia, Merekuria.
mercy. Aloha. *Mercy seat,* noho aloha. *God of mercy,* Lono-iki-aweawe-aloha.
merely. Wale, nō, auane'i.
meridian. Melekiana, melikiana.
merit. Kūpono, kū. *Certificate of merit,* palapala ho'omaika'i. *Person of exceptional merit or lineage,* maka hihiu.
mermaid. Wahine hi'u i'a.
merman. Kanaka lu'u i ka hohonu.
merry. Le'ale'a, le'a, 'oli'oli, 'aka'aka; mele. *Also:* laupa'apa'ani, 'olina. *Merry Christmas,* Mele Kalikimaka. *Make merry,* le'ale'a, wela ka hao *(fig.).*
merry-go-round. Lio lā'au.
mesh. 1. *Nets.* Maka, maka 'upena. *Various sizes:* nae, nukuwā'ula, nukuā'ula, nukunukuwā'ula, nukunukuā'ula, mākahi, mākahi 'oene, mākahi hoene, mālua, mālua 'oā, mālua 'owā, mākolu, mākolu 'owā, mākolu 'oā, māhā, mahae, mālewa, makahune. *To make net meshes,* kā. *To knot or fasten net meshes,* hi'a. *An additional mesh,* pu'umana. **2.** *Mats.* Maka, maka moena. *Check plait,* maka moena. *Twill plait,* 'o'eno, ho'ohewahewa. *Mesh sizes:* makali'i, makahune; makapepe *(fine);* pū'ao *(coarse). Mesh width,* koana.
Mesopotamia. Mekopakamia.
mess. 1. *Disorder.* Mōkākī. **2.** *Dining.* 'Aina, papa 'aina, wahi 'aina.
message. 'Ōlelo ho'ouna 'ia; leo *(verbal);* 'elele waha 'ole *(written);* kauoha; 'ōlelo uea 'ole *(wireless);* pū'olo *(fig.).*

messenger. 'Elele. *Also:* lawe kauoha, kūkini, 'āha'ilono, 'āha'i 'ōlelo; 'aulani *(of a chief).* One accompanying a messenger, hoa una.
Messiah. Mekia.
Messina. Mekina, Mesina.
metal. Mekala; keleawe *(general name).*
metalsmith. Ku'i keleawe.
metamorphose. Ho'omalule *(from a caterpillar into a butterfly).* See **change.**
metaphor. 'Ōlelo ho'ohālike, mana'o ho'okūkū.
meteor. Akua lele, hōkū lele, koli.
meteorologist. Kilo 'ōuli i ke au o ka manawa. *God of meteorologists,* Kuhimana.
meter. 1. *Distance.* Mika, mekele. **2.** *For measuring.* Ana. *Water meter,* ana wai.
method. 'Ano hana, papa hana. *Without method,* kīpalalē.
Methodist. Mekekiko, Mekokiko.
methylated spirits. Mekulika, metulika.
meticulous. Maiau.
metric. Mekele.
metronome. Ana manawa.
metropolis. Kūlanakauhale nui.
mew. 'Oau, 'owau, nīao.
Mexico, Mexican. Mekiko.
mi. Lī *(in musical scale).*
Michigan. Mikikana.
microbe. Mū 'ike 'ole 'ia e ka maka.
Micronesia, Micronesian. Maikonekia, Maikonikia.
microphone. Mea ho'ōlele leo, lawe 'ōlelo.
microscope. 'Ohe nānā, 'ohe ho'onui 'ike, aniani ho'onui 'ike.
midday. Awakea. *Also:* lolokū, molokū, wekea. *See saying,* **lolo.**
middle. Waena, waenakonu, wālua.
middle-aged. Āo'o, o'o.
midget. Peke.
midnight. Aumoe, kuluaumoe, 'auinapō. See **'ālike.** *Period between midnight and dawn,* pilipuka.
midrib. Nī'au *(coconut frond and leaf);* kua, kuakua *(leaf);* iwi *(as of ti leaf or pili grass).*
midriff. Maka'upena.
mid-tide. Hōlūlū.
midway. Mawaena, waenakonu, 'ālike.
midwife. Pale keiki. *To act as midwife,* ho'ohānau.
midwinter. Ho'oilo kū waena.
might. 1. See **maybe. 2.** *Strength.* Ikaika, mana.
mighty. Ikaika loa, mana loa, pūkonakona, luaahi.
migratory. Noho pa'a 'ole i ka 'āina; leleaoa *(rare).*
Milan. Milana.
mild. 'Ūpalu; kolonahe *(of wind);* mālani. See **gentle.**
mildew. Auloli, kūkaeloli. *Also:* punahelu, pōukiuki.
mile. Mile *(statute);* mile loa *(nautical).*
mileage. Mile, heluna mile.
militaristic. Puni 'oihana kaua.
military. Koa, pū'ali koa.
military academy. Kula koa.
military forces. 'Oihana koa.
military police. Māka'i koa.
military sentry. Koa kia'i.
milk. Waiū *(cf. Haw.-Eng. entry and entries that follow it). Milk cow,* pipi waiū. *To milk,* 'uwī, 'uwī waiū. *To pinch or squeeze in milking,* pikipiki, 'uwī.
milkfish. Awa. *Growth stages:* pua awa, puawa, awa 'aua, awa, awa kalamoho.
milk shake. Waiū luliluli, waiū ho'oluliluli.
milkweed. Laulele, nu'umela.
Milky Way. Hōkū-noho-aupuni, I'a, I'a-lele-i-aka, Kau, Lālani, Lele-aka, Leleiona.
mill. 1. *Mechanical device.* Wili, hale wili. *Coffee mill,* wili kope. *Sugar mill,* hale wili kō, wili kō. *Planing mill,* hale wili papa, wili papa. *Flour mill,* hale wili palaoa, kāwili palaoa. **2.** *Move confusedly.* Ho'owili, ho'opākaka'a hele. **3.** *Money of account.* Mila *(1/10 cent).*

millennium. Melenio, milenio.
millipede. 'Aha.
miller. Kanaka wili palaoa.
millet. Mileka.
millimeter. Miliamekele.
millinery. Mea ho'onani pāpale.
million. Miliona.
millionaire. 'Ona miliona.
millstone. Pōhaku ka'a palaoa, pōhaku ka'a.
mimic. Ho'opili. *Also:* ho'omāhu'i, ho'oma'auwē, ho'opa'i ā pa'i; ma'ewa, ho'oma'ewa *(sarcastic).*
mimosa. Mimoka.
mince pie. Pai me nā mea 'ai 'oki'oki 'ia.
mind. 1. *Intellect.* Mana'o, waihona no'ono'o, na'au. *Broad-minded,* no'ono'o laulā. *Narrow-minded,* no'ono'o hāiki. *A well-filled mind,* 'umeke kā'eo *(fig.). An empty mind,* 'umeke pala 'ole *(fig.). To set the mind on,* kau ka mana'o. *To change the mind,* ho'ohuli i ka mana'o. **2.** *Obey.* Lohe; ho'olohe *(imperative);* wiwo. **3.** *Heed.* Mālama, maliu. *Never mind,* he mea 'ole, 'a'ole pilikia.
mine. 1. *Possessive.* No'u, na'u, ko'u, ka'u, ku'u, o'u, a'u. See **my. 2.** *Pit.* Lua, lua 'eli waiwai; lua lānahu *(coal);* lua 'eli gula *(gold);* maine, mine. **3.** *Military.* Pōkā pahū kai.
mineral. Pōhaku, minelala.
mineral water. Wai minelala.
mingle. Hui pū, kauwili. *Also:* pa'i, hui ka 'aha, holehole.
mingled. Hui, hui 'ia, huihui, kipona.
minimum. Hapa 'u'uku loa, ha'aha'a.
minister. 1. *Priest.* Kahuna, kahuna pule; kahuna a'o *(teaching);* kahu. **2.** *Statesman.* Kuhina *(for various kinds, see Haw.-Eng. entry and entries that follow it).* **3.** *Aid.* Lawelawe.
ministry. 'Oihana kahuna pule *(religious);* 'oihana, ke'ena *(agency).*
Minneapolis. Mineapoli.
Minnesota. Minekoka.
minnow. Minao. See **anchovy, silversides.**
minor. 1. *Small.* 'U'uku iho. **2.** *Underage.* O'o 'ole, keiki o'o 'ole.
minority. Hapa iki, hapa 'u'uku, hapa 'uku. *Minority party,* 'ao'ao kū'ē.
minstrel show. Keaka nika.
mint. 1. *Plant.* Mōhihi, ma'ohi'ohi, honohono, kīponapona, mineka. **2.** *Fiscal.* 'Oihana hana kālā.
minuend. Kumuho'ēmi.
minus. Ho'olawe, lawe. *Minus sign,* kaha ho'olawe, kaha emi. *Eight minus two is six,* 'ewalu lawe 'elua, koe 'eono.
minute. 1. *Time.* Minuke. *Five minutes until eight,* 'elima minuke i koe, hola 'ewalu; 'elima minuke i koe, kani ka hola 'ewalu. *Ten minutes after eight,* 'umi minuke i hala, kā ka hola 'ewalu; 'umi minuke i hala, kani ka hola 'ewalu. **2.** See **tiny.**
minutes. Mo'olelo, mo'o'ōlelo *(as of a meeting). To keep the minutes,* ho'opa'a mo'olelo.
minutia. Nā mea li'ili'i loa, huna, hunehune, nā mea makali'i.
miracle. Hana mana.
miraculous. Mana. *See* **legendary beings.**
mirage. Waili'ulā, waili'u, li'ulā, wai'ō'upē. *God of mirages,* Lima-loa.
mire. Kelekele, pihō, pohō, ki'o lepo, lepo pohō, nenelu, naele.
mirror. Aniani, aniani kilohi; aniani kū *(standing);* aniani pa'a lima *(hand);* kilo pōhaku *(stone under water);* aniani nānā.
mis-. Hewa. *See* **mislead, misnomer, misprint,** *and others.*
misanthrope. Na'au kopekope, 'ōpū kopekope, 'ōpū 'ino, kanaka nanau, mea lanau.
misbehave. Hana kolohe, kolohe.
miscarriage. He'e wale, poholo. *See* **abortion, fetus.**

...li, ʻulīʻulī. *Modern: see* **accordion, autoharp, ...gpipe, bass viol, clarinet, drum, fiddle, flute, ...itar, harmonica, harp, horn, jew's harp, melo-...on, mouth organ, organ, trumpet, ukulele, ...olin.**

...ician. Mea hoʻokani pila *(player);* mea hīmeni, ...ʻopaʻa, puʻukani *(singer);* haku mele *(composer).*

...k. Hualūkini.

...ket. Pū poʻohiwi.

...skmelon. Ipu ʻāwaʻawaʻa.

...slin. Keʻokeʻo *(white);* keʻokeʻo maoli *(bleached, ...ood);* keʻokeʻo pia *(bleached, inferior);* keʻokeʻo wai ...bleached);* leponalo, makalena.

...ss. Hoʻopūkalakī *(as hair);* hoʻominomino *(as a ...ress).*

...ssed. Pūkalakī *(as hair);* minomino *(as a dress).*

...lso: uluulu, ʻahulu.

...ssel. Kio nahawele, ʻōlepe.

...st. Pono. *You must go,* e pono ʻoe ke hele.

...stache. ʻUmiʻumi.

...ustard. Mākeke *(black).*

...uster. Hoʻākoakoa.

...usty. Pelekunu, punahelu, ʻīʻī, uweko, ueko, ...uwekoweko, uekoeko, weko, wilu, wiluwilu, polo-polona, pōukiuki, puleipulu. *See* **moldy.**

...utant. Kāhuli.

...ute. Mumule, mū, mūmū, mule. *Deaf-mutes,* poʻe kuli ā ʻaʻā.

mutilate. Hana ʻino, ʻoki ʻino, hoʻomumuku, hoʻokīnā, ʻeleheʻu.

mutineer. Mea kipi i luna o ka moku.

mutiny. ʻOlohani, mokuāhana, kipi i luna o ka moku. *To cause a mutiny,* hōʻolohani.

mutter. Namunamu, kūhipahipa. *See* **mumble.**

mutton. ʻIʻo hipa. *Leg of mutton,* ʻūhā hipa.

mutual. Like, kaulike, pānaʻi like. *Mutual friend,* hoaloha like. *Mutual admiration,* mahalo kekahi i kekahi.

muzzle. Pūnuku, waha. *To muzzle,* hoʻopaʻa.

my. 1. *Singular possessed object.* Koʻu, kaʻu, kuʻu. 2. *Plural possessed objects.* Oʻu, aʻu.

mynah. Manu-ʻai-pilau, pihaʻekelo.

myriad. Manomano, kinikini, lehulehu.

myrrh. Mula.

myrtle. Hakaka, hadasa, maile haole.

myself. ʻO wau nō, ʻo wau ponoʻī, ʻo wau iho nō. *With myself,* me aʻu iho nō. *For myself,* noʻu iho nō, naʻu iho nō.

mysterious. Āiwaiwa, hōʻeʻepa, pāhaʻohaʻo, hoʻopano, pohihihi, pōliu, poʻo huna; kapolakā.

mystery. Pohihihi, kumulipo, mikelio.

mystic. Mea punihei i nā mea āiwaiwa.

mystify. Hōʻāiwaiwa, hōʻeʻepa, hoʻopāhaʻohaʻo.

myth. Moʻolelo o nā wā kahiko, moʻolelo.

mythical. Mea hoʻokalakupua o nā ʻōlelo kahiko loa. *See* **legendary beings, legendary place.**

Miscarried fetus, keiki heʻe wale, keiki hāʻule wale, hua hāʻule. *Miscarriage of justice,* holo pono ʻole o ke kānāwai.

miscellaneous. Kēlā me kēia, kēlā mea kēia mea, nā mea like ʻole, kīkoʻolā, laukua.

miscellany. Nā mea like ʻole, pūlehulehu.

mischief. Kolohe *(bad or innocent);* ʻeu *(funny).* See **mischief-maker, mischievous.**

mischief-maker. Kolohe, ʻāpiki. *See* **parrot fish.**

mischievous. Kolohe. *Also:* hoʻokolohe, ʻāpiki, ʻeu, ʻepa, hūʻeu, lapa, maka leʻa, lapuwale, ʻeʻeʻe, honole. *See saying,* **makaʻā.**

misconstrue. Hoʻohepa, wehewehe hewa, koho hewa.

misdemeanor. Mikamina.

misdirect. Kuhi pāʻēʻē, kuhikuhi hewa.

miser. Pī. *See* **greed, miserly.**

miserly. *See* **miser.** *Also:* akaoʻo, pīpine, hoʻolaholaho, makauliʻi, minamina, pukumoa.

misery. Pōʻino oki loa, luʻuluʻu, māino, ʻīnea.

misfortune. Pōʻino, pōpilikia. *Also:* ʻawa *(fig.);* laʻa uli, make. *Predict misfortune,* hoʻoiloilo. *Gloat over misfortunes of others,* ʻaikola, hōʻaikola, ʻākola.

misinform. Hōʻike hewa, kuhi pāʻēʻē.

mislead. Alakaʻi hewa. *Also:* kuhi pāʻēʻē, hoʻopāʻēʻē, hoʻopouli, kanaleʻo.

misnomer. ʻŌlelo hewa i ka inoa.

misprint. Paʻi hewa.

mispronounce. Hewa ka hopuna, paʻewa ka hopuna, hewa ka hoʻopuka ʻana.

misrepresent. Hōʻike hewa, hoʻopāʻēʻē.

miss. 1. *Fail to hit.* Hala, hewa. *Also:* kāhewa, hāʻulehope, kapeke; muʻu *(in marbles);* halahī, halahū, holohuʻa, pāhiʻa, holohiʻa. *To miss the way,* hū, hūhewa, hili, halakī. 2. *Perceive absence.* Haʻo. 3. *Nostalgia.* Haʻo wale, minamina. 4. *Unmarried woman.* Wahine male ʻole. *No equivalent to the title.*

misshapen. ʻAluʻalu, ʻanakeʻe, kīnā, naele, ʻopaha, hoʻōpaha, paʻewa, pepeʻe.

missile. Mea pākī, mea kī ʻia. *Guided missile,* mea kī hoʻopololei loa ʻia.

missing. Nalowale, nalo, nano, koe.

mission. Huakaʻi, mikiona, hololani *(rare).*

missionary. Mikanele, mikionele, mikionali; aʻo hele *(itinerant).* *To act like a missionary,* hoʻomikanele.

Mississippi. Mikikipi, Misisipi.

Missouri. Mikouli, Misouri.

misstep. Kāhehi, hehi hewa, kupe.

mist. Uhiwai, noe, ʻohu, ʻehu, ʻehuehu *(in approximate order of decreasing denseness).* In songs, mist is associated with romance. *Also:* lelehuna, huna wai, kēhau, kīʻohuʻohu, pūnohu, uakea, aokū, ʻawa, uahi wai; uaoa. *Fine mist,* lilinoe, kili ʻohu. *See* **misty.** *Heavy mist,* uhiwai. *Creeping mist,* noe kolo, ua noe. *Pink mist,* noe ʻula. *Rainbow-hued mist,* koʻiʻula. *White mist,* uakea. *Love is mist, settles on all hills,* he ʻohu ke aloha, ʻaʻohe kuahiwi kau ʻole *(of love).* *Goddess of mists,* Lilinoe.

mistake. Hewa, kuhi hewa, paʻewa, lalau; kīnaʻu *(flaw).* *To cause or feign a mistake,* hoʻohewa. *To mistake a person for someone else,* kuhi hewa, hoʻomaopopo ʻole. *A mistake by many,* hehehewa.

mistaken. ʻOlalau. *See* **mistake.**

mister. *See* **Mr.**

mistletoe. Kaumahana, hulumoa.

mistreat, mistreatment. Hana ʻino, māuna, pāʻuluʻā. *See* **cruel.**

mistress. Wahine manuahi, ipo manuahi, wahine noho pū; kahu *(of a pet).* *Mistress of a house,* haku wahine o ka home.

misty. Paʻa i ka noe, uhi i ka noe. *Also:* kēwai, pōhina, polohina, hea, hōʻohu; kīʻohuʻohu, māohu, pōluluhi. *See* **glory, mist,** *and sayings,* **kīʻohuʻohu, māʻohu.**

misunderstand. Maopopo akaaka ʻole.

mite. 1. *Insect.* Ona, ane; ona moa *(chicken);* ʻuku hipa *(sheep).* 2. *Small sum.* Lepeka.

mitigated. Akakuʻu, emi.

mitre. Kalaunu pīhopa, pāpale hainikā.

mitten. Mīkini, mīkini lima.

mix. Hoʻohui, hui *(general);* hoʻowali *(as poi, dough).* *Also:* huihui, huikaʻi, hauhili, hauhauhili, hilikau, ʻānoni, hoʻōʻā, kake, kīkomo, ʻāwili, kauwili, wili, noni. *See* **mixture, mix-up.** *To mix ingredients,* kāwili, paʻi, hokahokai. *To mix relish,* poho ʻinamona. *Mixing board or tray,* papa wili, papa wili ʻai. *Poi mixer,* lāʻau hoʻowali ʻai.

mixed. Huikau. *Also:* huihui, hoʻohuihui, hauhili, hauhauhili, hilikau, ʻaluka, kipona, laukua, ʻānoni, ʻānoninoni, ʻānoni, ʻōnoninoni, paʻipaʻi; — *colors,* aʻeaʻe, ʻōʻā. *Mixed liquid,* wai paʻipaʻi. *Mixed drink,* wai paʻipaʻi; iaia, lama hoʻohuihui ʻia, mea inu hoʻohuihui. *Mixed blood,* koko ʻāwili, hapa, ʻōʻā.

mixture. Mea i kāwili pū ʻia, mea i hoʻohuihui ʻia.

mix-up. Huikau, hoʻohuikau, hōkai, hokahokai, kaʻahōkai.

moan. ʻŪ, ʻuhū, ʻuhūʻuhū, kaniʻū, kaniʻuhū, kaniāʻau, auē, nā, nū, nūnū, hoʻonū.

moaning bird. ʻUaʻu kani; hōʻio *(rare).*

moat. ʻAuwaha e hoʻopuni ana i ke kākela.

mob. Uluāoʻa, poʻe hoʻohaunaele.

Mobile. Mopile, Mobile.

mock. Hoʻohenehene, pāhenehene, henehene. *Also:* laumaʻewa, hoʻomaʻewa, maʻewa, hoʻomahua, hoʻomahuakala, hoʻomāʻauwē, hoʻomāʻauea. *See* **battle.**

mock orange. Alaheʻe haole.

mode. ʻAno.

model. Ana, ana hoʻohālike, kumu, kumu hoʻohālike, kumu alakaʻi.

moderate. Hoʻokanahaʻi, akahele.

modern. No kēia au, nupaikini.

modest. Waipahē, akahai, haʻahaʻa, pē, naʻau pē, pēpē, naʻau pēpē, hōʻoiʻoi ʻole. *Also:* kolokolohai, wiwo; ʻōheke *(somewhat).* *Saying: stay down in the green clumps, do not raise yourself,* e noho iho i ke ōpū weuweu, mai hoʻokiʻekiʻe *(see also* **hakalī).**

Mohammed, Mohammedan. Mahomeka, Mohameka.

moist. ʻŪ, maʻū, māʻūʻū, koʻū, maʻūmaʻū, koʻoū, paʻū, ʻūpolu, pulu, līhau, kilipohe. *Moist with fog,* kawaū. *Moist and fragrant,* noʻū.

moisten. Hoʻomaʻū, hoʻomāʻūʻū, hoʻoū, hōʻū, kau wai, kaiehu.

molar. Kuʻi. *Click the molars together,* ʻaʻaki ke kuʻi. *Gnash the molars, hands are slow,* nau ke kuʻi, lohi ka lima *(anger slows work).*

molasses. Malakeke.

mold. 1. *Shape.* ʻOmoʻomo, hoʻomoʻomo, ʻōmilo, ʻōmilomilo. 2. *Fungus.* Ā. *See* **moldy.**

molded. Hōʻomoʻomo ʻia, ʻōmilomilo ʻia. *Molded into an image,* hana ʻia ā kūlike me ke kiʻi.

molding. Mōlina.

moldy. Punahelu. *Also:* ʻīʻī, nehi, paʻū, pīlekaleka, pōukiuki. *See* **musty.** *Moldy odor,* kūnāhelu, pelekunu.

mole. 1. *Anatomical.* Puʻu, kūkaenalo, leponalo. 2. *Mammal.* Mole, kameleona.

mollified. Mānalo.

mollify. Hoʻomānalo, hoʻopalupalu, hoʻomalimali.

mollusk. *See* **shell.**

Molokaʻi. Molokaʻi. *Epithet: great Molokaʻi of Hina,* Molokaʻi nui a Hina *(Hina was the legendary mother of Molokaʻi).*

molt. Māunu, heleleʻi ka hulu; auhā *(rare).*

molten. Hoʻoheheʻe ʻia.

Moluccas. Moluka.

moment. Manawa iki. *Wait a moment,* kali iki, eia iho.

momentum. Momeneku, ke ʻano o ka neʻe ʻana i mua. *To gain momentum,* hoʻonui aku i ko holo ʻana.

monarch. Mōʻī, aliʻi.

monarchy. Aupuni mōʻī.

monastery. Hale mōneka, monekekeli.

Monday. Pō‘akahi. *Rare:* Monelē, Moneke, Monede.
money. Kālā, moni. *Sum of money,* pu‘u kālā, pōkeokeo. *Paper money,* kālā pepa. *Silver money,* kālā ke‘oke‘o, kakalama, hapawalu. *Gold money,* kālā ‘ula‘ula. *Money order,* pepa kīko‘o kālā. *Postal money order,* pila kīko‘o hale leka.
moneyed. Kālā, lako i ke kālā.
Mongolia, Mongolian. Monokolia, Monogolia.
mongoose. ‘Iole manakuke, manakuke.
monitor. Kahu nānā, kahu ho‘oponopono, mea ho‘olohe pono i ka mea e ‘ōlelo ‘ia ana, monika.
monk. Mōneka.
monkey. Keko, mākinikā. *Monkey-like in appearance,* mukeko.
monkeypod. ‘Ohai.
monopoly. Pō‘ai‘ālunu.
monotonous. Manakā.
monsoon. Monokune.
mons pubis. Hena, hene, pu‘ukole. *To see, feel, handle the mons pubis,* ho‘ohena.
monster. Pilikua nui.
Montana. Monekana, Monakana.
Monterey. Monekelei.
month. Mahina, malama. *According to Johnson and Mahelona (40), the months are male stars in the sixth generation after male* Ao *(day) and female* Pō *(night). Each star-month has one or more star-wives. The males are born in succeeding generations starting with* ‘Ikuwā (Pohā-kō‘ele‘ele), *followed by* Welehu, Makali‘i (‘Auhuhu-pa‘ina), Kā‘elo, Kaulua, Nana, Welo, Ikiiki, Ka‘aona, Hinaia‘ele‘ele, Māhoe Mua (Hilina Ehu), *and* Māhoe Hope (Hilina Mā). *Malo 30 equates* ‘Ikuwā *with October, but as shown in Emerson's note (Malo 33–5), correspondences with the Western calendar differed according to islands and individuals. Variants are in parentheses in the above list. Nights of the lunar month:* Hilo, Hoaka, Kū Kahi, Kū Lua, Kū Kolu, Kū Pau, ‘Ole Kū Kahi, ‘Ole Kū Lua, ‘Ole Kū Kolu, ‘Ole Kū Pau, Huna (Ho‘āo), Mohalu (Mōhaluhalu), Hua, Akua, Hoku, Māhealani, Kū Lua, Lā‘au Kū Kahi, Lā‘au Kū Lua, Lā‘au Pau, ‘Ole Kū Kahi, ‘Ole Kū Lua, ‘Ole Pau, Kāloa Kū Kahi, Kāloa Kū Lua, Kāloa Pau, Kāne, Lono, Mauli, Muku. *Months of pregnancy,* kū.
monthly. Kēlā mahina, kēia mahina. *Monthly issue,* puka mahina. *Monthly pay,* uku ma ka mahina.
monument. Kia ho‘omana‘o.
moo. Umō.
mood. **1**. *Disposition.* ‘Ano, na‘au. *See* **feelings, moody**. **2**. *Grammar.* ‘Ōuli. *Indicative mood,* ‘ōuli-ha‘i.
moody. Loli mau ke ‘ano o ka no‘ono‘o, nunuha.
moon. Mahina, malama. *New moon,* mahina hou. *Full moon,* mahina piha, mahina poepoe; Hoku Palemo *(which sets before daylight);* Hoku Ili *(which sets after daylight). Halo around moon,* luahoana, luakālai, luakālai lani. *Nights of full moon,* Hoku, Māhealani *(see* **month***). Waxing moon,* mahina hapalua mua. *Waning moon,* mahina hapalua hope. *Goddess of the moon,* Hina-i-ka-malama. *The moon is up,* kau ka mahina *(a bald man appears).*
moon flower. Koali pehu, koani pehu.
moonlight. Mālamalama o ka mahina. *Pale moonlight,* māhinahina. *The moonlight shines brightly,* ka pā kōnane a ka mahina.
moored. Lana, kū, ho‘opa‘a.
mooring rock. Pōhaku lana.
Moorish idol. Kihikihi.
mop. Lā‘au holoi papahele, kāwele wai. *Mop the floor,* holoi papahele, kalapu papahele.
moral. Pono, molala. *Moral deportment,* noho pono. *To cleanse and purify morally,* huikala. *Cf.* **kānana, kālana**.
morale. Kūlana.
morality. Pono, noho pono ‘ana, maika‘i.
morals. Lula o ka nohona.
moray eel. Puhi ao, puhi kauila.
more. Hou, keu. *See ex.,* **hala 2**. *More or less,* ‘oi ā emi mai. *More than,* mua. *More chicken?* I moa hou? I moa hou nāu? *Give me more,* hā‘awi hou mai. *More people came,* nui hou aku ka po‘e i hele mai.
moreover. Kekahi, eia kekahi, eia hou, koe kēia.
Morinda citrifolia. Noni.
Mormon. Molemona, Moremona.
morning. Kakahiaka. *See* **good morning**. *Early morning,* kakahiaka nui. *Later this morning,* kēia kakahiaka aku. *The dust of morning,* ‘ehu kakahiaka *(fig., dawn, youth, brief shower).*
morning-glory. Koali, koani, kowali *(for various kinds, see Haw.-Eng. entry and entries that follow it),* pōhuehue, hunakai, kūpala, paha, ‘uala koali, kuahulu (koali kuahulu), pa‘ali‘i. *A morning-glory, a twister,* he koali, he pāka‘awili *(of unstable persons).*
Morning Star. Hōkū-ao, Hōkū-loa, Ka-‘elele-o-ka-wana‘ao (?), Hōkū-komohana, Kukui Wana‘ao, Iao, Waileia.
Morocco. Moloko.
moronic. Hepa, kūhepa, ‘ōhepa, ‘ōpulepule.
morose. Nunuha, na‘ina‘i.
morsel. Wahi hakina iki, hakina ‘ai, ‘āmikamika.
mortal. **1**. Kanaka maoli. **2**. *See* **fatal**.
mortar. **1**. *Cement.* Puna, puna hamo, pālolo. **2**. *Vessel.* Poho, ipu ku‘i. **3**. *Ordnance.* Pū kī, pōkā pahū.
mortgage. Molaki. *Chattel mortgage,* molaki waiwai lewa.
mortgagee. Mea pa‘a molaki.
mortgager. Mea molaki.
mortise. Kohe.
mosaic. Mokaika.
Moscow. Mokekao.
mosque. Mokeko.
mosquito. Makika. *Mosquito larvae,* naio makika.
mosquito fish. I‘a makika.
mosquito net. Pākū makika.
moss. Limu *(for various kinds, see Haw.-Eng. entry and entries that follow it). Also:* ‘ēkaha, hinihini ‘ula, huluhulu-a-‘īlio, huluhulu-a-Ka‘au-hele-moa, iliohe, kalauipo, līpoa kuahiwi, mākole mākōpi‘i (mākōpi‘i, maka‘ōpi‘i, kala makapi‘i), ‘ōnohiawa, ‘ōpulepule, ‘owau, wāwae‘iole. *See* **Florida moss**. *Moss-grown,* limua, hākuma, pa‘a i ka limu. *The district is moss-covered,* limua ka moku *(of peace, since moss grows in damp places undisturbed by man).*
most. Hapa nui, nui, hapa loa, loa.
mote. La‘ola‘o, pāla‘ola‘o, pula. *Having something in the eye, as a mote or eyelash,* la‘o, la‘o ka maka, pula ka maka.
moth. Pulelehua, ‘ōka‘i; mū *(clothes moth). Larva and case of case moth,* ‘ōpūlauoho, pūlauoho.
moth-eaten. Ānea, nono, popopo; ‘ai ‘ia e ka mū *(Ioba 13:28).*
mother. Makuahine, māmā; lūau‘i makuahine; hulilau *(fig.). See saying,* **‘alalā**, *and* **godmother, gourd, stepmother**. *Mother of one's children,* hānau kama.
mother and child. Makua mea keiki.
Mother Hubbard. Holokū.
mother-in-law. Makuahūnōai wahine.
mother-of-pearl shell. *See* **pearl shell**.
Mother's Day. Lā o nā mākuahine.
mother tongue. ‘Ōlelo makua.
motion. **1**. *Movement.* ‘Oni, au, ne‘e, mōkio. *Motion of hands and fingers,* hei. *Repeated motion,* hulehulei. *Set in motion,* ho‘ohele. **2**. *Parliamentary.* Noi. *To second a motion,* kōkua.
motionless. ‘Onipa‘a, mālie, ‘oni ‘ole; kīpū lani *(as clouds, stars).*
motive. Kumu.
motor. Mīkini.
motorcycle. Mokokaikala, ka‘a mokokaikala.
mottled. ‘Ōpulepule, kikiko, ‘ōni‘o, ‘ōni‘oni‘o, ni‘o.
motto. Mākia. *"Stand firm" was Lili‘u-o-ka-lani's motto,* " ‘onipa‘a" kā Lili‘u-o-ka-lani mākia.

mound. Ahu, āhua, pu‘u; pu‘u lepo *(earth),* ‘āpu‘u; pu‘u pele *(volcanic);* hāpu‘upu‘u, ha‘apu‘u; ho‘opu‘u; — *up,* po‘i, ho‘āhu.
mount. Pi‘i, e‘e, hō‘e‘e, kau; — *high,* amoamo.
mountain. Mauna, kuahiwi; *verdant —,* kuaola; — *area,* uka, mauka, kuahea. *See* **ridge**. *Region near the mountaintop,* kualono. *Mountain climber,* hele mauna, e‘e kuahiwi, pi‘i mauna.
mountain apple. ‘Ōhi‘a ‘ai.
mountainous. Mauna, ‘ōpalipali.
Mount Carmel. Mauna Kalemela.
mounted police. Māka‘i kau lio.
Mount Hood. Mauna Huka.
Mount Hor. Mauna Hora.
Mount Souffrière. Mauna Kupalali.
mourn. Uē, uwē, ‘ū, kanikau. *Also:* pihe, na‘au‘auā, kūmākena, ka‘akūmākena, kania‘ā, kaniā‘au, kani‘uhū, kūpina‘i; — *extravagantly,* pākepa; — *in chanting,* kanikau, kanikaniā‘ula. *See* **wail**.
mourner. Mea kanikau.
mourning. Mākena, paumākō; mānewanewa, pānewanewa *(extravagantly, as before Christianity or for a chief). Period of mourning,* ka‘akūmākena. *Go mourning,* ‘ū hele.
mouse. ‘Iole, ‘iole li‘ili‘i.
mousetrap. ‘Ūmi‘i ‘iole, ‘ūpiki ‘iole.
mousy. ‘Io‘iole.
mouth. Waha; o‘a *(eel);* lehelehe *(net);* nuku *(harbor);* nuku wai *(stream);* muliwai *(river).*
mouth organ. Pilapuhipuhi.
mouthpiece. Waha ‘ōlelo.
move. Ne‘e *(intransitive);* ho‘one‘e *(transitive, as an object or a checker);* naue, nauwe; ka‘i hele *(in line or succession or as in checkers);* noi *(parliamentary);* peki *(step by step);* ku‘i *(in kōnane game);* kūwili *(restlessly);* ānehe, ānehenehe *(stealthily);* ‘anau *(with jerky motion);* kuekue‘o *(slightly);* palanehe *(daintily);* — *backwards,* ne‘ehope, mene; — *back and forth,* helo, helohelo, ku‘e, ku‘eku‘ena, uene, malewa, koni-ni, kaiue; — *up and down,* ho‘oholu, kaiue, panau; —*straight ahead,* ne‘e i mua, ne‘e pololei, kauaheahe; — *swiftly,* ne‘e ‘āwīwī, mio, miomio, ‘i‘ī, olo‘io, olo-hio, kāholo; — *cautiously and carefully,* akaluli, aka-hele, ka‘iawe, koene, palela, kūnoni, pāne‘ene‘e; — *easily and noiselessly,* palamimo, niau, ka‘a niau, hani, halolani; — *in a flock, herd, company, or together,* ka‘i ‘āuna, mālana, ne‘epū, ne‘epapa, kahe ā wai; — *to and fro or from place to place,* kālewa, koiele, ‘ōhelo, ‘a‘au. *Also:* uai, ho‘ouai, ‘oni, hō‘oni, ‘oni-‘oni, hō‘oni‘oni, ho‘one‘e, oi, uoi, hele, pūne‘e, ne‘eu, lele, au, nene, pane‘e, hulei, pāuma; kolo *(as breeze). On the move,* ki‘ihele, haulani. *Move, as to a new house,* ne‘e aku, komo hale. *First attempts of infant to move,* ene. *Hard to move,* ‘onipa‘a; lolohe *(rare). Your move (in checkers),* kou manawa.
movement. Au, ‘oni, ne‘ena; lawena *(as of dancing hands);* miona *(swift). See* **move**.
movie. Ki‘i ‘oni‘oni.
moving. **1**. *In motion.* Hele, ‘oni, ‘oni‘oni, niau, hāne‘ene‘e; kūlewa *(as clouds);* nauane *(rare). See* **move**. **2**. *Eloquent.* Mīkololohua.
moving picture. Ki‘i ‘oni‘oni.
mow. ‘Oki. *Mow the grass,* ‘oki mau‘u.
Mr. *No term today; formerly, but not used commonly:* Mī, Mika. *Mr. Coan,* Mī Koana. *Mr. Remy,* Mika Remi.
Mrs. *No term today; formerly, but not used commonly:* wahine. *Mrs. Smith,* Kamika Wahine.
much. Nui. *Also:* lau, lua, hālau, kūwaluwalu, makawalu, mākena, ‘oe, oki. *Very much,* nui ‘ino, nui hewahewa, nui loa, kai! *How much?* ‘Ehia? *No matter how much,* ‘ehia. *Twice as much,* pāpālua. *We have much to do,* nui loa kā kāua hana, ‘a‘ohe i laua aku kā kāua hana.
muck. ‘Ōpala, kelekele, ala‘alai.
mucus. Hūpē, ‘ūpē, hākelo, wale. *Also:* na‘o, walewale, wale kea, weka, wekaweka, pīheka. . pāpa‘a hūpē. *To draw in mucus,* h *mucus,* kākelokelo.
mud. Kelekele, pālolo, lepo ‘ūkele. lepo lo‘i.
muddy. Kele, kelekele, kūkele, ahu kele ‘ūkelekele, ‘ōkelekele, hānupa. *Mudd*
mud hen. ‘Alae; nūkea *(white-billed);* *called* ka manu ke‘u ahiahi, *the bird t evening (considered a bad omen).*
mud puddle. Ki‘o lepo.
mud wasp. Nalo lawe lepo.
muff. Huluhulu ho‘opumehana lima.
muffler. Kā‘ei ‘ā‘ī; pale kalukalu *(Biblica*
mug. Ipu, pola.
mulatto. Malaka.
mulberry. Wauke, wauke mālolo, po‘a‘a koaha; *black —,* kalika, kilika, kukami noni; — *bark,* kīwawā. *Mulberry leaf, paper mulberry of Kūlolia that stands al* kū kahi o Kūlolia *(of anything uniquely b*
mulch. Pulu, kīpulu, po‘i kalo. *To clear* kāhili pulu, lauhu‘e. *See saying,* **pulu**. *M ing mulch,* pāhala.
mule. Hoki, miula, piula.
mullet. ‘Ama‘ama *(see* **‘ama‘ama** *for sayin stages);* ‘anae, pahaha; *false —,* uouoa. ‘alihilele.
mull over. Nalu, ho‘omāuiui; piolo *(fig.).*
multiple. Helu komo ‘ia.
multiplicand. Helu ho‘onui ‘ia.
multiplication. Ho‘onui. *Multiplication sig* kaha ho‘onui. *Multiplication tables,* ‘ālualu
multiplier. Helu ho‘onui.
multiply. Ho‘omāhuahua, ho‘onui. *Also:* ho‘ māhua, ho‘omāhua, laupa‘i, kulukulu. *M by two,* ‘alua lua.
multitude. Lehulehu, nehunehu, kini, mū, laupa‘i, pū‘ali, nu‘a.
multitudinous. Kinikini. *Also:* mānu‘unu‘u, m hono.
mum. Mūmū, mū, ho‘omū, mumule, mūkei. *See*
mumble. Namunamu, namu, ho‘onamu, kapalalū.
mumble-the-peg. Kuwala pahi.
mummy. I‘aloa.
mumps. ‘Auwaepahāha, ‘ā‘īpahāha.
munch. Nau, naunau, nome.
munitions. Lako pono kaua.
murder. Pepehi kanaka, kā make loa. *His mur someone else),* kāna make. *His murder (of hi* kona make.
murderer. Pepehi kanaka, lima koko.
murky. Pōuliuli, lepolepo, ‘ōlepolepo, ‘ōmea, ‘ mea.
murmuring. Hamumu, hamumumu, nē, ‘owē, hē, ‘owē ha‘iha‘i. *See* **complain**.
muscle. ‘I‘o, ‘i‘o huki, olonā, oloolonā, makela; *(small);* kāhā po‘ohiwi *(on shoulder blade);* lolokū *back of head);* ‘uala *(of upper arm);* ‘ulu *(in cal leg).*
muscular. Wa‘awa‘a, ‘āwa‘awa‘a, kīwa‘awa‘a, ho‘o lawakua, pūkonakona, konakona.
museum. Hale hō‘ike‘ike. *See* **Bishop Museum**.
mush. Palaoa lūlū.
mushroom. Kūkaelio, māmalu. *Mushroom-shape* pokake.
mushroom coral. Ko‘a kohe, ‘āko‘ako‘a kohe.
music. Mele *(vocal);* pila ho‘okani *(instrumental). Se* **interval, musical instrument, note, scale, tone**. *T play music,* ho‘okani, ho‘okani pila. *To read music* heluhelu hua mele. *Play music!* Kani ka pila!
musical instrument. Pila ho‘okani *(modern). Ancien musical instruments:* hano, hōkeo kani, hōkiokio, ‘ili‘ili, ipu, kā‘eke‘eke (pahūpahū), kāla‘au, nī‘au kani, pahu, papa hehi, pū, pū‘ili, pū lā‘ī, pūniu, ‘ūkēkē,

N

n. Nū.

nag. Nē, ho'ohune, koi ho'ohune, noi mau, nuku, nuku-nuku. *Also:* none, me'o, hauwene, ho'ohana.

nail. 1. *Carpenter's.* Kui, kui nao, kui hao, kui kākia. *Also:* kākia, hākia, mākia, kia, heke, meki, pōheoheo. *Nail point,* maka kui. 2. *Human.* Mai'ao, miki'ao, māi'u'u. 3. *Measurement.* Nala.

nainsook. Nanakuka.

naked. Kohana. *Also:* 'ōlohe, 'ōlohelohe, 'ilikini, koaka, pōka'o, hāka'o, 'omimo. *To go naked,* hele wale, hele kohana.

nakedness. Kohana, kahi huna, hena.

name. 1. *Noun.* Inoa. *See saying, 'a'ala. Name given in a dream,* inoa pō, inoa mai ka pō mai. *Family name,* inoa 'ohana. *Chiefly name,* inoa kapa na ke ali'i. *Fictitious or pet name, nickname, pen name,* inoa kapakapa. 2. *Verb.* Hea, hea inoa, kapa, kāhea.

name chant. Inoa, mele inoa. *To recite a name chant,* hea, hea mele inoa.

name dropping. Pai ali'i.

namely. 'Oia ho'i.

namesake. Inoa.

nankeen. Naneki.

Nanking. Nanekina.

Nantucket. Nanikokeka, Nanikoteka; Nanikukeka, Nanituketa.

nap. Hiamoe iki.

nape. Hokua.

napkin. Kāwele. *Rare:* hainakā, kahakahana lole. *Paper napkin,* kāwele pepa. *Sanitary napkin,* mea hume, kīhamo.

Naples. Napela.

narcotic. Lā'au ho'ohiamoe, lā'au moe, lā'au ho'omalule kino, mea 'ona.

narrate. Ha'i, kūka'i 'ōlelo.

narrow. Lā'iki, hāiki, ho'ohāiki. *Also:* mio, miomio, lānihinihi, ma'awe, 'ōiki, kuhāiki, mo'olio, 'ololī. *Narrow-minded,* hāiki ka 'ike, hāiki ka no'ono'o, loko hāiki, mana'o hāiki. *Narrow escape,* pakele māhunehune; pakele mai make *(from death).*

narrowing. Olomio, mu'oiki, miomio.

nasal. Hanu mai ka ihu. *Nasal speech,* ihu hānuna.

Nashville. Nakawila, Nasavila; Nakiwile.

nasturtium. Pohe haole.

nasty. Pelapela, hauka'e, mākonā, koaea; kō'ā *(fig.). See* **malevolent.**

nation. Lāhui, aupuni. *To form a nation,* ho'olāhui.

national. Aupuni, lāhui.

National Guard. Koa Kia'i Lāhui.

nationality. Lāhui.

native. Kama'āina, maoli, 'ōiwi, kupa, keiki papa. *Also:* kulāiwi, 'āpa'akuma, mauki. *Native land,* one hānau, kulāiwi; kuapuiwi *(rare). Native son,* keiki hānau o ka 'āina, ēwe hānau o ka 'āina. *Native-born,* papa. *Native bird,* manu kama'āina. *Native plant,* lā'au kama'āina. *Native speaker,* mānaleo *(lit., inherited language, a term invented in the 1970s by Larry Kimura and William Wilson).*

natural. Kūpono.

naturalization. Ho'okupa 'ana.

naturalize. Ho'okupa, ho'ohiki.

nature. 1. *Kind.* 'Ano. *Also:* 'ōuli; hulu *(rare). Chiefly nature or character,* na'au ali'i. *Dual natured,* 'ano pāpālua. *In the nature of,* 'ā-, 'ano like me. *Change of nature,* loli 'ano. *Of similar nature,* 'ano like, ho'okahi nō 'ano. *To tell the nature,* hō'ike 'ano. *To attend the calls of nature,* ho'opau pilikia. 2. *No word for nature in the sense of outdoors.*

naughty. Kolohe, 'eu, 'āpiki.

nausea. Pailua, papailua. *Also:* 'ōlanalana, luea, naluea, poluea, poluwā, unea.

nauseated. Liliha, lihaliha, papailua.

nauseating. Pailua, ho'opailua. *Also:* nānue, lua'ikū, liliha, 'ōlanalana.

nautilus. 'Aumoana, 'au-wa'a-lā-lua, moamoa, moamoa wa'a, naukilo. *Cf.* **aniani.**

naval. 'Oihana moku. *Naval battle,* kaua moana.

navel. Piko.

navel string. Piko, ēwe, wewe, 'iewe, 'iawe.

navigate, navigator. Ho'okele.

navy. 'Oihana moku.

navy-blue cloth. 'Ainakini, lainakini.

Nazarite. Nakalike.

neap tide. *No equivalent; see* **tide.**

near. Kokoke, hi'ialo. *To draw near,* kokoke, ho'okokoke.

nearby. Kokoke, a'e, a'e nei, eia aku.

nearly. Kokoke, 'ane'ane, mai. *Nearly dead,* mai make.

nearsighted. 'Ike pōkole.

neat. Maiau, 'auli'i; mikioi *(in craftsmanship). Also:* palamimo, palamio, miomio, ponopono, pa'ihi, popohe, pālawaiki.

Nebraska. Nepalaka, Nebaraka.

necessary. Pono.

necessity. Pono. *Necessities of life,* mea ola o ke kino, nā pono o ka nohona.

neck. 'Ā'ī; waha *(of a dress). Also:* kani'ā'ī, 'ōhao *(rare). Front of neck,* puana'ī. *Slender or slim neck,* 'ā'ī oeoe. *Stiff neck,* 'ā'ī 'o'ole'a, 'ā'īkū, 'ā'ī uaua. *Stiffness or soreness in neck cords,* uauakaha. *Calloused neck,* 'ā'ī pu'u. *Scrofulous neck,* 'ā'ī 'ala'ala, 'ā'ī pala'e, pūlele. *To tie, as about the neck;* kā'awe; 'ōhao *(rare).*

neckerchief. Hainakā 'ā'ī, hinakā 'ā'ī, lei 'ā'ī, hainakā lei.

necklace. Lei. *See* **lei, whale tooth.** *Pearl necklace,* lei momi. *Diamond necklace,* lei kaimana. *Bead necklace,* lei kula *(gold);* akalei *(glass). Hog-tusk necklace,* lei hoaka. *Dogtooth necklace,* lei niho 'īlio. *"Puka" shell necklace,* lei pūpū puka.

necktie. Lei 'ā'ī.

necromancer. Kilo, kuhikuhipu'uone, nīnau 'uhane, nīnau kupapa'u.

need. 1. *Necessity.* Pono, pu'u. *I need to go,* pono 'o au ke hele. 2. *Lacks.* Nele, hemahema.

needle. 1. *Instrument.* Kui, kui kele, kui humuhumu; mānai, pahele, hānai, mākai, mōkila, mākila *(for stringing leis);* hi'a *(for nets);* 'ōhi'u *(for thatching);* kui pāuma *(for sewing gunny sacks);* pine *(of compass);* hou kui *(for injections);* mōlī *(for tattooing). Needle point,* maka kui. *Slot of sewing machine needle,* puka kui kele. *Eye of needle,* puka kui. *To thread a needle,* ho'opiha kui. *Needle-pointed,* huini. 2. *Plant.* Kī, kī nehe.

needlefish. 'Aha, 'aha mele; 'aha'aha *(young).*

needy. Nele, hemahema, 'ōlohe. *See* **poor.**

ne'er-do-well. *See* **vagabond.**

negative. 1. *Negate.* 'Ole, hō'ole. 2. *Of a picture.* Aka ki'i.

neglect. Mālama 'ole, waiho wale, ho'opalaleha, ho'ohemahema, ho'omaopopo 'ole, ha'alele kōkua 'ole, hā'ule.

neglected. Hoʻomaopopo ʻole ʻia. *See* **neglect.**
negligence. Mālama ʻole.
negligent. Hoʻohemahema, palaka, palaheha.
negotiate. Kūkākūkā, kūkā kamaʻilio.
Negro. Nekelo. *See* **black 2.**
negroid. Pāʻele; pūnika *(rare).*
neigh. Ihihī, ʻuhūʻuhū. *To imitate neighing,* hōʻihihī.
neighbor. Hoa noho, hoalauna.
neighborhood. Wahi noho kokoke, kaulu, kaiāulu.
neither. ʻAʻole, ʻaʻole hoʻi. *Neither he nor I,* ʻaʻole ʻoia, ʻaʻole nō ʻo au. *Neither was any good,* ʻaʻole maikaʻi ʻo lāua ā ʻelua.
nephew. Keiki (ke keiki kāne a ke kaikuaʻana, ke kaikaina, ke kaikunāne, ke kaikuahine), keiki hanauna.
Nerita. Pipipi. *See saying,* **iʻa 1.**
nerve. Aʻa, aʻalolo; aʻalolo lohe *(auditory). Such nerve!* Wini ʻiʻo nō *(slang)!*
nervous. Pīhoihoi wale, haʻalulu o loko. *Also:* ulukū, palalū.
nervous system. Nā aʻalolo apau; lolokū; molokū *(rare).*
nervy. Mahaʻoi, wini.
nest. Pūnana.
net. *The most common kinds are* ʻupena *(see Haw.-Eng. entry and entries that follow it),* kōkō. *See* **float, mesh, seine.** *Various kinds: Throwing net,* ʻupena kiloi, ʻupena hoʻolei, ʻupena kiola, uhina. *Drag net,* lau, laukō, ʻalihilele. *Gill net,* kuʻu, ʻupena kuʻu, ʻupena hoʻolewalewa, pahu. *Set net,* ʻupena kuʻu, ʻupena hoʻomoemoe. *Dip net,* ʻākiʻikiʻi, pākiʻikiʻi. *Bag net,* ʻeke, hului, huli, papa, papa hului, hano, lauahi, luelue, nae kuku, papa waha nui, ʻupena kolo, pōuouo. *Mosquito net,* pākū makika. *Other kinds:* ʻaʻei, ʻakuʻikuʻi, pākuʻikuʻi, aumaiewa, hākaʻokaʻo, hei, hihi, hihi manō, holoholo, holowaʻa, holoaʻa, hoʻolewalewa, hukiheʻe, kāʻeʻe, kāhala, kāʻihī, kaʻiʻi, kāʻili, kākā, kākā uhu, kīholo, kōkō puʻupuʻu, kūpō, lau ʻōpae, maiewa, mala lua, mākolu, mālua, maoloha, nae, naepuni, nukuwāʻula, nukuāʻula, pākuʻipai, pāloa, papa, papa hoʻolewalewa *(rare),* pepeiao, pouono, puni, uluulu, ulūlu. Hau-*wood net handles:* hau ō ʻiao, hau ō mālolo. *Other net parts:* hāwele *(lashing);* hoene *(mesh);* kuku puhi, puhi nui, puhi ʻuʻuku, puhi iki *(stick supports);* aʻa puʻupuʻu, ʻaea *(rare),* ʻalihi, hānai, holokuku, hopeʻaʻei, kahahānai, lā, mole, ʻōkaʻi, pā, papa, piko, pīkoni, puʻumana, uluna, ununa. *Net spacer, gauge,* haha kā ʻupena, una. *Net mender,* kīʻoʻe. *To set a net,* kuʻu, kuʻuna, hoʻomoe, hoʻomoemoe. *To throw a net,* kiloi (kiola,hoʻolei) ʻupena. *To draw a net,* ani. *To make net meshes,* kā. *Place for setting a net,* moena, kuʻuna. *Net owner's canoe,* pokiʻi *(rare). Types of net fishing:* lawaiʻa kōkō, hukilau, laulele, kāheʻe, kahekahe, holoholo, mōkū.
nether world. Ke ao o Milu, Milu, Ka-paʻa-heo, poheue.
nettle. Nahele maneʻo.
network. Nae *(base of feather capes);* hiʻa, kōkō ʻula.
neuralgia. Huʻi ma nā aʻalolo.
neuritis. Lumakika, kālawa, hālawa.
neutral. Kāʻokoʻa, komo ʻole i ke kaua.
neutralize. Hoʻomānalo, kāʻokoʻa.
Nevada. Newaka, Newada, Nevada.
never. ʻAʻole, ʻaʻole loa. *Never before,* ʻakahi . . . ā, ʻaʻole i . . . mamua. *I've never been there before,* ʻakahi au ā hele malaila. *Never mind!* ʻAʻole pilikia! He mea ʻole!
nevertheless. Akā, akā hoʻi, naʻe.
new. Hou. *Also:* mea hou, ʻano hou, malihini. *New-fashioned,* ʻano hou; nupaikini *(rare). This is new to me,* he mea malihini kēia i kuʻu maka *(see* **malihini***). What's new?* He aha ka mea hou?
New Bedford. Nū Pelepeki, Nu Belefedi; Nū Pepeki; Nū Pekepoka, Nu Bedefoda.
New Caledonia. Nū Kalekonia, Nu Kaledonia.
newcomer. Malihini.

Newfoundland. Nūpounelana, Nufounelana.
New Guinea. Nū Kini, Nu Gini.
New Hampshire. Nū Hamekia, Nu Hamesia.
New Haven. Nū Hawena.
New Hebrides. Nū Hepeke, Nu Hebede, ʻĀina wohi.
New Holland. Nū Holani.
New Jersey. Nū ʻIeleke, Nu Ierese.
New London. Nū Lalana.
newly. ʻAkahi nō.
New Mexico. Nū Mekiko.
New Orleans. Nū ʻOlina.
news. Mea hou, nū hou, nū, lono; ʻanoʻai *(rare). Foreign news,* nū hou kūwaho. *Local news,* nū hou kūloko. *Bits of news,* hunahuna mea hou, hunehune mea hou. *News item,* ikamu mea hou. *To tell news, bringing of news,* ʻahaʻilono, haʻilono. *To hear sudden news,* lono honua. *The news spread,* kuʻi ka lono.
New South Wales. Nū Wale Hema.
newspaper. Nūpepa. *Daily newspaper,* nūpepa puka lā. *Newspaper carrier or subscriber,* mea lawe nūpepa.
New Testament. Kauoha Hou.
new year. Makahiki hou. *Happy New Year,* hauʻoli makahiki hou, hapenūia.
New Year's Eve. Ahiahi Makahiki Hou.
New York. Nuioka.
New Zealand. Nukīlani.
next. Aʻe, hope, hiki. *Next week,* kēia pule aʻe. *Week after next,* kēia pule aʻe ā ia pule aku. *What next?* Ā he aha aʻe? *The next house,* kekahi hale aku nō, kekahi hale aʻe.
Niagara. Niakala, Niagara.
nibble. Nali, nalinali, ʻaʻaki, ʻakiʻaki, nome. *Also:* namu, namunamu, mīkole, wahaʻula, pākukui, hōleha, mīkoi, mīkoikoi, mīkokoi.
Nicaragua. Nikalakua, Nikaragua.
nice. ʻAuliʻi; ʻoluʻolu *(pleasant);* maikaʻi.
nicked. Manumanu. *See saying,* **whittle.**
nickel. Hapaʻumi. *See* **five cents.**
nickers. Kākalaioa *(plant).*
nickname. Inoa kapakapa.
niece. Kaikamahine (ke kaikamahine a ke kaikuaʻana, ke kaikaina, ke kaikunāne, ke kaikuahine), keiki hanauna.
niggardly. Pī, kulipaʻa.
nigger. Nika.
night. Pō. *Divisions of the night: beginning,* kihi o ka pō; *late night,* aumoe, pili aumoe, kuluaumoe, kau; pōlalouli *(rare); period from midnight to dawn,* pilipuka. *To count the nights of the moon,* helu pō. *Last night,* ka pō nei. *To pass the night,* hōʻaumoe. *Dark night,* pouli, pō kinikini. *Many nights,* pō kinikini, pō mano. *For nights of the month, see* **month.**
night-blooming cereus. Pānini-o-Ka-puna-hou.
night cestrum. ʻAlaaumoe, kūpaoa, onaona Iāpana.
nightfall. Ka pili o ke ahiahi, pō ka lā. *See saying,* **ʻēheu 1.**
nightgown. Muʻumuʻu moe pō, lole moe pō.
nighthawk. Kama, tama.
nightmare. Moehewa, moe ʻino, moe kāhua, pahulu. *To have a nightmare,* moehewa, moe ʻino, hoʻopahulu. *God of nightmares,* Pahulu.
night school. Kula pō.
nightshade. Pōpolo (polopolo), kīkānia lei, ʻīnika.
night watchman. Kiaʻi pō, mākaʻi pō.
Niʻihau. Niʻihau. *Niʻihau person,* Niʻihau, kanaka Niʻihau. *Epithets: Niʻihau of Ka-hele-lani,* Niʻihau a Ka-hele-lani *(name of a chief); Niʻihau leans back firmly (independent),* Niʻihau i ke kīkū; *see also,* **kō 1.**
Nile. Nile.
nilga. Nileka.
nimble. ʻEleu, miki, māmā. *Also:* kaʻukaʻulele, kāholo, ʻākepa, ʻakakē, ʻuleulele.
nine. ʻEiwa, iwa. *Nine times, nine at a time,* pāiwa. *See Gram.* 10.3.
ninepins. Kulakula.

nineteen. 'Umi kūmāiwa, 'umi kumamāiwa.
ninety, ninetieth. Kanaiwa.
ninety-eight. Kanaiwa kūmāwalu, kanaiwa kumamāwalu.
ninety-five. Kanaiwa kūmālima, kanaiwa kumamālima.
ninety-four. Kanaiwa kūmāhā, kanaiwa kumamāhā.
ninety-nine. Kanaiwa kūmāiwa, kanaiwa kumamāiwa.
ninety-one. Kanaiwa kūmākahi, kanaiwa kumamākahi.
ninety-seven. Kanaiwa kūmāhiku, kanaiwa kumamāhiku.
ninety-six. Kanaiwa kūmāono, kanaiwa kumamāono.
ninety-three. Kanaiwa kūmākolu, kanaiwa kumamākolu.
ninety-two. Kanaiwa kūmālua, kanaiwa kumamālua.
ninth. Iwa. *One-ninth,* hapa iwa.
nip. Hō'aki, 'a'aki, 'aki, 'akipohe, 'ini'iniki; — *off,* 'ōmu'o, 'ōmaka, 'ō'ū.
nipped. 'Ōmu'o. *That project was nipped in the bud,* 'ōmu'o 'ia a'e ia hana.
nippers. Niho 'aki, 'ūpā 'ume.
nipple. Maka waiū, maka, maka pua'a, maka mino, 'ōmaka. *Sucking nipple, as for infants,* omo, omo waiū.
Nippon. Nīpona, Nipoa.
nit. Liha, lia.
nitrate. Nikelake.
no. 'A'ole, 'a'ohe. *Rare:* 'a'oe, 'e'oe.
noble. Ali'i, lani, hie, hiehie, hano, hanohano. *Noble bearing,* kohu ali'i, kapukapu. *House of Nobles,* Hale 'Aha'ōlelo Ali'i.
nobody. 'A'ohe mea, 'a'ohe kanaka. *Those nobodies!* 'O 'ole wale mā!
nod. Kūnou, kūlou, kū'ou, kimo.
noddy tern. Noio kōhā, kōhā.
node. Aka.
Noel. Noela.
noise. Hana kuli, kulikuli, wā, wawā, kani, kulina, halulu, ho'ohalulu, kakani, hauwawā, ho'ohauwawā, 'ikuwā.
noiseless. Palanehe, leo 'ole, hāmau.
noisy. Hana kuli, kulikuli, wā, wawā, āwā, ahu wawā. *Also:* ho'ohalulu, kakani, ko'ele, ho'ohauwawā, 'ikuwā. *Rare:* 'ea, kowowowo. *Don't be noisy,* kulikuli.
nolle prosequi. Ho'opau wale.
nomadic. Hele mau, kīhoe. *Nomadic people,* lāhui hele mau, lāhui ae'a.
nominate. Koho, wae, waiho inoa.
nomination. Koho 'ana, wae 'ana.
nominative case. 'Auikumu.
non-. 'Ole.
nonconformer. Kūlana kūlike 'ole, lelepā.
none. 'A'ohe mea, 'a'ohe, 'a'ole. *None whatsoever,* 'ole loa.
nonporous. Pa'apū.
nonsense. 'Ano 'ole, kohu 'ole. *See* **stuff.** *To talk nonsense,* lalau ka 'ōlelo. *Nonsense!* He lalau!
nonspiritual. Kino, kō 'ē kino.
noodle. *No known name.*
nook. Kū'ono, ke'ena, ke'e, po'opo'o, kīpolipoli.
noon. Awakea; kau ka lā i ka lolo *(see* **lolo***);* na'uwā *(rare).*
noose. Pahele, hele, 'ahele. *Also:* holo, puka lou, 'alehe.
nor. 'A'ole nō. *See* **neither.**
Norfolk. Nolepoka, Norefoka.
normal. Kūlike me ke 'ano mau, 'ano mau.
normal school. Kula kumu.
Normandy. Nolemaneki, Noremanedi.
north. 'Ākau. *Rare:* 'elekū, kuanalio.
North America. 'Amelika 'Ākau.
North Carolina. Kalolaina 'Ākau.
North Dakota. Kakoka 'Ākau.
northeast. Hikina 'ākau, noliki.
northern lights. Mālamalama o ka 'ākau.
North Pole. Wēlau 'Ākau.

North Star. Kio-pa'a, Hōkū-pa'a. *Also:* Kia-pa'akai, Noho-loa, Kū-mau.
northwest. Komohana 'ākau, noweke.
Norway. Nolewai, Norewai.
Norwegian. Nolewai, Noloweke.
Norwich. Nouaiki.
nose. Ihu *(descriptive terms,* ihu*).* See **nahunahuihu, contemptuous, lunkhead, quarrelsome, scorn, scornful, snobbish, snore, wise.** *A large, sharp nose,* 'o'oma. *An elevated nose,* pinana ka ihu. *Irregular bridge of nose,* 'ami. *To touch noses in greeting,* honi. *To blow nose,* ho'okē ihu. *A sniffling nose,* pipī ka ihu. *Barely able to breathe through the nose,* ihu pī. *Talk through the nose,* hānuna ka 'ōlelo.
nosebleed. Kahe ke koko o ka ihu.
nose flute. Hano, kōheoheo, 'ohe hano ihu. *Sound of nose flute,* hoehoe.
nostril. Pukaihu.
not. 'A'ole; 'ole, 'a'ohe. *Rare:* 'a'oe, 'e'oe. *Not in the least, not at all, certainly not,* 'a'ole loa, 'ole loa, 'ole wale. *If it were not for you,* e 'ole nō 'oe.
notarize, notary. Nōkali, nōkele.
notary public. Nōkali no ka lehulehu.
notch. Pū'ali, 'auwae, kepa, kepakepa, waha, niho mole; hana *(rare).*
notched. Nihoniho, nihoa, pū'ali, mākinikini, mā'oi'oi, kepa, kepakepa.
note. 1. *Letter.* Leka pōkole, 'ōlelo ho'omana'o, 'ōlelo wehewehe; kauhua *(rare).* 2. *Financial.* Palapala 'ai'ē, pila hō'ai'ē; noka, noka kālā, nota dala. 3. *Musical.* Leo mele, hua, hua mele. *Rare:* kānāwai hīmeni, kānāwai mele. *Grace note,* hua li'ili'i, hua kōkua. *Leading note,* hua alaka'i. *Lowest or highest note (do),* pā. *Whole note,* hua 'oko'a, po'o. *Half note,* po'olima, hua hapa. *Quarter note,* hua hapahā, po'o'ele. *Second note (re),* kō. *Third note (mi),* lī. *Fourth note (fa),* hā. *Sixth note,* lā. *Seventh note (ti),* mī. *Eighth note,* po'omana. *Sixteenth note,* po'omanalua. *Thirty-second note,* po'omanakolu.
notebook. Kālana kākau, kānana kākau.
noted. 'Ike laula 'ia, kaulana. *Noted place,* pana.
nothing. 'Ole, mea 'ole, 'a'ohe mea, nele; neo, 'alaneo, 'ōmilu. *See saying,* **goose.** *Better than nothing,* ma'ū nō ka 'ole; ma'ū nō ka nele. *Nothing doing,* e ahu ana, 'ole wale, 'ole loa.
notice. Hō'ike, 'ōlelo hō'ike, 'ōlelo ho'olaha. *Notice of sale,* ho'olaha kū'ai. *To notice,* nānā.
notify. Hō'ike. *You are hereby notified,* eia 'oe ke hō'ike 'ia aku nei.
notion. Mana'o ulu wale. *Don't get the notion of going,* mai make hele 'oe.
notorious. Kaulana i ka pono 'ole.
Nottingham. Nokinihama, Notinihama.
notwithstanding. Akā, 'a'ole na'e, koe kēia.
nought. 'Ole, neo, ho'oneo.
noun. Ha'iinoa. *See* **common noun, proper noun.** *Noun complement,* ukali ha'iinoa.
nourish. Hānai.
Nova Scotia. Nowa Kekokia, Nova Sekotia.
novel. 1. *Story.* Ka'ao. 2. *Strange.* 'Ano 'ē.
November. Nowemapa.
novice. 'Akahi akahi, ma'a 'ole, hōlona. *See saying,* **kā'e'a'e'a.** *The novice must be cautious,* e akahele ka mea 'akahi akahi.
now. I kēia manawa, 'ānō; inā *(rare). Just now,* a'e nei. *Now and then,* i kēlā manawa i kēia manawa, aia aku aia mai.
nozzle. Kī'amo.
nude. *See* **naked.**
nudge. Koke, ho'okeku, kekukeku, kuke, kukekuke; peu, ho'opeu *(upward).*
Nudibranchia. Lepelepe-o-Hina.
nuggets. Pu'upu'u kula *(gold).*
nuisance. Pilikia, mea ho'opilikia wale, ho'oluhi, mea ho'ouluhua wale, mea 'ino wale, hōkai.

Nukuhiva. Nuʻuhiwa.

null and void. Mea ʻole.

nullify. Hoʻolilo i mea ʻole, hōʻole, pale; luʻi *(rare)*.

numb. Lōlō, māʻeʻele, māʻele. *Also:* mānoanoa, nokule, ʻōpili, kūnāhihi, piliʻaikū, piliāʻaikū, manunu.

number. Helu, heluna, nui *(quantity);* hua helu *(figure).* *See* **numerous.** *Class number,* heluna papa. *Even number,* helu kaulike. *Odd number,* helu paʻewa. *Dual number,* helu lua. *Plural number,* helu nui. *Whole number,* helu ʻokoʻa. *Prime number,* helu kumu. *Perfect number,* helu poʻokela. *Reciprocal number,* hakina pānaʻi. *Mixed number,* hakina pili.

numbered. Helu ʻia.

numeral. Numela.

numerator. Hoʻohelu *(in fractions).*

numerous. Lau, hoʻolau, mano, manoa, lehu, lehulehu, nehunehu, kinikini, kini lau. *Also:* hālau, hoʻohālau, kūhaluka, kuapapa, makawalu, laha, mākena, pupu-pu, pākī, weliweli, weweli, pakapaka, kāʻele, pūlehulehu, kanalani.

numskull. Poʻo ʻolohaka.

nun. Wilikina, nuna.

nunnery. Nunele.

nurse. Kahu maʻi, kahu mālama maʻi; kahu keiki *(of a child).* *Wet nurse,* kahu waiū, kahu wale, nuʻakea, poliwaiū. *To nurse or suckle,* ʻai waiū, omo waiū, poli ʻai *(intransitive);* hānai i ka poli *(transitive).* *To nurse or care for, as an infant,* hiʻi, hiʻilani, hoʻokāpuhi.

nursery. 1. *Children's.* Wahi mālama keiki. **2.** *Garden.* Kīhāpai hoʻoulu mea kanu.

nut. Kukui haole. *Pandanus nut,* hala hua.

nutcracker. ʻŪmiʻi kukui haole.

nutmeg. Huaʻala.

Nuʻu-anu. Nuʻu-anu *(literally, cool height).* The wind comes down bearing the flowers of Nuʻu-anu *(PH 168),* ke iho lā ka makani halihali pua o Nuʻu-anu.

O

o. 1. *The letter.* 'Ō. 2. *Vocative.* Ē, ē . . . ē.

O'ahu. O'ahu. *Epithets: O'ahu, child of Lua,* O'ahu a Lua *[Lua slept with Papa after Papa became angry about husband Wākea's infidelity: HM 302].* The sands of Kā-kuhihewa *[an important O'ahu chief],* ke one o Kā-kuhihewa. *The chief destroying sands of Kā-kuhihewa,* ke one 'ai ali'i o Kā-kuhihewa.

oak. 'Oka. *See* silky oak.

Oakland. 'Okalana.

oakum. Ukamu.

oar. Hoe. *Steering oar,* hoe uli.

oarsman. Mea hoe wa'a, hoe wa'a.

oasis. Wahi uliuli ma ka wao one.

oath. 1. *In court.* Ho'ohiki, 'ōlelo ho'ohiki, 'ōlelo pa'a. *A Hawaiian oath:* pau Pele, pau manō *(see* manō*).* 2. *See* swear.

oatmeal. *No equivalent; see* breakfast food.

oats. 'Oka.

obedient. Ho'olono, ho'olohe, lohena, wiwo.

obese. Momona loa, pūhalalū. *Rare:* uhalalē, kualakai.

obey. Lohe, ho'olono, wiwo.

obituary. Mo'olelo o ka mea 'akahi nō ā make.

object. 1. *Thing.* Mea. *Object of a sentence,* hope ha'ina. 2. *Purpose.* Kumu, mea; mea i kaulona 'ia *(rare).* 3. *See* oppose.

objection. Kū'ē, kumu ho'ohalahala.

obligation. 'Ai'ē *(debt).*

oblige. Koi. *Much obliged,* mahalo nui.

obliging. 'Olu'olu, lokomaika'i.

oblique. Hiō, lala, ākepakepa, pala'ewa, kū'ewa, a'e, hīhe'e. *Cut obliquely,* kepa, ho'okepa, pāhi'a. *To strike obliquely, us wind or wave,* pā lala.

oblivious. Palaka, nānā 'ole.

oblong. Oloolo, olōlo.

obscene. Pelapela, haumia, ho'ohilahila. *Obscene language,* 'ōlelo haumia.

obscure. Poahi, pōahiahi, poehi, powehi, pōehiehi, pōwehiwehi, pohihihi, pōhihi, pohihiu, pō, kōli'u, kōli'uli'u. *Also:* pano, panopano, maka pōniuniu, āhiahia, ho'āhiahia, hea, palaweka, pālauweka, pālaueka, hāpu'upu'u, 'e'a'e'a, pōnalo, 'a'aki, pinao. *Obscure and difficult to understand,* 'ike pohihihi, maopopo pohihihi, akaaka 'ole.

observant. 'I'ike, maka kilo.

observation. Nānā 'ana, mana'o, loina.

observation point. Hālōna, 'īmaka.

observatory. Hale kilo hōkū. *Star observatory,* hale kilolani, kilolani.

observe. Nānā, nānā pono, hākilo, kilo malama, kilo, haka pono, aua; *to — an order,* mālama kauoha; — *closely,* kaulona, pau kilo. *To observe clouds,* nānā ao. *To observe fish,* kilo i'a. *To observe stars,* kilo hōkū. *To observe the seas,* kilo moana. *To observe the winds, as for navigation,* kilo makani.

obsession. Pulakaumaka.

obsidian. *No Hawaiian term noted.*

obsolete. Make.

obstacle. Ālaina, mea ala'alai, mea ke'ake'a, pu'upā. *Fig.,* pu'u, pali. *To meet an obstacle,* ku'ia.

obstetrician. Kauka ho'ohānau, kauka pale keiki.

obstinate. Pa'akikī, 'o'ole'a, pa'a loa, po'o pa'a, 'a'ī 'o'ole'a, lae pa'a. *Also:* hukihuki, ho'olehelehe nui, uaua, koe'ā, kā'ape.

obstreperous. Waha kole, nui ka wala'au, waha wala'au, ho'ohaunaele.

obstruct. Ālai, ānai, ke'a, ho'oke'a, ho'okāpae, 'āke'ake'a, kualo; pōhāko'i *(rare).*

obstruction. *See* obstruct. *To remove obstruction,* ho'okuakahi.

obtain. Loa'a.

obtrusive. Hō'oi'oi, maha'oi.

obtuse. Kūmūmū, lohi ka no'ono'o 'ana. *Obtuse angle,* huina peleleu.

obvious. Maopopo le'a, aniani, aliali, a'ia'i, mōakaaka, moakaka, mālani, waiho akaaka, ahuwale, waihokāka.

occasion. Wā, hanana.

occasionally. Aia aku aia mai, kūikawā.

occupant. Mea noho. *House occupant,* noho hale.

occupation. 'Oihana, hana. *Favorite occupation,* hana punahele, me'e.

occupied. Lilo, pa'a.

occupy. Noho, ho'onoho *(as a house).*

occur. Kupu, hiki mai; 'owālala, 'oālala *(as a thought).*

occurrence. Hanana.

ocean. Moana *(open);* kai. *Ocean depths,* hohonu kai. *Ocean floor,* papakū.

oceanographer, oceanography. Kilo moana.

ocher. Ma'alaea, 'okele; īhe'ekai *(used ceremoniously).*

o'clock. Hola. *Two o'clock,* hola 'elua.

octagon. Huinawalu.

octave. Pi'i pāwalu, lelepuni.

October. 'Okakopa.

octopus. He'e *(for various kinds, see Haw.-Eng. entry and entries that follow it).* See cowry shell, cuttle-fish, squid. *Octopus tentacle,* 'awe'awe, 'awe, 'awe ule, 'awe puhi. *Octopus beak,* niho. *Octopus ink,* weka. *Octopus ink sac,* 'ala'ala. *Octopus flesh,* iho. *Other parts:* pu he'e, pikapīka, pilipili. *To fish for octopus,* lūhe'e, kilo he'e, 'ōkilo he'e, 'ō he'e. *Octopus lure,* lūhe'e. *Octopus season,* wā he'e. *Slightly decomposed octopus,* mākole, he'e mākole, he'e puhi. *Mark left on skin by octopus tentacle,* 'ōpikopiko. *Octopus mouth,* waha o ka he'e *(liar).* A slice of octopus, poke he'e *(a chubby person).*

odd. 'Ano 'ē, pa'ewa, pau'aka. *Odd number,* helu pa'ewa. *Odds and ends,* 'o kēlā me kēia; kēlā mea kēia mea; hi'uhi'u *(as of ropes).*

Odessa. 'Okeka, Odesa.

odious. 'Ino'ino.

odor. *See* smell.

of. O, a, kō, kā, no. *Afraid of death,* maka'u i ka make.

off. Mai *(from);* 'ē *(away).* To fall off a box, hā'ule mai ka pahu. *Be off!* Hele i kahi 'ē! Hele pēlā! Hemū! *Off-balance,* kūlike 'ole.

offal. Moka, poka.

offend. Ho'ohuhū, ho'onāukiuki, ho'oma'au; 'ōlepolepo *(fig.).* See pulapula 3.

offended. Uluhua, ukiuki, kā'eko.

offense. Hewa, hala, lawehala, 'openi. *First offense,* hewa mua.

offer. Hā'awi, hō.

offering. Mōhai *(for various kinds, see Haw.-Eng. entry and entries that follow it);* church —, lūlū, ho'okupu, mahina hou, hānai pule. *Also:* hai, haina, hai 'ai, kaumaha, kaumaha 'ai, hāuna, hauhāuna, hua mua, ulu-'ālana; 'ālana, 'ālana aloha, 'ālana kuni, 'umihau, ho'āli, hi'ali, mua kau, kahukahu, 'onou, mea hana, kāmauli, hānai kuahu, pāpāi'awa, maukoli, papaio, pāpāia, puku.

office. 1. *Position.* Hana, 'oihana. 2. *Room.* Ke'ena, ke'ena hana.

office holder. Noho 'oihana.

officer. Ali'i, luna. *See* warrant officer. *High or impor-*

tant officer, luna nui, ali'i ki'eki'e, luna ko'iko'i. *Presiding officer,* ali'i ho'omalu. *Military officer,* ali-'ikoa, luna koa, luna kaua. *Communications officer,* luna'ōlelo. *Officers in the monarchy and in ancient Hawai'i:* kuhina, kuhina nui, kālaimoku, ilāmuku; kualanapuhi, ikū *(see Haw.-Eng. entries and those that follow them for these rare terms),* oma.

official. *See* **officer.** *Official business,* hana o ke aupuni.

offspring. Keiki, hānau, pua, pulapula, kupu, hua; hauloli'i *(rare). Fig.:* 'ano'ano, 'ohā, makalau, a'a. *One with many offspring,* kū ā makalau, lālā ola. *Without offspring,* lālā 'ole.

often. Pinepine, nui. *Also:* maumau, mākena, alapine.

ogle. 'Āwihi, kāluhe.

ogo *(seaweed).* Manauea.

oh. Auē, auē noho'i ē, auwē, kā, ā; kāhūhū, kāhāhā, kāhīhī, kāhōhō *(exclamations of surprise or indignation). To oh and ah,* ahē.

Ohio. 'Ohaio.

oil. 'Aila, hinu, mano'i, kelekele, kelema, poni. *To rub with oil,* kākele, kāhinu, poni.

oilcan. Kānuku 'aila.

oilcloth. Pale pākaukau 'aila.

oilfish. Walu, wolu. *Cf.* **maku'u 3.**

oily. Hinuhinu, hinu, kūhinu, kelekele, kele, 'ūkele, liliha, lihaliha, niuniu, likoliko.

ointment. Mea hamo, 'aila hamo, lā'au hamo, hinu, mea poni, mea 'ala, nini, ki'ikea.

O.K. Hiki, hiki nō, pololei.

Oklahoma. 'Okalahoma.

old. Kahiko *(usually not of people);* o'o, 'elemakule, luahine. *Also:* mākuakua, makua lua, 'alu'a, 'ele-, makule, kolo'u'a, kolopupū, 'āleuleu, pāleuleu, pāwelu, māuaua, kū'olo, 'āpela, pane'e, kolepeia'alu. *See* **old age, old man, old woman.** *To cling to old customs,* ho'okahiko.

old age. Wā 'elemakule, wā luahine, kolopupū. *See sayings,* **'auwae 1, hui 6, bone, chin, cowry shell, feeble, rat.** *Fig. and poetic terms:* 'ehu ahiahi, haumaka-'iole, pala lau hala, ka'ikōkō, kauko'o, kaniko'o, lā'ele, ō kō kea, puaaneane, puāneane. *Esteemed terms:* hulu, hulu kupuna, hulu makua. *Derisive terms:* 'auwae lenalena, kolepeia'alu, ku'i lena, nenanena 'auwae, niho lena, niho kahi.

older. Mua, hiapo *(of children in a family).*

oldest. Makua, kuapapa.

old-fashioned. Ho'okahiko, 'ano o ke au kahiko.

old fellow. 'Elekule, 'olopala.

old maid. 'Olomeka. *See* **spinster.**

old man. 'Elemakule, 'olomana. *To become an old man,* 'elemakule. *To behave like an old man,* hō'elemakule.

old soldier. Koa kahiko.

Old Testament. Kauoha Kahiko.

old woman. Luahine; 'elehine *(rare). See* **hag.**

oleander. 'Oliana, 'oliwa, nohomālie.

olive. 'Oliwa, oliva.

olivine. *No equivalent. Rock with olivine,* pōhaku pele 'ōma'o. *Sand with olivine,* one 'ōma'o.

Olympia. 'Olumepia.

Omega. 'Omeka.

omelet. Hua pākā, hua palai i ka'awili 'ia.

omen. 'Ōuli, hō'ailona. *See* **mud hen, thunder.** *To tell omens,* ha'i 'ōuli, nānā uli, kilo.

ominous. Hō'ailona pō'ino.

omission. Mea i waiho 'ia, mea i kāpae 'ia, hō'alo, 'alo 'ana.

omit. Waiho, kāpae, hō'alo.

omnipotent. Mana loa.

on. I, ma, maluna o, maluna, luna, nuna, luna o.

onanism. Pīkoikoi. *See* **masturbate.** *To practice onanism,* ha'akoi.

once. Ho'okahi wā, kekahi wā, pākahi, kuakahi. *Once upon a time,* i ho'okahi manawa.

one. 'Ekahi, 'akahi *(counting in a series);* ho'okahi, kahi, kekahi; hapa- *(in fractions). One quarter,* hapahā. *One eighth,* hapawalu. *The one who,* ka mea i, ka,

ke, ka i, ka e. *One at a time, one by one,* pākahi. *To make as one,* ho'okahi.

one-masted vessel. Kia kahi.

oneness. Ho'okahi.

onerous. Lu'ulu'u, kaumaha.

one-sided. Kapakahi, hō'ewa; pā'ao'ao *(rare).*

onion. 'Aka'akai *(for various kinds, see Haw.-Eng. entry and entries that follow it);* naku, mahina.

only. Wale nō, wale. *One only,* ho'okahi wale nō, kiakahi. *Only if, only when,* aia nō ā.

onomatopoeia. Hua'ōlelo ho'opilipili leo. *Examples of sounds believed onomatopoeic:* 'ekelo *(mynah bird);* ō *(peacock);* kokō *(hen, as after laying an egg);* pūkōkō *(hen in alarm);* kōlea, kolekolea *(kōlea bird);* kolokolo *(turkey gobbler);* pōkeokeo *(turkey hen);* laweke ō *(stilt bird);* li'oli'o *(li'o bird);* ōwī *('ō'ū bird);* 'ūlili *('ūlili bird);* kue *(petrel bird);* 'owā *('auku'u bird);* mā'ā'ā *(sheep, goat);* nū, hū *(pig);* 'olā'olā *(water);* kuekue *(tapping). See* **baa, bowwow, bray, cluck, cock-a-doodle-doo, coo, grunt, heehaw, honk, mew, moo, neigh, peep, quack, shish.**

onset. Ho'omaka 'ana, 'iliki.

onslaught. Po'ipū, pua'ō, 'ūpā.

Ontario. 'Onekalio, Onetario.

onward. I mua, mamua, hele i mua, holo i mua.

onyx. 'Onika, kalekonuka.

oo. *See* **digging stick, honey eater.**

ooze. Ū, nō, nono, hānono, hānonono, pīpī wai, pāhūhū.

open. *There is no general term; the main usages follow:* **1.** *Usually intransitive, a state of being open, as a crack.* Hāmama; makili, mikili, nakili, ho'omakili *(as a crack);* kūnihi; ka'aka'a *(as eyes);* ākea. *Also:* poale, pōaleale, ulehe, ulehelehe, kauhola, 'uhola, hoaka, hunāhunā 'ole, 'ōwehewehe, wahalehe, uhalehe, 'oma. *Open to the public (as open house),* ho'ohāmama 'ia i ka lehulehu. **2.** *As a flower.* Mōhala, ho'omōhala, mōhalu, molokala, pohala, makala, mokala, ōpū, 'ōme'o. **3.** *Transitive, as a door, package.* Wehe, 'uwehe, 'uehe, weke, wekeweke, hemo, maweke, māweke; hu'e *(as an oven);* 'ūpā, hā'upā; ho'ohāmama, 'ōlepe; ho'oka'aka'a *(as eyes).*

opener. *See* **can opener.**

openhanded. Lima hāmama, hā'awi lokomaika'i.

openhearted. Pu'uwai hāmama.

open house. *See* **open.**

opening. Puka, wehena, wehe 'ana, waha, ho'owaha, mōhala, 'īpuka; hu'ena *(as of oven);* 'uiki, 'uwiki, hua'ina, puma. *See* **open.**

opera. Keaka mele.

operate. 'Oki, kaha *(surgically);* hana *(do).*

operation. 'Oki.

operculum. Pani pūpū.

'opihi. *See* **limpet.**

opinion. Mana'o. *To state opinion,* ha'i mana'o. *To seek or change an opinion,* huli mana'o. *In my private opinion,* i ku'u mana'o wale nō.

opinions. Nā mana'o, manana'o.

opium. 'Opiuma.

opossum. 'Opakuma, 'opekama.

opponent. Hoa paio, mea kū'ē, 'ao'ao kū'ē.

opportunity. Manawa kūpono.

oppose. Kū'ē, ālai, ānai, ke'a, ke'ake'a. *Also:* pāku'i, kē, pūkani lua, 'ā'ume'ume, 'auwaepu'u. *Rare:* kēueue, na'ina'i.

opposite. Kū'ē, 'ē'ē, hulina alo. *See* **opposition.** *Opposite meaning,* mana'o kū'ē.

opposition. Kū'ē'ē, 'ao'ao kū'ē, hana kū'ē, 'ā'ume-'ume, noho ke'e. *To stir up opposition,* ho'okū'ē'ē.

oppress. Ho'olu'ulu'u, ho'oluhi hewa, ho'okaumaha, ho'oko'iko'i, ho'okuapa'a, hō'eha. *Also:* ho'olaukōnā, pāku'i, ho'okāuha, ho'okākāuha, 'a'e, ho'omauleho, kala'ihi, ho'omauha'alina.

or. Ai'ole, ā . . . paha; o *(lest). Two or three,* 'elua ā 'ekolu paha.

oracle. Haka *(medium).*

oracle gourd. Ipu 'ōlelo.
oracle tower. Lananu'u mamao, nananu'u mamao, lananu'u, nu'u, lana, 'anu'u *(on heiau). A part of the tower,* lewaanu'u *(rare).*
oral. Ha'i waha.
orange. 'Alani *(the fruit or tree).*
orange-yellow. Melemele 'ili 'alani.
orangutan. 'Oulanakana.
orate. Kākā'ōlelo, ha'i'ōlelo.
oration. Ha'i'ōlelo ho'ohanohano *(eulogistic).*
orator. Kākā'ōlelo, ha'i'ōlelo.
oratory. Kākā'ōlelo.
orbit. Ala pō'ai, apo hele.
orchard. Māla lā'au hua 'ai, kīhāpai.
orchestra. Hui ho'okani pila, pāna. *Cf.* hui puhi 'ohe.
orchid. 'Okika; 'okika honohono; 'awapuhi-a-Kanaloa.
ordain. Poni, ho'oponi, ho'okahuna.
ordeal. Pōpilikia, hana nui, hana pū'ika'ika, hana 'eha-'eha, 'awa.
order. 1. *Command.* Kauoha *(general; to send for, as groceries);* kēnā, ho'okēnākēnā, 'ōlelo kauoha, ho'opa'a. *Money order,* pepa kīko'o kālā. *Postal money order,* pila kīko'o hale leka. *By order of,* ma ke kauoha a. *To give orders,* kauoha, kuhikuhi. **2.** *Arrangement.* Ho'onohonoho 'ana, papa, noho papa, ho'onoho papa, ponopono, ka'ina, moekahi. *In perfect order,* pono. *To put to order,* ho'oponopono, ho'opapa, kuene; haku, hakuhaku *(rare). Word order,* ka'ina o nā hua 'ōlelo. *To call to order, as a meeting,* ho'omalu. **3.** *See* **in order to.**
ordinance. 'Ōlelo kūpa'a, kānāwai.
ordinary. Ma'amau, laha, mea loa'a wale, a'e nei, pākūwā, pākūā. *Ordinary person,* kanaka a'e nei nō; ki'i maka li'ili'i. *Having ways of ordinary folk,* ha'aha'a; waikanaka *(rare).*
ordination. 'Olinakio.
Oregon. 'Olekona, Oregona.
organ. 1. *Musical instrument.* 'Okana. *Hand organ,* 'okana wili lima. *Mouth organ,* pilapuhipuhi. **2.** *Part.* Mahele. *Internal organs,* loko.
organdy. 'Okanaki.
organic. 'Okanika.
Organic Act. Kānāwai Kumu, Kānāwai 'Okanika.
organization. Hui, 'ahahui, kūkulu 'ana, kūkunu 'ana, ho'onoho 'ana.
organize. Kūkulu, kūkunu, ho'ohui, ho'onohonoho.
orgasm. Le'a.
Orient. Hikina.
origin. Kinohi, ho'omaka 'ana, kumu; kumu honua *(of the earth);* kumulipo.
original. Kumu. *Original document,* palapala kumu.
originate. *See* **begin.**
Orion. 'Oliona. *Stars in Orion's belt,* Maiakū. *Stars in Orion's belt and sword,* Nā-kao.
ornament. Wehi, kāhiko, kīnohi, ho'okāhiko; *beautiful —,* linohau.
orphan. Keiki makua 'ole, kama lele. *Weeping for an orphan child, no parents, woe!* e uē nō anei, he keiki makua 'ole, 'a'ohe mākua, uē ho'i ē!
orthography. *See* **spelling.**
oscillate. Lewalewa, lewa, uene, uwene.
osprey. 'Okepela.
ossifrage. 'Okepelaka.
osteomalacia. 'Ea wāhi pa'a.
osteopath. Kauka lomilomi.
ostrich. 'Akolika, 'okekelika, oseterika, 'okelekelika.
other. Kekahi, 'ē a'e, 'ē.
otherwise. Akā na'e, ma kekahi 'ano 'ē a'e. *There was much rain, otherwise everything was fine,* ua nui ka ua, akā na'e maika'i nō nā mea apau.
ouch. Auē, auwē, auwī.
ought. Pono. *You ought to go,* he mea pono iā'oe ke hele.
ounce. 'Aunaki, 'aunake, 'auneki.
our. 1. *Singular possessed object, dual, inclusive.* Kō kāua *(o-class);* kā kāua *(a-class).* **2.** *Singular possessed*

object, dual, exclusive. Kō māua *(o-class);* kā māua *(a-class).* **3.** *Singular possessed object, plural, inclusive.* Kō kākou *(o-class);* kā kākou *(a-class).* **4.** *Singular possessed object, plural, exclusive.* Kō mākou *(o-class);* kā mākou *(a-class).* **5.** *Plural possessed objects, dual, inclusive.* O kāua *(o-class);* a kāua *(a-class).* **6.** *Plural possessed objects, dual, exclusive.* O māua *(o-class);* a māua *(a-class).* **7.** *Plural possessed objects, plural, inclusive.* O kākou *(o-class);* a kākou *(a-class).* **8.** *Plural possessed objects, plural, exclusive.* O mākou *(o-class);* a mākou *(a-class). There are 16 common translations of English "our." For other uses of k-less (zero-type) possessives, Gram. 9.6.3.*
ours. No kāua, no māua, no kākou, no mākou, na kāua, na māua, na kākou, na mākou. *See* **our.**
oust. Kipaku, ho'okuke, ualehe, kūlē.
out. Waho, i waho, mawaho; pio *(extinguished). Rare:* hauka, 'auka *(in games).*
outburst. Hū, pahū.
outcast. Kauā, kauwā *(for various qualifiers, see Haw.-Eng. entry and entries that follow it; also see* **lae** *and qualifiers). Uncomplimentary epithets:* heana kanaka *(intended for human sacrifice);* makawela, limu pae, lua'i pō, lau'ī pekepeke, lele koa'e, palani, pie ueue, auwehekika, hūpoenui, 'ōhao 'īlio. *See* **vagabond.** *Places where outcasts were drowned:* kai hehe'e.
outcrop. Mea hū honua.
outcry. Oho, ho'ōho, ohooho, ho'ōhooho.
outdo. Ho'okela; oko *(rare).*
outdoors. O waho.
outer. Waho, o waho, kūwaho.
outfitted. Ho'olako 'ia; lilihua *(rare).*
outhouse. Wahi ho'opau pilikia, hale li'ili'i, lua li'ili'i, lua, hale lua. *Rare:* luahaka, auolo, 'auwaha, auhā.
outlet. Pukana, puka wai, makawai. *Electric outlet,* kumu ho'opuka uila.
outrigger boom. 'Iako.
outrigger canoe. Wa'a.
outrigger float. Ama, iama. *End of float,* lupe. *Leaping float end,* lele lupe *(emotion). Kī-lau-ea is overturned like a canoe outrigger,* kahull Kī-lau-ea mehe ama wa'a lā.
outside. Waho, i waho, mawaho, kō waho, kūwaho.
outsider. Kanaka 'ē, kanaka o waho; lauhulu *(fig.).*
outstanding. Po'okela, kau i ka wēkiu, kū kahi. *Also:* kūlia, kakahi. *Outstanding debt,* 'ai'ē ka'a 'ole.
outstretched. Kākāuha.
outward. *See* **outer.**
outwit. Lanakila.
oval. Oloolo, olōlo, 'omo'omo, pō'ai lō'ihi, poepoehāwa'e, poepoepīkoi, hualala.
oven. Imu *(for various kinds, see Haw.-Eng. entry and entries that follow it);* umu, 'oma, 'oma Pukikī; umu pao, imu pao *(above ground); umu lepo (earth). Oven house,* hale umu. *To lay, as an oven,* haka. *To tend an oven, oven tender,* kahu umu. *Oven cooking,* kahuna. *Leaf lining of oven,* pale.
over. 1. *Above.* Luna, i luna, maluna, i nuna. *Over and above,* 'oi aku, pākeu, ā 'oi. **2.** *Completed.* Pau. **3.** *Again.* Hou. *Do over,* hana hou. *Do over and over,* hana hou ā hana hou; ka'awelekā *(rare).*
overactive. Lapa.
overalls. Lole wāwae 'epane.
overbearing. Ho'okelakela, ho'oki'eki'e, 'a'ano. *Also:* ka'aluna *(fig.),* kanaie, ho'okanaie, ho'olanakila, mahalua.
overboard. I ke kai. *Jump overboard,* lele i ke kai. *Throw overboard,* kiloi i loko o ke kai, kāwa'a.
overcast. 'Ōmalu, 'ōmalumalu, 'omamalu, ho'omalu, ho'ōmalumalu, lāuli, ho'ohaha.
overcome. 1. *To defeat.* Lanakila, ho'opio, holopapa. **2.** *Defeated.* Pio, puni. **3.** *Possessed, as by emotion, as fear, passion, joy, grief.* Lo'ohia, ilihia, ulupuni, 'ōkā, auālipo.
overcooked. Mo'a loa; mo'a palahē, palakahuki, paluhē *(as meat). Also:* ahulu, wahulu.

overeat. Pākela 'ai, ahu 'ai, kuenenu'u. *See* **eat.** *Discomfort from overeating,* 'ōpihapiha.
overfamiliarity. Pākela maha'oi; nole *(rare).*
overflow. Hū, hālana, hālanalana, hānana, hanini, ho'ohanini, pi'ipi'i, wai pi'i, waikahe, wai hū, huana, 'olo'olo, holomoku, holomokuna, kūmoho.
overgrowth. Uluāhewa, hihipe'a.
overhang. Luhe, lo'u.
overheated. Ahuli'u, hahana.
overladen. Lu'ulu'u, 'olo'olōna.
overlap. Kau iho kekahi maluna o kekahi, 'ili'ili; 'unu-'unu *(in sewing);* kuipapa *(as feathers in a lei).*
overlay. Pale; ho'opapa *(as shingles).*
overload. Ho'ouka nui, ho'olu'ulu'u loa.
overlook. 1. *Look over.* Nānā maluna a'e, hālō. **2.** *Miss.* Hala, palaka. **3.** *Condone.* Waiho mālie, kaumalumalu.
overpowering. Mana nui, po'ikū.
override. Mau'a'e *(as a veto).*
overripe. *See* **ripe.**
overrun. Holopapa.
overseer. Luna, luna hana, luna kia'i, luna ho'ohana, nuna, haku, haku hana.
oversexed. Kola mau; puni kāne *(of females);* puni wahine *(of males);* kuko makapehu, pākīai.
overshadow. Ho'omalumalu, ho'oūmalu, pāpale, 'e'a-'e'a.
oversight. 'Alo 'ana.
oversized. Nui loa, nui maluna o ka mea ma'amau, hālala.
oversleep. Hiamoe loa, moe loa.
overthrow. Kahuli, ho'okahuli, hiolo, ho'ohiolo, kula'i, kula'ina, huli pū, hulihia. *Also:* 'ōpe'a, auhuli, olopē, pōluku.

overtime pay. Uku kaulele.
overturn. Kahuli, huli pau, huli pū, hulihia, ho'ohuli, auhuli. *Also:* lumi, me'ea, 'ōpe'a, 'ōlepe, kīpau, kualono. *See ex.,* **outrigger float.**
overturning. Hulina.
overwhelm. Po'ipū, popo'i, uhi, lalawe, luma'i, holomoku, holomokuna. *Suffering of love is overwhelming, here in my heart (PH 178),* 'o ka 'eha a ke aloha ke lalawe nei, eia lā i loko, i ku'u manawa.
overwhelmed. Pa'uhia, lo'ohia, lumi, pōka'aka'a, kapakū.
overwork. Ho'opa'u. *Also:* ho'okauā, ho'omauleho, ho'opa'aua.
ovum. Hua.
owe. 'Ai'ē.
owl. Pueo, ululā, iana, mo'o lele. *Owl snare,* pehe.
own. Pono'ī, kuleana, kipona, 'ona. *I own the house,* no'u pono'ī ka hale. *This is my own,* na'u pono'ī. *Own native land,* 'āina kulāiwi. *Your own book,* kā kō iwi puke.
owner. Mea, 'ona, haku. *House owner,* mea hale, ka mea nona ka hale. *Canoe owner,* mea wa'a.
ownership. No . . . ka mea, kuleana. *Common ownership,* kuleana waiwai like.
ox. Pipi kauō, pipi kauwō.
oxalic acid. 'Okakalika 'akika.
Oxford. 'Okapoka, Okafoda. *Oxford University,* Kulanui o 'Okapoka.
oxygen. Ea ola māmā, 'okikene.
oyster. 'Ōlepe. *See* **pearl oyster.**
oyster plant. Kalapī.
ozena. I'akui, ihukilu, ihupilau.

P

p. Pī.
pace. Ka'ina wāwae, peki. *Full pace,* ke'ehi lō'ihi. *Pacing horse,* lio peki.
pacific. 1. *Calm.* Malino, la'i, mālie. *See* **calm.** 2. *Ocean.* Pākīpika, Moana Pākīpika.
Pacific Yacht Club. Hui Heihei Moku Pākīpika.
pacified. Nā.
pacify. Hō'olu, ho'onā, ho'oma'alili.
pack. Ho'okomo *(as a trunk);* 'awe, 'awe'awe, hā'awe *(carry). Also:* ho'onoho, ho'oukana; ho'opapa *(neatly);* ho'ohakē *(full).*
package. Pū'olo. *Also:* pū'ā, 'ope, 'ope'ope, pela; pī'ao *(of folded ti leaves);* pena, pu'uwai.
packed. Ho'okomo 'ia. *Also:* hakē, piha'ū, pihaku'i, 'ūpili, pū'uki'uki, piha pūku'iku'i, piha pū, pū'ika'ika; —, *as in a crowd,* pōlumilumi, kūpiliki'i. *Rare:* lē'ī, neki, noke'a, kuenenu'u.
packet. 1. *Small package.* Pū'olo. 2. *A ship.* Pākeke, moku lawe leka.
pad. Pale po'ohiwi *(shoulder).*
padded. Pulu; ho'onui 'ōlelo *(as of speech).*
paddle. Hoe. *See* **Māmala-hoe** *and sayings,* **hoe, swim, tongue.** *Paddle types:* hoe uli *(steering; fig., tongue);* hoe nanue, hoe nenue, hoe kala. *Paddle parts:* laulau, lauhoe, pālaulau *(blade);* hua *(bulge in blade);* 'au, kū'au *(shaft);* 'upe, io *(rib);* alelo, koho, 'oupē *(tip);* pu'ukole *(upper part of blade). To paddle,* hoe, pāhoe; lauhoe *(of several);* akahoe *(carefully);* puna, kiele *(rare). To have a canoe paddled,* ho'ohoe. *Paddle back and forth,* hoehoe.
paddler. Hoe wa'a.
paddling. Hoena.
paddy. Lo'i, pāki.
padlock. Laka.
Paducah. Pakuka.
pagan. Pekana.
page. 'Ao'ao. *Page reference,* kuhikuhi i ka 'ao'ao.
pageant. Kapalō, hō'ike'ike, hana keaka.
pagoda flower. Lau'awa.
paid. Ka'a. *Paid entirely,* ka'a'oko'a. *My debt is paid,* ua ka'a ku'u ai'ē.
pail. Pela, kini, kini pela, pākeke; kini kākai *(with a handle). To hold and carry, as a pail,* kālawe.
pain. 'Eha; hu'i *(tooth, bones);* nalulu *(dull, in stomach, head);* 'ūmi'i *(side). Also:* nahu *(stomach);* 'ōpū-ha'o, ho'īlewa *(hunger—rare);* holopani *(cutting off of breath);* ho'onākū, ikiiki, lou, walania, ho'owalania, walawalania, walenia, welenia, wawalania, nao, luhi; manawahua kai ko'o; 'ō, 'o'e *(sharp, darting). See* **kipona.** *Great pain or many small pains,* 'eha'eha. *To inflict pain,* hō'eha. *To shrink away in pain,* mū'e'eke.
painful. 'Eha'eha, hu'i. *See* **pain.**
painkiller. Penikila.
paint. Pena. *House paint,* pena hale. *To paint,* pena, kāpala; pālani *(lightly);* puhi'ōni'o *(spotted);* — *thinner,* 'aila ho'owali pena. *To paint pictures,* pena ki'i, kaha ki'i, kākau kaha.
paintbrush. Hulu pena.
painter. Kaha ki'i *(artist);* mea pena *(as of houses). House painter,* pena hale.
painting. Ki'i pena.
pair. Pa'a, kaulua. *To pair,* kaulua. *Pairing off,* kūlua. *Two pairs, as in poker,* kūpē, kūpea. *Pair of shoes,* pa'a kāma'a.
pajamas. Lole moe pō.
pal. *See* **friend.**

palace. Hale ali'i. *See* **castle.**
palanquin. Mānele, hale 'auamo, 'auamo.
palate. Luna o ka waha; kīleo *(soft).*
pale. Hākea. *Also:* haikea, ha'akea, nanakea, lanakea, hananakea, 'ōlohe, kuakea, puakea, laukea, mamae, onena, 'īkoko, pākea. *See* **yellow.**
Palermo. Palemo.
Palestine. Palekekine, Palesetine.
pali. *See* **cliff.**
pallor. Hailepo. *See* **pale.**
palm** 1. *Tree.* Pāma, pālama; niu *(coconut). See* **fan palm. 2. *Surface of hand.* Poho, poho lima. *Center of palm,* poli lima. *Solid palm of hand,* poho kano *(fig., stingy).*
palmer worm. 'Ūhini-hulu-'ole.
palmist, palmistry. Kilo nānā lima, kilokilo nānā lima.
Palm Sunday. Kominika o nā Lālā Lā'au.
Palmyra. Palamila, Palamira; Palamola, Palamora.
palpitate. Konikoni. *Also:* 'api, hāku'i, ho'olele, nape, kapalili.
palsy. Ma'i lōlō.
pamper. Ho'okamalani, pai. *See saying,* **welu 1.**
pan. Pā. *Rare:* pani, pana. *See* **saucepan.** *Baking pan,* 'oma. *Fire pan,* pā ahi. *Frying pan,* pā palai. *Iron pan,* pā hao. *Stew pan,* kū pana. *Tin pan,* pā kini. *Wash pan,* pā holoi, pā kini holoi.
Panama. Panamā. *Panama hat,* pāpale waiokila.
panax. Lapalapa.
pancake. Palaoa palai, palaoa linalina; papa palaoa *(rare).*
pancreas. Mālama.
pandanus. Hala *(for various kinds, see Haw.-Eng. entry and entries that follow it). See sayings,* **hala iwi nui, pala lau hala.** *Pandanus tree,* pū hala. *Pandanus trunk,* kumu hala. *Male pandanus tree,* hala hīnano, hala hīnalo. *Female pandanus tree,* hala hua. *Pandanus leaf,* lau hala; ko'o, 'i'oko'o, mu'o hala, pū'awa, pūkani; pilila'ele *(young);* lā'ele *(old);* pala lau hala, pa'ilau'ula *(dry). Bundle of forty leaves,* kī. *Male blossom, bracts,* hīnano, polohīnano. *Pandanus fruit,* 'āhui hala; polopoloua *(unripe);* polokā *(ripe);* kā'ao, kāō *(very ripe). Pandanus fruit stem,* polope'a. *Pandanus key,* hala; pani *(at bottom of cluster);* hala 'i'o *(ripe);* hala iwi nui *(upper hard portion);* pua hala *(yellow base). Nut in key,* hala hua, 'i'o hala. *Pandanus fruit core,* 'īkoi. *Pandanus root tip,* mu'o hala. *Pandanus aerial root,* ule hala, uleule hala. *Lumps on pandanus trunk,* pu'upu'u hala. *Width of pandanus plaiting strip,* koana. *Pandanus lei,* lei hala *(not worn by some because of double meaning; see* **hala 1, 2).** *Puna, where sea blasts amid pandanus (PH 2),* 'o Puna kai kuwā i ka hala.
pane. 'Āpana aniani.
pang. 'Ūmi'i, 'eha koni, 'a'aki, ha'awina.
panic. Maka'u kūhewa, haunaele. *Panic-stricken,* 'ā'ā. *To run in panic,* holo 'ā'ā.
panorama. Waihona 'āina, nānaina.
panoramic view. Waiho helahela 'ana.
pansy. Pāneki, po'okanaka.
pant. Haha, ahaaha, ehaha, nae, naenae, pauaho, paupauaho, manawaea, 'ā'ili, 'ā'ili'ili, ka'ahili, uhāuhā, nawe. *Pant for breath,* ka'apā ka hanu i ka houpo.
panther. Paneka.
panties. Lole wāwae (wahine).
pantry. Lumi waiho pā.
pants. Lole wāwae.

papa. Pāpā.
papaya. Mīkana, hē'ī, milikana, papaia. *Male papaya,* mīkana kāne. *Female papaya,* mīkana wahine.
papaya bird. Manu-'ai-mīkana, manu-'ai-papaia, 'ai-mīkana.
paper. Pepa *(for various kinds, see Haw.-Eng. entry and entries that follow it);* kānana, kālana *(for writing).* See **newspaper.** *Pile of paper,* pu'u pepa.
paper boy. Keiki lawe nūpepa.
paper clip. 'Ūmi'i pepa.
paper knife. Pahi 'oki pepa.
paper nautilus. 'Au-wa'a-lā-lua, moamoa.
papist. Pope.
papyrus. Kaluhā, papulo, kome *(RSV).*
parable. Nane, 'ōlelo nane. *To illustrate with parable,* ho'opilipili 'ōlelo.
parade. Huaka'i, ka'i huaka'i; paikau *(as of military);* ho'okahakaha. *Also:* kōheo, ho'ohaha. *Parade rest (military command),* hō'olu'olu.
paradise. Palekaiko, 'iu lani. See **Pali-uli.**
paragraph. Paukū, palekalapa. *Symbol of paragraph,* po'o hou.
Paraguay. Palakuae, Paraguae.
parallel. Kaulike, moe like, 'iliwai like. *Parallel line,* kaha kaulike.
parallelepiped. Pa'a'ili kaulike hiō *(oblique);* pa'a'ili kūpono *(cube or rectangular).*
parallelogram. Huinahā hiō lō'ihi.
paralysis. Lōlō, ma'i lōlō; hepa *(partial paralysis of vocal chords). Paralysis of tongue,* alelo pu'u.
paraphimosis. Hāko'i.
parasite. **1.** *Plant.* Lā'au kumu 'ole. **2.** *Person.* Kū 'īpuka hale *(see* **'īpuka***),* kūkake, lelewa, ho'opili wale, ho'opilimea'ai, pilimea'ai, ōkea pili mai. *See* **kauna'oa, vagabond,** *and sayings,* **limpet.**
parasol. Māmalu, loulu, noulu.
parcel. Pū'olo. *See* **package.**
parched. Malo'o loa. *Also:* anoa, 'ānia, kū'āno'a, pāpa'a, pāpa'alā, pīka'o, hākonakona, hākona, 'ōlino, 'āpa'apa'a, 'a'aka, pā, pākī'ai, kuapa'a.
parchment. 'Ili palapala.
pardon. Kala, huikala, kalakala; palapala huikala *(document);* pale'ōpua *(rare). Pardon me,* kala mai ia'u.
pare. Koli, pehē. *To pare nails,* koli miki'ao.
parent. Makua, makua mea keiki; lūau'i makua *(true, contrasting with foster).* See **stepparent.** *Foster parent,* makua hānai, kahu hānai *(from infancy);* makua ho'okama *(of an older child or adult). Parents,* mākua. *Precious parents,* mākua. *To act the part of a parent,* ho'omakua. *To address as parent,* ho'omakua.
parentheses. Kahaapo, apowaena.
parent-in-law. Makuahūnōai.
pariah. Kauā. *See* **outcast.**
parietal bone. Iwi 'ōpe'ape'a.
Paris, Parisian. Palika, Parisa.
parish. Kīhāpai.
park. **1.** *Recreation area.* Pāka. *Ka-pi'o-lani Park,* Ka-pi'o-lani Pāka. **2.** *To station.* Ho'okū, kūkulu. *To park a car,* ho'okū i ke ka'a. *Parked,* kū. *Parking lot,* wahi kūkulu ka'a.
parlor. Lumi ho'okipa, pala.
Parnassus. Panakuka.
parole. Palola.
parrot. Manu aloha.
parrot fish. Uhu *(for various kinds, growth stages, and fig. meanings, see* **uhu***). Also:* lauia, pāuhuuhu, 'ōhi-'uhi'u. *See slippery. Young parrot fish,* 'ōhua palemo *(fig., mischief-maker).*
parry. Pale, kaupale, ho'okāpae, kokope.
parsnip. Pakanika.
parson. Kahuna pule.
part. Mahele, mokuna, hapa, 'āpana. *Part-white,* hapa haole. *Part-Hawaiian,* hapa Hawai'i. *Take the part of Frank,* ho'olilo 'oe iā'oe iho 'o Palani.
partaker. Hoa loa'a.

partial. Kaulike 'ole, pā'ewa'ewa, ho'owae, ho'okēāmaka, lawe kapakahi; puni *(fond of);* hapa *(portion).*
participle. Hō'ailona o ka wā 'ānō *(present);* hō'ailona o ka wā i hala *(past).*
particle. Huna, māhune, pula, lihi; hunahuna 'ōlelo *(unit of speech). Particles,* hunahuna, huhuna, ko'ana.
particular. **1.** *Special.* Nō. *That special occasion,* kēlā hanana nō. **2.** *Exacting.* 'Ano waewae, ho'owae, 'eke'eke, 'e'eke, kamalani.
partition. Pale, ho'opale, kau pale, pākū, papa pale.
partitioning. Palena.
partner. Hoa, hoa hana, kōko'o, pakanā.
partnership. Hui; kōko'olua *(of two);* kōko'okolu *(of three);* kōko'ohā *(of four).*
part of speech. 'Ano hua 'ōlelo. *No generally used Hawaiian term for parts of speech. Andrews 1854 introduced terms as for ablative, accusative, agentive, dative, genitive, possessive, and various pronouns, but they seem to have been rarely if ever used.*
partridge. Manu 'aihue.
party. **1.** *Group.* 'Aha *(for various kinds, see Haw.-Eng. entry and entries that follow it);* 'ao'ao *(political). Liberal party,* 'ao'ao lipelala. **2.** *Festivity.* Ho'olaule'a *(large);* pā'ina *(dinner or supper);* 'aha inu *(drinking). See* **dinner. 3.** *Person.* Kanaka, mea, po'e.
par value. Waiwai inoa, waiwai kaulike.
pass. **1.** *Movement.* Mā'alo, kā'alo, 'aui, kaha, hala *(pass by);* holo, hala, kūnewa, au, uhaiāholo *(as time);* mā'alo'alo, ho'okā'alo, paikau *(to and fro);* ho'oholo, kau, 'āpono *(as a bill);* — *away,* hala, nalo, nalohia, ha'alele i ke ola, mā *(death); come to* —, kō, kau, ho'okau. *Also:* pāhiki, mao, ka'a, ka'a hope, āmio, kīhēhē, malewa, niau, hōla'o, pūlō. *Passed,* holo, 'āpono 'ia *(as a bill);* loa'a ka helu holo mua *(as an examination). Please pass the salt,* 'olu'olu e hā'awi mai i ka pa'akai. **2.** *Permission.* Palapala ho'oku'u. *Entrance pass,* palapala komo. *Free pass,* palapala komo wale. **3.** *See* **gap, passage.**
passage. Awa *(as through a reef).*
passenger. 'Ōhua. *Cabin passenger,* 'ōhua kāpena. *Deck passenger,* 'ōhua 'oneki. *Ship passenger,* e'e moku, holomoku. *Passenger conveyance,* ka'a hali 'ōhua.
passer-by. Ka'alo, mea mā'alo, malewa.
passion. Konikoni, koni, kaunu; hekili *(fig.). The Passion of Christ,* ka 'Eha'eha o ka Haku. *Burst of passion,* kīkīao. *Culmination of sexual passion,* le'a, huahua'i. *Passion calmed with her (UL 166),* la'i ai ke kaunu me ia lā.
passionate. Ko'iko'i, 'ino. *Passionate anger,* huhū 'ino, hae manawa 'ino. *See ex.,* **'īloli.**
passion fruit. Liliko'i, lemi wai, lemona, pohāpohā, huehue haole.
passion play. Hō'ike'ike i nā 'eha'eha o ka Haku.
Passion Sunday. Kominika o ka 'Eha.
passive voice. Leo pili 'ia mai. *See* **verb.**
passover. Pakoa, mōliaola.
passport. Palapala ho'āpono, palapala kuhikuhi kino, palapala 'ae e holo.
past. Hala, ka'a; wā'ae'oia, lā'ae'oia *(past days of youth, beauty, prosperity). Past time,* wā i hala, wā mamua. *To recall the past,* ho'omana'o i nā wā i hala, huliau, 'āla'apapa.
paste. Ho'opipili, mea ho'opipili; palaholo *(made of sap from 'ama'u fern fronds).*
pastime. Ho'ohala manawa, hana ho'ohala manawa. *Favorite pastime,* hana punahele. *Pleasant pastime,* hana ho'onanea.
pastor. Kahuna pule, kahu; kahu 'ekalekia, ekalesia.
pastry. Mea 'ono.
pasture. Kula, ho'oholohona, kula holoholona.
pasty. Pipili, kuhua.
pat. Hamohamo *(as a dog);* pa'ipa'i mālie.
patch. **1.** *Mending.* Poho, pāhono, pāhonohono, hono; pewa, kiki, kihi, pīna'i *(as in wood, see* **huini***).* **2.** *Garden.* Mahi, māla. *Also:* kūlana, kūnana, kīhāpai, ulu

kanu; 'e'a, palakei *(rare)*. *Taro patch,* lo'i kalo. *Arable patch surrounded by lava,* kīpuka, kīpohopoho.
patched. Pohopoho.
patchwork quilt. *See* **quilt.** *Patchwork cover or spread,* uhi 'āpana.
patella. Kuapo'i.
patent. Kila, palapala kila, palapala ho'okuleana.
patent leather. 'Ili hinuhinu, 'ili pahinu.
paternal. Makua kāne, ma ka 'ao'ao o ka makua kāne.
path. Ala, alahula. *See* **trail.**
pathetic. Kū i ke aloha, menemene, walohia.
pathos. Walohia.
patience. Ahonui, 'ōpū ahonui, ho'omanawanui. *To try one's patience,* ho'omanawanui, none.
patient. 1. *Forbearance.* Ahonui, 'ōpū ahonui, ho'omanawanui, 'a'au loa. *Be patient,* e ho'omanawanui. **2.** *Sick person.* Ma'i, mea ma'i.
patio. Pā.
patriarch. Makua ali'i, makuali'i.
patriotism. Aloha 'āina, make'e pono aupuni.
patrol. Kia'i ka'ahele, māka'i ka'ahele.
patron. Pakelona. *Patron saint,* pakelona.
patter. Nakulu, nū, hawewe, paka; kili nahe *(pleasant).* *See* **pitter patter.**
pattern. Ana, ana ho'ohālike; pākana, wai; lau *(as in quilts). See* **mat, model, tapa.**
pauper. 'Ilikole, 'ilikone, manu hulu 'ole. *Cf.* **poor.**
pause. Ho'omaha, ho'omalolo; 'ume *(in music). Pause a moment.* luana iki.
pave. Ho'omoe kimeki, kīpapa, ho'ounu.
pavement. Kīpapa, paepae, kīpaepae, nini, papahola.
paw. Wāwae, kapua'i. *To paw,* helu *(as the earth);* pīhole *(as a drunk).*
pawnbroker. Mea hō'ai'ē no ka uku pane'e.
pawnshop. Hale hō'ai'ē.
pay. Uku, ka'a, ho'oka'a, pē. *See* **installment, revenge.** *Pay in full,* ho'oka'a piha. *Pay on time,* uku manawa. *Pay damages,* uku pohō. *Pay out money,* kīko'o. *Refuse to pay losses or forfeit,* kā'ihi. *Pay attention,* nānā. *Pay out, as fishline,* ho'oku'uku'u; kāwa'ewa'e *(rare).*
payment. Uku. *See* **installment.** *Cash payment,* uku kū'ike. *Gift payment,* uku makana. *Arrears in a payment,* ka'a hope. *Partial payment,* ho'oka'a hapa.
pea. Pī, pāpapa.
peace. Malu, maluhia, la'i. *Also:* lulu, la'ikū, laule'a, kōnale, kuapapa, ku'ikahi like, luluka, kuakapu, niau, ku'u; *quiet —,* kīpū aheahe. *See* **pu'uhonua** *and sayings,* **chief, forecast, moss, poise.** *To make peace,* ho'omalu, ho'omaluhia, ho'oku'ikahi. *Rest in peace,* e ho'omaha me ka maluhia. *Peace after passion,* la'i ke kaunu. *Calm in Kona's peace (UL 66),* malino i ka la'i o Kona.
peacemaker. 'Uao, 'uwao.
peach. Piki.
peacock, peafowl. Pīkake.
peak. Pu'u 'oi'oi, pu'u, wēkiu, 'oi'oina, pū'o'a, lele ho'okau; 'ou *(high). Sharply peaked, as a mountain,* niolo.
peal. Kani, kani 'a'ina, ku'ina. *Long-drawn-out peal,* kani kō. *Pealing,* kakani.
peanut. Pineki. *Peanut oil,* 'aila pineki.
pear. Pea.
pearl. Momi.
pearl oyster. Pipi. *See sayings,* **i'a hāmau leo, kuhi 1.**
pearl shell. Pā, uhi, kea, kuwala, lehua; kā'ope *(rare).*
peasant. Lōpā.
pease-porridge-hot. Pahipahi *(a game).*
pebble. 'Ili'ili. *Also:* unu, 'ili, mā'ili, mā'ili'ili, kanawao. *Heap of pebbles,* pu'u 'ili'ili, pe'ape'a pōhaku. *Pebble hula,* hula 'ili'ili. *Rat-pelting pebble,* unu pehi 'iole *(insult). Trashy pebbles,* 'ōpalapala unu *(worthless person). Birth pebbles,* 'ili'ili hānau.
pebbly. 'Ili'ili, mā'ili.
peccary. Pekale.

peck. Kiko, kīkoni, kiki, pao, makiki. *To peck repeatedly,* kikokiko.
peculiar. 'Ē, 'ē'ē, 'ano 'ē, 'e'epa, 'āpiki.
pedal. Hehi wāwae. *To pedal,* hehi.
peddle. Kālepa, kālewa, piele, ma'au'auwā; mālaulau *(rare).*
peddler. *See* **peddle.**
pedestal. Kū.
pedestrian. Kanaka hele wāwae.
pedigree. Kū'auhau, mo'o kū'auhau.
peek. 'Āiki, ho'āiki. *See* **peep, peer.**
peel. 1. *Skin.* 'Ili. **2.** *To remove skin.* Māihi; koli *(pare). Also:* ihi, hole, 'a'aka, 'ōlepe, pehē, naka, unahipi'i, 'āka'a, mahiki, ho'ohiki, lole, puāhilo, 'alu'alu, pahelo, ho'opohole, ohi, ho'opaiho, pā'ē.
peep. 1. *Look.* Ki'ei, hālō; hā'ei *(rare).* **2.** *Chirp.* 'Io, mā'io'io, pio. *Peeping,* 'io'io, piopio.
peer. 1. *Look.* Ki'ei, hālō, 'āiki. *Place from which to peer,* hālona. **2.** *Associate.* Hoa. **3.** *Noble.* Ali'i.
peeved. Ukiuki, nuha. *Also:* kā'eko, ka'eo, ho'opalaka'eo.
peevish. 'A'aka, huhū wale, nuha, nuhanuha.
peewee. Ke'a lā'au *(game).*
peg. Kui lā'au, huini, pine, pine lā'au. *See* **wedge.**
Peking. Pekina.
pelargoniums. Laniuma.
Pele. *See* **volcano.**
Pele's hair. Lauoho-o-Pele.
Pele's tears. Waimaka-o-Pele.
pelican. Pelikana, pelekana.
pellet. Pōkā. *Pellet-shaped,* 'ana'ana.
pellmell. 'Āwīwī na'aupō, 'āwīwī ā mōkākī. *To run pellmell,* holo na'aupō, holo pupule.
pelt. 1. *Skin.* 'Ili. **2.** *To throw, hit.* Pehi, pehia, nou. *Also:* hīkau, kīpehi, kūpehi, kāpehi, nahu, nahunahu, hiu; ka'alina *(as rain);* kīpē *(as with stones). To pelt repeatedly,* hiuhiu.
pelvic bone. Iwi pūhaka, kā.
pen. 1. *Enclosure.* Pā. **2.** *Writing instrument.* Peni, hulu kākau; peni kila *(steel):* maka kila. *Pen point,* maka peni.
penal code. Kānāwai ho'opa'i kalaima.
penal laws. Kānāwai kalaima, kānāwai ho'opa'i kalaima.
penalty. Ho'opa'i, uku hala.
penance. Mihi hō'eha'eha, ho'opa'i mihi.
pencil. Penikala, peni.
pendant. 'Olo. *Whale-tooth pendant,* niho palaoa, lei palaoa, 'ōpu'u, lei 'ōpu'u. *Wiliwili wood pendant,* lei wiliwili.
pending. E kali ana, manawa kali.
pendulous. Lewalewa, lewa, uleule, 'olo.
penetrate. Komo, ho'okomo, hulā. *Also:* 'akiu, koili; kūli'u; konāhau *(as wind);* 'a'aki *(fig.).*
penguin. Manu-hele-kū, penekuina.
peninsula. 'Ānemoku.
penis. Ule. *Rare:* 'auwiniwini, kalohi, po'o. *See* **erect, foreskin, genital.** *Head of penis,* pōheo, heo, kole ka'aka, po'o kole ka'aka, pokake; hā'ali'ali *(rare). Dangling penis,* ma'i lewalewa. *Stripped-back penis,* ule hole *(insult).*
penknife. Pahi pelu.
penmanship. Kākau lima.
pen name. Inoa kapakapa.
Pennsylvania. Penekelewinia, Peneselevinia.
penny. Keneka, kenali, peni; hapahaneli *(issued in 1847).*
pennywort. Pohe, pohepohe, pohe kula.
pension. Uku ho'omau, ha'awina ho'omau.
Pension Board. Ke'ena Uku Ho'omau.
pentagon. Huinalima.
Pentecost. Penekekoka.
penurious. Kulio'o, kulipa'a.
people. Po'e, lāhui, lāhui kanaka, maka kanaka, kānaka; lehulehu, nehunehu *(multitude);* nui manu *(poetic). Many people,* lau kanaka. *To people,* ho'oulu lāhui.

Peoria. Peolia.
pepper. Pepa; nīoi *(for various kinds, see Haw.-Eng. entry and entries that follow it).* Cayenne pepper, pepakene.
peppergrass. 'Ānaunau.
peppermint. Pepamina.
peppery. Pika.
percale. 'Ula palani *(bright red).*
perceive. 'Ike, 'apo, kaunānā.
per cent. Pakeneka.
percentage. Pakeneka, hapahaneli.
perceptive. 'Ike.
perch. 1. *Rest.* Kau, haka, haka kau, peloka. *To perch,* kau, halakau, halahalakau, 'ō'ū, 'ōku'u, kī'ililī. *Perched,* kaumo'o. 2. *Surveying.* Peleka.
percolate. Pīpī wai *(of water);* hū, paila.
perfect. Hemolele, kīnā 'ole, pono loa. *Also:* pala 'ole, 'auli'i, kulukeoe, kaekae, kīkīko'ele. *See saying,* aukahi. *Perfect number,* helu po'okela. *To perfect,* ho'omaika'i. *To seek flaws in order to perfect,* paka.
perfectionist. 'Ano 'eke'eke,
perforate. Ho'opuka.
perforation. Puka.
perform. Lawelawe, hana, ho'okō, ho'okūpa'a. *To perform well,* kākela.
performance. Lawelawe 'ana, ho'okō 'ana, holona, hana 'ana.
perfume. Lūkini, wai lūkini, wai 'ala, wai hō'a'ala, 'a'ala, mea 'ala, onaona, puīa, moani, moaniani, mano'i. *Perfume container,* ipu 'ala. *Perfumed,* pē, 'ala. *To perfume,* hō'ala, ho'opē, ho'opuīa. *To issue perfume,* pō. *Perfume plants, as used to scent tapa:* ihuanu, mokihana, maile, 'iliahi, 'awapuhi, kolū, kamani, laua'e, kūpaoa. *Puna is overwhelmed with fragrance,* niniu Puna pō i ke 'ala *(see pō).* *(Puna is famous for fragrant pandanus.)*
perhaps. Paha, pēlā paha, malia, malia paha, ā . . . paha, mali'a, inā paha, mea paha. *Rare:* 'ano'ai, māki'a, malama, 'āpaha. *Perhaps not,* 'a'ole paha. - *Perhaps so,* pēlā paha.
peril. Make, pō'ino, maka'u.
perimeter. Anapuni.
period. 1. *Punctuation.* Kiko kahi, kiko ho'omaha. 2. *Time.* Wā, manawa, au.
periphery. Pelihele.
perished. Make, pau i ka make, mā.
peritoneum. Nikiniki.
periwinkle. 1. *Marine snail.* 'Ākōlea (kōlealea, pipipi 'ākōlea, pipipi kōlea, pipipi kōlea ihiloa, kūkaekōlea, pūpū kōlea). See i'a 1. 2. *Plant.* Kīhāpai *(Madagascar periwinkle).*
perjury. Hō'ike wahahe'e, ho'ohiki wahahe'e, hō'ike ho'opunipuni, ho'opilimea'ai, pilimea'ai.
permanent. Pa'a, loa, mau, mau loa. *Also:* kūpene, kulekule, ho'omakua. *To stay permanently,* noho loa, noho pa'a.
permanent wave. 'Ōwiliwili me ka uila, lauoho 'ōwiliwili 'ia me ka uila.
permeate. Punia. *See* **pervade.**
permission. 'Ae. *To use another's property without permission,* kā'ihi. *To pick flowers without permission,* 'ako kū i kā ha'i pua.
permissive. Ho'oku'uku'u.
permit. 'Ae, ho'oku'u. *Written permit,* palapala 'ae.
perpendicular. Kūpono, kū, 'ao'ao kūpono, kū pololei.
perpetual. Mau, mau loa.
perpetuate. Mau, ho'omau. *See saying,* **righteousness.**
perplex. Ho'ohihia, ho'ohuikau.
perplexed. Hihia, nāhili, noni.
perplexity. Hihia, kāhihi, 'ānoni, 'ānoninoni, 'anononi.
persecute. Ho'omāino, ho'omāinoino, māino, hō'ino, ho'oma'au; ho'ope'a *(fig.).*
persevere. Ho'omanawanui, ho'omau, mau, noke. *Also:* kaunaloa, oia, kāmau, kaukahi, mīkole; kaukolo

(in making a request); ho'okua *(in working without interest);* maukoli; ma'iha.
Persia. Pelekia, Peresia.
persist. Ho'omau, ho'opa'a, ho'okūpa'a, noke, unonoke, ho'olā'au, ho'ohune, ho'okina, ho'ohu'a, kakano, kā'i'ī, kinai.
person. Kanaka, mea, kama. *Also:* maka, kino; ka'aka *(slang);* pelekona. *Fig.:* manu, ulua. *Distinguished person,* mea hanohano, ao loa. *Beloved person,* mea nui, lei hulu, lei 'ā'ī, hulu 'aina 'ole, pua laha 'ole. *First person,* kino mua, kino kahi. *Second person,* kino lua. *Third person,* kino kolu. *The person who,* ka i, ke. *This person,* ia nei. *Divine or godly person,* mea akua. *Unusual person, one of another race,* mea 'ē. *Person one thinks of constantly,* pulakaumaka. *Mature person,* kanaka makua.
personal. Pilikino, kino, pono'ī. *Personal talk,* 'ōlelo pilikino. *Personal friend,* hoa pili. *Personal things,* nā mea pilikino.
personality. Kūlana o ke kanaka.
personally. Iho, pono'ī.
personal pronoun. Paniinoa pilikino.
personnel. Po'e hana.
persons. Po'e, kānaka, po'e kānaka.
perspiration. Hou. *Unpleasant odor of perspiration,* hohono. *Perspiration poured,* kikī ka hou.
perspire. Hou.
persuade. Koi; mali *(gently);* 'onou.
pertain. Pili.
perturbation. Ka'a ka lolo, hikilele, pilikia.
perturbed. Ulukū, pi'oloke, pīhoihoi, hopohopo, kaumaha.
Peru. Pelū.
pervade. Puni, ho'opiha.
perverse. Hō'oko'a i ka hana. *Also:* kewe, kīke'e, kāpae, na'ina'i, pau'ali.
pervert. Hō'oko'a i ka hana. *Also:* ho'okeke'e, kāpae, ho'okāhuli; kanaka 'ē *(noun).* *See* **homosexual.**
pessimist. Kūlana hoihoi 'ole.
pest. 1. *Nuisance.* Mea ho'ūluhua, mea ho'opilikia. 2. *See* **pestilence.**
pestilence. Ma'i ahulau, ahulau, ma'i pālahalaha. *Ancient pestilences:* ikipuahola, hailepo.
pestle. Mea ku'i. *Whale-tooth pestle,* palaoa ku'i. *Wooden palu pestle,* lā'au ku'i palu.
pet. 1. *Favorite.* Punahele, milimili; hānai ā huhu *(animal).* *To make a pet,* ho'opunahele; hānai ā huhu *(of an animal);* paikano *(rare).* *One who has a pet,* kahu. 2. *To caress.* Hamo, hamohamo. *Also:* mili, milimili, kūwili, ho'oka'awili.
petal. Lihilihi.
Petersburg. Pekelopolo, Peteroboro.
petite. 'Ūli'i, 'ō'uku'uku, 'uku li'i.
petition. Palapala ho'opi'i, palapala noi. *To petition,* noi, ho'opi'i, kauoko.
petitioner. Ka mea noi.
petrel. 'Ua'u, 'uwa'u, 'ua'u kēwai. *Bulwer's petrel,* 'ou, 'ou'ou. *Hawaiian stormy petrel,* 'akē'akē, lupe'akeke, oeoe. *Stormy petrel,* 'akihi ke'ehi 'ale. *Call to attract petrels, believed in imitation of their cry,* kue.
petrify. Ho'opōhaku.
petroglyph. Ki'i pōhaku, ki'i.
petticoat. Palekoki.
petty. Li'ili'i loa. *Petty officer,* ali'i palapala ho'okohu 'ole.
petulant. Ukiuki, kaki.
petunia. Pekunia.
pew. Noho.
pewter. Piula, kēpau.
phalanx. Pū'ulu kaua.
phantom. Lapu, kāhoaka, mākūkoa'e.
Pharaoh. Parao.
pharmacist. Kāwili lā'au, ho'ohuihui lā'au.
pharmacy. Hale kāwili lā'au, hale kū'ai lā'au.
pheasant. Kolohala.

'ūlili, 'ulī'ulī. *Modern: see* **accordion, autoharp, bagpipe, bass viol, clarinet, drum, fiddle, flute, guitar, harmonica, harp, horn, jew's harp, melodeon, mouth organ, organ, trumpet, ukulele, violin.**

musician. Mea ho'okani pila *(player);* mea hīmeni, ho'opa'a, pu'ukani *(singer);* haku mele *(composer).*

musk. Hualūkini.

musket. Pū po'ohiwi.

muskmelon. Ipu 'āwa'awa'a.

muslin. Ke'oke'o *(white);* ke'oke'o maoli *(bleached, good);* ke'oke'o pia *(bleached, inferior);* ke'oke'o wai *(bleached);* leponalo, makalena.

muss. Ho'opūkalakī *(as hair);* ho'ominomino *(as a dress).*

mussed. Pūkalakī *(as hair);* minomino *(as a dress). Also:* uluulu, 'ahulu.

mussel. Kio nahawele, 'ōlepe.

must. Pono. *You must go,* e pono 'oe ke hele.

mustache. 'Umi'umi.

mustard. Mākeke *(black).*

muster. Ho'ākoakoa.

musty. Pelekunu, punahelu, 'Ī'ī, uweko, ueko, uwekoweko, uekoeko, weko, wilu, wiluwilu, polopolona, pōukiuki, puleipulu. *See* **moldy.**

mutant. Kāhuli.

mute. Mumule, mū, mūmū, mule. *Deaf-mutes,* po'e kuli ā 'ā'ā.

mutilate. Hana 'ino, 'oki 'ino, ho'omumuku, ho'okīnā, 'elehe'u.

mutineer. Mea kipi i luna o ka moku.

mutiny. 'Olohani, mokuāhana, kipi i luna o ka moku. *To cause a mutiny,* hō'olohani.

mutter. Namunamu, kūhipahipa. *See* **mumble.**

mutton. 'I'o hipa. *Leg of mutton,* 'ūhā hipa.

mutual. Like, kaulike, pāna'i like. *Mutual friend,* hoaloha like. *Mutual admiration,* mahalo kekahi i kekahi.

muzzle. Pūnuku, waha. *To muzzle,* ho'opa'a.

my. 1. *Singular possessed object.* Ko'u, ka'u, ku'u. **2.** *Plural possessed objects.* O'u, a'u.

mynah. Manu-'ai-pilau, piha'ekelo.

myriad. Manomano, kinikini, lehulehu.

myrrh. Mula.

myrtle. Hakaka, hadasa, maile haole.

myself. 'O wau nō, 'o wau pono'ī, 'o wau iho nō. *With myself,* me a'u iho nō. *For myself,* no'u iho nō, na'u iho nō.

mysterious. Āiwaiwa, hō'e'epa, pāha'oha'o, ho'opano, pohihihi, pōliu, po'o huna; kapolakā.

mystery. Pohihihi, kumulipo, mikelio.

mystic. Mea punihei i nā mea āiwaiwa.

mystify. Hō'āiwaiwa, hō'e'epa, ho'opāha'oha'o.

myth. Mo'olelo o ka wā kahiko, mo'olelo.

mythical. Mea ho'okalakupua o nā 'ōlelo kahiko loa. *See* **legendary beings, legendary place.**

mound. Ahu, āhua, puʻu; puʻu lepo *(earth),* ʻapuʻu; puʻu pele *(volcanic);* hāpuʻupuʻu, haʻapuʻu; hoʻopuʻu; — *up,* poʻi, hoʻāhu.
mount. Piʻi, eʻe, hōʻeʻe, kau; — *high,* amoamo.
mountain. Mauna, kuahiwi; *verdant* —, kuaola; — *area,* uka, mauka, kuahea. *See* **ridge.** *Region near the mountaintop,* kualono. *Mountain climber,* hele mauna, eʻe kuahiwi, piʻi mauna.
mountain apple. ʻŌhiʻa ʻai.
mountainous. Mauna, ʻōpalipali.
Mount Carmel. Mauna Kalemela.
mounted police. Mākaʻi kau lio.
Mount Hood. Mauna Huka.
Mount Hor. Mauna Hora.
Mount Souffrière. Mauna Kupalali.
mourn. Uē, uwē, ʻū, kanikau. *Also:* pihe, naʻauʻauā, kūmākena, kaʻakūmākena, kaniaʻā, kaniāʻau, kaniʻuhū, kūpinaʻi; — *extravagantly,* pākepa; — *in chanting,* kanikau, kanikaniāʻula. *See* **wail.**
mourner. Mea kanikau.
mourning. Mākena, paumākō; mānewanewa, pānewanewa *(extravagantly, as before Christianity or for a chief).* *Period of mourning,* kaʻakūmākena. *Go mourning,* ʻū hele.
mouse. ʻIole, ʻiole liʻiliʻi.
mousetrap. ʻŪmiʻi ʻiole, ʻūpiki ʻiole.
mousy. ʻIoʻiole.
mouth. Waha; oʻa *(eel);* lehelehe *(net);* nuku *(harbor);* nuku wai *(stream);* muliwai *(river).*
mouth organ. Pilapuhipuhi.
mouthpiece. Waha ʻōlelo.
move. Neʻe *(intransitive);* hoʻoneʻe *(transitive, as an object or a checker);* naue, nauwe; kaʻi hele *(in line or succession or as in checkers);* noi *(parliamentary);* peki *(step by step);* kuʻi *(in kōnane game);* kūwili *(restlessly);* ānehe, ānehenehe *(stealthily);* ʻanau *(with jerky motion);* kuekueʻo *(slightly);* palanehe *(daintily);* — *backwards,* neʻehope, mene; — *back and forth,* helo, helohelo, kuʻe, kuʻekuʻena, uene, malewa, konini, kaiue; — *up and down,* hoʻoholu, kaiue, panau; —*straight ahead,* neʻe i mua, neʻe pololei, kaʻaheahe; — *swiftly,* neʻe ʻāwīwī, mio, miomio, ʻiʻī, oloʻio, olohio, kāholo; — *cautiously and carefully,* akaluli, akahele, kaʻiawe, kuene, palela, kūnoni, pāneʻeneʻe; — *easily and noiselessly,* palamimo, niau, kaʻa niau, hani, halolani; — *in a flock, herd, company, or together,* kaʻi ʻāuna, mālana, neʻepū, neʻepapa, kahe ā wai; — *to and fro or from place to place,* kālewa, koiele, ʻōhelo, ʻaʻau. *Also:* uai, hoʻouai, ʻoni, hōʻoni, ʻoniʻoni, hōʻoniʻoni, hoʻoneʻe, oi, uoi, hele, pūneʻe, neʻeu, lele, au, nene, paneʻe, hulei, pāuma; kolo *(as breeze).* *On the move,* kiʻihele, haulani. *Move, as to a new house,* kiʻi aku, komo hale. *First attempts of infant to move,* ene. *Hard to move,* ʻonipaʻa; lolohe *(rare).* *Your move (in checkers),* kou manawa.
movement. Au, ʻoni, neʻeau; lawena *(as of dancing hands);* miona *(swift).* *See* **move.**
movie. Kiʻi ʻoniʻoni.
moving. **1.** *In motion.* Hele, ʻoni, ʻoniʻoni, niau, hāneʻeneʻe; kūlewa *(as clouds);* nauane *(rare).* *See* **move. 2.** *Eloquent.* Mīkololohua.
moving picture. Kiʻi ʻoniʻoni.
mow. ʻOki. *Mow the grass,* ʻoki mauʻu.
Mr. *No term today; formerly, but not used commonly:* Mī, Mika. *Mr. Coan,* Mī Koana. *Mr. Remy,* Mika Remi.
Mrs. *No term today; formerly, but not used commonly:* wahine. *Mrs. Smith,* Kamika Wahine.
much. Nui. *Also:* lau, lua, hālau, kūwaluwalu, makawalu, mākena, ʻoe, oki. *Very much,* nui ʻino, nui hewahewa, nui loa, kai! *How much?* ʻEhia? *No matter how much,* ʻehia. *Twice as much,* pāpālua. *We have much to do,* nui loa kā kāua hana, ʻaʻohe i laua aku kā kāua hana.
muck. ʻŌpala, kelekele, alaʻalai.
mucus. Hūpē, ʻūpē, hākelo, wale. *Also:* naʻo, walewale,

wale kea, weka, wekaweka, pīheka. *Dried nasal mucus,* pāpaʻa hūpē. *To draw in mucus,* hohō. *To hang, as mucus,* kākelokelo.
mud. Kelekele, pālolo, lepo ʻūkele. *Taro-patch mud,* lepo loʻi.
muddy. Kele, kelekele, kūkele, ahu kele, kele lua, ʻūkele, ʻūkelekele, ʻōkelekele, hānupa. *Muddy water,* kele wai.
mud hen. ʻAlae; nūkea *(white-billed);* koki. *The ʻalae is called* ka manu keʻu ahiahi, *the bird that croaks in the evening (considered a bad omen).*
mud puddle. Kiʻo lepo.
mud wasp. Nalo lawe lepo.
muff. Huluhulu hoʻopumehana lima.
muffler. Kāʻei ʻāʻī; pale kalukalu *(Biblical).*
mug. Ipu, pola.
mulatto. Malaka.
mulberry. Wauke, wauke mālolo, poʻaʻaha; kaumanu, koaha; *black* —, kalika, kilika, kukamino; *Indian* —, noni; — *bark,* kīwawā. *Mulberry leaf,* lau lole. *The paper mulberry of Kūlolia that stands alone,* ka wauke kū kahi o Kūlolia *(of anything uniquely beautiful).*
mulch. Pulu, kīpulu, poʻi kalo. *To clear away mulch,* kāhili pulu, lauhuʻe. *See saying,* **pulu.** *Method of making mulch,* pāhala.
mule. Hoki, miula, piula.
mullet. ʻAmaʻama *(see* ʻama ʻama *for saying and growth stages);* ʻanae, pahaha; *false* —, uouoa. *Mullet net,* ʻalihilele.
mull over. Nalu, hoʻomāuiui; piolo *(fig.).*
multiple. Helu komo ʻia.
multiplicand. Helu hoʻonui ʻia.
multiplication. Hoʻonui. *Multiplication sign,* kahahiō, kaha hoʻonui. *Multiplication tables,* ʻālualua.
multiplier. Helu hoʻonui.
multiply. Hoʻomāhuahua, hoʻonui. *Also:* hoʻopulapula, māhua, hoʻomāhua, laupaʻi, kulukulu. *Multiply two by two,* ʻalua lua.
multitude. Lehulehu, nehunehu, kini, mū, hoʻomū, laupaʻi, pūʻali, nuʻa.
multitudinous. Kinikini. *Also:* mānuʻunuʻu, mokuāwai, hono.
mum. Mūmū, mū, hoʻomū, mumule, mūkei. *See* **silent.**
mumble. Namunamu, namu, hoʻonamu, naunau, kapalalū.
mumble-the-peg. Kuwala pahi.
mummy. Iʻaloa.
mumps. ʻAuwaepahāha, ʻāʻīpahāha.
munch. Nau, naunau, nome.
munitions. Lako pono kaua.
murder. Pepehi kanaka, kā make loa. *His murder (of someone else),* kāna make. *His murder (of himself),* kona make.
murderer. Pepehi kanaka, lima koko.
murky. Pōuliuli, lepolepo, ʻōlepolepo, ʻōmea, ʻōmeamea.
murmuring. Hamumu, hamumumu, nē, ʻowē, hē, lauʻowē haʻihaʻi. *See* **complain.**
muscle. ʻIʻo, ʻiʻo huki, olonā, oloolonā, makela; aʻa *(small);* kāhā poʻohiwi *(on shoulder blade);* lolokū *(on back of head);* ʻuala *(of upper arm);* ʻulu *(in calf of leg).*
muscular. Waʻawaʻa, ʻāwaʻawaʻa, kīwaʻawaʻa, hoʻolua, lawakua, pūkonakona, konakona.
museum. Hale hōʻikeʻike. *See* **Bishop Museum.**
mush. Palaoa lūlū.
mushroom. Kūkaelio, māmalu. *Mushroom-shaped,* pokake.
mushroom coral. Koʻa kohe, ʻākoʻakoʻa kohe.
music. Mele *(vocal);* pila hoʻokani *(instrumental).* *See* **interval, musical instrument, note, scale, tone.** *To play music,* hoʻokani pila. *To read music,* heluhelu hua mele. *Play music!* Kani ka pila!
musical instrument. Pila hoʻokani *(modern).* *Ancient musical instruments:* hano, hōkeo kani, hōkiokio, ʻiliʻili, ipu, kāʻekeʻeke *(pahūpahū),* kālaʻau, nīʻau kani, pahu, papa hehi, pū, pūʻili, pū lāʻī, pūniu, ʻūkēkē,

Monday. Pōʻakahi. *Rare:* Monelē, Moneke, Monede.
money. Kālā, moni. *Sum of money,* puʻu kālā, pōkeokeo. *Paper money,* kālā pepa. *Silver money,* kālā keʻokeʻo, kakalama, hapawalu. *Gold money,* kālā ʻulaʻula. *Money order,* pepa kīkoʻo kālā. *Postal money order,* pila kīkoʻo hale leka.
moneyed. Kālā, lako i ke kālā.
Mongolia, Mongolian. Monokolia, Monogolia.
mongoose. ʻIole manakuke, manakuke.
monitor. Kahu nānā, kahu hoʻoponopono, mea hoʻolohe pono i ka mea e ʻōlelo ʻia ana, monika.
monk. Mōneka.
monkey. Keko, mākinikā. *Monkey-like in appearance,* mukeko.
monkeypod. ʻŌhai.
monopoly. Pōʻaiʻālunu.
monotonous. Manakā.
monsoon. Monokune.
mons pubis. Hena, hene, puʻukole. *To see, feel, handle the mons pubis,* hoʻohena.
monster. Pilikua nui.
Montana. Monekana, Monakana.
Monterey. Monekelei.
month. Mahina, malama. *According to Johnson and Mahelona (40), the months are male stars in the sixth generation after male* Ao *(day) and female* Pō *(night). Each star-month has one or more star-wives. The males are born in succeeding generations starting with* ʻIkuwā (Pohā-kō-ʻeleʻele), *followed by* Welehu, Makaliʻi (ʻAuhuhu-paʻina), Kāʻelo, Kaulua, Nana, Welo, Ikiiki, Kaʻaona, Hinaiaʻeleʻele, Māhoe Mua (Hilina Ehu), *and* Māhoe Hope (Hilina Mā). *Malo 30 equates* ʻIkuwā *with October, but as shown in Emerson's note (Malo 33–5), correspondences with the Western calendar differed according to islands and individuals. Variants are in parentheses in the above list. Nights of the lunar month:* Hilo, Hoaka, Kū Kahi, Kū Lua, Kū Kolu, Kū Pau, ʻOle Kū Kahi, ʻOle Kū Lua, ʻOle Kū Kolu, ʻOle Kū Pau, Huna (Hoʻāo), Mohalu (Mōhaluhalu), Hua, Akua, Hoku, Māhealani, Kū Lua, Lāʻau Kū Kahi, Lāʻau Kū Lua, Lāʻau Pau, ʻOle Kū Kahi, ʻOle Kū Lua, ʻOle Pau, Kāloa Kū Kahi, Kāloa Kū Lua, Kāloa Pau, Kāne, Lono, Mauli, Muku. *Months of pregnancy,* kū.
monthly. Kēlā mahina, kēia mahina. *Monthly issue,* puka mahina. *Monthly pay,* uku ma ka mahina.
monument. Kia hoʻomanaʻo.
moo. Umō.
mood. 1. *Disposition.* ʻAno, naʻau. *See* **feelings, moody.** 2. *Grammar.* ʻŌuli. *Indicative mood,* ʻōuli-haʻi.
moody. Loli mau ke ʻano o ka noʻonoʻo, nunuha.
moon. Mahina, malama. *New moon,* mahina hou. *Full moon,* mahina piha, mahina poepoe; Hoku Palemo *(which sets before daylight);* Hoku Ili *(which sets after daylight). Halo around moon,* luahoana, luakālai, luakālai lani. *Nights of full moon,* Hoku, Māhealani *(see* **month***). Waxing moon,* mahina hapalua mua. *Waning moon,* mahina hapalua hope. *Goddess of the moon,* Hina-i-ka-malama. *The moon is up,* kau ka mahina *(a bald man appears).*
moon flower. Koali pehu, koani pehu.
moonlight. Mālamalama o ka mahina. *Pale moonlight,* māhinahina. *The moonlight shines brightly,* ka pā kōnane a ka mahina.
moored. Lana, kū, hoʻopaʻa.
mooring rock. Pōhaku lana.
Moorish idol. Kihikihi.
mop. Lāʻau holoi papahele, kāwele wai. *Mop the floor,* holoi papahele, kalapu papahele.
moral. Pono, molala. *Moral deportment,* noho pono. *To cleanse and purify morally,* huikala. *Cf.* **kānana, kālana.**
morale. Kūlana.
morality. Pono, noho pono ʻana, maikaʻi.
morals. Lula o ka nohona.

moray eel. Puhi ao, puhi kauila.
more. Hou, keu. *See ex.,* **hala 2.** *More or less,* ʻoi ā emi mai. *More than,* mua. *More chicken?* I moa hou? I moa hou nāu? *Give me more,* hāʻawi hou mai. *More people came,* nui hou aku ka poʻe i hele mai.
moreover. Kekahi, eia kekahi, eia hou, koe kēia.
Morinda citrifolia. Noni.
Mormon. Molemona, Moremona.
morning. Kakahiaka. *See* **good morning.** *Early morning,* kakahiaka nui. *Later this morning,* kēia kakahiaka aku. *The dust of morning,* ʻehu kakahiaka *(fig., dawn, youth, brief shower).*
morning-glory. Koali, koani, kowali *(for various kinds, see Haw.-Eng. entry and entries that follow it),* pōhuehue, hunakai, kūpala, paha, ʻuala koali, kuahulu (koali kuahulu), paʻaliʻi. *A morning-glory, a twister,* he koali, he pākaʻawili *(of unstable persons).*
Morning Star. Hōkū-ao, Hōkū-loa, Ka-ʻelele-o-ka-wanaʻao (?), Hōkū-komohana, Kukui Wanaʻao, Iao, Waileia.
Morocco. Moloko.
moronic. Hepa, kūhepa, ʻōhepa, ʻōpulepule.
morose. Nunuha, naʻinaʻi.
morsel. Wahi hakina iki, hakina ʻai, ʻāmikamika.
mortal. 1. Kanaka maoli. 2. *See* **fatal.**
mortar. 1. *Cement.* Puna, puna hamo, pālolo. 2. *Vessel.* Poho, ipu kuʻi. 3. *Ordnance.* Pū kī, pōkā pahū.
mortgage. Molaki. *Chattel mortgage,* molaki waiwai lewa.
mortgagee. Mea paʻa molaki.
mortgager. Mea molaki.
mortise. Kohe.
mosaic. Mokaika.
Moscow. Mokekao.
mosque. Mokeko.
mosquito. Makika. *Mosquito larvae,* naio makika.
mosquito fish. Iʻa makika.
mosquito net. Pākū makika.
moss. Limu *(for various kinds, see Haw.-Eng. entry and entries that follow it). Also:* ʻēkaha, hinihini ʻula, huluhulu-a-ʻīlio, huluhulu-a-Kaʻau-hele-moa, iliohe, kalauipo, līpoa kuahiwi, mākole mākōpiʻi (mākōpiʻi, makaʻōpiʻi, kala makapiʻi), ʻōnohiawa, ʻōpulepule, ʻowau, wāwaeʻiole. *See* **Florida moss.** *Moss-grown,* limua, hākuma, paʻa i ka limu. *The district is moss-covered,* limua ka moku *(of peace, since moss grows in damp places undisturbed by man).*
most. Hapa nui, nui, hapa loa, loa.
mote. Laʻolaʻo, pālaʻolaʻo, pula. *Having something in the eye, as a mote or eyelash,* laʻo, laʻo ka maka, pula ka maka.
moth. Pulelehua, ʻōkaʻi; mū *(clothes moth). Larva and case of case moth,* ʻōpūlauoho, pūlauoho.
moth-eaten. Ānea, nono, popopo; ʻai ʻia e ka mū *(Ioba 13:28).*
mother. Makuahine, māmā; lūauʻi makuahine; hulilau *(fig.). See saying,* **ʻalalā,** *and* **godmother, gourd, stepmother.** *Mother of one's children,* hānau kama.
mother and child. Makua mea keiki.
Mother Hubbard. Holokū.
mother-in-law. Makuahūnōai wahine.
mother-of-pearl shell. *See* **pearl shell.**
Mother's Day. Lā o nā mākuahine.
mother tongue. ʻŌlelo makua.
motion. 1. *Movement.* ʻOni, au, neʻe, mōkio. *Motion of hands and fingers,* hei. *Repeated motion,* hulehulei. *Set in motion.* hoʻohele. 2. *Parliamentary.* Noi. *To second a motion,* kōkua.
motionless. ʻOnipaʻa, mālie, ʻoni ʻole, kīpū lani *(as clouds, stars).*
motive. Kumu.
motor. Mīkini.
motorcycle. Mokokaikala, kaʻa mokokaikala.
mottled. ʻŌpulepule, kikiko, ʻōniʻo, ʻōniʻoniʻo, niʻo.
motto. Mākia. *"Stand firm" was Liliʻu-o-ka-lani's motto,* " ʻonipaʻa" kā Liliʻu-o-ka-lani mākia.

Miscarried fetus, keiki he'e wale, keiki hā'ule wale, hua hā'ule. *Miscarriage of justice,* holo pono 'ole o ke kānāwai.

miscellaneous. Kēlā me kēia, kēlā mea kēia mea, nā mea like 'ole, kīko'olā, laukua.

miscellany. Nā mea like 'ole, pūlehulehu.

mischief. Kolohe *(bad or innocent);* 'eu *(funny). See* **mischief-maker, mischievous.**

mischief-maker. Kolohe, 'āpiki. *See* **parrot fish.**

mischievous. Kolohe. *Also:* ho'okolohe, 'āpiki, 'eu, 'epa, hū'eu, lapa, maka le'a, lapuwale, 'e'e'e, honole. *See saying,* **maka'ā.**

misconstrue. Ho'ohepa, wehewehe hewa, koho hewa.

misdemeanor. Mikamina.

misdirect. Kuhi pā'ē'ē, kuhikuhi hewa.

miser. Pī. *See* **greed, miserly.**

miserly. *See* **miser.** *Also:* akao'o, pīpine, ho'olaholaho, makauli'i, minamina, pukumoa.

misery. Pō'ino oki loa, lu'ulu'u, māino, 'īnea.

misfortune. Pō'ino, pōpilikia. *Also:* 'awa *(fig.);* la'a uli, make. *Predict misfortune,* ho'oiloilo. *Gloat over misfortunes of others,* 'aikola, hō'aikola, 'ākola.

misinform. Hō'ike hewa, kuhi pā'ē'ē.

mislead. Alaka'i hewa. *Also:* kuhi pā'ē'ē, ho'opā'ē'ē, ho'opouli, kanale'o.

misnomer. 'Ōlelo hewa i ka inoa.

misprint. Pa'i hewa.

mispronounce. Hewa ka hopuna, pa'ewa ka hopuna, hewa ka ho'opuka 'ana.

misrepresent. Hō'ike hewa, ho'opā'ē'ē.

miss. 1. *Fail to hit.* Hala, hewa. *Also:* kāhewa, hā'ulehope, kapeke; mu'u *(in marbles);* halahī, halahū, holohu'a, pāhi'a, holohi'a. *To miss the way,* hū, hūhewa, hili, halakī. **2.** *Perceive absence.* Ha'o. **3.** *Nostalgia.* Ha'o wale, minamina. **4.** *Unmarried woman.* Wahine male 'ole. *No equivalent for the title.*

misshapen. 'Alu'alu, 'anake'e, kīnā, naele, 'ōpaha, ho'ōpaha, pa'ewa, pepe'e.

missile. Mea pākī, mea kī 'ia. *Guided missile,* mea kī ho'opololei loa 'ia.

missing. Nalowale, nalo, nano, koe.

mission. Huaka'i, mikiona; hololani *(rare).*

missionary. Mikanele, mikionele, mikionali; a'o hele *(itinerant). To act like a missionary,* ho'omikanele.

Mississippi. Mikikipi, Misisipi.

Missouri. Mikouli, Misouri.

misstep. Kāhehi, hehi hewa, kupe.

mist. Uhiwai, noe, 'ohu, 'ehu, 'ehuehu *(in approximate order of decreasing denseness). In songs, mist is associated with romance. Also:* lelehuna, huna wai, kēhau, kī'ohu'ohu, pūnohu, uakea, akū, 'awa, uahi wai; ua-oa. *Fine mist,* lilinoe, kili 'ohu. *See* **misty.** *Heavy mist,* uhiwai. *Creeping mist,* noe kolo, ua noe. *Pink mist,* noe 'ula. *Rainbow-hued mist,* ko'i'ula. *White mist,* uakea. *Love is mist, settles on all hills,* he 'ohu ke aloha, 'a'ohe kuahiwi kau 'ole *(of love). Goddess of mists,* Lilinoe.

mistake. Hewa, kuhi hewa, pa'ewa, lalau; kīnā'u *(flaw). To cause or feign a mistake,* ho'ohewa. *To mistake a person for someone else,* kuhi hewa, ho'omaopopo 'ole. *A mistake by many,* hehehewa.

mistaken. 'Olalau. *See* **mistake.**

mister. *See* **Mr.**

mistletoe. Kaumahana, hulumoa.

mistreat, mistreatment. Hana 'ino, māuna, pā'ulu'ā. *See* **cruel.**

mistress. Wahine manuahi, ipo manuahi, wahine noho pū; kahu *(of a pet). Mistress of a house,* haku wahine o ka home.

misty. Pa'a i ka noe, uhi i ka noe. *Also:* kēwai, pōhina, polohina, hea, hō'ohu; kī'ohu'ohu, māohu, poluluhi. *See glory, mist, and sayings,* **kī'ohu'ohu, mā'ohu.**

misunderstand. Maopopo akaaka 'ole.

mite. 1. *Insect.* Ona, ane; ona moa *(chicken);* 'uku hipa *(sheep).* **2.** *Small sum.* Lepeka.

mitigated. Akaku'u, emi.

mitre. Kalaunu pīhopa, pāpale hainikā.

mitten. Mīkini, mīkini lima.

mix. Ho'ohui, hui *(general);* ho'owali *(as poi, dough). Also:* huihui, huika'i, hauhili, hauhauhili, hilikau, 'ānoni, ho'ō'ā, kake, kīkomo, 'āwili, kauwili, wili, noni. *See* **mixture, mix-up.** *To mix ingredients,* kāwili, pa'i, hokahokai. *To mix relish,* poho 'inamona. *Mixing board or tray,* papa wili, papa wili 'ai. *Poi mixer,* lā'au ho'owali 'ai.

mixed. Huikau. *Also:* huihui, ho'ohuihui, hauhili, hauhauhili, hilikau, 'aluka, kipona, laukua, 'ānoni, 'ānoninoni, 'ānononi, 'ōnoninoni, pa'ipa'i; — *colors,* a'ea'e, 'ō'ā. *Mixed liquid,* wai pa'ipa'i. *Mixed drink,* wai pa'ipa'i, lama pa'ipa'i 'ia, lama ho'ohuihui 'ia, mea inu ho'ohuihui. *Mixed blood,* koko 'āwili, hapa, 'ō'ā.

mixture. Mea i kāwili pū 'ia, mea i ho'ohuihui 'ia.

mix-up. Huikau, ho'ohuikau, hōkai, hokahokai, ka'ahōkai.

moan. 'Ū, 'uhū, 'uhū'uhū, kani'ū, kani'uhū, kaniā'au, auē, nā, nū, nūnū, ho'onū.

moaning bird. 'Ua'u kani; hō'io *(rare).*

moat. 'Auwaha e ho'opuni ana i ke kākela.

mob. Uluao'a, po'e ho'ohaunaele.

Mobile. Mopile, Mobile.

mock. Ho'ohenehene, pāhenehene, henehene. *Also:* lauma'ewa, ho'oma'ewa, ma'ewa, ho'omahua, ho'omahuakala, ho'omā'auwē, ho'omā'auea. *See* **battle.**

mock orange. Alahe'e haole.

mode. 'Ano.

model. Ana, ana ho'ohālike, kumu, kumu ho'ohālike, kumu alaka'i.

moderate. Ho'okanaha'i, akahele.

modern. No kēia au, nupaikini.

modest. Waipahē, akahai, ha'aha'a, pē, na'au pē, pēpē, na'au pēpē, hō'oi'oi 'ole. *Also:* kolokolohai, wiwo; 'ōheke *(somewhat). Saying: stay down in the green clumps, do not raise yourself,* e noho iho i ke ōpū weuweu, mai ho'oki'eki'e *(see also* **hakalī***).*

Mohammed, Mohammedan. Mahomeka, Mohameka.

moist. 'Ū, mā'ū, mā'ū'ū, ko'ū, ma'ūma'ū, ko'oū, pa'ū, 'ūpolu, pulu, līhau, kilipohe. *Moist with fog,* kawaū. *Moist and fragrant,* no'ū.

moisten. Ho'oma'ū, ho'omā'ū'ū, ho'oū, hō'ū, kau wai, kaiehu.

molar. Ku'i. *Click the molars together,* 'a'aki ke ku'i. *Gnash the molars, hands are slow,* nau ke ku'i, lohi ka lima *(anger slows work).*

molasses. Malakeke.

mold. 1. *Shape.* 'Omo'omo, hō'omo'omo, 'ōmilo, 'ōmilomilo. **2.** *Fungus.* Ā. *See* **moldy.**

molded. Hō'omo'omo 'ia, 'ōmilomilo 'ia. *Molded into an image,* hana i ā ā kūlike me ke ki'i.

molding. Mōlina.

moldy. Punahelu. *Also:* 'ī'ī, nehi, pa'ū, pīlekaleka, pōukiuki. *See* **musty.** *Moldy odor,* kūnāhelu, pelekunu.

mole. 1. *Anatomical.* Pu'u, kūkaenalo, leponalo. **2.** *Mammal.* Mole, kameleona.

mollified. Mānalo.

mollify. Ho'omānalo, ho'opalupalu, ho'omalimali.

mollusk. *See* **shell.**

Moloka'i. Moloka'i. *Epithet: great Moloka'i of Hina,* Moloka'i nui a Hina *(Hina was the legendary mother of Moloka'i).*

molt. Māunu, helele'i ka hulu; auhā *(rare).*

molten. Ho'ohehe'e 'ia.

Moluccas. Moluka.

moment. Manawa iki. *Wait a moment,* kali iki, eia iho.

momentum. Momeneku, ke 'ano o ka ne'e 'ana i mua. *To gain momentum,* ho'onui aku i ka holo 'ana.

monarch. Mō'ī, ali'i.

monarchy. Aupuni mō'ī.

monastery. Hale mōneka, monekekeli.

N

n. Nū.

nag. Nē, hoʻohune, koi hoʻohune, noi mau, nuku, nukunuku. *Also:* none, meʻo, hauwene, hoʻohana.

nail. 1. *Carpenter's.* Kui, kui nao, kui hao, kui kākia. *Also:* kākia, hākia, mākia, kia, heke, meki, pōheoheo. *Nail point,* maka kui. **2.** *Human.* Maiʻao, mikiʻao, māiʻuʻu. **3.** *Measurement.* Nala.

nainsook. Nanakuka.

naked. Kohana. *Also:* ʻōlohe, ʻōlohelohe, ʻilikini, koaka, pōkaʻo, hākaʻo, ʻomimo. *To go naked,* hele wale, hele kohana.

nakedness. Kohana, kahi huna, hena.

name. 1. *Noun.* Inoa. *See saying, 'aʻala. Name given in a dream,* inoa pō, inoa mai ka pō mai. *Family name,* inoa ʻohana. *Chiefly name,* inoa kapa na ke aliʻi. *Fictitious or pet name, nickname, pen name,* inoa kapakapa. **2.** *Verb.* Hea, hea inoa, kapa, kāhea.

name chant. Inoa, mele inoa. *To recite a name chant,* hea, hea mele inoa.

name dropping. Pai aliʻi.

namely. ʻOia hoʻi.

namesake. Inoa.

nankeen. Naneki.

Nanking. Nanekina.

Nantucket. Nanikokeka, Nanikoteka; Nanikukeka, Nanituketa.

nap. Hiamoe iki.

nape. Hokua.

napkin. Kāwele. *Rare:* hainakā, kahakahana lole. *Paper napkin,* kāwele pepa. *Sanitary napkin,* mea hume, kīhamo.

Naples. Napela.

narcotic. Lāʻau hoʻohiamoe, lāʻau moe, lāʻau hoʻomalule kino, mea ʻona.

narrate. Haʻi, kūkaʻi ʻōlelo.

narrow. Lāʻiki, hāiki, hoʻohāiki. *Also:* mio, miomio, lānihinihi, maʻawe, ʻōiki, kuhāiki, moʻolio, ʻololī. *Narrow-minded,* hāiki ka ʻike, hāiki ka noʻonoʻo, loko hāiki, manaʻo hāiki. *Narrow escape,* pakele māhunehune; pakele mai make *(from death).*

narrowing. Olomio, muʻoiki, miomio.

nasal. Hanu mai ka ihu. *Nasal speech,* ihu hānuna.

Nashville. Nakawila, Nasavila; Nakiwile.

nasturtium. Pohe haole.

nasty. Pelapela, haukaʻe, mākonā, koaea; kōʻā *(fig.). See* **malevolent.**

nation. Lāhui, aupuni. *To form a nation,* hoʻolāhui.

national. Aupuni, lāhui.

National Guard. Koa Kiaʻi Lāhui.

nationality. Lāhui.

native. Kamaʻāina, maoli, ʻōiwi, kupa, keiki papa. *Also:* kulāiwi, ʻāpaʻakuma, mauki. *Native land,* one hānau, kulāiwi; kuapuiwi *(rare). Native son,* keiki hānau o ka ʻāina, ēwe hānau o ka ʻāina. *Native-born,* papa. *Native bird,* manu kamaʻāina. *Native plant,* lāʻau kamaʻāina. *Native speaker,* mānaleo *(lit., inherited language, a term invented in the 1970s by Larry Kimura and William Wilson).*

natural. Kūpono.

naturalization. Hoʻokupa ʻana.

naturalize. Hoʻokupa, hoʻohiki.

nature. 1. *Kind.* ʻAno. *Also:* ʻōuli; hulu *(rare). Chiefly nature or character,* naʻau aliʻi. *Dual natured,* ʻano pāpālua. *In the nature of,* ʻā-, ʻano like me. *Change of nature,* loli ʻano. *Of similar nature,* ʻano like, hoʻokahi nō ʻano. *To tell the nature,* hōʻike ʻano. *To attend the calls of nature,* hoʻopau pilikia. **2.** *No word for nature in the sense of outdoors.*

naughty. Kolohe, ʻeu, ʻāpiki.

nausea. Pailua, papailua. *Also:* ʻōlanalana, luea, naluea, poluea, poluwā, unea.

nauseated. Liliha, lihaliha, papailua.

nauseating. Pailua, hoʻopailua. *Also:* nānue, luaʻikū, liliha, ʻōlanalana.

nautilus. ʻAumoana, ʻau-waʻa-lā-lua, moamoa, moamoa waʻa, naukilo. *Cf.* **aniani.**

naval. ʻOihana moku. *Naval battle,* kaua moana.

navel. Piko.

navel string. Piko, ēwe, wewe, ʻiewe, ʻiawe.

navigate, navigator. Hoʻokele.

navy. ʻOihana moku.

navy-blue cloth. ʻAinakini, lainakini.

Nazarite. Nakalike.

neap tide. *No equivalent; see* **tide.**

near. Kokoke, hiʻialo. *To draw near,* kokoke, hoʻokokoke.

nearby. Kokoke, aʻe, aʻe nei, eia aku.

nearly. Kokoke, ʻaneʻane, mai. *Nearly dead,* mai make.

nearsighted. ʻIke pōkole.

neat. Maiau, ʻauliʻi; mikioi *(in craftsmanship). Also:* palamimo, palamio, miomio, ponopono, paʻihi, popohe, pālawaiki.

Nebraska. Nepalaka, Nebaraka.

necessary. Pono.

necessity. Pono. *Necessities of life,* mea ola o ke kino, nā pono o ka nohona.

neck. ʻĀʻī; waha *(of a dress). Also:* kaniʻāʻī, ʻōhao *(rare). Front of neck,* puanaʻī. *Slender or slim neck,* ʻāʻī oeoe. *Stiff neck,* ʻāʻī ʻoʻoleʻa, ʻāʻīkū, ʻāʻī uaua. *Stiffness or soreness in neck cords,* uauakaha. *Calloused neck,* ʻāʻī puʻu. *Scrofulous neck,* ʻāʻī ʻalaʻala, ʻāʻī palaʻe, pūlele. *To tie, as about the neck;* kāʻawe; ʻōhao *(rare).*

neckerchief. Hainakā ʻāʻī, hinakā ʻāʻī, lei ʻāʻī, hainakā lei.

necklace. Lei. *See* **lei, whale tooth.** *Pearl necklace,* lei momi. *Diamond necklace,* lei kaimana. *Bead necklace,* lei kula *(gold);* akalei *(glass). Hog-tusk necklace,* lei hoaka. *Dogtooth necklace,* lei niho ʻīlio. *"Puka" shell necklace,* lei pūpū puka.

necktie. Lei ʻāʻī.

necromancer. Kilo, kuhikuhipuʻuone, nīnau ʻuhane, nīnau kupapaʻu.

need. 1. *Necessity.* Pono, puʻu. *I need to go,* pono ʻo au ke hele. **2.** *Lacks.* Nele, hemahema.

needle. 1. *Instrument.* Kui, kui kele, kui humuhumu; mānai, pahele, hānai, mākai, mōkila, mākila *(for stringing leis);* hiʻa *(for nets);* ʻōhiʻu *(for thatching);* kui pāuma *(for sewing gunny sacks);* pine *(of compass);* hou kui *(for injections);* mōlī *(for tattooing). Needle point,* maka kui. *Slot of sewing machine needle,* puka kui kele. *Eye of needle,* puka kui. *To thread a needle,* hoʻopiha kui. *Needle-pointed,* huini. **2.** *Plant.* Kī, kī nehe.

needlefish. ʻAha, ʻaha mele; ʻahaʻaha *(young).*

needy. Nele, hemahema, ʻōlohe. *See* **poor.**

ne'er-do-well. *See* **vagabond.**

negative. 1. *Negate.* ʻOle, hōʻole. **2.** *Of a picture.* Aka kiʻi.

neglect. Mālama ʻole, waiho wale, hoʻopalaleha, hoʻohemahema, hoʻomaopopo ʻole, haʻalele kōkua ʻole, hāʻule.

neglected. Hoʻomaopopo ʻole ʻia. *See* **neglect.**
negligence. Mālama ʻole.
negligent. Hoʻohemahema, palaka, palaheha.
negotiate. Kūkākūkā, kūkā kamaʻilio.
Negro. Nekelo. *See* **black 2.**
negroid. Pāʻele; pūnika *(rare).*
neigh. Ihihī, ʻuhūʻuhū. *To imitate neighing,* hōʻihihī.
neighbor. Hoa noho, hoalauna.
neighborhood. Wahi noho kokoke, kaulu, kaiāulu.
neither. ʻAʻole, ʻaʻole hoʻi. *Neither he nor I,* ʻaʻole ʻoia, ʻaʻole nō ʻo au. *Neither was any good,* ʻaʻole maikaʻi ʻo lāua ā ʻelua.
nephew. Keiki (ke keiki kāne a ke kaikuaʻana, ke kaikaina, ke kaikunāne, ke kaikuahine), keiki hanauna.
Nerita. Pipipi. *See saying,* iʻa **1.**
nerve. Aʻa, aʻalolo; aʻalolo lohe *(auditory). Such nerve!* Wini ʻiʻo nō *(slang)!*
nervous. Pīhoihoi wale, haʻalulu o loko. *Also:* ulukū, palalū.
nervous system. Nā aʻalolo apau; lolokū; molokū *(rare).*
nervy. Mahaʻoi, wini.
nest. Pūnana.
net. *The most common kinds are* ʻupena *(see Haw.-Eng. entry and entries that follow it),* kōkō. *See* **float, mesh, seine.** *Various kinds: Throwing net,* ʻupena kiloi, ʻupena hoʻolei, ʻupena kiola, uhina. *Drag net,* lau, laukō, ʻalihilele. *Gill net,* kuʻu, ʻupena kuʻu, ʻupena hoʻolewalewa, pahu. *Set net,* ʻupena kuʻu, ʻupena hoʻomoemoe. *Dip net,* ʻākiʻikiʻi, pākiʻikiʻi. *Bag net,* ʻeke, hului, huli, papa, papa hului, hano, lauahi, luelue, nae kuku, papa waha nui, ʻupena kolo, pōuouo. *Mosquito net,* pākū makika. *Other kinds:* ʻaʻei, ʻakuʻikuʻi, pākuʻikuʻi, aumaiewa, hākaʻokaʻo, hei, hihi, hihi manō, holoholo, holowaʻa, holoaʻa, hoʻolewalewa, hukiheʻe, kāʻeʻe, kāhala, kāʻihi, kaʻiʻi, kāʻili, kākā, kākā uhu, kīholo, kōkō hoʻupuʻu, kūpō, lau ʻōpae, maiewa, maka lua, mākolu, mālua, maoloha, nae, naepuni, nukuwāʻula, nukuāʻula, pākuʻipai, pāloa, papa, papa hoʻolewalewa *(rare),* pepeiao, pouono, pouno, puni, uluulu, ulūlu. *Hau-wood net handles:* hau ō ʻiao, hau ō mālolo. *Other net parts:* hāwele *(lashing);* hoene *(mesh);* kuku puhi, puhi nui, puhi ʻuʻuku, puhi iki *(stick supports);* aʻa puʻupuʻu, ʻaea *(rare),* ʻalihi, hānai, holokuku, hopeʻaʻei, kahahānai, lā, mole, ʻōkaʻi, pā, papa, piko, pīkoni, puʻumana, uluna, ununa. *Net spacer, gauge,* haha kā ʻupena, una. *Net mender,* kīʻoʻe. *To set a net,* kuʻu, kuʻuna, hoʻomoe, hoʻomoemoe. *To throw a net,* kiloi (kiola,hoʻolei) ʻupena. *To draw a net,* ani. *To make net meshes,* kā. *Place for setting a net,* moena, kuʻuna. *Net owner's canoe,* pokiʻi *(rare). Types of net fishing:* lawaiʻa kōkō, hukilau, laulele, kāheʻe, kahekahe, holoholo, mōkū.
nether world. Ke ao o Milu, Milu, Ka-paʻa-heo, poheue.
nettle. Nahele maneʻo.
network. Nae *(base of feather capes);* hiʻa, kōkō ʻula.
neuralgia. Huʻi ma nā aʻalolo.
neuritis. Lumakika, kālawa, hālawa.
neutral. Kāʻokoʻa, komo ʻole i ke kaua.
neutralize. Hoʻomānalo, kāʻokoʻa.
Nevada. Newaka, Newada, Nevada.
never. ʻAʻole, ʻaʻole loa. *Never before,* ʻakahi . . . ā, ʻaʻole i . . . mamua. *I've never been there before,* ʻakahi au ā hele malaila. *Never mind!* ʻAʻole pilikia! He mea ʻole!
nevertheless. Akā, akā hoʻi, naʻe.
new. Hou. *Also:* mea hou, ʻano hou, malihini. *New-fashioned,* ʻano hou; nupaikini *(rare). This is new to me,* he mea malihini kēia i kuʻu maka *(see* **malihini***). What's new?* He aha ka mea hou?
New Bedford. Nū Pelepeki, Nu Belefedi; Nū Pepeki; Nū Pekepoka, Nu Bedefoda.
New Caledonia. Nū Kalekonia, Nu Kaledonia.
newcomer. Malihini.

Newfoundland. Nūpounelana, Nufounelana.
New Guinea. Nū Kini, Nu Gini.
New Hampshire. Nū Hamekia, Nu Hamesia.
New Haven. Nū Hawena.
New Hebrides. Nū Hepeke, Nu Hebede, ʻĀina wohi.
New Holland. Nū Holani.
New Jersey. Nū ʻIeleke, Nu Ierese.
New London. Nū Lalana.
newly. ʻAkahi nō.
New Mexico. Nū Mekiko.
New Orleans. Nū ʻOlina.
news. Mea hou, nū hou, nū, lono; ʻanoʻai *(rare). Foreign news,* nū hou kūwaho. *Local news,* nū hou kūloko. *Bits of news,* hunahuna mea hou, hunehune mea hou. *News item,* ikamu mea hou. *To tell news, bringing of news,* ʻāhaʻilono, haʻilono. *To hear sudden news,* lono honua. *The news spread,* kuʻi ka lono.
New South Wales. Nū Wale Hema.
newspaper. Nūpepa. *Daily newspaper,* nūpepa puka lā. *Newspaper carrier or subscriber,* mea lawe nūpepa.
New Testament. Kauoha Hou.
new year. Makahiki hou. *Happy New Year,* hauʻoli makahiki hou, hapenūia.
New Year's Eve. Ahiahi Makahiki Hou.
New York. Nuioka.
New Zealand. Nukīlani.
next. Aʻe, hope, hiki. *Next week,* kēia pule aʻe. *Week after next,* kēia pule aʻe ā ia pule aku. *What next? Ā* he aha aʻe? *The next house,* kekahi hale aku nō, kekahi hale aʻe.
Niagara. Niakala, Niagara.
nibble. Nali, nalinali, ʻaʻaki, ʻakiʻaki, nome. *Also:* namu, namunamu, mīkole, wahaʻula, pākukui, hōleha, mīkoi, mīkoikoi, mīkokoi.
Nicaragua. Nikalakua, Nikaragua.
nice. ʻAuliʻi; ʻoluʻolu *(pleasant);* maikaʻi.
nicked. Manumanu. *See saying,* **whittle.**
nickel. Hapaʻumi. *See* **five cents.**
nickers. Kākalaioa *(plant).*
nickname. Inoa kapakapa.
niece. Kaikamahine (ke kaikamahine a ke kaikuaʻana, ke kaikaina, ke kaikunāne, ke kaikuahine), keiki hanauna.
niggardly. Pī, kulipaʻa.
nigger. Nika.
night. Pō. *Divisions of the night: beginning,* kihi o ka pō; *late night,* aumoe, pili aumoe, kuluaumoe, kau; pōlalouli *(rare); period from midnight to dawn,* pilipuka. *To count the nights of the moon,* helu pō. *Last night,* ka pō nei. *To pass the night,* hōʻaumoe. *Dark night,* pouli, pō kinikini. *Many nights,* pō kinikini, pō mano. *For nights of the month, see* **month.**
night-blooming cereus. Pānini-o-Ka-puna-hou.
night cestrum. ʻAlaaumoe, kūpaoa, onaona Iāpana.
nightfall. Ka pili o ke ahiahi, pō ka lā. *See saying,* ʻēheu **1.**
nightgown. Muʻumuʻu moe pō, lole moe pō.
nighthawk. Kama, tama.
nightmare. Moehewa, moe ʻino, moe kāhua, pahulu. *To have a nightmare,* moehewa, moe ʻino, hoʻopahulu. *God of nightmares,* Pahulu.
night school. Kula pō.
nightshade. Pōpolo (polopolo), kīkānia lei, ʻīnika.
night watchman. Kiaʻi pō, mākaʻi pō.
Niʻihau. Niʻihau. *Niʻihau person,* Niʻihau, kanaka Niʻihau. *Epithets: Niʻihau of Ka-hele-lani,* Niʻihau a Ka-hele-lani *(name of a chief); Niʻihau leans back firmly (independent),* Niʻihau i ke kīkū; *see also,* **kō 1.**
Nile. Nile.
nilga. Nileka.
nimble. ʻEleu, miki, māmā. *Also:* kaʻukaʻulele, kāholo, ʻākepa, ʻakakē, ʻuleulele.
nine. ʻEiwa, iwa, ʻaiwa. *Nine times, nine at a time,* pāiwa. *See Gram.* 10.3.
ninepins. Kulakula.

nineteen. 'Umi kūmāiwa, 'umi kumamāiwa.
ninety, ninetieth. Kanaiwa.
ninety-eight. Kanaiwa kūmāwalu, kanaiwa kumamāwalu.
ninety-five. Kanaiwa kūmālima, kanaiwa kumamālima.
ninety-four. Kanaiwa kūmāhā, kanaiwa kumamāhā.
ninety-nine. Kanaiwa kūmāiwa, kanaiwa kumamāiwa.
ninety-one. Kanaiwa kūmākahi, kanaiwa kumamākahi.
ninety-seven. Kanaiwa kūmāhiku, kanaiwa kumamāhiku.
ninety-six. Kanaiwa kūmāono, kanaiwa kumamāono.
ninety-three. Kanaiwa kūmākolu, kanaiwa kumamākolu.
ninety-two. Kanaiwa kūmālua, kanaiwa kumamālua.
ninth. Iwa. *One-ninth,* hapa iwa.
nip. Hō'aki, 'a'aki, 'aki, 'akipohe, 'ini'iniki; — *off,* 'ōmu'o, 'ōmaka, 'ō'ū.
nipped. 'Ōmu'o. *That project was nipped in the bud,* 'ōmu'o 'ia a'e ia hana.
nippers. Niho 'aki, 'ūpā 'ume.
nipple. Maka waiū, maka, maka pua'a, maka mino, 'ōmaka. *Sucking nipple, as for infants,* omo, omo waiū.
Nippon. Nīpona, Nipoa.
nit. Liha, lia.
nitrate. Nikelake.
no. 'A'ole, 'a'ohe. *Rare:* 'a'oe, 'e'oe.
noble. Ali'i, lani, hie, hiehie, hano, hanohano. *Noble bearing,* kohu ali'i, kapukapu. *House of Nobles,* Hale 'Aha'ōlelo Ali'i.
nobody. 'A'ohe mea, 'a'ohe kanaka. *Those nobodies!* 'O 'ole wale mā!
nod. Kūnou, kūlou, kū'ou, kimo.
noddy tern. Noio kōhā, kōhā.
node. Aka.
Noel. Noela.
noise. Hana kuli, kulikuli, wā, wawā, kani, kulina, halulu, ho'ohalulu, kakani, hauwawā, ho'ohauwawā, 'ikuwā.
noiseless. Palanehe, leo 'ole, hāmau.
noisy. Hana kuli, kulikuli, wā, wawā, āwā, ahu wawā. *Also:* ho'ohalulu, kakani, ko'ele, ho'ohauwawā, 'ikuwā. *Rare:* 'ea, kowowowo. *Don't be noisy,* kulikuli.
nolle prosequi. Ho'opau wale.
nomadic. Hele mau, kīhoe. *Nomadic people,* lāhui hele mau, lāhui ae'a.
nominate. Koho, wae, waiho inoa.
nomination. Koho 'ana, wae 'ana.
nominative case. 'Auikumu.
non-. 'Ole.
nonconformer. Kūlana kūlike 'ole, lelepā.
none. 'A'ohe mea, 'a'ohe, 'a'ole. *None whatsoever,* 'ole loa.
nonporous. Pa'apū.
nonsense. 'Ano 'ole, kohu 'ole. *See* **stuff.** *To talk nonsense,* lalau ka 'ōlelo. *Nonsense!* He lalau!
nonspiritual. Kino, kō ke kino.
noodle. *No known name.*
nook. Kū'ono, ke'ena, ke'e, po'opo'o, kīpolipoli.
noon. Awakea; kau ka lā i ka lolo *(see* **lolo**); na'uwā *(rare).*
noose. Pahele, hele, 'ahele. *Also:* holo, puka lou, 'alehe.
nor. 'A'ole nō. *See* **neither.**
Norfolk. Nolepoka, Norefoka.
normal. Kūlike me ke 'ano mau, 'ano mau.
normal school. Kula kumu.
Normandy. Nolemaneki, Noremanedi.
north. 'Ākau. *Rare:* 'elekū, kuanalio.
North America. 'Amelika 'Ākau.
North Carolina. Kalolaina 'Ākau.
North Dakota. Kakoka 'Ākau.
northeast. Hikina 'ākau, noliki.
northern lights. Mālamalama o ka 'ākau.
North Pole. Wēlau 'Ākau.

North Star. Kio-pa'a, Hōkū-pa'a. *Also:* Kia-pa'akai, Noho-loa, Kū-mau.
northwest. Komohana 'ākau, noweke.
Norway. Nolewai, Norewai.
Norwegian. Nolewai, Noloweke.
Norwich. Nouaiki.
nose. Ihu *(descriptive terms,* **ihu***). See* **nahunahuihu, contemptuous, lunkhead, quarrelsome, scorn, scornful, snobbish, snore, wise.** *A large, sharp nose,* 'o'oma. *An elevated nose,* pinana ka ihu. *Irregular bridge of nose,* 'ami. *To touch noses in greeting,* honi. *To blow nose,* ho'okē ihu. *A sniffling nose,* pipī ka ihu. *Barely able to breathe through the nose,* ihu pī. *Talk through the nose,* hānuna ka 'ōlelo.
nosebleed. Kahe ke koko o ka ihu.
nose flute. Hano, kōheoheo, 'ohe hano ihu. *Sound of nose flute,* hoehoe.
nostril. Pukaihu.
not. 'A'ole; 'ole, 'a'ohe. *Rare:* 'a'oe, 'e'oe. *Not in the least, not at all, certainly not,* 'a'ole loa, 'ole loa, 'ole wale. *If it were not for you,* e 'ole nō 'oe.
notarize, notary. Nōkali, nōkele.
notary public. Nōkali no ka lehulehu.
notch. Pū'ali, 'auwae, kepa, kepakepa, waha, niho mole; hana *(rare).*
notched. Nihoniho, nihoa, pū'ali, mākinikini, mā'oi'oi, kepa, kepakepa.
note. 1. *Letter.* Leka pōkole, 'ōlelo ho'omana'o, 'ōlelo wehewehe; kauhua *(rare).* 2. *Financial.* Palapala 'ai'ē, pila hō'ai'ē; noka, noka kālā, nota dala. 3. *Musical.* Leo mele, hua, hua mele. *Rare:* kānāwai hīmeni, kānāwai mele. *Grace note,* hua li'ili'i, hua kōkua. *Leading note,* hua alaka'i. *Lowest or highest note (do),* pā. *Whole note,* hua 'oko'a, po'o. *Half note,* po'olima, hua hapa. *Quarter note,* hua hapahā, po'o'ele. *Second note (re),* kō. *Third note (mi),* lī. *Fourth note (fa),* hā. *Sixth note,* lā. *Seventh note (ti),* mī. *Eighth note,* po'omana. *Sixteenth note,* po'omanalua. *Thirty-second note,* po'omanakolu.
notebook. Kālana kākau, kānana kākau.
noted. 'Ike laulā 'ia, kaulana. *Noted place,* pana.
nothing. 'Ole, mea 'ole, 'a'ohe mea, nele; neo, 'alaneo, 'ōmilu. *See saying,* **goose.** *Better than nothing,* ma'ū nō ka 'ole; ma'ū nō ka nele. *Nothing doing,* e ahu ana, 'ole wale, 'ole loa.
notice. Hō'ike, 'ōlelo hō'ike, 'ōlelo ho'olaha. *Notice of sale,* ho'olaha kū'ai. *To notice,* nānā.
notify. Hō'ike. *You are hereby notified,* eia 'oe ke hō'ike 'ia aku nei.
notion. Mana'o ulu wale. *Don't get the notion of going,* mai make hele 'oe.
notorious. Kaulana i ka pono 'ole.
Nottingham. Nokinihama, Notinihama.
notwithstanding. Akā, 'a'ole na'e, koe kēia.
nought. 'Ole, neo, ho'oneo.
noun. Ha'iinoa. *See* **common noun, proper noun.** *Noun complement,* ukali ha'iinoa.
nourish. Hānai.
Nova Scotia. Nowa Kekokia, Nova Sekotia.
novel. 1. *Story.* Ka'ao. 2. *Strange.* 'Ano 'ē.
November. Nowemapa.
novice. 'Akahi akahi, ma'a 'ole, hōlona. *See saying,* **kā'e'a'e'a.** *The novice must be cautious,* e akahele ka mea 'akahi akahi.
now. I kēia manawa, 'ānō; inā *(rare). Just now,* a'e nei. *Now and then,* i kēlā manawa i kēia manawa, aia aku aia mai.
nozzle. Kī'amo.
nude. *See* **naked.**
nudge. Keku, ho'okeku, kekukeku, kuke, kukekuke; peu, ho'opeu *(upward).*
Nudibranchia. Lepelepe-o-Hina.
nuggets. Pu'upu'u kula *(gold).*
nuisance. Pilikia, mea ho'opilikia wale, ho'oluhi, mea ho'ouluhua wale, mea 'ino wale, hōkai.

Nukuhiva. Nu'uhiwa.

null and void. Mea 'ole.

nullify. Ho'olilo i mea 'ole, hō'ole, pale; lu'i *(rare).*

numb. Lōlō, mā'e'ele, mā'ele. *Also:* mānoanoa, nokule, 'ōpili, kūnāhihi, pili'aikū, piliā'aikū, manunu.

number. Helu, heluna, nui *(quantity);* hua helu *(figure). See* **numerous.** *Class number,* heluna papa. *Even number,* helu kaulike. *Odd number,* helu pa'ewa. *Dual number,* helu lua. *Plural number,* helu nui. *Whole number,* helu 'oko'a. *Prime number,* helu kumu. *Perfect number,* helu po'okela. *Reciprocal number,* hakina pāna'i. *Mixed number,* hakina pili.

numbered. Helu 'ia.

numeral. Numela.

numerator. Ho'ohelu *(in fractions).*

numerous. Lau, ho'olau, mano, manoa, lehu, lehulehu, nehunehu, kinikini, kini lau. *Also:* hālau, ho'ohālau, kūhaluka, kuapapa, makawalu, laha, mākena, pupu-pu, pākī, weliweli, weweli, pakapaka, kā'ele, pūlehulehu, kanalani.

numskull. Po'o 'olohaka.

nun. Wilikina, nuna.

nunnery. Nunele.

nurse. Kahu ma'i, kahu mālama ma'i; kahu keiki *(of a child). Wet nurse,* kahu waiū, kahu wale, nu'akea, poliwaiū. *To nurse or suckle,* 'ai waiū, omo waiū, poli 'ai *(intransitive);* hānai i ka poli *(transitive). To nurse or care for, as an infant,* hi'i, hi'ilani, ho'okāpuhi.

nursery. 1. *Children's.* Wahi mālama keiki. 2. *Garden.* Kīhāpai ho'oulu mea kanu.

nut. Kukui haole. *Pandanus nut,* hala hua.

nutcracker. 'Ūmi'i kukui haole.

nutmeg. Hua'ala.

Nu'u-anu. Nu'u-anu *(literally, cool height). The wind comes down bearing the flowers of Nu'u-anu (PH 168),* ke iho lā ka makani halihali pua o Nu'u-anu.

O

o. 1. *The letter.* 'Ō. 2. *Vocative.* Ē, ē . . . ē.
O'ahu. Hoʻahu. *Epithets: O'ahu, child of Lua,* O'ahu a Lua *[Lua slept with Papa after Papa became angry about husband Wākea's infidelity: HM 302].* The sands of Kā-kuhihewa *[an important O'ahu chief],* ke one o Kā-kuhihewa. *The chief destroying sands of Kā-kuhihewa,* ke one 'ai ali'i o Kā-kuhihewa.
oak. 'Oka. *See* **silky oak.**
Oakland. 'Okalana.
oakum. Ukamu.
oar. Hoe. *Steering oar,* hoe uli.
oarsman. Mea hoe wa'a, hoe wa'a.
oasis. Wahi uliuli ma ka wao one.
oath. 1. *In court.* Hoʻohiki, 'ōlelo hoʻohiki, 'ōlelo pa'a. *A Hawaiian oath:* pau Pele, pau manō *(see* **manō***).* 2. *See* **swear.**
oatmeal. *No equivalent; see* **breakfast food.**
oats. 'Oka.
obedient. Hoʻolono, hoʻolohe, lohena, wiwo.
obese. Momona loa, pūhalalū. *Rare:* uhalalē, kualakai.
obey. Lohe, hoʻolono, wiwo.
obituary. Moʻolelo o ka mea 'akahi nō ā make.
object. 1. *Thing.* Mea. *Object of a sentence,* hope ha'ina. 2. *Purpose.* Kumu, mea; mea i kaulona 'ia *(rare).* 3. *See* **oppose.**
objection. Kū'ē, kumu hoʻohalahala.
obligation. 'Ai'ē *(debt).*
oblige. Koi. *Much obliged,* mahalo nui.
obliging. 'Olu'olu, lokomaika'i.
oblique. Hiō, lala, ākepakepa, pala'ewa, kū'ewa, a'e, hī-he'e. *Cut obliquely,* kepa, hoʻokepa, pāhi'a. *To strike obliquely, as wind or wave,* pā lala.
oblivious. Palaka, nānā 'ole.
oblong. Oloolo, olōlo.
obscene. Pelapela, haumia, hoʻohilahila. *Obscene language,* 'ōlelo haumia.
obscure. Poahi, pōahiahi, poehi, powehi, pōehiehi, pō-wehiwehi, pohihihi, pohihi, pohihiu, pō, kōli'u, kōli'u-li'u. *Also:* pano, panopano, maka pōniuniu, āhiahia, hoʻāhiahia, hea, palaweka, pālauweka, pālaueka, hāpuʻupu'u, 'e'a'e'a, pōnalo, 'a'aki, pinao. *Obscure and difficult to understand,* 'ike pohihihi, maopopo pohi-hihi, akaaka 'ole.
observant. 'I'ike, maka kilo.
observation. Nānā 'ana, manaʻo, loina.
observation point. Hālōna, 'īmaka.
observatory. Hale kilo hōkū. *Star observatory,* hale kilolani, kilolani.
observe. Nānā, nānā pono, hākilo, kilo malama, kilo, haka pono, aua; *to — an order,* mālama kauoha; — *closely,* kaulona, pau kilo. *To observe clouds,* nānā ao. *To observe fish,* kilo i'a. *To observe stars,* kilo hōkū. *To observe the seas,* kilo moana. *To observe the winds, as for navigation,* kilo makani.
obsession. Pulakaumaka.
obsidian. *No Hawaiian term noted.*
obsolete. Make.
obstacle. Ālaina, mea ala'alai, mea ke'ake'a, pu'upā. *Fig., (see).* To meet an obstacle, ku'ia.
obstetrician. Kauka hoʻohānau, kauka pale keiki.
obstinate. Pa'akikī, 'oʻole'a, pa'a loa, poʻo pa'a, 'ā'ī 'oʻole'a, lae pa'a. *Also:* hukihuki, hoʻolehelehe nui, uaua, koe'ā, kā'ape.
obstreperous. Waha kole, nui ka wala'au, waha wala-'au, hoʻohaunaele.
obstruct. Ālai, ānai, ke'a, hoʻoke'a, hoʻokāpae, 'āke-'ake'a, kualo; pōhāko'i *(rare).*

obstruction. *See* **obstruct.** *To remove obstruction,* hoʻokuakahi.
obtain. Loa'a.
obtrusive. Hōʻoiʻoi, maha'oi.
obtuse. Kūmūmū, lohi ka noʻonoʻo 'ana. *Obtuse angle,* huina peleleu.
obvious. Maopopo le'a, aniani, aliali, a'ia'i, mōakaaka, moakaka, mālani, waiho akaaka, ahuwale, waiho-kāka.
occasion. Wā, hanana.
occasionally. Aia aku aia mai, kūikawā.
occupant. Mea noho. *House occupant,* noho hale.
occupation. 'Oihana, hana. *Favorite occupation,* hana punahele, me'e.
occupied. Lilo, pa'a.
occupy. Noho, hoʻonoho *(as a house).*
occur. Kupu, hiki mai; 'owālala, 'oālala *(as a thought).*
occurrence. Hanana.
ocean. Moana *(open);* kai. *Ocean depths,* hohonu kai. *Ocean floor,* papakū.
oceanographer, oceanography. Kilo moana.
ocher. Ma'alaea, 'okele; īhe'ekai *(used ceremoniously).*
o'clock. Hola. *Two o'clock,* hola 'elua.
octagon. Huinawalu.
octave. Pi'i pāwalu, lelepuni.
October. 'Okakopa.
octopus. He'e *(for various kinds, see Haw.-Eng. entry and entries that follow it). See* **cowry shell, cuttle-fish, squid.** *Octopus tentacle,* 'awe'awe, 'awe, 'awe ule, 'awe puhi. *Octopus beak,* niho. *Octopus ink,* we-ka. *Octopus ink sac,* 'ala'ala. *Octopus flesh,* iho. *Other parts:* pū he'e, pikapika, pilipili. *To fish for octopus,* lūhe'e, kilo he'e, 'ōkilo he'e, 'ō he'e. *Octopus lure,* lū-he'e. *Octopus season,* wā he'e. *Slightly decomposed octopus,* mākole, he'e mākole, he'e puhi. *Mark left on skin by octopus tentacle,* 'ōpikopiko. *Octopus mouth,* waha o ka he'e *(liar). A slice of octopus,* poke he'e *(a chubby person).*
odd. 'Ano 'ē, pa'ewa, pau'aka. *Odd number,* helu pa-'ewa. *Odds and ends,* 'o kēlā me kēia; kēlā mea kēia mea; hi'uhi'u *(as of ropes).*
Odessa. 'Okeka, Odesa.
odious. 'Inoʻino.
odor. *See* **smell.**
of. O, a, kō, kā, no. *Afraid of death,* maka'u i ka make.
off. Mai *(from);* 'ē *(away). To fall off a box,* hā'ule mai ka pahu. *Be off!* Hele i kahi 'ē! Hele pēlā! Hemū! *Off-balance,* kūlike 'ole.
offal. Moka, poka.
offend. Hoʻohuhū, hoʻonāukiuki, hoʻomaʻau; 'ōlepo-lepo *(fig.). See* **pulapula 3.**
offended. Uluhua, ukiuki, kā'eko.
offense. Hewa, hala, lawehala, 'openi. *First offense,* hewa mua.
offer. Hā'awi, hō.
offering. Mōhai *(for various kinds, see Haw.-Eng. entry and entries that follow it); church —,* lūlū, hoʻokupu, mahina hou, hānai kahu. *Also:* hai, haina, hai 'ai, kau-maha, kaumaha 'ai, hāuna, hauhāuna, hua mua, ulu-'alana; 'ālana, 'ālana aloha, 'ālana kuni, 'umihau, hoʻāli, hi'ali, mua kau, kahukahu, 'onou, mea hana, kāmauli, hānai kuahu, pāpāi'awa, maukoli, papaio, pāpāia, puku.
office. 1. *Position.* Hana, 'oihana. 2. *Room.* Ke'ena, ke-'ena hana.
office holder. Noho 'oihana.
officer. Ali'i, luna. *See* **warrant officer.** *High or impor-*

tant officer, luna nui, aliʻi kiʻekiʻe, luna koʻikoʻi. *Presiding officer,* aliʻi hoʻomalu. *Military officer,* aliʻikoa, luna koa, luna kaua. *Communications officer,* lunaʻōlelo. *Officers in the monarchy and in ancient Hawaiʻi:* kuhina, kuhina nui, kālaimoku, ilāmuku; kualanapuhi, ikū *(see Haw.-Eng. entries and those that follow them for these rare terms),* oma.

official. *See* **officer.** *Official business,* hana o ke aupuni.

offspring. Keiki, hānau, pua, pulapula, kupu, hua; hauloliʻi *(rare). Fig.:* ʻanoʻano, ʻohā, makalau, aʻa. *One with many offspring,* kū ā makalau, lālā ola. *Without offspring,* lālā ʻole.

often. Pinepine, nui. *Also:* maumau, mākena, alapine.

ogle. ʻĀwihi, kāluhe.

ogo *(seaweed).* Manauea.

oh. Auē, auē nohoʻi ē, auwē, kā, ā; kāhūhū, kāhāhā, kāhīhī, kāhōhō *(exclamations of surprise or indignation). To oh and ah,* ahē.

Ohio. ʻOhaio.

oil. ʻAila, hinu, manoʻi, kelekele, kelema, poni. *To rub with oil,* kākele, kāhinu, poni.

oilcan. Kānuku ʻaila.

oilcloth. Pale pākaukau ʻaila.

oilfish. Walu, wolu. *Cf.* **makuʻu 3.**

oily. Hinuhinu, hinu, kūhinu, kelekele, kele, ʻūkele, liliha, lihaliha, niuniu, likoliko.

ointment. Mea hamo, ʻaila hamo, lāʻau hamo, hinu, mea poni, mea ʻala, nini, kiʻikea.

O.K. Hiki, hiki nō, pololei.

Oklahoma. ʻOkalahoma.

old. Kahiko *(usually not of people);* oʻo, ʻelemakule, luahine. *Also:* mākuakua, makua lua, ʻāluʻa, ʻele-, makule, koloʻuʻa, kolopupū, ʻāleuleu, pāleuleu, pāwelu, māuaua, kūʻolo, ʻāpela, paneʻe, kolepeiaʻalu. *See* **old age, old man, old woman.** *To cling to old customs,* hoʻokahiko.

old age. Wā ʻelemakule, wā luahine, kolopupū. *See sayings,* ʻauwae 1, hui 6, bone, chin, cowry shell, feeble, rat. *Fig. and poetic terms:* ʻehu ahiahi, haumakaʻiole, pala lau hala, kaʻikōkō, kaukoʻo, kanikoʻo, lāʻele, ō kō kea, puaaneane, puāneane. *Esteemed terms:* hulu, hulu kupuna, hulu makua. *Derisive terms:* ʻauwae lenalena, kolepeiaʻalu, kuʻi lena, nenanena ʻauwae, niho lena, niho kahi.

older. Mua, hiapo *(of children in a family).*

oldest. Makua, kuapapa.

old-fashioned. Hoʻokahiko, ʻano o ke au kahiko.

old fellow. ʻElekule, ʻolopala.

old maid. ʻOlomeka. *See* **spinster.**

old man. ʻElemakule, ʻolomana. *To become an old man,* ʻelemakule. *To behave like an old man,* hoʻelemakule.

old soldier. Koa kahiko.

Old Testament. Kauoha Kahiko.

old woman. Luahine; ʻelehine *(rare). See* **hag.**

oleander. ʻOliana, ʻoliwa, nohomālie.

olive. ʻOliwa, oliva.

olivine. *No equivalent. Rock with olivine,* pōhaku pele ʻōmaʻo. *Sand with olivine,* one ʻōmaʻo.

Olympia. ʻOlumepia.

Omega. ʻOmeka.

omelet. Hua pākā, hua palai i kaʻawili ʻia.

omen. ʻŌuli, hōʻailona. *See* **mud hen, thunder.** *To tell omens,* haʻi ʻōuli, nānā uli, kilo.

ominous. Hōʻailona pōʻino.

omission. Mea i waiho ʻia, mea i kāpae ʻia, hōʻalo, ʻalo ʻana.

omit. Waiho, kāpae, hōʻalo.

omnipotent. Mana loa.

on. I, ma, maluna o, maluna, luna, nuna, luna o.

onanism. Pīkoikoi. *See* **masturbate.** *To practice onanism,* haʻakoi.

once. Hoʻokahi wā, kekahi wā, pākahi, kuakahi. *Once upon a time,* i hoʻokahi manawa.

one. ʻEkahi, ʻakahi *(counting in a series);* hoʻokahi, kahi, kekahi; hapa- *(in fractions). One quarter,* hapahā. *One eighth,* hapawalu. *The one who,* ka mea i, ka,

ke, ka i, ka e. *One at a time, one by one,* pākahi. *To make as one,* hoʻokahi.

one-masted vessel. Kia kahi.

oneness. Hoʻokahi.

onerous. Luʻuluʻu, kaumaha.

one-sided. Kapakahi, hōʻewa; pāʻaoʻao *(rare).*

onion. ʻAkaʻakai *(for various kinds, see Haw.-Eng. entry and entries that follow it);* naku, mahina.

only. Wale nō, wale. *One only,* hoʻokahi wale nō, kiakahi. *Only if, only when,* aia nō ā.

onomatopoeia. Huaʻōlelo hoʻopilipili leo. *Examples of sounds believed onomatopoeic:* ʻekelo *(mynah bird);* ō *(peacock);* kokō *(hen, as after laying an egg);* pūkōkō *(hen in alarm);* kōlea, kolekolea *(kōlea bird);* kolokolo *(turkey gobbler);* pōkeokeo *(turkey hen);* lawekeō *(stilt bird);* liʻoliʻo *(liʻo bird);* ōwī *(ʻōʻū bird);* ʻūlili *(ʻūlili bird);* kue *(petrel bird);* ʻowā *(ʻaukuʻu bird);* māʻaʻā *(sheep, goat);* nū, hū *(pig);* ʻolāʻolā *(water);* kuekue *(tapping). See* **baa, bowwow, bray, cluck, cock-a-doodle-doo, coo, grunt, heehaw, honk, mew, moo, neigh, peep, quack, shish.**

onset. Hoʻomaka ʻana, ʻiliki.

onslaught. Poʻipū, puaʻō, ʻūpā.

Ontario. ʻOnekalio, Onetario.

onward. I mua, mamua, hele i mua, holo i mua.

onyx. ʻOnika, kalekonuka.

oo. *See* **digging stick, honey eater.**

ooze. Ū, nō, nono, hānono, hānonono, pīpī wai, pāhūhū.

open. *There is no general term; the main usages follow:* **1.** *Usually intransitive, a state of being open, as a door.* Hāmama; makili, mikili, nakili, hoʻomakili *(as a crack);* kūnihi; kaʻakaʻa *(as eyes);* ākea. *Also:* poale, pōaleale, ulehe, ulehelehe, kauhola, ʻuhola, hoaka, hunāhunā ʻole, ʻōwehewehe, wahalehe, uhalehe, ʻoma. *Open to the public (as open house),* hoʻohāmama ʻia i ka lehulehu. **2.** *As a flower.* Mōhala, hoʻomōhala, mōhalu, molokala, pohala, makala, mokala, ōpū, ʻōmeʻo. **3.** *Transitive, as a door, package.* Wehe, ʻuwehe, ʻuehe, weke, wekeweke, hemo, māwehe, māweke; huʻe *(as an oven);* ʻūpā, hāʻupā; hoʻohāmama, ʻōlepe; hoʻokaʻakaʻa *(as eyes).*

opener. *See* **can opener.**

openhanded. Lima hāmama, hāʻawi lokomaikaʻi.

openhearted. Puʻuwai hāmama.

open house. *See* **open.**

opening. Puka, wehena, wehe ʻana, waha, hoʻowaha, mōhala, ʻīpuka; huʻena *(as of oven);* ʻuiki, ʻuwiki, huaʻina, puma. *See* **open.**

opera. Keaka mele.

operate. ʻOki, kaha *(surgically);* hana *(do).*

operation. ʻOki.

operculum. Pani pūpū.

ʻopihi. *See* **limpet.**

opinion. Manaʻo. *To state opinion,* haʻi manaʻo. *To seek or change an opinion,* huli manaʻo. *In my private opinion,* i kuʻu manaʻo wale nō.

opinions. Nā manaʻo, mananaʻo.

opium. ʻOpiuma.

opossum. ʻOpakuma, ʻopekama.

opponent. Hoa paio, mea kūʻē, ʻaoʻao kūʻē.

opportunity. Manawa kūpono.

oppose. Kūʻē, ālai, ānai, keʻa, keʻakeʻa. *Also:* pākuʻi, kē, pākani lua, ʻaʻumeʻume, ʻauwaepuʻu. *Rare:* kēueue, naʻinaʻi.

opposite. Kūʻē, ēʻē, hulina alo. *See* **opposition.** *Opposite meaning,* manaʻo kūʻē.

opposition. Kūʻēʻē, ʻaoʻao kūʻē, hana kūʻē, ʻaʻumeʻume, noho keʻe. *To stir up opposition,* hoʻokūʻēʻē.

oppress. Hoʻoluʻuluʻu, hoʻoluhi hewa, hoʻokaumaha, hoʻokoʻikoʻi, hoʻokuapaʻa, hōʻeha. *Also:* hoʻolaukōnā, pākuʻi, hoʻokē, hoʻopaʻu, hoʻokākāuha, ʻaʻe, hoʻomauluhi, ʻaaʻihi, hoʻomauhaʻalina.

or. Aiʻole, ā . . . paha; o *(lest). Two or three,* ʻelua ā ʻekolu paha.

oracle. Haka *(medium).*

oracle gourd. Ipu 'ōlelo.
oracle tower. Lananu'u mamao, nananu'u mamao, lananu'u, nu'u, lana, 'anu'u *(on heiau).* A part of the tower, lewaanu'u *(rare).*
oral. Ha'i waha.
orange. 'Alani *(the fruit or tree).*
orange-yellow. Melemele 'ili 'alani.
orangutan. 'Oulanakana.
orate. Kākā'ōlelo, ha'i'ōlelo.
oration. Ha'i'ōlelo ho'ohanohano *(eulogistic).*
orator. Kākā'ōlelo, ha'i'ōlelo.
oratory. Kākā'ōlelo.
orbit. Ala pō'ai, apo hele.
orchard. Māla lā'au hua 'ai, kīhāpai.
orchestra. Hui ho'okani pila, pāna. *Cf.* hui puhi 'ohe.
orchid. 'Okika; 'okika honohono; 'awapuhi-a-Kanaloa.
ordain. Poni, ho'oponi, ho'okahuna.
ordeal. Pōpilikia, hana nui, hana pū'ika'ika, hana 'eha-'eha, 'awa.
order. 1. *Command.* Kauoha *(general; to send for, as groceries);* kēnā, ho'okēnākēnā, 'ōlelo kauoha, ho'opa'a. *Money order,* pepa kīko'o kālā. *Postal money order,* pila kīko'o hale leka. *By order of,* ma ke kauoha a. *To give orders,* kauoha, kuhikuhi. **2.** *Arrangement.* Ho'onohonoho 'ana, papa, noho papa, ho'onoho papa, ponopono, ka'ina, moekahi. *In perfect order,* pono. *To put to order,* ho'oponopono, ho'opapa, kuene; haku, hakuhaku *(rare).* *Word order,* ka'ina o nā hua 'ōlelo. *To call to order, as a meeting,* ho'omalu. **3.** *See* **in order to.**
ordinance. 'Ōlelo kūpa'a, kānāwai.
ordinary. Ma'amau, laha, mea loa'a wale, a'e nei, pākūwā, pākūā. *Ordinary person,* kanaka a'e nei nō; ki'i maka li'ili'i. *Having ways of ordinary folk,* ha'aha'a; waikanaka *(rare).*
ordination. 'Olinakio.
Oregon. 'Olekona, Oregona.
organ. 1. *Musical instrument.* 'Okana. *Hand organ,* 'okana wili lima. *Mouth organ,* pilapuhipuhi. **2.** *Part.* Mahele. *Internal organs,* loko.
organdy. 'Okanaki.
organic. 'Okanika.
Organic Act. Kānāwai Kumu, Kānāwai 'Okanika.
organization. Hui, 'ahahui, kūkulu 'ana, kūkunu 'ana, ho'onoho 'ana.
organize. Kūkulu, kūkunu, ho'ohui, ho'onohonoho.
orgasm. Le'a.
Orient. Hikina.
origin. Kinohi, ho'omaka 'ana, kumu; kumu honua *(of the earth);* kumulipo.
original. Kumu. *Original document,* palapala kumu.
originate. *See* **begin.**
Orion. 'Oliona. *Stars in Orion's belt,* Maiakū. *Stars in Orion's belt and sword,* Nā-kao.
ornament. Wehi, kāhiko, kīnohi, ho'okāhiko; *beautiful —,* linohau.
orphan. Keiki makua 'ole, kama lele. *Weeping for an orphan child, no parents, woe!* e uē nō anei, he keiki makua 'ole, 'a'ohe mākua, uē ho'i ē!
orthography. *See* **spelling.**
oscillate. Lewalewa, lewa, uene, uwene.
osprey. 'Okepela.
ossifrage. 'Okepelaka.
osteomalacia. 'Ea wāhi pa'a.
osteopath. Kauka lomilomi.
ostrich. 'Akolika, 'okekelika, oseterika, 'okelekelika.
other. Kekahi, 'ē a'e, 'ē.
otherwise. Akā na'e, ma kekahi 'ano 'ē a'e. *There was much rain, otherwise everything was fine,* ua nui ka ua, akā na'e maika'i nō nā mea apau.
ouch. Auē, auwē, auwī.
ought. Pono. *You ought to go,* he mea pono iā'oe ke hele.
ounce. 'Aunaki, 'aunake, 'auneki.
our. 1. *Singular possessed object, dual, inclusive.* Kō kāua *(o-class);* kā kāua *(a-class).* **2.** *Singular possessed*

object, dual, exclusive. Kō māua *(o-class);* kā māua *(a-class).* **3.** *Singular possessed object, plural, inclusive.* Kō kākou *(o-class);* kā kākou *(a-class).* **4.** *Singular possessed object, plural, exclusive.* Kō mākou *(o-class);* kā mākou *(a-class).* **5.** *Plural possessed objects, dual, inclusive.* O kāua *(o-class);* a kāua *(a-class).* **6.** *Plural possessed objects, dual, exclusive.* O māua *(o-class);* a māua *(a-class).* **7.** *Plural possessed objects, plural, inclusive.* O kākou *(o-class);* a kākou *(a-class).* **8.** *Plural possessed objects, plural, exclusive.* O mākou *(o-class);* a mākou *(a-class).* There are 16 common translations of English "our." For other uses of k-less (zero-type) possessives, Gram. 9.6.3.
ours. No kāua, no māua, no kākou, no mākou, na kāua, na māua, na kākou, na mākou. *See* **our.**
oust. Kipaku, ho'okuke, ualehe, kūlē.
out. Waho, i waho, mawaho; pio *(extinguished). Rare:* hauka, 'auka *(in games).*
outburst. Hū, pahū.
outcast. Kauā, kauwā *(for various qualifiers, see Haw.-Eng. entry and entries that follow it; also see* **lae** *and qualifiers). Uncomplimentary epithets:* heana kanaka *(intended for human sacrifice);* makawela, limu pae, lua'i pō, lau'ī pekepeke, lele koa'e, palani, pie ueue, auwehekika, hūpoenui, 'ōhao 'īlio. *See* **vagabond.** *Places where outcasts were drowned:* kai hehe'e.
outcrop. Mea hū honua.
outcry. Oho, ho'ōho, ohooho, ho'ōhooho.
outdo. Ho'okela; oko *(rare).*
outdoors. O waho.
outer. Waho, o waho, kūwaho.
outfitted. Ho'olako 'ia; lilihua *(rare).*
outhouse. Wahi ho'opau pilikia, hale li'ili'i, lua li'ili'i, lua, hale lua. *Rare:* luahaka, auolo, 'auwaha, auhā.
outlet. Pukana, puka wai, makawai. *Electric outlet,* kumu ho'opuka uila.
outrigger boom. 'Iako.
outrigger canoe. Wa'a.
outrigger float. Ama, iama. *End of float,* lupe. *Leaping float end,* lele lupe *(emotion).* Kī-lau-ea is overturned like a canoe outrigger, kahuli Kī-lau-ea mehe ama wa'a lā.
outside. Waho, i waho, mawaho, kō waho, kūwaho.
outsider. Kanaka 'ē, kanaka o waho; lauhulu *(fig.).*
outstanding. Po'okela, kau i ka wēkiu, kū kahi. *Also:* kūlia, kakahi. *Outstanding debt,* 'ai'ē ka'a 'ole.
outstretched. Kākāuha.
outward. *See* **outer.**
outwit. Lanakila.
oval. Oloolo, olōlo, 'omo'omo, pō'ai lō'ihi, poepoehāwa'e, poepoepīkoi, hualala.
oven. Imu *(for various kinds, see Haw.-Eng. entry and entries that follow it);* umu, 'oma, 'oma Pukikī; umu pao, imu pao *(above ground);* umu lepo *(earth). Oven house,* hale umu. *To lay, as an oven,* haka. *To tend an oven, oven tender,* kahu umu. *Oven cooking,* kahuna. *Leaf lining of oven,* pale.
over. 1. *Above.* Luna, i luna, maluna, i nuna. *Over and above,* 'oi aku, pākeu, ā 'oi. **2.** *Completed.* Pau. **3.** *Again.* Hou. *Do over,* hana hou. *Do over and over,* hana hou ā hana hou; ka'awelekā *(rare).*
overactive. Lapa.
overalls. Lole wāwae 'epane.
overbearing. Ho'okelakela, ho'oki'eki'e, 'a'ano. *Also:* ka'aluna *(fig.),* kanaie, ho'okanaie, ho'olanakila, mahalua.
overboard. I ke kai. *Jump overboard,* lele i ke kai. *Throw overboard,* kiloi i loko o ke kai, kīwae.
overcast. 'Ōmalu, 'ōmalumalu, 'omamalu, ho'omalu, ho'ōmalumalu, lāuli, ho'ohaha.
overcome. 1. *To defeat.* Lanakila, ho'opio, holopapa. **2.** *Defeated.* Pio, puni. **3.** *Possessed, as by emotion, as fear, passion, joy, grief.* Lo'ohia, ilihia, ulupuni, 'ōkā, auālipo.
overcooked. Mo'a loa; mo'a palahē, palakahuki, paluhē *(as meat). Also:* ahulu, wahulu.

overeat. Pākela 'ai, ahu 'ai, kuenenu'u. *See* **eat.** *Discomfort from overeating,* 'ōpihapiha.
overfamiliarity. Pākela maha'oi; nole *(rare).*
overflow. Hū, hālana, hālanalana, hānana, hanini, ho'ohanini, pi'ipi'i, wai pi'i, waikahe, wai hū, huana, 'olo'olo, holomoku, holomokuna, kūmoho.
overgrowth. Uluāhewa, hihipe'a.
overhang. Luhe, lo'u.
overheated. Ahuli'u, hahana.
overladen. Lu'ulu'u, 'olo'olōna.
overlap. Kau iho kekahi maluna o kekahi, 'ili'ili; 'unu-'unu *(in sewing);* kuipapa *(as feathers in a lei).*
overlay. Pale; ho'opapa *(as shingles).*
overload. Ho'ouka nui, ho'olu'ulu'u loa.
overlook. 1. *Look over.* Nānā maluna a'e, hālō. **2.** *Miss.* Hala, palaka. **3.** *Condone.* Waiho mālie, kaumalumalu.
overpowering. Mana nui, po'ikū.
override. Mau'a'e *(as a veto).*
overripe. *See* **ripe.**
overrun. Holopapa.
overseer. Luna, luna hana, luna kia'i, luna ho'ohana, nuna, haku, haku hana.
oversexed. Kola mau; puni kāne *(of females);* puni wahine *(of males);* kuko makapehu, pākīai.
overshadow. Ho'omalumalu, ho'oūmalu, pāpale, 'e'a-'e'a.
oversight. 'Alo 'ana.
oversized. Nui loa, nui maluna o ka mea ma'amau, hālala.
oversleep. Hiamoe loa, moe loa.
overthrow. Kahuli, ho'okahuli, hiolo, ho'ohiolo, kula'i, kula'ina, huli pū, hulihia. *Also:* 'ōpe'a, auhuli, olopē, pōluku.

overtime pay. Uku kaulele.
overturn. Kahuli, huli pau, huli pū, hulihia, ho'ohuli, auhuli. *Also:* lumi, me'ea, 'ōpe'a, 'ōlepe, kīpau, kualono. *See ex.,* **outrigger float.**
overturning. Hulina.
overwhelm. Po'ipū, popo'i, uhi, lalawe, luma'i, holomoku, holomokuna. *Suffering of love is overwhelming, here in my heart (PH 178),* 'o ka 'eha a ke aloha ke lalawe nei, eia lā i loko, i ku'u manawa.
overwhelmed. Pa'uhia, lo'ohia, lumi, pōka'aka'a, kapakū.
overwork. Ho'opa'u. *Also:* ho'okauā, ho'omauleho, ho'opa'aua.
ovum. Hua.
owe. 'Ai'ē.
owl. Pueo, ululā, iana, mo'o lele. *Owl snare,* pehe.
own. Pono'ī, kuleana, kipona, 'ona. *I own the house,* no'u pono'ī ka hale. *This is my own,* na'u pono'ī. *Own native land,* 'āina kulāiwi. *Your own book,* kā kō iwi puke.
owner. Mea, 'ona, haku. *House owner,* mea hale, ka mea nona ka hale. *Canoe owner,* mea wa'a.
ownership. No . . . ka mea, kuleana. *Common ownership,* kuleana waiwai like.
ox. Pipi kauō, pipi kauwō.
oxalic acid. 'Okakalika 'akika.
Oxford. 'Okapoka, Okafoda. *Oxford University,* Kulanui o 'Okapoka.
oxygen. Ea ola māmā, 'okikene.
oyster. 'Ōlepe. *See* **pearl oyster.**
oyster plant. Kalapī.
ozena. I'akui, ihukilu, ihupilau.

P

p. Pī.
pace. Ka'ina wāwae, peki. *Full pace,* ke'ehi lō'ihi. *Pacing horse,* lio peki.
pacific. 1. *Calm.* Malino, la'i, mālie. *See* calm. 2. *Ocean.* Pākīpika, Moana Pākīpika.
Pacific Yacht Club. Hui Heihei Moku Pākīpika.
pacified. Nā.
pacify. Hō'olu, ho'onā, ho'oma'alili.
pack. Ho'okomo *(as a trunk);* 'awe, 'awe'awe, hā'awe *(carry). Also:* ho'onoho, ho'oukana; ho'opapa *(neatly);* ho'ohakē *(full).*
package. Pū'olo. *Also:* pū'ā, 'ope, 'ope'ope, pela; pī'ao *(of folded ti leaves);* pena, pu'uwai.
packed. Ho'okomo 'ia. *Also:* hakē, piha'ū, pihaku'i, 'ūpili, pū'uki'uki, piha pūku'iku'i, piha pū, pū'ika'ika; —, *as in a crowd,* pōlumilumi, kūpiliki'i. *Rare:* lē'ī, neki, noke'a, kuenenu'u.
packet. 1. *Small package.* Pū'olo. 2. *A ship.* Pākeke, moku lawe leka.
pad. Pale po'ohiwi *(shoulder).*
padded. Pulu; ho'onui 'ōlelo *(as of speech).*
paddle. Hoe. *See* Māmala-hoe *and sayings,* hoe, swim, tongue. *Paddle types:* hoe uli *(steering; fig., tongue);* hoe nanue, hoe nenue, hoe kala. *Paddle parts:* laulau, lauhoe, pālaulau *(blade);* hua *(bulge in blade);* 'au, kū'au *(shaft);* 'upe, io *(rib);* alelo, koho, 'oupē *(tip);* pu'ukole *(upper part of blade). To paddle,* hoe, pāhoe; lauhoe *(of several);* akahoe *(carefully);* puna, kiele *(rare). To have a canoe paddled,* ho'ohoe. *Paddle back and forth,* hoehoe.
paddler. Hoe wa'a.
paddling. Hoena.
paddy. Lo'i, pāki.
padlock. Laka.
Paducah. Pakuka.
pagan. Pekana.
page. 'Ao'ao. *Page reference,* kuhikuhi i ka 'ao'ao.
pageant. Kapalō, hō'ike'ike, hana keaka.
pagoda flower. Lau'awa.
paid. Ka'a. *Paid entirely,* ka'a'oko'a. *My debt is paid,* ua ka'a ku'u 'ai'ē.
pail. Pela, kini, kini pela, pākeke; kini kākai *(with a handle). To hold and carry, as a pail,* kālawe.
pain. 'Eha; hu'i *(tooth, bones);* nalulu *(dull, in stomach, head);* 'ūmi'i *(side). Also:* nahu *(stomach);* 'ōpū-ha'o, ho'īlewa *(hunger—rare);* holopani *(cutting off of breath);* ho'onākū, ikiiki, lou, walania, ho'owalania, walawalania, walenia, welenia, wawalania, nao, luhi, manawahua kai ko'o; 'ō, 'o'e *(sharp, darting). See* kipona. *Great pain or many small pains,* 'eha'eha. *To inflict pain,* hō'eha. *To shrink away in pain,* mū'e'eke.
painful. 'Eha'eha, hu'i. *See* pain.
painkiller. Penikila.
paint. Pena. *House paint,* pena hale. *To paint,* pena, kāpala; pālani *(lightly);* puhi'ōni'o *(spotted); — thinner,* 'aila ho'owali pena. *To paint pictures,* pena ki'i, kaha ki'i, kākau kaha.
paintbrush. Hulu pena.
painter. Kaha ki'i *(artist);* mea pena *(as of houses). House painter,* pena hale.
painting. Ki'i pena.
pair. Pa'a, kaulua. *To pair,* kaulua. *Pairing off,* kūlua. *Two pairs, as in poker,* kūpē, kūpea. *Pair of shoes,* pa'a kāma'a.
pajamas. Lole moe pō.
pal. *See* friend.

palace. Hale ali'i. *See* castle.
palanquin. Mānele, hale 'auamo, 'auamo.
palate. Luna o ka waha; kīleo *(soft).*
pale. Hākea. *Also:* haikea, ha'akea, nanakea, lanakea, nananakea, 'ōlohe, kuakea, puakea, laukea, mamae, onena, 'īkoko, pākea. *See* yellow.
Palermo. Palemo.
Palestine. Palekekine, Palesetine.
pali. *See* cliff.
pallor. Hailepo. *See* pale.
palm. 1. *Tree.* Pāma, pālama; niu *(coconut). See* fan palm. 2. *Surface of hand.* Poho, poho lima. *Center of palm,* poli lima. *Solid palm of hand,* poho kano *(fig., stingy).*
palmer worm. 'Ūhini-hulu-'ole.
palmist, palmistry. Kilo nānā lima, kilokilo nānā lima.
Palm Sunday. Kominika o nā Lālā Lā'au.
Palmyra. Palamila, Palamira; Palamola, Palamora.
palpitate. Konikoni. *Also:* 'api, hāku'i, ho'olele, nape, kapalili.
palsy. Ma'i lōlō.
pamper. Ho'okamalani, pai. *See saying,* welu 1.
pan. Pā. *Rare:* pani, pana. *See* saucepan. *Baking pan,* 'oma. *Fire pan,* pā ahi. *Frying pan,* pā palai. *Iron pan,* pā hao. *Stew pan,* kū pana. *Tin pan,* pā kini. *Wash pan,* pā holoi, pā kini holoi.
Panama. Panamā. *Panama hat,* pāpale waiokila.
panax. Lapalapa.
pancake. Palaoa palai, palaoa linalina; papa palaoa *(rare).*
pancreas. Mālama.
pandanus. Hala *(for various kinds, see Haw.-Eng. entry and entries that follow it). See sayings,* hala iwi nui, pala lau hala. *Pandanus tree,* pū hala. *Pandanus trunk,* kumu hala. *Male pandanus tree,* hala hīnano, hala hīnalo. *Female pandanus tree,* hala hua. *Pandanus leaf,* lau hala; ko'o, 'i'oko'o, mu'o hala, pū'awa, pūkani; pilila'ele *(young);* lā'ele *(old);* lau hala, pa'ilau'ula *(dry). Bundle of forty leaves,* kī. *Male blossom, bracts,* hīnano, polohīnano. *Pandanus fruit,* 'āhui hala; polopoloua *(unripe);* polokā *(ripe);* kā'ao, kāō *(very ripe). Pandanus fruit stem,* polope'a. *Pandanus key,* hala; pani *(at bottom of cluster);* hala 'i'o *(ripe);* hala iwi nui *(upper hard portion);* pua hala *(yellow base). Nut in key,* hala hua, 'i'o hala. *Pandanus fruit core,* 'īkoi. *Pandanus root tip,* mu'o hala. *Pandanus aerial root,* ule hala, uleule hala. *Lumps on pandanus trunk,* pu'upu'u hala. *Width of pandanus plaiting strip,* koana. *Pandanus lei,* lei hala *(not worn by some because of double meaning; see* hala 1, 2). *Puna, where sea blasts amid pandanus (PH 2),* 'o Puna kai kuwā i ka hala.
pane. 'Āpana aniani.
pang. 'Ūmi'i, 'eha koni, 'a'aki, ha'awina.
panic. Maka'u kūhewa, haunaele. *Panic-stricken,* 'ā'ā. *To run in panic,* holo 'ā'ā.
panorama. Waihona 'āina, nānaina.
panoramic view. Waiho helahela 'ana.
pansy. Pāneki, po'okanaka.
pant. Haha, ahaaha, ehaha, nae, naenae, pauaho, paupauaho, manawaea, 'ā'ili, 'ā'ili'ili, ka'ahili, uhāuhā, nawe. *Pant for breath,* ka'apā ka hanu i ka houpo.
panther. Paneka.
panties. Lole wāwae (wahine).
pantry. Lumi waiho pā.
pants. Lole wāwae.

papa. Pāpā.
papaya. Mīkana, hēʻī, milikana, papaia. *Male papaya,* mīkana kāne. *Female papaya,* mīkana wahine.
papaya bird. Manu-ʻai-mīkana, manu-ʻai-papaia, ʻai-mīkana.
paper. Pepa *(for various kinds, see Haw.-Eng. entry and entries that follow it);* kānana, kālana *(for writing).* See **newspaper.** *Pile of paper,* puʻu pepa.
paper boy. Keiki lawe nūpepa.
paper clip. ʻUmiʻi pepa.
paper knife. Pahi ʻoki pepa.
paper nautilus. ʻAu-waʻa-lā-lua, moamoa.
papist. Pope.
papyrus. Kaluhā, papulo, kome *(RSV).*
parable. Nane, ʻōlelo nane. *To illustrate with parable,* hoʻopilipili ʻōlelo.
parade. Huakaʻi, kaʻi huakaʻi; paikau *(as of military);* hoʻokahakaha. *Also:* kōheo, hoʻohaha. *Parade rest (military command),* hōʻoluʻolu.
paradise. Palekaiko, ʻiu lani. See **Pali-uli.**
paragraph. Paukū, palekalapa. *Symbol of paragraph,* poʻo hou.
Paraguay. Palakuae, Paraguae.
parallel. Kaulike, moe like, ʻiliwai like. *Parallel line,* kaha kaulike.
parallelepiped. Paʻaʻili kaulike hiō *(oblique);* paʻaʻili kūpono *(cube or rectangular).*
parallelogram. Huinahā hiō lōʻihi.
paralysis. Lōlō, maʻi lōlō; hepa *(partial paralysis of vocal chords). Paralysis of tongue,* alelo puʻu.
paraphimosis. Hākoʻi.
parasite. 1. *Plant.* Lāʻau kumu ʻole. **2.** *Person.* Kū ʻīpuka hale *(see* **ʻīpuka***),* kūkake, lelewa, hoʻopili wale, hoʻopilimeaʻai, pilimeaʻai, ōkea pili mai. *See* **kaunaʻoa, vagabond,** *and sayings,* **limpet.**
parasol. Māmalu, loulu, noulu.
parcel. Pūʻolo. *See* **package.**
parched. Maloʻo loa. *Also:* anoa, ʻānia, kūʻānoʻa, pāpaʻa, pāpaʻalā, pīkaʻo, hākonakona, hākona, ʻōlino, ʻāpaʻapaʻa, ʻaʻaka, pā, pākīʻai, kuapaʻa.
parchment. ʻIli palapala.
pardon. Kala, huikala, kalakala; palapala huikala *(document);* paleʻōpua *(rare). Pardon me,* kala mai iaʻu.
pare. Koli, pehē. *To pare nails,* koli mikiʻao.
parent. Makua, makua mea keiki; lūauʻi makua *(true, contrasting with foster). See* **stepparent.** *Foster parent,* makua hānai, kahu hānai *(from infancy);* makua hoʻokama *(of an older child or adult). Parents,* mākua. *Precious parents,* hulu mākua. *To act the part of a parent,* hoʻomakua. *To address as parent,* hoʻomakua.
parentheses. Kahaapo, apowaena.
parent-in-law. Makuahūnōai.
pariah. Kauā. *See* **outcast.**
parietal bone. Iwi ʻōpeʻapeʻa.
Paris, Parisian. Palika, Parisa.
parish. Kīhāpai.
park. 1. *Recreation area.* Pāka. *Ka-piʻo-lani Park,* Ka-piʻo-lani Pāka. **2.** *To station.* Hoʻokū, kūkulu. *To park a car,* hoʻokū i ke kaʻa. *Parked,* kū. *Parking lot,* wahi kūkulu kaʻa.
parlor. Lumi hoʻokipa, pala.
Parnassus. Panakuka.
parole. Palola.
parrot. Manu aloha.
parrot fish. Uhu *(for various kinds, growth stages, and fig. meanings, see* **uhu***). Also:* lauia, pāuhuuhu, ʻōhiʻuhiʻu. *See slippery. Young parrot fish,* ʻōhua palemo *(fig., mischief-maker).*
parry. Pale, kaupale, hoʻokāpae, kokope.
parsnip. Paanika.
parson. Kahuna pule.
part. Mahele, mokuna, hapa, ʻāpana. *Part-white,* hapa haole. *Part-Hawaiian,* hapa Hawaiʻi. *Take the part of Frank,* hoʻolilo ʻoe iāʻoe iho ʻo Palani.
partaker. Hoa loaʻa.

partial. Kaulike ʻole, pāʻewaʻewa, hoʻowae, hoʻokēāmaka, lawe kapakahi; puni *(fond of);* hapa *(portion).*
participle. Hōʻailona o ka wā ʻānō *(present);* hōʻailona o ka wā i hala *(past).*
particle. Huna, māhune, pula, lihi; hunahuna ʻōlelo *(unit of speech). Particles,* hunahuna, huhuna, koʻana.
particular. 1. *Special.* Nō. *That special occasion,* kēlā hanana nō. **2.** *Exacting.* ʻAno waewae, hoʻowae, ʻekeʻeke, ʻeʻeke, kamalani.
partition. Pale, hoʻopale, kau pale, pākū, papa pale.
partitioning. Palena.
partner. Hoa, hoa hana, kōkoʻo, pakanā.
partnership. Hui; kōkoʻolua *(of two);* kōkoʻokolu *(of three);* kōkoʻohā *(of four).*
part of speech. ʻAno hua ʻōlelo. *No generally used Hawaiian term for parts of speech. Andrews 1854 introduced terms as for ablative, accusative, agentive, dative, genitive, possessive, and various pronouns, but they seem to have been rarely if ever used.*
partridge. Manu ʻaihue.
party. 1. *Group.* ʻAha *(for various kinds, see Haw.-Eng. entry and entries that follow it). Liberal party,* ʻaoʻao lipelala *(political).* **2.** *Festivity.* Hoʻolauleʻa *(large);* pāʻina *(dinner or supper);* ʻaha inu *(drinking). See* **dinner. 3.** *Person.* Kanaka, mea, poʻe.
par value. Waiwai inoa, waiwai kaulike.
pass. 1. *Movement.* Māʻalo, kāʻalo, ʻaui, kaha, hala *(pass by);* holo, hala, kūnewa, au, uhaiāholo *(as time);* māʻaloʻalo, hoʻokāʻalo, paikau *(to and fro);* hoʻoholo, kau, ʻāpono *(as a bill);* — *away,* hala, nalo, nalohia, haʻaleke i ke ola, mā *(death);* come to —, kō, kau, hoʻokau. *Also:* pāhiki, mao, kaʻa, kaʻa hope, āmio, kīhēhē, malewa, niau, hōlaʻo, pūlō. *Passed,* holo, ʻāpono ʻia *(as a bill);* loaʻa ka helu holo mua *(as an examination). Please pass the salt,* ʻoluʻolu e hāʻawi mai i ka paʻakai. **2.** *Permission.* Palapala hoʻokuʻu. *Entrance pass,* palapala komo. *Free pass,* palapala komo wale. **3.** *See* **gap, passage.**
passage. Awa *(as through a reef).*
passenger. ʻŌhua. *Cabin passenger,* ʻōhua ʻoneki. *Ship passenger,* eʻe moku, holomoku. *Passenger conveyance,* kaʻa hali ʻōhua.
passer-by. Kaʻalo, mea māʻalo, malewa.
passion. Konikoni, koni, kaunu; hekili *(fig.). The Passion of Christ,* ka ʻEhaʻeha o ka Haku. *Burst of passion,* kīkīao. *Culmination of sexual passion,* leʻa, huahuaʻi. *Passion calmed with her (UL 166),* laʻi ai ke kaunu me ia lā.
passionate. Koʻikoʻi, ʻino. *Passionate anger,* huhū ʻino, hae manawa ʻino. *See ex.,* **ʻīloli.**
passion fruit. Likoʻi, lemi wai, lemona, pohāpohā, huehue haole.
passion play. Hōʻikeʻike i nā ʻehaʻeha o ka Haku.
Passion Sunday. Kominika o ka ʻEha.
passive voice. Leo pili ʻia mai. *See* **verb.**
passover. Pakoa, mōliaola.
passport. Palapala hoʻāpono, palapala kuhikuhi kino, palapala ʻae e holo.
past. Hala, kaʻa; wāʻaeʻoia, lāʻaeʻoia *(past days of youth, beauty, prosperity). Past time,* wā i hala, wā mamua. *To recall the past,* hoʻomanaʻo i nā wā i hala, huliau, ʻālaʻapapa.
paste. Hoʻopipili, mea hoʻopipili; palaholo *(made of sap from* ʻamaʻu *fern fronds).*
pastime. Hoʻohala manawa, hana hoʻohala manawa. *Favorite pastime,* hana punahele. *Pleasant pastime,* hana hoʻonanea.
pastor. Kahuna pule, kahu; kahu ʻekalekia, ekalesia.
pastry. Mea ʻono.
pasture. Kula, pā holoholona, kula holoholona.
pasty. Pipili, kuhua.
pat. Hamohamo *(as a dog);* paʻipaʻi mālie.
patch. 1. *Mending.* Poho, pāhono, pāhonohono, hono; pewa, kiki, kihi, pīnaʻi *(as in wood, see* **huini***).* **2.** *Garden.* Mahi, māla. *Also:* kūlana, kūnana, kīhāpai, ulu

Philippines. 'Āina Pilipino.
philosopher. Akeakamai, kanaka 'imi na'auao.
philosophy. Akeakamai, 'imi na'auao. *Moral philosophy,* huli kanaka. *Philosophy of life,* mana'o nui i ke 'ano o ka noho 'ana. *To take life philosophically,* kaiewa *(cf.* **easygoing***).*
phlegm. Male, na'o.
Phoenicia. Poinikia.
phonograph. Pahu 'ōlelo, ponokalapa; ipu uila 'ōlelo, pahu uila *(names used for an early phonograph said to have recorded Ka-lā-kaua's voice as he lay dying in 1891 in San Francisco). Phonograph record,* pā, pā ho'okani.
phosphorescence. Weli, kai kū weli, makaihuwa'a, pokepola.
phosphorus. Pokepola.
photograph. Ki'i. *To photograph,* pa'i ki'i.
photographer. Pa'i ki'i.
phrase. Māmala'ōlelo. *Phrases,* 'ōlelokīkēkē.
Phrygia. Pelukia, Perugia.
phylactery. 'Āpana kānāwai.
physic. Lā'au ho'onahā. *See* **emetic.**
physical. Kino, pilikino.
physician. Kauka, kauka lapa'au, kahuna lapa'au.
physic nut. Kuku'ihi.
physiology. 'Ike na'auao i mea kino ola.
physique. Kino, kanaka, 'ōiwi. *Fine physique,* kino maika'i, mōhā, mōhāhā. *Large muscular physique,* pūkonakona.
piano. Piano.
pick. 'Ohi, 'ako *(gather);* wae, koho *(select);* — *up,* hao, lapulapu; lālau *(as a fallen object);* akahao *(carefully);* kiko, pikawai *(as chickens);* — *at, as food,* niole, 'oninini; — *out,* 'ōhiki. *Pick breadfruit with a pole,* lou 'ulu.
pickaxe. Kipikua.
picket. 1. *Stake.* Pine. *Picket fence,* pā pine. **2.** *Guard.* Kia'i.
pickle. Pīkala.
pickleweed. 'Ākulikuli kai.
picnic. Pikiniki.
picture. Ki'i, ki'i ho'ākaaka. *His picture,* kona ki'i *(of him);* kāna ki'i *(by him). To draw or paint a picture,* kaha ki'i. *To paint a picture,* pena ki'i. *To take pictures,* pa'i ki'i. *Picture frame,* lā'au. *Picture projector,* mea ho'olele ki'i.
picul. Pika, pekula.
pidgin English. 'Ōlelo pa'i 'ai, namu pa'i 'ai, namu pa'i kalo.
pie. Pai. *Apple pie,* pai 'āpala. *Coconut pie,* pai niu. *Custard, egg, or fruit pie,* pai hua. *Pumpkin pie,* pai pū, pai pala'ai. *Hot mince pie,* pai wela me nā mea 'ai 'oki'oki 'ia.
piece. 'Āpana, paukū, māmala, mahele, poke. *See* **pieces.** *A short piece,* 'āpoke. *Broken piece,* hakina. *Piece labor or work,* ukupau. *Thirty pieces of silver (Mat. 26:15),* nā wahi moni he kanakolu.
piecemeal. Li'ili'i. *To give piecemeal,* hā'awi pākalikali.
pieces. Oka, okaoka *(as broken glass);* 'āpa'apana *(larger);* momoku *(severed objects);* mahele, iwi.
pier. Uwapo, uapo.
pierce. 'Ō, hou, pahu. *Also:* 'ō'ō, hulā, kīkoni. *Pierced by the needle,* kū i ke kui. *Pierced,* pōaleale, aleale.
piercing. Pahuna, 'ō, 'ou.
piety. Haipule.
pig. Pua'a. *See* **bracelet, eat, lecherous.** *Small pig,* pua'a māiki. *Old tough pig,* pua'a 'ā'aua. *Young female pig,* pua'a ohi. *Greasy pig,* pua'a hinu. *Hairless pig,* pua'a hulu 'ole. *Bloodstained pig,* pua'a he'a. *Pig offered as sacrifice,* pua'a kau, pua'a ūkō. *Wooden image of pig,* po'opua'a. *Pig tusk,* niho pua'a, ku'i pua'a. *Striped pig,* pua'a olomea. *Spotted pig,* pua'a pūko'a. *Pig with spot on one shoulder,* kīkepa, hahei. *Solidblack pig,* pua'a hiwa. *All black pig with white hoofs and white tips of tail, ears, and nose,* hiwa kea.

Pig, reddish-colored about the hams, hulu'iwi. *Cartilage of a pig's nose,* peu. *Roast pig reserved for priests,* hainaki. *Pig demigod,* Kama-pua'a *(noted for lechery). A descendant of Pig-man,* he mamo na Kama-pua'a *(a lascivious male). Call to pigs,* kō.
pigeon. Nūnū, manu kū. *Carrier pigeon,* manu-nūnū-lawe-leka.
pigeon pea. Pī nūnū, pī Pokoliko.
pigeon-toed. 'Ōnaha.
piglet. Pua pua'a, pua'a keiki.
pile. Ahu, pu'u, kūāhua. *Also:* āhua, kuapapa, anu'a, kūpa'i, 'ili'ili, paila; hu'a *(as of mats, tapa);* mahena. *To pile up,* ho'āhu, kuapapa, hō'ili'ili, kūkulu papa, ho'onoho papa, miho, ho'opu'u. *Pile of paper,* pu'u pepa. *Garbage pile,* pu'u 'ōpala. *Pile of rocks placed in sea,* umu. *To pile such rocks,* ho'oumu.
piled. Ho'āhua 'ia, ho'opu'u 'ia, ho'opu'upu'u 'ia, paila 'ia, pu'u, kūāhua, ho'okūāhua.
piles. Uha hemo *(hemorrhoids).*
pilfer. 'Aihue, palamimo, palamio, lālama, lawelawe, limalima.
pilferer. Lima lawelawe.
pilgrims. Po'e lewa.
Pilgrim's Progress. Ka Hele Malihini 'ana mai Kēia Ao aku ā Kēlā Ao *(see* **malihini***).*
pill. Huaale.
pillage. *See* **plunder** *and saying,* **Inu-wai.**
pillar. Kūkulu, kūkunu, kia, 'eho, oeoe, pou. *Upper part of pillar,* luna kia.
pill bug. Pokipoki.
pillow. Uluna, ununa, pela uluna, 'aki, 'ope'ope. *See saying,* **paka 3.**
pillowcase. Pale uluna.
pilot. Pailaka.
pilot fish. Nenue, manaloa.
pimento. Pimeneko.
pimp. We'a, we'awe'a; limalima pilau *(fig.).*
pimple. Pu'u, ane. *Pimples,* huehue. *Pimpled,* hāpu'u-pu'u, kukuku, pu'upu'u, 'āpu'upu'u, 'uluhaku. *No pimples, no crooks,* 'a'ohe pu'u, 'a'ohe ke'e *(of a handsome person).*
pin. Kui, pine, mākia, hākia, kākia, 'ō, poheoheo, heke. *See* **brooch.** *Common pin,* kui pine, kui 'ōmou. *Safety pin,* pine kaiapa. *Clothespin,* pine kaula'i. *Breast pin,* pine umauma. *Stick pin,* kui 'ōmou, pine 'ōmou. *Hog's tooth pin,* pine niho pua'a, pine hoaka. *Pincushion,* pulu kui. *To pin on,* 'ōmou, 'ōmau.
pince-nez. Makaaniani 'ūmi'i.
pinch. 'Iniki, 'ūmi'i, 'ini'iniki, niki, 'umiki, pāniki; pikipiki *(as in milking);* — *off,* 'ōniki, 'ō'ū; — *between fingers,* 'ūpiki, 'ōpiki.
pine. 1. *See* **pine tree. 2.** *Lament.* Lu'ulu'u, kanikau, mae.
pineapple. Hala kahiki, hala 'ai, hala kea, hala 'ula. *Pineapple cannery,* hale hana hala kahiki.
pine tree. Lā'au paina, paina, kikala, keakula.
pinfeathers. Hulu kupu.
ping-pong paddle. Lā'au pa'i kinipōpō.
pinguecula. Momi.
pink. 1. *Color.* 'Ākala, 'ōhelohelo, hā'ula'ula. *Pink mist,* noe 'ula. **2.** *Shrub of the pink family.* Laulihilihi.
pinkeye. Maka 'ula'ula.
pinkish. 'Ākalakala *(rare). To turn pinkish, as octopus,* mākole, he'e pulu.
pinnacle. Ni'o, panepo'o, 'ou. *To reach the pinnacle,* kū i ka ni'o.
pint. Paina.
pintail duck. Koloa māpu.
pinwheel. Huila makani; ahi pōka'uwili *(firework).*
pinworm. Naio, naio 'ai kae. *Pinworm daub,* pala naio *(insult).*
pioneer. Paionia.
pious. Haipule. *See* **sanctimonious.**
pipe. 'Ohe, paipu; ipu *(smoking). Water pipe,* hā wai, 'ohe wai. *Sewer pipe,* paipu lawe 'ino. *Tobacco pipe,*

ipu paka. *Chief's pipe lighter,* mūkī paka. *Musical pipes,* hōkio, hōkiokio; kā'eke'eke, 'ohe kā'eke'eke, pahūpahū *(bamboo)*. *To pipe on a flute-like instrument,* pio, piopio, ho'opiopio, hōpiopio.
Piper methysticum. *See* **kava**.
piping. 'Uiki, 'uwiki *(dress trimming)*.
pirate. Pōwā, pōwā moku, pōwā ma ka moana.
pistachio. Pikekakia.
pistil. Kukuna.
pistol. Pū, pūpanapana.
piston. Hao ku'e, ku'e, naku'e.
pit. Lua. *Also:* meki, hālua, pao; poho *(as for planting breadfruit trees);* kālua *(rare)*. *Deep pit,* lua meki, maka hakahaka. *Slime pit,* lua pikumena. *Pit in the* luakini *temple,* luapa'ū. *Woman of the pit (PH 25),* wahine o ka lua *(Pele)*.
pitch. 1. *Throw*. Nou, ho'olei, kiloi, kā. *To pitch in and help,* lawelawe lima. 2. *Motion of a vessel*. Luli, luliluli, kulana. *Also:* aukū, kaiue, hulei, 'okū'okū, kīhā, 'aui. 3. *Resin*. Hū lā'au, kēpau, kēpau hamo. 4. *Music*. Kī, ki'ina o ka leo, kani. *High pitch,* ki'ina leo ki'eki'e. *Low pitch,* leo ha'aha'a.
pitcher. 1. *Vessel*. Pika, kī'aha, kī'aha 'o'oma; pikele *(rare)*. *Water pitcher,* pika wai, kī'aha 'o'oma wai. 2. *Thrower*. Nou, mea nou.
pitchfork. 'Ō.
pitfall. Luahele.
pith. Iho, māhao, kōkōwaikī.
pitiful. Kū i ke aloha, māna'ona'o, lihaliha wale.
pitiless. Aloha 'ole, aloha menemene 'ole.
pittance. Pālau'eka, lau'eka, mā'ilu, mā'ilu'ilu, 'u'uku ka loa'a.
pitted. 'Ālualua, hālua, hākuma, kīpo'opo'o, 'ālo'alo'a, 'āpoho; 'āpukapuka *(rare)*.
pitter patter. 'Owē. *See* **patter**.
pity. Aloha, aloha menemene, mokuāhua, polohina. *What a pity!* Aloha 'ino!
placate. Ho'onā, ho'omālielie.
place. 1. *Locality*. Wahi, kahi, kaha, kauwahi. *Also:* kūlana, kūnana, kaulu, kaunu. *Place at sea where canoes stop,* kaulana wa'a. *Evil place,* wahi 'ino, kaha'ino. *Surf-riding place,* kūlana nalu, kūlana kai. *Legendary place,* wahi pana. *Place for urinating,* mīana. *Place of torment,* ki'o ahi. *Of or belonging to that place,* kō laila, o laila. *From place to place,* mai kahi wahi ā kahi wahi (Kel. 59). 2. *To put*. Kau *(for various uses, see* **kau**; ho'okau, waiho. *Also:* ho'okaukau, pākau; pēkau *(rare);* — *under,* ho'opili malalo a'e, hālalo; — *on the side,* kau ha'ao'ao; — *one-sided,* kīkepa. *To place flowers as on graves,* kau pua. *To place in authority,* ho'omana, ho'onoho. *Placed,* kau 'ia, kaulei. *Placed in rows, as soldiers,* noho papa.
placement. Kauna, kaulana.
placenta. 'Īewe, wewe, ēwe.
plague. Ma'i ahulau. *Black plague,* piwa 'ele'ele.
plaid. Papamū.
plain. 1. *Level land*. 'Āina pālahalaha, kula, papa, pāpū; pa'akō *(dry);* unana. 2. *Clear*. Mōakaaka, moaka, akaaka, maopopo, molale. 3. *Simple*. 'A'ohe i ho'onani 'ia *(unadorned);* u'i 'ole *(not beautiful)*.
plaintiff. Po'e (mea) ho'opi'i.
plait. Ulana, nala, nana. *Also:* unana, nanala, nanana, hi'i; kūpoki *(a process)*. *See* **mat, weft**. *Plaited, as helmet,* 'ie. *Check plait,* maka moena. *Twill plait,* 'o'eno, ho'ohewahewa. *Decorative plaiting,* ho'oheno *(rare)*. *To plait feathers,* haku hulu.
plan. Ho'olālā, kālai, ana; papa hana. *To draw plans,* kaha ki'i. *To plan slaughter,* makaluku.
plane. Ko'i kahi, ko'i kāholo, ko'i kāhela *(carpenter's)*.
plane tree. Pelekano, pelane.
planet. Hōkū hele, hōkū 'ae'a, hōkū lewa. *See* **Jupiter, Mars, Mercury, Saturn, Uranus, Venus**.
planing mill. Hale wili papa, wili papa.
plank. Papa lā'au, papa lā'au mānoanoa, papa mānoanoa.
planner. Mea ho'olālā; lelehua *(rare)*.

plans. Ki'i *(as for a house)*.
plant. Lā'au, mea ulu, lau nahele; mea kanu *(cultivated); tender* —, 'ohā; *thrifty* —, kawowo; — *propagated by slips or scions,* kūlālā, kumulā; *fallen* —, mauā; — *in lava bed,* makana'ā; *general name for underwater* —, limu. *Trailing plant,* lā'au hihi; pōlumu *(rare)*. *Creeping plant,* lā'au kolo. *Introduced plant,* lā'au malihini, lā'au lawe 'ia mai, lā'au mai nā 'āina 'ē. *To plant,* kanu; haiwā *(rare)*.
plantain. Mai'a; *broad-leafed* —, laukahi, laukahi kuahiwi, laukahi lau nui; manene. *See* **banana**.
plantation. Mahi, māla, māla 'ai, mahi 'ai, mahana, mahina 'ai. *Sugar plantation,* mahi kō.
planter. Kanaka mahi 'ai, mea kanu.
plant louse. 'Eleao.
plaster. Puna, hamo puna. *To plaster,* hamo, hamo puna, pa'i puna, kāpili.
plasterer. Hamo puna.
plastic. 'Ūlina *(malleable)*.
plate. Pā, papa. *Paper plate,* pā pepa. *Soup plate,* pā hohonu. *Wall plate and gable of a house,* lohelau.
platform. Kahua, haka, paepae. *To build a platform,* ho'opaepae. *Altar platform,* haka lele. *Platform between canoes of a double canoe,* pola. *Platform for drying fish,* hakakū. *Speaker's platform,* 'āwai. *Political platform,* kahua, papahana. *National platform (political),* kahua hana lāhui.
platonic wife. Wahine ho'owahine.
platoon. Mokuna.
platter. Pā pālahalaha; papa lā'au *(wooden);* kāloa *(oval wooden);* pā loloa *(long)*.
play. 1. *Recreation*. Pā'ani; pili *(gamble)*. *Also:* pa'apa'ani, upa'apa'ani. *Play ball,* pā'ani kinipōpō. *Play cards,* pā'ani pepa, hahau pepa. 2. *Music*. Ho'okani, ho'okani pila; puhi 'ohe *(wind instrument);* mūkī *(the* hōkiokio). 3. *Drama*. Hana keaka, hō'ike'ike.
player. Mea pā'ani. *Ballplayer,* pā'ani kinipōpō. *Player of the* pūhenehene *game,* kē.
playful. Pā'ani, ho'opā'ani, 'eu. *Also:* pa'apa'ani, laupa'apa'ani.
playground. Kahua, kahua pā'ani, kahua le'a, kahua le'ale'a.
playing cards. Pepa, pepa pā'ani, pepa hahau.
play language. *See* **language**.
playmate. Hoa pā'ani; hoa kamali'i *(childhood)*.
plaything. Mea pā'ani, milimili. *A water plaything,* kō-'ie'ie.
plea. Noi.
pleasant. 'Olu'olu, wai'olu. *Also:* 'olu, māhie, luakaha, la'ela'e, la'e, 'inā'inau, 'akeu, mōpua.
please. Hō'olu, hō'olu'olu, ho'ole'a, ho'ohoihoi; 'olu-'olu *(command)*. *Please do me a favor,* e 'olu'olu 'oe i ko'u mana'o. *Do as you please,* hana nō e like me kou makemake.
pleased. Hoihoi, ohohia, hia'ai. *Greatly pleased or delighted,* hia'ai'ono, piha i ka hoihoi.
pleasing. Hia'ai, le'a, wai'olu, kohu, mīkololohua, mīkolohua, mīkolelehua, lupea.
pleasure. Le'ale'a, mea ho'ohau'oli, mea e hoihoi ai, le'a, 'oli'oli, hoihoi, 'oli. *See ex.,* **duty**. *To go out for pleasure,* hoholo. *Place of pleasure, comfort, happiness,* kahua o Mali'o *(ancient)*.
pleat. 'Āpikipiki, 'unu'unu. *Pleated ruffle,* pihapiha 'ō koholā. *To lay on in folds, as pleats,* ko'o.
pledge. 'Ōlelo ho'ohiki, ho'ohiki. *See saying,* **manō**. *Pledge of allegiance,* ho'ohiki kūpa'a.
Pleiades. *Many names, most of them concerned with* Makali'i, *a deified Kaua'i chief:* Nā- (Ka-) huihui-o-Makali'i, Huihui-kōkō-a-Makali'i-kau-i-luna, Nā-kā-a-Makali'i, Nā-kōkō-a-Makali'i, Nā-wāhine-a-Makali'i, Ke-aweawe-Makali'i, Ka-lālani-a-Makali'i. *Also:* Huihui, Kūpuku, Peleiake.
plentiful. *See* **plenty**. *Overplentiful,* pākī.
plenty. Lawa pono, nui, lako.
pliable. Holu, kāluhi, lu'a, nīnole, hainole; 'ae wale *(to agree easily)*.

pliers. 'Ūpā 'ūmi'i.

plop. Kuhō, haluku.

plot. 1. *Conspiracy.* Kipi, 'ōhumu, 'ōhumu kipi, ho'okahua kipi; waohua *(rare).* *To plot evil,* kālai 'ino, ho'omakakī. **2.** *See* **lot. 3.** *Plot of story.* Kahua o ka mo'olelo.

plover. Kōlea. *The plover flies here, and when his breast is fat, returns,* lele mai nō ke kōlea, ā kāpule ka umauma, ho'i *(of carpetbaggers and some white sojourners in Hawai'i).* *Plover eggs are in foreign places (UL 220),* 'o ka hua o ke kōlea, aia i kahiki. *See sayings,* **kōlea.**

plow. 'Ō'ō hao, 'ō'ō palau, 'ō'ō hou, palau, kūpele.

pluck. Unuunu, uluulu *(as fowl);* 'ako *(as flowers).* *See* **gather, pick.**

plug. Pani, 'umoki. *Also:* kiki, kī'amo, 'omo, kui kākia. *Tobacco plug,* pōpō paka, pepe'e paka. *To plug, as a hole,* ho'opa'a, kiki; kihi *(rare).*

plum. Palama, puluma.

plumage. Hulu.

plumbago. 'Ilie'e.

plumber, plumbing. Palama.

plumeria. Melia; hae Hawai'i *(a variety).*

plummet. Walawalakī.

plump. Nepunepu, pu'ipu'i. *Also:* hananu'u, pau hananu'u, huakē, ōhāhā, pōkeokeo, polohuku, ponohuku, 'uheke, heke, hekekē, hekeheke, pōhekeheke, poheke, kaekae, kāhā, nenelu, newe, halakū, 'aka'ika'i, 'a'alakai, nopu, nepu, nepue, no'u, nuka, konopue, pōlunu, palaiki, palamea, hahei, hakakī, polo, mumuhu. *Cf.* **fat.** *Evenly plump,* holokū.

plunder. Waiwai pio, waiwai hao. *To plunder,* hao, pōwā, kā'ilikū, kā'ili wale, kaha, pākaha, mahi'ili, moluna.

plunge. Lu'u. *Also:* kimo, hou, ho'opalemo; haulani *(as a canoe);* kūpenu.

plural. Helu nui. *The common plural markers are:* nā (nā hale, *houses),* mau (kēlā mau hale, *those houses), and the k-less possessive* ('elua ona hale, *he has two houses).* *Inclusive plural (grammar),* helu nui pili. *Exclusive plural (grammar),* helu nui ka'awale.

plus. Ā me. *Plus sign,* kahahui, hui. *Two plus two is four,* 'elua ā me 'elua, 'ehā.

ply. Ka'ā. *Two-ply,* ka'ā lua. *To ply back and forth,* haulani. *Ply with frivolous questions,* nīele, nieniele.

Plymouth. Pelimuka, Pelimuta.

P.M. 'Auinalā *(afternoon);* ahiahi *(evening);* pō *(night).*

pneumonia. Numonia; hanu pau *(perhaps).*

pocket. Pākeke, pa'eke, 'eke'eke, 'eke, 'a'a. *In the pocket,* 'inipākeke.

pocketbook. Puke pākeke, paiki. *See* **purse.**

pockmarked. Pukapuka, hākuma, hakuhana, hākumakuma.

pod. Wahī o waho; hua keratio *(Luka 15.16, RSV).*

poem. Mele.

poet. Haku mele.

poetic. Pa'a i nā mele.

poetry. Mele.

poi. Poi, 'ai; kāpiki *(inferior).* *See* **pounder** *and saying,* **welcome.** *Thin poi,* 'ai kakake. *Lumpy poi,* 'ai pu'upu'u *(fig., unsociable);* 'ai hakuhaku *(due to mixing).* *Fresh poi,* 'ai hou; 'aka'akai *(bulrush, so-called because fresh poi was not liked);* miki pololei, pololei, polokē. *Poi beginning to ferment,* pohā ka 'ai. *Sour poi,* poi 'awa'awa *(fig., unpleasant disposition),* kahania. *Breadfruit poi,* poi 'ulu. *Sweet-potato poi,* pa'i 'uala, pa'i 'uwala, poi 'uala, poi 'uwala, 'uala ho'omalamala. *Flour poi,* poi palaoa. *Pumpkin poi,* poi pala'ai. *Poi cocktail,* 'ai kakake. *Poi concoction,* kūpele. *Stages of poi pounding:* pāku'iku'i, pākī, pākī'ai, pili, hui ka 'ai, ho'opohā; poho, pele, kūpele; ho'owali, moku. *Poi-pounding board,* papa ku'i 'ai. *Unmixed poi, small package,* pūkele'ai. *Hard, pounded, undiluted poi,* pa'i 'ai. *Ti-leaf bundle of hard poi,* holo 'ai. *Watery residue on poi-pounding board,* pīkale, kale 'ai. *Film of poi adhering to walls of the container,* pala'ai. *To scrape poi from*

the sides of the bowl with the fingers, kahi. *Single dip of poi,* kī'o'e poi. *To dip poi with fingers,* miki; miki pākahi, miki pāpākahi *(one finger);* miki pāpālua *(two fingers).* *To pound poi,* ku'i 'ai, ku'i poi; lua'a.

poinciana. 'Ohai 'ula.

point. Kiko *(dot);* lae *(of land);* wēlau, 'ēlau, welelau *(tip);* maka, 'oi'oina. *See* **fishhook.** *Sharp point,* pu'u 'oi'oi. *Highest point,* kaupoku, wēkiu. *Steel point,* maka kila. *Starting point,* kupuna. *Turning point,* kahana. *Point at canoe bow,* maka ihu. *Point of* 'ō'ō *digging stick,* maka ole *(fig.).* *Point of bonito lure or composite hook,* lālā. *To score a point,* 'ai. *To point,* kuhi, kuhikuhi, ho'okuhi; kuhikau *(rare).* *To ask pointblank,* noi kū. *To the point of,* ā, hele ā. *To shape into a point,* 'ōmu'o. *To point, as a pointer dog,* ho'opololei ka huelo.

pointed. Miomio, 'oi'oi. *Also:* wanawana *(spiked);* wakawaka *(as teeth);* wana, wawana, winiwini. *Any pointed instrument,* kui. *Pointed shoes,* kāma'a miomio. *Pointed remark,* 'ōlelo houhou, 'ōlelo pahupahu.

pointer. 1. *Stick.* Lā'au kuhikuhi. **2.** *Dog.* 'Īlio hahai manu.

pointing out. Kuhikuhina.

poi pounder. *See* **pounder.**

poise. Kūlana, kūnana, kaha, kīkaha, ho'ola'i. *Also:* 'iolana, lāhai, lahaina, ānehe. *Birds poise quietly in the gentle breeze,* ho'ola'i nā manu i ke aheahe *(of peaceful persons).*

poison. Lā'au make; ahulu *(fig.);* pōpō 'auhuhu, 'apu kōheoheo.

poisonous. Make, 'awa, kōheoheo. *Poisonous fang or tooth,* niho 'awa. *Poisonous-natured person,* kōheoheo.

poke. 'Ō'ō, hou, 'o'e; polo *(rare);* — *through,* me'ome'o; — *sideways, as in digging,* kaiehu; — *a fire,* 'ō'ōahi, hoelo. *See* **poker.**

pokeberry. Pōpolo, pōpolo kū mai.

poker. 1. *Implement.* Ulu ahi, 'ō'ōahi, 'ōhelo. **2.** *Card game.* Konoki.

Poland, Pole, Polish. Pōlani.

polar bear. Pea o ke Kā'ei-anu.

Polaris. *See* **North Star.**

pole. Pou, lā'au, peloka, pahu. *See* **fish, fishing pole, flagpole.** *Carrying pole,* 'auamo. *Fruit-plucking pole,* lou. *Bird-catching pole,* alakō, 'auku'u, pokia. *Surveying pole,* poloka kuea. *Telephone pole,* pou kelepona. *Pole indicative of taboo,* kaununu. *Pole for roof frame,* holo. *Pole for canoe protection,* kau ko'o.

pole vault. Lele lā'au, kūpololū.

police. Māka'i. *Chief of police,* luna māka'i. *Police matron,* māka'i wahine. *Police station,* hale māka'i. *Police whistle,* 'ūlili. *Mounted police,* māka'i kau lio. *To police,* māka'i. *Patrolling night police,* māka'i ho'omalu pō.

police court. 'Aha ho'okolokolo ho'omalu.

policeman. Māka'i; kaiko *(rare).* *To appoint as a policeman,* ho'omāka'i. *Traffic policeman,* māka'i kū huina. *Policeman's club,* newa, lā'au māka'i.

policy. 1. *Plan.* Mana'o ho'okō, kahua, papa hana; kālai 'ana *(fig.).* **2.** *Document.* Palapala. *Insurance policy,* palapala 'inikua, palapala ho'opa'a.

polish. 'Ānai, ho'ohinuhinu. *Also:* kūhinu, kuai, kuolo, halo, hē, au, ho'onemo, kahiau. *See* **bootblack, rub.** *Fingernail polish,* pena miki'ao. *Polishing stone,* noninui. *To polish with pumice or sand,* ho'ōne.

polished. Pala hinu, hinua, kūhinu. *Also:* kaekae, kamani, nemo, hinu, huali, pīkaka.

polite. 'Olu'olu, 'olu, waipahē, waipehē.

political. Kālai'āina, kalakalaiaupuni, polikika, polokika. *Political party,* 'ao'ao kālai'āina. *Political expert,* kilo aupuni.

political economy. 'Ike kālai'āina.

politician. Loea kālai'āina.

politics. Kālai'āina, polokika, hana kālai'āina.

poll. Pāloka, wahi koho pāloka.

pollen. 'Ehu, ehu. *Flower pollen,* 'ehu pua. Hīnano *blossom pollen,* 'ehu hīnano.
poll tax. 'Auhau kino, 'auhau po'o.
pollute. Ho'ohaumia, ho'opaumā'ele, ho'opelapela. *Polluted,* pilo, pino, pinopino. *Polluted water,* wai puna pilopilo.
pollution. Ho'ohaumia 'ana, ho'opelapela 'ana, 'ino, pilo.
Pollux. Nānā-hope. *See* **Castor.**
polo. Polo. *Water polo,* polo wai.
polyandry. Male lehulehu 'ana o ka wahine i ka manawa ho'okahi.
polygamy. Male lehulehu 'ana o ke kāne i ka manawa ho'okahi.
Polynesia, Polynesian. Polenekia.
polyp. 'Uku ko'ako'a.
pomegranate. Pomeikalana, pomekelane, pomegerane, pomelaike, pomeraite.
pomelo. No known Hawaiian name.
pommel. Pāluku, ku'i pehi, hāku'i. *See* **beat, saddle horn.**
pomp. Ho'okahakaha, hanohano.
pompano. Ulua.
pompous. Halalina, ho'okeha. *To strut pompously,* kā-'i'ī. *See* **proud.**
poncho. Kīpuka.
pond. Loko, ki'o, hāloko, hālokoloko, luawai, lau wai. *See* **pool.** *Salt pond,* loko pa'akai, loko li'u. *Manmade pond,* loko ku'i. *Pond near the shore,* pu'uone. *Pond reserved for a chief,* kō'ele. *Mythical pond,* Kūlani-hāko'i. *Fresh-water pond,* loko wai. *Fishpond,* loko i'a.
ponder. Nalu, kākepakepa, mana'ona'o.
poniard. Poniaka.
pontiff. Pope, kumukauoha.
pony. Pone, lio 'u'uku.
pool. 1. *Pond.* Ki'o, ki'o wai. *Also:* loko, hāloko, hālokoloko, luawai, huinawai, wai ahu, hāpuna, kīpoho, lahalaha wai, lau wai, huawaimaka, hakuone, ko'ana wai, kuki'o, pōnaha wai. *Sea pool,* kāheka; kāhekaheka *(small). Dirty pool,* ki'o lepo. *Pool for leaping,* ki'o kawa. *Pools,* lokoloko, lo'ilo'i, mālo'i. *Forest pool where rubbish collects,* ākuli. *To form a pool,* hāloko. *To settle in pools,* pāki'o, hālo'i. **2.** *A game.* Pahupahu. *To play pool,* pahupahu.
poor. 1. *Impoverished.* 'Ilihune. *Also:* hune, hō'ilihune, 'akole, puhikole, 'ilikole, 'ilikone, hō'ilikole, akakole; ka'a'owē, ka'a ka lolo *(fig.; see* **ka'a 1**); pakaneo. *See* **pauper** *and insulting epithets,* **laho kole, laho pōka'oka'o,** *and saying,* **manu 1. 2.** *Quality.* 'Ino'ino; kakakē *(rare).*
pop. Pohāpohā, ho'opakūpakū, pa'ina, pohā, kani kohā. *See* **soda.** *Sound of lips popped open,* mūkā.
popcorn. Kūlina pohāpohā.
pope. Pope, kumukauoha.
poplar. Popela.
poppy. Pua kala, pokalakala, pope, naule.
populace. Maka'āinana.
popular. Makemake nui 'ia, nui nā makamaka.
populated. Noho 'ia. *See saying,* **lē'ī.** *Densely populated,* laukanaka, noho nui 'ia.
population. Heluna kānaka, po'e, lehulehu, kānaka.
porch. Lānai. *Porch railing,* pale lānai. *Porch of pillars,* hale kia.
porcupine. Kīpoka, pua'a 'ili 'oi'oi.
porcupine fish. Kōkala, hoana.
pore. Pukapakī *(skin).*
porgy fish. Mū *(perhaps).*
pork. Pua'a, 'i'o pua'a. *Slab of salted pork,* pākākā, kākā pua'a. *Pork grease,* 'aila pua'a.
pornography. Nā mea pelapela, nā mea pelapela like 'ole ma nā puke, nā ki'i, nā ki'i 'oni'oni.
porous. Pukapuka.
porpoise. Nai'a, nu'ao.
port. Awa, awa kū moku. *Port side,* 'ao'ao hema.

portable. Lawe, hiki ke lawe 'ia.
portend. 'Ōuli.
portent. 'Ōuli, hō'ailona.
porter. Hali ukana, kanaka hali ukana; kia'i puka *(doorman).*
porthole. Puka ma ka 'ao'ao o ka moku.
portico. Hale kia.
portion. 'Āpana, mahele, kuleana, ha'awina, 'okana, hapa, hakina, pu'u; ka'ipu'u *(rare). Small portion,* hapa iki, hapa 'u'uku. *Greatest portion,* hapa loa, hapa nui. *Main portion,* kino. *Severed portion,* moku, mō, mokuna. *In two portions,* hapa lua. *To be a portion,* hapa.
portrait. Ki'i.
Portugal. Pokukala, Potugala.
Portuguese. Pukikī.
Portuguese man-of-war. Pa'imalau, po'imalau.
portulaca. 'Ākulikuli.
pose. 1. *As for pictures.* Kū mai no ka pa'i 'ana o ke ki'i *(standing).* **2.** *Pretend.* Ho'okohukohu.
position. Kūlana, kūnana, kuana, wahi; 'oihana *(occupation). Position of the land,* waihona 'āina. *Lying down position,* moena.
positive. 'Ike loa.
possess. 1. *See* **have, own. 2.** *As by a spirit.* Noho, ho'okomokomo. *Spirit that possesses,* akua noho, 'uhane noho.
possessive case. 'Auikōha'i, 'auipili. *See* **genitive case.** *O-form possessive,* 'auipili laulā. *A-form possessive,* 'auipili pa'a. *Possessive markers:* o, a, ō, ā.
possessor. Mea, haku, 'ona.
possible. Hiki. *When possible,* ke hiki. *Any possible time,* ka manawa e hiki ana. *Any possible day,* ka lā e hiki ana.
possibly. Paha, mali'a, auane'i. *Possibly not,* 'a'ole paha.
post. 1. *Pole.* Pou, pahu, kia, kūkulu, kūkunu, lā'au kū. *House post,* pou, pouomanu, kukuna, he'epālaha. *Gable post,* pou kukuna. *Supporting ridgepole post,* pouhana. *Front post,* pou alo. *Back post,* pou kua. *Corner post,* pou kihi. *Heiau posts,* nanahua, kikihi. *Post in a grass house,* konakū. *Post marking harbor,* ulehole. *Post designating place of human sacrifice,* pouomanu, pouamanu. *Post for hanging goods,* oleole. **2.** *To deposit.* Ho'ouna; ho'okomo *(as mail);* kū *(as a bond).* **3.** *Military. See* **fort.**
postage. Uku leka, uku leta. *Postage stamp,* po'oleka.
postal. 'Oihana leka. *Postal law,* kānāwai o ka 'oihana leka. *Postal department,* 'oihana leka.
postcard. Pepa po'oleka.
poster. Ki'i ho'olaha.
posterior. Hope.
posterity. Mo'opuna, mamo.
postlude. Ho'opau 'ana.
postman. Lawe leka.
postmark. Kuni.
postmaster. Luna leka.
postmaster general. Kuhina hale leka.
post office. Hale leka.
postpone. Pane'e, ho'opane'e, ho'omoe.
postponement. Pane'e 'ana.
postscript. 'Ōlelo pāku'i, mana'o poina.
posture. Kūlana, kūnana.
pot. Ipu. *Cooking pot,* ipu hao. *Flower pot,* poho mea kanu. *Earthenware pot,* kelemānia, ipu lepo.
"pot." Paka lōlō.
potable. Manalo, kūpono i ka inu.
potash. Pokaka.
potato. 'Uala kahiki *(Irish). See* **sweet potato.** *Wild potato,* 'ae'ahauka'e.
potbellied. 'Ōpū pala'ai *(term of ridicule);* 'ōpū palula, kēkē, ākēkē, na'ana'a, leholeho, 'alakai, 'āka'ika'i, nanae.
potent. Ikaika.
pot holder. Mea pa'a ipu hao.

potion. Mea inu. *Medical potion,* 'apu.
potluck. 'Ai i ka mea e loa'a ana, pū 'ai, pū pa'akai, kū-pu'u, kupupu'u, pono 'ai.
Potomac. Pokomaka, Potomaka.
potsherd. 'Āpana ipu lepo.
potter. Pokela.
potter's vessel. Ipu lepo.
pottery. Pokela.
pouch. Poho. *See* **bag.**
poultice. Kāpa'i. *Cf.,* **pūko'ako'a 2.**
poultry. Nā manu 'ai 'ia e like me ka moa, ka pelehū, a me ke kakā.
pounce. Po'i, 'āpo'ipo'i.
pound. 1. *To strike.* Ku'i. *Also:* ho'oku'i, ku'i pehi, hāku'i, pāku'i, 'aku'i, kīmō, kīmōmō, kīpō, kīkēkē; kāpa'i *(as a masseur);* 'āpohopoho, lumi *(as surf);* ho'ohāhā, pākī, pāluku; luluā'ina *(as sea urchins);* ku'ikā *(smooth). Pounded by the sea,* pāpā kai. *To pound into fine bits,* ku'i palu, napo, pākaikai. *To pound poi or food,* ku'i 'ai. *Poi pounder (person),* ku'i 'ai. *To pound iron,* ku'i hao. **2.** *Unit of weight or currency.* Paona.
pounder. Mea ku'i. *Poi pounder,* pōhaku ku'i 'ai, pōhaku ku'i poi. *Ring poi pounder,* pōhaku ku'i 'ai puka. *Whale-tooth pounder,* pōhaku ku'i palaoa. *Top of poi pounder,* pōheoheo.
pour. Ninini. *Also:* hanini, nini, ninini, loku, ho'oloku, 'iliki *(as rain); — forth,* hua'i, ukuhi; *— down, as the sun,* hawewe; kī'aha'aha *(out of a cup);* manini. *To pour out water,* kau wai. *Evil words poured out, poured back and forth,* manini aku ā manini mai nā 'ōlelo 'ino *(see* **manini***).*
pout. Ho'olehelehe nui, nuku pu'u, nunuha, nuha, 'e'ewa. *See saying,* **puna 8.**
poverty. *See* **poor.** *Poverty-stricken,* 'ilikole, pakaneo.
powder. Pauka, paoka, pouka, paula. *Container for powder,* poho pauka. *Face powder,* pauka maka. *To powder,* pauka.
powder horn. 'Ōwili, kākai pauka, holowa'a 'ōwili.
powdery. Huna, wali.
power. Mana, lima ikaika. *Supernatural power,* mana. *Guardian power,* mana kia'i. *Power to fly,* kino lele. *The power of the press,* ka mana o ka papa pa'i. *Power of attorney,* palapala ho'āmana. *Under control of a supernatural power,* kalakupua. *Great power,* 'āina nui *(nation).*
powerful. Mana, ikaika. *Also:* konapiliahi, ehuehu, maua'ālina.
powerhouse. Hale hana uila.
practice. 1. *Train.* Ho'oma'ama'a, ho'oma'a; kāhe'e *(rare).* **2.** *See* **procedure.**
prairie. Kula ākea.
prairie dog. 'Īlio kula 'olohelohe.
praise. Mahalo, ho'omaika'i, ho'onani, kaena. *Also:* mililani, hi'ilani, ho'ole'a, mailani, pailani, ho'olanilani, lele pailani, pai, pai ali'i, ho'okapukapu, akena, ho'ohilu, hūlani, hila'i, hāpaimemeue. *See saying,* **hapahapai.** *Word of praise, as for a place,* 'ōlelo kaena. *Chant of praise,* kānaenae *(see ex.,* **kānaenae***);* kauwōlani, pa'ipunahele.
praiseworthy. Kū i ka mahalo.
prance. Ka'inapu. *See* **gambol.**
prankster. Kolohe, 'eu. *To play pranks,* ho'okolohe, hone.
prattling. 'Ama'ama, 'ama.
pray. Pule, 'āmama.
prayer. Pule *(for various kinds, see Haw.-Eng. entry and entries that follow it). Christian prayers:* pule a ka Haku *(Lord's);* pule 'ohana *(family);* pule ho'omaka *(beginning);* pule ho'oku'u *(closing);* pule hāmau *(silent);* pule ho'ola'i *(dedicatory);* pule ho'omaika'i *(thanks). Pre-Christian prayers:* pule ho'ouluulu 'ai, pule ho'omau *(for crops);* pule ho'oulu 'āina *(increased productivity of land);* pule ho'ōla, pule ho'ouluulu *(healing);* pule pale, pule kala, kalakū *(to ward off evil);* pule ho'onoa *(to lift taboo);* pule 'anā'anā, pule kuni, pule

'umi, pule kameha'i, pule ho'ounauna, oneone-i-honua, kīpolo *(sorcery);* kānaenae *(of eulogy). Also:* wailana, wau'aha, waipā, waihā, lelea, le'ale'a, kai-o-Kauakahi, kai-a-pō-kea, kai-o-pō-keo, kaukau, kākua, 'aha, uhauhui, hahauhui, limalima, 'ōkalakala, kāhea 'ai, kāhoaka, kanilāhuluhulu, pale lau'ī, 'ulonokū, ho'oulu i'a, ho'oulu kauō, 'oki i ka moe'uhane, kāle'a, kuili, mōliaola, hui-o-Papa, kāmakamaka, kauō, kuwā, kuoha, 'ulono pule, pule polo, mauha'ale'a, pūpūweuweu. *Long conversational prayer,* kalokalo. *Long repetitious prayer,* kuawili. *To offer food and prayers,* kahukahu, kaumaha 'ai. *Words at end of prayers:* lele wale, 'eli'eli, 'āmama. *Prayer service,* kūlana pule *(Christian);* malu ko'i, malu 'ōhi'a *(other). Presentation of prayers,* haipule, pule, ha'ina pule, uhauhui. *Prayer drum,* pahu kanaloa. *Prayer gourd,* pule ipu.
preach. Ha'i'ōlelo. *Preach salvation,* ha'i ola. *Preach the gospel,* ha'i 'euanelio.
preacher. Kahuna pule, kahu. *Preacher of salvation,* ha'i ola. *Traveling preacher,* kahuna pule ka'ahele. *Teaching preacher,* kahuna a'o, kahuna ha'i'i'ōlelo *(especially an itinerant one).*
preadolescent. Poke'o; keiki ma'i lewalewa *(boy, see* **lewalewa***);* 'ulapa'a *(girl).*
precarious. Kūnihi, kūnihinihi, 'anihinihi, nihi, maka'u, kūlihi, kūlihilihi.
precaution. Hana ho'omākaukau mamua o ka pōpilikia, no'ono'o mua e pale i ka pōpilikia. *To take precautions,* ho'ākahele.
precautionary. Akahele.
precede. Hele mamua, hele mua.
precedent. Nā hana i ho'olaha mua 'ia.
precept. Loina, 'ōlelo a'o, 'ōlelo pa'a, kauoha.
precinct. Mahele, 'āpana. *Combined precincts,* mahele i hui 'ia.
precious. Makamae, hiwahiwa, nēnē hiwa, 'alamea, hulu, liho.
precipice. Pali, kawa. *A series of precipices,* kaka'i pali, 'opāpali, 'ōpalipali, pali ku'i.
precipitous. Palipali, kūnihinihi, kūlihilihi, kūlono, oheohe.
precise. Kūlike loa, miomio.
predawn. Pawa, paoa.
predicate, predication. Mana'oha'i.
predict. Wānana; *— misfortune,* ho'oiloilo.
preen. Wae, waewae; kanu'e'e'ina *(rare).*
preface. 'Ōlelo ha'i mua, 'ōlelo ho'ākaaka mua, 'ōlelo mua.
prefer. 'Oi ka makemake.
preferable. Aho.
prefix. Hua pāku'i mamua o ka hua'ōlelo.
pregnancy. Hapaina, kauhua. *See saying,* **hakē.** *Pregnancy sickness,* ho'okauhua, ma'i keiki, 'īloli, ho'īloli. *Pregnancy craving,* ho'okauhua. *To cause pregnancy,* ho'ohāpai.
pregnant. Hāpai. *Also:* pu'u, kauka, kōkō, piha, newe, ūkō, laulau, kō. *See saying,* **hakē.**
prejudice. Mana'o kū'ē, ho'okae. *Race prejudice,* ho'okae 'ili, kaupale 'ili.
prelude. Wehe 'ana.
premature. 'Ē, mamua o ka wā kūpono. *Premature baby,* keiki ala'i, keiki hānau 'ē, mumuku. *Premature birth,* hānau ēwe, 'ō'ili wale. *To speak or act prematurely,* lele 'ē.
premeditate. No'ono'o mua, nalu mua.
premier. Kuhina, kuhina nui.
premium. Uku kaulele. *Insurance premium,* uku ho'opa'a, uku 'inikua.
premonition. Haili moe, hali'a.
preparation. Mākaukau, ho'omākaukau 'ana.
preparatory school. Kula ho'omākaukau.
prepare. Ho'omākaukau, hana, ho'oliuliu.
prepared. Mākaukau. *Also:* liuliu, kū, lilihua.
preposition. 'Inaleo, 'inawaena *(part of speech).*
prepuce. Heo. *See* **foreskin.**

Presbyterian. Pelekepulikano.
presbytery. 'Aha lunakahiko.
prescribe. Kuhikuhi, ho'ākaaka, a'o.
prescription. Kuhikuhi; kuhikuhi nō ka lā'au e pa'i-pa'i ai.
presence. Alo. *In the presence of,* i mua o; me ka 'ike maka o. *Presence of mind,* no'ono'o pono i ka wā ulia.
present. 1. *Now.* 'Ānō, kēia manawa, kēia ao. 2. *At hand.* Ma'ane'i, 'ane'i; eia *(as response to roll call).* 3. *Gift.* Makana. *See* **gift.** *Presents at birth of a child,* makana hānau; maihuli *(rare).* 4. *To present.* Hā'awi, waiho.
presentation. Hā'awi 'ana.
presently. Kokoke, auane'i.
preservation. Mālama 'ana, mau.
preserve. Mālama, mau.
preserver. Mea kia'i, mea mālama.
preside. Ho'omalu *(as at a meeting). Presiding officer,* luna ho'omalu.
president. Pelekikena, palekikena, ikū lani.
presidential. Pelekikena, palekikena.
press. 1. *Exert pressure.* Kaomi, kahi; 'aiana *(as clothes);* — *hard,* kālele kū; — *out,* kāwī, kōwī. *Also:* lomi, kōmi, uma, 'ōpā, lumi, kāpā, mīkā. *Press, as for clamping material or pressing clothes,* mīkini kaomi. 2. *Printing press.* Pa'i palapala, papa pa'i. *See ex.,* **power.**
pressed. Ūkūkua *(with work). Hard-pressed,* pili pū i ka paia *(see* **pili pū***);* pāiki *(rare).*
presser foot. Kaomi lole, pale *(on a sewing machine).*
pressure. Ho'okaomi.
prestige. Kūlana hanohano.
presto. Ko'ihonua.
presume. Kuhi, kainō, kainoa, mana'o wale. *The accused party shall be presumed a good man,* 'o ka mea i ho'opi'i 'ia e mana'o 'ia nō 'oia he kanaka maika'i nō.
presumption. Mana'o koho, ho'okohu.
presumptuous. Maha'oi; hala'o'a *(fig.).*
pretend. Ho'omeamea, ho'okohukohu, ho'okamani; ho'o- *(as in* ho'ohāmama, ho'onou), ho- *(as in* ho'ōla), hō- *(as in* hō'ike). *Also:* kāma'e, ho'ohele, kanale'o. *See* **feign.** *Cf.* Gram. 6.4.
pretense. Ho'okohu, ho'omeamea; noho ni'o, poupou noho ni'o *(of knowledge or skill).*
pretentious. Hō'oi'oi, ho'olae. *See* **pretense.**
pretext. Kumu e 'alo ai. *See* **excuse.**
pretty. 1. *Attractive.* Nani, maika'i, u'i, nohea, huapala. 2. *Somewhat.* 'Ano. *Pretty good,* 'ano maika'i.
prevail. Lanakila, holopapa; īhe'e *(rare).*
prevent. Kāohi, pale, ke'ake'a.
previous. Mua, mamua a'e.
prey. Pio.
price. Kumu kū'ai, kumu, 'auhau, kālā, make. *Bid price,* huina koho. *What is the price?* He aha ke kumu kū'ai? 'Ehia kālā? *High price,* kumu kū'ai nui.
prick. 'Ō, 'o'e, hou.
prickly. 'O'oi, kukū; mane'o *(as some clothes).*
prickly heat. 'Ōhune wela.
prickly pear. *See* **cactus.**
prickly poppy. Pua kala, pōkalakala.
pride. Ha'aheo, kei, keha *(favorable);* mana'o ki'eki'e, ho'oki'eki'e, pehu *(conceit). See* **proud.** *Pride in ancestry,* he'e hōlua *(see* **hōlua***). Pride of the homeland,* maka lehua no ke one hānau.
pride of Barbados. 'Ohai ali'i.
pride of India. 'Inia, 'ilinia.
priest. Kahuna *(for various kinds, see Haw.-Eng. entry and entries that follow it);* kahuna pule, kahu akua; papahola *(rare). See saying,* '*olol*ī. *High priest,* kahuna nui, kahuna po'o. *Medical priest,* kahuna lapa'au. *Priest of the lineage of Lono,* mo'o Lono. *Priest of Lono,* palikū, kuhi 'alaea. *Priest of the lineage of Kū,* mo'o Kū. *Catholic priest,* makua 'uhane. *Priests versed in all branches of the profession,* puhi okaoka. *Priestly class,* papa kahuna, papa huli honua.

priestess. Kahuna pule wahine, kāula wahine; malū kua *(epithet).*
priesthood. 'Oihana kahuna; mo'o kahuna *(succession).*
primary. Mua. *Primary election,* koho wae moho, koho mua. *Primary school,* kula kamali'i.
prime. Nui, ko'iko'i, po'okela. *Prime number,* helu kumu. *Prime factor,* heluhana kumu.
prime minister. Kuhina nui.
primer. A'o heluhelu, kumu, palima. *To study a primer,* palima.
primitive. I ke 'ano kinohi.
primrose willow. Kāmole.
prince. Keiki ali'i, kamāli'i kāne. *Crown prince,* ho'oilina mō'ī.
princess. Kamāli'i wahine. *Crown princess,* ho'oilina mō'ī wahine.
principal. 1. *Main, head.* Nui, mua, po'o. *School principal,* po'o kumu. 2. *Capital sum.* Kumupa'a.
principle. Loina, kahua hana.
print. Pa'i, kikiko, kākau kaha, kākau. *See* **footprint, printing, printing press, type.** *Print shop,* hale pa'i. *Block-print cloth,* palaka. *Printed cloth,* lau, lole kalakoa. *To print, as tapa,* ho'ōni'o, no'eno'e, kāpala, palapala.
printer. Kanaka pa'i.
printing. Pa'i hakahaka *(as contrasted with handwriting). First printing,* ho'okahi o ka pa'i 'ana.
printing press. Mīkini pa'i palapala, pa'i palapala, papa pa'i; mīkini pa'i nūpepa *(newspaper).*
print shop. Hale pa'i.
prior. Mamua a'e.
prism. 'Ōpaka.
prison. Hale pa'ahao, hale wai. *To put in prison,* ho'opa'ahao.
prisoner. Pa'ahao, pio.
private. Pilikino, pono'ī. *See ex.,* **opinion.** *Private rights,* pono pilikino. *Private school,* kula uku. *Your private parts,* kou wahi hilahila.
privilege. Mana, kuleana. *See* **dream.**
privy. 1. *See* **private.** 2. *Toilet.* Lua, ki'ona.
privy council. 'Aha kūkā malū.
prize. Makana, uku. *See* **cherish.** *To prize,* minamina, mana'o nui, make'e, kau nui ka mana'o; ho'ohulu *(for choiceness and rarity).*
prized. Makamae, nēnē hiwa, wehiwa.
prize fight. Ku'iku'i, mokomoko, ku'iku'i pu'upu'u, pelēpelē *(for sport).*
probably. Paha, pēlā paha, malia, auane'i, mali'a, māki'a. *Probably not,* 'a'ole paha.
probate. Ho'okō.
probate court. 'Aha kauoha, 'aha ho'okō kauoha.
probation. Ho'omalu. *Probation officer,* māka'i ho'omalu.
probe. 'Ōhiki; 'o'e *(upward);* hō'o'e, 'akiu, nao.
problem. 1. *Difficulty.* Pilikia, hihia; 'ai pa'a, pu'u *(fig.). No problem,* 'a'ole pilikia. 2. *Mental.* Mana-'oha'i, naneha'i.
procedure. Hana, hana 'ana, lawelawe 'ana. *Correct procedure,* hana pono.
proceed. Hele mua, holo mua; ka'i like, ka'i hele *(in line).*
process. Hana, 'ano o ka hana 'ana, holo 'ana; palapala ki'i *(legal document). Due process of law,* kū i ke kānāwai.
procession. Huaka'i, ka'i huaka'i, kaka'i, 'ōka'i, ka'i. *See* **ghost.**
proclaim. Kūkala, kala, kalakū, ho'opuka, kuahaua, polo'ai; — *a law,* lāhui *(rare).*
proclaimer. Mea kala, mea kūkala, luna'ōlelo.
proclamation. Palapala kūkala, kala, kākālana, kuahaua. *To call out a proclamation,* kalahea. *To go forth, issuing a proclamation,* kala hele.
procrastinate. Ho'opane'e. *Also:* ka'uka'u, ka'ulua, ho'olohi, 'apa'apa, ho'oli'uli'u, ho'onāhili, ho'olalau, napa, ho'onapa, 'āpa'apāna.

procreate. Hoʻopulapula.
procure. Kiʻi, loaʻa. *Also:* weʻa, weʻaweʻa.
procurer. Weʻa, weʻaweʻa.
prod. ʻŌhiki, ʻoʻe, kuʻi, huʻe, hulā, peu, lūkē; — *loose, or sideways,* kaiehu.
prodigal. Hoʻomāunauna, ʻuhaʻuha.
produce. Hua. *To produce,* loaʻa, hoʻohua.
product. Mea i hana ʻia; hua loaʻa, loaʻa *(as in arithmetic).*
productive. Huahua, māhuahua, hua nui. *Productive or prolific family,* welo hānau.
profane. 1. *See* **blaspheme. 2.** *Not sacred.* Noa, laʻa ʻole, kapu ʻole.
profanity. *See* **blaspheme.**
profess. Hōʻoia.
profession. ʻOihana hoʻonaʻauao. *One without a profession,* kahua ʻole.
professional. ʻOihana. *Professional knowledge,* ʻike pili ʻoihana. *Professional certificate,* palapala hōʻoia mākaukau.
professor, professorial. Polopeka.
proficiency. Mākaukau.
proficient. Mākaukau, ʻailolo.
profit. Loaʻa, puka, waiwai hoʻopuka, pōmaikaʻi, huina loaʻa. *Profit and loss,* ka puka ā me ka pohō, ke kumuloaʻa ā me ke kumulilo. *Without profit,* makehewa, pohō wale.
profitable. Makepono, puka pono.
profiteer. Hoʻopukapuka hewa.
profitless. Makehewa, ʻuʻa, pauʻaka, maʻū wale, pohō wale.
profound. Hohonu, kūliʻu, kūkonukonu, kūʻono, liʻu; ʻeliʻeli, ʻaliʻali *(as taboo).*
progenitor. Makua aliʻi, makualiʻi, makua.
progeny. Welo, pua, kamaliʻi, keiki, kawowo, ʻanoʻano. *Source of progeny,* kumu hoʻolaha.
prognosticate. ʻŌuli, haʻi ʻōuli, ʻōuli hiki, wānana.
prognostication. ʻŌuli, ʻōuli hiki, wānana.
program. Papa kuhikuhi, papa hōʻike, papa hana, kuhikuhina.
progress. Holomua, holo i mua, neʻemua, paneʻe i mua, neʻe i mua, hiki mua, hoʻokāʻoi, laua; kāholo *(rapidly);* kūnoni *(slowly). To cause progress,* hoʻoholo i mua.
progressive. Hoʻokāʻoi; ulupono *(rare). See* **progress.**
prohibit. Pāpā, hoʻokapu, lāhui, hōʻole.
prohibition. Kapu, pāpā ʻana. *Prohibition of intoxicants,* hōʻole wai ʻona.
project. 1. *Protrude.* Kela. *Also:* kihikihi; ʻau *(into the sea);* ʻōmuku, hoʻokio, mūkoʻi, halaʻoʻa, wanaoʻa, peleleu, huku, kualapa, ʻōlapalapa, ʻioʻio, ʻou, hōʻouʻou, hōʻoi, koʻi, keʻo; hoʻolele *(as pictures). Rock that projects,* iwi honua. **2.** *Plan.* Papa hana.
projector. Mea hoʻolele kiʻi.
prolific. Hānau nui, huahua, weliweli, weweli.
prolix. Hoʻonui ʻōlelo.
prolong. Hoʻolōʻihi, hoʻoloa. *Also:* hoʻōeoe, kō, kōloa, hoʻokauwō *(as vowels or sounds);* nāʻū *(breathing);* hoʻoliʻuliʻu, aeae, hoʻoniau.
promenade. Holoholo.
prominent. ʻOi, kiʻekiʻe, ahuwale. *Also:* koʻikoʻi, keha, kūlana, meʻe, lae lua, ʻōʻili lua, kalalea, kaʻokaʻo, kiʻi maka nunui. *See saying,* **kalalea.**
promiscuous. Pili me kēlā me kēia. *Also:* pipine, palemo, kuʻulala, lelele; ʻŌ-lau-niu *(fig.). See saying,* **lelepā.** *Promiscuous male,* puaʻa laho, lahokū, mamo na Kama-puaʻa. *Promiscuous female,* haka kau a ka manu *(see* **haka***).*
promise. ʻŌlelo paʻa, ʻōlelo hoʻohiki. *To promise,* hoʻohiki.
promissory note. Pila hōʻaiʻē, palapala hōʻaiʻē.
promontory. Lae, ʻōlae, ʻoiʻoina.
promote. Hoʻopiʻi, piʻi aʻe *(as in a job);* hoʻoholo i mua, hoʻokiʻekiʻe, hoʻopaipai. *See* **advertise.**
promotion. Hoʻopiʻi, hoʻokiʻekiʻe, hoʻopaipai.

prompt. Hikiwawe, ʻeleu, mikiʻala, miki; kono *(remind).*
promulgate. Hoʻolaha.
prone. Moe pālaha, moe, kīpapa, kāhela.
pronoun. Paniinoa *(for various types, see Haw.-Eng. entry).*
pronounce. Hoʻopuka.
pronunciation. Hopuna, hopuna ʻōlelo, hoʻopuka ʻana, puana.
proof. Hōʻoiaʻiʻo, hōʻike.
proofread. Heluhelu hoʻoponopono.
proofs. Paʻi ʻana no ka hoʻoponopono *(of printing).*
prop. Koʻo, kia, unu, paepae, kākoʻo. *To prop with a pole,* hoʻokoʻo.
propaganda. Hoʻolaha manaʻo.
propagate, propagation. Hoʻolaha, hoʻoulu. *Means of propagation,* kumu hoʻolaha. *Propagation of the faith,* hoʻolaha manaʻoʻiʻo.
propeller. Huila hoʻoneʻe; pelemakani *(Niʻihau).*
propeller blade. Epaepa huila.
proper. Kūpono, kū, pono, nihinihi.
proper noun. Haʻiinoa pili kahi.
property. Waiwai, pono, kuleana, loaʻa; ʻano pili *(as of a number). See saying,* **heaven.** *Inherited property,* waiwai hoʻoilina. *Personal property,* waiwai lewa. *Stripped of property,* huhuhune.
prophecy, prophesy. Wānana; wālana, ulana *(rare).*
prophet. Kāula, makāula. *Prophet of evil,* waha ʻawa.
prophetess. Kāula wahine.
propitiate. *See* **placate.**
proportion. Lakio like. *Simple proportion,* lakio like kaukahi. *Well-proportioned,* kolopū, huakē.
proposal. Noi. *See* **propose.** *Proposal of marriage,* noi male.
propose. Hoʻolale, noi. *Propose marriage,* noi male.
proposition. Kumumanaʻo.
proprietor. Haku, ʻona, mea.
pro rata. ʻAwelika.
prosecute. Hoʻopiʻi.
prosecutor. Loiu hoʻokolokolo, mea hoʻopiʻi.
proselyte. Hoʻohulihuli, kāʻana.
prosit! Kāmau!
prosper. Hoʻowaiwai, lako, hoʻokūʻonoʻono. *Also:* pōmaikaʻi, lālāwai, kūloaʻa, polohuku, pōkeokeo, koʻū. *See saying,* **manu 1.**
prostitute. *No equivalent in ancient times.* Wahine hoʻokamakama, wahine laikini, wahine pākaukau, wahine moekolohe. *See* **kūkaeuli.**
prostrate. Moe.
prostration. Moe. *Prostration taboo,* kapu moe, kapu ā moe.
protect. Hoʻomalu, hoʻomāmalu, hoʻomaluhia, hoʻopakele, pale, palekana, panekana; hoʻopālama, mālama.
protected. Hoʻomaluhia, māmalu, malu; ʻōpele *(by taboo);* mālama ʻia, pale ʻia, aumoa.
protection. Malu. *Also:* māmalu, malumalu, ʻalama, mea kiaʻi, pale, lulu. *Protection of the gods,* malumalu akua. *It is protection for going in the sun,* he malumalu hele lā. *Protection of the house of Kū,* māmalu hale o Kū. *Chiefly protection,* lulu aliʻi. *Fire protection,* pale ahi. *To bring under the care or protection of,* hoʻomalu.
protectorate. Hoʻomalu ʻana.
protégé. Luhi.
protest. Kūʻē, hōʻole, kē, keʻu, kīpoʻi, hoʻokē.
Protestant. Hōʻole Pope, kūʻē i ka Pope.
protrude. ʻOiʻoi, huku, hoʻohuku, ʻou. *Also:* kiʻei, ʻōkū, ʻōhū, puʻu, manana, hākau, naʻanaʻa, hoʻonaʻanaʻa, kio, ʻoʻoi, puʻuhaku, hakē, kalalea, pōhuku, waka. *Protruding tooth,* niho keu. *Protruding lips,* nuku puʻu, puʻu ka nuku, kalalea.
protuberance. Puʻu. *Also:* kio, huku, pēheu, maka, lanahua, ʻōhū, ōnū, muni; hukuliʻi *(small).*
proud. Haʻaheo, haʻakei, hākei, kaena *(usually favorable);* hoʻokano, hoʻokiʻekiʻe, naʻau hoʻokiʻekiʻe *(usu-*

ally unfavorable). Also: heo, hoʻoheo, haʻakoi, kalalī, hoʻēheu, hoʻokehakeha, kaha, haha, hoʻohehelo, pahilolo, keʻo, keʻokeʻo, piʻilae, kū ka ihu. *See* pride. *The cloud billow stands proudly in the high air,* ʻōpua haʻaheo i ka lewa.

prove. Hōʻoiaʻiʻo, hoʻokūʻiʻo.

proverb. ʻŌlelo noʻeau, ʻōlelo akamai.

provide. Hoʻolako, hoʻonoho; hoʻākaaka *(state). Provided for by this law,* hoʻomākaukau ʻia ma kēia kānāwai *(see* **mākaukau***).*

provided. Eia nō naʻe hoʻi *(legal).*

provident. Makauliʻi.

provider. Mea hoʻolako, hānai, kāpuhi; makua *(fig.).*

province. Panalāʻau *(colony),* mokuʻāina *(as in Canada);* kuleana *(affair).*

provisional. Kūikawā. *Provisional government,* aupuni kūikawā.

provisions. Lako, ō. *To issue provisions,* hoʻolako, hoʻāʻīpuʻupuʻu.

provoke. Hoʻoukiuki, hoʻonāukiuki, hoʻohae, nanā, hoʻohana, hoʻolale, hoʻonāulu, hoʻohoa. *To provoke trouble,* hālua; hoʻohaunaele *(panic).*

prow. Ihu.

proxy. Hope, pani hakahaka.

prudent. Akahele, nihi.

prune. 1. *Fruit.* Puluna. 2. *Trim.* Paʻipaʻi, ʻokiʻoki.

Prussia, Prussian. Pelukia.

pry. Une, ʻōhiki. *Also:* ue, uma, ʻoʻe, hulā, ina, ine, hoʻomahiki, hoʻohiki, kuʻu; — *open,* ʻuwehe. *To pry limpets loose,* kuʻi ʻopihi. *To pry into the bad of the past,* ʻōhikihiki. *To pry into others' affairs,* ʻonou wale aku nō i kō haʻi kuleana; pāhiʻuhiʻu.

pshaw. Chā, kā. *(Gram. 7.5, 12.)*

psalm. Halelū; Samori *(1823, rare). To sing psalms,* halelū.

psaltery. Pekalakelia, kuolokani, wiola ʻumi.

pseudonym. Inoa kapakapa.

psychiatrist. Kauka hoʻoponopono noʻonoʻo *(see* **hoʻoponopono***).*

psychosis. Maʻi ʻōhewahewa; nahoa *(rare).*

psychotic. ʻŌpulepule, ʻōhewahewa.

pubescence. Hoʻoheu. *See saying,* **limu 1.**

public. Lehulehu; ākea. *Open to the public,* hāmama ʻia i ka lehulehu. *Public school,* kula aupuni. *To lay before the public,* hōʻike ākea, hoʻākea, hōʻike i mua o ka lehulehu. *To take a public stand,* kū ākea.

publican. Luna ʻauhau.

publication. Puke i paʻi ʻia, paʻi ʻana.

publicity. Hoʻolaha, hoʻolaulaha. *Publicity seeker,* imi hoʻokaulana.

publicize. Hoʻolaulaha, hoʻokū ākea, paʻēpaʻē.

publicly. Laulā, ākea.

publish. Paʻi, hoʻolaha. *Who published the book?* Na wai i paʻi i ka puke?

publisher. Mea paʻi, luna hoʻopuka.

publishing house. Hale paʻi.

pucker. Puku, puʻu. *Also:* mōkio, liki, ʻānuhenuhe, hoʻoʻiʻika, hōʻekekeʻi. *To pucker the lips,* puʻu ka waha, minoi, mīnoinoi, kaniuli. *To pucker and unpucker the lips,* piolo.

pudding. Pūkini *(Eng.). Kinds of Hawaiian puddings:* haupia, ʻaʻahokau *(coconut cream and cornstarch, formerly arrowroot);* kūlolo, piele *(taro, sweet potato, yam, banana, breadfruit with coconut cream);* pālau, kōʻelepālau *(sweet potato and coconut cream);* haukō *(arrowroot, coconut cream, sugar-cane juice).*

puddle. Kiʻo. *Also:* hāloko, lahalaha wai, hāpuna. *Puddles,* māloʻi, lokoloko. *Mud puddle,* kiʻo lepo, āloʻi.

Pueblo. Puepelo, Puebelo.

Puerto Rican, Puerto Rico, Porto Rico. Pokoliko, Poto Riko.

puff. Haʻu, haʻuhaʻu, nui ka hanu, puhi; ʻumoʻumoki *(as on a cigar or pipe);* hakuʻi *(as smoke);* uhāuhā *(as a dog or wind);* — *sonorously,* ʻūhīʻūhā; — *for breath,* nae, naenae; — *out,* puhaʻu, ʻolopū, nunu. *Puff of smoke,* pōpō uahi.

puffer fish. Ākēkē, ʻoʻopu hue, puʻuōlaʻi.

puffin. ʻAʻo. *See saying,* **ʻaʻo.**

pug dog. ʻĪlio koki.

pugilist. Kuʻi lima, mokomoko, kualapehu.

pugnacious. Puni hakakā.

pug nose. Ihu kū, kekeko, keko, nūkoki.

"puka shells." *See* **lei pūpū puka.**

pull. Huki; — *up,* uhuki, ʻunuʻunu; — *obliquely,* kiwi; — *away from,* nanahuki; — *back steadily, as a line,* ʻawala; — *taut, as a fishline,* kōmi; — *along,* kaualakō, alakō; — *hard or frequently,* huhuki, uhuki, hukihuki; — *together,* huki like, ʻunu; — *away, as in anger,* oi; — *out, as hairs or beard,* muʻo koli, melu, ʻōhuʻi; — *down, as eyelid,* hoʻohelei, helei *(a sign of contempt). Also:* kō, kōkō, lolia, hulei, pane, uhu, ʻuʻu, ʻumi, ue, koi, alaʻume; kolo *(as a seine);* ʻāʻili, kaʻi *(as weeds). To pull opening of the net,* hukia ka waha o ka ʻupena. *To pull on a paddle,* kā i ka hoe. *Pull a tooth,* huki i ka niho.

pullet. Piopio moa wahine, ohi moa wahine, ʻouo.

pulley. Kaʻa, pokakaʻa.

pulling. Hukina, kāʻiliʻili.

pulp. ʻIʻo, pahē *(of fruit). Reduced to a pulp,* paluhē.

pulpit. ʻĀwai.

pulsate. Pana, koni, konikoni, panau.

pulse. Pana, aʻa koni, aʻalele. *To take the pulse,* nānā i ka pana.

pulverize. Hoʻōkaoka, hoʻopē, hōʻae, hoʻopuhalu.

pulverized. Palahē, pīhelehele, paluhē; punapuna *(rare). See bait.*

pumice. ʻAna, ʻana ōlaʻi, ōlaʻi, huleʻia. *Also:* hāpou, lei ole, au, hoʻōne, hau; ʻana ʻalaea *(red);* ōahi *(pink);* elehu *(ash-colored).*

pummel. Kuʻi pehi, hākuʻi. *See* **saddle horn.**

pump. Pauma. *Water pump,* pauma wai. *Bilge pump,* omo liu.

pumpkin. Palaʻai, ipu pū, pū. *See* **pie.** *Pumpkin-bellied,* ʻōpū palaʻai. *Pumpkin poi,* poi palaʻai.

pun. Hoʻopili ʻōlelo ʻano like. *See ex.,* **hoi 1, pulu 5.**

Puna. Puna. *See* **carefully, kava, pandanus, perfume, sea,** *UL 104.*

punch. 1. *Strike.* Kuʻi, kuʻina, kukuʻi. *Paper punch,* pāniki. *Metal punch,* hao pana. *Punch doubly hard,* kuʻi lua, hiu i ka puʻupuʻu. 2. *Beverage.* Mea inu; wai hua ʻai *(fruit).*

punctual. Kū i ka manawa kūpono.

punctuate. Hoʻokomo kiko.

punctuation. Kiko. *Punctuation mark,* kiko, kaha; kiko hoʻomaha *(indicative of a pause). Manual of punctuation,* aʻo kiko.

puncture. Puka, ʻou; kū i ke kui *(as a tire punctured by a nail);* moku *(as a cut tire).*

punish. Hoʻopaʻi; pāniki *(rare).*

punk. Lāʻau pauka makika *(for mosquitoes).*

punning. Hoʻopilipili ʻōlelo. *See* **pun.**

puny. ʻUkiki, ʻōwali, ʻōmali, palakai, hōmī, hīnawenawe, holili, hua liʻi.

pup, puppy. ʻĪlio keiki.

pupil. 1. *Scholar.* Haumana, haumāna. *New pupil,* haumana komo hou. *Head pupil in a hula school,* poʻopuaʻa. 2. *Part of eye.* ʻŌnohi maka, kuʻi ʻōnohi. *Dark pupil of the eye,* kāhiwa uli *(rare).*

purchase. Mea kūʻai. *To purchase,* kūʻai mai. *Purchased,* lilo.

pure. Maʻemaʻe. *Also:* hemolele, huali, ʻano lani, aʻiaʻi, pōlani. *Pure-blooded,* piha. *Pure Hawaiian,* Hawaiʻi piha.

purgative. Lāʻau nahā, pakelo. *See* **laxative, medicine.** *Among the plants listed by Blaisdell used as purgatives are* ʻākia, ʻaloe, hala, hau, ʻilima, ipu ʻawaʻawa, kāʻeʻe, kaliko, kalo, koali ʻawa, kuawa, kukui, maiʻa, moa, pānini ʻawaʻawa, pilikai, pōhuehue. *To act as a purgative,* nahā. *Purgatives:* kūkapihe, welo, hoʻoilo.

purgatory. Lua ahi hoʻomaʻemaʻe, kahi hoʻomaʻemaʻe, pulekakoli.

purge. 1. *Biblical.* Hoʻomaʻemaʻe *(Oihn. 2.34.5),* huikala *(Hal. 51.7)*, holoi *(Ezek. 20.38)*. **2.** *Of bowels.* Ho'o-hī, hī, hahu, hahuhahu, hehu, haha, ho'ohahu, lele wai.

purification. Ho'oma'ema'e 'ana. *See* **purify.** *Purification day,* lā huikala. *Purification festivities,* hi'uwai.

purify. Ho'oma'ema'e. *Also:* huikala, lele uli; ho'opapa *(as a woman after childbirth);* — *with water,* lele wai, hāwai, kai 'ōlena; — *with salt water,* kapu kai, kapukapu kai, pī kai, pī kai 'ōlena, pī kai kea.

Puritan. Pulikana.

purity. Ma'ema'e.

purlin. 'Aho. *Main house purlin,* ke'a, 'ahopueo. *Horizontal purlin,* 'ahokele. *Thatch support purlin,* 'a'aho, 'ahopi'o kuahui, 'ahohui.

purple. Poni, māku'e. *See* **lavender.** *Purplish-blue (as sea, clouds),* pōpolohua.

purpose. Kumu. *Also:* mea, pono, mākia, hope. *One purpose, person of fixed purpose,* kiakahi. *To go without purpose,* hele wale.

purr. Nonolo, nīao.

purse. 1. *Bag.* 'Eke'eke, 'eke'eke pa'a lima, 'eke kālā, 'a'a moni, hīpu'u, paiki. **2.** *See* **pucker.**

purser. Kupakako *(ship).*

purslane. Po'e, 'ākulikuli kula.

pursue. Hahai, hai, alualu. *Also:* hiu *(with energy);* uhai ā holo *(swiftly);* kauholo *(to harm). See saying,* pī-'oe'oe.

pursuit. 'Āha'i 'ana.

pus. Palahēhē.

push. Pahu; — *along,* ne'e, pane'e, ne'ene'e; — *with elbows and shoulders,* kuke kū, ku'e, ho'oku'eku'e; — *over,* kula'i, kūna'i, ho'opalaha, kūna'ina, kula'ina; — *up,* peu *(but see* **push-up***);* — *aside,* pale, lū, ho'okē,

ho'okō, hu'e a'e, uai, papalena, ku'eku'ena; — *with a pole,* ko'o. *Also:* papahu, pāuma, uma, hu'e, ho'ohakē, kē, ho'okē, kō, kōkō; lale, ho'olale *(urge);* naku, nakunaku *(as through mud);* ho'oko'oko'o, hou, kula'ilua, kuke, 'onou. *To push ahead, regardless of consequences,* 'onou po'o, oko.

pushcart. Ka'a pahu.

pushing. Hu'ena; pahuna *(as a spear);* kula'ina *(over). Jerky pushing motion,* helo.

push-up. Ko'o lima.

put. Kau *(for various uses, see* kau 1*);* — *on, as clothes,* komo, komo lole, komo ā pa'a, 'a'ahu; kā'ai *(as armor);* — *out, as a fire,* kinai, ho'opio; — *down,* waiho, ho'oku'u, ku'u; — *up,* kūkulu; — *in,* ho'okomo, ho'okomokomo, 'ō'ō, ho'ō, hahao; — *forward,* kaupē; — *together,* ho'opili, uhaku; — *on wrong,* komohewa; komo humuhumu *(inside out);* — *aside, as for safekeeping,* ho'āhu; kīloa *(rare). Put out fires,* kinai ahi. *Put on a hat,* pāpale, kau pāpale. *Put on glasses,* kāpili makaaniani. *Put out a light,* kinai i ke kukui. *Put on the light,* hō'ā i ke kukui.

putrid. Pilau, palahō.

putty. Pake.

puzzle. Ho'opohihihi, ho'opāha'oha'o, nane, pā'ani kohokoho.

puzzled. Kāhāhā, kūnānā, ha'oha'o. *To make puzzled,* ho'oha'oha'o.

puzzling. Ho'onanenane, ha'oha'o, pāha'oha'o.

pyelitis. Kīkala hāne'ene'e.

pygarg. Kikona.

pyorrhea. Waina. *Medicine for pyorrhea,* kuakala.

pyramid. Pū'o'a, pelamika, pa'a'ili hā *(old term). Pyramid of Egypt,* pu'u pelamika o 'Aikupika.

Q

q. *No Hawaiian term.*

quack. Kakā.

quadrangle. Huinahā, huinahā like 'ole, huinahā lua like.

quadrilateral. Huinahā.

quadrille dance. Ho'owilimo'o.

quadruplets. Hānau pāhā.

quagga. Kuaka.

quail. Manu kapalulu. *Rare:* kakakō, kēlū, pau'aka.

quaint. 'Ano 'ē. *See* **old-fashioned.**

quake. Ha'alulu, naue, naka, kualakai, kūhulukū. *See* **earthquake.** *The earth quakes,* nei ke 'ōla'i.

Quaker. Kueka.

qualifications. Nā mea e kūpono ai; nā ho'okūpono 'ana.

qualified. Mākaukau, kūpono.

quality. 'Ano, kūlana. *Poor quality,* 'ano maika'i 'ole; kakakē *(rare). Moral qualities,* pono.

qualmish. Pāma'i, poluea.

quantity. Nui. *Also:* kuaniki, pu'u. *Great quantities,* laupa'i, 'a'ole i laua aku, 'a'ole o kana mai, ā hewa. *Small quantity,* 'a'ohe nui, lihi, iki.

quarantine. Ho'omalu ma'i. *Quarantine station,* hale ho'omalu. *Animal quarantine station,* wahi ho'omalu holoholona.

quarrel. Ho'opa'apa'a, paio, pāonioni, pāoni, kū'ē'ē, pā'ume'ume, hukihuki, hakakā, hākā 'ōlelo. *Also:* 'āpuni, pa'apa'a, kāmoko.

quarrelsome. Nanā, ihu nanā; kole ka waha *(see* **kole***);* nahunahuihu, kāpēke'u, wawa'u.

quarry. Lua 'eli pōhaku, lua ko'i *(adze).*

quart. Kuaka.

quarter. Hapahā; koaka *(rare). Quarter to five,* hapahā i koe, kani ka hola 'elima.

quarterly. Hapahā. *Quarterly report,* hō'ike hapahā.

quartermaster. Kūhoe.

quarter note. Po'o'ele.

quartet. Pū'ulu hīmeni pāhā, leokū pāhā.

quavering. Ha'alulu, ha'iha'i.

quay. Uwapo, uapo.

Quebec. Kuipeka, Kuibeka.

queen. Mō'ī wahine, ali'i wahine, kuini; wahine *(in playing cards).*

queen bee. Nalo meli mō'ī wahine.

queer. 'Ano 'ē. *See* **homosexual** *for slang usage.*

quench. Kinai.

quenched. Kena, kinai 'ia.

query. Ui, nīnau.

question. Nīnau, ui. *To question repeatedly,* ninaninau, nīele, neno. *To ask a leading question,* nīnau pākākā. *To question indirectly,* ho'ohuahualau, ho'onīnau.

question mark. Kiko nīnau.

questionnaire. Palapala ninaninau, pepa ho'opihapiha, pa'i hakahaka.

quick. 'Āwīwī, koke, māmā, wiki, wikiwiki, wawe, hikiwawe, 'eleu, 'emo 'ole, alawiki. *Also:* ala-, miki, 'āwiki, 'ākepa, 'akeu, hue, ka'uka'u lua 'ole, kāholo,

alapine, alapinepine, elemimo, alamimo, lauahi, ho'okanahē, kō'ala, kō'ala'ala, ālulu, ulele, akeake, 'akakē, 'e'ea, puahia, muku, panehū, panale'a, na'ena'e. *To learn quickly,* 'a'apo. *To make off with quickly,* mio, miomio, alamio.

quicksand. One pohō, one mimiki.

quicksilver. Waikāla, heu.

quick step. Hele wiki.

quick-tempered. Huhū wale, pōkole ka na'au, na'au pōkole, lelepī, nonohuwā, pīkananā, pīkanalā, ioiole'a. *See* **hot.**

quick time. Hele wiki.

quiet. 1. *Quality.* Mālie, ho'omālie, hilu, wailana, malu, maluhia, ho'omalu, ho'ola'i, la'i, pohu, malino. *Also:* kuapapa, nihi, kaulana, hālana, ōpūhea, ku'inehe, kuakapu, la'ikū, palanehe, kōnale, kāpehe, kūpalaiki, haumalu, maialile, no'eno'e, mimo, miha, hāmiha, mahū, pū. *To move quietly,* hele mālie, nihi ka hele, ka'a niau. *To do quietly,* hana mālie, kakakihi. *Wierdly quiet,* ano, ku'inehe. *To think quietly,* lana mālie ka mana'o. *To keep quiet,* noho mālie. *Quiet sea,* kai malino, mālie ke kai, kai kū. *Be quiet!* Kulikuli! **2.** *Transitive.* Ho'onā, ho'onānā, ho'omalimali, ho'oma'alili.

quieted. Akaku'u, nā. *See* **quiet.**

quill. Hulu, hulu kākau *(for writing).*

quills. Wanawana.

quilt. Kapa kuiki; kapa 'āpana, kapa lau *(with appliquéd designs);* kapa pulu *(padded);* kapa pohopoho, kapa poho *(patchwork, crazy);* kīhei pili, kapa pili *(lined). Base of quilt on which pattern is appliquéd,* kahua, honua. *Poles used in quilt making,* kua. *To quilt,* kuiki. *Quilt patterns or designs,* lau, kuiki. *For names of designs see* **kuiki.** *Other designs:* hae-Hawai'i, hala kahiki, kua-honu, kuli-pu'u, laia, makani-kā'ili-aloha, niho-wili-hemo, pika-waiohinu, 'ulu-hua-i-ka-hāpapa *(see* **'ulu***). To follow designs in quilting,* kuiki lau. *To quilt in a direction away from the quilter,* ho'opi'ipi'i. *To finish a space in a quilt,* ho'opaepae.

quintet. Pū'ulu hīmeni pālima, kuinikeke.

quintuplet. Hānau pālima.

quit. Ha'alele, waiho. *Quit it!* Uoki! *To quit work,* ha'alele i ka hana; 'olohani.

quitclaim. Palapala ho'olilo.

quite. Nō, wale. *Quite good,* maika'i nō, maika'i wale.

quiver. 1. *Shake.* Kapalili, ha'alulu, naka, kualakai, lī'ō, lule, lulelule, hālulelule. *Also:* ha'ukeke, 'api, pilu, 'olokā. **2.** *Arrow case,* 'A'a pua.

quiz. Hō'ike pōkole, nīnau hō'ike, nīele, ho'onīele, ho'ohuahualau.

quoits. Kilu, 'ume.

quorum. Hapa nui, kolamu.

quota. Mahele *(share);* ka mea i makemake 'ia, ka heluna i makemake 'ia *(desired quantity).*

quotation. Ka mea i 'ōlelo 'ia, 'ōlelo.

quotation marks. Kauna koma.

quote. 'Ōlelo, wahi.

quotient. Helu puka.

R

r. *No Hawaiian term.*
rabbet. ʻAi kepa.
rabbi. Lapi, rabi.
rabbit. Lāpaki, ʻiole lāpaki. *See* hare.
raccoon. Lakuna.
race. 1. *People.* Lāhui. 2. *Contest.* Heihei. *See* canoe race, foot race, horse race, sack race. *Goal or starting place of race,* pahu, pahukū. *Swimming race,* heihei ʻau. *Race with a burden,* heihei hāʻawe. *To practice racing,* hoʻokāholoholo, kōheʻe.
race horse. Lio heihei.
race prejudice. Hoʻokae ʻili, kaupale ʻili.
race track. Kahua heihei, lina heihei, lina.
racial. Lāhui.
rack. Haka, holopapa; heke *(for hanging);* oleole *(for storage);* haka kaulaʻi *(for drying);* kau mōkoi *(for fish poles).*
racket. Hana kuli, wawā, ʻuwā, halulu. *See* tennis racket.
raconteur. Kākāʻōlelo.
radiant. Mālamalama, ʻālohilohi, ʻōlinolino, ʻula.
radiate. Puka mai, puaʻi mai, kukuna, wanaoʻa. *To radiate happiness,* puka mai ka hauʻoli.
radical. Kūlike ʻole me ka mea maʻamau.
radio. Lekiō.
radio broadcast. Hoʻolele leo.
radio broadcasting station. Kahua hoʻolele leo.
radiogram. Kelekalapa, kelekalama.
radius. Kahahānai, kukuna.
radix. Lakika.
raffle. Lūlū.
raft. Huinalāʻaulana, huinapapalana.
rafter. Kua, oʻa. *Head of rafter,* pōheoheo. *Neck at rafter end,* pauʻakaʻaka.
rag. Welu, kapa peʻa. *Heap of rags,* puʻu welu.
rage, raging. Huhū loa, piʻi ka huhū wela loa, inaina, hae, ʻena, ʻenaʻena, ʻoʻolokū, pīkananā, pīkanalā, kūpikiʻō. *Rare:* ʻulupā, kuapuʻe, hekili, kū kākalaioa, āulu, kahu, puoko, kuke kū. *See saying.* hoahoa.
ragged. Weluwelu, pāwelu, ʻāwelu, welu.
raid. Pākaha, hoʻouka kaua. *Air raid,* pākaha mai ka lewa.
rail. 1. *Bar.* Pale, kaola, kālele; pale kai *(of a vessel);* ʻaʻaho *(fence). See* railing. 2. *Bird.* Moho, mohoea.
railing. Pale. *Porch railing,* pale lānai.
railroad. Kaʻaahi. *Railroad track.* alahao.
rain. Ua. *See sayings that are tributes to rain* (ʻāpaʻa, ʻehu 4, kāhiko) *and other poetic references* (lū lehua, poʻi 1, pūʻukiʻuki). *See* Kū-lani-hākoi, ua, downpour, Hilo, *and chant,* lolohe 1. *In poetry, rain or rains may signify joy, life, growth, greenery; good fortune (light rains, mist); grief, sorrow, and tears (heavy rains); the presence of gods or royalty, sexual relations, beauty; hardship. Fine light rain (much beloved),* kili, hoʻokili, kilihune, lilinoe, kili noe, līhau, kilikili noe, kilikilioe, kili nahe, uaoa. *Light moving rain,* koʻiawe. *Fine windblown rain,* lelehuna, lelehune, lele ua, leleaka. *Chilly rain,* kili hau, ua ʻawa. *Rain spray,* ehu. *Showery rain,* ua nāulu, pākiʻo, pākiʻokiʻo. *Drenching rain,* ua hōʻeʻele. *The bitter rain,* ka ua ʻawa *(of grief, tragedy, hardship). Rain downpour,* ua lani pili, ua loku. *Continuous rain,* ua hoʻokina, pīpīnoke. *Rain with large drops,* ua hekili, pakakū. *Slanting rain,* ua hikikiʻi. *Unexpected rain,* ililani. *Rainbow-hued rain,* uakoko, koʻiʻula. *Spring rain,* kuāua hope, *latter rain,* kuāua hope *(Biblical). Rain gauge,* ana ua. *Heiau with offerings for rain,* heiau hoʻoulu ua. *Thunder without

rain,* hekili pāmalō. *Darkness of rain,* ʻeleua. *Hilo is famous for rain, as in this saying:* ʻeleʻele Hilo, panopano i ka ua, *Hilo is black, dark with rain (hardship, grief, trouble). Many rains are named, usually associated with particular places, some on the same island and some on different islands. Some winds and rains have the same name (as* Kani-koʻo, Kīpuʻupuʻu, Lauʻawaʻawa, Līlī-lehua, *and probably* Moaniani-lehua); *winds seem to bring the rains. Of the rains identified with islands, 15 are on Oʻahu, 12 on Maui, 9 on Hawaiʻi, and 4 on Kauaʻi. They are nearly always in wet coastal areas (except Lahaina), and almost none in the uninhabited wet areas. The* lehua *flower is associated with rain and occurs in six of the rains listed here.*

RAINS COMMONLY MENTIONED IN CHANTS AND SONGS *(meanings that are obvious, associated places, and name variations are in parentheses):* ʻĀpua-kea *(Koʻolau Poko, Oʻahu),* Kani-lehua *(lehua sounding; Hilo),* Kinai-lehua *(quenching lehua; Pana-ʻewa, Hawaiʻi),* Kīpuʻupuʻu *(Wai-mea, Hawaiʻi), also a wind,* Laniha-ʻahaʻa *(low heavens; Hāna, Maui),* Mololani *(well-kept; Kaha-lu-u, Oʻahu),* Tuahine *or* Kuahine *(sister; Mānoa, Oʻahu),* Waʻahila *(Mānoa and Nu-ʻu-anu, Oʻahu).*

OTHER RAINS: Heʻe-nehu (nehu *fish run; Hilo),* Hehipua-hala *(stepping on pandanus flowers; Poʻo-kū, Kauaʻi),* Hōliʻoliʻo *(or* Hōliʻo; *Hawaiʻi and Oʻahu),* Kaʻau *(Kohala, Hawaiʻi),* Kaʻele-loli *(or* Kaʻekelo; *Makiki, Oʻahu),* Kani-koʻo *(cane tapping, with Koʻolau wind),* Kini-maka-lehua *(many lehua),* Kiʻo-wao *(upland; Nu-ʻu-anu, Oʻahu, and Wai-ʻaleʻale, Kauaʻi),* Kui-ʻilima *(Honolulu),* Kūkala-hale *(Honolulu), also wind name,* Lani-paʻina *(crackling heavens;* ʻUlu-palakua, *Maui),* Lēhei *(leaping; Maka-wao, Maui),* Lena *(yellow; Maui and Hanalei, Kauaʻi),* Līlī-lehua *(lehua chill; Pālolo, Oʻahu; and Wai-ehu, Maui),* Lū-lau-kō *(scattering cane leaves; Kauaʻi),* Maka-lau-koa, Malu-koʻi *(Kaha-lu-u, Oʻahu),* Moaniani-lehua *(wafted lehua fragrance; Puna, Hawaiʻi),* Moe-lehua *(sleeping lehua),* Nōweo-ʻula *(red brightness; Nā-pili, Maui),* Ōnini-puaʻiʻo *(Hāna, Maui),* Pali-loa *(long cliff),* Papa-wai *(Olo-walu, Maui),* Paʻū-pili *(moistening pili grass; Lahaina, Maui),* Peʻe-pā-pōhaku *(hide* [*at*] *stone wall; Kau-pō, Maui),* Peʻe-pūhala-hīnano *(hiding pandanus male flowers),* Pili-nahe, Pō-ʻai-hala *(surrounding pandanus; Kaha-lu-u, Oʻahu; also* Pōʻai-hale, Poʻo-kole, Poʻo-lipilipi *(adze-head; Kalihi, Oʻahu, and Hilo),* Poʻo-nui *(big head),* Pōpō-kapa *(tapa bundle; also* Pōpō-ua, *rain bundle),* Pūnāwai-ea *(rain spray),* Pupū-hale *(remaining near house; Hāmākua, Hawaiʻi),* Ua-a-ka-līpoa *(rain of the* līpoa *seaweed),* Ua-ma-ka-lau-koa *(rain on koa leaves; Nu-ʻu-anu, Oʻahu),* ʻUla-lena *(yellow red; Kaʻala mountain, Oʻahu and Haʻi-kū, Maui), also a wind.*

rain belt. Māʻau.
rainbow. Ānuenue. *Fig.:* ao akua, haka ʻula a Kāne. *See* alaea 1, arch. *The rainbow symbolized the presence of gods or chiefs. Rainbow fragment,* ʻōnohi, ʻōnohi ʻula, pūloʻu, ala muku. *Greenish rainbow,* hakahakaea *(rare). Earth-clinging rainbow,* uakoko, lehopulu. *Standing rainbow shaft,* kāhili. *Rainbow around sun or moon,* luahoano, luakālai, luakālai lani. *Rainbow-sparkling rainbow,* uakoko. *Lunar rainbow,* ānuenue kau pō; pō mākole *(night of lunar rainbow). Barely visible rainbow,* punakea.
rainbow runner. Kamanu *(a fish).*

raincoat. Kuka ua, kuka ʻaila, kukaweke. *Old kind of ti-leaf raincoat or cape,* ʻahu lāʻī, ʻahu ua, kapa ua, kui lāʻī.
raindrops. Paka ua, paka, kili, kikili, hākikili.
rain forest. Maʻukele, wao kele, māʻau.
rain spray. Noe, ua noe; lelehuna (lelehune, *wind-blown*).
rain tree. ʻŌhai.
rain water. Wai lani, wai hua, huawaimaka.
rainy. Ua, ʻōuaua; pahululu *(rare).*
rainy season. Wā ua, hoʻoilo, laʻa ua.
raise. 1. *Lift.* Hāpai, pai, ea, ʻaʻe, aea. *Also:* hoʻāla, kaʻikaʻi, hulei, amoamo, aukū, moala. *To raise a bet,* kaleʻoa. 2. *Bring up a child.* Hānai.
raisin. Hua waina maloʻo.
rake. Kope, ʻōʻō kope, kope ahi, kope lehu, mākoe, māhelu, maheu.
Raleigh. Lalei, Ralei.
rally. Hālāwai hōʻeuʻeu; haʻikūumauma *(rare).*
ram. 1. *Sheep.* Hipa kāne. 2. *Shove.* Hou, pahu, kipi, ʻōhelo.
ramble. ʻAuana; *to — verbally,* puaʻohi, ʻohipua; kiʻilau *(rare). Also:* lanaau, hiliau, kākele, kākākiʻi.
ramie. Lamie.
ramrod. ʻŌhelo, helo, nīʻau.
ranch. Wahi hānai holoholona, wahi hānai pipi; kuleana *(small holding).*
rancher. Kahu pipi *(cattle).*
rancid. ʻĪʻī, palanioa, polopolona, palani; puleipulu *(rare). See* **smell.**
random. Wale. *To read at random,* heluhelu kaulele. *To select at random,* ʻohi kaulele.
randy. Ake hoʻoipoipo, piha kuko, makeʻe ai. *See* **concupiscent, lustful.**
rank. 1. *Grade.* Kūlana, kiʻekiʻe, papa. *High rank,* kūlana aliʻi, kūlana kiʻekiʻe, hulinuʻu, leʻolani *(see sayings,* **kamahele, mānoanoa.***) Low rank,* kūlana haʻahaʻa, kupaliʻi, ʻalu. *To marry a close relative in order to increase rank of offspring,* hoʻi. *To claim high rank,* piʻikoi. *To arrange by rank,* noho papa. 2. *Formation.* Lālani, papa, papa poʻo, hunalewa. *To stand in ranks,* kūkū papa. 3. *Of growth.* Uluāhewa, ulu nui, hanahihi, hihia; ʻohaohala *(rare). See* **lush.**
ransack. Kuekaʻa. *Cf.* **plunder.**
ransom. Hoʻōla pānaʻi, ola pānaʻi, uku pānaʻi, kumu pānaʻi, kumu hoʻōla, kūʻai hoʻōla, kalahala.
rant. Nuku, wawaha, hoʻonui ʻōlelo, waha kole, ʻolēʻolē, kūkahalakē. *See saying,* **bristle.** *Shameless ranting,* nuku hilahila ʻole.
rap. Kīkē, kīkēkē, kīkoni; ʻukē *(rare).*
rapacious. Hao wale, ʻālunu, ʻānunu, ʻānulu, nunu; ʻenuhe *(fig.).*
rape. Puʻe, puʻe wale.
rape victim. Lolokukui *(rare).*
rapid. *See* **fast.**
rapt. Lilo i ka hoʻolohe, nanea i ka hoʻolohe.
rare. 1. *Infrequent.* Kakaʻikahi, ʻaʻole hana mau ʻia, laha ʻole, mea laha ʻole. *Also:* hihiu, pānoanoa, malihini. 2. *Underdone.* Moʻa iki, moʻa maka, moʻa hapa, moʻa kolekole, hoʻokolekole, kokoko *(as steak),* pala, makali.
Rarotonga. Lalakoʻa. *Cf. Gram. 2.9.4.*
rascal. Kolohe, kupuʻeu, ʻeu, ʻāpiki. *See* **idiom, parrot fish.**
rash. 1. *Bold.* ʻAʻa makehewa, ʻakūʻakū. 2. *Of skin.* ʻŌhune. *Heat rash,* ʻōhune wela.
rasp. Hole, apuapu, walu, ʻuwalu, waluhia, waluwalu, waʻu, uwaʻu, waʻuwaʻu, wawalu; ʻiʻi *(sound in chanting).*
raspberry. ʻĀkala, kala, ʻākalakala, ōlaʻa.
rat. ʻIole. *Large rat,* ʻiole nui, ʻiole poʻo wai. *See* **ratlike** *and sayings,* **piko pau ʻiole, pebble.** *Food left by rats,* pāʻiole. *Rat shooting,* pana ʻiole *(with bow and arrow). Blurred eyes of a rat,* haumakaʻiole *(of old age).*
rate. Helu, ana, nui. *See* **price.** *Interest rate,* helu kuala.
rather. 1. *Quite.* ʻAno. 2. *Prefer.* ʻOi aʻe ka makemake.
ratification. ʻĀpono ʻana.

ratify. ʻĀpono.
rating. Kūlana, papa.
ratio. Lakio.
ration. Kaupalena, hāʻawi kaupalena. *Also:* maukoli, kīhau.
rational. Maikaʻi ka noʻonoʻo, noʻonoʻo kūpono, aokanaka.
rations. Ō *(sea rations).*
ratlike. Hōʻiole, ʻioʻiole *(fig., steal, cheat).*
rat terrier. ʻĪlio ʻiole.
rattle. Koʻele, nakeke, hoʻonakeke, nakulu, haluku, kapa, ʻulīʻulī. *See* **rattles.**
rattlebox. Pikakani.
rattlepod. Kūkaehoki.
rattles. Pūʻili *(bamboo);* ʻulīʻulī *(gourd).*
rattlesnake. Naheka huelo kani.
rattrap. ʻŪpiki ʻiole, ʻūmiʻi ʻiole.
ravage. Luku, hao wale, hoʻoneoneo, apu, humuhumu, hākuma.
rave. *See* **rant.**
raven. Kolaka.
ravenous. Hae ka puʻu.
ravine. Kahawai, awaawa, awāwa, ʻōpaka, ʻaʻalu, ʻalu, pūʻali; *deep —,* kūhohō. *Many ravines,* ʻōlapalapa.
ravish. Puʻe, lima ikaika.
raw. Maka, makamaka; kole, kolekole *(as meat);* mūkole *(inflamed). Almost raw,* moʻa maka. *Raw fish,* iʻa maka; kualakai *(rare).*
rawness. Kolekole; hela *(of skin). See* **raw.**
ray. 1. *Spoke.* Kukuna, wana, manamana. *Rays of the sun,* kukuna o ka lā. 2. *Fish.* Hīhīmanu, hailepo *(sting ray);* hāhālua *(manta).*
raze. Kuʻikē, hoʻohiolo, ʻulupā. *See* **demolish.**
razor. Pahi ʻumiʻumi, pahi kahi, pahi āmū.
razorback. Kua kulilipi *(as of a pig).*
re. 1. *Regarding.* E pili ana. 2. *Note in music.* Kō.
re-. Hou. *Cf.* **recount 2.**
reach. Hiki, kū, loaʻa *(arrive at);* pā, ʻō, kaʻa, huki; *to — out, extend,* lālau, kīkoʻo, māʻaʻā, oni; *to — up or high,* hoʻōeoe, kela; *to — in,* hoʻō; *to — far for,* koʻokoʻona; *to — around,* apo; *to — the summit,* niʻo; *to — a goal,* kūkawowo. *To reach a house,* hiki i ka hale; loaʻa ka hale; hoʻea i ka hale.
read. Heluhelu. *To read in turn,* heluhelu kaʻahele.
reader. Mea heluhelu, poʻe heluhelu *(person);* puke heluhelu, aʻo heluhelu *(book). Reader of omens,* kilo.
ready. Mākaukau. *Also:* kū, liuliu, ʻeʻea. *Get ready,* hoʻomākaukau, i kū.
ready-made. Paʻa mua *(clothes).*
real. Maoli, ʻiʻo, ʻoiaʻiʻo.
real estate. Waiwai paʻa. *Real estate business,* ʻoihana kūʻai ʻāina.
realize. Hoʻomaopopo, maopopo.
really. ʻĀ ʻoia, oia, ʻiʻo, maoli. *Not really?* ʻAʻohe ʻiʻo hoʻi?
realm. Aupuni, ao.
ream. ʻĀpā.
reap. ʻOhi *(as grain).*
rear. 1. *Back.* Hope, kua. *Rear of an army, rear guard,* hunapaʻa. 2. *Raise, as a child.* Hānai. *One who helps rear a child,* mea nāna i luhi. *One who rears a child,* kahu mānai, i kū. 3. *As a horse.* ʻŌwala, wala kua, ʻokūʻokū.
rear admiral. Liaʻakimalala.
reason. Kumu, mea, kuleana, kau. *Without reason,* wale, honua, kumu ʻole. *For this reason,* no ia mea, no laila. *For what reason,* aha, no ke aha, no ke kumu hea.
reasonable. 1. *Sensible.* Kaulike ka noʻonoʻo. 2. *Not expensive.* Makepono.
rebel. Kipi, keʻehi, kīmopō, kūʻē aupuni, ʻāpua.
rebellion. Kipi.
rebirth. Hānau hou.
reborn. Hānau hou.
rebuke. Nuku, huhū; pukapai *(mildly).*
rebuked. Pā i ka leo.
rebuttal. Hōʻike pākuʻi.
recall. Hoʻomanaʻo. *Also:* hāʻupu, hāʻupuʻupu, hoʻo-

hā'upu, hō'upu'upu, haili, hali'a, hāli'ali'a, ho'o-no'ono'o, ho'omaopopo; kāwelewele *(something for-gotten);* mali'a.

recede. Emi, ho'i i hope, laumeki, mū'ekeke'i, nioke.

receipt. Palapala ho'oka'a, likiki ho'oka'a, palapala loa'a.

receipts. Loa'a.

receive. Loa'a mai. *To receive guests,* ho'okipa malihini. *To receive without giving,* maua.

recent. Hou.

recently. 'Ānō iho nei.

receptacle. Waihona. *Also:* wa'a, kino, poho, haona.

reception. Kipa 'ana. *Wedding reception,* pā'ina male. *Royal reception,* anaina 'ike ali'i.

receptionist. Mea kia'i ke'ena hana *(of an office).*

reception room. Lumi ho'oluana.

recess. Ho'omalolo.

recession. Au nele.

recipe. Lula no ke kuke 'ana.

recipient. Haka, ilina.

reciprocal proportion. Lakio like huli hope.

reciprocate, reciprocity. Pāna'i.

Reciprocity Treaty. Ku'ikahi Pāna'i Like.

recite. Ha'i walewaha mai, kuku'i 'ōlelo, heluhelu. *To recite in order,* helu papa. *To recite first lines of a stanza, by the dancer,* kāhea. *To recite rhythmically, as Bible passages,* ho'āeae.

reckless. 'A'a no'ono'o 'ole, nānā 'ole i ka pono, ho'o-ponopono 'ole. *To run recklessly,* holo pūpule.

reckoning. Helu, no'ono'o.

recline. Kāmoe, momoe.

recognition. Ho'omaopopo, 'ike. *Recognition token,* hō'ailona.

recognize. Ho'omaopopo, 'ike, 'i'ike. *To recognize at sight,* ho'okū'ike. *To recognize one another,* 'ike aku, 'ike mai. *To fail to recognize,* ho'ohewahewa; hōla'o *(rare).*

recoil. Kuemi; pinau *(rare).*

recollect. *See* **recall.**

recommend. 'Āpono.

recommendation. Kāko'o *(support). Letter of recom-mendation,* palapala kāko'o, palapala 'āpono.

recompense. Uku. *To go without recompense,* hele wale.

reconcile. Ho'oku'ikahi, 'uao.

reconnoiter. Ho'omakākiu, hākilo.

record. 1. *Account.* Mo'olelo. *Continuous record,* kua-mo'o 'ōlelo. *Congressional record,* mo'olelo 'aha'ōlelo lāhui. *To record a story,* ho'opa'a mo'olelo. *To keep a record,* ho'opa'a mana'o. *To record a voice,* 'apo leo. *To record music,* ho'opa'a mele. **2.** *Phonograph.* Pā, pā ho'okani. **3.** *See* **best.**

recorder. Kākau inoa, kākau mo'olelo, kākau hana; mīkini 'apo leo *(voice).*

recorder's office. Ke'ena kākau kope.

recording machine. Mīkini ho'opa'a.

recount. 1. *Tell.* Kūka'i 'ōlelo, helu. **2.** *Count again.* Helu hou.

recover. Ola, ola hou, ola loa, pohala, polapola, pale-kana, panekana. *Rare:* kū hou, ho'omōhala, kōnea, pāola, kūpaku.

recreation. Mea ho'onanea, mea le'ale'a. *Board of Parks and Recreation,* Papa o nā Pāka a me nā Hana Ho'onanea.

recruit. Koa komo mua.

rectal nozzle. Kī'amo.

rectangle. Huinahā loa, 'ahalualike.

rectify. Ho'oponopono.

rectum. 'Ōkole, 'amo, 'amo hulu.

red. 'Ula, 'ula'ula *(a sacred color associated with roy-alty);* wena, weo. *Also:* mā'ula'ula, pū'ula'ula, 'ōweo, kole, mākole, mūkole, hā'ena, nono, kūnono, heka, hela, ma'alaea, puakō'ula, nao, 'āpane, nāweo. *See* **reddish, reddish-brown.** *Shades of red:* 'ula 'ōkoko, 'ula kīna'u, he'a, pūkoko *(blood);* 'ula palani *(brandy);* pala'ā *(brownish);* hilihili, 'ula weo, 'ula wena, 'ula māku'e, māku'a, 'ula hiwa, 'ulaahiwa, nao, hi'ohi'o

(dark); 'ulahea *(faded);* pūnono *(gorgeous);* moano *(pale);* 'ula māku'e *(purplish);* 'ula waina *(wine). Red of natural phenomena:* 'alaea *(of rainbow or dark meat of fish);* helo *(of* 'ōhelo *berries);* pūkoko, mākole *(of tinted cloud);* nono, manono, makou, mōhiohio *(rare) (of sunburn). Red of tapa:* pūnoni *(see* **pūnoni***),* puakai, pūkohukohu. *Red hair,* po'o 'ula'ula *(of Cau-casians);* 'ehu *(of Polynesians).*

redbird. Manu 'ula'ula.

Red Cross. Hui Ke'a 'Ula'ula, Ke'a 'Ula'ula.

redden. Hō'ula'ula, hō'ula, 'ōwea, he'a, nononea.

reddish. Hā'ula, hā'ula'ula, 'ā'ula, 'ōmea, mākoko, 'e'ehu, nonomea, hehelo, 'iwi; — *tinge in hair,* 'ehu.

reddish-brown. Hā'ehu'ehu, mea, kama'ehu, 'ehu, 'ea; 'i'i *(as a dog);* ka'aona.

reddish-purple. Kai 'ina.

reddish-yellow. Pala 'ehu.

redeem, redemption. Uku pāna'i.

redeemer. Ho'ōla pāna'i, pu'ukalahala.

red-eyed. Mākole, noe'ula.

red-hot. 'Ena, 'ena'ena, hā'ea, mākole, kāoko.

red pepper. Nīoi *(for various kinds, see Haw.-Eng. entry and entries that follow it).*

Red River. Muliwai 'Ula'ula.

Red Sea. Kai 'Ula.

red snappers. 'Ula'ula; ko'i *(young stage).*

reduce. Ho'ēmi, ho'o'u'uku, ho'owīwī, emi; ho'ēmi kino, ho'ēmi momona *(lose weight).*

reduced. Emi.

reduction. Emi; ho'olilo *(fractions). Reduction sale,* kū'ai ho'ēmi.

reed. 'Ohe, he'upueo.

re-edit. Ho'oponopono hou.

reef. 1. *Coral.* Kohola *(outer);* papaioa, papa, laupapa, hāpapa. *See* **coral. 2.** *Sail.* Lī.

reel. 1. *Whirl.* Kunewa, newa, kāhulihuli, kulana, ku-lanalana, hīkākā. *Also:* hilala, ka'alele, kiwi, mahīkā-kā. **2.** *Spool.* Pōka'a; mīkini ho'owili lawai'a *(fishing).*

refer. Pili *(intransitive);* waiho *(as to a committee). Refer concisely or exactly,* pili pono.

referee. 'Uao, luna kānāwai.

reference committee. Kōmike hulihuli, kōmike noi'i.

referendum. Koho kūikawā a ka po'e koho pāloka.

refine. Hō'ae'ae, hō'ae. *Refine sugar,* ho'oke'oke'o i ke kōpa'a 'ula'ula.

reflect. 1. *To cast a reflection.* Noho ke aka, ili ke aka. *Also:* ho'ohuaka, huaka, 'ākuli. *If the pupil is un-skilled, the errors reflect on the teacher,* i hemahema ka haumana, ili ka 'āhewa i ke kumu. **2.** *Think.* No'ono'o, nalu, wae.

reflection. Aka, wai aka, no'ono'o, anahā. *See* **reflect.**

reflexive pronoun. Paniinoa pelu hope, paniinoa huli 'auikumu.

reform. Ho'opololei, ho'ohuli.

reform party. 'Ao'ao ho'oma'ema'e.

reform school. Kula ho'opololei.

refrain. 1. *Abstain.* Ho'ōki, ho'oka'oko'a. **2.** *Song.* Puana. *Tell the refrain,* ha'ina 'ia mai ana ka puana. *Some refrains in chants and songs (Gram. 12):* āēī, āēīē, eā eā, ēhā ēhē, ehehe, ehehene, ha'uha'u ē, la'ehana, lae lā lae, 'uhē'uhene.

refreshing. 'Olu'olu, 'olu, aniani, ma'ū, ho'ōpio.

refreshment. Mea 'ai. *Light refreshment,* mea 'ai māmā.

refrigerator. Pahu hau.

refuge. Pu'uhonua, wahi kanaaho, kanaaho, kanāho, wahi palekana.

refugee. Mea pakele.

refund. Uku pāna'i, ho'iho'i hou i ke kālā.

refusal. Hō'ole.

refuse. 1. *Deny.* Hō'ole, kē; — *to part with,* 'au'a; — *to see,* nā'i'ike; hōla'o *(rare);* — *to speak,* 'au'a, 'a'ole makemake e kama'ilio, nūkuke. **2.** *See* **rubbish.**

refute. Pale 'ōlelo, pane, ho'okāpae.

regain. Loa'a hou.

regal. Ali'i, ho'āli'i, ho'ohie, hanohano; 'ula, pali loa *(fig.);* kapukapu. *See saying,* **holowa'a 1.**

regalia. 'A'ahu 'oihana piha, nā kāhiko, nā mea ho'o-hanohano.
regard. Hāliu.
regardless. I loko o, 'oia ana nō.
regards. Aloha, mahalo. *Best regards,* me ke aloha, me ka mahalo.
regatta. Heihei wa'apā.
regatta day. Lā ho'oheihei wa'apā.
regent. Kuhina, kahu. *Board of regents of the university,* papa o nā kahu kula o ke kulanui.
regiment. Pū'ali koa; lekimana *(rare).*
region. *See* land, place.
register. Kākau ho'opa'a, kākau inoa, papa inoa, ho'o-pa'a, kākau hō'ike 'ana. *Registered letter,* leka i ho'o-pa'a 'ia.
registrar. Mea kākau kope.
registration. Kākau inoa, ho'opa'a inoa. *Registration office,* 'oihana kākau kope. *Registration of partnership,* kākau kope 'ana o nā hui. *Registration of voters,* kākau inoa 'ana o ka po'e koho. *Board of registration,* papa ho'opa'a inoa.
regret. Mihi. *Also:* aumihi, mimihi, mihimihi, mimimihi; minamina, mamina *(regret a loss).*
regrets. Hiki 'ole *(unable to accept an invitation).*
regular. Ma'amau, pa'a mau, kūmau, kaukahi.
regulate. Ho'oponopono, ho'onoho.
regulation. Lula, kānāwai.
regulator. Huila nihoniho *(stitch).*
regurgitate. Ho'olualua'i, ho'opi'ipi'i.
rehabilitate, rehabilitation. Ho'opulapula.
rehearsal. Ho'oma'ama'a, ho'oma'a, ho'oma'ama'a hō'ike'ike *(for show).*
rehearse. Ho'oma'ama'a, ho'oma'a.
reign. Noho ali'i, noho aupuni, noho, 'ai, kū.
reincarnation. Ho'okino hou 'ia, hānau wawā.
reindeer. Leinekia.
reins. Kaula waha, laina kaula waha, 'ili, 'ili kauwō, kaula kāohi.
reject. Hō'ole, ha'alele. *Also:* hulā, kamalole.
rejoice. 'Oli, hau'oli, 'oli'oli, 'olina.
rejuvenate. Ho'ōpiopio, ho'ōpio.
relate. 1. *See* tell. **2.** *Refer.* Pili.
related. Pili, 'ohana, pili 'ohana; pili ma ka hanauna *(see* hanauna*). People related for generations,* lepo 'ula-'ula *(fig.).*
relation. *See* relative.
relationship. Pili, pilina, pilikana. *See* relative. *Relationship by blood,* pili koko, pili 'ohana. *Loving relationship,* pilialoha. *Relationship by friendship,* hale aikāne, pili kāmau. *Relationship to one of high rank,* pili ali'i, pilipili 'ula. *To claim relationship,* ho'opili, ho'opilipili. *Inseparable relationship,* pili wehena 'ole, pili wehe 'ana 'ole. *To abolish relationship,* wehe i ka pili, hehi i ka pili, mō ka piko, moku ka piko.
relative. 'Ohana *(family, clan),* kini *(kin);* 'ohana ho-lo'oko'a *(extended family, clan);* pili koko, 'i'o, 'i'o pono'ī, wena *(blood relatives);* 'alaea, ēwe, ēweewe, 'iewe, auahi, aupo'ipū, hanauna, pilikana, pili ma nā kūpuna, kuleana *(remote relatives);* inoa *(see* inoa **3***);* hale aikāne *(often affinal);* pili kāmau, pilialoha, pili loko, 'auwaepili, hale aikāne *(close friends who are considered relatives; see* friend*);* elder relative, pili mua. *Relative of one's own generation,* hoa hanauna, hanauna like. *To talk about relatives,* kaula'i iwi, pā-kōlea, holehole iwi, welewele iwi *(mostly pejorative). Trusted relative of a chief,* iwikuamo'o, ka'iewe, pe'a-kua. *Without relatives,* 'ohana 'ole, kūloli.
relevant. E pili ana. *Relevant questions,* nā nīele e pili ana.
relax. Ku'u aku, ho'onanea, luana, ku'una, 'alu, ho'o-malule, ho'owalea. *Also:* ho'opaulinalina, ho'omō-halu, puhalu, halu, uhalu, hikiki'i, hi'olani, kālele-muku, lōli'i, 'oluea, 'a'ama. *See* saying, huli **1.**
release. Kala, ku'u, ho'oku'u, kalakū. *Also:* puhemo, ho'opuhemo, kalana, hō'ai'ai. *Released from taboo,* noa. *Certificate of release,* palapala ho'oku'u.

reliable. Kūpono. *See* trustworthy.
relief. Kōkua, kanaaho, pu'uho'omaha, pohala.
relief society. Hui manawale'a.
relieved. Maha ka no'ono'o, pohala, ku'una.
religion. Ho'omana *(for various kinds, see* mana*).*
religious. Haipule. *See* irreligious. *Religious meeting,* anaina pule.
relinquish. Lilo, ho'oku'u.
relish. Pūpū, mea hō'ono'ono. *To relish,* 'ono, 'ono ka pu'u, mo'ala. *Kinds of Hawaiian relish,* 'inamona, palu.
reluctance. Kānalua, mana'o ho'oka'uka'u, holo pono 'ole ka mana'o; ho'omomole *(rare).*
rely. Paulele, hilina'i, kauko'o, kaulani.
remain. Koe, noho loa, waiho, keu, ō, kū. *Also:* pupū, kīpū, 'oi, ho'opōhaku, mo'i. *To remain constantly at home,* ki'inoho.
remainder. Koena, koena 'oi, koe, puehu. *A large remainder,* koehonua.
remains. Koena; kupapa'u, heana, wailua *(corpse).*
remark. *See* cruel, say.
remarkable. *See* surprising.
remedy. Lā'au *(medicine);* ke'ehina hana *(solution, as to a problem).*
remember. Ho'omana'o, ho'omaopopo, hā'upu, hali'a, hāli'ali'a, haili, ho'ono'ono'o, pa'ana'au. *See* recall. *Fondly remember,* hali'a aloha. *Remember imperfectly,* pa'a pāhemohemo.
remembrance. *See* memory.
remind. Ho'omana'o mai, ho'omaopopo, ho'āla mana'o. *Also:* hō'upu'upu, ho'ohali'a, ho'ohāli'ali'a, kono.
reminder. Mea ho'omana'o.
reminiscent. Ho'ono'ono'o, ho'ohāli'ali'a, ho'āla mana'o.
remission of sins. Kalahala, ho'okalahala, wehe hala, wehewehe hala.
remit. Send. *To remit sins,* kalahala.
remittance. Uku, kālā i ho'ouna 'ia.
remnant. Koena. *Also:* koehonua, hakina, puehu, iwi, hi'uhi'u; 'ai paia niho *(food).*
remora. Omo, leleiona.
remorse. Mihi, mihi kaumaha, mihi 'eha'eha.
remote. Mamao, kūli'u, auwaea.
remove. Lawe i kahi 'ē, lawe aku, kāpae, kala, wehe, wehewehe, ho'omamao, hu'e, mahu'e, ihi. *Also:* 'oloka'a, olohi'a, kūlē, nāi'i.
remunerate, remuneration. Uku.
renew. Hana hou, ho'omau hou, ho'omaka hou, ho'āla.
renounce. Hō'ole.
renowned. *See* famous.
rent. Ho'olimalima.
reorganize. Ho'onohonoho hou, ho'oponopono hou.
repair. Pāhonohono, pāhono, kāpili, hana hou.
repartee. Pane ho'ākamai, ho'opāpā, 'ōlelokīkē; 'āpa-'apani *(pun). Amusing repartee,* pane ho'omāke'aka.
repeal. Ho'opau, ho'onoa.
repeat. 'Ōlelo hou, hana hou. *Also:* ho'olua, noke, ho'o-mano, kuawili, pīna'i, hono, milika'a, ka'awelekā, kō-lea, ho'opokaka'a, ho'opōka'aka'a, kuili, ho'opākū-wā, kaiua. *Repeat sound in music,* ho'i hou, pale kōkō, pale kiko.
repel. Pale, pahukū.
repent. Mihi, mimihi, mimimihi, mihimihi.
repetitious. Kuawili, kūālauwili, laukua, pepelu, mau-mau, manakā.
replace. Pani, pani hakahaka, pāna'i.
replacement. Pani hakahaka.
replant. Kanu hou.
reply. *See* answer.
report. 1. *Message.* Hō'ike, palapala hō'ike; lono *(news). Quarterly report,* hō'ike hapahā. *Financial report,* palapala hō'ike waiwai. *Series of reports,* mo'o lono. *To spread a report,* ha'ilono. **2.** *Sound.* 'A'ina, 'u'ina, kohā, kani kohā.
reporter. Kākau nūpepa, haku 'ōlelo, 'aha'ilono.

repose. Maha, nanea, hoʻonanea, walea.
represent. Kū no haʻi, pani, pani ma kahi o. *The comma represents a pause,* ʻo ke koma, he hōʻailona o ka hoʻomaha.
representation. Hōʻailona. *See* **represent.**
representative. Lunamakaʻāinana. *Also:* moho, ʻelele, luna wehe pilikia, hope. *Chosen representatives,* poʻe i koho ʻia.
repress. ʻUmi, kāohi.
repressed. Paʻapū o loko, kāohi.
reprieve. Kāohi, ʻōlelo hoʻoholo.
reprint. Paʻi hou, kākākau.
reproach. Hoʻāhewa, hoʻohalahala, ʻaʻahuā, hoʻomaʻewa, maʻewa, laumaʻewa.
reproduce. Hoʻohānau, hoʻolaupaʻi, hoʻohua.
reproducing pebbles. ʻIliʻili hānau.
reptile. Moʻo, moʻo kiha, moʻo kiha, kiha. *See* **snake.**
republic. Aupuni pelekikena, lepupalika.
Republican. Lepupalika, Repubalika. *National Republican party,* ʻaoʻao Lepupalika lāhui.
repudiate. Hōʻole, hehi, keʻehi.
repulse. Pale, keku, hoʻokeku.
reputation. Kūlana.
request. Noi, nonoi. *To deny a request,* hōʻole, kāʻiʻī.
requiem. Leo mele kanikau.
require. Koi, konokono.
requirement. Koi.
requisition. Pila koi.
rescue. Hoʻopakele, hoʻopalekana.
rescued. Palekana.
research. ʻImi i ke kumu; huli puke *(literary);* ʻimi naʻauao, noiʻi.
resemblance. Hoʻohālikelike, ʻano, hālina. *See* **resemble.**
resemble. Kohu like, kohu, like, kū, kūlike, hoʻohālikelike, pili ʻano, ʻoe. *To resemble somewhat,* ʻano like, kūhapa.
resent. Ukiuki, mauhala. *Also:* hoʻāhu, kamaniha, ʻāniha, hoʻokamaniha, ninihua, naluā, hoʻomakekeʻeo, kaʻeo, keʻeo, kuapuʻe, hoʻohuakeʻeo, hoʻopalakaʻeo, hoʻopuʻu.
reserve. Hoʻokaʻawale, hoʻopaʻa, mālama, kauoha, hoʻokoe, pahukū; hoʻokaʻawale *(as land). Reserve officer,* aliʻikoa ukali.
reserved. Malu, laʻa; hōʻiu, hilu *(modest);* hoʻokaʻawale ʻia *(set aside).*
reservoir. Luawai, luawai hoʻokiʻo, kūmano.
reside. Noho. *Reside permanently,* noho paʻa. *Reside for a long time at a place,* pene, penekū.
residence. Hale noho, kahi noho, nohona. *Residence for several generations,* wahi kupa.
residue. Koena. *See* **dregs, remainder.**
resign. Haʻalele, waiho.
resignation. Haʻalele ʻana, waiho ʻana. *Letter of resignation,* palapala haʻalele ʻoihana.
resilient. Holu.
resin. Kēpau, kēpau kaʻa, kaʻa, hūkaʻa, hū lāʻau, pīlali.
resist. Kūʻē, pale, kipi, ʻalo, hōʻoleʻa, hoʻokoʻokoʻo. *To stir up to resist,* hoʻokūʻē.
resolute. Manaʻopaʻa, ʻonipaʻa, kūpaʻa.
resolution. ʻŌlelo hoʻoholo, ʻōlelo ʻaelike. *Joint resolution,* ʻōlelo hoʻoholo hui.
resolved. Hoʻoholo. *Be it resolved,* hoʻoholo ʻia.
resonance. Ō, kani, kuolo; poʻohū *(rare). See* **reverberate.**
resound. Kani, walo, uwalo, wawalo, walowalo, kohā, olo, paʻina, kuwā, kaʻiahea. *See* **reverberate.**
resources. Kumu waiwai, pono.
respect. Mahalo, ʻihi, hōʻihi. *With respect to,* pili i.
respectable. Hoʻopono, kū i ka pono.
respected. Mahalo ʻia, hoʻohanohano ʻia; ʻōmea, kūanoano *(rare).*
respectfully. Me ka mahalo, me ka pono *(ending in letters). I am, respectfully,* ʻo au me ka haʻahaʻa *(see also* iho 7*). Respectfully yours,* me ka manaʻo nui.
respective. Pākahi.

respiration. Hanu, ea.
resplendent. *See* **splendor.**
response. Pane.
responsibility. Kuleana, kuleana hana, koʻikoʻi, amo. *To give or delegate responsibility,* hoʻokuleana, hoʻākuleana, ʻākuleana. *To live without sense of responsibility,* nohona hoʻomaopopo ʻole; pakaulei *(rare).*
responsive reading. Heluhelu kīkē.
rest. 1. *Stop work.* Maha, hoʻomaha, mahana, malolo, kuʻu ka nae, kuʻu ka luhi, kanaaho, hōʻoluʻolu, ōpū, pohala, oʻioʻi. *See saying,* **paka 3.** *To come to rest,* kau. **2.** *Placed on.* Kau. *Also:* kaulei, koili, koʻokoʻona. **3.** *Remainder.* Koe, koena. **4.** *In music.* Hoʻomaha.
restaurant. Hale ʻaina, hale ʻahaʻaina.
restful. Maluhia, kaulana.
resthouse. Hale hoʻomaha.
resting place. Oʻioʻina, puʻu oʻioʻina, puʻuhoʻomaha, moena, hipū, kaulana, kaunana.
restless. Pīhole, hīʻō, ulukū. *Also:* uilani, haulani, kīkaʻelekē, panau, leleiona. *To sleep restlessly,* moe pono ʻole, moehewa.
Restoration Day. Lā Hoʻihoʻi Ea.
restore. Hoʻihoʻi hou ā ke kūlana mua, hoʻihoʻi, hoʻāla. *Restored to health,* ola hou, konekonea, kōnea, kōneanea.
restrain. Kāohi. *Also:* kōhi, hoʻopaʻa, hoʻālia, ʻiʻiʻī.
restraint. Kāohi. *To give without restraint,* hāʻawi hemolele.
restrict. Kaupalena, hoʻomalu, hoʻohaiki.
rest room. Lumi hoʻomaha, wahi hoʻopau pilikia.
result. Hopena, hope, hua, haʻawina. *The results of your work,* ka hua o kā ʻoukou hana. *The result of being old,* hopena ʻelemakule, hopena luahine.
resume. Hoʻomaka hou.
resumé. Hōʻuluʻulu pōkole, hōʻike hoʻopōkole.
resurrect. Ala hou, kū hou, hoʻōla hou.
resurrection. Ola hou, ala hou, kū hou ʻana.
resuscitate. Hoʻohanu, ola hou, kūpaku.
retail. Kūʻai liʻiliʻi.
retained. Paʻa.
retainer. ʻŌhua, kanaka, haiā kāne, haiā wahine. *See* **servant.**
retarded. ʻAno hepa, lohi, lohiʻau, mau, mūnō.
retch. Luaʻi, ʻowā, hoʻowā, ʻaukuʻu, poluwā.
retinue. Poʻe ukali, pūʻulu.
retire. Hoʻomaha loa, hōʻoluʻolu *(to rest).*
retort. Panepane. *Rude retort,* pane kū.
retreat. Neʻehope, hoʻi hope, kuemi, hoʻēmiemi.
return. Hoʻi hou *(intransitive);* hoʻihoʻi *(transitive). Also:* emi hope, hoʻi hope, hoʻina. *To return often or persistently,* hohoʻi, nē.
reveal. Hōʻike, hōʻike ā maka. *Also:* hoʻomāʻikeʻike, huaʻi, ʻuwehe, kū.
revealed. Hōʻike ʻia, ʻike ʻia, kapeke.
revel. Anaina ʻuhaʻuha, anaina hoʻoipoipo, anaina hoʻohauʻoli ā kulikuli.
revelation. Puana, haʻawina, ʻike, palo *(rare).*
Revelation. Hōʻike ʻAna *(Biblical).*
revenge. Hoʻopaʻi, pānaʻi, hoʻopānaʻi, uku. *Also:* mākaia, mauhala, hoʻomauhala, hoʻomakakī.
revenue. Loaʻa.
reverberate. Kani, kani kō, nunulu, nākolo. *See* **resound.** *Also:* kūpinaʻi, lele wawalo, kūpaukolo, hākuʻi, kiliwehi.
revered. Mahalo ʻia, ʻiu, ʻihiʻihi, kapukapu, weliweli.
reverence. Ano, hoʻāno, ʻihi, hōʻihi, ʻihi lani, ʻeʻehia, ilihia; eliʻeli *(fig.).*
reverend. Kahu. *The Reverend Mr. Smith,* ke kahu Kamika.
reverent. Haipule, manaʻo haipule, manaʻo hoʻoʻihiʻihi.
reverse. Huli, lole, hoʻi i hope; pūlepe *(rare).*
revert. Hoʻi hope.
review. Hoʻomaʻamaʻa hou, kauʻeliʻeli. *Also see* **show 2.** *Book review,* hōʻike ʻano o ka puke.
revile. ʻŌlelo hōʻino, amu, kūamuamu, amuamu, ʻaʻana, hāʻiliʻili, pāleoleowā.

revise. Hoʻoponopono hou, hoʻololi hou.
revival. Hōʻeuʻeu ʻeuanelio.
revival committee. Kōmike hōʻeu.
revive. Ola hou, hoʻōla hou, hoʻāla hou, hoʻūlu hou; pohala, hoʻopohala *(after fainting).*
revoke. Hoʻopau, hoʻonoa.
revolt. Kipi, hoʻokipi. *Also:* ala kūʻē, hū honua.
revolting. Hoʻopailua, liliha.
revolution. Hoʻāuhuli ʻana, kipi ʻana, kahuli aupuni, hoʻokahuli aupuni *(uprising);* kaʻapuni ʻana *(revolving motion).*
revolutionary war. Kaua hoʻokahuli aupuni, kaua hulihia, kaua auhulihia.
revolutionist. Kahuli aupuni, hoʻokahuli aupuni.
revolve. Kaʻa, kaʻapuni, kakaʻa. *Also:* kaʻalewa, kaʻalelewa, naue, pokakaʻa, pōkaʻa, ʻōkaʻa, pōniu, mimilo, nome, hoʻokāpōʻai. *Revolving doors,* puka pokakaʻa. *To revolve hips, as in a hula,* ʻami hoʻolewa, haʻalewa, poahi.
revolver. Pūpanapana.
revulsion. Hoʻopailua; *sensation of —,* manene, ʻeʻeu.
reward. Makana, uku, uku pānaʻi; ahu ili *(rare).*
rewrite. Kākau hou, kākākau.
rheumatism. Lumakika.
Rhine River. Muliwai Lino, Muliwai Rino.
rhinoceros. Laehaokela.
rhizome. Aʻa kolo.
Rhode Island. Loke ʻAilana, Rode ʻAilana.
rhombus. Huinahā hiō.
Rhone River. Muliwai Lone, Muliwai Rone.
rhubarb. Lupepa.
rhyme. ʻAno like ka leo o nā panina laina i ka mele.
rhythm. Pana o ka mele, pā.
rib. Iwi ʻaoʻao *(human);* nīʻau *(coconut leaf or frond or umbrella);* oʻa, wae *(ship);* ʻupe, io *(paddle).*
ribbon. Lipine. *Typewriter ribbon,* lipine kikokiko.
rib bone. Iwi ʻaoʻao, iwi hilo.
rice. Laiki.
ricebird. Manu-ʻai-laiki.
rice bran. Pale laiki.
rich. 1. *Wealthy.* Waiwai, lako, kūʻonoʻono. *Rare:* koʻakoʻa, polohuku, ponohuku, ponopono, kapakapa, lālāwai; hoʻohonua, honu *(fig.).* *See saying,* eel. *Rich person,* kanaka waiwai, kiʻi maka nunui. **2.** *Of food.* Liliha, lihaliha, momona, kelekele. *Also:* kuhinia, kōhi, lololo, ʻokukuli. **3.** *Of soil.* Momona; mona *(rare).*
Richmond. Likemona, Rikemona.
rickety. Paʻa ʻole, kāhulihuli, kiolea, wīwī; pīlaliʻohe *(rare).*
ricochet. ʻŌhua *(as an arrow).*
rid. Hoʻokaʻawale aku, kipaku, hoʻopau.
riddle. Nane, ʻōlelo nane, nane huna, nanehaʻi. *Example of a riddle: A tree that goes to war* (he lāʻau hele i ke kaua). *Answer* (haʻina): Koa *(koa is the name of a tree and means soldier).* *See* **imu kālua loa, kalalī, pueo 3, puka 2, give, scrotum.**
riddling. Nanenane, nane, hoʻopāpā.
ride. Holo, holoholo, kau, holoholona. *To go for a ride,* holoholo. *To ride in a car,* holo kaʻa, holoholo kaʻa. *To ride free of charge,* kau wale, holo wale.
ride horseback. Holo lio, kau lio, holoholo lio; to — holo; to —, wearing a pāʻū, holo pāʻū; to — bareback, kau wale; to — sitting astride, kiomana; to — sidesaddle, noho kāpae; to — until horse is dead or exhausted, pākī lio.
rider. 1. *One who rides.* Holo lio, kau lio. *Car rider,* mea holo kaʻa. **2.** *Supplement.* Pākuʻi ʻena.
ridge. Kualapa, kualono, lapa; pou *(of a nose);* — between flutes of a column, ʻaukā; — with irregular projections, kiokio pali. *Also:* kūnihi, kūlihi, hālapa, nao, iwi, poʻo huku, moʻo, ʻōmoʻomoʻo, lipi, hiwi, uhaʻi.
ridged. Hāluʻa, lapalapa, ʻōlapalapa, moʻomoʻo, winiwini, kulilipi.
ridgepole. Kaupoku, kaupokuʻiole, kauhuhu, kuaʻiole, ʻauʻau. *Supports of ridgepole,* halakeʻa, hānā.
ridicule. Hoʻohenehene, henehene, hoʻowahāwahā, pāhenehene, hōʻakaʻaka. *Also:* hoʻomāʻauea, hoʻomahu-

akala, hoʻomaʻewa, hoʻopuʻukahua; hakukole *(in fig. language or chant).*
ridiculous. Kohu ʻole, kū i ka pāhenehene. *See* **adze.**
riding horse. Lio kau.
riffraff. ʻŌpala.
rifle. Pū laipala, pū laipela.
rig. Kūkulu i ka likini, hoa, hoʻoneʻe i loko.
Rigel. Puana-kau.
rigging. Kaula likini, likini, hoa, hoa waʻa; pākaula *(rare).*
right. 1. *Direction.* ʻĀkau. *Right, face,* ma ka ʻākau, huli. **2.** *Correct.* Pololei, pololoi, pono. *That's right,* pēlā nō, pēlā ʻiʻo nō, ā ʻoia. *Right away,* kēia manawa. *To right a canoe,* kama-i-huli-pū, kama-i-kahuli-waʻa. *To right a boat,* hoʻohuli hou i ka waʻapā. **3.** *Privilege.* Kuleana. *See* **rights.** *Right of way,* pono ala hele, mana ma ka hele ʻana. *Right of way of access,* kuleana ala hele e hiki aku ai.
right angle. Huina kūpono.
righteous. Pono, niolo, maikaʻi. *To strive to be righteous,* ʻimi pono.
righteousness. Pono. *The life of the land is perpetuated in righteousness,* ua mau ke ea o ka ʻāina i ka pono *(motto of Hawaiʻi).*
right-minded. Naʻau pono.
rights. Pono. *See* **human rights.** *Civil rights,* pono kīwila. *Women's rights,* nā pono o nā wāhine. *Equal rights,* pono kaulike. *Bill of rights,* palapala o nā pono pilikino o ke kanaka. *Private rights,* pono pilikino. *To put to rights,* hoʻoponopono.
rigid. ʻOʻoleʻa. *Also:* kola, kalaʻihi, kākāuha, kāʻiʻī, lāʻau, nanauha, wīkani, wīkaʻo. *Rigid observance,* nihinihi.
rigor. ʻOʻoleʻa. *To treat with rigor,* hoʻokoʻikoʻi.
rigor mortis. Lāʻau ke kino.
rim. Lihi, nihi, kaʻe, huʻa; nīao *(as of a bowl);* mōlina *(of a wheel);* ʻēheu *(of a hat).* *Also:* kīkepa, mūkaʻe.
rind. ʻIli, ʻaluʻalu.
ring. 1. *Jewelry.* Komo, apo. *Gold ring,* komo kula. **2.** *Circle.* Pōʻai, pōʻaha, lina; — about a drake's neck, lei; —, as in a game of ringtoss, pōkaʻa kaula. **3.** *To sound.* Kani, hoʻokani, kakani. *Also:* kuʻikē, kōluilui. *To ring in the ears,* ʻula. *To ring up, as on the telephone,* hoʻokani, wili, kāhea.
ring and ball game. Palaʻie.
ringtoss. Kīolaola lina.
ringworm. Ane, hāʻueʻue, hāʻukeʻuke, hāʻukaʻuka.
rinse. Mūmū *(mouth);* kaka *(fish, clothing).*
Rio Grande. Lio Kelaneke, Rio Geranede.
riot. Haunaele, anaina hoʻohaunaele. *Also:* uluāoʻa, ʻolohani.
rip. Nahae, nohae. *See* **tear.**
ripe. Pala. *Stages of ripeness:* oʻo *(fully formed but not ripe);* pala hāʻama, pala pono *(exactly ripe);* palakū *(dead ripe);* palahū, palahuki, pala ila, palaheʻe, palakāhela, kāpule, napele *(overripe).* *Also:* maka pala, hāpala, ʻalamea; kāʻao, kāō *(of pandanus);* kāhala *(of gourds).* *A spindly banana . . , not ripe in ten days* (For. 5:441), he līlā maiʻa . . , ʻaʻole e pala i ke anahulu *(a taunt).*
ripen. Pala, oʻo, hoʻāma, hoʻomāui.
ripple. ʻAle, ʻaleʻale, holu, lapalapa. *Also:* hāʻale, ʻowē, mimilo, nahenahe, hoʻolili, haʻakuʻe, hāluʻa, hāloku, nao, ʻaʻau.
rise. 1. *To rise up.* Ala, piʻi, aea, ea, kau, hoʻāla, hoʻolapa; ʻae *(as tide);* hū *(as yeast);* kū *(as dust);* pūnohu, pūkoʻa, pōnulu, nulu, nanulu *(as smoke);* piʻi ʻipiʻi kai *(of a strong sea);* ōpū, ʻōhū, kumoho *(rare, as water);* ulu, puka, piʻi *(as the sun);* hoʻēʻe *(as surf);* — in station, kaʻa maluna; — in horror, ʻeʻeu; to — frequently, eʻea; to — again, ala hou, kū hou. *Also:* ʻeu, māealani, māea, kūāhua, ihuihu, peu, meʻeu; huhulu kū *(as hair of a dog);* pulelo *(as a flag or fire);* hoʻokōkōliʻi, lei *(as a cloud);* hakū *(as the moon);* papaiāulu *(as a breeze).* *To rise and fall,* lele lupe, nunuki. *Rising sun,* lā hiki. *Prices rise,* piʻi nā kumu kūʻai. **2.** *An incline.* Piʻina, alana, kiʻekiʻena, ōnū.

pork, kāpī

ai.
r the sea).
o'ai.
i ka hō'ailona
ū ho'ohanohano.
ae.
alawekoa, Salawe-

o'okahi. *Same as ever,*
ame to you, me 'oe pū.
makua kāne. *At the same*
ho'okahi. *It's the same*

mea Kāmoa.
ku.
'a, ho'āno.
pule i ke 'ano ho'okamani,

o, ke'ena kapu, wahi kanaaho,
nua.
d, one kea, ōkea, kea. *Black cin-*
. *Black lava sand,* one 'ā. *Fine sand,*
one. *Sand beach,* kahaone, 'ae one,
heap, pu'u one. *Sand pellets,* kūkae
, one maka. *Sand washed by the sea,*
piopio. *Sand near fresh water,* one wai.
ne. *Sands of my birth,* ku'u one hānau

a hāwele, kāma'a hakahaka, pale wāwae,
wāwae; kāma'a 'ie *(braided);* kāma'a lā'ī,
naka *(ti-leaf).*
. 'Iliahi, 'aoa, lā'au 'ala, 'iliahi-a-lo'e,
, hua'ula'ula. *False or bastard sandalwood,*
ood of naio, 'a'aka. *Scion or shoot of sandal-*
aahi.
k. Āhua one, kumuone.
. Pu'e one.
ab. 'Ōhiki.
une. Pu'e one, pu'u one, āhua one.
rling. Hunakai.
hopper. 'Uku kai, 'uku limu.
dpaper. Pepa kalakala.
dpiper. Upupā.
d spurry. Mimi'īlio.
ndstone. Kumuone.
andwich. Nā palaoa me nā mea hō'ono'ono i waena.
sandy. Oneone, 'āone, one; onena *(rare).*
sane. Maika'i ka no'ono'o.
San Francisco. Kapalakiko.
sanitarium. *See* **hospital.**
sanitary. Ma'ema'e loa.
sanitary napkin. Kī'amo, mea hume.
sanitation. Kūlana o ke ola.
San Joaquin. Kāna 'Iōkina, Sana Iokina; Waikini.
San Miguel. Kāna Mikuela, Sana Miguela.
San Pedro. Kāna Pekelo, Sana Petero.
Santa Barbara. Kāna Palapala, Sana Barabara.
Santa Clara. Kāna Kalala, Sana Kalara.
Santa Claus. Kanakaloka.
Santa Cruz. Kāna Kaluka, Sana Karuza.
sap. Kohu, wai, wale, wale hau, wai lā'au, kaikea; 'ae *(from seaweed or leaves);* pēka'a, kulukulu'ā *(from green* kukui *nuts).*
sapphire. Kapaea, sapaea; kapeila, kapeilo, sapeiro, kapila, sapira.
Saracen. Kalekena.
sarcasm. 'Ōlelo hō'eha 'ano 'uhi'uhi 'ia, kū'akū.
sarcastic. Kīko'olā, pākīkē. *Also:* hō'aikola, ho'onā'ai-kola, kīkoi, kū'akū.
sardine. Makalē; kālina *(rare).*
Sardinia. Kakinia, Sadinia.
sardius. Kalekio.
sardonyx. Kalekonuka.
sarong. Pā'ū, kīkepa; lukaluka *(for men);* hau'ina *(dyed with* 'ōlena*). See ex.,* **sea.** *Sarong festooned with leaves or ferns,* pā'ū heihei. *To bind on a sarong,* kākua; kihi o ka mahina *(a special way).*
sash. Kā'ai, kā'ei.
Satan. Kākana.
satchel. Paiki; kī'eke *(rare).*
sateen. Kākīnia, kākini.
satellite star. Hōkū ukali.
satiated. Ho'olawa 'ana; mā'ona piha, ana, kenakena, 'okukuli *(with food);* 'aikena *(to the point of sickness)*
satiety. Lawa pono, mā'ona ho'oili, mā'ona piha. *See idiom,* **hewa 4.**
satin. Pāhoehoe. *Brocaded satin,* pāhoehoe lau.
satire. 'Ōlelo pāhenehene.
satisfaction. 'Olu'olu, ho'olaule'a. *Lack of satisfaction,* 'olu'olu 'ole, la'ola'o.
satisfactorily. Pono, kūpono, kohu pono.
satisfied. Ana, lawa, mā'ona *(after eating);* kena, kena-kena *(after drinking). See saying,* **pi'ikoi.** *Be satisfied with what you have got,* e 'olu'olu i ka mea i loa'a.
satisfy. Hō'olu'olu, ho'okō.
saturate. Ho'oma'ū, pulu, ho'opulu, pulu pē, kē'ae, polokake, kawakawa. *See* **moisten.**
Saturday. Pō'aono, lā ho'omalolo, Kakuke, Satude.
Saturn. Makulu, Mākulukulu, Kakulena.
satyr. Kao hihiu, kao kanaka.
sauce. Kai. *Various kinds:* kai helo *(of crushed shrimp and coconut cream);* 'ae limu *(seaweed juice);* kai 'ina *(sea-urchin);* kai ko'ako'a *(rich, as of parrot-fish liver). To mix or stew with sauce,* kākele.
saucepan. Pā ho'olapalapa, ipu hao.
saucer. Pā li'ili'i.
saucy. Pākīkē, kīko'olā, maha'oi, mahalua, honekoa.
saunter. Holoholo ho'onanea, ho'olalau, palela, kūo'e.
sausage. Na'aukake.
savage. Hihiu loa, hae, mākaha, iō'cna.
Savannah. Kawana, Savana.
save. 1. *As a life.* Ola, ho'ōla, ho'opakele, ho'opalekana. *God save the king,* ola ka mō'ī i ke Akua. *God save me,* e ola au i ke Akua. **2.** *Keep.* Mālama, pūlama, ho'īli, ho'oili, hō'ili'ili, ho'okoe, ana'ē.
saved. Ola, ola pāna'i, palekana, panekana.
saving. Makauli'i, minamina. *Also:* ko'ako'ana, kīhau, pukumoa. *See* **thrifty.**
savings. Loa'a hō'ili'ili, waihona, kālā ho'āhu.
savings bank. Panakō ho'āhu.
savior. Ho'ōla, palekana.
savor. 'Ono.
savory. 'Ono.
Savoy. 1. *The country.* Kawoe, Savoe. **2.** *(Not cap.) A kind of cabbage.* Kawoa.
saw. 1. *Tool.* Pahi olo, olo. *To saw,* olo, oloolo, piolo; helo *(with jerky motion);* olokīkī *(rare). To saw wood,* olo papa. **2.** *See* **see.** *I saw,* ua 'ike au.
sawdust. Oka lā'au.
sawhorse. Lio lā'au.
sawmill. Hale olo papa.
Saxon. Kakona, Sakona.
say. 'Ōlelo, ha'i, 'ī. *Also:* mea, mea mai, wahi a, pēlā, pēia, ho'opuka. *To say little,* 'ekemu, molu. *The chief said,* wahi a ke ali'i; 'ōlelo mai ke ali'i.
saying. 'Ōlelo no'eau. *Also:* 'ōlelo kaena *(of praise, as for a place or person);* ha'ina, kāleo.
scab. Pāpa'a, 'ōkohe, pihi.
scabbard. 'Ili wahī, wahī pahi kaua.
scabies. Kunakuna, ane.
scad. Akule; halalū, hahalalū, pā'ā'ā *(young).*
Scaevola. Naupaka.

risk. Maka'u, 'a'a, ho'ā'o me ka nānā 'ole, ho'ā'o me ka hopohopo. *To take a great risk,* hō'a'ano.
rite, ritual. *See* **ceremony.**
rival. Hoa paio, hoa pāonioni.
river. Kahawai, muliwai.
roach. 'Elelū; la'aloa *(slim-bodied).*
road. Ala, alanui, ala hele. *Also:* mo'o hele, kuamo'o, kumeheu. *Cleared road,* ala waele. *Road cut,* ala 'oki. *Belt road,* alaloa. *Unfinished or dead-end road,* ala muku. *Long road,* ala loa. *Circular road,* ala pō'ai. *Steep road,* alapi'i kū. *Winding road,* alanui kīke'e-ke'e. *Curve in a road,* kālawa, hālawa. *Road following cliffs,* ala kaka'i pali.
roadside. Pīpā alanui.
roan. Lokia.
roar. Wawā, wā, ho'owā, uwō, halulu, nākolokolo; ho'okani pihe *(as a crowd);* kapalulu, ho'okapalulu *(as an airplane);* kamumu, haukamumu *(as approaching rain);* kawewe *(as a downpour);* ho'okāwōwō, nū *(as wind);* kūwō *(as a lion); a prolonged* —, kōloa. *Also:* hū, nāku'i, kanulu, puwō, 'u'inakolo, wōwō, hauka-wewe, ku'inē, kahakikī, pa'ē pū, 'owā.
roast. 'Oma, loke, 'ōhinu. *See* **bake, broil.** *Roast turkey,* pelehū 'oma. *Roast beef,* pipi loke.
roasted. Ho'ō 'oma, 'oma, 'ōhinu.
rob. 'Aihue, pōwā. *Also:* pākaha, hao wale, kā'ilikū, kā-'ili wale, moluna.
robber. *See* **rob.**
robbery. 'Aihue, pākaha.
robe. 'A'ahu, lole ho'olu'elu'e.
robin. Lopine.
Rochester. Lokeka, Rokeka.
rock. 1. *Stone.* Pōhaku, 'ā, 'alā, hālelo. *Kinds:* 'a'ā, 'a'ā pu'upu'u, 'ā pele, pāhoehoe, kaiali'i, humu'ula, maki-ki, kei, lelekepue, pa'alā, pikapika, pīwai, uliuli. *See* **basalt, stone. 2.** *Motion.* Kulana, ho'oluli, naue, ho'onaue, kāhulihuli, paipai, pueo, pūeoeo.
rock borer. 'Ōlepe waha nui.
rock crevice. Naele.
rocket. Kao lele, 'ōahi; ahikao lele. *To send up rockets,* ho'olele kao.
rocking chair. Noho paipai.
rockskipper. Pao'o.
rock stratum. Hāpapa.
rocky. Nui ka pōhaku, pōhaku. *Also:* hālelo, mākō, hao'a, kō'ā.
Rocky Mountains. Mauna Pōhaku.
rod. Lā'au, 'ōhelo, loka, roda, kālī, ko'oko'o, peloka; kia, 'ōhelo huki manu, maile *(for snaring birds);* kāni'o *(supporting a house);* kā'aha *(priest's).*
rodent. *See* **'iole.**
roebuck. Pāpulō, 'anekelopa.
rogue. 'Eu, piha 'eu, kolohe, 'āpiki; lonu *(rare).*
roil. Hōlapu, naku, ho'onaku, 'a'aka, mōioio, hōkake-kake, mimiki.
roll. 1. *Turn.* Kaka'a, ka'a, 'ōka'a, kūka'a, kūpola; 'olo-ka'a *(as a wheel);* kāka'a *(as eyes);* luli *(as a ship);* 'aui *(as the sea);* mimilo *(as to induce abortion);* mākī *(as a mat);* — *beneath,* ka'a malalo; — *diagonally,* ka'a kepa; — *over backwards,* ka'akua; — *up,* wahī, kī, wili, uhaku, nunu. *To roll in salt,* ka'a pa'akai. *To fall down and roll,* ka'ahina. *To roll freely or without control,* ka'a wale. **2.** *Bundle.* Lola, 'ōwili, 'āpā, pōka'a. *Roll of rope,* pōka'a kaula. **3.** *Bread.* Palaoa li'ili'i. **4.** *Sound.* Kā'eleloi, palalū, pākīko'ele. *See* **ruffle.**
roll call. Hea inoa.
roller. 1. *Stick.* Lā'au ho'oka'a, lola ho'opalaha, ipuwai. *See* **steam roller. 2.** *Wave.* 'Aui, 'aui 'ale.
rolling. Ka'a, ka'ana; — *along, as a wheel,* nome. *See* **roll.**
rolling grindstone. Hoana ka'a.
rolling pin. Lā'au ho'oka'a, lola.
Roman Catholic. Kakōlika Loma.
romance. 1. *Novel.* Ka'ao. **2.** *Love affair.* Pili ho'oipo-ipo, pilialoha; hana kalakalai *(trifling).*
romantic. Ho'oipoipo.
Rome, Roman. Loma, Roma.
romp. Lelele, 'oehu.
rood. Luka.
roof. Kaupoku, kaupaku. *Temporary roofed construction,* lānai.
roofing. Pili. *Shingle roofing,* pili papa. *Corrugated iron roofing,* pili hao, pili piula.
room. 1. *Part of a house.* Lumi, ke'ena. *Private room,* ke'ena malu, ke'ena kapu. **2.** *Space.* Hakahaka. *Plenty of room,* nui ka lumi.
roommate. Hoa lumi.
roost. Haka.
rooster. Moa kāne.
root. 1. *Of plant.* A'a, mole, weli; — *with many sprouts,* kumulau; — *of* koali *vine,* kalēhuna. *Aerial root,* ma'alewa, a'a lewalewa, a'a kiolea, mahulukū; ule ha-la, uleule hala *(of pandanus). Root system,* pa'i a'a. *Root cutting,* kā. *Tip of pandanus root,* mu'o, mu'o hala. *Creeping root,* a'a kolo. *To take root,* ho'oa'a. *Root used in love sorcery,* hua nanai. **2.** *Source.* Kumu; mole *(as of a word).* **3.** *Dig.* 'Eku, naku, haunaku, peu. *Also:* 'e'eku, 'eku'eku, nakunaku.
root beer. Lukapia.
rootlet. Huluhulu, a'a; piko *(of* wauke*),* ki'u *(of sweet potato).*
rope. Kaula *(see Haw.-Eng. entry and entries that follow it),* kāwelewele. *Also:* 'umi'umi, kī'aho. *End of rope,* piko. *Leather rope,* kaula 'ili. *Rope tether,* kaula kū-pe'e. *Rope at bottom of net,* lio. *To rope,* ho'ohei *(see* **lasso***).*
rosary. Lei kolona, kolona, lōkālio.
rose. Loke *(see Haw.-Eng. entry and entries that follow it),* loke lani, roselani. *See* **green rose.**
rose apple. 'Ōhi'a loke.
rosewood. Lā'au loke.
rostrum. 1. *Pulpit.* 'Āwai. **2.** *Beak.* Kākala *(as of a shrimp).*
rosy. Loke, 'ōhelohelo, helo, nono.
rot. *See* **rotten.**
rotate. Ka'apuni, ka'a, pōniu, poahi, ho'okāpō'ai.
rote. Walewaha.
rotten. Pilau, palahū, 'ino'ino, palahō; popopo *(of wood, paper);* ēlo, lāla'au *(of eggs; fig., spoiled, worthless);* milu *(as fruit);* pala, palakiu, alapuka *(rare, as taro);* palahuki *(as banana stump). Also:* huhu, hu-huhu, pele'ū, peluluka, pūnonu, 'ūki'ukiu, 'ūkiukiu, nehi, 'oke, hahalu, māhao, nā'ele'ele, poholawa. *See* **decomposed.**
rouge. Mea hō'ula'ula papālina.
rough. 1. *As terrain.* Ho'olua, 'ālualua, mālualua, lua-lua, ho'opupū, 'āpu'upu'u, hāpu'upu'u, 'ōpu'upu'u, kīwa'awa'a. **2.** *As cloth or skin.* 'Ōkala, kala, kākala, pākala, hākuma, 'ōkuma, 'ōpakapaka, ooolo, ulu-ha'o, konakona, manumanu, 'āpulu. **3.** *As sea or wind.* Pikipiki'ō, 'ālo'alo'a, lo'alo'a, la'ola'o, hālo-'alo'a, āulu, olohi'a, pūkalakī, kū'ulukū, nalunalu, 'ōnalunalu, puleileho, maleuwō. *Rough sea,* kai ko'o, 'ōkaikai. **4.** *Manner.* 'Ōkalakala, kākala, kalakala, 'o'ole'a.
roughhouse. Limanui, haunaele, lapa, kolohe, mā-'ewa'ewa.
round. Poepoe, popohe, kūpoepoe; molea, mole, momo-le, kūmole, nemo, ka'anemo, polipoli *(smooth);* mūmū *(blunt);* nepu *(bulging). Also:* nia, 'akipohe, hūalakē, kōnunu, peo. *See* **around, circuit.** *Round object, as pill or bead,* hua. *Round mass,* pōpō, pōheoheo. *To form a round shape,* ho'opoe. *To go round and round,* ka'anini.
roundabout. Ho'olalau, lauwili, loloiāhili. *Roundabout way to lead up to a subject,* ho'ohelehele 'ōlelo.
round-shouldered. 'O'ohu; hanunu *(rare).*
roundup. Ho'ohuli pipi, ho'ā pipi.
roundworm. Ko'e kai.
rouse. Hō'eu'eu, ho'āla, ho'ouluulu, ho'opi'ipi'i, ho'o-lalelale. *Also:* ho'ohahana, ho'okokonoi'e, pai.
rout. Hō'auhe'e, ho'ohe'e, ho'opuehu, ho'ohū, 'āha'i, kipaku.
route. Ala hele.

routed. 'Auhe'e, puehu, kipaku 'ia.
rove. *See* **wander.**
row. 1. *Paddle.* Hoe. *To row here and there,* hoehoe, pā-nānā. **2.** *Line.* Pae, lālani, laina. **3.** *See* **riot.**
rowboat. Wa'apā.
rows. Paepae, lālani, laina. *To place in rows,* ho'onoho papa.
royal. Ali'i, lani, ho'āli'i, 'ano lani. *Also:* 'ula, 'a'ala *(fig.);* auali'i, wai 'ihi, wā'ihi. *See saying,* **'ie 1.** *Royal robe,* 'a'ahu ali'i. *Poetic references to rain, rainbow, height in general, red, hawk* ('io) *may signify royalty.*
royalist. Aloha ali'i, loialiki; 'āne'e ali'i *(disparaging).*
royal poinciana. 'Ohai 'ula.
rub. 1. *Friction.* 'Ānai, kuai, kuolo, hoana; 'upa'upā *(as clothes on washboard). Also:* olo, oloolo, piolo, halo, holoi, kaekae, walu, 'uwalu, waluhia, wa'uwa'u, wawalu, waluwalu, oloi, olokīkī. *See* **polish.** *To stretch by rubbing,* kahi kālena. *To rub with elbows,* neku'e. *To rub, as tapa on grass to gather moisture,* kā kēhau. *Rub with oil,* kāhinu, hinu *(as with oil). See* **rub.**
massage.
rubbed. Māhinu, hinu *(as with oil). See* **rub.**
rubber. 1. *Elastic.* Laholio. **2.** *Stone polisher.* Pōhaku 'ānai, pōhaku pahe'e 'ānai. *Buck lists six kinds:* puna *(coral);* 'elekū, 'ō'io *(basalt);* 'ana *(pumice); also:* 'ōahi, 'ōla'i.
rubber band. Laholio ho'opa'a.
rubbers. Kāma'a laholio.
rubbery. 'Ōuaua, laholio, 'ūlina, 'ūlinalina, 'ūnina.
rubbing oil. 'Aila hamo.
rubbish. 'Ōpala. *Also:* lepo, lepo hānai, kae, lemu'ā.
rubbish container. Kini 'ōpala, ipu 'aina.
rubbish pit. Lua 'ōpala. *Also:* luaunu, olomehani.
rudder. Hoe uli.
rudder fish. Nenue.
ruddy. 'Ehu; hi'ohi'o *(rare).*
ruddy turnstone. 'Akekeke.
rude. Kiko'olā, maha'oi, pākīkē, kekē niho, ho'okano. *Also:* waha 'ā, 'āwaha, kīkoi, kū, kō'ā, koaea, ha'akei, 'u'u, mahalua, pūhi'u, kakana, kakana'i'i, kū kakalaioa, kalakala, 'āpali, meku. mahi'opu. *See* **kio, nīele, pāhi'uhi'u.** *Speak rudely,* 'ōlelo kū, ho'opuka kū, ho'oku'iku'i 'ōlelo, 'ōlelo kohā, pua'ō, kīkahō, kala-'ea. *Ask rudely,* noi kū.
rue. Lue.
ruff. Pihapiha 'ā'ī *(neck),* 'alu.
ruffle. 1. *Folds, as in a garment.* 'Alu, pihapiha, pihapiha 'ō koholā, kauwawe, kauwewe, kauawe, 'ā'īlepe; — *and tucks,* hu'a. **2.** *Wrinkle.* 'A'apu, 'āka'a, uluulu, unuunu, pūkalakī. **3.** *Sound, as of drums.* Kā'eleloi.
ruffler. Ho'opihapiha *(as on a sewing machine).*
rug. *See* **carpet.**
ruin. Pilikia, hō'ino'ino, mā'ino'ino. *Rare:* apu, olopē, pahu'a.
ruins. Koena.

rule. 1. *A regulation.* Lula, loina, kānāwai. *Fundamental rule,* lula kumu. **2.** *To govern.* Noho ali'i, 'ai, noho aupuni, ho'omalu, ho'ohaku, ea, ka'a maluna.
ruler. 1. *Leader.* Ali'i; — *of an ahupua'a,* 'ai ahupua'a; — *of an* 'ili, 'ai 'ili; — *of a district,* 'ai moku. *See* **king.** **2.** *Measuring stick.* Lula, lā'au ana.
rum. Lama, rama.
rumble. Halalū, nāku'i, nākolo, kamumu, kani. *Also:* palalū, nei; kolokolo; 'ōlapa, nakulu *(as stomach);* nehe, haukamumu, pākīko'ele, hawewe, kiliwehi. *See* **roar, roll.**
rumor. Lono *(see* **lono 1),** lono wale. *Also:* lohe lau āhea, nēnē, ho'onēnē, lonowā, lonoā, nonoā, wawā, lauāhea, hūhā. *To hear rumors,* lohe wale.
rump. Puapua *(of a chicken). Rump bone of a chicken,* ke'emoa.
run. 1. *Move swiftly.* Holo, hoholo, ho'oholo, ka'aholo; —, *as for office,* holo, alualu; — *fast,* holo māmā, holo kikī, kikī holo, ho'oheihei; — *here and there,* holokē, holo hele, holo lua; holowā *(rare);* — *aground,* ili; oloi *(rare);* — *over,* ili; — *cautiously,* akaholo; — *lightly,* kakakihi; —, *as a messenger,* kūkini; — *of fish,* kahe, kū, he'e i'a; — *away, see* **flee;** — *after, see* **chase.** *To make a horse run,* ho'oholo lio. **2.** *Manage.* Ho'oholo, ka'a.
runner. 1. *Messenger.* Kūkini. *See saying,* **welo 1. 2.** *Of a vine.* 'Awe'awe, hā'awe'awe; kāili, kālī *(sweet potato).* **3.** *Of a sled.* Kāma'a loa.
running. Holona, uhaiāholo. *Running nose,* hūpēkole. *Running sore,* pala he'e.
running board. 'A'e ka'a *(of an automobile).*
runt. Hua li'i, keiki 'u'uku loa.
rupture. Pu'ulele, laho he'e, hoaka.
rural. Kua'āina.
ruse. Hei. *See* **trick.**
rush. 1. *Move swiftly.* Holo 'ino, holo 'āwīwī, lele'ino, auau, pūlale, holomoku, haluku, hakuko'i; — *out,* lele; —, *as water,* kokoi, kō'ie'ie; kūkawowo *(rare);* —, *as in battle,* olowalu, ho'ouka; —, *as a crowd,* mokuāwai, kokoi. **2.** *Plant.* Papulo *(papyrus);* mau'u. *See* **bulrush.**
Russia. Lukia, Rusia.
Russian. Lūkini, Lukia.
rust. Kūkaehao, lepohao; popopo *(Biblical). See* **rusty.**
rustic. Kua'āina; koai'e *(fig.).*
rustle. Hoene, nehe, 'u'inakolo, 'owē, nakeke, ho'onakeke, kapa. *To roll with a rustling sound,* ka'a'owē. *Rustling of the sea on the pebbles,* nehe a ke kai i ka 'ili'ili.
rusty. Kūkaehao, lepohao. *See* **rust.** *To become rusty,* ki'o kūkaehao.
rut. Kapo'o, napo'o, mō'ali. *Full of ruts,* mālualua, helehele, kīwa'awa'a, kāpo'opo'o.
ruthless. Ho'okaumaha; ho'oluhi hewa *(Biblical).*
rye. Lai, rai; huapalaoa 'ele'ele.

S

s. *No Hawaiian [...]*
-s. *The plural is [...]* nāhi, mau, po'e, [...] *(Gram. 9.6.3., 10.4.[...]*
-'s. *See* **of.**
Sabaoth. Kāpāōka.
Sabbath. Kāpaki, Sabati.
sabotage. Ho'opō'ino malū[...]
sack. 1. *Bag.* 'Eke; 'eke'eke [...] *(flour, unbleached muslin).* **2.** [...]
sackcloth. Kapa 'ino'ino, lole lau[...]
sack race. Heihei 'eke.
sacrament. Kakelema, kakelemenek[...] **Holy Communion.**
Sacramento. Kakalameko.
sacred. Kapu. *Also:* la'a, la'ahia, ano, ho'a[...] 'ihi, 'iu, hō'iu, po'iu, 'ula. *Sacred things o[...]* kea. *Sacred enclosure,* pālama. *Sacred pla[...]* kapu, hei kapu, wahi la'a.
Sacred Heart. Pu'uwai Ho'āno, Pu'uwai La'ahia.
sacrifice. Mōhai *(for various types, see Haw.-Eng. en[...] and entries that follow it). Also:* kaumaha, mōlia, mū liaola, haina, hai, hei, hai ao, papaiō; 'ōlapa *(for sorcery);* he'a *(blood);* kākū'ai *(food). Human sacrifice,* kanaka, ulua, heana, pua'a he'a, pua'a hinu, hinu, pua'a wāwae loa *(see* **wāwae),** 'oma, ha'alelea, uko'o. *Place of sacrifice,* heiau, haiau, lele, 'aoa. *One who sacrifices himself,* mōliaola. *Seekers of sacrifice,* makāla ulua. *Rod held by priest in sacrifice,* kā'aha.
sacrilege. Hehi kū i ke kapu; kakilileke *(Catholic).*
sacroiliac strain. Kīkala hāne'ene'e.
sad. Kaumaha, lu'ulu'u, 'aoa, 'ino'ino, 'EHA'eha; kaumaha lua *(extremely). See* **grief.** *Also:* pilihua, niniu, niuaua, malāoa. *To cause sadness,* ho'okaumaha.
saddle. Noho lio; *pack —,* noho 'āmana. *To saddle,* hauhoa.
saddle blanket. Pale lio.
saddle horn. Maku'u, ōmuku, 'ōkumu.
saddle horse. Lio holo noho.
safe. 1. *Not in danger.* Palekana, panekana, malu, maluhia. *Also:* kūola, mānalo, kuakapu, kūka'awe. **2.** *Depository.* Pahu hao, pahu pā, pahu kālā, halepā.
safety. Maluhia, palekana, panekana, malu. *Place of safety,* pu'uhonua.
safety pin. Kui kaiapa, pine kaiapa.
safflower. Mamo.
saffron. Keloko. *See* **turmeric.**
sag. 'Alu, 'alu'alu. *Also:* 'olo, 'olo'olo, he'e, hehe'e, lu'a, kū'olo, luhe; 'ōluheluhe *(as a potbelly);* lule, mū'olo; 'olo'olōna *(under a weight);* hūalakē, ho'okalekale, kalekale, 'ope'alu, paleha, pēheu, kōkīkī, puhalu, halu, uhalu.
sage. 1. *Wise man.* 'Elemakule 'imi loa. *See* **seer. 2.** *Plant.* Kako, līlīlehua.
sagittal. Hoai kaupaku.
sago. Keko.
said. *See* **say.** *It is said,* 'ōlelo 'ia. *Said to be,* pau *(see idiom,* **pau).**
sail. 1. *As a ship.* Holo, ho'oholo, hoholo, kele, ho'okele; ho'okelekele *(frequently);* holomoku, ho'oholomoku, holokai, holomoana. *Also:* kūkele, kikihi, leleaoa. *See* **drift.** *To go for a sail,* holoholo. *To sail to leeward,* ka'alalo. *To sail to windward,* ka'aluna, ho'opi'ipi'i; ho'opāhu'a *(rare). To sail around,* holo puni. *To sail swiftly,* holo kikī. *To sail aimlessly,* holoholo wale, auhele. *To sail cautiously,* akaholo. *To sail off*

[torn corner — partially legible diagonal text]

salt pork. Pua'a pa'akai, pua'a kāpī. *To sa[...]* pua'a. Hau'eli. *See* **smelling salts.** [...] pua'a. Poho lūlū pa'akai, poho pa'a[...] **salts.** Li'u, ālia, ālialia; 'ōmiko *(as soil ne[...]* **salt shaker.** [...] **salty.** Li'u, ālia, ālialia; 'ōmiko *(as soil ne[...]* **salutation.** Aloha. *Also:* ho'omaika'i, hā'aw[...] **salute.** Ho'āilona ho'omaika'i, pū aloha, [...] ho'omaika'i. *Gun salute,* ho'omaika'i i ka [...] *To salute the flag,* ho'omaika'i i ka [...] **Salvador.** Kalawakoa, Salawadoa[...]
salvation. Ola, ola mau loa, [...] doa.
Salvation Army. Pū'ali Ho'ōla, [...]
salve. Lā'au hamo, 'oia mau nō. [...]
same. Like, like pū, kohu like, [...] *same as usual,* 'oia mau nō. [...] *The same father,* ho'okahi nō [...] *time,* ho'okahi, 'i ka manawa [...] *result,* 'oia ana nō. [...]
Samoa. Kāmoa, Ha'amoa. [...]
Samoan. Kāmoa, Ha'amoa, [...]
sample. Mea ho'ike'ike 'u[...] **sanctify.** Ho'okapu, ho'o[...] **sanctimonious.** Ho'āpono [...] **sanction.** Ho'āpono. Wahi ho'ā[...] **sanctuary.** Wahi kanaho, pu'uh[...] wahi kanaho. *White sand,* [...] **sand.** One. *White sand,* [...] *dery sand,* pa'u ana[...] one 'ae'ae, hune[...] papa kea. *Sand[...]* 'ōhiki. *Wet sand,* [...] one hali, one '[...] *To sand,* [...] *(poetic).* Kāma[...] **sandal.** Kāma'a pale[...] palaha, kua[...] **sandalwood.** [...] wahic 'ala[...] naio. [...] wood, [...] **sandb[...]** sand[...] sand[...] sand[...] sand[...] sand[...] sand[...] sand[...] sand[...] sand[...]

s[...]
sa[...]
sc[...]
sale. [...] *sale).* [...] 'ēmi kū[...]
Salem. Kal[...]
salesman. K[...] **salesman.**
sales tax. 'Auhau [...]
saline. Pa'akai; 'ō[...]
saliva. Kuha, hā'ae, [...]
sallow. 'Ōlenalena.
sally over. Kale'oa.
salmon. Kāmano. *Canned [...]* salmon, kāmano pa'akai. [...] lomi. *Sea salmon,* kamanu. [...] kāmano, 'amo kāmano *[both [...]* white people];* 'amo, anal open[...] 'ōkole *because* amo *occurs in the [...]* Klamath, Oregon, where Hawaiian[...] fishing]. (Salmon was used in sorcery[...] of the similarity of its name to kāmano[...] used in love magic.) Compare* -mano, mar[...]
Salonika. Kalonika, Salonika.
saloon. Hale inu lama.
salsify. Kalapī.
salt. Pa'akai. *To salt,* kāpī, kōpī, ho'omiko, kān[...] *Ocherous earth used to color and flavor salt,* 'ala[...] *Salt thus treated,* pa'akai 'ula'ula. *Salt bed,* ālialia, ālia, hāhāpa'akai. *Salt flat,* papa pa'akai *(fig., sour disposition). Salt-encrusted,* ālia, ālialia, pa'apa'akai, pāpa'a kai, ni'i. *Sea water left in pool to form a salt crust by evaporation,* kai ho'olulu. *Salt container, saltcellar,* poho pa'akai, ipu kūli'u. *To salt pork,* kāpī pua'a. *To roll in salt,* ka'a pa'akai. *To gather salt,* hāhāpa'akai.
salted. Miko, mali'u *(well salted);* mikomiko *(lightly). Salted meat,* kākāmaka *(raw);* kākāmo'a *(cooked).*
Salt Lake City. Loko Pa'akai.
salt pan. Kāheka, makapāpipi *(natural);* kāhekaheka *(artificial).*

scaffold. 'Oloke'a.
scalawag. 'Alapu'u mo'o.
scald. Welaahi.
scale. 1. *Measure.* Alapi'i; *musical —,* alapi'i mele, pākōlī. *See* note, scales. **2.** *Fish.* Unahi, unahinahi. *To scale,* unaunahi. *The Kula people scale squids, the Kula people paddle awkwardly,* ka po'e unaunahi he'e o Kula, 'o Kula hoe hewa *(of ignorance).*
scaleless. Unahi 'ole.
scales. Kaupaona, paona, paona kaulike, ana paona *(weighing).* *Baby scales,* paona keiki.
scalloped. Nihoniho.
scallops. Nihoniho, pepeiao.
scalp. 'Ili po'o. *To scalp,* lole. *Crusty scalp, eczema of scalp,* pāpa'a piele, piele.
scaly. Unahi, unahinahi *(as fish);* māhuna, pakapaka, luehu *(as skin).*
scamp. 'Eu, piha 'eu, kupu'eu, kolohe.
scandal. Hana i wā 'ia. *See saying,* **māmane.**
scandalous. Kū i ka wā 'ia.
scanty. Lawa 'ole, hemo'ē.
scapegoat. Kao hele, mea i ho'opa'i 'ia no nā hewa o ha'i.
scar. 'Ālina, linalina, lina. *Also:* pihi, pihipihi, mō'ali, 'ali, 'ali'ali, kākala wela, pa'awela *(from burning);* pala'e *(on neck from glandular disease);* ko'ako'a, 'ala-'ala. *To scar,* hō'ali'ali, ho'olina, kākala wela.
scarce. Kaka'ikahi, pānoanoa.
scarcely. 'Ane'ane.
scare. Ho'omaka'u, ho'opū'iwa; — *away,* ho'ohemū.
scarecrow. Ki'i ho'oweliweli.
scarf. Lei 'ā'ī, kākai.
scarify. Kahakaha.
scarlet. 'Ula. *See* red.
scarlet fever. Piwa 'ula'ula.
scarred. 'A'alina, 'a'ali, hō'ali'ali, 'ali'ali, pihipihi, manu, manumanu, ko'ako'a, 'ālina.
scat. Hele ma kahi 'ē, hemū.
scatter. Ho'opuehu, lū, lūlū, lū helele'i, nū. *Also:* kau li'ili'i, ho'ohelele'i, lele li'ili'i, kāpī, kūlele, ho'oleilei, kaiehu, kōlū, kī'ope, ho'omalele. *Scatter in every direction,* ho'opuehu li'ili'i. *Scatter in excitement,* holo pū'ā'ā. *The crowd scatters,* ho'i nui ka lehulehu.
scattered. Puehu, helele'i, luehu. *Also:* malele, pākikokiko, pūlunaluna, pākakahi, nūpolupolu, nūponuponu, mōkākī, kāwala, pūkākā, kūka'ikahi, kūkāka'ikahi, punapuna, pū'ā'ā.
scavenger. 'Ai pilau, 'ai pala maunu, 'ai pala niho. *See saying,* **crab.**
scavenger bird. Manu-'ai-pilau.
scene. Nānaina; mahele, pale, moku *(in a play).*
scenery. Nānaina, 'ikena, waihona 'āina.
scent. *See* smell.
sceptical. Hilina'i 'ole, ho'omahuakala, mana'o'i'o 'ole, ho'opāhala, maloka, ho'omaloka.
sceptre. Hō'ailona ali'i pa'a lima, hō'ailona mō'ī.
schedule. Papa kuhikuhi, papa hō'ike, papa kuhikuhi manawa, papa.
scheme. Ho'olālā 'ana.
scholar. Mea 'imi na'auao, akeakamai.
scholarship. 1. *Pursuit of knowledge.* Hana 'imi na'auao, huli *(followed by qualifier; see* huli 2 *and below).* **2.** *Student aid.* Waihona kōkua ho'ona'auao, ha'awina kōkua ho'ona'auao.
scholium. Mana'o wehewehe.
school. 1. *Educational.* Kula. *See* high school, manual, preparatory school, private, reform school, select school, teacher, university. *Go to school,* hele kula, kukula. *Hold school,* kula. *School supplies,* lako kula. **2.** *Fish.* I'a kū, kū, he'e, kahe, kauhulu.
school child. Keiki hele kula.
schoolhouse. Hale kula.
schoolmaster. Kahu kula, luna kula.
schoolmate. Hoa kula.
schoolteacher. Kumu kula, kumu a'o.

schooner. Moku; moku kia lua *(two-masted);* kuna.
science. Akeakamai, hana 'imi na'auao, huli kanaka, 'ike no'eau.
scientific. *See* science. *Scientific name,* inoa Lākina.
scientist. Mea 'imi na'auao, akeakamai.
scion. Weli, weweli, weliweli.
scissors. 'Ūpā; 'ūpā miki'ao *(fingernail).*
scoff. Pāhenehene. *See* jeer.
scold. Nuku, ke'u, ho'okekē, ho'okekē niho, huhū. *Also:* ho'okekē nuku, ha'akekē, hae, kolokolo, waha lapalapa, meku, pakake'u, kūkahalakē, kekē.
scoop. Kī'o'e, kūpā, hao, kope, kope 'ana; — *out,* pō-'alo, pao, kī'alo, olohi'a. *Also:* po'o, kūpele, kīpaopao, hōuna, haohana.
scoopful. Haona.
scoop net. 'Upena uluulu, 'upena kā'e'e.
scope. Nui, laulā.
scorch. Kuni, pāpa'a wela, eina, 'ānia. *Also:* pāwela, lili'u, haulalapa, uno'o; pākī'ai, nikipa'u, haoa, 'ōhaoa.
score. 1. *Count.* Helu, 'ai. *To keep score,* helu 'ai. **2.** *See* twenty.
scoreboard. Papa helu.
scorekeeper. Helu 'ai.
scoreless. 'Ai 'ole; 'ōhule *(slang).*
scorn. Ho'owahāwahā, ho'okae, wahāwahā, kae. *Also:* ha'akei, ihu 'e'eke, pinana ka ihu, 'ōkoleoioi, ho'oma'ewa, ho'okē. *See* exclamation.
scornful. Ma'ewa; ihuihu, 'auwae, hō'auwae. *See* scorn.
scorpion. Mo'o-niho-'awa, mo'o-huelo-'awa, kopena, kopiana.
scorpionfish. Nohu *(see Haw.-Eng. entry and entries that follow it).*
Scotch, Scotland, Scottish. Kekokia.
Scotia. Sekotia.
scoundrel. Lapuwale, pu'uwai 'ele'ele.
scour. Kuai, 'ānai, kuolo, holoi.
scouring stone. Nohu.
scout. Kiu; 'oumuamua *(rare).*
scow. Kao.
scowl. Ho'oku'eku'emaka, ho'oku'eku'emaka nui, ho'opupuku, ho'o'i'ika. *Also:* 'i'ī, māku'e, makaku'iku'i, ho'onohu.
scraggly. Kīwalawala, kīwalawala'ō, hao'a.
scramble. Huikau, ho'ohuikau *(mix);* pākā. *Scrambled eggs,* hua kai, hua pākā.
scrap. 1. *Remnant.* Huna, hakina, hunahuna, 'āpana li'ili'i. **2.** *See* fight.
scrap bowl. Ipu 'aina.
scrape. Wa'u, wawa'u, wa'uwa'u, koe, kuai, kahi, pohole. *Also:* uwa'u, kāwa'u, walu, 'uwalu, mākoe, mahole, mohole, hē, kepa, mōholehole, kele.
scraper. Kahi, wa'u, uwa'u, wawa'u, wa'uwa'u; uhi *(of turtle shell);* kalepa.
scrap iron. Pāpa'a hao.
scraps. Koena, hakina 'ai, 'āmikamika, 'ōpilopilo, kō-'ala'ala.
scratch. Walu, wawalu, 'uwalu *(as a cat);* koe; helu *(as a hen).* *Also:* heluhelu, waluhia, waluwalu, wa'u, uwa'u, wawa'u, wa'uwa'u, kuolo, kope, kaha, kahakaha, kīhelu, māhelu, moku'oi, neneke.
scratched. Koea, waluhia. *See* scratch.
scratchings. Kahakahana, waluna, koena. *See* scratch.
scratch paper. Pepa kahakaha.
scrawly. Kiwala'ō *(as writing).*
scream. 'Alalā, pū'alalā, walā'au nui, kolopā. *See* roar.
screech. Alalī, kīkīko'u, kani 'ōkalakala.
screen. Pākū, pālulu, ālai, ānai, wahamana. *Wire screen,* uwea hamana. *Window screen,* uwea hakahaka, pālulu pukaaniani. *Screen for projecting pictures or movies,* wahi ho'olele ki'i.
screw. Kui nao, kui, kolū. *To screw,* wili.
screw auger. Wilipua'a, ulepua'a.
screwdriver. Kuikala, kala, kala nao.
scribble. Kākau wale, kopekope.

scribe. Kākau ʻōlelo. *Royal scribe,* kākau aliʻi.
Scriptures. Palapala Hemolele.
scrofula. ʻĀʻī palaʻe, ʻāʻī ʻalaʻala.
scroll. ʻŌwili palapala.
scrotum. Laho *(for various idioms and insults, see* laho *and entries that follow it). Also:* ʻeke, ʻekeʻeke, ʻōpeʻa, ʻolo. *Bull scrotum,* laho pipi. *Raw scrotum,* laho kole. *My man with big voice whose scrotum sounds,* kuʻu kanaka leo nui, na ka laho e hoʻokani *(a riddle: a bell is the answer).*
scrub. ʻĀnai, holoi, kuolo *(verb).*
scrubbing brush. Palaki ʻānai.
scrubby. ʻIʻi, kāiʻoiʻo.
scrutinize. Nānā pono, loi, hoʻomakauliʻi.
scrutiny. Loina. *See* **scrutinize.**
scud. Kaʻa.
sculptor. Mea kālai kiʻi, kuʻekepa.
scum. Huʻa, huʻahuʻa. *A few scums:* limu kalawai (pālāwai), pāwai, nehe.
scurvy. Pehu pala, puʻupuʻu.
scythe. Pahi kākiwi.
sea. Kai; moana *(open);* malo, pāʻū *(poetic). See sayings,* **pūnoni, forecast.** *Calm, quiet sea,* kai mālie, kai malino, kai malolo, kai hoʻolulu, kai pū, kai wahine, kai kalamania, kaiolohia. *Strong sea,* kai koʻo, kai kāne, kai nui, kai nuʻu, ʻōkaikai. *Rough or raging sea,* kai pupule, kai puʻeone, kai akua, ʻōkaikai. *Deep sea,* kai hohonu, kai ʻau, kai hoʻēʻe, kai lū heʻe *(fig.). Restless sea with undercurrent,* kai kuolo, kai holo, kai lewa, lapa kai, kai kō, kai au. *Dark blue sea,* moana uli, moauli. *Streaked sea, associated with Kona,* kai māʻokiʻoki. *Whispering sea, associated with Kawaihae,* kai hāwanawana. *Salt sea,* kai paʻakai. *Shallow or reef sea,* kai kohola, kai koʻele. *Rippled sea,* kai hoʻolili. *Receding or ebbing sea,* kai heʻe, kai emi, kai mimiki, kai hoʻi, kai nuʻu aku. *Western sea,* kai lalo. *High sea,* kai piha, kai nuʻu. *Of the sea,* o kai. *Towards the sea,* i kai, makai. *Place where sea and land meet,* ʻae kai. *By the sea,* a kai. *Sea almost surrounded by land,* kai hāloko. *The eight seas,* nā kai ʻewalu *(seas about the Hawaiian Islands, poetic). Puna with its sea rustling over pebbles,* Puna i ke kai nehe i ka ʻiliʻili. *My sea, concealing sarong (UL 124),* kuʻu kai, pāʻū halakā. *Black sea, yellow sea, Kāne's purplish-blue red-brown sea . . . silent sea, swinging sea (PH 237),* kai ʻeleʻele, kai melemele, kai pōpolohua mea a Kāne . . . kai mū, kai lewa.
sea area. Kai.
sea bean. Kāʻeʻe, maunaloa. *Seeds of* kāʻeʻe, pīpā, pēkaʻa.
seacoast. Kahakai.
sea cucumber. Loli *(for various kinds, see* loli *and entries that follow it),* weli, weliweli, maʻihole, kūnounou, hulali, hūlalilali, ʻūpalu, kūneuneu, ʻunae, kaʻukama kai. *See ex. of word magic,* ʻiloli. *Catch the sea cucumber by mistake, a blind fish,* hopu hewa i ka loli, ka iʻa makapō *(of disappointment, a worthless catch, or ignorance).*
sea dog. ʻĪlio ʻaukai.
sea elephant. ʻElepani kai.
seafarer. Holomoana, holokai, ʻaukai.
sea foam. Ehu kai.
sea gull. Nēnē ʻau kai, ʻōpaʻipaʻi.
sea horse. Moʻo lio.
Sea Island cotton. Kiʻailana.
seal. 1. *Emblem.* Kila. *Also:* uwepa, hoʻopaʻa, kuni. *Seal of office,* sila o ke keʻena. *To fix a seal,* kila. 2. *Mammal.* ʻĪlio-holo-i-ka-uaua, hulu *(rare).*
sea lettuce. ʻĪlioha, līpaha, līpahapaha, pahapaha, līpālahalaha, pakaiea, pālahalaha. *See* **seaweed.**
sealing wax. Kēpau kāpili palapala.
seam. Kuʻina, kuʻi, humu, humuhumu, humuna.
seaman. *See* **sailor.**
seamed. Hāluʻa.
sear. Kuni. *Also:* haulalapa, kā liliko.

search. ʻImi, huli; ʻimina, hulina *(nouns). Also:* holi, ʻakiu. *To search repeatedly,* hulihuli, huli hele. *To search, as for knowledge,* noiʻi, noiʻina.
search warrant. Palapala huli.
sea shell. Pūpū *(for various kinds, see* pūpū *and entries that follow it). See* **shell.**
seashore. Kahakai, kapa kai.
seasick. Poluea, luea, hoʻopapailua, ʻōlanalana. *See* **nausea.**
seaside. Kapa kai, kahakai, kai.
sea slug. *See* **sea cucumber.**
season. 1. *Time,* Kau. *Also:* wā, manawa, laʻa, kikina. *See* **fall, spring, summer, winter.** *Rainy season,* wā ua, manawa ua, laʻa ua. *Fruit season,* kau hua. *Season of dying plants,* laʻa make. *Octopus season,* wā heʻe. *Season after season,* kau ā kau. *To season, as lumber,* hoʻomaloʻo. 2. *Impart taste.* Hōʻono, hōʻonoʻono, hoʻomiko, kāmala. *Seasoned,* miko, liʻu, maliʻu.
seasoning. Mea hōʻonoʻono, mea hoʻomikomiko, liʻu, kūliʻu.
sea spray. Ehu kai.
seat. Noho, nohona, hoʻonoho. *High, rickety seat,* kiolea. *Seat cover,* pale noho.
sea urchin. Wana, wanawana, wana kauila; ʻina. *Various kinds:* hāʻukeʻuke *(also, name of a tapa design);* hāʻuke iwi loloa, hāʻuke, hāʻukaʻuka, hāʻueʻue, hākuʻekuʻe, hāluʻe, hālula, pūnohu, huluʻanai, niho, hailimoa. *Sea-urchin meat,* alelo, poke ʻina. *Sea-urchin sauce,* kai ʻina. *To remove sea-urchin flesh,* poke ʻina. *See saying,* **hāwaʻe.**
sea wall. Pani kai.
seaward. Makai, i kai, o kai.
sea water. Kai.
seaweed. Limu, lī-. *See Haw.-Eng. entries and the entries that follow them for various kinds.* Limu *and* lī- *are sometimes omitted. Some names vary according to islands. See lists below, also* **moss, scum, sea lettuce, vagabond.** *Ball of seaweed, as sold for food,* pōpō limu; *to gather seaweed,* ʻaku limu.
COMMON EDIBLE SEAWEEDS *(following Abbott and Williamson; var. names are in parentheses, but see Haw.-Eng. entries for other names):* ʻakiʻaki (kōʻeleʻele), ʻeleʻele, huluhulu waena (pakele-a-waʻa), limu kala, limu kohu (līpehe, līpehu, līpaʻakai), līpahapaha (pahapaha, pāpahapaha, līpaha, pālahalana, pakaiea, ʻīlioʻa), līpeʻepeʻe, līpoa, manauea, māneʻoneʻo, paheʻe (pāheʻeheʻe, limu lūʻau), wawaeʻiole (ʻaʻala, ʻaʻalaʻula, ʻalaʻula).
LESS COMMON SEAWEEDS *(alternate names are in parentheses; see also Haw.-Eng. entries beginning* limu *and* lī-*):* ʻākaʻakoʻa, alani, ʻānapanapa (limu loloa), ʻāpiʻipiʻi, ʻaʻula (hāʻula?), ʻawa, ʻāweʻaweʻa, ʻāweoweo, ʻekoʻelo (pīpīlani), hāwane, hinaʻula, hoʻonunu, huʻahuʻakai, hūai, huihui, huihui maka liʻi, hulu ʻiʻi, hulu ʻīlio (hulu, hulu pāhuluhulu, ʻīlio, nahawele, pūhuluhulu), hulu manu (ʻai-a-ka-honu, manu a, līmoa), huna (hunehune), huna pakēpakē, hūpēkohola, kāʻapeʻape, kāʻele, kāhili, kaunoʻa, kaupau, kāwelu, kihe (akula), kīkalamoa (kīkala), kīkī, kilihune, kōʻeleʻele (kōʻele, ʻāwikiwiki, ʻēkahakaha, limu-uaua-loli, nei), lauoho-o-Pele, lelepo, lepe-o-Hina (lehelehe-ʻīlio, lepelepe-o-Hina), leponalo, lolekalua, lupe, maka, makaloa, mākole, makua-o-ka-limu-kohu, manamana-ʻula, māwaewae-kilihune, moʻopuna-a-ka-līpoa (aupūpū), naio, nakeke, nane, nanea, nanoʻo, nene (nenue), nē, nuʻa, ʻōhelo-huihui, ʻōhiʻohiʻo, ʻōhune, ʻōkala, ʻōmaʻomaʻo, oneone, ʻoʻolu, ʻopiʻopi, pahapaha-o-Polihale, pahapaha-wai, pākalakala, pakelo, pakēpakē, pakūpakū, pala, pala pōhaku, pala ʻula, pale wāwae, paninikū, pānohonoho, pānoʻonoʻo, pāpaʻakea, pāʻū-o-Hiʻiaka, pehu, pepe-o-Hina, pīlali, pilikoʻa, pohāpohā (pohā), popohe-Makaliʻi, puakī, pūhā, pūkoʻakoʻa, pūʻula, ʻūnoko, wāwahi-waʻa, weluwelu.
sea worm. Koʻe kai.
Sechem. Kekema, Sekema.

second. Lua, kualua; kekona *(time unit);* kōko'olua *(in a duel). To second a motion,* kōkua. *The second time,* ka lua o ka manawa.
secondary. Lua.
second-degree murder. 'Elua kekele o ka pepehi kanaka.
secondhand. Mea i ho'ohana mua 'ia, hana mua 'ia.
secondly. Lua.
second sight. Maka 'ike, 'ike pāpālua. *Gift of second sight,* ha'awina 'ike.
secret. Mea huna, huna, malū, 'ōhuna. *To hide or keep in secret,* hūnā, hūnākele, 'ekepue. *To do evil in secret,* kāmalū. *Secret languages:* wehiwa, nehiwa, kake.
secretary. 1. *Clerical aid.* Kākau 'ōlelo, kākau mo'olelo; ikū kau *(rare). Private secretary,* kākau 'ōlelo pilikino. **2.** *High official.* Kuhina.
secretary of interior. Kuhina kālai'āina.
secretary of state. Kuhina moku'āina.
secretary of war. Kuhina kaua.
secretive. Pe'e poli, malū, 'ekepue, hō'ekepue, hūnā. *See saying,* **kio 2.**
secretly. Hunāhunā, malū. *Take secretly,* lawe malū.
secret service. 'Oihana kiu.
secret society. 'Ahahui malū; nauwā *(formed by Ka-lā-kaua).*
sect. Ho'omana, mahele ho'omana.
section. Paukū, moku, mokuna, 'āpana, mahele; mahele hana *(work section). Also:* mō, hakina; puna *(between joints);* kiko *(of a story);* huli *(as of town or place);* poke; hā'ao *(in chief's procession);* nanaka *(marked).*
sector. 'Āpana.
secure. Pa'a. *Also:* papa'a, kuapapa, kulekule. *See* **safe.** *To make secure,* ho'opa'a, hana pa'a, hoa, 'ōmau. *Not secure,* pa'a 'ole, holokake.
security. Palekana, panekana, maluhia, kahua pa'a; waiwai ho'opa'a *(investment). See saying,* **heaven.**
security bank. Panakō ho'omalu 'ia.
security guard. Kia'ipo'o.
sedan chair. Mənele.
sedate. Kūo'o, no'eno'e.
sedges. Mau'u. *Varieties:* 'ahaniu, 'ahu'awa, 'ehu'awa, kāluhāluhā, kiolohia, kohekohe, kuolohia, makaloa, manunēnē, mokae, pīpīwai, pōpōhau-o-Ni'ihau, pu'uka'a, 'uki.
sediment. Oka, ko'ana, mākū.
sedition libel. Laipila ho'ālaala kipi.
seditious. Kipi. *Seditious offenses,* hewa ho'ālaala kipi.
seduce. Ho'owalewale hewa, alaka'i hewa, luahele.
see. 'Ike; 'ike *(look at). To see clearly, well, keenly,* 'ike pono, 'ike le'a, maka 'ike, 'i'ike, 'ike kōnale. *To see personally,* 'ike maka. *To see double,* 'ike pāpālua. *To see supernatural things,* maka 'ike. *To see indistinctly,* hala'o'a, pāwao *(rare). To see but disregard,* nānā kuli. *Let me see!* 'Oliana! 'Oiana! 'Oia ana! Aliana! Inane!
seed. 'Ano'ano, hua; hua kanu *(for planting);* lū *(of beach poppy). To bear seed,* hua. *Seed of* loulu *palm,* wāhane, hāwane. *Seed of* 'āweoweo *(a shrub),* mokiweo. *Seed of* kā'e'e, pēka'a, pīpā.
seedbed. Wahi kanu 'ano'ano. *Also:* loko ulu, haokanu.
seedling. Kawowo, hehu. *Also:* ila, 'ōilo.
seeing. 'Ikena.
seek. 'Imi, huli. *Also:* huhuli, huhuhuli, 'i'imi *(of many and repeatedly);* 'akiu, nowelo. *To seek far,* 'imi loa. *To seek money,* 'imi kālā. *To seek work,* 'imi hana. *To seek information or knowledge,* noi'i, 'imi 'ike, 'imi na'auao. *To seek for sexual ends,* ki'i. *To seek revenge,* ho'opa'i, ho'opāna'i, 'imi i kahi e kū ai ka mākaia.
seeking. 'Imina, hulina.
seems. 'Amo, mehe mea lā. *It seems good,* he 'ano maika'i ia.
seen. 'Ike 'ia, kūmaka. *Plainly seen,* 'ike maopopo 'ia, kaula'ela'e, 'ō'ili lua.
seepage. Nono, nō, manono.

seer. Kāula, kilo, kuhikuhipu'uone, nānā ao, 'imi loa. *God of seers,* Kuhimana. *Hi'iaka, seer with power (PH 151),* 'O Hi'iaka, kāula mana.
seesaw. Papa hulei *(board). To seesaw,* hulehulei. *Also:* mahiki, panau, ho'opanau, mākoiele.
segment. 'Āpana; 'āpana pō'ai *(of a circle).*
segregate. Ho'oka'awale.
segregation. Ho'oka'awale 'ana.
seine. Hukilau, lau, 'upena kō lau, lau kapalili, lau'apo-'apo, pāloa.
seismograph. Ana ōla'i, mīkini ana ōla'i.
seize. Hopu, 'apo, lālau, kā'ili. *Also:* ho'oki'iki'i, kā'ilikū, 'apakau, kāpe'a, lelemū, kūlē, lauhulu.
seizing. 'Uo *(lashing).*
seldom. Kaka'ikahi.
select. Koho, wae, 'ohi. *Also:* waewae, ho'owae, māwae, mōwae, mōae, 'ele'ī.
selection. Koho 'ana, wae 'ana, 'ohina.
selection board. Papa 'ohi.
selective. Kamawae, wae, waewae.
select school. Kula wae.
self. Iho, kino, pono'ī, 'ōiwi. *See* **bone.** *For myself,* no'u iho.
self-control. Kāohi iho.
selfish. 'Au'a; no'ono'o iāia wale iho nō, ho'okēāmaka.
self-satisfied. 'Olu'olu nō iāia iho.
sell. Kū'ai aku. *Also:* kālepa, ho'olilo, ma'au'auwā; ku'aku'ai, ho'oku'aku'ai *(sell repeatedly, buy and sell);* pākaukau *(over the counter). To sell leis,* kau lei.
seller. Mea kū'ai aku. *Lei seller,* mea kau lei, wahine kau lei.
selvage. Ka'e pa'a *(of cloth).*
semen. Keakea. *Also:* wai o ke kāne, wai. *See saying,* **keakea.**
semester. Kau.
semiannual. Hapa makahiki.
semicircle. Pō'ai hapalua.
semicolon. Kiko ho'omaha, kiko koma.
semiconscious. Ho'olana i ka wai ke ola.
senate. 'Aha kenekoa.
senator. Kenekoa.
send. Ho'ouna; — *on an errand,* kēnā; — *for,* ki'i, ho'oki'i, kauoha; — *back,* ho'iho'i; — *away,* kipaku, paku.
senior. Mua, makua, hele mua, hānau mua. *See saying,* **wawaele.** *Senior class,* papa ki'eki'e loa, papa e puka aku ana. *Smith, Senior,* Kamika Makua. *Senior branch (of a family),* nā hele mua, lālā hele mua. *To act as senior,* ho'omuamua.
sennit. 'Aha. *To braid sennit,* hō'aha.
sensation. Mea ho'okāhāhā. *See* **manene, sense.**
sensational. Kū i ke kāhāhā.
sense. 1. *Faculty.* 'Ike. *Sense of taste,* 'ike i ka 'ono. *Sense of pain,* 'ike i ka 'eha. *Sense of sight,* 'ike i ka maka. *Common sense,* no'ono'o kūpono. **2.** *Import.* Mana'o nui.
sensible. No'ono'o pono.
sensitive. 1. *Perceptive.* 'Ike ho'omaopopo. **2.** *As to criticism.* 'Eha wale, ku'ia wale. *Also:* heke, lili.
sensitive plant. Pua hilahila.
sensory. 'Ike. *Extrasensory perception,* 'ike pāpālua.
sensual. Kuko i kō ke kino; pākīai *(rare).*
sentence. Māmala'ōlelo *(words);* 'ōlelo ho'opa'i *(penalty).*
sentiment. Aloha.
sentimental. Pakela ho'ālohaloha loa.
sentinel. Koa kia'i, kū uwaki.
separate. Ka'awale, kau 'oko'a, kā'oko'a, hemo, lele, ho'oka'awale. *Also:* ho'oka'a'oko'a, hō'oko'a, kauko'a, ho'okaupale, wae, waewae, māwae, mahae, weke, wekeweke, māwehe, māweke, mōwae, mōae, ho'opale, kōhikōhi, 'oki. *See* **kai'okia.** *To separate by space,* ho'okōwā. *To separate taro corm from stalk,* kōhi 'ai.
separately. Pākahi, ho'oka'awale 'ia, ho'okahi, 'oko'a. *Considered separately,* no'ono'o pākahi 'ia.

separation. Ka'awale 'ana, 'okina, ho'omoku, palena, hemohemo, 'akaka.
September. Kepakemapa.
sepulcher. Hale kupapa'u, ilina kupapa'u, ilina.
sequel. Hope, hopena.
sequence. Noho papa 'ana, ho'onoho papa 'ana, kaka-'ina, ka'ina, kekahi mahope mai o kekahi, moekahi. *See* **succession.**
seraphim. Kelapima.
serenade. Mele ho'oipoipo, mele ho'ālohaloha *(romantic).*
serene. Maluhia, la'i, mālie, la'ela'e, māla'e. *Also:* la'ikū, kohea, pālūlā, 'alaneo. *Serene weather,* kohea.
serge. 'Alapia, paina *(resembling).*
sergeant. Kakiana. *Sergeant major,* kakiana mekia.
sergeant-at-arms. Mālama puka.
sergeant fish. Mamo.
serial. Helu.
serial bond. Pona helu.
series. Mahele *(as of books);* mo'o. *See* **sequence, set.** *One of a series,* kaka'ina.
serious. Kūo'o. *Also:* hō'i'o, hana'i'o, kūkonukonu. *See* **important.**
sermon. Ha'i'ōlelo, ha'i a'o.
serpent. Mo'o, mo'o kiha, mo'olele. *See* **snake.**
Serpentine River. Muliwai Kepenakina.
serrated. Wakawaka, nihoniho, nihoa, 'ōniho.
servant. Kanaka hana *(male);* wahine hana *(female);* kanaka lawelawe, kanaka, 'ōhua. *See* **outcast, retainer.** *Anciently, attendants to a chief were privileged blood relatives who might not be dismissed;* kauā *(Biblical, servant) were despised outcasts not permitted access to chiefs; the Euro-American idea of the inferior status of servants was unknown. Your humble servant,* kāu kauā ha'aha'a. *Your obedient servant,* kāu kauā ho'olohe. *Servant of God,* kauā a ke Akua.
serve. Lawelawe. *Also:* ho'okō *(as a warrant);* mālama, ka'a malalo. *Serves you right!* Alolo! 'Aikola! Lolo! Ā la'a lā!
service. Lawelawe *(assistance);* hana, 'oihana *(occupation, division, department). Service charge,* uku lawelawe. *Military service,* 'oihana koa. *Church service,* pule, hālāwai haipule, haipule, haipule 'ana.
service of process. Ho'okō 'ana i ka palapala kēnā.
servile. Ha'aha'a loa, ka'apē, kuapa'a.
sesban. 'Ohai ke'oke'o, 'ohai 'ula'ula.
session. Kau. *Regular session,* kau mau *(of legislature). Special session,* kau kūikawā. *To be in session,* noho.
set. 1. *To place.* Kau; ho'onoho *(as table, bones, type);* ho'omoe, ho'omoemoe, ku'u, au *(as line or net);* 'ōniu, ulele *(as type);* mau *(as a wager);* napo'o, welo *(of sun);* kōkō *(bones by applying pressure);* pa'ihi, hao ā pa'ihi *(as sails);* kāpili *(as precious stones). To set on fire,* hō'ā, puhi ahi. *To set firmly,* pa'akūkū, ho'opa'a. *To set apart,* ho'oka'awale, hō'oko'a, kai'okia; mōlia *(for gods). To set aside,* kāpae, waiho. *To set up,* kūkulu, ho'okū. *To set off, explode,* ho'opahū. *To set free,* ho'oku'u, makala, mokala, puhemo. *To set apart for sacred purposes,* ho'ola'a, ho'okapu. *To set a table,* ho'onoho i ka pākaukau. **2.** *Assortment.* Nā mea kohu like o ke 'ano ho'okahi, kaina. *Tea set,* kaina ho'okahi o nā mea inu kī.
settee. Kokī, noho lō'ihi. *See* **couch.**
setting. Kahua, wahi; 'ōnohi *(as of a ring). Diamond setting,* 'ōpu'u kaimana, 'ōnohi kaimana. *Setting sun,* napo'ona lā, lā kau. *The setting of the moon (Kep. 105),* ka napo'ona mahina.
settle. Kau; mākū, ko'ana, ho'oko'ana, ki'o *(as dregs);* kiki'o, pāki'o, ho'oki'o, ki'o wai *(as water in a pond);* ku'u, emi iho, pohō, pohī *(as earth);* 'ōku'u, noe *(as mist);* ho'onā *(as a claim);* ho'oholo *(as a problem);* akaku'u *(as wind). To settle down, stay,* noho pa'a, ho'okahua.
settled. Kau, nā, holo, akaku'u. *See* **settle.**
settlement. Kauhale, aukanaka. *See* **agreement.**
seven. Hiku, 'ehiku, 'ahiku. *Seven times,* 'ehiku, 'ahiku,

pāhiku. *Seven years,* 'ehiku makahiki, hepekoma. *Seven times seven,* hiku hiku.
sevenfold. Pāhiku.
seventeen. 'Umi kūmāhiku, 'umi kumamāhiku.
seventh. Hiku. *One-seventh,* hapahiku.
Seventh-day Adventist. Ho'omana Pō'aono.
seventy. Kanahiku.
seventy-eight. Kanahiku kūmāwalu, kanahiku kumamāwalu.
seventy-five. Kanahiku kūmālima, kanahiku kumamālima.
seventy-four. Kanahiku kūmāhā, kanahiku kumamāhā.
seventy-nine. Kanahiku kūmāiwa, kanahiku kumamāiwa.
seventy-one. Kanahiku kūmākahi, kanahiku kumamākahi.
seventy-seven. Kanahiku kūmāhiku, kanahiku kumamāhiku.
seventy-six. Kanahiku kūmāono, kanahiku kumamāono.
seventy-three. Kanahiku kūmākolu, kanahiku kumamākolu.
seventy-two. Kanahiku kūmālua, kanahiku kumamālua.
sever. 'Oki, moku. *Also:* mō, muku, mukumuku, mokumoku, momoku, 'āmokumoku. *Severed,* moku, pahupū, lele loa, po'omuku, mokuna.
several. Kekahi, kekahi mau.
severance. 'Okina, mokuna.
severe. 'O'ole'a, 'a'aka, uahoa, ko'iko'i. *Also:* kūpiliki'i; lo'a'ā *(as taboo);* pā'ea'ea. *To treat severely,* ho'oko'iko'i.
Seville. Kewila, Sevila.
sew. Humuhumu. *Also:* hono, ku'i, holoholo, 'ōmau; pāhono *(as a tear);* holo *(as a break in a gourd);* kāholo *(with long stitches). To sew sails,* humu pe'a, uhauhumu *(rare). To sew in a diagonal line,* humu lala.
sewer. 'Auwai, kua, hā wai, 'auwai lawe mea 'ino.
sewer pipe. Paipu lawe 'ino, hā wai lawe 'ino.
sewing. Humuna. *See* **sew.**
sewing machine. Mīkini humuhumu, kāwiliwili humuhumu. *For parts, see* **huila, kā'ei, kanokaomi, pane'e'ūpiki, papa hehi, papa ho'oholo, bobbin winder, clamp, feed dog, gatherer, gauge, latch, presser foot, shuttle, spool.**
sex. *No Hawaiian term. See* **lascivious, lecherous, randy,** *and sayings,* **hua 4, ko'okā 1, pī'oe'oe, wa'uwa'u.** *Masculine sex,* keka kāne. *Feminine sex,* keka wahine.
sexual. *No Hawaiian term (but sexual innuendos are enjoyed);* pili i ke kāne me ka wahine. *See* **game** *and sayings,* **wali, cowry shell.** *Sexual passion,* kola, huahua'i. *Sexual excitement,* mane'o, kola. *Sexual part,* ma'i, wahi huna. *Sexually unattractive,* lemukū. *The hidden meaning of this song is sexual,* ke kaona o kēia mele, pili i ke kāne me ka wahine. *Beautiful but without sexual appeal,* he u'i kū i ki'ona (lit., *a beauty fit for the dung heap). Sexual attraction or relationship may be shown poetically by references to rain, mist, spray, coolness.*
sexual intercourse. Ai, ei, hana ma'i, moe, pi'i, panipani, aina. *Motions of sexual intercourse,* kū'ami'ami. *To have had sexual intercourse, of a female,* pā kanaka. *Sexual intercourse with a menstruating woman,* kokokohe.
shabby. Hāpa'upa'u, kuhā'eka, lu'a.
shack. Hale 'āpulu, kamala.
shaddock. 'Alani Pākē.
shade. Malu, māmalu; pālulu *(for protection). Shade under cliff or hill,* 'ūmalu. *To shade,* ho'omalumalu, ho'oma'ū, 'ūmalu, ho'o'ūmalu. *Eye shade,* pālulu maka. *Lamp shade,* pālulu kukui. *Window shade,* pākū pouli, pālulu pukaaniani. *Deep shade, as of trees,* malu hālau loa, malu ko'i, mālipolipo.
shadow. Aka, huaka, 'ūmalu. *See saying,* **aka 1.** *To cast a shadow,* ho'oaka, ili i ke aka, ho'ohuaka, ho'o'ūma-

lu; malila *(rare). To fall, as one shadow on another,* pi'i. *The valley of the shadow of death,* ke awāwa malu o ka make.

shady. Malumalu. *Also:* lāuli, 'ōmalu, 'ōmalumalu, ho'omalumalu, mālipolipo, milumilu, 'e'a'e'a; pololuhi *(rare). To make shady,* ho'omāmalu.

shaft. 1. *Column.* Kia, pou. **2.** *See* **handle.**

shaggy. Pūhuluhulu, 'ōhuluhulu, huluhulu.

shake. Naue, nauwe, nāueue, lūlū, hō'oni, ho'oluliluli, luli, luliluli *(as the head);* ho'oluli *(as a drink);* lūlū, nāueue, 'ōla'i, 'ōpa'ipa'i *(as the earth);* — *jerkily,* kūkū; — *as with palsy,* kuolo; — *as with cold or fear,* ulupi'i; — *badly,* 'oni 'ino. *Also:* ha'alulu, 'api, kuehu, kuekueni, lū, nū, naka, noiele, pilu, 'ōlūlū *(with fat),* 'olokā, paleha, ho'onāueue. *Shake hands,* lūlū lima.

shaky. Kulana, kulanalana, naluli, kāhulihuli.

shall. E . . . ana, e. *Gram. 5.2.*

shallow. Pāpa'u, hāpapa; mālānai, mānānai, pānānai, nānai *(rare). Shallow-rooted,* mālana, pūhai. *Sea too shallow to float a canoe in,* kai ko'ele.

sham. Ho'okamani. *Sham battle,* kaua kio, pahukala, kānekupua *(with spears).*

shame. Hilahila, waia. *To put to shame,* ho'ohilahila, ho'owaia, ho'ohoka. *What a shame!* Aloha 'ino!

shamefaced. Palai maka.

shameful. Ho'ohilahila.

shameless. Hilahila 'ole, 'uhane 'ole; mākolea *(rare).*

shampoo. Holoi lauoho. *Shampoo liquid,* mea holoi lauoho.

shamrock. 'Ihi pua kea.

Shanghai. Kainahai, Kanahai. *To shanghai,* kanahai.

shank. 1. *Fishhook part.* Kū'au. *Tail or small end of bonito lure,* muli. *Head or large end,* ihu. *Shank of octopus lure,* pou lua. **2.** *Leg.* Wāwae, lapawāwae.

shanty. Hale lālā lā'au, kāmala, hale pupupu.

shape. 'Ano, hō'omo'omo; kālai, 'ōmilo *(as a canoe hull);* ho'opololei, kālai *(as a policy or enterprise). Irregular in shape,* pā'ewa, pū'ali. *To take shape,* ho'okino. *To put in shape,* ho'oponopono, ho'opololei.

share. Mahele, pu'u; kea *(stocks). To share,* mahele; ka'ana, ho'oka'ana *(equally);* pu'unaue, 'alo. *Share food,* pū 'ai.

sharer. Hoa loa'a, hoa lawe pū.

shark. Manō *(for various kinds, sayings, fig. meanings, see Haw.-Eng. entry and entries that follow it). Also:* lālākea, laukāhi'u, leleiwi, lelewa'a, luhia, niuhi. *See saying,* **holopapa 2,** *and idiom,* **eat.** *Line of shark fins protruding above the water,* lālani kalalea. *To catch sharks with bait and noose,* kūmanō. *Shark-tooth weapon,* leiomano. *Shark-tooth knife,* niho 'oki. *To behave as a shark, to act like a shark, to pursue women,* ho'omanō. *The wiliwili blooms, sharks bite,* pua ka wiliwili, nanahu ka manō *(of a girl reaching maturity).*

shark sucker. Leleiona, moelawa *(remora).*

Sharon. Kalona. *The rose of Sharon,* ka loke o Kalona.

sharp. 1. *Not dull.* 'Oi, 'āwini. *Also:* 'oi'oi, kōī, ko'i, mūko'i, 'ou, kākala, kulilipi, nihoa, huini, waka, wakawaka, wana, wanawana, wawana. *Long and sharp,* pīoeoe. *Any sharp edge,* lipi. *Sharp point,* wini, winiwini. *Sharp nose,* ihu winiwini. *Sharp, shrill sounds,* huini. *Sharp-edged,* ka'e 'oi, 'ōniho. *Sharp-lipped,* lehe 'oi *(of one who makes cutting remarks).* **2.** *In music.* 'Oi.

sharpen. Ho'okala, hō'oi. *Also:* hō'oi'oi, hana ho'owini, koli, 'oi.

sharpener. Ho'okala, mea ho'okala.

sharpness. 'Oi.

sharpshooter. Kī pololei.

sharp-tongued. Kekē, kekē nuku, lehe 'oi, waha 'ā.

shatter. Wāwahi, nahā, nāhāhā, kā, ho'okā, kāpa'i.

shave. Kahi, āmū, koli. *To shave whiskers,* kahi 'umi-'umi. *To shave half the head in mourning,* kahi kīhapa. *Smooth-shaven,* kahania, kanekanea.

shavings. Oka lā'au, kahina; hānā *(rare).*

shawl. Kīhei. Kīhei *dyed with sandalwood,* peluliahi. *To wear a shawl,* kīheihei.

she. *Same as* **he.**

sheaf. Pū'ā, pū'ala. *We were binding sheaves,* i ka pū'ā 'ana a kākou i nā pū'ā.

shear. 'Ako, 'oki, āmū. *To shear sheep,* 'ako hulu hipa.

shearer. Mea 'ako. *Sheep shearer,* mea 'ako hulu hipa.

shears. 'Ūpā, 'ūpā nui. *Grass shears,* 'ūpā mau'u. *Pinking shears,* 'ūpā nihoniho.

shearwater. 'Ua'u kani (hō'io), 'a'o.

sheath. Pale, wahī, 'ili wahī. *Coconut-flower sheath,* holowa'a, holoa'a, lolo, lolo niu. *Coconut-sheath canoe,* wa'a lolo niu. *Banana-bud sheath,* 'ōpu'u mai'a.

shed. 1. *Building.* Hale ho'āhu. *Also:* hale pupupu, auolo, hale malu, hale malumalu, hale kāmala, lānai. **2.** *Throw off.* Helele'i, helelei *(as a dog's hair);* lū, nū; hāliko, ho'omalule *(as a crab sheds its shell);* auhā *(rare). Shed blood,* ho'okahe koko.

sheep. Hipa. *Flock of sheep,* kumu hipa, pū'ā hipa. *To tend sheep,* kahu hipa.

sheep dog. 'Īlio hipa, 'īlio kia'i hipa.

sheepfold. Pā hipa.

sheep market. Pūkahipa.

sheepskin. 'Ili hipa.

sheer. 1. *Perpendicular, steep.* Kū pololei, kūnihinihi. *Also:* kahakō, ku'i, kūlono, kūmole, laumania, nienie; lele koa'e *(poetic).* **2.** *Complete.* Loa, maoli. *Sheer nonsense,* kohu 'ole loa.

sheet. Lau, papa, pale. *Sheet of paper,* 'āpana pepa. *Bed sheet,* uhi pela, hāli'i moe, pale moe.

shekel. Kekela.

shelf. Haka, haka kau, papa, kumuhaka, holopapa, kaola. *Rare:* olo, olo'ewa. *Shelf for food containers,* haka ipu, papa ipu. *High shelf or place,* kauwōlani.

shell. 1. *Marine shell.* Pūpū *(see Haw.-Eng. entry and entries that follow it),* iwi. *Also:* 'ākōlea (pipipi 'ākōlea, kōlea), ālealea, 'aoa (maka 'aoa), apuhihi, 'āunauna, hailimoa, hau, hīhīwai (hapawai), hūai, kahelelani, kauna'oa (kio, una'oa), koholua, kuanaka, kuapo'i, kūpe'e, makahālili, makaloa (aupūpū, pūpū 'awa), moa (kāmoa), momi (pūpū Ni'ihau), nahawele (mahawele), naka 'ōni'oni'o, naunau (ānaunau), nene, 'ōlepe *and below,* pā, pā hau, pipi, pipipi *and below,* po'opalaoa, pūhali, pū'ōni'oni'o. *See* **barnacle, bivalve, conch shell, cowry shell, helmet shell, land shell, limpet, Nerita, oyster, pearl shell, sea urchin, snail, sundial shell, Trochus shell, turbo shell.** *Turtle or tortoise shell,* una, kua honu. *Shell on back of crab or turtle,* kuapo'i. *Shell for a lei,* pūpū lei. *Shell lei,* lei pūpū, lei leho, lei pipipi. **2.** *Hard case.* Iwi. *Shell of hiwa coconut,* ipu o Kāne. *Shell of lelo coconut used ceremonially,* ipu o Lono. *To shell,* poke, pō'alo, 'ōhiki. **3.** *Projectile.* Pōkā, pōkā pū, pōkā pahū *(bomb);* pōkā pōpō ahi *(incendiary bomb);* pōkā pū kuni ahi *(cannon ball).*

shelter. Wahi lulu, wahi ho'omalu, hale, hale kāmala, hale pupupu, lo'u pali, auolo, pāpa'i, malumalu, auhā. *In the shelter of his wings,* ma ka malu o kona 'ēheu. *This house is not very good, still it is a shelter,* 'a'ole maika'i loa 'o kēia hale, akā he malumalu.

shepherd. Kahu hipa.

shepherd dog. 'Īlio hipa, 'īlio kia'i hipa.

sheriff. Māka'i nui, ilāmuku. *District sheriff,* luna māka'i.

Shetland. Kekalana.

shewbread. Pelena hō'ike.

shield. Pālulu, pale, pu'upale; pale kaua *(Biblical);* pale lima, lulu, uhikino, pākū; 'a'ahu a po'o *(head). To shield,* pālulu, pale, lulu; kōlulu *(rare);* — *modestly with the hand,* pā'ūhalakā.

shift. Ho'one'e, 'oni, huli lua, ha'aku'e. *Work shift,* manawa hana, mahele hana.

shiftless. 'Ae'a, pālau'eke, 'akole, 'alopalopā, hīlea, lōpā, pākukui, pono nō i ka noho; moelepo *(fig.);* kūelekā *(rare). See saying,* **goat.**

shilling. Kilina.

shifty-eyed. Maka 'alo'alo, maka kāka̱'a.

Shiloh. Kilo, Silo.

shimmering. 'Olili, 'oliliko. *See* **shine.**

shin. Lapawāwae.

shinbone. Kū'auwāwae.

shine. *Common forms are derivatives of* lali, hinu, lohi, lino, napa, hulali, hūlalilali; liko *(as with dew).* *Also:* 'anapa, 'ānapanapa, 'alohi, hinuhinu, ho'ohinuhinu, 'ōhinu, 'ōhinuhinu, pahinu, pua, pūwā, hoaka, akaaka, akaka, huaka, kuali, mālamalama, mōhala, lapalapa, ho'ā'ia'i, a'ia'i, ho'āliali, ho'opuakea, lala, 'ōlali, la'ela'e, lile, 'olili, 'oliko, nōlinolino, nōweo, kamani, mohā. *To shine brightly, as moon or stars,* 'ā akaaka, pā, kōnane, pā kōnane, papā. *To shine shoes,* ho'ohinuhinu kāma'a. *The sun shines,* pā ka lā. *The Lord make his face to shine upon you (Nah. 6:25),* na Iēhowa e kau mai i ka mālamalama o kona maka maluna iho ou.

shingle. Pili, pili hale. *Wooden shingle,* pili lā'au. *To shingle,* kāpili.

ship. Moku *(for various kinds, see Haw.-Eng. entry and entries that follow it);* hale lana i ke kai *(fig.).* *To ship,* ho'ouna ma ka moku.

shipbuilder, shipbuilding. Kāpili moku.

shipmate. Hoa wa'a, hoa holomoku.

shipping clerk. Kanaka helu ukana.

shipwreck. Ili *(go aground);* nāhāhā *(broken to bits);* piholo *(sunk);* alapoki *(rare).* *Shipwrecked person,* 'ōlulo.

shipwright. Kāpili moku, kamanā kāpili moku.

shirring. 'Alu.

shirt. Pālule, 'ahu. *Shirt of block-print cloth,* palaka. *Aloha shirt,* palaka aloha.

shirtwaist. Pākana.

shish, shish shish. 'Ūhī'ūhā, mākēhā, ka'uka'ulī.

shiver. Ha'ukeke, naka, kū'ululū, ha'ulili, hulilī, kalakū, ulupi'i.

shoal. Hāpapa, kākaha, pāpa'u.

shock. 1. *Alarm.* Puoho, hikilele, ho'ohikilele, ho'olele hauli. **2.** *Sheaves.* Pu'u. **3.** *Electric shock.* Loa'a i ka uila.

shocked. Kūnāhihi, mā'e'ele, māna'ona'o, lele ka hauli, kāhāhā i ka 'ino.

shocking. Māna'ona'o. *Shocking news,* he mea hou ho'ohikilele.

shoe. Kāma'a. *See* **horseshoe.** *Pair of shoes,* pa'a kāma'a. *Patent-leather shoes,* kāma'a pāhinu. *Openwork shoes,* kāma'a hakahaka. *Leather shoes,* kāma'a 'ili. *To put on shoes,* ho'okāma'a, komo kāma'a. *To shoe, as a horse,* kāpili.

shoelace. Lī kāma'a, kaula lī kāma'a.

shoemaker. Kūmeka.

shoo. Ho'ohū, ho'okuke, ho'ēhu. *Also:* emu, hemū, hehu, kīpa'i.

shoot. 1. *Discharge.* Pana, kī. *Shoot with bow and arrow,* pana pua, pāpua, kakaka, kīko'o, 'umoki; pana i'a *(fish);* pana 'iole *(rats).* *Shoot arrows of sugar-cane tassels,* ke'a pua. *Shoot a coconut-leaf midrib,* panapana nī'au. *Shoot a gun,* kī, kī pū, kī pōkā, kīkī; kīkī manu *(birds).* *Shoot with a sling,* ma'aalaioa *(rare).* *Shoot marbles,* pana kinikini. **2.** *Sprout.* Keiki, 'ao, ilo, kawowo, 'ohā, pōhuli, pūliko, weli; koaha *(mulberry plant).* *To send forth shoots,* kā, kupu. *Shoot for planting,* makailo.

shooting star. Hōkū lele.

shop. Hale kū'ai *(store);* hale 'oihana *(workshop).*

shopping. Kū'ai hele, māka'ika'i hale kū'ai.

shore. Kahakai, kapa kai, kai, 'ae kai, makālae, pili'āina, pilikahakai. *Strip of barren land near the shore,* kākaha. *Hot, dry shore (in legends),* kaha. *Shore dweller,* kō a kai, kanaka o kai.

shoreward. Uka *(from sea);* kai *(from land).*

short. Pōkole, poko; 'ekeke'i, mū'ekeke'i *(as a dress).* *Also:* pōko'u, hāpokopoko, hanu'u, hananu'u, pouhananu'u, poupou, hāpou, hāpoupou, 'eleke'i, 'elehe'i, konopue, muku, mū'ou'ou, nukunuku, no'u, pāno'uno'u, ne'ine'i, pāha'a, paiaha'a, peke, pekepeke, popoki, pueo. *Rare:* 'apuki, ha'ako'a, pinauea, paku-

paku, pāna'e, pōlunu, pōnulu, ponululu, ponununu. *Cut short,* muku, pahupū. *Too short,* kaumuku, pakaulei, kaulei, kau 'ekeke'i. *Short cut,* ala 'oki, ka'akepa, ho'opōkole. *To hang short,* kau 'ekeke'i.

shortage. Pōkole.

shorten. Ho'opōkole. *Also:* hō'ekeke'i, ho'opoupou, pu'e'eke, 'unu, 'unua, 'ulua, na'ina'i.

shortened. Muku, po'omuku. *Also:* mu'umu'u, menui, piki.

shorthand. Kākau hua li'ili'i.

shortly. Kokoke, auane'i, a'uane'i.

shortness. Pōkole. *Shortness of breath,* nae, naenae, 'oaikū.

shorts. Lole wāwae pōkole, lole wāwae 'ekeke'i.

shot. Pōkā i maika *(shot-put).* *Bird shot, buckshot, grapeshot,* pōkā lū.

shotgun. Pū kī lū.

shot-put. Maika, kiola pōkā.

should. Pono e, pono ke, pono. *(Gram. 5.4.)*

shoulder. Po'ohiwi, hokua; 'ūhā mua *(of animal).* *Shoulder above armpit,* kīpō'ae'ae. *Points or edges of the shoulders,* kihi po'ohiwi, kīpo'ohiwi. *Shoulder to shoulder,* he kīpo'ohiwi i ke kīpo'ohiwi. *Shoulder pads or protection,* pale po'ohiwi. *Shoulder of a mountain,* kihi po'ohiwi, kīpo'ohiwi. *Shoulder arms!* E amo pū! *To hoist the shoulders,* ho'opahāha. *To shoulder aside,* ho'okē. *To carry on the shoulder,* 'auamo, pōhāki'iki'i. *To place on the shoulder,* kau po'ohiwi.

shoulder blade. Hoehoe, iwi hoehoe. *Fat or muscle on the shoulder blade,* kāhā po'ohiwi.

shout. 'Uwā, ho'ōho. *Also:* kani ka pihe, olo pihe, ho'okani pihe, wala'au. *Shout with derision,* 'uwā ho'ohilahila.

shove. Pahu, kē, hou, kula'i, kūna'i, kula'ilua, 'onou; — *away,* keku, ho'okeku. *Shove ahead, regardless of consequences,* 'onou po'o.

shovel. Kopalā, kope; hāpale *(rare).* *Fire shovel,* kope ahi, kope lehu.

shoveler. Koloa mōhā *(bird).*

show. 1. *Demonstrate.* Hō'ike, ho'omā'ike, ho'omā'ike-'ike, kuhikuhi, kū, makili, nene; ohiohi *(of wood grain).* *To show the sights,* ho'omāka'ika'i. *Show me!* 'Oliana! 'Oiana! 'Oia ana! Aliana! Inane! **2.** *Spectacle.* Hala keaka, hō'ike'ike, hō'ike 'ana.

shower. Kuāua; ua nāulu, nāulu *(sudden);* kualau, kuakualau *(with sea wind);* ko'iawe. *Light shower,* ua kilihune, kilihune; kilika'i; 'ehu kakahiaka *(see* **morning).**

showery. 'Ōuaua.

shoyu. Koiū.

shrapnel. Pōkā 'āpanapana.

shred. Welu, kīhae *(as ti leaves).*

shredded. Weluwelu.

Shreveport. Kaliwapoka.

shrewd. Ma'alea.

shriek. Pū'alalā, alawī. *Shriek angrily,* kekē, kekē niho, kekē nuku.

shrill. Alawī, huini, kōī, palalī, wī.

shrimp. 'Ōpae *(for various kinds, see Haw.-Eng. entry and entries that follow it);* mahiki *(used ceremonially).* *See saying,* **panau.** *Leaf container for shrimps,* pū'olo 'ōpae, ki'o'ōpae. *Shrimp head,* po'o 'ōpae *(insult).*

shrine. Heiau, haiau, ahu; ko'a *(fishing).* *See* **heiau** *(Eng.-Haw.).* *Shrine where bones of dead chiefs were kept,* hale poki.

shrink. 1. *Contract.* Miki. *Also:* ho'ohāiki, ho'o'i'ika, kīkenenei, lele, ne'ine'i, piki, pipiki, puku. **2.** *Recoil.* 'Eke, 'ekeke'i, mū'e'eke, pu'e'eke, kuemi, mene, pipika, kaumuku; kūpau *(rare).*

shriveling. Mino, mimino, minomino, 'ānuhenuhe, hōmī, 'i'ika, miki, pī'ao, pōnalo, 'ōmino, 'ōmali *(as fruit).* *Shriveled coconut meat,* niu 'ōka'a.

shroud. Pueo, kaula pū *(of a ship or canoe);* kapa olonā *(Biblical).*

shrub. *No equivalent:* la'alā'au, nahele.

shrug. Ho'ēheu *(the shoulders).*

risk. Maka'u, 'a'a, ho'ā'o me ka nānā 'ole, ho'ā'o me ka hopohopo. *To take a great risk,* hō'a'ano.

rite, ritual. *See* **ceremony.**

rival. Hoa paio, hoa pāonioni.

river. Kahawai, muliwai.

roach. 'Elelū; la'aloa *(slim-bodied).*

road. Ala, alanui, ala hele. *Also:* mo'o hele, kuamo'o, kumeheu. *Cleared road,* ala waele. *Road cut,* ala 'oki. *Belt road,* alaloa. *Unfinished or dead-end road,* ala muku. *Long road,* ala loa. *Circular road,* ala pō'ai. *Steep road,* alapi'i kū. *Winding road,* alanui kīke'eke'e. *Curve in a road,* kālawa, hālawa. *Road following cliffs,* ala kaka'i pali.

roadside. Pīpā alanui.

roan. Lokia.

roar. Wawā, wā, ho'owā, uwō, halulu, nākolokolo; ho'okani pihe *(as a crowd);* kapalulu, ho'okapalulu *(as an airplane);* kamumu, haukamumu *(as approaching rain);* kawewe *(as a downpour);* ho'okāwōwō, nū *(as wind);* kūwō *(as a lion); a prolonged —,* kōloa. *Also:* hū, nāku'i, kanulu, puwō, 'u'inakolo, wōwō, haukawewe, ku'inē, kahakikī, pa'ē pū, 'owā.

roast. 'Oma, loke, 'ōhinu. *See* **bake, broil.** *Roast turkey,* pelehū 'oma. *Roast beef,* pipi loke.

roasted. Ho'ō 'oma, 'oma, 'ōhinu.

rob. 'Aihue, pōwā. *Also:* pākaha, hao wale, kā'ilikū, kā-'ili wale, moluna.

robber. *See* **rob.**

robbery. 'Aihue, pākaha.

robe. 'A'ahu, lole ho'olu'elu'e.

robin. Lopine.

Rochester. Lokeka, Rokeka.

rock. 1. *Stone.* Pōhaku, 'ā, 'alā, hālelo. *Kinds:* 'a'ā, 'a'ā pu'upu'u, 'ā pele, pāhoehoe, kaiali'i, humu'ula, makiki, kei, lelekepue, pa'alā, pikapika, pīwai, uliuli. *See* **basalt, stone. 2.** *Motion.* Kulana, ho'oluli, naue, ho'onaue, kāhulihuli, paipai, pueo, pūeoeo.

rock borer. 'Ōlepe waha nui.

rock crevice. Naele.

rocket. Kao lele, 'ōahi; ahikao lele. *To send up rockets,* ho'olele kao.

rocking chair. Noho paipai.

rockskipper. Pao'o.

rock stratum. Hāpapa.

rocky. Nui ka pōhaku, pōhaku. *Also:* hālelo, mākō, hao'a, kō'ā.

Rocky Mountains. Mauna Pōhaku.

rod. Lā'au, 'ōhelo, loka, roda, kālī, ko'oko'o, peloka; kia, 'ōhelo huki manu, maile *(for snaring birds);* kāni'o *(supporting a house);* kā'aha *(priest's).*

rodent. *See* **'iole.**

roebuck. Pāpulō, 'anekelopa.

rogue. Lū, piha 'eu, kolohe, 'āpiki; lonu *(rare).*

roil. Hōlapu, naku, ho'onaku, 'a'aka, mōioio, hōkakekake, mimiki.

roll. 1. *Turn.* Kaka'a, ka'a, 'ōka'a, kūka'a, kūpola; 'oloka'a *(as a wheel);* kāka'a *(as eyes);* luli *(as a ship);* 'aui *(as the sea);* mimilo *(as to induce abortion);* mākī *(as a mat);* — *beneath,* ka'a malalo; — *diagonally,* ka'a kepa; — *over backwards,* ka'akua; — *up,* wahī, kī, wili, uhaku, nunu. *To roll in salt,* ka'a pa'akai. *To fall down and roll,* ka'a 'ahina. *To roll freely or without control,* ka'a wale. **2.** *Bundle.* Lola, 'ōwili, 'āpā, pōka'a. *Roll of rope,* pōka'a kaula. **3.** *Bread.* Palaoa li'ili'i. **4.** *Sound.* Kā'eleloi, palalū, pākīko'ele. *See* **ruffle.**

roll call. Hea inoa.

roller. 1. *Stick.* Lā'au ho'oka'a, lola ho'opalaha, ipuwai. *See* **steam roller. 2.** *Wave.* 'Aui, 'aui 'ale.

rolling. Ka'a, ka'ana; — *along, as a wheel,* nome. *See* **roll.**

rolling grindstone. Hoana ka'a.

rolling pin. Lā'au ho'oka'a, lola.

Roman Catholic. Kakōlika Loma.

romance. 1. *Novel.* Ka'ao. **2.** *Love affair.* Pili ho'oipoipo, pilialoha; hana kalakalai *(trifling).*

romantic. Ho'oipoipo.

Rome, Roman. Loma, Roma.

romp. Lelele, 'oehu.

rood. Luka.

roof. Kaupoku, kaupaku. *Temporary roofed construction,* lānai.

roofing. Pili. *Shingle roofing,* pili papa. *Corrugated iron roofing,* pili hao, pili piula.

room. 1. *Part of a house.* Lumi, ke'ena. *Private room,* ke'ena malu, ke'ena kapu. **2.** *Space.* Hakahaka. *Plenty of room,* nui ka lumi.

roommate. Hoa lumi.

roost. Haka.

rooster. Moa kāne.

root. 1. *Of plant.* A'a, mole, weli; — *with many sprouts,* kumulau; — *of koali vine,* kalēhuna. *Aerial root,* ma'alewa, a'a lewalewa, a'a kiolea, mahulukū; ule hala, uleule hala *(of pandanus). Root system,* pa'i a'a. *Root cutting,* kā. *Tip of pandanus root,* mu'o, mu'o hala. *Creeping root,* a'a kolo. *To take root,* ho'oa'a. *Root used in love sorcery,* hua nanai. **2.** *Source.* Kumu; mole *(as of a word).* **3.** *Dig.* 'Eku, naku, haunaku, peu. *Also:* 'e'eku, 'eku'eku, nakunaku.

root beer. Lukapia.

rootlet. Huluhulu, a'a; piko *(of wauke),* ki'u *(of sweet potato).*

rope. Kaula *(see Haw.-Eng. entry and entries that follow it),* kāwelewele. *Also:* 'umi'umi, kī'aho. *End of rope,* piko. *Leather rope,* kaula 'ili. *Rope tether,* kaula kūpe'e. *Rope at bottom of net,* lio. *To rope,* ho'ohei *(see* **lasso).**

rosary. Lei kolona, kolona, lōkālio.

rose. Loke *(see Haw.-Eng. entry and entries that follow it),* loke lani, roselani. *See* **green rose.**

rose apple. 'Ōhi'a loke.

rosewood. Lā'au loke.

rostrum. 1. *Pulpit.* 'Āwai. **2.** *Beak.* Kākala *(as of a shrimp).*

rosy. Loke, 'ōhelohelo, helo, nono.

rot. *See* **rotten.**

rotate. Ka'apuni, ka'a, pōniu, puahi, ho'okāpō'ai.

rote. Walewaha.

rotten. Pilau, palahū, 'ino'ino, palahō; popopo *(of wood, paper);* āelo, lāla'au *(of eggs; fig., spoiled, worthless);* milu *(as fruit);* pala, palakiu, alapuka *(rare, as taro);* palahuki *(as banana stump). Also:* huhu, huhuhu, pele'ū, peluluka, pūnonu, 'ūki'ukiu, 'ūkiukiu, nehi, 'oke, hahalu, māhao, nā'ele'ele, poholawa. *See* **decomposed.**

rouge. Mea hō'ula'ula papālina.

rough. 1. *As terrain.* Ho'olua, 'ālualua, mālualua, lualua, ho'opupū, 'āpu'upu'u, hāpu'upu'u, 'ōpu'upu'u, kīwa'awa'a. **2.** *As cloth or skin.* 'Ōkala, kala, kākala, pākala, hākuma, 'ōkuma, 'ōpakapaka, oloolo, uluha'o, konakona, manumanu, 'āpala. **3.** *As sea or wind.* Pikipiki'ō, 'alo'alo'a, lo'alo'a, la'ola'o, hālo-'alo'a, āulu, olohi'a, pūkalakī, kū'ulukū, nalunalu, 'ōnalunalu, puleileho, maleuwō. *Rough sea,* kai ko'o, 'ōkaikai. **4.** *Manner.* 'Ōkalakala, kākala, kalakala, 'o'ole'a.

roughhouse. Limanui, haunaele, lapa, kolohe, mā'ewa'ewa.

round. Poepoe, popohe, kūpoepoe; molea, mole, momole, kūmole, nemo, ka'anemo, polipoli *(smooth); (blunt);* nepu *(bulging). Also:* nia, 'akipohe, hūalakē, kōnunu, peo. *See* **around, circuit.** *Round object, as pill or bead,* hua. *Round mass,* pōpō, pōheoheo. *To form a round shape,* ho'opoe. *To go round and round,* ka'anini.

roundabout. Ho'olalau, lauwili, loloiāhili. *Roundabout way to lead up to a subject,* ho'ohelehele 'ōlelo.

round-shouldered. 'O'ohu; hanunu *(rare).*

roundup. Ho'ohuli pipi, ho'ā pipi.

roundworm. Ko'e kai.

rouse. Hō'eu'eu, ho'āla, ho'ouluulu, ho'opi'ipi'i, ho'olalelale, ho'ohahana, ho'okokonoi'e, pai.

rout. Hō'auhe'e, ho'ohe'e, ho'opuehu, ho'ohū, 'āha'i, kipaku.

route. Ala hele.

routed. 'Auhe'e, puehu, kipaku 'ia.
rove. *See* **wander.**
row. 1. *Paddle.* Hoe. *To row here and there,* hoehoe, pā-nānā. **2.** *Line.* Pae, lālani, laina. **3.** *See* **riot.**
rowboat. Wa'apā.
rows. Paepae, lālani, laina. *To place in rows,* ho'onoho papa.
royal. Ali'i, lani, ho'āli'i, 'ano lani. *Also:* 'ula, 'a'ala *(fig.);* auali'i, wai 'ihi, wā'ihi. *See saying,* **'ie 1.** *Royal robe,* 'a'ahu ali'i. *Poetic references to rain, rainbow, height in general, red, hawk* ('io) *may signify royalty.*
royalist. Aloha ali'i, loialiki; 'āne'e ali'i *(disparaging).*
royal poinciana. 'Ohai 'ula.
rub. 1. *Friction.* 'Ānai, kuai, kuolo, hoana; 'upa'upā *(as clothes on washboard).* *Also:* olo, oloolo, piolo, halo, holoi, kaekae, walu, 'uwalu, waluhia, wa'uwa'u, wa-walu, waluwalu, oloi, olokīkī. *See* **polish.** *To stretch by rubbing,* kahi kālena. *To rub with elbows,* neku'e. *To rub, as tapa on grass to gather moisture,* kā kēhau. *Rub with oil,* kūhinu, kāhinu, hamo, kākele. **2.** *See* **massage.**
rubbed. Māhinu, hinu *(as with oil).* *See* **rub.**
rubber. 1. *Elastic.* Laholio. **2.** *Stone polisher.* Pōhaku 'ānai, pōhaku pahe'e 'ānai. *Buck lists six kinds:* puna *(coral);* 'elekū, 'ō'io *(basalt);* 'an? *(pumice); also:* 'ōahi, 'ola'i.
rubber band. Laholio ho'opa'a.
rubbers. Kāma'a laholio.
rubbery. 'Ōuaua, laholio, 'ūlina, 'ūlinalina, 'ūnina.
rubbing oil. 'Aila hamo.
rubbish. 'Ōpala. *Also:* lepo, lepo hānai, kae, lemu'ā.
rubbish container. Kini 'ōpala, ipu 'aina.
rubbish pit. Lua 'ōpala. *Also:* luaunu, olomehani.
rudder. Hoe uli.
rudder fish. Nenue.
ruddy. 'Ehu; hi'ohi'o *(rare).*
ruddy turnstone. 'Akekeke.
rude. Kiko'olā, maha'oi, pākīkē, kekē niho, ho'okano. *Also:* waha 'ā, 'āwaha, kīkoi, kū, kō'ā, koaea, ha'akei, 'u'u, mahalua, pūhi'u, kakana, kakana'i'i, kū kakalai-oa, kalakala, 'āpali, meku. mahi'opu. *See* **kio, nīele, pāhi'uhi'u.** *Speak rudely,* 'ōlelo kū, ho'opuka kū, ho'oku'iku'i 'ōlelo, 'ōlelo kohā, pua'ō, kīkahō, kala-'ea. *Ask rudely,* noi kū.
rue. Lue.
ruff. Pihapiha 'ā'ī *(neck),* 'alu.
ruffle. 1. *Folds, as in a garment.* 'Alu, pihapiha, piha-piha 'ō koholā, kauwawe, kauwewe, kauawe, 'ā'īlepe; — *and tucks,* hu'a. **2.** *Wrinkle.* 'A'apu, 'āka'a, uluulu, unuunu, pūkalakī. **3.** *Sound, as of drums.* Kā'eleloi.
ruffler. Ho'opihapiha *(as on a sewing machine).*
rug. *See* **carpet.**
ruin. Pilikia, hō'ino'ino, mā'ino'ino. *Rare:* apu, olopē, pahu'a.
ruins. Koena.

rule. 1. *A regulation.* Lula, loina, kānāwai. *Fundamental rule,* lula kumu. **2.** *To govern.* Noho ali'i, kū, 'ai, noho aupuni, ho'omalu, ho'ohaku, ea, ka'a maluna.
ruler. 1. *Leader.* Ali'i; — *of an* ahupua'a, 'ai ahupua'a; — *of an* 'ili, 'ai 'ili; — *of a district,* 'ai moku. *See* **king.** **2.** *Measuring stick.* Lula, lā'au ana.
rum. Lama, rama.
rumble. Halalū, nāku'i, nākolo, kamumu, kani. *Also:* palalū, nei; kolokolo; 'ōlapa, nakulu *(as stomach);* nehe, haukamumu, pākīko'ele, hawewe, kiliwehi. *See* **roar, roll.**
rumor. Lono *(see* **lono 1***),* lono wale. *Also:* lohe lau āhea, nēnē, ho'onēnē, lonowā, lonoā, nonoā, wawā, lauāhea, hūhā. *To hear rumors,* lohe wale.
rump. Puapua *(of a chicken).* *Rump bone of a chicken,* ke'emoa.
run. 1. *Move swiftly.* Holo, hoholo, ho'oholo, ka'aholo; —, *as for office,* holo, alualu; — *fast,* holo māmā, holo kikī, kikī holo, ho'oheihei; — *here and there,* holokē, holo hele, holo lua; holowā *(rare);* — *aground,* ili; oloi *(rare);* — *over,* ili; — *cautiously,* akaholo; — *lightly,* kakakihi; —, *as a messenger,* kūkini; — *of fish,* kahe, kū, he'e i'a; — *away, see* **flee;** — *after, see* **chase.** *To make a horse run,* ho'oholo lio. **2.** *Manage.* Ho'oholo, ka'a.
runner. 1. *Messenger.* Kūkini. *See saying,* **welo 1. 2.** *Of a vine.* 'Awe'awe, hā'awe'awe; kāili, kālī *(sweet potato).* **3.** *Of a sled.* Kāma'a loa.
running. Holona, uhaiāholo. *Running nose,* hūpēkole. *Running sore,* pala he'e.
running board. 'A'e ka'a *(of an automobile).*
runt. Hua li'i, keiki 'u'uku loa.
rupture. Pu'ulele, laho he'e, hoaka.
rural. Kua'āina.
ruse. Hei. *See* **trick.**
rush. 1. *Move swiftly.* Holo 'ino, holo 'āwīwī, lele'ino, auau, pūlale, holomoku, haluku, hakuo'i; — *out,* lele; —, *as water,* kokoi, kō'ie'ie; kūkawowo *(rare);* —, *as in battle,* olowalu, ho'ouka; —, *as a crowd,* mokuā-wai, kokoi. **2.** *Plant.* Papulo *(papyrus);* mau'u. *See* **bulrush.**
Russia. Lukia, Rusia.
Russian. Lūkini, Lukia.
rust. Kūkaehao, lepohao; popopo *(Biblical).* *See* **rusty.**
rustic. Kua'āina; koai'e *(fig.).*
rustle. Hoene, nehe, 'u'inakolo, 'owē, nakeke, ho'o-nakeke, kapa. *To roll with a rustling sound,* ka'a'owē. *Rustling of the sea on the pebbles,* nehe a ke kai i ka 'ili'ili.
rusty. Kūkaehao, lepohao. *See* **rust.** *To become rusty,* ki'o kūkaehao.
rut. Kapo'o, napo'o, mō'ali. *Full of ruts,* mālualua, hele-hele, kīwa'awa'a, kāpo'opo'o.
ruthless. Ho'okaumaha; ho'oluhi hewa *(Biblical).*
rye. Lai, rai; huapalaoa 'ele'ele.

S

s. *No Hawaiian term.*
-s. *The plural is shown in Hawaiian by the particles* nā, nāhi, mau, po'e, kau, wahi, ona, *and the 0-possessives. (Gram. 9.6.3., 10.4.)*
-'s. *See* of.
Sabaoth. Kāpāōka.
Sabbath. Kāpaki, Sabati.
sabotage. Ho'opō'ino malū.
sack. **1.** *Bag.* 'Eke; 'eke'eke *(small);* 'eke kūkaenalo *(flour, unbleached muslin).* **2.** *Plunder.* Pōwā, luku.
sackcloth. Kapa 'ino'ino, lole lauoho.
sack race. Heihei 'eke.
sacrament. Kakelema, kakelemeneka, kakalema. *See* Holy Communion.
Sacramento. Kakalameko.
sacred. Kapu. *Also:* la'a, la'ahia, ano, ho'āno, 'ihi, hō-'ihi, 'iu, hō'iu, po'iu, 'ula. *Sacred things of day,* la'a kea. *Sacred enclosure,* pālama. *Sacred place,* wahi kapu, hei kapu, wahi la'a.
Sacred Heart. Pu'uwai Ho'āno, Pu'uwai La'ahia.
sacrifice. Mōhai *(for various types, see Haw.-Eng. entry and entries that follow it).* *Also:* kaumaha, mōlia, mō-liaola, haina, hai, hei, hai ao, papaiō; 'ōlapa *(for sorcery);* he'a *(blood);* kākū'ai *(food). Human sacrifice,* kanaka, ulua, heana, pua'a he'a, pua'a hinu, hinu, pua'a wāwae loa *(see* wāwae*),* 'oma, ha'alelea, uko'o. *Place of sacrifice,* heiau, haiau, lele, 'aoa. *One who sacrifices himself,* mōliaola. *Seekers of sacrifice,* ma-kāla ulua. *Rod held by priest in sacrifice,* kā'aha.
sacrilege. Hehi kū i ke kapu; kakilileke *(Catholic).*
sacroiliac strain. Kīkala hāne'ene'e.
sad. Kaumaha, lu'ulu'u, 'aoa, 'ino'ino, 'EHA'eha; kau-maha lua *(extremely). See* grief. *Also:* pilihua, niniu, niuaua, malāoa. *To cause sadness,* ho'okaumaha.
saddle. Noho lio; *pack —,* noho 'āmana. *To saddle,* hauhoa.
saddle blanket. Pale lio.
saddle horn. Maku'u, ōmuku, 'ōkumu.
saddle horse. Lio holo noho.
safe. **1.** *Not in danger.* Palekana, panekana, malu, malu-hia. *Also:* kūola, mānalo, kuakapu, kūka'awe. **2.** *Depository.* Pahu hao, pahu pā, pahu kālā, halepā.
safety. Maluhia, palekana, panekana, malu. *Place of safety,* pu'uhonua.
safety pin. Kui kaiapa, pine kaiapa.
safflower. Mamo.
saffron. Keloko. *See* turmeric.
sag. 'Alu, 'alu'alu. *Also:* 'olo, 'olo'olo, he'e, hehe'e, lu'a, kū'olo, luhe; 'ōluheluhe *(as a potbelly);* lule, mū-'olo; 'olo'olōna *(under a weight);* hūalakē, ho'okale-kale, kalekale, 'ope'alu, paleha, pēheu, kōkīkī, puhalu, halu, uhalu.
sage. **1.** *Wise man.* 'Elemakule 'imi loa. *See* seer. **2.** *Plant.* Kako, līlīlehua.
sagittal. Hoai kaupaku.
sago. Keko.
said. *See* say. *It is said,* 'ōlelo 'ia. *Said to be,* pau *(see* idiom, pau*).*
sail. **1.** *As a ship.* Holo, ho'oholo, hoholo, kele, ho'o-kele; ho'okelekele *(frequently);* holomoku, ho'oholo-moku, holokai, holomoana. *Also:* kūkele, kikihi, lelea-oa. *See* drift. *To go for a sail,* holoholo. *To sail to leeward,* ka'alalo. *To sail to windward,* ka'aluna, ho'o-pi'ipi'i; ho'opāhu'a *(rare). To sail around,* holo puni. *To sail swiftly,* holo kikī. *To sail aimlessly,* holoholo wale, auhele. *To sail cautiously,* akaholo. *To sail off*

and on, pō'ala, ka'alewa. *To sail to foreign parts,* holokahiki. *Sail on distant seas,* 'au i ke kai loa *(of one who travels far).* **2.** *Noun.* Lā, pe'a. *Also:* lauoha, 'ōpe'ape'a; kālepa, 'ōpihipihi *(mats). See* jib sail, mainsail, topsail. *Long sail,* pe'a oe. *To make sails,* humu pe'a.
sailfish. A'u, a'u lepe.
sail ho! Kēlō!
sailing. Holona, niau. *See* sail. *Sailing regulations,* nā lula e pili ana i nā moku.
sailing vessel. Moku pe'a.
sailor. Kelamoku, kela, holomoku. *Also:* luina, 'aukai, 'aumoana, holokahiki, holokai. *Experienced sailor,* 'īlio 'aukai.
saint. Kaneka, Saneta; Kāna, Sana; po'e hemolele. *Patron saint,* pakelona.
Saint Helena. Kāna Helena, Sana Helena.
Saint Joseph. Kāna 'Iokepa, Sana Iosepa.
Saint Louis. Kāna Lui, Sana Lui. *Saint Louis High School,* ke Kula Ki'eki'e o Kāna Lui.
Saint Peter. Kāna Pekelo, Sana Petero.
saintly. Hemolele.
sake. Pono.
salad. Lau 'ai.
salad dressing. Mea hō'ono'ono lau 'ai.
salary. Uku hana. *To pay salary,* uku hana. *Salary schedule,* papa kuhikuhi uku.
sale. Kū'ai aku, kū'ai ho'olilo; kū'ai ho'ēmi *(reduction sale). For sale,* mea kū'ai aku. *Special sale,* kū'ai ho-'ēmi kūikawā.
Salem. Kalema, Salema.
salesman. Kanaka kū'ai aku, kālepa. *See* traveling salesman.
sales tax. 'Auhau no nā mea kū'ai.
saline. Pa'akai; 'ōmiko *(as soil near the sea).*
saliva. Kuha, hā'ae, 'ae, wale wai.
sallow. 'Ōlenalena.
sally over. Kale'oa.
salmon. Kāmano. *Canned salmon,* kāmano kini. *Salted salmon,* kāmano pa'akai. *Mashed salmon,* kāmano lomi. *Sea salmon,* kamanu. *Salmon buttocks,* 'ōkole kāmano, 'amo kāmano *[both names mock the skin of white people];* 'amo, *anal opening [jokingly replaces* 'ōkole *because* amo *occurs in the name* Keamolewa, Klamath, Oregon, where Hawaiians went for salmon fishing]. (Salmon was used in sorcery, perhaps because of the similarity of its name to* kāmanomano, *a weed used in love magic.) Compare* -mano, many.
Salonika. Kalonika, Salonika.
saloon. Hale inu lama.
salsify. Salapī.
salt. Pa'akai. *To salt,* kāpī, kōpī, ho'omiko, kāmala. *Ocherous earth used to color and flavor salt,* 'alaea. *Salt thus treated,* pa'akai 'ula'ula. *Salt bed,* alialia, ālia, hāhāpa'akai. *Salt flat,* papa pa'akai *(fig., sour disposition).* *Salt-encrusted,* ālia, alialia, pa'apa'akai, pāpa'a kai, ni'i. *Sea water left in pool to form a salt crust by evaporation,* kai ho'olulu. *Salt container, saltcellar,* poho pa'akai, ipu kūli'u. *To salt pork,* kāpī pua'a. *To roll in salt,* ka'a pa'akai. *To gather salt,* hā-hāpa'akai.
salted. Miko, mali'u *(well salted);* mikomiko *(lightly). Salted meat,* kākāmaka *(raw);* kākāmo'a *(cooked).*
Salt Lake City. Loko Pa'akai.
salt pan. Kāheka, makapāpipi *(natural);* kāhekaheka *(artificial).*

salt pork. Pua'a pa'akai, pua'a kāpī. *To salt pork,* kāpī pua'a.
salts. Hau'eli. *See* **smelling salts.**
salt shaker. Poho lūlū pa'akai, poho pa'akai.
salty. Li'u, ālia, ālialia; 'ōmiko *(as soil near the sea).*
salutation. Aloha. *Also:* welina, weli, 'ano'ai.
salute. Hō'ailona ho'omaika'i, hā'awi i ka hō'ailona ho'omaika'i. *Gun salute,* pū aloha, pū ho'ohanohano. *To salute the flag,* ho'omaika'i i ka hae.
Salvador. Kalawakoa, Salawadoa; Kalawekoa, Salawedoa.
salvation. Ola, ola mau loa.
Salvation Army. Pū'ali Ho'ōla.
salve. Lā'au hamo.
same. Like, like pū, kohu like, ho'okahi. *Same as ever, same as usual,* 'oia mau nō. *Same to you,* me 'oe pū. *The same father,* ho'okahi nō makua kāne. *At the same time,* ho'okahi, i ka manawa ho'okahi. *It's the same result,* 'oia ana nō.
Samoa. Kāmoa, Ha'amoa.
Samoan. Kāmoa, Ha'amoa, mea Kāmoa.
sample. Mea hō'ike'ike 'u'uku.
sanctify. Ho'okapu, ho'ola'a, ho'āno.
sanctimonious. Ho'ohaipule i ke 'ano ho'okamani, ho'omikanele.
sanction. Ho'āpono.
sanctuary. Wahi ho'āno, ke'ena kapu, wahi kanaaho, wahi kanaho, pu'uhonua.
sand. One. *White sand,* one kea, ōkea, kea. *Black cindery sand,* pa'u ahi. *Black lava sand,* one 'ā. *Fine sand,* one 'ae'ae, hune one. *Sand beach,* kahaone, 'ae one, papa kea. *Sand heap,* pu'u one. *Sand pellets,* kūkae 'ōhiki. *Wet sand,* one maka. *Sand washed by the sea,* one hali, one 'ōpiopio. *Sand near fresh water,* one wai. *To sand,* ho'ōne. *Sands of my birth,* ku'u one hānau *(poetic).*
sandal. Kāma'a hāwele, kāma'a hakahaka, pale wāwae, kāma'a pale wāwae; kāma'a 'ie *(braided);* kāma'a lā'ī, pālaha, kuanaka *(ti-leaf).*
sandalwood. 'Iliahi, 'aoa, lā'au 'ala, 'iliahi-a-lo'e, wahie'ala, hua'ula'ula. *False or bastard sandalwood,* naio. *Wood of* naio, 'a'aka. *Scion or shoot of sandalwood,* a'aahi.
sandbank. Āhua one, kumuone.
sand bar. Pu'e one.
sand crab. 'Ōhiki.
sand dune. Pu'e one, pu'u one, āhua one.
sanderling. Hunakai.
sand hopper. 'Uku kai, 'uku limu.
sandpaper. Pepa kalakala.
sandpiper. Upupā.
sand spurry. Mimi'īlio.
sandstone. Kumuone.
sandwich. Nā palaoa me nā mea hō'ono'ono i waena.
sandy. Oneone, 'āone, one; onena *(rare).*
sane. Maika'i i ka no'ono'o.
San Francisco. Kapalakiko.
sanitarium. *See* **hospital.**
sanitary. Ma'ema'e loa.
sanitary napkin. Kī'amo, mea hume.
sanitation. Kūlana o ke ola.
San Joaquin. Kāna 'Iōkina, Sana Iokina; Waikini.
San Miguel. Kāna Mikuela, Sana Miguela.
San Pedro. Kāna Pekelo, Sana Petero.
Santa Barbara. Kāna Palapala, Sana Barabara.
Santa Clara. Kāna Kalala, Sana Kalara.
Santa Claus. Kanakaloka.
Santa Cruz. Kāna Kaluka, Sana Karuza.
sap. Kohu, wai, wale, wale hau, wai lā'au, kaikea; 'ae *(from seaweed or leaves);* pēka'a, kulukulu'ā *(from green* kukui *nuts).*
sapphire. Kapaea, sapaea; kapeila, kapeilo, sapeiro, kapila, sapira.
Saracen. Kalekena.
sarcasm. 'Ōlelo hō'eha 'ano 'uhi'uhi 'ia, kū'akū.

sarcastic. Kīko'olā, pākīkē. *Also:* hō'aikola, ho'onā'aikola, kīkoi, kū'akū.
sardine. Makalē; kālina *(rare).*
Sardinia. Kakinia, Sadinia.
sardius. Kalekio.
sardonyx. Kalekonuka.
sarong. Pā'ū, kīkepa; lukaluka *(for men);* hau'ina *(dyed with* 'ōlena*). See ex., sea. Sarong festooned with leaves or ferns,* pā'ū heihei. *To bind on a sarong,* kākua; kihi o ka mahina *(a special way).*
sash. Kā'ai, kā'ei.
Satan. Kākana.
satchel. Paiki; kī'eke *(rare).*
sateen. Kākīnia, kākini.
satellite star. Hōkū ukali.
satiated. Ho'olawa 'ana; mā'ona piha, ana, kenakena, 'okukui *(with food);* 'aikena *(to the point of sickness).*
satiety. Lawa pono, mā'ona ho'oili, mā'ona piha. *See idiom,* **hewa 4.**
satin. Pāhoehoe. *Brocaded satin,* pāhoehoe lau.
satire. 'Ōlelo pāhenehene.
satisfaction. 'Olu'olu, ho'olaule'a. *Lack of satisfaction,* 'olu'olu 'ole, la'ola'o.
satisfactorily. Pono, kūpono, kohu pono.
satisfied. Ana, lawa, mā'ona *(after eating);* kena, kenakena *(after drinking). See saying,* **pi'ikoi.** *Be satisfied with what you have got,* e 'olu'olu i ka mea i loa'a.
satisfy. Hō'olu'olu, ho'okō.
saturate. Ho'oma'ū, pulu, ho'opulu, pulu pē, kē'ae, polokake, kawakawa. *See* **moisten.**
Saturday. Pō'aono, lā ho'omalolo, Kakuke, Satude.
Saturn. Makulu, Mākulukulu, Kakulena.
satyr. Kao hihiu, kao kanaka.
sauce. Kai. *Various kinds:* kai helo *(of crushed shrimp and coconut cream);* 'ae limu *(seaweed juice);* kai 'ina *(sea-urchin);* kai ko'ako'a *(rich, as of parrot-fish liver). To mix or stew with sauce,* kākele.
saucepan. Pā ho'olapalapa, ipu hao.
saucer. Pā li'ili'i.
saucy. Pākīkē, kīko'olā, maha'oi, mahalua, honekoa.
saunter. Holoholo ho'onanea, ho'olalau, palela, kūo'e.
sausage. Na'aukake.
savage. Hihiu loa, hae, mākaha, iō'ena.
Savannah. Kawana, Savana.
save. 1. *As a life.* Ola, ho'ōla, ho'opakele, ho'opalekana. *God save the king,* ola ka mō'ī i ke Akua. *God save me,* e ola au i ke Akua. 2. *Keep.* Mālama, pūlama, ho'ili, ho'oili, hō'ili'ili, ho'okoe, ana'ē.
saved. Ola, ola pāna'i, palekana, panekana.
saving. Makauli'i, minamina. *Also:* ko'ako'ana, kīhau, pukumoa. *See* **thrifty.**
savings. Loa'a hō'ili'ili, waihona, kālā ho'āhu.
savings bank. Panakō ho'āhu.
savior. Ho'ōla, palekana.
savor. 'Ono.
savory. 'Ono.
Savoy. 1. *The country.* Kawoe, Savoe. 2. *(Not cap.) A kind of cabbage.* Kawoa.
saw. 1. Pahi olo, olo. *To saw,* olo, oloolo, piolo; helo *(with jerky motion);* olokīkī *(rare). To saw wood,* olo papa. 2. *See* **see.** *I saw,* ua 'ike au.
sawdust. Oka lā'au.
sawhorse. Lio lā'au.
sawmill. Hale olo papa.
Saxon. Kakona, Sakona.
say. 'Ōlelo, ha'i, 'ī. *Also:* mea, mea mai, wahi a, pēlā, pēia, ho'opuka. *To say little,* 'ekemu, molu. *The chief said,* wahi a ke ali'i; 'ōlelo mai ke ali'i.
saying. 'Ōlelo no'eau. *Also:* 'ōlelo kaena *(of praise, as for a place or person);* ha'ina, kāleo.
scab. Pāpa'a, 'ōkohe, pihi.
scabbard. 'Ili wahī, wahī pahi kaua.
scabies. Kunakuna, ane.
scad. Akule; halalū, hahalalū, pā'ā'ā *(young).*
Scaevola. Naupaka.

scaffold. 'Oloke'a.
scalawag. 'Alapu'u mo'o.
scald. Welaahi.
scale. 1. *Measure.* Alapi'i; *musical* —, alapi'i mele, pā-kōlī. *See* note, scales. 2. *Fish.* Unahi, unahinahi. *To scale,* unaunahi. *The Kula people scale squids, the Kula people paddle awkwardly,* ka po'e unaunahi he'e o Kula, 'o Kula hoe hewa *(of ignorance).*
scaleless. Unahi 'ole.
scales. Kaupaona, paona, paona kaulike, ana paona *(weighing).* *Baby scales,* paona keiki.
scalloped. Nihoniho.
scallops. Nihoniho, pepeiao.
scalp. 'Ili po'o. *To scalp,* lole. *Crusty scalp, eczema of scalp,* pāpa'a piele, piele.
scaly. Unahi, unahinahi *(as fish);* māhuna, pakapaka, luehu *(as skin).*
scamp. 'Eu, piha 'eu, kupu'eu, kolohe.
scandal. Hana i wā 'ia. *See saying,* **māmane.**
scandalous. Kū i ka wā 'ia.
scanty. Lawa 'ole, hemo'ē.
scapegoat. Kao hele, mea i ho'opa'i 'ia no nā hewa o ha'i.
scar. 'Ālina, linalina, lina. *Also:* pihi, pihipihi, mō'ali, 'ali, 'ali'ali, kākala wela, pa'awela *(from burning);* pala'e *(on neck from glandular disease);* ko'ako'a, 'ala-'ala. *To scar,* hō'ali'ali, ho'olina, kākala wela.
scarce. Kaka'ikahi, pānoanoa.
scarcely. 'Ane'ane.
scare. Ho'omaka'u, ho'opū'iwa; — *away,* ho'ohemū.
scarecrow. Ki'i ho'oweliweli.
scarf. Lei 'ā'ī, kākai.
scarify. Kahakaha.
scarlet. 'Ula. *See* red.
scarlet fever. Piwa 'ula'ula.
scarred. 'A'alina, 'a'ali, hō'ali'ali, 'ali'ali, pihipihi, manu, manumanu, ko'ako'a, 'ālina.
scat. Hele ma kahi 'ē, hemū.
scatter. Ho'opuehu, lū, lūlū, lū helele'i, nū. *Also:* kau li'ili'i, ho'ohelele'i, lele li'ili'i, kāpī, kūlele, ho'oleilei, kaiehu, kōlū, kī'ope, ho'omalele. *Scatter in every direction,* ho'opuehu li'ili'i. *Scatter in excitement,* holo pū'ā'ā. *The crowd scatters,* ho'i nui ka lehulehu.
scattered. Puehu, helele'i, luehu. *Also:* malele, pākikokiko, pūlunaluna, pākakahi, nūpolupolu, nūponuponu, mōkākī, kāwala, pūkākā, kūka'ikahi, kūkāka'ikahi, punapuna, pū'ā'ā.
scavenger. 'Ai pilau, 'ai pala maunu, 'ai pala niho. *See saying,* **crab.**
scavenger bird. Manu-'ai-pilau.
scene. Nānaina; mahele, pale, moku *(in a play).*
scenery. Nānaina, 'ikena, waihona 'āina.
scent. *See* smell.
sceptical. Hilina'i 'ole, ho'omahuakala, mana'o'i'o 'ole, ho'opāhala, maloka, ho'omaloka.
sceptre. Hō'ailona ali'i pa'a lima, hō'ailona mō'ī.
schedule. Papa kuhikuhi, papa hō'ike, papa kuhikuhi manawa, papa.
scheme. Ho'olālā 'ana.
scholar. Mea 'imi na'auao, akeakamai.
scholarship. 1. *Pursuit of knowledge.* Hana 'imi na'auao, huli *(followed by qualifier; see* huli 2 *and below).* 2. *Student aid.* Waihona kōkua ho'ona'auao, ha'awina kōkua ho'ona'auao.
scholium. Mana'o wehewehe.
school. 1. *Educational.* Kula. *See* high school, manual, preparatory school, private, reform school, select school, township, university. *Go to school,* hele kula, kukula. *Hold school,* kula. *School supplies,* lako kula. 2. *Fish.* I'a kū, kū, he'e, kahe, kauhulu.
school child. Keiki hele kula.
schoolhouse. Hale kula.
schoolmaster. Kahu kula, luna kula.
schoolmate. Hoa kula.
schoolteacher. Kumu kula, kumu a'o.

schooner. Moku; moku kia lua *(two-masted);* kuna.
science. Akeakamai, hana 'imi na'auao, huli kanaka, 'ike no'eau.
scientific. *See* science. *Scientific name,* inoa Lākina.
scientist. Mea 'imi na'auao, akeakamai.
scion. Weli, weweli, weliweli.
scissors. 'Ūpā; 'ūpā miki'ao *(fingernail).*
scoff. Pāhenehene. *See* jeer.
scold. Nuku, ke'u, ho'okekē, ho'okekē niho, huhū. *Also:* ho'okekē nuku, ha'akekē, hae, kolokolo, waha lapalapa, meku, pakake'u, kūkahalakē, kekē.
scoop. Kī'o'e, kūpā, hao, kope, kope 'ana; — *out,* pō-'alo, pao, kī'alo, olohi'a. *Also:* po'o, kūpele, kīpaopao, hōuna, haohana.
scoopful. Haona.
scoop net. 'Upena uluulu, 'upena kā'e'e.
scope. Nui, laulā.
scorch. Kuni, pāpa'a wela, eina, 'ānia. *Also:* pāwela, lili'u, haulalapa, uno'o; pākī'ai, nikipa'u, haoa, 'ōhaoa.
score. 1. *Count.* Helu, 'ai. *To keep score,* helu 'ai. 2. *See* twenty.
scoreboard. Papa helu.
scorekeeper. Helu 'ai.
scoreless. 'Ai 'ole; 'ōhule *(slang).*
scorn. Ho'owahāwahā, ho'okae, wahāwahā, kae. *Also:* ha'akei, ihu 'e'eke, pinana ka ihu, 'ōkoleoioi, ho'oma'ewa, ho'okē. *See* exclamation.
scornful. Ma'ewa; ihuihu, 'auwae, hō'auwae. *See* scorn.
scorpion. Mo'o-niho-'awa, mo'o-huelo-'awa, kopena, kopiana.
scorpionfish. Nohu *(see Haw.-Eng. entry and entries that follow it).*
Scotch, Scotland, Scottish. Kekokia.
Scotia. Sekotia.
scoundrel. Lapuwale, pu'uwai 'ele'ele.
scour. Kuai, 'ānai, kuolo, holoi.
scouring stone. Nohu.
scout. Kiu; 'oumuamua *(rare).*
scow. Kao.
scowl. Ho'oku'eku'emaka, ho'oku'eku'emaka nui, ho'opupuku, ho'o'i'ika. *Also:* 'i'ī, māku'i, makaku'iku'i, ho'onohu.
scraggly. Kīwalawala, kīwalawala'ō, hao'a.
scramble. Huikau, ho'ohuikau *(mix);* pākā. *Scrambled eggs,* hua kai, hua pākā.
scrap. 1. *Remnant.* Huna, hakina, hunahuna, 'āpana li'ili'i. *See* scraps. 2. *See* fight.
scrap bowl. Ipu 'aina.
scrape. Wa'u, wawa'u, wa'uwa'u, koe, kuai, kahi, pohole. *Also:* uwa'u, kāwa'u, walu, 'uwalu, mākoe, mahole, mohole, hē, kepa, mōholehole, kele.
scraper. Kahi, wa'u, uwa'u, wawa'u, wa'uwa'u; uhi *(of turtle shell);* kalepa.
scrap iron. Pāpa'a hao.
scraps. Koena, hakina 'ai, 'āmikamika, 'ōpilopilo, kō-'ala'ala.
scratch. Walu, wawalu, 'uwalu *(as a cat);* koe; helu *(as a hen).* *Also:* heluhelu, waluhia, waluwalu, wa'u, uwa'u, wawa'u, wa'u, kuolo, kope, kaha, kahakaha, kīhelu, māhelu, moku'oi, neneke.
scratched. Koea, waluhia. *See* scratch.
scratchings. Kahakahana, waluna, koena. *See* scratch.
scratch paper. Pepa kahakaha.
scrawly. Kiwala'ō *(as writing).*
scream. 'Alalā, pū'alalā, wala'au nui, kolopā. *See* roar.
screech. Alalī, kīkīko'u, kani 'ōkalakala.
screen. Pākū, pālulu, ālai, ānai, wahamana. *Wire screen,* uwea hakahaka. *Window screen,* uwea hakahaka, pālulu pukaaniani. *Screen for projecting pictures or movies,* wea hakahaka.
screw. Kui nao, kui, kolū. *To screw,* wili.
screw auger. Wilipua'a, ulepua'a.
screwdriver. Kuikala, kala, kala nao.
scribble. Kākau wale, kopekope.

scribe. Kākau ʻōlelo. *Royal scribe,* kākau aliʻi.
Scriptures. Palapala Hemolele.
scrofula. ʻĀʻī palaʻe, ʻaʻī ʻalaʻala.
scroll. ʻŌwili palapala.
scrotum. Laho *(for various idioms and insults, see* **laho** *and entries that follow it). Also:* ʻeke, ʻekeʻeke, ʻōpeʻa, ʻolo. *Bull scrotum,* laho pipi. *Raw scrotum,* laho kole. *My man with big voice whose scrotum sounds,* kuʻu kanaka leo nui, na ka laho e hoʻokani *(a riddle: a bell is the answer).*
scrub. ʻĀnai, holoi, kuolo *(verb).*
scrubbing brush. Palaki ʻānai.
scrubby. ʻIʻi, kāiʻoiʻo.
scrutinize. Nānā pono, loi, hoʻomakauliʻi.
scrutiny. Loina. *See* **scrutinize.**
scud. Kaʻa.
sculptor. Mea kālai kiʻi, kuʻekepa.
scum. Huʻa, huʻahuʻa. *A few scums:* limu kalawai (pālāwai), pāwai, nehe.
scurvy. Pehu pai, puʻupuʻu.
scythe. Pahi kākiwi.
sea. Kai; moana *(open);* malo, pāʻū *(poetic). See sayings,* **pūnoni, forecast.** *Calm, quiet sea,* kai mālie, kai malino, kai malolo, kai hoʻolulu, kai pū, kai wahine, kai kalamania, kaiolohia. *Strong sea,* kai koʻo, kai kāne, kai nui, kai nuʻu, ʻōkaikai. *Rough or raging sea,* kai pupule, kai puʻeone, kai akua, ʻōkaikai. *Deep sea,* kai hohonu, kai ʻau, kai hoʻēʻe, kai lū heʻe *(fig.). Restless sea with undercurrent,* kai kuolo, kai holo, kai lewa, lapa kai, kai kō, kai au. *Dark blue sea,* moana uli, moauli. *Streaked sea, associated with Kona,* kai māʻokiʻoki. *Whispering sea, associated with Kawaihae,* kai hāwanawana. *Salt sea,* kai paʻakai. *Shallow or reef sea,* kai kohola, kai koʻele. *Rippled sea,* kai hoʻolili. *Receding or ebbing sea,* kai heʻe, kai emi, kai mimiki, kai hoʻi, kai nuʻu aku. *Western sea,* kai lalo. *High sea,* kai piha, kai nuʻu. *Of the sea,* o kai. *Towards the sea,* i kai, makai. *Place where sea and land meet,* ʻae kai. *By the sea,* a kai. *Sea almost surrounded by land,* kai hāloko. *The eight seas,* nā kai ʻewalu *(seas about the Hawaiian Islands, poetic). Puna with its sea rustling over pebbles,* Puna i ke kai nehe i ka ʻiliʻili. *My sea, concealing sarong (UL 124),* kuʻu kai, pāʻū halakā. *Black sea, yellow sea, Kāne's purplish-blue red-brown sea . . . silent sea, swinging sea (PH 237),* kai ʻeleʻele, kai melemele, kai pōpolohua mea a Kāne . . . kai mū, kai lewa.
sea area. Kai.
sea bean. Kāʻeʻe, maunaloa. *Seeds of kāʻeʻe,* pīpā, pēkaʻa.
seacoast. Kahakai.
sea cucumber. Loli *(for various kinds, see* **loli** *and entries that follow it),* weli, weliweli, maʻihole, kūnounou, hulali, hūlalilali, ʻūpalu, kūneuneu, ʻunae, kaʻukama kai. *See ex. of word magic,* ʻiloli. *Catch the sea cucumber by mistake, a blind fish,* hopu hewa i ka loli, ka iʻa makapō *(of disappointment, a worthless catch, or ignorance).*
sea dog. ʻĪlio ʻaukai.
sea elephant. ʻElepani kai.
seafarer. Holomoana, holokai, ʻaukai.
sea foam. Ehu kai.
sea gull. Nēnē ʻau kai, ʻōpaʻipaʻi.
sea horse. Moʻo lio.
Sea Island cotton. Kiʻailana.
seal. 1. *Emblem.* Kila. *Also:* uwepa, hoʻopaʻa, kuni. *Seal of office,* sila o ke keʻena. *To fix a seal,* kila. **2.** *Mammal.* ʻĪlio-holo-i-ka-uaua, hulu *(rare).*
sea lettuce. ʻĪliohaʻa, līpaha, līpahapaha, pahapaha, līpālahalaha, pakaiea, pālahalaha. *See* **seaweed.**
sealing wax. Kēpau kāpili palapala.
seam. Kuʻina, kuʻi, humu, humuhumu, humuna.
seaman. *See* **sailor.**
seamed. Hāluʻa.
sear. Kuni. *Also:* haulalapa, kā liliko.

search. ʻImi, huli; ʻimina, hulina *(nouns). Also:* holi, ʻakiu. *To search repeatedly,* hulihuli, huli hele. *To search, as for knowledge,* noiʻi, noiʻina.
search warrant. Palapala huli.
sea shell. Pūpū *(for various kinds, see* **pūpū** *and entries that follow it). See* **shell.**
seashore. Kahakai, kapa kai.
seasick. Poluea, luea, hoʻopapailua, ʻōlanalana. *See* **nausea.**
seaside. Kapa kai, kahakai, kai.
sea slug. *See* **sea cucumber.**
season. 1. *Time,* Kau. *Also:* wā, manawa, laʻa, kikina. *See* **fall, spring, summer, winter.** *Rainy season,* wā ua, manawa ua, laʻa ua. *Fruit season,* kau hua. *Season of dying plants,* laʻa make. *Octopus season,* wā heʻe. *Season after season,* kau ā kau. *To season, as lumber,* hoʻomaloʻo. **2.** *Impart taste.* Hōʻono, hōʻonoʻono, hoʻomiko, kāmala. *Seasoned,* miko, liʻu, maliʻu.
seasoning. Mea hōʻonoʻono, mea hoʻomikomiko, liʻu, kūliʻu.
sea spray. Ehu kai.
seat. Noho, nohona, hoʻonoho. *High, rickety seat,* kiolea. *Seat cover,* pale noho.
sea urchin. Wana, wanawana, wana kauila; ʻina. *Various kinds:* hāʻukeʻuke *(also, name of a tapa design);* hāʻukeʻuke iwi loloa, hāʻuke, hāʻukaʻuka, hāʻueʻue, hākuʻekuʻe, hāwaʻe, hālula, pūnohu, huluʻanai, niho, hailimoa. *Sea-urchin meat,* alelo, poke ʻina. *Sea-urchin sauce,* kai ʻina. *To remove sea-urchin flesh,* poke ʻina. *See saying,* **hāwaʻe.**
sea wall. Pani kai.
seaward. Makai, i kai, o kai.
sea water. Kai.
seaweed. Limu, lī-. *See Haw.-Eng. entries and the entries that follow them for various kinds.* Limu *and* lī- *are sometimes omitted. Some names vary according to islands. See lists below, also* **moss, scum, sea lettuce, vagabond.** *Ball of seaweed, as sold for food,* pōpō limu; *to gather seaweed,* ʻaku limu.
COMMON EDIBLE SEAWEEDS *(following Abbott and Williamson; var. names are in parentheses, but see Haw.-Eng. entries for other names):* ʻakiʻaki (kōʻeleʻele), ʻeleʻele, huluhulu waena (pakele-a-waʻa), limu kala, limu kohu (līpehe, līpehu, līpaʻakai), līpahapaha (pahapaha, pāpahapaha, līpaha, pālahalana, pakaiea, ʻīliohaʻa), līpeʻepeʻe, līpoa, manauea, māneʻoneʻo, paheʻe (pāheʻeheʻe, limu lūʻau), wawaeʻiole (ʻaʻala, ʻaʻalaʻula, ʻalaʻula).
LESS COMMON SEAWEEDS *(alternate names are in parentheses; see also Haw.-Eng. entries beginning* limu *and* lī-*):* ʻākaʻakoʻa, alani, ʻānapanapa (limu loloa), ʻāpiʻipiʻi, ʻaʻula (hāʻula?), ʻawa, ʻaweʻaweʻa, ʻāweoweo, ʻeloʻelo (pīpīlani), hāwane, hinaʻula, hoʻonunu, huʻahuʻakai, hūai, huihui, huihui maka liʻi, hulu ʻiʻi, hulu ʻīlio (hulu, hulu pāhuluhulu, ʻīlio, nahawele, pūhuluhulu), hulu manu (ʻai-a-ka-honu, hulu moa, līmoa), huna (hunehune), huna pakēpakē, hūpēkohola, kāʻapeʻape, kāʻele, kāhili, kaunoʻa, kaupau, kāwelu, kihe (ʻakali, kīkalamoa (kīkala), kīkī, kilihune, kōʻeleʻele (kōʻele, ʻāwikiwiki, ʻēkahakaha, limu-uaua-loli, nei), lauoho-o-Pele, lelepo, lepe-o-Hina (lehelehe-ʻīlio, lepelepe-o-Hina), leponalo, likolehua, lupe, maka, makaloa, mākole, makua-o-ka-limu-kohu, manamana-ʻula, māwaewae-kilihune, moʻopuna-a-ka-līpoa (aupūpū), naio, nakeke, nane, nanea, nanoʻo, nanue (nenue), nē, nuʻa, ʻōhelo-huihui, ʻōhiʻohiʻo, ʻōhune, ʻōkala, ʻōmaʻomaʻo, oneone, ʻoʻolu, ʻopiʻopi, pahapaha-o-Polihale, pahapaha-wai, pākalakala, pakelo, pakēpakē, pakūpakū, pala, pala pōhaku, pala ʻula, pale wāwae, paninikū, pānohonoho, pānoʻonoʻo, pāpaʻakea, pāʻiā-o-Hiʻiaka, pehu, pepe-o-Hina, pīlali, pilikoʻa, pohāpohā (pohā), popohe-Makaliʻi, puakī, pūhā, pūkoʻakoʻa, pūʻula, ʻūnoko, wāwahi-waʻa, weluwelu.
sea worm. Koʻe kai.
Sechem. Kekema, Sekema.

second. Lua, kualua; kekona *(time unit); kōko'olua (in a duel). To second a motion,* kōkua. *The second time,* ka lua o ka manawa.
secondary. Lua.
second-degree murder. 'Elua kekele o ka pepehi kanaka.
secondhand. Mea i ho'ohana mua 'ia, hana mua 'ia.
secondly. Lua.
second sight. Maka 'ike, 'ike pāpālua. *Gift of second sight,* ha'awina 'ike.
secret. Mea huna, huna, malū, 'ōhuna. *To hide or keep in secret,* hūnā, hūnākele, 'ekepue. *To do evil in secret,* kāmalū. *Secret languages:* wehiwa, nehiwa, kake.
secretary. 1. *Clerical aid.* Kākau 'ōlelo, kākau mo'olelo; ikū kau *(rare). Private secretary,* kākau 'ōlelo pilikino. 2. *High official.* Kuhina.
secretary of interior. Kuhina kālai'āina.
secretary of state. Kuhina moku'āina.
secretary of war. Kuhina kaua.
secretive. Pe'e poli, malū, 'ekepue, hō'ekepue, hūnā. *See saying,* kio 2.
secretly. Hunāhunā, malū. *Take secretly,* lawe malū.
secret service. 'Oihana kiu.
secret society. 'Ahahui malū; nauwā *(formed by Ka-lā-kaua).*
sect. Ho'omana, mahele ho'omana.
section. Paukū, moku, mokuna, 'āpana, mahele; mahele hana *(work section). Also:* mō, hakina; puna *(between joints);* kiko *(of a story);* huli *(as of town or place);* poke; hā'ao *(in chief's procession);* nanaka *(marked).*
sector. 'Āpana.
secure. Pa'a. *Also:* papa'a, kuapapa, kulekule. *See* **safe.** *To make secure,* ho'opa'a, hana pa'a, hoa, 'ōmau. *Not secure,* pa'a 'ole, holokake.
security. Palekana, panekana, maluhia, kahua pa'a; waiwai ho'opa'a *(investment). See saying,* **heaven.**
security bank. Panakō ho'omalu 'ia.
security guard. Kia'ipo'o.
sedan chair. Manele.
sedate. Kūo'o, no'eno'e.
sedges. Mau'u. *Varieties:* 'ahaniu, 'ahu'awa, 'ehu'awa, kāluhāluhā, kiolohia, kohekohe, kuolohia, makaloa, manunēnē, mokae, pīpīwai, pōpōhau-o-Ni'ihau, pu'uka'a, 'uki.
sediment. Oka, ko'ana, mākū.
sedition libel. Laipila ho'ālaala kipi.
seditious. Kipi. *Seditious offenses,* hewa ho'ālaala kipi.
seduce. Ho'owalewale hewa, alaka'i hewa, luahele.
see. 'Ike; nānā *(look at). To see clearly, well, keenly,* 'ike pono, 'ike le'a, maka 'ike, 'i'ike, 'ike kōnale. *To see personally,* 'ike maka. *To see double,* 'ike pāpālua. *To see supernatural things,* maka 'ike. *To see indistinctly,* hala'o'a, pāwao *(rare). To see but disregard,* nānā kuli. *Let me see!* 'Oliana! 'Oiana! 'Oia ana! Aliana! Inane!
seed. 'Ano'ano, hua; hua kanu *(for planting);* lū *(of beach poppy). To bear seed,* hua. *Seed of* loulu *palm,* wāhane, hāwane. *Seed of* 'āweoweo *(a shrub),* mokiweo. *Seed of* kā'e'e, pēka'a, pīpā.
seedbed. Wahi kanu 'ano'ano. *Also:* loko ulu, haokanu.
seedling. Kawowo, hehu. *Also:* ila, 'ōilo.
seeing. 'Ikena.
seek. 'Imi, huli. *Also:* huhuli, huhuhuli, 'i'imi *(of many and repeatedly);* 'akiu, nowelo. *To seek far,* 'imi loa. *To seek money,* 'imi kālā. *To seek work,* 'imi hana. *To seek information or knowledge,* noi'i, 'imi 'ike, 'imi na'auao. *To seek for sexual ends,* ki'i. *To seek revenge,* ho'opa'i, ho'opāna'i, 'imi i kahi e kū ai ka mākaia.
seeking. 'Imina, hulina.
seems. 'Amo, mehe mea lā. *It seems good,* he 'ano mai-ka'i ia.
seen. 'Ike 'ia, kūmaka. *Plainly seen,* 'ike maopopo 'ia, kaula'ela'e, 'ō'ili lua.
seepage. Nono, nō, manono.

seer. Kāula, kilo, kuhikuhipu'uone, nānā ao, 'imi loa. *God of seers,* Kuhimana. *Hi'iaka, seer with power (PH 151),* 'O Hi'iaka, kāula mana.
seesaw. Papa hulei *(board). To seesaw,* hulehulei. *Also:* mahiki, panau, ho'opanau, mākoiele.
segment. 'Āpana; 'āpana pō'ai *(of a circle).*
segregate. Ho'oka'awale.
segregation. Ho'oka'awale 'ana.
seine. Hukilau, lau, 'upena kō lau, lau kapalili, lau'apo-'apo, pāloa.
seismograph. Ana ōla'i, mīkini ana ōla'i.
seize. Hopu, 'apo, lālau, kā'ili. *Also:* ho'oki'iki'i, kā'ilikū, 'apakau, kāpe'a, lelemū, kūlē, lauhulu.
seizing. 'Uo *(lashing).*
seldom. Kaka'ikahi.
select. Koho, wae, 'ohi. *Also:* waewae, ho'owae, māwae, mōwae, mōae, 'ele'ī.
selection. Koho 'ana, wae 'ana, 'ohina.
selection board. Papa 'ohi.
selective. Kamawae, wae, waewae.
select school. Kula wae.
self. Iho, kino, pono'ī, 'ōiwi. *See* **bone.** *For myself,* no'u iho.
self-control. Kāohi iho.
selfish. 'Au'a; no'ono'o iāia wale iho nō, ho'okeāmaka.
self-satisfied. 'Olu'olu nō iāia iho.
sell. Kū'ai aku. *Also:* kālepa, ho'olilo, ma'au'auwā; ku'aku'ai, ho'oku'aku'ai *(sell repeatedly, buy and sell);* pākaukau *(over the counter). To sell leis,* kau lei.
seller. Mea kū'ai aku. *Lei seller,* mea kau lei, wahine kau lei.
selvage. Ka'e pa'a *(of cloth).*
semen. Keakea. *Also:* wai o ke kāne, wai. *See saying,* **keakea.**
semester. Kau.
semiannual. Hapa makahiki.
semicircle. Pō'ai hapalua.
semicolon. Kiko ho'omaha, kiko koma.
semiconscious. Ho'olana i ka wai ke ola.
senate. 'Aha kenekoa.
senator. Kenekoa.
send. Ho'ouna; — *on an errand,* kēnā; — *for,* ki'i, ho'o-ki'i, kauoha; — *back,* ho'iho'i; — *away,* kīpaku, paku.
senior. Mua, makua, hele mua, hānau mua. *See saying,* **wawaele.** *Senior class,* papa ki'eki'e loa, papa e puka aku ana. *Smith, Senior,* Kamika Makua. *Senior branch (of a family),* nā hele mua, lālā hele mua. *To act as senior,* ho'omuamua.
sennit. 'Aha. *To braid sennit,* hō'aha.
sensation. Mea ho'okāhāhā. *See* **manene, sense.**
sensational. Kū i ke kāhāhā.
sense. 1. *Faculty.* 'Ike. *Sense of taste,* 'ike i ka 'ono. *Sense of pain,* 'ike i ka 'eha. *Sense of sight,* 'ike i ka maka. *Common sense,* no'ono'o kūpono. 2. *Import.* Mana'o nui.
sensible. No'ono'o pono.
sensitive. 1. *Perceptive.* 'Ike ho'omaopopo. 2. *As to criticism.* 'Eha wale, ku'ia wale. *Also:* heke, lili.
sensitive plant. Pua hilahila.
sensory. 'Ike. *Extrasensory perception,* 'ike pāpālua.
sensual. Kuko i kō ke kino; pākīai *(rare).*
sentence. Māmala'ōlelo *(words);* 'ōlelo ho'opa'i *(penalty).*
sentiment. Aloha.
sentimental. Pakela ho'ālohaloha loa.
sentinel. Koa kia'i, kū uwaki.
separate. Ka'awale, kau 'oko'a, kā'oko'a, hemo, lele, ho'oka'awale, wae. *Also:* ho'oka'a'oko'a, hō'oko'a, kauko'a, ho'okaupale, wae, waewae, māwae, mahae, weke, wekewele, māwehe, māweke, mōwae, mōae, ho'opale, kōhikōhi, 'oki. *See* **kai'ōkia.** *To separate by space,* ho'okōwā. *To separate taro corm from stalk,* kōhi 'ai.
separately. Pākahi, ho'oka'awale 'ia, ho'okahi, 'oko'a. *Considered separately,* no'ono'o pākahi 'ia.

separation. Ka'awale 'ana, 'okina, ho'omoku, palena, hemohemo, 'akaka.
September. Kepakemapa.
sepulcher. Hale kupapa'u, ilina kupapa'u, ilina.
sequel. Hope, hopena.
sequence. Noho papa 'ana, ho'onoho papa 'ana, kaka-'ina, ka'ina, kekahi mahope mai o kekahi, moekahi. *See* **succession.**
seraphim. Kelapima.
serenade. Mele ho'oipoipo, mele ho'ālohaloha *(romantic).*
serene. Maluhia, la'i, mālie, la'ela'e, māla'e. *Also:* la'ikū, kohea, pālūlā, 'alaneo. *Serene weather,* kohea.
serge. 'Alapia, paina *(resembling).*
sergeant. Kakiana. *Sergeant major,* kakiana mekia.
sergeant-at-arms. Mālama puka.
sergeant fish. Mamo.
serial. Helu.
serial bond. Pona helu.
series. Mahele *(as of books);* mo'o. *See* **sequence, set.** *One of a series,* kaka'ina.
serious. Kūo'o. *Also:* hō'i'o, hana'i'o, kūkonukonu. *See* **important.**
sermon. Ha'i'ōlelo, ha'i a'o.
serpent. Mo'o, mo'o kiha, mo'olele. *See* **snake.**
Serpentine River. Muliwai Kepenakina.
serrated. Wakawaka, nihoniho, nihoa, 'ōniho.
servant. Kanaka hana *(male);* wahine hana *(female);* kanaka lawelawe, kanaka, 'ōhua. *See* **outcast, retainer.** *Anciently, attendants to a chief were privileged blood relatives who might not be dismissed;* kauā *(Biblical, servant) were despised outcasts not permitted access to chiefs; the Euro-American idea of the inferior status of servants was unknown. Your humble servant,* kāu kauā ha'aha'a. *Your obedient servant,* kāu kauā ho'olohe. *Servant of God,* kauā a ke Akua.
serve. Lawelawe. *Also:* ho'okō *(as a warrant);* mālama, ka'a malalo. *Serves you right!* Alolo! 'Aikola! Lolo! Ā la'a lā!
service. Lawelawe *(assistance);* hana, 'oihana *(occupation, division, department). Service charge,* uku lawelawe. *Military service,* 'oihana koa. *Church service,* pule, hālāwai haipule, haipule, haipule 'ana.
service of process. Ho'okō 'ana i ka palapala kēnā.
servile. Ha'aha'a loa, ka'apē, kuapa'a.
sesban. 'Ohai ke'oke'o, 'ohai 'ula'ula.
session. Kau. *Regular session,* kau mau *(of legislature). Special session,* kau kūikawā. *To be in session,* noho.
set. 1. *To place.* Kau; ho'onoho *(as table, bones, type);* ho'omoe, ho'omoemoe, ku'u, au *(as line or net);* 'ōniu, ulele *(as type);* mau *(as a wager);* napo'o, welo *(of sun);* kōkō *(bones by applying pressure);* pa'ihi, hao ā pa'ihi *(as sails);* kāpili *(as precious stones). To set on fire,* hō'ā, puhi ahi. *To set firmly,* pa'akūkū, ho'opa'a. *To set apart,* ho'oka'awale, hō'oko'a, kai'okia; mōlia *(for gods). To set aside,* kāpae, waiho. *To set up,* kūkulu, ho'okū. *To set off, explode,* ho'opahū. *To set free,* ho'oku'u, makala, puhemo. *To set apart for sacred purposes,* ho'ola'a, ho'okapu. *To set a table,* ho'onoho i ka pākaukau. 2. *Assortment.* Nā mea kohu like o ke 'ano ho'okahi, kaina. *Tea set,* kaina ho'okahi o nā mea inu kī.
settee. Kokī, noho lō'ihi. *See* **couch.**
setting. Kahua, wahi; 'ōnohi *(as of a ring). Diamond setting,* 'ōpu'u kaimana, 'ōnohi kaimana. *Setting sun,* napo'ona lā, lā kau. *The setting of the moon (Kep. 105),* ka napo'ona mahina.
settle. Kau; mākū, ko'ana, ho'oko'ana, ki'o *(as dregs);* kiki'o, pāki'o, ho'oki'o, ki'o wai *(as water in a pond);* ku'u, emi iho, pohō, pohī *(as earth);* 'ōku'u, noe *(as mist);* ho'onā *(as a claim);* ho'oholo *(as a problem);* akaku'u *(as wind). To settle down, stay,* noho pa'a, ho'okahua.
settled. Kau, nā, holo, akaku'u. *See* **settle.**
settlement. Kauhale, aukanaka. *See* **agreement.**
seven. Hiku, 'ehiku, 'ahiku. *Seven times,* 'ehiku, 'ahiku,

pāhiku. *Seven years,* 'ehiku makahiki, hepekoma. *Seven times seven,* hiku hiku.
sevenfold. Pāhiku.
seventeen. 'Umi kūmāhiku, 'umi kumamāhiku.
seventh. Hiku. *One-seventh,* hapahiku.
Seventh-day Adventist. Ho'omana Pō'aono.
seventy. Kanahiku.
seventy-eight. Kanahiku kūmāwalu, kanahiku kumamāwalu.
seventy-five. Kanahiku kūmālima, kanahiku kumamālima.
seventy-four. Kanahiku kūmāhā, kanahiku kumamāhā.
seventy-nine. Kanahiku kūmāiwa, kanahiku kumamāiwa.
seventy-one. Kanahiku kūmākahi, kanahiku kumamākahi.
seventy-seven. Kanahiku kūmāhiku, kanahiku kumamāhiku.
seventy-six. Kanahiku kūmāono, kanahiku kumamāono.
seventy-three. Kanahiku kūmākolu, kanahiku kumamākolu.
seventy-two. Kanahiku kūmālua, kanahiku kumamālua.
sever. 'Oki, moku. *Also:* mō, muku, mukumuku, mokumoku, momoku, 'āmokumoku. *Severed,* moku, pahupū, lele loa, po'omuku, mokuna.
several. Kekahi, kekahi mau.
severance. 'Okina, mokuna.
severe. 'O'ole'a, 'a'aka, uahoa, ko'iko'i. *Also:* kūpiliki'i; lo'a'ā *(as taboo);* pā'ea'ea. *To treat severely,* ho'oko'iko'i.
Seville. Kewila, Sevila.
sew. Humuhumu. *Also:* hono, ku'i, holoholo, 'ōmau; pāhono *(as a tear);* holo *(as a break in a gourd);* kāholo *(with long stitches). To sew sails,* humu pe'a, uhauhumu *(rare). To sew in a diagonal line,* humu lala.
sewer. 'Auwai, kua, hā wai, 'auwai lawe mea 'ino.
sewer pipe. Paipu lawe 'ino, hā wai lawe 'ino.
sewing. Humuna. *See* **sew.**
sewing machine. Mīkini humuhumu, kāwiliwili humuhumu. *For parts, see* **huila, kā'ei, kanokaomi, pane'e'ūpiki, papa hehi, papa ho'oholo, bobbin winder, clamp, feed dog, gatherer, gauge, latch, presser foot, shuttle, spool.**
sex. *No Hawaiian term. See* **lascivious, lecherous, randy,** *and sayings,* hua 4, ko'okā 1, pī'oe'oe, wa'uwa'u. *Masculine sex,* keka kāne. *Feminine sex,* keka wahine.
sexual. *No Hawaiian term (but sexual innuendos are enjoyed);* pili i ke kāne me ka wahine. *See* **game** *and sayings,* **wali, cowry shell.** *Sexual passion,* kola, huahua'i. *Sexual excitement,* mane'o, kola. *Sexual part,* ma'i, wahi huna. *Sexually unattractive,* lemukū. *The hidden meaning of this song is sexual,* ke kaona o kēia mele, pili i ke kāne me ka wahine. *Beautiful but without sexual appeal,* he u'i kū i ki'ona *(lit., a beauty fit for the dung heap). Sexual attraction or relationship may be shown poetically by references to rain, mist, spray, coolness.*
sexual intercourse. Ai, ei, hana ma'i, moe, pi'i, panipani, aina. *Motions of sexual intercourse,* kū'ami'ami. *To have had sexual intercourse, of a female,* pā kanaka. *Sexual intercourse with a menstruating woman,* kokokohe.
shabby. Hāpa'upa'u, kuhā'eka, lu'a.
shack. Hale 'āpulu, kāmala.
shaddock. 'Alani Pākē.
shade. Malu, māmalu; palulu *(for protection). Shade under cliff or hill,* 'ūmalu. *To shade,* ho'omalumalu, ho'oma'ū, 'ūmalu, ho'o'ūmalu. *Eye shade,* palulu maka. *Lamp shade,* palulu kukui. *Window shade,* pākū pouli, palulu pukaaniani. *Deep shade, as of trees,* malu hālau loa, malu ko'i, mālipolipo.
shadow. Aka, huaka, 'ūmalu. *See saying,* **aka** 1. *To cast a shadow,* ho'oaka, ili i ke aka, ho'ohuaka, ho'o'ūma-

lu; malila *(rare)*. *To fall, as one shadow on another,* pi'i. *The valley of the shadow of death,* ke awāwa malu o ka make.

shady. Malumalu. *Also:* lāuli, 'ōmalu, 'ōmalumalu, ho'omalumalu, mālipolipo, milumilu, 'e'a'e'a; pololuhi *(rare)*. *To make shady,* ho'omāmalu.

shaft. 1. *Column.* Kia, pou. 2. *See* **handle.**

shaggy. Pūhuluhulu, 'ōhuluhulu, huluhulu.

shake. Naue, nauwe, nāueue, lūlū, hō'oni, ho'oluliluli, luli, luliluli *(as the head)*; ho'oluli *(as a drink)*; lūlū, nāueue, 'ōla'i, 'ōpa'ipa'i *(as the earth)*; — *jerkily,* kūkū; — *as with palsy,* kuolo; — *as with cold or fear,* ulupi'i; — *badly,* 'oni 'ino. *Also:* ha'alulu, 'api, kuehu, kuekueni, lū, nū, naka, noiele, pilu, 'ōlūlū *(with fat)*, 'oloka, paleha, ho'onāueue. *Shake hands,* lūlū lima.

shaky. Kulana, kulanalana, naluli, kāhulihuli.

shall. E . . . ana, e. *Gram. 5.2.*

shallow. Pāpa'u, hāpapa; mālānai, mānānai, pānānai, nānai *(rare)*. *Shallow-rooted,* mālana, pūhai. *Sea too shallow to float a canoe in,* kai ko'ele.

sham. Ho'okamani. *Sham battle,* kaua kio, pahukala, kānekupua *(with spears)*.

shame. Hilahila, waia. *To put to shame,* ho'ohilahila, ho'owaia, ho'ohoka. *What a shame!* Aloha 'ino!

shamefaced. Palai maka.

shameful. Ho'ohilahila.

shameless. Hilahila 'ole, 'uhane 'ole; mākolea *(rare)*.

shampoo. Holoi lauoho. *Shampoo liquid,* mea holoi lauoho.

shamrock. 'Ihi pua kea.

Shanghai. Kainahai, Kanahai. *To shanghai,* kanahai.

shank. 1. *Fishhook part.* Kū'au. *Tail or small end of bonito lure,* muli. *Head or large end,* ihu. *Shank of octopus lure,* pou lua. 2. *Leg.* Wāwae, lapawāwae.

shanty. Hale lālā lā'au, kāmala, hale pupupu.

shape. 'Ano, hō'omo'omo; kālai, 'ōmilo *(as a canoe hull)*; ho'opololei, kālai *(as a policy or enterprise)*. *Irregular in shape,* pā'ewa, pū'ali. *To take shape,* ho'okino. *To put in shape,* ho'oponopono, ho'opololei.

share. Mahele, pu'u; kea *(stocks)*. *To share,* mahele; ka'ana, ho'oka'ana *(equally)*; pu'unaue, 'alo. *Share food,* pū 'ai.

sharer. Hoa loa'a, hoa lawe pū.

shark. Manō *(for various kinds, sayings, fig. meanings, see Haw.-Eng. entry and entries that follow it)*. *Also:* lālākea, laukāhi'u, leleiwi, lelewa'a, luhia, niuhi. *See saying,* **holopapa** 2, *and idiom,* **eat.** *Line of shark fins protruding above the water,* lālani kalalea. *To catch sharks with bait and noose,* kūmanō. *Shark-tooth weapon,* leiomano. *Shark-tooth knife,* niho 'oki. *To behave as a shark, to act like a shark, to pursue women,* ho'omanō. *The wiliwili blooms, sharks bite,* pua ka wiliwili, nanahu ka manō *(of a girl reaching maturity)*.

shark sucker. Leleiona, moelawa *(remora)*.

Sharon. Kalona. *The rose of Sharon,* ka loke o Kalona.

sharp. 1. *Not dull.* 'Oi, 'āwini. *Also:* 'oi'oi, kōī, ko'i, mūko'i, 'ou, kākala, kulilipi, nihoa, huini, waka, wakawaka, wana, wanawana, wawana. *Long and sharp,* pīoeoe. *Any sharp edge,* lipi. *Sharp point,* wini, winiwini. *Sharp nose,* ihu winiwini. *Sharp, shrill sounds,* huini. *Sharp-edged,* ka'e 'oi, 'ōniho. *Sharp-lipped,* lehe 'oi *(of one who makes cutting remarks)*. 2. *In music.* 'Oi.

sharpen. Ho'okala, hō'oi. *Also:* hō'oi'oi, hana ho'owini, koli, 'oi.

sharpener. Ho'okala, mea ho'okala.

sharpness. 'Oi.

sharpshooter. Kī pololei.

sharp-tongued. Kekē, kekē nuku, lehe 'oi, waha 'ā.

shatter. Wāwahi, nahā, nāhāhā, kā, ho'okā, kāpa'i.

shave. Kahi, āmū, koli. *To shave whiskers,* kahi 'umi'umi. *To shave half the head in mourning,* kahi kīhapa. *Smooth-shaven,* kahania, kanekanea.

shavings. Oka lā'au, kahina; hānā *(rare)*.

shawl. Kīhei. Kīhei *dyed with sandalwood,* peluliahi. *To wear a shawl,* kīheihei.

she. *Same as* **he.**

sheaf. Pū'ā, pū'ala. *We were binding sheaves,* i ka pū'ā 'ana a kākou i nā pū'ā.

shear. 'Ako, 'oki, āmū. *To shear sheep,* 'ako hulu hipa.

shearer. Mea 'ako. *Sheep shearer,* mea 'ako hulu hipa.

shears. 'Ūpā, 'ūpā nui. *Grass shears,* 'ūpā mau'u. *Pinking shears,* 'ūpā nihoniho.

shearwater. 'Ua'u kani (hō'io), 'a'o.

sheath. Pale, wahī, 'ili wahī. *Coconut-flower sheath,* holowa'a, holoa'a, lolo, lolo niu. *Coconut-sheath canoe,* wa'a lolo niu. *Banana-bud sheath,* 'ōpu'u mai'a.

shed. 1. *Building.* Hale ho'āhu. *Also:* hale pupupu, auolo, hale malu, hale malumalu, hale kāmala, lānai. 2. *Throw off.* Helele'i, helelei *(as a dog's hair)*; lū, nū; hāliko, ho'omalule *(as a crab sheds its shell)*; auhā *(rare)*. *Shed blood,* ho'okahe koko.

sheep. Hipa. *Flock of sheep,* kumu hipa, pū'ā hipa. *To tend sheep,* kahu hipa.

sheep dog. 'Īlio hipa, 'īlio kia'i hipa.

sheepfold. Pā hipa.

sheep market. Pukahipa.

sheepskin. 'Ili hipa.

sheer. 1. *Perpendicular, steep.* Kū pololei, kūnihinihi. *Also:* kahakō, ku'i, kūlono, kūmole, laumania, nienie; lele koa'e *(poetic)*. 2. *Complete.* Loa, maoli. *Sheer nonsense,* kohu 'ole loa.

sheet. Lau, papa, pale. *Sheet of paper,* 'āpana pepa. *Bed sheet,* uhi pela, hāli'i moe, pale moe.

shekel. Kekela.

shelf. Haka, haka kau, papa, kumuhaka, holopapa, kaola. *Rare:* olo, olo'ewa. *Shelf for food containers,* haka ipu, papa ipu. *High shelf or place,* kauwōlani.

shell. 1. *Marine shell.* Pūpū *(see Haw.-Eng. entry and entries that follow it)*, iwi. *Also:* 'ākōlea (pipipi 'ākōlea, kōlea), ālealea, 'aoa (maka 'aoa), apuhihi, 'āunauna, hailimoa, hau, hīhīwai (hapawai), hūai, kahelelani, kauna'oa (kio, una'oa), koholua, kuanaka, kuapo'i, kūpe'e, makahālili, makaloa (aupūpū, pūpū 'awa), moa (kāmoa), momi (pūpū Ni'ihau), nahawele (mahawele), alaea 'ōni'oni'o, naunau (ānaunau), nene, 'ōlepe *and below,* pā, pā hau, pipi, pipipi *and below,* po'opalaoa, pūhali, pū'ōni'oni'o. *See* **barnacle, bivalve, conch shell, cowry shell, helmet shell, land shell, limpet, Nerita, oyster, pearl shell, sea urchin, snail, sundial shell, Trochus shell, turbo shell.** *Turtle or tortoise shell,* una, kua honu. *Shell on back of crab or turtle,* kuapo'i. *Shell for a lei,* pūpū lei. *Shell lei,* lei pūpū, lei leho, lei pipipi. 2. *Any hard case.* Iwi. *Shell of hiwa coconut,* ipu o Kāne. *Shell of lelo coconut used ceremonially,* ipu o Lono. *To shell,* poke, pō'alo, 'ōhiki. 3. *Projectile.* Pōkā, pōkā pū, pōkā pahū *(bomb)*; pōkā pōpō ahi *(incendiary bomb)*; pōkā pū kuni ahi *(cannon ball)*.

shelter. Wahi lulu, wahi ho'omalu, hale, hale kāmala, hale pupupu, lo'u pali, auolo, pāpa'i, malumalu, auhā. *In the shelter of his wings,* ma ka malu o kona 'ēheu. *This house is not very good, still it is a shelter,* 'a'ole maika'i loa 'o kēia hale, akā he malumalu.

shepherd. Kahu hipa.

shepherd dog. 'Īlio hipa, 'īlio kia'i hipa.

sheriff. Māka'i nui, ilāmuku. *District sheriff,* luna māka'i.

Shetland. Kekalana.

shewbread. Pelena hō'ike.

shield. Pālulu, pale, pu'upale; pale kaua *(Biblical)*; pale lima, lulu, uhikino, pākū; 'a'ahu a po'o *(head)*. *To shield,* pālulu, pale, lulu; kōlulu *(rare)*; — *modestly with the hand,* pa'ūhalakā.

shift. Ho'one'e, 'oni, huli lua, ha'aku'e. *Work shift,* manawa hana, mahele hana.

shiftless. 'Ae'a, pālau'eke, 'akole, alopalopā, hīlea, lōpā, pākukui, pono nō i ka noho; moelepo *(fig.)*; kūelekā *(rare)*. *See saying,* **goat.**

shilling. Kilina.

shifty-eyed. Maka 'alo'alo, maka kāka'a.

Shiloh. Kilo, Silo.

shimmering. 'Olili, 'oliliko. *See* **shine.**

shin. Lapawāwae.

shinbone. Kū'auwāwae.

shine. *Common forms are derivatives of* lali, hinu, lohi, lino, napa, hulali, hūlalilali; liko *(as with dew).* Also: 'anapa, 'ānapanapa, 'alohi, hinuhinu, ho'ohinuhinu, 'ōhinu, 'ōhinuhinu, pahinu, pua, pūwā, hoaka, akaaka, akaka, huaka, kuali, mālamalama, mōhala, lapalapa, ho'ā'ia'i, a'ia'i, ho'āliali, ho'opuakea, lala, 'ōlali, la'ela'e, lile, 'olili, 'oliko, nōlinolino, nōweo, kamani, mohā. *To shine brightly, as moon or stars,* 'ā akaaka, pā, kōnane, pā kōnane, papā. *To shine shoes,* ho'ohinuhinu kāma'a. *The sun shines,* pā ka lā. *The Lord make his face to shine upon you (Nah. 6:25),* na Iēhowa e kau mai i ka mālamalama o kona maka maluna iho ou.

shingle. Pili, pili hale. *Wooden shingle,* pili lā'au. *To shingle,* pili.

ship. Moku *(for various kinds, see Haw.-Eng. entry and entries that follow it);* hale lana i ke kai *(fig.).* To *ship,* ho'ouna ma ka moku.

shipbuilder, shipbuilding. Kāpili moku.

shipmate. Hoa wa'a, hoa holomoku.

shipping clerk. Kanaka helu ukana.

shipwreck. Ili *(go aground);* nāhāhā *(broken to bits);* piholo *(sunk);* alapoki *(rare). Shipwrecked person,* 'ōlulo.

shipwright. Kāpili moku, kamanā kāpili moku.

shirring. 'Alu.

shirt. Pālule, 'ahu. *Shirt of block-print cloth,* palaka. *Aloha shirt,* palaka aloha.

shirtwaist. Pākana.

shish, shish shish. 'Ūhī'ūhā, mākēhā, ka'uka'ulī.

shiver. Ha'ukeke, naka, kū'ululū, ha'ulili, hulilī, kalakū, ulupi'i.

shoal. Hāpapa, kākaha, pāpa'u.

shock. 1. *Alarm.* Puoho, hikilele, ho'ohikilele, ho'olele hauli. **2.** *Sheaves.* Pu'u. **3.** *Electric shock.* Loa'a i ka uila.

shocked. Kūnāhihi, mā'e'ele, māna'ona'o, lele ka hauli, kāhāhā i ka 'ino.

shocking. Māna'ona'o. *Shocking news,* he mea hou ho'ohikilele.

shoe. Kāma'a. *See* **horseshoe.** *Pair of shoes,* pa'a kāma'a. *Patent-leather shoes,* kāma'a pāhinu. *Openwork shoes,* kāma'a hakahaka. *Leather shoes,* kāma'a 'ili. *To put on shoes,* ho'okāma'a, komo kāma'a. *To shoe, as a horse,* kāpili.

shoelace. Lī kāma'a, kaula lī kāma'a.

shoemaker. Kūmeka.

shoo. Ho'ohū, ho'okuke, ho'ēhu. *Also:* emu, hemū, hehu, kīpa'i.

shoot. 1. *Discharge.* Pana, kī. *Shoot with bow and arrow,* pana pua, pāpua, kakaka, kīko'o, 'umoki; pana i'a *(fish); Shoot arrows of sugar-cane tassels,* ke'a pua. *Shoot a coconut-leaf midrib,* panapana nī'au. *Shoot a gun,* kī, kī pū, kī pōkā, kīkī; kīkī manu *(birds). Shoot with a sling,* ma'aalaioa *(rare). Shoot marbles,* pana kinikini. **2.** *Sprout.* Keiki, 'ao, ilo, kawowo, 'ohā, pōhuli, pūliko, weli; koaha *(mulberry plant). To send forth shoots,* kā, kupu. *Shoot for planting,* makailo.

shooting star. Hōkū lele.

shop. Hale kū'ai *(store);* hale 'oihana *(workshop).*

shopping. Kū'ai hele, māka'ika'i hale kū'ai.

shore. Kahakai, kapa kai, kai, 'ae kai, makālae, pili'āina, pilikahakai. *Strip of barren land near the shore,* kākaha. *Hot, dry shore (in legends),* kaha. *Shore dweller,* kō a kai, kanaka o kai.

shoreward. Uka *(from sea);* kai *(from land).*

short. Pōkole, poko; 'ekeke'i, mū'ekeke'i *(as a dress). Also:* pōko'u, hāpokopoko, hanu'u, hananu'u, pohananu'u, poupou, hāpou, hāpoupou, 'eleke'i, 'elehe'i, konopue, muku, mū'ou'ou, nukunuku, no'u, pāno'uno'u, ne'ine'i, pāha'a, paiaha'a, peke, pekepeke, popoki, pueo. *Rare:* 'apuki, ha'ako'a, pinauea, paku-

paku, pāna'e, pōlunu, pōnulu, ponululu, ponununu. *Cut short,* muku, pahupū. *Too short,* kaumuku, pakaulei, kaulei, kau 'ekeke'i. *Short cut,* ala 'oki, ka'akepa, ho'opōkole. *To hang short,* kau 'ekeke'i.

shortage. Pōkole.

shorten. Ho'opōkole. *Also:* hō'ekeke'i, ho'opoupou, pu'e'eke, 'unu, 'unua, 'ulua, na'ina'i.

shortened. Muku, po'omuku. *Also:* mu'umu'u, menui, piki.

shorthand. Kākau hua li'ili'i.

shortly. Kokoke, auane'i, a'uane'i.

shortness. Pōkole. *Shortness of breath,* nae, naenae, 'oaikū.

shorts. Lole wāwae pōkole, lole wāwae 'ekeke'i.

shot. Pōkā i maika *(shot-put). Bird shot, buckshot, grapeshot,* pōkā lū.

shotgun. Pū kī lū.

shot-put. Maika, kiola pōkā.

should. Pono e, pono ke, pono. *(Gram. 5.4.)*

shoulder. Po'ohiwi, hokua; 'ūhā mua *(of animal). Shoulder above armpit,* kīpō'ae'ae. *Points or edges of the shoulders,* kihi po'ohiwi, kīpo'ohiwi. *Shoulder to shoulder,* he kīpo'ohiwi i ke kīpo'ohiwi. *Shoulder pads or protection,* pale po'ohiwi. *Shoulder of a mountain,* kihi po'ohiwi, kīpo'ohiwi. *Shoulder arms!* E amo pū! *To hoist the shoulders,* ho'opahāha. *To shoulder aside,* ho'okē. *To carry on the shoulder,* 'auamo, pōhāki'iki'i. *To place on the shoulder,* kau po'ohiwi.

shoulder blade. Hoehoe, iwi hoehoe. *Fat or muscle on the shoulder blade,* kāhā po'ohiwi.

shout. 'Uwā, ho'ōho. *Also:* kani ka pihe, olo pihe, ho'o-kani pihe, wala'au. *Shout with derision,* 'uwā ho'ohila-hila.

shove. Pahu, kē, hou, kula'i, kūna'i, kula'ilua, 'onou; — *away,* keku, ho'okeku. *Shove ahead, regardless of consequences,* 'onou po'o.

shovel. Kopalā, kope; hāpale *(rare). Fire shovel,* kope ahi, kope lehu.

shoveler. Koloa mōhā *(bird).*

show. 1. *Demonstrate.* Hō'ike, ho'omā'ike, ho'omā'ike-'ike, kuhikuhi, kū, makili, nene; ohiohi *(of wood grain). To show the sights,* ho'ike. *Show me!* 'Oliana! 'Oiana! 'Oia ana! Aliana! Inane! **2.** *Spectacle.* Hala keaka, hō'ike'ike, hō'ike 'ana.

shower. Kuāua; ua nāulu, nāulu *(sudden);* kualau, kuakualau *(with sea wind);* ko'iawe. *Light shower,* ua kilihune, kilihune; kilika'i; 'ehu kakahiaka *(see* **morning***).*

showery. 'Ōuaua.

shoyu. Koiū.

shrapnel. Pōkā 'āpanapana.

shred. Welu, kīhae *(as ti leaves).*

shredded. Weluwelu.

Shreveport. Kaliwapoka.

shrewd. Ma'alea.

shriek. Pū'alalā, alawī. *Shriek angrily,* kekē, kekē niho, kekē nuku.

shrill. Alawī, huini, kōī, palalī, wī.

shrimp. 'Ōpae *(for various kinds, see Haw.-Eng. entry and entries that follow it);* mahiki *(used ceremonially). See saying,* **panau.** *Leaf container for shrimps,* pū'olo 'ōpae, ki'o'ōpae. *Shrimp head,* po'o 'ōpae *(insult).*

shrine. Heiau, haiau, ahu; ko'a *(fishing). See* **heiau** *(Eng.-Haw.). Shrine where bones of dead chiefs were kept,* hale poki.

shrink. 1. *Contract.* Miki. *Also:* ho'ohāiki, ho'o'i'ika, kīkenenei, lele, ne'ine'i, piki, pipiki, puku. **2.** *Recoil.* 'Eke, 'ekeke'i, mū'e'eke, pu'e'eke, kuemi, mene, pipika, kaumuku; kūpau *(rare).*

shriveling. Mino, mimino, minomino, 'ānuhenuhe, hōmī, 'i'ika, miki, pī'ao, pōnalo, 'ōmino, 'ōmali *(as fruit). Shriveled coconut meat,* niu 'ōka'a.

shroud. Pueo, kaula pū *(of a ship or canoe);* kapa olonā *(Biblical).*

shrub. *No equivalent:* la'alā'au, nahele.

shrug. Ho'ēheu *(the shoulders).*

pahipahi *(as hands)*. *To slap the chest in grief,* pa'i ā uma, pā umauma. *Chest-slapping hula,* pa'i umauma. *Slapping sound,* kohā.

slash. 'Oki'oki wale; kuapā *(as waves)*.

slate. Papa kākau, papa pōhaku.

slattern. Wahine kāpulu.

slaughter. Luku, lukuna, luku wale, pōluku. *To plan slaughter,* makaluku.

slaughterhouse. Hale pepehi holoholona, hale lole holoholona.

slave. Kauā *(for various kinds, see Haw.-Eng. entry and entries that follow it)*; kuapa'a. *Slave labor,* hana kauā kuapa'a.

slaving. Pa'u, ho'okuapa'a. *See* **slave.**

sled. Hōlua, papa hōlua, ka'a holo hau. *See saying,* **hōlua.** *To ride a sled,* he'e hōlua. *Sled course,* hōlua, holo hōlua, kahua hōlua.

sledge hammer. Hāmale ku'i hao.

sleek. Nuka, nemonemo, pawa; kāhā *(Biblical)*; mahamoe.

sleep. Moe, hiamoe. *Also:* momoe, momomoe, hi'olani. *See* **asleep** *and sayings,* **lihilihi 2, moe 1, niolopua 2, uha'i.** *Sleep late,* moe awakea, moe loa. *Overcome with sleep,* pa'uhia. *Indisposed to sleep,* hia'ā. *Sleep with,* moe me. *Sleep alone,* moekahi. *Sleep in a reclining position,* moe hilina'i. *Sleep on the ground,* moe lepo. *Eternal sleep,* hiamoe loa. *A little sleep,* hiamoe iki. *God of sleep,* Niolopua. *Sleeping place,* moe, kahi moe; ka'anu'a *(in a grasshouse)*. *To lull to sleep,* ho'ohiamoe. *To pretend to sleep,* ho'omoemoe, ho'ohiamoe. *To put to sleep,* ho'omoe, ho'omoemoe, ho'ohiamoe. *To sleep quickly,* moe koke. *To sleep restlessly,* moehewa. *To sleep deeply,* hiamoe loa, kāia i ka hiamoe. *To sleep in death,* hiamoe i ka make.

sleeping companion. Hoa moe.

sleeping drug. Lā'au ho'ohiamoe, huaale ho'omoe.

sleepless. Hia'ā, makahia, makalahia.

sleepy. Maka hiamoe, molohai, molohi, malohi. *Also:* mania; maniawai *(especially after bathing)*; mōlelehu, 'olelehu, lelehu, poluhi, niolo, nipo. *Sleepy day,* 'ōheahea ka lā. *To cause to be sleepy,* ho'omania.

sleet. Ua me ka hau.

sleeve. Lima, lima 'eke'eki *(short)*; lima pihapiha *(ruffled)*; lima pūha'uha'u *(puffed)*; lima pa'i 'ai *(looseflowing)*; lima lā'iki *(long, narrow)*; lima 'ūhā hipa *(leg-of-mutton)*.

sleigh. Wa'a holo hau.

sleight-of-hand trick. Kēpuka.

slender. Wīwī. *Also:* kioea *(person)*; 'ōeoeo, puāhilo, 'ūhini, hīnawenawe; makikoe *(as a tree)*. *See* **slim.**

slenderize. Ho'owīwī.

slice. Poke, 'āpana; kaha *(lengthwise, as fish)*; paukū *(in sections)*; pāpa'a *(bread)*. *Slice of bread,* pāpa'a palaoa. *To slice bread,* 'oki'oki palaoa.

slick. Mania, nemonemo, hinuhinu. *See* **slip, slippery, smooth.**

slide. He'e, pahe'e, holo. *Also:* hāne'e, hehe'e, ka'a *(as earth)*; ho'ohehe'e *(by jerks)*; ho'ohe'ehe'e, kākele, kūkele, pakelo, pakika, uai, olokīkī. *See* **slip.** *Projection slide picture,* ki'i ho'olele aka. *Ti-leaf slide,* ho'ohe'e kī, hōlua kī. *Sliding game,* kōī.

slight. Lihi, iki. *Slight knowledge,* 'ike nāwele, 'ike mālani. *To slight,* ho'okē'ē. *Slight touch of sickness,* loa'a mahu'i i ka ma'i.

slim. Wīwī. *Also:* pīlahilahi, pīlahi, pālanaiki, paioa, pānānai. *See* **slender.** *Slim-waisted and broadshouldered,* polinahe.

slime. Wale, walewale; 'a'amo'o *(as on fresh water)*; walewalena, hākelo, pe'ape'a. *Slime pit,* lua pikumena.

slimy. Hākelo, kelo, kākelokelo *(as mucus)*; pīlalilali, na'o, kika, kika, 'ū'ua, wale wai.

sling. Ma'a, ma'akū, kā'alā; ma'aalaioa *(rare)*. *Pocket in sling holding the stone,* 'eke'eke ma'a.

slingshot. Ma'aalaioa *(rare)*.

slingstone. 'Alā o ka ma'a.

slip. 1. *Slide.* He'e, pahe'e, pakika, poholo, hāne'e, 'ōhua; pāhi'a *(obliquely)*; kake *(back and forth)*; palaha *(stumble)*; ho'ohe'ehe'e; 'anu'u *(fig.)*; — *away,* palemo; — *off,* pahemo; — *out, as a fish from the hand,* pakelo; — *through,* poholopū. *Slip of the tongue,* hepa ka 'ōlelo, 'ōlelo hewa, ho'opuka hewa. 2. *Scion.* Lālā, lālā ho'oulu. 3. *Garment.* Mu'umu'u.

slipknot. Pikoholo, kākolea.

slipped disk. 'Anu'u ka 'ā'ī, 'anu'u ke kua, kīkala hāne'ene'e.

slipper. Kāma'a pale wāwae, pale wāwae.

slippery. Pahe'e, palaha, pakelo, pākelokelo, pakika, lali, lalilali, hānupa, hānupanupa; kelo *(as mucus)*; kika, kikika, kūkele, nakele, kūmole, polokake, 'ū'ua, ho'owale hau. *See* **slick, slip.** *Slippery parrot fish,* uhu pakelo *(a wily person)*.

slipshod. Kāpulu, palalē; manuea *(rare)*.

slit. 'Oki, kahe, puka, 'owā.

slobber. Hā'ae; kahe ka hā'ae; pu'awai *(rare)*.

slogan. 'Ōlelo hō'eu'eu *(lit., stimulating word)*.

sloop. Kia kahi, moku kia kahi.

slop. Wai mea 'ino; — *over,* halalē, hanini.

slop basin. Ipu 'aina.

slope. Ihona, lapa, papali. *Also:* hene, henehene, ho'oihona, ku'una, 'auina, ka'a, hiō, ho'oku'u.

slosh. *See* **empty.**

sloth. Holoholona hiamoe.

slouch. Noho pololei 'ole; oi, uoi *(rare)*.

slough. *See* **swamp.**

slovenly. Kāpulu, ho'oponopono 'ole.

slow. Lohi. *Also:* ho'olohi; pupū *(in movement or learning)*; akahele, 'ūlōlohi, kali, ho'okali, hākālia, hākupe, hakupehe, hō'apa'apa, ho'ohākālia, kā'ele, ka'unē, kūloma, lelemu, li'u, lōiele, loma, manukā, mili, mili 'apa, naua, nohili, none, pānauea. *Rare:* nopa; poholelua *(as a vessel)*. *See* **slowly.** *Slow-moving,* ka'alolohi, kupa'eli, lemu, palela. *His work is certainly slow and careless,* manukā noho'i kāna hana.

slowly. Mālie, aka-. *Eat slowly,* 'ai mālie. *Speak slowly,* 'ōlelo lohi. *Work slowly,* hana lohi, kawele, manukā.

slowpoke. Lolohi, lelemu; kālona *(horse)*. *To be a slowpoke,* ho'omoe.

slug. *See* **sea cucumber.**

sluggish. Malohi, lōiele, lelemu, lola, kūlola, pālīlea, pū, kālē, pāpālole.

sluice. Pani wai, hā, ki'o.

sluice gate. Mākāhā.

slur. 1. *Indistinct speech.* Ho'opuka pono 'ole, ho'ohui i nā hua 'ōlelo. 2. *Insult.* 'Ōlelo hō'ino ho'onalonalo. 3. *In music.* Huina.

slurp. Halalē *(as soup)*.

slush. Kelekele, hau hehe'e, 'ūkele.

sly. Ma'alea. *See* **cunning.**

smack. Mūkā, lūkā, mūkī; 'ukā *(to eat loudly, as pigs)*; kanono.

small. Iki, li'i, li'ili'i, lili'i, 'uku, 'u'uku, 'uku li'i. *Also:* ho'okanaha'i, hua li'i, hukiki, hukuli'i, huna, 'i'i, kupali'i, kūpihipihi, ma'awe, māiki, mamamala, maukoli, mō'ali, mo'o'ali, mo'olio, mo'owini, nāwele, ne'ine'i, no'ino'i; 'ōiki, 'ō'uku'uku *(somewhat)*; pālanaiki, pānanaiki, pīkanele; pikanini *(slang)*; pīloli, poki, pū'uku'uku; 'alapu'u *(of creatures)*; komoi'i'i, 'ā'ā *(of stature)*; kekeko *(and ugly)*. *See saying,* **bowl 2.** *Very small,* makali'i. *Small thing,* 'ōpihipihi. *Small bit,* ne'ine'i. *Small fragments,* ko'ana. *Small and close together,* pipipi. *To make small,* ho'oli'ili'i, ho'oiki, ho'omākoli.

smaller. 'U'uku mai, emi mai.

smallpox. Ma'i pu'upu'u li'ili'i, ma'i Hepela, hanakapahu, kapuahikuni, kamolapoki.

smart. 1. *Intelligent.* Akamai; ho'okāpuhi *(fig.)*. *See* **wise.** *Act smart,* ho'olae. 2. *Pain.* Lili'u; mane'o *(as the throat after eating raw taro or certain fish)*; walania, wawalania, walawalania, māhanahana, walenia, welenia, okooko, wi'u.

smash. Nahā, hoʻonahā, palahē, kīmō, kīpō, pākī. *See* **split.**

smear. Pala, kāpala, hāpala, palaheʻa, kīpalaheʻa; heʻaheʻa *(as with red earth);* haukaʻe, hōkaʻe, hoʻopaumā-ʻele, hamo.

smell. Honi, honihoni *(transitive). Also:* hanu, ea, ʻea. *See saying,* **goat.** *Sweet-smelling,* ʻala, ʻaʻala; onaona *(soft);* paoa, kūpaoa *(strong);* māpu, moani *(wafted);* anuhea, waianuhea *(cool, soft);* kolopua, hōʻala, kānaʻe, nae, kaluhea, pē, puīa. *Bad-smelling,* pilau *(as of rotten flesh);* pilapilau *(somewhat pilau);* ʻenaʻena pilau *(strongly pilau, unbearable stench);* ʻōhonohono, ʻōpilopilo, palani, malani, ʻuaʻuala *(rancid);* pilo, pelekunu, polopolona, kūnāhelu, kilu *(musty, swampy);* hauna, hauhau, hauhauna *(fishy, sulphur);* hohono, honohono, maea, pilo, puluea *(body);* hanahana, māhanahana, kākā *(excreta, flatulence);* ekikilau *(drawing flies);* lāhea, eko, ekoeko, neko, weko, uweko, ʻino, wilu, niku, māʻā *(stench). Rare:* ʻokaʻoka, ʻonaʻona, mōuki, piena, ʻukī, ʻikuʻiku *(bad). Strong smell, good or foul,* pākuʻi. *The bad smell arises,* kū ka lāhea.

smelling salts. Paʻakai hoʻohanuhanu.

smile. Minoʻaka.

smite. Kuʻi, kā, kākā, kākiʻi, hau, hahau, hauhia, hili, paʻi, welokā. *See* **hit, strike.**

smith. 1. *Blacksmith.* Kuʻi hao, ʻāmala. **2.** *Family name. (Cap.)* Kamika.

smoke. Uahi. *To smoke,* hoʻouahi, pua, hoʻopipī *(as a ham). To smoke tobacco,* puhi, puhi paka. *Smoke-colored, as clouds,* lālauahi.

smokestack. Puka uahi.

smoky. Uauahi, paʻapū i ka uahi. *Also:* hea, polohina; pōhūhū *(rare).*

smolder. Pipī, pī *(as green firewood).*

smooth. Malino *(as the sea, any surface);* paheʻe *(as skin);* ʻaeʻae *(as poi, dough);* ʻōmolemole *(as glass). Also:* palaha, pakika, mole, momole, molemole, molea, kūmole, hāmole, ʻōmole, nemo, nemonemo, kaʻanemo, niau, nia, ania, āniania, alania, kahania, kalamania, kalania, laumania, māniania, ʻāpole, aukahi, aulike, pāeaea, hahu, hukiheʻe, kaekae, nienie, kamani, māhola, mehani, mani, paniʻo, wawali, waliwali, kaʻiʻiʻi, hinu. *Rare:* kānaʻi, kanuʻeʻeʻina, kīauau, mahamoe, ʻōniki, ʻōpapa, pawa, pīkaka, polohi. *See* **slick, slip, slippery.** *To smooth fresh cement,* palaina kimeki. *To smooth and finish, as a canoe,* kahi ā malino; kīkoni. *Smooth, planed lumber,* papa hole. *Smooth-shaven,* kahania.

smother. ʻUmi; poʻipoʻi *(cover);* paʻa ka hanu.

smudge. Kaʻe, haukaʻe, pala, kāpala, paʻu; hāʻekaʻeka *(as with smoke).*

smuggle. Hoʻopae malū, pale hewa i ke kuke. *Smuggled goods,* waiwai hoʻopae malū. *Lawsuit involving smuggling,* hihia waiwai kolohe.

smutty. Hauʻeka, haukaʻe, penopeno. *Smutty language,* ʻōlelo haumia.

snack. ʻAi māmā.

snag. Hoʻomau, hoʻouluulu.

snagged. Mau *(as a hook);* uluulu, unuunu.

snail. Kamaloli, pūpū, homeka. *See* **shell.** *Fresh-water snail,* hīhīwai, wī. *Chinese snail,* pūpū Pākē, pūpū loʻi.

snake. Naheka, nahesa, moʻo.

snake charmer. Mea hoʻowalewale i nā nahesa.

snake mackerel. Hāuliuli puhi, hāuliuli.

snakeskin. ʻIli naheka, ʻaʻamoʻo.

snap. 1. *Break.* Haʻi, haki, hahaki, uhaki, kepa. **2.** *Bite.* ʻAki, ʻakiʻaki, apu, kīkepa; hae *(as a dog);* ʻai kepakepa *(as the jaws);* ʻūpiki *(as a trap).* **3.** *Sharp sound.* ʻUʻina, ʻaʻina, ʻaʻaʻina, paʻina, pāpaʻaʻina, paʻapaʻaʻina, kawewe, kanapi; pinau *(rare). Snap the whip,* hoʻokani i ka uwepa. *Snap the fingers,* pana i nā manamana. **4.** *Speak curtly.* Pīkananā, pīkanalā, keʻu, ʻōlelo kaki, ʻaki, ʻakiʻaki.

snapdragon. Nani-o-Olaʻa.

snapper. 1. *Fish.* ʻUlaʻula *(red; varieties are qualified by*

hiwa, koaʻe, maoli, ʻōpūlauoho*);* ʻōpakapaka *(blue; the four stages are* ʻūkīkiki, pākale, ʻōpakapaka, kalekale*);* uku, uku palu *(deep-sea); early growth stage of both* ʻulaʻula *and* ʻōpakapaka *is* ʻūkīkiki *—also called* ʻakiki, kiki, koʻi, ʻukiki. *Also:* āhunihuni. **2.** *End of whip.* ʻElau, hoʻa.

snapshot. Kiʻi.

snare. Hei, ʻalehe, ʻahele, hele, pahele; pāhelehele *(example, For. 5:85);* ʻūpiki, ʻōpiki, hihi; *crab —,* kao, paeaea; *shrimp —,* puluʻaha; *bird —,* ʻaukuʻu, kāpiʻo, kaukau; puʻu *(plover);* kīpuka *(owl);* hīpuka, pehe. *To snare birds,* kono, kāwili *(with gum);* kia, kā, kā manu, pēkeu. *Snaring stick for birds,* lāʻau kia manu.

snared. Hei ʻia, hihia, helea. *See* **snare.**

snarl. 1. *Growl, snap.* Nunulu *(dog);* nanā, kekē niho. **2.** *Tangle.* Hihia, hauhili, hauhauhili, hauhilikī, hauhalakī, auwalakī, mauwelekā, mauhili, hilikau, kauhihi; wilikāʻeka *(of hair);* uluulu, unuunu, miko.

snatch. Kāʻili, kāʻiliʻili; apu *(as with the teeth),* poʻi. *To snatch away ruthlessly,* kīpuka. *Lālau ʻino. To snatch without being seen, as by a thief,* ʻelemio, palamimo. *To snatch souls by sorcery,* poʻi ʻuhane.

sneer. ʻAka hoʻomaʻewa, ʻaka pāhenehene. *Also:* maʻewa, hoʻomaʻewa, laumaʻewa.

sneeze. Kihe. *See* **Gesundheit!**

snell. Kaʻā.

snicker. ʻAka iki, hene iki, henehene.

sniff. Hanu, honi, honihoni.

sniffle. Pī, pipī, hanu pī, hūpēkole. *The nose sniffles,* pipī ka ihu.

snip. ʻOki, ʻako.

snobbish. Hukikū, ihu piʻi, kū ka ihu, hoʻokeikei.

snood. Kaʻā, kaʻi. *Part of snood lashing on composite hooks, as for bonitos,* pou.

snoop. Hākilo. *See saying,* **pāhiʻuhiʻu.**

snooty. Ihu piʻi, haʻakei, ihu kū.

snore. Nonō, hohō, hānuna, ihu hānuna, ʻolāʻolā ka ihu; ihu ʻolāʻolā *(with short puffs);* ihu nā *(with prolonged sounds).*

snort. Hohō, haʻu, haʻuhaʻu, hoʻokī; pī *(as a horse).*

snotter. Pū.

snotty. Hūpēkole, hākelo. *See* **mucus.**

snout. Nuku, ihu. *See idiom,* **lightning.**

snow. Hau, hau kea. *Goddess of snow,* Poliʻahu. *See saying,* ʻale.

snowball. Pōpōhau.

snowbush. Laukalakoa.

snowflake. Hau pūehuehu.

snowshed. Hale pale hau.

snub. 1. *Avoid.* Hoʻopāweo. **2.** *Make fast.* Hoʻopaʻa, hāwele *(as a rope).*

snub-nosed. Nūkoki, ihu meumeu; ihu ʻū; koki *(as of a bulldog).*

snuff. 1. *Tobacco.* Paka hanuhanu, paka honihoni. **2.** *Extinguish.* Kinai, hoʻopio. *Snuffing out, as life,* kinaina.

snuffer. ʻŪpā koli kukui *(candle).*

snuggle. Neʻeneʻe ā pili.

so. 1. *Similar.* Penei, pēlā, pe, laʻa. *That's so,* pēlā nō; ʻoiaʻiʻo kā hoʻi. *So do I,* ʻo au pū. *Maybe so,* pēlā paha *(very common);* ʻoia paha. *And so on,* ā pēlā aku. *So that is your opinion,* pēlā kou manaʻo ʻea. **2.** *Therefore.* No laila. *See* **in order to.** *So that not,* iʻole. **3.** *Interjection.* Kā, kā hoʻi, oia hoʻi, āhē. *Is that so!* ʻOia ʻea! ʻOiaʻiʻo kā hoʻi! Pēlā ʻea! Pēlā anei! **4.** *Fifth note in musical scale.* Nō.

soak. Hoʻomaʻū, hoʻopaʻū, hoʻoū, hōʻū, ū, paʻū, pā-ʻūʻū, pē, pulu pē, pulu ʻū, pulu, pulukā, pelepulu, peno, ʻeʻelo, hōʻeʻelo, kēʻae; hoʻokelekele *(as pandanus leaves);* kū *(as clothes);* kū i ka wai *(in water);* paʻi *(clothes in soapy water);* pelu *(as in preparing pia). Rain-soaked,* nolu ehu, nolu pē, ū, noʻū.

so-and-so. Mea, hikaua.

soap. Kopa. *Powdered soap,* kopa pauka. *Laundry soap,* kopa holoi. *Bath soap,* kopa ʻauʻau. *Perfumed soap,* kopa 'ala. *Liquid soap,* wai ho'oma'ema'e. *Soap bubble,* hu'a kopa.

soapberry. A'e, mānele, māhoe.

soap plant. 'Ānapanapa, kukuku.

soapsuds. Hu'ahu'a kopa.

soar. Kīkaha, lele ho'olahalaha, kaulele, 'ēheu, 'iolana; ka'alele, kaha.

sob. Ha'uha'u uwē.

sociable. Laulauna, launa, naho, maka launa, 'akeu.

social. *See* **sociable.** *Social club,* kalapu ho'ohau'oli.

social science. Huli kanaka.

society. 1. *Club.* 'Ahahui *(for various kinds, see Haw.-Eng. entry and entries that follow it).* *Also:* hui; hui malū *(secret);* kalapu. **2.** *Companionship.* Launa 'ana.

sock. Kākini *(stocking). See* **hit.**

socket. Pona, puka ho'okomo iho, kumu; nāpana *(rare).* *Eye socket,* pona, maka lua. *Socket at a joint,* iwi pona.

soda. Koka.

soda water. Kolowaka, wai momona.

Sodom. Kokoma, Sodoma.

sodomy. Kokomi, kohe lemu, moc aikāne.

soft. Palupalu, palu; nahe, nahenahe, lahe, hone, hoene, polinahe *(as sound);* 'ōlū, hōlū, hōlule, hōlulo, 'ōlulo, 'ōluheluhe *(as a crab that has shed its shell);* 'ōninanina, lina, nina *(as cheeks);* pala, palapū, maka pala *(as a boil);* 'ae *(as down);* pahē, milu *(as fruit);* momona *(as wood). Also:* wali, waliwali, wawali; awe, puawe, hani, hāpele, hāwali, hō'alu'alu, hōninanina, huki, halu, uhalu, puhalu, hulina, kāpehe, kololū, lu'a, mahāha, malule, melu, mona, nāeheehe, naele, nakele, napele, nāpelepele, nāwele, nenelu, nolu, nu'anu'a, pahe'e, palakea, pēheu, pele, puhalu, pulu, 'ūlika, 'ūlina, 'ūnina, 'ūpalu, uwa'uwali, wai'olu.

soft-boiled. Mo'a hapa.

soften. Ho'opalupalu, ho'owali. *Also:* hō'ae, hō'olu, ho'ohehe'e; kīkoni *(wauke bark),* ho'opaluhē; 'upi'upī *(an octopus). Softened and wet,* nolu ehu.

softhearted. Na'au palupalu.

softly. Mālie, nihi; hoene *(sound).*

soft-mannered. Pahē.

softness. Walina, nāwele, 'olu. *See* **soft.**

soft palate. Kīleo *(including uvula).*

soft-shelled. *See* **soft.**

soft-spoken. Nahenahe, 'ōlelo palupalu, 'ūpalu, pahē, waipahē.

soggy. Hōwai, 'elo, napele, ū wai; loliloli 'ōloliloli, palakē *(as taro). See* **swamp.**

soil. 1. *Earth.* Lepo. *See* **limestone.** *Sandy soil,* 'āone, lauone, makaili. *Fertile soil,* lepo momona. *Poor soil,* lepo momona 'ole, kaha 'eka. *Stony soil,* lepo 'ā, lepo 'a'ā. *Red soil,* lepo 'ula. *Cindery soil,* lepo 'ākeke. *Exhausted soil,* pahulu, kīpahulu. *To fallow soil,* ho'opahulu. **2.** *Verb.* Lepo, 'eka. *To soil,* ho'olepo, hō'eka, ho'oniku, ho'ōpala, ho'opaumā'ele, ho'opelapela, ho'opōneko, hōka'e, ho'owi'u.

sojourn. Noho, noho hele, noho malihini.

sojourner. 'Ōhua.

solace. Hō'olu, hō'olu'olu, ho'onā, la'i.

solar. Lā. *Solar system,* kahua o nā hōkū.

solar plexus. Houpo. *Pulsation in the solar plexus,* houpo 'ume pau.

sold. *See* **sell.** *All sold,* pau i ka lilo.

solder. Kēpau kāpili mekala, kāpili mekala.

soldier. Koa, pū'ali.

sole. 1. *Bottom surface.* Kapua'i *(of food);* 'ili pale o kāma'a *(of shoe).* **2.** *Only.* Ho'okahi, wale nō.

solemn. 'E'ehia, kūo'o, milumilu, ho'āno.

solicit. Noi, noi ā koi. *Libidinous soliciting,* ho'owalewale moekolohe.

solid. Pa'a, mānoa, pa'apū. *Solid-black,* hiwa pa'a. *Geometric solid,* pa'a, pa'a'ili *(for various kinds, see Haw.-Eng. entry and entries that follow it).*

solidified. Pa'a, mākū.

solitary. Mehameha, kakahi, kaukahi.

solitude. Ho'okahi, mehameha, noho ho'okahi, nohona mehameha; ano *(weird).*

solo. Leokū pākahi, hīmeni kū pākahi *(vocal).*

solon. Kolona.

solution. 1. *Explanation.* Ha'ina, wehewehe 'ana, wehena, loa'a, ha'iloa'a, ke'ehina hana. **2.** *Liquid.* Wai pa'ipa'i.

solve. Loa'a ka ha'ina, wehe.

somber. 'Āhiwa. *See* **dark.**

some. Kekahi, wahi. *Also:* kahi, kauwahi, nāhi, ona. *Give me some,* na'u kahi. *Some other day,* kekahi lā. *Some other time,* kekahi manawa. *Some place,* kauwahi.

somebody. Kekahi kanaka, kekahi mea.

somehow. Pehea lā, i kekahi 'ano.

someone. Kahi, kekahi. *Someone else,* ha'i.

somersault. Kuwala, 'owala, wala kua *(backwards). To somersault,* kuwala po'o, 'owala. *To turn a somersault,* ho'okaka'a.

something. Kekahi mea. *Also:* kauwahi.

sometime. Kckahi manawa, kekahi wā.

somewhat. 'Ano, ho'o-, 'ō-. *Somewhat good,* 'ano maika'i.

somewhere. Aia nō i kahi e hele ai, ma kekahi wahi.

son. Keiki, keiki kāne, kama kāne.

song. Mele. *Also:* hula *(for dancing);* hīmeni *(not for dancing);* leokū *(sung to an audience);* lei, inoa, mele ma'i, wehi. *Song of praise,* leo ho'onani. *Hawaiian type of song with English words,* mele hapa haole. *Words of a song,* hua mele. *Division of a hula song,* 'oki. *Beginning and theme of a song,* puana. *Two or more last verses of a song,* ha'ina. *Song leader,* alaka'i hīmeni, alaka'i mele. *Song contest,* ho'okūkū hīmeni. *Song festival,* 'aha mele.

songbird. Manu mele.

son-in-law. Hūnōna kāne.

son of a bitch. Kanapapiki.

Sons and Daughters of Hawaiian Warriors. 'Ahahui Māmakakaua.

soon. Koke, auane'i, koe, aku, eia aku. *As soon as,* i, iā, hākālia nō ā, lawa; loa *(rare). As soon as I,* ia'u. *No sooner than,* i. *No sooner than I,* ia'u. *As soon as the sun shines, let's go,* aia ā pā ka lā, hele kāua.

soot. Pa'u, pa'u ahi.

soothe. Ho'omālie, ho'onā. *Also:* nā, ho'onānā, ho'oka'ahea, kūpalaiki, mali, malimali, ho'omalimali, pohu, ho'omā'alili; pa'apa'anā *(rare).*

soothing. Hō'olu'olu, malina, hamohamo.

soothsayer. Kilo lani, kuhikuhipu'uone, ha'i 'ōuli. *See* **seer.**

sooty. Pa'u, hāpa'upa'u.

sooty tern. 'Ewa'ewa.

sop. Penu *(as gravy); — up,* kūpenu.

soporific. Ho'ohiamoe; lā'au ho'ohiamoe, lā'au moe *(drug).*

soprano. Leo wahine, kopolano.

sorcerer. Kahuna, po'oko'i; *malevolent —,* kahuna 'anā'anā, kahuna ho'opi'opi'o, kahuna 'ai pilau, mo'okiko. *See* **Hāwa'e** *and saying,* 'ololī. *Teaching sorcerer,* kahuna a'o. *A warning to avoid sorcerers:* e mālama o loa'a i ka niho, *be careful or (you will be) caught in the teeth.*

sorcery. Hana kahuna *(general);* 'anā'anā, ho'ounauna, ho'opi'opi'o, kuni, kuni ola, 'ō, hi'u, ka'a lā'au, kuehu kapa, pāhi'uhi'u *(usually malevolent);* hana aloha, kala aloha *(love);* kala, pale, ho'iho'i, 'a'e *(counter). See* **prayer** *and sayings,* niho **1**, o'o. *Sanctified stone used in sorcery,* kahalili. *Objects used in sorcery,* maunu. *Name of* manulele *sugar cane used in* hana aloha *sorcery,* kā'awe, kā'awe 'ā'ī. *To induce by sorcery,* hana. *To destroy by sorcery,* 'ai hamu, kālai 'ino, lumi, mākia, kā'ina. *To make a cross or an X in sorcery,* kaha pe'a. *Death from sorcery,* kā ha'i make mai ho'i.

sordid. Paumā'ele, hauka'e, pā'ele, haumia.

sore. 'Eha; hēhē, pala he'e, hilo *(running). Also:* mala, heka; 'ūkihi *(at corner of mouth);* 'ainā, aleale, pōaleale, mālani, mauwā, pohole, pōholehole; ukokole *(as eyes);* pūhā *(burst);* pūlele *(on neck). Rare:* po'ana, ponanā, alapuka. *See* **boil** 2. *Eating, spreading, as a sore,* 'a'ai. *To become sore from rubbing,* maoa. *Sore-eyed,* noe'ula, mākole.

soreness. 'Eha; maoa *(from rubbing). To cause soreness of the eyes,* ho'omākole.

sorrel. 'Ihi *(for various kinds, see Haw.-Eng. entry and entries that follow it).*

sorrow. Kaumaha. *Also:* minamina, mānewanewa, kani 'uhū, mokuāhua, pu'u, 'ū, lu'ulu'u, manoni. *Poetic references to heavy rain and tears may signify sorrow. See saying,* **lu'ulu'u.**

sorrowful. Lu'ulu'u, kaumaha, pilihua; malāoa *(rare).*

sorry. Kaumaha. *Also:* minamina, mihi, mimihi, mimimihi, aumihi; menemene. *I'm sorry for you,* kaumaha au nou. *Don't be sorry,* mai ho'okaumaha. *I'm sorry,* kala mai ia'u.

sort. 1. *Select.* Wae, waewae, māwae, mōwae, ho'oka'awale; kī *(pandanus leaves).* **2.** *Kind.* 'Ano.

sough. Nei, hihio, 'owē, hoene, 'iolo, hē.

soul. 'Uhane. *Soul snatching, as by sorcery,* po'i 'uhane. *Tarrying place of souls,* pu'u kū 'akahi.

soulless. 'Uhane 'ole.

sound. 1. *Noise.* Leo, kani, pā, papā, olokani; wawā, 'uwā, wawalo, walo *(loud);* nei, puō *(muffled, indistinct);* oe, oeoe, aeae, hoehoe, kōloa, olo *(prolonged);* nahenahe, nahe, lahe, aheahe, hone, honehone, hihio *(soft);* po'a, kani pē *(hollow);* wī *(shrill);* 'ou, 'ou'ou *(sharp);* 'owē *(of tearing);* kani wahie *(hard, ringing);* leo 'oko'a *(as in language);* 'a'aea *(of infants). Rare:* laolao, lu'i, 'ōhāhā, palaiki, palalā, palalū. *See* **n-** *(Haw.-Eng.),* **bang, boom, letter, roar, rumble, shrill, tone.** *Simultaneous sounds,* olowalu. **2.** *Flawless.* Kīnā 'ole, pa'a. **3.** *Fathom (verb).* Ana i ka hohonu.

soup. Kai, kupa.

soupbone. Ku'eku'e pipi.

sour. 'Awa, 'awa'awa, 'awa'awahua, 'awa'awahia. *Also:* mala, malaia, malailena, 'ākia, mulemule, 'ī'ī, hanahana, halahala; 'awa'awa 'ākia *(as acid, or extremely sour);* kahania, mamalahia, hua'ā *(as poi). See* **disposition.** *Sour smell,* kūālani, palani, palanioa.

source. Kumu, mole. *Also:* momole, molemole, kula, kupuna, maka. *Water source,* kula wai, māno wai, po'o wai, pukana wai, 'ōmaka. *Source of income or livelihood,* kula waiwai. *Source of life,* māno wai *(fig.).*

south. Hema. *Also:* kaunalipo, lalo; 'elemoe *(priestly name). Go south,* hele iho i ka hema, iho, ho'oihona.

South America. 'Amelika Hema.

South Carolina. Kalolaina Hema.

southeast. Hikina hema, kauliki.

southern. Hema, lalo. *Southern sky,* lipo, kaunalipo, Liolio-i-Wawau.

Southern Cross. Hōkū-ke'a, Ka-pe'a, Newa, Newe, Kaulu, Hānai-a-ka-malama.

South Hampton. Kau Hamekona.

South Pole. Wēlau Hema.

southwest. Komohana hema, kauweke.

souvenir. Mea ho'omana'o. *Also:* pukana, pa'aloha. *Souvenir of a beloved,* pukana aloha.

sovereign. Mō'ī.

sovereignty. Ea.

Soviet Union. *See* **Russia.**

sow. 1. *Pig.* Pua'a wahine. *Old sow,* kolo'u'a, pua'a kumulau. **2.** *Scatter.* Lū, nū, lūlū, ho'ohelele'i.

sow bug. Pokipoki.

sower. Lūlū hua.

soy sauce. *See* **shoyu.**

space. Lewa, haka, wahi hakahaka, wahi ka'awale, wā, kōwā, koana, olowā; apoālewa *(where birds soar).*

Outer space, lewa mawaho, lewa lilo loa, lewa luna lilo. *To make spaces,* ho'okuakua.

spacer. Haha kā 'upena, una *(for making nets).*

spacious. Ākea.

spade. 1. *Shovel.* 'Ō'ō, 'ō'ōpē. **2.** *Playing card.* Peki. *King of spades,* kini peki. *Ace of spades,* 'eki peki, 'eki pihulu.

spadix. Iho, 'īkoi pua.

Spain. Kepania, Sepania.

span. Apo, kaulua, kīko'o. *For life span, see* **sunrise.**

Spaniard. Paniolo.

Spanish. Kepania, Sepania, Paniolo. *Spanish clover,* kīkānia pipili.

spank. Pa'i, pa'i i ka pāpākole.

spanner. Paniani, paaniani.

spar. 'Ōpe'a, o'a pe'a, o'a moku; kia *(mast);* pumi *(boom).*

spare. 1. *Save.* Ola, ho'ōla, kāpae. *See ex.,* **ka'a'oko'a.** *To spare life,* ola, waiho ola. *Spare my life,* e ola au iā 'oe. **2.** *Extra.* Keu, koe, ka'awale, kai'okia.

spareribs. Iwi 'ao'ao o ka pua'a.

sparingly. 'Au'a, kīhau; muni *(rare). To eat sparingly,* 'ai pākiko, ho'okāwala.

spark. Hunaahi *(of fire).*

sparkle. 'Ā *(as a fire or gem);* hulali, hulili, lohi, 'alohi, 'ōnohinohi. *See* **glitter, shine.**

sparrow. Manu li'ili'i, kepola.

sparse. Kāwala, kaka'ikahi; namauahi *(rare). See* **inhabited.**

Sparta. Kepalake, Separate; Kapaka, Sapata. *A Spartan existence,* he nohona puni kaua ā ho'owahāwahā i nā mea e ho'ohiwahiwa ai i ka noho 'ana.

spasm. Oikū, huki, 'a'ili'ili, ka'apā.

spatter. Pakī, ho'opakī, mahiki, palalē, kikiko.

spawn. Pua i'a, 'āhua.

speak. 'Ōlelo, wala'au, namu, 'ī, ho'opuka, leo, kala-'au, pane, pua, hua, hōpilo, kūpā'oi, pāo'io'i; hewa ka waha *(hastily, too much). See* **chat, garrulous, gibberish, indistinct, jabber, rude, speech.** *Speak loudly,* leo nui, leoleo, leoleowā, ōleoleo, pakakī, ka'aleo; pūhāhā *(fig.). Speak softly,* leo iki. *Speak with force,* ko'iko'i ka 'ōlelo, ha'ano'u. *Speak harshly, bluntly,* 'āwaha, ho'okala, 'o'ole'a nā 'ōlelo, kīpehi, paopao, ho'opukakū, pūhāhā. *Speak largely unintelligibly, as with impediment or a foreign language,* namu, palalē, hīkapalalē, hapaku'e, hāpu'upu'u. *Speak vaguely,* kāholo ka 'ōlelo. *Speak cautiously, deliberately,* 'ōlelo akahele, aka'ōlelo. *Speak brokenly,* pāhemahema i ka ho'onohonoho 'ana i nā hua 'ōlelo. *Speak but little,* 'ōlelo iki; 'ekemu.

speaker. Ka mea e 'ōlelo ana *(the one talking),* ha'i'ōlelo *(lecturer, orator),* luna ho'omalu *(chairman). To the honorable speaker,* i ka mea hanohano, ka luna ho'omalu.

spear. Ihe, ihe pahe'e, 'ēlau *(short);* pololū *(long);* ihe laumeki *(barbed);* ihe 'ō *(piercing);* 'au hau *(of hibiscus wood);* 'au'au *(of loulu palm wood);* kao, 'ō, 'ōkoholua *(fishing);* pōluhi, polokāwa'e. *See* **bath.** *Cluster of spears,* makalau, mākini. *Fish spear shot from bow,* pana i'a. *Spear point,* 'ēlau, maka ihe. *Spear thrust,* 'ai, pahuna. *Throwing of spears at a chief as test of courage and skill,* kā ali'i, kāli'i. *Art of spear throwing,* lono-maka-ihe. *Sport of spear throwing,* 'ō'ō ihe, pahe'e, kāhau. *Spear fencing,* kākā lā'au. *God of spear fighters,* Lono-maka-ihe. *To spear seals,* 'ō hulu. *To spear octopuses,* 'ō he'e.

spearfish. A'u.

spearmint. Kepemineka.

special. Kūikawā, mea i wae 'ia. *Special or occasional report,* hō'ike kūikawā. *Special order,* kauoha nui.

specialty. 'Oihana mākaukau loa, mea mākaukau loa. *Specialty of the house (restaurant),* mea 'ai po'okela o ka hale 'aina.

species. Lāhui.

specific. Kuhikuhi pono 'ia.

specifications. Nā kuhikuhi pono.
specified. I 'ōlelo 'ia. *At a specified time,* i kekahi manawa i 'ōlelo 'ia.
specimen. Mea hō'ike'ike.
speck. Kiko, huna, māhune, pula.
speckled. Kiko, kikokiko, loli, 'īloli, pulepule, 'ōpulepule.
spectacles. Makaaniani; makaaniani 'ūmi'i *(pince-nez).*
spectator. Māka'ika'i.
specter. Lapu, akua lapu, kāhoaka. *Specter of the Brocken,* 'Akakū ānuenue.
speculate. Ho'opukapuka *(invest).* See **conjecture.**
speech. 'Ōlelo, ha'i'ōlelo; pepelu *(repetitious);* 'ōlelo lolelole *(roundabout, twisted);* ha'i'ōlelo kānaenae ā ho'ole'a *(eulogistic);* kākāki'i *(blundering);* pua'o *(rude, abrupt).* See **waha** *and below,* **indistinct, speak, language.**
speechless. 'Ōlelo 'ole, leo 'ole, mū, mumule, 'ōkā, waha pio.
speed. 'Āwīwī, māmā, wikiwiki. *Also:* ka'aholo, ho'o-kāholo, hikiwawe, paukikī, miki, haulani. See *sayings,* **pola 1, fast.** *To speed recklessly, as an auto,* holo pupule, holo 'ino, holo akahele 'ole, holo nui, ho'okele 'ino.
spell. 1. *Orthography.* Pela, kepela, kauhua, ho'oku'i. *How is your name spelled?* Pehea e pela ai kou inoa? **2.** *Charm, power.* Mana, pule. *Under the spell of,* malalo o ka mana o, pa'a i ka mana o. **3.** *Magical.* Pule. *To cast a spell,* ho'ohei mana'o.
spellbound. Hei 'ia.
spelling. Kepela, kepela 'ana.
spelling book. Puke a'o kepela, palapala pī'āpā.
spend. Ho'olilo; ho'omauna, lū *(wastefully).*
spendthrift. Mea lū wale. See *saying,* **'ākau 1.**
sperm. 1. See **semen. 2.** *Whale.* Kēpama, koholā kēpama, pāma. *Sperm oil,* 'aila kēpama, 'aila pāma.
sphere. Poepoe, poepoepīkoi, pa'a poepoe; poepoehāwa'e *(flat).*
spice. Mea ho'omiko 'ai, mea hō'ono'ono mea 'ai; hua 'ala *(Biblical).*
spider. Lanalana, lalana, nananana; ku'uku'u *(variety). Spinning spider,* pūnāwelewele. *Large house spider,* pe'epe'emakawalu. *Spider, hit by the southerly wind, turns over (FS 183),* lanalana, pā 'ia i ke Kona, huli pū *(of a weakling).*
spider dance. Hula pe'cpe'emakawalu.
spiderflower. Honohina, 'ili'ohu.
spider web. Hihi pūnāwelewele, 'upena nananana, pūnāwelewele.
spike. Kia, hākia, mākia, kui, meki, wana; kukuna, hākui *(as of sea urchin);* kao *(as on the tail of a sting ray);* puapua *(in the back of sphinx moth). Spike on a spur,* kui kēpā.
spiked. Wanawana, 'o'e.
spikenard. Naleko.
spill. Hanini, nini, palalē; manini *(rare); — over,* halalē.
spin. Niniu, ho'oniniu. *Also:* molo, mola, 'ōka'a, niu, liua, pōniu, 'ōniu, poahi, ho'oniua, pokaka'a; milo, 'ōmilo, lōmilo, hilo *(as thread);* kūwili *(as in a dance). To spin a top,* ho'oniniu i ka hū, 'ōniu; pūniu *(rare). The brain spins,* ka'a ka lolo.
spinach. 'Īnika.
spindle. Kālī, kui wili lopi. *Spindlelegs,* 'auhaka.
spindling. Hīnawenawe, hīnawe, nānawaū, hīnewanewaū.
spindly. Āewa, holili, līlā, lolopaioea, lolopaioa.
spine. Iwikuamo'o, kuamo'o *(backbone);* kukū, kālī, wanawana. *Spines on fish fin,* iwi kā, iwi kala, iwi kā lalo, iwi kala kua, kākala, pola, kōkala.
spinster. Wahine kāne 'ole, kāne 'ole, wahine male 'ole. *See* **old maid.**
spinsterhood. Noho male 'ole.
spiny. Wanawana.
spiral. 'Oni *(of colors in a lei);* pāka'awili, pāka'uwili. *A spiral design,* mo'oni *(in featherwork).*

spirit. 'Uhane, wailua; akua *(for various types, see Haw.-Eng. entry and entries that follow it). Also:* ea, haili, hoaka, kupu, makani, mauli, 'ula. *Cf.* **'aumakua,** *Nānā 193–195. Holy Spirit,* 'Uhane Hemolele. *Unclean, evil spirit,* 'uhane 'ino *(Biblical);* nukumane'o, aumiha. *Disembodied spirit,* 'ula lele. *Spirit of dead,* kino wailua, 'unihipili, 'uhinipili. *Spirit of living,* kino aka, kāhoaka, makuakeahu; kakaola *(visible). To feed spirits of the dead,* kākū'ai. *Traveling spirit,* 'uhane hele. *Guardian spirit,* 'uhane kia'i. *The multitudinous spirits.* kini akua. *Abode of the spirits,* kaha akua. *People familiar with spirits, people who seek familiar spirits,* po'e nīnau kupapa'u. *Possession by spirits,* noho. *Spirit possessing a person,* 'uhane noho, akua noho. *Spirit possessing partially,* akua kī-hei pua, 'uhane kīhei pua. *Spirit that possesses a medium and speaks through him,* makani noho. *Calling voices of the spirit,* leo wawalo o ka hanehane. *One who consults the dead or spirits,* nīnau kupapa'u. *To summon spirits,* ho'onoho. *To communicate with spirits,* kilo 'uhane. *To speak through familiar spirits,* nīnau 'uhane. *Blessed are the poor in spirit (Mat. 5:3),* pōmaika'i ka po'e i ha'aha'a ka na'au.
spirited. Hō'eu'eu, kā'eu'eu, piha 'eu, ioiole'a, uilani.
spiritless. Loha, kā'eu'eu 'ole, kūpolō.
spirits. Wai 'ona.
spiritual. Mana, lani, 'uhane, pili 'uhane. *Spiritual powers,* mana 'uhane, papa lani. *Spiritual things,* kō ka 'uhane.
spiritualism, spiritualist. Kilo 'uhane.
spit. Kuha, pupuhi; kī *(cat). Spit constantly,* pakī ke kuha. *To make a cat spit,* ho'okī.
spite. Mauhala, na'au kopekope. *In spite of,* i loko o, me ka nānā 'ole.
spittle. Kuha, hā'ae, na'o; pu'awai, hikianakopili *(rare).*
spittoon. Ipu kuha.
Spitzbergen. Kapikapakena, Sapitabagena.
splash. Pakī. *Also:* kāpeku, po'o, pāku'iku'i, ho'opakī, kuhō, kīkahō, hohō, māpu; kapau'u *(as fish);* kapakapa, kapakē, kapa *(as raindrops on water);* 'olo'ā *(as surf on rocks). Sound of splashing,* 'u'ina.
spleen. Akeloa, akenī'au.
splendid. Kamaha'o, hiehie.
splendor. Nani, nani kamaha'o, hinuhinu. *Also:* 'alohi, hine, hoaka, kamahoi, polina. *Heavenly splendor,* 'ihi lani.
splice. Ku'i, ho'oku'i; — *on,* pāku'i. *Also:* ku'ika'a, kaumo'o, pāna'i, 'uo; malina *(as rope).*
splint. Lā'au ho'opololei.
splinter. Māmala, huluhulu, lā'au. *I have a splinter in my hand,* ua kū ko'u lima i ka lā'au.
split. Wāhi. *Also:* wāhia, wāwahia, 'akaka, mahae, nahā, ho'onahā, 'owā; kōhi *(as breadfruit);* 'ōwae *(as dry earth); — open,* makili, kūlepe. *Rare:* lepeulu, muaiwa, 'uwia. *Splitting of a breadfruit,* kōhina. *Split hairs,* 'ainemanema.
splitter. Kōhi.
splotch. Pōhaka.
spoil. 1. *Decay.* 'Ino, 'ino'ino, mā'ino'ino, pilau; pilapilau *(not quite spoiled);* palahū, palakāhela, nehi, kēwai, pōniuniu; kiohoa *(as flowers);* malau *(rare).* **2.** *Mar.* Hōkai, pahu'a, ho'opahu'a; ho'ohauka'e *(as a ballot).* See **damage. 3.** *Pamper.* Pai, mailani, pailani, ho'okamalani *(as a child).* **4.** *Booty.* Waiwai kaua, waiwai pio, loa'a, waiwai i hao 'ia.
spoiled. See **worthless.**
spoilsport. Pepehi i ka mana'olana.
spoke. Kukuna *(as of a wheel).* See **speak.**
spokesman. Waha 'ōlelo.
sponge. Hu'akai, hu'ahu'akai, 'ūpī; 'ana *(stony).* *Coconut sponge,* lolo niu, iho.
spongy. Kalekale, naele.
sponsor. Mea kāko'o.
spontaneous. Kupu wale, ulu wale. *Spontaneous combustion,* 'ā wale.

spool. Pōka'a. *Spool of thread,* pōka'a lopi. *Spool pins on sewing machine,* pou.

spoon. Puna. *Coconut-shell spoon,* kī'o'e. *Spoon for pālau pudding,* kī'o'e pālau. *Large or serving spoon,* puna nui.

spoonbill. Koloa mōhā.

spoonful. Piha puna.

sport. Mea pā'ani ho'oikaika kino *(body strengthening).* See **archery, baseball, basketball, box, cockfighting, dive, fence, football, foot race, game, kite, pole vault, shot-put, sled, slide, surf, weight, wrestling.**

spot. Kiko, kīkohu, kāpala, pōhaka, we'awe'a, 'āwe'awe'a; pūhā'a'ā *(rare).* *To imprint with spots,* he'ahe'a.

spotted. Kikokiko, kikiko, pākikokiko, ni'o, nini'o, paninini'o, pāni'o; 'ōni'o *(as a pig);* kīnohi, loli, 'īloli; nokea *(white);* kāpule *(black);* pulepule, 'ōpulepule, pikapika, 'āpikapika; 'ōpikopiko *(as with tattoo marks);* pūko'a; pona *(as the sea with various shades).*

spouse. Kāne, wahine, kekahi, kahi; punalua *(spouses sharing a spouse);* 'epukane, hoa 'inau; wai 'apo *(fig.);* pili'ao'ao, moe mau. *How is your spouse?* Pehea kahi o 'olua?

spout. Kīkī, kānuku, nuku, 'o'oma; puhi *(as a whale).* See **waterspout.**

sprain. Māui, ho'omāui, 'anu'u.

sprawl. Moe pāki'i, kūpeleleu, kāhelahela *(as a person).* *Fall sprawling,* hina pālaha.

spray. 'Ehu, ehu, 'ehu kai, huna kai, hune kai, makakai, huna wai, huna wailele, uahi wai, 'ehu wai, 'ea, kāhilihili, lelehuna, lelehune, 'ūpī, wai puhia, wai ehu, pu'awai, pōhūhū *(rare).* *White spray, white caps,* 'ale kuakea, papākea. *Wind-blown spray,* kilihune, kaiehu, wai puhia. *The spray of surfing arises,* ea mai ka makakai he'e nalu. *Poetic references to spray may signify sexual relations.*

spread. Hāli'i, laha. *Also:* 'a'ai *(as a sore);* 'a'ama *(the fingers);* 'apakau *(as sunlight);* hāli'i pili *(as rain over pili grass);* hela *(as the arms);* hola, hohola, pāhola, 'uhola, holopapa, hihi, hihina; pa'ahihi, malele *(here and there);* pāhihi, oha, hīkākā *(as vines);* hamo, hāpola *(as butter);* hikiki'i *(as mist);* hōlapu, ho'olapa *(as fire);* ho'okio; ka'apeha *(wings or tail feathers);* kāhela, kūkawowo, ho'olaha, ho'olaulaha, laulaha, pālaha, ma'au, mo'au, mana; manana *(as octopus tentacles);* moana, moanaana, mahola, māholahola, mōhā, mōhāhā, mohala, mōhalahala, mohahala, mōhola, nakulu, nana, ne'epapa, nene'e; pāki'i *(flat);* peleleu, puakea, pūnohu, uhi, ulu. *Rare:* īhe'e, nana'i, ualei. *Patchwork spread or quilt,* uhi 'āpana. *Spread the knees,* hāli'i kuli. *Spread the news,* ku'i ka lono, lonopapa, laulaha. *Spread gossip,* holoholo 'ōlelo.

spreader. Wae, waewae *(in canoe).*

sprightly. 'Eleu, mikimiki, 'uleu, miki. *Also:* kili, 'ākepa, 'ouo, 'inā'inau.

spring. 1. *Water source.* Puna, kumu wai, hāpuna, pūnāwai; wai hū, māpuna, māpunapuna *(bubbling);* 'ele *(covered with growth);* pūhau *(cool).* *Spring water,* wai māpuna. *Spring tide,* kai piha. 2. *Season. No Hawaiian word; terms sometimes used:* kupulau, la'a ulu, kau o makalapua. 3. *Coil.* Pilina. See **bedsprings.** *The springs are broken,* pili pū ka pilina.

springboard. Papa lele kawa *(for diving).*

Springfield. Kepilepila, Sepirefila.

springy. Nolu, 'api'api, holu, 'olu, napa, nape, nenelu.

sprinkle. 1. *Scatter.* Pīpī, pīpī wai, pī, pī wai, pī kai, pī kai 'ōlena, kāpīpī, kūpīpī, ho'okelekele; kaiehu *(as poi being pounded);* — *with salt,* kāpī, kāpīpī, kōpī, kōpīpī, kāhunahuna. 2. *Rain.* Ua kilikili, ua kilikilihune.

sprinkler. Wiliwiliwai *(lawn).*

sprit. Ko'o, ō. *Sprit line,* kaula ō.

sprout. Kupu. *Also:* 'ōkupu, ēwe, heu, ho'oheu, 'ōheu, holi, ho'oulu, ilo, iloilo, ho'oilo, mā'au, ma'ū, mā'i'i, me'o, 'ōme'o, nopu, oho, 'ōilo, 'ō'ili ka maka, palupalu; polapola *(as a bud);* pōhuli, pu'u.

spruce. Lā'au hū.

spry. 'Eleu. *Also:* 'akakē, 'ele'io, puahia, 'uleulele.

spun yarn. Pāniani.

spur. Kēpā, kākala. *Sharp spurs of fighting cock,* kākala-pī-ka-wai. *Budding spur of young cock,* 'ōpu'u. *To strike with spurs, as fighting cocks,* kīkākala.

spurge. Kokokahiki; kaliko *(wild variety).*

spurn. Hō'ole 'ino.

spurt. Kikī, mokī, mokīmokī, pakī, hanu'u, kokoi.

sputtering. Pī, kukukū.

sputum. Kuha, hā'ae.

spy. Kiu. *Also:* 'akiu, hākiu, makākiu, kilo, hākilo, hālua, ho'omahua; ka'ukoe, ka'uō *(unarmed);* māka'i; — *cunningly,* kiuho'opulu. *See saying,* **heron.** *To act as a spy,* ho'omakākiu.

spyglass. 'Ohe nānā.

squad. Paukū, kuea. *Cf.* **platoon.**

squadron. Mahele 'aumoku, mahele koa.

squall. Kīkīao, kaumuku.

squander. 'Uha'uha, ho'omāunauna, 'uha 'ai, lū.

square. Huinahā kaulike, huinahā like, kuea; 'ili *(in measurements).* *Square foot,* kapua'i kuea, kapua'i 'ili. *Square root,* kumu kuea.

squash. 1. *Vegetable.* Pū, ipu pū, pala'ai, pū kualau. 2. See **smash.**

squat. 'Ōku'u, kī'enenei, kī'elelei, kīkenenei, kī'elei, kī'olei, kikanalei, kī'ililī, 'auwae pu'u, ne'ine'i.

squatter. Mea noho kuleana 'ole; lōpālau'eka *(insulting term).*

squatty. Pepe.

squawk. Kohā, kani halalē.

squeak. 'Uwī'uwī, kakani, po'o, wī.

squeal. 'Alalā, 'uwī'uwī, wī, wīwī.

squeeze. 'Uwī, 'ōpā, kaomi, lomi. *Also:* 'umiki, 'ūmi'i, 'ūpī, kōwī, kāwī, hoka; pahūpahū *(as fish);* pikipiki, 'uwī *(in milking);* — *out,* pakū, kāwī, kōwī, ho'opoheke. *Rare:* kāpā, kūpī. *To soak and squeeze, as in preparing* pia, peluluka.

squid. Mūhe'e. See **'ala'ala, octopus.**

squint. Pipī, pipipi, maka pili.

squirm. Pīhole, hole. *Also:* ka'anini, laumilo, ueue, oioi, 'oni, ne'e.

squirrel. Kiulela.

squirrelfish. 'Ū'ū, 'ala'ihi; 'a'ala'ihi *(young).*

squirt. Pakī, 'ūpī, kī, mūkī.

squish. 'Ūpī.

stab. Hou, 'ō; polo *(rare).* *To stab with a knife,* hou pahi.

stable. 1. See **barn.** 2. See **firm.**

staccato. Kī ho'oikaika *(music).*

stack. Pu'u, kūpa'i.

stadia. Kekakia.

stadium. Kahua pā'ani.

staff. 1. *Stick.* Ko'oko'o, pahu, 'au; *music —,* ko'oko'o, kumu pākōlī, o'a. *Small staff,* 'auli'i. *To lean upon a staff,* kālele. 2. *Workers.* Po'e kōkua, po'e hana.

stage. 1. *Theatrical.* Kahua *(platform).* 2. *Period.* Wā.

stagecoach. Ka'a 'ōhua.

stagger. Kunewa, newa, kūnewanewa; — *forward,* kikiwi. *Also:* hīkākā, kanali'o, kūpou, ho'ohiō, ho'okiwi, pāhila; mahīkākā *(rare).*

staghorn. Uluhe, unuhe.

stagnant. Lana mālie ā 'ōpilopilo; 'ona'ona, kupalaka. *Stagnant water,* wai kū.

stain. Kohu, kāpala, hauka'e, kīkohu, palahe'a, kīpalahe'a, kīna'u. *Stained red,* kāhe'a, he'a, kilihe'a, kīhe'ahe'a, mā; hamo 'ula *(as tapa).* *To stain,* kūhili, he'ahe'a, uhi, waiho'olu'u. *Octopus tentacle stain,* 'ōpikopiko.

stairs. Ala'alapa'i, 'anu'u.

stake. 1. *Staff.* Pahu, papahu, mākia. *Stake taboo sign,* pahu kapu. *Goal stake,* pahu hope, pahu hopu. *Stake in owl trap,* 'oloka'a. 2. *Wager.* Pili.

stale. Malo'o *(as bread);* polopolona *(as air).*

stalk. 1. *Stem.* Hā, 'au, kū'au, ko'o. *Also:* hākai, 'au'au. *Stalk with many branches,* pū manamana. *Hereditary* *stalk,* hāhoʻoili *(of a family long-established).* **2.** *To follow.* Hahai malū, uhai mālie, hoʻomoho, hakupehe.

stall. 1. *Compartment.* Keʻena; kāmala *(for horses or cattle).* *Market stall,* pākaukau makeke. **2.** *To stop.* Mamau, hoʻomamau, nuha, pupū. *Stalled, as a car,* mau.

stallion. Lio laho, lio keʻa.

stalwart. Uʻi, ikaika, meʻe.

stammer. *See* **stutter.**

stamp. 1. *Symbol of paid money.* Poʻoleka *(postage).* *War-savings stamp,* poʻoleka kaua. *Stamp collection,* hōʻiliʻili poʻoleka. *To put on a stamp,* kau i ka poʻoleka. **2.** *Imprint.* Hōʻailona paʻi *(printed).* *Bamboo stamp for printing tapa,* ʻohe kāpala. **3.** *To bring down with force.* Hehi, hehi ʻino, keʻehi *(as with feet);* pahūpahū *(with force);* kuni *(burn, brand).*

stampede. ʻAuheʻe pūʻiwa, hulimoku, holo pūʻaʻā.

stance. Kūlana, kūnana, keʻehina.

stanchion. Pine.

stand. 1. *Upright position.* Kū, kukū, kūlia; — *apart, separate,* kū kaʻawale, kū kahi, kūkākaʻikahi, kūkaʻikahi; — *with legs apart,* kiʻihelei, kiʻelei; — *erect,* ʻōkū, ʻūlepe; ʻōkala *(as hair);* — *rudely with hands on hips or crossed,* kūākiʻi, kū ʻahaʻaha; — *together or in rows,* kūlike; — *watching, or on cliff edge,* hakakaupili. *Stand at the top,* kū i ke ʻaki. *Stand up for Jesus,* kū no Iesu. **2.** *Table.* Pākaukau, paka. **3.** *Platform.* Kahua.

standard. 1. *Emblem.* Kāhili *(tall staff, as of kauila wood, with feathers of tropic bird, frigate bird,* ʻōʻō, ʻiʻiwi, *chicken; symbols of royalty);* kāhili paʻa lima *(carried in the hand).* *Standard-bearer,* lawe kāhili, paʻa kāhili. **2.** *Criterion.* Kūlana paʻa *(as weight or money);* ana. *Standard of living,* kūlana (ʻano) o ka nohona.

standing. Kuana, kū. *Standing committee,* kōmike mau. *See* **stand.**

stanza. Paukū, ʻoki; ʻepe *(rare).*

staple. 1. *Nail.* Kui piʻo. *To staple,* ʻūmiʻi. **2.** *Principal food.* ʻAi nui.

stapler. Mea hoʻopaʻa ʻūmiʻi; ʻūmiʻi pepa *(paper).*

star. Hōkū. *For stars tentatively identified see* **Aldebaran, Altair, Antares, Arcturus, Betelgeuse, Canopus, Castor, Evening Star, Lyra, Morning Star, North Star, Pollux, Rigel, Sirius, Vega.** *See also* **constellation, month, planet.**

UNIDENTIFIED STARS *(alternate names are in parentheses):* ʻAeʻae-a-hiwa, ʻAi-kanaka, Ala-kea, Aniani-ika lani, Au-haele, Au-haku, Haʻilono, Haka-lau-ʻai, Haku-pō-kano, Hālau-lani, Hā-loa, Hana-ka-lau-ʻai, Hana-kauluna, Haʻo, Hauna-kelekele, Hiʻikua, Hiʻilei, Hikianalia, Hiki-au-moana, Hiki-kau-e-lono (ʻĀiki-kau-e-lono), Hiki-kau-lono-meha, Hilina-ehu, Hinaia-ʻeleʻele, Hina-lani, Hinaliʻi, Hina-mālailena (Hinaonalailena), Hōʻeu, Hōkū-pōkano, Holu, Hoʻokele-ʻale, Hoʻoleia, Hoʻomālama, Hoʻomaliu, Hua, Huo, Ihu-kū, Ihu-moe, I-ka-wao-lani, ʻIli-ʻula, Iwi-kau-i-ka-ua, Kaʻaʻei,

Kaʻakaʻa, Kaʻa-lolo, Kaʻaona, Kaekae, Kāʻelo, Kaha-i-Kahaʻi, Kāhela, Kahiki-nui, Ka-hoana-kū, Kahoʻea, Kāholo, Kahuʻa, Ka-huelo-iki, Ka-huelo-kū, Kahuli-aliʻi, Kaiehu, Ka-ʻili-ʻula, Kākaʻe, Kākaihili, Ka-lālani-a-Makaliʻi, Ka-lua-o-ka-ʻohe, Ka-lua-okaoka, Ka maile-hope, Ka-maile-mua, Kamaʻiʻo, Ka-maka-Unulau, Ka-malama, Kama-lei, Ka-mālie, Ka-mālie Hope, Ka-mālie Mua, Kanameʻe, Kāne, Kani-haʻalilo, Kanikani, Kanikaniāʻula, Kani-ʻōʻū, Ka-noe-Makaliʻi, Ka-ʻōnohi-aliʻi, Kapakapa, Ka-pawa, Ka-pohā-kōʻeleʻele, Ka-pola, Kapuahi, Ka-pua-lalo-ka-lani, Ka-pūlehu, Kau, Kau-aka-puʻu, Kau-ano-meha, Kau-ka-liʻa, Kau-ka-malama, Kaʻu-lama-ʻākala, Kaulana-a-ka-lā, Kaulia, Kauliolio-i-Wawau, Kaulu-i-kua, Kaulu-wena, Kau-ʻōpae, Kau-ʻōpua, Kāwaʻe, Ka-waewae-ka-hōkū-e-kau-i-luna-o-he-lani, Ka-wao-nui-a-Ola, Kāwaʻu, Ka-welo Aliʻi, Ka-welo Lani, Ka-weo, Ke-ahi-lele, Ke-ala-kaʻa, (Ke)-aliʻi-i-o-Kona-i-ka-lewa, Ke-ʻalohi, Ke-ʻalohi-lani, Keawe, Ke-

ʻehu-hiwa, Kēhela, Ke-kai-hili, Ke-kau-hiwa-kā, Kēkēpue, Ke-ola, Ke-ō-lewa, Ke-pani-paʻa, Ke-paniwai-o-loko-o-Kahiki, Kīkīʻula, Koko-iki, Kona, Koʻolua, Kōwā, Kua-ʻie, Kuānea, Kūea, Kukui, Kukui-a-kona-mau-kuku (Kona-mau-kuku), Kumukoʻa, Kūpoʻi-lani-ua, Kupua-lalo-o-ka-lani,

Laʻelaʻe, Lālani, Lana-ka-malama, Lani-kū-hana, Lea, Lehua-kona, Lena, Lewa, Liolio-i-Wawau (Wawau), Lipo, Lono, Lua-hoʻomoe, Maha-pili, Mahi-ʻai, Maiakū, Maiao, Māʻiʻo, Maka-ʻālohilohi, Maka-ʻamoʻamo, Makaha, Maka-hai-aku, Maka-hai-waʻa, Mākaha Kona, Maka-holo-waʻa, Maka-ihu-waʻa, Maka-ʻio-lani, Makao, Mākaukau, Maka-ʻUnulau, Makeaupeʻa (Mekeaupeʻa), Mākohi-lani, Makua-ka-ʻūmana, Mālama-i-haneʻelekia, Malamaiku, Mālamalama, Mālana, Malu-lani, Manakū, Mānalo Kai, Mānana-kea, Mana-wahine, Maukuku, Māui, Melemele, Mūlehu, Naʻau-ake-ʻai-haku, Nāholoholo, Na-ka-uilani-ʻelua, Na-lālani-a-pili-lua, Nana, Nāpēhā, Naue-a-ke-au-haku(?), Nēnēhua-ka-wāwae, Nēnēhua Kea, Nēnēhua Uli, Nui, Nuku-loa, Nuʻu-anu,

ʻOea, ʻOlolū, ʻŌmaʻo, Pāʻao, Pae-loa-hiki, Paʻi-kauhale, Pa-kōnane, Pāmāʻele, Pāʻōpua, Pāpolohiwa, Pau-ahi, Pau-ahi Lani, Pāuli-kū-aliʻi, Pau-maka, Pau-makua, Pau-makua-lani, Pawa, Pili-lua, Pīpā, Polapola, Polo-ahi-lani (Pōhina, Polohilani, Polo-ʻula, Polo-wehi-lani), Pou-hānuʻu, Pua-ahi, Pua-nane, Pūkōloa, Pupue, Puʻuwepa (Pūwepa), Uliuli, Ulu-koa, Ulu-loa, Unu-lau, ʻŪʻū, Waia, Waileia, Wai-loa, Wai-naku, Wehewehe, Welo, Welo-ʻula, Wikiwiki.

starboard. ʻAoʻao ʻākau. *Starboard ends of outrigger booms,* muku *(hence also starboard side of canoe).* *Starboard hull of double canoe,* waʻa ʻākea, waʻa kea.

starch. Pia. *Manioc starch,* pia manioka. *Starched clothes,* lole pia.

stare. Nānā pono, haka pono, haka, hōʻaʻā maka, ʻaʻā, ʻaʻā maka.

starfish. Peʻa, peʻapeʻa, ʻōpeʻapeʻa, hōkū kai.

stargazer. Kilo hōkū, kilo, kilo lani.

start. Hoʻomaka, maka hou, kū, hoʻokumu; hoʻohele *(as a clock);* ʻoia *(as a command to race);* — *and not finish,* lemukū; — *up and fly,* lehei. *Let's get started,* e hoʻomaka kākou; hoe aku i ka waʻa *(see* **hoe***);* hoea.

startle. Hoʻopūʻiwa, hoʻohikilele.

startled. Pūʻiwa, piʻolole, puoho, lele ka hauli, hoʻolele ka hauli, meʻu.

starve. Make pōloli.

state. 1. *Condition.* ʻAno, kūlana, kū, hele ā, pō-, kaʻa. **2.** *Political unit.* Mokuʻāina. **3.** *To say,* Haʻi, haʻi manaʻo, hōʻike. *Publicly stated,* ʻōlelo laulā ʻia.

stately. Hanohano, kohu aliʻi. *Also:* hoʻohie, niolo.

statement. ʻŌlelo, haʻina. *Bank statement,* hōʻike panakō. *True statement,* ʻōlelo ʻoiaʻiʻo, ʻōlelo kūʻiʻo.

statesman. Loea kālai aupuni; makou *(rare).*

station. Hale, hale hoʻolulu, kūlana. *See* **terminal.** *Stations of the cross,* alanui o ke keʻa. *To station,* hoʻonoho, hoʻokahua.

stationary. Paʻa, mau. *Also:* kūpene, mōkū, pōhaku.

stationery. Kālana, kānana. *Stationery supplies,* lako kākau.

statistics. Helu; papa helu *(tables).*

statue. Kiʻi, kiʻi kālai ʻia. *His statue (of him),* kona kiʻi. *A statue (by him),* kāna kiʻi.

stature. Kiʻekiʻe.

statute. Kānāwai *(for various kinds, see* **kānāwai** *and below);* ʻōlelopaʻa, ʻōlelo kūpaʻa.

stay. 1. *Remain.* Noho, kū; hoʻopōhaku *(rare). Staying,* noho ʻana. **2.** *Line, support.* Kaula koʻo, koʻo, heʻe.

steadfast. Kūpaʻa, ʻonipaʻa, ʻoni ʻole, paʻa, mau, kūkia, hoʻomānea, paʻamua.

steady. *See* **steadfast.** *To steady,* hoʻokūpaʻa.

steak. Pipi kōʻala *(broiled);* pipi palai *(fried).*

steal. ʻAihue. *Also:* hue, ʻaihuehua, ʻaihuelia, ʻaihuenia, hoʻopuhi, mio, huhuhue; mōkio, pūheʻemiki *(and run);* molulo, mōlulolulo. *See* **ratlike, thief.**

stealthily. Nihi, malū.

steam. Māhu, hoʻomāhu, uahi wai, pūholo. *To generate steam,* hāwai. *To steam food,* hākui.

steam bath. Pūloʻuloʻu. *To take a steam bath,* hoʻopūloʻuloʻu. *See* **sweat bath.**

steam roller. Lola māhu hana alanui, kimalola.

steamship. Mokuahi, mokumāhu, moku holo ahi. *Steamship line,* laina mokuahi.

steamy. Kūmahumahu.

steel. Kila. *Heart of steel,* puʻuwai hao kila.

steep. Laumania, kū, kūnihi, kūlihi, kūnihinihi. *Also:* nihi, kahakō, oheohe, kūmole, kuʻi, ʻūlili; lele koaʻe *(fig.); — as house roof,* kūkūohi. *Rare:* hanunu, kūʻoʻili. *See* **towering.**

steeple. Pūʻoʻa.

steer. 1. *To direct.* Uli, hoʻokele, kia, kupe. *Steering paddle,* hoe uli *(see* **tongue**). *Steering rules,* lula nō nā hoe uli. **2.** *Male bovine.* Pipi poʻa.

steersman. Uli, hoʻokele, kīpū.

stem. *See* **stalk.** *Also:* kū *(as of a goblet); kano (as on a banana bunch); ʻamokiʻi (as of fruits, tubers); ʻaukā (long);* hokua, hiʻanakiʻu *(of vine); iwi (stem and midrib, as of ti leaf). Ti stem,* ʻau kī. *Gourd-leaf stem,* hā ipu. *Place of attachment of stem to leaf,* piko.

stench. *See* **smell.**

stenographer. Kākau ʻōlelo pōkole, kākau pōkole.

step. 1. *Foot movement.* Keʻehi, kaʻi, neʻe *(to step);* kaʻina wāwae *(footstep); — on,* hehi, ʻeʻehi; *— firmly,* hehi ʻino; *— back,* kuemi; *— over,* ʻaʻe, mauʻaʻe; *— lightly,* hani, kakakihi. *Short step,* keʻehi pōkole, eʻe pōkole. *Long step,* keʻehi loa, eʻe loa. *In step,* kaʻi like. *Out of step,* paʻewa ke kaʻi ʻana. *Half step (military),* keʻehi pōkole. **2.** *A rest for the foot.* Alapiʻi, ʻaʻe, ʻanuʻu; kaulu *(as in a cliff);* kīpaepae. *Too many steps,* nui loa nā alapiʻi.

stepfather. Makua kāne kōlea.

stepmother. Makuahine kōlea.

stepparent. Makua kōlea.

stepping. Hehina, kaʻi ʻana.

sterile. Pā *(of females),* hua ʻole. *Also:* maʻiʻawa, lolena. *For a sign of future sterility, see* **ōpūlauoho.**

sterilize. *See* **castrate, disinfect.**

stern. 1. *Severe.* ʻOleʻa, kūoʻo. **2.** *Rear end of a vessel.* Muli, hope; kīkala; uma *(of a canoe, rare).*

sternum. Iwi umauma.

stevedore. Poʻolā.

stew. Kupa, kū. *Chicken stew,* moa kū. *Beef stew,* pipi kū. *To mix or stew with sauce or gravy,* kākele.

steward. Kuene, ʻāʻīpuʻupuʻu, puʻukū, kanaka lawelawe. *See* **attendant.**

stewardess. Wahine lawelawe, kuene wahine. *See* **attendant.**

stick. 1. *Wood.* Lāʻau. *Also:* kūʻau, ʻauʻau; pahu *(staff);* koʻo. *Small sticks,* laʻalāʻau. *Digging stick,* ʻōʻō, ʻālaʻa. *Pointed stick,* ʻō, kuʻia. *Stick dancing,* kālaʻau. *Carrying stick,* ʻauamo, amo kau, māmaka. *Stick for husking coconuts,* ʻō, ʻōniu. *Stick snare for birds,* lāʻau kia, kia manu, kia. *Stick or spear used in game,* ihe paheʻe. *Stick held by priest while sacrificing,* kāʻaha. *Stick lure,* melomelo, mākālei. *Stick for spreading oven stones,* ulu. *Stick vise to hold a canoe,* kīwaʻa *(mōlī).* **2.** *To adhere.* Pili, hoʻopili, pipili, hoʻopipili, pilipili, hoʻopilipili; pili paʻa *(firmly).* **3.** *See* **stick out.**

stick image. Akua kāʻai.

stick out. ʻOiʻoi, kīkoʻo, koʻokū; *— tongue,* hoʻopakeʻo, ʻoiʻoi.

stickpin. Kui ʻōmou, pine ʻōmou.

sticky. Pipili, hoʻopili. *Also:* pīlalilali, pīlali, lali, aweawe, ʻuoʻuo; ʻālikalika *(fig., stingy);* ʻūlika, ʻūlikalika, pīkekaleka, leka, pālololo, lina; pīkale *(as water on a poi board). Any sticky matter,* pilipili. *Sticky juice,* kēpau. *Sticky mud,* pālolo. *Not sticky,* maumau *(as poi of medium texture).*

stiff. ʻOleʻa; māloʻeloʻe, loʻeloʻe, ʻainā *(as from exercise);* mākū *(as molasses);* uāniʻi *(as salted fish);* lāʻau *(as wood);* liki *(as a limb). Also:* kaʻeʻe, ʻeʻe, mauwā, māʻuluʻulu, mala, ʻiʻī, ponanā, piliʻaikū. *Stiff with cold,* make anu, hauʻoki. *Joints are stiff,* ʻoʻoleʻa nā ʻami. *Stiff-backed,* nanai, lanai.

stiffen. Hōʻoʻoleʻa, hoʻouāniʻi, paʻakukū, kano.

stiff neck. ʻĀʻīkū, ʻāʻī ʻoʻoleʻa, ʻāʻī uaua, uakaha, uauakaha.

stifle. ʻUmi, ʻuʻumi, paʻapū; ikiiki, kikiki. *Stifling sensation of inhaling smoke,* kenakena.

stile. Alapiʻi *(steps);* puka pokakaʻa *(revolving).*

still. 1. *Motionless, silent.* Mālie; lana, wailana *(as water);* hoʻomalu *(as during taboo). Also:* lūlā, ʻāʻā, kuaehu, ʻelemoe, maialile, ulana. *Keep still,* kulikuli *(silent);* noho mālie *(motionless, silent). Still waters,* wailana mālie, wailana. *See ex.,* **know.** **2.** *Yet.* Naʻe, koe, ā hiki i kēia wā. *Still here,* eia a nō kā; ke koe nei nō. **3.** *Distilling apparatus.* Ipu hao puhi ʻōkolehao.

stilt. Kukuluaeʻo, aeʻo. *To walk on stilts,* kukuluaeʻo, aeʻo. *To stand on stilts,* hakakē.

stimulant. Mea hoʻoikaika, mea hoʻopaipai.

stimulate. Hoʻoulu, hoʻūlu, hoʻoikaika, hōʻeuʻeu, hoʻopaipai, hoʻolalelale; haʻinole *(rare).*

stimulus. Kumu hoʻolalelale.

sting. Kiki, kikikiki, kui, nahu, ʻō, ʻoʻoi, hueloʻawa.

stinging fly. Nalo nahu.

sting ray. Hīhīmanu, lupe.

stingy. Pī, ʻauʻa. *Also:* hōʻāpī, pīpine, lauʻauʻa, akaoʻo, kulipaʻa, kūkoʻo, hāliʻi kuli, kāʻiʻī, ʻī, oʻoʻo, maua; manini *(modern slang);* wekaweka; linu, puʻaki *(rare). See saying,* **uoʻo** *and fig. idioms,* **palm, sticky, strain 2.**

stink. *See* **smell.**

stinkbug. Puʻu.

stink vine. Maile pilau.

stipulation. ʻŌlelo hoʻopaʻa, ʻano kumu ʻaelike.

stipule. Pepeiao *(as of noni leaf).*

stir. ʻOni *(move);* kāwili *(as ingredients); — up (excite),* hoʻopiʻipiʻi, hōʻeu, hōʻeuʻeu, hōʻeleu, hoʻoulu, hoʻūlu, hoʻouluulu, hoʻouluaoʻa, pai, hoʻopai, hoʻopaipai, hoʻāla, hoʻālaala, ui; kuehu, kaiehu *(as dust);* hoʻohaunaele *(as trouble). Also:* ʻoai, hoʻāli, kōʻai, ʻapi, nene, hānene, au, wiliau, ʻale, hoʻoniua, hoʻolepe; ulu imu *(an oven);* hoʻēhu, hoelo, ʻōhani, hiʻali *(as a fire). Heart-stirring,* hōʻoni puʻuwai. *To stir with life,* ʻīnana.

stirrup. Keʻehi, ʻili keʻehi, hao keʻehi; pēkeu *(rare). Leather covering for stirrups,* pale wāwae, ʻoʻoma noho.

stitch. Humu *(for various kinds, see* **humu**, *and entries that follow it);* kuʻi, hono; hoʻopihapiha *(solid);* kā *(cross);* hoʻoihoiho *(running, in quilting);* humuhumu, maka. *To sew with long stitches,* kāholo, hoʻoholoholo, hoʻoioio. *To sew a quilt so that stitches settle in grooves,* hoʻoioio.

stock. Waihona, kumupaʻa; kea *(in the stock market);* poʻo lāʻau *(as of a gun). See* **livestock.** *To stock,* hoʻopiha, hoʻolako.

stockade. Pā, pā kaua.

Stockholm. Kekokehome, Sekotehome.

stocking. Kākini.

stocks. Lāʻau kūpeʻe *(fetters).*

stocky. Puʻipuʻi, poupou, noʻu.

stoke. Pao, pao ahi.

stoker. Pao ahi.

stomach. ʻŌpū. *Also:* ʻōpū ʻaiʻai, puʻuʻaiʻai; puʻu *(as of some fish). Stomach disorders:* ʻeha ka ʻōpū, hālapa ka ʻōpū, pualewa ka ʻōpū, nalulu ka ʻōpū, puʻu makani, ʻōpū ʻaki, ʻōpū huli, hoaka, lūmanawahua, manawahua. *Lines on stomach of pregnant woman,* alawela. *To move the stomach muscles, as in certain hula dances,* papaʻi. *The stomach is full,* piha ka ʻōpū; paʻa ka houpo. *(see* **houpo.**)

stone. *The common names are* pōhaku *(for various kinds, see* **pōhaku** *and entries that follow it);* ʻiliʻili *(pebbles);* ʻalā *(dense basaltic);* ʻaʻā, pāhoehoe *(volcanic). Precious stone,* pōhaku makamae. *Soft porous stones used for polishing or scouring:* nohu, noninui, pōhuehue, polipoli, hiena, kauaʻula; kohenalo *(corru-*

gated). *Porous stones:* maheu, maka'āwela, ka'ulaiki; 'oai, hau *(rare).* *Hard dense stones as used for adzes:* 'alāmea, laekoloa (kalaniā'ula, kalama'ula), lelekepue, ke'e, 'awali'i, ha'iali'i, ehuehu, 'alā; haumekū *(rare).* See **basalt, chalk, checkers, coral, emerald, flint, lava, limestone, marble, onyx, pebble, pumice, rock, sinker, topaz** *and below. Stone container used for sorcery,* poho kuni 'anā'anā. *Stone lamp,* poho kukui, pohokano. *Stone bowl,* poho pōhaku. *Stone table,* papa pōhaku. *Stone statue,* ki'i pōhaku, 'eho. *Stone anchor,* hekau, heleuma. *Stone to sharpen tools, as adzes,* pōhaku hoana. *Stone used in games of* pūhenehene *and* no'a, no'a. *Red-hot stones put inside animals for cooking,* 'eho. *Stones marking land boundary,* iwi. *Stone pile,* pu'u pōhaku, 'eho. *A row of stones,* pae pōhaku, nini, niho ka'i. *Stone wall,* pā pōhaku. *Rough or jagged stone,* 'ōahi, lo'a'ā. *Type of stone laid near coral pile to attract fish,* hinakea. *Stone for chipping,* haku kā ko'i. *Birth stones,* 'ili'ili hānau. *Stones that break in fire, not desirable for the* imu, makapā. *To set stones,* ho'oniho. *To stone,* hailuku, pehi, pehi i ka pōhaku, ahukū. *To carve or hew stone,* kālai pōhaku. *Stone weighing down a mat,* pōhaku kaomi moena *[a homebody].*

LESS COMMON NAMES OF STONES *(alternate names are in parentheses):* 'alā po'o malu, 'elekū, 'ele'ū, haku, ho'okele, hui'apa, huipa, humu'ula (kalaniā'ula), ihu-o-ka-pua'a, ikimakua, 'ina, ka'au'aupu'u, kahakaha, kalapaiki, kauila, kāwa'ewa'e, kāwa'upu'u, kepue, kumuma'o, kumuone, kūpaoa, laukea, lū'au, luehu, māhikihiki (makai'a), makahinu, makawela, makawī *(Kaua'i),* makiki, māono, mauna, pahapaha (māono, O'ahu), pākea, pala'ā, pe'ahi, pia, waianu'ukole, waimano.

stony. Nui nā pōhaku, nui ka 'a'ā, nui ka pāhoehoe.

stool. 1. *Seat.* Noho, paepae, noho li'ili'i. See **footstool.** **2.** *Feces.* Hana lepo, 'aukā.

stool pigeon. Pekapeka.

stoop. Kūlou, kūnou, kū'ou. *Also:* ho'opoupou, 'alu, 'āluna, pahlō. *Stooped, stoop-shouldered,* 'o'ohu, kanahua, āhua, 'anahua, kua pipi'o, 'ōnaha, palakā hela, hanunu, kakaki.

stop. 1. *Cease.* Ho'opau; ho'oku'u *(disperse);* waiho *(leave off);* kū *(as a car). Also:* alia, oki, ho'ōki, ho'ālia, kākona; — *up,* 'umoki. *Stop it!* Uoki! *Stopped,* kū, ho'oku'u, mau, ho'omau; 'ōmu'o. *Stop the car,* ho'okū i ke ka'a. *Stop work,* ho'opau i ka hana. **2.** See **stay.**

stopper. 'Umoki, popo'i, mea ho'opa'a, pani, kī'amo. *Bottle stopper,* pani 'ōmole.

storage. Kahi e waiho ai.

store. Hale kū'ai; — *away,* hō'ili'ili, ho'āhu. *To store in a house,* ho'ohale papa'a.

storehouse. Hale ho'āhu, hale ahu waiwai, hale ukana, hale papa'a, waihona; olowalu *(as for chief's property). To serve as a storehouse, to convert into a storehouse,* ho'ohale papa'a.

storeroom. Lumi ho'āhu, lumi waiho ukana.

stork. Kikonia, pia, kekoleka.

storm. 'Ino. *Also:* 'ino'ino, 'ihi'awa'awa, 'o'olokū, puleileho. See **hurricane** *and sayings,* **nahoa 1, bird, weather.** *Storm-beset at sea,* 'ōlulo. *Threatening thunderstorm,* ho'ohekili. *Time of storm,* manawa 'ino. *Southerly storm,* Kona Hea (Kona Hea Puka), Konanui-a-niho. *For the first time have I seen a Hilo storm,* 'akahi au a 'ike i ka 'ino o Hilo *(of evil).*

stormy. 'Ino, 'ino'ino. *Also:* 'o'olokū, 'ole'ole'o, ho'ole'ole'o, 'o'ele, pōlua, pikipiki'ō, pūkīkī, 'e'elekoa. *Stormy appearance,* lālauahi.

stormy petrel. See **petrel.**

story. 1. *Narrative.* Mo'olelo. *Also:* ka'ao *(fiction);* mo'o'ōlelo, mo'o, kuamo'o 'ōlelo, kole. *Short story,* mo'olelo pōkole. *To tell stories,* ha'i mo'olelo. *To put several stories into one,* huika'i 'ōlelo. *To record a story,* ho'opa'a mo'olelo. *Telling stories all night,*

kuku'i wana'ao. **2.** See **lie. 3.** *Floor.* Papahele, papa. *Middle story or floor,* papa waena. *Second story,* papa lua. *Building with many stories,* haleku'i.

storyteller. Ha'i mo'olelo *Also:* kākā'ōlelo, kuku'i 'ōlelo, makou.

story writer. Haku mo'olelo.

stout. Pu'ipu'i, poupou. *Rare:* pouhananu'u, nuka, kila; — *and symmetrical,* holokū.

stove. Kapuahi. *Kerosene stove,* kapuahi 'aila māhu. *Gas stove,* kapuahi ea. *Electric stove,* kapuahi uila.

stow. Ho'āhu, waiho, kau, kāpae.

stowaway. Mea pe'e malū maluna o ka moku.

straddle. Kiomana. *Also:* kūkīhelei, ki'ihelei, helei; kaiena *(as on a horse);* hakakau *(rare).*

straggler. Mea hili i hope; pu'u welu *(fig.).*

straight. Pololei. *Also:* kālole *(as hair);* mālō, niolo; kolihana, oheohe, mā'ohe'ohe *(and tall). Straight body,* kino pololei, kino mālō. *Stand straight,* kū pololei, kū ā mālō. *Straight chair,* noho kū. *Straight to the point,* kuakahi. *To go straight ahead,* hele pololei, kāmoe, moena; moc, moea *(rare). Vote a straight ticket,* koho pololei.

straighten. Ho'opololei, lala.

strain. 1. *Filter.* Kānana, kālana, kā'e'e; paka *(as dregs from medicinal herbs);* 'ānana *(as juice or poi);* hoka, pākā *(as kava).* **2.** *Exert.* Ho'oikaika; — *and grunt,* hō'i'ī *(fig., stingy). Also:* oikū, uhu, 'anu'u, ho'onou. **3.** *Hereditary character.* Welo.

strainer. Kānana, kālana. *Poi strainer,* kānana 'ai. *Kava strainer,* hoka 'awa, mau'u.

strait. 1. *Channel.* Kōwā, kaikōwā. **2.** *Trouble.* Pōpilikia, pilikia. *In straitened circumstances,* kuhāiki.

strand. 1. *Fiber.* Ma'awe, awe, mō'ali, mo'o'ali, ka'ā. *Two-stranded,* kālua, ka'ā lua. *Three-stranded,* kākolu, ka'ā kolu. *Strand of pandanus plaiting,* mau'u. *Strand of hair,* wili oho. **2.** *Shore.* Kahakai, one.

stranded. Ili.

strange. 'Ē, 'ano 'ē, mea 'ē, kupaianaha, kupanaha, ha'oha'o, hilu.

stranger. Malihini, mea 'ē, kanaka 'ē. *To be as a stranger,* ho'omalihini.

strangle. 'Umi, 'u'umi, kā'awe; 'ahamaka *(in lua fighting). Strangled,* pu'ua. *Strangling,* 'umina. *Strangling cord,* ka'ane. *Strangling, choking sensation,* kā'awe-'awe.

strap. Kaula, kaula 'ili, 'ili, kalapu. *To strap,* kalapu. *Tail strap,* kaula huelo. *Straps to carry a bundle,* 'awe'awe.

stratagem. Papahana, lālā, a'oa'o, hei.

strategist. 'Alihikaua, ka'a kaua, 'ike ka'a kaua, lau'au'a.

strategy. Ka'a kaua *(war).*

stratosphere. Lewa mawaho, lewa luna lilo.

stratum. Papa, 'āpapa, nu'u, pa'a. *Horizontal stratum,* papa moe. *Heavenly stratum,* mā'ohe'ohe, papa lani. *Highest stratum of the heavens,* lewa lani. *Lower stratum,* papa lalo.

stratus cloud. Ao loa.

straw. Mau'u malo'o. *Drinking straw,* mea omo. *To draw straws,* koho lā'au.

strawberry. 'Ōhelo papa *(native). Strawberry shortcake,* mea 'ono 'ōhelo papa.

strawberry guava. Waiawī.

strawflower. Nani mau loa, pua pepa.

stray. 'Auwana, lalau, 'ae'a. *Also:* holoholo wale, hō-'ā'ā, loloiāhili, lolohili, kū'ae'a, ewa, hili. *Stray cat,* pōpoki pae hewa.

streak. Wana; no'a *(colored);* kiawe; kāhe'a *(red, as at dawn).* See **stripe.** *Streak of gray in hair,* wana hina. *Flying streak, as tail of a comet,* welowelo.

streaked. Mā'oki'oki, ma'oki, ni'o, 'ōni'o, kāni'o, nini'o, 'āwe'awe'a, we'awe'a; mo'o *(as dog or tabby cat).* See **sea.**

stream. 1. *Water.* Kahawai. *Also:* wai, waikahe, lau wai, kahena wai. *Main stream,* kahawai nui, moloalo.

Small stream, ʻaʻalu. *Stream source*, kumu wai, māno. *See* **Hilo, river. 2.** *To flow.* Kahe, kōwelo, welo, wewelo, welowelo, ʻōwelo, hoʻohuelo, pāhihi, kiawe, hoʻokiawe.
streamer. Kīlepalepa, mea hoʻowewelo, kaula lei, puapua, alia.
street. Alanui. *Street corner*, kihi alanui, huina alanui.
streetcar. Kaʻa uila.
strength. Ikaika. *Also:* iwi kani, malu, lāʻau, ʻoʻoleʻa; kamaehu *(rare). See saying*, **ila.** *Past days of strength*, lāʻaeʻoia. *Limited strength*, ʻōpū ʻukuʻuku. *Extraordinary or supernatural strength*, ikaika hoʻokalakupua. *Of superior strength, to exercise strength*, mauaʻālina *(rare). To display strength*, kākāuha. *To conceal strength*, lauʻauʻa *(fig.).*
strengthen. Hoʻoikaika. *Also:* hōʻikaika, hoʻokūpaʻa, hoʻomānea, hōʻoʻoleʻa. *Strengthen the body*, hōʻoʻoleʻa kino, hoʻoikaika kino.
strenuous. Hana luhi, hana ikaika, ʻoʻoleʻa.
stress. Koʻikoʻi, hoʻokālele, kālele leo, kālele manaʻo, kaulele, hoʻokoʻikoʻi. *Cf.* **kahakō.** *Stressing*, koʻikoʻina, hoʻokoʻikoʻina. *Secondary stress in music*, kaulele iki. *Diacritic marking stress*, kālele leo.
stretch. Kīkoʻo, kīkoʻokoʻo, hoʻonaele. *Also:* hoʻoloa, aeae, huki, hoʻolei, kīkiʻi, hohola, kioea, kualapa, manana, malana, naele, hoʻomanana, nīao, koloau; hoʻohelei, hoʻowahalele *(as the mouth);* hoʻoeoe *(as the neck);* nanā *(as muscles); — taut*, hoʻomāloʻeloʻe, hoʻolilio, lena, kualena, kālena, paulinalina. *Stretch the rubber*, hoʻonaele i ka laholio.
stretched. Naele, hekau, lehe, moʻou, kākāuha; helei *(sideways). To lie stretched out*, moe kāhelahela. *He stretched his arms*, kīkoʻokoʻo ʻoia i nā lima.
stretcher. Mānele, moe hoʻolewa. *To carry on a stretcher*, mānele, hoʻolewa.
strew. Lū heleleʻi.
stricken. Loʻohia, kūpouli. *Stricken with sickness*, loʻohia i ka maʻi.
strict. Aʻo ikaika, hoʻokuʻukuʻu ʻole, ʻoʻoleʻa, nihinihi.
strife. ʻĀʻumeʻume, paio, mokuāhana, hakakā.
strike. 1. *Hit.* Kuʻi, pepehi, hau, hahau, uhau, kā; kāhoa *(as a fish on a hook);* kani, kē *(as a clock);* koe *(as a match).* Also: kākā, hoa, hoahoa, kū, kūhewa, kua, hekau, kīpē, kākiʻi, ʻiliki, pūkē, kōkē, kāpehi, hoʻoīkā; panapana *(gently);* paʻē *(as distant sounds on the ear);* haluku *(as canoe sides with a paddle);* kāʻina *(in sorcery); — indiscriminately*, kuʻikē; — *down*, kua; — *against*, keʻehi, īkā; — *with a side stroke or obliquely*, pā lala, kākiwi; — *from the back*, kālawa kua; — *with wings, as an angry bird*, kīpaʻi. *Rare:* hoko, oloʻū, oma. *To strike with the fist*, kuʻi lima. *To strike with a net*, uhau ʻupena. *To strike with sticks*, ʻōlāʻau. **2.** *Work stoppage.* ʻOlohana, ʻolohani. *To cause a strike*, hōʻolohani.
string. Kaula, aho *(cord);* ʻaha *(as for musical instruments);* kuaina *(twine). Also:* hili; kālī, kāili *(as for threading things);* maʻa. *See* **string figure.** *To string*, kui, kōī, māka, mākila, mōkila *(as leis);* hili, ʻuo. *String of fish*, kālī iʻa, kāili iʻa. *String of beads*, akalei. *To string leis*, kui lei. *A stringing together*, kuina. *String trick*, pūkaula, ʻoki kaula. *To tie strings*, kōkō.
stringed instrument. Pila ʻaha.
string figure. Hei, uene. *To make string figures*, hei. *Twist of fingers in string figures*, lumahaʻi. *Dickey describes 115 Hawaiian figures (not including slip tricks).*
stringy. Kaʻakaʻalina, ʻaʻaʻa.
strip. 1. *A length.* ʻĀpana *(as of paper);* mōlina *(as of cloth, wood);* kuakua *(as of fish netting). Strip of pandanus leaf*, kīhae lau hala. **2.** *To tear.* Holehole *(as sugar cane);* ʻuʻu *(as maile);* uhole *(as tough skin);* kīhae *(as leaves, and as thorns from pandanus leaves);* koe, mākoe *(as pandanus leaves). Also:* ihi, pehē, hahae, māihi, lole, hole, paʻipaʻi. *To strip flesh from bones*, holehole iwi, welewele iwi, pūholoholo, pāʻiʻo, waimāhoehoe. *To strip naked*, wehe o kohana. *To strip ʻieʻie roots*, hole ʻie. **3.** *See* **undress.**
stripe. Kaha *(as on a flag or military insignia);* hāluʻa,

haua, kahakahana. *Stars and stripes*, nā hōkū a me nā kaha.
striped. ʻŌniʻoniʻo, kahakaha, hāluʻa, kīʻoki; peʻelua, moelua *(double);* moekolu *(triple);* kāniʻo *(crosswise). See* **streaked.**
stripper. Koe *(of pandanus leaves).*
strip tease. Hana keaka wehe nā lole apau.
strive. Hoʻoikaika, hōʻikaika, hoʻāʻo. *Also:* ʻāpuʻepuʻe, naʻi, kūlia, mākia.
stroke. 1. *Blow.* Hāuna, hauhāuna, hahau, hau, uhau, lāʻau, hili; pā, ʻai, kiʻina *(of an instrument). For lua strokes see* **fight.** *Fighting club strokes:* hāuna lāʻau, lāʻau, māmala *(general names);* kāwala-kiʻi, laumaki, wahie-ʻekeʻeke *(particular strokes). Breast stroke (swimming),* ʻau umauma. *Crawl stroke,* ʻau kolo. *How many club strokes did you strike?* ʻEhia māmala newa āu i hahau ai? **2.** *To touch lightly.* Kahi, hamo. **3.** *Sudden attack.* Huki, kūhewa, kauhola, ulupō, huki leo paʻa.
stroll. Mākaʻikaʻi, holoholo.
strong. Ikaika. *Also:* mahi, kani, wīkani, lawa, lawakua, konakona, pūkonakona, ʻoʻoleʻa, kāʻeo, paʻa, konapiliahi, pūkīkī, hoʻolehua, hoʻolua, pūkani lua, ʻuoʻuo, kilakila, mōkila, kila, konāhao, kūlepe, ika. *Rare:* wīkaʻo, pūlawa, kīkā, mauaʻālina. *Very strong,* ikaika loa, lawa lua. *Strong arm,* lima akaika. *Strong of limb,* ʻoʻoleʻa nā lālā, lālākoʻa. *Strong-backed,* lawakua. *Strong sea,* kai koʻo, huliāmahi. *To grow strong, as after weakness,* piʻi hou ka ikaika, polapola, kokonoiʻe.
strongbox. Pahu hao.
stronghold. Wahi paʻa, puʻukaua; pā kaua *(Biblical).*
struck. Pā ʻia; kāina *(rare). See* **strike.**
structure. Ke ʻano o ke kūkulu ʻia ʻana. *Word or sentence structure,* pilina ʻōlelo. *Family or social structure,* pili nohona.
struggle. Paio, ʻaʻumeʻume. *Also:* kaʻahili, ʻāpuʻepuʻe, kūpāpā, kūlapa, kūpaka, kē, naku, hamo, kuanui, hoʻokuanui.
strum. Koekoe.
strut. Hoʻokahakaha, hele haʻaheo. *Also:* haukalalī, nanā, nanai, hananai, kōheo, haʻaheo, hoʻohaha, kāʻiʻī, heheo; pahāha, pahilolo.
strychnine. Kikanaine.
stub. Hoʻokuʻi. *Stub the toe,* hoʻokuʻi i ka manamana.
stubble. Kumukumu *(as of beard);* ʻōkupu.
stubborn. Paʻakikī. *Also:* poʻo paʻa, paʻa, lae paʻa, koniā, kananuha, nuha, haʻi ʻole, kanū, lolohe, kūnono, hoʻopōhaku, uhakole, aʻī uaua, hoʻouaua, ʻoʻoleʻa.
stubby. Mūʻouʻou. *See* **short.**
stuck. Paʻa, pupū, hoʻomamau; mau *(as a car). Stuck in the mud,* paʻa i ka ʻūkele.
student. Haumāna, haumana, māna. *See* **reflect.**
studio. Keʻena. *Painting studio,* keʻena kaha kiʻi. *Photographic studio,* keʻena paʻi kiʻi. *Studio apartment,* keʻena noho ʻuʻuku. *Hula studio,* hālau, pā hula, keʻena aʻo hula.
studious. Hoʻopaʻa haʻawina, puni hoʻopaʻa haʻawina.
study. Hoʻopaʻa haʻawina, hoʻopaʻa, huli.
stuff. 1. *Matter.* Mea, waiwai o kēlā me kēia ʻano. *Stuff and nonsense,* mea kū i ke kohu ʻole, i ka ʻī. **2.** *Fill.* Hoʻopiha, kūpalu; iʻaloa *(as an animal). See* **eat, gag.**
stuffed. Piha loa, māʻona loa, māʻona piha *(with food). Also:* lāʻiki, kuenenuʻu, kinanape, kūpalu.
stuffing. Mea hoʻopihapiha. *Chicken stuffing,* mea hoʻopihapiha moa.
stuffy. Paʻapū; ikiiki *(and hot). Stuffy odor,* polopolona.
stumble. Kuʻia ka wāwae, hilikau nā wāwae. *Also:* ʻōkupe, hoʻōkupe, kupe, kalepa, palaha, kulipeʻe, kāhehi, hili hewa ka wāwae, ʻanuʻu.
stump. ʻŌmuku, ʻōkumu, ʻaukā. *Stumps,* kumukumu. *Full of stumps,* ʻāmokumoku, ʻāmukumuku.
stumpy. ʻŌkumu, ʻakumu, ʻākumukumu, pānoʻunoʻu; pōnulu *(rare).*
stunted. Kanaliʻi, kakanaliʻi, ʻanaliʻi, ʻaʻanaliʻi, hōmīmī. *Also:* hōmī, ʻiʻi, ʻomino, palakai, ʻukiki, lākī, ha-

nu'u; mālili *(as fruits);* mōlili, 'ōlili, hāla'ola'o, ho'o-kanaha'i; 'ōlala *(as plants). Rare:* 'anini, no'ino'i.

stupefied. Kūpouli; pāhola, hola *(as fish by drugging).*

stupid. Hūpō. *Also:* wa'awa'a, wa'awa'a iki; Wa'awa'a-iki-na'aupō *(ignorant stupid one, name of a legendary simpleton);* pūwa'awa'a, mānoanoa, ihu papa'a, kū-loma, peue. *See saying,* gourd.

sturdy. Ikaika, pa'a, pu'ipu'i, kā'ala'ala. *To make sturdy, as a plant (in ancient prayers),* hāluapou.

stutter. 'Ū'ū, mā'ū'ū; 'ā'ā *(as a dumb person).*

sty. 1. *Enclosure.* Pā. **2.** *Swelling on eyelid.* Uleule.

style. Paikini, kaila, 'ano; 'ai *(dancing).* 'Ōlapa *style,* ke 'ano 'ōlapa.

stylish. Kaila, kū i ke kaila.

suave. Nahenahe, aukahi, akahai.

subdistrict. 'Okana.

subdue. Ho'okūlou, ho'opio. *See* conquer.

subincise. *Same as* circumcise.

subject. 1. *Citizen.* Maka'āinana, kanaka; uli, 'ūhā kā-kau *(of chief).* **2.** *Topic.* Kumumana'o, kahua hana, kumuhana. *Subject of a sentence,* kumu'ōlelo, ku-muha'i.

subjective. Pilikino.

sublease. Ho'olimalima hou.

submarine. Mokulu'u.

submarine base. Kahua mokulu'u.

submissive. Noho malalo *(Biblical),* ha'aha'a.

submit. Waiho.

subordinate. Malalo, o lalo; loha *(fig.).*

subpoena. Palapala kēnā, palapala ki'i, kūpina.

subscribe. Kākau inoa, ho'opa'a, kauoho.

subsequent. Hope, mahope.

subside. Emi, iho, ku'u, numi.

subsidy. Uku kāko'o.

substance. 'I'o.

substitute. Pani hakahaka, pani, hope, pāna'i; kala *(Biblical). See* teacher.

subtract, subtraction. Ho'olawe.

subtrahend. Helu ho'olawe.

suburb. Hu'a. *Cf.* huli 3.

succeed. 1. *Accomplish.* Holomua, holo i mua, holo le'a, holo pono, kō, loa'a. *We have succeeded,* ua pono kāua. **2.** *Follow.* Ukali, pani, hahai.

successful. Holo i mua, holomua. *Also:* holopono, holo le'a, lele pono, pono, loa'a, ho'oholo i mua, kūle'a, lālāwai, ka'aka'ahiki, ulupono. *See sayings,* 'aki 2, uene 1, top. *Our work is successful,* ua pono kā kāua hana.

succession. Ka'ina. *Also:* kaka'ina, mo'o, mō, 'āma-'amau. *Succession of people,* mo'o kanaka. *See* se-quence. *Genealogical succession,* mo'o kū'auhau; mo'o ali'i *(chiefly).*

successor. Ho'oilina, ho'īlina, hope, pani hakahaka.

succulent. Mea ulu wai nui *(plant),* 'ākulikuli *(general name);* 'oliwa kū kahakai, 'ala'ala-wai-nui *(varieties).*

such. Like. *Such as this, such and such, such as,* e like me kēia, e la'a me kēia, penei ke 'ano. *Such a,* keu ā. *This is such a lazy cat,* he keu kēia ā ka pōpoki molowā.

suck. Omo, omoomo, mōmo, minoi, mīnoinoi, mūkī; — *in,* miki, mimiki. *Sucking noise,* mūkī. *To suck blood,* omo koko.

sucker. Keiki, weli, kawowo, hehu; 'ohā *(taro);* pōhuli *(banana);* maka ('awapuhi); 'umi'umi *(attaching bi-valves to rocks).*

sucking fish. Omo.

suckle. 'Ai waiū, omo, omo waiū. *Suckling child,* keiki 'ai waiū, keiki omo waiū.

suckling. Waiū *(nursing).*

suction. Omo. *Suction cups on octopus tentacles,* pika-pika, 'āpikapika. *Suction tube,* 'ili omo wai.

suddenly. 'Emo 'ole, hikiwawe, honua, poni, aia ho'i. *See saying,* lani 1.

suds. Hu'a.

sue. Ho'opi'i. *Sue for damages,* koi pohō.

Suez. Kueka, Sueza.

suffer. 'Eha, 'eha'eha. *Also:* 'īnea, ikiiki, polikia.

sufficient. Lawa, ka'a i ka lawa.

suffix. Hua pāku'i mahope o ka hua 'ōlelo.

suffocate. 'Umi, 'ai pō'ala. *Suffocated,* pu'ua. *Suffoca-tion from smoke,* kenakena.

Suffolk. Kupaka, Sufaka.

suffrage. Koho pāloka. *Right of suffrage,* pono koho pāloka.

sugar. Kōpa'a. *Powdered sugar,* kōpa'a hō'ae'ae. *Lump sugar,* kōpa'a pu'upu'u, pu'upu'u kōpa'a. *Coarse sugar,* kōpa'a mānoanoa. *Brown sugar,* kōpa'a 'ula-'ula. *Refined sugar,* kōpa'a ho'oke'oke'o.

sugar cane. Kō. *See* bagasse *and sayings,* kea 3, pū kō. *Clump of sugar cane,* pū kō. *Cane leaf,* lau kō, lau'ō, lākō, lā'ō. *Sugar-cane tassel,* kīlepalepa kō. *Sugar-cane stem and tassel,* pua kō. *Cane growing along a border,* pae kō. *Sugar-cane refuse,* kō 'aina, laina. *Sugar cane held up with sticks,* pū kō ko'o, pū ko'o.

SUGAR CANES USED IN MEDICINE: kō kea, kō honua 'ula, 'ainakea (pū kea) manulele.

CANES USED IN LOVE MAGIC: manulele, papa'a, pilimai, laukona.

OTHER CANES *(alternate names are in parentheses):* 'aina kea, 'aina kea melemele, 'akilolo, 'akilolo 'ula-'ula *(nānahu, red mutant),* 'akoki, 'ala'ihi, 'āwela (pua'ole), 'āwela melemele (pua'ole), 'āweoweo, halā-li'i, hinahina, hou, 'ili'ōpua, kāni'o, kauila, kea (kō kea), kihe, kōaki, kō Pākē, kō Palani, lahaina (keni-keni), lahi, lahi kahakaha 'ākala, lauloa, lehu, māiko-iko (kō 'ele'ele), māikoiko kahakaha, maka'ā, manini, mā'ohe'ohe, mīkokoi, moano, nika, 'ōhi'a, 'oliana, opukea, pa'apa'a (ho'opa'apa'a), pailolo, pakaiea, pa-kaweli, pakē, piliko'a, pōhina, puahala, uahi-a-Pele (na'aukake), 'uala, 'uala lehu, uhu, 'ula'ula, ule'ohi'u ('āwela melemele, uluhui), wai'ōhi'a, wehe hala (wehe-wehe hala).

sugar grinder. Wili kō.

sugar mill. Wili kō, hale wili kō, hale puhi kō.

sugar plantation. Mahi kō.

suggest. Ho'upuka mana'o; ho'olale *(as action). Also:* ho'ohelehele 'ōlelo, ho'oloko, hani, ho'ohali 'ōlelo, ho'omaoe.

suggestion. 'Ōlelo ho'ohali. *Cf.* mana'o.

suit. 1. *Clothing.* Pa'a, pa'a lole, pa'a lole komo. **2.** *Court action.* Ho'opi'i, hihia. *Suit over land,* ho'opi'i 'āina. *Damage suit,* ho'opi'i pohō. *Suit involving smuggling,* hihia waiwai kolohe. **3.** *To please or satis-fy.* Kū i ka makemake, kū pono i ka mana'o, kohu po-no. *Suit yourself,* aia nō ia iā 'oe *(see* aia). *Not suiting,* kū 'ole i ka hoi *(see* hoi). *This suits me fine,* kohu pono kēia ia'u; kū kēia i ko'u makemake.

suitable. Kūpono, kū, kohu, kohu pono.

suitcase. Paiki.

suitor. Mea noi male.

sulk. Nuha, nunuha, nuhanuha, naluā, ho'okololohe, ka'e.

sulky. Nuha. *Also:* kananuha, nunuha, ho'okananuha, ho'okololohe, kanū, ka'e, ho'olehelehe nui, mumule, koniā, monū, naluā; hō'e'elo *(tearfully);* uhelehe.

sullen. *See* head, sulky. *Also:* ka'e, kūkona, hakanū, kanū, niha, nihaniha, maniha, ho'okamaniha, kama-niha, mumule, loha.

sully. 'Ōlepolepo. *See* dirt.

sulphate of soda. Hau'eli.

sulphur. Kūkaepele, lepopele, kalapa, kulepa, lua'i pele. *Sulphur smoke,* uahi 'awa.

sultan. Kulekana.

sultana. Kulekana wahine.

sultry. Hahana, kō'eha'eha, ikiiki.

sum. Huina helu, huina, heluna; melehuka *(rare). Sum of money,* pu'u kālā.

sumach. Neleau.

Sumatra. Kumakala, Sumatara.

summarize. Hō'ulu'ulu ā ho'opōkole i ke kumuhana, ha'i pōkole, hō'ulu'ulu mana'o.

summary. Hō'ike ho'opōkole, hō'ulu'ulu pōkole *(syn-opsis).*

summer. Kau, kau wela.

summit. Wēkiu, piko, poʻo, puʻu ʻoiʻoi, niʻo, panepoʻo, pane, nuʻu. *Strive to reach the summit (Queen Ka-piʻo-laniʻs motto),* kūlia i ka nuʻu.

summon. Kiʻi, kēnā, kāhea. *Also:* kauoha, poloʻai, kapakapa, hāluna. *To summon a spirit to possess,* hoʻonoho.

summons. Palapala kiʻi, palapala kēnā, palapala hopu.

sun. Lā; kahikole *(early morning);* kahikū *(before noon). Sun heat,* lā. *To sun,* hoʻolā, kaulaʻi lā, lalala, ʻōmea; lōlā *(rare). Circle around sun,* lua kālai lani, luakālai, luahoana.

sunbath. Kaulaʻi lā.

sunbeam. Pōhaka lā.

sunbonnet. Pāpale ʻoʻoma.

sunburned. Pāpaʻa lā, ʻōwela, nono, ʻai lā, pākīʻai. *Sunburned skin,* ʻili pāpaʻa, ʻili pāpaʻa lā.

Sunday. Lāpule; Kuneke, Sunede *(rare). See* **Sabbath.** *Communion Sunday,* Lāpule ʻAi Pelena.

Sunday school. Kula Kāpaki.

sundew. Mikinalo.

sundial. Mea hōʻike kekele *(Biblical),* pā kuhikuhi manawa.

sundial shell. Pūpū puhi, hālili, pūlewa.

sunfish. Kūnehi, ʻāpahu, mākua, mākuakua.

sunflower. Pua nānā lā, nānālā.

sunk. Palemo, piholo.

sunken. Poʻopoʻo, ʻolohaka, hakahaka *(as facial features);* puhalu, halu, uhalu, pohō; ʻopi *(as a jaw);* pōlea.

sunlight. Mālamalama o ka lā.

sunny. Lā.

sunrise. Pukana lā, puka ʻana o ka lā. *From sunrise to sunset (a whole day or whole life span),* mai ka lā hiki ā ka lā kau.

sunset. Napoʻo ʻana o ka lā. *See saying,* **welo.** *Sunset glow,* alaula. *Red sunset,* akaʻula.

sunshine. Pā ʻana a ka lā.

superb. Poʻokela, hiehie, hoʻokahakaha, kamahaʻo. *See* **splendor.**

supercargo. Kupakako.

superficial. Mālani; ihupōhue, hāpapa *(fig.). See saying,* **pūhue.** *He has a superficial knowledge of the hula,* he ʻike mālani kona i ka hula.

superintend. Hoʻoponopono.

superintendent. Haku hana, luna nui. *School superintendent,* kahu kula nui. *Superintendent of the Water Works,* luna nui o ka ʻOihana Wai.

superior. ʻOi aʻe, poʻokela. *Also:* kilohana, ʻoiʻoi, hoʻokela, lua ʻole, ana ʻole, launa ʻole. *To act superior,* hoʻokano, hōʻoio, hōʻoiʻoi, lanahaʻakei, kū ka ihu.

Superior Court. Same as **Supreme Court** in Hawaiian.

superlative. ʻOi loa, launa ʻole, oki, ʻaʻole e kana mai ka maikaʻi, neʻeneʻeu. *Superlative degree,* anuʻu loa.

supermarket. Mākeke nui.

supernatural. Hoʻokalakupua. *Also:* akua, hoʻākua, pāʻēʻē. *See* **legendary beings.** *Supernatural deed,* hana mana. *Supernatural forms, as of Pele,* kino lau, kino pāʻēʻē. *Supernatural knowledge,* ʻike pāpālua. *Under control of the supernatural,* kalakupua.

superstitious. Hoʻomanamana.

supervise. Hoʻoponopono.

supervisor. Luna, luna kiaʻi, luna hoʻoponopono. *Female supervisor,* haku wahine. *School supervisor,* kahu kula. *Board of Supervisors,* Papa Luna Kiaʻi.

supper. ʻAina ahiahi, pāʻina ahiahi. *Poi supper,* pāʻina ʻai poi.

supple. Palupalu, ʻolu. *Also:* wali, waliwali, wawali.

supplement. Hope, pākuʻi, kaulele. *Word supplements,* ʻōlelo pākuʻi hou.

supplied. Hoʻolako ʻia; lilihua *(rare). Well-supplied,* lako, lawa puni, pākī, laupaʻi, pūlawa *(rare).*

supplies. Lako *(for various kinds, see* **lako** *and entries that follow it);* kuleana lako, ukana. *Office supplies,* lako keʻena.

supply. Lako, hoʻolako, hoʻolawa, hoʻolawalawa, hoʻolaupaʻi; momoa, moamoa *(with food). Supply and de-*

mand, ka nui a me ka makemake ʻia. *Well supplied,* lako, lawa puni, pākī, koʻakoʻa, laupaʻi, pūlawa.

support. Kākoʻo, hāpai. *Also:* koʻokoʻo, koʻo, kaʻikaʻi, kōkua, mālama, kālele, paepae; kaulani *(a chief). Support for birds,* koʻo manu. *Support for chickens,* koʻo moa. *Means of support,* mālama ola. *He was sued for nonsupport,* ua hoʻopiʻi ʻia ʻo ia no ka mālama ola ʻole. *Person with no property or means of support,* kaʻaʻowē. *Visible means of support,* mea e akaaka ai ka loaʻa ʻana o ke ola.

supporter. Kākoʻo, hope. *Male supporter,* ʻeke hoʻopaʻa laho.

suppose. Manaʻo, kuhi, mahuʻi, ʻī, manaʻo wale. *See* **presume.** *To suppose wrongly,* kainō, kainoa, kuhi hewa.

supposition. Manaʻo koho.

suppress. Kaomi, hoʻopau, kinai, ʻuʻumi. *Suppression of crime,* kinai i ka hewa.

supreme. Poʻokela, kiʻekiʻe loa. *Also:* holoʻokoʻa, ʻī, kiakahi.

Supreme Court. ʻAha Hoʻokolokolo Kiʻekiʻe, ʻAha Kiʻekiʻe.

sure. ʻOiaʻiʻo. *Are you sure?* He ʻoiaʻiʻo kēnā? *Make sure,* hōʻoiaʻiʻo. *Sure indeed,* sure maoli nō *(in songs).*

surely. Hiki, hiki nō, ʻiʻo. *Iʻll surely come,* e hiki ʻiʻo mai ana au.

surety. Pānaʻi, hope. *I will be surety for him,* ʻo wau nō ka pānaʻi nona.

surf. Nalu, nanu. *See* **surfboard, surfer, wave,** *and sayings,* **kāʻeʻaʻeʻa, lalilali, makakai.** *Some types of surf:* ʻōpuʻu, kakala, lala, lauloa, muku, ʻōhū. *Surf just before breaking point,* kua nalu, kūlana nalu. *Breaking surf,* kai poʻi, kuapā. *To rise and swell, of surf,* lālahalaha. *To surf,* heʻe, heʻe nalu. *To surf to mouth of stream,* heʻe puʻewai. *To mount or catch a wave,* pae. *To ride a wave into shore,* pae i ka nalu. *To surf, as with canoe, body, board,* pākā, kaha. *Surf rider,* heʻe nalu. *Body surfing,* kaha nalu, heʻe umauma. *Surfs were named in ancient Hawaii. Finney (pp. 26–31) lists and locates 86 sites, most of which were named. Pukui, Elbert, and Mookini 1974 (especially p. 243) list many more, including modern names such as Avalanche, Banzai Pipeline, Flies, Incinerators, Populars, Slaughterhouse, and Turtle. More than 1,700 surfing sites have been identified.*

surface. ʻIli, ʻiliwai, lau; papa *(flat);* alo *(upper). Surface of the earth,* ʻili honua, papakū. *Surface of the sea,* ʻilikai.

surfboard. Papa heʻe nalu. *Of special kinds, the most common were olo (of* wiliwili *wood, as long as 5.5 m, for chiefs) and* alaia *(of* koa *or breadfruit wood). Other names:* kīkoʻo, kīoe, omo, ʻonini, ʻōwili, paha, puʻua. *To ride a surfboard,* heʻe nalu. *Prone position on a surfboard,* kīpapa.

surfeit. Ana, kenakena, ʻaikena. *Also:* noneā, pākī.

surfer. Heʻe nalu. *See sayings,* **kāʻeʻaʻeʻa, lalilali.** *The unskilled surfer tumbles,* he ʻō ʻia ka mea hāwāwā i ka heʻe nalu *(of any lack of skill).*

surge. Hū, hōʻale, hānupa, hānupanupa, haulani, haʻi ale, hakukoʻi, haʻanopu, kāhela, māpu, loku, hoʻonuʻa, nape, kuahaka, hoʻoui, kāhela, maʻalewa, paiāhaʻa. *Her love surges forth,* māpu mai kona aloha, hū aʻela kona aloha.

surgeon. Kauka kaha.

surgeonfish. Kala, manini, ʻapi, kakakī; kole *(see saying* **kole**; mahaha, naʻenaʻe; māʻiʻiʻi; pākuʻikuʻi, palani, pualu, puwalu.

surly. Nuha, ʻaʻaka, naʻau kopekope, kekē, kekē niho. *Also:* keʻemoa, kakana, hoʻokeʻekeʻe, hōʻaʻaka, nau.

surmise. Kuhi, mahuʻi, hoʻohuoi, hōʻopuʻopu.

surmullet. Weke *(for various kinds, see* Haw.-Eng. *entry and entries that follow it).*

surname. Inoa ʻohana.

surpass. Hoʻokela, pākela, puka, pākeu, holo i mua, holomua, oko.

surplus. Koe, koena, keu.

leaves, laupa'e, laupa'i. *Young leaves,* paha. *Un-expanded taro leaf,* lū'au, 'ao lū'au. *Taro top,* huli; huli mio *(spent strength). Taro shoot,* 'ohā. *Center of taro corm,* 'aihē. *Taro where corm is cut away,* kōhina. *Taro plant after half of young leaf is removed,* 'ōpe'a-pe'a. *Small tubers,* 'ala'ala'a. *Taro stalk,* hā. *Last of taro crop.* 'oene. *Worn-out ratoon crops,* palili, pau-nihinihi, 'ōnihinihi, 'ānihinihi, pahūpahū. *Cooked un-pounded taro,* kalo pa'a, 'ai 'oko'a, kūpu'u, kuwala, kuelo, nē'ū. *Dried taro,* 'ao. *Cooked taro leaves,* lū'au, pē'ū. *Cooked, pounded but undiluted taro,* pa'i 'ai, 'ai pa'a. *Taro pudding,* kūlolo, piele. *Taro baked in ti leaves,* 'ai lau, 'oana. *Cooked taro that has fermented,* 'ī'īaao. *To peel, as taro stems,* ihi, 'āpikipiki. *To pound taro,* ku'i 'ai, ku'i poi. *To break up cooked taro in first stage of poi making,* pākī'ai. *To pull taro,* huhuki 'ai, huhuki i ke kalo. *Taro patch,* lo'i kalo, lo'i-lo'i, māla 'ai, ala'alai, aualalo'i, kipi, hakupa'a. *Divi-sion between taro patches,* pale kōhina, kuāuna, kaikā, īkā. *Series of taro patches,* kuapapa lo'i. *To eat cooked taro,* 'ai i kalo mo'a *(enjoy a tranquil life of ease).*

KINDS OF TAROS *(alternate names are in parentheses):* 'a'ae ('ae, wa'e), 'āhē, 'ala, 'ala-o-Puna (welowelolā), 'ao'ao-leo-nui, 'āpi'i, 'apo, 'apowale, 'apu, 'apuwai ('a'apuwai), 'awapuhi, 'āweu ('āweuweu), 'eka'eka, 'ele'ele (hinupua'a, naioea), 'ele'ele mākoko, 'ele'ele 'ōma'o, 'ele'ele 'ula, ēulu, haehae, haokea ('ahakea, ha'akea, hā'awikea, lūkea), hāpu'upu'u (hāpu'u), he-kili, helemauna, hi'iaka, hinalea, hinapū, hona, ho'o-leinawao, hulipūloa, humuhumu, 'ie'ie, iheihe, iheihe lei, 'ili'ā, 'iliuaua, 'i'oaweawe, ipu-o-Lono, ka'eolau, ka'eonui, kāī, kalalau, kāmau, kanaio, kāni'o, kele, kihi-lau-nui, ki'i-hekekē, kīkīpalapala, koa'e, kuamū, kūkae'iole, kūmū, kū'oho, lapa, lauloa (hāloa; *see* **palakea**), launui, lehua *(see Haw.-Eng. entry for variet-ies),* lehua ke'oke'o (waiakea), lehua maoli, lehua pala-'i'i ('i'i, pala'i'i), le'o, lī'apu, lihilihi molina, līlīlehua, lola, māea, mahakea, mahamaha, mahiki, māhuna, maihua, mā'i'i'i, mā'ili, mā'i'o, maka'ōpio, makaua, mākohi, mākoko (kia'i-ma-ka-lae), mana *(see Haw.-Eng. entry and entries that follow it),* mana kukula hema (manua), manini, manini 'ōpelu, manini 'ōwali, mimi'iole, moano, mokihana, nahiolea, naio, nalili ko'i, nana, nanapikoa, nao, naua, nāwao (kanawao), ne'ene'e (moi), nihopu'u, nina, nohu, nuku 'e'ehu (nuku 'ehu), nukukau, nukumanu, oalu, oalu nui, 'oā-'oā, 'o'au, 'o'au alu niu, 'ohe, 'ōhi'a, ola'aloa (la'a-loa), 'o'olu, 'o'opukai, 'ōpelu, 'ōpelu haole, pa'akai, pa'akai mikomiko, pa'apa'a'ina, pa'ea, pa'ele-hili-mā-noanoa, pa'iaha, pakaiea, pākea, pala, palakea (lauloa hā'ele'ele, lauloa palakea), palakea 'ele'ele, palakea ke'oke'o, pala mahiki, pālau, pani'ole, pāpākole-kā-wa'a, pāpākole koa'e, pāpalakea, papamū, papapueo, paua, pau'iole, pā'ū-o-Hi'iaka, pehua, peluhā'ele, pia, piapia, pi'iali'i, pi'ihālāwai, piko *(see Haw.-Eng. entry and entries that follow it),* pilimai, pōhina, poni, pua-kawaihae, pu'ukōnane, uahi-a-Pele, ualehu, uaua, uia, 'ula'ula, wehiwa (wewehiwa).

tarpaulin. Kapolena.

tarry. Kali iki, 'apa, noho iki.

tart. 1. *Pie.* Pai. **2.** *Sour.* 'Awa'awa, māniani, kīko'olā.

tartar. Pala niho *(of teeth).*

task. Hana, ha'awina.

taskmaster. Luna ho'oluhi.

tassel. Ku'uwelu, kīlepalepa; pua *(of sugar cane). To tassel, as sugar cane,* 'ō.

taste. Ho'ā'o. *To taste food,* 'ai, ho'opā i ka 'ai. *Taste bud,* a'alolo ho'ā'o. *To have a taste for,* makemake, paoa. *In good taste,* kohu, pālawaiki. *In poor taste,* kohu 'ole; 'a'ohe kohu iki; ua 'ewa ka pilina a ka niho-niho *(see* **pilina***). How does the food taste?* Pehea ka 'ono o ka 'ai 'ana?

tasteless. Ko'eko'e, hūkākai, hūkaikai, 'ōkākai, pō-ka'o, mūhea. *Also:* kāhalahala, pu'apu'a, mu'umūnā, 'a'alakai, 'oka'okai, kai, ānea, 'ōhea, maika. *See* **in-sipid.**

---

surprise. Pū'iwa, ho'opū'iwa, ho'oha'oha'o. *See* **excla-mation, surprising, unexpected.**

surprising. Kupaianaha, kupanaha, kamaha'o, ho'opū-'iwa, pū'iwa, ha'oha'o, ha'o, ho'oha'oha'o, ho'okāhā-hā, kāhāhā, kāmeha'i.

surrender. Hā'awipio, hā'ulepio; *unconditional* —, hā-'awipio 'oko'u.

surround. Ka'apuni, ho'opuni. *Also:* ho'opō'ai, pō'ai, kīpuni, kūpuni, puana, kalawai, puni.

surrounded. Ho'opuni pō'ai pū 'ia.

survey. Ana; 'imi ā ho'ākoakoa *(lit., look for and as-semble);* ana 'āina *(land).*

surveying rod. Lā'au ana.

surveyor. Mea ana 'āina.

surveyor general. Luna ana 'āina nui.

survive. Ola, ō. *Barely surviving,* pipī *(fig.).*

survivor. Mea ola. *Sole survivor who reports news (in legends),* 'aha'ilono.

susceptible. Pāma'i *(to disease).*

suspect. Ho'ohuoi, mahu'i.

suspend. 1. *Hang.* Kau, kaulia, ho'olewa, kau lewa; pūailewa *(in air);* wele, welehia. **2.** *Abrogate.* Kāpae, ho'omalu.

suspenders. Kāliki.

suspense. *See* **anxiety.**

suspicious. Ho'ohuoi, kīkāmū. *Suspicious glance,* maka lena.

sustain. Paepae, ko'o *(support);* hānai *(feed).*

suture. Hoai *(for various kinds, see Haw.-Eng entry and entries that follow it).*

swagger. *See* **strut.**

swallow. 1. *Ingest.* Ale; ala *(rare);* moni, monia, moni-moni, momoni, momomoni; — *whole,* alaō, alapoho. *Sound of swallowing,* 'u'ina ka pu'u. **2.** *Bird.* Manu 'io'io, kualo.

swallow-tailed coat. Kuka puapua.

swamp. 1. *Marsh.* Pohō, naele. *Also:* kele, 'olokele, ki'o lepo, 'alē, nāpele, nenelu. *Swampy foul odor,* pilo. **2.** *Founder.* Pihō, pihōpihō, piholo.

swan. Nokekula.

swap. Kuapo. *See* **trade.**

swarm. Huhui, huihui, mumulu. *Also:* kauluwela, ne'e-papa, nunu'a, pōnalo, pīkokoi, muhu, mumuhu, mī-noinoi, mōnoinoi. *Swarm of bees (Lunk. 14:08),* po'e nalo meli.

swarthy. Hāuli, hāuliuli.

swathe. Wahī, nunu.

sway. Kāhulihuli, luliluli, māewa. *Also:* 'akū'akū, ewa, āewa, akalewa, pōlewa, malewa, ho'olewa, ha'anapu, ha'i, ho'ohihina, holu, ho'oholu, ho'oluli, ho'oluliluli, holunape, nape, ka'alele, kaiue, kiawe, kulana, kū-lanalana, kūlewa, ho'okalahē, luli, 'āluli, kāluli, ho'o-kāluli, laumāewa, luaiele, naluli, naue, ho'onaue, mī-nole, ninipo, nolu pē, puni wale, oioi, ue, 'ukē, 'u'upekupeku, kohai.

swear. 1. *Vow.* Ho'ohiki. *(See* **manō***).* **2.** *See* **curse.** *Also:* kuea *(Eng.). Gram. 12. No swearwords existed other than exclamations and insults, and from English:* kanapapiki *(son of a bitch),* Kokami *(God damn),* and kokahele iā Paka *(go to hell, you bugger).*

sweat. Hou; ho'opuluea *(offensive).*

sweatband. Pale hou.

sweat bath. Imu loa, umu loa, pūholo. *Cf.* **steam bath.**

sweater. Kueka.

Swede, Sweden, Swedish. Kuekena, Suedena.

sweep. Pūlumi, kāhili; hio, kālu'u, puhohō *(as the wind);* kāhela, kūhela *(as waves).*

sweet. Momona, mona, kuhikuhi, mōkuhikuhi; hone, nahenahe, polinahe *(as music);* laua'e, henoheno *(as a lover);* onaona *(as eyes or disposition);* 'a'ala, hone, 'ala, nae, anuhea, onaona *(as fragrance).*

sweet basil. Kī'a'ala, kīpaoa.

sweet calamus, sweet cane. 'Ohe 'ala.

sweeten. Ho'omomona.

sweetheart. Ipo. *Also:* aloha, kāne, huapala, wai puna,

---

hoa 'inau, 'ano'i pua. *See sayings,* **kāī, maka lena 2, pūnua, uhu 1, endearing, flower.** *In songs, a sweet-heart may be likened to flowers* (pua); *to any particular flower (as* 'awapuhi, 'ilima, kalaunu, kiele, kukui, laniuma, lehua, maile, mamo, melia, pīkake); *buds* (liko); *leis; fragrance* ('ala, 'a'ala, onaona); *ferns* (laua'e, palai); *birds* ('i'iwi, ka'upu, manu, 'ō'ō, pū-nua); *fish* (kole, kūmū, manō, ulua); *and spring water* (wai puna). *Gone to pull in an ulua fish,* aia i ka huki ulua *(a man).*

sweetheart vine. Huapala.

sweet pea. Pī wai anuhea, pī anuhea.

sweet pepper. Nīoi pūha'uha'u, nīoi pū'alu'alu, nīoi 'alu'alu.

sweet potato. 'Uala *(for various kinds, see Haw.-Eng. entry and entries that follow it). Sweet-potato vine or slip,* lau. *Planted sweet-potato vine,* lau kanu. *Collect-ed sweet-potato vines,* puku kālina. *Sweet-potato sprouts,* hāpu'upu'u, hā'upu'upu, hā'apu'apu, hā-wa'e, hāwa'ewa'e. *Root connecting sweet potato to vine,* 'āni'uni'u. *To hill up sweet potatoes,* pu'e 'uala, kaiue. *Small sweet potato removed in thinning a hill,* hahae. *Sweet potato from branch vine,* lālā, ālalā. *Sweet potato grown on old vines,* pu'ukōlea. *First har-vest,* kauaiki. *To grow a second crop,* kā'io'io. *Volun-teer sweet potato,* pahulu. *Small, poor sweet potato,* au. *Dried sweet potato,* 'ao. *Broken fragments,* kū'ō'ō, pā'ō'ō. *Method of preparing sweet potatoes,* kūpu'u. *Sweet-potato pudding,* piele. *Cooked and fermented sweet potato,* pa'i 'uala, poi 'uala, 'ī'īaao. *Cooked sweet-potato leaves,* palula. *Sweet-potato beer,* 'uala 'awa'awa.

SWEET POTATOES IN ADDITION TO 'uala: 'ae'ahauka'e, 'āpō, 'aumakiki, 'awapuhi, 'ele'ele, hā'ae, hā'elelepo, hāloa, hālonaipu, hamo, hā'ulelani, hāwai, hē'ī, hekili, hi'iaka, hilo, hinapū, hōkeo, hōlei, hōlule, ho'ohamo, ho'omanamana, ho'omanana, ho'omau, hualani, hua-moa, hua'ono, ka'eumu, kahalui, kakaka, kake, kā-konakona, kala, kala ke'oke'o, kala poni, kalia, kalika, kalika lau ke'oke'o, kalika 'ula'ula, kalikole-hua, kamalino, kāmau, kāne'ohe, kāpanekeoe, kau-aheahe, kāwao, kawelo, kawelo kupa, keaumahina, keoe, kihe, kihi, kihikihi, kihi lau nui, ki'ikekekē, kī-papa, kipawale, koa'e, koali, kokoko'ohā (koko'ohā), koko-o-Keawe, kome'ula'ula, konapākeke, ko'okā, ku'ipopo, kūpala, la'ela'e, lahaina, lahalile, la'ila'i, la'i-o-Kona, laloloa, lāna'i, lapa, laumanamana, lau'u-la'ula, lehelehenui, līhau, lihilihi, likolehua, limawīwī, mahiki, mahina, mahinakēhau, ma'ihu'i ke'oke'o, ma'ihu'i 'ula'ula, mā'i'o, maka, māka'a, maka kila, maka koali, maka nui, manamana, manini, maoli, maui, moe'āhua, mōhihi, moi, mokiawe, mōlina, moloka'i, nakulehu, nanani 'ele'ele, nanani ke'oke'o, nā'ū, nauewai, ne'ene'e, nenewai, nihopopo, nukukau, nukulehu, 'ohe'ohe, 'okilipi, 'ōkoholā, 'ōmealani, 'ōnohinohi, pa'a, pa'apa'a'ina, pa'auhau, pā'ele (nika), pā'ele hili mānoanoa, paioea, pākeke, pala, palakaia, pala mahiki, palani, palikea, pānini, pani'ole, pāpa'akoali, pā'ū-o-Hi'iaka, pā'ū'ū, pehu, pia, piapia, pilimai, poe, pōhina, pōhuehue, poni, pū, puakawaihae, pulakamaka, pūnana, pu'u, uahi-a-Pele, unahiuhu, waianiani, wailua, waipalupalu, wehiwa.

sweet-toned. Pu'ukani, nahenahe.

sweet-voiced. Pu'ukani, 'ale'a.

sweet william. Ponimō'ī li'ili'i.

swell. 1. *See* **swelling.** **2.** *Wave.* 'Ōhū, 'ōhuku. *Also:* āhua, 'aiō, 'ako'ako, 'aui, ha'anopu, ho'ohua, kua-haka, kūhela, nu'a, ōnū, 'ōpu'u, ōpū.

swellfish. 'O'opu hue.

swelling. Pehu, hū. *Also:* ōnū, 'ōhū, hūalakē, lalahū, kāla'e, me'ome'o, 'ōhao, pēheu, polohuku, ponohuku, 'u'ulukai; 'anako'i *(lymph gland);* 'ea kūka'a *(disease);* po'ohū *(as on the head);* 'eho *(under the arm or be-tween the legs);* awaihiki, auko'i, 'auwaihiki, wawai, 'ēwai, haha'i, hauhauko'i *(in the groin);* ho'ohū, kū-ka'a; ho'olapa *(as a blister);* kālunu *(as with moisture);*

kēkewe (as with dropsy): nopu, nunu, lunu, puha'u, kūhela, pu'upu'u, hakē, hānupa, hānupanupa, ki'ima-nana, kōlikoliko, nepu, pele, 'ōpele, makapehu, pehu, 'ūpehupehu; ho'opehupehu (as a cloud); pōhuku, nupa, nupanupa, lōnū, ponaha. *Rare:* kualakai, mana-na, nanana, 'oai, pā'ili, hakakai, kūhākakai, pahāha. *Swelling tonsils,* pu'u 'ōkohekohe. *Swelling with pride or conceit,* pehu.

swift. 'Āwīwī, 'āwiki, wiki, wikiwiki, kikī, māmā. *Also:* ho'olehua, kāholo, kulu, lauhulu, palamimo (pala-mio), niau. *Swift runner,* kūkini koke. *Swift disappear-ance or movement,* miona. *To do swiftly,* kikī. *To move swiftly,* mio, miomio.

swim. 'Au, 'aukai; panau (as a lobster). See **stroke.** *Go swimming,* 'au, 'aukai; hō'au. *Swim evenly or abreast,* 'au like. *To teach or learn to swim,* 'au like. *Swim with a drowning person,* hō'au. *Swim like a fish,* holo ā i'a. *Swim with paddling motions, as in learning,* manahalo halo ā 'ike i ke 'au. *Paddle until you know how to swim, e mana-(rare).*

swindle. 'Āpuka.

swine. Pua'a.

swing. Lele, lele koali, lewa, kālewa. *Also:* 'ōlewa, mā-ewa, ma'alewa; pūlewa (as a ship at anchor): koali, ku'uwelu, 'ai'aiele, ho'oleilei, huleilua; 'ukē (pendu-lously): — the arms, kā, kāia; — and hit, 'ukē (pendu-back and forth, kaiue, ho'ohilala, kuekuene, ha'ukē. 'ukē. *Rare:* pūka'ika'i, mākoiele. *Swing a rope (as for jumping),* kā i ke kaula. *To ride in a swing,* lele koali, lelepinao. *Kind of swinging game,* lele pīna'i.

swipes. 'Uwī'uwī, kuaipa.

swirl. Ho'owiliwili, ho'oheheo; hē (as of a whip); halalē (as full skirt); wai au.

swish. Heheo, ho'oheheo; pūheheo, pōheheo (as the sea); mūmū (as water in the mouth); halalē (as skyrockets).

swiss cloth. Makalena pu'u (dotted); 'ulāli'i (dotted with red).

switch. 1. *Stick.* Lā'au hili, 'uwī'uwī. 2. *Beat.* Hahau, hau, uhau, hili, 'uwī'uwī, kāhili. 3. *Wig.* 'Akī, lauoho ku'i, ohoku'i.

Switzerland, Swiss. Kuikilana, Suizilana.

swivel. Poka'a.

swivel adze. Kūpā.

swivel chair. Noho poka'a.

swivel rope. Kaula kī.

swollen. See **swell.**

swoop. Māpu, māpumāpu; kaha (as a kite). *The hawk that flies swooping,* 'o ka 'io lele māpumāpu.

sword. Pahi kaua. *Flaming sword (Biblical),* pahi waka-waka.

sword fern. Kupukupu, 'ōkupukupu.

swordfish. A'u; a'u kū (broadbill); a'ua'u (young stage).

sycamine. Kukamino.

sycamore. Kukomolea.

Sydney. Kikinē.

syllable. Leo, hakina 'ōlelo, hopuna'ōlelo.

symbol. Hō'ailona.

sympathy. Aloha, aloha menemene.

symptom. 'Ōuli, 'ōuli hiki, ha'awina.

synagogue. Hale hālāwai.

synonym. Hua 'ōlelo like 'ole me ka mana'o ho'okahi, ho'okahi nō 'ano.

synonymous. Ho'okahi nō 'ano.

synopsis. See **summary.**

syntax. Huipa'a.

syphilis. Kaokao, waikūlono 'ako'ako'a. See **ihu 'ole.** *venereal disease. Secondary syphilis,* puhi kaokao.

Syracuse. Kulakuke, Surakuse.

syringe. Hano, 'āpī. *To use a syringe,* hano.

system. Ho'onohonoho 'ana, kahua. *Solar system,* ke kanua o nā hōkū.

T

table... ne'e... 'aina.

table... Table...

papa helu...

tableau. U...

tablecloth. U...

table mat. Mo...

tablet. Kālana... (pill); papa pōh... mana'o.

taboo. Kapu, pāpā... 'ānoho, kapu moe... kua'a, kuapala, kua... pu'ukoāmaka, kua... mau'u mae. *Taboo pla-*ma, humu, paehumu, ka... ka'ani'au. *Taboo mark,* pūlo'ulo'u, pahu kapu, pāh... *Taboo ceremony,* kauila... hu'a kapu. *Taboo-surrounde-*kuapola, ka'apola; pō kūloa... taboo, hō'auwae. *Without obser-*lay a taboo, ho'okapu, ho'olāh... move a taboo, ho'onoa, ho'olāh... stretch the taboo cord, kākai. *To b-*break. Taboo on approaching the... kua'a, kua liholiho, kua kapu, kua...

hono-i-ka-pa'a.

tabret. Pahu kani.

tache. Lou.

tacit. 'Ekemu 'ole.

taciturn. Mumule, molu, koe'a, 'ekemu. cal. 1. *Small nail.* Kui kākia. *To tack.* 2.

tack. 1. *Seize.* Pūnini.

tackle. 1. *Seize.* Lawelawe lima, lālau lima, lālau. 2. paratus. Hoa wa'a (canoe rigging). *Fishing tackle,* lawai'a.

Tacoma. Kakoma, Takoma.

tact. No'ono'o pono i ka mea e 'ōlelo ai.

tactless. Kama'ilio no'ono'o 'ole, pi'oā'ea.

taffeta. Kilika nehe, nehe, waili'ulā.

taffrail. Pale kai.

tag. 1. *Game.* 'Io, pio. 2. *Symbol.* Hō'ailona; mekala (as of a dog). 3. *Follow.* Hahai mahope.

Tahiti. Kahiki; Polapola, Borabora.

Tahitian. Kahiki, kanaka Kahiki, Polapola.

tail. 1. *End piece.* Huelo (of fish, shrimp, lobster); hi'u (of fish); pewa (of animal); hi'u (of a bird); pola, kākaiāpola (of a malo). *Part of fishtail above and below the cleft,* epa-epa. *Taillike,* hueloelo. *At the tail end,* huelo māewa, huehuelo. *To spread wing or tail feathers,* ka'apeha. *Consumed head, consumed tail,* pau po'o, pau hi'u (of complete destruction). 2. *To follow secretly.* Hahai malū.

tailfish. Lai, palailai.

tailor. Kela, kela lole.

tailorbird. Manu humuhumu.

"tails." Pupua moa.

tainted. Hauna, 'ōnuhenuhe.

ho'ola. *Tapa garments:* pā'ū, malo, kīkepa, kīhei, ha... 'ina, palelei. *Decorated outer tapa sheet,* kilohana. *In-ner layers of sleeping tapa,* iho. *Tapa bed coveri-*ku'inakapa, kapa ku'ina. *Pile of tapa,* hu'a kapa... *To cut tapa fringe,* palalei. *Tapa beater,* i'e kuku, i'e k... ho'oki, 'ole, pepehi, hohoa, hohoa, uananal... *Tapa beater part,* mole hālu'a. *Grooved boar-*making ribbed tapa, 'ohe kāpala, lā'au kāpalapal... nao. *Tapa stamp,* 'ohe kāpala, papa hole. *Ridges in tapa h-*ki. *Tapa dye,* wai 'ele. *Tapa ball of cord to ca-*welu ahi. *House for beating tapa,* kua. *Tapa s-*lauhuki. *Tapa holder,* hō'ihi. *Tapa bast or p-*pulu. *Tapa fragment hung as taboo sign,* we... used for tapa, wauke, māmaki, 'oloa, ma... *To beat tapa,* kuku, ho'omo'omo'o. *To pa-*lani. *To dry and bleach tapa,* ki'olena. *To-*kākau. *To unite portions of tapa by beatin-*plants used to scent tapa, see **perfume.**

KINDS OF TAPA (alternate names are in... 'a'ahu ali'i, 'aekai-mokiha, 'ae-o-kaha-l... pālau-anahu), 'ahapi'i, ahunāli'i, aka-'a'ih... 'akaha-ka-na'i, 'ākala, 'āpikipiki, 'ele'ele, 'eleul... alo, 'ape'ula, 'āpikipiki, hili, hōle... manawa, halakea, hamo'ula, hili, hōle... la, hūlili, hunakāha'i, i'e-ioio-kaha-loa... kalukalu, kapa-aho, kelewai, kikama,... wa'a, kōpili, kuamū, kua'ula, kū'ou... huna, mālolo, mālua'ula, maolua,... lola, ninikea, 'oloa, olomea, 'ōma'o... holo-wai-o-La'a, pa'iua, pa'i'ula, pakē, pa'i kuku... pa'i-niu, pa'iua, pa'i'ula, pehu-a-koa,... palūpalū, pa'ūpa'ū, pehu-a-koa, puakai, p... pilipuka, pipi, po'ipū, puakai, pūnana, pūna... niu, puela, pūlo'u, pūnana, pūnana, pu'u... pu'uko'a, pu'ukohukohu, pu'u... u'au'a, 'ula'ula, ulu, wai'ele, w... 'opu, wai-palupalu.

TAPA DESIGNS OR PATTERNS:... 'āpi'i, 'ekaha-loa, hā'ao (na... Haw.-Eng. entry and entries... (hā'uka'uka, hā'uke), ho'o... puhi, kapua'i-koloa, ko'eau... also quilts), la'i-o-Kona,... niu, lei-hala, lelepe, lū... quilts), na'ena'e, nao (see... that follow it), niho-li'i... lupalupa, 'ohu'ohu, o... pua-hala (also a quilt des... try and entries that foll... Eng. entry and entries...

PLANTS USED FOR TA... ma'u (red), hōlei (yell... (black, red), ma'o (g... (red, yellow), 'ōlena... (pale blue).

tape. Leki. *Bias tap-*ho'okani. *Tape me-*

tapering. Olomio, 'u... 'io'io, 'ōmilo, 'ūhini... fine point, 'ūhini...

tapioca. Kapioka....

tapping sound. K...

taproot. Mole, m...

tar. Kā, kēpau,...

tarantula. Kala...

tardy. Lohi,...

tares. Kīkān...

target. Mā... shootin...

tariff. K...

taro. h...

tapa. Kapa. See **anvi**... 155–157. *Piece of tap.*

taster. Hamuʻili.
tasty. ʻOno. *Also:* miko, kuhikuhi, mokae, mōkaekae; kaekae *(as a sweet potato);* lololo *(rare).*
tattered. Weluwelu, peʻa.
tatting. Lihilihi hana lima.
tattle. Holoholoʻōlelo. *Also:* waha nui, pekapeka, ʻioʻiolepo, lawe ʻōlelo, ili ʻōlelo, ʻama, ʻahiʻahi.
tattler. ʻŪlili. *A tattler running on the beach, struck by a big sea, falls,* he ʻūlili holoholo kahakai, pā i ke kai nui, hina *(of weaklings).*
tattoo. Kākau, kākau kaha; — *with dots and spots,* kiko, kikiko, — *solid black without design,* pāʻele; pāʻelekūlani *(one side only);* uhi, kākau uhi. *Long stripe tattoo,* alaniho. *Tattoo brand on the forehead of a* kauā, *or on the forehead of the seducer of a high chief's wife,* hikoni. *Tattooed eyelid, as a humiliating sign of a warrior's defeat,* maka uhi. *Tattooing ink,* paʻu. *Bone tattooing needle,* mōlī. *Straight line in tattoo pattern,* mōlī, mōlina. *To tattoo with* mōlī *needle,* molimolī.
taught. Aʻo ʻia, ua aʻo. *See* **teach.**
taunt. Hoʻouluulu, hoʻopāpā, kūʻē akena, ʻōlelokīkē. *Anciently, stylized taunts and boasts preceded combat; see* **boast, ripe, spider.**
taut. Māloʻeloʻe.
tavern. Hale inu lama.
tax. ʻAuhau *(for various kinds, see* **ʻauhau***);* hoʻokupu, uku, hoʻouku. *Gift or tax given to a chief at the birth of a child,* pālala. *Tax collector,* luna ʻauhau, luna ʻohi kālā ʻauhau. *Tax building,* hale ʻauhau.
taxable. Kū i ka ʻauhau.
taxi. Kaʻa ʻōhua, kaʻa hoʻolimalima.
tea. Kī, wai kī. *Tea leaf,* lau kī. *Tea tree or shrub (tea family),* ānini, wānini. *Plants used for tea,* nehe, kīnehe, koʻokoʻolau.
teach. Aʻo. *Also:* kula, paka, kuhikuhi.
teacher. Kumu, kumu aʻo. *See* **assistant teacher** *and saying,* **reflect.** *School teacher,* kumu kula. *Itinerant teacher,* aʻo hele. *Substitute teacher,* kōkua kumu, kumu pani hakahaka, hope kumu. *Teachers' training school,* kula kumu, kula aʻo kumu. *My teacher,* kaʻu kumu.
teaching. Aʻo, kumu aʻo. *Innermost teacning,* aʻo loko.
teacup. Kīʻaha kī.
teahouse. Hale inu kī.
teakettle. Kikila kī.
team. 1. *Group.* Hui, ʻaoʻao. 2. *Draft animals.* Paʻa, pūkolo.
teapot. Ipu kī, kikila kī.
tear. 1. *Weeping.* Waimaka; pūkai *(rare).* See **Hilo** *(Eng.-Haw.).* *Tear duct,* luaʻuhane. *In poetry, rain may signify tears. Tears of heaven,* nā waimaka o ka lani *(of showers at a funeral: gods wept).* 2. *Sunder.* Hae, nahae, haehae. *Also:* hahae, uhae, haena, hoʻopōhae, nāhaehae, mahae, māhaehae, hoʻōlepe, ʻōlepe, ʻāwelu, hoʻokepa, ʻai kepa; kīhae *(as leaves);* — *off,* ihi. *See* **torn.** 3. *To run.* Holo pupule, holo ʻāwīwī.
tearful. Hāloʻiloʻi, halahalawai.
tease. Hoʻohenehene, hoʻohene. *Also:* henehene, ʻuhene, hoʻohaehae, ahahana, hoʻohene, hauwene, hoʻohauwene, hoʻohae, hone, meʻo, hoʻohana, hana wale, wahapaʻa, hoʻomaʻau, kauloloa, none. *Rare:* pūhene, honole, hoʻouhuhī. *Vexed by teasing,* nāulu. *To tease for something,* nē, hoʻonē.
teashop. Hale inu kī.
teaspoon. Puna kī.
teat. Ū, maka.
technical. Loea, noʻeau. *Technical knowledge,* ʻike loea.
technique. Loea, noʻeau.
tedious. Luhi, kua nui, hoʻokuanui, none, nohili, paʻu.
teeming. Pupupu, paʻapū.
teeter. ʻUʻupekupeku. *See* **seesaw.**
teeth. Niho. *See* **tooth.**
teethe. Puka ka niho.
teetotaler. Hōʻole lama.
telegram. Kelekalama.
telegraph. Kelekalapa.

telephone. Kelepona. *To telephone,* kelepona, kāhea ma ke kelepona. *Telephone operator,* kikowaena. *Telephone book,* puke kelepona. *The telephone is busy,* paʻa ke kelepona.
telescope. ʻOhe nānā, aniani hoʻonui ʻike.
tell. Haʻi, haʻina, hōʻike, ʻōlelo. *To tell tales,* haʻi moʻolelo, kole, pālau, pākaʻa; hoʻoholo ʻōlelo, pekapeka *(gossip). To tell of the times,* haʻi manawa. *To tell woes,* ʻōhumuhumu. *To tell evil,* holehole *(fig.). To tell of ancestors,* haʻi kupuna.
teller. Helu. *Bank teller,* luna helu kālā. *Election teller,* helu pāloka (balota).
temper. Naʻau, ʻano o ka naʻau. *See* **piʻi 1, 2, ashes, control.** *Good temper,* ʻoluʻolu ka naʻau. *Bad temper,* huhū wale, ʻaʻaka, lelepī, pīʻena, pīkananā, ʻainiha, ʻōkaikai, ʻawaʻawa, hoahoa, pūkalakī. *Short temper,* pōkole ka naʻau, lele koke, puhipuhi ahi. *To lose one's temper,* piʻi ka huhū, kū ka ʻehu, piʻi ke kai, lelepī.
temperance. Pākiko. *Temperance songs:* mele kinai ʻona, mele kinai rama, mele hōʻole lama, mele hōʻole wai ʻona. *Temperance union,* ʻahahui hōʻole wai ʻona. *Temperance society,* pūʻali inu wai.
temperature. Anu, wela, welawela, ka wela a me ke anu. *To take temperature,* ana piwa.
tempest. *See* **storm.**
temple. 1. *Edifice.* Luakini. *See* **heiau.** 2. *Part of head.* Maha. *Bald temple,* hiʻaloa. *Temple muscle,* ʻiʻo maha. *Back of the temple,* kua maha. *Soft spot in temple,* ʻapi.
tempo marker. Ana manawa *(music).*
temporal suture. Hoai maha.
temporary. Kūikawā, no ka manawa pōkole, manawa; pā *(rare). Temporary house or shelter,* hale pupupu, kāmala.
tempt. Hoʻowalewale, hoʻāʻo, weʻa, weʻaweʻa.
temptation, tempter. Hoʻowalewale.
ten. ʻUmi. *Ten times, tenfold, by tens, to divide by tens,* pāʻumi. *Ten days,* anahulu. *See* **tens.**
tenacious. Pipili, pili paʻa. *Also:* aweawe, ʻālikalika, lina.
tenant. Hoaʻāina, mea hoʻolimalima, mea hoʻolimalima hale, lōpā.
tend. Mālama, lawelawe; kahu *(an oven).*
tendency. ʻAno.
tender. 1. *Not tough.* Palupalu. *Also:* ʻūpalu, huki, mahāha, pūloku. *Tender-eyed,* maka wai, maka onaona. *Tender feet,* manene ka wāwae. *Tender vegetables,* lāʻau palupalu. 2. *To offer.* Hāʻawi. 3. *Currency.* Kālā. *Legal tender,* kālā ma ke kānāwai. 4. *Ship.* Moku lawelawe.
tenderloin. ʻIʻoliu; uhao *(rare).*
tendon. Aʻahuki; *small —,* aʻa.
tendril. ʻUmiʻumi, ʻōkaʻi.
tenfold. Pāʻumi.
Tennessee. Kenekī, Tenesi.
tennis. Kenika.
tennis court. Kahua kenika, kahua kinipōpō.
tennis racket. Lāʻau paʻi kinipōpō.
tenon. Komo, ule, home, kumu, maʻi.
tenor. Leo kāne kiʻekiʻe.
ten-pounder. *See* **milkfish.**
tens. Kana. *Count by tens,* helu pāʻumi.
tense. 1. *Taut.* ʻIhaʻiha, liolio; paʻapū o loko *(repressed).* 2. *Grammar.* Wā *(cf. Gram. 5.2, 5.3). Present tense,* wā e hiki mai ana. *Future tense,* wā e hiki mai ana. *Past tense,* wā i hala.
tent. Hale lole, hale peʻa. *Also:* halelewa, uhi, pūʻoʻa.
tentacle. ʻAwe. *Tentacles,* ʻaweʻawe. *Thin end of octopus tentacles,* pilipili heʻe.
tenth. ʻUmi. *Tenth part, one tenth,* hapaʻumi.
tentmakers. Poʻe humuhumu hale lole.
tenure. Kuleana.
tepid. Mūhea, heahea. *Tepid water,* wai anuhea.
teredo. Mū wāwahi waʻa.
term. 1. *Period of time.* Kau, mahele manawa, wā. *Office term,* noho ʻana. 2. *Expression.* Inoa, ʻōlelo, hua

'ōlelo. *Terms of a fraction,* palena. *To term,* kapa. *See* **terms.**
terminal. Hale ho'olulu. *Air terminal,* hale ho'olulu mokulele. *Bus terminal,* hale ho'olulu ka'a. *Train terminal,* hale ho'olulu ka'aahi. *Terminal disease,* ma'i make.
terminate. Ho'opau, ho'ōki.
terminated. Pau. *Completely terminated,* pau pono.
terminus. Hopena alahao *(railroad).*
termite. Naonao lele, huhu.
terms. Nā mea 'aelike *(conditions). See* **term.**
tern. Noio, 'eki'eki *(Hawaiian);* kenola, tenora. *Noddy tern,* noio kōhā. *Gray-backed tern (bridled, spectacled, or gray wide-awake tern),* pākalakala, kala. *Sooty tern,* 'ewa'ewa. *Sea tern,* hoi'a *(Ni'ihau). White or fairy tern,* manu-o-Kū. *The tern that treads the billows of the distant sea,* he noio 'a'e 'ale no ke kai loa *(in admiration of a wise person).*
terrace. Lānai kaupoko 'ole, 'anu'u, kaulu 'anu'u, pali kāmoe. *Level terrace,* kīpapa. *Irrigated terrace,* lo'i.
terra firma. Kahua pa'a.
terrible. Weliweli.
terrify. Ho'oweli, ho'oweliweli, ho'omaka'u. *Also:* hō-'upu'upu, ho'omā'e'ele.
territorial. Kelikoli.
territory. Kelikoli, panalā'au. *Territory of Hawai'i,* Panalā'au o Hawai'i.
terror. Weli, weliweli, 'e'ehia.
terrorist. Kanaka ho'omake huna.
terror-stricken. Kau ka weli, 'e'ehia, kū i ka weli.
test. Hō'ike. *To test,* hō'ike, ho'ā'o, hailona, ho'opā.
testament. Kauoha. *Last will and testament,* palapala kauoha, palapala ho'oilina. *Old Testament,* Kauoha Kahiko. *New Testament,* Kauoha Hou.
testicles. Hua, huahua, kowaū. *See* **scrotum.** *Broken testicles,* hua pēpē 'ia.
testify. Hō'ike, ha'i mana'o.
testimony. Hō'ike, 'ōlelo hō'ike.
tether. Kūkulu, ho'opa'a, mūki'i, hīki'i, nāki'i, nīki'i.
Texas. Kekeka, Teseta.
text. Po'o'ōlelo, kumumana'o.
textbook. Puke a'o.
textile. Mea ulana 'ia. *Plaited ti-leaf textile,* kapa lau'ī.
Thames. Kameka, Tamesa.
than. *No Hawaiian term. This is bigger than that,* nui kēia mamua o kēlā.
thank. Mahalo, ho'omaika'i. *Thanks,* mahalo. *To give thanks,* ho'omaika'i, mililani.
thankful. Ho'omaika'i, mahalo nui. *See* **grateful.**
Thanksgiving Day. Lā Ho'omaika'i. *Also:* Lā Ho'ālohaloha, Lā 'Ai Pelehū.
that. Kēlā, lā *(far);* kēnā, nā *(near the person addressed); cf. Gram. 8.3);* ia, ua . . . lā. *That way, in that way,* pēlā. *Is that so?* Pēlā anei? *Is that how? So that's it! Isn't it?* Pēlā, 'ea? *That's right,* pēlā 'i'o nō, 'oia, 'a 'oia, 'oia nō. *That's so, that's it,* pēlā nō. *That very day,* o ia lā ho'okahi nō.
thatch. Ako, pili; ka'a lau niu *(coconut-leaf);* lolelau. *Thatch needle,* 'ōhi'u. *Thatch purlin,* 'aho, 'a'aho, lolo, lolo 'iole. *Thatch purlin support,* 'ahopi'o kuahui. *Thatch above a door,* piko. *To cut this thatch,* 'oki i ka piko, mō ka piko. *To thatch,* ako, kaupoku, 'ōhi'u, pa'i. *To thatch the inside of the house,* kā lau. *To tie a thatch purlin to roof frame,* ho'opa'a.
the. Ka, ke *(singular);* nā *(plural), but see Gram. 10.2. Rare:* nāhi.
theater. Keaka. *Theater building,* hale keaka. *To act in the theater,* hana keaka.
theatrical. Keaka.
Thebes. Kepeka, Tebesa.
theft. 'Aihue; hue *(rare).*
their. 1. *Singular possessed object, dual.* Kō lāua *(o-class);* kā lāua *(a-class).* 2. *Singular possessed object, plural.* Kō lākou *(o-class);* kā lākou *(a-class).* 3. *Plural possessed objects, dual.* O lāua *(o-class);* a lāua *(a-class).* 4. *Plural possessed objects, plural.* O lākou *(o-*

class); a lākou *(a-class). For other uses of k-less (zero-type) possessives, see Gram. 9.6.3.*
theirs. No lāua, no lākou, na lāua, na lākou. *See* **their.**
them. Iā lāua *(dual),* iā lākou *(plural).*
theme. Po'omana'o; — *of a song,* puana.
themselves. Lāua iho, lāua pono'ī *(dual);* lākou iho, lākou pono'ī *(plural).*
then. Ā laila, ia wā, ia manawa, ia manawa nō, ā, eia kā, inā. *The chief then came,* ā laila, hele mai ke ali'i; hele maila ke ali'i.
thence. Mai laila, mai laila aku, no laila aku.
theological seminary. Kula kahuna pule.
theorem. Mana'oha'i.
theorist. Ho'ākamai.
theory. Mana'o, kumumana'o.
therapy. Ho'oponopono *(family).*
there. Laila, malaila, i laila *(general);* lā, ala, maila *(not specific);* 'ō, ma'ō, i 'ō *(far);* ai. *There!* Aia lā! *There it is,* aia. *See there!* Aia ho'i! *There now!* Aia kā! *There, I told you so!* Aia lā! *To be there,* ai laila, aia i laila. *Down there,* ai lalo, aia i lalo. *Up there,* ai luna, aia i luna. *You, there!* Eia ala!
thereabouts. Ma ia mau wahi.
thereby. Pēlā nō, no ka mea.
therefore. No laila, no ia mea.
thermometer. Kelemomeka, ana wela, mea ana wela, ana pīwa.
these. Kēia mau; ua . . . nei. *These books,* kēia mau puke.
thesis. 1. *Dissertation.* Mea e kākau 'ia no he kekele ki'eki'e. 2. *See* **theme.**
they. Lāua *(dual),* lākou *(plural),* mea mā.
thick. Mānoanoa, pepe'ekue, pe'ekue; kūpū *(of liquids). Also:* mānoa, mano, maho'a, mākolu, mākū, honu pe'ekue, pāno'uno'u, hānu'u, nu'a, halu'a, mākuakua, kūpuku, pupupu, popoki, polo, pe'e; 'a'aki *(fig.);* pa'apū *(as a crowd);* hākuma, mākuma *(as clouds);* mākolukolu *(as a board). Thick-growing,* nu'a, papa, nūpolupolu, nūponuponu, pō.
thicken. Ho'omānoa, kuhua; ho'okūpū, ho'omākū *(as cream).*
thicket. Ōpū nāhelehele, hihia, lā'au, lā'au kukū, puo'a. *Tangled thicket,* hihipe'a. *See* **clump.** *The dense thicket of the forest,* ka hihia pa'a o ka nahele.
thickset. Poupou, no'u.
thief. 'Aihue. *Rare:* molulo, mōlulolulo, moluna, lima 'āpā. *See* **ratlike,** *and sayings,* '**ā 5, 'iwa 1, piko pau 'iole, po'i 4.**
thigh. 'Ūhā. *Inner side of thighs,* hene 'ūhā. *Hollow of thigh,* hena.
thighbone. Iwi hilo. *Throbbing in the thighbone,* konikoni lua i ka iwi hilo *(thrilled to the very depths).*
thimble. Komo, komo humuhumu; komo lima *(rare).*
thimbleberries. 'Ākala.
thin. 1. *As the human torso.* Wīwī, hakahaka; emi *(to have lost weight);* ho'owīwī, hōki'i, ho'okilo, hōmali, hōmale; māilo, māio *(tubercular). Also:* hiwi, hiwihiwi; pili ke kua me ke alo *(see kua),* kekē, nāeheehe, lolopaioea, lolopaioa, paioa, paioea, leioa, lolio, loio, puaki'i, hāla'ola'o, lala, 'ōlala, 'ukiki, pānauea, 'o'olu, 'aka'aka'a, kawane, hīnawe, 'amopu'u, pīlahi, kakakī, holowī, mālalaioa, kōlīlā, homa, haho. 2. *As cloth, paper.* Lahi, lahilahi, nahi, nahinahi, lau lahilahi, lālahi, ho'olahi, makae'e, nanahe. 3. *Wispy, threadlike.* Puawe, maukoli 2, awe, 'ae'ae, ma'awe, hīnawenawe, āewa, wele, welehia, nāwele, namauahi, hīnau, puināwele, hīnale, puela, koloau. 4. *As poi, watery.* Wali, waliwali, wawali, kele, kakale, ho'okalekale. 5. *Spindly.* Pīoeoe, līlā. 6. *Ridged.* Lānihinihi.
thing. Mea.
think. Mana'o, no'ono'o. *Also:* hō'opu'opu, piolo, kākepakepa; — *deeply,* ho'okuano'o, lololo; — *with affection,* hali'a aloha, ho'omana'o aloha, nēnē. *See* **nalu, thought.** *I think,* mana'o au, ku'u mana'o. *To think much,* kau nui ka mana'o.
thinker. Po'o no'o, po'o no'ono'o; lelehua *(rare).*

third. Hapakolu, kolu. *Two thirds,* 'elua hapakolu. *Third mate on a ship,* kolomeki.
thirst. Make wai. *See saying,* burn.
thirsty. Make wai, 'ono wai, 'a'aka, hae i ka wai.
thirteen, thirteenth. 'Umi kūmākolu, 'umi kumamākolu.
thirtieth, thirty. Kanakolu.
thirty-eight. Kanakolu kūmāwalu, kanakolu kumamāwalu.
thirty-five. Kanakolu kūmālima, kanakolu kumamālima.
thirty-four. Kanakolu kūmāhā, kanakolu kumamāhā.
thirty-nine. Kanakolu kūmāiwa, kanakolu kumamāiwa.
thirty-one. Kanakolu kūmākahi, kanakolu kumamākahi.
thirty-seven. Kanakolu kūmāhiku, kanakolu kumamāhiku.
thirty-six. Kanakolu kūmāono, kanakolu kumamāono.
thirty-three. Kanakolu kūmākolu, kanakolu kumamākolu.
thirty-two. Kanakolu kūmālua, kanakolu kumamālua.
this. Kēia, ia, 'oia, nei, neia, ua . . . nei. *This way, like this,* penei. *This and that,* kēlā me kēia.
thistle. Puakala, pualele.
Thomas Square. Kamaki Kuea.
thong. Hāwele, kaula, lī, aho.
thorn. Kukū, 'oi'oi, kākala; kōkala *(as on pandanus leaf).* *Thorn hedge,* pā lā'au 'oi'oi.
thorny. Kukū, wanawana, 'oi'oi, kākala, kākalaioa, kalakala; pōniho *(as cactus).* *Thorny tree,* lā'au kukū, lā'au 'o'oi.
thorough. Pau pono, piha pono. *Also:* le'a, maiau. *A thorough talk,* ho'onoho papa i ka 'ōlelo.
thoroughfare. Alanui.
thoroughwort. Pāmakani haole.
those. Kēlā mau; ua . . . lā. *Those of that place,* kō laila. *Those books,* kēlā mau puke.
thou. 'Oe.
though. I loko o. *See* although. *As though,* mehe, mai, mehe mea lā, me.
thought. Mana'o, no'ono'o, 'upu. *See* corrode, think. *Train of thought,* ka helena o ka no'ono'o, au. *Subject for thought,* kumuno'ono'o. *Random thought,* mana'o ulu wale. *Explanatory thought,* mana'o wehewehe. *Evil thought,* mana'o 'ino. *I thought (but it was not so),* kainō, kainoa, kuhi. *I thought you had gone,* kainō ua hele 'oe. *Constantly in mind and thought,* mea mana'o nui 'ia, pulakaumaka; hōlio *(rare).*
thoughtful. No'ono'o. *Also:* kuano'o, lana ka mana'o, kolokolohai, na'au ali'i.
thoughtless. No'ono'o 'ole, na'au kūhili, ho'oponopono 'ole.
thousand. Kaukani. *By thousands, to distribute to thousands,* pākaukani.
thousandfold. Pākaukani.
Thrace. Kelake, Terake.
thrash. Hahau, pāluku, kūpaka, hili, welokā.
thread. Lopi. *Also:* ka'ā, awe, ma'awe, mō'ali, mo'o-'ali. *Basting thread,* lopi kāholo, lopi ho'oholoholo. *Embroidery thread,* lopi humulau. *Twisted thread,* lopi huluhulu. *Spool of thread,* pōka'a lopi. *To thread, as a needle,* ho'opiha, 'uo; kui *(as beads).*
threadfish. Moi *(for growth stages and sayings, see* moi*).*
threadlike. Aweawe, nāwele, hilo.
threadworms. Ko'e kai.
threat. 'Ōlelo ho'oweliweli, ho'oweliweli; pu'u make *(dire).*
threaten. 'Ōlelo ho'oweliweli, ho'oweliweli. *Also:* kekē niho, ke'eke'e nuku, ho'onuinui, hoana; hoko *(rare).* *Threaten to throw, as at a dog,* ho'āni, ho'āni pākī.
three. Kolu, 'ekolu, 'akolu. *Three times,* 'ekolu, 'akolu, kuakolu, pākolu. *Three in one,* kahikolu. *Three-masted vessel,* kia kolu.
threefold. Pākolu, ka'ā kolu.
three fourths. 'Ekolu hapahā.

thresh. Kākā, ku'i palu, welokā. *To thresh wheat,* hehi palaoa. *Threshing floor,* kahua hehi.
threshold. Paepae puka, ni'o.
thrice. 'Ekolu manawa, kuakolu.
thrifty. Makauli'i, ho'omakauli'i. *Also:* ko'ako'ana; pānuhu *(as of plants, rare).*
thrill. Kapalili ka houpo. *Also:* nāku'i; ilihia *(as by beauty);* lalawe. *See* mane'o, thighbone. *Thrill in the heart,* konikoni lua i ka pu'uwai.
thrive. Ulu pono, lupalupa, nupanupa, oha. *Also:* māhua, māhuahua, ahuahu, ola nō, ko'ū.
throat. Pu'u, pu'umoni, pu'umoni'ai, kani'a'ī. *Front of throat,* puana'ī. *Sore throat,* pu'u 'eha, pu'upau. *Throat irritation,* 'ako. *Throat cancer,* pu'upau.
throb. Koni, konikoni, kapalili. *Also:* pana, 'api, hula; pākoni *(as teeth);* a'a koni. *Throbbing ache, as of love,* 'eha koni. *Throbbing in the heart,* konikoni lua i ka pu'uwai.
throne. Noho ali'i.
throne room. Ke'ena kalaunu.
throng. Pū'ulu, kūpina'i. *See* crowd. *To throng,* 'ākoakoa, kūpipipi, kūpina'i.
throttle. 'Umi.
through. 1. *Finished.* Pau. 2. *In.* Ma, ma loko o. 3. *By means of.* Ma o, no ka mea o.
throw. Nou, ho'olei, kiola; pehi *(pelt);* lū, nū *(scatter).* *Also:* pākī, ho'ohina, hīkau; — *at,* kāpehi, kīpehi, kūpehi; — *away,* kiloi, kiola, ho'olei wale; — *down, as a fighter,* hina; — *aimlessly, carelessly,* hikua; — *with force,* ho'okāwala, hiu; — *backwards,* wala, walawala, wala kua, 'āwala. *Throw stones,* nou pōhaku, pākī pōhaku; mano *(rare).* *Throw a spear,* 'ō'ō, 'ō'ō ihe, pahu ihe.
throwing net. *See* net.
thrush. 1. *Bird.* Kāma'o, 'ōma'o, keluka. *Hawaiian thrush,* 'āmaui, 'ōma'o. *Small Kaua'i thrush,* puaiohi. *Lāna'i and Moloka'i thrush,* oloma'o. 2. *Disease.* 'Ea *(for various kinds, see* 'ea *and entries that follow it).*
thrust. Hou, 'ō, kā, nao; pahu, pahuna, pakelo *(as a spear);* holowā *(rare);* — *aside,* kaupale, pale, ho'okāpae; — *on,* 'onou; — *up,* peu; — *in,* ho'ō. *Thrust of war club,* hāuna lā'au.
thud. Kamumu, mumu, haukamumu, pahū, haluku, palunu, 'ukē.
thumb. Manamana lima nui, lima nui. *Green thumb,* lima ulu.
thumbtack. Kui pahu, kui 'onou.
Thummim. Kumina, Tumima.
thump. Nāku'i, hāku'i, ko'ele, neneke; kamumu, haukamumu *(as footsteps);* pā, po'a'ala *(as a drum).* *Rare:* mukikiki, mūkekeke.
thunder. Hekili. *Also:* hekikili, kili, ku'i ka hekili, 'u'ina pōhaku a Kāne, pōhaku, pohāka'a, ka'a ka pōhaku. *To cause thunder,* ho'ohekili. *To thunder without rain,* pāmalō, hekili pāmalō, hekili pāmalo'o *(considered an omen).* *Peal of thunder,* ku'i hekili, kili.
thunderbolt. Ku'i ikaika ka hekili me ka lapa uila.
thunderclap. Ku'i hekili.
thundercloud. Ao hākuma me ka lapa uila; manuhekili *(rare).*
Thursday. Pō'ahā; Kaleke, Tarede *(rare).*
thus. Pēlā, pēia, pe, penei, pe kēia, 'oia, e la'a me kēia.
thwart. 1. *Frustrate.* Ho'ohoka, ho'opūhili. 2. *Canoe thwart.* Wae, wae wa'a.
thwarted. Hoka, pūhili, kāhewa.
thyme. Kaima.
thyroid. 'Ā'īpau.
ti. 1. *Plant.* Kī *(for various uses, see Haw.-Eng. entry),* kī'ula'ula *(ornamental),* 'āpi'i. *See* raincoat, sandal, skirt. *Ti leaf,* lā'ī, lau'ī, lau kī, lākī; lau'ī pekepeke *(short, stunted);* lau kī pala *(yellowed).* *Ti flower,* pua kī. *Ti-blossom stem,* pū'au *(rare).* *Shredded ti stalk,* kī-lau. *Brew from ti root,* 'ōkolehao, lolo. *Ti root as used for stain,* mole kī. *Fine pieces of ti root, as in the oven,* 'ae kī. *Ti-root oven,* imu kī, umu kī. *Glaze of ti-root*

juice, liki. *Providers of ti,* kumulau. *Place where ti grows,* wahi ulu o ke kī, 'ekī. **2.** *Music.* Mī.

Tibet. Kipeka, Tibeta.

tick. 1. *Sound.* Kani. *Also:* ko'ele, pa'ina; 'ukē *(rare).* **2.** *Insect.* 'Uku hipa, nalo paka. **3.** *Mattress cover.* Hulumanu.

ticket. Kikiki, likiki.

tickle, ticklish. Ho'omāne'one'o, māne'one'o, mane'o, ho'omane'o.

tidal wave. Kai e'e, kai ho'ē'e, kai a Pele. *Receding sea, as before a tidal wave,* kai mimiki. *Cf.* **Kahinali'i.**

tide. Au, kai. *Low tide,* kai make, kai malo'o, kai malolo, kai a malō. *Mid-tide,* hōlūlū, kai kū, kai maumau, kai pū. *Rising tide,* kai pi'i, kai apo, kai ea, kai nu'u mai, kai kī, 'ae. *High tide,* kai nui, kai ulu, kai piha. *Turn of the tide,* kai moku, kai ho'i, nioke, kai emi, kai nu'u aku.

tidings. 'Ōlelo *(Biblical);* nū hou *(news),* lono.

tidy. Maiau, ponopono, pa'ihi, pālawaiki.

tie. 1. *To bind.* Hīki'i, nīki'i, hāki'i, nāki'i, mūki'i, pūki'i, lawa, hele, ho'opa'a, hoa; lī *(as shoelace);* 'ope, pa'i *(as a package);* hīpu'u, nīpu'u, ho'ohīpu'u, nakinaki *(as a knot);* — *loosely,* hūalakē, kāmola, naia *(all are rare);* — *about neck,* kā'awe; — *as a slip knot,* kākolea; — *round,* kā'ai; — *bundles of stripped pandanus leaves,* kīmo'o. *Also:* kama, hāwele, 'āwele, 'ālikiliki, polikia, 'a'a, hauhoa, hauhō, molo, pākōlea, kalapu, ma'a, lapulapu, lino, mali, nikiniki, kūkulu, mīnoinoi, pu'aka, 'ōhao; nīpe'a *(Kaua'i).* *See* **bind.** *Tied to a stake,* mōkū. **2.** *A draw.* Pa'i, pa'i wale, pa'i ā pa'i. **3.** *In music.* Huina.

tie beam. 'Īlio.

Tierra del Fuego. 'Āina Ahi.

tiger. Kika.

tiger's-claw. Wiliwili haole.

tight. Likiliki, kūlikiliki, ho'olikiliki *(as a dress);* pa'a, 'i'ī *(as a cork);* pū'ika'ika *(packed);* lā'iki. *Also:* 'ālikiliki, papa'a, ha'apapa'a, pipiki, 'iha'iha, mālena, mū'ekeke'i, ho'omālō, kāo'o, lena. *See* **taut.**

tighten. Ho'olikiliki, nāki'i ā pa'a, huki ā mālo'elo'e.

Tigris. Kikelika, Tigerisa.

tile. Pōhaku 'ula.

till. 1. *Until.* 'Ā, ā hiki i. **2.** *Farm.* Mahi.

tiller. 1. *See* **rudder.** **2.** *See* **farmer.**

tilt. Kīki'i, wala, walawala, kulana, 'o'upe, ho'okapeke; — *back, as the head,* hīka'a. *Tilted nose,* ihu kū. *Tilt the chair,* ho'okīki'i i ka noho.

timber. Lā'au; hūka'a *(resinous).*

timbrel. Kuolokani.

time. Wā, manawa, au; hola *(o'clock).* *See* **times.** *Also:* hanana, la'a, la'ahia; ano *(in songs);* mawa *(rare);* pale, lele *(time interval in music).* *At a time,* pā- *(followed by a numeral).* *At the time that,* i, iā, i . . . hana. *At the time that I,* ia'u. *At the time that he,* iāia. *By the time that,* hele ā *(see* **hele 3).** *Passing of much time on a piece of land, as an old family,* au 'āpa'apa'a. *First time,* 'akahi nō . . . ā *(see* **'akahi);** maka mua. *In no time at all,* 'a'ole 'emo, manawa 'ole, 'emo 'ole, 'a'ole i 'ū. *For a short time, for the time being,* no ka manawa; kūikawā. *Any possible time,* ka manawa e hiki mai ana. *Time-consuming,* lohi, none. *Regular or usual time,* manawa pa'a mau. *Free time,* manawa ka'awale. *A long time, to take a long time,* li'u, li'uli'u, kūlō'ihi. *At the same time,* ho'okahi, like. *Portion of time,* paukū manawa. *From time to time,* i kēlā manawa i kēia manawa. *A long time ago, see* **ago.** *Distant time,* kikilo, kikiloa. *To waste time,* ho'opaumanawa. *To pass the time,* ho'ohala manawa; ho'olalau. *To pass time pleasantly,* ho'onanea, walea, luakaha, ho'okā'au. *To have a good time,* le'ale'a, nanea. *To beat time with hands,* pā. *To speak of old times,* ho'okahiko. *What time is it?* Hola 'ehia kēia?

timekeeper. Kikolā.

times. Wā, au. *Ancient times,* wā kahiko. *Good times,* wā maika'i. *Bad times, times of trouble,* wā pōpilikia. *Times sign (in multiplication),* kahahiō. *The Times (publication),* Ha'i Manawa.

timetable. Papa kuhikuhi, papa hō'ike, palapala hō'ike manawa, papa helu ka'aahi.

timid. Maka'u. *Also:* 'āhē, wiwo, ho'ohilahila, 'e'ena, kaupē.

tin. Kini, keleawe, piula. *Tin pan or plate,* pā kini.

tinder. Pulu, pulupulu. *Tinder resulting from plowing with the fire plow,* 'āhia.

tinea. Kane.

tingle. Koni.

tingling. Konikoni, 'ini'iniki, hu'ihu'i, houhou 'ili.

tinkle. Kani, wī, ō.

tinsmith. Ku'i keleawe.

tint. Ho'olu'u lahilahi.

tiny. 'U'uku, 'uku, 'uku li'i, li'i. *Also:* 'i'i, 'i'i'i, pū'uku-'uku, makali'i, lili'i, 'ūli'i, kikiki, hune, komoi'i'i, 'ōpihipihi, peke, kūpīhipihi. *Rare:* unana, 'anini. *Tiny bit,* mea hunahuna, huna, mākoli, mea hunehune, hune, oka li'ili'i, okaoka.

-tion. 'Ana, -na.

tip. 1. *Top.* Wēkiu, wēlau, welelau, 'ēlau, 'elelau, welewelelau, kihi, 'aki, nuku, piko. *See* **tongue.** **2.** *To tilt.* Kāhulihuli; wehe, wehewehe *(as a hat).* **3.** *Gratuity.* Uku lawelawe.

tipple. Wala kī'aha.

tipsy. 'Ona li'i.

tiptoe. Nihi, nīao.

tiptop. Maluna loa, kōkī.

tire. 1. *See* **tired.** **2.** *Of an automobile.* Laholio ho'opa'a huila.

tired. Luhi, māluhiluhi. *Also:* piula *(slang);* maka luhi *(of people, eyes);* kaea; mā'opa'opa *(as legs);* moluhi, luhi hewa, uihā, ma'uhā, 'ainea, pō'ie'ie, maika.

tiresome. Māluhiluhi, manakā, ho'omāluhiluhi, uihā.

tissue. 'A'a'a. *Tissue paper,* pepa lahilahi. *Cleaning tissue,* hainakā pepa.

tithe. Hapa'umi, waiwai hapa'umi.

titillate. Mane'o, ho'omāne'one'o, ho'okola.

title. 1. *Rank.* Kūlana. **2.** *Right.* Kuleana; 'alolio *(in fee simple).* *Certificate of title (land),* palapala ho'onā. *See* **land title.** **3.** *Heading, as of an article.* Po'o, po'o-'ōlelo, po'omana'o, inoa.

titter. 'Aka hene iki.

to. I, iā, iō; ā, ā hiki i; e, no *(purpose).* *To and fro,* i 'ō i 'ane'i, ha'aku'e. *I want to go,* makemake au e hele.

toad. Poloka.

toadstool. Kūkaelio.

toast. 1. *Bread.* Palaoa ho'opāpa'a, palaoa pāpa'a, palaoa pūlehu, lānia. *See* **broil.** *To toast bread,* ho'opāpa'a palaoa. **2.** *Drinking.* Inu ho'omaika'i. *A toast!* Kāmau! Huli pau! 'Ōkole maluna!

toaster. Mea ho'opāpa'a palaoa.

toastmaster. Luna 'aha'aina.

tobacco. Paka. *Smoking tobacco,* paka puhi. *Plug tobacco,* pepe'e paka. *Chewing tobacco,* paka nau. *Wild tobacco,* mākahala. *Tobacco pipe,* ipu paka. *Tobacco pouch or container,* poho paka, hano paka, pahu paka. *Guardian of high chief's tobacco and pipes,* kahu paka. *To smoke tobacco,* puhi paka.

today. Kēia lā.

toe. Manamana wāwae. *Big toe,* manamana nui. *Toe of a shoe,* ihu, ihu kāma'a.

toenail. Mai'ao, mānea o ka manamana wāwae, māi'u'u.

together. Pū. *Also:* like, ho'okahi, kūmaumau, la'a. *To do together,* hana like, 'ilau. *To paddle together,* hoe like, 'ilau hoe. *All together,* papau, pau pū, papa. *Close together,* pili, pīna'i. *To put or bring together,* ho'opili, kāpili. *Let's be together,* e pili kāua. *Let us live together,* ho'okahi nō kō kāua noho pū 'ana. *To pull together or cooperate,* huki like, alu like.

toil. Luhi, luhi 'ana, hana luhi, pa'i.

toilet. 1. *Bathroom.* Lua, wahi ho'opau pilikia, lua li'ili'i, ki'ona. *Outside toilet,* hale li'ili'i. *Go to the toilet,* hele i ka lua. **2.** *Adornment.* Ho'oma'ema'e a hō'a'ahu i ke kino. *Toilet water,* wai 'ala. *Toilet articles,* nā mea ho'onani (ho'oma'ema'e) kino.

toilet paper. Pepa hāleu, hāleu.

toilsome. Hana luhi, māluhiluhi, pa'u.

token. Hō'ike, hō'ailona.

told. *See* **tell.** *I told you so!* 'Aikola! Alolo! Ā la'a lā! Lolo! 'Ailolo!

tolerant. Mana'o laulā, 'olu'olu me ka ho'āhewa 'ole i kō ha'i mana'o.

tolerate. *See* **endure.**

toll. **1.** *Tax or due.* 'Auhau, uku. **2.** *To sound.* Ho'okani, kani, ku'ikē, kanikē, ho'ōeoe, ō.

tomato. 'Ōhi'a, 'ōhi'a lomi, 'ōhi'a haole, kamako, komako; 'ōhi'a ma ka nahele *(currant).*

tomb. Hale kupapa'u, lua kupapa'u, ilina.

tomorrow. 'Apōpō. *Day after tomorrow,* 'apōpō ā ia lā aku.

ton. Kana, kona.

tone. Leo, kani o ka leo; hua kani *(in music). Deep tone,* leo halulu, mali'u; kīkīko'u *(rare). Full tone,* leo lele puni.

tongs. 'Ūpā, 'ūpā ahi.

tongue. Alelo, elelo, lelo. *Tongue tip,* 'ēlau alelo, wēlau alelo, lau alelo. *Coated tongue,* alelo pala. *Doubletongued,* elelo lua. *To stick out the tongue, as in contempt,* ho'opake'o i ke alelo. *Sharp-tongued,* kekē, waha 'ā. *The tongue, steering paddle of the words of the mouth,* 'o ke alelo, ka hoe uli o ka 'ōlelo a ka waha *(advice to speak cautiously).*

tongue-tied. Alelo pelu, pu'u ke alelo; hiki 'ole ke pane *(unable to answer).*

tonic. **1.** *Medicine.* Lā'au ho'oikaika. **2.** *Music.* Kī alaka'i, puana.

tonight. Kēia pō, i kēia pō.

tonnage. Huina o nā kona.

tonsils. Pu'u. *Swollen tonsils,* pu'u 'ōkohekohe, pu'u kohekohe.

tonsillitis. Pu'u kohekohe. *Bilateral tonsillitis,* kohekohe papa.

too. **1.** *Also.* Kekahi, kahi, ho'i. *Me too,* 'o au pū. *I'm going too,* 'o au kahi e hele. **2.** *Excessive.* No Hawaiian equivalents except intensifiers nui, nui loa; keu *(often followed by ā).*

tool. Mea hana, mea ho'ohana, mea pa'ahana. *Tools,* pono hana, nā mea ho'ohana. *Tool house,* hale pa'ahana.

tooth. Niho *(for various kinds, see* **niho** *and entries that follow it). New tooth,* niho hou, niho peku. *Eye tooth,* maka ole. *Back tooth,* ku'i; ku'i lena *(yellowed, symbol of old age). False tooth,* niho ku'i, niho ho'okomo. *Loose tooth,* niho naue. *Decayed tooth,* niho popo. *Tooth tartar,* pala niho. *Worn teeth,* mauole. *Row or set of teeth,* papa niho, pae niho. *Point of a dog's tooth,* maka ole. *Whale tooth,* niho palaoa; palaoa pae *(washed ashore). Whale-tooth pendant,* lei palaoa, niho palaoa. *Tooth of deceased beloved,* heia. *To pull a tooth,* huki i ka niho. *To fill a tooth,* ho'opiha i ka niho. *To expose teeth,* ho'okekē niho, ha'akekē niho *(scold). Eye for an eye, tooth for a tooth* (Oihk. 14:20), he maka no ka maka, he niho no ka niho.

toothache. Niho hu'i, niho ka'i, pākoni.

toothbrush. Palaki niho.

toothed. Niho, nihoniho, nihoa, 'ōniho.

toothless. Niho 'ole, 'ūka'e. *Toothless gums,* ka'e, mūka'e.

toothpick. Lā'au 'ōhikihiki niho, 'ōhi'u niho.

top. 1. *Uppermost.* Wēkiu, wēlau, luna. *Also:* welelau, 'ēlau, lau, 'aki, piko, kilohana; po'o huku *(of a hill);* pane, kuamauna *(as of a mountain);* pā *(of a hat);* miona *(as of a hanging valley);* lau'eki *(as of sugarcane tassel or shell ginger about to bloom). To top, as top branches,* ēulu. *To get on top of,* pi'i, 'a'e, e'e. *To have reached the top,* kū i ke 'aki *(success). Strive to reach the top,* kūlia i ka nu'u. **2.** *Toy.* Hū, 'ōniu, 'ōka'a, 'ūlili. *Cord for spinning top,* kaula hū.

topaz. Kopako.

Topeka. Kopika.

top-heavy. Po'onui.

topic. Kumuhana, kumumana'o, po'omana'o; pū'olo *(fig.).*

topknot. Pū. *Also:* pūpū lauoho, maku'u, kā'eo, nīheu. *To tie the hair in a topknot,* pū i ka lauoho, hamaku'u, kīkī.

topmast. Kia luna.

topmost. Wēkiu, panepo'o, kōkī, maluna loa.

topographer. Mea kaha palapala'āina.

topography. Waihona 'āina, ke 'ano o ka moe 'ana o ka 'āina.

topple. Hina pū, pōhina, hina.

topsail. Heke, pe'a heke.

topsy-turvy. Kapakahi, kūwalawala, kīko'olā.

torch. Lama, lamakū, kālama, pūlama, kukui, ihoiho. *Torch fishing,* lamalama i'a. *Many torches stand,* kū ka lau lama *(symbol of victory).*

torment. Hō'eha'eha, 'eha nui, hana 'ino. *Also:* ho'oma'au, walania, walawalania, walenia, wawalania, welenia, poheue, pōlio. *See* **torture.**

torn. *See* **tear.**

tornado. Makani ka'a wiliwili.

torpedo. Kōpiko.

torpid. *See* **sluggish.**

torrent. Waikahe nui, holomoku.

torrential. Lanipili, loku, nu'u.

torso. Paukū kino.

torticollis. 'Ā'īkū.

tortoise. Honu. *Land tortoise,* 'ea kua neneke. *Tortoise shell,* una.

torture. Ho'omāinoino. *Also:* laumilo, ho'oka'awili. *See* **torment.**

toss. Ho'olei, kiola; — *about or back and forth,* ho'oleilei, kīolaola, walakīkē, huhuhulei, 'akūkū, ka'apā; —, *as a ship,* hulei, huleilua, kāhulihuli, ka'inapu, paiāha'a, paialewa, kulana; —, *as with palm of hand up,* kuwala, kuala; — *up,* hapahapai *(as a child);* kuehu, kaiehu *(as spray);* ho'oheheo. *Also:* lei, kā, hāuna, hauhāuna. *To toss while sleeping,* moe 'ino, moe kāhua.

total. Huina, huina helu; heluna *(sum);* holo'oko'a, helu.

tote. Paialewa. *See* **carry.**

totter. Ha'alulu, luli, kāhulihuli, kūlanalana, hīkākā, kunewa, kāpekepeke, kūhau, pananā.

touch. Pā, ho'opā, pili, meu, hani, ho'ohani; ho'opā iki, makahani, pā lihi *(graze);* —, *as of two objects,* pāpā; — *repeatedly,* ho'opāpā. *To touch the skin,* pā 'ili. *Touch and gone (as of a stolen object)!* Pā nō lilo!

touching. *See* **pathetic.**

touchstone. Pōhaku ho'opā.

tough. Pa'akikī, māuaua, uaua. *Also:* ho'ouaua, 'uo'uo, uo'o, laukani, pūkonakona, oloolonā, kani, 'ālikalika; ka'aka'alina *(as banana skin). Somewhat tough,* 'ōuaua.

toughen. Ho'ouaua; makauaua *(by drying).*

tour. Ka'apuni, ka'ahele, huaka'i ka'apuni, hele māka'ika'i. *Tour group,* po'e māka'ika'i like.

tourists. Po'e māka'ika'i, malihini māka'ika'i, malihini.

tousled. Puehuehu, pūkalakī *(as hair);* māewaewa, huhulu *(as feathers). See ex.,* **pāuma.**

tow. Kolo, kō, hekau, kauō. *To tow or drag a canoe,* kō wa'a. *To tow a ship,* kōlomoku.

towards. I, iā, iō.

towel. Kāwele. *Dish towel,* kāwele pā, pale 'umeke. *Bath towel,* kāwele 'au'au. *Paper towel,* kāwele pepa. *To wipe dishes with a towel,* kāwele pā.

tower. 'Ale'o, pā'o'a, haleku'i, hale pāku'i, hūlili, hale kaua, hale pūkaua, kowela. *See* **oracle tower.** *Watchtower,* hale kia'i.

towering. 'Ale'o, oeoe, halehale.

Tower of Babel. Haleku'i o Papela.

Tower of London. Kowela o Lākana, Towera o Ladana.

towhead. Po'o kea.

towline. Kaula kauō, kaula kolo, hekau.

town. Kūlanakauhale, kūnanahale, kaona.

toy. Mea pā'ani, milimili; kō'ie'ie *(water).*

trace. Meheu, we'awe'a, 'āwe'awe'a, nāwele. *To trace,* ho'okolo, ho'omeheu.

trachea. Kani'ā'ī.

track. 1. *Mark, course.* Meheu, kapua'i, mō'ali, mo'o-'ali, ma'awe, ho'oma'awe; mo'o, mo'owā *(narrow);* alahao *(railroad).* *Track of a god,* kaha akua. *To track,* ho'okolo, ho'omeheu, kolokolo. *To make a track,* ho'omeheu. 2. *Athletics.* Nā heihei a me nā ho'okūkū like 'ole e ikaika ai ke kino ma ke kahua pā'ani.

tract. 1. *Pamphlet.* Palapala, kelaka. 2. *Land.* 'Āpana 'āina.

tractor. Ka'a kauō.

trade. 1. *Barter.* Kālepa. *Also:* ku'aku'ai, kū'ai aku kū'ai mai, ho'oku'aku'ai, piele, ma'au'auwā, kuapo, mālaulau. *Trade ship,* moku kālepa. 2. *Occupation.* 'Oihana, 'oihana hana lima. *One without a trade,* kahua 'ole.

trader. Kālepa, piele. *Trading company,* hui kālepa.

trade school. Kula a'o 'oihana.

tradewind. *See* **wind.**

tradition. Mo'olelo, mo'o'ōlelo, mo'o, 'ōlelo mai nā kūpuna mai, nā hana a ka wā kahiko.

traditional. Mai nā kūpuna mai, ku'una.

Trafalgar. Kalapalaka, Tarafalaga.

traffic. 1. *Of pedestrians, vehicles.* Ne'e 'ana i ke alahele. *Heavy traffic,* nui nā ka'a *(motor).* *Traffic policeman,* māka'i kū huina. 2. *See* **trade.**

tragedy. Mea kaumaha loa; keaka hopena kaumaha *(theatrical).* *In poetry, heavy rain may represent tears and tragedy.*

tragic. Kaumaha loa, hō'eha'eha na'au, 'awa'awa, 'awa'awahia.

trail. Ala, ala hele. *Also:* mo'o hele, meheu, kumeheu, kuamo'o, maka ala, makala, mokala, kaolo; *steep* —, hūlili, ala 'ūlili; — *or follow behind,* ho'okolo, hahai, ho'omoho *(transitive);* kōwelo, kōwelokā, kāwelokā *(as a dress train).* *Trailing plant,* lā'au kolo, pō'aha.

trailer. Ka'a kauō. *House trailer,* ka'a hale.

train. 1. *Teach.* A'o, ho'oma'ama'a. *To train as a* kahuna, ho'okahuna, a'o i ka 'oihana kahuna. *To train to grow straight, as an infant's crooked limb, or as a plant,* 'ōmilomilo, pākolea, ho'oulu pono. *Trained,* 'ailolo, lae 'ula; hialoa *(rare).* 2. *See* **railroad.** 3. *Of a dress.* Hu'a, huelo.

trainee. Haumana a'o 'oihana.

trait. Welo, ēwe, māna. *True to the family traits,* kū nō i ke ēwe. *See ex.,* **māna.**

traitor. Kumakaia, mākaia, paoke'e. *See* **treachery.**

tra-la-la. 'Eā, 'eā 'eā, eā, eā eā, 'uhe'uhene.

tramp. 1. *See* **vagabond.** 2. *See* **trample, walk.**

trample. Hehi, hahi, ke'ehia, hehikū, naku. *Rain trampling on the breadfruit leaves (FS 285),* ka ua hehi lau 'ulu.

trance. Akakū.

tranquil. La'i.

tranquilizer. Lā'au ho'omālielie.

tranquillity. Mālie, la'i, nanea, walea, maluhia. *Also:* ōpūhea, kōnale, pālūlā, kuapapa, māaniani, kīpū, hālala'i. *Tranquillity of eventide,* kīpū ahiahi. *See phrases,* **calm, peace, taro.**

transact. Lawelawe, hana ho'okō.

transfer. Ho'olilo, ho'oʻīli, ho'oili, hō; 'oloka'a *(as a debt).* *Bus or streetcar transfer,* pepa ho'ololi ka'a, palapala ho'olilo.

transfiguration. Ho'opāha'oha'o 'ia 'ana, kākū'ai.

transform. Loli, kū.

transformation. Loli 'ana, kūākino.

transgress. Lawehala, mau'a'e, hape, kolohe, āneho.

transient. Kūikawā, mea kipa mai no ka manawa.

transit. Kūikawā, mā'alo. *Transit goods,* waiwai mā'alo.

transitive. *See* **verb.**

translate. Unuhi, unuhi 'ōlelo, mahele, mahele 'ōlelo.

translation. Unuhina. *Literal translation,* unuhi kūlike loa, unuhi pili. *Free translation,* unuhi laulā loa.

translator. Mea unuhi, unuhi 'ōlelo, mahele 'ōlelo.

transmit. Ho'ouna, ho'oʻīli, ho'oili, halihali.

transparent. Aniani, akaaka; māliko *(as fish of some species);* kaka'e *(rare).*

transpiration. Hanu, pi'ikū.

transpire. *See* **happen.**

transplant. Kanu ma kahi 'ē, uai i kahi kanu.

transport. Halihali, lawe. *Transport ship,* mokuahi lawe 'ōhua; mokuahi lawe koa *(troops);* mokuahi lawe ukana *(merchandise).* *Transported with emotion,* lalawe i ke kino.

transportation. Halihali 'ana, lawe 'ana.

transship. Lawe mai kahi moku ā kahi moku; mā'alo moku.

transshipment. Lawe i ka waiwai mai kahi moku ā kahi moku.

transubstantiation. Ho'okūākino.

Transvaal. Kanawaala.

trap. 'Ūmi'i, 'umiki, 'ūpiki, pahele, 'ōpiki. *Kinds of fish traps include:* hīna'i, hānai, kia, imu, 'ie, 'ie kala, mākālei, naomakalua, hā, hāhā, pai, kula. *See sayings,* **'auwaha 1.** *Mousetrap,* 'ūmi'i 'iole. *Owl trap,* pēkeu. *Place where a trap is set,* heau.

trapezoid. Huinahā lua like.

trash. 'Ōpala, la'ola'o. *Trash heap,* pu'u 'ōpala, ho'oleina. *Wind-blown trash,* wilikōī *(rare).*

travail. Ho'okōhi, ha'akōhi, kōhi, kuakoko *(of childbirth).*

travel. Ka'ahele, ka'apuni, huaka'i hele, huaka'i, māhoa; hoe *(fig.);* — *around,* ka'apuni, holopuni; — *with brief stopovers,* noho hele; — *by sea,* 'au, aukai, 'aumoana; — *in the mountains,* hele mauna; — *together, of two,* hele lua. *Fond of travel,* puni hele.

traveler. Kama hele. *See saying,* **sail.** *Fellow traveler,* hoa hele. *Commercial traveler, traveling salesman,* 'ākena kālepa ka'ahele. *Traveling company,* po'e ka'ahele, ka'iālana.

tray. Pā halihali. *Mixing tray,* papa wili, papa wili 'ai. *Wooden tray,* pā lā'au. *Ash tray,* pā lehu.

treachery. 'Āpiki, 'ūpiki, mākaia, kumakaia, kipi, 'ōpe'a, ho'ōpe'a, pahele. *To plot treachery,* kālai 'ino.

tread. Hehi, hehihehi, hahi, hahihahi, ke'ehi, ma'awe, naku, meheu, kapua'i; — *upon,* 'a'e; — *along,* peki. *To tread water,* 'au kū, kū'au'au.

treading. Hehina.

treadle. Papa hehi. *Treadle-board hula,* hula papa hehi.

treason. *See* **treachery.**

treasure. Mea makamae. *To treasure,* pūlama.

treasurer. Pu'ukū, ikūone, kuene. *Acting or deputy treasurer,* hope pu'ukū.

treasury. Waihona, waihona kālā, waihona waiwai, waihona moni.

treat. 1. *Attend to.* Lapa'au *(as the sick);* hana; wehewehe *(explain);* — *as a parent,* ho'omakua. *Treat your young brother kindly,* hana maika'i 'oe i kou pōki'i. 2. *Pleasure.* Mea ho'ohau'oli, mea e hoihoi ai. *My treat,* na'u e uku *(for me to pay).*

treaty. Palapala 'aelike, ku'ikahi.

treble. Pākolu.

tree. Lā'au, kumulā'au. *Main stalk of a tree, trunk,* kumu. *Tree or plant consisting of several stalks or roots, as banana, pandanus, kava,* pū, ōpū. *Top part of tree, above ground,* ēlau. *Fallen tree,* kumu hina, mauwā. *Gather in trees, as birds,* ho'olā'au. *The tree of life,* ka lā'au o ke ola.

tree fern. *See* **fern.**

tremble. Ha'alulu, kapalili. *Also:* naka, ulupi'i *(as with cold or fear);* naue, kuekueni, 'api, 'ōpa'ipa'i.

tremendous. Nui lua 'ole, nui hewahewa, 'a'ole o kana mai ka nui, 'a'ole o ka'e mai ka nui.

tremor. 'Ōla'i, 'i'i, manunu, āhua. *See* **earthquake.**

tremulous. Napa. *See* **quiver.**

trench. 'Auwaha, 'āwa'a, wa'a, wa'awa'a. *To dig a trench,* 'eli, hō'auwaha, 'āwa'a, ho'owa'a, ho'owa'alia, uwa'a.

trend. 'Ano, au.

trepang. Loli *(for various kinds, see* **loli** *and entries that follow it).* *See* **sea cucumber.**

trespass. Komo hewa, komo wale, 'ae'a hauka'e, kahakū, 'a'e, 'a'e kū, hehikū. *See* **sin.** *Forgive us our trespasses as we forgive those who trespass against us (Mat. 6.12),* e kala mai ho'i iā mākou i kā mākou lawehala 'ana, me mākou e kala nei i ka po'e i lawehala i kā mākou.

trespasser. 'Ae'a hauka'e, 'a'e kapu.

trespassing. *See* **trespass.** *No trespassing,* kapu.

trestle. Haka 'ūlili, hūlili, alahaka, kaulanahaka.

trial. Ho'okolokolo *(court);* ho'ā'o *(attempt);* pōpilikia *(hardship). Poetic references to rain and storms may signify trial and tribulation. See* **Hilo** *(Eng.-Haw.).*

triangle. Huinakolu. *Right-angle triangle,* huinakolu kūpono. *Obtuse triangle,* huinakolu peleleu. *Irregular triangle,* huinakolu 'ao'ao like 'ole. *Isosceles triangle,* huinakolu 'elua 'ao'ao like. *Acute triangle,* huinakolu 'oi. *Equilateral triangle,* huinakolu like. *Triangle design on Ni'ihau mats,* nānānu'u. *Triangular sail,* heke.

tribe. *No Hawaiian term in the anthropological sense; see* **'alaea, clan, family.**

tribulation. Pōpilikia, 'eha'eha. *See* **trial.**

tribute. Ho'okupu, uku, 'auhau, 'auwae'āina. *Tribute to a high chief,* kuapōla'o. *To assemble such tribute,* ho'okuapōla'o. *Tribute from uplands,* waiwai maloko. *We pay tribute to Ceasar (Luka 20:22),* ho'okupu mākou iā Kaisara.

trick. Hana ma'alea; hana 'āpiki *(bad);* hana kolohe, hana 'epa. *Rare:* 'ōpe'a, 'oeha'a, limu. *Card trick,* hana ma'alea me ka pu'u pepa. *See saying,* **ho'oko'iko'i.**

trickle. Kahe, kulu; paihī *(rare).*

tricycle. Ka'a hehi wāwae.

Tridacna. 'Olepe nui.

trifle. Mea 'ole, mea 'ano 'ole, mea iki, mea li'ili'i, iki. *Also:* 'ōpihipihi, pālau'eka, mā'ilu, 'ōmilu. *See* **gourd.** *A trifle larger,* nui iki. *Trifling affair,* hana kalakalai. *To trifle,* kolohe wale, pā'ani wale, ho'omea.

trigger. Kī, kīleo, kiko.

triggerfish. Humuhumu *(for various kinds, see* **humuhumu** *and entries that follow it). Also:* mukumukuwahanui, 'uwī'uwī, 'uwī'uwī lua.

trigonometry. Ana huinakolu.

trill. Kapalili, kūolokū, kūpaloloi, kī'ililī, ha'alulu. *Trilling voice,* leo ho'ānu'unu'u *(Hawaiian style).*

trillion. Kiliona, keliliona.

trim. 1. *Cut.* 'Oki, 'oki'oki, pa'ipa'i. *Also:* pa'i koli, mu'o koli, 'ako, kipikipi, āmū; mōlina *(as the edge of a dress).* **2.** *Decorate.* Ho'onani, ho'okāhiko. **3.** *Neat.* 'Auli'i, mikioi, popohe, pālanaiki, miomio.

trimmings. 1. *Decorations.* Nā mea ho'onani, nā mea kīnohinohi; 'uiki *(pipings).* **2.** *Cuttings.* Nā mea i 'oki'oki 'ia. *Thatched-house trimmings,* loha.

trinity. Kahikolu, kolukahi, kaukolu. *Holy Trinity,* Akua Kahikolu, Kolukahi Hemolele. *See* **Kū-kauakahi.**

trinket. Mea li'ili'i ho'okīnohinohi *(ornamental);* mea li'ili'i milimili *(toy).*

trio. Pūkolu. *Music trio,* hīmeni kū pākolu, leokū pākolu.

trip. 1. *Voyage.* Huaka'i. **2.** *Stumble.* 'Ōkupe, ho'ōkupe, ho'ohilikau i nā wāwae. *Don't trip him,* mai ho'ōkupe iāia.

tripe. 'Ōpū, 'ōpū 'āpikapika, 'ōpū huluhulu, 'ōpū 'opi-'opi, 'ōpū maka 'upena. *Beef tripe,* 'ōpū pipi. *Pig tripe,* 'ōpū pua'a.

triple. Kaukolu.

triplet. Pūkolu.

triplets. Hānau pākolu.

tripper. Pīkoi, 'īkoi.

trite. Pākūwā.

triumph. Lanakila, 'ō'ili pulelo. *See* **firebrand, torch.**

trivial. 'Ano 'ole, mea 'ole. *See* **trifle.**

Trochus shell. Pūpū-o-Hā'upu.

troll. Hī *(as for bonito,* 'ahi *and* kala). *Trolling line,* aho kālewa, aho kakele.

trolley. Ka'a uila *(electric).*

trollop. Wahine moekolohe wale.

troops. Pū'ali koa.

troopship. Moku halihali koa, moku lawe koa.

trophy. Hō'ailona lanakila.

tropic bird. Koa'e, 'ula, koa'e 'ula, koa'e kea. *See sayings,* **kahakō, pāuma, cliff.**

Tropic of Cancer. Pō'ai-'olu 'Ākau.

Tropic of Capricorn. Pō'ai-'olu Hema.

trot. Holo kūkū, holopeki, hulei, huleilua. *Trotting,* huhuhulei.

trouble. Pilikia, pōpilikia. *Also:* hihia, kauhihi, ho'oluhi, pu'u, la'a, la'ahia, no'ono'o 'iha'iha, 'ōupē, olohi'a. *To cause trouble,* ho'opilikia, ho'ohihia, ho'opōpilikia, 'imi hana, ho'ouluāo'a, ho'ononi. *See* **difficulties** *and sayings,* **hekau 2, Ko'olau 1, la'a 2, mano 1, paehumu, palahuli, po'o 1, puluea, bird, wall.** *In trouble,* kū i ka pilikia, 'āpikipiki, 'ō'ili, noni, makaua; kūpiliki'i *(in dire trouble). Poetic references to rain or storms may signify trouble.*

troubled. Kaumaha, lu'ulu'u, pilikia, 'āpikipiki, noni, makaua, no'ono'o 'iha'iha *(see* **'iha'iha***).*

troublemaker. Mea ho'opilikia, mea ho'oulu pilikia, 'imi 'epa, 'eleao.

trough. Holowa'a, holoa'a, hā. *Water trough,* kula wai, hā wai; pā wai *(rare). Food trough, kneading trough,* papa wili 'ai.

troupe. Hui. *Hula troupe,* pā hula.

trousers. Lole wāwae. *See* **shorts.** *Long trousers,* lole wāwae loloa. *Short trousers,* lole wāwae pōkole. *Linen trousers,* wāwae olonā. *Triangular piece inserted at base of bell-bottom trousers,* pi'i.

trowel. 'Ō'ō pālahalaha, kila pa'i puna, hamo puna, hāpale.

truce. Ho'opau kaua, ho'omalolo kaua. *Truce-breakers,* pale pelika.

truck. Kalaka, ka'a kalaka, ka'a ukana.

truck farm. Wahi ho'oulu mea 'ai no ka mākeke, mahina 'ai.

trudge. Ko'ele, ko'ele wāwae, kūo'e; — *along,* peki.

true. 'Oia'i'o. *Also:* 'i'o, oia, kū'i'o, maoli. *Come true, as a prophesy,* kō 'i'o.

truly. Maoli, 'i'o, 'oia'i'o. *Yours truly,* me ka 'oia'i'o.

trump. Huli *(in cards). To trump,* kāmau, hahau. *No trumps,* 'a'ohe huli. *Spades are trumps,* he peki ka huli.

trumpet. Pū, pū ho'okani, pū kani, 'olē. *Conch-shell trumpet,* pū puhi. *Trumpet of animal horn,* pepeiaohao. *Trumpet leading an army,* pū ka'i.

trumpet fish. Nūnū, nuhu.

trumpet vine. Huapala.

trundle bed. Moeka'a.

trunk. Pahu, pahu lole *(clothes);* kumu *(tree);* ihu *(elephant);* paukū kino *(body).*

trunkfish. Pahu, moa, moamoa.

trust. Hilina'i, kālele, paulele, lelepau.

trustee. Kahu waiwai, mālama waiwai, luna mālama waiwai, luna ho'oponopono waiwai.

trust territory. Nā 'āina noho kahu 'ia.

trustworthy. Paulele 'ia.

truth. 'Oia'i'o, oia. *Partial truth,* 'ohaohala *(rare).*

try. Ho'ā'o *(sample);* ho'oikaika, hō'ikaika, kūlia *(make effort);* ho'opā; — *in court,* ho'okolokolo.

T-shaped. 'Āmana.

tsunami. *See* **Kahinali'i, tidal wave.**

tub. Kapu.

tube. 'Ohe. *Suction tube,* omo, 'ili omo wai.

tuber. Hua; 'āla'a *(as of taro, rare); bitter yam aerial —,* 'ala'ala. *From a tuber,* hua, hō'i'o.

tuberculosis. Ma'i-'ai-ake, akepau, hōki'i, leiowī, wai-'ōpua. *Cf.* **thin.** *Tuberculosis adenitis,* 'ala'ala.

tuberose. Kupaloke.

tuck. 'Alu *(as in a dress);* hu'a *(as in a dress or mat). To take a tuck, tuck in,* 'ōmau, pelu. *Tuck creaser,* hō'ailona 'alu. *To tuck under, as a hen with chicks,* pāpio. *The dog tucked in his tail,* pelu ka huelo o ka 'īlio.

Tuesday. Pō'alua; Kukeke, Tusede *(rare).*

tuff cone. Pu'u lehu.

tuft. Pūpū. *Tuft of dried ti leaves on octopus lure,* pupua. *Tufted,* moa.

tug. Hiuhiu, koni, kō, huki.
tugboat. Moku kolo, kolomoku.
tug-of-war. Hukihuki, pāʻumeʻume.
tuition. Uku. *School tuition,* uku kula.
tulip. Kulipa.
tumble. Hāʻule *(from a height);* hina *(topple);* — *down, collapse,* hiolo.
tumbler. Kīʻaha.
tumor. ʻIʻo ulu, puʻupuʻu koko, kuaʻeho, ʻeho. *Venereal tumor,* ʻanakoʻi.
tumult. Haunaele, pōnaʻanaʻa, kīpalalē, uluāoʻa, ʻeleʻelepī, wawā. *To cause tumult,* hoʻūluāoʻa, hoʻouluāoʻa, hoʻohaunaele, hōʻaleʻale.
tuna. ʻAhi, hiʻuwīwī, kahauli, aku, kawakawa; pālaha *(small variety).*
tune. Leo, leo mele. *To tune,* hoʻokani pono, hoʻoponopono.
tunnel. Ana puka, alapao, konela, konela puka.
turban. Kāʻei poʻo, pāpale hainikā.
turbid. Lepolepo, lepo huaʻi. *To render turbid,* haluku.
turbo shell. ʻAlīlea, pūpū makua.
turbulent. Hāloʻaloʻa, ʻāloʻaloʻa, ʻeleʻelepī, wiliau; kūpikiʻō *(as wind or storm).*
Turin. Kulino, Turino.
Turk. Kuleke, Tureke.
Turkey. 1. *The country.* Kuleke, Tureke. 2. *(Not cap.) Fowl.* Pelehū, palahū, pōkeokeo.
turmeric. ʻŌlena, lena; īheʻekai *(used ceremonially).*
turn. 1. *Move.* Huli; kā *(as a rope for jumping);* — *around, twist, revolve,* wili, kaʻa, kaʻawili, kūlapa, molo, hole, wilimoʻo, palawili, ʻōlepe, ʻōmilo, laumilo, ue, oi, kaʻamola, kaʻa wale, kīoe; — *aside,* ʻaui, hili, hoʻoiala, hoʻokihi, kihi, kāpae, kakaʻa, hoʻohala, kipa, kīkaha, kepa, kīkepa, kaha, kaha loa, kahakū, peʻa, pelu, peʻu, pelukua, pipika, palai, pāweo, īkā, pinanaʻiea; — *over,* kāhuli pū, ʻowala; kūwalawala *(repeatedly);* palahuli, kakaʻa, pūlepe; — *inside out,* lole; — *towards,* maliu, kālelei; — *this way and that,* hou hewa; — *and rush,* hulimoku; — *into,* lilo, kū ā. *Also:* hāliu, huhuli, huhuhuli, hoʻohuli, loli, hoʻokeʻe, pāuma. *Turn the back,* huli kua; ʻōkoleoioi *(as in anger). Turn back,* huli. *Turn in two ways or twice,* huli lua. *Turn and toss in sleep,* moe ʻino, moekāhua. *Right, turn,* ma ka ʻākau, wili. 2. *Time.* Manawa. *In turn, take turns,* kaʻahele, i kekahi ā i kekahi aku. *This is your turn,* kou manawa kēia, iāʻoe ia wahi. *To read in turn,* heluhelu kaʻahele.
turncoat. Lolelua, mākaia, kumakaia; lepelua *(rare).*
turning. Hulina, kaʻa, lauwili, mola, molamola. *Motions of turning hinges,* kūʻamiʻami, ʻōlepelepe. *Turning point,* huliau, kahana.
turnip. ʻUala pilau, ananū.
turnkey. Wilikī.
turnstile. Puka poniniu, puka uai.
turnstone. ʻAkekeke, keke.
turpentine. Kapenekine, tapenetine, ʻaila hoʻomaloʻo pena.
turtle. Honu, ʻea. *See sayings,* **honu** *and* **turtledove.** *Dark greenish meat in a turtle,* lūʻau, ʻiʻo lūʻau. *Turtle shell,* una, ʻea. *Turtle coloring,* hilihili honu. *Turtle markings on back,* nanaka. *Turtle back,* makauliʻi. *Turtle, turtle, come up to breathe,* ē honu, ē honu, e pūhā *(turtle hula).*
turtledove. Kuhukukū. *See* **dove.** *The voice of the turtle, (archaic for turtledove),* ka leo o ke kuhukukū.
Tuscaloosa. Kukakaluka, Tusakalusa.
Tuscany. Kukekani, Tusekani.
tusk. Niho, kuʻi. *Pig tusk,* niho puaʻa.
tutor. Kumu aʻo, kumu. *To tutor,* aʻo.

twelve. ʻUmi kūmālua, ʻumi kumamālua; ʻekolu kāuna.
twenty, twentieth. Iwakālua.
twenty-eight. Iwakālua kūmāwalu, iwakālua kumamāwalu.
twenty-five. Iwakālua kūmālima, iwakālua kumamālima. *Twenty-five cents,* hapahā.
twenty-four. Iwakālua kūmāhā, iwakālua kumamāhā.
twenty-nine. Iwakālua kūmāiwa, iwakālua kumamāiwa.
twenty-one. Iwakālua kūmākahi, iwakālua kumamākahi.
twenty-seven. Iwakālua kūmāhiku, iwakālua kumamāhiku.
twenty-six. Iwakālua kūmāono, iwakālua kumamāono.
twenty-three. Iwakālua kūmākolu, iwakālua kumamākolu.
twenty-two. Iwakālua kūmālua, iwakālua kumamālua.
twice. Pālua, lua, ʻelua, ʻalua, ʻelua manawa, kualua. *See ex.,* **pālua.** *To do twice,* hoʻolua. *Twice as much,* pāpālua.
twig. Lālā ʻuʻuku. *Twigs,* laʻalāʻau.
twilight. Mōlehu, mōlehulehu, pōlehulehu, pūlehulehu, liʻulā, maliʻo. *Rare:* mālehulehu, mālaʻolaʻo; ʻehu ahiahi *(fig.).*
twill. ʻOʻeno, hoʻohewahewa, kuila.
twin. Māhoe, māhana, kūlua. *Twin peaks,* māhana puʻu.
twine. Kuaina, kaula kuaina. *To twine,* ʻoai, ʻowai, koali, hihi, hoʻohihi.
twinkle. ʻImo, ʻamo, ʻamoʻamo, ʻuiki, pipī; nakili *(rare). Twinkling star,* hōkū ʻimoʻimo.
twirl. Koali.
twist. Wili, kaʻawili, lauwili; milo *(as thread, rope);* kupe, ʻōkupe *(as ankle);* hilo *(braid). Also:* wilinau, palawili, ʻōwili; nūkeʻe, ʻūkeʻe *(as the mouth);* kaʻa, kaʻā; ʻōmilo, lōmilo, laumilo, hoʻomimilo, milo, mimilo, milomilo; wilimoʻo, hoʻowilimoʻo, napanapa *(as an eel);* kekeʻe, hoʻokekeʻe *(out of shape);* hoʻōai, ʻuwī, hoʻopepeʻe, pepeʻe, ue, kūlapa, mola, molamola, kūpaka, lino, molo, hole, lepeʻa, ʻōhuʻi, ʻōpeʻa, kāʻekā, huki, hualala, lolelole.
twitch. Kapalili; hula, hulahula *(rare);* ʻiwi *(as the eye);* huki *(as the mouth);* ʻāʻili.
twitter. ʻIoʻio.
two. Lua, ʻelua, ʻalua. *Two by two, double, twofold, twice, two at a time, by twos,* pālua. *Two of a kind,* kaulua. *In two portions,* hapalua. *Two-sided or two-faced,* alolua, maka lua, kiʻilua. *Twofold, as a plaited mat,* maka lua. *Two-ply,* mālua, kaʻā lua. *Two-edged,* ʻoi lua, naomakalua. *Two-minded,* naʻau lua, kaulua. *Two-thirty o'clock,* hapalua hola ʻelua. *Two-masted schooner,* kia lua. *Two-by-four lumber,* papa lua hā. *To count by twos,* helu pālua. *To divide in two parts,* hoʻopālua.
two thirds. ʻElua hapakolu.
type. 1. *Kind.* ʻAno. 2. *Print.* Hua, hua hoʻonoho. *Printer's type,* huakēpau. *To set type,* hoʻonoho hua, ʻōniu huakēpau, hoʻolele huakēpau, kūkulu kēpau, ulele kēpau. *To type,* kikokiko.
Typee. Kaipī, Taipi.
typesetter. Ulele kēpau. *See* **type.**
typewriter. Mīkini kikokiko hua. *To typewrite,* kikokiko hua, kikokiko.
typhoid. Piwa hoʻonāwaliwali.
typhoon. Kaipuni.
typhus. Maʻi kuni.
typist. Kikokiko hua.
typographical error. Paʻi hewa.
tyrant. Haku ikaika ā hainā.

U

u. 'Ū.

udder. Ū.

ugly. Pupuka. *Also:* 'ino, mumuka, mākinikā, haumanumanu *(see saying)*; pōuhu *(rare)*. *To make ugly,* ho'opupuka.

ukulele. 'Ukulele.

ulcer. Pūhā, pūhō, hēhē, me'eau. *Stomach ulcer,* 'ōpū pūhā; iki'alamea *(rare)*. *Bleeding ulcer,* hī koko *(RSV)*. *Medicine for ulcers,* kuakala.

ulcerous. 'A'ai hele, hēhē.

ultimate. Hope loa.

ultraviolet rays. Kuawehi.

umbilical cord. Piko. *Small hard spots on an umbilical cord,* kūkae'iole.

umbrella. Māmalu, loulu. *Umbrella rib,* nī'au.

umbrella plant. 'Ahu'awa haole.

umbrella shell. 'Opihi kapua'i lio.

umpire. 'Uao.

un-. 'Ole, hiki 'ole ke, 'a'ole, 'a'ohe.

unable. Hiki 'ole.

unaccommodating. Na'au kōkua 'ole, naua.

unaccountable. Maopopo 'ole, kupaianaha, kupanaha, hiki 'ole ke wehewehe.

unaccustomed. Ma'a 'ole, mamalihini.

unafraid. Maka'u 'ole. *Also:* maka koa.

unanimous. Mana'o lōkahi. *To do with unanimity,* komo 'oko'a, huliāmahi.

unapproachable. Hiki 'ole ke hele aku. *Also:* mehani, pano; kū ma kapa *(see* **kapa***)*. *Taboo on approaching a chief from behind,* kua'ā.

unassuming. Akahai, ha'aha'a; mimo *(rare)*.

unattractive. U'i 'ole, pupuka, 'ano 'ole. *Sexually unattractive,* lemukū, he u'i kū i ki'ona *(lit., a beauty fit for the dung heap)*.

unavoidable. 'A'ole hiki ke alo a'e, hiki 'ole ke kāpae.

unaware. 'Ike 'ole, maopopo 'ole.

unbelieving. Hilina'i 'ole, maloka, ho'omaloka, ho'omalau, 'aiā.

unbleached muslin. Kūkaenalo. *Flour sack or sack of unbleached muslin, as formerly used for poi,* 'eke kūkaenalo.

unbound. Pa'a 'ole, ulehelehe.

unbreakable. Hiki 'ole ke nahā (ha'i, wāhi), ha'i 'ole.

unburden. Ku'u i ka lu'ulu'u, kala.

unbutton. Wehe i ka pihi.

unceasing. Mau, pau 'ole.

unceremoniously. Kū; 'o kū, 'o kā *(see* **kū** . . . **kā***)*; me ka ho'ohiwahiwa 'ole; pōnolu *(rare)*.

uncertain. Kānalua, kūlanalana, kūnānā. *Also:* hopohopo, kākālule, ku'ihē, kaumo'o, 'ōhio, kāpekepeke, pākole. *Particles expressing uncertainty,* ho'i, lā.

uncircumcised. Kahe 'ole, olomu'o. *Uncircumcised foreskin,* puhi.

uncivil. Ho'opuka kū, ho'okamaniha, hanahihi.

uncivilized. Ho'ona'auao 'ole 'ia, na'aupō; 'a'alaioa *(rare)*.

uncle. Makua kāne, 'anakala. *Younger brother or cousin of the father or mother,* makua kāne 'ōpio. *Older brother or cousin of the father or mother,* makua kāne makua. *Parents' brothers and male cousins,* makua kāne hanauna.

unclean. Ma'ema'e 'ole, haumia, kāpulu, hawa, 'ino, pe'a, pe'ape'a, pauma'ele, pelapela.

unclear. Akaaka 'ole. *Also:* niniu; halalē *(as speech)*.

unclouded. Kāla'e, 'alaneo, kahania, palakea.

uncombed. Kahi 'ole 'ia, pūkalakī.

uncomfortable. 'Olu'olu 'ole, ho'o'iha'iha; 'ōpihapiha *(after overeating)*; 'ano 'ē.

uncommon. Laha 'ole, hana mau 'ole 'ia, 'ano 'ē, kaka'ikahi, pākuwā 'ole, hihiu. *Uncommon word,* hua 'ōlelo hana mau 'ole 'ia.

uncomplaining. Leo 'ole, ho'ohalahala 'ole, 'ōhumuhumu 'ole.

unconcerned. Me ka no'ono'o 'ole, wale.

unconditional. Kaupalena 'ole 'ia, me nā kaupalena 'ole. *Unconditional surrender,* hā'awipio 'oko'a.

unconscious. Pau ka 'ike, pau ka lohe *(see* **'ike***)*; pau ka ho'omaopopo 'ana. *See* **unaware.**

unconstitutional. Kū'ē kumukānāwai.

uncooked. Maka.

uncooperative. Hukikū, laulima 'ole, na'au kōkua 'ole.

uncouth. Lula 'ole, pa'a lula 'ole; kākāki'i *(rare)*.

uncover. 'Uwehe, hu'e, hua'i, wehe.

uncovering. Wehe 'ana, hua'ina, wehena.

unction. Ukione *(extreme)*.

uncultured. Kahua 'ole.

undecided. Kānalua, na'au lua, kūnānā, ku'ihē.

under. Lalo, malalo, i lalo.

underclothes. Pale'a'ahu.

undercut. Poholalo.

underdone. *See* **rare.**

underdrawers. Palema'i, palema'i o lalo, pale'ili, pale'ili o lalo.

underground. Malalo o ka honua. *Underground stream,* ilina wai.

undergrowth. Nāhelehele; ulueki *(rare)*.

underhanded. Poholalo, ka'alalo, kīmopō.

underline. Kaha lalo.

underling. Mea noho malalo aku o kekahi; mānea *(fig)*.

undermine. Poholalo, po'a, pao.

underneath. Malalo iho.

underrate. Ho'oha'aha'a, kāwa'e.

undershirt. Pale'ili, pale'ili o luna, palema'i o luna.

undersigned. Ka mea i kākau inoa malalo iho.

undersized. 'U'uku iho, 'ā'ā, 'i'i.

underslip. Mu'umu'u.

understand. Maopopo, ho'omaopopo, 'ike. *I understand,* maopopo ia'u; ho'omaopopo au.

undertake. Ho'ā'o, lawe, lele. *To undertake wholeheartedly,* komo 'oko'a.

undertaker. Kanaka ho'olewa. *Undertaker's establishment,* hale ho'olewa, hale kupapa'u.

undertow. Kai miki, kai huki, kai kuolo, au kō malalo.

underwear. Pale'a'ahu.

underworld. Malalo iho.

undesirable. Makemake 'ole 'ia, kū 'ole i ka makemake, ho'opaumanawa.

undo. Wehe, wehewehe, wehe hou, ho'ohemo, kala, mokala, makala, molokala; — *evil by prayer,* kakakū.

undone. Māwehe, māweke, kō 'ole 'ia.

undoubtedly. 'A'ole e 'ole, pēlā 'i'o nō.

undress. Wehe i ka lole.

undulate. Ho'ānu'unu'u, ho'olili. *Also:* kauha'a, ānu'unu'u, ho'āli, hulili, 'ulili, 'ale'ale, paiāha'a.

uneasy. 'Ano pīhoihoi, panau, hopohopo. *Uneasy stomach,* nalulu ka 'ōpū.

unemployed. Nele i ka hana, po'e nele i ka hana, noho hana 'ole, 'a'ohe hana.

unenlightened. Na'aupō.

unenthusiastic. Hoihoi 'ole, puhalu, halu, uhalu.

unequalled. 'A'ohe lua, lua 'ole, ana 'ole, launa 'ole, 'a'ole e loa'a.

unethical. Kū 'ole i ka lula maika'i, kolohe, pono 'ole.

uneven. Kaulike 'ole. *Also:* lualua, mālualua, 'āwa'awa'a, kīwa'awa'a, kanapu'u, 'anapu'u, 'āmokemoke, 'alu'alu, 'ahulu, 'ōkumukumu, pa'ewa, mā'oi-

'oi, napa, nāpai, ho'ole'ole'o, kīlepa, nānai. *Uneven tooth,* niho keu.

unexpected. Mahu'i 'ole 'ia, 'ano'ai.

unfaithful. Kūpa'a 'ole, 'auana; lepelua *(rare).*

unfamiliar. Malihini, ma'a 'ole, 'a'ole i ma'ama'ahia. *This is unfamiliar to me,* he mea malihini kēia ia'u.

unfasten. Wehe, ho'ohemo, ulehelehe.

unfastening. Wehena, wehe 'ana.

unfavorable. Kūpono 'ole. *Cf.* **lele 'opu.**

unfeigned. Ho'okamani 'ole.

unfermented. Hū 'ole.

unfold. Lole; hohola, kauhola *(as a tapa);* makala, 'ōme'o, mōhala *(as a blossom);* 'uhola, mohahala, mōhalahala, mōhola.

unforgiving. Huikala 'ole, mauhala.

unfortunate. Pō'ino, pōpilikia, make, niuniu, pōmaika'i 'ole.

unfriendly. Laulauna 'ole. *Also:* maka lena, 'āniha, makaua, auakua, konā, kūkona, laukōnā; 'auwae o'o *(fig.);* lanau, nanau.

unfurl. Wehe, ho'olu'e; hohola *(as tapa).*

unfurnished. 'A'ohe lako hale, 'a'ohe pono hale.

ungainly. 'Oeha'a. *See* **awkward.**

ungodly. 'Aiā, 'aiāhulu, aiāhua, haihaiā.

ungracious. 'Olu'olu 'ole, kakana, ho'okēāmaka; linu *(rare).*

ungrateful. Aloha 'ole, maua. *See sayings,* **au 4, gouge.**

unhampered. Hihia 'ole, kuakahi.

unhappy. Hau'oli 'ole; manoni *(rare). See* **sad.**

unharness. Wehewehe i ka mea ho'opa'a.

unholy. Haihaiā.

unhook. Wehe i ke kīlou, wehe i ka lou.

unicorn. Laehaokela, le'ema.

unicorn fish. Kala.

uniform. 1. *Similar.* Kohu like, like. 2. *Dress.* Makalike, pa'a lole makalike. *Full-dress uniform,* 'a'ahu 'oihana piha.

unimportant. Mea 'ole.

uninhabited. Noho 'ole 'ia, kanaka 'ole. *Also:* kōkeāno, wa'awa'a; kōkahe *(rare).*

uninhibited. Ho'okō wale i ka mana'o e 'upu a'e ana, ho'oponopono 'ole, ku'upau.

unintelligent. Hūpō, kuānea.

unintelligible. Maopopo 'ole. *See* **gibberish.** *Also:* kāwala, kāwalawala, kīwawā, waha pu'u. *To talk unintelligibly,* ho'okāwala.

uninterested. Manakā, palaka, hoihoi 'ole; ma'oeā, kūkaikea *(rare).*

union. Hui, pilina, ho'ohui 'ana; uniona *(labor);* — *under a single ruler,* kuapapa; — *of two,* kōko'olua.

unique. Laha 'ole, lua 'ole. *Also:* kū kahi, kiakahi, kakahi. *See saying,* **mulberry.**

unison. Lōkahi. *Also:* ne'epapa, papa, kāpapa, kiakahi, puwalu; lile *(rare).*

Unitarian. Unikalio.

unite. Hui, hui pū, pili pū, kāpili, ho'ohui, ho'oku'īku'i, ho'okahi, hū, ku'i, ho'oku'ikahi.

united. Hui pū 'ia, huihui, hui kahi, hui 'ia. *Also:* ne'epapa, papau, pūpūkahi, aukahi, wai kahi, ku'ikahi, 'āpipi, puwalu; ho'opili *(as friends). See saying,* **umauma.**

United Nations. Nā Lāhui Huipū.

United States of America. 'Amelika Hui, 'Amelika Huipū.

unity. Lōkahi, ku'ikahi. *See* **unite** *and saying,* **wai 1.**

universal. Ma nā wahi a pau, ma nā 'āina a pau.

universe. Ao holo'oko'a.

university. Kulanui.

unjust. Kaulike 'ole, pono 'ole, ho'opono 'ole, 'ewa'ewa.

unkempt. Kāpulu, ākepakepa, kiwala'ō.

unkind. Loko 'ino, mānewanewa, ho'omānewanewa.

unknown. 'Ike 'ole 'ia, la'a uli.

unlawful. Kū'ē kānāwai.

unleavened. Hū 'ole. *Unleavened bread,* pelena hū 'ole, perena hū 'ole, pōpō palaoa hū 'ole.

unless. Ke 'ole, inā 'a'ole. *Unless you work hard, (you) won't get your grade,* ke 'ole (inā 'a'ole) 'oe e hō'ika-ika, 'a'ole e loa'a ana kou heluna.

unlike. Like 'ole.

unlikely. 'A'ole paha.

unlimited. Palena 'ole, kaupalena 'ole 'ia.

unload. Wehewehe i ka ukana, ho'olei ukana, hu'e.

unloading. Hu'ena.

unlock. Wehe me ke kī.

unlucky. Pōmaika'i 'ole, pakalaki. *Also:* paoa, niuaua, niuniu, pahulu; lolomū *(rare). See sayings,* **'ole 2, unele, mudhen.**

unmarried. Male 'ole. *To remain unmarried,* noho male 'ole.

unmerciful. Aloha 'ole, loko 'ino, hainā.

unnecessary. Ho'opaumanawa, waiwai 'ole, pono 'ole.

unobstructed. Ke'ake'a 'ole. *Also:* kuakahi, pāpū, ākea, molale, mōla'e, mōla'ela'e.

unobtrusive. Ha'aha'a, akahai, hilu, nihi, hō'oi'oi 'ole.

unoccupied. Ka'awale, 'a'ole noho 'ia.

unpalatable. *See* **distasteful.**

unpleasant. Hoihoi 'ole, 'olu'olu 'ole. *See* **disagreeable.**

unprepared. Hemahema, mākaukau 'ole.

unpretentious. Na'au pēpē, ha'aha'a. *See* **modest.**

unprincipled. Pono 'ole, 'ino nā hana, kolohe. *See* **unethical.**

unproductive. Hua 'ole. *Also:* lolena, pau'aka, aukaha.

unqualified. Mākaukau 'ole, kūpono 'ole.

unreasonable. 1. *Unfair.* Kaulike 'ole. 2. *Exorbitant.* 'Oi mamua o ka mea kūpono. 3. *Not amenable to change.* Ho'opa'akikī, pa'akikī, po'o pa'a.

unreceptive. Ho'olohe 'ole, ho'opa'akikī, kū ma kapa.

unrelated. 'Oko'a, pili 'ole.

unreliable. Hiki 'ole ke paulele 'ia, kūpono 'ole. *Also:* pau'aka; ho'owale hau, hoeha'a *(fig.).*

unresponsive. Lohe 'ole, pane 'ole. *Also:* kukule, kūpolō.

unrestrained. Hiki 'ole ke kāohi; ku'ulala *(wild);* lelepā *(wanton);* mōhalu, mōhaluhalu *(relaxed).*

unrewarding. Hua 'ole, waiwai 'ole, pau'aka.

unrighteous. Pono 'ole, hewa; keke'e *(fig.).*

unripe. Maka, o'o 'ole, 'ōpiopio; kākāhou *(rare).*

unroll. Ho'omahola.

unsaddle. Wehewehe i ka noho lio.

unsafe. Malu 'ole, pilikia, maka'u.

unsavory. 'Ōnuhenuhe, 'a'alakai, ko'eko'e, haumia. *One of unsavory reputation,* lāhea.

unseemly. Pupuka. *See* **improper.**

unsettled. Kau lewa, pualewa, kālewa, kāhulihuli, kūlanalana; ku'una 'ole *(not relaxed);* ku'ia *(mentally).*

unsheath. 'U'u, unuhi, wehe.

unsightly. Pupuka.

unskilled. Hemahema, pāhemahema, kue'o. *Also:* kaialile, hāwāwā, mā'uka'uka, hōlona, 'onana; neki, poholelua *(rare). Unskilled laborer,* limahana mā'uka'uka. *See saying,* **surfer.**

unsociable. Laulauna 'ole. *Also:* laule'a 'ole, waiakua, koe'ā, monū, 'iolea, lanau, nanau. *See* **chin, head, poi.**

unstable. Loli wale, huli lua, lauwili wale. *Also:* ewa, pūlewa, lewa, kuewa, māena, lolelua, lolilua, mola, molamola, 'ae'a, kūlanalana, ho'owale hau, limu, hoeha'a, malana'opi. *See* **morning-glory, uncertain.**

unsteady. Luliluli, kāhulihuli, kulana, kūlanalana, ānewa. *Also:* naluli, pōlewa, pālokeloke, mūhe'e, naka, kāpekepeke, ka'amola, kūnapa, hīkākā, 'ona, 'ai'aiele, māena, kue'o, luni, pehe.

unsuccessful. Pohō, kō 'ole 'ia, holole'a 'ole. *Also:* pahu'a, paoa, lolomū, lihili.

unsuitable. Kohu 'ole, kūpono 'ole, 'a'ohe kohu iki. *See saying,* **pilina.**

unsurpassed. Palena 'ole, lua 'ole, ana 'ole, launa 'ole. *Unsurpassed knowledge,* palena 'ole ka 'ike.

unsymmetrical. Pā'ewa'ewa; nui pahupū *(of size).*

unsystematic. Kīpalalē, malele. *To farm scattered patches unsystematically,* mahi kīkoi.

untamed. Hihiu, 'āhiu, iō'ena, 'e'ena, 'eno, makanahele, ho'omakanahele, hanahihi.
untidy. Mōkākī, kāpulu, kiwala'ō, hauhalakī, ho'oponopono 'ole. *See saying,* **candlenut.**
untie. Wehe, 'uwehe, wehewehe, kala, molokala, mokala, makala; palahemo *(rare).*
untied. Hemo, wehe 'ia, ulehelehe.
until. Ā, ā hiki i.
untouchable. Kauā *(for various kinds, see* **kauā** *and entries that follow it).*
untrue. 'Oia'i'o 'ole, ho'opunipuni, hewa, pahilau.
unusual. Mea 'ē, 'ano 'ē, 'ē, 'ano hou, malihini, ma'amau 'ole, kūha'o, kāmeha'i. *Unusual or rare work,* hana hihiu. *How unusual!* He ha'o wale ho'i!
unweaned. Ukuhi 'ole, 'ai waiū.
unwedded. Male 'ole, kuakahi.
unwell. 'Ōma'ima'i, 'oma'i.
unwholesome. 'Ino, kūpono 'ole.
unwilling. Kū'ē.
unwrap. Wehe, wehewehe.
unwrinkled. Malino; ka'i'i *(rare).*
unwritten. Kākau 'ole.
unyielding. Pa'akikī. *Also:* konā, konākonā, mākonā, koniā, kūna'e.
up. Luna, i luna, maluna, nuna. *To come up from under,* ka'a maluna. *Up-and-down motion, as of a trip hammer,* kimokimo. *Up there,* aia i luna.
uphill. I luna, maluna. *To walk or go uphill,* pi'i.
uphold. Kāko'o, ko'o.
upland. Uka. *Upland dweller,* noho uka, kō a uka, kō kula uka.
uplands. Uka; 'umeke 'ai *(fig.).*
upon. I luna o, maluna o.
upper. Luna, maluna a'e, kōkī.
upright. **1.** *Erect.* Kū, kūpono, niolo, uluo'a; kāpi'o *(supports for a house).* **2.** *Moral.* Na'au pono, kohu pono, ho'opono, pololei. *Also:* papakū, nakulu'ai.
uprising. Kipi, ala hou.
uproot. 'Ula'a, hula'a, hehu, hulā, peu, 'āka'a; kula'a *(rare).*
upset. **1.** *Capsize.* Ho'okahuli, auhuli, kahuli, luma'i, 'ōlepe. *Upset stomach,* nahu ka 'ōpū, pualewa, 'o'olokū. **2.** *Worried.* Pīhoihoi ka mana'o, pīhoihoi, pono 'ole ka mana'o, hopohopo; ulukū *(extreme).*

upside down. Hulihia, kahuli pū.
upstairs. Papahele o luna.
upstart. Hō'oi'oi, mī'oi'oi, kupu.
upward. A'e, i luna a'e.
Uranus. Heleekela, Hereekela.
urge. Koi, ha'akoi, ho'okina, ho'okikina, pai, ho'opai, lale, ho'olale, ho'olalelale, kauleo, une; — *persistently,* ho'olā'au, ho'okonokono.
urgent. Ko'iko'i, mea 'ano nui.
urging. Kōina, koikoi.
Urim. 'Ulima, Urima.
urinal. Mīana.
urinate. Mimi. *Also:* mī, pīpī, hanawai; kama, kamahānau *(rare).* *To urinate repeatedly,* mimi helele'i, mimi hono. *To urinate painfully,* mimi 'eha. *Desire to urinate,* pu'u mimi, pu'amimi. *Inability to urinate,* mimi pa'a. *Urinating contest (as of small boys),* ho'okahekahe wai, na'ina'i mimi.
urine. Mimi. *Also:* wai mimi, mī, hanawai; mimi 'awa *(bad-smelling);* kamahānau *(rare).*
urn. Ipu.
urticaria. Laina.
us. Iā kāua, iā māua *(dual);* iā kākou, iā mākou *(plural).* *He saw us,* 'ike 'oia iā mākou.
usage. Hana ma'a, hana mau.
use. **1.** *Value.* Waiwai, pono; 'uko *(rare).* *Of no use,* waiwai 'ole, pau'aka, 'uko 'ole. *Of little use but better than nothing,* ma'ū. **2.** *Utilize.* Ho'ohana.
used to. Ma'a, ma'ama'a, ma'ama'ahia.
useful. Waiwai, mea kōkua.
useless. Waiwai 'ole, makehewa, 'u'a, 'ole wale, 'uko 'ole, pohō wale. *Also:* hāloli'ili, pau'aka, hakanele. *See* **worthless** *and idioms,* **'ala'ala, hāwa'e.**
usher. Kuhikuhi i kahi e noho ai.
usual. Ma'amau, mea mau. *Also:* pa'a mau, kūmau, kuluma, hana mau 'ia. *Same as usual,* 'oia mau nō.
usurer, usurious. Puni kuala.
usurp. Kā'ili hewa, lawe 'āpiki, kā'ihi.
usury. Uku ho'opane'e, kuala.
Utah. Uka, Uta; Mauna Pōhaku *(poetic).*
utensil. Ipu, mea pa'ahana.
utmost. Po'okela, nui loa.
utter. Ho'opuka, pua'i. *See* **say.**
utterance. 'Ōlelo, māpuna leo, māpuna 'ōlelo, puana.

V

v. *No Hawaiian term.*
vacancy. Haka, hakahaka, wahi kaʻawale.
vacant. Hakahaka, haka, kāwaha.
vacation. Wā hoʻomaha, hoʻomahana, maha.
vaccinate. ʻŌ.
vaccination. ʻŌ lima *(arm)*.
vacuum cleaner. Mīkini hoʻomaʻemaʻe hale, wākiuma.
vagabond. Kanaka ʻaeʻa, kuewa, lewa. *Also:* ʻaeʻa haukaʻe, limu pae, limu lana, puewa, pālauʻeka, kālole, kīhoe, akauahelo, kualana, lau hala lana, pākukui, ānea, ʻōlemukaʻa, peʻe pao, kea pili mai, kūelekā, pakaulei, pakauhelo. *See* **outcast, parasite.**
vagina. Kohe. *Also:* ʻamo, ʻamo hulu, peo, kali; pīnēnē *(rare);* osseous —, pukapaʻa. *Cavity of vagina,* poholua. *Division between the vagina and anus,* kohe lemu.
vague. Pōwehiwehi, pōwehi, akaaka ʻole, kāpekepeke, ʻōhio.
vain. **1.** *Proud.* Hoʻokano, hoʻokiʻekiʻe, hoʻoheo, kanaʻie, hoʻokanaʻie, haʻakei, hakalina. **2.** *Without results.* Pohō, makehewa, ʻuʻa, Hikauhi, wale; hua āelo *(fig.).*
vale. *Same as* **valley.** *Vale of tears,* ʻowāwa o nā waimaka.
Valentine's Day. Ka Lā o Lono-i-ke-aweawe-aloha *(i.e., the day of the god of love and mercy; a term coined in 1980).*
valiant. Koa, ʻaʻa; koʻakā *(fig.);* koapaka.
valley. Awaawa, awāwa, kahawai, ʻowāwa, ʻoawa, ʻōawaawa, ʻaʻalu; hēkuawa, hekuawawa, kuawa *(used poetically);* Hono-, Hana- *(used only in place names).* *Valley bottom,* papa lalo. *See ex.,* **shadow.**
valuable. Waiwai, makamae.
value. Waiwai, minamina, waiwai kaulike, waiwai ʻiʻo. *Of some little value,* maʻū. *See* **par value.**
valueless. Waiwai ʻole, ʻole wale, lapuwale, ʻole loa. *To keep doing something that is valueless,* milikaʻa.
valve. Pani; pepeiao *(of the heart);* aʻapau *(of a vein);* kuapuʻu *(as of clams).*
vamp. Kāholo *(hula step).* *See also* **flirt.**
van. Kaʻa; hunalewa *(of army).* *See* **truck.**
vandal. Kolohe, mea luku wale.
vandalism. Luku wale.
vanilla. Wanila.
vanish. Nalowale, nalo, nalohia. *Also:* olomio, poholo, palemo, pio loa, ʻāhaʻikapupuhi.
vanity. Haʻaheo, hoʻokahakaha. *Biblical:* lapuwale, hanu.
vanity case. Poho pauka.
vapor. Ea, noe, ʻohu, māhu.
variable. Lolilua, lolelua, loli wale, lauwili, kākālule, ʻōlewa, kāhulihuli.
variant. Mana.
variation. Loli ʻana, ʻaui ʻana. *Variation of form,* kīpuka.
varicose veins. Aʻa kūkūkū, ʻaʻahuʻi.
variegated. Kiʻokiʻo, pikapika, lolohuamea, kalakoa, ponapona.
variety. ʻAno, kēlā me kēia ʻano. *Great variety,* nui nā ʻano like ʻole.
various. Like ʻole, kēlā me kēia.
varnish. Waniki, ʻiliki.
vary. Loli aʻe, pūlewa; ʻanini *(rare).* *To vary in appearance,* kūhapa; mikololia *(rare).* *To vary in color or texture,* kipona.
vase. Pika; pika pua *(flower);* kīʻaha ʻoʻoma.
vassal. Kauā hoʻoluhi. *See* **outcast.**

vast. Nui ʻino, nui loa. *Also:* palena ʻole, mānoa, kūāhewa, nui hewahewa, mānuʻunuʻu, oneʻula.
Vatican. Wakikana.
vault. Waihona, keʻena. *Burial vault,* waihona kupapaʻu. *See* **fireproof, pole vault.**
veal. ʻIʻo pipi keiki.
veer. Huli, kīkaha; holohiʻa *(at an angle);* pūhili, ʻōkeʻe *(as the wind).*
Vega. Keoe *(probably).*
vegetable. *No Hawaiian equivalent; early Hawaiians distinguished poi* (ʻai, poi) *and accompaniments to poi* (iʻa, ʻīnaʻi). *Nearest equivalents to English term:* mea ulu, mea kanu, mea ʻai launahele, lāʻau palupalu.
vegetation. Nahele, nāhelehele.
vehicle. Kaʻa *(for various kinds, see Haw.-Eng. entry and entries that follow it).*
veil. Uhi, pale uhi, uhi maka, pale maka, pākū.
vein. Aʻa koko, aʻa; paʻi aʻa koko *(small);* hōʻaʻa. *See* **varicose veins.** *Network of veins,* aʻaʻaʻa. *Valve of a vein,* aʻapau. *Vein of metal,* au metala.
velocity. Welokike. *See* **fast.**
velvet. Weleweka.
velvet grass. Mauʻu Kepanī.
venerated. Mahalo ʻia, hōʻihi ʻia, mōʻiu, mōʻiuʻiu.
venereal disease. Maʻi ʻino *(general name),* maʻi hilo, hilo, maʻi wili, ʻako, kulu, waikī, palakiʻo; kohe ʻako *(females),* ule hilo *(males).* *Rare:* kūʻoha, hahaʻianana, ʻōpikopiko. *See* **ʻāhui hala 2, gonorrhea, syphilis, tumor.**
Venetian blinds. ʻŌpeʻapeʻa, ʻōlepelepe.
vengeance. Hoʻopaʻi, mākaia, pānaʻi i ka ʻino.
venomous. Make. *Venomous mouth,* waha okooko *(fig.).*
vent. Puka; miona *(in stomach of fish).*
ventilate. Hoʻokomo makani, hoʻokomo ea.
ventriloquism, ventriloquist. Hoʻolele leo.
venture. ʻAʻa, hoʻāʻo.
Venus. *Many names have been listed, some probably doubtful;* Hōkū-ahiahi, Hōkū-kau-ahiahi, Hōkū-kauʻōpae, Hōkū-aliʻi, Hōkū-aliʻi-wahine, Hōkū-komohana, Hōkū-loa (Kūloa), Holo-i-kahiti, Mānanalo, Mūlehu, Nā-holoholo (?), Wenuka. *See* **Jupiter.**
Venus's-flytrap. Mikinalo.
Vera Cruz. Wela Kaluka, Vera Karuza.
veranda. Lānai; hale kia *(with pillars).*
verb. Haʻina, haʻihana. *Kinds:* haʻina pili, haʻina pili aku *(active);* haʻina kōkua *(auxiliary);* haʻina ʻokoʻa, haʻina pili ʻole aku *(intransitive);* haʻina kekeʻe *(irregular);* haʻina ʻokoʻa *(neuter);* haʻina pili, haʻina pili aku *(transitive);* haʻina pili iā haʻi *(transitive active);* haʻina pili ʻia mai *(transitive passive);* ka haʻi ʻana i ka hana aku *(active verb);* ka haʻi ʻana i ka hana ʻia mai *(passive verb).*
verbal. ʻŌlelo, haʻi waha. *Verbal will,* hoʻoilina ʻōlelo.
verbatim. Haʻi e like loa me ka mea i lohe ʻia.
verbena. Ōwī, haʻuōwī; wāpine, vabine *(lemon).*
verbose. Hoʻonui ʻōlelo. *Verbose and idle,* palaualelo.
verdict. ʻŌlelohoʻoholo, palapala hoʻokō.
verdure. Uluwehi, uluwehiwehi, uliuli.
verification. Hōʻoiaʻiʻo.
verify. Hōʻoia, hōʻoiaʻiʻo, hoʻokūʻiʻo.
verily. ʻOiaʻiʻo.
Vermont. Welemoneka, Veremoneta.
versatile. Mākaukau i nā mea like ʻole.
verse. Laina, lālani *(line);* paukū, ʻoki *(stanza).*
versed. ʻIke loa, ʻike noʻeau, paʻa, mākaukau. *Well*

versed, ka'a. *Versed in lore or legends,* pa'a mo'olelo. *Versed in songs,* pa'a mele.
version. Mana *(as of a tale).*
versus. Kū'ē.
vertebra. Paukū iwi o ka iwikuamo'o; 'anu'u *(disjointed).*
vertical. Kū pololei.
vertigo. Niniu, newa, pōniu, pōniuniu, 'ea pōniu. *See* **dizzy.**
very. Loa, nō, wale, maoli, pau, 'ino, ho'ikau, hewahewa. *Very good,* maika'i nō, maika'i loa, maika'i maoli. *Very, very many,* nui 'ino. *Very much,* 'ino. *Very, very much,* ā nui, nui 'ino. *How very!* Kai! *Thanks very, very, very much,* mahalo ā nui loa.
vesper. Wepele, mele ahiahi.
vessel. **1.** *Container.* Ipu; 'umeke *(circular);* ipu lepo *(earth);* hue *(narrow-necked).* **2.** *Ship.* Moku. **3.** *Anatomy.* A'a koko *(blood).*
vest. Pūliki.
Vesuvius. Wekuwia, Vesuvia.
veteran. Koa kahiko.
veterinary. Kauka holoholona.
veto. Hō'ole, wiko.
vex. Ho'onāukiuki, ho'ouluhua, 'ō'upē; ho'ouhuhī *(rare).*
vexed. Nāuki, ukiuki, uluhua, nāulu, pi'oloke, makaua; uhelehe *(rare).*
vibrate. Hulili, 'ulili. *Also:* ho'olili, kuekueni, naue, 'ānu'unu'u, ho'ānu'unu'u, kuolo, kūpaloloi, 'iolo, mahiki, nakulu, 'ōnini, kanulu, pilu. *Heat vibrating,* hawewe, kolilili, ānea.
vice. Hewa, hala, 'ino, hana haumia.
vice-. Hope, pani.
vice-president. Hope pelekikena.
viceroy. Ali'i ho'omalu.
vicinity. Kahi kokoke.
vicious. 'Ino, hae.
Vicksburg. Wikapuka, Vikabuga.
victim. Luaahi, pio, heana. *Also:* moepu'u, kama; lua-'oni *(the second).*
victor. Mea lanakila, mea eo.
victory. Lanakila, eo. *See sayings,* **moi 1, torch.**
view. 'Ikena, nānaina, maka; — *down,* hālona; — *out,* kilohana.
vigil. Wikilia, wigilia.
vigilant. Maka'ala.
vigor. Ikaika; u'i *(youthful). Also:* ehuehu, ahuahu, kā-'ala'ala, pa'a.
vile. Haumia, nonohua, 'ala'uka.
village. Kūlanakauhale, kaiāulu.
vine. Lā'au hihi; *creeping —,* 'āhihi, kolokolo; *long —,* kālī, kālina, kā *(as of sweet potato). Sacred vine,* kā hiwa. *To send out a vine,* kā.
vinegar. Pinika, wīneka.
vineyard. Māla waina, pā waina, mahi waina.
viol. Wiola.
violate. 'A'e, hehikū, 'a'e kū, 'a'e kapu. *See* **kolohe, rape.**
violation. Hana kū'ē, 'a'e kapu, hehikū.
violent. Weliweli, uluulu, ehuehu, hao wale, hanahana.
violet. Waioleka, aupaka. *Kinds:* 'olopū, nani Wai'ale-'ale, kalili, liliwai, pohe hiwa; pāmakani *(Moloka'i);* pakalana *(Chinese). For the color, see* **lavender, purple.**
violin. Pila kuolo, pila, waiolina.
VIP. Mea 'ano nui, ki'i maka nunui.
viper. Mo'o make, mo'o niho 'awa.
virgin. Pu'upa'a *(female);* ulepa'a *(male).*
Virginia. Wilikinia, Viriginia, Wilikine.
virginity. Pu'upa'a.

virile. Ke'a, pūkonakona.
virtue, virtuous. Hemolele, pono.
virus. Mea ho'oma'i.
viscid. Uaua, pipili, pilipili, ka'aka'alina; maka piapia, moekuhua *(of eyes).*
vise. 'Ūmi'i.
visible. Kūmaka, 'ike maka. *Also:* akaaka, pāpū, 'ō'ili lua, kō'iu'iu.
vision. Haili moe, hihi'o, 'ike. *Rare:* akakū, pinauea, 'ea kai wawaka.
visit. Māka'ika'i, kipa, launa. *To visit unasked or by chance,* kipa wale. *To visit from district to district,* komo 'āpana. *To visit from place to place,* kipa hele. *Visiting committee,* kōmike komo 'āpana.
visitor. Mea māka'ika'i, mea kipa.
visitors' bureau. Pulo ho'okipa malihini.
visor. Lala, pālulu *(sun).*
vital. 'Ano nui, ko'iko'i.
vitriol. Wikiliola.
vivacious. 'Ele'eleu, hō'eu'eu, hō'ele'eleu, lamalama.
vivid. 'A'ai, nohi.
vocabulary. Papa 'ōlelo *(list);* huina 'ōlelo *(word totality).*
vocation. 'Oihana.
vocative case. 'Auihea.
voice. **1.** *Physical.* Leo. *Distinct voice,* leo akaaka. *Harsh voice,* leo kākala. *Loud voice,* leo nui. *Low voice,* leo iki, pihano. *Male voice,* leo kāne. *Middle voice,* leo waena. *Sweet voice,* leo nahenahe, 'ale'a, leo kani. *Wafted voice,* māpuna leo, māpuna 'ōlelo. *Voice or authority and respect,* leo hano. *Voices of the gods,* 'ikuwā. *Voices of the spirits,* nā leo wawalo o ka hanehane, 'ulaleo, hakahaka leo. *Din of voices,* pihe. *Rising and falling of the voice,* ha'iha'i. *Snatching the voice (by sorcery, to prevent speaking),* 'apo leo. *To deepen the voice,* ho'oko'iko'i. *To record the voice,* 'apo leo. *See saying,* **eat. 2.** *Grammar.* Leo pili. *Active voice,* leo pili aku, ka ha'i 'ana i ka hana aku. *Passive voice,* leo pili 'ia mai, ka ha'i 'ana i ka hana 'ia mai.
void. 'Ole loa *(not in effect);* hahalu *(empty). See* **excrete.**
volcanic. Pele, 'a'ā pele. *Volcanic flow,* lua'i pele, 'ā pele. *Volcanic ejecta,* pōhāhā. *Volcanic haze,* noeuahi.
volcano. Lua pele, pele, ahi 'ai honua. *Volcano goddess,* Pele; *epithets for Pele:* earth-eating woman, wahine 'ai honua; *woman of the pit,* wahine o ka lua; *foreign woman,* wahine malihini *[she came from Kahiki]; woman of the white garment,* wahine o ka 'a'ahu ke'oke'o.
volume. 1. *Quantity.* Nui. **2.** *Literary.* Puke, helu.
voluntary. Makemake iho, koho e hana.
volunteer. 'A'a.
vomit. Lua'i, pua'i. *Also:* hō'owā, 'auku'u; lua'i koko *(blood).*
voracious. Pākela 'ai, ho'onu'u nui. *Also:* haupa, 'ai ā manō, kāpapa, 'a'ao.
vote. Koho, koho pāloka. *Vote of confidence,* 'ōlelo ho-'oholo hilina'i. *To vote for the sake of voting, without forethought,* koho honua. *To vote a straight ticket,* koho pololei.
voter. Mea koho. *Voters,* po'e koho pāloka, manakoho.
voting. Koho pāloka.
voting booth. Ke'ena koho pāloka.
voucher. Pila 'ai'ē, palapala hō'oia'i'o.
vow. Ho'ohiki, 'ōlelo ho'ohiki, 'ōlelo pa'a.
vowel. Hua palapala leo kahi, hua leo kahi, leokani.
voyage. Huaka'i, holomoana, holokai.
vulgar. Pelapela.
Vulgate. Wulekake.
vulture. Wulekula, vuletula, 'aekelona, aeselona.

W

w. Wē.

wad. Pōpō. *Wad of tobacco,* pōpō paka. *Gun wad,* ʻumoki, panipū. *Wad discharged from a weapon,* pōkā ukali.

waddle. ʻOehaʻa, pau hananuʻu.

wade. Hele wāwae i loko o ke kai (ka wai), helekū.

wafer. Pāpaʻa pelena, uwepa; papa palaoa *(rare).*

waft. Māpu, māpuana, aheahe, ahe; — *off to sleep,* kuluhio. *Wafted fragrance,* moani. *White wafted smoke,* ʻo ka uahi māpu kea. *The fragrance of the maile wafts in the breeze,* ke māpu nei ke ʻala o ka maile.

wag. Luli, kolili, konini, ʻoniʻoni. *The dog wags the tail,* hoʻokonini ka ʻīlio i ka huelo.

wage. Uku. *See* **wage war.** *Wages of sin (Roma 6:23),* ka uku no ka hewa.

wager. Pili, piliwaiwai, ʻai. *To wager one's bones,* pili i nā iwi.

wagered. Mau, hoʻomau.

wages. Uku, uku hana. *To pay wages,* uku hana.

wage war. Hoʻouka kaua, kaua.

wagon. Kaʻa. *Horse-drawn wagon,* kaʻa lio. *Wagon tongue or shafts,* kolo, kolo kaʻa.

wahoo. Ono.

Wai-kīkī. Waikīkī *(lit., spouting water).*

wail. Uē, ʻalalā, kanikau; uē helu, uē kaukau *(and weep in mourning). Also:* pihe, olo pihe, kūmakena, puwō, puō, makena, kaʻakūmakena, kūpinaʻi, kūwō, kūō, aeae, leoleo, nā, kaniāʻau.

Wai-luku. Wailuku *(lit., waters of destruction).*

Wai-mea. Waimea *(lit., reddish-brown waters).*

Wai-piʻo. Waipiʻo *(lit., curved water). See saying,* **drowsy.**

waist. Pūhaka, ʻaʻa, pākana. *Tight waist binder,* kāliki. *To gird the waist tightly,* paulinalina.

wait. Kali, kakali, alia, hoʻālia; kapakaʻi *(rare);* — *on tables,* lawelawe, kuene. *Wait a moment,* kali iki, eia iho, pēlā iho. *Wait a long time,* kūlōʻihi. *Wait patiently and you shall receive what you crave,* hoʻomanawanui i ka ʻono. *Wait for you,* kala iāʻoe. *Wait on you,* lawelawe iāʻoe.

waiter. Kuene, kanaka lawelawe, mea lawelawe. *House waiter,* kuene hale.

waiting. Kalina, ʻemo. *Waiting station,* hale hoʻolulu.

waitress. Wahine lawelawe, kuene wahine.

waiver. Hōʻole ʻana.

wake. 1. *Awaken.* Ala. *To awaken someone,* hoʻāla, hoʻālahia. *To wake suddenly,* puoho. *To wake up the child,* hoʻāla i ke keiki. *Wake, it is light, it is bright (UL 197),* e ala, ua ao, ua mālamalama. **2.** *Prefuneral vigil.* Anaina hoʻolewa, kiaʻi kupapaʻu. **3.** *Track.* Awe, aweawe.

wakeful. Hiaʻā, hoʻālahia.

Wales. Wāle. *Prince of Wales,* Keiki aliʻi o Wāle.

walk. Hele wāwae, hele; piʻi *(towards mountains or uphill);* iho *(towards the sea or downhill). Also:* wāwae, au. *To take a walk,* holoholo, mākaʻikaʻi. *To walk slowly, quietly,* hele mālie, nihi ka hele; kaʻa niau, kuoni, keni *(rare). To help walk, as a child,* hoʻoholoholo, hoʻohelehele, hoʻohele. *To walk in line or succession,* kaʻi hele, kaʻi, kakaʻi. *To walk with a stiff back,* nanai, lanai. *To walk with legs wide apart,* kiʻihelei, kaiena. *To walk lightly and swiftly,* hele ʻāwīwī, auau, kīau. *To walk backward,* kuemi. *To walk with a cane,* kaukoʻo, hoʻokaukoʻo. *Ungainly walk,* ʻoehaʻa. *To walk along absent-mindedly,* kīkaha. *To walk unstead-*

ily, kaʻi hele, kūpehe, hakupehe, kaupē. *To endeavor to walk in spite of weakness,* hoʻokoene. *To sway the hips in walking,* hele kaiue. *To walk upright,* helekū. *To walk in a brisk, haughty manner,* kalalī. *To walk proudly,* hele kīkahakaha; pahāha *(rare). Walked on,* hehe ʻia, meheu.

walking stick. *See* **cane.**

wall. Pā; paia *(of house). Stone wall,* pā pōhaku. *Adobe wall,* pā lepo. *Wall of a fishpond,* kuapā; pā puni *(circular or surrounding). Sea wall,* pani kai, pale kai. *Interlocking stones, as in a wall,* niho. *Long, straight stone wall,* kuaiwi *(Niʻihau). Walled city,* kūlanakauhale (kūnanakauhale) i paʻa i ka pā. *Pressed hard to the wall,* pili pū i ka paia *(in trouble).*

wallet. ʻEke kālā, ʻekeʻeke kālā.

walleyed. Maka ʻāhewa.

wallop. Hahau ikaika.

wallow. Naku, kaʻa. *Also:* haunaku, oikū; haluku *(as a hog). To wallow in a mud puddle,* kaʻa i ke kiʻo lepo.

wallpaper. Pepa hale, pepa hoʻonani hale.

wall plate. Kaola, lohelau.

walnut. Walanuka.

walrus. Palaʻo, waleluka, walerusa, wolu.

wan. Nanakea, lanakea, hākeakea, mamae; ʻīkoko *(rare).*

wand. Koʻo, lāʻau; maile *(in games of pūhenehene and* ʻume); kāʻaha *(held by priest while sacrificing).*

wander. ʻAuana, kiʻihele, lalau, hoʻolalau, ʻaeʻa, kuewa. *Also:* hili, nāhili, kakahili, auhili, loloiāhili, kuawili, kualana, lanaau, ʻaʻau, lewa, ewa, māewa, kūʻaeʻa, hōʻaeʻa, hōʻaʻā, kūhilo, kakaʻi ā hele, kīhoe, hoʻopanau, pakauhelo. *See* **vagabond.** *Wander mentally,* lalau ka noʻonoʻo, lauele. *Wander in sin,* lalau hewa. *Wander in the dark,* hili pō.

wandering Jew. Honohono, mākolokolo.

wandering tattler. ʻŪlili.

wane. Emi, manono *(as the moon). Waning moon,* mahina hapalua hope.

want. 1. *Desire.* Makemake; mamake *(colloquial). Also:* make, lana ka manaʻo, manaʻo, hōʻopuʻopu. *See* **wish. 2.** *Lack.* Nele, hemahema.

wanton. ʻUhaʻuha wale, maka leho. *Also:* lelepā, kuʻulala, pākukui, pākaukau, pakaulei, pākiʻakiʻa. *Cf.* **pākīai.**

war. Kaua; paomomi *(rare). Civil war,* kaua kūloko. *Revolutionary war,* kaua hulihia, kaua auhulihia. *War finery (formerly helmet, feather cape),* kāhiko kaua. *War maneuvers,* kaʻa kaua. *War tank or chariot,* kaʻa kaua. *War strategist,* kaʻa kaua. *Heiau for success in war,* heiau waikaua. *See saying,* **bath.**

warble. Kūolokū; nunulu *(rare).*

war club. *See* **club.**

ward. 1. *Fend off.* Pale, hoʻopale. *Also:* kūpale, palekana, panekana, hoaka; hoʻoheihei *(as sorcery);* kōlulu *(rare). Warding off,* pale ʻana, papalena. *Ward off clubs,* ʻōniu lāʻau. **2.** *Person under guardianship.* Mea hoʻokahu ʻia. **3.** *Precinct.* ʻĀpana.

warden. Kahu mālama paʻahao *(prison);* kahu mālama ʻāpana *(district);* kahu.

wardrobe. Nā ʻaʻahu apau *(clothes);* keʻena waihona ʻaʻahu *(clothes closet).*

wardrobe mistress. Wahine mālama kapa.

wardroom. Lumi ʻaina o nā aliʻikoa.

warehouse. Hale ukana, hale hoʻāhu.

warlike. Puni kaua, makekau.

warm. Mahana, pumehana. *Also:* hahana, hana, hana-

hana, mehana, hoʻomāhanahana, māhanahana, hoʻopumehana, kōhanahana, pūwelawela, ʻōwela, ʻōikiiki,
lānia, kohea, heahea, ʻaheahea, mule, ʻōhea. *See* **hot.**
Warm over a fire, hoʻomahana, lala, ʻōlani. *Warm
spring,* wai welawela. *Warm aloha,* aloha pumehana.

warmth. Mahana, pumehana.

warn. Aʻo, kāmalū, hōʻike e mālama pono.

warning. Aʻo ʻana. *Siren warning of disaster,* oeoe
haʻina pōpilikia.

warp. 1. *Contract.* ʻAʻapu, napa. *Also:* ʻaʻapi, nenehū,
nāpai, hualala, ʻehipa, popoli, manawai. **2.** *Lengthwise
threads.* Maʻawe loloa. **3.** *Nautical.* Hekau, kaula
hoʻokolo moku.

war party. Pūʻulu kaua, kaua.

warrant. 1. *Document.* Palapala, palapala kiʻi, palapala
hoʻokō. *Bank warrant,* palapala kīkoʻo. *Blanket warrant,* pila kīkoʻo hoʻohuihui ʻia. *Warrant for arrest,*
palapala hoʻopiʻi, palapala hopu. **2.** *See* **justify.**

warrant officer. Aliʻikoa uku.

warrior. Koa, pūʻali. *Fig.:* au *(strong);* moa mahi, moa
kākala, lehua, kāpiʻi; lau ʻaua *(experienced). See sayings and epithets,* **ʻaʻaliʻi, ʻaʻama, ʻahi kananā, au 2,
ʻeʻa 1, holopapa 2, laumeke, ʻolelepā, puhi 4, pū
kō, pūkoʻa 1, ʻulaʻa, wakawaka 1, crab.** *Leader of
warriors,* papa poʻo. *Special warriors in Kamehameha's time,* Kīpuʻupuʻu. *God of warriors,* Lono-
maka-ihe.

warship. Moku kaua, manuā, ʻīlio ʻaukai.

wart. ʻIlikona, puʻu.

Warwick. Waleweki.

wary. ʻEʻena, ʻāhē. *Also:* ualehe *(as a fish);* pā i ka
ʻupena, pā i ka makau *(see* **pā 4);** kīkāmū, hōʻeno
(rare).

was. *No equivalent; see* **ua, be.**

wash. Holoi. *To have washed, pretend to wash,* hoʻoholoi. *To wash clothes,* holoi lole. *To wash hands,* holoi lima.

washbasin. Ipu holoi, ipu ʻauʻau, ipu wai ʻauʻau, poʻi
wai holoi, kapu holoi maka.

washboard. Papa holoi.

washcloth. Kāwele holoi.

washer. Pihipihi, mea holoi.

washing. Lole holoi, mea holoi *(clothes).*

washing machine. Mīkini holoi.

washing stick. Hoahoa, hohoa *(beating).*

Washington. Wakinekona, Wasinetona.

washout. Lilo i ka wai.

washpan. Pā kini holoi.

washtub. Kapu wai, kapu holoi.

wasp. Hopeʻō, kopena; nalo lawe lepo *(mud). Slender
abdominal part of wasp,* pūʻali.

waste. Hoʻomāunauna, hoʻopau, ʻuhaʻuha. *Also:* hoʻomāuna, māuna, ʻuha, kae; — *away,* emi, hōkiʻi, māilo,
hoʻomāilo, māio, hoʻomāilo, hoʻokilo, mae. *Waste
matter,* nā mea ʻino, ʻōpala, moka. *To eat wastefully,*
ʻai ʻuhaʻuha. *To waste food,* hoʻopau ʻai *(fig., worthless person). To waste time,* hoʻopaumanawa, ʻapa,
hoʻopaulina, hoʻopaulinalina.

wastebasket. ʻIe ʻōpala.

wastrel. ʻUhaʻuha.

watch. 1. *Observe.* Kiaʻi, hoʻokiaʻi; kaʻakaʻa *(rare).
Watch carefully,* nānā pono, maka kilo, kilo, hakakaupili. *Watch or you'll be hurt,* mālama o pā *(see* **pā 4).**
Watch out! Mālama pono! **2.** *Timepiece.* Uwaki, uaki.
Wrist watch, uwaki pūlima. *Face of a watch or clock,*
papahola. **3.** *Guardianship.* Uwaki. *To stand watch,* kū
uwaki.

watchful. Makaʻala, miki, makaʻina. *Watchful eyes,*
maka kilo.

watchman. Kiaʻi, kū uwaki. *Watchman's stand,* pā
kiaʻi.

watchtower. Hale kiaʻi, ʻīmaka.

water. Wai *(fresh; for various kinds, see* **wai 1** *and entries that follow it);* kai *(salt). See* **coconut, waterfall.**
To water, ninini wai, hoʻokahe wai, hoʻokahekahe wai,
hoʻokele wai, hanawai. *Spring water,* wai puna, wai

māpuna. *Water source,* māno wai, poʻo wai, makawai.
Abundance of water, lau wai, lawe wai. *Charged
water,* wai pipiʻi, wai piʻipiʻi. *Trickling water,* paihī.
Place with water, waina. *Flowing water,* wai kahe, wai
aulia. *Faucet water,* wai piula. *Ice water,* wai hau. *Potable water,* wai mānalo. *Brackish water,* wai kai, wai
ʻawaʻawa. *Polluted water,* wai pilopilo. *Sparkling
water,* wai lohia. *Agitated water,* lapa wai, puʻewai.
Water rights, kuleana wai. *One in charge of water
rights,* kahu wai. *To sprinkle with water,* pī wai. *To
mix with water, as poi,* hoʻokele wai; emōwai *(Kauaʻi).*
To water at the mouth, moni i ka hāʻae, kahe ka hāʻae.
To backwater in a canoe, hoʻēmi hope i ka waʻa. *A
water game,* pōhā kīhelei. *A water toy,* kōʻieʻie. *Water
given by Kāne and Kanaloa, spring water, water to
drink, water for power, water for life, may there be life
(UL 258),* i ka wai kau a Kāne me Kanaloa, he wai
puna, he wai e inu, he wai e mana, he wai e ola, e ola
nō.

water bottle. *See* **water gourd.**

water bubble. Huʻa o ka wai.

water buffalo. Pipi Pākē.

water chestnut. Ulu kai.

water colors. Pena kiʻi.

water container. Ipu wai, hue wai.

watercourse. Holowai. *See* **ditch, sluice.**

watercress. Lēkō. *Kinds:* lēkō ʻeleʻele, lēkō keʻokeʻo,
ʻihi kū kēpau, pāʻihi.

waterfall. Wailele; — *trickling, as down a cliff,* wai hī
(also: ʻōhāwai, hei, wai paihī). *Upside-down waterfall,*
wai puhia.

water gourd. Ipu wai, hue wai, nuku pueo.

water hole. Lua wai, kiʻo wai, ʻele.

water lemon. Lilikoʻi, lemi wai, laniwai, lemona.

Waterloo. Wakalū, Watalu.

watermaster. Luna wai, kahu wai.

watermelon. Ipu *(various kinds are listed);* ipu haole,
ipu huluhulu, ipu oloolo, ipu poʻo kanaka, ipu kāniʻo.

water meter. Ana wai.

water pistol. Pū kikī wai.

water polo. Polo wai.

waterproof. Komo ʻole ka wai.

water spirit. Moʻo, moʻo kiha.

waterspout. Waipuʻilani, waikōʻihi; pūlehu *(rare).*

waterway. Alawai, makawai.

water wheel. Huila wai.

water works. ʻOihana wai.

watery. Hōwai, kakale, kalekale, kale, kele wai. *Also:*
hoʻokakale, ukalekale, ʻōkalekale, hōkale, kele, kelekele, halahalawai, kēwai, holowai, wawai, ʻōhulu,
palakē. *To make watery,* hoʻokalekale, hoʻokakale,
kaiaka, pīholoholo.

wattles. Lepelepe, ʻolo, ʻaʻali, lepe, kīlepe.

wave. 1. *Ocean.* Nalu, nanu, ʻale. *See* **surf, swell 2,
tidal wave.** *High waves,* kai piʻi, eaea, huia, nalu pū
kī. *Breaking wave,* nalu haʻi, kai poʻi; papākolea
(rare). Receding wave, kai emi, kai heʻe, nalu miki.
Long wave, nalu kua loloa, lauloa, ʻonaulu loa. *Waves
that rise and fall without breaking,* nalu ʻaiō. *A surfing
wave,* huia. *Wave that breaks diagonally,* nalu haʻi
lala. *Broken section of wave,* nalu muku, muku.
Rough wave, nalunalu. *Base of a breaker,* honua nalu.
Bend of a wave, ʻopi nalu. *Tip of high waves,* hokua. *A
long-backed wave from the open sea,* he ʻale kua loloa
no ka moana *(boast of a hero).* **2.** *Motion.* Ani, peʻahi,
ani peʻahi; welo, welowelo, ʻōwelo, kōwelo, kōwelo-
welo, kālepa, kālepalepa *(as a flag). Also:* hoʻāni,
hoʻāli; hoʻokolili, kapalili *(shake);* konini, kuehu,
pulelo, holu, holunape, kiani. *Long may it wave,* e ani
mau loa ia.

wavy. ʻĀnuʻunuʻu, ʻāpiʻipiʻi, piʻipiʻi, nalu, hoʻāli. *Wavy
hair,* lauoho piʻipiʻi lau nui.

wax. 1. *To increase.* Māhuahua, hoʻonui. *See* **moon. 2.**
Substance. Pīlali, pīlali pālolo. *See* **beeswax, earwax.**
Wax seal, to seal with wax, uwepa.

waxflower. Pua hōkū hihi.

way. 1. *Route.* Ala, ala hele, alanui; ala waʻa *(canoe).* *Right of way,* pono ala hele. *Miss the way,* lalau, hala-kī. *This way and that way,* i ʻō, i ʻō. 2. *Manner, custom.* ʻAno, ʻaoʻao, kuamoʻo. *Way of life,* nohona. *That way,* pēlā. *This way,* penei.

waylay. Pōwā, hoʻohālua; kīmopō *(at night).* See **hālua, abduct.**

we. Kāua *(dual, inclusive);* kākou *(plural, inclusive);* māua *(dual, exclusive);* mākou *(plural, exclusive).*

weak. Nāwaliwali; lahilahi, nahinahi *(as coffee). Also:* palupalu, nāwali, ʻōnāwali, ʻōnāwaliwali, ʻōmaʻimaʻi, ikaika ʻole, uwaʻuwali, hāwali, ʻōwali, ʻōmali, lule, malule, haʻimalule, maʻule, hemo, puhemo, palalū, halalū; ʻōhemo *(as from dysentery);* hākalalū *(as from age or sickness);* ʻaʻalina *(as a fat person);* kololū, nanaiea, lanaiea, puanaiea, pīnauea, pānauea, hini, ʻuhinipili, ʻunihipili, nanahe, hakakaʻe, hākaneno, pananā, ʻonana, mahāha, aheahe, nīnole, hālina, kole, kūnāhihi, manuʻu, kūhau, maʻawe, kūhelahela, ʻalalehe, hānewanewa, nāwele, puaināwele, pūhalu, ʻōhea, ʻaʻaiole, holili, pūlewa, puhalu, halu, uhalu. *Rare:* mahū, hoʻomānewanewa, uhanui, uheule, ʻōmaʻi, hakalunu, hakaneno, hakanelo, pīloli, pēluʻe, nīpolo, pakē. *Too weak to stand alone,* hinapē, hinapā. *Weak-voiced,* leo iki, hano pilo, pihano.

weaken. Hoʻōnāwaliwali, hoʻomalule, hoʻomamae, hoʻonānawaū.

weakling. ʻŌmali, ʻōpalupalu. *See sayings,* **pēpē 1, pōpoki, banana, spider, tattler.**

wealth. Waiwai, lako, loaʻa. *See sayings,* **hilihili, pakī.** *Source of wealth,* kumu waiwai. *To hide wealth,* ʻaweka.

wealthy. *See* **rich** *and sayings,* **hilihili, eel.**

wean. Ukuhi *(as a child).*

weapon. Mea kaua, mea make, mea pepehi kanaka, mea hōʻeha. *See* **club, dagger, shark, sling, spear.** *Coming prepared for war, long spears, short spears* (ʻēlau, ihe), *clubs, shark teeth, daggers, feather cloaks, helmets, all weapons* (For. *5:321),* hele me ka mākaukau no ke kaua, ka pololū, ka ʻēlau, ka ihe, ka newa, ka niho manō, ka pāhoa, ka ʻahu ʻula, ka mahiole, nā mea make apau loa.

wear. Komo; — *a skirt,* pāʻū; — *a hat,* pāpale, pāpale i ka pāpale; — *finery,* kāhiko; — *well,* paʻa. *To wear out, as old clothes,* komo maʻuʻa.

weariness. Luhi, kunewa. *Weariness is released, there is rest,* kuʻu ka luhi, ua maha *(of death).*

wearisome. Māluhiluhi, manakā, mākoeā, uihā, makaʻeleʻele.

weary. Luhi, māluhiluhi, paʻa luhi, pauaho. *Also:* luhi hewa, luhina, moluhi, uluhua, hoʻouluhua, pilihua, kunewa; heha *(following sexual gratification);* maʻuhā, uihā, ʻainea, unā, kena, ikiiki, auka, maika, poʻana, pōʻieʻie.

weasel. Mukuela, mutuela.

weather. Ke ʻano o ka manawa; au *(rare).* There is no general name; the type of weather may be specified, as in this saying: hiki mai ka mālie, ā hiki mai nō ka ʻino, *fair weather comes, storms come too. Forecast of weather,* wānana i ke au o ka manawa.

weatherboard. Kuapoʻi.

weathered. Lolea, nalukai.

weave. *See* **plait.** *Also:* lino, kāmola *(tie, twist).*

weaver. Mea ulana lole.

web. ʻUpena, hihi. *Spider web,* ʻupena nananana, pūnanana, pūnāwelewele. *Weblike,* ʻūhini, puaināwele.

wed. *See* **marry.**

wedding. Male ʻana. *Wedding feast,* ʻahaʻaina male. *Come to our wedding,* hele mai ʻoe i kō māua male ʻana.

wedge. Unu, mākia; pewa, kepa, kepakepa *(as for mending bowls).*

wedlock. Noho male, nohona male. *To live with a mate out of wedlock,* moe mau, noho manuahi.

Wednesday. Pōʻakolu. *Ash Wednesday,* Pōʻakolu Kau Lehu.

wee. ʻUku liʻi, ʻūliʻi. *Also:* pūʻukuʻuku, ʻanaliʻi, kanaliʻi, kakanaliʻi, ʻaʻanaliʻi, makaliʻi, māiki, unana.

weed. Nahele, nāhelehele. *Also:* maʻau, kūkanawao, kīkānia. *Choked, as by weeds,* kāhihi. *To weed,* waele, wawaele, wele, welewele, welehia, au, emu, kaʻi, mahi waena, ʻōheu, kīheu, kāheu, ʻōlaʻo, ʻōlaʻolaʻo, olohiʻo.

week. Pule, hepekoma. *Next week,* kēia pule aʻe. *Week after next,* kēia pule aʻe a ia pule aku. *Last week,* kēlā pule aku nei. *Week before last,* kēlā pule aku nei a ia pule aku.

weekday. Lā noa.

weekly. I kēlā me kēia pule, kēlā pule kēia pule; puka pule *(as a journal);* ma ka pule.

weep. Uē; uwē helu *(and wail in mourning);* makena *(lamentation);* loku. *See sayings,* **māmane.** *The heavens weep, the land lives,* uwē ka lani, ola ka honua. *In poetry, rain and tears symbolize weeping.*

weeping willow. Wīlou lohaloha.

weevil. Mū.

weft. Koana; alokahi *(single);* alolua *(double);* makaliʻi *(narrow);* kākū *(working);* kāmoe *(recumbent). To add a new weft,* hāunu.

weigh. Kaupaona, ana kaumaha, ana paona, mahiki. *To weigh anchor,* huki i ka heleuma.

weight. Kaupaona, kaumaha, ana kaumaha, paona, weka; koʻikoʻi *(fig.). Metric weight,* ana mekela. *To lose weight,* hōʻemi, emi pū, hoʻowīwī. *To gain weight,* hoʻonui nā paona, polapola. *Weighted down,* kau i ka mea kaumaha; mauhaʻalina, pōhaku *(rare). Weights for lifting,* pōhaku hoʻoikaika. *What is your weight?* ʻEhia ou paona?

weighty. Koʻikoʻi *(profound).*

weir. Pākolokolo *(probably).*

weird. Ano, ʻeʻehia, āiwaiwa.

welcome. Heahea. *There is no equivalent to the English; one may say* hale: he hale kou, *you have a house (you are always welcome there). Call of welcome,* heahea, kāhea, pā kāhea. *To welcome guests,* hoʻokipa i ka malihini. *Welcoming song,* mele komo. *You are welcome,* he mea iki, he mea ʻole *(lit., a little thing, nothing; modern). Expression of welcome:* should [*you wish to*] *come to the land, there is a house, poi, fish for you, the land is for you,* i kū ā hele mai i ka ʻāina, he hale, he ʻai, he iʻa nou, nou ka ʻāina. *To wear out a welcome,* uluhua i ka pīnaʻi. *Welcome!* E komo mai! Mai! He mai!

weld. Hoʻopaʻa hao, hoʻokuʻi. *Weld silver,* kuʻi kālā.

welfare. Pono, pōmaikaʻi. *Public welfare,* pono o ka lehulehu. *Spiritual welfare,* pono ʻuhane. *Welfare committee,* kōmike ola.

well. 1. *Good.* Maikaʻi, pono, ahona. *He is well,* maikaʻi ʻoia. *He works well,* hana maikaʻi ʻoia. *Well done,* moʻa leʻa *(cooked);* maikaʻi ka hana *(well executed).* 2. *Source of water.* Luawai, wai ʻeli. *Artesian well,* luawai aniani. *To well up, as tears in eyes,* māloʻi, hāloʻi, ʻale. 3. *Exclamation.* ʻĀ!.

well-being. Ola, maikaʻi, pono, ahona.

Wellington. Welinakona, Welinatona.

well-known. ʻIke nui ʻia, kaulana.

well-off. *See* **rich.**

Welsh. Wale.

welt. Mōʻali.

were. *No equivalent; see* **e** *(verb)* **ana, ua 3, be.**

Wessex. Wekeka, Weseka.

west. Komohana. *Rare:* kaulana a Kāne *(poetic),* ʻeleiālani *(priests' name),* hikimoe, Kāne-neʻeneʻe, ʻelehonua. *See saying,* **Lehua.**

Western Hemisphere. ʻAoʻao Komohana.

West Indies. ʻĪnia Komohana.

Westminster. Wekaminika.

West Virginia. Wilikinia Komohana.

wet. Pulu, pulu pē, maʻū, ʻelo, paʻū. *Also:* hoʻomāʻūʻū, peleʻū, hoʻoū, hōʻū, noʻū, ʻeloʻelo, hoʻelo, kele, kele lua, kilipohe; palapī *(as green wood);* hakukele, halahalawai, panopaʻū, pānoʻūnoʻū, ʻueʻuele, ʻuhē. *Wet and softened with mist or rain,* nolu ehu. *Wet with* *cold,* kawaū. *Wet bundle, as of laundry,* pōpō pulu. *Symbolic connotations of wet are similar to those of rain.*

wet nurse. Kahu waiū, kahu wale, poliwaiū, waiū; nu'akea *(for chiefly infants).*

whack. Kanono. *See* **beat.**

whale. Koholā *(humpbacked),* palaoa *(sperm whale). To whale,* 'ō koholā.

whaleboat. Huelopoki.

whale tooth. Niho palaoa, lei palaoa. *Whale tooth washed ashore,* palaoa pae. *Whale-tooth pendant,* lei palaoa. *Convex curve of lower portion of whale-tooth pendant,* alelo.

whaling. 'Ō koholā. *Whaling ship,* moku 'ō koholā.

wharf. Uwapo, uapo.

what. 1. *Relative pronoun.* Mea *(Gram. 11.3). I don't know what he wants,* 'a'ole au i 'ike i kāna mea i makemake ai. **2.** *Exclamation.* Keu ā, auwē, auē. *What a nuisance!* He keu ā ka ho'oluhi! **3.** *Interrogative.* Aha *(for idioms, see* **aha** *and Gram. 8.5). What?* He aha? Pehea? *What does he have? What's his opinion? What* [business] *is it of his?* He aha kāna? *What's that?* He aha kēlā? *What of it? What's that?* He aha ia mea? *What are you doing?* E aha ana 'oe? *Lest what?* O aha? *Lest what happen?* O aha'ina? *What-d'you-call-it,* mea. *What time is it?* Hola 'ehia? *What page?* Ka 'ao-'ao 'ehia? Ka 'ao'ao hea?

whatever. Nā mea, nā mea like 'ole, aia. *Whatever you ask I'll do,* nā mea āu e noi mai nei, 'o au e hana.

whatsoever. Nā mea like 'ole. *Any whatsoever,* 'a'ohe pilo.

wheat. Huika, huapalaoa, palaoa.

wheedle. Nē ho'ohune, ho'omalimali. *Bragging and wheedling,* ke ā nui, ke ā iki. *(see* **ā** *1).*

wheel. Huila, pokaka'a. *Water wheel,* huila wai. *Disc wheel,* huila kaulike. *Wheel axis,* iho huila. *Ferris wheel,* huila pōniuniu, ka'a pōniuniu. *Wheel chair,* noho huila. *To wheel a wheel chair,* ho'oholo i ka noho huila.

wheelbarrow. Huilapalala, huilabalala, huilapalela, ka'a huila kahi. *Wheelbarrow race,* heihei huilapalala.

wheeze. Hānō, hō, huene, hanopilo. *Rare:* pōhānō, hohoiea.

when. 1. *Declarative past.* I ka manawa . . . i, i ka wā . . . i, i . . . ka hana; i *(see* **i** *5). When you lived at Kailua,* i ka manawa ou i noho ai i Kailua; i kou manawa i noho ai i Kailua. *When he looked down (For. 4:225),* a i nānā iho ka hana. **2.** *Declarative future.* I ka manawa . . . e, i ka wā . . . e, ke, ā, aia; hele *(see* **hele** *3). When he arrives,* ā hiki mai ia; aia hiki mai 'oia; ke hiki mai 'oia. *When I,* ia'u. **3.** *Interrogative future.* Āhea? I ka manawa hea . . . e? I ka wā hea . . . e? **4.** *Interrogative past.* Ināhea? I ka manawa hea . . . i? I ka wā hea . . . i?

whence. 1. *Declarative.* No laila, mai laila. **2.** *Interrogative.* No hea? Mai hea mai?

whenever. Aia nō, aia ā, i ka wā, i ka manawa. *Whenever finished, ask again,* aia nō ā pau, noi hou mai.

where. 1. *Declarative.* Kahi. **2.** *Interrogative.* Aia i hea? 'Auhea? Ai hea? Mahea? I hea? Hea? *Where is the place to go?* 'Auhea kahi e hele ai? *From where?* Mai hea mai? No hea?

whereas. No ka mea, 'oiai.

whereby. Mamuli o, mamuli o ia mea.

wherever. Ma nā wahi apau. *Wherever you go,* ma kahi āu e hele aku ai.

wherewithal. Ka mea; ka mea e hiki ai *(lit., the thing able to do with).*

whether. Inā. *Whether . . . not,* inā . . . 'ole. *Whether you work or don't work,* inā 'oe e hana ā e hana 'ole. *Whether it rains or not,* inā e ua, ā ua 'ole.

whetstone. Hoana.

which. 1. *Declarative.* Ka mea i, ka i *(past);* ka mea e, ke *(future). The thing which he will see,* ka mea āna e 'ike aku ai. *The thing which he saw,* ka mea āna i 'ike ai.

Which is often untranslated: the house which was sold, ka hale i kū'ai 'ia. *See* **who. 2.** *Interrogative.* Hea? Ka mea hea?

whichever. Ka mea nō.

whiff. Uifi.

whiffle. Pūnohu, 'iolo.

while. 'Oiai, 'oi, i, i ka manawa, i ka wā. *See* **during,** *Gram. 11.1. While I,* ia'u. *A while ago,* aku nei. *To while away the time,* ho'ohala manawa; kūkahekahe *(pleasantly). While there is time,* 'oi ola honua.

whim. Mana'o ulu wale, mana'o kupu wale.

whimpering. Nēnē.

whine. 'Uhī'uhī *(as a child);* 'owē *(as a bullet).*

whinny. Ihihī.

whip. Hahau, hau, uhau, uwepa, uepa, huipa, 'uwī'uwī; wili mawaho *(as in sewing machines). Flexible hand whip,* uwepa kiani. *To whip,* hahau, hau, uhau, haua, hili, hilikua; kāwelowelo *(as a flag in the wind). To whip gently or pretend to whip,* ho'ohili.

whiplash. 'Ōmua *(for dart throwing).*

whipsaw. Pahi olo lua.

whir. Kapalulu, kani.

whirl. Niniu. *Also:* ho'ōniu, ho'oniua, pōniu, kaka'a, pūhihio, heheo, milo, mimilo, milomilo, wili'ōka'i, pokaka'a, 'ōniu, niu, niuniu.

whirlpool. Wiliwai, mimilo.

whirlwind. Puahiohio, makani wili.

whisk. Puehu, ho'opuehu, lawe hikiwawe.

whisk broom. Pūlumi ehu lepo.

whiskers. 'Umi'umi. *To shave whiskers,* kahi 'umi'umi.

whiskey. Wekekē, waikekē, wikeke.

whisper. Hāwanawana, hāwana, hamumu; hōpilo *(rare).* Kawaihae, *whispering sea,* Kawaihae, kai hāwanawana.

whist. 'Uwiki, kāmau.

whistle. Hōkio, hōkiokio *(with lips);* pio *(with fingers);* hōkio pūeoeo *(with hands);* hū *(as wind or top);* oeoe *(as steamer or train siren);* 'ūlili *(as of bamboo or police). Gourd whistle,* nokea. *To play the* hōkiokio, mūkī. *Ti-leaf whistle,* pū lā'ī. *Sound of whistle,* ō.

white. Ke'oke'o, ke'o, kea; hina *(of hair). Also:* hākea, lākea, palakea, kuali, huali, aliali, a'ia'i, huaka; lawa, uakea *(as a chicken);* uakea *(as mist, snow). White-haired,* hina, 'āhina, ko'okea, po'o kea, po'o ke'oke'o, po'o hina. *White of an egg,* kauō ke'oke'o, ēwe o ka hua moa. *White-hot,* lehuli'u. *White mixed with a darker color,* lawaa'ea'e. *White and salt-encrusted,* kuakea. *White-spotted,* nokea. *White of a blind person's eye,* makai'a. *White tapa,* ninikea. *White muslin,* ke'oke'o *(usually followed by* maoli, pia *or* wai*). White lime,* hāwena. *Whitecaps,* 'ale kuakea, papākea, kai 'ūpoho, ehu kai. *White-beaked, white around animal's snout,* nūkea.

white man. Haole, 'ilipuakea; hauhole *(slang). To act like a white man, to ape white people or assume superior airs,* ho'ohaole. *Sayings about white men:* haole kī kōlea *(see* **kōlea***); 'elelū kea, white cockroach (insulting); see* **plover, salmon.**

whiten. Ho'oke'o, ho'okuakea, ho'okuali, ho'āliali, ho'a'ia'i.

whitewash. Pa'i puna, puna, hamo puna, palaina puna, ho'ā'ia'i; ho'ōhule *(keep opponent scoreless, slang).*

whither. *See* **where.**

whitish. Ha'akea, hākea, hākeakea.

whittle. Kalakalai, kolikoli, koli. *Much whittling, nicked product,* nui kalakalai, manumanu ka loa'a *(see* **kalakalai***).*

whiz. Kapalulu; — *by,* pūhalahio, halahī.

who. 1. *Declarative.* I, e, nāna *(Gram. 9.11). The one who did,* ka mea i, ka i, kai. *The one who will,* ka mea e, ke *(Gram. 10.2). See* **which. 2.** *Interrogative.* Wai? 'O wai, na wai *(subject,* **wai** *5)?* Iā wai *(object)? See Gram. 7.5.*

whoa. Wō, kū.

whoever. Ka mea nō.

whole. Holo'oko'a, kā'oko'a, 'oko'a, pa'a. *Whole note*

in music, hua ʻokoʻa. *Whole number,* helu ʻokoʻa. *To bake whole,* kālua paʻa.

wholesale. Kūʻai nui, kūʻai kāʻokoʻa, kūkaʻa. *Wholesale clothing,* lole kūkaʻa. *Wholesale buying,* kūʻai kūkaʻa, kūʻai nui.

wholesome. Pono no ke olakino.

whole step. Kanipiha *(music).*

whom. Iā wai. *By whom?* Na wai? *For whom?* Na wai? No wai? *(Gram. 9.11.)*

whoop. ʻŌ, hoʻōho, kalea; ʻea *(rare).*

Whoopee! Wela ka hao!

whooping cough. Kalea, kunu kalea.

whore. *See* **prostitute.**

whorish. Kūakalikea *(rare). Whorish heart,* naʻau moekolohe.

whose. 1. *Declarative.* Nona, nāna *(Gram. 11.3.) The man whose hat was taken,* ke kanaka nona ka pāpale i lawe ʻia. **2.** *Interrogative.* Na wai? No wai?

why. 1. *Declarative.* Ke kumu, ka mea. **2.** *Interrogative.* Aha? No ke aha? I ke aha? He mea aha? Hea? *Why not?* Hea? Kainō? Kainoa? *Why don't you come?* Kainō hoʻi e hele mai ʻolua? *Why go?* I aha ai ka hele ʻana? *Why indeed!* He aha iho la! No ke aha lā! *(Gram. 7.5.)*

wick. ʻUwiki, kaula ahi.

wicked. ʻIno, hana ʻino. *Also:* ʻinoʻino, ʻaiā, ʻaiāhulu, haihaiā, kūāʻino, pupuka, hewa, kīnā. *To act wickedly or presumptuously,* ʻaʻa hewa, ʻā hewa.

wicker. ʻIe. *Wicker chair,* noho ʻie.

wide. Ākea, laulā. *Also:* pālaha, pālahalaha, pālālā, kīlaha, moana, moanaana, peleleu.

widen. Hoʻolaulā.

widespread. Laha, laulaha *(prevalent);* waiho kāhela *(spread out).*

widow. Wahine kāne make.

widowed. Kāne make.

widower. Kāne wahine make.

widowhood. Nohona kāne make.

width. Ākea, laulā. *Width of mesh of pandanus plaiting strips,* koana.

wield. Kaʻa, hahau. *To wield a war club,* kaʻa lāʻau. *Wield power,* noho mana, hoʻohana i ka mana.

wiener. Naʻaukake.

wife. Wahine. *Also:* wahine male, pilialo, hānau kama, kahi. *Fig.:* lei, hulilau. *His wife,* kāna wahine. *To take as a wife,* hoʻowahine. *Wife of a chief,* haku wahine. *Wife other than your own,* aliʻi wahine *(polite term). Common-law wife,* wahine manuahi, wahine noho pū.

wig. Lauoho kuʻi, ohokuʻi. *See* **switch.**

wiggle. ʻOniʻoni. *See* **squirm.**

wigwam. Wikiwama.

wild. ʻĀhiu, hihiu. *Also:* hae, makanahele, hoʻomakanahele, hewahewa, ʻeʻena, ʻeno, iōʻena, hanahihi, kū kākalaioa, makapā, ʻaʻalaioa. *Wild pig,* puaʻa ʻāhiu, puaʻa makanahele. *Papaya growing wild,* mīkana makanahele. *To let a garden grow wild,* hoʻomakanahele. *To act wild, as a frightened animal,* līʻō.

wilderness. Wao akua, wao nahele, nahele, ulunahele.

wild-goose chase. Hahai loaʻa ʻole; piʻi ka lapa manu ʻole *(climb a ridge without birds). See sayings,* **ʻalaʻala pū loa, manu.**

wildness. Haena. *See* **wild.**

wile. Hana maʻalea. *See* **crafty** *and saying,* **uhu 1.**

will. 1. *Testament.* Kauoha, palapala hoʻoilina, palapala kauoha. *To make a will verbally,* kaulanaʻōlelo. *To will,* hoʻīli, hoʻoili. **2.** *Desire.* Makemake, manaʻo. *Thy will be done,* e mālama ʻia kou makemake. **3.** *Verb markers.* E . . . ana *(future);* e *(imperative). I will go,* e hele aku ana au. *See* **be.**

willful. Naʻau hoʻokiʻekiʻe, uhu, wale. *Also:* uaua, kūnono, hoʻohuki, koeʻā, kāʻape, hoʻolana, hanaea. *See* **stubborn** *and saying,* **kaupoku 1.**

willing. Makemake, ʻoluʻolu.

willow. Wīlou.

Wilmington. Wilemikona, Wilemitona.

wilt. Mae. *Also:* kāmae, ʻōlala, laumeki, mio, miomio,

luhe, loha, ʻōmali, mā, mamake, ʻāheahea, make wale, nikipaʻu. *See* **wither.** *The flower that never wilts,* ka pua mae ʻole.

win. Lanakila, eo, loaʻa, puka.

wince. ʻEʻeke, ʻeke.

wind *(air movement).* Makani *(for fig. meanings and types of winds, see Haw.-Eng. entry and entries that follow it). See* **break wind.** *Variable wind,* makani pālua. *Fair wind,* makani ʻoluʻolu, peawini. *Wind puff,* ahe lau makani, ʻōnini. *Wind-borne,* pā makani, māpu, lele, kūpani, kō. *Icy wind,* hauʻoki. *Sound of wind,* wī. *Blowing of wind,* pā, loku. *Gust or draft of wind,* hihio, kīkīao, kūhewa; limu *(rare). Wind-resisting,* kūmakani. *Strong wind,* makani ikaika, makani pāhili. *Increase or rising of wind,* ulu, pehuea. *Stormy wind,* ʻena makani; puku kālina *(poetical). To turn into the wind,* hoʻopiʻi, kaʻaluna; kūpapaula *(rare). Northeast trade wind,* Moaʻa, Moaʻe Kū, Moaʻe Pehu, Moaʻe Lehua, Aʻe, Aʻe Loa, Kaiāulu, Kaomi, Noe. *Southerly or leeward wind,* Kona. *Usual wind of a place,* makani kamaʻāina. *Goddess of winds,* Laʻamaomao. *Many wind names are associated with places, especially those chanted by the* keiki hoʻopāpā *(a wit, riddler, bag wonder),* Kū-a-Pākaʻa, *who names more than 100 winds (For. 5:93–103) or more than 200 (Nak. 53–60, 67–71), some being gentle breezes and others wintry gales. These and other names are listed below. Many names are widespread, but some are in special areas. In Honolulu 6 winds are listed, 5 in Hilo, and 2 in the Molokaʻi valley of Hālawa, the home of the boy wonder previously mentioned.*

WIND NAMES *(alternate names are in parentheses; islands and places where the names are known follow):* ʻĀhiu, *Oʻahu;* ʻAi-koʻo, *Kauaʻi;* ʻAi-loli, *Kaupō [Maui];* ʻAi-maunu, *Hāna;* ʻAki-pohe, *Maui;* Ala-ʻeli, *Honolulu;* ʻAla-honua (ʻAʻala-honua), *Hilo;* Ala-hou, *Molokaʻi;* Ala-ʻoli, *Kauaʻi;* Amu, *Kauaʻi;* ʻAoa (ʻAoaoa, Ulu-mano), *Hawaiʻi, Oʻahu.* ʻAoa-laenihi, *Niʻihau, also a rain;* ʻĀpaʻapaʻa, *Hawaiʻi;* ʻEhu-kai, *Hālawa [Molokaʻi];* ʻEka (ʻEʻeka), *Hawaiʻi;* ʻEkeʻeke, *Kaʻula Island;* ʻEke-loa;

Hakaʻano, *Hālawa [Molokaʻi];* Hale-mauʻu, *Hāna;* Hauna-ʻīloli; Haunone; Hiki-pua, *Hālawa [Molokaʻi];* Holo-poʻopoʻo, *Hawaiʻi;* Hoʻoheu; Hoʻolapa, *Hawaiʻi;* Hoʻolua (Kiu Inu Wai, Mālua Kiʻi Wai), *Kauaʻi, Hāna, Hālawa [Molokaʻi];* Huli-alo-pali, *Lahaina;* Huli-lua, *Kauaʻi;* Iʻa-iki, *Maui, Molokaʻi;* Ihu-anu, *Oʻahu;* ʻImi-hau, *Lahaina;* Inu-wai.

Kaʻao, *Hālawa [Molokaʻi];* Kaʻele (Kaʻeʻele), *Molokaʻi;* Kaiāulu, *Maui, Oʻahu;* Kākea, *Honolulu;* Ka-laʻiākea, *Hawaiʻi;* Kanomi, *Hāna;* Kāpae, *Hawaiʻi;* Ka-ua-hae, *Kauaʻi;* Ka-ua-ʻula, *Lahaina;* Kaʻula, *Maui;* Kēhau, *in many areas;* Kēpia, *Hilo;* Kēwai, *Hilo;* Kia-lehua, *Niʻihau;* Kīhae-lāʻī, *Hilo;* Kiliʻoʻopu (Kili-ʻopu), *Molokaʻi;* Kili-poe; Kili-ua, *Oʻahu;* Kinai-lehua, *Hawaiʻi;* Kīpuʻupuʻu, *Hawaiʻi, also a rain;* Kiu (Mālualua, Mālua Kiʻi Wai, Hoʻolua), *in many areas;* Kiu Anu, *Kauaʻi;* Kiu Inu Wai (Huehu); Kiu Kai Nui, *Kauaʻi;* Kiu Keʻe, *Kauaʻi;* Kiu Wai Lehua (Kiu Lehua); Koa, *Molokaʻi;* Koholā Lele (Kiu, Koholā Pehu), *in many areas;* Koi-pali, *Hālawa [Molokaʻi];* Kolo-ʻāpuʻupuʻu, *Hawaiʻi;* Kololio, *Kauaʻi, Maui;* Kolo-puʻepuʻe; Kō-momona, *Honolulu;* Kona, *in all areas;* Kona Hea (Kona Hea Puka), *Hawaiʻi;* Kona Hili Maiʻa, *also a rain;* Kona Kū; Kona Lani; Kona Moae; Kona Moe; Kona-nui-a-niho; Koʻolau, *between Kauaʻi and Niʻihau;* Koʻolau-wahine, *Niʻihau;* Koʻo-makani, *Kauaʻi;* Koʻopali, *Hālawa [Molokaʻi];* Kuamū *also a rain;* Kuapā, *Molokaʻi;* Kuehu Kai, *Kauaʻi;* Kuehu Lepo, *Kaʻū, Oʻahu;* Kuʻi-a-manini, *Kauaʻi;* Kuʻi-lehua, *Niʻihau;* Kūkala-hale, *Oʻahu, also a rain;* Kūlōlio, *Maui;* Kumuma-ʻoma'o, *Kauaʻi;* Kuʻuanu, *Kauaʻi;*

Laʻi-kū, *Hālawa [Molokaʻi];* Lanakila, *Oʻahu;* Laniku'u-waʻa, *Kauaʻi;* Lauaʻe, *Kauaʻi;* Lau-kamani, *Hālawa [Molokaʻi];* Lau-kō-wai, *Maui;* Lau-maʻomaʻo, *Molokaʻi;* Lawakua, *Kauaʻi;* Lehua, *Lehua Island;*

Lele-ku'i-lua; Lele-uli; Lī-anu, *Hālawa [Moloka'i]*; Līlī-lehua, *Maui, O'ahu, also a rain;* Lima-huli, *Kaua'i;* Luha, *Kaua'i;* Lū-hau-pua, *Hawai'i;* Lū-pua, *Kaua'i;*

Ma'a'a ('A'a), *Lahaina;* Ma'a'a Kua Lapu, *Hawai'i;* Ma'a'a Pa'imalau; Maka-iki-o-Lea, *Kaua'i (?);* Makani-hānai-loli, *Maui;* Malailua, *Honolulu;* Mālama-lama-iki, *Kaua'i;* Malanai, *Kaua'i, Maui, O'ahu;* Mālua; Malua Hele, *Kaua'i;* Malua Kele, *Kaua'i;* Mālua Ki'i Wai (Mālualua Ki'i Wai), *Hilo;* Mālualua, *Maui, Moloka'i, O'ahu;* Māunuunu, *O'ahu;* Meheu, *Kaua'i;* Mikioi, *Ni'ihau;* Moa'e (A'e at Kaua'i, A'e Loa, *Moloka'i);* Moa'e Lehua; Moani-'ala, *Hawai'i;* Moa-'ula, *Hālawa [Moloka'i]*; Moeāhua, *Kaua'i;* Mumuku (Muku), *Hawai'i;* Nahua, *Maui;* Nāulu, *in many areas;* 'Okia, *Hālawa [Moloka'i]*; 'Ō-lau-niu, *Hawai'i, Honolulu;* One-hali, *Kaua'i;* 'O'opu, *Maui;*

Pa'alā (Pa'ala'a); Pahele-hala, *Kaua'i, O'ahu;* Pakaiea, *O'ahu;* Pā-kololio-kaiāulu, *Maui;* Papa, *Maui;* Pāpa'a; Papa'a Inu Wai, *Kaua'i, Ni'ihau;* Pāpa'a Lā, *Maui;* Pe'e-hala, *Hawai'i;* Pili-'ā, *Hawai'i;* Pohu, *Hawai'i;* Pu'u-Ka'ala, *O'ahu;* Pu'u-ka-pele (Pu'u-pele), *Kaua'i;* Pu'u-lena, *Hawai'i;* Pu'u-kōlea, *Hawai'i;* Pu'u-nahele, *Kaua'i;* Pu'u-o-Kona, *Honolulu;*

Uahi-a-Pele, *Hawai'i;* 'Ūkiu ('Ūkiukiu), *Maui;* 'Ulalena, *Maui, also a rain;* Ulu-au, *Hilo;* Ulu-au-nui, *Maui;* Unulau, *Kaua'i, Ni'ihau, Maui;* Unuloa, *Hawai'i;* Wai-'ōpua, *Kaua'i;* Wai-pao (Wai-paoa), *Kaua'i;* Wai-uli, *Maui;* Wehe-lau-niu, *Maui.*

wind *(to twist).* Wili, pōka'a, ka'a, pō'ai, kōke'e; *— around,* kō'ai; *— or set, as a clock,* kī.

windbag. Palaualelo.

windbreak. Kūmakani, pālulu, pālulu makani. *Rare:* pa'amua, honomakani.

wind instrument. Pū kani. *To play a wind instrument, player of a wind instrument,* puhi 'ohe. *Cf.* **ho'ohiliu.**

windless. Pohu, lūlā.

windmill. Wili makani, huila wai; 'ena makani *(rare).*

window. Pukaaniani, puka hale, puka makani. *See* **curtain.**

window sill. Paepae pukaaniani.

windshield. Pale makani, pālulu.

Windsor Castle. Kākela Winikoa, Kākela Winisoa.

windward. 'Ao'ao Ko'olau, 'ao'ao makani, kua, na'e.

windy. Makani, 'ōhio, puhohō. *The windy cloud,* ke ao makani.

wine. Waina. *Wine-colored,* 'ea 'ula. *Wine press,* kaomi waina.

winebibber. Pākela inu waina.

wineglass. Kī'aha inu waina.

wing. 'Ēheu; maha *(of flying fish). Wing feathers,* hulu 'ekekeu. *Wings,* 'ekekeu, pekekeu, 'eheheu. *Wing on stem of plant,* mōlina. *Wing of house,* pāku'i. *Wing of army,* mahele, lālā. *To stretch or flap wings,* ho'ēheu. *To spread wings or tail feathers,* ka'apeha.

winged. 'Ēheu.

wink. 'Imo, ho'imo, 'amo, 'āwihi.

winner. Mea lanakila, mea eo.

winnings. Puka, loa'a. *To take or grab, as winnings,* hului.

winnow. Kānana, kālana. *Also:* pe'ahi, lūlū.

winter. Ho'oilo *(see saying,* **ho'oilo***);* ho'īlo, kau anu.

wipe. Kāwele, holoi, ho'okāwele; ka'a *(Ka'ū);* ka'a malo'o; hāleu *(as with toilet paper).*

wire. Uwea, uea. *Wire screen,* uwea hakahaka. *Telephone wire,* uwea kelepona. *Chicken wire,* uwea maka 'upena. *Telegraph wire,* uwea 'ōlelo. *Smooth wire,* uwea poepoe. *Barbed wire,* uwea kukū.

wire grass. Mānienie ali'i.

wireless. Uwea 'ole. *Wireless message,* 'ōlelo uwea 'ole.

Wisconsin, Wikonekina, Wikonesina.

wisdom. Na'auao. *Also:* lae, ihupani, mahao'o, lawa. *See saying,* **li'u 3.** *Spirit of wisdom,* mana'o akamai. *Torch of wisdom,* lamakū o ka na'auao. *Seasoned with wisdom,* mali'u.

wise. Na'auao, no'eau, 'ike loa, mahao'o, ihupani. *See*

saying, **tern.** *Wise thought,* mana'o akamai. *To pretend to be wise,* ho'olae, hō'oi'oi.

wish. *No exact equivalent other than the words for desire, hope, want. Best wishes,* e pili mau nā pōmaika'i me 'oe. *Dream of a cherished wish,* moemoeā. *Best wishes for health,* nā kalokalo leo 'ana no ke ola *(rare).*

wishbone. Iwi 'ō.

wisp. Uahi iki *(as smoke);* ehu *(as mist, spray);* mā'awe iki *(as hair).*

wit. 1. *Sagacity.* Akamai, na'auao. **2.** *See* **witty.**

witch. *No exact equivalent; see* **kupua.**

witchcraft. Hana mana, ho'okalakupua. *See* **sorcery.**

with. Me. *To associate with, be with,* pili. *With me,* me a'u. *With him,* me ia. *He went with Kū,* hele lāua 'o Kū; hele 'oia me Kū.

withdraw. 1. *Go back.* Emi hope, ho'i, ho'oka'awale, kuemi, ha'alele. **2.** *To take back.* Unuhi. *Withdraw money,* unuhi kālā.

wither. Mālili. *Also:* 'ōmino, hōmī, mōlili, 'ōlili, palakai, ka'e'e, mae, mamae, 'omī, 'ōmīmī, mīmī, mīmino, luhe. *See* **wilt.**

withhold. 'Au'a, lau'au'a, kāohi, hō'āpī, pa'a.

within. I loko, maloko.

without. Nele, 'ole, kā i ka nele loa.

witness. Hō'ike, hō'ike pa'a *(as in court). To witness personally,* 'ike maka. *False witness,* hō'ike ho'opunipuni.

witticism. 'Ōlelo hō'aka'aka, 'ōlelo ho'omāke'aka.

witty. Ho'omāke'aka, hū'eu, laupa'apa'ani, ho'okā'au.

wizard. Kahuna ho'okalakupua.

wobbly. Kūlanalana. *Also:* polokake, pāloke, pōloke, pālokeloke, kaupē.

woe. Pōpilikia nui, kaumaha nui. *Also:* walania, walawalania, walenia, wawalania, welenia. *See* **grief, rain.** *To relate woes,* 'ōhumuhumu. *Woe!* Auwē! Auē! *Woe is me!* 'Ehia ua mea aloha, 'o wau! Auwē (Auē) ho'i au!

woeful. Lu'ulu'u, kaumaha, uwē.

wolf. 'Īlio hae, 'īlio hihiu hae, lupo. *To wolf food,* 'ai ā pua'a.

woman. Wahine *(for various kinds, see Haw-Eng. entry and entries that follow it). Fig. references, see* **canoe, gourd;** *also see* **old woman, women.** *Chiefly woman,* ali'i wahine, haku wahine. *Woman easily taken,* wahine pānoa. *To behave as a woman,* ho'owahine. *Unattractive woman,* wahine lau'au'a, lemukū.

womanliness. Wahine.

womb. Pū'ao, 'ōpū, waihona keiki, pupu'u, a'a. *Orifice of womb,* lapa. *Fallen womb,* pū'ao pelu.

women. Wāhine. *The women,* nā wāhine, ka po'e wāhine.

women's rights. Nā pono o nā wāhine.

wonder. Kāhāhā, pāha'oha'o, āiwaiwa, ha'oha'o. *Also:* makahehi, nūnē. *To arouse wonder,* ho'oha'oha'o, ho'opāha'oha'o. *To look, as in wonder,* maka leha. *A wonder,* he mea 'ē.

wonderful. Kupaianaha, kupanaha, kamaha'o, kamahoi, mea 'ē, āiwaiwa, makahehi. *To be or do something wonderful,* ho'okamaha'o.

wondrous. Kamaha'o, oki, oki pau.

won't. 'A'ole e. *I won't go,* 'a'ole loa au e hele.

woo. Ho'oipo, ho'oipoipo, ho'onipo, ho'opilipili.

wood. Lā'au.

wood borer. Huhu-pao-lā'au *(of a slanderer, defamer).*

woodcutter. Kālai lā'au.

wooded. Pa'apū i ka ulu lā'au.

wooden. Lā'au, papa. *Wooden building,* hale lā'au.

woodpile. Pu'u wahie, paila wahie.

wood rose. Pilikai.

woods. *See* **forest.**

woody. Lā'au.

woof. Ma'awe pokopoko.

wool. Hulu, pili. *Sheep wool,* hulu hipa. *Wool on base of tree-fern leaf stalks,* pulu.

wool carder. Koe.

woolen. Huluhulu.

Worcestershire. Wolekeka, Woreseta.
word. 'Ōlelo, hua 'ōlelo, hua, lokou. *Word-of-mouth,* ha'i waha. *Word play,* ho'opilipili 'ōlelo. *Words of a song,* hua mele. *I give my word,* ke ho'opa'a nei au i ka'u 'ōlelo. *Life is in the word, death is in the word,* i ka 'ōlelo nō ke ola, i ka 'ōlelo nō ka make *(saying).*
wordy. Ho'onui 'ōlelo.
work. Hana, hahahana. *See sayings,* **hoe, keha, pa'i 5, pī 2, pīkoikoi 2;** *see* **unemployed.** *To work carefully,* akahana. *Tedious, prolonged work,* pa'u hana. *Work with hands (manual),* hana lima. *Unusual or rare work,* hana hihiu. *Work section,* mahele hana. *Work for a chief,* kō'ele, Pō'alima. *To work hard,* ho'oikaika, hō'ikaika, hana 'o'ole'a, pa'aua, pu'aka. *To look for work,* huli hana. *To work aimlessly, uselessly,* hana wale. *To work together,* ho'olaulima, huki like; menehune, kuahui, kāwao *(rare). To put to work,* ho'ohana. *To work slowly,* hana lohi, ho'onone, kalana'e. *Working bit by bit,* mīkole. *No work is left!* 'A'ohe hana i koe! *Get going with the work,* 'a'ako aku i ka hana.
workbench. Papa hana.
workday. Lā hana.
worker. Kanaka hana, limahana, pa'ahana. *Fellow worker,* hoa hana, hoa pa'ahana, hoa luhi, hoa lawehana. *Feast for workers,* 'aha'aina maka luhi.
workman. Pa'ahana, lawehana.
workmanship. 'Ano o ka hana. *Good workmanship,* no'eau ka hana 'ana. *Poor workmanship,* kāpulu ka hana 'ana.
work program. Papa hana, kuhikuhi hana.
workshop. Ke'ena hana, hale hana, hale pa'ahana, wahi hana.
world. Ao, honua. *Beginning of the world,* kumu honua. *World's fair,* hō'ike'ike honua nui.
worldly. Puni i kō ke ao nei, pili kino.
world war. Kaua honua. *World War II,* Kaua Honua 'Elua.
worm. Ko'e, ilo. *See* **army worm, bristle worm, cutworm, maggot, measuring worm, pinworm.** *Annelid worm,* muiona. *Small worm in sand,* moeone. *Worm offal,* popopo. *Worm-eaten,* huhuhu. *A worm shell,* po'apo'ai.
wormy. Iloilo, huhuhu.
worn-out. 1. *As a garment.* 'Āpulu; pāwelu *(ragged);* 'alu'a *(faded);* 'unae *(as a mattress). Also:* 'āleuleu, pāleuleu, 'u'a, kolo'u'a, lu'a, lohelau, pane'e, pō'ie'ie, pau ka pono. 2. *As a person.* Māluhiluhi, pauaho, pākī, mauole, lohelau. *See saying,* Hilo *(Eng.-Haw.).*
worried. Pīhoihoi, pono 'ole ka mana'o. *Also:* niniu, kapau'u.
worry. Ho'opīhoihoi, pīhoihoi o ka na'au, po'o nui, ho'okūpouli, ho'okaumaha, ka 'eha 'ana o ka na'au. *Marks of worry, as on the face,* kahakahana kaumaha. *Without worry,* lana ka mana'o, lōli'i. *Don't worry,* mai ho'okaumaha.
worse. 'Oi aku ka 'ino. *To grow worse, as sickness,* ho'olawehala.
worship. Ho'omana, haipule, pule; kākua *(especially with food offerings). See* **heiau, church.** *Image worship,* ho'omana ki'i. *Place of worship in a private house,* kua'aha.
worth. Waiwai, waiwai 'i'o, waiwai kaulike, minamina.
worthless. Lapuwale, waiwai 'ole, hakanele. *Also:* hua 'ole, 'ole loa, 'uka, 'ala'uka, hana 2, kole ka'aka, pāwelu; hua āelo *(fig.). See* **useless** *and sayings,* **'ala-'ala, mai'a, mat, pebble, rotten, sea cucumber, waste.**

worthy. Kūpono.
would. *No equivalent term, and no conditional mood. English conditionals may often be translated by* inā *(see ex.,* **inā** *and Gram. 11.1).*
wound. Palapū. *Also:* po'ohū, nāpele, paopao, nahoa, aleale, pōaleale. *See saying,* **manuā.** *To wound,* hō-'eha, 'eha, ho'owalania.
woven. Ulana 'ia. *See* **plait, weave.**
wrangle. Uluulu, 'āpuni; kole ka waha *(see* **kole**). *See* **bickering, herd** *(verb).*
wrap. 1. *Bind.* Wahī. *Also:* lauhulu, laulau, kama, kīpola, kāpola; — *around,* kīpuni; — *wet, as laundry,* pōpō pulu. 2. *Garment.* 'A'ahu, kuka.
wrapper. Wahī, pālaulau, pālau, kīpola, laulau. *Paper wrapper,* wahī pepa.
wrasses. Hīnālea *(for various types, see* **hīnālea** *and entries that follow it). Also:* 'a'awa *(for various types, see* **'a'awa);** po'ou, 'ōpule, 'akilolo, pāniholoa, 'ōhua, pa'awela.
wrath. Inaina. *See* **anger.**
wreath. Lei. *See* **lei** *(Haw.-Eng. and Eng.-Haw.).*
wreck. Wāwahi *(break);* ho'opahu'a. *See* **shipwreck.**
wrench. Wili, hao wili *(tool). See* **sprain.**
wrestler. Mea hākōkō.
wrestling. Hākōkō. *See* **fight.** *Hand wrestling,* uma, pa'a uma, huinalima. *Sitting wrestling,* hākōkō noho, kula'i wāwae, kulakula'i. *Standing wrist wrestling,* pā uma.
wretch. Lapuwale, ka'aka *(see* **mahumahu).** *Also:* kūmahumahu kole, limalima pilau, kāpī pua'a.
wretched. Kaumaha, lu'ulu'u, 'ino'ino.
wriggle. 'Oni'oni, ueue, wilinau.
wring. 'Uwī, 'uī, 'ūkī, 'ūpī; hūpī *(rare);* — *out,* kāwī, kōwī. *Wring the neck of a chicken,* wili i ka 'ā'ī o ka moa.
wringer. Mea 'uwī.
wrinkle. Minomino. *Also:* 'ānuhenuhe, ho'o'i'ika; — *the nose,* hō'ekeke'i, pu'e'eke, ihu 'e'eke; — *the eyelids,* mīoioi.
wrinkled. Minomino. *Also:* 'alu'alu, 'ālu'a, pī'alu, hālu'a, lu'a, 'ānuhenuhe, mino, mimino, pakalua, 'ōmino, 'opi, 'aua, 'uka, 'a'aka, 'ōpukupuku, pukupuku, pakapaka, 'ōpakapaka, pākāeaea, lulumi, pākā, kolepeia'alu.
wrinkles. 'Uka.
wrist. Pūlima. *Wrist joints,* pu'ulima.
wristbone. Ku'eku'e.
wrist watch. Uwaki pūlima.
writ. Palapala, palapala ki'i. *See* **habeas corpus.** *Writ of error,* palapala kuhikuhi hewa, palapala ha'i a kuhikuhi hewa, palapala ha'i hewa.
write. Kākau, kākau lima, palapala, kauhua.
writer. Mea kākau, haku 'ōlelo. *Writer of stories,* kākau mo'olelo. *Writer about chiefs,* kākau ali'i.
writhe. Ka'anini, laumilo, ka'awili, napanapa, wili, wilinau, kūlapa, kūpaka; wilimo'o *(as a reptile).*
writing. Palapala, kākau. *Writing desk,* papa palapala.
written. Kākau lima *(by hand). Written message,* 'elele waha 'ole.
wrong. Hewa, pono 'ole, pa'ewa, 'olalau. *To do wrong,* hana hewa. *To be in the wrong,* kū i ka hewa. *To go wrong,* hele hewa. *To cause one to do wrong,* ho'ohewa. *To abet in doing wrong,* kōkua i ka hewa.
wrought. Hana 'ia. *What hath God wrought (Nah. 23:23),* kupaianaha ka hana 'ana a ke Akua.
Wyoming. Waiomina.

X

x. *No Hawaiian term.*
xerox. Pepa kope.

X-ray. Nānā i loko o ke kino.
X-ray machine. Mīkini nānā iā loko o ke kanaka.

Y

y. *No Hawaiian term.*
yacht. Moku pe'a.
yak. Iaka.
yam. Uhi *(Oceanic; for various kinds, see* **uhi** *and entries that follow it; not to be confused with sweet potato). Also:* pālau, ulehihi, ho'onohonoho, lehua, pi'a, poni, laha, ni'ihau, 'ālela, uhi 'ālela. *Bitter yam,* hoi; pi'oi *(Kaua'i; cf.* **'ala'ala**). *Yam pudding,* piele.
yard. 1. *Unit of measure.* Iā, iwilei, pio. **2.** *Spar.* Iā. **3.** *Enclosure.* Pā. *House yard,* pā hale.
yardstick. Lā'au ana.
yarn. 1. *Spun material.* Pāniani, lopi huluhulu. **2.** *Story.* Kole, mo'olelo.
yawn. Hāmama, ho'ohāmama.
yaws. *See* **ulcer**.
ye. 'Olua, 'oukou.
year. Makahiki. *New Year,* Makahiki Hou. *Leap year,* makahiki lele 'oi, makahiki lā keu. *Happy New Year,* Hau'oli Makahiki Hou.
yearling. Pipi kolo *(beef)*.
yearly. Makahiki, kūmakahiki, i kēlā me kēia makahiki.
yearn. Ake, 'i'ini, nipo, ninipo, niponipo, li'a, ha'e, 'īloli, ho'īloli.
yeast. Ho'ohū, hū.
yell. 'Uwā, ho'ōho; 'ea *(rare)*.
yellow. Melemele, lena, 'ōlena, 'ōlenalena, lenalena. *Also:* mālena, pualena, kamalena, mele, memele, pua hau; pala *(as leaves)*. *Pale yellow,* hālena, pia, hēpia, nā'ū. *Golden yellow,* pala luhiehu. *Reddish-yellow,* pala 'ehu. *To begin to turn yellow,* hā'ama.
yellowfin tuna. 'Ahi.
yellowish. Hālenalena, hālena, lenalena, nenanena, hālelo, 'ano melemele. *Also:* lena, lelo, pōlena, mea; kēhue *(as soil)*.
yellow jacket. Hope'ō.
yellow red. 'Ula lena.
Yellow Sea. Kai Melemele.
yellowtail. *Same as* **amberjack**.
yelp. 'Alalā, 'alalī.
yes. 'Ae, 'ē; ō *(giving permission);* eō *(in answer to a call by name, or to acknowledge a name chant in one's honor);* 'ū *(signifying listening)*.
yesterday. Nehinei, inehinei. *Day before yesterday,* nehinei ā ia lā aku.

yet. 1. *Still.* Na'e. *Not yet,* koe, 'a'ole. **2.** *See* **but**.
yield. 1. *To produce.* Hua, ho'ohua; hua loa'a. **2.** *To agree.* 'Ae, ku'u.
ylang-ylang. Lanalana.
yodel. Ho'ōeoe.
yoke. Kua *(of a holokū). Also:* 'auamo, lei. *To yoke or harness together,* kaulua. *Ox yoke,* kua pipi, lei pipi.
yokefellow. Hoa pa'ahana.
yolk. Kauō melemele *(of an egg)*.
yonder. 'Ō, i 'ō, ma'ō.
Yorktown. Iōkakaona, Iokataona.
you. 'Oe *(singular);* 'olua *(dual);* 'oukou *(plural);* kēuā; iū *(rare). Vocative,* ē, 'ea. *You here (sometimes affectionate),* eia nei, ei nei. *You over there,* eia ala, eia lā. *For, by you,* nāu. *To, toward, for you,* nou, i ou, iā 'oe.
young. 'Ōpio, 'ōpiopio. *Also:* kiokio; kaekae *(as an attractive woman);* mo'o, mo'omo'o, 'alapu'u; 'ouo *(of animals);* pua, 'ōhua *(of certain fish);* 'ōilo *(as of* 'ō'io *or eel). Young people,* po'e 'ōpiopio, po'e u'i.
younger. Muli, muli iho, hope, 'ōpio. *Younger branch of family,* mu'o.
youngest. Hope loa, muli loa.
Young People's Christian Endeavor Society. Hō'ikaika Kalikiano; 'Ahahui 'Ōpiopio 'Imi Pono o Karisto *(old name)*.
youngster. Keiki, 'ōpio, 'ohā.
your. 1. *Singular possessed object, singular.* Kou *(o-class);* kāu *(a-class);* kō *(neutral class)*. **2.** *Singular possessed object, dual.* Kō 'olua *(o-class);* kā 'olua *(a-class)*. **3.** *Singular possessed object, plural.* Kō 'oukou *(o-class);* kā 'oukou *(a-class)*. **4.** *Plural possessed objects, singular.* Ou *(o-class);* āu *(a-class)*. **5.** *Plural possessed objects, dual.* O 'olua *(o-class);* a 'olua *(a-class)*. **6.** *Plural possessed objects, plural.* O 'oukou *(o-class);* a 'oukou *(a-class). For other uses of k-less (zero-type) possessives, see Gram. 8.4.2.*
yours. Nou, no 'olua, no 'oukou, nāu, na 'olua, na 'oukou. *See* **your**.
yourself. 'Oe iho, 'oe pono'ī. *See* **bone**.
youth. 'Ōpio, 'ōpiopio, u'i, ohi, 'ouo; liko *(fig.). See sayings,* **lana 1**, **wini 1**, **morning**. *Time of youth,* wā 'ōpiopio, wā u'i, wā heu 'ole, 'ehu kakahiaka.
youthful. 'Ōpiopio, u'i, 'ouo.

Z

z. *No Hawaiian term.*
zeal. Manaʻo ikaika, ʻiʻini loa.
zebra. Kepela, kuaka.
zebu. Kēpū.
zenith. Hoʻokuʻi, lolopua, Kahiki-kapu-i-Hōlani-ke-ku-ʻina; hikialoalo, wekea *(rare). See ex., * **hālāwai.**
zephyr. *See* **breeze.**
zero. ʻOle.
zigzag. Kīkeʻekeʻe, kihikihi, māʻoiʻoi, hoʻokeʻekeʻe. *To go zigzag,* hoʻokīkeʻe, kanaliʻo. *Zigzag lines,* laina hoʻokeʻekeʻe, kīkeʻekeʻe.

zinc. Kini.
zinnia. Pua pihi.
Zion. Kiona, Ziona.
Zizania. Kīkānia.
zodiac. Kokiaka, hōʻike no ka helena a ka lā.
zone. Kāʻei, wahi i hoʻokaʻawale ʻia, mahele.
zoo. Kahua hōʻikeʻike holoholona laka ʻole, kahi hōʻikeʻike holoholona laka ʻole.
zoology. ʻIke noʻeau i ke ʻano o nā holoholona.
zoom. Holo kapalulu.
Zurich. Kulika, Zurika.

References

Books and Articles

Abbott, Isabella Aiona, and Eleanor Horswill Williamson. 1974. *Limu. An Ethnobotanical Study of Some Edible Hawaiian Seaweeds.* Lawai, Hawaii: Pacific Tropical Botanical Garden.

Akana-Gooch, Collette L. 1980. "The Discrepancies between *Hawaiian Antiquities* and 'Ka Moolelo Hawaii'." Bernice P. Bishop Museum Library, Honolulu. Manuscript.

Alexander, W. D. 1968. *A Short Synopsis of the Most Essential Points in Hawaiian Grammar.* Rutland, Vt.: Charles E. Tuttle Co. (First published in 1864.)

Andrews, Lorrin. 1974. *A Dictionary of the Hawaiian Language, to which is Appended an English-Hawaiian Vocabulary and a Chronological Table of Remarkable Events.* Rutland, Vt.: Charles E. Tuttle Co. (First published in 1865.)

————. 1922. *A Dictionary of the Hawaiian Language.* Revised by Henry H. Parker. Honolulu: Board of Commissioners of the Public Archives of the Territory of Hawaii.

Arago, J. 1823. *Narrative of a Voyage round the World, in the Uranie and Physicienne Corvettes, Commanded by Captain Freycinet, during the Years 1817, 1818, 1819, and 1820,* pp. 291–294. London.

Barrère, Dorothy B. 1969. *The Kumuhonua Legends: A Study of Late 19th Century Hawaiian Stories of Creation and Origins.* Honolulu: Pacific Anthropological Records no. 3, Department of Anthropology, Bernice P. Bishop Museum.

Beaglehole, J. C., ed. 1967. *The Voyage of the* Resolution *and* Discovery, *1776–1780.* Part 2. Cambridge, England: Cambridge University Press. (Published for the Hakluyt Society.)

Beckwith, Martha W., ed. 1932. "Kepelino's Traditions of Hawaii." Bernice P. Bishop Museum Bulletin 95. Honolulu.

Berger, Andrew J. 1981. *Hawaiian Birdlife.* 2nd ed. Honolulu: University Press of Hawaii.

Biggs, Bruce. 1972. "Proto Polynesian Wordlist, with Supporting Data from Nine Languages." University of Auckland, computer printout.

————. 1978. "The History of Polynesian Phonology." In *Second International Conference on Austronesian Linguistics. Proceedings* (ed. S. A. Wurm and L. Carrington), no. 2, pp. 691–716.

Blaisdell, Richard K. 1982. "Ka Lapa'au Kahiko: Notions and Misnotions about Ancient Hawaiian Medicine." Paper presented at the Hawaiian Historical Society membership meeting, Honolulu, March 18.

Blixan, Olaf. 1972. "La Oclusión Glótica del Pascuense y Algunas Observaciones sobre la Posición del Pascuense dentro del Grupo Polinesias." *Moana, Estudios de Antropología Oceánica* 1(5). Montevideo.

Brigham, William T. 1906. *Mat and Basket Weaving of the Ancient Hawaiians.* Bernice P. Bishop Memoirs, vol. 2. Honolulu.

Buck, Peter H. See Te Rangi Hiroa.

Buniana, Ioane [John Bunyan]. 1842. *Ka Hele Malihini Ana Mai keia Ao aku a Hiki i kela Ao; he Olelonane Hoohalikeia me he Moeuhane la* [Pilgrim's progress from this world to that world, a parable like a dream]. Honolulu.

Carroll, Vern, and Tobias Soulik. 1973. *Nukuoro Lexicon.* Honolulu: The University Press of Hawaii.

Chamisso, Adelbert von. 1969. *Über die Hawaiische Sprache.* Facsimile edition with a critical introduction and an annotated bibliography of literature relating to the Hawaiian language, by Samuel H. Elbert. Amsterdam: Philo Press. (First published in 1837.)

Churchward, C. Maxwell. 1959. *Tongan Dictionary (Tongan-English and English-*

Tongan). London: Oxford University Press.

Clark, Ephraim W. 1903. *Buke Wehewehe Huaolelo Baibala me na Palapalaaina a me na Kii* [Book explaining Biblical words with maps and illustrations]. New York.

Clark, Ross. 1976. "Aspects of Proto-Polynesian Syntax." *Te Reo Monographs,* Linguistic Society of New Zealand.

Cleghorn, A. S. 1887. *Memorial Volume in Honor of H.R.H. Princess Miriam Likelike.*

Cook, James. 1785. *A Voyage to the Pacific Ocean, Undertaken by the Command of His Majesty, for Making Discoveries in the Northern Hemisphere,* vol. 3, pp. 547–551. London.

Daws, Gavan. 1974. *Shoal of Time: A History of the Hawaiian Islands.* Honolulu: The University Press of Hawaii. (First published in 1968 by Macmillan Co., New York.)

Dickey, Lyle A. 1928. "String Figures from Hawaii, Including Some from New Hebrides and Gilbert Islands." Bernice P. Bishop Museum Bulletin 54. Honolulu.

Dordillon, I. R. 1904. *Grammaire et Dictionnaire de la Langue des Iles Marquises.* Paris: Imprimerie Belin Frères.

Dordillon, René Ildefonse. 1931. *Grammaire et dictionnaire de la langue des Iles Marquises, Marquisien-Français.* Paris: Institut d'Ethnologie.

———. 1932. *Dictionnaire de la langue des Iles Marquises, Français-Marquisien.* Paris: Institut d'Ethnologie.

Elbert, Samuel H. 1954. "The Hawaiian Dictionaries, Past and Future." *In* Sixty-second Annual Report of the Hawaiian Historical Society, for the Year 1953, pp. 5–18.

———, ed. 1959. *Selections from Fornander's Hawaiian Antiquities and Folk-lore.* Honolulu: University of Hawaii Press.

———. 1962. "Symbolism in Hawaiian Poetry." *Etc.: A Review of General Semantics* 18:389–400.

———. 1964. "Hawaiian Reflexes of Proto-Malayo-Polynesian and Proto-Polynesian Reconstructed Forms." *Journal of the Polynesian Society* 73:399–410.

———. 1970. *Spoken Hawaiian.* Honolulu: University of Hawaii Press.

———. 1975. *Dictionary of the Language of Rennell and Bellona.* Copenhagen: National Museum of Denmark.

———. 1982. "Lexical Diffusion in Polynesia and the Marquesan-Hawaiian Relationship." *Journal of the Polynesian Society* 91:499–517.

Elbert, Samuel H., and Edgar C. Knowlton, Jr. 1962. " 'Ukulele." *American Speech* 32:307–310.

———. 1984. "Hawaiian Loanwords from Classical Languages." Hamilton Library, University of Hawaii at Manoa. Manuscript.

Elbert, Samuel H., and Noelani Mahoe. 1970. *Nā Mele o Hawai'i Nei: 101 Hawaiian Songs.* Honolulu: University of Hawaii Press.

Elbert, Samuel H., and Mary Kawena Pukui. 1979. *Hawaiian Grammar.* Honolulu: The University Press of Hawaii.

Ellis, William. 1827. *Narrative of a Tour through Owhyhee,* 2nd ed. London: H. Fisher, Son, and P. Jackson.

Emerson, J. [John] S. 1845. *He Hoakakaolelo no na Huaolelo Beritania, i Mea Kokua i na Kanaka Hawaii e Ao ana ia Olelo* [An explanation of English words, as an aid to Hawaiians learning this language]. Lahainaluna, Hawaii.

Emerson, J. [Joseph] S. 1892. "The Lesser Hawaiian Gods." *Hawaiian Historical Society Papers,* no. 2.

———. 1918. *Selections from a Kahuna's Book of Prayers.* Twenty-sixth Annual Report of the Hawaiian Historical Society, for the Year 1917, pp. 17–39. Honolulu: Paradise of the Pacific Press.

Emerson, N. [Nathaniel] B. 1893. "The Long Voyages of the Ancient Hawaiians." *Hawaiian Historical Society Papers,* no. 5.

———. 1965. *Unwritten Literature of Hawaii: The Sacred Songs of the Hula, Collected and Translated with Notes and an Account of the Hula.* Rutland, Vt.:

Charles E. Tuttle Co. (First published in 1909 as Bureau of American Ethnology Bulletin 38, Washington, D.C.)

———. 1978. *Pele and Hiiaka, a Myth of Hawaii*. With an introduction to the new edition by Terence Barrow. Rutland, Vt.: Charles E. Tuttle Co. (First published in 1915.)

Emory, Kenneth P. 1972. "Easter Island's Position in the Prehistory of Polynesia." *Journal of the Polynesian Society* 81:57–69.

Emory, Kenneth P., William J. Bonk, and Yoshiko H. Sinoto. 1959. *Fishhooks*. Bernice P. Bishop Museum Special Publication 47.

Englert, Sebastián. 1978. *Idioma Rapanui, Gramatica y Diccionario del Antiguo Idioma de la Isla de Pascua*. Universidad de Chile, Santiago.

Finney, Ben R. 1959. "Surfing in Ancient Hawaii." *Journal of the Polynesian Society* 68:327–347.

Fornander, Abraham. 1917–1920. *Hawaiian Antiquities and Folk-lore*. Bernice P. Bishop Museum Memoirs, vols. 4, 5, 6. Honolulu.

Fuentes, Jordi. 1960. *Diccionario y Gramática de la Lengua de la Isla de Pascua, Pascuense-Castellano, Castellano-Pascuense; Dictionary & Grammar of the Easter Island Language, Pascuense-English, English-Pascuense*. Santiago, Chile: Editorial Andres Bello.

Gosline, William A., and Vernon E. Brock. 1960. *Handbook of Hawaiian Fishes*. Honolulu: University of Hawaii Press.

Green, Laura C. S., and Mary Kawena Pukui. 1936. *The Legend of Kawelo and other Hawaiian Folk Tales*. Honolulu, Territory of Hawaii. Privately printed.

Green, Roger. 1966. "Linguistic Subgrouping within Polynesia: The Implications for Prehistoric Settlement." *Journal of the Polynesian Society* 75:6–38.

Hale, Horatio. 1968. "Ethnography and Philology." In *United States Exploring Expedition during the Years 1838, 1839, 1840, 1841, 1842, under the Command of Charles Wilkes, U.S.N.* Ridgewood, N.J.: The Gregg Press. (First published in 1846.)

Handy, E. S. Craighill. 1940. *The Hawaiian Planter, His Plants, Methods and Areas of Cultivation*. Bernice P. Bishop Museum Bulletin 161. Honolulu.

Handy, E. S. Craighill, and Elizabeth Green Handy (with Mary Kawena Pukui, collaborator). 1972. *Native Planters in Old Hawaii, Their Life, Lore, and Environment*. Bernice P. Bishop Museum Bulletin 233. Honolulu.

Handy, E. S. Craighill, and Mary Kawena Pukui. 1958. *The Polynesian Family System in Ka-'u, Hawaii*. Wellington: The Polynesian Society.

Handy, E. S. Craighill, Mary Kawena Pukui, and Katherine Livermore. 1934. *Outline of Hawaiian Physical Therapeutics*. Bernice P. Bishop Museum Bulletin 126. Honolulu.

Harper's Bible Dictionary. See Miller, M. S.

Hawkins, Emily A. 1982. *Pedagogical Grammar of Hawaiian, Recurrent Problems*. Honolulu: Hawaiian Studies Program, University of Hawai'i at Mānoa.

Hawkins, Emily A., and William H. Wilson. 1978. "Recommendations and Comments on the 'Ahahui 'Ōlelo Hawai'i 1978 Spelling Project." Hamilton Library, University of Hawaii at Manoa. Manuscript.

He Buke no ke Ola Kino no na Kamalii, e Pili Ana i na Poino i Loaa i ke Kino o na Kanaka ma na Wai Ona a me na Laau Hoohiamoe [A book about the health of children, pertaining to harm done to man's body by intoxicating liquors and drugs]. 1887. New York.

He Kumu Paikau no na Koa Hele Wawae o ke Aupuni Hawaii [A manual of arms for the infantry soldiers of the Hawaiian Kingdom]. 1854. Honolulu.

Hervey, Wesley D. 1968. "A History of the Adaptations of an Orthography for the Hawaiian Language." Ph.D. dissertation, University of Oregon.

Hillebrand, W. F. 1888. *Flora of the Hawaiian Islands*. Heidelberg.

Hitchcock, H. R. 1887. *An English-Hawai-*

ian Dictionary; with Various Useful Tables: Prepared for the Use of Hawaiian-English School.* San Francisco.

Holy Bible, Containing Old and New Testaments (King James Version).

Holy Bible, Revised Standard Version Containing the Old and New Testaments. Old Testament 1952. New Testament, 2nd ed., 1971. Grand Rapids, Michigan: Zondervan Bible Publishers.

Ii, John Papa. 1959. *Fragments of Hawaii History.* Honolulu: Bernice P. Bishop Museum.

Indices of Awards Made by the Board of Commissioners to Quiet Land Titles in the Hawaiian Islands. Compiled and published by the Office of the Commissioner of Public Lands of the Territory of Hawaii, 1929. Honolulu.

Johnson, Rubellite [Kawena] Kinney, ed. 1976. *Kukini 'Aha'ilono* [Carry on the news]: *Over a Century of Native Hawaiian Life and Thought from the Hawaiian Language Newspapers of 1834 to 1948.* Honolulu: Topgallant Publishing Co.

————. 1982. *Kumulipo: The Hawaiian Hymn of Creation.* Honolulu: Topgallant Publishing Co.

Johnson, Rubellite Kawena, and John Kaipo Mahelona. 1975. *Nā Inoa Hōkū: A Catalogue of Hawaiian and Pacific Star Names.* Honolulu: Topgallant Publishing Co.

Judd, Henry P. 1930. *Hawaiian Proverbs and Riddles.* Bernice P. Bishop Museum Bulletin 77. Honolulu.

Judd, Henry P., Mary Kawena Pukui, and John F. G. Stokes. 1945. *Introduction to the Hawaiian Language (an English-Hawaiian Vocabulary).* Honolulu: Tongg Publishing Co.

Ka Baibala Hemolele o ke Kauoha Kahiko a me ke Kauoha Hou; i Unuhiia Mailoko mai o na Olelo Kahiko, a Hooponopono Hou ia [The Holy Bible of the Old Testament and the New Testament; translated from ancient tongues and revised]. New York: American Bible Society, 1941.

Ka Buke Ao Heluhelu; i Hooponoponoia no

na Kula Hawaii ma Keia Aupuni* [The book instructing reading; arranged for the Hawaiian schools in this nation]. 2nd ed. 1876. Honolulu.

Kaeppler, Adrienne. 1981. "Hula and Ha'a, Hawaiian Dance in Historic Perspective." Paper presented at the Hawaiian Historical Society membership meeting, September 24.

Kamakau, Samuel M. 1961. *Ruling Chiefs of Hawaii.* Honolulu: Kamehameha Schools Press.

————. 1964. *Ka Po'e Kahiko, the People of Old.* Translated from the newspaper *Ke Au 'Oko'a* by Mary Kawena Pukui, arranged and edited by Dorothy B. Barrère. Bernice P. Bishop Museum Special Publication 51. Honolulu.

————. 1976. *The Works of the People of Old, Na Hana a ka Po'e Kahiko.* Translated from the newspaper *Ke Au 'Oko'a* by Mary Kawena Pukui, arranged and edited by Dorothy B. Barrère. Bernice P. Bishop Museum Special Publication 61. Honolulu.

Kamakau o Ka-'awa-loa. 1919–1920. *No ka 'Oihana Kahuna Kahiko* [Concerning ancient priestly works]. (From Fornander, vol. 6, pp. 1–45.)

Kanahele, George S., ed. 1979. *Hawaiian Music and Musicians: An Illustrated History.* Honolulu: The University Press of Hawaii.

Ka Palapala Hemolele a Iehova ko Kakou Akua o ke Kauoha Kahiko a me ke Kauoha Hou; i Unuhiia Mailoko mai o na Olelo Kahiko [The holy document of Jehovah our God, the New Testament and the Old Testament, translated from ancient languages]. 1843. Honolulu.

Kay, E. Alison. 1979. *Hawaiian Marine Shells, Reef and Shore Fauna of Hawaii.* Section 4, *Mollusca.* Bernice P. Bishop Museum Special Publication 64(4). Honolulu: Bishop Museum Press.

Ke Alanui o ka Lani, Oia ka Manuale Kakolika i Paiia ma ke Kauoha o Gulekana, ep. o Panopolis, vic. ap. [The path to Heaven, the Catholic manual published by order of

Gulstan, Bishop of Panopolis, Vicar Apostolic]. 1896. Paris.

Kelekona, Kahikona [W. J. Sheldon]. 1906. *Kaluaikoolau, Piilani, Alo Ehu Poka* [Dodging sprays of bullets]. Hoopaaia ke Kuleana Mana Hoolaha iloko o ke Keena Puuku o ka Teritore o Hawaii [Copyrighted and distributed within the treasurer's office of the Territory of Hawaii].

Kepelino. See Beckwith 1932.

Kinney, Ruby Kawena. 1956. "A Non-purist View of Morphomorphemic Variations in Hawaiian Speech." *Journal of the Polynesian Society* 65:282–286.

Korn, Alfons L. 1976. "Some Notes on the Origin of Certain Hawaiian Shirts: Frock, Smock-frock, Block, and Palaka." *Oceanic Linguistics* 15:14–38.

Krauss, Beatrice H. n.d. "Ethnobotany of Hawaii." Department of Botany, University of Hawaii, Honolulu. Manuscript.

Kuhelani, J. W. 1856. "Kekahi mau Mea a ka Poe Kahiko [Several things about the old people]." *Ka Hae Hawaii,* November 19.

Kuykendall, Ralph S. 1947. *The Hawaiian Kingdom.* Vol. 1, *1778–1854: Foundation and Transformation.* Honolulu: University of Hawaii Press.

———. 1953. *The Hawaiian Kingdom.* Vol. 2, *1854–1874: Twenty Critical Years.* Honolulu: University of Hawaii Press.

———. 1967. *The Hawaiian Kingdom.* Vol. 3, *1874–1893: The Kalakaua Dynasty.* Honolulu: University of Hawaii Press.

Lavondès, Henri. 1975. *Terre et Mer pour une Lecture de quelques Mythes Polynésiens.* Hamilton Library, University of Hawaii at Manoa. Mimeo.

Lemaître, Yves. 1973. *Lexique Tahitien contemporain, Tahitien-Français, Français-Tahitien.* Paris: Office de la Recherche Scientifique et Technique Outre-Mer.

Lieber, Michael, and Kalio D. Dikepa. 1974. *Kapingamarangi Lexicon.* Honolulu: The University Press of Hawaii.

Lisiansky, Urey. 1814. *A voyage round the World in the Years 1803, 4, 5, 6, Performed by Order of His Imperial Majesty,* *Alexander the First, Emperor of Russia, in the Ship Neva,* pp. 326–328. London.

Luomala, Katharine. 1949. *Maui-of-a-Thousand-Tricks: His Oceanic and European Biographers.* Bernice P. Bishop Museum Bulletin 198. Honolulu.

———. 1951. *The Menehune of Polynesia and Other Mythical Little People of Oceania.* Bernice P. Bishop Museum Bulletin 203. Honolulu.

Macdonald, Gordon A., Agatin T. Abbott, and Frank L. Peterson. 1983. *Volcanoes in the Sea: The Geology of Hawaii.* 2nd ed. Honolulu: University of Hawaii Press.

McEwen, J. M. 1970. *Niue Dictionary.* Wellington, N.Z.: Hutcheson, Bowman and Stewart.

McGuire, James W. L. 1938. *He Moolelo Pokole o ka Huakai Hele a ka Moiwahine Kapiolani i Enelani i ka Makahiki 1887 i ka Iubile o ka Moiwahine Vitoria o Beretania Nui* [A short account of the journey of Queen Kapiolani to England in the year 1887 for the Jubilee of Queen Victoria of Great Britain]. Honolulu: Collegiate Press.

McKeown, Sean. 1978. *Hawaiian Reptiles and Amphibians.* Honolulu: Oriental Publishing Co.

Makemson, Maud Worcester. 1941. *The Morning Star Rises: An Account of Polynesian Astronomy.* New Haven: Yale University Press.

Malo, David. 1951. *Hawaiian Antiquities (Moolelo Hawaii).* Translated by Nathaniel B. Emerson, 1898. Bernice P. Bishop Museum Special Publications 2. 2nd ed. Honolulu.

Manuokekula, G. W. K. 1871. "Ka Hanau Ana o na Malama." *Ka Hoku o ka Pakipika,* October 14.

Métraux, Alfred. 1971. *Ethnology of Easter Island.* Bishop Museum Press Reprints, Honolulu. (First published in 1940 as Bernice P. Bishop Museum Bulletin 160.)

Miller, M. S., and J. L. Miller. 1952. *Harper's Bible Dictionary.* New York: Harper Brothers.

Milner, G. B. 1966. *Samoan Dictionary: Samoan-English, English-Samoan.* London: Oxford University Press.

Mitchell, Donald D. Kilolani. 1975. *Hawaiian Games for Today: Descriptions of Sixty Hawaiian Games with Full Directions for Playing Thirty.* Honolulu: Kamehameha Schools Press.

Mookini, Esther K. 1974. *The Hawaiian Newspapers.* Honolulu: Topgallant Publishing Co.

Moolelo o na Hana o ka Hale o na Lunamakaainana, Kau Mau o 1905, Ahaolelo o ka Teritore o Hawaii [Journal of the House of Representatives, Regular Session of 1905, Legislature of the Territory of Hawaii]. 1905. Honolulu.

Mosblech, Boniface. 1843. *Vocabulaire océanien-français et français-océanien des dialectes parlés aux îles Marquises, Sandwich, Gambier, etc., d'après les documens recueillis sur les lieux par les missionaires catholiques et les ministres protestans.* Paris.

Na Kanawai Karaima o ko Hawaii Pae Aina, 1897, i Hoouluuluia mai ke Kanawai Hoopai Karaima mai o 1859 [i.e. 1869] *ame na Kanawai o na Kau Ahaolelo mai 1870 a 1896* [Penal laws of the Hawaiian Islands, 1897, compiled from the Penal Code from 1859 and the laws of the legislative sessions from 1870 to 1896]. 1897. Honolulu: Hawaiian Gazette.

Nakuina, Moses K., ed. n.d. [probably early 1900s]. *Moolelo Hawaii o Pakaa a me Kua-Pakaa* [Hawaiian account of Pakaa and Ku-a-Paka'a]. Hamilton Library, University of Hawaii. Privately printed.

Neal, Marie C. 1965. *In Gardens of Hawaii.* New and revised edition. Bernice P. Bishop Museum Special Publication 50. Honolulu: Bishop Museum Press. (First published in 1948.)

Neves, Paki. 1976. "Some Problems with Orthography Encountered by the Reader of Old Hawaiian Texts." *Oceanic Linguistics* 15:51–74.

Newbrand, Helene Luise. 1951. "A Phonemic Analysis of Hawaiian." Master's thesis, University of Hawaii.

Pawley, Andrew. 1966. "Polynesian Languages: A Subgrouping Based on Shared Innovations in Morphology." *Journal of the Polynesian Society* 75:39–64.

The Penal Laws of the Hawaiian Islands, 1897, Compiled from the Penal Code of 1869 and the Session Laws of 1870 to 1896 Inclusive. 1897. Honolulu: Hawaiian Gazette.

Pratt, George. 1960. *Pratt's Grammar and Dictionary of the Samoan Language.* Malua, Western Samoa: Malua Printing Press.

Pope, W. T. 1926. *Banana Culture in Hawaii.* Hawaiian Agricultural Experiment Station Bulletin 55.

Pukui, Mary Kawena. 1983. *'Ōlelo No'eau: Hawaiian Proverbs and Poetical Sayings.* Bernice P. Bishop Museum Special Publication 71. Honolulu.

Pukui, Mary Kawena, and Samuel H. Elbert. 1964. *English-Hawaiian Dictionary.* Honolulu: University of Hawaii Press.

———. 1965. *Hawaiian-English Dictionary.* 3rd ed. Honolulu: University of Hawaii Press. (First published in 1957.)

Pukui, Mary Kawena, E. W. Haertig, and Cathering A. Lee. 1972. *Nānā i ke Kumu* [Look to the source]. Honolulu: Hui Hānai.

Pukui, Mary Kawena, and Alfons L. Korn. 1973. *The Echo of Our Song: Chants and Poems of the Hawaiians.* Honolulu: The University Press of Hawaii.

Pukui, Mary Kawena, Samuel H. Elbert, and Esther T. Mookini. 1974. *Place Names of Hawaii.* Revised and expanded edition. Honolulu: The University Press of Hawaii.

———. 1975. *The Pocket Hawaiian Dictionary, with a Concise Hawaiian Grammar.* Honolulu: The University Press of Hawaii.

Pyle, Robert L. 1977. "Preliminary List of the Birds of Hawaii." *Elepaio* 37:110–121.

Reed, Minnie. 1907. "The Economic Seaweeds of Hawaii." Washington: U.S. Government Printing Office. (First published in 1906 as Hawaii Agricultural Experiment Station Annual Report, Honolulu.)

Remy, M. Jules. 1893. "L'île de Molokai avant la leproserie." Arcis-sur-Aube, France: Imprimerie Leon Fremont, Ed.

Roberts, Helen H. 1967. *Ancient Hawaiian Music*. New York: Dover Publications. (First published in 1926 as Bernice P. Bishop Museum Bulletin 29.)

Rock, J. F. 1913. *List of Hawaiian Names of Plants*. Territory of Hawaii Board of Agriculture and Forestry. Botanical Bulletin no. 2. Honolulu.

Sahlins, Marshall. 1981. *Historical Metaphors and Mythical Realities: Structure in the Early History of the Sandwich Islands Kingdom*. Association for Social Anthropology in Oceania, Special Publication 1. Ann Arbor: University of Michigan Press.

Savage, Stephen. 1962. *A Dictionary of the Maori Language of Rarotonga*. Department of Island Territories, Wellington.

Schütz, Albert J. 1976. "Take My Word for It: Missionary Influence on Borrowings in Hawaiian." *Oceanic Linguistics* 15:75–92.

———. 1981. "A Reanalysis of the Hawaiian Vowel System." *Oceanic Linguistics* 20:1–43.

St. John, Harold. 1975a. "The Variability of the Hawaiian *Maile*." *Phytologia* 32:377–386.

———. 1975b. *List and Summary of the Flowering Plants in the Hawaiian Islands*. Pacific Tropical Botanical Garden Memoir no. 1. Lawai, Hawaii.

———. 1982. *Vernacular Plant Names Used on Niʻihau Island*. Hawaiian Plant Studies 69. Bernice P. Bishop Museum Occasional Papers vol. 25, no. 3. Honolulu.

Stimson, J. Frank (with Donald Stanley Marshall, collaborator). 1964. *A Dictionary of some Tuamotuan Dialects of the Polynesian Language*. The Hague: Martinus Nijhoff.

Stokes, John F. G. 1932. "The Hawaiian King (Mo-i, alii-aimoku, alii-kapu)." *Hawaiian Historical Society Papers* 19:1–28.

Summers, Catherine C. 1964. *Hawaiian Fishponds*. Bernice P. Bishop Museum Special Publication 52. Honolulu.

———. 1971. *Molokai: A Site Survey*. Bernice P. Bishop Museum, Pacific Anthropological Records no. 10. Honolulu.

The Taro Collection. 1970. Honolulu: Harold L. Lyon Arboretum, University of Hawaii.

Te Rangi Hiroa [Peter H. Buck]. 1957. *Arts and Crafts of Hawaii*. Bernice P. Bishop Museum Special Publication 45. Honolulu.

Thomson, James B. 1870. *Ka Huinahelu Hou: Oia Hoi ka Arimatika Kulanui; Malaila i Aoia ai ke Ano a me ka Hoopiliia ana o na Helu* [The new combined arithmetic; or an arithmetic for the high school, in which the kind and properties of the numbers are taught]. Translated by C. J. Lyons. Honolulu.

Thrum, T. G. 1896. *The Hawaiian Almanac and Annual for 1896*. Honolulu: Thos. G. Thrum.

———. 1906. *The Hawaiian Almanac and Annual for 1906*. Honolulu: Thos. G. Thrum.

———. 1924. *Hawaiian Annual for 1925*. Honolulu: Thos. G. Thrum.

Titcomb, Margaret. 1948. "Kava in Hawaii." *Journal of the Polynesian Society* 57:105–171.

———. 1969. *Dog and Man in the Ancient Pacific*. Bernice P. Bishop Museum Special Publication 59.

——— (with Mary Kawena Pukui, collaborator). 1972. *Native Use of Fish in Hawaii*. Honolulu: The University Press of Hawaii. (First published in 1952 by the Avery Press, New Plymouth, New Zealand.)

Whitney, Leo D., F. A. I. Bowers, and M. Takahashi. 1939. *Taro Varieties in Hawaii*. University of Hawaii Agricultural Experiment Station Bulletin 84. Honolulu.

Williams, Herbert W. 1932. *A Dictionary*

of the Maori Language. Wellington: W. A. G. Skinner, Government Printer.

Wilson, William H. 1976. "The *o/a* Distinction in Hawaiian Possessives." *Oceanic Linguistics* 15:39–50.

Yasuda, Ayako. 1968. *The Structure of the Penrhyn Phrase.* Master's thesis, University of Hawaii.

Hawaiian Newspapers

Ka Elele Hawaii (The Hawaiian Messenger). Honolulu, 1845–1855.

Ka Elele Poakolu (The Wednesday Messenger). Honolulu, 1880–1881.

Ka Hae Hawaii (The Hawaiian Flag). Honolulu, 1856–1861.

Ka Hoku o Hawaii (The Star of Hawaii). Hilo, 1906–1948.

Ka Lama Hawaii (The Hawaiian Luminary). Lahainaluna, 1834.

Ka Leo o ka Lahui (The Voice of the Nation). Honolulu, 1889–1896.

Ka Loea Kalaiaina (The Political Expert). Honolulu, 1897–1900.

Ka Naʻi Aupuni (The National Conqueror). Honolulu, 1905–1908.

Ka Nonanona (The Ant: see *ʻānonanona*). Honolulu, 1841–1854.

Ka Nupepa Kuokoa (The Independent Newspaper). Honolulu, 1861–1927.

Ke Aloha Aina (The Patriot). Honolulu, 1895–1920.

Ke Au Okoa (The Independent Era). Honolulu, 1865–1873.

Ke Kumu Hawaii (The Hawaiian Teacher). Honolulu, 1834–1839.

Lahui Hawaii (Hawaiian Nation). Honolulu, 1875–1877.

HAWAII **Production Notes**

This book was designed by Roger Eggers. Composition and typesetting were done on Compugraphic equipment by the design and production staff of University of Hawaii Press.

The text typeface is Compugraphic Times Roman and the display typeface is Univers 65.

Offset presswork and binding were done by Vail-Ballou Press, Inc. Text paper is Glatfelter Offset Vellum, basis 45.